College Edition

HARPER COLLINS PORTUGUESE DICTIONARY

ENGLISH • PORTUGUESE   PORTUGUESE • ENGLISH

John Whitlam   Vitoria Davies
Mike Harland

<comment>HarperCollins logo</comment>

HarperCollins*Publishers*

First published 1991

© Copyright 1991 HarperCollins Publishers

Latest reprint 1996

HarperCollins Publishers
PO Box, Glasgow G4 ONB, Great Britain

ISBN 0 00 433225-3

_____

10 East 53rd Street, New York, NY 10022

ISBN 0-06-273489-X (paperback)

First HarperCollins edition published 1997

_____

Library of Congress Cataloging-in-Publication Data

Whitlam, John.
  Harper Collins Portuguese dictionary : English-Portuguese
Portuguese-English / John Whitlam, Vitoria Davies, Mike Harland, –
College ed.
     p.   cm.
  Updated ed. of: Collins Portuguese dictionary. 1991.
  ISBN 0-06-273489-X
  1. Portuguese language–Dictionaries–English.   2. English
language–Dictionaries–Portuguese.   I. Davies, Vitoria.
II. Harland, Mike.   III. Whitlam, John. Collins Portuguese
dictionary.   IV. Title.
PC5333.W45   1997
469.3'21–dc20   96-44948

_____

96 97 98 99 00 CIBM 10 9 8 7 6 5 4 3 2 1

Printed and bound in Great Britain by
Caledonian International Book Manufacturing Ltd, Glasgow, G64

ÍNDICE

CONTENTS

contributors/colaboradores
Carlos Ramires,
Nelly Wanderley Fernandes Porto,
Ana Maria de Mello e Souza,
Adriana Ceschin Rieche, Lígia Xavier,
Amos Maidantchik, Helio Leoncio Martins,
Jane Horwood

consultant/assessor
Dr Euzi Rodrigues Moraes

editorial staff/redação
Gerry Breslin, Lesley Johnston,
Irene Lakhani

INTRODUÇÃO

Para compreender o inglês

Este novo dicionário, completamente atualizado, fornece ao leitor uma cobertura ampla e prática dos usos lingüísticos mais comuns, incluindo a terminologia relativa à área empresarial e à microinformática, além de uma seleção abrangente de abreviaturas, siglas e topônimos encontrados freqüentemente na imprensa. Para facilitar as consultas do leitor, as formas irregulares de verbos e substantivos ingleses foram incluídas, com indicações que fazem referência à forma básica, onde uma tradução é dada.

Para expressar-se em inglês

A fim de ajudar o leitor a expressar-se correta e idiomaticamente em inglês, foram incluídas várias indicações para orientá-lo quanto à tradução mais apropriada em um determinado contexto. Todas as palavras de uso mais comum receberam um tratamento detalhado, com muitos exemplos de utilização típica.

Um companheiro de trabalho

Todo o cuidado foi tomado para fazer deste novo dicionário da editora Collins uma obra totalmente confiável, fácil de ser usada e útil para o trabalho e estudos do leitor. Esperamos que ele seja um companheiro de longos anos no atendimento das necessidades de expressão numa língua estrangeira.

Understanding Portuguese

This new and thoroughly up-to-date dictionary provides the user with wide-ranging, practical coverage of current usage, including terminology relevant to business and office automation, and a comprehensive selection of abbreviations, acronyms and geographical names commonly found in the press. You will also find, for ease of consultation, irregular forms of Portuguese verbs and nouns with a cross-reference to the basic form where a translation is given.

Self-expression in Portuguese

To help you express yourself correctly and idiomatically in Portuguese, numerous indications — think of them as signposts — guide you to the most appropriate translation for your context. All the most commonly used words are given detailed treatment, with many examples of typical usage.

A working companion

Much care has been taken to make this new Collins dictionary thoroughly reliable, easy to use and relevant to your work and study. We hope it will become a long-serving companion for all your foreign language needs.

ABREVIATURAS

ABBREVIATIONS

abreviatura	**ab(b)r**	abbreviation
adjetivo	**adj**	adjective
administração	**ADMIN**	administration
advérbio, locução adverbial	**adv**	adverb, adverbial phrase
aeronáutica	**AER**	flying, air travel
agricultura	**AGR**	agricultura
anatomia	**ANAT**	anatomy
arquitetura	**ARQ, ARCH**	architecture
artigo definido	**art def**	definite article
artigo indefinido	**art indef**	indefinite article
uso atributivo do substantivo	**atr**	compound element
automobilismo	**AUT(O)**	the motor car and motoring
auxiliar	**aux**	auxiliary
aeronáutica	**AVIAT**	flying, air travel
biologia	**BIO**	biology
botânica, flores	**BOT**	botany
português do Brasil	**BR**	Brazilian
inglês britânico	**BRIT**	British English
química	**CHEM**	chemistry
linguagem coloquial (! chulo)	**col(!)**	colloquial usage (! particularly offensive)
comércio, finanças, bancos	**COM(M)**	commerce, finance, banking
comparativo	**compar**	comparative
computação	**COMPUT**	computing
conjunção	**conj**	conjunction
construção	**CONSTR**	building
uso atributivo do substantivo	**cpd**	compound element
cozinha	**CULIN**	cookery
artigo definido	**def art**	definite article
economia	**ECON**	economics
educação, escola e universidade	**EDUC**	schooling, schools and universities
eletricidade, eletrônica	**ELET, ELEC**	electricity, electronics
especialmente	**esp**	especially
exclamação	**excl**	exclamation
feminino	**f**	feminine
ferrovia	**FERRO**	railways
uso figurado	**fig**	figurative use
física	**FÍS**	physics
fisiologia	**FISIOL**	physiology
fotografia	**FOTO**	photography
(verbo inglês) do qual a partícula é inseparável	**fus**	(phrasal verb) where the particle is inseparable
geralmente	**gen**	generally
geografia, geologia	**GEO**	geography, geology
geometria	**GEOM**	geometry
geralmente	**ger**	generally
impessoal	**impess, impers**	impersonal
artigo indefinido	**indef art**	indefinite article
linguagem coloquial (! chulo)	**inf (!)**	informal usage (! particularly offensive)
infinitivo	**infin**	infinitive
invariável	**inv**	invariable
irregular	**irreg**	irregular

ABREVIATURAS

ABBREVIATIONS

jurídico	**JUR**	law
gramática, lingüística	**LING**	grammar, linguistics
masculino	**m**	masculine
matemática	**MAT(H)**	mathematics, calculus
medicina	**MED**	medicine
ou masculino ou feminino, dependendo do sexo da pessoa	**m/f**	masculine/feminine
militar, exército	**MIL**	military matters
música	**MÚS, MUS**	music
substantivo	**n**	noun
navegação, náutica	**NÁUT, NAUT**	sailing, navigation
adjetivo ou substantivo numérico	**num**	numeral adjective or noun
	o.s.	oneself
pejorativo	**pej**	pejorative
fotografia	**PHOT**	photography
física	**PHYS**	physics
fisiologia	**PHYSIOL**	physiology
plural	**pl**	plural
política	**POL**	politics
particípio passado	**pp**	past participle
preposição	**prep**	preposition
pronome	**pron**	pronoun
psicologia, psiquiatria	**PSICO, PSYCH**	psychology, psychiatry
português de Portugal	**PT**	European Portuguese
pretérito	**pt**	past tense
química	**QUÍM**	chemistry
religião e cultos	**REL**	religion, church services
	sb	somebody
educação, escola e universidade	**SCH**	schooling, schools and universities
singular	**sg**	singular
	sth	something
sujeito (gramatical)	**su(b)j**	(grammatical) subject
subjuntivo, conjuntivo	**sub(jun)**	subjunctive
superlativo	**superl**	superlative
também	**tb**	also
técnica, tecnologia	**TEC(H)**	technical term, technology
telecomunicações	**TEL**	telecommunications
tipografia, imprensa	**TIP**	typography, printing
televisão	**TV**	television
tipografia, imprensa	**TYP**	typography, printing
inglês americano	**US**	American English
ver	**V**	see
verbo	**vb**	verb
verbo intransitivo	**vi**	intransitive verb
verbo reflexivo	**vr**	reflexive verb
verbo transitivo	**vt**	transitive verb
zoologia	**ZOOL**	zoology
marca registrada	**®**	registered trademark
indica um equivalente cultural	**≈**	introduces a cultural equivalent

PORTUGUESE PRONUNCIATION

The rules given below refer to Portuguese as spoken in the city and surrounding region of Rio de Janeiro, Brazil. In general, the pronunciation of each entry is given in square brackets in the text after the word in question. However, where an entry is composed of two or more words, each of which is given elsewhere in the dictionary, you will find the pronunciation of each word in its alphabetical position.

Consonants

c	[k]	café	c before a, o, u is pronounced as in cat
ce, ci	[s]	cego	c before e or i, as in receive
ç	[s]	raça	ç is pronounced as in receive
ch	[ʃ]	chave	ch is pronounced as in shock
d	[d]	data	as in English EXCEPT
de, di	[dʒ]	difícil	d before an i sound or final unstressed e is
		cidade	pronounced as in judge
g	[g]	gado	g before a, o or u, as in gap
ge, gi	[ʒ]	giria	g before e or i, as s in leisure
h		humano	h is always silent in Portuguese
j	[ʒ]	jogo	j is pronounced as s in leisure
l	[w]	falta, total	l after a vowel tends to become w
lh	[ʎ]	trabalho	lh is pronounced like the lli in million
m	[m]	animal, massa	as in English EXCEPT
	[ãw]	cantam	m at the end of a syllable preceded by a
	[ĩ]	sim	vowel nasalizes the preceding vowel
n	[n]	nadar, penal	as in English EXCEPT
	[ã]	cansar	n at the end of a syllable, preceded by a
	[ẽ]	alento	vowel and followed by a consonant, nasalizes the preceding vowel
nh	[ɲ]	tamanho	nh is pronounced like the ni in onion
q	[k]	queijo	qu before e or i is pronounced as in kick
q	[kw]	quanto	qu before a or o, or qü before e or i, is
		cinqüenta	pronounced as in quoits
-r-	[r]	compra	r preceded by a consonant (except n) and followed by a vowel is pronounced with a single trill
r-, -r-	[x]	rato, arpão	initial r, r followed by a consonant and rr are
rr	[x]	bexerro	pronounced similar to the Scottish ch in loch
-r	[*]	pintar, dizer	word-final r before a word beginning with a consonant or at the end of a sentence is pronounced [x]; before a word beginning with a vowel it is pronounced [r]. In colloquial speech this variable sound is often not pronounced at all.
s-	[s]	sol	as in English EXCEPT
-s-	[z]	mesa	intervocalic s is pronounced as in rose
-s-	[ʒ]	rasgar, desmaio	s before b, d, g, l, m, n, r and v, as in leisure
-s-, -s	[ʃ]	escada, livros	s before c, f, p, qu, t and finally, as in sugar
-ss-	[s]	nosso	double s is always pronounced as in boss

t	[t]	*t*odo	as in English, EXCEPT
te, ti	[tʃ]	aman*t*e *t*ipo	*t* followed by an *i* sound or final unstressed *e* is pronounced as *ch* in *ch*eer
x-	[ʃ]	*x*arope e*x*plorar	initial *x* or *x* before a consonant (except *c*) is pronounced as in *s*ugar
-xce-, -xci-	[s]	e*x*ceto, e*x*citar	*x* before *ce* or *ci* is unpronounced
ex-	[z]	e*x*ame	*x* in the prefix *ex* before a vowel is pronounced as *z* in squee*z*e
-x-	[ʃ]	ri*x*a	*x* in any other position may be pronounced
	[ks]	fi*x*o	as in *s*ugar, a*x*e or *s*ail
	[s]	au*x*iliar	
z-, -z-	[z]	*z*angar	as in English EXCEPT
-z	[ʒ]	carta*z*	final *z* is pronounced as in lei*s*ure

b, f, k, p, v, w are prounced as in English.

Vowels

a, á, à, â	[a]	m*a*ta	*a* is normally pronounced as in f*a*ther
ã	[ã]	irm*ã*	*ã* is pronounced approximately as in s*u*ng
e	[e]	v*e*jo	unstressed (except final) *e* is pronounced like *e* in th*ey*; stressed *e* is pronounced either as in th*ey* or as in b*e*t
-e	[i]	fom*e*	final *e* is pronounced as in mon*ey*
é	[ɛ]	mis*é*ria	*é* is pronounced as in b*e*t
ê	[e]	p*ê*lo	*ê* is pronounced as in th*ey*
i	[i]	v*i*da	*i* is pronounced as in m*ea*n
o	[o]	loc*o*motiva	unstressed (except final) *o* is pronounced as in l*o*cal; stressed *o* can
	[ɔ]	l*o*ja	be pronounced either as in l*o*cal or as in r*o*ck
	[o]	gl*o*bo	
-o	[u]	livr*o*	final *o* is pronounced as in f*oo*t
ó	[ɔ]	*ó*leo	*o* is pronounced as in r*o*ck
ô	[o]	col*ô*nia	*ô* is pronounced as in l*o*cal
u	[u]	l*u*va	*u* is pronounced as in r*u*le; it is silent in *gue, gui, que* and *qui*

Semivowels

e	[j]	t*e*atro	occasionally before a stressed *a, e* is pronounced as *y* in *y*acht
i	[j]	cí*u*me, silênc*i*o	unstressed *i* before a vowel is pronounced as *y* in *y*acht
u	[w]	ág*u*a, aq*u*ático ag*ü*entar	*u* is pronounced *w* in q*ua*, q*uo* and g*ua*, and when marked with a dieresis

Dipthongs

ãe	[aj]	m*ãe*	nasalized, approximately as in fly*i*ng
ai	[aj]	v*ai*	as in r*i*de
ao, au	[aw]	*ao*s, *au*xílio	as in sh*ou*t
ão	[ãw]	v*ão*	nasalized, approximately as in r*ou*nd
ei	[ej]	f*ei*ra	as in th*ey*
eu	[ew]	d*eu*sa	both elements pronounced
oi	[oj]	b*oi*	as in t*oy*
ou	[o]	cen*ou*ra	as in l*o*cal
õe	[õj]	avi*õe*s	nasalized, approximately as in "b*oi*ng!"

Stress

The rules of stress in Portuguese are as follows:

(a) when a word ends in *a, e, o, m* (except *im, um* and their plural forms) or *s*, the second last syllable is stressed; cama*ra*da, cama*ra*das, *par*te, *par*tem
(b) when a word ends in *i, u, im* (and plural), *um* (and plural), *n* or a consonant other than *m* or *s*, the stress falls on the last syllable: ven*di*, al*gum*, al*guns*, fa*lar*
(c) when the rules set out in (a) and (b) are not applicable, an acute or circumflex accent appears over the stressed vowel: *ó*tica, *â*nimo, in*glês*

In the phonetic transcription, the symbol ['] precedes the syllable on which the stress falls.

EUROPEAN PRONUNCIATION

The pronunciation of Brazilian Portuguese differs quite markedly from the Portuguese spoken in Portugal itself and in the African and island states. The more phonetic nature of Brazilian means that words nearly always retain their set pronunciation; in European Portuguese, on the other hand, vowels can often be unpronounced or weakened and consonants can change their sound, all depending on their position within a word or whether they are being elided with a following word. The major differences in pronunciation of European Portuguese are as follows:

Consonants: as in Brazilian, except:

-b-	[β]	cu*b*a	*b* between vowels is a softer sound, closer to ha*v*e
d	[d]	*d*ança, *d*ifícil	as in English, *EXCEPT*
-d-	[ð]	fa*d*o, ci*d*a*d*e	*d* between vowels is softer, approximately as in *th*e
-g-	[ɣ]	sa*g*a	*g* between vowels is a softer sound, approximately as in la*g*er
gu	[ɣw]	a*gu*entar	in certain words *gu* is pronounced as in *Gw*ent
qu	[kw]	tran*qu*ilo	in certain words *qu* is pronounced as in *qu*oits
r-, rr	[ʀ]		initial *r* and double *r* are pronounced either
	[rr]		like the French *r* or strongly trilled as in Scottish *R*ory; pronunciation varies according to region
-r-, -r	[r]	*r*ato, a*r*ma	*r* in any other position is slightly trilled
t	[t]	*t*odo, aman*t*e	*t* is pronounced as in English
z	[z]	*z*angar	as in English *EXCEPT*
	[ʃ]	carta*z*	final *z* is pronounced as *sh* in fla*sh*

Vowels: as in Brazilian, except:

a	[a]	fal*a*r	stressed *a* is pronounced either as in f*a*ther
	[ɐ]	c*a*ma	or as *u* in f*u*rther
-a-, -a	[ə]	f*a*lar, fal*a*	unstressed or final *a* is pronounced as *e* in furth*e*r
e	[ə]	m*e*dir	unstressed *e* is a very short *i* sound as in rabb*i*t
-e	[ə]	art*e*, regim*e*	final *e* is barely pronounced; these would sound like English *art* and *regime*
o	[u]	poç*o*, p*o*der	unstressed or final *o* is pronounced as in f*oo*t

PRONÚNCIA INGLESA

Em geral, damos a pronúncia de cada verbete em colchetes logo após a palavra em questão. Todavia, quando a verbete for composto de duas ou mais palavras, e cada uma delas aparecer em outro lugar no dicionário, o leitor encontrará a pronúncia de cada palavra na sua posição alfabética.

Vogais e ditongos

	Exemplo Inglês	Explicação
[aː]	father	Entre o *a* de p*a*dre e o *o* de n*ó*; como en f*a*da
[ʌ]	b*u*t, c*o*me	Aproximadamente como o primeiro *a* de c*a*ma
[æ]	m*a*n, c*a*t	Som entre o *a* de l*á* e o *e* de p*é*
[ə]	fath*er*, *a*go	Som parecido com o *e* final pronunciado em Portugal
[əː]	b*i*rd, h*ea*rd	Entre o *e* aberto e o *o* fechado
[ɛ]	g*e*t, b*e*d	Como em p*é*
[ɪ]	*i*t, b*i*g	Mais breve do que em s*i*
[iː]	t*ea*, s*ee*	Como em f*i*no
[ɔ]	h*o*t, w*a*sh	Como em p*ó*
[ɔː]	s*aw*, *a*ll	Como o *o* de p*o*rte
[u]	p*u*t, b*oo*k	Som breve e mais fechado do que em b*u*rro
[uː]	t*oo*, y*ou*	Som aberto como em j*u*ro
[aɪ]	fl*y*, h*igh*	Como em b*ai*le
[au]	h*ow*, h*ou*se	Como em c*au*sa
[ɛə]	th*ere*, b*ear*	Como o *e* de a*e*roporte
[eɪ]	d*ay*, ob*ey*	Como o *ei* de l*ei*
[ɪə]	h*ere*, h*ear*	Como *ia* de companh*ia*
[əu]	g*o*, n*o*te	[ə] seguido de um *u* breve
[ɔɪ]	b*oy*, *oi*l	Como em b*ói*a
[uə]	p*oor*, s*ure*	Como *ua* em s*ua*

Consoantes

	Exemplo Inglés	*Explicação*
[d]	men*d*ed	Como em *d*ado, an*d*ar
[g]	*g*et, bi*g*	Como em *g*rande
[dʒ]	*g*in, *j*u*dg*e	Como em ida*d*e
[ŋ]	si*ng*	Como em ci*n*co
[h]	*h*ouse, *h*e	*h* aspirado
[j]	*y*oung, *y*es	Como em *i*ogurte
[k]	*c*ome, mo*ck*	Como em *c*ama
[r]	*r*ed, t*r*ead	*r* como em para, mas pronunciado no céu da boca
[s]	*s*and, ye*s*	Como em *s*ala
[z]	ro*s*e, *z*ebra	Como em *z*ebra
[ʃ]	*sh*e, ma*ch*ine	Como em *ch*apéu
[tʃ]—	*ch*in, ri*ch*	Como *t* em *t*imbre
[w]	*w*ater, *w*hich	Como o *u* em ág*u*a
[ʒ]	vi*s*ion	Como em *j*á
[θ]	*th*ink, my*th*	Sem equivalente, aproximadamente como um *s* pronunciado entre os dentes
[ð]	*th*is, *th*e	Sem equivalente, aproximadamente como um *z* pronunciado entre os dentes

b, f, l, m, n, p, t, v pronunciam-se como em português.

O signo [*] indica que o r final escrito pronuncia-se apenas em inglês britânico, excepto quando a palavra seguinte começa por uma vogal. O signo ['] indica a sílaba acentuada.

EUROPEAN PORTUGUESE

The spelling of European Portuguese differs significantly from that of Brazilian. The differences, which affect consonant groups and accents, follow general patterns but do not on the whole conform to fixed rules. Limited space makes it impossible to cover all European forms in the dictionary text, but major differences in spelling and vocabulary have been included. In addition, the following guide is intended as a broad outline of these differences.

The following orthographic changes are consistent:

Brazilian *gü* and *qü* become European *gu* and *qu*, e.g. ag*ü*entar (*BR*), ag*u*entar (*PT*), cinq*ü*enta (*BR*), cinq*u*enta (*PT*)

Brazilian -*éia* becomes European -*eia*, e.g. id*éia* (*BR*), id*eia* (*PT*)

European spelling links forms of the verb *haver de* with a hyphen, e.g. *hei de* (*BR*), *hei-de* (*PT*)

The numbers dez*e*sseis (*BR*), dez*e*ssete (*BR*), dez*e*nove (*BR*) become dez*a*sseis (*PT*), dez*a*ssete (*PT*), dez*a*nove (*PT*)

Adverbial forms of adjectives ending in *m* take double *m* in European spelling, single *m* in Brazilian, e.g. comum*m*ente (*BR*), comum*mm*ente (*PT*)

European spelling adds an acute accent to the final *a* in first person plural preterite forms of regular -*ar* verbs to distinguish them from the present tense, e.g. am*a*mos (*BR*), am*á*mos (*PT*)

Brazilian co*n*osco becomes European co*nn*osco.

The following changes may take place, but are not consistent:

Consonant changes

Brazilian *c* and *ç* double to *cc* and *cç*, e.g. a*c*ionista (*BR*), a*cc*ionista (*PT*), se*ç*ão (*BR*), se*cç*ão (*PT*)

Brazilian *t* becomes *ct*, e.g. fa*t*o (*BR*), fa*ct*o (*PT*), edi*t*o (*BR*), edi*ct*o (*PT*)

European spelling adds *b* to certain words, e.g. sú*d*to (*BR*), su*bd*ito (*PT*), su*t*ilizar (*BR*), su*bt*ilizar (*PT*)

European spelling changes *ç*, *t* to *pç*, *pt*, e.g. exce*ç*ão (*BR*), exce*pç*ão (*PT*), ó*t*ico (*BR*), ó*pt*ico (*PT*)

Brazilian -*n*- becomes -*mn*-, e.g. a*n*istia (*BR*), a*mn*istia (*PT*)

Brazilian *tr* becomes *t*, e.g. regis*tr*o (*BR*), regis*t*o (*PT*)

Accentuation changes

Brazilian *ôo* loses circumflex accent, e.g. v*ôo* (*BR*), v*oo* (*PT*)

European spelling changes circumflex accent on *e* and *o* to acute, e.g. t*ê*nis (*BR*), t*é*nis (*PT*), abd*ô*men (*BR*), abd*ó*men (*PT*)

PORTUGUESE VERB FORMS

1 Gerund. 2 Imperative. 3 Present. 4 Imperfect. 5 Preterite. 6 Future. 7 Present subjunctive. 8 Imperfect subjunctive. 9 Future subjunctive. 10 Past participle. 11 Pluperfect. 12 Personal infinitive.

Etc indicates that the irregular root is used for all persons of the tense, e.g. **ouvir: 7** ouça, ouças, ouça, ouçamos, ouçais, ouçam.

abrir 10 aberto
acudir 2 acode **3** acudo, acodes, acode, acodem
aderir 3 adiro **7** adira
aduzir 2 aduz **3** aduzo, aduzes, aduz
advertir 3 advirto **7** advirta *etc*
agir 3 ajo **7** aja *etc*
agradecer 3 agradeço **7** agradeça *etc*
agredir 2 agride **3** agrido, agrides, agride, agridem **7** agrida *etc*
AMAR 1 amando **2** ama, amai **3** amo, amas, ama, amamos, amais, amam **4** amava, amavas, amava, amávamos, amáveis, amavam **5** amei, amaste, amou, amamos (*PT*: amá-), amastes, amaram **6** amarei, amarás, amará, amaremos, amareis, amarão **7** ame, ames, ame, amemos, ameis, amem **8** amasse, amasses, amasse, amássemos, amásseis, amassem **9** amar, amares, amar, ámarmos, amardes, amarem **10** amado **11** amara, amaras, amara, amáramos, amáreis, amaram **12** amar, amares, amar, amarmos, amardes, amarem
ansiar 2 anseia **3** anseio, anseias, anseia, anseiam **7** anseie *etc*
aprazer 2 apraz **3** aprazo, aprazes, apraz **5** aprouve *etc* **8** aprouvesse *etc* **9** aprouver *etc* **11** aprouvera *etc*
apreçar 7 aprece *etc*
arrancar 7 arranque *etc*
arruinar 2 arruína **3** arruíno, arruínas, arruína, arruínam **7** arruíne, arruínes, arruíne, arruínem
aspergir 3 aspirjo **7** aspirja *etc*
averiguar 7 averigúe, avergúes, averigúe, averigúem
boiar 2 bóia, bóias, bóia, bóiam **7** bóie, bóies, bóie, bóiem
bulir 2 bole **3** bulo, boles, bole, bolem
caber 3 caibo **5** coube *etc* **7** caiba *etc* **8** coubesse *etc* **9** couber *etc*
cair 2 cai **3** caio, cais, cai, caímos, caís, caem **4** caía *etc* **5** caí, caíste **7** caia *etc* **8** caísse *etc*
cobrir 3 cubro **7** cubra *etc* **10** coberto
colorir 3 coluro **7** colura *etc*
compelir 3 compilo **7** compila *etc*
crer 3 crê **3** creio, crês, crê, cremos, credes, crêem **5** cri, creste, creu, cremos, crestes, creram **7** creia *etc*

cuspir 2 cospe **3** cuspo, cospes, cospe, cospem
dar 2 dá **3** dou, dás, dá, damos, dais, dão **5** dei, deste, deu, demos, destes, deram **7** dê, dês, dê, demos, deis, dêem **8** desse *etc* **9** der *etc* **11** dera *etc*
denegrir 2 denigre **3** denigro, denigres, denigre, denigrem **7** denigra *etc*
despir 3 dispo **7** dispa *etc*
dizer 2 diz (dize) **3** digo, dizes, diz, dizemos, dizeis, dizem **5** disse *etc* **6** direi *etc* **7** diga *etc* **8** dissesse *etc* **9** disser *etc* **10** dito
doer 2 dói **3** dôo (*BR*), doo (*PT*), dóis, dói
dormir 3 durmo **7** durma *etc*
escrever 10 escrito
ESTAR 2 está **3** estou, estás, está, estamos, estais, estão **4** estava *etc* **5** estive, estiveste, esteve, estivemos, estivestes, estiveram **7** esteja *etc* **8** estivesse *etc* **9** estiver *etc* **11** estivera *etc*
extorquir 3 exturco **7** exturca *etc*
FAZER 3 faço **5** fiz, fizeste, fez, fizemos, fizestes, fizeram **6** farei *etc* **7** faça *etc* **8** fizesse *etc* **9** fizer *etc* **10** feito **11** fizera *etc*
ferir 3 firo **7** fira *etc*
flectir 3 flito **7** flita *etc*
fluir 3 fluo, fluis, flui, fluímos, fluís, fluem
fremir 3 frimo **7** frima *etc*
fruir 3 fruo, fruis, frui, fruímos, fruís, fruem
fugir 2 foge **3** fujo, foges, foge, fogem, fogem **7** fuja *etc*
ganhar 10 ganho
gastar 10 gasto
gerir 3 giro **7** gira *etc*
haver 2 há **3** hei, hás, há, havemos, haveis, hão **4** havia *etc* **5** houve, houveste, houve, houvemos, houvestes, houveram **7** haja *etc* **8** houvesse *etc* **9** houver *etc* **11** houvera *etc*
ir 1 indo **2** vai **3** vou, vais, vai, vamos, ides, vão **4** ia *etc* **5** fui, foste, foi, fomos, fostes, foram **7** vá, vás, vá, vamos, vades, vão **8** fosse, fosses, fosse, fôssemos, fôsseis, fossem **9** for *etc* **10** ido **11** fora *etc*
jazer 3 jazo, jazes, jaz
ler 2 lê **3** leio, lês, lê, lemos, ledes, lêem **5** li, leste, leu, lemos, lestes, leram **7** leia *etc*
medir 3 meço **7** meça *etc*
mentir 3 minto **7** minta *etc*
ouvir 3 ouço **7** ouça *etc*

pagar 10 pago
parar 2 pára 3 paro, paras, pára
parir 3 pairo 7 paira *etc*
pecar 7 peque *etc*
pedir 3 peço 7 peça *etc*
perder 3 perco 7 perca *etc*
poder 3 pesso 5 pude, pudeste, pôde, pudemos, pudestes, puderam 7 possa *etc* 8 pudesse *etc* 9 puder *etc* 11 pudera *etc*
polir 2 pule 3 pulo, pules, pule, pulem 7 pula *etc*
pôr 1 pondo 2 põe 3 ponho, pões, põe, pomos, pondes, põem 4 punha *etc* 5 pus, puseste, pôs, pusemos, pusestes, puseram 6 porei *etc* 7 ponha *etc* 8 pusesse *etc* 9 puser *etc* 10 posto 11 pusera *etc*
preferir 3 prefiro 7 prefire *etc*
premir 2 prime 3 primo, primes, prime, primem 7 prima *etc*
prevenir 2 previne 3 previno, prevines, previne, previnem 7 previna *etc*
prover 2 provê 3 provejo, provês, provê, provemos, provedes, provêem 5 provi, proveste, proveu, provemos, provestes, proveram 7 proveja *etc* 8 provesse *etc* 9 prover *etc*
provir 2 provém 3 provenho, provéns, provém, provimos, provindes, provêm 4 provinha *etc* 5 provim, provieste, proveio, proviemos, proviestes, provieram 7 provenha *etc* 8 proviesse *etc* 9 provier *etc* 10 provindo 11 proviera *etc*
querer 3 quero, queres, quer 5 quis, quiseste, quis, quisemos, quisestes, quiseram 7 queira *etc* 8 quisesse *etc* 9 quiser *etc* 11 quisera *etc*
repetir 3 repito 7 repita *etc*
requerer 3 requeiro, requeres, requer 7 requeira *etc*
retorquir 3 returco 7 returca *etc*
reunir 2 reúne 3 reúno, reúnes, reúne, reúnem 7 reúna *etc*
rir 2 ri 3 rio, ris, ri, rimos, rides, riem 5 ri, riste, riu, rimos, ristes, riram 7 ria *etc*
saber 3 sei, sabes, sabe, sabemos, sabeis, sabem 5 soube, soubeste, soube, soubemos, soubestes, souberam 7 saiba *etc* 8 soubesse *etc* 9 souber *etc* 11 soubera *etc*
seguir 3 sigo 7 siga *etc*
sentir 3 sinto 7 sinta *etc*
ser 2 sê 3 sou, és, é, somos, sois, são 4 era *etc* 5 fui, foste, foi, fomos, fostes, foram 7 seja *etc* 8 fosse *etc* 9 for *etc* 11 fora *etc*
servir 3 sirvo 7 sirva *etc*

subir 2 sobe 3 subo, sobes, sobe, sobem
suster 2 sustém 3 sustenho, sustens, sustém, sustendes, sustêm 5 sustive, sustiveste, susteve, sustivemos, sustivestes, sustiveram 7 sustenha *etc*
ter 2 tem 3 tenho, tens, tem, temos, tendes, têm 4 tinha *etc* 5 tive, tiveste, teve, tivemos, tivestes, tiveram 6 terei *etc* 7 tenha *etc* 8 tivesse *etc* 8 tiver *etc* 11 tivera *etc*
torcer 3 torço 7 torça *etc*
tossir 3 tusso 7 tussa *etc*
trair 2 trai 3 traio, trais, trai, traímos, traís, traem 7 traia *etc*
trazer 2 (traze) traz 3 trago, trazes, traz 5 trouxe, trouxeste, trouxe, trouxemos, trouxestes, trouxeram 6 trarei *etc* 7 traga *etc* 8 trouxesse *etc* 9 trouxer *etc* 11 trouxera *etc*
UNIR 1 unindo 2 une, uni 3 uno, unes, une, unimos, unis, unem 4 unia, unias, unia, uníamos, uníeis, uniam 5 uni, uniste, uniu, unimos, unistes, uniram 6 unirei, unirás, unirá, uniremos, unireis, unirão 7 una, unas, una, unamos, unais, unam 8 unisse, unisses, unisse, uníssemos, unísseis, unissem 9 unir, unires, unir, unirmos, unirdes, unirem 10 unido 11 unira, uniras, unira, uníramos, uníreis, uniram 12 unir, unires, unir, unirmos, unirdes, unirem
valer 3 valho 7 valha *etc*
ver 2 vê 3 vejo, vês, vê, vemos, vedes, vêem 4 via *etc* 5 vi, viste, viu, vimos, vistes, viram 7 veja *etc* 8 visse *etc* 9 vir *etc* 10 visto 11 vira
vir 1 vindo 2 vem 3 venho, vens, vem, vimos, vindes, vêm 4 vinha *etc* 5 vim, vieste, veio, viemos, viestes, vieram 7 venha *etc* 8 viesse *etc* 9 vier *etc* 10 vindo 11 viera *etc*
VIVER 1 vivendo 2 vive, vivei 3 vivo, vives, vive, vivemos, viveis, vivem 4 vivia, vivias, vivia, vivíamos, vivíeis, viviam 5 vivi, viveste, viveu, vivemos, vivestes, viveram 6 viverei, viverás, viverá, viveremos, vivereis, viverão 7 viva, vivas, viva, vivamos, vivais, vivam 8 vivesse, vivesses, vivesse, vivêssemos, vivêsseis, vivessem 9 viver, viveres, viver, vivermos, viverdes, viverem 10 vivido 11 vivera, viveras, vivera, vivêramos, vivêreis, viveram 12 viver, viveres, viver, vivermos, viverdes, viverem

VERBOS INGLESES

present	pt	pp	present	pt	pp
arise (arising)	arose	arisen	eat	ate	eaten
			fall	fell	fallen
awake (awaking)	awoke	awaked	feed	fed	fed
			feel	felt	felt
be (am, is, are, being)	was, were	been	fight	fought	fought
			find	found	found
bear	bore	born(e)	flee	fled	fled
beat	beat	beaten	fling	flung	flung
become (becoming)	became	become	fly (flies)	flew	flown
			forbid (forbidding)	forbade	forbidden
befall	befell	befallen			
begin (beginning)	began	begun	forecast	forecast	forecast
			forego	forewent	foregone
behold	beheld	beheld	foresee	foresaw	foreseen
bend	bent	bent	foretell	foretold	foretold
beseech	besought	besought	forget (forgetting)	forgot	forgotten
beset (besetting)	beset	beset	forgive (forgiving)	forgave	forgiven
bet (betting)	bet (also betted)	bet (also betted)	forsake (forsaking)	forsook	forsaken
bid (bidding)	bid (also bade)	bid (also bidden)	freeze (freezing)	froze	frozen
bind	bound	bound			
bite (biting)	bit	bitten	get (getting)	got	got, (US) gotten
bleed	bled	bled			
blow	blew	blown	give (giving)	gave	given
break	broke	broken	go (goes)	went	gone
breed	bred	bred	grind	ground	ground
bring	brought	brought	grow	grew	grown
build	built	built	hang	hung (also hanged)	hung (also hanged)
burn	burnt (also burned)	burnt (also burned)	have (has; having)	had	had
burst	burst	burst			
buy	bought	bought	hear	heard	heard
can	could	(been able)	hide (hiding)	hid	hidden
cast	cast	cast	hit (hitting)	hit	hit
catch	caught	caught	hold	held	held
choose (choosing)	chose	chosen	hurt	hurt	hurt
			keep	kept	kept
cling	clung	clung	kneel	knelt (also kneeled)	knelt (also kneeled)
come (coming)	came	come			
			know	knew	known
cost	cost	cost	lay	laid	laid
creep	crept	crept	lead	led	led
cut (cutting)	cut	cut	lean	leant (also leaned)	leant (also leaned)
deal	dealt	dealt			
dig (digging)	dug	dug	leap	leapt (also leaped)	leapt (also leaped)
do (3rd person: he/she/it/does)	did	done	learn	learnt (also learned)	learnt (also learned)
draw	drew	drawn	leave (leaving)	left	left
dream	dreamed (also dreamt)	dreamed (also dreamt)	lend	lent	lent
			let (letting)	let	let
drink	drank	drunk	lie (lying)	lay	lain
drive (driving)	drove	driven	light	lit (also lighted)	lit (also lighted)
dwell	dwelt	dwelt	lose (losing)	lost	lost

present	pt	pp	present	pt	pp
make (making)	made	made	spell	spelt (*also* spelled)	spelt (*also* spelled)
may	might	—	spend	spent	spent
mean	meant	meant	spill	spilt (*also* spilled)	spilt (*also* spilled)
meet	met	met			
mistake (mistaking)	mistook	mistaken	spin (spinning)	spun	spun
mow	mowed	mown (*also* mowed)	spit (spitting)	spat	spat
			split (splitting)	split	split
must	(had to)	(had to)	spoil	spoiled (*also* spoilt)	spoiled (*also* spoilt)
pay	paid	paid			
put (putting)	put	put	spread	spread	spread
quit (quitting)	quit (*also* quitted)	quit (*also* quitted)	spring	sprang	sprung
read	read	read	stand	stood	stood
rend	rent	rent	steal	stole	stolen
rid (ridding)	rid	rid	stick	stuck	stuck
ride (riding)	rode	ridden	sting	stung	stung
ring	rang	rung	stink	stank	stunk
rise (rising)	rose	risen	stride (striding)	strode	stridden
run (running)	ran	run	strike (striking)	struck	struck (*also* stricken)
saw	sawed	sawn			
say	said	said	strive (striving)	strove	striven
see	saw	seen			
seek	sought	sought	swear	swore	sworn
sell	sold	sold	sweep	swept	swept
send	sent	sent	swell	swelled	swollen (*also* swelled)
set (setting)	set	set			
shake (shaking)	shook	shaken	swim (swimming)	swam	swum
shall	should	—			
shear	sheared	shorn (*also* sheared)	swing	swung	swung
			take (taking)	took	taken
shed (shedding)	shed	shed	teach	taught	taught
			tear	tore	torn
shine (shining)	shone	shone	tell	told	told
			think	thought	thought
shoot	shot	shot	throw	threw	thrown
show	showed	shown	thrust	thrust	thrust
shrink	shrank	shrunk	tread	trod	trodden
shut (shutting)	shut	shut	wake (waking)	woke (*also* waked)	woken (*also* waked)
sing	sang	sung	waylay	waylaid	waylaid
sink	sank	sunk	wear	wore	worn
sit (sitting)	sat	sat	weave (weaving)	wove (*also* weaved)	woven (*also* weaved)
slay	slew	slain			
sleep	slept	slept	wed (wedding)	wedded (*also* wed)	wedded (*also* wed)
slide (sliding)	slid	slid			
sling	slung	slung	weep	wept	wept
slit (slitting)	slit	slit	win (winning)	won	won
smell	smelled, (*BRIT*) smelt	smelled, (*BRIT*) smelt	wind	wound	wound
			withdraw	withdrew	withdrawn
sow	sowed	sown (*also* sowed)	withhold	withheld	withheld
			withstand	withstood	withstood
speak	spoke	spoken	wring	wrung	wrung
speed	sped (*also* speeded)	sped (*also* speeded)	write (writing)	wrote	written

NÚMEROS

NUMBERS

um (uma)*	1	one
dois (duas)*	2	two
três	3	three
quatro	4	four
cinco	5	five
seis	6	six
sete	7	seven
oito	8	eight
nove	9	nine
dez	10	ten
onze	11	eleven
doze	12	twelve
treze	13	thirteen
catorze	14	fourteen
quinze	15	fifteen
dezesseis (BR), dezasseis (PT)	16	sixteen
dezessete (BR), dezassete (PT)	17	seventeen
dezoito	18	eighteen
dezenove (BR), dezanove (PT)	19	nineteen
vinte	20	twenty
vinte e um (uma)*	21	twenty-one
trinta	30	thirty
quarenta	40	forty
cinqüenta (BR), cinquenta (PT)	50	fifty
sessenta	60	sixty
setenta	70	seventy
oitenta	80	eighty
noventa	90	ninety
cem (cento)**	100	a hundred
cem e um (uma)*	101	a hundred and one
duzentos/as*	200	two hundred
trezentos/as*	300	three hundred
quinhentos/as*	500	five hundred
mil	1 000	a thousand
un milhão	1 000 000	a million

primeiro/a, 1º/1ª	first, 1st	trigésimo/a	thirtieth
segundo/a, 2º/2ª	second, 2nd	quadragésimo/a	fortieth
terceiro/a, 3º/3ª	third, 3rd	qüinquagésimo/a (BR), quinquagésimo/a (PT)	fiftieth
quarto/a, 4º/4ª	fourth, 4th		
quinto/a	fifth	sexagésimo/a	sixtieth
sexto/a	sixth	setuagésimo/a (BR), septuagésimo/a (PT)	seventieth
sétimo/a	seventh		
oitavo/a	eighth	octagésimo/a	eightieth
nono/a	ninth	nonagésimo/a	ninetieth
décimo/a	tenth	centésimo/a	hundredth
décimo primeiro/a	eleventh	milésimo/a	thousandth
vigésimo/a	twentieth		

* "um" *etc*, "dois" *etc* and the hundreds (duzentos *etc*) agree in gender with their noun: trinta e uma pessoas. NB: 2 000 is **duas** mil before a feminine noun.

** "cem" is used when not followed by a lower number: cem mil, cem mulheres *etc*; "cento e" is used when a lower follows: cento e vinte dias.

ENGLISH-PORTUGUESE
INGLÊS-PORTUGUÊS

A

A, a [eɪ] *n* (*letter*) A, a *m*; (*MUS*): **A** lá *m*; **A for Andrew** (*BRIT*) *or* **Able** (*US*) A de Antônio; **A road** (*BRIT*: *AUT*) via expressa; **A shares** (*BRIT*: *STOCK EXCHANGE*) ações *fpl* preferenciais.

a [eɪ, ə] (*before vowel or silent h*: **an**) *indef art* um(a); **an apple** uma maçã; **I haven't got ~ car** não tenho carro; **he's ~ doctor** ele é médico; **3 a day/week** 3 por dia/semana; **10 km an hour** 10 km por hora.

a. *abbr* = **acre**.

AA *n abbr* (*BRIT*: = *Automobile Association*) ≈ TCB *m* (*BR*), ≈ ACP *m* (*PT*); (*US*: = *Associate in/of Arts*) título universitário; (= *Alcoholics Anonymous*) AA *m*; (= *antiaircraft*) AA.

AAA *n abbr* (= *American Automobile Association*) ≈ TCB *m* (*BR*), ≈ ACP *m* (*PT*); (*BRIT*) = **Amateur Athletics Association**.

AAUP *n abbr* (= *American Association of University Professors*) sindicato universitário.

AB *abbr* (*BRIT*) = **able-bodied seaman**; (*CANADA*) = **Alberta**.

aback [ə'bæk] *adv*: **to be taken ~** ficar surpreendido, sobressaltar-se.

abaci ['æbəsaɪ] *npl of* **abacus**.

abacus ['æbəkəs] (*pl* **abaci**) *n* ábaco.

abandon [ə'bændən] *vt* abandonar ♦ *n* desenfreamento; **to ~ ship** abandonar o navio.

abandoned [ə'bændənd] *adj* (*child, house*) abandonado; (*unrestrained*) desenfreado.

abase [ə'beɪs] *vt*: **to ~ o.s. (so far as to do)** rebaixar-se (até o ponto de fazer).

abashed [ə'bæʃt] *adj* envergonhado.

abate [ə'beɪt] *vi* (*lessen*) diminuir; (*calm down*) acalmar-se.

abatement [ə'beɪtmənt] *n see* **noise**.

abattoir ['æbətwɑː*] (*BRIT*) *n* matadouro.

abbey ['æbɪ] *n* abadia, mosteiro.

abbot ['æbət] *n* abade *m*.

abbreviate [ə'briːvɪeɪt] *vt* abreviar.

abbreviation [əbriːvɪ'eɪʃən] *n* (*short form*) abreviatura; (*act*) abreviação *f*.

ABC *n abbr* (= *American Broadcasting Company*) rede de televisão.

abdicate ['æbdɪkeɪt] *vt* abdicar, renunciar a ♦ *vi* abdicar, renunciar ao trono.

abdication [æbdɪ'keɪʃən] *n* abdicação *f*.

abdomen ['æbdəmən] *n* abdômen *m*.

abdominal [æb'dɔmɪnl] *adj* abdominal.

abduct [æb'dʌkt] *vt* seqüestrar.

abduction [æb'dʌkʃən] *n* seqüestro.

Aberdonian [æbə'dəunɪən] *adj* de Aberdeen ♦ *n* natural *m/f* de Aberdeen.

aberration [æbə'reɪʃən] *n* aberração *f*; **in a moment of mental ~** num momento de desatino.

abet [ə'bɛt] *vt see* **aid**.

abeyance [ə'beɪəns] *n*: **in ~** (*law*) em desuso; (*matter*) suspenso.

abhor [əb'hɔː*] *vt* detestar, odiar.

abhorrent [əb'hɔrənt] *adj* detestável, repugnante.

abide [ə'baɪd] *vt* agüentar, suportar.

abide by *vt fus* (*promise, word*) cumprir; (*law, rules*) ater-se a.

ability [ə'bɪlɪtɪ] *n* habilidade *f*, capacidade *f*; (*talent*) talento; **to the best of my ~** o melhor que eu puder *or* pudesse.

abject ['æbdʒɛkt] *adj* (*poverty*) miserável; (*coward*) desprezível, vil; **an ~ apology** um pedido de desculpa humilde.

ablaze [ə'bleɪz] *adj* em chamas; **~ with light** resplandecente.

able ['eɪbl] *adj* capaz; (*skilled*) hábil, competente; **to be ~ to do sth** poder fazer alguma coisa.

able-bodied [-'bɔdɪd] *adj* são/sã; **~ seaman** (*BRIT*) marinheiro experimentado.

ably ['eɪblɪ] *adv* habilmente.

ABM *n abbr* = **anti-ballistic missile**.

abnormal [æb'nɔːməl] *adj* anormal.

abnormality [æbnɔː'mælɪtɪ] *n* anormalidade *f*.

aboard [ə'bɔːd] *adv* a bordo ♦ *prep* a bordo de; (*train*) dentro de.

abode [ə'bəud] *n* (*old*) residência, domicílio; (*LAW*): **of no fixed ~** sem domicílio fixo.

abolish [ə'bɔlɪʃ] *vt* abolir.

abolition [æbə'lɪʃən] *n* abolição *f*.

abominable [ə'bɔmɪnəbl] *adj* abominável, detestável.

aborigine [æbə'rɪdʒɪnɪ] *n* aborígene *m/f*.

abort [ə'bɔːt] *vt* abortar.

abortion [ə'bɔːʃən] *n* aborto; **to have an ~** fazer um aborto.

abortive [ə'bɔːtɪv] *adj* (*failed*) fracassado; (*fruitless*) inútil.

abound [ə'baund] *vi*: **to ~ (in)** abundar (em).

about [ə'baut] *prep* (*subject*) acerca de, sobre; (*place*) em redor de, por ♦ *adv* mais ou menos; **do something ~ it!** faça alguma coisa!; **it takes ~ 10 hours** leva mais ou menos 10 horas; **at ~ 2 o'clock** aproximadamente às duas; **it's just ~ finished** está quase

terminado; **is Paul ~?** (BRIT) o Paulo está
por aí?; **it's the other way ~** (BRIT) está
pelo avesso; **it's ~ here** é por aqui; **to walk
~ the town** andar pela cidade; **to run ~**
(BRIT) correr por todos os lados; **they left all
their things lying ~** eles deixaram suas coisas espalhadas por toda parte; **to be ~ to**
estar a ponto de; **I'm not ~ to do all that for
nothing** (inf) não estou disposto a fazer tudo
isso de graça; **what** or **how ~ doing this?**
que tal se fizermos isso?
about face n (MIL) meia-volta; (fig) reviravolta.
about turn n (MIL) meia-volta; (fig) reviravolta.
above [əˈbʌv] adv em/por cima, acima ♦ prep
acima de, por cima de; **mentioned ~** acima
mencionado; **costing ~ £10** que custa mais
de £10; **~ all** sobretudo.
aboveboard [əˈbʌvˈbɔːd] adj legítimo, limpo.
abrasion [əˈbreɪʒən] n (on skin) esfoladura.
abrasive [əˈbreɪzɪv] adj abrasivo; (fig) cáustico, mordaz.
abreast [əˈbrest] adv lado a lado; **to keep ~
of** estar a par de.
abridge [əˈbrɪdʒ] vt resumir, abreviar.
abroad [əˈbrɔːd] adv (to be) no estrangeiro;
(to go) ao estrangeiro; **there is a rumour ~
that ...** (fig) corre o boato de que ....
abrupt [əˈbrʌpt] adj (sudden) brusco, inesperado; (gruff) áspero.
abruptly [əˈbrʌptlɪ] adv bruscamente.
abscess [ˈæbsɪs] n abscesso (BR), abcesso (PT).
abscond [əbˈskɒnd] vi fugir, sumir.
absence [ˈæbsəns] n ausência; **in the ~ of**
(person) na ausência de; (thing) na falta de.
absent [ˈæbsənt] adj ausente; **~ without leave**
ausente sem permissão oficial; **to be ~**
faltar.
absentee [æbsənˈtiː] n ausente m/f.
absenteeism [æbsənˈtiːɪzəm] n absenteísmo.
absent-minded adj distraído.
absent-mindedness [-ˈmaɪndɪdnɪs] n distração f.
absolute [ˈæbsəluːt] adj absoluto.
absolutely [æbsəˈluːtlɪ] adv absolutamente;
oh, yes, ~! claro que sim!
absolve [əbˈzɒlv] vt: **to ~ sb (from)** (sin etc)
absolver alguém (de); **to ~ sb from** (oath)
desobrigar alguém de.
absorb [əbˈzɔːb] vt absorver; **to be ~ed in a
book** estar absorvido num livro.
absorbent [əbˈzɔːbənt] adj absorvente.
absorbent cotton (US) n algodão m hidrófilo.
absorbing [əbˈzɔːbɪŋ] adj (book, film etc) absorvente, cativante.
absorption [əbˈzɔːpʃən] n absorção f.
abstain [əbˈsteɪn] vi: **to ~ (from)** abster-se
(de).
abstemious [əbˈstiːmɪəs] adj abstinente.
abstention [əbˈstenʃən] n abstenção f.
abstinence [ˈæbstɪnəns] n abstinência, sobriedade f.
abstract [adj, n ˈæbstrækt, vt æbˈstrækt] adj abs-

trato ♦ n resumo ♦ vt (remove) abstrair;
(summarize) resumir; (steal) surripiar.
absurd [əbˈsɔːd] adj absurdo.
absurdity [əbˈsɔːdɪtɪ] n absurdo.
ABTA [ˈæbtə] n abbr = **Association of British
Travel Agents.**
Abu Dhabi [ˈæbuːˈdɑːbɪ] n Abu Dabi (no article).
abundance [əˈbʌndəns] n abundância.
abundant [əˈbʌndənt] adj abundante.
abuse [n əˈbjuːs, vt əˈbjuːz] n (insults) insultos
mpl, injúrias fpl; (misuse) abuso ♦ vt (ill-
treat) maltratar; (take advantage of) abusar
de; **open to ~** aberto ao abuso.
abusive [əˈbjuːsɪv] adj ofensivo.
abysmal [əˈbɪzməl] adj (ignorance) profundo,
total; (very bad) péssimo.
abyss [əˈbɪs] n abismo.
AC n abbr (US) = **athletic club** ♦ abbr (=
alternating current) CA.
a/c abbr (BANKING etc: = account) c/.
academic [ækəˈdemɪk] adj acadêmico, universitário; (pej: issue) teórico ♦ n
universitário/a; **~ freedom** liberdade de cátedra.
academic year n ano letivo.
academy [əˈkædəmɪ] n (learned body) academia; (school) instituto, academia, colégio;
military/naval ~ academia militar/escola naval; **~ of music** conservatório.
ACAS [ˈeɪkæs] (BRIT) n abbr (= Advisory, Conciliation and Arbitration Service) ≈ Justiça
do Trabalho.
accede [ækˈsiːd] vi: **to ~ to** (request)
consentir em, aceder a; (throne) subir a.
accelerate [ækˈseləreɪt] vt acelerar ♦ vi
apressar-se.
acceleration [ækseləˈreɪʃən] n aceleração f.
accelerator [ækˈseləreɪtə*] n acelerador m.
accent [ˈæksent] n (stress, written) acento;
(pronunciation) sotaque m.
accentuate [ækˈsentjueɪt] vt (syllable)
acentuar; (need, difference etc) ressaltar, salientar.
accept [əkˈsept] vt aceitar.
acceptable [əkˈseptəbl] adj aceitável.
acceptance [əkˈseptəns] n aceitação f; **to
meet with general ~** ter aprovação geral.
access [ˈækses] n acesso ♦ vt (COMPUT)
acessar; **to have ~ to** ter acesso a; **the
burglars gained ~ through a window** os ladrões conseguiram entrar por uma janela.
accessible [ækˈsesəbl] adj acessível.
accession [ækˈseʃən] n acessão f; (of king)
elevação f ao trono; (to library) aquisição f.
accessory [ækˈsesərɪ] n acessório; **toilet
accessories** (BRIT) artigos de toalete.
access road n via de acesso.
access time n (COMPUT) tempo de acesso.
accident [ˈæksɪdənt] n acidente m; (chance)
casualidade f; **to meet with** or **have an ~**
sofrer or ter um acidente; **~s at work** acidentes de trabalho; **by ~** (unintentionally)
sem querer; (by coincidence) por acaso.
accidental [æksɪˈdentl] adj acidental.

accidentally [æksɪ'dɛntəlɪ] *adv* (*by accident*) sem querer; (*by chance*) casualmente.

accident insurance *n* seguro contra acidentes.

accident-prone *adj* com tendência para sofrer *or* causar acidente, desastrado.

acclaim [ə'kleɪm] *vt* aclamar ♦ *n* aclamação *f*.

acclamation [æklə'meɪʃən] *n* (*approval*) aclamação *f*; (*applause*) aplausos *mpl*.

acclimate [ə'klaɪmət] (*US*) *vt* = **acclimatize**.

acclimatize [ə'klaɪmətaɪz] (*BRIT*) *vt*: **to become ~d** aclimatar-se.

accolade ['ækəleɪd] *n* louvor *m*, honra.

accommodate [ə'kɒmədeɪt] *vt* alojar, hospedar; (*reconcile*) conciliar; (*oblige, help*) comprazer a; (*adapt*): **to ~ one's plans to** acomodar seus projetos a; **this car ~s 4 people** este carro tem lugar para 4 pessoas.

accommodating [ə'kɒmədeɪtɪŋ] *adj* complacente, serviçal.

accommodation [əkɒmə'deɪʃən] (*BRIT*) *n* alojamento; (*space*) lugar *m* (*BR*), sítio (*PT*); **he's found ~** ele já encontrou um lugar para morar; **"~ to let"** "aluga-se (apartamento *etc*)"; **they have ~ for 500** têm lugar para 500 pessoas; **seating ~** lugares *mpl* sentados.

accommodations [əkɒmə'deɪʃənz] (*US*) *npl* = **accommodation**.

accompaniment [ə'kʌmpənɪmənt] *n* acompanhamento.

accompanist [ə'kʌmpənɪst] *n* acompanhador(a) *m/f*, acompanhante *m/f*.

accompany [ə'kʌmpənɪ] *vt* acompanhar.

accomplice [ə'kʌmplɪs] *n* cúmplice *m/f*.

accomplish [ə'kʌmplɪʃ] *vt* (*achieve*) realizar, levar a cabo.

accomplished [ə'kʌmplɪʃt] *adj* ilustre, talentoso.

accomplishment [ə'kʌmplɪʃmənt] *n* (*bringing about*) realização *f*; (*achievement*) proeza; **~s** *npl* (*skills*) talentos *mpl*.

accord [ə'kɔːd] *n* acordo ♦ *vt* conceder; **of his own ~** por sua iniciativa; **with one ~** de comum acordo.

accordance [ə'kɔːdəns] *n*: **in ~ with** de acordo com, conforme.

according [ə'kɔːdɪŋ]: **~ to** *prep* segundo; (*in accordance with*) conforme; **~ to plan** como previsto.

accordingly [ə'kɔːdɪŋlɪ] *adv* (*thus*) por conseguinte, conseqüentemente.

accordion [ə'kɔːdɪən] *n* acordeão *m*.

accost [ə'kɒst] *vt* abordar.

account [ə'kaunt] *n* (*COMM*) conta; (*report*) relato; **~s** *npl* (*books, department*) contabilidade *f*; **"~ payee only"** (*BRIT*) "cheque não endossável"** (*a ser creditado na conta do favorecido*); **to keep an ~ of** anotar, registrar; **to bring sb to ~ for sth/for having done sth** chamar alguém a contas por algo/ por ter feito algo; **by all ~s** segundo dizem todos; **of little ~** sem importância; **on his own ~** por sua conta; **to pay £5 on ~** pagar £5 por conta; **to buy sth on ~** comprar algo a crédito; **on no ~** de modo nenhum; **on ~ of** por causa de; **to take into ~, take ~ of** levar em conta.

account for *vt fus* prestar contas de; **all the children were ~ed for** nenhuma das crianças faltava; **4 people are still not ~ed for** 4 pessoas ainda não foram encontradas.

accountability [əkauntə'bɪlɪtɪ] *n* responsabilidade *f*.

accountable [ə'kauntəbl] *adj* responsável.

accountancy [ə'kauntənsɪ] *n* contabilidade *f*.

accountant [ə'kauntənt] *n* contador(a) *m/f* (*BR*), contabilista *m/f* (*PT*).

accounting [ə'kauntɪŋ] *n* contabilidade *f*.

accounting period *n* exercício.

account number *n* número de conta.

account payable *n* conta a pagar.

account receivable *n* conta a receber.

accredited [ə'krɛdɪtɪd] *adj* (*person*) autorizado.

accretion [ə'kriːʃən] *n* acresção *f*.

accrue [ə'kruː] *vi* aumentar; (*mount up*) acumular-se; **to ~ to** advir a; **~d interest** juros *mpl* acumulados.

accumulate [ə'kjuːmjuleɪt] *vt* acumular, amontoar ♦ *vi* acumular-se.

accumulation [əkjuːmju'leɪʃən] *n* acumulação *f*.

accuracy ['ækjurəsɪ] *n* exatidão *f*, precisão *f*.

accurate ['ækjurɪt] *adj* (*number*) exato; (*answer*) correto; (*shot*) certeiro.

accurately ['ækjurətlɪ] *adv* com precisão.

accusation [ækju'zeɪʃən] *n* acusação *f*.

accusative [ə'kjuːzətɪv] *n* (*LING*) acusativo.

accuse [ə'kjuːz] *vt* acusar.

accused [ə'kjuːzd] *n* acusado/a.

accustom [ə'kʌstəm] *vt* acostumar; **to ~ o.s. to sth** acostumar-se a algo.

accustomed [ə'kʌstəmd] *adj* (*usual*) habitual; **~ to** acostumado a.

AC/DC *abbr* (= *alternating current/direct current*) CA/CC.

ACE [eɪs] *n abbr* = **American Council on Education**.

ace [eɪs] *n* ás *m*; **to be** *or* **come within an ~ of doing** (*BRIT*) não fazer por um triz.

acerbic [ə'sɜːbɪk] *adj* (*also fig*) acerbo.

acetate ['æsɪteɪt] *n* acetato.

ache [eɪk] *n* dor *f* ♦ *vi* doer; (*yearn*): **to ~ to do sth** ansiar por fazer algo; **I've got (a) stomach ~** eu estou com dor de barriga; **my head ~s** dói-me a cabeça; **I'm aching all over** estou todo dolorido.

achieve [ə'tʃiːv] *vt* (*reach*) alcançar; (*realize*) realizar; (*victory, success*) obter.

achievement [ə'tʃiːvmənt] *n* (*of aims*) realização *f*; (*success*) proeza.

acid ['æsɪd] *adj* ácido; (*bitter*) azedo ♦ *n* ácido.

acidity [ə'sɪdɪtɪ] *n* acidez *f*.

acid rain *n* chuva ácida.

NB: European Portuguese adds the following consonants to certain words: **b** (sú(b)dito, su(b)til); **c** (a(c)ção, a(c)cionista, a(c)to); **m** (inde(m)ne); **p** (ado(p)ção, ado(p)tar); *for further details see p. xiii.*

acknowledge [ək'nɔlɪdʒ] *vt* reconhecer; (*also:* ~ *receipt of*) acusar o recebimento de (*BR*) *or* a recepção de (*PT*); (*fact*) admitir.

acknowledgement [ək'nɔlɪdʒmənt] *n* reconhecimento, notificação *f* de recebimento; ~**s** *npl* (*in book*) agradecimentos *mpl*.

ACLU *n abbr* (= *American Civil Liberties Union*) *associação que defende os direitos humanos*.

acme ['ækmɪ] *n* acme *m*.

acne ['æknɪ] *n* acne *f*.

acorn ['eɪkɔ:n] *n* bolota.

acoustic [ə'ku:stɪk] *adj* acústico.

acoustic coupler *n* (*COMPUT*) acoplador *m* acústico.

acoustics [ə'ku:stɪks] *n, npl* acústica.

acoustic screen *n* divisória.

acquaint [ə'kweɪnt] *vt*: **to ~ sb with sth** (*inform*) pôr alguém ao corrente de alguma coisa; **to be ~ed with** (*person*) conhecer; (*fact*) saber.

acquaintance [ə'kweɪntəns] *n* conhecimento; (*person*) conhecido/a; **to make sb's ~** conhecer alguém.

acquiesce [ækwɪ'es] *vi*: **to ~ (in)** condescender (com).

acquire [ə'kwaɪə*] *vt* adquirir.

acquired [ə'kwaɪəd] *adj* adquirido; **an ~ taste** um gosto cultivado.

acquisition [ækwɪ'zɪʃən] *n* aquisição *f*.

acquisitive [ə'kwɪzɪtɪv] *adj* cobiçoso.

acquit [ə'kwɪt] *vt* absolver; **to ~ o.s. well** desempenhar-se bem.

acquittal [ə'kwɪtəl] *n* absolvição *f*.

acre ['eɪkə*] *n* acre *m* (= 4047*m²*).

acreage ['eɪkərɪdʒ] *n* extensão *f* (em acres).

acrid ['ækrɪd] *adj* (*smell*) acre, pungente; (*fig*) mordaz.

acrimonious [ækrɪ'məʊnɪəs] *adj* (*remark*) mordaz; (*argument*) acrimonioso.

acrobat ['ækrəbæt] *n* acrobata *m/f*.

acrobatic [ækrə'bætɪk] *adj* acrobático.

acrobatics [ækrə'bætɪks] *npl* acrobacia.

Acropolis [ə'krɔpəlɪs] *n*: **the ~** a Acrópole.

across [ə'krɔs] *prep* (*on the other side of*) no outro lado de; (*crosswise*) através de ♦ *adv* transversalmente, de um lado ao outro; **to walk ~ (the road)** atravessar (a rua); **to run/swim ~** atravessar correndo/a nado; **the lake is 12 km ~** o lago tem 12 km de largura; **~ from** em frente de; **to get sth ~ (to sb)** conseguir comunicar algo (a alguém).

acrylic [ə'krɪlɪk] *adj, n* acrílico.

ACT *n abbr* (= *American College Test*) ≈ vestibular *m*.

act [ækt] *n* ação *f*; (*THEATRE*) ato; (*in music-hall etc*) número; (*LAW*) lei *f* ♦ *vi* (*THEATRE*) representar; (*pretend*) fingir; (*take action*) tomar atitude ♦ *vt* (*part*) representar; **~ of God** (*LAW*) força maior; **to catch sb in the ~** apanhar alguém em flagrante, flagrar alguém; **it's only an ~** é só encenação; **to ~ Hamlet** (*BRIT*) representar Hamlet; **to ~ the fool** (*BRIT*) fazer-se de bobo; **to ~ as** servir de; **it ~s as a deterrent** serve para dissua-

dir; **~ing in my capacity as chairman, I ...** na qualidade de presidente, eu ....

act on *vt fus*: **to ~ on sth** agir de acordo com algo.

act out *vt* (*event*) representar; (*fantasy*) realizar.

acting ['æktɪŋ] *adj* interino ♦ *n* (*performance*) representação *f*, atuação *f*; (*activity*): **to do some ~** fazer teatro.

action ['ækʃən] *n* ação *f*; (*MIL*) batalha, combate *m*; (*LAW*) ação judicial; **to bring an ~ against sb** (*LAW*) intentar ação judicial contra alguém; **killed in ~** (*MIL*) morto em combate; **out of ~** fora de combate; (*machine*) com defeito; **to take ~** tomar atitude; **to put a plan into ~** pôr um plano em ação.

action replay (*BRIT*) *n* (*TV*) replay *m*.

activate ['æktɪveɪt] *vt* (*mechanism*) acionar; (*CHEM, PHYS*) ativar.

active ['æktɪv] *adj* ativo; (*volcano*) em atividade.

active duty (*US*) *n* (*MIL*) ativa.

actively ['æktɪvlɪ] *adv* ativamente.

active partner *n* (*COMM*) comanditado/a.

active service (*BRIT*) *n* (*MIL*) ativa.

activist ['æktɪvɪst] *n* ativista *m/f*, militante *m/f*.

activity [æk'tɪvɪtɪ] *n* atividade *f*.

actor ['æktə*] *n* ator *m*.

actress ['æktrɪs] *n* atriz *f*.

ACTT (*BRIT*) *n abbr* (= *Association of Cinematographic, Television and Allied Technicians*) *sindicato dos técnicos do cinema e da televisão*.

actual ['æktjuəl] *adj* real.

actually ['æktjuəlɪ] *adv* realmente; (*in fact*) de fato.

actuary ['æktjuərɪ] *n* atuário/a.

actuate ['æktjueɪt] *vt* atuar, acionar.

acuity [ə'kju:ɪtɪ] *n* acuidade *f*.

acumen ['ækjumən] *n* perspicácia; **business ~** tino para os negócios.

acupuncture ['ækjupʌŋktʃə*] *n* acupuntura.

acute [ə'kju:t] *adj* agudo.

AD *adv abbr* (= *Anno Domini*) d.C. ♦ *n abbr* (*US*: *MIL*) = **active duty**.

ad [æd] *n abbr* = **advertisement**.

adamant ['ædəmənt] *adj* inflexível.

Adam's apple ['ædəmz-] *n* pomo-de-Adão *m* (*BR*), maçã-de-Adão *f* (*PT*).

adapt [ə'dæpt] *vt* adaptar ♦ *vi*: **to ~ (to)** adaptar-se (a).

adaptability [ədæptə'bɪlɪtɪ] *n* adaptabilidade *f*.

adaptable [ə'dæptəbl] *adj* (*device*) ajustável; (*person*) adaptável.

adaptation [ædæp'teɪʃən] *n* adaptação *f*.

adapter [ə'dæptə*] *n* (*ELEC*) adaptador *m*.

ADC *n abbr* (*MIL*) = **aide-de-camp**; (*US*: = *Aid to Dependent Children*) *auxílio a crianças dependentes*.

add [æd] *vt* acrescentar; (*figures*: *also*: ~ *up*) somar ♦ *vi*: **to ~ to** (*increase*) aumentar ♦

add on *vt* acrescentar, adicionar.

add up *vt* (*figures*) somar ♦ *vi* (*fig*): **it doesn't ~ up** não faz sentido; **it doesn't ~**

up to much é pouca coisa.
adder ['ædə*] *n* víbora.
addict ['ædɪkt] *n* viciado/a; **heroin** ~ viciado/a em heroína; **drug** ~ toxicômano/a.
addicted [ə'dɪktɪd] *adj*: **to be/become** ~ **to** ser/ficar viciado em.
addiction [ə'dɪkʃən] *n* (*MED*) dependência.
adding machine ['ædɪŋ-] *n* máquina de somar.
Addis Ababa ['ædɪs'æbəbə] *n* Adis-Abeba.
addition [ə'dɪʃən] *n* (*adding up*) adição *f*; (*thing added*) acréscimo; **in** ~ além disso; **in** ~ **to** além de.
additional [ə'dɪʃənl] *adj* adicional.
additive ['ædɪtɪv] *n* aditivo.
addled ['ædld] (*BRIT*) *adj* (*egg*) podre, estragado.
address [ə'drɛs] *n* endereço; (*speech*) discurso ♦ *vt* (*letter*) endereçar; (*speak to*) dirigir-se a, dirigir a palavra a; **form of** ~ tratamento; **to** ~ (**o.s. to**) (*problem, issue*) enfocar; **absolute/relative** ~ (*COMPUT*) endereço absoluto/relativo.
addressee [ædrɛ'siː] *n* destinatário/a.
Aden ['eɪdən] *n* Áden (*no article*); **Gulf of** ~ golfo de Áden.
adenoids ['ædɪnɔɪdz] *npl* adenóides *fpl*.
adept ['ædɛpt] *adj*: ~ **at** hábil *or* competente em.
adequate ['ædɪkwɪt] *adj* (*enough*) suficiente; (*suitable*) adequado; **to feel** ~ **to the task** sentir-se à altura da tarefa.
adequately ['ædɪkwɪtlɪ] *adv* adequadamente.
adhere [əd'hɪə*] *vi*: **to** ~ **to** aderir a; (*fig: abide by*) ater-se a.
adherent [əd'hɪərənt] *n* partidário/a.
adhesion [əd'hiːʒən] *n* adesão *f*.
adhesive [əd'hiːzɪv] *adj*, *n* adesivo; ~ **tape** (*BRIT*) durex *m* ®, fita adesiva; (*US*) esparadrapo.
ad hoc [-hɔk] *adj* (*decision*) para o caso; (*committee*) ad hoc.
ad infinitum [-ɪnfɪ'naɪtəm] *adv* ad infinitum.
adjacent [ə'dʒeɪsənt] *adj*: ~ (**to**) adjacente (a), contíguo (a).
adjective ['ædʒɛktɪv] *n* adjetivo.
adjoin [ə'dʒɔɪn] *vt* ser contíguo a.
adjoining [ə'dʒɔɪnɪŋ] *adj* adjacente, contíguo.
adjourn [ə'dʒəːn] *vt* (*postpone*) adiar; (*session*) suspender ♦ *vi* encerrar a sessão; (*go*) deslocar-se; **they** ~**ed to the pub** (*BRIT: inf*) deslocaram-se para o bar.
adjournment [ə'dʒəːnmənt] *n* (*period*) recesso.
Adjt *abbr* (*MIL*: = *adjutant*) Ajte.
adjudicate [ə'dʒuːdɪkeɪt] *vt*, *vi* julgar.
adjudication [ədʒuːdɪ'keɪʃən] *n* julgamento.
adjudicator [ə'dʒuːdɪkeɪtə*] *n* juíza *m/f*.
adjust [ə'dʒʌst] *vt* (*change*) ajustar; (*clothes*) arrumar; (*machine*) regular ♦ *vi*: **to** ~ (**to**) adaptar-se (a).
adjustable [ə'dʒʌstəbl] *adj* ajustável.

adjuster [ə'dʒʌstə*] *n see* **loss**.
adjustment [ə'dʒʌstmənt] *n* ajuste *m*; (*of engine*) regulagem *f*; (*of prices, wages*) reajuste *m*; (*of person*) adaptação *f*.
adjutant ['ædʒətənt] *n* ajudante *m*.
ad-lib [-lɪb] *vt*, *vi* improvisar ♦ *n* improviso; (*THEATRE*) caco ♦ *adv*: **ad lib** à vontade.
adman ['ædmæn] (*inf*; *irreg*) *n* publicitário.
admin ['ædmɪn] (*inf*) *n* *abbr* = **administration**.
administer [əd'mɪnɪstə*] *vt* administrar.
administration [ədmɪnɪs'treɪʃən] *n* administração *f*; (*US*: *government*) governo.
administrative [əd'mɪnɪstrətɪv] *adj* administrativo.
administrator [əd'mɪnɪstreɪtə*] *n* administrador(a) *m/f*.
admirable ['ædmərəbl] *adj* admirável.
admiral ['ædmərəl] *n* almirante *m*.
Admiralty ['ædmərəltɪ] (*BRIT*) *n* (*also*: ~ *Board*) Ministério da Marinha, Almirantado.
admiration [ædmə'reɪʃən] *n* admiração *f*.
admire [əd'maɪə*] *vt* admirar.
admirer [əd'maɪrə*] *n* admirador(a) *m/f*.
admission [əd'mɪʃən] *n* (*entry*) entrada, ingresso; (*enrolment*) admissão *f*; (*confession*) confissão *f*; **"~ free"**, **"free ~"** "entrada gratuita", "ingresso gratuito"; **by his own** ~ **he drinks too much** ele mesmo reconhece que bebe demais.
admit [əd'mɪt] *vt* admitir; (*acknowledge*) reconhecer; (*accept*) aceitar; (*confess*) confessar; **"children not** ~**ted"** "entrada proibida a menores de idade"; **this ticket** ~**s two** este ingresso é válido para duas pessoas; **I must** ~ **that** ... devo admitir *or* reconhecer que ....
admit of *vt fus* admitir.
admit to *vt fus* confessar.
admittance [əd'mɪtəns] *n* entrada; **"no** ~**"** "entrada proibida".
admittedly [əd'mɪtədlɪ] *adv* evidentemente.
admonish [əd'mɔnɪʃ] *vt* admoestar.
ad nauseam [æd'nɔːsɪæm] *adv* sem parar.
ado [ə'duː] *n*: **without further** *or* (**any**) **more** ~ sem mais cerimônias.
adolescence [ædəu'lɛsns] *n* adolescência.
adolescent [ædəu'lɛsnt] *adj*, *n* adolescente *m/f*.
adopt [ə'dɔpt] *vt* adotar.
adopted [ə'dɔptɪd] *adj* adotivo.
adoption [ə'dɔpʃən] *n* adoção *f*.
adorable [ə'dɔːrəbl] *adj* encantador(a).
adoration [ædə'reɪʃən] *n* adoração *f*.
adore [ə'dɔː*] *vt* adorar.
adoring [ə'dɔːrɪŋ] *adj* devotado.
adoringly [ə'dɔːrɪŋlɪ] *adv* com adoração.
adorn [ə'dɔːn] *vt* adornar, enfeitar.
adornment [ə'dɔːnmənt] *n* enfeite *m*, adorno.
ADP *n* *abbr* = **automatic data processing**.
adrenalin [ə'drɛnəlɪn] *n* adrenalina.
Adriatic (Sea) [eɪdrɪ'ætɪk-] *n* (mar *m*) Adriático.

NB: European Portuguese adds the following consonants to certain words: **b** (sú(b)dito, su(b)til); **c** (a(c)ção, a(c)cionista, a(c)to); **m** (inde(m)ne); **p** (ado(p)ção, ado(p)tar); *for further details see p. xiii.*

adrift [ə'drɪft] *adv* à deriva; **to come** ~ desprender-se.

adroit [ə'drɔɪt] *adj* hábil.

ADT (*US*) *abbr* (= *Atlantic Daylight Time*) *hora de verão de Nova Iorque*.

adult ['ædʌlt] *n* adulto/a.

adult education *n* educação *f* de adultos.

adulterate [ə'dʌltəreɪt] *vt* adulterar.

adulterer [ə'dʌltərə*] *n* adúltero.

adulteress [ə'dʌltərɪs] *n* adúltera.

adultery [ə'dʌltərɪ] *n* adultério.

adulthood ['ædʌlthud] *n* idade *f* adulta.

advance [əd'vɑːns] *n* avanço; (*money: payment in advance*) adiantamento; (: *loan*) empréstimo; (*MIL*) avançada ♦ *vt* (*develop*) desenvoiver, promover; (*lend*) adiantar ♦ *vi* avançar; **in** ~ com antecedência; (*pay*) adiantado; **to make** ~s **to sb** (*gen*) fazer propostas a alguém; (*amorously*) fazer propostas amorosas a alguém.

advanced [əd'vɑːnst] *adj* avançado; (*SCH*: *studies*) adiantado; ~ **in years** de idade avançada.

advancement [əd'vɑːnsmənt] *n* avanço, progresso; (*in rank*) promoção *f*, ascenção *f*.

advance notice *n* aviso prévio.

advantage [əd'vɑːntɪdʒ] *n* vantagem *f*; **to take** ~ **of** (*use*) aproveitar, aproveitar-se de; (*gain by*) tirar proveito de; **it's to our** ~ **(to do)** é vantajoso para nós (fazer).

advantageous [ædvən'teɪdʒəs] *adj* vantajoso.

advent ['ædvənt] *n* vinda, chegada; **A**~ (*REL*) Advento.

Advent calendar *n* calendário do Advento.

adventure [əd'ventʃə*] *n* aventura.

adventurer [əd'ventʃərə*] *n* aventureiro/a.

adventurous [əd'ventʃərəs] *adj* aventuroso; (*person*) aventureiro.

adverb ['ædvə:b] *n* advérbio.

adversary ['ædvəsərɪ] *n* adversário/a.

adverse ['ædvə:s] *adj* adverso, contrário; ~ **to** contrário a.

adversity [əd'və:sɪtɪ] *n* adversidade *f*.

advert ['ædvə:t] (*BRIT*) *n abbr* = **advertisement**.

advertise ['ædvətaɪz] *vi* anunciar, fazer propaganda; (*in newspaper etc*) anunciar ♦ *vt* (*in newspaper*) anunciar; (*product*) fazer a propaganda de; **to** ~ **for** (*staff*) procurar.

advertisement [əd'və:tɪsmənt] *n* (*classified*) anúncio; (*display, TV*) propaganda, anúncio.

advertiser ['ædvətaɪzə*] *n* anunciante *m/f*.

advertising ['ædvətaɪzɪŋ] *n* publicidade *f*.

advertising agency *n* agência de publicidade.

advertising campaign *n* campanha publicitária.

advice [əd'vaɪs] *n* conselhos *mpl*; (*notification*) aviso; **piece of** ~ conselho; **to ask (sb) for** ~ pedir conselho (a alguém); **to take legal** ~ consultar um advogado.

advice note (*BRIT*) *n* aviso.

advisable [əd'vaɪzəbl] *adj* aconselhável.

advise [əd'vaɪz] *vt* aconselhar; (*inform*): **to** ~ **sb of sth** avisar alguém de algo; **to** ~ **sb**

against sth desaconselhar algo a alguém; **to** ~ **sb against doing sth** aconselhar alguém a não fazer algo; **you would be well/ill** ~**d to** go seria melhor você ir/você não ir.

advisedly [əd'vaɪzɪdlɪ] *adv* de propósito.

adviser [əd'vaɪzə*] *n* conselheiro/a; (*business adviser*) consultor(a) *m/f*; (*political*) assessor(a) *m/f*.

advisory [əd'vaɪzərɪ] *adj* consultivo; **in an** ~ **capacity** na qualidade de assessor(a) *or* consultor(a).

advocate [*vt* 'ædvəkeɪt, *n* 'ædvəkɪt] *vt* advogar, defender ♦ *n* advogado/a, defensor(a) *m/f*.

advt. *abbr* = **advertisement**.

AEA (*BRIT*) *n abbr* (= *Atomic Energy Authority*) ≈ CNEN *f*.

AEC (*US*) *n abbr* (= *Atomic Energy Commission*) ≈ CNEN *f*.

Aegean (Sea) [iː'dʒiːən-] *n* (mar *m*) Egeu *m*.

aegis ['iːdʒɪs] *n*: **under the** ~ **of** sob a égide de.

aeon ['iːən] *n* eternidade *f*.

aerial ['ɛərɪəl] *n* antena ♦ *adj* aéreo.

aerobatics [ɛərəu'bætɪks] *npl* acrobacias *fpl* aéreas.

aerobics [ɛə'rəubɪks] *n* ginástica.

aerodrome ['ɛərədrəum] (*BRIT*) *n* aeródromo.

aerodynamic [ɛərəudaɪ'næmɪk] *adj* aerodinâmico.

aerodynamics [ɛərəudaɪ'næmɪks] *n*, *npl* aerodinâmica.

aeronautics [ɛərə'nɔːtɪks] *n* aeronáutica.

aeroplane ['ɛərəpleɪn] *n* avião *m*.

aerosol ['ɛərəsɔl] *n* aerossol *m*.

aerospace industry ['ɛərəuspeɪs-] *n* indústria aeroespacial.

aesthetic [iːs'θetɪk] *adj* estético.

aesthetics [iːs'θetɪks] *n*, *npl* estética.

AEU (*BRIT*) *n abbr* (= *Amalgamated Engineering Union*) sindicato dos operários técnicos.

afar [ə'fɑː*] *adv*: **from** ~ de longe.

AFB (*US*) *n abbr* = **Air Force Base**.

AFDC (*US*) *n abbr* (= *Aid to Families with Dependent Children*) auxílio-família *m*.

affable ['æfəbl] *adj* afável, simpático.

affair [ə'fɛə*] *n* negócio; (*also: love* ~) caso; ~**s** (*matters*) assuntos *mpl*; (*personal concerns*) vida; **that is my** ~ isso é comigo; **the Watergate** ~ o caso Watergate.

affect [ə'fɛkt] *vt* afetar; (*move*) comover.

affectation [æfɛk'teɪʃən] *n* afetação *f*.

affected [ə'fɛktɪd] *adj* afetado.

affection [ə'fɛkʃən] *n* afeto, afeição *f*.

affectionate [ə'fɛkʃənət] *adj* afetuoso, carinhoso.

affectionately [ə'fɛkʃənətlɪ] *adv* carinhosamente.

affidavit [æfɪ'deɪvɪt] *n* (*LAW*) declaração *f* escrita e juramentada.

affiliated [ə'fɪlɪeɪtɪd] *adj*: ~ **(to)** afiliado (a); ~ **company** filial *f*.

affinity [ə'fɪnɪtɪ] *n* afinidade *f*.

affirm [ə'fə:m] *vt* afirmar.

affirmation [æfə'meɪʃən] *n* afirmação *f*.

affirmative [əˈfɔːmətɪv] *adj* afirmativo ♦ *n*: **in the ~** afirmativamente.

affix [əˈfɪks] *vt* (*signature*) apor; (*stamp*) afixar, colar.

afflict [əˈflɪkt] *vt* afligir; **to be ~ed with** sofrer de.

affliction [əˈflɪkʃən] *n* aflição *f*; (*illness*) doença.

affluence [ˈæfluəns] *n* riqueza, opulência.

affluent [ˈæfluənt] *adj* rico, opulento; (*person*) rico; **the ~ society** a sociedade de abundância.

afford [əˈfɔːd] *vt* (*provide*) fornecer, dar; (*goods etc*) ter o dinheiro *or* os recursos para; **can we ~ a car?** temos dinheiro para comprar um carro?; **I can't ~ the time** não tenho tempo; **we can ~ to wait** podemos permitir-nos esperar.

affray [əˈfreɪ] (*BRIT*) *n* (*LAW*) desordem *f*, tumulto.

affront [əˈfrʌnt] *n* afronta, ofensa.

affronted [əˈfrʌntɪd] *adj* afrontado, ofendido.

Afghan [ˈæfgæn] *adj, n* afegão/gã *m/f*.

Afghanistan [æfˈgænɪstæn] *n* Afeganistão *m*.

afield [əˈfiːld] *adv*: **far ~** muito longe.

AFL-CIO *n abbr* (= *American Federation of Labor and Congress of Industrial Organizations*) *confederação sindical.*

afloat [əˈfləut] *adv* (*floating*) flutuando; (*at sea*) no mar; **to stay ~** continuar flutuando; **to keep/get ~** (*business*) manter financeiramente equilibrado/estabelecer.

afoot [əˈfut] *adv*: **there is something ~** está acontecendo algo.

aforementioned [əˈfɔːmɛnʃənd] *adj* acima mencionado.

aforesaid [əˈfɔːsɛd] *adj* supracitado, referido.

afraid [əˈfreɪd] *adj* (*frightened*) assustado; (*fearful*) receoso; **to be ~ of/to** ter medo de; **I am ~ that** lamento que; **I'm ~ so/not** receio que sim/não.

afresh [əˈfrɛʃ] *adv* de novo, outra vez.

Africa [ˈæfrɪkə] *n* África.

African [ˈæfrɪkən] *adj, n* africano/a.

Afrikaans [æfrɪˈkɑːns] *n* (*LING*) afrikaan *m*.

Afrikaner [æfrɪˈkɑːnə*] *n* africânder *m/f*.

Afro-American [ˈæfrəu-] *adj* afro-americano.

AFT *n abbr* (= *American Federation of Teachers*) *sindicato dos professores.*

aft [ɑːft] *adv* a ré.

after [ˈɑːftə*] *prep* (*time*) depois de ♦ *adv* depois ♦ *conj* depois que; **~ dinner** depois do jantar; **the day ~ tomorrow** depois de amanhã; **day ~ day** dia após dia; **time ~ time** repetidas vezes; **a quarter ~ two** (*US*) duas e quinze; **what are you ~?** o que você quer?; **who are you ~?** quem procura?; **the police are ~ him** a polícia está atrás dele; **to ask ~ sb** perguntar por alguém; **~ all** afinal (de contas); **~ you!** passe primeiro!

afterbirth [ˈɑːftəbɜːθ] *n* placenta.

aftercare [ˈɑːftəkɛə*] (*BRIT*) *n* (*MED*) assistência pós-operatória.

after-effects *npl* repercussões *fpl*; (*of drug*) efeitos *mpl* secundários.

afterlife [ˈɑːftəlaɪf] *n* vida após a morte.

aftermath [ˈɑːftəmæθ] *n* conseqüências *fpl*; **in the ~ of** no período depois de.

afternoon [ɑːftəˈnuːn] *n* tarde *f*; **good ~!** boa tarde!

afters [ˈɑːftəz] (*BRIT*: *inf*) *n* (*dessert*) sobremesa.

after-sales service *n* serviço pós-vendas; (*of computers etc*) assistência técnica.

after-shave (lotion) [ˈɑːftəʃeɪv] *n* loção *f* após-barba.

aftershock [ˈɑːftəʃɔk] *n* abalo secundário.

afterthought [ˈɑːftəθɔːt] *n* reflexão *f* posterior *or* tardia.

afterwards [ˈɑːftəwədz] *adv* depois; **immediately ~** logo depois.

again [əˈgɛn] *adv* outra vez, de novo; **to do sth ~** voltar a fazer algo; **~ and ~** repetidas vezes; **now and ~** de vez em quando.

against [əˈgɛnst] *prep* contra; **~ a blue background** sobre um fundo azul; **(as) ~** (*BRIT*) em contraste com.

age [eɪdʒ] *n* idade *f*; (*old ~*) velhice *f*; (*period*) época ♦ *vt, vi* envelhecer; **he's 20 years of ~** ele tem 20 anos de idade; **at the ~ of 20** aos 20 anos de idade; **under ~** menor de idade; **to come of ~** atingir a maioridade; **it's been ~s since I saw him** faz muito tempo *or* um tempão (*BR*: *inf*) que eu não o vejo.

aged¹ [eɪdʒd] *adj*: **~ 10** de 10 anos de idade.

aged² [ˈeɪdʒɪd] *adj* idoso ♦ *npl*: **the ~** os idosos.

age group *n* faixa etária; **the 40 to 50 ~** a faixa etária dos 40 aos 50 anos.

ageless [ˈeɪdʒlɪs] *adj* (*eternal*) eterno; (*ever young*) sempre jovem.

age limit *n* idade *f* mínima/máxima.

agency [ˈeɪdʒənsɪ] *n* agência; **through** *or* **by the ~ of** por meio de.

agenda [əˈdʒɛndə] *n* ordem *f* do dia.

agent [ˈeɪdʒənt] *n* agente *m/f*.

aggravate [ˈægrəveɪt] *vt* agravar; (*annoy*) irritar.

aggravation [ægrəˈveɪʃən] *n* irritação *f*.

aggregate [ˈægrɪgət] *n* (*whole*) conjunto; **on ~** (*SPORT*) no total dos pontos.

aggression [əˈgrɛʃən] *n* agressão *f*.

aggressive [əˈgrɛsɪv] *adj* agressivo.

aggressiveness [əˈgrɛsɪvnɪs] *n* agressividade *f*.

aggrieved [əˈgriːvd] *adj* aflito.

aghast [əˈgɑːst] *adj* horrorizado.

agile [ˈædʒaɪl] *adj* ágil.

agitate [ˈædʒɪteɪt] *vt* (*shake*) agitar; (*trouble*) perturbar ♦ *vi*: **to ~ for** fazer agitação em prol de *or* a favor de.

agitation [ædʒɪˈteɪʃən] *n* agitação *f*.

agitator [ˈædʒɪteɪtə*] *n* agitador(a) *m/f*.

AGM *n abbr* (= *annual general meeting*)

NB: *European Portuguese adds the following consonants to certain words:* **b** (sú(b)dito, su(b)til); **c** (a(c)ção, a(c)cionista, a(c)to); **m** (inde(m)ne); **p** (ado(p)ção, ado(p)tar); *for further details see p. xiii.*

AGO *f*.

ago [ə'gəu] *adv*: **2 days** ~ há 2 dias (atrás); **not long** ~ há pouco tempo; **as long** ~ **as 1960** já em 1960; **how long** ~? há quanto tempo?

agog [ə'gɔg] *adj* (*impatient*): ~ **to** ansioso para; (*excited*): **(all)** ~ empolgado, entusiasmado.

agonize ['ægənaɪz] *vi*: **to** ~ **over sth** agoniar-se *or* angustiar-se com algo.

agonizing ['ægənaɪzɪŋ] *adj* (*pain*) agudo; (*suspense*) angustiante.

agony ['ægənɪ] *n* (*pain*) dor *f*; (*distress*) angústia; **to be in** ~ sofrer dores terríveis.

agony column *n* correspondência sentimental.

agree [ə'griː] *vt* (*price*) combinar, ajustar ♦ *vi* (*statements etc*) combinar; **to** ~ **(with)** (*person*, *LING*) concordar (com); **to** ~ **to do** aceitar fazer; **to** ~ **to sth** consentir algo; **to** ~ **that** (*admit*) concordar *or* admitir que; **it was** ~**d that** ... foi combinado que ...; **they** ~ **on this** concordam *or* estão de acordo nisso; **garlic doesn't** ~ **with me** não me dou bem com o alho.

agreeable [ə'griːəbl] *adj* agradável; (*willing*) disposto; **are you** ~ **to this?** você concorda *or* está de acordo com isso?

agreed [ə'griːd] *adj* (*time*, *place*) combinado; **to be** ~ concordar, estar de acordo.

agreement [ə'griːmənt] *n* acordo; (*COMM*) contrato; **in** ~ de acordo; **by mutual** ~ de comum acordo.

agricultural [ægrɪ'kʌltʃərəl] *adj* (*of crops*) agrícola; (*of crops and cattle*) agropecuário.

agriculture ['ægrɪkʌltʃə*] *n* (*of crops*) agricultura; (*of crops and cattle*) agropecuária.

aground [ə'graund] *adv*: **to run** ~ encalhar.

ahead [ə'hɛd] *adv* adiante; **go right** *or* **straight** ~ continue sempre em frente; **go** ~! (*fig*) vá la!; (: *speak*) pode falar!; ~ **of** à frente de; (*fig*: *schedule etc*) antes de; ~ **of time** antes do tempo; **to go** ~ **(with)** prosseguir (com); **to be** ~ **of sb** (*fig*) ter vantagem sobre alguém.

AI *n abbr* = **Amnesty International**; (*COMPUT*) = **artificial intelligence**.

AIB (*BRIT*) *n abbr* (= *Accident Investigation Bureau*) *comissão de inquérito sobre acidentes*.

AID *n abbr* = **artificial insemination by donor**; (*US*) = **Agency for International Development**.

aid [eɪd] *n* ajuda, auxílio ♦ *vt* ajudar, auxiliar; **with the** ~ **of** com a ajuda de; **in** ~ **of** em benefício de; **to** ~ **and abet** (*LAW*) ser cúmplice de.

aide [eɪd] *n* (*person*) assessor(a) *m/f*.

AIDS [eɪdz] *n abbr* (= *acquired immune deficiency syndrome*) AIDS *f* (*BR*), SIDA *f* (*PT*).

AIH *n abbr* = **artificial insemination by husband**.

ailment ['eɪlmənt] *n* achaque *m*.

aim [eɪm] *vt*: **to** ~ **sth at** (*gun*, *camera*, *blow*) apontar algo para; (*missile*, *remark*) dirigir algo a ♦ *vi* (*also*: *take* ~) apontar ♦ *n* (*accuracy*) pontaria; (*objective*) objetivo, meta; **to** ~ **at** (*objective*) visar; **to** ~ **to do** pretender fazer.

aimless ['eɪmlɪs] *adj* à toa.

aimlessly ['eɪmlɪslɪ] *adv* à toa.

ain't [eɪnt] (*inf*) = **am not; aren't; isn't**.

air [ɛə*] *n* ar *m*; (*appearance*) aparência, aspeto ♦ *vt* arejar; (*grievances*, *ideas*) discutir ♦ *cpd* (*currents*, *attack etc*) aéreo; **by** ~ (*travel*) de avião; (*send*) por via aérea; **to be on the** ~ (*RADIO*, *TV*: *programme*, *station*) estar no ar.

air base *n* base *f* aérea.

airbed ['ɛəbɛd] (*BRIT*) *n* colchão *m* de ar.

airborne ['ɛəbɔːn] *adj* (*in the air*) no ar; (*plane*) em vôo; (*troops*) aerotransportado.

air cargo *n* frete *m* aéreo.

air-conditioned [-kən'dɪʃənd] *adj* com ar condicionado.

air conditioning [-kən'dɪʃənɪŋ] *n* ar condicionado.

air-cooled [-kuːld] *adj* refrigerado a ar.

aircraft ['ɛəkrɑːft] *n inv* aeronave *f*.

aircraft carrier *n* porta-aviões *m inv*.

air cushion *n* almofada de ar.

airfield ['ɛəfiːld] *n* campo de aviação.

Air Force *n* Força Aérea, Aeronáutica.

air freight *n* frete *m* aéreo.

airgun ['ɛəgʌn] *n* espingarda de ar comprimido.

air hostess (*BRIT*) *n* aeromoça (*BR*), hospedeira (*PT*).

airily ['ɛərɪlɪ] *adv* levianamente.

airing ['ɛərɪŋ] *n*: **to give an** ~ **to** arejar; (*fig*: *ideas*, *views*) discutir.

air letter (*BRIT*) *n* aerograma *m*.

airlift ['ɛəlɪft] *n* ponte aérea.

airline ['ɛəlaɪn] *n* linha aérea.

airliner ['ɛəlaɪnə*] *n* avião *m* de passageiros.

airlock ['ɛəlɔk] *n* (*blockage*) entupimento de ar.

airmail ['ɛəmeɪl] *n*: **by** ~ por via aérea.

air mattress *n* colchão *m* de ar.

airplane ['ɛəpleɪn] (*US*) *n* avião *m*.

air pocket *n* bolsa de ar.

airport ['ɛəpɔːt] *n* aeroporto.

air raid *n* ataque *m* aéreo.

airsick ['ɛəsɪk] *adj*: **to be** ~ enjoar-se (no avião).

airstrip ['ɛəstrɪp] *n* pista (de aterrissar).

air terminal *n* terminal *m* aéreo.

airtight ['ɛətaɪt] *adj* hermético.

air traffic control *n* controle *m* de tráfego aéreo.

air traffic controller *n* controlador(a) *m/f* de tráfego aéreo.

air waybill *n* conhecimento aéreo.

airy ['ɛərɪ] *adj* (*room*) arejado, ventilado; (*person*) leviano.

aisle [aɪl] *n* (*of church*) nave *f*; (*of theatre*, *plane*) corredor *m*, coxia.

ajar [ə'dʒɑː*] *adj* entreaberto.

AK (*US*) *abbr* (*POST*) = **Alaska**.

aka *abbr* (= *also known as*) vulgo.
akin [ə'kın] *adj*: ~ **to** parecido com.
AL (*US*) *abbr* (*POST*) = **Alabama**.
ALA *n abbr* = **American Library Association**.
à la carte [ælɑː'kɑːt] *adj*, *adv* à la carte.
alacrity [ə'lækrıtı] *n*: **with** ~ prontamente.
alarm [ə'lɑːm] *n* alarme *m*; (*anxiety*) inquietação *f* ♦ *vt* alarmar, inquietar.
alarm clock *n* despertador *m*.
alarming [ə'lɑːmıŋ] *adj* alarmante.
alarmist [ə'lɑːmıst] *adj*, *n* alarmista *m/f*.
alas [ə'læs] *excl* ai, ai de mim.
Alaska [ə'læskə] *n* Alasca *m*.
Albania [æl'beınıə] *n* Albânia.
Albanian [æl'beınıən] *adj* albanês/esa ♦ *n* albanês/esa *m/f*; (*LING*) albanês *m*.
albeit [ɔːl'biːıt] *conj* embora.
album ['ælbəm] *n* álbum *m*; (*record*) elepê *m*, álbum.
albumen ['ælbjumın] *n* albumina; (*of egg*) albume *m*.
alchemy ['ælkımı] *n* alquimia.
alcohol ['ælkəhɔl] *n* álcool *m*.
alcoholic [ælkə'hɔlık] *adj* alcoólico ♦ *n* alcoólatra *m/f*.
alcoholism ['ælkəhɔlızəm] *n* alcoolismo.
alcove ['ælkəuv] *n* alcova.
Ald. *abbr* = **alderman**.
alderman ['ɔːldəmən] (*irreg*) *n* vereador *m*.
ale [eıl] *n* cerveja.
alert [ə'lɔːt] *adj* atento; (*sharp*) esperto; (*watchful*) vigilante ♦ *n* alerta ♦ *vt*: **to** ~ **sb** (**to sth**) alertar alguém (de *or* sobre algo); **on the** ~ de sobreaviso *or* alerta.
Aleutian Islands [ə'luːʃən-] *npl* ilhas *fpl* Aleútas.
Alexandria [ælıg'zɑːndrıə] *n* Alexandria.
alfresco [æl'freskəu] *adj*, *adv* ao ar livre.
Algarve [æl'gɑːv] *m*: **the** ~ o Algarve.
algebra ['ældʒıbrə] *n* álgebra.
Algeria [æl'dʒıərıə] *n* Argélia.
Algerian [æl'dʒıərıən] *adj*, *n* argelino/a.
Algiers [æl'dʒıəz] *n* Argel *f*.
algorithm ['ælgərıðəm] *n* algoritmo.
alias ['eılıəs] *adv* também chamado ♦ *n* outro nome, pseudônimo.
alibi ['ælıbaı] *n* álibi *m*.
alien ['eılıən] *n* estrangeiro/a; (*from space*) alienígena *m/f* ♦ *adj*: ~ **to** estranho a, alheio a.
alienate ['eılıəneıt] *vt* alienar.
alienation [eılıə'neıʃən] *n* alienação *f*.
alight [ə'laıt] *adj* aceso ♦ *vi* (*passenger*) apear; (*bird*) pousar.
align [ə'laın] *vt* alinhar.
alignment [ə'laınmənt] *n* alinhamento.
alike [ə'laık] *adj* (*identical*) igual; (*similar*) parecido ♦ *adv* igualmente, do mesmo modo; **to look** ~ parecer-se.
alimony ['ælımənı] *n* (*payment*) pensão *f* alimentícia, sustento.
alive [ə'laıv] *adj* vivo; **to be** ~ **with** fervilhar

de; ~ **to** sensível a.
alkali ['ælkəlaı] *n* álcali *m*.
all [ɔːl] *adj* todo; (*pl*) todos/as ♦ *pron* tudo; (*pl*: *pessoas*) todos/as ♦ *adv* todo, completamente; ~ **alone** completamente só; ~ **the time/his life** o tempo todo/toda a sua vida; ~ **five** (**of them**) todos os cinco; ~ **of them** todos eles; ~ **of it** tudo; **we** ~ **went**, ~ **of us went** nós fomos todos; ~ **day** o dia inteiro; **is that** ~? é só isso?; **for** ~ **their efforts** apesar de seus esforços; **not as hard** *etc* **as** ~ **that** não tão difícil *etc* assim; **not at** ~ (*in answer to question*) em absoluto, absolutamente não; (*after thanks*) de nada; **I'm not at** ~ **tired** não estou nada cansada; **anything at** ~ **will do** qualquer coisa serve; ~ **but** quase; **to be** ~ **in** (*BRIT*: *inf*) estar exausto; ~ **in** ~ ao todo; ~ **out** com toda a energia; **it's** ~ **the same** dá no mesmo.
allay [ə'leı] *vt* (*fears*) acalmar; (*pain*) aliviar.
all clear *n* sinal *m* de tudo limpo; (*after air raid*) sinal de fim de alerta aérea.
allegation [ælı'geıʃən] *n* alegação *f*, afirmação *f*.
allege [ə'ledʒ] *vt* alegar, afirmar; **he is** ~**d to have said** afirma-se que ele disse.
alleged [ə'ledʒd] *adj* pretenso.
allegedly [ə'ledʒıdlı] *adv* segundo dizem.
allegiance [ə'liːdʒəns] *n* lealdade *f*.
allegory ['ælıgərı] *n* alegoria.
all-embracing [-ım'breısıŋ] *adj* universal.
allergic [ə'lɔːdʒık] *adj*: ~ **to** alérgico a.
allergy ['ælədʒı] *n* alergia.
alleviate [ə'liːvıeıt] *vt* aliviar.
alley ['ælı] *n* (*street*) viela, beco; (*in garden*) passeio.
alliance [ə'laıəns] *n* aliança.
allied ['ælaıd] *adj* aliado; (*related*) afim, aparentado.
alligator ['ælıgeıtə*] *n* aligátor *m*; (*in Brazil*) jacaré *m*.
all-important *adj* importantíssimo.
all-in (*BRIT*) *adj*, *adv* (*charge*) tudo incluído.
all-in wrestling (*BRIT*) *n* luta livre.
alliteration [əlıtə'reıʃən] *n* aliteração *f*.
all-night *adj* (*café*) aberto toda a noite; (*party*) que dura toda a noite.
allocate ['æləkeıt] *vt* (*share out*) distribuir; (*devote*) designar.
allocation [ælə'keıʃən] *n* (*of money*) repartição *f*; (*distribution*) distribuição *f*; (*money*) verbas *fpl*.
allot [ə'lɔt] *vt* distribuir, repartir; (*devote*) designar; **in the** ~**ted time** no tempo designado.
allotment [ə'lɔtmənt] *n* distribuição *f*, partilha; (*garden*) lote *m*.
all-out *adj* (*effort etc*) máximo; (*attack etc*) irrestrito.
allow [ə'lau] *vt* (*practice, behaviour*) permitir; (*sum to spend etc*) dar, conceder; (*claim*) admitir; (*sum, time estimated*) calcular;

NB: European Portuguese adds the following consonants to certain words: **b** (sú(b)dito, su(b)til); **c** (a(c)ção, a(c)cionista, a(c)to); **m** (inde(m)ne); **p** (ado(p)ção, ado(p)tar); *for further details see p. xiii.*

(*concede*): **to ~ that** reconhecer que; **to ~ sb to do** permitir a alguém fazer; **he is ~d to do** é permitido que ele faça, ele pode fazer; **smoking is not ~ed** é proibido fumar; **we must ~ 3 days for the journey** temos que calcular três dias para a viagem.

allow for *vt fus* levar em conta.

allowance [ə'lauəns] *n* concessão *f*; (*payment*) pensão *f*, subsídio; (: *for expenses*) ajuda de custo; (*discount*) desconto; (*TAX*) abatimento; **to make ~s for** levar em consideração.

alloy ['ælɔɪ] *n* liga.

all right *adv* (*well*) bem; (*as answer*) está bem!

all-round *adj* (*view*) geral, amplo; (*person*) consumado.

all-rounder (*BRIT*) *n*: **to be a good ~** ser homem/mulher para tudo.

allspice ['ɔːlspaɪs] *n* pimenta da Jamaica.

all-time *adj* (*record*) de todos os tempos.

allude [ə'luːd] *vi*: **to ~ to** aludir a.

alluring [ə'ljuərɪŋ] *adj* tentador(a), sedutor(a).

allusion [ə'luːʒən] *n* alusão *f*.

alluvium [ə'luːvɪəm] *n* aluvião *m*.

ally [*n* 'ælaɪ, *vt* ə'laɪ] *n* aliado ♦ *vt*: **to ~ o.s. with** aliar-se com.

almighty [ɔːl'maɪtɪ] *adj* onipotente, todo-poderoso.

almond ['ɑːmənd] *n* (*fruit*) amêndoa; (*tree*) amendoeira.

almost ['ɔːlməust] *adv* quase.

alms [ɑːmz] *npl* esmolas *fpl*, esmola.

aloft [ə'lɔft] *adv* em cima, no alto.

alone [ə'ləun] *adj* só, sozinho ♦ *adv* só, somente; **to leave sb ~** deixar alguém em paz; **to leave sth ~** não tocar em algo; **let ~ ...** sem falar em ....

along [ə'lɔŋ] *prep* por, ao longo de ♦ *adv*: **is he coming ~?** ele vem conosco?; **he was limping ~** ia coxeando; **~ with** junto com.

alongside [əlɔŋ'saɪd] *prep* ao lado de ♦ *adv* (*NAUT*) encostado.

aloof [ə'luːf] *adj* afastado, altivo ♦ *adv*: **to stand ~** afastar-se.

aloofness [ə'luːfnɪs] *n* afastamento, altivez *f*.

aloud [ə'laud] *adv* em voz alta.

alphabet ['ælfəbet] *n* alfabeto.

alphabetical [ælfə'betɪkəl] *adj* alfabético; **in ~ order** em ordem alfabética.

alphanumeric ['ælfənjuː'merɪk] *adj* alfanumérico.

alpine ['ælpaɪn] *adj* alpino, alpestre.

Alps [ælps] *npl*: **the ~** os Alpes.

already [ɔːl'redɪ] *adv* já.

alright [ɔːl'raɪt] (*BRIT*) *adv* = **all right**.

Alsatian [æl'seɪʃən] (*BRIT*) *n* (*dog*) pastor *m* alemão.

also ['ɔːlsəu] *adv* também.

altar ['ɔltə*] *n* altar *m*.

alter ['ɔltə*] *vt* alterar, modificar ♦ *vi* alterar-se, modificar-se.

alteration [ɔltə'reɪʃən] *n* alteração *f*, modificação *f*; **~s** *npl* (*SEWING*) consertos *mpl*; (*ARCHIT*) reformas *fpl*; **timetable subject to**

~ horário sujeito a mudanças.

alternate [*adj* ɔl'təːnɪt, *vi* 'ɔltəːneɪt] *adj* alternado ♦ *vi* alternar-se; **on ~ days** em dias alternados.

alternately [ɔl'təːnɪtlɪ] *adv* alternadamente.

alternating ['ɔltəːneɪtɪŋ] *adj*: **~ current** corrente *f* alternada.

alternative [ɔl'təːnətɪv] *adj* alternativo ♦ *n* alternativa.

alternatively [ɔl'təːnətɪvlɪ] *adv*: **~ one could ...** por outro lado se podia ....

alternator ['ɔltəːneɪtə*] *n* (*AUT*) alternador *m*.

although [ɔːl'ðəu] *conj* embora; (*given that*) se bem que.

altitude ['æltɪtjuːd] *n* altitude *f*.

alto ['æltəu] *n* (*female*) contralto *f*; (*male*) alto.

altogether [ɔːltə'gɛðə*] *adv* (*completely*) totalmente, de todo; (*on the whole, in all*) no total, ao todo; **how much is that ~?** qual é a soma total?

altruistic [æltru'ɪstɪk] *adj* (*person*) altruísta; (*act*) altruístico.

aluminium [ælju'mɪnɪəm] (*BRIT*) *n* alumínio.

aluminum [ə'luːmɪnəm] (*US*) *n* = **aluminium**.

always ['ɔːlweɪz] *adv* sempre.

AM *abbr* = **amplitude modulation**.

am [æm] *vb see* **be**.

a.m. *adv abbr* (= *ante meridiem*) da manhã.

AMA *n abbr* = **American Medical Association**.

amalgam [ə'mælgəm] *n* amálgama *m*.

amalgamate [ə'mælgəmeɪt] *vi* amalgamar-se, unir-se ♦ *vt* amalgamar, unir.

amalgamation [əmælgə'meɪʃən] *n* (*COMM*) amalgamação *f*, união *f*.

amass [ə'mæs] *vt* acumular, amontoar.

amateur ['æmətə*] *adj*, *n* amador(a) *m/f*; **~ dramatics** teatro amador.

amateurish ['æmətərɪʃ] (*pej*) *adj* amador(a).

amaze [ə'meɪz] *vt* assombrar, espantar; **to be ~d (at)** espantar-se (de or com).

amazement [ə'meɪzmənt] *n* assombro, espanto; **to my ~** para o meu espanto.

amazing [ə'meɪzɪŋ] *adj* (*surprising*) surpreendente; (*incredible*) incrível.

amazingly [ə'meɪzɪŋlɪ] *adv* (*surprisingly*) surpreendentemente; (*incredibly*) incrivelmente.

Amazon ['æməzən] *n* (*GEO*) Amazonas *m*; (*MYTHOLOGY*) amazona *f* ♦ *cpd* amazônico, do Amazonas; **the ~ basin** a bacia amazônica; **the ~ jungle** a selva amazônica.

Amazonian [æmə'zeunɪən] *adj* (*of river, region*) amazônico; (*of state*) amazonense ♦ *n* amazonense *m/f*.

ambassador [æm'bæsədə*] *n* embaixador/embaixatriz *m/f*.

amber ['æmbə*] *n* âmbar *m*; **at ~** (*BRIT: AUT*) em amarelo.

ambidextrous [æmbɪ'dekstrəs] *adj* ambidestro.

ambience ['æmbɪəns] *n* ambiente *m*.

ambiguity [æmbɪ'gjuɪtɪ] *n* ambigüidade *f*.

ambiguous [æm'bɪgjuəs] *adj* ambíguo.

ambition [æm'bɪʃən] *n* ambição *f*.

ambitious [æm'bɪʃəs] *adj* ambicioso; *(plan)* grandioso.

ambivalent [æm'bɪvələnt] *adj* ambivalente; *(pej)* equívoco.

amble ['æmbl] *vi (also: ~ along)* andar a furta-passo.

ambulance ['æmbjuləns] *n* ambulância.

ambush ['æmbuʃ] *n* emboscada ♦ *vt* emboscar.

ameba [ə'miːbə] *(US) n* = **amoeba**.

ameliorate [ə'miːlɪəreɪt] *vt* melhorar.

amen ['ɑː'mɛn] *excl* amém.

amenable [ə'miːnəbl] *adj*: ~ **to** *(advice etc)* receptivo a.

amend [ə'mɛnd] *vt (law, text)* emendar; *(habits)* corrigir.

amendment [ə'mɛndmənt] *n (to law etc)* emenda; *(in text)* correção *f.*

amends [ə'mɛndz] *n*: **to make** ~ reparar seus erros; **to make** ~ **to sb for sth** compensar alguém por algo.

amenity [ə'miːnɪtɪ] *n* amenidade *f*; **amenities** *npl* atrações *fpl*, comodidades *fpl.*

America [ə'mɛrɪkə] *n (continent)* América; *(USA)* Estados Unidos *mpl.*

American [ə'mɛrɪkən] *adj* americano; *(from USA)* norte-americano, estadunidense ♦ *n* americano/a; *(from USA)* norte-americano/a.

americanize [ə'mɛrɪkənaɪz] *vt* americanizar.

amethyst ['æmɪθɪst] *n* ametista.

Amex ['æmɛks] *n abbr* = **American Stock Exchange.**

amiable ['eɪmɪəbl] *adj* amável, simpático.

amicable ['æmɪkəbl] *adj* amigável; *(person)* amigo.

amid(st) [ə'mɪd(st)] *prep* em meio a.

amiss [ə'mɪs] *adv*: **to take sth** ~ levar algo a mal; **there's something** ~ aí tem coisa.

ammo ['æməu] *(inf) n abbr* = **ammunition.**

ammonia [ə'məunɪə] *n (gas)* amoníaco; *(liquid)* amônia.

ammunition [æmju'nɪʃən] *n* munição *f*; *(fig)* argumentos *mpl.*

ammunition dump *n* depósito de munições.

amnesia [æm'niːzɪə] *n* amnésia.

amnesty ['æmnɪstɪ] *n* anistia; **to grant an** ~ **to** anistiar.

amoeba [ə'miːbə] *(US* **ameba)** *n* ameba.

amok [ə'mɔk] *adv*: **to run** ~ enlouquecer.

among(st) [ə'mʌŋ(st)] *prep* entre, no meio de.

amoral [æ'mɔrəl] *adj* amoral.

amorous ['æmərəs] *adj* amoroso; *(in love)* apaixonado, enamorado.

amorphous [ə'mɔːfəs] *adj* amorfo.

amortization [əmɔːtaɪ'zeɪʃən] *n* amortização *f.*

amount [ə'maunt] *n* quantidade *f*; *(of money etc)* quantia, importância, montante *m* ♦ *vi*: **to** ~ **to** *(reach)* chegar a; *(total)* montar a; *(be same as)* equivaler a, significar; **this** ~**s to a refusal** isto equivale a uma recusa; **the total** ~ *(of money)* o total.

amp(ère) ['æmp(ɛə*)] *n* ampère *m*; **a 13 amp**

plug um pino de tomada de 13 ampères.

ampersand ['æmpəsænd] *n* "e" *m* comercial.

amphibian [æm'fɪbɪən] *n* anfíbio.

amphibious [æm'fɪbɪəs] *adj* anfíbio.

amphitheatre ['æmfɪθɪətə*] *(US* **amphitheater)** *n* anfiteatro.

ample ['æmpl] *adj* amplo; *(enough)* suficiente; **this is** ~ isso é mais do que suficiente; **to have** ~ **time/room** ter tempo/lugar de sobra.

amplifier ['æmplɪfaɪə*] *n* amplificador *m.*

amplify ['æmplɪfaɪ] *vt* amplificar.

amply ['æmplɪ] *adv* amplamente.

ampoule ['æmpuːl] *(US* **ampule)** *n (MED)* ampola.

amputate ['æmpjuteɪt] *vt* amputar.

Amsterdam ['æmstədæm] *n* Amsterdá *(BR)*, Amsterdão *(PT).*

amt *abbr* = **amount.**

amuck [ə'mʌk] *adv* = **amok.**

amuse [ə'mjuːz] *vt* divertir; **to** ~ **o.s. with sth/by doing sth** divertir-se com algo/em fazer algo; **to be** ~**d at** achar graça em; **he was not** ~**d** ele ficou sem graça.

amusement [ə'mjuːzmənt] *n* diversão *f*, divertimento; *(pastime)* passatempo; *(laughter)* riso; **much to my** ~ para grande diversão minha.

amusement arcade *n* fliperama *m.*

amusing [ə'mjuːzɪŋ] *adj* divertido.

an [æn, ən, n] *indef art see* **a.**

ANA *n abbr* = **American Newspaper Association; American Nurses Association.**

anachronism [ə'nækrənɪzəm] *n* anacronismo.

anaemia [ə'niːmɪə] *(US* **anemia)** *n* anemia.

anaemic [ə'niːmɪk] *(US* **anemic)** *adj* anêmico.

anaesthetic [ænɪs'θɛtɪk] *(US* **anesthetic)** *adj, n* anestésico; **under** ~ sob anestesia; **local/general** ~ anestesia local/geral.

anaesthetist [æ'niːsθɪtɪst] *(US* **anesthetist)** *n* anestesista *m/f.*

anagram ['ænəgræm] *n* anagrama *m.*

analgesic [ænæl'dʒiːsɪk] *adj, n* analgésico.

analog(ue) ['ænəlɔg] *adj (watch, computer)* analógico.

analogy [ə'nælədʒɪ] *n* analogia; **to draw** *or* **make an** ~ **between** fazer uma analogia entre.

analyse ['ænəlaɪz] *(US* **analyze)** *vt* analisar.

analyses [ə'næləsiːz] *npl of* **analysis.**

analysis [ə'næləsɪs] *(pl* **analyses)** *n* análise *f*; **in the last** *or* **final** ~ em última análise.

analyst ['ænəlɪst] *n* analista *m/f*; *(psychoanalyst)* psicanalista *m/f.*

analytic(al) [ænə'lɪtɪk(əl)] *adj* analítico.

analyze ['ænəlaɪz] *(US) vt* = **analyse.**

anarchic [æ'nɑːkɪk] *adj* anárquico.

anarchist ['ænəkɪst] *adj, n* anarquista *m/f.*

anarchy [ˈænəkɪ] *n* anarquia.

anathema [ə'næθɪmə] *n*: **it is** ~ **to him** ele tem horror disso.

anatomical [ænə'tɔmɪkəl] *adj* anatômico.

anatomy [ə'nætəmɪ] *n* anatomia.

NB: European Portuguese adds the following consonants to certain words: **b** (sú(b)dito, su(b)til); **c** (a(c)ção, a(c)cionista, a(c)to); **m** (inde(m)ne); **p** (ado(p)ção, ado(p)tar); *for further details see p. xiii.*

ANC *n abbr* (= *African National Congress*) CNA *m*.
ancestor ['ænsɪstə*] *n* antepassado.
ancestral [æn'sɛstrəl] *adj* ancestral.
ancestry ['ænsɪstrɪ] *n* ascendência, ancestrais *mpl*.
anchor ['æŋkə*] *n* âncora ♦ *vi* (*also*: *to drop* ~) ancorar, fundear ♦ *vt* (*boat*) ancorar; (*fig*) segurar, firmar; **to weigh** ~ levantar âncoras; **to drop** ~ fundear.
anchorage ['æŋkərɪdʒ] *n* ancoradouro.
anchovy ['æntʃəvɪ] *n* enchova.
ancient ['eɪnʃənt] *adj* antigo, velho; ~ **monument** monumento antigo.
ancillary [æn'sɪlərɪ] *adj* auxiliar.
and [ænd] *conj* e; ~ **so on** e assim por diante; **try** ~ **come** tente vir; **come** ~ **sit here** vem sentar aqui; **better** ~ **better** cada vez melhor; **more** ~ **more** cada vez mais.
Andes ['ændiːz] *npl*: **the** ~ os Andes.
anecdote ['ænɪkdəʊt] *n* anedota.
anemia [ə'niːmɪə] (*US*) *n* = **anaemia**.
anemic [ə'niːmɪk] (*US*) *adj* = **anaemic**.
anemone [ə'nɛmənɪ] *n* (*BOT*) anêmona.
anesthetic [ænɪs'θɛtɪk] (*US*) *adj*, *n* = **anaesthetic**.
anesthetist [æ'niːsθɪtɪst] (*US*) *n* = **anaesthetist**.
anew [ə'njuː] *adv* de novo, novamente.
angel ['eɪndʒəl] *n* anjo.
anger ['æŋgə*] *n* raiva ♦ *vt* zangar.
angina [æn'dʒaɪnə] *n* angina (de peito).
angle ['æŋgl] *n* ângulo ♦ *vi*: **to** ~ **for** (*fish*, *compliments*) pescar; **from their** ~ do ponto de vista deles.
angler ['æŋglə*] *n* pescador(a) *m/f* de vara (*BR*), pescador(a) *m/f* à linha (*PT*).
Anglican ['æŋglɪkən] *adj*, *n* anglicano/a.
anglicize ['æŋglɪsaɪz] *vt* anglicizar.
angling ['æŋglɪŋ] *n* pesca à vara (*BR*), pesca à linha (*PT*).
Anglo- ['æŋgləʊ] *prefix* anglo-.
Anglo-Brazilian *adj* anglo-brasileiro.
Anglo-Portuguese *adj* anglo-português/esa.
Anglo-Saxon [-'sæksən] *adj* anglo-saxão/xôni(c)a ♦ *n* anglo-saxão/xôni(c)a *m/f*; (*LING*) anglo-saxão *m*.
Angola [æŋ'gəʊlə] *n* Angola (*no article*).
Angolan [æŋ'gəʊlən] *adj*, *n* angolano/a.
angrily ['æŋgrɪlɪ] *adv* com raiva, zangadamente.
angry ['æŋgrɪ] *adj* zangado; **to be** ~ **with sb/ at sth** estar zangado com alguém/algo; **to get** ~ zangar-se; **to make sb** ~ zangar alguém.
anguish ['æŋgwɪʃ] *n* (*physical*) dor *f*, sofrimento; (*mental*) angústia.
angular ['æŋgjʊlə*] *adj* (*shape*) angular; (*features*) anguloso.
animal ['ænɪməl] *n* animal *m*, bicho ♦ *adj* animal.
animal spirits *npl* vivacidade *f*.
animate [*vt* 'ænɪmeɪt, *adj* 'ænɪmɪt] *vt* animar ♦ *adj* animado.
animated ['ænɪmeɪtɪd] *adj* animado.

animation [ænɪ'meɪʃən] *n* animação.
animosity [ænɪ'mɔsɪtɪ] *n* animosidade *f*.
aniseed ['ænɪsiːd] *n* erva-doce *f*, anis *f*.
Ankara ['æŋkərə] *n* Ancara.
ankle ['æŋkl] *n* tornozelo.
ankle socks *npl* soquetes *fpl*.
annex [*n* 'ænɛks, *vt* æ'nɛks] *n* (*also*: *BRIT*: *annexe*) (*building*) anexo ♦ *vt* anexar.
annexation [ænɛks'eɪʃən] *n* anexação *f*.
annexe ['ænɛks] (*BRIT*) *n* = **annex**.
annihilate [ə'naɪəleɪt] *vt* aniquilar.
anniversary [ænɪ'vɜːsərɪ] *n* aniversário.
annotate ['ænəʊteɪt] *vt* anotar.
announce [ə'naʊns] *vt* anunciar; **he** ~**ed that he wasn't going** ele declarou que não iria.
announcement [ə'naʊnsmənt] *n* anúncio; (*official*) comunicação *f*; (*letter*, *card*) aviso; **to make an** ~ anunciar alguma coisa.
announcer [ə'naʊnsə*] *n* (*RADIO*, *TV*) locutor(a) *m/f*.
annoy [ə'nɔɪ] *vt* aborrecer, irritar; **to be** ~**ed (at sth/with sb)** aborrecer-se *or* irritar-se (com algo/alguém); **don't get** ~**ed!** não se aborreça!
annoyance [ə'nɔɪəns] *n* aborrecimento; (*thing*) moléstia.
annoying [ə'nɔɪɪŋ] *adj* aborrecido; (*person*) importuno.
annual ['ænjʊəl] *adj* anual ♦ *n* (*BOT*) anual *f*; (*book*) anuário.
annual general meeting (*BRIT*) *n* assembléia geral ordinária.
annually ['ænjʊəlɪ] *adv* anualmente, cada ano.
annual report *n* relatório anual.
annuity [ə'njuːɪtɪ] *n* anuidade *f* *or* renda anual; **life** ~ renda vitalícia.
annul [ə'nʌl] *vt* anular; (*law*) revogar.
annulment [ə'nʌlmənt] *n* anulação *f*; (*of law*) revogação *f*.
annum ['ænəm] *n see* **per annum**.
Annunciation [ənʌnsɪ'eɪʃən] *n* Anunciação *f*.
anode ['ænəʊd] *n* anodo.
anoint [ə'nɔɪnt] *vt* ungir.
anomalous [ə'nɔmələs] *adj* anômalo.
anomaly [ə'nɔməlɪ] *n* anomalia.
anon [ə'nɔn] *adv* daqui a pouco.
anon. [ə'nɔn] *abbr* = **anonymous**.
anonymity [ænə'nɪmɪtɪ] *n* anonimato.
anonymous [ə'nɔnɪməs] *adj* anônimo; **to remain** ~ ficar no anonimato.
anorak ['ænəræk] *n* anoraque *m* (*BR*), anorak *m* (*PT*).
anorexia [ænə'rɛksɪə] *n* (*MED*: *also*: ~ *nervosa*) anorexia.
another [ə'nʌðə*] *adj*: ~ **book** (*one more*) outro livro, mais um livro; (*a different one*) um outro livro, um livro diferente ♦ *pron* outro; ~ **drink?** outra bebida?, mais uma bebida?; **in** ~ **5 years** daqui a 5 anos; *see also* **one**.
ANSI *n abbr* (= *American National Standards Institute*) instituto de padrões.
answer ['ɑːnsə*] *n* resposta; (*to problem*) solução *f* ♦ *vi* responder ♦ *vt* (*reply to*) responder a; (*problem*) resolver; **to** ~ **the phone** atender o telefone; **in** ~ **to your letter**

em resposta *or* respondendo à sua carta; **to ~ the bell** *or* **the door** atender à porta.

answer back *vi* replicar, retrucar.

answer for *vt fus* responder por, responsabilizar-se por.

answer to *vt fus (description)* corresponder a; *(needs)* satisfazer.

answerable ['ɑːnsərəbl] *adj*: ~ **(to sb/for sth)** responsável (perante alguém/por algo); **I am ~ to no-one** não tenho que dar satisfações a ninguém.

answering machine ['ɑːnsərɪŋ-] *n* secretária eletrônica.

ant [ænt] *n* formiga.

ANTA *n abbr* = **American National Theatre and Academy.**

antacid [ænt'æsɪd] *adj* antiácido.

antagonism [æn'tægənɪzəm] *n* antagonismo.

antagonist [æn'tægənɪst] *n* antagonista *m/f*, adversário/a.

antagonistic [æntægə'nɪstɪk] *adj* antagônico, hostil; *(opposed)* oposto, contrário.

antagonize [æn'tægənaɪz] *vt* contrariar, hostilizar.

Antarctic [ænt'ɑːktɪk] *adj* antártico ♦ *n*: **the ~** o Antártico.

Antarctica [ænt'ɑːktɪkə] *n* Antártica.

Antarctic Circle *n* Círculo Polar Antártico.

Antarctic Ocean *n* oceano Antártico.

ante ['æntɪ] *n*: **to up the ~** apostar mais alto.

ante... ['æntɪ] *prefix* ante..., pré....

anteater ['æntiːtə*] *n* tamanduá *m*.

antecedent [æntɪ'siːdənt] *n* antecedente *m*.

antechamber ['æntɪtʃeɪmbə*] *n* antecâmara.

antelope ['æntɪləup] *n* antílope *m*.

antenatal ['æntɪ'neɪtl] *adj* pré-natal; ~ **clinic** clínica pré-natal.

antenna [æn'tɛnə] *(pl ~e) n* antena.

antennae [æn'tɛniː] *npl of* **antenna**.

anthem ['ænθəm] *n* motete *m*; *see also* **national anthem.**

ant hill *n* formigueiro.

anthology [æn'θɒlədʒɪ] *n* antologia.

anthropologist [ænθrə'pɒlədʒɪst] *n* antropologista *m/f*, antropólogo/a.

anthropology [ænθrə'pɒlədʒɪ] *n* antropologia.

anti... [æntɪ] *prefix* anti....

anti-aircraft *adj* antiaéreo.

anti-aircraft defence *n* defesa antiaérea.

anti-ballistic missile ['æntɪbə'lɪstɪk-] *n* míssil *m* antimíssil.

antibiotic [æntɪbaɪ'ɒtɪk] *adj, n* antibiótico.

antibody ['æntɪbɒdɪ] *n* anticorpo.

anticipate [æn'tɪsɪpeɪt] *vt (foresee)* prever; *(expect)* esperar; *(forestall)* antecipar; *(look forward to)* aguardar, esperar; **this is worse than I ~d** isso é pior do que eu esperava; **as ~d** como previsto.

anticipation [æntɪsɪ'peɪʃən] *n* expectativa; **thanking you in ~** antecipadamente grato(s), agradeço *(or* agradecemos) antecipadamente a atenção de V.Sª.

anticlimax [æntɪ'klaɪmæks] *n* desapontamento, desilusão *f*.

anticlockwise [æntɪ'klɔkwaɪz] *adv* em sentido anti-horário.

antics ['æntɪks] *npl* bobices *fpl*; *(of child)* travessuras.

anticyclone [æntɪ'saɪkləun] *n* anticiclone *m*.

antidote ['æntɪdəut] *n* antídoto.

antifreeze ['æntɪfriːz] *n* anticongelante *m*.

antihistamine [æntɪ'hɪstəmiːn] *n* anti-histamínico.

Antilles [æn'tɪliːz] *npl*: **the ~** as Antilhas.

antipathy [æn'tɪpəθɪ] *n* antipatia.

Antipodean [æntɪpə'diːən] *adj* australiano e neozelandês.

Antipodes [æn'tɪpədiːz] *npl*: **the ~** a Austrália e a Nova Zelândia.

antiquarian [æntɪ'kwɛərɪən] *adj*: ~ **bookshop** livraria de livros usados, sebo *(BR)* ♦ *n* antiquário/a.

antiquated ['æntɪkweɪtɪd] *adj* antiquado.

antique [æn'tiːk] *n* antiguidade *f*, antigualha ♦ *adj* antigo.

antique dealer *n* antiquário/a.

antique shop *n* loja de antiguidades.

antiquity [æn'tɪkwɪtɪ] *n* antiguidade *f*.

anti-Semitic [-sɪ'mɪtɪk] *adj (person)* anti-semita; *(views, publications etc)* anti-semítico.

anti-Semitism [-'sɛmɪtɪzəm] *n* anti-semitismo.

antiseptic [æntɪ'sɛptɪk] *adj, n* anti-séptico.

antisocial [æntɪ'səuʃəl] *adj* insociável; *(against society)* anti-social.

antitank ['æntɪ'tæŋk] *adj* antitanque *inv*.

antitheses [æn'tɪθɪsiːz] *npl of* **antithesis.**

antithesis [æn'tɪθɪsɪs] *(pl* **antitheses)** *n* antítese *f*.

antitrust legislation ['æntɪ'trʌst-] *n* legislação *f* antitruste.

antlers ['æntləz] *npl* esgalhos *mpl*, chifres *mpl*.

Antwerp ['æntwɔːp] *n* Antuérpia.

anus ['eɪnəs] *n* ânus *m*.

anvil ['ænvɪl] *n* bigorna.

anxiety [æŋ'zaɪətɪ] *n (worry)* inquietude *f*; *(eagerness)* ânsia; *(MED)* ansiedade *f*; ~ **to do** ânsia de fazer.

anxious ['æŋkʃəs] *adj (worried)* inquieto, apreensivo; *(moment)* angustiante; *(keen)* ansioso; ~ **to do/for sth** ansioso para fazer/ por algo; **to be ~ that** desejar que; **I'm very ~ about you** estou muito preocupado com você.

anxiously ['æŋkʃəslɪ] *adv* ansiosamente.

any ['ɛnɪ] *adj (in negative and interrogative sentences = some)* algum(a); *(negative sense)* nenhum(a); *(no matter which)* qualquer; *(each and every)* todo/a ♦ *pron (some)* algum(a); *(none)* nenhum(a) ♦ *adv (in negative sentences)* nada; *(in interrogative and conditional constructions)* algo; **I haven't ~ money/books** não tenho dinheiro/ livros; **have you ~ butter/children?** você

NB: European Portuguese adds the following consonants to certain words: **b** (sú(b)dito, su(b)til); **c** (a(c)ção, a(c)cionista, a(c)to); **m** (inde(m)ne); **p** (ado(p)ção, ado(p)tar); *for further details see p. xiii.*

tem manteiga/filhos?; **without ~ difficulty** sem problema nenhum; **at ~ moment** a qualquer momento; **come (at) ~ time** venha a qualquer hora; **~ day now** qualquer dia desses; **in ~ case** em todo o caso; **at ~ rate** de qualquer modo; **I haven't ~** não tenho nenhum; **have you got ~?** tem algum?; **can ~ of you sing?** algum de vocês sabe cantar?; **I can't hear him ~ more** não consigo mais ouvi-lo; **do you want ~ more soup?** quer mais sopa?; **are you feeling ~ better?** você se está sentindo melhor?

anybody ['ɛnɪbɔdɪ] *pron* qualquer um, qualquer pessoa; (*in interrogative sentences*) alguém; (*in negative sentences*): **I don't see ~** não vejo ninguém.

anyhow ['ɛnɪhau] *adv* de qualquer modo; (*carelessly*) descuidadamente; **I shall go ~** eu irei de qualquer jeito.

anyone ['ɛnɪwʌn] *pron* qualquer um, qualquer pessoa; (*in interrogative sentences*) alguém; (*in negative sentences*): **I don't see ~** não vejo ninguém.

anyplace ['ɛnɪpleɪs] (*US*) *adv* em qualquer parte; (*negative sense*) em parte nenhuma; (*everywhere*) em *or* por toda a parte.

anything ['ɛnɪθɪŋ] *pron* qualquer coisa; (*in interrogative sentences*) alguma coisa; (*in negative sentences*) nada; (*everything*) tudo.

anytime ['ɛnɪtaɪm] *adv* (*at any moment*) a qualquer momento; (*whenever*) não importa quando.

anyway ['ɛnɪweɪ] *adv* de qualquer modo.

anywhere ['ɛnɪwɛə*] *adv* em qualquer parte; (*negative sense*) em parte nenhuma; (*everywhere*) em *or* por toda a parte; **I don't see him ~** não o vejo em parte nenhuma; **~ in the world** em qualquer lugar do mundo.

Anzac ['ænzæk] *n abbr* (= *Australia-New Zealand Army Corps*) soldado da tropa ANZAC.

apart [ə'pɑ:t] *adv* à parte, de lado; (*separately*) separado; **10 miles ~** separados por 10 milhas; **they are living ~** estão separados; **~ from** além de, à parte de.

apartheid [ə'pɑ:teɪt] *n* apartheid *m*.

apartment [ə'pɑ:tmənt] (*US*) *n* apartamento.

apartment building (*US*) *n* prédio *or* edifício (de apartamentos).

apathetic [æpə'θɛtɪk] *adj* apático, indiferente.

apathy ['æpəθɪ] *n* apatia, indiferença.

APB (*US*) *n abbr* (= *all points bulletin*) expressão usada pela polícia significando "descubram e prendam o suspeito".

ape [eɪp] *n* macaco ♦ *vt* macaquear, imitar.

Apennines ['æpənaɪnz] *npl*: **the ~** os Apeninos.

aperitif [ə'pɛrɪtɪv] *n* aperitivo.

aperture ['æpətʃjuə*] *n* orifício; (*PHOT*) abertura.

APEX ['eɪpɛks] *n* (*BRIT*: = *Association of Professional, Executive, Clerical and Computer Staff*) sindicato de funcionários comerciais; (*AVIAT*: = *advance passenger excursion*) APEX *f*.

apex ['eɪpɛks] *n* ápice *m*.

aphid ['eɪfɪd] *n* pulgão *m*.

aphrodisiac [æfrəu'dɪzɪæk] *adj, n* afrodisíaco.

API *n abbr* = **American Press Institute**.

apiece [ə'pi:s] *adv* (*for each person*) cada um, por cabeça; (*for each item*) cada.

aplomb [ə'plɔm] *n* desenvoltura.

APO (*US*) *n abbr* (= *Army Post Office*) serviço postal do exército.

apocalypse [ə'pɔkəlɪps] *n* apocalipse *m*.

apolitical [eɪpə'lɪtɪkl] *adj* apolítico.

apologetic [əpɔlə'dʒɛtɪk] *adj* cheio de desculpas.

apologetically [əpɔlə'dʒɛtɪklɪ] *adv* (*say*) desculpando-se; (*smile*) como quem pede desculpas.

apologize [ə'pɔlədʒaɪz] *vi*: **to ~ (for sth to sb)** desculpar-se *or* pedir desculpas (por *or* de algo a alguém).

apology [ə'pɔlədʒɪ] *n* desculpas *fpl*; **please accept my apologies for ...** peço desculpas por ...; **to send one's apologies** apresentar desculpas.

apoplectic [æpə'plɛktɪk] *adj* (*MED*) apopléctico; (*inf*): **~ with rage** enraivecido.

apoplexy ['æpəplɛksɪ] *n* (*MED*) apoplexia.

apostle [ə'pɔsl] *n* apóstolo.

apostrophe [ə'pɔstrəfɪ] *n* apóstrofo.

appal [ə'pɔ:l] *vt* horrorizar.

Appalachian Mountains [æpə'leɪʃən-] *npl*: **the ~** os montes Apalaches.

appalling [ə'pɔ:lɪŋ] *adj* horrível; **she's an ~ cook** ela é uma péssima cozinheira.

apparatus [æpə'reɪtəs] *n* aparelho; (*in gym*) aparelhos *mpl*.

apparel [ə'pærl] (*US*) *n* vestuário, roupa.

apparent [ə'pærənt] *adj* aparente; (*obvious*) claro, patente; **it is ~ that ...** é claro *or* evidente que ....

apparently [ə'pærəntlɪ] *adv* aparentemente, pelo(s) visto(s).

apparition [æpə'rɪʃən] *n* aparição *f*; (*ghost*) fantasma *m*.

appeal [ə'pi:l] *vi* (*LAW*) apelar, recorrer ♦ *n* (*LAW*) recurso, apelação *f*; (*request*) pedido; (*plea*) súplica; (*charm*) encanto, atração *f*; **to ~ for** solicitar; **to appeal to** (*subj: person*) suplicar a; (: *thing*) atrair, agradar a; **to ~ to sb for mercy** pedir misericórdia a alguém; **it doesn't ~ to me** não me atrai; **right of ~** direito a recorrer *or* apelar.

appealing [ə'pi:lɪŋ] *adj* (*nice*) atraente; (*touching*) comovedor(a), comovente.

appear [ə'pɪə*] *vi* (*come into view*) aparecer; (*be present*) comparecer; (*LAW*) apresentar-se, comparecer; (*publication*) ser publicado; (*seem*) parecer; **it would ~ that** pareceria que; **to ~ in Hamlet** trabalhar em Hamlet; **to ~ on TV** (*person, news item*) sair na televisão; (*programme*) passar na televisão.

appearance [ə'pɪərəns] *n* (*coming into view*) aparecimento; (*presence*) comparecimento; (*look, aspect*) aparência; **to put in** *or* **make an ~** comparecer; **in order of ~** (*THEATRE*) por ordem de entrar em cena; **to keep up**

~s manter as aparências; **to all** ~s ao que tudo indica.

appease [ə'piːz] vt (pacify) apaziguar; (satisfy) satisfazer.

appeasement [ə'piːzmənt] n apaziguamento.

append [ə'pɛnd] vt anexar.

appendage [ə'pɛndɪdʒ] n apêndice m.

appendices [ə'pɛndɪsiːz] npl of **appendix**.

appendicitis [əpɛndɪ'saɪtɪs] n apendicite f.

appendix [ə'pɛndɪks] (pl **appendices**) n apêndice m; **to have one's** ~ **out** tirar o apêndice.

appetite ['æpɪtaɪt] n apetite m; **that walk has given me an** ~ essa caminhada me abriu o apetite.

appetizer ['æpɪtaɪzə*] n (food) tira-gosto; (drink) aperitivo.

appetizing ['æpɪtaɪzɪŋ] adj apetitoso.

applaud [ə'plɔːd] vt, vi aplaudir.

applause [ə'plɔːz] n aplausos mpl.

apple ['æpl] n maçã f; (also: ~ **tree**) macieira; **she's the** ~ **of his eye** ela é a menina dos olhos dele.

apple tree n macieira.

apple turnover n pastel m de maçã.

appliance [ə'plaɪəns] n (TECH) aparelho; **electrical** or **domestic** ~s eletrodomésticos mpl.

applicable [ə'plɪkəbl] adj aplicável; (relevant) apropriado; **the law is** ~ **from January** a lei entrará em vigor a partir de janeiro; **to be** ~ **to** valer para.

applicant ['æplɪkənt] n: ~ **(for)** (for post) candidato/a (a); (ADMIN: for benefit etc) requerente m/f (de).

application [æplɪ'keɪʃən] n aplicação f; (for a job, a grant etc) candidatura, requerimento; **on** ~ a pedido.

application form n (formulário de) requerimento.

application program n (COMPUT) aplicativo.

applications package n (COMPUT) pacote m de aplicações.

applied [ə'plaɪd] adj aplicado.

apply [ə'plaɪ] vt: **to** ~ **(to)** aplicar (a) ♦ vi: **to** ~ **to** apresentar-se a; (be suitable for) ser aplicável a; (be relevant to) dizer respeito a; **to** ~ **for** (permit, grant, job) solicitar, pedir; **to** ~ **the brakes** frear (BR), travar (PT); **to** ~ **o.s. to** aplicar-se a, dedicar-se a.

appoint [ə'pɔɪnt] vt (to post) nomear; (date, place) marcar.

appointee [əpɔɪn'tiː] n nomeado/a.

appointment [ə'pɔɪntmənt] n (engagement) encontro, marcado, compromisso; (at doctors etc) hora marcada; (act) nomeação f; (post) cargo; **to make an** ~ **(with)** marcar um encontro (com); (with doctor, hairdresser etc) marcar hora (com); "~s **(vacant)"** (PRESS) "ofertas de emprego"; **by** ~ com hora marcada.

apportion [ə'pɔːʃən] vt repartir, distribuir; (blame) pôr; **to** ~ **sth to sb** atribuir algo a alguém.

appraisal [ə'preɪzl] n avaliação f, estimatura.

appraise [ə'preɪz] vt avaliar.

appreciable [ə'priːʃəbl] adj apreciável, notável.

appreciate [ə'priːʃɪeɪt] vt (like) apreciar, estimar; (be grateful for) agradecer; (be aware of) compreender, perceber ♦ vi (COMM) valorizar-se; **I** ~ **your help** agradeço-lhe a or pela sua ajuda.

appreciation [əpriːʃɪ'eɪʃən] n apreciação f, estima; (gratitude) agradecimento; (FINANCE) valorização f.

appreciative [ə'priːʃɪətɪv] adj (person) agradecido; (comment) elogioso.

apprehend [æprɪ'hɛnd] vt (understand) perceber, compreender; (arrest) prender.

apprehension [æprɪ'hɛnʃən] n apreensão f.

apprehensive [æprɪ'hɛnsɪv] adj apreensivo, receoso.

apprentice [ə'prɛntɪs] n aprendiz m/f ♦ vt: **to be** ~**d to** ser aprendiz de.

apprenticeship [ə'prɛntɪsʃɪp] n aprendizado, aprendizagem f; **to serve one's** ~ fazer seu aprendizado.

appro. ['æprəu] (BRIT: inf) abbr (COMM) = **approval**.

approach [ə'prəutʃ] vi aproximar-se ♦ vt aproximar-se de; (be approximate) aproximar-se a; (ask, apply to) dirigir-se a; (subject, passer-by) abordar ♦ n aproximação f; (access) acesso; (proposal) proposição f; (way of handling) enfoque m; **to** ~ **sb about sth** falar com alguém sobre algo.

approachable [ə'prəutʃəbl] adj (person) tratável; (place) acessível.

approach road n via de acesso.

approbation [æprə'beɪʃən] n aprovação f.

appropriate [vt ə'prəuprɪeɪt, adj ə'prəuprɪɪt] vt (take) apropriar-se de; (allot): **to** ~ **sth for** destinar algo a ♦ adj (apt) apropriado, próprio; (relevant) adequado; **it would not be** ~ **for me to comment** não seria conveniente eu comentar.

appropriately [ə'prəuprɪɪtlɪ] adv adequadamente.

appropriation [əprəuprɪ'eɪʃən] n (confiscation) apropriação f; (of funds for sth) dotação f.

approval [ə'pruːvəl] n aprovação f; **on** ~ (COMM) a contento; **to meet with sb's** ~ (proposal etc) ser aprovado por alguém, obter a aprovação de alguém.

approve [ə'pruːv] vt aprovar.

approve of vt fus aprovar.

approved school [ə'pruːvd-] (BRIT) n reformatório.

approvingly [ə'pruːvɪŋlɪ] adv com aprovação.

approx. abbr = **approximately**.

approximate [adj ə'prɔksɪmɪt, vt ə'prɔksɪmeɪt] adj aproximado ♦ vt aproximar.

approximately [ə'prɔksɪmɪtlɪ] adv aproxima-

*NB: European Portuguese adds the following consonants to certain words: **b** (sú(b)dito, su(b)til); **c** (a(c)ção, a(c)cionista, a(c)to); **m** (inde(m)ne); **p** (ado(p)ção, ado(p)tar); for further details see p. xiii.*

damente.
approximation [əprɔksɪ'meɪʃən] *n* aproximação *f*.
apr *n abbr* (= *annual percentage rate*) taxa de juros anual.
Apr. *abbr* = **April**.
apricot ['eɪprɪkɔt] *n* damasco.
April ['eɪprəl] *n* abril *m*; *see also* **July**.
April Fool's Day *n* Primeiro-de-abril *m*.
apron ['eɪprən] *n* avental *m*; (*AVIAT*) pátio de estacionamento.
apse [æps] *n* (*ARCHIT*) abside *f*.
APT (*BRIT*) *n abbr* = **advanced passenger train**.
apt [æpt] *adj* (*suitable*) adequado; (*appropriate*) a propósito, apropriado; (*likely*): ~ **to do** sujeito a fazer.
Apt. *abbr* (= *apartment*) ap., apto.
aptitude ['æptɪtjuːd] *n* aptidão *f*, talento.
aptitude test *n* teste *m* de aptidão.
aptly ['æptlɪ] *adv* (*express*) acertadamente; ~ **named** apropriadamente chamado.
aqualung ['ækwəlʌŋ] *n* aparelho respiratório autônomo.
aquarium [ə'kwɛərɪəm] *n* aquário.
Aquarius [ə'kwɛərɪəs] *n* Aquário.
aquatic [ə'kwætɪk] *adj* aquático.
aqueduct ['ækwɪdʌkt] *n* aqueduto.
AR (*US*) *abbr* (*POST*) = **Arkansas**.
ARA (*BRIT*) *n abbr* = **Associate of the Royal Academy**.
Arab ['ærəb] *adj*, *n* árabe *m/f*.
Arabia [ə'reɪbɪə] *n* Arábia.
Arabian [ə'reɪbɪən] *adj* árabe.
Arabian Desert *n* deserto da Arábia.
Arabian Sea *n* mar *m* Arábico.
Arabic ['ærəbɪk] *n* árabe *m* ♦ *adj* árabe.
Arabic numerals *npl* algarismos *mpl* arábicos.
arable ['ærəbl] *adj* cultivável.
ARAM (*BRIT*) *n abbr* = **Associate of the Royal Academy of Music**.
arbiter ['ɑːbɪtə*] *n* árbitro.
arbitrary ['ɑːbɪtrərɪ] *adj* arbitrário.
arbitrate ['ɑːbɪtreɪt] *vi* arbitrar.
arbitration [ɑːbɪ'treɪʃən] *n* arbitragem *f*; **the dispute went to** ~ o litígio foi submetido a arbitragem.
arbitrator ['ɑːbɪtreɪtə*] *n* árbitro.
ARC *n abbr* = **American Red Cross**.
arc [ɑːk] *n* arco.
arcade [ɑː'keɪd] *n* arcada; (*round a square*) arcos *mpl*; (*passage with shops*) galeria.
arch [ɑːtʃ] *n* arco ♦ *vt* arquear, curvar ♦ *adj* malicioso ♦ *prefix*: ~(-) arce..., arqui...; **pointed** ~ ogiva.
archaeological [ɑːkɪə'lɔdʒɪkl] (*US* **archeological**) *adj* arqueológico.
archaeologist [ɑːkɪ'ɔlədʒɪst] (*US* **archeologist**) *n* arqueólogo/a.
archaeology [ɑːkɪ'ɔlədʒɪ] (*US* **archeology**) *n* arqueologia.
archaic [ɑː'keɪɪk] *adj* arcaico.
archangel ['ɑːkeɪndʒəl] *n* arcanjo.
archbishop [ɑːtʃ'bɪʃəp] *n* arcebispo.

arch-enemy *n* arquiinimigo/a.
archeology *etc* [ɑːkɪ'ɔlədʒɪ] (*US*) = **archaeology** *etc*.
archer ['ɑːtʃə*] *n* arqueiro/a.
archery ['ɑːtʃərɪ] *n* tiro de arco.
archetypal ['ɑːkɪtaɪpəl] *adj* arquetípico.
archetype ['ɑːkɪtaɪp] *n* arquétipo.
archipelago [ɑːkɪ'pɛlɪgəʊ] *n* arquipélago.
architect ['ɑːkɪtɛkt] *n* arquiteto/a.
architectural [ɑːkɪ'tɛktʃərəl] *adj* arquitetônico.
architecture ['ɑːkɪtɛktʃə*] *n* arquitetura.
archives ['ɑːkaɪvz] *npl* arquivo.
archivist ['ɑːkɪvɪst] *n* arquivista *m/f*.
archway ['ɑːtʃweɪ] *n* arco.
ARCM (*BRIT*) *n abbr* = **Associate of the Royal College of Music**.
Arctic ['ɑːktɪk] *adj* ártico ♦ *n*: **the** ~ o Ártico.
Arctic Circle *n* Círculo Polar Ártico.
Arctic Ocean *n* oceano Ártico.
ARD (*US*) *n abbr* (*MED*) = **acute respiratory disease**.
ardent ['ɑːdənt] *adj* (*passionate*) ardente, apaixonado; (*fervent*) fervoroso.
ardour ['ɑːdə*] (*US* **ardor**) *n* (*passion*) ardor *m*; (*fervour*) fervor *m*.
arduous ['ɑːdjuəs] *adj* árduo.
are [ɑː*] *vb see* **be**.
area ['ɛərɪə] *n* área; (*MAT*) superfície *f*, extensão *f*; (*zone*) zona, região *f*; **dining** ~ área de jantar; **the London** ~ a região de Londres.
area code (*US*) *n* (*TEL*) código DDD *or* de área.
arena [ə'riːnə] *n* arena; (*of circus*) picadeiro (*BR*), pista (*PT*); (*for bullfight*) arena (*BR*), praça (*PT*).
aren't [ɑːnt] = **are not**.
Argentina [ɑːdʒən'tiːnə] *n* Argentina.
Argentinian [ɑːdʒən'tɪnɪən] *adj*, *n* argentino/a.
arguable ['ɑːgjuəbl] *adj* discutível.
arguably ['ɑːgjuəblɪ] *adv* possivelmente.
argue ['ɑːgjuː] *vi* (*quarrel*) discutir; (*reason*) argumentar; **to** ~ **about sth (with sb)** discutir sobre algo (com alguém); **to** ~ **that** sustentar que.
argument ['ɑːgjumənt] *n* (*reasons*) argumento, razão *f*; (*quarrel*) briga, discussão *f*; (*debate*) debate *m*; ~ **for/against** argumento a favor de/contra.
argumentative [ɑːgju'mɛntətɪv] *adj* discutidor(a).
aria ['ɑːrɪə] *n* (*MUS*) ária.
ARIBA (*BRIT*) *n abbr* = **Associate of the Royal Institute of British Architects**.
arid ['ærɪd] *adj* árido.
aridity [ə'rɪdɪtɪ] *n* aridez *f*.
Aries ['ɛərɪz] *n* Áries *m*.
arise [ə'raɪz] (*irreg*: *like* **rise**) *vi* (*rise up*) levantar-se, erguer-se; (*emerge*) surgir; **to** ~ **from** resultar de; **should the need** ~ se for necessário.
aristocracy [ærɪs'tɔkrəsɪ] *n* aristocracia.
aristocrat ['ærɪstəkræt] *n* aristocrata *m/f*.
aristocratic [ærɪstə'krætɪk] *adj* aristocrático.
arithmetic [ə'rɪθmətɪk] *n* aritmética.

arithmetical [ærɪθ'metɪkl] *adj* aritmético.

ark [ɑːk] *n*: **Noah's A~** arca de Noé.

arm [ɑːm] *n* (*ANAT*) braço ♦ *vt* armar; **~s** *npl* (*weapons*) armas *fpl*; (*HERALDRY*) brasão *m*; **~ in ~** de braços dados.

armaments ['ɑːməmənts] *npl* (*weapons*) armamento.

armband ['ɑːmbænd] *n* faixa de braço, braçadeira; (*for swimming*) bóia de braço.

armchair ['ɑːmtʃeə*] *n* poltrona.

armed [ɑːmd] *adj* armado; **the ~ forces** as forças armadas.

armed robbery *n* assalto à mão armada.

Armenia [ɑː'miːnɪə] *n* Armênia.

Armenian [ɑː'miːnɪən] *adj* armênio ♦ *n* armênio/a; (*LING*) armênio.

armful ['ɑːmful] *n* braçada.

armistice ['ɑːmɪstɪs] *n* armistício.

armour ['ɑːmə*] (*US* **armor**) *n* armadura; (*also*: **~ plating**) blindagem *f*.

armo(u)red car ['ɑːməd-] *n* carro blindado.

armo(u)ry ['ɑːmərɪ] *n* arsenal *m*.

armpit ['ɑːmpɪt] *n* sovaco.

armrest ['ɑːmrest] *n* braço (de poltrona).

arms control *n* controle *m* de armas.

arms race *n* corrida armamentista.

army ['ɑːmɪ] *n* exército.

aroma [ə'rəumə] *n* aroma.

aromatic [ærə'mætɪk] *adj* aromático.

arose [ə'rəuz] *pt of* **arise**.

around [ə'raund] *adv* em volta; (*in the area*) perto ♦ *prep* em redor de, em volta de; (*fig*: *about*) cerca de; **is he ~?** ele está por aí?

arouse [ə'rauz] *vt* despertar.

arpeggio [ɑː'pedʒɪəu] *n* arpejo.

arrange [ə'reɪndʒ] *vt* arranjar; (*programme*) organizar ♦ *vi*: **we have ~d for a car to pick you up** providenciamos um carro para buscá-lo; **it was ~d that ...** foi combinado que ...; **to ~ to do sth** combinar em *or* ficar de fazer algo.

arrangement [ə'reɪndʒmənt] *n* arranjo; (*agreement*) acordo; **~s** *npl* (*plans*) planos *mpl*; (*preparations*) preparativos *mpl*; **to come to an ~ (with sb)** chegar a um acordo (com alguém); **home deliveries by ~** entregas a domicílio por convênio; **I'll make all the necessary ~s** eu vou tomar todas as providências necessárias.

array [ə'reɪ] *n* (*variety*) leque *m*; (*MATH*, *COMPUT*) tabela.

arrears [ə'rɪəz] *npl* atrasos *mpl*; **to be in ~ with one's rent** atrasar o aluguel.

arrest [ə'rest] *vt* prender, deter; (*sb's attention*) chamar, prender ♦ *n* detenção *f*, prisão *f*; **under ~** preso.

arresting [ə'restɪŋ] *adj* (*fig*: *beauty*) cativante; (: *painting*, *novel*) impressionante.

arrival [ə'raɪvəl] *n* chegada; **new ~** recém-chegado.

arrive [ə'raɪv] *vi* chegar.

  arrive at *vt fus* (*fig*) chegar a.

arrogance ['ærəgəns] *n* arrogância.

arrogant ['ærəgənt] *adj* arrogante.

arrow ['ærəu] *n* flecha, seta.

arse [ɑːs] (*BRIT*: *inf!*) *n* cu *m* (*!*).

arsenal ['ɑːsɪnl] *n* arsenal *m*.

arsenic ['ɑːsnɪk] *n* arsênico.

arson ['ɑːsn] *n* incêndio premeditado.

art [ɑːt] *n* arte *f*; (*craft*) ofício; (*skill*) habilidade *f*, jeito; **~s** *npl* (*SCH*) letras *fpl*; **work of ~** obra de arte.

artefact ['ɑːtɪfækt] *n* artefato.

arterial [ɑː'tɪərɪəl] *adj* (*ANAT*) arterial; **~ road** estrada mestra.

artery ['ɑːtərɪ] *n* (*MED*) artéria; (*fig*) estrada principal.

artful ['ɑːtful] *adj* ardiloso, esperto.

art gallery *n* museu *m* de belas artes; (*small*, *private*) galeria de arte.

arthritis [ɑː'θraɪtɪs] *n* artrite *f*.

artichoke ['ɑːtɪtʃəuk] *n* alcachofra; *see also* **Jerusalem**.

article ['ɑːtɪkl] *n* artigo; (*BRIT*: *LAW*: *training*): **~s** *npl* contrato de aprendizagem; **~s of clothing** peças *fpl* de vestuário.

articles of association *npl* (*COMM*) estatutos *mpl* sociais.

articulate [*adj* ɑː'tɪkjulɪt, *vt* ɑː'tɪkjuleɪt] *adj* (*person*) que se expressa com clareza e desenvoltura; (*speech*) bem articulado ♦ *vt* articular, pronunciar.

articulated lorry [ɑː'tɪkjuleɪtɪd-] (*BRIT*) *n* caminhão (*PT*: camião) *m* articulado, jamanta.

artifice ['ɑːtɪfɪs] *n* ardil *m*, artifício.

artificial [ɑːtɪ'fɪʃəl] *adj* artificial; (*teeth etc*) postiço.

artificial insemination [-ɪnsemɪ'neɪʃən] *n* inseminação *f* artificial.

artificial intelligence *n* inteligência artificial.

artificial respiration *n* respiração *f* artificial.

artillery [ɑː'tɪlərɪ] *n* artilharia.

artisan ['ɑːtɪzæn] *n* artesão/sã *m/f*.

artist ['ɑːtɪst] *n* artista *m/f*; (*MUS*) intérprete *m/f*.

artistic [ɑː'tɪstɪk] *adj* artístico.

artistry ['ɑːtɪstrɪ] *n* arte *f*, mestria.

artless ['ɑːtlɪs] *adj* (*innocent*) natural, simples; (*clumsy*) desajeitado.

art school *n* ≈ escola de artes.

ARV *n abbr* (= *American Revised Version*) tradução norte-americana da Bíblia.

AS (*US*) *n abbr* (*SCH*: = *Associate in/of Science*) título universitário ♦ *abbr* (*POST*) = **American Samoa**.

as [æz, əz] *conj* (*cause*) como, já que; (*time*: *moment*) quando; (*duration*) enquanto; (*manner*) como ♦ *prep* (*in the capacity of*) como; **~ big ~** tão grande como; **twice ~ big ~** duas vezes maior que; **much ~ I like them, I ...** por mais que eu goste deles, eu ...; **strong ~ he is, he won't be able to ...** por mais forte que seja, não poderá ...; **~ the years went by** no decorrer dos anos; **~ she**

NB: European Portuguese adds the following consonants to certain words: **b** (sú(b)dito, su(b)til); **c** (a(c)ção, a(c)cionista, a(c)to); **m** (inde(m)ne); **p** (ado(p)ção, ado(p)tar); *for further details see p. xiii.*

said como ela disse; **he gave me this** ~ **a present** ele me deu isso de presente; ~ **if** *or* **though** como se; ~ **for** *or* **to** quanto a; ~ *or* **so long** ~ desde que, contanto que; ~ **much/many ...** (~) tanto/s ... (como); ~ **soon** ~ logo que, assim que; ~ **soon** ~ **possible** o mais cedo possível; ~ **such** como tal; ~ **well** também; ~ **well** ~ assim como; *see also* **so**; **such**.
ASA *n abbr* (= *American Standards Association*) *associação de padronização*.
a.s.a.p. *abbr* = **as soon as possible**.
asbestos [æz'bɛstəs] *n* asbesto, amianto.
ascend [ə'sɛnd] *vt* ascender, subir.
ascendancy [ə'sɛndənsɪ] *n* predomínio, ascendência.
ascendant [ə'sɛndənt] *n*: **to be in the** ~ estar em alta.
Ascension [ə'sɛnʃən] *n* (*REL*): **the** ~ a Ascensão.
Ascension Island *n* ilha da Ascensão.
ascent [ə'sɛnt] *n* subida; (*slope*) rampa; (*promotion*) ascensão *f*.
ascertain [æsə'teɪn] *vt* averiguar, verificar.
ascetic [ə'sɛtɪk] *adj* ascético.
asceticism [ə'sɛtɪsɪzəm] *n* ascetismo.
ASCII ['æskiː] *n abbr* (= *American Standard Code for Information Interchange*) ASCII *m*.
ascribe [ə'skraɪb] *vt*: **to** ~ **sth to** atribuir algo a.
ASCU (*US*) *n abbr* = **Association of State Colleges and Universities**.
ASE *n abbr* = **American Stock Exchange**.
ASH [æʃ] (*BRIT*) *n abbr* (= *Action on Smoking and Health*) liga antitabagista.
ash [æʃ] *n* cinza; (*also*: ~ **tree**) freixo.
ashamed [ə'ʃeɪmd] *adj* envergonhado; **to be** ~ **of** ter vergonha de; **to be** ~ (**of o.s.**) **for having done** ter vergonha de ter feito.
ashen ['æʃn] *adj* cinzento.
ashore [ə'ʃɔː*] *adv* em terra; **to go** ~ descer à terra, desembarcar.
ashtray ['æʃtreɪ] *n* cinzeiro.
Ash Wednesday *n* quarta-feira de cinzas.
Asia ['eɪʃə] *n* Ásia.
Asia Minor *n* Ásia Menor.
Asian ['eɪʃən] *adj, n* asiático/a.
Asiatic [eɪsɪ'ætɪk] *adj* asiático/a.
aside [ə'saɪd] *adv* à parte, de lado ♦ *n* aparte *m*; ~ **from** além de.
ask [ɑːsk] *vt* perguntar; (*invite*) convidar; **to** ~ **sb sth** perguntar algo a alguém; **to** ~ **sb for sth** pedir algo a alguém; **to** ~ **sb to do sth** pedir para alguém fazer algo; **to** ~ **sb the time** perguntar as horas a alguém; **to** ~ **sb about sth** perguntar a alguém sobre algo; **to** ~ **about the price** perguntar pelo preço; **to** ~ (**sb**) **a question** fazer uma pergunta (a alguém); **to** ~ **sb out to dinner** convidar alguém para jantar.
ask after *vt fus* perguntar por.
ask for *vt fus* pedir; **it's just** ~**ing for it** *or* **trouble** é procurar encrenca.
askance [ə'skɑːns] *adv*: **to look** ~ **at sb** olhar alguém de soslaio.

askew [ə'skjuː] *adv* torto, de esguelha.
asking price ['ɑːskɪŋ-] *n* preço pedido.
asleep [ə'sliːp] *adj* dormindo; **to fall** ~ dormir, adormecer.
ASLEF ['æzlɛf] (*BRIT*) *n abbr* (= *Associated Society of Locomotive Engineers and Firemen*) sindicato dos ferroviários.
asp [æsp] *n* áspide *f or m*.
asparagus [əs'pærəgəs] *n* aspargo (*PT*: esp-).
asparagus tips *npl* aspargos *mpl*.
ASPCA *n abbr* = **American Society for the Prevention of Cruelty to Animals**.
aspect ['æspɛkt] *n* aspecto; (*direction in which a building etc faces*) orientação *f*.
aspersions [əs'pɜːʃənz] *npl*: **to cast** ~ **on** difamar, caluniar.
asphalt ['æsfælt] *n* asfalto.
asphyxiate [æs'fɪksɪeɪt] *vt* asfixiar ♦ *vi* asfixiar-se.
asphyxiation [æsfɪksɪ'eɪʃən] *n* asfixia.
aspirate [*vt* 'æspəreɪt, *adj* 'æspərɪt] *vt* aspirar ♦ *adj* aspirado.
aspiration [æspə'reɪʃən] *n* aspiração *f*.
aspire [əs'paɪə*] *vi*: **to** ~ **to** aspirar a.
aspirin ['æsprɪn] *n* aspirina.
ass [æs] *n* jumento, burro; (*inf*) imbecil *m/f*; (*US: inf!*) cu *m* (!).
assail [ə'seɪl] *vt* assaltar, atacar.
assailant [ə'seɪlənt] *n* (*attacker*) assaltante *m/f*, atacante *m/f*; (*aggressor*) agressor(a) *m/f*.
assassin [ə'sæsɪn] *n* assassino/a.
assassinate [ə'sæsɪneɪt] *vt* assassinar.
assassination [əsæsɪ'neɪʃən] *n* assassinato, assassínio.
assault [ə'sɔːlt] *n* assalto; (*LAW*): ~ (**and battery**) vias *fpl* de fato ♦ *vt* assaltar, atacar; (*sexually*) agredir, violar.
assemble [ə'sɛmbl] *vt* reunir; (*TECH*) montar ♦ *vi* reunir-se.
assembly [ə'sɛmblɪ] *n* (*meeting*) reunião *f*, assembléia; (*people*) congregação *f*; (*construction*) montagem *f*.
assembly language *n* (*COMPUT*) linguagem *f* de montagem.
assembly line *n* linha de montagem.
assent [ə'sɛnt] *n* assentimento, aprovação *f* ♦ *vi*: **to** ~ (**to sth**) consentir *or* assentir (em algo).
assert [ə'sɜːt] *vt* afirmar; (*claim etc*) fazer valer; **to** ~ **o.s.** impor-se.
assertion [ə'sɜːʃən] *n* afirmação *f*.
assertive [ə'sɜːtɪv] *adj* (*vigorous*) enérgico; (*forceful*) agressivo; (*dogmatic*) peremptório.
assess [ə'sɛs] *vt* avaliar; (*tax, damages*) fixar; (*property etc: for tax*) taxar.
assessment [ə'sɛsmənt] *n* avaliação *f*.
assessor [ə'sɛsə*] *n* avaliador(a) *m/f*; (*of tax*) avaliador(a) do fisco.
asset ['æsɛt] *n* (*property*) bem *m*; (*quality*) vantagem *f*, trunfo; ~**s** *npl* (*of company*) ativo; (*of person*) bens *mpl*.
asset-stripping [-'strɪpɪŋ] *n* (*COMM*) venda em parcelas do patrimônio social.
assiduous [ə'sɪdjuəs] *adj* assíduo.

assign [ə'saɪn] vt (date) fixar; **to ~ sth to** (task) designar algo a; (resources) destinar algo a; (cause, meaning) atribuir algo a.

assignment [ə'saɪnmənt] n tarefa.

assimilate [ə'sɪmɪleɪt] vt assimilar.

assimilation [əsɪmɪ'leɪʃən] n assimilação f.

assist [ə'sɪst] vt ajudar; (progress etc) auxiliar; (injured person etc) socorrer.

assistance [ə'sɪstəns] n ajuda, auxílio; (welfare) subsídio; (to injured person) socorro.

assistant [ə'sɪstənt] n assistente m/f, auxiliar m/f; (BRIT: also: shop ~) vendedor(a) m/f.

assistant manager n subgerente m/f.

assizes [ə'saɪzɪz] npl sessão f de tribunal superior.

associate [adj, n ə'səuʃɪɪt, vt, vi ə'səuʃɪeɪt] adj associado ♦ n (colleague) colega m/f; (partner) sócio/a; (in crime) cúmplice m/f; (member) sócio/a ♦ vt associar ♦ vi: **to ~ with sb** associar-se com alguém; **~ company** companhia ligada; **~ director** diretor(a) m/f associado/a.

associated company [ə'səuʃɪeɪtɪd-] n companhia ligada.

association [əsəusɪ'eɪʃən] n associação f; (COMM) sociedade f; **in ~ with** em parceria com.

association football (BRIT) n futebol m.

assorted [ə'sɔːtɪd] adj sortido; **in ~ sizes** em vários tamanhos.

assortment [ə'sɔːtmənt] n sortimento.

Asst. abbr = **assistant**.

assuage [ə'sweɪdʒ] vt (grief, pain) aliviar, abrandar; (thirst) matar.

assume [ə'sjuːm] vt (suppose) supor, presumir; (responsibilities etc) assumir; (attitude, name) adotar, tomar.

assumed name [ə'sjuːmd-] n nome m falso.

assumption [ə'sʌmpʃən] n (supposition) suposição f, presunção f; **on the ~ that** na suposição or hipótese que; (on condition that) com a condição de que.

assurance [ə'ʃuərəns] n garantia; (confidence) confiança; (insurance) seguro.

assure [ə'ʃuə*] vt assegurar; **to ~ sb that** garantir or assegurar a alguém que.

AST (US) abbr (= Atlantic Standard Time) hora de inverno de Nova Iorque.

asterisk ['æstərɪsk] n asterisco.

astern [ə'stɜːn] adv à popa; (direction) à ré.

asteroid ['æstərɔɪd] n asteróide m.

asthma ['æsmə] n asma.

asthmatic [æs'mætɪk] adj, n asmático/a.

astigmatism [ə'stɪgmətɪzəm] n astigmatismo.

astir [ə'stɜː*] adv em agitação.

ASTMS (BRIT) n abbr (= Association of Scientific, Technical and Managerial Staffs) sindicato dos empregados científicos, técnicos e administrativos.

astonish [ə'stɔnɪʃ] vt assombrar, espantar.

astonishing [ə'stɔnɪʃɪŋ] adj espantoso, surpreendente.

astonishingly [ə'stɔnɪʃɪŋlɪ] adv surpreendentemente.

astonishment [ə'stɔnɪʃmənt] n assombro, espanto; **to my ~** para minha grande surpresa.

astound [ə'staund] vt pasmar, estarrecer.

astray [ə'streɪ] adv: **to go ~** (person) perder-se; (letter etc) extraviar-se; **to go ~ in one's calculations** cometer um erro em seus cálculos; **to lead ~** desencaminhar.

astride [ə'straɪd] prep a cavalo or montado sobre.

astringent [ə'strɪndʒənt] adj adstringente ♦ n adstringente m.

astrologer [əs'trɔlədʒə*] n astrólogo/a.

astrology [əs'trɔlədʒɪ] n astrologia.

astronaut ['æstrənɔːt] n astronauta m/f.

astronomer [əs'trɔnəmə*] n astrônomo/a.

astronomical [æstrə'nɔmɪkəl] adj astronômico.

astronomy [əs'trɔnəmɪ] n astronomia.

astrophysics ['æstrəu'fɪzɪks] n astrofísica.

astute [əs'tjuːt] adj astuto, esperto.

asunder [ə'sʌndə*] adv: **to put ~** separar; **to tear ~** rasgar.

ASV n abbr (= American Standard Version) tradução da Bíblia.

asylum [ə'saɪləm] n (refuge) asilo; (hospital) manicômio; see also **political asylum**.

asymmetric(al) [eɪsɪ'mɛtrɪk(l)] adj assimétrico.

at [æt] prep em, a; (because of): **he was surprised/annoyed ~** ele ficou surpreso/chateado com; **~ the top** em cima; **~ John's** na casa de João; **~ the baker's** na padaria; **~ times** às vezes; **~ 4 o'clock** às quatro; **~ night** à noite; **~ £1 a kilo** a uma libra o quilo; **~ a stroke** de um golpe; **two ~ a time** de dois em dois.

ate [eɪt] pt of **eat**.

atheism ['eɪθɪɪzəm] n ateísmo.

atheist ['eɪθɪɪst] n ateu/atéia m/f.

Athenian [ə'θiːnɪən] adj, n ateniense m/f.

Athens ['æθɪnz] n Atenas f.

athlete ['æθliːt] n atleta m/f.

athletic [æθ'lɛtɪk] adj atlético.

athletics [æθ'lɛtɪks] n atletismo.

Atlantic [ət'læntɪk] adj atlântico ♦ n: **the ~ (Ocean)** o (oceano) Atlântico.

atlas ['ætləs] n atlas m.

Atlas Mountains npl: **the ~** os montes Atlas.

A.T.M. abbr (= Automatic Telling Machine) caixa automática or eletrônica.

atmosphere ['ætməsfɪə*] n atmosfera; (fig) ambiente m.

atmospheric [ætməs'fɛrɪk] adj atmosférico.

atmospherics [ætməs'fɛrɪks] npl (RADIO) estática.

atoll ['ætɔl] n atol m.

atom ['ætəm] n átomo.

atomic [ə'tɔmɪk] adj atômico.

atom(ic) bomb n bomba atômica.

---

*NB: European Portuguese adds the following consonants to certain words: **b** (sú(b)dito, su(b)til); **c** (a(c)ção, a(c)cionista, a(c)to); **m** (inde(m)ne); **p** (ado(p)ção, ado(p)tar); for further details see p. xiii.*

atomizer ['ætəmaɪzə*] n atomizador m, pulverizador m.

atone [ə'təʊn] vi: **to ~ for** expiar.

atonement [ə'təʊnmənt] n expiação f.

ATP n abbr (= Association of Tennis Professionals) Associação f de Tenistas Profissionais.

atrocious [ə'trəʊʃəs] adj atroz; (very bad) péssimo.

atrocity [ə'trɒsɪtɪ] n atrocidade f.

atrophy ['ætrəfɪ] n atrofia ♦ vt atrofiar ♦ vi atrofiar-se.

attach [ə'tætʃ] vt (fix) prender; (document, letter) juntar, anexar; (employee, troops) adir; **to be ~ed to sb/sth** (to like) ter afeição por alguém/algo; **the ~ed letter** a carta junta or anexa.

attaché [ə'tæʃeɪ] n adido/a.

attaché case n pasta.

attachment [ə'tætʃmənt] n (tool) acessório; (love): **~ (to)** afeição f (por).

attack [ə'tæk] vt atacar; (subj: criminal) assaltar; (task etc) empreender ♦ n ataque m; (mugging etc) assalto; (on sb's life) atentado; (also: heart ~) ataque cardíaco or de coração.

attacker [ə'tækə*] n agressor(a) m/f; (criminal) assaltante m/f.

attain [ə'teɪn] vt (also: ~ to) alcançar, atingir.

attainments [ə'teɪnmənts] npl dotes mpl, talento.

attempt [ə'tɛmpt] n tentativa ♦ vt tentar; **~ed theft** etc (LAW) tentativa de roubo etc; **to make an ~ on sb's life** atentar contra a vida de alguém; **he made no ~ to help** ele não fez nada para ajudar.

attend [ə'tɛnd] vt (meeting, talk) assistir a; (party) presenciar; (school) cursar; (church) ir a; (course) fazer; (patient) tratar; **to ~ (up)on** acompanhar, servir.

attend to vt fus (matter) encarregar-se de; (speech etc) prestar atenção a; (needs, customer) atender a.

attendance [ə'tɛndəns] n (being present) comparecimento; (people present) assistência.

attendant [ə'tɛndənt] n servidor(a) m/f; (THEATRE) arrumador(a) m/f ♦ adj concomitante.

attention [ə'tɛnʃən] n atenção f; **~!** (MIL) sentido!; **at ~** (MIL) em posição de sentido; **for the ~ of ...** (ADMIN) atenção ...; **it has come to my ~ that ...** constatei que ....

attentive [ə'tɛntɪv] adj atento; (polite) cortês.

attentively [ə'tɛntɪvlɪ] adv atentamente.

attenuate [ə'tɛnjueɪt] vt atenuar ♦ vi atenuar-se.

attest [ə'tɛst] vi: **to ~ to** atestar.

attic ['ætɪk] n sótão m.

attire [ə'taɪə*] n traje m, roupa.

attitude ['ætɪtjuːd] n atitude f; (view): **~ (to)** atitude (para com).

attorney [ə'tɜːnɪ] n (US: lawyer) advogado/a; (having proxy) procurador(a) m/f.

Attorney General n procurador(a) m/f geral da Justiça.

attract [ə'trækt] vt atrair; (attention) chamar.

attraction [ə'trækʃən] n atração f; (good point) atrativo; **~ towards sth** atração por algo.

attractive [ə'træktɪv] adj atraente.

attribute [n 'ætrɪbjuːt, vt ə'trɪbjuːt] n atributo ♦ vt: **to ~ sth to** atribuir algo a.

attrition [ə'trɪʃən] n see **war**.

Atty. Gen. abbr = **Attorney General**.

ATV n abbr (= all terrain vehicle) veículo todo-terreno.

aubergine ['əʊbəʒiːn] n berinjela.

auburn ['ɔːbən] adj castanho-avermelhado.

auction ['ɔːkʃən] n (also: sale by ~) leilão m ♦ vt leiloar; **to sell by ~** vender em leilão; **to put up for ~** pôr em leilão.

auctioneer [ɔːkʃə'nɪə*] n leiloeiro/a.

auction room n local m de leilão.

audacious [ɔː'deɪʃəs] adj audaz, atrevido; (pej) descarado.

audacity [ɔː'dæsɪtɪ] n audácia, atrevimento; (pej) descaramento.

audible ['ɔːdɪbl] adj audível.

audience ['ɔːdɪəns] n (in theatre, concert etc) platéia; (of TV, radio programme) audiência; (of speech etc) auditório; (of writer, magazine) público; (interview) audiência.

audio typist ['ɔːdɪəʊ-] n datilógrafo/a (de textos ditados em fita).

audiovisual [ɔːdɪəʊ'vɪzjuəl] adj audiovisual; **~ aids** recursos mpl audiovisuais.

audit ['ɔːdɪt] vt fazer a auditoria de ♦ n auditoria.

audition [ɔː'dɪʃən] n audição f.

auditor ['ɔːdɪtə*] n auditor(a) m/f.

auditoria [ɔːdɪ'tɔːrɪə] npl of **auditorium**.

auditorium [ɔːdɪ'tɔːrɪəm] (pl **~s** or **auditoria**) n auditório.

AUEW (BRIT) n abbr (= Amalgamated Union of Engineering Workers) sindicato das indústrias mecânicas.

Aug. abbr = **August**.

augment [ɔːg'mɛnt] vt, vi aumentar.

augur ['ɔːgə*] vi: **it ~s well** é de bom augúrio ♦ vt (be a sign of) augurar, pressagiar.

August ['ɔːgəst] n agosto; see also **July**.

august [ɔː'gʌst] adj augusto, imponente.

aunt [ɑːnt] n tia.

auntie ['ɑːntɪ] n titia.

aunty ['ɑːntɪ] n = **auntie**.

au pair ['əʊ'pɛə*] n (also: ~ girl) au pair f.

aura ['ɔːrə] n (of person) ar m, aspecto; (of place) ambiente m.

auspices ['ɔːspɪsɪz] npl: **under the ~ of** sob os auspícios de.

auspicious [ɔːs'pɪʃəs] adj propício.

Aussie ['ɒzɪ] (inf) adj, n australiano/a.

austere [ɒs'tɪə*] adj austero; (manner) severo.

austerity [ɒ'stɛrɪtɪ] n austeridade f.

Australasia [ɒːstrə'leɪzɪə] n Australásia.

Australia [ɒs'treɪlɪə] n Austrália.

Australian [ɒs'treɪlɪən] adj, n australiano/a.

Austria ['ɒstrɪə] n Áustria.

Austrian ['ɔstrɪən] *adj, n* austríaco/a.
AUT (*BRIT*) *n abbr* (= *Association of University Teachers*) *sindicato universitário*.
authentic [ɔː'θɛntɪk] *adj* autêntico.
authenticate [ɔː'θɛntɪkeɪt] *vt* autenticar.
authenticity [ɔːθɛn'tɪsɪtɪ] *n* autenticidade *f*.
author ['ɔːθə] *n* autor(a) *m/f*.
authoritarian [ɔːθɔrɪ'tɛərɪən] *adj* autoritário.
authoritative [ɔː'θɔrɪtɪtɪv] *adj* autorizado; (*manner*) autoritário.
authority [ɔː'θɔrɪtɪ] *n* autoridade *f*; (*permission*) autorização *f*; **the authorities** *npl* as autoridades; **to have** ~ **to do sth** ter autorização para fazer algo.
authorization [ɔːθəraɪ'zeɪʃən] *n* autorização *f*.
authorize ['ɔːθəraɪz] *vt* autorizar.
authorized capital ['ɔːθəraɪzd-] *n* (*COMM*) capital *m* autorizado.
authorship ['ɔːθəʃɪp] *n* autoria.
autistic [ɔː'tɪstɪk] *adj* autista.
auto ['ɔːtəu] (*US*) *n* carro, automóvel *m* ♦ *cpd* (*industry*) automobilístico.
autobiographical [ɔːtəbaɪə'græfɪkl] *adj* autobiográfico.
autobiography [ɔːtəbaɪ'ɔgrəfɪ] *n* autobiografia.
autocratic [ɔːtə'krætɪk] *adj* autocrático.
autograph ['ɔːtəgrɑːf] *n* autógrafo ♦ *vt* (*photo etc*) autografar.
automat ['ɔːtəmæt] *n* (*vending machine*) autômato; (*US: restaurant*) restaurante *m* automático.
automata [ɔː'tɔmətə] *npl of* **automaton**.
automated ['ɔːtəmeɪtɪd] *adj* automatizado.
automatic [ɔːtə'mætɪk] *adj* automático ♦ *n* (*gun*) pistola automática; (*washing machine*) máquina de lavar roupa automática; (*BRIT*: *AUT*) carro automático.
automatically [ɔːtə'mætɪklɪ] *adv* automaticamente.
automatic data processing *n* processamento automático de dados.
automation [ɔːtə'meɪʃən] *n* automação *f*.
automaton [ɔː'tɔmətən] (*pl* **automata**) *n* autômato.
automobile ['ɔːtəməbiːl] (*US*) *n* carro, automóvel *m* ♦ *cpd* (*industry*, *accident*) automobilístico.
autonomous [ɔː'tɔnəməs] *adj* autônomo.
autonomy [ɔː'tɔnəmɪ] *n* autonomia.
autopsy ['ɔːtɔpsɪ] *n* autópsia.
autumn ['ɔːtəm] *n* outono.
auxiliary [ɔːg'zɪlɪərɪ] *adj, n* auxiliar *m/f*.
AV *n abbr* (= *Authorized Version*) *tradução inglesa da Bíblia* ♦ *abbr* = **audiovisual**.
Av. *abbr* (= *avenue*) Av., Avda.
avail [ə'veɪl] *vt*: **to** ~ **o.s. of** aproveitar, valer-se de ♦ *n*: **to no** ~ em vão, inutilmente.
availability [əveɪlə'bɪlɪtɪ] *n* disponibilidade *f*.
available [ə'veɪləbl] *adj* disponível; **every** ~ **means** todos os recursos à sua (*or* nossa *etc*) disposição; **is the manager** ~? o gerente

pode me atender?; (*on phone*) queria falar com o gerente; **to make sth** ~ **to sb** pôr algo à disposição de alguém.
avalanche ['ævəlɑːnʃ] *n* avalanche *f*, alude *m*.
avant-garde ['ævãŋ'gɑːd] *adj* de vanguarda.
avaricious [ævə'rɪʃəs] *adj* avarento, avaro.
avdp. *abbr* = **avoirdupois**.
Ave. *abbr* (= *avenue*) Av., Avda.
avenge [ə'vɛndʒ] *vt* vingar.
avenue ['ævənjuː] *n* avenida; (*fig*) caminho.
average ['ævərɪdʒ] *n* média ♦ *adj* (*mean*) médio; (*ordinary*) regular ♦ *vt* (*calculate*) calcular a média de; (*a certain figure*) alcançar uma média de; **on** ~ em média; **above/below (the)** ~ acima/abaixo da média.
average out *vt* calcular a média de ♦ *vi*: **to** ~ **out at** dar uma média de.
averse [ə'vɜːs] *adj*: **to be** ~ **to sth/doing** ser avesso *or* pouco disposto a algo/a fazer algo; **I wouldn't be** ~ **to a drink** eu aceitaria uma bebida.
aversion [ə'vɜːʃən] *n* aversão *f*.
avert [ə'vɜːt] *vt* prevenir; (*blow, one's eyes*) desviar.
aviary ['eɪvɪərɪ] *n* aviário, viveiro de aves.
aviation [eɪvɪ'eɪʃən] *n* aviação *f*.
avid ['ævɪd] *adj* ávido.
avidly ['ævɪdlɪ] *adv* avidamente.
avocado [ævə'kɑːdəu] *n* (*also: BRIT*: ~ *pear*) abacate *m*.
avoid [ə'vɔɪd] *vt* evitar.
avoidable [ə'vɔɪdəbl] *adj* evitável.
avoidance [ə'vɔɪdəns] *n* evitação *f*.
avowed [ə'vaud] *adj* confesso, declarado.
AVP (*US*) *n abbr* = **assistant vice-president**.
AWACS ['eɪwæks] *n abbr* (= *airborne warning and control system*) AWACS *m* (*sistema aerotransportado de alerta e de controle*).
await [ə'weɪt] *vt* esperar, aguardar; ~**ing attention/delivery** (*COMM*) a ser(em) atendido(s)/entregue(s); **long** ~**ed** longamente esperado.
awake [ə'weɪk] (*pt* **awoke**, *pp* **awoken** *or* ~**d**) *adj* acordado ♦ *vt* despertar, acordar ♦ *vi* despertar, acordar; ~ **to** atento a.
awakening [ə'weɪkənɪŋ] *n* despertar *m*.
award [ə'wɔːd] *n* (*prize*) prêmio, condecoração *f*; (*LAW*) sentença; (*act*) concessão *f* ♦ *vt* (*prize*) outorgar, conceder; (*LAW: damages*) adjudicar.
aware [ə'wɛə*] *adj*: ~ **of** (*conscious*) consciente de; (*informed*) informado de *or* sobre; **to become** ~ **of** reparar em, saber de; **politically/socially** ~ conscientizado politicamente/socialmente; **I am fully** ~ **that** ... eu compreendo perfeitamente que ....
awareness [ə'wɛənɪs] *n* consciência; (*knowledge*) conhecimento; **to develop people's** ~ **(of)** conscientizar o público (de).
awash [ə'wɔʃ] *adj* inundado.
away [ə'weɪ] *adv* fora; (*far* ~) muito longe;

NB: European Portuguese adds the following consonants to certain words: **b** (sú(b)dito, su(b)til); **c** (a(c)ção, a(c)cionista, a(c)to); **m** (inde(m)ne); **p** (ado(p)ção, ado(p)tar); *for further details see p. xiii.*

two kilometres ~ a dois quilômetros de distância; **two hours** ~ **by car** a duas horas de carro; **the holiday was two weeks** ~ faltavam duas semanas para as férias; ~ **from** longe de; **he's** ~ **for a week** está ausente uma semana; **he's** ~ **in Miami** ele foi para Miami; **to take** ~ levar; **to work/pedal** ~ trabalhar/pedalar sem parar; **to fade** ~ desvanecer-se.

away game *n* (*SPORT*) jogo de fora.

away match *n* (*SPORT*) jogo de fora.

awe [ɔː] *n* temor *m* respeitoso.

awe-inspiring *adj* imponente.

awesome ['ɔːsəm] *adj* imponente.

awestruck ['ɔːstrʌk] *adj* pasmado.

awful ['ɔːfəl] *adj* terrível, horrível; **an** ~ **lot of** um monte de.

awfully ['ɔːfəlɪ] *adv* (*very*) muito.

awhile [ə'waɪl] *adv* por algum tempo, um pouco.

awkward ['ɔːkwəd] *adj* (*clumsy*) desajeitado; (*shape*) incômodo; (*problem*) difícil; (*embarrassing*) embaraçoso, delicado.

awkwardness ['ɔːkwədnəs] *n* (*embarrassment*) embaraço.

awl [ɔːl] *n* sovela.

awning ['ɔːnɪŋ] *n* toldo.

awoke [ə'wəuk] *pt of* **awake**.

awoken [ə'wəukən] *pp of* **awake**.

AWOL ['eɪwɔl] *abbr* (*MIL*) = **absent without leave**.

awry [ə'raɪ] *adv*: **to be** ~ estar de viés *or* de esguelha; **to go** ~ sair mal.

axe [æks] (*US* **ax**) *n* machado ♦ *vt* (*employee*) despedir; (*project etc*) abandonar; (*jobs*) reduzir; **to have an** ~ **to grind** (*fig*) ter interesse pessoal, puxar a brasa para a sua sardinha (*inf*).

axes¹ ['æksɪz] *npl of* **axe**; **ax**.

axes² ['æksiːz] *npl of* **axis**.

axiom ['æksɪəm] *n* axioma *m*.

axiomatic [æksɪəu'mætɪk] *adj* axiomático.

axis ['æksɪs] (*pl* **axes**) *n* eixo.

axle ['æksl] *n* (*also:* ~ *tree*) eixo.

ay(e) [aɪ] *excl* (*yes*) sim ♦ *n*: **the ayes** os votos a favor.

AYH *n abbr* = **American Youth Hostels**.

AZ (*US*) *abbr* (*POST*) = **Arizona**.

azalea [ə'zeɪlɪə] *n* azaléia.

Azores [ə'zɔːz] *npl*: **the** ~ os Açores.

Aztec ['æztɛk] *adj*, *n* asteca *m/f*.

azure ['eɪʒə*] *adj* azul-celeste *inv*.

B

B, b [biː] *n* (*letter*) B, b *m*; (*MUS*): **B** si *m*; **B for Benjamin** (*BRIT*) *or* **Baker** (*US*) B de Beatriz; **B road** (*BRIT*: *AUT*) via secundária.

b. *abbr* = **born**.

BA *n abbr* = **British Academy**; (*SCH*) = **Bachelor of Arts**.

babble ['bæbl] *vi* balbuciar ♦ *n* balbucio.

baboon [bə'buːn] *n* babuíno.

baby ['beɪbɪ] *n* neném *m/f*, nenê *m/f*, bebê *m/f*.

baby carriage (*US*) *n* carrinho de bebê.

baby grand *n* (*also:* ~ *piano*) piano de ¼ de cauda.

babyhood ['beɪbɪhud] *n* primeira infância.

babyish ['beɪbɪʃ] *adj* infantil.

baby-minder (*BRIT*) *n* ≈ babá *f*.

baby-sit (*irreg*) *vi* tomar conta da(s) criança(s).

baby-sitter *n* baby-sitter *m/f*.

bachelor ['bætʃələ*] *n* solteiro; (*SCH*): **B~ of Arts/Science** ≈ bacharel *m* em Letras/Ciências; **B~ of Arts/Science degree** ≈ bacharelado em Letras/Ciências.

bachelorhood ['bætʃələhud] *n* celibato.

bachelor party (*US*) *n* despedida de solteiro.

back [bæk] *n* (*of person*) costas *fpl*; (*of animal*) lombo; (*of hand*) dorso; (*of car, train*) parte *f* traseira; (*of house*) fundos *mpl*; (*of chair*) encosto; (*of page*) verso; (*of coin*) reverso; (*FOOTBALL*) zagueiro (*BR*), defesa *m* (*PT*) ♦ *vt* (*financially*) patrocinar; (*candidate: also:* ~ *up*) apoiar; (*horse: at races*) apostar em; (*car*) recuar ♦ *vi* (*car etc*) recuar, dar ré (*BR*), fazer marcha atrás (*PT*) ♦ *adj* (*in compounds*) traseiro, de trás ♦ *adv* (*not forward*) para trás; (*returned*) de volta; **he's** ~ ele voltou; **when will you be** ~? quando você estará de volta?; **he ran** ~ recuou correndo; **throw the ball** ~ devolva a bola; **can I have it** ~? pode devolvê-lo?; **he called** ~ chamou de novo; **to have one's** ~ **to the wall** (*fig*) estar acuado; **to break the** ~ **of a job** (*BRIT*) fazer o mais difícil de um trabalho; **at the** ~ **of my mind was the thought that ...** no meu íntimo havia a idéia que ...; ~ **to front** pelo avesso, às avessas; ~ **garden/room** jardim *m*/quarto dos fundos; ~ **seats/wheels** (*AUT*) assentos *mpl*/rodas *fpl* de trás; **to take a** ~ **seat** (*fig*) colocar-se em segundo plano; ~ **payments/rent** pagamentos *mpl* atrasados/aluguel *m* atrasado.

back down *vi* desistir.

back on to *vt fus*: **the house** ~**s on to the golf course** a casa dá fundas para o campo de golfe.

back out *vi* (*of promise*) voltar atrás, recuar.

back up *vt* (*COMPUT*) tirar um backup de.

backache ['bækeɪk] *n* dor *f* nas costas.

backbencher [bæk'bentʃə*] (*BRIT*) *n* membro do parlamento sem pasta.

backbiting ['bækbaɪtɪŋ] *n* maledicência.

backbone ['bækbəun] *n* coluna vertebral; **he's the** ~ **of the organization** ele é o pilar *or* esteio da organização.

backchat ['bæktʃæt] (*BRIT*: *inf*) *n* insolências *fpl*.

back-cloth (*BRIT*) *n* pano de fundo.

backcomb ['bækəum] (*BRIT*) *vt* encrespar.

backdate [bæk'deɪt] vt (letter) antedatar; ~d **pay rise** aumento de vencimento com efeito retroativo.

backdrop ['bækdrɔp] n pano de fundo.

backer ['bækə*] n (supporter) partidário/a; (COMM: in partnership) comanditário/a; (: financier) financiador(a) m/f.

backfire [bæk'faɪə*] vi (AUT) engasgar; (plan) sair pela culatra.

backgammon [bæk'gæmən] n gamão m.

background ['bækgraund] n fundo; (of events) antecedentes mpl; (basic knowledge) bases fpl; (experience) conhecimentos mpl, experiência ♦ cpd (noise, music) de fundo; ~ **reading** leitura de fundo; **family** ~ antecedentes mpl familiares.

backhand ['bækhænd] n (TENNIS: also: ~ stroke) revés m.

backhanded ['bækhændɪd] adj (fig) ambíguo, insincero.

backhander ['bækhændə*] (BRIT) n (bribe) propina, peita (PT).

backing ['bækɪŋ] n (fig) apoio; (COMM) patrocínio; (MUS) fundo (musical).

backlash ['bæklæʃ] n reação f.

backlog ['bæklɔg] n: ~ **of work** atrasos mpl.

back number n (of magazine etc) número atrasado.

backpack ['bækpæk] n mochila.

backpacker ['bækpækə*] n excursionista m/f com mochila.

back pay n salário atrasado.

backpedal ['bækpedl] vi (fig) recuar, voltar atrás.

backside [bæk'saɪd] (inf) n traseiro.

backslash ['bækslæʃ] n contrabarra.

backslide ['bækslaɪd] (irreg) vi ter uma recaída.

backsliding ['bækslaɪdɪŋ] n recaídas fpl.

backspace ['bækspeɪs] vi (TYPING) retroceder.

backstage [bæk'steɪdʒ] adv nos bastidores.

back-street adj (abortion) clandestino; ~ **abortionist** aborteiro/a.

backstroke ['bækstrəuk] n nado de costas.

backtrack ['bæktræk] vi (fig) = **backpedal.**

backup ['bækʌp] adj (train, plane) reserva inv; (COMPUT) de backup ♦ n (support) apoio; (COMPUT: also: ~ file) backup m; (US: congestion) congestionamento.

backward ['bækwəd] adj (movement) para trás; (person, country) atrasado; (shy) tímido; ~ **and forward movement** movimento de vaivém.

backwards ['bækwədz] adv (move, go) para trás; (read a list) às avessas; (fall) de costas; **to know sth** ~ (BRIT) or ~ **and forwards** (US) (inf) saber algo de cor e salteado.

backwater ['bækwɔːtə*] n (fig: backward place) lugar m atrasado; (: remote place) fim-do-mundo m.

backyard [bæk'jɑːd] n quintal m.

bacon ['beɪkən] n toucinho, bacon m.

bacteria [bæk'tɪərɪə] npl bactérias fpl.

bacteriology [bæktɪərɪ'ɔlədʒɪ] n bacteriologia.

bad [bæd] adj mau/má, ruim; (child) levado; (serious) grave; (meat, food) estragado; **his** ~ **leg** sua perna machucada; **to go** ~ estragar-se; **to have a** ~ **time of it** passar um mau pedaço; **I feel** ~ **about it** (guilty) eu me sinto culpado (por isso); **in** ~ **faith** de má fé.

bade [bæd] pt of **bid.**

badge [bædʒ] n (emblem) emblema m; (to wear) crachá m.

badger ['bædʒə*] n texugo ♦ vt acossar.

badly ['bædlɪ] adv (work, dress etc) mal; ~ **wounded** gravemente ferido; **he needs it** ~ faz-lhe grande falta; **things are going** ~ as coisas vão mal; **to be** ~ **off (for money)** estar com pouco dinheiro.

bad-mannered [-'mænəd] adj mal-educado, sem modas.

badminton ['bædmɪntən] n badminton m.

bad-tempered adj mal humorado; (temporary) de mau humor.

baffle ['bæfl] vt (puzzle) deixar perplexo, desconcertar.

baffled ['bæfld] adj perplexo.

baffling ['bæflɪŋ] adj desconcertante.

bag [bæg] n saco, bolsa; (handbag) bolsa; (satchel, shopping ~) sacola; (case) mala; (of hunter) caça ♦ vt (inf: take) pegar; (game) matar; (TECH) ensacar; ~s **of** ... (inf: lots of) ... de sobra; **to pack one's** ~s fazer as malas; ~s **under the eyes** olheiras fpl.

bagful ['bægful] n saco cheio.

baggage ['bægɪdʒ] n bagagem f.

baggage checkroom [-'tʃekruːm] (US) n depósito de bagagem.

baggage claim n (at airport) recebimento de bagagem.

baggy ['bægɪ] adj folgado, largo.

bagpipes ['bægpaɪps] npl gaita de foles.

Baghdad [bæg'dæd] n Bagdá f.

bag-snatcher [-'snætʃə*] (BRIT) n trombadinha m.

bag-snatching [-'snætʃɪŋ] (BRIT) n roubo de bolsa.

Bahamas [bə'hɑːməz] npl: **the** ~ as Bahamas.

Bahrain [bɑː'reɪn] n Barein m.

bail [beɪl] n fiança ♦ vt (prisoner: also: grant ~ to) libertar sob fiança; (boat: also: ~ out) baldear a água de; **to be released on** ~ ser posto em liberdade mediante fiança; see also **bale.**

bail out vt (prisoner) afiançar; (fig: help out) socorrer.

bailiff ['beɪlɪf] n oficial m/f de justiça (BR) or de diligências (PT).

bait [beɪt] n isca, engodo ♦ vt iscar, cevar; (fig) apoquentar.

bake [beɪk] vt cozinhar ao forno ♦ vi (cook:

NB: European Portuguese adds the following consonants to certain words: **b** (sú(b)dito, su(b)til); **c** (a(c)ção, a(c)cionista, a(c)to); **m** (inde(m)ne); **p** (ado(p)ção, ado(p)tar); for further details see p. xiii.

cake, person) cozinhar; *(be hot)* fazer um calor terrível.

baked beans [beɪkt-] *npl* feijão *m* cozido com molho de tomate.

baker ['beɪkə*] *n* padeiro/a.

bakery ['beɪkərɪ] *n (for bread)* padaria; *(for cakes)* confeitaria.

baking ['beɪkɪŋ] *n (act)* cozimento; *(batch)* fornada.

baking powder *n* fermento em pó.

baking tin *n (for cake)* fôrma; *(for meat)* assadeira.

baking tray *n* tabuleiro.

balaclava [bælə'klɑːvə] *n (also: ~ helmet)* capuz *f*.

balance ['bæləns] *n* equilíbrio; *(scales)* balança; *(COMM)* balanço; *(remainder)* resto, saldo ♦ *vt* equilibrar; *(budget)* nivelar; *(account)* fazer o balanço de; *(compensate)* contrabalançar; *(pros and cons)* pesar; **~ of trade/payments** balança comercial/balanço de pagamentos; **~ carried forward** transporte; **~ brought forward** transporte; **to ~ the books** fazer o balanço dos livros.

balanced ['bælənst] *adj (personality, diet)* equilibrado.

balance sheet *n* balanço geral.

balance wheel *n* balanceiro.

balcony ['bælkənɪ] *n (open)* varanda; *(closed)* galeria.

bald [bɔːld] *adj* calvo, careca; *(tyre)* careca.

baldness ['bɔːldnɪs] *n* calvície *f*.

bale [beɪl] *n (AGR)* fardo.

bale out *vi (of a plane)* atirar-se de pára-quedas ♦ *vt (NAUT: water)* baldear; *(: boat)* baldear a água de.

Balearic Islands [bælɪ'ærɪk-] *npl*: **the ~ as** ilhas Baleares.

baleful ['beɪlful] *adj (look)* triste; *(sinister)* funesto, sinistro.

balk [bɔːk] *vi*: **to ~ (at)** *(subj: person)* relutar (contra); *(: horse)* refugar, empacar (diante de); **to ~ at doing** relutar em fazer.

Balkan ['bɔːlkən] *adj* balcânico ♦ *n*: **the ~s** os Balcãs.

ball [bɔːl] *n* bola; *(dance)* baile *m*; **~s** *npl (inf!)* colhões *mpl (!)*, ovos *mpl (!)*; **to play ~ with sb** jogar bola com alguém; *(fig)* fazer o jogo de alguém; **to be on the ~** *(fig: competent)* ser competente *or* batuta *(inf)*; *(: alert)* estar alerta; **to start the ~ rolling** *(fig)* dar começo, dar o pontapé inicial; **the ~ is in their court** *(fig)* é a vez deles de agir.

ballad ['bæləd] *n* balada.

ballast ['bæləst] *n* lastro.

ball bearing *n* rolamento de esferas, rolimã *m*.

ball cock *n* torneira com bóia.

ballerina [bælə'riːnə] *n* bailarina.

ballet ['bæleɪ] *n* balé *m*.

ballet dancer *n* bailarino/a.

ballistic [bə'lɪstɪk] *adj* balístico.

ballistics [bə'lɪstɪks] *n* balística.

balloon [bə'luːn] *n* balão *m* ♦ *vi (sails etc)* inflar(-se); *(prices)* disparar.

balloonist [bə'luːnɪst] *n* aeróstata *m/f*.

ballot ['bælət] *n* votação *f*.

ballot box *n* urna.

ballot paper *n* cédula eleitoral.

ballpark ['bɔːlpɑːk] *(US) n* estádio de beisebol.

ballpark figure *(inf) n* número aproximado.

ball-point pen *n (caneta)* esferográfica.

ballroom ['bɔːlrum] *n* salão *m* de baile.

balm [bɑːm] *n* bálsamo.

balmy ['bɑːmɪ] *adj (breeze, air)* suave, fragrante; *(BRIT: inf)* = **barmy**.

BALPA ['bælpə] *n abbr (= British Airline Pilots' Association) sindicato dos aeronautas.*

balsam ['bɔːlsəm] *n* bálsamo.

balsa (wood) ['bɔːlsə-] *n* pau-de-balsa *m*.

Baltic ['bɔːltɪk] *n*: **the ~ (Sea)** o *(mar)* Báltico.

balustrade ['bæləstreɪd] *n* balaustrada.

bamboo [bæm'buː] *n* bambu *m*.

bamboozle [bæm'buːzl] *(inf) vt* embromar, trapacear.

ban [bæn] *n* proibição *f*, interdição *f* ♦ *vt* proibir, interditar; *(exclude)* excluir; **he was ~ned from driving** *(BRIT)* cassaram-lhe a carteira de motorista.

banal [bə'nɑːl] *adj* banal, vulgar.

banana [bə'nɑːnə] *n* banana.

band [bænd] *n (group)* bando, banda; *(gang)* quadrilha, bando; *(strip)* faixa, cinta; *(at a dance)* orquestra; *(MIL)* banda.

band together *vi* juntar-se, associar-se.

bandage ['bændɪdʒ] *n* atadura *(BR)*, ligadura *(PT)* ♦ *vt* enfaixar.

Band-Aid ['bændeɪd] ® *(US) n* esparadrapo.

bandit ['bændɪt] *n* bandido.

bandstand ['bændstænd] *n* coreto.

bandwagon ['bændwægən] *n*: **to jump on the ~** *(fig)* entrar na roda, ir na onda.

bandy ['bændɪ] *vt (jokes, insults)* trocar.

bandy about *vt* usar a torto e a direito.

bandy-legged ['bændɪ'legɪd] *adj* cambaio, de pernas tortas.

bane [beɪn] *n*: **it** *(or he etc)* **is the ~ of my life** é a maldição da minha vida.

bang [bæŋ] *n* estalo; *(of door)* estrondo; *(blow)* pancada ♦ *vt* bater com força; *(door)* fechar com violência ♦ *vi* produzir estrondo; *(door)* bater ♦ *adv (BRIT: inf)*: **to be ~ on time** chegar na hora exata; **~s** *npl (US: fringe)* franja; **to ~ at the door** bater à porta com violência; **to ~ into sth** bater em algo.

banger ['bæŋə*] *n (BRIT: car: also: old ~)* calhambeque *m*, lata-velha; *(: inf: sausage)* salsicha; *(firework)* bomba *(de São João)*.

Bangkok [bæŋ'kɔk] *n* Bangcoc.

Bangladesh [bæŋglə'dɛʃ] *n* Bangladesh *m (no article)*.

bangle ['bæŋgl] *n* bracelete *m*, pulseira.

banish ['bænɪʃ] *vt* banir.

banister(s) ['bænɪstə(z)] *n(pl)* corrimão *m*.

banjo ['bændʒəu] *(pl ~es or ~s) n* banjo.

bank [bæŋk] *n (COMM)* banco; *(of river, lake)* margem *f*; *(of earth)* rampa, ladeira ♦ *vi (AVIAT)* ladear-se; *(COMM)*: **they ~ with Pitt's** eles têm conta no banco Pitt's.

bank on *vt fus* contar com, apostar em.
bank account *n* conta bancária.
bank card *n* cartão *m* de garantia de cheques.
bank charges (*BRIT*) *npl* encargos *mpl* bancários.
bank draft *n* saque *m* bancário.
banker ['bæŋkə*] *n* banqueiro/a; ~'s **card** (*BRIT*) cartão *m* de garantia de cheques; ~'s **order** (*BRIT*) ordem *f* bancária.
bank giro *n* transferência bancária.
Bank holiday (*BRIT*) *n* feriado nacional.
banking ['bæŋkɪŋ] *n* transações *fpl* bancárias; (*job*) profissão *f* de banqueiro.
banking hours *npl* horário de banco.
bank loan *n* empréstimo bancário.
bank manager *n* gerente *m/f* de banco.
banknote ['bæŋknəut] *n* nota (bancária).
bank rate *n* taxa bancária.
bankrupt ['bæŋkrʌpt] *n* falido/a, quebrado/a ♦ *adj* falido, quebrado; **to go** ~ falir; **to be** ~ estar falido/quebrado.
bankruptcy ['bæŋkrʌptsɪ] *n* falência; (*fraudulent*) bancarrota.
bank statement *n* extrato bancário.
banner ['bænə*] *n* bandeira; (*in demonstration*) estandarte *m*.
bannister(s) ['bænɪstə(z)] *n(pl)* = **banister(s)**.
banns [bænz] *npl* proclamas *fpl*.
banquet ['bæŋkwɪt] *n* banquete *m*.
bantam-weight ['bæntəm-] *n* peso-galo.
banter ['bæntə*] *n* caçoada.
BAOR *n abbr* (= *British Army of the Rhine*) forças armadas britânicas na Alemanha.
baptism ['bæptɪzəm] *n* batismo.
Baptist ['bæptɪst] *n* batista *m/f*.
baptize [bæp'taɪz] *vt* batizar.
bar [bɑ:*] *n* (*gen*, *MUS*, *of chocolate*) barra; (*of window etc*) tranca; (*fig: hindrance*) obstáculo; (*prohibition*) impedimento; (*pub*) bar *m*; (*counter: in pub*) balcão *m* ♦ *vt* (*road*) obstruir; (*window*) trancar; (*person*) excluir; (*activity*) proibir ♦ *prep*: ~ **none** sem exceção; ~ **of soap** sabonete *m*; **behind** ~s (*prisoner*) atrás das grades; **the B**~ (*LAW*) (*profession*) a advocacia; (*people*) o corpo de advogados.
Barbados [bɑ:'beɪdɔs] *n* Barbados *m* (*no article*).
barbaric [bɑ:'bærɪk] *adj* bárbaro.
barbarous ['bɑ:bərəs] *adj* bárbaro.
barbecue ['bɑ:bɪkju:] *n* churrasco.
barbed wire ['bɑ:bd-] *n* arame *m* farpado.
barber ['bɑ:bə*] *n* barbeiro, cabeleireiro.
barbiturate [bɑ:'bɪtjurɪt] *n* barbitúrico.
Barcelona [bɑ:sə'ləunə] *n* Barcelona.
bar chart *n* gráfico de barras.
bar code *n* código de barras.
bare [bɛə*] *adj* nu; (*head*) descoberto ♦ *vt* desnudar, descobrir; **to** ~ **one's teeth** mostrar os dentes; **the** ~ **essentials** o imprescindível.

bareback ['bɛəbæk] *adv* em pêlo, sem arreios.
barefaced ['bɛəfeɪst] *adj* descarado.
barefoot ['bɛəfut] *adj, adv* descalço.
bareheaded [bɛə'hedɪd] *adj, adv* de cabeça descoberta.
barely ['bɛəlɪ] *adv* apenas, mal.
Barents Sea ['bærənts-] *n*: **the** ~ o mar de Barents.
bargain ['bɑ:gɪn] *n* (*deal*) negócio; (*good buy*) pechincha ♦ *vi* (*trade*) negociar; (*haggle*) regatear; **into the** ~ ainda por cima.
bargain for (*inf*) *vt fus*: **he got more than he** ~**ed for** ele conseguiu mais do que pediu.
bargaining ['bɑ:gənɪŋ] *n* (*haggling*) regateio; (*talks*) negociações *fpl*.
barge [bɑ:dʒ] *n* barcaça.
barge in *vi* irromper.
barge into *vt fus* (*collide with*) atropelar; (*interrupt*) intrometer-se em.
baritone ['bærɪtəun] *n* barítono.
barium meal ['bɛərɪəm-] *n* contraste *m* de bário.
bark [bɑ:k] *n* (*of tree*) casca; (*of dog*) latido ♦ *vi* latir.
barley ['bɑ:lɪ] *n* cevada.
barley sugar *n* maltose *f*.
barmaid ['bɑ:meɪd] *n* garçonete *f* (*BR*), empregada (de bar) (*PT*).
barman ['bɑ:mən] (*irreg*) *n* garçom *m* (*BR*), empregado (de bar) (*PT*).
barmy ['bɑ:mɪ] (*BRIT*: *inf*) *adj* maluco.
barn [bɑ:n] *n* celeiro.
barnacle ['bɑ:nəkl] *n* craca.
barometer [bə'rɔmɪtə*] *n* barômetro.
baron ['bærən] *n* barão *m*; **the press/oil** ~s os magnatas da imprensa/do petróleo.
baroness ['bærənɪs] *n* baronesa.
barracks ['bærəks] *npl* quartel *m*, caserna.
barrage ['bærɑ:ʒ] *n* (*MIL*) fogo de barragem; (*dam*) barragem *f*; **a** ~ **of questions** uma saraivada de perguntas.
barrel ['bærəl] *n* barril *m*, barrica; (*of gun*) cano.
barrel organ *n* realejo.
barren ['bærən] *adj* (*sterile*) estéril; (*land*) árido.
barricade [bærɪ'keɪd] *n* barricada ♦ *vt* barricar.
barrier ['bærɪə*] *n* barreira; (*obstacle*) obstáculo; (*BRIT*: *also*: **crash** ~) cerca entre as pistas.
barrier cream (*BRIT*) *n* creme *m* protetor.
barring ['bɑ:rɪŋ] *prep* exceto, salvo.
barrister ['bærɪstə*] (*BRIT*) *n* advogado/a, causídico/a.
barrow ['bærəu] *n* (*cart*) carrinho (de mão).
barstool ['bɑ:stu:l] *n* tamborete *m* de bar.
Bart. (*BRIT*) *abbr* = **baronet**.
bartender ['bɑ:tendə*] (*US*) *n* garçom *m* (*BR*), empregado (de bar) (*PT*).
barter ['bɑ:tə*] *n* permuta, troca ♦ *vt*: **to** ~ **sth for sth** trocar algo por algo.

NB: European Portuguese adds the following consonants to certain words: **b** (sú(b)dito, su(b)til); **c** (a(c)ção, a(c)cionista, a(c)to); **m** (inde(m)ne); **p** (ado(p)ção, ado(p)tar); *for further details see p. xiii.*

base [beɪs] n base f ♦ vt (troops): **to be ~d at** estar estacionado em; (opinion, belief): **to ~ sth on** basear or fundamentar algo em ♦ adj baixo, vil; **coffee-~d** à base de café; **a Rio-~d firm** uma empresa sediada no Rio; **I'm ~d in London** estou sediado em Londres.

baseball ['beɪsbɔːl] n beisebol m.

baseboard ['beɪsbɔːd] (US) n rodapé m.

base camp n base f de operações.

Basel ['bɑːzl] n = **Basle**.

basement ['beɪsmənt] n (in house) porão m; (in shop etc) subsolo.

base rate n taxa de base.

bases[1] ['beɪsɪz] npl of **base**.

bases[2] ['beɪsiːz] npl of **basis**.

bash [bæʃ] (inf) vt (with fist) dar soco or murro em; (with object) bater em ♦ n (BRIT): **I'll have a ~ (at it)** vou tentar (fazê-lo); **~ed in** amassado.

   bash up (inf) vt (car) arrebentar; (BRIT: person) dar uma surra em, espancar.

bashful ['bæʃful] adj tímido, envergonhado.

bashing ['bæʃɪŋ] (inf) n surra; **Paki-~** espancamento de asiáticos por motivos racistas; **queer-~** espancamento de homossexuais.

BASIC ['beɪsɪk] n (COMPUT) BASIC m.

basic ['beɪsɪk] adj básico; (vocabulary, rate) de base.

basically ['beɪsɪkəlɪ] adv fundamentalmente, basicamente; (really) no fundo.

basic rate n (of tax) alíquota de base.

basil ['bæzl] n manjericão m.

basin ['beɪsn] n (vessel) bacia; (dock, GEO) bacia; (also: wash~) pia.

basis ['beɪsɪs] (pl **bases**) n base f; **on the ~ of what you've said** com base no que você disse.

bask [bɑːsk] vi: **to ~ in the sun** tomar sol.

basket ['bɑːskɪt] n cesto; (with handle) cesta.

basketball ['bɑːskɪtbɔːl] n basquete(bol) m.

basketball player n jogador(a) m/f de basquete.

basketwork ['bɑːskɪtwɜːk] n obra de verga, trabalho de vime.

Basle [bɑːl] n Basiléia.

Basque [bæsk] adj, n basco/a.

Basque Country n: **the ~** o País Basco.

bass [beɪs] n (MUS) baixo.

bass clef n clave f de fá.

bassoon [bə'suːn] n fagote m.

bastard ['bɑːstəd] n bastardo/a; (inf!) filho-da-puta (!).

baste [beɪst] vt (CULIN) untar; (SEWING) alinhavar.

bastion ['bæstɪən] n baluarte m.

BASW n abbr (= British Association of Social Workers) sindicato dos assistentes sociais.

bat [bæt] n (ZOOL) morcego; (for ball games) bastão m; (for table tennis) raquete f ♦ vt: **he didn't ~ an eyelid** ele nem pestanejou; **off one's own ~** por iniciativa própria.

batch [bætʃ] n (of bread) fornada; (pile of papers) monte m; (lot) remessa, lote m.

batch processing n (COMPUT) processamento

batch or em lote.

bated ['beɪtɪd] adj: **with ~ breath** contendo a respiração.

bath [bɑːθ, pl bɑːðz] n banho; (bathtub) banheira ♦ vt banhar; **~s** npl banhos mpl públicos; (also: swimming ~s) piscina; **to have a ~** tomar banho (de banheira).

bathchair [bɑːθ'tʃeə*] n cadeira de rodas.

bathe [beɪð] vi banhar-se ♦ vt banhar; (wound) lavar.

bather ['beɪðə*] n banhista m/f.

bathing ['beɪðɪŋ] n banho.

bathing cap n touca de banho.

bathing costume (US **bathing suit**) n (woman's) maiô m (BR), fato de banho (PT).

bathmat ['bɑːθmæt] n tapete m de banheiro.

bathrobe ['bɑːθrəub] n roupão m de banho.

bathroom ['bɑːθrum] n banheiro (BR), casa de banho (PT).

bath towel n toalha de banho.

bathtub ['bɑːθtʌb] n banheira.

batman ['bætmən] (irreg) (BRIT) n ordenança m.

baton ['bætən] n (MUS) batuta; (truncheon) cassetete m.

battalion [bə'tælɪən] n batalhão m.

batten ['bætn] n (CARPENTRY) caibro.

   batten down vt (NAUT): **to ~ down the hatches** correr as escotilhas.

batter ['bætə*] vt espancar, bater em; (wife, child) seviciar ♦ n massa (mole).

battered ['bætəd] adj (hat, pan) amassado, surrado; **~ wife/child** mulher/criança seviciada.

battering ram ['bætərɪŋ] n aríete m.

battery ['bætərɪ] n bateria; (of torch) pilha.

battery charger n carregador m de bateria.

battery farming n criação f intensiva.

battle ['bætl] n batalha; (fig) luta ♦ vi lutar; **that's half the ~** (fig) é meio caminho andado; **it's a** or **we're fighting a losing ~** estamos lutando em vão.

battle dress n uniforme m de combate.

battlefield ['bætlfiːld] n campo de batalha.

battlements ['bætlmənts] npl ameias fpl.

battleship ['bætlʃɪp] n couraçado.

bauble ['bɔːbl] n bugiganga.

baud [bɔːd] n (COMPUT) baud m.

baud rate n (COMPUT) índice m de baud, taxa de transmissão.

baulk [bɔːlk] vi = **balk**.

bauxite ['bɔːksaɪt] n bauxita.

bawdy ['bɔːdɪ] adj indecente; (joke) imoral.

bawl [bɔːl] vi gritar, berrar.

bay [beɪ] n (GEO) baía; (BOT) louro; (BRIT: for parking) área de estacionamento; (: for loading) vão m de carregamento ♦ vi ladrar; **to hold sb at ~** manter alguém a distância; **the B~ of Biscay** o golfo de Biscaia.

bay leaf (irreg) n louro.

bayonet ['beɪənɪt] n baioneta.

bay tree n loureiro.

bay window n janela saliente.

bazaar [bə'zɑː*] n bazar m.

bazooka [bə'zuːkə] n bazuca.

BB (BRIT) n abbr (= Boys' Brigade) movimento de meninos.

B & B n abbr = **bed and breakfast**.

BBB (US) n abbr (= Better Business Bureau) organização de defesa ao consumidor.

BBC n abbr (= British Broadcasting Corporation) companhia britânica de rádio e televisão.

BBE (US) n abbr (= Benevolent and Protective Order of Elks) associação beneficente.

BC adv abbr (= before Christ) a.C. ♦ abbr (CANADA) = **British Columbia**.

BCG n abbr (= Bacillus Calmette-Guérin) BCG m.

BD n abbr (= Bachelor of Divinity) título universitário.

B/D abbr = **bank draft**.

BDS n abbr (= Bachelor of Dental Surgery) título universitário.

be [bi:] (pt **was, were**, pp **been**) vi (of permanent place/state) ser; (of temporary place/condition) estar; **I am English** sou inglês; **I am tired** estou cansado; **how are you?** como está?; **who is it?** quem é?; **it's me** sou eu; **it is raining** está chovendo (BR) or a chover (PT); **I am warm** estou com calor; **it is cold** está frio; **where is the bank?** onde é o banco?; **how much is it?** quanto é or custa?; **he is four (years old)** ele tem quatro anos; **it's 8 o'clock** são 8 horas; **2 and 2 are 4** dois e dois são quatro; **where have you been?** (recently) onde você tem estado?; (at a certain time) onde você estava?; **I've been waiting for her for two hours** há or faz duas horas que eu espero por ela; **to ~ killed** ser morto; **he is nowhere to ~ found** ninguém sabe o paradeiro dele; **the car is to ~ sold** o carro está a venda; **he was to have come yesterday** ele devia ter vindo ontem, era para ele vir ontem; **if I were you, I ...** se eu fosse você, eu ...; **am I to understand that ...?** devo então concluir que ...?

B/E abbr = **bill of exchange**.

beach [bi:tʃ] n praia ♦ vt puxar para a terra or praia, encalhar.

beachcomber ['bi:tʃkəumə*] n vagabundo/a de praia.

beachwear ['bi:tʃwɛə*] n roupa de praia.

beacon ['bi:kən] n (lighthouse) farol m; (marker) baliza; (also: radio ~) radiofarol m.

bead [bi:d] n (of necklace) conta; (of sweat) gota; **~s** npl (necklace) colar m.

beady ['bi:dɪ] adj: **~ eyes** olhinhos vivos.

beagle ['bi:gl] n bigle m.

beak [bi:k] n bico.

beaker ['bi:kə*] n copo com bico.

beam [bi:m] n (ARCH) viga; (of light) raio; (NAUT) través m; (RADIO) feixe m direcional ♦ vi brilhar; (smile) sorrir; **to drive on full** or **main ~** (BRIT), **to drive on high ~** (US) transitar com os faróis altos.

beaming ['bi:mɪŋ] adj (sun, smile) radiante.

bean [bi:n] n feijão m; (of coffee) grão m.

beanshoots ['bi:nʃu:ts] npl brotos mpl de feijão.

beansprouts ['bi:nsprauts] npl brotos mpl de feijão.

bear [bɛə*] (pt **bore**, pp **borne**) n urso; (STOCK EXCHANGE) baixista m/f ♦ vt (carry) carregar; (cost) arcar com; (endure, support) suportar, agüentar; (fruit) dar; (name, title) trazer; (traces, signs) apresentar, trazer; (children) ter, dar à luz; (COMM: interest) render ♦ vi: **to ~ right/left** virar à direita/à esquerda; **to ~ the responsibility of** assumir a responsabilidade de; **to ~ comparison with** comparar-se a; **I can't ~ him** eu não o agüento; **to bring pressure to ~ on sb** exercer pressão sobre alguém.

bear out vt (theory, suspicion) confirmar, corroborar.

bear up vi agüentar, resistir.

bear with vt fus (sb's moods, temper) ter paciência com; **~ with me a minute** só um momentinho, por favor.

bearable ['bɛərəbl] adj suportável, tolerável.

beard [bɪəd] n barba.

bearded ['bɪədɪd] adj barbado, barbudo.

bearer ['bɛərə*] n portador(a) m/f.

bearing ['bɛərɪŋ] n porte m, comportamento; (connection) relação f; (TECH): (ball) **~** rolamento de esferas; **to take a ~** fazer marcação; **to find one's ~s** orientar-se.

beast [bi:st] n besta, bicho; (inf) fera.

beastly ['bi:stlɪ] adj horrível.

beat [bi:t] (pt **beat**, pp **beaten**) n (of heart) batida; (MUS) ritmo, compasso; (of policeman) ronda ♦ vt (hit) bater em; (eggs) bater; (defeat) vencer, derrotar; (better) superar, ultrapassar; (drum) tocar; (rhythm) marcar ♦ vi (heart) bater; **off the ~en track** fora de mão; **to ~ about the bush** falar com rodeios (BR), fazer rodeios (PT); **to ~ it** (inf) cair fora; **to ~ time** marcar o compasso; **that ~s everything!** isso é o cúmulo!

beat down vt (door) arrombar; (price) conseguir que seja abatido; (seller) conseguir que abata o preço ♦ vi (rain) cair a cântaros; (sun) bater de chapa.

beat off vt repelir.

beat up vt (inf: person) espancar; (eggs) bater.

beaten ['bi:tn] pp of **beat**.

beater ['bi:tə*] n (for eggs, cream) batedeira.

beating ['bi:tɪŋ] n batida; (of person) sova, surra; **to take a ~** levar uma surra.

beat-up (inf) adj (car) caindo aos pedaços; (suitcase etc) surrado.

beautician [bju:'tɪʃən] n esteticista m/f.

beautiful ['bju:tɪful] adj belo, lindo, formoso.

beautifully ['bju:tɪfulɪ] adv maravilhosamente, lindamente.

beautify ['bju:tɪfaɪ] vt embelezar.

NB: European Portuguese adds the following consonants to certain words: **b** (sú(b)dito, su(b)til); **c** (a(c)ção, a(c)cionista, a(c)to); **m** (inde(m)ne); **p** (ado(p)ção, ado(p)tar); *for further details see p. xiii.*

beauty ['bjuːtɪ] n beleza; (person) beldade f, beleza; **the ~ of it is that** ... o atrativo disso é que ....

beauty contest n concurso de beleza.

beauty queen n miss f, rainha de beleza.

beauty salon [-sælɔ̃ːŋ] n salão m de beleza.

beauty spot n sinal m (de beleza na pele); (BRIT: TOURISM) lugar m de beleza excepcional.

beaver ['biːvə*] n castor m.

becalmed [bɪ'kɑːmd] adj parado devido a calmaria.

became [bɪ'keɪm] pt of **become**.

because [bɪ'kɔz] conj porque; ~ **of** por causa de.

beck [bɛk] n: **to be at sb's ~ and call** estar às ordens de alguém.

beckon ['bɛkən] vt (also: ~ **to**) chamar com sinais, acenar para.

become [bɪ'kʌm] (irreg: like **come**) vt (suit) favorecer a ♦ vi (+ n) virar, fazer-se, tornar-se; (+ adj) tornar-se, ficar; **to ~ fat** engordar, ficar gordo; **to ~ angry** zangar-se, ficar com raiva; **it became known that** soube-se que; **what has ~ of him?** o que é feito dele?, o que aconteceu a ele?

becoming [bɪ'kʌmɪŋ] adj (behaviour) decoroso; (clothes) favorecedor(a), elegante.

BEd n abbr (= Bachelor of Education) habilitação ao magistério.

bed [bɛd] n cama; (of flowers) canteiro; (of coal, clay) camada, base f; (of sea, lake) fundo; (of river) leito; **to go to ~** ir dormir, deitar(-se).

bed down vi dormir.

bed and breakfast n (terms) cama e café da manhã (BR) or pequeno almoço (PT); (place) pensão f.

bedbug ['bɛdbʌg] n percevejo.

bedclothes ['bɛdkləuðz] npl roupa de cama.

bedcover ['bɛdkʌvə*] n colcha.

bedding ['bɛdɪŋ] n roupa de cama.

bedevil [bɪ'dɛvl] vt (harass) acossar; **to be ~led by** ser vítima de.

bedfellow ['bɛdfɛləu] n: **they are strange ~s** (fig) eles formam uma dupla estranha.

bedlam ['bɛdləm] n confusão f.

bedpan ['bɛdpæn] n comadre f.

bedpost ['bɛdpəust] n pé m de cama.

bedraggled [bɪ'drægld] adj molhado, ensopado; (dirty) enlameado.

bedridden ['bɛdrɪdn] adj acamado.

bedrock ['bɛdrɔk] n (fig) fundamento, alicerce m; (GEO) leito de rocha firme.

bedroom ['bɛdrum] n quarto, dormitório.

Beds (BRIT) abbr = **Bedfordshire**.

bedside ['bɛdsaɪd] n: **at sb's ~** à cabeceira de alguém ♦ cpd (book, lamp) de cabeceira.

bedsit(ter) ['bɛdsɪt(ə*)] (BRIT) n conjugado.

bedspread ['bɛdsprɛd] n colcha.

bedtime ['bɛdtaɪm] n: **it's ~** está na hora de ir para a cama.

bee [biː] n abelha; **to have a ~ in one's bonnet (about sth)** estar obcecado (por algo).

beech [biːtʃ] n faia.

beef [biːf] n carne f de vaca.

beef up (inf) vt (support) reforçar; (essay) desenvolver mais.

beefburger ['biːfbəːgə*] n hambúrguer m.

beefeater ['biːfiːtə*] n alabardeiro (da guarda da Torre de Londres).

beehive ['biːhaɪv] n colméia.

beeline ['biːlaɪn] n: **to make a ~ for** ir direto a.

been [biːn] pp of **be**.

beer [bɪə*] n cerveja.

beer can n lata de cerveja.

beet [biːt] (US) n beterraba.

beetle ['biːtl] n besouro.

beetroot ['biːtruːt] (BRIT) n beterraba.

befall [bɪ'fɔːl] (irreg: like **fall**) vt acontecer a.

befit [bɪ'fɪt] vt convir a.

before [bɪ'fɔː*] prep (of time) antes de; (of space) diante de ♦ conj antes que ♦ adv (time) antes, anteriormente; ~ **going** antes de sair; ~ **she goes** antes dela sair; **the week ~** a semana anterior; **I've seen it ~** eu já vi isso (antes); **I've never seen it ~** nunca vi isso antes.

beforehand [bɪ'fɔːhænd] adv antes.

befriend [bɪ'frɛnd] vt fazer amizade com.

befuddled [bɪ'fʌdld] adj atordoado, aturdido.

beg [bɛg] vi mendigar, pedir esmola ♦ vt (as beggar) mendigar; (favour) pedir; (entreat) suplicar; **that ~s the question of** ... isso dá por resolvida a questão de ....

began [bɪ'gæn] pt of **begin**.

beggar ['bɛgə*] n (also: ~**man**; ~**woman**) mendigo/a.

begin [bɪ'gɪn] (pt **began**, pp **begun**) vt, vi começar, iniciar; **to ~ doing** or **to do sth** começar a fazer algo; ~**ning (from) Monday** a partir de segunda-feira; **I can't ~ to thank you** não sei como agradecer-lhe; **to ~ with** em primeiro lugar.

beginner [bɪ'gɪnə*] n principiante m/f.

beginning [bɪ'gɪnɪŋ] n início, começo; **right from the ~** desde o início.

begrudge [bɪ'grʌdʒ] vt: **to ~ sb sth** (envy) invejar algo de alguém; (give grudgingly) dar algo a alguém de má vontade.

beguile [bɪ'gaɪl] vt (enchant) encantar.

beguiling [bɪ'gaɪlɪŋ] adj (charming) sedutor(a), encantador(a).

begun [bɪ'gʌn] pp of **begin**.

behalf [bɪ'hɑːf] n: **on** (BRIT) or **in** (US) ~ **of** em nome de; (in aid of) em favor de.

behave [bɪ'heɪv] vi comportar-se; (well: also: ~ **o.s.**) comportar-se (bem).

behaviour [bɪ'heɪvjə*] (US **behavior**) n comportamento.

behead [bɪ'hɛd] vt decapitar, degolar.

beheld [bɪ'hɛld] pt, pp of **behold**.

behind [bɪ'haɪnd] prep atrás de ♦ adv atrás; (move) para trás ♦ n traseiro; ~ **(time)** atrasado; ~ **the scenes** nos bastidores; **to leave sth ~** (forget) esquecer algo; (run ahead of) deixar algo para trás; **to be ~ (schedule) with sth** estar atrasado or com atraso em algo.

behold [bɪ'həuld] (irreg: like **hold**) vt contemplar.

beige [beɪʒ] adj bege.

being ['biːɪŋ] n (state) existência; (entity) ser m; **to come into** ~ nascer, aparecer.

Beirut [beɪ'ruːt] n Beirute.

belated [bɪ'leɪtɪd] adj atrasado, tardio.

belch [beltʃ] vi arrotar ♦ vt (also: ~ out: smoke etc) vomitar.

beleaguered [bɪ'liːgəd] adj (city, fig) assediado; (army) cercado.

Belfast ['belfɑːst] n Belfast.

belfry ['belfrɪ] n campanário.

Belgian ['beldʒən] adj, n belga m/f.

Belgium ['beldʒəm] n Bélgica.

Belgrade [bel'greɪd] n Belgrado.

belie [bɪ'laɪ] vt (invalidate) desmentir; (obscure) ocultar.

belief [bɪ'liːf] n (opinion) opinião f; (trust, faith) fé f; (acceptance as true) crença, convicção f; **it's beyond** ~ é inacreditável; **in the** ~ **that** na convicção de que.

believable [bɪ'liːvəbl] adj crível, acreditável.

believe [bɪ'liːv] vt: **to** ~ **sth/sb** acreditar algo/em alguém ♦ vi: **to** ~ **in** (God, ghosts) crer em; (method, person) acreditar em; **I believe (that)** ... (think) eu acho que ...; **I don't** ~ **in corporal punishment** não sou partidário de castigos corporais; **he is** ~**d to be abroad** acredita-se que ele esteja no exterior.

believer [bɪ'liːvə*] n (REL) crente m/f, fiel m/f; (in idea, activity): ~ **in** partidário/a de.

belittle [bɪ'lɪtl] vt diminuir, depreciar.

Belize [be'liːz] n Belize m (no article).

bell [bel] n sino; (small, door~) campainha; (animal's, on toy) guizo, sininho; **that rings a** ~ (fig) tenho uma vaga lembrança disso; **the name rings a** ~ o nome não me é estranho.

bell-bottoms npl calça boca-de-sino.

bellboy ['belbɔɪ] (BRIT) n boy m (de hotel) (BR), groom m (PT).

bellhop ['belhɔp] (US) n = **bellboy**.

belligerent [bɪ'lɪdʒərənt] adj (at war) beligerante; (fig) agressivo.

bellow ['beləu] vi berrar, mugir; (person) bramar ♦ vt (orders) gritar, berrar; ~**s** npl fole m.

bell push (BRIT) n botão m de campainha.

belly ['belɪ] n barriga, ventre m.

bellyache ['belɪeɪk] (inf) n dor f de barriga ♦ vi bufar.

belly button ['belɪbʌtn] n umbigo.

belong [bɪ'lɔŋ] vi: **to** ~ **to** pertencer a; (club etc) ser sócio de; **the book** ~**s on the shelf** o livro fica guardado na estante.

belongings [bɪ'lɔŋɪŋz] npl pertences mpl.

beloved [bɪ'lʌvɪd] adj querido, amado ♦ n bem-amado/a.

below [bɪ'ləu] prep (lower than, less than) abaixo de; (covered by) debaixo de ♦ adv em

baixo; **see** ~ ver abaixo; **temperatures** ~ **normal** temperaturas abaixo da normal.

belt [belt] n cinto; (area) faixa; (TECH) correia ♦ vt (thrash) surrar ♦ vi (BRIT: inf): **to** ~ **along** ir a toda, correr; **industrial** ~ zona industrial.

belt out vt (song) cantar a plenos pulmões.

belt up (BRIT: inf) vi calar a boca.

beltway ['beltweɪ] (US) n via circular.

bemoan [bɪ'məun] vt lamentar.

bemused [bɪ'mjuːzd] adj bestificado, estupidificado.

bench [bentʃ] n banco; **the B**~ (LAW) o tribunal; (people) os magistrados, o corpo de magistrados.

bench mark n referência.

bend [bend] (pt, pp **bent**) vt dobrar, curvar; (leg, arm) dobrar ♦ vi dobrar-se, inclinar-se ♦ n curva; ~**s** n mal-dos-mergulhadores m.

bend down vi abaixar-se; (squat) agachar-se.

bend over vi debruçar-se.

beneath [bɪ'niːθ] prep (lower than, less than) abaixo de; (covered by) debaixo de; (unworthy of) indigno de ♦ adv em baixo.

benefactor ['benɪfæktə*] n benfeitor(a) m/f.

benefactress ['benɪfæktrɪs] n benfeitora.

beneficial [benɪ'fɪʃəl] adj: ~ **(to)** benéfico (a).

beneficiary [benɪ'fɪʃərɪ] n (LAW) beneficiário/a.

benefit ['benɪfɪt] n benefício, proveito; (as part of salary etc) benefício; (money) subsídio, auxílio ♦ vt beneficiar ♦ vi: **to** ~ **from sth** beneficiar-se de algo.

benefit (performance) n apresentação f beneficente.

Benelux ['benɪlʌks] n Benelux m.

benevolent [bɪ'nevələnt] adj benévolo.

BEng n abbr (= Bachelor of Engineering) título universitário.

benign [bɪ'naɪn] adj (person, smile) afável, bondoso; (MED) benigno.

bent [bent] pt, pp of **bend** ♦ n inclinação f ♦ adj (wire, pipe) torto; (inf: dishonest) corrupto; **to be** ~ **on** estar empenhado em; **to have a** ~ **for** ter queda para.

bequeath [bɪ'kwiːð] vt legar.

bequest [bɪ'kwest] n legado.

bereaved [bɪ'riːvd] npl: **the** ~ os enlutados ♦ adj enlutado.

bereavement [bɪ'riːvmənt] n luto.

beret ['bereɪ] n boina.

Bering Sea ['beɪrɪŋ-] n: **the** ~ o mar de Bering.

Berks (BRIT) abbr = **Berkshire**.

Berlin [bəː'lɪn] n Berlim; **East/West** ~ Berlim Oriental/Ocidental.

berm [bəːm] (US) n acostamento (BR), berma (PT).

Bermuda [bəː'mjuːdə] n Bermudas fpl.

Bermuda shorts npl bermuda.

Bern [bəːn] n Berna.

NB: European Portuguese adds the following consonants to certain words: **b** (sú(b)dito, su(b)til); **c** (a(c)ção, a(c)cionista, a(c)to); **m** (inde(m)ne); **p** (ado(p)ção, ado(p)tar); for further details see p. xiii.

berry ['bɛrɪ] *n* baga.

berserk [bə'sɜːk] *adj*: **to go** ~ perder as estribeiras.

berth [bɜːθ] *n* (*on ship*) beliche *m*; (*on train*) leito; (*for ship*) ancoradouro ♦ *vi* (*in harbour*) atracar, encostar-se; (*at anchor*) ancorar; **to give sb a wide** ~ (*fig*) evitar alguém.

beseech [bɪ'siːtʃ] (*pt, pp* **besought**) *vt* suplicar, implorar.

beset [bɪ'sɛt] (*irreg*: *like* **set**) *vt* (*subj*: *problems, difficulties*) acossar ♦ *adj*: **a policy** ~ **with dangers** uma política cercada de perigos.

besetting [bɪ'sɛtɪŋ] *adj*: **his** ~ **sin** seu grande vício.

beside [bɪ'saɪd] *prep* (*next to*) junto de, ao lado de, ao pé de; (*compared with*) em comparação com; **that's** ~ **the point** isso não tem nada a ver; **to be** ~ **o.s.** (**with anger**) estar fora de si.

besides [bɪ'saɪdz] *adv* além disso ♦ *prep* (*as well as*) além de; (*except*) salvo, exceto.

besiege [bɪ'siːdʒ] *vt* (*town*) sitiar, pôr cerco a; (*fig*) assediar.

besotted [bɪ'sɔtɪd] (*BRIT*) *adj*: ~ **with** gamado em, louco por.

besought [bɪ'sɔːt] *pt, pp of* **beseech**.

bespectacled [bɪ'spɛktɪkld] *adj* de óculos.

bespoke [bɪ'spəuk] (*BRIT*) *adj* (*garment*) feito sob medida; ~ **software** software *m* sob medida; ~ **tailor** alfaiate *m* que confecciona roupa sob medida.

best [bɛst] *adj* melhor ♦ *adv* (o) melhor; **the** ~ **part of** (*quantity*) a maior parte de; **at** ~ na melhor das hipóteses; **to make the** ~ **of sth** tirar o maior partido possível de algo; **to do one's** ~ fazer o possível; **to the** ~ **of my knowledge** que eu saiba; **to the** ~ **of my ability** o melhor que eu puder; **he's not exactly patient at the** ~ **of times** mesmo nos seus melhores momentos ele não é muito paciente; **the** ~ **thing to do is** ... o melhor é ....

best man *n* padrinho de casamento.

bestow [bɪ'stəu] *vt* outorgar; (*affection*) dar, oferecer.

bestseller ['bɛst'sɛlə*] *n* (*book*) best-seller *m*.

bet [bɛt] (*pt, pp* **bet** *or* ~**ted**) *n* aposta ♦ *vt, vi*: **to** ~ **(on)** apostar (em); **it's a safe** ~ (*fig*) é coisa segura, é dinheiro ganho.

Bethlehem ['bɛθlɪhɛm] *n* Belém.

betray [bɪ'treɪ] *vt* trair, atraiçoar; (*denounce*) delatar.

betrayal [bɪ'treɪəl] *n* traição *f*.

better ['bɛtə*] *adj, adv* melhor ♦ *vt* melhorar; (*go above*) superar ♦ *n*: **to get the** ~ **of sb** vencer alguém; **you had** ~ **do it** é melhor você fazer isso; **he thought** ~ **of it** pensou melhor, mudou de opinião; **to get** ~ melhorar; **that's** ~! isso!; ~ **off** em melhor situação; **you'd be** ~ **off this way** (*fig*) seria melhor para você assim.

betting ['bɛtɪŋ] *n* jogo.

betting shop (*BRIT*) *n* agência de apostas.

between [bɪ'twiːn] *prep* no meio de, entre ♦ *adv* no meio; **the road** ~ **here and London** a estrada daqui a Londres; **we only had 5** ~ **us** juntos só tínhamos 5; ~ **you and me** cá entre nós.

bevel ['bɛvəl] *n* (*also*: ~ *edge*) bisel *m*.

beverage ['bɛvərɪdʒ] *n* bebida.

bevy ['bɛvɪ] *n*: **a** ~ **of** um grupo *or* bando de.

bewail [bɪ'weɪl] *vt* lamentar.

beware [bɪ'wɛə*] *vt, vi*: **to** ~ **(of)** precaver-se (de), ter cuidado (com) ♦ *excl* cuidado!

bewildered [bɪ'wɪldəd] *adj* confuso, desnorteado.

bewildering [bɪ'wɪldərɪŋ] *adj* atordoador(a), desnorteante.

bewitching [bɪ'wɪtʃɪŋ] *adj* encantador(a), sedutor(a).

beyond [bɪ'jɔnd] *prep* (*in space*) além de; (*exceeding*) acima de, fora de ♦ *adv* além.

b/f *abbr* = **brought forward**.

BFPO *n abbr* (= *British Forces Post Office*) serviço postal do exército.

bhp *n abbr* (*AUT*: *brake horsepower*) potência efetiva ao freio.

bi... [baɪ] *prefix* bi....

biannual [baɪ'ænjuəl] *adj* semestral.

bias ['baɪəs] *n* (*prejudice*) preconceito; (*preference*) prevenção *f*.

bias(s)ed ['baɪəst] *adj* parcial; **to be** ~ **against** ter preconceito contra.

bib [bɪb] *n* babadouro, babador *m*.

Bible ['baɪbl] *n* Bíblia.

bibliography [bɪblɪ'ɔgrəfɪ] *n* bibliografia.

bicarbonate of soda [baɪ'kɑːbənɪt-] *n* bicarbonato de sódio.

bicentenary [baɪsɛn'tiːnərɪ] *n* bicentenário.

bicentennial [baɪsɛn'tɛnɪəl] *n* bicentenário.

biceps ['baɪsɛps] *n* bíceps *m inv*.

bicker ['bɪkə*] *vi* brigar.

bicycle ['baɪsɪkl] *n* bicicleta.

bicycle path *n* ciclovia.

bicycle pump *n* bomba de bicicleta.

bicycle track *n* ciclovia.

bid [bɪd] (*pt* **bade** *or* **bid**, *pp* **bidden** *or* **bid**) *n* oferta; (*at auction*) lance *m*; (*attempt*) tentativa ♦ *vi* fazer uma oferta; (*COMM*) licitar, fazer uma licitação ♦ *vt* (*price*) oferecer; (*order*) mandar, ordenar; **to** ~ **sb good day** dar bom dia a alguém.

bidder ['bɪdə*] *n* (*COMM*) licitante *m*; **the highest** ~ quem oferece mais.

bidding ['bɪdɪŋ] *n* (*at auction*) lances *mpl*; (*COMM*) licitação *f*; (*order*) ordem *f*.

bide [baɪd] *vt*: **to** ~ **one's time** esperar o momento adequado.

bidet ['biːdeɪ] *n* bidê *m*.

bidirectional ['baɪdɪ'rɛkʃənl] *adj* bidirecional.

biennial [baɪ'ɛnɪəl] *adj* bienal ♦ *n* (*plant*) planta bienal.

bier [bɪə*] *n* féretro.

bifocals [baɪ'fəuklz] *npl* óculos *mpl* bifocais.

big [bɪg] *adj* grande; **to do things in a** ~ **way** fazer as coisas em grande escala.

bigamy ['bɪgəmɪ] *n* bigamia.

big business *n* alto comércio.

big dipper [-'dɪpə*] *n* montanha-russa.
big end *n* (*AUT*) cabeça de biela.
bigheaded ['bɪg'hɛdɪd] *adj* vaidoso.
big-hearted ['bɪg'hɑːtɪd] *adj* magnânimo.
bigot ['bɪgət] *n* fanático, intolerante *m/f*.
bigoted ['bɪgətɪd] *adj* fanático, intolerante.
bigotry ['bɪgətrɪ] *n* fanatismo, intolerância.
big toe *n* dedão *m* do pé.
big top *n* tenda de circo.
big wheel *n* (*at fair*) roda gigante.
bigwig ['bɪgwɪg] (*inf*) *n* mandachuva *m*.
bike [baɪk] *n* bicicleta.
bikini [bɪ'kiːnɪ] *n* biquíni *m*.
bilateral [baɪ'lætrəl] *adj* bilateral.
bile [baɪl] *n* bílis *f*.
bilingual [baɪ'lɪŋgwəl] *adj* bilíngüe.
bilious ['bɪlɪəs] *adj* bilioso.
bill [bɪl] *n* (*account*) conta; (*invoice*) fatura;
(*POL*) projeto de lei; (*US*: *banknote*) bilhete
m, nota; (*in restaurant*) conta, notinha; (*notice*) cartaz *m*; (*of bird*) bico ♦ *vt* (*item*) faturar; (*customer*) enviar fatura a; **may I
have the ~ please?** a conta *or* a notinha, por
favor?; **"stick** *or* **post no ~s"** "é proibido
afixar cartazes"; **to fit** *or* **fill the ~** (*fig*)
servir; **~ of exchange** letra de câmbio; **~ of
lading** conhecimento de carga; **~ of sale**
nota de venda; (*formal*) escritura de venda.
billboard ['bɪlbɔːd] *n* quadro para cartazes.
billet ['bɪlɪt] *n* alojamento ♦ *vt* alojar, quarte-
lar.
billfold ['bɪlfəuld] (*US*) *n* carteira (para notas).
billiards ['bɪlɪədz] *n* bilhar *m*.
billion ['bɪlɪən] *n* (*BRIT*: = 1,000,000,000,000) trilhão *m*; (*US*: = 1,000,000,000) bilhão *m*.
billow ['bɪləu] *n* (*of smoke*) bulcão *m* ♦ *vi*
(*smoke*) redemoinhar; (*sail*) enfunar-se.
billy goat ['bɪlɪ-] *n* bode *m*.
bin [bɪn] *n* caixa; (*BRIT*: *also*: *dust~*; *litter ~*)
lata de lixo; *see also* **breadbin**.
binary ['baɪnərɪ] *adj* binário.
bind [baɪnd] (*pt*, *pp* **bound**) *vt* atar, amarrar;
(*wound*) enfaixar; (*book*) encadernar;
(*oblige*) obrigar.
bind over *vt* (*LAW*) pôr em liberdade condicional.
bind up *vt* (*wound*) enfaixar; **to be bound
up with** estar vinculado a.
binder ['baɪndə*] *n* (*file*) fichário.
binding ['baɪndɪŋ] *adj* (*contract*) sujeitante ♦
n (*of book*) encadernação *f*.
binge [bɪndʒ] (*inf*) *n*: **(to go on a) ~** (cair
na) farra.
bingo ['bɪŋgəu] *n* bingo.
binoculars [bɪ'nɔkjuləz] *npl* binóculo.
biochemistry [baɪə'kɛmɪstrɪ] *n* bioquímica.
biodegradable ['baɪəudɪ'greɪdəbl] *adj* biodegradável.
biographer [baɪ'ɔgrəfə*] *n* biógrafo/a.
biographic(al) [baɪə'græfɪk(l)] *adj* biográfico.
biography [baɪ'ɔgrəfɪ] *n* biografia.
biological [baɪə'lɔdʒɪkəl] *adj* biológico.

biologist [baɪ'ɔlədʒɪst] *n* biólogo/a.
biology [baɪ'ɔlədʒɪ] *n* biologia.
biophysics ['baɪəu'fɪzɪks] *n* biofísica.
biopsy ['baɪɔpsɪ] *n* biopsia.
biotechnology ['baɪəutɛk'nɔlədʒɪ] *n* biotecnia.
birch [bɜːtʃ] *n* bétula; (*cane*) vara de vidoeiro.
bird [bɜːd] *n* ave *f*, pássaro; (*BRIT*: *inf*: *girl*)
gatinha.
birdcage ['bɜːdkeɪdʒ] *n* gaiola.
bird's-eye view *n* vista aérea; (*fig*) vista geral.
bird watcher [-'wɔtʃə*] *n* ornitófilo/a.
Biro ['baɪərəu] ® *n* caneta esferográfica.
birth [bɜːθ] *n* nascimento; (*MED*) parto; **to
give ~ to** dar à luz, parir.
birth certificate *n* certidão *f* de nascimento.
birth control *n* controle *m* de natalidade;
(*methods*) métodos *mpl* anticoncepcionais.
birthday ['bɜːθdeɪ] *n* aniversário (*BR*), dia *m*
de anos (*PT*).
birthmark ['bɜːθmɑːk] *n* nevo.
birthplace ['bɜːθpleɪs] *n* lugar *m* de nascimento.
birth rate *n* (índice *m* de) natalidade *f*.
Biscay ['bɪskeɪ] *n*: **the Bay of ~** o golfo de
Biscaia.
biscuit ['bɪskɪt] *n* (*BRIT*) bolacha, biscoito; (*US*)
pão *m* doce.
bisect [baɪ'sɛkt] *vt* dividir ao meio.
bishop ['bɪʃəp] *n* bispo.
bit [bɪt] *pt of* **bite** ♦ *n* pedaço, bocado; (*of tool*)
broca; (*of horse*) freio; (*COMPUT*) bit *m*; **a ~
of** (*a little*) um pouco de; **a ~ mad** um pouco
or meio doido; **~ by ~** pouco a pouco; **to
come to ~s** (*break*) cair aos pedaços; **bring
all your ~s and pieces** traz todos os teus troços; **to do one's ~** fazer sua parte.
bitch [bɪtʃ] *n* (*dog*) cadela, cachorra; (*inf!*)
cadela (*!*), vagabunda (*!*).
bite [baɪt] (*pt* **bit**, *pp* **bitten**) *vt*, *vi* morder;
(*insect etc*) picar ♦ *n* mordida; (*insect ~*) picada; (*mouthful*) bocado; **let's have a ~ (to
eat)** vamos comer algo; **to ~ one's nails**
roer as unhas.
biting ['baɪtɪŋ] *adj* (*wind*) penetrante; (*wit*)
mordaz.
bit part *n* (*THEATRE*) ponta.
bitten ['bɪtn] *pp of* **bite**.
bitter ['bɪtə*] *adj* amargo; (*wind*, *criticism*)
cortante, penetrante; (*battle*) encarniçado ♦
n (*BRIT*: *beer*) cerveja amarga; **to the ~ end**
até o fim.
bitterly ['bɪtəlɪ] *adv* (*complain*, *weep*) amarga-
mente; (*criticize*) asperamente; (*oppose*) im-
placavelmente; (*jealous*, *disappointed*) extremamente; **it's ~ cold** faz um frio glacial.
bitterness ['bɪtənɪs] *n* amargor *m*; (*anger*)
rancor *m*.
bittersweet ['bɪtəswiːt] *adj* agridoce.
bitty ['bɪtɪ] (*BRIT*: *inf*) *adj* sem nexo.
bitumen ['bɪtjumɪn] *n* betume *m*.
bivouac ['bɪvuæk] *n* bivaque *m*.

NB: *European Portuguese adds the following consonants to certain words:* **b** (sú(b)dito, su(b)til); **c** (a(c)ção,
a(c)cionista, a(c)to); **m** (inde(m)ne); **p** (ado(p)ção, ado(p)tar); *for further details see p. xiii.*

bizarre [bɪ'zɑː*] *adj* esquisito.
bk *abbr* = **bank**; **book.**
BL *n abbr* (= *Bachelor of Laws*; *Bachelor of Letters*) título universitário; (*US*: = *Bachelor of Literature*) título universitário.
bl *abbr* = **bill of lading.**
blab [blæb] *vi* dar *or* bater com a língua nos dentes ♦ *vt* (*also*: ~ *out*) revelar, badalar.
black [blæk] *adj* preto ♦ *n* (*colour*) cor *f* preta; (*person*): **B~** negro/a, preto/a ♦ *vt* (*shoes*) lustrar (*BR*), engraxar (*PT*); (*BRIT*: *INDUSTRY*) boicotar; **to give sb a ~ eye** esmurrar alguém e deixá-lo de olho roxo; ~ **coffee** café *m* preto; **there it is in ~ and white** (*fig*) aí está preto no branco; **to be in the ~** (*in credit*) estar com saldo credor; ~ **and blue** contuso, contundido.
black out *vi* (*faint*) desmaiar.
black belt (*US*) *n* zona de negros.
blackberry ['blækbərɪ] *n* amora preta (*BR*), amora silvestre (*PT*).
blackbird ['blækbɜːd] *n* melro.
blackboard ['blækbɔːd] *n* quadro(-negro).
black box *n* (*AVIAT*) caixa preta.
Black Country (*BRIT*) *n*: **the ~** zona industrial na região central da Inglaterra.
blackcurrant [blæk'kʌrənt] *n* groselha negra.
black economy (*BRIT*) *n* economia invisível.
blacken ['blækən] *vt* enegrecer; (*fig*) denegrir.
Black Forest *n*: **the ~** a Floresta Negra.
blackhead ['blækhɛd] *n* cravo.
black ice *n* gelo negro.
blackjack ['blækdʒæk] *n* (*CARDS*) vinte-e-um *m*; (*US*: *truncheon*) cassetete *m*.
blackleg ['blæklɛg] (*BRIT*) *n* fura-greve *m/f*.
blacklist ['blæklɪst] *n* lista negra ♦ *vt* colocar na lista negra.
blackmail ['blækmeɪl] *n* chantagem *f* ♦ *vt* fazer chantagem a.
blackmailer ['blækmeɪlə*] *n* chantagista *m/f*.
black market *n* mercado *or* câmbio negro.
blackout ['blækaut] *n* blecaute *m*; (*fainting*) desmaio; (*of radio signal*) desvanecimento.
Black Sea *n*: **the ~** o mar Negro.
black sheep *n* (*fig*) ovelha negra.
blacksmith ['blæksmɪθ] *n* ferreiro.
black spot *n* (*AUT*) lugar *m* perigoso.
bladder ['blædə*] *n* bexiga.
blade [bleɪd] *n* folha; (*cutting edge*) lâmina; (*of oar, rotor*) pá *f*; **a ~ of grass** uma folha de relva.
blame [bleɪm] *n* culpa ♦ *vt*: **to ~ sb for sth** culpar alguém por algo; **to be to ~** ter a culpa.
blameless ['bleɪmlɪs] *adj* (*person*) inocente.
blanch [blɑːntʃ] *vi* (*person, face*) empalidecer ♦ *vt* (*CULIN*) escaldar.
bland [blænd] *adj* suave; (*taste*) brando.
blank [blæŋk] *adj* em branco; (*shot*) sem bala; (*look*) sem expressão ♦ *n* lacuna, espaço em branco; (*cartridge*) bala de festim; **we drew a ~** (*fig*) chegamos a lugar nenhum.
blank cheque (*US* **blank check**) *n* cheque *m* em branco; **to give sb a ~ to do ...** dar

carta branca a alguém para fazer ....
blanket ['blæŋkɪt] *n* (*for bed*) cobertor *m*; (*for travelling etc*) manta ♦ *adj* (*statement, agreement*) global, geral; **to give ~ cover** (*subj: insurance policy*) dar cobertura geral.
blare [blɛə*] *vi* (*horn, radio*) clangorar.
blarney ['blɑːnɪ] *n* bajulação *f*.
blasé ['blɑːzeɪ] *adj* indiferente.
blasphemous ['blæsfɪməs] *adj* blasfemo.
blasphemy ['blæsfɪmɪ] *n* blasfêmia.
blast [blɑːst] *n* (*of wind*) rajada; (*of whistle*) toque *m*; (*of explosive*) explosão *f*; (*shock wave*) sopro; (*of air, steam*) jato ♦ *vt* (*blow up*) fazer voar; (*blow open*) abrir com uma carga explosiva ♦ (*BRIT*: *inf*) *excl* droga!; **(at) full ~** (*play music etc*) no volume máximo; (*fig*) a todo vapor.
blast off *vi* (*SPACE*) decolar.
blast furnace *n* alto forno.
blast-off *n* (*SPACE*) lançamento.
blatant ['bleɪtənt] *adj* descarado.
blatantly ['bleɪtəntlɪ] *adv* (*lie*) descaradamente; **it's ~ obvious** é de toda a evidência, está na cara.
blaze [bleɪz] *n* (*fire*) fogo; (*in building etc*) incêndio; (*flames*) chamas *fpl*; (*of sun etc*) esplendor *m*; (*fig*) explosão *f* ♦ (*fire*) arder; (*fig*) resplandecer ♦ *vt*: **to ~ a trail** (*fig*) abrir (um) caminho; **in a ~ of publicity** numa explosão de publicidade.
blazer ['bleɪzə*] *n* casaco esportivo, blazer *m*.
bleach [bliːtʃ] *n* (*also: household ~*) água sanitária ♦ *vt* (*linen*) branquear.
bleached [bliːtʃt] *adj* (*hair*) oxigenado; (*linen*) branqueado, alvejado.
bleachers ['bliːtʃəz] (*US*) *npl* (*SPORT*) arquibancada descoberta.
bleak [bliːk] *adj* (*countryside*) desolado; (*prospect*) desanimador(a), sombrio; (*weather*) ruim; (*smile*) sem graça, amarelo.
bleary-eyed ['blɪərɪ'aɪd] *adj* de olhos injetados.
bleat [bliːt] *vi* balir ♦ *n* balido.
bled [blɛd] *pt, pp of* **bleed.**
bleed [bliːd] (*pt, pp* **bled**) *vt, vi* sangrar; **my nose is ~ing** eu estou sangrando do nariz.
bleeper ['bliːpə*] *n* (*of doctor etc*) bip *m*.
blemish ['blɛmɪʃ] *n* mancha, falha.
blend [blɛnd] *n* mistura ♦ *vt* misturar ♦ *vi* (*colours etc*) combinar-se, misturar-se.
blender ['blɛndə*] *n* (*CULIN*) liquidificador *m*.
bless [blɛs] (*pt, pp* **blessed** *or* **blest**) *vt* abençoar.
blessed¹ [blɛst] *pt, pp of* **bless; to be ~ with** estar dotado de.
blessed² ['blɛsɪd] *adj* (*REL*: *holy*) bendito, bento; (*happy*) afortunado; **it rains every ~ day** chove cada santo dia.
blessing ['blɛsɪŋ] *n* bênção *f*; (*advantage*) benefício, vantagem *f*; **to count one's ~s** dar graças a Deus; **it was a ~ in disguise** Deus escreve certo por linhas tortas.
blest [blɛst] *pt, pp of* **bless.**
blew [bluː] *pt of* **blow.**
blight [blaɪt] *vt* (*hopes etc*) frustrar, gorar ♦ *n*

(*of plants*) ferrugem *f*.
blimey ['blaɪmɪ] (*BRIT: inf*) *excl* nossa!
blind [blaɪnd] *adj* cego ♦ *n* (*for window*)
persiana ♦ *vt* cegar; (*dazzle*) deslumbrar; **to
turn a ~ eye** (**on** *or* **to**) fazer vista grossa
(a).
blind alley *n* beco-sem-saída *m*.
blind corner (*BRIT*) *n* curva sem visibilidade.
blindfold ['blaɪndfəʊld] *n* venda ♦ *adj, adv*
com os olhos vendados, às cegas ♦ *vt* vendar
os olhos a.
blindly ['blaɪndlɪ] *adv* às cegas, cegamente.
blindness ['blaɪndnɪs] *n* cegueira.
blind spot *n* ponto cego; (*fig*) cegueira.
blink [blɪŋk] *vi* piscar ♦ (*inf*) *n*: **the TV's on
the ~** a TV está com defeito.
blinkers ['blɪŋkəz] *npl* antolhos *mpl*.
blinking ['blɪŋkɪŋ] (*BRIT: inf*) *adj*: **this ~** ...
este danado ....
bliss [blɪs] *n* felicidade *f*.
blissful ['blɪsful] *adj* (*event, day*) maravilhoso;
(*sigh, smile*) contente; **in ~ ignorance** numa
bendita ignorância.
blissfully ['blɪsfulɪ] *adv* (*smile*) ditosamente;
(*happy*) maravilhosamente.
blister ['blɪstə*] *n* (*on skin*) bolha, empola ♦ *vi*
(*paint*) empolar-se.
blistering ['blɪstərɪŋ] *adj* (*heat*) causticante.
blithe [blaɪð] *adj* alegre.
blithely ['blaɪðlɪ] *adv* (*unconcernedly*) tranqüilamente; (*joyfully*) alegremente.
blithering ['blɪðərɪŋ] (*inf*) *adj*: **this ~ idiot**
esta besta quadrada.
BLit(t) *n abbr* (= *Bachelor of Literature*) título
universitário.
blitz [blɪts] *n* bombardeio aéreo; (*fig*): **to have
a ~ on sth** dar um jeito em algo.
blizzard ['blɪzəd] *n* nevasca.
BLM (*US*) *n abbr* = **Bureau of Land Management**.
bloated ['bləʊtɪd] *adj* inchado.
blob [blɔb] *n* (*drop*) gota; (*stain, spot*) mancha.
bloc [blɔk] *n* (*POL*) bloco.
block [blɔk] *n* bloco; (*in pipes*) entupimento;
(*toy*) cubo; (*of buildings*) quarteirão *m* ♦ *vt*
obstruir, bloquear; (*pipe*) entupir; (*progress*)
impedir; (*COMPUT*) blocar; **~ of flats** (*BRIT*)
prédio (de apartamentos); **3 ~s from here** a
três quarteirões daqui; **mental ~** bloqueio; **~
and tackle** (*TECH*) talha.
block up *vt* (*hole*) tampar; (*pipe*) entupir;
(*road*) bloquear.
blockade [blɔ'keɪd] *n* bloqueio ♦ *vt* bloquear.
blockage ['blɔkɪdʒ] *n* obstrução *f*.
block booking *n* reserva em bloco.
blockbuster ['blɔkbʌstə*] *n* grande sucesso.
block capitals *npl* letras *fpl* de forma.
blockhead ['blɔkhɛd] *n* imbecil *m/f*.
block letters *npl* letras *fpl* maiúsculas.
block release (*BRIT*) *n* licença para fins de
aperfeiçoamento profissional.

block vote (*BRIT*) *n* voto em bloco.
bloke [bləʊk] (*BRIT: inf*) *n* cara *m* (*BR*), gajo
(*PT*).
blond(e) [blɔnd] *adj, n* louro/a.
blood [blʌd] *n* sangue *m*.
bloodcurdling ['blʌdkɔːdlɪŋ] *adj* horripilante,
de fazer gelar o sangue nas veias.
blood donor *n* doador(a) *m/f* de sangue.
blood group *n* grupo sangüíneo.
bloodhound ['blʌdhaund] *n* sabujo.
bloodless ['blʌdlɪs] *adj* (*victory*) incruento;
(*pale*) pálido.
bloodletting ['blʌdletɪŋ] *n* (*MED*) sangria;
(*fig*) derramamento de sangue.
blood poisoning *n* toxemia.
blood pressure *n* pressão *f* arterial *or*
sangüínea.
bloodshed ['blʌdʃɛd] *n* matança, carnificina.
bloodshot ['blʌdʃɔt] *adj* (*eyes*) injetado.
bloodstained ['blʌdsteɪnd] *adj* manchado de
sangue.
bloodstream ['blʌdstriːm] *n* corrente *f* sangüínea.
blood test *n* exame *m* de sangue.
bloodthirsty ['blʌdθɜːstɪ] *adj* sangüinário.
blood transfusion *n* transfusão *f* de sangue.
blood vessel *n* vaso sangüíneo.
bloody ['blʌdɪ] *adj* sangrento; (*BRIT: inf!*):
this ~ ... essa droga de ..., esse maldito ... ♦
adv (*BRIT: inf!*): **~ strong/good** forte/bom
pra burro (*inf*).
bloody-minded ['blʌdɪ'maɪndɪd] (*BRIT: inf*)
adj espírito de porco *inv*.
bloom [bluːm] *n* flor *f*; (*fig*) florescimento, viço ♦ *vi* florescer.
blooming ['bluːmɪŋ] (*inf*) *adj*: **this ~** ... esse
maldito ..., esse miserável ....
blossom ['blɔsəm] *n* flor *f* ♦ *vi* florescer; (*fig*)
desabrochar-se; **to ~ into** (*fig*) tornar-se.
blot [blɔt] *n* borrão *m* ♦ *vt* borrar; (*ink*) secar; **a ~ on the landscape** um aleijão na
paisagem; **to ~ one's copy book** (*fig*) manchar sua reputação.
blot out *vt* (*view*) tapar; (*memory*) apagar.
blotchy ['blɔtʃɪ] *adj* (*complexion*) cheio de
manchas.
blotter ['blɔtə*] *n* mata-borrão *m*.
blotting paper ['blɔtɪŋ-] *n* mata-borrão *m*.
blouse [blauz] *n* blusa.
blow [bləʊ] (*pt* **blew**, *pp* **blown**) *n* golpe *m* ♦
vi soprar ♦ *vt* (*glass*) soprar; (*fuse*) queimar; (*instrument*) tocar; **to ~ one's nose**
assoar o nariz; **to come to ~s** chegar às
vias de fato.
blow away *vt* levar, arrancar ♦ *vi* ser levado pelo vento.
blow down *vt* derrubar.
blow off *vt* levar ♦ *vi* ser levado.
blow out *vi* (*candle*) apagar; (*tyre*) estourar ♦ *vt* (*candle*) apagar.
blow over *vi* passar, ser esquecido.

NB: European Portuguese adds the following consonants to certain words: **b** (sú(b)dito, su(b)til); **c** (a(c)ção,
a(c)cionista, a(c)to); **m** (inde(m)ne); **p** (ado(p)ção, ado(p)tar); *for further details see p. xiii.*

blow up vi explodir; (fig) perder a paciência ♦ vt dinamitar; (tyre) encher; (PHOT) ampliar.
blow-dry n escova ♦ vt fazer escova em.
blowlamp ['bləʊlæmp] (BRIT) n maçarico.
blow-out n (of tyre) furo, estouro; (inf: big meal) rega-bofe m.
blowtorch ['bləʊtɔːtʃ] n maçarico.
blowzy ['blaʊzɪ] (BRIT) adj balofa.
BLS (US) n abbr = **Bureau of Labor Statistics**.
blubber ['blʌbə*] n óleo de baleia ♦ vi (pej) choramingar.
blue [bluː] adj azul; ~s npl: **the ~s** (MUS) o blues; **to have the ~s** (inf: feeling) estar na fossa, estar de baixo astral; ~ **film/joke** filme/anedota picante; **(only) once in a ~ moon** uma vez na vida e outra na morte; **out of the** ~ (fig) de estalo, inesperadamente.
blue baby n criança azul.
bluebell ['bluːbɛl] n campainha (azul), campânula.
bluebottle ['bluːbɔtl] n varejeira azul.
blue cheese n queijo tipo roquefort.
blue-chip adj: ~ **investment** investimento de primeira ordem.
blue-collar worker n operário/a.
blue jeans npl jeans m (BR), jeans mpl (PT).
blueprint ['bluːprɪnt] n anteprojeto; (fig): ~ **(for)** esquema m (de).
bluff [blʌf] vi blefar ♦ n blefe m; (crag) penhasco ♦ adj (person) brusco; **to call sb's** ~ pagar para ver alguém.
blunder ['blʌndə*] n gafe f ♦ vi cometer or fazer uma gafe; **to** ~ **into sb/sth** esbarrar com alguém/algo.
blunt [blʌnt] adj (blade) cego, embotado; (pencil) rombudo; (person) franco, direto ♦ vt embotar; ~ **instrument** (LAW) arma imprópria.
bluntly ['blʌntlɪ] adv sem rodeios.
bluntness ['blʌntnɪs] n (of person) franqueza, rudeza.
blur [blə:*] n borrão m, nebulosidade f ♦ vt borrar, nublar.
blurb [blə:b] n (for book) dizeres mpl de propaganda.
blurred [blə:d] adj indistinto, borrado.
blurt [blə:t]: **to** ~ **out** vt (reveal) deixar escapar; (say) balbuciar.
blush [blʌʃ] vi corar, ruborizar-se ♦ n rubor m, vermelhidão f.
blusher ['blʌʃə*] n blusher m.
bluster ['blʌstə*] n fanfarronada, bazófia ♦ vi fanfarronar.
blustering ['blʌstərɪŋ] adj (person) fanfarrão/rona.
blustery ['blʌstərɪ] adj (weather) borrascoso, tormentoso.
Blvd abbr = **boulevard**.
BM n abbr = **British Museum**; (SCH: = Bachelor of Medicine) título universitário.
BMA n abbr = **British Medical Association**.
BMJ n abbr = **British Medical Journal**.
BMus n abbr (= Bachelor of Music) título universitário.

BO n abbr (inf: = body odour) fartum m, c.c. m; (US) = **box office**.
boar [bɔ:*] n javali m.
board [bɔ:d] n tábua; (on wall) quadro; (for chess etc) tabuleiro; (committee) junta, conselho; (in firm) diretoria, conselho administrativo ♦ vt embarcar em; **on** ~ (NAUT, AVIAT) a bordo; **full** ~ (BRIT) pensão f completa; **half** ~ (BRIT) meia-pensão; ~ **and lodging** casa e comida; **above** ~ (fig) limpo; **across the** ~ adj geral ♦ adv de uma maneira geral; **to go by the** ~ ficar abandonado, dançar (inf).
board up vt (door) entabuar.
boarder ['bɔ:də*] n hóspede m/f; (SCH) interno/a.
board game n jogo de tabuleiro.
boarding card ['bɔ:dɪŋ-] n (AVIAT, NAUT) cartão m de embarque.
boarding house ['bɔ:dɪŋ-] (irreg) n pensão m.
boarding pass ['bɔ:dɪŋ-] (BRIT) n cartão m de embarque.
boarding school ['bɔ:dɪŋ-] n internato.
board meeting n reunião f da diretoria.
board room n sala da diretoria.
boardwalk ['bɔ:dwɔ:k] (US) n passeio de tábuas.
boast [bəʊst] vi contar vantagem; **to** ~ **(about or of)** gabar-se (de), jactar-se (de) ♦ vt ostentar ♦ n jactância, bazófia.
boastful ['bəʊstful] adj vaidoso, jactancioso.
boastfulness ['bəʊstfulnɪs] n bazófia, jactância.
boat [bəʊt] n barco; (small) bote m; (big) navio; **to go by** ~ ir de barco; **to be in the same** ~ (fig) estar no mesmo barco.
boater ['bəʊtə*] n (hat) chapéu m de palha.
boating ['bəʊtɪŋ] n passeio de barco.
boatman ['bəʊtmən] (irreg) n barqueiro.
boatswain ['bəʊsn] n contramestre m.
bob [bɔb] vi (boat, cork on water: also: ~ up and down) balouçar-se ♦ n (BRIT: inf) = **shilling**.
bob up vi aparecer, surgir.
bobbin ['bɔbɪn] n bobina, carretel m.
bobby ['bɔbɪ] (BRIT: inf) n policial m/f (BR), polícia m (PT).
bobsleigh ['bɔbsleɪ] n bob m, trenó m duplo.
bode [bəʊd] vi: **to** ~ **well/ill (for)** ser de bom/mau agouro (para).
bodice ['bɔdɪs] n corpete m.
bodily ['bɔdɪlɪ] adj corpóreo, corporal; (pain) físico; (needs) material ♦ adv (lift) em peso.
body ['bɔdɪ] n corpo; (corpse) cadáver m; (of car) carroceria; (of plane) fuselagem f; (fig: society) órgão m; (: quantity) conjunto; (of wine) corpo; **in a** ~ todos juntos.
body-building n musculação f.
bodyguard ['bɔdɪgɑ:d] n guarda-costas m inv.
body repairs npl lanternagem f.
bodywork ['bɔdɪwɔ:k] n lataria.
boffin ['bɔfɪn] (BRIT) n cientista m/f.
bog [bɔg] n pântano, atoleiro ♦ vt: **to get ~ged down (in)** (fig) atolar-se (em).

bogey ['bəugɪ] *n* (*worry*) espectro; (*BRIT*: *inf*: *dried mucus*) meleca.

boggle ['bɔgl] *vi*: **the mind ~s** (*wonder*) não dá para imaginar; (*innuendo*) nem quero pensar.

bogie ['bəugɪ] *n* (*RAIL*) truque *m*.

Bogotá [bɔgə'tɑ:] *n* Bogotá.

bogus ['bəugəs] *adj* falso; (*person*) fingido, farsante.

Bohemia [bəu'hi:mɪə] *n* Boêmia.

Bohemian [bəu'hi:mɪən] *adj*, *n* boêmio/a.

boil [bɔɪl] *vt* ferver; (*eggs*) cozinhar ♦ *vi* ferver ♦ *n* (*MED*) furúnculo; **to come to the** (*BRIT*) **or a** (*US*) **~** começar a ferver; **to bring to the** (*BRIT*) **or a** (*US*) **~** deixar ferver; **~ed egg** (*hard*) ovo cozido; (*soft*) ovo quente; **~ed potatoes** batatas *fpl* cozidas.
  boil down *vi* (*fig*): **to ~ down to** reduzir-se a.
  boil over *vi* transbordar.

boiler ['bɔɪlə*] *n* caldeira; (*for central heating*) boiler *m*.

boiler suit (*BRIT*) *n* macacão *m* (*BR*), fato macaco (*PT*).

boiling ['bɔɪlɪŋ] *adj*: **it's ~** (*weather*) está um calor horrível; **I'm ~** (*hot*) (*inf*) estou morrendo de calor.

boiling point *n* ponto de ebulição.

boisterous ['bɔɪstərəs] *adj* (*noisy*) barulhento; (*excitable*) agitado; (*crowd*) turbulento.

bold [bəuld] *adj* audacioso, corajoso; (*pej*) atrevido, insolente; (*outline, colour*) forte.

boldness ['bəuldnɪs] *n* arrojo, coragem *f*; (*cheek*) audácia, descaramento.

bold type *n* (*TYP*) negrito.

Bolivia [bə'lɪvɪə] *n* Bolívia.

Bolivian [bə'lɪvɪən] *adj*, *n* boliviano/a.

bollard ['bɔləd] *n* (*BRIT*: *AUT*) poste *m* de sinalização; (*NAUT*) poste de amarração.

bolster ['bəulstə*] *n* travesseiro.
  bolster up *vt* sustentar.

bolt [bəult] *n* (*lock*) trinco, ferrolho; (*with nut*) parafuso, cavilha ♦ *adv*: **~ upright** direito como um fuso ♦ *vt* (*door*) fechar a ferrolho, trancar; (*food*) engolir às pressas ♦ *vi* fugir; (*horse*) disparar; **to be a ~ from the blue** (*fig*) cair como uma bomba, ser uma bomba.

bomb [bɔm] *n* bomba ♦ *vt* bombardear.

bombard [bɔm'bɑ:d] *vt* bombardear.

bombardment [bɔm'bɑ:dmənt] *n* bombardeio.

bombastic [bɔm'bæstɪk] *adj* empolado, bombástico; (*person*) pomposo.

bomb disposal *n*: **~ expert** perito/a em desmontagem de explosivos; **~ unit** unidade *f* de desmontagem de explosivos.

bomber ['bɔmə*] *n* (*AVIAT*) bombardeiro; (*terrorist*) terrorista *m/f*.

bombing ['bɔmɪŋ] *n* bombardeio; (*by terrorists*) atentado a bomba.

bombshell ['bɔmʃɛl] *n* granada de artilharia;

(*fig*) bomba.

bomb site *n* zona bombardeada.

bona fide ['bəunə'faɪdɪ] *adj* genuíno, autêntico.

bonanza [bə'nænzə] *n* boom *m*.

bond [bɔnd] *n* (*binding promise*) compromisso; (*FINANCE*) obrigação *f*; (*link*) vínculo, laço; **in ~** (*goods*) retido sob caução na alfândega.

bondage ['bɔndɪdʒ] *n* escravidão *f*.

bonded warehouse ['bɔndɪd-] (*irreg*) *n* depósito da alfândega, entreposto aduaneiro.

bone [bəun] *n* osso; (*of fish*) espinha ♦ *vt* (*fish*) tirar as espinhas de; (*meat*) desossar.

bone china *n* porcelana com mistura de cinza de ossos.

bone-dry *adj* completamente seco.

bone idle *adj* preguiçoso.

boner ['bəunə*] (*US*) *n* gafe *f*.

bonfire ['bɔnfaɪə*] *n* fogueira.

Bonn [bɔn] *n* Bonn.

bonnet ['bɔnɪt] *n* toucado; (*BRIT*: *of car*) capô *m*.

bonny ['bɔnɪ] (*SCOTTISH*) *adj* bonitinho.

bonus ['bəunəs] *n* bônus *m*, prêmio; (*on salary*) prêmio, gratificação *f*.

bony ['bəunɪ] *adj* (*arm, face*, *MED*: *tissue*) ossudo; (*meat*) cheio de ossos; (*fish*) cheio de espinhas.

boo [bu:] *vt* vaiar ♦ *n* vaia ♦ *excl* ruuh!, bu!

boob [bu:b] (*inf*) *n* (*breast*) seio; (*BRIT*: *mistake*) besteira, gafe *f*.

booby prize ['bu:bɪ-] *n* prêmio de consolação.

booby trap ['bu:bɪ-] *n* armadilha explosiva.

booby-trapped ['bu:bɪtræpt] *adj* que tem armadilha explosiva.

book [buk] *n* livro; (*notebook*) caderno; (*COMM*): **~s** *npl* contas *fpl*, contabilidade *f* ♦ *vt* reservar; (*driver*) autuar; (*football player*) mostrar o cartão amarelo a; **to keep the ~s** fazer a escrituração or contabilidade; **by the ~** de acordo com o regulamento, corretamente; **to throw the ~ at sb** condenar alguém à pena máxima.

book in (*BRIT*) *vi* (*at hotel*) registrar (*BR*), registar (*PT*).

book up *vt* reservar; **all seats are ~ed up** todos os lugares estão tomados; **the hotel is ~ed up** o hotel está lotado.

bookable ['bukəbl] *adj*: **seats are ~** lugares podem ser reservados.

bookcase ['bukkeɪs] *n* estante *f* (para livros).

book ends *npl* suportes *mpl* de livros.

booking ['bukɪŋ] (*BRIT*) *n* reserva.

booking office (*BRIT*) *n* (*RAIL, THEATRE*) bilheteria (*BR*), bilheteira (*PT*).

book-keeping *n* escrituração *f*, contabilidade *f*.

booklet ['buklɪt] *n* livrinho, brochura.

bookmaker ['bukmeɪkə*] *n* book(maker) *m* (*BR*), agenciador *m* de apostas (*PT*).

bookseller ['buksɛlə*] *n* livreiro/a.

NB: *European Portuguese adds the following consonants to certain words:* **b** (sú(b)dito, su(b)til); **c** (a(c)ção, a(c)cionista, a(c)to); **m** (inde(m)ne); **p** (ado(p)ção, ado(p)tar); *for further details see p. xiii.*

bookshop ['bukʃɔp] n livraria.
bookstall ['bukstɔːl] n banca de livros.
bookstore ['bukstɔː*] n livraria.
book token n vale m para livro.
book value n valor m contábil.
boom [buːm] n (noise) barulho, estrondo; (in sales etc) aumento rápido; (ECON) boom m, fase f or aumento de prosperidade ♦ vi (sound) retumbar, ribombar; (business) tomar surto.
boomerang ['buːməræŋ] n bumerangue m.
boom town n cidade f de rápido crescimento econômico.
boon [buːn] n benefício.
boorish ['buərɪʃ] adj rude.
boost [buːst] n estímulo ♦ vt estimular; **to give a ~ to sb's spirits** or **to sb** dar uma força a alguém.
booster ['buːstə*] n (MED) revacinação f; (TV) amplificador m (de sinal); (ELEC) sobrevoltador m; (also: ~ rocket) foguete m auxiliar.
booster seat n (AUT: for children) assento de carro para crianças maiores.
boot [buːt] n bota; (for football) chuteira; (ankle ~) botina; (BRIT: of car) porta-malas m (BR), mala (BR: inf), porta-bagagem m (PT) ♦ vt (kick) dar pontapé em; (COMPUT) dar carga em; **to ~** (in addition) ainda por cima; **to give sb the ~** (inf) botar alguém na rua.
booth [buːð] n (at fair) barraca; (telephone ~, voting ~) cabine f.
bootleg ['buːtlɛg] adj de contrabando; **~ recording** gravação f pirata.
booty ['buːtɪ] n despojos mpl, pilhagem f.
booze [buːz] (inf) n bebida alcoólica ♦ vi embebedar-se.
boozer ['buːzə*] (inf) n (person) beberrão/beberrona m/f; (BRIT: pub) pub m.
border ['bɔːdə*] n margem f, borda; (of a country) fronteira ♦ cpd (town, region) fronteiriço; **the B~s** a região fronteiriça entre a Escócia e a Inglaterra.
border on vt fus limitar-se com; (fig) chegar às raias de.
borderline ['bɔːdəlaɪn] n (fig) fronteira ♦ adj: **~ case** caso-limite m.
bore [bɔː*] pt of **bear** ♦ vt (hole) abrir; (person) aborrecer ♦ n (person) chato, maçante; (of gun) calibre m; **what a ~!** que chato! (BR), que saco! (BR), que maçada! (PT); **to be ~d to tears** or **~d to death** or **~d stiff** estar muito entediado.
bored [bɔːd] adj entediado.
boredom ['bɔːdəm] n tédio, aborrecimento.
boring ['bɔːrɪŋ] adj chato, maçante.
born [bɔːn] adj: **to be ~** nascer; **I was ~ in 1960** nasci em 1960; **~ blind** cego de nascença; **a ~ leader** um líder nato.
borne [bɔːn] pp of **bear**.
Borneo ['bɔːnɪəu] n Bornéu.
borough ['bʌrə] n município.
borrow ['bɔrəu] vt: **to ~ sth (from sb)** pedir algo emprestado a alguém; **may I ~ your car?** você pode me emprestar o seu carro?

borrower ['bɔrəuə*] n tomador(a) m/f de empréstimo.
borrowing ['bɔrəuɪŋ] n empréstimo(s) m(pl).
borstal ['bɔːstl] (BRIT) n reformatório (de menores).
bosom ['buzəm] n peito.
bosom friend n amigo/a íntimo/a or do peito.
boss [bɔs] n chefe m/f; (employer) patrão/troa m/f; (in agriculture, industry etc) capataz m ♦ vt (also: ~ around) mandar em.
bossy ['bɔsɪ] adj mandão/dona.
bosun ['bəusn] n contramestre m.
botanical [bə'tænɪkl] adj botânico.
botanist ['bɔtənɪst] n botânico/a.
botany ['bɔtənɪ] n botânica.
botch [bɔtʃ] vt (also: ~ up) estropiar, atamancar.
both [bəuθ] adj, pron ambos/as, os dois/as duas ♦ adv: **~ A and B** tanto A como B; **~ of us went, we ~ went** nós dois fomos, ambos fomos.
bother ['bɔðə*] vt (worry) preocupar; (irritate) incomodar, molestar; (disturb) atrapalhar ♦ vi (also: ~ o.s.) preocupar-se ♦ n: **a ~ to have to do** é chato ter que fazer ♦ excl bolas!; **to ~ doing** dar-se ao trabalho de fazer; **to ~ about** preocupar-se com; **I'm sorry to ~ you** lamento incomodá-lo; **please don't ~** por favor, não se preocupe, não se dê ao trabalho; **don't ~** não vale a pena; **it's no ~** não tem problema.
Botswana [bɔt'swɑːnə] n Botsuana.
bottle ['bɔtl] n garrafa; (of perfume, medicine) frasco; (baby's) mamadeira (BR), biberão m (PT) ♦ vt engarrafar.
bottle up vt conter, refrear.
bottleneck ['bɔtlnɛk] n (traffic) engarrafamento; (of bottle, fig) gargalo.
bottle-opener n abridor m (de garrafas) (BR), abre-garrafas m inv (PT).
bottom ['bɔtəm] n (of box, sea) fundo; (buttocks) traseiro, bunda (inf); (of page, list) pé m; (of mountain, hill) sopé m ♦ adj (low) inferior, mais baixo; (last) último; **to get to the ~ of sth** (fig) tirar algo a limpo.
bottomless ['bɔtəmlɪs] adj sem fundo, (fig) insondável.
bough [bau] n ramo.
bought [bɔːt] pt, pp of **buy**.
boulder ['bəuldə*] n pedregulho, matacão m.
bounce [bauns] vi (ball) saltar, quicar; (cheque) ser devolvido (por insuficiência de fundos) ♦ vt fazer saltar ♦ n (rebound) salto; **he's got plenty of ~** (fig) ele tem pique.
bouncer ['baunsə*] (inf) n leão-de-chácara m.
bound [baund] pt, pp of **bind** ♦ n (leap) pulo, salto; (gen pl: limit) limite m ♦ vt (limit) limitar ♦ vi (leap) pular, saltar ♦ adj: **~ by** (limited by) limitado por; **to be ~ to do sth** (obliged) ter a obrigação de fazer algo; (likely) na certa ir fazer algo; **~ for** com destino a; **out of ~s** fora dos limites.
boundary ['baundrɪ] n limite m, fronteira.
boundless ['baundlɪs] adj ilimitado.
bountiful ['bauntɪful] adj (person) generoso;

(*supply*) farto.

bounty ['baunti] *n* (*generosity*) generosidade *f*; (*wealth*) fartura.

bouquet ['bukei] *n* (*of flowers*) buquê *m*, ramalhete *m*; (*of wine*) buquê *m*, aroma *m*.

bourbon ['buəbən] (*US*) *n* (*also*: ~ *whiskey*) uísque *m* (*BR*) *or* whisky (*PT*) (norteamericano).

bourgeois ['bueʒwɑ:] *adj* burguês/guesa.

bout [baut] *n* período; (*of malaria etc*) ataque *m*; (*BOXING etc*) combate *m*.

boutique [bu:'ti:k] *n* butique *f*.

bow¹ [bəu] *n* (*knot*) laço; (*weapon*, *MUS*) arco.

bow² [bau] *n* (*of the body*) reverência; (*of the head*) inclinação *f*; (*NAUT*: *also*: ~s) proa ♦ *vi* curvar-se, fazer uma reverência; (*yield*): **to ~ to** *or* **before** ceder ante, submeter-se a; **to ~ to the inevitable** curvar-se ao inevitável.

bowels ['bauəlz] *npl* intestinos *mpl*, tripas *fpl*; (*fig*) entranhas *fpl*.

bowl [bəul] *n* tigela; (*for washing*) bacia; (*ball*) bola; (*of pipe*) fornilho; (*US*: *stadium*) estádio ♦ *vi* (*CRICKET*) arremessar a bola; ~s *n* (*game*) jogo de bolas.

bowl over *vt* (*fig*) impressionar, comover.

bow-legged *adj* cambaio, de pernas tortas.

bowler ['bəulə*] *n* jogador(a) *m/f* de bolas; (*CRICKET*) lançador *m* (da bola); (*BRIT*: *also*: ~ *hat*) chapéu-coco *m*.

bowling ['bəuliŋ] *n* (*game*) boliche *m*.

bowling alley *n* boliche *m*.

bowling green *n* gramado (*BR*) *or* relvado (*PT*) para jogo de bolas.

bow tie ['bəu-] *n* gravata-borboleta.

box [bɔks] *n* caixa; (*crate*) caixote *m*; (*for jewels*) estojo; (*for money*) cofre *m*; (*THEATRE*) camarote *m* ♦ *vt* encaixotar; (*SPORT*) boxear contra ♦ *vi* (*SPORT*) boxear.

boxer ['bɔksə*] *n* (*person*) boxeador *m*, pugilista *m*; (*dog*) boxer *m*.

boxer shorts *npl* cueca samba-canção.

boxing ['bɔksiŋ] *n* (*SPORT*) boxe *m*, pugilismo.

Boxing Day (*BRIT*) *n* Dia de Santo Estêvão, *26 de dezembro*.

boxing gloves *npl* luvas *fpl* de boxe.

boxing ring *n* ringue *m* de boxe.

box number *n* (*for advertisements*) caixa postal.

box office *n* bilheteria (*BR*), bilheteira (*PT*).

boxroom ['bɔksrum] *n* quarto pequeno.

boy [bɔi] *n* (*young*) menino, garoto; (*older*) moço, rapaz *m*; (*servant*) criado.

boycott ['bɔikɔt] *n* boicote *m*, boicotagem *f* ♦ *vt* boicotar.

boyfriend ['bɔifrend] *n* namorado.

boyish ['bɔiiʃ] *adj* de menino, pueril.

Bp *abbr* = **bishop**.

BR *abbr* = **British Rail**.

bra [brɑ:] *n* sutiã (*PT*: soutien) *s*.

brace [breis] *n* reforço, braçadeira; (*on teeth*) aparelho; (*tool*) arco de pua; (*TYP*: *also*: ~ *bracket*) chave *f* ♦ *vt* firmar, reforçar; ~s *npl* (*BRIT*) suspensórios *mpl*; **to ~ o.s.** (*fig*) preparar-se.

bracelet ['breislit] *n* pulseira.

bracing ['breisiŋ] *adj* tonificante.

bracken ['brækən] *n* samambaia (*BR*), feto (*PT*).

bracket ['brækit] *n* (*TECH*) suporte *m*; (*group*) classe *f*, categoria; (*also*: **brace** ~) chave *f*; (*also*: **round** ~) parêntese *m*; (*gen*: **square** ~) colchete *m* ♦ *vt* pôr entre parênteses; (*fig*: *also*: ~ *together*) agrupar; **in** ~s entre parênteses (*or* colchetes).

brackish ['brækiʃ] *adj* (*water*) salobro.

brag [bræg] *vi* gabar-se, contar vantagem.

braid [breid] *n* (*trimming*) galão *m*; (*of hair*) trança.

Braille [breil] *n* braile *m*.

brain [brein] *n* cérebro; ~s *npl* inteligência, miolos *mpl*; **he's got** ~s ele é inteligente.

brainchild ['breintʃaild] *n* idéia original.

brainless ['breinlis] *adj* estúpido, desmiolado.

brainstorm ['breinstɔ:m] *n* (*fig*) momento de distração; (*US*: *brainwave*) idéia luminosa.

brainwash ['breinwɔʃ] *vt* fazer uma lavagem cerebral em.

brainwave ['breinweiv] *n* inspiração *f*, idéia luminosa *or* brilhante.

brainy ['breini] *adj* inteligente.

braise [breiz] *vt* estufar.

brake [breik] *n* (*on vehicle*) freio (*BR*), travão *m* (*PT*) ♦ *vt*, *vi* frear (*BR*), travar (*PT*).

brake drum *n* tambor *m* de freio (*BR*) *or* de travão (*PT*).

brake fluid *n* óleo de freio (*BR*) *or* dos travões (*PT*).

brake light *n* farol *m* do freio (*BR*), farolim *m* de travagem (*PT*).

brake pedal *n* pedal *m* do freio (*BR*), travão *m* de pé (*PT*).

bramble ['græmbl] *n* amora-preta.

bran [bræn] *n* farelo.

branch [brɑ:ntʃ] *n* ramo, galho; (*road*) ramal *m*; (*COMM*) sucursal *f*, filial *f*; (: *bank*) agência ♦ *vi* bifurcar-se.

branch out *vi* diversificar suas atividades; **to ~ out into** estender suas atividades a.

branch line *n* (*RAIL*) ramal *m*.

branch manager *n* gerente *m/f* de sucursal *or* filial.

brand [brænd] *n* marca ♦ *vt* (*cattle*) marcar com ferro quente; (*fig*: *pej*): **to ~ sb a communist** *etc* estigmatizar alguém de comunista *etc*.

brandish ['brændiʃ] *vt* brandir.

brand name *n* marca de fábrica, griffe *f*.

brand-new *adj* novo em folha, novinho.

brandy ['brændi] *n* conhaque *m*.

brash [bræʃ] *adj* (*rough*) grosseiro; (*cheeky*) descarado.

Brasilia [brə'ziliə] *n* Brasília.

NB: *European Portuguese adds the following consonants to certain words:* **b** (sú(b)dito, su(b)til); **c** (a(c)ção, a(c)cionista, a(c)to); **m** (inde(m)ne); **p** (ado(p)ção, ado(p)tar); *for further details see p. xiii.*

brass [brɑːs] n latão m; **the** ~ (MUS) os metais; **the top** ~ as altas patentes.
brass band n banda de música.
brassiere ['bræsɪə*] n sutiã m (BR), soutien m (PT).
brass tacks npl: **to get down to** ~ passar ao que interessa, entrar no assunto principal.
brat [bræt] (pej) n pirralho, fedelho, malcriado.
bravado [brə'vɑːdəu] n bravata.
brave [breɪv] adj valente, corajoso ♦ n guerreiro pele-vermelha ♦ vt (challenge) desafiar; (resist) encarar.
bravery ['breɪvərɪ] n coragem f, bravura.
bravo [brɑː'vəu] excl bravo!
brawl [brɔːl] n briga, pancadaria ♦ vi brigar.
brawn [brɔːn] n força; (meat) patê m de carne.
brawny ['brɔːnɪ] adj musculoso, carnudo.
bray [breɪ] n zurro, ornejo ♦ vi zurrar, ornejar.
brazen ['breɪzn] adj descarado ♦ vt: **to** ~ **it out** defender-se descaradamente.
brazier ['breɪzɪə*] n braseiro.
Brazil [brə'zɪl] n Brasil m.
Brazilian [brə'zɪljən] adj, n brasileiro/a.
Brazil nut n castanha-do-pará f.
breach [briːtʃ] vt abrir brecha em ♦ n (gap) brecha; (estrangement) rompimento; (breaking): ~ **of contract** inadimplência (BR), inadimplemento (PT); ~ **of the peace** perturbação f da ordem pública; ~ **of trust** abuso de confiança.
bread [brɛd] n pão m; (inf: money) grana; ~ **and butter** pão com manteiga; (fig) ganhapão m; **to earn one's daily** ~ ganhar o pão or a vida; **to know which side one's** ~ **is buttered (on)** saber o que lhe convém.
breadbin ['brɛdbɪn] (BRIT) n caixa de pão.
breadboard ['brɛdbɔːd] n tábua de pão; (COMPUT) breadboard m.
breadbox ['brɛdbɔks] (US) n caixa de pão.
breadcrumbs ['brɛdkrʌmz] npl migalhas fpl; (CULIN) farinha de rosca.
breadline ['brɛdlaɪn] n: **to be on the** ~ viver na miséria.
breadth [brɛtθ] n largura; (fig) amplitude f.
breadwinner ['brɛdwɪnə*] n arrimo de família.
break [breɪk] (pt broke, pp broken) vt quebrar (BR), partir (PT); (split) partir; (promise) quebrar; (word) faltar a; (fall) amortecer; (journey) interromper; (law) violar, transgredir; (record) bater; (news) revelar ♦ vi quebrar-se, partir-se; (storm) estalar ♦ n (gap) abertura; (crack) fenda; (fracture) fratura; (breakdown) ruptura, rompimento; (rest) descanso; (time) intervalo; (at school) recreio; (chance) oportunidade f; **to** ~ **one's leg** etc quebrar a perna etc; **to** ~ **with sb** romper com alguém; **to** ~ **even** sair sem ganhar nem perder; **to** ~ **free** or **loose** soltar-se; **to take a** ~ (few minutes) descansar um pouco, fazer uma pausa; (holiday) tirar férias para descansar; **without a** ~ sem parar.
break down vt (door etc) arrombar; (fig-

ures, data) analisar; (resistance) acabar com ♦ vi (go awry) desarranjar-se; (machine, AUT) enguiçar, pifar (inf); (MED) sofrer um colapso; (cry) desatar a chorar.
break in vt (horse etc) domar; (US: car) fazer a rodagem de ♦ vi (burglar) forçar uma entrada.
break into vt fus (house) arrombar.
break off vi (speaker) parar-se, deter-se; (branch) partir ♦ vt (talks) suspender; (relations) cortar; (engagement) terminar, acabar com.
break open vt (door etc) arrombar.
break out vi (war) estourar; (prisoner) libertar-se; **to** ~ **out in spots** aparecer coberto de manchas.
break through vi: **the sun broke through** o sol apareceu, o tempo abriu ♦ vt fus (defences, barrier) transpor; (crowd) abrir passagem por.
break up vi despedaçar-se; (partnership) acabar; (marriage) desmanchar-se; (friends) separar-se, brigar ♦ vt romper; (intervene) intervir em; (marriage) desmanchar.
breakable ['breɪkəbl] adj quebradiço, frágil ♦ n: ~**s** artigos mpl frágeis.
breakage ['breɪkɪdʒ] n quebradura; (COMM) quebra; **to pay for** ~**s** pagar indenização por quebras.
breakaway ['breɪkəweɪ] adj (group etc) dissidente.
breakdown ['breɪkdaun] n (AUT) enguiço, avaria; (in communications) interrupção f; (machine) enguiço; (MED: also: nervous ~) esgotamento nervoso; (of figures) discriminação f, desdobramento.
breakdown service (BRIT) n auto-socorro (BR), pronto socorro (PT).
breakdown van (BRIT) n reboque m (BR), pronto socorro (PT).
breaker ['breɪkə*] n onda grande.
breakeven ['breɪk'iːvn] cpd: ~ **chart** gráfico do ponto de equilíbrio; ~ **point** ponto de equilíbrio.
breakfast ['brɛkfəst] n café m da manhã (BR), pequeno almoço (PT).
breakfast cereal n cereais mpl.
break-in n roubo com arrombamento.
breaking point ['breɪkɪŋ-] n limite m.
breakthrough ['breɪkθruː] n ruptura; (fig) avanço.
break-up n (of partnership, marriage) dissolução f.
break-up value n (COMM) valor m de liquidação.
breakwater ['breɪkwɔːtə*] n quebra-mar m.
breast [brɛst] n (of woman) peito, seio; (chest) peito.
breast-feed (irreg) vt, vi amamentar.
breast pocket n bolso sobre o peito.
breaststroke ['brɛststrəuk] n nado de peito.
breath [brɛθ] n fôlego, hálito, respiração f; **to go out for a** ~ **of air** sair para tomar fôlego; **out of** ~ ofegante, sem fôlego.
Breathalyser ['brɛθəlaɪzə*] ® n bafômetro.

breathe [bri:ð] *vt, vi* respirar; **I won't ~ a word about it** não vou abrir a boca, eu sou um túmulo.
breathe in *vt, vi* inspirar.
breathe out *vt, vi* expirar.
breather ['bri:ðə*] *n* pausa.
breathing ['bri:ðɪŋ] *n* respiração *f*.
breathing space *n* (*fig*) descanso, repouso.
breathless ['brɛθlɪs] *adj* sem fôlego, ofegante.
breathtaking ['brɛθteɪkɪŋ] *adj* empolgante.
bred [brɛd] *pt, pp of* **breed**.
-bred [brɛd] *suffix*: **well/ill~** bem-/mal-educado.
breed [bri:d] (*pt, pp* **bred**) *vt* (*animals*) criar; (*hate, suspicion*) gerar ♦ *vi* reproduzir-se, procriar-se ♦ *n* raça.
breeder ['bri:də*] *n* (*person*) criador(a) *m/f*; (*PHYS: also:* ~ **reactor**) reator *m* regenerador.
breeding ['bri:dɪŋ] *n* reprodução *f*; (*raising*) criação *f*; (*of person: culture*) educação *f*, cultura.
breeze [bri:z] *n* brisa, aragem *f*.
breezeblock ['bri:zblɔk] (*BRIT*) *n* bloco pré-moldado.
breezy ['bri:zɪ] *adj* ventoso; (*person*) despreocupado, animado.
Breton ['brɛtən] *adj* bretão/tã ♦ *n* bretão/tã; (*LING*) bretão *m*.
brevity ['brɛvɪtɪ] *n* brevidade *f*.
brew [bru:] *vt* (*tea*) fazer; (*beer*) fermentar; (*plot*) armar, tramar ♦ *vi* (*tea*) fazer-se, preparar-se; (*beer*) fermentar; (*fig*) armar-se.
brewer ['bru:ə*] *n* cervejeiro/a.
brewery ['bruərɪ] *n* cervejaria.
briar ['braɪə*] *n* (*thorny bush*) urze-branca *f*; (*wild rose*) roseira-brava.
bribe [braɪb] *n* suborno ♦ *vt* subornar; **to ~ sb to do sth** subornar alguém para fazer algo.
bribery ['braɪbərɪ] *n* suborno.
bric-a-brac ['brɪkəbræk] *n* bricabraque *m*.
brick [brɪk] *n* tijolo.
bricklayer ['brɪkleɪə*] *n* pedreiro.
brickwork ['brɪkwə:k] *n* alvenaria.
brickworks ['brɪkwə:kz] *n* fábrica de tijolos.
bridal ['braɪdl] *adj* nupcial.
bride [braɪd] *n* noiva.
bridegroom ['braɪdgrum] *n* noivo.
bridesmaid ['braɪdzmeɪd] *n* dama de honra.
bridge [brɪdʒ] *n* ponte *f*; (*NAUT*) ponte de comando; (*CARDS*) bridge *m*; (*of nose*) cavalete *m*; (*DENTISTRY*) ponte *f* ♦ *vt* (*river*) lançar uma ponte sobre; (*gap*) transpor.
bridgehead ['brɪdʒhɛd] *n* cabeça-de-ponte *f*.
bridging loan ['brɪdʒɪŋ-] (*BRIT*) *n* empréstimo a curto prazo.
bridle ['braɪdl] *n* cabeçada, freio ♦ *vt* enfrear; (*fig*) refrear, conter.
bridle path *n* senda.
brief [bri:f] *adj* breve ♦ *n* (*LAW*) causa ♦ *vt* (*inform*) informar; (*instruct*) instruir; **~s**

npl (*for men*) cueca (*BR*), cuecas *fpl* (*PT*); (*for women*) calcinha (*BR*), cuecas *fpl* (*PT*); **in ~ ... em resumo ...; to ~ sb about sth** informar alguém sobre algo.
briefcase ['bri:fkeɪs] *n* pasta.
briefing ['bri:fɪŋ] *n* (*PRESS*) instruções *fpl*.
briefly ['bri:flɪ] *adv* brevemente; **to glimpse ~** vislumbrar.
briefness ['bri:fnɪs] *n* brevidade *f*.
Brig. *abbr* (= *brigadier*) brig.
brigade [brɪ'geɪd] *n* (*MIL*) brigada.
brigadier [brɪgə'dɪə*] *n* general *m* de brigada, brigadeiro.
bright [braɪt] *adj* claro, brilhante; (*weather*) resplandecente; (*person: clever*) inteligente; (: *lively*) alegre, animado; (*colour*) vivo; **to look on the ~ side** considerar o lado positivo.
brighten ['braɪtən] *vt* (*room: also:* ~ **up**) tornar mais alegre ♦ *vi* (*weather*) clarear; (*person: also:* ~ **up**) animar-se, alegrar-se.
brightly ['braɪtlɪ] *adv* brilhantemente.
brightness ['braɪtnɪs] *n* claridade *f*.
brilliance ['brɪljəns] *n* brilho, claridade *f*.
brilliant ['brɪljənt] *adj* brilhante; (*clever*) inteligente; (*inf: great*) sensacional.
brim [brɪm] *n* borda; (*of hat*) aba.
brimful ['brɪmful] *adj* cheio até as bordas; (*fig*) repleto.
brine [braɪn] *n* (*CULIN*) salmoura.
bring [brɪŋ] (*pt, pp* **brought**) *vt* trazer; **to ~ sth to an end** acabar com algo; **I can't ~ myself to fire him** não posso me resolver a despedi-lo.
bring about *vt* ocasionar, produzir.
bring back *vt* trazer de volta; (*return*) devolver.
bring down *vt* (*lower*) abaixar; (*shoot down*) abater; (*government*) derrubar.
bring forward *vt* adiantar; (*BOOKKEEPING*) transportar.
bring in *vt* (*person*) fazer entrar; (*object*) trazer; (*POL: legislation*) introduzir; (: *bill*) apresentar; (*LAW: verdict*) pronunciar; (*produce: income*) render; (*harvest*) recolher.
bring off *vt* (*task, plan*) levar a cabo; (*deal*) fechar.
bring out *vt* (*object*) tirar; (*meaning*) salientar; (*new product, book*) lançar.
bring round *vt* (*unconscious person*) fazer voltar a si; (*convince*) convencer.
bring to *vt* (*unconscious person*) fazer voltar a si.
bring up *vt* (*person*) educar, criar; (*carry up*) subir; (*question*) introduzir; (*food*) vomitar.
brink [brɪŋk] *n* beira; **on the ~ of doing** a ponto de fazer, à beira de fazer; **she was on the ~ of tears** ela estava à beira de desatar em prantos.
brisk [brɪsk] *adj* vigoroso; (*speedy*) rápido; (*trade, business*) ativo.

NB: European Portuguese adds the following consonants to certain words: **b** (sú(b)dito, su(b)til); **c** (a(c)ção, a(c)cionista, a(c)to); **m** (inde(m)ne); **p** (ado(p)ção, ado(p)tar); *for further details see p. xiii.*

brisket ['brɪskɪt] *n* carne *f* de vaca para assar.
bristle ['brɪsl] *n* cerda ♦ *vi* eriçar-se; **to ~ with** estar cheio de.
bristly ['brɪslɪ] *adj* (*beard, hair*) eriçado.
Brit [brɪt] (*inf*) *n abbr* (= *British person*) britânico/a.
Britain ['brɪtən] *n* (*also*: *Great* ~) Grã-Bretanha; **in** ~ na Grã-Bretanha.
British ['brɪtɪʃ] *adj* britânico; **the** ~ *npl* os britânicos; **the** ~ **Isles** as ilhas Británicas.
British Rail *n* companhia ferroviária británica.
Briton ['brɪtən] *n* britânico/a.
Brittany ['brɪtənɪ] *n* Bretanha.
brittle ['brɪtl] *adj* quebradiço, frágil.
Br(o). *abbr* (*REL*: = *brother*) Fr.
broach [brəutʃ] *vt* (*subject*) abordar, tocar em.
broad [brɔːd] *adj* amplo, largo; (*distinction, outline*) geral; (*accent*) carregado ♦ *n* (*US: inf*) sujeita; ~ **hint** indireta transparente; **in** ~ **daylight** em pleno dia.
broad bean *n* fava.
broadcast ['brɔːdkɑːst] (*pt, pp* **broadcast**) *n* transmissão *f* ♦ *vt* (*RADIO, TV*) transmitir ♦ *vi* transmitir.
broadcasting ['brɔːdkɑːstɪŋ] *n* radiodifusão *f*, transmissão *f*.
broadcasting station *n* emissora.
broaden ['brɔːdən] *vt* alargar ♦ *vi* alargar-se, ampliar-se.
broadly ['brɔːdlɪ] *adv* em geral.
broad-minded *adj* tolerante, liberal.
broccoli ['brɔkəlɪ] *n* brócolis *mpl* (*BR*), brócolos *mpl* (*PT*).
brochure ['brəuʃjuə*] *n* folheto, brochura.
brogue [brəug] *n* (*accent*) sotaque *m* regional; (*shoe*) chanca.
broil [brɔɪl] (*US*) *vt* grelhar.
broiler ['brɔɪlə*] *n* (*fowl*) ave *f* (*a ser grelhada*).
broke [brəuk] *pt of* **break** ♦ *adj* (*inf*) sem um vintém, duro; **to go** ~ (*business*) quebrar.
broken ['brəukən] *pp of* **break** ♦ *adj* (*leg, promise etc*) quebrado; (*marriage*) desfeito; **a** ~ **home** um lar desfeito; **children from** ~ **homes** filhos de pais separados; **in** ~ **English** num inglês mascavado.
broken-down *adj* (*car*) enguiçado; (*machine*) com defeito; (*house*) desmoronado, caindo aos pedaços.
broken-hearted *adj* com o coração partido.
broker ['brəukə*] *n* corretor(a) *m/f*.
brokerage ['brəukrɪdʒ] *n* corretagem *f*.
brolly ['brɔlɪ] (*BRIT: inf*) *n* guarda-chuva *m*.
bronchitis [brɔŋ'kaɪtɪs] *n* bronquite *f*.
bronze [brɔnz] *n* bronze *m*.
bronzed ['brɔnzd] *adj* bronzeado.
brooch [brəutʃ] *n* broche *m*.
brood [bruːd] *n* ninhada; (*children*) filhos *mpl*; (*pej*) prole *f* ♦ *vi* (*hen*) chocar; (*person*) cismar, parafusar, matutar.
broody ['bruːdɪ] *adj* (*fig*) taciturno, melancólico.
brook [bruk] *n* arroio, ribeiro.

broom [brum] *n* vassoura; (*BOT*) giesta.
broomstick ['brumstɪk] *n* cabo de vassoura.
Bros. *abbr* (*COMM*: = *brothers*) Irmãos.
broth [brɔθ] *n* caldo.
brothel ['brɔθl] *n* bordel *m*.
brother ['brʌðə*] *n* irmão *m*.
brotherhood ['brʌðəhud] *n* (*association, REL*) confraria.
brother-in-law (*pl* **brothers-in-law**) *n* cunhado.
brotherly ['brʌðəlɪ] *adj* fraternal, fraterno.
brought [brɔːt] *pt, pp of* **bring**.
brow [brau] *n* (*forehead*) fronte *f*, testa; (*rare*: *gen*: *eye*~) sobrancelha; (*of hill*) cimo, cume *m*.
browbeat ['braubiːt] (*irreg*: *like* **beat**) *vt* intimidar, amedrontar.
brown [braun] *adj* marrom (*BR*), castanho (*PT*); (*hair*) castanho; (*tanned*) bronzeado, moreno; (*rice, bread, flour*) integral ♦ *n* (*colour*) cor *f* marrom (*BR*) *or* castanha (*PT*) ♦ *vt* tostar; (*tan*) bronzear; (*CULIN*) dourar; **to go** ~ (*person*) bronzear-se, ficar moreno; (*leaves*) secar.
brownie ['braunɪ] *n* fadinha de bandeirante.
brown paper *n* papel *m* pardo.
brown sugar *n* açúcar *m* mascavo.
browse [brauz] *vi* (*in shop*) dar uma olhada; (*among books*) folhear livros; (*animal*) pastar; **to** ~ **through a book** folhear um livro.
bruise [bruːz] *n* hematoma *m*, contusão *f* ♦ *vt* machucar, contundir; (*fig*) magoar ♦ *vi* (*fruit*) amassar.
Brum [brʌm] (*inf*) *n abbr* = **Birmingham**.
Brummagem ['brʌmədʒəm] (*inf*) *n* = **Birmingham**.
Brummie ['brʌmɪ] (*inf*) *n* natural *m/f* de Birmingham.
brunch [brʌntʃ] *n* brunch *m*.
brunette [bruː'net] *n* morena.
brunt [brʌnt] *n*: **the** ~ **of** (*greater part*) a maior parte de.
brush [brʌʃ] *n* escova; (*for painting, shaving etc*) pincel *m*; (*BOT*) mato rasteiro; (*quarrel*) bate-boca *m* ♦ *vt* escovar; (*also*: ~ *past*, ~ *against*) tocar ao passar, roçar; **to have a** ~ **with sb** bater boca com alguém; **to have a** ~ **with the police** ser indiciado pela polícia.
brush aside *vt* afastar, não fazer caso de.
brush up *vt* (*knowledge*) retocar, revisar.
brushed [brʌʃt] *adj* (*TECH*: *steel, chrome etc*) escovado; (*nylon, denim etc*) felpudo.
brush-off (*inf*) *n*: **to give sb the** ~ dar o fora em alguém.
brushwood ['brʌʃwud] *n* (*bushes*) mato; (*sticks*) lenha, gravetos *mpl*.
brusque [bruːsk] *adj* brusco, áspero.
Brussels ['brʌslz] *n* Bruxelas.
Brussels sprout *n* couve-de-bruxelas *f*.
brutal ['bruːtl] *adj* brutal.
brutality [bruː'tælɪtɪ] *n* brutalidade *f*.
brute [bruːt] *n* bruto; (*person*) animal *m* ♦ *adj*: **by** ~ **force** por força bruta.
brutish ['bruːtɪʃ] *adj* grosseiro, bruto.

BS (*US*) *n abbr* = **Bachelor of Science**.
bs *abbr* = **bill of sale**.
BSA *n abbr* = **Boy Scouts of America**.
BSc *n abbr* = **Bachelor of Science**.
BSI *n abbr* (= *British Standards Institution*) instituto britânico de padrões.
BST *abbr* (= *British Summer Time*) hora de verão.
Bt. (*BRIT*) *abbr* = **baronet**.
btu *n abbr* (= *British thermal unit*) BTU *f* (= *1054.2 joules*).
bubble ['bʌbl] *n* bolha (*BR*), borbulha (*PT*) ♦ *vi* borbulhar.
bubble bath *n* banho de espuma.
bubble gum *n* chiclete *m* (de bola) (*BR*), pastilha elástica (*PT*).
Bucharest [buːkə'rest] *n* Bucareste.
buck [bʌk] *n* macho; (*US*: *inf*) dólar *m* ♦ *vi* corcovear; **to pass the** ~ fazer o jogo de empurra.
buck up *vi* (*cheer up*) animar-se, cobrar ânimo ♦ *vt*: **to** ~ **one's ideas up** tomar jeito.
bucket ['bʌkɪt] *n* balde *m* ♦ *vi* (*BRIT*: *inf*): **the rain is ~ing down** está chovendo a cântaros.
buckle ['bʌkl] *n* fivela ♦ *vt* afivelar ♦ *vi* torcer-se, cambar-se.
buckle down *vi* empenhar-se.
Bucks [bʌks] (*BRIT*) *abbr* = **Buckinghamshire**.
bud [bʌd] *n* broto, rebento; (*of flower*) botão *m* ♦ *vi* brotar, desabrochar; (*fig*) florescer.
Budapest [bjuːdə'pest] *n* Budapeste.
Buddha ['budə] *n* Buda *m*.
Buddhism ['budɪzəm] *n* budismo.
Buddhist ['budɪst] *adj* (*person*) budista; (*scripture, thought etc*) budístico ♦ *n* budista *m/f*.
budding ['bʌdɪŋ] *adj* (*flower*) em botão; (*passion etc*) nascente; (*poet etc*) em ascensão.
buddy ['bʌdɪ] (*US*) *n* camarada *m*, companheiro.
budge [bʌdʒ] *vt* mover ♦ *vi* mexer-se.
budgerigar ['bʌdʒərɪɡɑ:*] *n* periquito.
budget ['bʌdʒɪt] *n* orçamento ♦ *vi*: **to** ~ **for sth** incluir algo no orçamento; **I'm on a tight** ~ estou com o orçamento apertado.
budgie ['bʌdʒɪ] *n* = **budgerigar**.
Buenos Aires ['bwenə'saɪrɪz] *n* Buenos Aires.
buff [bʌf] *adj* (*colour*) cor *f* de camurça ♦ *n* (*enthusiast*) aficionado/a.
buffalo ['bʌfələu] (*pl* ~ *or* ~**es**) *n* búfalo.
buffer ['bʌfə*] *n* pára-choque *m*; (*COMPUT*) buffer *m*, memória intermediária.
buffering ['bʌfərɪŋ] *n* (*COMPUT*) buffering *m*, armazenamento intermediário.
buffer state *n* estado-tampão *m*.
buffet [*n* 'bufeɪ, *vt* 'bʌfɪt] *n* (*BRIT*: *bar*) bar *m*, cafeteria; (*food*) bufê *m* ♦ *vt* (*strike*) esbofetear; (*subj*: *wind etc*) fustigar.
buffet car (*BRIT*) *n* vagão-restaurante *m*.
buffet lunch *n* almoço americano.
buffoon [bə'fuːn] *n* bufão *m*.
bug [bʌg] *n* (*insect*) bicho; (*fig*: *germ*) micró-

bio; (*spy device*) microfone *m* oculto; (*tap*) escuta clandestina; (*COMPUT*: *of program*) erro; (: *of equipment*) defeito ♦ *vt* (*inf*: *annoy*) apoquentar, incomodar; (*room*) colocar microfones em; (*phone*) grampear; **I've got the travel** ~ peguei a mania de viajar.
bugbear ['bʌgbeə*] *n* pesadelo, fantasma *m*.
bugger ['bʌgə*] (*inf!*) *n* filho-da-puta *m* (*!*) ♦ *vt*: ~ (**it**)! merda! (*!*); ~ **all** (*nothing*) chongas (*!*).
bugger off (*inf!*) *vi*: ~ **off!** vai a merda! (*!*).
bugle ['bjuːgl] *n* trompa, corneta.
build [bɪld] (*pt, pp* **built**) *n* (*of person*) talhe *m*, estatura ♦ *vt* construir, edificar.
build on *vt fus* (*fig*) explorar, aproveitar.
build up *vt* (*MED*) fortalecer; (*stocks*) acumular; (*business*) desenvolver; (*reputation*) estabelecer.
builder ['bɪldə*] *n* (*contractor*) construtor(a) *m/f*, empreiteiro/a *m/f*; (*worker*) pedreiro.
building ['bɪldɪŋ] *n* (*act*) construção *f*; (*residential, offices*) edifício, prédio.
building contractor *n* empreiteiro/a de obras; (*company*) construtora.
building industry *n* construção *f*.
building site *n* terreno de construção.
building society (*BRIT*) *n* sociedade *f* de crédito imobiliário, financiadora.
building trade *n* construção *f*.
build-up *n* (*of gas etc*) acumulação *f*; (*publicity*): **to give sb/sth a good** ~ fazer muita propaganda de alguém/algo.
built [bɪlt] *pt, pp of* **build**.
built-in *adj* (*cupboard*) embutido; (*device*) incorporado, embutido.
built-up area *n* zona urbanizada.
bulb [bʌlb] *n* (*BOT*) bulbo; (*ELEC*) lâmpada.
bulbous ['bʌlbəs] *adj* bojudo.
Bulgaria [bʌl'geərɪə] *n* Bulgária.
Bulgarian [bʌl'geərɪən] *adj* búlgaro ♦ *n* búlgaro/a; (*LING*) búlgaro.
bulge [bʌldʒ] *n* bojo, saliência; (*in birth rate, sales*) disparo ♦ *vi* inchar-se; (*pocket etc*) fazer bojo; **to be bulging with** estar abarrotado de.
bulk [bʌlk] *n* (*mass*) massa, volume *m*; **in** ~ (*COMM*) a granel; **the** ~ **of** a maior parte de.
bulk buying [-'baɪɪŋ] *n* compra a granel.
bulkhead ['bʌlkhed] *n* anteparo.
bulky ['bʌlkɪ] *adj* volumoso; (*person*) corpulento.
bull [bul] *n* touro; (*STOCK EXCHANGE*) altista *m/f*; (*REL*) bula.
bulldog ['buldɔg] *n* buldogue *m*.
bulldoze ['buldəuz] *vt* arrasar (com buldôzer); **I was ~d into doing it** (*fig*: *inf*) fui forçado *or* obrigado a fazê-lo.
bulldozer ['buldəuzə*] *n* buldôzer *m*, escavadora.
bullet ['bulɪt] *n* bala.
bulletin ['bulɪtɪn] *n* boletim *m*.

NB: European Portuguese adds the following consonants to certain words: **b** (sú(b)dito, su(b)til); **c** (a(c)ção, a(c)cionista, a(c)to); **m** (inde(m)ne); **p** (ado(p)ção, ado(p)tar); *for further details see p. xiii.*

bulletin board n (US) quadro de anúncios; (COMPUT) informativo.
bulletproof ['bulıtpru:f] adj à prova de balas; ~ **vest** colete m à prova de balas.
bullet wound n ferida de bala.
bullfight ['bulfaɪt] n tourada.
bullfighter ['bulfaɪtə*] n toureiro.
bullfighting ['bulfaɪtıŋ] n (art) tauromaquia.
bullion ['buljən] n ouro (or prata) em barras.
bullock ['bulək] n boi m, novilho.
bullring ['bulrıŋ] n praça de touros.
bull's-eye n centro do alvo, mosca (do alvo) (BR).
bully ['bulı] n fanfarrão m, valentão m ♦ vt intimidar, tiranizar.
bullying ['bulıŋ] n provocação f, implicância.
bum [bʌm] n (inf: backside) traseiro, bunda; (tramp) vagabundo/a, vadio/a.
bum around (inf) vi vadiar.
bumblebee ['bʌmblbi:] n (ZOOL) mamangaba.
bumf [bʌmf] (inf) n (forms etc) papelada.
bump [bʌmp] n (blow) choque m, embate m, baque m; (jolt) sacudida; (on head) galo, inchaço; (sound) baque ♦ vt (strike) bater contra, dar encontrão em ♦ vi dar sacudidas.
bump along vi mover-se aos solavancos.
bump into vt fus chocar-se com or contra, colidir com; (inf: person) dar com, topar com.
bumper ['bʌmpə*] n (BRIT) pára-choque m ♦ adj: ~ **crop/harvest** supersafra.
bumper cars npl carros mpl de trombada.
bumph [bʌmf] n = **bumf**.
bumptious ['bʌmpʃəs] adj presunçoso.
bumpy ['bʌmpı] adj (road) acidentado, cheio de altos e baixos; (journey) cheio de solavancos; (flight) turbulento.
bun [bʌn] n pão m doce (BR), pãozinho (PT); (in hair) coque m.
bunch [bʌntʃ] n (of flowers) ramo; (of keys) molho; (of bananas, grapes) cacho; (of people) grupo.
bundle ['bʌndl] n trouxa; (tied up) embrulho; (of sticks) feixe m; (of papers) maço ♦ vt (also: ~ up) embrulhar, atar; (put): **to ~ sth/sb into** meter or enfiar algo/alguém correndo em.
bundle off vt (person) despachar sem cerimônia.
bundle out vt expulsar sem cerimônia.
bung [bʌŋ] n tampão m, batoque m ♦ vt (also: ~ up: pipe, hole) tapar; (BRIT: inf: throw) jogar; **my nose is ~ed up** estou com o nariz entupido.
bungalow ['bʌŋgələu] n bangalô m, chalé m.
bungle ['bʌŋgl] vt estropear, estragar.
bunion ['bʌnjən] n joanete m.
bunk [bʌŋk] n beliche m.
bunk beds npl beliche m, cama-beliche f.
bunker ['bʌŋkə*] n (coal store) carvoeira; (MIL) abrigo, casamata; (GOLF) bunker m.
bunny ['bʌnı] n (also: ~ rabbit) coelhinho.
bunny girl (BRIT) n coelhinha.
bunny hill (US) n (SKI) pista para principiantes.

bunting ['bʌntıŋ] n bandeiras fpl.
buoy [bɔı] n bóia.
buoy up vt fazer boiar; (fig) animar.
buoyancy ['bɔıənsı] n flutuabilidade f.
buoyant ['bɔıənt] adj flutuante; (person) alegre; (COMM: market) animado; (: currency, prices) firme.
burden ['bə:dn] n carga; (fig) fardo ♦ vt carregar; (oppress) sobrecarregar; **to be a ~** ser um fardo para alguém.
bureau [bjuə'rəu] (pl ~s) n (BRIT: desk) secretária, escrivaninha; (US: chest of drawers) cômoda; (office) escritório, agência.
bureaucracy [bjuə'rɔkrəsı] n burocracia.
bureaucrat ['bjuərəkræt] n burocrata m/f.
bureaucratic [bjuərə'krætık] adj burocrático.
bureaux [bjuə'rəuz] npl of **bureau**.
burgeon ['bə:dʒən] vi florescer.
burglar ['bə:glə*] n ladrão/ladrona m/f.
burglar alarm n alarma de roubo.
burglarize ['bə:gləraız] (US) vt assaltar, arrombar.
burglary ['bə:glərı] n roubo.
burgle ['bə:gl] vt assaltar, arrombar.
Burgundy ['bə:gəndı] n (wine) borgonha m.
burial ['berıəl] n enterro.
burial ground n cemitério.
burlesque [bə:'lesk] n paródia.
burly ['bə:lı] adj robusto, forte.
Burma ['bə:mə] n Birmânia.
Burmese [bə:'mi:z] adj birmanês/esa ♦ n inv birmanês/esa m/f; (LING) birmanês m.
burn [bə:n] (pt, pp ~ed or burnt) vt queimar ♦ vi queimar-se, arder; (sting) arder, picar ♦ n queimadura; **the cigarette ~t a hole in her dress** o cigarro fez um buraco no vestido dela; **I've ~t myself!** eu me queimei!
burn down vt incendiar.
burn out vt (subj: writer etc): **to ~ o.s. out** desgastar-se.
burner ['bə:nə*] n (gas) bico de gás, fogo.
burning ['bə:nıŋ] adj ardente.
burnish ['bə:nıʃ] vt polir, lustrar.
burnt [bə:nt] pt, pp of **burn**.
burnt sugar (BRIT) n caramelo.
burp [bə:p] (inf) n arroto ♦ vi arrotar.
burrow ['bʌrəu] n toca, lura ♦ vt fazer uma toca, cavar.
bursar ['bə:sə*] n tesoureiro/a; (BRIT: student) bolsista m/f (BR), bolseiro/a (PT).
bursary ['bə:sərı] (BRIT) n (grant) bolsa.
burst [bə:st] (pt, pp burst) vt (balloon, pipe) arrebentar; (banks etc) romper ♦ vi estourar; (bomb) estourar, explodir ♦ n estouro m; (of shots) rajada; **a ~ of energy** uma explosão de energia; **a ~ of applause** uma salva de palmas; **a ~ of speed** uma arrancada; **to ~ into flames** incendiar-se de repente; **to ~ out laughing** cair na gargalhada; **to ~ into tears** desatar a chorar; **to be ~ing with** (crammed with) estar abarrotado de; **to be ~ing with health/energy** estar esbanjando saúde/energia; **the door ~ open** a porta abriu-se de repente.
burst into vt fus (room etc) irromper em.

burst out of vt fus sair precipitadamente de.

bury ['bɛrɪ] vt enterrar; (body) enterrar, sepultar; to ~ one's head in one's hands cobrir o rosto com as mãos; to ~ one's head in the sand (fig) bancar avestruz; to ~ the hatchet (fig) fazer as pazes.

bus [bʌs] n ônibus m inv (BR), autocarro (PT).

bush [buʃ] n arbusto, mata; (scrub land) sertão m.

bushel ['buʃl] n alqueire m.

bushy ['buʃɪ] adj (thick) espesso, denso.

busily ['bɪzɪlɪ] adv atarefadamente.

business ['bɪznɪs] n (matter) negócio; (trading) comércio, negócios mpl; (firm) empresa; (occupation) profissão f; (affair) assunto; to travel on ~ viajar a negócios; he's in the insurance ~ ele trabalha com seguros; to do ~ with sb fazer negócios com alguém; it's my ~ to ... encarrego-me de ...; it's none of my ~ eu não tenho nada com isto; that's my ~ isso é cá comigo; he means ~ fala a sério.

business address n endereço profissional.

business card n cartão m de visita.

businesslike ['bɪznɪslaɪk] adj eficiente, metódico, sério.

businessman ['bɪznɪsmən] (irreg) n homem m de negócios.

business trip n viagem f de negócios.

businesswoman ['bɪznɪswumən] (irreg) n mulher f de negócios.

busker [bʌskə*] (BRIT) n artista m/f de rua.

bus lane n pista reservada aos ônibus (BR) or autocarros (PT).

bus shelter n abrigo.

bus station n rodoviária.

bus stop n ponto de ônibus (BR), paragem f de autocarro (PT).

bust [bʌst] n (ANAT) busto ♦ adj (inf: broken) quebrado ♦ vt (inf: POLICE: arrest) prender, grampear; to go ~ falir.

bustle ['bʌsl] n animação f, movimento ♦ vi apressar-se, andar azafamado.

bustling ['bʌslɪŋ] adj (town) animado, movimentado.

bust-up (BRIT: inf) n bate-boca m.

busy ['bɪzɪ] adj (person) ocupado, atarefado; (shop, street) animado, movimentado; (US: TEL) ocupado (BR), impedido (PT) ♦ vt: to ~ o.s. with ocupar-se em or de.

busybody ['bɪzɪbɒdɪ] n intrometido/a.

busy signal (US) n sinal m de ocupado (BR) or impedido (PT).

but [bʌt] conj mas ♦ prep exceto, menos; **nothing** ~ só, somente; ~ **for** sem, se não fosse; **no-one** ~ **him** só ele, ninguém a não ser ele; **the last** ~ **one** (BRIT) o/a penúltimo/a; **all** ~ **finished** quase acabado; **anything** ~ **finished** tudo menos acabado.

butane ['bjuːteɪn] n butano.

butcher ['butʃə*] n açougueiro (BR), homem m do talho (PT) ♦ vt chacinar; (cattle etc for meat) abater e carnear; ~'s (shop) açougue m (BR), talho (PT).

butler ['bʌtlə*] n mordomo.

butt [bʌt] n (cask) tonel m; (for rain) barril m; (thick end) cabo, extremidade f; (of gun) coronha; (of cigarette) toco (BR), ponta (PT); (BRIT: fig: target) alvo ♦ vt dar uma cabeçada em.

butt in vi (interrupt) interromper.

butter ['bʌtə*] n manteiga ♦ vt untar com manteiga.

butter bean n fava.

buttercup ['bʌtəkʌp] n botão-de-ouro m, ranúnculo.

butter dish n manteigueira.

butterfingers ['bʌtəfɪŋgəz] (inf) n mão-furada m/f.

butterfly ['bʌtəflaɪ] n borboleta; (SWIMMING: also: ~ stroke) nado borboleta.

buttocks ['bʌtəks] npl nádegas fpl.

button ['bʌtn] n botão m ♦ vt (also: ~ up) abotoar ♦ vi ter botões.

buttonhole ['bʌtnhəʊl] n casa de botão, botoeira; (flower) flor f na lapela ♦ vt obrigar a ouvir.

buttress ['bʌtrɪs] n contraforte m.

buxom ['bʌksəm] adj (baby) saudável; (woman) rechonchudo.

buy [baɪ] (pt, pp bought) vt comprar ♦ n compra; to ~ sb sth/sth from sb comprar algo para alguém/algo a alguém.

buy back vt comprar de volta; (COMM) recomprar.

buy in (BRIT) vt (goods) comprar, abastecer-se com.

buy into (BRIT) vt fus (COMM) comprar ações de.

buy off vt (partner) comprar a parte de; (business) comprar o fundo de comércio de.

buy up vt comprar em grande quantidade.

buyer ['baɪə*] n comprador(a) m/f; ~'s **market** mercado de comprador.

buzz [bʌz] n zumbido; (inf: phone call) ligada ♦ vi zumbir ♦ vt (call on intercom) chamar no interfone; (AVIAT: plane, building) voar baixo sobre.

buzz off (inf) vi cair fora.

buzzard ['bʌzəd] n abutre m, urubu m.

buzzer ['bʌzə*] n cigarra; (doorbell) campainha.

buzz word n modismo.

by [baɪ] prep por; (beside) perto de, ao pé de, ao lado de; (according to) segundo, de acordo com; (before): ~ **4 o'clock** antes das quatro ♦ adv see **pass, go** etc; **a picture** ~ **Picasso** um quadro de Picasso; **surrounded** ~ **enemies** cercado de inimigos; ~ **bus/car** de ônibus/carro; **paid** ~ **the hour** pago por hora; **to increase** etc ~ **the hour** aumentar etc de hora em hora; ~ **the kilo/metre** por quilo/metro; ~ **night/day** de noite/dia; **to**

NB: European Portuguese adds the following consonants to certain words: b (sú(b)dito, su(b)til); c (a(c)ção, a(c)cionista, a(c)to); m (inde(m)ne); p (ado(p)ção, ado(p)tar); for further details see p. xiii.

pay ~ cheque pagar com cheque; **a room 3 metres ~ 4** um cômodo medindo 3 metros por 4; **the bullet missed him ~ inches** por pouco a bala não acertou nele; **~ saving hard, he …** economizando muito, ele …; **(all) ~ oneself** (completamente) só, sozinho; **~ the way** a propósito; **~ and large** em geral; **~ and ~ logo**, mais tarde; **~ this time tomorrow** esta mesma hora amanhã.

bye(-bye) ['baı('baı)] *excl* até logo *(BR)*, tchau *(BR)*, adeus *(PT)*.

by(e)-law *n* lei *f* de município.

by-election *(BRIT)* *n* eleição *f* parlamentar complementar.

bygone ['baıgɔn] *adj* passado, antigo ♦ *n*: **let ~s be ~s** que passou passou, águas passadas não movem moinhos.

bypass ['baıpɑːs] *n* via secundária, desvio; *(MED)* ponte *f* de safena ♦ *vt* evitar.

by-product *n* subproduto, produto derivado.

byre ['baıə*] *(BRIT)* *n* estábulo (de vacas).

bystander ['baıstændə*] *n* circunstante *m/f*; *(observer)* espectador(a); **a crowd of ~s** um grupo de curiosos.

byte [baıt] *n (COMPUT)* byte *m*.

byway ['baıweı] *n* caminho secundário.

byword ['baıwɔːd] *n*: **to be a ~ for** ser sinônimo de.

by-your-leave *n*: **without so much as a ~** sem mais aquela.

C

C, c [siː] *n (letter)* C, c *m*; *(SCH: mark)* ≈ 5, 6; *(MUS)*: **C** dó *m*; **C for Charlie** C de Carlos.

C *abbr* (= *Celsius*; *centigrade*) C.

c *abbr* (= *century*) séc.; (= *circa*) ca.; *(US etc:* = *cent*) cent.

CA *n abbr* = **Central America**; *(BRIT)* = **chartered accountant** ♦ *abbr (US: POST)* = **California**.

ca. *abbr* (= *circa*) ca.

c/a *abbr* = **capital account**; **credit account**; (= *current account*) c/c.

CAA *n abbr* (= *Civil Aviation Authority (BRIT)*; *Civil Aeronautics Authority (US)*) ≈ DAC *m*.

CAB *(BRIT)* *n abbr* (= *Citizens' Advice Bureau*) serviço de informação do consumidor.

cab [kæb] *n* táxi *m*; *(of truck)* boléia; *(horse-drawn)* cabriolé *m*.

cabaret ['kæbəreı] *n* cabaré *m*.

cabbage ['kæbıdʒ] *n* repolho *(BR)*, couve *f (PT)*.

cabin ['kæbın] *n* cabana; *(on ship)* camarote *m*.

cabin cruiser *n* lancha a motor com cabine.

cabinet ['kæbınıt] *n (POL)* gabinete *m*; *(furni-*

ture) armário; *(also: display ~)* armário com vitrina; **~ reshuffle** reforma ministerial.

cabinet-maker *n* marceneiro/a.

cabinet minister *n* ministro/a *(integrante do gabinete)*.

cable ['keıbl] *n* cabo; *(telegram)* cabograma *m* ♦ *vt* enviar cabograma para.

cable-car *n* bonde *m (BR)*, teleférico *(PT)*.

cablegram ['keıblgræm] *n* cabograma *m*.

cable railway *(BRIT)* *n* funicular *m*.

cable television *n* televisão *f* a cabo.

cache [kæʃ] *n* esconderijo; **a ~ of arms** *etc* um depósito secreto de armas *etc*.

cackle ['kækl] *vi* cacarejar.

cacti ['kæktaı] *npl of* **cactus**.

cactus ['kæktəs] *(pl* **cacti***)* *n* cacto.

CAD *n abbr* (= *computer-aided design*) CAD *m*.

caddie ['kædı] *n* caddie *m*.

cadet [kə'det] *n (MIL)* cadete *m*.

cadge [kædʒ] *(inf)* *vt* filar.

cadger ['kædʒə*] *n* filante *m/f*.

cadre ['kɑːdə*] *n* funcionários *mpl* qualificados.

Caesarean [siː'zɛərıən] *(US* **Cesarean***)* *adj*, *n*: **~ (section)** cesariana.

CAF *(BRIT)* *abbr* (= *cost and freight*) custo e frete.

café ['kæfeı] *n* café *m*.

cafeteria [kæfı'tıərıə] *n* lanchonete *f*.

caffein(e) ['kæfiːn] *n* cafeína.

cage [keıdʒ] *n (bird ~)* gaiola; *(for large animals)* jaula ♦ *vt* engaiolar; enjaular.

cagey ['keıdʒı] *(inf)* *adj* cuidadoso, reservado, desconfiado.

cagoule [kə'guːl] *n* casaco de náilon.

CAI *n abbr* (= *computer-aided instruction*) CAI *m*.

Cairo ['kaıərəu] *n* o Cairo.

cajole [kə'dʒəul] *vt* lisonjear.

cake [keık] *n (large)* bolo; *(small)* doce *m*, bolinho; **~ of soap** sabonete *m*; **it's a piece of ~** *(inf)* é moleza *or* sopa; **he wants to have his ~ and eat it (too)** *(fig)* ele quer chupar cana e assoviar ao mesmo tempo; **~ mix** massa pronta de bolo.

caked [keıkt] *adj*: **~ with** empastado de.

cake shop *n* confeitaria.

calamitous [kə'læmıtəs] *adj* calamitoso.

calamity [kə'læmıtı] *n* calamidade *f*.

calcium ['kælsıəm] *n* cálcio.

calculate ['kælkjuleıt] *vt* calcular; *(estimate: chances, effect)* avaliar.

calculate on *vt fus*: **to ~ on sth/on doing sth** contar com algo/em fazer algo.

calculated ['kælkjuleıtıd] *adj (insult, action)* intencional; **a ~ risk** um risco calculado.

calculating ['kælkjuleıtıŋ] *adj (clever)* matreiro, calculista; *(devious)* esperto.

calculation [kælkju'leıʃən] *n* cálculo.

calculator ['kælkjuleıtə*] *n* calculador *m*.

calculus ['kælkjuləs] *n* cálculo; **integral/differential** ~ cálculo integral/diferencial.

calendar ['kæləndə*] *n* calendário.

calendar month *n* mês *m* civil.

calendar year *n* ano civil.

calf [kɑːf] (*pl* **calves**) *n* (*of cow*) bezerro, vitela; (*of other animals*) cria; (*also*: ~*skin*) pele *f or* couro de bezerro; (*ANAT*) barriga-da-perna.

caliber ['kælɪbə*] (*US*) *n* = **calibre**.

calibrate ['kælɪbreɪt] *vt* calibrar.

calibre ['kælɪbə*] (*US* **caliber**) *n* calibre *m*.

calico ['kælɪkəu] *n* (*BRIT*) morim *m*; (*US*) chita.

California [kælɪ'fɔːnɪə] *n* Califórnia.

calipers ['kælɪpəz] (*US*) *npl* = **callipers**.

call [kɔːl] *vt* chamar; (*telephone*) telefonar a, ligar para; (*announce*: *flight*) anunciar; (*meeting*, *strike*) convocar ♦ *vi* chamar; (*visit*: *also*: ~ *in*, ~ *round*) dar um pulo ♦ *n* (*shout*, *announcement*) chamada; (*also*: *telephone* ~) telefonema *m*; (*of bird*) canto; (*visit*) visita; (*fig*: *appeal*) chamamento, apelo; **to** ~ **(for)** passar (para buscar); **to be on** ~ estar de prontidão; **she's** ~**ed Suzana** ela se chama Suzana; **who is** ~**ing?** (*TEL*) quem fala?; **London** ~**ing** (*RADIO*) aqui fala Londres; **please give me a** ~ **at 7** acorde-me às 7.00 por favor; **to make a** ~ telefonar; **to pay a** ~ **on sb** visitar alguém, dar um pulo na casa de alguém; **there's not much** ~ **for these items** não há muita procura para esses artigos.

call at *vt fus* (*subj*: *ship*) fazer escala em; (: *train*) parar em.

call back *vi* (*return*) voltar, passar de novo; (*TEL*) ligar de volta ♦ *vt* (*TEL*) ligar de volta para.

call for *vt fus* (*demand*) requerer, exigir; (*fetch*) ir buscar.

call in *vt* (*doctor*, *expert*, *police*) chamar.

call off *vt* (*cancel*) cancelar.

call on *vt fus* (*visit*) visitar; (*turn to*) recorrer a; **to** ~ **on sb to do** pedir para alguém fazer.

call out *vi* gritar, bradar ♦ *vt* (*doctor*, *police*, *troops*) chamar.

call up *vt* (*MIL*) chamar às fileiras.

callbox ['kɔːlbɔks] (*BRIT*) *n* cabine *f* telefônica.

caller ['kɔːlə*] *n* visita *m/f*; (*TEL*) chamador(a) *m/f*.

call girl *n* call girl *f*, prostituta.

call-in (*US*) *n* (*RADIO*) programa com participação dos ouvintes; (*TV*) programa com participação dos espectadores.

calling ['kɔːlɪŋ] *n* vocação *f*; (*trade*) profissão *f*.

calling card (*US*) *n* cartão *m* de visita.

callipers ['kælɪpəz] (*US* **calipers**) *npl* (*MATH*) compasso de calibre; (*MED*) aparelho ortopédico.

callous ['kæləs] *adj* cruel, insensível.

callousness ['kæləsnɪs] *n* crueldade *f*, insensibilidade *f*.

callow ['kæləu] *adj* inexperiente.

calm [kɑːm] *n* calma ♦ *vt* acalmar ♦ *adj* tranqüilo; (*sea*) calmo, sereno.

calm down *vi* acalmar-se, tranqüilizar-se ♦ *vt* acalmar, tranqüilizar.

calmly ['kɑːmlɪ] *adv* tranqüilamente, com calma.

calmness ['kɑːmnɪs] *n* tranqüilidade *f*.

Calor gas ['kælə*-] ® (*BRIT*) *n* butano.

calorie ['kælərɪ] *n* caloria.

calve [kɑːv] *vi* parir.

calves [kɑːvz] *npl of* **calf**.

CAM *n abbr* (= *computer-aided manufacture*) CAM *m*.

camber ['kæmbə*] *n* (*of road*) abaulamento.

Cambodia [kæm'bəudjə] *n* Camboja.

Cambodian [kæm'bəudɪən] *adj*, *n* cambojano/a.

Cambs (*BRIT*) *abbr* = **Cambridgeshire**.

came [keɪm] *pt of* **come**.

camel ['kæməl] *n* camelo.

cameo ['kæmɪəu] *n* camafeu *m*.

camera ['kæmərə] *n* máquina fotográfica; (*CINEMA*, *TV*) câmera; **in** ~ em câmara.

cameraman ['kæmərəmən] (*irreg*) *n* camaraman *m*.

Cameroon [kæmə'ruːn] *n* Camarões *m*.

Cameroun [kæmə'ruːn] *n* = **Cameroon**.

camouflage ['kæməflɑːʒ] *n* camuflagem *f* ♦ *vt* camuflar.

camp [kæmp] *n* campo, acampamento ♦ *vi* acampar ♦ *adj* afetado, afeminado; **to go** ~**ing** fazer camping (*BR*), fazer campismo (*PT*).

campaign [kæm'peɪn] *n* (*MIL*, *POL etc*) campanha ♦ *vi* fazer campanha.

campaigner [kæm'peɪnə*] *n*: ~ **for** partidário/a de; ~ **against** oponente *m/f* de.

campbed ['kæmpbed] *n* cama de campanha.

camper ['kæmpə*] *n* campista *m/f*; (*vehicle*) reboque *m*.

camping ['kæmpɪŋ] *n* camping *m* (*BR*), campismo (*PT*).

camping site *n* camping *m* (*BR*), parque *m* de campismo (*PT*).

campsite ['kæmpsaɪt] *n* camping *m* (*BR*), parque *m* de campismo (*PT*).

campus ['kæmpəs] *n* campus *m*, cidade *f* universitária.

camshaft ['kæmʃɑːft] *n* eixo de ressaltos.

can¹ [kæn] *n* (*of oil*, *food*) lata ♦ *vt* enlatar; (*preserve*) conservar em latas; **to carry the** ~ (*BRIT*: *inf*) assumir a responsabilidade.

can² [kæn] (*conditional* **could**) *aux vb* (*gen*) poder; (*know how to*) saber; **I** ~ **swim** eu sei nadar; **I** ~ **speak Portuguese** eu falo português; ~ **you hear me?** você está me ouvindo?; **could I have a word with you?** será que eu podia falar com você?; **he could be in the library** ele talvez esteja na biblioteca; **they could have forgotten** eles podiam ter esquecido.

Canada ['kænədə] *n* Canadá *m*.

Canadian [kə'neɪdɪən] *adj*, *n* canadense *m/f*.

canal [kə'næl] *n* canal *m*.

NB: European Portuguese adds the following consonants to certain words: **b** (sú(b)dito, su(b)til); **c** (a(c)ção, a(c)cionista, a(c)to); **m** (inde(m)ne); **p** (ado(p)ção, ado(p)tar); *for further details see p. xiii.*

Canaries [kə'nεərız] *npl* = **Canary Islands.**

canary [kə'nεərı] *n* canário.

Canary Islands *npl*: **the** ~ as (ilhas) Canárias.

Canberra ['kænbərə] *n* Canberra.

cancel ['kænsəl] *vt* (*gen, train, cheque*) cancelar; (*appointment*) desmarcar; (*cross out*) riscar, invalidar; (*stamp*) contra-selar.

cancel out *vt* anular; **they** ~ **each other out** eles se anulam.

cancellation [kænsə'leıʃən] *n* cancelamento; (*of contract*) anulação *f*.

cancer ['kænsə*] *n* câncer *m* (*BR*), cancro (*PT*); **C**~ (*ASTROLOGY*) Câncer.

cancerous ['kænsrəs] *adj* canceroso.

cancer patient *n* canceroso/a.

cancer research *n* pesquisa sobre o câncer (*BR*) or cancro (*PT*).

C and F (*BRIT*) *abbr* (= *cost and freight*) custo e frete.

candid ['kændıd] *adj* franco, sincero.

candidacy ['kændıdəsı] *n* candidatura.

candidate ['kændıdeıt] *n* candidato/a.

candidature ['kændıdətʃə*] (*BRIT*) *n* = **candidacy.**

candied ['kændıd] *adj* cristalizado; ~ **apple** (*US*) maçã *f* do amor.

candle ['kændl] *n* vela; (*in church*) círio.

candle holder *n* (*single*) castiçal *m*; (*bigger, more ornate*) candelabro, lustre *m*.

candlelight ['kændllaıt] *n*: **by** ~ à luz de vela; (*dinner*) à luz de velas.

candlestick ['kændlstık] *n* (*single*) castiçal *m*; (*bigger, ornate*) candelabro, lustre *m*.

candour ['kændə*] (*US* **candor**) *n* franqueza.

candy ['kændı] *n* açúcar *m* cristalizado; (*US*) bala (*BR*), rebuçado (*PT*).

candy floss [-flɔs] (*BRIT*) *n* algodão-doce *m*.

candy store (*US*) *n* confeitaria.

cane [keın] *n* (*BOT*) cana; (*stick*) bengala; (*for chairs etc*) palhinha ♦ *vt* (*BRIT: SCH*) castigar (com bengala).

canine ['kænaın] *adj* canino.

canister ['kænıstə*] *n* lata.

cannabis ['kænəbıs] *n* (*also:* ~ *plant*) cânhamo; (*drug*) maconha.

canned [kænd] *adj* (*food*) em lata, enlatado; (*inf: music*) gravado; (*BRIT: inf: drunk*) bêbado; (*US: inf: worker*) despedido.

cannibal ['kænıbəl] *n* canibal *m/f*.

cannibalism ['kænıbəlızəm] *n* canibalismo.

cannon ['kænən] (*pl inv or* ~**s**) *n* canhão *m*.

cannonball ['kænənbɔːl] *n* bala (de canhão).

cannon fodder *n* bucha para canhão.

cannot ['kænɔt] = **can not.**

canny ['kænı] *adj* astuto.

canoe [kə'nuː] *n* canoa.

canoeing [kə'nuːıŋ] *n* (*SPORT*) canoagem *f*.

canoeist [kə'nuːıst] *n* canoísta *m/f*.

canon ['kænən] *n* (*clergyman*) cônego; (*standard*) cânone *m*.

canonize ['kænənaız] *vt* canonizar.

can opener *n* abridor *m* de latas (*BR*), abrelatas *m inv* (*PT*).

canopy ['kænəpı] *n* dossel *m*; (*ARCH*) baldaquino.

cant [kænt] *n* jargão *m*.

can't [kaːnt] = **can not.**

Cantab. (*BRIT*) *abbr* (= *cantabrigiensis*) = **of Cambridge.**

cantankerous [kæn'tæŋkərəs] *adj* rabugento, irritável.

canteen [kæn'tiːn] *n* cantina; (*bottle*) cantil *m*; (*of cutlery*) jogo (de talheres).

canter ['kæntə*] *n* meio galope ♦ *vi* ir a meio galope.

cantilever ['kæntıliːvə*] *n* cantiléver *m*.

canvas ['kænvəs] *n* (*material*) lona; (*for painting*) tela; (*NAUT*) velas *fpl*; **under** ~ (*camping*) em barracas.

canvass ['kænvəs] *vt* (*POL: district*) fazer campanha em; (: *person*) angariar; (: *opinion*) sondar.

canvasser ['kænvəsə*] *n* cabo eleitoral.

canvassing ['kænvəsıŋ] *n* (*POL*) angariação *f* de votos; (*COMM*) pesquisa de mercado.

canyon ['kænjən] *n* canhão *m*, garganta, desfiladeiro.

CAP *n abbr* (= *Common Agricultural Policy*) PAC *f*.

cap [kæp] *n* gorro; (*peaked*) boné *m*; (*of pen, bottle*) tampa; (*BRIT: contraceptive: also: Dutch* ~) diafragma *m*; (: *FOOTBALL*): **he won his England** ~ ele foi escalado para jogar na seleção inglesa ♦ *vt* rematar; (*outdo*) superar; **and to** ~ **it all, he** ... (*BRIT*) e para completar or culminar, ele ....

capability [keıpə'bılıtı] *n* capacidade *f*.

capable ['keıpəbl] *adj* (*of sth*) capaz; (*competent*) competente, hábil; ~ **of** (*interpretation etc*) susceptível de, passível de.

capacious [kə'peıʃəs] *adj* vasto.

capacity [kə'pæsıtı] *n* capacidade *f*; (*role*) condição *f*; **filled to** ~ lotado; **in his** ~ **as** em sua condição de; **this work is beyond my** ~ este trabalho está além das minhas limitações; **in an advisory** ~ na condição de consultor; **to work at full** ~ trabalhar com máximo rendimento.

cape [keıp] *n* capa; (*GEO*) cabo.

Cape of Good Hope *n* Cabo da Boa Esperança.

caper ['keıpə*] *n* (*CULIN: gen:* ~**s**) alcaparra; (*prank*) travessura.

Cape Town *n* Cidade *f* do Cabo.

capita ['kæpıtə] *see* **per capita.**

capital ['kæpıtl] *n* (*also:* ~ *city*) capital *f*; (*money*) capital *m*; (*also:* ~ *letter*) maiúscula.

capital account *n* conta de capital.

capital allowance *n* desconto para depreciação.

capital assets *npl* bens *mpl* imobilizados, ativo fixo.

capital expenditure *n* despesas *fpl* or dispêndio de capital.

capital gains tax *n* imposto sobre ganhos de capital.

capital goods *npl* bens *mpl* de capital.

capital-intensive *adj* intensivo de capital.

capitalism ['kæpɪtəlɪzəm] *n* capitalismo.
capitalist ['kæpɪtəlɪst] *adj*, *n* capitalista *m/f*.
capitalize ['kæpɪtəlaɪz] *vt* capitalizar.
  capitalize on *vt fus* (*fig*) aproveitar, explorar.
capital punishment *n* pena de morte.
capital transfer tax (*BRIT*) *n* imposto sobre transferências de capital.
capitulate [kə'pɪtjuleɪt] *vi* capitular.
capitulation [kəpɪtju'leɪʃən] *n* capitulação *f*.
capricious [kə'prɪʃəs] *adj* caprichoso.
Capricorn ['kæprɪkɔːn] *n* Capricórnio.
caps [kæps] *abbr* = **capital letters**.
capsize [kæp'saɪz] *vt*, *vi* emborcar, virar.
capstan ['kæpstən] *n* cabrestante *m*.
capsule ['kæpsjuːl] *n* cápsula.
Capt. *abbr* (= *captain*) Cap.
captain ['kæptɪn] *n* capitão *m* ♦ *vt* capitanear, ser o capitão de.
caption ['kæpʃən] *n* (*heading*) título; (*to picture*) legenda.
captivate ['kæptɪveɪt] *vt* cativar.
captive ['kæptɪv] *adj*, *n* cativo/a.
captivity [kæp'tɪvɪtɪ] *n* cativeiro.
captor ['kæptə*] *n* capturador(a) *m/f*.
capture ['kæptʃə*] *vt* prender, aprisionar; (*place*) tomar; (*attention*) captar, chamar ♦ *n* captura; (*of place*) tomada; (*thing taken*) presa.
car [kɑː*] *n* carro, automóvel *m*; (*US: RAIL*) vagão *m*; **by** ~ de carro.
Caracas [kə'rækəs] *n* Caracas.
carafe [kə'ræf] *n* garrafa de mesa.
caramel ['kærəməl] *n* caramelo.
carat ['kærət] *n* quilate *m*; **18** ~ **gold** ouro de 18 quilates.
caravan ['kærəvæn] *n* reboque *m* (*BR*), trailer *m* (*BR*), rulote *f* (*PT*); (*of camels*) caravana.
caravan site (*BRIT*) *n* camping *m* para reboques (*BR*), parque *m* de campismo (*PT*).
caraway ['kærəweɪ] *n*: ~ **seed** sementes *fpl* de alcaravia.
carbohydrate [kɑːbəu'haɪdreɪt] *n* hidrato de carbono; (*food*) carboidrato.
carbolic acid [kɑː'bɔlɪk-] *n* ácido carbólico, fenol *m*.
carbon ['kɑːbən] *n* carbono.
carbonated ['kɑːbəneɪtɪd] *adj* (*drink*) gasoso.
carbon copy *n* cópia de papel carbono.
carbon dioxide *n* dióxido de carbono.
carbon monoxide *n* monóxido de carbono.
carbon paper *n* papel *m* carbono.
carbon ribbon *n* fita carbono.
carburettor [kɑːbju'rɛtə*] (*US* **carburetor**) *n* carburador *m*.
carcass ['kɑːkəs] *n* carcaça.
carcinogenic [kɑːsɪnə'dʒɛnɪk] *adj* carcinogênico.
card [kɑːd] *n* (*also: playing* ~) carta; (*visiting* ~, *post*~ *etc*) cartão *m*; (*membership* ~ *etc*) carteira; (*thin cardboard*) cartolina; **to play** ~**s** jogar cartas.

cardamom ['kɑːdəməm] *n* cardamomo.
cardboard ['kɑːdbɔːd] *n* cartão *m*, papelão *m*.
cardboard box *n* caixa de papelão.
card-carrying member [-'kærɪŋ-] *n* membro ativo.
card game *n* jogo de cartas.
cardiac ['kɑːdɪæk] *adj* cardíaco.
cardigan ['kɑːdɪgən] *n* casaco de lã, cardigã *m*.
cardinal ['kɑːdɪnl] *adj* cardeal; (*MATH*) cardinal ♦ *n* (*REL*) cardeal *m*; (*MATH*) número cardinal.
card index *n* fichário.
Cards (*BRIT*) *abbr* = **Cardiganshire**.
cardsharp ['kɑːdʃɑːp] *n* batoteiro/a, trapaceiro/a.
card vote (*BRIT*) *n* votação *f* de delegados.
CARE [kɛə*] *n abbr* (= *Cooperative for American Relief Everywhere*) associação beneficente.
care [kɛə*] *n* cuidado; (*worry*) preocupação *f*; (*charge*) encargo, custódia ♦ *vi*: **to** ~ **about** preocupar-se com, ter interesse em; **would you** ~ **to/for ...?** você quer ...?; **I wouldn't** ~ **to do it** eu não gostaria de fazê-lo; **in sb's** ~ a cargo de alguém; ~ **of** (*on letter*) aos cuidados de; **"with** ~**"** "frágil"; **to take** ~ **to** cuidar-se *or* ter o cuidado de; **to take** ~ **of** cuidar de; **the child has been taken into** ~ a criança foi entregue aos cuidados da Assistência Social; **I don't** ~ não me importa; **I couldn't** ~ **less** não dou a mínima.
  care for *vt fus* cuidar de; (*like*) gostar de.
careen [kə'riːn] *vi* (*ship*) dar de quilha, querenar ♦ *vt* querenar.
career [kə'rɪə*] *n* carreira ♦ *vi* (*also:* ~ *along*) correr a toda velocidade.
career girl *n* moça disposta a fazer carreira.
careers officer *n* orientador(a) *m/f* vocacional.
carefree ['kɛəfriː] *adj* despreocupado.
careful ['kɛəful] *adj* cuidadoso; (*cautious*) cauteloso; **(be)** ~**!** tenha cuidado!
carefully ['kɛəfulɪ] *adv* com cuidado, cuidadosamente; (*cautiously*) cautelosamente.
careless ['kɛəlɪs] *adj* descuidado; (*heedless*) desatento.
carelessly ['kɛəlɪslɪ] *adv* sem cuidado; (*without worry*) sem preocupação.
carelessness ['kɛəlɪsnɪs] *n* descuido, falta de atenção.
caress [kə'rɛs] *n* carícia ♦ *vt* acariciar.
caretaker ['kɛəteɪkə*] *n* zelador(a) *m/f*.
caretaker government (*BRIT*) *n* governo interino.
car-ferry *n* barca para carros (*BR*), barco de passagem (*PT*).
cargo ['kɑːgəu] (*pl* ~**es**) *n* carregamento, carga; (*freight*) frete *m*.
cargo boat *n* cargueiro.
cargo plane *n* avião *m* de carga.

NB: *European Portuguese adds the following consonants to certain words:* **b** (sú(b)dito, su(b)til); **c** (a(c)ção, a(c)cionista, a(c)to); **m** (inde(m)ne); **p** (ado(p)ção, ado(p)tar); *for further details see p. xiii.*

car hire (BRIT) n aluguel m (BR) or aluguer m (PT) de carros.

Caribbean [kærɪ'biːən] adj caraíba; **the ~ (Sea)** o Caribe.

caricature ['kærɪkətjuə*] n caricatura.

caring ['kɛərɪŋ] adj (person) bondoso; (society) humanitário.

carnage ['kɑːnɪdʒ] n carnificina, matança.

carnal ['kɑːnl] adj carnal.

carnation [kɑː'neɪʃən] n cravo.

carnival ['kɑːnɪvəl] n carnaval m; (US: funfair) parque m de diversões.

carnivore ['kɑːnɪvɔː*] n carnívoro.

carnivorous [kɑː'nɪvərəs] adj carnívoro.

carol ['kærəl] n: **(Christmas)** ~ cântico de Natal.

carouse [kə'rauz] vi farrear.

carousel [kærə'sɛl] (US) n carrossel m.

carp [kɑːp] n inv (fish) carpa.

  carp at vt fus criticar.

car park n estacionamento.

carpenter ['kɑːpɪntə*] n carpinteiro.

carpentry ['kɑːpɪntrɪ] n carpintaria.

carpet ['kɑːpɪt] n tapete m ♦ vt atapetar; (with fitted ~) acarpetar; **fitted** ~ (BRIT) carpete m.

carpet slippers npl chinelos mpl.

carpet sweeper [-'swiːpə*] n limpador m de tapetes.

car rental (US) n aluguel m (BR) or aluguer m (PT) de carros.

carriage ['kærɪdʒ] n carruagem f, coche m; (RAIL) vagão m; (of goods) transporte m; (: cost) porte m; (of typewriter) carro; (bearing) porte m; ~ **forward** frete a pagar; ~ **free** franco de porte; ~ **paid** frete or porte pago.

carriage return n retorno do carro.

carriageway ['kærɪdʒweɪ] (BRIT) n (part of road) pista.

carrier ['kærɪə*] n transportador(a) m/f; (company) empresa de transportes, transportadora; (MED) portador(a) m/f; (NAUT) porta-aviões m inv.

carrier bag n saco, sacola.

carrier pigeon n pombo-correio.

carrion ['kærɪən] n carniça.

carrot ['kærət] n cenoura.

carry ['kærɪ] vt carregar; (take) levar; (transport) transportar; (a motion, bill) aprovar; (involve: responsibilities etc) implicar; (MATH: figure) levar; (COMM: interest) render ♦ vi (sound) projetar-se; **to get carried away** (fig) exagerar.

  carry forward vt transportar.

  carry on vi (continue) seguir, continuar; (inf: complain) queixar-se, criar caso ♦ vt prosseguir, continuar.

  carry out vt (orders) cumprir; (investigation) levar a cabo, realizar; (idea, threat) executar.

carrycot ['kærɪkɔt] (BRIT) n moisés m inv.

carry-on (inf) n alvoroço, rebuliço.

cart [kɑːt] n carroça, carreta; (US: for luggage) carrinho ♦ vt transportar (em carroça).

carte blanche ['kɑːt'blɒnʃ] n: **to give sb** ~ dar carta branca a alguém.

cartel [kɑː'tɛl] n (COMM) cartel m.

cartilage ['kɑːtɪlɪdʒ] n cartilagem f.

cartographer [kɑː'tɔgrəfə*] n cartógrafo/a.

cartography [kɑː'tɔgrəfɪ] n cartografia.

carton ['kɑːtən] n (box) caixa (de papelão); (of yogurt) pote m; (packet) pacote m.

cartoon [kɑː'tuːn] n (PRESS) charge f; (satirical) caricatura; (comic strip) história em quadrinhos (BR), banda desenhada (PT); (film) desenho animado.

cartoonist [kɑː'tuːnɪst] n caricaturista m/f, cartunista m/f; (PRESS) chargista m/f.

cartridge ['kɑːtrɪdʒ] n cartucho; (of record player) cápsula.

cartwheel ['kɑːtwiːl] n pirueta, cabriola; **to turn a** ~ fazer uma pirueta.

carve [kɑːv] vt (meat) trinchar; (wood, stone) cinzelar, esculpir; (on tree) gravar; **to ~ up** dividir, repartir.

carving ['kɑːvɪŋ] n (in wood etc) escultura, obra de talha or de entalhe.

carving knife (irreg) n trinchante m, faca de trinchar.

car wash n lavagem f de carros.

cascade [kæs'keɪd] n cascata ♦ vi cascatear, cair em cascata.

case [keɪs] n (container) caixa, estojo; (instance, affair, MED) caso; (for jewels etc) estojo; (LAW) causa; (BRIT: also: suit~) mala; (TYP): **lower/upper** ~ caixa baixa/alta; **to have a good** ~ ter bons argumentos; **there's a strong** ~ **for ...** há bons argumentos para ...; **in** ~ **(of)** em caso (de); **in any** ~ em todo o caso; **just in** ~ conj se por acaso ♦ adv por via das dúvidas.

case-hardened adj calejado.

case history n (MED) anamnese f.

case study n (MED) caso clínico; (SOCIOLOGY) estudo sociológico.

cash [kæʃ] n dinheiro (em espécie) ♦ vt descontar; **to pay (in)** ~ pagar em dinheiro; ~ **on delivery** pagamento contra entrega; **to be short of** ~ estar sem dinheiro.

  cash in vt (insurance policy etc) resgatar.

  cash in on vt fus lucrar com, explorar.

cash account n conta de caixa.

cashbook ['kæʃbuk] n livro-caixa m.

cash box n cofre m.

cash card n cartão m de saque.

cashdesk ['kæʃdɛsk] (BRIT) n caixa.

cash discount n desconto por pagamento à vista.

cash dispenser n caixa automática or eletrônica.

cashew [kæ'ʃuː] n (also: ~ nut) castanha de caju.

cash flow n fluxo de caixa.

cashier [kæ'ʃɪə*] n caixa m/f ♦ vt (MIL) exonerar.

cashmere ['kæʃmɪə*] n caxemira, cachemira.

cash payment n (in money) pagamento em dinheiro; (in one go) pagamento à vista.

cash price n preço à vista.

cash register n caixa registradora.
cash sale n venda à vista.
casing ['keɪsɪŋ] n invólucro; (of boiler etc) revestimento.
casino [kə'siːnəu] n casino.
cask [kɑːsk] n barril m, casco.
casket ['kɑːskɪt] n cofre m, porta-jóias m inv; (US: coffin) caixão m.
Caspian Sea ['kæspɪən-] n: the ~ o mar Cáspio.
casserole ['kæsərəul] n panela de ir ao forno; (food) ensopado (BR) no forno, guisado (PT) no forno.
cassette [kæ'sɛt] n fita-cassete f.
cassette deck n toca-fitas m inv.
cassette player n toca-fitas m inv.
cassette recorder n gravador m.
cassock ['kæsək] n sotaina, batina.
cast [kɑːst] (pt, pp cast) vt (throw) lançar, atirar; (skin) mudar, perder; (metal) fundir; (THEATRE): to ~ sb as Hamlet dar a alguém o papel de Hamlet ♦ vi (FISHING) lançar ♦ n (THEATRE) elenco; (mould) forma, molde m; (also: plaster ~) gesso; to ~ loose soltar; to ~ one's vote votar.
cast aside vt rejeitar.
cast away vt desperdiçar.
cast down vt abater, desalentar.
cast off vi (NAUT) soltar o cabo; (KNITTING) rematar os pontos ♦ vt (KNITTING) rematar.
cast on vt (KNITTING) montar ♦ vi montar os pontos.
castanets [kæstə'nɛts] npl castanholas fpl.
castaway ['kɑːstəwəɪ] n náufrago/a.
caste [kɑːst] n casta.
caster sugar ['kɑːstə*-] (BRIT) n acuçar m branco refinado.
casting vote ['kɑːstɪŋ-] (BRIT) n voto decisivo, voto de minerva.
cast iron n ferro fundido ♦ adj: **cast-iron** (fig: will) de ferro; (: alibi) forte.
castle ['kɑːsl] n castelo; (CHESS) torre f.
castor ['kɑːstə*] n (wheel) rodízio.
castor oil n óleo de rícino.
castor sugar (BRIT) n = **caster sugar**.
castrate [kæs'treɪt] vt castrar.
casual ['kæʒjul] adj (by chance) fortuito; (irregular: work etc) eventual; (unconcerned) despreocupado; (informal: atmosphere etc) descontraído; ~ **wear** roupas fpl esportivas.
casual labour n mão-de-obra f ocasional.
casually ['kæʒjulɪ] adv (by chance) casualmente; (informally) informalmente.
casualty ['kæʒjultɪ] n (wounded) ferido/a; (dead) morto/a; (MIL) baixa; **casualties** npl perdas fpl.
casualty ward (BRIT) n setor m de emergência, pronto-socorro.
cat [kæt] n gato.
catacombs ['kætəkuːmz] npl catacumbas fpl.
Catalan ['kætəlæn] adj catalão/lã ♦ n catalão/lã m/f; (LING) catalão m.
catalogue ['kætələɔg] (US **catalog**) n catálogo ♦ vt catalogar.
Catalonia [kætə'ləunɪə] n Catalunha.
catalyst ['kætəlɪst] n catalisador m.
catapult ['kætəpʌlt] n catapulta; (child's toy) atiradeira.
cataract ['kætərækt] n (also: MED) catarata.
catarrh [kə'tɑː*] n catarro.
catastrophe [kə'tæstrəfɪ] n catástrofe f.
catastrophic [kætə'strɔfɪk] adj catastrófico.
catcall ['kætkɔːl] n assobio.
catch [kætʃ] (pt, pp **caught**) vt (ball, train, flu) pegar (BR), apanhar (PT); (arrest) deter; (person: by surprise) flagrar, surpreender; (understand) compreender; (get entangled) prender; (also: ~ up) alcançar ♦ vi (fire) pegar; (in branches etc) ficar preso, prender-se ♦ n (fish etc) pesca; (act of ~ing) captura; (trap) manha, armadilha; (of lock) trinco, lingüeta; to ~ sb's attention or eye chamar a atenção de alguém; to ~ fire pegar fogo; (building) incendiar-se; to ~ sight of avistar.
catch on vi (understand) entender (BR), perceber (PT); (grow popular) pegar.
catch out (BRIT) vt (with trick question) apanhar em erro.
catch up vi equiparar-se; (make up for lost time) recuperar o tempo perdido ♦ vt (also: ~ up with) alcançar.
catching ['kætʃɪŋ] adj (MED) contagioso.
catchment area ['kætʃmənt-] n área atendida por um hospital, uma escola etc.
catch phrase n clichê m, slogan m.
catch-22 [-twentɪ'tuː] n: **it's a ~ situation** é uma situação do tipo se correr, o bicho pega, se ficar, o bicho come.
catchy ['kætʃɪ] adj (tune) que pega fácil, que gruda no ouvido.
catechism ['kætɪkɪzəm] n (REL) catecismo.
categoric(al) [kætɪ'gɔrɪk(əl)] adj categórico, terminante.
categorize ['kætɪgəraɪz] vt classificar.
category ['kætɪgɔrɪ] n categoria.
cater ['keɪtə*] vi preparar comida.
cater for vt fus (needs) atender a; (consumers) satisfazer.
caterer ['keɪtərə*] n (service) serviço de bufê.
catering ['keɪtərɪŋ] n serviço de bufê; (trade) abastecimento.
caterpillar ['kætəpɪlə*] n lagarta ♦ cpd (vehicle) de lagartas; ~ **track** lagarta.
cathedral [kə'θiːdrəl] n catedral f.
cathode ['kæθəud] n cátodo.
cathode ray tube n tubo de raios catódicos.
Catholic ['kæθəlɪk] adj, n (REL) católico/a.
catholic ['kæθəlɪk] adj eclético.
cat's eye (BRIT) n (AUT) catadióptrico.
catsup ['kætsəp] (US) n ketchup m.
cattle ['kætl] npl gado.
catty ['kætɪ] adj malicioso, rancoroso.

m/f; (LING) catalão m.

NB: European Portuguese adds the following consonants to certain words: **b** (sú(b)dito, su(b)til); **c** (a(c)ção, a(c)cionista, a(c)to); **m** (inde(m)ne); **p** (ado(p)ção, ado(p)tar); *for further details see p. xiii.*

Caucasian [kɔː'keɪʒn] *adj, n* caucasóide *m/f.*
Caucasus ['kɔːkəsəs] *n* Cáucaso.
caucus ['kɔːkəs] *n* (*US: POL*) comitê *m* eleitoral (para indicar candidatos); (*BRIT: POL: group*) panelinha (de políticos).
caught [kɔːt] *pt, pp of* **catch.**
cauliflower ['kɔlɪflaʊə*] *n* couve-flor *f.*
cause [kɔːz] *n* causa; (*reason*) motivo, razão *f* ♦ *vt* causar, provocar; **there is no ~ for concern** não há motivo de preocupação; **to ~ sth to be done** fazer com que algo seja feito; **to ~ sb to do sth** fazer com que alguém faça algo.
causeway ['kɔːzweɪ] *n* (*road*) calçada; (*embankment*) banqueta.
caustic ['kɔːstɪk] *adj* cáustico; (*fig*) mordaz.
caution ['kɔːʃən] *n* cautela, prudência; (*warning*) aviso ♦ *vt* acautelar, avisar.
cautious ['kɔːʃəs] *adj* cauteloso, prudente, precavido.
cautiously ['kɔːʃəslɪ] *adv* com cautela.
cautiousness ['kɔːʃəsnɪs] *n* cautela, prudência.
cavalier [kævə'lɪə*] *adj* arrogante, descortês ♦ *n* (*knight*) cavaleiro.
cavalry ['kævəlrɪ] *n* cavalaria.
cave [keɪv] *n* caverna, gruta ♦ *vi*: **to go caving** fazer espeleologia.
cave in *vi* dar de si; (*roof etc*) ceder.
caveman ['keɪvmæn] (*irreg*) *n* troglodita *m*, homem *m* das cavernas.
cavern ['kævən] *n* caverna.
caviar(e) ['kævɪɑː*] *n* caviar *m.*
cavity ['kævɪtɪ] *n* cavidade *f.*
cavort [kə'vɔːt] *vi* cabriolar.
caw [kɔː] *vi* grasnar.
cayenne [keɪ'ɛn] *n* (*also: ~ pepper*) pimenta-de-caiena.
CB *n abbr* = **Citizens' Band (Radio)**; (*BRIT*: = *Companion of (the Order of) the Bath*) título honorífico.
CBC *n abbr* = **Canadian Broadcasting Corporation.**
CBE *n abbr* (= *Companion of (the Order of) the British Empire*) título honorífico.
CBI *n abbr* = *Confederation of British Industry*) federação de indústria.
CBS (*US*) *n abbr* (= *Columbia Broadcasting System*) emissora de televisão.
CC (*BRIT*) = **County Council.**
cc *abbr* (= *cubic centimetre*) cc; (*on letter etc*) = **carbon copy.**
CCA (*US*) *n abbr* (= *Circuit Court of Appeals*) tribunal de recursos itinerante.
CCU (*US*) *n abbr* (= *coronary care unit*) unidade de cardiologia.
CD *n abbr* (= *compact disc*) disco laser; (*MIL*) = **Civil Defence (Corps)** (*BRIT*); **Civil Defense** (*US*) ♦ *abbr* (*BRIT*: = *Corps Diplomatique*) CD.
CDC (*US*) *n abbr* = **center for disease control.**
CD player *n* toca-discos *m inv* laser.
Cdr. *abbr* (= *commander*) Com.
CDT (*US*) *n abbr* (= *Central Daylight Time*) hora de verão do centro.

cease [siːs] *vt, vi* cessar.
ceasefire [siːs'faɪə*] *n* cessar-fogo *m.*
ceaseless ['siːslɪs] *adj* contínuo, incessante.
ceaselessly ['siːslɪslɪ] *adv* sem parar, sem cessar.
CED (*US*) *n abbr* = **Committee for Economic Development.**
cedar ['siːdə*] *n* cedro.
cede [siːd] *vt* ceder.
cedilla [sɪ'dɪlə] *n* cedilha.
CEEB (*US*) *n abbr* (= *College Entry Examination Board*) comissão de admissão ao ensino superior.
ceiling ['siːlɪŋ] *n* (*also fig*) teto.
celebrate ['sɛlɪbreɪt] *vt* celebrar ♦ *vi* celebrar, festejar.
celebrated ['sɛlɪbreɪtɪd] *adj* célebre.
celebration [sɛlɪ'breɪʃən] *n* (*act*) celebração *f*; (*party*) festa.
celebrity [sɪ'lɛbrɪtɪ] *n* celebridade *f.*
celeriac [sə'lɛrɪæk] *n* aipo-rábano.
celery ['sɛlərɪ] *n* aipo.
celestial [sɪ'lɛstɪəl] *adj* (*of sky*) celeste; (*divine*) celestial.
celibacy ['sɛlɪbəsɪ] *n* celibato.
cell [sɛl] *n* cela; (*BIO*) célula; (*ELEC*) pilha, elemento.
cellar ['sɛlə*] *n* porão *m*; (*for wine*) adega.
'cellist ['tʃɛlɪst] *n* violoncelista *m/f.*
'cello ['tʃɛləu] *n* violoncelo.
cellophane ['sɛləfeɪn] *n* celofane *m.*
cellular ['sɛljulə*] *adj* celular.
Celluloid ['sɛljulɔɪd] ® *n* celulóide *m* ®.
cellulose ['sɛljuləus] *n* celulose *f.*
Celsius ['sɛlsɪəs] *adj* Célsius *inv.*
Celt [kɛlt, sɛlt] *adj, n* celta *m/f.*
Celtic ['kɛltɪk, 'sɛltɪk] *adj* celta ♦ *n* (*LING*) celta *m.*
cement [sə'mɛnt] *n* cimento ♦ *vt* cimentar; (*fig*) cimentar, fortalecer.
cement mixer *n* betoneira.
cemetery ['sɛmɪtrɪ] *n* cemitério.
cenotaph ['sɛnətɑːf] *n* cenotáfio.
censor ['sɛnsə*] *n* (*person*) censor(a) *m/f*; (*concept*): **the ~** a censura ♦ *vt* censurar.
censorship ['sɛnsəʃɪp] *n* censura.
censure ['sɛnʃə*] *vt* censurar.
census ['sɛnsəs] *n* censo.
cent [sɛnt] (*US*) *n* (*coin*) cêntimo; *see also* **per.**
centenary [sɛn'tiːnərɪ] *n* centenário.
centennial [sɛn'tɛnɪəl] *n* centenário.
center *etc* ['sɛntə*] (*US*) = **centre** *etc.*
centigrade ['sɛntɪgreɪd] *adj* centígrado.
centilitre ['sɛntɪliːtə*] (*US* **centiliter**) *n* centilitro.
centimetre ['sɛntɪmiːtə*] (*US* **centimeter**) *n* centímetro.
centipede ['sɛntɪpiːd] *n* centopéia.
central ['sɛntrəl] *adj* central.
Central African Republic *n* República Centro-Africana.
Central America *n* América Central.
Central American *adj* centro-americano.
central heating *n* aquecimento central.
centralize ['sɛntrəlaɪz] *vt* centralizar.

central processing unit *n* (*COMPUT*) unidade *f* central de processamento.

central reservation (*BRIT*) *n* (*AUT*) canteiro divisor.

centre ['sɛntə*] (*US* **center**) *n* centro ♦ *vt* centrar ♦ *vi* (*concentrate*): **to ~ (on)** concentrar (em).

centrefold ['sɛntəfəuld] (*US* **centerfold**) *n* poster *m* central.

centre-forward *n* (*SPORT*) centro-avante *m*, centro.

centre-half *n* (*SPORT*) (centro) médio.

centrepiece ['sɛntəpiːs] (*US* **centerpiece**) *n* centro de mesa.

centre spread (*BRIT*) *n* páginas *fpl* centrais.

centrifugal [sɛntrɪ'fjuːgl] *adj* centrífugo.

centrifuge ['sɛntrɪfjuːʒ] *n* centrífuga.

century ['sɛntjurɪ] *n* século; **20th ~** século vinte.

CEO (*US*) *n abbr* = **chief executive officer**.

ceramic [sɪ'ræmɪk] *adj* cerâmico.

ceramics [sɪ'ræmɪks] *n* cerâmica.

cereal ['siːrɪəl] *n* cereal *m*.

cerebral ['sɛrɪbrəl] *adj* cerebral.

ceremonial [sɛrɪ'məunɪəl] *n* cerimonial *m*; (*rite*) rito.

ceremony ['sɛrɪmənɪ] *n* cerimônia; **to stand on ~** fazer cerimônia.

cert [səːt] (*BRIT*: *inf*) *n*: **it's a dead ~** é barbada, é coisa certa.

certain ['səːtən] *adj* certo; (*person: sure*) seguro; **to make ~ of** assegurar-se de; **for ~** com certeza.

certainly ['səːtənlɪ] *adv* certamente, com certeza.

certainty ['səːtəntɪ] *n* certeza.

certificate [sə'tɪfɪkɪt] *n* certificado.

certified letter ['səːtɪfaɪd-] (*US*) *n* carta registrada.

certified public accountant ['səːtɪfaɪd-] (*US*) *n* perito-contador *m*/perita-contadora *f*.

certify ['səːtɪfaɪ] *vt* certificar ♦ *vi*: **to ~ to** atestar.

cervical ['səːvɪkl] *adj*: **~ cancer** câncer *m* (*BR*) *or* cancro (*PT*) do colo do útero; **~ smear** exame *m* de lâmina, esfregaço.

cervix ['səːvɪks] *n* cerviz *f*.

Cesarean [sɪ'zɛərɪən] (*US*) *adj*, *n* = **Caesarean**.

cessation [sə'seɪʃən] *n* cessação *f*, suspensão *f*.

cesspit ['sɛspɪt] *n* fossa séptica.

CET *abbr* (= *Central European Time*) hora da Europa Central.

Ceylon [sɪ'lɔn] *n* (*old*) Ceilão *m*.

cf. *abbr* (= *compare*) cf.

c/f *abbr* (*COMM*: = *carry forward*) a transportar.

CG (*US*) *n abbr* = **coastguard**.

cg *abbr* (= *centigram*) cg.

CH (*BRIT*) *n abbr* (= *Companion of Honour*) título honorífico.

ch (*BRIT*) *abbr* = **central heating**.

ch. *abbr* (= *chapter*) cap.

Chad [tʃæd] *n* Chad *m*.

chafe [tʃeɪf] *vt* (*rub*) roçar; (*wear*) gastar; (*irritate*) irritar ♦ *vi* (*fig*): **to ~ at sth** irritar-se com algo.

chaffinch ['tʃæfɪntʃ] *n* tentilhão *m*.

chagrin ['ʃægrɪn] *n* desgosto.

chain [tʃeɪn] *n* corrente *f*; (*of shops*) cadeia ♦ *vt* (*also*: **~ up**) encadear.

chain reaction *n* reação *f* em cadeia.

chain-smoke *vi* fumar um (cigarro) atrás do outro.

chain store *n* magazine *m* (*BR*), grande armazem *f* (*PT*).

chair [tʃɛə*] *n* cadeira; (*armchair*) poltrona; (*of university*) cátedra ♦ *vt* (*meeting*) presidir; **the ~** (*US*: *electric ~*) a cadeira elétrica.

chairlift ['tʃɛəlɪft] *n* teleférico.

chairman ['tʃɛəmən] (*irreg*) *n* presidente *m*.

chairperson ['tʃɛəpəːsn] *n* presidente *m*/*f*.

chairwoman ['tʃɛəwumən] (*irreg*) *n* presidenta, presidente *f*.

chalet ['ʃæleɪ] *n* chalé *m*.

chalice ['tʃælɪs] *n* cálice *m*.

chalk [tʃɔːk] *n* (*GEO*) greda; (*for writing*) giz *m*.

chalk up *vt* escrever a giz; (*fig: success*) obter.

challenge ['tʃælɪndʒ] *n* desafio ♦ *vt* desafiar; (*statement, right*) disputar, contestar; **to ~ sb to sth/to do sth** desafiar alguém para algo/a fazer algo.

challenger ['tʃælɪndʒə*] *n* (*SPORT*) competidor(a) *m*/*f*.

challenging ['tʃælɪndʒɪŋ] *adj* desafiante; (*tone*) de desafio.

chamber ['tʃeɪmbə*] *n* câmara; **~ of commerce** câmara de comércio.

chambermaid ['tʃeɪmbəmeɪd] *n* arrumadeira (*BR*), empregada (*PT*).

chamber music *n* música de câmara.

chamberpot ['tʃeɪmbəpɔt] *n* urinol *m*.

chameleon [kə'miːlɪən] *n* camaleão *m*.

chamois ['ʃæmwɑː] *n* camurça.

chamois leather ['ʃæmɪ-] *n* camurça.

champagne [ʃæm'peɪn] *n* champanhe *m or f*.

champion ['tʃæmpɪən] *n* campeão/peã *m*/*f* ♦ *vt* defender, lutar por.

championship ['tʃæmpɪənʃɪp] *n* campeonato.

chance [tʃɑːns] *n* (*luck*) acaso, casualidade *f*; (*opportunity*) oportunidade, ocasião *f*; (*likelihood*) chance *f*; (*risk*) risco ♦ *vt* arriscar ♦ *adj* fortuito, casual; **there is little ~ of his coming** é pouco provável que ele venha; **to take a ~** arriscar-se; **it's the ~ of a lifetime** é uma chance que só se tem uma vez na vida; **by ~** por acaso **to ~ it** arriscar-se; **to ~ to do** fazer por acaso.

chance (up)on *vt fus* dar com, encontrar por acaso.

chancel ['tʃɑːnsəl] *n* coro, capela-mor *f*.

chancellor ['tʃɑːnsələ*] *n* chanceler *m*; **C~ of**

NB: European Portuguese adds the following consonants to certain words: **b** (sú(b)dito, su(b)til); **c** (a(c)ção, a(c)cionista, a(c)to); **m** (inde(m)ne); **p** (ado(p)ção, ado(p)tar); *for further details see p. xiii.*

the **Exchequer** (*BRIT*) Ministro da Economia (Fazenda e Planejamento).

chandelier [ʃændə'lɪə*] *n* lustre *m*.

change [tʃeɪndʒ] *vt* (*move, alter*) mudar; (*exchange*) trocar; (*replace*) substituir; (*gear, clothes, house*) mudar de, trocar de; (*transform*): **to ~ sb into** transformar alguém em ♦ *vi* (*gen*) mudar(-se); (*change clothes*) trocar de roupa; (*trains*) fazer baldeação (*BR*), mudar (*PT*) ♦ *n* mudança; (*exchange, money returned*) troca; (*modification*) modificação *f*; (*transformation*) transformação *f*; (*coins: also: small ~*) trocado; **for a ~** para variar; **to ~ into** transformar-se em; **to ~ one's mind** mudar de idéia; **she ~d into an old skirt** ela (trocou de roupa e) vestiu uma saia velha; **a ~ of clothes** uma muda de roupa; **to give sb ~ for** *or* **of £10** trocar £10 para alguém.

changeable ['tʃeɪndʒəbl] *adj* (*weather*) variável, instável; (*person*) inconstante, volúvel.

changeless ['tʃeɪndʒlɪs] *adj* imutável.

change machine *n* máquina que fornece trocado.

changeover ['tʃeɪndʒəuvə*] *n* (*to new system*) mudança.

changing ['tʃeɪndʒɪŋ] *adj* variável.

changing room (*BRIT*) *n* (*SPORT*) vestiário; (*in shop*) cabine *f* de provas.

channel ['tʃænl] *n* (*TV*) canal *m*; (*of river*) leito; (*of sea*) canal, estreito; (*groove*) ranhura; (*fig: medium*) meio, via ♦ *vt* (*also fig*): **to ~ (into)** canalizar (para); **to go through the usual ~s** seguir os trâmites normais; **green/red ~** (*CUSTOMS*) canal verde/vermelho; **the (English) C~** o Canal da Mancha.

Channel Islands *npl*: **the ~** as ilhas Anglo-Normandas.

chant [tʃɑːnt] *n* cântico ♦ *vt* cantar; (*fig*) entoar.

chaos ['keɪɔs] *n* caos *m*.

chaotic [keɪ'ɔtɪk] *adj* caótico.

chap [tʃæp] *n* (*BRIT: inf: man*) sujeito (*BR*), tipo (*PT*); (*term of address*): **old ~** meu velho ♦ *vt* (*skin*) rachar.

chapel ['tʃæpəl] *n* capela.

chaperon(e) ['ʃæpərəun] *n* mulher *f* acompanhante ♦ *vt* acompanhar.

chaplain ['tʃæplɪn] *n* capelão *m*.

chapter ['tʃæptə*] *n* capítulo.

char [tʃɑː*] *vt* (*burn*) tostar, queimar ♦ *vi* (*BRIT*) trabalhar como diarista ♦ *n* (*BRIT*) = **charlady.**

character ['kærɪktə*] *n* caráter *m*; (*in novel, film*) personagem *m/f*; (*role*) papel *m*; (*eccentric*): **to be a (real) ~** ser um número; **a person of good ~** uma pessoa de bom caráter.

character code *n* (*COMPUT*) código de caráter.

characteristic [kærɪktə'rɪstɪk] *adj* característico ♦ *n* característica.

characterize ['kærɪktəraɪz] *vt* caracterizar.

charade [ʃə'rɑːd] *n* charada.

charcoal ['tʃɑːkəul] *n* carvão *m* de lenha; (*ART*) carvão *m*.

charge [tʃɑːdʒ] *n* (*of gun, electrical, MIL: attack*) carga; (*LAW*) encargo, acusação *f*; (*cost*) preço, custo; (*responsibility*) encargo; (*task*) incumbência ♦ *vt* (*LAW*): **to ~ sb (with)** acusar alguém (de); (*gun, battery*) carregar; (*MIL: enemy*) atacar; (*price*) cobrar; (*customer*) cobrar dinheiro de; (*sb with task*) incumbir, encarregar ♦ *vi* precipitar-se; (*make pay*) cobrar; **~s** *npl*: **bank/labour ~s** taxas *fpl* cobradas pelo banco/custos *mpl* de mão-de-obra; **free of ~** grátis; **is there a ~?** se tem que pagar?; **there's no ~** é de graça; **extra ~** sobretaxa; **to reverse the ~s** (*BRIT: TEL*) ligar a cobrar; **to take ~ of** encarregar-se de, tomar conta de; **to be in ~ of** estar a cargo de *or* encarregado de; **they ~d us £10 for the dinner** eles nos cobraram £10 pelo jantar; **how much do you ~?** quanto você cobra?; **to ~ an expense (up) to sb's account** pôr a despesa na conta de alguém; **to ~ in/out** precipitar-se para dentro/fora.

charge account *n* conta de crédito.

charge card *n* cartão *m* de crédito (*emitido por uma loja*).

chargé d'affaires ['ʃɑːʒeɪdæ'feə*] *n* encarregado/a de negócios.

chargehand ['tʃɑːdʒhænd] (*BRIT*) *n* capataz *m*.

charger ['tʃɑːdʒə*] *n* (*also: battery ~*) carregador *m*; (*old: warhorse*) cavalo de batalha.

charitable ['tʃærɪtəbl] *adj* caritativo; (*organization*) beneficente.

charity ['tʃærɪtɪ] *n* caridade *f*; (*sympathy*) compaixão *f*; (*organization*) obra *f* de caridade.

charlady ['tʃɑːleɪdɪ] (*BRIT*) *n* diarista.

charm [tʃɑːm] *n* (*quality*) charme *m*; (*attraction*) encanto, atrativo; (*spell*) feitiço; (*object*) amuleto ♦ *vt* encantar, enfeitiçar.

charm bracelet *n* pulseira de berloques.

charming ['tʃɑːmɪŋ] *adj* encantador(a), simpático, charmoso.

chart [tʃɑːt] *n* (*table*) quadro; (*graph*) gráfico; (*map*) carta de navegação; (*weather ~*) carta meteorológica *or* de tempo ♦ *vt* fazer um gráfico de; (*course, progress*) traçar; **to be in the ~s** (*record, pop group*) estar nas paradas (de sucesso).

charter ['tʃɑːtə*] *vt* fretar ♦ *n* (*document*) carta, alvará *m*; **on ~** (*plane*) fretado.

chartered accountant ['tʃɑːtəd-] (*BRIT*) *n* perito-contador *m*/perita-contadora *f*.

charter flight *n* vôo charter *or* fretado.

charwoman ['tʃɑːwumən] (*BRIT: irreg*) *n* diarista.

chase [tʃeɪs] *vt* (*follow*) perseguir; (*hunt*) caçar, dar caça a ♦ *vi*: **to ~ after** correr atrás de ♦ *n* perseguição *f*, caça.

chase down (*US*) *vt* = **chase up.**

chase up (*BRIT*) *vt* (*person*) ficar atrás de; (*information*) pesquisar.

chasm ['kæzəm] *n* abismo.

chassis ['ʃæsɪ] *n* chassi *m*.

chaste [tʃeɪst] *adj* casto.

chastened ['tʃeɪsnd] *adj*: **to be ~ by an experience** aprender uma lição com uma experiência.

chastening ['tʃeɪsnɪŋ] *adj*: **it was a ~ experience** foi uma lição.

chastise [tʃæs'taɪz] *vt* castigar.

chastity ['tʃæstɪtɪ] *n* castidade *f*.

chat [tʃæt] *vi* (*also: have a ~*) conversar, bater papo (*BR*), cavaquear (*PT*) ♦ *n* conversa, bate-papo *m* (*BR*), cavaqueira (*PT*).

chat up (*BRIT: inf*) *vt* (*girl*) paquerar.

chat show (*BRIT*) *n* programa *m* de entrevistas.

chattel ['tʃætl] *n see* **goods**.

chatter ['tʃætə*] *vi* (*person*) tagarelar; (*teeth*) tiritar ♦ *n* (*of birds*) chilro; (*of people*) tagarelice *f*.

chatterbox ['tʃætəbɔks] *n* tagarela *m/f*.

chatty ['tʃætɪ] *adj* (*style*) informal; (*person*) conversador(a).

chauffeur ['ʃəʊfə*] *n* chofer *m*, motorista *m/f*.

chauvinism ['ʃəʊvɪnɪzəm] *n* (*also: male ~*) machismo; (*nationalism*) chauvinismo.

chauvinist ['ʃəʊvɪnɪst] *n* (*also: male ~*) machista *m*; (*nationalist*) chauvinista *m/f*.

ChE *abbr* = **chemical engineer**.

cheap [tʃiːp] *adj* barato; (*ticket etc*) a preço reduzido; (*joke*) de mau gosto; (*poor quality*) barato, de pouca qualidade ♦ *adv* barato; **a ~ trick** uma sujeira, uma sacanagem.

cheapen ['tʃiːpən] *vt* baixar o preço de, rebaixar; **to ~ o.s.** rebaixar-se.

cheaply ['tʃiːplɪ] *adv* barato, por baixo preço.

cheat [tʃiːt] *vi* trapacear; (*at cards*) roubar (*BR*), fazer batota (*PT*); (*in exam*) colar (*BR*), cabular (*PT*) ♦ *vt* defraudar, enganar ♦ *n* fraude *f*; (*person*) trapaceiro/a; **to ~ on sb** (*inf: husband, wife etc*) passar alguém para trás.

cheating ['tʃiːtɪŋ] *n* trapaça.

check [tʃɛk] *vt* (*examine*) controlar; (*facts*) verificar; (*count*) contar; (*halt*) impedir, deter; (*restrain*) parar, refrear ♦ *vi* verificar ♦ *n* (*inspection*) controle *m*, inspeção *f*; (*curb*) freio; (*bill*) conta; (*CHESS*) xeque *m*; (*token*) ficha, talão *m*; (*pattern: gen pl*) xadrez *m*; (*US*) = **cheque** ♦ *adj* (*also: ~ed: pattern, cloth*) xadrez *inv*; **to ~ with sb** perguntar a alguém; **to keep a ~ on sb/sth** controlar alguém/algo.

check in *vi* (*in hotel*) registrar-se; (*in airport*) apresentar-se ♦ *vt* (*luggage*) entregar.

check off *vt* checar.

check out *vi* (*of hotel*) pagar a conta e sair ♦ *vt* (*story*) verificar; (*person*) investigar; **~ it out** (*see for yourself*) confira.

check up *vi*: **to ~ up on sth** verificar algo; **to ~ up on sb** investigar alguém.

checkbook ['tʃɛkbuk] (*US*) *n* = **chequebook**.

checkered ['tʃɛkəd] (*US*) *adj* = **chequered**.

checkers ['tʃɛkəz] (*US*) *n* (jogo de) damas *fpl*.

check guarantee card (*US*) *n* cartão *m* (de garantia) de cheques.

check-in *n* (*also: ~ desk: at airport*) check-in *m*.

checking account ['tʃɛkɪŋ-] (*US*) *n* conta corrente.

checklist ['tʃɛklɪst] *n* lista de conferência.

checkmate ['tʃɛkmeɪt] *n* xeque-mate *m*.

checkout ['tʃɛkaut] *n* caixa.

checkpoint ['tʃɛkpɔɪnt] *n* (ponto de) controle *m*.

checkup ['tʃɛkʌp] *n* (*MED*) check-up *m*; (*of machine*) revisão *f*.

cheek [tʃiːk] *n* bochecha; (*impudence*) folga, descaramento; **what a ~!** que folga!

cheekbone ['tʃiːkbəun] *n* maçã *f* do rosto.

cheeky ['tʃiːkɪ] *adj* insolente, descarado.

cheep [tʃiːp] *n* (*of bird*) pio ♦ *vi* piar.

cheer [tʃɪə*] *vt* dar vivas a, aplaudir; (*gladden*) alegrar, animar ♦ *vi* aplaudir, gritar com entusiasmo ♦ *n* (*gen pl*) aplausos *mpl*; **~s!** saúde!

cheer on *vt* torcer por.

cheer up *vi* animar-se, alegrar-se ♦ *vt* alegrar, animar.

cheerful ['tʃɪəful] *adj* alegre.

cheerfulness ['tʃɪəfulnɪs] *n* alegria.

cheerio [tʃɪərɪ'əu] (*BRIT*) *excl* tchau (*BR*), adeus (*PT*).

cheerless ['tʃɪəlɪs] *adj* triste, sombrio.

cheese [tʃiːz] *n* queijo.

cheeseboard ['tʃiːzbɔːd] *n* (*in restaurant*) sortimento de queijos.

cheesecake ['tʃiːzkeɪk] *n* queijada, torta de queijo.

cheetah ['tʃiːtə] *n* chitá *m*.

chef [ʃɛf] *n* cozinheiro-chefe/cozinheira-chefe *m/f*.

chemical ['kɛmɪkəl] *adj* químico ♦ *n* produto químico.

chemist ['kɛmɪst] *n* (*BRIT: pharmacist*) farmacêutico/a; (*scientist*) químico/a; **~'s (shop)** (*BRIT*) farmácia.

chemistry ['kɛmɪstrɪ] *n* química.

cheque [tʃɛk] (*US* **check**) *n* cheque *m*; **to pay by ~** pagar com cheque.

chequebook ['tʃɛkbuk] (*US* **checkbook**) *n* talão *m* (*BR*) *or* livro (*PT*) de cheques.

cheque card (*BRIT*) *n* cartão *m* (de garantia) de cheques.

chequered ['tʃɛkəd] (*US* **checkered**) *adj* (*fig*) variado, acidentado.

cherish ['tʃɛrɪʃ] *vt* (*love*) apreciar; (*protect*) cuidar; (*hope etc*) acalentar.

cheroot [ʃə'ruːt] *n* charuto.

cherry ['tʃɛrɪ] *n* cereja.

Ches (*BRIT*) *abbr* = **Cheshire**.

chess [tʃɛs] *n* xadrez *m*.

chessboard ['tʃɛsbɔːd] *n* tabuleiro de xadrez.

chessman ['tʃɛsmæn] (*irreg*) *n* peça, pedra (de xadrez).

NB: European Portuguese adds the following consonants to certain words: **b** (sú(b)dito, su(b)til); **c** (a(c)ção, a(c)cionista, a(c)to); **m** (inde(m)ne); **p** (ado(p)ção, ado(p)tar); *for further details see p. xiii.*

chessplayer ['tʃɛspleɪə*] n xadrezista m/f.

chest [tʃɛst] n (ANAT) peito; (box) caixa, cofre m; **to get sth or it off one's ~** (inf) desabafar; **~ of drawers** cômoda.

chest measurement n medida de peito.

chestnut ['tʃɛsnʌt] n castanha; (also: ~ tree) castanheiro; (colour) castanho ♦ adj castanho.

chew [tʃuː] vt mastigar.

chewing gum ['tʃuːŋ-] n chiclete m (BR), pastilha elástica (PT).

chic [ʃɪk] adj elegante, chique.

chick [tʃɪk] n pinto; (US: inf) broto.

chicken ['tʃɪkɪn] n galinha; (food) galinha, frango; (inf: coward) covarde m/f, galinha.

chicken out (inf) vi agalinhar-se.

chicken feed n (fig) dinheiro miúdo.

chickenpox ['tʃɪkɪnpɔks] n catapora (BR), varicela (PT).

chickpea ['tʃɪkpiː] n grão-de-bico m.

chicory ['tʃɪkərɪ] n chicória.

chide [tʃaɪd] vt repreender, censurar.

chief [tʃiːf] n chefe m/f ♦ adj principal; **C~ of Staff** (MIL) chefe m do Estado-Maior.

chief constable (BRIT) n chefe m/f de polícia.

chief executive (US **chief executive officer**) n diretor(a) m/f geral.

chiefly ['tʃiːflɪ] adv principalmente.

chiffon ['ʃɪfɔn] n gaze f.

chilblain ['tʃɪlbleɪn] n frieira.

child [tʃaɪld] (pl ~ren) n criança; (offspring) filho/a.

childbirth ['tʃaɪldbəːθ] n parto.

childhood ['tʃaɪldhud] n infância.

childish ['tʃaɪldɪʃ] adj infantil, pueril.

childless ['tʃaɪldlɪs] adj sem filhos.

childlike ['tʃaɪldlaɪk] adj infantil, ingênuo.

childminder ['tʃaɪld'maɪndə*] (BRIT) n cuidadora de crianças.

children ['tʃɪldrən] npl of **child**.

Chile ['tʃɪlɪ] n Chile m.

Chilean ['tʃɪlɪən] adj, n chileno/a.

chili ['tʃɪlɪ] (US) n = **chilli**.

chill [tʃɪl] n frio; (MED) resfriamento ♦ vt esfriar; (CULIN) semi-congelar ♦ adj frio, glacial; **"serve ~ed"** "servir fresco".

chilli ['tʃɪlɪ] (US **chili**) n pimentão m picante.

chilly ['tʃɪlɪ] adj frio; (sensitive to cold) friorento; **to feel ~** estar com frio.

chime [tʃaɪm] n (peal) repique m, som m ♦ vi repicar, soar.

chimney ['tʃɪmnɪ] n chaminé f.

chimney sweep n limpador m de chaminés.

chimpanzee [tʃɪmpæn'ziː] n chimpanzé m.

chin [tʃɪn] n queixo.

China ['tʃaɪnə] n China f.

china ['tʃaɪnə] n porcelana; (crockery) louça fina.

Chinese [tʃaɪ'niːz] adj chinês/esa ♦ n inv chinês/esa m/f; (LING) chinês m.

chink [tʃɪŋk] n (opening) fresta, abertura; (noise) tinir m.

chip [tʃɪp] n (gen pl: BRIT: CULIN) batata frita; (: US: also: **potato ~**) batatinha frita; (of wood) lasca; (of glass, stone) lasca, pedaço;

(at poker) ficha; (also: ~micro~) chip m ♦ vt (cup, plate) lascar; **when the ~s are down** (fig) na hora H.

chip in (inf) vi interromper; (contribute) compartilhar as despesas.

chipboard ['tʃɪpbɔːd] n compensado.

chipmunk ['tʃɪpmʌŋk] n tâmia m.

chippings ['tʃɪpɪŋz] npl: **"loose ~"** "projeção de cascalho".

chiropodist [kɪ'rɔpədɪst] (BRIT) n pedicuro/a.

chiropody [kɪ'rɔpədɪ] (BRIT) n quiropodia.

chirp [tʃəːp] vi chilrar, piar; (cricket) chilrear ♦ n chilro.

chirpy ['tʃəːpɪ] adj alegre, animado.

chisel ['tʃɪzl] n (for wood) formão m; (for stone) cinzel m.

chit [tʃɪt] n talão m.

chitchat ['tʃɪttʃæt] n conversa fiada.

chivalrous ['ʃɪvəlrəs] adj cavalheiresco.

chivalry ['ʃɪvəlrɪ] n cavalaria.

chives [tʃaɪvz] npl cebolinha.

chloride ['klɔːraɪd] n cloreto.

chlorinate ['klɔrɪneɪt] vt clorar.

chlorine ['klɔːriːn] n cloro.

chock [tʃɔk] n cunha.

chock-a-block adj abarrotado, apinhado.

chock-full adj abarrotado, apinhado.

chocolate ['tʃɔklɪt] n chocolate m.

choice [tʃɔɪs] n escolha; (preference) preferência ♦ adj seleto, escolhido; **by or from ~** de preferência; **a wide ~** uma grande variedade.

choir ['kwaɪə*] n coro.

choirboy ['kwaɪəbɔɪ] n menino de coro.

choke [tʃəuk] vi sufocar-se; (on food) engasgar ♦ vt afogar, sufocar; (block) obstruir ♦ n (AUT) afogador m (BR), ar m (PT).

choker ['tʃəukə*] n (necklace) colar m curto.

cholera ['kɔlərə] n cólera m.

cholesterol [kə'lestərɔl] n colesterol m.

choose [tʃuːz] (pt **chose**, pp **chosen**) vt escolher ♦ vi: **to ~ between** escolher entre; **to ~ to do** optar por fazer.

choosy ['tʃuːzɪ] adj exigente.

chop [tʃɔp] vt (wood) cortar, talhar; (CULIN: also: ~ **up**) cortar em pedaços; (meat) picar ♦ n golpe m; (CULIN) costeleta; **~s** npl (jaws) beiços mpl; **to get the ~** (BRIT: inf: project) ser cancelado; (: person: be sacked) ser posto na rua.

chop down vt (tree) abater, derrubar.

chopper ['tʃɔpə*] n (helicopter) helicóptero.

choppy ['tʃɔpɪ] adj (sea) agitado.

chopsticks ['tʃɔpstɪks] npl pauzinhos mpl, palitos mpl.

choral ['kɔːrəl] adj coral.

chord [kɔːd] n (MUS) acorde m.

chore [tʃɔː*] n tarefa; (routine task) trabalho de rotina; **household ~s** afazeres mpl domésticos.

choreographer [kɔrɪ'ɔɡrəfə*] n coreógrafo/a.

chorister ['kɔrɪstə*] n corista m/f.

chortle ['tʃɔːtl] vi rir, gargalhar.

chorus ['kɔːrəs] n coro; (repeated part of song) estribilho.

chose [tʃəuz] *pt of* **choose**.
chosen ['tʃəuzn] *pp of* **choose**.
chow [tʃau] *n* (*dog*) chow *m* (*raça de cão*).
chowder ['tʃaudə*] *n* sopa (de peixe).
Christ [kraɪst] *n* Cristo.
christen ['krɪsn] *vt* batizar.
christening ['krɪsnɪŋ] *n* batismo.
Christian ['krɪstɪən] *adj, n* cristão/tã *m/f*.
Christianity [krɪstɪ'ænɪtɪ] *n* cristianismo.
Christian name *n* prenome *m*, nome *m* de batismo.
Christmas ['krɪsməs] *n* Natal *m*; **happy** *or* **merry** ~! Feliz Natal!
Christmas card *n* cartão *m* de Natal.
Christmas Day *n* dia *m* de Natal.
Christmas Eve *n* véspera de Natal.
Christmas Island *n* ilha de Christmas.
Christmas tree *n* árvore *f* de Natal.
chrome [krəum] *n* cromo.
chromium ['krəumɪəm] *n* cromo.
chromosome ['krəuməsəum] *n* cromossomo.
chronic ['krɒnɪk] *adj* crônico; (*fig: smoker, liar*) inveterado.
chronicle ['krɒnɪkl] *n* crônica.
chronological [krɒnə'lɒdʒɪkəl] *adj* cronológico.
chrysanthemum [krɪ'sænθəməm] *n* crisântemo.
chubby ['tʃʌbɪ] *adj* roliço, gorducho.
chuck [tʃʌk] *vt* jogar (*BR*), deitar (*PT*); **to** ~ **(up** *or* **in)** (*BRIT: job*) largar; (: *person*) acabar com.
chuck out *vt* (*thing*) jogar (*BR*) *or* deitar (*PT*) fora; (*person*) expulsar.
chuckle ['tʃʌkl] *vi* rir.
chug [tʃʌg] *vi* andar fazendo ruído da descarga.
chug along *vi* (*fig*) ir indo.
chum [tʃʌm] *n* camarada *m/f*.
chump [tʃʌmp] (*inf*) *n* imbecil *m/f*, boboca *m/f*.
chunk [tʃʌŋk] *n* pedaço, naco.
chunky ['tʃʌŋkɪ] *adj* (*furniture*) pesado; (*person*) atarracado; (*knitwear*) grosso.
church [tʃəːtʃ] *n* igreja; **the C~ of England** a Igreja Anglicana.
churchyard ['tʃəːtʃjɑːd] *n* adro, cemitério.
churlish ['tʃəːlɪʃ] *adj* grosseiro, rude.
churn [tʃəːn] *n* (*for butter*) batedeira; (*for milk*) lata, vasilha ♦ *vt* bater, agitar.
churn out *vt* produzir em série.
chute [ʃuːt] *n* rampa; (*also: rubbish* ~) despejador *m*.
chutney ['tʃʌtnɪ] *n* conserva picante.
CIA (*US*) *n abbr* (= *Central Intelligence Agency*) CIA *f*.
CID (*BRIT*) *n abbr* = **Criminal Investigation Department**.
cider ['saɪdə*] *n* sidra.
CIF *abbr* (= *cost, insurance and freight*) CIF.
cigar [sɪ'gɑː*] *n* charuto.
cigarette [sɪgə'rɛt] *n* cigarro.
cigarette case *n* cigarreira.

cigarette end *n* ponta de cigarro, guimba (*BR*).
cigarette holder *n* piteira (*BR*), boquilha (*PT*).
C-in-C *abbr* = **commander-in-chief**.
cinch [sɪntʃ] (*inf*) *n*: **it's a** ~ é sopa, é moleza.
cinder ['sɪndə*] *n* cinza.
Cinderella [sɪndə'rɛlə] *n* Gata Borralheira.
cine-camera ['sɪnɪ-] (*BRIT*) *n* câmera (cinematográfica).
cine-film ['sɪnɪ-] (*BRIT*) *n* filme *m* cinematográfico.
cinema ['sɪnəmə] *n* cinema *m*.
cine-projector ['sɪnɪ-] (*BRIT*) *n* projetor *m* cinematográfico.
cinnamon ['sɪnəmən] *n* canela.
cipher ['saɪfə*] *n* cifra; **in** ~ cifrado.
circa ['səːkə] *prep* cerca de.
circle ['səːkl] *n* círculo; (*in cinema*) balcão *m* ♦ *vi* dar voltas ♦ *vt* (*surround*) rodear, cercar; (*move round*) dar a volta de.
circuit ['səːkɪt] *n* circuito; (*tour, lap*) volta; (*track*) pista.
circuit board *n* placa.
circuitous [səː'kjuɪtəs] *adj* tortuoso, indireto.
circular ['səːkjulə*] *adj* circular ♦ *n* circular *f*.
circulate ['səːkjuleɪt] *vi* circular ♦ *vt* pôr em circulação, espalhar.
circulation [səːkju'leɪʃən] *n* circulação *f*; (*of newspaper*) tiragem *f*.
circumcise ['səːkəmsaɪz] *vt* circuncidar.
circumference [sə'kʌmfərəns] *n* circunferência.
circumflex ['səːkəmflɛks] *n* (*also:* ~ *accent*) (acento) circunflexo.
circumscribe ['səːkəmskraɪb] *vt* circunscrever.
circumspect ['səːkəmspɛkt] *adj* circunspeto, prudente.
circumstances ['səːkəmstənsɪz] *npl* circunstâncias *fpl*; (*financial condition*) situação *f* econômica; **in the** ~ em tais circunstâncias, assim sendo, neste caso; **under no** ~ de modo algum, de jeito nenhum.
circumstantial [səːkəm'stænʃl] *adj* (*report*) circunstanciado; ~ **evidence** prova circunstancial.
circumvent [səːkəm'vɛnt] *vt* (*rule etc*) driblar, burlar.
circus ['səːkəs] *n* circo; (*also: C~: in place names*) praça.
cistern ['sɪstən] *n* tanque *m*, reservatório; (*in toilet*) caixa d'água.
citation [saɪ'teɪʃən] *n* (*commendation*) menção *f*; (*US: LAW*) intimação *f*; (*quotation*) citação *f*.
cite [saɪt] *vt* citar.
citizen ['sɪtɪzn] *n* (*POL*) cidadão/dã *m/f*; (*resident*) habitante *m/f*.
citizenship ['sɪtɪznʃɪp] *n* cidadania.
citric acid ['sɪtrɪk-] *n* ácido cítrico.
citrus fruit ['sɪtrəs-] *n* citrino.

NB: European Portuguese adds the following consonants to certain words: **b** (sú(b)dito, su(b)til); **c** (a(c)ção, a(c)cionista, a(c)to); **m** (inde(m)ne); **p** (ado(p)ção, ado(p)tar); *for further details see p. xiii.*

city ['sɪtɪ] n cidade f; **the C~** centro financeiro de Londres.

city centre n centro (da cidade).

civic ['sɪvɪk] adj cívico, municipal.

civic centre (BRIT) n sede f do município.

civil ['sɪvɪl] adj civil; (polite) delicado, cortês.

civil disobedience n resistência passiva.

civil engineer n engenheiro/a civil.

civil engineering n engenharia civil.

civilian [sɪ'vɪlɪən] adj, n civil m/f, paisano/a.

civilization [sɪvɪlaɪ'zeɪʃən] n civilização f.

civilized ['sɪvɪlaɪzd] adj civilizado.

civil law n direito civil.

civil rights npl direitos mpl civis.

civil servant n funcionário/a público/a.

Civil Service n administração f pública.

civil war n guerra civil.

cl abbr (= centilitre) cl.

clad [klæd] adj: ~ **(in)** vestido (de).

claim [kleɪm] vt exigir, reclamar; (rights etc) reivindicar; (assert) afirmar, alegar ♦ vi (for insurance) reclamar ♦ n reclamação f; (LAW) direito; (pretension) pretensão f; (wage ~ etc) reivindicação f; **(insurance)** ~ reclamação f; **to put in a** ~ **for** (pay rise etc) reivindicar.

claimant ['kleɪmənt] n (ADMIN, LAW) requerente m/f.

claim form n formulário de requerimento; (INSURANCE) formulário para reclamações.

clairvoyant [klɛə'vɔɪənt] n clarividente m/f.

clam [klæm] n molusco.

clam up (inf) vi ficar calado.

clamber ['klæmbə*] vi subir.

clammy ['klæmɪ] adj (cold) frio e úmido; (sticky) pegajoso.

clamour ['klæmə*] (US clamor) n clamor m ♦ vi: **to** ~ **for sth** clamar algo.

clamp [klæmp] n grampo ♦ vt segurar.

clamp down on vt fus suprimir, proibir.

clan [klæn] n clã m.

clandestine [klæn'dɛstɪn] adj clandestino.

clang [klæŋ] n retintim m, som metálico ♦ vi retinir.

clansman ['klænzmən] (irreg) n membro de um clã escocês.

clap [klæp] vi bater palmas, aplaudir ♦ vt (performer) aplaudir ♦ n (of hands) palmas fpl; **to** ~ **one's hands** bater palmas; **a** ~ **of thunder** uma trovoada.

clapping ['klæpɪŋ] n aplausos mpl, palmas fpl.

claret ['klærət] n clarete m.

clarification [klærɪfɪ'keɪʃən] n esclarecimento.

clarify ['klærɪfaɪ] vt esclarecer, aclarar.

clarinet [klærɪ'nɛt] n clarinete m.

clarity ['klærɪtɪ] n claridade f.

clash [klæʃ] n (of metal) estridor m; (with police, fig) choque m ♦ vi (fight) chocar-se; (disagree) entrar em conflito, ter uma desavença; (colours) não combinar; (dates, events) coincidir.

clasp [klɑːsp] n fecho ♦ vt afivelar; (hand) apertar; (embrace) abraçar.

class [klɑːs] n classe f; (lesson) aula ♦ cpd de classe ♦ vt classificar.

class-conscious adj que tem consciência de classe.

class consciousness n consciência de classe.

classic ['klæsɪk] adj clássico ♦ n (author, work, race etc) clássico; ~**s** npl (SCH) línguas fpl clássicas.

classical ['klæsɪkl] adj clássico.

classification [klæsɪfɪ'keɪʃən] n classificação f.

classified ['klæsɪfaɪd] adj (information) secreto; ~ **ads** classificados mpl.

classify ['klæsɪfaɪ] vt classificar.

classmate ['klæsmeɪt] n colega m/f de aula.

classroom ['klæsrum] n sala de aula.

classy ['klɑːsɪ] (inf) adj (person) classudo; (flat, clothes) chique, incrementado.

clatter ['klætə*] n ruído, estrépito ♦ vi fazer barulho or ruído.

clause [klɔːz] n cláusula; (LING) oração f.

claustrophobia [klɔːstrə'fəubɪə] n claustrofobia.

claw [klɔː] n (of cat) pata, unha; (of bird of prey) garra; (of lobster) pinça; (TECH) unha ♦ vt arranhar.

claw at vt fus arranhar; (tear) rasgar.

clay [kleɪ] n argila.

clean [kliːn] adj limpo; (clear) nítido, bem definido ♦ vt limpar ♦ adv: **he** ~ **forgot** ele esqueceu completamente; **to come** ~ (inf: own up) abrir o jogo; **to** ~ **one's teeth** (BRIT) escovar os dentes; ~ **driving licence** (BRIT), ~ **record** (US) carteira de motorista sem infrações.

clean off vt tirar.

clean out vt limpar.

clean up vt limpar, assear ♦ vi (fig: make profit): **to** ~ **up on** faturar com, lucrar com.

clean-cut adj (person) alinhado.

cleaner ['kliːnə*] n (person) faxineiro/a; (also: dry ~) tintureiro/a; (product) limpador m.

cleaning ['kliːnɪŋ] n limpeza.

cleaning lady n faxineira.

cleanliness ['klɛnlɪnɪs] n limpeza.

cleanly ['kliːnlɪ] adv perfeitamente; (without mess) limpamente.

cleanse [klɛnz] vt limpar; (fig) purificar.

cleanser ['klɛnzə*] n limpador m; (for face) creme m de limpeza.

clean-shaven [-'ʃeɪvn] adj sem barba, de cara raspada.

cleansing department ['klɛnzɪŋ-] (BRIT) n departamento de limpeza.

clean-up n limpeza geral.

clear [klɪə*] adj claro; (road, way) limpo, livre; (profit) líquido; (majority) absoluto ♦ vt (space) abrir; (desk etc) limpar; (room) esvaziar; (LAW: suspect) absolver; (obstacle) salvar, passar sobre; (debt) liquidar; (woodland) desmatar; (cheque) compensar; (COMM: goods) liquidar ♦ vi (weather) abrir, clarear; (fog etc) dissipar-se ♦ adv: ~ **of** a salvo de ♦ n: **to be in the** ~ (out of debt) estar sem dívidas; (out of suspicion) estar livre de suspeita; (out of danger) estar fora de perigo; **to** ~ **the table** tirar a mesa; **to** ~

one's throat pigarrear; **to ~ a profit** fazer um lucro líquido; **let me make myself ~** deixe-me explicar melhor; **do I make myself ~?** entendeu?; **to make o.s. ~** fazer-se entender bem; **to make it ~ to sb that ...** deixar bem claro para alguém que; **I have a ~ day tomorrow** (BRIT) não tenho compromisso amanhã; **to keep ~ of sb/sth** evitar alguém/algo.

clear off (inf) vi (leave) cair fora.

clear up vt limpar; (mystery) resolver, esclarecer.

clearance ['klɪərəns] n (removal) despejo; (permission) permissão f.

clearance sale n (COMM) liquidação f.

clear-cut adj bem definido, nítido.

clearing ['klɪərɪŋ] n (in wood) clareira; (BRIT: BANKING) compensação f.

clearing bank (BRIT) n câmara de compensação.

clearly ['klɪəlɪ] adv claramente.

clearway ['klɪəweɪ] (BRIT) n estrada onde não se pode estacionar.

cleavage ['kliːvɪdʒ] n (of dress) decote m; (of woman) colo.

cleaver ['kliːvə] n cutelo (de açougueiro).

clef [klɛf] n (MUS) clave f.

cleft [klɛft] n (in rock) fissura.

clemency ['klɛmənsɪ] n clemência.

clement ['klɛmənt] adj (weather) ameno.

clench [klɛntʃ] vt apertar, cerrar.

clergy ['klɜːdʒɪ] n clero.

clergyman ['klɜːdʒɪmən] (irreg) n clérigo, pastor m.

clerical ['klɛrɪkəl] adj de escritório; (REL) clerical.

clerk [klɑːk, (US) klɜːrk] n auxiliar m/f de escritório; (US: salesman/woman) balconista m/f; **C~ of Court** (LAW) escrivão/vã m/f (do tribunal).

clever ['klɛvə] adj (mentally) inteligente; (deft, crafty) hábil; (device, arrangement) engenhoso.

clew [kluː] (US) n = **clue**.

cliché ['kliːʃeɪ] n clichê m, frase f feita.

click [klɪk] vt (tongue) estalar; (heels) bater ♦ vi estalar.

client ['klaɪənt] n cliente m/f.

clientele [kliːɑːn'tɛl] n clientela.

cliff [klɪf] n penhasco.

cliffhanger ['klɪfhæŋə] n (TV, fig) história de suspense.

climactic [klaɪ'mæktɪk] adj culminante.

climate ['klaɪmɪt] n clima m.

climax ['klaɪmæks] n clímax m, ponto culminante; (sexual) clímax.

climb [klaɪm] vi subir, trepar; (plane) ganhar altitude ♦ vt (stairs) subir; (tree) trepar em; (hill) escalar ♦ n subida; **to ~ over a wall** passar por cima de um muro.

climb down vi descer; (BRIT: fig) recuar, ceder.

climbdown ['klaɪmdaun] (BRIT) n recuo.

climber ['klaɪmə] n alpinista m/f.

climbing ['klaɪmɪŋ] n alpinismo.

clinch [klɪntʃ] vt (deal) fechar; (argument) decidir, resolver.

cling [klɪŋ] (pt, pp clung) vi: **to ~ to** pegar-se a, aderir a; (hold on to: object, idea) agarrar-se a; (clothes) ajustar-se a.

clinic ['klɪnɪk] n clínica; (consultation) consulta.

clinical ['klɪnɪkl] adj clínico; (fig) frio, impessoal.

clink [klɪŋk] vi tinir.

clip [klɪp] n (for hair) grampo (BR), gancho (PT); (also: paper ~) mola, clipe m; (on necklace etc) fecho; (AUT: holding hose etc) braçadeira ♦ vt (cut) cortar; (shorten, trim) aparar; (also: ~ together: papers) grampear.

clippers ['klɪpəz] npl (for gardening) podadeira; (for hair) máquina; (for nails) alicate m de unhas.

clipping ['klɪpɪŋ] n recorte m.

clique [kliːk] n panelinha.

cloak [kləuk] n capa, manto ♦ vt (fig) encobrir.

cloakroom ['kləukrum] n vestiário; (BRIT: WC) sanitários mpl (BR), lavatórios mpl (PT).

clock [klɔk] n relógio; (in taxi) taxímetro; **round the ~** (work etc) dia e noite, ininterruptamente; **30,000 on the ~** (BRIT: AUT) 30,000 km rodados; **to work against the ~** trabalhar contra o tempo.

clock in (BRIT) vi assinar o ponto na entrada.

clock off (BRIT) vi assinar o ponto na saída.

clock on (BRIT) vi assinar o ponto na entrada.

clock out (BRIT) vi assinar o ponto na saída.

clock up vt (miles, hours etc) fazer.

clockwise ['klɔkwaɪz] adv em sentido horário.

clockwork ['klɔkwɜːk] n mecanismo de relógio ♦ adj de corda.

clog [klɔg] n tamanco ♦ vt entupir ♦ vi entupir-se, emperrar.

cloister ['klɔɪstə] n claustro.

clone [kləun] n clone m.

close [adj, adv kləus, vb, n kləuz] adj próximo; (print, weave) denso, compacto; (friend) íntimo; (connection) estreito; (examination) minucioso; (weather) abafado; (atmosphere) sufocante; (room) mal arejado ♦ adv perto ♦ vt (shut) fechar; (end) acabar, concluir ♦ vi (shop, door etc) fechar; (end) concluir-se, terminar-se ♦ n (end) fim m, conclusão f, terminação f; **~ by, ~ at hand** perto, pertinho; **how ~ is Edinburgh to Glasgow?** qual é a distância entre Edimburgo e Glasgow?; **to have a ~ shave** (fig) livrar-se por um triz; **at ~ quarters** de perto; **to bring sth to a ~** dar fim a algo.

NB: European Portuguese adds the following consonants to certain words: **b** (sú(b)dito, su(b)til); **c** (a(c)ção, a(c)cionista, a(c)to); **m** (inde(m)ne); **p** (ado(p)ção, ado(p)tar); *for further details see p. xiii.*

close down *vt*, *vi* fechar definitivamente.

close in *vi* (*hunters*) apertar o cerco; (*night*, *fog*) cair; **the days are closing in** os dias estão ficando mais curtos; **to ~ in on sb** aproximar-se de alguém, cercar alguém.

close off *vt* (*area*) isolar.

closed [kləuzd] *adj* (*shop etc*) fechado.

closed-circuit *adj*: **~ television** televisão *f* de circuito fechado.

closed shop *n* *estabelecimento industrial que só admite empregados sindicalizados.*

close-knit *adj* (*family*, *community*) muito unido.

closely ['kləuslı] *adv* (*exactly*) fielmente; (*carefully*) rigorosamente; (*watch*) de perto; **we are ~ related** somos parentes próximos; **a ~ guarded secret** um segredo bem guardado.

closet ['klɔzɪt] *n* (*cupboard*) armário; (*walk-in*) closet *m*.

close-up [kləus-] *n* close *m*, close-up *m*.

closing ['kləuzıŋ] *adj* (*stages*, *remarks*) final; **~ price** (*STOCK EXCHANGE*) cotação *f* de fechamento.

closing-down sale (*BRIT*) *n* liquidação *f* (por motivo de fechamento).

closure ['kləuʒə*] *n* (*close-down*) encerramento, fechamento.

clot [klɔt] *n* (*gen*: *blood* ~) coágulo; (*inf*: *idiot*) imbecil *m/f* ♦ *vi* (*blood*) coagular-se, coalhar-se.

cloth [klɔθ] *n* (*material*) tecido, fazenda; (*rag*) pano; (*also*: *table*~) toalha.

clothe [kləuð] *vt* vestir; (*fig*) revestir.

clothes [kləuðz] *npl* roupa; **to put one's ~ on** vestir-se; **to take one's ~ off** tirar a roupa.

clothes brush *n* escova (para a roupa).

clothes line *n* corda (para estender a roupa).

clothes peg (*US* **clothes pin**) *n* pregador *m*.

clothing ['kləuðıŋ] *n* vestuário.

clotted cream ['klɔtɪd-] (*BRIT*) *n* creme *m* coalhado.

cloud [klaud] *n* nuvem *f* ♦ *vt* (*liquid*) turvar; **to ~ the issue** confundir *or* complicar as coisas; **every ~ has a silver lining** (*proverb*) Deus escreve certo por linhas tortas.

cloud over *vi* (*also*: *fig*) fechar.

cloudburst ['klaudbə:st] *n* aguaceiro.

cloud-cuckoo-land (*BRIT*) *n*: **to live in ~** viver no mundo da lua.

cloudy ['klaudı] *adj* nublado; (*liquid*) turvo.

clout [klaut] *vt* dar uma bofetada em ♦ *n* (*blow*) bofetada; (*fig*) influência.

clove [kləuv] *n* cravo; **~ of garlic** dente *m* de alho.

clover ['kləuvə*] *n* trevo.

cloverleaf ['kləuvəli:f] (*irreg*) *n* (*AUT*) trevo rodoviário.

clown [klaun] *n* palhaço ♦ *vi* (*also*: **~ about**; **~ around**) fazer palhaçadas.

cloying ['klɔɪıŋ] *adj* (*taste*, *smell*) enjoativo, nauseabundo.

club [klʌb] *n* (*society*) clube *m*; (*weapon*) cacete *m*; (*also*: *golf* ~) taco ♦ *vt* esbordoar ♦ *vi*: **to ~ together** cotizar-se; **~s** *npl* (*CARDS*) paus *mpl*.

club car (*US*) *n* vagão-restaurante *m*.

clubhouse ['klʌbhaus] (*irreg*) *n* sede *f* do clube.

cluck [klʌk] *vi* cacarejar.

clue [klu:] *n* indício, pista; (*in crossword*) definição *f*; **I haven't a ~** não faço idéia.

clued in [klu:d-] (*US* **clued in**) (*inf*) *adj* entendido.

clueless ['klu:lıs] (*inf*) *adj* burro.

clump [klʌmp] *n* (*of trees*) grupo.

clumsy ['klʌmzı] *adj* (*person*) desajeitado; (*movement*) deselegante, mal-feito.

clung [klʌŋ] *pt*, *pp of* **cling**.

cluster ['klʌstə*] *n* grupo; (*BOT*) cacho, ramo ♦ *vi* agrupar-se, apinhar-se.

clutch [klʌtʃ] *n* (*grip*, *grasp*) garra; (*AUT*) embreagem *f* (*BR*), embraiagem *f* (*PT*); (*pedal*) pedal *m* de embreagem (*BR*) *or* embraiagem (*PT*) ♦ *vt* empunhar, pegar em ♦ *vi*: **to ~ at** agarrar-se a.

clutter ['klʌtə*] *vt* abarrotar, encher desordenadamente ♦ *n* bagunça, desordem *f*.

CM (*US*) *abbr* (*POST*) = **North Mariana Islands**.

cm *abbr* (= *centimetre*) cm.

CNAA (*BRIT*) *n abbr* (= *Council for National Academic Awards*) órgão não universitário que outorga diplomas.

CND *n abbr* = **Campaign for Nuclear Disarmament**.

CO *n abbr* (= *commanding officer*) Com.; (*BRIT*) = **Commonwealth Office** ♦ *abbr* (*US*: *POST*) = **Colorado**.

Co. *abbr* = **county**; (= *company*) Cia.

c/o *abbr* (= *care of*) a/c.

coach [kəutʃ] *n* (*bus*) ônibus *m* (*BR*), autocarro (*PT*); (*horse-drawn*) carruagem *f*, coche *m*; (*of train*) vagão *m*; (*SPORT*) treinador(a) *m/f*, instrutor(a) *m/f* ♦ *vt* (*SPORT*) treinar; (*student*) preparar, ensinar.

coach trip *n* passeio de ônibus (*BR*) *or* autocarro (*PT*).

coagulate [kəu'ægjuleıt] *vi* coagular-se ♦ *vt* coagular.

coal [kəul] *n* carvão *m*.

coal face *n* frente *f* de carvão.

coalfield ['kəulfi:ld] *n* região *f* carbonífera.

coalition [kəuə'lıʃən] *n* coalizão *f*, coligação *f*.

coalman ['kəulmæn] (*irreg*) *n* carvoeiro.

coal merchant *n* carvoeiro.

coalmine ['kəulmaın] *n* mina de carvão.

coal miner *n* mineiro de carvão.

coal mining *n* mineração *f* de carvão.

coarse [kɔ:s] *adj* grosso, áspero; (*vulgar*) grosseiro, ordinário.

coast [kəust] *n* costa, litoral *m* ♦ *vi* (*AUT*) ir em ponto morto.

coastal ['kəustəl] *adj* costeiro, litorâneo.

coaster ['kəustə*] *n* embarcação *f* costeira, barco de cabotagem; (*for glass*) descanso.

coastguard ['kəustgɑ:d] *n* guarda costeira.

coastline ['kəustlaın] *n* litoral *m*.

coat [kəut] *n* (*jacket*) casaco; (*overcoat*) sobretudo; (*of animal*) pelo; (*of paint*) demão *f*, camada ♦ *vt* cobrir, revestir.

coat hanger *n* cabide *m*.
coating ['kəutɪŋ] *n* camada, revestimento.
coat of arms *n* brasão *m*.
co-author [kəu-] *n* co-autor(a) *m/f*.
coax [kəuks] *vt* persuadir com meiguice.
cob [kɔb] *n see* corn.
cobbler ['kɔblə*] *n* sapateiro.
cobbles ['kɔblz] *npl* pedras *fpl* arredondadas.
cobblestones ['kɔblstəunz] *npl* pedras *fpl* arredondadas.
COBOL ['kəubɔl] *n* COBOL *m*.
cobra ['kəubrə] *n* naja.
cobweb ['kɔbwɛb] *n* teia de aranha.
cocaine [kɔ'keɪn] *n* cocaína.
cock [kɔk] *n* (*rooster*) galo; (*male bird*) macho ♦ *vt* (*gun*) engatilhar; to ~ one's ears (*fig*) prestar atenção.
cock-a-hoop *adj* exultante, eufórico.
cockatoo [kɔkə'tuː] *n* cacatua.
cockerel ['kɔkərəl] *n* frango, galo pequeno.
cock-eyed [-aɪd] *adj* (*crooked*) torto; (*fig*: *scheme*) absurdo.
cockle ['kɔkl] *n* berbigão *m*.
cockney ['kɔknɪ] *n* londrino/a (*nativo dos bairros populares do leste de Londres*).
cockpit ['kɔkpɪt] *n* (*in aircraft*) cabina.
cockroach ['kɔkrəutʃ] *n* barata.
cocktail ['kɔkteɪl] *n* coquetel (*PT*: cocktail) *m*; prawn (*BRIT*) *or* shrimp (*US*) ~ coquetel de camarão (*BR*), cocktail de gambas (*PT*).
cocktail cabinet *n* móvel-bar *m*.
cocktail party *n* coquetel (*PT*: cocktail) *m*.
cocktail shaker [-ʃeɪkə*] *n* coqueteleira.
cocoa ['kəukəu] *n* cacau *m*; (*drink*) chocolate *m*.
coconut ['kəukənʌt] *n* coco.
cocoon [kə'kuːn] *n* casulo.
COD *abbr* = cash (*BRIT*) *or* collect (*US*) on delivery.
cod [kɔd] *n inv* bacalhau *m*.
code [kəud] *n* código; ~ of behaviour código de comportamento; ~ of practice deontologia.
codeine ['kəudiːn] *n* codeína.
code name *n* codinome *m*.
codicil ['kɔdɪsɪl] *n* codicilo.
codify ['kəudɪfaɪ] *vt* codificar.
cod-liver oil *n* óleo de fígado de bacalhau.
co-driver [kəu-] *n* (*in race*) co-piloto; (*in lorry*) segundo motorista *m*.
co-ed ['kəu'ɛd] *adj abbr* = coeducational ♦ *n* (*US*: *female student*) aluna de escola mista; (*BRIT*: *school*) escola mista.
coeducational ['kəuɛdju'keɪʃənl] *adj* misto.
coerce [kəu'əːs] *vt* coagir.
coercion [kəu'əːʃən] *n* coerção *f*.
coexistence ['kəuɪg'zɪstəns] *n* coexistência.
C. of C. *n abbr* = chamber of commerce.
C of E *abbr* = Church of England.
coffee ['kɔfɪ] *n* café *m*; white ~ (*BRIT*) *or* ~ with cream (*US*) café com leite.
coffee bar (*BRIT*) *n* café *m*, lanchonete *f*.

coffee bean *n* grão *m* de café.
coffee break *n* hora do café.
coffeecake ['kɔfɪkeɪk] (*US*) *n* pão *m* doce com passas.
coffee cup *n* xícara (*BR*) *or* chávena (*PT*) de café.
coffee grounds *npl* borras *fpl* de café.
coffee plant *n* pé *m* de café.
coffee plantation *n* cafezal *m*.
coffeepot ['kɔfɪpɔt] *n* cafeteira.
coffee table *n* mesinha de centro.
coffin ['kɔfɪn] *n* caixão *m*.
C of I *abbr* = Church of Ireland.
C of S *abbr* = Church of Scotland.
cog [kɔg] *n* (*tooth*) dente *m*; (*wheel*) roda dentada.
cogent ['kəudʒənt] *adj* convincente.
cognac ['kɔnjæk] *n* conhaque *m*.
cogwheel ['kɔgwiːl] *n* roda dentada.
cohabit [kəu'hæbɪt] *vi* (*formal*): to ~ (with sb) coabitar (com alguém).
coherent [kəu'hɪərənt] *adj* coerente.
cohesion [kəu'hiːʒən] *n* coesão *f*.
cohesive [kəu'hiːsɪv] *adj* coeso.
COHSE ['kəuzi] (*BRIT*) *n abbr* (= *Confederation of Health Service Employees*) sindicato dos empregados do serviço de saúde.
COI (*BRIT*) *n abbr* (= *Central Office of Information*) serviço de informação governamental.
coil [kɔɪl] *n* rolo; (*rope*) corda enrolada; (*of smoke*) espiral *f*; (*ELEC*) bobina; (*contraceptive*) DIU *m* ♦ *vt* enrolar, enroscar ♦ *vi* enrolar-se, espiralar-se.
coin [kɔɪn] *n* moeda ♦ *vt* (*word*) cunhar, criar.
coinage ['kɔɪnɪdʒ] *n* moeda, sistema *m* monetário.
coin-box (*BRIT*) *n* telefone *m* público.
coincide [kəuɪn'saɪd] *vi* coincidir.
coincidence [kəu'ɪnsɪdəns] *n* coincidência.
coin-operated [-'ɔpəreɪtɪd] *adj* (*machine, laundry*) automático, que funciona com moedas.
Coke [kəuk] ® *n* (*drink*) coca.
coke [kəuk] *n* (*coal*) coque *m*.
Col. *abbr* (= *colonel*) Cel.
COLA (*US*) *n abbr* (= *cost-of-living adjustment*) ≈ URP *f*.
colander ['kɔləndə*] *n* coador *m*, passador *m*.
cold [kəuld] *adj* frio ♦ *n* frio; (*MED*) resfriado (*BR*), constipação *f* (*PT*); it's ~ está frio; to be ~ estar com frio; to catch ~ resfriar-se (*BR*), apanhar constipação (*PT*); in ~ blood a sangue frio; to have ~ feet (*fig*) estar com medo; to give sb the ~ shoulder tratar alguém com frieza, dar uma fria em alguém (*inf*).
cold-blooded [-'blʌdɪd] *adj* (*ZOOL*) de sangue frio; (*murder*) a sangue frio.
cold cream *n* creme *m* de limpeza.
coldly ['kəuldlɪ] *adv* friamente.
cold sore *n* herpes *m* labial.

NB: European Portuguese adds the following consonants to certain words: **b** (sú(b)dito, su(b)til); **c** (a(c)ção, a(c)cionista, a(c)to); **m** (inde(m)ne); **p** (ado(p)ção, ado(p)tar); *for further details see p. xiii.*

coleslaw ['kəulslɔ:] *n* salada de repolho cru.

colic ['kɔlık] *n* cólica.

collaborate [kə'læbəreıt] *vi* colaborar.

collaboration [kəlæbə'reıʃən] *n* colaboração *f*.

collaborator [kə'læbəreıtə*] *n* colaborador(a) *m/f*.

collage [kɔ'lɑ:ʒ] *n* colagem *f*.

collagen ['kɔlədʒən] *n* colágeno.

collapse [kə'læps] *vi* cair, tombar; (*roof*) dar de si, desabar; (*building*) desabar; (*MED*) desmaiar ♦ *n* desabamento, desmoronamento; (*of government*) queda; (*MED*) colapso.

collapsible [kə'læpsəbl] *adj* dobrável.

collar ['kɔlə*] *n* (*of shirt*) colarinho; (*of coat etc*) gola; (*for dog*) coleira; (*TECH*) aro, colar *m* ♦ *vt* (*inf: person*) prender.

collarbone ['kɔləbəun] *n* clavícula.

collate [kɔ'leıt] *vt* cotejar.

collateral [kɔ'lætrəl] *n* garantia subsidiária *or* pignoratícia.

collation [kə'leıʃən] *n* colação *f*.

colleague ['kɔli:g] *n* colega *m/f*.

collect [kə'lɛkt] *vt* reunir; (*as a hobby*) colecionar; (*pick up*) recolher; (*wages, debts*) cobrar; (*donations, subscriptions*) colher; (*mail*) coletar; (*BRIT: call for*) (ir) buscar ♦ *vi* (*people*) reunir-se; (*dust, dirt*) acumular-se ♦ *adv*: **to call ~** (*US: TEL*) ligar a cobrar; **to ~ one's thoughts** refletir; **~ on delivery** (*US: COMM*) pagamento na entrega.

collected [kə'lɛktıd] *adj*: **~ works** obra completa.

collection [kə'lɛkʃən] *n* coleção *f*; (*of people*) reunião *f*, grupo; (*of donations*) arrecadação *f*; (*of post, in church*) coleta; (*of writings*) coletânea.

collective [kə'lɛktıv] *adj* coletivo.

collective bargaining *n* negociação *f* coletiva.

collector [kə'lɛktə*] *n* colecionador(a) *m/f*; (*of taxes etc*) cobrador(a) *m/f*; **~'s item** *or* **piece** peça de coleção.

college ['kɔlıdʒ] *n* colégio; (*faculty*) faculdade *f*; (*of technology, agriculture*) instituto, escola; **to go to ~** fazer faculdade; **~ of education** ≈ faculdade *f* de educação.

collide [kə'laıd] *vi*: **to ~ (with)** colidir (com).

collie ['kɔlı] *n* collie *m*.

colliery ['kɔlıərı] (*BRIT*) *n* mina de carvão.

collision [kə'lıʒən] *n* choque *m*; **to be on a ~ course** estar em curso de colisão.

colloquial [kə'ləukwıəl] *adj* familiar, coloquial.

collusion [kə'lu:ʒən] *n* colusão *f*, conluio; **in ~ with** em conluio com.

cologne [kə'ləun] *n* (*also: eau-de-~*) (água de) colônia.

Colombia [kə'lɔmbıə] *n* Colômbia.

Colombian [kə'lɔmbıən] *adj*, *n* colombiano/a.

colon ['kəulən] *n* (*sign*) dois pontos; (*MED*) cólon *m*.

colonel ['kɔ:nl] *n* coronel *m*.

colonial [kə'ləunıəl] *adj* colonial.

colonize ['kɔlənaız] *vt* colonizar.

colony ['kɔlənı] *n* colônia.

color *etc* ['kʌlə*] (*US*) = **colour** *etc*.

Colorado beetle [kɔlə'rɑ:dəu-] *n* besouro da batata, dorífora.

colossal [kə'lɔsl] *adj* colossal.

colour ['kʌlə*] (*US* **color**) *n* cor *f* ♦ *vt* colorir; (*with crayons*) colorir, pintar; (*dye*) tingir; (*news*) falsear ♦ *vi* (*blush*) corar ♦ *cpd* (*photograph etc*) a cores; **~s** *npl* (*of party, club*) cores *fpl*.

colo(u)r bar *n* discriminação *f* racial.

colo(u)r-blind ['kʌləblaınd] *adj* daltônico.

colo(u)red ['kʌləd] *adj* colorido; (*person*) de cor.

colo(u)reds ['kʌlədz] *npl* gente *f* de cor.

colo(u)r film *n* filme *m* a cores.

colo(u)rful ['kʌləful] *adj* colorido; (*personality*) vivo, animado.

colo(u)ring ['kʌlərıŋ] *n* colorido; (*complexion*) tez *f*.

colo(u)rless ['kʌləlıs] *adj* sem cor, pálido.

colo(u)r scheme *n* distribuição *f* de cores.

colour supplement (*BRIT*) *n* (*PRESS*) revista, suplemento a cores.

colo(u)r television *n* televisão *f* a cores.

colt [kəult] *n* potro.

column ['kɔləm] *n* coluna; **the editorial ~** o editorial.

columnist ['kɔləmnıst] *n* cronista *m/f*.

coma ['kəumə] *n* coma *m*.

comb [kəum] *n* pente *m*; (*of cock*) crista ♦ *vt* (*hair*) pentear; (*area*) vasculhar.

combat ['kɔmbæt] *n* combate *m* ♦ *vt* combater.

combination [kɔmbı'neıʃən] *n* combinação *f*; (*of safe*) segredo.

combination lock *n* fechadura de combinação.

combine [*vt*, *vi* kəm'baın, *n* 'kɔmbaın] *vt* combinar; (*qualities*) reunir ♦ *vi* combinar-se ♦ *n* (*ECON*) associação *f*; (*pej*) monopólio; **a ~d effort** um esforço conjunto.

combine (harvester) *n* ceifeira debulhadora.

combo ['kɔmbəu] *n* (*JAZZ etc*) conjunto.

combustible [kəm'bʌstıbl] *adj* combustível.

combustion [kəm'bʌstʃən] *n* combustão *f*.

come [kʌm] (*pt* **came**, *pp* **come**) *vi* vir; (*inf: sexually*) gozar; **he is coming with us to Paris** ele vai a Paris com a gente; **... what might ~ of it** ... o que poderia resultar disso; **to ~ into sight** *or* **view** aparecer; **to ~ to** (*conclusion etc*) chegar a; **to ~ undone/ loose** desfazer-se/soltar-se; **coming!** já vou!; **it if ~s to it** em último caso.

come about *vi* suceder, acontecer.

come across *vt fus* (*person*) topar com; (*thing*) encontrar ♦ *vi*: **to ~ across well/ badly** fazer uma boa/má impressão.

come along *vi* (*pupil, work*) ir bem; **~ along!** vem!

come apart *vi* desfazer-se.

come away *vi* ir-se embora; (*become detached*) desprender-se, soltar-se.

come back *vi* voltar; (*reply*): **can I ~ back to you on that one?** posso lhe dar uma resposta sobre isso mais tarde?

come by *vt fus* (*acquire*) conseguir.

come down *vi* descer; (*prices*) baixar; (*crash*) desabar; (*buildings*) desmoronar-se; (: *be demolished*) ser derrubado.

come forward *vi* apresentar-se; (*move forward*) avançar.

come from *vt fus* vir de; (*place: subj: person*) ser de; (: *thing*) originar-se de.

come in *vi* entrar; (*train*) chegar; (*fashion*) entrar na moda.

come in for *vt fus* (*criticism etc*) merecer.

come into *vt fus* (*money*) herdar.

come off *vi* (*button*) desprender-se, soltar-se; (*attempt*) dar certo.

come on *vi* (*pupil, undertaking*) avançar, fazer progressos; (*lights, heating*) ser ligado ♦ *vt fus* (*find*) encontrar; ~ **on!** vamos!, vai!

come out *vi* sair; (*book*) ser publicado; (*be revealed*) revelar-se; (*strike*) entrar em greve; **to** ~ **out for/against** declarar-se por/contra.

come over *vt fus*: **I don't know what's** ~ **over him!** eu não sei o que deu nele.

come round *vi* (*after faint etc*) voltar a si.

come through *vi* (*survive*) sobreviver; (*telephone call*) ser completado.

come to *vi* voltar a si ♦ *vt fus* (*total*) somar.

come under *vt fus* (*heading*) incluir-se em, estar sob; (*influence*) estar sujeito a.

come up *vi* subir; (*sun*) nascer; (*problem*) surgir.

come up against *vt fus* (*resistance, difficulties*) tropeçar com, esbarrar em.

come up to *vt fus* alcançar; (*expectations*) corresponder a.

come up with *vt fus* (*idea*) propor, sugerir.

come upon *vt fus* encontrar, achar.

comeback ['kʌmbæk] *n* (*THEATRE*) reaparição *f*; (*reaction*) reação *f*; (*response*) resposta.

Comecon ['kɔmɪkɔn] *n abbr* (= *Council for Mutual Economic Aid*) COMECON *m*.

comedian [kə'miːdɪən] *n* cômico, humorista *m*.

comedienne [kəmi:dɪ'ɛn] *n* cômica, humorista.

comedown ['kʌmdaun] (*inf*) *n* revés *m*, humilhação *f*.

comedy ['kɔmɪdɪ] *n* comédia.

comet ['kɔmɪt] *n* cometa *m*.

comeuppance [kʌm'ʌpəns] *n*: **to get one's** ~ **(for sth)** pagar (por algo).

comfort ['kʌmfət] *n* comodidade *f*, conforto; (*well-being*) bem-estar *m*; (*solace*) consolo; (*relief*) alívio ♦ *vt* consolar, confortar; ~s *npl* conforto.

comfortable ['kʌmfətəbl] *adj* confortável; **I don't feel very** ~ **about it** não estou completamente conformado com isso.

comfortably ['kʌmfətəblɪ] *adv* confortavelmente.

comforter ['kʌmfətə*] (*US*) *n* edredom (*PT*: -dão) *m*.

comfort station (*US*) *n* banheiro (*BR*), lavatórios *mpl* (*PT*).

comic ['kɔmɪk] *adj* cômico ♦ *n* (*person*) cômico/a, humorista *m/f*; (*magazine*) revista em quadrinhos (*BR*), revista de banda desenhada (*PT*), gibi *m* (*BR: inf*).

comical ['kɔmɪkl] *adj* engraçado, cômico.

comic strip *n* história em quadrinhos (*BR*), banda desenhada (*PT*).

coming ['kʌmɪŋ] *n* vinda, chegada ♦ *adj* que vem, vindouro; ~**(s) and going(s)** *n*(*pl*) vaivém *m*, azáfama; **in the** ~ **weeks** nas próximas semanas.

Comintern ['kɔmɪntɜːn] *n* Comintern *m*.

comma ['kɔmə] *n* vírgula.

command [kə'mɑːnd] *n* ordem *f*, mandado; (*MIL: authority*) comando; (*mastery*) domínio; (*COMPUT*) comando ♦ *vt* (*troops*) mandar; (*give orders to*) mandar, ordenar; (*dispose of*) dispor de; (*deserve*) merecer; **to** ~ **sb to do** mandar alguém fazer; **to have/take** ~ **of** ter/assumir o controle de; **to have at one's** ~ (*money, resources etc*) dispor de.

commandeer [kɔmən'dɪə*] *vt* requisitar.

commander [kə'mɑːndə*] *n* (*MIL*) comandante *m/f*.

commander-in-chief *n* (*MIL*) comandante-em-chefe *m/f*, comandante-chefe *m/f*.

commanding [kə'mɑːndɪŋ] *adj* (*appearance*) imponente; (*voice, tone*) autoritário, imperioso; (*lead, position*) dominante.

commanding officer *n* comandante *m/f*.

commandment [kə'mɑːndmənt] *n* (*REL*) mandamento.

command module *n* (*SPACE*) módulo de comando.

commando [kə'mɑːndəu] *n* comando.

commemorate [kə'mɛməreɪt] *vt* comemorar.

commemoration [kəmɛmə'reɪʃən] *n* comemoração *f*.

commemorative [kə'mɛmərətɪv] *adj* comemorativo.

commence [kə'mɛns] *vt, vi* começar, iniciar.

commend [kə'mɛnd] *vt* (*praise*) elogiar, louvar; (*recommend*) recomendar; (*entrust*) encomendar.

commendable [kə'mɛndəbl] *adj* louvável.

commendation [kɔmɛn'deɪʃən] *n* elogio, louvor *m*.

commensurate [kə'mɛnʃərɪt] *adj*: ~ **with** compatível com.

comment ['kɔmɛnt] *n* comentário ♦ *vi* fazer comentários, comentar; **to** ~ **on sth** comentar algo; **to** ~ **that** observar que; **"no** ~**"** "sem comentário".

commentary ['kɔməntərɪ] *n* comentário.

commentator ['kɔməntɛɪtə*] *n* comentarista *m/f*.

commerce ['kɔmə:s] *n* comércio.

commercial [kə'mə:ʃəl] *adj* comercial ♦ *n*

anúncio, comercial *m*; ~ **break** intervalo para os comerciais.
commercial bank *n* banco comercial.
commercial college *n* escola de comércio.
commercialism [kə'mə:ʃəlɪzəm] *n* mercantilismo.
commercialize [kə'mə:ʃəlaɪz] *vt* comercializar.
commercial television *n* televisão *f* comercial.
commercial traveller *n* caixeiro/a-viajante *m/f*.
commercial vehicle *n* (veículo) utilitário.
commiserate [kə'mɪzəreɪt] *vi*: **to** ~ **with** comiserar-se de, condoer-se de.
commission [kə'mɪʃən] *n* (*body*, *fee*) comissão *f*; (*act*) incumbência; (*order for work of art etc*) empreitada, encomenda ♦ *vt* (*MIL*) dar patente oficial a; (*work of art*) encomendar; (*artist*) incumbir; **out of** ~ (*NAUT*) fora do serviço ativo; (*machine*) com defeito; **to** ~ **sb to do sth** mandar alguém fazer algo; **to** ~ **sth from sb** encomendar algo a alguém; ~ **of inquiry** (*BRIT*) comissão de inquérito.
commissionaire [kəmɪʃə'nɛə*] (*BRIT*) *n* porteiro.
commissioner [kə'mɪʃənə*] *n* comissário/a.
commit [kə'mɪt] *vt* (*act*) cometer; (*to sb's care*) entregar; **to** ~ **o.s. (to do)** comprometer-se (a fazer); **to** ~ **suicide** suicidar-se; **to** ~ **to writing** pôr por escrito, pôr no papel; **to** ~ **sb for trial** levar alguém a julgamento.
commitment [kə'mɪtmənt] *n* (*obligation*) compromisso; (*political etc*) engajamento.
committed [kə'mɪtɪd] *adj* (*writer*, *politician etc*) engajado.
committee [kə'mɪtɪ] *n* comitê *m*; **to be on a** ~ ser membro de um comitê.
committee meeting *n* reunião *f* de comitê.
commodity [kə'mɔdɪtɪ] *n* mercadoria; **commodities** *npl* (*COMM*) commodities *mpl*.
commodity exchange *n* bolsa de mercadorias.
common ['kɔmən] *adj* comum; (*pej*) ordinário ♦ *n* terrenos baldios *mpl*; **C~s** *npl* (*BRIT*: *POL*): **the (House of) C~s** a Câmara dos Comuns; **in** ~ em comum; **in** ~ **use** de uso corrente; **it's** ~ **knowledge that** todos sabem que; **to the** ~ **good** para o bem comum.
commoner ['kɔmənə*] *n* plebeu/béia *m/f*.
common ground *n* (*fig*) consenso.
common law *n* lei *f* consuetudinária ♦ *adj*: **common-law wife** concubina.
commonly ['kɔmənlɪ] *adv* geralmente.
Common Market *n* Mercado Comum.
commonplace ['kɔmənpleɪs] *adj* vulgar, trivial ♦ *n* lugar-comum *m*.
common room *n* sala comum; (*SCH*) sala dos professores (*or* estudantes).
common sense *n* bom senso.
Commonwealth ['kɔmənwɛlθ] *n*: **the** ~ a Comunidade Britânica.
commotion [kə'məuʃən] *n* tumulto, confusão

f.
communal ['kɔmju:nl] *adj* (*life*) comunal; (*bathroom etc*) social.
commune [*n* 'kɔmju:n, *vi* kə'mju:n] *n* (*group*) comuna ♦ *vi*: **to** ~ **with** conversar com.
communicate [kə'mju:nɪkeɪt] *vt* comunicar ♦ *vi*: **to** ~ **(with)** comunicar-se (com).
communication [kəmju:nɪ'keɪʃən] *n* comunicação *f*.
communication cord (*BRIT*) *n* sinal *m* de alarme.
communications network *n* rede *f* de comunicações.
communications satellite *n* satélite *m* de comunicações.
communicative [kə'mju:nɪkətɪv] *adj* comunicativo.
communion [kə'mju:nɪən] *n* (*also*: *Holy C~*) comunhão *f*.
communiqué [kə'mju:nɪkeɪ] *n* comunicado.
communism ['kɔmjunɪzəm] *n* comunismo.
communist ['kɔmjunɪst] *adj*, *n* comunista *m/f*.
community [kə'mju:nɪtɪ] *n* comunidade *f*.
community centre *n* centro social.
community chest (*US*) *n* fundo de assistência social.
community health centre *n* centro de saúde comunitário.
community service *n* serviços *mpl* comunitários.
community spirit *n* espírito comunitário.
commutation ticket [kɔmju'teɪʃən-] (*US*) *n* passe *m*, bilhete *m* de assinatura.
commute [kə'mju:t] *vi* viajar diariamente ♦ *vt* comutar.
commuter [kə'mju:tə*] *n* viajante *m/f* habitual.
compact [*adj* kəm'pækt, *n* 'kɔmpækt] *adj* compacto; (*style*) conciso ♦ *n* (*pact*) pacto; (*for powder*) estojo.
compact disk *n* disco laser.
companion [kəm'pænɪən] *n* companheiro/a.
companionship [kəm'pænɪənʃɪp] *n* companhia; (*spirit*) camaradagem *f*.
companionway [kəm'pænjənweɪ] *n* (*NAUT*) escada de tombadilho.
company ['kʌmpənɪ] *n* companhia; (*COMM*) sociedade *f*, companhia; **he's good** ~ ele é uma boa companhia; **we have** ~ temos visita; **to keep sb** ~ fazer companhia a alguém; **to part** ~ **with** separar-se de; **Smith and C~** Smith e Companhia.
company car *n* carro da companhia.
company director *n* administrador(a) *m/f* de companhia.
company secretary (*BRIT*) *n* (*COMM*) secretário/a geral (*de uma companhia*).
comparable ['kɔmpərəbl] *adj* comparável.
comparative [kəm'pærətɪv] *adj* comparativo; (*relative*) relativo.
comparatively [kəm'pærətɪvlɪ] *adj* (*relatively*) relativamente.
compare [kəm'pɛə*] *vt* (*set side by side*) cotejar; (*contrast*): **to** ~ **(to/with)** comparar (a/ com) ♦ *vi*: **to** ~ **with** comparar-se com; **how**

do the prices ~? qual é a diferença entre os preços?; **~d with** or **to** em comparação com.

comparison [kəm'pærɪsn] n comparação f; **in ~ with** em comparação com, comparado com.

compartment [kəm'pɑːtmənt] n (also: RAIL) compartimento.

compass ['kʌmpəs] n bússola; **within the ~ of** no âmbito de.

compasses ['kʌmpəsiz] npl compasso.

compassion [kəm'pæʃən] n compaixão f.

compassionate [kəm'pæʃənət] adj compassivo; **on ~ grounds** por motivos humanitários.

compatibility [kəmpætɪ'bɪlɪtɪ] n compatibilidade f.

compatible [kəm'pætɪbl] adj compatível.

compel [kəm'pɛl] vt obrigar.

compelling [kəm'pɛlɪŋ] adj (fig: argument) convincente.

compendium [kəm'pɛndɪəm] n compêndio.

compensate ['kɔmpənseɪt] vt (financially) indenizar ♦ vi: **to ~ for** compensar.

compensation [kɔmpən'seɪʃən] n compensação f; (damages) indenização f.

compère ['kɔmpɛə*] n apresentador(a) m/f.

compete [kəm'piːt] vi (take part) competir, concorrer; (vie): **to ~ (with)** competir (com), fazer competição (com).

competence ['kɔmpɪtəns] n competência, capacidade f.

competent ['kɔmpɪtənt] adj competente.

competition [kɔmpɪ'tɪʃən] n (contest) concurso; (ECON) concorrência; (rivalry) competição f; **in ~ with** em competição com.

competitive [kəm'pɛtɪtɪv] adj (ECON, sport) competitivo; (spirit) competidor(a), de rivalidade.

competitive examination n concurso.

competitor [kəm'pɛtɪtə*] n (rival) competidor(a) m/f; (participant, ECON) concorrente m/f; **our ~s** (COMM) a (nossa) concorrência.

compile [kəm'paɪl] vt compilar, compor.

complacency [kəm'pleɪsnsɪ] n satisfação f consigo mesmo.

complacent [kəm'pleɪsənt] adj relaxado, acomodado.

complain [kəm'pleɪn] vi: **to ~ (about)** queixar-se (de); (in shop etc) reclamar (de). **complain of** vt fus (MED) sofrer de.

complaint [kəm'pleɪnt] n queixa; (in shop etc) reclamação f; (JUR) querela; (MED) achaque m, doença.

complement ['kɔmplɪmənt] n complemento; (esp ship's crew) tripulação f ♦ vt complementar.

complementary [kɔmplɪ'mɛntərɪ] adj complementar.

complete [kəm'pliːt] adj (full) completo; (finished) acabado ♦ vt (fulfil) completar; (finish) acabar; (a form) preencher; **a ~ disaster** um desastre total.

completely [kəm'pliːtlɪ] adv completamente.

completion [kəm'pliːʃən] n conclusão f, término; (of contract etc) realização f; **to be nearing ~** estar quase pronto; **on ~ of contract** na assinatura do contrato; (for house) na escritura.

complex ['kɔmplɛks] adj complexo ♦ n (PSYCH, of ideas etc) complexo; (of buildings) conjunto.

complexion [kəm'plɛkʃən] n (of face) cor f, tez f; (fig) aspecto.

complexity [kəm'plɛksɪtɪ] n complexidade f.

compliance [kəm'plaɪəns] n (submission) submissão f; (agreement) conformidade f; **in ~ with** de acordo com, conforme.

compliant [kəm'plaɪənt] adj complacente, submisso.

complicate ['kɔmplɪkeɪt] vt complicar.

complicated ['kɔmplɪkeɪtɪd] adj complicado.

complication [kɔmplɪ'keɪʃən] n complicação f.

complicity [kəm'plɪsɪtɪ] n cumplicidade f.

compliment [n 'kɔmplɪmənt, vt 'kɔmplɪmɛnt] n (formal) cumprimento; (praise) elogio ♦ vt elogiar; **~s** npl cumprimentos mpl; **to pay sb a ~** elogiar alguém; **to ~ sb (on sth/on doing sth)** cumprimentar or elogiar alguém (por algo/por ter feito algo).

complimentary [kɔmplɪ'mɛntərɪ] adj lisonjeiro; (free) gratuito.

complimentary ticket n entrada de favor or de cortesia.

compliments slip n memorando.

comply [kəm'plaɪ] vi: **to ~ with** cumprir com.

component [kəm'pəunənt] adj componente ♦ n (TECH) peça; (element) componente m.

compose [kəm'pəuz] vt compor; **to be ~d of** compor-se de; **to ~ o.s.** tranqüilizar-se.

composed [kəm'pəuzd] adj calmo.

composer [kəm'pəuzə*] n (MUS) compositor(a) m/f.

composite ['kɔmpəzɪt] adj composto.

composition [kɔmpə'zɪʃən] n composição f.

compost ['kɔmpɔst] n adubo.

composure [kəm'pəuʒə*] n serenidade f, calma.

compound [n, adj 'kɔmpaund, vt kəm'paund] n (CHEM, LING) composto; (enclosure) recinto ♦ adj composto; (fracture) complicado ♦ vt (fig: problem etc) agravar.

compound interest n juro composto.

comprehend [kɔmprɪ'hɛnd] vt compreender.

comprehension [kɔmprɪ'hɛnʃən] n compreensão f.

comprehensive [kɔmprɪ'hɛnsɪv] adj abrangente.

comprehensive insurance policy n apólice f de seguro com cobertura total.

comprehensive (school) (BRIT) n escola secundária de amplo programa.

compress [vt kəm'prɛs, n 'kɔmprɛs] vt comprimir ♦ n (MED) compressa.

compression [kəm'prɛʃən] n compressão f.

---

comprise [kəm'praız] *vt* (*also: be ~d of*) compreender, constar de.

compromise ['kɔmprəmaız] *n* meio-termo ♦ *vt* comprometer ♦ *vi* chegar a um meio-termo ♦ *cpd* (*decision, solution*) de meio-termo.

compulsion [kəm'pʌlʃən] *n* compulsão *f*; **under** ~ sob coação, à força.

compulsive [kəm'pʌlsıv] *adj* (*PSYCH*) compulsório; **he's a** ~ **smoker** ele não pode deixar de fumar.

compulsory [kəm'pʌlsərı] *adj* obrigatório.

compulsory purchase *n* compra compulsória.

compunction [kəm'pʌŋkʃən] *n* compunção; **to have no** ~ **about doing sth** não hesitar em fazer algo.

computer [kəm'pjuːtə*] *n* computador *m*.

computerize [kəm'pjuːtəraız] *vt* informatizar, computadorizar.

computer language *n* linguagem *f* de máquina.

computer peripheral *n* periférico.

computer program *n* programa *m* de computador.

computer progra(m)mer *n* programador(a) *m/f*.

computer program(m)ing *n* programação *f*.

computer science *n* informática, computação *f*.

computer scientist *n* cientista *m/f* da computação.

computing [kəm'pjuːtıŋ] *n* informática, computação *f*.

comrade ['kɔmrıd] *n* camarada *m/f*.

comradeship ['kɔmrıdʃıp] *n* camaradagem *f*.

comsat ['kɔmsæt] *n abbr* = **communications satellite**.

con [kɔn] *vt* enganar ♦ *n* vigarice *f*; **~s** *npl see* **convenience**; **pro**; **to** ~ **sb into doing sth** convencer alguém a fazer algo (por artimanhas).

concave [kɔn'keıv] *adj* côncavo.

conceal [kən'siːl] *vt* ocultar.

concede [kən'siːd] *vt* conceder ♦ *vi* ceder.

conceit [kən'siːt] *n* presunção *f*.

conceited [kən'siːtıd] *adj* presunçoso.

conceivable [kən'siːvəbl] *adj* concebível; **it is** ~ **that** é possível que.

conceivably [kən'siːvəblı] *adv*: **he may** ~ **be right** é possível que ele tenha razão.

conceive [kən'siːv] *vt* conceber ♦ *vi*: **to** ~ **of sth/of doing sth** conceber algo/fazer idéia de fazer algo.

concentrate ['kɔnsəntreıt] *vi* concentrar-se ♦ *vt* concentrar.

concentration [kɔnsən'treıʃən] *n* concentração *f*.

concentration camp *n* campo de concentração.

concentric [kɔn'sɛntrık] *adj* concêntrico.

concept ['kɔnsɛpt] *n* conceito.

conception [kən'sɛpʃən] *n* (*idea*) conceito, idéia; (*BIO*) concepção *f*.

concern [kən'sɔːn] *n* (*matter*) assunto;

(*COMM*) empresa; (*anxiety*) preocupação *f* ♦ *vt* dizer respeito a; **to be** ~**ed (about)** preocupar-se (com); "**to whom it may** ~" "a quem interessar possa"; **as far as I'm** ~**ed** no que me diz respeito, quanto a mim; **to be** ~**ed with** (*person: involved with*) ocupar-se de; (*book: be about*) tratar de; **the department** ~**ed** (*under discussion*) o departamento em questão; (*relevant*) o departamento competente.

concerning [kən'sɔːnıŋ] *prep* sobre, a respeito de, acerca de.

concert ['kɔnsət] *n* concerto; **in** ~ de comum acordo.

concerted [kən'sɔːtıd] *adj* (*joint*) conjunto; (*strong*) sério.

concert hall *n* sala de concertos.

concertina [kɔnsə'tiːnə] *n* sanfona, concertina ♦ *vi* engavetar-se.

concert master (*US*) *n* primeiro violino de uma orquestra.

concerto [kən'tʃɔːtəu] *n* concerto.

concession [kən'sɛʃən] *n* concessão *f*.

concessionaire [kənsɛʃə'nɛə*] *n* concessionário/a.

concessionary [kən'sɛʃənrı] *adj* (*ticket, fare*) a preço reduzido.

conciliation [kənsılı'eıʃən] *n* conciliação *f*.

conciliatory [kən'sılıətrı] *adj* conciliador(a).

concise [kən'saıs] *adj* conciso.

conclave ['kɔnkleıv] *n* conclave *m*.

conclude [kən'kluːd] *vt* (*finish*) acabar, concluir; (*treaty etc*) firmar; (*agreement*) chegar a; (*decide*): **to** ~ **that** chegar à conclusão de que ♦ *vi* terminar, acabar.

conclusion [kən'kluːʒən] *n* conclusão *f*; **come to the** ~ **that** chegar à conclusão de que.

conclusive [kən'kluːsıv] *adj* conclusivo, decisivo.

concoct [kən'kɔkt] *vt* confeccionar; (*plot*) fabricar, tramar.

concoction [kən'kɔkʃən] *n* (*food, drink*) mistura.

concord ['kɔŋkɔːd] *n* (*harmony*) concórdia; (*treaty*) acordo.

concourse ['kɔŋkɔːs] *n* (*hall*) saguão *m*; (*crowd*) multidão *f*.

concrete ['kɔnkriːt] *n* concreto (*BR*), betão *m* (*PT*) ♦ *adj* concreto.

concrete mixer *n* betoneira.

concur [kən'kɔː*] *vi* estar de acordo, concordar.

concurrently [kən'kʌrntlı] *adv* ao mesmo tempo, simultaneamente.

concussion [kən'kʌʃən] *n* (*MED*) concussão *f* cerebral.

condemn [kən'dɛm] *vt* condenar.

condemnation [kɔndɛm'neıʃən] *n* condenação *f*; (*blame*) censura.

condensation [kɔndɛn'seıʃən] *n* condensação *f*.

condense [kən'dɛns] *vi* condensar-se ♦ *vt* condensar.

condensed milk [kən'dɛnst-] *n* leite *m*

condensado.

condescend [kɔndɪ'send] *vi* condescender, dignar-se; **to ~ to do sth** condescender a fazer algo.

condescending [kɔndɪ'sendɪŋ] *adj* condescendente.

condition [kən'dɪʃən] *n* condição *f*; (*health*) estado de saúde ♦ *vt* condicionar; **on ~ that** com a condição (de) que; **in good/poor ~** em bom/mau estado (de conservação); **a heart ~** um problema no coração; **weather ~s** condições *fpl* meteorológicas.

conditional [kən'dɪʃənl] *adj* condicional; **to be ~ upon** depender de.

conditioner [kən'dɪʃənə*] *n* (*for hair*) condicionador *m*.

condo ['kɔndəu] (*US*: *inf*) *n abbr* = **condominium**.

condolences [kən'dəulənsɪz] *npl* pêsames *mpl*.

condom ['kɔndɔm] *n* preservativo, camisa-de-Venus *f*.

condominium [kɔndə'mɪnɪəm] (*US*) *n* (*building*) edifício; (*rooms*) apartamento.

condone [kən'dəun] *vt* admitir, aceitar.

conducive [kən'djuːsɪv] *adj*: **~ to** conducente para *or* a.

conduct [*n* 'kɔndʌkt, *vt*, *vi* kən'dʌkt] *n* conduta, comportamento ♦ *vt* (*lead*) conduzir; (*manage*) dirigir; (*MUS*) reger ♦ *vi* (*MUS*) reger uma orquestra; **to ~ o.s.** comportar-se.

conducted tour [kən'dʌktɪd-] *n* viagem *f* organizada; (*of building etc*) visita guiada.

conductor [kən'dʌktə*] *n* (*of orchestra*) regente *m/f*; (*on bus*) cobrador(a) *m/f*; (*RAIL*) revisor(a) *m/f*; (*ELEC*) condutor *m*.

conductress [kən'dʌktrɪs] *n* (*on bus*) cobradora.

conduit ['kɔndɪt] *n* conduto.

cone [kəun] *n* cone *m*; (*for ice-cream*) casquinha; **pine ~** pinha.

confectioner [kən'fekʃənə*] *n* confeiteiro/a (*BR*), pasteleiro/a (*PT*); **~'s (shop)** confeitaria (*BR*), pastelaria (*PT*); (*sweet shop*) confeitaria.

confectionery [kən'fekʃnərɪ] *n* (*cakes*) bolos *mpl*; (*sweets*) doces *mpl*.

confederate [kən'fedrɪt] *adj* confederado ♦ *n* cúmplice *m/f*; (*US*: *HISTORY*) confederado/a (sulista).

confederation [kənfedə'reɪʃən] *n* confederação *f*.

confer [kən'fəː*] *vt*: **to ~ on** outorgar a ♦ *vi* conferenciar.

conference ['kɔnfərns] *n* (*meeting*) congresso; **to be in ~** estar em conferência.

conference room *n* sala de conferência.

confess [kən'fes] *vt* confessar ♦ *vi* confessar-se.

confession [kən'feʃən] *n* confissão *f*.

confessional [kən'feʃənl] *n* confessionário.

confessor [kən'fesə*] *n* confessor *m*.

confetti [kən'fetɪ] *n* confete *m*.

confide [kən'faɪd] *vi*: **to ~ in** confiar em, fiar-se em.

confidence ['kɔnfɪdns] *n* confiança; (*secret*) confidência; **to have (every) ~ that** ter certeza de que; **motion of no ~** moção de não confiança; **in ~** em confidência.

confidence trick *n* conto do vigário.

confident ['kɔnfɪdnt] *adj* confiante, convicto.

confidential [kɔnfɪ'denʃəl] *adj* confidencial; (*secretary*) de confiança.

confidentiality ['kɔnfɪdenʃɪ'ælɪtɪ] *n* sigilo.

configuration [kən'fɪgju'reɪʃən] *n* (*also*: *COMPUT*) configuração *f*.

confine [kən'faɪn] *vt* (*limit*) limitar; (*shut up*) encarcerar; **to ~ o.s. to (doing) sth** limitar-se a (fazer) algo.

confined [kən'faɪnd] *adj* (*space*) reduzido, retido.

confinement [kən'faɪnmənt] *n* (*prison*) prisão *f*; (*enclosure*) reclusão *f*; (*MED*) parto.

confines ['kɔnfaɪnz] *npl* confins *mpl*.

confirm [kən'fɔːm] *vt* confirmar.

confirmation [kɔnfə'meɪʃən] *n* confirmação *f*.

confirmed [kən'fɔːmd] *adj* inveterado.

confiscate ['kɔnfɪskeɪt] *vt* confiscar.

confiscation [kɔnfɪs'keɪʃən] *n* confiscação *f*.

conflagration [kɔnflə'greɪʃən] *n* conflagração *f*.

conflict [*n* 'kɔnflɪkt, *vi* kən'flɪkt] *n* conflito ♦ *vi* estar em conflito; (*opinions*) divergir.

conflicting [kən'flɪktɪŋ] *adj* (*views*) divergente; (*interests*) oposto; (*account*) discrepante.

conform [kən'fɔːm] *vi* conformar-se; **to ~ to** ajustar-se a, acomodar-se a.

conformist [kən'fɔːmɪst] *n* conformista *m/f*.

confound [kən'faund] *vt* confundir; (*amaze*) desconcertar.

confounded [kən'faundɪd] *adj* maldito.

confront [kən'frʌnt] *vt* (*problems*) enfrentar; (*enemy, danger*) defrontar-se com.

confrontation [kɔnfrən'teɪʃən] *n* confrontação *f*.

confuse [kən'fjuːz] *vt* (*perplex*) desconcertar; (*mix up*) confundir, misturar.

confused [kən'fjuːzd] *adj* confuso; (*person*) perplexo, confuso.

confusing [kən'fjuːzɪŋ] *adj* confuso.

confusion [kən'fjuːʒən] *n* confusão *f*.

congeal [kən'dʒiːl] *vi* (*freeze*) congelar-se; (*coagulate*) coagular-se.

congenial [kən'dʒiːnɪəl] *adj* simpático, agradável.

congenital [kən'dʒenɪtl] *adj* congênito.

conger eel ['kɔŋgə*-] *n* congro.

congested [kən'dʒestɪd] *adj* (*gen*) congestionado.

congestion [kən'dʒestʃən] *n* (*MED*) congestão *f*; (*traffic*) congestionamento.

conglomerate [kən'glɔmərɪt] *n* (*COMM*) conglomerado.

conglomeration [kənglɔmə'reɪʃən] *n* conglo-

NB: *European Portuguese adds the following consonants to certain words:* **b** (sú(b)dito, su(b)til); **c** (a(c)ção, a(c)cionista, a(c)to); **m** (inde(m)ne); **p** (ado(p)ção, ado(p)tar); *for further details see p. xiii.*

meração f, aglomeração f.
Congo ['kɔŋgəu] n (state) Congo.
congratulate [kən'grætjuleɪt] vt: **to ~ sb (on)** felicitar or parabenizar alguém (por).
congratulations [kəngrætju'leɪʃənz] npl: ~ **(on)** parabéns mpl (por) ♦ excl parabéns!
congregate ['kɔŋgrɪgeɪt] vi reunir-se.
congregation [kɔŋgrɪ'geɪʃən] n (in church) fiéis mpl; (assembly) congregação f, reunião f.
congress ['kɔŋgrɛs] n congresso.
congressman ['kɔŋgrɛsmən] (US: irreg) n deputado.
congresswoman ['kɔŋgrɛswumən] (US: irreg) n deputada.
conical ['kɔnɪkl] adj cônico.
conifer ['kɔnɪfə*] n conífera.
coniferous [kə'nɪfərəs] adj (forest) conífero.
conjecture [kən'dʒɛktʃə*] n conjetura ♦ vt, vi conjeturar.
conjugal ['kɔndʒugl] adj conjugal.
conjugate ['kɔndʒugeɪt] vt conjugar.
conjugation [kɔndʒu'geɪʃən] n conjugação f.
conjunction [kən'dʒʌŋkʃən] n conjunção f; **in ~ with** junto com.
conjunctivitis [kəndʒʌŋktɪ'vaɪtɪs] n conjuntivite f.
conjure ['kʌndʒə*] vi fazer truques ♦ vt fazer aparecer.
conjure up vt (ghost, spirit) fazer aparecer, invocar; (memories) evocar.
conjurer ['kʌndʒərə*] n mágico/a, prestidigitador(a) m/f.
conjuring trick ['kʌndʒərɪŋ-] n mágica.
conker ['kɔŋkə*] (BRIT) n castanha-da-índia.
conk out [kɔŋk-] (inf) vi pifar.
con man ['kɔn-] (irreg) n vigarista m.
connect [kə'nɛkt] vt juntar, unir; (ELEC) ligar, conectar; (fig) relacionar, unir ♦ vi: **to ~ with** (train) conectar com; **to be ~ed with** estar relacionado com; **I'm trying to ~ you** (TEL) estou tentando completar a ligação.
connection [kə'nɛkʃən] n ligação f; (ELEC, RAIL) conexão f; (TEL) ligação f; (fig) relação f; **in ~ with** com relação a; **what is the ~ between them?** qual é a relação entre eles?; **business ~s** contatos de trabalho.
connexion [kə'nɛkʃən] (BRIT) n = **connection**.
conning tower ['kɔnɪŋ-] n torre f de comando.
connive [kə'naɪv] vi: **to ~ at** ser conivente em.
connoisseur [kɔnɪ'sə*] n conhecedor(a) m/f, apreciador(a) m/f.
connotation [kɔnə'teɪʃən] n conotação f.
connubial [kə'njuːbɪəl] adj conjugal.
conquer ['kɔŋkə*] vt conquistar; (enemy) vencer; (feelings) superar.
conqueror ['kɔŋkərə*] n conquistador(a) m/f.
conquest ['kɔŋkwɛst] n conquista.
conscience ['kɔnʃəns] n consciência; **in all ~** em sã consciência.
conscientious [kɔnʃɪ'ɛnʃəs] adj consciencioso; (objection) de consciência.

conscientious objector n aquele que faz uma objeção de consciência à sua participação nas forças armadas.
conscious ['kɔnʃəs] adj consciente; (deliberate: insult, error) intencional; **to become ~ of** tornar-se consciente de, conscientizar-se de.
consciousness ['kɔnʃəsnɪs] n consciência; **to lose/regain ~** perder/recuperar os sentidos.
conscript ['kɔnskrɪpt] n recruta m/f.
conscription [kən'skrɪpʃən] n serviço militar obrigatório.
consecrate ['kɔnsɪkreɪt] vt consagrar.
consecutive [kən'sɛkjutɪv] adj consecutivo, sucessivo, seguido.
consensus [kən'sɛnsəs] n consenso; **the ~ (of opinion)** o consenso (de opiniões).
consent [kən'sɛnt] n consentimento ♦ vi: **to ~ to** consentir em; **age of ~** maioridade; **by common ~** de comum acordo.
consequence ['kɔnsɪkwəns] n conseqüência; **in ~** por conseqüência.
consequently ['kɔnsɪkwəntlɪ] adv por conseguinte.
conservation [kɔnsə'veɪʃən] n conservação f; (also: **nature ~**) proteção f do meio ambiente; **energy ~** conservação da energia.
conservationist [kɔnsə'veɪʃənɪst] n conservacionista m/f.
Conservative [kən'sə:vətɪv] (BRIT) adj, n (POL) conservador(a) m/f.
conservative [kən'sə:vətɪv] adj conservador(a); (cautious) moderado.
conservatory [kən'sə:vətrɪ] n conservatório; (greenhouse) estufa.
conserve [kən'sə:v] vt conservar ♦ n conserva.
consider [kən'sɪdə*] vt considerar; (take into account) levar em consideração; (study) estudar, examinar; **to ~ doing sth** pensar em fazer algo; **~ yourself lucky** dê-se por sortudo; **all things ~ed** afinal de contas.
considerable [kən'sɪdərəbl] adj considerável; (sum) importante.
considerably [kən'sɪdərəblɪ] adv consideravelmente.
considerate [kən'sɪdərɪt] adj atencioso.
consideration [kənsɪdə'reɪʃən] n consideração f; (reward) remuneração f; **out of ~ for** em consideração a; **to be under ~** estar em apreciação; **my first ~ is my family** minha maior preocupação é a minha família.
considering [kən'sɪdərɪŋ] prep em vista de ♦ conj: **~ (that)** apesar de que, considerando que.
consign [kən'saɪn] vt consignar.
consignee [kɔnsaɪ'niː] n consignatário/a.
consignment [kən'saɪnmənt] n consignação f.
consignment note n (COMM) guia de remessa.
consignor [kən'saɪnə*] n consignador(a) m/f.
consist [kən'sɪst] vi: **to ~ of** consistir em, compor-se de.
consistency [kən'sɪstənsɪ] n (of person etc) coerência; (thickness) consistência.
consistent [kən'sɪstənt] adj (person) compatí-

vel, coerente; (even) constante; ~ **with** compatível com, de acordo com.

consolation [kɔnsə'leɪʃən] n consolação f, consolo.

console [vt kən'səul, n 'kɔnsəul] vt consolar ♦ n consolo.

consolidate [kən'sɔlideɪt] vt consolidar.

consols ['kɔnsɔlz] (BRIT) npl (STOCK EX- CHANGE) consolidados mpl.

consommé [kən'sɔmeɪ] n consomê m, caldo.

consonant ['kɔnsənənt] n consoante f.

consort [n 'kɔnsɔːt, vi kən'sɔːt] n consorte m/f ♦ vi: **to** ~ **with** ter ligações com, conviver com; **prince** ~ príncipe m consorte.

consortia [kən'sɔːtɪə] npl of **consortium**.

consortium [kən'sɔːtɪəm] (pl ~**s** or **consortia**) n consórcio.

conspicuous [kən'spɪkjuəs] adj (visible) visível; (garish) berrante; (outstanding) notável; **to make o.s.** ~ fazer-se notar.

conspiracy [kən'spɪrəsɪ] n conspiração f, trama.

conspiratorial [kən'spɪrə'tɔːrɪəl] adj conspirador(a).

conspire [kən'spaɪə*] vi conspirar.

constable ['kʌnstəbl] (BRIT) n policial m/f (BR), polícia m/f (PT); **chief** ~ chefe m/f de polícia.

constabulary [kən'stæbjulərɪ] n polícia (distrital).

constant ['kɔnstənt] adj constante; (loyal) leal, fiel.

constantly ['kɔnstəntlɪ] adv constantemente.

constellation [kɔnstə'leɪʃən] n constelação f.

consternation [kɔnstə'neɪʃən] n consternação f.

constipated ['kɔnstɪpeɪtəd] adj com prisão de ventre.

constipation [kɔnstɪ'peɪʃən] n prisão f de ventre.

constituency [kən'stɪtjuənsɪ] n (POL) distrito eleitoral; (people) eleitorado.

constituency party n partido local.

constituent [kən'stɪtjuənt] n (POL) eleitor(a) m/f; (part) componente m.

constitute ['kɔnstɪtjuːt] vt constituir.

constitution [kɔnstɪ'tjuːʃn] n constituição f.

constitutional [kɔnstɪ'tjuːʃənl] adj constitucional.

constrain [kən'streɪn] vt obrigar.

constrained [kən'streɪnd] adj: **to feel** ~ **to ...** sentir-se compelido a ....

constraint [kən'streɪnt] n (force) força, coação f; (restraint) limitação f; (shyness) constrangimento.

constrict [kən'strɪkt] vt apertar, constringir.

construct [kən'strʌkt] vt construir.

construction [kən'strʌkʃən] n construção f; (fig: interpretation) interpretação f; **under** ~ em construção.

construction industry n construção f.

constructive [kən'strʌktɪv] adj construtivo.

construe [kən'struː] vt interpretar.

consul ['kɔnsl] n cônsul m/f.

consulate ['kɔnsjulɪt] n consulado.

consult [kən'sʌlt] vt, vi consultar.

consultancy [kən'sʌltənsɪ] n consultoria.

consultancy fee n honorário de consultor.

consultant [kən'sʌltənt] n (MED) (médico/a) especialista m/f; (other specialist) assessor(a) m/f, consultor(a) m/f ♦ cpd: ~ **engineer** engenheiro-consultor/engenheira-consultora m/f; ~ **paediatrician** pediatra m/f; **legal/management** ~ assessor jurídico/ consultor em administração.

consultation [kɔnsəl'teɪʃən] n consulta; **in** ~ **with** em consulta com.

consulting room [kən'sʌltɪŋ-] (BRIT) n consultório.

consume [kən'sjuːm] vt (eat) comer; (drink) beber; (fire etc, COMM) consumir.

consumer [kən'sjuːmə*] n consumidor(a) m/f.

consumer credit n crédito ao consumidor.

consumer durables npl bens mpl de consumo duráveis.

consumer goods npl bens mpl de consumo.

consumerism [kən'sjuːmərɪzəm] n (ECON) consumismo; (consumer protection) proteção f ao consumidor.

consumer society n sociedade f de consumo.

consummate ['kɔnsʌmeɪt] vt consumar.

consumption [kən'sʌmpʃən] n consumo; (MED) tuberculose f; **not fit for human** ~ impróprio para consumo.

cont. abbr = **continued**.

contact ['kɔntækt] n contato ♦ vt entrar or pôr-se em contato com; **to be in** ~ **with sb** estar em contato com alguém; **he has good** ~**s** tem boas relações.

contact lenses npl lentes fpl de contato.

contagious [kən'teɪdʒəs] adj contagioso.

contain [kən'teɪn] vt conter; **to** ~ **o.s.** conter-se.

container [kən'teɪnə*] n recipiente m; (for shipping etc) container m, cofre m de carga.

containerize [kən'teɪnəraɪz] vt containerizar.

contaminate [kən'tæmɪneɪt] vt contaminar.

contamination [kəntæmɪ'neɪʃən] n contaminação f.

cont'd abbr = **continued**.

contemplate ['kɔntəmpleɪt] vt contemplar; (expect) contar com; (intend) pretender, pensar em.

contemplation [kɔntəm'pleɪʃən] n contemplação f.

contemporary [kən'tempərərɪ] adj contemporâneo; (design) moderno ♦ n contemporâneo/a.

contempt [kən'tempt] n desprezo; ~ **of court** (LAW) desacato à autoridade do tribunal.

contemptible [kən'temptəbl] adj desprezível.

contemptuous [kən'temptjuəs] adj desdenhoso.

contend [kən'tend] vt (argue) afirmar ♦ vi

NB: *European Portuguese adds the following consonants to certain words:* **b** (sú(b)dito, su(b)til); **c** (a(c)ção, a(c)cionista, a(c)to); **m** (inde(m)ne); **p** (ado(p)ção, ado(p)tar); *for further details see p. xiii.*

(*struggle*) lutar; **to have to ~ with** arcar com, lidar com; **he has a lot to ~ with** ele tem muito o que enfrentar.

contender [kən'tendə*] *n* contendor(a) *m/f*.

content [*adj, vt* kən'tɛnt, *n* 'kɔntɛnt] *adj* (*happy*) contente; (*satisfied*) satisfeito ♦ *vt* contentar, satisfazer ♦ *n* conteúdo; **~s** *npl* conteúdo; **(table of) ~s** índice *m* das matérias; **to be ~ with** estar contente *or* satisfeito com; **to ~ o.s. with/with doing sth** contentar-se com algo/em fazer algo.

contented [kən'tɛntɪd] *adj* contente, satisfeito.

contentedly [kən'tɛntɪdlɪ] *adv* contentemente.

contention [kən'tɛnʃən] *n* contenda; (*argument*) afirmação *f*; **bone of ~** pomo da discórdia.

contentious [kən'tɛnʃəs] *adj* controvertido.

contentment [kən'tɛntmənt] *n* contentamento.

contest [*n* 'kɔntɛst, *vt* kən'tɛst] *n* contenda; (*competition*) concurso ♦ *vt* (*dispute*) disputar; (*legal case*) defender; (*POL*) ser candidato a, disputar.

contestant [kən'tɛstənt] *n* competidor(a) *m/f*; (*in fight*) adversário/a.

context ['kɔntɛkst] *n* contexto; **in/out of ~** em/fora de contexto.

continent ['kɔntɪnənt] *n* continente *m*; **the C~** (*BRIT*) o continente europeu; **on the C~** na Europa (continental).

continental [kɔntɪ'nɛntl] *adj* continental ♦ *n* (*BRIT*) europeu/péia *m/f*.

continental breakfast *n* café *m* da manhã (*BR*), pequeno almoço (*PT*) (*de pão, geléia e café*).

continental quilt (*BRIT*) *n* edredom (*PT: -dão*) *m*.

contingency [kən'tɪndʒənsɪ] *n* contingência.

contingency plan *n* plano de contingência.

contingent [kən'tɪndʒənt] *n* contingente *m* ♦ *adj* contingente; **to be ~ upon** depender de.

continual [kən'tɪnjuəl] *adj* contínuo.

continually [kən'tɪnjuəlɪ] *adv* constantemente.

continuation [kəntɪnju'eɪʃən] *n* prolongamento; (*after interruption*) continuação *f*, retomada.

continue [kən'tɪnjuː] *vi* prosseguir, continuar ♦ *vt* continuar; (*start again*) recomeçar, retomar; **to be ~d** (*story*) segue; **~d on page 10** continua na página 10.

continuity [kɔntɪ'njuɪtɪ] *n* (*also: CINEMA*) continuidade *f*.

continuity girl *n* (*CINEMA*) continuista.

continuous [kən'tɪnjuəs] *adj* contínuo; **~ performance** (*CINEMA*) sessão *f* contínua; **~ stationery** (*COMPUT*) formulários *mpl* contínuos.

continuously [kən'tɪnjuəslɪ] *adv* (*repeatedly*) repetidamente; (*uninterruptedly*) continuamente.

contort [kən'tɔːt] *vt* retorcer.

contortion [kən'tɔːʃən] *n* contorção *f*.

contortionist [kən'tɔːʃənɪst] *n* contorcionista *m/f*.

contour ['kɔntuə*] *n* contorno; (*also: ~ line*) curva de nível.

contraband ['kɔntrəbænd] *n* contrabando ♦ *adj* de contrabando, contrabandeado.

contraception [kɔntrə'sɛpʃən] *n* anticoncepção *f*.

contraceptive [kɔntrə'sɛptɪv] *adj* anticoncepcional ♦ *n* anticoncepcional *f*.

contract [*n, cpd* 'kɔntrækt, *vi, vi* kən'trækt] *n* contrato ♦ *cpd* (*price, date*) contratual; (*work*) de empreitada ♦ *vi* (*become smaller*) contrair-se, encolher-se; (*COMM*): **to ~ to do sth** comprometer-se por contrato a fazer algo ♦ *vt* contrair; **~ of employment** *or* **service** contrato de trabalho, ≈ vínculo empregatício.

contract in *vi* comprometer-se por contrato.

contract out *vi* desobrigar-se por contrato; (*from pension scheme*) optar por não participar.

contraction [kən'trækʃən] *n* contração *f*.

contractor [kən'træktə*] *n* contratante *m/f*.

contractual [kən'træktʃuəl] *adj* contratual.

contradict [kɔntrə'dɪkt] *vt* (*deny*) desmentir; (*be contrary to*) contradizer.

contradiction [kɔntrə'dɪkʃən] *n* contradição *f*; **to be in ~ with** contradizer.

contradictory [kɔntrə'dɪktərɪ] *adj* contraditório.

contralto [kən'træltəu] *n* contralto.

contraption [kən'træpʃən] (*pej*) *n* engenhoca, geringonça.

contrary¹ ['kɔntrərɪ] *adj, n* contrário; **on the ~** muito pelo contrário; **unless you hear to the ~** salvo aviso contrário; **~ to what we thought** ao contrário do que pensamos.

contrary² [kən'trɛərɪ] *adj* teimoso.

contrast [*n* 'kɔntrɑːst, *vt* kən'trɑːst] *n* contraste *m* ♦ *vt* contrastar, comparar; **in ~ to** *or* **with** em contraste com, ao contrário de.

contrasting [kən'trɑːstɪŋ] *adj* oposto.

contravene [kɔntrə'viːn] *vt* infringir.

contravention [kɔntrə'vɛnʃən] *n* contravenção *f*, infração *f*.

contribute [kən'trɪbjuːt] *vt* contribuir ♦ *vi*: **to ~ to** contribuir para; (*newspaper*) escrever para; (*discussion*) participar de.

contribution [kɔntrɪ'bjuːʃən] *n* (*money*) contribuição *f*; (*to debate*) intervenção *f*; (*to journal*) colaboração *f*.

contributor [kən'trɪbjuːtə*] *n* (*to newspaper*) colaborador(a) *m/f*.

contributory [kən'trɪbjutərɪ] *adj*: **it was a ~ factor in ...** era um fator que contribuiu para ....

contributory pension scheme (*BRIT*) *n* sistema *m* de pensão contributária.

contrite ['kɔntraɪt] *adj* arrependido, contrito.

contrivance [kən'traɪvəns] *n* (*scheme*) maquinação *f*; (*device*) aparelho, dispositivo.

contrive [kən'traɪv] *vt* (*invent*) idealizar; (*carry out*) efetuar; (*plot*) tramar ♦ *vi*: **to ~ to do** chegar a fazer.

control [kən'trəul] *vt* controlar; (*traffic etc*) dirigir; (*machinery*) regular; (*temper*) dominar ♦ *n* (*command*) controle *m*, autoridade *f*; (*of car*) direção *f* (*BR*), condução *f* (*PT*); (*check*) freio, controle; **~s** *npl* mando; **to**

take ~ of assumir o controle de; **to be in ~ of** ter o controle de; (*in charge of*) ser responsável por; **to ~ o.s.** controlar-se; **out of/under** ~ descontrolado/sob controle; **through circumstances beyond our ~** por motivos alheios à nossa vontade.
control key n (*COMPUT*) tecla de controle.
controller [kən'trəʊlə*] n controlador(a) m/f.
controlling interest [kən'trəʊlɪŋ-] n (*COMM*) controle m acionário.
control panel n painel m de instrumentos.
control point n ponto de controle.
control room n sala de comando; (*RADIO, TV*) sala de controle.
control tower n (*AVIAT*) torre f de controle.
control unit n (*COMPUT*) unidade f de controle.
controversial [kɒntrə'vəːʃl] adj controvertido, polêmico.
controversy ['kɒntrəvəːsɪ] n controvérsia, polêmica.
conurbation [kɒnə'beɪʃən] n conurbação f.
convalesce [kɒnvə'lɛs] vi convalescer.
convalescence [kɒnvə'lɛsns] n convalescença.
convalescent [kɒnvə'lɛsnt] adj, n convalescente m/f.
convector [kən'vɛktə*] n (*heater*) aquecedor m de convecção.
convene [kən'viːn] vt convocar ♦ vi reunir-se.
convener [kən'viːnə*] n organizador(a) m/f.
convenience [kən'viːnɪəns] n (*comfort*) comodidade f; (*advantage*) vantagem f, conveniência; **at your ~** quando lhe convier; **at your earliest ~** (*COMM*) o mais cedo que lhe for possível; **all modern ~s** (*also: BRIT: all mod cons*) com todos os confortos.
convenience foods npl alimentos mpl semiprontos.
convenient [kən'viːnɪənt] adj cômodo; (*useful*) útil; (*place*) acessível; (*time*) oportuno, conveniente; **if it is ~ to you** se isso lhe convier, se isso não lhe for incômodo.
conveniently [kən'viːnɪəntlɪ] adv convenientemente.
convent ['kɒnvənt] n convento.
convention [kən'vɛnʃən] n convenção f; (*meeting*) assembléia.
conventional [kən'vɛnʃənl] adj convencional.
convent school n colégio de freiras.
converge [kən'vəːdʒ] vi convergir.
conversant [kən'vəːsnt] adj: **to be ~ with** estar familiarizado com.
conversation [kɒnvə'seɪʃən] n conversação f, conversa.
conversational [kɒnvə'seɪʃənl] adj (*familiar*) familiar; (*talkative*) loquaz; (*COMPUT*) conversacional, interativo.
conversationalist [kɒnvə'seɪʃnəlɪst] n conversador(a) m/f; **she's a good ~** ela tem muita conversa.
converse [n 'kɒnvəːs, vi kən'vəːs] n inverso ♦ vi conversar.

conversely [kɒn'vəːslɪ] adv pelo contrário, inversamente.
conversion [kən'vəːʃən] n conversão f; (*BRIT: of house*) transformação f.
conversion table n tabela de conversão.
convert [vt kən'vəːt, n 'kɒnvəːt] vt (*REL, COMM*) converter; (*alter*) transformar ♦ n convertido/a.
convertible [kən'vəːtəbl] adj convertível ♦ n conversível m.
convex [kɒn'vɛks] adj convexo.
convey [kən'veɪ] vt transportar, levar; (*thanks*) comunicar; (*idea*) exprimir.
conveyance [kən'veɪəns] n (*of goods*) transporte m; (*vehicle*) meio de transporte, veículo.
conveyancing [kən'veɪənsɪŋ] n (*LAW*) transferência de bens imóveis.
conveyor belt [kənveɪə*-] n correia transportadora.
convict [vt kən'vɪkt, n 'kɒnvɪkt] vt condenar; (*sentence*) declarar culpado ♦ n presidiário.
conviction [kən'vɪkʃən] n condenação f; (*belief*) convicção f.
convince [kən'vɪns] vt convencer; **to ~ sb of sth/that** convencer alguém de algo/de que.
convincing [kən'vɪnsɪŋ] adj convincente.
convincingly [kən'vɪnsɪŋlɪ] adv convincentemente.
convivial [kən'vɪvɪəl] adj jovial, alegre.
convoluted ['kɒnvəluːtɪd] adj (*shape*) curvilíneo; (*argument*) complicado.
convoy ['kɒnvɔɪ] n escolta.
convulse [kən'vʌls] vt convulsionar; **to be ~d with laughter** morrer de rir.
convulsion [kən'vʌlʃən] n convulsão f; (*laughter*) ataque m, acesso.
coo [kuː] vi arrulhar.
cook [kuk] vt cozinhar; (*meal*) preparar ♦ vi cozinhar ♦ n cozinheiro/a.
cook up (*inf*) vt (*excuse, story*) bolar.
cookbook ['kukbuk] n livro de receitas.
cooker ['kukə*] n fogão m.
cookery ['kukərɪ] n (*dishes*) cozinha; (*art*) (arte f) culinária.
cookery book (*BRIT*) n livro de receitas.
cookie ['kukɪ] (*US*) n bolacha, biscoito.
cooking ['kukɪŋ] n cozinha ♦ cpd (*apples, chocolate*) para cozinhar; (*utensils, salt*) de cozinha.
cookout ['kukaut] (*US*) n churrasco.
cool [kuːl] adj fresco; (*not hot*) tépido; (*not afraid*) calmo; (*unfriendly*) frio ♦ vt, vi esfriar; **it's ~** (*weather*) está fresco.
cool down vi esfriar; (*fig: person, situation*) acalmar-se.
cool box (*BRIT*) n mala frigorífica.
cooler ['kuːlə*] (*US*) n mala frigorífica.
cooling tower ['kuːlɪŋ-] n torre f de esfriamento.
coolly ['kuːlɪ] adv (*calmly*) calmamente; (*audaciously*) descaradamente; (*unenthusiasti-*

*NB: European Portuguese adds the following consonants to certain words: **b** (sú(b)dito, su(b)til); **c** (a(c)ção, a(c)cionista, a(c)to); **m** (inde(m)ne); **p** (ado(p)ção, ado(p)tar); for further details see p. xiii.*

cally) friamente.

coolness ['ku:lnɪs] *n* frescura; (*hostility*) frieza; (*indifference*) indiferença.

coop [ku:p] *n* galinheiro, capoeira.

coop up *vt* (*fig*) confinar.

co-op ['kəuɔp] *n abbr* = **cooperative (society)**.

cooperate [kəu'ɔpəreɪt] *vi* cooperar, colaborar.

cooperation [kəuɔpə'reɪʃən] *n* cooperação *f*, colaboração *f*.

cooperative [kəu'ɔpərətɪv] *adj* cooperativo ♦ *n* cooperativa.

coopt [kəu'ɔpt] *vt*: **to ~ sb onto a committee** cooptar alguém para fazer parte de um comitê.

coordinate [*vt* kəu'ɔ:dɪneɪt, *n* kəu'ɔdɪnət] *vt* coordenar ♦ *n* (*MATH*) coordenada *f*; **~s** *npl* (*clothes*) coordenados *mpl*.

coordination [kəuɔ:dɪ'neɪʃən] *n* coordenação *f*.

coot [ku:t] *n* galeirão *m*.

co-ownership [kəu-] *n* co-propriedade *f*, condomínio.

cop [kɔp] (*inf*) *n* policial *m/f* (*BR*), polícia *m/f* (*PT*), tira *m* (*inf*).

cope [kəup] *vi* sair-se, dar-se; **to ~ with** poder com, arcar com; (*problem*) estar à altura de.

Copenhagen ['kəupn'heɪgən] *n* Copenhague.

copier ['kɔpɪə*] *n* (*also: photo~*) copiador *m*.

co-pilot [kəu-] *n* co-piloto/a.

copious ['kəupɪəs] *adj* copioso, abundante.

copper ['kɔpə*] *n* (*metal*) cobre *m*; (*inf: policeman*) polícia *m*; **~s** *npl* moedas *fpl* de pouco valor.

copper sulphate *n* sulfato de cobre.

coppice ['kɔpɪs] *n* bosquete *m*.

copse [kɔps] *n* bosquete *m*.

copulate ['kɔpjuleɪt] *vi* copular.

copulation [kɔpju'leɪʃən] *n* cópula.

copy ['kɔpɪ] *n* cópia; (*of book etc*) exemplar *m*; (*of writing*) originais *mpl* ♦ *vt* copiar; (*imitate*) imitar; **to make good ~** (*PRESS*) fazer uma boa matéria.

copy out *vt* copiar.

copycat ['kɔpɪkæt] (*inf*) *n* macaco.

copyright ['kɔpɪraɪt] *n* direitos *mpl* de autor, direitos autorais, copirraite *m*; **~ reserved** todos os direitos reservados.

copy typist *n* datilógrafo/a.

copywriter ['kɔpɪraɪtə*] *n* redator(a) *m/f* de material publicitário.

coral ['kɔrəl] *n* coral *m*.

coral reef *n* recife *m* de coral.

Coral Sea *n*: **the ~** o mar de Coral.

cord [kɔ:d] *n* corda; (*ELEC*) fio, cabo; (*fabric*) veludo cotelê; **~s** *npl* (*trousers*) calça (*BR*) *or* calças *fpl* (*PT*) de veludo cotelê.

cordial ['kɔ:dɪəl] *adj* cordial ♦ *n* cordial *m*.

cordless ['kɔ:dlɪs] *adj* sem fio.

cordon ['kɔ:dn] *n* cordão *m*.

cordon off *vt* isolar.

corduroy ['kɔ:dərɔɪ] *n* veludo cotelê.

CORE [kɔ:*] (*US*) *n abbr* = **Congress of Racial Equality**.

core [kɔ:*] *n* centro, núcleo; (*of fruit*) caroço; (*of problem*) âmago ♦ *vt* descaroçar; **rotten to the ~** completamente podre.

Corfu [kɔ:'fu:] *n* Corfu *f* (*no article*).

coriander [kɔrɪ'ændə*] *n* coentro.

cork [kɔ:k] *n* rolha; (*tree*) cortiça.

corkage ['kɔ:kɪdʒ] *n* taxa cobrada num restaurante pela abertura das garrafas levadas pelo cliente.

corked [kɔ:kt] (*BRIT*) *adj* que tem gosto de rolha.

corkscrew ['kɔ:kskru:] *n* saca-rolhas *m inv*.

corky ['kɔ:kɪ] (*US*) *adj* que tem gosto de rolha.

corm [kɔ:m] *n* cormo.

cormorant ['kɔ:mərnt] *n* cormorão *m*, corvo marinho.

Corn (*BRIT*) *abbr* = **Cornwall**.

corn [kɔ:n] *n* (*BRIT: wheat*) trigo; (*US: maize*) milho; (*cereals*) grão *m*, cereal *m*; (*on foot*) calo; **~ on the cob** (*CULIN*) espiga de milho.

cornea ['kɔ:nɪə] *n* córnea.

corned beef ['kɔ:nd-] *n* carne *f* de boi enlatada.

corner ['kɔ:nə*] *n* (*outside*) esquina; (*inside*) canto; (*in road*) curva; (*FOOTBALL*) córner *m* ♦ *vt* (*trap*) encurralar; (*COMM*) açambarcar, monopolizar ♦ *vi* (*in car*) fazer uma curva; **to cut ~s** (*fig*) matar o serviço.

corner flag *n* (*FOOTBALL*) bandeira de escanteio.

corner kick *n* (*FOOTBALL*) córner *m*.

cornerstone ['kɔ:nəstəun] *n* pedra angular.

cornet ['kɔ:nɪt] *n* (*MUS*) cornetim *m*; (*BRIT: of ice-cream*) casquinha.

cornflakes ['kɔ:nfleɪks] *npl* flocos *mpl* de milho.

cornflour ['kɔ:nflauə*] (*BRIT*) *n* farinha de milho, maisena ®.

cornice ['kɔ:nɪs] *n* cornija.

Cornish ['kɔ:nɪʃ] *adj* de Cornualha ♦ *n* (*LING*) córnico.

corn oil *n* óleo de milho.

cornstarch ['kɔ:nstɑ:tʃ] (*US*) *n* farinha de milho, maisena ®.

cornucopia [kɔ:nju'kəupɪə] *n* cornucópia.

Cornwall ['kɔ:nwəl] *n* Cornualha.

corny ['kɔ:nɪ] (*inf*) *adj* velho, gasto.

corollary [kə'rɔlərɪ] *n* corolário.

coronary ['kɔrənərɪ] *n*: **~ (thrombosis)** trombose *f* (coronária).

coronation [kɔrə'neɪʃən] *n* coroação *f*.

coroner ['kɔrənə*] *n* magistrado que investiga mortes suspeitas.

coronet ['kɔrənɪt] *n* coroa aberta, diadema *m*.

Corp. *abbr* = **corporation**.

corporal ['kɔ:pərl] *n* cabo ♦ *adj* corpóreo; **~ punishment** castigo corporal.

corporate ['kɔ:pərɪt] *adj* corporativo; (*COMM: of a company*) da empresa.

corporate body *n* (*LAW*) pessoa jurídica.

corporate identity *n* imagem *f* da empresa.

corporate image *n* imagem *f* da empresa.

corporation [kɔ:pə'reɪʃən] *n* (*of town*) município, junta; (*COMM*) sociedade *f*.

corporation tax *n* imposto sobre a renda de

sociedades.

corps [kɔː*, *pl* kɔːz] (*pl* **corps**) *n* corpo; **the press** ~ a imprensa.

corpse [kɔːps] *n* cadáver *m*.

corpuscle ['kɔːpʌsl] *n* corpúsculo.

corral [kəˈrɑːl] *n* curral *m*.

correct [kəˈrɛkt] *adj* correto ♦ *vt* corrigir; **you are** ~ você tem razão.

correction [kəˈrɛkʃən] *n* correção *f*, retificação *f*; (*erasure*) emenda.

correlate ['kɔrɪleɪt] *vt* correlacionar ♦ *vi*: **to** ~ **with** corresponder a.

correlation [kɔrɪˈleɪʃən] *n* correlação *f*.

correspond [kɔrɪsˈpɒnd] *vi* (*write*) corresponder-se, escrever-se; (*be equal to*): **to** ~ **to** *or* **with** corresponder a.

correspondence [kɔrɪsˈpɒndəns] *n* correspondência.

correspondence column *n* (*PRESS*) seção *f* de cartas.

correspondence course *n* curso por correspondência.

correspondent [kɔrɪsˈpɒndənt] *n* correspondente *m/f*.

corresponding [kɔrɪsˈpɒndɪŋ] *adj* correspondente.

corridor ['kɔrɪdɔː*] *n* corredor *m*.

corroborate [kəˈrɒbəreɪt] *vt* corroborar.

corrode [kəˈrəud] *vt* corroer ♦ *vi* corroer-se.

corrosion [kəˈrəuʒən] *n* corrosão *f*.

corrosive [kəˈrəuzɪv] *adj* corrosivo.

corrugated ['kɔrəgeɪtɪd] *adj* ondulado.

corrugated iron *n* chapa ondulada *or* corrugada.

corrupt [kəˈrʌpt] *adj* corrupto ♦ *vt* corromper; (*bribe*) subornar; (*data*) corromper, destruir; ~ **practices** corrupção *f*.

corruption [kəˈrʌpʃən] *n* corrupção *f*; (*of data*) destruição *f*.

corset ['kɔːsɪt] *n* espartilho.

Corsica ['kɔːsɪkə] *n* Córsega.

Corsican ['kɔːsɪkən] *adj*, *n* córsico/a.

cortège [kɔːˈteɪʒ] *n* séquito, cortejo.

cortisone ['kɔːtɪzəun] *n* cortisona.

coruscating ['kɔrəskeɪtɪŋ] *adj* cintilante.

c.o.s. *abbr* (= *cash on shipment*) pagamento na expedição.

cosh [kɔʃ] (*BRIT*) *n* cassetete *m*.

cosignatory ['kəuˈsɪgnətərɪ] *n* co-signatário/a.

cosiness ['kəuzɪnɪs] (*US* **coziness**) *n* conforto; (*atmosphere*) aconchego, conforto.

cos lettuce [kɔs-] *n* alface *m* (cos).

cosmetic [kɔzˈmɛtɪk] *n* cosmético ♦ *adj* (*preparation*) cosmético; (*fig: reforms*) simbólico, superficial; ~ **surgery** cirurgia plástica embelezadora.

cosmic ['kɔzmɪk] *adj* cósmico.

cosmonaut ['kɔzmənɔːt] *n* cosmonauta *m/f*.

cosmopolitan [kɔzməˈpɒlɪtn] *adj* cosmopolita.

cosmos ['kɔzmɒs] *n* cosmo.

cost [kɔst] (*pt*, *pp* **cost**) *n* (*gen*) custo; (*price*) preço ♦ *vi* custar ♦ *vt* custar; (*determine cost of*) determinar o custo de; ~**s** *npl* (*LAW*) custas *fpl*; **at the** ~ **of** à custa de; **how much does it** ~? quanto custa?; **it** ~**s £5/too much** custa £5/é muito caro; **it** ~ **him his life/job** custou-lhe a vida/o emprego; **the** ~ **of living** o custo de vida; **at all** ~**s** custe o que custar.

cost accountant *n* contador(a) *m/f* de custos.

co-star [kəu-] *n* co-estrela *m/f*.

Costa Rica ['kɔstəˈriːkə] *n* Costa Rica.

Costa Rican ['kɔstəˈriːkən] *adj*, *n* costarriquenho/a.

cost centre *n* centro de custo.

cost control *n* controle *m* dos custos.

cost-effective *adj* rentável.

cost-effectiveness *n* rentabilidade *f*.

costly ['kɔstlɪ] *adj* (*expensive*) caro, custoso; (*valuable*) suntuoso.

cost-of-living *adj*: ~ **allowance** ajuda de custo; ~ **index** índice *m* de preços ao consumidor.

cost price (*BRIT*) *n* preço de custo.

costume ['kɔstjuːm] *n* traje *m*; (*BRIT: also*: **swimming** ~) (*woman's*) maiô *m* (*BR*), fato de banho (*PT*); (*man's*) calção *m* (de banho) (*BR*), calções *mpl* de banho (*PT*).

costume jewellery *n* bijuteria.

cosy ['kəuzɪ] (*US* **cozy**) *adj* cômodo; (*atmosphere*) aconchegante; (*life*) folgado, confortável.

cot [kɔt] *n* (*BRIT: child's*) cama (de criança), berço; (*US: campbed*) cama de lona.

Cotswolds ['kɔtswəuldz] *npl*: **the** ~ região de colinas em Gloucestershire.

cottage ['kɔtɪdʒ] *n* casa de campo; (*rustic*) cabana.

cottage cheese *n* ricota (*BR*), queijo creme (*PT*).

cottage industry *n* indústria artesanal.

cottage pie *n* prato de carne picada com batata.

cotton ['kɔtn] *n* algodão *m*; (*thread*) fio, linha ♦ *cpd* de algodão.

cotton on (*inf*) *vi*: **to** ~ **on (to sth)** sacar (algo).

cotton wool (*BRIT*) *n* algodão *m* (hidrófilo).

couch [kautʃ] *n* sofá *m*; (*doctor's*) cama; (*psychiatrist's*) divã *m* ♦ *vt* formular.

couchette [kuːˈʃɛt] *n* leito.

cough [kɔf] *vi* tossir ♦ *n* tosse *f*.

cough up *vt* expelir; (*inf: money*) desembolsar.

cough drop *n* pastilha para a tosse.

cough mixture *n* xarope *m* (para a tosse).

cough syrup *n* xarope *m* (para a tosse).

could [kud] *conditional of* **can**.

couldn't ['kudnt] = **could not**.

council ['kaunsl] *n* conselho; **city** *or* **town** ~ câmara municipal; **C**~ **of Europe** Conselho da Europa.

council estate (*BRIT*) *n* conjunto habitacio-

NB: *European Portuguese adds the following consonants to certain words:* **b** (sú(b)dito, su(b)til); **c** (a(c)ção, a(c)cionista, a(c)to); **m** (inde(m)ne); **p** (ado(p)ção, ado(p)tar); *for further details see p. xiii.*

nal.

council house (*BRIT*: *irreg*) *n* casa popular.

councillor ['kaunsələ*] *n* vereador(a) *m/f*.

counsel ['kaunsl] *n* (*advice*) conselho; (*lawyer*) advogado/a ♦ *vt*: **to ~ sth/sb to do sth** aconselhar algo/alguém a fazer algo; **~ for the defence/the prosecution** advogado/a de defesa/promotor(a) *m/f* público/a.

counsellor ['kaunsələ*] *n* (*US* **counselor**) conselheiro/a; (*US*: *LAW*) advogado/a.

count [kaunt] *vt* contar ♦ *vi* contar ♦ *n* conta; (*of votes*) contagem *f*; (*nobleman*) conde *m*; (*sum*) total *m*, soma; **not ~ing the children** sem contar as crianças; **10 ~ing him** 10 contando com ele; **it ~s for very little** conta muito pouco; **~ yourself lucky** considere-se sortudo; **that doesn't ~!** isso não vale!

count on *vt fus* contar com; **to ~ on doing sth** contar em fazer algo.

count up *vt* contar.

countdown ['kauntdaun] *n* contagem *f* regressiva.

countenance ['kauntɪnəns] *n* expressão *f* ♦ *vt* aprovar.

counter ['kauntə*] *n* (*in shop*) balcão *m*; (*in post office etc*: *window*) guichê *m*; (*in games*) ficha ♦ *vt* contrariar; (*blow*) parar ♦ *adv*: **~ to** ao contrário de; **to buy under the ~** (*fig*) comprar por baixo do pano *or* da mesa.

counteract [kauntər'ækt] *vt* neutralizar.

counterattack ['kauntərətæk] *n* contra-ataque *m* ♦ *vi* contra-atacar.

counterbalance [kauntə'bæləns] *n* contrapeso.

counter-clockwise *adv* ao contrário dos ponteiros do relógio.

counter-espionage *n* contra-espionagem *f*.

counterfeit ['kauntəfɪt] *n* falsificação *f* ♦ *vt* falsificar ♦ *adj* falso, falsificado.

counterfoil ['kauntəfɔɪl] *n* canhoto (*BR*), talão *m* (*PT*).

counterintelligence ['kauntərɪn'tɛlɪdʒəns] *n* contra-informação *f*.

countermand ['kauntəmɑːnd] *vt* revogar.

countermeasure ['kauntəmɛʒə*] *n* contramedida.

counteroffensive ['kauntərə'fɛnsɪv] *n* contraofensiva.

counterpane ['kauntəpeɪn] *n* colcha.

counterpart ['kauntəpɑːt] *n* contrapartida; (*of person*) sósia *m/f*; (: *opposite number*) homólogo/a.

counterproductive ['kauntəprə'dʌktɪv] *adj* contraproducente.

counterproposal ['kauntəprə'pəuzl] *n* contraproposta.

counter-revolution *n* contra-revolução *f*.

countersign ['kauntəsaɪn] *vt* referendar.

countersink ['kauntəsɪŋk] (*irreg*: *like* **sink**) *vt* escarear.

countess ['kauntɪs] *n* condessa.

countless ['kauntlɪs] *adj* inumerável.

countrified ['kʌntrɪfaɪd] *adj* bucólico, rústico.

country ['kʌntrɪ] *n* país *m*; (*native land*) terra; (*as opposed to town*) campo; (*region*) região *f*, terra; **in the ~** no campo; (*esp in Brazil*) no interior; **mountainous ~** região montanhosa.

country and western (music) *n* música country.

country dancing (*BRIT*) *n* dança regional.

country house (*irreg*) *n* casa de campo.

countryman ['kʌntrɪmən] (*irreg*) *n* (*national*) compatriota *m*; (*rural*) camponês *m*.

countryside ['kʌntrɪsaɪd] *n* campo.

country-wide *adj* em todo o país; (*problem*) de escala nacional ♦ *adv* em todo o país.

county ['kauntɪ] *n* condado.

county town (*BRIT*) *n* capital *f* do condado.

coup [kuː] *n* golpe *m* de mestre; (*also*: **~ d'état**) golpe (de estado).

coupé ['kuːpeɪ] *n* (*AUT*) cupê *m*.

couple ['kʌpl] *n* (*of things*, *people*) par *m*; (*married ~*, *courting ~*) casal *m* ♦ *vt* (*ideas*, *names*) unir, juntar; (*machinery*) ligar, juntar; **a ~ of** um par de; (*a few*) alguns/algumas.

couplet ['kʌplɪt] *n* dístico.

coupling ['kʌplɪŋ] *n* (*RAIL*) engate *m*.

coupon ['kuːpɔn] *n* cupom (*PT*: -pão) *m*; (*pools ~*) talão *m*; (*voucher*) vale *m*; (*FINANCE*) cupom (*PT*: -pão).

courage ['kʌrɪdʒ] *n* coragem *f*.

courageous [kə'reɪdʒəs] *adj* corajoso, valente.

courgette [kuə'ʒɛt] (*BRIT*) *n* abobrinha.

courier ['kurɪə*] *n* (*messenger*) correio; (*diplomatic*) mala; (*for tourists*) guia *m/f*, agente *m/f* de turismo.

course [kɔːs] *n* (*direction*) direção *f*, caminho; (*of river*, *SCH*) curso; (*of ship*) rumo; (*of bullet*) trajetória; (*fig*) procedimento; (*GOLF*) campo; (*part of meal*) prato; **of ~** claro, naturalmente; **of ~!** claro!, lógico!; **(no) of ~ not!** claro que não!; **in due ~** oportunamente, no devido tempo; **first ~** entrada; **in the ~ of the next few days** no decorrer dos próximos dias; **~ (of action)** atitude *f*; **the best ~ would be to do** ... o melhor seria fazer ...; **we have no other ~ but to** ... não temos nenhuma outra opção, senão ...; **~ of lectures** série de palestras; **~ of treatment** (*MED*) tratamento.

court [kɔːt] *n* (*royal*) corte *f*; (*LAW*) tribunal *m*; (*TENNIS*) quadra ♦ *vt* (*woman*) cortejar, namorar; (*danger etc*) procurar; **out of ~** (*LAW*: *settle*) extrajudicialmente; **to take to ~** demandar, levar a julgamento; **~ of appeal** tribunal de recursos.

courteous ['kɔːtɪəs] *adj* cortês/esa.

courtesan [kɔːtɪ'zæn] *n* cortesã *f*.

courtesy ['kɔːtəsɪ] *n* cortesia; **by ~ of** com permissão de.

courtesy coach *n* ônibus *m* (*BR*) *or* autocarro (*PT*) gratuito.

courtesy light *n* (*AUT*) luz *f* interior.

court-house (*US*: *irreg*) *n* palácio de justiça.

courtier ['kɔːtɪə*] *n* cortesão *m*.

court martial (*pl* **courts martial**) *n* conselho de guerra ♦ *vt* submeter a conselho de guerra.

courtroom ['kɔːtrum] *n* sala de tribunal.

court shoe n escarpim m.

courtyard ['kɔːtjɑːd] n pátio.

cousin ['kʌzn] n primo/a m/f; **first** ~ primo/a irmão/mã.

cove [kəuv] n angra, enseada.

covenant ['kʌvənənt] n convênio ♦ vt: **to ~ £2000 per year to a charity** comprometer-se a doar £2000 por ano para uma obra de caridade.

Coventry ['kɔvəntrɪ] n: **to send sb to ~** (fig) relegar alguém ao ostracismo.

cover ['kʌvə*] vt (gen, PRESS, costs) cobrir; (with lid) tapar; (chairs etc) revestir; (distance) percorrer; (include) abranger; (protect) abrigar; (issues) tratar ♦ n (gen, PRESS, comm) cobertura; (lid) tampa; (for chair etc) capa; (for bed) cobertor m; (envelope) envelope m; (for book) capa, forro; (of magazine) capa; (shelter) abrigo; (insurance) cobertura; **to take** ~ abrigar-se; **under** ~ (indoors) abrigado; **under** ~ **of** sob o abrigo de; (fig) sob capa de; **under separate** ~ (comm) em separado; **£10 will** ~ **everything** £10 vão dar para tudo.

cover up vt (person, object): **to ~ up** (with) cobrir (com); (fig: truth, facts) abafar, encobrir ♦ vi: **to ~ up for sb** (fig) cobrir alguém.

coverage ['kʌvərɪdʒ] n (PRESS, INSURANCE) cobertura.

cover charge n couvert m.

covering ['kʌvərɪŋ] n cobertura, invólucro.

covering letter (US **cover letter**) n carta de cobertura.

cover note n (INSURANCE) nota de cobertura.

cover price n preço de capa.

covert ['kʌuvɔːt] adj (threat) velado; (action) oculto, secreto.

cover-up n encobrimento (dos fatos).

covet ['kʌvɪt] vt cobiçar.

cow [kau] n vaca ♦ cpd fêmea ♦ vt intimidar.

coward ['kauəd] n covarde m/f.

cowardice ['kauədɪs] n covardia.

cowardly ['kauədlɪ] adj covarde.

cowboy ['kaubɔɪ] n vaqueiro.

cower ['kauə*] vi encolher-se (de medo).

cowshed ['kauʃed] n estábulo.

cowslip ['kauslɪp] n (BOT) primavera.

cox [kɔks] n abbr = **coxswain**.

coxswain ['kɔksn] n timoneiro/a m/f.

coy [kɔɪ] adj tímido.

coyote [kɔɪ'əutɪ] n coiote m.

coziness ['kəuzɪnɪs] (US) n = **cosiness**.

cozy ['kəuzɪ] (US) adj = **cosy**.

CP n abbr (= Communist Party) PC m.

cp. abbr (= compare) cp.

c/p (BRIT) abbr = **carriage paid**.

CPA (US) n abbr = **certified public accountant**.

CPI n abbr (= Consumer Price Index) IPC m.

Cpl. abbr = **Corporal**.

CP/M n abbr (= Central Program for Micro-processors) CP/M m.

c.p.s. abbr (= characters per second) c.p.s.

CPSA (BRIT) n abbr (= Civil and Public Services Association) sindicato dos funcionários públicos.

CPU n abbr (= Central Processing Unit) CPU f.

cr. abbr = **credit**; **creditor**.

crab [kræb] n caranguejo.

crab apple n maçã ácida.

crack [kræk] n rachadura, arranhão m; (noise) estalo; (joke) piada; (DRUGS) crack m; (inf: attempt): **to have a ~ (at sth)** tentar (fazer algo) ♦ vt quebrar; (nut) partir, descascar; (safe) arrombar; (whip etc) estalar; (knuckles) estalar, partir; (joke) soltar; (mystery) resolver; (code) decifrar ♦ cpd (expert) excelente; **to get ~ing** (inf) pôr mãos à obra.

crack down on vt fus (crime) ser linha dura com; (spending) cortar.

crack up vi (MED) sofrer um colapso nervoso.

crackdown ['krækdaun] n: ~ **(on)** (on crime) endurecimento (em relação a); (on spending) arrocho (a).

cracked [krækt] (inf) adj doido.

cracker ['krækə*] n (biscuit) biscoito; (Christmas ~) busca-pé-surpresa m; (firework) busca-pé m; **a ~ of a** ... (BRIT: inf) um(a) ... sensacional.

crackers ['krækəz] (BRIT: inf) adj: **he's** ~ ele é maluco.

crackle ['krækl] vi crepitar.

crackling ['kræklɪŋ] n (of fire) crepitação f; (of leaves etc) estalidos mpl; (of pork) torresmo.

cradle ['kreɪdl] n berço ♦ vt (child) embalar; (object) segurar com cuidado.

craft [krɑːft] n (skill) arte f; (trade) ofício; (cunning) astúcia; (boat) barco.

craftsman ['krɑːftsmən] (irreg) n artífice m, artesão m.

craftsmanship ['krɑːftsmənʃɪp] n artesanato.

craftsmen ['krɑːftsmɛn] npl of **craftsman**.

crafty ['krɑːftɪ] adj astuto, malandro, esperto.

crag [kræg] n penhasco.

craggy ['krægɪ] adj escarpado.

cram [kræm] vt (fill): **to ~ sth with** encher or abarrotar algo de; (put): **to ~ sth into** enfiar algo em.

crammed [kræmd] adj abarrotado.

cramming ['kræmɪŋ] n (for exams) virada final.

cramp [kræmp] n (MED) cãibra; (TECH) grampo ♦ vt (limit) restringir; (annoy) estorvar.

cramped [kræmpt] adj apertado, confinado.

crampon ['kræmpən] n gato de ferro.

cranberry ['krænbərɪ] n oxicoco.

crane [kreɪn] n (TECH) guindaste m; (bird) grou m ♦ vt, vi: **to ~ forward**, **to ~ one's**

NB: European Portuguese adds the following consonants to certain words: **b** (sú(b)dito, su(b)til); **c** (a(c)ção, a(c)cionista, a(c)to); **m** (inde(m)ne); **p** (ado(p)ção, ado(p)tar); for further details see p. xiii.

neck espichar-se, espichar o pescoço.
crania ['kreınıə] *npl* of **cranium**.
cranium ['kreınıəm] (*pl* **crania**) *n* crânio.
crank [kræŋk] *n* manivela; (*person*) excêntrico/a.
crankshaft ['kræŋkʃɑːft] *n* virabrequim *m*.
cranky ['kræŋkı] *adj* (*eccentric*) excêntrico; (*bad-tempered*) irritadiço.
cranny ['krænı] *n see* **nook**.
crap [kræp] (*inf!*) *n* papo furado; **to have a ~** cagar (*!*).
crash [kræʃ] *n* (*noise*) estrondo; (*of cars etc*) choque *m*, batida; (*of plane*) desastre *m* de avião; (*COMM*) falência, quebra; (*STOCK EXCHANGE*) craque *m* ♦ *vt* (*plane*) espatifar ♦ *vi* (*plane*) cair, espatifar-se; (*two cars*) colidir, bater; (*fall noisily*) cair (com estrondo); (*fig*) despencar; **to ~ into** bater em; **he ~ed into a wall** ele bateu com o carro num muro.
crash barrier (*BRIT*) *n* (*AUT*) cerca de proteção.
crash course *n* curso intensivo.
crash helmet *n* capacete *m*.
crash landing *n* aterrissagem *f* forçada (*BR*), aterragem *f* forçosa (*PT*).
crass [kræs] *adj* crasso.
crate [kreıt] *n* caixote *m*; (*inf: old car*) lata-velha; (*of beer*) engradado.
crater ['kreıtə*] *n* cratera.
cravat(e) [krə'væt] *n* gravata.
crave [kreıv] *vt, vi*: **to ~ for** ansiar por.
craving ['kreıvıŋ] *n* (*of pregnant woman*) desejo.
crawl [krɔːl] *vi* arrastar-se; (*child*) engatinhar; (*vehicle*) arrastar-se a passo de tartaruga ♦ *n* rastejo; (*SWIMMING*) crawl *m*; **to ~ to sb** (*inf*) puxar o saco de alguém.
crayfish ['kreıfıʃ] *n inv* lagostim *m*.
crayon ['kreıən] *n* lápis *m* de cera, crayon *m*.
craze [kreız] *n* mania; (*fashion*) moda.
crazed [kreızd] *adj* (*look, person*) enlouquecido; (*pottery, glaze*) craquelê.
crazy ['kreızı] *adj* (*person*) louco, maluco, doido; (*idea*) disparatado; **to go ~** enlouquecer; **to be ~ about sth** (*inf*) ser louco por algo.
crazy paving (*BRIT*) *n* pavimento irregular.
creak [kriːk] *vi* chiar, ranger; (*door etc*) ranger.
cream [kriːm] *n* (*of milk*) nata; (*gen*) creme *m*; (*fig*): **the ~ of** a fina flor de ♦ *adj* (*colour*) creme *inv*.
cream off *vt* (*fig*) tirar.
cream cake *n* bolo de creme.
cream cheese *n* ricota (*BR*), queijo creme (*PT*).
creamery ['kriːmərı] *n* (*shop*) leiteria; (*factory*) fábrica de laticínios.
creamy ['kriːmı] *adj* cremoso.
crease [kriːs] *n* (*fold*) dobra, vinco; (*in trousers*) vinco; (*wrinkle*) ruga ♦ *vt* (*fold*) dobrar, vincar; (*wrinkle*) amassar, amarrotar ♦ *vi* (*wrinkle up*) amassar-se, amarrotar-se.
crease-resistant *adj*: **a ~ fabric** um tecido que não amarrota.

create [kriː'eıt] *vt* criar.
creation [kriː'eıʃən] *n* criação *f*.
creative [kriː'eıtıv] *adj* criativo.
creativity [kriːeı'tıvıtı] *n* criatividade *f*.
creator [kriː'eıtə*] *n* criador(a) *m/f*.
creature ['kriːtʃə*] *n* (*animal*) animal *m*, bicho; (*living thing*) criatura.
creche [krɛʃ] *n* creche *f*.
crèche [krɛʃ] *n* = **creche**.
credence ['kriːdns] *n* crédito.
credentials [krı'dɛnʃlz] *npl* credenciais *fpl*.
credibility [krɛdı'bılıtı] *n* credibilidade *f*.
credible ['krɛdıbl] *adj* crível.
credit ['krɛdıt] *n* (*gen, SCH*) crédito; (*merit*) mérito, honra ♦ *vt* (*believe: also: give ~ to*) acreditar; (*COMM*) creditar ♦ *cpd* creditício; **~s** *npl* (*CINEMA*) crédito; **to ~ sb with sth** (*fig*) atribuir algo a alguém; **to ~ £5 to sb** creditar £5 a alguém; **to be in ~** (*person, bank account*) ter fundos; **on ~** a crédito; **to one's ~** honra lhe seja; **to take the ~ for sth** atribuir-se o mérito de; **it does him ~** é motivo de honra para ele; **he's a ~ to his family** ele é um orgulho para a família.
creditable ['krɛdıtəbl] *adj* louvável.
credit account *n* conta de crédito.
credit agency (*BRIT*) *n* agência de crédito.
credit balance *n* saldo credor.
credit bureau (*US: irreg*) *n* agência de crédito.
credit card *n* cartão *m* de crédito.
credit control *n* controle *m* de crédito.
credit facilities *npl* crediário.
credit limit *n* limite *m* de crédito.
credit note *n* nota de crédito.
creditor ['krɛdıtə*] *n* credor(a) *m/f*.
credit transfer *n* transferência.
creditworthy ['krɛdıtwəːðı] *adj* merecedor(a) de crédito.
credulity [krı'djuːlıtı] *n* credulidade *f*.
creed [kriːd] *n* credo.
creek [kriːk] *n* enseada; (*US*) riacho.
creel [kriːl] *n* cesto de pescador.
creep [kriːp] (*pt, pp* **crept**) *vi* (*animal*) rastejar; (*person*) deslizar(-se), andar na ponta dos pés; (*plant*) trepar ♦ *n* (*inf*) puxa-saco *m*; **it gives me the ~s** me dá arrepios; **to ~ up on sb** pegar alguém de surpresa.
creeper ['kriːpə*] *n* trepadeira; **~s** *npl* (*US: for baby*) macacão *m* (*BR*), fato macaco (*PT*).
creepy ['kriːpı] *adj* (*frightening*) horripilante.
creepy-crawly [-'krɔːlı] (*inf*) *n* bichinho.
cremate [krı'meıt] *vt* cremar.
cremation [krə'meıʃən] *n* cremação *f*.
crematoria [krɛmə'tɔːrıə] *npl* of **crematorium**.
crematorium [krɛmə'tɔːrıəm] (*pl* **crematoria**) *n* crematório.
creosote ['krıəsəut] *n* creosoto.
crêpe [kreıp] *n* (*fabric*) crepe *m*; (*paper*) papel crepom *m*.
crêpe bandage *n* atadura de crepe.
crêpe paper *n* papel *m* crepom.
crêpe sole *n* sola de crepe.
crept [krɛpt] *pt, pp* of **creep**.
crescendo [krı'ʃɛndəu] *n* crescendo.
crescent ['krɛsnt] *n* meia-lua; (*street*) rua se-

micircular.
cress [krɛs] *n* agrião *m*.
crest [krɛst] *n* (*of bird*) crista; (*of hill*) cimo, topo; (*of helmet*) cimeira; (*of coat of arms*) timbre *m*.
crestfallen ['krɛstfɔːlən] *adj* abatido, cabisbaixo.
Crete [kriːt] *n* Creta.
crevasse [krɪ'væs] *n* fenda.
crevice ['krɛvɪs] *n* fenda, greta.
crew [kruː] *n* (*of ship etc*) tripulação *f*; (*gang*) bando, quadrilha; (*MIL*) guarnição *f*; (*CINEMA*) equipe *f*.
crew-cut *n* corte *m* à escovinha.
crew-neck *n* gola arredondada.
crib [krɪb] *n* manjedoira, presépio; (*US: cot*) berço ♦ *vt* (*inf*) colar.
cribbage ['krɪbɪdʒ] *n jogo de cartas*.
crick [krɪk] *n* cãibra; ~ **in the neck** torcicolo.
cricket ['krɪkɪt] *n* (*insect*) grilo; (*game*) criquete *m*, cricket *m*.
cricketer ['krɪkɪtə*] *n* jogador(a) *m/f* de criquete.
crime [kraɪm] *n* crime *m*; (*less serious*) delito; (~ *in general*) criminalidade *f*.
crime wave *n* onda de criminalidade.
criminal ['krɪmɪnl] *n* criminoso ♦ *adj* criminal; (*law*) penal; **the C~ Investigation Department** (*BRIT*) a Brigada de Investigação Criminal.
crimp [krɪmp] *vt* (*hair*) frisar.
crimson ['krɪmzn] *adj* carmesim *inv*.
cringe [krɪndʒ] *vi* agachar-se, encolher-se.
crinkle ['krɪŋkl] *vt* amassar, enrugar.
cripple ['krɪpl] *n* coxo/a, aleijado/a ♦ *vt* aleijar; (*ship, plane*) inutilizar; (*industry, exports*) paralisar.
crippling ['krɪplɪŋ] *adj* (*disease*) devastador(a); (*taxation, debts*) excessivo.
crises ['kraɪsiːz] *npl of* **crisis**.
crisis ['kraɪsɪs] (*pl* **crises**) *n* crise *f*.
crisp [krɪsp] *adj* (*crunchy*) crocante; (*vegetables, fruit*) fresco; (*cooked*) torrado; (*manner*) seco.
crisps [krɪsps] (*BRIT*) *npl* batatinhas *fpl* fritas.
criss-cross [krɪs-] *adj* (*lines*) entrecruzado; (*pattern*) em xadrez ♦ *vt* entrecruzar; ~ **pattern** (padrão *m* em) xadrez *m*.
criteria [kraɪ'tɪərɪə] *npl of* **criterion**.
criterion [kraɪ'tɪərɪən] (*pl* **criteria**) *n* critério.
critic ['krɪtɪk] *n* crítico/a.
critical ['krɪtɪkl] *adj* crítico; (*illness*) grave; **to be** ~ **of sth/sb** criticar algo/alguém.
critically ['krɪtɪkəlɪ] *adv* (*examine*) criteriosamente; (*speak*) criticamente; (*ill*) gravemente.
criticism ['krɪtɪsɪzm] *n* crítica.
criticize ['krɪtɪsaɪz] *vt* criticar.
critique [krɪ'tiːk] *n* crítica.
croak [krəuk] *vi* (*frog*) coaxar; (*raven*) crocitar ♦ *n* grasnido.
crochet ['krəuʃeɪ] *n* crochê *m*.

crock [krɔk] *n* jarro; (*inf: also: old* ~: *person*) caco velho; (: *car*) calhambeque *m*.
crockery ['krɔkərɪ] *n* louça.
crocodile ['krɔkədaɪl] *n* crocodilo.
crocus ['krəukəs] *n* açafrão-da-primavera *m*.
croft [krɔft] (*BRIT*) *n* pequena chácara.
crofter ['krɔftə*] (*BRIT*) *n* arrendatário.
croissant ['krwasã] *n* croissant *m*.
crone [krəun] *n* velha encarquilhada.
crony ['krəunɪ] *n* camarada *m/f*, compadre *m*.
crook [kruk] *n* (*inf: criminal*) vigarista *m/f*; (*of shepherd*) cajado; (*of arm*) curva.
crooked ['krukɪd] *adj* torto; (*path*) tortuoso; (*action*) desonesto.
crop [krɔp] *n* (*species*) colheita; (*quantity*) safra; (*riding* ~) chicotinho; (*of bird*) papo ♦ *vt* cortar, ceifar.
crop up *vi* surgir.
cropper ['krɔpə*] *n*: **to come a** ~ (*inf*) dar com os burros n'água, entrar pelo cano.
crop spraying [-'spreɪŋ] *n* pulverização *f* das culturas.
croquet ['krəukeɪ] *n* croquet *m*, croquê *m*.
croquette [krə'kɛt] *n* croquete *m*.
cross [krɔs] *n* cruz *f*; (*BIO*) cruzamento ♦ *vt* cruzar; (*street etc*) atravessar; (*thwart: person, plan*) contrariar ♦ *vi* atravessar ♦ *adj* zangado, mal-humorado; **to** ~ **o.s.** persignar-se; **they've got their lines** ~**ed** eles têm um mal-entendido.
cross out *vt* riscar.
cross over *vi* atravessar.
crossbar ['krɔsbɑː*] *n* travessa; (*SPORT*) barra transversal.
crossbreed ['krɔsbriːd] *n* raça cruzada.
cross-Channel ferry *n* barca que faz a travessia do Canal da Mancha.
cross-check *n* conferição *f* ♦ *vt* conferir.
cross-country (race) *n* corrida pelo campo.
cross-examination *n* interrogatório; (*LAW*) repergunta.
cross-examine *vt* interrogar; (*LAW*) reperguntar.
cross-eyed [-aɪd] *adj* vesgo.
crossfire ['krɔsfaɪə*] *n* fogo cruzado.
crossing ['krɔsɪŋ] *n* (*road*) cruzamento; (*rail*) passagem *f* de nível; (*sea-passage*) travessia; (*also: pedestrian* ~) faixa (para pedestres) (*BR*), passadeira (*PT*).
cross-purposes *npl*: **to be at** ~ (**with sb**) não entender-se (com alguém); **we're (talking) at** ~ não falamos da mesma coisa.
cross-reference *n* referência remissiva.
crossroads ['krɔsrəudz] *n* cruzamento.
cross section *n* (*BIO*) corte *m* transversal; (*of population*) grupo representativo.
crosswalk ['krɔswɔːk] (*US*) *n* faixa (para pedestres) (*BR*), passadeira (*PT*).
crosswind ['krɔswɪnd] *n* vento costal.
crosswise ['krɔswaɪz] *adv* transversalmente.
crossword ['krɔswɔːd] *n* palavras *fpl* cruzadas.

NB: *European Portuguese adds the following consonants to certain words:* **b** (sú(b)dito, su(b)til); **c** (a(c)ção, a(c)cionista, a(c)to); **m** (inde(m)ne); **p** (ado(p)ção, ado(p)tar); *for further details see p. xiii.*

crotch [krɔtʃ] n (of garment) fundilho.
crotchet ['krɔtʃɪt] n (MUS) semínima.
crotchety ['krɔtʃɪtɪ] adj (person) rabugento.
crouch [krautʃ] vi agachar-se.
croup [kru:p] n (MED) crupe m.
croupier ['kru:pɪə] n crupiê m/f.
crouton ['kru:tɔn] n crouton m.
crow [krəu] n (bird) corvo; (of cock) canto, cocoricó m ♦ vi (cock) cantar, cocoricar; (fig) contar vantagem.
crowbar ['krəuba:*] n pé-de-cabra m.
crowd [kraud] n multidão f; (SPORT) público, galera (inf); (unruly) tropel m; (common herd) turba, vulgo ♦ vt (fill) apinhar ♦ vi (gather) reunir-se; ~s of people um grande número de pessoas.
crowded ['kraudɪd] adj (full) lotado; (well-attended) concorrido.
crowd scene n (CINEMA, THEATRE) cena de multidão.
crown [kraun] n coroa; (of head) topo, alta; (of hat) copa; (of hill) cume m ♦ vt coroar; (tooth) pôr uma coroa artificial em.
crown court (BRIT) n Tribunal m de Justiça.
crowning ['kraunɪŋ] adj (achievement, glory) supremo.
crown jewels npl jóias fpl reais.
crown prince n príncipe m herdeiro.
crow's-feet npl pés-de-galinha mpl.
crow's-nest n (on ship) cesto de gávea.
crucial ['kru:ʃl] adj decisivo; ~ **to** vital para.
crucifix ['kru:sɪfɪks] n crucifixo.
crucifixion [kru:sɪ'fɪkʃən] n crucificação f.
crucify ['kru:sɪfaɪ] vt crucificar.
crude [kru:d] adj (materials) bruto; (fig: basic) tosco; (: vulgar) grosseiro.
crude (oil) n petróleo em bruto.
cruel ['kruəl] adj cruel.
cruelty ['kruəltɪ] n crueldade f.
cruet ['kru:ɪt] n galheta.
cruise [kru:z] n cruzeiro ♦ vi (ship) fazer um cruzeiro; (aircraft) voar; (car): **to** ~ **at** ... **km/h** ir a ... km por hora.
cruise missile n míssil m Cruise.
cruiser ['kru:zə*] n cruzador m.
cruising speed ['kru:zɪŋ-] n velocidade f de cruzeiro.
crumb [krʌm] n migalha.
crumble ['krʌmbl] vt esmigalhar ♦ vi desintegrar-se; (building, fig) desmoronar-se.
crumbly ['krʌmblɪ] adj friável.
crummy ['krʌmɪ] (inf) adj mixa; (unwell) podre.
crumpet ['krʌmpɪt] n bolo leve.
crumple ['krʌmpl] vt (paper) amassar; (material) amarrotar.
crunch [krʌntʃ] vt (food etc) mastigar; (underfoot) esmagar ♦ n (fig) crise f.
crunchy ['krʌntʃɪ] adj crocante.
crusade [kru:'seɪd] n cruzada ♦ vi (fig): **to** ~ **for/against** batalhar por/contra.
crusader [kru:'seɪdə*] n cruzado; (fig): ~ **(for)** batalhador(a) m/f (por).
crush [krʌʃ] n (people) esmagamento; (crowd) aglomeração f; (love): **to have a** ~

on sb ter um rabicho por alguém; (drink): **lemon** ~ limonada ♦ vt (gen) esmagar; (paper) amassar; (cloth) enrugar; (fruit) espremer.
crushing ['krʌʃɪŋ] adj (burden) esmagador(a).
crust [krʌst] n côdea; (MED) crosta.
crustacean [krʌs'teɪʃən] n crustáceo.
crusty ['krʌstɪ] adj cascudo.
crutch [krʌtʃ] n muleta; (of garment: also: crotch) fundilho.
crux [krʌks] n ponto crucial.
cry [kraɪ] vi chorar; (shout) gritar ♦ n grito; **to** ~ **for** gritar por socorro; **it's a far** ~ **from** ... (fig) é totalmente diferente de ....
cry off vi desistir.
crying ['kraɪɪŋ] adj (fig) flagrante.
crypt [krɪpt] n cripta.
cryptic ['krɪptɪk] adj enigmático.
crystal ['krɪstl] n cristal m.
crystal-clear adj cristalino, claro.
crystallize ['krɪstəlaɪz] vt cristalizar ♦ vi cristalizar-se.
CSA n abbr = **Confederate States of America.**
CSC n abbr (= Civil Service Commission) comissão de recrutamento de funcionários públicos.
CSE (BRIT) n abbr = **Certificate of Secondary Education.**
CSEU (BRIT) n abbr (= Confederation of Shipbuilding and Engineering Unions) confederação dos sindicatos da construção naval e da engenharia.
CS gas (BRIT) n gás m CS.
CST (US) n abbr (= Central Standard Time) fuso horário.
CSU (BRIT) n abbr (= Civil Service Union) sindicato de funcionários públicos.
CT (US) abbr (POST) = **Connecticut.**
ct abbr = **carat.**
cu. abbr = **cubic.**
cub [kʌb] n filhote m; (also: ~ scout) lobinho.
Cuba ['kju:bə] n Cuba.
Cuban ['kju:bən] adj, n cubano/a.
cubbyhole ['kʌbɪhəul] n esconderijo.
cube [kju:b] n cubo ♦ vt (MATH) elevar ao cubo.
cube root n raiz f cúbica.
cubic ['kju:bɪk] adj cúbico; ~ **metre** etc metro etc cúbico; ~ **capacity** (AUT) cilindrada.
cubicle ['kju:bɪkl] n cubículo; (shower ~) boxe m.
cuckoo ['kuku:] n cuco.
cuckoo clock n relógio de cuco.
cucumber ['kju:kʌmbə*] n pepino.
cud [kʌd] n: **to chew the** ~ ruminar.
cuddle ['kʌdl] vt abraçar ♦ vi abraçar-se.
cuddly ['kʌdlɪ] adj fofo.
cudgel ['kʌdʒəl] n cacete m ♦ vt: **to** ~ **one's brains** quebrar a cabeça.
cue [kju:] n (SNOOKER) taco; (THEATRE etc) deixa.
cuff [kʌf] n (of shirt, coat etc) punho; (US: on trousers) bainha; (blow) bofetada ♦ vt esbofetear; **off the** ~ de improviso.

cufflinks ['kʌflɪŋks] *npl* abotoaduras *fpl*.
cu. in. *abbr* = **cubic inches**.
cuisine [kwɪ'ziːn] *n* cozinha.
cul-de-sac ['kʌldəsæk] *n* beco sem saída.
culinary ['kʌlɪnərɪ] *adj* culinário.
cull [kʌl] *vt* (*flowers*) escolher; (*select*) selecionar; (*kill*) matar seletivamente.
culminate ['kʌlmɪneɪt] *vi*: **to ~ in** terminar em; (*lead to*) resultar em.
culmination [kʌlmɪ'neɪʃən] *n* culminação *f*, auge *m*.
culottes [kjuː'lɒts] *npl* saia-calça.
culpable ['kʌlpəbl] *adj* culpável.
culprit ['kʌlprɪt] *n* culpado/a.
cult [kʌlt] *n* culto.
cult figure *n* ídolo.
cultivate ['kʌltɪveɪt] *vt* (*also fig*) cultivar.
cultivation [kʌltɪ'veɪʃən] *n* cultivo; (*fig*) cultura.
cultural ['kʌltʃərəl] *adj* cultural.
culture ['kʌltʃə*] *n* (*also fig*) cultura.
cultured ['kʌltʃəd] *adj* culto.
cumbersome ['kʌmbəsəm] *adj* pesado, incômodo.
cumin ['kʌmɪn] *n* cominho.
cumulative ['kjuːmjulətɪv] *adj* cumulativo.
cunning ['kʌnɪŋ] *n* astúcia ♦ *adj* astuto, malandro; (*clever*: *device*, *idea*) engenhoso.
cup [kʌp] *n* xícara (*BR*), chávena (*PT*); (*prize*, *event*) taça.
cupboard ['kʌbəd] *n* armário; (*for crockery*) guarda-louça.
cup final (*BRIT*) *n* final *f*.
Cupid ['kjuːpɪd] *n* Cupido.
cupidity [kjuː'pɪdɪtɪ] *n* cupidez *f*.
cupola ['kjuːpələ] *n* cúpula.
cup-tie *n* jogo eliminatório.
cur [kɜː] *n* cão *m* vadio, vira-latas *m inv*; (*person*) patife *m/f*.
curable ['kjuərəbl] *adj* curável.
curate ['kjuəːrɪt] *n* coadjutor *m*.
curator [kjuə'reɪtə*] *n* diretor(a) *m/f*, curador(a) *m/f*.
curb [kɜːb] *vt* refrear ♦ *n* freio; (*US*) = **kerb**.
curdle ['kɜːdl] *vi* coalhar.
curds [kɜːdz] *npl* coalho.
cure [kjuə*] *vt* curar ♦ *n* tratamento, cura; **to be ~d of sth** sarar(-se) de algo.
cure-all *n* (*also*: *fig*) panacéia.
curfew ['kɜːfjuː] *n* hora de recolher.
curio ['kjuərɪəu] *n* antiguidade *f*.
curiosity [kjuərɪ'ɒsɪtɪ] *n* curiosidade *f*.
curious ['kjuərɪəs] *adj* curioso.
curiously ['kjuərɪəslɪ] *adv* curiosamente; **~ enough**, ... por estranho que pareça, ...
curl [kɜːl] *n* anel *m*, caracol *m* ♦ *vt* (*hair*) frisar, encrespar; (*paper*) enrolar; (*lip*) torcer ♦ *vi* (*hair*) encaracolar.
curl up *vi* frisar-se; (*person*) encaracolar-se.
curler ['kɜːlə*] *n* rolo, bobe *m*.
curlew ['kɜːluː] *n* maçarico.

curling ['kɜːlɪŋ] *n* (*SPORT*) curling *m*.
curling tongs (*US* **curling irons**) *npl* ferros *mpl* de frisar cabelo.
curly ['kɜːlɪ] *adj* frisado, crespo.
currant ['kʌrnt] *n* passa de corinto; (*black*, *red*) groselha.
currency ['kʌrnsɪ] *n* moeda; **foreign ~** câmbio, divisas; **to gain ~** (*fig*) consagrar-se.
current ['kʌrnt] *n* (*ELEC*) corrente *f*; (*in river*) correnteza ♦ *adj* corrente; (*present*) atual; **in ~ usage** de uso corrente.
current account *n* conta corrente.
current affairs *npl* atualidades *fpl*.
current assets *npl* (*COMM*) ativo corrente.
current liabilities *npl* (*COMM*) passivo corrente.
currently ['kʌrntlɪ] *adv* atualmente.
curricula [kə'rɪkjulə] *npl of* **curriculum**.
curriculum [kə'rɪkjuləm] (*pl* **~s** *or* **curricula**) *n* programa *m* de estudos.
curriculum vitae [-'viːtaɪ] *n* curriculum vitae *m*, currículo.
curry ['kʌrɪ] *n* caril *m* ♦ *vt*: **to ~ favour with** captar simpatia de.
curry powder *n* pós *mpl* de caril, curry *m*.
curse [kɜːs] *vi* xingar (*BR*), praguejar (*PT*) ♦ *vt* amaldiçoar, xingar (*BR*) ♦ *n* maldição *f*; (*swearword*) palavrão *m* (*BR*), baixo calão *m* (*PT*).
cursor ['kɜːsə*] *n* (*COMPUT*) cursor *m*.
cursory ['kɜːsərɪ] *adj* rápido, superficial.
curt [kɜːt] *adj* seco, brusco.
curtail [kɜː'teɪl] *vt* (*visit etc*) abreviar, encurtar; (*expenses etc*) reduzir.
curtain ['kɜːtn] *n* cortina; (*THEATRE*) pano.
curtain call *n* (*THEATRE*) chamada à ribalta.
curtain ring *n* argola.
curts(e)y ['kɜːtsɪ] *n* mesura, reverência ♦ *vi* fazer reverência.
curvature ['kɜːvətʃə*] *n* curvatura.
curve [kɜːv] *n* curva ♦ *vt* encurvar, torcer ♦ *vi* encurvar-se, torcer-se; (*road*) fazer (uma) curva.
curved [kɜːvd] *adj* curvado, curvo.
cushion ['kuʃən] *n* almofada; (*SNOOKER*) tabela ♦ *vt* (*seat*) escorar com almofada; (*shock*) amortecer.
cushy ['kuʃɪ] (*inf*) *adj*: **a ~ job** uma boca; **to have a ~ time** estar na moleza.
custard ['kʌstəd] *n* (*for pouring*) nata, creme *m*.
custard powder (*BRIT*) *n* pó *m* para fazer creme.
custodian [kʌs'təudɪən] *n* guarda *m/f*.
custody ['kʌstədɪ] *n* custódia; (*for offenders*) prisão *f* preventiva; **to take into ~** deter.
custom ['kʌstəm] *n* costume *m*; (*COMM*) clientela; **~s** *npl* alfândega.
customary ['kʌstəmərɪ] *adj* costumeiro; **it is ~ to do it** é costume fazê-lo.
custom-built *adj* feito sob encomenda.

NB: *European Portuguese adds the following consonants to certain words:* **b** (sú(b)dito, su(b)til); **c** (a(c)ção, a(c)cionista, a(c)to); **m** (inde(m)ne); **p** (ado(p)ção, ado(p)tar); *for further details see p. xiii.*

customer ['kʌstəmə*] *n* cliente *m/f*; **he's an awkward ~** (*inf*) ele é um cara difícil.
custom-made *adj* feito sob encomenda; (*clothes*) feito sob medida.
Customs and Excise (*BRIT*) *n* autoridades *fpl* alfandegárias.
customs duty *n* imposto alfandegário.
customs officer *n* inspetor(a) *m/f* da alfândega, aduaneiro/a.
cut [kʌt] (*pt, pp* **cut**) *vt* cortar; (*price*) baixar; (*record*) gravar; (*reduce*) reduzir; (*inf: class*) matar ♦ *vi* cortar; (*intersect*) interceptar-se ♦ *n* corte *m*; **cold ~s** *npl* (*US*) frios *mpl* sortidos; **to ~ a tooth** estar com um dente nascendo; **to ~ one's finger** cortar o dedo; **to get one's hair ~** cortar o cabelo; **to ~ sth short** abreviar algo; **to ~ sb dead** fingir que não conhece alguém.
cut back *vt* (*plants*) podar; (*production, expenditure*) cortar.
cut down *vt* (*tree*) derrubar; (*reduce*) reduzir; **to ~ sb down to size** (*fig*) abaixar a crista de alguém, colocar alguém no seu lugar.
cut in *vi*: **to ~ in (on)** interromper; (*AUT*) cortar.
cut off *vt* cortar; (*retreat*) impedir; (*troops*) cercar; **we've been ~ off** (*TEL*) fomos cortados.
cut out *vt* (*shape*) recortar; (*delete*) suprimir.
cut through *vi* abrir caminho.
cut up *vt* cortar em pedaços.
cut-and-dried *adj* (*also: cut-and-dry*) todo resolvido.
cutaway ['kʌtəweɪ] *adj, n*: **~ (drawing)** vista diagramática.
cutback ['kʌtbæk] *n* redução *f*, corte *m*.
cute [kjuːt] *adj* bonitinho, gracinha; (*shrewd*) astuto.
cut glass *n* cristal *m* lapidado.
cuticle ['kjuːtɪkl] *n* cutícula; **~ remover** produto para tirar as cutículas.
cutlery ['kʌtlərɪ] *n* talheres *mpl*.
cutlet ['kʌtlɪt] *n* costeleta.
cutoff ['kʌtɔf] *n* (*also: ~ point*) ponto de corte.
cutoff switch *n* interruptor *m*.
cutout ['kʌtaut] *n* figura para recortar; (*ELEC*) interruptor *m*.
cut-price (*US* **cut-rate**) *adj* a preço reduzido.
cut-throat *n* assassino/a ♦ *adj* impiedoso, feroz.
cutting ['kʌtɪŋ] *adj* cortante; (*remark*) mordaz ♦ *n* (*BRIT: from newspaper*) recorte *m*; (: *RAIL*) corte *m*; (*CINEMA*) corte *m*.
cuttlefish ['kʌtlfɪʃ] (*pl inv or ~es*) *n* sita.
cut-up *adj* arrasado, aflito.
CV *n abbr* = **curriculum vitae**.
C & W *n abbr* = **country and western** (music).
cwo *abbr* (*COMM*) = **cash with order**.
cwt *abbr* = **hundredweight**.
cyanide ['saɪənaɪd] *n* cianeto.
cybernetics [saɪbə'nɛtɪks] *n* cibernética.
cyclamen ['sɪkləmən] *n* cíclame *m*.

cycle ['saɪkl] *n* ciclo; (*bicycle*) bicicleta ♦ *vi* andar de bicicleta.
cycle race *n* corrida de bicicletas.
cycle rack *n* engradado para guardar bicicletas.
cycling ['saɪklɪŋ] *n* ciclismo.
cyclist ['saɪklɪst] *n* ciclista *m/f*.
cyclone ['saɪkləun] *n* ciclone *m*.
cygnet ['sɪgnɪt] *n* cisne *m* novo.
cylinder ['sɪlɪndə*] *n* cilindro.
cylinder block *n* bloco de cilindros.
cylinder capacity *n* capacidade *f* cilíndrica, cilindrada.
cylinder head *n* cilíndrico.
cylinder-head gasket *n* culatra.
cymbals ['sɪmblz] *npl* pratos *mpl*.
cynic ['sɪnɪk] *n* cínico/a.
cynical ['sɪnɪkl] *adj* cínico, sarcástico.
cynicism ['sɪnɪsɪzəm] *n* cinismo.
CYO (*US*) *n abbr* = **Catholic Youth Organization**.
cypress ['saɪprɪs] *n* cipreste *m*.
Cypriot ['sɪprɪət] *adj, n* cipriota *m/f*.
Cyprus ['saɪprəs] *n* Chipre *f*.
cyst [sɪst] *n* cisto.
cystitis [sɪs'taɪtɪs] *n* cistite *f*.
CZ (*US*) *n abbr* (= *Canal Zone*) zona do canal do Panamá.
czar [zɑ:*] *n* czar *m*.
Czech [tʃɛk] *adj* tcheco ♦ *n* tcheco/a; (*LING*) tcheco.
Czechoslovak [tʃɛkə'sləuvæk] *adj, n* = **Czechoslovakian**.
Czechoslovakia [tʃɛkəslə'vækɪə] *n* Tchecoslováquia.
Czechoslovakian [tʃɛkəslə'vækɪən] *adj, n* tchecoslovaco/a.

D

D, d [di:] *n* (*letter*) D, d *m*; (*MUS*): **D** ré *m*; **D for David** (*BRIT*) *or* **Dog** (*US*) D de dado.
D (*US*) *abbr* (*POL*) = **democrat(ic)**.
d (*BRIT*) *abbr* (*old*) = **penny**.
d. *abbr* = **died**.
DA (*US*) *n abbr* = **district attorney**.
dab [dæb] *vt* (*eyes, wound*) tocar (de leve); (*paint, cream*) aplicar de leve ♦ *n* (*of paint*) pincelada; (*of liquid*) gota; (*amount*) pequena quantidade *f*.
dabble ['dæbl] *vi*: **to ~ in** interessar-se por.
dachshund ['dækshund] *n* bassê *m*.
dad [dæd] *n* papai *m*.
daddy ['dædɪ] *n* = **dad**.
daddy-long-legs *n inv* pernilongo.
daffodil ['dæfədɪl] *n* narciso-dos-prados *m*.
daft [dɑːft] *adj* bobo, besta; **to be ~ about** ser louco por.

dagger ['dægə*] n punhal m, adaga; **to look ~s at sb** olhar feio para alguém; **to be at ~s drawn with sb** andar às turras com alguém.

dahlia ['deɪljə] n dália.

daily ['deɪlɪ] adj diário, cotidiano ♦ n (paper) diário; (BRIT: domestic help) diarista (BR), mulher f a dias (PT) ♦ adv diariamente, todo dia; **twice ~** duas vezes por dia.

dainty ['deɪntɪ] adj delicado; (tasteful) elegante, gracioso.

dairy ['dɛərɪ] n leiteria ♦ adj (industry) de laticínios; (cattle) leiteiro.

dairy cow n vaca leiteira.

dairy farm n fazenda de gado leiteiro.

dairy produce n laticínios mpl.

dais ['deɪɪs] n estrado.

daisy ['deɪzɪ] n margarida.

daisy wheel n (on printer) margarida.

daisy-wheel printer n impressora margarida.

Dakar ['dækə*] n Dacar.

dale [deɪl] n vale m.

dally ['dælɪ] vi vadiar.

dalmatian [dæl'meɪʃən] n (dog) dálmata m.

dam [dæm] n represa, barragem f ♦ vt represar.

damage ['dæmɪdʒ] n (physical) danos mpl; (harm) prejuízo; (to machine) avaria ♦ vt (physically) danificar; (harm) prejudicar; **~s** npl (LAW) indenização f por perdas e danos; **to pay £5,000 in ~s** pagar £5,000 de indenização; **~ to property** danos materiais.

damaging ['dæmɪdʒɪŋ] adj: **~ (to)** prejudicial (a).

Damascus [də'mɑːskəs] n Damasco.

dame [deɪm] n (title) título honorífico dado a uma membra da Ordem do Império Britânico; título honorífico dado à esposa de um cavalheiro ou baronete; (US: inf) dona; (THEATRE) dama.

damn [dæm] vt condenar; (curse) maldizer ♦ n (inf): **I don't give a ~** não dou a mínima, estou me lixando ♦ adj (inf) (que) droga de; **~ (it)!** (que) droga!

damnable ['dæmnəbl] (inf) adj (behaviour) condenável; (weather) horrível.

damnation [dæm'neɪʃən] n (REL) danação f ♦ excl (inf) droga!

damning ['dæmɪŋ] adj (evidence) prejudicial; (criticism) condenador(a).

damp [dæmp] adj úmido ♦ n umidade f ♦ vt (also: ~en: cloth, rag) umedecer; (enthusiasm etc) jogar água fria em.

dampcourse ['dæmpkɔːs] n impermeabilização f.

damper ['dæmpə*] n (MUS) abafador m; (of fire) registro; **to put a ~ on** (fig: atmosphere) criar um mal-estar em; (: party) acabar com a animação de; (: enthusiasm) cortar.

dampness ['dæmpnɪs] n umidade f.

damson ['dæmzən] n ameixa pequena.

dance [dɑːns] n dança; (party) baile m ♦ vi dançar; **to ~ about** saltitar.

dance hall n salão m de baile.

dancer ['dɑːnsə*] n dançarino/a; (professional) bailarino/a.

dancing ['dɑːnsɪŋ] n dança.

D and C n abbr (MED: = dilation and curettage) dilatação f e curetagem f.

dandelion ['dændɪlaɪən] n dente-de-leão m.

dandruff ['dændrəf] n caspa.

dandy ['dændɪ] n dândi m ♦ adj (US: inf) bacana.

Dane [deɪn] n dinamarquês/esa m/f.

danger ['deɪndʒə*] n perigo; **to be in ~ of** correr o risco de; **in ~** em perigo; **out of ~** fora de perigo; **~ money** (BRIT) adicional m por insalubridade.

danger list n (MED): **on the ~** na lista dos pacientes graves.

dangerous ['deɪndʒərəs] adj perigoso.

dangerously ['deɪndʒərəslɪ] adv perigosamente; **~ ill** gravemente doente.

danger zone n zona de perigo.

dangle ['dæŋgl] vt balançar ♦ vi pender balançando.

Danish ['deɪnɪʃ] adj dinamarquês/esa ♦ n (LING) dinamarquês m.

Danish pastry n doce m (de massa com frutas).

dank [dæŋk] adj frio e úmido.

Danube ['dænjuːb] n: **the ~** o Danúbio.

dapper ['dæpə*] adj garboso.

dare [dɛə*] vt: **to ~ sb to do sth** desafiar alguém a fazer algo ♦ vi: **to ~ (to) do sth** atrever-se a fazer algo, ousar fazer algo; **I ~n't tell him** (BRIT) eu não ouso dizê-lo a ele; **I ~ say he'll turn up** acho provável que ele venha.

daredevil ['dɛədɛvl] n intrépido, atrevido.

Dar-es-Salaam ['dɑːrɛssə'lɑːm] n Dar-es-Salaam.

daring ['dɛərɪŋ] adj atrevido, ousado ♦ n atrevimento, audácia, ousadia.

dark [dɑːk] adj (gen, hair) escuro; (complexion) moreno; (cheerless) triste, sombrio; (fig) sombrio ♦ n escuro; **in the ~** no escuro; **in the ~ about** (fig) no escuro sobre; **after ~** depois de escurecer; **it is/is getting ~** está escuro/está escurecendo.

dark chocolate n chocolate m amargo.

darken ['dɑːkən] vt escurecer; (colour) fazer mais escuro ♦ vi escurecer(-se).

dark glasses npl óculos mpl escuros.

darkly ['dɑːklɪ] adv (gloomily) sombriamente; (in a sinister way) sinistramente.

darkness ['dɑːknɪs] n escuridão f, trevas fpl.

dark room n câmara escura.

darling ['dɑːlɪŋ] adj, n querido/a.

darn [dɑːn] vt remendar, cerzir.

dart [dɑːt] n dardo; ♦ vi precipitar-se; **~s** n jogo de dardos; **to ~ away/along** ir-se/seguir

precipitadamente.
dartboard ['dɑːtbɔːd] *n* alvo (para jogo de dardos).
dash [dæʃ] *n* (*sign*) hífen *m*; (: *long*) travessão *m*; (*rush*) correria; (*small quantity*) pontinha ♦ *vt* (*throw*) arremessar; (*hopes*) frustrar ♦ *vi* precipitar-se, ir depressa.
dash away *vi* sair apressado.
dash off *vt* (*letter*, *essay*) escrever a toda ♦ *vi* sair apressado.
dashboard ['dæʃbɔːd] *n* painel *m* de instrumentos.
dashing ['dæʃɪŋ] *adj* arrojado.
dastardly ['dæstədlɪ] *adj* vil.
data ['deɪtə] *npl* dados *mpl*.
database ['deɪtəbeɪs] *n* banco de dados.
data capture *n* entrada de dados.
data processing *n* processamento de dados.
data transmission *n* transmissão *f* de dados.
date [deɪt] *n* (*day*) data; (*with friend*) encontro; (*fruit*) tâmara; (*tree*) tamareira ♦ *vt* datar; (*inf*: *go out with*) namorar; **what's the ~ today?** que dia é hoje?; **~ of birth** data de nascimento; **closing ~** data de encerramento; **to ~** até agora; **out of ~** desatualizado; **up to ~** (*correspondence etc*) em dia; (*dictionary*, *phone book etc*) atualizado; (*method*, *technology*) moderno; **to bring up to ~** (*correspondence*, *person*) pôr em dia; (*method*) modernizar; **letter ~d 5th July** (*BRIT*) *or* **July 5th** (*US*) carta datada de 5 de julho.
dated ['deɪtɪd] *adj* antiquado.
dateline ['deɪtlaɪn] *n* meridiano *or* linha de data.
date stamp *n* carimbo datador.
daub [dɔːb] *vt* borrar.
daughter ['dɔːtə*] *n* filha.
daughter-in-law (*pl* **daughters-in-law**) *n* nora.
daunt [dɔːnt] *vt* desalentar, desencorajar.
daunting ['dɔːntɪŋ] *adj* desalentador(a).
dauntless ['dɔːntlɪs] *adj* intrépido, destemido.
dawdle ['dɔːdl] *vi* (*waste time*) fazer cera; (*go slow*) vadiar.
dawn [dɔːn] *n* alvorada, amanhecer *m* ♦ *vi* (*day*) amanhecer; (*fig*): **it ~ed on him that ...** começou a perceber que ...; **at ~** ao amanhecer; **from ~ to dusk** de manhã à noite.
dawn chorus (*BRIT*) *n* canto dos pássaros na alvorada.
day [deɪ] *n* dia *m*; (*working ~*) jornada, dia útil; **the ~ before** a véspera; **the ~ after**, **the following ~** o dia seguinte; **the ~ before yesterday** anteontem; **the ~ after tomorrow** depois de amanhã; **(on) the ~ that ...** (n)o dia em que ...; **~ by ~** dia a dia; **by ~** de dia; **paid by the ~** pago por dia; **these ~s**, **in the present ~** hoje em dia.
daybook ['deɪbuk] (*BRIT*) *n* diário.
day boy *n* (*SCH*) externo.
daybreak ['deɪbreɪk] *n* amanhecer *m*.
daydream ['deɪdriːm] *n* devaneio ♦ *vi* devanear.
day girl *n* (*SCH*) externa.

daylight ['deɪlaɪt] *n* luz *f* (do dia).
Daylight Saving Time (*US*) *n* hora de verâo.
day release *n*: **to be on ~** ter licença de um dia por semana para fins de aperfeiçoamento profissional.
day return (ticket) (*BRIT*) *n* bilhete *m* de ida e volta no mesmo dia.
day shift *n* turno diurno.
daytime ['deɪtaɪm] *n* dia *m* ♦ *adj* de dia, diurno.
day-to-day *adj* (*life*, *expenses*) cotidiano; **the ~ routine** o dia-a-dia; **on a ~ basis** dia a dia, diariamente.
day trip *n* excursão *f* (de um dia).
day tripper *n* excursionista *m/f*.
daze [deɪz] *vt* (*stun*) aturdir ♦ *n*: **in a ~** aturdido.
dazzle ['dæzl] *vt* deslumbrar, ofuscar.
dazzling ['dæzlɪŋ] *adj* deslumbrante, ofuscante.
DC *abbr* (*ELEC*) = **direct current**; (*US*: *POST*) = **District of Columbia**.
DD *n* *abbr* (= *Doctor of Divinity*) título universitário.
dd. *abbr* (*COMM*: = *delivered*) entregue.
D/D *abbr* = **direct debit**.
D-day ['diːdeɪ] *n* o dia D.
DDS (*US*) *n* *abbr* (= *Doctor of Dental Science*; *Doctor of Dental Surgery*) títulos universitários.
DDT *n* *abbr* (= *dichlorodiphenyltrichloroethane*) DDT *m*.
DE (*US*) *abbr* (*POST*) = **Delaware**.
DEA (*US*) *n* *abbr* (= *Drug Enforcement Administration*) ≈ Conselho Nacional de Entorpecentes.
deacon ['diːkən] *n* diácono.
dead [dɛd] *adj* morto; (*deceased*) falecido; (*telephone*) cortado; (*ELEC*) sem corrente ♦ *adv* (*very*) totalmente; (*exactly*) absolutamente ♦ *npl*: **the ~** os mortos; **~ tired** morto de cansado; **to stop ~** estacar; **he was shot ~** ele foi morto a tiro; **~ on time** na hora em ponto; **the line has gone ~** (*TEL*) caiu a ligação.
deaden ['dɛdn] *vt* (*blow*, *sound*) amortecer; (*make numb*) anestesiar.
dead end *n* beco sem saída ♦ *adj*: **a dead-end job** um emprego sem perspectivas.
dead heat *n* (*SPORT*) empate *m*; **to finish in a ~** (*race*) ser empatado.
dead-letter office *n* seção *f* de cartas não reclamadas.
deadline ['dɛdlaɪn] *n* prazo final; **to work to a ~** trabalhar com prazo estabelecido.
deadlock ['dɛdlɔk] *n* impasse *m*.
dead loss (*inf*) *n*: **to be a ~** não ser de nada.
deadly ['dɛdlɪ] *adj* mortal, fatal; (*weapon*) mortífero ♦ *adv*: **~ dull** tediosíssimo, chatíssimo.
deadpan [dɛd'pæn] *adj* sem expressão.
Dead Sea *n*: **the ~** o mar Morto.
dead season *n* (*TOURISM*) baixa estação *f*.
deaf [dɛf] *adj* surdo.
deaf-aid (*BRIT*) *n* aparelho para a surdez.

deaf-and-dumb *adj* surdo-mudo; ~ **alphabet** alfabeto de surdos-mudos.

deafen ['dɛfn] *vt* ensurdecer.

deafening ['dɛfnɪŋ] *adj* ensurdecedor(a).

deaf-mute *n* surdo-mudo/surda-muda.

deafness ['dɛfnɪs] *n* surdez *f*.

deal [diːl] (*pt, pp* **dealt**) *n* (*agreement*) acordo; (*business*) negócio ♦ *vt* (*cards, blows*) dar; **to strike a ~ with sb** fechar um negócio com alguém; **it's a ~!** (*inf*) negócio fechado; **he got a fair/bad ~ from them** ele foi/não foi bem tratado por eles; **a good ~** bastante; **a good** *or* **great ~ (of)** bastante, muito.

deal in *vt fus* (*COMM*) negociar em *or* com.

deal with *vt fus* (*people*) tratar com; (*problem*) ocupar-se de; (*be about: book etc*) tratar de; (*COMM*) negociar com; (*punish*) castigar.

dealer ['diːlə*] *n* negociante *m/f*; (*for cars*) concessionário/a; (*for products*) revendedor(a) *m/f*; (*CARDS*) carteador(a) *m/f*, banqueiro/a.

dealership ['diːləʃɪp] *n* concesionária.

dealings ['diːlɪŋz] *npl* transações *fpl*; (*relations*) relações *fpl*.

dealt [dɛlt] *pt, pp of* **deal**.

dean [diːn] *n* (*REL*) decano; (*BRIT: SCH*) reitor(a) *m/f*; (*US: SCH*) orientador(a) *m/f* de estudos.

dear [dɪə*] *adj* querido; (*expensive*) caro ♦ *n*: **my ~** meu querido/minha querida; **~ me!** ai, meu Deus!; **D~ Sir/Madam** (*in letter*) Ilmo. Senhor/Exma. Senhora (*BR*), Exmo. Senhor/Exma. Senhora (*PT*).

dearly ['dɪəlɪ] *adv* (*love*) ternamente; (*pay*) caro.

dearth [dɜ:θ] *n* escassez *f*.

death [dɛθ] *n* morte *f*; (*ADMIN*) óbito.

deathbed ['dɛθbɛd] *n* leito de morte.

death certificate *n* certidão *f* de óbito.

death duties *npl* (*BRIT*) impostos *mpl* sobre inventário.

deathly ['dɛθlɪ] *adj* mortal; (*silence*) profundo ♦ *adv* (*quiet*) completamente.

death penalty *n* pena de morte.

death rate *n* (índice *m* de) mortalidade *f*.

death sentence *n* sentença de morte.

deathtrap ['dɛθtræp] *n* perigo.

deb [dɛb] (*inf*) *n abbr* = **debutante**.

debar [dɪ'bɑ:*] *vt* (*exclude*) excluir; **to ~ sb from doing sth** proibir a alguém fazer algo *or* que faça algo.

debase [dɪ'beɪs] *vt* degradar; (*currency*) desvalorizar.

debatable [dɪ'beɪtəbl] *adj* discutível.

debate [dɪ'beɪt] *n* debate *m* ♦ *vt* debater ♦ *vi* (*consider*): **to ~ whether** perguntar-se se.

debauchery [dɪ'bɔːtʃərɪ] *n* libertinagem *f*.

debenture [dɪ'bɛntʃə*] *n* (*COMM*) debênture *f*.

debilitate [dɪ'bɪlɪteɪt] *vt* debilitar.

debit ['dɛbɪt] *n* débito ♦ *vt*: **to ~ a sum to sb** *or* **to sb's account** lançar uma quantia ao débito de alguém *or* à conta de alguém.

debit balance *n* saldo devedor.

debit note *n* nota de débito.

debrief [di:'bri:f] *vt* interrogar.

debriefing [di:'bri:fɪŋ] *n* interrogatório.

debris ['dɛbri:] *n* escombros *mpl*.

debt [dɛt] *n* dívida; **to be in ~** ter dívidas, estar endividado; **bad ~** dívida incobrável.

debt collector *n* cobrador(a) *m/f* de dívidas.

debtor ['dɛtə*] *n* devedor(a) *m/f*.

debug ['di:'bʌg] *vt* (*COMPUT*) depurar.

debunk [di:'bʌŋk] *vt* (*theory, claim*) desacreditar, desmerecer.

début ['deɪbju:] *n* estréia.

debutante ['dɛbjutænt] *n* debutante *f*.

Dec. *abbr* (= *December*) dez.

decade ['dɛkeɪd] *n* década.

decadence ['dɛkədəns] *n* decadência.

decadent ['dɛkədənt] *adj* decadente.

decaffeinated [dɪ'kæfɪneɪtɪd] *adj* descafeinado.

decamp [dɪ'kæmp] (*inf*) *vi* safar-se.

decant [dɪ'kænt] *vt* (*wine*) decantar.

decanter [dɪ'kæntə*] *n* garrafa ornamental.

decarbonize [di:'kɑ:bənaɪz] *vt* (*AUT*) descarbonizar.

decay [dɪ'keɪ] *n* decadência; (*of building*) ruína; (*fig*) deterioração *f*; (*rotting*) podridão *f*; (*also: tooth ~*) cárie *f* ♦ *vi* (*rot*) apodrecerse; (*fig*) decair.

decease [dɪ'si:s] *n* falecimento, óbito.

deceased [dɪ'si:st] *n*: **the ~** o/a falecido/a.

deceit [dɪ'si:t] *n* engano.

deceitful [dɪ'si:tful] *adj* enganador(a).

deceive [dɪ'si:v] *vt* enganar.

decelerate [di:'sɛləreɪt] *vt* moderar a marcha de, desacelerar ♦ *vi* diminuir a velocidade.

December [dɪ'sɛmbə*] *n* dezembro; *see also* **July**.

decency ['di:sənsɪ] *n* decência.

decent ['di:sənt] *adj* (*proper*) decente; (*person*) honesto, amável.

decently ['di:səntlɪ] *adv* (*respectably*) decentemente; (*kindly*) gentilmente.

decentralization ['di:sɛntrəlaɪ'zeɪʃən] *n* descentralização *f*.

decentralize [di:'sɛntrəlaɪz] *vt* descentralizar.

deception [dɪ'sɛpʃən] *n* engano, fraude *f*.

deceptive [dɪ'sɛptɪv] *adj* enganador(a).

decibel ['dɛsɪbɛl] *n* decibel *m*.

decide [dɪ'saɪd] *vt* (*person*) decidir; (*question, argument*) resolver ♦ *vi* decidir; **to ~ to do/ that** decidir fazer/que; **to ~ on sth** decidir-se por algo; **to ~ on doing** decidir fazer; **to ~ against doing** decidir não fazer.

decided [dɪ'saɪdɪd] *adj* (*resolute*) decidido; (*clear, definite*) claro, definido.

decidedly [dɪ'saɪdɪdlɪ] *adv* decididamente.

deciding [dɪ'saɪdɪŋ] *adj* decisivo.

deciduous [dɪ'sɪdjuəs] *adj* decíduo, caduco.

decimal ['dɛsɪməl] *adj* decimal ♦ *n* decimal *m*;

NB: *European Portuguese adds the following consonants to certain words:* **b** (sú(b)dito, su(b)til); **c** (a(c)ção, a(c)cionista, a(c)to); **m** (inde(m)ne); **p** (ado(p)ção, ado(p)tar); *for further details see p. xiii.*

to 3 ~ **places** com 3 casas decimais.
decimalize ['dɛsɪmɔlaɪz] (*BRIT*) *vt* decimalizar.
decimal point *n* vírgula de decimais.
decimate ['dɛsɪmeɪt] *vt* dizimar.
decipher [dɪ'saɪfɔ*] *vt* decifrar.
decision [dɪ'sɪʒən] *n* decisão *f*; **to make a** ~ tomar uma decisão.
decisive [dɪ'saɪsɪv] *adj* decisivo; (*conclusive*) decidido, terminante; (*manner, reply*) categórico.
deck [dɛk] *n* (*NAUT*) convés *m*; (*of bus*) andar *m*; (*of cards*) baralho; **to go up on** ~ subir ao convés; **below** ~ abaixo do convés principal; **record/cassette** ~ toca-discos *m* *inv*/toca-fitas *m* *inv*.
deckchair ['dɛktʃɛɔ*] *n* cadeira de lona, espreguiçadeira.
deck hand *n* taifeiro/a.
declaration [dɛklɔ'reɪʃən] *n* declaração *f*.
declare [dɪ'klɛɔ*] *vt* declarar.
declassify [diː'klæsɪfaɪ] *vt* tornar público.
decline [dɪ'klaɪn] *n* declínio, decadência; (*lessening*) diminuição *f*, baixa ♦ *vt* recusar ♦ *vi* decair, diminuir; (*fall*) baixar; ~ **in living standards** queda dos padrões de vida; **to** ~ **to do sth** recusar-se a fazer algo.
declutch ['diː'klʌtʃ] (*BRIT*) *vi* debrear.
decode [diː'kəud] *vt* decifrar; (*TV signal etc*) decodificar.
decoder [diː'kəudə*] *n* decodificador *m*.
decompose [diːkəm'pəuz] *vi* decompor-se.
decomposition [diːkɔmpə'zɪʃən] *n* decomposição *f*.
decompression [diːkəm'prɛʃən] *n* descompressão *f*.
decompression chamber *n* câmara de descompressão.
decongestant [diːkən'dʒɛstənt] *n* descongestionante *m*.
decontaminate [diːkən'tæmɪneɪt] *vt* descontaminar.
decontrol [diːkən'trəul] *vt* (*prices etc*) liberar.
décor ['deɪkɔː*] *n* decoração *f*; (*THEATRE*) cenário.
decorate ['dɛkəreɪt] *vt* (*adorn*) enfeitar, decorar; (*give medal to*) condecorar; (*paint*) pintar; (*paper*) decorar com papel.
decoration [dɛkə'reɪʃən] *n* decoração *f*, adorno; (*act*) decoração; (*medal*) condecoração *f*.
decorative ['dɛkərətɪv] *adj* decorativo.
decorator ['dɛkəreɪtə*] *n* (*painter*) pintor(a) *m/f*.
decorum [dɪ'kɔːrəm] *n* decoro.
decoy ['diːkɔɪ] *n* engodo, chamariz *m*.
decrease [*n* 'diːkriːs, *vt, vi* diː'kriːs] *n* diminuição *f* ♦ *vt* diminuir, reduzir ♦ *vi* diminuir; **to be on the** ~ estar diminuindo.
decreasing [diː'kriːsɪŋ] *adj* decrescente.
decree [dɪ'kriː] *n* decreto ♦ *vt*: **to** ~ **(that)** decretar (que); ~ **absolute** sentença final de divórcio; ~ **nisi** ordem *f* provisória de divórcio.
decrepit [dɪ'krɛpɪt] *adj* decrépito, caduco; (*building*) (que está) caindo aos pedaços.

decry [dɪ'kraɪ] *vt* execrar; (*disparage*) denegrir.
dedicate ['dɛdɪkeɪt] *vt* dedicar.
dedicated ['dɛdɪkeɪtɪd] *adj* (*person*, *COMPUT*) dedicado; ~ **word processor** processador *m* de texto dedicado.
dedication [dɛdɪ'keɪʃən] *n* (*devotion*) dedicação *f*; (*in book*) dedicatória.
deduce [dɪ'djuːs] *vt* deduzir.
deduct [dɪ'dʌkt] *vt* deduzir; (*from wage etc*) descontar.
deduction [dɪ'dʌkʃən] *n* (*deducting*) redução *f*, dedução *f*; (*from wage etc*) desconto; (*conclusion*) conclusão *f*, dedução *f*.
deed [diːd] *n* feito, ato; (*feat*) façanha; (*LAW*) escritura, título; ~ **of covenant** escritura de transferência.
deem [diːm] *vt* julgar, estimar; **to** ~ **it wise to do** julgar prudente fazer.
deep [diːp] *adj* profundo; (*voice*) baixo, grave; (*person*) fechado ♦ *adv*: **the spectators stood 20** ~ os espectadores formaram-se em 20 fileiras; **knee-**~ **in water** com água até os joelhos; **to be 4 metres** ~ ter 4 metros de profundidade; **he took a** ~ **breath** ele respirou fundo.
deepen ['diːpən] *vt* aprofundar ♦ *vi* (*mystery*) aumentar.
deep-freeze (*irreg*) *vt* congelar ♦ *n* congelador *m*, freezer *m* (*BR*).
deep-fry *vt* fritar em recipiente fundo.
deeply ['diːplɪ] *adv* profundamente.
deep-rooted [-'ruːtɪd] *adj* (*prejudice*) enraizado; (*affection*) profundo.
deep-sea diver *n* escafandrista *m/f*.
deep-sea diving *n* mergulho com escafandro.
deep-sea fishing *n* pesca de alto-mar.
deep-seated [-'siːtɪd] *adj* (*beliefs*) arraigado.
deep-set *adj* (*eyes*) fundo.
deer [dɪə*] *n* *inv* veado, cervo.
deerskin ['dɪəskɪn] *n* camurça, pele *f* de cervo.
deerstalker ['dɪəstɔːkə*] *n* tipo de chapéu, como o de Sherlock Holmes.
deface [dɪ'feɪs] *vt* desfigurar, deformar.
defamation [dɛfə'meɪʃən] *n* difamação *f*.
defamatory [dɪ'fæmətrɪ] *adj* difamatório.
default [dɪ'fɔːlt] *vi* (*LAW*) inadimplir; (*SPORT*) não comparecer ♦ *n* (*COMPUT*) default *m*; **by** ~ (*LAW*) à revelia; (*SPORT*) por ausência; **to** ~ **on a debt** deixar de pagar uma dívida.
defaulter [dɪ'fɔːltə*] *n* (*in debt*) devedor(a) *m/f* inadimplente.
default option *n* (*COMPUT*) opção *f* de default.
defeat [dɪ'fiːt] *n* derrota ♦ *vt* derrotar, vencer; (*fig: efforts*) frustrar.
defeatism [dɪ'fiːtɪzm] *n* derrotismo.
defeatist [dɪ'fiːtɪst] *adj*, *n* derrotista *m/f*.
defect [*n* 'diːfɛkt, *vi* dɪ'fɛkt] *n* defeito ♦ *vi* desertar; **physical/mental** ~ defeito físico/mental.
defective [dɪ'fɛktɪv] *adj* defeituoso.
defector [dɪ'fɛktə*] *n* trânsfuga *m/f*.
defence [dɪ'fɛns] (*US* **defense**) *n* defesa; **in** ~ **of** em defesa de; **witness for the** ~ testemu-

nha de defesa; **the Ministry of D~** (*BRIT*), **the Department of Defense** (*US*) o Ministério da Defesa.
defenceless [dɪ'fɛnslɪs] *adj* indefeso.
defend [dɪ'fɛnd] *vt* defender.
defendant [dɪ'fɛndənt] *n* acusado/a; (*in civil case*) réu/ré *m/f*.
defender [dɪ'fɛndə*] *n* defensor(a) *m/f*.
defending champion [dɪ'fɛndɪŋ-] *n* (*SPORT*) atual campeão/peã *m/f*.
defending counsel [dɪ'fɛndɪŋ-] *n* (*LAW*) advogado/a de defesa.
defense [dɪ'fɛns] *n* = **defence**.
defensive [dɪ'fɛnsɪv] *adj* defensivo ♦ *n*: **on the ~** na defensiva.
defer [dɪ'fəː*] *vt* (*postpone*) adiar ♦ *vi* (*submit*): **to ~ to** submeter-se a.
deference ['dɛfərəns] *n* deferência, respeito; **out of** *or* **in ~ to** por *or* em deferência a.
defiance [dɪ'faɪəns] *n* desafio, desrespeito; **in ~ of** sem respeito por; (*despite*) a despeito de.
defiant [dɪ'faɪənt] *adj* (*insolent*) desafiante, insolente; (*challenging*) desafiador(a).
defiantly [dɪ'faɪəntlɪ] *adv* desafiadoramente.
deficiency [dɪ'fɪʃənsɪ] *n* (*lack*) deficiência, falta; (*defect*) defeito; (*COMM*) déficit *m*.
deficiency disease *n* doença de carência.
deficient [dɪ'fɪʃənt] *adj* (*lacking*) deficiente; (*incomplete*) incompleto; (*defective*) imperfeito; **~ in** falto de, carente de.
deficit ['dɛfɪsɪt] *n* déficit *m*.
defile [*vt*, *vi* dɪ'faɪl, *n* 'diːfaɪl] *vt* sujar, profanar ♦ *vi* desfilar ♦ *n* desfile *m*.
define [dɪ'faɪn] *vt* definir.
definite ['dɛfɪnɪt] *adj* (*fixed*) definitivo; (*clear*, *obvious*) claro, categórico; (*LING*) definido; **he was ~ about it** ele foi categórico.
definitely ['dɛfɪnɪtlɪ] *adv* sem dúvida.
definition [dɛfɪ'nɪʃən] *n* definição *f*.
definitive [dɪ'fɪnɪtɪv] *adj* definitivo.
deflate [diː'fleɪt] *vt* esvaziar; (*person*) fazer perder o rebolado; (*ECON*) deflacionar.
deflation [diː'fleɪʃən] *n* (*ECON*) deflação *f*.
deflationary [diː'fleɪʃənrɪ] *adj* (*ECON*) deflacionário.
deflect [dɪ'flɛkt] *vt* desviar.
defog ['diː'fɔg] (*US*) *vt* desembaçar.
defogger ['diː'fɔgə*] (*US*) *n* (*AUT*) desembaçador *m*.
deform [dɪ'fɔːm] *vt* deformar.
deformed [dɪ'fɔːmd] *adj* deformado.
deformity [dɪ'fɔːmɪtɪ] *n* deformidade *f*.
defraud [dɪ'frɔːd] *vt* defraudar.
defray [dɪ'freɪ] *vt* (*costs*, *expenses*) correr com.
defrost [diː'frɔst] *vt* descongelar.
deft [dɛft] *adj* destro, hábil.
defunct [dɪ'fʌŋkt] *adj* extinto.
defuse [diː'fjuːz] *vt* tirar o estopim *or* a espoleta de.
defy [dɪ'faɪ] *vt* (*resist*) opor-se a; (*challenge*)

desafiar; (*order*) desobedecer.
degenerate [*vi* dɪ'dʒɛnəreɪt, *adj* dɪ'dʒɛnərɪt] *vi* degenerar ♦ *adj* degenerado.
degradation [dɛgrə'deɪʃən] *n* degradação *f*.
degrade [dɪ'greɪd] *vt* degradar.
degrading [dɪ'greɪdɪŋ] *adj* degradante.
degree [dɪ'griː] *n* grau *m*; (*SCH*) diploma *m*, título; **~ in maths** formatura em matemática; **10 ~s below (zero)** 10 graus abaixo de zero; **a considerable ~ of risk** um grau considerável de risco; **by ~s** (*gradually*) pouco a pouco; **to some ~**, **to a certain ~** até certo ponto.
dehydrated [diːhaɪ'dreɪtɪd] *adj* desidratado; (*milk*) em pó.
dehydration [diːhaɪ'dreɪʃən] *n* desidratação *f*.
de-ice *vt* (*windscreen*) descongelar.
de-icer [-'aɪsə*] *n* descongelador *m*.
deign [deɪn] *vi*: **to ~ to do** dignar-se a fazer.
deity ['diːɪtɪ] *n* divindade *f*, deidade *f*.
dejected [dɪ'dʒɛktɪd] *adj* abatido, desanimado; (*face*) triste.
dejection [dɪ'dʒɛkʃən] *n* desânimo.
del. *abbr* = **delete**.
delay [dɪ'leɪ] *vt* retardar, atrasar; (*trains*) atrasar ♦ *vi* retardar-se ♦ *n* demora, atraso; **without ~** sem demora *or* atraso.
delayed-action [dɪ'leɪd-] *adj* de retardo, de ação retardada.
delectable [dɪ'lɛktəbl] *adj* deleitável.
delegate [*n* 'dɛlɪgɪt, *vt* 'dɛlɪgeɪt] *n* delegado/a ♦ *vt* delegar; **to ~ sth to sb/sb to do sth** delegar algo a alguém/alguém para fazer algo.
delegation [dɛlɪ'geɪʃən] *n* delegação *f*.
delete [dɪ'liːt] *vt* eliminar, riscar; (*COMPUT*) deletar.
Delhi ['dɛlɪ] *n* Délhi.
deliberate [*adj* dɪ'lɪbərɪt, *vi* dɪ'lɪbəreɪt] *adj* (*intentional*) intencional; (*slow*) pausado, lento ♦ *vi* deliberar.
deliberately [dɪ'lɪbərɪtlɪ] *adv* (*on purpose*) de propósito; (*slowly*) lentamente.
deliberation [dɪlɪbə'reɪʃən] *n* deliberação *f*.
delicacy ['dɛlɪkəsɪ] *n* delicadeza; (*choice food*) iguaria.
delicate ['dɛlɪkɪt] *adj* delicado; (*fragile*) frágil; (*skilled*) fino.
delicately ['dɛlɪkɪtlɪ] *adv* delicadamente.
delicatessen [dɛlɪkə'tɛsn] *n* delicatessen *m*.
delicious [dɪ'lɪʃəs] *adj* delicioso, saboroso.
delight [dɪ'laɪt] *n* (*feeling*) prazer *m*, deleite *m*; (*object*) encanto, delícia ♦ *vt* encantar, deleitar; **to take ~ in** deleitar-se com.
delighted [dɪ'laɪtɪd] *adj*: **~ (at** *or* **with sth)** encantado (com algo); **to be ~ to do sth/that** ter muito prazer em fazer algo/ficar muito contente que; **I'd be ~** eu adoraria.
delightful [dɪ'laɪtful] *adj* encantador(a), delicioso.
delimit [diː'lɪmɪt] *vt* delimitar.
delineate [dɪ'lɪnɪeɪt] *vt* delinear; (*fig*: *describe*) descrever, definir.

delinquency [dɪ'lɪŋkwənsɪ] n delinqüência.
delinquent [dɪ'lɪŋkwənt] adj, n delinqüente m/f.
delirious [dɪ'lɪrɪəs] adj delirante; **to be ~** delirar.
delirium [dɪ'lɪrɪəm] n delírio.
deliver [dɪ'lɪvə*] vt (mail) distribuir; (goods) entregar; (message) comunicar; (speech) proferir; (free) livrar; (MED) partejar; **to ~ the goods** (fig) dar conta do recado.
deliverance [dɪ'lɪvrəns] n libertação f, livramento.
delivery [dɪ'lɪvərɪ] n entrega; (of mail) distribuição f; (of speaker) enunciação f; (MED) parto; **to take ~ of** receber.
delivery note n guia or nota de entrega.
delivery van (US **delivery truck**) n furgão m de entrega.
delouse ['di:'laus] vt espiolhar.
delta ['dɛltə] n delta m.
delude [dɪ'lu:d] vt iludir, enganar; **to ~ o.s.** iludir-se.
deluge ['dɛlju:dʒ] n dilúvio ♦ vt (fig): **to ~ (with)** inundar (de).
delusion [dɪ'lu:ʒən] n ilusão f; **to have ~s of grandeur** ter mania de grandeza.
de luxe [də'lʌks] adj de luxo.
delve [dɛlv] vi: **to ~ into** investigar, pesquisar.
Dem. (US) abbr (POL) = **democrat(ic)**.
demagogue ['dɛməgɔg] n demagogo/a.
demand [dɪ'mɑ:nd] vt exigir; (rights) reivindicar, reclamar ♦ n exigência; (claim) reivindicação f; (ECON) procura; **to ~ sth (from or of sb)** exigir algo (de alguém); **to be in ~** ser muito solicitado; **on ~** à vista.
demanding [dɪ'mɑ:ndɪŋ] adj (boss) exigente; (work) absorvente.
demarcation [di:mɑ:'keɪʃən] n demarcação f.
demarcation dispute n (INDUSTRY) dissídio coletivo.
demean [dɪ'mi:n] vt: **to ~ o.s.** rebaixar-se.
demeanour [dɪ'mi:nə*] (US **demeanor**) n conduta, comportamento.
demented [dɪ'mɛntɪd] adj demente, doido.
demilitarized zone [di:'mɪlɪtəraɪzd-] n zona desmilitarizada.
demise [dɪ'maɪz] n falecimento.
demist [di:'mɪst] (BRIT) vt desembaçar.
demister [di:'mɪstə*] (BRIT) n (AUT) desembaçador m de pára-brisa.
demo ['dɛməu] (inf) n abbr (= **demonstration**) passeata.
demobilize [di:'məubɪlaɪz] vt desmobilizar.
democracy [dɪ'mɔkrəsɪ] n democracia.
democrat ['dɛməkræt] n democrata m/f.
democratic [dɛmə'krætɪk] adj democrático.
demography [dɪ'mɔgrəfɪ] n demografia.
demolish [dɪ'mɔlɪʃ] vt demolir, derrubar.
demolition [dɛmə'lɪʃən] n demolição f.
demon ['di:mən] n demônio ♦ cpd: **a ~ squash player** um(a) craque em squash.
demonstrate ['dɛmənstreɪt] vt demonstrar ♦ vi: **to ~ (for/against)** manifestar-se (a favor de/contra).

demonstration [dɛmən'streɪʃən] n (POL) manifestação f; (: march) passeata; (proof) demonstração f; **to hold a ~** realizar uma passeata.
demonstrative [dɪ'mɔnstrətɪv] adj demonstrativo.
demonstrator ['dɛmənstreɪtə*] n (POL) manifestante m/f; (COMM: sales person) demonstrador(a) m/f; (: car, computer etc) modelo de demonstração
demoralize [dɪ'mɔrəlaɪz] vt desmoralizar.
demote [dɪ'məut] vt rebaixar de posto.
demotion [dɪ'məuʃən] n rebaixamento.
demur [dɪ'mə:*] vi: **to ~ (at sth)** objetar (a algo), opor-se (a algo) ♦ n: **without ~** sem objeção.
demure [dɪ'mjuə*] adj recatado.
demurrage [dɪ'mʌrɪdʒ] n sobreestadia.
den [dɛn] n (of animal) covil m; (room) aposento privado, cantinho.
denationalization ['di:næʃnəlaɪ'zeɪʃən] n desnacionalização f, desestatização f.
denationalize [di:'næʃnəlaɪz] nt desnacionalizar, desestatizar.
denial [dɪ'naɪəl] n (refusal) negativa; (of report etc) desmentido.
denier ['dɛnɪə*] n denier m; **15 ~ stockings** meias de 15 denieres.
denigrate ['dɛnɪgreɪt] vt denegrir.
denim ['dɛnɪm] n brim m, zuarte m; **~s** npl jeans m (BR), jeans mpl (PT).
denim jacket n jaqueta de brim.
denizen ['dɛnɪzn] n habitante m/f.
Denmark ['dɛnmɑ:k] n Dinamarca.
denomination [dɪnɔmɪ'neɪʃən] n valor m, denominação f; (REL) confissão f, seita.
denominator [dɪ'nɔmɪneɪtə*] n denominador m.
denote [dɪ'nəut] vt (indicate) denotar, indicar; (mean) significar.
denounce [dɪ'nauns] vt denunciar.
dense [dɛns] adj (thick) denso, espesso; (: foliage etc) denso; (inf: stupid) estúpido, bronco.
densely ['dɛnslɪ] adv: **~ populated** com grande densidade de população; **~ wooded** coberto de florestas densas.
density ['dɛnsɪtɪ] n densidade f; **single/double ~ disk** (COMPUT) disco de densidade simples/dupla.
dent [dɛnt] n amolgadura, depressão f ♦ vt (also: **make a ~ in**) amolgar, dentar; **to make a ~ in** (fig) reduzir.
dental ['dɛntl] adj dental.
dental surgeon n cirurgião/giã m/f dentista.
dentifrice ['dɛntɪfrɪs] n dentifrício.
dentist ['dɛntɪst] n dentista m/f; **~'s surgery** (BRIT) consultório dentário.
dentistry ['dɛntɪstrɪ] n odontologia.
dentures ['dɛntʃəz] npl dentadura.
denunciation [dɪnʌnsɪ'eɪʃən] n denúncia.
deny [dɪ'naɪ] vt negar; (report) desmentir; **he denies having said it** ele nega ter dito isso.
deodorant [di:'əudərənt] n desodorante m (BR), desodorizante m (PT).

depart [dɪ'pɑːt] *vi* ir-se, partir; (*train*) sair; **to ~ from** (*fig*: *differ from*) afastar-se de.

department [dɪ'pɑːtmənt] *n* departamento; (*COMM*) seção *f*; (*POL*) repartição *f*; **that's not my ~** (*fig*) este não é o meu departamento; **D~ of State** (*US*) Departamento de Estado.

departmental [diːpɑːt'mɛntl] *adj* departamental; **~ manager** chefe *m/f* de serviço.

department store *n* magazine *m* (*BR*), grande armazém *m* (*PT*).

departure [dɪ'pɑːtʃə*] *n* partida, ida; (*of train*) saída; (*fig*): **~ from** afastamento de; **a new ~** uma nova orientação.

departure lounge *n* sala de embarque.

departures board (*US* **departure board**) *n* horário de saídas.

depend [dɪ'pɛnd] *vi*: **to ~ (up)on** depender de; (*rely on*) contar com; **it ~s** depende; **~ing on the result** ... dependendo do resultado ....

dependable [dɪ'pɛndəbl] *adj* (*person*) de confiança, seguro.

dependant [dɪ'pɛndənt] *n* dependente *m/f*.

dependence [dɪ'pɛndəns] *n* dependência.

dependent [dɪ'pɛndənt] *adj*: **to be ~ (on)** depender (de), ser dependente (de) ♦ *n* = **dependant**.

depict [dɪ'pɪkt] *vt* (*in picture*) retratar, representar; (*describe*) descrever.

depilatory [dɪ'pɪlətrɪ] *n* (*also*: **~ cream**) depilatório.

depleted [dɪ'pliːtɪd] *adj* depauperado.

deplorable [dɪ'plɔːrəbl] *adj* (*disgraceful*) deplorável; (*regrettable*) lamentável.

deplore [dɪ'plɔː*] *vt* (*condemn*) deplorar; (*regret*) lamentar.

deploy [dɪ'plɔɪ] *vt* dispor; (*missiles*) instalar.

depopulate [diː'pɔpjuleɪt] *vt* despovoar.

depopulation ['diːpɔpjuˈleɪʃən] *n* despovoamento.

deport [dɪ'pɔːt] *vt* deportar.

deportation [dɪpɔːˈteɪʃən] *n* deportação *f*.

deportation order *n* ordem *f* de deportação.

deportment [dɪ'pɔːtmənt] *n* comportamento.

depose [dɪ'pəuz] *vt* depor.

deposit [dɪ'pɔzɪt] *n* (*COMM*, *GEO*) depósito; (*CHEM*) sedimento; (*of ore, oil*) jazida; (*part payment*) sinal *m*; (*for hired goods etc*) caução *f* ♦ *vt* depositar; **to put down a ~ of £50** pagar um sinal de £50.

deposit account *n* conta de depósito a prazo.

depositor [dɪ'pɔzɪtə*] *n* depositante *m/f*.

depository [dɪ'pɔzɪtərɪ] *n* (*person*) depositário/a; (*place*) depósito.

depot ['dɛpəu] *n* (*storehouse*) depósito, armazém *m*; (*for vehicles*) garagem *f*, parque *m*.

depraved [dɪ'preɪvd] *adj* depravado, viciado.

depravity [dɪ'prævɪtɪ] *n* depravação *f*, vício.

deprecate ['dɛprɪkeɪt] *vt* desaprovar.

deprecating ['dɛprɪkeɪtɪŋ] *adj* desaprovador(a).

depreciate [dɪ'priːʃɪeɪt] *vt* depreciar ♦ *vi* depreciar-se, desvalorizar-se.

depreciation [dɪpriːʃɪ'eɪʃən] *n* depreciação *f*.

depress [dɪ'prɛs] *vt* deprimir; (*press down*) apertar.

depressant [dɪ'prɛsnt] *n* (*MED*) depressor *m*.

depressed [dɪ'prɛst] *adj* (*person*) deprimido; (*area, market, trade*) em depressão.

depressing [dɪ'prɛsɪŋ] *adj* deprimente.

depression [dɪ'prɛʃən] *n* (*also*: *ECON*) depressão *f*.

deprivation [dɛprɪ'veɪʃən] *n* privação *f*; (*loss*) perda.

deprive [dɪ'praɪv] *vt*: **to ~ sb of** privar alguém de.

deprived [dɪ'praɪvd] *adj* carente.

dept. *abbr* (= *department*) depto.

depth [dɛpθ] *n* profundidade *f*; (*of room etc*) comprimento; **in the ~s of** nas profundezas de; **at a ~ of 3 metres** a uma profundidade de 3 metros; **to be out of one's ~** (*BRIT*: *swimmer*) estar sem pé; (*fig*) estar voando; **to study sth in ~** estudar algo em profundidade.

depth charge *n* carga de profundidade.

deputation [dɛpju'teɪʃən] *n* delegação *f*.

deputize ['dɛpjutaɪz] *vi*: **to ~ for sb** substituir alguém.

deputy ['dɛpjutɪ] *adj*: **~ chairman** vice-presidente/a *m/f* ♦ *n* (*replacement*) substituto/a, suplente *m/f*; (*POL*: *MP*) deputado/a; (*second in command*) vice *m/f*; **~ head** (*SCH*) diretor adjunto/diretora adjunta *m/f*; **~ leader** (*BRIT*: *POL*) vice-líder *m/f*.

derail [dɪ'reɪl] *vt* descarrilhar; **to be ~ed** descarrilhar.

derailment [dɪ'reɪlmənt] *n* descarrilhamento.

deranged [dɪ'reɪndʒd] *adj* (*person*) louco, transtornado.

derby ['dɑːbɪ] (*US*) *n* chapéu-coco.

Derbys (*BRIT*) *abbr* = **Derbyshire**.

deregulate [dɪ'rɛgjuleɪt] *vt* liberar.

deregulation [dɪ'rɛgjuˈleɪʃən] *n* liberação *f*.

derelict ['dɛrɪlɪkt] *adj* abandonado.

deride [dɪ'raɪd] *vt* ridicularizar, zombar de.

derision [dɪ'rɪʒən] *n* irrisão *f*, escárnio.

derisive [dɪ'raɪsɪv] *adj* zombeteiro.

derisory [dɪ'raɪsərɪ] *adj* (*sum*) irrisório; (*person, smile*) zombeteiro.

derivation [dɛrɪ'veɪʃən] *n* derivação *f*.

derivative [dɪ'rɪvətɪv] *n* derivado ♦ *adj* derivado; (*work*) pouco original.

derive [dɪ'raɪv] *vt* derivar ♦ *vi*: **to ~ from** derivar-se de.

dermatitis [dəːmə'taɪtɪs] *n* dermatite *f*.

dermatology [dəːmə'tɔlədʒɪ] *n* dermatologia.

derogatory [dɪ'rɔgətərɪ] *adj* depreciativo.

derrick ['dɛrɪk] *n* (*crane*) guindaste *m*; (*oil ~*) torre *f* de perfurar.

derv [dəːv] (*BRIT*) *n* gasóleo.

DES (*BRIT*) *n abbr* (= *Department of Education and Science*) Ministério da Educação e *das Ciências.*

desalination [diːsælɪˈneɪʃən] *n* dessalinização
f.

descend [dɪˈsɛnd] *vt, vi* descer; **to ~ from**
descer de; **in ~ing order** em ordem decrescente.

descend on *vt fus* (*subj: enemy, angry
person*) cair sobre; (: *misfortune*) abater-se
sobre; (: *gloom, silence*) invadir; **visitors
~ed (up)on us** visitas invadiram nossa casa.

descendant [dɪˈsɛndənt] *n* descendente *m/f.*

descent [dɪˈsɛnt] *n* descida; (*slope*) declive *m*,
ladeira; (*origin*) descendência.

describe [dɪsˈkraɪb] *vt* descrever.

description [dɪsˈkrɪpʃən] *n* descrição *f*; (*sort*)
classe *f*, espécie *f*; **of every ~** de toda a
sorte, de todo o tipo.

descriptive [dɪsˈkrɪptɪv] *adj* descritivo.

desecrate [ˈdɛsɪkreɪt] *vt* profanar.

desert [*n* ˈdɛzət, *vt, vi* dɪˈzɜːt] *n* deserto ♦ *vt*
abandonar ♦ *vi* (*MIL*) desertar.

deserter [dɪˈzɜːtə*] *n* desertor *m.*

desertion [dɪˈzɜːʃən] *n* deserção *f.*

desert island *n* ilha deserta.

deserts [dɪˈzɜːts] *npl*: **to get one's just ~** receber o que merece.

deserve [dɪˈzɜːv] *vt* merecer.

deservedly [dɪˈzɜːvɪdlɪ] *adj* merecidamente.

deserving [dɪˈzɜːvɪŋ] *adj* (*person*) merecedor(a), digno; (*action, cause*) meritório.

desiccated [ˈdɛsɪkeɪtɪd] *adj* dessecado.

design [dɪˈzaɪn] *n* (*sketch*) desenho, esboço;
(*layout, shape*) plano, projeto; (*pattern*) desenho, padrão *m*; (*of dress, car etc*) modelo;
(*art*) design *m*; (*intention*) propósito,
intenção *f* ♦ *vt* desenhar; (*plan*) projetar; **to
have ~s on** ter a mira em; **well-~ed** bem
projetado; **to be ~ed for sb/sth** (*intended*)
ser destinado a alguém/algo.

designate [*vt* ˈdezɪgneɪt, *adj* ˈdezɪgnɪt] *vt*
(*point to*) apontar; (*appoint*) nomear; (*destine*) designar ♦ *adj* designado.

designation [dezɪgˈneɪʃən] *n* (*appointment*)
nomeação *f*; (*name*) designação *f.*

designer [dɪˈzaɪnə*] *n* (*ART*) artista *m/f*
gráfico/a; (*TECH*) desenhista *m/f*, projetista
m/f; (*fashion ~*) estilista *m/f.*

desirability [dɪzaɪrəˈbɪlɪtɪ] *n* necessidade *f.*

desirable [dɪˈzaɪərəbl] *adj* (*proper*) desejável;
(*attractive*) atraente.

desire [dɪˈzaɪə*] *n* desejo ♦ *vt* desejar; **to ~ to
do sth/that** desejar fazer algo/que.

desirous [dɪˈzaɪərəs] *adj*: **~ of** desejoso de.

desk [dɛsk] *n* (*in office*) mesa, secretária; (*for
pupil*) carteira *f*; (*at airport*) balcão *m*; (*in
hotel*) recepção *f*; (*BRIT: in shop, restaurant*)
caixa.

desk-top publishing *n* editoração *f* eletrônica, desktop publishing *m.*

desolate [ˈdɛsəlɪt] *adj* (*place*) deserto;
(*person*) desolado.

desolation [dɛsəˈleɪʃən] *n* (*of place*) desolação
f; (*of person*) aflição *f.*

despair [dɪsˈpɛə*] *n* desespero ♦ *vi*: **to ~ of**
desesperar-se de; **to be in ~** estar desespera-

do.

despatch [dɪsˈpætʃ] *n, vt* = **dispatch.**

desperate [ˈdɛspərɪt] *adj* desesperado.

desperately [ˈdɛspərɪtlɪ] *adv* desesperadamente; (*very*) terrívelmente, gravemente.

desperation [dɛspəˈreɪʃən] *n* desespero,
desesperança; **in ~** desesperado.

despicable [dɪsˈpɪkəbl] *adj* desprezível.

despise [dɪsˈpaɪz] *vt* desprezar.

despite [dɪsˈpaɪt] *prep* apesar de, a despeito
de.

despondent [dɪsˈpɔndənt] *adj* abatido, desanimado.

despot [ˈdɛspɔt] *n* déspota *m/f.*

dessert [dɪˈzɜːt] *n* sobremesa.

dessertspoon [dɪˈzɜːtspuːn] *n* colher *f* de sobremesa.

destabilize [diːˈsteɪbɪlaɪz] *vt* desestabilizar.

destination [dɛstɪˈneɪʃən] *n* destino.

destine [ˈdɛstɪn] *vt* destinar.

destined [ˈdɛstɪnd] *adj*: **~ to do sth** destinado
a fazer algo; **~ for London** com destino a
Londres.

destiny [ˈdɛstɪnɪ] *n* destino.

destitute [ˈdɛstɪtjuːt] *adj* indigente, necessitado; **~ of** desprovido de.

destroy [dɪsˈtrɔɪ] *vt* destruir.

destroyer [dɪsˈtrɔɪə*] *n* (*NAUT*) contratorpedeiro.

destruction [dɪsˈtrʌkʃən] *n* destruição *f.*

destructive [dɪsˈtrʌktɪv] *adj* destrutivo, destruidor(a).

desultory [ˈdɛsəltərɪ] *adj* (*reading, conversation*) desconexo; (*contact*) irregular.

detach [dɪˈtætʃ] *vt* separar; (*unstick*) desprender.

detachable [dɪˈtætʃəbl] *adj* separável; (*TECH*)
desmontável.

detached [dɪˈtætʃt] *adj* (*attitude*) imparcial,
objetivo; (*house*) independente, isolado.

detachment [dɪˈtætʃmənt] *n* separação *f*;
(*MIL*) destacamento; (*fig*) objetividade *f*,
imparcialidade *f.*

detail [ˈdiːteɪl] *n* detalhe *m*; (*MIL*) destacamento ♦ *vt* detalhar; (*MIL*): **to ~ sb (for)**
destacar alguém (para); **in ~** pormenorizado, em detalhe; **to go into ~(s)** entrar em
detalhes.

detailed [ˈdiːteɪld] *adj* detalhado.

detain [dɪˈteɪn] *vt* deter; (*in hospital*) hospitalizar.

detainee [diːteɪˈniː] *n* detido/a.

detect [dɪˈtɛkt] *vt* descobrir; (*MED, POLICE*)
identificar; (*MIL, RADAR, TECH*) detectar.

detection [dɪˈtɛkʃən] *n* descobrimento; (*MED,
POLICE*) identificação *f*; (*MIL, RADAR, TECH*)
detecção *f*; **to escape ~** evitar ser descoberto; **crime ~** investigação *f* de crimes.

detective [dɪˈtɛktɪv] *n* detetive *m/f*; **private ~**
detetive particular.

detective story *n* romance *m* policial.

detector [dɪˈtɛktə*] *n* detetor *m.*

détente [deɪˈtɑːnt] *n* distensão *f* (de relações),
détente *f.*

detention [dɪˈtɛnʃən] *n* detenção *f*, prisão *f*;

(SCH) castigo.

deter [dɪ'tə:*] vt (discourage) desanimar; (dissuade) dissuadir; (prevent) impedir.

detergent [dɪ'tə:dʒənt] n detergente m.

deteriorate [dɪ'tɪərɪəreɪt] vi deteriorar-se.

deterioration [dɪtɪərɪə'reɪʃən] n deterioração f.

determination [dɪtə:mɪ'neɪʃən] n determinação f; (resolve) resolução f.

determine [dɪ'tə:mɪn] vt determinar; **to ~ to do** resolver fazer, determinar-se de fazer.

determined [dɪ'tə:mɪnd] adj (person) resoluto, decidido; (quantity) determinado; (effort) grande.

deterrence [dɪ'tɛrəns] n dissuasão f.

deterrent [dɪ'tɛrənt] n dissuasivo.

detest [dɪ'tɛst] vt detestar.

detestable [dɪ'tɛstəbl] adj detestável.

detonate ['dɛtəneɪt] vi explodir, estalar ♦ vt detonar.

detonator ['dɛtəneɪtə*] n detonador m.

detour ['di:tuə*] n desvio.

detract [dɪ'trækt] vi: **to ~ from** (merits, reputation) depreciar; (quality, pleasure) diminuir.

detractor [dɪ'træktə*] n detrator(a) m/f.

detriment ['dɛtrɪmənt] n: **to the ~ of** em detrimento de; **without ~ to** sem detrimento de.

detrimental [dɛtrɪ'mɛntl] adj: **~ (to)** prejudicial (a).

deuce [dju:s] n (TENNIS) empate m, iguais.

devaluation [dɪvælju:'eɪʃən] n desvalorização f.

devalue [dɪ'vælju:] vt desvalorizar.

devastate ['dɛvəsteɪt] vt devastar; **he was ~d by the news** as notícias deixaram-no desolado.

devastating ['dɛvəsteɪtɪŋ] adj devastador(a); (fig) assolador(a).

devastation [dɛvəs'teɪʃən] n devastação f.

develop [dɪ'vɛləp] vt desenvolver; (PHOT) revelar; (disease) contrair; (resources) explotar; (engine trouble) começar a ter ♦ vi desenvolver-se; (advance) progredir; (appear) aparecer.

developer [dɪ'vɛləpə*] n (PHOT) revelador m; (also: property ~) empresário/a de imóveis.

developing country [dɪ'vɛləpɪŋ-] país m em desenvolvimento.

development [dɪ'vɛləpmənt] n desenvolvimento; (advance) progresso; (of land) urbanização f.

development area n zona a ser urbanizada.

deviate ['di:vɪeɪt] vi desviar-se.

deviation [di:vɪ'eɪʃən] n desvio.

device [dɪ'vaɪs] n (scheme) estratagema m, plano; (apparatus) aparelho, dispositivo; **explosive ~** dispositivo explosivo.

devil ['dɛvl] n diabo.

devilish ['dɛvlɪʃ] adj diabólico.

devil-may-care adj despreocupado.

devious ['di:vɪəs] adj (means) intricado, indi-

reto; (person) malandro, esperto.

devise [dɪ'vaɪz] vt idear, inventar.

devoid [dɪ'vɔɪd] adj: **~ of** destituído de.

devolution [di:və'lu:ʃən] n (POL) descentralização f.

devolve [dɪ'vɔlv] vi: **to ~ (up)on** passar a ser da competência de.

devote [dɪ'vəut] vt: **to ~ sth to** dedicar algo a.

devoted [dɪ'vəutɪd] adj (loyal) leal, fiel; **the book is ~ to politics** o livro trata de política; **to be ~ to** (love) estar devotado a.

devotee [dɛvəu'ti:] n adepto/a, entusiasta m/f.

devotion [dɪ'vəuʃən] n dedicação f; (REL) devoção f.

devour [dɪ'vauə*] vt devorar.

devout [dɪ'vaut] adj devoto.

dew [dju:] n orvalho.

dexterity [dɛks'tɛrɪtɪ] n destreza.

dext(e)rous ['dɛkstrəs] adj destro.

dg abbr (= decigram) dg.

Dhaka ['dækə] n Daca.

diabetes [daɪə'bi:ti:z] n diabete f.

diabetic [daɪə'bɛtɪk] adj (person) diabético; (chocolate, jam) para diabéticos ♦ n diabético/a.

diabolical [daɪə'bɔlɪkl] adj diabólico; (inf: dreadful) terrível, horrível.

diaeresis [daɪ'ɛrɪsɪs] n diérese f.

diagnose [daɪəg'nəuz] vt diagnosticar.

diagnoses [daɪəg'nəsi:z] npl of **diagnosis**.

diagnosis [daɪəg'nəusɪs] (pl **diagnoses**) n diagnóstico.

diagonal [daɪ'ægənl] adj diagonal ♦ n diagonal f.

diagram ['daɪəgræm] n diagrama m, esquema m.

dial ['daɪəl] n disco ♦ vt (number) discar (BR), marcar (PT); **to ~ a wrong number** discar (BR) or marcar (PT) um número errado; **can I ~ London direct?** é possível discar direto para Londres?

dial. abbr = **dialect**.

dial code (US) n = **dialling code**.

dialect ['daɪəlɛkt] n dialeto.

dialling code ['daɪəlɪŋ-] (BRIT) n código.

dialling tone ['daɪəlɪŋ-] (BRIT) n sinal m de discar (BR) or de marcar (PT).

dialogue ['daɪəlɔg] n diálogo.

dial tone (US) n = **dialling tone**.

dialysis [daɪ'ælɪsɪs] n diálise f.

diameter [daɪ'æmɪtə*] n diâmetro.

diametrically [daɪə'mɛtrɪklɪ] adv: **~ opposed (to)** diametralmente oposto (a).

diamond ['daɪəmənd] n diamante m; (shape) losango, rombo; **~s** npl (CARDS) ouros mpl.

diamond ring n anel m de brilhante.

diaper ['daɪəpə*] (US) n fralda.

diaphragm ['daɪəfræm] n diafragma m.

diarrhoea [daɪə'rɪə] (US **diarrhea**) n diarréia.

diary ['daɪərɪ] n (daily account) diário; (book)

---

*NB: European Portuguese adds the following consonants to certain words: **b** (sú(b)dito, su(b)til); **c** (a(c)ção, a(c)cionista, a(c)to); **m** (inde(m)ne); **p** (ado(p)ção, ado(p)tar); for further details see p. xiii.*

agenda; **to keep a** ~ ter um diário.
diatribe ['daɪətraɪb] *n* diatribe *f*.
dice [daɪs] *npl of* **die** ♦ *n inv* dado ♦ *vt* (*CULIN*) cortar em cubos.
dicey ['daɪsɪ] (*inf*) *adj*: **it's a bit** ~ é um pouco arriscado.
dichotomy [daɪ'kɔtəmɪ] *n* dicotomia.
Dictaphone ['dɪktəfəun] ® *n* ditafone *m* ®, máquina de ditar.
dictate [dɪk'teɪt] *vt* ditar ♦ *vi*: **to** ~ **to** (*person*) dar ordens a; **I won't be** ~**d to** não vou acatar ordens.
dictates ['dɪkteɪts] *npl* ditames *npl*.
dictation [dɪk'teɪʃən] *n* ditado; **at** ~ **speed** com a velocidade de ditado.
dictator [dɪk'teɪtə*] *n* ditador(a) *m/f*.
dictatorship [dɪk'teɪtəʃɪp] *n* ditadura.
diction ['dɪkʃən] *n* dicção *f*.
dictionary ['dɪkʃənrɪ] *n* dicionário.
did [dɪd] *pt of* **do**.
didactic [daɪ'dæktɪk] *adj* didático.
die [daɪ] (*pl* **dice**) *vi* morrer ♦ *n* dado; (*pl*: **dies**) cunho, molde *m*; **to** ~ **of** *or* **from** morrer de; **to be dying for sth** estar louco por algo; **to be dying to do sth** estar morrendo de vontade de fazer algo.
die away *vi* (*sound, light*) extinguir-se lentamente.
die down *vi* apagar-se; (*wind*) abrandar.
die out *vi* desaparecer, apagar-se.
diehard ['daɪhɑːd] *n* reacionário/a, reaça *m/f* (*inf*).
diesel ['diːzl] *n* diesel *m*.
diesel engine ['diːzəl-] *n* motor *m* diesel.
diesel (fuel) *n* óleo diesel.
diesel (oil) *n* óleo diesel.
diet ['daɪət] *n* dieta; (*restricted food*) regime *m* ♦ *vi* (*also: be on a* ~) estar de dieta, fazer regime; **to live on a** ~ **of** alimentar-se de.
dietician [daɪə'tɪʃən] *n* dietista *m/f*.
differ ['dɪfə*] *vi*: **to** ~ **from sth** (*be different*) ser diferente de algo, diferenciar-se de algo; **to** ~ **from sb over sth** discordar de alguém em algo.
difference ['dɪfərəns] *n* diferença; (*quarrel*) desacordo; **it makes no** ~ **to me** não faz diferença para mim, para mim dá no mesmo; **to settle one's** ~**s** resolver as diferenças.
different ['dɪfərənt] *adj* diferente.
differential [dɪfə'renʃəl] *n* (*AUT*) diferencial *m*; **wage/price** ~**s** diferenças de salário/preço.
differentiate [dɪfə'renʃɪeɪt] *vt* diferenciar, distinguir ♦ *vi* diferenciar-se; **to** ~ **between** distinguir entre.
differently ['dɪfərəntlɪ] *adv* de outro modo, de forma diferente.
difficult ['dɪfɪkəlt] *adj* difícil; ~ **to understand** difícil de (se) entender.
difficulty ['dɪfɪkəltɪ] *n* dificuldade *f;* **to have difficulties with** ter problemas com; **to be in** ~ estar em dificuldade.
diffidence ['dɪfɪdəns] *n* timidez *f*.
diffident ['dɪfɪdənt] *adj* tímido.
diffuse [*adj* dɪ'fjuːs, *vt* dɪ'fjuːz] *adj* difuso ♦ *vt*

difundir.
dig [dɪg] (*pt, pp* **dug**) *vt* (*hole, garden*) cavar; (*coal*) escavar; (*nails etc*) cravar ♦ *n* (*prod*) pontada; (*archaeological*) excavação *f*; (*remark*) alfinetada; ~**s** *npl* (*BRIT: inf*) pensão *f*, alojamento; **to** ~ **into one's pockets for sth** enfiar as mãos nos bolsos à procura de algo; **to** ~ **one's nails into** cravar as unhas em.
dig in *vi* (*MIL*) cavar trincheiras; (*inf: eat*) atacar ♦ *vt* (*compost*) misturar; (*knife, claw*) cravar; **to** ~ **in one's heels** (*fig*) bater o pé; ~ **in!** vai lá!
dig out *vt* escavar.
dig up *vt* desenterrar; (*plant*) arrancar.
digest [*vt* daɪ'dʒɛst, *n* 'daɪdʒɛst] *vt* (*food*) digerir; (*facts*) assimilar ♦ *n* sumário.
digestible [dɪ'dʒɛstəbl] *adj* digerível.
digestion [dɪ'dʒɛstʃən] *n* digestão *f*.
digestive [dɪ'dʒɛstɪv] *adj* digestivo.
digit ['dɪdʒɪt] *n* (*MATH, finger*) dígito.
digital ['dɪdʒɪtəl] *adj* digital.
dignified ['dɪgnɪfaɪd] *adj* digno.
dignitary ['dɪgnɪtərɪ] *n* dignitário/a.
dignity ['dɪgnɪtɪ] *n* dignidade *f*.
digress [daɪ'grɛs] *vi*: **to** ~ **from** afastar-se de.
digression [daɪ'grɛʃən] *n* digressão *f*.
dilapidated [dɪ'læpɪdeɪtɪd] *adj* arruinado.
dilate [daɪ'leɪt] *vt* dilatar ♦ *vi* dilatar-se.
dilatory ['dɪlətərɪ] *adj* retardio.
dilemma [daɪ'lɛmə] *n* dilema *m*; **to be in a** ~ estar num dilema.
diligent ['dɪlɪdʒənt] *adj* diligente.
dill [dɪl] *n* endro, aneto.
dilly-dally ['dɪlɪ'dælɪ] *vi* (*loiter*) vadiar; (*hesitate*) vacilar.
dilute [daɪ'luːt] *vt* diluir ♦ *adj* diluído.
dim [dɪm] *adj* (*light, eyesight*) fraco; (*outline*) indistinto; (*memory*) vago; (*stupid*) burro; (*room*) escuro ♦ *vt* (*light*) diminuir; (*US: AUT: headlights*) baixar; **to take a** ~ **view of sth** desaprovar algo.
dime [daɪm] (*US*) *n moeda de dez centavos*.
dimension [dɪ'mɛnʃən] *n* dimensão *f*.
-dimensional [dɪ'mɛnʃənl] *suffix*: **two**~ bidimensional.
diminish [dɪ'mɪnɪʃ] *vt, vi* diminuir.
diminished [dɪ'mɪnɪʃt] *adj*: ~ **responsibility** (*LAW*) responsabilidade *f* reduzida.
diminutive [dɪ'mɪnjutɪv] *adj* diminuto ♦ *n* (*LING*) diminutivo.
dimly ['dɪmlɪ] *adv* fracamente; (*not clearly*) indistintamente.
dimmers ['dɪməz] (*US*) *npl* (*AUT*) faróis *mpl* baixos.
dimple ['dɪmpl] *n* covinha.
dim-witted [-'wɪtɪd] (*inf*) *adj* burro.
din [dɪn] *n* zoeira ♦ *vt*: **to** ~ **sth into sb** (*inf*) meter algo na cabeça de alguém, repisar algo a alguém.
dine [daɪn] *vi* jantar.
diner ['daɪnə*] *n* (*person*) comensal *m/f*; (*RAIL*) vagão-restaurante *m*; (*US: eating place*) lanchonete *f*.
dinghy ['dɪŋgɪ] *n* dingue *m*, bote *m*; **rubber** ~

bote de borracha; (also: sailing ~) barco a vela.

dingy ['dɪndʒɪ] adj (room) sombrio, lúgubre; (dirty) esquálido; (dull) descolorido.

dining car ['daɪnɪŋ-] n vagão-restaurante m.

dining room ['daɪnɪŋ-] n sala de jantar.

dinner ['dɪnə*] n (evening meal) jantar m; (lunch) almoço; (public) jantar, banquete m; ~'s ready! está na mesa!

dinner jacket n smoking m.

dinner party n jantar m.

dinner time n hora de jantar or almoçar.

dinosaur ['daɪnəsɔ:*] n dinossauro.

dint [dɪnt] n: **by ~ of (doing) sth** à força de (fazer) algo.

diocese ['daɪəsɪs] n diocese f.

dioxide [daɪ'ɔksaɪd] n dióxido.

Dip. (BRIT) abbr = **diploma.**

dip [dɪp] n (slope) inclinação f; (in sea) mergulho ♦ vt (in water) mergulhar; (ladle etc) meter; (BRIT: AUT: lights) baixar ♦ vi mergulhar.

diphtheria [dɪf'θɪərɪə] n difteria.

diphthong ['dɪfθɔŋ] n ditongo.

diploma [dɪ'pləumə] n diploma m.

diplomacy [dɪ'pləuməsɪ] n diplomacia.

diplomat ['dɪpləmæt] n diplomata m/f.

diplomatic [dɪplə'mætɪk] adj diplomático; **to break off ~ relations (with)** romper relações diplomáticas (com).

dipstick ['dɪpstɪk] n (AUT) vareta medidora.

dipswitch ['dɪpswɪtʃ] (BRIT) n (AUT) interruptor m de luz alta e baixa.

dire [daɪə*] adj terrível; (very bad) péssimo.

direct [daɪ'rekt] adj direto ♦ vt dirigir; **can you ~ me to ...?** pode me indicar o caminho a ...?; **to ~ sb to do sth** mandar alguém fazer algo.

direct cost n (COMM) custo direto.

direct current n (ELEC) corrente f contínua.

direct debit n (BANKING) débito direto.

direct dialling n (TEL) discagem f direta (BR), marcação f directa (PT).

direct hit n (MIL) acerto direto.

direction [dɪ'rekʃən] n direção f; ~s npl (to a place) indicação f; (instructions) instruções fpl; ~s for use modo de usar; **to ask for ~s** pedir uma indicação, perguntar o caminho; **sense of ~** senso de direção; **in the ~ of** na direção de.

directive [dɪ'rektɪv] n diretriz f.

direct labour n mão-de-obra direta.

directly [dɪ'rektlɪ] adv (in straight line) diretamente; (at once) imediatamente.

direct mail n mala direta.

direct mailshot (BRIT) n mailing m.

directness [daɪ'rektnɪs] n (of person, speech) franqueza.

director [dɪ'rektə*] n diretor m; **D~ of Public Prosecutions** (BRIT) ≈ procurador(a) m/f da República.

directory [dɪ'rektərɪ] n (TEL) lista (telefôni-

ca); (also: street ~) lista de endereços; (also: trade ~) anuário comercial; (COMPUT) diretório.

directory enquiries (US **directory assistance**) n (serviço de) informações fpl (BR), serviço informativo (PT).

dirt [dɜ:t] n sujeira (BR), sujidade (PT); **to treat sb like ~** espezinhar alguém.

dirt-cheap adj baratíssimo.

dirt road n estrada de terra.

dirty ['dɜ:tɪ] adj sujo; (joke) indecente ♦ vt sujar; ~ **trick** golpe m baixo, sujeira.

disability [dɪsə'bɪlɪtɪ] n incapacidade f.

disability allowance n pensão f de invalidez.

disable [dɪs'eɪbl] vt (subj: illness, accident) incapacitar; (tank, gun) inutilizar.

disabled [dɪs'eɪbld] adj incapacitado, deficiente.

disadvantage [dɪsəd'vɑ:ntɪdʒ] n desvantagem f, inconveniente m.

disadvantaged [dɪsəd'vɑ:ntɪdʒd] adj (person) menos favorecido.

disadvantageous [dɪsædvɑːn'teɪdʒəs] adj desvantajoso.

disaffected [dɪsə'fektɪd] adj: ~ **(to** or **towards)** descontente (de).

disaffection [dɪsə'fekʃən] n descontentamento.

disagree [dɪsə'gri:] vi (differ: accounts) diferir; (be against, think otherwise): **to ~ (with)** não concordar (com), discordar (de); **garlic ~s with me** o alho me faz mal, o alho não me convém.

disagreeable [dɪsə'grɪəbl] adj desagradável.

disagreement [dɪsə'gri:mənt] n desacordo; (quarrel) desavença.

disallow ['dɪsə'lau] vt não admitir; (BRIT: goal) anular.

disappear [dɪsə'pɪə*] vi desaparecer, sumir.

disappearance [dɪsə'pɪərəns] n desaparecimento, desaparição f.

disappoint [dɪsə'pɔɪnt] vt (cause to regret) desapontar; (let down) decepcionar; (hopes) frustrar.

disappointed [dɪsə'pɔɪntɪd] adj decepcionado; (with oneself) desapontado.

disappointing [dɪsə'pɔɪntɪŋ] adj decepcionante.

disappointment [dɪsə'pɔɪntmənt] n decepção f; (regret) desapontamento.

disapproval [dɪsə'pru:vəl] n desaprovação f.

disapprove [dɪsə'pru:v] vi: **to ~ of** desaprovar.

disapproving [dɪsə'pru:vɪŋ] adj desaprovativo, de desaprovação.

disarm [dɪs'ɑːm] vt desarmar.

disarmament [dɪs'ɑːməmənt] n desarmamento.

disarming [dɪs'ɑːmɪŋ] adj (smile) encantador(a).

disarray [dɪsə'reɪ] n desordem f; **in ~** (troops) desbaratado; (thoughts) confuso; (clothes) em desalinho; **to throw into ~** (troops)

NB: European Portuguese adds the following consonants to certain words: **b** (sú(b)dito, su(b)til); **c** (a(c)ção, a(c)cionista, a(c)to); **m** (inde(m)ne); **p** (ado(p)ção, ado(p)tar); for further details see p. xiii.

desbaratar; (government etc) deixar em polvorosa.

disaster [dɪ'zɑːstə*] n (accident) desastre m; (natural) catástrofe f.

disastrous [dɪ'zɑːstrəs] adj desastroso.

disband [dɪs'bænd] vt dispersar ♦ vi dispersar-se, desfazer-se.

disbelief [dɪsbə'liːf] n incredulidade f; in ~ com incredulidade, incrédulo.

disbelieve ['dɪsbə'liːv] vt não acreditar em.

disc [dɪsk] n disco.

disc. abbr (COMM) = **discount**.

discard [dɪs'kɑːd] vt (old things) desfazer-se de; (fig) descartar.

disc brake n freio de disco (BR), travão m de discos (PT).

discern [dɪ'sɜːn] vt perceber.

discernible [dɪ'sɜːnəbl] adj perceptível; (object) visível.

discerning [dɪ'sɜːnɪŋ] adj perspicaz.

discharge [vt dɪs'tʃɑːdʒ, n 'dɪstʃɑːdʒ] vt (duties) cumprir, desempenhar; (settle: debt) saldar, quitar; (patient) dar alta a; (employee) despedir; (soldier) dar baixa em, dispensar; (defendant) pôr em liberdade; (waste etc) descarregar, despejar ♦ n (ELEC) descarga; (dismissal) despedida; (of duty) desempenho; (of debt) quitação f; (from hospital) alta; (from army) baixa; (LAW) absolvição f; (MED) secreção f; (also: vaginal ~) corrimento; to ~ one's gun descarregar a arma, disparar; ~d bankrupt falido/a reabilitado/a.

disciple [dɪ'saɪpl] n discípulo/a.

disciplinary ['dɪsɪplɪnərɪ] adj disciplinar; to take ~ action against sb mover ação disciplinar contra alguém.

discipline ['dɪsɪplɪn] n disciplina ♦ vt disciplinar; (punish) punir; to ~ o.s. to do sth disciplinar-se para fazer algo.

disc jockey n (on radio) radialista m/f; (in discothèque) discotecário/a.

disclaim [dɪs'kleɪm] vt negar.

disclaimer [dɪs'kleɪmə*] n desmentido; to issue a ~ publicar um desmentido.

disclose [dɪs'kləʊz] vt revelar.

disclosure [dɪs'kləʊʒə*] n revelação f.

disco ['dɪskəʊ] n abbr = **discothèque**.

discolour [dɪs'kʌlə*] (US discolor) vt descolorar; (fade: fabric) desbotar; (yellow: teeth) amarelar; (stain) manchar ♦ vi (fabric) desbotar; (teeth etc) amarelar.

discolo(u)ration [dɪskʌlə'reɪʃən] n (of fabric) desbotamento; (stain) mancha.

discolo(u)red [dɪs'kʌləd] adj descolorido; (teeth etc) amarelado.

discomfort [dɪs'kʌmfət] n desconforto; (unease) inquietação f; (physical) mal-estar m.

disconcert [dɪskən'sɜːt] vt desconcertar.

disconnect [dɪskə'nɛkt] vt desligar; (gas, water) cortar.

disconnected [dɪskə'nɛktɪd] adj (speech, thoughts) desconexo, incoerente.

disconsolate [dɪs'kɒnsəlɪt] adj desconsolado, inconsolável.

discontent [dɪskən'tɛnt] n descontentamento.

discontented [dɪskən'tɛntɪd] adj descontente.

discontinue [dɪskən'tɪnjuː] vt interromper; (payments) suspender; "~d" (COMM) "fora de linha".

discord ['dɪskɔːd] n discórdia; (MUS) dissonância.

discordant [dɪs'kɔːdənt] adj dissonante.

discothèque ['dɪskəʊtɛk] n discoteca.

discount [n 'dɪskaunt, vt dɪs'kaunt] n desconto ♦ vt descontar; to give sb a ~ on sth dar or conceder um desconto a alguém por algo; ~ for cash desconto por pagamento à vista; at a ~ com desconto.

discount house (irreg) n (FINANCE) agência corretora de descontos; (COMM: also: discount store) loja de descontos.

discount rate n taxa de desconto.

discourage [dɪs'kʌrɪdʒ] vt (dishearten) desanimar; (dissuade) dissuadir; (deter) desincentivar; (theft etc) desencorajar.

discouragement [dɪs'kʌrɪdʒmənt] n (depression) desânimo, desalento; to act as a ~ to sb dissuadir alguém.

discouraging [dɪs'kʌrɪdʒɪŋ] adj desanimador(a).

discourteous [dɪs'kɜːtɪəs] adj descortês.

discover [dɪs'kʌvə*] vt descobrir.

discovery [dɪs'kʌvərɪ] n (act) descobrimento, descoberta; (thing discovered) descoberta.

discredit [dɪs'krɛdɪt] vt desacreditar ♦ n descrédito.

discreet [dɪ'skriːt] adj discreto.

discreetly [dɪ'skriːtlɪ] adv discretamente.

discrepancy [dɪ'skrɛpənsɪ] n (difference) diferença; (disagreement) discrepância.

discretion [dɪ'skrɛʃən] n discrição f; use your ~ aja segundo o seu critério.

discretionary [dɪ'skrɛʃənrɪ] adj (powers) discricionário.

discriminate [dɪ'skrɪmɪneɪt] vi: to ~ between fazer distinção entre; to ~ against discriminar contra.

discriminating [dɪ'skrɪmɪneɪtɪŋ] adj acurado, criterioso.

discrimination [dɪskrɪmɪ'neɪʃən] n (discernment) discernimento; (bias) discriminação f; racial/sexual ~ discriminação racial/sexual.

discus ['dɪskəs] n disco; (event) arremesso do disco.

discuss [dɪ'skʌs] vt discutir.

discussion [dɪ'skʌʃən] n discussão f; under ~ em discussão.

disdain [dɪs'deɪn] n desdém m ♦ vt desdenhar.

disease [dɪ'ziːz] n moléstia.

diseased [dɪ'ziːzd] adj doente.

disembark [dɪsɪm'bɑːk] vt, vi desembarcar.

disembarkation [dɪsɛmbɑː'keɪʃən] n desembarque m.

disembodied ['dɪsɪm'bɒdɪd] adj desencarnado.

disembowel ['dɪsɪm'bauəl] vt estripar, eviscerar.

disenchanted ['dɪsɪn'tʃɑːntɪd] adj: ~ (with) desencantado (de).

disenfranchise ['dɪsɪn'fræntʃaɪz] vt privar do

privilégio do voto; (*COMM*) retirar a concessão de.

disengage [dɪsɪn'geɪdʒ] *vt* soltar; (*TECH*) desengrenar; **to ~ the clutch** (*AUT*) desembrear.

disengagement [dɪsɪn'geɪdʒmənt] *n* (*POL*) desengajamento.

disentangle [dɪsɪn'tæŋgl] *vt* desenredar.

disfavour [dɪs'feɪvə*] (*US* **disfavor**) *n* desfavor *m*.

disfigure [dɪs'fɪgə*] *vt* desfigurar.

disgorge [dɪs'gɔːdʒ] *vt* descarregar, despejar.

disgrace [dɪs'greɪs] *n* ignomínia; (*downfall*) queda; (*shame*) vergonha, desonra ♦ *vt* desonrar.

disgraceful [dɪs'greɪsful] *adj* vergonhoso; (*behaviour*) escandaloso.

disgruntled [dɪs'grʌntld] *adj* descontente.

disguise [dɪs'gaɪz] *n* disfarce *m* ♦ *vt* disfarçar; **in ~** disfarçado; **to ~ o.s. as** disfarçar-se de; **there's no disguising the fact that ...** não há como esconder o fato de que ....

disgust [dɪs'gʌst] *n* repugnância ♦ *vt* repugnar a, dar nojo em.

disgusting [dɪs'gʌstɪŋ] *adj* repugnante, nojento.

dish [dɪʃ] *n* prato; (*serving ~*) travessa; **to do** *or* **wash the ~es** lavar os pratos *or* a louça.

dish out *vt* repartir.

dish up *vt* servir; (*facts, statistics*) apresentar.

dishcloth ['dɪʃklɔθ] *n* pano de prato *or* de louça.

dishearten [dɪs'hɑːtn] *vt* desalentar.

dishevelled [dɪ'ʃevəld] (*US* **disheveled**) *adj* despenteado, desgrenhado.

dishonest [dɪs'ɔnɪst] *adj* (*person*) desonesto; (*means*) fraudulento.

dishonesty [dɪs'ɔnɪstɪ] *n* desonestidade *f*.

dishonour [dɪs'ɔnə*] (*US* **dishonor**) *n* desonra.

dishono(u)rable [dɪs'ɔnərəbl] *adj* desonroso.

dish soap (*US*) *n* detergente *m*.

dishtowel [dɪʃ'tauəl] (*US*) *n* pano de prato.

dishwasher ['dɪʃwɔʃə*] *n* máquina de lavar louça *or* pratos.

disillusion [dɪsɪ'luːʒən] *vt* desiludir ♦ *n* desilusão *f*; **to become ~ed** ficar desiludido, desiludir-se.

disillusionment [dɪsɪ'luːʒənmənt] *n* desilusão *f*.

disincentive [dɪsɪn'sentɪv] *n* desincentivo; **to be a ~ to sb** desincentivar alguém.

disinclined ['dɪsɪn'klaɪnd] *adj*: **to be ~ to do** estar pouco disposto a fazer.

disinfect [dɪsɪn'fekt] *vt* desinfetar.

disinfectant [dɪsɪn'fektənt] *n* desinfetante *m*.

disinflation [dɪsɪn'fleɪʃən] *n* desinflação *f*.

disinherit [dɪsɪn'herɪt] *vt* deserdar.

disintegrate [dɪs'ɪntɪgreɪt] *vi* desagregar-se, desintegrar-se.

disinterested [dɪs'ɪntrəstɪd] *adj* desinteressado.

disjointed [dɪs'dʒɔɪntɪd] *adj* desconexo.

disk [dɪsk] *n* (*COMPUT*) disco; **single-/double-sided ~** disquete de face simples/dupla.

disk drive *n* unidade *f* de disco.

diskette [dɪs'ket] *n* (*COMPUT*) disquete *m*.

disk operating system *n* sistema *m* operacional residente em disco.

dislike [dɪs'laɪk] *n* antipatia, aversão *f* ♦ *vt* antipatizar com, não gostar de; **to take a ~ to sb/sth** tomar antipatia por alguém/algo; **I ~ the idea** não gosto da idéia.

dislocate ['dɪsləkeɪt] *vt* deslocar; **he has ~d his shoulder** ele deslocou o ombro.

dislodge [dɪs'lɔdʒ] *vt* desentocar; (*enemy*) desalojar.

disloyal [dɪs'lɔɪəl] *adj* desleal.

dismal ['dɪzml] *adj* (*dull*) sombrio, lúgubre; (*depressing*) deprimente; (*very bad*) horrível.

dismantle [dɪs'mæntl] *vt* desmontar, desmantelar.

dismay [dɪs'meɪ] *n* consternação *f* ♦ *vt* consternar; **much to my ~** para minha grande consternação.

dismiss [dɪs'mɪs] *vt* (*worker*) despedir; (*official*) demitir; (*idea*) descartar; (*LAW, possibility*) rejeitar ♦ *vi* (*MIL*) sair de forma.

dismissal [dɪs'mɪsəl] *n* (*of worker*) despedida; (*of official*) demissão *f*.

dismount [dɪs'maunt] *vi* desmontar.

disobedience [dɪsə'biːdɪəns] *n* desobediência.

disobedient [dɪsə'biːdɪənt] *adj* desobediente.

disobey [dɪsə'beɪ] *vt* desobedecer a; (*rules*) transgredir, desrespeitar.

disorder [dɪs'ɔːdə*] *n* desordem *f*; (*rioting*) distúrbios *mpl*, tumulto; (*MED*) distúrbio; **stomach ~** problema estomacal.

disorderly [dɪs'ɔːdəlɪ] *adj* (*untidy*) desordenado; (*crowd*) tumultuado; (*behaviour*) escandaloso.

disorderly conduct *n* (*LAW*) perturbação *f* da ordem, ofensa à moral.

disorganized [dɪs'ɔːgənaɪzd] *adj* desorganizado.

disorientated [dɪs'ɔːrɪenteɪtəd] *adj* desorientado.

disown [dɪs'əun] *vt* repudiar.

disparaging [dɪs'pærɪdʒɪŋ] *adj* depreciativo; **to be ~ about sb/sth** fazer pouco de alguém/algo, depreciar alguém/algo.

disparate ['dɪspərɪt] *adj* diverso, desigual.

disparity [dɪs'pærɪtɪ] *n* desigualdade *f*.

dispassionate [dɪs'pæʃənət] *adj* (*calm*) calmo, controlado; (*impartial*) desinteressado, imparcial.

dispatch [dɪs'pætʃ] *vt* (*person, business*) despachar; (*send: parcel etc*) expedir ♦ *n* (*sending*) remessa; (*speed*) rapidez *f*, urgência; (*PRESS*) comunicado; (*MIL*) parte *f*.

dispatch department *n* (serviço de) expedição *f*.

dispatch rider *n* (*MIL*) estafeta *m/f*.

NB: *European Portuguese adds the following consonants to certain words:* **b** (sú(b)dito, su(b)til); **c** (a(c)ção, a(c)cionista, a(c)to); **m** (inde(m)ne); **p** (ado(p)ção, ado(p)tar); *for further details see p. xiii.*

dispel [dɪs'pel] *vt* dissipar.

dispensary [dɪs'pensərɪ] *n* dispensário, farmácia.

dispense [dɪs'pens] *vt* (*give out*) dispensar; (*medicine*) preparar (e vender); **to ~ sb from** dispensar alguém de.

dispense with *vt fus* prescindir de.

dispenser [dɪs'pensə*] *n* (*device*) distribuidor *m* automático.

dispensing chemist [dɪs'pensɪŋ-] (*BRIT*) *n* farmacêutico/a.

dispersal [dɪs'pəːsl] *n* dispersão *f*.

disperse [dɪs'pəːs] *vt* dispersar ♦ *vi* dispersar-se.

dispirited [dɪs'pɪrɪtɪd] *adj* desanimado.

displace [dɪs'pleɪs] *vt* (*shift*) deslocar.

displaced person [dɪs'pleɪst-] *n* (*POL*) deslocado/a de guerra.

displacement [dɪs'pleɪsmənt] *n* deslocamento.

display [dɪs'pleɪ] *n* (*exhibition*) exposição *f*; (*computer ~: information*) apresentação *f* visual; (: *device*) display *m*; (*MIL*) parada; (*of feeling*) manifestação *f*; (*pej*) ostentação *f*; (*show, spectacle*) espetáculo ♦ *vt* (*goods*) expor; (*feelings, tastes*) manifestar; (*ostentatiously*) ostentar; (*results, departure times*) expor; **on ~** (*visible*) à mostra; (*goods, paintings etc*) em exposição.

display advertising *n* anúncios *mpl*.

displease [dɪs'pliːz] *vt* desagradar, desgostar; **~d with** descontente com.

displeasure [dɪs'pleʒə*] *n* desgosto.

disposable [dɪs'pəuzəbl] *adj* (*pack etc*) descartável; (*income*) disponível; **~ nappy** (*BRIT*) fralda descartável.

disposal [dɪs'pəuzl] *n* (*availability, arrangement*) disposição *f*; (*of rubbish*) destruição *f*; (*of property etc: by selling*) venda, traspasse *m*; (: *by giving away*) cessão *f*; **at sb's ~** à disposição de alguém; **to put sth at sb's ~** pôr algo à disposição de alguém.

dispose [dɪs'pəuz] *vt* dispor.

dispose of *vt fus* (*time, money*) dispor de; (*unwanted goods*) desfazer-se de; (*throw away*) jogar (*BR*) *or* tirar (*PT*) fora; (*COMM: stock*) vender; (*problem, task*) expedir.

disposed [dɪs'pəuzd] *adj*: **~ to do** disposto a fazer.

disposition [dɪspə'zɪʃən] *n* disposição *f*; (*temperament*) índole *f*.

dispossess ['dɪspəzɛs] *vt*: **to ~ sb (of)** despojar alguém (de).

disproportion [dɪsprə'pɔːʃən] *n* desproporção *f*.

disproportionate [dɪsprə'pɔːʃənət] *adj* desproporcionado.

disprove [dɪs'pruːv] *vt* refutar.

dispute [dɪs'pjuːt] *n* disputa; (*verbal*) discussão *f*; (*also: industrial ~*) conflito, disputa ♦ *vt* disputar; (*argue*) discutir; (*question*) questionar; **to be in** *or* **under ~** (*matter*) estar em discussão; (*territory*) estar em disputa, ser disputado.

disqualification [dɪskwɔlɪfɪ'keɪʃən] *n* (*LAW*) inabilitação *f*, incapacitação *f*; (*SPORT*) des-

classificação *f*; **~ (from driving)** (*BRIT*) cassação *f* da carteira (de motorista).

disqualify [dɪs'kwɔlɪfaɪ] *vt* (*SPORT*) desclassificar; **to ~ sb for sth/from doing sth** desqualificar alguém para algo/de fazer algo; **to ~ sb (from driving)** (*BRIT*) cassar a carteira (de motorista) a alguém.

disquiet [dɪs'kwaɪət] *n* inquietação *f*.

disquieting [dɪs'kwaɪətɪŋ] *adj* inquietante, alarmante.

disregard [dɪsrɪ'gaːd] *vt* desconsiderar ♦ *n* (*indifference*): **~ (for)** (*feelings*) desconsideração *f* (por); (*danger*) indiferença (a); (*money*) menosprezo (por).

disrepair [dɪsrɪ'pɛə*] *n*: **to fall into ~** ficar dilapidado.

disreputable [dɪs'rɛpjutəbl] *adj* (*person*) de má fama; (*behaviour*) vergonhoso.

disrepute ['dɪsrɪ'pjuːt] *n* descrédito, desonra; **to bring into ~** desacreditar, desprestigiar.

disrespect [dɪsrɪ'spɛkt] *n*: **~ (for)** desrespeito (por).

disrespectful [dɪsrɪ'spɛktful] *adj* desrespeitoso.

disrupt [dɪs'rʌpt] *vt* (*plans*) desfazer; (*meeting, process*) perturbar, interromper.

disruption [dɪs'rʌpʃən] *n* transtorno, perturbação *f*.

disruptive [dɪs'rʌptɪv] *adj* (*influence*) maléfico; (*strike*) perturbador(a).

dissatisfaction [dɪssætɪs'fækʃən] *n* descontentamento.

dissatisfied [dɪs'sætɪsfaɪd] *adj*: **~ (with)** descontente (com).

dissect [dɪ'sɛkt] *vt* dissecar.

disseminate [dɪ'sɛmɪneɪt] *vt* disseminar.

dissent [dɪ'sɛnt] *n* dissensão *f*.

dissenter [dɪ'sɛntə*] *n* (*REL, POL etc*) dissidente *m/f*.

dissertation [dɪsə'teɪʃən] *n* (*SCH*) dissertação *f*, tese *f*.

disservice [dɪs'səːvɪs] *n*: **to do sb a ~** prejudicar alguém.

dissident ['dɪsɪdnt] *adj, n* dissidente *m/f*.

dissimilar [dɪ'sɪmɪlə*] *adj*: **~ (to)** dessemelhante (de), diferente (de).

dissipate ['dɪsɪpeɪt] *vt* dissipar ♦ *vi* dissipar-se.

dissipated ['dɪsɪpeɪtɪd] *adj* (*person*) dissoluto.

dissociate [dɪ'səuʃɪeɪt] *vt* dissociar, separar; **to ~ o.s. from** desassociar-se de, distanciar-se de.

dissolute ['dɪsəluːt] *adj* dissoluto.

dissolution [dɪsə'luːʃən] *n* dissolução *f*.

dissolve [dɪ'zɔlv] *vt* dissolver ♦ *vi* dissolver-se; (*fig: problem etc*) desaparecer.

dissuade [dɪ'sweɪd] *vt*: **to ~ sb (from)** dissuadir alguém (de).

distaff ['dɪstaːf] *n*: **~ side** lado materno.

distance ['dɪstns] *n* distância; **in the ~** ao longe; **what's the ~ to London?** qual é a distância daqui a Londres?; **it's within walking ~** pode-se ir a pé, dá para ir a pé (*inf*).

distant ['dɪstnt] *adj* distante; (*manner*) afastado, reservado.

distaste [dɪs'teɪst] *n* repugnância.
distasteful [dɪs'teɪstful] *adj* repugnante, desagradável.
Dist. Atty. (*US*) *abbr* = **district attorney**.
distemper [dɪs'tɛmpə*] *n* (*paint*) tinta plástica; (*of dogs*) cinomose *f*.
distended [dɪs'tɛndɪd] *adj* inchado.
distil [dɪs'tɪl] *vt* destilar.
distillery [dɪs'tɪlərɪ] *n* destilaria.
distinct [dɪs'tɪŋkt] *adj* (*different*) distinto; (*clear*) claro; (*unmistakeable*) nítido; **as ~ from** em oposição a.
distinction [dɪs'tɪŋkʃən] *n* distinção *f*; **to draw a ~ between** fazer distinção entre; **a writer of ~** um escritor de destaque.
distinctive [dɪs'tɪŋktɪv] *adj* distintivo.
distinctly [dɪs'tɪŋktlɪ] *adv* claramente, nitidamente.
distinguish [dɪs'tɪŋgwɪʃ] *vt* distinguir ♦ *vi*: **to ~ between** (*concepts*) distinguir entre, fazer distinção entre; **to ~ o.s.** distinguir-se.
distinguished [dɪs'tɪŋgwɪʃt] *adj* (*eminent*) eminente, distinto; (*career*) notável.
distinguishing [dɪs'tɪŋgwɪʃɪŋ] *adj* (*feature*) distintivo.
distort [dɪs'tɔːt] *vt* alterar.
distortion [dɪs'tɔːʃən] *n* deformação *f*; (*of sound*) deturpação *f*.
distract [dɪs'trækt] *vt* distrair; (*attention*) desviar; (*bewilder*) aturdir.
distracted [dɪs'træktɪd] *adj* distraído.
distraction [dɪs'trækʃən] *n* distração *f*; (*confusion*) aturdimento, perplexidade *f*; (*amusement*) divertimento; **to drive sb to ~** deixar alguém louco.
distraught [dɪs'trɔːt] *adj* desesperado.
distress [dɪs'trɛs] *n* (*anguish*) angústia; (*misfortune*) desgraça; (*want*) miséria; (*pain*) dor *f* ♦ *vt* (*cause anguish*) afligir; **in ~** (*ship*) em perigo; **~ed area** (*BRIT*) área de baixo nível socio-econômico.
distressing [dɪs'trɛsɪŋ] *adj* aflitivo, angustioso.
distress signal *n* sinal *m* de socorro.
distribute [dɪs'trɪbjuːt] *vt* distribuir.
distribution [dɪstrɪ'bjuːʃən] *n* distribuição *f*.
distribution cost *n* custo de distribuição.
distributor [dɪ'strɪbjutə*] *n* (*AUT*) distribuidor *m*; (*COMM*) distribuidor(a) *m/f*; (: *company*) distribuidora.
district ['dɪstrɪkt] *n* (*of country*) região *f*; (*of town*) zona; (*ADMIN*) distrito.
district attorney (*US*) *n* promotor(a) *m/f* público/a.
district council (*BRIT*) *n* ≈ município (*BR*), câmara municipal (*PT*).
district nurse (*BRIT*) *n* enfermeiro/a do *Serviço Nacional que visita os pacientes em casa*.
distrust [dɪs'trʌst] *n* desconfiança ♦ *vt* desconfiar de.
distrustful [dɪs'trʌstful] *adj* desconfiado.
disturb [dɪs'tɜːb] *vt* perturbar; (*bother*) inco-

modar; (*interrupt*) atrapalhar; **sorry to ~ you** desculpe incomodá-lo.
disturbance [dɪs'tɜːbəns] *n* perturbação *f*; (*political etc*) distúrbio; (*violence*) agitação *f*; (*of mind*) transtorno; **to cause a ~** perturbar a ordem.
disturbed [dɪs'tɜːbd] *adj* perturbado; **to be mentally/emotionally ~** ter problemas psicológicos/emocionais.
disturbing [dɪs'tɜːbɪŋ] *adj* perturbador(a), inquietante.
disuse [dɪs'juːs] *n*: **to fall into ~** cair em desuso.
disused [dɪs'juːzd] *adj* desusado, abandonado.
ditch [dɪtʃ] *n* fosso; (*irrigation ~*) rego ♦ *vt* (*inf*) desfazer-se de.
dither ['dɪðə*] *vi* vacilar.
ditto ['dɪtəʊ] *adv* idem.
divan [dɪ'væn] *n* divã *m*.
divan bed *n* divã *m*.
dive [daɪv] *n* (*from board*) salto; (*underwater, of submarine*) mergulho; (*AVIAT*) picada; (*pej: café, bar etc*) espelunca ♦ *vi* saltar; mergulhar; picar.
diver ['daɪvə*] *n* (*SPORT*) saltador(a) *m/f*; (*underwater*) mergulhador(a) *m/f*.
diverge [daɪ'vɜːdʒ] *vi* divergir.
divergent [daɪ'vɜːdʒənt] *adj* divergente.
diverse [daɪ'vɜːs] *adj* diverso; (*group*) heterogêneo.
diversification [daɪvɜːsɪfɪ'keɪʃən] *n* diversificação *f*.
diversify [daɪ'vɜːsɪfaɪ] *vt, vi* diversificar.
diversion [daɪ'vɜːʃən] *n* (*BRIT: AUT*) desvio; (*distraction, MIL*) diversão *f*.
diversity [daɪ'vɜːsɪtɪ] *n* diversidade *f*.
divert [daɪ'vɜːt] *vt* (*change course of*) desviar; (*amuse*) divertir.
divest [daɪ'vɛst] *vt*: **to ~ sb of sth** privar alguém de algo.
divide [dɪ'vaɪd] *vt* dividir; (*separate*) separar ♦ *vi* dividir-se; (*road*) bifurcar-se; **to ~ (between** *or* **among)** dividir *or* repartir (entre); **40 ~d by 5** 40 dividido por 5.
divide out *vt*: **to ~ out (between** *or* **among)** distribuir *or* repartir (entre).
divided [dɪ'vaɪdɪd] *adj* (*fig*) dividido.
divided highway (*US*) *n* pista dupla.
divided skirt *n* saia-calça.
dividend ['dɪvɪdɛnd] *n* dividendo; (*fig*) lucro.
dividend cover *n* cobertura para pagamento de dividendos.
dividers [dɪ'vaɪdəz] *npl* compasso de ponta seca; (*between pages*) divisórias *fpl*.
divine [dɪ'vaɪn] *adj* divino ♦ *vt* (*future, truth*) adivinhar; (*water, metal*) descobrir.
diving ['daɪvɪŋ] *n* (*SPORT*) salto; (*underwater*) mergulho.
diving board *n* trampolim *m*.
diving suit *n* escafandro.
divinity [dɪ'vɪnɪtɪ] *n* divindade *f*; (*SCH*) teologia.

NB: *European Portuguese adds the following consonants to certain words:* **b** (sú(b)dito, su(b)til); **c** (a(c)ção, a(c)cionista, a(c)to); **m** (inde(m)ne); **p** (ado(p)ção, ado(p)tar); *for further details see p. xiii.*

division [dɪ'vɪʒən] n (also: BRIT: FOOTBALL) divisão f; (sharing out) repartição f; (disagreement) discórdia; (BRIT: POL) votação f; ~ **of labour** divisão do trabalho.

divisive [dɪ'vaɪsɪv] adj que causa divisão.

divorce [dɪ'vɔːs] n divórcio ♦ vt divorciar-se de.

divorced [dɪ'vɔːst] adj divorciado.

divorcee [dɪvɔː'siː] n divorciado/a.

divulge [daɪ'vʌldʒ] vt divulgar, revelar.

DIY (BRIT) adj, n abbr = **do-it-yourself.**

dizziness ['dɪzɪnɪs] n vertigem f, tontura.

dizzy ['dɪzɪ] adj (person) tonto; (height) vertiginoso; **to feel** ~ sentir-se tonto, sentir-se atordoado; **to make sb** ~ dar vertigem a alguém.

DJ n abbr = **disc jockey.**

Djakarta [dʒə'kɑːtə] n Jacarta.

DJIA (US) n abbr (STOCK EXCHANGE) = **Dow Jones Industrial Average.**

dl abbr (= decilitre) dl.

DLit(t) n abbr (= Doctor of Literature; Doctor of Letters) títulos universitários.

DLO n abbr = **dead-letter office.**

dm abbr (= decimetre) dm.

DMus n abbr (= Doctor of Music) título universitário.

DMZ n abbr = **demilitarized zone.**

DNA n abbr (= deoxyribonucleic acid) ADN m.

do [duː] (pt did, pp done) vt, vi (gen) fazer; (speed) ir a; (visit: city, museum) visitar; (THEATRE) representar ♦ n (inf: party) festa; (: formal gathering) recepção f; **he didn't laugh** ele não riu; ~ **you want any?** você quer?; **she swims better than I** ~ ela nada melhor que eu; **he laughed, didn't he?** ele riu, não foi?; ~ **they?** ah, é?; **who broke it?** — **I did** quem quebrou isso? — (fui) eu; ~ **you agree?** — **I** ~ você concorda? — concordo; **so does he** ele também; **DO come!** venha mesmo!; **I DO wish I could go** eu gostaria tanto de ir; **but I DO like it!** mas claro que eu gosto!; **to** ~ **one's nails/teeth** fazer as unhas/escovar os dentes; **to** ~ **one's hair** (comb) pentear-se; (style) fazer um penteado; **will it** ~**?** (is it enough?) dá?, chega?; (is it suitable?) serve?; **that will** ~**!** basta!, chega!; **to** ~ **well** prosperar, ter êxito; **to make** ~ **with** contentar-se com; **to** ~ **without sth** passar sem algo; **what did he** ~ **with the cat?** o que é que ele fez com o gato?; **what has that got to** ~ **with it?** o que é que isso tem a ver?

do away with vt fus (kill) matar; (suppress) suprimir.

do for (BRIT: inf) vt fus (clean for) fazer o serviço de casa para.

do up vt (laces) atar; (room) arrumar, renovar; **to** ~ **o.s. up** arrumar-se.

do with vt fus: **I could** ~ **with a drink** eu bem que gostaria de tomar alguma coisa; **I could** ~ **with some help** eu bem que precisaria de uma ajuda; **it could** ~ **with a wash** seria bom lavá-lo.

do. abbr = **ditto.**

DOA abbr (= dead on arrival) ≈ já era cadáver.

d.o.b. abbr = **date of birth.**

docile ['dəʊsaɪl] adj dócil.

dock [dɒk] n (NAUT) doca; (wharf) cais m; (LAW) banco (dos réus); ~**s** npl docas fpl ♦ vi (arrive) chegar; (enter ~) entrar no estaleiro ♦ vt (pay etc) deduzir.

dock dues npl direitos mpl portuários.

docker ['dɒkə*] n portuário, estivador m.

docket ['dɒkɪt] n (of delivery etc) guia.

dockyard ['dɒkjɑːd] n estaleiro.

doctor ['dɒktə*] n médico/a; (Ph.D. etc) doutor(a) m/f ♦ vt (fig) tratar, falsificar; (drink etc) falsificar; (cat) castrar; ~**'s office** (US) consultório; **D**~ **of Philosophy** (degree) doutorado; (person) doutor(a) m/f.

doctorate ['dɒktərɪt] n doutorado.

doctrine ['dɒktrɪn] n doutrina.

document [n 'dɒkjʊmənt, vt 'dɒkjʊment] n documento ♦ vt documentar.

documentary [dɒkjʊ'mentərɪ] adj documental ♦ n documentário.

documentation [dɒkjʊmen'teɪʃən] n documentação f.

DOD (US) n abbr = **Department of Defense.**

doddering ['dɒdərɪŋ] adj (senile) caquético, caduco.

Dodecanese (Islands) [dəʊdɪkə'niːz-] n(pl) (ilhas fpl do) Dodecaneso.

dodge [dɒdʒ] n (of body) evasiva; (fig) trapaça ♦ vt esquivar-se de, evitar; (blow) furtar-se a ♦ vi: **to** ~ **out of the way** esquivar-se; **to** ~ **the traffic** ziguezaguear por entre os carros.

dodgems ['dɒdʒəmz] (BRIT) npl carros mpl de choque.

dodgy ['dɒdʒɪ] adj arriscado.

DOE n abbr (BRIT) = **Department of the Environment;** (US) = **Department of Energy.**

doe [dəʊ] n corça.

does [dʌz] see **do.**

doesn't ['dʌznt] = **does not.**

dog [dɒg] n cachorro, cão m ♦ vt acossar; **to go to the** ~**s** (nation etc) degringolar.

dog biscuits npl biscoitos mpl para cachorro.

dog collar n coleira de cachorro; (fig: of priest) gola de padre.

dog-eared [-ɪəd] adj surrado.

dog food n ração f para cachorro.

dogged ['dɒgɪd] adj tenaz, persistente.

dogma ['dɒgmə] n dogma m.

dogmatic [dɒg'mætɪk] adj dogmático.

do-gooder [-'gʊdə*] (pej) n bom/boa samaritano/a.

dogsbody ['dɒgzbɒdɪ] (BRIT) n faz-tudo m/f.

doing ['duːɪŋ] n: **this is your** ~ foi você que fez isso; ~**s** npl (events) acontecimentos mpl; (acts) atos mpl.

do-it-yourself n sistema m faça-você-mesmo ♦ adj do tipo faça-você-mesmo.

doldrums ['dɒldrəmz] npl: **to be in the** ~ (person) estar abatido; (business) estar parado or estagnado.

dole [dəul] (_BRIT_) _n_ (_payment_) subsídio de desemprego; **on the ~** desempregado.
dole out _vt_ repartir.
doleful ['dəulful] _adj_ triste, lúgubre.
doll [dɔl] _n_ boneca.
doll up _vt_: **to ~ o.s. up** embonecar-se (_BR_), ataviar-se (_PT_).
dollar ['dɔlə*] _n_ dólar _m_.
dollar area _n_ zona do dólar.
dolphin ['dɔlfɪn] _n_ golfinho.
domain [də'meɪn] _n_ domínio; (_fig_) campo.
dome [dəum] _n_ (_ARCH_) cúpula; (_shape_) abóbada.
domestic [də'mestɪk] _adj_ (_gen_) doméstico; (_national_) nacional; (_home-loving_) caseiro; (_strife_) interno.
domesticated [də'mestɪkeɪtɪd] _adj_ domesticado; **he's very ~** ele é muito prendado (no lar).
domesticity [dɔmɛs'tɪsɪtɪ] _n_ vida caseira.
domestic servant _n_ empregado/a doméstico/a.
domicile ['dɔmɪsaɪl] _n_ domicílio.
dominant ['dɔmɪnənt] _adj_ dominante.
dominate ['dɔmɪneɪt] _vt_ dominar.
domination [dɔmɪ'neɪʃən] _n_ dominação _f_.
domineering [dɔmɪ'nɪərɪŋ] _adj_ dominante, mandão/dona.
Dominican Republic [də'mɪnɪkən-] _n_ República Dominicana.
dominion [də'mɪnɪən] _n_ domínio.
domino ['dɔmɪnəu] (_pl_ ~**es**) _n_ peça de dominó; ~**es** _n_ (_game_) dominó _m_.
don [dɔn] _n_ (_BRIT_) professor(a) _m/f_ universitário/a ♦ _vt_ vestir.
donate [də'neɪt] _vt_ doar.
donation [də'neɪʃən] _n_ doação _f_.
done [dʌn] _pp of_ **do**.
donkey ['dɔŋkɪ] _n_ burro.
donkey-work (_BRIT_: _inf_) _n_ labuta.
donor ['dəunə*] _n_ doador(a) _m/f_.
don't [dəunt] = **do not**.
doodle ['duːdl] _n_ rabisco ♦ _vi_ rabiscar.
doom [duːm] _n_ (_fate_) destino; (_ruin_) ruína ♦ _vt_: **to be ~ed to failure** estar destinado _or_ fadado ao fracasso.
doomsday ['duːmzdeɪ] _n_ o Juízo Final.
door [dɔː*] _n_ porta; (_entry_) entrada; **next ~** na casa ao lado; **to go from ~ to ~** ir de porta em porta.
doorbell ['dɔːbel] _n_ campainha.
door handle _n_ maçaneta (_BR_), puxador _m_ (_PT_); (_of car_) maçaneta.
door knocker _n_ aldrava.
doorman ['dɔːmæn] (_irreg_) _n_ porteiro.
doormat ['dɔːmæt] _n_ capacho.
doormen ['dɔːmen] _npl of_ **doorman**.
doorpost ['dɔːpəust] _n_ batente _m_ da porta.
doorstep ['dɔːstep] _n_ degrau _m_ da porta, soleira.
door-to-door _adj_: ~ **selling** venda de porta em porta.

doorway ['dɔːweɪ] _n_ vão _m_ da porta, entrada.
dope [dəup] _n_ (_inf_: _person_) imbecil _m/f_ (: _drugs_) maconha; (: _information_) dica, macete _m_ ♦ _vt_ (_horse etc_) dopar.
dopey ['dəupɪ] _adj_ (_dizzy_) zonzo.
dormant ['dɔːmənt] _adj_ inativo; (_latent_) latente.
dormer ['dɔːmə*] _n_ (_also:_ ~ _window_) águafurtada, trapeira.
dormice ['dɔːmaɪs] _npl of_ **dormouse**.
dormitory ['dɔːmɪtrɪ] _n_ dormitório.
dormouse ['dɔːmaus] (_pl_ **dormice**) _n_ rato (de campo).
Dors (_BRIT_) _abbr_ = **Dorset**.
DOS [dɔs] _n_ _abbr_ (= _disk operating system_) DOS _m_.
dosage ['dəusɪdʒ] _n_ dose _f_; (_on label_) posologia.
dose [dəus] _n_ dose _f_; (_BRIT_: _bout_) ataque _m_ ♦ _vt_: **to ~ o.s.** medicar-se; **a ~ of flu** uma gripe.
doss house ['dɔs-] (_BRIT_: _irreg_) _n_ pensão _f_ barata _or_ de malta (_PT_).
dossier ['dɔsɪeɪ] _n_ dossiê.
DOT (_US_) _n_ _abbr_ = **Department of Transportation**.
dot [dɔt] _n_ ponto ♦ _vt_: ~**ted with** salpicado de; **on the ~** em ponto.
dot command _n_ (_COMPUT_) comando precedido de um ponto.
dote on [dəut-] _vt fus_ adorar, idolatrar.
dot-matrix printer _n_ impressora matricial.
dotted line ['dɔtɪd-] _n_ linha pontilhada; **to sign on the ~** (_fig_) firmar o compromisso.
dotty ['dɔtɪ] (_inf_) _adj_ lelé, doido.
double ['dʌbl] _adj_ duplo ♦ _adv_ (_twice_): **to cost ~ (sth)** custar o dobro (de algo) ♦ _n_ dobro; (_person_) duplo/a; (_CINEMA_) substituto/a ♦ _vt_ dobrar; (_efforts_) duplicar ♦ _vi_ duplicar(-se); (_have two uses_): **to ~ as** servir também de; ~**s** _n_ (_TENNIS_) dupla; ~ **five two six (5526)** (_BRIT_: _TEL_) cinco cinco dois meia; **it's spelt with a ~ "l"** escreve-se com dois ls; **at the ~** (_BRIT_), **on the ~** em passo acelerado.
double back _vi_ (_person_) voltar atrás.
double up _vi_ (_bend over_) dobrar-se; (_share room_) dividir o quarto.
double bass _n_ contrabaixo.
double bed _n_ cama de casal.
double bend (_BRIT_) _n_ curva dupla, curva em "s".
double-breasted [-'brestɪd] _adj_ trespassado.
double-check _vt_, _vi_ verificar de novo.
double-clutch (_US_) _vi_ fazer embreagem dupla.
double cream (_BRIT_) _n_ creme _m_ de leite.
doublecross [dʌbl'krɔs] _vt_ (_trick_) enganar; (_betray_) atraiçoar.
doubledecker [dʌbl'dekə*] _n_ ônibus _m_ (_BR_) _or_ autocarro (_PT_) de dois andares.
double declutch (_BRIT_) _vi_ fazer embreagem

dupla.

double exposure *n* (*PHOT*) dupla exposição *f*.

double glazing [-'gleɪzɪŋ] (*BRIT*) *n* (janelas *fpl* de) vidro duplo.

double-page spread *n* anúncio (*or* reportagem *f etc*) de página dupla.

double-park *vi*, *vt* estacionar em fila dupla.

double room *n* quarto de casal.

doubly ['dʌblɪ] *adv* duplamente.

doubt [daut] *n* dúvida ♦ *vt* duvidar; (*suspect*) desconfiar de; **without (a)** ~ sem dúvida; **beyond** ~ *adv* sem dúvida alguma ♦ *adj* indubitável; **there is no** ~ **that** não há dúvida que; **to** ~ **that** duvidar que; **I** ~ **it very much** duvido muito.

doubtful ['dautful] *adj* duvidoso; **to be** ~ **about sth** ter dúvidas *or* estar em dúvida sobre algo; **I'm a bit** ~ duvido.

doubtless ['dautlɪs] *adv* sem dúvida.

dough [dəu] *n* massa; (*inf*: *money*) grana.

doughnut ['dəunʌt] *n* sonho (*BR*), bola de Berlim (*PT*).

dour [duə*] *adj* austero.

douse [dauz] *vt* (*with water*) encharcar; (*flames*) apagar.

dove [dʌv] *n* pomba.

dovetail ['dʌvteɪl] *vi* (*fig*) encaixar-se ♦ *n*: ~ **joint** sambladura em cauda de andorinha.

dowager ['dauədʒə*] *n* mulher que herda o título do marido falecido.

dowdy ['daudɪ] *adj* desalinhado; (*inelegant*) deselegante, pouco elegante.

Dow-Jones average ['dau'dʒəunz-] (*US*) *n* índice *m* da bolsa de valores de Nova Iorque.

down [daun] *n* (*fluff*) lanugem *f*; (*feathers*) penugem *f*; (*hill*) colina ♦ *adv* abaixo; (~*wards*) para baixo; (*on the ground*) por terra ♦ *prep* por, abaixo ♦ *vt* (*inf*: *drink*) tomar de um gole só; (: *food*) devorar; **D~s** *npl* (*BRIT*): **the** ~ chapada gredosa do sul da Inglaterra; ~ **there** lá em baixo; ~ **here** aqui em baixo; **the price of meat is** ~ o preço da carne baixou; **I've got it** ~ **in my diary** já o anotei na minha agenda; **to pay £2** ~ pagar £2 de entrada; **England are two goals** ~ a Inglaterra está perdendo por dois gols; **to** ~ **tools** (*BRIT*) cruzar os braços; ~ **with X!** abaixo X!

down-and-out *n* (*tramp*) vagabundo/a.

down-at-heel *adj* descuidado, desmazelado; (*appearance*) deselegante.

downbeat ['daunbiːt] *n* (*MUS*) tempo forte ♦ *adj* sombrio, negativo.

downcast ['daunkɑːst] *adj* abatido.

downer ['daunə*] (*inf*) *n* (*drug*) calmante *m*; **to be on a** ~ (*depressed*) estar na fossa, estar de baixo astral.

downfall ['daunfɔːl] *n* queda, ruína.

downgrade ['daungreɪd] *vt* (*reduce*) reduzir; (*devalue*) desvalorizar, depreciar.

downhearted [daun'hɑːtɪd] *adj* desanimado.

downhill ['daun'hɪl] *adv* para baixo ♦ *n* (*SKI*) *also*: ~ *race*) descida; **to go** ~ descer, ir morro abaixo; (*fig*: *business*) degringolar.

Downing Street ['daunɪŋ-] (*BRIT*) *n*: **10** ~ residência *do primeiro-ministro*.

download ['daunləud] *vt* (*COMPUT*) baixar.

down-market *adj* destinado a consumidores de renda baixa.

down payment *n* entrada, sinal *m*.

downplay ['daunpleɪ] (*US*) *vt* minimizar.

downpour ['daunpɔ:*] *n* aguaceiro.

downright ['daunraɪt] *adj* (*lie*) patente ♦ *adv* francamente.

downstairs ['daun'stɛəz] *adv* (*below*) (lá) em baixo; (*downwards*) para baixo; **to come** ~, **to go** ~ descer.

downstream ['daun'striːm] *adv* água *or* rio abaixo.

downtime ['dauntaɪm] *n* (*of machine*, *person*) tempo ocioso.

down-to-earth *adj* prático, realista.

downtown ['daun'taun] *adv* no centro da cidade ♦ *adj* (*US*): ~ **Chicago** o centro comercial de Chicago.

downtrodden ['dauntrɔdn] *adj* oprimido.

down under *adv* na Austrália (*or* Nova Zelândia).

downward ['daunwəd] *adj* para baixo; **a** ~ **trend** uma tendência para a baixa.

downward(s) ['daunwəd(z)] *adv* para baixo.

dowry ['daurɪ] *n* dote *m*.

doz. *abbr* (= *dozen*) dz.

doze [dəuz] *vi* dormitar.

doze off *vi* cochilar.

dozen ['dʌzn] *n* dúzia; **a** ~ **books** uma dúzia de livros; **80p a** ~ 80p a dúzia; **~s of times** milhares de vezes.

DPh *n abbr* (= *Doctor of Philosophy*) título *universitário*.

DPhil *n abbr* = **DPh**.

DPP (*BRIT*) *n abbr* = **Director of Public Prosecutions**.

DPT *n abbr* (*MED*: = *diphtheria*, *pertussis*, *tetanus*) espécie de vacina.

DPW (*US*) *n abbr* = **Department of Public Works**.

Dr *abbr* (= *doctor*) Dr(a).

Dr. *abbr* (*in street names*) = **drive**; (= *doctor*) Dr(a).

dr *abbr* (*COMM*) = **debtor**.

drab [dræb] *adj* monótono, sombrio.

draft [drɑːft] *n* (*first copy*) rascunho; (*COMM*) saque *m*, letra; (*US*: *call-up*) recrutamento ♦ *vt* (*plan*) esboçar; (*speech*, *letter*) rascunhar; *see also* **draught**.

draftsman *etc* ['drɑːftsmən] (*US*) *n* = **draughtsman** *etc*.

drag [dræg] *vt* arrastar; (*river*) dragar ♦ *vi* arrastar-se ♦ *n* (*inf*) chatice *f* (*BR*), maçada (*PT*); (*of cigarette*) tragada; (*AVIAT*, *NAUT*) resistência; (*women's clothing*): **in** ~ em travesti.

drag away *vt*: **to** ~ **away (from)** desgrudar (de).

drag on *vi* arrastar-se.

dragnet ['drægnɛt] *n* rede *f* de arrasto; (*by police*) diligência policial.

dragon ['drægən] *n* dragão *m*.

dragonfly ['drægənflaɪ] n libélula.
dragoon [drə'guːn] n (cavalryman) dragão m ♦ vt: **to ~ sb into doing sth** (BRIT) forçar alguém a fazer algo.
drain [dreɪn] n (~ pipe) cano de esgoto; (underground) esgoto; (in street) bueiro; (on resources) sorvedouro ♦ vt (land, marshes, MED) drenar; (reservoir) esvaziar; (vegetables) coar; (fig) esgotar ♦ vi (water) escorrer, escoar-se; **to feel ~ed** sentir-se esgotado or estafado.
drainage ['dreɪnɪdʒ] n (act) drenagem f; (MED, AGR) dreno; (sewage) esgoto.
drainboard ['dreɪnbɔːd] (US) n = **draining board**.
draining board ['dreɪnɪŋ-] (BRIT) n escorredor m.
drainpipe ['dreɪnpaɪp] n cano de esgoto.
drake [dreɪk] n pato (macho).
dram [dræm] n (drink) trago.
drama ['drɑːmə] n (art) teatro; (play, event) drama m.
dramatic [drə'mætɪk] adj dramático.
dramatically [drə'mætɪklɪ] adv dramaticamente.
dramatist ['dræmətɪst] n dramaturgo/a.
dramatize ['dræmətaɪz] vt dramatizar.
drank [dræŋk] pt of **drink**.
drape [dreɪp] vt ornar, cobrir ♦ vi cair.
draper ['dreɪpə*] (BRIT) n fanqueiro/a.
drapes [dreɪps] (US) npl cortinas fpl.
drastic ['dræstɪk] adj drástico.
drastically ['dræstɪklɪ] adv drasticamente.
draught [drɑːft] (US **draft**) n (of air) corrente f; (drink) trago; (NAUT) calado; (beer) chope m; **~s** n (BRIT) (jogo de) damas fpl; **on ~** (beer) de barril.
draughtboard ['drɑːftbɔːd] (BRIT) n tabuleiro de damas.
draughtsman ['drɑːftsmən] (US **draftsman**) (irreg) n desenhista m/f industrial.
draughtsmanship ['drɑːftsmənʃɪp] (US **draftsmanship**) n (art) desenho industrial; (technique) habilidade f de desenhista.
draughtsmen ['drɑːftsmɛn] (US **draftsmen**) npl of **draughtsman**.
draw [drɔː] (pt **drew**, pp **drawn**) vt (pull) tirar; (take out) retirar; (attract) atrair; (picture) desenhar; (money) tirar, receber (: from bank) sacar; (comparison, distinction) fazer ♦ vi (SPORT) empatar ♦ n (SPORT) empate m; (lottery) sorteio; (attraction) atração f; **to ~ to a close** tender para o fim; **to ~ near** aproximar-se.
draw back vi (move back): **to ~ back (from)** recuar (de).
draw in vi (BRIT: car) encostar; (: train) entrar na estação ♦ vt (involve) envolver.
draw on vt fus (resources) recorrer a, lançar mão de; (person, imagination) recorrer a.
draw out vi (car, train) sair ♦ vt

(lengthen) esticar, alargar; (money) sacar; (confession, truth) arrancar; (shy person) desacanhar, desinibir.
draw up vi (stop) parar(-se) ♦ vt (document) redigir; (plans) esboçar.
drawback ['drɔːbæk] n inconveniente m, desvantagem f.
drawbridge ['drɔːbrɪdʒ] n ponte f levadiça.
drawee [drɔː'iː] n sacado.
drawer¹ [drɔː*] n gaveta.
drawer² ['drɔːə*] n (of cheque) sacador(a) m/f, emitente m/f.
drawing ['drɔːɪŋ] n desenho.
drawing board n prancheta.
drawing pin (BRIT) n tachinha (BR), pionés m (PT).
drawing room n sala de visitas.
drawl [drɔːl] n fala arrastada.
drawn [drɔːn] pp of **draw** ♦ adj (haggard) abatido.
drawstring ['drɔːstrɪŋ] n cordão m.
dread [drɛd] n medo, pavor m ♦ vt temer, recear, ter medo de.
dreadful ['drɛdful] adj terrível.
dream [driːm] (pt, pp ~**ed** or **dreamt**) n sonho ♦ vt, vi sonhar; **to have a ~ about sb/sth, to ~ about sb/sth** sonhar com alguém/algo; **sweet ~s!** sonha com os anjos!
dream up vt inventar, bolar (inf).
dreamer ['driːmə*] n sonhador(a) m/f.
dreamt [drɛmt] pt, pp of **dream**.
dream world n mundo da fantasia.
dreamy ['driːmɪ] adj (distracted) sonhador(a), distraído; (music) sentimental.
dreary ['drɪərɪ] adj (boring) monótono; (bad) sombrio.
dredge [drɛdʒ] vt dragar.
dredge up vt tirar do fundo; (fig: unpleasant facts) trazer à tona, descobrir.
dredger ['drɛdʒə*] n (ship) draga; (BRIT: also: sugar ~) polvilhador m.
dregs [drɛgz] npl lia.
drench [drɛntʃ] vt encharcar; **to get ~ed** encharcar-se.
dress [drɛs] n vestido; (clothing) traje m ♦ vt vestir; (wound) pensar; (CULIN) preparar, temperar ♦ vi vestir-se; **to ~ o.s., to get ~ed** vestir-se; **to ~ a shop window** adornar uma vitrina.
dress up vi vestir-se com elegância; (in fancy dress) fantasiar-se.
dress circle n balcão m nobre.
dress designer n estilista m/f.
dresser ['drɛsə*] n (THEATRE) camareiro/a; (also: window ~) vitrinista m/f; (furniture) aparador m; (: US) cômoda de espelho.
dressing ['drɛsɪŋ] n (MED) penso; (CULIN) molho.
dressing gown (BRIT) n roupão m; (woman's) peignoir m.
dressing room n (THEATRE) camarim m; (SPORT) vestiário.

NB: European Portuguese adds the following consonants to certain words: **b** (sú(b)dito, su(b)til); **c** (a(c)ção, a(c)cionista, a(c)to); **m** (inde(m)ne); **p** (ado(p)ção, ado(p)tar); for further details see p. xiii.

dressing table n penteadeira (BR), toucador m (PT).

dressmaker ['drɛsmeɪkə*] n costureiro/a.

dressmaking ['drɛsmeɪkɪŋ] n (arte f da) costura.

dress rehearsal n ensaio geral.

dress shirt n camisa social.

dressy ['drɛsɪ] (inf) adj (clothes) chique.

drew [druː] pt of **draw**.

dribble ['drɪbl] vi gotejar, pingar; (baby) babar ♦ vt (ball) driblar.

dried [draɪd] adj seco; (eggs, milk) em pó.

drier ['draɪə*] n = **dryer**.

drift [drɪft] n (of current etc) força; (of snow, sand etc) monte m; (distance off course) deriva; (meaning) sentido ♦ vi (boat) derivar; (sand, snow) amontoar-se; **to let things ~** deixar o barco correr; **to ~ apart** (friends, lovers) afastar-se um do outro; **I get** or **catch your ~** eu entendo mais ou menos o que você está dizendo.

drifter ['drɪftə*] n nômade m/f.

driftwood ['drɪftwud] n madeira flutuante.

drill [drɪl] n furadeira; (bit, of dentist) broca; (for mining etc) broca, furadeira; (MIL) exercícios mpl militares ♦ vt furar, brocar; (MIL) exercitar ♦ vi (for oil) perfurar.

drilling ['drɪlɪŋ] n (for oil) perfuração f.

drilling rig n torre f de perfurar.

drily ['draɪlɪ] adv = **dryly**.

drink [drɪŋk] (pt **drank**, pp **drunk**) n bebida ♦ vt, vi beber; **to have a ~** tomar uma bebida; **a ~ of water** um copo d'água; **would you like something to ~?** você quer beber or tomar alguma coisa?; **to ~ to sb/sth** brindar alguém/algo.

drink in vt embeber-se em.

drinkable ['drɪŋkəbl] adj (not dangerous) potável; (palatable) bebível.

drinker ['drɪŋkə*] n bebedor(a) m/f.

drinking ['drɪŋkɪŋ] n (drunkenness) alcoolismo.

drinking fountain n bebedouro.

drinking water n água potável.

drip [drɪp] n (act) gotejar m; (one ~) gota, pingo; (MED) gota a gota m; (inf: person) mané m, banana m ♦ vi gotejar, pingar.

drip-dry adj (shirt) de lavar e vestir.

drip-feed (irreg) vt alimentar intravenosamente.

dripping ['drɪpɪŋ] n gordura ♦ adj: **~ wet** encharcado.

drive [draɪv] (pt **drove**, pp **driven**) n passeio (de automóvel); (journey) trajeto, percurso; (also: ~way) entrada; (energy) energia, vigor m; (PSYCH) impulso; (SPORT) drive m; (push) campanha; (TECH) propulsão f; (COMPUT: also: disk ~) unidade f de disco ♦ vt conduzir; (car) dirigir (BR), guiar (PT); (urge) fazer trabalhar; (by power) impelir; (nail) cravar; (push) empurrar; (TECH: motor) acionar ♦ vi (AUT: at controls) dirigir (BR), guiar (PT); (: travel) ir de carro; **to go for a ~** dar um passeio (de carro); **it's 3 hours' ~ from London** são 3 horas de carro

de lá a Londres; **left-/right-hand ~** direção à esquerda/direita; **front-/rear-wheel ~** (AUT) tração dianteira/traseira; **to ~ sb to do sth** impelir alguém a fazer algo; **to ~ sb mad** deixar alguém louco.

drive at vt fus (fig: intend, mean) querer dizer; **what are you driving at?** onde é que voce queria chegar?

drive on vi seguir adiante ♦ vt impelir.

drive-in adj drive-in ♦ n (cinema) drive-in m.

drive-in window (US) n balcão m drive-in.

drivel ['drɪvl] (inf) n bobagem f, besteira.

driven ['drɪvn] pp of **drive**.

driver ['draɪvə*] n motorista m/f.

driver's license (US) n carteira de motorista (BR), carta de condução (PT).

driveway ['draɪvweɪ] n entrada.

driving ['draɪvɪŋ] n direção f (BR), condução f (PT) ♦ adj: **~ rain** chuva torrencial.

driving belt n correia de transmissão.

driving force n (fig) mola.

driving instructor n instrutor(a) m/f de auto-escola (BR) or de condução (PT).

driving lesson n aula de direção (BR) or de condução (PT).

driving licence (BRIT) n carteira de motorista (BR), carta de condução (PT).

driving mirror (BRIT) n retrovisor m.

driving school n auto-escola f.

driving test n exame m de motorista.

drizzle ['drɪzl] n chuvisco ♦ vi chuviscar.

droll [drəul] adj engraçado.

dromedary ['drɔmədərɪ] n dromedário.

drone [drəun] n (sound) zumbido; (male bee) zangão m ♦ vi (bee, engine) zumbir; (also: ~ on) falar monotonamente.

drool [druːl] vi babar(-se); **to ~ over sth** babar por algo.

droop [druːp] vi pender.

drop [drɔp] n (of water) gota; (fall: in prices) baixa, queda; (: in salary) redução f; (of cliff) escarpa, declive m; (also: parachute ~) salto ♦ vt (allow to fall) deixar cair; (voice, eyes, price) baixar; (set down from car) deixar (saltar/descer); (omit) omitir ♦ vi cair; (price, temperature) baixar; (wind) parar; **~s** npl (MED) gotas fpl; **cough ~s** pastilhas para tosse; **a ~ of 10%** uma queda de 10%; **to ~ sb a line** escrever (umas linhas) para alguém.

drop in (inf) vi (visit): **to ~ in (on)** dar um pulo (na casa de).

drop off vi (sleep) cochilar ♦ vt (passenger) deixar (saltar).

drop out vi (withdraw) retirar-se; (student etc) largar tudo.

droplet ['drɔplɪt] n gotícula.

drop-out n pessoa que abandona o trabalho/os estudos, etc.

dropper ['drɔpə*] n conta-gotas m inv.

droppings ['drɔpɪŋz] npl fezes fpl (de animal).

dross [drɔs] n escória.

drought [draut] n seca.

drove [drəuv] pt of **drive** ♦ n: **~s of people** uma quantidade de gente.

drown [draun] *vt* afogar; (*also:* ~ **out**: *sound*) encobrir ♦ *vi* afogar-se.

drowse [drauz] *vi* dormitar.

drowsy ['drauzɪ] *adj* sonolento; **to be** ~ estar com sono.

drudge [drʌdʒ] *n* burro-de-carga *m*.

drudgery ['drʌdʒərɪ] *n* labuta.

drug [drʌg] *n* remédio, medicamento; (*narcotic*) droga; (: *MED, ADMIN*) entorpecente *m* ♦ *vt* drogar; **he's on** ~**s** (*an addict*) ele é um viciado em drogas; (*MED*) ele está sob medicação.

drug addict *n* toxicômano/a.

druggist ['drʌgɪst] (*US*) *n* farmacêutico/a.

drug peddler *n* traficante *m/f* de drogas.

drugstore ['drʌgstɔː] (*US*) *n* drogaria.

drum [drʌm] *n* tambor *m*; (*large*) bombo; (*for oil, petrol*) tambor, barril *m* ♦ *vi* (*with fingers*) tamborilar ♦ *vt*: **to** ~ **sth into sb** incutir algo em alguém; ~**s** *npl* (*in band*) bateria.

drum up *vt* (*enthusiasm, support*) angariar.

drummer ['drʌmə*] *n* baterista *m/f*.

drum roll *n* rufo de tambor.

drumstick ['drʌmstɪk] *n* (*MUS*) baqueta; (*of chicken*) perna.

drunk [drʌŋk] *pp* **of drink** ♦ *adj* bêbado ♦ *n* bêbado/a; **to get** ~ ficar bêbado, encher a cara (*inf*).

drunkard ['drʌŋkəd] *n* beberrão/beberrona *m/ f*.

drunken ['drʌŋkən] *adj* bêbado; ~ **driving** embriaguez *f* no volante.

drunkenness ['drʌŋkənnɪs] *n* embriaguez *f*.

dry [draɪ] *adj* seco; (*day*) sem chuva; (*uninteresting*) insípido; (*humour*) irônico; ♦ *vt* secar, enxugar; (*tears*) limpar ♦ *vi* secar; **on** ~ **land** em terra firme; **to** ~ **one's hands/ hair/eyes** enxugar as maôs o cabelo/as lágrimas.

dry up *vi* secar completamente; (*supply*) esgotar-se; (*in speech*) calar-se; (*dishes*) enxugar (a louça).

dry-clean *vt* lavar a seco.

dry-cleaner *n* tintureiro/a.

dry-cleaner's *n* tinturaria, lavanderia.

dry-cleaning *n* lavagem *f* a seco.

dry dock *n* (*NAUT*) dique *m* seco.

dryer ['draɪə*] *n* secador *m*; (*also:* spin-~) secadora.

dry goods *npl* (*COMM*) fazendas *fpl* e artigos *mpl* de armarinho.

dry goods store (*US*) *n* armarinho.

dry ice *n* gelo seco.

dryness ['draɪnɪs] *n* secura.

dry rot *n* putrefação *f* fungosa.

dry run *n* (*fig*) ensaio, prova.

dry ski slope *n* pista de esqui artificial.

DSc *n abbr* (= *Doctor of Science*) *título universitário*.

DSS (*BRIT*) *n abbr* (= *Department of Social Security*) ≈ INAMPS *m*.

DST (*US*) *abbr* (= *Daylight Saving Time*) hora de verão.

DT *n abbr* (*COMPUT*) = **data transmission**.

DTI (*BRIT*) *n* = **Department of Trade and Industry**.

DT's (*inf*) *npl abbr* (= *delirium tremens*) delirium tremens *m*.

dual ['djuəl] *adj* dual, duplo.

dual carriageway (*BRIT*) pista dupla.

dual-control *adj* de duplo comando.

dual nationality *n* dupla nacionalidade *f*.

dual-purpose *adj* de duplo uso.

dubbed [dʌbd] *adj* (*CINEMA*) dublado; (*nicknamed*) apelidado.

dubious ['djuːbɪəs] *adj* duvidoso; (*reputation, company*) suspeitoso; **I'm very** ~ **about it** eu tenho muitas dúvidas a respeito.

Dublin ['dʌblɪn] *n* Dublin.

Dubliner ['dʌblɪnə*] *n* natural *m/f* de Dublin.

duchess ['dʌtʃɪs] *n* duquesa.

duck [dʌk] *n* pato ♦ *vi* abaixar-se repentinamente ♦ *vt* mergulhar.

duckling ['dʌklɪŋ] *n* patinho.

duct [dʌkt] *n* conduto, canal *m*; (*ANAT*) ducto.

dud [dʌd] *n* (*shell*) bomba falhada; (*object, tool*): **it's a** ~ não presta ♦ *adj* (*BRIT: coin, note*) falso; ~ **cheque** cheque sem fundos, cheque voador (*inf*).

due [djuː] *adj* (*proper*) devido; (*expected*) esperado; (*fitting*) conveniente, oportuno ♦ *n* (*deserts*) aquilo que foi merecido ♦ *adv*: ~ **north** exatamente ao norte; ~**s** *npl* (*for club, union*) quota; (*in harbour*) direitos *mpl*; **in** ~ **course** no devido tempo; ~ **to** devido a; **the rent is** ~ **on the 30th** o aluguel vence no dia 30; **the train is** ~ **at 8** o trem deve chegar às 8; **I am** ~ **6 days' leave** eu tenho direito a 6 dias de folga.

due date *n* (data de) vencimento.

duel ['djuəl] *n* duelo.

duet [djuː'ɛt] *n* dueto.

duff [dʌf] (*BRIT: inf*) *adj* de nada.

duffelbag ['dʌflbæg] *n* mochila.

duffelcoat ['dʌflkəut] *n* casaco de baeta.

duffer ['dʌfə*] (*inf*) *n* zero (à esquerda).

duffle bag ['dʌfl-] *n* = **duffelbag**.

duffle coat ['dʌfl-] *n* = **duffelcoat**.

dug [dʌg] *pt, pp* **of dig**.

duke [djuːk] *n* duque *m*.

dull [dʌl] *adj* (*light*) sombrio; (*slow*) lento; (*boring*) enfadonho; (*sound, pain*) surdo; (*weather, day*) nublado, carregado; (*blade*) embotado, cego ♦ *vt* (*pain, grief*) aliviar; (*mind, senses*) entorpecer.

duly ['djuːlɪ] *adv* devidamente; (*on time*) no devido tempo.

dumb [dʌm] *adj* mudo; (*stupid*) estúpido; **to be struck** ~ (*fig*) ficar pasmo.

dumbbell ['dʌmbɛl] *n* (*SPORT*) haltere *m*.

dumbfounded [dʌm'faundɪd] *adj* pasmado.

dummy ['dʌmɪ] *n* (*tailor's model*) boneco, manequim *m*; (*BRIT: for baby*) chupeta; (*CARDS*)

NB: European Portuguese adds the following consonants to certain words: **b** (sú(b)dito, su(b)til); **c** (a(c)ção, a(c)cionista, a(c)to); **m** (inde(m)ne); **p** (ado(p)ção, ado(p)tar); *for further details see p. xiii.*

morto ♦ adj falso, postiço.
dummy run n prova, ensaio.
dump [dʌmp] n (heap) montão m; (place) depósito de lixo; (inf) chiqueiro; (MIL) depósito; (COMPUT) dump m, descarga ♦ vt (put down) depositar, descarregar; (get rid of) desfazer-se de; (COMM: goods) fazer dumping de; (COMPUT) tirar um dump de; **to be (down) in the ~s** (inf) estar na fossa.
dumping ['dʌmpɪŋ] n (ECON) dumping m; (of rubbish): **"no ~"** "proibido jogar lixo" (BR), "proibido deitar lixo" (PT).
dumpling ['dʌmplɪŋ] n bolinho cozido.
dumpy ['dʌmpɪ] adj gorducho.
dunce [dʌns] n burro, ignorante.
dune [djuːn] n duna.
dung [dʌŋ] n estrume m.
dungarees [dʌŋgə'riːz] npl macacão m (BR), fato macaco (PT).
dungeon ['dʌndʒən] n calabouço.
dunk [dʌŋk] vt mergulhar.
duo ['djuːəu] n (MUS) duo; (gen) dupla.
duodenal [djuːə'diːnl] adj duodenal.
dupe [djuːp] n (victim) otário/a, trouxa m/f ♦ vt enganar.
duplex ['djuːplɛks] (US) n (also: ~ apartment) duplex m.
duplicate [n 'djuːplɪkət, vt 'djuːplɪkeɪt] n duplicado, duplicata ♦ vt duplicar; (on machine) multigrafar; (reproduce) reproduzir; **in ~** em duplicata; **~ key** cópia de chave.
duplicating machine ['djuːplɪkeɪtɪŋ-] n duplicador m.
duplicator ['djuːplɪkeɪtə*] n duplicador m.
duplicity [djuː'plɪsɪtɪ] n duplicidade f, falsidade f.
Dur (BRIT) abbr = **Durham**.
durability [djuərə'bɪlɪtɪ] n durabilidade f, solidez f.
durable ['djuərəbl] adj durável; (clothes, metal) resistente.
duration [djuə'reɪʃən] n duração f.
duress [djuə'rɛs] n: **under ~** sob coação.
Durex ['djuərɛks] ® (BRIT) n preservativo, camisinha (inf), camisa-de-venus f.
during ['djuərɪŋ] prep durante.
dusk [dʌsk] n crepúsculo, anoitecer m.
dusky ['dʌskɪ] adj (sky, room) sombrio; (person, complexion) moreno.
dust [dʌst] n pó m, poeira ♦ vt (furniture) tirar o pó de; (cake etc): **to ~ with** polvilhar com.
dust off vt (dirt) tirar.
dustbin ['dʌstbɪn] n (BRIT) lata de lixo.
duster ['dʌstə*] n espanador m de pó, pano de pó.
dust jacket n sobrecapa.
dustman ['dʌstmən] (BRIT: irreg) n lixeiro, gari m (BR: inf).
dustpan ['dʌstpæn] n pá f de lixo.
dusty ['dʌstɪ] adj empoeirado.
Dutch [dʌtʃ] adj holandês/esa ♦ n (LING) holandês m ♦ adv: **let's go ~** or **d~** cada um paga o seu, vamos rachar; **the ~** npl os holandeses.

Dutch auction leilão m em que os ofertantes oferecem cada vez menos.
Dutchman ['dʌtʃmən] (irreg) n holandês m.
Dutchwoman ['dʌtʃwumən] (irreg) n holandesa.
dutiable ['djuːtɪəbl] adj (taxable) tributável; (by customs) sujeito a impostos alfandegários.
dutiful ['djuːtɪful] adj (child) respeitoso; (husband, wife) atencioso; (employee) zeloso, consciente.
duty ['djuːtɪ] n dever m; (tax) taxa; (customs) taxa alfandegária; **duties** npl funções fpl; **to make it one's ~ to do sth** dar-se a responsabilidade de fazer algo; **to pay ~ on sth** pagar imposto sobre algo; **on ~** de serviço; (at night etc) de plantão; **off ~** de folga.
duty-free adj livre de impostos; **~ shop** duty-free f.
duty officer n (MIL etc) oficial m de serviço.
duvet ['duːveɪ] (BRIT) n edredom (PT: -dão) m.
DV abbr (= Deo volente) se Deus quiser.
DVLC (BRIT) n abbr (= Driver and Vehicle Licensing Centre) ≈ Contran m.
DVM (US) n abbr (= Doctor of Veterinary Medicine) título universitário.
dwarf [dwɔːf] (pl **dwarves**) n anão/anã m/f ♦ vt ananicar.
dwarves [dwɔːvz] npl of **dwarf**.
dwell [dwɛl] (pt, pp **dwelt**) vi morar.
dwell on vt fus estender-se sobre.
dweller ['dwɛlə*] n habitante m/f.
dwelling ['dwɛlɪŋ] n residência.
dwelt [dwɛlt] pt, pp of **dwell**.
dwindle ['dwɪndl] vi minguar, diminuir.
dwindling ['dwɪndlɪŋ] adj descrescente, minguante.
dye [daɪ] n tintura, tinta ♦ vt tingir; **hair ~** tintura para o cabelo.
dyestuffs ['daɪstʌfs] npl corantes mpl.
dying ['daɪɪŋ] adj moribundo, agonizando; (moments) final; (words) último.
dyke [daɪk] n (embankment) dique m.
dynamic [daɪ'næmɪk] adj dinâmico.
dynamics [daɪ'næmɪks] n, npl dinâmica.
dynamite ['daɪnəmaɪt] n dinamite f ♦ vt dinamitar.
dynamo ['daɪnəməu] n dínamo m.
dynasty ['dɪnəstɪ] n dinastia.
dysentery ['dɪsntrɪ] n disenteria.
dyslexia [dɪs'lɛksɪə] n dislexia.
dyslexic [dɪs'lɛksɪk] adj, n dislético/a, disléxico/a.
dyspepsia [dɪs'pɛpsɪə] n dispepsia.
dystrophy ['dɪstrəfɪ] n distrofia; see also **muscular dystrophy**.

E

E, e [i:] *n* (*letter*) E, e *m*; (*MUS*): **E** mi *m*; **E for Edward** (*BRIT*) *or* **Easy** (*US*) E de Eliane.
E *abbr* (= *east*) E.
E111 *n abbr* (*also*: *form* ~) formulário E111.
ea. *abbr* = **each**.
E.A. (*US*) *n abbr* (= *educational age*) idade educacional.
each [i:tʃ] *adj* cada *inv* ♦ *pron* cada um(a); ~ **one** cada um; ~ **other** um ao outro; **they hate** ~ **other** (eles) se odeiam; **you are jealous of** ~ **other** vocês têm ciume um do outro; ~ **day** cada dia; **they have 2 books** ~ eles têm 2 livros cada um; **they cost £5** ~ custam £5 cada; ~ **of us** cada um de nós.
eager ['i:gə*] *adj* ávido; (*hopeful*) desejoso; (*ambitious*) ambicioso; (*pupil*) empolgado; **to be** ~ **to do sth** ansiar por fazer algo; **to be** ~ **for** ansiar por.
eagle ['i:gl] *n* águia.
E and OE *abbr* (= *errors and omissions excepted*) SEO.
ear [ɪə*] *n* (*external*) orelha; (*inner*, *fig*) ouvido; (*of corn*) espiga; **to play by** ~ tocar de ouvido; **up to one's** ~**s in debt** endividado até o pescoço.
earache ['ɪəreɪk] *n* dor *f* de ouvidos.
eardrum ['ɪədrʌm] *n* tímpano.
earl [ə:l] *n* conde *m*.
earlier ['ə:lɪə*] *adj* (*date etc*) mais adiantado; (*edition etc*) anterior ♦ *adv* mais cedo.
early ['ə:lɪ] *adv* cedo; (*before time*) com antecedência ♦ *adj* prematuro; (*reply*) pronto; (*Christians*, *settlers*) primeiro; (*man*) primitivo; (*life*, *work*) juvenil; **have an** ~ **night/start** vá para cama cedo/saia de manhã cedo; **in the** ~ *or* ~ **in the spring/19th century** no princípio da primavera/do século dezenove; **as** ~ **as possible** o mais cedo possível; **you're** ~! você chegou cedo!; ~ **in the morning** de manhã cedo; **she's in her** ~ **forties** ela tem pouco mais de 40 anos; **at your earliest convenience** (*COMM*) o mais cedo que lhe for possível.
early retirement *n* aposentadoria antecipada.
early warning system *n* sistema *m* de alerta antecipado.
earmark ['ɪəmɑ:k] *vt*: **to** ~ **sth for** reservar *or* destinar algo para.
earn [ə:n] *vt* ganhar; (*COMM*: *yield*) render; (*praise*, *reward*) merecer; **to** ~ **one's living** ganhar a vida.
earned income [ə:nd-] *n* rendimento do trabalho individual.
earnest ['ə:nɪst] *adj* sério ♦ *n* (*also*: ~ *money*) sinal *m* em dinheiro; **in** ~ a sério.
earnings ['ə:nɪŋz] *npl* (*personal*) vencimentos *mpl*, salário, ordenado; (*of company*) lucro.
ear nose and throat specialist *n* otorrinolaringologista *m/f*, otorrino *m/f*.
earphones ['ɪəfəunz] *npl* fones *mpl* de ouvido.
earplugs ['ɪəplʌgz] *npl* borrachinhas *fpl* (de ouvido).
earring ['ɪərɪŋ] *n* brinco.
earshot ['ɪəʃɔt] *n*: **out of/within** ~ fora do/ao alcance do ouvido *or* da voz.
earth [ə:θ] *n* terra; (*BRIT*: *ELEC*) fio terra ♦ *vt* (*BRIT*: *ELEC*) ligar à terra; **what on** ~! que diabo!
earthenware ['ə:θənwɛə*] *n* louça de barro ♦ *adj* de barro.
earthly ['ə:θlɪ] *adj* terrestre; ~ **paradise** paraíso terrestre; **there is no** ~ **reason to think** ... não há a mínima razão para se pensar que ....
earthquake ['ə:θkweɪk] *n* terremoto (*BR*), terramoto (*PT*).
earth tremor tremor *m*, abalo sísmico.
earthworks ['ə:θwə:ks] *npl* trabalhos *mpl* de terraplenagem.
earthworm ['ə:θwə:m] *n* minhoca.
earthy ['ə:θɪ] *adj* (*fig*: *vulgar*) grosseiro; (: *natural*) natural.
earwax ['ɪəwæks] *n* cerume *m*.
earwig ['ɪəwɪg] *n* lacrainha.
ease [i:z] *n* facilidade *f*; (*relaxed state*) sossego ♦ *vt* facilitar; (*relieve*: *pressure*) afrouxar; (*soothe*) aliviar; (*help pass*): **to** ~ **sth in/out** meter/tirar algo com cuidado ♦ *vi* (*situation*) abrandar; **at** ~! (*MIL*) descansar!; **to be at** ~ estar à vontade; **with** ~ com facilidade.
ease off *vi* acalmar-se; (*at work*) deixar de trabalhar tanto; (*wind*) baixar; (*rain*) moderar-se.
ease up *vi* acalmar-se; (*at work*) deixar de trabalhar tanto; (*wind*) baixar; (*rain*) moderar-se.
easel ['i:zl] *n* cavalete *m*.
easily ['i:zɪlɪ] *adv* facilmente, fácil (*inf*).
easiness ['i:zɪnɪs] *n* facilidade *f*; (*of manner*) desenvoltura.
east [i:st] *n* leste *m*, este *m* ♦ *adj* oriental, do leste ♦ *adv* para o leste; **the E**~ o Oriente; (*POL*) o Leste.
Easter ['i:stə*] *n* Páscoa ♦ *adj* (*holidays*) da Páscoa; (*traditions*) pascal.
Easter egg *n* ovo de Páscoa.
Easter Island *n* ilha da Páscoa.
easterly ['i:stəlɪ] *adj* (*to the east*) para o leste; (*from the east*) do Leste.
Easter Monday *n* Segunda-Feira da Páscoa.
eastern ['i:stən] *adj* do leste, oriental; **E**~ **Europe** a Europa Oriental; **the E**~ **bloc** (*POL*) o Bloco Oriental.

NB: European Portuguese adds the following consonants to certain words: **b** (sú(b)dito, su(b)til); **c** (a(c)ção, a(c)cionista, a(c)to); **m** (inde(m)ne); **p** (ado(p)ção, ado(p)tar); *for further details see p. xiii.*

Easter Sunday n Domingo da Páscoa.
East Germany n Alemanha Oriental.
eastward(s) ['i:stwəd(z)] adv ao leste.
easy ['i:zı] adj fácil; (comfortable) folgado, cômodo; (relaxed) natural, complacente ♦ adv: **to take it** or **things ~** (not worry) levar as coisas com calma; (go slowly) ir devagar; (rest) descansar; **payment on ~ terms** (COMM) pagamento facilitado; **that's easier said than done** é mais fácil falar do que fazer; **I'm ~** (inf) para mim, tanto faz.
easy chair n poltrona.
easy-going adj pacato, fácil.
eat [i:t] (pt ate, pp eaten) vt, vi comer.
  eat away vt corroer.
  eat away at vt fus corroer.
  eat into vt fus corroer.
  eat out vi jantar fora.
  eat up vt (food) acabar; **it ~s up electricity** consome eletricidade demais.
eatable ['i:təbl] adj comestível.
eau-de-cologne [əudə-] n (água de) Colônia.
eaves [i:vz] npl beira, beiral m.
eavesdrop ['i:vzdrɔp] vi: **to ~ (on sb)** escutar (alguém) às escondidas.
ebb [εb] n refluxo ♦ vi baixar; (fig: also: ~ away) declinar; **the ~ and flow** o fluxo e refluxo; **to be at a low ~** (fig: person) estar de maré baixa; (: business, relations etc) ir mal.
ebb tide n baixa-mar f, maré f vazante.
ebony ['εbənı] n ébano.
ebullient [ı'bʌlıənt] adj vivo, enérgico.
EC n abbr (= European Community) CE f.
eccentric [ık'sεntrık] adj, n excêntrico/a.
ecclesiastic(al) [ıkli:zı'æstık(əl)] adj eclesiástico.
ECG n abbr (= electrocardiogram) eletro.
ECGD n abbr (= Export Credits Guarantee Department) serviço de garantia financeira para exportações.
echo ['εkəu] (pl ~es) n eco ♦ vt (sound) ecoar, repetir ♦ vi ressoar, repetir.
éclair [eı'klεə*] n (CULIN) bomba.
eclipse [ı'klıps] n eclipse m ♦ vt eclipsar.
ECM (US) n abbr = **European Common Market.**
ecologist [ı'kɔlədʒıst] n ecologista m/f.
ecology [ı'kɔlədʒı] n ecologia.
economic [i:kə'nɔmık] adj econômico; (proposition etc) rentável.
economical [i:kə'nɔmıkəl] adj econômico; (proposition etc) rentável.
economically [i:kə'nɔmıklı] adv economicamente.
economics [i:kə'nɔmıks] n economia ♦ npl aspectos mpl econômicos.
economist [ı'kɔnəmıst] n economista m/f.
economize [ı'kɔnəmaız] vi economizar, fazer economias.
economy [ı'kɔnəmı] n economia; **economies of scale** economias de escala.
economy class n (AVIAT etc) classe f econômica.
economy size n tamanho econômico.

ECSC n abbr (= European Coal and Steel Community) CECA f.
ecstasy ['εkstəsı] n êxtase m; **to go into ecstasies over** extasiar-se com.
ecstatic [εks'tætık] adj extasiado.
ECT n abbr = **electroconvulsive therapy.**
ECU n abbr (= European Currency Unit) ECU f.
Ecuador ['εkwədɔ:*] n Equador m.
Ecuadorian [εkwə'dɔ:rıən] adj, n equatoriano/a.
ecumenical [i:kju'mεnıkl] adj ecumênico.
eczema ['εksımə] n eczema m.
eddy ['εdı] n rodamoinho.
edge [εdʒ] n (of knife etc) fio; (of object) borda; (of lake etc) margem f ♦ vt (SEWING) embainhar ♦ vi: **to ~ forward** avançar pouco a pouco; **to ~ away from** afastar-se pouco a pouco de; **on ~** (fig) nervoso, inquieto; **to have the ~ on** (fig) levar vantagem sobre.
edgeways ['εdʒweız] adv lateralmente; **he couldn't get a word in ~** não pôde entrar na conversa.
edging ['εdʒıŋ] n (SEWING) debrum m; (of path) borda.
edgy ['εdʒı] adj nervoso, inquieto.
edible ['εdıbl] adj comestível.
edict ['i:dıkt] n édito.
edifice ['εdıfıs] n edifício.
edifying ['εdıfaıŋ] adj edificante.
Edinburgh ['εdınbərə] n Edimburgo.
edit ['εdıt] vt (be editor of) dirigir; (cut) cortar, redigir; (COMPUT, TV) editar; (CINEMA) montar.
edition [ı'dıʃən] n (gen) edição f; (number printed) tiragem f.
editor ['εdıtə*] n redator(a) m/f; (of newspaper) diretor(a) m/f; (of book) organizador(a) m/f da edição; (also: film ~) montador(a) m/f.
editorial [εdı'tɔ:rıəl] adj editorial ♦ n editorial m; **the ~ staff** a redação.
EDP n abbr = **electronic data processing.**
EDT (US) abbr (= Eastern Daylight Time) hora de verão de Nova Iorque.
educate ['εdjukeıt] vt educar; **~d at ... que cursou ....**
education [εdju'keıʃən] n educação f; (schooling) ensino; (science) pedagogia; **primary** (BRIT) or **elementary** (US)/ **secondary ~** ensino de 1°/2° grau.
educational [εdju'keıʃənl] adj (policy etc) educacional; (teaching) docente; (instructive) educativo; **~ technology** tecnologia educacional.
Edwardian [εd'wɔ:dıən] adj da época do rei Eduardo VII, dos anos 1900.
EE abbr = **electrical engineer.**
EEC n abbr (= European Economic Community) CEE f.
EEG n abbr (= electroencephalogram) eletro.
eel [i:l] n enguia.
EENT (US) n abbr (MED) = **eye, ear, nose and throat.**
EEOC (US) n abbr = **Equal Employment**

Opportunity Commission.

eerie ['ɪərɪ] *adj* (*strange*) estranho; (*mysterious*) misterioso.

EET *n abbr* (= *Eastern European Time*) hora da Europa Oriental.

effect [ɪ'fɛkt] *n* efeito ♦ *vt* efetuar; **~s** *npl* (*THEATRE*) efeitos *mpl*; (*property*) bens *mpl* móveis, pertences *mpl*; **to take ~** (*LAW*) entrar em vigor; (*drug*) fazer efeito; **to put into ~** (*plan*) pôr em ação *or* prática; **to have an ~ on sb/sth** produzir efeito em alguém/algo; **in ~** na realidade; **his letter is to the ~ that ...** a carta dele informa que ....

effective [ɪ'fɛktɪv] *adj* eficaz; (*striking*) impressionante; (*real*) efetivo; **to become ~** (*LAW*) entrar em vigor; **~ date** data de entrada em vigor.

effectively [ɪ'fɛktɪvlɪ] *adv* (*efficiently*) eficazmente; (*in reality*) efetivamente.

effectiveness [ɪ'fɛktɪvnɪs] *n* eficácia.

effeminate [ɪ'fɛmɪnɪt] *adj* efeminado.

effervescent [ɛfə'vɛsnt] *adj* efervescente.

efficacy ['ɛfɪkəsɪ] *n* eficácia.

efficiency [ɪ'fɪʃənsɪ] *n* eficiência; (*of machine*) rendimento.

efficiency apartment (*US*) *n* kitchenette *f*.

efficient [ɪ'fɪʃənt] *adj* eficiente.

efficiently [ɪ'fɪʃəntlɪ] *adv* eficientemente.

effigy ['ɛfɪdʒɪ] *n* efígie *f*.

effluent ['ɛfluənt] *n* efluente *m*.

effort ['ɛfət] *n* esforço; **to make an ~ to** esforçar-se para.

effortless ['ɛfətlɪs] *adj* com desenvoltura.

effrontery [ɪ'frʌntərɪ] *n* descaramento.

effusive [ɪ'fjuːsɪv] *adj* efusivo; (*welcome*) caloroso.

EFL *n abbr* (*SCH*) = **English as a foreign language.**

EFTA ['ɛftə] *n abbr* (= *European Free Trade Association*) AELC *f*.

e.g. *adv abbr* (= *exempli gratia*) p. ex.

egalitarian [ɪgælɪ'tɛərɪən] *adj* igualitário.

egg [ɛg] *n* ovo.

egg on *vt* incitar.

eggcup ['ɛgkʌp] *n* oveiro.

eggplant ['ɛgplɑːnt] (*US*) *n* beringela.

eggshell ['ɛgʃɛl] *n* casca de ovo.

egg white *n* clara (de ovo).

egg yolk *n* gema.

ego ['iːgəu] *n* ego.

egoism ['iːgəuɪzəm] *n* egoísmo.

egoist ['iːgəuɪst] *n* egoísta *m/f*.

egotism ['ɛgəutɪzəm] *n* egotismo *m*.

egotist ['ɛgəutɪst] *n* egotista *m/f*.

Egypt ['iːdʒɪpt] *n* Egito.

Egyptian [ɪ'dʒɪpʃən] *adj*, *n* egípcio/a.

eiderdown ['aɪdədaun] *n* edredom (*PT*: -dão) *m*.

eight [eɪt] *num* oito; *see also* **five.**

eighteen ['eɪ'tiːn] *num* dezoito; *see also* **five.**

eighth [eɪtθ] *num* oitavo; *see also* **fifth.**

eighty ['eɪtɪ] *num* oitenta; *see also* **fifty.**

Eire ['ɛərə] *n* (República da) Irlanda.

EIS *n abbr* (= *Educational Institute of Scotland*) sindicato dos professores escoceses.

either ['aɪðə*] *adj* (*each*) cada; (*any*) qualquer; (*both*) ambos ♦ *pron*: **~ (of them)** qualquer (dos dois) ♦ *adv*: **no, I don't ~** eu também não ♦ *conj*: **~ yes or no** ou sim ou não; **on ~ side** de ambos os lados; **I don't like ~** não gosto nem de um nem do outro; **I haven't seen ~ one or the other** eu não vi nem um nem o outro.

ejaculation [ɪdʒækju'leɪʃən] *n* (*PHYSIOLOGY*) ejaculação *f*.

eject [ɪ'dʒɛkt] *vt* expulsar ♦ *vi* (*pilot*) ser ejetado.

ejector seat [ɪ'dʒɛktə*-] *n* assento ejetor.

eke [iːk]: **to ~ out** *vt* (*money*) economizar; (*food*) economizar em; (*add to*) complementar.

EKG (*US*) *n abbr* (= *electrocardiogram*) eletro.

el [ɛl] (*US*: *inf*) *n abbr* = **elevated railroad.**

elaborate [*adj* ɪ'læbərɪt, *vt*, *vi* ɪ'læbəreɪt] *adj* complicado; (*decorated*) rebuscado ♦ *vt* elaborar ♦ *vi* entrar em detalhes.

elapse [ɪ'læps] *vi* decorrer.

elastic [ɪ'læstɪk] *adj*, *n* elástico.

elastic band (*BRIT*) *n* elástico.

elasticity [ɪlæs'tɪsɪtɪ] *n* elasticidade *f*.

elated [ɪ'leɪtɪd] *adj*: **to be ~** rejubilar-se.

elation [ɪ'leɪʃən] *n* exaltação *f*.

elbow ['ɛlbəu] *n* cotovelo ♦ *vt*: **to ~ one's way through the crowd** abrir passagem pela multidão com os cotovelos.

elbow room *n* (*fig*) liberdade *f*.

elder ['ɛldə*] *adj* mais velho ♦ *n* (*tree*) sabugueiro; (*person*) o/a mais velho/a; (*of tribe*) ancião; (*of church*) presbítero.

elderly ['ɛldəlɪ] *adj* idoso, de idade ♦ *npl*: **the ~** as pessoas de idade, os idosos.

eldest ['ɛldɪst] *adj* mais velho ♦ *n* o/a mais velho/a.

elect [ɪ'lɛkt] *vt* eleger; (*choose*): **to ~ to do** optar por fazer ♦ *adj*: **the president ~** o presidente eleito.

election [ɪ'lɛkʃən] *n* eleição *f*; **to hold an ~** realizar uma eleição.

election campaign *n* campanha eleitoral.

electioneering [ɪlɛkʃə'nɪərɪŋ] *n* campanha *or* propaganda eleitoral.

elector [ɪ'lɛktə*] *n* eleitor(a) *m/f*.

electoral [ɪ'lɛktərəl] *adj* eleitoral.

electoral college *n* colégio eleitoral.

electoral roll (*BRIT*) *n* lista de eleitores.

electorate [ɪ'lɛktərɪt] *n* eleitorado.

electric [ɪ'lɛktrɪk] *adj* elétrico.

electrical [ɪ'lɛktrɪkəl] *adj* elétrico.

electrical engineer *n* engenheiro/a eletricista.

electrical failure *n* pane *f* elétrica.

electric blanket *n* cobertor *m* elétrico.

electric chair *n* cadeira elétrica.

electric cooker *n* fogão *m* elétrico.

NB: European Portuguese adds the following consonants to certain words: **b** (sú(b)dito, su(b)til); **c** (a(c)ção, a(c)cionista, a(c)to); **m** (inde(m)ne); **p** (ado(p)ção, ado(p)tar); *for further details see p. xiii.*

electric current *n* corrente *f* elétrica.
electric fire (*BRIT*) *n* aquecimento elétrico.
electrician [ɪlɛk'trɪʃən] *n* eletricista *m/f*.
electricity [ɪlɛk'trɪsɪtɪ] *n* eletricidade *f*.
electricity board (*BRIT*) *n* empresa de energia elétrica.
electric light *n* luz *f* elétrica.
electric shock *n* choque *m* elétrico.
electrify [ɪ'lɛktrɪfaɪ] *vt* (*RAIL*) eletrificar; (*audience*) eletrizar.
electro... [ɪ'lɛktrəu] *prefix* eletro....
electrocardiogram [ɪ'lɛktrəu'kɑːdɪəgræm] *n* eletrocardiograma *m*.
electro-convulsive therapy *n* eletrochoques *mpl*.
electrocute [ɪ'lɛktrəkjuːt] *vt* eletrocutar.
electrode [ɪ'lɛktrəud] *n* eletrodo (*BR*), eléctrodo (*PT*).
electroencephalogram [ɪ'lɛktrəuen'sɛfələgræm] *n* eletroencefalograma *m*.
electrolysis [ɪlɛk'trɔlɪsɪs] *n* eletrólise *f*.
electromagnetic [ɪlɛktrəumæg'nɛtɪk] *adj* eletromagnético.
electron [ɪ'lɛktrɔn] *n* elétron *m* (*BR*), electrão *m* (*PT*).
electronic [ɪlɛk'trɔnɪk] *adj* eletrônico.
electronic data processing *n* processamento de dados eletrônico.
electronic mail *n* correio eletrônico.
electronics [ɪlɛk'trɔnɪks] *n* eletrônica.
electron microscope *n* microscópio eletrônico.
electroplated [ɪ'lɛktrəu'pleɪtɪd] *adj* galvanizado.
electrotherapy [ɪ'lɛktrəu'θɛrəpɪ] *n* eletroterapia.
elegance ['ɛlɪgəns] *n* elegância.
elegant ['ɛlɪgənt] *adj* elegante.
element ['ɛlɪmənt] *n* elemento; **to brave the ~s** enfrentar intempérie.
elementary [ɛlɪ'mɛntərɪ] *adj* (*gen*) elementar; (*primitive*) rudimentar; (*school, education*) primário.
elephant ['ɛlɪfənt] *n* elefante *m*.
elevate ['ɛlɪveɪt] *vt* elevar; (*in rank*) promover.
elevated railroad (*US*) *n* ferrovia elevada.
elevation [ɛlɪ'veɪʃən] *n* elevação *f*; (*land*) eminência; (*height*) altura.
elevator ['ɛlɪveɪtəª] (*US*) *n* elevador *m*.
eleven [ɪ'lɛvn] *num* onze; *see also* **five**.
elevenses [ɪ'lɛvənzɪz] (*BRIT*) *npl* refeição leve da manhã.
eleventh [ɪ'lɛvnθ] *num* décimo-primeiro; **at the ~ hour** (*fig*) no último momento, na hora H; *see also* **fifth**.
elf [ɛlf] (*pl* **elves**) *n* elfo, duende *m*.
elicit [ɪ'lɪsɪt] *vt*: **to ~ (from)** arrancar (de), eliciar (de).
eligible ['ɛlɪdʒəbl] *adj* elegível, apto; **to be ~ for sth** (*job etc*) ter qualificações para algo; (*pension etc*) ter direito a algo.
eliminate [ɪ'lɪmɪneɪt] *vt* eliminar; (*strike out*) suprimir; (*suspect*) eliminar, excluir.
elimination [ɪlɪmɪ'neɪʃən] *n* eliminação *f*; **by a process of ~** por eliminação.

élite [eɪ'liːt] *n* elite *f*.
élitist [eɪ'liːtɪst] (*pej*) *adj* elitista.
elixir [ɪ'lɪksəª] *n* elixir *m*.
Elizabethan [ɪlɪzə'biːθən] *adj* elisabetano.
ellipse [ɪ'lɪps] *n* elipse *f*.
elliptical [ɪ'lɪptɪkl] *adj* elíptico.
elm [ɛlm] *n* olmo.
elocution [ɛlə'kjuːʃən] *n* elocução *f*.
elongated ['iːlɔŋgeɪtɪd] *adj* alongado.
elope [ɪ'ləup] *vi* fugir.
elopement [ɪ'ləupmənt] *n* fuga do lar paterno.
eloquence ['ɛləkwəns] *n* eloqüência.
eloquent ['ɛləkwənt] *adj* eloqüente.
else [ɛls] *adv* outro, mais; **something ~** outra coisa; **somewhere ~** em outro lugar (*BR*), noutro sítio (*PT*); **everywhere ~** por todo o lado (menos aqui); **everyone ~** todos os outros; **where ~?** onde mais?; **what ~ can we do?** que mais podemos fazer?; **or ~** senão; **there was little ~ to do** não havia outra coisa a fazer; **nobody ~ spoke** ninguém mais falou.
elsewhere [ɛls'wɛəª] *adv* (*be*) em outro lugar (*BR*), noutro sítio (*PT*); (*go*) para outro lugar (*BR*), a outro sítio (*PT*).
ELT *n abbr* (*SCH*) = **English Language Teaching**.
elucidate [ɪ'luːsɪdeɪt] *vt* esclarecer, elucidar.
elude [ɪ'luːd] *vt* (*pursuer*) escapar de, esquivar-se de; (*question*) evadir.
elusive [ɪ'luːsɪv] *adj* esquivo; (*answer*) evasivo.
elves [ɛlvz] *npl of* **elf**.
emaciated [ɪ'meɪsɪeɪtɪd] *adj* emaciado, macilento.
emanate ['ɛməneɪt] *vi* emanar.
emancipate [ɪ'mænsɪpeɪt] *vt* emancipar.
emancipated [ɪ'mænsɪpeɪtɪd] *adj* emancipado.
emancipation [ɪmænsɪ'peɪʃən] *n* emancipação *f*.
emasculate [ɪ'mæskjuleɪt] *vt* emascular.
embalm [ɪm'bɑːm] *vt* embalsamar.
embankment [ɪm'bæŋkmənt] *n* aterro; (*riverside*) dique *m*.
embargo [ɪm'bɑːgəu] (*pl* **~es**) *n* (*NAUT*) embargo; (*COMM*) proibição *f* ♦ *vt* boicotear; **to put an ~ on sth** proibir algo.
embark [ɪm'bɑːk] *vi* embarcar ♦ *vt* embarcar; **to ~ on** (*fig*) empreender, começar.
embarkation [ɛmbɑː'keɪʃən] *n* (*of people, goods*) embarque *m*.
embarkation card *n* cartão *m* de embarque.
embarrass [ɪm'bærəs] *vt* embaraçar, constranger; **to be financially ~ed** estar com dificuldades financeiras.
embarrassing [ɪm'bærəsɪŋ] *adj* embaraçoso, constrangedor(a).
embarrassment [ɪm'bærəsmənt] *n* embaraço, constrangimento; (*financial*) dificuldades *fpl*.
embassy ['ɛmbəsɪ] *n* embaixada.
embed [ɪm'bɛd] *vt* embutir; (*teeth etc*) cravar.
embellish [ɪm'bɛlɪʃ] *vt* embelezar; (*fig: story*) florear.

embers ['embəz] *npl* brasa, borralho, cinzas *fpl*.

embezzle [ɪm'bezl] *vt* desviar.

embezzlement [ɪm'bezlmənt] *n* desvio (de fundos).

embezzler [ɪm'bezlə*] *n* malversador(a) *m/f*.

embitter [ɪm'bɪtə*] *vt* (*person*) amargurar; (*relations*) azedar.

embittered [ɪm'bɪtəd] *adj* amargurado.

emblem ['embləm] *n* emblema *m*.

embodiment [ɪm'bɔdɪmənt] *n* encarnação *f*.

embody [ɪm'bɔdɪ] *vt* (*features*) incorporar; (*ideas*) expressar.

embolden [ɪm'bəuldn] *vt* encorajar, animar.

embolism ['embəlɪzəm] *n* embolia.

embossed [ɪm'bɔst] *adj* realçado; ~ **with** ornado com relevos de.

embrace [ɪm'breɪs] *vt* abraçar, dar um abraço em; (*include*) abarcar, abranger; (*adopt*: *idea*) adotar ♦ *vi* abraçar-se ♦ *n* abraço.

embroider [ɪm'brɔɪdə*] *vt* bordar; (*fig*: *story*) florear.

embroidery [ɪm'brɔɪdərɪ] *n* bordado.

embroil [ɪm'brɔɪl] *vt*: **to become** ~**ed (in sth)** ficar envolvido (em algo).

embryo ['embrɪəu] *n* (*also*: *fig*) embrião *m*.

emend [ɪ'mend] *vt* emendar.

emerald ['emərəld] *n* esmeralda.

emerge [ɪ'mɔːdʒ] *vi* sair, aparecer; (*arise*) surgir; **it** ~**s that** ... (*BRIT*) veio à tona que ....

emergence [ɪ'mɔːdʒəns] *n* surgimento, aparecimento; (*of a nation*) nascimento.

emergency [ɪ'mɔːdʒənsɪ] *n* emergência; **in an** ~ em caso de urgência; **state of** ~ estado de emergência.

emergency exit *n* saída de emergência.

emergency landing *n* aterrissagem *f* forçada (*BR*), aterragem *f* forçosa (*PT*).

emergency lane (*US*) *n* (*AUT*) acostamento (*BR*), berma (*PT*).

emergency meeting *n* reunião *f* extraordinária.

emergency road service (*US*) *n* autosocorro (*BR*), pronto socorro (*PT*).

emergency service *n* serviço de emergência.

emergency stop (*BRIT*) *n* (*AUT*) parada de emergência.

emergent [ɪ'mɔːdʒənt] *adj*: ~ **nation** país *m* em desenvolvimento.

emery board ['emərɪ-] *n* lixa de unhas.

emery paper ['emərɪ-] *n* lixa *or* papel *m* de esmeril.

emetic [ɪ'metɪk] *n* emético.

emigrant ['emɪgrənt] *n* emigrante *m/f*.

emigrate ['emɪgreɪt] *vi* emigrar.

emigration [emɪ'greɪʃən] *n* emigração *f*.

émigré ['emɪgreɪ] *n* emigrado/a.

eminence ['emɪnəns] *n* eminência.

eminent ['emɪnənt] *adj* eminente.

eminently ['emɪnəntlɪ] *adv* eminentemente.

emirate ['emɪrɪt] *n* emirado.

emission [ɪ'mɪʃən] *n* emissão *f*.

emit [ɪ'mɪt] *vt* (*gen*) emitir; (*smoke*) soltar; (*smell*) exalar; (*sound*) produzir.

emolument [ɪ'mɔljumənt] *n* (*often pl*: *formal*: *fee*) honorário; (*salary*) remuneração *f*.

emotion [ɪ'məuʃən] *n* emoção *f*.

emotional [ɪ'məuʃənəl] *adj* (*person*) sentimental, emotivo; (*scene*) comovente; (*problem*) emocional; (*tone*) emocionante.

emotionally [ɪ'məuʃənəlɪ] *adv* (*disturbed*, *involved*) emocionalmente; (*behave*) emotivamente; (*speak*) com emoção.

emotive [ɪ'məutɪv] *adj* que sensibiliza; ~ **power** capacidade *f* de comover.

empathy ['empəθɪ] *n* empatia; **to feel** ~ **with sb** ter afinidade com alguém.

emperor ['empərə*] *n* imperador *m*.

emphases ['emfəsiːz] *npl of* **emphasis**.

emphasis ['emfəsɪs] (*pl* **emphases**) *n* ênfase *f*; **to lay** *or* **place** ~ **on sth** dar ênfase a; **the** ~ **is on reading** a leitura ocupa um lugar de destaque.

emphasize ['emfəsaɪz] *vt* (*word*, *point*) enfatizar, acentuar; (*feature*) salientar.

emphatic [em'fætɪk] *adj* (*strong*) enérgico; (*unambiguous*, *clear*) enfático.

emphatically [em'fætɪkəlɪ] *adv* com ênfase.

empire ['empaɪə*] *n* império.

empirical [em'pɪrɪkl] *adj* empírico.

employ [ɪm'plɔɪ] *vt* empregar; **he's** ~**ed in a bank** ele trabalha num banco.

employee [ɪmplɔɪ'iː] *n* empregado/a.

employer [ɪm'plɔɪə*] *n* empregador(a) *m/f*, patrão/troa *m/f*.

employment [ɪm'plɔɪmənt] *n* (*gen*) emprego; (*work*) trabalho; **to find** ~ encontrar um emprego; **without** ~ sem emprego, desempregado; **place of** ~ local de trabalho.

employment agency *n* agência de empregos.

employment exchange (*BRIT*) *n* bolsa de trabalho.

empower [ɪm'pauə*] *vt*: **to** ~ **sb to do sth** autorizar alguém para fazer algo.

empress ['emprɪs] *n* imperatriz *f*.

emptiness ['emptɪnɪs] *n* vazio, vácuo.

empty ['emptɪ] *adj* vazio; (*place*) deserto; (*house*) desocupado; (*threat*) vão/vã ♦ *n* (*bottle*) vazio ♦ *vt* esvaziar; (*place*) evacuar ♦ *vi* esvaziar-se; (*place*) ficar deserto; **on an** ~ **stomach** em jejum, com o estômago vazio; **to** ~ **into** (*river*) desaguar em.

empty-handed [-'hændɪd] *adj* de mãos vazias.

empty-headed [-'hedɪd] *adj* de cabeça oca.

EMS *n abbr* (= *European Monetary System*) SME *m*.

EMT *n abbr* = **emergency medical technician**.

emulate ['emjuleɪt] *vt* (*person*) emular com.

emulsion [ɪ'mʌlʃən] *n* emulsão *f*; (*also*: ~ *paint*) tinta plástica.

NB: European Portuguese adds the following consonants to certain words: **b** (sú(b)dito, su(b)til); **c** (a(c)ção, a(c)cionista, a(c)to); **m** (inde(m)ne); **p** (ado(p)ção, ado(p)tar); *for further details see p. xiii.*

enable [ɪ'neɪbl] *vt*: **to ~ sb to do sth** (*allow*) permitir que alguém faça algo; (*prepare*) capacitar alguém para fazer algo.

enact [ɪn'ækt] *vt* (*LAW*) pôr em vigor, promulgar; (*play*) representar; (*role*) fazer.

enamel [ɪ'næməl] *n* esmalte *m*.

enamel paint *n* esmalte *m*.

enamoured [ɪ'næməd] *adj*: **to be ~ of** (*person*) estar apaixonado por; (*activity etc*) ser louco por; (*idea*) encantar-se com.

encampment [ɪn'kæmpmənt] *n* acampamento.

encased [ɪn'keɪst] *adj*: **~ in** (*enclosed*) encaixado em; (*covered*) revestido de.

encash [ɪn'kæʃ] (*BRIT*) *vt* descontar.

enchant [ɪn'tʃɑːnt] *vt* encantar.

enchanting [ɪn'tʃɑːntɪŋ] *adj* encantador(a).

encircle [ɪn'səːkl] *vt* cercar, circundar; (*waist*) rodear.

enc(l). *abbr* (*in letters etc*) = **enclosed; enclosure.**

enclose [ɪn'kləuz] *vt* (*land*) cercar; (*with letter etc*) anexar (*BR*), enviar junto (*PT*); **please find ~d** segue junto.

enclosure [ɪn'kləuʒə*] *n* cercado; (*COMM*) documento anexo.

encoder [ɪn'kəudə*] *n* (*COMPUT*) codificador *m*.

encompass [ɪn'kʌmpəs] *vt* abranger, encerrar.

encore [ɔŋ'kɔː*] *excl* bis!, outra! ♦ *n* bis *m*.

encounter [ɪn'kauntə*] *n* encontro ♦ *vt* encontrar, topar com; (*difficulty*) enfrentar.

encourage [ɪn'kʌrɪdʒ] *vt* encorajar, animar; (*growth*) estimular; **to ~ sb to do sth** animar alguém a fazer algo.

encouragement [ɪn'kʌrɪdʒmənt] *n* estímulo.

encouraging [ɪn'kʌrɪdʒɪŋ] *adj* animador(a).

encroach [ɪn'krəutʃ] *vi*: **to ~ (up)on** invadir; (*time*) ocupar.

encrusted [ɪn'krʌstəd] *adj*: **~ with** incrustado de.

encumber [ɪn'kʌmbə*] *vt*: **to be ~ed with** (*carry*) estar carregado de; (*debts*) estar sobrecarregado de.

encyclop(a)edia [ɛnsaɪkləu'piːdɪə] *n* enciclopédia.

end [ɛnd] *n* (*in time; also: aim*) fim *m*; (*of table, line, rope etc*) ponta; (*of street*) final *m*; (*SPORT*) ponta ♦ *vt* acabar, terminar; (*also: bring to an ~, put an ~ to*) acabar com, pôr fim a ♦ *vi* terminar, acabar; **from ~ to ~** de ponta a ponta; **to come to an ~** acabar; **to be at an ~** estar no fim, estar terminado; **in the ~** ao fim, por fim, finalmente; **on ~** (*object*) na ponta; **to stand on ~** (*hair*) arrepiar-se; **for hours on ~** por horas a fio; **at the ~ of the day** (*BRIT: fig*) no final das contas; **to this ~, with this ~ in view** a este fim.

end up *vi*: **to ~ up in** terminar em; (*place*) ir parar em.

endanger [ɪn'deɪndʒə*] *vt* pôr em perigo; **an ~ed species** uma espécie ameaçada de extinção.

endear [ɪn'dɪə*] *vt*: **to ~ o.s. to sb** conquistar a afeição de alguém, cativar alguém.

endearing [ɪn'dɪərɪŋ] *adj* simpático, atrativo.

endearment [ɪn'dɪəmənt] *n*: **to whisper ~s** sussurrar palavras carinhosas; **term of ~** palavra carinhosa.

endeavour [ɪn'dɛvə*] (*US* **endeavor**) *n* esforço; (*attempt*) tentativa; (*striving*) empenho ♦ *vi*: **to ~ to do** esforçar-se para fazer; (*try*) tentar fazer.

endemic [ɛn'dɛmɪk] *adj* endêmico.

ending ['ɛndɪŋ] *n* fim *m*, conclusão *f*; (*of book*) desenlace *m*; (*LING*) terminação *f*.

endive ['ɛndaɪv] *n* (*curly*) chicória; (*smooth, flat*) endívia.

endless ['ɛndlɪs] *adj* interminável; (*possibilities*) infinito.

endorse [ɪn'dɔːs] *vt* (*cheque*) endossar; (*approve*) aprovar.

endorsee [ɪndɔː'siː] *n* endossado/a, endossatário/a.

endorsement [ɪn'dɔːsmənt] *n* (*BRIT: on driving licence*) descrição *f* das multas; (*approval*) aval *m*; (*signature*) endosso.

endorser [ɪn'dɔːsə*] *n* endossante *m/f*, endossador(a) *m/f*.

endow [ɪn'dau] *vt* (*provide with money*) dotar; (: *institution*) fundar; **to be ~ed with** ser dotado de.

endowment [ɪn'daumənt] *n* dotação *f*.

endowment assurance *n* seguro dotal.

end product *n* (*INDUSTRY*) produto final; (*fig*) resultado.

end result *n* resultado final.

endurable [ɪn'djuərəbl] *adj* suportável.

endurance [ɪn'djuərəns] *n* resistência.

endurance test teste *m* de resistência.

endure [ɪn'djuə*] *vt* (*bear*) agüentar, suportar ♦ *vi* (*last*) durar; (*resist*) resistir.

end user *n* (*COMPUT*) usuário/a (*BR*) *or* utente *m/f* (*PT*) final.

enema ['ɛnɪmə] *n* (*MED*) enema *m*, clister *m*.

enemy ['ɛnəmɪ] *adj, n* inimigo/a; **to make an ~ of sb** fazer de alguém um inimigo.

energetic [ɛnə'dʒɛtɪk] *adj* energético.

energy ['ɛnədʒɪ] *n* energia; **Department of E~** Ministério da Energia.

energy crisis *n* crise *f* de energia.

energy-saving *adj* (*policy*) de economia de energia; (*device*) que economiza energia.

enervating ['ɛnəveɪtɪŋ] *adj* enervante.

enforce [ɪn'fɔːs] *vt* (*LAW*) fazer cumprir.

enforced [ɪn'fɔːst] *adj* forçoso.

enfranchise [ɪn'fræntʃaɪz] *vt* conferir o direito de voto a; (*set free*) emancipar.

engage [ɪn'geɪdʒ] *vt* (*attention*) chamar; (*lawyer*) contratar; (*clutch*) engrenar ♦ *vi* (*TECH*) engrenar; **to ~ in** dedicar-se a, ocupar-se com; **to ~ sb in conversation** travar conversa com alguém.

engaged [ɪn'geɪdʒd] *adj* (*BRIT: phone*) ocupado (*BR*), impedido (*PT*); (: *toilet*) ocupado; (*betrothed*) noivo; **to get ~** ficar noivo; **he is ~ in research** dedica-se à pesquisa.

engaged tone (*BRIT*) *n* (*TEL*) sinal *m* de ocupado (*BR*) *or* de impedido (*PT*).

engagement [ɪn'geɪdʒmənt] n (appointment) encontro; (battle) combate m; (to marry) noivado; **I have a previous** ~ já tenho compromisso.

engagement ring n aliança de noivado.

engaging [ɪn'geɪdʒɪŋ] adj atraente, simpático.

engender [ɪn'dʒendə*] vt engendrar, gerar.

engine ['endʒɪn] n (AUT) motor m; (RAIL) locomotiva.

engine driver (BRIT) n maquinista m/f.

engineer [endʒɪ'nɪə*] n engenheiro/a; (US: RAIL) maquinista m/f; (BRIT: for domestic appliances) consertador(a) m/f (de aparelhos domésticos).

engineering [endʒɪ'nɪərɪŋ] n engenharia ♦ cpd: ~ **works** or **factory** fábrica de construção de máquinas.

engine failure n falha do motor.

engine trouble n enguiço.

England ['ɪŋglənd] n Inglaterra.

English ['ɪŋglɪʃ] adj inglês/esa ♦ n (LING) inglês m; **the ~** npl os ingleses; **an ~ speaker** uma pessoa de língua inglesa.

English Channel n: **the ~** o Canal da Mancha.

Englishman ['ɪŋglɪʃmən] (irreg) n inglês m.

English-speaking adj de língua inglesa.

Englishwoman ['ɪŋglɪʃwumən] (irreg) n inglesa.

engrave [ɪn'greɪv] vt gravar.

engraving [ɪn'greɪvɪŋ] n gravura, gravação f.

engrossed [ɪn'grəust] adj: ~ **in** absorto em.

engulf [ɪn'gʌlf] vt engolfar, tragar.

enhance [ɪn'hɑːns] vt (gen) ressaltar, salientar; (beauty) realçar; (position) melhorar; (add to) aumentar.

enigma [ɪ'nɪgmə] n enigma m.

enigmatic [enɪg'mætɪk] adj enigmático.

enjoy [ɪn'dʒɔɪ] vt (like) gostar de; (have: health, privilege) desfrutar de; (food) comer com gosto; **to ~ o.s.** divertir-se.

enjoyable [ɪn'dʒɔɪəbl] adj (pleasant) agradável; (amusing) divertido.

enjoyment [ɪn'dʒɔɪmənt] n (joy) prazer m; (use) gozo.

enlarge [ɪn'lɑːdʒ] vt aumentar; (broaden) estender, alargar; (PHOT) ampliar ♦ vi: **to ~ on** (subject) desenvolver, estender-se sobre.

enlarged [ɪn'lɑːdʒd] adj (edition) ampliado; (MED: organ, gland) dilatado, hipertrofiado.

enlargement [ɪn'lɑːdʒmənt] n (PHOT) ampliação f.

enlighten [ɪn'laɪtn] vt (inform) informar, instruir.

enlightened [ɪn'laɪtnd] adj (cultured) culto; (knowledgeable) bem informado; (tolerant) compreensivo.

enlightening [ɪn'laɪtnɪŋ] adj esclarecedor(a).

enlightenment [ɪn'laɪtənmənt] n esclarecimento; (HISTORY): **the E~** o Século das Luzes.

enlist [ɪn'lɪst] vt alistar; (support) conseguir,

aliciar ♦ vi alistar-se; ~**ed man** (US: MIL) praça m.

enliven [ɪn'laɪvn] vt animar, agitar.

enmity ['enmɪtɪ] n inimizade f.

ennoble [ɪ'nəubl] vt (with title) nobilitar.

enormity [ɪ'nɔːmɪtɪ] n enormidade f.

enormous [ɪ'nɔːməs] adj enorme.

enormously [ɪ'nɔːməslɪ] adv imensamente.

enough [ɪ'nʌf] adj: ~ **time/books** tempo suficiente/livros suficientes ♦ n: **have you got** ~? você tem o suficiente? ♦ adv: **big** ~ suficientemente grande; **will 5 be** ~? 5 chegam?; ~**!** basta!, chega!; **that's** ~, **thanks** chega, obrigado; **I've had** ~**!** não agüento mais!; **I've had** ~ **of him** estou farto dele; **he has not worked** ~ não tem trabalhado o suficiente; **it's hot** ~ **(as it is)!** já está tão quente!; **he was kind** ~ **to lend me the money** ele teve a gentileza de me emprestar o dinheiro; **which, funnily** ~ ... o que, por estranho que pareça ....

enquire [ɪn'kwaɪə*] vt, vi = inquire.

enrage [ɪn'reɪdʒ] vt enfurecer, enraivecer.

enrich [ɪn'rɪtʃ] vt enriquecer.

enrol [ɪn'rəul] (US **enroll**) vt inscrever; (SCH) matricular ♦ vi inscrever-se; (SCH) matricular-se.

enrol(l)ment [ɪn'rəulmənt] n inscrição f; (SCH) matrícula.

en route [ɔn-] adv (on the way) no caminho; ~ **for** or **to** a caminho de.

ensconced [ɪn'skɔnst] adj: ~ **in** acomodado em.

enshrine [ɪn'ʃraɪn] vt (fig) conservar, resguardar.

ensign ['ensaɪn] n (flag) bandeira; (MIL) insígnia; (US: NAUT) guarda-marinha m.

enslave [ɪn'sleɪv] vt escravizar.

ensue [ɪn'sjuː] vi seguir-se; (result) resultar; (happen) acontecer.

ensure [ɪn'ʃuə*] vt assegurar; **to ~ that** verificar-se que.

ENT n abbr (= Ear, Nose & Throat) otorrinolaringologia.

entail [ɪn'teɪl] vt (imply) implicar; (result in) acarretar.

entangle [ɪn'tæŋgl] vt enredar, emaranhar; **to get ~d in sth** (fig) ficar enrolado em algo.

entanglement [ɪn'tæŋglmənt] n emaranhado.

enter ['entə*] vt (room) entrar em; (club) ficar or fazer-se sócio de; (army) alistar-se em; (competition) inscrever-se em; (sb for a competition) inscrever; (write down) anotar; (COMPUT) entrar com ♦ vi entrar.

enter for vt fus inscrever-se em.

enter into vt fus (relations) estabelecer; (plans) fazer parte de; (debate, negotiations) entrar em; (agreement) chegar a, firmar.

enter up vt lançar.

enter (up)on vt fus (career) entrar para.

enteritis [entə'raɪtɪs] n enterite f.

enterprise ['entəpraɪz] n empresa; (spirit) iniciativa.

enterprising ['ɛntəpraızıŋ] *adj* empreendedor(a).

entertain [ɛntə'teɪn] *vt* (*amuse*) divertir, entreter; (*receive: guest*) receber (em casa); (*idea, plan*) estudar.

entertainer [ɛntə'teɪnə*] *n* artista *m/f*.

entertaining [ɛntə'teɪnɪŋ] *adj* divertido ♦ *n*: **to do a lot of** ~ receber com freqüência.

entertainment [ɛntə'teɪnmənt] *n* (*amusement*) entretenimento, diversão *f*; (*show*) espetáculo.

entertainment allowance *n* verba de representação.

enthralled [ɪn'θrɔːld] *adj* encantado, cativado.

enthralling [ɪn'θrɔːlɪŋ] *adj* cativante, encantador(a).

enthuse [ɪn'θuːz] *vi*: **to** ~ **about** *or* **over** entusiasmar-se com *or* por.

enthusiasm [ɪn'θuːzɪæzəm] *n* entusiasmo.

enthusiast [ɪn'θuːzɪæst] *n* entusiasta *m/f*; **a jazz** *etc* ~ um(a) aficionado/a de jazz *etc*.

enthusiastic [ɪnθuːzɪ'æstɪk] *adj* entusiástico; **to be** ~ **about** entusiasmar-se por.

entice [ɪn'taɪs] *vt* atrair, tentar; (*seduce*) seduzir.

enticing [ɪn'taɪsɪŋ] *adj* sedutor(a), tentador(a).

entire [ɪn'taɪə*] *adj* inteiro.

entirely [ɪn'taɪəlɪ] *adv* totalmente, completamente.

entirety [ɪn'taɪərətɪ] *n*: **in its** ~ na sua totalidade.

entitle [ɪn'taɪtl] *vt*: **to** ~ **sb to sth** dar a alguém direito a algo; **to** ~ **sb to do** dar a alguém direito de fazer.

entitled [ɪn'taɪtld] *adj* (*book*) intitulado; **to be** ~ **to sth/to do sth** ter direito a algo/de fazer algo.

entity ['ɛntɪtɪ] *n* ente *m*.

entourage [ɔntuˈrɑːʒ] *n* séquito.

entrails ['ɛntreɪlz] *npl* entranhas *fpl*.

entrance [*n* 'ɛntrəns, *vt* ɪn'trɑːns] *n* entrada ♦ *vt* encantar, fascinar; **to gain** ~ **to** (*university etc*) ser admitido em.

entrance examination *n* exame *m* de admissão.

entrance fee *n* jóia; (*to museum etc*) (preço da) entrada.

entrance ramp (*US*) *n* (*AUT*) entrada (para a rodovia).

entrancing [ɪn'trɑːnsɪŋ] *adj* encantador(a), fascinante.

entrant ['ɛntrənt] *n* participante *m/f*; (*BRIT: in exam*) candidato/a.

entreat [ɛn'triːt] *vt* rogar, suplicar.

entreaty [ɛn'triːtɪ] *n* rogo, súplica.

entrée ['ɔntreɪ] *n* (*CULIN*) entrada.

entrenched [ɛn'trɛntʃd] *adj* entrincheirado.

entrepreneur [ɔntrəprə'nəː] *n* empresário/a.

entrepreneurial [ɔntrəprə'nəːrɪəl] *adj* empreendedor(a).

entrust [ɪn'trʌst] *vt*: **to** ~ **sth to sb** confiar algo a alguém.

entry ['ɛntrɪ] *n* entrada; (*permission to enter*) acesso; (*in register*) registro, assentamento; (*in account*) lançamento; (*in dictionary*) verbete *m*; **"no** ~**"** "entrada proibida"; (*AUT*) "contramão" (*BR*), "entrada proibida" (*PT*); **single/double** ~ **book-keeping** escrituração por partidas simples/dobradas.

entry form *n* formulário de inscrição.

entry phone (*BRIT*) *n* interfone *m* (em apartamento).

entwine [ɪn'twaɪn] *vt* entrelaçar.

enumerate [ɪ'njuːməreɪt] *vt* enumerar.

enunciate [ɪ'nʌnsɪeɪt] *vt* pronunciar; (*principle etc*) enunciar.

envelop [ɪn'vɛləp] *vt* envolver.

envelope ['ɛnvələup] *n* envelope *m*.

enviable ['ɛnvɪəbl] *adj* invejável.

envious ['ɛnvɪəs] *adj* invejoso; (*look*) de inveja.

environment [ɪn'vaɪərnmənt] *n* meio ambiente *m*; **Department of the E**~ (*BRIT*) ≈ Ministério da Habitação, Urbanismo e Meio Ambiente.

environmental [ɪnvaɪərn'mɛntl] *adj* ambiental; ~ **studies** (*SCH*) ecologia.

environmentalist [ɪnvaɪərn'mɛntəlɪst] *n* ecologista *m/f*.

Environmental Protection Agency (*US*) *n* ≈ Secretaria Especial do Meio Ambiente.

envisage [ɪn'vɪzɪdʒ] *vt* (*foresee*) prever; (*imagine*) conceber, imaginar.

envision [ɪn'vɪʒən] (*US*) *vt* = **envisage**.

envoy ['ɛnvɔɪ] *n* enviado/a.

envy ['ɛnvɪ] *n* inveja ♦ *vt* ter inveja de; **to** ~ **sb sth** invejar alguém por algo, cobiçar algo de alguém.

enzyme ['ɛnzaɪm] *n* enzima.

EPA (*US*) *n abbr* (= *Environmental Protection Agency*) ≈ SEMA.

ephemeral [ɪ'fɛmərl] *adj* efêmero.

epic ['ɛpɪk] *n* epopéia ♦ *adj* épico.

epicentre ['ɛpɪsɛntə*] (*US* **epicenter**) *n* epicentro.

epidemic [ɛpɪ'dɛmɪk] *n* epidemia.

epilepsy ['ɛpɪlɛpsɪ] *n* epilepsia.

epileptic [ɛpɪ'lɛptɪk] *adj, n* epilético/a.

epilogue ['ɛpɪlɔg] *n* epílogo.

episcopal [ɪ'pɪskəpl] *adj* episcopal.

episode ['ɛpɪsəud] *n* episódio.

epistle [ɪ'pɪsl] *n* epístola.

epitaph ['ɛpɪtɑːf] *n* epitáfio.

epithet ['ɛpɪθɛt] *n* epíteto.

epitome [ɪ'pɪtəmɪ] *n* epítome *m*.

epitomize [ɪ'pɪtəmaɪz] *vt* epitomar, resumir.

epoch ['iːpɔk] *n* época.

epoch-making *adj* que marca época, marcante.

eponymous [ɪ'pɔnɪməs] *adj* epônimo.

equable ['ɛkwəbl] *adj* uniforme, igual; (*character*) tranqüilo, calmo.

equal ['iːkwl] *adj* igual; (*treatment*) equitativo, equivalente ♦ *n* igual *m/f* ♦ *vt* ser igual a; **to be** ~ **to** (*task*) estar à altura de; ~ **to doing** capaz de fazer.

equality [iːˈkwɔlɪtɪ] *n* igualdade *f*.

equalize ['iːkwəlaɪz] *vt, vi* igualar; (*SPORT*)

empatar.

equalizer ['iːkwəlaɪzə*] *n* gol (*PT*: golo) *m* de empate.

equally ['iːkwəlɪ] *adv* igualmente; (*share etc*) por igual.

Equal Opportunities Commission (*US* **Equal Employment Opportunity Commission**) *n* comissão para a não-discriminação no trabalho.

equal(s) sign *n* sinal *m* de igualdade.

equanimity [ɛkwə'nɪmɪtɪ] *n* equanimidade *f*.

equate [ɪ'kweɪt] *vt*: **to ~ sth with** equiparar algo com; **to ~ sth to** igualar algo a.

equation [ɪ'kweɪʒən] *n* (*MATH*) equação *f*.

equator [ɪ'kweɪtə*] *n* equador *m*.

equatorial [ɛkwə'tɔːrɪəl] *adj* equatorial.

Equatorial Guinea *n* Guiné *f* Equatorial.

equestrian [ɪ'kwɛstrɪən] *adj* eqüestre; (*sport*) hípico ♦ *n* (*man*) ginete *m*; (*woman*) amazona.

equilibrium [iːkwɪ'lɪbrɪəm] *n* equilíbrio.

equinox ['iːkwɪnɔks] *n* equinócio.

equip [ɪ'kwɪp] *vt* equipar; (*person*) prover, munir; **to ~ sb/sth with** equipar alguém/ algo com, munir alguém/algo de; **to be well ~ped** estar bem preparado *or* equipado.

equipment [ɪ'kwɪpmənt] *n* equipamento; (*machines etc*) equipamentos *mpl*, aparelhagem *f*.

equitable ['ɛkwɪtəbl] *adj* equitativo.

equities ['ɛkwɪtɪz] (*BRIT*) *npl* (*COMM*) ações *fpl* ordinárias.

equity capital *n* capital *m* próprio.

equivalent [ɪ'kwɪvəlnt] *adj* equivalente ♦ *n* equivalente *m*; **to be ~ to** ser equivalente a.

equivocal [ɪ'kwɪvəkl] *adj* equívoco; (*open to suspicion*) ambíguo.

equivocate [ɪ'kwɪvəkeɪt] *vi* sofismar.

equivocation [ɪkwɪvə'keɪʃən] sofismas *mpl*.

ER (*BRIT*) *abbr* (= *Elizabeth Regina*) a rainha Elisabete.

ERA (*US*) *n* *abbr* (*POL*: = *equal rights amendment*) emenda sobre a igualdade das mulheres.

era ['ɪərə] *n* era, época.

eradicate [ɪ'rædɪkeɪt] *vt* erradicar, eliminar.

erase [ɪ'reɪz] *vt* apagar.

eraser [ɪ'reɪzə*] *n* borracha (de apagar).

erect [ɪ'rɛkt] *adj* erguido, ereto ♦ *vt* erigir, levantar; (*assemble*) montar; (*tent*) armar.

erection [ɪ'rɛkʃən] *n* construção *f*; (*assembly*) montagem *f*; (*structure*) edifício; (*PHYSIOLOGY*) ereção *f*.

ergonomics [əːgə'nɔmɪks] *n* ergonomia.

ERISA (*US*) *n* *abbr* (= *Employee Retirement Income Security Act*) lei referente às aposentadorias.

ermine ['əːmɪn] *n* arminho.

ERNIE ['əːnɪ] (*BRIT*) *n* *abbr* (= *Electronic Random Number Indicator Equipment*) computador que serve para o sorteio dos "premium bonds".

erode [ɪ'rəud] *vt* (*GEO*) causar erosão em; (*salary*) corroer.

erosion [ɪ'rəuʒən] *n* erosão *f*; (*fig*) corrosão *f*.

erotic [ɪ'rɔtɪk] *adj* erótico.

eroticism [ɪ'rɔtɪsɪzm] *n* erotismo.

err [əː*] *vi* errar, enganar-se; (*REL*) pecar.

errand ['ɛrnd] *n* recado, mensagem *f*; **to run ~s** fazer incumbências; **~ of mercy** missão *f* de caridade.

errand boy *n* mensageiro.

erratic [ɪ'rætɪk] *adj* irregular.

erroneous [ɪ'rəunɪəs] *adj* errôneo.

error ['ɛrə*] *n* erro; **typing/spelling ~** erro de datilografia/ortografia; **in ~** por engano; **~s and omissions excepted** salvo erro ou omissão.

error message *n* (*COMPUT*) mensagem *f* de erro.

erstwhile ['əːstwaɪl] *adj* antigo.

erudite ['ɛrjudaɪt] *adj* erudito.

erupt [ɪ'rʌpt] *vi* entrar em erupção; (*fig*) explodir, estourar.

eruption [ɪ'rʌpʃən] *n* erupção *f*; (*fig*) explosão *f*.

ESA *n* *abbr* (= *European Space Agency*) AEE *f*.

escalate ['ɛskəleɪt] *vi* intensificar-se; (*costs, prices*) disparar.

escalation [ɛskə'leɪʃən] *n* escalada, intensificação *f*.

escalation clause *n* cláusula de reajustamento.

escalator ['ɛskəleɪtə*] *n* escada rolante.

escapade [ɛskə'peɪd] *n* peripécia.

escape [ɪ'skeɪp] *n* fuga; (*from duties*) escapatória; (*from chase*) fuga, evasão *f* ♦ *vi* escapar; (*flee*) fugir, evadir-se; (*leak*) vazar, escapar ♦ *vt* evitar, fugir de; (*consequences*) fugir de; **to ~ from** (*place*) escapar de; (*person*) escapulir de; (*clutches*) livrar-se de; **to ~ to** fugir para; **to ~ to safety** salvar-se; **to ~ notice** passar despercebido.

escape artist *n* ilusionista *m/f*.

escape clause *n* cláusula que permite revogação do contrato.

escape key *n* (*COMPUT*) tecla de saída.

escape route *n* (*from fire*) saída de emergência; (*of prisoners*) roteiro da fuga.

escapism [ɪ'skeɪpɪzəm] *n* escapismo, fuga à realidade.

escapist [ɪ'skeɪpɪst] *adj* (*person*) que foge da realidade; (*literature*) de evasão.

escapologist [ɛskə'pɔlədʒɪst] (*BRIT*) *n* ilusionista *m/f*.

escarpment [ɪs'kɑːpmənt] *n* escarpa.

eschew [ɪs'tʃuː] *vt* evitar.

escort [*n* 'ɛskɔːt, *vt* ɪ'skɔːt] *n* acompanhante *m/f*; (*MIL, NAUT*) escolta ♦ *vt* acompanhar; (*MIL, NAUT*) escoltar.

escort agency *n* agência de escorte.

Eskimo ['ɛskɪməu] *adj* esquimó ♦ *n* esquimó *m/f*; (*LING*) esquimó *m*.

ESL n abbr (SCH) = **English as a Second Language.**

esophagus [iːˈsɔfəgəs] (US) n = **oesophagus.**

esoteric [ɛsəˈtɛrɪk] adj esotérico.

ESP n abbr = **extrasensory perception.**

esp. abbr = **especially.**

especially [ɪˈspɛʃlɪ] adv (gen) especialmente; (above all) sobretudo; (particularly) em particular.

espionage [ˈɛspɪənɑːʒ] n espionagem f.

esplanade [ɛspləˈneɪd] n (by sea) avenida beira-mar, esplanada.

espouse [ɪˈspauz] vt (cause) abraçar.

Esq. (BRIT) abbr (= Esquire) Sr.

Esquire [ɪˈskwaɪə*] (BRIT) n: **J. Brown,** ~ Sr. J. Brown.

essay [ˈɛseɪ] n (SCH) ensaio.

essence [ˈɛsns] n essência; **in** ~ em sua essência; **speed is of the** ~ a rapidez é fundamental.

essential [ɪˈsɛnʃl] adj (necessary) indispensável; (basic) essencial ♦ n elemento essencial; **it is** ~ **that** é indispensável que + sub.

essentially [ɪˈsɛnʃəlɪ] adv essencialmente.

EST (US) abbr (= Eastern Standard Time) hora de inverno de Nova Iorque.

est. abbr = **established; estimate(d).**

establish [ɪˈstæblɪʃ] vt estabelecer; (facts) verificar; (proof) demonstrar; (relations) fundar.

established [ɪˈstæblɪʃt] adj consagrado; (staff) fixo.

establishment [ɪˈstæblɪʃmənt] n estabelecimento; **the E~** a classe dirigente.

estate [ɪˈsteɪt] n (land) fazenda (BR), propriedade f (PT); (property) propriedade; (inheritance) herança; (POL) estado; (BRIT: also: housing ~) conjunto habitacional.

estate agency (BRIT) n imobiliária, corretora de imóveis.

estate agent (BRIT) n corretor(a) m/f de imóveis (BR), agente m/f imobiliário/a (PT).

estate car (BRIT) n perua (BR), canadiana (PT).

esteem [ɪˈstiːm] n estima ♦ vt estimar; **to hold sb in high** ~ estimar muito alguém.

esthetic [ɪsˈθɛtɪk] (US) adj **aesthetic.**

estimate [n ˈɛstɪmət, vt, vi ˈɛstɪmeɪt] n estimativa; (assessment) avaliação f, cálculo; (COMM) orçamento ♦ vt estimar, avaliar, calcular ♦ vi (BRIT: COMM): **to** ~ **for a job** orçar uma obra; **at a rough** ~ numa estimativa aproximada.

estimation [ɛstɪˈmeɪʃən] n estimação f, opinião f; (esteem) apreço; **in my** ~ na minha opinião.

estimator [ˈɛstɪmeɪtə*] n avaliador(a) m/f.

Estonia [ɛˈstəunɪə] n Estônia.

estranged [ɪˈstreɪndʒd] adj (couple) separado; (husband, wife) de quem se separou.

estrangement [ɪˈstreɪndʒmənt] n separação f.

estrogen [ˈiːstrəudʒɛn] (US) n = **oestrogen.**

estuary [ˈɛstjuərɪ] n estuário.

ET (US) abbr (= Eastern Time) hora de Nova Iorque.

ETA n abbr = **estimated time of arrival.**

et al. abbr (= et alii: and others) e outras pessoas.

etc. abbr (= et cetera) etc.

etch [ɛtʃ] vt gravar com água-forte.

etching [ˈɛtʃɪŋ] n água-forte f.

ETD n abbr = **estimated time of departure.**

eternal [ɪˈtəːnl] adj eterno.

eternity [ɪˈtəːnɪtɪ] n eternidade f.

ether [ˈiːθə*] n éter m.

ethereal [ɪˈθɪərɪəl] adj etéreo.

ethical [ˈɛθɪkl] adj ético; (honest) honrado.

ethics [ˈɛθɪks] n ética ♦ npl moral f.

Ethiopia [iːθɪˈəupɪə] n Etiópia.

Ethiopian [iːθɪˈəupɪən] adj, n etíope m/f.

ethnic [ˈɛθnɪk] adj étnico; (clothes) folclórico; (food) exótico.

ethnology [ɛθˈnɔlədʒɪ] n etnologia.

ethos [ˈiːθɔs] n sistema m de valores.

etiquette [ˈɛtɪkɛt] n etiqueta.

ETU (BRIT) n abbr (= Electrical Trades Union) sindicato dos eletricistas.

ETV (US) n abbr (= Educational Television) TV f educativa.

etymology [ɛtɪˈmɔlədʒɪ] n etimologia.

eucalyptus [juːkəˈlɪptəs] n eucalipto.

euphemism [ˈjuːfəmɪzm] n eufemismo.

euphemistic [juːfəˈmɪstɪk] adj eufêmico.

euphoria [juːˈfɔːrɪə] n euforia.

Eurasia [juəˈreɪʃə] n Eurásia.

Eurasian [juəˈreɪʃən] adj (person) eurasiático; (continent) eurásio ♦ n eurasiático/a.

Euratom [juəˈrætəm] n abbr (= European Atomic Energy Community) EURATOM f.

Eurocheque [ˈjuərəutʃɛk] n eurocheque m.

Eurocrat [ˈjuərəukræt] n eurocrata m/f, funcionário/a da CEE.

Eurodollar [ˈjuərəudɔlə*] n eurodólar m.

Europe [ˈjuərəp] n Europa.

European [juərəˈpiːən] adj, n europeu/péia.

European Court of Justice n Tribunal m Europeu de Justiça.

euthanasia [juːθəˈneɪzɪə] n eutanásia.

evacuate [ɪˈvækjueɪt] vt evacuar.

evacuation [ɪvækjuˈeɪʃən] n evacuação f.

evade [ɪˈveɪd] vt evadir, evitar; (duties) esquivar-se de, escapar a.

evaluate [ɪˈvæljueɪt] vt avaliar; (evidence) interpretar.

evangelist [ɪˈvændʒəlɪst] n evangelista m/f; (preacher) evangelizador(a) m/f.

evangelize [ɪˈvændʒəlaɪz] vt evangelizar.

evaporate [ɪˈvæpəreɪt] vi evaporar-se ♦ vt evaporar.

evaporated milk [ɪˈvæpəreɪtɪd-] n leite m condensado.

evaporation [ɪvæpəˈreɪʃən] n evaporação f.

evasion [ɪˈveɪʒən] n evasão f, fuga; (fig) evasiva.

evasive [ɪˈveɪsɪv] adj evasivo.

eve [iːv] n: **on the** ~ **of** na véspera de.

even [ˈiːvn] adj (level) plano; (smooth) liso; (speed, temperature) uniforme; (number) par; (nature) equilibrado; (SPORT) igual ♦ adv até, mesmo; ~ **if** mesmo que; ~ **though**

mesmo que, embora; ~ **more** ainda mais; ~ **faster** ainda mais rápido, mais rápido ainda; ~ **so** mesmo assim; **never** ~ nem sequer; **not** ~ nem; ~ **he was there** até ele esteve ali; ~ **on Sundays** até nos domingos; **to get** ~ **with sb** ficar quite com alguém; **to break** ~ sair sem lucros nem prejuízos.
even out *vi* nivelar-se.

evening ['iːvnɪŋ] *n* noite *f*; *(before six)* tarde *f*; *(event)* noitada; **in the** ~ à noite; **this** ~ hoje à noite; **tomorrow/yesterday** ~ amanhã/ontem à noite.

evening class *n* aula noturna.

evening dress *n* *(man's)* traje *m* de rigor *(BR) or* de cerimónia *(PT)*; *(woman's)* vestido de noite.

evenly ['iːvnlɪ] *adv* uniformemente; *(space)* regularmente; *(divide)* por igual.

evensong ['iːvnsɔŋ] *n* oração *f* da tarde.

event [ɪ'vɛnt] *n* acontecimento; *(SPORT)* prova; **in the course of** ~s no decorrer dos acontecimentos; **in the** ~ **of** no caso de; **in the** ~ **de** fato, na realidade; **at all** ~s *(BRIT)*, **in any** ~ em todo o caso.

eventful [ɪ'vɛntful] *adj* cheio de acontecimentos; *(game etc)* cheio de emoção, agitado.

eventing [ɪ'vɛntɪŋ] *n* *(HORSERIDING)* concurso completo *(hipismo)*.

eventual [ɪ'vɛntʃuəl] *adj* *(last)* final; *(resulting)* definitivo.

eventuality [ɪvɛntʃu'ælɪtɪ] *n* eventualidade *f*.

eventually [ɪ'vɛntʃuəlɪ] *adv* *(finally)* finalmente; *(in time)* por fim.

ever ['ɛvə*] *adv* já, alguma vez; *(in negative)* nunca, jamais; *(at all times)* sempre; **the best** ~ o melhor que já se viu; **have you** ~ **seen it?** você alguma vez já viu isto?; **better than** ~ melhor que nunca; **for** ~ para sempre; **hardly** ~ quase nunca; ~ **since** *adv* desde então ♦ *conj* depois que; ~ **so pretty** tão bonitinho; **thank you** ~ **so much** muitíssimo obrigado, obrigadão *(inf)*; **yours** ~ *(BRIT: in letters)* sempre seu/sua.

Everest ['ɛvərɪst] *n* *(also: Mount* ~*)* o monte Everest.

evergreen ['ɛvəgriːn] *n* sempre-verde *f*.

everlasting [ɛvə'lɑːstɪŋ] *adj* eterno, perpétuo.

every ['ɛvrɪ] *adj* *(each)* cada; *(all)* todo; ~ **day** todo dia; ~ **other/third day** cada dois/três dias; ~ **other car** cada dois carros; ~ **now and then** de vez em quando; ~ **3 weeks** de 3 em 3 semanas; **I have** ~ **confidence in him** tenho absoluta confiança nele.

everybody ['ɛvrɪbɔdɪ] *pron* todos, todo mundo *(BR)*, toda a gente *(PT)*; ~ **knows about it** todo o mundo já sabe; ~ **else** todos os outros.

everyday ['ɛvrɪdeɪ] *adj* *(daily)* diário; *(usual)* corrente; *(common)* comum; *(routine)* rotineiro.

everyone ['ɛvrɪwʌn] *pron* todos, todo o mundo *(BR)*, toda a gente *(PT)*.

everything ['ɛvrɪθɪŋ] *pron* tudo; ~ **is ready** tudo está pronto; **he did** ~ **possible** ele fez todo o possível.

everywhere ['ɛvrɪwɛə*] *adv* *(be)* em todo lugar *(BR)*, em toda a parte *(PT)*; *(go)* a todo lugar *(BR)*, a toda a parte *(PT)*; ~ **you go you meet** ... aonde quer que se vá, encontra-se ....

evict [ɪ'vɪkt] *vt* despejar.

eviction [ɪ'vɪkʃən] *n* despejo.

eviction notice *n* notificação *f* de despejo.

evidence ['ɛvɪdəns] *n* *(proof)* prova(s) *f(pl)*; *(of witness)* testemunho, depoimento; *(facts)* dados *mpl*, evidência; **to give** ~ testemunhar, prestar depoimento; **in** ~ *(obvious)* em evidência, evidente.

evident ['ɛvɪdənt] *adj* evidente.

evidently ['ɛvɪdəntlɪ] *adv* evidentemente.

evil ['iːvl] *adj* mau/má; *(influence)* funesto; *(smell)* horrível ♦ *n* mal *m*, maldade *f*.

evildoer ['iːvlduːə*] *n* malfeitor(a) *m/f*.

evince [ɪ'vɪns] *vt* evidenciar.

evocative [ɪ'vɔkətɪv] *adj* evocativo, sugestivo.

evoke [ɪ'vəuk] *vt* evocar.

evolution [iːvə'luːʃən] *n* evolução *f*.

evolve [ɪ'vɔlv] *vt* desenvolver ♦ *vi* desenvolver-se.

ewe [juː] *n* ovelha.

ex- [ɛks] *prefix* *(former)* ex-; *(out of)*: **the price** ~ **works** o preço na porta da fábrica.

exacerbate [ɛks'æsəbeɪt] *vt* *(pain, illness)* exacerbar; *(fig)* agravar.

exact [ɪg'zækt] *adj* exato ♦ *vt*: **to** ~ **sth (from)** exigir algo (de).

exacting [ɪg'zæktɪŋ] *adj* exigente; *(conditions)* difícil.

exactitude [ɪg'zæktɪtjuːd] *n* exatidão *f*.

exactly [ɪg'zæktlɪ] *adv* exatamente; *(time)* em ponto.

exaggerate [ɪg'zædʒəreɪt] *vt, vi* exagerar.

exaggeration [ɪgzædʒə'reɪʃən] *n* exagero.

exalted [ɪg'zɔːltɪd] *adj* exaltado.

exam [ɪg'zæm] *n abbr* = **examination**.

examination [ɪgzæmɪ'neɪʃən] *n* *(SCH, MED)* exame *m*; *(LAW)* inquirição *f*; *(inquiry)* investigação *f*; **to sit** *(BRIT) or* **take an** ~ submeter-se a um exame; **the matter is under** ~ o assunto está sendo examinado.

examine [ɪg'zæmɪn] *vt* examinar; *(inspect)* inspecionar; *(SCH, LAW: person)* interrogar; *(at customs: luggage)* revistar; *(passport)* controlar.

examiner [ɪg'zæmɪnə*] *n* examinador(a) *m/f*.

example [ɪg'zɑːmpl] *n* exemplo; **for** ~ por exemplo; **to set a good/bad** ~ dar um bom/mau exemplo.

exasperate [ɪg'zɑːspəreɪt] *vt* exasperar, irritar.

exasperating [ɪg'zɑːspəreɪtɪŋ] *adj* irritante.

exasperation [ɪgzɑːspə'reɪʃən] *n* exasperação *f*, irritação *f*.

excavate ['ɛkskəveɪt] *vt* escavar.

NB: *European Portuguese adds the following consonants to certain words:* **b** (sú(b)dito, su(b)til); **c** (a(c)ção, a(c)cionista, a(c)to); **m** (inde(m)ne); **p** (ado(p)ção, ado(p)tar); *for further details see p. xiii.*

excavation [ɛkskə'veɪʃən] *n* escavação *f*.

excavator ['ɛkskəveɪtə*] *n* (*machine*) escavadeira.

exceed [ɪk'siːd] *vt* exceder; (*number*) ser superior a; (*speed limit*) ultrapassar; (*limits*) ir além de; (*powers*) exceder-se em; (*hopes*) superar.

exceedingly [ɪk'siːdɪŋlɪ] *adv* extremamente.

excel [ɪk'sɛl] *vi* sobressair, distinguir-se ♦ *vt* superar; **to ~ o.s.** (*BRIT*) destacar-se.

excellence ['ɛksələns] *n* excelência.

Excellency ['ɛksələnsɪ] *n*: **His ~** Sua Excelência.

excellent ['ɛksələnt] *adj* excelente.

except [ɪk'sɛpt] *prep* (*also*: **~ for**, **~ing**) exceto, a não ser ♦ *vt* excetuar, excluir; **~ if/ when** a menos que, a não ser que; **~ that** exceto que.

exception [ɪk'sɛpʃən] *n* exceção *f*; **to take ~ to** ressentir-se de; **with the ~ of** à exceção de; **to make an ~** fazer exceção.

exceptional [ɪk'sɛpʃənl] *adj* excepcional.

excerpt ['ɛksəːpt] *n* trecho.

excess [ɪk'sɛs] *n* excesso; (*COMM*) excedente *m*; **in ~ of** mais de.

excess baggage *n* excesso de bagagem.

excess fare *n* sobretaxa de excesso.

excessive [ɪk'sɛsɪv] *adj* excessivo.

excess supply *n* oferta excedente.

exchange [ɪks'tʃeɪndʒ] *n* permuta, câmbio; (*of goods, of ideas*) troca; (*also*: **telephone ~**) estação *f* telefônica (*BR*), central *f* telefónica (*PT*) ♦ *vt*: **to ~ (for)** trocar (por); **in ~ for** em troca de; **foreign ~** (*COMM*) divisas *fpl*, câmbio.

exchange control *n* controle *m* de câmbio.

exchange market *n* mercado cambial *or* de câmbio.

exchange rate *n* (taxa de) câmbio.

exchequer [ɪks'tʃɛkə*] (*BRIT*) *n* ≈ Tesouro Nacional.

excisable [ɪk'saɪzəbl] *adj* tributável.

excise [*n* 'ɛksaɪz, *vt* ɛk'saɪz] *n* imposto de consumo ♦ *vt* cortar (fora).

excise duties *npl* impostos *mpl* indiretos.

excitable [ɪk'saɪtəbl] *adj* excitável; (*edgy*) nervoso.

excite [ɪk'saɪt] *vt* (*stimulate*) excitar; (*awaken*) despertar; (*move*) entusiasmar; **to get ~d** entusiasmar-se.

excitement [ɪk'saɪtmənt] *n* emoções *fpl*; (*anticipation*) expectativa; (*agitation*) agitação *f*.

exciting [ɪk'saɪtɪŋ] *adj* emocionante, empolgante.

excl. *abbr* = **excluding**; **exclusive (of)**.

exclaim [ɪk'skleɪm] *vi* exclamar.

exclamation [ɛksklə'meɪʃən] *n* exclamação *f*.

exclamation mark *n* ponto de exclamação.

exclude [ɪk'skluːd] *vt* excluir; (*except*) excetuar.

excluding [ɪk'skluːdɪŋ] *prep*: **~ tax** imposto excluído.

exclusion [ɪk'skluːʒən] *n* exclusão *f*; **to the ~ of** a ponto de excluir.

exclusion clause *n* cláusula de exclusão.

exclusive [ɪk'skluːsɪv] *adj* exclusivo; (*club, district*) privativo; (*item of news*) com exclusividade ♦ *adv* (*COMM*): **~ of tax** sem incluir os impostos; **~ of postage** tarifas postais excluídas; **from 1st to 15th March ~** entre o dia 1º e 15 de março; **~ rights** (*COMM*) exclusividade *f*.

exclusively [ɪk'skluːsɪvlɪ] *adv* unicamente.

excommunicate [ɛkskə'mjuːnɪkeɪt] *vt* excomungar.

excrement ['ɛkskrəmənt] *n* excremento.

excrete [ɪk'skriːt] *vi* excretar.

excruciating [ɪk'skruːʃɪeɪtɪŋ] *adj* (ex)cruciante, torturante.

excursion [ɪk'skəːʃən] *n* excursão *f*.

excursion ticket *n* passagem *f* de excursão.

excusable [ɪk'skjuːzəbl] *adj* perdoável, excusável.

excuse [*n* ɪk'skjuːs, *vt* ɪk'skjuːz] *n* desculpa; (*evasion*) pretexto ♦ *vt* desculpar, perdoar; **to ~ sb from doing sth** dispensar alguém de fazer algo; **~ me!** (*calling attention*) desculpe!; (*asking permission*) (com) licença; **if you will ~ me** com a sua licença; **to make ~s for sb** apresentar desculpas por alguém; **to ~ o.s. for sth/for doing sth** desculpar-se de algo/de fazer algo.

ex-directory (*BRIT*) *adj*: **~ (phone) number** número que não figura na lista telefônica.

execute ['ɛksɪkjuːt] *vt* (*plan*) realizar; (*order*) cumprir; (*person*) executar.

execution [ɛksɪ'kjuːʃən] *n* realização *f*; (*killing*) execução *f*.

executioner [ɛksɪ'kjuːʃənə*] *n* verdugo, carrasco.

executive [ɪg'zɛkjutɪv] *n* (*COMM, POL*) executivo ♦ *adj* executivo.

executive director *n* diretor(a) *m/f* executivo/a.

executor [ɪg'zɛkjutə*] *n* executor(a) *m/f* testamentário/a, testamenteiro/a.

exemplary [ɪg'zɛmplərɪ] *adj* exemplar.

exemplify [ɪg'zɛmplɪfaɪ] *vt* exemplificar.

exempt [ɪg'zɛmpt] *adj*: **~ from** isento de ♦ *vt*: **to ~ sb from** dispensar or isentar alguém de.

exemption [ɪg'zɛmpʃən] *n* (*from taxes etc*) isenção *f*; (*from military service*) dispensa; (*immunity*) imunidade *f*.

exercise ['ɛksəsaɪz] *n* exercício ♦ *vt* exercer; (*right*) valer-se de; (*dog*) levar para passear ♦ *vi* (*also*: **to take ~**) fazer exercício.

exercise book *n* caderno.

exert [ɪg'zəːt] *vt* exercer; **to ~ o.s.** esforçar-se, empenhar-se.

exertion [ɪg'zəːʃən] *n* esforço.

ex gratia [-'greɪʃə] *adj*: **~ payment** gratificação *f*.

exhale [ɛks'heɪl] *vt*, *vi* expirar.

exhaust [ɪg'zɔːst] *n* (*pipe*) escape *m*, exaustor *m*; (*fumes*) escapamento (de gás) ♦ *vt* esgotar; **to ~ o.s.** esgotar-se; **~ manifold** (*AUT etc*) cano de descarga.

exhausted [ɪg'zɔːstɪd] *adj* esgotado.

exhausting [ɪg'zɔːstɪŋ] *adj* exaustivo, estafante.

exhaustion [ɪɡ'zɔːstʃən] n exaustão f.

exhaustive [ɪɡ'zɔːstɪv] adj exaustivo.

exhibit [ɪɡ'zɪbɪt] n (ART) obra exposta; (LAW) objeto exposto ♦ vt (courage etc) manifestar, mostrar; (emotion) demonstrar; (film) apresentar; (paintings) expor.

exhibition [ɛksɪ'bɪʃən] n exposição f.

exhibitionist [ɛksɪ'bɪʃənɪst] n exibicionista m/f.

exhibitor [ɪɡ'zɪbɪtə*] n expositor(a) m/f.

exhilarating [ɪɡ'zɪləreɪtɪŋ] adj estimulante, tônico.

exhilaration [ɪɡzɪlə'reɪʃən] n euforia.

exhort [ɪɡ'zɔːt] vt exortar.

exile ['ɛksaɪl] n exílio; (person) exilado/a ♦ vt desterrar, exilar; **in ~** em exílio, exilado.

exist [ɪɡ'zɪst] vi existir; (live) viver.

existence [ɪɡ'zɪstəns] n existência; (life) vida; **to be in ~** existir.

existentialism [ɛɡzɪs'tɛnʃlɪzəm] n existencialismo.

existing [ɪɡ'zɪstɪŋ] adj (laws) existente; (system, regime) atual.

exit ['ɛksɪt] n saída ♦ vi (COMPUT, THEATRE) sair.

exit ramp (US) n (AUT) saída da rodovia.

exit visa n visto de saída.

exodus ['ɛksədəs] n êxodo.

ex officio [-ə'fɪʃɪəu] adj, adv ex-officio, por dever do cargo.

exonerate [ɪɡ'zɔnəreɪt] vt: **to ~ from** absolver de.

exorbitant [ɪɡ'zɔːbɪtənt] adj exorbitante.

exorcize ['ɛksɔːsaɪz] vt exorcizar.

exotic [ɪɡ'zɔtɪk] adj exótico.

expand [ɪk'spænd] vt (widen) ampliar; (number) aumentar; (influence etc) estender ♦ vi (population, production) aumentar; (trade, gas, etc) expandir-se; (metal) dilatar-se; **to ~ on** (notes, story etc) estender-se sobre.

expanse [ɪk'spæns] n extensão f.

expansion [ɪk'spænʃən] n (of town) desenvolvimento; (of trade) expansão f; (of population) aumento; (of metal) dilatação f.

expansionism [ɪk'spænʃənɪzəm] n expansionismo.

expansionist [ɪk'spænʃənɪst] adj expansionista.

expatriate [n ɛks'pætrɪət, vt ɛks'pætrɪeɪt] n expatriado/a ♦ vt expatriar.

expect [ɪk'spɛkt] vt (gen) esperar; (count on) contar com; (suppose) supor; (require) exigir ♦ vi: **to be ~ing** estar grávida; **to ~ sb to do** (anticipate) esperar que alguém faça; (demand) esperar de alguém que faça; **to ~ to do sth** esperar fazer algo; **as ~ed** como previsto; **I ~ so** suponho que sim.

expectancy [ɪks'pɛktənsɪ] n expectativa; **life ~** expectativa de vida.

expectant [ɪk'spɛktənt] adj expectante; **~ mother** gestante f.

expectantly [ɪk'spɛktəntlɪ] adv cheio de expectativa.

expectation [ɛkspɛk'teɪʃən] n esperança, expectativa; **in ~ of** na expectativa de; **against or contrary to all ~(s)** contra todas as expectativas; **to come or live up to one's ~s** corresponder à expectativa de alguém.

expedience [ɛk'spiːdɪəns] n conveniência; **for the sake of ~** por ser mais conveniente.

expediency [ɛk'spiːdɪənsɪ] n = **expedience**.

expedient [ɛk'spiːdɪənt] adj conveniente, oportuno ♦ n expediente m, recurso.

expedite ['ɛkspədaɪt] vt acelerar.

expedition [ɛkspə'dɪʃən] n expedição f.

expeditionary force [ɛkspə'dɪʃənrɪ-] n força expedicionária.

expeditious [ɛkspə'dɪʃəs] adj eficiente.

expel [ɪk'spɛl] vt expelir; (SCH) expulsar.

expend [ɪk'spɛnd] vt gastar; (use up) consumir.

expendable [ɪk'spɛndəbl] adj prescindível.

expenditure [ɪk'spɛndɪtʃə*] n gastos mpl.

expense [ɪk'spɛns] n gasto, despesa; (high cost) custo; **~s** npl (COMM: costs) despesas fpl; (: paid to employee) ajuda de custo; **at the ~ of** à custa de; **to go to the ~ of** fazer a despesa de; **to meet the ~ of** arcar com a despesa de.

expense account n relatório de despesas.

expensive [ɪk'spɛnsɪv] adj caro.

experience [ɪk'spɪərɪəns] n experiência ♦ vt experimentar; (suffer) sofrer; **to learn by ~** aprender com a experiência.

experienced [ɪk'spɪərɪənst] adj experimentado, experiente.

experiment [ɪk'spɛrɪmənt] n experimento, experiência ♦ vi fazer experiências.

experimental [ɪkspɛrɪ'mɛntl] adj experimental.

expert ['ɛkspɜːt] adj hábil, perito ♦ n perito/a; (specialist) especialista m/f; **~ in or at doing sth** perito em fazer algo; **an ~ on sth** um perito em algo; **~ witness** (LAW) perito/a.

expertise [ɛkspɜː'tiːz] n perícia.

expire [ɪk'spaɪə*] vi (gen) expirar; (end) terminar; (run out) vencer.

expiry [ɪk'spaɪərɪ] n expiração f, vencimento.

explain [ɪk'spleɪn] vt explicar; (clarify) esclarecer; (demonstrate) expor.

explain away vt justificar.

explanation [ɛksplə'neɪʃən] n explicação f; **to find an ~ for sth** achar uma explicação para algo.

explanatory [ɪk'splænətrɪ] adj explicativo.

explicit [ɪk'splɪsɪt] adj explícito.

explode [ɪk'spləud] vi estourar, explodir; (with anger) rebentar ♦ vt detonar, fazer explodir; (fig: theory) derrubar; (: myth) destruir.

exploit [n 'ɛksplɔɪt, vt ɪk'splɔɪt] n façanha ♦ vt explorar.

exploitation [ɛksplɔɪ'teɪʃən] n exploração f.

exploration [ɛksplə'reɪʃən] n exploração f.
exploratory [ɪk'splɔrətrɪ] adj (fig: talks) exploratório, de pesquisa; (MED: operation) exploratório.
explore [ɪk'splɔ:*] vt explorar; (fig) examinar, pesquisar.
explorer [ɪk'splɔːrə*] n explorador(a) m/f.
explosion [ɪk'spləuʒən] n explosão f.
explosive [ɪk'spləusɪv] adj, n explosivo.
exponent [ɪk'spəunənt] n representante m/f, expoente m/f; (MATH) expoente m.
export [vt ɛk'spɔːt, n, cpd 'ɛkspɔːt] vt exportar ♦ n exportação f ♦ cpd de exportação.
exportation [ɛkspɔː'teɪʃən] n exportação f.
exporter [ɛk'spɔːtə*] n exportador(a) m/f.
export licence n licença de exportação.
expose [ɪk'spəuz] vt expor; (unmask) desmascarar.
exposed [ɪk'spəuzd] adj exposto; (position) desabrigado; (wire) descascado; (pipes, beams) aparente.
exposition [ɛkspə'zɪʃən] n exposição f.
exposure [ɪk'spəuʒə*] n exposição f; (PHOT) revelação f; (: shot) fotografia; **to die from ~** (MED) morrer de frio.
exposure meter n fotômetro.
expound [ɪk'spaund] vt expor, explicar.
express [ɪk'sprɛs] adj (definite) expresso, explícito; (BRIT: letter etc) urgente ♦ n (train) rápido ♦ adv (send) por via expressa ♦ vt exprimir, expressar; **to ~ o.s.** expressar-se.
expression [ɪk'sprɛʃən] n expressão f.
expressionism [ɪk'sprɛʃənɪzəm] n expressionismo.
expressive [ɪk'sprɛsɪv] adj expressivo.
expressly [ɪk'sprɛslɪ] adv expressamente.
expressway [ɪk'sprɛsweɪ] (US) n rodovia (BR), auto-estrada (PT).
expropriate [ɛks'prəuprɪeɪt] vt expropriar.
expulsion [ɪk'spʌlʃən] n expulsão f.
exquisite [ɛk'skwɪzɪt] adj requintado.
ex-serviceman (irreg) n veterano (de guerra).
ext. abbr (TEL: = extension) r. (BR), int. (PT).
extemporize [ɪk'stɛmpəraɪz] vi improvisar.
extend [ɪk'stɛnd] vt (visit, street) prolongar; (building) aumentar; (offer) fazer; (COMM: credit) conceder; (: period of loan) prorrogar ♦ vi (land) estender-se.
extension [ɪk'stɛnʃən] n extensão f; (building) acréscimo, expansão f; (TEL) ramal m (BR), extensão f (PT); (of deadline) prolongamento, prorrogação f.
extension cable n cabo de extensão.
extensive [ɪk'stɛnsɪv] adj extenso; (damage) considerável; (broad) vasto, amplo; (frequent) geral, comum.
extensively [ɪk'stɛnsɪvlɪ] adv (altered, damaged etc) amplamente; **he's travelled ~** ele já viajou bastante.
extent [ɪk'stɛnt] n (breadth) extensão f; (of damage etc) dimensão f; (scope) alcance m; **to some** or **to a certain ~** até certo ponto; **to the ~ of ...** a ponto de ...; **to a large ~** em grande parte; **to what ~?** até que

ponto?; **to such an ~ that** ... a tal ponto que ...; **debts to the ~ of £5,000** dívidas da ordem de £5,000.
extenuating [ɪks'tɛnjueɪtɪŋ]: **~ circumstances** circunstâncias fpl atenuantes.
exterior [ɛk'stɪərɪə*] adj exterior, externo ♦ n exterior m; (appearance) aspecto.
exterminate [ɪk'stəːmɪneɪt] vt exterminar.
extermination [ɪkstəːmɪ'neɪʃən] n extermínio.
external [ɛk'stəːnl] adj externo; (foreign) exterior ♦ n: **the ~s** as aparências; **for ~ use only** (MED) exclusivamente para uso externo.
externally [ɛk'stəːnəlɪ] adv por fora.
extinct [ɪk'stɪŋkt] adj extinto.
extinction [ɪk'stɪŋkʃən] n extinção f.
extinguish [ɪk'stɪŋgwɪʃ] vt extinguir.
extinguisher [ɪk'stɪŋgwɪʃə*] n extintor m.
extol [ɪk'stəul] (US **extoll**) vt (merits) exaltar; (person) elogiar.
extort [ɪk'stɔːt] vt: **to ~ sth (from sb)** extorquir algo (a or de alguém).
extortion [ɪk'stɔːʃən] n extorsão f.
extortionate [ɪk'stɔːʃnət] adj extorsivo, excessivo.
extra ['ɛkstrə] adj adicional; (excessive) de mais, extra; (bonus: payment) extraordinário ♦ adv (in addition) adicionalmente ♦ n (addition) extra m, suplemento; (THEATRE) figurante m/f; (newspaper) edição f extra; **the wine will cost ~** o vinho não está incluído no preço; **~ large sizes** tamanhos extra grandes.
extra... [ɛkstrə] prefix extra....
extract [vt ɪk'strækt, n 'ɛkstrækt] vt tirar, extrair; (tooth) arrancar; (confession) arrancar, obter ♦ n extrato.
extraction [ɪk'strækʃən] n extração f; (of tooth) arrancamento; (descent) descendência.
extracurricular ['ɛkstrəkə'rɪkjulə*] adj (SCH) extracurricular.
extradite ['ɛkstrədaɪt] vt (from country) extraditar; (to country) obter a extradição de.
extradition [ɛkstrə'dɪʃən] n extradição f.
extramarital [ɛkstrə'mærɪtl] adj extramatrimonial.
extramural [ɛkstrə'mjuərl] adj (course) de extensão universitária.
extraneous [ɛk'streɪnɪəs] adj: **~ to** alheio a.
extraordinary [ɪk'strɔːdnrɪ] adj extraordinário; (odd) estranho.
extraordinary general meeting n assembléia geral extraordinária.
extrapolation [ɛkstræpə'leɪʃən] n extrapolação f.
extrasensory perception ['ɛkstrə'sɛnsərɪ-] n percepção f extra-sensorial.
extra time n (FOOTBALL) prorrogação f.
extravagance [ɪk'strævəgəns] n extravagância; (spending) esbanjamento.
extravagant [ɪk'strævəgənt] adj (lavish) extravagante; (wasteful) gastador(a), esbanjador(a); (price) exorbitante; (praise) excessivo; (odd) excêntrico, estranho.

extreme [ɪk'striːm] *adj* extremo; *(case)* excessivo ♦ *n* extremo, extremidade *f*; **the ~ left/right** *(POL)* a extrema esquerda/direita; **~s of temperature** temperaturas extremas.
extremely [ɪk'striːmlɪ] *adv* muito, extremamente.
extremist [ɪk'striːmɪst] *adj, n* extremista *m/f*.
extremity [ɪk'strɛmətɪ] *n* extremidade *f*; *(need)* apuro, necessidade *f*.
extricate ['ɛkstrɪkeɪt] *vt*: **to ~ sth (from)** soltar algo (de).
extrovert ['ɛkstrəvəːt] *n* extrovertido/a.
exuberance [ɪg'zjuːbərəns] *n* exuberância.
exuberant [ɪg'zjuːbərnt] *adj (person)* eufórico; *(style)* exuberante.
exude [ɪg'zjuːd] *vt* exsudar; *(fig)* esbanjar; **the charm *etc* he ~s** o charme *etc* que emana dele.
exult [ɪg'zʌlt] *vi* regozijar-se.
exultant [ɪg'zʌltənt] *adj* exultante, triunfante.
exultation [ɛgzʌl'teɪʃən] *n* exultação *f*, regozijo.
eye [aɪ] *n* olho; *(of needle)* buraco ♦ *vt* olhar, observar; **as far as the ~ can see** a perder de vista; **to keep an ~ on** vigiar, ficar de olho em; **to have an ~ for sth** ter faro para algo; **in the public ~** conhecido pelo público; **with an ~ to doing** *(BRIT)* com vista a fazer; **there's more to this than meets the ~** a coisa é mais complicada do que parece.
eyeball ['aɪbɔːl] *n* globo ocular.
eyebath ['aɪbɑːθ] *(BRIT)* *n* copinho *(para lavar o olho)*.
eyebrow ['aɪbrau] *n* sobrancelha.
eyebrow pencil *n* lápis *m* de sobrancelha.
eye-catching *adj* chamativo, vistoso.
eye cup *(US)* *n* copinho *(para lavar o olho)*.
eyedrops ['aɪdrɔps] *npl* gotas *fpl* para os olhos.
eyeglass ['aɪglɑːs] *n* monóculo; **~es** *npl* *(US)* óculos *mpl*.
eyelash ['aɪlæʃ] *n* cílio.
eyelet ['aɪlɪt] *n* ilhós *m*.
eye-level *adj* à altura dos olhos.
eyelid ['aɪlɪd] *n* pálpebra.
eyeliner ['aɪlaɪnə*] *n* delineador *m*.
eye-opener *n* revelação *f*, grande surpresa.
eyeshadow ['aɪʃædəu] *n* sombra de olhos.
eyesight ['aɪsaɪt] *n* vista, visão *f*.
eyesore ['aɪsɔː*] *n* monstruosidade *f*.
eyestrain ['aɪstreɪn] *n* cansaço ocular.
eyetooth ['aɪtuːθ] *(irreg)* *n* dente *m* canino superior; **to give one's eyeteeth for sth/to do sth** *(fig)* dar tudo por algo/para fazer algo.
eyewash ['aɪwɔʃ] *n* colírio; *(fig)* disparates *mpl*, maluquices *fpl*.
eye witness *n* testemunha *f* ocular.
eyrie ['ɪərɪ] *n* ninho de ave de rapina.

F

F, f [ɛf] *n (letter)* F, f *m*; *(MUS)*: **F** fá *m*; **F for Frederick** *(BRIT)* *or* **Fox** *(US)* F de Francisco.
F *abbr* = **Fahrenheit**.
FA *(BRIT)* *n abbr* (= *Football Association*) *confederação de futebol.*
FAA *(US)* *n abbr* = **Federal Aviation Administration.**
fable ['feɪbl] *n* fábula.
fabric ['fæbrɪk] *n* tecido, pano; *(of building)* estrutura.
fabricate ['fæbrɪkeɪt] *vt* inventar.
fabrication [fæbrɪ'keɪʃən] *n* invencionice *f*.
fabric conditioner *n* amaciante *m* de pano.
fabulous ['fæbjuləs] *adj* fabuloso; *(inf: super)* sensacional.
façade [fə'sɑːd] *n* fachada.
face [feɪs] *n* *(ANAT)* cara, rosto; *(grimace)* careta; *(of clock)* mostrador *m*; *(side, surface)* superfície *f* ♦ *vt* *(person, reality, facts)* encarar; *(subj: building)* dar para, ter frente para; *(problems)* enfrentar; **to lose ~** perder o prestígio; **to save ~** salvar as aparências, livrar a cara; **to pull a ~** fazer careta; **in the ~ of** *(difficulties etc)* diante de, à vista de; **on the ~ of it** a julgar pelas aparências, à primeira vista; **~ to ~** cara a cara; **~ down** *(person)* de bruços; *(card)* virado para baixo; **we are ~d with serious problems** estamos enfrentando sérios problemas, temos problemas pela frente.
face up to *vt fus* enfrentar.
face cloth *(BRIT)* *n* pano de rosto.
face cream *n* creme *m* facial.
face lift *n* (operação *f*) plástica; *(of façade)* remodelamento.
face powder *n* pó *m* de arroz.
face-saving *adj* para salvar as aparências.
facet ['fæsɪt] *n* faceta.
facetious [fə'siːʃəs] *adj* engraçado, faceto.
face-to-face *adv* face a face, cara a cara.
face value *n* *(of stamp)* valor *m* nominal; **to take sth at ~** *(fig)* tomar algo em sentido literal.
facia ['feɪʃə] *n* = **fascia**.
facial ['feɪʃəl] *adj* facial.
facile ['fæsaɪl] *adj* superficial.
facilitate [fə'sɪlɪteɪt] *vt* facilitar.
facility [fə'sɪlɪtɪ] *n* facilidade *f*; **facilities** *npl* facilidades *fpl*, instalações *fpl*; **credit facilities** crediário.
facing ['feɪsɪŋ] *prep* de frente para ♦ *n* *(of wall etc)* revestimento; *(SEWING)* forro.

*NB: European Portuguese adds the following consonants to certain words: **b** (sú(b)dito, su(b)til); **c** (a(c)ção, a(c)cionista, a(c)to); **m** (inde(m)ne); **p** (ado(p)ção, ado(p)tar); for further details see p. xiii.*

facsimile [fæk'sɪmɪlɪ] n (copy, machine, document) fac-símile m.
fact [fækt] n fato; **in** ~ realmente, na verdade; **to know for a** ~ **that** ... saber com certeza que ...; ~**s and figures** dados e números.
fact-finding adj: **a** ~ **tour** or **mission** uma missão de pesquisa.
faction ['fækʃən] n facção f.
factor ['fæktə*] n fator m; (COMM) comissário financiador, empresa que compra contas a receber; (: agent) corretor(a) m/f ♦ vi comprar contas a receber; **safety** ~ fator de segurança.
factory ['fæktərɪ] n fábrica.
factory farming (BRIT) n criação f intensiva.
factory ship n navio-fábrica m.
factual ['fæktjuəl] adj real, fatual.
faculty ['fækəltɪ] n faculdade f; (US: teaching staff) corpo docente.
fad [fæd] (inf) n mania, modismo.
fade [feɪd] vi (colour, cloth) desbotar; (sound, hope) desvanecer-se; (light) apagar-se; (flower) murchar.
fade in vt (sound) subir; (picture) clarear.
fade out vt (sound) abaixar; (picture) escurecer.
faeces ['fiːsɪz] (US **feces**) npl fezes fpl.
fag [fæg] (inf) n (cigarette) cigarro; (US: homosexual) bicha; (chore): **what a** ~! que saco!
fag end (BRIT: inf) n ponta de cigarro, guimba.
fagged out [fægd-] (BRIT: inf) adj estafado.
fail [feɪl] vt (candidate) reprovar; (exam) não passar em, ser reprovado em ♦ vi (person) fracassar; (business) falir; (supply) acabar; (engine, brakes, voice) falhar; (patient) enfraquecer-se; **to** ~ **to do sth** (neglect) deixar de fazer algo; (be unable) não conseguir fazer algo; **without** ~ sem falta.
failing ['feɪlɪŋ] n defeito ♦ prep na or à falta de; ~ **that** senão.
failsafe ['feɪlseɪf] adj (device etc) de segurança contra falhas.
failure ['feɪljə*] n fracasso; (in exam) reprovação f; (of crop) perda; (mechanical etc) falha; **his** ~ **to turn up** o fato dele não ter vindo; **heart** ~ parada cardíaca; ~ **rate** taxa de reprovados.
faint [feɪnt] adj fraco; (recollection) vago; (mark) indistinto; (smell, trace) leve; (dizzy) tonto ♦ n desmaio ♦ vi desmaiar.
faint-hearted adj pusilânime.
faintly ['feɪntlɪ] adv indistintamente, vagamente.
faintness ['feɪntnɪs] n fraqueza.
fair [fɛə*] adj justo; (colour: hair) louro; (: complexion) branco; (weather) bom; (good enough) razoável; (sizeable) considerável ♦ adv: **to play** ~ fazer jogo limpo ♦ n feira; (BRIT: funfair) parque m de diversões; **a** ~ **amount of time** bastante tempo; **it's not** ~! não é justo!
fair copy n cópia a limpo.
fair-haired adj (de cabelo) louro.

fairly ['fɛəlɪ] adv (justly) com justiça; (share) igualmente; (quite) bastante; **I'm** ~ **sure** tenho quase certeza.
fairness ['fɛənɪs] n justiça; (impartiality) imparcialidade f; **in all** ~ com toda a justiça.
fair play n jogo limpo.
fairy ['fɛərɪ] n fada.
fairy godmother n fada-madrinha.
fairy lights (BRIT) npl lâmpadas fpl coloridas de enfeite.
fairy tale n conto de fadas.
faith [feɪθ] n fé f; (trust) confiança; (denomination) seita; **to have** ~ **in sb/sth** ter fé or confiança em alguém/algo.
faithful ['feɪθful] adj fiel.
faithfully ['feɪθfulɪ] adv fielmente; **yours** ~ (BRIT: in letters) atenciosamente.
faith healer n curandeiro/a.
fake [feɪk] n (painting etc) falsificação f; (person) impostor(a) m/f ♦ adj falso ♦ vt fingir; (painting etc) falsificar; **his illness is a** ~ sua doença é fingimento or um embuste.
falcon ['fɔːlkən] n falcão m.
Falkland Islands ['fɔːlklənd-] npl: **the** ~ **as** (ilhas) Malvinas or Falkland.
fall [fɔːl] (pt **fell**, pp **fallen**) n queda; (US: autumn) outono ♦ vi cair; (price) baixar; ~**s** npl (waterfall) cascata, queda d'água; **to** ~ **flat** (on one's face) cair de cara no chão; (plan) falhar; (joke) não agradar; **to** ~ **short of** (sb's expectations) não corresponder a, ficar abaixo de; **a** ~ **of snow** (BRIT) uma nevasca.
fall apart vi cair aos pedaços; (inf: emotionally) descontrolar-se completamente.
fall back vi retroceder.
fall back on vt fus (remedy etc) recorrer a.
fall behind vi ficar para trás.
fall down vi (person) cair; (building) desabar; (hopes) cair por terra.
fall for vt fus (trick) cair em; (person) enamorar-se de.
fall in vi (roof) ruir; (MIL) alinhar-se.
fall in with vt fus (sb's plans etc) conformar-se com.
fall off vi cair; (diminish) declinar, diminuir.
fall out vi (friends etc) brigar; (MIL) sair da fila.
fall over vi cair por terra, tombar.
fall through vi (plan, project) furar.
fallacy ['fæləsɪ] n (error) erro; (lie) mentira, falácia.
fallback ['fɔːlbæk] adj: ~ **position** alternativa.
fallen ['fɔːlən] pp of **fall**.
fallible ['fæləbl] adj falível.
falling-off ['fɔːlɪŋ-] n declínio.
fallopian tube [fə'ləupɪən-] n (ANAT) trompa de Falópio.
fallout ['fɔːlaut] n chuva radioativa.
fallout shelter n refúgio contra chuva radioativa.
fallow ['fæləu] adj alqueivado, de pousio.
false [fɔːls] adj falso; (hair, teeth etc) postiço;

(disloyal) desleal, traidor(a); **under ~ pretences** sob falsos pretextos.
false alarm *n* alarme *m* falso.
falsehood ['fɔːlshud] *n* (*lie*) mentira; *(falseness)* falsidade *f*.
falsely ['fɔːlslɪ] *adv* falsamente.
false teeth *(BRIT)* *npl* dentadura postiça.
falsify ['fɔːlsɪfaɪ] *vt* falsificar.
falter ['fɔːltə*] *vi* vacilar.
fame [feɪm] *n* fama.
familiar [fə'mɪlɪə*] *adj* (*well-known*) conhecido; *(tone)* familiar, íntimo; **to be ~ with** *(subject)* estar familiarizado com; **to make o.s. ~ with sth** familiarizar-se com algo; **to be on ~ terms with sb** ter intimidade com alguém.
familiarity [fəmɪlɪ'ærɪtɪ] *n* familiaridade *f*.
familiarize [fə'mɪlɪəraɪz] *vt*: **to ~ o.s. with** familiarizar-se com.
family ['fæmɪlɪ] *n* família.
family allowance *(BRIT)* *n* abono-família *m*.
family business *n* negócio familiar.
family doctor *n* médico/a da família.
family life *n* vida familiar.
family planning *n* planejamento familiar; **~ clinic** clínica de planejamento familiar.
family tree *n* árvore *f* genealógica.
famine ['fæmɪn] *n* fome *f*.
famished ['fæmɪʃt] *adj* faminto; **I'm ~!** *(inf)* estou morrendo de fome.
famous ['feɪməs] *adj* famoso, célebre.
famously ['feɪməslɪ] *adv* (*get on*) maravilhosamente.
fan [fæn] *n* (*hand-held*) leque *m*; *(ELEC)* ventilador *m*; *(person)* fã *(PT:* fan*)* *m/f*; *(SPORT)* torcedor(a) *m/f* *(BR)*, adepto/a *(PT)* ♦ *vt* abanar; *(fire, quarrel)* atiçar.
fan out *vi* espalhar-se.
fanatic [fə'nætɪk] *n* fanático/a.
fanatical [fə'nætɪkəl] *adj* fanático.
fan belt *n* correia do ventilador *(BR)* or da ventoinha *(PT)*.
fancied ['fænsɪd] *adj* imaginário.
fanciful ['fænsɪful] *adj* fantástico; *(imaginary)* imaginário.
fancy ['fænsɪ] *n* (*whim*) capricho; *(taste)* inclinação *f*, gosto; *(imagination)* imaginação *f* ♦ *adj* (*decorative*) ornamental; *(luxury)* luxuoso; *(as decoration)* como decoração ♦ *vt* (*feel like, want*) desejar, querer; *(imagine)* imaginar; **to take a ~** to tomar gosto por; **it took** *or* **caught my ~** gostei disso; **when the ~ takes him** quando lhe dá na veneta; **to ~ that ...** imaginar que ...; **he fancies her** ele está a fim dela.
fancy dress *n* fantasia.
fancy-dress ball *n* baile *m* à fantasia.
fancy goods *npl* artigos *mpl* de fantasia.
fanfare ['fænfeə*] *n* fanfarra.
fanfold paper ['fænfəuld-] *n* formulários *mpl* contínuos.
fang [fæŋ] *n* presa.

fan heater *(BRIT)* *n* aquecedor *m* de ventoinha.
fanlight ['fænlaɪt] *n* (*window*) basculante *f*.
fantasize ['fæntəsaɪz] *vi* fantasiar.
fantastic [fæn'tæstɪk] *adj* fantástico.
fantasy ['fæntəsɪ] *n* fantasia.
FAO *n* *abbr* (= *Food and Agriculture Organization*) FAO *f*.
FAQ *abbr* (= *free at quay*) posto no cais.
far [fɑː*] *adj* (*distant*) distante ♦ *adv* (*also ~ away*; ~ *off*) longe; **the ~ side/end** o lado de lá/a outra ponta; **the ~ left/right** *(POL)* a extrema esquerda/direita; **is it ~ to London?** Londres é longe daqui?; **it's not ~ (from here)** não é longe (daqui); **~ better** muito melhor; **~ from** longe de; **by ~** de longe; **go as ~ as the farm** vá até a *(BR)* or à *(PT)* fazenda; **as ~ as I know** que eu saiba; **as ~ as possible** na medida do possível; **how ~?** até onde?; *(fig)* até que ponto?
faraway ['fɑːrəweɪ] *adj* remoto, distante.
farce [fɑːs] *n* farsa.
farcical ['fɑːsɪkəl] *adj* farsante.
fare [feə*] *n* (*on trains, buses*) preço (da passagem); *(in taxi: cost)* tarifa; (: *passenger*) passageiro/a; *(food)* comida ♦ *vi* sair-se.
Far East *n*: **the ~** o Extremo Oriente.
farewell [feə'wel] *excl* adeus ♦ *n* despedida ♦ *cpd* (*party etc*) de despedida.
far-fetched [-fetʃt] *adj* inverossímil.
farm [fɑːm] *n* fazenda *(BR)*, quinta *(PT)* ♦ *vt* cultivar.
farm out *vt* (*work etc*) dar de empreitada.
farmer ['fɑːmə*] *n* fazendeiro/a, agricultor *m*.
farmhand ['fɑːmhænd] *n* lavrador(a) *m/f*, trabalhador(a) *m/f* rural.
farmhouse ['fɑːmhaus] *(irreg)* *n* casa da fazenda *(BR)* or da quinta *(PT)*.
farming ['fɑːmɪŋ] *n* agricultura; *(tilling)* cultura; **intensive ~** cultura intensiva; **sheep ~** criação de ovelhas, ovinocultura.
farm labourer *n* lavrador(a) *m/f*, trabalhador(a) *m/f* rural.
farmland ['fɑːmlænd] *n* terra de cultivo.
farm produce *n* produtos *mpl* agrícolas.
farm worker *n* lavrador(a) *m/f*, trabalhador(a) *m/f* rural.
farmyard ['fɑːmjɑːd] *n* curral *m*.
Faroe Islands ['feərəu-] *npl*: **the ~ as** (ilhas) Faroë.
Faroes ['feərəuz] *npl* = **Faroe Islands**.
far-reaching [-'riːtʃɪŋ] *adj* de grande alcance, abrangente.
far-sighted *adj* presbita; *(fig)* previdente.
fart [fɑːt] *(inf!)* *n* peido (!) ♦ *vi* soltar um peido (!), peidar (!).
farther ['fɑːðə*] *adv* mais longe ♦ *adj* mais distante, mais afastado.
farthest ['fɑːðɪst] *superl of* **far**.
FAS *(BRIT)* *abbr* (= *free alongside ship*) FAS.
fascia ['feɪʃə] *n* *(AUT)* painel *m*.
fascinate ['fæsɪneɪt] *vt* fascinar.

fascinating ['fæsɪneɪtɪŋ] *adj* fascinante.
fascination [fæsɪ'neɪʃən] *n* fascinação *f*, fascínio.
fascism ['fæʃɪzəm] *n* fascismo.
fascist ['fæʃɪst] *adj*, *n* fascista *m/f*.
fashion ['fæʃən] *n* moda; *(manner)* maneira ♦ *vt* amoldar; **in** ~ na moda; **out of** ~ fora da moda; **in the Greek** ~ à grega, à maneira dos gregos; **after a** ~ *(finish, manage etc)* até certo ponto.
fashionable ['fæʃənəbl] *adj* na moda, elegante; *(writer, café)* da moda.
fashion designer *n* estilista *m/f*.
fashion parade *(BRIT)* *n* desfile *m* de modas.
fashion show *n* desfile *m* de modas.
fast [faːst] *adj* rápido; *(dye, colour)* firme, permanente; *(PHOT: film)* de alta sensibilidade; *(clock)*: **to be** ~ estar adiantado ♦ *adv* rápido, rapidamente, depressa; *(stuck, held)* firmemente ♦ *n* jejum *m* ♦ *vi* jejuar; **my watch is 5 minutes** ~ meu relógio está 5 minutos adiantado; ~ **asleep** dormindo profundamente; **as** ~ **as I can** o mais rápido possível; **to make a boat** ~ *(BRIT)* amarrar um barco.
fasten ['faːsn] *vt* fixar, prender; *(coat)* fechar; *(belt)* apertar, atar ♦ *vi* prender-se, fixar-se.
fasten (up)on *vt fus (idea)* agarrar-se a.
fastener ['faːsnə*] *n* presilha, fecho; *(of door etc)* fechadura; **zip** ~ *(BRIT)* fecho ecler *(BR)* or éclair *(PT)*.
fastening ['faːsnɪŋ] *n* presilha, fecho; *(of door etc)* fechadura.
fast food *n* fast food *f*.
fastidious [fæs'tɪdɪəs] *adj (fussy)* meticuloso; *(demanding)* exigente.
fast lane *n (AUT)* pista de velocidade.
fat [fæt] *adj* gordo; *(meat)* com muita gordura; *(greasy)* gorduroso ♦ *n (on person)* gordura; *(lard)* banha, gordura; **to live off the** ~ **of the land** viver na abundância.
fatal ['feɪtl] *adj* fatal; *(injury)* mortal; *(consequence)* funesto.
fatalism ['feɪtəlɪzəm] *n* fatalismo.
fatality [fə'tælɪtɪ] *n (road death etc)* vítima *m/f*.
fatally ['feɪtəlɪ] *adv*: ~ **injured** mortalmente ferido.
fate [feɪt] *n* destino; *(of person)* sorte *f*.
fated ['feɪtɪd] *adj (person)* condenado; *(project)* fadado ao fracasso.
fateful ['feɪtful] *adj* fatídico.
father ['faːðə*] *n* pai *m*.
Father Christmas *n* Papai *m* Noel.
fatherhood ['faːðəhud] *n* paternidade *f*.
father-in-law *(pl* **fathers-in-law***) n* sogro.
fatherland ['faːðəlænd] *n* pátria.
fatherly ['faːðəlɪ] *adj* paternal.
fathom ['fæðəm] *n* braça ♦ *vt (NAUT)* sondar; *(unravel)* penetrar, deslindar; *(understand)* compreender.
fatigue [fə'tiːg] *n* fadiga, cansaço; *(MIL)* faxina; **metal** ~ fadiga do metal.
fatness ['fætnɪs] *n* gordura.
fatten ['fætn] *vt*, *vi* engordar; **chocolate is**

~**ing** o chocolate engorda.
fatty ['fætɪ] *adj (food)* gorduroso ♦ *n (inf)* gorducho/a.
fatuous ['fætjuəs] *adj* fátuo.
faucet ['fɔːsɪt] *(US) n* torneira.
fault [fɔːlt] *n (error)* defeito, falta; *(blame)* culpa; *(defect)* defeito; *(GEO)* falha ♦ *vt* criticar; **it's my** ~ é minha culpa; **to find** ~ **with** criticar, queixar-se de; **at** ~ culpado; **to a** ~ em demasia.
faultless ['fɔːltlɪs] *adj (action)* impecável; *(person)* irrepreensível.
faulty ['fɔːltɪ] *adj* defeituoso.
fauna ['fɔːnə] *n* fauna.
faux pas ['fəu'paː] *n inv* gafe *f*.
favour ['feɪvə*] *(US* **favor***) n* favor *m* ♦ *vt (proposition)* favorecer, aprovar; *(person etc)* favorecer; *(assist)* auxiliar; **to ask a** ~ **of** pedir um favor a; **to do sb a** ~ fazer favor a alguém; **to be in** ~ **of sth/of doing sth** estar a favor de algo/de fazer algo; **to find** ~ **with** cair nas boas graças de; **in** ~ **of** em favor de.
favo(u)rable ['feɪvərəbl] *adj* favorável.
favo(u)rably ['feɪvərəblɪ] *adv* favoravelmente.
favo(u)rite ['feɪvərɪt] *adj* predileto ♦ *n* favorito/a.
favo(u)ritism ['feɪvərɪtɪzəm] *n* favoritismo.
fawn [fɔːn] *n* cervo novo, cervato ♦ *adj (also:* ~**-coloured***)* castanho-claro *inv* ♦ *vi*: **to** ~ **(up)on** bajular.
fax [fæks] *n (document, machine)* fax *m*, fac-símile *m* ♦ *vt* enviar por fax *or* fac-símile.
FBI *(US) n abbr (= Federal Bureau of Investigation)* FBI *m*.
FCC *(US) n abbr* = **Federal Communications Commission**.
FCO *(BRIT) n abbr (= Foreign and Commonwealth Office)* ministério das Relações Exteriores.
FD *(US) n abbr* = **fire department**.
FDA *(US) n abbr (= Food and Drug Administration)* órgão controlador de medicamentos e gêneros alimentícios.
fear [fɪə*] *n* medo; *(misgiving)* temor *m* ♦ *vt* ter medo de, temer ♦ *vi*: **to** ~ **for** recear *or* temer por; **to** ~ **that** temer que; ~ **of heights** medo das alturas, vertigem *f*; **for** ~ **of** com medo de.
fearful ['fɪəful] *adj* medonho, temível; *(cowardly)* medroso; *(awful)* terrível; **to be** ~ **of** temer, ter medo de.
fearfully ['fɪəfəlɪ] *adv (timidly)* timidamente; *(inf: very)* muito, terrivelmente.
fearless ['fɪəlɪs] *adj* sem medo, intrépido; *(bold)* audaz.
fearsome ['fɪəsəm] *adj (opponent)* medonho, temível; *(sight)* espantoso.
feasibility [fiːzə'bɪlɪtɪ] *n* viabilidade *f*.
feasibility study *n* estudo de viabilidade.
feasible ['fiːzəbl] *adj* viável, praticável.
feast [fiːst] *n* banquete *m*; *(REL: also:* ~ **day***)* festa ♦ *vi* banquetear-se.
feat [fiːt] *n* façanha, feito.
feather ['fɛðə*] *n* pena ♦ *vt*: **to** ~ **one's nest**

(fig) acumular riquezas ♦ cpd (bed etc) de penas.

feather-weight n (BOXING) peso-pena m.

feature ['fi:tʃə*] n característica; (ANAT) feição f, traço; (article) reportagem f ♦ vt (subj: film) apresentar ♦ vi figurar; ~s npl (of face) feições fpl; **it ~d prominently in ...** ocupou um lugar de destaque em ....

feature film n longa-metragem m.

featureless ['fi:tʃəlɪs] adj anônimo.

Feb. abbr (= February) fev.

February ['fɛbruərɪ] n fevereiro; see also **July**.

feces ['fi:si:z] (US) npl = **faeces**.

feckless ['fɛklɪs] adj displicente.

Fed (US) abbr = **federal; federation**.

fed [fɛd] pt, pp of **feed; to be ~ up** estar (de saco) cheio (BR), estar farto (PT).

Fed. [fɛd] (US: inf) n abbr = **Federal Reserve Board**.

federal ['fɛdərəl] adj federal.

Federal Reserve Board (US) n órgão controlador do banco central dos EUA.

Federal Trade Commission (US) n órgão regulador de práticas comerciais.

federation [fɛdə'reɪʃən] n federação f.

fee [fi:] n taxa (BR), propina (PT); (of school) matrícula; (of doctor, lawyer) honorários mpl; **entrance ~** (to club) jóia; (to museum etc) entrada; **membership ~** (to join) jóia; (annual etc) quota; **for a small ~** em troca de uma pequena taxa.

feeble ['fi:bl] adj fraco, débil.

feeble-minded adj imbecil.

feed [fi:d] (pt, pp **fed**) n comida; (of baby) alimento infantil; (of animal) ração f; (on printer) mecanismo alimentador ♦ vt (gen, machine) alimentar; (baby: breastfeed) amamentar; (animal) dar de comer a; (data, information): **to ~ into** introduzir em.

feed on vt fus alimentar-se de.

feedback ['fi:dbæk] m (ELEC) feedback m; (from person) reação f.

feeder ['fi:də*] n (bib) babador m.

feeding bottle ['fi:dɪŋ-] (BRIT) n mamadeira.

feel [fi:l] (pt, pp **felt**) n (sensation) sensação f; (sense of touch) tato ♦ vt (touch) tocar, apalpar; (cold, pain etc) sentir; (think, believe) achar, acreditar; **to get the ~ of sth** (fig) acostumar-se a algo; **to ~ (that)** achar (que); **I ~ that you ought to do it** eu acho que você deveria fazê-lo; **to ~ hungry/cold** estar com fome/frio (BR), ter fome/frio (PT); **to ~ lonely/better** sentir-se só/melhor; **to ~ sorry for** ter pena de; **it ~s soft** é macio; **it ~s colder here** sente-se mais frio aqui; **it ~s like velvet** parece veludo; **to ~ like** (want) querer; **to ~ about** or **around** apalpar, tatear; **I'm still ~ing my way** (fig) ainda estou me ambientando.

feeler ['fi:lə*] n (of insect) antena; **to put out ~s** or **a ~** (fig) sondar opiniões, lançar um balão-de-ensaio.

feeling ['fi:lɪŋ] n sensação f; (foreboding) pressentimento; (opinion) opinião f; (emotion) sentimento; **to hurt sb's ~s** magoar alguém; **~s ran high about it** os sentimentos se esquentaram a respeito disso; **what are your ~s about the matter?** qual é a sua opinião sobre o assunto?; **my ~ is that ...** eu acho que ...; **I have a ~ that ...** tenho a impressão de que ....

feet [fi:t] npl of **foot**.

feign [feɪn] vt fingir.

felicitous [fɪ'lɪsɪtəs] adj feliz.

feline ['fi:laɪn] adj felino.

fell [fɛl] pt of **fall** ♦ vt (tree) lançar por terra, derrubar ♦ n (BRIT: mountain) montanha; (: moorland): **the ~s** a charneca ♦ adj: **with one ~ blow** de um só golpe.

fellow ['fɛləu] n (gen) camarada m/f; (inf: man) cara m (BR), tipo (PT); (of learned society) membro; (of university) membro do conselho universitário ♦ cpd: **~ students** colegas m/fpl de curso; **his ~ workers** seus colegas de trabalho.

fellow citizen n concidadão/dã m/f.

fellow countryman (irreg) n compatriota m.

fellow feeling n simpatia.

fellow men npl semelhantes mpl.

fellowship ['fɛləuʃɪp] n (comradeship) amizade f; (grant) bolsa de estudo; (society) associação f.

fellow traveller (US **fellow traveler**) n companheiro/a de viagem; (POL) simpatizante m/f.

fell-walking (BRIT) n caminhadas fpl nas montanhas.

felon ['fɛlən] n (LAW) criminoso/a.

felony ['fɛlənɪ] n (LAW) crime m.

felt [fɛlt] pt, pp of **feel** ♦ n feltro.

felt-tip pen n caneta pilot ® (BR) or de feltro (PT).

female ['fi:meɪl] n (woman) mulher f; (ZOOL) fêmea ♦ adj (BIO, ELEC) fêmeo/a; (sex, character) feminino; (vote etc) das mulheres; (child etc) de sexo feminino; **male and ~ teachers** professores e professoras.

female impersonator n (THEATRE) travesti m.

feminine ['fɛmɪnɪn] adj feminino; (womanly) feminil ♦ n feminino.

femininity [fɛmɪ'nɪnɪtɪ] n feminilidade f.

feminism ['fɛmɪnɪzəm] n feminismo.

feminist ['fɛmɪnɪst] n feminista m/f.

fen [fɛn] (BRIT) n: **the F~s** os pântanos de Norfolk.

fence [fɛns] n cerca; (SPORT) obstáculo; (inf: person) receptor(a) m/f ♦ vt (also: ~ in) cercar ♦ vi esgrimir; **to sit on the ~** (fig) ficar no muro.

fencing ['fɛnsɪŋ] n (sport) esgrima.

fend [fɛnd] vi: **to ~ for o.s.** defender-se, virar-se.

NB: European Portuguese adds the following consonants to certain words: **b** (sú(b)dito, su(b)til); **c** (a(c)ção, a(c)cionista, a(c)to); **m** (inde(m)ne); **p** (ado(p)ção, ado(p)tar); *for further details see p. xiii.*

fend off vt (attack, attacker) defender-se de.

fender ['fɛndə*] n (of fireplace) guarda-fogo m; (US: AUT) pára-lama m; (: RAIL) limpa-trilhos m inv.

fennel ['fɛnl] n erva-doce f, funcho.

ferment [vi fə'mɛnt, n 'fɔːmɛnt] vi fermentar ♦ n (fig) agitação f.

fermentation [fɔːmən'teɪʃən] n fermentação f.

fern [fɔːn] n samambaia (BR), feto (PT).

ferocious [fə'rəuʃəs] adj feroz.

ferocity [fə'rɔsɪtɪ] n ferocidade f.

ferret ['fɛrɪt] n furão m.

   ferret about (BRIT) vi = **ferret around**.

   ferret around vi: **to ~ around in sth** vasculhar algo.

   ferret out vt (information) desenterrar, descobrir.

ferry ['fɛrɪ] n (small) barco (de travessia); (ship) balsa ♦ vt transportar; **to ~ sth/sb across** or **over** transportar algo/alguém para o outro lado.

ferryman ['fɛrɪmən] (irreg) n barqueiro, balseiro.

fertile ['fɔːtaɪl] adj fértil; (BIO) fecundo.

fertility [fə'tɪlɪtɪ] n fertilidade f; (BIO) fecundidade f.

fertility drug n droga que propicia a fecundação.

fertilize ['fɔːtɪlaɪz] vt fertilizar, fecundar; (AGR) adubar.

fertilizer ['fɔːtɪlaɪzə*] n adubo, fertilizante m.

fervent ['fɔːvənt] adj ardente, apaixonado.

fervour ['fɔːvə*] (US **fervor**) n fervor m.

fester ['fɛstə*] vi inflamar-se.

festival ['fɛstɪvəl] n (REL) festa; (ART, MUS) festival m.

festive ['fɛstɪv] adj festivo; **the ~ season** (BRIT: Christmas) a época do Natal.

festivities [fɛs'tɪvɪtɪz] npl festas fpl, festividades fpl.

festoon [fɛs'tuːn] vt: **to ~ with** engrinaldar de or com.

fetch [fɛtʃ] vt ir buscar, trazer; (BRIT: sell for) alcançar; **how much did it ~?** quanto rendeu?, por quanto foi vendido?

   fetch up (US) vi ir parar.

fetching ['fɛtʃɪŋ] adj atraente.

fête [feɪt] n festa.

fetid ['fɛtɪd] adj fétido.

fetish ['fɛtɪʃ] n fetiche m.

fetter ['fɛtə*] vt restringir, refrear.

fetters ['fɛtəz] npl grilhões mpl.

fettle ['fɛtl] (BRIT) n: **in fine ~** (car etc) em bom estado; (person) em forma.

fetus ['fiːtəs] (US) n = **foetus**.

feud [fjuːd] n (hostility) inimizade f; (quarrel) disputa, rixa ♦ vi brigar; **a family ~** uma briga de família.

feudal ['fjuːdl] adj feudal.

feudalism ['fjuːdəlɪzəm] n feudalismo.

fever ['fiːvə*] n febre f; **he has a ~** ele está com febre.

feverish ['fiːvərɪʃ] adj febril.

few [fjuː] adj, pron poucos/as; **a ~ ...** alguns/ algumas ...; **I know a ~** conheço alguns; **quite a ~ ...** vários/as ...; **in the next ~ days** nos próximos dias; **in the past ~ days** nos últimos dias; **every ~ days/months** cada dois ou três dias/meses; **a ~ more ...** mais alguns/algumas ....

fewer ['fjuːə*] adj, pron menos.

fewest ['fjuːɪst] adj o menor número de.

FFA n abbr = **Future Farmers of America**.

FH (BRIT) abbr = **fire hydrant**.

FHA (US) n abbr (= Federal Housing Administration) secretaria federal da habitação.

fiancé [fɪ'ãːŋseɪ] n noivo.

fiancée [fɪ'ãːŋseɪ] n noiva.

fiasco [fɪ'æskəu] n fiasco.

fib [fɪb] n lorota.

fibre ['faɪbə*] (US **fiber**) n fibra.

fibreboard ['faɪbəbɔːd] (US **fiberboard**) n madeira compensada, compensado.

fibre-glass (US **fiber-glass**) n fibra de vidro.

fibrositis [faɪbrə'saɪtɪs] n aponeurosite f.

FICA (US) n abbr = **Federal Insurance Contributions Act**.

fickle ['fɪkl] adj inconstante.

fiction ['fɪkʃən] n ficção f.

fictional ['fɪkʃənl] adj de ficção.

fictionalize ['fɪkʃnəlaɪz] vt romancear.

fictitious [fɪk'tɪʃəs] adj fictício.

fiddle ['fɪdl] n (MUS) violino; (cheating) fraude f, embuste m; (swindle) trapaça ♦ vt (BRIT: accounts) falsificar.

   fiddle with vt fus brincar com.

fiddler ['fɪdlə*] n violinista m/f.

fiddly ['fɪdlɪ] adj (task) espinhoso.

fidelity [fɪ'dɛlɪtɪ] n fidelidade f.

fidget ['fɪdʒɪt] vi estar irrequieto, mexer-se.

fidgety ['fɪdʒɪtɪ] adj inquieto, nervoso.

fiduciary [fɪ'djuːʃɪərɪ] n fiduciário/a.

field [fiːld] n campo; (fig) área, esfera, especialidade f; **to lead the ~** (SPORT) tomar a dianteira; (COMM) liderar; **to have a ~ day** (fig) fazer a festa.

field glasses npl binóculo.

field marshal n marechal-de-campo.

fieldwork ['fiːldwɜːk] n trabalho de campo.

fiend [fiːnd] n demônio.

fiendish ['fiːndɪʃ] adj diabólico.

fierce [fɪəs] adj feroz; (wind, attack) violento; (heat) intenso; (fighting, enemy) feroz, violento.

fiery ['faɪərɪ] adj (burning) ardente; (temperament) fogoso.

FIFA ['fiːfə] n abbr (= Fédération Internationale de Football Association) FIFA.

fifteen [fɪf'tiːn] num quinze; see also **five**.

fifth [fɪfθ] num quinto; **I was (the) ~ to arrive** eu fui o quinto a chegar; **he came ~ in the competition** ele tirou o quinto lugar; (in race) ele chegou em quinto lugar; **Henry the F~** Henrique Quinto; **the ~ of July, July the ~** dia cinco de julho; **I wrote to him on the ~** eu lhe escrevi no dia cinco.

fiftieth ['fɪftɪɪθ] num qüinquagésimo; see also **fifth**.

fifty ['fɪftɪ] num cinqüenta; **about ~ people**

umas cinqüenta pessoas; **he'll be ~ (years old) next birthday** ele fará cinqüenta anos no seu próximo aniversário; **he's about ~** ele tem uns cinqüenta anos; **the fifties** os anos 50; **to be in one's fifties** estar na casa dos cinqüenta anos; **the temperature was in the fifties** a temperatura estava na faixa dos cinqüenta graus; **to do ~** (AUT) ir a 50 (quilômetros por hora).

fifty-fifty ['fɪftɪ'fɪftɪ] *adv*: **to share** *or* **go ~ with sb** dividir meio a meio com alguém, rachar com alguém ♦ *adj*: **to have a ~ chance** ter 50% de chance.

fig [fɪg] *n* figo.

fight [faɪt] (*pt*, *pp* **fought**) *n* briga; (MIL) combate *m*; (*struggle: against illness etc*) luta ♦ *vt* lutar contra; (*cancer, alcoholism*) combater; (LAW: *case*) defender ♦ *vi* brigar, bater-se; (*fig*): **to ~ (for/against)** lutar (por/contra).

fight back *vi* revidar; (SPORT, *from illness etc*) reagir ♦ *vt* (*tears*) tentar reter.

fight off *vt* (*attack, attacker*) repelir; (*illness, sleep, urge*) lutar contra.

fight out *vt*: **to ~ it out** resolver a questão pela briga.

fighter ['faɪtə*] *n* combatente *m/f*; (*fig*) lutador(a) *m/f*; (*plane*) caça *m*.

fighter pilot *n* piloto de caça.

fighting ['faɪtɪŋ] *n* luta, briga; (*battle*) batalha.

figment ['fɪgmənt] *n*: **a ~ of the imagination** um produto da imaginação.

figurative ['fɪgjurətɪv] *adj* figurado, figurativo.

figure ['fɪgə*] *n* (DRAWING, MATH) figura, desenho; (*numeral*) algarismo; (*number, cipher*) número, cifra; (*outline*) forma; (*of woman*) corpo; (*person*) personagem *m* ♦ *vt* (*esp US*) imaginar ♦ *vi* (*appear*) figurar; (US: *make sense*) fazer sentido; **public ~** personalidade *f*; **~ of speech** figura de linguagem.

figure on (US) *vt fus*: **to ~ on doing** contar em fazer.

figure out *vt* (*understand*) compreender.

figurehead ['fɪgəhɛd] *n* (NAUT) carranca de proa; (*fig*) chefe *m* nominal.

figure skating *n* movimentos *mpl* de patinação.

Fiji (Islands) ['fiːdʒiː-] *n(pl)* (ilhas *fpl*) Fiji (*no article*).

filament ['fɪləmənt] *n* filamento.

filch [fɪltʃ] (*inf*) *vt* furtar, abafar.

file [faɪl] *n* (*tool*) lixa; (*dossier*) dossiê *m*, pasta; (*folder*) pasta; (: *binder*) fichário; (COMPUT) arquivo; (*row*) fila, coluna ♦ *vt* lixar; (*papers*) arquivar; (LAW: *claim*) apresentar, dar entrada em; (*store*) arquivar ♦ *vi*: **to ~ in/out** entrar/sair em fila; **to ~ past** desfilar em frente de; **to ~ a suit against sb** (LAW) abrir processo contra alguém.

file name *n* (COMPUT) nome *m* do arquivo.

filibuster ['fɪlɪbʌstə*] (*esp US*) *n* (POL) obstrucionista *m/f* ♦ *vi* obstruir.

filing ['faɪlɪŋ] *n* arquivamento; **~s** *npl* (*of iron etc*) limalha.

filing cabinet *n* fichário, arquivo.

filing clerk *n* arquivista *m/f*.

Filipino [fɪlɪ'piːnəu] *n* (*person*) filipino/a; (LING) filipino.

fill [fɪl] *vt* encher; (*vacancy*) preencher; (*order*) atender ♦ *n*: **to eat one's ~** encher-se *or* fartar-se de comer; **~ed with admiration** cheio de admiração.

fill in *vt* (*form*) preencher; (*hole*) tapar; (*details, report*) escrever ♦ *vi*: **to ~ in for sb** substituir alguém; **to ~ sb in on sth** (*inf*) dar as dicas a alguém sobre algo.

fill out *vt* preencher.

fill up *vt* encher ♦ *vi* (AUT) abastecer o carro; **~ it up, please** (AUT) pode encher (o tanque), por favor.

fillet ['fɪlɪt] *n* filete *m*, filé *m* ♦ *vt* preparar em filés.

fillet steak *n* filé *m*.

filling ['fɪlɪŋ] *n* (CULIN) recheio; (*for tooth*) obturação *f* (BR), chumbo (PT).

filling station *n* posto de gasolina.

fillip ['fɪlɪp] *n* estímulo, incentivo.

filly ['fɪlɪ] *n* potranca.

film [fɪlm] *n* filme *m* ♦ *vt* (*scene*) rodar, filmar ♦ *vi* filmar.

film star *n* astro/estrela do cinema.

filmstrip ['fɪlmstrɪp] *n* diafilme *m*.

film studio *n* estúdio (de cinema).

filter ['fɪltə*] *n* filtro ♦ *vt* filtrar.

filter coffee *n* café *m* filtro.

filter lane (BRIT) *n* (AUT) pista para se dobrar à esquerda (*or* à direita).

filter tip *n* filtro.

filth [fɪlθ] *n* sujeira (BR), sujidade *f* (PT).

filthy ['fɪlθɪ] *adj* sujo; (*language*) indecente, obsceno.

fin [fɪn] *n* barbatana.

final ['faɪnl] *adj* (*last*) final, último; (*definitive*) definitivo ♦ *n* (SPORT) final *f*; **~s** *npl* (SCH) exames *mpl* finais; **~ demand** (*on invoice etc*) demanda final.

finale [fɪ'nɑːlɪ] *n* final *m*.

finalist ['faɪnəlɪst] *n* (SPORT) finalista *m/f*.

finalize ['faɪnəlaɪz] *vt* concluir, completar.

finally ['faɪnəlɪ] *adv* (*lastly*) finalmente, por fim; (*eventually*) por fim; (*irrevocably*) definitivamente.

finance [faɪ'næns] *n* (*money*) fundos *mpl* ♦ *vt* financiar; **~s** *npl* finanças *fpl*.

financial [faɪ'nænʃəl] *adj* financeiro; **~ statement** demonstração financeira.

financially [faɪ'nænʃəlɪ] *adv* financeiramente.

financial year *n* ano fiscal, exercício.

financier [fɪ'nænsɪə*] *n* financista *m/f*; (*backer*) financiador(a) *m/f*.

find [faɪnd] (*pt*, *pp* **found**) *vt* encontrar, achar ♦ *n* achado, descoberta; **to ~ sb guilty** (LAW) declarar alguém culpado.

NB: *European Portuguese adds the following consonants to certain words:* **b** (sú(b)dito, su(b)til); **c** (a(c)ção, a(c)cionista, a(c)to); **m** (inde(m)ne); **p** (ado(p)ção, ado(p)tar); *for further details see p. xiii.*

find out *vt* descobrir; *(person)* desmascarar ♦ *vi*: **to ~ out about** informar-se sobre; *(by chance)* saber de.

findings ['faɪndɪŋz] *npl* (*LAW*) veredito, decisão *f*; *(of report)* constatações *fpl*.

fine [faɪn] *adj* *(delicate, refined, thin)* fino; *(good)* bom/boa; *(beautiful)* bonito ♦ *adv* *(well)* muito bem ♦ *n* (*LAW*) multa ♦ *vt* (*LAW*) multar; **to be ~** *(weather)* estar bom; **you're doing ~** você se dá bem; **to cut it ~** deixar pouca margem; *(arrive just in time)* chegar em cima da hora.

fine arts *npl* belas artes *fpl*.

finely ['faɪnlɪ] *adv* *(tune)* finamente; **~ chopped** picado.

finery ['faɪnərɪ] *n* enfeites *mpl*.

finesse [fɪ'nɛs] *n* sutileza.

fine-tooth comb *n*: **to go through sth with a ~** *(fig)* passar o pente fino em algo.

finger ['fɪŋgə*] *n* dedo ♦ *vt* *(touch)* manusear; *(MUS)* dedilhar; **little/index ~** dedo mínimo/indicador.

fingering ['fɪŋgərɪŋ] *n* (*MUS*) dedilhado.

fingermark ['fɪŋgəmɑːk] *n* dedada.

fingernail ['fɪŋgəneɪl] *n* unha.

fingerprint ['fɪŋgəprɪnt] *n* impressão *f* digital ♦ *vt* *(person)* tirar as impressões digitais de.

fingerstall ['fɪŋgəstɔːl] *n* dedeira.

fingertip ['fɪŋgətɪp] *n* ponta do dedo; **to have sth at one's ~s** ter algo à sua disposição, dispor de algo; *(knowledge)* saber algo na ponta da língua.

finicky ['fɪnɪkɪ] *adj* *(fussy)* fresco, cheio de coisas.

finish ['fɪnɪʃ] *n* *(end)* fim *m*; *(SPORT)* chegada; *(on wood etc)* acabamento ♦ *vt, vi* terminar, acabar; **to ~ doing sth** terminar de fazer algo; **to ~ with sb** *(end relationship)* acabar com alguém; **to ~ third** chegar no terceiro lugar.

finish off *vt* terminar; *(kill)* liquidar.

finish up *vt* acabar ♦ *vi* acabar; *(in place)* ir parar.

finished product ['fɪnɪʃt-] *n* produto acabado.

finishing line ['fɪnɪʃɪŋ-] *n* linha de chegada, meta.

finishing school ['fɪnɪʃɪŋ-] *n* escola de aperfeiçoamento (para moças).

finishing touches ['fɪnɪʃɪŋ-] *npl* últimos retoques *mpl*.

finite ['faɪnaɪt] *adj* finito.

Finland ['fɪnlənd] *n* Finlândia.

Finn [fɪn] *n* finlandês/esa *m/f*.

Finnish ['fɪnɪʃ] *adj* finlandês/esa ♦ *n* (*LING*) finlandês *m*.

fiord [fjɔːd] *n* fiorde *m*.

fir [fəː*] *n* abeto.

fire ['faɪə*] *n* fogo; *(accidental)* incêndio ♦ *vt* *(gun)* disparar; *(interest)* despertar; *(dismiss)* despedir; *(excite)*: **to ~ sb with enthusiasm** encher alguém de entusiasmo ♦ *vi* disparar ♦ *cpd*: **~ hazard, ~ risk** perigo *or* risco de incêndio; **on ~** em chamas; **to set ~ to sth, set sth on ~** incendiar algo; **insured against ~** segurado contra fogo; **to**

come under ~ (from) *(fig)* ser atacado (por).

fire alarm *n* alarme *m* de incêndio.

firearm ['faɪərɑːm] *n* arma de fogo.

fire brigade *n* (corpo de) bombeiros *mpl*.

fire chief (*US*) *n* = **fire master**.

fire department (*US*) *n* = **fire brigade**.

fire drill *n* treinamento de incêndio.

fire engine *n* carro de bombeiro.

fire escape *n* escada de incêndio.

fire extinguisher *n* extintor *m* de incêndio.

fireguard ['faɪəgɑːd] (*BRIT*) *n* guarda-fogo *m*.

fire insurance *n* seguro contra fogo.

fireman ['faɪəmɛn] *(irreg)* *n* bombeiro.

fire master (*BRIT*) *n* capitão *m* dos bombeiros.

firemen ['faɪəmɛn] *npl of* **fireman**.

fireplace ['faɪəpleɪs] *n* lareira.

fireproof ['faɪəpruːf] *adj* à prova de fogo.

fire regulations *npl* normas *fpl* preventivas contra incêndio.

fire screen *n* guarda-fogo *m*.

fireside ['faɪəsaɪd] *n* lugar *m* junto à lareira.

fire station *n* posto de bombeiros.

firewood ['faɪəwud] *n* lenha.

fireworks ['faɪəwəːks] *npl* fogos *mpl* de artifício.

firing ['faɪərɪŋ] *n* (*MIL*) tiros *mpl*, tiroteio.

firing line *n* (*MIL*) linha de fogo; **to be in the ~** *(fig)* estar na linha de frente.

firing squad *n* pelotão *m* de fuzilamento.

firm [fəːm] *adj* firme ♦ *n* firma; **to be a ~ believer in sth** ser partidário perseverante de algo; **to stand ~** *or* **take a ~ stand on sth** *(fig)* manter-se firme em algo.

firmly ['fəːmlɪ] *adv* firmemente.

firmness ['fəːmnɪs] *n* firmeza.

first [fəːst] *adj* primeiro ♦ *adv* *(before others)* primeiro; *(when listing reasons etc)* em primeiro lugar ♦ *n* *(person: in race)* primeiro/a; *(AUT)* primeira; *(BRIT: SCH)* menção *f* honrosa; **the ~ of January** primeiro de janeiro *(BR)*, dia um de Janeiro *(PT)*; **at ~** no início; **~ of all** antes de tudo, antes de mais nada; **in the ~ place** em primeiro lugar; **I'll do it ~ thing tomorrow** vou fazê-lo amanhã cedo; **head ~** com a cabeça para a frente; **for the ~ time** pela primeira vez; **from the (very) ~** desde o início; *see also* **fifth**.

first aid *n* pronto socorro.

first-aid kit *n* estojo de pronto socorro.

first-aid post *n* pronto-socorro.

first-class *adj* de primeira classe.

first-class mail *n* correspondência prioritária.

first-hand *adj* de primeira mão.

first lady (*US*) *n* primeira dama.

firstly ['fəːstlɪ] *adv* primeiramente, em primeiro lugar.

first name *n* primeiro nome *m*.

first night *n* (*THEATRE*) estréia.

first-rate *adj* de primeira categoria.

fir tree *n* abeto.

FIS (*BRIT*) *n abbr* (= *Family Income Supplement*) abono-família *m*.

fiscal ['fɪskəl] *adj* fiscal; **~ year** ano-fiscal.

fish [fɪʃ] *n inv* peixe *m* ♦ *vt, vi* pescar; **to go ~ing** ir pescar.
fish out *vt* (*from water*) pescar; (*from box etc*) tirar.
fishbone ['fɪʃbəun] *n* espinha de peixe.
fisherman ['fɪʃəmən] (*irreg*) *n* pescador *m*.
fishery ['fɪʃərɪ] *n* pescaria.
fish factory (*BRIT*) *n* fábrica de processamento de pescados.
fish farm *n* viveiro (de piscicultura).
fish fingers (*BRIT*) *npl* filezinhos *mpl* de peixe.
fish hook *n* anzol *m*.
fishing boat ['fɪʃɪŋ-] *n* barco de pesca.
fishing industry ['fɪʃɪŋ-] *n* indústria da pesca.
fishing line ['fɪʃɪŋ-] *n* linha de pesca.
fishing net ['fɪʃɪŋ-] *n* rede *f* de pesca.
fishing rod ['fɪʃɪŋ-] *n* vara (de pesca).
fishing tackle ['fɪʃɪŋ-] *n* apetrechos *mpl* (de pesca).
fish market *n* mercado de peixe.
fishmonger ['fɪʃmʌŋgə*] *n* peixeiro/a; **~'s (shop)** peixaria.
fish sticks (*US*) *npl* filezinhos *mpl* de peixe.
fishy ['fɪʃɪ] *adj* (*fig*) suspeito.
fission ['fɪʃən] *n* fissão *f*; **nuclear ~** fissão nuclear.
fissure ['fɪʃə*] *n* fenda, fissura.
fist [fɪst] *n* punho.
fistfight ['fɪstfaɪt] *n* briga de socos.
fit [fɪt] *adj* (*MED, SPORT*) em (boa) forma; (*proper*) adequado, apropriado ♦ *vt* (*clothes*) caber em; (*try on: clothes*) experimentar, provar; (*facts*) enquadrar-se *or* condizer com; (*accommodate*) ajustar, adaptar; (*correspond exactly*) encaixar em; (*put in, attach*) colocar; (*equip*) equipar ♦ *vi* (*clothes*) servir; (*in space, gap*) caber; (*correspond*) encaixar-se ♦ *n* (*MED*) ataque *m*; **~ to** bom para; **~ for** adequado para; **this dress is a good/tight ~** este vestido tem um bom corte/está um pouco justo; **a ~ of anger** um acesso de raiva; **to have a ~** (*MED*) sofrer *or* ter um ataque; (*fig: inf*) fazer escândalo; **do as you think** *or* **see ~** faça como você achar melhor; **by ~s and starts** espasmodicamente.
fit in *vi* encaixar-se; (*fig: person*) dar-se bem (com todos).
fit out (*BRIT*) *vt* (*also: ~ up*) equipar.
fitful ['fɪtful] *adj* espasmódico, intermitente.
fitment ['fɪtmənt] *n* móvel *m*.
fitness ['fɪtnɪs] *n* (*MED*) saúde *f*, boa forma; (*of remark*) conveniência.
fitted ['fɪtɪd] *adj* (*cupboards*) embutido; (*kitchen*) com armários embutidos; **~ carpet** carpete *m*.
fitter ['fɪtə*] *n* ajustador(a) *m/f*, montador(a) *m/f*; (*also: gas ~*) gasista *m/f*.
fitting ['fɪtɪŋ] *adj* próprio, apropriado ♦ *n* (*of dress*) prova; **~s** *npl* instalações *fpl*, acessó-

rios *mpl*.
fitting room *n* (*in shop*) cabine *f* (para experimentar roupa).
five [faɪv] *num* cinco; **she is ~ (years old)** ela tem cinco anos; **they live at number ~/at ~ Green Street** eles moram no número cinco/na Green Street número cinco; **there are ~ of us** somos cinco; **all ~ of them came** todos os cinco vieram; **it costs ~ pounds** custa cinco libras; **~ and a quarter/half** cinco e um quarto/e meio; **it's ~ (o'clock)** são cinco horas; **to divide sth into ~** dividir algo em cinco partes; **they are sold in ~s** eles são vendidos em pacotes de cinco.
five-day week *n* semana de cinco dias.
fiver ['faɪvə*] (*inf*) *n* (*BRIT*) nota de cinco libras; (*US*) nota de cinco dólares.
fix [fɪks] *vt* (*secure*) fixar, colocar; (*arrange*) arranjar; (*mend*) consertar; (*meal, drink*) preparar; (*inf: game etc*) arranjar ♦ *n*: **to be in a ~** estar em apuros; **the fight was a ~** a luta foi uma marmelada; **to ~ sth in one's mind** gravar algo.
fix up *vt* (*meeting*) marcar; **to ~ sb up with sth** arranjar algo para alguém.
fixation [fɪk'seɪʃən] *n* fixação *f*.
fixative ['fɪksətɪv] *n* fixador *m*.
fixed [fɪkst] *adj* (*prices etc*) fixo; **how are you ~ for money?** (*inf*) a quantas anda você em matéria de dinheiro?
fixed assets *npl* ativo fixo.
fixture ['fɪkstʃə*] *n* coisa fixa; (*furniture*) móvel *m* fixo; (*SPORT*) desafio, encontro.
fizz [fɪz] *vi* efervescer.
fizzle ['fɪzl] *vi* chiar.
fizzle out *vi* fracassar, falhar.
fizzy ['fɪzɪ] *adj* (*drink*) com gás, gasoso; (*gen*) efervescente.
fjord [fjɔːd] *n* = **fiord**.
FL (*US*) *abbr* (*POST*) = **Florida**.
flabbergasted ['flæbəgɑːstɪd] *adj* pasmado.
flabby ['flæbɪ] *adj* flácido.
flag [flæg] *n* bandeira; (*stone*) laje *f* ♦ *vi* acabar-se, descair; **~ of convenience** bandeira de conveniência.
flag down *vt*: **to ~ sb down** fazer sinais a alguém para que pare.
flagon ['flægən] *n* garrafão *m*.
flagpole ['flægpəul] *n* mastro de bandeira.
flagrant ['fleɪgrənt] *adj* flagrante.
flagship ['flægʃɪp] *n* nau *f* capitânia.
flag stop (*US*) *n* (*for bus*) parada facultativa.
flair [flɛə*] *n* jeito, habilidade *f*.
flak [flæk] *n* (*MIL*) fogo antiaéreo; (*inf: criticism*) críticas *fpl*.
flake [fleɪk] *n* (*of rust, paint*) lasca; (*of snow, soap powder*) floco ♦ *vi* (*also: ~ off*) lascar, descamar-se.
flaky ['fleɪkɪ] *adj* (*paintwork*) laminoso; (*skin*) escamoso; (*pastry*) folhado.
flamboyant [flæm'bɔɪənt] *adj* (*dress*) espalhafatoso; (*person*) extravagante.

NB: European Portuguese adds the following consonants to certain words: **b** (sú(b)dito, su(b)til); **c** (a(c)ção, a(c)cionista, a(c)to); **m** (inde(m)ne); **p** (ado(p)ção, ado(p)tar); *for further details see p. xiii.*

flame [fleɪm] n chama; **to burst into** ~s irromper em chamas; **old** ~ (inf) velha paixão f.

flamingo [fləˈmɪŋɡəu] (pl ~es) n flamingo.

flammable [ˈflæməbl] adj inflamável.

flan [flæn] n torta.

flange [flændʒ] n flange m.

flank [flæŋk] n flanco; (of person) lado ♦ vt ladear.

flannel [ˈflænl] n (also: face ~) pano; (fabric) flanela; (BRIT: inf) conversa fiada; ~s npl calça (BR) or calças fpl (PT) de flanela.

flannelette [flænəˈlet] n baetilha.

flap [flæp] n (of pocket, table) aba; (of envelope) dobra; (wing movement) bater m; (AVIAT) flap m ♦ vt (wings) bater ♦ vi (sail, flag) ondular; (inf: also: be in a ~) estar atarantado.

flapjack [ˈflæpdʒæk] n (US: pancake) panqueca; (BRIT: biscuit) biscoito de aveia.

flare [flɛə*] n fogacho, chama; (MIL) sinal m luminoso; (in skirt etc) folga.

flare up vi chamejar; (fig: person) encolerizar-se; (: revolt) irromper.

flared [ˈflɛəd] adj (trousers) com roda; (skirt) rodado.

flash [flæʃ] n relâmpago; (also: news ~) notícias fpl de última hora; (PHOT) flash m; (of inspiration) lampejo ♦ vt (light, headlights) piscar; (torch) acender; (send: message) transmitir ♦ vi brilhar, relampejar; **in a** ~ num instante; **he** ~**ed by** or **past** passou como um raio; **to** ~ **sth about** (fig: inf) ostentar or exibir algo.

flashback [ˈflæʃbæk] n flashback m.

flashbulb [ˈflæʃbʌlb] n lâmpada de flash.

flash card n (SCH) cartão m.

flashcube [ˈflæʃkjuːb] n cubo de flash.

flasher [ˈflæʃə*] n (AUT) pisca-pisca m.

flashlight [ˈflæʃlaɪt] n lanterna de bolso.

flashpoint [ˈflæʃpɔɪnt] n ponto de centelha.

flashy [ˈflæʃɪ] (pej) adj espalhafatoso.

flask [flɑːsk] n frasco; (also: vacuum ~) garrafa térmica (BR), termo (PT).

flat [flæt] adj chato, plano; (smooth) liso; (battery) descarregado; (tyre) vazio; (beer) choco; (denial) categórico; (MUS) abemolado; (: voice) desafinado ♦ n (BRIT: apartment) apartamento; (MUS) bemol m; (AUT) pneu m furado; ~ **out** (work) a toque de caixa; (race) a toda; ~ **rate of pay** (COMM) salário fixo.

flat-footed [-ˈfutɪd] adj de pés chatos.

flatly [ˈflætlɪ] adv terminantemente.

flatmate [ˈflætmeɪt] (BRIT) n companheiro/a de apartamento.

flatness [ˈflætnɪs] n (of land) planura, lisura.

flatten [ˈflætən] vt (also: ~ out) aplanar; (smooth out) alisar; (demolish) arrasar; (defeat) derrubar.

flatter [ˈflætə*] vt lisonjear; (show to advantage) favorecer.

flatterer [ˈflætərə*] n lisonjeador(a) m/f.

flattering [ˈflætərɪŋ] adj lisonjeiro; (clothes etc) favorecedor(a).

flattery [ˈflætərɪ] n bajulação f.

flatulence [ˈflætjuləns] n flatulência.

flaunt [flɔːnt] vt ostentar, pavonear.

flavour [ˈfleɪvə*] (US **flavor**) n sabor m ♦ vt condimentar, aromatizar; **vanilla-**~**ed** com sabor de baunilha.

flavo(u)ring [ˈfleɪvərɪŋ] n condimento; (synthetic) aromatizante m.

flaw [flɔː] n defeito.

flawless [ˈflɔːlɪs] adj impecável.

flax [flæks] n linho.

flaxen [ˈflæksən] adj de cor de linho.

flea [fliː] n pulga.

flea market n feira de quinquilharias.

fleapit [ˈfliːpɪt] n (cinema) pulgueiro.

fleck [flɛk] n (of dust) partícula; (of mud) salpico; (of paint) pontinho ♦ vt salpicar; **brown** ~**ed with white** marrom salpicado de branco.

fled [flɛd] pt, pp of **flee**.

fledg(e)ling [ˈflɛdʒlɪŋ] n ave f recém-emplumada.

flee [fliː] (pt, pp **fled**) vt fugir de ♦ vi fugir.

fleece [fliːs] n velo; (wool) lã f ♦ vt (inf) pelar, depenar.

fleecy [ˈfliːsɪ] adj (blanket) felpudo; (cloud) fofo.

fleet [fliːt] n (gen, of lorries etc) frota; (of ships) esquadra.

fleeting [ˈfliːtɪŋ] adj fugaz.

Flemish [ˈflɛmɪʃ] adj flamengo ♦ n (LING) flamengo; **the** ~ npl os flamengos.

flesh [flɛʃ] n carne f; (of fruit) polpa; **of** ~ **and blood** de carne e osso.

flesh wound n ferimento de superfície.

flew [fluː] pt of **fly**.

flex [flɛks] n fio ♦ vt (muscles) flexionar.

flexibility [flɛksɪˈbɪlɪtɪ] n flexibilidade f.

flexible [ˈflɛksɪbl] adj flexível.

flick [flɪk] n pancada leve; (with finger) peteleco, piparote m; (with whip) chicotada ♦ vt dar pancada leve em; ~**s** npl (BRIT: inf) cinema m.

flick through vt fus folhear.

flicker [ˈflɪkə*] vi (light) tremeluzir; (flame) tremular ♦ n tremulação f; **a** ~ **of light** um fio de luz.

flick knife (BRIT: irreg) n canivete m de mola.

flier [ˈflaɪə*] n aviador(a) m/f.

flight [flaɪt] n vôo m; (escape) fuga; (of steps) lance m; **to take** ~ fugir, pôr-se em fuga; **to put to** ~ pôr em fuga.

flight attendant (US) n comissário/a de bordo.

flight crew n tripulação f.

flight deck n (AVIAT) cabine f do piloto; (NAUT) pista de aterrissagem (BR) or aterragem (PT).

flight recorder n gravador m de vôo.

flimsy [ˈflɪmzɪ] adj (thin) delgado, franzino; (weak) débil; (excuse) fraco.

flinch [flɪntʃ] vi encolher-se; **to** ~ **from sth/ from doing sth** vacilar diante de algo/em fazer algo.

fling [flɪŋ] (*pt*, *pp* **flung**) *vt* lançar ♦ *n* (*love affair*) caso.

flint [flɪnt] *n* pederneira; (*in lighter*) pedra.

flip [flɪp] *vt* (*turn over*) dar a volta em; (*throw*) jogar; **to ~ a coin** tirar cara ou coroa.

flip through *vt fus* folhear.

flippant ['flɪpənt] *adj* petulante, irreverente.

flipper ['flɪpə*] *n* (*of animal*) nadadeira; (*for swimmer*) pé-de-pato, nadadeira.

flip side *n* (*of record*) outro lado.

flirt [fləːt] *vi* flertar ♦ *n* namorador(a) *m/f*, paquerador(a) *m/f*.

flirtation [fləːˈteɪʃən] *n* flerte *m*, paquera.

flit [flɪt] *vi* esvoaçar.

float [fləut] *n* bóia; (*in procession*) carro alegórico; (*sum of money*) caixa ♦ *vi* flutuar; (*swimmer*) boiar ♦ *vt* fazer flutuar; (*company*) lançar (na Bolsa).

floating ['fləutɪŋ] *adj* flutuante; **~ vote** voto oscilante; **~ voter** indeciso/a.

flock [flɔk] *n* (*of sheep*) rebanho; (*of birds*) bando; (*of people*) multidão *f*.

floe [fləu] *n* (*also: ice ~*) banquisa.

flog [flɔg] *vt* açoitar; (*inf*) vender.

flood [flʌd] *n* enchente *f*, inundação *f*; (*of words, tears etc*) torrente *m* ♦ *vt* inundar, alagar; (*AUT: carburettor*) afogar; **to ~ the market** (*COMM*) inundar o mercado; **in ~** transbordante.

flooding ['flʌdɪŋ] *n* inundação *f*.

floodlight ['flʌdlaɪt] (*irreg: like light*) *n* refletor *m*, holofote *m* ♦ *vt* iluminar com holofotes.

floodlit ['flʌdlɪt] *pt*, *pp of* **floodlight** ♦ *adj* iluminado (por holofotes).

flood tide *n* maré *f* enchente.

floor [flɔː*] *n* chão *m*; (*in house*) soalho; (*storey*) andar *m*; (*of sea*) fundo; (*dance ~*) pista de dança ♦ *vt* (*fig: confuse*) confundir, pasmar; **ground ~** (*BRIT*) *or* **first ~** (*US*) andar térreo (*BR*), rés-do-chão (*PT*); **first ~** (*BRIT*) *or* **second ~** (*US*) primeiro andar; **top ~** último andar; **to have the ~** (*speaker*) ter a palavra.

floorboard ['flɔːbɔːd] *n* tábua de assoalho.

flooring ['flɔːrɪŋ] *n* piso.

floor lamp (*US*) *n* abajur *m* de pé.

floor show *n* show *m*.

floorwalker ['flɔːwɔːkə*] (*esp US*) *n* supervisor(a) *m/f* (numa loja de departamentos).

flop [flɔp] *n* fracasso ♦ *vi* (*fail*) fracassar.

floppy ['flɔpɪ] *adj* frouxo, mole.

floppy disk *n* disquete *m*.

flora ['flɔːrə] *n* flora.

floral ['flɔːrl] *adj* floral.

Florence ['flɔrəns] *n* Florença.

florid ['flɔrɪd] *adj* (*style*) florido; (*complexion*) corado.

florist ['flɔrɪst] *n* florista *m/f*; **~'s (shop)** floricultura.

flotation [fləuˈteɪʃən] *n* (*of shares*) emissão *f*;

(*of company*) lançamento (na Bolsa).

flounce [flauns] *n* babado, debrum *m*.

flounce out *vi* sair indignado.

flounder ['flaundə*] (*pl ~ or ~s*) *n* (*ZOOL*) linguado ♦ *vi* atrapalhar-se.

flour ['flauə*] *n* farinha.

flourish ['flʌrɪʃ] *vi* florescer ♦ *vt* brandir, menear ♦ *n* floreio; (*of trumpets*) fanfarra.

flourishing ['flʌrɪʃɪŋ] *adj* próspero.

flout [flaut] *vt* (*law*) desrespeitar; (*offer*) desprezar.

flow [fləu] *n* (*movement, tide*) fluxo; (*direction*) curso; (*of river*) corrente *f*; (*ELEC, of blood*) circulação *f* ♦ *vi* correr, fluir; (*traffic, blood*) circular; (*robes, hair*) flutuar.

flow chart *n* fluxograma *m*.

flow diagram *n* fluxograma *m*.

flower ['flauə*] *n* flor *f* ♦ *vi* florescer, florir; **in ~** em flor.

flower bed *n* canteiro.

flowerpot ['flauəpɔt] *n* vaso.

flowery ['flauərɪ] *adj* florido.

flown [fləun] *pp of* **fly**.

flu [fluː] *n* gripe *f*.

fluctuate ['flʌktjueɪt] *vi* flutuar, variar.

fluctuation [flʌktjuˈeɪʃən] *n* flutuação *f*, oscilação *f*.

flue [fluː] *n* fumeiro.

fluency ['fluːənsɪ] *n* fluência.

fluent ['fluːənt] *adj* (*speech*) fluente; **he speaks ~ French, he's ~ in French** ele fala francês fluentemente.

fluently ['fluːəntlɪ] *adv* fluentemente.

fluff [flʌf] *n* felpa, penugem *f*.

fluffy ['flʌfɪ] *adj* macio, fofo; **~ toy** brinquedo de pelúcia.

fluid ['fluːɪd] *adj* fluido ♦ *n* fluido; (*in diet*) líquido.

fluid ounce (*BRIT*) *n* = 0.028 *l*; 0.05 *pints*.

fluke [fluːk] (*inf*) *n* sorte *f*.

flummox ['flʌməks] *vt* desconcertar.

flung [flʌŋ] *pt*, *pp of* **fling**.

flunky ['flʌŋkɪ] *n* lacaio.

fluorescent [fluəˈrɛsnt] *adj* fluorescente.

fluoride ['fluəraɪd] *n* fluoreto ♦ *cpd*: **~ toothpaste** pasta de dentes com flúor.

fluorine ['fluəriːn] *n* flúor *m*.

flurry ['flʌrɪ] *n* (*of snow*) lufada; (*haste*) agitação *f*; **~ of activity** muita atividade.

flush [flʌʃ] *n* (*on face*) rubor *m*; (*plenty*) abundância ♦ *vt* lavar com água; (*also: ~ out*) levantar ♦ *vi* ruborizar-se; **~ with** rente com; **to ~ the toilet** dar descarga; **hot ~es** (*MED*) calores.

flushed [flʌʃt] *adj* ruborizado, corado.

fluster ['flʌstə*] *n* agitação *f* ♦ *vt* atrapalhar, desconcertar.

flustered ['flʌstəd] *adj* atrapalhado.

flute [fluːt] *n* flauta.

fluted ['fluːtɪd] *adj* acanelado.

flutter ['flʌtə*] *n* agitação *f*; (*of wings*) bater *m*; (*inf: bet*) aposta ♦ *vi* esvoaçar.

NB: European Portuguese adds the following consonants to certain words: **b** (sú(b)dito, su(b)til); **c** (a(c)ção, a(c)cionista, a(c)to); **m** (inde(m)ne); **p** (ado(p)ção, ado(p)tar); *for further details see p. xiii.*

flux [flʌks] *n* fluxo; **in a state of** ~ mudando continuamente.

fly [flaɪ] (*pt* **flew**, *pp* **flown**) *n* (*insect*) mosca; (*on trousers*: *also*: *flies*) braguilha ♦ *vt* (*plane*) pilotar; (*passengers*, *cargo*) transportar (de avião); (*flag*) hastear; (*distances*) percorrer; (*kite*) soltar, empinar ♦ *vi* voar; (*passengers*) ir de avião; (*escape*) fugir; (*flag*) hastear-se; **to** ~ **open** abrir-se bruscamente; **to** ~ **off the handle** perder as estribeiras.

fly away *vi* ir-se.

fly in *vi* chegar.

fly off *vi* ir-se.

fly out *vi* sair (de avião).

fly-fishing *n* pesca com iscas artificiais.

flying [ˈflaɪɪŋ] *n* (*activity*) aviação *f* ♦ *adj*: ~ **visit** visita de médico; **with** ~ **colours** brilhantemente; **he doesn't like** ~ ele não gosta de andar de avião.

flying buttress *n* arcobotante *m*.

flying saucer *n* disco voador.

flying start *n*: **to get off to a** ~ (*in race*) disparar; (*fig*) começar muito bem.

fly leaf [ˈflaɪliːf] (*irreg*) *n* guarda (*num livro*).

flyover [ˈflaɪəʊvə*] (*BRIT*) *n* (*bridge*) viaduto.

flypast [ˈflaɪpɑːst] *n* desfile *m* aéreo.

flysheet [ˈflaɪʃiːt] *n* (*for tent*) duplo teto.

flywheel [ˈflaɪwiːl] *n* volante *m*.

FM *abbr* (*BRIT*: *MIL*) = **field marshal**; (*RADIO*: = *frequency modulation*) FM.

FMB (*US*) *n abbr* = **Federal Maritime Board**.

FMCS (*US*) *n abbr* (= *Federal Mediation and Conciliation Service*) ≈ Justiça do Trabalho.

FO (*BRIT*) *n abbr* = **Foreign Office**.

foal [fəʊl] *n* potro.

foam [fəʊm] *n* espuma ♦ *vi* espumar.

foam rubber *n* espuma de borracha.

FOB *abbr* (= *free on board*) FOB.

fob [fɔb] *vt*: **to** ~ **sb off with sth** despachar alguém com algo; **to** ~ **sth off on sb** impingir algo a alguém.

foc (*BRIT*) *abbr* = **free of charge**.

focal [ˈfəʊkəl] *adj* focal.

focal point *n* foco.

focus [ˈfəʊkəs] (*pl* ~**es**) *n* foco ♦ *vt* (*field glasses etc*) enfocar ♦ *vi*: **to** ~ **on** enfocar, focalizar; **in/out of** ~ enfocado/desenfocado, em foco/fora de foco.

fodder [ˈfɔdə*] *n* forragem *f*.

FOE *n abbr* (= *Friends of the Earth*) organização ecologista; (*US*: = *Fraternal Order of Eagles*) associação beneficente.

foe [fəʊ] *n* inimigo.

foetus [ˈfiːtəs] (*US* **fetus**) *n* feto.

fog [fɔg] *n* nevoeiro.

fogbound [ˈfɔgbaʊnd] *adj* imobilizado pelo nevoeiro.

foggy [ˈfɔgɪ] *adj* nevoento.

fog lamp (*US* **fog light**) *n* farol *m* de neblina.

foible [ˈfɔɪbl] *n* fraqueza, ponto fraco.

foil [fɔɪl] *vt* frustrar ♦ *n* folha metálica; (*also*: *kitchen* ~) folha or papel *m* de alumínio; (*FENCING*) florete *m*; **to act as a** ~ **to** (*fig*) dar realce a.

foist [fɔɪst] *vt*: **to** ~ **sth on sb** impingir algo a alguém.

fold [fəʊld] *n* (*bend*, *crease*) dobra, vinco, prega; (*of skin*) ruga; (*AGR*) redil *m*, curral *m* ♦ *vt* dobrar; **to** ~ **one's arms** cruzar os braços.

fold up *vi* (*map etc*) dobrar; (*business*) abrir falência ♦ *vt* (*map etc*) dobrar.

folder [ˈfəʊldə*] *n* (*for papers*) pasta; (: *binder*) fichário; (*brochure*) folheto.

folding [ˈfəʊldɪŋ] *adj* (*chair*, *bed*) dobrável.

foliage [ˈfəʊlɪɪdʒ] *n* folhagem *f*.

folk [fəʊk] *npl* gente *f* ♦ *adj* popular, folclórico; ~**s** *npl* (*family*) família, parentes *mpl*; (*people*) gente *f*.

folklore [ˈfəʊklɔː*] *n* folclore *m*.

folksong [ˈfəʊksɔŋ] *n* canção *f* popular *or* folclórica.

follow [ˈfɔləʊ] *vt* seguir ♦ *vi* seguir; (*result*) resultar; **to** ~ **sb's advice** seguir o conselho de alguém; **I don't quite** ~ **you** não consigo acompanhar o seu raciocínio; **to** ~ **in sb's footsteps** seguir os passos de alguém; **it doesn't** ~ **that** ... (isso) não quer dizer que ...; **he** ~**ed suit** ele fez o mesmo.

follow out *vt* (*idea*, *plan*) levar a cabo, executar.

follow through *vt* levar a cabo, executar.

follow up *vt* (*letter*) responder a; (*offer*) levar adiante; (*case*) acompanhar.

follower [ˈfɔləʊə*] *n* seguidor(a) *m/f*; (*POL*) partidário/a.

following [ˈfɔləʊɪŋ] *adj* seguinte ♦ *n* séquito, adeptos *mpl*.

follow-up *n* continuação *f* ♦ *cpd*: ~ **letter** carta suplementar de reforço.

folly [ˈfɔlɪ] *n* loucura.

fond [fɔnd] *adj* (*loving*) amoroso, carinhoso; **to be** ~ **of** gostar de.

fondle [ˈfɔndl] *vt* acariciar.

fondly [ˈfɔndlɪ] *adv* (*lovingly*) afetuosamente; (*naïvely*): **he** ~ **believed that** ... ele acreditava piamente que ....

fondness [ˈfɔndnɪs] *n* (*for things*) gosto, afeição *f*; (*for people*) carinho.

font [fɔnt] *n* (*REL*) pia batismal; (*TYP*) fonte *f*, família.

food [fuːd] *n* comida.

food mixer *n* batedeira.

food poisoning *n* intoxicação *f* alimentar.

food processor *n* multiprocessador *m* de cozinha.

foodstuffs [ˈfuːdstʌfs] *npl* gêneros *mpl* alimentícios.

fool [fuːl] *n* tolo/a; (*HISTORY*: *of king*) bobo; (*CULIN*) purê *m* de frutas com creme ♦ *vt* enganar ♦ *vi* (*gen*: ~ *around*) brincar; (*waste time*) fazer bagunça; **to make a** ~ **of sb** (*ridicule*) ridicularizar alguém; (*trick*) fazer alguém de bobo; **to make a** ~ **of o.s.** fazer papel de bobo, fazer-se de bobo; **you can't** ~ **me** você não pode me fazer de bobo.

fool about (*pej*) *vi* (*waste time*) fazer bagunça; (*behave foolishly*) fazer-se de bobo.

fool around (*pej*) *vi* (*waste time*) fazer bagunça; (*behave foolishly*) fazer-se de

bobo.
foolhardy ['fu:lhɑːdɪ] *adj* temerário.
foolish ['fu:lɪʃ] *adj* bobo; (*stupid*) burro; (*careless*) imprudente.
foolishly ['fu:lɪʃlɪ] *adv* imprudentemente.
foolishness ['fu:lɪʃnɪs] *n* tolice *f*.
foolproof ['fu:lpruːf] *adj* (*plan etc*) infalível.
foolscap ['fu:lskæp] *n* papel *m* ofício.
foot [fut] (*pl* **feet**) *n* pé *m*; (*measure*) pé (=*304 mm*; *12 inches*); (*of animal*) pata ♦ *vt* (*bill*) pagar; **on ~** a pé; **to find one's feet** (*fig*) ambientar-se; **to put one's ~ down** (*AUT*) acelerar; (*say no*) bater o pé.
footage ['futɪdʒ] *n* (*CINEMA: length*) ≈ metragem *f*; (: *material*) seqüências *fpl*.
foot and mouth (disease) *n* febre *f* aftosa.
football ['futbɔːl] *n* bola; (*game: BRIT*) futebol *m*; (: *US*) futebol norte-americano.
footballer ['futbɔːlə*] *n* futebolista *m*, jogador *m* de futebol.
football ground *n* campo de futebol.
football match (*BRIT*) *n* partida de futebol.
football player *n* jogador *m* de futebol.
footbrake ['futbreɪk] *n* freio (*BR*) or travão *m* (*PT*) de pé.
footbridge ['futbrɪdʒ] *n* passarela.
foothills ['futhɪlz] *npl* contraforte *m*.
foothold ['futhəuld] *n* apoio para o pé.
footing ['futɪŋ] *n* (*fig*) posição *f*; **to lose one's ~** escorregar; **on an equal ~** em pé de igualdade.
footlights ['futlaɪts] *npl* ribalta.
footman ['futmən] (*irreg*) *n* lacaio.
footnote ['futnəut] *n* nota ao pé da página, nota de rodapé.
footpath ['futpɑːθ] *n* senda, vereda, caminho; (*pavement*) calçada.
footprint ['futprɪnt] *n* pegada.
footrest ['futrest] *n* suporte *m* para os pés.
footsore ['futsɔː*] *adj* com os pés doloridos.
footstep ['futstɛp] *n* passo.
footwear ['futwɛə*] *n* calçados *mpl*.
FOR *abbr* (= *free on rail*) franco sobre vagão.
for [fɔː*] *prep* (*gen*) para; (*as, in exchange for, because of*) por; (*during*) durante; (*in spite of*): **~ all that** apesar de tudo isso ♦ *conj* pois, porque; **I haven't seen him ~ a week** faz uma semana que não o vejo; **he was away ~ 2 years** esteve fora 2 anos; **he went ~ the paper** foi pegar o jornal; **it was sold ~ £100** foi vendido por £100; **~ sale** vende-se; **the train ~ London** o trem para Londres; **it's time ~ lunch** é hora de almoçar; **what ~?** (*why*) por quê?; (*to what end*) para quê?; **what's it ~?** para que serve?; **there's nothing ~ it but to jump** (*BRIT*) não há outra solução senão saltar; **the campaign ~** a campanha pró *or* a favor de.
forage ['fɔrɪdʒ] *n* forragem *f* ♦ *vi* ir à procura de alimentos.
forage cap *n* casquete *m*.
foray ['fɔreɪ] *n* incursão *f*.

forbad(e) [fə'bæd] *pt of* **forbid**.
forbearing [fɔː'bɛərɪŋ] *adj* indulgente.
forbid [fə'bɪd] (*pt* **forbad(e)**, *pp* **forbidden**) *vt* proibir; **to ~ sb to do** proibir alguém de fazer.
forbidden [fə'bɪdn] *pp of* **forbid** ♦ *adj* proibido.
forbidding [fə'bɪdɪŋ] *adj* (*gloomy*) lúgubre; (*severe*) severo.
force [fɔːs] *n* força ♦ *vt* (*gen, smile*) forçar; (*confession*) arrancar à força; **the F~s** *npl* (*BRIT*) as Forças Armadas; **to ~ sb to do** forçar alguém a fazer; **in ~** em vigor; **to come into ~** entrar em vigor; **a ~ 5 wind** um vento força 5; **the sales ~** (*COMM*) a equipe de vendas; **to join ~s** unir forças; **by ~** à força.
force back *vt* (*crowd, enemy*) fazer recuar; (*tears*) reprimir.
force down *vt* (*food*) forçar-se a comer.
forced [fɔːst] *adj* forçado.
force-feed ['fɔːsfiːd] (*irreg*) *vt* alimentar à força.
forceful ['fɔːsful] *adj* enérgico, vigoroso.
forcemeat ['fɔːsmiːt] (*BRIT*) *n* (*CULIN*) recheio.
forceps ['fɔːsɛps] *npl* fórceps *m inv*.
forcibly ['fɔːsəblɪ] *adv* à força.
ford [fɔːd] *n* vau *m* ♦ *vt* vadear.
fore [fɔː*] *n*: **to bring to the ~** pôr em evidência; **to come to the ~** (*person*) salientar-se.
forearm ['fɔːrɑːm] *n* antebraço.
forebear ['fɔːbɛə*] *n* antepassado.
foreboding [fɔː'bəudɪŋ] *n* mau presságio.
forecast ['fɔːkɑːst] (*irreg: like* **cast**) *n* prognóstico, previsão *f*; (*also: weather ~*) previsão do tempo ♦ *vt* prognosticar, prever.
foreclose [fɔː'kləuz] *vt* (*LAW: also: ~ on*) executar.
foreclosure [fɔː'kləuʒə*] *n* execução *f* de uma hipoteca.
forecourt ['fɔːkɔːt] *n* (*of garage*) área de estacionamento.
forefathers ['fɔːfɑːðəz] *npl* antepassados *mpl*.
forefinger ['fɔːfɪŋɡə*] *n* (dedo) indicador *m*.
forefront ['fɔːfrʌnt] *n*: **in the ~ of** em primeiro plano em.
forego (*irreg: like* **go**) *vt* = **forgo**.
foregoing ['fɔːɡəuɪŋ] *adj* acima mencionado ♦ *n*: **the ~** o supracitado.
foregone ['fɔːɡɔn] *pp of* **forego** ♦ *adj*: **it's a ~ conclusion** é uma conclusão inevitável.
foreground ['fɔːɡraund] *n* primeiro plano ♦ *cpd* (*COMPUT*) de primeiro plano.
forehand ['fɔːhænd] *n* (*TENNIS*) golpe *m* de frente.
forehead ['fɔrɪd] *n* testa.
foreign ['fɔrɪn] *adj* estrangeiro; (*trade*) exterior.
foreign body *n* corpo estranho.
foreign currency *n* câmbio, divisas *fpl*.
foreigner ['fɔrɪnə*] *n* estrangeiro/a.

NB: *European Portuguese adds the following consonants to certain words*: **b** (sú(b)dito, su(b)til); **c** (a(c)ção, a(c)cionista, a(c)to); **m** (inde(m)ne); **p** (ado(p)ção, ado(p)tar); *for further details see p. xiii.*

foreign exchange n (*system*) câmbio; (*money*) divisas *fpl*.
foreign exchange market n mercado de câmbio.
foreign exchange rate n taxa de câmbio.
foreign investment n investimento estrangeiro.
Foreign Office (*BRIT*) n Ministério das Relações Exteriores.
foreign secretary (*BRIT*) n ministro das Relações Exteriores.
foreleg ['fɔːleg] n perna dianteira.
foreman ['fɔːmən] (*irreg*) n capataz m; (*in construction*) contramestre m; (*LAW: of jury*) primeiro jurado.
foremost ['fɔːməust] adj principal ♦ adv: **first and** ~ antes de mais nada.
forename ['fɔːneɪm] n prenome m.
forensic [fə'rensɪk] adj forense; ~ **medicine** medicina legal; ~ **expert** perito/a criminal.
forerunner ['fɔːrʌnə*] n precursor(a) m/f.
foresee [fɔː'siː] (*irreg: like* **see**) vt prever.
foreseeable [fɔː'siːəbl] adj previsível.
foreshadow [fɔː'fædəu] vt prefigurar.
foreshorten [fɔː'fɔːtn] vt escorçar.
foresight ['fɔːsaɪt] n previdência.
foreskin ['fɔːskɪn] n (*ANAT*) prepúcio.
forest ['fɔrɪst] n floresta.
forestall [fɔː'stɔːl] vt prevenir.
forestry ['fɔrɪstrɪ] n silvicultura.
foretaste ['fɔːteɪst] n antegosto, antegozo; (*sample*) amostra.
foretell [fɔː'tel] (*irreg: like* **tell**) vt predizer, profetizar.
forethought ['fɔːθɔːt] n previdência.
forever [fə'rɛvə*] adv para sempre; (*a long time*) muito tempo, um tempão (*inf*); **he's** ~ **forgetting my name** ele vive esquecendo o meu nome.
forewarn [fɔː'wɔːn] vt prevenir.
forewent pt of **forego**.
foreword ['fɔːwəːd] n prefácio.
forfeit ['fɔːfɪt] n prenda, perda; (*fine*) multa ♦ vt perder (direito a); (*one's life, health*) pagar com.
forgave [fə'geɪv] pt of **forgive**.
forge [fɔːdʒ] n forja; (*smithy*) ferraria ♦ vt (*signature, money*) falsificar; (*metal*) forjar.
forge ahead vi avançar constantemente.
forger ['fɔːdʒə*] n falsificador(a) m/f.
forgery ['fɔːdʒərɪ] n falsificação f.
forget [fə'get] (*pt* **forgot**, *pp* **forgotten**) vt, vi esquecer.
forgetful [fə'getful] adj esquecido.
forgetfulness [fə'getfulnɪs] n esquecimento.
forget-me-not n miosótis m.
forgive [fə'gɪv] (*irreg: like* **give**) vt perdoar; **to** ~ **sb for sth** perdoar algo a alguém, perdoar alguém de algo.
forgiveness [fə'gɪvnɪs] n perdão m.
forgiving [fə'gɪvɪŋ] adj clemente.
forgo [fɔː'gəu] (*irreg: like* **go**) vt (*give up*) renunciar a; (*go without*) abster-se de.
forgot [fə'gɔt] pt of **forget**.
forgotten [fə'gɔtn] pp of **forget**.

fork [fɔːk] n (*for eating*) garfo; (*for gardening*) forquilha; (*of roads*) bifurcação f ♦ vi (*road*) bifurcar-se.
fork out (*inf*) vt (*pay*) desembolsar, morrer em ♦ vi (*pay*) descolar uma grana.
forked [fɔːkt] adj (*lightning*) em ziguezague.
fork-lift truck n empilhadeira.
forlorn [fə'lɔːn] adj desesperado; (*abandoned*) abandonado; (*attempt*) desesperado; (*hope*) último.
form [fɔːm] n forma; (*SCH*) série f; (*questionnaire*) formulário ♦ vt formar; **in the** ~ **of** na forma de; **to** ~ **part of sth** fazer parte de algo; **to** ~ **a queue** (*BRIT*) fazer fila; **to be in good** ~ (*SPORT, fig*) estar em forma; **in top** ~ em plena forma.
formal ['fɔːməl] adj (*offer, receipt*) oficial; (*person etc*) cerimonioso; (*occasion, dinner*) formal; (*dress*) a rigor (*BR*), de cerimônia (*PT*); (*ART, PHILOSOPHY*) formal.
formality [fɔː'mælɪtɪ] n (*of person*) formalismo; (*formal requirement*) formalidade f; (*ceremony*) cerimônia; **formalities** npl formalidades.
formalize ['fɔːməlaɪz] vt formalizar.
formally ['fɔːməlɪ] adv oficialmente, formalmente; (*in a formal way*) formalmente.
format ['fɔːmæt] n formato ♦ vt (*COMPUT*) formatar.
formation [fɔː'meɪʃən] n formação f.
formative ['fɔːmətɪv] adj (*years*) formativo.
former ['fɔːmə*] adj anterior; (*earlier*) antigo; (*ex*) ex-; **the** ~ ... **the latter** ... aquele ... este ...; **the** ~ **president** o ex-presidente.
formerly ['fɔːməlɪ] adv antigamente.
form feed n (*on printer*) alimentar formulário.
formidable ['fɔːmɪdəbl] adj terrível, temível.
formula ['fɔːmjulə] n fórmula; **F~ One** (*AUT*) Fórmula Um.
formulate ['fɔːmjuleɪt] vt formular.
fornicate ['fɔːnɪkeɪt] vi fornicar.
forsake [fə'seɪk] (*pt* **forsook**, *pp* **forsaken**) vt abandonar; (*plan*) renunciar a.
forsaken [fə'seɪkən] pp of **forsake**.
forsook [fə'suk] pt of **forsake**.
fort [fɔːt] n forte m; **to hold the** ~ (*fig*) agüentar a mão.
forte ['fɔːtɪ] n forte m.
forth [fɔːθ] adv para adiante; **back and** ~ de cá para lá; **and so** ~ e assim por diante.
forthcoming ['fɔːθ'kʌmɪŋ] adj próximo, que está para aparecer; (*character*) comunicativo; (*book*) a ser publicado.
forthright ['fɔːθraɪt] adj franco.
forthwith ['fɔːθ'wɪθ] adv em seguida.
fortieth ['fɔːtɪɪθ] num quadragésimo; *see also* **fifth**.
fortification [fɔːtɪfɪ'keɪʃən] n fortificação f.
fortified wine ['fɔːtɪfaɪd-] n vinho generoso.
fortify ['fɔːtɪfaɪ] vt fortalecer.
fortitude ['fɔːtɪtjuːd] n fortaleza.
fortnight ['fɔːtnaɪt] n quinzena, quinze dias mpl.
fortnightly ['fɔːtnaɪtlɪ] adj quinzenal ♦ adv

quinzenalmente.

FORTRAN ['fɔːtræn] n FORTRAN m.

fortress ['fɔːtrɪs] n fortaleza.

fortuitous [fɔːˈtjuːɪtəs] adj fortuito.

fortunate ['fɔːtʃənɪt] adj: **to be ~** ter sorte; **it is ~ that** ... é uma sorte que ....

fortunately ['fɔːtʃənɪtlɪ] adv felizmente.

fortune ['fɔːtʃən] n sorte f; (wealth) fortuna; **to make a ~** fazer fortuna.

fortune-teller n adivinho/a.

forty ['fɔːtɪ] num quarenta; see also **fifty**.

forum ['fɔːrəm] n foro.

forward ['fɔːwəd] adj (movement) para a frente; (position) avançado; (front) dianteiro; (not shy) imodesto, presunçoso; (COMM: delivery) futuro; (: sales, exchange) a termo ♦ n (SPORT) atacante m ♦ adv para a frente ♦ vt (letter) remeter; (goods, parcel) expedir; (career) promover; **to move ~** avançar; **"please ~"** "por favor remeta a novo endereço"; **~ planning** planejamento para o futuro.

forward(s) ['fɔːwəd(z)] adv para a frente.

forwent [fɔːˈwɛnt] pt of **forgo**.

fossil ['fɔsl] n fóssil m; **~ fuel** combustível m fóssil.

foster ['fɔstə*] vt fomentar.

foster brother n irmão m de criação.

foster child (irreg) n filho adotivo.

foster mother n mãe f adotiva.

fought [fɔːt] pt, pp of **fight**.

foul [faul] adj sujo, porco; (food) podre; (weather) horrível; (smell etc) nojento; (language) obsceno; (deed) infame ♦ n (FOOTBALL) falta ♦ vt (dirty) sujar; (block) entupir; (football player) cometer uma falta contra; (entangle: anchor, propeller) enredar.

foul play n (SPORT) jogada suja; (LAW) crime m.

found [faund] pt, pp of **find** ♦ vt (establish) fundar.

foundation [faunˈdeɪʃən] n (act) fundação f; (basis) base f; (also: ~ cream) creme m base; **~s** npl (of building) alicerces mpl; **to lay the ~s** (fig) lançar os alicerces.

foundation stone n pedra fundamental.

founder ['faundə*] n fundador(a) m/f ♦ vi naufragar.

founding ['faundɪŋ] n fundação f ♦ adj fundador(a).

foundry ['faundrɪ] n fundição f.

fount [faunt] n fonte f.

fountain ['fauntɪn] n chafariz m.

fountain pen n caneta-tinteiro f.

four [fɔː*] num quatro; **on all ~s** de quatro; see also **five**.

four-poster n (also: ~ bed) cama com colunas.

foursome ['fɔːsəm] n grupo de quatro pessoas.

fourteen ['fɔːˈtiːn] num catorze; see also **five**.

fourteenth ['fɔːˈtiːnθ] num décimo-quarto; see

also **fifth**.

fourth [fɔːθ] adj quarto ♦ n (AUT: also: ~ gear) quarta; see also **fifth**.

four-wheel drive n (AUT): **with ~** com tração nas quatro rodas.

fowl [faul] n ave f (doméstica).

fox [fɔks] n raposa ♦ vt deixar perplexo.

fox fur n raposa.

foxglove ['fɔksglʌv] n (BOT) dedaleira.

fox-hunting n caça à raposa.

foxtrot ['fɔkstrɔt] n foxtrote m.

foyer ['fɔɪeɪ] n vestíbulo, saguão m.

FP n abbr (BRIT) = **former pupil**; (US) = **fire-plug**.

FPA (BRIT) n abbr = **Family Planning Association**.

Fr. abbr (REL: = father) P.; (: = friar) Fr.

fr. abbr (= franc) fr.

fracas ['fræːkɑː] n desordem f, rixa.

fraction ['frækʃən] n fração f.

fractionally ['frækʃnəlɪ] adv: **~ smaller** etc um pouquinho menor etc.

fractious ['frækʃəs] adj irascível.

fracture ['fræktʃə*] n fratura ♦ vt fraturar.

fragile ['frædʒaɪl] adj frágil.

fragment ['frægmənt] n fragmento.

fragmentary ['frægməntərɪ] adj fragmentário.

fragrance ['freɪgrəns] n fragrância.

fragrant ['freɪgrənt] adj fragrante, perfumado.

frail [freɪl] adj (fragile) frágil, quebradiço; (weak) delicado.

frame [freɪm] n (of building) estrutura; (body) corpo; (TECH) armação f; (of picture, door) moldura; (of spectacles: also: ~s) armação f, aro ♦ vt enquadrar, encaixilhar; (reply) formular; (inf) incriminar; **~ of mind** estado de espírito.

framework ['freɪmwɜːk] n armação f; (fig) sistema m, quadro.

France [frɑːns] n França.

franchise ['fræntʃaɪz] n (POL) direito de voto; (COMM) concessão f.

franchisee [fræntʃaɪˈziː] n concessionário/a.

franchiser ['fræntʃaɪzə*] n concedente m/f.

frank [fræŋk] adj franco ♦ vt (letter) franquear.

Frankfurt ['fræŋkfəːt] n Frankfurt (BR), Francoforte (PT).

frankfurter ['fræŋkfəːtə*] n salsicha de cachorro quente.

franking machine ['fræŋkɪŋ-] n máquina de selagem.

frankly ['fræŋklɪ] adv francamente.

frankness ['fræŋknɪs] n franqueza.

frantic ['fræntɪk] adj frenético; (person) fora de si.

frantically ['fræntɪklɪ] adv freneticamente.

fraternal [frəˈtəːnl] adj fraterno.

fraternity [frəˈtəːnɪtɪ] n (club) fraternidade f; (US) clube m de estudantes; (guild) confraria.

fraternize ['frætənaɪz] vi confraternizar.

NB: European Portuguese adds the following consonants to certain words: **b** (sú(b)dito, su(b)til); **c** (a(c)ção, a(c)cionista, a(c)to); **m** (inde(m)ne); **p** (ado(p)ção, ado(p)tar); *for further details see p. xiii.*

fraud [frɔːd] *n* fraude *f*; (*person*) impostor(a) *m/f*.

fraudulent ['frɔːdjulənt] *adj* fraudulento.

fraught [frɔːt] *adj* tenso; ~ **with** repleto de.

fray [freɪ] *n* combate *m*, luta ♦ *vt* esfiapar ♦ *vi* esfiapar-se; **tempers were** ~**ed** estavam com os nervos em frangalhos.

FRB (*US*) *n abbr* = **Federal Reserve Board**.

FRCM (*BRIT*) *n abbr* = **Fellow of the Royal College of Music**.

FRCO (*BRIT*) *n abbr* = **Fellow of the Royal College of Organists**.

FRCP (*BRIT*) *n abbr* = **Fellow of the Royal College of Physicians**.

FRCS (*BRIT*) *n abbr* = **Fellow of the Royal College of Surgeons**.

freak [friːk] *n* (*person*) anormal *m/f*; (*event*) anomalia; (*thing*) aberração *f*; (*inf: enthusiast*): **health** ~ maníaco/a com a saúde.

freak out (*inf*) *vi* (*on drugs*) baratinar-se; (*get angry*) ficar uma fera.

freakish ['friːkɪʃ] *adj* anormal.

freckle ['frɛkl] *n* sarda.

free [friː] *adj* livre; (*not fixed*) solto; (*gratis*) gratuito; (*liberal*) generoso ♦ *vt* (*prisoner etc*) pôr em liberdade; (*jammed object*) soltar; **to give sb a** ~ **hand** dar carta branca a alguém; ~ **and easy** informal; **admission** ~ entrada livre; ~ (**of charge**) grátis, de graça.

freebie ['friːbɪ] (*inf*) *n* brinde *m*; (*trip etc*): **it's a** ~ está tudo pago.

freedom ['friːdəm] *n* liberdade *f*.

freedom fighter *n* lutador(a) *m/f* pela liberdade.

free enterprise *n* livre iniciativa.

free-for-all *n* quebra-quebra *m*.

free gift *n* brinde *m*.

freehold ['friːhəuld] *n* propriedade *f* livre e alodial.

free kick *n* (tiro) livre *m*.

freelance ['friːlɑːns] *adj* autônomo.

freelancer ['friːlɑːnsə*] *n* free-lance *m/f*.

freeloader ['friːləudə*] (*pej*) *n* sanguessuga *m*.

freely ['friːlɪ] *adv* livremente.

freemason ['friːmeɪsən] *n* maçom *m*.

freemasonry ['friːmeɪsnrɪ] *n* maçonaria.

freepost ['friːpəust] *n* porte *m* pago.

free-range *n* (*egg*) caseiro.

free sample *n* amostra grátis.

free speech *n* liberdade *f* de expressão.

free trade *n* livre comércio.

freeway ['friːweɪ] (*US*) *n* auto-estrada.

freewheel [friː'wiːl] *vi* ir em ponto morto.

freewheeling [friː'wiːlɪŋ] *adj* independente, livre.

free will *n* livre arbítrio; **of one's own** ~ por sua própria vontade.

freeze [friːz] (*pt* **froze**, *pp* **frozen**) *vi* gelar (-se), congelar-se ♦ *vt* gelar; (*prices, food, salaries*) congelar ♦ *n* geada, congelamento.

freeze over *vi* (*lake, river*) gelar; (*windscreen*) cobrir-se de gelo.

freeze up *vi* gelar.

freeze-dried *adj* liofilizado.

freezer ['friːzə*] *n* congelador *m*, freezer *m* (*BR*).

freezing ['friːzɪŋ] *adj*: ~ (**cold**) (*room etc*) glacial; (*person, hands*) gelado ♦ *n*: **3 degrees below** ~ 3 graus abaixo de zero.

freezing point *n* ponto de congelamento.

freight [freɪt] *n* (*goods*) carga; (*money charged*) frete *m*; ~ **forward** frete pago na chegada; ~ **inward** frete incluído no preço.

freight car (*US*) *n* vagão *m* de carga.

freighter ['freɪtə*] *n* cargueiro.

freight forwarder [-'fɔːwədə*] *n* despachante *m/f*.

freight train (*US*) *n* trem *m* de carga.

French [frɛntʃ] *adj* francês/esa ♦ *n* (*LING*) francês *m*; **the** ~ *npl* os franceses.

French bean *n* feijão *m* comum.

French-Canadian *adj* franco-canadense ♦ *n* canadense *m/f* francês/esa *or* da parte francesa; (*LING*) francês *m* do Canadá.

French dressing *n* (*CULIN*) molho francês (de salada).

French fried potatoes (*US* **French fries**) *npl* batatas *fpl* fritas.

French Guiana [-gaɪ'ænə] *n* Guiana Francesa.

Frenchman ['frɛntʃmən] (*irreg*) *n* francês *m*.

French Riviera *n*: **the** ~ a Costa Azul.

French window *n* porta-janela, janela de batente.

Frenchwoman ['frɛntʃwumən] (*irreg*) *n* francesa.

frenetic [frə'nɛtɪk] *adj* frenético.

frenzy ['frɛnzɪ] *n* frenesi *m*.

frequency ['friːkwənsɪ] *n* freqüência.

frequency modulation *n* freqüência modulada.

frequent [*adj* 'friːkwənt, *vt* frɪ'kwɛnt] *adj* freqüente ♦ *vt* freqüentar.

frequently ['friːkwəntlɪ] *adv* freqüentemente, a miúdo.

fresco ['frɛskəu] *n* fresco.

fresh [frɛʃ] *adj* fresco; (*new*) novo; (*cheeky*) atrevido; **to make a** ~ **start** começar de novo.

freshen ['frɛʃən] *vi* (*wind, air*) tornar-se mais forte.

freshen up *vi* (*person*) lavar-se, refrescar-se.

freshener ['frɛʃnə*] *n*: **skin** ~ refrescante *m* da pele; **air** ~ purificador *m* de ar.

fresher ['frɛʃə*] (*BRIT: inf*) *n* (*SCH*) calouro/a.

freshly ['frɛʃlɪ] *adv* (*newly*) novamente; (*recently*) recentemente.

freshman ['frɛʃmən] (*irreg*) *n* (*SCH*) calouro/a.

freshness ['frɛʃnɪs] *n* frescura.

freshwater ['frɛʃwɔːtə*] *adj* de água doce.

fret [frɛt] *vi* afligir-se.

fretful ['frɛtful] *adj* irritável.

Freudian ['frɔɪdɪən] *adj* freudiano; ~ **slip** ato falho.

FRG *n abbr* (= *Federal Republic of Germany*) RFA *f*.

Fri. *abbr* (= *Friday*) sex.

friar ['fraɪə*] *n* frade *m*; (*before name*) frei *m*.

friction ['frɪkʃən] *n* fricção *f*.

friction feed n (on printer) alimentação f por fricção.

Friday ['fraɪdɪ] n sexta-feira f; see also **Tuesday**.

fridge [frɪdʒ] n geladeira (BR), frigorífico (PT).

fried [fraɪd] pt, pp of **fry** ♦ adj frito; ~ **egg** ovo estrelado or frito.

friend [frend] n amigo/a; **to make ~s with sb** fazer amizade com alguém.

friendliness ['frendlɪnɪs] n simpatia.

friendly ['frendlɪ] adj (kind) simpático; (relations, behaviour) amigável ♦ n (also: ~ match) amistoso; **to be ~ with** ser amigo de; **to be ~ to** ser simpático com.

friendly society n sociedade f mutuante, mútua.

friendship ['frendʃɪp] n amizade f.

frieze [friːz] n friso.

frigate ['frɪgɪt] n fragata.

fright [fraɪt] n susto; **to take ~** assustar-se.

frighten ['fraɪtən] vt assustar.

frighten away vt espantar.

frighten off vt espantar.

frightened ['fraɪtnd] adj: **to be ~ of** ter medo de.

frightening ['fraɪtnɪŋ] adj assustador(a).

frightful ['fraɪtful] adj terrível, horrível.

frightfully ['fraɪtfulɪ] adv terrivelmente.

frigid ['frɪdʒɪd] adj (MED) frígido, frio.

frigidity [frɪ'dʒɪdɪtɪ] n (MED) frigidez f.

frill [frɪl] n babado; **without ~s** (fig: car) sem nenhum luxo; (: dinner) simples; (: service) sem mordomias; (: holiday) sem extras.

fringe [frɪndʒ] n franja; (edge: of forest etc) orla, margem f; (fig): **on the ~ of** à margem de.

fringe benefits npl benefícios mpl adicionais.

fringe theatre n teatro de vanguarda.

frisk [frɪsk] vt revistar.

frisky ['frɪskɪ] adj alegre, brincalhão/lhona.

fritter ['frɪtə*] n bolinho frito.

fritter away vt desperdiçar.

frivolity [frɪ'vɔlɪtɪ] n frivolidade f.

frivolous ['frɪvələs] adj frívolo.

frizzy ['frɪzɪ] adj frisado.

fro [frəu] see **to**.

frock [frɔk] n vestido.

frog [frɔg] n rã f; **to have a ~ in one's throat** ter pigarro.

frogman ['frɔgmən] (irreg) n homem-rã m.

frogmarch ['frɔgmɑːtʃ] (BRIT) vt: **to ~ sb in/out** arrastar alguém para dentro/para fora.

frogmen ['frɔgmən] npl of **frogman**.

frolic ['frɔlɪk] vi brincar.

from [frɔm] prep de; **~ January (on)** a partir de janeiro; **where ~?** de onde?, daonde? (inf); **where is he ~?** ele é de onde?; **(as) ~ Friday** a partir de sexta-feira; **prices range ~ £10 to £50** os preços vão de £10 a £50; **~ what he says** pelo que ele diz.

frond [frɔnd] n fronde f.

front [frʌnt] n (foremost part) frente f, parte f dianteira; (of house) fachada; (of book) capa; (promenade: also: sea ~) orla marítima; (MIL, POL, METEOROLOGY) frente f; (fig: appearances) fachada ♦ adj dianteiro, da frente ♦ vi: **to ~ onto sth** dar para algo; **in ~ (of)** em frente (de).

frontage ['frʌntɪdʒ] n frontaria.

frontal ['frʌntəl] adj frontal.

front bench (BRIT) n (POL) os dirigentes do partido no poder ou da oposição.

front desk (US) n (in hotel, at doctor's) recepção f.

front door n porta principal; (of car) porta dianteira.

frontier ['frʌntɪə*] n fronteira.

frontispiece ['frʌntɪspiːs] n frontispício.

front page n primeira página.

front room (BRIT) n salão m, sala de estar.

front runner n (fig) favorito/a.

front-wheel drive n tração f dianteira.

frost [frɔst] n geada; (also: hoar~) gelo.

frostbite ['frɔstbaɪt] n ulceração f produzida pelo frio.

frosted ['frɔstɪd] adj (glass) fosco; (esp US: cake) com cobertura.

frosting ['frɔstɪŋ] (esp US) n (on cake) glace f.

frosty ['frɔstɪ] adj (window) coberto de geada; (welcome) glacial.

froth [frɔθ] n espuma.

frown [fraun] n olhar m carrancudo, cara amarrada ♦ vi franzir as sobrancelhas, amarrar a cara.

frown on vt fus (fig) desaprovar, não ver com bons olhos.

froze [frəuz] pt of **freeze**.

frozen ['frəuzn] pp of **freeze** ♦ adj congelado; **~ foods** congelados mpl.

FRS n abbr (BRIT: = Fellow of the Royal Society) membro de associação promovedora de pesquisa científica; (US: = Federal Reserve System) banco central dos EUA.

frugal ['fruːgəl] adj frugal.

fruit [fruːt] n inv fruta; (fig: pl ~s) fruto.

fruiterer ['fruːtərə*] n fruteiro/a; **~'s (shop)** fruteiro (BR), frutaria (PT).

fruitful ['fruːtful] adj proveitoso.

fruition [fruː'ɪʃən] n: **to come to ~** realizar-se.

fruit juice n suco (BR) or sumo (PT) de frutas.

fruitless ['fruːtlɪs] adj inútil, vão/vã.

fruit machine n caça-níqueis m inv (BR), máquina de jogo (PT).

fruit salad n salada de frutas.

frump [frʌmp] n careta (mulher antiquada).

frustrate [frʌs'treɪt] vt frustrar.

frustrated [frʌs'treɪtɪd] adj frustrado.

frustrating [frʌs'treɪtɪŋ] adj frustrante.

frustration [frʌs'treɪʃən] n frustração f.

fry [fraɪ] (pt, pp **fried**) vt fritar ♦ npl: **small ~** gente f insignificante.

frying pan ['fraɪɪŋ-] n frigideira.

FT (BRIT) n abbr (= Financial Times) jornal

NB: European Portuguese adds the following consonants to certain words: **b** (sú(b)dito, su(b)til); **c** (a(c)ção, a(c)cionista, a(c)to); **m** (inde(m)ne); **p** (ado(p)ção, ado(p)tar); for further details see p. xiii.

financeiro; **the** ~ **index** o índice da Bolsa de Valores de Londres.

ft. *abbr* = **foot; feet.**

FTC *(US)* *n* *abbr* = **Federal Trade Commission.**

fuchsia ['fjuːʃə] *n* fúcsia.

fuck [fʌk] *(inf!)* *vi* trepar(*!*) ♦ *vt* trepar com *(!)*; ~ **off**! vai tomar no cu!(*!*).

fucking ['fʌkɪŋ] *(inf!)* *adj*: **this** ~ ... essa merda de ... *(!)*; ~ **hell** puta que pariu *(!)*.

fuddled ['fʌdld] *adj (muddled)* confuso, enrolado.

fuddy-duddy ['fʌdɪdʌdɪ] *adj, n* careta *m/f*.

fudge [fʌdʒ] *n (CULIN)* ≈ doce *m* de leite ♦ *vt (issue, problem)* evadir.

fuel [fjuəl] *n (gen, for heating)* combustível *m*; *(for propelling)* carburante *m*.

fuel oil *n* óleo combustível.

fuel pump *n (AUT)* bomba de gasolina.

fuel tank *n* depósito de combustível.

fug [fʌg] *(BRIT)* *n* bafio.

fugitive ['fjuːdʒɪtɪv] *n* fugitivo/a.

fulfil [ful'fɪl] *(US* **fulfill**) *vt (function)* cumprir; *(condition)* satisfazer; *(wish, desire)* realizar.

fulfilled [ful'fɪld] *adj (person)* realizado.

fulfil(l)ment [ful'fɪlmənt] *n* satisfação *f*; *(of wish, desire)* realização *f*.

full [ful] *adj* cheio; *(fig)* pleno; *(complete)* completo; *(information)* detalhado; *(price)* integral; *(skirt)* folgado ♦ *adv*: ~ **well** perfeitamente; **I'm** ~ estou satisfeito; ~ **(up)** *(hotel etc)* lotado; ~ **employment** pleno emprego; ~ **fare** passagem completa; **a** ~ **two hours** duas horas completas; **at** ~ **speed** a toda a velocidade; **in** ~ *(reproduce, quote)* integralmente; *(name)* por completo.

fullback ['fulbæk] *n* zagueiro *(BR)*, defesa *m (PT)*.

full-blooded [-'blʌdɪd] *adj (vigorous)* vigoroso.

full-cream *(BRIT)* *adj*: ~ **milk** leite *m* integral.

full-grown *adj* crescido, adulto.

full-length *adj (portrait)* de corpo inteiro; ~ **(feature) film** longa-metragem *m*.

full moon *n* lua cheia.

full-scale *adj (model)* em tamanho natural; *(search, retreat)* em grande escala.

full-sized [-saɪzd] *adj (portrait etc)* em tamanho natural.

full stop *n* ponto (final).

full-time *adj (work)* de tempo completo *or* integral ♦ *n*: **full time** *(SPORT)* final *m*.

fully ['fulɪ] *adv* completamente; *(at least)*: ~ **as big as** pelo menos tão grande como.

fully-fledged [-fledʒd] *adj (teacher, barrister)* diplomado; *(citizen, member)* verdadeiro.

fulsome ['fulsəm] *(pej)* *adj* extravagante.

fumble ['fʌmbl] *vi* atrapalhar-se ♦ *vt (ball)* atrapalhar-se com, apanhar de *(inf)*.

fumble with *vt fus* atrapalhar-se com, apanhar de *(inf)*.

fume [fjuːm] *vi* fumegar; *(be angry)* estar com raiva; ~**s** *npl* gases *mpl*.

fumigate ['fjuːmɪgeɪt] *vt* fumigar; *(against*

pests etc) pulverizar.

fun [fʌn] *n (amusement)* divertimento; *(joy)* alegria; **to have** ~ divertir-se; **for** ~ de brincadeira; **it's not much** ~ não tem graça; **to make** ~ **of** fazer troça de, zombar de.

function ['fʌŋkʃən] *n* função *f*; *(reception, dinner)* recepção *f* ♦ *vi* funcionar; **to** ~ **as** funcionar como.

functional ['fʌŋkʃənəl] *adj* funcional.

function key *n (COMPUT)* tecla de função.

fund [fʌnd] *n* fundo; *(source, store)* fonte *f*; ~**s** *npl* fundos *mpl*.

fundamental [fʌndə'mɛntl] *adj* fundamental.

fundamentalist [fʌndə'mɛntəlɪst] *n* fundamentalista *m/f*.

fundamentally [fʌndə'mɛntəlɪ] *adv* fundamentalmente.

fundamentals [fʌndə'mɛntlz] *npl* fundamentos *mpl*.

fund-raising [-'reɪzɪŋ] *n* angariação *f* de fundos.

funeral ['fjuːnərəl] *n (burial)* enterro; *(ceremony)* exéquias *fpl*.

funeral director *n* agente *m/f* funerário/a.

funeral parlour *n* casa funerária.

funeral service *n* missa fúnebre.

funereal [fjuː'nɪərɪəl] *adj* fúnebre, funéreo.

funfair ['fʌnfɛə*] *(BRIT)* *n* parque *m* de diversões.

fungi ['fʌŋgaɪ] *npl of* **fungus.**

fungus ['fʌŋgəs] *(pl* **fungi**) *n* fungo; *(mould)* bolor *m*, mofo.

funicular [fjuː'nɪkjulə*] *n (also:* ~ **railway**) funicular *m*.

funnel ['fʌnl] *n* funil *m*; *(of ship)* chaminé *m*.

funnily ['fʌnɪlɪ] *adv*: ~ **enough** por incrível que pareça.

funny ['fʌnɪ] *adj* engraçado, divertido; *(strange)* esquisito, estranho.

funny bone *n* parte sensível do cotovelo.

fur [fəː*] *n* pele *f*; *(BRIT: in kettle etc)* depósito, crosta.

fur coat *n* casaco de peles.

furious ['fjuərɪəs] *adj* furioso; *(effort)* violento.

furiously ['fjuərɪəslɪ] *adv* com fúria; *(argue)* com violência.

furl [fəːl] *vt* enrolar; *(NAUT)* colher.

furlong ['fəːlɔŋ] *n* = 201.17*m*.

furlough ['fəːləu] *n* licença.

furnace ['fəːnɪs] *n* forno.

furnish ['fəːnɪʃ] *vt* mobiliar *(BR)*, mobilar *(PT)*; *(supply)*: **to** ~ **with** fornecer de; ~**ed flat** *(BRIT)* *or* **apartment** *(US)* apartamento mobiliado *(BR)* *or* mobilado *(PT)*.

furnishings ['fəːnɪʃɪŋz] *npl* mobília.

furniture ['fəːnɪtʃə*] *n* mobília, móveis *mpl*; **piece of** ~ móvel.

furniture polish *n* cera de lustrar móveis.

furore [fjuə'rɔːrɪ] *n* furor *m*.

furrier ['fʌrɪə*] *n* peleiro/a.

furrow ['fʌrəu] *n* sulco.

furry ['fəːrɪ] *adj* peludo; *(toy)* de pelúcia.

further ['fəːðə*] *adj (new)* novo, adicional ♦ *adv* mais longe; *(more)* mais; *(moreover)* além disso ♦ *vt* promover; **how much** ~ **is**

it? quanto mais tem que se ir?; **until** ~ notice até novo aviso; ~ **to your letter of** ... (COMM) em resposta à sua carta do ....

further education n educação f superior.

furthermore [fɜːðə'mɔː*] adv além disso.

furthermost ['fɜːðəməust] adj mais distante.

furthest ['fɜːðɪst] superl of **far**.

furtive ['fɜːtɪv] adj furtivo.

furtively ['fɜːtɪvlɪ] adv furtivamente.

fury ['fjuərɪ] n fúria.

fuse [fjuːz] (US **fuze**) n fusível m; (for bomb etc) espoleta, mecha ♦ vt (metal) fundir; (fig) unir ♦ vi (metal) fundir-se; (fig) unir-se; (ELEC): **to** ~ **the lights** queimar as luzes; **a** ~ **has blown** queimou um fusível.

fuse box n caixa de fusíveis.

fuselage ['fjuːzəlɑːʒ] n fuselagem f.

fuse wire n fio fusível.

fusillade [fjuːzɪ'leɪd] n fuzilada; (fig) saraivada.

fusion ['fjuːʒən] n fusão f.

fuss [fʌs] n (uproar) rebuliço; (excitement) espalhafato; (complaining) escândalo ♦ vi criar caso; **to make a** ~ criar caso; **to make a** ~ **of sb** paparicar alguém.

fuss over vt fus (person) paparicar.

fussy ['fʌsɪ] adj (person) exigente, complicado, cheio de coisas (inf); (dress, style) espalhafatoso; **I'm not** ~ (inf) para mim, tanto faz.

futile ['fjuːtaɪl] adj (frivolous) fútil; (useless) inútil, vão/vã.

futility [fjuː'tɪlɪtɪ] n inutilidade f.

future ['fjuːtʃə*] adj, n futuro ~**s** npl (COMM) operações fpl a termo; **in (the)** ~ no futuro; **in the near/immediate** ~ em futuro próximo/imediato.

futuristic [fjuːtʃə'rɪstɪk] adj futurístico.

fuze [fjuːz] (US) n, vi, vt = **fuse**.

fuzzy ['fʌzɪ] adj (PHOT) indistinto; (hair) frisado, encrespado.

fwd. abbr = **forward**.

fwy (US) abbr = **freeway**.

FY abbr = **fiscal year**.

FYI abbr (= for your information) para seu conhecimento.

G

G, g [dʒiː] n (letter) G, g m; (MUS): **G** sol m; **G for George** G de Gomes.

G n abbr (BRIT: SCH) = **good**; (US: CINEMA: = general (audience)) livre.

g abbr (= gram; gravity) g.

GA (US) abbr (POST) = **Georgia**.

gab [gæb] (inf) n: **to have the gift of the** ~ ter

lábia, ser bom de bico.

gabble ['gæbl] vi tagarelar.

gaberdine [gæbə'diːn] n gabardina, gabardine f.

gable ['geɪbl] n cumeeira.

Gabon [gə'bɔn] n Gabão m.

gad about [gæd-] (inf) vi badalar.

gadget ['gædʒɪt] n aparelho, engenhoca; (in kitchen) pequeno utensílio.

Gaelic ['geɪlɪk] adj gaélico/a ♦ n (LING) gaélico.

gaffe [gæf] n gafe f.

gag [gæg] n (on mouth) mordaça; (joke) piada ♦ vt amordaçar.

gaga ['gɑːgɑː] adj: **to go** ~ ficar gagá.

gaiety ['geɪɪtɪ] n alegria.

gaily ['geɪlɪ] adv alegremente.

gain [geɪn] n lucro, ganho ♦ vt ganhar ♦ vi (watch) adiantar-se; **to** ~ **by sth** tirar proveito de algo; **to** ~ **on sb** aproximar-se de alguém; **to** ~ **3lbs (in weight)** engordar 3 libras; **to** ~ **ground** ganhar terreno.

gainful ['geɪnful] adj lucrativo, proveitoso.

gainsay [geɪn'seɪ] (irreg: like **say**) vt (contradict) contradizer; (deny) negar.

gait [geɪt] n modo de andar.

gal. abbr = **gallon**.

gala ['gɑːlə] n festa, gala; **swimming** ~ festival de natação.

Galapagos (Islands) [gə'læpəgəs-] npl: **the** ~ as ilhas Galápagos.

galaxy ['gæləksɪ] n galáxia.

gale [geɪl] n (wind) ventania; ~ **force 10** vento de força 10.

gall [gɔːl] n (ANAT) fel m, bílis f; (fig) descaramento ♦ vt irritar.

gall. abbr = **gallon**.

gallant ['gælənt] adj valente; (towards ladies) galante.

gallantry ['gæləntrɪ] n valentia; (courtesy) galanteria.

gall-bladder n vesícula biliar.

galleon ['gælɪən] n galeão m.

gallery ['gælərɪ] n (in theatre etc) galeria; (also: art ~) galeria (de arte).

galley ['gælɪ] n (ship's kitchen) cozinha; (ship) galé f; (also: ~ proof) paquê m.

Gallic ['gælɪk] adj francês/esa.

galling ['gɔːlɪŋ] adj irritante.

gallon ['gæln] n galão m (BRIT = 4.543 l; US = 3.785 l).

gallop ['gæləp] n galope m ♦ vi galopar; ~**ing inflation** inflação galopante.

gallows ['gæləuz] n forca.

gallstone ['gɔːlstəun] n cálculo biliar.

galore [gə'lɔː*] adv à beça.

galvanize ['gælvənaɪz] vt galvanizar; (fig): **to** ~ **sb into action** galvanizar or eletrizar alguém.

Gambia ['gæmbɪə] n Gâmbia (no article).

gambit ['gæmbɪt] n (fig): (opening) ~ início (de conversa).

NB: European Portuguese adds the following consonants to certain words: **b** (sú(b)dito, su(b)til); **c** (a(c)ção, a(c)cionista, a(c)to); **m** (inde(m)ne); **p** (ado(p)ção, ado(p)tar); for further details see p. xiii.

gamble ['gæmbl] *n* (*risk*) risco; (*bet*) aposta ♦ *vt*: **to ~ on** apostar em; ♦ *vi* jogar, arriscar; (*COMM*) especular.

gambler ['gæmblə*] *n* jogador(a) *m/f*.

gambling ['gæmblɪŋ] *n* jogo.

gambol ['gæmbl] *vi* cabriolar.

game [geɪm] *n* jogo; (*of cards, football*) partida; (*HUNTING*) caça ♦ *adj* valente; (*ready*): **to be ~ for anything** topar qualquer parada; **~s** *npl* (*SCH*) esporte *m* (*BR*), desporto (*PT*); **I'm ~** eu topo; **big ~** caça grossa.

game bird *n* ave *f* de caça.

gamekeeper ['geɪmkiːpə*] *n* guarda-caça *m*.

gamely ['geɪmlɪ] *adv* valentemente.

game reserve *n* reserva de caça.

gamesmanship ['geɪmzmənʃɪp] *n* tática.

gammon ['gæmən] *n* (*bacon*) toucinho (defumado); (*ham*) presunto.

gamut ['gæmət] *n* gama.

gang [gæŋ] *n* bando, grupo; (*of workmen*) turma ♦ *vi*: **to ~ up on sb** conspirar contra alguém.

Ganges ['gændʒiːz] *n*: **the ~** o Ganges.

gangling ['gæŋglɪŋ] *adj* desengonçado.

gangplank ['gæŋplæŋk] *n* prancha (de desembarque).

gangrene ['gæŋgriːn] *n* gangrena.

gangster ['gæŋstə*] *n* gângster *m*, bandido.

gangway ['gæŋweɪ] *n* (*in theatre etc*) passagem *f*, coxia; (*on ship*) passadiço; (*on dock*) portaló *m*.

gantry ['gæntrɪ] *n* pórtico; (*for rocket*) guindaste *m*.

GAO (*US*) *n abbr* (= *General Accounting Office*) ≈ Tribunal *m* de Contas da União.

gaol [dʒeɪl] (*BRIT*) *n*, *vt* = **jail**.

gap [gæp] *n* brecha, fenda; (*in trees, traffic*) abertura; (*in time*) intervalo; (*fig*) lacuna.

gape [geɪp] *vi* estar *or* ficar boquiaberto.

gaping ['geɪpɪŋ] *adj* (*hole*) muito aberto.

garage ['gærɑːʒ] *n* garagem *f*.

garb [gɑːb] *n* traje *m*.

garbage ['gɑːbɪdʒ] *n* lixo; (*fig: inf*) disparates *mpl*; **the book/film is ~** o livro/filme é uma droga.

garbage can (*US*) *n* lata de lixo.

garbage disposal (unit) *n* triturador *m* de lixo.

garbled ['gɑːbld] *adj* (*distorted*) adulterado, deturpado.

garden ['gɑːdn] *n* jardim *m* ♦ *vi* jardinar; **~s** *npl* jardim público, parque *m*.

garden centre *n* loja de jardinagem.

gardener ['gɑːdnə*] *n* jardineiro/a.

gardening ['gɑːdnɪŋ] *n* jardinagem *f*.

gargle ['gɑːgl] *vi* gargarejar ♦ *n* gargarejo.

gargoyle ['gɑːgɔɪl] *n* gárgula.

garish ['gɛərɪʃ] *adj* vistoso, chamativo; (*colour*) berrante.

garland ['gɑːlənd] *n* guirlanda.

garlic ['gɑːlɪk] *n* alho.

garment ['gɑːmənt] *n* peça de roupa.

garner ['gɑːnə*] *vt* acumular, amontoar.

garnish ['gɑːnɪʃ] *vt* adornar; (*CULIN*) enfeitar.

garret ['gærət] *n* mansarda.

garrison ['gærɪsn] *n* guarnição *f* ♦ *vt* guarnecer.

garrulous ['gærjuləs] *adj* tagarela.

garter ['gɑːtə*] *n* liga.

garter belt (*US*) *n* cinta-liga.

gas [gæs] *n* gás *m*; (*US: gasoline*) gasolina ♦ *vt* asfixiar com gás; (*MIL*) gasear.

gas cooker (*BRIT*) *n* fogão *m* a gás.

gas cylinder *n* bujão *m* de gás.

gaseous ['gæsɪəs] *adj* gasoso.

gas fire (*BRIT*) *n* aquecedor *m* a gás.

gash [gæʃ] *n* talho; (*on face*) corte *m* ♦ *vt* talhar; (*with knife*) cortar.

gasket ['gæskɪt] *n* (*AUT*) junta, gaxeta.

gas mask *n* máscara antigás.

gas meter *n* medidor *m* de gás.

gasoline ['gæsəliːn] (*US*) *n* gasolina.

gasp [gɑːsp] *n* arfada ♦ *vi* arfar.

gasp out *vt* (*say*) dizer com voz entrecortada.

gas ring *n* boca de gás.

gas station (*US*) *n* posto de gasolina.

gas stove *n* (*cooker*) fogão *m* a gás; (*heater*) aquecedor *m* a gás.

gassy ['gæsɪ] *adj* gasoso.

gas tank (*US*) *n* (*AUT*) tanque *m* de gasolina.

gas tap *n* torneira do gás.

gastric ['gæstrɪk] *adj* gástrico.

gastric ulcer *n* úlcera gástrica.

gastroenteritis ['gæstrəuɛntə'raɪtɪs] *n* gastrenterite *f*.

gastronomy [gæs'trɔnəmɪ] *n* gastronomia.

gasworks ['gæswɔːks] *n*, *npl* usina de gás, gasômetro.

gate [geɪt] *n* portão *m*; (*RAIL*) barreira; (*of town, castle*) porta; (*at airport*) portão *m*; (*of lock*) comporta.

gateau ['gætəu] (*pl* **-x**) *n* bolo com creme e frutas.

gateaux ['gætəuz] *npl of* **gateau**.

gatecrash ['geɪtkræʃ] *vt* entrar de penetra em.

gatecrasher ['geɪtkræʃə*] *n* penetra *m/f*.

gateway ['geɪtweɪ] *n* portão *m*, passagem *f*.

gather ['gæðə*] *vt* (*flowers, fruit*) colher; (*assemble*) reunir; (*pick up*) colher; (*SEWING*) franzir; (*understand*) compreender ♦ *vi* (*assemble*) reunir-se; (*dust, clouds*) acumular-se; **to ~ (from/that)** concluir *or* depreender (de/que); **as far as I can ~** ao que eu entendo; **to ~ speed** acelerar(-se).

gathering ['gæðərɪŋ] *n* reunião *f*, assembléia.

GATT [gæt] *n* (= *General Agreement on Tariffs and Trade*) GATT *m*.

gauche [gəuʃ] *adj* desajeitado.

gaudy ['gɔːdɪ] *adj* chamativo; (*pej*) cafona.

gauge [geɪdʒ] *n* (*instrument*) medidor *m*; (*measure, fig*) medida; (*RAIL*) bitola; ♦ *vt* medir; (*fig: sb's capabilities, character*) avaliar; **to ~ the right moment** calcular o momento azado; **petrol** (*BRIT*) *or* **gas** (*US*) **~** medidor de gasolina.

Gaul [gɔːl] *n* (*country*) Gália; (*person*) gaulês/esa *m/f*.

gaunt [gɔːnt] *adj* descarnado; (*grim, desolate*) desolado.

gauntlet ['gɔːntlɪt] n (fig): **to throw down the ~** lançar um desafio; **to run the ~** expôr-se (à crítica).

gauze [gɔːz] n gaze f.

gave [geɪv] pt of **give**.

gavel ['gævl] n martelo.

gawky ['gɔːkɪ] adj desengonçado.

gawp [gɔːp] vi: **to ~ at** olhar boquiaberto para.

gay [geɪ] adj (homosexual) gay; (old-fashioned: person) alegre; (colour) vistoso, vivo.

gaze [geɪz] n olhar m fixo ♦ vi: **to ~ at sth** fitar algo.

gazelle [gə'zɛl] n gazela.

gazette [gə'zɛt] n (newspaper) jornal m; (official publication) boletim m oficial.

gazetteer [gæzə'tɪə*] n dicionário geográfico.

gazumping [gə'zʌmpɪŋ] n o fato de um vendedor quebrar uma promessa de venda para conseguir uma preço mais alto.

GB abbr = **Great Britain**.

GBH (BRIT: inf) n abbr (LAW) = **grievous bodily harm**.

GC (BRIT) n abbr (= George Cross) distinção militar.

GCE (BRIT) n abbr = **General Certificate of Education**.

GCHQ (BRIT) n abbr (= Government Communications Headquarters) centro de intercepção de radiotransmissões estrangeiras.

GCSE (BRIT) n abbr = **General Certificate of Secondary Education**.

Gdns abbr = **gardens**.

GDP n abbr = **gross domestic product**.

GDR n abbr (= German Democratic Republic) RDA f.

gear [gɪə*] n equipamento; (TECH) engrenagem f; (AUT) velocidade f, marcha (BR), mudança (PT) ♦ vt: **our service is ~ed to meet the needs of the disabled** o nosso serviço está adequado às necessidades dos deficientes físicos; **top** (BRIT) or **high** (US)/**low ~** quarta/primeira (marcha); **in ~** engrenado; **out of ~** desengrenado.

gear up vi: **to ~ up to do** preparar-se para fazer.

gear box n caixa de mudança (BR) or velocidades (PT).

gear lever (US **gear shift**) n alavanca de mudança (BR) or mudanças (PT).

gear wheel n roda de engrenagem.

GED (US) n abbr (SCH) = **general educational development**.

geese [giːs] npl of **goose**.

Geiger counter ['gaɪgə-] n contador m Geiger.

gel [dʒɛl] n gel m.

gelatin(e) ['dʒɛlətiːn] n gelatina.

gelignite ['dʒɛlɪgnaɪt] n gelignite f.

gem [dʒɛm] n jóia, gema.

Gemini ['dʒɛmɪnaɪ] n Gêminis m, Gêmeos mpl.

gen [dʒɛn] (BRIT: inf) n: **to give sb the ~ on sth** pôr alguém a par de algo.

Gen. abbr (MIL: = general) Gen.

gen. abbr (= general; generally) ger.

gender ['dʒɛndə*] n gênero.

gene [dʒiːn] n (BIO) gene m.

genealogy [dʒiːnɪ'ælədʒɪ] n genealogia.

general ['dʒɛnərl] n general m ♦ adj geral; **in ~** em geral; **the ~ public** o grande público; **~ audit** (COMM) exame m geral de auditoria.

general anaesthetic (US **general anesthetic**) n anestesia geral.

general election n eleições fpl gerais.

generalization [dʒɛnrəlaɪ'zeɪʃən] n generalização f.

generalize ['dʒɛnrəlaɪz] vi generalizar.

generally ['dʒɛnrəlɪ] adv geralmente.

general manager n diretor(a) m/f geral.

general practitioner n clínico/a geral.

general strike n greve f geral.

generate ['dʒɛnəreɪt] vt (ELEC) gerar; (fig) produzir.

generation [dʒɛnə'reɪʃən] n geração f.

generator ['dʒɛnəreɪtə*] n gerador m.

generic [dʒə'nɛrɪk] adj genérico.

generosity [dʒɛnə'rɒsɪtɪ] n generosidade f.

generous ['dʒɛnərəs] adj generoso; (helping etc) abundante.

genesis ['dʒɛnəsɪs] n gênese f.

genetic [dʒə'nɛtɪk] adj genético; **~ engineering** engenharia genética.

genetics [dʒɪ'nɛtɪks] n genética.

Geneva [dʒɪ'niːvə] n Genebra.

genial ['dʒiːnɪəl] adj jovial, simpático.

genitals ['dʒɛnɪtlz] npl órgãos mpl genitais.

genitive ['dʒɛnɪtɪv] n genitivo.

genius ['dʒiːnɪəs] n gênio.

genocide ['dʒɛnəusaɪd] n genocídio.

gent [dʒɛnt] (BRIT: inf) n abbr = **gentleman**.

genteel [dʒɛn'tiːl] adj fino, elegante.

gentle ['dʒɛntl] adj (sweet) amável, doce; (touch etc) leve, suave; (animal) manso.

gentleman ['dʒɛntlmən] (irreg) n senhor m; (well-bred man) cavalheiro; **~'s agreement** acordo de cavalheiros.

gentlemanly ['dʒɛntlmənlɪ] adj cavalheiresco.

gentlemen ['dʒɛntlmen] npl of **gentleman**.

gentleness ['dʒɛntlnɪs] n doçura, meiguice f; (of touch) suavidade f; (of animal) mansidão f.

gently ['dʒɛntlɪ] adv suavemente.

gentry ['dʒɛntrɪ] n pequena nobreza.

gents [dʒɛnts] n banheiro de homens (BR), casa de banho dos homens (PT).

genuine ['dʒɛnjuɪn] adj autêntico; (person) sincero.

genuinely ['dʒɛnjuɪnlɪ] adj sinceramente, realmente.

geographer [dʒɪ'ɒgrəfə*] n geógrafo/a.

geographic(al) [dʒɪə'græfɪk(l)] adj geográfico.

---

*NB: European Portuguese adds the following consonants to certain words: **b** (sú(b)dito, su(b)til); **c** (a(c)ção, a(c)cionista, a(c)to); **m** (inde(m)ne); **p** (ado(p)ção, ado(p)tar); for further details see p. xiii.*

geography [dʒɪˈɔgrəfɪ] *n* geografia.
geological [dʒɪəˈlɔdʒɪkl] *adj* geológico.
geologist [dʒɪˈɔlədʒɪst] *n* geólogo/a.
geology [dʒɪˈɔlədʒɪ] *n* geologia.
geometric(al) [dʒɪəˈmɛtrɪk(l)] *adj* geométrico.
geometry [dʒɪˈɔmətrɪ] *n* geometria.
Geordie [ˈdʒɔːdɪ] (*BRIT*: *inf*) *n* natural *m/f* da cidade de Newcastle-upon-Tyne.
geranium [dʒɪˈreɪnjəm] *n* gerânio.
geriatric [dʒɛrɪˈætrɪk] *adj* geriátrico.
germ [dʒɜːm] *n* micróbio, bacilo; (*BIO*, *fig*) germe *m*.
German [ˈdʒɜːmən] *adj* alemão/mã ♦ *n* alemão/mã *m/f*; (*LING*) alemão *m*.
German measles *n* rubéola.
Germany [ˈdʒɜːmənɪ] *n* Alemanha.
germination [dʒɜːmɪˈneɪʃən] *n* germinação *f*.
germ warfare *n* guerra bacteriológica.
gerrymandering [ˈdʒɛrɪmændərɪŋ] *n* reorganização dos distritos eleitorais para garantir a vitória do próprio partido.
gestation [dʒɛsˈteɪʃən] *n* gestação *f*.
gesticulate [dʒɛsˈtɪkjuleɪt] *vi* gesticular.
gesture [ˈdʒɛstjə*] *n* gesto; **as a ~ of friendship** em sinal de amizade.
get [gɛt] (*pt*, *pp* **got**, (*US*) *pp* **gotten**) *vt* (*obtain*) obter, arranjar; (*receive*) receber; (*achieve*) conseguir; (*find*) encontrar; (*catch*) pegar; (*fetch*) ir buscar; (*understand*) compreender; (*inf*: *annoy*): **he really ~s me!** ele me enche o saco! ♦ *vi* (*become*) ficar, tornar-se; (*go*): **to ~ to** (*place*) chegar a ♦ *modal aux vb*: **you've got to do it** você tem que fazê-lo; **to have got** ter; **to ~ old** envelhecer; **he got under the fence** passou por baixo da cerca; **to ~ sth for sb** arranjar algo para alguém; (*fetch*) ir buscar algo para alguém; **~ me Mr Jones, please** (*TEL*) pode chamar o Sr Jones por favor; **can I ~ you a drink?** você está a fim do?; **to ~ ready** preparar-se; **to ~ washed** lavar-se; **to ~ sth done** (*do*) fazer algo; (*have done*) mandar fazer algo; **to ~ one's hair cut** cortar o cabelo; **to ~ sb to do sth** convencer alguém a fazer algo; **I can't ~ it in/out/through** não consigo enfiá-lo/tirá-lo/passá-lo; **to ~ sth out of sth** (*fig*) tirar proveito de algo; **let's ~ going** *or* **started** vamos lá!
get about *vi* sair muito, viajar muito; (*news*) espalhar-se.
get across *vt*: **to ~ across (to)** (*message*, *meaning*) comunicar (a) ♦ *vi*: **to ~ across to** (*subj*: *speaker*) fazer-se entender por.
get along *vi* (*agree*) entender-se; (*depart*) ir embora; (*manage*) = **get by**.
get at *vt fus* (*attack*) atacar; (*reach*) alcançar; (*the truth*) descobrir; **what are you ~ting at?** o que você está querendo dizer?
get away *vi* partir; (*on holiday*) ir-se de férias; (*escape*) escapar.
get away with *vt fus* conseguir fazer impunemente.
get back *vi* (*return*) regressar, voltar ♦ *vt*

receber de volta, recobrar; **to ~ back to** (*return*) voltar a; (*contact again*) estar em contato novamente com.
get back at (*inf*) *vt fus*: **to ~ back at sb** ir à forra com alguém.
get by *vi* (*manage*) virar-se; **I can ~ by in Dutch** eu me viro em holandês.
get down *vi* descer ♦ *vt* (*object*) abaixar, descer; (*depress*) deprimir.
get down to *vt fus* (*work*) pôr-se a (fazer); **to ~ down to business** entrar no assunto.
get in *vi* (*train*) chegar; (*arrive home*) voltar para casa ♦ *vt* (*bring in*: *harvest*) colher; (: *supplies*) abastecer-se de *or* com ♦ *vt fus* (*car etc*) subir em.
get into *vt fus* entrar em; (*vehicle*) subir em; (*clothes*) pôr, vestir, enfiar; **to ~ into bed** meter-se na cama; **to ~ into a rage** ficar com raiva.
get off *vi* (*from train etc*) saltar (*BR*), descer (*PT*); (*depart*: *person*, *car*) sair ♦ *vt* (*remove*: *clothes*, *stain*) tirar; (*send off*) mandar; (*have as leave*: *day*, *time*): **we got 2 days off** tivemos 2 dias de folga ♦ *vt fus* (*train*, *bus*) saltar de (*BR*), sair de (*PT*); **to ~ off to a good start** (*fig*) começar bem.
get on *vi* (*at exam etc*) ter sucesso; (*agree*) entender-se ♦ *vt fus* (*train etc*) subir em (*BR*), subir para (*PT*); (*horse*) montar em; **how are you ~ting on?** como vai?
get on to (*BRIT*) *vt fus* (*deal with*: *problem*) lidar com; (*contact*: *person*) entrar em contato com.
get out *vi* (*of place*, *vehicle*) sair; (*news*) vir a público ♦ *vt* (*take out*) tirar.
get out of *vt fus* sair de; (*duty etc*) escapar de.
get over *vt fus* (*illness*) restabelecer-se de ♦ *vt* (*communicate*: *idea etc*) fazer compreender, comunicar; (*finish*): **let's ~ it over (with)** vamos acabar com isso.
get round *vt fus* rodear; (*fig*: *person*) convencer ♦ *vi*: **to ~ round to doing sth** conseguir fazer algo.
get through *vi* (*TEL*) completar a ligação ♦ *vt fus* (*finish*: *work*, *book*) terminar.
get through to *vt fus* (*TEL*) comunicar-se com.
get together *vi* reunir-se ♦ *vt* reunir.
get up (*inf*) *vi* (*rise*) levantar(-se) ♦ *vt fus* levantar.
get up to *vt fus* (*reach*) chegar a; (*BRIT*: *prank etc*) fazer.
getaway [ˈgɛtəweɪ] *n* fuga, escape *m*.
getaway car *n* carro de fuga.
get-together *n* reunião *f*.
get-up (*inf*) *n* (*outfit*) roupa.
get-well card *n* cartão *m* com votos de melhoras.
geyser [ˈgiːzə*] *n* aquecedor *m* de água; (*GEO*) gêiser *m*.
Ghana [ˈgɑːnə] *n* Gana (*no article*).
Ghanaian [gɑːˈneɪən] *adj*, *n* ganense *m/f*.
ghastly [ˈgɑːstlɪ] *adj* horrível; (*pale*) pálido.

gherkin ['gə:kɪn] n pepino em vinagre.
ghetto ['gɛtəu] n gueto.
ghost [gəust] n fantasma m ♦ vt (sb else's book) escrever.
ghostly ['gəustlɪ] adj fantasmal.
ghostwriter ['gəustraɪtə*] n escritor(a) m/f cujos trabalhos são assinados por outrem.
ghoul [gu:l] n assombração f.
ghoulish ['gu:lɪʃ] adj (tastes etc) macabro.
GHQ n abbr (MIL) = **general headquarters**.
GI (US: inf) n abbr (= government issue) soldado do exército americano.
giant ['dʒaɪənt] n gigante m ♦ adj gigantesco, gigante; ~ **(size) packet** pacote tamanho gigante.
gibber ['dʒɪbə*] vi algaraviar.
gibberish ['dʒɪbərɪʃ] n algaravia.
gibe [dʒaɪb] n deboche m ♦ vi: **to ~ at** debochar de.
giblets ['dʒɪblɪts] npl miúdos mpl.
Gibraltar [dʒɪ'brɔːltə*] n Gibraltar m (no article).
giddiness ['gɪdɪnɪs] n vertigem f.
giddy ['gɪdɪ] adj (dizzy) tonto; (speed) vertiginoso; (frivolous) frívolo; **it makes me ~** me dá vertigem; **to be ~** estar com vertigem.
gift [gɪft] n presente m, dádiva; (offering) oferta; (ability) dom m, talento; (COMM: also: free ~) brinde m; **to have a ~ for sth** ter o dom de algo, ter facilidade para algo.
gifted ['gɪftɪd] adj dotado.
gift token n vale m para presente.
gift voucher n vale m para presente.
gig [gɪg] (inf) n (of musician) show m.
gigantic [dʒaɪ'gæntɪk] adj gigantesco.
giggle ['gɪgl] vi dar risadinha boba ♦ n risadinha boba.
GIGO ['gaɪgəu] (inf) abbr (COMPUT: = garbage in, garbage out) qualidade de entrada, qualidade de saída.
gild [gɪld] vt dourar.
gill [dʒɪl] n (measure) = 0.25 pints (BRIT = 0.148 l; US = 0.118 l).
gills [gɪlz] npl (of fish) guelras fpl, brânquias fpl.
gilt [gɪlt] adj, n dourado.
gilt-edged [-'ɛdʒd] adj (stocks, securities) do Estado, de toda confiança.
gimlet ['gɪmlɪt] n verruma.
gimmick ['gɪmɪk] n truque m or macete m (publicitário).
gin [dʒɪn] n gim m, genebra.
ginger ['dʒɪndʒə*] n gengibre m.
ginger up vt animar.
ginger ale n cerveja de gengibre.
ginger beer n cerveja de gengibre.
gingerbread ['dʒɪndʒəbrɛd] n pão m de gengibre.
ginger-haired adj ruivo.
gingerly ['dʒɪndʒəlɪ] adv cuidadosamente.
gingham ['gɪŋəm] n riscadinho.
gipsy ['dʒɪpsɪ] n cigano ♦ cpd (caravan, camp)

de ciganos.
giraffe [dʒɪ'rɑːf] n girafa.
girder ['gə:də*] n viga, trave f.
girdle ['gə:dl] n (corset) cinta ♦ vt cintar.
girl [gə:l] n (small) menina (BR), rapariga (PT); (young woman) jovem f, moça; **an English ~** uma moça inglesa.
girlfriend ['gə:lfrɛnd] n (of girl) amiga; (of boy) namorada.
girlish ['gə:lɪʃ] adj ameninado, de menina.
Girl Scout (US) n escoteira.
Giro ['dʒaɪrəu[n: **the National ~** (BRIT) serviço bancário do correio.
giro ['dʒaɪrəu] n (bank ~) transferência bancária; (post office ~) transferência postal.
girth [gə:θ] n circunferência; (stoutness) gordura; (of horse) cilha.
gist [dʒɪst] n essencial m.
give [gɪv] (pt gave, pp given) vt dar; (deliver) entregar; (as gift) oferecer ♦ vi (break) dar folga; (stretch: fabric) dar de si; **to ~ sb sth, ~ sth to sb** dar algo a alguém; **to ~ a cry/sigh** dar um grito/suspiro; **how much did you ~ for it?** quanto você pagou por isso?; **12 o'clock, ~ or take a few minutes** por volta do meio-dia; **to ~ way** ceder; (BRIT: AUT) dar a preferência (BR), dar prioridade (PT).
give away vt (give free) dar de graça; (betray) traiçoar; (disclose) revelar; (bride) conduzir ao altar.
give back vt devolver.
give in vi ceder ♦ vt entregar.
give off vt soltar.
give out vt (food etc) distribuir; (news) divulgar ♦ vi (be exhausted: strength, supplies) esgotar-se; (fail) falhar.
give up vi desistir, dar-se por vencido ♦ vt renunciar a; **to ~ up smoking** deixar de fumar; **to ~ o.s. up** entregar-se.
give-and-take n toma-lá-dá-cá m.
giveaway ['gɪvəweɪ] cpd: ~ **prices** preços de liquidação ♦ n (inf): **her expression was a ~** a expressão dela a atraiçoava; **the exam was a ~!** o exame foi sopa!
given ['gɪvn] pp of **give** ♦ adj (fixed: time, amount) dado, determinado ♦ conj: ~ **the circumstances ...** dadas as circunstâncias ...; ~ **that ...** dado que ..., já que ....
glacial ['gleɪsɪəl] adj (GEO) glaciário; (wind, weather) glacial.
glacier ['glæsɪə*] n glaciar m, geleira.
glad [glæd] adj contente; **to be ~ about sth/that** estar contente com algo/contente que; **I was ~ of his help** eu lhe agradeci (por) sua ajuda.
gladden ['glædən] vt alegrar.
glade [gleɪd] n clareira.
gladioli [glædɪ'əulaɪ] npl gladíolos mpl.
gladly ['glædlɪ] adv com muito prazer.
glamorous ['glæmərəs] adj encantador(a), glamoroso.

NB: *European Portuguese adds the following consonants to certain words:* **b** (sú(b)dito, su(b)til); **c** (a(c)ção, a(c)cionista, a(c)to); **m** (inde(m)ne); **p** (ado(p)ção, ado(p)tar); *for further details see p. xiii.*

glamour ['glæmə*] n encanto, glamour m.

glance [glɑ:ns] n relance m, vista de olhos ♦ vi: to ~ at olhar (de relance).

glance off vt fus (bullet) ricochetear de.

glancing ['glɑ:nsɪŋ] adj (blow) oblíquo.

gland [glænd] n glândula.

glandular fever ['glændjulə*-] (BRIT) adj mononucleose f infecciosa.

glare [glɛə*] n luz f, brilho ♦ vi deslumbrar; to ~ at olhar furiosamente para.

glaring ['glɛərɪŋ] adj (mistake) notório.

glass [glɑ:s] n vidro, cristal m; (for drinking) copo; (: with stem) cálice m; (also: looking ~) espelho; ~es npl óculos mpl.

glass-blowing [-bləʊɪŋ] n modelagem f de vidro a quente.

glass fibre n fibra de vidro.

glasshouse ['glɑ:shaʊs] (irreg) n estufa.

glassware ['glɑ:swɛə*] n objetos mpl de cristal.

glassy ['glɑ:sɪ] adj (eyes) vidrado.

Glaswegian [glæs'wi:dʒən] adj de Glasgow ♦ n natural m/f de Glasgow.

glaze [gleɪz] vt (door) envidraçar; (pottery) vitrificar; (CULIN) glaçar ♦ n verniz m; (CULIN) glacê m.

glazed [gleɪzd] adj (eye) vidrado; (pottery) vitrificado.

glazier ['gleɪzɪə*] n vidraceiro/a.

GLC (BRIT) n abbr (old: = Greater London Council) o município de Grande Londres.

gleam [gli:m] n brilho ♦ vi brilhar; a ~ of hope um fio de esperança.

gleaming ['gli:mɪŋ] adj brilhante.

glean [gli:n] vt (information) colher.

glee [gli:] n alegria, regozijo.

gleeful ['gli:ful] adj alegre.

glen [glɛn] n vale m.

glib [glɪb] adj (answer) pronto; (politician) labioso.

glibness ['glɪbnɪs] n verbosidade f, lábia; (of answer) facilidade f.

glide [glaɪd] vi deslizar; (AVIAT, birds) planar ♦ n deslizamento; (AVIAT) vôo planado.

glider ['glaɪdə*] n (AVIAT) planador m.

gliding ['glaɪdɪŋ] n (AVIAT) vôo sem motor.

glimmer ['glɪmə*] n luz f trêmula ♦ vi tremeluzir.

glimpse [glɪmps] n olhar m de relance, vislumbre m ♦ vt vislumbrar, ver de relance; to catch a ~ of vislumbrar.

glint [glɪnt] n brilho; (in the eye) cintilação f ♦ vi cintilar.

glisten ['glɪsn] vi cintilar, resplandecer.

glitter ['glɪtə*] vi reluzir, brilhar ♦ n brilho.

glitz [glɪts] (inf) n cafonice f.

gloat [gləʊt] vi: to ~ (over) exultar (com).

global ['gləʊbl] adj (worldwide) mundial; (overall) global.

globe [gləʊb] n globo, esfera.

globetrotter ['gləʊbtrɔtə*] n pessoa que corre mundo.

globule ['glɔbju:l] n glóbulo.

gloom [glu:m] n escuridão f; (sadness) tristeza.

gloomy ['glu:mɪ] adj (dark) escuro; (sad) triste; (pessimistic) pessimista; to feel ~ estar abatido.

glorification [glɔ:rɪfɪ'keɪʃən] n glorificação f.

glorify ['glɔ:rɪfaɪ] vt glorificar; (praise) adorar.

glorious ['glɔ:rɪəs] adj glorioso; (splendid) excelente.

glory ['glɔ:rɪ] n glória ♦ vi: to ~ in gloriar-se de.

glory hole (inf) n zona.

Glos (BRIT) abbr = **Gloucestershire**.

gloss [glɔs] n (shine) brilho; (also: ~ paint) pintura brilhante, esmalte m.

gloss over vt fus encobrir.

glossary ['glɔsərɪ] n glossário.

glossy ['glɔsɪ] adj lustroso ♦ n (also: ~ magazine) revista de luxo.

glove [glʌv] n luva.

glove compartment n (AUT) porta-luvas m inv.

glow [gləʊ] vi (shine) brilhar; (fire) arder ♦ n brilho.

glower ['glaʊə*] vi: to ~ at olhar de modo ameaçador.

glowing ['gləʊɪŋ] adj (fire) ardente; (complexion) afogueado; (report, description etc) entusiástico.

glow-worm n pirilampo, vaga-lume m.

glucose ['glu:kəʊs] n glicose f.

glue [glu:] n cola ♦ vt colar.

glue-sniffing [-'snɪfɪŋ] n cheira-cola m.

glum [glʌm] adj (mood) abatido; (person, tone) triste.

glut [glʌt] n abundância, fartura ♦ vt (market) saturar.

glutinous ['glu:tɪnəs] adj glutinoso.

glutton ['glʌtn] n glutão/ona m/f; a ~ for work um trabalhador incansável.

gluttonous ['glʌtənəs] adj glutão/ona.

gluttony ['glʌtənɪ] n gula.

glycerin(e) ['glɪsəri:n] n glicerina.

gm abbr (= gram) g.

GMAT (US) n abbr (= Graduate Management Admissions Test) exame de admissão aos cursos de pós-graduação.

GMB (BRIT) n abbr (= General Municipal Boilermakers and Allied Trade Union) sindicato dos empregados dos municípios.

GMT abbr (= Greenwich Mean Time) GMT m.

gnarled [nɑ:ld] adj nodoso.

gnash [næʃ] vt: to ~ one's teeth ranger os dentes.

gnat [næt] n mosquito.

gnaw [nɔ:] vt roer.

gnome [nəʊm] n gnomo.

GNP n abbr = **gross national product**.

go [gəʊ] (pt went, pp gone, pl ~es) vi ir; (travel) viajar; (depart) partir, ir-se; (work) funcionar; (be sold): to ~ for £10 ser vendido por £10; (time) passar; (become) ficar; (break) romper-se; (suit): to ~ with acompanhar, combinar com ♦ n: to have a ~ (at) tentar a sorte (com); to be on the ~ ter muito para fazer; **whose ~ is it?** de quem é a vez?; **to ~ by car/on foot** ir de carro/a pé; **he's ~ing to do it** ele vai fazê-lo; **to ~ for a walk** ir passear; **to ~ dancing** ir dançar; **to ~ to sleep** adormecer, dormir; **to ~ and see sb, to ~ to see sb** ir visitar alguém; **how is it ~ing?** como vai?; **how did it ~?** como foi?; **my voice has gone** fiquei afônico; **the cake is all gone** o bolo acabou; **I'll take whatever is ~ing** (*BRIT*) eu aceito o que tem; **... to ~** (*US: food*) ... para levar.

go about *vi* (*also*: ~ *around*) andar por aí; (*rumour*) espalhar-se ♦ *vt fus*: **how do I ~ about this?** como é que eu faço isso?; **to ~ about one's business** ocupar-se de seus afazeres.

go after *vt fus* (*pursue*) perseguir, ir atrás de; (*job, record etc*) tentar conseguir.

go against *vt fus* (*be unfavourable to*) ser desfavorável a; (*be contrary to*) ser contrário a.

go ahead *vi* (*make progress*) progredir; (*be realized*) efetuar-se.

go along *vi* (*go too*) ir também; (*continue*) continuar, prosseguir ♦ *vt fus* ladear; **correct as you ~ along** corrija na hora; **to ~ along with** (*accompany*) acompanhar; (*agree with*) concordar com.

go away *vi* ir-se, ir embora.

go back *vi* voltar.

go back on *vt fus* (*promise*) faltar com.

go by *vi* (*years, time*) passar ♦ *vt fus* guiar-se por; (*believe*) acreditar em.

go down *vi* descer, baixar; (*ship*) afundar; (*sun*) pôr-se ♦ *vt fus* descer; **that should ~ down well with him** (*fig*) isso deve agradar-lhe.

go for *vt fus* (*fetch*) ir buscar; (*like*) gostar de; (*attack*) atacar.

go in *vi* entrar.

go in for *vt fus* (*competition*) inscrever-se em; (*like*) gostar de.

go into *vt fus* entrar em; (*investigate*) investigar; (*embark on*) embarcar em.

go off *vi* ir-se; (*food*) estragar, apodrecer; (*explode*) explodir; (*lights etc*) apagar-se; (*event*) realizar-se ♦ *vt fus* deixar de gostar de; **the gun went off** o revólver disparou; **to ~ off to sleep** adormecer; **the party went off well** a festa foi um sucesso.

go on *vi* seguir, continuar; (*happen*) acontecer, ocorrer; (*lights*) acender-se ♦ *vt fus* (*be guided by*: *evidence etc*) basear-se em; **to ~ on doing** continuar fazendo *or* a fazer; **what's ~ing on here?** o que é que está acontecendo aqui?

go on at *vt fus* (*nag*) bronquear com.

go on with *vt fus* continuar com.

go out *vi* sair; (*fire, light*) apagar-se; (*tide*) baixar; **to ~ out with sb** (*boyfriend, girlfriend*) namorar alguém.

go over *vi* (*ship*) soçobrar ♦ *vt fus* (*check*)

revisar; **to ~ over sth in one's mind** refletir sobre algo.

go round *vi* (*circulate*: *news, rumour*) circular; (*revolve*) girar; (*suffice*) bastar, dar (para todos); (*visit*): **to ~ round to sb's** ir à casa de alguém; (*make a detour*): **to ~ round (by)** fazer um desvio (por).

go through *vt fus* (*town etc*) atravessar; (*search through*) vasculhar; (*examine*: *list, book*) percorrer de cabo a rabo: (*carry out*) executar.

go through with *vt fus* (*plan, crime*) levar a cabo.

go together *vi* combinar.

go under *vi* (*sink*) afundar; (*fail*: *company*) falir; (: *person*) sucumbir.

go up *vi* subir; (*price*) aumentar ♦ *vt fus* subir; **to ~ up in flames** incendiar-se, pegar fogo.

go without *vt fus* passar sem.

goad [gəud] *vt* aguilhoar.

go-ahead *adj* empreendedor(a), dinâmico ♦ *n* luz *f* verde.

goal [gəul] *n* meta, alvo; (*SPORT*) gol *m* (*BR*), golo (*PT*).

goalkeeper ['gəulkiːpə*] *n* goleiro/a (*BR*), guarda-redes *m/f inv* (*PT*).

goal post *n* trave *f*.

goat [gəut] *n* cabra; (*also*: *billy ~*) bode *m*.

gobble ['gɔbl] *vt* (*also*: ~ *down*, ~ *up*) engolir rapidamente, devorar.

go-between *n* intermediário/a.

Gobi Desert ['gəubɪ-] *n* Deserto de Gobi.

goblet ['gɔblɪt] *n* cálice *m*.

goblin ['gɔblɪn] *n* duende *m*.

go-cart *n* kart *m* ♦ *cpd*: ~ **racing** kartismo.

god [gɔd] *n* deus *m*; **G~** Deus.

godchild ['gɔdtʃaɪld] (*irreg*) *n* afilhado/a.

goddaughter ['gɔddɔːtə*] *n* afilhada.

goddess ['gɔdɪs] *n* deusa.

godfather ['gɔdfɑːðə*] *n* padrinho.

godforsaken ['gɔdfəseɪkən] *adj* miserável, abandonado.

godmother ['gɔdmʌðə*] *n* madrinha.

godparents ['gɔdpɛərənts] *npl* padrinhos *mpl*.

godsend ['gɔdsend] *n* dádiva do céu.

godson ['gɔdsʌn] *n* afilhado.

goes [gəuz] *vb see* **go**.

go-getter [-'gɛtə*] *n* pessoa dinâmica, pessoa furona (*inf*).

goggle ['gɔgl] *vi*: **to ~ at** olhar de olhos esbugalhados.

goggles ['gɔglz] *npl* óculos *mpl* de proteção.

going ['gəuɪŋ] *n* (*conditions*) estado do terreno ♦ *adj*: **the ~ rate** tarifa corrente *or* em vigor; **a ~ concern** empresa em funcionamento, empresa com fundo de comérico; **it was slow ~** ia devagar.

goings-on (*inf*) *npl* maquinações *fpl*.

go-kart [-kɑːt] *n* = **go-cart**.

gold [gəuld] *n* ouro ♦ *adj* de ouro.

golden ['gəuldən] *adj* (*made of gold*) de ouro;

NB: *European Portuguese adds the following consonants to certain words:* **b** (sú(b)dito, su(b)til); **c** (a(c)ção, a(c)cionista, a(c)to); **m** (inde(m)ne); **p** (ado(p)ção, ado(p)tar); *for further details see p. xiii.*

(*gold in colour*) dourado.
golden age *n* idade *f* de ouro.
golden handshake (*BRIT*) *n* bolada.
golden rule *n* regra de ouro.
goldfish ['gəuldfɪʃ] *n inv* peixe-dourado *m*.
gold leaf *n* ouro em folha.
gold medal *n* (*SPORT*) medalha de ouro.
goldmine ['gəuldmaɪn] *n* mina de ouro.
gold-plated [-'pleɪtɪd] *adj* plaquê *inv*.
gold-rush *n* corrida do ouro.
goldsmith ['gəuldsmɪθ] *n* ourives *m/f inv*.
gold standard *n* padrão-ouro *m*.
golf [gɔlf] *n* golfe *m*.
golf ball *n* bola de golfe; (*on typewriter*) esfera.
golf club *n* clube *m* de golfe; (*stick*) taco.
golf course *n* campo de golfe.
golfer ['gɔlfə*] *n* jogador(a) *m/f* de golfe, golfista *m/f*.
gondola ['gɔndələ] *n* gôndola.
gondolier [gɔndə'lɪə*] *n* gondoleiro.
gone [gɔn] *pp of* go.
gong [gɔŋ] *n* gongo.
gonorrhea [gɔnə'rɪə] *n* gonorréia.
good [gud] *adj* bom/boa; (*kind*) bom, bondoso; (*well-behaved*) educado; (*useful*) útil ♦ *n* bem *m*; ~**s** *npl* (*possessions*) bens *mpl*; (*COMM*) mercadorias *fpl*; ~**s and chattels** bens móveis; ~**!** bom!; **to be ~ at** ser bom em; **to be ~ for** servir para; **it's ~ for you** faz-lhe bem; **it's a ~ thing you were there** ainda bem que você estava lá; **she is ~ with children/her hands** ela tem habilidade com crianças/com as mãos; **to feel ~** sentir-se bem, estar bom; **it's ~ to see you** é bom ver você; (*formal*) prazer em vê-lo; **he's up to no ~** ele tem más intenções; **it's no ~ complaining** não adianta se queixar; **for the common ~** para o bem comum; **would you be ~ enough to ...?** podia fazer-me o favor de ...?, poderia me fazer a gentileza de ...?; **that's very ~ of you** é muita bondade sua; **is this any ~?** (*will it do?*) será que isso serve?; (*what's it like?*) será que vale a pena?; **a ~ deal (of)** muito; **a ~ many** muitos; **to make ~** reparar; **for ~** (*forever*) para sempre, definitivamente; (*once and for all*) de uma vez por todas; ~ **morning/afternoon!** bom dia/boa tarde!; ~ **evening!** boa noite!; ~ **night!** boa noite!
goodbye [gud'baɪ] *excl* até logo (*BR*), adeus (*PT*); **to say ~** despedir-se.
good faith *n* boa fé.
good-for-nothing *adj* imprestável.
Good Friday *n* Sexta-Feira Santa.
good-humoured [-'hju:məd] *adj* (*person*) alegre; (*remark, joke*) sem malícia.
good-looking [-'lukɪŋ] *adj* bonito.
good-natured *adj* (*person*) de bom gênio; (*discussion*) cordial.
goodness ['gudnɪs] *n* (*of person*) bondade *f*; **for ~ sake!** pelo amor de Deus!; ~ **gracious!** meu Deus do céu!, nossa (senhora)!
goods train (*BRIT*) *n* trem *m* de carga.
goodwill [gud'wɪl] *n* boa vontade *f*; (*COMM*)

fundo de comércio, aviamento.
goody-goody ['gudɪgudɪ] (*pej*) *n* puxa-saco *m*.
goose [gu:s] (*pl* geese) *n* ganso.
gooseberry ['guzbərɪ] *n* groselha; **to play ~** ficar de vela, segurar a vela.
gooseflesh ['gu:sflɛʃ] *n* pele *f* arrepiada.
goosepimples ['gu:spɪmplz] *npl* pele *f* arrepiada.
goose step *n* (*MIL*) passo de ganso.
GOP (*US: inf*) *n abbr* (*POL*: = *Grand Old Party*) partido republicano.
gore [gɔ:*] *vt* escornar ♦ *n* sangue *m*.
gorge [gɔ:dʒ] *n* desfiladeiro ♦ *vt*: **to ~ o.s. (on)** empanturrar-se (de).
gorgeous ['gɔ:dʒəs] *adj* magnífico, maravilhoso; (*woman*) lindo.
gorilla [gə'rɪlə] *n* gorila *m*.
gormless ['gɔ:mlɪs] (*BRIT: inf*) *adj* burro.
gorse [gɔ:s] *n* tojo.
gory ['gɔ:rɪ] *adj* sangrento.
go-slow (*BRIT*) *n* greve *f* de trabalho lento, operação *f* tartaruga.
gospel ['gɔspl] *n* evangelho.
gossamer ['gɔsəmə*] *n* (*cobweb*) teia de aranha; (*cloth*) tecido diáfano, gaze *f* fina.
gossip ['gɔsɪp] *n* (*scandal*) fofocas *fpl* (*BR*), mexericos *mpl* (*PT*); (*chat*) conversa; (*scandalmonger*) fofoqueiro/a (*BR*), mexeriqueiro/a (*PT*) ♦ *vi* (*spread scandal*) fofocar (*BR*), mexericar (*PT*); (*chat*) bater (um) papo (*BR*), cavaquear (*PT*); **a piece of ~** uma fofoca (*BR*), um mexerico (*PT*).
gossip column *n* (*PRESS*) coluna social.
got [gɔt] *pt, pp of* get.
Gothic ['gɔθɪk] *adj* gótico.
gotten ['gɔtn] (*US*) *pp of* get.
gouge [gaudʒ] *vt* (*also*: ~ **out**: *hole etc*) abrir; (: *initials*) talhar: **to ~ sb's eyes out** arrancar os olhos de alguém.
gourd [guəd] *n* cabaça, cucúrbita.
gourmet ['guəmeɪ] *n* gourmet *m*, gastrônomo/a.
gout [gaut] *n* gota.
govern ['gʌvən] *vt* governar.
governess ['gʌvənɪs] *n* governanta.
governing ['gʌvənɪŋ] *adj* (*POL*) no governo, ao poder; ~ **body** conselho de administração.
government ['gʌvnmənt] *n* governo ♦ *cpd* (*of administration*) governamental; (*of state*) do Estado; **local ~** governo municipal.
governmental [gʌvn'mɛntl] *adj* governamental.
government housing (*US*) *n* casas *fpl* populares.
government stock *n* títulos *mpl* do governo.
governor ['gʌvənə*] *n* governador(a) *m/f*; (*of school, hospital, jail*) diretor(a) *m/f*.
Govt *abbr* = government.
gown [gaun] *n* vestido; (*of teacher, judge*) toga.
GP *n abbr* (*MED*) = general practitioner.
GPO *n abbr* (*BRIT: old*) = General Post Office; (*US*) = Government Printing Office.
gr. *abbr* (*COMM*) = gross.

grab [græb] *vt* agarrar ♦ *vi*: **to ~ at** tentar agarrar.

grace [greɪs] *n* (*REL*) graça; (*gracefulness*) elegância, fineza ♦ *vt* (*favour*) honrar; **5 days' ~** um prazo de 5 dias; **to say ~** dar graças (antes de comer); **with a good/bad ~** de bom/mau grado; **his sense of humour is his saving ~** seu único mérito é seu senso de humor.

graceful ['greɪsful] *adj* elegante, gracioso.

gracious ['greɪʃəs] *adj* gracioso, afável; (*benevolent*) bondoso, complacente; (*formal*: *God*) misericordioso ♦ *excl*: **(good) ~!** meu Deus do céu!, nossa (senhora)!

gradation [grə'deɪʃn] *n* gradação *f*.

grade [greɪd] *n* (*quality*) classe *f*, qualidade *f*; (*degree*) grau *m*; (*US*: *SCH*) série *f*, classe; (: *gradient*) declive *m* ♦ *vt* classificar; **to make the ~** (*fig*) ter sucesso.

grade crossing (*US*) *n* passagem *f* de nível.

grade school (*US*) *n* escola primária.

gradient ['greɪdɪənt] *n* declive *m*; (*GEOM*) gradiente *m*.

gradual ['grædjuəl] *adj* gradual, gradativo.

gradually ['grædjuəlɪ] *adv* gradualmente, gradativamente, pouco a pouco.

graduate [*n* 'grædjuɪt, *vi* 'grædjueɪt] *n* graduado, licenciado; (*US*) diplomado do colégio ♦ *vi* formar-se, licenciar-se.

graduated pension ['grædjueɪtɪd-] *n* aposentadoria calculada em função dos últimos salários.

graduation [grædju'eɪʃən] *n* formatura.

graffiti [grə'fiːtɪ] *n* pichações *fpl*.

graft [grɑːft] *n* (*AGR*, *MED*) enxerto; (*bribery*) suborno ♦ *vt* enxertar; **hard ~** (*inf*) labuta.

grain [greɪn] *n* grão *m*; (*corn*) cereais *mpl*; (*US*: *corn*) trigo; (*in wood*) veio, fibra; **it goes against the ~** é contra a sua (*or* minha *etc*) natureza.

gram [græm] *n* grama *m*.

grammar ['græmə*] *n* gramática.

grammar school *n* (*BRIT*) ≈ liceo, ≈ ginásio.

grammatical [grə'mætɪkl] *adj* gramatical.

gramme [græm] *n* = **gram**.

gramophone ['græməfəun] (*BRIT*) *n* toca-discos *m inv* (*BR*), gira-discos *m inv* (*PT*).

granary ['grænərɪ] *n* celeiro.

grand [grænd] *adj* grande, magnífico ♦ *n* (*inf*: *thousand*) mil libras *fpl* (*or* dólares *mpl*).

grandchild ['græntʃaɪld] (*irreg*) *n* neto/a.

granddad ['grændæd] *n* vovô *m*.

granddaughter ['grændɔːtə*] *n* neta.

grandeur ['grændjə*] *n* grandeza, magnificência; (*of event*) grandiosidade *f*; (*of house*, *style*) imponência.

grandfather ['grænfɑːðə*] *n* avô *m*.

grandiose ['grændɪəuz] *adj* grandioso; (*pej*) pomposo; (*house*, *style*) imponente.

grand jury (*US*) *n* júri *m* de instrução.

grandma ['grænmɑː] *n* avó *f*, vovó *f*.

grandmother ['grænmʌðə*] *n* avó *f*.

grandpa ['grænpɑː] *n* = **granddad**.

grandparents ['grændpeərənts] *npl* avós *mpl*.

grand piano *n* piano de cauda.

Grand Prix ['grɑ̃:'priː] *n* (*AUT*) Grande Prêmio.

grandson ['grænsʌn] *n* neto.

grandstand ['grænstænd] *n* (*SPORT*) tribuna principal.

grand total *n* total *m* geral *or* global.

granite ['grænɪt] *n* granito.

granny ['grænɪ] *n* avó *f*, vovó *f*.

grant [grɑːnt] *vt* (*concede*) conceder; (*a request etc*) anuir a; (*admit*) admitir ♦ *n* (*SCH*) bolsa; (*ADMIN*) subvenção *f*, subsídio; **to take sth for ~ed** dar algo por certo; **to ~ that** admitir que.

granulated sugar ['grænjuleɪtɪd-] *n* açúcar *m* granulado.

granule ['grænjuːl] *n* grânulo.

grape [greɪp] *n* uva; **sour ~s** (*fig*) inveja; **a bunch of ~s** um cacho de uvas.

grapefruit ['greɪpfruːt] *n* toranja, grapefruit *m* (*BR*).

grapevine ['greɪpvaɪn] *n* parreira; **I heard it on *or* through the ~** (*fig*) um passarinho me contou.

graph [grɑːf] *n* gráfico.

graphic ['græfɪk] *adj* gráfico.

graphic designer *n* desenhista *m/f* industrial.

graphics ['græfɪks] *n* (*art*) artes *fpl* gráficas ♦ *npl* (*drawings*) dessenhos *mpl*; (: *COMPUT*) gráficos *mpl*.

graphite ['græfaɪt] *n* grafita.

graph paper *n* papel *m* quadriculado.

grapple ['græpl] *vi*: **to ~ with sth** estar às voltas com algo.

grappling iron ['græplɪŋ-] *n* (*NAUT*) arpéu *m*.

grasp [grɑːsp] *vt* agarrar, segurar; (*understand*) compreender, entender ♦ *n* (*grip*) agarramento; (*reach*) alcance *m*; (*understanding*) compreensão *f*; **to have sth within one's ~** ter algo ao seu alcance; **to have a good ~ of sth** (*fig*) ter um bom domínio de algo, dominar algo.

grasp at *vt fus* (*rope etc*) tentar agarrar; (*opportunity*) agarrar.

grasping ['grɑːspɪŋ] *adj* avaro.

grass [grɑːs] *n* grama (*BR*), relva (*PT*); (*uncultivated*) cupim *m*; (*lawn*) gramado (*BR*), relvado (*PT*); (*BRIT*: *inf*: *informer*) dedo-duro *m*.

grasshopper ['grɑːshɔpə*] *n* gafanhoto.

grassland ['grɑːslænd] *n* pradaria.

grass roots *npl* (*fig*) raízes *fpl*, base *f* ♦ *adj*: **grass-roots** popular.

grass snake *n* serpente *f*.

grassy ['grɑːsɪ] *adj* coberto de grama (*BR*) *or* de relva (*PT*).

grate [greɪt] *n* (*fireplace*) lareira; (*of iron*) grelha ♦ *vi* ranger ♦ *vt* (*CULIN*) ralar.

grateful ['greɪtful] *adj* agradecido, grato.

gratefully ['greɪtfəlɪ] *adv* agradecidamente.

NB: *European Portuguese adds the following consonants to certain words:* **b** *(sú(b)dito, su(b)til);* **c** *(a(c)ção, a(c)cionista, a(c)to);* **m** *(inde(m)ne);* **p** *(ado(p)ção, ado(p)tar); for further details see p. xiii.*

grater ['greɪtə*] n ralador m, ralo.
gratification [grætɪfɪ'keɪʃən] n satisfação f.
gratify ['grætɪfaɪ] vt gratificar; (whim) satisfazer.
gratifying ['grætɪfaɪɪŋ] adj gratificante.
grating ['greɪtɪŋ] n (iron bars) grade f ♦ adj (noise) áspero.
gratitude ['grætɪtjuːd] n agradecimento.
gratuitous [grə'tjuːɪtəs] adj gratuito.
gratuity [grə'tjuːɪtɪ] n gratificação f, gorjeta.
grave [greɪv] n cova, sepultura ♦ adj sério, grave.
gravedigger ['greɪvdɪgə*] n coveiro.
gravel ['grævl] n cascalho.
gravely ['greɪvlɪ] adv gravemente; ~ ill gravemente doente.
gravestone ['greɪvstəun] n lápide f.
graveyard ['greɪvjɑːd] n cemitério.
gravitate ['græviteɪt] vi: to ~ towards ser atraído por.
gravity ['grævɪtɪ] n (PHYS) gravidade f; (seriousness) seriedade f, gravidade f.
gravy ['greɪvɪ] n molho (de carne).
gravy boat n molheira.
gravy train (inf) n: to be on or ride the ~ ter achado uma mina.
gray [greɪ] adj = grey.
graze [greɪz] vi pastar ♦ vt (touch lightly) roçar; (scrape) raspar; (MED) esfolar ♦ n (MED) esfoladura, arranhadura.
grazing ['greɪzɪŋ] n (pasture) pasto, pastagem f.
grease [griːs] n (fat) gordura; (lubricant) graxa, lubrificante m ♦ vt (CULIN: dish) untar; (TECH: brakes etc) lubrificar, engraxar.
grease gun n bomba de graxa.
greasepaint [griːspeɪnt] n maquilagem f (para o teatro).
greaseproof paper ['griːspruːf-] n papel m de cera (vegetal).
greasy ['griːzɪ] adj gordurento, gorduroso; (hands, clothes) engordurado; (BRIT: road, surface) escorregadio.
great [greɪt] adj grande; (inf) ótimo; (pain, heat) forte; **they're** ~ **friends** eles são grandes amigos; **we had a** ~ **time** nos divertimos à beça; **it was** ~! foi ótimo, foi um barato (inf); **the** ~ **thing is that** ... o melhor é que ....
Great Barrier Reef n: the ~ a Grande Barreira.
Great Britain n Grã-Bretanha.
great-grandchild (irreg) n bisneto/a.
great-grandfather n bisavô m.
great-grandmother n bisavó f.
Great Lakes npl: the ~ os Grandes Lagos.
greatly ['greɪtlɪ] adv imensamente, muito.
greatness ['greɪtnɪs] n grandeza.
Grecian ['griːʃən] adj grego.
Greece [griːs] n Grécia.
greed [griːd] n (also: ~iness) avidez f, cobiça; (for food) gula.
greedily ['griːdɪlɪ] adv com avidez; (eat) gulosamente.
greedy ['griːdɪ] adj avarento; (for food) gulo-

so.
Greek [griːk] adj grego ♦ n grego/a; (LING) grego; **ancient/modern** ~ grego clássico/moderno.
green [griːn] adj verde; (inexperienced) inexperiente, ingênuo ♦ n verde m; (stretch of grass) gramado (BR), relvado (PT); (on golf course) green m; (also: village ~) ≈ praça; ~s npl verduras fpl; **to have** ~ **fingers** (BRIT) or **a** ~ **thumb** (US) ter mão boa (para plantar).
green belt n (round town) cinturão m verde.
green card n (BRIT: AUT) carta verde; (US) autorização f de residência.
greenery ['griːnərɪ] n verdura.
greenfly ['griːnflaɪ] (BRIT) n pulgão m.
greengage ['griːngeɪdʒ] n rainha-cláudia.
greengrocer ['griːngrəusə*] n (BRIT) verdureiro/a.
greenhouse ['griːnhaus] (irreg) n estufa.
greenish ['griːnɪʃ] adj esverdeado.
Greenland ['griːnlənd] n Groenlândia.
Greenlander ['griːnləndə*] n groenlandês/esa m/f.
green pepper n pimentão m verde.
greet [griːt] vt saudar; (welcome) acolher.
greeting ['griːtɪŋ] n cumprimento; (welcome) acolhimento; **Christmas/birthday** ~s votos de boas festas/feliz aniversário.
greeting(s) card n cartão m comemorativo.
gregarious [grə'geərɪəs] adj gregário.
grenade [grə'neɪd] n (also: hand ~) granada.
grew [gruː] pt of **grow**.
grey [greɪ] adj cinzento; (dismal) sombrio; **to go** ~ (hair, person) ficar grisalho.
grey-haired adj grisalho.
greyhound ['greɪhaund] n galgo.
grid [grɪd] n grade f; (ELEC) rede f; (US: AUT) cruzamento.
griddle [grɪdl] n (on cooker) chapa de assar.
gridiron ['grɪdaɪən] n grelha; (US: FOOTBALL) campo.
grief [griːf] n dor f, pena; **to come to** ~ fracassar.
grievance ['griːvəns] n motivo de queixa, agravo.
grieve [griːv] vi afligir-se, sofrer ♦ vt dar pena a, afligir; **to** ~ **for** chorar por.
grievous ['griːvəs] adj penoso; ~ **bodily harm** (LAW) lesão f corporal (grave).
grill [grɪl] n (on cooker) grelha ♦ vt (BRIT) grelhar; (question) interrogar cerradamente.
grille [grɪl] n grade f; (AUT) grelha.
grill(room) ['grɪl(rum)] n grill-room m, ≈ churrascaria.
grim [grɪm] adj sinistro, lúgubre; (inf: dreadful) horrível.
grimace [grɪ'meɪs] n careta ♦ vi fazer caretas.
grime [graɪm] n (BR) sujeira (BR), sujidade f (PT).
grimy ['graɪmɪ] adj sujo, encardido.
grin [grɪn] n sorriso largo ♦ vi sorrir abertamente; **to** ~ **(at)** dar um sorriso largo (para).
grind [graɪnd] (pt, pp **ground**) vt (mangle) triturar; (coffee, pepper etc) moer; (make

sharp) afiar; (*US*: *meat*) picar; (*polish*: *gem*) lapidar; (: *lens*) polir ♦ *vi* (*car gears*) ranger ♦ *n* (*work*) labuta; **to ~ one's teeth** os dentes; **to ~ to a halt** (*vehicle*) parar com um ranger de freios; (*fig*: *work*, *production*) paralisar-se; (: *talks*, *process*) empacar; **the daily ~** (*inf*) a labuta diária.

grinder ['graɪndə*] *n* (*machine*: *for coffee*) moinho; (: *for waste disposal*) triturador *m*.

grindstone ['graɪndstəʊn] *n*: **to keep one's nose to the ~** trabalhar sem descanso.

grip [grɪp] *n* (*of hands*) aperto; (*handle*) punho; (*of racquet etc*) cabo; (*holdall*) valise *f* ♦ *vt* agarrar; **to come** or **get to ~s with** arcar com; **to ~ the road** (*AUT*) aderir à estrada; **to lose one's ~** perder a pega; (*fig*) perder a eficiência.

gripe [graɪp] *n* (*MED*) cólicas *fpl*; (*inf*: *complaint*) queixa ♦ *vi* (*inf*) bufar.

gripping ['grɪpɪŋ] *adj* absorvente, emocionante.

grisly ['grɪzlɪ] *adj* horrendo, medonho.

grist [grɪst] *n* (*fig*): **it's (all) ~ to his mill** ele se vale de tudo.

gristle ['grɪsl] *n* cartilagem *f*.

grit [grɪt] *n* areia, grão *m* de areia; (*courage*) coragem *f* ♦ *vt* (*road*) pôr areia em; **~s** *npl* (*US*) canjica; **to ~ one's teeth** cerrar os dentes; **to have a piece of ~ in one's eye** ter uma pedrinha no olho.

grizzle ['grɪzl] (*BRIT*) *vi* choramingar.

grizzly ['grɪzlɪ] *n* (*also*: **~ bear**) urso pardo.

groan [grəʊn] *n* gemido ♦ *vi* gemer.

grocer ['grəʊsə*] *n* dono/a de mercearia.

grocer's (shop) *n* mercearia.

grocery ['grəʊsərɪ] *n* mercearia; **groceries** *npl* comestíveis *mpl*.

grog [grɒg] grogue *m*.

groggy ['grɒgɪ] *adj* grogue.

groin [grɔɪn] *n* virilha.

groom [gruːm] *n* cavalariço; (*also*: *bride~*) noivo ♦ *vt* (*horse*) tratar; (*fig*): **to ~ sb for sth** preparar alguém para algo; **well-~ed** bem-posto.

groove [gruːv] *n* ranhura, entalhe *m*.

grope [grəʊp] *vi* tatear.

grope for *vt fus* procurar às cegas.

grosgrain ['grəʊgreɪn] *n* gorgorão *m*.

gross [grəʊs] *adj* grosso; (*COMM*) bruto ♦ *n inv* (*twelve dozen*) grosa ♦ *vt* (*COMM*): **to ~ £500,000** dar uma receita bruta de £500,000.

gross domestic product *n* produto interno bruto.

grossly ['grəʊslɪ] *adv* (*greatly*) enormemente, gritantemente.

gross national product *n* produto nacional bruto.

grotesque [grə'tɛsk] *adj* grotesco.

grotto ['grɒtəʊ] *n* gruta.

grotty ['grɒtɪ] (*BRIT*: *inf*) *adj* (*room etc*) mixa; **I'm feeling ~** estou me sentindo podre.

grouch [graʊtʃ] (*inf*) *vi* ralhar ♦ *n* (*person*) pessoa geniosa, rabugento/a.

ground [graʊnd] *pt*, *pp of* **grind** ♦ *n* terra, chão *m*; (*SPORT*) campo; (*land*) terreno; (*reason*: *gen pl*) motivo, razão *f* (*US*: *also*: *~wire*) (ligação *f* à) terra, fio-terra *m* ♦ *vt* (*plane*) manter em terra; (*US*: *ELEC*) ligar à terra ♦ *vi* (*ship*) encalhar ♦ *adj* (*coffee etc*) moído; (*US*: *meat*) picado; **~s** *npl* (*of coffee etc*) borra; (*gardens etc*) jardins *mpl*, parque *m*; **on the ~** no chão; **to the ~** por terra; **below ~** embaixo da terra; **to gain/lose ~** ganhar/perder terreno; **common ~** consenso; **he covered a lot of ~ in his lecture** sua palestra cobriu uma área considerável.

ground cloth (*US*) *n* = **groundsheet**.

ground control *n* (*AVIAT*, *SPACE*) controle *m* de solo or terra.

ground floor *n* andar *m* térreo (*BR*), rés-do-chão *m* (*PT*).

grounding ['graʊndɪŋ] *n* (*SCH*) conhecimentos *mpl* básicos.

groundless ['graʊndlɪs] *adj* infundado.

groundnut ['graʊndnʌt] *n* amendoim *m*.

ground rent (*BRIT*) *n* foro.

groundsheet ['graʊndʃiːt] *n* capa impermeável.

groundskeeper ['graʊndziːpə*] (*US*) *n* (*SPORT*) zelador *m* de um campo esportivo.

groundsman ['graʊndzmən] (*irreg*) *n* (*SPORT*) zelador *m* de um campo esportivo.

ground staff *n* pessoal *m* de terra.

groundswell ['graʊndswɛl] *n* vagalhão *m*.

ground-to-ground missile *n* míssil *m* terra-terra.

groundwork ['graʊndwɜːk] *n* base *f*, preparação *f*.

group [gruːp] *n* grupo; (*musical*) conjunto ♦ *vt* (*also*: **~ together**) agrupar ♦ *vi* (*also*: **~ together**) agrupar-se.

grouse [graʊs] *n inv* (*bird*) tetraz *m*, galo-silvestre *m* ♦ *vi* (*complain*) queixar-se, resmungar.

grove [grəʊv] *n* arvoredo.

grovel ['grɒvl] *vi* (*fig*) humilhar-se; **to ~ (before)** abaixar-se (diante de).

grow [grəʊ] (*pt* **grew**, *pp* **grown**) *vi* crescer; (*increase*) aumentar; (*become*) tornar-se ♦ *vt* cultivar; **to ~ rich/weak** enriquecer(-se)/enfraquecer-se.

grow apart *vi* (*fig*) afastar-se (um do outro).

grow away from *vt fus* (*fig*) afastar-se de.

grow on *vt fus*: **that painting is ~ing on me** estou gostando cada vez mais daquele quadro.

grow out of *vt fus* (*clothes*) ficar muito grande para; (*habit*) superar com or perder o tempo.

grow up *vi* crescer, fazer-se homem/mulher.

grower ['grəʊə*] *n* cultivador(a) *m/f*, produtor(a) *m/f*.

NB: *European Portuguese adds the following consonants to certain words:* **b** (sú(b)dito, su(b)til); **c** (a(c)ção, a(c)cionista, a(c)to); **m** (inde(m)ne); **p** (ado(p)ção, ado(p)tar); *for further details see p.* xiii.

growing ['grəuıŋ] *adj* crescente; ~ **pains** (*MED*) dores *fpl* do crescimento; (*fig*) dificuldades *fpl* iniciais.

growl [graul] *vi* rosnar.

grown [grəun] *pp of* **grow** ♦ *adj* crescido, adulto.

grown-up *n* adulto/a, pessoa mais velha.

growth [grəuθ] *n* crescimento, desenvolvimento; (*what has grown*) crescimento; (*increase*) aumento; (*MED*) abcesso, tumor *m*.

growth rate *n* taxa de crescimento.

GRSM (*BRIT*) *n abbr* = **Graduate of the Royal Schools of Music.**

grub [grʌb] *n* larva, lagarta; (*inf: food*) comida, rango (*BR*).

grubby ['grʌbı] *adj* encardido.

grudge [grʌdʒ] *n* motivo de rancor ♦ *vt*: **to** ~ **sb sth** dar algo a alguém de má vontade, invejar algo a alguém; **to bear sb a** ~ **for sth** guardar rancor a alguém por algo; **he** ~**s (giving) the money** ele dá dinheiro de má vontade.

grudgingly ['grʌdʒıŋlı] *adv* de má vontade.

gruelling ['gruəlıŋ] *adj* duro, árduo.

gruesome ['gru:səm] *adj* horrível.

gruff [grʌf] *adj* (*voice*) rouco; (*manner*) brusco.

grumble ['grʌmbl] *vi* resmungar, bufar.

grumpy ['grʌmpı] *adj* rabugento.

grunt [grʌnt] *vi* grunhir ♦ *n* grunhido.

G-string *n* (*garment*) tapa-sexo *m*.

GSUSA *n abbr* = **Girl Scouts of the United States of America.**

GU (*US*) *abbr* (*POST*) = **Guam.**

guarantee [gærən'ti:] *n* garantia ♦ *vt* garantir.

guarantor [gærən'tɔ:*] *n* fiador(a) *m/f*.

guard [gɑ:d] *n* guarda; (*one man*) guarda *m*; (*BRIT: RAIL*) guarda-freio; (*safety device*) dispositivo de segurança; (*also: fire* ~) guarda-fogo ♦ *vt* guardar; (*protect*): **to** ~ **sth (against** *or* **from)** proteger algo de *or* contra; **to be on one's** ~ estar prevenido.

guard against *vt fus*: **to** ~ **against doing sth** guardar-se de fazer algo.

guard dog *n* cão *m* de guarda.

guarded ['gɑ:dıd] *adj* (*fig*) cauteloso.

guardian ['gɑ:dıən] *n* protetor(a) *m/f*; (*of minor*) tutor(a) *m/f*.

guard's van (*BRIT*) *n* (*RAIL*) vagão *m* de freio.

Guatemala [gwɔtə'mɑ:lə] *n* Guatemala.

Guatemalan [gwɔtə'mɑ:lən] *adj*, *n* guatemalteco/a.

Guernsey ['gə:nzı] *n* Guernsey *f* (*no article*).

guerrilla [gə'rılə] *n* guerrilheiro/a.

guerrilla warfare *n* guerrilha.

guess [gɛs] *vt*, *vi* adivinhar; (*US: suppose*) achar, supor ♦ *n* suposição *f*, conjetura; **to take** *or* **have a** ~ adivinhar, chutar (*inf*); **to keep sb** ~**ing** não contar a alguém; **my** ~ **is that ...** meu palpite é que ...; **to** ~ **right/wrong** acertar/errar.

guesstimate ['gɛstımıt] (*inf*) *n* estimativa aproximada.

guesswork ['gɛswə:k] *n* conjeturas *fpl*; **I got**

the answer by ~ obtive a resposta por adivinhação.

guest [gɛst] *n* convidado/a; (*in hotel*) hóspede *m/f*; **be my** ~ fique à vontade.

guest-house (*irreg*) *n* pensão *f*.

guest room *n* quarto de hóspedes.

guffaw [gʌ'fɔ:] *n* gargalhada ♦ *vi* dar gargalhadas.

guidance ['gaıdəns] *n* orientação *f*; (*advice*) conselhos *mpl*; **under the** ~ **of** sob a direção de, orientado por; **vocational** *or* **careers** ~ orientação vocacional; **marriage** ~ aconselhamento conjugal.

guide [gaıd] *n* (*person*) guia *m/f*; (*book, fig*) guia *m*; (*also: girl* ~) escoteira ♦ *vt* guiar; **to be** ~**d by sb/sth** orientar-se com alguém/por algo.

guidebook ['gaıdbuk] *n* guia *m*.

guided missile ['gaıdıd-] *n* (*internally controlled*) míssil *m* guiado; (*remote-controlled*) míssil *m* teleguiado.

guide dog *n* cão *m* de guia.

guidelines ['gaıdlaınz] *npl* (*fig*) princípios *mpl* gerais, diretrizes *fpl*.

guild [gıld] *n* grêmio.

guildhall ['gıldhɔ:l] (*BRIT*) *n* sede *f* da prefeitura.

guile [gaıl] *n* astúcia.

guileless ['gaıllıs] *adj* ingênuo, cândido.

guillotine ['gıləti:n] *n* guilhotina.

guilt [gılt] *n* culpa.

guilty ['gıltı] *adj* culpado; **to plead** ~**/not** ~ declarar-se culpado/inocente.

Guinea ['gını] *n*: **Republic of** ~ (República da) Guiné *f*.

guinea ['gını] (*BRIT*) *n* guinéu *m* (= *21 shillings*: *antiga unidade monetária equivalente a £1.05*).

guinea pig ['gınıpıg] *n* porquinho-da-Índia *m*, cobaia; (*fig*) cobaia.

guise [gaız] *n*: **in** *or* **under the** ~ **of** sob a aparência de.

guitar [gı'tɑ:*] *n* violão *m*.

guitarist [gı'tɑ:rıst] *n* violonista *m/f*.

gulch [gʌltʃ] (*US*) *n* ravina.

gulf [gʌlf] *n* golfo; (*abyss*) abismo; **the (Persian) G** ~ o Golfo Pérsico.

Gulf States *npl*: **the** ~ (*in Middle East*) os países do Golfo Pérsico.

Gulf Stream *n*: **the** ~ a corrente do Golfo.

gull [gʌl] *n* gaivota.

gullet ['gʌlıt] *n* esôfago.

gullibility [gʌlə'bılıtı] *n* credulidade *f*.

gullible ['gʌlıbl] *adj* crédulo.

gully ['gʌlı] *n* barranco.

gulp [gʌlp] *vi* engolir em seco ♦ *vt* (*also:* ~ *down*) engolir ♦ *n* (*of drink*) gole *m*; **at one** ~ de um gole só.

gum [gʌm] *n* (*ANAT*) gengiva; (*glue*) goma; (*also: chewing-*~) chiclete *m* (*BR*), pastilha elástica (*PT*) ♦ *vt* colar.

gum up *vt*: **to** ~ **up the works** (*inf*) estragar tudo.

gumboil ['gʌmbɔıl] *n* abscesso gengival, parúlide *f*.

gumboots ['gʌmbuːts] (*BRIT*) *npl* botas *fpl* de borracha, galochas *fpl*.

gumption ['gʌmpʃən] *n* juízo, bom senso.

gun [gʌn] *n* (*gen*) arma (de fogo); (*revolver*) revólver *m*; (*small*) pistola; (*rifle*) espingarda; (*cannon*) canhão *m* ♦ *vt* (*also*: ~ *down*) balear; **to stick to one's** ~**s** (*fig*) não dar o braço a torcer, ser durão (*inf*).

gunboat ['gʌnbəut] *n* canhoneira.

gun dog *n* cão *m* de caça.

gunfire ['gʌnfaɪə*] *n* tiroteio.

gunk [gʌŋk] (*inf*) *n* sujeira (*BR*), sujidade *f* (*PT*).

gunman ['gʌnmən] (*irreg*) *n* pistoleiro.

gunner ['gʌnə*] *n* artilheiro.

gunpoint ['gʌnpɔɪnt] *n*: **at** ~ sob a ameaça de uma arma.

gunpowder ['gʌnpaudə*] *n* pólvora.

gunrunner ['gʌnrʌnə*] *n* contrabandista *m/f* de armas.

gunrunning ['gʌnrʌnɪŋ] *n* contrabando de armas.

gunshot ['gʌnʃɔt] *n* tiro (de arma de fogo); **within** ~ ao alcance do tiro.

gunsmith ['gʌnsmɪθ] *n* armeiro/a.

gurgle ['gəːgl] *vi* gorgolejar ♦ *n* gorgolejo.

guru ['guruː] *n* guru *m*.

gush [gʌʃ] *vi* jorrar; (*fig*) alvoroçar-se ♦ *n* jorro.

gusset ['gʌsɪt] *n* nesga; (*of tights, pants*) entreperna.

gust [gʌst] *n* (*of wind*) rajada.

gusto ['gʌstəu] *n* entusiasmo, garra.

gut [gʌt] *n* intestino, tripa; (*MUS etc*) corda de tripa ♦ *vt* (*poultry, fish*) estripar; (*building*) destruir o interior de; ~**s** *npl* (*courage*) coragem *f*, raça (*inf*); **to hate sb's** ~**s** ter alguém atravessado na garganta, não poder ver alguém nem pintado.

gut reaction *n* reação *f* instintiva.

gutter ['gʌtə*] *n* (*of roof*) calha; (*in street*) sarjeta.

guttural ['gʌtərl] *adj* gutural.

guy [gaɪ] *n* (*also*: ~*rope*) corda; (*inf: man*) cara *m* (*BR*), tipo (*PT*).

Guyana [gaɪˈænə] *n* Guiana.

Guyanese [gaɪəˈniːz] *adj*, *n* guianense *m/f*.

guzzle ['gʌzl] *vi* comer *or* beber com gula ♦ *vt* engolir com gula.

gym [dʒɪm] *n* (*also: gymnasium*) ginásio; (*also: gymnastics*) ginástica.

gymkhana [dʒɪmˈkɑːnə] *n* gincana.

gymnasium [dʒɪmˈneɪzɪəm] *n* ginásio.

gymnast ['dʒɪmnæst] *n* ginasta *m/f*.

gymnastics [dʒɪmˈnæstɪks] *n* ginástica.

gym shoes *npl* tênis *mpl*.

gym slip (*BRIT*) *n* uniforme *m* escolar.

gynaecologist [gaɪnɪˈkɔlədʒɪst] (*US* **gynecologist**) *n* ginecologista *m/f*.

gynaecology [gaɪnəˈkɔlədʒɪ] (*US* **gynecology**) *n* ginecologia.

gypsy ['dʒɪpsɪ] *n*, *cpd* = **gipsy**.

gyrate [dʒaɪˈreɪt] *vi* girar.

gyroscope ['dʒaɪərəskəup] *n* giroscópio.

H

H, h [eɪtʃ] *n* (*letter*) H, h *m*; **H for Harry** (*BRIT*) *or* **How** (*US*) H de Henrique.

habeas corpus ['heɪbɪəsˈkɔːpəs] *n* (*LAW*) habeas-corpus *m*.

haberdashery ['hæbəˈdæʃərɪ] (*BRIT*) *n* armarinho.

habit ['hæbɪt] *n* hábito, costume *m*; (*costume*) hábito; **to get out of/into the** ~ **of doing sth** perder/criar o hábito de fazer algo.

habitable ['hæbɪtəbl] *adj* habitável.

habitat ['hæbɪtæt] *n* habitat *m*.

habitation [hæbɪˈteɪʃən] *n* habitação *f*.

habitual [həˈbɪtjuəl] *adj* habitual, costumeiro; (*drinker, liar*) inveterado.

habitually [həˈbɪtjuəlɪ] *adv* habitualmente.

hack [hæk] *vt* (*cut*) cortar; (*chop*) talhar ♦ *n* corte *m*; (*axe blow*) talho; (*pej: writer*) escrevinhador(a) *m/f*; (*old horse*) metungo.

hackles ['hæklz] *npl*: **to make sb's** ~ **rise** (*fig*) enfurecer alguém.

hackney cab ['hæknɪ-] *n* fiacre *m*.

hackneyed ['hæknɪd] *adj* corriqueiro, batido.

had [hæd] *pt, pp of* **have**.

haddock ['hædək] (*pl inv or* ~**s**) *n* hadoque *m* (*BR*), eglefim *m* (*PT*).

hadn't ['hædnt] = **had not**.

haematology ['hiːməˈtɔlədʒɪ] (*US* **hematology**) *n* hematologia.

haemoglobin ['hiːməˈgləubɪn] (*US* **hemoglobin**) *n* hemoglobina.

haemophilia ['hiːməˈfɪlɪə] (*US* **hemophilia**) *n* hemofilia.

haemorrhage ['hɛmərɪdʒ] (*US* **hemorrhage**) *n* hemorragia.

haemorrhoids ['hɛmərɔɪdz] (*US* **hemorrhoids**) *npl* hemorróidas *fpl*.

hag [hæg] *n* (*ugly*) bruxa; (*nasty*) megera; (*witch*) bruxa.

haggard ['hægəd] *adj* emaciado, macilento.

haggis ['hægɪs] *n* miúdos de carneiro com aveia, cozidos no estômago do animal.

haggle ['hægl] *vi* (*bargain*) pechinchar, regatear; **to** ~ **over** discutir sobre.

haggling ['hæglɪŋ] *n* regateio.

Hague [heɪg] *n*: **The** ~ Haia.

hail [heɪl] *n* (*weather*) granizo ♦ *vt* (*greet*) cumprimentar, saudar; (*call*) chamar ♦ *vi* chover granizo; (*originate*): **he** ~**s from Scotland** ele é originário da Escócia.

hailstone ['heɪlstəun] *n* pedra de granizo.

hailstorm ['heɪlstɔːm] *n* tempestade *f* de granizo.

hair [heə*] *n* (*of human*) cabelo; (*of animal, on legs*) pêlo; (*one* ~) fio de cabelo, pêlo; (*head of* ~) cabeleira; **grey** ~ cabelo grisalho; **to do one's** ~ pentear-se.

hairbrush ['heəbrʌʃ] *n* escova de cabelo.

haircut ['heəkʌt] *n* corte *m* de cabelo.

hairdo ['heədu:] *n* penteado.

hairdresser ['heədresə*] *n* cabeleireiro/a.

hairdresser's *n* cabeleireiro.

hair-dryer *n* secador *m* de cabelo.

-haired [heəd] *suffix*: **fair/long**~ de cabelo louro/comprido.

hairgrip ['heəgrɪp] *n* grampo (*BR*), gancho (*PT*).

hairline ['heəlaɪn] *n* contorno do couro cabeludo.

hairline fracture *n* fratura muito fina.

hairnet ['heənet] *n* rede *f* de cabelo.

hair oil *n* óleo para o cabelo.

hairpiece ['heəpi:s] *n* aplique *m*.

hairpin ['heəpɪn] *n* grampo (*BR*), gancho (*PT*), pinça.

hairpin bend (*US* **hairpin curve**) *n* curva fechada.

hair-raising [-'reɪzɪŋ] *adj* horripilante, de arrepiar os cabelos.

hair remover *n* (creme *m*) depilatório.

hair spray *n* laquê *m* (*BR*), laca (*PT*).

hairstyle ['heəstaɪl] *n* penteado.

hairy ['heərɪ] *adj* cabeludo, peludo; (*fig*) perigoso.

Haiti ['heɪtɪ] *n* Haiti *m*.

hake [heɪk] (*pl inv or* ~**s**) *n* abrótea.

halcyon ['hælsɪən] *adj* tranqüilo.

hale [heɪl] *adj*: ~ **and hearty** robusto, em ótima forma.

half [hɑːf] (*pl* **halves**) *n* metade *f*; (*SPORT: of match*) tempo; (*of ground*) lado ♦ *adj* meio ♦ *adv* meio, pela metade; ~**-an-hour** meia hora; ~ **a pound** meia libra; **two and a** ~ dois e meio; **a week and a** ~ uma semana e meia; ~ (**of it**) a metade; ~ (**of**) a metade de; ~ **the amount of** a metade de; **to cut sth in** ~ cortar algo ao meio; ~ **past three** três e meia; ~ **asleep/empty/closed** meio adormecido/vazio/fechado; **to go halves (with sb)** rachar as despesas (com alguém).

half-back *n* (*SPORT*) meio-de-campo.

half-baked (*inf*) *adj* (*idea, scheme*) mal planejado.

half-breed *n* mestiço/a.

half-brother *n* meio-irmão *m*.

half-caste *n* mestiço/a.

half-hearted *adj* irresoluto, indiferente.

half-hour *n* meia hora.

half-mast *n*: **at** ~ (*flag*) a meio-pau.

halfpenny ['heɪpnɪ] *n* meio pêni *m*.

half-price *adj* pela metade do preço ♦ *adv* (*also: at* ~) pela metade do preço.

half term (*BRIT*) *n* (*SCH*) dias de folga no meio do semestre.

half-time *n* meio tempo.

halfway ['hɑːf'weɪ] *adv* a meio caminho; **to**

meet sb ~ (*fig*) chegar a um meio-termo com alguém.

half-yearly *adv* semestralmente ♦ *adj* semestral.

halibut ['hælɪbət] *n inv* hipoglosso.

halitosis [hælɪ'təʊsɪs] *n* halitose *f*, mau hálito.

hall [hɔːl] *n* (*for concerts*) sala; (*entrance way*) hall *m*, entrada; (*corridor*) corredor *m*; **town** ~ prefeitura (*BR*), câmara municipal (*PT*); ~ **of residence** (*BRIT*) residência universitária.

hallmark ['hɔːlmɑːk] *n* (*also fig*) marca.

hallo [hə'ləʊ] *excl* = **hello**.

Hallowe'en ['hæləu'iːn] *n* Dia *m* das Bruxas (*31 de outubro*).

hallucination [həlu:sɪ'neɪʃən] *n* alucinação *f*.

hallway ['hɔːlweɪ] *n* hall *m*, entrada; (*corridor*) corredor *m*.

halo ['heɪləu] *n* (*of saint*) auréola; (*of sun*) halo.

halt [hɔːlt] *n* (*stop*) parada (*BR*), paragem *f* (*PT*); (*RAIL*) pequena parada; (*MIL*) alto ♦ *vi* parar; (*MIL*) fazer alto ♦ *vt* deter; (*process*) interromper; **to call a** ~ **to sth** (*fig*) pôr um fim a algo.

halter ['hɔːltə*] *n* (*for horse*) cabresto.

halterneck ['hɔːltənek] *adj* (*dress*) frente-única *inv*.

halve [hɑːv] *vt* (*divide*) dividir ao meio; (*reduce by half*) reduzir à metade.

halves [hɑːvz] *npl of* **half**.

ham [hæm] *n* presunto, fiambre *m* (*PT*); (*inf: actor, actress*) canastrão/trona *m/f*; (*: also: radio* ~) rádio-amador/a *m/f*.

hamburger ['hæmbɜːgə*] *n* hambúrguer *m*.

ham-fisted [-'fɪstɪd] (*BRIT*) *adj* desajeitado.

ham-handed [-'hændɪd] (*US*) *adj* desajeitado.

hamlet ['hæmlɪt] *n* aldeola, lugarejo.

hammer ['hæmə*] *n* martelo ♦ *vt* martelar; (*fig*) dar uma surra em ♦ *vi* (*on door*) bater insistentemente; **to** ~ **a point home to sb** fincar uma idéia na mente de alguém.

hammer out *vt* (*metal*) malhar; (*fig: solution*) elaborar.

hammock ['hæmək] *n* rede *f*.

hamper ['hæmpə*] *vt* dificultar, atrapalhar ♦ *n* cesto.

hamster ['hæmstə*] *n* hamster *m*.

hamstring ['hæmstrɪŋ] *n* (*ANAT*) tendão *m* do jarrete.

hand [hænd] *n* mão *f*; (*of clock*) ponteiro; (*writing*) letra; (*applause*) aplauso; (*at cards*) cartas *fpl*; (*worker*) trabalhador *m*; (*measurement*) palmo ♦ *vt* (*give*) dar, passar; (*deliver*) entregar; **to give sb a** ~ dar uma mãozinha a alguém, dar uma ajuda a alguém; **at** ~ à mão, disponível; **in** ~ sob controle; (*COMM*) em caixa, à disposição; **to be on** ~ (*person*) estar disponível; (*emergency services*) estar num estado de prontidão; **to** ~ (*information*) à mão; **to force sb's** ~ forçar alguém a agir; **to have a free** ~ ter carta branca; **to have sth in one's** ~ ter algo na mão; **on the one** ~ ..., **on the other** ~ ... por um lado ..., por outro (lado) ....

hand down vt passar; (tradition, heirloom) transmitir; (US: sentence, verdict) proferir.

hand in vt entregar.

hand out vt distribuir.

hand over vt (deliver) entregar; (surrender) ceder; (powers etc) transmitir.

hand round (BRIT) vt (information) fazer circular; (chocolates) oferecer.

handbag ['hændbæg] n bolsa.

handball ['hændbɔ:l] n handebol m.

handbasin ['hændbeɪsn] n pia (BR), lavatório (PT).

handbook ['hændbuk] n manual m.

handbrake ['hændbreɪk] n freio (BR) or travão m (PT) de mão.

hand cream n creme m para as mãos.

handcuffs ['hændkʌfs] npl algemas fpl.

handful ['hændful] n punhado.

handicap ['hændɪkæp] n (MED) incapacidade f; (disadvantage) desvantagem f ♦ vt prejudicar; **mentally/physically ~ped** deficiente mental/físico.

handicraft ['hændɪkrɑːft] n artesanato, trabalho manual.

handiwork ['hændɪwəːk] n obra; **this looks like his ~** (pej) isso parece coisa dele.

handkerchief ['hæŋkətʃɪf] n lenço.

handle ['hændl] n (of door etc) maçaneta; (of bag etc) alça; (of cup etc) asa; (of knife etc) cabo; (for winding) manivela; (inf: name) título ♦ vt (touch) manusear; (deal with) tratar de; (treat: people) lidar com; "~ with care" "cuidado — frágil"; **to fly off the ~** perder as estribeiras.

handlebar(s) ['hɑːndlbɑː(z)] n(pl) guidom (PT: -dão) m.

handling charges ['hændlɪŋ-] npl taxa de manuseio; (BANKING) comissão f.

hand-luggage n bagagem f de mão.

handmade ['hændmeɪd] adj feito a mão.

handout ['hændaut] n (charity) doação f, esmola; (leaflet) folheto; (university) apostila.

hand-picked [-'pɪkt] adj (fruit) colhido à mão; (staff) escolhido a dedo.

handrail ['hændreɪl] n (on staircase) corrimão m.

handshake ['hændʃeɪk] n aperto de mão; (COMPUT) handshake m.

handsome ['hænsəm] adj bonito; (gift) generoso; (profit) considerável.

handstand ['hændstænd] n: **to do a ~** plantar bananeira.

hand-to-mouth adj (existence) ao deus-dará.

handwriting ['hændraɪtɪŋ] n letra, caligrafia.

handwritten ['hændrɪtn] adj escrito à mão, manuscrito.

handy ['hændɪ] adj (close at hand) à mão; (convenient) útil, prático; (skilful) habilidoso, hábil; **to come in ~** ser útil.

handyman ['hændɪmæn] (irreg) n biscateiro,

faz-tudo m.

hang [hæŋ] (pt, pp hung) vt pendurar; (on wall etc) prender; (head) baixar; (criminal: pt, pp ~ed) enforcar ♦ vi estar pendurado; (hair, drapery) cair ♦ n (inf): **to get the ~ of (doing) sth** pegar o jeito de (fazer) algo.

hang about vi vadiar, vagabundear; ~ **about!** (inf) 'pera aí!

hang back vi (hesitate): **to ~ back from (doing) sth** vacilar em (fazer) algo.

hang on vi (wait) esperar ♦ vt fus (depend on) depender de; **to ~ on to** (keep hold of) não soltar, segurar; (keep) ficar com.

hang out vt (washing) estender ♦ vi (be visible) aparecer; (inf: spend time) fazer ponto.

hang together vi (argument etc) ser coerente.

hang up vi (TEL) desligar ♦ vt (coat) pendurar; **to ~ up on sb** (TEL) bater o telefone na cara de alguém.

hangar ['hæŋə*] n hangar m.

hangdog ['hæŋdɔg] adj (look, expression) envergonhado.

hanger ['hæŋə*] n cabide m.

hanger-on n parasita m/f, filão/filona m/f.

hang-gliding n vôo livre.

hanging ['hæŋɪŋ] n enforcamento.

hangman ['hæŋmən] (irreg) n carrasco.

hangover ['hæŋəuvə*] n (after drinking) ressaca; **to have a ~** estar de ressaca.

hang-up n mania, grilo.

hank [hæŋk] n meada.

hanker ['hæŋkə*] vi: **to ~ after** (miss) sentir saudade de; (long for) ansiar por.

hankie ['hæŋkɪ] n abbr = **handkerchief**.

hanky ['hæŋkɪ] n abbr = **handkerchief**.

Hants (BRIT) abbr = **Hampshire**.

haphazard [hæp'hæzəd] adj (random) fortuito; (disorganized) desorganizado.

hapless ['hæplɪs] adj desafortunado.

happen ['hæpən] vi acontecer; **what's ~ing?** o que é que está acontecendo?; **she ~ed to be in London** aconteceu que estava em Londres; **if anything ~ed to him** se lhe acontecesse alguma coisa; **as it ~s** ... acontece que ....

happen (up)on vt fus dar com.

happening ['hæpənɪŋ] n acontecimento, ocorrência.

happily ['hæpɪlɪ] adv (luckily) felizmente; (cheerfully) alegremente.

happiness ['hæpɪnɪs] n felicidade f; (joy) alegria.

happy ['hæpɪ] adj feliz, contente; **to be ~ (with)** estar contente (com); **to be ~** ser feliz; **yes, I'd be ~ to** sim, com muito prazer; ~ **birthday!** feliz aniversário; (said to somebody) parabéns!; ~ **Christmas/New Year** feliz Natal/Ano Novo.

happy-go-lucky adj despreocupado.

harangue [hə'ræŋ] vt arengar.

harass ['hærəs] vt (bother) importunar;

NB: European Portuguese adds the following consonants to certain words: **b** (sú(b)dito, su(b)til); **c** (a(c)ção, a(c)cionista, a(c)to); **m** (inde(m)ne); **p** (ado(p)ção, ado(p)tar); for further details see p. xiii.

(*pursue*) acossar.
harassed ['hærəst] *adj* chateado.
harassment ['hærəsmənt] *n* perseguição *f*; (*worry*) preocupação *f*.
harbour ['hɑːbə*] (*US* **harbor**) *n* porto ♦ *vt* (*hope etc*) abrigar; (*hide*) esconder; **to ~ a grudge against sb** guardar rancor a alguém.
harbo(u)r dues *npl* direitos *mpl* portuários.
harbo(u)r master *n* capitão *m* do porto.
hard [hɑːd] *adj* duro; (*difficult*) difícil; (*work*) árduo; (*person*) severo, cruel ♦ *adv* (*work*) muito, diligentemente; (*think, try*) seriamente; **to look ~ at** olhar firme *or* fixamente para; **~ luck!** azar!; **no ~ feelings!** sem ressentimentos!; **to be ~ of hearing** ser surdo; **to be ~ done by** ser tratado injustamente; **to be ~ on sb** ser rigoroso com alguém; **I find it ~ to believe that ...** acho difícil acreditar que ....
hard-and-fast *adj* rígido.
hardback ['hɑːdbæk] *n* livro de capa dura.
hardboard ['hɑːdbɔːd] *n* madeira compensada.
hard-boiled egg [-'bɔɪld-] *n* ovo cozido.
hard cash *n* dinheiro vivo *or* em espécie.
hard copy *n* (*COMPUT*) cópia impressa.
hard-core *adj* (*pornography*) pesado; (*supporters*) ferrenho.
hard court *n* (*TENNIS*) quadra de cimento.
hard disk *n* (*COMPUT*) disco rígido.
harden ['hɑːdən] *vt* endurecer; (*steel*) temperar; (*fig*) tornar insensível ♦ *vi* endurecer-se.
hardened ['hɑːdnd] *adj* (*criminal, drinker*) inveterado; **to be ~ to sth** ser insensível a algo.
hardening ['hɑːdnɪŋ] *n* endurecimento.
hard-headed [-'hedɪd] *adj* prático, pouco sentimental.
hard-hearted *adj* empedernido, insensível.
hard labour *n* trabalhos *mpl* forçados.
hardliner [hɑːd'laɪnə*] *n* intransigente *m/f*.
hardly ['hɑːdlɪ] *adv* (*scarcely*) apenas, mal; **that can ~ be true** dificilmente pode ser verdade; **~ ever** quase nunca; **I can ~ believe it** mal posso acreditar nisso.
hardness ['hɑːdnɪs] *n* dureza.
hard sell *n* venda agressiva.
hardship ['hɑːdʃɪp] *n* (*troubles*) sofrimento; (*financial*) privação *f*.
hard shoulder (*BRIT*) *n* (*AUT*) acostamento (*BR*), berma (*PT*).
hard-up (*inf*) *adj* duro (*BR*), liso (*PT*).
hardware ['hɑːdwɛə*] *n* ferragens *fpl*, maquinaria; (*COMPUT*) hardware *m*.
hardware shop *n* loja de ferragens.
hard-wearing [-'wɛərɪŋ] *adj* resistente.
hard-working *adj* trabalhador(a).
hardy ['hɑːdɪ] *adj* forte; (*plant*) resistente.
hare [heə*] *n* lebre *f*.
hare-brained [-breɪnd] *adj* estonteado, desatinado.
harelip ['heəlɪp] *n* (*MED*) lábio leporino.
harem [hɑː'riːm] *n* harém *m*.
hark back [hɑːk-] *vi*: **to ~ back to** (*reminisce*) recordar; (*be reminiscent of*) lembrar.

harm [hɑːm] *n* mal *m*, dano ♦ *vt* (*person*) fazer mal a, prejudicar; (*thing*) danificar; **to mean no ~** ter boas intenções; **there's no ~ in trying** não faz mal tentar; **out of ~'s way** a salvo.
harmful ['hɑːmful] *adj* prejudicial; (*plant, weed*) daninho.
harmless ['hɑːmlɪs] *adj* inofensivo.
harmonic [hɑː'mɔnɪk] *adj* harmônico.
harmonica [hɑː'mɔnɪkə] *n* gaita de boca, harmônica.
harmonics [hɑː'mɔnɪks] *npl* harmônicos *mpl*.
harmonious [hɑː'məunɪəs] *adj* harmonioso.
harmonium [hɑː'məunɪəm] *n* harmônio.
harmonize ['hɑːmənaɪz] *vt, vi* harmonizar.
harmony ['hɑːmənɪ] *n* harmonia.
harness ['hɑːnɪs] *n* arreios *mpl* ♦ *vt* (*horse*) arrear, pôr arreios em; (*resources*) aproveitar.
harp [hɑːp] *n* harpa ♦ *vi*: **to ~ on about** bater sempre na mesma tecla sobre.
harpist ['hɑːpɪst] *n* harpista *m/f*.
harpoon [hɑː'puːn] *n* arpão *m* ♦ *vt* arpoar.
harpsichord ['hɑːpsɪkɔːd] *n* cravo, clavecino.
harrow ['hærəu] *n* (*AGR*) grade *f*, rastelo.
harrowing ['hærəuɪŋ] *adj* doloroso, pungente.
harry ['hærɪ] *vt* (*MIL, fig*) assolar.
harsh [hɑːʃ] *adj* (*hard*) duro, severo; (*rough: surface, taste*) áspero; (: *sound*) desarmonioso.
harshly ['hɑːʃlɪ] *adv* severamente.
harshness ['hɑːʃnɪs] *n* dureza, severidade *f*; (*roughness*) aspereza.
harvest ['hɑːvɪst] *n* colheita; (*of grapes*) vindima ♦ *vt, vi* colher.
harvester ['hɑːvɪstə*] *n* (*machine*) segadora; (*also: combine ~*) ceifeira-debulhadora; (*person*) segador(a) *m/f*.
has [hæz] *vb see* **have**.
has-been (*inf*) *n* (*person*): **he/she's a ~** ele/ela já era.
hash [hæʃ] *n* (*CULIN*) picadinho; (*fig: mess*) confusão *f*, bagunça ♦ *n abbr* (*inf*) = **hashish**.
hashish ['hæʃɪʃ] *n* haxixe *m*.
hasn't ['hæznt] = **has not**.
hassle ['hæsl] (*inf*) *n* (*fuss, problems*) complicação *f* ♦ *vt* molestar, chatear.
haste [heɪst] *n* pressa; **in ~** às pressas.
hasten ['heɪsn] *vt* acelerar ♦ *vi* apressar-se; **I ~ to add that ...** eu me apresso a acrescentar que ....
hastily ['heɪstɪlɪ] *adv* depressa.
hasty ['heɪstɪ] *adj* apressado.
hat [hæt] *n* chapéu *m*.
hatbox ['hætbɔks] *n* chapeleira.
hatch [hætʃ] *n* (*NAUT: also: ~way*) escotilha; (*BRIT: also: service ~*) comunicação *f* entre a cozinha e a sala de jantar ♦ *vi* sair do ovo, chocar ♦ *vt* chocar; (*plot*) tramar, arquitetar.
hatchback ['hætʃbæk] *n* (*AUT*) camionete *f*, hatch *m*.
hatchet ['hætʃɪt] *n* machadinha.
hate [heɪt] *vt* odiar, detestar ♦ *n* ódio; **to ~ to do** *or* **doing** odiar *or* detestar fazer; **I ~ to trouble you, but ...** desculpe incomodá-lo,

mas ....

hateful ['heɪtful] *adj* odioso.

hatred ['heɪtrɪd] *n* ódio.

hat trick (*BRIT*) *n* (*SPORT, also fig*) três vitórias (*or* gols *etc*) consecutivas.

haughty ['hɔːtɪ] *adj* soberbo, arrogante.

haul [hɔːl] *vt* puxar; (*by lorry*) carregar, fretar; (*NAUT*) levar à orça ♦ *n* (*of fish*) redada; (*of stolen goods etc*) pilhagem *f*, presa.

haulage ['hɔːlɪdʒ] *n* transporte *m* (rodoviário); (*costs*) gasto com transporte.

haulage contractor (*BRIT*) *n* (*firm*) transportadora; (*person*) transportador(a) *m/f*.

hauler ['hɔːlə*] (*US*) *n* = **haulier**.

haulier ['hɔːljə*] (*BRIT*) *n* (*firm*) transportadora; (*person*) transportador(a) *m/f*.

haunch [hɔːntʃ] *n* anca, quadril *m*; (*of meat*) quarto traseiro.

haunt [hɔːnt] *vt* (*subj: ghost*) assombrar; (*frequent*) freqüentar; (*obsess*) obcecar ♦ *n* lugar *m* freqüentado.

haunted ['hɔːntɪd] *adj* (*castle etc*) malassombrado.

haunting ['hɔːntɪŋ] *adj* (*sight, music*) obcecante.

Havana [hə'vænə] *n* Havana.

have [hæv] (*pt, pp* **had**) *vt* ter; (*possess*) possuir; (*shower*) tomar; (*meal*) comer ♦ *aux vb*: **he has gone** foi embora ♦ *n*: **the ~s and ~-nots** (*inf*) os ricos e os pobres; **I don't ~ any money (on me)** estou sem dinheiro; **to ~ breakfast** tomar café (*BR*), tomar o pequeno almoço (*PT*); **to ~ lunch** almoçar; **to ~ dinner** jantar; **I'll ~ a coffee** vou tomar um café; **to ~ a baby** dar à luz, ter um nenê (*BR*) *or* bebé (*PT*); **to ~ an operation** fazer uma operação; **to ~ a party** fazer uma festa; **to ~ sth done** mandar fazer algo; **he had a suit made** ele mandou fazer um terno; **let me ~ a try** deixe-me tentar; **she has to do it** ela tem que fazê-lo; **I had better leave** é melhor que eu vá embora; **I won't ~ it** não vou agüentar isso; **he's been had** (*inf*) ele comprou gato por lebre; **rumour has it (that)** ... dizem os boatos que ....

have in *vt*: **to ~ it in for sb** (*inf*) estar com implicância *or* de pinimba com alguém.

have on *vt*: **~ you anything on tomorrow?** (*BRIT*) você tem compromisso amanhã?; **to ~ sb on** (*BRIT*) brincar com alguém.

have out *vt*: **to ~ it out with sb** explicar-se com alguém.

haven ['heɪvn] *n* porto; (*fig*) abrigo, refúgio.

haven't ['hævnt] = **have not**.

haversack ['hævəsæk] *n* mochila.

havoc ['hævək] *n* destruição *f*: **to play ~ with** (*fig*) estragar.

Hawaii [hə'waiiː] *n* Havaí *m*.

Hawaiian [hɑ'waɪjən] *adj, n* havaiano/a.

hawk [hɔːk] *n* falcão *m* ♦ *vt* (*goods for sale*) mascatear.

hawker ['hɔːkə*] *n* camelô *m*, mascate *m*.

hawthorn ['hɔːθɔːn] *n* pilriteiro, estripeiro.

hay [heɪ] *n* feno.

hay fever *n* febre *f* do feno.

haystack ['heɪstæk] *n* palheiro.

haywire ['heɪwaɪə*] (*inf*) *adj*: **to go ~** (*person*) ficar maluco; (*plan*) desorganizar-se, degringolar.

hazard ['hæzəd] *n* (*danger*) perigo, risco; (*chance*) acaso ♦ *vt* aventurar, arriscar; **to be a health/fire ~** ser um risco para a saúde/de incêndio; **to ~ a guess** arriscar um palpite.

hazardous ['hæzədəs] *adj* (*dangerous*) perigoso; (*risky*) arriscado.

hazard pay (*US*) *n* adicional *m* por insalubridade.

hazard warning lights *npl* (*AUT*) pisca-alerta *m*.

haze [heɪz] *n* névoa, neblina.

hazel ['heɪzl] *n* (*tree*) aveleira ♦ *adj* (*eyes*) castanho-claro *inv*.

hazelnut ['heɪzlnʌt] *n* avelã *f*.

hazy ['heɪzɪ] *adj* nublado; (*idea*) confuso.

H-bomb *n* bomba de hidrogênio.

h & c (*BRIT*) *abbr* = **hot and cold (water)**.

HE *abbr* = **high explosive**; (*REL, DIPLOMACY*) = **His** (*or* **Her**) **Excellency**.

he [hiː] *pron* ele; **~ who** ... quem ..., aquele que ....; **~-bear** *etc* urso *etc* macho.

head [hɛd] *n* cabeça; (*leader*) chefe *m/f*, líder *m/f* ♦ *vt* (*list*) encabeçar; (*group*) liderar; **~s or tails** cara ou coroa; **~ first** de cabeça; **~ over heels** de pernas para o ar; **~ over heels in love** apaixonadíssimo; **to ~ the ball** cabecear a bola; **£10 a** *or* **per ~** £10 por pessoa *or* cabeça; **to sit at the ~ of the table** sentar-se à cabeceira da mesa; **to have a ~ for business** ter tino para negócios; **to have no ~ for heights** não suportar alturas; **to come to a ~** (*fig: situation etc*) chegar a um ponto crítico; **on your ~ be it** você que arque com as conseqüências.

head for *vt fus* dirigir-se a.

head off *vt* (*danger, threat*) desviar.

headache ['hɛdeɪk] *n* dor *f* de cabeça; **to have a ~** estar com dor de cabeça.

head cold *n* resfriado (*BR*), constipação *f* (*PT*).

headdress ['hɛddrɛs] *n* (*of Indian etc*) cocar *m*; (*of bride*) grinalda.

header ['hɛdə*] *n* (*BRIT: inf: FOOTBALL*) cabeçada; (*on page*) cabeçalho.

headhunter ['hɛdhʌntə*] *n* caçador *m* de cabeças.

heading ['hɛdɪŋ] *n* título, cabeçalho; (*subject title*) rubrica.

headlamp ['hɛdlæmp] (*BRIT*) *n* farol *m*.

headland ['hɛdlənd] *n* promontório.

headlight ['hɛdlaɪt] *n* farol *m*.

headline ['hɛdlaɪn] *n* manchete *f*.

headlong ['hɛdlɔŋ] *adv* (*fall*) de cabeça;

NB: European Portuguese adds the following consonants to certain words: **b** (sú(b)dito, su(b)til); **c** (a(c)ção, a(c)cionista, a(c)to); **m** (inde(m)ne); **p** (ado(p)ção, ado(p)tar); *for further details see p. xiii.*

(*rush*) precipitadamente.

headmaster [hɛd'mɑːstə*] n diretor m (de escola).

headmistress [hɛd'mɪstrɪs] n diretora f (de escola).

head office n matriz f.

head-on adj (*collision*) de frente.

headphones ['hɛdfəunz] npl fones mpl de ouvido.

headquarters [hɛd'kwɔːtəz] npl (*of business etc*) sede f; (*MIL*) quartel m general.

head-rest n apoio para a cabeça.

headroom ['hɛdrum] n (*in car*) espaço (para a cabeça); (*under bridge*) vão m livre.

headscarf ['hɛdskɑːf] (*irreg*) n lenço de cabeça.

headset ['hɛdsɛt] n fones mpl de ouvido.

headstone ['hɛdstəun] n lápide f de ponta cabeça.

headstrong ['hɛdstrɔŋ] adj voluntarioso, teimoso.

head waiter n maitre m (*BR*), chefe m de mesa (*PT*).

headway ['hɛdweɪ] n progresso; **to make ~** avançar.

headwind ['hɛdwɪnd] n vento contrário.

heady ['hɛdɪ] adj (*exciting*) emocionante; (*intoxicating*) estonteante.

heal [hiːl] vt curar ♦ vi cicatrizar.

health [hɛlθ] n saúde f; **good ~!** saúde!; **Department of H~** (*US*) ≈ Ministério da Saúde.

health centre (*BRIT*) n posto de saúde.

health food(s) n(pl) alimentos mpl naturais.

health food shop n loja de comida natural.

health hazard n risco para a saúde.

Health Service (*BRIT*) n: **the ~** o Serviço Nacional da Saúde, ≈ a Previdência Social.

healthy ['hɛlθɪ] adj saudável, sadio; (*economy*) próspero, forte.

heap [hiːp] n pilha, montão m ♦ vt amontoar, empilhar; (*plate*) encher; **~s (of)** (*inf: lots*) um monte de; **to ~ favours/praise/gifts etc on sb** cobrir or cumular alguém de favores/elogios/presentes etc.

hear [hɪə*] (*pt, pp* **heard**) vt ouvir; (*listen to*) escutar; (*news*) saber; (*lecture*) assistir a ♦ vi ouvir; **to ~ about** ouvir falar de; **when did you ~ about this?** quando você soube disso?; **to ~ from sb** ter notícias de alguém; **I've never heard of the book** eu nunca ouvi falar no livro.

hear out vt ouvir sem interromper.

heard [hɜːd] pt, pp of **hear**.

hearing ['hɪərɪŋ] n (*sense*) audição f; (*LAW*) audiência; **to give sb a ~** (*BRIT*) ouvir alguém.

hearing aid n aparelho para a surdez.

hearsay ['hɪəseɪ] n boato, ouvir-dizer m; **by ~** por ouvir dizer.

hearse [hɜːs] n carro fúnebre.

heart [hɑːt] n coração m; **~s** npl (*CARDS*) copas fpl; **at ~** no fundo; **by ~** (*learn, know*) de cor; **to lose ~** perder o ânimo; **to take ~** criar coragem; **to set one's ~ on sth/on**

doing sth decidir-se por algo/a fazer algo; **the ~ of the matter** a essência da questão.

heart attack n ataque m de coração.

heartbeat ['hɑːtbiːt] n batida do coração.

heartbreak ['hɑːtbreɪk] n desgosto, dor f.

heartbreaking ['hɑːtbreɪkɪŋ] adj desolador(a).

heartbroken ['hɑːtbrəukən]: **to be ~** estar inconsolável.

heartburn ['hɑːtbɜːn] n azia.

-hearted ['hɑːtɪd] suffix: **kind~** bondoso.

heartening ['hɑːtnɪŋ] adj animador(a).

heart failure n parada cardíaca.

heartfelt ['hɑːtfɛlt] adj (*cordial*) cordial; (*deeply felt*) sincero.

hearth [hɑːθ] n lar m; (*fireplace*) lareira.

heartily ['hɑːtɪlɪ] adv sinceramente, cordialmente; (*laugh*) a gargalhadas, com vontade; (*eat*) apetitosamente; **I ~ agree** concordo completamente; **to be ~ sick of** (*BRIT*) estar farto de.

heartland ['hɑːtlænd] n coração m (do país).

heartless ['hɑːtlɪs] adj cruel, sem coração.

heart-to-heart adj (*conversation*) franco, sincero ♦ n conversa franca.

heart transplant n transplante m de coração.

heartwarming ['hɑːtwɔːmɪŋ] adj emocionante.

hearty ['hɑːtɪ] adj cordial, sincero.

heat [hiːt] n calor m; (*ardour*) ardor m; (*SPORT: also: qualifying ~*) (prova) eliminatória; (*ZOOL*): **in ~, on ~** (*BRIT*) no cio ♦ vt esquentar; (*room, house*) aquecer; (*fig*) acalorar.

heat up vi aquecer-se, esquentar ♦ vt esquentar.

heated ['hiːtɪd] adj aquecido; (*fig*) acalorado.

heater ['hiːtə*] n aquecedor m.

heath [hiːθ] (*BRIT*) n charneca.

heathen ['hiːðn] adj, n pagão/pagã m/f.

heather ['hɛðə*] n urze f.

heating ['hiːtɪŋ] n aquecimento, calefação f.

heat-resistant adj resistente ao calor.

heatstroke ['hiːtstrəuk] n insolação f.

heatwave ['hiːtweɪv] n onda de calor.

heave [hiːv] vt (*pull*) puxar; (*push*) empurrar (com esforço); (*lift*) levantar (com esforço) ♦ vi (*water*) agitar-se; (*retch*) ter ânsias de vômito ♦ n puxão m; empurrão m; **to ~ a sigh** soltar um suspiro.

heave to vi (*NAUT*) capear.

heaven ['hɛvn] n céu m, paraíso; **~ forbid!** Deus me livre!; **thank ~!** graças a Deus!; **for ~'s sake!** pelo amor de Deus!

heavenly ['hɛvnlɪ] adj celestial; (*REL*) divino.

heavily ['hɛvɪlɪ] adv pesadamente; (*drink, smoke*) excessivamente; (*sleep, sigh*) profundamente.

heavy ['hɛvɪ] adj pesado; (*work*) duro; (*sea*) violento; (*rain, meal*) forte; (*drinker, smoker*) inveterado; **it's ~ going** é difícil.

heavy cream (*US*) n creme de leite.

heavy-duty adj de serviço pesado.

heavy goods vehicle (*BRIT*) n caminhão m de carga pesada.

heavy-handed [-'hændɪd] adj (*fig*) desajeitado, sem tato.

heavyweight ['hɛvɪweɪt] *n* (*SPORT*) peso-pesado.

Hebrew ['hiːbruː] *adj* hebreu/hebréia; (*LING*) hebraico ♦ *n* (*LING*) hebraico.

Hebrides ['hɛbrɪdiːz] *n*: **the ~ as** (ilhas) Hé-bridas.

heckle ['hɛkl] *vt* apartear.

heckler ['hɛklə*] *n* pessoa que aparteia.

hectare ['hɛktɛə*] (*BRIT*) *n* hectare *m*.

hectic ['hɛktɪk] *adj* febril, agitado.

hector ['hɛktə*] *vt* importunar, implicar com.

he'd [hiːd] = **he would**; **he had**.

hedge [hɛdʒ] *n* cerca viva, sebe *f* ♦ *vi* dar evasivas ♦ *vt*: **to ~ one's bets** (*fig*) resguardar-se; **as a ~ against inflation** para precaver-se da inflação.

hedge in *vt* cercar com uma sebe.

hedgehog ['hɛdʒhɔg] *n* ouriço.

hedgerow ['hɛdʒrəu] *n* cercas *fpl* vivas, sebes *fpl*.

hedonism ['hiːdənɪzm] *n* hedonismo.

heed [hiːd] *vt* (*also: take ~ of: attend to*) prestar atenção a; (: *bear in mind*) levar em consideração.

heedless ['hiːdlɪs] *adj* desatento, negligente.

heel [hiːl] *n* (*of shoe*) salto; (*of foot*) calcanhar *m* ♦ *vt* (*shoe*) pôr salto em; **to take to one's ~s** dar no pé *or* aos calcanhares.

hefty ['hɛftɪ] *adj* (*person*) robusto; (*piece*) grande; (*price*) alto.

heifer ['hɛfə*] *n* novilha, bezerra.

height [haɪt] *n* (*of person*) estatura; (*of building*) altura; (*high ground*) monte *m*; (*altitude*) altitude *f*; (*fig: of glory*) cume *m*; (: *of stupidity*) cúmulo; **what ~ are you?** quanto você tem de altura?; **of average ~** de estatura mediana; **to be afraid of ~s** ter medo de alturas; **it's the ~ of fashion** é a última palavra *or* moda.

heighten ['haɪtən] *vt* elevar; (*fig*) aumentar.

heinous ['hiːnəs] *adj* hediondo, abominável.

heir [ɛə*] *n* herdeiro.

heir apparent *n* herdeiro presuntivo.

heiress ['ɛərɪs] *n* herdeira.

heirloom ['ɛəluːm] *n* relíquia de família.

heist [haɪst] (*US: inf*) *n* (*hold-up*) assalto.

held [hɛld] *pt, pp of* **hold**.

helicopter ['hɛlɪkɔptə*] *n* helicóptero.

heliport ['hɛlɪpɔːt] *n* (*AVIAT*) heliporto.

helium ['hiːliəm] *n* hélio.

hell [hɛl] *n* inferno; **a ~ of a ...** (*inf*) um ... da-nado; **oh ~!** (*inf*) droga!

he'll [hiːl] = **he will**; **he shall**.

hellish ['hɛlɪʃ] *adj* infernal; (*inf*) terrível.

hello [hə'ləu] *excl* oi! (*BR*), olá! (*PT*); (*on phone*) alô! (*BR*), está! (*PT*); (*surprise*) ora essa!

helm [hɛlm] *n* (*NAUT*) timão *m*, leme *m*.

helmet ['hɛlmɪt] *n* capacete *m*.

helmsman ['hɛlmzmən] (*irreg*) *n* timoneiro.

help [hɛlp] *n* ajuda; (*charwoman*) faxineira;

(*assistant etc*) auxiliar *m/f* ♦ *vt* ajudar; **~!** socorro!; **~ yourself** sirva-se; **can I ~ you?** (*in shop*) deseja alguma coisa?; **with the ~ of** com a ajuda de; **to be of ~ to sb** ajudar alguém, ser útil a alguém; **to ~ sb (to) do sth** ajudar alguém a fazer algo; **he can't ~ it** não tem culpa.

helper ['hɛlpə*] *n* ajudante *m/f*.

helpful ['hɛlpful] *adj* (*thing*) útil, benéfico; (*person*) prestativo.

helping ['hɛlpɪŋ] *n* porção *f*.

helpless ['hɛlplɪs] *adj* (*incapable*) incapaz; (*defenceless*) indefeso; (*baby*) desamparado.

helplessly ['hɛlplɪslɪ] *adv* (*watch*) sem poder fazer nada.

Helsinki [hɛl'sɪŋkɪ] *n* Helsinque.

helter-skelter ['hɛltə'skɛltə*] (*BRIT*) *n* (*at amusement park*) tobogã *m*.

hem [hɛm] *n* bainha ♦ *vt* embainhar.

hem in *vt* cercar, encurralar; **to feel ~med in** sentir-se acuado.

he-man (*irreg*) *n* macho.

hematology ['hiːmə'tɔlədʒɪ] (*US*) *n* = **haematology**.

hemisphere ['hɛmɪsfɪə*] *n* hemisfério.

hemlock ['hɛmlɔk] *n* cicuta.

hemoglobin ['hiːmə'gləubɪn] (*US*) *n* = **haemoglobin**.

hemophilia ['hiːmə'fɪlɪə] (*US*) *n* = **haemophilia**.

hemorrhage ['hɛmərɪdʒ] (*US*) *n* = **haemorrhage**.

hemorrhoids ['hɛmərɔɪdʒ] (*US*) *npl* = **haemorrhoids**.

hemp [hɛmp] *n* cânhamo.

hen [hɛn] *n* galinha; (*female bird*) fêmea.

hence [hɛns] *adv* (*therefore*) daí, portanto; **2 years ~** daqui a 2 anos.

henceforth ['hɛns'fɔːθ] *adv* de agora em diante, doravante.

henchman ['hɛntʃmən] (*irreg*) *n* jagunço, ca-panga *m*.

henna ['hɛnə] *n* hena.

hen party (*inf*) *n* reunião *f* de mulheres.

henpecked ['hɛnpɛkt] *adj* dominado pela esposa.

hepatitis [hɛpə'taɪtɪs] *n* hepatite *f*.

her [həː*] *pron* (*direct*) a; (*indirect*) lhe; (*stressed, after prep*) ela ♦ *adj* seu/sua, dela; **~ name** o nome dela; **I see ~** vejo-a, vejo ela; (*BR: inf*); **give ~ a book** dá-lhe um livro, dá um livro a ela.

herald ['hɛrəld] *n* (*forerunner*) precursor(a) *m/f* ♦ *vt* anunciar.

heraldic [hɛ'rældɪk] *adj* heráldico.

heraldry ['hɛrəldrɪ] *n* heráldica.

herb [həːb] *n* erva.

herbaceous [həː'beɪʃəs] *adj* herbáceo.

herbal ['həːbəl] *adj* herbáceo; **~ tea** tisana.

herd [həːd] *n* rebanho ♦ *vt* (*drive: animals, people*) conduzir; (*gather*) arrebanhar.

here [hɪə*] *adv* aqui; (*to this place*) para cá ♦

NB: European Portuguese adds the following consonants to certain words: **b** (sú(b)dito, su(b)til); **c** (a(c)ção, a(c)cionista, a(c)to); **m** (inde(m)ne); **p** (ado(p)ção, ado(p)tar); *for further details see p. xiii.*

excl toma!; ~! *(present)* presente!; ~ **he/ she is** aqui está ele/ela; ~ **she comes** lá vem ela; **come** ~! vem cá!; ~ **and there** aqui e ali.

hereabouts ['hɪərə'bauts] *adv* por aqui.

hereafter [hɪər'ɑːftə*] *adv* daqui por diante ♦ *n*: **the** ~ a vida de além-túmulo.

hereby [hɪə'baɪ] *adv (in letter)* por este meio.

hereditary [hɪ'redɪtrɪ] *adj* hereditário.

heredity [hɪ'redɪtɪ] *n* hereditariedade *f*.

heresy ['herəsɪ] *n* heresia.

heretic ['herətɪk] *n* herege *m/f*.

heretical [hɪ'retɪkl] *adj* herético.

herewith [hɪə'wɪð] *adv* em anexo, junto.

heritage ['herɪtɪdʒ] *n* herança; *(fig)* patrimônio; **our national** ~ nosso patrimônio nacional.

hermetically [həː'metɪklɪ] *adv* hermeticamente; ~ **sealed** hermeticamente fechado.

hermit ['həːmɪt] *n* eremita *m/f*.

hernia ['həːnɪə] *n* hérnia.

hero ['hɪərəu] *(pl* ~es) *n* herói *m*; *(of book, film)* protagonista *m*.

heroic [hɪ'rəuɪk] *adj* heróico.

heroin ['herəuɪn] *n* heroína.

heroin addict *n* viciado/a em heroína.

heroine ['herəuɪn] *n* heroína; *(of book, film)* protagonista.

heroism ['herəuɪzm] *n* heroísmo.

heron ['herən] *n* garça.

hero worship *n* culto de heróis.

herring ['herɪŋ] *(pl inv or* ~s) *n* arenque *m*.

hers [həːz] *pron* (o) seu/(a) sua, (o/a) dela; **a friend of** ~ uma amiga dela; **this is** ~ isto é dela.

herself [həː'self] *pron (reflexive)* se; *(emphatic)* ela mesma; *(after prep)* si (mesma).

Herts *(BRIT) abbr* = **Hertfordshire**.

he's [hiːz] = **he is; he has**.

hesitant ['hezɪtənt] *adj* hesitante, indeciso; **to be** ~ **about doing sth** hesitar em fazer algo.

hesitate ['hezɪteɪt] *vi* hesitar; **to** ~ **to do** hesitar em fazer; **don't** ~ **to phone** não deixe de telefonar.

hesitation [hezɪ'teɪʃən] *n* hesitação *f*, indecisão *f*; **I have no** ~ **in saying (that)** ... não hesito em dizer (que) ....

hessian ['hesɪən] *n* aniagem *f*.

heterogeneous ['hetərə'dʒiːnɪəs] *adj* heterogêneo.

heterosexual ['hetərəu'seksjuəl] *adj, n* heterossexual *m/f*.

het up [het-] *(inf) adj* excitado.

HEW *(US) n abbr (= Department of Health, Education and Welfare)* ministério da saúde, da educação e da previdência social.

hew [hjuː] *vt* cortar (com machado).

hex [heks] *(US) n* feitiço ♦ *vt* enfeitiçar.

hexagon ['heksəgən] *n* hexágono.

hexagonal [hek'sægənl] *adj* hexagonal.

hey [heɪ] *excl* eh! ei!

heyday ['heɪdeɪ] *n*: **the** ~ **of** o auge *or* apogeu de.

HF *n abbr (= high frequency)* HF *f*.

HGV *(BRIT) n abbr* = **heavy goods vehicle**.

HI *(US) abbr (POST)* = **Hawaii**.

hi [haɪ] *excl* oi!

hiatus [haɪ'eɪtəs] *n* hiato.

hibernate ['haɪbəneɪt] *vi* hibernar.

hibernation [haɪbə'neɪʃən] *n* hibernação *f*.

hiccough ['hɪkʌp] *vi* soluçar ♦ *n* soluço; **to have (the)** ~**s** estar com soluço.

hiccup ['hɪkʌp] *vi, n* = **hiccough**.

hid [hɪd] *pt of* **hide**.

hidden ['hɪdn] *pp of* **hide** ♦ *adj (costs)* oculto.

hide [haɪd] *(pt* **hid**, *pp* **hidden**) *n (skin)* pele *f* ♦ *vt* esconder, ocultar ♦ *vi*: **to** ~ **(from sb)** esconder-se *or* ocultar-se (de alguém).

hide-and-seek *n* esconde-esconde *m*.

hideaway ['haɪdəweɪ] *n* esconderijo.

hideous ['hɪdɪəs] *adj* horrível.

hide-out *n* esconderijo.

hiding ['haɪdɪŋ] *n (beating)* surra; **to be in** ~ *(concealed)* estar escondido.

hiding place *n* esconderijo.

hierarchy ['haɪərɑːkɪ] *n* hierarquia.

hieroglyphic [haɪərə'glɪfɪk] *adj* hieroglífico.

hieroglyphics [haɪərə'glɪfɪks] *npl* hieroglifos *mpl*.

hi-fi ['haɪfaɪ] *abbr (= high fidelity) n* alta-fidelidade *f*; *(system)* som *m* ♦ *adj* de alta-fidelidade.

higgledy-piggledy ['hɪgldɪ'pɪgldɪ] *adv* desordenadamente.

high [haɪ] *adj (gen, speed)* alto; *(number)* grande; *(price)* alto, elevado; *(wind)* forte; *(voice)* agudo; *(inf: person: on drugs)* alto, baratinado; *(BRIT: CULIN: meat, game)* faisandé *inv*; (: *spoilt)* estragado ♦ *adv* alto, a grande altura ♦ *n*: **exports have reached a new** ~ as exportações atingiram um novo pico; **it is 20 m** ~ tem 20 m de altura; ~ **in the air** nas alturas; **to pay a** ~ **price for sth** pagar caro por algo.

highball ['haɪbɔːl] *(US) n* uísque com soda.

highboy ['haɪbɔɪ] *(US) n* comoda alta.

highbrow ['haɪbrau] *adj* intelectual, erudito.

highchair ['haɪtʃɛə*] *n* cadeira alta (para criança).

high-class *adj (neighbourhood)* nobre; *(hotel)* de primeira categoria; *(person)* da classe alta; *(performance etc)* de alto nível.

high court *n (LAW)* tribunal *m* superior.

higher ['haɪə*] *adj (form of life, study etc)* superior ♦ *adv* mais alto.

higher education *n* ensino superior.

high finance *n* altas finanças *fpl*.

high-flier *n* estudante *m/f (or* empregado/a) talentoso/a e ambicioso/a.

high-flying *adj (fig)* ambicioso, talentoso.

high-handed [-'hændɪd] *adj* despótico.

high-heeled [-'hiːld] *adj* de salto alto.

highjack ['haɪdʒæk] *n, vt* = **hijack**.

high jump *n (SPORT)* salto em altura.

highlands ['haɪləndz] *npl* serrania, serra; **the H**~ *(in Scotland)* a Alta Escócia.

high-level *adj* de alto nível; ~ **language** *(COMPUT)* linguagem *f* de alto nível.

highlight ['haɪlaɪt] *n (fig: of event)* ponto alto ♦ *vt* realçar, ressaltar; ~**s** *npl (in hair)* mechas *fpl*; **the ~s of the match** os melhores lances do jogo.

highlighter ['haɪlaɪtə*] *n* (*pen*) caneta marcatexto.

highly ['haɪlɪ] *adv* altamente; (*very*) muito; **~ paid** muito bem pago; **to speak ~ of** falar elogiosamente de.

highly-strung *adj* tenso, irritadiço.

High Mass *n* missa cantada.

highness ['haɪnɪs] *n* altura; **Her H~** Sua Alteza.

high-pitched *adj* agudo.

high-powered *adj* (*engine*) muito potente, de alta potência; (*fig: person*) dinâmico; (: *job*, *businessman*) muito importante.

high-pressure *adj* de alta pressão.

high-rise block *n* edifício alto, espigão *m*.

high school *n* (*BRIT*) escola secundária; (*US*) científico.

high season (*BRIT*) *n* alta estação *f*.

high spirits *npl* alegria; **to be in ~** estar alegre.

high street (*BRIT*) *n* rua principal.

highway ['haɪweɪ] *n* estrada, rodovia.

Highway Code (*BRIT*) *n* Código Nacional de Trânsito.

highwayman ['haɪweɪmən] (*irreg*) *n* salteador *m* de estrada.

hijack ['haɪdʒæk] *vt* seqüestrar ♦ *n* (*also*: **~ing**) seqüestro (de avião).

hijacker ['haɪdʒækə*] *n* seqüestrador(a) *m/f* (de avião).

hike [haɪk] *vi* (*go walking*) caminhar; ♦ *n* caminhada, excursão *f* a pé; (*inf: in prices etc*) aumento ♦ *vt* (*inf*) aumentar.

hiker ['haɪkə*] *n* caminhante *m/f*, andarilho/a.

hiking ['haɪkɪŋ] *n* excursões *fpl* a pé, caminhar *m*.

hilarious [hɪ'lɛərɪəs] *adj* (*behaviour*, *event*) hilariante.

hilarity [hɪ'lærɪtɪ] *n* hilaridade *f*.

hill [hɪl] *n* colina; (*high*) montanha; (*slope*) ladeira, rampa.

hillbilly ['hɪlbɪlɪ] (*US*) *n* montanhês/esa *m/f*; (*pej*) caipira *m/f*, jeca *m/f*.

hillock ['hɪlək] *n* morro pequeno.

hillside ['hɪlsaɪd] *n* vertente *f*.

hill start *n* (*AUT*) partida em ladeira.

hilly ['hɪlɪ] *adj* montanhoso; (*uneven*) acidentado.

hilt [hɪlt] *n* (*of sword*) punho, guarda; **to the ~** plenamente.

him [hɪm] *pron* (*direct*) o; (*indirect*) lhe; (*stressed, after prep*) ele; **I see ~** vejo-o, vejo ele (*BR: inf*); **give ~ a book** dá-lhe um livro, dá um livro a ele.

Himalayas [hɪmə'leɪəz] *npl*: **the ~** o Himalaia.

himself [hɪm'sɛlf] *pron* (*reflexive*) se; (*emphatic*) ele mesmo; (*after prep*) si (mesmo).

hind [haɪnd] *adj* traseiro ♦ *n* corça.

hinder ['hɪndə*] *vt* atrapalhar; (*delay*) re-

tardar.

hindquarters ['haɪnd'kwɔːtəz] *npl* (*ZOOL*) quartos *mpl* traseiros.

hindrance ['hɪndrəns] *n* impedimento, estorvo.

hindsight ['haɪndsaɪt] *n*: **with the benefit of ~** em retrospecto.

Hindu ['hɪnduː] *n* hindu *m/f*.

hinge [hɪndʒ] *n* dobradiça ♦ *vi* (*fig*): **to ~ on** depender de.

hint [hɪnt] *n* insinuação *f*; (*advice*) palpite *m*, dica ♦ *vt*: **to ~ that** insinuar que ♦ *vi* dar indiretas; **to ~ at** fazer alusão a; **to drop a ~** dar uma indireta; **give me a ~** (*clue*) me dá uma pista.

hip [hɪp] *n* quadril *m*.

hip flask *n* cantil *m*.

hippie ['hɪpɪ] *n* hippie *m/f*.

hip pocket *n* bolso traseiro.

hippopotami [hɪpə'pɔtəmaɪ] *npl of* **hippopotamus**.

hippopotamus [hɪpə'pɔtəməs] (*pl* **~es** *or* **hippopotami**) *n* hipopótamo.

hippy ['hɪpɪ] *n* = **hippie**.

hire ['haɪə*] *vt* (*BRIT: car, equipment*) alugar; (*worker*) contratar ♦ *n* aluguel *m*; (*of person*) contratação *f*; **for ~** aluga-se; (*taxi*) livre; **on ~** alugado.

hire out *vt* alugar.

hire(d) car ['haɪə(d)-] (*BRIT*) *n* carro alugado.

hire purchase (*BRIT*) *n* compra a prazo; **to buy sth on ~** comprar algo a prazo *or* pelo crediário.

his [hɪz] *pron* (o) seu/(a) sua, (o/a) dele ♦ *adj* seu/sua *or* dele; **~ name** o nome dele; **it's ~** é dele.

Hispanic [hɪs'pænɪk] *adj* hispânico.

hiss [hɪs] *vi* silvar; (*boo*) vaiar ♦ *n* silvo; vaia.

histogram ['hɪstəgræm] *n* histograma *m*.

historian [hɪ'stɔːrɪən] *n* historiador(a) *m/f*.

historic(al) [hɪ'stɔrɪk(l)] *adj* histórico.

history ['hɪstərɪ] *n* história; (*of illness etc*) histórico; **medical ~** (*of patient*) histórico médico.

histrionics [hɪstrɪ'ɔnɪks] *n* teatro.

hit [hɪt] (*pt, pp* **hit**) *vt* (*strike*) bater em; (*reach: target*) acertar, alcançar; (*collide with: car*) bater em, colidir com; (*fig: affect*) atingir ♦ *n* (*blow*) golpe *m*; (*success*) sucesso, grande êxito; (*song*) sucesso; **to ~ it off with sb** dar-se bem com alguém; **to ~ the headlines** virar *or* fazer manchete; **to ~ the road** (*inf*) dar o fora, mandar-se.

hit back *vi*: **to ~ back at sb** revidar ao ataque (*or* à crítica *etc*) de alguém.

hit out at *vt fus* tentar bater em; (*fig*) criticar veementemente.

hit (up)on *vt fus* (*answer*) descobrir.

hit-and-run driver *n* motorista que atropela alguém *e* foge da cena do acidente.

hitch [hɪtʃ] *vt* (*fasten*) atar, amarrar; (*also*: **~ up**) levantar ♦ *n* (*difficulty*) dificuldade *f*; **to ~ a lift** pegar carona (*BR*), arranjar uma boleia (*PT*); **technical** ~ probleminha técnico.

hitch up *vt* (*horse, cart*) atrelar; *see also* **hitch**.

hitch-hike *vi* pegar carona (*BR*), andar à boleia (*PT*).

hitch-hiker *n* pessoa que pega carona (*BR*) *or* anda à boleia (*PT*).

hi-tech *adj* tecnologicamente avançado ♦ *n* alta tecnologia.

hitherto [hɪðə'tuː] *adv* até agora.

hitman ['hɪtmæn] (*irreg*) *n* sicário.

hit-or-miss *adj* aleatório; **it's** ~ **whether** ... não é nada certo que ....

hit parade *n* parada de sucessos.

hive [haɪv] *n* colméia; **the shop was a** ~ **of activity** (*fig*) a loja fervilhava de atividade.

hive off (*inf*) *vt* transferir.

hl *abbr* (= *hectolitre*) hl.

HM *abbr* (= *His* (*or Her*) *Majesty*) SM.

HMG (*BRIT*) *abbr* = **His** (*or* **Her**) **Majesty's Government**.

HMI (*BRIT*) *abbr* (*SCH*) = **His** (*or* **Her**) **Majesty's Inspector**.

HMO (*US*) *n abbr* (= *health maintenance organization*) órgão que garante a manutenção de saúde.

HMS (*BRIT*) *abbr* = **His** (*or* **Her**) **Majesty's Ship**.

HMSO *n abbr* (= *His* (*or Her*) *Majesty's Stationery Office*) imprensa do governo.

HNC (*BRIT*) *n abbr* = **Higher National Certificate**.

HND (*BRIT*) *n abbr* = **Higher National Diploma**.

hoard [hɔːd] *n* provisão *f*; (*of money*) tesouro ♦ *vt* acumular.

hoarding ['hɔːdɪŋ] (*BRIT*) *n* tapume *m*, outdoor *m*.

hoarfrost ['hɔːfrɒst] *n* geada.

hoarse [hɔːs] *adj* rouco.

hoax [həuks] *n* trote *m*.

hob [hɒb] *n* mesa (do fogão).

hobble ['hɒbl] *vi* coxear.

hobby ['hɒbɪ] *n* hobby *m*, passatempo predileto.

hobby-horse *n* cavalinho-de-pau; (*fig*) tema *m* favorito.

hobnob ['hɒbnɒb] *vi*: **to** ~ **with** ter intimidade com.

hobo ['həubəu] (*pl* ~s *or* ~es) (*US*) *n* vagabundo.

hock [hɒk] *n* (*BRIT*: *wine*) vinho branco do Reno; (*of animal*, *CULIN*) jarrete *m*; (*inf*): **to be in** ~ (*person*) estar endividado; (*object*) estar no prego *or* empenhado.

hockey ['hɒkɪ] *n* hóquei *m*.

hocus-pocus ['həukəs'pəukəs] *n* (*trickery*) tapeação *f*; (*words*) embromação *f*.

hodgepodge ['hɒdʒpɒdʒ] *n* = **hotchpotch**.

hoe [həu] *n* enxada ♦ *vt* trabalhar com enxada, capinar.

hog [hɒg] *n* porco; (*person*) glutão/ona *m/f* ♦ *vt* (*fig*) monopolizar; **to go the whole** ~ ir até o fim.

hoist [hɔɪst] *n* (*lift*) guincho; (*crane*)

guindaste *m* ♦ *vt* içar.

hold [həuld] (*pt, pp* **held**) *vt* segurar; (*contain*) conter; (*keep back*) reter; (*believe*) sustentar; (*have*) ter; (*record etc*) deter; (*take weight*) agüentar; (*meeting*) realizar ♦ *vi* (*withstand pressure*) resistir; (*be valid*) ser válido ♦ *n* (*handle*) apoio (para a mão); (*fig: grasp*) influência, domínio; (*NAUT*) porão *m* de navio; **to catch** *or* **get (a)** ~ **of** agarrar, pegar; **to get** ~ **of** (*fig*) arranjar; **to get** ~ **of o.s.** controlar-se; ~ **the line!** (*TEL*) não desligue!; **to** ~ **one's own** (*fig*) virar-se, sair-se bem; **to** ~ **office** (*POL*) exercer um cargo; **to** ~ **firm** *or* **fast** agüentar; **he** ~**s the view that** ... ele sustenta que ...; **to** ~ **sb responsible for sth** responsabilizar alguém por algo.

hold back *vt* reter; (*secret*) manter, guardar; **to** ~ **sb back from doing sth** impedir alguém de fazer algo.

hold down *vt* (*person*) segurar; (*job*) manter.

hold forth *vi* discursar, deitar falação.

hold off *vt* (*enemy*) afastar, repelir ♦ *vi* (*rain*): **if the rain** ~**s off** se não chover.

hold on *vi* agarrar-se; (*wait*) esperar; ~ **on!** espera aí!; (*TEL*) não desligue!

hold on to *vt fus* agarrar-se a; (*keep*) guardar, ficar com.

hold out *vt* estender ♦ *vi* (*resist*) resistir; **to** ~ **out** (**against**) defender-se (contra).

hold over *vt* (*meeting etc*) adiar.

hold up *vt* (*raise*) levantar; (*support*) apoiar; (*delay*) atrasar; (*traffic*) reter; (*rob*) assaltar.

holdall ['həuldɔːl] (*BRIT*) *n* bolsa de viagem.

holder ['həuldə*] *n* (*of ticket*) portador(a) *m/f*; (*of record*) detentor(a) *m/f*; (*of office, title etc*) titular *m/f*.

holding ['həuldɪŋ] *n* (*share*) participação *f*; ~**s** *npl* posses *fpl*.

holding company *n* holding *f*.

holdup ['həuldʌp] *n* (*robbery*) assalto; (*delay*) demora; (*BRIT*: *in traffic*) engarrafamento.

hole [həul] *n* buraco ♦ *vt* esburacar; ~ **in the heart** (*MED*) defeito na membrana cardíaca; **to pick** ~**s (in)** (*fig*) botar defeito (em).

hole up *vi* esconder-se.

holiday ['hɒlədɪ] *n* (*BRIT*: *vacation*) férias *fpl*; (*day off*) dia *m* de folga; (*public*) feriado; **to be on** ~ estar de férias; **tomorrow is a** ~ amanhã é feriado.

holiday camp (*BRIT*) *n* colônia de férias.

holiday-maker (*BRIT*) *n* pessoa (que está) de férias.

holiday pay salário de férias.

holiday resort *n* local *m* de férias.

holiday season *n* temporada de férias.

holiness ['həulɪnɪs] *n* santidade *f*.

Holland ['hɒlənd] *n* Holanda.

hollow ['hɒləu] *adj* oco, vazio; (*eyes*) fundo; (*sound*) surdo; (*doctrine*) falso ♦ *n* buraco; (*in ground*) cavidade *f*, depressão *f* ♦ *vt*: **to** ~ **out** escavar.

holly ['hɒlɪ] *n* azevinho.

hollyhock ['hɒlɪhɒk] n malva-rosa.
holocaust ['hɒləkɔːst] n holocausto.
holster ['həʊlstə*] n coldre m.
holy ['həʊlɪ] adj santo, sagrado; (water) bento.
Holy Communion n Sagrada Comunhão f.
Holy Ghost n Espírito Santo.
Holy Land n: the ~ a Terra Santa.
holy orders npl ordens fpl sacras.
Holy Spirit n = Holy Ghost.
homage ['hɒmɪdʒ] n homenagem f; **to pay** ~ **to** prestar homenagem a, homenagear.
home [həʊm] n casa, lar m; (country) pátria; (institution) asilo ♦ cpd (domestic) caseiro, doméstico; (of family) familiar; (heating, computer etc) residencial; (ECON, POL) nacional, interno (SPORT: team) de casa; (: win, match) no próprio campo ♦ adv (direction) para casa; (right in: nail etc) até o fundo; **at** ~ em casa; **to go/come** ~ ir/vir para casa; **make yourself at** ~ fique à vontade; **near my** ~ perto da minha casa.
  home in on vt fus (missiles) dirigir-se automaticamente para.
home address n endereço residencial.
home-brew n (wine) vinho feito em casa; (beer) cerveja feita em casa.
homecoming ['həʊmkʌmɪŋ] n regresso ao lar.
home computer n computador m residencial.
Home Counties npl os condados por volta de Londres.
home economics n economia doméstica.
home-grown adj (not foreign) nacional; (from garden) plantado em casa.
homeland ['həʊmlænd] n terra (natal).
homeless ['həʊmlɪs] adj sem casa, desabrigado ♦ npl: the ~ os desabrigados.
home loan n crédito imobiliário, financiamento habitacional.
homely ['həʊmlɪ] adj (domestic) caseiro; (simple) simples inv.
home-made adj caseiro.
Home Office (BRIT) n Ministério do Interior.
homeopathy etc [həʊmɪ'ɒpəθɪ] (US) = homoeopathy etc.
home rule n autonomia.
Home Secretary (BRIT) n Ministro do Interior.
homesick ['həʊmsɪk] adj: **to be** ~ estar com saudades (do lar).
homestead ['həʊmstɛd] n propriedade f; (farm) fazenda.
home town n cidade f natal.
homeward ['həʊmwəd] adj (journey) para casa, para a terra natal.
homeward(s) ['həʊmwəd(z)] adv para casa.
homework ['həʊmwɜːk] n dever m de casa.
homicidal [hɒmɪ'saɪdl] adj homicida.
homicide ['hɒmɪsaɪd] (US) n homicídio.
homily ['hɒmɪlɪ] n homilia.
homing ['həʊmɪŋ] adj (device, missile) de correção de rumo; ~ **pigeon** pombo- correio.

homoeopath ['həʊmɪəpæθ] (US **homeopath**) n homeopata m/f.
homoeopathic [həʊmɪə'pæθɪk] (US **homeopathic**) adj homeopático.
homoeopathy [həʊmɪ'ɒpəθɪ] (US **homeopathy**) n homeopatia.
homogeneous [hɒməʊ'dʒiːnɪəs] adj homogêneo.
homogenize [hə'mɒdʒənaɪz] vt homogeneizar.
homosexual [hɒməʊ'sɛksjʊəl] adj, n homossexual m/f.
homosexuality [hɒməsɛksjʊ'ælətɪ] n homossexualismo.
Hon. abbr = honourable; honorary.
Honduran [hɒn'djʊərən] adj, n hondurenho/a.
Honduras [hɒn'djʊərəs] n Honduras (no article).
hone [həʊn] vt amolar, afiar.
honest ['ɒnɪst] adj honesto; (sincere) sincero, franco; **to be quite** ~ **with you** ... para falar a verdade ....
honestly ['ɒnɪstlɪ] adv honestamente, francamente.
honesty ['ɒnɪstɪ] n honestidade f, sinceridade f.
honey ['hʌnɪ] n mel m; (US: inf: darling) querido/a.
honeycomb ['hʌnɪkəʊm] n favo de mel; (pattern) em forma de favo ♦ vt (fig): **to** ~ **with** crivar de.
honeymoon ['hʌnɪmuːn] n lua-de-mel f; (trip) viagem f de lua-de-mel.
honeysuckle ['hʌnɪsʌkl] n madressilva.
Hong Kong ['hɒŋ'kɒŋ] n Hong Kong (no article).
honk [hɒŋk] n buzinada ♦ vi (AUT) buzinar.
Honolulu [hɒnə'luːluː] n Honolulu.
honor ['ɒnə*] (US) vt, n = honour.
honorary ['ɒnərərɪ] adj (unpaid) não remunerado; (duty, title) honorário.
honour ['ɒnə*] (US **honor**) vt honrar ♦ n honra; **in** ~ **of** em honra de.
hono(u)rable ['ɒnərəbl] adj honrado.
hono(u)r-bound adj: **to be** ~ **to do** estar moralmente obrigado a fazer.
hono(u)rs degree n (SCH) diploma m com distinção.
Hons. abbr (SCH) = hono(u)rs degree.
hood [hʊd] n capuz m, touca; (BRIT: AUT) capota; (US: AUT) capô m; (inf: hoodlum) pinta-brava m.
hooded ['hʊdɪd] adj encapuzado, mascarado.
hoodlum ['huːdləm] n pinta-brava m.
hoodwink ['hʊdwɪŋk] vt tapear.
hoof [huːf] (pl ~s or **hooves**) n casco, pata.
hook [hʊk] n gancho; (on dress) colchete m; (for fishing) anzol m ♦ vt enganchar, fisgar; ~ **and eye** colchete m; **by** ~ **or by crook** custe o que custar; **to be** ~**ed (on)** (inf) estar viciado (em); (person) estar fissurado (em).
  hook up vt ligar.

NB: European Portuguese adds the following consonants to certain words: **b** (sú(b)dito, su(b)til); **c** (a(c)ção, a(c)cionista, a(c)to); **m** (inde(m)ne); **p** (ado(p)ção, ado(p)tar); for further details see p. xiii.

hooligan ['hu:lɪgən] *n* desordeiro/a, bagunceiro/a.

hooliganism ['hu:lɪgənɪzm] *n* vandalismo.

hoop [hu:p] *n* arco.

hoot [hu:t] *vi* (*AUT*) buzinar; (*siren*) tocar; (*owl*) piar ♦ *vt* (*jeer at*) vaiar ♦ *n* buzinada; toque *m* de sirena; **to ~ with laughter** morrer de rir.

hooter ['hu:tə*] *n* (*BRIT*: *AUT*) buzina; (*NAUT*, *factory*) sirena.

hoover ['hu:və*] (*BRIT*) ® *n* aspirador *m* (de pó) ♦ *vt* passar o aspirador em.

hooves [hu:vz] *npl of* **hoof**.

hop [hɔp] *vi* saltar, pular; (*on one foot*) pular num pé só ♦ *n* salto, pulo; **~s** *npl* lúpulo.

hope [həup] *vi* esperar ♦ *n* esperança; **I ~ so/not** espero que sim/não.

hopeful ['həupful] *adj* (*person*) otimista, esperançoso; (*situation*) promissor(a); **I'm ~ that she'll manage to come** acredito que ela conseguirá vir.

hopefully ['həupfulɪ] *adv* (*with hope*) esperançosamente; **~, they'll come back** é de esperar *or* esperamos que voltem.

hopeless ['həuplɪs] *adj* desesperado, irremediável; (*useless*) inútil; (*bad*) péssimo.

hopelessly ['həupləslɪ] *adv* (*confused*, *involved*) irremediavelmente.

hopper ['hɔpə*] *n* tremonha.

horde [hɔ:d] *n* horda.

horizon [hə'raɪzn] *n* horizonte *m*.

horizontal [hɔrɪ'zɔntl] *adj* horizontal.

hormone ['hɔ:məun] *n* hormônio.

horn [hɔ:n] *n* corno, chifre *m*; (*MUS*) trompa; (*AUT*) buzina.

horned [hɔ:nd] *adj* (*animal*) com chifres, chifrudo.

hornet ['hɔ:nɪt] *n* vespão *m*.

horn-rimmed [-rɪmd] *adj* com aro de chifre *or* de tartaruga.

horny ['hɔ:nɪ] *adj* (*material*) córneo; (*hands*) calejado; (*inf*: *aroused*) tarado, com tesão (*BR*: !).

horoscope ['hɔrəskəup] *n* horóscopo.

horrendous [hə'rendɔs] *adj* horrível, terrível.

horrible ['hɔrɪbl] *adj* horrível.

horrid ['hɔrɪd] *adj* antipático, horrível.

horrific [hə'rɪfɪk] *adj* horroroso.

horrify ['hɔrɪfaɪ] *vt* horrorizar.

horrifying ['hɔrɪfaɪɪŋ] *adj* horripilante.

horror ['hɔrə*] *n* horror *m*.

horror film *n* filme *m* de terror.

horror-striken *adj* = **horror-struck**.

horror-struck *adj* horrorizado.

hors d'œuvre [ɔ:'də:vrə] *n* entrada.

horse [hɔ:s] *n* cavalo.

horseback ['hɔ:sbæk] : **on ~** *adv* a cavalo.

horsebox ['hɔ:sbɔks] *n* reboque *m* (para transportar cavalos).

horse chestnut *n* castanha-da-índia.

horse-drawn *adj* puxado a cavalo.

horsefly ['hɔ:sflaɪ] *n* mutuca.

horseman ['hɔ:smən] (*irreg*) *n* cavaleiro; (*skilled*) ginete *m*.

horsemanship ['hɔ:smənʃɪp] *n* equitação *f*.

horsemen ['hɔ:smən] *npl of* **horseman**.

horseplay ['hɔ:spleɪ] *n* zona, bagunça (*brincadeiras etc*).

horsepower ['hɔ:spauə*] *n* cavalo-vapor *m*.

horse-racing *n* corridas *fpl* de cavalo, turfe *m*.

horseradish ['hɔ:srædɪʃ] *n* rábano-bastardo.

horseshoe ['hɔ:sʃu:] *n* ferradura.

horse show *n* concurso hípico.

horse-trading *n* regateio.

horse trials *npl* = **horse show**.

horsewhip ['hɔ:swɪp] *vt* chicotear.

horsewoman ['hɔ:swumən] (*irreg*) *n* amazona.

horsey ['hɔ:sɪ] *adj* aficionado por cavalos; (*appearance*) com cara de cavalo.

horticulture ['hɔ:tɪkʌltʃə*] *n* horticultura.

hose [həuz] *n* (*also*: **~pipe**) mangueira.

hose down *vt* lavar com mangueira.

hosiery ['həuzɪərɪ] *n* meias *fpl* e roupa de baixo.

hospice ['hɔspɪs] *n* asilo.

hospitable ['hɔspɪtəbl] *adj* hospitaleiro.

hospital ['hɔspɪtl] *n* hospital *m*.

hospitality [hɔspɪ'tælɪtɪ] *n* hospitalidade *f*.

hospitalize ['hɔspɪtəlaɪz] *vt* hospitalizar.

host [həust] *n* anfitrião *m*; (*in hotel etc*) hospedeiro; (*TV*) animador(a) *m/f*; (*REL*) hóstia; (*large number*): **a ~ of** uma multidão de ♦ *vt* (*TV programme*) apresentar, animar.

hostage ['hɔstɪdʒ] *n* refém *m*.

host country *n* país *m* anfitrião.

hostel ['hɔstl] *n* hospedaria; (*for students*, *tramps*) residência; (*also*: **youth ~**) albergue *m* de juventude.

hostelling ['hɔstlɪŋ] *n*: **to go (youth) ~** *viajar de férias pernoitando em albergues de juventude*.

hostess ['həustɪs] *n* anfitriã *f*; (*air ~*) aeromoça (*BR*), hospedeira de bordo (*PT*); (*in nightclub*) taxi-girl *f*.

hostile ['hɔstaɪl] *adj* hostil.

hostility [hɔ'stɪlɪtɪ] *n* hostilidade *f*.

hot [hɔt] *adj* quente; (*as opposed to only warm*) muito quente, ardente; (*spicy*) picante; (*fig*) ardente, veemente; **to be ~** (*person*) estar com calor; (*thing*, *weather*) estar quente.

hot up (*BRIT*: *inf*) *vi* (*party*, *debate*) esquentar ♦ *vt* (*pace*) acelerar; (*engine*) envenenar.

hot-air balloon *n* balão *m* de ar quente.

hotbed ['hɔtbed] *n* (*fig*) faco, ninho.

hotchpotch ['hɔtʃpɔtʃ] (*BRIT*) *n* mixórdia, salada.

hot dog *n* cachorro-quente *m*.

hotel [həu'tel] *n* hotel *m*.

hotelier [hə'telɪeɪ] *n* hoteleiro/a.

hotel industry *n* indústria hoteleira.

hotel room *n* quarto de hotel.

hotfoot ['hɔtfut] *adv* a mil, a toda.

hotheaded [hɔt'hedɪd] *adj* impetuoso, fogoso.

hothouse ['hɔthaus] (*irreg*) *n* estufa.

hot line *n* (*POL*) telefone *m* vermelho, linha direta.

hotly ['hɔtlɪ] adv ardentemente, apaixonadamente.

hotplate ['hɔtpleɪt] n (on cooker) chapa elétrica.

hotpot ['hɔtpɔt] (BRIT) n (CULIN) ragu m.

hot seat n (fig) posição f de responsabilidade.

hot spot n área de tensão.

hot spring n fonte f termal.

hot-tempered adj esquentado, de pavio curto.

hot-water bottle n bolsa de água quente.

hound [haund] vt acossar, perseguir ♦ n cão m de caça, sabujo.

hour ['auə*] n hora; **at 30 miles an** ~ ≈ a 50 km por hora; **lunch** ~ hora do almoço; **to pay sb by the** ~ pagar alguém por hora.

hourly ['auəlɪ] adv de hora em hora ♦ adj de hora em hora; (rate) por hora.

house [n haus, pl hauzɪz, vt hauz] n (gen, firm) casa; (POL) câmara; (THEATRE) assistência, lotação f ♦ vt (person) alojar; **to/at my** ~ para a/na minha casa; **the H** ~ **(of Commons)** (BRIT) a Câmara dos Comuns; **the H** ~ **(of Representatives)** (US) a Câmara de Deputados; **on the** ~ (fig) por conta da casa.

house arrest n prisão f domiciliar.

houseboat ['hausbəut] n casa flutuante.

housebound ['hausbaund] adj preso em casa.

housebreaking ['hausbreɪkɪŋ] n arrombamento de domicílio.

house-broken (US) adj = **house-trained**.

housecoat ['hauskəut] n roupão m.

household ['haushəuld] n família; (house) casa; ~ **name** nome m conhecido por todos.

householder ['haushəuldə*] n (owner) dono/a de casa; (head of family) chefe m/f de família.

househunting ['haushʌntɪŋ] n: **to go** ~ procurar casa para morar.

housekeeper ['hauski:pə*] n governanta.

housekeeping ['hauski:pɪŋ] n (work) trabalhos mpl domésticos; (also: ~ money) economia doméstica; (COMPUT) gestão f dos discos.

houseman ['hausmən] (BRIT: irreg) n (MED) interno.

house-proud adj preocupado com a aparência da casa.

house-to-house adj (enquiries) de porta em porta; (search) de casa em casa.

house-trained (BRIT) adj (animal) domesticado.

house-warming (party) [-'wɔ:mɪŋ-] n festa de inauguração de uma casa.

housewife ['hauswaɪf] (irreg) n dona de casa.

housework ['hauswə:k] n trabalhos mpl domésticos.

housing ['hauzɪŋ] n (act) alojamento m; (houses) residências fpl; (as issue) habitação f ♦ cpd (problem, shortage) habitacional.

housing association n organização beneficente que vende ou aluga casas.

housing conditions npl condições fpl de habitação.

housing development (BRIT **housing estate**) n conjunto residencial.

hovel ['hɔvl] n choupana, casebre m.

hover ['hɔvə*] vi pairar; (person) rondar.

hovercraft ['hɔvəkrɑ:ft] n aerobarco.

hoverport ['hɔvəpɔ:t] n porto para aerobarcos.

how [hau] adv como; ~ **are you?** como vai?; ~ **do you do?** (muito) prazer; ~ **far is it to** ...? qual é a distância daqui a ...?; ~ **long have you been here?** quanto tempo você está aqui?; ~ **lovely!** que lindo!; ~ **many/much?** quantos/quanto?; ~ **old are you?** quantos anos você tem?; ~'**s school?** como vai a escola?; ~ **about a drink?** que tal beber alguma coisa?; ~ **is it that** ...? por que é que ...?

however [hau'evə*] adv de qualquer modo; (+ adj) por mais ... que; (in questions) como ♦ conj no entanto, contudo, todavia.

howitzer ['hauɪtsə*] n (MIL) morteiro, obus m.

howl [haul] n uivo ♦ vi uivar.

howler ['haulə*] n besteira, erro.

HP (BRIT) n abbr = **hire purchase**.

hp abbr (AUT: = horsepower) CV.

HQ n abbr (= headquarters) QG m.

HR (US) n abbr = **House of Representatives**.

HRH abbr (= His (or Her) Royal Highness) SAR.

hr(s) abbr (= hour(s)) h(s).

HS (US) abbr = **high school**.

HST (US) abbr (= Hawaiian Standard Time) hora do Havaí.

hub [hʌb] n (of wheel) cubo; (fig) centro.

hubbub ['hʌbʌb] n algazarra, vozerio.

hubcap ['hʌbkæp] n (AUT) calota.

HUD (US) n abbr (= Department of Housing and Urban Development) ministério do urbanismo e da habitação.

huddle ['hʌdl] vi: **to** ~ **together** aconchegar-se.

hue [hju:] n cor f, matiz m; ~ **and cry** clamor m público.

huff [hʌf] n: **in a** ~ com raiva; **to take the** ~ ficar sem graça.

hug [hʌg] vt abraçar ♦ n abraço; **to give sb a** ~ dar um abraço em alguém, abraçar alguém.

huge [hju:dʒ] adj enorme, imenso.

hulk [hʌlk] n (wreck) navio velho; (hull) casco, carcaça; (person) brutamontes m inv.

hulking ['hʌlkɪŋ] adj pesado, grandão/ona.

hull [hʌl] n (of ship) casco.

hullabaloo ['hʌləbə'lu:] (inf) n algazarra.

hullo [hə'ləu] excl = **hello**.

hum [hʌm] vt (tune) cantarolar ♦ vi cantarolar; (insect, machine etc) zumbir ♦ n zumbido.

human ['hju:mən] adj humano ♦ n (also: ~ being) ser m humano.

humane [hju:'meɪn] adj humano, humanitário.

humanism ['hju:mənɪzm] *n* humanismo.
humanitarian [hju:mænɪ'tɛərɪən] *adj* humanitário.
humanity [hju:'mænɪtɪ] *n* humanidade *f*.
humanly ['hju:mənlɪ] *adv* humanamente.
humanoid ['hju:mənɔɪd] *adj, n* humanóide *m/f*.
humble ['hʌmbl] *adj* humilde ♦ *vt* humilhar.
humbly ['hʌmblɪ] *adv* humildemente.
humbug ['hʌmbʌg] *n* fraude *f*, embuste *m*; (*BRIT*: *sweet*) bala de hortelã.
humdrum ['hʌmdrʌm] *adj* (*boring*) monótono, enfadonho; (*routine*) rotineiro.
humid ['hju:mɪd] *adj* úmido.
humidifier [hju:'mɪdɪfaɪə*] *n* umidificador *m*.
humidity [hju:'mɪdɪtɪ] *n* umidade *f*.
humiliate [hju:'mɪlɪeɪt] *vt* humilhar.
humiliation [hju:mɪlɪ'eɪʃən] *n* humilhação *f*.
humility [hju:'mɪlɪtɪ] *n* humildade *f*.
humorist ['hju:mərɪst] *n* humorista *m/f*.
humor ['hju:mə*] (*US*) *n, vt* = **humour**.
humorous ['hju:mərəs] *adj* humorístico.
humour ['hju:mə*] (*US* **humor**) *n* humorismo, senso de humor; (*mood*) humor *m* ♦ *vt* (*person*) fazer a vontade de; **sense of** ~ senso de humor; **to be in a good/bad** ~ estar de bom/mau humor.
humo(u)rless ['hju:mələs] *adj* sem senso de humor.
hump [hʌmp] *n* (*in ground*) elevação *f*; (*camel's*) corcova, giba.
humpback ['hʌmpbæk] *n* corcunda *m/f* ♦ *cpd*: ~ **bridge** (*BRIT*) *ponte pequena e muito arqueada*.
humus ['hju:məs] *n* húmus *m*, humo.
hunch [hʌntʃ] *n* (*premonition*) pressentimento, palpite *m*.
hunchback ['hʌntʃbæk] *n* corcunda *m/f*.
hunched [hʌntʃt] *adj* corcunda.
hundred ['hʌndrəd] *num* cem; (*before lower numbers*) cento; (*collective*) centena; **~s of people** centenas de pessoas; **I'm a** ~ **per cent sure** tenho certeza absoluta.
hundredweight ['hʌndrədweɪt] *n* (*BRIT*) = *50.8 kg; 112 lb*; (*US*) = *45.3 kg; 100 lb*.
hung [hʌŋ] *pt, pp of* **hang**.
Hungarian [hʌŋ'gɛərɪən] *adj* húngaro ♦ *n* húngaro/a; (*LING*) húngaro.
Hungary ['hʌŋgərɪ] *n* Hungria.
hunger ['hʌŋgə*] *n* fome *f* ♦ *vi*: **to** ~ **for** ter fome de; (*desire*) desejar ardentemente.
hunger strike *n* greve *f* de fome.
hungrily ['hʌŋgrəlɪ] *adv* (*eat*) vorazmente; (*fig*) avidamente.
hungry ['hʌŋgrɪ] *adj* faminto, esfomeado; **to be** ~ estar com fome; ~ **for** (*fig*) ávido de, ansioso por.
hung up (*inf*) *adj* complexado, grilado.
hunk [hʌŋk] *n* naco *m*; (*inf*: *man*) gatão *m*.
hunt [hʌnt] *vt* (*seek*) buscar, perseguir; (*SPORT*) caçar ♦ *vi* caçar ♦ *n* caça, caçada.
hunt down *vt* acossar.
hunter ['hʌntə*] *n* caçador(a) *m/f*; (*BRIT*: *horse*) cavalo de caça.
hunting ['hʌntɪŋ] *n* caça.

hurdle ['hə:dl] *n* (*SPORT*) barreira; (*fig*) obstáculo.
hurl [hə:l] *vt* arremessar, lançar.
hurrah [hu'rɑ:] *excl* viva!, hurra!
hurray [hu'reɪ] *excl* = **hurrah**.
hurricane ['hʌrɪkən] *n* furacão *m*.
hurried ['hʌrɪd] *adj* (*fast*) apressado; (*rushed*) feito às pressas.
hurriedly ['hʌrɪdlɪ] *adv* depressa, apressadamente.
hurry ['hʌrɪ] *n* pressa ♦ *vi* apressar-se ♦ *vt* (*person*) apressar; (*work*) acelerar; **to be in a** ~ estar com pressa; **to do sth in a** ~ fazer algo às pressas; **to** ~ **in/out** entrar/sair correndo; **to** ~ **home** correr para casa.
hurry along *vi* andar às pressas.
hurry away *vi* sair correndo.
hurry off *vi* sair correndo.
hurry up *vi* apressar-se.
hurt [hə:t] (*pt, pp* **hurt**) *vt* machucar; (*injure*) ferir; (*damage*: *business etc*) prejudicar; (*fig*) magoar ♦ *vi* doer ♦ *adj* machucado, ferido; **I** ~ **my arm** machuquei o braço; **where does it** ~? onde é que dói?
hurtful ['hə:tful] *adj* (*remark*) que magoa, ofensivo.
hurtle ['hə:tl] *vi* correr; **to** ~ **past** passar como um raio; **to** ~ **down** cair com violência.
husband ['hʌzbənd] *n* marido, esposo.
hush [hʌʃ] *n* silêncio, quietude *f* ♦ *vt* silenciar, fazer calar; ~! silêncio!, psiu!
hush up *vt* (*fact*) abafar, encobrir.
hushed [hʌʃt] *adj* (*tone*) baixo.
hush-hush *adj* secreto.
husk [hʌsk] *n* (*of wheat*) casca; (*of maize*) palha.
husky ['hʌskɪ] *adj* rouco; (*burly*) robusto ♦ *n* cão *m* esquimó.
hustings ['hʌstɪŋz] (*BRIT*) *npl* (*POL*) campanha (eleitoral).
hustle ['hʌsl] *vt* (*push*) empurrar; (*hurry*) apressar ♦ *n* agitação *f*, atividade *f* febril; ~ **and bustle** grande movimento.
hut [hʌt] *n* cabana, choupana; (*shed*) alpendre *m*.
hutch [hʌtʃ] *n* coelheira.
hyacinth ['haɪəsɪnθ] *n* jacinto.
hybrid ['haɪbrɪd] *adj, n* híbrido.
hydrant ['haɪdrənt] *n* (*also*: *fire* ~) hidrante *m*.
hydraulic [haɪ'drɔ:lɪk] *adj* hidráulico.
hydraulics [haɪ'drɔ:lɪks] *n* hidráulica.
hydrochloric acid ['haɪdrəu'klɔrɪk-] *n* ácido clorídrico.
hydroelectric [haɪdrəuɪ'lɛktrɪk] *adj* hidroelétrico.
hydrofoil ['haɪdrəfɔɪl] *n* hidrofoil *m*, aliscafo.
hydrogen ['haɪdrədʒən] *n* hidrogênio.
hydrogen bomb *n* bomba de hidrogênio.
hydrolysis [haɪ'drɔləsɪs] *n* hidrólise *f*.
hydrophobia ['haɪdrə'fəubɪə] *n* hidrofobia.
hydroplane ['haɪdrəpleɪn] *n* lancha planadora.
hyena [haɪ'i:nə] *n* hiena.
hygiene ['haɪdʒi:n] *n* higiene *f*.

hygienic [haɪ'dʒiːnɪk] *adj* higiênico.
hymn [hɪm] *n* hino.
hype [haɪp] *(inf)* *n* tititi *m*, falatório.
hyperactive ['haɪpər'æktɪv] *adj* hiperativo.
hypermarket ['haɪpəmɑːkɪt] *n* hipermercado.
hypertension ['haɪpə'tenʃən] *n* (*MED*) hipertensão *f*.
hyphen ['haɪfn] *n* hífen *m*.
hypnosis [hɪp'nəʊsɪs] *n* hipnose *f*.
hypnotic [hɪp'nɒtɪk] *adj* hipnótico.
hypnotism ['hɪpnətɪzm] *n* hipnotismo.
hypnotist ['hɪpnətɪst] *n* hipnotizador(a) *m/f*.
hypnotize ['hɪpnətaɪz] *vt* hipnotizar.
hypoallergenic ['haɪpəʊæləˈdʒenɪk] *adj* hipoalergênico.
hypochondriac [haɪpə'kɒndrɪæk] *n* hipocondríaco/a.
hypocrisy [hɪ'pɒkrɪsɪ] *n* hipocrisia.
hypocrite ['hɪpəkrɪt] *n* hipócrita *m/f*.
hypocritical [hɪpə'krɪtɪkl] *adj* hipócrita.
hypodermic [haɪpə'dɜːmɪk] *adj* hipodérmico ♦ *n* seringa hipodérmica.
hypothermia [haɪpə'θɜːmɪə] *n* hipotermia.
hypotheses [haɪ'pɒθɪsiːz] *npl of* **hypothesis**.
hypothesis [haɪ'pɒθɪsɪs] *(pl* **hypotheses**) *n* hipótese *f*.
hypothetic(al) [haɪpə'θetɪk(l)] *adj* hipotético.
hysterectomy [hɪstə'rektəmɪ] *n* histerectomia.
hysteria [hɪ'stɪərɪə] *n* histeria.
hysterical [hɪ'sterɪkl] *adj* histérico.
hysterics [hɪ'sterɪks] *npl* (*nervous*) crise *f* histérica; (*laughter*) ataque *m* de riso.
Hz *abbr* (= *hertz*) Hz.

I

I, i [aɪ] *n* (*letter*) I, i *m*; **I for Isaac** (*BRIT*) *or* **Item** (*US*) I de Irene.
I [aɪ] *pron* eu ♦ *abbr* (= *island; isle*) I.
IA (*US*) *abbr* (*POST*) = **Iowa**.
IAEA *n abbr* (= *International Atomic Energy Agency*) IAEA *f*.
IBA (*BRIT*) *n* (= *Independent Broadcasting Authority*) *órgão que supervisiona as emissoras comerciais de TV*.
Iberian [aɪ'bɪərɪən] *adj* ibérico.
Iberian Peninsula *n*: **the** ~ a península Ibérica.
IBEW (*US*) *n abbr* (= *International Brotherhood of Electrical Workers*) *sindicato internacional dos eletricistas*.
i/c (*BRIT*) *abbr* = **in charge**.
ICC *n abbr* = **International Chamber of Commerce**; (*US*) = **Interstate Commerce Commission**.

ice [aɪs] *n* gelo ♦ *vt* (*cake*) cobrir com glacê; (*drink*) gelar ♦ *vi* (*also*: ~ *over*, ~ *up*) gelar; **to put sth on** ~ (*fig*) engavetar algo.
ice age *n* era glacial.
ice axe *n* picareta para o gelo.
iceberg ['aɪsbɜːg] *n* iceberg *m*; **this is just the tip of the** ~ isso é só a ponta do iceberg.
icebox ['aɪsbɒks] *n* (*US*) geladeira; (*BRIT*: in *fridge*) congelador *m*.
icebreaker ['aɪsbreɪkə*] *n* navio quebra-gelo *m*.
ice bucket *n* balde *m* de gelo.
ice-cold *adj* gelado.
ice cream *n* sorvete *m* (*BR*), gelado (*PT*).
ice cube *n* pedra de gelo.
iced [aɪst] *adj* (*drink*) gelado; (*cake*) glaçado.
ice hockey *n* hóquei *m* sobre o gelo.
Iceland ['aɪslənd] *n* Islândia.
Icelander ['aɪsləndə*] *n* islandês/esa *m/f*.
Icelandic [aɪs'lændɪk] *adj* islandês/esa ♦ *n* (*LING*) islandês *m*.
ice lolly (*BRIT*) *n* picolé *m*.
ice pick *n* furador *m* de gelo.
ice rink *n* pista de gelo, rinque *m*.
ice-skate *n* patim *m* (para o gelo) ♦ *vi* patinar no gelo.
ice-skating *n* patinação *f* no gelo.
icicle ['aɪsɪkl] *n* pingente *m* de gelo.
icing ['aɪsɪŋ] *n* (*CULIN*) glacê *m*; (*AVIAT etc*) formação *f* de gelo.
icing sugar (*BRIT*) *n* açúcar *m* glacê.
ICJ *n abbr* = **International Court of Justice**.
icon ['aɪkɒn] *n* ícone *m*.
ICR (*US*) *n abbr* = **Institute for Cancer Research**.
ICU *n abbr* (= *intensive care unit*) UTI *f*.
icy ['aɪsɪ] *adj* (*road*) gelado; (*fig*) glacial, indiferente.
ID (*US*) *abbr* (*POST*) = **Idaho**.
I'd [aɪd] = **I would; I had**.
ID card *n* = **identity card**.
IDD (*BRIT*) *n abbr* (*TEL*: = *international direct dialling*) DDI *f*.
idea [aɪ'dɪə] *n* idéia; **good** ~! boa idéia!; **to have an** ~ **that** ... ter a impressão de que ...; **I haven't the least** ~ não tenho a mínima idéia.
ideal [aɪ'dɪəl] *n* ideal *m* ♦ *adj* ideal.
idealist [aɪ'dɪəlɪst] *n* idealista *m/f*.
ideally [aɪ'dɪəlɪ] *adv* de preferência; ~ **the book should have** ... seria ideal que o livro tivesse ....
identical [aɪ'dentɪkl] *adj* idêntico.
identification [aɪdentɪfɪ'keɪʃən] *n* identificação *f*; **means of** ~ documentos pessoais.
identify [aɪ'dentɪfaɪ] *vt* identificar ♦ *vi*: **to** ~ **with** identificar-se com.
Identikit picture [aɪ'dentɪkɪt-] ® *n* retrato falado.
identity [aɪ'dentɪtɪ] *n* identidade *f*.
identity card *n* carteira de identidade.
identity parade (*BRIT*) *n* identificação *f*.

NB: European Portuguese adds the following consonants to certain words: **b** (sú(b)dito, su(b)til); **c** (a(c)ção, a(c)cionista, a(c)to); **m** (inde(m)ne); **p** (ado(p)ção, ado(p)tar); *for further details see p. xiii.*

ideological [aɪdɪə'lɔdʒɪkəl] *adj* ideológico.
ideology [aɪdɪ'ɔlədʒɪ] *n* ideologia.
idiocy ['ɪdɪəsɪ] *n* idiotice *f*; *(stupid act)* estupidez *f*.
idiom ['ɪdɪəm] *n* expressão *f* idiomática; *(style of speaking)* idioma *m*, linguagem *f*.
idiomatic [ɪdɪə'mætɪk] *adj* idiomático.
idiosyncrasy [ɪdɪəʊ'sɪŋkrəsɪ] *n* idiossincrasia.
idiot ['ɪdɪət] *n* idiota *m/f*.
idiotic [ɪdɪ'ɔtɪk] *adj* idiota.
idle ['aɪdl] *adj* ocioso; *(lazy)* preguiçoso; *(unemployed)* desempregado; *(pointless)* inútil, vão/vã ♦ *vi (machine)* funcionar com a transmissão desligada.
   idle away *vt*: **to ~ away the time** perder *or* desperdiçar tempo.
idleness ['aɪdlnɪs] *n* ociosidade *f*; preguiça; *(pointlessness)* inutilidade *f*.
idler ['aɪdlə*] *n* preguiçoso/a.
idle time *n (COMM)* tempo ocioso.
idol ['aɪdl] *n* ídolo.
idolize ['aɪdəlaɪz] *vt* idolatrar.
idyllic [ɪ'dɪlɪk] *adj* idílico.
i.e. *abbr* (= *id est: that is*) i.e., isto é.
if [ɪf] *conj* se ♦ *n*: **there are a lot of ~s and buts** não está nada decidido; **I'd be pleased ~ you could do it** ficaria satisfeito se você pudesse fazê-lo; **~ necessary** se necessário; **~ only he were here** se pelo menos ele estivesse aqui; **even ~** mesmo que.
igloo ['ɪgluː] *n* iglu *m*.
ignite [ɪg'naɪt] *vt* acender; *(set fire to)* incendiar ♦ *vi* acender.
ignition [ɪg'nɪʃən] *n (AUT)* ignição *f*; **to switch on/off the ~** ligar/desligar o motor.
ignition key *n (AUT)* chave *f* de ignição.
ignoble [ɪg'nəʊbl] *adj* ignóbil.
ignominious [ɪgnə'mɪnɪəs] *adj* vergonhoso, humilhante.
ignoramus [ɪgnə'reɪməs] *n* ignorante *m/f*.
ignorance ['ɪgnərəns] *n* ignorância; **to keep sb in ~ of sth** deixar alguém na ignorância de algo.
ignorant ['ɪgnərənt] *adj* ignorante; **to be ~ of** ignorar.
ignore [ɪg'nɔː*] *vt (person)* não fazer caso de; *(fact)* não levar em consideração, ignorar.
ikon ['aɪkɔn] *n* = **icon**.
IL *(US) abbr (POST)* = **Illinois**.
ILA *(US) n abbr* (= *International Longshoremen's Association*) *sindicato internacional dos portuários*.
ILEA ['ɪlɪə] *(BRIT) n abbr* (= *Inner London Education Authority*) *órgão administrador de ensino em Grande Londres*.
ILGWU *(US) n abbr* (= *International Ladies' Garment Workers' Union*) *sindicato dos trabalhadores na área de roupa feminina*.
I'll [aɪl] = **I will; I shall**.
ill [ɪl] *adj* doente; *(slightly ~)* indisposto; *(bad)* mau/má ♦ *n* mal *m*; *(fig)* desgraça ♦ *adv*: **to speak/think ~ of sb** falar/pensar mal de alguém; **to take** *or* **be taken ~** ficar doente.
ill-advised [-əd'vaɪzd] *adj* pouco recomendado; *(misled)* mal aconselhado.

ill-at-ease *adj* constrangido, pouco à vontade.
ill-considered [-kən'sɪdəd] *adj (plan)* imponderado.
ill-disposed *adj*: **to be ~ towards sb/sth** ser desfavorável a alguém/algo.
illegal [ɪ'liːgl] *adj* ilegal.
illegally [ɪ'liːgəlɪ] *adv* ilegalmente.
illegible [ɪ'ledʒɪbl] *adj* ilegível.
illegitimate [ɪlɪ'dʒɪtɪmət] *adj* ilegítimo.
ill-fated *adj* malfadado, azarento.
ill-favoured [-'feɪvəd] *(US* **ill-favored)** *adj* desagradável.
ill feeling *n* má vontade *f*, rancor *m*.
ill-gotten *adj (gains etc)* mal adquirido.
illicit [ɪ'lɪsɪt] *adj* ilícito.
ill-informed *adj* mal informado.
illiterate [ɪ'lɪtərət] *adj* analfabeto.
ill-mannered [-'mænəd] *adj* mal-educado, grosseiro.
illness ['ɪlnɪs] *n* doença.
illogical [ɪ'lɔdʒɪkl] *adj* ilógico.
ill-suited [-'suːtɪd] *adj (couple)* desajustado; **he is ~ to the job** ele é inadequado para o cargo.
ill-timed [-taɪmd] *adj* inoportuno.
ill-treat *vt* maltratar.
ill-treatment *n* maus tratos *mpl*.
illuminate [ɪ'luːmɪneɪt] *vt (room, street)* iluminar, clarear; *(subject)* esclarecer; **~d sign** anúncio luminoso.
illuminating [ɪ'luːmɪneɪtɪŋ] *adj* esclarecedor.
illumination [ɪluːmɪ'neɪʃən] *n* iluminação *f*; **~s** *npl* luminárias *fpl*.
illusion [ɪ'luːʒən] *n* ilusão *f*; **to be under the ~ that** ... estar com a ilusão de que ....
illusive [ɪ'luːsɪv] *adj* ilusório.
illusory [ɪ'luːsərɪ] *adj* ilusório.
illustrate ['ɪləstreɪt] *vt* ilustrar; *(subject)* esclarecer; *(point)* exemplificar.
illustration [ɪlə'streɪʃən] *n (example)* exemplo; *(explanation)* esclarecimento; *(in book)* gravura, ilustração *f*.
illustrator ['ɪləstreɪtə*] *n* ilustrador(a) *m/f*.
illustrious [ɪ'lʌstrɪəs] *adj* ilustre.
ill will *n* animosidade *f*, má vontade *f*.
ILO *n abbr* (= *International Labour Organization*) OIT *f*.
ILWU *(US) n abbr* (= *International Longshoremen's and Warehousemen's Union*) *sindicato dos portuários*.
I'm [aɪm] = **I am**.
image ['ɪmɪdʒ] *n* imagem *f*.
imagery ['ɪmɪdʒərɪ] *n* imagens *fpl*.
imaginable [ɪ'mædʒɪnəbl] *adj* imaginável, concebível.
imaginary [ɪ'mædʒɪnərɪ] *adj* imaginário.
imagination [ɪmædʒɪ'neɪʃən] *n* imaginação *f*; *(inventiveness)* inventividade *f*; *(illusion)* fantasia.
imaginative [ɪ'mædʒɪnətɪv] *adj* imaginativo.
imagine [ɪ'mædʒɪn] *vt* imaginar; *(delude o.s.)* fantasiar.
imbalance [ɪm'bæləns] *n* desequilíbrio; *(inequality)* desigualdade *f*.
imbecile ['ɪmbəsiːl] *n* imbecil *m/f*.

imbue [ɪm'bjuː] *vt*: **to ~ sth with** imbuir *or* impregnar algo de.

IMF *n abbr* (= *International Monetary Fund*) FMI *m*.

imitate ['ɪmɪteɪt] *vt* imitar.

imitation [ɪmɪ'teɪʃən] *n* imitação *f*; (*copy*) cópia; (*mimicry*) mímica.

imitator ['ɪmɪteɪtə*] *n* imitador(a) *m/f*.

immaculate [ɪ'mækjulət] *adj* impecável; (*REL*) imaculado.

immaterial [ɪmə'tɪərɪəl] *adj* imaterial; **it is ~ whether** ... é indiferente se ....

immature [ɪmə'tjuə*] *adj* (*person*) imaturo; (*of one's youth*) juvenil.

immaturity [ɪmə'tjuərɪtɪ] *n* imaturidade *f*.

immeasurable [ɪ'meʒrəbl] *adj* incomensurável, imensurável.

immediacy [ɪ'miːdɪəsɪ] *n* (*of events etc*) proximidade *f*; (*of needs*) urgência.

immediate [ɪ'miːdɪət] *adj* imediato; (*pressing*) urgente, premente.

immediately [ɪ'miːdɪətlɪ] *adv* (*at once*) imediatamente; **~ next to** bem junto a.

immense [ɪ'mens] *adj* imenso, enorme.

immensity [ɪ'mensətɪ] *n* imensidade *f*.

immerse [ɪ'mɜːs] *vt* (*submerge*) submergir; (*sink*) imergir, mergulhar; **to be ~d in** (*fig*) estar absorto em.

immersion heater [ɪ'mɜːʃn-] (*BRIT*) *n* aquecedor *m* de imersão.

immigrant ['ɪmɪgrənt] *n* imigrante *m/f*.

immigrate ['ɪmɪgreɪt] *vi* imigrar.

immigration [ɪmɪ'greɪʃən] *n* imigração *f*.

immigration authorities *npl* fiscais *mpl* de imigração, ≈ polícia federal.

immigration laws *npl* leis *fpl* imigratórias.

imminent ['ɪmɪnənt] *adj* iminente.

immobile [ɪ'məubaɪl] *adj* imóvel.

immobilize [ɪ'məubɪlaɪz] *vt* imobilizar.

immoderate [ɪ'mɒdərət] *adj* imoderado.

immodest [ɪ'mɒdɪst] *adj* (*indecent*) indecente, impudico; (*person: boasting*) presumido, arrogante.

immoral [ɪ'mɒrl] *adj* imoral.

immorality [ɪmə'rælɪtɪ] *n* imoralidade *f*.

immortal [ɪ'mɔːtl] *adj* imortal.

immortalize [ɪ'mɔːtəlaɪz] *vt* imortalizar.

immovable [ɪ'muːvəbl] *adj* (*object*) imóvel, fixo; (*person*) inflexível.

immune [ɪ'mjuːn] *adj*: **~ to** imune a, imunizado contra.

immunity [ɪ'mjuːnɪtɪ] *n* (*MED*) imunidade *f*; (*COMM*) isenção *f*; **diplomatic ~** imunidade diplomática.

immunization [ɪmjunaɪ'zeɪʃən] *n* imunização *f*.

immunize ['ɪmjunaɪz] *vt* imunizar.

imp [ɪmp] *n* diabinho, criança levada.

impact ['ɪmpækt] *n* impacto (*PT*: impacte *m*).

impair [ɪm'peə*] *vt* prejudicar.

impale [ɪm'peɪl] *vt* perfurar, empalar.

impart [ɪm'paːt] *vt* dar, comunicar.

impartial [ɪm'paːʃl] *adj* imparcial.

impartiality [ɪmpaːʃɪ'ælɪtɪ] *n* imparcialidade *f*.

impassable [ɪm'paːsəbl] *adj* (*barrier, river*) intransponível; (*road*) intransitável.

impasse [æm'paːs] *n* (*fig*) impasse *m*.

impassioned [ɪm'pæʃənd] *adj* ardente, veemente.

impassive [ɪm'pæsɪv] *adj* impassível.

impatience [ɪm'peɪʃəns] *n* impaciência.

impatient [ɪm'peɪʃənt] *adj* impaciente; **to get** *or* **grow ~** impacientar-se.

impeach [ɪm'piːtʃ] *vt* impugnar; (*public official*) levar a juízo.

impeachment [ɪm'piːtʃmənt] *n* (*LAW*) impeachment *m*.

impeccable [ɪm'pekəbl] *adj* impecável.

impecunious [ɪmpə'kjuːnɪəs] *adj* impecunioso, sem recursos.

impede [ɪm'piːd] *vt* impedir, estorvar.

impediment [ɪm'pedɪmənt] *n* obstáculo, impedimento; (*also: speech ~*) defeito (de fala).

impel [ɪm'pel] *vt* (*force*): **to ~ sb (to do sth)** impelir alguém (a fazer algo).

impending [ɪm'pendɪŋ] *adj* (*near*) iminente, próximo.

impenetrable [ɪm'penɪtrəbl] *adj* impenetrável; (*unfathomable*) incompreensível.

imperative [ɪm'perətɪv] *adj* (*tone*) imperioso, obrigatório; (*necessary*) indispensável; (*pressing*) premente ♦ *n* (*LING*) imperativo.

imperceptible [ɪmpə'septɪbl] *adj* imperceptível.

imperfect [ɪm'pəːfɪkt] *adj* imperfeito; (*goods etc*) defeituoso ♦ *n* (*LING*: also: **~ tense**) imperfeito.

imperfection [ɪmpə'fekʃən] *n* (*blemish*) defeito; (*state*) imperfeição *f*.

imperial [ɪm'pɪərɪəl] *adj* imperial.

imperialism [ɪm'pɪərɪəlɪzəm] *n* imperialismo.

imperil [ɪm'perɪl] *vt* pôr em perigo, arriscar.

imperious [ɪm'pɪərɪəs] *adj* imperioso.

impersonal [ɪm'pəːsənl] *adj* impessoal.

impersonate [ɪm'pəːsəneɪt] *vt* fazer-se passar por, personificar; (*THEATRE*) imitar.

impersonation [ɪmpəːsə'neɪʃən] *n* (*LAW*) impostura; (*THEATRE*) imitacão *f*.

impersonator [ɪm'pəːsəneɪtə*] *n* impostor(a) *m/f*; (*THEATRE*) imitador(a) *m/f*.

impertinence [ɪm'pəːtɪnəns] *n* impertinência, insolência.

impertinent [ɪm'pəːtɪnənt] *adj* impertinente, insolente.

imperturbable [ɪmpə'təːbəbl] *adj* imperturbável, inabalável.

impervious [ɪm'pəːvɪəs] *adj* impenetrável; (*fig*): **~ to** insensível a.

impetuous [ɪm'petjuəs] *adj* impetuoso, precipitado.

impetus ['ɪmpətəs] *n* ímpeto; (*fig*) impulso.

impinge [ɪm'pɪndʒ]: **to ~ on** *vt fus* impressionar, impingir em; (*affect*) afetar.

impish ['ɪmpɪʃ] *adj* levado, travesso.

NB: *European Portuguese adds the following consonants to certain words:* **b** (sú(b)dito, su(b)til); **c** (a(c)ção, a(c)cionista, a(c)to); **m** (inde(m)ne); **p** (ado(p)ção, ado(p)tar); *for further details see p. xiii.*

implacable [ɪm'plækəbl] *adj* implacável, impiedoso.

implant [*vt* ɪm'plɑːnt, *n* 'ɪmplɑːnt] *vt* (*MED*) implantar; (*fig*) inculcar ♦ *n* implante *m*.

implausible [ɪm'plɔːzɪbl] *adj* inverossímil (*PT*: -osí-).

implement [*n* 'ɪmplɪmənt, *vt* 'ɪmplɪment] *n* instrumento, ferramenta; (*for cooking*) utensílio ♦ *vt* efetivar; (*carry out*) realizar, executar.

implicate ['ɪmplɪkeɪt] *vt* (*compromise*) comprometer; (*involve*) implicar, envolver.

implication [ɪmplɪ'keɪʃən] *n* implicação *f*, conseqüência; **by ~** por conseqüência.

implicit [ɪm'plɪsɪt] *adj* implícito; (*complete*) absoluto.

implicitly [ɪm'plɪsɪtlɪ] *adv* implicitamente; (*completely*) completamente.

implore [ɪm'plɔː*] *vt* (*person*) implorar, suplicar.

imply [ɪm'plaɪ] *vt* (*involve*) implicar; (*mean*) significar; (*hint*) dar a entender que; **it is implied** se subentende.

impolite [ɪmpə'laɪt] *adj* indelicado, ineducado.

imponderable [ɪm'pɒndərəbl] *adj* imponderável.

import [*vt* ɪm'pɔːt, *n, cpd* 'ɪmpɔːt] *vt* importar ♦ *n* (*COMM*) importação *f*; (: *article*) mercadoria importada; (*meaning*) significado, sentido ♦ *cpd* (*duty, licence etc*) de importação.

importance [ɪm'pɔːtəns] *n* importância; **to be of great/little ~** ser de grande/pouca importância.

important [ɪm'pɔːtənt] *adj* importante; **it is ~ that ...** é importante *or* importa que ...; **it's not ~** não tem importância, não importa.

importantly [ɪm'pɔːtəntlɪ] *adv*: **but, more ~** ... mas, o que é mais importante, ...

importation [ɪmpɔː'teɪʃən] *n* importação *f*.

imported [ɪm'pɔːtɪd] *adj* importado.

importer [ɪm'pɔːtə*] *n* importador(a) *m/f*.

impose [ɪm'pəʊz] *vt* impor ♦ *vi*: **to ~ on sb** abusar de alguém.

imposing [ɪm'pəʊzɪŋ] *adj* imponente.

imposition [ɪmpə'zɪʃən] *n* (*of tax etc*) imposição *f*; **to be an ~ on sb** (*person*) abusar de alguém.

impossibility [ɪmpɒsɪ'bɪlɪtɪ] *n* impossibilidade *f*.

impossible [ɪm'pɒsɪbl] *adj* impossível; (*person*) insuportável; **it's ~ for me to leave** é-me impossível sair, não dá para eu sair (*inf*).

impostor [ɪm'pɒstə*] *n* impostor(a) *m/f*.

impotence ['ɪmpətəns] *n* impotência.

impotent ['ɪmpətənt] *adj* impotente.

impound [ɪm'paʊnd] *vt* confiscar.

impoverished [ɪm'pɒvərɪʃt] *adj* empobrecido; (*land*) esgotado.

impracticable [ɪm'præktɪkəbl] *adj* impraticável, inexeqüível.

impractical [ɪm'præktɪkl] *adj* pouco prático.

imprecise [ɪmprɪ'saɪs] *adj* impreciso, vago.

impregnable [ɪm'prɛgnəbl] *adj* invulnerável; (*castle*) inexpugnável.

impregnate ['ɪmprɛgneɪt] *vt* (*gen*) impregnar; (*soak*) embeber; (*fertilize*) fecundar.

impresario [ɪmprɪ'sɑːrɪəʊ] *n* empresário/a.

impress [ɪm'prɛs] *vt* impressionar; (*mark*) imprimir ♦ *vi* causar boa impressão; **to ~ sth on sb** inculcar algo em alguém; **it ~ed itself on me** fiquei com isso gravado (na memória).

impression [ɪm'prɛʃən] *n* impressão *f*; (*footprint etc*) marca; (*print run*) edição *f*; **to make a good/bad ~ on sb** fazer boa/má impressão em alguém; **to be under the ~ that** estar com a impressão de que.

impressionable [ɪm'prɛʃənəbl] *adj* impressionável; (*sensitive*) sensível.

impressionist [ɪm'prɛʃənɪst] *n* impressionista *m/f*.

impressive [ɪm'prɛsɪv] *adj* impressionante.

imprint ['ɪmprɪnt] *n* impressão *f*, marca; (*PUBLISHING*) nome *m* (da coleção).

imprinted [ɪm'prɪntɪd] *adj*: **~ on** imprimido em; (*fig*) gravado em.

imprison [ɪm'prɪzn] *vt* encarcerar.

imprisonment [ɪm'prɪzənmənt] *n* prisão *f*.

improbable [ɪm'prɒbəbl] *adj* improvável; (*story*) inverossímil (*PT*: -osí-).

impromptu [ɪm'prɒmptjuː] *adj* improvisado ♦ *adv* de improviso.

improper [ɪm'prɒpə*] *adj* (*incorrect*) impróprio; (*unseemly*) indecoroso; (*indecent*) indecente.

impropriety [ɪmprə'praɪətɪ] *n* falta de decoro, inconveniência; (*indecency*) indecência; (*of language*) impropriedade *f*.

improve [ɪm'pruːv] *vt* melhorar ♦ *vi* melhorar; (*pupils*) progredir.

improve (up)on *vt fus* melhorar.

improvement [ɪm'pruːvmənt] *n* melhora; (*of pupils*) progresso; **to make ~s to** melhorar.

improvisation [ɪmprəvaɪ'zeɪʃən] *n* improvisação *f*.

improvise ['ɪmprəvaɪz] *vt, vi* improvisar.

imprudence [ɪm'pruːdns] *n* imprudência.

imprudent [ɪm'pruːdnt] *adj* imprudente.

impudent ['ɪmpjudnt] *adj* insolente, impudente.

impugn [ɪm'pjuːn] *vt* impugnar, contestar.

impulse ['ɪmpʌls] *n* impulso, ímpeto; **to act on ~** agir sem pensar *or* num impulso.

impulse buy *n* compra por impulso.

impulsive [ɪm'pʌlsɪv] *adj* impulsivo.

impunity [ɪm'pjuːnɪtɪ] *n*: **with ~** impunemente.

impure [ɪm'pjʊə*] *adj* (*adulterated*) adulterado; (*not pure*) impuro.

impurity [ɪm'pjʊərɪtɪ] *n* impureza.

IN (*US*) *abbr* (*POST*) = **Indiana**.

in [ɪn] *prep em*; (*within*) dentro de; (*with time*: *during, within*): **~ 2 days** em *or* dentro de 2 dias; (: *after*): **~ 2 weeks** daqui a 2 semanas; (*with town, country*): **it's ~ France** é *or* fica na França ♦ *adv* dentro, para dentro; (*fashionable*) na moda ♦ *n*: **the ~s and outs** os cantos e recantos, os pormenores; **is he ~?** ele está?; **~ the United States** nos Estados Unidos; ~ **1986** em 1986; ~ **May** em maio; ~ **spring/autumn** na primavera/no outono; ~ **the morning** de manhã; ~ **the distance** ao longe; ~ **the country** no campo; ~ **town** no centro (da cidade); ~ **the sun** ao or sob o sol; ~ **the rain** na chuva; ~ **French** em francês; ~ **writing** por escrito; **written** ~ **pencil** escrito a lápis; **to pay** ~ **dollars** pagar em dólares; **1** ~ **10** 1 em 10, 1 em cada 10; ~ **hundreds** às centenas; **the best pupil** ~ **the class** o melhor aluno da classe; **to be** ~ **teaching/publishing** ser professor/ trabalhar numa editora; ~ **saying this** ao dizer isto; ~ **that** ... já que ...; **their party is** ~ seu partido chegou ao poder; **to ask sb** ~ convidar alguém para entrar; **to run/limp** ~ entrar correndo/mancando.

in. *abbr* = **inch(es)**.

inability [ɪnə'bɪlɪtɪ] *n* incapacidade *f*; ~ **to pay** impossibilidade de pagar.

inaccessible [ɪnək'sɛsɪbl] *adj* inacessível.

inaccuracy [ɪn'ækjurəsɪ] *n* inexatidão *f*, imprecisão *f*.

inaccurate [ɪn'ækjurət] *adj* inexato, impreciso.

inaction [ɪn'ækʃən] *n* inação *f*.

inactivity [ɪnæk'tɪvɪtɪ] *n* inatividade *f*.

inadequacy [ɪn'ædɪkwəsɪ] *adj* (*insufficiency*) insuficiência.

inadequate [ɪn'ædɪkwət] *adj* (*insufficient*) insuficiente; (*unsuitable*) inadequado; (*person*) impróprio.

inadmissible [ɪnəd'mɪsəbl] *adj* inadmissível.

inadvertent [ɪnəd'vɜːtənt] *adj* (*mistake*) cometido sem querer.

inadvertently [ɪnəd'vɜːtntlɪ] *adv* inadvertidamente, sem querer.

inadvisable [ɪnəd'vaɪzəbl] *adj* não aconselhável, inoportuno.

inane [ɪ'neɪn] *adj* tolo; (*fatuous*) vazio.

inanimate [ɪn'ænɪmət] *adj* inanimado.

inapplicable [ɪn'æplɪkəbl] *adj* inaplicável.

inappropriate [ɪnə'prəuprɪət] *adj* inadequado, inconveniente; (*word, expression*) impróprio.

inapt [ɪn'æpt] *adj* inapto.

inaptitude [ɪn'æptɪtjuːd] *n* incapacidade *f*, inaptidão *f*.

inarticulate [ɪnɑː'tɪkjulət] *adj* (*person*) incapaz de expressar-se (bem); (*speech*) inarticulado.

inasmuch as [ɪnəz'mʌtʃ-] *conj* (*given that*) visto que; (*since*) desde que, já que.

inattention [ɪnə'tɛnʃən] *n* inatenção *f*.

inattentive [ɪnə'tɛntɪv] *adj* desatento.

inaudible [ɪn'ɔːdɪbl] *adj* inaudível.

inaugural [ɪ'nɔːgjurəl] *adj* (*speech*) inaugural; (: *of president*) de posse.

inaugurate [ɪ'nɔːgjureɪt] *vt* inaugurar; (*president, official*) empossar.

inauguration [ɪnɔːgju'reɪʃən] *n* inauguração *f*; (*of president, official*) posse *f*.

inauspicious [ɪnɔːs'pɪʃəs] *adj* infausto.

in-between *adj* intermediário, entre dois extremos.

inborn [ɪn'bɔːn] *adj* (*feeling*) inato; (*defect*) congênito.

inbred [ɪn'brɛd] *adj* inato; (*family*) de procriação consangüínea.

inbreeding [ɪn'briːdɪŋ] *n* endogamia.

Inc. *abbr* = **incorporated**.

Inca ['ɪŋkə] *adj* (*also: ~n*) inca, incaico ♦ *n* inca *m/f*.

incalculable [ɪn'kælkjuləbl] *adj* incalculável.

incapability [ɪnkeɪpə'bɪlɪtɪ] *n* incapacidade *f*.

incapable [ɪn'keɪpəbl] *adj* incapaz.

incapacitate [ɪnkə'pæsɪteɪt] *vt* incapacitar.

incapacitated [ɪnkə'pæsɪteɪtɪd] *adj* (*LAW*) incapacitado.

incapacity [ɪnkə'pæsɪtɪ] *n* (*inability*) incapacidade *f*.

incarcerate [ɪn'kɑːsəreɪt] *vt* encarcerar.

incarnate [*adj* ɪn'kɑːnɪt, *vt* 'ɪnkɑːneɪt] *adj* encarnado, personificado ♦ *vt* encarnar.

incarnation [ɪnkɑː'neɪʃən] *n* encarnação *f*.

incendiary [ɪn'sɛndɪərɪ] *adj* incendiário ♦ *n* (*bomb*) bomba incendiária.

incense [*n* 'ɪnsɛns, *vt* ɪn'sɛns] *n* incenso ♦ *vt* (*anger*) exasperar, enraivecer.

incense burner *n* incensório.

incentive [ɪn'sɛntɪv] *n* incentivo, estímulo.

incentive scheme *n* plano de incentivos.

inception [ɪn'sɛpʃən] *n* começo, início.

incessant [ɪn'sɛsnt] *adj* incessante, contínuo.

incessantly [ɪn'sɛsntlɪ] *adv* constantemente.

incest ['ɪnsɛst] *n* incesto.

inch [ɪntʃ] *n* polegada (= *25 mm*; *12 in a foot*); **to be within an** ~ **of** estar a um passo de; **he didn't give an** ~ ele não cedeu nem um milímetro.

inch forward *vi* avançar palmo a palmo.

inch tape (*BRIT*) *n* fita métrica.

incidence ['ɪnsɪdns] *n* (*of crime, disease*) incidência.

incident ['ɪnsɪdnt] *n* incidente *m*, evento; (*in book*) episódio.

incidental [ɪnsɪ'dɛntl] *adj* acessório, não essencial; (*unplanned*) acidental, casual; ~ **expenses** despesas *fpl* adicionais.

incidentally [ɪnsɪ'dɛntəlɪ] *adv* (*by the way*) a propósito.

incidental music *n* música de cena or de fundo.

incinerate [ɪn'sɪnəreɪt] *vt* incinerar.

incinerator [ɪn'sɪnəreɪtə*] *n* incinerador *m*.

incipient [ɪn'sɪpɪənt] *adj* incipiente.

incision [ɪn'sɪʒən] *n* incisão *f*.

incisive [ɪn'saɪsɪv] *adj* (*mind*) penetrante, perspicaz; (*tone*) mordaz, sarcástico; (*remark etc*) incisivo.

incisor [ɪn'saɪzə*] *n* incisivo.

incite [ɪn'saɪt] *vt* incitar, provocar.

incl. *abbr* = **including; inclusive (of)**.

inclement [ɪn'klɛmənt] *adj* (*weather*) inclemente.

inclination [ɪnklɪ'neɪʃən] *n* (*tendency*)

tendência, inclinação *f*.

incline [*n* 'ınklaın, *vt*, *vi* ın'klaın] *n* inclinação *f*, ladeira ♦ *vt* (*slope*) inclinar; (*head*) curvar, inclinar ♦ *vi* inclinar-se; **to be ~d to** (*tend*) tender a, ser propenso a; (*be willing*) estar disposto a.

include [ın'kluːd] *vt* incluir; **the service is/is not ~d** o serviço está/não está incluído.

including [ın'kluːdıŋ] *prep* inclusive; **~ tip** gorjeta incluída.

inclusion [ın'kluːʒən] *n* inclusão *f*.

inclusive [ın'kluːsıv] *adj* incluído, incluso ♦ *adv* inclusive; **£50 ~ of all surcharges** £50, incluídas todas as sobretaxas.

inclusive terms (*BRIT*) *npl* preço global.

incognito [ınkɔg'niːtəu] *adv* incógnito.

incoherent [ınkəu'hıərənt] *adj* incoerente.

income ['ıŋkʌm] *n* (*earnings*) renda, rendimentos; (*unearned*) renda; (*profit*) lucro; **gross/net ~** renda bruta/líquida; **~ and expenditure account** conta de receitas e despesas; **~ bracket** faixa salarial.

income tax *n* imposto de renda (*BR*), imposto complementar (*PT*).

income tax inspector *n* fiscal *m/f* do imposto de renda.

income tax return *n* declaração *f* do imposto de renda.

incoming ['ınkʌmıŋ] *adj* (*flight*, *passenger*) de chegada; (*mail*) de entrada; (*government*, *tenant*) novo; **~ tide** maré enchente.

incommunicado [ınkəmjunı'kɑːdəu] *adj* incomunicável.

incomparable [ın'kɔmpərəbl] *adj* incomparável.

incompatible [ınkəm'pætıbl] *adj* incompatível.

incompetence [ın'kɔmpıtəns] *n* incompetência.

incompetent [ın'kɔmpıtənt] *adj* incompetente.

incomplete [ınkəm'pliːt] *adj* incompleto; (*unfinished*) por terminar.

incomprehensible [ınkɔmprı'hensıbl] *adj* incompreensível.

inconceivable [ınkən'siːvəbl] *adj* inconcebível.

inconclusive [ınkən'kluːsıv] *adj* inconclusivo; (*argument*) pouco convincente.

incongruous [ın'kɔŋgruəs] *adj* (*foolish*) ridículo, absurdo; (*remark*, *act*) incongruente, ilógico.

inconsequential [ınkɔnsı'kwenʃl] *adj* sem importância.

inconsiderable [ınkən'sıdərəbl] *adj*: **not ~** importante.

inconsiderate [ınkən'sıdərət] *adj* sem consideração; **how ~ of him!** que falta de consideração (de sua parte)!

inconsistency [ınkən'sıstənsı] *n* inconsistência.

inconsistent [ınkən'sıstnt] *adj* inconsistente, incompatível; **~ with** (que) não está de acordo com.

inconsolable [ınkən'səuləbl] *adj* inconsolável.

inconspicuous [ınkən'spıkjuəs] *adj* não conspícuo; (*modest*) modesto; **to make o.s. ~** não chamar a atenção.

inconstant [ın'kɔnstnt] *adj* inconstante.

incontinence [ın'kɔntınəns] *n* incontinência.

incontinent [ın'kɔntınənt] *adj* incontinente.

incontrovertible [ınkɔntrə'vəːtəbl] *adj* incontestável.

inconvenience [ınkən'viːnjəns] *n* (*quality*) inconveniência; (*problem*) inconveniente *m* ♦ *vt* incomodar; **don't ~ yourself** não se incomode.

inconvenient [ınkən'viːnjənt] *adj* inconveniente, incômodo; (*time*, *place*) inoportuno; **that time is very ~ for me** esse horário me é muito inconveniente.

incorporate [ın'kɔːpəreıt] *vt* incorporar; (*contain*) compreender; (*add*) incluir.

incorporated company [ın'kɔːpəretıd-] (*US*) *n ≈* sociedade *f* anônima.

incorrect [ınkə'rekt] *adj* incorreto.

incorrigible [ın'kɔrıdʒıbl] *adj* incorrigível.

incorruptible [ınkə'rʌptıbl] *adj* incorruptível; (*not open to bribes*) insubornável.

increase [*n* 'ınkriːs, *vi*, *vt* ın'kriːs] *n* aumento ♦ *vi*, *vt* aumentar; **an ~ of 5%** um aumento de 5%; **to be on the ~** estar em crescimento *or* alta.

increasing [ın'kriːsıŋ] *adj* (*number*) crescente, em aumento.

increasingly [ın'kriːsıŋlı] *adv* cada vez mais.

incredible [ın'kredıbl] *adj* incrível.

incredulous [ın'kredjuləs] *adj* incrédulo.

increment ['ınkrımənt] *n* aumento, incremento.

incriminate [ın'krımıneıt] *vt* incriminar.

incriminating [ın'krımıneıtıŋ] *adj* incriminador(a).

incrust [ın'krʌst] *vt* = **encrust**.

incubate ['ınkjubeıt] *vt*, *vi* incubar.

incubation [ınkju'beıʃən] *n* incubação *f*.

incubation period *n* período de incubação.

incubator ['ınkjubeıtə*] *n* incubadora; (*for eggs*) chocadeira.

inculcate ['ınkʌlkeıt] *vt*: **to ~ sth in sb** inculcar algo a alguém.

incumbent [ın'kʌmbənt] *n* titular *m/f* ♦ *adj*: **it is ~ on him to ...** cabe a ele ....

incur [ın'kəː*] *vt* incorrer em; (*expenses*) contrair.

incurable [ın'kjuərəbl] *adj* incurável; (*fig*) irremediável.

incursion [ın'kəːʃən] *n* incursão *f*.

indebted [ın'detıd] *adj*: **to be ~ to sb** estar em dívida com alguém, dever obrigação a alguém.

indecency [ın'diːsnsı] *n* indecência.

indecent [ın'diːsnt] *adj* indecente.

indecent assault (*BRIT*) *n* atentado contra o pudor.

indecent exposure *n* exibição *f* obscena, exibicionismo.

indecipherable [ındı'saıfərəbl] *adj* indecifrável.

indecision [ındı'sıʒən] *n* indecisão *f*.

indecisive [ındı'saısıv] *adj* indeciso; (*discussion*) inconcludente, sem resultados.

indeed [ın'diːd] *adv* de fato, realmente;

(furthermore) aliás; **yes ~!** claro que sim!

indefatigable [ɪndɪˈfætɪgəbl] *adj* incansável.

indefensible [ɪndɪˈfɛnsɪbl] *adj* indefensível.

indefinable [ɪndɪˈfaɪnəbl] *adj* indefinível.

indefinite [ɪnˈdɛfɪnɪt] *adj* indefinido; *(uncertain)* impreciso; *(period, number)* indeterminado.

indefinitely [ɪnˈdɛfɪnɪtlɪ] *adv (wait)* indefinidamente.

indelible [ɪnˈdɛlɪbl] *adj* indelével.

indelicate [ɪnˈdɛlɪkɪt] *adj (tactless)* inábil; *(not polite)* indelicado, rude.

indemnify [ɪnˈdɛmnɪfaɪ] *vt* indenizar, compensar.

indemnity [ɪnˈdɛmnɪtɪ] *n (insurance)* garantia, seguro; *(compensation)* indenização *f*.

indent [ɪnˈdɛnt] *vt (text)* recolher ♦ *vi*: **to ~ for sth** *(COMM)* encomendar algo.

indentation [ɪndɛnˈteɪʃən] *n* entalhe *m*, recorte *m*; *(TYP)* parágrafo, recuo.

indenture [ɪnˈdɛntʃə*] *n* contrato de aprendizagem.

independence [ɪndɪˈpɛndns] *n* independência.

independent [ɪndɪˈpɛndnt] *adj* independente; **to become ~** tornar-se independente.

independently [ɪndɪˈpɛndntlɪ] *adv* independentemente.

indescribable [ɪndɪˈskraɪbəbl] *adj* indescritível.

indestructible [ɪndɪˈstrʌktəbl] *adj* indestrutível.

indeterminate [ɪndɪˈtə:mɪnɪt] *adj* indeterminado.

index [ˈɪndɛks] *(pl ~es) n (in book)* índice *m*; *(: in library etc)* catálogo; *(pl: indices: ratio, sign)* índice *m*, expoente *m*.

index card *n* ficha de arquivo.

indexed [ˈɪndɛkst] *(US) adj* = **index-linked**.

index finger *n* dedo indicador.

index-linked [-lɪŋkt] *(BRIT) adj* vinculado ao índice (do custo de vida).

India [ˈɪndɪə] *n* Índia.

Indian [ˈɪndɪən] *adj, n (from India)* indiano/a; *(American, Brazilian)* índio/a.

Indian ink *n* tinta nanquim.

Indian Ocean *n*: **the ~** o oceano Índico.

Indian summer *n (fig)* veranico.

India paper *n* papel *m* da China.

India rubber *n* borracha.

indicate [ˈɪndɪkeɪt] *vt* indicar ♦ *vi (BRIT: AUT)*: **to ~ left/right** indicar para a esquerda/direita.

indication [ɪndɪˈkeɪʃən] *n* indício, sinal *m*.

indicative [ɪnˈdɪkətɪv] *adj* indicativo ♦ *n (LING)* indicativo; **to be ~ of sth** ser sintomático de algo.

indicator [ˈɪndɪkeɪtə*] *n* indicador *m*; *(on car)* pisca-pisca *m*.

indices [ˈɪndɪsiːz] *npl of* **index**.

indict [ɪnˈdaɪt] *vt* acusar.

indictable [ɪnˈdaɪtəbl] *adj (person)* culpado; **~ offence** crime sujeito às penas da lei.

indictment [ɪnˈdaɪtmənt] *n* acusação *f*, denúncia.

indifference [ɪnˈdɪfrəns] *n* indiferença.

indifferent [ɪnˈdɪfrənt] *adj* indiferente; *(poor)* regular, medíocre.

indigenous [ɪnˈdɪdʒɪnəs] *adj* indígena, nativo.

indigestible [ɪndɪˈdʒɛstɪbl] *adj* indigesto.

indigestion [ɪndɪˈdʒɛstʃən] *n* indigestão *f*.

indignant [ɪnˈdɪgnənt] *adj*: **to be ~ about sth** estar indignado com algo, indignar-se de algo.

indignation [ɪndɪgˈneɪʃən] *n* indignação *f*.

indignity [ɪnˈdɪgnɪtɪ] *n* indignidade *f*; *(insult)* ultraje *m*, afronta.

indigo [ˈɪndɪgəu] *adj* cor de anil *inv* ♦ *n* anil *m*.

indirect [ɪndɪˈrɛkt] *adj* indireto.

indirectly [ɪndɪˈrɛktlɪ] *adv* indiretamente.

indiscreet [ɪndɪˈskriːt] *adj* indiscreto; *(rash)* imprudente.

indiscretion [ɪndɪˈskrɛʃən] *n* indiscrição *f*; imprudência.

indiscriminate [ɪndɪˈskrɪmɪnət] *adj* indiscriminado.

indispensable [ɪndɪˈspɛnsəbl] *adj* indispensável, imprescindível.

indisposed [ɪndɪˈspəuzd] *adj (unwell)* indisposto.

indisposition [ɪndɪspəˈzɪʃən] *n (illness)* mal-estar *m*, indisposição *f*.

indisputable [ɪndɪˈspjuːtəbl] *adj* incontestável.

indistinct [ɪndɪˈstɪŋkt] *adj* indistinto; *(memory, noise)* confuso, vago.

indistinguishable [ɪndɪˈstɪŋwɪʃəbl] *adj* indistinguível.

individual [ɪndɪˈvɪdjuəl] *n* indivíduo ♦ *adj* individual; *(personal)* pessoal; *(for/of one only)* particular.

individualist [ɪndɪˈvɪdjuəlɪst] *n* individualista *m/f*.

individuality [ɪndɪvɪdjuˈælɪtɪ] *n* individualidade *f*.

individually [ɪndɪˈvɪdjuəlɪ] *adv* individualmente, particularmente.

indivisible [ɪndɪˈvɪzɪbl] *adj* indivisível.

Indo-China [ˈɪndəu-] *n* Indochina.

indoctrinate [ɪnˈdɔktrɪneɪt] *vt* doutrinar.

indoctrination [ɪndɔktrɪˈneɪʃən] *n* doutrinação *f*.

indolent [ˈɪndələnt] *adj* indolente, preguiçoso.

Indonesia [ɪndəˈniːzɪə] *n* Indonésia.

Indonesian [ɪndəˈniːzɪən] *adj* indonésio ♦ *n* indonésio/a; *(LING)* indonésio.

indoor [ˈɪndɔː*] *adj (inner)* interno, interior; *(inside)* dentro de casa; *(swimming pool)* coberto; *(games, sport)* de salão.

indoors [ɪnˈdɔːz] *adv* em lugar fechado; *(at home)* em casa.

indubitable [ɪnˈdjuːbɪtəbl] *adj* indubitável.

induce [ɪnˈdjuːs] *vt* induzir; *(bring about)* causar, produzir; *(provoke)* provocar; **to ~ sb to do sth** induzir alguém a fazer algo.

NB: *European Portuguese adds the following consonants to certain words:* **b** (sú(b)dito, su(b)til); **c** (a(c)ção, a(c)cionista, a(c)to); **m** (inde(m)ne); **p** (ado(p)ção, ado(p)tar); *for further details see p. xiii.*

inducement [ɪn'djuːsmənt] n (incentive) incentivo, estímulo.

induct [ɪn'dʌkt] vt instalar.

induction [ɪn'dʌkʃən] n (MED: of birth) indução f.

induction course (BRIT) n curso de indução.

indulge [ɪn'dʌldʒ] vt (desire) satisfazer; (whim) condescender com; (person) comprazer; (child) fazer a vontade de ♦ vi: **to ~ in** entregar-se a, satisfazer-se com.

indulgence [ɪn'dʌldʒəns] n (of desire) satisfação f; (leniency) indulgência, tolerância.

indulgent [ɪn'dʌldʒənt] adj indulgente.

industrial [ɪn'dʌstrɪəl] adj industrial; (injury) de trabalho; (dispute) trabalhista.

industrial action n greve f.

industrial design n desenho industrial.

industrial estate (BRIT) n zona industrial.

industrialist [ɪn'dʌstrɪəlɪst] n industrial m/f.

industrialize [ɪn'dʌstrɪəlaɪz] vt industrializar.

industrial park (US) n parque m industrial.

industrial relations npl relações fpl industriais.

industrial tribunal (BRIT) n ≈ tribunal m do trabalho.

industrial unrest (BRIT) n agitação f operária.

industrious [ɪn'dʌstrɪəs] adj trabalhador(a); (student) aplicado.

industry ['ɪndəstrɪ] n indústria; (diligence) aplicação f, diligência.

inebriated [ɪ'niːbrɪeɪtɪd] adj embriagado, bêbado.

inedible [ɪn'ɛdɪbl] adj não-comestível.

ineffective [ɪnɪ'fɛktɪv] adj ineficaz.

ineffectual [ɪnɪ'fɛktʃuəl] adj ineficaz.

inefficiency [ɪnɪ'fɪʃənsɪ] n ineficiência.

inefficient [ɪnɪ'fɪʃənt] adj ineficiente.

inelegant [ɪn'ɛlɪgənt] adj deselegante.

ineligible [ɪn'ɛlɪdʒɪbl] adj (candidate) inelegível; **to be ~ for sth** não estar qualificado para algo.

inept [ɪ'nɛpt] adj inepto.

ineptitude [ɪ'nɛptɪtjuːd] n inépcia, incompetência.

inequality [ɪnɪ'kwɔlɪtɪ] n desigualdade f.

inequitable [ɪn'ɛkwɪtəbl] adj injusto, iníquo.

ineradicable [ɪnɪ'rædɪkəbl] adj inerradicável.

inert [ɪ'nəːt] adj inerte; (immobile) imóvel.

inertia [ɪ'nəːʃə] n inércia; (laziness) lerdeza.

inertia-reel seat belt n cinto de segurança retrátil.

inescapable [ɪnɪ'skeɪpəbl] adj inevitável.

inessential [ɪnɪ'sɛnʃl] adj desnecessário.

inestimable [ɪn'ɛstɪməbl] adj inestimável, incalculável.

inevitable [ɪn'ɛvɪtəbl] adj inevitável; (necessary) forçoso, necessário.

inevitably [ɪn'ɛvɪtəblɪ] adv inevitavelmente.

inexact [ɪnɪg'zækt] adj inexato.

inexcusable [ɪnɪks'kjuːzəbl] adj imperdoável, indesculpável.

inexhaustible [ɪnɪg'zɔːstɪbl] adj inesgotável, inexaurível.

inexorable [ɪn'ɛksərəbl] adj inexorável.

inexpensive [ɪnɪk'spɛnsɪv] adj barato, econômico.

inexperience [ɪnɪk'spɪərɪəns] n inexperiência, falta de experiência.

inexperienced [ɪnɪk'spɪərɪənst] adj inexperiente.

inexplicable [ɪnɪk'splɪkəbl] adj inexplicável.

inexpressible [ɪnɪk'sprɛsɪbl] adj inexprimível.

inextricable [ɪnɪk'strɪkəbl] adj inextricável.

infallibility [ɪnfælə'bɪlɪtɪ] n infalibilidade f.

infallible [ɪn'fælɪbl] adj infalível.

infamous ['ɪnfəməs] adj infame, abominável.

infamy ['ɪnfəmɪ] n infâmia.

infancy ['ɪnfənsɪ] n infância.

infant ['ɪnfənt] n (baby) bebê m; (young child) criança.

infantile ['ɪnfəntaɪl] adj infantil; (pej) acriançado.

infant mortality n mortalidade f infantil.

infantry ['ɪnfəntrɪ] n infantaria.

infantryman ['ɪnfəntrɪmən] (irreg) n soldado de infantaria.

infant school (BRIT) n pré-escola.

infatuated [ɪn'fætjueɪtɪd] adj: **~ with** apaixonado por.

infatuation [ɪnfætju'eɪʃən] n gamação f, paixão f louca.

infect [ɪn'fɛkt] vt (wound) infeccionar, infetar; (person) contagiar; (fig: pej) corromper, contaminar; **~ed with** (illness) contagiado por; **to become ~ed** (wound) infeccionar(-se), infetar(-se).

infection [ɪn'fɛkʃən] n infecção f; (fig) contágio.

infectious [ɪn'fɛkʃəs] adj contagioso; (also: fig) infeccioso.

infer [ɪn'fəː*] vt deduzir, inferir.

inference ['ɪnfərəns] n dedução f, inferência.

inferior [ɪn'fɪərɪə*] adj inferior; (goods) de qualidade inferior ♦ n inferior m/f; (in rank) subalterno/a; **to feel ~** sentir-se inferior.

inferiority [ɪnfɪərɪ'ɔrətɪ] n inferioridade f.

inferiority complex n complexo de inferioridade.

infernal [ɪn'fəːnl] adj infernal.

infernally [ɪn'fəːnəlɪ] adv (very) muito.

inferno [ɪn'fəːnəu] n inferno; (fig) inferno de chamas.

infertile [ɪn'fəːtaɪl] adj infértil, estéril.

infertility [ɪnfə'tɪlɪtɪ] n infertilidade f, esterilidade f.

infested [ɪn'fɛstɪd] adj: **~ (with)** infestado (de), assolado (por).

infidelity [ɪnfɪ'dɛlɪtɪ] n infidelidade f.

in-fighting n (fig) lutas fpl internas, conflitos mpl internos.

infiltrate ['ɪnfɪltreɪt] vt (troops etc) infiltrar-se em ♦ vi infiltrar-se.

infinite ['ɪnfɪnɪt] adj infinito; (time, money) ilimitado.

infinitely ['ɪnfɪnɪtlɪ] adv infinitamente.

infinitesimal [ɪnfɪnɪ'tɛsɪməl] adj infinitésimo.

infinitive [ɪn'fɪnɪtɪv] n infinitivo.

infinity [ɪn'fɪnɪtɪ] n (also: MATH) infinito; (an ~) infinidade f.

infirm [ɪn'fɔːm] adj enfermo, fraco.
infirmary [ɪn'fɔːmərɪ] n enfermaria, hospital m.
infirmity [ɪn'fɔːmɪtɪ] n fraqueza; (illness) enfermidade f, achaque m.
inflame [ɪn'fleɪm] vt inflamar.
inflamed [ɪn'fleɪmd] adj inflamado.
inflammable [ɪn'flæməbl] (BRIT) adj inflamável.
inflammation [ɪnflə'meɪʃən] n inflamação f.
inflammatory [ɪn'flæmətərɪ] adj (speech) incendiário.
inflatable [ɪn'fleɪtəbl] adj inflável.
inflate [ɪn'fleɪt] vt (tyre, balloon) inflar, encher; (fig) inchar.
inflated [ɪn'fleɪtɪd] adj (style) empolado, pomposo; (value) excessivo.
inflation [ɪn'fleɪʃən] n (ECON) inflação f.
inflationary [ɪn'fleɪʃənərɪ] adj inflacionário.
inflexible [ɪn'fleksɪbl] adj inflexível.
inflict [ɪn'flɪkt] vt: to ~ on infligir em; (tax etc) impor a.
infliction [ɪn'flɪkʃən] n imposição f, inflição f.
in-flight adj (refuelling) em vôo; (movie) exibido durante o vôo; (service) de bordo.
inflow ['ɪnfləu] n afluência.
influence ['ɪnfluəns] n influência ♦ vt influir em, influenciar; (persuade) persuadir; under the ~ of alcohol sob o efeito do álcool.
influential [ɪnflu'enʃl] adj influente.
influenza [ɪnflu'enzə] n gripe f.
influx ['ɪnflʌks] n afluxo, influxo.
inform [ɪn'fɔːm] vt: to ~ sb of sth informar alguém de algo; (warn) avisar alguém de algo; (communicate) comunicar algo a alguém ♦ vi: to ~ on sb delatar alguém; to ~ sb about informar alguém sobre.
informal [ɪn'fɔːml] adj (person, manner) sem formalidade; (language) informal; (visit, discussion) extra-oficial; (intimate) familiar; "dress ~" "traje de passeio".
informality [ɪnfɔː'mælɪtɪ] n falta de cerimônia; (intimacy) intimidade f; (familiarity) familiaridade f; (ease) informalidade f.
informally [ɪn'fɔːməlɪ] adv sem formalidade; (unofficially) não oficialmente.
informant [ɪn'fɔːmənt] n informante m/f; (to police) delator(a) m/f.
information [ɪnfə'meɪʃən] n informação f, informações fpl; (news) notícias fpl; (knowledge) conhecimento; a piece of ~ uma informação; for your ~ para a sua informação, para o seu governo.
information bureau n balcão m de informações.
information processing n processamento de informações.
information retrieval n recuperação f de informações.
information technology n informática.
informative [ɪn'fɔːmətɪv] adj informativo.
informed [ɪn'fɔːmd] adj informado; an ~

guess um palpite baseado em conhecimento dos fatos.
informer [ɪn'fɔːmə*] n delator(a) m/f.
infra dig ['ɪnfrə-] (inf) adj abbr (= infra dignitatem) abaixo da minha (or sua etc) dignidade.
infra-red ['ɪnfrə-] adj infravermelho.
infrastructure ['ɪnfrəstrʌktʃə*] n infraestrutura.
infrequent [ɪn'friːkwənt] adj infreqüente.
infringe [ɪn'frɪndʒ] vt infringir, transgredir ♦ vi: to ~ on invadir, violar.
infringement [ɪn'frɪndʒmənt] n transgressão f; (of rights) violação f; (SPORT) infração f.
infuriate [ɪn'fjuərɪeɪt] vt enfurecer, enraivecer.
infuriating [ɪn'fjuərɪeɪtɪŋ] adj de dar raiva, enfurecedor(a).
infuse [ɪn'fjuːz] vt: to ~ sb with sth (fig) inspirar or infundir algo em alguém.
infusion [ɪn'fjuːʒən] n (tea etc) infusão f.
ingenious [ɪn'dʒiːnjəs] adj engenhoso.
ingenuity [ɪndʒɪ'njuːɪtɪ] n engenho, habilidade f.
ingenuous [ɪn'dʒenjuəs] adj ingênuo.
ingot ['ɪŋgət] n lingote m.
ingrained [ɪn'greɪnd] adj arraigado, enraizado.
ingratiate [ɪn'greɪʃɪeɪt] vt: to ~ o.s. with cair nas (boas) graças de.
ingratiating [ɪn'greɪʃɪeɪtɪŋ] adj insinuante.
ingratitude [ɪn'grætɪtjuːd] n ingratidão f.
ingredient [ɪn'griːdɪənt] n ingrediente m.
ingrowing toenail ['ɪngrəuɪŋ-] n unha encravada.
ingrown toenail ['ɪngrəun-] n = ingrowing toenail.
inhabit [ɪn'hæbɪt] vt habitar; (occupy) ocupar.
inhabitable [ɪn'hæbɪtəbl] adj habitável.
inhabitant [ɪn'hæbɪtənt] n habitante m/f.
inhale [ɪn'heɪl] vt inalar ♦ vi (in smoking) aspirar.
inherent [ɪn'hɪərənt] adj: ~ in or to inerente a.
inherently [ɪn'hɪərəntlɪ] adv inerentemente, em si.
inherit [ɪn'herɪt] vt herdar.
inheritance [ɪn'herɪtəns] n herança; (fig) patrimônio.
inhibit [ɪn'hɪbɪt] vt inibir; to ~ sb from doing sth impedir alguém de fazer algo.
inhibited [ɪn'hɪbɪtɪd] adj inibido.
inhibiting [ɪn'hɪbɪtɪŋ] adj constrangedor(a).
inhibition [ɪnhɪ'bɪʃən] n inibição f.
inhospitable [ɪnhɔs'pɪtəbl] adj (person) inospitaleiro; (place) inóspito.
inhuman [ɪn'hjuːmən] adj inumano, desumano.
inhumane [ɪnhjuː'meɪn] adj desumano.
inimitable [ɪ'nɪmɪtəbl] adj inimitável.
iniquity [ɪ'nɪkwɪtɪ] n iniqüidade f; (injustice) injustiça.
initial [ɪ'nɪʃl] adj inicial; (first) primeiro ♦ n inicial f ♦ vt marcar com iniciais; ~s npl iniciais fpl; (abbreviation) abreviatura, sigla.

initialize [ɪ'nɪʃəlaɪz] vt (COMPUT) inicializar.
initially [ɪ'nɪʃəlɪ] adv inicialmente, no início.
initiate [ɪ'nɪʃɪeɪt] vt (start) iniciar, começar; (person) iniciar; **to ~ sb into a secret** revelar um segredo a alguém; **to ~ proceedings against sb** (LAW) abrir um processo contra alguém.
initiation [ɪnɪʃɪ'eɪʃən] n (into secret etc) iniciação f; (beginning) começo, início.
initiative [ɪ'nɪʃətɪv] n iniciativa; **to take the ~** tomar a iniciativa.
inject [ɪn'dʒɛkt] vt (liquid, fig: money) injetar; (person) dar uma injeção em; (fig: put in) introduzir.
injection [ɪn'dʒɛkʃən] n injeção f; **to have an ~** tomar uma injeção.
injudicious [ɪndʒu'dɪʃəs] adj imprudente.
injunction [ɪn'dʒʌŋkʃən] n injunção f, ordem f.
injure ['ɪndʒə*] vt ferir; (damage: reputation etc) prejudicar; (offend) ofender, magoar; **to ~ o.s.** ferir-se.
injured ['ɪndʒəd] adj (person, leg) ferido; (feelings) ofendido, magoado; **~ party** (LAW) parte f lesada.
injurious [ɪn'dʒuərɪəs] adj: **~ (to)** prejudicial (a).
injury ['ɪndʒərɪ] n ferida; (wrong) dano, prejuízo; **to escape without ~** escapar ileso.
injury time n (SPORT) desconto.
injustice [ɪn'dʒʌstɪs] n injustiça; **to do sb an ~** fazer mau juízo de alguém.
ink [ɪŋk] n tinta.
ink-jet printer n impressora a tinta.
inkling ['ɪŋklɪŋ] n suspeita; (idea) idéia vaga.
inkpad ['ɪŋkpæd] n almofada de tinta.
inky ['ɪŋkɪ] adj manchado de tinta.
inlaid ['ɪnleɪd] adj embutido; (table etc) marchetado.
inland [adj 'ɪnlənd, adv ɪn'lænd] adj interior, interno ♦ adv para o interior; **~ waterways** hidrovias fpl.
Inland Revenue (BRIT) n ≈ fisco, ≈ receita federal (BR).
in-laws npl sogros mpl.
inlet ['ɪnlɛt] n (GEO) enseada, angra; (TECH) entrada.
inlet pipe n tubo de admissão.
inmate ['ɪnmeɪt] n (in prison) presidiário/a; (in asylum) internado/a.
inmost ['ɪnməust] adj mais íntimo.
inn [ɪn] n hospedaria, taberna.
innards ['ɪnədʒ] (inf) npl entranhas fpl.
innate [ɪ'neɪt] adj inato.
inner ['ɪnə*] adj interno, interior.
inner city n aglomeração f urbana, metrópole f.
innermost ['ɪnəməust] adj mais íntimo.
inner tube n (of tyre) câmara de ar.
innings ['ɪnɪŋz] n (SPORT) turno; (BRIT: fig): **he's had a good ~** ele aproveitou bem a vida.
innocence ['ɪnəsns] n inocência.
innocent ['ɪnəsnt] adj inocente.
innocuous [ɪ'nɔkjuəs] adj inócuo.

innovation [ɪnəu'veɪʃən] n inovação f, novidade f.
innuendo [ɪnju'ɛndəu] (pl ~es) n insinuação f, indireta.
innumerable [ɪ'nju:mrəbl] adj inumerável.
inoculate [ɪ'nɔkjuleɪt] vt: **to ~ sb with sth** inocular algo em alguém; **to ~ sb against sth** vacinar alguém contra algo.
inoculation [ɪnɔkju'leɪʃən] n inoculação f, vacinação f.
inoffensive [ɪnə'fɛnsɪv] adj inofensivo.
inopportune [ɪn'ɔpətjuːn] adj inoportuno.
inordinate [ɪn'ɔːdɪnət] adj desmesurado, excessivo.
inordinately [ɪn'ɔːdɪnətlɪ] adv desmedidamente, excessivamente.
inorganic [ɪnɔː'gænɪk] adj inorgânico.
in-patient n paciente m/f interno/a.
input ['ɪnput] n (ELEC, COMPUT) entrada; (COMM) investimento ♦ vt (COMPUT) entrar com.
inquest ['ɪnkwɛst] n inquérito policial; (coroner's) inquérito judicial.
inquire [ɪn'kwaɪə*] vi pedir informação ♦ vt (ask) perguntar; **to ~ about** pedir informações sobre; **to ~ when/where/whether** perguntar quando/onde/se.
inquire after vt fus (person) perguntar por.
inquire into vt fus investigar, indagar.
inquiring [ɪn'kwaɪərɪŋ] adj (mind) inquiridor(a); (look) interrogativo.
inquiry [ɪn'kwaɪərɪ] n pergunta; (LAW) investigação f, inquérito; (commission) comissão f de inquérito; **to hold an ~ into sth** realizar uma investigação sobre algo.
inquiry desk (BRIT) n balcão m de informações.
inquiry office (BRIT) n seção f de informações.
inquisition [ɪnkwɪ'zɪʃən] n inquérito; (REL): **the I~** a Inquisição.
inquisitive [ɪn'kwɪzɪtɪv] adj (curious) curioso, perguntador(a); (prying) indiscreto, intrometido.
inroads ['ɪnrəudz] npl: **to make ~ into** (savings, supplies) consumir parte de.
ins. abbr = **inches**.
insane [ɪn'seɪn] adj louco, doido; (MED) demente, insano.
insanitary [ɪn'sænɪtərɪ] adj insalubre.
insanity [ɪn'sænɪtɪ] n (MED) insanidade f, demência; (folly) loucura.
insatiable [ɪn'seɪʃəbl] adj insaciável.
inscribe [ɪn'skraɪb] vt inscrever; (book etc): **to ~ (to sb)** dedicar (a alguém).
inscription [ɪn'skrɪpʃən] n inscrição f; (in book) dedicatória.
inscrutable [ɪn'skruːtəbl] adj inescrutável, impenetrável.
inseam measurement ['ɪnsiːm-] (US) n altura de entrepernas.
insect ['ɪnsɛkt] n inseto.
insect bite n picada de inseto.
insecticide [ɪn'sɛktɪsaɪd] n inseticida m.
insect repellent n repelente m contra inse-

tos, insetífugo.

insecure [ɪnsɪ'kjuə*] *adj* inseguro.

insecurity [ɪnsɪ'kjuərətɪ] *n* insegurança.

insensible [ɪn'sɛnsɪbl] *adj* impassível, insensível; (*unconscious*) inconsciente.

insensitive [ɪn'sɛnsɪtɪv] *adj* insensível.

insensitivity [ɪnsɛnsɪ'tɪvɪtɪ] *n* insensibilidade *f*.

inseparable [ɪn'sɛprəbl] *adj* inseparável.

insert [*vt* ɪn'sɜːt, *n* 'ɪnsɜːt] *vt* (*between things*) intercalar; (*into sth*) introduzir, inserir; (*in paper*) publicar; (: *advert*) pôr ♦ *n* folha solta.

insertion [ɪn'sɜːʃən] *n* inserção *f*; (*publication*) publicação *f*; (*of pages*) matéria inserida.

in-service *adj* (*training*) contínuo; (*course*) de aperfeiçoamento, de reciclagem.

inshore [ɪn'ʃɔː*] *adj* perto da costa, costeiro ♦ *adv* (*be*) perto da costa; (*move*) em direção à costa.

inside ['ɪnsaɪd] *n* interior *m*; (*lining*) forro; (*of road: in Britain*) lado esquerdo (da estrada); (: *in US, Europe etc*) lado direito (da estrada) ♦ *adj* interior, interno; (*secret*) secreto ♦ *adv* (*within*) (por) dentro; (*with movement*) para dentro; (*inf: in prison*) na prisão ♦ *prep* dentro de; (*of time*): ~ **10 minutes** em menos de 10 minutos; ~**s** *npl* (*inf*) entranhas *fpl*; ~ **out** às avessas; **to turn sth** ~ **out** virar algo pelo avesso; **to know sth** ~ **out** conhecer algo como a palma da mão; (*book etc*) conhecer algo a fundo; ~ **information** informação privilegiada; **the** ~ **story** a verdade sobre os fatos.

inside forward *n* (*SPORT*) centro avante.

inside lane *n* (*AUT: in Britain*) pista da esquerda; (: *in US, Europe etc*) pista da direita.

inside leg measurement (*BRIT*) *n* altura de entrepernas.

insider [ɪn'saɪdə*] *n* iniciado/a.

insider dealing *n* (*STOCK EXCHANGE*) uso de informações privilegiadas.

insidious [ɪn'sɪdɪəs] *adj* insidioso; (*underground*) clandestino.

insight ['ɪnsaɪt] *n* (*quality*) discernimento; **an** ~ **into sth** uma idéia de algo.

insignia [ɪn'sɪgnɪə] *npl* insígnias *fpl*.

insignificant [ɪnsɪg'nɪfɪknt] *adj* insignificante.

insincere [ɪnsɪn'sɪə*] *adj* insincero.

insincerity [ɪnsɪn'sɛrɪtɪ] *n* insinceridade *f*.

insinuate [ɪn'sɪnjueɪt] *vt* insinuar.

insinuation [ɪnsɪnju'eɪʃən] *n* insinuação *f*; (*hint*) indireta.

insipid [ɪn'sɪpɪd] *adj* insípido, insosso; (*person*) sem graça.

insist [ɪn'sɪst] *vi* insistir; **to** ~ **on doing** insistir em fazer; (*stubbornly*) teimar em fazer; **to** ~ **that** insistir em que; (*claim*) cismar que.

insistence [ɪn'sɪstəns] *n* insistência; (*stubbornness*) teimosia.

insistent [ɪn'sɪstənt] *adj* insistente, pertinaz.

insole ['ɪnsəul] *n* palmilha.

insolence ['ɪnsələns] *n* insolência, atrevimento.

insolent ['ɪnsələnt] *adj* insolente, atrevido.

insoluble [ɪn'sɔljubl] *adj* insolúvel.

insolvency [ɪn'sɔlvənsɪ] *n* insolvência.

insolvent [ɪn'sɔlvənt] *adj* insolvente.

insomnia [ɪn'sɔmnɪə] *n* insônia.

insomniac [ɪn'sɔmnɪæk] *n* insone *m/f*.

inspect [ɪn'spɛkt] *vt* inspecionar; (*building*) vistoriar; (*tickets*) fiscalizar; (*troops*) passar revista em.

inspection [ɪn'spɛkʃən] *n* inspeção *f*; vistoria; fiscalização *f*.

inspector [ɪn'spɛktə*] *n* inspetor(a) *m/f*; (*RAIL*) fiscal *m*.

inspiration [ɪnspə'reɪʃən] *n* inspiração *f*.

inspire [ɪn'spaɪə*] *vt* inspirar.

inspired [ɪn'spaɪəd] *adj* (*writer, book etc*) inspirado; **in an** ~ **moment** num momento de inspiração.

inspiring [ɪn'spaɪərɪŋ] *adj* inspirador(a).

inst. (*BRIT*) *abbr* (*COMM*) = **instant**.

instability [ɪnstə'bɪlɪtɪ] *n* instabilidade *f*.

install [ɪn'stɔːl] *vt* instalar.

installation [ɪnstə'leɪʃən] *n* instalação *f*.

installment [ɪn'stɔːlmənt] (*US*) *n* = **instalment**.

installment plan (*US*) *n* crediário.

instalment [ɪn'stɔːlmənt] (*BRIT*) *n* (*of money*) prestação *f*; (*of story*) fascículo; (*of TV serial etc*) capítulo; **in** ~**s** (*pay*) a prestações; (*receive*) em várias vezes.

instance ['ɪnstəns] *n* (*example*) exemplo; (*case*) caso; **for** ~ por exemplo; **in many** ~**s** em muitos casos; **in that** ~ naquele caso; **in the first** ~ em primeiro lugar.

instant ['ɪnstənt] *n* instante *m*, momento ♦ *adj* instantâneo, imediato; (*coffee*) instantâneo; **of the 10th** ~ (*BRIT: COMM*) de 10 do corrente.

instantaneous [ɪnstən'teɪnɪəs] *adj* instantâneo.

instantly ['ɪnstəntlɪ] *adv* imediatamente.

instant replay (*US*) *n* (*TV*) replay *m*.

instead [ɪn'stɛd] *adv* em vez disso; ~ **of** em vez de, em lugar de.

instep ['ɪnstɛp] *n* peito do pé.

instigate ['ɪnstɪgeɪt] *vt* (*rebellion, strike*) fomentar; (*new ideas*) suscitar.

instigation [ɪnstɪ'geɪʃən] *n* instigação *f*; **at sb's** ~ por incitação de alguém.

instil [ɪn'stɪl] *vt*: **to** ~ (**into**) infundir *or* incutir (em).

instinct ['ɪnstɪŋkt] *n* instinto.

instinctive [ɪn'stɪŋktɪv] *adj* instintivo.

instinctively [ɪn'stɪŋktɪvlɪ] *adv* por instinto, instintivamente.

institute ['ɪnstɪtjuːt] *n* instituto; (*professional body*) associação *f* ♦ *vt* (*inquiry*) começar, iniciar; (*proceedings*) instituir, estabelecer.

institution [ɪnstɪ'tjuːʃən] *n* instituição *f*; (*be-*

ginning) início; (*organization*) instituto; (*MED*: *home*) asilo; (*asylum*) manicômio; (*custom*) costume *m*.

institutional [ɪnstɪ'tjuːʃənəl] *adj* institucional.

instruct [ɪn'strʌkt] *vt*: **to ~ sb in sth** instruir alguém em *or* sobre algo; **to ~ sb to do sth** dar instruções a alguém para fazer algo.

instruction [ɪn'strʌkʃən] *n* (*teaching*) instrução *f*; **~s** *npl* ordens *fpl*; **~s (for use)** modo de usar.

instruction book *n* livro de instruções.

instructive [ɪn'strʌktɪv] *adj* instrutivo.

instructor [ɪn'strʌktə*] *n* instrutor(a) *m/f*.

instrument ['ɪnstrumənt] *n* instrumento.

instrumental [ɪnstru'mɛntl] *adj* (*MUS*) instrumental; **to be ~ in** contribuir para.

instrumentalist [ɪnstru'mɛntəlɪst] *n* instrumentalista *m/f*.

instrument panel *n* painel *m* de instrumentos.

insubordinate [ɪnsə'bɔːdənɪt] *adj* insubordinado.

insubordination [ɪnsəbɔːdə'neɪʃən] *n* insubordinação *f*.

insufferable [ɪn'sʌfrəbl] *adj* insuportável.

insufficient [ɪnsə'fɪʃənt] *adj* insuficiente.

insufficiently [ɪnsə'fɪʃəntlɪ] *adv* insuficientemente.

insular ['ɪnsjulə*] *adj* insular; (*outlook*) estreito; (*person*) de mente limitada.

insulate ['ɪnsjuleɪt] *vt* isolar.

insulating tape ['ɪnsjuleɪtɪŋ-] *n* fita isolante.

insulation [ɪnsju'leɪʃən] *n* isolamento.

insulin ['ɪnsjulɪn] *n* insulina.

insult [*n* 'ɪnsʌlt, *vt* ɪn'sʌlt] *n* insulto; (*offence*) ofensa ♦ *vt* insultar, ofender.

insulting [ɪn'sʌltɪŋ] *adj* insultante, ofensivo.

insuperable [ɪn'sjuːprəbl] *adj* insuperável.

insurance [ɪn'ʃuərəns] *n* seguro; **fire ~** seguro contra incêndio; **life ~** seguro de vida; **to take out ~ (against)** segurar-se *or* fazer seguro (contra).

insurance agent *n* agente *m/f* de seguros.

insurance broker *n* corretor(a) *m/f* de seguros.

insurance company *n* seguradora.

insurance policy *n* apólice *f* de seguro.

insurance premium *n* prêmio de seguro.

insure [ɪn'ʃuə*] *vt* segurar; **to ~ sb/sb's life** segurar alguém/a vida de alguém; **to be ~d for £5000** estar segurado em £5000.

insured [ɪn'ʃuəd] *n*: **the ~** o/a segurado/a.

insurer [ɪn'ʃuərə*] *n* (*person*) segurador(a) *m/f*; (*company*) seguradora.

insurgent [ɪn'sɔːdʒənt] *adj*, *n* insurgente *m/f*.

insurmountable [ɪnsə'mauntəbl] *adj* insuperável.

insurrection [ɪnsə'rɛkʃən] *n* insurreição *f*.

intact [ɪn'tækt] *adj* intacto, íntegro; (*unharmed*) ileso, são e salvo.

intake ['ɪnteɪk] *n* (*TECH*) entrada, tomada; (: *pipe*) tubo de entrada; (*of food*) quantidade *f* ingerida; (*SCH*): **an ~ of 200 a year** 200 matriculados por ano.

intangible [ɪn'tændʒɪbl] *adj* intangível.

integral ['ɪntɪgrəl] *adj* (*whole*) integral, total; (*part*) integrante.

integrate ['ɪntɪgreɪt] *vt* integrar ♦ *vi* integrar-se.

integrated circuit ['ɪntɪgreɪtɪd-] *n* (*COMPUT*) circuito integrado.

integration [ɪntɪ'greɪʃən] *n* integração *f*; **racial ~** integração racial.

integrity [ɪn'tɛgrɪtɪ] *n* integridade *f*, honestidade *f*, retidão *f*.

intellect ['ɪntəlɛkt] *n* intelecto.

intellectual [ɪntə'lɛktjuəl] *adj*, *n* intelectual *m/f*.

intelligence [ɪn'tɛlɪdʒəns] *n* inteligência; (*MIL etc*) informações *fpl*.

intelligence quotient *n* quociente *m* de inteligência.

Intelligence Service *n* Serviço de Informações.

intelligence test *n* teste *m* de inteligência.

intelligent [ɪn'tɛlɪdʒənt] *adj* inteligente.

intelligently [ɪn'tɛlɪdʒəntlɪ] *adv* inteligentemente.

intelligible [ɪn'tɛlɪdʒɪbl] *adj* inteligível, compreensível.

intemperate [ɪn'tɛmpərət] *adj* imoderado; (*with alcohol*) intemperado.

intend [ɪn'tɛnd] *vt* (*gift etc*): **to ~ sth for** destinar algo a; **to ~ to do sth** tencionar *or* pretender fazer algo.

intended [ɪn'tɛndɪd] *adj* (*effect*) desejado ♦ *n* noivo/a.

intense [ɪn'tɛns] *adj* intenso; (*person*) muito emotivo.

intensely [ɪn'tɛnslɪ] *adv* intensamente; (*very*) extremamente.

intensify [ɪn'tɛnsɪfaɪ] *vt* intensificar; (*increase*) aumentar.

intensity [ɪn'tɛnsɪtɪ] *n* intensidade *f*; (*of emotion*) força, veemência.

intensive [ɪn'tɛnsɪv] *adj* intensivo.

intensive care *n*: **to be in ~** estar na UTI.

intensive care unit *n* unidade *f* de tratamento intensivo.

intent [ɪn'tɛnt] *n* intenção *f* ♦ *adj* (*absorbed*) absorto; (*attentive*) atento; **to all ~s and purposes** para todos os efeitos; **to be ~ on doing sth** estar resolvido a fazer algo.

intention [ɪn'tɛnʃən] *n* intenção *f*, propósito.

intentional [ɪn'tɛnʃənl] *adj* intencional, proposital.

intentionally [ɪn'tɛnʃənəlɪ] *adv* de propósito.

intently [ɪn'tɛntlɪ] *adv* atentamente.

inter [ɪn'tɔː*] *vt* enterrar.

interact [ɪntər'ækt] *vi* interagir.

interaction [ɪntər'ækʃən] *n* interação *f*, ação *f* recíproca.

interactive [ɪntər'æktɪv] *adj* interativo.

intercede [ɪntə'siːd] *vi*: **to ~ with sb/on behalf of sb** interceder junto a alguém/em favor de alguém.

intercept [ɪntə'sɛpt] *vt* interceptar; (*person*) deter.

interception [ɪntə'sɛpʃən] *n* interceptação *f*; (*of person*) detenção *f*.

interchange [n 'ıntətʃeındʒ, vt ıntə'tʃeındʒ] n intercâmbio; (exchange) troca, permuta; (on motorway) trevo ♦ vt intercambiar, trocar.
interchangeable [ıntə'tʃeındʒəbl] adj permutável.
intercity (train) [ıntə'sıtı-] n expresso.
intercom ['ıntəkɔm] n interfone m.
interconnect [ıntəkə'nɛkt] vi interligar.
intercontinental [ıntəkɔntı'nɛntl] adj intercontinental.
intercourse ['ıntəkɔːs] n (social) relacionamento; **sexual** ~ relações fpl sexuais.
interdependent [ıntədı'pɛndənt] adj interdependente.
interest ['ıntrıst] n interesse m; (COMM: on loan etc) juros mpl; (: share) participação f ♦ vt interessar; **compound/simple** ~ juros compostos/simples; **British ~s in the Middle East** os interesses britânicos no Oriente Médio.
interested ['ıntrɛstıd] adj interessado; **to be** ~ **in** interessar-se por, estar interessado em.
interest-free adj sem juros.
interesting ['ıntrıstıŋ] adj interessante.
interest rate n taxa de juros.
interface ['ıntəfeıs] n (COMPUT) interface f.
interfere [ıntə'fıə*] vi: **to** ~ **in** (quarrel, other people's business) interferir or intrometer-se em; **to** ~ **with** (objects) mexer em; (hinder) impedir; **don't** ~ não se meta.
interference [ıntə'fıərəns] n intromissão f; (RADIO, TV) interferência.
interfering [ıntə'fıərıŋ] adj intrometido.
interim ['ıntərım] adj interino, provisório ♦ n: **in the** ~ neste ínterim, nesse meio tempo.
interior [ın'tıərıə*] n interior m ♦ adj interior.
interior decorator n decorador(a) m/f, arquiteto/a de interiores.
interior designer n arquiteto/a de interiores.
interject [ıntə'dʒɛkt] vt inserir, interpor.
interjection [ıntə'dʒɛkʃən] n interjeição f, exclamação f.
interlock [ıntə'lɔk] vi entrelaçar-se; (wheels etc) engatar-se, engrenar-se ♦ vt engrenar.
interloper ['ıntələupə*] n intruso/a.
interlude ['ıntəluːd] n interlúdio; (rest) descanso; (THEATRE) intervalo.
intermarry [ıntə'mærı] vi ligar-se por casamento.
intermediary [ıntə'miːdıərı] n intermediário/a.
intermediate [ıntə'miːdıət] adj intermédio, intermediário.
interminable [ın'təːmınəbl] adj interminável.
intermission [ıntə'mıʃən] n (THEATRE) intervalo.
intermittent [ıntə'mıtnt] adj intermitente.
intermittently [ıntə'mıtntlı] adv intermitentemente, a intervalos.
intern [vt ın'təːn, n 'ıntəːn] vt internar; (enclose) encerrar ♦ n (US) médico-interno/médica-interna.
internal [ın'təːnl] adj interno; ~ **injuries** feri-

mentos mpl internos.
internally [ın'təːnəlı] adv interiormente; **"not to be taken** ~" "uso externo".
Internal Revenue (Service) (US) n ≈ fisco, ≈ receita federal (BR).
international [ıntə'næʃənl] adj internacional ♦ (BRIT) n (SPORT: game) jogo internacional; (: player) jogador(a) m/f internacional.
International Atomic Energy Agency n Agência Internacional de Energia Atômica.
International Court of Justice n Corte f Internacional de Justiça.
international date line n linha internacional de mudança de data.
internationally [ıntə'næʃnəlı] adv internacionalmente.
International Monetary Fund n Fundo Monetário Internacional.
internecine [ıntə'niːsaın] adj mutuamente destrutivo.
internee [ıntəː'niː] n internado/a.
internment [ın'təːnmənt] n internamento.
interplay ['ıntəpleı] n interação f.
Interpol ['ıntəpɔl] n Interpol m.
interpret [ın'təːprıt] vt interpretar; (translate) traduzir ♦ vi interpretar.
interpretation [ıntəːprı'teıʃən] n interpretação f; (translation) tradução f.
interpreter [ın'təːprıtə*] n intérprete m/f.
interpreting [ın'təːprıtıŋ] n (profession) interpretação f.
interrelated [ıntərı'leıtıd] adj inter-relacionado.
interrogate [ın'tɛrəugeıt] vt interrogar.
interrogation [ıntɛrə'geıʃən] n interrogatório.
interrogative [ıntə'rɔgətıv] adj interrogativo ♦ n (LING) interrogativo.
interrogator [ın'tɛrəgeıtə*] n interrogador(a) m/f.
interrupt [ıntə'rʌpt] vt, vi interromper.
interruption [ıntə'rʌpʃən] n interrupção f.
intersect [ıntə'sɛkt] vt cruzar ♦ vi (roads) cruzar-se.
intersection [ıntə'sɛkʃən] n intersecção f; (of roads) cruzamento.
intersperse [ıntə'spəːs] vt entremear; **to** ~ **with** entremear com or de.
intertwine [ıntə'twaın] vt entrelaçar ♦ vi entrelaçar-se.
interval ['ıntəvl] n intervalo; (BRIT: SCH) recreio; (THEATRE, SPORT) intervalo; **sunny ~s** (in weather) períodos de melhoria; **at ~s** a intervalos.
intervene [ıntə'viːn] vi intervir; (occur) ocorrer.
intervention [ıntə'vɛnʃən] n intervenção f.
interview ['ıntəvjuː] n entrevista ♦ vt entrevistar.
interviewee [ıntəvjuː'iː] n entrevistado/a.
interviewer ['ıntəvjuːə*] n entrevistador(a) m/f.
intestate [ın'tɛsteıt] adj intestado.

NB: European Portuguese adds the following consonants to certain words: **b** (sú(b)dito, su(b)til); **c** (a(c)ção, a(c)cionista, a(c)to); **m** (inde(m)ne); **p** (ado(p)ção, ado(p)tar); *for further details see p. xiii.*

intestinal [ɪn'tɛstɪnl] *adj* intestinal.
intestine [ɪn'tɛstɪn] *n*: **large/small** ~ intestino grosso/delgado.
intimacy ['ɪntɪməsɪ] *n* intimidade *f*.
intimate [*adj* 'ɪntɪmət, *vt* 'ɪntɪmeɪt] *adj* íntimo; (*knowledge*) profundo ♦ *vt* insinuar, sugerir.
intimately ['ɪntɪmətlɪ] *adv* intimamente.
intimation [ɪntɪ'meɪʃən] *n* insinuação *f*, sugestão *f*.
intimidate [ɪn'tɪmɪdeɪt] *vt* intimidar, amedrontar.
intimidation [ɪntɪmɪ'deɪʃən] *n* intimidação *f*.
into ['ɪntu] *prep* em; ~ **3 pieces/French** em 3 pedaços/para o francês; **to change pounds** ~ **dollars** trocar libras por dólares.
intolerable [ɪn'tɔlərəbl] *adj* intolerável, insuportável.
intolerance [ɪn'tɔlərəns] *n* intolerância.
intolerant [ɪn'tɔlərənt] *adj*: ~ **of** intolerante com *or* para com.
intonation [ɪntəu'neɪʃən] *n* entonação *f*, inflexão *f*.
intoxicate [ɪn'tɔksɪkeɪt] *vt* embriagar.
intoxicated [ɪn'tɔksɪkeɪtɪd] *adj* embriagado.
intoxication [ɪntɔksɪ'keɪʃən] *n* intoxicação *f*, embriaguez *f*.
intractable [ɪn'træktəbl] *adj* (*child*) intratável; (*material*) difícil de trabalhar; (*problem*) espinhoso; (*illness*) intratável.
intransigent [ɪn'trænsɪdʒənt] *adj* intransigente.
intransitive [ɪn'trænsɪtɪv] *adj* intransitivo.
intra-uterine device ['ɪntrə'juːtəraɪn-] *n* dispositivo intra-uterino.
intravenous [ɪntrə'viːnəs] *adj* intravenoso.
in-tray *n* cesta para correspondência de entrada.
intrepid [ɪn'trepɪd] *adj* intrépido.
intricacy ['ɪntrɪkəsɪ] *n* complexidade *f*.
intricate ['ɪntrɪkət] *adj* complexo, complicado.
intrigue [ɪn'triːg] *n* intriga ♦ *vt* intrigar ♦ *vi* fazer intriga.
intriguing [ɪn'triːgɪŋ] *adj* intrigante.
intrinsic [ɪn'trɪnsɪk] *adj* intrínseco.
introduce [ɪntrə'djuːs] *vt* introduzir, inserir; **to** ~ **sb (to sb)** apresentar alguém (a alguém); **to** ~ **sb to** (*pastime, technique*) iniciar alguém em; **may I** ~ **...?** permita-me apresentar ....
introduction [ɪntrə'dʌkʃən] *n* introdução *f*; (*of person*) apresentação *f*; **a letter of** ~ uma carta de recomendação.
introductory [ɪntrə'dʌktərɪ] *adj* introdutório, preliminar; ~ **remarks** observações preliminares; ~ **offer** oferta de lançamento.
introspection [ɪntrəu'spekʃən] *n* introspecção *f*.
introspective [ɪntrəu'spektɪv] *adj* introspectivo.
introvert ['ɪntrəuvɜːt] *adj, n* introvertido/a.
intrude [ɪn'truːd] *vi*: **to** ~ **on** *or* **into** intrometer-se em.
intruder [ɪn'truːdə*] *n* intruso/a.
intrusion [ɪn'truːʒən] *n* intromissão *f*.
intrusive [ɪn'truːsɪv] *adj* intruso.

intuition [ɪntjuː'ɪʃən] *n* intuição *f*.
intuitive [ɪn'tjuːɪtɪv] *adj* intuitivo.
inundate ['ɪnʌndeɪt] *vt*: **to** ~ **with** inundar de.
inure [ɪn'juə*] *vt*: **to** ~ **(to)** habituar (a).
invade [ɪn'veɪd] *vt* invadir.
invader [ɪn'veɪdə*] *n* invasor(a) *m/f*.
invalid [*n* 'ɪnvəlɪd, *adj* ɪn'vælɪd] *n* inválido/a ♦ *adj* (*not valid*) inválido, nulo.
invalidate [ɪn'vælɪdeɪt] *vt* invalidar, anular.
invalid chair ['ɪnvəlɪd-] (*BRIT*) *n* cadeira de rodas.
invaluable [ɪn'væljuəbl] *adj* inestimável, impagável.
invariable [ɪn'vɛərɪəbl] *adj* invariável.
invariably [ɪn'vɛərɪəblɪ] *adv* invariavelmente; **she is** ~ **late** ela sempre chega atrasada.
invasion [ɪn'veɪʒən] *n* invasão *f*.
invective [ɪn'vɛktɪv] *n* invectiva.
inveigle [ɪn'viːgl] *vt*: **to** ~ **sb into (doing) sth** aliciar alguém para (fazer) algo.
invent [ɪn'vɛnt] *vt* inventar.
invention [ɪn'vɛnʃən] *n* invenção *f*; (*inventiveness*) engenho; (*lie*) ficção *f*, mentira.
inventive [ɪn'vɛntɪv] *adj* engenhoso.
inventiveness [ɪn'vɛntɪvnɪs] *n* engenhosidade *f*, inventiva.
inventor [ɪn'vɛntə*] *n* inventor(a) *m/f*.
inventory ['ɪnvəntrɪ] *n* inventário, relação *f*.
inventory control *n* (*COMM*) controle *m* de estoques.
inverse [ɪn'vɜːs] *adj, n* inverso; **in** ~ **proportion to** em proporção inversa a.
inversely [ɪn'vɜːslɪ] *adv* inversamente.
invert [ɪn'vɜːt] *vt* inverter.
invertebrate [ɪn'vɜːtɪbrət] *n* invertebrado.
inverted commas [ɪn'vɜːtɪd-] (*BRIT*) *npl* aspas *fpl*.
invest [ɪn'vɛst] *vt* investir; (*endow*): **to** ~ **sb with sth** conferir algo a alguém, investir alguém de algo ♦ *vi* investir; **to** ~ **in** investir em; (*acquire*) comprar.
investigate [ɪn'vɛstɪgeɪt] *vt* investigar; (*study*) estudar, examinar.
investigation [ɪnvɛstɪ'geɪʃən] *n* investigação *f*.
investigative journalism [ɪn'vɛstɪgətɪv-] *n* jornalismo de investigação.
investigator [ɪn'vɛstɪgeɪtə*] *n* investigador(a) *m/f*; **private** ~ detetive particular.
investiture [ɪn'vɛstɪtʃə*] *n* investidura.
investment [ɪn'vɛstmənt] *n* investimento.
investment income *n* rendimento de investimentos.
investment trust *n* fundo mútuo.
investor [ɪn'vɛstə*] *n* investidor(a) *m/f*.
inveterate [ɪn'vɛtərət] *adj* inveterado.
invidious [ɪn'vɪdɪəs] *adj* injusto; (*task*) desagradável.
invigilate [ɪn'vɪdʒɪleɪt] (*BRIT*) *vt* fiscalizar ♦ *vi* fiscalizar o exame.
invigilator [ɪn'vɪdʒɪleɪtə*] (*BRIT*) *n* fiscal *m/f* (de exame).
invigorating [ɪn'vɪgəreɪtɪŋ] *adj* revigorante.
invincible [ɪn'vɪnsɪbl] *adj* invencível.
inviolate [ɪn'vaɪələt] *adj* inviolado.
invisible [ɪn'vɪzɪbl] *adj* invisível.

invisible assets (*BRIT*) *npl* ativo intangível.
invisible ink *n* tinta invisível.
invisible mending *n* cerzidura.
invitation [ɪnvɪ'teɪʃən] *n* convite *m*; **by ~ only** estritamente mediante convite; **at sb's ~** a convite de alguém.
invite [ɪn'vaɪt] *vt* convidar; (*opinions etc*) solicitar, pedir; (*trouble*) pedir; **to ~ sb to do** convidar alguém para fazer; **to ~ sb to dinner** convidar alguém para jantar.
invite out *vt* convidar *or* chamar para sair.
invite over *vt* chamar.
inviting [ɪn'vaɪtɪŋ] *adj* convidativo.
invoice ['ɪnvɔɪs] *n* fatura ♦ *vt* faturar; **to ~ sb for goods** faturar mercadorias em nome de alguém.
invoke [ɪn'vəuk] *vt* invocar; (*aid*) implorar; (*law*) apelar para.
involuntary [ɪn'vɔləntrɪ] *adj* involuntário.
involve [ɪn'vɔlv] *vt* (*entail*) implicar; (*require*) exigir; **to ~ sb (in)** envolver alguém (em).
involved [ɪn'vɔlvd] *adj* envolvido; (*emotionally*) comprometido; (*complex*) complexo; **to be/get ~ in sth** estar/ficar envolvido em algo.
involvement [ɪn'vɔlvmənt] *n* envolvimento; (*obligation*) compromisso.
invulnerable [ɪn'vʌlnərəbl] *adj* invulnerável.
inward ['ɪnwəd] *adj* (*movement*) interior, interno; (*thought, feeling*) íntimo.
inwardly ['ɪnwədlɪ] *adv* (*feel, think etc*) para si, para dentro.
inward(s) ['ɪnwəd(z)] *adv* para dentro.
i/o *abbr* (*COMPUT*: = *input/output*) E/S, I/O.
IOC *n* *abbr* (= *International Olympic Committee*) COI *m*.
iodine ['aɪəudiːn] *n* iodo.
ion ['aɪən] *n* íon *m*, iâo *m* (*PT*).
Ionian Sea [aɪ'əunɪən-] *n*: **the ~** o mar Iônico.
iota [aɪ'əutə] *n* (*fig*) pouquinho, tiquinho.
IOU *n abbr* (= *I owe you*) vale *m*.
IOW (*BRIT*) *abbr* = **Isle of Wight**.
IPA *n abbr* (= *International Phonetic Alphabet*) AFI *m*.
IQ *n abbr* (= *intelligence quotient*) QI *m*.
IRA *n abbr* (= *Irish Republican Army*) IRA *m*; (*US*) = **individual retirement account**.
Iran [ɪ'rɑːn] *n* Irã (*PT*: Irão) *m*.
Iranian [ɪ'reɪnɪən] *adj* iraniano ♦ *n* iraniano/a; (*LING*) iraniano.
Iraq [ɪ'rɑːk] *n* Iraque *m*.
Iraqi [ɪ'rɑːkɪ] *adj* *n* iraquiano/a.
irascible [ɪ'ræsɪbl] *adj* irascível.
irate [aɪ'reɪt] *adj* irado, enfurecido.
Ireland ['aɪələnd] *n* Irlanda; **Republic of ~** República da Irlanda.
iris ['aɪrɪs] (*pl* **~es**) *n* íris *f*.
Irish ['aɪrɪʃ] *adj* irlandês/esa ♦ *n* (*LING*) irlandês *m*; **the ~** *npl* os irlandeses.
Irishman ['aɪrɪʃmən] (*irreg*) *n* irlandês *m*.

Irish Sea *n*: **the ~** o mar da Irlanda.
Irishwoman ['aɪrɪʃwumən] (*irreg*) *n* irlandesa.
irk [əːk] *vt* aborrecer.
irksome ['əːksəm] *adj* aborrecido.
IRN (*BRIT*) *n* *abbr* (= *Independent Radio News*) agência de notícias radiofônicas.
IRO (*US*) *n* *abbr* = **International Refugee Organization**.
iron ['aɪən] *n* ferro; (*for clothes*) ferro de passar roupa ♦ *adj* de ferro ♦ *vt* (*clothes*) passar; **~s** *npl* (*chains*) grilhões *mpl*.
iron out *vt* (*crease*) tirar; (*fig: problem*) resolver.
Iron Curtain *n*: **the ~** a cortina de ferro.
iron foundry *n* fundição *f*.
ironic(al) [aɪ'rɔnɪk(l)] *adj* irônico.
ironically [aɪ'rɔnɪklɪ] *adv* ironicamente.
ironing ['aɪənɪŋ] *n* (*ironed clothes*) roupa passada; (*to be ironed*) roupa a ser passada.
ironing board *n* tábua de passar roupa.
ironmonger ['aɪənmʌŋɡə*] (*BRIT*) *n* ferreiro/a; **~'s (shop)** loja de ferragens.
iron ore *n* minério de ferro.
ironworks ['aɪənwəːks] *n* siderúrgica.
irony ['aɪrənɪ] *n* ironia; **the ~ of it is that …** o irônico é que ....
irrational [ɪ'ræʃənl] *adj* irracional.
irreconcilable [ɪrekən'saɪləbl] *adj* irreconciliável, incompatível.
irredeemable [ɪrɪ'diːməbl] *adj* (*COMM*) irresgatável.
irrefutable [ɪrɪ'fjuːtəbl] *adj* irrefutável.
irregular [ɪ'reɡjulə*] *adj* irregular; (*surface*) desigual; (*illegal*) ilegal.
irregularity [ɪreɡju'lærɪtɪ] *n* irregularidade *f*; (*of surface*) desigualdade *f*.
irrelevance [ɪ'reləvəns] *n* irrelevância.
irrelevant [ɪ'reləvənt] *adj* irrelevante, descabido.
irreligious [ɪrɪ'lɪdʒəs] *adj* irreligioso.
irreparable [ɪ'repərəbl] *adj* irreparável.
irreplaceable [ɪrɪ'pleɪsəbl] *adj* insubstituível.
irrepressible [ɪrɪ'presəbl] *adj* irreprimível, irrefreável.
irreproachable [ɪrɪ'prəutʃəbl] *adj* irrepreensível.
irresistible [ɪrɪ'zɪstɪbl] *adj* irresistível.
irresolute [ɪ'rezəluːt] *adj* irresoluto.
irrespective [ɪrɪ'spektɪv]: **~ of** *prep* independente de, sem considerar.
irresponsible [ɪrɪ'spɔnsɪbl] *adj* (*act, person*) irresponsável.
irretrievable [ɪrɪ'triːvəbl] *adj* (*object*) irrecuperável; (*loss, damage*) irreparável.
irreverent [ɪ'revərnt] *adj* irreverente, desrespeitoso.
irrevocable [ɪ'revəkəbl] *adj* irrevogável.
irrigate ['ɪrɪɡeɪt] *vt* irrigar.
irrigation [ɪrɪ'ɡeɪʃən] *n* irrigação *f*.
irritable ['ɪrɪtəbl] *adj* irritável; (*mood*) de mal humor, nervoso.
irritate ['ɪrɪteɪt] *vt* irritar.

NB: European Portuguese adds the following consonants to certain words: **b** (sú(b)dito, su(b)til); **c** (a(c)ção, a(c)cionista, a(c)to); **m** (inde(m)ne); **p** (ado(p)ção, ado(p)tar); *for further details see p. xiii.*

irritation [ɪrɪ'teɪʃən] *n* irritação *f*.

IRS (*US*) *n abbr* = **Internal Revenue Service**.

is [ɪz] *vb see* **be**.

ISBN *n abbr* (= *International Standard Book Number*) ISBN *m*.

Islam ['ɪzlɑːm] *n* islamismo.

island ['aɪlənd] *n* ilha; (*also: traffic* ~) abrigo.

islander ['aɪləndə*] *n* ilhéu/ilhoa *m/f*.

isle [aɪl] *n* ilhota, ilha.

isn't ['ɪznt] = **is not**.

isolate ['aɪsəleɪt] *vt* isolar.

isolated ['aɪsəleɪtɪd] *adj* isolado.

isolation [aɪsə'leɪʃən] *n* isolamento.

isolationism [aɪsə'leɪʃənɪzm] *n* isolacionismo.

isotope ['aɪsəutəup] *n* isótopo.

Israel ['ɪzreɪl] *n* Israel *m* (*no article*).

Israeli [ɪz'reɪlɪ] *adj, n* israelense *m/f*.

issue ['ɪsjuː] *n* questão *f*, tema *m*; (*outcome*) resultado; (*of banknotes etc*) emissão *f*; (*of newspaper etc*) número; (*offspring*) sucessão *f*, descendência ♦ *vt* (*rations, equipment*) distribuir; (*orders*) dar; (*certificate*) emitir; (*decree*) promulgar; (*book*) publicar; (*cheques, banknotes, stamps*) emitir ♦ *vi*: **to** ~ **from** (*smell, liquid*) emanar de; **at** ~ em debate; **to avoid the** ~ contornar o problema; **to take** ~ **with sb (over sth)** discordar de alguém (sobre algo); **to make an** ~ **of sth** criar caso com algo; **to confuse** *or* **obscure the** ~ complicar as coisas.

Istanbul [ɪstæn'buːl] *n* Istambul.

isthmus ['ɪsməs] *n* istmo.

IT *n abbr* = **information technology**.

it [ɪt] *pron* (*subject*) ele/ela; (*direct object*) o/a; (*indirect object*) lhe; (*impers*) isto, isso; (*after prep*) ele, ela; **in front of/behind** ~ em frente/atrás; **who is** ~? quem é?; ~'s **me** sou eu; **what is** ~? o que é que é? **where is** ~? onde está? ~'s **Friday tomorrow** amanhã é sexta-feira; ~'s **raining** está chovendo (*BR*) *or* a chover (*PT*); ~'s **six o'clock** são seis horas; ~'s **two hours by train** são duas horas de trem; **he's proud of** ~ ele orgulha-se disso; **he agreed to** ~ ele consentiu.

ITA (*BRIT*) *n abbr* (= *initial teaching alphabet*) *alfabeto modificado utilizado na alfabetização*.

Italian [ɪ'tæljən] *adj* italiano ♦ *n* italiano/a; (*LING*) italiano.

italic [ɪ'tælɪk] *adj* itálico.

italics [ɪ'tælɪks] *npl* itálico.

Italy ['ɪtəlɪ] *n* Itália.

itch [ɪtʃ] *n* comichão *f*, coceira ♦ *vi* (*person*) estar com *or* sentir comichão *or* coceira; (*part of body*) comichar, coçar; **I'm** ~**ing to do sth** estou louco para fazer algo.

itching ['ɪtʃɪŋ] *n* comichão *f*, coceira.

itchy ['ɪtʃɪ] *adj* que coça; **to be** ~ coçar.

it'd ['ɪtd] = **it would**; **it had**.

item ['aɪtəm] *n* item *m*; (*on agenda*) assunto; (*in programme*) número; (*also: news* ~) notícia; ~**s of clothing** artigos de vestuário.

itemize ['aɪtəmaɪz] *vt* detalhar, especificar.

itinerant [ɪ'tɪnərənt] *adj* itinerante.

itinerary [aɪ'tɪnərərɪ] *n* itinerário.

it'll ['ɪtl] = **it will**; **it shall**.

ITN (*BRIT*) *n abbr* = *Independent Television News*) *agência de notícias televisivas*.

its [ɪts] *adj* seu/sua, dele/dela ♦ *pron* (o) seu/(a) sua, o dele/a dela.

it's [ɪts] = **it is**; **it has**.

itself [ɪt'self] *pron* (*reflexive*) si mesmo/a; (*emphatic*) ele mesmo/ela mesma.

ITV (*BRIT*) *n abbr* (= *Independent Television*) *canal de televisão comercial*.

IUD *n abbr* (= *intra-uterine device*) DIU *m*.

I've [aɪv] = **I have**.

ivory ['aɪvərɪ] *n* marfim *m*.

Ivory Coast *n* Costa do Marfim.

ivory tower *n* (*fig*) torre *f* de marfim.

ivy ['aɪvɪ] *n* hera.

Ivy League (*US*) *n* as grandes faculdades do nordeste dos EUA (*Harvard, Yale, Princeton etc*).

J

J, j [dʒeɪ] *n* (*letter*) J, j *m*; **J for Jack** (*BRIT*) *or* **Jig** (*US*) J de José.

JA *n abbr* = **judge advocate**.

J/A *abbr* = **joint account**.

jab [dʒæb] *vt* (*elbow*) cutucar; (*punch*) esmurrar, socar ♦ *n* cotovelada, murro; (*MED: inf*) injeção *f*; **to** ~ **sth into sth** cravar algo em algo.

jabber ['dʒæbə*] *vt, vi* tagarelar.

jack [dʒæk] *n* (*AUT*) macaco; (*BOWLS*) bola branca; (*CARDS*) valete *m*.

jack in (*inf*) *vt* largar.

jack up *vt* (*AUT*) levantar com macaco; (*raise: prices*) aumentar.

jackel ['dʒækl] *n* chacal *m*.

jackass ['dʒækæs] *n* (*also: fig*) burro.

jackdaw ['dʒækdɔː] *n* gralha.

jacket ['dʒækɪt] *n* jaqueta, casaco curto; (*of boiler etc*) capa, forro; (*of book*) sobrecapa; **potatoes in their** ~**s** (*BRIT*) batatas com casca.

jack-in-the-box *n* caixa de surpresas.

jack-knife (*irreg: like* **knife**) *n* canivete *m* ♦ *vi*: **the lorry** ~**d** o reboque do caminhão deu uma guinada.

jack-of-all-trades *n* pau *m* para toda obra, homem *m* dos sete instrumentos.

jack plug (*BRIT*) *n* pino.

jackpot ['dʒækpɔt] *n* bolada, sorte *f* grande.

jacuzzi [dʒə'kuːzɪ] ® *n* jacuzzi *m* ®, banheira de hidromassagem.

jade [dʒeɪd] *n* (*stone*) jade *m*.

jaded ['dʒeɪdɪd] *adj* (*tired*) cansado; (*fed-up*) aborrecido, amolado.

JAG *n abbr* = **Judge Advocate General**.

jagged ['dʒægɪd] *adj* dentado, denteado.

jaguar ['dʒægjuə*] *n* jaguar *m*.
jail [dʒeɪl] *n* prisão *f*, cadeia ♦ *vt* encarcerar.
jailbird ['dʒeɪlbəːd] *n* criminoso inveterado.
jailbreak ['dʒeɪlbreɪk] *n* fuga da prisão.
jailer ['dʒeɪlə*] *n* carcereiro.
jalopy [dʒə'lɒpɪ] (*inf*) *n* calhambeque *m*.
jam [dʒæm] *n* geléia; (*also: traffic* ~) engarrafamento; (*difficulty*) apuro ♦ *vt* (*passage etc*) obstruir, atravancar; (*mechanism*) emperrar; (*RADIO*) bloquear, interferir ♦ *vi* (*mechanism, drawer etc*) emperrar; **to get sb out of a** ~ (*inf*) tirar alguém de uma enrascada; **to** ~ **sth into sth** forçar algo dentro de algo; **the telephone lines are** ~**med** as linhas telefônicas estão congestionadas.
Jamaica [dʒə'meɪkə] *n* Jamaica.
Jamaican [dʒə'meɪkən] *adj, n* jamaicano/a *m/f*.
jamb ['dʒæm] *n* umbral *m*.
jam-packed *adj*: ~ (**with**) abarrotado (de).
jam session *n* jam session *m*.
Jan. *abbr* (= *January*) jan.
jangle ['dʒæŋgl] *vi* soar estridentemente, desafinar.
janitor ['dʒænɪtə*] *n* (*caretaker*) zelador *m*; (*doorman*) porteiro.
January ['dʒænjuərɪ] *n* janeiro; *see also* **July**.
Japan [dʒə'pæn] *n* Japão *m*.
Japanese [dʒæpə'niːz] *adj* japonês/esa ♦ *n inv* japonês/esa *m/f*; (*LING*) japonês *m*.
jar [dʒɑː*] *n* (*glass: large*) jarro; (*: small*) pote *m* ♦ *vi* (*sound*) ranger, chiar; (*colours*) destoar ♦ *vt* (*shake*) abalar.
jargon ['dʒɑːgən] *n* jargão *m*.
jarring ['dʒɑːrɪŋ] *adj* (*sound, colour*) destoante.
Jas. *abbr* = **James**.
jasmin(e) ['dʒæzmɪn] *n* jasmim *m*.
jaundice ['dʒɔːndɪs] *n* icterícia.
jaundiced ['dʒɔːndɪst] *adj* (*fig: embittered*) amargurado, despeitado; (*: disillusioned*) desiludido.
jaunt [dʒɔːnt] *n* excursão *f*.
jaunty ['dʒɔːntɪ] *adj* alegre, jovial.
Java ['dʒɑːvə] *n* Java (*no article*).
javelin ['dʒævlɪn] *n* dardo de arremesso.
jaw [dʒɔː] *n* mandíbula, maxilar *m*.
jawbone ['dʒɔːbəun] *n* osso maxilar, maxila.
jay [dʒeɪ] *n* gaio.
jaywalker ['dʒeɪwɔːkə*] *n* pedestre *m/f* imprudente (*BR*), peão *m* imprudente (*PT*).
jazz [dʒæz] *n* jazz *m*.
jazz up *vt* (*liven up*) animar, avivar.
jazz band *n* banda de jazz.
jazzy ['dʒæzɪ] *adj* (*of jazz*) jazzístico; (*bright*) de cor berrante.
JCS (*US*) *n abbr* = **Joint Chiefs of Staff.**
JD (*US*) *n abbr* (= *Doctor of Laws*) título universitário; (= *Justice Department*) ministério da Justiça.
jealous ['dʒɛləs] *adj* ciumento; (*envious*) invejoso; **to be** ~ estar com ciúmes.

jealously ['dʒɛləslɪ] *adv* (*enviously*) invejosamente; (*guard*) zelosamente.
jealousy ['dʒɛləsɪ] *n* ciúmes *mpl*; (*envy*) inveja.
jeans [dʒiːnz] *npl* jeans *m* (*BR*), jeans *mpl* (*PT*).
jeep [dʒiːp] *n* jipe *m*.
jeer [dʒɪə*] *vi*: **to** ~ (**at**) (*boo*) vaiar; (*mock*) zombar (de).
jeering ['dʒɪərɪŋ] *adj* vaiador(a) ♦ *n* vaias *fpl*.
jeers ['dʒɪəz] *npl* (*boos*) vaias *fpl*; (*mocking*) zombarias *fpl*.
jelly ['dʒɛlɪ] *n* geléia, gelatina.
jellyfish ['dʒɛlɪfɪʃ] *n inv* água-viva.
jeopardize ['dʒɛpədaɪz] *vt* arriscar, pôr em perigo.
jeopardy ['dʒɛpədɪ] *n*: **to be in** ~ estar em perigo, estar correndo risco.
jerk [dʒəːk] *n* (*jolt*) solavanco, sacudida; (*wrench*) puxão *m*; (*inf*) babaca *m* ♦ *vt* sacudir ♦ *vi* (*vehicle*) dar um solavanco.
jerkin ['dʒəːkɪn] *n* jaqueta.
jerky ['dʒəːkɪ] *adj* espasmódico, aos arrancos.
jerry-built ['dʒɛrɪ-] *adj* mal construído.
jerry can ['dʒɛrɪ-] *n* lata.
Jersey ['dʒəːzɪ] *n* Jersey (*no article*).
jersey ['dʒəːzɪ] *n* suéter *m or f* (*BR*), camisola (*PT*); (*fabric*) jérsei *m*, malha.
Jerusalem [dʒə'ruːsələm] *n* Jerusalém; ~ **artichoke** topinambo.
jest [dʒɛst] *n* gracejo, brincadeira; **in** ~ de brincadeira.
jester ['dʒɛstə*] *n* (*HISTORY*) bobo.
Jesus ['dʒiːzəs] *n* Jesus *m*; ~ **Christ** Jesus Cristo.
jet [dʒɛt] *n* (*of gas, liquid*) jato; (*AVIAT*) (avião *m* a) jato.
jet-black *adj* da cor do azeviche.
jet engine *n* motor *m* a jato.
jet lag *n* cansaço devido à diferença de fuso horário.
jetsam ['dʒɛtsəm] *n* objetos *mpl* alijados ao mar.
jettison ['dʒɛtɪsn] *vt* alijar.
jetty ['dʒɛtɪ] *n* quebra-mar *m*, cais *m*.
Jew [dʒuː] *n* judeu/dia *m/f*.
jewel ['dʒuːəl] *n* jóia; (*in watch*) rubi *m*.
jeweller ['dʒuːələ*] (*US* **jeweler**) *n* joalheiro/a; ~'**s (shop)** joalheria.
jewellery ['dʒuːəlrɪ] (*US* **jewelry**) *n* jóias *fpl*, pedrarias *fpl*.
Jewess ['dʒuːɪs] *n* (*offensive*) judia.
Jewish ['dʒuːɪʃ] *adj* judeu/judia.
JFK (*US*) *n abbr* = **John Fitzgerald Kennedy International Airport.**
jib [dʒɪb] *n* (*NAUT*) bujarrona; (*of crane*) lança ♦ *vi* (*horse*) empacar; **to** ~ **at doing sth** relutar em fazer algo.
jibe [dʒaɪb] *n* zombaria.
jiffy ['dʒɪfɪ] (*inf*) *n*: **in a** ~ num instante.
jig [dʒɪg] *n* jiga.
jigsaw ['dʒɪgsɔː] *n* (*also*: ~ *puzzle*) quebra-

cabeça *m*; *(tool)* serra de vaivém.
jilt [dʒɪlt] *vt* dar o fora em.
jingle ['dʒɪŋgl] *n* *(advert)* música de propaganda ♦ *vi* tilintar, retinir.
jingoism ['dʒɪŋgəʊɪzm] *n* jingoísmo.
jinx [dʒɪŋks] *(inf)* *n* caipora, pé *m* frio.
jitters ['dʒɪtəz] *(inf)* *npl*: **to get the ~** ficar muito nervoso.
jittery ['dʒɪtərɪ] *(inf)* *adj* nervoso.
jiu-jitsu [dʒuː'dʒɪtsuː] *n* jiu-jítsu *m*.
job [dʒɔb] *n* trabalho; *(task)* tarefa; *(duty)* dever *m*; *(post)* emprego; *(inf: difficulty)*: **you'll have a ~ to do that** não vai ser fácil você fazer isso; **a part-time/full-time ~** um trabalho de meio-expediente/de tempo integral; **it's a good ~ that ...** ainda bem que ...; **just the ~!** justo o que queria!
jobber ['dʒɔbə*] *(BRIT)* *n* *(STOCK EXCHANGE)* operador(a) *m/f* intermediário/a.
jobbing ['dʒɔbɪŋ] *(BRIT)* *adj* *(workman)* tarefeiro, pago por tarefa.
Jobcentre ['dʒɔbsɛntə*] *n* agência de emprego.
job creation scheme *n* plano para a criação de empregos.
job description *n* descrição *f* do cargo.
jobless ['dʒɔblɪs] *adj* desempregado.
job lot *n* lote *m* (de mercadorias variadas).
job satisfaction *n* satisfação *f* profissional.
job security *n* estabilidade *f* de emprego.
job specification *n* especificação *f* do cargo.
jockey ['dʒɔkɪ] *n* jóquei *m* ♦ *vi*: **to ~ for position** manobrar para conseguir uma posição.
jockey box *(US)* *n* *(AUT)* porta-luvas *m inv*.
jocular ['dʒɔkjulə*] *adj* *(humorous)* jocoso, divertido; *(merry)* alegre.
jog [dʒɔg] *vt* empurrar, sacudir ♦ *vi* *(run)* fazer jogging or cooper; **to ~ along** ir levando; **to ~ sb's memory** refrescar a memória de alguém.
jogger ['dʒɔgə*] *n* corredor(a) *m/f*, praticante *m/f* de jogging.
jogging ['dʒɔgɪŋ] *n* jogging *m*.
join [dʒɔɪn] *vt* *(things)* juntar, unir; *(become member of)* associar-se a, afiliar-se a; *(meet)* encontrar-se com; *(accompany)* juntar-se a ♦ *vi* *(roads, rivers)* confluir ♦ *n* junção *f*; **will you ~ us for dinner?** você janta conosco?; **I'll ~ you later** vou me encontrar com você mais tarde; **to ~ forces (with)** associar-se (com).
join in *vi* participar ♦ *vt fus* participar em.
join up *vi* unir-se; *(MIL)* alistar-se.
joiner ['dʒɔɪnə*] *n* marceneiro.
joinery ['dʒɔɪnərɪ] *n* marcenaria.
joint [dʒɔɪnt] *n* *(TECH)* junta, união *f*; *(wood)* encaixe *m*; *(ANAT)* articulação *f*; *(CULIN)* quarto; *(inf: place)* espelunca; (: *marijuana cigarette*) baseado ♦ *adj* *(common)* comum; *(combined)* conjunto; *(committee)* misto; **by ~ agreement** por comum acordo; **~ responsibility** co-responsabilidade *f*.
joint account *n* conta conjunta.
jointly ['dʒɔɪntlɪ] *adv* em comum; *(collectively)* coletivamente; *(together)* conjunta-

mente.
joint ownership *n* co-propriedade *f*, condomínio.
joint-stock company *n* sociedade *f* anônima por ações.
joint venture *n* joint venture *m*.
joist [dʒɔɪst] *n* barrote *m*.
joke [dʒəuk] *n* piada; *(also: practical ~)* brincadeira, peça ♦ *vi* brincar; **to play a ~ on** pregar uma peça em.
joker ['dʒəukə*] *n* piadista *m/f*, brincalhão/lhona *m/f*; *(CARDS)* curingão *m*.
joking ['dʒəukɪŋ] *n* brincadeira.
jollity ['dʒɔlɪtɪ] *n* alegria.
jolly ['dʒɔlɪ] *adj* *(merry)* alegre; *(enjoyable)* divertido ♦ *adv* *(BRIT: inf)* muito, extremamente ♦ *vt* *(BRIT)*: **to ~ sb along** animar alguém; **~ good!** *(BRIT)* excelente!
jolt [dʒəult] *n* *(shake)* sacudida, solavanco; *(shock)* susto ♦ *vt* sacudir, abalar.
Jordan ['dʒɔːdən] *n* Jordânia; *(river)* Jordão *m*.
Jordanian [dʒɔː'deɪnɪən] *adj, n* jordaniano/a.
joss stick [dʒɔs-] *n* palito perfumado.
jostle ['dʒɔsl] *vt* acotovelar, empurrar.
jot [dʒɔt] *n*: **not one ~** nem um pouquinho.
jot down *vt* anotar.
jotter ['dʒɔtə*] *(BRIT)* *n* bloco (de anotações).
journal ['dʒɔːnl] *n* *(paper)* jornal *m*; *(magazine)* revista; *(diary)* diário.
journalese [dʒɔːnə'liːz] *(pej)* *n* linguagem *f* jornalística.
journalism ['dʒɔːnəlɪzəm] *n* jornalismo.
journalist ['dʒɔːnəlɪst] *n* jornalista *m/f*.
journey ['dʒɔːnɪ] *n* viagem *f*; *(distance covered)* trajeto ♦ *vi* viajar; **return ~** volta; **a 5-hour ~** 5 horas de viagem.
jovial ['dʒəuvɪəl] *adj* jovial, alegre.
jowl [dʒaul] *n* papada.
joy [dʒɔɪ] *n* alegria.
joyful ['dʒɔɪful] *adj* alegre.
joyous ['dʒɔɪəs] *adj* alegre.
joy ride *n* passeio de carro; *(illegal)* passeio (com veículo roubado).
joystick ['dʒɔɪstɪk] *n* *(AVIAT)* manche *m*, alavanca de controle; *(COMPUT)* joystick *m*.
JP *n abbr* = **Justice of the Peace**.
Jr. *abbr* = **junior**.
JTPA *(US)* *n abbr* (= *Job Training Partnership*) *programa governamental de aprendizagem*.
jubilant ['dʒuːbɪlnt] *adj* jubilante.
jubilation [dʒuːbɪ'leɪʃən] *n* júbilo, regozijo.
jubilee ['dʒuːbɪliː] *n* jubileu *m*; **silver ~** jubileu de prata.
judge [dʒʌdʒ] *n* juiz/juíza *m/f* ♦ *vt* julgar; *(estimate: weight, size etc)* avaliar; *(consider)* considerar ♦ *vi*: **judging or to ~ by ...** a julgar por ...; **as far as I can ~** ao que me parece, no meu entender; **I ~d it necessary to inform him** julguei necessário informá-lo.
judge advocate *n* *(MIL)* auditor *m* de guerra.
Judge Advocate General *n* *(MIL)* procurador *m* geral da Justiça Militar.
judg(e)ment ['dʒʌdʒmənt] *n* juízo; *(pun-*

ishment) decisão *f*, sentença; **in my ~ na mi-nha opinião; to pass ~ on** (*LAW*) julgar, dar sentença sobre.

judicial [dʒuːˈdɪʃl] *adj* judicial; (*fair*) imparcial.

judiciary [dʒuːˈdɪʃɪərɪ[*n* poder *m* judiciário.

judicious [dʒuːˈdɪʃəs] *adj* judicioso.

judo [ˈdʒuːdəu] *n* judô *m*.

jug [dʒʌg] *n* jarro.

jugged hare [dʒʌgd-] (*BRIT*) *n* guisado de le-bre.

juggernaut [ˈdʒʌgənɔːt] (*BRIT*) *n* (*huge truck*) jamanta.

juggle [ˈdʒʌgl] *vi* fazer malabarismos.

juggler [ˈdʒʌglə*] *n* malabarista *m/f*.

Jugoslav [ˈjuːgəuslɑːv] *adj, n* = **Yugoslav**.

jugular (vein) [ˈdʒʌgjulə*-] *n* veia jugular.

juice [dʒuːs] *n* suco (*BR*), sumo (*PT*); (*inf: pet-rol*): **we've run out of ~** estamos sem gaso-lina.

juicy [ˈdʒuːsɪ] *adj* suculento.

jukebox [ˈdʒuːkbɔks] *n* juke-box *m*.

Jul. *abbr* (= *July*) jul.

July [dʒuːˈlaɪ] *n* julho; **the first of ~** dia pri-meiro de julho; **(on) the eleventh of ~** (no) dia onze de julho; **in the month of ~** no mês de julho; **at the beginning/end of ~** no começo/fim de julho; **in the middle of ~** em meados de julho; **during ~** durante o mês de julho; **in ~ of next year** em julho do ano que vem; **each** *or* **every ~** todo ano em julho; **~ was wet this year** choveu muito em julho deste ano.

jumble [ˈdʒʌmbl] *n* confusão *f*, mixórdia ♦ *vt* (*also*: **~ up**: *mix up*) misturar; (: *dis-arrange*) desorganizar.

jumble sale (*BRIT*) *n* venda de objetos usa-dos, bazar *m*.

jumbo [ˈdʒʌmbəu] *adj*: **~ jet** avião *m* jumbo; **~ size** tamanho gigante.

jump [dʒʌmp] *vi* saltar, pular; (*start*) sobressaltar-se; (*increase*) disparar ♦ *vt* pu-lar, saltar ♦ *n* pulo, salto; (*increase*) alta; (*fence*) obstáculo; **to ~ the queue** (*BRIT*) fu-rar a fila (*BR*), pôr-se à frente (*PT*); **to ~ for joy** pular de alegria.

jump about *vi* saltitar.

jump at *vt fus* (*accept*) aceitar imediata-mente; (*chance*) agarrar.

jump down *vi* pular para baixo.

jump up *vi* levantar-se num ímpeto.

jumped-up [dʒʌmpt-] (*BRIT*: *pej*) *adj* arri-vista.

jumper [ˈdʒʌmpə*] *n* (*BRIT*: *pullover*) suéter *m* or *f* (*BR*), camisola (*PT*); (*US*: *pinafore dress*) avental *m*; (*SPORT*) saltador(a) *m/f*.

jump leads (*US* **jumper cables**) *npl* cabos *mpl* para ligar a bateria.

jumpy [ˈdʒʌmpɪ] *adj* nervoso.

Jun. *abbr* = **June; junior**.

junction [ˈdʒʌŋkʃən] *n* (*BRIT*: *of roads*) cruza-mento; (: *on motorway*) trevo; (*RAIL*) en-troncamento.

juncture [ˈdʒʌŋktʃə*] *n*: **at this ~** neste mo-mento, nesta conjuntura.

June [dʒuːn] *n* junho; *see also* **July**.

jungle [ˈdʒʌŋgl] *n* selva, mato.

junior [ˈdʒuːnɪə*] *adj* (*in age*) mais novo *or* moço; (*competition*) juvenil; (*position*) sub-alterno ♦ *n* jovem *m/f*; (*SPORT*) júnior *m*; **he's ~ to me (by 2 years), he's (2 years) my ~** ele é (dois anos) mais novo do que eu; **he's ~ to me** (*seniority*) tenho mais antigui-dade do que ele.

junior executive *n* executivo/a júnior.

junior high school (*US*) *n* ≈ colégio (*2⁰ e 3⁰ ginasial*).

junior minister (*BRIT*) *n* ministro/a subalterno/a.

junior partner *n* sócio/a minoritário/a.

junior school (*BRIT*) *n* escola primária.

junior sizes *npl* (*COMM*) tamanhos *mpl* para crianças.

juniper [ˈdʒuːnɪpə*] *n* junípero.

junk [dʒʌŋk] *n* (*cheap goods*) tranqueira, ve-lharias *fpl*; (*lumber*) trastes *mpl*; (*rubbish*) lixo; (*ship*) junco ♦ *vt* (*inf*) jogar no lixo.

junk dealer *n* belchior *m*.

junket [ˈdʒʌŋkɪt] *n* (*CULIN*) coalhada; (*BRIT*: *inf*): **to go on a ~** viajar à custa do governo ♦ *vi* (*BRIT*: *inf*): **to go ~ing = to go on a ~**.

junk food *n* lanches *mpl*.

junkie [ˈdʒʌŋkɪ] (*inf*) *n* drogado/a.

junk room (*US*) *n* quarto de despejo.

junk shop *n* loja de objetos usados.

Junr *abbr* = **junior**.

junta [ˈdʒʌntə] *n* junta.

Jupiter [ˈdʒuːpɪtə*] *n* Júpiter *m*.

jurisdiction [dʒuərɪsˈdɪkʃən] *n* jurisdição *f*; **it falls** *or* **comes within/outside our ~** é/não é da nossa competência.

jurisprudence [dʒuərɪsˈpruːdəns] *n* jurispru-dência.

juror [ˈdʒuərə*] *n* jurado/a.

jury [ˈdʒuərɪ] *n* júri *m*.

jury box *n* banca dos jurados.

juryman [ˈdʒuərɪmən] (*irreg*) *n* = **juror**.

just [dʒʌst] *adj* justo ♦ *adv* (*exactly*) justa-mente, exatamente; (*only*) apenas, somente; **he's ~ done it/left** (*PT*: acaba) de fazê-lo/ir; **~ as I expected** exatamente como eu esperava; **~ right** perfeito; **~ two o'clock** duas (horas) em ponto; **I was ~ about to phone** eu já ia telefonar; **we were ~ leaving** estávamos de saída; **~ as he was leaving** no momento em que ele saía; **~ before/enough** justo antes/o suficiente; **~ here** bem aqui; **it's ~ a mistake** não passa de um erro; **he ~ missed** falhou por pouco; **~ listen** escute aqui!; **~ ask someone the way** é só pedir uma indicação; **it's ~ as good** é igualmente bom; **~ as well that ...** ainda bem que ...; **not ~ now** não neste mo-mento; **~ a minute!**, **~ one moment!** só um

NB: *European Portuguese adds the following consonants to certain words:* **b** (sú(b)dito, su(b)til); **c** (a(c)ção, a(c)cionista, a(c)to); **m** (inde(m)ne, (m)ne); **p** (ado(p)ção, ado(p)tar); *for further details see p. xiii.*

minuto!, espera aí!, peraí! (inf).

justice ['dʒʌstɪs] n justiça; **Lord Chief J~** (BRIT) presidente do tribunal de recursos; **this photo doesn't do you** ~ esta foto não te faz justiça.

Justice of the Peace n juiz/juíza m/f de paz.

justifiable [dʒʌstɪ'faɪəbl] adj justificável.

justifiably [dʒʌstɪ'faɪəblɪ] adv justificadamente.

justification [dʒʌstɪfɪ'keɪʃən] n (reason) justificativa; (action) justificação f.

justify ['dʒʌstɪfaɪ] vt justificar; **to be justified in doing sth** ter razão de fazer algo.

justly ['dʒʌstlɪ] adv justamente; (with reason) com razão.

justness ['dʒʌstnɪs] n justiça.

jut [dʒʌt] vi (also: ~ out) sobressair.

jute [dʒuːt] n juta.

juvenile ['dʒuːvənaɪl] adj juvenil; (court) de menores ♦ n jovem m/f; (LAW) menor m/f de idade.

juvenile delinquency n delinqüência juvenil.

juvenile delinquent n delinqüente m/f juvenil.

juxtapose ['dʒʌkstəpəuz] vt justapor.

juxtaposition [dʒʌkstəpə'zɪʃən] n justaposição f.

K

K, k [keɪ] n (letter) K, k m; **K for King** K de Kátia.

K abbr (= kilobyte) K; (BRIT: = Knight) título honorífico ♦ n abbr = **one thousand**.

kaftan ['kæftæn] n cafetã m.

Kalahari Desert [kælə'hɑːrɪ-] n deserto de Kalahari.

kale [keɪl] n couve f.

kaleidoscope [kə'laɪdəskəup] n calidoscópio, caleidoscópio.

Kampala [kæm'pɑːlə] n Campala.

Kampuchea [kæmpu'tʃɪə] n Kampuchea m, Camboja m.

kangaroo [kæŋgə'ruː] n canguru m.

kaput [kə'put] (inf) adj pifado.

karate [kə'rɑːtɪ] n karatê m.

Kashmir [kæʃ'mɪə*] n Cachemira.

KC (BRIT) n abbr (LAW: = King's Counsel) título dado a certos advogados.

kd abbr (= knocked down) em pedaços.

kebab [kə'bæb] n churrasquinho, espetinho.

keel [kiːl] n quilha; **on an even** ~ (fig) em equilíbrio.

keel over vi (NAUT) emborcar; (person) desmaiar.

keen [kiːn] adj (interest, desire) grande, vivo; (eye, intelligence) penetrante; (competition) acirrado, intenso; (edge) afiado; (eager)

entusiasmado; **to be** ~ **to do** or **on doing sth** sentir muita vontade de fazer algo; **to be** ~ **on sth/sb** gostar de algo/alguém; **I'm not** ~ **on going** não estou a fim de ir.

keenly ['kiːnlɪ] adv (enthusiastically) com entusiasmo; (feel) profundamente, agudamente.

keenness ['kiːnnɪs] n (eagerness) entusiasmo, interesse m; ~ **to do** vontade de fazer.

keep [kiːp] (pt, pp kept) vt (retain) ficar com; (look after) guardar; (preserve) conservar; (hold back) reter; (shop, diary) ter; (feed: family etc) manter; (promise) cumprir; (chickens, bees etc) criar ♦ vi (food) conservar-se; (remain) ficar ♦ n (of castle) torre f de menagem; (food etc): **to earn one's** ~ ganhar a vida; ~**s** n: **for** ~**s** (inf) para sempre; **to** ~ **doing sth** continuar fazendo algo; **to** ~ **sb from doing sth** impedir alguém de fazer algo; **to** ~ **sth from happening** impedir que algo aconteça; **to** ~ **sb happy** fazer alguém feliz; **to** ~ **a place tidy** manter um lugar limpo; **to** ~ **sb waiting** deixar alguém esperando; **to** ~ **an appointment** manter um compromisso; **to** ~ **a record of sth** anotar algo; **to** ~ **sth to o.s.** guardar algo para si mesmo; **to** ~ **sth (back) from sb** ocultar algo de alguém; **to** ~ **time** (clock) marcar a hora exata.

keep away vt: **to** ~ **sth/sb away from sb** manter algo/alguém afastado de alguém ♦ vi: **to** ~ **away (from)** manter-se afastado (de).

keep back vt (crowd, tears) conter; (money) reter ♦ vi manter-se afastado.

keep down vt (control: prices, spending) limitar, controlar ♦ vi não se levantar; **I can't** ~ **my food down** o que como não pára no estômago.

keep in vt (invalid, child) não deixar sair; (SCH) reter ♦ vi: **to** ~ **in with sb** manter boas relações com alguém.

keep off vi não se aproximar ♦ vt afastar; **"~ off the grass"** "não pise na grama"; ~ **your hands off!** tira a mão!

keep on vi: **to** ~ **on doing** continuar fazendo.

keep out vt impedir de entrar ♦ vi (stay out) permanecer fora; **"~ out"** "entrada proibida".

keep up vt manter ♦ vi não atrasar-se, acompanhar; **to** ~ **up with** (pace) acompanhar; (level) manter-se ao nível de.

keeper ['kiːpə*] n guarda m, guardião/diã m/f.

keep-fit n ginástica.

keeping ['kiːpɪŋ] n (care) cuidado; **in** ~ **with** de acordo com.

keepsake ['kiːpseɪk] n lembrança.

keg [kɛg] n barrilete m, barril m pequeno.

kennel ['kɛnl] n casa de cachorro; ~**s** npl canil m.

Kenya ['kɛnjə] n Quênia m.

Kenyan ['kɛnjən] adj, n queniano/a m/f.

kept [kɛpt] pt, pp of **keep**.

kerb [kəːb] n (BRIT) n meio-fio (BR), borda do passeio (PT).

kernel ['kə:nl] *n* amêndoa.
kerosene ['kɛrəsi:n] *n* querosene *m*.
ketchup ['kɛtʃəp] *n* molho de tomate, catsup *m*.
kettle ['kɛtl] *n* chaleira.
kettle drums *npl* tímpanos *mpl*.
key [ki:] *n* chave *f*; (*MUS*) clave *f*; (*of piano, typewriter*) tecla; (*on map*) legenda ♦ *cpd* (-) chave.
key in *vt* (*text*) digitar, teclar.
keyboard ['ki:bɔːd] *n* teclado ♦ *vt* (*text*) teclar, digitar.
keyed up [ki:d-] *adj*: **to be (all)** ~ estar excitado *or* ligado (*inf*).
keyhole ['ki:həul] *n* buraco da fechadura.
keynote ['ki:nəut] *n* (*MUS*) tônica; (*fig*) idéia fundamental ♦ *cpd*: ~ **speech** discurso programático.
keypad ['ki:pæd] *n* teclado complementar.
keyring ['ki:rɪŋ] *n* chaveiro.
keystone ['ki:stəun] *n* pedra angular.
keystroke ['ki:strəuk] *n* batida de tecla.
kg *abbr* (= *kilogram*) kg.
KGB *n abbr* KGB *f*.
khaki ['kɑːkɪ] *adj* cáqui.
kibbutz [kɪ'buts] (*pl* ~**im**) *n* kibutz *m*.
kibbutzim [kɪ'butsɪm] *npl of* **kibbutz**.
kick [kɪk] *vt* (*person*) dar um pontapé em; (*ball*) chutar ♦ *vi* (*horse*) dar coices ♦ *n* pontapé *m*, chute *m*; (*of rifle*) recuo; (*inf: thrill*): **he does it for** ~**s** faz isso para curtir.
kick around (*inf*) *vi* ficar por aí.
kick off *vi* (*SPORT*) dar o pontapé inicial.
kick-off *n* (*SPORT*) pontapé *m* inicial.
kick-start *n* (*also*: ~**er**) arranque *m* ♦ *vt* dar partida em.
kid [kɪd] *n* (*child*) criança; (*animal*) cabrito; (*leather*) pelica ♦ *vi* (*inf*) brincar.
kidnap ['kɪdnæp] *vt* seqüestrar.
kidnapper ['kɪdnæpə*] *n* seqüestrador(a) *m/f*.
kidnapping ['kɪdnæpɪŋ] *n* seqüestro.
kidney ['kɪdnɪ] *n* rim *m*.
kidney bean *n* feijão *m* roxo.
kidney machine *n* (*MED*) aparelho de hemodiálise.
Kilimanjaro [kɪlɪmən'dʒɑːrəu] *n*: **Mount** ~ Kilimanjaro.
kill [kɪl] *vt* matar; (*murder*) assassinar; (*destroy*) destruir; (*finish off*) acabar com, aniquilar ♦ *n* ato de matar; **to** ~ **time** matar o tempo.
kill off *vt* aniquilar; (*fig*) eliminar.
killer ['kɪlə*] *n* assassino/a.
killing ['kɪlɪŋ] *n* (*one*) assassinato; (*several*) matança; (*inf*): **to make a** ~ faturar uma boa nota ♦ *adj* (*funny*) divertido, engraçado.
kill-joy *n* desmancha-prazeres *m inv*.
kiln [kɪln] *n* forno.
kilo ['ki:ləu] *n* quilo.
kilobyte ['ki:ləubaɪt] *n* kilobyte *m*.
kilogram(me) ['kɪləugræm] *n* quilograma *m*.
kilometre ['kɪləmi:tə*] (*US* **kilometer**) *n* quilô-

metro.
kilowatt ['kɪləuwɔt] *n* quilowatt *m*.
kilt [kɪlt] *n* saiote *m* escocês.
kimono [kɪ'məunəu] *n* quimono.
kin [kɪn] *n* parentela; *see* **next**; **kith**.
kind [kaɪnd] *adj* (*friendly*) gentil; (*generous*) generoso; (*good*) bom/boa, bondoso, amável ♦ *n* espécie *f*, classe *f*; (*species*) gênero; **a** ~ **of** uma espécie de; **two of a** ~ dois da mesma espécie; **would you be** ~ **enough to ...?**, **would you be so** ~ **as to ...?** pode me fazer a gentileza de ...?; **it's very** ~ **of you (to do)** é muito gentil da sua parte (fazer); **in** ~ (*COMM*) em espécie; **to repay sb in** ~ (*fig*) pagar alguém na mesma moeda.
kindergarten ['kɪndəgɑːtn] *n* jardim *m* de infância.
kind-hearted *adj* de bom coração, bondoso.
kindle ['kɪndl] *vt* acender.
kindling ['kɪndlɪŋ] *n* gravetos *mpl*.
kindly ['kaɪndlɪ] *adj* (*good*) bom/boa, bondoso; (*gentle*) gentil, carinhoso ♦ *adv* bondosamente, amavelmente; **will you** ~ **...** você pode fazer o favor de ...; **he didn't take it** ~ não gostou.
kindness ['kaɪndnɪs] *n* bondade *f*, gentileza.
kindred ['kɪndrɪd] *adj* aparentado; ~ **spirit** pessoa com os mesmos gostos.
kinetic [kɪ'nɛtɪk] *adj* cinético.
king [kɪŋ] *n* rei *m*.
kingdom ['kɪŋdəm] *n* reino.
kingfisher ['kɪŋfɪʃə*] *n* martim-pescador *m*.
kingpin ['kɪŋpɪn] *n* (*TECH*) pino mestre; (*fig*) mandachuva *m*.
king-size(d) [-saɪz(d)] *adj* tamanho grande; (*cigarettes*) king-size.
kink [kɪŋk] *n* (*of rope*) dobra, coca; (*inf: fig*) mania.
kinky ['kɪŋkɪ] *adj* (*odd*) excêntrico, esquisito; (*pej*) pervertido.
kinship ['kɪnʃɪp] *n* parentesco.
kinsman ['kɪnzmən] (*irreg*) *n* parente *m*.
kinswoman ['kɪnzwumən] (*irreg*) *n* parenta.
kiosk ['ki:ɔsk] *n* banca (*BR*), quiosque *m* (*PT*); (*BRIT*: *also*: **telephone** ~) cabine *f*.
kipper ['kɪpə*] *n* tipo de arenque defumado.
kiss [kɪs] *n* beijo ♦ *vt* beijar; **to** ~ (**each other**) beijar-se; **to** ~ **sb goodbye** despedir-se de alguém com beijos; ~ **of life** (*BRIT*) respiração *f* boca-a-boca.
kit [kɪt] *n* apetrechos *mpl*; (*equipment*) equipamento; (*set of tools etc*) caixa de ferramentas; (*for assembly*) kit *m* para montar.
kit out (*BRIT*) *vt* equipar.
kitbag ['kɪtbæg] *n* saco de viagem.
kitchen ['kɪtʃɪn] *n* cozinha.
kitchen garden *n* horta.
kitchen sink *n* pia (de cozinha).
kitchen unit (*BRIT*) *n* módulo de cozinha.
kitchenware ['kɪtʃɪnwɛə*] *n* bateria de cozinha.
kite [kaɪt] *n* (*toy*) papagaio, pipa; (*ZOOL*) mi-

NB: European Portuguese adds the following consonants to certain words: **b** (sú(b)dito, su(b)til); **c** (a(c)ção, a(c)cionista, a(c)to); **m** (inde(m)ne); **p** (ado(p)ção, ado(p)tar); *for further details see p. xiii.*

lhafre *m*.
kith [kıθ] *n*: ~ **and kin** amigos e parentes *mpl*.
kitten ['kıtn] *n* gatinho.
kitty ['kıtı] *n* (*pool of money*) fundo comum, vaquinha; (*CARDS*) bolo.
KKK (*US*) *n abbr* = **Ku Klux Klan**.
Kleenex ['kliːnɛks] ® *n* lenço de papel.
kleptomaniac [klɛptəu'meɪnɪæk] *n* cleptomaníaco/a.
km *abbr* (= *kilometre*) km.
km/h *abbr* (= *kilometres per hour*) km/h.
knack [næk] *n*: **to have the** ~ **of doing sth** ter um jeito *or* queda para fazer algo; **there's a** ~ **(to it)** tem um jeito.
knapsack ['næpsæk] *n* mochila.
knave [neɪv] *n* (*CARDS*) valete *m*.
knead [niːd] *vt* amassar.
knee [niː] *n* joelho.
kneecap ['niːkæp] *n* rótula.
knee-deep *adj*: **the water was** ~ a água batia no joelho.
kneel [niːl] (*pt, pp* **knelt**) *vi* (*also:* ~ *down*) ajoelhar-se.
kneepad ['niːpæd] *n* joelheira.
knell [nɛl] *n* dobre *m* de finados.
knelt [nɛlt] *pt, pp of* **kneel**.
knew [njuː] *pt of* **know**.
knickers ['nɪkəz] *npl* calcinha (*BR*), cuecas *fpl* (*PT*).
knick-knack ['nɪk-] *n* bibelô *m*.
knife [naɪf] (*pl* **knives**) *n* faca ♦ *vt* esfaquear; ~, **fork and spoon** talher *m*.
knight [naɪt] *n* cavaleiro; (*CHESS*) cavalo.
knighthood ['naɪthud] *n* cavalaria; (*title*): **to get a** ~ receber o título de Sir.
knit [nɪt] *vt* tricotar; (*brows*) franzir ♦ *vi* tricotar (*BR*), fazer malha (*PT*); (*bones*) consolidar-se; **to** ~ **together** (*fig*) unir, juntar.
knitted ['nɪtɪd] *adj* de malha.
knitting ['nɪtɪŋ] *n* trabalho de tricô (*BR*), malha (*PT*).
knitting machine *n* máquina de tricotar.
knitting needle *n* agulha de tricô (*BR*) *or* de malha (*PT*).
knitting pattern *n* molde *m* para tricotar.
knitwear ['nɪtwɛə*] *n* roupa de malha.
knives [naɪvz] *npl of* **knife**.
knob [nɔb] *n* (*of door*) maçaneta; (*of drawer*) puxador *m*; (*of stick*) castão *m*; (*lump*) calombo; **a** ~ **of butter** (*BRIT*) uma porção de manteiga.
knobbly ['nɔblɪ] (*BRIT*) *adj* (*wood, surface*) nodoso; (*knees*) ossudo.
knobby ['nɔbɪ] (*US*) *adj* = **knobbly**.
knock [nɔk] *vt* (*strike*) bater em; (*bump into*) colidir com; (*fig: inf*) criticar, malhar ♦ *n* pancada, golpe *m*; (*on door*) batida ♦ *vi*: **to** ~ **at** *or* **on the door** bater à porta; **to** ~ **a hole in sth** abrir um buraco em algo; **to** ~ **a nail into** pregar um prego em.
knock down *vt* derrubar; (*price*) abater; (*pedestrian*) atropelar.
knock off *vi* (*inf: finish*) terminar ♦ *vt* (*inf: steal*) abafar; (*vase*) derrubar; (*fig: from*

price etc): **to** ~ **off £10** fazer um desconto de £10.
knock out *vt* pôr nocaute, nocautear.
knock over *vt* (*object*) derrubar; (*pedestrian*) atropelar.
knockdown ['nɔkdaun] *adj* (*price*) de liqüidação, de queima (*inf*).
knocker ['nɔkə*] *n* (*on door*) aldrava.
knock-for-knock (*BRIT*) *adj*: ~ **agreement** acordo entre seguradoras pelo qual cada uma se compromete a indenizar seu próprio cliente.
knocking ['nɔkıŋ] *n* pancadas *fpl*.
knock-kneed [-niːd] *adj* cambaio.
knockout ['nɔkaut] *n* (*BOXING*) nocaute *m*.
knockout competition (*BRIT*) *n* competição *f* com eliminatórias.
knock-up *n* (*TENNIS*) bate-bola *m*.
knot [nɔt] *n* nó *m* ♦ *vt* dar nó em; **to tie a** ~ dar *or* fazer um nó.
knotty ['nɔtı] *adj* (*fig*) cabeludo, espinhoso.
know [nəu] (*pt* **knew**, *pp* **known**) *vt* saber; (*person, author, place*) conhecer ♦ *vi*: **to** ~ **about** *or* **of sth** saber de algo; **to** ~ **that** ... saber que ...; **to** ~ **how to swim** saber nadar; **to get to** ~ **sth** (*fact*) saber, descobrir; (*place*) conhecer; **I don't** ~ **him** não o conheço; **to** ~ **right from wrong** saber distinguir o bem e o mal; **as far as I** ~ ... que eu saiba ....
know-all (*BRIT*: *pej*) *n* sabichão/chona *m/f*.
know-how *n* know-how *m*, experiência.
knowing ['nəuıŋ] *adj* (*look: of complicity*) de cumplicidade.
knowingly ['nəuıŋlı] *adv* (*purposely*) de propósito; (*spitefully*) maliciosamente.
know-it-all (*US*) *n* = **know-all**.
knowledge ['nɔlɪdʒ] *n* conhecimento; (*range of learning*) saber *m*, conhecimentos *mpl*; **to have no** ~ **of** não ter conhecimento de; **not to my** ~ que eu saiba, não; **without my** ~ sem eu saber; **to have a working** ~ **of Portuguese** ter um conhecimento básico do português; **it's common** ~ **that** ... todos sabem que ...; **it has come to my** ~ **that** ... chegou ao meu conhecimento que ....
knowledgeable ['nɔlɪdʒəbl] *adj* entendido, versado.
known [nəun] *pp of* **know** ♦ *adj* (*thief*) famigerado; (*fact*) conhecido.
knuckle ['nʌkl] *n* nó *m*.
knuckle under (*inf*) *vi* ceder.
knuckleduster ['nʌkldʌstə*] *n* soco inglês.
KO *n abbr* = **knockout** ♦ *vt* nocautear, pôr nocaute.
koala [kəu'ɑːlə] *n* (*also:* ~ *bear*) coala *m*.
kook [kuːk] (*US*: *inf*) *n* maluco/a, biruta (*inf*).
Koran [kɔ'rɑːn] *n* Alcorão *m*.
Korea [kə'rɪə] *n* Coréia; **North/South** ~ Coréia do Norte/Sul.
Korean [kə'rɪən] *adj* coreano ♦ *n* coreano/a; (*LING*) coreano.
kosher ['kəuʃə*] *adj* kosher *inv*.
kowtow ['kau'tau] *vi*: **to** ~ **to sb** bajular alguém.

Kremlin ['kremlɪn] *n*: **the ~** o Kremlin.
KS (*US*) *abbr* (*POST*) = **Kansas**.
Kt (*BRIT*) *abbr* (= *Knight*) título honorífico.
Kuala Lumpur ['kwɑːlə'lumpuə*] *n* Cuala Lumpur.
kudos ['kjuːdɔs] *n* glória, fama.
Kuwait [ku'weɪt] *n* Kuweit *m*.
Kuwaiti [ku'weɪtɪ] *adj*, *n* kuweitiano/a.
kW *abbr* (= *kilowatt*) kW.
KY (*US*) *abbr* (*POST*) = **Kentucky**.

L

L, l [ɛl] *n* (*letter*) L, l *m*; **L for Lucy** (*BRIT*) or **Love** (*US*) L de Lúcia.
L *abbr* (= *lake*) L; (= *large*) G; (= *left*) esq; (*BRIT*: *AUT*: = *learner*) (condutor(a) *m/f*) aprendiz *m/f*.
l *abbr* (= *litre*) l.
LA (*US*) *n* *abbr* = **Los Angeles** ♦ *abbr* (*POST*) = **Louisiana**.
lab [læb] *n* *abbr* = **laboratory**.
label ['leɪbl] *n* etiqueta, rótulo; (*brand*: *of record*) selo ♦ *vt* etiquetar, rotular; **to ~ sb a** ... rotular alguém de ....
labor *etc* ['leɪbə*] (*US*) = **labour** *etc*.
laboratory [lə'bɔrətərɪ] *n* laboratório.
Labor Day (*US*) *n* Dia *m* do Trabalho.
laborious [lə'bɔːrɪəs] *adj* laborioso.
labor union (*US*) *n* sindicato.
Labour ['leɪbə*] (*BRIT*) *n* (*POL*: *also*: **the ~ Party**) o partido trabalhista, os trabalhistas.
labour ['leɪbə*] (*US* **labor**) *n* (*task*) trabalho; (**~** *force*) mão-de-obra; (*workers*) trabalhadores *mpl*; (*MED*) (trabalho de) parto ♦ *vi*: **to ~ (at)** trabalhar (em) ♦ *vt* insistir em; **in ~** (*MED*) em trabalho de parto.
labo(u)r camp *n* campo de trabalhos forçados.
labo(u)r cost *n* custo de mão-de-obra.
labo(u)red ['leɪbəd] *adj* (*movement*) forçado; (*style*) elaborado.
labo(u)rer ['leɪbərə*] *n* operário; (*on farm*) trabalhador *m* rural, peão *m*; (*day* **~**) diarista *m*.
labo(u)r force *n* mão-de-obra *f*.
labo(u)r-intensive *adj* intensivo de mão-de-obra.
labo(u)r market *n* mercado de trabalho.
labo(u)r pains *npl* dores *fpl* do parto.
labo(u)r relations *npl* relações *fpl* trabalhistas.
labo(u)r-saving *adj* que poupa trabalho.
labo(u)r unrest *n* agitação *f* operária.
labyrinth ['læbɪrɪnθ] *n* labirinto.

lace [leɪs] *n* renda; (*of shoe etc*) cordão *m* ♦ *vt* (*shoe*) amarrar; (*drink*) misturar aguardente a.
lacemaking ['leɪsmeɪkɪŋ] *n* feitura de renda.
laceration [læsə'reɪʃən] *n* laceração *f*.
lace-up *adj* (*shoes etc*) de cordões.
lack [læk] *n* falta ♦ *vt* carecer de; **through** *or* **for ~ of** por falta de; **to be ~ing** faltar; **to be ~ing in** carecer de.
lackadaisical [lækə'deɪzɪkl] *adj* (*careless*) descuidado; (*indifferent*) apático, aéreo.
lackey ['lækɪ] *n* (*also*: *fig*) lacaio.
lacklustre ['læklʌstə*] *adj* sem brilho, insosso.
laconic [lə'kɔnɪk] *adj* lacônico.
lacquer ['lækə*] *n* laca; (*for hair*) fixador *m*.
lacy ['leɪsɪ] *adj* rendado.
lad [læd] *n* menino, rapaz *m*, moço; (*BRIT*: *in stable etc*) empregado.
ladder ['lædə*] *n* escada de mão *f*; (*BRIT*: *in tights*) (em forma de escada) ♦ *vt* (*BRIT*: *tights*) desfiar ♦ *vi* (*BRIT*: *tights*) desfiar.
laden ['leɪdn] *adj*: **~ (with)** carregado (de); **fully ~** (*truck*, *ship*) completamente carregado, com a carga máxima.
ladle ['leɪdl] *n* concha (de sopa).
lady ['leɪdɪ] *n* senhora; (*distinguished*, *noble*) dama; **young ~** senhorita; **L~ Smith** a lady Smith; **"ladies' (toilets)"** "senhoras"; **a ~ doctor** uma médica.
ladybird ['leɪdɪbəːd] (*BRIT*) *n* joaninha.
ladybug ['leɪdɪbʌg] (*US*) *n* joaninha.
lady-in-waiting *n* dama de companhia.
ladykiller ['leɪdɪkɪlə*] *n* mulherengo.
ladylike ['leɪdɪlaɪk] *adj* elegante, refinado.
ladyship ['leɪdɪʃɪp] *n*: **her ~** Sua Senhoria.
lag [læg] *n* = **time lag** ♦ *vi* (*also*: **~ behind**) ficar para trás ♦ *vt* (*pipes*) revestir com isolante térmico.
lager ['lɑːgə*] *n* cerveja leve e clara.
lagging ['lægɪŋ] *n* revestimento.
lagoon [lə'guːn] *n* lagoa.
Lagos ['leɪgɔs] *n* Lagos.
laid [leɪd] *pt*, *pp* *of* **lay**.
laid-back (*inf*) *adj* descontraído.
lain [leɪn] *pp* *of* **lie**.
lair [lɛə*] *n* covil *m*, toca.
laissez-faire [lɛseɪ'fɛə*] *n* laissez-faire *m*.
laity ['leɪətɪ] *n* leigos *mpl*.
lake [leɪk] *n* lago.
Lake District (*BRIT*) *n*: **the ~** a região dos Lagos.
lamb [læm] *n* cordeiro.
lamb chop *n* costeleta de cordeiro.
lambskin ['læmskɪn] *n* pele *f* de cordeiro.
lambswool ['læmzwul] *n* lã *f* de cordeiro.
lame [leɪm] *adj* coxo, manco; (*weak*) pouco convincente, fraco; **~ duck** (*fig*) pessoa incapaz.
lamely ['leɪmlɪ] *adv* (*fig*) sem convicção.
lament [lə'ment] *n* lamento, queixa ♦ *vt* lamentar-se de.

NB: European Portuguese adds the following consonants to certain words: **b** (sú(b)dito, su(b)til); **c** (a(c)ção, a(c)cionista, a(c)to); **m** (inde(m)ne); **p** (ado(p)ção, ado(p)tar); *for further details see p. xiii.*

lamentable ['læməntəbl] *adj* lamentável.
laminated ['læmɪneɪtɪd] *adj* laminado.
lamp [læmp] *n* lâmpada.
lamplight ['læmplaɪt] *n*: **by** ~ à luz da lâmpada.
lampoon [læm'puːn] *vt* satirizar.
lamppost ['læmppəust] (*BRIT*) *n* poste *m*.
lampshade ['læmpʃeɪd] *n* abajur *m*, quebra-luz *m*.
lance [lɑːns] *n* lança ♦ *vt* (*MED*) lancetar.
lance corporal (*BRIT*) *n* cabo.
lancet ['lɑːnsɪt] *n* (*MED*) bisturi, lanceta.
Lancs [læŋks] (*BRIT*) *abbr* = **Lancashire**.
land [lænd] *n* terra; (*country*) país *m*; (*piece of* ~) terreno; (*estate*) terras *fpl*, propriedades *fpl*; (*AGR*) solo ♦ *vi* (*from ship*) desembarcar; (*AVIAT*) pousar, aterrissar (*BR*), aterrar (*PT*); (*fig: fall*) cair, terminar ♦ *vt* (*obtain*) conseguir; (*passengers, goods*) desembarcar; **to go/travel by** ~ ir/viajar por terra; **to own** ~ ter propriedades; **to** ~ **on one's feet** (*fig*) dar-se bem, cair de pé.
land up *vi* ir parar.
landed gentry ['lændɪd-] *n* proprietários *mpl* de terras.
landing ['lændɪŋ] *n* (*from ship*) desembarque *m*; (*AVIAT*) pouso, aterrissagem *f* (*BR*), aterragem *f* (*PT*); (*of staircase*) patamar *m*.
landing card *n* cartão *m* de desembarque.
landing craft *n* navio para desembarque.
landing gear *n* trem *m* de aterrissagem (*BR*) *or* de aterragem (*PT*).
landing stage (*BRIT*) *n* cais *m* de desembarque.
landing strip *n* pista de aterrissagem (*BR*) *or* de aterragem (*PT*).
landlady ['lændleɪdɪ] *n* (*of boarding house*) senhoria; (*owner*) proprietária.
landlocked ['lændlɔkt] *adj* cercado de terra.
landlord ['lændlɔːd] *n* senhorio, locador *m*; (*of pub etc*) dono, proprietário.
landlubber ['lændlʌbə*] *n* pessoa desacostumada ao mar.
landmark ['lændmɑːk] *n* lugar *m* conhecido; (*fig*) marco.
landowner ['lændəunə*] *n* latifundiário/a.
landscape ['lændskeɪp] *n* paisagem *f*.
landscape architect *n* paisagista *m/f*.
landscaped ['lændskeɪpt] *adj* projetado paisagisticamente.
landscape gardener *n* paisagista *m/f*.
landscape painting *n* (*ART: genre*) paisagismo; (: *picture*) paisagem *f*.
landslide ['lændslaɪd] *n* (*GEO*) desmoronamento, desabamento; (*fig: POL*) vitória esmagadora.
lane [leɪn] *n* (*in country*) senda; (*in town*) ruela; (*AUT*) pista; (*in race*) raia; (*for air or sea traffic*) rota.
language ['læŋgwɪdʒ] *n* língua; (*way one speaks, COMPUT*) linguagem *f*; **bad** ~ palavrões *mpl*.
language laboratory *n* laboratório de línguas.
languid ['læŋgwɪd] *adj* lânguido.

languish ['læŋgwɪʃ] *vi* elanguescer, debilitar-se.
lank [læŋk] *adj* (*hair*) liso.
lanky ['læŋkɪ] *adj* magricela.
lanolin(e) ['lænəlɪn] *n* lanolina.
lantern ['læntn] *n* lanterna.
Laos [laus] *n* Laos *m*.
lap [læp] *n* (*of track*) volta; (*of body*): **to sit on sb's** ~ sentar-se no colo de alguém ♦ *vt* (*also*: ~ *up*) lamber ♦ *vi* (*waves*) marulhar.
lap up *vt* (*fig: food*) comer sofregamente; (: *compliments etc*) receber com sofreguidão.
La Paz [læ'pæz] *n* La Paz.
lapdog ['læpdɔg] *n* cãozinho de estimação.
lapel [lə'pɛl] *n* lapela.
Lapland ['læplænd] *n* Lapônia.
Lapp [læp] *adj*, *n* lapão/ona *m/f*.
lapse [læps] *n* lapso; (*in behaviour*) lapso, deslize *m* ♦ *vi* (*expire*) caducar; (*LAW*) prescrever; (*morally*) decair; **to** ~ **into bad habits** adquirir maus hábitos; ~ **of time** lapso, intervalo; **a** ~ **of memory** um lapso de memória.
larceny ['lɑːsənɪ] *n* furto; **petty** ~ delito leve.
lard [lɑːd] *n* banha de porco.
larder ['lɑːdə*] *n* despensa.
large [lɑːdʒ] *adj* grande; (*fat*) gordo; **at** ~ (*free*) em liberdade; (*generally*) em geral; **to make** ~**r** ampliar; **a** ~ **number of people** um grande número de pessoas; **by and** ~ de modo geral; **on a** ~ **scale** em grande escala.
largely ['lɑːdʒlɪ] *adv* em grande parte.
large-scale *adj* (*map*) em grande escala; (*fig*) importante, de grande alcance.
lark [lɑːk] *n* (*bird*) cotovia; (*joke*) brincadeira, peça.
lark about *vi* divertir-se, brincar.
larva ['lɑːvə] (*pl* **-vae**) *n* larva.
larvae ['lɑːviː] *npl of* **larva**.
laryngitis [lærɪn'dʒaɪtɪs] *n* laringite *f*.
larynx ['lærɪŋks] *n* laringe *f*.
lascivious [lə'sɪvɪəs] *adj* lascivo.
laser ['leɪzə*] *n* laser *m*.
laser beam *n* raio laser.
laser printer *n* impressora a laser.
lash [læʃ] *n* chicote *m*, açoite *m*; (*blow*) chicotada; (*also: eyelash*) pestana, cílio ♦ *vt* chicotear, açoitar; (*tie*) atar.
lash down *vt* atar, amarrar ♦ *vi* (*rain*) cair em bátegas.
lash out *vi*: **to** ~ **out at** *or* **against sb** atacar alguém violentamente; **to** ~ **out (on sth)** (*inf: spend*) esbanjar dinheiro (em algo).
lashings ['læʃɪŋz] (*BRIT: inf*) *npl*: ~ **of** (*cream etc*) montes *mpl* de, um montão de.
lass [læs] *n* moça.
lasso [læ'suː] *n* laço ♦ *vt* laçar.
last [lɑːst] *adj* (*gen*) último; (*final*) derradeiro ♦ *adv* em último lugar ♦ *vi* (*endure*) durar; (*continue*) continuar; ~ **week** na semana passada; ~ **night** ontem à noite; **at** ~ finalmente; **at** ~! até que enfim!; ~ **but one** penúltimo; **the** ~ **time** a última vez; **it** ~**s (for) 2 hours** dura 2 horas.
last-ditch *adj* desesperado, derradeiro.

lasting ['lɑːstɪŋ] *adj* durável, duradouro.
lastly ['lɑːstlɪ] *adv* por fim, por último.
last-minute *adj* de última hora.
latch [lætʃ] *n* trinco, fecho, tranca.
latch on to *vt fus* (*cling to: person*) grudar em; (: *idea*) agarrar-se a.
latchkey ['lætʃkiː] *n* chave *f* de trinco.
late [leɪt] *adj* (*not on time*) atrasado; (*far on in day etc*) tardio; (*hour*) avançado; (*recent*) recente; (*former*) antigo, ex-, anterior; (*dead*) falecido ♦ *adv* tarde; (*behind time, schedule*) atrasado; **to be ~** estar atrasado, atrasar; **to be 10 minutes ~** estar atrasado dez minutos; **to work ~** trabalhar até tarde; **~ in life** com idade avançada; **it was too ~** já era tarde; **of ~** recentemente; **in ~ May** no final de maio; **the ~ Mr X** o falecido Sr X.
latecomer ['leɪtkʌmə*] *n* retardatário/a.
lately ['leɪtlɪ] *adv* ultimamente.
lateness ['leɪtnɪs] *n* (*of person*) atraso; (*of event*) hora avançada.
latent ['leɪtnt] *adj* latente.
later ['leɪtə*] *adj* (*date etc*) posterior; (*version etc*) mais recente ♦ *adv* mais tarde, depois; **~ on today** hoje mais tarde.
lateral ['lætərl] *adj* lateral.
latest ['leɪtɪst] *adj* último; **the ~ news** as últimas novidades; **at the ~** no mais tardar.
latex ['leɪteks] *n* látex *m*.
lath [læθ, *pl* læðz] *n* ripa.
lathe [leɪð] *n* torno.
lather ['lɑːðə*] *n* espuma (de sabão) ♦ *vt* ensaboar ♦ *vi* fazer espuma.
Latin ['lætɪn] *n* latim *m* ♦ *adj* latino.
Latin America *n* América Latina.
Latin-American *adj*, *n* latino-americano/a.
latitude ['lætɪtjuːd] *n* (*also fig*) latitude *f*.
latrine [lə'triːn] *n* latrina.
latter ['lætə*] *adj* último; (*of two*) segundo ♦ *n*: **the ~** o último, este.
latterly ['lætəlɪ] *adv* ultimamente.
lattice ['lætɪs] *n* treliça.
lattice window *n* janela com treliça de chumbo.
Latvia ['lætvɪə] *n* Letônia.
laudable ['lɔːdəbl] *adj* louvável.
laudatory ['lɔːdətrɪ] *adj* laudatório, elogioso.
laugh [lɑːf] *n* riso, risada; (*loud*) gargalhada ♦ *vi* rir, dar risada (*or* gargalhada).
laugh at *vt fus* rir de.
laugh off *vt* disfarçar sorrindo.
laughable ['lɑːfəbl] *adj* risível, ridículo.
laughing ['lɑːfɪŋ] *adj* risonho; **this is no ~ matter** isto não é para rir.
laughing gas *n* gás *m* hilariante.
laughing stock *n* alvo de riso.
laughter ['lɑːftə*] *n* riso, risada; (*people laughing*) risos *mpl*.
launch [lɔːntʃ] *n* (*boat*) lancha; (*of rocket, book etc*) lançamento ♦ *vt* (*ship, rocket, plan*) lançar.

launch out *vi*: **to ~ out (into)** lançar-se (a).
launching ['lɔːntʃɪŋ] *n* (*of rocket etc*) lançamento.
launch(ing) pad *n* plataforma de lançamento.
launder ['lɔːndə*] *vt* lavar e passar; (*money*) lavar.
launderette [lɔːn'drɛt] (*BRIT*) *n* lavanderia automática.
laundromat ['lɔːndrəmæt] (*US*) *n* lavanderia automática.
laundry ['lɔːndrɪ] *n* lavanderia; (*clothes*) roupa para lavar; **to do the ~** lavar a roupa.
laureate ['lɔːrɪət] *adj see* **poet**.
laurel ['lɔrl] *n* louro; (*BOT*) loureiro; **to rest on one's ~s** dormir sobre os louros.
lava ['lɑːvə] *n* lava.
lavatory ['lævətərɪ] *n* privada (*BR*), casa de banho (*PT*); **lavatories** *npl* sanitários *mpl* (*BR*), lavabos *mpl* (*PT*).
lavatory paper (*BRIT*) *n* papel *m* higiênico.
lavender ['lævəndə*] *n* lavanda.
lavish ['lævɪʃ] *adj* profuso, perdulário; (*giving freely*): **~ with** pródigo em, generoso com ♦ *vt*: **to ~ sth on sb** encher *or* cobrir alguém de algo.
lavishly ['lævɪʃlɪ] *adv* (*give, spend*) prodigamente; (*furnished*) luxuosamente.
law [lɔː] *n* lei *f*; (*study*) direito; **against the ~** contra a lei; **to study ~** estudar direito; **to go to ~** (*BRIT*) recorrer à justiça; **~ and order** a ordem pública.
law-abiding [-ə'baɪdɪŋ] *adj* obediente à lei.
lawbreaker ['lɔːbreɪkə*] *n* infrator(a) *m/f* (de lei).
law court *n* tribunal *m* de justiça.
lawful ['lɔːful] *adj* legal, lícito.
lawfully ['lɔːfulɪ] *adv* legalmente.
lawless ['lɔːlɪs] *adj* (*act*) ilegal; (*person*) rebelde; (*country*) sem lei, desordenado.
lawmaker ['lɔːmeɪkə*] *n* legislador(a) *m/f*.
lawn [lɔːn] *n* gramado (*BR*), relvado (*PT*).
lawnmower ['lɔːnməuə*] *n* cortador *m* de grama (*BR*) *or* de relva (*PT*).
lawn tennis *n* tênis *m* de gramado (*BR*) *or* de relvado (*PT*).
law school *n* faculdade *f* de direito.
law student *n* estudante *m/f* de direito.
lawsuit ['lɔːsuːt] *n* ação *f* judicial, processo; **to bring a ~ against** mover processo contra.
lawyer ['lɔːjə*] *n* advogado/a; (*for sales, wills etc*) notário/a, tabelião/liã *m/f*.
lax [læks] *adj* (*discipline*) relaxado; (*person*) negligente.
laxative ['læksətɪv] *n* laxante *m*.
laxity ['læksɪtɪ] *n*: **moral ~** falta de escrúpulo *or* caráter.
lay [leɪ] (*pt, pp* **laid**) *pt of* **lie** ♦ *adj* leigo ♦ *vt* (*place*) colocar; (*eggs, table*) pôr; (*trap*) armar; (*plan*) traçar; **to ~ the table** pôr a mesa; **to ~ the facts/one's proposals before**

sb apresentar os fatos/suas propostas a alguém; **to get laid** (*inf!*) trepar (*!*).
lay aside *vt* pôr de lado.
lay by *vt* pôr de lado.
lay down *vt* (*pen etc*) depositar; (*flat*) deitar; (*arms*) depor; (*policy*) estabelecer; **to ~ down the law** impor regras.
lay in *vt* armazenar, abastecer-se de.
lay into (*inf*) *vt fus* (*attack*) surrar, espancar; (*scold*) dar uma bronca em.
lay off *vt* (*workers*) dispensar.
lay on *vt* (*water, gas*) instalar; (*provide*) prover; (*paint*) aplicar.
lay out *vt* (*design*) planejar; (*display*) expor; (*spend*) esbanjar.
lay up *vt* (*store*) estocar; (*ship*) pôr fora de serviço; (*subj: illness*) acometer.
layabout ['leɪəbaut] *n* vadio/a, preguiçoso/a.
lay-by (*BRIT*) *n* acostamento.
lay days *npl* (*NAUT*) dias *mpl* de estadia.
layer ['leɪə*] *n* camada.
layette [leɪ'ɛt] *n* enxoval *m* de bebê.
layman ['leɪmən] (*irreg*) *n* leigo.
lay-off *n* demissão *f*.
layout ['leɪaut] *n* (*design*) leiaute *m*, esquema *m*; (*disposition*) disposição *f*; (*PRESS*) composição *f*.
laze [leɪz] *vi* descansar; (*pej*) vadiar.
laziness ['leɪzɪnɪs] *n* preguiça.
lazy ['leɪzɪ] *adj* preguiçoso.
LB (*CANADA*) *abbr* = **Labrador**.
lb. *abbr* = **pound** (*weight*).
lbw *abbr* (*CRICKET*: = *leg before wicket*) falta em que o batedor está com a perna em frente da meta.
LC (*US*) *n abbr* = **Library of Congress**.
LCD *n abbr* = **liquid crystal display**.
Ld (*BRIT*) *abbr* (= *lord*) título honorífico.
LDS *n abbr* (= *Licentiate in Dental Surgery*) diploma universitário; (= *Latter-day Saints*) os Santos dos Últimos Dias.
LEA (*BRIT*) *n abbr* (= *local education authority*) departamento de ensino do município.
lead¹ [liːd] (*pt, pp* **led**) *n* (*front position*) dianteira; (*SPORT*) liderança; (*distance, time ahead*) vantagem *f*; (*clue*) pista; (*ELEC*) fio; (*for dog*) correia; (*THEATRE*) papel *m* principal ♦ *vt* conduzir; (*induce*) levar, induzir; (*be leader of*) chefiar, dirigir; (*SPORT*) liderar; (*orchestra*: *BRIT*) ser a primeira figura de; (: *US*) reger ♦ *vi* encabeçar; **to ~ to** levar a, conduzir a; (*result in*) resultar em; **to ~ sb astray** desencaminhar alguém; **to be in the ~** (*SPORT*: *in race*) estar na frente; (: *in match*) estar ganhando; **to take the ~** (*SPORT*) disparar na frente; (*fig*) tomar a dianteira; **to ~ sb to believe that** ... levar alguém a acreditar que ...; **to ~ sb to do sth** levar alguém a fazer algo.
lead away *vt* levar.
lead back *vt* levar de volta.
lead off *vi* (*in game etc*) começar.
lead on *vt* (*tease*) provocar; **to ~ sb on to** induzir alguém a.
lead up to *vt fus* conduzir a.

lead² [lɛd] *n* chumbo; (*in pencil*) grafite *f*.
leaded ['lɛdɪd] *adj* (*petrol*) com chumbo; **~ window** janela com pequenas lâminas de vidro presas por tiras de chumbo.
leader ['liːdə*] *n* líder *m/f*, chefe *m/f*; (*of party, union etc*) líder *m/f*; (*of gang*) cabeça *m/f*; (*of newspaper*) artigo de fundo; **they are ~s in their field** são os líderes na área em que atuam; **the L~ of the House** (*BRIT*) o chefe dos ministros na Câmara.
leadership ['liːdəʃɪp] *n* liderança, direção *f*; (*quality*) poder *m* de liderança; **under the ~ of** ... sob a liderança de ...; (*army*) sob o comando de ...; **qualities of ~** qualidades de liderança.
lead-free [lɛd-] *adj* sem chumbo.
leading ['liːdɪŋ] *adj* (*main*) principal; (*outstanding*) de destaque, notável; (*front*) dianteiro; **a ~ question** uma pergunta capciosa; **~ role** papel de destaque.
leading lady *n* (*THEATRE*) primeira atriz *f*.
leading light *n* (*person*) figura principal, destaque *m*.
leading man (*irreg*) *n* (*THEATRE*) ator *m* principal.
lead pencil [lɛd-] *n* lápis *f* de grafite.
lead poisoning [lɛd-] *n* saturnismo.
lead time [liːd-] *n* (*COMM*) prazo de entrega.
lead weight [lɛd-] *n* peso de chumbo.
leaf [liːf] (*pl* **leaves**) *n* folha; (*of table*) aba; **to turn over a new ~** mudar de vida, partir para outra (*inf*); **to take a ~ out of sb's book** (*fig*) seguir o exemplo de alguém.
leaf through *vt fus* (*book*) folhear.
leaflet ['liːflɪt] *n* folheto.
leafy ['liːfɪ] *adj* folhoso, folhudo.
league [liːg] *n* liga; (*FOOTBALL*: *championship*) campeonato; (: *table*) classificação *f*; **to be in ~ with** estar de comum acordo com.
leak [liːk] *n* (*of liquid, gas*) escape *m*, vazamento; (*hole*) buraco, rombo; (*in roof*) goteira; (*fig*: *of information*) vazamento ♦ *vi* (*ship*) fazer água; (*shoe*) deixar entrar água; (*roof*) gotejar; (*pipe, container, liquid etc*) vazar; (*gas*) escapar; (*fig*: *news*) vazar ♦ *vt* vazar; **the information was ~ed to the enemy** as informações foram passadas para o inimigo.
leak out *vi* vazar.
leakage ['liːkɪdʒ] *n* (*also*: *fig*) vazamento.
leaky ['liːkɪ] *adj* (*pipe, shoe, boat*) furado; (*roof*) com goteira.
lean [liːn] (*pt, pp* **~ed** *or* **leant**) *adj* magro ♦ *n* (*of meat*) carne *f* magra ♦ *vt*: **to ~ sth on** encostar *or* apoiar algo em ♦ *vi* (*slope*) inclinar-se; (*rest*): **to ~ against** encostar-se *or* apoiar-se contra; **to ~ on** encostar-se *or* apoiar-se em.
lean back *vi* (*move body*) inclinar-se para trás; (*against wall, in chair*) recostar-se.
lean forward *vi* inclinar-se para frente.
lean out *vi*: **to ~ out (of)** inclinar-se para fora (de).
lean over *vi* debruçar-se ♦ *vt fus* debruçar-

se sobre.

leaning ['liːnɪŋ] adj inclinado ♦ n: ~ **(towards)** inclinação f (para); **the L~ Tower of Pisa** a torre inclinada de Pisa.

leant [lɛnt] pt, pp of **lean**.

lean-to n alpendre m.

leap [liːp] (pt, pp ~ed or **leapt**) n salto, pulo ♦ vi saltar.

leap at vt fus: **to ~ at an offer** agarrar uma oferta.

leap up vi (person) levantar-se num ímpeto.

leapfrog ['liːpfrɔg] n jogo de pular carniça.

leapt [lɛpt] pt, pp of **leap**.

leap year n ano bissexto.

learn [ləːn] (pt, pp ~ed or **learnt**) vt aprender; (come to know of) saber, ficar sabendo ♦ vi aprender; **to ~ how to do sth** aprender a fazer algo; **we were sorry to ~ that ...** sentimos tomar conhecimento de que ...; **to ~ about sth** (SCH) instruir-se sobre algo; (hear) saber de algo.

learned ['ləːnɪd] adj erudito.

learner ['ləːnə*] n principiante m/f; (BRIT: also: ~ **driver**) (condutor(a) m/f) aprendiz m/f.

learning ['ləːnɪŋ] n (process) aprendizagem f; (quality) erudição f; (knowledge) saber m.

lease [liːs] n arrendamento ♦ vt arrendar, alugar; **on ~** em arrendamento.

lease back vt vender e alugar do comprador.

leaseback ['liːsbæk] n venda de uma propriedade com a condição do comprador alugá-la ao vendedor.

leasehold ['liːshəuld] n (contract) arrendamento ♦ adj arrendado.

leash [liːʃ] n correia.

least [liːst] adj: **the ~ + n** o/a menor; (smallest amount of) a menor quantidade de ♦ adv: **the ~ + adj** o/a menos ♦ pron: **not in the ~** de maneira nenhuma; **the ~ money** o menos dinheiro de todos; **the ~ expensive** o/a menos caro/a; **the ~ possible effort** o menor esforço possível; **at ~** pelo menos.

leather ['lɛðə*] n couro ♦ cpd de couro; ~ **goods** artigos mpl de couro.

leave [liːv] (pt, pp **left**) vt deixar; (go away from) abandonar ♦ vi ir-se, sair; (train) sair ♦ n (consent) permissão f, licença; (time off, MIL) licença; **to be left** sobrar; **there's some milk left over** sobrou um pouco de leite; **to ~ school** sair da escola; **~ it to me!** deixe comigo!; **on ~** de licença; **to take one's ~ of** despedir-se de; **~ of absence** licença excepcional.

leave behind vt (also fig) deixar para trás; (forget) esquecer.

leave off vt (lid, cover) não colocar; (heating) não ligar; (light) deixar apagado; (BRIT: inf: stop): **to ~ off (doing sth)** parar (de fazer algo).

leave on vt (coat etc) ficar com, não tirar;

(lid) não tirar; (light, fire) deixar aceso; (radio) deixar ligado.

leave out vt omitir.

leaves [liːvz] npl of **leaf**.

leavetaking ['liːvteɪkɪŋ] n despedida.

Lebanese [lɛbə'niːz] adj, n inv libanês/esa m/f.

Lebanon ['lɛbənən] n Líbano.

lecherous ['lɛtʃərəs] adj lascivo.

lectern ['lɛktəːn] n atril m.

lecture ['lɛktʃə*] n conferência, palestra; (SCH) aula ♦ vi dar aulas, lecionar ♦ vt (scold) passar um sermão em; **to give a ~ on** dar uma conferência sobre.

lecture hall n salão m de conferências, anfiteatro.

lecturer ['lɛktʃərə*] n conferencista m/f (BR), conferente m/f (PT); (BRIT: at university) professor(a) m/f; **assistant ~** (BRIT) assistente m/f; **senior ~** (BRIT) lente m/f.

lecture theatre n = **lecture hall**.

LED n abbr (= light-emitting diode) LED m.

led [lɛd] pt, pp of **lead**.

ledge [lɛdʒ] n (of window) peitoril m; (of mountain) saliência, proeminência.

ledger ['lɛdʒə*] n livro-razão m, razão m.

lee [liː] n sotavento; **in the ~ of** ao abrigo de.

leech [liːtʃ] n sanguessuga.

leek [liːk] n alho-poró m.

leer [lɪə*] vi: **to ~ at sb** olhar maliciosamente para alguém.

leeward ['liːwəd] adj de sotavento ♦ adv a sotavento ♦ n sotavento; **to ~** para sotavento.

leeway ['liːweɪ] n (fig): **to make up ~** reduzir o atraso; **to have some ~** ter certa liberdade de ação.

left [lɛft] pt, pp of **leave** ♦ adj esquerdo ♦ n esquerda ♦ adv à esquerda; **on the ~** à esquerda; **to the ~** para a esquerda; **the L~** (POL) a Esquerda.

left-hand drive (BRIT) n direção f do lado esquerdo.

left-handed [-'hændɪd] adj canhoto; (scissors etc) para canhotos.

left-hand side n esquerda, lado esquerdo.

leftist ['lɛftɪst] adj (POL) esquerdista.

left-luggage (office) (BRIT) n depósito de bagagem.

left-overs npl sobras fpl.

left wing n (MIL, SPORT) ala esquerda; (POL) esquerda ♦ adj: **left-wing** (POL) de esquerda, esquerdista.

left-winger n (POL) esquerdista m/f; (SPORT) ponta-esquerda m/f.

leg [lɛg] n perna; (of animal) pata; (of chair) pé m; (CULIN: of meat) perna; (of journey) etapa; **lst/2nd ~** (SPORT) primeiro/segundo turno; **to pull sb's ~** brincar or mexer com alguém; **to stretch one's ~s** esticar as pernas.

legacy ['lɛgəsɪ] n legado.

legal ['liːgl] adj (lawful, of law) legal; (terminology, enquiry etc) jurídico; **to take ~**

NB: European Portuguese adds the following consonants to certain words: **b** (sú(b)dito, su(b)til); **c** (a(c)ção, a(c)cionista, a(c)to); **m** (inde(m)ne); **p** (ado(p)ção, ado(p)tar); for further details see p. xiii.

proceedings *or* **action against sb** instaurar processo contra alguém.
legal adviser *n* consultor(a) *m/f* jurídico/a.
legality [lɪ'gælɪtɪ] *n* legalidade *f*.
legalize ['liːgəlaɪz] *vt* legalizar.
legally ['liːgəlɪ] *adv* legalmente; *(in terms of law)* de acordo com a lei.
legal tender *n* moeda corrente.
legation [lə'geɪʃən] *n* legação *f*.
legend ['lɛdʒənd] *n* lenda.
legendary ['lɛdʒəndərɪ] *adj* legendário.
-legged ['lɛgɪd] *suffix*: **two~** de duas patas *(or* pernas).
leggings ['lɛgɪŋz] *npl (overtrousers)* perneiras *fpl; (women's)* legging *f*.
legibility [lɛdʒɪ'bɪlɪtɪ] *n* legibilidade *f*.
legible ['lɛdʒəbl] *adj* legível.
legibly ['lɛdʒəblɪ] *adv* legivelmente.
legion ['liːdʒən] *n* legião *f*.
legionnaire [liːdʒə'nɛə*] *n* legionário; **~'s disease** doença rara parecida à pneumonia.
legislate ['lɛdʒɪsleɪt] *vi* legislar.
legislation [lɛdʒɪs'leɪʃən] *n* legislação *f*; **a piece of ~** uma lei.
legislative ['lɛdʒɪslətɪv] *adj* legislativo.
legislator ['lɛdʒɪsleɪtə*] *n* legislador(a) *m/f*.
legislature ['lɛdʒɪslətʃə*] *n* legislatura.
legitimacy [lɪ'dʒɪtɪməsɪ] *n* legitimidade *f*.
legitimate [lɪ'dʒɪtɪmət] *adj* legítimo.
legitimize [lɪ'dʒɪtɪmaɪz] *vt* legitimar.
leg-room *n* espaço para as pernas.
Leics *(BRIT) abbr* = **Leicestershire**.
leisure ['lɛʒə*] *n* lazer *m*; **at ~** desocupado, livre.
leisure centre *n* centro de lazer.
leisurely ['lɛʒəlɪ] *adj* calmo, vagaroso.
leisure suit *(BRIT) n* jogging *m*.
lemon ['lɛmən] *n* limão(-galego) *m*.
lemonade [lɛmə'neɪd] *n* limonada.
lemon cheese *n* coalho *or* pasta de limão.
lemon curd *n* coalho *or* pasta de limão.
lemon juice *n* suco *(BR) or* sumo *(PT)* de limão.
lemon squeezer [-'skwiːzə*] *n* espremedor *m* de limão.
lemon tea *n* chá *m* de limão.
lend [lɛnd] *(pt, pp* **lent)** *vt*: **to ~ sth to sb** emprestar algo a alguém; **to ~ a hand** dar uma ajuda.
lender ['lɛndə*] *n* emprestador(a) *m/f*.
lending library ['lɛndɪŋ] *n* biblioteca circulante.
length [lɛŋθ] *n* comprimento, extensão *f*; *(section: of road, pipe etc)* trecho; **~ of time** duração; **what ~ is it?** de que comprimento é?; **it is 2 metres in ~** tem dois metros de comprimento; **to fall full ~** cair estirado; **at ~** *(at last)* finalmente, afinal; *(lengthily)* por extenso; **to go to any ~(s) to do sth** fazer qualquer coisa para fazer algo.
lengthen ['lɛŋθən] *vt* encompridar, alongar ♦ *vi* encompridar-se.
lengthways ['lɛŋθweɪz] *adv* longitudinalmente, ao comprido.
lengthy ['lɛŋθɪ] *adj* comprido, longo; *(meet-*

ing) prolongado.
leniency ['liːnɪənsɪ] *n* indulgência.
lenient ['liːnɪənt] *adj* indulgente, clemente.
leniently ['liːnɪəntlɪ] *adv* com indulgência.
lens [lɛnz] *n (of spectacles)* lente *f*; *(of camera)* objetiva.
Lent [lɛnt] *n* Quaresma.
lent [lɛnt] *pt, pp of* **lend**.
lentil ['lɛntl] *n* lentilha.
Leo ['liːəu] *n* Leão *m*.
leopard ['lɛpəd] *n* leopardo.
leotard ['liːətɑːd] *n* collant *m*.
leper ['lɛpə*] *n* leproso/a.
leper colony *n* leprosário.
leprosy ['lɛprəsɪ] *n* lepra.
lesbian ['lɛzbɪən] *adj* lésbico ♦ *n* lésbica.
lesion ['liːʒən] *n (MED)* lesão *f*.
Lesotho [lɪ'suːtuː] *n* Lesoto.
less [lɛs] *adj* menos ♦ *pron, adv* menos; **~ than that/you** menos que isso/você; **~ than half** menos da metade; **~ than 1/a kilo/3 metres** menos de um/um quilo/3 metros; **~ and ~** cada vez menos; **the ~ he works ...** quanto menos trabalha ...; **income ~ expenses** renda menos despesas.
lessee [lɛ'siː] *n* arrendatário/a, locatário/a.
lessen ['lɛsn] *vi* diminuir, minguar ♦ *vt* diminuir, reduzir.
lesser ['lɛsə*] *adj* menor; **to a ~ extent** *or* **degree** nem tanto.
lesson ['lɛsn] *n* aula; *(in book etc)* lição *f*; **a maths ~** uma aula *or* uma lição de matemática; **to give ~s in** dar aulas de; **it taught him a ~** *(fig)* serviu-lhe de lição.
lessor ['lɛsə*] *n* arrendador(a) *m/f*, locador(a) *m/f*.
lest [lɛst] *conj*: **~ it happen** para que não aconteça; **I was afraid ~ he forget** temi que ele esquecesse.
let [lɛt] *(pt, pp* **let)** *vt (allow)* deixar; *(lease)* alugar; **to ~ sb do sth** deixar alguém fazer algo; **to ~ sb know sth** avisar alguém de algo; **he ~ me go** ele me deixou ir; **~ the water boil and ...** deixe ferver a água e ...; **~'s go!** vamos!; **~ him come!** deixa ele vir!; **"to ~"** "aluga-se".
let down *vt (lower)* abaixar; *(dress)* encompridar; *(BRIT: tyre)* esvaziar; *(hair)* soltar; *(disappoint)* desapontar.
let go *vt, vi* soltar.
let in *vt* deixar entrar; *(visitor etc)* fazer entrar; **what have you ~ yourself in for?** onde você foi se meter?
let off *vt (allow to leave)* deixar ir; *(not punish)* perdoar; *(subj: bus driver)* deixar (saltar); *(firework etc)* soltar; **to ~ off steam** *(fig)* desabafar.
let on *(inf) vt*: **to ~ on that ...** dizer por aí que ..., contar que ....
let out *vt* deixar sair; *(dress)* alargar; *(scream)* soltar; *(rent out)* alugar.
let up *vi* cessar, afrouxar.
let-down *n (disappointment)* decepção *f*.
lethal ['liːθl] *adj* letal; *(wound)* mortal.
lethargic [lɛ'θɑːdʒɪk] *adj* letárgico.

lethargy ['lεθədʒı] n letargia.
letter ['lεtə*] n (of alphabet) letra; (correspondence) carta; **small/capital** ~ minúscula/maiúscula; ~ **of credit** carta de crédito.
letter bomb n carta-bomba.
letterbox ['lεtəbɒks] (BRIT) n caixa do correio.
letterhead ['lεtəhεd] n cabeçalho.
lettering ['lεtərıŋ] n letras fpl.
letter opener n corta-papel m.
letterpress ['lεtəprεs] n (method) impressão f tipográfica.
letter quality n qualidade f carta.
letters patent n carta patente.
lettuce ['lεtıs] n alface f.
let-up n diminuição f, afrouxamento.
leukaemia [lu:'ki:mıə] (US **leukemia**) n leucemia.
level ['lεvl] adj (flat) plano; (flattened) nivelado; (uniform) uniforme ♦ adv no mesmo nível ♦ n nível m; (flat place) plano; (also: spirit ~) nível de bolha ♦ vt nivelar, aplanar; (gun) apontar; (accusation): **to** ~ **(against)** dirigir or lançar (contra) ♦ vi (inf): **to** ~ **with sb** ser franco com alguém; **"A"** ~s npl (BRIT) ≈ vestibular m; **"O"** ~s npl (BRIT) exames optativos feitos após o término do 1º Grau; **a** ~ **spoonful** (CULIN) uma colherada rasa; **to be** ~ **with** estar no mesmo nível que; **to draw** ~ **with** (team) empatar com; (runner, car) alcançar; **on the** ~ em nível; (fig: honest) sincero.
level off vi (prices etc) estabilizar-se ♦ vt (ground) nivelar, aplanar.
level out vi (prices etc) estabilizar-se ♦ vt (ground) nivelar, aplanar.
level crossing (BRIT) n passagem f de nível.
level-headed [-'hεdıd] adj sensato.
levelling ['lεvlıŋ] (US **leveling**) adj (process) de nivelamento; (effect) nivelador(a).
lever ['li:və*] n alavanca ♦ vt: **to** ~ **up** levantar com alavanca.
leverage ['li:vərıdʒ] n (fig: influence) influência.
levity ['lεvıtı] n leviandade f, frivolidade f.
levy ['lεvı] n imposto, tributo ♦ vt arrecadar, cobrar.
lewd [lu:d] adj obsceno, lascivo.
LI (US) abbr = **Long Island**.
liability [laıə'bılıtı] n responsabilidade f; (handicap) desvantagem f; **liabilities** npl (COMM) exigibilidades fpl, obrigações fpl; (on balance sheet) passivo.
liable ['laıəbl] adj (subject): ~ **to** sujeito a; (responsible): **to be** ~ **for** ser responsável por; **to be** ~ **to** (likely) ser capaz de; **to be** ~ **to a fine** ser passível de or sujeito a uma multa.
liaise [li:'eız] vi: **to** ~ **with** cooperar com.
liaison [li:'eızɒn] n (coordination) ligação f; (affair) relação f amorosa.
liar ['laıə*] n mentiroso/a.
libel ['laıbl] n difamação f ♦ vt caluniar, difa-

mar.
libellous ['laıbləs] (US **libelous**) adj difamatório.
liberal ['lıbərl] adj liberal; (generous): ~ **with** generoso com ♦ n: **L~** (POL) Liberal m/f.
liberality [lıbə'rælıtı] n (generosity) generosidade f.
liberalize ['lıbərəlaız] vt liberalizar.
liberal-minded adj liberal.
liberate ['lıbəreıt] vt liberar, libertar.
liberation [lıbə'reıʃən] n liberação f, libertação f.
Liberia [laı'bıərıə] n Libéria.
Liberian [laı'bıərıən] adj, n liberiano/a.
liberty ['lıbətı] n liberdade f; **to be at** ~ **to do** ser livre de fazer; **to take the** ~ **of doing sth** tomar a liberdade de fazer algo.
libido [lı'bi:dəu] n libido f.
Libra ['li:brə] n Libra, Balança.
librarian [laı'brεərıən] n bibliotecário/a.
library ['laıbrərı] n biblioteca.
library book n livro de biblioteca.
libretto [lı'brεtəu] n libreto.
Libya ['lıbıə] n Líbia.
Libyan ['lıbıən] adj, n líbio/a.
lice [laıs] npl of **louse**.
licence ['laısns] (US **license**) n (gen, COMM) licença; (also: **driving** ~ (BRIT), **driver's license** (US)) carteira de motorista (BR), carta de condução (PT); (excessive freedom) libertinagem f; **import** ~ licença de importação; **produced under** ~ fabricado sob licença.
licence number (BRIT) n (AUT) número da placa.
license ['laısns] n (US) = **licence** ♦ vt autorizar, licenciar; (car) licenciar.
licensed ['laısnst] adj (for alcohol) autorizado para vender bebidas alcoólicas.
licensee [laısən'si:] (BRIT) n (in a pub) dono/a.
license plate (esp US) n (AUT) placa (de identificação) (do carro).
licentious [laı'sεnʃəs] adj licencioso.
lichen ['laıkən] n líquen m.
lick [lık] vt lamber; (inf: defeat) arrasar, surrar ♦ n lambida; **a** ~ **of paint** uma mão de pintura.
licorice ['lıkərıs] n = **liquorice**.
lid [lıd] n (of box, case, pan) tampa; **to take the** ~ **off sth** (fig) desvendar algo.
lido ['laıdəu] n piscina pública ao ar livre.
lie [laı] (pt, pp ~**d**) n mentira ♦ vi (tell untruths) mentir; (pt **lay**, pp **lain**) (act) deitar-se; (state) estar deitado; (of object: be situated) estar, encontrar-se; **to** ~ **low** (fig) esconder-se; **to tell** ~**s** dizer mentiras, mentir.
lie about vi (things) estar espalhado; (people) vadiar.
lie around vi (things) estar espalhado; (people) vadiar.
lie back vi recostar-se.

NB: European Portuguese adds the following consonants to certain words: **b** (sú(b)dito, su(b)til); **c** (a(c)ção, a(c)cionista, a(c)to); **m** (inde(m)ne); **p** (ado(p)ção, ado(p)tar); for further details see p. xiii.

lie down *vi* deitar-se.
Liechtenstein ['lɪktənstaɪn] *n* Liechtenstein *m*.
lie detector *n* detector *m* de mentiras.
lie-down (*BRIT*) *n*: **to have a ~** descansar.
lie-in (*BRIT*) *n*: **to have a ~** dormir até tarde.
lieu [luː]: **in ~ of** *prep* em vez de.
Lieut. *abbr* (= *lieutenant*) Ten.
lieutenant [lɛf'tɛnənt, (*US*) luː'tɛnənt] *n* (*MIL*) tenente *m*.
lieutenant-colonel *n* tenente-coronel *m*.
life [laɪf] (*pl* **lives**) *n* vida ♦ *cpd* (*imprisonment*) perpétuo; (*style*) de vida; **true to ~** fiel à realidade; **to paint from ~** pintar copiando a natureza; **to be sent to prison for ~** ser condenado a prisão perpétua; **country/city ~** vida campestre/urbana.
life annuity *n* renda vitalícia.
life assurance (*BRIT*) *n* seguro de vida.
lifebelt ['laɪfbɛlt] (*BRIT*) *n* cinto salva-vidas.
lifeblood ['laɪfblʌd] *n* (*fig*) força vital.
lifeboat ['laɪfbəut] *n* barco salva-vidas.
lifebuoy ['laɪfbɔɪ] *n* bóia salva-vidas.
life expectancy *n* expectativa de vida.
lifeguard ['laɪfgɑːd] *n* (guarda *m*) salva-vidas *m/f*.
life imprisonment *n* prisão *f* perpétua.
life insurance *n* seguro de vida.
life jacket *n* colete *m* salva-vidas.
lifeless ['laɪflɪs] *adj* sem vida; (*dull*) sem graça.
lifelike ['laɪflaɪk] *adj* natural.
lifeline ['laɪflaɪn] *n* corda salva-vidas.
lifelong ['laɪflɔŋ] *adj* vitalício, perpétuo.
life preserver [-prɪ'zəːvə*] (*US*) *n* colete *m* salva-vidas.
life-raft *n* balsa salva-vidas.
life-saver [-'seɪvə*] *n* (guarda *m*) salva-vidas *m/f*.
life sentence *n* pena de prisão perpétua.
life-sized [-saɪzd] *adj* de tamanho natural.
life span *n* vida, duração *f*.
life style *n* estilo de vida.
life support system *n* (*MED*) sistema *m* de respiração artificial.
lifetime ['laɪftaɪm] *n*: **in his ~** durante a sua vida; **once in a ~** uma vez na vida; **the chance of a ~** uma oportunidade única.
lift [lɪft] *vt* levantar; (*steal*) roubar ♦ *vi* (*fog*) dispersar-se, dissipar-se ♦ *n* (*BRIT*: *elevator*) elevador *m*; **to give sb a ~** (*BRIT*) dar uma carona para alguém (*BR*), dar uma boleia a alguém (*PT*).
lift off *vi* (*rocket, helicopter*) decolar.
lift out *vt* tirar; (*troops etc*) evacuar de avião *or* helicóptero.
lift up *vt* levantar.
lift-off ['lɪftɔf] *n* decolagem *f*.
ligament ['lɪgəmənt] *n* ligamento.
light [laɪt] (*pt, pp* **~ed** *or* **lit**) *n* luz *f*; (*lamp*) luz, lâmpada; (*daylight*) luz do) dia *m*; (*headlight*) farol *m*; (*rear ~*) luz traseira; (*traffic ~*) sinal *m*; (*for cigarette etc*): **have you got a ~?** tem fogo? ♦ *vt* (*candle, cigarette, fire*) acender; (*room*) iluminar ♦ *adj* (*colour, room*) claro; (*not heavy, also: fig*)

leve ♦ *adv* (*travel*) com pouca bagagem; **to turn the ~ on/off** acender/apagar a luz; **to cast** *or* **shed** *or* **throw ~ on** esclarecer; **to come to ~** vir à tona; **in the ~ of ...** à luz de ...; **to make ~ of sth** (*fig*) não levar algo a sério, fazer pouco caso de algo.
light up *vi* (*smoke*) acender um cigarro; (*face*) iluminar-se ♦ *vt* (*illuminate*) iluminar; (*cigarette etc*) acender.
light bulb *n* lâmpada.
lighten ['laɪtən] *vi* (*grow light*) clarear ♦ *vt* (*give light to*) iluminar; (*make lighter*) clarear; (*make less heavy*) tornar mais leve.
lighter ['laɪtə*] *n* (*also: cigarette ~*) isqueiro, acendedor *m*; (*boat*) chata.
light-fingered [-'fɪŋgəd] *adj* gatuno; **to be ~** ter mão leve.
light-headed [-'hɛdɪd] *adj* (*dizzy*) aturdido, tonto; (*excited*) exaltado; (*by nature*) estouvado.
light-hearted *adj* alegre, despreocupado.
lighthouse ['laɪthaus] (*irreg*) *n* farol *m*.
lighting ['laɪtɪŋ] *n* (*act, system*) iluminação *f*.
lighting-up time (*BRIT*) *n* hora oficial do anoitecer.
lightly ['laɪtlɪ] *adv* (*touch*) ligeiramente; (*thoughtlessly*) despreocupadamente; (*slightly*) levemente; (*not seriously*) levianamente; **to get off ~** conseguir se safar, livrar a cara (*inf*).
light meter *n* (*PHOT*) fotômetro.
lightness ['laɪtnɪs] *n* claridade *f*; (*in weight*) leveza.
lightning ['laɪtnɪŋ] *n* relâmpago, raio.
lightning conductor (*US* **lightning rod**) *n* pára-raios *m inv*.
lightning strike (*BRIT*) *n* greve *f* relâmpago.
light pen *n* caneta leitora.
lightship ['laɪtʃɪp] *n* navio-farol *m*.
lightweight ['laɪtweɪt] *adj* (*suit*) leve; (*BOXING*) peso-leve.
light year *n* ano-luz *m*.
like [laɪk] *vt* gostar de ♦ *prep* como ♦ *adj* parecido, semelhante ♦ *n*: **the ~** coisas *fpl* parecidas; **his ~s and dislikes** seus gostos e aversões; **I would ~, I'd ~** (eu) gostaria de; **would you ~ a coffee?** você quer um café?; **to be** *or* **look ~ sb/sth** parecer-se com alguém/algo, parecer alguém/algo; **what's he ~?** como é que ele é?; **what's the weather ~?** como está o tempo?; **that's just ~ him** é típico dele; **something ~ that** uma coisa dessas; **I feel ~ a drink** estou com vontade de tomar um drinque; **if you ~** se você quiser; **it is nothing ~ ...** não se parece nada com ....
likeable ['laɪkəbl] *adj* simpático, agradável.
likelihood ['laɪklɪhud] *n* probabilidade *f*.
likely ['laɪklɪ] *adj* provável; (*excuse*) plausível; **he's ~ to leave** é provável que ele se vá; **not ~!** (*inf*) nem morto!
like-minded *adj* da mesma opinião.
liken ['laɪkən] *vt*: **to ~ sth to sth** comparar algo com algo.
likeness ['laɪknɪs] *n* semelhança.

likewise ['laɪkwaɪz] *adv* igualmente.
liking ['laɪkɪŋ] *n*: **to take a ~ to sb** simpatizar com alguém; **to his ~** ao seu gosto.
lilac ['laɪlək] *n* lilás *m* ♦ *adj* (*colour*) de cor lilás.
lilt [lɪlt] *n* cadência.
lilting ['lɪltɪŋ] *n* cadenciado.
lily ['lɪlɪ] *n* lírio, açucena; **~ of the valley** lírio-do-vale *m*.
Lima ['liːmə] *n* Lima.
limb [lɪm] *n* membro; **to be out on a ~** (*fig*) estar isolado.
limber up ['lɪmbə*-] *vi* (*SPORT*) fazer aquecimento.
limbo ['lɪmbəu] *n*: **to be in ~** (*fig*) viver na expectativa.
lime [laɪm] *n* (*tree*) limeira; (*fruit*) limão *m*; (*GEO*) cal *f*.
lime juice *n* suco (*BR*) *or* sumo (*PT*) de limão.
limelight ['laɪmlaɪt] *n*: **to be in the ~** (*fig*) ser o centro das atenções.
limerick ['lɪmərɪk] *n* quintilha humorística.
limestone ['laɪmstəun] *n* pedra calcária.
limit ['lɪmɪt] *n* limite *m* ♦ *vt* limitar; **weight/ speed ~** limite de peso/de velocidade.
limitation [lɪmɪ'teɪʃən] *n* limitação *f*.
limited ['lɪmɪtɪd] *adj* limitado; **to be ~ to** limitar-se a; **~ edition** edição *f* limitada.
limited (liability) company (*BRIT*) *n* ≈ sociedade *f* anônima.
limitless ['lɪmɪtlɪs] *adj* ilimitado.
limousine ['lɪməziːn] *n* limusine *f*.
limp [lɪmp] *n*: **to have a ~** mancar, ser coxo ♦ *vi* mancar ♦ *adj* frouxo.
limpet ['lɪmpɪt] *n* lapa.
limpid ['lɪmpɪd] *adj* límpido, cristalino.
linchpin ['lɪntʃpɪn] *n* cavilha; (*fig*) pivô *m*.
Lincs [lɪŋks] (*BRIT*) *abbr* = **Lincolnshire**.
line [laɪn] *n* linha; (*straight ~*) reta; (*rope*) corda; (*for fishing*) linha; (*US: queue*) fila (*BR*), bicha (*PT*); (*wire*) fio; (*row*) fila, fileira; (*of writing*) linha; (*on face*) ruga; (*speciality*) ramo (de negócio); (*COMM: type of goods*) linha ♦ *vt*: **to ~ (with)** (*coat etc*) forrar (de); **to ~ the streets** ladear as ruas; **to cut in ~** (*US*) furar a fila (*BR*), pôr-se à frente (*PT*); **in his ~ of business** no ramo dele; **on the right ~s** no caminho certo; **a new ~ in cosmetics** uma nova linha de cosméticos; **hold the ~ please** (*BRIT: TEL*) não desligue; **to be in ~ for sth** estar na bica para algo; **in ~ with** de acordo com; **to bring sth into ~ with sth** alinhar algo com algo; **to draw the ~ at doing sth** (*fig*) recusar-se a fazer algo; **to take the ~ that** ... ser de opinião que ....
line up *vi* enfileirar-se ♦ *vt* enfileirar; (*set up, have ready*) preparar, arranjar; **to have sth/sb ~d up** ter algo programado/alguém em vista.
linear ['lɪnɪə*] *adj* linear.
lined [laɪnd] *adj* (*face*) enrugado; (*paper*) pau-

tado; (*clothes*) forrado.
line feed *n* (*COMPUT*) entrelinha.
linen ['lɪnɪn] *n* roupa branca *or* de cama; (*cloth*) linho.
line printer *n* impressora de linha.
liner ['laɪnə*] *n* navio de linha regular.
linesman ['laɪnzmən] (*irreg*) *n* (*SPORT*) juiz *m* de linha.
line-up *n* formação *f* em linha, alinhamento; (*players*) escalação *f*.
linger ['lɪŋgə*] *vi* demorar-se, retardar-se; (*smell, tradition*) persistir.
lingerie ['lænʒəriː] *n* lingerie *f*, roupa de baixo (de mulher).
lingering ['lɪŋgərɪŋ] *adj* persistente; (*death*) lento, vagaroso.
lingo ['lɪŋgəu] (*pl ~es*) (*pej*) *n* língua.
linguist ['lɪŋgwɪst] *n* lingüista *m/f*.
linguistic [lɪŋ'gwɪstɪk] *adj* lingüístico.
linguistics [lɪŋ'gwɪstɪks] *n* lingüística.
lining ['laɪnɪŋ] *n* forro; (*TECH*) revestimento; (: *of brakes*) lona.
link [lɪŋk] *n* (*of a chain*) elo; (*connection*) conexão *f*; (*bond*) vínculo, laço ♦ *vt* vincular, unir; **~s** *npl* campo de golfe; **rail ~** ligação ferroviária.
link up *vt* acoplar ♦ *vi* unir-se.
link-up *n* ligação *f*; (*in space*) acoplamento; (*of roads*) junção *f*, confluência; (*RADIO, TV*) transmissão *f* em rede.
lino ['laɪnəu] *n* = **linoleum**.
linoleum [lɪ'nəuliəm] *n* linóleo.
linseed oil ['lɪnsiːd-] *n* óleo de linhaça.
lint [lɪnt] *n* fibra de algodão; (*thread*) fio.
lintel ['lɪntl] *n* verga.
lion ['laɪən] *n* leão *m*.
lion cub *n* filhote *m* de leão.
lioness ['laɪənɪs] *n* leoa.
lip [lɪp] *n* lábio; (*of jug*) bico; (*of cup etc*) borda; (*insolence*) insolência.
lipread ['lɪpriːd] (*irreg*) *vi* ler os lábios.
lip salve *n* pomada para os lábios.
lip service *n*: **to pay ~ to sth** devotar-se a *or* elogiar algo falsamente.
lipstick ['lɪpstɪk] *n* batom *m*.
liquefy ['lɪkwɪfaɪ] *vt* liquefazer ♦ *vi* liquefazer-se.
liqueur [lɪ'kjuə*] *n* licor *m*.
liquid ['lɪkwɪd] *adj, n* líquido.
liquid assets *npl* ativo disponível, disponibilidades *fpl*.
liquidate ['lɪkwɪdeɪt] *vt* liquidar.
liquidation [lɪkwɪ'deɪʃən] *n*: **to go into ~** entrar em liquidação.
liquidation sale (*US*) *n* liquidação *f* (por motivo de fechamento).
liquidator ['lɪkwɪdeɪtə*] *n* liquidador(a) *m/f*.
liquid crystal display *n* display *m* digital em cristal líquido.
liquidity [lɪ'kwɪdətɪ] *n* (*COMM*) liquidez *f*.
liquidize ['lɪkwɪdaɪz] (*BRIT*) *vt* (*CULIN*) liqüidificar, passar no liqüidificador.

NB: *European Portuguese adds the following consonants to certain words:* **b** (sú(b)dito, su(b)til); **c** (a(c)ção, a(c)cionista, a(c)to); **m** (inde(m)ne); **p** (ado(p)ção, ado(p)tar); *for further details see p. xiii.*

liquidizer ['lɪkwɪdaɪzə*] (BRIT) n (CULIN) liqüi-dificador m.

liquor ['lɪkə*] n licor m, bebida alcoólica.

liquorice ['lɪkərɪs] (BRIT) n alcaçuz m.

Lisbon ['lɪzbən] n Lisboa.

lisp [lɪsp] n ceceio ♦ vi cecear, falar com a língua presa.

lissom ['lɪsəm] adj gracioso, ágil.

list [lɪst] n lista; (of ship) inclinação f ♦ vt (write down) fazer uma lista or relação de; (enumerate) enumerar; (COMPUT) listar ♦ vi (ship) inclinar-se, adernar; **shopping** ~ lista de compras.

listed building ['lɪstɪd-] n prédio tombado.

listed company ['lɪstɪd-] n ≈ sociedade f de capital aberto, sociedade cotada na Bolsa.

listen ['lɪsn] vi escutar, ouvir; (pay attention) prestar atenção; **to** ~ **to** escutar.

listener ['lɪsnə*] n ouvinte m/f.

listing ['lɪstɪŋ] n (COMPUT) listagem f.

listless ['lɪstlɪs] adj apático, indiferente.

listlessly ['lɪstlɪslɪ] adv apaticamente.

list price n preço de tabela.

lit [lɪt] pt, pp of **light**.

litany ['lɪtənɪ] n ladainha, litania.

liter ['liːtə*] (US) n = **litre**.

literacy ['lɪtərəsɪ] n capacidade f de ler e es-crever, alfabetização f; ~ **campaign** campanha de alfabetização.

literal ['lɪtərl] adj literal.

literally ['lɪtərəlɪ] adv literalmente.

literary ['lɪtərərɪ] adj literário.

literate ['lɪtərət] adj alfabetizado, instruído; (fig) culto, letrado.

literature ['lɪtərɪtʃə*] n literatura; (brochures etc) folhetos mpl.

lithe [laɪð] adj ágil, flexível.

lithography [lɪ'θɔgrəfɪ] n litografia.

Lithuania [lɪθju'eɪnɪə] n Lituânia.

litigate ['lɪtɪgeɪt] vt, vi litigar.

litigation [lɪtɪ'geɪʃən] n litígio.

litmus paper ['lɪtməs-] n papel m de tornassol.

litre ['liːtə*] (US liter) n litro.

litter ['lɪtə*] n (rubbish) lixo; (paper) papéis mpl; (young animals) ninhada; (stretcher) maca, padiola ♦ vt (subj: person) jogar lixo em; (: papers etc) estar espalhado por; ~**ed with** (scattered) semeado de; (covered) co-berto de.

litter bin (BRIT) n lata de lixo.

litterbug ['lɪtəbʌg] n sujismundo.

litter lout (BRIT) n = **litterbug**.

little ['lɪtl] adj (small) pequeno; (not much) pouco; often translated by suffix: eg ~ **house** casinha ♦ adv pouco; **a** ~ um pouco (de); ~ **milk** pouco leite; **a** ~ **milk** um pouco de leite; **for a** ~ **while** por um instante; **with** ~ **difficulty** com pouca dificuldade; **as** ~ **as possible** o menos possível; ~ **by** ~ pouco a pouco; **to make** ~ **of** fazer pouco de.

little finger n dedo mindinho.

liturgy ['lɪtədʒɪ] n liturgia.

live [vi, vt lɪv, adj laɪv] vi viver; (reside) mo-rar ♦ vt (a life) levar; (experience) viver ♦

adj (animal) vivo; (wire) eletrizado; (broadcast) ao vivo; (shell) carregado; **to** ~ **in London** morar em Londres; **to** ~ **together** viver juntos; ~ **ammunition** munição de guerra.

live down vt redimir.

live in vi (maid) dormir no emprego; (stu-dent, nurse) ser interno/a.

live off vt fus (land, fish etc) viver de; (pej: parents etc) viver às custas de.

live on vt fus (food) viver de, alimentar-se de ♦ vi continuar vivo; **to** ~ **on £50 a week** viver com £50 por semana.

live out vi (BRIT: student) ser externo ♦ vt: **to** ~ **out one's days** or **life** viver o resto de seus dias.

live up (inf) vt: **to** ~ **it up** cair na farra.

live up to vt fus (fulfil) cumprir; (justify) justificar.

livelihood ['laɪvlɪhud] n meio de vida, sub-sistência.

liveliness ['laɪvlɪnɛs] n vivacidade f.

lively ['laɪvlɪ] adj vivo; (talk) animado; (pace) rápido; (party, tune) alegre.

liven up ['laɪvn-] vt (room) dar nova vida a; (discussion, evening) animar.

liver ['lɪvə*] n (ANAT) fígado.

liverish ['lɪvərɪʃ] adj (fig) rabugento, mal-humorado.

Liverpudlian [lɪvə'pʌdlɪən] adj de Liverpool ♦ n natural m/f de Liverpool.

livery ['lɪvərɪ] n libré f.

lives [laɪvz] npl of **life**.

livestock ['laɪvstɔk] n gado.

livid ['lɪvɪd] adj lívido; (furious) furioso.

living ['lɪvɪŋ] adj (alive) vivo ♦ n: **to earn** or **make a** ~ ganhar a vida; **cost of** ~ custo de vida; **within** ~ **memory** na memória de pessoas ainda vivas.

living conditions npl condições fpl de vida.

living expenses npl despesas fpl para sobre-vivência quotidiana.

living room n sala de estar.

living standards npl padrão m or nível m de vida.

living wage n salário de subsistência.

lizard ['lɪzəd] n lagarto.

llama ['lɑːmə] n lhama.

LLB n abbr (= Bachelor of Laws) título uni-versitário.

LLD n abbr (= Doctor of Laws) título universi-tário.

LMT (US) abbr (= Local Mean Time) hora lo-cal.

load [ləud] n carga; (weight) peso ♦ vt (gen, COMPUT) carregar; (fig) cumular, encher; **a** ~ **of**, ~**s of** (fig) um monte de, uma porção de.

loaded ['ləudɪd] adj (dice) viciado; (question, word) intencionado; (inf: rich) cheio da nota; (: drunk) de porre.

loading bay ['ləudɪŋ-] n vão m de carrega-mento.

loaf [ləuf] (pl loaves) n (bisnaga de) pão m ♦ vi (also: ~ about, ~ around) vadiar, vagabundar.

loam [ləum] n marga.

loan [ləun] n empréstimo ♦ vt emprestar; **on** ~ emprestado; **to raise a** ~ levantar um empréstimo.

loan account n conta de empréstimo.

loan capital n capital-obrigações m.

loath [ləuθ] adj: **to be** ~ **to do sth** estar pouco inclinado a or relutar em fazer algo.

loathe [ləuð] vt detestar, odiar.

loathing ['ləuðɪŋ] n ódio; **it fills me with** ~ me dá (um) ódio.

loathsome ['ləuðsəm] adj repugnante, asqueroso.

loaves [ləuvz] npl of **loaf**.

lob [lɔb] n (TENNIS) lobe m ♦ vt: **to** ~ **the ball** dar um lobe.

lobby ['lɔbɪ] n vestíbulo, saguão m; (POL: pressure group) grupo de pressão, lobby m ♦ vt pressionar.

lobbyist ['lɔbɪɪst] n membro de um grupo de pressão.

lobe [ləub] n lóbulo.

lobster ['lɔbstə*] n lagostim m; (large) lagosta.

lobster pot n armadilha para pegar lagosta.

local ['ləukl] adj local ♦ n (BRIT: inf: pub) bar m (local); **the** ~**s** npl os moradores locais.

local anaesthetic (US **local anesthetic**) n anestesia local.

local authority n município.

local call n (TEL) ligação f local.

local government n administração f municipal.

locality [ləu'kælɪtɪ] n localidade f.

localize ['ləukəlaɪz] vt localizar.

locally ['ləukəlɪ] adv nos arredores, na vizinhança.

locate [ləu'keɪt] vt (find) localizar, situar; (situate) colocar.

location [ləu'keɪʃən] n local m, posição f; **on** ~ (CINEMA) em externas.

loch [lɔx] n lago.

lock [lɔk] n (of door, box) fechadura; (of canal) eclusa; (of hair) anel m, mecha ♦ vt (with key) trancar; (immobilize) travar ♦ vi (door etc) fechar-se à chave; (wheels) travar-se; ~ **stock and barrel** (fig) com tudo; **on full** ~ (BRIT: AUT) com o volante virado ao máximo.

lock away vt (valuables) guardar a sete chaves; (person) encarcerar.

lock in vt trancar dentro.

lock out vt trancar no lado de fora; (on purpose) deixar na rua; (: workers) recusar trabalho a.

lock up vi fechar tudo.

locker ['lɔkə*] n compartimento com chave.

locket ['lɔkɪt] n medalhão m.

lockjaw ['lɔkdʒɔː] n trismo.

lockout ['lɔkaut] n greve f de patrões, lockout m.

locksmith ['lɔksmɪθ] n serralheiro/a.

lock-up n (prison) prisão f; (cell) cela; (also: ~ garage) compartimento seguro.

locomotive [ləukə'məutɪv] n locomotiva.

locum ['ləukəm] n (MED) (médico/a) interino/a.

locust ['ləukəst] n gafanhoto.

lodge [lɔdʒ] n casa do guarda, guarita; (porter's) portaria; (FREEMASONRY) loja ♦ vi (person): **to** ~ **(with)** alojar-se (na casa de) ♦ vt (complaint) apresentar; **to** ~ **(itself) in/between** cravar-se em/entre.

lodger ['lɔdʒə*] n inquilino/a, hóspede m/f.

lodging ['lɔdʒɪŋ] n alojamento; ~**s** npl quarto (mobiliado); see also **board**.

lodging house (BRIT: irreg) n casa de hóspedes.

loft [lɔft] n sótão m.

lofty ['lɔftɪ] adj alto, elevado; (haughty) altivo, arrogante; (sentiments, aims) nobre.

log [lɔg] n (of wood) tronco, lenho; (book) = **logbook** ♦ n abbr (= logarithm) log m ♦ vt registrar.

log in vi (COMPUT) iniciar o uso, logar.

log on vi (COMPUT) iniciar o uso, logar.

log off vi (COMPUT) encerrar o uso, dar logoff.

log out vi (COMPUT) encerrar o uso, dar logoff.

logarithm ['lɔgərɪðəm] n logaritmo.

logbook ['lɔgbuk] n (NAUT) diário de bordo; (AVIAT) diário de vôo; (of car) documentação f (do carro).

log cabin n cabana de madeira.

log fire n fogueira.

loggerheads ['lɔgəhɛdz] npl: **at** ~ **(with)** às turras (com).

logic ['lɔdʒɪk] n lógica.

logical ['lɔdʒɪkl] adj lógico.

logically ['lɔdʒɪkəlɪ] adv logicamente.

logistics [lɔ'dʒɪstɪks] n logística.

logo ['ləugəu] n logotipo.

loin [lɔɪn] n (CULIN) (carne de) lombo; ~**s** npl lombos mpl.

loin cloth n tanga.

loiter ['lɔɪtə*] vi perder tempo; (pej) vadiar, vagabundar.

loll [lɔl] vi (also: ~ about) refestelar-se, reclinar-se.

lollipop ['lɔlɪpɔp] n pirulito (BR), chupa-chupa m (PT); (iced) picolé m.

lollipop lady (BRIT) n mulher que ajuda as crianças a atravessarem a rua.

lollipop man (BRIT: irreg) n homem que ajuda as crianças a atravessarem a rua.

lollop ['lɔləp] (BRIT) vi andar com pachorra.

London ['lʌndən] n Londres.

Londoner ['lʌndənə*] n londrino/a.

lone [ləun] adj solitário.

loneliness ['ləunlɪnɪs] n solidão f, isolamento.

lonely ['ləunlɪ] adj (person) só; (place, childhood) solitário, isolado; **to feel** ~

NB: European Portuguese adds the following consonants to certain words: **b** (sú(b)dito, su(b)til); **c** (a(c)ção, a(c)cionista, a(c)to); **m** (inde(m)ne); **p** (ado(p)ção, ado(p)tar); for further details see p. xiii.

sentir-se só.

loner ['ləunə*] *n* solitário/a.

lonesome ['ləunsəm] *adj* (*person*) só; (*place*, *childhood*) solitário.

long [lɒŋ] *adj* comprido, longo ♦ *adv* muito tempo ♦ *n*: **the ~ and the short of it is that** ... (*fig*) em poucas palavras ... ♦ *vi*: **to ~ for sth** ansiar *or* suspirar por algo; **he had ~ understood that** ... fazia muito tempo que ele entendia ...; **how ~ is the street?** qual é a extensão da rua?; **how ~ is the lesson?** quanto dura a lição?; **6 metres ~** de 6 metros de extensão, que mede 6 metros; **6 months ~** de 6 meses de duração, que dura 6 meses; **all night ~** a noite inteira; **he no ~er comes** ele não vem mais; **~ before** muito antes; **before ~** (+ *future*) dentro de pouco; (+ *past*) pouco tempo depois; **~ ago** há muito tempo atrás; **don't be ~!** não demore!; **I shan't be ~** não vou demorar; **at ~ last** por fim, no final; **in the ~ run** no final de contas; **so** *or* **as ~ as** contanto que.

long-distance *adj* (*race*) de longa distância; (*call*) interurbano.

long-haired *adj* (*person*) cabeludo; (*animal*) peludo.

longhand ['lɒŋhænd] *n* escrita usual.

longing ['lɒŋɪŋ] *n* desejo, anseio; (*nostalgia*) saudade *f* ♦ *adj* saudoso.

longingly ['lɒŋɪŋlɪ] *adv* ansiosamente; (*nostalgically*) saudosamente.

longitude ['lɒŋgɪtjuːd] *n* longitude *f*.

long johns [-dʒɒnz] *npl* ceroulas *fpl*.

long jump *n* salto em distância.

long-lost *adj* perdido há muito (tempo).

long-playing record [-'pleɪɪŋ-] *n* elepê *m* (*BR*), LP *m* (*PT*).

long-range *adj* de longo alcance; (*weather forecast*) a longo prazo.

longshoreman ['lɒŋʃɔːmən] (*US*: *irreg*) *n* estivador *m*, portuário.

long-sighted *adj* (*BRIT*) presbita; (*fig*) previdente.

long-standing *adj* de muito tempo.

long-suffering *adj* paciente, resignado.

long-term *adj* a longo prazo.

long wave *n* (*RADIO*) onda longa.

long-winded [-'wɪndɪd] *adj* prolixo, cansativo.

loo [luː] (*BRIT*: *inf*) *n* banheiro (*BR*), casa de banho (*PT*).

loofah ['luːfə] *n* tipo de esponja.

look [luk] *vi* olhar; (*seem*) parecer; (*building etc*): **to ~ south/on to the sea** dar para o sul/o mar ♦ *n* olhar *m*; (*glance*) olhada, vista de olhos; (*appearance*) aparência, aspecto; (*style*) visual *m*; **~s** *npl* físico, aparência; **to ~ like sb** parecer-se com alguém; **it ~s like him** parece ele; **it ~s about 4 metres long** parece ter uns 4 metros de comprimento; **it ~s all right to me** para mim está bem; **to have a ~ at sth** dar uma olhada em algo; **to have a ~ for sth** procurar algo; **to ~ ahead** olhar para a frente; (*fig*) pensar no futuro.

look after *vt fus* cuidar de; (*luggage etc*: *watch over*) ficar de olho em.

look around *vi* olhar em torno; (*in shop*) dar uma olhada.

look at *vt fus* olhar (para); (*consider*) considerar.

look back *vi*: **to ~ back at sth/sb** voltar-se para ver algo/alguém; **to ~ back on** (*event*, *period*) recordar, rever.

look down on *vt fus* (*fig*) desdenhar, desprezar.

look for *vt fus* procurar.

look forward to *vt fus* aguardar com prazer, ansiar por; **to ~ forward to doing sth** não ver a hora de fazer algo; **I'm not ~ing forward to it** não estou nada animado com isso; **~ing forward to hearing from you** (*in letter*) no aguardo de suas notícias.

look in *vi*: **to ~ in on sb** dar uma passada na casa de alguém.

look into *vt fus* investigar.

look on *vi* assistir.

look out *vi* (*beware*): **to ~ out (for)** tomar cuidado (com).

look out for *vt fus* (*seek*) procurar; (*await*) esperar.

look over *vt* (*essay*) dar uma olhada em; (*town*, *building*) visitar; (*person*) olhar da cabeça aos pés.

look round *vi* virar a cabeça, voltar-se; **to ~ round for sth** procurar algo.

look through *vt fus* (*papers*, *book*) examinar; (: *briefly*) folhear; (*telescope*) olhar através de.

look to *vt fus* cuidar de; (*rely on*) contar com.

look up *vi* levantar os olhos; (*improve*) melhorar ♦ *vt* (*word*) procurar; (*friend*) visitar.

look up to *vt fus* admirar, respeitar.

look-out *n* (*tower etc*) posto de observação, guarita; (*person*) vigia *m*; **to be on the ~ for sth** estar na expectativa de algo.

look-up table *n* (*COMPUT*) tabela de pesquisa.

LOOM (*US*) *n abbr* (= *Loyal Order of Moose*) *associação beneficente*.

loom [luːm] *n* tear *m* ♦ *vi* assomar-se; (*threaten*) ameaçar.

loony ['luːnɪ] (*inf*) *adj* meio doido ♦ *n* debil *m*/*f* mental.

loony bin (*inf*) *n* hospício, manicômio.

loop [luːp] *n* laço; (*bend*) volta, curva; (*contraceptive*) DIU *m*.

loophole ['luːphəul] *n* escapatória.

loose [luːs] *adj* (*not fixed*) solto; (*not tight*) frouxo; (*animal*) solto; (*clothes*) folgado; (*morals*, *discipline*) relaxado; (*sense*) impreciso ♦ *vt* (*free*) soltar; (*slacken*) afrouxar; **~ connection** (*ELEC*) conexão solta; **to be at a ~ end** (*BRIT*) *or* **at ~ ends** (*US*) (*fig*) não ter o que fazer; **to tie up ~ ends (of sth)** (*fig*) amarrar (algo).

loose change *n* trocado.

loose-fitting *adj* (*clothes*) folgado, largo.

loose-leaf *adj*: **~ binder** *or* **folder** pasta de folhas soltas.

loose-limbed [-'lɪmd] *adj* ágil.

loosely ['luːslɪ] *adv* frouxamente, folgada-

mente; *(not closely)* aproximativamente.
loosen ['luːsən] *vt (free)* soltar; *(untie)* desatar; *(slacken)* afrouxar.
loosen up *vi (before game)* aquecer; *(inf: relax)* descontrair-se.
loot [luːt] *n* saque *m*, despojo ♦ *vt* saquear, pilhar.
looter ['luːtə*] *n* saqueador(a) *m/f*.
looting ['luːtɪŋ] *n* saque *m*, pilhagem *f*.
lop off [lɔp-] *vt* cortar; *(branches)* podar.
lop-sided [-'saɪdɪd] *adj* desequilibrado, torto.
lord [lɔːd] *n* senhor *m*; **L~ Smith** Lord Smith; **the L~** *(REL)* o Senhor; **the (House of) L~s** *(BRIT)* a Câmara dos Lordes.
lordly ['lɔːdlɪ] *adj* senhorial; *(arrogant)* arrogante.
lordship ['lɔːdʃɪp] *(BRIT)* *n*: **Your L~** Vossa senhoria.
lore [lɔː*] *n* sabedoria popular, tradições *fpl*.
lorry ['lɔrɪ] *(BRIT)* *n* caminhão *m (BR)*, camião *m (PT)*.
lorry driver *(BRIT)* *n* caminhoneiro *(BR)*, camionista *m/f (PT)*.
lorry load *(BRIT)* *n* carga de caminhão.
lose [luːz] *(pt, pp* **lost)** *vt, vi* perder; **to ~ (time)** *(clock)* atrasar-se; **to ~ no time (in doing sth)** não demorar (a fazer algo); **to get lost** *(person)* perder-se; *(thing)* extraviar-se.
loser ['luːzə*] *n* perdedor(a) *m/f*; **to be a good/bad ~** ser bom/mau perdedor.
loss [lɔs] *n* perda; **to cut one's ~es** reduzir os prejuízos; **to make a ~** sair com prejuízo; **to sell sth at a ~** vender algo com prejuízo; **to be at a ~** estar perplexo; **to be at a ~ to do** ser incapaz de fazer; **to be a dead ~** ser totalmente inútil.
loss adjuster *n (INSURANCE)* árbitro regulador de avarias.
loss leader *n (COMM)* chamariz *m*.
lost [lɔst] *pt, pp of* **lose** ♦ *adj* perdido; **~ in thought** perdido em seus pensamentos; **~ and found property** *(US)* (objetos *mpl*) perdidos e achados *mpl*; **~ and found** *(US)* (seção *f* de) perdidos e achados *mpl*.
lost property *(BRIT)* *n* (objetos *mpl*) perdidos e achados *mpl*; **~ office** *or* **department** (seção *f* de) perdidos e achados *mpl*.
lot [lɔt] *n (at auctions)* lote *m*; *(destiny)* destino, sorte *f*; **the ~** tudo, todos/as; **a ~** muito, bastante; **a ~ of, ~s of** muito(s); **to draw ~s** tirar à sorte; **I read a ~** leio bastante; **parking ~** *(US)* estacionamento.
lotion ['ləʊʃən] *n* loção *f*.
lottery ['lɔtərɪ] *n* loteria.
loud [laʊd] *adj (voice)* alto; *(shout)* forte; *(noisy)* barulhento; *(gaudy)* berrante ♦ *adv* alto; **out ~** alto.
loudhailer [laud'heɪlə*] *(BRIT)* *n* megafone *m*.
loudly ['laʊdlɪ] *adv (noisily)* ruidosamente; *(aloud)* em voz alta.
loudspeaker [laud'spiːkə*] *n* alto-falante *m*.

lounge [laundʒ] *n* sala de estar *f*; *(of airport)* salão *m* ♦ *vi* recostar-se, espreguiçar-se.
lounge bar *n* bar *m* social.
lounge suit *(BRIT)* *n* terno *(BR)*, fato *(PT)*.
louse [laus] *(pl* **lice)** *n* piolho.
louse up *(inf)* *vt* estragar.
lousy ['lauzɪ] *adj (fig)* ruim, péssimo.
lout [laut] *n* rústico, grosseiro.
louvre ['luːvə*] *(US* **louver)** *adj*: **~ door** porta de veneziana; **~ window** veneziana.
lovable ['lʌvəbl] *adj* adorável, simpático.
love [lʌv] *n* amor *m* ♦ *vt* amar, adorar; **I ~ coffee** adoro o café; **to ~ to do** gostar muito de fazer; **I'd ~ to come** gostaria muito de ir; **"15 ~"** *(TENNIS)* "15 a zero"; **to be in ~ with** estar apaixonado por; **to fall in ~ with sb** apaixonar-se por alguém; **to make ~** fazer amor; **~ at first sight** amor à primeira vista; **for the ~ of** pelo amor de; **to send one's ~ to sb** mandar um abraço para alguém; **~ from Anne, ~, Anne** um abraço *or* um beijo, Anne.
love affair *n* aventura (amorosa), caso (de amor).
love letter *n* carta de amor.
love life *(irreg)* *n* vida sentimental.
lovely ['lʌvlɪ] *adj (delightful)* encantador(a), delicioso; *(beautiful)* lindo, belo; *(holiday, surprise)* muito agradável, maravilhoso; **we had a ~ time** foi maravilhoso, nós nos divertimos muito.
lover ['lʌvə*] *n* amante *m/f*; *(amateur)*: **a ~ of** um(a) apreciador(a) de *or* um(a) amante de.
lovesick ['lʌvsɪk] *adj* perdido de amor.
lovesong ['lʌvsɔŋ] *n* canção *f* de amor.
loving ['lʌvɪŋ] *adj* carinhoso, afetuoso.
low [ləʊ] *adj, adv* baixo ♦ *n (METEOROLOGY)* área de baixa pressão ♦ *vi (cow)* mugir; **to feel ~** sentir-se deprimido; **to turn (down) ~** *vt* baixar, diminuir; **to reach a new** *or* **an all-time ~** cair para o seu nível mais baixo.
lowbrow ['ləʊbrau] *adj* sem pretensões intelectuais.
low-calorie *adj* baixo em calorias, de baixo teor calórico.
low-cut *adj (dress)* decotado.
low-down *n (inf)*: **he gave me the ~ on it** me deu a dica sobre isso ♦ *adj (mean)* vil, desprezível.
lower1 ['ləʊə*] *vt* abaixar; *(reduce)* reduzir, diminuir; **to ~ o.s. to** *(fig)* rebaixar-se a.
lower2 ['lauə*] *vi (sky, clouds)* escurecer; *(person)*: **to ~ at sb** olhar para alguém com raiva.
low-fat *adj* magro.
low-grade *adj* de baixa qualidade.
low-key *adj* discreto.
lowland ['ləʊlənd] *n* planície *f*.
low-level *adj* de baixo nível, baixo; *(flying)* a baixa altura.
lowly ['ləʊlɪ] *adj* humilde.

NB: *European Portuguese adds the following consonants to certain words:* **b** (sú(b)dito, su(b)til); **c** (a(c)ção, a(c)cionista, a(c)to); **m** (inde(m)ne); **p** (ado(p)ção, ado(p)tar); *for further details see p. xiii.*

low-lying *adj* de baixo nível.
low-paid *adj* (*person*) de renda baixa; (*work*) mal pago.
loyal ['lɔɪəl] *adj* leal.
loyalist ['lɔɪəlɪst] *n* legalista *m/f*.
loyalty ['lɔɪəltɪ] *n* lealdade *f*.
lozenge ['lɔzɪndʒ] *n* (*MED*) pastilha; (*GEOM*) losango, rombo.
LP *n abbr* = **long-playing record**.
L-plates ['ɛlpleɪts] (*BRIT*) *npl* placas *fpl* de aprendiz de motorista.
LPN (*US*) *n abbr* (= *Licensed Practical Nurse*) enfermeiro/a diplomado/a.
LRAM (*BRIT*) *n abbr* = **Licentiate of the Royal Academy of Music**.
LSAT (*US*) *n abbr* = **Law Schools Admissions Test**.
LSD *n abbr* (= *lysergic acid diethylamide*) LSD *m*; (*BRIT*: = *pounds, shillings and pence*) sistema monetário usado na Grã-Bretanha até 1971.
LSE *n abbr* = **London School of Economics**.
LT *abbr* (*ELEC*: = *low tension*) BT.
Lt. *abbr* (= *lieutenant*) Ten.
Ltd (*BRIT*) *abbr* (= *limited* (*liability*) *company*) SA.
lubricant ['lu:brɪkənt] *n* lubrificante *m*.
lubricate ['lu:brɪkeɪt] *vt* lubrificar.
lucid ['lu:sɪd] *adj* lúcido.
lucidity [lu:'sɪdɪtɪ] *n* lucidez *f*.
luck [lʌk] *n* sorte *f*; **bad** ~ azar *m*; **to be in** ~ ter *or* dar sorte; **to be out of** ~ ter azar; **good** ~! boa sorte!
luckily ['lʌkɪlɪ] *adv* por sorte, felizmente.
lucky ['lʌkɪ] *adj* (*person*) sortudo; (*coincidence*) feliz; (*number etc*) da sorte.
lucrative ['lu:krətɪv] *adj* lucrativo.
ludicrous ['lu:dɪkrəs] *adj* ridículo.
ludo ['lu:dəu] *n* ludo.
lug [lʌg] *vt* (*drag*) arrastar; (*pull*) puxar.
luggage ['lʌgɪdʒ] *n* bagagem *f*.
luggage car (*US*) *n* (*RAIL*) vagão *m* de bagagens.
luggage rack *n* (*in train*) rede *f* para bagagem; (*on car*) porta-bagagem *m*, bagageiro.
luggage van (*BRIT*) *n* (*RAIL*) vagão *m* de bagagens.
lugubrious [lu'gu:brɪəs] *adj* lúgubre.
lukewarm ['lu:kwɔ:m] *adj* morno, tépido; (*fig*) indiferente.
lull [lʌl] *n* calmaria ♦ *vt* (*child*) embalar, acalentar; (*person, fear*) acalmar.
lullaby ['lʌləbaɪ] *n* canção *f* de ninar.
lumbago [lʌm'beɪgəu] *n* lumbago.
lumber ['lʌmbə*] *n* (*junk*) trastes *mpl* velhos; (*wood*) madeira serrada, tábua ♦ *vt* (*BRIT*: *inf*): **to** ~ **sb with sth/sb** empurrar algo/ alguém para cima de alguém ♦ *vi* (*also*: ~ *about*, ~ *along*) mover-se pesadamente.
lumberjack ['lʌmbədʒæk] *n* madeireiro, lenhador *m*.
lumber room (*BRIT*) *n* quarto de despejo.
lumber yard *n* depósito de madeira.
luminous ['lu:mɪnəs] *adj* luminoso.
lump [lʌmp] *n* torrão *m*; (*fragment*) pedaço;

(*in sauce*) caroço; (*in throat*) nó *m*; (*swelling*) galo, caroço ♦ *vt* (*also*: ~ *together*) amontoar.
lump sum *n* quantia global.
lumpy ['lʌmpɪ] *adj* (*sauce*) encaroçado.
lunacy ['lu:nəsɪ] *n* loucura.
lunar ['lu:nə*] *adj* lunar.
lunatic ['lu:nətɪk] *adj*, *n* louco/a.
lunatic asylum *n* manicômio, hospício.
lunch [lʌntʃ] *n* almoço ♦ *vi* almoçar; **to invite sb for** ~ convidar alguém para almoçar.
luncheon ['lʌntʃən] *n* almoço formal.
luncheon meat *n* bolo de carne.
luncheon voucher *n* vale *m* para refeição, ticket *m* restaurante.
lunch hour *n* hora do almoço.
lunchtime ['lʌntʃtaɪm] *n* hora do almoço.
lung [lʌŋ] *n* pulmão *m*.
lung cancer *n* câncer *m* (*BR*) *or* cancro (*PT*) de pulmão.
lunge [lʌndʒ] *vi* (*also*: ~ *forward*) dar estocada *or* bote; **to** ~ **at** arremeter-se contra.
lupin ['lu:pɪn] *n* tremoço.
lurch [lə:tʃ] *vi* balançar ♦ *n* sacudida, solavanco; **to leave sb in the** ~ deixar alguém em apuros, deixar alguém na mão (*inf*).
lure [luə*] *n* (*bait*) isca; (*decoy*) chamariz *m*, engodo ♦ *vt* atrair, seduzir.
lurid ['luərɪd] *adj* (*account*) sensacional; (*detail*) horrível.
lurk [lə:k] *vi* (*hide*) esconder-se; (*wait*) estar à espreita.
luscious ['lʌʃəs] *adj* delicioso.
lush [lʌʃ] *adj* exuberante.
lust [lʌst] *n* luxúria; (*greed*) cobiça.
  lust after *vt fus* cobiçar.
luster ['lʌstə*] (*US*) *n* = **lustre**.
lustful ['lʌstful] *adj* lascivo, sensual.
lustre ['lʌstə*] (*US* **luster**) *n* lustre *m*, brilho.
lusty ['lʌstɪ] *adj* robusto, forte.
lute [lu:t] *n* alaúde *m*.
Luxembourg ['lʌksəmbə:g] *n* Luxemburgo.
luxuriant [lʌg'zjuərɪənt] *adj* luxuriante, exuberante.
luxurious [lʌg'zjuərɪəs] *adj* luxuoso.
luxury ['lʌkʃərɪ] *n* luxo ♦ *cpd* de luxo.
LV (*BRIT*) *n abbr* = **luncheon voucher**.
LW *abbr* (*RADIO*: = *long wave*) OL.
lying ['laɪɪŋ] *n* mentira(s) *f*(*pl*) ♦ *adj* mentiroso, falso.
lynch [lɪntʃ] *vt* linchar.
lynching ['lɪntʃɪŋ] *n* linchamento.
lynx [lɪŋks] *n* lince *m*.
lyre ['laɪə*] *n* lira.
lyric ['lɪrɪk] *adj* lírico.
lyrical ['lɪrɪkəl] *adj* lírico.
lyricism ['lɪrɪsɪzəm] *n* lirismo.
lyrics ['lɪrɪks] *npl* (*of song*) letra.

M

M, m [εm] *n* (*letter*) M, m *m*; **M for Mary** (*BRIT*) *or* **Mike** (*US*) M de Maria.
M *n abbr* (*BRIT*: = *motorway*): **the M8** ≈ BR 8 *f*; (= *medium*) M.
m *abbr* (= *metre*) m; (= *mile*) mil.; = **million.**
MA *abbr* (*SCH*) = **Master of Arts**; (*US*) = **military academy**; (: *POST*) = **Massachusetts.**
mac [mæk] (*BRIT*) *n* capa impermeável.
macabre [mə'kɑːbrə] *adj* macabro.
Macao [mə'kau] *n* Macau.
macaroni [mækə'rəunɪ] *n* macarrão *m*.
macaroon [mækə'ruːn] *n* biscoitinho de amêndoas.
mace [meɪs] *n* (*BOT*) macis *m*; (*sceptre*) bastão *m*.
machinations [mækɪ'neɪʃənz] *npl* maquinações *fpl*, intrigas *fpl*.
machine [mə'ʃiːn] *n* máquina ♦ *vt* (*dress etc*) costurar à máquina; (*TECH*) usinar.
machine code *n* (*COMPUT*) código de máquina.
machine gun *n* metralhadora.
machine language *n* (*COMPUT*) linguagem *f* de máquina.
machine readable *adj* (*COMPUT*) legível por máquina.
machinery [mə'ʃiːnərɪ] *n* maquinaria; (*fig*) mecanismo.
machine shop *n* oficina mecânica.
machine tool *n* máquina-ferramenta *f*.
machine washable *adj* (*garment*) lavável à máquina.
machinist [mə'ʃiːnɪst] *n* operário/a (de máquina); (*RAIL*) maquinista *m/f*.
macho ['mætʃəu] *adj* machista.
mackerel ['mækrl] *n inv* cavala.
mackintosh ['mækɪntɔʃ] (*BRIT*) *n* capa impermeável.
macro... ['mækrəu] *prefix* macro....
macro-economics *n* macroeconomia.
mad [mæd] *adj* louco; (*angry*) furioso, brabo; **to go ~** enlouquecer; **to be ~ (keen) about** *or* **on sth** (*inf*) ser louco por algo.
madam ['mædəm] *n* senhora, madame *f*; **yes, ~** sim, senhora; **M~ Chairman** Senhora Presidente; **can I help you, ~?** a senhora já foi atendida?
madden ['mædn] *vt* exasperar.
maddening ['mædnɪŋ] *adj* exasperante.
made [meɪd] *pt, pp of* **make**.

Madeira [mə'dɪərə] *n* (*GEO*) Madeira; (*wine*) (vinho) Madeira *m*.
Madeiran [mə'dɪərən] *adj, n* madeirense *m/f*.
made-to-measure (*BRIT*) *adj* feito sob medida.
madly ['mædlɪ] *adv* loucamente.
madman ['mædmən] (*irreg*) *n* louco.
madness ['mædnɪs] *n* loucura.
Madrid [mə'drɪd] *n* Madri (*BR*), Madrid (*PT*).
Mafia ['mæfɪə] *n* máfia.
mag. [mæg] (*BRIT*: *inf*) *n abbr* = **magazine** (*PRESS*).
magazine [mægə'ziːn] *n* (*PRESS*) revista; (*MIL*: *store*) depósito; (*of firearm*) câmara.
magazine rack *n* porta-revistas *m inv*.
maggot ['mægət] *n* larva de inseto.
magic ['mædʒɪk] *n* magia, mágica ♦ *adj* mágico.
magical ['mædʒɪkl] *adj* mágico.
magician [mə'dʒɪʃən] *n* mago/a; (*entertainer*) mágico/a.
magistrate ['mædʒɪstreɪt] *n* magistrado/a, juiz/juíza *m/f*.
magnanimous [mæg'nænɪməs] *adj* magnânimo.
magnate ['mægneɪt] *n* magnata *m*.
magnesium [mæg'niːzɪəm] *n* magnésio.
magnet ['mægnɪt] *n* ímã *m*, iman *m* (*PT*).
magnetic [mæg'nɛtɪk] *adj* magnético.
magnetic disk *n* (*COMPUT*) disco magnético.
magnetic tape *n* fita magnética.
magnetism ['mægnɪtɪzəm] *n* magnetismo.
magnification [mægnɪfɪ'keɪʃən] *n* aumento.
magnificence [mæg'nɪfɪsns] *n* magnificência.
magnificent [mæg'nɪfɪsnt] *adj* magnífico.
magnify ['mægnɪfaɪ] *vt* aumentar.
magnifying glass ['mægnɪfaɪɪŋ-] *n* lupa, lente *f* de aumento.
magnitude ['mægnɪtjuːd] *n* magnitude *f*.
magnolia [mæg'nəulɪə] *n* magnólia.
magpie ['mægpaɪ] *n* pega.
mahogany [mə'hɔgənɪ] *n* mogno, acaju *m* ♦ *cpd* de mogno *or* acaju.
maid [meɪd] *n* empregada; **old ~** (*pej*) solteirona.
maiden ['meɪdn] *n* moça, donzela ♦ *adj* (*aunt etc*) solteirona; (*speech, voyage*) inaugural.
maiden name *n* nome *m* de solteira.
mail [meɪl] *n* correio; (*letters*) cartas *fpl* ♦ *vt* (*post*) pôr no correio; (*send*) mandar pelo correio; **by ~** pelo correio.
mailbox ['meɪlbɔks] *n* (*US*: *for letters*) caixa do correio; (*COMPUT*) caixa de entrada.
mailing list ['meɪlɪŋ-] *n* lista de clientes, mailing list *m*.
mailman ['meɪlmæn] (*US*: *irreg*) *n* carteiro.
mail order *n* pedido por reembolso postal; (*business*) venda por correspondência ♦ *cpd*: **mail-order firm** *or* **house** firma de vendas por correspondência.
mailshot ['meɪlʃɔt] (*BRIT*) *n* mailing *m*.
mail train *n* trem-correio, trem *m* postal.

NB: European Portuguese adds the following consonants to certain words: **b** (sú(b)dito, su(b)til); **c** (a(c)ção, a(c)cionista, a(c)to); **m** (inde(m)ne); **p** (ado(p)ção, ado(p)tar); *for further details see p. xiii.*

mail truck (*US*) *n* (*AUT*) = **mail van**.
mail van (*BRIT*) *n* (*AUT*) furgão *m* do correio; (*RAIL*) vagão *m* postal.
maim [meɪm] *vt* mutilar, aleijar.
main [meɪn] *adj* principal ♦ *n* (*pipe*) cano *or* esgoto principal; **the ~s** *npl* (*ELEC*) a rede elétrica; **in the ~** na maior parte.
main course *n* (*CULIN*) prato principal.
mainframe ['meɪnfreɪm] *n* (*also:* ~ **computer**) mainframe *m*.
mainland ['meɪnlənd] *n* continente *m*.
mainline ['meɪnlaɪn] (*inf*) *vt* (*heroin*) picar-se com ♦ *vi* picar-se, aplicar-se.
main line *n* (*RAIL*) linha-tronco *f* ♦ *adj*: **main-line** de linha-tronco.
mainly ['meɪnlɪ] *adv* principalmente.
main road *n* estrada principal.
mainstay ['meɪnsteɪ] *n* (*fig*) esteio.
mainstream ['meɪnstriːm] *n* (*fig*) corrente *f* principal.
maintain [meɪn'teɪn] *vt* manter; (*keep up*) conservar (em bom estado); (*affirm*) sustentar, afirmar; **to ~ that ...** afirmar que ....
maintenance ['meɪntənəns] *n* manutenção *f*; (*LAW: alimony*) alimentos *mpl*, pensão *f* alimentícia.
maintenance contract *n* contrato de assistência técnica.
maintenance order *n* (*LAW*) ordem *f* de pensão.
maisonette [meɪzə'nɛt] (*BRIT*) *n* duplex *m*.
maize [meɪz] *n* milho.
Maj. *abbr* (*MIL*) = **major**.
majestic [mə'dʒɛstɪk] *adj* majestoso.
majesty ['mædʒɪstɪ] *n* majestade *f*.
major ['meɪdʒə*] *n* (*MIL*) major *m* ♦ *adj* (*main*) principal; (*considerable*) importante; (*great*) grande; (*MUS*) maior ♦ *vi* (*US: SCH*): **to ~ (in)** especializar-se (em); **a ~ operation** (*MED*) uma operação séria.
Majorca [mə'jɔːkə] *n* Maiorca.
major general *n* (*MIL*) general-de-divisão *m*.
majority [mə'dʒɒrɪtɪ] *n* maioria ♦ *cpd* (*verdict, holding*) majoritário.
make [meɪk] (*pt, pp* **made**) *n* marca ♦ *vt* fazer; (*manufacture*) fabricar, produzir; (*cause to be*): **to ~ sb sad** entristecer alguém, fazer alguém ficar triste; (*force*): **to ~ sb do sth** fazer com que alguém faça algo; (*equal*): **2 and 2 ~ 4** dois e dois são quatro; **to ~ do with** contentar-se com; **to ~ it** (*in time etc*) chegar; (*succeed*) ter sucesso; **what time do you ~ it?** que horas você tem?; **to ~ good** *vi* (*succeed*) dar-se bem ♦ *vt* (*losses*) indenizar; **to ~ a profit/loss** ter um lucro/uma perda.
make for *vt fus* (*place*) dirigir-se a.
make off *vi* fugir.
make out *vt* (*decipher*) decifrar; (*understand*) compreender; (*see*) divisar, avistar; (*write out: prescription*) escrever; (: *form, cheque*) preencher; (*claim, imply*) afirmar; (*pretend*) fazer de conta; **to ~ out a case for sth** argumentar em favor de algo,

defender algo.
make over *vt* (*assign*): **to ~ over (to)** transferir (para).
make up *vt* (*invent*) inventar; (*parcel*) embrulhar ♦ *vi* reconciliar-se; (*with cosmetics*) maquilar-se (*PT:* -lha-); **to be made up of** compor-se de, ser composto de; **to ~ up one's mind** decidir-se.
make up for *vt fus* compensar.
make-believe *adj* fingido, simulado ♦ *n*: **a world of ~** um mundo de faz-de-conta; **it's just ~** é pura ilusão.
maker ['meɪkə*] *n* fabricante *m/f*.
makeshift ['meɪkʃɪft] *adj* provisório.
make-up ['meɪkʌp] *n* maquilagem (*PT:* -lha-) *f*.
make-up bag *n* bolsa de maquilagem (*PT:* -lha-).
make-up remover *n* desmaquilante (*PT:* -lha-) *m*.
making ['meɪkɪŋ] *n* (*fig*): **in the ~** em vias de formação; **he has the ~s of an actor** ele tem tudo para ser ator.
maladjusted [mælə'dʒʌstɪd] *adj* inadaptado, desajustado.
malaise [mæ'leɪz] *n* mal-estar *m*, indisposição *f*.
malaria [mə'lɛərɪə] *n* malária.
Malawi [mə'lɑːwɪ] *n* Malavi *m*.
Malay [mə'leɪ] *adj* malaio ♦ *n* malaio/a; (*LING*) malaio.
Malaya [mə'leɪə] *n* Malaia.
Malayan [mə'leɪən] *adj, n* = **Malay**.
Malaysia [mə'leɪzɪə] *n* Malaísia (*BR*), Malásia (*PT*).
Malaysian [mə'leɪzɪən] *adj, n* malásio/a.
Maldives ['mɔːldaɪvz] *npl*: **the ~** as ilhas Maldivas.
male [meɪl] *n* (*BIO, ELEC*) macho ♦ *adj* (*sex, attitude*) masculino; (*animal*) macho; (*child etc*) do sexo masculino.
male chauvinist *n* machista *m*.
male nurse *n* enfermeiro.
malevolence [mə'lɛvələns] *n* malevolência.
malevolent [mə'lɛvələnt] *adj* malévolo.
malfunction [mæl'fʌŋkʃən] *n* funcionamento defeituoso.
malice ['mælɪs] *n* (*ill will*) malícia; (*rancour*) rancor *m*.
malicious [mə'lɪʃəs] *adj* malicioso, mal-intencionado; (*LAW*) com intenção criminosa.
malign [mə'laɪn] *vt* caluniar, difamar.
malignant [mə'lɪgnənt] *adj* (*MED*) maligno.
malingerer [mə'lɪŋgərə*] *n* doente *m/f* fingido/a.
mall [mɔːl] *n* (*also: shopping ~*) shopping *m*.
malleable ['mælɪəbl] *adj* maleável.
mallet ['mælɪt] *n* maço, marreta.
malnutrition [mælnjuː'trɪʃən] *n* desnutrição *f*.
malpractice [mæl'præktɪs] *n* falta profissional.
malt [mɔːlt] *n* malte *m* ♦ *cpd*: ~ **whisky** uísque *m* de malte.
Malta ['mɔːltə] *n* Malta.
Maltese [mɔːl'tiːz] *adj* maltês/esa ♦ *n inv* maltês/esa *m/f*; (*LING*) maltês *m*.

maltreat [mæl'triːt] *vt* maltratar.
mammal ['mæml] *n* mamífero.
mammoth ['mæməθ] *n* mamute *m* ♦ *adj* gigantesco, imenso.
man [mæn] (*pl* **men**) *n* homem *m*; (*CHESS*) peça ♦ *vt* (*NAUT*) tripular; (*MIL*) guarnecer; **an old** ~ um velho; **a young** ~ um jovem; ~ **and wife** marido e mulher.
manacles ['mænəklz] *npl* grilhões *mpl*.
manage ['mænɪdʒ] *vi* arranjar-se, virar-se ♦ *vt* (*be in charge of*) dirigir, administrar; (*business*) gerenciar; (*device*) manusear; (*carry*) carregar; **to** ~ **to do sth** conseguir fazer algo; **to** ~ **without sb/sth** passar sem alguém/algo; **can you** ~? você consegue?
manageable ['mænɪdʒəbl] *adj* manejável; (*task etc*) viável.
management ['mænɪdʒmənt] *n* administração *f*, direção *f*, gerência; "**under new** ~" "sob nova direção".
management accounting *n* contabilidade *f* administrativa *or* gerencial.
management consultant *n* consultor(a) *m/f* em administração.
manager ['mænɪdʒə*] *n* gerente *m/f*; (*SPORT*) técnico/a; (*of project*) superintendente *m/f*; (*of department*, *unit*) chefe *m/f*, diretor(a) *m/f*; (*of artist*) empresário/a; **sales** ~ gerente de vendas.
manageress [mænɪdʒə'rɛs] *n* gerente *f*.
managerial [mænə'dʒɪərɪəl] *adj* administrativo, gerencial.
managing director ['mænɪdʒɪŋ-] *n* diretor(a) *m/f* geral, diretor-gerente/diretora-gerente *m/f*.
Mancunian [mæŋ'kjuːnɪən] *adj* de Manchester ♦ *n* natural *m/f* de Manchester.
mandarin ['mændərɪn] *n* (*also:* ~ *orange*) tangerina; (*person*) mandarim *m*.
mandate ['mændeɪt] *n* mandato.
mandatory ['mændətərɪ] *adj* obrigatório; (*powers etc*) mandatório.
mandolin(e) ['mændəlɪn] *n* bandolim *m*.
mane [meɪn] *n* (*of horse*) crina; (*of lion*) juba.
maneuver *etc* [mə'nuːvə*] (*US*) = **manoeuvre** *etc*.
manfully ['mænfəlɪ] *adv* valentemente.
manganese ['mæŋɡəniːz] *n* manganês *m*.
mangle ['mæŋɡl] *vt* mutilar, estropiar ♦ *n* calandra.
mango ['mæŋɡəu] (*pl* ~**es**) *n* manga.
mangrove ['mæŋɡrəuv] *n* mangue *m*.
mangy ['meɪndʒɪ] *adj* sarnento, esfarrapado.
manhandle ['mænhændl] *vt* (*mistreat*) maltratar; (*move by hand*) manipular.
manhole ['mænhəul] *n* poço de inspeção.
manhood ['mænhud] *n* (*adulthood*) idade *f* adulta; (*masculinity*) virilidade *f*.
man-hour *n* hora-homem *f*.
manhunt ['mænhʌnt] *n* caça ao homem.
mania ['meɪnɪə] *n* mania.
maniac ['meɪnɪæk] *n* maníaco/a; (*fig*) louco/a.

manic ['mænɪk] *adj* maníaco.
manic-depressive *adj*, *n* maníaco-depressivo/a.
manicure ['mænɪkjuə*] *n* manicure (*PT*: -cura) *f* ♦ *vt* (*person*) fazer as unhas a.
manicure set *n* estojo de manicure (*PT*: -cura).
manifest ['mænɪfɛst] *vt* manifestar, mostrar ♦ *adj* manifesto, evidente ♦ *n* (*AVIAT*, *NAUT*) manifesto.
manifestation [mænɪfɛs'teɪʃən] *n* manifestação *f*.
manifesto [mænɪ'fɛstəu] (*pl* ~**s** *or* ~**es**) *n* manifesto.
manifold ['mænɪfəuld] *adj* múltiplo ♦ *n* (*AUT etc*) *see* **exhaust**.
Manila [mə'nɪlə] *n* Manilha.
manila [mə'nɪlə] *adj*: ~ **paper** papel-manilha *m*.
manipulate [mə'nɪpjuleɪt] *vt* manipular, manejar.
manipulation [mənɪpju'leɪʃən] *n* manipulação *f*.
mankind [mæn'kaɪnd] *n* humanidade *f*, raça humana.
manliness ['mænlɪnɪs] *n* virilidade *f*.
manly ['mænlɪ] *adj* másculo, viril.
man-made *adj* sintético, artificial.
manna ['mænə] *n* maná *m*.
mannequin ['mænɪkɪn] *n* manequim *m*.
manner ['mænə*] *n* modo, maneira; (*behaviour*) conduta, comportamento; (*type*) espécie *f*, gênero; (**good**) ~**s** *npl* boas maneiras *fpl*, educação *f*; **bad** ~**s** falta de educação; **all** ~ **of** todo tipo de.
mannerism ['mænərɪzəm] *n* maneirismo, hábito.
mannerly ['mænəlɪ] *adj* polido, educado.
manoeuvrable [mə'nuːvrəbl] (*US* **maneuverable**) *adj* manobrável.
manoeuvre [mə'nuːvə*] (*US* **maneuver**) *vt*, *vi* manobrar ♦ *n* manobra; **to** ~ **sb into doing sth** induzir alguém a fazer algo.
manor ['mænə*] *n* (*also*: ~ *house*) casa senhorial, solar *m*.
manpower ['mænpauə*] *n* potencial *m* humano, mão-de-obra.
manservant ['mænsəvənt] (*pl* **menservants**) *n* criado.
mansion ['mænʃən] *n* mansão *f*, palacete *m*.
manslaughter ['mænslɔːtə*] *n* homicídio involuntário.
mantelpiece ['mæntlpiːs] *n* consolo da lareira.
mantle ['mæntl] *n* manto; (*fig*) camada.
man-to-man *adj*, *adv* de homem para homem.
manual ['mænjuəl] *adj* manual ♦ *n* manual *m*; (*MUS*) teclado.
manual worker *n* trabalhador(a) *m/f* braçal.
manufacture [mænju'fæktʃə*] *vt* manufaturar, fabricar ♦ *n* fabricação *f*.
manufactured goods [mænju'fæktʃəd-] *npl*

NB: European Portuguese adds the following consonants to certain words: **b** (sú(b)dito, su(b)til); **c** (a(c)ção, a(c)cionista, a(c)to); **m** (inde(m)ne); **p** (ado(p)ção, ado(p)tar); *for further details see p. xiii.*

produtos *mpl* industrializados.

manufacturer [mænju'fæktʃərə*] *n* fabricante *m/f*.

manufacturing industries [mænju'fæktʃərɪŋ] *npl* indústrias *fpl* de transformação.

manure [mə'njuə*] *n* estrume *m*, adubo.

manuscript ['mænjuskrɪpt] *n* manuscrito.

many ['mɛnɪ] *adj*, *pron* muitos/as; **how ~?** quantos/as?; **a great ~** muitíssimos; **twice as ~** *adj* duas vezes mais ♦ *pron* o dobro; **~ a time** muitas vezes.

map [mæp] *n* mapa *m* ♦ *vt* fazer o mapa de.
map out *vt* traçar; (*fig*: *career, holiday*) planejar.

maple ['meɪpl] *n* bordo.

mar [mɑ:*] *vt* estragar.

Mar. *abbr* = **March**.

marathon ['mærəθən] *n* maratona ♦ *adj*: **a ~ session** uma sessão exaustiva.

marathon runner *n* corredor(a) *m/f* de maratona, maratonista *m/f*.

marauder [mə'rɔ:də*] *n* saqueador(a) *m/f*.

marble ['mɑ:bl] *n* mármore *m*; (*toy*) bola de gude; **~s** *n* (*game*) jogo de gude.

March [mɑ:tʃ] *n* março; *see also* **July**.

march [mɑ:tʃ] *vi* (*MIL*) marchar; (*demonstrators*) desfilar ♦ *n* marcha; (*demonstration*) passeata; **to ~ out of/into** *etc* sair de/entrar em *etc* marchando.

marcher ['mɑ:tʃə*] *n* (*demonstrator*) manifestante *m/f*.

marching ['mɑ:tʃɪŋ] *n*: **to give sb his ~ orders** (*fig*) dar um bilhete azul a alguém, mandar passear alguém.

march-past *n* desfile *m*.

mare [mɛə*] *n* égua.

marg. [mɑ:dʒ] (*inf*) *n abbr* = **margarine**.

margarine [mɑ:dʒə'ri:n] *n* margarina.

margin ['mɑ:dʒɪn] *n* margem *f*.

marginal ['mɑ:dʒɪnl] *adj* marginal; **~ seat** (*POL*) cadeira ganha por pequena maioria.

marginally ['mɑ:dʒɪnəlɪ] *adv* ligeiramente.

marigold ['mærɪɡəuld] *n* malmequer *m*.

marijuana [mærɪ'wɑ:nə] *n* maconha.

marina [mə'ri:nə] *n* marina.

marinade [*n* mærɪ'neɪd, *vt* 'mærɪneɪd] *n* escabeche *m* ♦ *vt* = **marinate**.

marinate ['mærɪneɪt] *vt* marinar, pôr em escabeche.

marine [mə'ri:n] *adj* (*in the sea*) marinho; (*of seafaring*) marítimo ♦ *n* fuzileiro naval.

marine insurance *n* seguro marítimo.

marital ['mærɪtl] *adj* matrimonial, marital; **~ status** estado civil.

maritime ['mærɪtaɪm] *adj* marítimo.

maritime law *n* direito marítimo.

marjoram ['mɑ:dʒərəm] *n* manjerona.

mark [mɑ:k] *n* marca, sinal *m*; (*imprint*) impressão *f*; (*stain*) mancha; (*BRIT*: *SCH*) nota; (*currency*) marco; (*BRIT*: *TECH*): **M~ 2** 2ª versão ♦ *vt* (*also*: *SPORT*: *player*) marcar; (*stain*) manchar; (*BRIT*: *SCH*: *grade*) dar nota em; (: *correct*) corrigir; **to ~ time** marcar passo; **to be quick off the ~ (in doing)** (*fig*) não perder tempo (para fazer); **up to the ~**

(*in efficiency*) à altura das exigências.

mark down *vt* (*prices, goods*) rebaixar, remarcar para baixo.

mark off *vt* (*tick off*) ticar.

mark out *vt* (*trace*) traçar; (*designate*) destinar.

mark up *vt* (*price*) aumentar, remarcar.

marked [mɑ:kt] *adj* marcado.

markedly ['mɑ:kɪdlɪ] *adv* marcadamente.

marker ['mɑ:kə*] *n* (*sign*) marcador *m*, marca; (*bookmark*) marcador.

market ['mɑ:kɪt] *n* mercado ♦ *vt* (*COMM*) comercializar; **to be on the ~** estar à venda; **on the open ~** no mercado livre; **to play the ~** especular na bolsa de valores.

marketable ['mɑ:kɪtəbl] *adj* comercializável.

market analysis *n* análise *f* de mercado.

market day *n* dia *m* de mercado.

market demand *n* procura de mercado.

market forces *npl* forças *fpl* do mercado.

market garden (*BRIT*) *n* horta.

marketing ['mɑ:kɪtɪŋ] *n* marketing *m*.

market leader *n* líder *m* do mercado.

marketplace ['mɑ:kɪtpleɪs] *n* mercado.

market price *n* preço de mercado.

market research *n* pesquisa de mercado.

market value *n* valor *m* de mercado.

marking ['mɑ:kɪŋ] *n* (*on animal*) marcação *f*; (*on road*) marca.

marksman ['mɑ:ksmən] (*irreg*) *n* bom atirador *m*.

marksmanship ['mɑ:ksmənʃɪp] *n* boa pontaria.

marksmen ['mɑ:ksmɛn] *npl of* **marksman**.

mark-up *n* (*COMM*: *margin*) margem *f* (de lucro), markup *m*; (: *increase*) remarcação *f*, aumento.

marmalade ['mɑ:məleɪd] *n* geléia de laranja.

maroon [mə'ru:n] *vt*: **to be ~ed** ficar abandonado (numa ilha) ♦ *adj* de cor castanho-avermelhado, vinho *inv*.

marquee [mɑ:'ki:] *n* toldo, tenda.

marquess ['mɑ:kwɪs] *n* marquês *m*.

marquis ['mɑ:kwɪs] *n* = **marquess**.

marriage ['mærɪdʒ] *n* casamento.

marriage bureau (*irreg*) *n* agência matrimonial.

marriage certificate *n* certidão *f* de casamento.

marriage counselling (*US*) *n* orientação *f* matrimonial.

marriage guidance (*BRIT*) *n* orientação *f* matrimonial.

married ['mærɪd] *adj* casado; (*life, love*) conjugal; **to get ~** casar(-se).

marrow ['mærəu] *n* medula; (*vegetable*) abóbora.

marry ['mærɪ] *vt* casar(-se) com; (*subj*: *father, priest etc*) casar, unir ♦ *vi* casar(-se).

Mars [mɑ:z] *n* (*planet*) Marte *m*.

marsh [mɑ:ʃ] *n* pântano; (*salt ~*) marisma.

marshal ['mɑ:ʃl] *n* (*MIL*) marechal *m*; (*at sports meeting etc*) oficial *m* ♦ *vt* (*facts*) dispor, ordenar; (*soldiers*) formar.

marshalling yard ['mɑ:ʃlɪŋ] *n* (*RAIL*) local *m*

de manobras.

marshmallow [maːʃ'mæləu] n espécie de doce de malvavisco.

marshy ['maːʃɪ] adj pantanoso.

marsupial [maː'suːpɪəl] adj marsupial ♦ n marsupial m.

martial ['maːʃl] adj marcial.

martial law n lei f marcial.

Martian ['maːʃən] n marciano/a.

martin ['maːtɪn] n (also: house ~) andorinha-de-casa.

martyr ['maːtə*] n mártir m/f ♦ vt martirizar.

martyrdom ['maːtədəm] n martírio.

marvel ['maːvl] n maravilha ♦ vi: to ~ (at) maravilhar-se (de or com).

marvellous ['maːvələs] (US **marvelous**) adj maravilhoso.

Marxism ['maːksɪzəm] n marxismo.

Marxist ['maːksɪst] adj, n marxista m/f.

marzipan ['maːzɪpæn] n maçapão m.

mascara [mæs'kaːrə] n rímel m.

mascot ['mæskət] n mascote f.

masculine ['mæskjulɪn] adj, n masculino.

masculinity [mæskju'lɪnɪtɪ] n masculinidade f.

MASH [mæʃ] (US) n abbr (MIL) = **mobile army surgical hospital**.

mash [mæʃ] vt (CULIN) fazer um purê de; (crush) amassar.

mashed potatoes [mæʃt-] n purê m de batatas.

mask [maːsk] n máscara ♦ vt mascarar.

masochism ['mæsəkɪzəm] n masoquismo.

masochist ['mæsəkɪst] n masoquista m/f.

mason ['meɪsn] n (also: stone~) pedreiro/a; (also: free~) maçom m.

masonic [mə'sɔnɪk] adj maçônico.

masonry ['meɪsənrɪ] n (also: free~) maçonaria; (building) alvenaria.

masquerade [mæskə'reɪd] n baile m de máscaras; (fig) farsa, embuste m ♦ vi: to ~ as disfarçar-se de, fazer-se passar por.

mass [mæs] n (people) multidão f; (PHYS) massa; (REL) missa; (great quantity) montão m ♦ vi reunir-se; (MIL) concentrar-se; **the ~es** npl as massas; **to go to ~** ir à missa.

massacre ['mæsəkə*] n massacre m, carnificina ♦ vt massacrar.

massage ['mæsaːʒ] n massagem f ♦ vt fazer massagem em, massagear.

masseur [mæ'səː*] n massagista m.

masseuse [mæ'səːz] n massagista.

massive ['mæsɪv] adj (large) enorme; (support) massivo.

mass market n mercado de consumo em massa.

mass media npl meios mpl de comunicação de massa, mídia.

mass meeting n concentração f de massa.

mass-produce vt produzir em massa, fabricar em série.

mass-production n produção f em massa, fabricação f em série.

mast [maːst] n (NAUT) mastro; (RADIO etc) antena.

master ['maːstə*] n mestre m; (landowner) senhor m, dono; (in secondary school) professor m; (title for boys): **M~ X** o menino X ♦ vt dominar; (learn) conhecer a fundo; **~ of ceremonies** mestre de cerimônias; **M~ of Arts/Science** detentor(a) m/f de mestrado em letras/ciências; **M~ of Arts/Science degree** mestrado; **M~'s degree** mestrado.

master disk n (COMPUT) disco mestre.

masterful ['maːstəful] adj autoritário, imperioso.

master key n chave f mestra.

masterly ['maːstəlɪ] adj magistral.

mastermind ['maːstəmaɪnd] n (fig) cabeça ♦ vt dirigir, planejar.

masterpiece ['maːstəpiːs] n obra-prima.

master plan n plano piloto.

master stroke n golpe m de mestre.

mastery ['maːstərɪ] n domínio.

mastiff ['mæstɪf] n mastim m.

masturbate ['mæstəbeɪt] vi masturbar-se.

masturbation [mæstə'beɪʃən] n masturbação f.

mat [mæt] n esteira; (also: door~) capacho ♦ adj = **matt**.

match [mætʃ] n fósforo; (game) jogo, partida; (fig) igual m/f ♦ vt casar, emparelhar; (go well with) combinar com; (equal) igualar ♦ vi casar-se, combinar; **to be a good ~** (people) formar um bom casal; (colours) combinar.

match up vt casar, emparelhar.

matchbox ['mætʃbɔks] n caixa de fósforos.

matching ['mætʃɪŋ] adj que combina (com).

matchless ['mætʃlɪs] adj sem igual, incomparável.

mate [meɪt] n (also: inf) colega m/f; (assistant) ajudante m/f; (CHESS) mate m; (animal) macho/fêmea; (in merchant navy) imediato ♦ vi acasalar-se ♦ vt acasalar.

material [mə'tɪərɪəl] n (substance) matéria; (equipment) material m; (cloth) pano, tecido; (data) dados mpl ♦ adj material; (important) importante; **~s** npl material; **reading ~** (material de) leitura.

materialistic [mətɪərɪə'lɪstɪk] adj materialista.

materialize [mə'tɪərɪəlaɪz] vi materializar-se, concretizar-se.

materially [mə'tɪərɪəlɪ] adv materialmente.

maternal [mə'təːnl] adj maternal.

maternity [mə'təːnɪtɪ] n maternidade f ♦ cpd de maternidade, de gravidez.

maternity benefit n auxílio-maternidade m.

maternity dress n vestido de gestante.

maternity hospital n maternidade f.

matey ['meɪtɪ] (BRIT: inf) adj chapinha.

math. [mæθ] (US) n abbr = **mathematics**.

mathematical [mæθə'mætɪkl] adj matemático.

mathematician [mæθəmə'tɪʃən] n matemático/a.

---

mathematics [mæθə'mætıks] *n* matemática.
maths [mæθs] (*BRIT*) *n abbr* = **mathematics**.
matinée ['mætıneı] *n* matinê *f*.
mating ['meıtıŋ] *n* acasalamento.
mating call *n* chamado do macho.
mating season *n* época de cio.
matriarchal [meıtrı'ɑːkl] *adj* matriarcal.
matrices ['meıtrısiːz] *npl of* **matrix**.
matriculation [mətrıkju'leıʃən] *n* matrícula.
matrimonial [mætrı'məunıəl] *adj* matrimonial.
matrimony ['mætrımənı] *n* matrimônio, casamento.
matrix ['meıtrıks] (*pl* **matrices**) *n* matriz *f*.
matron ['meıtrən] *n* (*in hospital*) enfermeira-chefe *f*; (*in school*) inspetora.
matronly ['meıtrənlı] *adj* matronal; (*fig: figure*) corpulento.
matt [mæt] *adj* fosco, sem brilho.
matted ['mætıd] *adj* emaranhado.
matter ['mætə*] *n* questão *f*, assunto; (*PHYS*) matéria, substância; (*content*) conteúdo; (*MED: pus*) pus *m* ♦ *vi* importar; **it doesn't ~** não importa; (*I don't mind*) tanto faz; **what's the ~?** o que (é que) há?, qual é o problema?; **no ~ what** aconteça o que acontecer; **as a ~ of course** o que é de se esperar; (*routine*) por rotina; **as a ~ of fact** na realidade, de fato; **it's a ~ of habit** é uma questão de hábito; **printed ~** impressos; **reading ~** (*BRIT*) (material de) leitura.
matter-of-fact [mætərə'fækt] *adj* prosaico, prático.
matting ['mætıŋ] *n* esteira.
mattress ['mætrıs] *n* colchão *m*.
mature [mə'tjuə*] *adj* maduro ♦ *vi* amadurecer.
maturity [mə'tjuərıtı] *n* maturidade *f*.
maudlin ['mɔːdlın] *adj* (*film, book*) piegas *inv*; (*person*) chorão/rona.
maul [mɔːl] *vt* machucar, maltratar.
Mauritania [mɔːrı'teınıə] *n* Mauritânia.
Mauritius [mə'rıʃəs] *n* Maurício *f* (*no article*).
mausoleum [mɔːsə'lıəm] *n* mausoléu *m*.
mauve [məuv] *adj* cor de malva *inv*.
maverick ['mævrık] *n* (*fig*) dissidente *m/f*.
mawkish ['mɔːkıʃ] *adj* piegas *inv*.
max. *abbr* = **maximum**.
maxim ['mæksım] *n* máxima.
maxima ['mæksımə] *npl of* **maximum**.
maximize ['mæksımaız] *vt* maximizar.
maximum ['mæksıməm] (*pl* **maxima**) *adj, n* máximo.
May [meı] *n* maio; *see also* **July**.
may [meı] (*pt, conditional* **might**) *aux vb* (*indicating possibility*): **he ~ come** pode ser que ele venha, é capaz de vir; (*be allowed to*): **~ I smoke?** posso fumar?; (*wishes*): **~ God bless you!** que Deus lhe abençoe; **he might be there** ele poderia estar lá, ele é capaz de estar lá; **I might as well go** mais vale que eu vá; **you might like to try** talvez você queira tentar.
maybe ['meıbiː] *adv* talvez; **~ he'll come** talvez ele venha; **~ not** talvez não.
May Day *n* dia *m* primeiro de maio.

mayday ['meıdeı] *n* S.O.S. *m* (*chamada de socorro internacional*).
mayhem ['meıhem] *n* caos *m*.
mayonnaise [meıə'neız] *n* maionese *f*.
mayor [meə*] *n* prefeito (*BR*), presidente *m* do município (*PT*).
mayoress ['meərıs] *n* prefeita (*BR*), presidenta do município (*PT*).
maypole ['meıpəul] *n* mastro erguido no dia primeiro de maio.
maze [meız] *n* labirinto.
MB *abbr* (*COMPUT*) = **megabyte**; (*CANADIAN*) = **Manitoba**.
MBA *n abbr* (= *Master of Business Administration*) *grau universitário*.
MBBS (*BRIT*) *n abbr* (= *Bachelor of Medicine and Surgery*) *grau universitário*.
MBChB (*BRIT*) *n abbr* (= *Bachelor of Medicine and Surgery*) *grau universitário*.
MBE (*BRIT*) *n abbr* (= *Member of the Order of the British Empire*) *título honorífico*.
MC *n abbr* = **master of ceremonies**.
MCAT (*US*) *n abbr* = **Medical College Admissions Test**.
MCP (*BRIT: inf*) *n abbr* (= *male chauvinist pig*) machista *m*.
MD *n abbr* = **Doctor of Medicine**; (*COMM*) = **managing director** ♦ *abbr* (*US: POST*) = **Maryland**.
MDT (*US*) *abbr* (= *Mountain Daylight Time*) *hora de verão nas montanhas Rochosas*.
ME (*US*) *abbr* (*POST*) = **Maine** ♦ *n abbr* (*MED*) = **medical examiner**.
me [miː] *pron* me; (*stressed, after prep*) mim; **with ~** comigo; **it's ~** sou eu.
meadow ['medəu] *n* prado, campina.
meagre ['miːgə*] (*US* **meager**) *adj* escasso.
meal [miːl] *n* refeição *f*; (*flour*) farinha; **to go out for a ~** jantar fora.
mealtime ['miːltaım] *n* hora da refeição.
mealy-mouthed ['miːlımauðd] *adj* insincero.
mean [miːn] (*pt, pp* **meant**) *adj* (*with money*) sovina, avarento, pão-duro *inv* (*BR*); (*unkind*) mesquinho; (*shabby*) surrado, miserável; (*of poor quality*) inferior; (*average*) médio ♦ *vt* (*signify*) significar, querer dizer; (*intend*): **~ to do sth** pretender *or* tencionar fazer algo ♦ *n* meio, meio termo; **~s** *npl* meio; **by ~s of** por meio de, mediante; **by all ~s!** claro que sim!, pois não; **to be meant for** estar destinado a; **do you ~ it?** você está falando sério?; **what do you ~?** o que você quer dizer?
meander [mı'ændə*] *vi* (*river*) serpentear; (*person*) vadiar, perambular.
meaning ['miːnıŋ] *n* sentido, significado.
meaningful ['miːnıŋful] *adj* significativo; (*relationship*) sério.
meaningless ['miːnıŋlıs] *adj* sem sentido.
meanness ['miːnnıs] *n* (*with money*) avareza, sovinice *f*; (*shabbiness*) vileza, baixeza; (*unkindness*) maldade *f*, mesquinharia.
means test *n* (*ADMIN*) avaliação *f* de rendimento.
meant [ment] *pt, pp of* **mean**.

meantime ['mi:ntaɪm] *adv* (*also*: *in the* ~) entretanto, enquanto isso.
meanwhile ['mi:nwaɪl] *adv* (*also*: *in the* ~) entretanto, enquanto isso.
measles ['mi:zlz] *n* sarampo.
measly ['mi:zlɪ] (*inf*) *adj* miserável.
measure ['mɛʒə*] *vt* medir; (*for clothes etc*) tirar as medidas de; (*consider*) avaliar, ponderar ♦ *vi* medir ♦ *n* medida; (*ruler*) régua; **a litre** ~ um litro; **some** ~ **of success** certo grau de sucesso; **to take** ~**s to do sth** tomar medidas *or* providências para fazer algo.
measure up *vi*: **to** ~ **up (to)** corresponder (a).
measured ['mɛʒəd] *adj* medido, calculado; (*tone*) ponderado.
measurement ['mɛʒəmənt] *n* (*act*) medição *f*; (*dimension*) medida; ~**s** *npl* medidas *fpl*; **to take sb's** ~**s** tirar as medidas de alguém; **chest/hip** ~ medida de peito/quadris.
meat [mi:t] *n* carne *f*; **cold** ~**s** (*BRIT*) frios; **crab** ~ caranguejo.
meatball ['mi:tbɔ:l] *n* almôndega.
meat pie *n* bolo de carne.
meaty ['mi:tɪ] *adj* carnudo; (*fig*) substancial.
Mecca ['mɛkə] *n* Meca; (*fig*): **a** ~ **(for)** a meca (de).
mechanic [mɪ'kænɪk] *n* mecânico; ~**s** *n* mecânica ♦ *npl* mecanismo.
mechanical [mɪ'kænɪkl] *adj* mecânico.
mechanical engineer *n* engenheiro/a mecânico/a.
mechanical engineering *n* (*science*) mecânica; (*industry*) engenharia mecânica.
mechanism ['mɛkənɪzəm] *n* mecanismo.
mechanization [mɛkənaɪ'zeɪʃən] *n* mecanização *f*.
MEd *n abbr* (= *Master of Education*) *grau universitário*.
medal ['mɛdl] *n* medalha.
medalist ['mɛdəlɪst] (*US*) *n* = **medallist**.
medallion [mɪ'dælɪən] *n* medalhão *m*.
medallist ['mɛdəlɪst] (*US* **medalist**) *n* (*SPORT*) ganhador(a) *m/f* de medalha.
meddle ['mɛdl] *vi*: **to** ~ **in** meter-se em, intrometer-se em; **to** ~ **with sth** mexer em algo.
meddlesome ['mɛdlsəm] *adj* intrometido.
meddling ['mɛdlɪŋ] *adj* intrometido.
media ['mi:dɪə] *npl* meios *mpl* de comunicação, mídia.
mediaeval [mɛdɪ'i:vl] *adj* = **medieval**.
median ['mi:dɪən] (*US*) *n* (*also*: ~ *strip*) canteiro divisor.
media research *n* pesquisa de audiência.
mediate ['mi:dɪeɪt] *vi* mediar.
mediation [mi:dɪ'eɪʃən] *n* mediação *f*.
mediator ['mi:dɪeɪtə*] *n* mediador(a) *m/f*.
medical ['mɛdɪkl] *adj* médico ♦ *n* (*also*: ~ *examination*) exame *m* médico.
medical certificate *n* atestado médico.

medical student *n* estudante *m/f* de medicina.
Medicare ['mɛdɪkɛə*] (*US*) *n* sistema federal de seguro saúde.
medicated ['mɛdɪkeɪtɪd] *adj* medicinal, higienizado.
medication [mɛdɪ'keɪʃən] *n* (*drugs etc*) medicação *f*.
medicinal [mɛ'dɪsɪnl] *adj* medicinal.
medicine ['mɛdsɪn] *n* medicina; (*drug*) remédio, medicamento.
medicine chest *n* armário de remédios.
medicine man (*irreg*) *n* curandeiro *m*, pajé *m*.
medieval [mɛdɪ'i:vl] *adj* medieval.
mediocre [mi:dɪ'əukə*] *adj* medíocre.
mediocrity [mi:dɪ'ɔkrɪtɪ] *n* mediocridade *f*.
meditate ['mɛdɪteɪt] *vi* meditar.
meditation [mɛdɪ'teɪʃən] *n* meditação *f*.
Mediterranean [mɛdɪtə'reɪnɪən] *adj* mediterrâneo; **the** ~ **(Sea)** o (mar) Mediterrâneo.
medium ['mi:dɪəm] (*pl* ~**s**) *adj* médio ♦ *n* (*pl*: **media**: *means*) meio; (*person*) médium *m/f*; **the happy** ~ o justo meio.
medium-sized [-saɪzd] *adj* de tamanho médio.
medium wave *n* (*RADIO*) onda média.
medley ['mɛdlɪ] *n* mistura; (*MUS*) pot-pourri *m*.
meek [mi:k] *adj* manso, dócil.
meet [mi:t] (*pt, pp* **met**) *vt* (*gen*) encontrar; (*accidentally*) topar com, dar de cara com; (*by arrangement*) encontrar-se com, ir ao encontro de; (*for the first time*) conhecer; (*go and fetch*) ir buscar; (*opponent*) enfrentar; (*obligations*) cumprir ♦ *vi* encontrar-se; (*in session*) reunir-se; (*join: objects*) unir-se; (*get to know*) conhecer-se ♦ *n* (*BRIT*: *HUNTING*) reunião *f* de caçadores; (*US*: *SPORT*) promoção *f*, competição *f*; **pleased to** ~ **you!** prazer em conhecê-lo/-la.
meet up *vi*: **to** ~ **up with sb** encontrar-se com alguém.
meet with *vt fus* reunir-se com; (*face: difficulty*) encontrar.
meeting ['mi:tɪŋ] *n* encontro; (*session: of club etc*) reunião *f*; (*interview*) entrevista; (*formal*) assembléia; (*SPORT*) corrida; **she's in** *or* **at a** ~ ela está em conferência; **to call a** ~ convocar uma reunião.
meeting place *n* ponto de encontro.
megabyte ['mɛgəbaɪt] *n* (*COMPUT*) megabyte *m*.
megalomaniac [mɛgələu'meɪnɪæk] *adj*, *n* megalomaníaco/a.
megaphone ['mɛgəfəun] *n* megafone *m*.
melancholy ['mɛlənkəlɪ] *n* melancolia ♦ *adj* melancólico.
melee ['mɛleɪ] *n* briga, refrega.
mellow ['mɛləu] *adj* (*sound*) melodioso, suave; (*colour*) suave; (*fruit*) maduro ♦ *vi* (*person*) amadurecer.

---

melodious [mɪˈləʊdɪəs] adj melodioso.
melodrama [ˈmɛləʊdrɑːmə] adj melodrama m.
melodramatic [mɛlədrəˈmætɪk] adj melodramático.
melody [ˈmɛlədɪ] n melodia.
melon [ˈmɛlən] n melão m.
melt [mɛlt] vi (metal) fundir-se; (snow) derreter; (fig) desvanecer-se ♦ vt derreter.
melt away vi desaparecer.
melt down vt fundir.
meltdown [ˈmɛltdaun] n fusão f.
melting point [ˈmɛltɪŋ-] n ponto de fusão.
melting pot [ˈmɛltɪŋ-] n (fig) cadinho.
member [ˈmɛmbə*] n (gen) membro/a; (of club) sócio/a ♦ cpd: ~ **state** estado membro; **M~ of Parliament** (BRIT) deputado/a; **M~ of the European Parliament** Membro/a do Parlamento Europeu; **M~ of the House of Representatives** (US) membro/a da Câmara dos representantes.
membership [ˈmɛmbəʃɪp] n (being a member) adesão f, condição f de membro; (of club) associação f; (members) número de sócios; **to seek ~ of** candidatar-se a sócio de.
membership card n carteira de sócio.
membrane [ˈmɛmbreɪn] n membrana.
memento [məˈmɛntəʊ] (pl ~s or ~es) n lembrança.
memo [ˈmɛməʊ] n memorando, nota.
memoirs [ˈmɛmwɑːz] npl memórias fpl.
memo pad n bloco de memorando.
memorable [ˈmɛmərəbl] adj memorável.
memoranda [mɛməˈrændə] npl of **memorandum**.
memorandum [mɛməˈrændəm] (pl **memoranda**) n memorando.
memorial [mɪˈmɔːrɪəl] n memorial m, monumento comemorativo ♦ adj comemorativo.
memorize [ˈmɛməraɪz] vt decorar, aprender de cor.
memory [ˈmɛmərɪ] n (faculty) memória; (recollection) lembrança; **to have a good/bad ~** ter memória boa/ruim; **loss of ~** perda de memória; **in ~ of** em memória de.
men [mɛn] npl of **man**.
menace [ˈmɛnəs] n ameaça; (inf: nuisance) droga ♦ vt ameaçar.
menacing [ˈmɛnəsɪŋ] adj ameaçador(a).
menagerie [məˈnædʒərɪ] n coleção f de animais.
mend [mɛnd] vt consertar, reparar; (darn) remendar ♦ n remendo; **to be on the ~** estar melhorando.
mending [ˈmɛndɪŋ] n reparação f; (clothes) roupas fpl por consertar.
menial [ˈmiːnɪəl] adj doméstico; (pej) baixo.
meningitis [mɛnɪnˈdʒaɪtɪs] n meningite f.
menopause [ˈmɛnəʊpɔːz] n menopausa.
menservants [ˈmɛnsəːvənts] npl of **manservant**.
menstruate [ˈmɛnstrueɪt] vi menstruar.
menstruation [mɛnstruˈeɪʃən] n menstruação f.

mental [ˈmɛntl] adj mental; **~ illness** doença mental.
mentality [mɛnˈtælɪtɪ] n mentalidade f.
mentally [ˈmɛntlɪ] adv: **to be ~ handicapped** ser deficiente mental.
menthol [ˈmɛnθɔl] n mentol m.
mention [ˈmɛnʃən] n menção f ♦ vt mencionar; (speak of) falar de; **don't ~ it!** não tem de quê!, de nada!; **I need hardly ~ that ...** não preciso dizer que ...; **not to ~ ...**, **without ~ing ...** para não falar de ..., sem falar de ....
mentor [ˈmɛntɔː*] n mentor m.
menu [ˈmɛnjuː] n (set ~, COMPUT) menu m; (printed) cardápio (BR), ementa (PT).
menu-driven adj (COMPUT) que se navega através de menus.
MEP n abbr = **Member of the European Parliament**.
mercantile [ˈməːkəntaɪl] adj mercantil; (law) comercial.
mercenary [ˈməːsɪnərɪ] adj, n mercenário.
merchandise [ˈməːtʃəndaɪz] n mercadorias fpl ♦ vt comercializar.
merchandiser [ˈməːtʃəndaɪzə*] n comerciante m/f.
merchant [ˈməːtʃənt] n comerciante m/f; **timber/wine ~** negociante de madeira/vinhos.
merchant bank (BRIT) n banco mercantil.
merchantman [ˈməːtʃəntmən] (irreg) n navio mercante.
merchant navy (US **merchant marine**) n marinha mercante.
merciful [ˈməːsɪful] adj piedoso, misericordioso.
mercifully [ˈməːsɪflɪ] adv misericordiosamente, generosamente; (fortunately) graças a Deus, felizmente.
merciless [ˈməːsɪlɪs] adj desapiedado, impiedoso.
mercurial [məːˈkjuərɪəl] adj volúvel; (lively) vivo.
mercury [ˈməːkjurɪ] n mercúrio.
mercy [ˈməːsɪ] n piedade f; (REL) misericórdia; **to have ~ on sb** apiedar-se de alguém; **at the ~ of** à mercê de.
mercy killing n eutanásia.
mere [mɪə*] adj mero, simples inv.
merely [ˈmɪəlɪ] adv simplesmente, somente, apenas.
merge [məːdʒ] vt (join) unir; (mix) misturar; (COMM) fundir; (COMPUT) intercalar ♦ vi unir-se; (COMM) fundir-se.
merger [ˈməːdʒə*] n (COMM) fusão f.
meridian [məˈrɪdɪən] n meridiano.
meringue [məˈræŋ] n suspiro, merengue m.
merit [ˈmɛrɪt] n mérito ♦ vt merecer.
meritocracy [mɛrɪˈtɔkrəsɪ] n sistema m social baseado no mérito.
mermaid [ˈməːmeɪd] n sereia.
merrily [ˈmɛrɪlɪ] adv alegremente, com alegria.
merriment [ˈmɛrɪmənt] n alegria.
merry [ˈmɛrɪ] adj alegre; **M~ Christmas!** Fe-

liz Natal!

merry-go-round n carrossel m.

mesh [mɛʃ] n malha; (TECH) engrenagem f ♦ vi (gears) engrenar.

mesmerize ['mɛzməraɪz] vt hipnotizar.

mess [mɛs] n (gen) confusão f; (of objects) desordem f; (tangle) bagunça; (MIL) rancho; **to be (in) a** ~ (house, room) ser uma bagunça, estar numa bagunça; (fig: marriage, life) estar bagunçado; **to be/get o.s. in a** ~ (fig) meter-se numa encrenca.

mess about (inf) vi perder tempo; (pass the time) vadiar.

mess about with (inf) vt fus mexer com.

mess around (inf) vi perder tempo; (pass the time) vadiar.

mess around with (inf) vi mexer com.

mess up vt (disarrange) desarrumar; (spoil) estragar; (dirty) sujar.

message ['mɛsɪdʒ] n recado, mensagem f; **to get the** ~ (fig: inf) sacar, pescar.

message switching [-'swɪtʃɪŋ] n (COMPUT) troca de mensagens.

messenger ['mɛsɪndʒə*] n mensageiro/a.

Messiah [mɪ'saɪə] n Messias m.

Messrs(.) ['mɛsəz] abbr (on letters: = messieurs) Srs.

messy ['mɛsɪ] adj (dirty) sujo; (untidy) desarrumado; (confused) bagunçado.

Met [mɛt] (US) n abbr = **Metropolitan Opera.**

met [mɛt] pt, pp of **meet** ♦ adj abbr = **meteorological.**

metabolism [mɛ'tæbəlɪzəm] n metabolismo.

metal ['mɛtl] n metal m ♦ vt (road) empedrar.

metallic [mɛ'tælɪk] adj metálico.

metallurgy [mɛ'tælədʒɪ] n metalurgia.

metalwork ['mɛtlwɜːk] n (craft) trabalho em metal.

metamorphoses [mɛtə'mɔːfəsiːz] npl of **metamorphosis.**

metamorphosis [mɛtə'mɔːfəsɪs] (pl **metamorphoses**) n metamorfose f.

metaphor ['mɛtəfə*] n metáfora.

metaphysics [mɛtə'fɪzɪks] n metafísica.

mete out [miːt-] vt fus infligir.

meteor ['miːtɪə*] n meteoro.

meteoric [miːtɪ'ɔrɪk] adj (fig) meteórico.

meteorite ['miːtɪəraɪt] n meteorito.

meteorological [miːtɪərə'lɒdʒɪkl] adj meteorológico.

meteorology [miːtɪə'rɒlədʒɪ] n meteorologia.

meter ['miːtə*] n (instrument) medidor m; (also: parking ~) parcômetro; (US) = **metre.**

methane ['miːθeɪn] n metano.

method ['mɛθəd] n método; ~ **of payment** modalidade de pagamento.

methodical [mɪ'θɒdɪkl] adj metódico.

Methodist ['mɛθədɪst] adj, n metodista m/f.

methylated spirit ['mɛθɪleɪtɪd-] n (also: BRIT: meths) álcool m metílico or desnaturado.

meticulous [mɛ'tɪkjuləs] adj meticuloso.

metre ['miːtə*] (US meter) n metro.

metric ['mɛtrɪk] adj métrico; **to go** ~ adotar o sistema métrico decimal.

metrical ['mɛtrɪkl] adj métrico.

metrication [mɛtrɪ'keɪʃən] n conversão f ao sistema métrico decimal.

metric system n sistema m métrico decimal.

metric ton n tonelada (métrica).

metronome ['mɛtrənəum] n metrônomo.

metropolis [mɪ'trɒpəlɪs] n metrópole f.

metropolitan [mɛtrə'pɒlɪtən] adj metropolitano.

Metropolitan Police (BRIT) n: **the** ~ a polícia de Londres.

mettle ['mɛtl] n (spirit) caráter m, têmpera; (courage) coragem f.

mew [mjuː] vi (cat) miar.

mews [mjuːz] (BRIT) n: ~ **cottage** pequena casa resultante de reforma de antigos estábulos.

Mexican ['mɛksɪkən] adj, n mexicano/a.

Mexico ['mɛksɪkəu] n México.

Mexico City n Cidade f do México.

mezzanine ['mɛtsəniːn] n sobreloja, mezanino.

MFA (US) n abbr (= Master of Fine Arts) grau universitário.

mfr abbr = **manufacture; manufacturer.**

mg abbr (= milligram) mg.

Mgr abbr = **Monseigneur; Monsignor;** (= manager) dir.

MHR (US) n abbr = **Member of the House of Representatives.**

MHz abbr (= megahertz) MHz.

MI (US) abbr (POST) = **Michigan.**

MI5 (BRIT) n abbr (= Military Intelligence 5) ≈ SNI m.

MI6 (BRIT) n abbr (= Military Intelligence 6) ≈ SNI m.

MIA abbr = **missing in action.**

miaow [miː'au] vi miar.

mice [maɪs] npl of **mouse.**

microbe ['maɪkrəub] n micróbio.

microbiology [maɪkrəubaɪ'ɔlədʒɪ] n microbiologia.

microchip ['maɪkrəutʃɪp] n (ELEC) microchip m.

micro(computer) ['maɪkrəu(kəm'pjuːtə*)] n micro(computador) m.

microcosm ['maɪkrəukɔzəm] n microcosmo.

microeconomics [maɪkrəuiːkə'nɔmɪks] n microeconomia.

microfiche ['maɪkrəufiːʃ] n microficha.

microfilm ['maɪkrəufɪlm] n microfilme m ♦ vt microfilmar.

microlight ['maɪkrəulaɪt] n ultraleve m.

micrometer [maɪ'krɔmɪtə*] n micrômetro.

microphone ['maɪkrəfəun] n microfone m.

microprocessor [maɪkrəu'prəusesə*] n microprocessador m.

microscope ['maɪkrəskəup] n microscópio; **under the** ~ com microscópio.

microscopic [maɪkrə'skɔpɪk] adj microscópico.

microwave ['maɪkrəuweɪv] n (also: ~ oven)

NB: European Portuguese adds the following consonants to certain words: **b** (sú(b)dito, su(b)til); **c** (a(c)ção, a(c)cionista, a(c)to); **m** (inde(m)ne); **p** (ado(p)ção, ado(p)tar); for further details see p. xiii.

forno microondas.

mid [mɪd] *adj*: **in ~ May** em meados de maio; **in ~ afternoon** no meio da tarde; **in ~ air** em pleno ar; **he's in his ~ thirties** ele tem por volta de trinta e cinco anos.

midday ['mɪddeɪ] *n* meio-dia *m*.

middle ['mɪdl] *n* meio; (*waist*) cintura ♦ *adj* meio; (*quantity, size*) médio, mediano; **in the ~ of the night** no meio da noite; **I'm in the ~ of reading it** estou no meio da leitura.

middle age *n* meia-idade *f* ♦ *cpd*: **middle-age spread** barriga de meia-idade.

middle-aged *adj* de meia-idade.

Middle Ages *npl*: **the ~** a Idade Média.

middle class *n*: **the ~(es)** a classe média ♦ *adj* (*also*: *middle-class*) de classe média.

Middle East *n*: **the ~** o Oriente Médio.

middleman ['mɪdlmæn] (*irreg*) *n* intermediário; (*COMM*) atravessador *m*.

middle management *n* escalão gerencial intermediário.

middlemen ['mɪdlmɛn] *npl of* **middleman**.

middle name *n* segundo nome *m*.

middle-of-the-road *adj* (*policy*) de meio-termo; (*music*) romântico.

middleweight ['mɪdlweɪt] *n* (*BOXING*) peso médio.

middling ['mɪdlɪŋ] *adj* mediano.

Middx (*BRIT*) *abbr* = **Middlesex**.

midge [mɪdʒ] *n* mosquito.

midget ['mɪdʒɪt] *n* anão/anã *m/f* ♦ *adj* minúsculo.

Midlands ['mɪdləndz] *npl* região central da Inglaterra.

midnight ['mɪdnaɪt] *n* meia-noite *f*; **at ~** à meia-noite.

midriff ['mɪdrɪf] *n* barriga.

midst [mɪdst] *n*: **in the ~ of** no meio de, entre.

midsummer [mɪd'sʌmə*] *n*: **a ~ day** um dia em pleno verão.

midway [mɪd'weɪ] *adj, adv*: **~ (between)** no meio do caminho (entre).

midweek [mɪd'wiːk] *adv* no meio da semana.

midwife ['mɪdwaɪf] (*irreg*) *n* parteira.

midwifery ['mɪdwɪfərɪ] *n* trabalho de parteira, obstetrícia.

midwinter [mɪd'wɪntə*] *n*: **in ~** em pleno inverno.

midwives ['mɪdwaɪvz] *npl of* **midwife**.

might [maɪt] *pt, conditional of* **may** ♦ *n* poder *m*, força.

mighty ['maɪtɪ] *adj* poderoso, forte ♦ *adv* (*inf*): **~ ...** ... pra burro.

migraine ['miːgreɪn] *n* enxaqueca.

migrant ['maɪgrənt] *n* (*bird*) ave *f* de arribação; (*person*) emigrante *m/f*; (*fig*) nômade *m/f* ♦ *adj* migratório; (*worker*) emigrante.

migrate [maɪ'greɪt] *vi* emigrar; (*birds*) arribar.

migration [maɪ'greɪʃən] *n* emigração *f*; (*of birds*) arribação *f*.

mike [maɪk] *n abbr* = **microphone**.

mild [maɪld] *adj* (*character*) pacífico; (*climate*) temperado; (*slight*) ligeiro; (*taste*)

suave; (*illness*) leve, benigno ♦ *n* cerveja ligeira.

mildew ['mɪldjuː] *n* mofo; (*BOT*) míldio.

mildly ['maɪldlɪ] *adv* brandamente; (*slightly*) ligeiramente, um tanto; **to put it ~** (*inf*) para não dizer coisa pior.

mildness ['maɪldnɪs] *n* (*softness*) suavidade *f*; (*gentleness*) doçura; (*quiet character*) brandura.

mile [maɪl] *n* milha (= *1609 m*); **to do 30 ~s per gallon** ≈ fazer 10.64 quilômetros por litro.

mileage ['maɪlɪdʒ] *n* número de milhas; (*AUT*) ≈ quilometragem *f*.

mileage allowance *n* ≈ ajuda de custo com base na quilometragem rodada.

mileometer [maɪ'lɔmɪtə*] (*BRIT*) *n* ≈ contaquilômetros *m inv*.

milestone ['maɪlstəun] *n* marco miliário; (*event*) marco.

milieu ['miːljə:] (*pl* **~s** *or* **~x**) *n* meio, meio social.

milieux ['miːljə:z] *npl of* **milieu**.

militant ['mɪlɪtnt] *adj, n* militante *m/f*.

militarism ['mɪlɪtərɪzəm] *n* militarismo.

militaristic [mɪlɪtə'rɪstɪk] *adj* militarista.

military ['mɪlɪtərɪ] *adj* militar ♦ *n*: **the ~** as forças armadas, os militares.

militate ['mɪlɪteɪt] *vi*: **to ~ against** militar contra.

militia [mɪ'lɪʃə] *n* milícia.

milk [mɪlk] *n* leite *m* ♦ *vt* (*cow*) ordenhar; (*fig*) explorar, chupar.

milk chocolate *n* chocolate *m* de leite.

milk float (*BRIT*) *n* furgão *m* de leiteiro.

milking ['mɪlkɪŋ] *n* ordenhação *f*, ordenha.

milkman ['mɪlkmən] (*irreg*) *n* leiteiro.

milk shake *n* milk-shake *m*, leite *m* batido com sorvete.

milk tooth (*irreg*) *n* dente *m* de leite.

milk truck (*US*) *n* = **milk float**.

milky ['mɪlkɪ] *adj* leitoso.

Milky Way *n* Via Láctea.

mill [mɪl] *n* (*windmill etc*) moinho; (*coffee ~*) moedor *m* de café; (*factory*) moinho, engenho; (*spinning ~*) fábrica de tecelagem, fiação *f* ♦ *vt* moer ♦ *vi* (*also*: **~ about**) aglomerar-se, remoinhar.

millennia [mɪ'lɛnɪə] *npl of* **millennium**.

millennium [mɪ'lɛnɪəm] (*pl* **~s** *or* **millennia**) *n* milênio, milenário.

miller ['mɪlə*] *n* moleiro/a.

millet ['mɪlɪt] *n* milhete *m*.

milli... ['mɪlɪ] *prefix* mili....

milligram(me) ['mɪlɪgræm] *n* miligrama *m*.

millilitre ['mɪlɪliːtə*] (*US* **milliliter**) *n* mililitro.

millimetre ['mɪlɪmiːtə*] (*US* **millimeter**) *n* milímetro.

milliner ['mɪlɪnə*] *n* chapeleiro/a de senhoras.

millinery ['mɪlɪnərɪ] *n* chapelaria de senhoras.

million ['mɪljən] *n* milhão *m*; **a ~ times** um milhão de vezes.

millionaire [mɪljə'nɛə*] *n* milionário/a.

millipede ['mɪlɪpiːd] *n* embuá *m*.

millstone ['mɪlstəun] *n* mó *f*, pedra (de moinho).

millwheel ['mɪlwiːl] n roda de azenha.

milometer [maɪˈlɒmɪtə*] n = **mileometer**.

mime [maɪm] n mimo; (actor) mímico/a, comediante m/f ♦ vt imitar ♦ vi fazer mímica.

mimic ['mɪmɪk] n mímico/a, imitador(a) m/f ♦ vt imitar, parodiar.

mimicry ['mɪmɪkrɪ] n imitação f; (ZOOL) mimetismo.

Min. (BRIT) abbr (POL) = **ministry**.

min. abbr (= minute; minimum) min.

minaret [mɪnəˈrɛt] n minarete m.

mince [mɪns] vt moer ♦ vi (in walking) andar com afetação ♦ n (BRIT: CULIN) carne f moída; **he does not ~ (his) words** ele não tem papas na língua.

mincemeat ['mɪnsmiːt] n recheio de sebo e frutas picadas.

mince pie n pastel com recheio de sebo e frutas picadas.

mincer ['mɪnsə*] n moedor m de carne.

mincing ['mɪnsɪŋ] adj afetado (PT: -ct-).

mind [maɪnd] n mente f ♦ vt (attend to, look after) tomar conta de, cuidar de; (be careful of) ter cuidado com; (object to): **I don't ~ the noise** não me importa o ruído; **do you ~ if ...?** você se incomoda se ...?; **I don't ~** (it doesn't worry me) eu nem ligo; (it's all the same to me) para mim tanto faz; **~ you,** ... se bem que ...; **never ~!** não faz mal, não importa!; (don't worry) não se preocupe!; **it is on my ~** não me sai da cabeça; **to change one's ~** mudar de idéia; **to be in two ~s about sth** (BRIT) estar dividido em relação a algo; **to my ~** a meu ver; **to be out of one's ~** estar fora de si; **to bear** or **keep sth in ~** levar algo em consideração, não esquecer-se de algo; **to have sb/sth in ~** ter alguém/algo em mente; **to have in ~ to do** pretender fazer; **it went right out of my ~** saiu-me totalmente da cabeça; **to bring** or **call sth to ~** lembrar algo; **to make up one's ~** decidir-se; **"~ the step"** "cuidado com o degrau".

-minded ['maɪndɪd] suffix: **fair~** imparcial, justo; **an industrially~ nation** uma nação de vocação industrial.

minder ['maɪndə*] n (child~) cuidadora de crianças; (bodyguard) guarda-costas m/f inv.

mindful ['maɪndful] adj: **~ of** consciente de, atento a.

mindless ['maɪndlɪs] adj estúpido; (violence, crime) insensato.

mine [maɪn] pron (o) meu/(a) minha etc ♦ n mina ♦ vt (coal) extrair, explorar; (ship, beach) minar.

mine detector n detector m de minas.

minefield ['maɪnfiːld] n campo minado.

miner ['maɪnə*] n mineiro.

mineral ['mɪnərəl] adj mineral ♦ n mineral m; **~s** npl (BRIT: soft drinks) refrigerantes mpl.

mineralogy [mɪnəˈrælədʒɪ] n mineralogia.

mineral water n água mineral.

minesweeper ['maɪnswiːpə*] n caça-minas m inv.

mingle ['mɪŋgl] vt misturar ♦ vi: **to ~ with** misturar-se com.

mingy ['mɪndʒɪ] (inf) adj sovina, pão-duro (BR) inv.

miniature ['mɪnətʃə*] adj em miniatura ♦ n miniatura.

minibus ['mɪnɪbʌs] n microônibus m.

minicab ['mɪnɪkæb] (BRIT) n ≈ (táxi m) cooperativado.

minicomputer ['mɪnɪkəmˈpjuːtə*] n minicomputador m, míni m.

minim ['mɪnɪm] n (MUS) mínima.

minima ['mɪnɪmə] npl of **minimum**.

minimal ['mɪnɪml] adj mínimo.

minimize ['mɪnɪmaɪz] vt minimizar.

minimum ['mɪnɪməm] (pl **minima**) adj, n mínimo; **to reduce to a ~** reduzir ao mínimo.

minimum lending rate n (ECON) taxa mínima de empréstimos.

minimum wage n salário mínimo.

mining ['maɪnɪŋ] n exploração f de minas ♦ adj mineiro.

minion ['mɪnjən] (pej) n lacaio.

miniskirt ['mɪnɪskəːt] n minissaia.

minister ['mɪnɪstə*] n (POL) ministro/a; (REL) pastor m ♦ vi: **to ~ to sb** prestar assistência a alguém; **to ~ to sb's needs** atender às necessidades de alguém.

ministerial [mɪnɪsˈtɪərɪəl] adj (POL) ministerial.

ministry ['mɪnɪstrɪ] n ministério; (REL): **to go into the ~** ingressar no sacerdócio.

mink [mɪŋk] n marta.

mink coat n casaco de marta.

minnow ['mɪnəu] n peixinho (de água doce).

minor ['maɪnə*] adj menor; (unimportant) de pouca importância; (inferior) inferior; (MUS) menor ♦ n (LAW) menor m/f de idade.

Minorca [mɪˈnɔːkə] n Minorca.

minority [maɪˈnɔrɪtɪ] n minoria; (age) menoridade f; **to be in a ~** estar em minoria.

minster ['mɪnstə*] n catedral f.

minstrel ['mɪnstrəl] n menestrel m.

mint [mɪnt] n (plant) hortelã f; (sweet) bala de hortelã ♦ vt (coins) cunhar; **the (Royal) M~** (BRIT) or **the (US) M~** (US) ≈ a Casa da Moeda; **in ~ condition** em perfeito estado.

mint sauce n molho de hortelã.

minuet [mɪnjuˈɛt] n minueto.

minus ['maɪnəs] n (also: **~ sign**) sinal m de subtração ♦ prep menos; (without) sem.

minute [n 'mɪnɪt, adj maɪˈnjuːt] n minuto; (official record) ata ♦ adj miúdo, diminuto; (search) minucioso; **~s** npl atas fpl; **it is 5 ~s past 3** são 3 e 5; **wait a ~!** (espere) um minuto or minutinho!; **at the last ~** no último momento; **to leave sth till the last ~** deixar algo até em cima da hora; **up to the ~** (fashion) último; (news) de última hora; **up to the ~ technology** a última tecnologia; **in**

NB: European Portuguese adds the following consonants to certain words: **b** (sú(b)dito, su(b)til); **c** (a(c)ção, a(c)cionista, a(c)to); **m** (inde(m)ne); **p** (ado(p)ção, ado(p)tar); for further details see p. xiii.

~ **detail** por miúdo, em miúdos.
minute book *n* livro de atas.
minute hand *n* ponteiro dos minutos.
minutely [maɪ'njuːtlɪ] *adv* (*by a small amount*) ligeiramente; (*in detail*) minuciosamente.
miracle ['mɪrəkl] *n* milagre *m*.
miraculous [mɪ'rækjuləs] *adj* milagroso.
mirage ['mɪrɑːʒ] *n* miragem *f*.
mire ['maɪə*] *n* lamaçal *m*.
mirror ['mɪrə*] *n* espelho; (*in car*) retrovisor *m* ♦ *vt* refletir.
mirror image *n* imagem *f* de espelho.
mirth [mɜːθ] *n* alegria; (*laughter*) risada.
misadventure [mɪsəd'vɛntʃə*] *n* desgraça, infortúnio; **death by** ~ (*BRIT*) morte acidental.
misanthropist [mɪ'zænθrəpɪst] *n* misantropo/a.
misapply [mɪsə'plaɪ] *vt* empregar mal.
misapprehension [mɪsæprɪ'hɛnʃən] *n* malentendido, equívoco.
misappropriate [mɪsə'prəuprɪeɪt] *vt* desviar.
misappropriation [mɪsəprəuprɪ'eɪʃən] *n* desvio.
misbehave [mɪsbɪ'heɪv] *vi* comportar-se mal.
misbehaviour [mɪsbɪ'heɪvjə*] (*US* **misbehavior**) *n* mau comportamento.
misc. *abbr* = **miscellaneous**.
miscalculate [mɪs'kælkjuleɪt] *vt* calcular mal.
miscalculation [mɪskælkju'leɪʃən] *n* erro de cálculo.
miscarriage ['mɪskærɪdʒ] *n* (*MED*) aborto (espontâneo); ~ **of justice** erro judicial.
miscarry [mɪs'kærɪ] *vi* (*MED*) abortar espontaneamente; (*fail: plans*) fracassar.
miscellaneous [mɪsɪ'leɪnɪəs] *adj* (*items, expenses*) diverso; (*selection*) variado.
miscellany [mɪ'sɛlənɪ] *n* coletânea.
mischance [mɪs'tʃɑːns] *n* infelicidade *f*, azar *m*.
mischief ['mɪstʃɪf] ~ (*naughtiness*) travessura; (*harm*) dano, prejuízo; (*maliciousness*) malícia.
mischievous ['mɪstʃɪvəs] *adj* malicioso; (*naughty*) travesso.
misconception [mɪskən'sɛpʃən] *n* concepção *f* errada, conceito errado.
misconduct [mɪs'kɔndʌkt] *n* comportamento impróprio; **professional** ~ má conduta profissional.
misconstrue [mɪskən'struː] *vt* interpretar mal.
miscount [mɪs'kaunt] *vt, vi* contar mal.
misdeed [mɪs'diːd] *n* delito, ofensa.
misdemeanour [mɪsdɪ'miːnə*] (*US* **misdemeanor**) *n* má ação, contravenção *f*.
misdirect [mɪsdɪ'rɛkt] *vt* (*person*) orientar *or* informar mal; (*letter*) endereçar mal.
miser ['maɪzə*] *n* avaro/a, sovina *m/f*.
miserable ['mɪzərəbl] *adj* (*unhappy, of weather*) triste; (*wretched*) miserável; (*despicable*) desprezível; **to feel** ~ estar na fossa, estar de baixo astral.
miserably ['mɪzərəblɪ] *adv* (*smile, answer*) tristemente; (*fail, live, pay*) miseravelmente.
miserly ['maɪzəlɪ] *adj* avarento, mesquinho.

misery ['mɪzərɪ] *n* (*unhappiness*) tristeza; (*wretchedness*) miséria.
misfire [mɪs'faɪə*] *vi* falhar.
misfit ['mɪsfɪt] *n* (*person*) inadaptado/a, deslocado/a.
misfortune [mɪs'fɔːtʃən] *n* desgraça, infortúnio.
misgiving(s) [mɪs'gɪvɪŋ(z)] *n(pl)* (*mistrust*) desconfiança, receio; (*apprehension*) mau pressentimento; **to have** ~**s about sth** ter desconfianças em relação a algo.
misguided [mɪs'gaɪdɪd] *adj* enganado.
mishandle [mɪs'hændl] *vt* (*treat roughly*) maltratar; (*mismanage*) manejar mal.
mishap ['mɪshæp] *n* desgraça, contratempo.
mishear [mɪs'hɪə*] (*irreg*) *vt* ouvir mal.
mishmash ['mɪʃmæʃ] (*inf*) *n* mixórdia, salada.
misinform [mɪsɪn'fɔːm] *vt* informar mal.
misinterpret [mɪsɪn'tɜːprɪt] *vt* interpretar mal.
misinterpretation [mɪsɪntɜːprɪ'teɪʃən] *n* interpretação *f* errônea.
misjudge [mɪs'dʒʌdʒ] *vt* fazer um juízo errado de, julgar mal.
mislay [mɪs'leɪ] (*irreg*) *vt* extraviar, perder.
mislead [mɪs'liːd] (*irreg*) *vt* induzir em erro, enganar.
misleading [mɪs'liːdɪŋ] *adj* enganoso, errôneo.
misled [mɪs'lɛd] *pt, pp* of **mislead**.
mismanage [mɪs'mænɪdʒ] *vt* administrar mal.
mismanagement [mɪs'mænɪdʒmənt] *n* má administração *f*.
misnomer [mɪs'nəumə*] *n* termo impróprio *or* errado.
misogynist [mɪ'sɔdʒɪnɪst] *n* misógino.
misplace [mɪs'pleɪs] *vt* (*lose*) extraviar, perder; (*wrongly*) colocar em lugar errado; **to be** ~**d** (*trust etc*) ser imerecido.
misprint ['mɪsprɪnt] *n* erro tipográfico.
mispronounce [mɪsprə'nauns] *vt* pronunciar mal.
misquote [mɪs'kwəut] *vt* citar incorretamente.
misread [mɪs'riːd] (*irreg*) *vt* interpretar *or* ler mal.
misrepresent [mɪsreprɪ'zɛnt] *vt* desvirtuar, deturpar.
Miss [mɪs] *n* Senhorita (*BR*), a menina (*PT*); **Dear** ~ **Smith** Ilma. Srta. Smith (*BR*), Exma. Sra. Smith (*PT*).
miss [mɪs] *vt* (*train, appointment, class*) perder; (*fail to hit*) errar, não acertar em; (*notice loss of: money etc*) dar por falta de; (*regret the absence of*): **I** ~ **him** sinto a falta dele ♦ *vi* falhar ♦ *n* (*shot*) tiro perdido *or* errado; (*fig*): **that was a near** ~ (*near accident*) essa foi por pouco; **the bus just** ~**ed the wall** o ônibus por pouco não bateu no muro; **you're** ~**ing the point** você não está entendendo.
miss out (*BRIT*) *vt* omitir.
miss out on *vt fus* perder, ficar por fora de.
missal ['mɪsl] *n* missal *m*.
misshapen [mɪs'ʃeɪpən] *adj* disforme.

missile ['mɪsaɪl] n (AVIAT) míssil m; (object thrown) projétil m.

missile base n base f de mísseis.

missile launcher [-'lɔːntʃə*] n plataforma para lançamento de mísseis.

missing ['mɪsɪŋ] adj (pupil) ausente; (thing) perdido; (after escape, disaster: person) desaparecido; **to go** ~ desaparecer; ~ **person** pessoa desaparecida.

mission ['mɪʃən] n missão f; **on a** ~ **to sb** em missão a alguém.

missionary ['mɪʃənərɪ] n missionário/a.

missive ['mɪsɪv] n missiva.

misspell [mɪs'spɛl] vt (irreg: like spell) escrever errado, errar na ortografia de.

misspent [mɪs'spɛnt] adj: **his** ~ **youth** sua juventude desperdiçada.

mist [mɪst] n (light) neblina; (heavy) névoa; (at sea) bruma ♦ vi (also: ~ over; ~ up) enevoar-se; (BRIT: windows) embaçar.

mistake [mɪs'teɪk] (irreg: like take) n erro, engano ♦ vt entender or interpretar mal; **to** ~ **A for B** confundir A com B; **by** ~ por engano; **to make a** ~ fazer or cometer um erro; **to make a** ~ **about sb/sth** enganar-se a respeito de alguém/algo.

mistaken [mɪs'teɪkən] pp of **mistake** ♦ adj (idea etc) errado; (person) enganado; **to be** ~ enganar-se, equivocar-se.

mistaken identity n identidade f errada.

mistakenly [mɪs'teɪkənlɪ] adv por engano.

mister ['mɪstə*] (inf) n senhor m; see **Mr**.

mistletoe ['mɪsltəʊ] n visco.

mistook [mɪs'tuk] pt of **mistake**.

mistranslation [mɪstræns'leɪʃən] n erro de tradução, tradução f incorreta.

mistreat [mɪs'triːt] vt maltratar.

mistreatment [mɪs'triːtmənt] n maus tratos mpl.

mistress ['mɪstrɪs] n (lover) amante f; (of house) dona (da casa); (BRIT: in school) professora, mestra; see **Mrs**.

mistrust [mɪs'trʌst] vt desconfiar de ♦ n: ~ **(of)** desconfiança (em relação a).

mistrustful [mɪs'trʌstful] adj: ~ **(of)** desconfiado (em relação a).

misty ['mɪstɪ] adj enevoado, nebuloso; (day) nublado; (glasses) embaçado.

misty-eyed [-aɪd] adj (fig) sentimental.

misunderstand [mɪsʌndə'stænd] (irreg) vt, vi entender or interpretar mal.

misunderstanding [mɪsʌndə'stændɪŋ] n malentendido.

misunderstood [mɪsʌndə'stud] pt, pp of **misunderstand**.

misuse [n mɪs'juːs, vt mɪs'juːz] n uso impróprio; (of power) abuso ♦ vt (use wrongly) empregar mal; (power) abusar de; (funds) desviar.

MIT (US) n abbr = **Massachusetts Institute of Technology**.

mite [maɪt] n (small quantity) pingo; (BRIT:

small child) criancinha.

miter ['maɪtə*] (US) n = **mitre**.

mitigate ['mɪtɪgeɪt] vt mitigar, atenuar; **mitigating circumstances** circunstâncias fpl atenuantes.

mitigation [mɪtɪ'geɪʃən] n abrandamento, mitigação f.

mitre ['maɪtə*] (US **miter**) n mitra; (CARPENTRY) meia-esquadria.

mitt(en) ['mɪt(n)] n mitene f.

mix [mɪks] vt (gen) misturar; (combine) combinar ♦ vi misturar-se; (people) entrosar-se ♦ n mistura; **to** ~ **sth with sth** misturar algo com algo; **to** ~ **business with pleasure** misturar trabalho com divertimento.

mix in vt misturar.

mix up vt misturar; (confuse) confundir, misturar; **to be** ~**ed up in sth** estar envolvido or metido em algo.

mixed [mɪkst] adj (assorted) sortido, variado; (school etc) misto.

mixed doubles npl (SPORT) duplas fpl mistas.

mixed economy n economia mista.

mixed grill (BRIT) n carnes fpl grelhadas.

mixed-up adj (confused) confuso.

mixer ['mɪksə*] n (for food) batedeira; (person) pessoa sociável.

mixture ['mɪkstʃə*] n mistura; (MED) preparado.

mix-up n trapalhada, confusão f.

Mk (BRIT) abbr (TECH) = **mark**.

mk abbr = **mark** (currency).

mkt abbr = **market**.

MLitt n abbr (= Master of Literature; Master of Letters) grau universitário.

MLR (BRIT) n abbr = **minimum lending rate**.

mm abbr (= millimetre) mm.

MN abbr (BRIT) = **merchant navy**; (US: POST) = **Minnesota**.

MO n abbr (MED) = **medical officer**; (US: inf: = modus operandi) método ♦ abbr (US: POST) = **Missouri**.

M.O. abbr = **money order**.

moan [məʊn] n gemido ♦ vi gemer; (inf: complain): **to** ~ **(about)** queixar-se (de), bufar (sobre) (inf).

moaning ['məʊnɪŋ] n gemidos mpl; (inf: complaining) queixas fpl.

moat [məʊt] n fosso.

mob [mɔb] n multidão f; (pej): **the** ~ (masses) o povinho; (mafia) a máfia ♦ vt cercar.

mobile ['məʊbaɪl] adj móvel ♦ n móvel m; **applicants must be** ~ (BRIT) os candidatos devem estar dispostos a aceitar qualquer deslocamento.

mobile home n trailer m, casa móvel.

mobile shop (BRIT) n loja circulante.

mobility [məʊ'bɪlɪtɪ] n mobilidade f.

mobilize ['məʊbɪlaɪz] vt mobilizar ♦ vi

mobilizar-se; (*MIL*) ser mobilizado.

moccasin ['mɒkəsɪn] *n* mocassim *m*.

mock [mɒk] *vt* (*make ridiculous*) ridicularizar; (*laugh at*) zombar de, gozar de ♦ *adj* falso, fingido.

mockery ['mɒkərɪ] *n* zombaria; **to make a** ~ **of sth** ridicularizar algo.

mocking ['mɒkɪŋ] *adj* zombeteiro.

mockingbird ['mɒkɪŋbəːd] *n* tordo-dos-remédios *m*.

mock-up *n* maqueta, modelo.

MOD (*BRIT*) *n abbr* = **Ministry of Defence**.

mod cons (*BRIT*) *npl abbr* (= *modern conveniences*) *see* **convenience**.

mode [məud] *n* modo; (*of transport*) meio.

model ['mɒdl] *n* (*gen*) modelo; (*ARCH*) maqueta; (*person: for fashion, ART*) modelo *m/f* ♦ *adj* (*car, toy*) de brinquedo; (*child, factory*) modelar ♦ *vt* modelar ♦ *vi* servir de modelo; (*in fashion*) trabalhar como modelo; ~ **railway** trenzinho de brinquedo; **to** ~ **clothes** desfilar apresentando modelos; **to** ~ **sb/sth on** modelar alguém/algo a *or* por.

modeller ['mɒdlə*] (*US* **modeler**) *n* modelador(a) *m/f*; (*model maker*) maquetista *m/f*.

modem ['məudɛm] *n* modem *m*.

moderate [*adj, n* 'mɒdərət, *vi, vt* 'mɒdəreɪt] *adj, n* moderado/a ♦ *vi* moderar-se, acalmar-se ♦ *vt* moderar.

moderately ['mɒdərətlɪ] *adv* (*act*) com moderação, moderadamente; (*pleased, happy*) razoavelmente; ~ **priced** de preço médio *or* razoável.

moderation [mɒdə'reɪʃən] *n* moderação *f*; **in** ~ com moderação.

modern ['mɒdən] *adj* moderno; ~ **languages** línguas *fpl* vivas.

modernization [mɒdənaɪ'zeɪʃən] *n* modernização *f*.

modernize ['mɒdənaɪz] *vt* modernizar, atualizar.

modest ['mɒdɪst] *adj* modesto.

modesty ['mɒdɪstɪ] *n* modéstia.

modicum ['mɒdɪkəm] *n*: **a** ~ **of** um mínimo de.

modification [mɒdɪfɪ'keɪʃən] *n* modificação *f*.

modify ['mɒdɪfaɪ] *vt* modificar.

Mods [mɒdz] (*BRIT*) *n abbr* (= *Honour Moderations*) *primeiro exame universitário* (*em Oxford*).

modular ['mɒdjulə*] *adj* (*filing, unit*) modular.

modulate ['mɒdjuleɪt] *vt* modular.

modulation [mɒdju'leɪʃən] *n* modulação *f*.

module ['mɒdjuːl] *n* módulo.

mogul ['məugl] *n* (*fig*) magnata *m*.

MOH (*BRIT*) *n abbr* = **Medical Officer of Health**.

mohair ['məuhɛə*] *n* mohair *m*, angorá *m*.

Mohammed [mə'hæmɪd] *n* Maomé *m*.

moist [mɔɪst] *adj* úmido (*PT*: hú-), molhado.

moisten ['mɔɪsn] *vt* umedecer (*PT*: hu-).

moisture ['mɔɪstʃə*] *n* umidade *f* (*PT*: hu-).

moisturize ['mɔɪstʃəraɪz] *vt* (*skin*) hidratar.

moisturizer ['mɔɪstʃəraɪzə*] *n* creme *m* hidratante.

molar ['məulə*] *n* molar *m*.

molasses [məu'læsɪz] *n* melaço, melado.

mold [məuld] (*US*) *n, vt* = **mould**.

mole [məul] *n* (*animal*) toupeira; (*spot*) sinal *m*, lunar *m*.

molecule ['mɒlɪkjuːl] *n* molécula.

molehill ['məulhɪl] *n* montículo (feito por uma toupeira).

molest [məu'lɛst] *vt* molestar, importunar.

mollusc ['mɒləsk] *n* molusco.

mollycoddle ['mɒlɪkɒdl] *vt* mimar.

molt [məult] (*US*) *vi* = **moult**.

molten ['məultən] *adj* fundido; (*lava*) liquefeito.

mom [mɒm] (*US*) *n* = **mum**.

moment ['məumənt] *n* momento; (*importance*) importância; **at the** ~ neste momento; **for the** ~ por enquanto; **in a** ~ num instante; **"one** ~ **please"** (*TEL*) "não desligue".

momentarily ['məuməntrɪlɪ] *adv* momentaneamente; (*US: soon*) daqui a pouco.

momentary ['məuməntərɪ] *adj* momentâneo.

momentous [məu'mɛntəs] *adj* importantíssimo.

momentum [məu'mɛntəm] *n* momento; (*fig*) ímpeto; **to gather** ~ ganhar ímpeto.

mommy ['mɒmɪ] (*US*) *n* = **mummy**.

Mon. *abbr* (= *Monday*) seg., 2ª.

Monaco ['mɒnəkəu] *n* Mônaco (*no article*).

monarch ['mɒnək] *n* monarca *m/f*.

monarchist ['mɒnəkɪst] *n* monarquista *m/f*.

monarchy ['mɒnəkɪ] *n* monarquia.

monastery ['mɒnəstərɪ] *n* mosteiro, convento.

monastic [mə'næstɪk] *adj* monástico.

Monday ['mʌndɪ] *n* segunda-feira; *see also* **Tuesday**.

monetarist ['mʌnɪtərɪst] *n* monetarista *m/f*.

monetary ['mʌnɪtərɪ] *adj* monetário.

money ['mʌnɪ] *n* dinheiro; **to make** ~ ganhar dinheiro; **I've got no** ~ **left** não tenho mais dinheiro.

moneyed ['mʌnɪd] *adj* rico, endinheirado.

moneylender ['mʌnɪlɛndə*] *n* agiota *m/f*.

moneymaking ['mʌnɪmeɪkɪŋ] *adj* lucrativo, rendoso.

money market *n* mercado financeiro.

money order *n* vale *m* (postal).

money-spinner (*inf*) *n* mina.

money supply *n* meios *mpl* de pagamento, suprimento monetário.

Mongol ['mɒŋgəl] *n* mongol *m/f*; (*LING*) mongol *m*.

mongol ['mɒŋgəl] *adj, n* (*offensive*) mongolóide *m/f*.

Mongolia [mɒŋ'gəulɪə] *n* Mongólia.

Mongolian [mɒŋ'gəulɪən] *adj* mongol ♦ *n* mongol *m/f*; (*LING*) mongol *m*.

mongoose ['mɒŋguːs] *n* mangusto.

mongrel ['mʌŋgrəl] *n* (*dog*) vira-lata *m*.

monitor ['mɒnɪtə*] *n* (*SCH*) monitor(a) *m/f*; (*TV, COMPUT*) terminal *m* de vídeo ♦ *vt* controlar; (*foreign station*) controlar, monitorar.

monk [mʌŋk] *n* monge *m*.

monkey ['mʌŋkɪ] *n* macaco.

monkey business n trapaça, travessura.
monkey nut (*BRIT*) n amendoim m.
monkey tricks npl trapaça, travessura.
monkey wrench n chave f inglesa.
mono ['mɔnəu] adj mono inv.
mono... ['mɔnəu] prefix mono....
monochrome ['mɔnəkrəum] adj monocromático.
monocle ['mɔnəkl] n monóculo.
monogram ['mɔnəgræm] n monograma m.
monolith ['mɔnəliθ] n monólito.
monologue ['mɔnələg] n monólogo.
monoplane ['mɔnəplein] n monoplano.
monopolize [mə'nɔpəlaiz] vt monopolizar.
monopoly [mə'nɔpəli] n monopólio; **Monopolies and Mergers Commission** (*BRIT*) comissão de inquérito sobre os monopólios.
monorail ['mɔnəureil] n monotrilho.
monosodium glutamate [mɔnə'sɔudiəm 'glu:təmeit] n glutamato de monossódio.
monosyllabic [mɔnəusi'læbik] adj monossilábico; (*person*) lacônico.
monosyllable ['mɔnəsiləbl] n monossílabo.
monotone ['mɔnətəun] n monotonia; **to speak in a** ~ falar num tom monótono.
monotonous [mə'nɔtənəs] adj monótono.
monotony [mə'nɔtəni] n monotonia.
monoxide [mɔ'nɔksaid] n see **carbon monoxide**.
monsoon [mɔn'su:n] n monção f.
monster ['mɔnstə*] n monstro.
monstrosity [mɔns'trɔsiti] n monstruosidade f.
monstrous ['mɔnstrəs] adj (*huge*) descomunal; (*atrocious*) monstruoso.
montage [mɔn'tɑ:ʒ] n montagem f.
Mont Blanc [mɔ̃blɑ̃] n Monte m Branco.
Montevideo ['mɔnteivi'deiəu] n Montevidéu.
month [mʌnθ] n mês m; **every** ~ todo mês; **300 dollars a** ~ 300 dólares mensais or por mês.
monthly ['mʌnθli] adj mensal ♦ adv mensalmente ♦ n (*magazine*) revista mensal; **twice** ~ duas vezes por mês.
monument ['mɔnjumənt] n monumento.
monumental [mɔnju'mentl] adj monumental.
monumental mason n marmorista m/f.
moo [mu:] vi mugir.
mood [mu:d] n humor m; **to be in a good/bad** ~ estar de bom/mau humor; **to be in the** ~ **for** estar a fim or com vontade de.
moody ['mu:di] adj (*variable*) caprichoso, de veneta; (*sullen*) rabugento.
moon [mu:n] n lua.
moonbeam ['mu:nbi:m] n raio de lua.
moon landing n alunissagem f.
moonlight ['mu:nlait] n luar m ♦ vi ter dois empregos, ter um bico.
moonlighting ['mu:nlaitiŋ] n trabalho adicional, bico.
moonlit ['mu:nlit] adj enluarado; **a** ~ **night** uma noite de lua.
moonshot ['mu:nʃɔt] n (*SPACE*) lançamento de

nave para a lua.
moonstruck ['mu:nstrʌk] adj lunático, aluado.
Moor [muə*] n mouro/a.
moor [muə*] n charneca ♦ vt (*ship*) amarrar ♦ vi fundear, atracar.
mooring ['muəriŋ] n (*place*) ancoradouro; ~s npl (*chains*) amarras fpl.
Moorish ['muəriʃ] adj mouro; (*architecture*) mourisco.
moorland ['muələnd] n charneca.
moose [mu:s] n inv alce m.
moot [mu:t] vt levantar ♦ adj: ~ **point** ponto discutível.
mop [mɔp] n esfregão m; (*of hair*) grenha ♦ vt esfregar.
mop up vt limpar.
mope [məup] vi estar or andar deprimido or desanimado.
mope about vi andar por aí desanimado.
mope around vi andar por aí desanimado.
moped ['məuped] (*BRIT*) (*BR*), motorizada (*PT*) n moto f pequena.
moquette [mɔ'kɛt] n moquete f.
moral ['mɔrl] adj moral ♦ n moral f; ~s npl moralidade f, costumes mpl.
morale [mɔ'rɑ:l] n moral f, estado de espírito.
morality [mɔ'ræliti] n moralidade f.
moralize ['mɔrəlaiz] vi: **to** ~ (**about**) dar lições de moral (sobre).
morally ['mɔrəli] adv moralmente.
morass [mɔ'ræs] n pântano, brejo.
moratoria [mɔrə'tɔ:riə] npl of **moratorium**.
moratorium [mɔrə'tɔ:riəm] (pl ~s or **moratoria**) n moratória.
morbid ['mɔ:bid] adj mórbido.
more [mɔ:*] adj, adv mais; ~ **money** mais dinheiro; **I want** ~ quero mais; **is there any** ~? tem ainda?; **many/much** ~ muitos/muito mais; ~ **and** ~ cada vez mais; **once** ~ outra vez; **no** ~, **not any** ~ não ... mais; **and what's** ~ ... além do mais ..., aliás ...; ~ **dangerous than** mais perigoso do que; ~ **or less** mais ou menos; ~ **than ever** mais do que nunca.
moreover [mɔ:'rəuvə*] adv além do mais, além disso.
morgue [mɔ:g] n necrotério.
MORI ['mɔri] (*BRIT*) n abbr (= *Market and Opinion Research Institute*) ≈ IBOPE m.
moribund ['mɔribʌnd] adj moribundo, agonizante.
Mormon ['mɔ:mən] n mórmon m/f.
morning ['mɔ:niŋ] n manhã f; (*early* ~) madrugada; **good** ~ bom dia; **in the** ~ de manhã; **7 o'clock in the** ~ (às) 7 da manhã; **3 o'clock in the** ~ (às) 3 da madrugada; **tomorrow** ~ amanhã de manhã; **this** ~ hoje de manhã.
morning sickness n náusea matinal.
Moroccan [mə'rɔkən] adj, n marroquino/a.
Morocco [mə'rɔkəu] n Marrocos m.
moron ['mɔ:rɔn] n débil mental m/f, idiota m/

f.

moronic [mə'rɒnɪk] *adj* imbecil, idiota.

morose [mə'rəus] *adj* taciturno, rabugento.

morphine ['mɔːfiːn] *n* morfina.

Morse [mɔːs] *n (also: ~ code)* código Morse.

morsel ['mɔːsl] *n (of food)* bocado.

mortal ['mɔːtl] *adj, n* mortal *m/f.*

mortality [mɔː'tælɪtɪ] *n* mortalidade *f.*

mortality rate *n* (taxa de) mortalidade *f.*

mortar ['mɔːtə*] *n* argamassa; *(dish)* pilão *m*, almofariz *m.*

mortgage ['mɔːgɪdʒ] *n* hipoteca; *(for house)* financiamento ♦ *vt* hipotecar; **to take out a ~** fazer um crédito imobiliário.

mortgage company *(US) n* sociedade *f* de crédito imobiliário.

mortgagee [mɔːgə'dʒiː] *n* credor(a) *m/f* hipotecário/a.

mortgagor ['mɔːgədʒə*] *n* devedor(a) *m/f* hipotecário/a.

mortician [mɔː'tɪʃən] *(US) n* agente *m/f* funerário/a.

mortified ['mɔːtɪfaɪd] *adj* morto de vergonha.

mortise lock ['mɔːtɪs-] *n* fechadura embutida.

mortuary ['mɔːtjuərɪ] *n* necrotério.

mosaic [məu'zeɪɪk] *n* mosaico.

Moscow ['mɒskəu] *n* Moscou *(BR)*, Moscovo *(PT).*

Moslem ['mɒzləm] *adj, n* = **Muslim**.

mosque [mɒsk] *n* mesquita.

mosquito [mɒs'kiːtəu] *(pl ~es) n* mosquito.

mosquito net *n* mosquiteiro.

moss [mɒs] *n* musgo.

mossy ['mɒsɪ] *adj* musgoso, musguento.

most [məust] *adj* a maior parte de, a maioria de ♦ *pron* a maior parte a, a maioria ♦ *adv* o mais; *(very)* muito; **the ~** *(also: + adj)* o mais; **~ fish** a maioria dos peixes; **~ of them** a maioria deles; **I saw (the) ~** *vi* mais; **at the (very) ~** quando muito, no máximo; **to make the ~ of** aproveitar ao máximo; **a ~ interesting book** um livro interessantíssimo.

mostly ['məustlɪ] *adv* principalmente, na maior parte.

MOT *(BRIT) n abbr (= Ministry of Transport)*: **the ~ (test)** *vistoria anual dos veículos automotores.*

motel [məu'tɛl] *n* motel *m.*

moth [mɒθ] *n* mariposa; *(clothes ~)* traça.

mothball ['mɒθbɔːl] *n* bola de naftalina.

moth-eaten *adj* roído pelas traças.

mother ['mʌðə*] *n* mãe *f* ♦ *adj* materno ♦ *vt (care for)* cuidar de (como uma mãe).

mother board *n (COMPUT)* placa-base *f.*

motherhood ['mʌðəhud] *n* maternidade *f.*

mother-in-law *(pl* **mothers-in-law)** *n* sogra.

motherly ['mʌðəlɪ] *adj* maternal.

mother-of-pearl *n* madrepérola.

mother's help *n* babá *f.*

mother-to-be *(pl* **mothers-to-be)** *n* futura mamãe *f.*

mother tongue *n* língua materna.

mothproof ['mɒθpruːf] *adj* à prova de traças.

motif [məu'tiːf] *n* motivo.

motion ['məuʃən] *n* movimento; *(gesture)* gesto, sinal *m*; *(at meeting)* moção *f*; *(BRIT: of bowels)* fezes *fpl* ♦ *vt, vi*: **to ~ (to) sb to do sth** fazer sinal a alguém para que faça algo; **to be in ~** *(vehicle)* estar em movimento; **to set in ~** pôr em movimento; **to go through the ~s of doing sth** *(fig)* fazer algo automaticamente ou sem convicção.

motionless ['məuʃənlɪs] *adj* imóvel.

motion picture *n* filme *m* (cinematográfico).

motivate ['məutɪveɪt] *vt* motivar.

motivated ['məutɪveɪtɪd] *adj* motivado.

motivation [məutɪ'veɪʃən] *n* motivação *f.*

motive ['məutɪv] *n* motivo ♦ *adj* motor/motriz; **from the best (of) ~s** com as melhores intenções.

motley ['mɒtlɪ] *adj* variado, heterogêneo.

motor ['məutə*] *n* motor *m*; *(BRIT: inf: vehicle)* carro, automóvel *m* ♦ *adj* motor/motriz.

motorbike ['məutəbaɪk] *n* moto(cicleta) *f*, motoca *(inf).*

motorboat ['məutəbəut] *n* barco a motor.

motorcar ['məutəkɑː] *(BRIT) n* carro, automóvel *m.*

motorcoach ['məutəkəutʃ] *n* ônibus *m* turístico.

motorcycle ['məutəsaɪkl] *n* motocicleta.

motorcyclist ['məutəsaɪklɪst] *n* motociclista *m/f.*

motoring ['məutərɪŋ] *(BRIT) n* automobilismo ♦ *adj (accident, offence)* de trânsito; **~ holiday** passeio de carro.

motorist ['məutərɪst] *n* motorista *m/f.*

motorize ['məutəraɪz] *vt* motorizar.

motor oil *n* óleo de motor.

motor racing *(BRIT) n* corrida de carros, automobilismo.

motor scooter *n* lambreta *(BR)*, motoreta *(PT).*

motor vehicle *n* automóvel *m*, veículo automotor.

motorway ['məutəweɪ] *(BRIT) n* rodovia *(BR)*, autoestrada *(PT).*

mottled ['mɒtld] *adj* mosqueado, em furtacores.

motto ['mɒtəu] *(pl ~es) n* lema *m.*

mould [məuld] *(US* **mold)** *n* molde *m*; *(mildew)* mofo, bolor *m* ♦ *vt* moldar; *(fig)* modelar, plasmar.

mo(u)lder ['məuldə*] *vi (decay)* desfazer-se.

mo(u)lding ['məuldɪŋ] *n* moldura.

mo(u)ldy ['məuldɪ] *adj* mofado.

moult [məult] *(US* **molt)** *vi* mudar (de penas etc).

mound [maund] *n* montão *m*, montículo.

mount [maunt] *n* monte *m*; *(horse)* montaria; *(for jewel etc)* engaste *m*; *(for picture)* moldura ♦ *vt (horse etc)* montar em, subir a; *(stairs)* subir; *(exhibition)* montar; *(attack)* montar, desfechar; *(picture)* emoldurar ♦ *vi (also: ~ up)* aumentar.

mountain ['mauntɪn] *n* montanha ♦ *cpd* de montanha; **to make a ~ out of a molehill** *(fig)* fazer um bicho de sete cabeças ou um cavalo de batalha (de algo).

mountaineer [mauntɪ'nɪə*] *n* alpinista *m/f*, montanhista *m/f*.
mountaineering [mauntɪ'nɪərɪŋ] *n* alpinismo; **to go ~** praticar o alpinismo.
mountainous ['mauntɪnəs] *adj* montanhoso.
mountain rescue team *n* equipe *m* de socorro para alpinistas.
mountainside ['mauntɪnsaɪd] *n* lado da montanha.
mounted ['mauntɪd] *adj* montado.
Mount Everest *n* monte *m* Everest.
mourn [mɔːn] *vt* chorar, lamentar ♦ *vi*: **to ~ for** chorar *or* lamentar a morte de.
mourner ['mɔːnə*] *n* parente/a *m/f or* amigo/a do defunto.
mournful ['mɔːnful] *adj* desolado, triste.
mourning ['mɔːnɪŋ] *n* luto ♦ *cpd* (*dress*) de luto; **(to be) in ~** (estar) de luto.
mouse [maus] (*pl* **mice**) *n* camundongo (*BR*), rato (*PT*).
mousetrap ['maustræp] *n* ratoeira.
mousse [muːs] *n* musse *f*.
moustache [məs'tɑːʃ] *n* bigode *m*.
mousy ['mausɪ] *adj* (*person*) tímido; (*hair*) pardacento.
mouth [mauθ, *pl* mauðz] *n* boca; (*of river*) desembocadura.
mouthful ['mauθful] *n* bocado.
mouth organ *n* gaita.
mouthpiece ['mauθpiːs] *n* (*of musical instrument*) bocal *m*; (*representative*) porta-voz *m/f*.
mouth-to-mouth *adj*: **~ resuscitation** respiração *f* boca-a-boca.
mouthwash ['mauθwɔʃ] *n* colutório.
mouth-watering *adj* de dar água na boca.
movable ['muːvəbl] *adj* móvel.
move [muːv] *n* (*movement*) movimento; (*in game*) lance *m*, jogada; (: *turn to play*) turno, vez *f*; (*change of house*) mudança ♦ *vt* (*hand etc*) mexer, mover; (*from one place to another*) deslocar; (*emotionally*) comover; (*POL: resolution etc*) propor ♦ *vi* (*gen*) mexer-se, mover-se; (*traffic*) circular; (*also:* **~ house**) mudar-se; **to ~ sb to do sth** convencer alguém a fazer algo; **to get a ~ on** apressar-se; **to be ~d** (*emotionally*) ficar comovido.
move about *vi* (*fidget*) mexer-se; (*travel*) deslocar-se.
move along *vi* avançar.
move around *vi* (*fidget*) mexer-se; (*travel*) deslocar-se.
move away *vi* afastar-se.
move back *vi* (*step back*) recuar; (*return*) voltar.
move down *vt* abaixar; (*demote*) rebaixar.
move forward *vi* avançar ♦ *vt* adiantar.
move in *vi* (*to a house*) instalar-se (numa casa).
move off *vi* partir.

move on *vi* ir andando ♦ *vt* (*onlookers*) afastar.
move out *vi* (*of house*) sair (de uma casa).
move over *vi* afastar-se; **~ over!** (*towards speaker*) chega mais para cá!; (*away from speaker*) chega mais para lá!
move up *vi* subir; (*employee*) ser promovido; (**~ aside**) chegar mais para lá *or* cá.
movement ['muːvmənt] *n* movimento; (*TECH*) mecanismo; (*MED: also: bowel ~*) defecação *f*.
mover ['muːvə*] *n* autor(a) *m/f* de proposta.
movie ['muːvɪ] *n* filme *m*; **the ~s** o cinema.
movie camera *n* câmara cinematográfica.
moviegoer ['muːvɪgəuə*] (*US*) *n* freqüentador(a) *m/f* de cinema.
moving ['muːvɪŋ] *adj* (*emotional*) comovente; (*mobile*) móvel; (*in motion*) em movimento ♦ *n* (*US*) mudança.
mow [məu] (*pt* **~ed**, *pp* **~ed** *or* **mown**) *vt* (*grass*) cortar; (*corn*) ceifar.
mow down *vt* ceifar; (*massacre*) chacinar.
mower ['məuə*] *n* ceifeira; (*also: lawn~*) cortador *m* de grama (*BR*) *or* de relva (*PT*).
mown [məun] *pp of* **mow**.
Mozambique [məuzəm'biːk] *n* Moçambique *m* (*no article*) ♦ *adj* moçambicano.
MP *n abbr* (= *Military Police*) PM *f*; (*BRIT*) = **Member of Parliament**; (*CANADIAN*) = **Mounted Police.**
mpg *n abbr* = **miles per gallon** (*30 mpg = 10.64 km/l*).
mph *abbr* = **miles per hour** (*60 mph = 96 km/h*).
MPhil *n abbr* (= *Master of Philosophy*) grau universitário.
MPS (*BRIT*) *n abbr* = **Member of the Pharmaceutical Society.**
Mr(.) ['mɪstə*] *n*: **~ Smith** (o) Sr. Smith.
MRC (*BRIT*) *n abbr* = **Medical Research Council.**
MRCP (*BRIT*) *n abbr* = **Member of the Royal College of Physicians.**
MRCS (*BRIT*) *n abbr* = **Member of the Royal College of Surgeons.**
MRCVS (*BRIT*) *n abbr* = **Member of the Royal College of Veterinary Surgeons.**
Mrs(.) ['mɪsɪz] *n*: **~ Smith** (a) Sra. Smith.
MS *n abbr* (= *manuscript*) ms; = **multiple sclerosis**; (*US: = Master of Science*) grau universitário ♦ *abbr* (*US: POST*) = **Mississippi.**
Ms(.) [mɪz] *n* (= *Miss or Mrs*): **~ X** (a) Sa X.
MSA (*US*) *n abbr* (= *Master of Science in Agriculture*) grau universitário.
MSc *n abbr* = **Master of Science.**
MSG *n abbr* = **monosodium glutamate.**
MST (*US*) *abbr* (= *Mountain Standard Time*) hora de inverno das montanhas Rochosas.
MSW (*US*) *n abbr* (= *Master of Social Work*) grau universitário.
MT *n abbr* = **machine translation** ♦ *abbr* (*US:*

NB: European Portuguese adds the following consonants to certain words: **b** (sú(b)dito, su(b)til); **c** (a(c)ção, a(c)cionista, a(c)to); **m** (inde(m)ne); **p** (ado(p)ção, ado(p)tar); *for further details see p. xiii.*

POST) = **Montana**.

Mt *abbr* (*GEO*: = *mount*) Mt.

much [mʌtʃ] *adj, adv, pron* muito ♦ *n* muito, grande parte *f*; **how ~ is it?** quanto é?, quanto custa?; **it's not ~** não é muito; **too ~** demais; **so ~** tanto; **as ~ as** tanto como; **I like it very/so ~** gosto muito/tanto disso; **thank you very ~** muito obrigado/a; **however ~ he tries** por mais que tente.

muck [mʌk] *n* (*dirt*) sujeira (*BR*), sujidade *f* (*PT*); (*manure*) estrume *m*; (*fig*) porcaria.

muck about (*inf*) *vi* (*be silly*) fazer besteiras; (*waste time*) fazer cera; (*tinker*) mexer.

muck in (*BRIT*: *inf*) *vi* dar uma ajuda.

muck out *vt* (*stable*) limpar.

muck up (*inf*) *vt* (*ruin*) estragar; (*dirty*) sujar.

muckraking ['mʌkreɪkɪŋ] (*inf*) *n* (*PRESS*) sensacionalismo.

mucky ['mʌkɪ] *adj* (*dirty*) sujo.

mucus ['mjuːkəs] *n* muco.

mud [mʌd] *n* lama.

muddle ['mʌdl] *n* confusão *f*, bagunça; (*mixup*) trapalhada ♦ *vt* (*also*: **~ up**) confundir, misturar; **to be in a ~** (*person*) estar confuso; **to get in a ~** (*while explaining etc*) enrolar-se.

muddle along *vi* viver sem rumo.

muddle through *vi* virar-se.

muddle-headed [-'hedɪd] *adj* (*person*) confuso.

muddy ['mʌdɪ] *adj* (*road*) lamacento; (*person, clothes*) enlameado.

mud flats *npl* extensão *f* de terra lamacenta.

mudguard ['mʌdgɑːd] *n* pára-lama *m*.

mudpack ['mʌdpæk] *n* máscara (de beleza).

mud-slinging [-slɪŋɪŋ] *n* difamação *f*, injúria.

muff [mʌf] *n* regalo ♦ *vt* (*chance*) desperdiçar, perder; (*lines*) estropiar.

muffin ['mʌfɪn] *n* bolinho redondo e chato.

muffle ['mʌfl] *vt* (*sound*) abafar; (*against cold*) agasalhar.

muffled ['mʌfld] *adj* abafado, surdo.

muffler ['mʌflə*] *n* (*scarf*) cachecol *m*; (*US: AUT*) silencioso (*BR*), panela de escape (*PT*).

mufti ['mʌftɪ] *n*: **in ~** vestido à paisana.

mug [mʌg] *n* (*cup*) caneca; (: *for beer*) caneco, canecão; (*inf*: *face*) careta; (: *fool*) bobo/a ♦ *vt* (*assault*) assaltar.

mug up (*BRIT*: *inf*) *vt* (*also*: **~ up on**) decorar.

mugger ['mʌgə*] *n* assaltante *m/f*.

mugging ['mʌgɪŋ] *n* assalto.

muggy ['mʌgɪ] *adj* abafado.

mulatto [mjuː'lætəu] (*pl* **~es**) *n* mulato/a.

mulberry ['mʌlbrɪ] *n* (*fruit*) amora; (*tree*) amoreira.

mule [mjuːl] *n* mula.

mull over [mʌl-] *vt* meditar sobre.

mulled [mʌld] *adj*: **~ wine** quentão *m*.

multi... [mʌltɪ] *prefix* multi....

multi-access *adj* (*COMPUT*) de múltiplo acesso.

multicoloured ['mʌltɪkʌləd] (*US* **multicolored**) *adj* multicolor.

multifarious [mʌltɪ'fɛərɪəs] *adj* diverso, variado.

multilateral [mʌltɪ'lætrəl] *adj* (*POL*) multilateral.

multi-level (*US*) *adj* de vários andares.

multimillionaire [mʌltɪmɪljə'nɛə*] *n* multimilionário/a.

multinational [mʌltɪ'næʃənl] *n* multinacional *f* ♦ *adj* multinacional.

multiple ['mʌltɪpl] *adj, n* múltiplo.

multiple choice *n* múltipla escolha.

multiple crash *n* engavetamento.

multiple sclerosis *n* esclerose *f* múltipla.

multiple store *n* cadeia de lojas.

multiplication [mʌltɪplɪ'keɪʃən] *n* multiplicação *f*.

multiplication table *n* tabela de multiplicação.

multiplicity [mʌltɪ'plɪsɪtɪ] *n* multiplicidade *f*.

multiply ['mʌltɪplaɪ] *vt* multiplicar ♦ *vi* multiplicar-se.

multiracial [mʌltɪ'reɪʃl] *adj* multirracial.

multistorey ['mʌltɪ'stɔːrɪ] (*BRIT*) *adj* de vários andares.

multitude ['mʌltɪtjuːd] *n* multidão *f*.

mum [mʌm] *n* (*BRIT*) mamãe *f* ♦ *adj*: **to keep ~** ficar calado; **~'s the word!** bico calado!

mumble ['mʌmbl] *vt, vi* resmungar, murmurar.

mummify ['mʌmɪfaɪ] *vt* mumificar.

mummy ['mʌmɪ] *n* (*BRIT*: *mother*) mamãe *f*; (*embalmed*) múmia.

mumps [mʌmps] *n* caxumba.

munch [mʌntʃ] *vt, vi* mascar.

mundane [mʌn'deɪn] *adj* banal, mundano.

municipal [mjuː'nɪsɪpl] *adj* municipal.

municipality [mjuːnɪsɪ'pælɪtɪ] *n* municipalidade *f*; (*area*) município.

munitions [mjuː'nɪʃənz] *npl* munições *fpl*.

mural ['mjuərl] *n* mural *m*.

murder ['məːdə*] *n* assassinato; (*LAW*) homicídio ♦ *vt* assassinar; (*spoil*) estragar; **to commit ~** cometer um assassinato.

murderer ['məːdərə*] *n* assassino.

murderess ['məːdərɪs] *n* assassina.

murderous ['məːdərəs] *adj* homicida.

murk [məːk] *n* escuridão *f*.

murky ['məːkɪ] *adj* escuro; (*fig*) sombrio.

murmur ['məːmə*] *n* murmúrio ♦ *vt, vi* murmurar; **heart ~** (*MED*) sopro cardíaco or no coração.

MusB(ac) *n abbr* (= *Bachelor of Music*) grau universitário.

muscle ['mʌsl] *n* músculo; (*fig*: *strength*) força (*muscular*).

muscle in *vi* imiscuir-se, impor-se.

muscular ['mʌskjulə*] *adj* muscular; (*person*) musculoso.

muscular dystrophy *n* distrofia muscular.

MusD(oc) *n abbr* (= *Doctor of Music*) grau universitário.

muse [mjuːz] *vi* meditar ♦ *n* musa.

museum [mjuː'zɪəm] *n* museu *m*.

mush [mʌʃ] *n* pasta, papa; (*fig*) pieguice *f*.

mushroom ['mʌʃrum] *n* cogumelo ♦ *vi* (*fig*)

crescer da noite para o dia, pipocar.
mushy ['mʌʃɪ] *adj* mole; *(pej)* piegas *inv*.
music ['mjuːzɪk] *n* música.
musical ['mjuːzɪkl] *adj* *(of music, person)* musical; *(harmonious)* melodioso ♦ *n* *(show)* musical *m*.
music(al) box *n* caixinha de música.
musical instrument *n* instrumento musical.
music hall *n* teatro de variedades.
musician [mjuː'zɪʃən] *n* músico/a.
music stand *n* atril *m*, estante *f* de música.
musk [mʌsk] *n* almíscar *m*.
musket ['mʌskɪt] *n* mosquete *m*.
muskrat ['mʌskræt] *n* rato almiscarado.
musk rose *n* *(BOT)* rosa-moscada.
Muslim ['mʌzlɪm] *adj, n* muçulmano/a.
muslin ['mʌzlɪn] *n* musselina.
musquash ['mʌskwɔʃ] *n* rato almiscarado; *(fur)* pele *f* de rato almiscarado.
mussel ['mʌsl] *n* mexilhão *m*.
must [mʌst] *aux vb* *(obligation)*: **I ~ do it** tenho que *or* devo fazer isso; *(probability)*: **he ~ be there by now** ele já deve estar lá ♦ *n* *(necessity)*: **it's a ~** é imprescindível; **I ~ have made a mistake** eu devo ter feito um erro.
mustache ['mʌstæʃ] *(US)* *n* = **moustache**.
mustard ['mʌstəd] *n* mostarda.
mustard gas *n* gás *m* de mostarda.
muster ['mʌstə*] *vt* reunir, juntar; *(also: ~ up: strength, courage)* criar, juntar.
mustiness ['mʌstɪnɪs] *n* mofo.
mustn't ['mʌsnt] = **must not**.
musty ['mʌstɪ] *adj* mofado, com cheiro de bolor.
mutant ['mjuːtənt] *adj, n* mutante *m/f*.
mutate [mjuː'teɪt] *vi* sofrer mutação genética.
mutation [mjuː'teɪʃən] *n* mutação *f*.
mute [mjuːt] *adj, n* mudo/a.
muted ['mjuːtɪd] *adj* *(noise, MUS)* abafado; *(criticism)* velado.
mutilate ['mjuːtɪleɪt] *vt* mutilar.
mutilation [mjuːtɪ'leɪʃən] *n* mutilação *f*.
mutinous ['mjuːtɪnəs] *adj* *(troops)* amotinado; *(attitude)* rebelde.
mutiny ['mjuːtɪnɪ] *n* motim *m*, rebelião *f* ♦ *vi* amotinar-se.
mutter ['mʌtə*] *vt, vi* resmungar, murmurar.
mutton ['mʌtn] *n* carne *f* de carneiro.
mutual ['mjuːtʃuəl] *adj* mútuo; *(shared)* comum.
mutually ['mjuːtʃuəlɪ] *adv* mutuamente, reciprocamente.
muzzle ['mʌzl] *n* *(of animal)* focinho; *(protective device)* focinheira; *(of gun)* boca ♦ *vt* *(press etc)* amordaçar; *(dog)* pôr focinheira em.
MVP *(US)* *n abbr* *(SPORT)* = **most valuable player**.
MW *abbr* (= *medium wave*) OM.
my [maɪ] *adj* meu/minha ♦ *excl*: **~!** meu Deus!

mynah bird ['maɪnə-] *n* mainá *m*.
myopic [maɪ'ɔpɪk] *adj* míope.
myriad ['mɪrɪəd] *n* miríade *f*.
myself [maɪ'self] *pron* *(reflexive)* me; *(emphatic)* eu mesmo; *(after prep)* mim mesmo.
mysterious [mɪs'tɪərɪəs] *adj* misterioso.
mystery ['mɪstərɪ] *n* mistério.
mystery story *n* romance *m* policial.
mystic ['mɪstɪk] *adj, n* místico/a.
mystical ['mɪstɪkl] *adj* místico.
mystify ['mɪstɪfaɪ] *vt* *(perplex)* mistificar, confundir; *(disconcert)* desconcertar.
mystique [mɪs'tiːk] *n* mística.
myth [mɪθ] *n* mito.
mythical ['mɪθɪkəl] *adj* mítico.
mythological [mɪθə'lɔdʒɪkl] *adj* mitológico.
mythology [mɪ'θɔlədʒɪ] *n* mitologia.

N

N, n [ɛn] *n* *(letter)* N, n *m*; **N for Nellie** *(BRIT)* *or* **Nan** *(US)* N de Nair.
N *abbr* (= *north*) N.
NA *(US)* *n abbr* (= *Narcotics Anonymous*) associação de assistência aos toxicômanos; = **National Academy**.
n/a *abbr* = **not applicable**; *(COMM etc)* = **no account**.
NAACP *(US)* *n abbr* = **National Association for the Advancement of Colored People**.
NAAFI ['næfɪ] *(BRIT)* *n abbr* (= *Navy, Army & Air Force Institute*) órgão responsável pelas lojas e cantinas do exército.
nab [næb] *(inf)* *vt* pegar, prender.
NACU *(US)* *n abbr* = **National Association of Colleges and Universities**.
nadir ['neɪdɪə*] *n* *(ASTRONOMY, fig)* nadir *m*.
nag [næg] *n* *(pej: horse)* rocim *m* ♦ *vt* ralhar, apoquentar.
nagging ['nægɪŋ] *adj* *(doubt)* persistente; *(pain)* contínuo ♦ *n* queixas *fpl*, censuras *fpl*, apoquentação *f*.
nail [neɪl] *n* *(human)* unha; *(metal)* prego ♦ *vt* pregar; **to ~ sb down to a date/price** conseguir que alguém se defina sobre a data/o preço; **to pay cash on the ~** *(BRIT)* pagar na bucha.
nailbrush ['neɪlbrʌʃ] *n* escova de unhas.
nailfile ['neɪlfaɪl] *n* lixa de unhas.
nail polish *n* esmalte *m* *(BR)* *or* verniz *m* *(PT)* de unhas.
nail polish remover *n* dissolvente *m* de esmalte *(BR)* *or* verniz *(PT)*.
nail scissors *npl* tesourinha de unhas.
nail varnish *(BRIT)* *n* esmalte *m* *(BR)* *or*

NB: European Portuguese adds the following consonants to certain words: **b** (sú(b)dito, su(b)til); **c** (a(c)ção, a(c)cionista, a(c)to); **m** (inde(m)ne); **p** (ado(p)ção, ado(p)tar); *for further details see p. xiii.*

verniz *m* (*PT*) de unhas.

Nairobi [naɪˈrəʊbɪ] *n* Nairóbi.

naïve [naɪˈiːv] *adj* ingênuo.

naïveté [naɪˈiːvteɪ] *n* = **naivety**.

naïvety [naɪˈiːvətɪ] *n* ingenuidade *f*.

naked [ˈneɪkɪd] *adj* (*nude*) nu/nua; **with the ~ eye** a olho nu.

nakedness [ˈneɪkɪdnɪs] *n* nudez *f*.

NALGO [ˈnælgəʊ] (*BRIT*) *n abbr* (= *National and Local Government Officers' Association*) sindicato dos funcionários públicos.

NAM (*US*) *n abbr* = **National Association of Manufacturers**.

name [neɪm] *n* nome *m*; (*surname*) sobrenome *m*; (*reputation*) reputação *f*, fama ♦ *vt* (*child*) pôr nome em; (*criminal*) apontar; (*appoint*) nomear; (*price*) fixar; (*date*) marcar; **by ~** de nome; **in the ~ of** em nome de; **what's your ~?** qual é o seu nome?, como (você) se chama?; **my ~ is Peter** eu me chamo Peter; **to take sb's ~ and address** anotar o nome e o endereço de alguém; **to make a ~ for o.s.** fazer nome; **to get (o.s.) a bad ~** fazer má reputação; **to call sb ~s** xingar alguém.

name-dropping [-ˈdrɒpɪŋ] *n*: **she loves ~ ela** adora esnobar conhecimento de gente importante.

nameless [ˈneɪmlɪs] *adj* sem nome, anônimo.

namely [ˈneɪmlɪ] *adv* a saber, isto é.

nameplate [ˈneɪmpleɪt] *n* (*on door etc*) placa.

namesake [ˈneɪmseɪk] *n* xará *m/f* (*BR*), homónimo/a (*PT*).

nanny [ˈnænɪ] *n* babá *f*.

nanny goat *n* cabra.

nap [næp] *n* (*sleep*) soneca; (*cloth*) felpa ♦ *vi*: **to be caught ~ping** ser pego de surpresa.

NAPA (*US*) *n abbr* (= *National Association of Performing Artists*) sindicato dos artistas de teatro e de cinema.

napalm [ˈneɪpɑːm] *n* napalm *m*.

nape [neɪp] *n*: **~ of the neck** nuca.

napkin [ˈnæpkɪn] *n* (*also: table ~*) guardanapo.

nappy [ˈnæpɪ] (*BRIT*) *n* fralda.

nappy liner (*BRIT*) *n* gaze *f*.

nappy rash (*BRIT*) *n* assadura.

narcissi [nɑːˈsɪsaɪ] *npl of* **narcissus**.

narcissistic [nɑːsɪˈsɪstɪk] *adj* narcisista.

narcissus [nɑːˈsɪsəs] (*pl* **narcissi**) *n* narciso.

narcotic [nɑːˈkɒtɪk] *n* (*MED*) narcótico; **~s** *npl* (*drugs*) entorpecentes *mpl*.

nark [nɑːk] (*BRIT: inf*) *vt* encher o saco de.

narrate [nəˈreɪt] *vt* narrar, contar.

narration [nəˈreɪʃən] *n* narração *f*.

narrative [ˈnærətɪv] *n* narrativa ♦ *adj* narrativo.

narrator [nəˈreɪtə*] *n* narrador(a) *m/f*.

narrow [ˈnærəʊ] *adj* estreito; (*shoe*) apertado; (*fig*) intolerante, limitado ♦ *vi* estreitar-se; **to have a ~ escape** escapar por um triz; **to ~ sth down to** restringir *or* reduzir algo a.

narrow gauge *adj* (*RAIL*) de bitola estreita.

narrowly [ˈnærəʊlɪ] *adv* (*miss*) por pouco; **he ~ missed injury/the tree** por pouco não se

machucou/não bateu na árvore.

narrow-minded [-ˈmaɪndɪd] *adj* de visão limitada, bitolado.

NAS (*US*) *n abbr* = **National Academy of Sciences**.

NASA [ˈnæsə] (*US*) *n abbr* (= *National Aeronautics and Space Administration*) NASA *f*.

nasal [ˈneɪzl] *adj* nasal.

Nassau [ˈnæsɔː] *n* (*in Bahamas*) Nassau.

nastily [ˈnɑːstɪlɪ] *adv* (*say, act*) maldosamente.

nastiness [ˈnɑːstɪnɪs] *n* (*malice*) maldade *f*; (*rudeness*) grosseria.

nasturtium [nəsˈtəːʃəm] *n* chagas *fpl*, capuchinha.

nasty [ˈnɑːstɪ] *adj* (*unpleasant: remark*) desagradável; (: *person*) mau, ruim; (*malicious*) maldoso; (*rude*) grosseiro, obsceno; (*revolting: taste, smell*) repugnante, asqueroso; (*wound, disease etc*) grave, sério; **to turn ~** (*situation, weather*) ficar feio; (*person*) engrossar.

NAS/UWT (*BRIT*) *n abbr* (= *National Association of Schoolmasters/Union of Women Teachers*) sindicato dos professores.

nation [ˈneɪʃən] *n* nação *f*.

national [ˈnæʃənl] *adj*, *n* nacional *m/f*.

national anthem *n* hino nacional.

national debt *n* dívida pública.

national dress *n* traje *m* nacional.

National Guard (*US*) *n* guarda nacional.

National Health Service (*BRIT*) *n* serviço nacional de saúde, ≈ Instituto Nacional de Assistência Médica e Previdência Social.

National Insurance (*BRIT*) *n* previdência social.

nationalism [ˈnæʃənəlɪzəm] *n* nacionalismo.

nationalist [ˈnæʃənəlɪst] *adj*, *n* nacionalista *m/f*.

nationality [næʃəˈnælɪtɪ] *n* nacionalidade *f*.

nationalization [næʃənəlaɪˈzeɪʃən] *n* nacionalização *f*.

nationalize [ˈnæʃənəlaɪz] *vt* nacionalizar.

nationally [ˈnæʃənəlɪ] *adv* (*nationwide*) de âmbito nacional; (*as a nation*) nacionalmente, como nação.

national park *n* parque *m* nacional.

national press *n* imprensa nacional.

National Security Council (*US*) *n* conselho nacional de segurança.

national service *n* (*MIL*) serviço militar.

nationwide [ˈneɪʃənwaɪd] *adj* de âmbito or a nível nacional ♦ *adv* em todo o país.

native [ˈneɪtɪv] *n* (*local inhabitant*) natural *m/f*, nativo/a; (*in colonies*) indígena *m/f*, nativo/a ♦ *adj* (*indigenous*) indígena; (*of one's birth*) natal; (*language*) materno; (*innate*) inato, natural; **a ~ of Russia** um natural da Rússia; **a ~ speaker of Portuguese** uma pessoa de língua materna portuguesa.

Nativity [nəˈtɪvɪtɪ] *n* (*REL*): **the ~** a Natividade.

NATO [ˈneɪtəʊ] *n abbr* (= *North Atlantic Treaty Organization*) OTAN *f*.

NATSOPA [nætˈsəʊpə] (*BRIT*) *n abbr* (= *National Society of Operative Printers,*

Graphical and Media Personnel) sindicato da imprensa e das indústrias gráficas.

natter ['nætə*] *(BRIT) vi* conversar fiado.

NATTKE *(BRIT) n abbr* (= *National Association of Television, Theatrical and Kinematographic Employees) sindicato dos empregados de televisão, de teatro e de cinema.*

natural ['nætʃrəl] *adj* natural; **death from ~ causes** morte *f* natural.

natural childbirth *n* parto natural.

natural gas *n* gás *m* natural.

naturalist ['nætʃrəlɪst] *n* naturalista *m/f*.

naturalization [nætʃrəlaɪ'zeɪʃən] *n* naturalização *f*.

naturalize ['nætʃrəlaɪz] *vt*: **to become ~d** *(person)* naturalizar-se.

naturally ['nætʃrəlɪ] *adv* naturalmente; *(of course)* claro, evidentemente; *(instinctively)* por instinto, espontaneamente.

naturalness ['nætʃrəlnɪs] *n* naturalidade *f*.

natural resources *npl* recursos *mpl* naturais.

natural wastage *n (INDUSTRY)* afastamentos *mpl* naturais e voluntários.

nature ['neɪtʃə*] *n* natureza; *(character)* caráter *m*, índole *f*; **by ~** por natureza; **documents of a confidential ~** documentos de caráter confidencial.

-natured ['neɪtʃəd] *suffix*: **ill~** de mau caráter.

nature reserve *(BRIT) n* reserva natural.

nature trail *n* trilha de descoberta da natureza.

naturist ['neɪtʃərɪst] *n* naturista *m/f*.

naught [nɔːt] *n* = **nought**.

naughtiness ['nɔːtɪnɪs] *n (of child)* travessura, mau comportamento; *(of story etc)* picante *m*.

naughty ['nɔːtɪ] *adj (child)* travesso, levado; *(story, film)* picante.

nausea ['nɔːsɪə] *n* náusea.

nauseate ['nɔːsɪeɪt] *vt* dar náuseas a; *(fig)* repugnar.

nauseating ['nɔːsɪeɪtɪŋ] *adj* nauseabundo, enjoativo; *(fig)* nojento, repugnante.

nauseous ['nɔːsɪəs] *adj (nauseating)* nauseabundo, enjoativo; *(feeling sick)*: **to be ~** estar enjoado.

nautical ['nɔːtɪkl] *adj* náutico.

nautical mile *n* milha marítima (= *1853 m*).

naval ['neɪvl] *adj* naval.

naval officer *n* oficial *m* de marinha.

nave [neɪv] *n* nave *f*.

navel ['neɪvl] *n* umbigo.

navigable ['nævɪɡəbl] *adj* navegável.

navigate ['nævɪɡeɪt] *vt (ship)* pilotar; *(sea)* navegar ♦ *vi* navegar; *(AUT)* ler o mapa.

navigation [nævɪ'ɡeɪʃən] *n (action)* navegação *f*; *(science)* náutica.

navigator ['nævɪɡeɪtə*] *n* navegante *m/f*, navegador(a) *m/f*.

navvy ['nævɪ] *(BRIT) n* trabalhador *m* braçal, cavouqueiro.

navy ['neɪvɪ] *n* marinha (de guerra); *(ships)* armada, frota; **Department of the N~** *(US)* ministério da Marinha.

navy(-blue) *adj* azul-marinho *inv*.

Nazareth ['næzərəθ] *n* Nazaré.

Nazi ['nɑːtsɪ] *adj, n* nazista *m/f*.

Nazism ['nɑːtsɪzəm] *n* nazismo.

NB *abbr* (= *nota bene*) NB; *(CANADA)* = **New Brunswick**.

NBA *(US) n abbr* = **National Basketball Association**; **National Boxing Association**.

NBC *(US) n abbr* (= *National Broadcasting Company)* rede de televisão.

NBS *(US) n abbr* (= *National Bureau of Standards)* órgão de padronização.

NC *abbr (COMM etc)* = **no charge**; *(US: POST)* = **North Carolina**.

NCB *(BRIT) n abbr (old)* = **National Coal Board**.

NCC *n abbr (BRIT: = Nature Conservancy Council) órgão de proteção à natureza; (US)* = **National Council of Churches**.

NCCL *(BRIT) n abbr* (= *National Council for Civil Liberties) associação de defesa das liberdades civis.*

NCO *n abbr* = **non-commissioned officer**.

ND *(US) abbr (POST)* = **North Dakota**.

NE *(US) abbr (POST)* = **Nebraska; New England**.

NEA *(US) n abbr* = **National Education Association**.

neap tide [niːp-] *n* maré *f* morta.

near [nɪə*] *adj (place)* vizinho; *(time)* próximo; *(relation)* íntimo ♦ *adv* perto ♦ *prep (also: ~ to) (space)* perto de; *(time)* perto de, quase ♦ *vt* aproximar-se de, abeirar-se de; **~ here/there** aqui/ali perto; **£25,000 or ~est offer** *(BRIT)* £25,000 ou melhor oferta; **in the ~ future** no próximo futuro; **the building is ~ing completion** o edifício está quase pronto; **to come ~** aproximar-se.

nearby [nɪə'baɪ] *adj* próximo, vizinho ♦ *adv* à mão, perto.

Near East *n*: **the ~** o Oriente Próximo.

nearer ['nɪərə*] *adj* que fica mais perto ♦ *adv* mais perto.

nearly ['nɪəlɪ] *adv* quase; **I ~ fell** quase que caí; **it's not ~ big enough** é pequeno demais.

near miss *n (of planes)* quase-colisão *f*; *(shot)* tiro que passou de raspão.

nearness ['nɪənɪs] *n* proximidade *f*; *(relationship)* intimidade *f*.

nearside ['nɪəsaɪd] *n (AUT: right-hand drive)* lado esquerdo (: *left-hand drive)* lado direito ♦ *adj* esquerdo; direito.

near-sighted [-'saɪtɪd] *adj* míope.

neat [niːt] *adj (place)* arrumado, em ordem; *(person)* asseado, arrumado; *(skilful)* hábil; *(plan)* engenhoso, bem bolado; *(spirits)* puro.

neatly ['niːtlɪ] *adv* caprichosamente, com capricho; *(avoid etc)* habilmente.

neatness ['niːtnɪs] *n (tidiness)* asseio;

NB: *European Portuguese adds the following consonants to certain words:* **b** *(sú(b)dito, su(b)til);* **c** *(a(c)ção, a(c)cionista, a(c)to);* **m** *(inde(m)ne);* **p** *(ado(p)ção, ado(p)tar); for further details see p. xiii.*

(skilfulness) habilidade *f*.

nebulous ['nɛbjuləs] *adj* nebuloso; *(fig)* vago, confuso.

necessarily ['nɛsɪsrɪlɪ] *adv* necessariamente; **not** ~ não necessariamente.

necessary ['nɛsɪsrɪ] *adj* necessário; **he did all that was** ~ fez tudo o que foi necessário; **if** ~ se necessário for.

necessitate [nɪ'sɛsɪteɪt] *vt* exigir, tornar necessário.

necessity [nɪ'sɛsɪtɪ] *n (thing needed)* necessidade *f*, requisito; *(compelling circumstances)* necessidade; **necessities** *npl* artigos *mpl* de primeira necessidade; **in case of** ~ em caso de necessidade.

neck [nɛk] *n (ANAT)* pescoço; *(of garment)* gola; *(of bottle)* gargalo ♦ *vi (inf)* ficar de agarramento; ~ **and** ~ emparelhados; **to stick one's** ~ **out** *(inf)* arriscar-se.

necklace ['nɛklɪs] *n* colar *m*.

neckline ['nɛklaɪn] *n* decote *m*.

necktie ['nɛktaɪ] *(esp US) n* gravata.

nectar ['nɛktə*] *n* néctar *m*.

nectarine ['nɛktərɪn] *n* nectarina.

NEDC *(BRIT) n abbr* = **National Economic Development Council**.

Neddy ['nɛdɪ] *(BRIT: inf) n abbr* = **NEDC**.

née [neɪ] *adj:* ~ **Scott** em solteira Scott.

need [niːd] *n (lack)* falta, carência; *(necessity)* necessidade *f*; *(thing needed)* requisito, necessidade ♦ *vt (require)* precisar de; **I** ~ **to do it** preciso fazê-lo; **you don't** ~ **to go** você não precisa ir; **a signature is** ~**ed** é necessária uma assinatura; **to be in** ~ **of** *or* **have** ~ **of** estar precisando de; **£10 will meet my immediate** ~**s** £10 atenderão minhas necessidades mais prementes; **in case of** ~ em caso de necessidade; **there's no** ~ **to do ...** não é preciso fazer ...; **there's no** ~ **for that** isso não é necessário.

needle ['niːdl] *n* agulha ♦ *vt (inf)* provocar, picar, alfinetar.

needlecord ['niːdlkɔːd] *(BRIT) n* veludo cotelê.

needless ['niːdlɪs] *adj* inútil, desnecessário; ~ **to say ...** desnecessário dizer que ....

needlessly ['niːdlɪslɪ] *adv* desnecessariamente, à toa.

needlework ['niːdlwəːk] *n* trabalho de agulha, costura.

needn't ['niːdnt] = **need not**.

needy ['niːdɪ] *adj* necessitado, carente.

negation [nɪ'geɪʃən] *n* negação *f*.

negative ['nɛgətɪv] *n (PHOT)* negativo; *(answer)* negativa ♦ *adj* negativo; **to answer in the** ~ responder negativamente.

neglect [nɪ'glɛkt] *vt (one's duty)* negligenciar, não cumprir com; *(child)* descuidar, esquecer-se de ♦ *n* descuido, desatenção *f*; *(personal)* desleixo; *(of duty)* negligência; **(state of)** ~ abandono; **to** ~ **to do sth** omitir de fazer algo.

neglected [nɪ'glɛktɪd] *adj* abandonado.

neglectful [nɪ'glɛktful] *adj* negligente; **to be** ~ **of sb/sth** descuidar de alguém/algo.

negligee ['nɛglɪʒeɪ] *n* négligé *m*.

negligence ['nɛglɪdʒəns] *n* negligência, descuido.

negligent ['nɛglɪdʒənt] *adj* negligente.

negligently ['nɛglɪdʒəntlɪ] *adv* por negligência; *(offhandedly)* negligentemente.

negligible ['nɛglɪdʒɪbl] *adj* insignificante, desprezível, ínfimo.

negotiable [nɪ'gəuʃɪəbl] *adj (cheque)* negociável; *(road)* transitável.

negotiate [nɪ'gəuʃɪeɪt] *vi* negociar ♦ *vt (treaty)* negociar; *(obstacle)* contornar; **to** ~ **with sb for sth** negociar com alguém para obter algo.

negotiation [nɪgəuʃɪ'eɪʃən] *n* negociação *f*; **to enter into** ~**s with sb** entrar em negociações com alguém.

negotiator [nɪ'gəuʃɪeɪtə*] *n* negociador(a) *m/f*.

Negress ['niːgrɪs] *n* negra.

Negro ['niːgrəu] *(pl* ~**es**) *adj* negro ♦ *n* negro/a.

Negroes ['niːgrəuz] *npl of* **Negro**.

neigh [neɪ] *n* relincho ♦ *vi* relinchar.

neighbour ['neɪbə*] *(US* **neighbor**) *n* vizinho/a.

neighbo(u)rhood ['neɪbəhud] *n (place)* vizinhança, bairro; *(people)* vizinhos *mpl*.

neighbo(u)ring ['neɪbərɪŋ] *adj* vizinho.

neighbo(u)rly ['neɪbəlɪ] *adj* amistoso, prestativo.

neither ['naɪðə*] *conj:* **I didn't move and** ~ **did he** não me movi nem ele ♦ *adj, pron* nenhum (dos dois), nem um nem outro ♦ *adv:* ~ **good nor bad** nem bom nem mau.

neo... [niːəu] *prefix* neo-.

neolithic [niːəu'lɪθɪk] *adj* neolítico.

neologism [nɪ'ɔlədʒɪzəm] *n* neologismo.

neon ['niːɔn] *n* neônio, néon *m*.

neon light *n* luz *f* de neônio.

neon sign *n* anúncio luminoso a neônio.

Nepal [nɪ'pɔːl] *n* Nepal *m*.

nephew ['nɛvjuː] *n* sobrinho.

nepotism ['nɛpətɪzm] *n* nepotismo.

nerve [nəːv] *n (ANAT)* nervo; *(courage)* coragem *f*; *(impudence)* descaramento, atrevimento; **he gets on my** ~**s** ele me irrita, ele me dá nos nervos; **to have a fit of** ~**s** ter uma crise nervosa; **to lose one's** ~ *(self-confidence)* perder o sangue frio.

nerve centre *(US* **nerve center**) *n (ANAT)* centro nervoso; *(fig)* centro de operações.

nerve gas *n* gás *m* tóxico.

nerve-racking [-'rækɪŋ] *adj* angustiante.

nervous ['nəːvəs] *adj (anxious, ANAT)* nervoso; *(timid)* tímido, acanhado; ~ **exhaustion** esgotamento nervoso.

nervous breakdown *n* esgotamento nervoso.

nervously ['nəːvəslɪ] *adv* nervosamente; *(timidly)* timidamente.

nervousness ['nəːvəsnɪs] *n* nervosismo; *(timidity)* timidez *f*.

nest [nɛst] *vi* aninhar-se ♦ *n (of bird)* ninho; *(of wasp)* vespeiro; ~ **of tables** jogo de mesinhas.

nest egg *n (fig)* pé-de-meia *m*.

nestle ['nɛsl] *vi:* **to** ~ **up to sb** aconchegar-se a alguém.

nestling ['nɛstlɪŋ] n filhote m (de passarinho).

net [nɛt] n rede f ♦ adj (COMM) líquido ♦ vt pegar na rede; (money: subj: person) faturar; (: deal, sale) render; ~ **of tax** isento de impostos; **he earns £10,000 ~ per year** ele ganha £10,000 líquidas por ano.

netball ['nɛtbɔːl] n (espécie de) basquetebol.

net curtains npl cortinas fpl de voile.

Netherlands ['nɛðələndz] npl: **the ~** os Países Baixos.

net profit n lucro líquido.

nett [nɛt] adj = **net**.

netting ['nɛtɪŋ] n rede f, redes fpl; (fabric) voile m.

nettle ['nɛtl] n urtiga.

network ['nɛtwɔːk] n rede f ♦ vt (RADIO, TV) transmitir em rede; (computers) interligar.

neuralgia [njuə'rældʒə] n neuralgia.

neuroses [njuə'rəusiːz] npl of **neurosis**.

neurosis [njuə'rəusɪs] (pl **neuroses**) n neurose f.

neurotic [njuə'rɔtɪk] adj, n neurótico/a.

neuter ['njuːtə*] adj neutro ♦ n neutro ♦ vt (cat etc) castrar, capar.

neutral ['njuːtrəl] adj neutro ♦ n (AUT) ponto morto.

neutrality [njuː'trælɪtɪ] n neutralidade f.

neutralize ['njuːtrəlaɪz] vt neutralizar.

neutron ['njuːtrɔn] n nêutron (PT: neutrão) m.

neutron bomb n bomba de nêutrons (PT: neutrões).

never ['nɛvə*] adv nunca; **I ~ went** nunca fui; **~ again** nunca mais; **~ in my life** nunca na minha vida; see also **mind**.

never-ending [-'ɛndɪŋ] adj sem fim, interminável.

nevertheless [nɛvəðə'lɛs] adv todavia, contudo.

new [njuː] adj novo; **as good as ~** tal como novo.

newborn ['njuːbɔːn] adj recém-nascido.

newcomer ['njuːkʌmə*] n recém-chegado/a.

new-fangled [-'fæŋgld] (pej) adj ultramoderno.

new-found adj (friend) novo; (enthusiasm) recente.

Newfoundland ['njuːfənlənd] n Terra Nova.

New Guinea n Nova Guiné f.

newly ['njuːlɪ] adv recém, novamente.

newly-weds npl recém-casados mpl.

new moon n lua nova.

newness ['njuːnɪs] n novidade f.

news [njuːz] n notícias fpl; (RADIO, TV) noticiário; **a piece of ~** uma notícia; **good/bad ~** boa/má notícia; **financial ~** noticiário financeiro.

news agency n agência de notícias.

newsagent ['njuːzeɪdʒənt] (BRIT) n jornaleiro/a.

news bulletin n (RADIO, TV) noticiário.

newscaster ['njuːzkɑːstə*] n (RADIO, TV) noticiarista m/f.

newsdealer ['njuːzdiːlə*] (US) n jornaleiro/a.

news flash n notícia de última hora.

newsletter ['njuːzlɛtə*] n boletim m informativo.

newspaper ['njuːzpeɪpə*] n jornal m; (material) papel m de jornal; **daily ~** diário; **weekly ~** semanário.

newsprint ['njuːzprɪnt] n papel m de jornal.

newsreader ['njuːzriːdə*] n noticiarista.

newsreel ['njuːzriːl] n jornal m cinematográfico, atualidades fpl.

newsroom ['njuːzruːm] n (PRESS) sala de redação; (TV) estúdio.

newsstand ['njuːzstænd] n banca de jornais.

newt [njuːt] n tritão m.

New Year n ano novo; **Happy ~!** Feliz Ano Novo!; **to wish sb a happy ~** desejar feliz ano novo a alguém.

New Year's Day n dia m de ano novo.

New Year's Eve n véspera de ano novo.

New York [-jɔːk] n Nova Iorque.

New Zealand [-'ziːlənd] n Nova Zelândia ♦ cpd neozelandês/esa.

New Zealander [-'ziːləndə*] n neozelandês/esa m/f.

next [nɛkst] adj (in space) próximo, vizinho; (in time) seguinte, próximo ♦ adv (place) depois; (time) depois, logo; ~ **to** ao lado de; ~ **to nothing** quase nada; ~ **time** na próxima vez; **the ~ day** o dia seguinte; ~ **year** (n)o ano que vem; "**turn to the ~ page**" "vire para a página seguinte"; **who's ~?** quem é o próximo?; **the week after ~** sem ser a semana que vem, a outra; **when do we meet ~?** quando é que nós nos reencontramos?

next door adv na casa do lado ♦ adj vizinho.

next-of-kin n parentes mpl mais próximos.

NF n abbr (BRIT: POL: = National Front) partido político da extrema direita ♦ abbr (CANADA) = **Newfoundland**.

NFL (US) n abbr = **National Football League**.

NFU (BRIT) n abbr (= National Farmers' Union) sindicato dos fazendeiros.

NG (US) abbr = **National Guard**.

NGA (BRIT) n abbr (= National Graphical Association) sindicato das indústrias gráficas.

NGO (US) n abbr = **non-governmental organization**.

NH (US) abbr (POST) = **New Hampshire**.

NHL (US) n abbr = **National Hockey League**.

NHS (BRIT) n abbr = **National Health Service**.

NI abbr = **Northern Ireland**; (BRIT) = **National Insurance**.

Niagara Falls [naɪ'ægrə-] npl: **the ~** as cataratas do Niagara.

nib [nɪb] n ponta or bico da pena.

nibble ['nɪbl] vt mordiscar, beliscar; (ZOOL) roer.

Nicaragua [nɪkə'rægjuə] n Nicarágua.

Nicaraguan [nɪkə'rægjuən] adj, n nicaragüense m/f.

NB: European Portuguese adds the following consonants to certain words: **b** (sú(b)dito, su(b)til); **c** (a(c)ção, a(c)cionista, a(c)to); **m** (inde(m)ne); **p** (ado(p)ção, ado(p)tar); *for further details see p. xiii.*

nice [naɪs] *adj* (*likeable*) simpático; (*kind*) amável, atencioso; (*pleasant*) agradável; (*flat, picture*) bonito; (*subtle*) sutil, fino.

nice-looking [-'lukɪŋ] *adj* bonito.

nicely ['naɪslɪ] *adv* agradavelmente, bem; **that will do** ~ isso será perfeito.

niceties ['naɪsɪtɪz] *npl* sutilezas *fpl*.

niche [niːʃ] *n* nicho.

nick [nɪk] *n* (*wound*) corte *m*; (*cut, indentation*) entalhe *m*, incisão *f*; (*BRIT: inf*): **in good** ~ em bom estado ♦ *vt* (*cut*) entalhar; (*inf: steal*) furtar; (: *BRIT: arrest*) prender, arrochar; **in the** ~ **of time** na hora H, no momento exato; **to** ~ **o.s.** cortar-se.

nickel ['nɪkl] *n* níquel *m*; (*US*) moeda de 5 centavos.

nickname ['nɪkneɪm] *n* apelido (*BR*), alcunha (*PT*) ♦ *vt* apelidar de (*BR*), alcunhar de (*PT*).

Nicosia [nɪkə'siːə] *n* Nicósia.

nicotine ['nɪkətiːn] *n* nicotina.

niece [niːs] *n* sobrinha.

nifty ['nɪftɪ] (*inf*) *adj* (*car, jacket*) chique; (*gadget, tool*) jeitoso.

Niger ['naɪdʒəˣ] *n* (*country, river*) Níger *m*.

Nigeria [naɪ'dʒɪərɪə] *n* Nigéria.

Nigerian [naɪ'dʒɪərɪən] *adj, n* nigeriano/a.

niggardly ['nɪgədlɪ] *adj* (*person*) avarento, sovina; (*amount*) miserável.

nigger ['nɪgəˣ] (*inf!*) *n* (*highly offensive*) crioulo/a, baiano/a.

niggle ['nɪgl] *vi* (*find fault*) botar defeito; (*fuss*) fazer histórias ♦ *vt* irritar.

niggling ['nɪglɪŋ] *adj* (*trifling*) insignificante, mesquinho; (*annoying*) irritante; (*pain, doubt*) persistente.

night [naɪt] *n* noite *f*; **at** *or* **by** ~ à *or* de noite; **in** *or* **during the** ~ durante a noite; **last** ~ ontem à noite; **the** ~ **before last** anteontem à noite; **good** ~! boa noite!

night-bird *n* (*ZOOL*) ave *f* noturna; (*fig*) noctívago/a *m*.

nightcap ['naɪtkæp] *n* (*drink*) *bebida tomada antes de dormir*.

night club *n* boate *f*.

nightdress ['naɪtdrɛs] *n* camisola (*BR*), camisa de noite (*PT*).

nightfall ['naɪtfɔːl] *n* anoitecer *m*.

nightgown ['naɪtgaun] *n* camisola (*BR*), camisa de noite (*PT*).

nightie ['naɪtɪ] *n* camisola (*BR*), camisa de noite (*PT*).

nightingale ['naɪtɪŋgeɪl] *n* rouxinol *m*.

night life *n* vida noturna.

nightly ['naɪtlɪ] *adj* noturno, de noite ♦ *adv* todas as noites, cada noite.

nightmare ['naɪtmɛəˣ] *n* pesadelo.

night porter *n* porteiro da noite.

night safe *n* cofre *m* noturno.

night school *n* escola noturna.

nightshade ['naɪtʃeɪd] *n*: **deadly** ~ (*BOT*) beladona.

nightshift ['naɪtʃɪft] *n* turno da noite.

night-time *n* noite *f*.

night watchman (*irreg*) *n* vigia *m*, guarda-noturno *m*.

nihilism ['naɪɪlɪzm] *n* niilismo.

nil [nɪl] *n* nada; (*BRIT: SPORT*) zero.

Nile [naɪl] *n*: **the** ~ o Nilo.

nimble ['nɪmbl] *adj* (*agile*) ágil, ligeiro; (*skilful*) hábil, esperto.

nine [naɪn] *num* nove; *see also* **five**.

nineteen [naɪn'tiːn] *num* dezenove (*BR*), dezanove (*PT*); *see also* **five**.

ninety ['naɪntɪ] *num* noventa; *see also* **fifty**.

ninth [naɪnθ] *num* nono; *see also* **fifth**.

nip [nɪp] *vt* (*pinch*) beliscar; (*bite*) morder ♦ *vi* (*BRIT: inf*): **to** ~ **out/down/up** dar uma saidinha/descida/subida ♦ *n* (*drink*) gole *m*, trago; **to** ~ **into a shop** dar um pulo numa loja.

nipple ['nɪpl] *n* (*ANAT*) bico do seio, mamilo; (*of bottle*) bocal *m*, bico; (*TECH*) bocal (roscado).

nippy ['nɪpɪ] (*BRIT*) *adj* (*person*) rápido, ágil; (*cold*) friozinho.

nit [nɪt] *n* (*in hair*) lêndea, ovo de piolho; (*inf: idiot*) imbecil *m/f*, idiota *m/f*.

nit-pick (*inf*) *vi* ser implicante.

nitrate ['naɪtreɪt] *n* nitrato.

nitrogen ['naɪtrədʒən] *n* nitrogênio.

nitroglycerin(e) [naɪtrəu'glɪsəriːn] *n* nitroglicerina.

nitty-gritty ['nɪtɪ'grɪtɪ] (*inf*) *n*: **to get down to the** ~ chegar ao âmago.

nitwit ['nɪtwɪt] (*inf*) *n* pateta *m/f*, bobalhão/ona *m/f*.

NJ (*US*) *abbr* (*POST*) = **New Jersey**.

NLF *n abbr* = **National Liberation Front**.

NLQ *abbr* (= *near letter quality*) qualidade *f* carta.

NLRB (*US*) *n abbr* (= *National Labor Relations Board*) órgão de proteção aos trabalhadores.

NM (*US*) *abbr* (*POST*) = **New Mexico**.

no [nəu] *adv* não ♦ *adj* nenhum(a), não ... algum ♦ *n* não *m*, negativa; **I have** ~ **more wine** não tenho mais vinho; "~ **entry**" "entrada proibida"; "~ **dogs**" "proibido a cães"; **I won't take** ~ **for an answer** não aceitarei um não como resposta.

no. *abbr* (= *number*) nº.

nobble ['nɔbl] (*BRIT: inf*) *vt* (*bribe*) subornar; (*person: speak to*) agarrar; (*RACING: horse*) incapacitar (*com drogas*).

Nobel prize [nəu'bel-] *n* prêmio Nobel.

nobility [nəu'bɪlɪtɪ] *n* nobreza.

noble ['nəubl] *adj* (*person*) nobre; (*title*) de nobreza.

nobleman ['nəublmən] (*irreg*) *n* nobre *m*, fidalgo.

nobly ['nəublɪ] *adv* nobremente.

nobody ['nəubədɪ] *pron* ninguém (*with negative*).

no-claims bonus *n* bonificação *f* (*por não ter reclamado indenização*).

nocturnal [nɔk'təːnəl] *adj* noturno.

nod [nɔd] *vi* (*greeting*) cumprimentar com a cabeça; (*in agreement*) acenar (que sim) com a cabeça; (*doze*) cochilar, dormitar ♦ *vt*: **to** ~ **one's head** inclinar a cabeça ♦ *n* inclinação *f* da cabeça; **they ~ded their agreement** inclinaram a cabeça afirmando seu acordo.

nod off *vi* cochilar.

noise [nɔɪz] *n* barulho; **~ abatement** luta contra a poluição sonora.

noiseless ['nɔɪzlɪs] *adj* silencioso.

noisily ['nɔɪzɪlɪ] *adv* ruidosamente, com muito barulho.

noisy ['nɔɪzɪ] *adj* barulhento.

nomad ['nəʊmæd] *n* nômade *m/f*.

nomadic [nəʊ'mædɪk] *adj* nômade.

no man's land *n* terra de ninguém.

nominal ['nɒmɪnl] *adj* nominal.

nominate ['nɒmɪneɪt] *vt* (*propose*) propor; (*appoint*) nomear.

nomination [nɒmɪ'neɪʃən] *n* nomeação *f*; (*proposal*) proposta.

nominee [nɒmɪ'niː] *n* pessoa nomeada, candidato/a.

non- [nɒn] *prefix* não-, des..., in..., anti-....

non-alcoholic *adj* não-alcoólico.

nonaligned [-ə'laɪnd] *adj* não-alinhado.

non-breakable *adj* inquebrável.

nonce word ['nɒns-] *n* palavra criada para a ocasião.

nonchalant ['nɒnʃələnt] *adj* despreocupado.

non-commissioned [-kə'mɪʃənd] *adj*: **~ officer** oficial *m* subalterno.

non-committal [-kə'mɪtl] *adj* (*uncommitted*) evasivo.

nonconformist [nɒnkən'fɔːmɪst] *adj* não-conformista, dissidente ♦ *n* não-conformista *m/f*.

non-contributory *adj*: **~ pension scheme** (*BRIT*) *or* **plan** (*US*) caixa de aposentadoria não-contributária.

non-cooperation *n* não-cooperação *f*.

nondescript ['nɒndɪskrɪpt] *adj* qualquer; (*pej*) medíocre.

none [nʌn] *pron* (*person*) ninguém; (*thing*) nenhum(a), nada; **~ of you** nenhum de vocês; **I have ~** não tenho; **I have ~ left** não tenho mais; **~ at all** (*not one*) nem um só; **how much milk? - ~ at all** quanto leite? - nada; **he's ~ the worse for it** isso não o afetou.

nonentity [nɒ'nentɪtɪ] *n* nulidade *f*, zero à esquerda *m*.

non-essential *adj* não essencial, dispensável ♦ *npl*: **~s** desnecessários *mpl*.

nonetheless [nʌnðə'les] *adv* no entanto, apesar disso, contudo.

non-executive *adj*: **~ director** administrador(a) *m/f*, conselheiro/a.

non-existent [-ɪg'zɪstənt] *adj* inexistente.

non-fiction *n* literatura de não-ficção.

non-flammable *adj* não inflamável.

non-intervention *n* não-intervenção *f*.

non obst. *abbr* (= *non obstante*; *notwithstanding*) não obstante.

non-payment *n* falta de pagamento.

nonplussed [nɒn'plʌst] *adj* perplexo, pasmado.

non-profit-making *adj* sem fins lucrativos.

nonsense ['nɒnsəns] *n* disparate *m*, besteira, absurdo; **~!** bobagem!, que nada!; **it's ~ to say ...** é um absurdo dizer que ....

non-shrink (*BRIT*) *adj* que não encolhe.

non-skid *adj* antiderrapante.

non-smoker *n* não-fumador(a) *m/f*.

non-stick *adj* tefal ®, não-aderente.

non-stop *adj* ininterrupto; (*RAIL*) direto; (*AVIAT*) sem escala ♦ *adv* sem parar.

non-taxable income *n* renda não-tributável.

non-U (*BRIT*: *inf*) *adj abbr* (= *non-upper class*) que não se diz (*or* se faz).

non-volatile memory *n* (*COMPUT*) memória não volátil.

non-voting shares *npl* ações *fpl* sem direito de voto.

non-white *adj*, *n* não-branco/a.

noodles ['nuːdlz] *npl* talharim *m*.

nook [nʊk] *n* canto, recanto; **~s and crannies** esconderijos *mpl*.

noon [nuːn] *n* meio-dia *m*.

no-one *pron* (*with negative*) ninguém.

noose [nuːs] *n* laço corrediço; (*hangman's*) corda da forca.

nor [nɔː*] *conj* = **neither** ♦ *adv* see **neither**.

Norf (*BRIT*) *abbr* = **Norfolk**.

norm [nɔːm] *n* norma.

normal ['nɔːml] *adj* normal ♦ *n*: **to return to ~** normalizar-se.

normality [nɔː'mælɪtɪ] *n* normalidade *f*.

normally ['nɔːməlɪ] *adv* normalmente.

Normandy ['nɔːməndɪ] *n* Normandia.

north [nɔːθ] *n* norte *m* ♦ *adj* do norte, setentrional ♦ *adv* ao *or* para o norte.

North Africa *n* África do Norte.

North African *adj*, *n* norte-africano/a.

North America *n* América do Norte.

North American *adj*, *n* norte-americano/a.

Northants [nɔː'θænts] (*BRIT*) *abbr* = **Northamptonshire**.

northbound ['nɔːθbaʊnd] *adj* em direção norte.

Northd (*BRIT*) *abbr* = **Northumberland**.

north-east *n* nordeste *m*.

northerly ['nɔːðəlɪ] *adj* (*wind*, *course*) norte.

northern ['nɔːðən] *adj* do norte, setentrional.

Northern Ireland *n* Irlanda do Norte.

North Pole *n*: **the ~** o Pólo Norte.

North Sea *n*: **the ~** o Mar do Norte.

North Sea oil *n* petróleo do Mar do Norte.

northward(s) ['nɔːθwəd(z)] *adv* em direção norte.

north-west *n* noroeste *m*.

Norway ['nɔːweɪ] *n* Noruega.

Norwegian [nɔː'wiːdʒən] *adj* norueguês/esa ♦ *n* norueguês/esa *m/f*; (*LING*) norueguês *m*.

nos. *abbr* (= *numbers*) n°.

nose [nəʊz] *n* (*ANAT*) nariz *m*; (*ZOOL*) focinho; (*sense of smell*) faro, olfato ♦ *vi* (*also*: **~ one's way**) avançar cautelosamente; **to turn**

up one's ~ at desdenhar; **to pay through the ~ (for sth)** (*inf*) pagar os olhos da cara (por algo).

nose about *vi* bisbilhotar.

nose around *vi* bisbilhotar.

nosebleed ['nəuzbli:d] *n* hemorragia nasal.

nose-dive *n* (*deliberate*) vôo picado; (*involuntary*) parafuso.

nose drops *npl* gotas *fpl* para o nariz.

nosey ['nəuzɪ] *adj* intrometido, abelhudo.

nostalgia [nɔs'tældʒɪə] *n* nostalgia.

nostalgic [nɔs'tældʒɪk] *adj* nostálgico.

nostril ['nɔstrɪl] *n* narina.

nosy ['nəuzɪ] *adj* = **nosey**.

not [nɔt] *adv* não; **~ at all** não ... de modo nenhum; (*after thanks*) de nada; **~ that he knows** não que ele o saiba; **~ yet** ainda não; **~ now** agora não; **why ~?** por que não?; **I hope ~** espero que não.

notable ['nəutəbl] *adj* notável.

notably ['nəutəblɪ] *adv* notavelmente.

notary ['nəutərɪ] *n* (*also*: **~ public**) tabelião/tabelioa *m/f*, notário/a.

notation [nəu'teɪʃən] *n* notação *f*.

notch [nɔtʃ] *n* entalhe *m*, corte *m*.

notch up *vt* (*score*) marcar; (*victory*) registrar.

note [nəut] *n* (*MUS*, *bank* **~**) nota; (*letter*) nota, bilhete *m*; (*record*) nota, anotação *f*; (*tone*) tom *m* ♦ *vt* (*observe*) observar, reparar em; (*also*: **~ down**) anotar, tomar nota de; **just a quick ~ to let you know** ... apenas um bilhete rápido para avisá-lo ...; **to take ~s** tomar notas; **to compare ~s** (*fig*) trocar impressões; **to take ~ of** fazer caso de; **a person of ~** uma pessoa eminente.

notebook ['nəutbuk] *n* caderno.

note-case (*BRIT*) *n* carteira.

noted ['nəutɪd] *adj* célebre, conhecido.

notepad ['nəutpæd] *n* bloco de anotações.

notepaper ['nəutpeɪpə*] *n* papel *m* de carta.

noteworthy ['nəutwə:ðɪ] *adj* notável.

nothing ['nʌθɪŋ] *n* nada; (*zero*) zero; **he does ~** ele não faz nada; **~ new** nada de novo; **for ~** (*free*) de graça, grátis; (*in vain*) em vão, por nada; **~ at all** absolutamente nada, coisa nenhuma.

notice ['nəutɪs] *n* (*sign*) aviso, anúncio; (*warning*) aviso; (*of leaving*) aviso prévio; (*BRIT*: *review*: *of play etc*) resenha ♦ *vt* (*observe*) reparar em, notar; **without ~** sem aviso prévio; **advance ~** aviso prévio, preaviso; **to give sb ~ of sth** dar aviso a alguém de algo; **at short ~** a curto prazo; **until further ~** até nova ordem; **to hand in or give one's ~** (*subj*: *employee*) demitir, pedir a demissão; **to take ~ of** prestar atenção a, fazer caso de; **to bring sth to sb's ~** levar algo ao conhecimento de alguém; **it has come to my ~ that** ... tornei-me ciente que ...; **to escape** *or* **avoid ~** passar desapercebido.

noticeable ['nəutɪsəbl] *adj* evidente, sensível.

notice board (*BRIT*) *n* quadro de avisos.

notification [nəutɪfɪ'keɪʃən] *n* aviso, notifica-

ção *f*.

notify ['nəutɪfaɪ] *vt* avisar, notificar; **to ~ sth to sb** notificar algo a alguém; **to ~ sb of sth** avisar alguém de algo.

notion ['nəuʃən] *n* noção *f*, idéia.

notions ['nəuʃənz] (*US*) *npl* miudezas *fpl*.

notoriety [nəutə'raɪətɪ] *n* notoriedade *f*, má fama.

notorious [nəu'tɔ:rɪəs] *adj* notório.

notoriously [nəu'tɔ:rɪəslɪ] *adv* notoriamente.

Notts [nɔts] (*BRIT*) *abbr* = **Nottinghamshire**.

notwithstanding [nɔtwɪθ'stændɪŋ] *adv* no entanto, não obstante ♦ *prep*: **~ this** apesar disto.

nougat ['nu:gɑ:] *n* torrone *m*, nugá *m*.

nought [nɔ:t] *n* zero.

noun [naun] *n* substantivo.

nourish ['nʌrɪʃ] *vt* nutrir, alimentar; (*fig*) fomentar, alentar.

nourishing ['nʌrɪʃɪŋ] *adj* nutritivo, alimentício.

nourishment ['nʌrɪʃmənt] *n* alimento, nutrimento.

Nov. *abbr* (= *November*) nov.

Nova Scotia ['nəuvə'skəuʃə] *n* Nova Escócia.

novel ['nɔvl] *n* romance *m*; (*short*) novela ♦ *adj* (*new*) novo, recente; (*unexpected*) insólito.

novelist ['nɔvəlɪst] *n* romancista *m/f*.

novelty ['nɔvəltɪ] *n* novidade *f*.

November [nəu'vɛmbə*] *n* novembro; *see also* **July**.

novice ['nɔvɪs] *n* principiante *m/f*, novato/a; (*REL*) noviço/a.

NOW [nau] (*US*) *n abbr* = **National Organization for Women**.

now [nau] *adv* (*at the present time*) agora; (*these days*) atualmente, hoje em dia ♦ *conj*: **~ (that)** agora que; **right ~** agora mesmo; **that's the fashion just ~** é a moda atualmente; **I saw her just ~** eu a vi agora, acabei de vê-la; **~ and then**, **~ and again** de vez em quando; **from ~ on** de agora em diante; **in 3 days from ~** daqui a 3 dias; **between ~ and Monday** até segunda-feira; **that's all for ~** por agora é tudo.

nowadays ['nauədeɪz] *adv* hoje em dia.

nowhere ['nəuwɛə*] *adv* (*direction*) a lugar nenhum; (*location*) em nenhum lugar; **~ else** em nenhum outro lugar.

noxious ['nɔkʃəs] *adj* nocivo.

nozzle ['nɔzl] *n* bico, bocal *m*; (*TECH*) tubeira; (: *hose*) agulheta.

NP *n abbr* = **notary public**.

NS (*CANADA*) *abbr* = **Nova Scotia**.

NSC (*US*) *n abbr* = **National Security Council**.

NSF (*US*) *n abbr* = **National Science Foundation**.

NSPCC (*BRIT*) *n abbr* = **National Society for the Prevention of Cruelty to Children**.

NSW (*AUSTRALIA*) *abbr* = **New South Wales**.

NT *n abbr* (= *New Testament*) NT.

nth [ɛnθ] *adj*: **for the ~ time** pela enésima vez.

NUAAW (*BRIT*) *n abbr* (= *National Union of*

Agricultural and Allied Workers) sindicato da agropecuária.

nuance ['njuːɑ̃ːns] *n* nuança, matiz *m*.

NUBE (*BRIT*) *n abbr* (= *National Union of Bank Employees*) *sindicato dos bancários.*

nubile ['njuːbaɪl] *adj* (*attractive*) jovem e bela.

nuclear ['njuːklɪə*] *adj* nuclear.

nuclear disarmament *n* desarmamento nuclear.

nuclei ['njuːklɪaɪ] *npl of* **nucleus**.

nucleus ['njuːklɪəs] (*pl* **nuclei**) *n* núcleo.

nude [njuːd] *adj* nu/nua ♦ *n* (*ART*) nu *m*; **in the ~** nu, pelado.

nudge [nʌdʒ] *vt* acotovelar, cutucar (*BR*).

nudist ['njuːdɪst] *n* nudista *m/f*.

nudist colony *n* colonia nudista.

nudity ['njuːdɪtɪ] *n* nudez *f*.

nugget ['nʌgɪt] *n* pepita.

nuisance ['njuːsns] *n* amolação *f*, aborrecimento; (*person*) chato; **what a ~!** que saco! (*BR*), que chatice! (*PT*).

NUJ (*BRIT*) *n abbr* (= *National Union of Journalists*) *sindicato dos jornalistas.*

nuke [njuːk] (*inf*) *n* usina nuclear.

null [nʌl] *adj*: **~ and void** írrito e nulo.

nullify ['nʌlɪfaɪ] *vt* anular, invalidar.

NUM (*BRIT*) *n abbr* (= *National Union of Mineworkers*) *sindicato dos mineiros.*

numb [nʌm] *adj* dormente, entorpecido; (*fig*) insensível ♦ *vt* adormecer, entorpecer; **~ with cold** tolhido de frio; **~ with fear** paralisado de medo.

number ['nʌmbə*] *n* número; (*numeral*) algarismo ♦ *vt* (*pages etc*) numerar; **a ~ of** vários, muitos; **to be ~ed among** figurar entre; **they were ten in ~** eram em número de dez; **wrong ~** (*TEL*) engano.

numbered account ['nʌmbəd-] *n* (*in bank*) conta numerada.

number plate (*BRIT*) *n* placa (do carro).

Number Ten (*BRIT*) *n* (= *10 Downing Street*) *residência do primeiro-ministro.*

numbness ['nʌmnɪs] *n* torpor *m*, dormência; (*fig*) insensibilidade *f*.

numeral ['njuːmərəl] *n* algarismo.

numerate ['njuːmərɪt] (*BRIT*) *adj*: **to be ~** ter uma noção básica da aritmética.

numerical [njuː'merɪkl] *adj* numérico.

numerous ['njuːmərəs] *adj* numeroso.

nun [nʌn] *n* freira.

NUPE ['njuːpɪ] (*BRIT*) *n abbr* (= *National Union of Public Employees*) *sindicato dos funcionários públicos.*

nuptial ['nʌpʃəl] *adj* nupcial.

NUR (*BRIT*) *n abbr* (= *National Union of Railwaymen*) *sindicato dos ferroviários.*

nurse [nɜːs] *n* enfermeiro/a; (*nanny*) amaseca, babá *f* ♦ *vt* (*patient*) cuidar de, tratar de; (*baby: feed*) criar, amamentar; (: *BRIT: rock*) embalar; (*fig*) alimentar; **wet ~** ama de leite.

nursery ['nɜːsərɪ] *n* (*institution*) creche *f*; (*room*) quarto das crianças; (*for plants*) viveiro.

nursery rhyme *n* poesia infantil.

nursery school *n* escola maternal.

nursery slope (*BRIT*) *n* (*SKI*) rampa para principiantes.

nursing ['nɜːsɪŋ] *n* (*profession*) enfermagem *f*; (*care*) cuidado, assistência ♦ *adj* (*mother*) amamentadora.

nursing home *n* sanatório, clínica de repouso.

nurture ['nɜːtʃə*] *vt* alimentar.

NUS (*BRIT*) *n abbr* (= *National Union of Seamen*) *sindicato dos marinheiros*; (= *National Union of Students*) *sindicato dos estudantes.*

NUT (*BRIT*) *n abbr* (= *National Union of Teachers*) *sindicato dos professores.*

nut [nʌt] *n* (*TECH*) porca; (*BOT*) noz *f* ♦ *cpd* (*chocolate etc*) de nozes.

nutcase ['nʌtkeɪs] (*inf*) *n* doido/a, biruta *m/f*.

nutcrackers ['nʌtkrækəz] *npl* quebra-nozes *m inv*.

nutmeg ['nʌtmɛg] *n* noz-moscada.

nutrient ['njuːtrɪənt] *n* nutrimento ♦ *adj* nutritivo.

nutrition [njuː'trɪʃən] *n* nutrição *f*, alimentação *f*.

nutritionist [njuː'trɪʃənɪst] *n* nutricionista *m/f*.

nutritious [njuː'trɪʃəs] *adj* nutritivo.

nuts [nʌts] (*inf*) *adj*: **he's ~** ele é doido.

nutshell ['nʌtʃɛl] *n* casca de noz; **in a ~** em poucas palavras.

nuzzle ['nʌzl] *vi*: **to ~ up to** aconchegar-se com.

NV (*US*) *abbr* (*POST*) = **Nevada**.

NWT (*CANADA*) *abbr* = **Northwest Territories**.

NY (*US*) *abbr* (*POST*) = **New York**.

NYC (*US*) *abbr* (*POST*) = **New York City**.

nylon ['naɪlɔn] *n* náilon *m* (*BR*), nylon *m* (*PT*) ♦ *adj* de náilon; **~s** *npl* meias *fpl* (de náilon).

nymph [nɪmf] *n* ninfa.

nymphomaniac [nɪmfəu'meɪnɪæk] *n* ninfômana.

NYSE (*US*) *n abbr* = **New York Stock Exchange**.

NZ *abbr* = **New Zealand**.

O

O, o [əu] *n* (*letter*) O, o *m*; (*US: SCH*) = **outstanding**; **O for Olive** (*BRIT*) *or* **Oboe** (*US*) O de Osvaldo.

oaf [əuf] *n* imbecil *m/f*.

oak [əuk] *n* carvalho ♦ *cpd* de carvalho.

OAP (*BRIT*) *n abbr* = **old-age pensioner**.

NB: European Portuguese adds the following consonants to certain words: b (sú(b)dito, su(b)til); c (a(c)ção, a(c)cionista, a(c)to); m (inde(m)ne); p (ado(p)ção, ado(p)tar); for further details see p. xiii.

oar [ɔ:*] *n* remo; **to put** *or* **shove one's ~ in** (*fig*: *inf*) meter o bedelho *or* a colher.
oarsman ['ɔ:zmən] (*irreg*) *n* remador *m*.
oarswoman ['ɔ:zwumən] (*irreg*) *n* remadora.
OAS *n abbr* (= *Organization of American States*) OEA *f*.
oases [əu'eɪsi:z] *npl of* **oasis**.
oasis [əu'eɪsɪs] (*pl* **oases**) *n* oásis *m inv*.
oath [əuθ] *n* juramento; (*swear word*) palavrão *m*; (*curse*) praga; **on** (*BRIT*) *or* **under ~** sob juramento; **to take an ~** prestar juramento.
oatmeal ['əutmi:l] *n* farinha *or* mingau *m* de aveia.
oats [əuts] *n* aveia.
OAU *n abbr* (= *Organization of African Unity*) OUA *f*.
obdurate ['ɔbdjurɪt] *adj* (*obstinate*) teimoso; (*sinner*) empedernido; (*unyielding*) inflexível.
obedience [ə'bi:dɪəns] *n* obediência; **in ~ to** em conformidade com.
obedient [ə'bi:dɪənt] *adj* obediente; **to be ~ to sb/sth** obedecer a alguém/algo.
obelisk ['ɔbɪlɪsk] *n* obelisco.
obese [əu'bi:s] *adj* obeso.
obesity [əu'bi:sɪtɪ] *n* obesidade *f*.
obey [ə'beɪ] *vt* obedecer a; (*instructions, regulations*) cumprir ♦ *vi* obedecer.
obituary [ə'bɪtjuərɪ] *n* necrológio.
object [*n* 'ɔbdʒɪkt, *vi* əb'dʒektɪ] *n* (*gen, LING*) objeto; (*purpose*) objetivo ♦ *vi*: **to ~ to** (*attitude*) desaprovar, objetar a; (*proposal*) opor-se a; **I ~!** protesto!; **he ~ed that ...** ele objetou que ...; **do you ~ to my smoking?** você se incomoda que eu fume?; **what's the ~ of doing that?** qual o objetivo de fazer isso?; **money is no ~** o dinheiro não tem importância.
objection [əb'dʒekʃən] *n* objeção *f*; (*drawback*) inconveniente *m*; **I have no ~ to ...** não tenho nada contra ...; **to make** *or* **raise an ~** fazer *or* levantar uma objeção.
objectionable [əb'dʒekʃənəbl] *adj* desagradável; (*conduct*) censurável.
objective [əb'dʒektɪv] *adj, n* objetivo.
objectivity [ɔbdʒɪk'tɪvɪtɪ] *n* objetividade *f*.
object lesson *n* (*fig*): **~ (in)** demonstração *f* (de).
objector [əb'dʒektə*] *n* opositor(a) *m/f*.
obligation [ɔblɪ'geɪʃən] *n* obrigação *f*; (*debt*) dívida (de gratidão); **without ~** sem compromisso; **to be under an ~ to do sth** ser obrigado a fazer algo.
obligatory [ə'blɪgətərɪ] *adj* obrigatório.
oblige [ə'blaɪdʒ] *vt* (*do a favour for*) obsequiar, fazer um favor a; (*force*): **to ~ sb to do sth** obrigar *or* forçar alguém a fazer algo; **I should be ~d if ...** agradeceria muito se ...; **anything to ~!** (*inf*) estou à sua disposição!
obliging [ə'blaɪdʒɪŋ] *adj* amável, prestativo.
oblique [ə'bli:k] *adj* oblíquo; (*allusion*) indireto ♦ *n* (*BRIT: TYP*): **~ (stroke)** barra.
obliterate [ə'blɪtəreɪt] *vt* (*erase*) apagar; (*destroy*) destruir.

oblivion [ə'blɪvɪən] *n* esquecimento.
oblivious [ə'blɪvɪəs] *adj*: **~ of** inconsciente de, esquecido de.
oblong ['ɔblɔŋ] *adj* oblongo, retangular ♦ *n* retângulo.
obnoxious [əb'nɔkʃəs] *adj* odioso, detestável; (*smell*) enjoativo.
o.b.o (*US*) *abbr* (= *or best offer*) ou melhor oferta.
oboe ['əubəu] *n* oboé *m*.
obscene [əb'si:n] *adj* obsceno.
obscenity [əb'senɪtɪ] *n* obscenidade *f*.
obscure [əb'skjuə*] *adj* obscuro, pouco claro ♦ *vt* ocultar, escurecer; (*hide*: *sun etc*) esconder.
obscurity [əb'skjuərɪtɪ] *n* obscuridade *f*; (*darkness*) escuridão *f*.
obsequious [əb'si:kwɪəs] *adj* obsequioso, servil.
observable [əb'zə:vəbl] *adj* observável; (*appreciable*) perceptível.
observance [əb'zə:vns] *n* observância, cumprimento; (*ritual*) prática, hábito; **religious ~s** observância religiosa.
observant [əb'zə:vnt] *adj* observador(a).
observation [ɔbzə'veɪʃən] *n* observação *f*; (*by police etc*) vigilância; (*MED*) exame *m*.
observation post *n* (*MIL*) posto de observação.
observatory [əb'zə:vətrɪ] *n* observatório.
observe [əb'zə:v] *vt* observar; (*rule*) cumprir.
observer [əb'zə:və*] *n* observador(a) *m/f*.
obsess [əb'ses] *vt* obsedar, obcecar; **to be ~ed by** *or* **with sb/sth** estar obcecado por *or* com alguém/algo.
obsession [əb'seʃən] *n* obsessão *f*, idéia fixa.
obsessive [əb'sesɪv] *adj* obsessivo.
obsolescence [ɔbsə'lesns] *n* obsolescência; **built-in** *or* **planned ~** (*COMM*) obsolescência pré-incorporada.
obsolescent [ɔbsə'lesnt] *adj* obsolescente, antiquado.
obsolete ['ɔbsəli:t] *adj* obsoleto; **to become ~** cair em desuso.
obstacle ['ɔbstəkl] *n* obstáculo; (*hindrance*) estorvo, impedimento.
obstacle race *n* corrida de obstáculos.
obstetrician [ɔbstə'trɪʃən] *n* obstetra *m/f*.
obstetrics [ɔb'stetrɪks] *n* obstetrícia.
obstinacy ['ɔbstɪnəsɪ] *n* teimosia, obstinação *f*.
obstinate ['ɔbstɪnɪt] *adj* teimoso, obstinado; (*determined*) pertinaz.
obstreperous [əb'strepərəs] *adj* turbulento.
obstruct [əb'strʌkt] *vt* obstruir; (*block*: *pipe*) entupir; (*hinder*) estorvar.
obstruction [əb'strʌkʃən] *n* obstrução *f*; (*hindrance*) estorvo, obstáculo.
obstructive [əb'strʌktɪv] *adj* obstrutor(a).
obtain [əb'teɪn] *vt* (*get*) obter; (*achieve*) conseguir ♦ *vi* prevalecer.
obtainable [əb'teɪnəbl] *adj* disponível.
obtrusive [əb'tru:sɪv] *adj* (*person*) intrometido, intruso; (*building etc*) que dá muito na vista.
obtuse [əb'tju:s] *adj* obtuso.

obverse ['ɔbvəːs] n (of medal, coin) obverso; (fig) contrapartida.

obviate ['ɔbvɪeɪt] vt obviar a, prevenir.

obvious ['ɔbvɪəs] adj (clear) óbvio, evidente; (unsubtle) nada sutil.

obviously ['ɔbvɪəslɪ] adv evidentemente; ~, he was not drunk or he was ~ not drunk certamente ele não estava bêbado; **he was not ~ drunk** ele não aparentava estar bêbado; ~**!** claro!, lógico!; ~ **not!** (é) claro que não!

OCAS n abbr (= Organization of Central American States) ODECA f.

occasion [ə'keɪʒən] n ocasião f; (event) acontecimento ♦ vt ocasionar, causar; **on that ~** naquela ocasião; **to rise to the ~** mostrar-se à altura da situação.

occasional [ə'keɪʒənl] adj (feito etc) de vez em quando.

occasionally [ə'keɪʒənəlɪ] adv de vez em quando; **very ~** raramente.

occasional table n mesinha.

occult [ɔ'kʌlt] adj oculto ♦ n: **the ~** as ciências ocultas.

occupancy ['ɔkjupənsɪ] n ocupação f, posse f.

occupant ['ɔkjupənt] n (of house) inquilino/a; (of car) ocupante m/f.

occupation [ɔkju'peɪʃən] n ocupação f; (job) profissão f; **unfit for ~** (house) inabitável.

occupational [ɔkju'peɪʃənl] adj (accident) de trabalho; (disease) profissional.

occupational guidance (BRIT) n orientação f vocacional.

occupational hazard n risco profissional.

occupational pension n pensão f profissional.

occupational therapy n terapia ocupacional.

occupier ['ɔkjupaɪə*] n inquilino/a.

occupy ['ɔkjupaɪ] vt ocupar; (house) morar em; (time) encher; **to ~ o.s. with** or **by doing** (as job) dedicar-se a fazer; (to pass time) ocupar-se de fazer; **to be occupied with sth** ocupar-se de algo.

occur [ə'kəː*] vi ocorrer, acontecer; (difficulty, opportunity) surgir; (phenomenon) encontrar-se; **to ~ to** ocorrer a, vir à mente de; **it ~s to me that ...** ocorre-me que ....

occurrence [ə'kʌrəns] n (event) ocorrência, acontecimento; (existence) existência.

ocean ['əuʃən] n oceano; ~**s of** (inf) um monte de.

ocean bed n fundo do oceano.

ocean-going [-'gəuɪŋ] adj de longo curso.

Oceania [əuʃɪ'eɪnɪə] n Oceania.

ocean liner n transatlântico.

ochre ['əukə*] (US **ocher**) adj cor de ocre inv.

o'clock [ə'klɔk] adv: **it is 5 ~** são cinco horas.

OCR n abbr = **optical character reader**; **optical character recognition**.

Oct. abbr (= October) out.

octagonal [ɔk'tægənl] adj octogonal.

octane ['ɔkteɪn] n octano; **high-~ petrol**

(BRIT) or **gas** (US) gasolina de alto índice de octana.

octave ['ɔktɪv] n oitava.

October [ɔk'təubə*] n outubro; see also **July**.

octogenarian [ɔktəudʒɪ'nɛərɪən] n octogenário/a.

octopus ['ɔktəpəs] n polvo.

odd [ɔd] adj (strange) estranho, esquisito; (number) ímpar; (left over) avulso, de sobra; **60-~** 60 e tantos; **at ~ times** às vezes, de vez em quando; **to be the ~ one out** ficar sobrando, ser a exceção.

oddball ['ɔdbɔːl] (inf) n excêntrico/a, esquisitão/ona m/f.

oddity ['ɔdɪtɪ] n coisa estranha, esquisitice f; (person) excêntrico/a.

odd-job man (irreg) n faz-tudo m.

odd jobs npl biscates mpl, bicos mpl.

oddly ['ɔdlɪ] adv curiosamente.

oddments ['ɔdmənts] (BRIT) npl (COMM) retalhos mpl.

odds [ɔdz] npl (in betting) pontos mpl de vantagem; **the ~ are against his coming** é pouco provável que ele venha; **it makes no ~** dá no mesmo; **to succeed against all the ~** conseguir contra todas as expectativas; ~ **and ends** miudezas fpl; **at ~** brigados/as, de mal.

ode [əud] n ode f.

odious ['əudɪəs] adj odioso.

odometer [əu'dɔmɪtə*] n conta-quilômetros m inv.

odour ['əudə*] (US **odor**) n odor m, cheiro.

odo(u)rless ['əudəlɪs] adj inodoro.

OECD n abbr (= Organization for Economic Cooperation and Development) OCDE f.

oesophagus [iː'sɔfəgəs] (US **esophagus**) n esôfago.

oestrogen ['iːstrəudʒən] (US **estrogen**) n estrogênio.

of [ɔv, əv] prep de; **a friend ~ ours** um amigo nosso; **3 ~ them** 3 deles; **the 5th ~ July** dia 5 de julho; **a boy ~ 10** um menino de 10 anos; **made ~ wood** feito de madeira; **a kilo ~ flour** um quilo de farinha; **that was very kind ~ you** foi muito gentil da sua parte; **a quarter ~ 4** (US) quinze para as 4.

off [ɔf] adj, adv (engine, radio) desligado; (light) apagado; (tap) fechado; (BRIT: food: bad) passado; (: milk) talhado; (cancelled) anulado; (removed): **the lid was ~** estava destampado ♦ prep de; **to be ~** (to leave) ir(-se) embora; **I must be ~** devo ir-me; **to be ~ sick** estar ausente por motivo de saúde; **a day ~** um dia de folga or livre; **today I had an ~ day** hoje não foi o meu dia; **he had his coat ~** ele havia tirado o casaco; **10% ~** (COMM) 10% de abatimento or desconto; **to be 5 km ~** estar a 5 km de distância; **5 km ~ (the road)** a 5 km (da estrada); ~ **the coast** em frente à costa; **a house ~ the main road** uma casa afastada

---

NB: European Portuguese adds the following consonants to certain words: **b** (sú(b)dito, su(b)til); **c** (a(c)ção, a(c)cionista, a(c)to); **m** (inde(m)ne); **p** (ado(p)ção, ado(p)tar); for further details see p. xiii.

da estrada principal; **it's a long way** ~ fica bem longe; **I'm** ~ **meat** não como mais carne; **on the** ~ **chance** ao acaso; **to be well/badly** ~ estar em boa/má situação; ~ **and on, on and** ~ de vez em quando; **I'm afraid the chicken is** ~ (*BRIT: not available*) sinto muito, mas frango não tem mais; **that's a bit** ~ (*fig: inf*) o que é que isso?, isso não se faz.

offal ['ɔfl] *n* (*CULIN*) sobras *fpl*, restos *mpl*.

offbeat ['ɔfbiːt] *adj* excêntrico.

off-centre (*US* **off-center**) *adj* descentrado, excêntrico.

off-colour (*BRIT*) *adj* (*ill*) indisposto.

offence [ə'fɛns] (*US* **offense**) *n* (*crime*) delito; (*insult*) insulto, ofensa; **to give** ~ **to** ofender; **to take** ~ **at** ofender-se com, melindrar-se com; **to commit an** ~ cometer uma infração.

offend [ə'fɛnd] *vt* (*person*) ofender ♦ *vi*: **to** ~ **against** (*law, rule*) pecar contra, transgredir.

offender [ə'fɛndə*] *n* delinqüente *m/f*; (*against regulations*) infrator(a) *m/f*.

offense [ə'fɛns] (*US*) *n* = **offence**.

offensive [ə'fɛnsɪv] *adj* (*weapon, remark*) ofensivo; (*smell etc*) repugnante ♦ *n* (*MIL*) ofensiva.

offer ['ɔfə*] *n* oferta; (*proposal*) proposta ♦ *vt* oferecer; (*opportunity*) proporcionar; **to make an** ~ **for sth** fazer uma oferta por algo; **to** ~ **sth to sb,** ~ **sb sth** oferecer algo a alguém; **to** ~ **to do sth** oferecer-se para fazer algo; **"on** ~**"** (*COMM*) "em oferta".

offering ['ɔfərɪŋ] *n* oferenda.

offertory ['ɔfətərɪ] *n* (*REL*) ofertório.

offhand [ɔf'hænd] *adj* informal ♦ *adv* de improviso; **I can't tell you** ~ não posso te dizer assim de improviso.

office ['ɔfɪs] *n* (*place*) escritório; (*room*) gabinete *m*; (*position*) cargo, função *f*; **to take** ~ tomar posse; **doctor's** ~ (*US*) consultório; **through his good** ~**s** (*fig*) graças aos grandes préstimos dele; **O**~ **of Fair Trading** (*BRIT*) órgão de proteção ao consumidor.

office automation *n* automação *f* de escritórios.

office bearer *n* (*of club etc*) detentor(a) *m/f* de um cargo.

office block (*BRIT*) *n* conjunto de escritórios.

office boy *n* contínuo, bói *m*.

office building (*US*) *n* conjunto de escritórios.

office hours *npl* (*horas fpl* de) expediente *m*; (*US: MED*) horas *fpl* de consulta.

office manager *n* gerente *m/f* de escritório.

officer ['ɔfɪsə*] *n* (*MIL etc*) oficial *m/f*; (*of organization*) diretor(a) *m/f*; (*also: police* ~) agente *m/f* policial *or* de polícia.

office work *n* trabalho de escritório.

office worker *n* empregado/a *or* funcionário/a de escritório.

official [ə'fɪʃl] *adj* oficial ♦ *n* oficial *m/f*; (*civil servant*) funcionário/a (público/a).

officialdom [ə'fɪʃldəm] *n* burocracia.

officially [ə'fɪʃəlɪ] *adv* oficialmente.

official receiver *n* síndico/a de massa falida.

officiate [ə'fɪʃɪeɪt] *vi* (*REL*) oficiar; **to** ~ **as Mayor** exercer as funções de prefeito; **to** ~ **at a marriage** celebrar um casamento.

officious [ə'fɪʃəs] *adj* intrometido.

offing ['ɔfɪŋ] *n*: **in the** ~ (*fig*) em perspectiva.

off-key *adj, adv* desafinado.

off-licence (*BRIT*) *n* (*shop*) loja de bebidas alcoólicas.

off-limits (*esp US*) *adj* proibido.

off line *adj* (*COMPUT*) fora de linha; (: *switched off*) desligado.

off-load *vt*: **to** ~ **sth (onto)** (*goods*) descarregar algo (sobre); (*job*) descarregar algo (em).

off-peak *adj* de temporada de pouco consumo *or* pouca atividade.

off-putting [-'putɪŋ] (*BRIT*) *adj* desconcertante.

off-season *adj, adv* fora de estação *or* temporada.

offset ['ɔfsɛt] (*irreg: like* **set**) *vt* (*counteract*) compensar, contrabalançar ♦ *n* (*also:* ~ *printing*) ofsete *m*.

offshoot ['ɔfʃuːt] (*fig*) *n* desdobramento.

offshore [ɔf'ʃɔː*] *adv* a pouca distância da costa, ao largo ♦ *adj* (*breeze*) de terra; (*island*) perto do litoral; (*fishing*) costeiro; ~ **oilfield** campo petrolífero ao largo.

offside ['ɔf'saɪd] *n* (*AUT*) lado do motorista ♦ *adj* (*SPORT*) impedido; (*AUT*) do lado do motorista.

offspring ['ɔfsprɪŋ] *n* descendência, prole *f*.

offstage ['ɔf'steɪdʒ] *adv* nos bastidores.

off-the-cuff *adj* improvisado ♦ *adv* de improviso.

off-the-job training *n* treinamento fora do local de trabalho.

off-the-peg (*US* **off-the-rack**) *adj* pronto.

off-white *adj* quase branco.

often ['ɔfn] *adv* muitas vezes, freqüentemente; **how** ~ **do you go?** quantas vezes *or* com que freqüência você vai?; **as** ~ **as not** quase sempre; **very** ~ com muita freqüência.

ogle ['əugl] *vt* comer com os olhos.

ogre ['əugə*] *n* ogre *m*.

OH (*US*) *abbr* (*POST*) = **Ohio**.

oh [əu] *excl* oh!, ó!, ah!

OHMS (*BRIT*) *abbr* = **On His** (*or* **Her**) **Majesty's Service**.

oil [ɔɪl] *n* óleo; (*petroleum*) petróleo; (*CULIN*) azeite *m* ♦ *vt* (*machine*) lubrificar.

oilcan ['ɔɪlkæn] *n* almotolia; (*for storing*) lata.

oil change *n* mudança de óleo.

oilfield ['ɔɪlfiːld] *n* campo petrolífero.

oil filter *n* (*AUT*) filtro de óleo.

oil-fired [-'faɪəd] *adj* que usa óleo combustível.

oil gauge *n* indicador *m* do nível de óleo.

oil industry *n* indústria petroleira.

oil level *n* nível *m* de óleo.

oil painting *n* pintura a óleo.

oil refinery *n* refinaria de petróleo.

oil rig *n* torre *f* de perfuração.

oilskins ['ɔɪlskɪnz] *npl* capa de oleado.

oil slick *n* mancha de óleo.

oil tanker *n* petroleiro.

oil well n poço petrolífero.
oily ['ɔɪlɪ] adj oleoso; (food) gorduroso.
ointment ['ɔɪntmənt] n pomada.
OK (US) abbr (POST) = **Oklahoma**.
O.K. = **okay**.
okay ['əu'keɪ] excl está bem, está bom, tá
(bem or bom) (inf) ♦ adj bom; (correct)
certo ♦ vt aprovar ♦ n: **to give sth the ~**
dar luz verde a algo; **is it ~?** tá bom?; **are**
you ~? você está bem?; **are you ~ for**
money? você está bem de dinheiro?; **it's ~**
with or **by me** para mim tudo bem.
old [əuld] adj velho; (former) antigo, anterior;
how ~ are you? quantos anos você tem?;
he's 10 years ~ ele tem 10 anos; **~er**
brother irmão mais velho; **any ~ thing will**
do qualquer coisa serve.
old age n velhice f.
old-age pensioner (BRIT) n aposentado/a
(BR), reformado/a (PT).
old-fashioned [-'fæʃnd] adj antiquado, fora de
moda; (person) careta.
old maid n solteirona.
old people's home n asilo de velhos.
old-time adj antigo, do tempo antigo.
old-timer n veterano.
old wives' tale n conto da carochinha.
olive ['ɔlɪv] n (fruit) azeitona; (tree) oliveira ♦
adj (also: **~-green**) verde-oliva inv.
olive oil n azeite m de oliva.
Olympic [əu'lɪmpɪk] adj olímpico; **the ~**
Games, the ~s os Jogos Olímpicos, as
Olimpíadas.
OM (BRIT) n abbr (= Order of Merit) título honorífico.
O&M n abbr = **organization and method**.
Oman [əu'mɑːn] n Omã (PT: Oman) m.
OMB (US) n abbr (= Office of Management
and Budget) serviço que assessora o presidente em assuntos orçamentários.
omelet(te) ['ɔmlɪt] n omelete f (BR), omeleta
(PT).
omen ['əumən] n presságio, agouro.
ominous ['ɔmɪnəs] adj (menacing) ameaça-
dor(a); (event) de mau agouro.
omission [əu'mɪʃən] n omissão f; (error)
descuido, negligência.
omit [əu'mɪt] vt omitir; (by mistake) esquecer; **to ~ to do sth** deixar de fazer algo.
omnivorous [ɔm'nɪvərəs] adj onívoro.
ON (CANADA) abbr = **Ontario**.
on [ɔn] prep sobre, em (cima de) ♦ adv (machine) em funcionamento; (light) aceso; (radio) ligado; (tap) aberto; **~ to** em, para, em
direção a; **is the meeting still ~?** ainda vai
haver reunião?; **when is this film ~?** quando
vão passar este filme?; **~ the train** no trem;
~ the wall na parede; **~ television** na televisão; **~ the Continent** no continente; **a book**
~ physics um livro sobre física; **~ seeing**
this ao ver isto; **~ arrival** ao chegar; **~ the**
left à esquerda; **~ Friday** na sexta-feira; **~**

Fridays nas sextas-feiras; **a week ~ Friday**
sem ser esta sexta-feira, a outra; **~ holiday**
(BRIT) or **vacation** (US) de férias; **I haven't**
any money ~ me estou sem dinheiro; **this**
round's ~ me esta rodada é por minha
conta; **to have one's coat ~** estar de casaco; **to go ~** continuar (em frente); **from**
that day ~ daquele dia em diante; **it was**
well ~ in the evening a noite estava
adiantada; **we're ~ irregular verbs** estamos
tratando de verbos irregulares; **she's ~**
£20,000 a year ela ganha £20.000 por ano; **it's**
not ~! isso não se faz!; **~ and off** de vez em
quando.
ONC (BRIT) n abbr = **Ordinary National**
Certificate.
once [wʌns] adv uma vez; (formerly) outrora
♦ conj depois que; **~ he had left** depois que
ele saiu; **at ~** imediatamente; (simultaneously) de uma vez, ao mesmo tempo; **all at**
~ de repente; **~ a week** uma vez por semana; **~ more** mais uma vez; **I knew him ~** eu
o conheci antigamente; **~ and for all** uma
vez por todas, definitivamente; **~ upon a**
time era uma vez.
oncoming ['ɔnkʌmɪŋ] adj (traffic) que vem de
frente.
OND (BRIT) n abbr = **Ordinary National Di-**
ploma.
one [wʌn] adj, num um/uma ♦ pron um/uma;
(+ vb: impers) se; **this ~** este/esta; **that ~**
esse/essa, aquele/aquela; **~ by ~** um por
um; **~ never knows** nunca se sabe; **~**
another um ao outro; **the ~ book which ...** o
único livro que ...; **it's ~** (o'clock) é uma
(hora); **which ~ do you want?** qual você
quer?; **to be ~ up on sb** levar vantagem a
alguém; **to be at ~ (with sb)** estar de
acordo (com alguém); see also **five**.
one-armed bandit n caça-níqueis m inv.
one day excursion (US) n bilhete m de ida e
volta.
one-man adj (business) individual.
one-man band n homem-orquestra m.
one-off (BRIT: inf) n exemplar m único ♦ adj
único.
one-piece adj: **~ bathing suit** maiô inteiro.
onerous ['ɔunərəs] adj (task, duty) incômodo;
(responsibility) pesado.
oneself [wʌn'self] pron se; (after prep, also
emphatic) si (mesmo/a); **by ~** sozinho/a.
one-sided [-'saɪdɪd] adj (decision) unilateral;
(judgement, account) parcial; (contest) desigual.
one-time adj antigo.
one-to-one adj (relationship) individual.
one-upmanship [-'ʌpmənʃɪp] n: **the art of ~**
a arte de aparentar ser melhor do que os outros.
one-way adj (street, traffic) de mão única
(BR), de sentido único (PT).
ongoing ['ɔngəuɪŋ] adj contínuo, em anda-

NB: European Portuguese adds the following consonants to certain words: **b** (sú(b)dito, su(b)til); **c** (a(c)ção,
a(c)cionista, a(c)to); **m** (inde(m)ne); **p** (ado(p)ção, ado(p)tar); *for further details see p. xiii.*

mento.

onion ['ʌnjən] *n* cebola.

on line *adj* (*COMPUT*) on-line, em linha; (: *switched on*) ligado.

onlooker ['ɔnlukə*] *n* espectador(a) *m/f*.

only ['əunlɪ] *adv* somente, apenas ♦ *adj* único, só ♦ *conj* só que, porém; **an ~ child** um filho único; **not ~ ... but also ...** não só ... mas também ...; **I ~ ate one** eu comi só um; **I saw her ~ yesterday** apenas ontem eu a vi; **I'd be ~ too pleased to help** eu teria muitíssimo prazer em ajudar; **I would come, ~ I'm very busy** eu iria, porém estou muito ocupado.

ono *abbr* (= *or nearest offer*) ou melhor oferta.

onset ['ɔnsɛt] *n* (*beginning*) começo; (*attack*) ataque *m*.

onshore ['ɔnʃɔː*] *adj* (*wind*) do mar.

onslaught ['ɔnslɔːt] *n* investida, arremetida.

on-the-job training *n* treinamento no serviço.

onto ['ɔntu] *prep* = **on to**.

onus ['əunəs] *n* responsabilidade *f*; **the ~ is upon him to prove it** cabe a ele comprová-lo.

onward(s) ['ɔnwəd(z)] *adv* (*move*) para diante, para a frente; **from this time ~** de (ag)ora em diante.

onyx ['ɔnɪks] *n* ônix *m*.

ooze [uːz] *vi* ressumar, filtrar-se; **to ~ a feeling** mostrar um sentimento exagerado.

opacity [əu'pæsɪtɪ] *n* opacidade *f*.

opal ['əupl] *n* opala.

opaque [əu'peɪk] *adj* opaco, fosco.

OPEC ['əupɛk] *n abbr* (= *Organization of Petroleum-Exporting Countries*) OPEP *f*.

open ['əupn] *adj* aberto; (*car*) descoberto; (*road*) livre; (*meeting*) público; (*admiration*) declarado; (*question*) discutível; (*enemy*) assumido ♦ *vt* abrir ♦ *vi* (*gen*) abrir(-se); (*shop*) abrir; (*book etc*: *commence*) começar; **in the ~ (air)** ao ar livre; **the ~ sea** o largo; **~ ground** (*among trees*) clareira, abertura; (*waste ground*) terreno baldio; **to have an ~ mind (on sth)** ter uma cabeça aberta (a respeito de algo).

open on to *vt fus* (*subj*: *room, door*) dar para.

open out *vt* abrir ♦ *vi* abrir-se.

open up *vt* abrir; (*blocked road*) desobstruir ♦ *vi* abrir-se.

open-air *adj* a céu aberto.

open-and-shut *adj*: **~ case** caso evidente.

open day (*BRIT*) *n* dia *m* de visita.

open-ended [-'ɛndɪd] *adj* (*fig*) não limitado.

opener ['əupnə*] *n* (*also*: *can ~, tin ~*) abridor *m* de latas (*BR*), abre-latas *m inv* (*PT*).

open-heart surgery *n* cirurgia de coração aberto.

opening ['əupnɪŋ] *n* abertura; (*start*) início; (*opportunity*) oportunidade *f*; (*job*) vaga.

opening night *n* (*THEATRE*) estréia.

openly ['əupnlɪ] *adv* abertamente.

open-minded [-'maɪndɪd] *adj* aberto, imparcial.

open-necked [-nɛkt] *adj* aberto no colo.

openness ['əupnnɪs] *n* abertura, sinceridade *f*.

open-plan *adj* sem paredes divisórias.

open sandwich *n* canapê *m*.

open shop *n* empresa que admite trabalhadores não sindicalizados.

Open University (*BRIT*) *n universidade que oferece curso universitário por correspondência.*

opera ['ɔpərə] *n* ópera.

opera glasses *npl* binóculo de teatro.

opera house (*irreg*) *n* teatro lírico *or* de ópera.

opera singer *n* cantor(a) *m/f* de ópera.

operate ['ɔpəreɪt] *vt* (*machine*) fazer funcionar, pôr em funcionamento; (*company*) dirigir ♦ *vi* funcionar; (*drug*) fazer efeito; **to ~ on sb** (*MED*) operar alguém.

operatic [ɔpə'rætɪk] *adj* lírico, operístico.

operating ['ɔpəreɪtɪŋ] *adj* (*COMM*: *costs*, *profit*) operacional.

operating system *n* (*COMPUT*) sistema *m* operacional.

operating table *n* mesa de operações.

operating theatre *n* sala de operações.

operation [ɔpə'reɪʃən] *n* operação *f*; (*of machine*) funcionamento; **to have an ~** fazer uma operação; **to be in ~** (*system*) estar em vigor; (*machine*) estar funcionando.

operational [ɔpə'reɪʃənl] *adj* operacional; **when the service is fully ~** quando o serviço estiver com toda a sua eficácia.

operative ['ɔpərətɪv] *adj* (*measure*) em vigor ♦ *n* (*in factory*) operário/a; **the ~ word** a palavra mais importante *or* atuante.

operator ['ɔpəreɪtə*] *n* (*of machine*) operador(a) *m/f*, manipulador(a) *m/f*; (*TEL*) telefonista *m/f*.

operetta [ɔpə'rɛtə] *n* opereta.

ophthalmic [ɔf'θælmɪk] *adj* oftálmico.

ophthalmologist [ɔfθæl'mɔlədʒɪst] *n* oftalmologista *m/f*, oftalmólogo/a.

opinion [ə'pɪnɪən] *n* opinião *f*; **in my ~** na minha opinião, a meu ver; **to seek a second ~** procurar uma segunda opinião.

opinionated [ə'pɪnɪəneɪtɪd] *adj* opinioso.

opinion poll *n* pesquisa, levantamento.

opium ['əupɪəm] *n* ópio.

opponent [ə'pəunənt] *n* adversário/a, oponente *m/f*.

opportune ['ɔpətjuːn] *adj* oportuno.

opportunist [ɔpə'tjuːnɪst] *n* oportunista *m/f*.

opportunity [ɔpə'tjuːnɪtɪ] *n* oportunidade *f*; **to take the ~ to do** *or* **of doing** aproveitar a oportunidade para fazer.

oppose [ə'pəuz] *vt* opor-se a; **to be ~d to sth** opor-se a algo, estar contra algo; **as ~d to** em oposição a.

opposing [ə'pəuzɪŋ] *adj* (*side*) oposto, contrário.

opposite ['ɔpəzɪt] *adj* oposto; (*house etc*) em frente ♦ *adv* (lá) em frente ♦ *prep* em frente de, defronte de ♦ *n* oposto, contrário.

opposite number (*BRIT*) *n* homólogo/a.

opposite sex n: **the** ~ o sexo oposto.
opposition [ɔpə'zɪʃən] n oposição f.
oppress [ə'prɛs] vt oprimir.
oppression [ə'prɛʃən] n opressão f.
oppressive [ə'prɛsɪv] adj opressivo.
opprobrium [ə'prəubrɪəm] n (formal) opróbrio.
opt [ɔpt] vi: **to** ~ **for** optar por; **to** ~ **to do** optar por fazer; **to** ~ **out of doing sth** optar por não fazer algo.
optical ['ɔptɪkl] adj ótico.
optical character reader n leitora de caracteres óticos.
optical character recognition n reconhecimento de caracteres óticos.
optical fibre n fibra ótica.
optician [ɔp'tɪʃən] n oculista m/f.
optics ['ɔptɪks] n ótica.
optimism ['ɔptɪmɪzəm] n otimismo.
optimist ['ɔptɪmɪst] n otimista m/f.
optimistic [ɔptɪ'mɪstɪk] adj otimista.
optimum ['ɔptɪməm] adj ótimo.
option ['ɔpʃən] n opção f; **to keep one's** ~**s open** (fig) manter as opções em aberto; **I have no** ~ não tenho opção or escolha.
optional ['ɔpʃənəl] adj opcional, facultativo; ~ **extras** acessórios mpl opcionais.
opulence ['ɔpjuləns] n opulência.
opulent ['ɔpjulənt] adj opulento.
OR (US) abbr (POST) = **Oregon.**
or [ɔː*] conj ou; (with negative): **he hasn't seen** ~ **heard anything** ele não viu nem ouviu nada; ~ **else** senão; **either ...,** ~ **else** ou ..., ou (então).
oracle ['ɔrəkl] n oráculo.
oral ['ɔːrəl] adj oral ♦ n exame m oral.
orange ['ɔrɪndʒ] n (fruit) laranja ♦ adj cor de laranja inv, alaranjado.
orangeade [ɔrɪndʒ'eɪd] n laranjada.
oration [ɔː'reɪʃən] n oração f.
orator ['ɔrətə*] n orador(a) m/f.
oratorio [ɔrə'tɔːrɪəu] n oratório.
orb [ɔːb] n orbe m.
orbit ['ɔːbɪt] n órbita ♦ vt, vi orbitar; **to be/go into** ~ **(around)** estar/entrar em órbita (em torno de).
orchard ['ɔːtʃəd] n pomar m; **apple** ~ pomar de macieiras.
orchestra ['ɔːkɪstrə] n orquestra; (US: seating) platéia.
orchestral [ɔː'kɛstrəl] adj orquestral; (concert) sinfônico.
orchestrate ['ɔːkɪstreɪt] vt (MUS, fig) orquestrar.
orchid ['ɔːkɪd] n orquídea.
ordain [ɔː'deɪn] vt (REL) ordenar, decretar; (decide) decidir, mandar.
ordeal [ɔː'diːl] n experiência penosa, provação f.
order ['ɔːdə*] n (gen) ordem f; (COMM) encomenda ♦ vt (also: put in ~) pôr em ordem, arrumar; (in restaurant) pedir; (COMM)

encomendar; (command) mandar, ordenar; **in** ~ em ordem; **out of** ~ com defeito, enguiçado; **a machine in working** ~ uma máquina em bom estado; **in** ~ **of preference** por ordem de preferência; **in** ~ **to do/that** para fazer/que + sub; **to** ~ **sb to do sth** mandar alguém fazer algo; **to place an** ~ **for sth with sb** fazer uma encomenda a alguém para algo, encomendar algo a alguém; **made to** ~ feito sob encomenda; **to be under** ~s to do sth ter ordens para fazer algo; **a point of** ~ uma questão de ordem; **to the** ~ **of** (BANKING) à ordem de.
order book n livro de encomendas.
order form n impresso para encomendas.
orderly ['ɔːdəlɪ] n (MIL) ordenança m; (MED) servente m/f ♦ adj (room) arrumado, ordenado; (person) metódico.
order number n número de encomenda.
ordinal ['ɔːdɪnl] adj (number) ordinal.
ordinary ['ɔːdnrɪ] adj comum, usual; (pej) ordinário, medíocre; **out of the** ~ fora do comum, extraordinário.
ordinary seaman (BRIT: irreg) n marinheiro de segunda classe.
ordinary shares npl ações fpl ordinárias.
ordination [ɔːdɪ'neɪʃən] n ordenação f.
ordnance ['ɔːdnəns] n (MIL: unit) artilharia.
Ordnance Survey (BRIT) n serviço oficial de topografia e cartografia.
ore [ɔː*] n minério.
organ ['ɔːgən] n (gen) órgão m.
organic [ɔː'gænɪk] adj orgânico.
organism ['ɔːgənɪzəm] n organismo.
organist ['ɔːgənɪst] n organista m/f.
organization [ɔːgənaɪ'zeɪʃən] n organização f.
organization chart n organograma m.
organize ['ɔːgənaɪz] vt organizar; **to get** ~**d** organizar-se.
organized labour ['ɔːgənaɪzd-] n mão-de-obra sindicalizada.
organizer ['ɔːgənaɪzə*] n organizador(a) m/f.
orgasm ['ɔːgæzəm] n orgasmo.
orgy ['ɔːdʒɪ] n orgia.
Orient ['ɔːrɪənt] n: **the** ~ o Oriente.
oriental [ɔːrɪ'ɛntl] adj, n oriental m/f.
orientate ['ɔːrɪənteɪt] vt orientar.
orifice ['ɔrɪfɪs] n orifício.
origin ['ɔrɪdʒɪn] n origem f; (point of departure) procedência; **country of** ~ país de origem.
original [ə'rɪdʒɪnl] adj original ♦ n original m.
originality [ərɪdʒɪ'nælɪtɪ] n originalidade f.
originally [ə'rɪdʒɪnəlɪ] adv (at first) originalmente; (with originality) com originalidade.
originate [ə'rɪdʒɪneɪt] vi: **to** ~ **from** originar-se de, surgir de; **to** ~ **in** ter origem em.
originator [ə'rɪdʒɪneɪtə*] n iniciador(a) m/f.
Orkneys ['ɔːknɪz] npl: **the** ~ (also: the Orkney Islands) as ilhas Órcadas.
ornament ['ɔːnəmənt] n ornamento; (trinket)

quinquilharia.

ornamental [ɔːnə'mɛntl] *adj* decorativo, ornamental.

ornamentation [ɔːnəmɛn'teɪʃən] *n* ornamentação *f*.

ornate [ɔː'neɪt] *adj* enfeitado, requintado.

ornithologist [ɔːnɪ'θɔlədʒɪst] *n* ornitólogo/a.

ornithology [ɔːnɪ'θɔlədʒɪ] *n* ornitologia.

orphan ['ɔːfn] *n* órfão/órfã *m/f* ♦ *vt*: **to be ~ed** ficar orfão.

orphanage ['ɔːfənɪdʒ] *n* orfanato.

orthodox ['ɔːθədɔks] *adj* ortodoxo.

orthodoxy ['ɔːθədɔksɪ] *n* ortodoxia.

orthopaedic [ɔːθə'piːdɪk] (*US* **orthopedic**) *adj* ortopédico.

orthop(a)edics [ɔːθə'piːdɪks] *n* ortopedia.

OS (*BRIT*) *abbr* = **Ordnance Survey**; (*NAUT*) = **ordinary seaman**; (*DRESS*) = **outsize**.

O/S *abbr* = **out of stock**.

oscillate ['ɔsɪleɪt] *vi* oscilar; (*person*) vacilar, hesitar.

OSHA (*US*) *n abbr* (= *Occupational Safety and Health Administration*) órgão que supervisiona a higiene e a segurança do trabalho.

Oslo ['ɔzləu] *n* Oslo.

ostensible [ɔs'tɛnsɪbl] *adj* aparente.

ostensibly [ɔs'tɛnsɪblɪ] *adv* aparentemente.

ostentation [ɔstɛn'teɪʃən] *n* ostentação *f*.

ostentatious [ɔstɛn'teɪʃəs] *adj* aparatoso, pomposo; (*person*) ostentoso.

osteopath ['ɔstɪəpæθ] *n* osteopata *m/f*.

ostracize ['ɔstrəsaɪz] *vt* condenar ao ostracismo.

ostrich ['ɔstrɪtʃ] *n* avestruz *m/f*.

OT *n abbr* (= *Old Testament*) AT *m*.

OTB (*US*) *n abbr* (= *off-track betting*) apostas tomadas fora da pista de corridas.

other ['ʌðə*] *adj* outro ♦ *pron*: **the ~ (one)** o outro/a outra; **~s** (*~ people*) outros; **some ~ people have still to arrive** outras pessoas ainda não chegaram; **the ~ day** outro dia; **~ than** (*in another way*) de outro modo que; (*apart from*) além de; **some actor or ~** um certo ator; **somebody or ~** não sei quem, alguém; **the car was none ~ than John's** o carro não era nenhum outro senão o de João.

otherwise ['ʌðəwaɪz] *adv* de outra maneira ♦ *conj* (*if not*) senão; **an ~ good piece of work** sob outros aspectos, um trabalho bem feito.

OTT (*inf*) *abbr* = **over the top**; *see* **top**.

otter ['ɔtə*] *n* lontra.

OU (*BRIT*) *n abbr* = **Open University**.

ouch [autʃ] *excl* ai!

ought [ɔːt] (*pt* **ought**) *aux vb*: **I ~ to do it** eu deveria fazê-lo; **this ~ to have been corrected** isto deveria ter sido corrigido; **he ~ to win** (*probability*) ele deve ganhar; **you ~ to go and see it** você deveria ir vê-lo.

ounce [auns] *n* onça (= *28.35g*; *16 in a pound*).

our ['auə*] *adj* nosso.

ours ['auəz] *pron* (o) nosso/(a) nossa *etc*.

ourselves [auə'sɛlvz] *pron pl* (*reflexive, after prep*) nós; (*emphatic*) nós mesmos/as; **we did it (all) by ~** nós fizemos isso sozinhos.

oust [aust] *vt* desalojar, expulsar.

out [aut] *adv* fora; (*not at home*) fora (de casa); (*light, fire*) apagado; (*on strike*) em greve; **~ there** lá fora; **~ here** aqui fora; **he's ~** (*absent*) não está, saiu; (*unconscious*) está inconsciente; **get ~!** fora!; **to be ~ in one's calculations** enganar-se nos cálculos; **to run ~** sair correndo; **to be ~ and about** (*BRIT*) or **around** (*US*) **again** estar com a saúde refeita; **before the week was ~** antes da semana acabar; **the journey ~** a ida; **the boat was 10 km ~** o barco estava a 10 km da costa; **~ loud** em voz alta; **~ of** (*outside*) fora de; (*because of: anger etc*) por; **~ of petrol** sem gasolina; *"~ of order"* "não funciona", "avariado"; **made ~ of wood** de madeira; **~ of stock** (*COMM*) esgotado.

outage ['autɪdʒ] (*esp US*) *n* (*power failure*) blecaute *m*.

out-and-out *adj* acabado, rematado.

outback ['autbæk] *n* interior *m*.

outbid [aut'bɪd] (*pt, pp* **outbid** or **~ded**) *vt* sobrepujar.

outboard motor ['autbɔːd-] *n* motor *m* de popa.

outbreak ['autbreɪk] *n* (*of war*) deflagração *f*; (*of disease*) surto; (*of violence etc*) explosão *f*.

outbuilding ['autbɪldɪŋ] *n* dependência.

outburst ['autbɜːst] *n* explosão *f*.

outcast ['autkɑːst] *n* pária *m/f*.

outclass [aut'klɑːs] *vt* ultrapassar, superar.

outcome ['autkʌm] *n* resultado.

outcrop ['autkrɔp] *n* afloramento.

outcry ['autkraɪ] *n* clamor *m* (de protesto).

outdated [aut'deɪtɪd] *adj* antiquado, fora de moda.

outdistance [aut'dɪstəns] *vt* deixar para trás.

outdo [aut'duː] (*irreg*) *vt* ultrapassar, exceder.

outdoor [aut'dɔː*] *adj* ao ar livre.

outdoors [aut'dɔːz] *adv* ao ar livre.

outer ['autə*] *adj* exterior, externo.

outer space *n* espaço (exterior).

outfit ['autfɪt] *n* equipamento; (*clothes*) roupa, traje *m*; (*inf*: *COMM*) firma.

outfitter's ['autfɪtəz] (*BRIT*) *n* fornecedor *m* de roupas.

outgoing ['autgəuɪŋ] *adj* (*president, tenant*) de saída; (*character*) extrovertido, sociável.

outgoings ['autgəuɪŋz] (*BRIT*) *npl* despesas *fpl*.

outgrow [aut'grəu] (*irreg*) *vt*: **he has ~n his clothes** a roupa ficou pequena para ele.

outhouse ['authaus] (*irreg*) *n* anexo.

outing ['autɪŋ] *n* (*going out*) saída; (*excursion*) excursão *f*.

outlandish [aut'lændɪʃ] *adj* estranho, bizarro.

outlast [aut'lɑːst] *vt* sobreviver a.

outlaw ['autlɔː] *n* fora-da-lei *m/f* ♦ *vt* (*person*) declarar fora da lei; (*practice*) declarar ilegal.

outlay ['autleɪ] *n* despesas *fpl*.

outlet ['autlɛt] *n* saída, escape *m*; (*of pipe*) desagüe *m*, escoadouro; (*US: ELEC*) tomada;

(also: retail ~) posto de venda.

outline ['aʊtlaɪn] *n (shape)* contorno, perfil *m;* *(of plan)* traçado; *(sketch)* esboço, linhas *fpl* gerais.

outlive [aʊt'lɪv] *vt* sobreviver a.

outlook ['aʊtluk] *n* perspectiva; *(opinion)* ponto de vista.

outlying ['aʊtlaɪɪŋ] *adj* afastado, remoto.

outmanoeuvre [aʊtmə'nuːvə*] *(US* **outmaneuver)** *vt (rival etc)* passar a perna em.

outmoded [aʊt'məʊdɪd] *adj* antiquado, fora de moda, obsoleto.

outnumber [aʊt'nʌmbə*] *vt* exceder em número.

out-of-date *adj (passport, ticket)* sem validade; *(theory, idea)* antiquado, superado; *(custom)* antiquado; *(clothes)* fora de moda.

out-of-the-way *adj* remoto, afastado; *(fig)* insólito.

outpatient ['aʊtpeɪʃənt] *n* paciente *m/f* externo/a *or* de ambulatório.

outpost ['aʊtpəʊst] *n* posto avançado.

output ['aʊtpʊt] *n (volume m* de) produção *f;* *(TECH)* rendimento ♦ *vt (COMPUT)* liberar.

outrage ['aʊtreɪdʒ] *n (scandal)* escândalo; *(atrocity)* atrocidade *f* ♦ *vt* ultrajar.

outrageous [aʊt'reɪdʒəs] *adj* ultrajante, escandaloso.

outrider ['aʊtraɪdə*] *n (on motorcycle)* batedor(a) *m/f.*

outright [*adv* aʊt'raɪt, *adj* 'aʊtraɪt] *adv* completamente ♦ *adj* completo.

outrun [aʊt'rʌn] *(irreg) vt* ultrapassar.

outset ['aʊtsɛt] *n* início, princípio.

outshine [aʊt'ʃaɪn] *(irreg) vt (fig)* eclipsar.

outside [aʊt'saɪd] *n* exterior *m* ♦ *adj* exterior, externo; *(contractor etc)* de fora ♦ *adv* (lá) fora ♦ *prep* fora de; *(beyond)* além (dos limites) de; **at the ~** *(fig)* no máximo; **an ~ chance** uma possibilidade remota; **~ left/right** *(FOOTBALL)* ponta *m* esquerdo/direito.

outside broadcast *n (RADIO, TV)* transmissão *f* de exteriores.

outside lane *n (AUT: in Britain)* pista da direita; *(: in US, Europe etc)* pista da esquerda.

outside line *n (TEL)* linha de saída.

outsider [aʊt'saɪdə*] *n (stranger)* estranho/a, forasteiro/a; *(in race etc)* outsider *m.*

outsize ['aʊtsaɪz] *adj* enorme; *(clothes)* de tamanho extra-grande *or* especial.

outskirts ['aʊtskɜːts] *npl* arredores *mpl,* subúrbios *mpl.*

outsmart [aʊt'smɑːt] *vt* passar a perna em.

outspoken [aʊt'spəʊkən] *adj* franco, sem rodeios.

outspread [aʊt'sprɛd] *adj* estendido.

outstanding [aʊt'stændɪŋ] *adj* excepcional, saliente; *(unfinished, debt)* pendente; **your account is still ~** a sua conta ainda não está liquidada.

outstay [aʊt'steɪ] *vt:* **to ~ one's welcome**

abusar da hospitalidade (demorando mais tempo).

outstretched [aʊt'strɛtʃt] *adj (hand)* estendido; *(body)* esticado.

outstrip [aʊt'strɪp] *vt (also: fig)* ultrapassar.

out-tray *n* cesta de saída.

outvote [aʊt'vəʊt] *vt:* **to ~ sb (by ...)** vencer alguém (por ... votos); **to ~ sth (by ...)** rejeitar algo (por ... votos).

outward ['aʊtwəd] *adj (sign, appearances)* externo; *(journey)* de ida.

outwardly ['aʊtwədlɪ] *adv* para fora.

outweigh [aʊt'weɪ] *vt* ter mais valor do que.

outwit [aʊt'wɪt] *vt* passar a perna em.

oval ['əʊvl] *adj* ovalado ♦ *n* oval *m.*

ovary ['əʊvərɪ] *n* ovário.

ovation [əʊ'veɪʃən] *n* ovação *f.*

oven ['ʌvn] *n* forno.

ovenproof ['ʌvnpruːf] *adj* refratário.

oven-ready *adj* pronto para o forno.

ovenware ['ʌvnwɛə*] *n* louça refratária.

over ['əʊvə*] *adv* por cima; *(excessively)* muito, demais ♦ *adj (or adv) (finished)* acabado; *(too much)* a mais ♦ *prep* por cima de; *(above)* acima de; *(on the other side of)* do outro lado de; *(more than)* mais de; *(during)* durante; *(about, concerning):* **they fell out ~ money** eles se desentenderam por dinheiro; **~ here** por aqui, cá; **~ there** por ali, lá; **all ~** *(everywhere)* por todos os lados; *(finished)* acabado; **~ and ~ (again)** repetidamente; **~ and above** além de; **to ask sb ~** convidar alguém; **to bend ~** inclinar-se (sobre); **to go ~ to sb's** passar na casa de alguém; **now ~ to our Paris correspondent** com a palavra o nosso correspondente em Paris; **the world ~** no mundo inteiro; **she's not ~ intelligent** *(BRIT)* ela não é superdotada.

over... [əʊvə*] *prefix* sobre..., super....

overabundant [əʊvərə'bʌndənt] *adj* superabundante.

overact [əʊvər'ækt] *vi (THEATRE)* exagerar.

overall [*n, adj* 'əʊvərɔːl, *adv* əʊvər'ɔːl] *adj (length)* total; *(study)* global ♦ *adv* globalmente; **~s** *npl* macacão *m (BR),* (fato) macaco *(PT).*

overanxious [əʊvər'æŋkʃəs] *adj* muito ansioso.

overawe [əʊvər'ɔː] *vt* intimidar.

overbalance [əʊvə'bæləns] *vi* perder o equilíbrio, desequilibrar-se.

overbearing [əʊvə'bɛərɪŋ] *adj* autoritário, dominador(a); *(arrogant)* arrogante.

overboard ['əʊvəbɔːd] *adv (NAUT)* ao mar; **man ~!** homem ao mar!; **to go ~ for sth** *(fig)* empolgar-se com algo.

overbook [əʊvə'buk] *vi* fazer reservas em excesso.

overcapitalize [əʊvə'kæpɪtəlaɪz] *vt* sobrecapitalizar.

overcast ['əʊvəkɑːst] *adj* nublado, fechado.

overcharge [əʊvə'tʃɑːdʒ] *vt:* **to ~ sb** cobrar

NB: European Portuguese adds the following consonants to certain words: **b** (sú(b)dito, su(b)til); **c** (a(c)ção, a(c)cionista, a(c)to); **m** (inde(m)ne); **p** (ado(p)ção, ado(p)tar); *for further details see p. xiii.*

em excesso a alguém.

overcoat ['əuvəkəut] n sobretudo.

overcome [əuvə'kʌm] (irreg) vt vencer, dominar; (difficulty) superar ♦ adj (emotionally) assolado; ~ **with grief** tomado pela dor.

overconfident [əuvə'kɔnfɪdənt] adj confiante em excesso.

overcrowded [əuvə'kraudɪd] adj superlotado; (country) superpovoado.

overcrowding [əuvə'kraudɪŋ] n superlotação f; (in country) superpovoamento .

overdo [əuvə'du:] (irreg) vt exagerar; (overcook) cozinhar demais; **to ~ it, to ~ things** (work too hard) exceder-se; (go too far) exagerar.

overdose ['əuvədəus] n overdose f, dose f excessiva.

overdraft ['əuvədrɑːft] n saldo negativo.

overdrawn [əuvə'drɔːn] adj (account) sem fundos, a descoberto.

overdue [əuvə'djuː] adj atrasado; (COMM) vencido; (recognition) tardio; **that change was long ~** essa mudança foi muito protelada.

overestimate [əuvər'ɛstɪmeɪt] vt sobrestimar.

overexcited [əuvərɪk'saɪtɪd] adj superexcitado.

overexertion [əuvərɪg'zəːʃən] n estafa.

overexpose [əuvərɪk'spəuz] vt (PHOT) expor demais (à luz).

overflow [vi əuvə'fləu, n 'əuvəfləu] vi transbordar ♦ n (excess) excesso; (also: ~ pipe) tubo de descarga, ladrão m.

overfly [əuvə'flaɪ] (irreg) vt sobrevoar.

overgenerous [əuvə'dʒɛnərəs] adj pródigo; (offer) excessivo.

overgrown [əuvə'grəun] adj (garden) coberto de vegetação; **he's just an ~ schoolboy** (fig) ele é apenas um garotão de escola.

overhang [vt, vi əuvə'hæŋ, n 'əuvəhæŋ] (irreg) vt sobrepairar ♦ vi sobressair ♦ n saliência, ressalto.

overhaul [vt əuvə'hɔːl, n 'əuvəhɔːl] vt examinar, revisar ♦ n revisão f.

overhead [adv əuvə'hɛd, adj, n 'əuvəhɛd] adv por cima, em cima ♦ adj aéreo, elevado; (railway) suspenso ♦ n (US) (also: BRIT: ~s npl) despesas fpl gerais.

overhear [əuvə'hɪə*] (irreg) vt ouvir por acaso.

overheat [əuvə'hiːt] vi ficar superaquecido; (engine) aquecer demais.

overjoyed [əuvə'dʒɔɪd] adj maravilhado, cheio de alegria.

overkill ['əuvəkɪl] n (fig): **it would be ~** seria exagero, seria matar mosquito com tiro de canhão.

overland ['əuvəlænd] adj, adv por terra.

overlap [vi əuvə'læp, n 'əuvəlæp] vi coincidir or sobrepor-se em parte ♦ n sobreposição f.

overleaf [əuvə'liːf] adv no verso.

overload [əuvə'ləud] vt sobrecarregar.

overlook [əuvə'luk] vt (have view on) dar para; (miss) omitir; (forgive) fazer vista grossa a.

overlord ['əuvəlɔːd] n suserano.

overmanning [əuvə'mænɪŋ] n excesso de pessoal.

overnight [adv əuvə'naɪt, adj 'əuvənaɪt] adv durante a noite; (fig: suddenly) da noite para o dia ♦ adj de uma (or de) noite; (decision) tomada da noite para o dia; **to stay ~** passar a noite, pernoitar; **if you travel ~ ...** se você viajar de noite ...; **he'll be away ~** ele não voltará hoje.

overpaid [əuvə'peɪd] pt, pp of **overpay**.

overpass ['əuvəpɑːs] n (road) viaduto; (US) passagem f superior.

overpay [əuvə'peɪ] (irreg) vt: **to ~ sb by £50** pagar £50 em excesso a alguém.

overpower [əuvə'pauə*] vt dominar, subjugar; (fig) assolar.

overpowering [əuvə'pauərɪŋ] adj (heat, stench) sufocante.

overproduction [əuvəprə'dʌkʃən] n superprodução f.

overrate [əuvə'reɪt] vt sobrestimar, supervalorizar.

overreach [əuvə'riːtʃ] vt: **to ~ o.s.** exceder-se.

overreact [əuvəriː'ækt] vi reagir com exagero.

override [əuvə'raɪd] (irreg) vt (order, objection) não fazer caso de, ignorar; (decision) anular.

overriding [əuvə'raɪdɪŋ] adj primordial.

overrule [əuvə'ruːl] vt (decision) anular; (claim) indeferir.

overrun [əuvə'rʌn] (irreg) vt (MIL: country etc) invadir; (time limit) ultrapassar, exceder ♦ vi ultrapassar o devido tempo; **the town is ~ with tourists** a cidade está infestada de turistas.

overseas [əuvə'siːz] adv ultra-mar; (abroad) no estrangeiro, no exterior ♦ adj (trade) exterior; (visitor) estrangeiro.

overseer ['əuvəsiə*] n (in factory) superintendente m/f; (foreman) capataz m.

overshadow [əuvə'ʃædəu] vt (fig) eclipsar, ofuscar.

overshoot [əuvə'ʃuːt] (irreg) vt passar.

oversight ['əuvəsaɪt] n descuido; **due to an ~** devido a um descuido or uma inadvertência.

oversimplify [əuvə'sɪmplɪfaɪ] vt simplificar demais.

oversleep [əuvə'sliːp] (irreg) vi dormir além da hora.

overspend [əuvə'spɛnd] (irreg) vi gastar demais; **we have overspent by $5000** gastamos $5000 além dos nossos recursos.

overspill ['əuvəspɪl] n excesso (de população).

overstaffed [əuvə'stɑːft] adj: **to be ~** ter um excesso de pessoal.

overstate [əuvə'steɪt] vt exagerar.

overstatement [əuvə'steɪtmənt] n exagero.

overstep [əuvə'stɛp] vt: **to ~ the mark** ultrapassar o limite.

overstock [əuvə'stɔk] vt estocar em excesso.

overstrike [n 'əuvəstraɪk, vt əuvə'straɪk] (irreg: like **strike**) n (on printer) batida múltipla ♦ vt sobreimprimir.

overt [əu'vəːt] *adj* aberto, indissimulado.
overtake [əuvə'teɪk] *(irreg)* *vt* ultrapassar.
overtaking [əuvə'teɪkɪŋ] *n* *(AUT)* ultrapassagem *f*.
overtax [əuvə'tæks] *vt* *(ECON)* sobrecarregar de impostos; *(fig: strength, patience)* abusar de; (: *person*) exigir demais de; **to ~ o.s.** exceder-se.
overthrow [əuvə'θrəu] *(irreg)* *vt* *(government)* derrubar.
overtime ['əuvətaɪm] *n* horas *fpl* extras; **to do** *or* **work ~** fazer horas extras.
overtime ban *n* recusa de fazer horas extras.
overtone ['əuvətəun] *n* *(fig)* implicação *f*, tom *m*.
overture ['əuvətʃuə*] *n* *(MUS)* abertura; *(fig)* proposta, oferta.
overturn [əuvə'təːn] *vt* virar; *(accidentally)* derrubar; *(decision)* anular ♦ *vi* virar; *(car)* capotar.
overweight [əuvə'weɪt] *adj* gordo demais, com excesso de peso; *(luggage)* com excesso de peso.
overwhelm [əuvə'wɛlm] *vt* esmagar, assolar.
overwhelming [əuvə'wɛlmɪŋ] *adj* *(victory, defeat)* esmagador(a); *(desire)* irresistível; **one's ~ impression is of heat** a impressão mais forte é de calor.
overwhelmingly [əuvə'wɛlmɪŋlɪ] *adv* *(vote)* em massa; *(win)* esmagadoramente.
overwork [əuvə'wəːk] *n* excesso de trabalho ♦ *vt* sobrecarregar de trabalho ♦ *vi* trabalhar demais.
overwrite [əuvə'raɪt] *(irreg)* *vt* *(COMPUT)* gravar em cima de.
overwrought [əuvə'rɔːt] *adj* extenuado, superexcitado.
ovulation [ɔvju'leɪʃən] *n* ovulação *f*.
owe [əu] *vt* dever; **to ~ sb sth, to ~ sth to sb** dever algo a alguém.
owing to ['əuɪŋ-] *prep* devido a, por causa de.
owl [aul] *n* coruja.
own [əun] *adj* próprio ♦ *vi* *(BRIT)*: **to ~ to (having done) sth** confessar (ter feito) algo ♦ *vt* possuir, ter; **a room of my ~** meu próprio quarto; **can I have it for my (very) ~?** posso ficar com isso para mim?; **to get one's ~ back** ir à forra; **on one's ~** sozinho; **to come into one's ~** revelar-se.
own up *vi*: **to ~ up to sth** confessar algo; **to ~ up to having done sth** confessar ter feito algo.
own brand *n* *(COMM)* marca de distribuidora.
owner ['əunə*] *n* dono/a, proprietário/a.
owner-occupier *n* proprietário/a com posse e uso.
ownership ['əunəʃɪp] *n* posse *f*; **it's under new ~** *(shop etc)* está sob novo proprietário.
ox [ɔks] *(pl ~en)* *n* boi *m*.
oxen ['ɔksn] *npl of* **ox**.
Oxfam ['ɔksfæm] *(BRIT)* *n abbr* (= *Oxford Committee for Famine Relief*) associação de

assistência.
oxide ['ɔksaɪd] *n* óxido.
Oxon. ['ɔksn] *(BRIT)* *abbr* (= *Oxoniensis*) = *of Oxford.*
oxtail soup ['ɔksteɪl-] *n* rabada.
oxyacetylene [ɔksɪə'sɛtɪliːn] *n* oxiacetileno ♦ *cpd*: **~ burner, ~ torch** maçarico oxiacetilênico.
oxygen ['ɔksɪdʒən] *n* oxigênio.
oxygen mask *n* máscara de oxigênio.
oxygen tent *n* tenda de oxigênio.
oyster ['ɔɪstə*] *n* ostra.
oz. *abbr* = **ounce(s)**.
ozone ['əuzəun] *n* ozônio.
ozone layer *n* camada de ozônio.

P

P, p [piː] *n* *(letter)* P, p *m*; **P for Peter** P de Pedro.
P *abbr* = **president; prince**.
p [piː] *abbr* (= *page*) p; *(BRIT)* = **penny; pence**.
PA *n abbr* = **personal assistant; public address system** ♦ *abbr* *(US: POST)* = **Pennsylvania**.
pa [pɑː] *(inf)* *n* papai *m*.
p.a. *abbr* = **per annum**.
PAC *(US)* *n abbr* = **political action committee**.
pace [peɪs] *n* *(step)* passo; *(rhythm)* ritmo ♦ *vi*: **to ~ up and down** andar de um lado para o outro; **to keep ~ with** acompanhar o passo de; *(events)* manter-se inteirado de *or* atualizado com; **to set the ~** *(running)* regular a marcha; *(fig)* dar o tom; **to put sb through his ~s** *(fig)* pôr alguém à prova.
pacemaker ['peɪsmeɪkə*] *n* *(MED)* marca-passo *m*.
pacific [pə'sɪfɪk] *adj* pacífico ♦ *n*: **the P~ (Ocean)** o (Oceano) Pacífico.
pacification [pæsɪfɪ'keɪʃən] *n* pacificação *f*.
pacifier ['pæsɪfaɪə*] *(US)* *n* chupeta.
pacifist ['pæsɪfɪst] *n* pacifista *m/f*.
pacify ['pæsɪfaɪ] *vt* *(soothe)* acalmar, serenar; *(country)* pacificar.
pack [pæk] *n* pacote *m*, embrulho; *(US: packet)* pacote *m*; *(of cigarettes)* maço; *(of hounds)* matilha; *(of thieves etc)* bando, quadrilha; *(of cards)* baralho; *(bundle)* trouxa; *(back ~)* mochila ♦ *vt* *(wrap)* empacotar, embrulhar; *(fill)* encher; *(in suitcase etc)* arrumar (na mala); *(cram)* entupir, entulhar; *(fig: room etc)* lotar; *(COMPUT)* compactar ♦ *vi*: **to ~ (one's bags)** fazer as

malas; **to ~ into** (room, stadium) apinhar-se em; **to send sb ~ing** (inf) dar o fora em alguém.

pack in (BRIT: inf) vi (machine) pifar ♦ vt (boyfriend) dar o fora em; **~ it in!** pára com isso!

pack off vt (person) despedir.

pack up vi (BRIT: inf: machine) pifar; (: person) desistir, parar ♦ vt (belongings) arrumar; (goods, presents) empacotar, embrulhar.

package ['pækɪdʒ] n pacote m; (bulky) embrulho, fardo; (also: ~ deal) acordo global, pacote; (COMPUT) pacote ♦ vt (goods) empacotar, acondicionar.

package holiday (BRIT) n férias fpl organizadas.

package tour n excursão f organizada.

packaging ['pækɪdʒɪŋ] n embalagem f.

packed [pækt] adj (crowded) lotado, apinhado; **~ lunch** (BRIT) merenda.

packer ['pækə*] n (person) empacotador(a) m/f.

packet ['pækɪt] n pacote m; (of cigarettes) maço; (NAUT) paquete m.

packet switching [-'swɪtʃɪŋ] n (COMPUT) chaveamento de pacote.

pack ice n gelo flutuante.

packing ['pækɪŋ] n embalagem f; (internal) enchimento.

packing case n caixa de embalagem.

pact [pækt] n pacto; (COMM) convênio.

pad [pæd] n (of paper) bloco; (for inking) almofada; (launching ~) plataforma (de lançamento); (inf: home) casa ♦ vt acolchoar, enchumaçar ♦ vi: **to ~ in/about** etc entrar/andar etc sem ruído.

padding ['pædɪŋ] n enchimento, recheio; (fig) palavreado inútil.

paddle ['pædl] n (oar) remo curto ♦ vt remar ♦ vi (with feet) patinhar.

paddle steamer n vapor m movido a rodas.

paddling pool ['pædlɪŋ-] n lago de recreação.

paddock ['pædək] n cercado, paddock m.

paddy ['pædɪ] n (also: ~ field) arrozal m.

padlock ['pædlɔk] n cadeado ♦ vt fechar com cadeado.

padre ['pɑːdrɪ] n capelão m, padre m.

paediatrics [piːdɪ'ætrɪks] (US pediatrics) n pediatria.

pagan ['peɪgən] adj, n pagão/pagã m/f.

page [peɪdʒ] n página; (also: ~ boy) mensageiro; (at wedding) pajem m ♦ vt (in hotel etc) mandar chamar.

pageant ['pædʒənt] n (procession) cortejo suntuoso; (show) desfile m alegórico.

pageantry ['pædʒəntrɪ] n pompa, fausto.

page break n quebra de página.

pager ['peɪdʒə*] n bip m.

paginate ['pædʒɪneɪt] vt paginar.

pagination [pædʒɪ'neɪʃən] n paginação f.

pagoda [pə'gəudə] n pagode m.

paid [peɪd] pt, pp of **pay** ♦ adj (work) remunerado; (official) assalariado; **to put ~ to** (BRIT) acabar com.

paid-up (US **paid-in**) adj (member) efetivo; (shares) integralizado; **~ capital** capital m realizado.

pail [peɪl] n balde m.

pain [peɪn] n dor f; **to be in ~** sofrer or sentir dor; **to have a ~ in** estar com uma dor em; **on ~ of death** sob pena de morte; **to take ~s to do sth** dar-se ao trabalho de fazer algo.

pained [peɪnd] adj (expression) magoado, aflito.

painful ['peɪnful] adj doloroso; (difficult) penoso; (disagreeable) desagradável.

painfully ['peɪnfulɪ] adv (fig: very) terrivelmente.

painkiller ['peɪnkɪlə*] n analgésico, calmante m.

painless ['peɪnlɪs] adj sem dor, indolor.

painstaking ['peɪnzteɪkɪŋ] adj esmerado, meticuloso.

paint [peɪnt] n pintura ♦ vt pintar; **to ~ the door blue** pintar a porta de azul; **to ~ the town red** (fig) cair na farra.

paintbox ['peɪntbɔks] n estojo de tintas.

paintbrush ['peɪntbrʌʃ] n (artist's) pincel m; (decorator's) broxa.

painter ['peɪntə*] n pintor(a) m/f.

painting ['peɪntɪŋ] n pintura; (picture) tela, quadro.

paint-stripper n removedor m de tinta.

paintwork ['peɪntwɔːk] (BRIT) n pintura.

pair [peə*] n (of shoes, gloves etc) par m; (of people) casal m; (twosome) dupla; **a ~ of scissors** uma tesoura; **a ~ of trousers** uma calça (BR), umas calças (PT).

pair off vi formar pares.

pajamas [pɪ'dʒɑːməz] (US) npl pijama m.

Pakistan [pɑːkɪ'stɑːn] n Paquistão m.

Pakistani [pɑːkɪ'stɑːnɪ] adj, n paquistanês/esa m/f.

PAL [pæl] n abbr (TV: phase alternation line) PAL m.

pal [pæl] (inf) n camarada m/f, colega m/f.

palace ['pæləs] n palácio.

palatable ['pælɪtəbl] adj saboroso, apetitoso; (acceptable) aceitável.

palate ['pælɪt] n paladar m.

palatial [pə'leɪʃəl] adj suntuoso, magnífico.

palaver [pə'lɑːvə*] n (fuss) confusão f; (hindrances) complicação f.

pale [peɪl] adj pálido; (colour) claro ♦ vi empalidecer ♦ n: **to be beyond the ~** passar dos limites; **to grow** or **turn ~** empalidecer; **~ blue** azul claro inv; **to ~ into insignificance (beside)** perder a importância (diante de).

paleness ['peɪlnɪs] n palidez f.

Palestine ['pælɪstaɪn] n Palestina.

Palestinian [pælɪs'tɪnɪən] adj, n palestino/a.

palette ['pælɪt] n palheta.

paling ['peɪlɪŋ] n (stake) estaca; (fence) cerca.

palisade [pælɪ'seɪd] n paliçada.

pall [pɔːl] n (of smoke) manto ♦ vi perder a graça.

pallet ['pælɪt] n (for goods) paleta.
pallid ['pælɪd] adj pálido, descorado.
pallor ['pælə*] n palidez f.
pally ['pælɪ] (inf) adj chapinha.
palm [pɑːm] n (hand, leaf) palma; (also: ~ tree) palmeira ♦ vt: **to ~ sth off on sb** (inf) impingir algo a alguém.
palmist ['pɑːmɪst] n quiromante m/f.
Palm Sunday n Domingo de Ramos.
palpable ['pælpəbl] adj palpável.
palpitation [pælpɪ'teɪʃən] n palpitação f; **to have ~s** sentir palpitações.
paltry ['pɔːltrɪ] adj irrisório.
pamper ['pæmpə*] vt paparicar, mimar.
pamphlet ['pæmflət] n panfleto.
pan [pæn] n (also: sauce~) panela (BR), caçarola (PT); (also: frying ~) frigideira; (of lavatory) vaso ♦ vi (CINEMA) tomar uma panorâmica ♦ vt (inf: book, film) arrasar com; **to ~ for gold** batear à procura de ouro.
panacea [pænə'sɪə] n panacéia.
Panama ['pænəmɑː] n Panamá m.
Panama Canal n canal m do Panamá.
pancake ['pænkeɪk] n panqueca.
Pancake Day (BRIT) n terça-feira de Carnaval.
pancreas ['pæŋkrɪəs] n pâncreas m inv.
panda ['pændə] n panda m/f.
panda car (BRIT) n patrulhinha, carro policial.
pandemonium [pændɪ'məunɪəm] n (noise) pandemônio; (mess) caos m.
pander ['pændə*] vi: **to ~ to** favorecer.
pane [peɪn] n vidraça, vidro.
panel ['pænl] n (of wood, RADIO, TV) painel m; (of cloth) pano.
panel game (BRIT) n jogo em painel.
panelling ['pænəlɪŋ] (US **paneling**) n painéis mpl.
panellist ['pænəlɪst] (US **panelist**) n convidado/a, integrante m/f do painel.
pang [pæŋ] n: **~s of conscience** dor f de consciência; **~s of hunger** fome aguda.
panic ['pænɪk] n pânico ♦ vi entrar em pânico.
panicky ['pænɪkɪ] adj (person) assustadiço, apavorado.
panic-stricken [-'strɪkən] adj tomado de pânico.
pannier ['pænɪə*] n (on bicycle) cesta; (on mule etc) cesto, alcofa.
panorama [pænə'rɑːmə] n panorama m.
panoramic [pænə'ræmɪk] adj panorâmico.
pansy ['pænzɪ] n (BOT) amor-perfeito; (inf) bicha (BR), maricas m (PT).
pant [pænt] vi arquejar, ofegar.
pantechnicon [pæn'teknɪkən] (BRIT) n caminhão m de mudanças.
panther ['pænθə*] n pantera.
panties ['pæntɪz] npl calcinha (BR), cuecas fpl (PT).
pantihose ['pæntɪhəuz] (US) n meia-calça (BR), collants mpl (PT).

pantomime ['pæntəmaɪm] (BRIT) n pantomima, revista musical montada na época de Natal, baseada em contos de fada.
pantry ['pæntrɪ] n despensa.
pants [pænts] npl (BRIT: woman's) calcinha (BR), cuecas fpl (PT); (: man's) cueca (BR), cuecas (PT); (US: trousers) calça (BR), calças fpl (PT).
pantsuit ['pæntsuːt] (US) n terninho (de mulher).
papacy ['peɪpəsɪ] n papado.
papal ['peɪpəl] adj papal.
paper ['peɪpə*] n papel m; (also: news~) jornal m; (study, article) artigo, dissertação f; (exam) exame m, prova ♦ adj de papel ♦ vt empapelar; **~s** npl (also: identity ~s) documentos mpl; **a piece of ~** um papel; **to put sth down on ~** pôr algo por escrito.
paper advance n (on printer) avançar formulário.
paperback ['peɪpəbæk] n livro de capa mole ♦ adj: **~ edition** edição f brochada.
paper bag n saco de papel.
paperboy ['peɪpəbɔɪ] n jornaleiro.
paper clip n clipe m.
paper handkerchief n lenço de papel.
paper mill n fábrica de papel.
paper money n papel-moeda m.
paper profit n lucro fictício.
paperweight ['peɪpəweɪt] n pesa-papéis m inv.
paperwork ['peɪpəwɔːk] n trabalho burocrático; (pej) papelada.
papier-mâché ['pæpɪeɪ'mæʃeɪ] n papel m machê.
paprika ['pæprɪkə] n páprica, pimentão-doce m.
Pap smear [pæp-] n (MED) esfregaço.
Pap test [pæp-] n (MED) esfregaço.
par [pɑː*] n par m; (GOLF) média f; **to be on a ~ with** estar em pé de igualdade com; **at ~** ao par; **above/below ~** acima/abaixo do par; **to feel below** or **under** or **not up to ~** estar aquém das suas possibilidades.
parable ['pærəbl] n parábola.
parabola [pə'ræbələ] n parábola.
parachute ['pærəʃuːt] n pára-quedas m inv ♦ vi saltar de pára-quedas.
parachute jump n salto de pára-quedas.
parachutist ['pærəʃuːtɪst] n pára-quedista m/f.
parade [pə'reɪd] n desfile m ♦ vt desfilar; (show off) exibir ♦ vi desfilar; (MIL) passar revista.
parade ground n praça de armas.
paradise ['pærədaɪs] n paraíso.
paradox ['pærədɔks] n paradoxo.
paradoxical [pærə'dɔksɪkl] adj paradoxal.
paradoxically [pærə'dɔksɪklɪ] adv paradoxalmente.
paraffin ['pærəfɪn] (BRIT) n: **~ (oil)** querosene m; **liquid ~** óleo de parafina.
paraffin heater (BRIT) n aquecedor m a pa-

NB: European Portuguese adds the following consonants to certain words: **b** (sú(b)dito, su(b)til); **c** (a(c)ção, a(c)cionista, a(c)to); **m** (inde(m)ne); **p** (ado(p)ção, ado(p)tar); for further details see p. xiii.

rafina.
paraffin lamp (BRIT) n lâmpada de parafina.
paragon ['pærəgən] n modelo.
paragraph ['pærəgrɑːf] n parágrafo.
Paraguay ['pærəgwaɪ] n Paraguai m.
Paraguayan [pærə'gwaɪən] adj, n paraguaio/a.
parallel ['pærəlɛl] adj: ~ (with or to) paralelo (a); (fig) correspondente (a) ♦ n (line) paralela; (fig, GEO) paralelo.
paralyses [pə'rælɪsiːz] npl of **paralysis**.
paralysis [pə'rælɪsɪs] (pl **paralyses**) n paralisia.
paralytic [pærə'lɪtɪk] adj paralítico; (BRIT: inf: drunk) de cara cheia.
paralyze ['pærəlaɪz] vt paralisar.
parameter [pə'ræmɪtə*] n parâmetro.
paramilitary [pærə'mɪlɪtərɪ] adj paramilitar.
paramount ['pærəmaunt] adj: of ~ importance de suma importância, primordial.
paranoia [pærə'nɔɪə] n paranóia.
paranoid ['pærənɔɪd] adj paranóico.
paranormal [pærə'nɔːməl] adj paranormal.
paraphernalia [pærəfə'neɪlɪə] n (gear) acessórios mpl, equipamento.
paraphrase ['pærəfreɪz] vt parafrasear.
paraplegic [pærə'pliːdʒɪk] n paraplégico/a.
parapsychology [pærəsaɪ'kɔlədʒɪ] n parapsicologia.
parasite ['pærəsaɪt] n parasito/a.
parasol ['pærəsɔl] n guarda-sol m, sombrinha.
paratrooper ['pærətruːpə*] n pára-quedista m/f.
parcel ['pɑːsl] n pacote m ♦ vt (also: ~ up) embrulhar, empacotar.
parcel out vt repartir, distribuir.
parcel bomb (BRIT) n pacote-bomba m.
parcel post n serviço de encomenda postal.
parch [pɑːtʃ] vt secar, ressecar.
parched [pɑːtʃt] adj (person) morto de sede.
parchment ['pɑːtʃmənt] n pergaminho.
pardon ['pɑːdn] n perdão m; (LAW) indulto ♦ vt perdoar; (LAW) indultar; ~! desculpe!; ~ me!, I beg your ~ (apologizing) desculpe(-me); (I beg your) ~? (BRIT), ~ me? (US) (not hearing) como?, como disse?
pare [pɛə*] vt (BRIT: nails) aparar; (fruit etc) descascar; (fig: costs etc) reduzir, cortar.
parent ['pɛərənt] n pai m (or mãe f); ~s npl pais mpl.
parentage ['pɛərəntɪdʒ] n ascendência; of unknown ~ de pais desconhecidos.
parental [pə'rɛntl] adj paternal (or maternal), dos pais.
parent company n (empresa) matriz f.
parentheses [pə'rɛnθɪsiːz] npl of **parenthesis**.
parenthesis [pə'rɛnθɪsɪs] (pl **parentheses**) n parêntese m; in parentheses entre parênteses.
parenthood ['pɛərənthud] n paternidade f (or maternidade f).
parenting ['pɛərəntɪŋ] n trabalho de ser pai (or mãe).
Paris ['pærɪs] n Paris.
parish ['pærɪʃ] n paróquia, freguesia ♦ adj pa-

roquial.
parish council (BRIT) n ≈ junta da freguesia.
parishioner [pə'rɪʃənə*] n paroquiano/a.
Parisian [pə'rɪzɪən] adj, n parisiense m/f.
parity ['pærɪtɪ] n paridade f, igualdade f.
park [pɑːk] n parque m ♦ vt, vi estacionar.
parka ['pɑːkə] n parka m.
parking ['pɑːkɪŋ] n estacionamento; "no ~" "estacionamento proibido".
parking lights npl luzes fpl de estacionamento.
parking lot (US) n (parque de) estacionamento.
parking meter n parquímetro.
parking offence (BRIT) n infração f por estacionamento não permitido.
parking place n vaga.
parking ticket n multa por estacionamento proibido.
parking violation (US) n infração f por estacionamento não permitido.
parkway ['pɑːkweɪ] (US) n rodovia arborizada.
parlance ['pɑːləns] n: in common/modern ~ na linguagem cotidiana or corrente/moderna.
parliament ['pɑːləmənt] n parlamento.
parliamentary [pɑːlə'mɛntərɪ] adj parlamentar.
parlour ['pɑːlə*] (US parlor) n sala de visitas, salão m, saleta.
parlous ['pɑːləs] adj (formal) precário.
Parmesan [pɑːmɪ'zæn] n (also: ~ cheese) parmesão m.
parochial [pə'rəukɪəl] adj paroquial; (pej) provinciano.
parody ['pærədɪ] n paródia ♦ vt parodiar.
parole [pə'rəul] n: on ~ em liberdade condicional, sob promessa.
paroxysm ['pærəksɪzəm] n (MED, of grief) paroxismo; (of anger, coughing) acesso.
parquet ['pɑːkeɪ] n: ~ floor(ing) parquete m, assoalho de tacos.
parrot ['pærət] n papagaio.
parrot fashion adv mecanicamente, feito papagaio.
parry ['pærɪ] vt aparar, desviar.
parsimonious [pɑːsɪ'məunɪəs] adj parco.
parsley ['pɑːslɪ] n salsa.
parsnip ['pɑːsnɪp] n chirivia, pastinaga.
parson ['pɑːsn] n padre m, clérigo; (Church of England) pastor m.
parsonage ['pɑːsnɪdʒ] n presbitério.
part [pɑːt] n (gen, MUS) parte f; (of machine) peça; (THEATRE etc) papel m; (of serial) capítulo; (US: in hair) risca, repartido ♦ adj parcial ♦ adv em parte ♦ vt dividir; (break) partir; (hair) repartir ♦ vi (people) separar-se; (roads) bifurcar-se; (crowd) dispersar-se; (break) partir-se; to take ~ in participar de, tomar parte em; to take sb's ~ defender alguém; on his ~ da sua parte; for my ~ pela minha parte; for the most ~ na maior parte; for the better ~ of the day durante a maior parte do dia; to be ~ and parcel of fazer parte de; to take sth in good ~ não se ofender com algo; ~ of speech (LING) cate-

goria gramatical.
part with *vt fus* ceder, entregar; *(money)* pagar.
partake [pɑː'teɪk] *(irreg)* *vi* *(formal)*: **to ~ of sth** participar de algo.
part exchange *(BRIT)* *n*: **in ~** como parte do pagamento.
partial ['pɑːʃl] *adj* parcial; **to be ~ to** gostar de, ser apreciador(a) de.
partially ['pɑːʃlɪ] *adv* parcialmente.
participant [pɑː'tɪsɪpənt] *n* *(in competition)* participante *m/f*.
participate [pɑː'tɪsɪpeɪt] *vi*: **to ~ in** participar de.
participation [pɑːtɪsɪ'peɪʃən] *n* participação *f*.
participle ['pɑːtɪsɪpl] *n* particípio.
particle ['pɑːtɪkl] *n* partícula; *(of dust)* grão *m*.
particular [pə'tɪkjulə*] *adj* *(special)* especial; *(specific)* específico; *(given)* determinado; *(fussy)* exigente, minucioso; **in ~** em particular; **I'm not ~** para mim tanto faz.
particularly [pə'tɪkjulənlɪ] *adv* em particular, especialmente.
particulars [pə'tɪkjuləz] *npl* detalhes *mpl*.
parting ['pɑːtɪŋ] *n* *(act of)* separação *f*; *(farewell)* despedida; *(BRIT: in hair)* risca, repartido ♦ *adj* de despedida; **~ shot** *(fig)* flecha de parto.
partisan [pɑːtɪ'zæn] *adj* partidário ♦ *n* partidário/a; *(in war)* guerrilheiro/a.
partition [pɑː'tɪʃən] *n* *(POL)* divisão *f*; *(wall)* tabique *m*, divisória ♦ *vt* separar com tabique; *(fig)* dividir.
partly ['pɑːtlɪ] *adv* em parte.
partner ['pɑːtnə*] *n* *(COMM)* sócio/a; *(SPORT)* parceiro/a; *(at dance)* par *m*; *(spouse)* cônjuge *m/f*; *(friend etc)* companheiro/a ♦ *vt* acompanhar.
partnership ['pɑːtnəʃɪp] *n* associação *f*, parceria; *(COMM)* sociedade *f*; **to go into** *or* **form a ~ (with)** associar-se (com), formar sociedade (com).
partook [pɑː'tuk] *pt of* **partake**.
part payment *n* parcela, prestação *f*.
partridge ['pɑːtrɪdʒ] *n* perdiz *f*.
part-time *adj, adv* de meio expediente.
part-timer *n* *(also: part-time worker)* trabalhador(a) *m/f* de meio expediente.
party ['pɑːtɪ] *n* *(POL)* partido; *(celebration)* festa; *(group)* grupo; *(LAW)* parte *f* interessada, litigante *m/f* ♦ *adj* *(POL)* do partido, partidário; *(dress etc)* de gala, de luxo; **dinner ~** jantar *m*; **to give** *or* **have** *or* **throw a ~** dar uma festa; **to be a ~ to a crime** ser cúmplice num crime.
party line *n* *(POL)* linha partidária; *(TEL)* linha compartilhada.
par value *n* *(of share, bond)* valor *m* nominal.
pass [pɑːs] *vt* *(time, object)* passar; *(exam)* passar em; *(place)* passar por; *(overtake, surpass)* ultrapassar; *(approve)* aprovar;

(candidate) aprovar ♦ *vi* passar; *(SCH)* ser aprovado, passar ♦ *n* *(permit)* passe *m*; *(membership card)* carteira; *(in mountains)* desfiladeiro; *(SPORT)* passe *m*; *(SCH: also: ~ mark)*: **to get a ~ in** ser aprovado em; **she could ~ for 25/a singer** ela podia passar por 25 anos/cantora; **to ~ sth through sth** passar algo por algo; **things have come to a pretty ~** *(BRIT)* as coisas ficaram pretas; **to make a ~ at sb** tomar liberdade com alguém.
pass away *vi* falecer.
pass by *vi* passar ♦ *vt* *(ignore)* passar por cima de.
pass down *vt* *(customs, inheritance)* passar.
pass on *vi* *(die)* falecer ♦ *vt* *(hand on)*: **to ~ on (to)** transmitir (a); *(: price rises)* repassar (a).
pass out *vi* desmaiar; *(BRIT: MIL)* sair *(de uma escola militar)*.
pass over *vt* *(ignore)* passar por cima de.
pass up *vt* deixar passar.
passable ['pɑːsəbl] *adj* *(road)* transitável; *(work)* aceitável.
passage ['pæsɪdʒ] *n* *(also: ~way)* corredor *m*; *(act of passing)* trânsito; *(in book)* passagem *f*, trecho; *(fare)* passagem *(BR)*, bilhete *m* *(PT)*; *(by boat)* travessia; *(MECHANICS, MED)* conduto.
passbook ['pɑːsbuk] *n* caderneta.
passenger ['pæsɪndʒə*] *n* passageiro/a.
passer-by ['pɑːsə*-] *n* transeunte *m/f*.
passing ['pɑːsɪŋ] *adj* *(fleeting)* passageiro, fugaz; **in ~** de passagem.
passing place *n* trecho de ultrapassagem.
passion ['pæʃən] *n* paixão *f*; **to have a ~ for sth** ser aficionado/a de algo.
passionate ['pæʃənɪt] *adj* apaixonado.
passive ['pæsɪv] *adj* *(also: LING)* passivo.
passkey ['pɑːskiː] *n* chave *f* mestra.
Passover ['pɑːsəuvə*] *n* Páscoa *(dos judeus)*.
passport ['pɑːspɔːt] *n* passaporte *m*.
passport control *n* controle *m* dos passaportes.
password ['pɑːswɜːd] *n* senha, contra-senha.
past [pɑːst] *prep* *(further than)* para além de; *(later than)* depois de ♦ *adj* passado; *(president etc)* ex-, anterior ♦ *n* passado; **quarter/ half ~ four** quatro e quinze/meia; **ten/ twenty ~ four** quatro e dez/vinte; **he's ~ forty** ele tem mais de quarenta anos; **for the ~ few days** nos últimos dias; **to run ~** passar correndo (por); **it's ~ midnight** é mais de meia-noite; **in the ~** no passado; **I'm ~ caring** já não ligo mais; **he's ~ it** *(BRIT: inf: person)* ele já passou da idade.
pasta ['pæstə] *n* massa.
paste [peɪst] *n* *(gen)* pasta; *(glue)* grude *m*, cola; *(jewellery)* vidro ♦ *vt* *(stick)* grudar; *(glue)* colar; **tomato ~** massa de tomate.
pastel ['pæstl] *adj* pastel; *(painting)* a pastel.
pasteurized ['pæstəraɪzd] *adj* pasteurizado.

NB: *European Portuguese adds the following consonants to certain words:* **b** *(sú(b)dito, su(b)til);* **c** *(a(c)ção, a(c)cionista, a(c)to);* **m** *(inde(m)ne);* **p** *(ado(p)ção, ado(p)tar); for further details see p. xiii.*

pastille ['pæstl] *n* pastilha.
pastime ['pɑ:staɪm] *n* passatempo.
past master (*BRIT*) *n*: **to be a ~ at** ser perito em.
pastor ['pɑ:stə*] *n* pastor(a) *m/f*.
pastoral ['pɑ:stərl] *adj* pastoral.
pastry ['peɪstrɪ] *n* massa; (*cake*) bolo.
pasture ['pɑ:stʃə*] *n* (*grass*) pasto; (*land*) pastagem *f*, pasto.
pasty [*n* 'pæstɪ, *adj* 'peɪstɪ] *n* empadão *m* de carne ♦ *adj* pastoso; (*complexion*) pálido.
pat [pæt] *vt* dar palmadinhas em; (*dog etc*) fazer festa em ♦ *n* (*of butter*) porção *f* ♦ *adv*: **he knows it off ~** (*BRIT*), **he has it down ~** (*US*) ele sabe isso de cor; **to give sb a ~ on the back** (*fig*) animar alguém.
patch [pætʃ] *n* (*of material*) retalho; (*spot*) mancha; (*mend*) remendo; (*of land*) lote *m*, terreno ♦ *vt* (*clothes*) remendar; **a bad ~** (*BRIT*) um mau pedaço.
patch up *vt* (*mend temporarily*) consertar provisoriamente; (*quarrel*) resolver.
patchwork ['pætʃwɜ:k] *n* colcha de retalhos ♦ *adj* (feito) de retalhos.
patchy ['pætʃɪ] *adj* desigual.
pate [peɪt] *n*: **a bald ~** uma calva, uma careca.
pâté ['pæteɪ] *n* patê *m*.
patent ['peɪtnt] *n* patente *f* ♦ *vt* patentear ♦ *adj* patente, evidente.
patent leather *n* verniz *m*.
patently ['peɪtntlɪ] *adv* claramente.
patent medicine *n* medicamento registrado.
patent office *n* escritório de registro de patentes.
paternal [pə'tɜ:nl] *adj* paternal; (*relation*) paterno.
paternity [pə'tɜ:nɪtɪ] *n* paternidade *f*.
paternity suit *n* (*LAW*) processo de paternidade.
path [pɑ:θ] *n* caminho; (*trail, track*) trilha, senda; (*of missile*) trajetória; (*of planet*) órbita.
pathetic [pə'θetɪk] *adj* (*pitiful*) patético, digno de pena; (*very bad*) péssimo; (*moving*) comovente.
pathological [pæθə'lɔdʒɪkl] *adj* patológico.
pathologist [pə'θɔlədʒɪst] *n* patologista *m/f*.
pathology [pə'θɔlədʒɪ] *n* patologia.
pathos ['peɪθɔs] *n* patos *m*, patético.
pathway ['pɑ:θweɪ] *n* caminho, trilha.
patience ['peɪʃns] *n* paciência; **to lose one's ~** perder a paciência.
patient ['peɪʃnt] *n* paciente *m/f* ♦ *adj* paciente.
patiently ['peɪʃntlɪ] *adv* pacientemente.
patio ['pætɪəu] *n* pátio.
patriot ['peɪtrɪət] *n* patriota *m/f*.
patriotic [pætrɪ'ɔtɪk] *adj* patriótico.
patriotism ['pætrɪətɪzəm] *n* patriotismo.
patrol [pə'trəul] *n* patrulha ♦ *vt* patrulhar; **to be on ~** fazer ronda, patrulhar.
patrol boat *n* barco de patrulha.
patrol car *n* carro de patrulha, radiopatrulha.
patrolman [pə'trəulmən] (*US*: *irreg*) guarda *m*, policial *m* (*BR*), polícia *m* (*PT*).

patron ['peɪtrən] *n* (*in shop*) cliente *m/f*; (*of charity*) benfeitor(a) *m/f*; **~ of the arts** mecenas *m*.
patronage ['pætrənɪdʒ] *n* patrocínio *m*.
patronize ['pætrənaɪz] *vt* (*shop*) ser cliente de; (*business*) patrocinar; (*look down on*) tratar com ar de superioridade.
patronizing ['pætrənaɪzɪŋ] *adj* condescendente.
patron saint *n* (santo/a) padroeiro/a.
patter ['pætə*] *n* tamborilada; (*of feet*) passos miúdos *mpl*; (*sales talk*) jargão *m* profissional ♦ *vi* correr dando passinhos; (*rain*) tamborilar.
pattern ['pætən] *n* modelo, padrão *m*; (*SEWING*) molde *m*; (*design*) desenho; (*sample*) amostra; **behaviour ~** modo de comportamento.
patterned ['pætənd] *adj* padronizado.
paucity ['pɔ:sɪtɪ] *n* penúria, escassez *f*.
paunch [pɔ:ntʃ] *n* pança, barriga.
pauper ['pɔ:pə*] *n* pobre *m/f*; **~'s grave** vala comum.
pause [pɔ:z] *n* pausa; (*interval*) intervalo ♦ *vi* fazer uma pausa; **to ~ for breath** tomar fôlego; (*fig*) fazer uma pausa.
pave [peɪv] *vt* pavimentar; **to ~ the way for** preparar o terreno para.
pavement ['peɪvmənt] *n* (*BRIT*) calçada (*BR*), passeio (*PT*); (*US*) pavimento.
pavilion [pə'vɪlɪən] *n* pavilhão *m*; (*for band etc*) coreto; (*SPORT*) barraca.
paving ['peɪvɪŋ] *n* pavimento, calçamento.
paving stone *n* laje *f*, paralelepípedo.
paw [pɔ:] *n* pata; (*of cat*) garra ♦ *vt* passar a pata em; (*touch*) manusear; (*amorously*) apalpar.
pawn [pɔ:n] *n* (*CHESS*) peão *m*; (*fig*) títere *m* ♦ *vt* empenhar.
pawnbroker ['pɔ:nbrəukə*] *n* agiota *m/f*.
pawnshop ['pɔ:nʃɔp] *n* loja de penhores.
pay [peɪ] (*pt*, *pp* **paid**) *n* salário; (*of manual worker*) paga ♦ *vt* pagar; (*debt*) liquidar, saldar; (*visit*) fazer; (*respect*) apresentar ♦ *vi* pagar; (*be profitable*) valer a pena, render; **how much did you ~ for it?** quanto você pagou por isso?; **I paid £5 for that record** paguei *or* dei £5 por esse disco; **to ~ one's way** pagar sua parte; (*company*) render; **to ~ dividends** (*fig*) trazer vantagens *or* benefícios; **it won't ~ you to do that** não vale a pena você fazer isso; **to ~ attention (to)** prestar atenção (a).
pay back *vt* (*money*) devolver; (*person*) pagar; (*debt*) saldar.
pay in *vt* depositar.
pay off *vt* (*debts*) saldar, liquidar; (*mortgage*) resgatar; (*creditor*) pagar, reembolsar; (*worker*) despedir ♦ *vi* (*plan, patience*) valer a pena; **to ~ sth off in instalments** pagar algo a prazo.
pay out *vt* (*money*) pagar, desembolsar; (*rope*) dar.
pay up *vt* (*debts*) pagar, liquidar; (*amount*) pagar.
payable ['peɪəbl] *adj* pagável; **to make a**

cheque ~ to sb emitir um cheque nominal em favor de alguém.
pay day n dia m do pagamento.
PAYE (BRIT) n abbr (= pay as you earn) tributação na fonte.
payee [peɪ'iː] n beneficiário/a.
pay envelope (US) n envelope m de pagamento.
paying ['peɪɪŋ] adj pagador(a); (business) rendoso; ~ **guest** pensionista m/f.
payload ['peɪləud] n carga paga.
payment ['peɪmənt] n pagamento; (of debt, bill) liquidação f; **advance ~** (part sum) entrada; (total sum) pagamento adiantado; **deferred ~, ~ by instalments** pagamento a prazo; **monthly ~** mensalidade f; **in ~ for** or **of** em pagamento por; **on ~ of £5** contra pagamento de £5.
pay packet (BRIT) n envelope m de pagamento.
payphone ['peɪfəun] n telefone m público.
payroll ['peɪrəul] n folha de pagamento; **to be on a firm's ~** fazer parte do quadro de pessoal assalariado de uma firma.
pay slip (BRIT) n contracheque m.
pay station (US) n cabine f telefônica, orelhão m (BR).
PBS (US) n abbr = Public Broadcasting Service.
PC n abbr (= personal computer) PC m; (BRIT) = **police constable** ♦ abbr (BRIT) = **Privy Councillor.**
pc abbr = **per cent; postcard.**
p/c abbr = **petty cash.**
PCB n abbr = **printed circuit board.**
PD (US) n abbr = **police department.**
pd abbr = **paid.**
PDSA (BRIT) n abbr = **People's Dispensary for Sick Animals.**
PDT (US) abbr (= Pacific Daylight Time) hora de verão do Pacífico.
PE n abbr = **physical education** ♦ abbr (CANADA) = **Prince Edward Island.**
pea [piː] n ervilha.
peace [piːs] n paz f; (calm) tranqüilidade f, quietude f; **to be at ~ with sb/sth** estar em paz com alguém/algo; **to keep the ~** (subj: policeman) manter a ordem; (: citizen) não perturbar a ordem pública.
peaceable ['piːsəbl] adj pacato.
peaceful ['piːsful] adj (gentle) pacífico; (calm) tranqüilo, sossegado.
peace-keeping [-'kiːpɪŋ] n pacificação f.
peace offering n proposta de paz.
peach [piːtʃ] n pêssego.
peacock ['piːkɔk] n pavão m.
peak [piːk] n (of mountain: top) cume m; (: point) pico; (of cap) pala, viseira; (fig: of career, fame) apogeu m; (: highest level) máximo.
peak-hour adj (traffic etc) no horário de maior movimento, na hora de pique.

peak hours npl horário de maior movimento.
peak period n período de pique.
peaky ['piːkɪ] (BRIT: inf) adj adoentado.
peal [piːl] n (of bells) repique m, toque m; ~ **of laughter** gargalhada.
peanut ['piːnʌt] n amendoim m.
peanut butter n manteiga de amendoim.
pear [pɛə*] n pêra; ~ **tree** pereira.
pearl [pɜːl] n pérola.
peasant ['pɛznt] n camponês/esa m/f.
peat [piːt] n turfa.
pebble ['pɛbl] n seixo, calhau m.
peck [pɛk] vt (also: ~ at) bicar, dar bicadas em; (food) beliscar ♦ n bicada; (kiss) beijoca.
pecking order ['pɛkɪŋ-] n ordem f de hierarquia.
peckish ['pɛkɪʃ] (BRIT: inf) adj: **I feel ~** estou a fim de comer alguma coisa.
peculiar [pɪ'kjuːlɪə*] adj (odd) estranho, esquisito; (typical) próprio, característico; (marked) especial; ~ **to** próprio de.
peculiarity [pɪkjuːlɪ'ærɪtɪ] n peculiaridade f; (oddity) excentricidade f, singularidade f.
pecuniary [pɪ'kjuːnɪərɪ] adj pecuniário.
pedal ['pɛdl] n pedal m ♦ vi pedalar.
pedal bin (BRIT) n lata de lixo com pedal.
pedantic [pɪ'dæntɪk] adj pedante.
peddle ['pɛdl] vt vender nas ruas, mascatear; (drugs) traficar, fazer tráfico de.
peddler ['pɛdlə*] n mascate m/f, camelô m.
pedestal ['pɛdəstl] n pedestal m.
pedestrian [pɪ'dɛstrɪən] n pedestre m/f (BR), peão m (PT) ♦ adj pedestre (BR), para peões (PT); (fig) prosaico.
pedestrian crossing (BRIT) n passagem f para pedestres (BR), passadeira (PT).
pedestrian precinct (BRIT) n zona para pedestres (BR) or peões (PT), calçadão m (BR).
pediatrics [piːdɪ'ætrɪks] (US) n = **paediatrics.**
pedigree ['pɛdɪgriː] n genealogia; (of animal) raça ♦ cpd (animal) de raça.
pedlar ['pɛdlə*] n = **peddler.**
pee [piː] (inf) vi fazer xixi, mijar.
peek [piːk] vi espiar, espreitar.
peel [piːl] n casca ♦ vt descascar ♦ vi (paint etc) descascar; (wallpaper) desprender-se.
peel back vt descascar.
peeler ['piːlə*] n (potato etc ~) descascador m.
peelings ['piːlɪŋz] npl cascas fpl.
peep [piːp] n (BRIT: look) espiadela; (sound) pio ♦ vi (BRIT: look) espreitar; (sound) piar.
peep out (BRIT) vi mostrar-se, surgir.
peephole ['piːphəul] n vigia.
peer [pɪə*] vi: **to ~** at perscrutar, fitar ♦ n (noble) par m/f; (equal) igual m/f.
peerage ['pɪərɪdʒ] n pariato.
peerless ['pɪəlɪs] adj sem igual.
peeved [piːvd] adj irritado.
peevish ['piːvɪʃ] adj rabugento.
peg [pɛg] n cavilha; (for coat etc) cabide m;

NB: European Portuguese adds the following consonants to certain words: **b** (sú(b)dito, su(b)til); **c** (a(c)ção, a(c)cionista, a(c)to); **m** (inde(m)ne); **p** (ado(p)ção, ado(p)tar); *for further details see p. xiii.*

(BRIT: also: clothes ~) pregador m; (tent ~) estaca ♦ vt (clothes) prender; (BRIT: groundsheet) segurar com estacas; (fig: prices, wages) fixar, tabelar.

pejorative [pɪ'dʒɔrətɪv] adj pejorativo.

Pekin [piː'kɪn] n Pequim.

Peking [piː'kɪŋ] n = **Pekin**.

pekingese [piːkɪ'niːz] n pequinês m.

pelican ['pɛlɪkən] n pelicano.

pelican crossing (BRIT) n (AUT) passagem f protegida de pedestres (BR), passadeira para peões (PT).

pellet ['pɛlɪt] n bolinha; (bullet) pelota de chumbo.

pell-mell ['pɛl'mɛl] adv a esmo.

pelmet ['pɛlmɪt] n sanefa.

pelt [pɛlt] vt: **to ~ sb with sth** atirar algo em alguém ♦ vi (rain) chover a cântaros ♦ n pele f (não curtida).

pelvis ['pɛlvɪs] n pelvis f, bacia.

pen [pɛn] n caneta; (for sheep) redil m, cercado; (US: inf: prison) cadeia; **to put ~ to paper** escrever.

pen in vt encurralar.

penal ['piːnl] adj penal.

penalize ['piːnəlaɪz] vt impor penalidade a; (SPORT) penalizar; (fig) prejudicar.

penal servitude [-'sɜːvɪtjuːd] n pena de trabalhos forçados.

penalty ['pɛnltɪ] n pena, penalidade f; (fine) multa; (SPORT) punição f; (FOOTBALL) pênalti m; **to take a ~** cobrar um pênalti.

penalty area (BRIT) n área de pênalti.

penalty clause n cláusula penal.

penalty kick n (FOOTBALL) cobrança de pênalti.

penance ['pɛnəns] n penitência.

pence [pɛns] (BRIT) npl of **penny**.

penchant ['pɑːʃɑːŋ] n pendor m, queda.

pencil ['pɛnsl] n lápis m ♦ vt: **to ~ sth in** anotar algo a lápis.

pencil case n lapiseira, porta-lápis m inv.

pencil sharpener n apontador m (de lápis) (BR), apara-lápis m inv (PT).

pendant ['pɛndnt] n pingente m.

pending ['pɛndɪŋ] prep (during) durante; (until) até ♦ adj pendente.

pendulum ['pɛndjuləm] n pêndulo.

penetrate ['pɛnɪtreɪt] vt penetrar.

penetrating ['pɛnɪtreɪtɪŋ] adj penetrante.

penetration [pɛnɪ'treɪʃən] n penetração f.

penfriend ['pɛnfrɛnd] (BRIT) n amigo/a por correspondência, correspondente m/f.

penguin ['pɛŋgwɪn] n pingüim m.

penicillin [pɛnɪ'sɪlɪn] n penicilina.

peninsula [pə'nɪnsjulə] n península.

penis ['piːnɪs] n pênis m.

penitence ['pɛnɪtns] n penitência.

penitent ['pɛnɪtnt] adj arrependido; (REL) penitente.

penitentiary [pɛnɪ'tɛnʃərɪ] (US) n penitenciária, presídio.

penknife ['pɛnnaɪf] (irreg) n canivete m.

pen name n pseudônimo.

pennant ['pɛnənt] n flâmula.

penniless ['pɛnɪlɪs] adj sem dinheiro, sem um tostão.

Pennines ['pɛnaɪnz] npl: **the ~** as Pennines.

penny ['pɛnɪ] (pl **pennies** or **pence**) n pêni m (new: 100 in a pound; old: 12 in a shilling; a tendência é de se utilizar "pennies" ou "twopence piece" etc para as moedas, "pence" para o valor); (US) = **cent**.

penpal ['pɛnpæl] n amigo/a por correspondência, correspondente m/f.

pension ['pɛnʃən] n pensão f; (old-age ~) aposentadoria f; (MIL) reserva.

pension off vt aposentar.

pensionable ['pɛnʃnəbl] adj (person) com direito a uma pensão; (age) de aposentadoria.

pensioner ['pɛnʃənə*] (BRIT) n aposentado/a (BR), reformado/a (PT).

pension fund n fundo da aposentadoria.

pensive ['pɛnsɪv] adj pensativo; (withdrawn) absorto.

pentagon ['pɛntəgən] n pentágono.

Pentecost ['pɛntɪkɔst] n Pentecostes m.

penthouse ['pɛnthaus] (irreg) n cobertura.

pent-up [pɛnt-] adj (feelings) reprimido.

penultimate [pɪ'nʌltɪmət] adj penúltimo.

penury ['pɛnjurɪ] n pobreza, miséria.

people ['piːpl] npl gente f, pessoas fpl; (citizens) povo ♦ n (nation, race) povo ♦ vt povoar; **several ~ came** vieram várias pessoas; **I know ~ who ...** conheço gente que ...; **~ say that ...** dizem que ...; **old ~** os idosos; **young ~** os jovens; **a man of the ~** um homem do povo.

pep [pɛp] (inf) n pique m, energia, dinamismo.

pep up vt animar.

pepper ['pɛpə*] n pimenta; (vegetable) pimentão m ♦ vt apimentar; (fig) salpicar.

peppermint ['pɛpəmɪnt] n hortelã-pimenta; (sweet) bala de hortelã.

pepperpot ['pɛpəpɔt] n pimenteiro.

peptalk ['pɛptɔːk] (inf) n conversa para levantar o espírito.

per [pɜː*] prep por; **~ day/person** por dia/pessoa; **as ~ your instructions** conforme suas instruções.

per annum adv por ano.

per capita adj, adv per capita, por pessoa.

perceive [pə'siːv] vt perceber.

per cent adv por cento; **a 20 ~ discount** um desconto de 20 por cento.

percentage [pə'sɛntɪdʒ] n porcentagem f, percentagem f; **on a ~ basis** na base de percentagem.

perceptible [pə'sɛptɪbl] adj perceptível, sensível.

perception [pə'sɛpʃən] n percepção f; (insight) perspicácia.

perceptive [pə'sɛptɪv] adj perceptivo.

perch [pɜːtʃ] (pl ~es) n (for bird) poleiro; (pl: inv or ~es: fish) perca ♦ vi empoleirar-se, pousar.

percolate ['pɜːkəleɪt] vt, vi passar.

percolator ['pɜːkəleɪtə*] n cafeteira de filtro.

percussion [pə'kʌʃən] n percussão f.

peremptory [pə'rɛmptərɪ] adj peremptório;

(*person: imperious*) autoritário.

perennial [pə'renɪəl] *adj* perene ♦ *n* planta perene.

perfect [*adj, n* 'pɔːfɪkt, *vt* pə'fekt] *adj* perfeito ♦ *n* (*also*: ~ *tense*) perfeito ♦ *vt* aperfeiçoar; **a ~ stranger** uma pessoa completamente desconhecida.

perfection [pə'fekʃən] *n* perfeição *f*.

perfectionist [pə'fekʃənɪst] *n* perfeccionista *m/f*.

perfectly ['pɔːfɪktlɪ] *adv* perfeitamente; **I'm ~ happy with the situation** estou completamente satisfeito com a situação; **you know ~ well** você sabe muito bem.

perforate ['pɔːfəreɪt] *vt* perfurar.

perforated ['pɔːfəreɪtɪd] *adj* (*stamp*) picotado.

perforated ulcer *n* (*MED*) úlcera perfurada.

perforation [pɔːfə'reɪʃən] *n* perfuração *f*; (*line of holes*) picote *m*.

perform [pə'fɔːm] *vt* (*carry out*) realizar, fazer; (*concert etc*) executar; (*piece of music*) interpretar ♦ *vi* (*animal*) fazer truques de amestramento; (*THEATRE*) representar; (*TECH*) funcionar.

performance [pə'fɔːməns] *n* (*of task*) cumprimento, realização *f*; (*of artist, player etc*) atuação *f*; (*of car engine, function*) desempenho; (*of car*) performance *f*.

performer [pə'fɔːmə*] *n* (*actor*) artista *m/f*, ator/atriz *m/f*; (*MUS*) intérprete *m/f*.

performing [pə'fɔːmɪŋ] *adj* (*animal*) amestrado, adestrado.

perfume ['pɔːfjuːm] *n* perfume *m* ♦ *vt* perfumar.

perfunctory [pə'fʌŋktərɪ] *adj* superficial, negligente.

perhaps [pə'hæps] *adv* talvez; **~ he'll come** talvez ele venha; **~ so/not** talvez seja assim/talvez não.

peril ['perɪl] *n* perigo, risco.

perilous ['perɪləs] *adj* perigoso.

perilously ['perɪləslɪ] *adv*: **they came ~ close to being caught** não foram presos por um triz.

perimeter [pə'rɪmɪtə*] *n* perímetro.

perimeter wall *n* muro periférico.

period ['pɪərɪəd] *n* período; (*HISTORY*) época; (*time limit*) prazo; (*SCH*) aula; (*full stop*) ponto final; (*MED*) menstruação *f*, regra ♦ *adj* (*costume, furniture*) da época; **for a ~ of three weeks** por um período de três semanas; **the holiday ~** (*BRIT*) o período de férias.

periodic [pɪərɪ'ɔdɪk] *adj* periódico.

periodical [pɪərɪ'ɔdɪkl] *adj, n* periódico.

periodically [pɪərɪ'ɔdɪklɪ] *adv* periodicamente, de vez em quando.

period pains (*BRIT*) *npl* cólicas *fpl* menstruais.

peripatetic [perɪpə'tetɪk] *adj* (*salesman*) viajante; (*teacher*) que trabalha em vários lugares.

peripheral [pə'rɪfərəl] *adj* periférico ♦ *n* (*COMPUT*) periférico.

periphery [pə'rɪfərɪ] *n* periferia.

periscope ['perɪskəup] *n* periscópio.

perish ['perɪʃ] *vi* perecer; (*decay*) deteriorar-se, estragar.

perishable ['perɪʃəbl] *adj* perecível, deteriorável.

perishables ['perɪʃəblz] *npl* perecíveis *mpl*.

perishing ['perɪʃɪŋ] (*BRIT: inf*) *adj* (*cold*) gelado, glacial.

peritonitis [perɪtə'naɪtɪs] *n* peritonite *f*.

perjure ['pɔːdʒə*] *vt*: **to ~ o.s.** prestar falso testemunho.

perjury ['pɔːdʒərɪ] *n* (*LAW*) perjúrio, falso testemunho.

perk [pɔːk] (*inf*) *n* mordomia, regalia.

perk up (*inf*) *vi* (*cheer up*) animar-se; (*in health*) recuperar-se.

perky ['pɔːkɪ] *adj* (*cheerful*) animado, alegre.

perm [pɔːm] *n* permanente *f* ♦ *vt*: **to have one's hair ~ed** fazer permanente (no cabelo).

permanence ['pɔːmənəns] *n* permanência, continuidade *f*.

permanent ['pɔːmənənt] *adj* permanente; **I'm not ~ here** não estou aqui em caráter permanente.

permanently ['pɔːmənəntlɪ] *adv* permanentemente.

permeable ['pɔːmɪəbl] *adj* permeável.

permeate ['pɔːmɪeɪt] *vi* difundir-se ♦ *vt* penetrar.

permissible [pə'mɪsɪbl] *adj* permissível, lícito.

permission [pə'mɪʃən] *n* permissão *f*; (*authorization*) autorização *f*; **to give sb ~ to do sth** dar permissão a alguém para fazer algo.

permissive [pə'mɪsɪv] *adj* permissivo.

permit [*n* 'pɔːmɪt, *vt* pə'mɪt] *n* permissão *f*; (*for fishing, export etc*) licença; (*to enter*) passe *m* ♦ *vt* permitir; (*authorize*) autorizar; **to ~ sb to do sth** permitir a alguém fazer *or* que faça algo; **weather ~ting** se o tempo permitir.

permutation [pɔːmju'teɪʃən] *n* permutação *f*.

pernicious [pɔː'nɪʃəs] *adj* nocivo; (*MED*) pernicioso, maligno.

pernickety [pə'nɪkɪtɪ] (*inf*) *adj* cheio de novehoras *or* luxo; (*task*) minucioso.

perpendicular [pɔːpən'dɪkjulə*] *adj* perpendicular ♦ *n* perpendicular *f*.

perpetrate ['pɔːpɪtreɪt] *vt* cometer.

perpetual [pə'petjuəl] *adj* perpétuo.

perpetuate [pə'petjueɪt] *vt* perpetuar.

perpetuity [pɔːpɪ'tjuːɪtɪ] *n*: **in ~** para sempre.

perplex [pə'pleks] *vt* deixar perplexo.

perplexing [pɔː'pleksɪŋ] *adj* desconcertante.

perquisites ['pɔːkwɪzɪts] *npl* (*also: perks*) mordomias *fpl*, regalias *fpl*.

persecute ['pɔːsɪkjuːt] *vt* (*pursue*) perseguir; (*harass*) importunar.

persecution [pɔːsɪ'kjuːʃən] *n* perseguição *f*.

NB: *European Portuguese adds the following consonants to certain words:* **b** (sú(b)dito, su(b)til); **c** (a(c)ção, a(c)cionista, a(c)to); **m** (inde(m)ne); **p** (ado(p)ção, ado(p)tar); *for further details see p. xiii.*

perseverance [pɔːsɪ'vɪərəns] *n* perseverança.
persevere [pɔːsɪ'vɪə*] *vi* perseverar.
Persia ['pɔːʃə] *n* Pérsia.
Persian ['pɔːʃən] *adj* persa ♦ *n* (*LING*) persa *m*; **the (~) Gulf** o golfo Pérsico.
persist [pɔ'sɪst] *vi*: **to ~ (in doing sth)** persistir (em fazer algo).
persistence [pɔ'sɪstəns] *n* persistência; (*of disease*) insistência; (*obstinacy*) teimosia.
persistent [pɔ'sɪstənt] *adj* persistente; (*determined*) teimoso; (*disease*) insistente, persistente; **~ offender** (*LAW*) infrator(a) *m/f* contumaz.
persnickety [pɔ'snɪkɪtɪ] (*US*: *inf*) *adj* = **pernickety**.
person ['pɔːsn] *n* pessoa; **in ~** em pessoa; **on** *or* **about one's ~** consigo; **~ to ~ call** (*TEL*) chamada pessoal.
personable ['pɔːsənəbl] *adj* atraente, bem apessoado.
personal ['pɔːsənl] *adj* pessoal; (*private*) particular; (*visit*) em pessoa, pessoal; **~ belongings** *or* **effects** pertences *mpl* particulares; **~ hygiene** higiene *f* íntima; **a ~ interview** uma entrevista particular.
personal allowance *n* (*TAX*) abatimento da renda de pessoa física.
personal assistant *n* secretário/a particular.
personal call *n* (*TEL*) chamada pessoal.
personal column *n* anúncios *mpl* pessoais.
personal computer *n* computador *m* pessoal.
personal details *npl* (*on form etc*) dados *mpl* pessoais.
personal identification number *n* (*COMPUT*, *BANKING*) senha, número de identificação individual.
personality [pɔːsə'nælɪtɪ] *n* personalidade *f*.
personally ['pɔːsənəlɪ] *adv* pessoalmente.
personal property *n* bens *mpl* móveis.
personify [pɔː'sɔnɪfaɪ] *vt* personificar.
personnel [pɔːsə'nel] *n* pessoal *m*.
personnel department *n* departamento de pessoal.
personnel manager *n* gerente *m/f* de pessoal.
perspective [pɔ'spektɪv] *n* perspectiva; **to get sth into ~** colocar algo em perspectiva.
perspex ['pɔːspeks] ® (*BRIT*) *n* Blindex *m* ®.
perspicacity [pɔːspɪ'kæsɪtɪ] *n* perspicácia.
perspiration [pɔːspɪ'reɪʃən] *n* transpiração *f*.
perspire [pɔ'spaɪə*] *vi* transpirar.
persuade [pɔ'sweɪd] *vt* persuadir; **to ~ sb to do sth** persuadir alguém a fazer algo; **to ~ sb that/of sth** persuadir alguém que/de algo.
persuasion [pɔ'sweɪʒən] *n* persuasão *f*; (*persuasiveness*) poder *m* de persuasão; (*creed*) convicção *f*, crença.
persuasive [pɔ'sweɪsɪv] *adj* persuasivo.
pert [pɔːt] *adj* atrevido, descarado.
pertaining to [pɔː'teɪnɪŋ-] *prep* relativo a.
pertinent ['pɔːtɪnənt] *adj* pertinente, a propósito.
perturb [pɔ'tɔːb] *vt* inquietar.
perturbing [pɔ'tɔːbɪŋ] *adj* inquietante.

Peru [pɔ'ruː] *n* Peru *m*.
perusal [pɔ'ruːzl] *n* leitura.
peruse [pɔ'ruːz] *vt* ler com atenção, examinar.
Peruvian [pɔ'ruːvjən] *adj*, *n* peruano/a.
pervade [pɔ'veɪd] *vt* impregnar, penetrar em.
pervasive [pɔ'veɪsɪv] *adj* (*smell*) penetrante; (*influence*, *ideas*, *gloom*) difundido.
perverse [pɔ'vɔːs] *adj* perverso; (*stubborn*) teimoso; (*wayward*) caprichoso.
perversion [pɔ'vɔːʃən] *n* perversão *f*.
perversity [pɔ'vɔːsɪtɪ] *n* perversidade *f*.
pervert [*n* 'pɔːvɔːt, *vt* pɔ'vɔːt] *n* pervertido/a ♦ *vt* perverter, corromper.
pessary ['pesərɪ] *n* pessário.
pessimism ['pesɪmɪzəm] *n* pessimismo.
pessimist ['pesɪmɪst] *n* pessimista *m/f*.
pessimistic [pesɪ'mɪstɪk] *adj* pessimista.
pest [pest] *n* peste *f*, praga; (*insect*) inseto nocivo; (*fig*) peste *f*.
pest control *n* dedetização *f*; (*for mice*) desratização *f*.
pester ['pestə*] *vt* incomodar.
pesticide ['pestɪsaɪd] *n* pesticida *m*.
pestilent ['pestɪlənt] (*inf*) *adj* (*exasperating*) chato.
pestilential [pestɪ'lenʃəl] (*inf*) *adj* (*exasperating*) chato.
pestle ['pesl] *n* mão *f* (de almofariz).
pet [pet] *n* animal *m* de estimação; (*favourite*) preferido/a ♦ *vt* acariciar ♦ *vi* acariciar-se, emburrar ♦ *adj*: **~ lion** *etc* leão *m etc* de estimação; **my ~ hate** a coisa que eu mais odeio.
petal ['petl] *n* pétala.
peter out ['piːtə*-] *vi* esgotar-se, acabar-se.
petite [pɔ'tiːt] *adj* diminuto.
petition [pɔ'tɪʃən] *n* petição *f*; (*list of signatures*) abaixo-assinado ♦ *vt* apresentar uma petição a ♦ *vi*: **to ~ for divorce** requerer divórcio.
pet name (*BRIT*) *n* apelido carinhoso.
petrified ['petrɪfaɪd] *adj* (*fig*) petrificado, paralisado.
petrify ['petrɪfaɪ] *vt* paralisar; (*frighten*) petrificar.
petrochemical [petrɔ'kemɪkl] *adj* petroquímico.
petrodollars ['petrɔudɔləz] *npl* petrodólares *mpl*.
petrol ['petrɔl] (*BRIT*) *n* gasolina.
petrol can (*BRIT*) *n* lata de gasolina.
petrol engine (*BRIT*) *n* motor *m* a gasolina.
petroleum [pɔ'trɔulɪəm] *n* petróleo.
petroleum jelly *n* vaselina.
petrol pump (*BRIT*) *n* (*in car*, *at garage*) bomba de gasolina.
petrol station (*BRIT*) *n* posto (*BR*) *or* bomba (*PT*) de gasolina.
petrol tank (*BRIT*) *n* tanque *m* de gasolina.
petticoat ['petɪkəut] *n* anágua; (*slip*) combinação *f*.
pettifogging ['petɪfɔgɪŋ] *adj* chicaneiro.
pettiness ['petɪnɪs] *n* mesquinharia *f*.
petty ['petɪ] *adj* (*mean*) mesquinho; (*unimportant*) insignificante.

petty cash n fundo para despesas miúdas, caixa pequena, fundo de caixa.

petty officer n suboficial m da marinha.

petulant ['petjulənt] adj irascível.

pew [pju:] n banco (de igreja).

pewter ['pju:tə*] n peltre m.

Pfc (US) abbr (MIL) = **private first class.**

PG n abbr (CINEMA: = parental guidance) aviso dos pais recomendado.

PGA n abbr = **Professional Golfers' Association.**

PH (US) n abbr (MIL: = Purple Heart) condecoração para feridos em combate.

p & h (US) abbr = **postage and handling.**

PHA (US) n abbr (= Public Housing Administration) órgão que supervisiona a construção.

phallic ['fælɪk] adj fálico.

phantom ['fæntəm] n fantasma m.

Pharaoh ['fɛərəu] n faraó m.

pharmaceutical [fɑːmə'sju:tɪkl] adj farmacêutico.

pharmaceuticals [fɑːmə'sju:tɪklz] npl farmacêuticos mpl.

pharmacist ['fɑːməsɪst] n farmacêutico/a.

pharmacy ['fɑːməsɪ] n farmácia.

phase [feɪz] n fase f ♦ vt: **to ~ sth in/out** introduzir/retirar algo por etapas.

PhD abbr = **Doctor of Philosophy** ♦ n ≈ doutorado.

pheasant ['feznt] n faisão m.

phenomena [fə'nɔmɪnə] npl of **phenomenon.**

phenomenon [fə'nɔmɪnən] (pl **phenomena**) n fenômeno.

phew [fju:] excl ufa!

phial ['faɪəl] n frasco.

philanderer [fɪ'lændərə*] n mulherengo.

philanthropic [fɪlən'θrɔpɪk] adj filantrópico.

philanthropist [fɪ'lænθrəpɪst] n filantropo/a.

philatelist [fɪ'lætəlɪst] n filatelista m/f.

philately [fɪ'lætəlɪ] n filatelia.

Philippines ['fɪlɪpi:nz] npl (also: **Philippine Islands**): **the ~** as Filipinas.

philosopher [fɪ'lɔsəfə*] n filósofo/a.

philosophical [fɪlə'sɔfɪkl] adj filosófico.

philosophy [fɪ'lɔsəfɪ] n filosofia.

phlegm [flɛm] n fleuma.

phlegmatic [flɛg'mætɪk] adj fleumático.

phobia ['fəubjə] n fobia.

phone [fəun] n telefone m ♦ vt telefonar a, ligar para ♦ vi telefonar, ligar; **to be on the ~** ter telefone; (be calling) estar no telefone.

phone back vt, vi ligar de volta.

phone book n lista telefônica.

phone booth n cabine f telefônica.

phone box n cabine f telefônica.

phone call n telefonema m, ligada.

phone-in (BRIT) n (RADIO) programa com participação dos ouvintes; (TV) programa com participação dos espectadores.

phonetics [fə'netɪks] n fonética.

phoney ['fəunɪ] adj falso; (person) fingido ♦ n (person) impostor(a) m/f.

phonograph ['fəunəgrɑːf] (US) n vitrola.

phony ['fəunɪ] adj, n = **phoney.**

phosphate ['fɔsfeɪt] n fosfato.

phosphorus ['fɔsfərəs] n fósforo.

photo ['fəutəu] n foto f.

photo... ['fəutəu] prefix foto....

photocopier ['fəutəukɔpɪə*] n fotocopiadora f.

photocopy ['fəutəukɔpɪ] n fotocópia, xerox m ♦ vt fotocopiar, xerocar.

photoelectric [fəutəuɪ'lɛktrɪk] adj fotoelétrico; **~ cell** célula fotoelétrica.

photogenic [fəutəu'dʒɛnɪk] adj fotogênico.

photograph ['fəutəgrɑːf] n fotografia ♦ vt fotografar; **to take a ~ of sb** bater or tirar uma foto de alguém.

photographer [fə'tɔgrəfə*] n fotógrafo/a.

photographic [fəutə'græfɪk] adj fotográfico.

photography [fə'tɔgrəfɪ] n fotografia.

photostat ['fəutəustæt] n cópia fotostática.

photosynthesis [fəutəu'sɪnθəsɪs] n fotossíntese f.

phrase [freɪz] n frase f ♦ vt expressar; (letter) redigir.

phrasebook ['freɪzbuk] n livro de expressões idiomáticas (para turistas).

physical ['fɪzɪkl] adj físico; **~ examination** exame m físico; **~ education** educação f física; **~ exercise** exercício físico, movimento.

physically ['fɪzɪklɪ] adv fisicamente.

physician [fɪ'zɪʃən] n médico/a.

physicist ['fɪzɪsɪst] n físico/a.

physics ['fɪzɪks] n física.

physiological [fɪzɪə'lɔdʒɪkl] adj fisiológico.

physiology [fɪzɪ'ɔlədʒɪ] n fisiologia.

physiotherapist [fɪzɪəu'θɛrəpɪst] n fisioterapeuta m/f.

physiotherapy [fɪzɪəu'θɛrəpɪ] n fisioterapia.

physique [fɪ'zi:k] n físico.

pianist ['pi:ənɪst] n pianista m/f.

piano [pɪ'ænəu] n piano.

piano accordion (BRIT) n acordeão m, sanfona.

piccolo ['pɪkələu] n flautim m.

pick [pɪk] n (tool: also: **~-axe**) picareta ♦ vt (select) escolher, selecionar; (gather) colher; (lock) forçar; **take your ~** escolha o que quiser; **the ~ of** o melhor de; **to ~ a bone** roer um osso; **to ~ one's nose** colocar o dedo no nariz; **to ~ one's teeth** palitar os dentes; **to ~ sb's brains** aproveitar os conhecimentos de alguém; **to ~ pockets** roubar or bater carteira; **to ~ a quarrel or a fight with sb** comprar uma briga com alguém; **to ~ and choose** ser exigente.

pick off vt (kill) matar de um tiro.

pick on vt fus (person) azucrinar, aporrinhar.

pick out vt escolher; (distinguish) distinguir.

pick up vi (improve) melhorar ♦ vt (from floor) apanhar; (telephone) atender, tirar do gancho; (collect) buscar; (learn) aprender;

NB: European Portuguese adds the following consonants to certain words: **b** (sú(b)dito, su(b)til); **c** (a(c)ção, a(c)cionista, a(c)to); **m** (inde(m)ne); **p** (ado(p)ção, ado(p)tar); for further details see p. xiii.

(*RADIO, TV, TEL*) pegar; **to ~ up speed** acelerar; **to ~ o.s. up** levantar-se; **to ~ up where one left off** continuar do ponto onde se parou.

pickaxe ['pɪkæks] (*US* **pickax**) *n* picareta.

picket ['pɪkɪt] *n* (*in strike*) piquete *m*; (*person*) piqueteiro/a ♦ *vt* formar piquete em frente de.

picket line *n* piquete *m*.

pickings ['pɪkɪŋz] *npl*: **there are rich ~ to be had for investors in gold** os investidores em ouro vão se dar bem.

pickle ['pɪkl] *n* (*also*: ~s: *as condiment*) picles *mpl*; (*fig*: *mess*) apuro ♦ *vt* (*in vinegar*) conservar em vinagre.

pick-me-up *n* estimulante *m*.

pickpocket ['pɪkpɔkɪt] *n* batedor(a) *m/f* de carteira (*BR*), carteirista *m/f* (*PT*).

pickup ['pɪkʌp] *n* (*on record player*) pick-up *m*; (*small truck*: *also*: ~ **truck**, ~ **van**) camioneta, pick-up *m*.

picnic ['pɪknɪk] *n* piquenique *m* ♦ *vi* fazer um piquenique.

picnicker ['pɪknɪkə*'] *n* pessoa que faz piquenique.

pictorial [pɪk'tɔːrɪəl] *adj* pictórico; (*magazine etc*) ilustrado.

picture ['pɪktʃə*'] *n* quadro; (*TV*) imagem *f*; (*painting*) pintura; (*drawing*) desenho; (*photograph*) foto(grafia) *f*; (*film*) filme *m* ♦ *vt* imaginar-se; (*describe*) retratar; **the ~s** *npl* (*BRIT*) o cinema; **to take a ~ of sb/sth** tirar uma foto de alguém/algo; **the overall ~** o quadro geral; **to put sb in the ~** pôr alguém a par da situação.

picture book *n* livro de figuras.

picturesque [pɪktʃə'resk] *adj* pitoresco.

picture window *n* janela panorâmica.

piddling ['pɪdlɪŋ] (*inf*) *adj* irrisório.

pidgin ['pɪdʒɪn] *adj*: ~ **English** *forma achinesada do inglês usada entre comerciantes.*

pie [paɪ] *n* pastelão *m*; (*open*) torta; (*of meat*) empadão *m*.

piebald ['paɪbɔːld] *adj* malhado.

piece [piːs] *n* pedaço; (*of land*) lote *m*, parcela; (*CHESS etc*) peça; (*item*): **a ~ of furniture/advice** um móvel/um conselho ♦ *vt*: **to ~ together** juntar; (*TECH*) montar; **in ~s** (*broken*) em pedaços; (*not yet assembled*) desmontado; **to fall to ~s** cair aos pedaços; **to take to ~s** desmontar; **in one ~** (*object*) inteiro; (*person*) ileso; **a 10p ~** (*BRIT*) uma moeda de 10p; ~ **by ~** pedaço por pedaço; **a six-~ band** um sexteto; **to say one's ~** vender o seu peixe.

piecemeal ['piːsmiːl] *adv* pouco a pouco.

piece rate *n* salário por peça.

piecework ['piːswəːk] *n* trabalho por empreitada *or* peça.

pie chart *n* gráfico de setores.

pier [pɪə*'] *n* cais *m*; (*jetty*) embarcadouro, molhe *m*; (*of bridge etc*) pilar *m*, pilastra.

pierce [pɪəs] *vt* furar, perfurar; **to have one's ears ~d** furar as orelhas.

piercing ['pɪəsɪŋ] *adj* (*cry*) penetrante, agudo.

piety ['paɪətɪ] *n* piedade *f*.

piffling ['pɪflɪŋ] *adj* irrisório.

pig [pɪg] *n* porco; (*fig*) porcalhão/lhona *m/f*.

pigeon ['pɪdʒən] *n* pombo.

pigeonhole ['pɪdʒənhəul] *n* escaninho.

pigeon-toed [-təud] *adj* com pé de pombo.

piggy bank ['pɪgɪ-] *n* cofre em forma de porquinho.

pigheaded ['pɪg'hɛdɪd] *adj* teimoso, cabeçudo.

piglet ['pɪglɪt] *n* porquinho, leitão *m*.

pigment ['pɪgmənt] *n* pigmento.

pigmentation [pɪgmən'teɪʃən] *n* pigmentação *f*.

pigmy ['pɪgmɪ] *n* = **pygmy**.

pigskin ['pɪgskɪn] *n* couro de porco.

pigsty ['pɪgstaɪ] *n* chiqueiro.

pigtail ['pɪgteɪl] *n* (*girl's*) trança; (*Chinese*) rabicho, rabo-de-cavalo.

pike [paɪk] *n* (*pl* ~**s**) (*spear*) lança, pique *m*; (*pl*: *inv*: *fish*) lúcio.

pilchard ['pɪltʃəd] *n* sardinha.

pile [paɪl] *n* (*of books*) pilha; (*heap*) monte *m*; (*of carpet*) pêlo; (*of cloth*) lado felpudo; (*support*: *in building*) estaca ♦ *vt* (*also*: ~ **up**) empilhar; (*heap*) amontoar; (*fig*) acumular ♦ *vi* (*also*: ~ **up**) amontoar-se; ~**s** *npl* (*MED*) hemorróidas *fpl*; **in a ~** numa pilha.

pile on *vt*: **to ~ it on** (*inf*) exagerar.

pileup ['paɪlʌp] *n* (*AUT*) engavetamento.

pilfer ['pɪlfə*'] *vt*, *vi* furtar, afanar, surripiar.

pilfering ['pɪlfərɪŋ] *n* furto.

pilgrim ['pɪlgrɪm] *n* peregrino/a.

pilgrimage ['pɪlgrɪmɪdʒ] *n* peregrinação *f*, romaria.

pill [pɪl] *n* pílula; **the ~** a pílula; **to be on the ~** usar *or* tomar a pílula.

pillage ['pɪlɪdʒ] *vt* saquear, pilhar.

pillar ['pɪlə*'] *n* pilar *m*; (*concrete*) coluna.

pillar box (*BRIT*) *n* caixa coletora (do correio) (*BR*), marco do correio (*PT*).

pillion ['pɪljən] *n* (*of motor cycle*) garupa ♦ *adv*: **to ride ~** andar na garupa.

pillory ['pɪlərɪ] *n* pelourinho ♦ *vt* expor ao ridículo.

pillow ['pɪləu] *n* travesseiro (*BR*), almofada (*PT*).

pillowcase ['pɪləukeɪs] *n* fronha.

pillowslip ['pɪləuslɪp] *n* fronha.

pilot ['paɪlət] *n* piloto/a ♦ *cpd* (*scheme etc*) piloto *inv* ♦ *vt* pilotar; (*fig*) guiar.

pilot boat *n* barco-piloto.

pilot light *n* piloto.

pimento [pɪ'mɛntəu] *n* pimentão-doce *m*.

pimp [pɪmp] *n* cafetão *m* (*BR*), cáften *m* (*PT*).

pimple ['pɪmpl] *n* espinha.

pimply ['pɪmplɪ] *adj* espinhento.

PIN *n abbr* = **personal identification number**.

pin [pɪn] *n* alfinete *m*; (*TECH*) cavilha; (*wooden*, *BRIT*: *ELEC*: *of plug*) pino ♦ *vt* alfinetar; ~**s and needles** comichão *f*, sensação *f* de formigamento; **to ~ sb against** *or* **to** apertar alguém contra; **to ~ sth on sb** (*fig*) culpar alguém de algo.

pin down *vt* (*fig*): **to ~ sb down** conseguir

que alguém se defina *or* tome atitude; **there's something strange here but I can't quite ~ it down** há alguma coisa estranha aqui, mas não consigo precisar o quê.
pinafore ['pɪnəfɔ:*] *n* avental *m*.
pinafore dress *n* avental *m*.
pinball ['pɪnbɔ:l] *n* fliper *m*, fliperama *m*.
pincers ['pɪnsəz] *npl* pinça, tenaz *f*.
pinch [pɪntʃ] *n* beliscão *m*; *(of salt etc)* pitada ♦ *vt* beliscar; *(inf: steal)* furtar ♦ *vi (shoe)* apertar; **at a ~** em último caso; **to feel the ~** *(fig)* apertar o cinto, passar por um aperto.
pinched [pɪntʃt] *adj (drawn)* abatido; **~ with cold** transido de frio; **~ for money** desprovido de dinheiro; **to be ~ for space** não dispor de muito espaço.
pincushion ['pɪnkuʃən] *n* alfineteira.
pine [paɪn] *n (also: ~ tree)* pinho ♦ *vi:* **to ~ for** ansiar por.
pine away *vi* consumir-se, definhar.
pineapple ['paɪnæpl] *n* abacaxi *m (BR)*, ananás *m (PT)*.
ping [pɪŋ] *n (noise)* silvo, sibilo.
ping-pong *n* pingue-pongue *m*.
pink [pɪŋk] *adj* cor de rosa *inv* ♦ *n (colour)* cor *f* de rosa; *(BOT)* cravo, cravina.
pinking scissors ['pɪŋkɪŋ-] *npl* tesoura para picotar.
pinking shears ['pɪŋkɪŋ-] *npl* tesoura para picotar.
pin money *(BRIT)* *n* dinheiro extra.
pinnacle ['pɪnəkl] *n* cume *m*; *(fig)* auge *m*.
pinpoint ['pɪnpɔɪnt] *vt* localizar com precisão.
pinstripe ['pɪnstraɪp] *n* tecido listrado ♦ *adj* listrado.
pint [paɪnt] *n* quartilho; **to go for a ~** *(BRIT: inf)* ir tomar uma cerveja.
pin-up *n* pin-up *f*, retrato de mulher atraente.
pioneer [paɪə'nɪə*] *n* pioneiro/a ♦ *vt* ser pioneiro de.
pious ['paɪəs] *adj* pio, devoto.
pip [pɪp] *n (seed)* caroço, semente *f*; *(BRIT: time signal on radio)*: **the ~s** ≈ o tope de oito segundos.
pipe [paɪp] *n* cano, tubo; *(for smoking)* cachimbo; *(MUS)* flauta ♦ *vt* canalizar, encanar; **~s** *npl (also: bag~s)* gaita de foles.
pipe down *(inf)* *vi* calar o bico, meter a viola no saco.
pipe cleaner *n* limpa-cachimbo.
piped music [paɪpt-] *n* música enlatada.
pipe dream *n* sonho impossível, castelo no ar.
pipeline ['paɪplaɪn] *n (for oil)* oleoduto; *(for gas)* gaseoduto; **it's in the ~** *(fig)* está na bica *(inf)*.
piper ['paɪpə*] *n (gen)* flautista *m/f*; *(of bagpipes)* gaiteiro/a.
pipe tobacco *n* fumo *(BR) or* tabaco *(PT)* para cachimbo.
piping ['paɪpɪŋ] *adv:* **~ hot** chiando de quente.

piquant ['pi:kənt] *adj* picante.
pique [pi:k] *n* ressentimento, melindre *m*.
piracy ['paɪrəsɪ] *n* pirataria.
pirate ['paɪərət] *n* pirata *m* ♦ *vt (record, video, book)* piratear.
pirate radio *(BRIT)* *n* rádio pirata.
pirouette [pɪru'et] *n* pirueta ♦ *vi* fazer pirueta(s).
Pisces ['paɪsi:z] *n* Pisces *m*, Peixes *mpl*.
piss [pɪs] *(col!)* *vi* mijar; **~ off!** vai à merda *(!)*.
pissed [pɪst] *(BRIT: inf)* *adj (drunk)* bêbado, de porre.
pistol ['pɪstl] *n* pistola.
piston ['pɪstən] *n* pistão *m*, êmbolo.
pit [pɪt] *n* cova, fossa; *(also: coal ~)* mina de carvão; *(also: orchestra ~)* fosso ♦ *vt:* **to ~ A against B** opor A a B; **~s** *npl (AUT)* box *m*; **to ~ o.s. against** opor-se a.
pitapat ['pɪtə'pæt] *(BRIT)* *adv:* **to go ~** *(heart)* disparar; *(rain)* tiquetaquear.
pitch [pɪtʃ] *n (throw)* arremesso, lance *m*; *(MUS)* tom *m*; *(of voice)* altura; *(fig: degree)* intensidade *f*; *(also: sales ~)* papo (de vendedor); *(SPORT)* campo; *(tar)* piche *m*, breu *m*; *(NAUT)* arfada; *(in market etc)* barraca ♦ *vt (throw)* arremessar, lançar; *(tent)* armar; *(set: price, message)* adaptar ♦ *vi (fall)* tombar, cair; *(NAUT)* jogar, arfar; **to be ~ed forward** ser jogado para frente; **at this ~** neste pique *or* ritmo; **to ~ one's aspirations too high** colocar as aspirações alto demais.
pitch in *vi* contribuir.
pitch-black [pɪtʃ'blæk] *adj* escuro como o breu.
pitched battle [pɪtʃt-] *n* batalha campal.
pitcher ['pɪtʃə*] *n* jarro, cântaro; *(US: BASEBALL)* arremessador *m*.
pitchfork ['pɪtʃfɔ:k] *n* forcado.
piteous ['pɪtɪəs] *adj* lastimável.
pitfall ['pɪtfɔ:l] *n* perigo (imprevisto), armadilha.
pith [pɪθ] *n (of orange)* casca interna e branca; *(fig)* essência, parte *f* essencial.
pithead ['pɪthed] *(BRIT)* *n* boca do poço.
pithy ['pɪθɪ] *adj* substancial, rico.
pitiable ['pɪtɪəbl] *adj* deplorável.
pitiful ['pɪtɪful] *adj (touching)* comovente, tocante; *(contemptible)* desprezível, lamentável.
pitifully ['pɪtɪfəlɪ] *adv* lamentavelmente, deploravelmente.
pitiless ['pɪtɪlɪs] *adj* impiedoso.
pittance ['pɪtns] *n* ninharia, miséria.
pitted ['pɪtɪd] *adj:* **~ with** *(chickenpox)* marcado com; *(rust)* picado de; **~ with potholes** esburacado.
pity ['pɪtɪ] *n (compassion)* compaixão *f*, piedade *f*; *(shame)* pena ♦ *vt* ter pena de, compadecer-se de; **what a ~!** que pena!; **it's a ~ (that) you can't come** é uma pena que você não possa vir; **to have** *or* **take ~ on sb**

ter pena de alguém.

pitying ['pɪtɪɪŋ] adj compassivo, compadecido.

pivot ['pɪvət] n pino, eixo; (fig) pivô m ♦ vi: to ~ on girar sobre; (fig) depender de.

pixel ['pɪksl] n (COMPUT) píxel m.

pixie ['pɪksɪ] n duende m.

pizza ['piːtsə] n pizza.

P&L abbr = profit and loss.

placard ['plækɑːd] n (sign) placar m; (in march etc) cartaz m.

placate [plə'keɪt] vt apaziguar, aplacar.

placatory [plə'keɪtərɪ] adj apaziguador(a), aplacador(a).

place [pleɪs] n lugar m; (rank) posição f; (post) posto; (home): at/to his ~ na/para a casa dele ♦ vt (object) pôr, colocar; (identify) identificar, situar; (find a post for) colocar; to take ~ realizar-se; (occur) ocorrer; from ~ to ~ de lugar em lugar; all over the ~ em tudo quanto é lugar; out of ~ (not suitable) fora de lugar, deslocado; I feel out of ~ here eu me sinto deslocado aqui; in the first ~ em primeiro lugar; to change ~s with sb trocar de lugar com alguém; to put sb in his ~ (fig) pôr alguém no seu lugar; he's going ~s (fig) ele vai se dar bem; it's not my ~ to do it não me compete fazê-lo; to ~ an order with sb for sth (COMM) encomendar algo a alguém; to be ~d (in race, exam) classificar-se; how are you ~d next week? você tem tempo na semana que vem?

placebo [plə'siːbəu] n placebo.

place mat n descanso.

placement ['pleɪsmənt] n (placing) colocação f; (job) cargo.

place name n topônimo.

placenta [plə'sɛntə] n placenta.

placid ['plæsɪd] adj plácido, sereno.

placidity [plə'sɪdɪtɪ] n placidez f.

plagiarism ['pleɪdʒərɪzm] n plágio.

plagiarist ['pleɪdʒərɪst] n plagiário/a.

plagiarize ['pleɪdʒəraɪz] vt plagiar.

plague [pleɪg] n praga; (MED) peste f ♦ vt (fig) atormentar, importunar; to ~ sb with questions importunar alguém com perguntas.

plaice [pleɪs] n inv solha.

plaid [plæd] n (material) tecido enxadrezado; (pattern) xadrez m escocês.

plain [pleɪn] adj (clear) claro, evidente; (simple) simples inv, despretensioso; (frank) franco, sem rodeios; (not handsome) sem atrativos; (pure) puro, natural; (in one colour) liso ♦ adv claramente, com franqueza ♦ n planície f, campina; in ~ clothes (police) à paisana; to make sth ~ to sb dar claramente a entender algo a alguém.

plain chocolate n chocolate m amargo.

plainly ['pleɪnlɪ] adv claramente, obviamente; (frankly) francamente, sem rodeios.

plainness ['pleɪnnɪs] n clareza; (simplicity) simplicidade f; (frankness) franqueza.

plaintiff ['pleɪntɪf] n querelante m/f, queixoso/a.

plaintive ['pleɪntɪv] adj (voice, tone) queixoso;

(song) lamentoso; (look) tristonho.

plait [plæt] n trança, dobra ♦ vt trançar.

plan [plæn] n plano; (scheme) projeto; (schedule) programa m ♦ vt planejar (BR), planear (PT), programar ♦ vi fazer planos; to ~ to do tencionar fazer, propor-se fazer; how long do you ~ to stay? quanto tempo você pretende ficar?

plane [pleɪn] n (AVIAT) avião m; (tree) plátano; (tool) plaina; (ART, MATH) plano ♦ adj plano ♦ vt (with tool) aplainar.

planet ['plænɪt] n planeta m.

planetarium [plænɪ'tɛərɪəm] n planetário.

plank [plæŋk] n tábua; (POL) item m da plataforma política.

plankton ['plæŋktən] n plâncton m.

planner ['plænə*] n planejador(a) m/f (BR), planeador(a) m/f (PT); (chart) agenda (quadro); town (BRIT) or city (US) ~ urbanista m/f.

planning ['plænɪŋ] n planejamento (BR), planeamento (PT).

planning permission (BRIT) n autorização f para construir.

plant [plɑːnt] n planta; (machinery) maquinaria; (factory) usina, fábrica ♦ vt plantar; (field) semear; (bomb) colocar, pôr; (inf) pôr às escondidas.

plantation [plæn'teɪʃən] n plantação f; (estate) fazenda.

plant hire n locação f de equipamentos.

plant pot (BRIT) n vaso para planta.

plaque [plæk] n placa, insígnia; (also: dental ~) placa dental.

plasma ['plæzmə] n plasma m.

plaster ['plɑːstə*] n (for walls) reboco; (on leg etc) gesso; (BRIT: also: sticking ~) esparadrapo, band-aid m ♦ vt rebocar; (cover): to ~ with encher or cobrir de; in ~ (BRIT: leg etc) engessado; ~ of Paris gesso.

plaster cast n (MED) aparelho de gesso; (ART) molde m de gesso.

plastered ['plɑːstəd] (inf) adj bêbado, de porre.

plasterer ['plɑːstərə*] n rebocador(a) m/f, caiador(a) m/f.

plastic ['plæstɪk] n plástico ♦ adj de plástico; (flexible) plástico; (art) plástico.

plastic bag n sacola de plástico.

plasticine ['plæstɪsiːn] ® n plasticina ®.

plastic surgery n cirurgia plástica.

plate [pleɪt] n (dish) prato; (metal) placa, chapa; (PHOT, on door) chapa; (dental) dentadura; (TYP) clichê m; (in book) gravura; (AUT: number ~) placa; gold/silver ~ (dishes) baixela de ouro/prata.

plateau ['plætəu] (pl ~s or ~x) n planalto.

plateaux ['plætəuz] npl of **plateau**.

plateful ['pleɪtful] n pratada.

plate glass n vidro laminado.

platelayer ['pleɪtleɪə*] (BRIT) n (RAIL) assentador m de trilhos.

platen ['plætən] n (on typewriter, printer) rolo.

plate rack n escorredor m de pratos.

platform ['plætfɔːm] n (RAIL) plataforma (BR),

cais *m* (*PT*); (*stage*) estrado; (*at meeting*) tribuna; (*POL*) programa *m* partidário.

platform ticket (*BRIT*) *n* bilhete *m* de plataforma (*BR*) or cais (*PT*).

platinum ['plætɪnəm] *n* platina.

platitude ['plætɪtjuːd] *n* lugar *m* comum, chavão *m*.

platoon [plə'tuːn] *n* pelotão *m*.

platter ['plætə*] *n* travessa.

plaudits ['plɔːdɪts] *npl* aclamações *fpl*, aplausos *mpl*.

plausible ['plɔːzɪbl] *adj* plausível; (*person*) convincente.

play [pleɪ] *n* jogo; (*THEATRE*) obra, peça ♦ *vt* (*game*) jogar; (*team, opponent*) jogar contra; (*instrument, music*) tocar; (*THEATRE*) representar; (: *part*) fazer o papel de; (*fig*) desempenhar ♦ *vi* (*sport, game*) jogar; (*music*) tocar; (*frolic*) brincar; **to bring** or **call into** ~ (*plan*) acionar; (*emotions*) detonar; ~ **on words** jogo de palavras, trocadilho; **to** ~ **a trick on sb** pregar uma peça em alguém; **they're** ~**ing at soldiers** eles estão brincando de soldados; **to** ~ **for time** (*fig*) tentar ganhar tempo, protelar; **to** ~ **into sb's hands** (*fig*) fazer o jogo de alguém; **to** ~ **the fool/innocent** bancar o tolo/inocente.

play about *vi* brincar.

play along *vi* (*fig*): **to** ~ **along with sb** fazer o jogo de alguém ♦ *vt* (*fig*): **to** ~ **sb along** fazer alguém de criança.

play around *vi* brincar.

play back *vt* repetir.

play down *vt* minimizar.

play on *vt fus* (*sb's feelings, credulity*) tirar proveito de, usar.

play up *vi* (*person*) dar trabalho; (*TV, car*) estar com defeito.

playact ['pleɪækt] *vi* fazer fita.

playboy ['pleɪbɔɪ] *n* playboy *m*.

played-out [pleɪd-] *adj* gasto.

player ['pleɪə*] *n* jogador(a) *m/f*; (*THEATRE*) ator/atriz *m/f*; (*MUS*) músico/a.

playful ['pleɪful] *adj* brincalhão/lhona.

playgoer ['pleɪɡəuə*] *n* freqüentador(a) *m/f* de teatro.

playground ['pleɪɡraund] *n* pátio de recreio.

playgroup ['pleɪɡruːp] *n* espécie de jardim de infância.

playing card ['pleɪɪŋ-] *n* carta de baralho.

playing field ['pleɪɪŋ-] *n* campo de esportes (*BR*) or jogos (*PT*).

playmate ['pleɪmeɪt] *n* colega *m/f*, camarada *m/f*.

play-off ['pleɪɔf] *n* (*SPORT*) partida de desempate.

playpen ['pleɪpɛn] *n* cercado para crianças.

playroom ['pleɪruːm] *n* sala de jogos.

plaything ['pleɪθɪŋ] *n* brinquedo; (*fig*) joguete *m*.

playtime ['pleɪtaɪm] *n* (*SCH*) recreio.

playwright ['pleɪraɪt] *n* dramaturgo/a.

plc (*BRIT*) *abbr* = **public limited company**.

plea [pliː] *n* (*request*) apelo, petição *f*; (*excuse*) justificativa; (*LAW*: *defence*) defesa.

plead [pliːd] *vt* (*LAW*) defender, advogar; (*give as excuse*) alegar ♦ *vi* (*LAW*) declarar-se; (*beg*): **to** ~ **with sb (for sth)** suplicar or rogar (algo) a alguém; **to** ~ **guilty/not guilty** declarar-se culpado/inocente.

pleasant ['plɛznt] *adj* agradável; (*person*) simpático.

pleasantly ['plɛzntlɪ] *adv* agradavelmente.

pleasantness ['plɛzntnɪs] *n* (*of person*) amabilidade *f*, simpatia; (*of place*) encanto.

pleasantry ['plɛzntrɪ] *n* (*joke*) brincadeira; **pleasantries** *npl* (*polite remarks*) amenidades *fpl* (na conversa).

please [pliːz] *vt* (*give pleasure to*) agradar a, dar prazer a ♦ *vi* (*think fit*): **do as you** ~ faça o que or como quiser; ~! por favor!; ~ **yourself!** como você quiser!, você que sabe!

pleased [pliːzd] *adj* (*happy*) satisfeito, contente; ~ (**with**) satisfeito (com); ~ **to meet you** prazer (em conhecê-lo); **we are** ~ **to inform you that** ... temos a satisfação de informá-lo de que ....

pleasing ['pliːzɪŋ] *adj* agradável.

pleasurable ['plɛʒərəbl] *adj* agradável.

pleasure ['plɛʒə*] *n* prazer *m*; **it's a** ~ não tem de quê; **with** ~ com muito prazer; **is this trip for business or** ~? esta viagem é de negócios ou de recreio?

pleasure steamer *n* vapor *m* de recreio.

pleat [pliːt] *n* prega.

plebiscite ['plɛbɪsɪt] *n* plebiscito.

plebs [plɛbz] (*pej*) *npl* plebe *f*.

plectrum ['plɛktrəm] *n* plectro.

pledge [plɛdʒ] *n* (*object*) penhor *m*; (*promise*) promessa ♦ *vt* (*invest*) empenhar; (*promise*) prometer; **to** ~ **support for sb** empenhar-se a apoiar alguém; **to** ~ **sb to secrecy** comprometer alguém a guardar sigilo.

plenary ['pliːnərɪ] *adj*: **in** ~ **session** no plenário.

plentiful ['plɛntɪful] *adj* abundante, profuso.

plenty ['plɛntɪ] *n* abundância; ~ **of** (*enough*) bastante; (*many*) muitos/as; **we've got** ~ **of time** temos tempo de sobra.

pleurisy ['pluərɪsɪ] *n* pleurisia.

Plexiglas ['plɛksɪɡlɑːs] ® (*US*) *n* Blindex *m* ®.

pliable ['plaɪəbl] *adj* flexível.

pliers ['plaɪəz] *npl* alicate *m*.

plight [plaɪt] *n* situação *f* difícil, apuro.

plimsolls ['plɪmsəlz] (*BRIT*) *npl* tênis *mpl*.

PLO *n abbr* (= *Palestine Liberation Organization*) OLP *f*.

plod [plɔd] *vi* caminhar pesadamente; (*fig*) trabalhar laboriosamente.

plodder ['plɔdə*] *n* burro-de-carga *m*.

plodding ['plɔdɪŋ] *adj* mourejador(a).

plonk [plɔŋk] (*inf*) *n* (*BRIT*: *wine*) zurrapa ♦ *vt*: **to** ~ **sth down** deixar cair algo (pesada-

---

NB: European Portuguese adds the following consonants to certain words: **b** (sú(b)dito, su(b)til); **c** (a(c)ção, a(c)cionista, a(c)to); **m** (inde(m)ne); **p** (ado(p)ção, ado(p)tar); *for further details see p. xiii.*

mente).

plot [plɔt] *n* (*scheme*) conspiração *f*, complô *m*; (*of story, play*) enredo, trama; (*of land*) lote *m* ♦ *vt* (*mark out*) traçar; (*conspire*) tramar, planejar (*PT*: planear) ♦ *vi* conspirar; **a vegetable** ~ (*BRIT*) uma horta.

plotter ['plɔtə*] *n* conspirador(a) *m/f*; (*COMPUT*) plotter *f*, plotadora.

plough [plau] (*US* **plow**) *n* arado ♦ *vt* (*earth*) arar.

plough back *vt* (*COMM*) reinvestir.

plough through *vt fus* (*crowd*) abrir caminho por; (*snow*) avançar penosamente por.

ploughing ['plauɪŋ] (*US* **plowing**) *n* aradura.

ploughman ['plaumən] (*US* **plowman**) (*irreg*) *n* lavrador *m*; ~'s **lunch** (*BRIT*) lanche de pão, queijo e picles.

plow *etc* [plau] (*US*) = **plough** *etc*.

ploy [plɔɪ] *n* estratagema *m*.

pluck [plʌk] *vt* (*fruit*) colher; (*musical instrument*) dedilhar; (*bird*) depenar ♦ *n* coragem *f*, puxão *m*; **to** ~ **one's eyebrows** fazer as sobrancelhas; **to** ~ **up courage** criar coragem.

plucky ['plʌkɪ] *adj* corajoso, valente.

plug [plʌg] *n* tampão *m*; (*ELEC*) tomada (*BR*), ficha (*PT*); (*AUT: also: spark*(ing) ~) vela (de ignição) ♦ *vt* (*hole*) tapar; (*inf: advertise*) fazer propaganda de; **to give sb/sth a** ~ (*inf*) fazer propaganda de alguém/algo.

plug in *vt* (*ELEC*) ligar.

plughole ['plʌghəul] (*BRIT*) *n* (*in sink*) escoadouro.

plum [plʌm] *n* (*fruit*) ameixa ♦ *adj* (*inf*): **a** ~ **job** um emprego jóia.

plumage ['pluːmɪdʒ] *n* plumagem *f*.

plumb [plʌm] *adj* vertical ♦ *n* prumo ♦ *adv* (*exactly*) exatamente ♦ *vt* sondar.

plumb in *vt* (*washing machine*) instalar.

plumber ['plʌmə*] *n* bombeiro/a (*BR*), encanador(a) *m/f* (*BR*), canalizador(a) *m/f* (*PT*).

plumbing ['plʌmɪŋ] *n* (*trade*) ofício de encanador; (*piping*) encanamento.

plumbline ['plʌmlaɪn] *n* fio de prumo.

plume [pluːm] *n* pluma; (*on helmet*) penacho.

plummet ['plʌmɪt] *vi* despencar.

plump [plʌmp] *adj* roliço, rechonchudo ♦ *vt*: **to** ~ **sth (down) on** deixar cair algo em.

plump for (*inf*) *vt fus* (*choose*) optar por.

plump up *vt* (*cushion*) afofar.

plunder ['plʌndə*] *n* saque *m*, pilhagem *f*; (*loot*) despojo ♦ *vt* pilhar, espoliar.

plunge [plʌndʒ] *n* (*dive*) salto; (*submersion*) mergulho ♦ *vt* mergulhar, afundar ♦ *vi* (*fall*) despencar; (*dive*) mergulhar; **to take the** ~ topar a parada; **to** ~ **a room into darkness** mergulhar um aposento na escuridão.

plunger ['plʌndʒə*] *n* êmbolo; (*for blocked sink*) desentupidor *m*.

plunging ['plʌndʒɪŋ] *adj* (*neckline*) decotado.

pluperfect [pluː'pəːfɪkt] *n* mais-que-perfeito.

plural ['pluərl] *adj* plural ♦ *n* plural *m*.

plus [plʌs] *n* (*also:* ~ **sign**) sinal *m* de adição ♦ *prep* mais ♦ *adj*: **ten/twenty** ~ dez/vinte e tantos; **it's a** ~ é uma vantagem.

plus fours *npl* calça (*BR*) *or* calças *fpl* (*PT*) de golfe.

plush [plʌʃ] *adj* de pelúcia; (*fig*) suntuoso ♦ *n* pelúcia.

plutonium [pluː'təunɪəm] *n* plutônio.

ply [plaɪ] *n* (*of wool*) fio; (*of wood*) espessura ♦ *vt* (*a trade*) exercer ♦ *vi* (*ship*) ir e vir; **three** ~ (*wool*) de três fios; **to** ~ **sb with drink** dar muita bebida a alguém; **to** ~ **sb with questions** bombardear alguém com perguntas.

plywood ['plaɪwud] *n* madeira compensada.

PM (*BRIT*) *n abbr* = **Prime Minister**.

p.m. *adv abbr* (= *post meridiem*) da tarde, da noite.

pneumatic [njuː'mætɪk] *adj* pneumático; ~ **drill** perfuratriz *f*.

pneumonia [njuː'məunɪə] *n* pneumonia.

PO *n abbr* = **Post Office**; (*MIL*) = **petty officer**.

po *abbr* = **postal order**.

POA (*BRIT*) *n abbr* = **Prison Officers' Association**.

poach [pəutʃ] *vt* (*cook*) escaldar, escalfar; (*eggs*) fazer pochê (*BR*), escalfar (*PT*); (*steal*) furtar ♦ *vi* caçar (*or* pescar) em propriedade alheia.

poached [pəutʃt] *adj* (*egg*) pochê (*BR*), escalfado (*PT*).

poacher ['pəutʃə*] *n* caçador *m* (*or* pescador *m*) furtivo.

poaching ['pəutʃɪŋ] *n* caça (*or* pesca) furtiva.

PO Box *n abbr* = **Post Office Box**.

pocket ['pɔkɪt] *n* bolso; (*BILLIARDS*) caçapa, ventanilha ♦ *vt* embolsar, meter no bolso; (*BILLIARDS*) encaçapar; **to be out of** ~ (*BRIT*) perder, ter prejuízo; ~ **of resistance** foco de resistência.

pocketbook ['pɔkɪtbuk] *n* carteira.

pocket knife (*irreg*) *n* canivete *m*.

pocket money *n* dinheiro para despesas miúdas; (*for child*) mesada.

pockmarked ['pɔkmaːkt] *adj* (*face*) com marcas de varíola.

pod [pɔd] *n* vagem *f* ♦ *vt* descascar.

podgy ['pɔdʒɪ] *adj* nédio, mole.

podiatrist [pɔ'diːətrɪst] (*US*) *n* pedicuro/a.

podiatry [pɔ'diːətrɪ] (*US*) *n* podiatria.

podium ['pəudɪəm] *n* pódio.

POE *n abbr* = **port of embarkation**; **port of entry**.

poem ['pəuɪm] *n* poema *m*.

poet ['pəuɪt] *n* poeta/poetisa *m/f*.

poetess ['pəuɪtɪs] *n* poetisa.

poetic [pəu'etɪk] *adj* poético.

poet laureate [-'lɔːrɪət] *n* poeta *m* laureado.

poetry ['pəuɪtrɪ] *n* poesia.

POEU (*BRIT*) *n abbr* (= *Post Office Engineering Union*) sindicato dos técnicos do correio.

poignant ['pɔɪnjənt] *adj* comovente; (*sharp*) agudo.

point [pɔɪnt] *n* ponto; (*tip*) ponta; (*purpose*) finalidade *f*; (*BRIT*: *ELEC*: *also: power* ~) tomada; (*also: decimal* ~): **2** ~ **3 (2.3)** dois vírgula três ♦ *vt* (*window, wall*) tomar com

argamassa; (*gun etc*): **to ~ sth at sb** apontar algo para alguém ♦ *vi* apontar; **to ~ to** apontar para; (*fig*) indicar; **~s** *npl* (*AUT*) platinado, contato; (*RAIL*) agulhas *fpl*; **good ~s** qualidades; **to make a ~** fazer uma observação; **to make a ~ of** fazer questão de, insistir em; **to make one's ~** dar sua opinião; **you've made your ~** você já disse o que queria, você já falou (*inf*); **to get the ~** compreender; **to come to the ~** ir ao assunto; **when it comes to the ~** na hora; **there's no ~ (in doing)** não adianta nada (fazer); **to be on the ~ of doing sth** estar prestes a *or* a ponto de fazer algo; **that's the whole ~!** aí é que está a questão!, aí é que 'tá! (*inf*); **to be beside the ~** estar fora do assunto; **you've got a ~ there!** você tem razão!; **in ~ of fact** na verdade, na realidade; **~ of departure** ponto de partida; **~ of order** questão *f* de ordem; **~ of sale** (*COMM*) ponto de venda; **~ of view** ponto de vista.
 point out *vt* (*indicate*) indicar; (*emphasize*) ressaltar.
point-blank [pɔint'blæŋk] *adv* (*also: at ~ range*) à queima-roupa ♦ *adj* (*fig*) categórico.
point duty (*BRIT*) *n*: **to be on ~** estar de serviço no controle do trânsito.
pointed ['pɔintid] *adj* (*shape*) pontudo, aguçado; (*remark*) mordaz.
pointedly ['pɔintidli] *adv* sugestivamente.
pointer ['pɔintə*] *n* (*stick*) indicador *m*, ponteiro; (*needle*) agulha; (*dog*) pointer *m*; (*clue, advice*) dica.
pointless ['pɔintlis] *adj* (*useless*) inútil; (*senseless*) sem sentido; (*motiveless*) sem razão.
poise [pɔiz] *n* (*balance*) equilíbrio; (*of head, body*) porte *m*; (*calmness*) serenidade *f* ♦ *vt* pôr em equilíbrio; **to be ~d for** (*fig*) estar pronto para.
poison ['pɔizn] *n* veneno ♦ *vt* envenenar.
poisoning ['pɔizniŋ] *n* envenenamento.
poisonous ['pɔiznəs] *adj* venenoso; (*fumes etc*) tóxico; (*fig*) pernicioso.
poke [pəuk] *vt* (*fire*) atiçar; (*jab with finger, stick etc*) cutucar; (*put*): **to ~ sth in(to)** enfiar *or* meter algo em ♦ *n* (*to fire*) remexida; (*jab*) cutucada; (*with elbow*) cotovelada; **to ~ one's nose into** meter o nariz em; **to ~ one's head out of the window** meter a cabeça para fora da janela; **to ~ fun at sb** ridicularizar *or* fazer troça de alguém.
 poke about *vi* escarafunchar, espionar.
poker ['pəukə*] *n* atiçador *m*; (*CARDS*) pôquer *m*.
poker-faced [-feist] *adj* com rosto impassível.
poky ['pəuki] *adj* acanhado, apertado.
Poland ['pəulənd] *n* Polônia.
polar ['pəulə*] *adj* polar.
polar bear *n* urso polar.
polarize ['pəuləraiz] *vt* polarizar.
Pole [pəul] *n* polonês/esa *m/f*.

pole [pəul] *n* vara; (*GEO*) pólo; (*TEL*) poste *m*; (*flag~*) mastro; (*tent~*) estaca.
pole bean (*US*) *n* feijão-trepador *m*.
polecat ['pəulkæt] *n* furão-bravo.
Pol. Econ. ['pɔlikɔn] *n abbr* = **political economy**.
polemic [pə'lemik] *n* polêmica.
pole star *n* estrela Polar.
pole vault *n* salto com vara.
police [pə'liːs] *npl* polícia ♦ *vt* policiar.
police car *n* rádio-patrulha *f*.
police constable (*BRIT*) *n* policial *m/f* (*BR*), polícia *m/f* (*PT*).
police department (*US*) *n* polícia.
police force *n* polícia.
policeman [pə'liːsmən] (*irreg*) *n* policial *m* (*BR*), polícia *m* (*PT*).
police officer *n* policial *m/f* (*BR*), polícia *m/f* (*PT*).
police record *n* ficha na polícia.
police state *n* estado policial.
police station *n* delegacia (de polícia) (*BR*), esquadra (*PT*).
policewoman [pə'liːswumən] (*irreg*) *n* policial *f* (feminina) (*BR*), mulher *f* polícia (*PT*).
policy ['pɔlisi] *n* política; (*also: insurance ~*) apólice *f*; (*of newspaper, company*) orientação *f*; **to take out a ~** (*INSURANCE*) fazer uma apólice *or* um contrato de seguro.
policy holder *n* segurado/a.
polio ['pəuliəu] *n* poliomielite *f*, polio *f*.
Polish ['pəulif] *adj* polonês/esa ♦ *n* (*LING*) polonês *m*.
polish ['pɔlif] *n* (*for shoes*) graxa; (*for floor*) cera (para encerar); (*for nails*) esmalte *m*; (*shine*) brilho; (*fig: refinement*) refinamento, requinte *m* ♦ *vt* (*shoes*) engraxar; (*make shiny*) lustrar, dar brilho a; (*fig: improve*) refinar, polir.
 polish off *vt* (*work*) dar os arremates a; (*food*) raspar.
polished ['pɔlift] *adj* (*fig: person*) culto; (: *manners*) refinado.
polite [pə'lait] *adj* educado; (*formal*) cortês; **it's not ~ to do that** é falta de educação fazer isso.
politely [pə'laitli] *adv* educadamente.
politeness [pə'laitnis] *n* gentileza, cortesia.
politic ['pɔlitik] *adj* prudente.
political [pə'litikl] *adj* político.
political asylum *n* asilo político; **to seek ~** pedir asilo político.
politically [pə'litikli] *adv* politicamente.
politician [pɔli'tifən] *n* político.
politics ['pɔlitiks] *npl* política.
polka ['pɔlkə] *n* polca.
polka dot *n* bolinha.
poll [pəul] *n* (*votes*) votação *f*; (*also: opinion ~*) pesquisa, sondagem *f* ♦ *vt* (*votes*) receber, obter; **to go to the ~s** (*voters*) ir às urnas; (*government*) convocar eleições.
pollen ['pɔlən] *n* pólen *m*.

NB: *European Portuguese adds the following consonants to certain words:* **b** (sú(b)dito, su(b)til); **c** (a(c)ção, a(c)cionista, a(c)to); **m** (inde(m)ne); **p** (ado(p)ção, ado(p)tar); *for further details see p. xiii.*

pollen count *n* contagem *f* de pólen.
pollination [pɔlɪ'neɪʃən] *n* polinização *f*.
polling ['pəulɪŋ] *n* (*BRIT:* *POL*) votação *f*; (*TEL*) apuração *f*.
polling booth (*BRIT*) *n* cabine *f* de votar.
polling day (*BRIT*) *n* dia *m* de eleição.
polling station (*BRIT*) *n* centro eleitoral.
pollute [pə'luːt] *vt* poluir.
pollution [pə'luːʃən] *n* poluição *f*.
polo ['pəuləu] *n* (*sport*) pólo.
polo-neck *adj* de gola rolê ♦ *n* gola rolê.
poly ['pɔlɪ] (*BRIT*) *n* *abbr* = **polytechnic**.
polyester [pɔlɪ'ɛstə*] *n* poliéster *m*.
polyethylene [pɔlɪ'ɛθɪliːn] (*US*) *n* polietileno.
polygamy [pə'lɪgəmɪ] *n* poligamia.
Polynesia [pɔlɪ'niːzɪə] *n* Polinésia.
Polynesian [pɔlɪ'niːzɪən] *adj*, *n* polinésio/a.
polyp ['pɔlɪp] *n* (*MED*) pólipo.
polystyrene [pɔlɪ'staɪriːn] *n* isopor *m* ®.
polytechnic [pɔlɪ'tɛknɪk] *n* politécnico, escola politécnica.
polythene ['pɔlɪθiːn] (*BRIT*) *n* politeno.
polythene bag *n* bolsa de plástico.
polyurethane [pɔlɪ'juːrəθeɪn] *n* poliuretano.
pomegranate ['pɔmɪɡrænɪt] *n* (*fruit*) romã *f*.
pommel ['pɔml] *n* botão *m*; (*saddle*) maçaneta ♦ *vt* = **pummel**.
pomp [pɔmp] *n* pompa, fausto.
pompom ['pɔmpɔm] *n* pompom *m*.
pompon ['pɔmpɔn] *n* = **pompom**.
pompous ['pɔmpəs] *adj* pomposo.
pond [pɔnd] *n* (*natural*) lago pequeno; (*artificial*) tanque *m*.
ponder ['pɔndə*] *vt*, *vi* ponderar, meditar (sobre).
ponderous ['pɔndərəs] *adj* pesado.
pong [pɔŋ] (*BRIT:* *inf*) *n* fedor *m*, fartum *m* (*inf*), catinga (*inf*) ♦ *vi* feder.
pontiff ['pɔntɪf] *n* pontífice *m*.
pontificate [pɔn'tɪfɪkeɪt] *vi* (*fig*): **to ~ (about)** pontificar (sobre).
pontoon [pɔn'tuːn] *n* pontão *m*; (*BRIT:* *card game*) vinte-e-um *m*.
pony ['pəunɪ] *n* pônei *m*.
ponytail ['pəunɪteɪl] *n* rabo-de-cavalo.
pony trekking ['trɛkɪŋ] (*BRIT*) *n* excursão *f* em pônei.
poodle ['puːdl] *n* cão-d'água *m*.
pooh-pooh [puː'puː] *vt* desprezar.
pool [puːl] *n* (*of rain*) poça, charco; (*pond*) lago; (*also:* *swimming* ~) piscina; (*billiards*) sinuca; (*sth shared*) fundo comum; (*money at cards*) bolo; (*COMM:* *consortium*) consórcio, pool *m*; (*US:* *monopoly trust*) truste *m* ♦ *vt* juntar; (**football**) ~**s** *npl* (*BRIT*) loteria esportiva (*BR*), totobola (*PT*); **typing** (*BRIT*) *or* **secretary** (*US*) ~ seção *f* de datilografia.
poor [puə*] *adj* pobre; (*bad*) inferior, mau ♦ *npl*: **the** ~ os pobres.
poorly ['puəlɪ] *adj* adoentado, indisposto ♦ *adv* mal.
pop [pɔp] *n* (*sound*) estalo, estouro; (*MUS*) pop *m*; (*US:* *inf:* *father*) papai *m*; (*inf:* *lemonade*) bebida gasosa ♦ *vt* (*put*) pôr ♦ *vi*

estourar; (*cork*) saltar; **she ~ped her head out of the window** ela meteu a cabeça fora da janela.
pop in *vi* dar um pulo.
pop out *vi* dar uma saída.
pop up *vi* surgir, aparecer inesperadamente.
pop concert *n* concerto pop.
popcorn ['pɔpkɔːn] *n* pipoca.
pope [pəup] *n* papa *m*.
poplar ['pɔplə*] *n* álamo, choupo.
poplin ['pɔplɪn] *n* popeline *f*.
popper ['pɔpə*] (*BRIT*) *n* presilha.
poppy ['pɔpɪ] *n* papoula.
poppycock ['pɔpɪkɔk] (*inf*) *n* conversa fiada, papo furado.
popsicle ['pɔpsɪkl] ® (*US*) *n* picolé *m*.
populace ['pɔpjuləs] *n* povo.
popular ['pɔpjulə*] *adj* popular; (*fashionable*) badalado; **to be ~ (with)** (*person*) fazer sucesso (com); (*decision*) ser aplaudido (por).
popularity [pɔpju'lærɪtɪ] *n* popularidade *f*.
popularize ['pɔpjuləraɪz] *vt* popularizar; (*science*) vulgarizar.
populate ['pɔpjuleɪt] *vt* povoar.
population [pɔpju'leɪʃən] *n* população *f*.
population explosion *n* explosão *f* demográfica.
populous ['pɔpjuləs] *adj* populoso.
porcelain ['pɔːslɪn] *n* porcelana.
porch [pɔːtʃ] *n* pórtico; (*US:* *verandah*) varanda.
porcupine ['pɔːkjupaɪn] *n* porco-espinho.
pore [pɔː*] *n* poro ♦ *vi*: **to ~ over** examinar minuciosamente.
pork [pɔːk] *n* carne *f* de porco.
pork chop *n* costeleta de porco.
pornographic [pɔːnə'ɡræfɪk] *adj* pornográfico.
pornography [pɔː'nɔɡrəfɪ] *n* pornografia.
porous ['pɔːrəs] *adj* poroso.
porpoise ['pɔːpəs] *n* golfinho, boto.
porridge ['pɔrɪdʒ] *n* mingau *m* (de aveia).
port [pɔːt] *n* (*harbour*) porto; (*NAUT:* *left side*) bombordo; (*wine*) vinho do Porto; (*COMPUT*) porta, port *m* ♦ *cpd* portuário; **to ~** (*NAUT*) a bombordo; **~ of call** porto de escala.
portable ['pɔːtəbl] *adj* portátil.
portal ['pɔːtl] *n* portal *m*.
portcullis [pɔːt'kʌlɪs] *n* grade *f* levadiça.
portend [pɔː'tɛnd] *vt* pressagiar.
portent ['pɔːtɛnt] *n* presságio, portento.
porter ['pɔːtə*] *n* (*for luggage*) carregador *m*; (*doorkeeper*) porteiro.
portfolio [pɔːt'fəulɪəu] *n* pasta.
porthole ['pɔːthəul] *n* vigia.
portico ['pɔːtɪkəu] *n* pórtico.
portion ['pɔːʃən] *n* porção *f*, quinhão *m*; (*of food*) ração *f*.
portly ['pɔːtlɪ] *adj* corpulento.
portrait ['pɔːtreɪt] *n* retrato.
portray [pɔː'treɪ] *vt* retratar; (*in writing*) descrever.
portrayal [pɔː'treɪəl] *n* representação *f*.
Portugal ['pɔːtjuɡl] *n* Portugal *m* (*no article*).
Portuguese [pɔːtju'ɡiːz] *adj* português/esa ♦ *n*

inv português/esa *m/f*; (*LING*) português *m*.
Portuguese man-of-war (*irreg*: *like* **man**) *n* (*jellyfish*) urtiga-do-mar *f*, caravela.
pose [pəuz] *n* postura, pose *f*; (*pej*) pose, afetação *f* ♦ *vi* posar; (*pretend*): **to ~ as** fazer-se passar por ♦ *vt* (*question*) pôr; **to strike a ~** fazer pose.
poser ['pəuzə*] *n* problema *m*, abacaxi *m* (*BR*: *inf*); (*person*) = **poseur**.
poseur [pəu'zə:*] (*pej*) *n* posudo/a, pessoa afetada.
posh [pɔʃ] (*inf*) *adj* fino, chique; **to talk ~** falar com sotaque fino.
position [pə'zɪʃən] *n* posição *f*; (*job*) cargo ♦ *vt* colocar, situar; **to be in a ~ to do sth** estar em posição de fazer algo.
positive ['pɔzɪtɪv] *adj* positivo; (*certain*) certo; (*definite*) definitivo; **I'm ~** tenho certeza absoluta.
posse ['pɔsɪ] (*US*) *n* pelotão *m* de civis armados.
possess [pə'zɛs] *vt* possuir; **like one ~ed** como um possuído do demônio; **whatever can ~ed you?** o que é que te deu?
possession [pə'zɛʃən] *n* posse *f*, possessão *f*; (*object*) bem *m*, posse; **to take ~ of sth** tomar posse de algo.
possessive [pə'zɛsɪv] *adj* possessivo.
possessively [pə'zɛsɪvlɪ] *adv* possessivamente.
possessor [pə'zɛsə*] *n* possuidor(a) *m/f*.
possibility [pɔsɪ'bɪlɪtɪ] *n* possibilidade *f*.
possible ['pɔsɪbl] *adj* possível; **it is ~ to do it** é possível fazê-lo; **as far as ~** tanto quanto possível, na medida do possível; **if ~** se for possível; **as big as ~** o maior possível.
possibly ['pɔsɪblɪ] *adv* (*perhaps*) pode ser, talvez; **if you ~ can** se lhe for possível; **could you ~ come over?** será qué você podia vir para ca?; **I cannot ~ come** estou impossibilitado de vir.
post [pəust] *n* (*BRIT*: *mail*) correio; (*job, situation*) cargo, posto; (*pole*) poste *m*; (*trading ~*) entreposto comercial ♦ *vt* (*BRIT*: *send by ~*) pôr no correio; (: *MIL*) nomear; (*bills*) afixar, pregar; (*BRIT*: *appoint*): **to ~ to** destinar a; **by ~** (*BRIT*) pelo correio; **by return of ~** (*BRIT*) na volta do correio; **to keep sb ~ed** manter alguém informado.
post- [pəust] *prefix* pós...; **~1990** depois de 1990.
postage ['pəustɪdʒ] *n* porte *m*, franquia; **~ paid** porte pago; **~ prepaid** (*US*) franquia de porte.
postage stamp *n* selo postal.
postal ['pəustəl] *adj* postal.
postal order *n* vale *m* postal.
postbag ['pəustbæg] (*BRIT*) *n* mala de correio; (*postman's*) sacola.
postbox ['pəustbɔks] (*BRIT*) *n* caixa de correio.
postcard ['pəustka:d] *n* cartão *m* postal.
postcode ['pəustkəud] (*BRIT*) *n* código postal, ≈ CEP *m* (*BR*).

postdate [pəust'deɪt] *vt* (*cheque*) pós-datar.
poster ['pəustə*] *n* cartaz *m*; (*as decoration*) pôster *m*.
poste restante [pəust'rɛstã:nt] (*BRIT*) *n* posta-restante *f*.
posterior [pɔs'tɪərɪə*] (*inf*) *n* traseiro, nádegas *fpl*.
posterity [pɔs'tɛrɪtɪ] *n* posteridade *f*.
poster paint *n* guache *m*.
post exchange (*US*) *n* (*MIL*) loja do exército.
post-free (*BRIT*) *adj* franco de porte.
postgraduate [pəust'grædjuət] *n* pós-graduado/a.
posthumous ['pɔstjuməs] *adj* póstumo.
posthumously ['pɔstjuməslɪ] *adv* postumamente.
posting ['pəustɪŋ] (*BRIT*) *n* nomeação *f*.
postman ['pəustmən] (*irreg*) *n* carteiro.
postmark ['pəustma:k] *n* carimbo do correio.
postmaster ['pəustma:stə*] *n* agente *m* (*BR*) or chefe *m* (*PT*) do correio.
Postmaster General *n* ≈ Superintendente *m* Geral dos Correios.
postmen ['pəustmɛn] *npl of* **postman**.
postmistress ['pəustmɪstrɪs] *n* agente *f* (*BR*) or chefe *f* (*PT*) do correio.
post-mortem [-'mɔ:təm] *n* autópsia.
postnatal [pəust'neɪtl] *adj* pós-natal.
post office *n* (*building*) agência do correio, correio; (*organization*) Empresa Nacional dos Correios e Telégrafos (*BR*), Correios, Telégrafos e Telefones (*PT*).
post office box *n* caixa postal.
post-paid (*BRIT*) *adj* porte pago.
postpone [pəs'pəun] *vt* adiar.
postponement [pəs'pəunmənt] *n* adiamento.
postscript ['pəustskrɪpt] *n* pós-escrito.
postulate ['pɔstjuleɪt] *vt* postular.
posture ['pɔstʃə*] *n* postura, atitude *f* ♦ *vi* posar.
postwar [pəust'wɔ:*] *adj* de após-guerra.
posy ['pəuzɪ] *n* ramalhete *m*.
pot [pɔt] *n* (*for cooking*) panela; (*for flowers*) vaso; (*for jam, piece of pottery*) pote *m*; (*inf*: *marijuana*) maconha ♦ *vt* (*plant*) plantar em vaso; (*conserve*) pôr em conserva; **to go to ~** (*country, economy*) arruinar-se, degringolar; **the town has gone to ~** a cidade mixou; **~s of** ... (*BRIT*: *inf*) ... aos potes.
potash ['pɔtæʃ] *n* potassa.
potassium [pə'tæsɪəm] *n* potássio.
potato [pə'teɪtəu] (*pl ~es*) *n* batata.
potato crisps (*US* **potato chips**) *npl* batatinhas *fpl* fritas.
potato flour *n* fécula (de batata).
potato peeler *n* descascador *m* de batatas.
potbellied ['pɔtbɛlɪd] *adj* barrigudo.
potency ['pəutənsɪ] *n* potência; (*of drink*) teor *m* alcoólico.
potent ['pəutnt] *adj* potente, poderoso; (*drink*) forte.

NB: European Portuguese adds the following consonants to certain words: **b** (sú(b)dito, su(b)til); **c** (a(c)ção, a(c)cionista, a(c)to); **m** (inde(m)ne); **p** (ado(p)ção, ado(p)tar); *for further details see p. xiii.*

potentate ['pəutnteit] n potentado.
potential [pə'tɛnʃl] adj potencial, latente ♦ n potencial m; **to have** ~ ser promissor.
potentially [pə'tɛnʃəlɪ] adv potencialmente.
pothole ['pɔthəul] n (in road) buraco; (BRIT: underground) caldeirão m, cova.
potholer ['pɔthəulə*] (BRIT) n espeleologista m/f.
potholing ['pɔthəulɪŋ] (BRIT) n: **to go** ~ dedicar-se à espeleologia.
potion ['pəuʃən] n poção f.
potluck [pɔt'lʌk] n: **to take** ~ contentar-se com o que houver.
potpourri [pəu'purɪ:] n potpourri m (de pétalas e folhas secas para perfumar o ambiente).
pot roast n carne f assada.
potshot ['pɔtʃɔt] n: **to take a** ~ **at sth** atirar em algo a esmo.
potted ['pɔtɪd] adj (food) em conserva; (plant) de vaso; (fig: shortened) resumido.
potter ['pɔtə*] n (artistic) ceramista m/f; (artisan) oleiro/a ♦ vi (BRIT): **to** ~ **around**, ~ **about** ocupar-se com pequenos trabalhos; ~'s **wheel** roda or torno de oleiro.
pottery ['pɔtərɪ] n cerâmica, olaria; **a piece of** ~ uma cerâmica.
potty ['pɔtɪ] adj (BRIT: inf: mad) maluco, doido ♦ n penico.
potty-training n treino (da criança) para o uso do urinol.
pouch [pautʃ] n (ZOOL) bolsa; (for tobacco) tabaqueira.
pouf(fe) [pu:f] n pufe m.
poultice ['pəultɪs] n cataplasma.
poultry ['pəultrɪ] n aves fpl domésticas.
poultry farm n granja avícola.
poultry farmer n avicultor(a) m/f.
pounce [pauns] vi: **to** ~ **on** lançar-se sobre ♦ n salto, arremetida.
pound [paund] n libra (weight = 453g, 16 ounces; money = 100 pence); (for dogs) canil m; (for cars) depósito ♦ vt (beat) socar, esmurrar; (crush) triturar ♦ vi (beat) dar pancadas; **half a** ~ **(of)** meia libra (de); **a five-**~ **note** uma nota de cinco libras.
pounding ['paundɪŋ] n: **to take a** ~ (fig) levar uma surra.
pound sterling n libra esterlina.
pour [pɔ:*] vt despejar; (tea) servir ♦ vi fluir, correr; (rain) chover a cântaros.
pour away vt esvaziar, decantar.
pour in vi: **to come** ~**ing in** (water, people) entrar numa enxurrada; (letters) chegar numa enxurrada.
pour off vt esvaziar, decantar.
pour out vi (people) sair aos borbotões ♦ vt (drink) servir; (water etc) esvaziar.
pouring ['pɔ:rɪŋ] adj: ~ **rain** chuva torrencial.
pout [paut] vi fazer beicinho or biquinho.
poverty ['pɔvətɪ] n pobreza, miséria.
poverty-stricken adj indigente, necessitado.
poverty trap (BRIT) n armadilha da pobreza.
POW n abbr = prisoner of war.

powder ['paudə*] n pó m; (face ~) pó-de-arroz m; (gun~) pólvora ♦ vt pulverizar; (face) empoar, passar pó em; **to** ~ **one's nose** empoar-se; (euphemism) ir ao banheiro; ~**ed milk** leite m em pó.
powder compact n estojo (de pó-de-arroz).
powder puff n esponja de pó-de-arroz.
powder room n toucador m, banheiro de senhoras.
powdery ['paudərɪ] adj poeirento.
power ['pauə*] n poder m; (strength) força; (nation) potência; (ability, POL: of party, leader) poder, poderio; (of speech, thought) faculdade f; (MATH, TECH) potência; (ELEC) força ♦ vt (ELEC) alimentar; (engine, machine) acionar; (car, plane) propulsionar; **to do all in one's** ~ **to help sb** fazer tudo que tiver ao seu alcance para ajudar alguém; **the world** ~**s** as grandes potências; **to be in** ~ estar no poder; ~ **of attorney** procuração f.
powerboat ['pauəbəut] (BRIT) n barco a motor.
power cut (BRIT) n corte m de energia, blecaute m (BR).
power-driven adj movido a motor; (ELEC) elétrico.
powered ['pauəd] adj: ~ **by** movido a; **nuclear-**~ **submarine** submarino nuclear.
power failure n deficiência de força.
powerful ['pauəful] adj poderoso; (engine) potente; (build) vigoroso; (emotion) intenso.
powerhouse ['pauəhaus] (irreg) n (fig: person) poço de energia; **a** ~ **of ideas** um poço de idéias.
powerless ['pauəlɪs] adj impotente.
power line n fio de alta tensão.
power point (BRIT) n tomada.
power station n central f elétrica.
power steering n direção f hidráulica.
powwow ['pauwau] n reunião f.
pox [pɔks] (inf) n sífilis f; see also **chickenpox**; **smallpox**.
pp abbr (= per procurationem: by proxy) p.p.
p&p (BRIT) abbr (= postage and packing) porte e embalagem.
PPE (BRIT) n abbr (SCH) = **philosophy, politics and economics**.
PPS n abbr (= post postscriptum) PPS; (BRIT: = parliamentary private secretary) parlamentário no serviço de um ministro.
PQ (CANADA) abbr = **Province of Quebec**.
PR n abbr = **proportional representation**; **public relations** ♦ abbr (US: POST) = **Puerto Rico**.
Pr. abbr (= prince) Prínc.
practicability [præktɪkə'bɪlɪtɪ] n viabilidade f.
practicable ['præktɪkəbl] adj (scheme) praticável, viável.
practical ['præktɪkl] adj prático.
practicality [præktɪ'kælɪtɪ] n (of plan) viabilidade f; (of person) índole f prática; **practicalities** npl aspectos mpl práticos.
practical joke n brincadeira, peça.
practically ['præktɪkəlɪ] adv (almost) praticamente.

practice ['præktɪs] *n* (*habit*) costume *m*, hábito; (*exercise*) prática; (*of profession*) exercício; (*training*) treinamento; (*MED*) consultório ♦ *vt*, *vi* (*US*) = **practise; in** ~ (*in reality*) na prática; **out of** ~ destreinado; **it's common** ~ é comum; **to put sth into** ~ pôr algo em prática; **to set up in** ~ abrir consultório.

practice match *n* jogo de treinamento.

practise ['præktɪs] (*US* **practice**) *vt* praticar; (*profession*) exercer; (*train at*) treinar ♦ *vi* (*doctor, lawyer*) ter consultório; (*train*) treinar, praticar.

practised ['præktɪst] (*BRIT*) *adj* (*person*) experiente, experimentado; (*performance*) competente; (*liar*) contumaz; **with a** ~ **eye** com olhar de entendedor.

practising ['præktɪsɪŋ] *adj* (*Christian etc*) praticante; (*lawyer*) que exerce; (*homosexual*) assumido.

practitioner [præk'tɪʃənə*] *n* praticante *m/f*; (*MED*) médico/a.

pragmatic [præg'mætɪk] *adj* pragmático.

Prague [prɑːg] *n* Praga.

prairie ['prɛərɪ] *n* campina, pradaria.

praise [preɪz] *n* louvor *m*, elogio ♦ *vt* elogiar, louvar.

praiseworthy ['preɪzwɜːðɪ] *adj* louvável, digno de elogio.

pram [præm] (*BRIT*) *n* carrinho de bebê.

prance [prɑːns] *vi* (*horse*) curvetear, fazer cabriolas.

prank [præŋk] *n* travessura, peça.

prattle ['prætl] *vi* tagarelar; (*child*) balbuciar.

prawn [prɔːn] *n* pitu *m*; (*small*) camarão *m*.

pray [preɪ] *vi* rezar.

prayer [prɛə*] *n* oração *f*, prece *f*; (*entreaty*) súplica, rogo.

prayer book *n* missal *m*, livro de orações.

pre- ['priː] *prefix* pré-; ~**1970** antes de 1970.

preach [priːtʃ] *vt*, *vi* pregar; **to** ~ **at sb** fazer sermões a alguém.

preacher ['priːtʃə*] *n* pregador(a) *m/f*; (*US*: *clergyman*) pastor *m*.

preamble [prɪ'æmbl] *n* preâmbulo.

prearranged [priːə'reɪndʒd] *adj* combinado de antemão.

precarious [prɪ'kɛərɪəs] *adj* precário.

precaution [prɪ'kɔːʃən] *n* precaução *f*.

precautionary [prɪ'kɔːʃənrɪ] *adj* (*measure*) de precaução.

precede [prɪ'siːd] *vt*, *vi* preceder.

precedence ['prɛsɪdəns] *n* precedência; (*priority*) prioridade *f*.

precedent ['prɛsɪdənt] *n* precedente *m*; **to establish** *or* **set a** ~ estabelecer *or* abrir precedente.

preceding [prɪ'siːdɪŋ] *adj* precedente.

precept ['priːsɛpt] *n* preceito.

precinct ['priːsɪŋkt] *n* (*round church*) recinto; (*US*: *district*) distrito policial; ~**s** *npl* arredores *mpl*; **shopping** ~ (*BRIT*) zona comercial.

precious ['prɛʃəs] *adj* precioso; (*stylized*) afetado ♦ *adv* (*inf*): ~ **little** muito pouco, pouquíssimo; **your** ~ **dog** (*ironic*) seu adorado cãozinho.

precipice ['prɛsɪpɪs] *n* precipício.

precipitate [*adj* prɪ'sɪpɪtɪt, *vt* prɪ'sɪpɪteɪt] *adj* (*hasty*) precipitado, apressado ♦ *vt* (*hasten*) precipitar, acelerar; (*bring about*) causar.

precipitation [prɪsɪpɪ'teɪʃən] *n* precipitação *f*.

precipitous [prɪ'sɪpɪtəs] *adj* (*steep*) íngreme, escarpado.

précis ['preɪsiː, *pl* 'preɪsiːz] *n inv* resumo, sumário.

precise [prɪ'saɪs] *adj* exato, preciso; (*person*) escrupuloso, meticuloso.

precisely [prɪ'saɪslɪ] *adv* exatamente.

precision [prɪ'sɪʒən] *n* precisão *f*.

preclude [prɪ'kluːd] *vt* excluir; **to** ~ **sb from doing** impedir que alguém faça.

precocious [prɪ'kəʊʃəs] *adj* precoce.

preconceived [priːkən'siːvd] *adj* (*idea*) preconcebido.

preconception [priːkən'sɛpʃən] *n* preconceito.

precondition [priːkən'dɪʃən] *n* condição *f* prévia.

precursor [priː'kɜːsə*] *n* precursor(a) *m/f*.

predate ['priːdeɪt] *vt* (*precede*) preceder.

predator ['prɛdətə*] *n* predador *m*.

predatory ['prɛdətərɪ] *adj* predatório, rapace.

predecessor ['priːdɪsɛsə*] *n* predecessor(a) *m/f*, antepassado/a.

predestination [priːdɛstɪ'neɪʃən] *n* predestinação *f*, destino.

predetermine [priːdɪ'tɜːmɪn] *vt* predeterminar, predispor.

predicament [prɪ'dɪkəmənt] *n* situação *f* difícil, apuro.

predicate ['prɛdɪkɪt] *n* (*LING*) predicado.

predict [prɪ'dɪkt] *vt* prever, predizer, prognosticar.

predictable [prɪ'dɪktəbl] *adj* previsível.

predictably [prɪ'dɪktəblɪ] *adv* (*behave, react*) de maneira previsível; ~ **she didn't come** como era de se esperar, ela não veio.

prediction [prɪ'dɪkʃən] *n* previsão *f*, prognóstico.

predispose [priːdɪs'pəʊz] *vt* predispor.

predominance [prɪ'dɒmɪnəns] *n* predominância, preponderância.

predominant [prɪ'dɒmɪnənt] *adj* predominante, preponderante.

predominantly [prɪ'dɒmɪnəntlɪ] *adv* (*for the most part*) na maioria; (*above all*) sobretudo.

predominate [prɪ'dɒmɪneɪt] *vi* predominar.

pre-eminent *adj* preeminente.

pre-empt [-ɛmt] (*BRIT*) *vt* (*obtain*) adquirir por preempção *or* de antemão; (*fig*): **to** ~ **sb/sth** antecipar-se a alguém/antecipar algo.

pre-emptive [-ɛmtɪv] *adj*: ~ **strike** ataque *m* preventivo.

preen [priːn] *vt*: **to** ~ **itself** (*bird*) limpar e

NB: *European Portuguese adds the following consonants to certain words:* **b** (sú(b)dito, su(b)til); **c** (a(c)ção, a(c)cionista, a(c)to); **m** (inde(m)ne); **p** (ado(p)ção, ado(p)tar); *for further details see p. xiii.*

alisar as penas (com o bico); **to ~ o.s.** enfeitar-se, envaidecer-se.

prefab ['pri:fæb] *n* casa pré-fabricada.

prefabricated [pri:'fæbrɪkeɪtɪd] *adj* pré-fabricado.

preface ['prɛfəs] *n* prefácio.

prefect ['pri:fɛkt] *n* (*BRIT: SCH*) monitor(a) *m/f*, tutor(a) *m/f*; (*in Brazil*) prefeito/a.

prefer [prɪ'fɔː*] *vt* preferir; (*LAW*): **to ~ charges** intentar uma ação judicial; **to ~ coffee to tea** preferir café a chá.

preferable ['prɛfrəbl] *adj* preferível.

preferably ['prɛfrəblɪ] *adv* de preferência.

preference ['prɛfrəns] *n* preferência; **in ~ to sth** de preferência a algo.

preference shares (*BRIT*) *npl* ações *fpl* preferenciais.

preferential [prɛfə'rɛnʃəl] *adj* preferencial; **~ treatment** preferência.

preferred stock [prɪ'fɔːd-] (*US*) *npl* ações *fpl* preferenciais.

prefix ['pri:fɪks] *n* prefixo.

pregnancy ['prɛgnənsɪ] *n* gravidez *f*.

pregnant ['prɛgnənt] *adj* grávida; **3 months ~** grávida de 3 meses; **~ with** rico de, cheio de.

prehistoric [pri:hɪs'tɔrɪk] *adj* pré-histórico.

prehistory [pri:'hɪstərɪ] *n* pré-história.

prejudge [pri:'dʒʌdʒ] *vt* fazer um juízo antecipado de, prejulgar.

prejudice ['prɛdʒudɪs] *n* (*bias*) preconceito; (*harm*) prejuízo ♦ *vt* (*predispose*) predispor; (*harm*) prejudicar; **to ~ sb in favour of/against** predispor alguém a favor de/contra.

prejudiced ['prɛdʒudɪst] *adj* (*person*) cheio de preconceitos; (*view*) parcial, preconcebido; **to be ~ against sb/sth** estar com prevenção contra alguém/algo.

prelate ['prɛlət] *n* prelado.

preliminaries [prɪ'lɪmɪnərɪz] *npl* preliminares *fpl*.

preliminary [prɪ'lɪmɪnərɪ] *adj* preliminar, prévio.

prelude ['prɛljuːd] *n* prelúdio.

premarital [pri:'mærɪtl] *adj* pré-nupcial.

premature ['prɛmətʃuə*] *adj* prematuro, precoce; **to be ~ (in doing sth)** precipitar-se (em fazer algo).

premeditated [pri:'mɛdɪteɪtɪd] *adj* premeditado.

premeditation [pri:mɛdɪ'teɪʃən] *n* premeditação *f*.

premenstrual [pri:'mɛnstruəl] *adj* pré-menstrual.

premenstrual tension *n* tensão *f* pré-menstrual.

premier ['prɛmɪə*] *adj* primeiro, principal ♦ *n* (*POL*) primeiro-ministro/primeira-ministra.

première ['prɛmɪɛə*] *n* estréia.

premise ['prɛmɪs] *n* premissa; **~s** *npl* local *m*; (*house*) casa; (*shop*) loja; **on the ~s** no local; **business ~s** local utilizado para fins comerciais.

premium ['pri:mɪəm] *n* prêmio, recompensa; (*COMM*) prêmio; **to be at a ~** ser difícil de

obter; **to sell at a ~** (*shares*) vender acima do par.

premium bond (*BRIT*) *n* obrigação qué dá direito a prêmio mediante sorteio.

premium deal *n* (*COMM*) oferta especial.

premium gasoline (*US*) *n* gasolina azul *or* super.

premonition [prɛmə'nɪʃən] *n* presságio, pressentimento.

preoccupation [pri:ɔkju'peɪʃən] *n* preocupação *f*.

preoccupied [pri:'ɔkjupaɪd] *adj* (*worried*) preocupado, apreensivo; (*absorbed*) absorto.

prep [prɛp] *adj abbr*: **~ school = preparatory school** ♦ *n* (*SCH*: **~ = preparation**) deveres *mpl*.

prepackaged [pri:'pækɪdʒd] *adj* embalado para venda ao consumidor.

prepaid [pri:'peɪd] *adj* com porte pago.

preparation [prɛpə'reɪʃən] *n* preparação *f*; **~s** *npl* preparativos *mpl*; **in ~ for** em preparação para.

preparatory [prɪ'pærətərɪ] *adj* preparatório; **~ to antes de.**

preparatory school *n* escola preparatória.

prepare [prɪ'pɛə*] *vt* preparar ♦ *vi*: **to ~ for** preparar-se *or* aprontar-se para; (*make preparations*) fazer preparativos para.

prepared [prɪ'pɛəd] *adj*: **~ to** pronto para, disposto a.

preponderance [prɪ'pɔndərns] *n* preponderância, predomínio.

preposition [prɛpə'zɪʃən] *n* preposição *f*.

prepossessing [pri:pə'zɛsɪŋ] *adj* atraente.

preposterous [prɪ'pɔstərəs] *adj* absurdo, disparatado.

prep school *n* **= preparatory school.**

prerecorded ['pri:rɪ'kɔːdɪd] *adj* pré-gravado.

prerequisite [pri:'rɛkwɪzɪt] *n* pré-requisito, condição *f* prévia.

prerogative [prɪ'rɔgətɪv] *n* prerrogativa.

presbyterian [prɛzbɪ'tɪərɪən] *adj*, *n* presbiteriano/a.

presbytery ['prɛzbɪtərɪ] *n* presbitério.

preschool ['pri:'skuːl] *adj* (*education*) pré-escolar; (*child*) de idade pré-escolar.

prescribe [prɪ'skraɪb] *vt* prescrever; (*MED*) receitar; **~d books** (*BRIT: SCH*) livros *mpl* requisitados.

prescription [prɪ'skrɪpʃən] *n* prescrição *f*, ordem *f*; (*MED*) receita; **to make up** (*BRIT*) *or* **fill** (*US*) **a ~** aviar uma receita; **"only available on ~"** "venda exclusivamente mediante receita médica".

prescription charges (*BRIT*) *npl* participação *f* no preço das receitas médicas.

prescriptive [prɪ'skrɪptɪv] *adj* prescritivo.

presence ['prɛzns] *n* presença; **~ of mind** presença de espírito.

present [*adj*, *n* 'prɛznt, *vt* prɪ'zɛnt] *adj* (*in attendance*) presente; (*current*) atual ♦ *n* (*gift*) presente *m*; (*also: ~ tense*) presente *m* ♦ *vt* (*introduce*) apresentar; (*expound*) expor; (*prize*) entregar; (*THEATRE*) representar; **to ~ sb with sth** (*as gift*) presentear alguém com algo; *(as prize etc)* entregar algo a alguém; **at ~** no momento, agora; **for the ~** por enquanto; **to be ~ at** estar presente a, presenciar; **to give sb a ~** presentear alguém.

presentable [prɪ'zɛntəbl] *adj* apresentável.

presentation [prɛzn'teɪʃən] *n* apresentação *f*; *(gift)* presente *m*; *(ceremony)* entrega; *(of case)* exposição *f*; *(THEATRE)* representação *f*; **on ~ of** mediante apresentação de.

present-day ['prɛznt'deɪ] *adj* atual, de hoje.

presenter [prɪ'zɛntə*] *(BRIT) n (RADIO, TV)* apresentador(a) *m/f*.

presently ['prɛzntlɪ] *adv (soon)* logo, em breve; *(now)* atualmente.

preservation [prɛzə'veɪʃən] *n* conservação *f*, preservação *f*.

preservative [prɪ'zɔːvətɪv] *n* preservativo.

preserve [prɪ'zɔːv] *vt (keep safe)* preservar, proteger; *(maintain)* conservar, manter; *(food)* pôr em conserva; *(in salt)* conservar em sal, salgar ♦ *n (for game)* reserva de caça, coutada; *(often pl: jam)* geléia; *(: fruit)* compota, conserva.

preshrunk ['priː'ʃrʌŋk] *adj* pré-encolhido.

preside [prɪ'zaɪd] *vi* presidir.

presidency ['prɛzɪdənsɪ] *n* presidência.

president ['prɛzɪdənt] *n* presidente/a *m/f*.

presidential [prɛzɪ'dɛnʃl] *adj* presidencial.

press [prɛs] *n (tool, machine)* prensa; *(printer's)* imprensa, prelo; *(newspapers)* imprensa; *(crowd)* turba, apinhamento; *(of hand)* apertão *m* ♦ *vt (push)* apertar; *(squeeze: fruit etc)* espremer; *(clothes: iron)* passar; *(TECH)* prensar; *(harry)* assediar; *(insist)*: **to ~ sth on sb** insistir para que alguém aceite algo; *(urge)*: **to ~ sb to do or into doing sth** impelir *or* pressionar alguém a fazer algo ♦ *vi (squeeze)* apertar; *(pressurize)* fazer pressão, pressionar; **we are ~ed for time** estamos com pouco tempo; **to ~ for sth** pressionar por algo; **to ~ sb for an answer** pressionar alguém por uma resposta; **to ~ charges against sb** *(LAW)* intentar ação judicial contra alguém; **to go to ~** *(newspaper)* ir para o prelo; **to be in the ~** estar no prelo; **to appear in the ~** sair no jornal.

press on *vi* continuar.

press agency *n* agência de informações.

press clipping *n* recorte *m* de jornal.

press conference *n* entrevista coletiva (para a imprensa).

press cutting *n* recorte *m* de jornal.

press-gang *n* pelotão *de recrutamento da marinha* ♦ *vt*: **to be ~ed into doing** ser impelido a fazer.

pressing ['prɛsɪŋ] *adj* urgente ♦ *n* ação *f (or* serviço *etc)* de passar roupa.

pressman ['prɛsmæn] *(irreg) n* jornalista *m*.

press release *n* release *m or* comunicado à imprensa.

press stud *(BRIT) n* botão *m* de pressão.

press-up *(BRIT) n* flexão *f*.

pressure ['prɛʃə*] *n* pressão *f* ♦ *vt* = **to put ~ on**; **to put ~ on sb (to do sth)** pressionar alguém (a fazer algo).

pressure cooker *n* panela de pressão.

pressure gauge *n* manômetro.

pressure group *n* grupo de pressão.

pressurize ['prɛʃəraɪz] *vt* pressurizar; *(BRIT: fig)*: **to ~ sb (into doing sth)** pressionar alguém (a fazer algo).

pressurized ['prɛʃəraɪzd] *adj* pressurizado.

Prestel ['prɛstɛl] ® *n* serviço de videotexto.

prestige [prɛs'tiːʒ] *n* prestígio.

prestigious [prɛs'tɪdʒəs] *adj* prestigioso.

presumably [prɪ'zjuːməblɪ] *adv* presumivelmente, provavelmente; **~ he did it** é de se presumir que ele o fez.

presume [prɪ'zjuːm] *vt* presumir, supor; **to ~ to do** *(dare)* ousar fazer, atrever-se a fazer; *(set out to)* pretender fazer.

presumption [prɪ'zʌmpʃən] *n* suposição *f*; *(pretension)* presunção *f*; *(boldness)* atrevimento, audácia.

presumptuous [prɪ'zʌmpʃəs] *adj* presunçoso.

presuppose [priːsə'pəʊz] *vt* pressupor, implicar.

pre-tax *adj* antes de impostos.

pretence [prɪ'tɛns] *(US* **pretense)** *n (claim)* pretensão *f*; *(display)* ostentação *f*; *(pretext)* pretexto; *(make-believe)* fingimento; **on the ~ of** sob o pretexto de; **to make a ~ of doing** fingir fazer.

pretend [prɪ'tɛnd] *vt* fingir ♦ *vi (feign)* fingir; *(claim)*: **to ~ to sth** aspirar a *or* pretender a algo; **to ~ to do** fingir fazer.

pretense [prɪ'tɛns] *(US) n* = **pretence**.

pretension [prɪ'tɛnʃən] *n (presumption)* presunção *f*; *(claim)* pretensão *f*; **to have no ~s to sth/to being sth** não ter pretensão a algo/ a ser algo.

pretentious [prɪ'tɛnʃəs] *adj* pretensioso, presunçoso.

preterite ['prɛtərɪt] *n* pretérito.

pretext ['priːtɛkst] *n* pretexto; **on** *or* **under the ~ of doing sth** sob o *or* a pretexto de fazer algo.

pretty ['prɪtɪ] *adj* bonito ♦ *adv (quite)* bastante.

prevail [prɪ'veɪl] *vi (win)* triunfar; *(be current)* imperar; *(be usual)* prevalecer, vigorar; *(persuade)*: **to ~ (up)on sb to do sth** persuadir alguém a fazer algo.

prevailing [prɪ'veɪlɪŋ] *adj (dominant)* predominante; *(usual)* corrente.

prevalent ['prɛvələnt] *adj (dominant)* predominante; *(usual)* corrente; *(fashionable)* da moda.

prevarication [prɪværɪ'keɪʃən] *n* embromação *f*.

prevent [prɪ'vɛnt] *vt*: **to ~ sb from doing sth** impedir alguém de fazer algo.

NB: *European Portuguese adds the following consonants to certain words:* **b** (sú(b)dito, su(b)til); **c** (a(c)ção, a(c)cionista, a(c)to); **m** (inde(m)ne); **p** (ado(p)ção, ado(p)tar); *for further details see p. xiii.*

preventable [prɪ'vɛntəbl] *adj* evitável.
preventative [prɪ'vɛntətɪv] *adj* preventivo.
prevention [prɪ'vɛnʃən] *n* prevenção *f*.
preventive [prɪ'vɛntɪv] *adj* preventivo.
preview ['priːvjuː] *n* (*of film*) pré-estréia; (*fig*) antecipação *f*.
previous ['priːvɪəs] *adj* (*experience, notice*) prévio; (*earlier*) anterior; **I have a ~ engagement** já tenho compromisso; **~ to doing** antes de fazer.
previously ['priːvɪəslɪ] *adv* (*in advance*) previamente, antecipadamente; (*earlier*) antes, anteriormente.
prewar [priː'wɔː*] *adj* anterior à guerra.
prey [preɪ] *n* presa ♦ *vi*: **to ~ on** viver às custas de; (*feed on*) alimentar-se de; (*plunder*) saquear, pilhar; **it was ~ing on his mind** preocupava-o, atormentava-o.
price [praɪs] *n* preço; (*of shares*) cotação *f* ♦ *vt* (*goods*) fixar o preço de; **what is the ~ of ...?** qual é o preço de ...?, quanto é ...?; **to go up** *or* **rise in ~** subir de preço; **to put a ~ on sth** determinar o preço de algo; **to be ~d out of the market** (*article*) não ser competitivo; (*producer, country*) perder freguesia por causa de preços muito altos; **what ~ his promises now?** que valem suas promessas agora?; **he regained his freedom, but at a ~** ele recobrou a liberdade, mas pagou caro; **at any ~** por qualquer preço.
price control *n* controle *m* de preços.
price-cutting *n* corte *m* de preços.
priceless ['praɪslɪs] *adj* inestimável; (*inf: amusing*) impagável.
price list *n* lista *or* tabela de preços.
price range *n* gama de preços; **it's within my ~** está dentro do meu preço.
price tag *n* etiqueta de preço.
price war *n* guerra de preços.
pricey ['praɪsɪ] (*inf*) *adj* salgado.
prick [prɪk] *n* picada; (*with pin*) alfinetada; (*inf!: penis*) pau *m* (!); (*inf!: person*) filho-da-puta *m* (!) ♦ *vt* picar; **to ~ up one's ears** aguçar os ouvidos.
prickle ['prɪkl] *n* (*sensation*) comichão, ardência; (*BOT*) espinho.
prickly ['prɪklɪ] *adj* espinhoso; (*fig: person*) irritadiço.
prickly heat *n* brotoeja.
prickly pear *n* opúncia.
pride [praɪd] *n* orgulho; (*pej*) soberba ♦ *vt*: **to ~ o.s.** on orgulhar-se de; **to take (a) ~ in** orgulhar-se de, sentir orgulho em; **to have ~ of place** (*BRIT*) ocupar o lugar de destaque, ter destaque; **her ~ and joy** seu tesouro.
priest [priːst] *n* sacerdote *m*, padre *m*.
priestess ['priːstɪs] *n* sacerdotisa.
priesthood ['priːsthud] *n* (*practice*) sacerdócio; (*priests*) clero.
prig [prɪg] *n* pedante *m/f*.
prim [prɪm] *adj* (*formal*) empertigado; (*affected*) afetado.
prima facie ['praɪmə'feɪʃɪ] *adj*: **to have a ~ case** (*LAW*) ter uma causa convincente.
primarily ['praɪmərɪlɪ] *adv* (*above all*) princi-

palmente; (*firstly*) em primeiro lugar.
primary ['praɪmərɪ] *adj* primário; (*first in importance*) principal ♦ *n* (*US: election*) eleição *f* primária.
primary colour *n* cor *f* primária.
primary products *npl* produtos *mpl* básicos.
primary school (*BRIT*) *n* escola primária.
primate¹ ['praɪmɪt] *n* (*REL*) primaz *m*.
primate² ['praɪmeɪt] *n* (*ZOOL*) primata *m*.
prime [praɪm] *adj* primeiro, principal; (*basic*) fundamental, primário; (*excellent*) de primeira ♦ *vt* (*gun, pump*) escorvar; (*fig*) aprontar, preparar ♦ *n*: **in the ~ of life** na primavera da vida.
prime minister *n* primeiro-ministro/primeira-ministra.
primer ['praɪmə*] *n* (*book*) livro de leitura; (*paint*) pintura de base; (*of gun*) escorva.
prime time *n* (*RADIO, TV*) horário nobre.
primeval [praɪ'miːvl] *adj* primitivo.
primitive ['prɪmɪtɪv] *adj* primitivo; (*crude*) rudimentar; (*uncivilized*) grosseiro, inculto.
primrose ['prɪmrəuz] *n* prímula, primavera.
primus (stove) ['praɪməs-] ® (*BRIT*) *n* fogão *m* portátil a petróleo.
prince [prɪns] *n* príncipe *m*.
princess [prɪn'sɛs] *n* princesa.
principal ['prɪnsɪpl] *adj* principal ♦ *n* (*head teacher*) diretor(a) *m/f*; (*in play*) papel *m* principal; (*money*) principal *m*.
principality [prɪnsɪ'pælɪtɪ] *n* principado.
principally ['prɪnsɪplɪ] *adv* principalmente.
principle ['prɪnsɪpl] *n* princípio; **in ~** em princípio; **on ~** por princípio.
print [prɪnt] *n* (*impression*) impressão *f*, marca; (*letters*) letra de forma; (*fabric*) estampado; (*ART*) estampa, gravura; (*PHOT*) cópia ♦ *vt* imprimir; (*write in capitals*) escrever em letra de imprensa; **out of ~** esgotado.
print out *vt* (*COMPUT*) imprimir.
printed circuit board ['prɪntɪd-] *n* placa de circuito impresso.
printed matter ['prɪntɪd-] *n* impressos *mpl*.
printer ['prɪntə*] *n* impressor(a) *m/f*; (*machine*) impressora.
printhead ['prɪnthɛd] *n* cabeçote *m* de impressão.
printing ['prɪntɪŋ] *n* (*art*) imprensa; (*act*) impressão *f*; (*quantity*) tiragem *f*.
printing press *n* prelo, máquina impressora.
print-out *n* cópia impressa.
print wheel *n* margarida.
prior ['praɪə*] *adj* anterior, prévio ♦ *n* (*REL*) prior *m*; **~ to doing** antes de fazer; **without ~ notice** sem aviso prévio; **to have a ~ claim to sth** ter prioridade na reivindicação de algo.
priority [praɪ'ɔrɪtɪ] *n* prioridade *f*; **to have** *or* **take ~ over sth/sb** ter prioridade sobre algo/alguém.
priory ['praɪərɪ] *n* priorado.
prise [praɪz] *vt*: **to ~ open** arrombar.
prism ['prɪzəm] *n* prisma *m*.
prison ['prɪzn] *n* prisão *f* ♦ *cpd* carcerário.

prison camp n campo de prisioneiros.
prisoner ['prɪzənə*] n (in prison) preso/a, presidiário/a; (under arrest) detido/a; (in dock) acusado/a, réu/ré m/f; **to take sb ~** aprisionar alguém, prender alguém; **~ of war** prisioneiro de guerra.
prissy ['prɪsɪ] adj fresco, cheio de luxo.
pristine ['prɪstiːn] adj imaculado.
privacy ['prɪvəsɪ] n (seclusion) isolamento, solidão f; (intimacy) intimidade f, privacidade f.
private ['praɪvɪt] adj (personal) particular; (confidential) confidencial, reservado; (lesson, car) particular; (intimate) privado, íntimo; (sitting etc) a portas fechadas ♦ n soldado raso; "~" (on envelope) "confidencial"; (on door) "privativo"; **in ~** em particular; **in (his) ~ life** em (sua) vida particular; **he is a very ~ person** ele é uma pessoa muito reservada; **to be in ~ practice** ter clínica particular; **~ hearing** (LAW) audiência em segredo da justiça.
private enterprise n iniciativa privada.
private eye n detetive m/f particular.
private limited company (BRIT) n sociedade f anônima fechada.
privately ['praɪvɪtlɪ] adv em particular; (in oneself) no fundo.
private parts npl partes fpl (pudendas).
private property n propriedade f privada.
private school n escola particular.
privation [praɪ'veɪʃən] n privação f.
privatize ['praɪvɪtaɪz] vt privatizar.
privet ['prɪvɪt] n alfena.
privilege ['prɪvɪlɪdʒ] n privilégio.
privileged ['prɪvɪlɪdʒd] adj privilegiado.
privy ['prɪvɪ] adj: **to be ~ to** estar inteirado de.
Privy Council (BRIT) n Conselho Privado.
prize [praɪz] n prêmio ♦ adj (bull, novel) premiado; (first class) de primeira classe; (example) perfeito ♦ vt valorizar.
prize fight n luta de boxe profissional.
prize giving [-'gɪvɪŋ] n distribuição f dos prêmios.
prize money n dinheiro do prêmio.
prizewinner ['praɪzwɪnə*] n premiado/a.
prizewinning ['praɪzwɪnɪŋ] adj premiado.
PRO n abbr (= public relations officer) RP m/f inv.
pro [prəu] n (SPORT) profissional m/f; (advantage): **the ~s and cons** os prós e os contras.
pro- [prəu] prefix (in favour of) pró-.
probability [prɔbə'bɪlɪtɪ] n probabilidade f; **in all ~** com toda a probabilidade.
probable ['prɔbəbl] adj provável; (plausible) verossímil; **it is ~/hardly ~ that ...** é provável/pouco provável que ....
probably ['prɔbəblɪ] adv provavelmente.
probate ['prəubɪt] n (LAW) homologação f, legitimação f.

probation [prə'beɪʃən] n (in employment) estágio probatório; (LAW) liberdade f condicional; (REL) noviciado; **on ~** (employee) em estágio probatório; (LAW) em liberdade condicional.
probationary [prə'beɪʃənrɪ] adj (period) probatório.
probe [prəub] n (MED, SPACE) sonda; (enquiry) pesquisa ♦ vt sondar; (investigate) investigar, esquadrinhar.
probity ['prəubɪtɪ] n probidade f.
problem ['prɔbləm] n problema m; **what's the ~?** qual é o problema?; **I had no ~ in finding her** não foi difícil encontrá-la; **no ~!** não tem problema!
problematic [prɔblə'mætɪk] adj problemático.
procedure [prə'siːdʒə*] n (ADMIN, LAW) procedimento; (method) método, processo; **cashing a cheque is a simple ~** descontar um cheque é uma operação simples.
proceed [prə'siːd] vi proceder; (continue): **to ~ (with)** continuar or prosseguir (com); **to ~ to** passar a; **to ~ to do** passar a fazer; **I am not sure how to ~** não sei como proceder; **to ~ against sb** (LAW) processar alguém, instaurar processo contra alguém.
proceeding [prə'siːdɪŋ] n processo; **~s** npl procedimento; (lawsuit) processo.
proceeds ['prəusiːdz] npl produto, proventos mpl.
process [n, vt 'prəuses, vi prə'ses] n processo ♦ vt processar, elaborar ♦ vi (BRIT: formal: go in procession) desfilar; **in ~** em andamento; **we are in the ~ of moving to Rio** estamos em processo de mudança para o Rio.
processed cheese ['prəusest-] n ≈ requeijão m.
processing ['prəusesɪŋ] n processamento.
procession [prə'seʃən] n desfile m, procissão f; **funeral ~** cortejo fúnebre.
proclaim [prə'kleɪm] vt proclamar; (announce) anunciar.
proclamation [prɔklə'meɪʃən] n proclamação f; (written) promulgação f.
proclivity [prə'klɪvɪtɪ] n inclinação f.
procrastination [prəukræstɪ'neɪʃən] n protelação f.
procreation [prəukrɪ'eɪʃən] n procriação f.
procure [prə'kjuə*] vt obter.
procurement [prə'kjuəmənt] n obtenção f; (purchase) compra.
prod [prɔd] vt (push) empurrar; (with elbow) cutucar, acotovelar; (jab) espetar ♦ n empurrão m; cotovelada; espetada.
prodigal ['prɔdɪgl] adj pródigo.
prodigious [prə'dɪdʒəs] adj prodigioso, extraordinário.
prodigy ['prɔdɪdʒɪ] n prodígio.
produce [n 'prɔdjuːs, vt prə'djuːs] n (AGR) produtos mpl agrícolas ♦ vt produzir; (profit) render; (cause) provocar; (show) apresentar, exibir; (THEATRE) pôr em cena or em cartaz;

(offspring) dar à luz.

producer [prə'djuːsə*] *n* (*THEATRE*) diretor(a) *m/f*; (*AGR*, *CINEMA*) produtor(a) *m/f*.

product ['prɒdʌkt] *n* produto.

production [prə'dʌkʃən] *n* (*act*) produção *f*; (*thing*) produto; (*THEATRE*) encenação *f*; **to put into** ~ (*goods*) passar a fabricar.

production agreement (*US*) *n* acórdo sobre produtividade.

production control *n* controle *m* de produção.

production line *n* linha de produção *or* de montagem.

production manager *n* gerente *m/f* de produção.

productive [prə'dʌktɪv] *adj* produtivo.

productivity [prɒdʌk'tɪvɪtɪ] *n* produtividade *f*.

productivity agreement (*BRIT*) *n* acordo sobre produtividade.

productivity bonus *n* prêmio de produção.

Prof. [prɒf] *abbr* (= *professor*) Prof.

profane [prə'feɪn] *adj* profano; (*language etc*) irreverente, sacrílego.

profess [prə'fes] *vt* professar; (*regret*) manifestar; **I do not** ~ **to be an expert** não me tenho na conta de entendido.

professed [prə'fest] *adj* (*self-declared*) assumido.

profession [prə'feʃən] *n* profissão *f*; **the ~s** *npl* as profissões liberais.

professional [prə'feʃənl] *n* profissional *m/f* ♦ *adj* profissional; (*work*) de profissional; **he's a** ~ **man** ele exerce uma profissão liberal; **to take** ~ **advice** consultar um perito.

professionalism [prə'feʃnəlɪzm] *n* profissionalismo.

professionally [prə'feʃnəlɪ] *adv* profissionalmente; (*as a job*) de profissão; **I only know him** ~ eu só conheço ele pelo trabalho.

professor [prə'fesə*] *n* catedrático/a; (*US: teacher*) professor(a) *m/f*.

professorship [prə'fesəʃɪp] *n* cátedra.

proffer ['prɒfə*] *vt* (*hand*) estender; (*remark*) fazer; (*apologies*) apresentar.

proficiency [prə'fɪʃənsɪ] *n* competência, proficiência.

proficient [prə'fɪʃənt] *adj* competente, proficiente.

profile ['prəufaɪl] *n* perfil *m*; **to keep a high** ~ destacar-se; **to keep a low** ~ sair de circulação.

profit ['prɒfɪt] *n* (*COMM*) lucro; (*fig*) proveito, vantagem *f* ♦ *vi*: **to** ~ **by** *or* **from** (*financially*) lucrar com; (*benefit*) aproveitar-se de, tirar proveito de; ~ **and loss account** conta de lucros e perdas; **to make a** ~ lucrar; **to sell sth at a** ~ vender algo com lucro.

profitability [prɒfɪtə'bɪlɪtɪ] *n* rentabilidade *f*.

profitable ['prɒfɪtəbl] *adj* (*ECON*) lucrativo, rendoso; (*useful*) proveitoso.

profit centre *n* centro de lucro.

profiteering [prɒfɪ'tɪərɪŋ] *n* mercantilismo, exploração *f*.

profit-making *adj* com fins lucrativos.

profit margin *n* margem *f* de lucro.

profit-sharing [-'ʃɛərɪŋ] *n* participação *f* nos lucros.

profits tax (*BRIT*) *n* imposto sobre os lucros.

profligate ['prɒflɪgɪt] *adj* (*behaviour*, *person*) devasso; (*extravagant*): ~ **(with)** pródigo (de).

pro forma [-'fɔːmə] *adj*: ~ **invoice** fatura pro-forma *or* simulada.

profound [prə'faund] *adj* profundo.

profuse [prə'fjuːs] *adj* abundante.

profusely [prə'fjuːslɪ] *adv* profusamente.

profusion [prə'fjuːʒən] *n* profusão *f*, abundância.

progeny ['prɒdʒɪnɪ] *n* prole *f*, progênie *f*.

programme ['prəugræm] (*US* **program**) *n* programa *m* ♦ *vt* programar.

program(m)er ['prəugræmə*] *n* programador(a) *m/f*.

program(m)ing ['prəugræmɪŋ] *n* programação *f*.

program(m)ing language *n* linguagem *f* de programação.

progress [*n* 'prəugres, *vi* prə'gres] *n* progresso ♦ *vi* progredir, avançar; **in** ~ em andamento; **to make** ~ fazer progressos; **as the match** ~**ed** à medida que o jogo se desenvolvia.

progression [prə'greʃən] *n* progressão *f*.

progressive [prə'gresɪv] *adj* progressivo; (*person*) progressista.

progressively [prə'gresɪvlɪ] *adv* progressivamente.

progress report *n* (*MED*) boletim *m* médico; (*ADMIN*) relatório sobre o andamento dos trabalhos.

prohibit [prə'hɪbɪt] *vt* proibir; **to** ~ **sb from doing sth** proibir alguém de fazer algo; **"smoking ~ed"** "proibido fumar".

prohibition [prəuɪ'bɪʃən] *n* proibição *f*; (*US: ban on alcohol*) lei *f* seca.

prohibitive [prə'hɪbɪtɪv] *adj* (*price etc*) proibitivo.

project [*n* 'prɒdʒekt, *vt*, *vi* prə'dʒekt] *n* projeto; (*SCH: research*) pesquisa ♦ *vt* projetar ♦ *vi* (*stick out*) ressaltar, sobressair.

projectile [prə'dʒektaɪl] *n* projétil *m*.

projection [prə'dʒekʃən] *n* projeção *f*; (*overhang*) saliência.

projectionist [prə'dʒekʃənɪst] *n* operador(a) *m/f* de projetor.

projection room *n* (*CINEMA*) sala de projeção.

projector [prə'dʒektə*] *n* projetor *m*.

proletarian [prəulɪ'tɛərɪən] *adj*, *n* proletário/a.

proletariat [prəulɪ'tɛərɪət] *n* proletariado.

proliferate [prə'lɪfəreɪt] *vi* proliferar.

proliferation [prəlɪfə'reɪʃən] *n* proliferação *f*.

prolific [prə'lɪfɪk] *adj* prolífico.

prologue ['prəulɒg] *n* prólogo.

prolong [prə'lɒŋ] *vt* prolongar.

prom [prɒm] *n* *abbr* = **promenade**; **promenade concert**; (*US: ball*) baile *m* de estudantes.

promenade [prɒmə'nɑːd] *n* (*by sea*) passeio

(à orla marítima).

promenade concert *n* concerto (de música clássica).

promenade deck *n* (*NAUT*) convés *m* superior.

prominence ['prɒmɪnəns] *n* (*fig*) eminência, importância.

prominent ['prɒmɪnənt] *adj* (*standing out*) proeminente; (*important*) eminente, notório; **he is ~ in the field of** ... ele é muito conhecido no campo de ....

prominently ['prɒmɪnəntlɪ] *adv* (*display, set*) bem à vista; **he figured ~ in the case** ele teve um papel importante no caso.

promiscuity [prɒmɪ'skju:ɪtɪ] *n* promiscuidade *f*.

promiscuous [prə'mɪskjuəs] *adj* promíscuo.

promise ['prɒmɪs] *n* promessa ♦ *vt, vi* prometer; **to make sb a ~** fazer uma promessa a alguém; **to ~ (sb) to do sth** prometer (a alguém) fazer algo; **a young man of ~** um jovem que promete; **to ~ well** prometer.

promising ['prɒmɪsɪŋ] *adj* prometedor(a).

promissory note ['prɒmɪsərɪ-] *n* (nota) promissória.

promontory ['prɒməntrɪ] *n* promontório.

promote [prə'məut] *vt* promover; (*new product*) promover, fazer propaganda de; (*event*) patrocinar.

promoter [prə'məutə*] *n* (*of sporting event etc*) patrocinador(a) *m/f*; (*of cause etc*) partidário/a.

promotion [prə'məuʃən] *n* promoção *f*.

prompt [prɒmpt] *adj* pronto, rápido ♦ *n* (*COMPUT*) sinal *m* de orientação, prompt *m* ♦ *vt* (*urge*) incitar, impelir; (*cause*) provocar, ocasionar; (*THEATRE*) servir de ponto a; **to ~ sb to do sth** induzir alguém a fazer algo; **he's very ~** (*punctual*) ele é pontual; **at 8 o'clock ~** às 8 horas em ponto; **he was ~ to accept** ele não hesitou em aceitar.

prompter ['prɒmptə*] *n* (*THEATRE*) ponto.

promptly ['prɒmptlɪ] *adv* (*punctually*) pontualmente; (*rapidly*) rapidamente.

promptness ['prɒmptnɪs] *n* (*punctuality*) pontualidade *f*; (*rapidity*) rapidez *f*.

promulgate ['prɒməlgeɪt] *vt* promulgar.

prone [prəun] *adj* (*lying*) inclinado, de bruços; **~ to** propenso a, predisposto a; **she is ~ to burst into tears if** ... ela tende a desatar a chorar se ....

prong [prɒŋ] *n* ponta; (*of fork*) dente *m*.

pronoun ['prəunaun] *n* pronome *m*.

pronounce [prə'nauns] *vt* pronunciar; (*declare*) declarar ♦ *vi*: **to ~ (up)on** pronunciar-se sobre.

pronounced [prə'naunst] *adj* (*marked*) marcado, nítido.

pronouncement [prə'naunsmənt] *n* pronunciamento.

pronunciation [prənʌnsɪ'eɪʃən] *n* pronúncia.

proof [pru:f] *n* prova; (*of alcohol*) teor *m*

alcoólico ♦ *adj*: **~ against** à prova de ♦ *vt* (*BRIT*: *tent, anorak*) impermeabilizar; **to be 70° ~** ter 70° de gradação.

proofreader ['pru:fri:də*] *n* revisor(a) *m/f* de provas.

Prop. *abbr* (*COMM*) = **proprietor**.

prop [prɒp] *n* suporte *m*, escora; (*fig*) amparo, apoio ♦ *vt* (*also*: **~ up**) apoiar, escorar; (*lean*): **to ~ sth against** apoiar algo contra.

propaganda [prɒpə'gændə] *n* propaganda.

propagate ['prɒpəgeɪt] *vt* propagar.

propel [prə'pɛl] *vt* propelir, propulsionar.

propeller [prə'pɛlə*] *n* hélice *f*.

propelling pencil [prə'pɛlɪŋ-] (*BRIT*) *n* lapiseira.

propensity [prə'pɛnsɪtɪ] *n* propensão *f*.

proper ['prɒpə*] *adj* (*suited, right*) próprio; (*seemly*) correto, conveniente; (*authentic*) genuíno; (*inf*: *real*) autêntico; **physics ~** a física propriamente dita; **to go through the ~ channels** (*ADMIN*) seguir os trâmites oficiais.

properly ['prɒpəlɪ] *adv* direito; (*really*) bem.

proper noun *n* nome *m* próprio.

property ['prɒpətɪ] *n* (*possessions, quality*) propriedade *f*; (*goods*) posses *fpl*, bens *mpl*; (*buildings*) imóveis *mpl*; (*estate*) propriedade *f*, fazenda; **it's their ~** é deles, pertence a eles.

property developer (*BRIT*) *n* empresário/a de imóveis.

property owner *n* proprietário/a.

property tax *n* imposto predial e territorial.

prophecy ['prɒfɪsɪ] *n* profecia.

prophesy ['prɒfɪsaɪ] *vt* profetizar; (*fig*) predizer ♦ *vi* profetizar.

prophet ['prɒfɪt] *n* profeta *m/f*.

prophetic [prə'fɛtɪk] *adj* profético.

proportion [prə'pɔ:ʃən] *n* proporção *f*; (*share*) parte *f*, porção *f* ♦ *vt* proporcionar; **in ~ to** *or* **with sth** em proporção *or* proporcional a algo; **out of ~** desproporcionado; **to see sth in ~** (*fig*) ter a visão adequada de algo.

proportional [prə'pɔ:ʃənl] *adj* proporcional.

proportional representation *n* (*POL*) representação *f* proporcional.

proportionate [prə'pɔ:ʃənɪt] *adj* proporcionado.

proposal [prə'pəuzl] *n* proposta; (*of marriage*) pedido.

propose [prə'pəuz] *vt* propor ♦ *vi* propor casamento; **to ~ to do** propor-se fazer.

proposer [prə'pəuzə*] (*BRIT*) *n* (*of motion etc*) apresentador(a) *m/f*.

proposition [prɒpə'zɪʃən] *n* proposta, proposição *f*; **to make sb a ~** fazer uma proposta a alguém.

propound [prə'paund] *vt* propor.

proprietary [prə'praɪətrɪ] *adj*: **~ brand** marca registrada; **~ product** produto patenteado.

proprietor [prə'praɪətə*] *n* proprietário/a,

---

dono/a.
propriety [prə'praɪətɪ] n propriedade f.
propulsion [prə'pʌlʃən] n propulsão f.
pro rata [-'rɑːtə] adv pro rata, proporcionalmente.
prosaic [prəu'zeɪɪk] adj prosaico.
Pros. Atty. (US) abbr = **prosecuting attorney.**
proscribe [prə'skraɪb] vt proscrever.
prose [prəuz] n prosa.
prosecute ['prɒsɪkjuːt] vt (LAW) processar.
prosecuting attorney ['prɒsɪkjuːtɪŋ-] (US) n promotor(a) m/f público/a.
prosecution [prɒsɪ'kjuːʃən] n acusação f; (accusing side) autor m da demanda.
prosecutor ['prɒsɪkjuːtə*] n promotor(a) m/f; (also: public ~) promotor(a) m/f público/a.
prospect [n 'prɒspɛkt, vt, vi prə'spɛkt] n (chance) probabilidade f; (outlook, potential) perspectiva ♦ vt explorar ♦ vi prospectar; ~s npl perspectivas fpl; **we are faced with the ~ of ...** nós estamos diante da perspectiva de ...; **there is every ~ of an early victory** há toda probabilidade de uma vitória rápida.
prospecting [prə'spɛktɪŋ] n prospecção f.
prospective [prə'spɛktɪv] adj (possible) provável; (future) em perspectiva.
prospector [prə'spɛktə*] n garimpeiro/a.
prospectus [prə'spɛktəs] n prospecto, programa m.
prosper ['prɒspə*] vi prosperar.
prosperity [prɒ'spɛrɪtɪ] n prosperidade f.
prosperous ['prɒspərəs] adj próspero.
prostate ['prɒsteɪt] n (also: ~ gland) próstata.
prostitute ['prɒstɪtjuːt] n prostituta; **male ~** prostituto.
prostitution [prɒstɪ'tjuːʃən] n prostituição f.
prostrate [adj 'prɒstreɪt, vt prɒ'streɪt] adj prostrado; (fig) abatido, aniquilado ♦ vt: **to ~ o.s. (before sb)** prostrar-se (diante de alguém).
protagonist [prə'tægənɪst] n protagonista m/f.
protect [prə'tɛkt] vt proteger.
protection [prə'tɛkʃən] n proteção f; **to be under sb's ~** estar sob a proteção de alguém.
protectionism [prə'tɛkʃənɪzm] n protecionismo.
protection racket n extorsão f.
protective [prə'tɛktɪv] adj protetor(a); **~ custody** (LAW) prisão f preventiva.
protector [prə'tɛktə*] n protetor(a) m/f.
protégé ['prəutɛʒeɪ] n protegido.
protégée ['prəutɛʒeɪ] n protegida.
protein ['prəutiːn] n proteína.
pro tem [-tɛm] adv abbr (= pro tempore: for the time being) provisoriamente.
protest [n 'prəutɛst, vi, vt prə'tɛst] n protesto ♦ vi protestar ♦ vt (affirm) afirmar, declarar.
Protestant ['prɒtɪstənt] adj, n protestante m/f.
protester [prə'tɛstə*] n manifestante m/f.
protest march n passeata.
protestor [prə'tɛstə*] n = **protester.**
protocol ['prəutəkɒl] n protocolo.
prototype ['prəutətaɪp] n protótipo.

protracted [prə'træktɪd] adj prolongado, demorado.
protractor [prə'træktə*] n (GEOM) transferidor m.
protrude [prə'truːd] vi projetar-se, sobressair, ressaltar.
protuberance [prə'tjuːbərəns] n protuberância.
proud [praud] adj orgulhoso; (pej) vaidoso, soberbo; **to be ~ to do sth** sentir-se orgulhoso de fazer algo; **to do sb ~** (inf) fazer muita festa a alguém.
proudly ['praudlɪ] adv orgulhosamente.
prove [pruːv] vt comprovar ♦ vi: **to ~ correct** vir a ser correto; **to ~ o.s.** pôr-se à prova; **to ~ itself (to be) useful** etc revelar-se or mostrar-se útil etc; **he was ~d right in the end** no final deram-lhe razão.
proverb ['prɒvəːb] n provérbio.
proverbial [prə'vəːbɪəl] adj proverbial.
provide [prə'vaɪd] vt fornecer, proporcionar; **to ~ sb with sth** fornecer alguém de algo, fornecer algo a alguém; **to be ~d with** estar munido de.
provide for vt fus (person) prover à subsistência de; (emergency) prevenir.
provided (that) [prə'vaɪdɪd-] conj contanto que + sub, sob condição de (que) + sub.
Providence ['prɒvɪdəns] n a Divina Providência.
providing [prə'vaɪdɪŋ] conj contanto que + sub.
province ['prɒvɪns] n província; (fig) esfera.
provincial [prə'vɪnʃəl] adj provincial; (pej) provinciano.
provision [prə'vɪʒən] n provisão f; (supply) fornecimento; (supplying) abastecimento; (in contract) cláusula, condição f; **~s** npl (food) mantimentos mpl; **to make ~ for** fazer provisão para; **there's no ~ for this in the contract** não há cláusula nesse sentido no contrato.
provisional [prə'vɪʒənl] adj provisório, interino; (agreement, licence) provisório ♦ n: **P~** (IRISH: POL) militante do braço armado do IRA.
provisional licence (BRIT) n (AUT) licença prévia para aprendizagem.
provisionally [prə'vɪʒnəlɪ] adv provisoriamente.
proviso [prə'vaɪzəu] n condição f; (reservation) ressalva; (LAW) cláusula; **with the ~ that** com a ressalva que.
Provo ['prɒvəu] (inf) n abbr = **Provisional.**
provocation [prɒvə'keɪʃən] n provocação f.
provocative [prə'vɒkətɪv] adj provocante; (stimulating) sugestivo.
provoke [prə'vəuk] vt provocar; **to ~ sb to sth/to do or into doing sth** provocar alguém a algo/a fazer algo.
provoking [prə'vəukɪŋ] adj provocante.
provost ['prɒvəst] n (BRIT: of university) reitor(a) m/f; (SCOTTISH) prefeito/a.
prow [prau] n proa.
prowess ['prauɪs] n destreza, perícia.

prowl [praul] *vi* (*also*: ~ *about*, ~ *around*) rondar, andar à espreita ♦ *n*: **on the** ~ de ronda, rondando.

prowler ['praulə*] *n* tarado/a.

proximity [prɔk'sımıtı] *n* proximidade *f*.

proxy ['prɔksɪ] *n* procuração *f*; (*person*) procurador(a) *m/f*; **by** ~ por procuração.

prude [pruːd] *n* pudico/a.

prudence ['pruːdns] *n* prudência.

prudent ['pruːdənt] *adj* prudente.

prudish ['pruːdɪʃ] *adj* pudico/a.

prune [pruːn] *n* ameixa seca ♦ *vt* podar.

pry [praɪ] *vi*: **to** ~ **into** intrometer-se em.

PS *n abbr* (= *postscript*) PS *m*.

psalm [sɑːm] *n* salmo.

PSAT (*US*) *n abbr* = **Preliminary Scholastic Aptitude Test.**

PSBR (*BRIT*) *n abbr* (= *public sector borrowing requirement*) necessidade *f* de empréstimos no setor público.

pseud [sjuːd] (*BRIT*: *inf*) *n* posudo/a.

pseudo- [sjuːdəu] *prefix* pseudo-.

pseudonym ['sjuːdənɪm] *n* pseudônimo.

PST (*US*) *abbr* (= *Pacific Standard Time*) *hora de inverno do Pacífico.*

PSV (*BRIT*) *n abbr* = **public service vehicle.**

psyche ['saɪkɪ] *n* psiquismo.

psychiatric [saɪkɪ'ætrɪk] *adj* psiquiátrico.

psychiatrist [saɪ'kaɪətrɪst] *n* psiquiatra *m/f*.

psychiatry [saɪ'kaɪətrɪ] *n* psiquiatria.

psychic ['saɪkɪk] *adj* (*also*: ~*al*) paranormal; (*person*) sensível a forças psíquicas ♦ *n* médium *m/f*.

psychoanalyse [saɪkəu'ænəlaɪz] *vt* psicanalisar.

psychoanalysis [saɪkəuə'nælɪsɪs] *n* psicanálise *f*.

psychoanalyst [saɪkəu'ænəlɪst] *n* psicanalista *m/f*.

psychological [saɪkə'lɔdʒɪkl] *adj* psicológico.

psychologist [saɪ'kɔlədʒɪst] *n* psicólogo/a.

psychology [saɪ'kɔlədʒɪ] *n* psicologia.

psychopath ['saɪkəupæθ] *n* psicopata *m/f*.

psychoses [saɪ'kəusiːz] *npl of* **psychosis.**

psychosis [saɪ'kəusɪs] (*pl* **psychoses**) *n* psicose *f*.

psychosomatic [saɪkəusə'mætɪk] *adj* psicossomático.

psychotherapy [saɪkəu'θerəpɪ] *n* psicoterapia.

psychotic [saɪ'kɔtɪk] *adj*, *n* psicótico/a.

PT (*BRIT*) *n abbr* = **physical training.**

Pt. *abbr* (*in place names* = *Point*) Pto.

pt *abbr* = pint; point.

PTA *n abbr* = **Parent-Teacher Association.**

Pte. (*BRIT*) *abbr* (*MIL*) = **private.**

PTO *abbr* (= *please turn over*) v.v., vire.

PTV (*US*) *n abbr* = **pay television; public television.**

pub [pʌb] *n abbr* (= *public house*) pub *m*, bar *m*, botequim *m*.

puberty ['pjuːbətɪ] *n* puberdade *f*.

pubic ['pjuːbɪk] *adj* púbico, pubiano.

public ['pʌblɪk] *adj*, *n* público; **in** ~ em público; **the general** ~ o grande público; **to be** ~ **knowledge** ser de conhecimento público; **to go** ~ (*COMM*) tornar-se uma companhia de capital aberto, passar a ser cotado na Bolsa de Valores.

public address system *n* sistema *m* (de reforço) de som.

publican ['pʌblɪkən] *n* dono/a de pub.

publication [pʌblɪ'keɪʃən] *n* publicação *f*.

public company *n* sociedade *f* anônima aberta.

public convenience (*BRIT*) *n* banheiro público.

public holiday (*BRIT*) *n* feriado.

public house (*BRIT*: *irreg*) *n* pub *m*, bar *m*, taberna.

publicity [pʌb'lɪsɪtɪ] *n* publicidade *f*.

publicize ['pʌblɪsaɪz] *vt* divulgar; (*product*) promover.

public limited company *n* sociedade *f* anônima aberta.

publicly ['pʌblɪklɪ] *adv* publicamente.

public opinion *n* opinião *f* pública.

public ownership *n*: **to be taken into** ~ ser estatizado.

public relations *n* relações *fpl* públicas.

public relations officer *n* relações-públicas *m/f inv*.

public school *n* (*BRIT*) escola particular; (*US*) escola pública.

public sector *n* setor *m* público.

public service vehicle (*BRIT*) *n* veículo para o transporte público.

public-spirited [-'spɪrɪtɪd] *adj* zeloso pelo bem-estar público.

public transport (*US* **public transportation**) *n* transporte *m* coletivo.

public utility *n* (serviço de) utilidade *f* pública.

public works *npl* obras *fpl* públicas.

publish ['pʌblɪʃ] *vt* publicar.

publisher ['pʌblɪʃə*] *n* editor(a) *m/f*; (*company*) editora.

publishing ['pʌblɪʃɪŋ] *n* (*industry*) a indústria editorial.

publishing company *n* editora.

puce [pjuːs] *adj* roxo.

puck [pʌk] *n* (*elf*) duende *m*; (*ICE HOCKEY*) disco.

pucker ['pʌkə*] *vt* (*fabric*) amarrotar; (*brow etc*) franzir.

pudding ['pudɪŋ] *n* (*BRIT*: *dessert*) sobremesa; (*cake*) pudim *m*, doce *m*; **black** (*BRIT*) or **blood** (*US*) ~ morcela; **rice** ~ pudim de arroz.

puddle ['pʌdl] *n* poça.

puerile ['pjuəraɪl] *adj* infantil.

Puerto Rico ['pwəːtəu'riːkəu] *n* Porto Rico (*no article*).

Puerto Rican ['pwəːtə'riːkən] *adj*, *n* portoriquenho/a.

NB: European Portuguese adds the following consonants to certain words: **b** (sú(b)dito, su(b)til); **c** (a(c)ção, a(c)cionista, a(c)to); **m** (inde(m)ne); **p** (ado(p)ção, ado(p)tar); *for further details see p. xiii.*

puff [pʌf] *n* sopro; *(from mouth)* baforada; *(gust)* rajada, lufada; *(sound)* sopro; *(also: powder ~)* pompom *m* ♦ *vt:* **to ~ one's pipe** tirar baforadas do cachimbo ♦ *vi* soprar; *(pant)* arquejar.
   puff out *vt (sails)* enfunar; *(cheeks)* encher; **to ~ out smoke** lançar baforadas.
   puff up *vt* inflar.
puffed [pʌft] *(inf) adj (out of breath)* sem fôlego.
puffin ['pʌfɪn] *n* papagaio-do-mar *m*.
puff pastry *(US* **puff paste)** *n* massa folhada.
puffy ['pʌfɪ] *adj* inchado, entumecido.
pugnacious [pʌg'neɪʃəs] *adj* pugnaz, brigão/ona.
pull [pul] *n (of magnet, sea etc)* atração *f*; *(influence)* influência; *(tug):* **to give sth a ~** dar um puxão em algo ♦ *vt* puxar; *(muscle)* distender ♦ *vi* puxar, dar um puxão; **to ~ a face** fazer careta; **to ~ to pieces** picar em pedacinhos; **to ~ one's punches** não usar toda a força; **to ~ one's weight** fazer a sua parte; **to ~ o.s. together** recompor-se; **to ~ sb's leg** *(fig)* brincar com alguém, sacanear alguém *(inf)*; **to ~ strings for sb** mexer os pauzinhos para alguém.
   pull about *(BRIT) vt (handle roughly)* maltratar.
   pull apart *vt* separar; *(break)* romper.
   pull down *vt* abaixar; *(house)* demolir, derrubar; *(tree)* abater, derrubar.
   pull in *vi (AUT: at the kerb)* encostar; *(RAIL)* chegar (na plataforma).
   pull off *vt* tirar; *(deal etc)* acertar.
   pull out *vi* arrancar, partir; *(withdraw)* retirar-se; *(AUT: from kerb)* sair ♦ *vt* tirar, arrancar; **to ~ out in front of sb** *(AUT)* dar uma fechada em alguém.
   pull over *vi (AUT)* encostar.
   pull round *vi (unconscious person)* voltar a si; *(sick person)* recuperar-se.
   pull through *vi* sair-se bem (de um aperto); *(MED)* sobreviver.
   pull up *vi (stop)* deter-se, parar ♦ *vt* levantar; *(uproot)* desarraigar, arrancar; *(stop)* parar.
pulley ['pulɪ] *n* roldana.
pull-out *n (withdrawal)* retirada; *(section: in magazine, newspaper)* encarte *m* ♦ *cpd (magazine, pages)* destacável.
pullover ['puləuvə*] *n* pulóver *m*.
pulp [pʌlp] *n (of fruit)* polpa; *(for paper)* pasta, massa; **to reduce sth to a ~** amassar algo.
pulpit ['pulpɪt] *n* púlpito.
pulsate [pʌl'seɪt] *vi* pulsar, palpitar; *(music)* vibrar.
pulse [pʌls] *n (ANAT)* pulso; *(of music, engine)* cadência; **~s** *npl (CULIN)* legumes *mpl*; **to feel** *or* **take sb's ~** tomar o pulso de alguém; **~ rate** freqüência de pulsos.
pulverize ['pʌlvəraɪz] *vt* pulverizar; *(fig)* esmagar, aniquilar.
puma ['pjuːmə] *n* puma, onça-parda.
pumice ['pʌmɪs] *n (also: ~ stone)* pedra-

pomes *f*.
pummel ['pʌml] *vt* esmurrar, socar.
pump [pʌmp] *n* bomba; *(shoe)* sapatilha (de dança) ♦ *vt* bombear; *(fig: inf)* sondar; **to ~ sb for information** tentar extrair informações de alguém.
   pump up *vt* encher.
pumpkin ['pʌmpkɪn] *n* abóbora.
pun [pʌn] *n* jogo de palavras, trocadilho.
punch [pʌntʃ] *n (blow)* soco, murro; *(tool)* punção *m*; *(for tickets)* furador *m*; *(drink)* ponche *m*; *(fig: force)* vigor *m*, força ♦ *vt (make a hole in)* perfurar, picotar; *(hit):* **to ~ sb/sth** esmurrar *or* socar alguém/algo.
   punch in *(US) vi* assinar o ponto na entrada.
   punch out *(US) vi* assinar o ponto na saída.
punch-drunk *(BRIT) adj* estupidificado.
punch(ed) card [pʌntʃ(t)-] *n* cartão *m* perfurado.
punch line *n (of joke)* remate *m*.
punch-up *(inf) n* briga.
punctual ['pʌŋktjuəl] *adj* pontual.
punctuality [pʌŋktju'ælɪtɪ] *n* pontualidade *f*.
punctually ['pʌŋktjuəlɪ] *adv* pontualmente; **it will start ~ at 6** começará às 6 horas em ponto.
punctuate ['pʌŋktjueɪt] *vt* pontuar.
punctuation [pʌŋktju'eɪʃən] *n* pontuação *f*.
punctuation marks *npl* sinais *mpl* de pontuação.
puncture ['pʌŋktʃə*] *(BRIT) n* picada, furo; *(flat tyre)* pneu *m* furado ♦ *vt* picar, furar; *(tyre)* furar; **I have a ~** *(AUT)* estou com um pneu furado.
pundit ['pʌndɪt] *n* entendedor(a) *m/f*.
pungent ['pʌndʒənt] *adj* pungente, acre; *(fig)* mordaz.
punish ['pʌnɪʃ] *vt* punir, castigar; **to ~ sb for sth/for doing sth** punir alguém por algo/por ter feito algo.
punishable ['pʌnɪʃəbl] *adj* punível, castigável.
punishing ['pʌnɪʃɪŋ] *adj (fig: exhausting)* desgastante ♦ *n* punição *f*.
punishment ['pʌnɪʃmənt] *n* castigo, punição *f*; *(fig: wear)* desgaste *m*.
punk [pʌŋk] *n (person: also: ~ rocker)* punk *m/f*; *(music: also: ~ rock)* punk *m*; *(US: inf: hoodlum)* pinta-brava *m*.
punt [pʌnt] *n (boat)* chalana.
punter ['pʌntə*] *(BRIT) n (gambler)* jogador(a) *m/f*; *(inf: client)* cliente *m/f*.
puny ['pjuːnɪ] *adj* débil, fraco.
pup [pʌp] *n (dog)* cachorrinho *(BR)*, cachorro *(PT)*; *(seal etc)* filhote *m*.
pupil ['pjuːpl] *n* aluno/a.
puppet ['pʌpɪt] *n* marionete *f*, títere *m*.
puppet government *n* governo fantoche *or* títere.
puppy ['pʌpɪ] *n* cachorrinho *(BR)*, cachorro *(PT)*.
purchase ['pəːtʃɪs] *n* compra; *(grip)* ponto de apoio ♦ *vt* comprar; **to get a ~ on** apoiar-se em.
purchase order *n* ordem *f* de compra.

purchase price *n* preço de compra.
purchaser ['pɔːtʃɪsə*] *n* comprador(a) *m/f*.
purchase tax (*BRIT*) *n* ≈ imposto de circulação de mercadorias.
purchasing power ['pɔːtʃɪsɪŋ-] *n* poder *m* aquisitivo.
pure [pjuə*] *adj* puro; **a ~ wool jumper** um pulôver de pura lã; **~ and simple** puro e simples.
purebred ['pjuəbred] *adj* de sangue puro.
purée ['pjuəreɪ] *n* purê *m*.
purely ['pjuəlɪ] *adv* puramente; (*only*) meramente.
purge [pɔːdʒ] *n* (*MED*) purgante *m*; (*POL*) expurgo ♦ *vt* purgar; (*POL*) expurgar.
purification [pjuərɪfɪ'keɪʃən] *n* purificação *f*, depuração *f*.
purify ['pjuərɪfaɪ] *vt* purificar, depurar.
purist ['pjuərɪst] *n* purista *m/f*.
puritan ['pjuərɪtən] *n* puritano/a.
puritanical [pjuərɪ'tænɪkl] *adj* puritano.
purity ['pjuərɪtɪ] *n* pureza *f*.
purl [pɔːl] *n* ponto reverso ♦ *vt* fazer ponto de tricô.
purloin [pɔː'lɔɪn] *vt* surripiar.
purple ['pɔːpl] *adj* roxo, purpúreo.
purport [pɔː'pɔːt] *vi*: **to ~ to be/do** dar a entender que é/faz.
purpose ['pɔːpəs] *n* propósito, objetivo; **on ~** de propósito; **for teaching ~s** para fins pedagógicos; **for the ~s of this meeting** para esta reunião; **to no ~** em vão.
purpose-built (*BRIT*) *adj* feito sob medida.
purposeful ['pɔːpəsful] *adj* decidido, resoluto.
purposely ['pɔːpəslɪ] *adv* de propósito.
purr [pɔː*] *n* ronrom *m* ♦ *vi* ronronar.
purse [pɔːs] *n* carteira; (*US: bag*) bolsa ♦ *vt* enrugar, franzir.
purser ['pɔːsə*] *n* (*NAUT*) comissário de bordo.
purse snatcher [-'snætʃə*] *n* trombadinha *m/f*.
pursue [pə'sjuː] *vt* perseguir; (*profession*) exercer; (*inquiry, matter*) prosseguir.
pursuer [pə'sjuːə*] *n* perseguidor(a) *m/f*.
pursuit [pə'sjuːt] *n* (*chase*) caça; (*persecution*) perseguição *f*; (*occupation*) ocupação *f*, atividade *f*; (*pastime*) passatempo; **in (the) ~ of sth** em busca de algo.
purveyor [pə'veɪə*] *n* fornecedor(a) *m/f*.
pus [pʌs] *n* pus *m*.
push [puʃ] *n* empurrão *m*; (*attack*) ataque *m*, arremetida; (*advance*) avanço ♦ *vt* empurrar; (*button*) apertar; (*promote*) promover; (*thrust*): **to ~ sth (into)** enfiar algo (em) ♦ *vi* empurrar; **to ~ a door open/shut** abrir/fechar uma porta empurrando-a; *"~"* (*on door*) "empurre"; (*on bell*) "aperte"; **to ~ for** (*better conditions, pay*) reivindicar; **to be ~ed for time/money** estar com pouco tempo/dinheiro; **she is ~ing fifty** (*inf*) ela está beirando os 50; **at a ~** (*BRIT: inf*) em último caso.

push aside *vt* afastar com a mão.
push in *vi* introduzir-se à força.
push off (*inf*) *vi* dar o fora.
push on *vi* (*continue*) prosseguir.
push over *vt* derrubar.
push through *vt* (*measure*) forçar a aceitação de.
push up *vt* (*total, prices*) forçar a alta de.
push-bike (*BRIT*) *n* bicicleta.
push-button *adj* por botões de pressão.
pushchair ['puʃtʃeə*] (*BRIT*) *n* carrinho.
pusher ['puʃə*] *n* (*also: drug ~*) traficante *m/f* or passador(a) *m/f* de drogas.
pushing ['puʃɪŋ] *adj* empreendedor(a).
pushover ['puʃəuvə*] (*inf*) *n*: **it's a ~** é sopa.
push-up (*US*) *n* flexão *f*.
pushy ['puʃɪ] (*pej*) *adj* intrometido, agressivo.
puss [pus] *n* gatinho.
pussy(-cat) ['pusɪ-] *n* gatinho.
put [put] (*pt, pp* **put**) *vt* (*place*) pôr, colocar; (*~ into*) meter; (*say*) dizer, expressar; (*a question*) fazer; (*estimate*) avaliar, calcular; **to ~ sb in a good/bad mood** deixar alguém de bom/mau humor; **to ~ sb to bed** pôr alguém para dormir; **to ~ sb to a lot of trouble** incomodar alguém; **how shall I ~ it?** como dizer?; **to ~ a lot of time into sth** investir muito tempo em algo; **to ~ money on a horse** apostar num cavalo; **I ~ it to you that ...** (*BRIT*) eu gostaria de colocar que ...; **to stay ~** não se mexer.
put about *vi* (*NAUT*) mudar de rumo ♦ *vt* (*rumour*) espalhar.
put across *vt* (*ideas etc*) comunicar.
put aside *vt* deixar de lado.
put away *vt* (*store*) guardar.
put back *vt* (*replace*) repor; (*postpone*) adiar; (*delay, also: watch, clock*) atrasar.
put by *vt* (*money*) poupar, pôr de lado.
put down *vt* (*parcel etc*) pôr no chão; (*pay*) pagar; (*animal*) sacrificar; (*in writing*) anotar, inscrever; (*suppress: revolt etc*) sufocar; (*attribute*) atribuir.
put forward *vt* (*ideas*) apresentar, propor; (*date, clock*) adiantar.
put in *vt* (*application, complaint*) apresentar; (*gas, electricity*) instalar.
put in for *vt fus* (*job*) candidatar-se a; (*promotion, pay rise*) solicitar.
put off *vt* (*light*) apagar; (*postpone*) adiar, protelar; (*discourage*) desencorajar.
put on *vt* (*clothes, lipstick etc*) pôr; (*light etc*) acender; (*play etc*) encenar; (*food, meal*) preparar; (*weight*) ganhar; (*brake*) aplicar; (*attitude*) fingir, simular; (*accent, manner*) assumir; (*inf: tease*) fazer de criança; (*inform*): **to ~ sb on to sth** indicar algo a alguém.
put out *vt* pôr para fora; (*fire, light*) apagar; (*one's hand*) estender; (*news*) anunciar; (*rumour*) espalhar; (*tongue etc*) mostrar; (*person: inconvenience*) incomodar;

*NB: European Portuguese adds the following consonants to certain words: **b** (sú(b)dito, su(b)til); **c** (a(c)ção, a(c)cionista, a(c)to); **m** (inde(m)ne); **p** (ado(p)ção, ado(p)tar); for further details see p. xiii.*

(*BRIT*: *dislocate*) deslocar ♦ *vi* (*NAUT*): **to ~ out to sea** fazer-se ao mar; **to ~ out from Plymouth** zarpar de Plymouth.

put through *vt* (*caller, call*) transferir; **I'd like to ~ a call through to Brazil** eu gostaria de fazer uma ligação para o Brasil.

put together *vt* colocar junto(s); (*assemble*) montar; (*meal*) preparar.

put up *vt* (*raise*) levantar, erguer; (*hang*) prender; (*build*) construir, edificar; (*tent*) armar; (*increase*) aumentar; (*accommodate*) hospedar; **to ~ sb up to doing sth** incitar alguém a fazer algo; **to ~ sth up for sale** pôr algo à venda.

put upon *vt fus*: **to be ~ upon** sofrer abusos.

put up with *vt fus* suportar, agüentar.

putrid ['pju:trɪd] *adj* pútrido, podre.

putt [pʌt] *vt* (*GOLF*) fazer um putt ♦ *n* putt *m*, tacada leve.

putter ['pʌtə*] *n* (*GOLF*) putter *m*.

putting green ['pʌtɪŋ-] *n* campo de golfe em miniatura.

putty ['pʌtɪ] *n* massa de vidraceiro, betume *m*.

put-up *adj*: **~ job** embuste *m*.

puzzle ['pʌzl] *n* (*riddle*) charada; (*jigsaw*) quebra-cabeça *m*; (*also*: *crossword* ~) palavras cruzadas *fpl*; (*mystery*) enigma *m* ♦ *vt* desconcertar, confundir ♦ *vi* estar perplexo; **to ~ over** tentar entender; **to be ~d about sth** estar perplexo com algo.

puzzling ['pʌzlɪŋ] *adj* (*mysterious*) enigmático, misterioso; (*unnerving*) desconcertante; (*incomprehensible*) incompreensível.

PVC *n abbr* (= *polyvinyl chloride*) PVC *m*.

Pvt. (*US*) *abbr* (*MIL*) = **private**.

pw *abbr* (= *per week*) por semana.

PX (*US*) *n abbr* (*MIL*) = **post exchange**.

pygmy ['pɪgmɪ] *n* pigmeu/méia *m/f*.

pyjamas [pɪ'dʒɑ:məz] (*BRIT*) *npl* pijama *m* or *f*.

pylon ['paɪlən] *n* pilono, poste *m*, torre *f*.

pyramid ['pɪrəmɪd] *n* pirâmide *f*.

Pyrenees [pɪrə'ni:z] *npl*: **the ~** os Pirineus.

Pyrex ['paɪrɛks] ® *n* Pirex *m* ® ♦ *cpd*: **a ~ dish** um pirex.

python ['paɪθən] *n* pitão *m*.

Q

Q, q [kju:] *n* (*letter*) Q, q *m*; **Q for Queen** Q de Quinteta.

Qatar [kæ'tɑ:*] *n* Catar *m*.

QC (*BRIT*) *n abbr* (= *Queen's Counsel*) título dado a certos advogados.

QED *abbr* (= *quod erat demonstrandum*) QED.

QM *n abbr* = **quartermaster**.

q.t. (*inf*) *n abbr* (= *quiet*): **on the ~** de fininho.

qty *abbr* (= *quantity*) quant.

quack [kwæk] *n* (*of duck*) grasnido; (*pej*: *doctor*) curandeiro/a, charlatão/tã *m/f* ♦ *vi* grasnar.

quad [kwɔd] *abbr* = **quadrangle**; **quadruplet**.

quadrangle ['kwɔdræŋgl] *n* (*courtyard*) pátio quadrangular.

quadruped ['kwɔdruped] *n* quadrúpede *m*.

quadruple [kwɔ'drupl] *adj*, *n* quádruplo ♦ *vt*, *vi* quadruplicar.

quadruplets [kwɔ:'dru:plɪts] *npl* quadrigêmeos *mpl*, quádruplos *mpl*.

quagmire ['kwægmaɪə*] *n* lamaçal *m*, atoleiro.

quail [kweɪl] *n* (*bird*) codorniz *f*, codorna (*BR*) ♦ *vi* acovardar-se.

quaint [kweɪnt] *adj* curioso, esquisito; (*picturesque*) pitoresco.

quake [kweɪk] *vi* tremer, estremecer ♦ *n abbr* = **earthquake**.

Quaker ['kweɪkə*] *n* quacre *m/f*.

qualification [kwɔlɪfɪ'keɪʃən] *n* (*reservation*) restrição *f*, ressalva; (*modification*) modificação *f*; (*act*) qualificação *f*; (*degree*) título, qualificação; **what are your ~s?** quais são as suas qualificações?

qualified ['kwɔlɪfaɪd] *adj* (*trained*) habilitado, qualificado; (*fit*) apto, capaz; (*limited*) limitado; (*professionally*) diplomado; **~ for/to do** credenciado *or* qualificado para/para fazer.

qualify ['kwɔlɪfaɪ] *vt* qualificar; (*capacitate*) capacitar; (*modify*) modificar; (*limit*) restringir, limitar ♦ *vi* (*SPORT*) classificar-se; **to ~ (as)** *vt* classificar (como) ♦ *vi* formar-se *or* diplomar-se (em); **to ~ (for)** reunir os requisitos (para).

qualifying ['kwɔlɪfaɪɪŋ] *adj*: **~ exam** exame *m* de habilitação; **~ round** eliminatórias *fpl*.

qualitative ['kwɔlɪteɪtɪv] *adj* qualitativo.

quality ['kwɔlɪtɪ] *n* qualidade *f* ♦ *cpd* de qualidade; **of good/poor ~** de boa/má qualidade.

quality control *n* controle *m* de qualidade.

quality papers (*BRIT*) *npl*: **the ~** os jornais de categoria.

qualm [kwɑ:m] *n* (*doubt*) dúvida; (*scruple*) escrúpulo; **to have ~s about sth** ter dúvidas sobre a retidão de algo.

quandary ['kwɔndrɪ] *n*: **to be in a ~** estar num dilema.

quango ['kwæŋgəu] (*BRIT*) *n abbr* (= *quasiautonomous non-governmental organization*) comissão nomeada pelo governo.

quantitative ['kwɔntɪtətɪv] *adj* quantitativo.

quantity ['kwɔntɪtɪ] *n* quantidade *f*; **in ~** em quantidade.

quantity surveyor (*BRIT*) *n* calculista *m/f* de obra.

quarantine ['kwɔrnti:n] *n* quarentena.

quarrel ['kwɔrl] *n* (*argument*) discussão *f*; (*fight*) briga *f* ♦ *vi* brigar, discutir; **to have a ~ with sb** ter uma briga *or* brigar com alguém; **I have no ~ with him** não tenho nada contra ele; **I can't ~ with that** não posso discordar disso.

quarrelsome ['kwɔrlsəm] adj brigão/gona.

quarry ['kwɔrɪ] n (for stone) pedreira; (animal) presa, caça ♦ vt (marble etc) extrair.

quart [kwɔːt] n quarto de galão (= 1.136 l).

quarter ['kwɔːtə*] n quarto, quarta parte f; (of year) trimestre m; (district) bairro; (US, CANADA: 25 cents) (moeda de) 25 centavos mpl de dólar ♦ vt dividir em quatro; (MIL: lodge) aquartelar; ~s npl (MIL) quartel m; (living ~s) alojamento; a ~ of an hour um quarto de hora; it's a ~ to (BRIT) or of (US) 3 são quinze para as três (BR), são três menos um quarto (PT); it's a ~ past (BRIT) or after (US) 3 são três e quinze (BR), são três e um quarto (PT); from all ~s de toda parte; at close ~s de perto.

quarter-deck n (NAUT) tombadilho superior.

quarter final n quarta de final.

quarterly ['kwɔːtəlɪ] adj trimestral ♦ adv trimestralmente ♦ n (PRESS) revista trimestral.

quartermaster ['kwɔːtəmɑːstə*] n (MIL) quartel-mestre m; (NAUT) contramestre m.

quartet(te) [kwɔːˈtɛt] n quarteto.

quarto ['kwɔːtəu] adj, n in-quarto inv.

quartz [kwɔːts] n quartzo ♦ cpd de quartzo.

quash [kwɔʃ] vt (verdict) anular.

quasi- ['kweɪzaɪ] prefix quase-.

quaver ['kweɪvə*] n (BRIT: MUS) colcheia ♦ vi tremer.

quay [kiː] n (also: ~side) cais m.

queasy ['kwiːzɪ] adj (sickly) enjoado.

Quebec [kwɪˈbɛk] n Quebec.

queen [kwiːn] n rainha; (CARDS etc) dama.

queen mother n rainha-mãe f.

queer [kwɪə*] adj (odd) esquisito, estranho; (suspect) suspeito, duvidoso; (BRIT: sick): I feel ~ não estou bem ♦ n (inf!: highly offensive) bicha m (BR), maricas m (PT).

quell [kwɛl] vt abrandar, acalmar; (put down) sufocar.

quench [kwɛntʃ] vt apagar; (thirst) matar.

querulous ['kwɛruləs] adj lamuriante.

query ['kwɪərɪ] n (question) pergunta; (doubt) dúvida; (question mark) ponto de interrogação ♦ vt questionar.

quest [kwɛst] n busca; (journey) expedição f.

question ['kwɛstʃən] n pergunta; (matter) questão f ♦ vt (plan, idea) duvidar, questionar; (person) interrogar, inquirir; to ask sb a ~, to put a ~ to sb fazer uma pergunta a alguém; to bring or call sth into ~ colocar algo em questão, pôr algo em dúvida; the ~ is ... a questão é ...; it is a ~ of ... é questão de; beyond ~ sem dúvida; out of the ~ fora de cogitação, impossível.

questionable ['kwɛstʃənəbl] adj discutível; (doubtful) duvidoso.

questioner ['kwɛstʃənə*] n pessoa que faz uma pergunta (or que fez a pergunta etc).

questioning ['kwɛstʃənɪŋ] adj interrogador(a)

♦ n interrogatório.

question mark n ponto de interrogação.

questionnaire [kwɛstʃəˈnɛə*] n questionário.

queue [kjuː] (BRIT) n fila (BR), bicha (PT) ♦ vi fazer fila (BR) or bicha (PT); to jump the ~ furar a fila (BR), pôr-se à frente (PT).

quibble ['kwɪbl] vi embromar, tergiversar.

quick [kwɪk] adj rápido; (temper) vivo; (agile) ágil; (mind) sagaz, despachado ♦ adv rápido ♦ n: to cut sb to the ~ ferir alguém; be ~! ande depressa!, vai rápido!; to be ~ to act agir com rapidez; she was ~ to see that ... ela não tardou a ver que ....

quicken ['kwɪkən] vt apressar ♦ vi apressar-se.

quicklime ['kwɪklaɪm] n cal f viva.

quickly ['kwɪklɪ] adv rapidamente, depressa.

quickness ['kwɪknɪs] n rapidez f; (agility) agilidade f; (liveliness) vivacidade f.

quicksand ['kwɪksænd] n areia movediça.

quickstep ['kwɪkstɛp] n dança de ritmo rápido.

quick-tempered adj irritadiço, de pavio curto.

quick-witted [-ˈwɪtɪd] adj perspicaz, vivo.

quid [kwɪd] (BRIT: inf) n inv libra.

quid pro quo [-kwəu] n contrapartida.

quiet ['kwaɪət] adj (tranquil) tranqüilo, calmo; (person: still) quieto; (not noisy: engine) silencioso; (: person) calado; (not busy: day, business) calmo; (ceremony, colour) discreto ♦ n sossego, quietude f ♦ vt, vi (US) = quieten; keep ~! cale-se!, fique quieto!; on the ~ de fininho.

quieten ['kwaɪətən] (also: ~ down) vi (grow calm) acalmar-se; (grow silent) calar-se ♦ vt (calm) tranqüilizar; (make quiet) fazer calar.

quietly ['kwaɪətlɪ] adv tranqüilamente; (silently) silenciosamente; (talk) baixo.

quietness ['kwaɪətnɪs] n (silence) quietude f; (calm) tranqüilidade f.

quill [kwɪl] n pena (de escrever).

quilt [kwɪlt] n acolchoado, colcha; (continental) ~ (BRIT) edredom (PT: -dão) m.

quin [kwɪn] n abbr = **quintuplet**.

quince [kwɪns] n (fruit) marmelo; (tree) marmeleiro.

quinine [kwɪˈniːn] n quinina.

quintet(te) [kwɪnˈtɛt] n quinteto.

quintuplets [kwɪnˈtjuːplɪts] npl quíntuplos mpl.

quip [kwɪp] n escárnio, dito espirituoso ♦ vt: ... he ~ped ... soltou.

quire ['kwaɪə*] n mão f (de papel).

quirk [kwɔːk] n peculiaridade f; by some ~ of fate por uma singularidade do destino, por uma dessas coisas que acontecem.

quit [kwɪt] (pt, pp quit or ~ted) vt deixar; (premises) desocupar ♦ vi parar; (give up) desistir; (resign) demitir-se; to ~ doing parar or deixar de fazer; ~ stalling! (US: inf) chega de evasivas!; notice to ~ (BRIT) aviso para desocupar (um imóvel).

quite [kwaɪt] *adv* (*rather*) bastante; (*entirely*) completamente, totalmente; ~ **new** novinho; **she's** ~ **pretty** ela é bem bonita; **I** ~ **understand** eu entendo completamente; ~ **a few of them** um bom número deles; **that's not** ~ **right** não é bem assim; **not** ~ **as many as last time** um pouco menos do que da vez passada; ~ **(so)!** exatamente!, isso mesmo!

Quito [ˈkiːtəu] *n* Quito.

quits [kwɪts] *adj*: ~ **(with)** quite (com); **let's call it** ~ ficamos quites.

quiver [ˈkwɪvə*] *vi* estremecer ♦ *n* (*for arrows*) carcás *m*, aljava.

quiz [kwɪz] *n* (*game*) concurso (de cultura geral); (*in magazine etc*) questionário, teste *m* ♦ *vt* interrogar.

quizzical [ˈkwɪzɪkəl] *adj* zombeteiro.

quoits [kwɔɪts] *npl* jogo de malha.

quorum [ˈkwɔːrəm] *n* quorum *m*.

quota [ˈkwəutə] *n* cota, quota.

quotation [kwəuˈteɪʃən] *n* citação *f*; (*estimate*) orçamento; (*of shares*) cotação *f*.

quotation marks *npl* aspas *fpl*.

quote [kwəut] *n* citação *f*; (*COMM*) orçamento ♦ *vt* (*sentence*) citar; (*price*) propor; (*shares*) cotar ♦ *vi*: **to** ~ **from** citar; ~**s** *npl* aspas *fpl*; **to** ~ **for a job** propor um preço para um trabalho; **in** ~**s** entre aspas; ~ ... **unquote** (*in dictation*) abre aspas ... fecha aspas.

quotient [ˈkwəuʃənt] *n* quociente *m*.

qv *abbr* (= *quod vide: which see*) vide.

qwerty keyboard [ˈkwɔːtɪ-] *n* teclado qwerty.

R

R, r [ɑː*] *n* (*letter*) R, r *m*; **R for Robert** (*BRIT*) *or* **Roger** (*US*) R de Roberto.

R *abbr* (= *right*) dir.; (= *river*) R.; (= *Réaumur* (*scale*)) R; (*US: CINEMA*: = *restricted*) *proibido para menores de 17 anos*; (*US: POL*) = **republican**; (*BRIT*) = **Rex; Regina.**

RA *abbr* = **rear admiral** ♦ *n abbr* (*BRIT*) = **Royal Academy; Royal Academician.**

RAAF *n abbr* = **Royal Australian Air Force.**

Rabat [rəˈbɑːt] *n* Rabat.

rabbi [ˈræbaɪ] *n* rabino.

rabbit [ˈræbɪt] *n* coelho ♦ *vi*: **to** ~ **(on)** (*BRIT*) tagarelar.

rabbit hole *n* toca, lura.

rabbit hutch *n* coelheira.

rabble [ˈræbl] (*pej*) *n* povinho, ralé *f*.

rabid [ˈræbɪd] *adj* raivoso.

rabies [ˈreɪbiːz] *n* raiva.

RAC (*BRIT*) *n abbr* (= *Royal Automobile Club*)

≈ TCB *m* (*BR*), ≈ ACP *m* (*PT*).

raccoon [rəˈkuːn] *n* mão-pelada *m*, guaxinim *m*.

race [reɪs] *n* (*competition, rush*) corrida; (*species*) raça ♦ *vt* (*person*) apostar corrida com; (*horse*) fazer correr; (*engine*) acelerar ♦ *vi* (*compete*) competir; (*run*) correr; (*pulse*) bater rapidamente; **the human** ~ a raça humana; **to** ~ **in/out** *etc* entrar/sair *etc* correndo.

race car (*US*) *n* = **racing car.**

race car driver (*US*) *n* = **racing driver.**

racecourse [ˈreɪskɔːs] *n* hipódromo.

racehorse [ˈreɪshɔːs] *n* cavalo de corridas.

race relations *npl* relações *fpl* entre as raças.

racetrack [ˈreɪstræk] *n* pista de corridas; (*for cars*) autódromo.

racial [ˈreɪʃl] *adj* racial.

racialism [ˈreɪʃəlɪzəm] *n* racismo.

racialist [ˈreɪʃəlɪst] *adj, n* racista *m/f*.

racing [ˈreɪsɪŋ] *n* corrida.

racing car (*BRIT*) *n* carro de corrida.

racing driver (*BRIT*) *n* piloto/a de corrida.

racism [ˈreɪsɪzəm] *n* racismo.

racist [ˈreɪsɪst] (*pej*) *adj, n* racista *m/f*.

rack [ræk] *n* (*also: luggage* ~) bagageiro; (*shelf*) estante *f*; (*also: roof* ~) xalmas *fpl*, porta-bagagem *m*; (*clothes* ~) cabide *m* ♦ *vt* (*cause pain to*) atormentar; **to** ~ **one's brains** quebrar a cabeça; **to go to** ~ **and ruin** (*building*) cair aos pedaços; (*business*) falir.

rack up *vt* acumular.

rack-and-pinion [-ˈpɪnjən] *n* (*TECH*) cremalheira e pinhão.

racket [ˈrækɪt] *n* (*for tennis*) raquete *f* (*BR*), raqueta (*PT*); (*noise*) barulheira, zoeira; (*swindle*) negócio ilegal, fraude *f*.

racketeer [rækɪˈtɪə*] (*esp US*) *n* chantagista *m/f*.

racoon [rəˈkuːn] *n* = **raccoon.**

racquet [ˈrækɪt] *n* raquete *f* (*BR*), raqueta (*PT*).

racy [ˈreɪsɪ] *adj* ousado, picante.

RADA [ˈrɑːdə] (*BRIT*) *n abbr* = **Royal Academy of Dramatic Art.**

radar [ˈreɪdɑː*] *n* radar *m* ♦ *cpd* de radar.

radar trap *n* radar *m* rodoviário.

radial [ˈreɪdɪəl] *adj* (*also:* ~*-ply*) radial.

radiance [ˈreɪdɪəns] *n* brilho, esplendor *m*.

radiant [ˈreɪdɪənt] *adj* radiante, brilhante; (*PHYS*) radiante.

radiate [ˈreɪdɪeɪt] *vt* (*heat*) irradiar; (*emit*) emitir ♦ *vi* (*lines*) difundir-se, estender-se.

radiation [reɪdɪˈeɪʃən] *n* radiação *f*.

radiation sickness *n* radiointoxicação *f*, intoxicação *f* radioativa.

radiator [ˈreɪdɪeɪtə*] *n* radiador *m*.

radiator cap *n* tampa do radiador.

radiator grill *n* (*AUT*) grade *f* do radiador.

radical [ˈrædɪkl] *adj* radical.

radii [ˈreɪdɪaɪ] *npl of* **radius.**

radio [ˈreɪdɪəu] *n* rádio ♦ *vi*: **to** ~ **to sb** comunicar com alguém por rádio ♦ *vt* (*informa-*

tion) transmitir por rádio; (*position*) comunicar por rádio; **on the** ~ no rádio.

radioactive [reɪdɪəʊ'æktɪv] *adj* radioativo.

radioactivity [reɪdɪəʊæk'tɪvɪtɪ] *n* radioatividade *f*.

radio announcer *n* locutor(a) *m/f* de rádio.

radio-controlled [-kən'trəʊld] *adj* controlado por rádio.

radiographer [reɪdɪ'ɔgrəfə*] *n* radiógrafo/a.

radiography [reɪdɪ'ɔgrəfɪ] *n* radiografia.

radiologist [reɪdɪ'ɔlədʒɪst] *n* radiologista *m/f*.

radiology [reɪdɪ'ɔlədʒɪ] *n* radiologia.

radio station *n* emissora, estação *f* de rádio.

radio taxi *n* rádio-táxi *m*.

radiotelephone [reɪdɪəʊ'tɛlɪfəʊn] *n* radiotelefone *m*.

radiotherapist [reɪdɪəʊ'θɛrəpɪst] *n* radioterapeuta *m/f*.

radiotherapy [reɪdɪəʊ'θɛrəpɪ] *n* radioterapia.

radish ['rædɪʃ] *n* rabanete *m*.

radium ['reɪdɪəm] *n* rádio.

radius ['reɪdɪəs] (*pl* **radii**) *n* raio; (*ANAT*) rádio; **within a 50-mile** ~ dentro de um raio de 50 milhas.

RAF (*BRIT*) *n abbr* = **Royal Air Force**.

raffia ['ræfɪə] *n* ráfia.

raffish ['ræfɪʃ] *adj* reles *inv*, ordinário.

raffle ['ræfl] *n* rifa ♦ *vt* rifar.

raft [rɑːft] *n* (*also*: *life* ~) balsa; (*logs*) flutuante *m* de árvores.

rafter ['rɑːftə*] *n* viga, caibro.

rag [ræg] *n* (*piece of cloth*) trapo; (*torn cloth*) farrapo; (*pej: newspaper*) jornaleco; (*for charity*) atividades estudantis beneficentes ♦ *vt* (*BRIT*) encarnar em, zombar de; ~**s** *npl* trapos *mpl*, farrapos *mpl*; **in** ~**s** em farrapos.

rag-and-bone man (*irreg*) *n* negociante *m* de trastes.

ragbag ['rægbæg] *n* (*fig*) salada.

rag doll *n* boneca de trapo.

rage [reɪdʒ] *n* (*fury*) raiva, furor *m* ♦ *vi* (*person*) estar furioso; (*storm*) bramar; **to fly into a** ~ enfurecer-se; **it's all the** ~ é a última moda.

ragged ['rægɪd] *adj* (*edge*) irregular, desigual; (*cuff*) puído, gasto; (*appearance*) esfarrapado, andrajoso; (*coastline*) acidentado.

raging ['reɪdʒɪŋ] *adj* furioso; (*fever, pain*) violento; ~ **toothache** dor de dente alucinante; **in a** ~ **temper** enfurecido.

ragman ['rægmæn] (*irreg*) *n* negociante *m* de trastes.

rag trade (*inf*) *n*: **the** ~ a confecção e venda de roupa.

raid [reɪd] *n* (*MIL*) incursão *f*; (*criminal*) assalto; (*attack*) ataque *m*; (*by police*) batida ♦ *vt* (*MIL*) invadir, atacar; (*bank etc*) assaltar; (*subj: police*) fazer uma batida em.

raider ['reɪdə*] *n* atacante *m/f*; (*criminal*) assaltante *m/f*.

rail [reɪl] *n* (*on stair*) corrimão *m*; (*on bridge*,

balcony) parapeito, anteparo; (*of ship*) amurada; ~**s** *npl* (*for train*) trilhos *mpl*; **by** ~ de trem (*BR*), por caminho de ferro (*PT*).

railing(s) ['reɪlɪŋ(z)] *n(pl)* grade *f*.

railroad ['reɪlrəʊd] (*US*) *n* estrada (*BR*) *or* caminho (*PT*) de ferro.

railway ['reɪlweɪ] *n* estrada (*BR*) *or* caminho (*PT*) de ferro.

railway engine *n* locomotiva.

railway line *n* linha de trem (*BR*) *or* de comboio (*PT*).

railwayman ['reɪlweɪmən] (*irreg*) *n* ferroviário.

railway station *n* estação *f* ferroviária (*BR*) *or* de caminho de ferro (*PT*).

rain [reɪn] *n* chuva ♦ *vi* chover; **in the** ~ na chuva; **it's** ~**ing** está chovendo (*BR*), está a chover (*PT*); **it's** ~**ing cats and dogs** chove a cântaros.

rainbow ['reɪnbəʊ] *n* arco-íris *m inv*.

raincoat ['reɪnkəʊt] *n* impermeável *m*, capa de chuva.

raindrop ['reɪndrɔp] *n* gota de chuva.

rainfall ['reɪnfɔːl] *n* chuva; (*measurement*) pluviosidade *f*.

rainproof ['reɪnpruːf] *adj* impermeável.

rainstorm ['reɪnstɔːm] *n* chuvada torrencial.

rainwater ['reɪnwɔːtə*] *n* água pluvial.

rainy ['reɪnɪ] *adj* chuvoso; **a** ~ **day** um dia de chuva.

raise [reɪz] *n* aumento ♦ *vt* (*lift*) levantar; (*end: siege, embargo*) levantar, terminar; (*build*) erguer, edificar; (*increase*) aumentar; (*doubts*) suscitar, despertar; (*a question*) fazer, expor; (*cattle, family*) criar; (*crop*) cultivar, plantar; (*army*) recrutar, alistar; (*funds*) angariar; (*loan*) levantar, obter; **to** ~ **one's voice** levantar a voz; **to** ~ **one's glass to sb/sth** brindar à saúde de alguém/brindar algo; **to** ~ **sb's hopes** dar esperanças a alguém; **to** ~ **a laugh/smile** provocar risada/sorrisos.

raisin ['reɪzn] *n* passa, uva seca.

Raj [rɑːdʒ] *n*: **the** ~ o império (na Índia).

rajah ['rɑːdʒə] *n* rajá *m*.

rake [reɪk] *n* (*tool*) ancinho; (*person*) libertino ♦ *vt* (*garden*) revolver *or* limpar com o ancinho; (*fire*) remover as cinzas de; (*with machine gun*) varrer ♦ *vi*: **to** ~ **through** (*fig: search*) vasculhar.

rake-off (*inf*) *n* comissão *f*.

rakish ['reɪkɪʃ] *adj* (*dissolute*) devasso, dissoluto; **at a** ~ **angle** de banda, inclinado.

rally ['rælɪ] *n* (*POL etc*) comício; (*AUT*) rally *m*, rali *m*; (*TENNIS*) rebatida ♦ *vt* reunir ♦ *vi* reorganizar-se; (*sick person, Stock Exchange*) recuperar-se.

rally round *vi* dar apoio ♦ *vt fus* dar apoio a.

rallying point ['rælɪŋ-] *n* (*POL, MIL*) ponto de encontro.

RAM [ræm] *n abbr* (*COMPUT: = random access*

memory) RAM *f*.

ram [ræm] *n* carneiro; (*TECH*) êmbolo, aríete *m* ♦ *vt* (*push*) cravar; (*crash into*) colidir com; (*tread down*) pisar, calcar.

ramble ['ræmbl] *n* caminhada, excursão *f* a pé ♦ *vi* (*pej: also:* ~ *on*) divagar.

rambler ['ræmblə*] *n* caminhante *m/f*; (*BOT*) roseira trepadeira.

rambling ['ræmblɪŋ] *adj* (*speech*) desconexo, incoerente; (*house*) cheio de recantos; (*plant*) rastejante ♦ *n* excursionismo.

RAMC (*BRIT*) *n abbr* = **Royal Army Medical Corps**.

ramification [ræmɪfɪ'keɪʃən] *n* ramificação *f*.

ramp [ræmp] *n* (*incline*) rampa; (*in road*) lombada.

rampage [ræm'peɪdʒ] *n*: **to be on the** ~ alvoroçar-se ♦ *vi*: **they went rampaging through the town** correram feito loucos pela cidade.

rampant ['ræmpənt] *adj* (*disease etc*) violento, implacável.

rampart ['ræmpɑːt] *n* baluarte *m*; (*wall*) muralha.

ramshackle ['ræmʃækl] *adj* caindo aos pedaços.

RAN *n abbr* = **Royal Australian Navy**.

ran [ræn] *pt of* **run**.

ranch [rɑːntʃ] *n* rancho, fazenda, estância.

rancher ['rɑːntʃə*] *n* rancheiro/a, fazendeiro/a.

rancid ['rænsɪd] *adj* rançoso, râncio.

rancour ['ræŋkə*] (*US* **rancor**) *n* rancor *m*.

random ['rændəm] *adj* ao acaso, casual, fortuito; (*COMPUT, MATH*) aleatório ♦ *n*: **at** ~ a esmo, aleatoriamente.

random access memory *n* (*COMPUT*) memória de acesso randômico *or* aleatório.

randy ['rændɪ] (*BRIT: inf*) *adj* de fogo.

rang [ræŋ] *pt of* **ring**.

range [reɪndʒ] *n* (*of mountains*) cadeia, cordilheira; (*of missile*) alcance *m*; (*of voice*) extensão *f*; (*series*) série *f*; (*of products*) gama, sortimento; (*MIL: also: shooting* ~) estande *m*; (*also: kitchen* ~) fogão *m* ♦ *vt* (*place*) colocar; (*arrange*) arrumar, ordenar ♦ *vi*: **to** ~ **over** (*wander*) percorrer; (*extend*) estender-se por; **to** ~ **from ... to ...** variar de ... a ..., oscilar entre ... e ...; **do you have anything else in this price** ~? você tem outras coisas dentro desta faixa de preço?; **within (firing)** ~ ao alcance de tiro; ~**d left/right** (*text*) alinhado à esquerda/ direita.

ranger ['reɪndʒə*] *n* guarda-florestal *m/f*.

Rangoon [ræŋ'guːn] *n* Rangum.

rank [ræŋk] *n* (*row*) fila, fileira; (*MIL*) posto; (*status*) categoria, posição *f*; (*BRIT: also: taxi* ~) ponto de táxi ♦ *vi*: **to** ~ **among** figurar entre ♦ *vt*: **I** ~ **him sixth** eu o coloco em sexto lugar ♦ *adj* (*stinking*) fétido, malcheiroso; (*hypocrisy, injustice*) total; **the** ~**s** *npl* (*MIL*) a tropa; **the** ~ **and file** (*fig*) a gente comum; **to close** ~**s** (*MIL, fig*) cerrar fileiras.

rankle ['ræŋkl] *vi* (*insult*) doer, magoar.

ransack ['rænsæk] *vt* (*search*) revistar;

(*plunder*) saquear, pilhar.

ransom ['rænsəm] *n* resgate *m*; **to hold sb to** ~ (*fig*) encostar alguém contra a parede.

rant [rænt] *vi* arengar.

ranting ['ræntɪŋ] *n* palavreado oco.

rap [ræp] *n* batida breve e seca, tapa ♦ *vt* bater de leve.

rape [reɪp] *n* estupro; (*BOT*) colza ♦ *vt* violentar, estuprar.

rape(seed) oil ['reɪp(siːd)-] *n* óleo de colza.

rapid ['ræpɪd] *adj* rápido.

rapidity [rə'pɪdɪtɪ] *n* rapidez *f*.

rapidly ['ræpɪdlɪ] *adv* rapidamente.

rapids ['ræpɪdz] *npl* (*GEO*) cachoeira.

rapist ['reɪpɪst] *n* estuprador *m*.

rapport [ræ'pɔː*] *n* harmonia, afinidade *f*.

rapt [ræpt] *adj* absorvido; **to be** ~ **in contemplation** estar contemplando embevecido.

rapture ['ræptʃə*] *n* êxtase *m*, arrebatamento; **to go into** ~**s over** extasiar-se com.

rapturous ['ræptʃərəs] *adj* extático; (*applause*) entusiasta.

rare [rɛə*] *adj* raro; (*CULIN: steak*) mal passado.

rarebit ['rɛəbɪt] *n see* **Welsh rarebit**.

rarefied ['rɛərɪfaɪd] *adj* (*air, atmosphere*) rarefeito.

rarely ['rɛəlɪ] *adv* raramente.

raring ['rɛərɪŋ] *adj*: **to be** ~ **to go** (*inf*) estar louco para começar.

rarity ['rɛərɪtɪ] *n* raridade *f*.

rascal ['rɑːskl] *n* maroto, malandro.

rash [ræʃ] *adj* impetuoso, precipitado ♦ *n* (*MED*) exantema *m*, erupção *f* cutânea; **he came out in a** ~ apareceu-lhe uma irritação na pele.

rasher ['ræʃə*] *n* fatia fina.

rashness ['ræʃnɪs] *n* impetuosidade *f*.

rasp [rɑːsp] *n* (*tool*) lima, raspadeira ♦ *vt* (*speak: also:* ~ *out*) falar em voz áspera.

raspberry ['rɑːzbərɪ] *n* framboesa.

raspberry bush *n* framboeseira.

rasping ['rɑːspɪŋ] *adj*: **a** ~ **noise** um ruído áspero *or* irritante.

rat [ræt] *n* rato (*BR*), ratazana (*PT*).

ratable ['reɪtəbl] *adj* = **rateable**.

ratchet ['rætʃɪt] *n* (*TECH*) roquete *m*, catraca.

rate [reɪt] *n* (*ratio*) razão *f*; (*percentage*) percentagem *f*, proporção *f*; (*price*) preço, taxa; (: *of hotel*) diária; (*of interest*) taxa; (*speed*) velocidade *f* ♦ *vt* (*value*) taxar; (*estimate*) avaliar; ~**s** *npl* (*BRIT*) imposto predial e territorial; **to** ~ **as** ser considerado como; **to** ~ **sb/sth as** considerar alguém/algo como; **to** ~ **sth among** considerar algo como um(a) dos/das; **to** ~ **sb/sth highly** valorizar alguém/algo; **at a** ~ **of 60 kph** à velocidade de 60 kph; **at any** ~ de qualquer modo; ~ **of exchange** taxa de câmbio; ~ **of growth** taxa de crescimento; ~ **of return** taxa de retorno.

rateable value ['reɪtəbl-] (*BRIT*) *n* valor *m* tributável (*de um imóvel*).

ratepayer ['reɪtpeɪə*] (*BRIT*) *n* contribuinte *m/f* de imposto predial.

rather ['rɑːðə*] *adv* (*somewhat*) um tanto,

meio; **it's ~ expensive** é meio caro; **there's ~ a lot** há bastante *or* muito; **~ than** em vez de; **I would** *or* **I'd ~ go** preferiria *or* preferia ir; **I'd ~ not leave** eu preferiria *or* preferia não sair; **or ~** (*more accurately*) ou melhor; **I ~ think he won't come** eu estou achando que ele não vem.

ratification [rætɪfɪ'keɪʃən] *n* ratificação *f*.

ratify ['rætɪfaɪ] *vt* ratificar.

rating ['reɪtɪŋ] *n* (*valuation*) avaliação *f*; (*value*) valor *m*; (*standing*) posição *f*; (NAUT: *category*) posto; (: *sailor*) marinheiro; **~s** *npl* (*RADIO, TV*) índice(s) *m(pl)* de audiência.

ratio ['reɪʃɪəu] *n* razão *f*, proporção *f*; **in the ~ of 100 to 1** na proporção *or* razão de 100 para 1.

ration ['ræʃən] *n* ração *f* ♦ *vt* racionar; **~s** *npl* mantimentos *mpl*, víveres *mpl*.

rational ['ræʃənl] *adj* racional; (*solution, reasoning*) lógico; (*person*) sensato, razoável.

rationale [ræʃə'nɑːl] *n* razão *f* fundamental.

rationalization [ræʃnəlaɪ'zeɪʃən] *n* racionalização *f*.

rationalize ['ræʃənəlaɪz] *vt* racionalizar.

rationally ['ræʃənəlɪ] *adv* racionalmente; (*logically*) logicamente.

rationing ['ræʃnɪŋ] *n* racionamento.

rat poison *n* raticida *m*.

rat race *n* corre-corre *m* diário.

rattan [ræ'tæn] *n* rotim *m*.

rattle ['rætl] *n* batida, rufar *m*; (*of train etc*) chocalhada; (*of hail*) saraivada; (*object: of baby*) chocalho; (: *of sports fan*) matraca; (*of snake*) guizo ♦ *vi* chocalhar; (*small objects*) tamborilar ♦ *vt* sacudir, fazer bater; (*inf: disconcert*) desconcertar; (: *annoy*) encher.

rattlesnake ['rætlsneɪk] *n* cascavel *f*.

ratty ['rætɪ] (*inf*) *adj* rabugento.

raucous ['rɔːkəs] *adj* áspero, rouco.

raucously ['rɔːkəslɪ] *adv* em voz rouca.

ravage ['rævɪdʒ] *vt* devastar, estragar.

ravages ['rævɪdʒɪz] *npl* estragos *mpl*.

rave [reɪv] *vi* (*in anger*) encolerizar-se; (*with enthusiasm, MED*) delirar ♦ *cpd*: **~ review** (*inf*) crítica estrondosa.

raven ['reɪvən] *n* corvo.

ravenous ['rævənəs] *adj* morto de fome, esfaimado.

ravine [rə'viːn] *n* ravina, barranco.

raving ['reɪvɪŋ] *adj*: **~ lunatic** doido/a varrido/a.

ravings ['reɪvɪŋz] *npl* delírios *mpl*.

ravioli [rævɪ'əulɪ] *n* ravióli *m*.

ravish ['rævɪʃ] *vt* arrebatar; (*delight*) encantar.

ravishing ['rævɪʃɪŋ] *adj* encantador(a).

raw [rɔː] *adj* (*uncooked*) cru; (*not processed*) bruto; (*sore*) vivo; (*inexperienced*) inexperiente, novato; **to get a ~ deal** (*inf*) levar a pior.

raw material *n* matéria-prima.

ray [reɪ] *n* raio; **~ of hope** fio de esperança.

rayon ['reɪən] *n* raiom *m*.

raze [reɪz] *vt* (*also*: **~ to the ground**) arrasar, aniquilar.

razor ['reɪzə*] *n* (*open*) navalha; (*safety ~*) aparelho de barbear.

razor blade *n* gilete *m* (BR), lâmina de barbear (PT).

razzle(-dazzle) ['ræzl-] (BRIT: *inf*) *n*: **to go on the ~** cair na farra.

razzmatazz ['ræzmə'tæz] (*inf*) *n* alvoroço.

R&B *n abbr* = **rhythm and blues**.

RC *abbr* = **Roman Catholic**.

RCAF *n abbr* = **Royal Canadian Air Force**.

RCMP *n abbr* = **Royal Canadian Mounted Police**.

RCN *n abbr* = **Royal Canadian Navy**.

RD (US) *abbr* (POST) = **rural delivery**.

Rd *abbr* = **road**.

R&D *n abbr* = **research and development**.

RDC (BRIT) *n abbr* = **rural district council**.

RE (BRIT) *n abbr* = **religious education**; (MIL) = **Royal Engineers**.

re [riː] *prep* referente a.

reach [riːtʃ] *n* alcance *m*; (BOXING) campo de ação; (*of river etc*) extensão *f* ♦ *vt* alcançar, atingir; (*arrive at*) chegar em; (*achieve*) conseguir; (*stretch out*) estender, esticar ♦ *vi* alcançar; (*stretch*) estender-se; **within ~** (*object*) ao alcance (da mão); **within easy ~ (of)** (*place*) ao alcance (de); **out of** *or* **beyond ~** fora de alcance; **to ~ out for sth** estender *or* esticar a mão para pegar (em) algo; **to ~ sb by phone** comunicar-se com alguém por telefone; **can I ~ you at your hotel?** posso entrar em contato com você no seu hotel?

react [riː'ækt] *vi* reagir.

reaction [riː'ækʃən] *n* reação *f*.

reactionary [riː'ækʃənrɪ] *adj*, *n* reacionário/a.

reactor [riː'æktə*] *n* reator *m*.

read [riːd, *pt, pp* red] *vi* ler ♦ *vt* ler; (*understand*) compreender; (*study*) estudar; **to take sth as read** (*fig*) considerar algo como garantido; **do you ~ me?** (TEL) está me ouvindo?; **to ~ between the lines** ler nas entrelinhas.

read out *vt* ler em voz alta.

read over *vt* reler.

read through *vt* (*quickly*) dar uma lida em; (*thoroughly*) ler até o fim.

read up (on) *vt fus* estudar.

readable ['riːdəbl] *adj* (*writing*) legível; (*book*) que merece ser lido.

reader ['riːdə*] *n* leitor(a) *m/f*; (*book*) livro de leituras; (BRIT: *at university*) professor(a) *m/f* adjunto/a.

readership ['riːdəʃɪp] *n* (*of paper: readers*) leitores *mpl*; (: *number of readers*) número de leitores.

readily ['redɪlɪ] *adv* (*willingly*) de boa vontade; (*easily*) facilmente; (*quickly*) sem demora, prontamente.

readiness ['rɛdɪnɪs] *n* boa vontade *f*, prontidão *f*; (*preparedness*) preparação *f*; **in ~** (*prepared*) preparado, pronto.

reading ['ri:dɪŋ] *n* leitura; (*understanding*) compreensão *f*; (*on instrument*) indicação *f*.

reading lamp *n* lâmpada de leitura.

reading room *n* sala de leitura.

readjust [ri:ə'dʒʌst] *vt* reajustar ♦ *vi* (*person*): **to ~ to** reorientar-se para.

ready ['rɛdɪ] *adj* pronto, preparado; (*willing*) disposto; (*available*) disponível ♦ *adv*: **~-cooked** pronto para comer ♦ *n*: **at the ~** (*MIL*) pronto para atirar; (*fig*) pronto; **~ for use** pronto para o uso; **to be ~ to do sth** estar pronto *or* preparado para fazer algo; **to get ~** *vi* preparar-se ♦ *vt* preparar.

ready cash *n* dinheiro vivo.

ready-made *adj* (já) feito; (*clothes*) pronto.

ready-mix *n* (*for cakes etc*) massa pronta.

ready reckoner [-'rɛkənə*] (*BRIT*) *n* tabela de cálculos feitos.

ready-to-wear *adj* pronto.

reaffirm [ri:ə'fə:m] *vt* reafirmar.

reagent [ri:'eɪdʒənt] *n* reagente *m*, reativo.

real [rɪəl] *adj* real; (*genuine*) verdadeiro, autêntico; (*proper*) de verdade ♦ *adv* (*US*: *inf*: *very*) bem; **in ~ life** na vida real; **in ~ terms** em termos reais.

real estate *n* bens *mpl* imobiliários *or* de raiz.

realism ['rɪəlɪzəm] *n* realismo.

realist ['rɪəlɪst] *n* realista *m/f*.

realistic [rɪə'lɪstɪk] *adj* realista.

reality [ri:'ælɪtɪ] *n* realidade *f*; **in ~** na verdade, na realidade.

realization [rɪəlaɪ'zeɪʃən] *n* (*fulfilment*) realização *f*; (*understanding*) compreensão *f*; (*COMM*) conversão *f* em dinheiro, realização.

realize ['rɪəlaɪz] *vt* (*understand*) perceber; (*a project, COMM*: *asset*) realizar; **I ~ that ...** eu concordo que ....

really ['rɪəlɪ] *adv* realmente, na verdade; **~?** é mesmo?

realm [rɛlm] *n* reino.

real-time *adj* (*COMPUT*) em tempo real.

realtor ['rɪəltə*] (*US*) *n* corretor(a) *m/f* de imóveis (*BR*), agente *m/f* imobiliário/a (*PT*).

ream [ri:m] *n* resma; **~s** *npl* (*fig*: *inf*) páginas *fpl* e páginas.

reap [ri:p] *vt* segar, ceifar; (*fig*) colher.

reaper ['ri:pə*] *n* segador(a) *m/f*, ceifeiro/a; (*machine*) segadora.

reappear [ri:ə'pɪə*] *vi* reaparecer.

reappearance [ri:ə'pɪərəns] *n* reaparição *f*.

reapply [ri:ə'plaɪ] *vi*: **to ~ for** requerer de novo; (*job*) candidatar-se de novo a.

reappraisal [ri:ə'preɪzl] *n* reavaliação *f*.

rear [rɪə*] *adj* traseiro, de trás ♦ *n* traseira; (*inf*: *bottom*) traseiro ♦ *vt* (*cattle, family*) criar ♦ *vi* (*also*: **~ up**: *animal*) empinar-se.

rear-engined [-'ɛndʒɪnd] *adj* (*AUT*) com motor traseiro.

rearguard ['rɪəgɑ:d] *n* retaguarda.

rearm [ri:'ɑ:m] *vt*, *vi* rearmar.

rearmament [ri:'ɑ:məmənt] *n* rearmamento *m*.

rearrange [ri:ə'reɪndʒ] *vt* arrumar de novo, reorganizar.

rear-view mirror *n* (*AUT*) espelho retrovisor.

reason ['ri:zn] *n* razão *f* ♦ *vi*: **to ~ with sb** argumentar com *or* persuadir alguém; **the ~ for/why** a razão de/pela qual; **to have ~ to think** ter motivo para pensar; **it stands to ~ that** é razoável *or* lógico que; **she claims with good ~ that ...** ela afirma com toda a razão que ...; **all the more ~ why you should not sell it** mais uma razão para você não vendê-lo.

reasonable ['ri:znəbl] *adj* razoável; (*sensible*) sensato.

reasonably ['ri:znəblɪ] *adv* razoavelmente; **one can ~ assume that ...** tudo indica que ....

reasoned ['ri:znd] *adj* (*argument*) fundamentado.

reasoning ['ri:znɪŋ] *n* raciocínio, argumentação *f*.

reassemble [ri:ə'sɛmbl] *vt* (*people*) reunir; (*machine*) montar de novo ♦ *vi* reunir-se de novo.

reassert [ri:ə'sə:t] *vt* reafirmar.

reassurance [ri:ə'ʃuərəns] *n* garantia; (*comfort*) reconforto.

reassure [ri:ə'ʃuə*] *vt* tranqüilizar, animar; **to ~ sb of** reafirmar a confiança de alguém acerca de.

reassuring [ri:ə'ʃuərɪŋ] *adj* animador(a), tranqüilizador(a).

reawakening [ri:ə'weɪknɪŋ] *n* despertar *m*.

rebate ['ri:beɪt] *n* (*on product*) abatimento; (*on tax etc*) devolução *f*; (*refund*) reembolso.

rebel [*n* 'rɛbl, *vi* rɪ'bɛl] *n* rebelde *m/f* ♦ *vi* rebelar-se.

rebellion [rɪ'bɛljən] *n* rebelião *f*, revolta.

rebellious [rɪ'bɛljəs] *adj* insurreto; (*child*) rebelde.

rebirth [ri:'bə:θ] *n* renascimento.

rebound [*vi* rɪ'baund, *n* 'ri:baund] *vi* (*ball*) ressaltar ♦ *n* ressalto.

rebuff [rɪ'bʌf] *n* repulsa, recusa ♦ *vt* repelir.

rebuild [ri:'bɪld] (*irreg*) *vt* reconstruir.

rebuke [rɪ'bju:k] *n* reprimenda, censura ♦ *vt* repreender.

rebut [rɪ'bʌt] *vt* refutar.

rebuttal [rɪ'bʌtl] *n* refutação *f*.

recalcitrant [rɪ'kælsɪtrənt] *adj* recalcitrante, teimoso.

recall [rɪ'kɔ:l] *vt* (*remember*) recordar, lembrar; (*ambassador etc*) mandar voltar ♦ *n* chamada (de volta); (*memory*) recordação *f*; **it is beyond ~** caiu no esquecimento.

recant [rɪ'kænt] *vi* retratar-se.

recap ['ri:kæp] *vt*, *vi* recapitular ♦ *n* recapitulação *f*.

recapture [ri:'kæptʃə*] *vt* (*town*) retomar, recobrar; (*atmosphere*) recriar.

recd. *abbr* = **received**.

recede [rɪ'si:d] *vi* (*go back*) retroceder; (*go*

away) afastar-se.

receding [rɪ'siːdɪŋ] *adj (forehead, chin)* metido *or* puxado para dentro; ~ **hairline** entradas *fpl* (no cabelo).

receipt [rɪ'siːt] *n (document)* recibo; *(act of receiving)* recebimento (*BR*), recepção *f (PT)*; ~**s** *npl (COMM)* receitas *fpl*; **on** ~ **of** ao receber; **to acknowledge** ~ **of** acusar o recebimento (*BR*) *or* a recepção *(PT)* de; **we are in** ~ **of** ... recebimos ....

receivable [rɪ'siːvəbl] *adj (COMM)* a receber.

receive [rɪ'siːv] *vt* receber; *(guest)* acolher; *(wound)* sofrer; "~**d with thanks**" *(COMM)* "recebido".

receiver [rɪ'siːvə*] *n (TEL)* fone *m (BR)*, auscultador *m (PT)*; *(RADIO)* receptor *m*; *(of stolen goods)* receptador(a) *m/f*; *(COMM)* curador(a) *m/f or* síndico/a de massa falida.

recent ['riːsnt] *adj* recente; **in** ~ **years** nos últimos anos.

recently ['riːsntlɪ] *adv (a short while ago)* recentemente; *(in recent times)* ultimamente; **as** ~ **as yesterday** ainda ontem; **until** ~ até recentemente.

receptacle [rɪ'sɛptɪkl] *n* receptáculo, recipiente *m*.

reception [rɪ'sɛpʃən] *n* recepção *f*; *(welcome)* acolhida.

reception centre (*BRIT*) *n* centro de recepção.

reception desk *n* (mesa de) recepção *f*.

receptionist [rɪ'sɛpʃənɪst] *n* recepcionista *m/f*.

receptive [rɪ'sɛptɪv] *adj* receptivo.

recess [rɪ'sɛs] *n (in room)* recesso, vão *m*; *(for bed)* nicho; *(secret place)* esconderijo; *(POL etc: holiday)* férias *fpl*; *(US: LAW: short break)* recesso; *(SCH: esp US)* recreio.

recession [rɪ'sɛʃən] *n* recessão *f*.

recharge [riː'tʃɑːdʒ] *vt (battery)* recarregar.

rechargeable [riː'tʃɑːdʒəbl] *adj* recarregável.

recipe ['rɛsɪpɪ] *n* receita.

recipient [rɪ'sɪpɪənt] *n* recipiente *m/f*, recebedor(a) *m/f*; *(of letter)* destinatário/a.

reciprocal [rɪ'sɪprəkl] *adj* recíproco.

reciprocate [rɪ'sɪprəkeɪt] *vt* retribuir ♦ *vi (in hospitality etc)* retribuir; *(in aggression etc)* revidar.

recital [rɪ'saɪtl] *n* recital *m*.

recite [rɪ'saɪt] *vt (poem)* recitar; *(complaints etc)* enumerar.

reckless ['rɛkləs] *adj (driver)* imprudente; *(speed)* imprudente, excessivo; *(spender)* irresponsável.

recklessly ['rɛkləslɪ] *adv* temerariamente, sem prudência; *(spend)* irresponsavelmente.

reckon ['rɛkən] *vt (count)* calcular, contar; *(consider)* considerar; *(think)*: **I** ~ **that** ... acho que ... ♦ *vi*: **he is somebody to be** ~**ed with** ele é alguém que não pode ser esquecido; **to** ~ **without sb/sth** não levar alguém/algo em conta, não contar com alguém/algo.

reckon on *vt fus* contar com.

reckoning ['rɛkənɪŋ] *n (calculation)* cálculo; **the day of** ~ o dia do Juízo Final.

reclaim [rɪ'kleɪm] *vt (get back)* recuperar; *(land)* desbravar; *(: from sea)* aterrar; *(demand back)* reivindicar.

reclamation [rɛklə'meɪʃən] *n* recuperação *f*; *(of land from sea)* aterro.

recline [rɪ'klaɪn] *vi* reclinar-se; *(lean)* apoiarse, recostar-se.

reclining [rɪ'klaɪnɪŋ] *adj (seat)* reclinável.

recluse [rɪ'kluːs] *n* recluso/a.

recognition [rɛkəg'nɪʃən] *n* reconhecimento; **transformed beyond** ~ tão transformado que está irreconhecível; **in** ~ **of** em reconhecimento de; **to gain** ~ ser reconhecido.

recognizable ['rɛkəgnaɪzəbl] *adj* reconhecível.

recognize ['rɛkəgnaɪz] *vt* reconhecer; *(accept)* aceitar; **to** ~ **by/as** reconhecer por/como.

recoil [*vi* rɪ'kɔɪl, *n* 'riːkɔɪl] *vi* recuar ♦ *n (of gun)* coice *m*; **to** ~ **from doing sth** recusar-se a fazer algo.

recollect [rɛkə'lɛkt] *vt* lembrar, recordar.

recollection [rɛkə'lɛkʃən] *n* recordação *f*, lembrança; **to the best of my** ~ se não me falha a memória.

recommend [rɛkə'mɛnd] *vt* recomendar; **she has a lot to** ~ **her** ela tem muito a seu favor.

recommendation [rɛkəmɛn'deɪʃən] *n* recomendação *f*.

recommended retail price [rɛkə'mɛndɪd-] (*BRIT*) *n* preço máximo consumidor.

recompense ['rɛkəmpɛns] *vt* recompensar ♦ *n* recompensa.

reconcilable [rɛkən'saɪləbl] *adj (ideas)* conciliável.

reconcile ['rɛkənsaɪl] *vt (two people)* reconciliar; *(two facts)* conciliar, harmonizar; **to** ~ **o.s. to sth** resignar-se a *or* conformar-se com algo.

reconciliation [rɛkənsɪlɪ'eɪʃən] *n* reconciliação *f*.

recondite [rɪ'kɔndaɪt] *adj* obscuro.

recondition [riːkən'dɪʃən] *vt* recondicionar.

reconnaissance [rɪ'kɔnɪsns] *n (MIL)* reconhecimento.

reconnoitre [rɛkə'nɔɪtə*] (*US* **reconnoiter**) *vt (MIL)* reconhecer ♦ *vi* fazer um reconhecimento.

reconsider [riːkən'sɪdə*] *vt* reconsiderar.

reconstitute [riː'kɔnstɪtjuːt] *vt* reconstituir.

reconstruct [riːkən'strʌkt] *vt* reconstruir.

reconstruction [riːkən'strʌkʃən] *n* reconstrução *f*.

record [*n, adj* 'rɛkɔːd, *vt* rɪ'kɔːd] *n (MUS)* disco; *(of meeting etc)* ata, minuta; *(register, proof, COMPUT)* registro (*BR*), registo (*PT*); *(file)* arquivo; *(also: police* ~*)* ficha na polícia; *(written)* história; *(SPORT)* recorde *m* ♦ *vt (set down)* assentar, registrar (*BR*), registar (*PT*); *(relate)* relatar, referir; *(MUS: song etc)* gravar ♦ *adj*: **in** ~ **time** num tempo recorde; **public** ~s arquivo público; **to keep a ~ of** anotar; **to put the ~ straight** (fig) corrigir um equívoco; **he is on ~ as saying that ...** ele declarou publicamente que ...; **Italy's excellent ~** o excelente desempenho da Itália; **off the ~** adj confidencial ♦ adv confidencialmente.

record card n (in file) ficha.

recorded delivery letter [rɪˈkɔːdɪd-] (BRIT) n (POST) ≈ carta registrada (BR) or registada (PT).

recorder [rɪˈkɔːdə*] n (MUS) flauta; (TECH) indicador m mecânico; (official) escrivão/vã m/f.

record holder n (SPORT) detentor(a) m/f do recorde.

recording [rɪˈkɔːdɪŋ] n (MUS) gravação f.

recording studio n estúdio de gravação.

record library n discoteca.

record player n toca-discos m inv (BR), gira-discos m inv (PT).

recount [rɪˈkaunt] vt relatar.

re-count [n ˈriːkaunt, vt riːˈkaunt] n (POL: of votes) nova contagem f, recontagem f ♦ vt recontar.

recoup [rɪˈkuːp] vt: **to ~ one's losses** recuperar-se dos prejuízos.

recourse [rɪˈkɔːs] n recurso; **to have ~ to** recorrer a.

recover [rɪˈkʌvə*] vt recuperar; (rescue) resgatar ♦ vi (from illness) recuperar-se; (from shock) refazer-se.

re-cover vt (chair etc) revestir.

recovery [rɪˈkʌvərɪ] n recuperação f, restabelecimento; (MED) melhora.

recreate [riːkrɪˈeɪt] vt recriar.

recreation [rɛkrɪˈeɪʃən] n recreação f; (play) recreio.

recreational [rɛkrɪˈeɪʃənl] adj recreativo.

recreational vehicle (US) n kombi m.

recrimination [rɪkrɪmɪˈneɪʃən] n recriminação f.

recruit [rɪˈkruːt] n recruta m/f ♦ vt recrutar.

recruiting office [rɪˈkruːtɪŋ-] n centro de recrutamento.

recruitment [rɪˈkruːtmənt] n recrutamento.

rectangle [ˈrɛktæŋgl] n retângulo.

rectangular [rɛkˈtæŋgjulə*] adj retangular.

rectify [ˈrɛktɪfaɪ] vt retificar.

rector [ˈrɛktə*] n (REL) pároco; (SCH) reitor(a) m/f.

rectory [ˈrɛktərɪ] n presbitério, residência paroquial.

rectum [ˈrɛktəm] n (ANAT) reto.

recuperate [rɪˈkuːpəreɪt] vi restabelecer-se, recuperar-se.

recur [rɪˈkə:*] vi repetir-se, ocorrer outra vez; (opportunity) surgir de novo; (symptoms) reaparecer.

recurrence [rɪˈkʌrəns] n repetição f; (of symptoms) reaparição f.

recurrent [rɪˈkʌrənt] adj repetido, periódico.

recurring [rɪˈkə:rɪŋ] adj (MATH) periódico.

red [rɛd] n vermelho; (POL: pej) vermelho/a ♦ adj vermelho; (hair) ruivo; **to be in the ~** (person) estar no vermelho; (account) não ter fundos.

red carpet treatment n: **she was given the ~** ela foi recebida com todas as honras.

Red Cross n Cruz f Vermelha.

redcurrant [ˈrɛdˈkʌrənt] n groselha.

redden [ˈrɛdən] vt avermelhar ♦ vi corar, ruborizar-se.

reddish [ˈrɛdɪʃ] adj avermelhado; (hair) arruivado.

redecorate [riːˈdɛkəreɪt] vt decorar de novo, redecorar.

redecoration [riːdɛkəˈreɪʃən] n remodelação f.

redeem [rɪˈdiːm] vt (REL) redimir; (sth in pawn) tirar do prego; (debt, shares, also: fig) resgatar.

redeemable [rɪˈdiːməbl] adj resgatável.

redeeming [rɪˈdiːmɪŋ] adj: **~ feature** lado bom or que salva.

redeploy [riːdɪˈplɔɪ] vt (resources, troops) redistribuir.

redeployment [riːdɪˈplɔɪmənt] n redistribuição f.

redevelop [riːdɪˈvɛləp] vt renovar.

redevelopment [riːdɪˈvɛləpmənt] n renovação f.

red-haired adj ruivo.

red-handed [-ˈhændɪd] adj: **to be caught ~** ser apanhado em flagrante, ser flagrado.

redhead [ˈrɛdhɛd] n ruivo/a.

red herring n (fig) pista falsa.

red-hot adj incandescente.

redid [riːˈdɪd] pt of **redo**.

redirect [riːdaɪˈrɛkt] vt (mail) endereçar de novo.

redistribute [riːdɪˈstrɪbjuːt] vt redistribuir.

red-letter day n dia m memorável.

red light n: **to go through a ~** (AUT) avançar o sinal.

red-light district n zona (de meretrício).

redness [ˈrɛdnɪs] n vermelhidão f.

redo [riːˈduː] (irreg) vt refazer.

redolent [ˈrɛdələnt] adj: **~ of** que cheira a; (fig) que evoca.

redone [riːˈdʌn] pp of **redo**.

redouble [riːˈdʌbl] vt: **to ~ one's efforts** redobrar os esforços.

redraft [riːˈdrɑːft] vt redigir de novo.

redress [rɪˈdrɛs] n reparação f ♦ vt retificar, remediar; **to ~ the balance** restituir o equilíbrio.

Red Sea n: **the ~** o mar Vermelho.

redskin [ˈrɛdskɪn] n pele-vermelha m/f.

red tape n (fig) papelada, burocracia.

reduce [rɪˈdjuːs] vt reduzir; (lower) rebaixar; **"~ speed now"** (AUT) "diminua a velocidade"; **to ~ sth by/to** diminuir algo em/reduzir algo a; **to ~ sb to tears/despair** levar alguém às lágrimas/ao desespero.

reduced [rɪˈdjuːst] adj: **"greatly ~ prices"** "preços altamente reduzidos"; **at a ~ price** a preço reduzido.

reduction [rɪˈdʌkʃən] n redução f; (of price) abatimento; (discount) desconto.

redundancy [rɪˈdʌndənsɪ] n redundância;

(*BRIT*: *of worker*) demissão *f*; **compulsory ~** demissão; **voluntary ~** demissão voluntária.

redundancy payment (*BRIT*) *n* indenização paga aos empregados dispensados sem justa causa.

redundant [rɪ'dʌndnt] *adj* (*BRIT*: *worker*) desempregado; (*detail*, *object*) redundante, supérfluo; **to be made ~** ficar sem trabalho or desempregado.

reed [riːd] *n* (*BOT*) junco; (*MUS*: *of clarinet etc*) palheta.

reedy ['riːdɪ] *adj* (*voice*, *instrument*) agudo.

reef [riːf] *n* (*at sea*) recife *m*.

reek [riːk] *vi*: **to ~ (of)** cheirar (a), feder (a).

reel [riːl] *n* carretel *m*, bobina; (*of film*) rolo, filme *m* ♦ *vt* (*TECH*) bobinar; (*also*: **~ up**) enrolar ♦ *vi* (*sway*) cambalear, oscilar; **my head is ~ing** estou completamente confuso.

reel off *vt* (*say*) enumerar, recitar.

re-election *n* reeleição *f*.

re-enter *vt* reentrar em.

re-entry *n* reentrada.

re-export [*vt* riːɪks'pɔːt, *n* riː'ekspɔːt] *vt* reexportar ♦ *n* reexportação *f*.

ref [ref] (*inf*) *n abbr* = **referee**.

ref. *abbr* (*COMM*: = *reference*) ref.

refectory [rɪ'fektərɪ] *n* refeitório.

refer [rɪ'fɜː*] *vt*: **to ~ sth to** (*dispute*, *decision*) submeter algo à apreciação de; **to ~ sb to** (*inquirer*: *for information*) encaminhar alguém a; (*reader*: *to text*) remeter alguém a.

refer to *vt fus* (*allude to*) referir-se or aludir a; (*apply to*) aplicar-se a; (*consult*) recorrer a; **~ring to your letter** (*COMM*) com referência à sua carta.

referee [refə'riː] *n* árbitro/a; (*BRIT*: *for job application*) referência ♦ *vt* arbitrar; (*football match*) apitar.

reference ['refrəns] *n* referência; **with ~ to** com relação a; (*COMM*: *in letter*) com referência a; **"please quote this ~"** (*COMM*) "queira citar esta referência".

reference book *n* livro de consulta.

reference number *n* (*COMM*) número de referência.

referenda [refə'rendə] *npl of* **referendum**.

referendum [refə'rendəm] (*pl* **referenda**) *n* referendum *m*, plebiscito.

refill [*vt* riː'fɪl, *n* 'riːfɪl] *vt* reencher; (*lighter etc*) reabastecer ♦ *n* (*for pen*) carga nova; (*COMM*) refill *m*.

refine [rɪ'faɪn] *vt* (*sugar*, *oil*) refinar.

refined [rɪ'faɪnd] *adj* (*person*, *taste*) refinado, culto.

refinement [rɪ'faɪnmənt] *n* (*of person*) cultura, refinamento, requinte *m*.

refinery [rɪ'faɪnərɪ] *n* refinaria.

refit [*n* 'riːfɪt, *vt* riː'fɪt] *n* (*NAUT*) reequipamento ♦ *vt* reequipar.

reflate [riː'fleɪt] *vt* (*economy*) reflacionar.

reflation [riː'fleɪʃən] *n* reflação *f*.

reflationary [riː'fleɪʃənrɪ] *adj* reflacionário.

reflect [rɪ'flekt] *vt* (*light*, *image*) refletir ♦ *vi* (*think*) refletir, meditar.

reflect on *vt fus* (*discredit*) prejudicar.

reflection [rɪ'flekʃən] *n* (*act*) reflexão *f*; (*image*) reflexo; (*criticism*): **~ on** crítica de; **on ~** pensando bem.

reflector [rɪ'flektə*] *n* (*also*: *AUT*) refletor *m*.

reflect stud (*US*) *n* (*AUT*) olho de gato.

reflex ['riːfleks] *adj*, *n* reflexo.

reflexive [rɪ'fleksɪv] *adj* (*LING*) reflexivo.

reform [rɪ'fɔːm] *n* reforma ♦ *vt* reformar.

reformat [riː'fɔːmæt] *vt* (*COMPUT*) reformatar.

Reformation [refə'meɪʃən] *n*: **the ~** a Reforma.

reformatory [rɪ'fɔːmətərɪ] (*US*) *n* reformatório.

reformed [rɪ'fɔːmd] *adj* emendado, reformado.

reformer [rɪ'fɔːmə*] *n* reformador(a) *m/f*.

reformist [rɪ'fɔːmɪst] *n* reformista *m/f*.

refrain [rɪ'freɪn] *vi*: **to ~ from doing** abster-se de fazer ♦ *n* estribilho, refrão *m*.

refresh [rɪ'freʃ] *vt* refrescar.

refresher course [rɪ'freʃə*-] (*BRIT*) *n* curso de reciclagem.

refreshing [rɪ'freʃɪŋ] *adj* refrescante; (*sleep*) repousante; (*change*) agradável; (*idea*, *thought*) original.

refreshment [rɪ'freʃmənt] *n* (*eating*): **for some ~** para comer alguma coisa; (*resting etc*): **in need of ~** precisando se refazer, precisando refazer as suas forças; **~s** *npl* (*drinks*) refrescos *mpl*.

refrigeration [rɪfrɪdʒə'reɪʃən] *n* refrigeração *f*.

refrigerator [rɪ'frɪdʒəreɪtə*] *n* refrigerador *m*, geladeira (*BR*), frigorífico (*PT*).

refuel [riː'fjuəl] *vt*, *vi* reabastecer.

refuge ['refjuːdʒ] *n* refúgio; **to take ~ in** refugiar-se em.

refugee [refju'dʒiː] *n* refugiado/a.

refugee camp *n* campo de refugiados.

refund [*n* 'riːfʌnd, *vt* riː'fʌnd] *n* reembolso ♦ *vt* devolver, reembolsar.

refurbish [riː'fɜːbɪʃ] *vt* renovar.

refurnish [riː'fɜːnɪʃ] *vt* colocar móveis novos em.

refusal [rɪ'fjuːzəl] *n* recusa, negativa; **first ~** primeira opção.

refuse [*n* 'refjuːs, *vt*, *vi* rɪ'fjuːz] *n* refugo, lixo ♦ *vt* recusar; (*order*) recusar-se a ♦ *vi* recusar-se, negar-se; **to ~ to do sth** recusar-se a fazer algo.

refuse bin *n* lata de lixo.

refuse collection *n* remoção *f* de lixo.

refuse collector *n* lixeiro/a, gari *m/f* (*BR*).

refuse disposal *n* destruição *f* de lixo.

refuse tip *n* depósito de lixo.

refute [rɪ'fjuːt] *vt* refutar.

regain [rɪ'geɪn] *vt* recuperar, recobrar.

regal ['riːgl] *adj* real, régio.

regale [rɪ'geɪl] *vt*: **to ~ sb with sth** regalar alguém com algo.

regalia [rɪ'geɪlɪə] *n*, *npl* insígnias *fpl* reais.

NB: European Portuguese adds the following consonants to certain words: **b** (sú(b)dito, su(b)til); **c** (a(c)ção, a(c)cionista, a(c)to); **m** (inde(m)ne); **p** (ado(p)ção, ado(p)tar); *for further details see p. xiii.*

regard [rɪ'gɑːd] *n* (*aspect*) respeito; (*attention*) atenção *f*; (*esteem*) estima, consideração *f* ♦ *vt* (*consider*) considerar; **to give one's ~s to** dar lembranças a; **"with kindest ~s"** "cordialmente"; **as ~s, with ~ to** com relação a, com respeito a, quanto a.

regarding [rɪ'gɑːdɪŋ] *prep* com relação a.

regardless [rɪ'gɑːdlɪs] *adv* apesar de tudo; ~ **of** apesar de.

regatta [rɪ'gætə] *n* regata.

regency ['riːdʒənsɪ] *n* regência.

regenerate [rɪ'dʒɛnəreɪt] *vt* regenerar ♦ *vi* regenerar-se.

regent ['riːdʒənt] *n* regente *m/f*.

régime [reɪ'ʒiːm] *n* regime *m*.

regiment [*n* 'rɛdʒɪmənt, *vt* 'rɛdʒɪmɛnt] *n* regimento ♦ *vt* regulamentar; (*children etc*) subordinar a disciplina rígida.

regimental [rɛdʒɪ'mɛntl] *adj* regimental.

regimentation [rɛdʒɪmɛn'teɪʃən] *n* organização *f*.

region ['riːdʒən] *n* região *f*; **in the ~ of** (*fig*) por volta de, ao redor de.

regional ['riːdʒənl] *adj* regional.

regional development *n* desenvolvimento regional.

register ['rɛdʒɪstə*] *n* registro (*BR*), registo (*PT*); (*list*) lista ♦ *vt* registrar (*BR*), registar (*PT*); (*subj: instrument*) marcar, indicar ♦ *vi* (*at hotel*) registrar-se (*BR*), registar-se (*PT*); (*sign on*) inscrever-se; (*make impression*) causar impressão; **to ~ for a course** matricular-se num curso; **to ~ a protest** registrar (*BR*) or registar (*PT*) uma queixa.

registered ['rɛdʒɪstəd] *adj* (*design, letter*) registrado (*BR*), registado (*PT*); (*student*) matriculado; (*voter*) inscrito.

registered company *n* sociedade *f* registrada (*BR*) or registada (*PT*).

registered nurse (*US*) *n* enfermeiro/a formado/a.

registered office *n* sede *f* social.

registered trademark *n* marca registrada (*BR*) or registada (*PT*).

registrar ['rɛdʒɪstrɑː*] *n* oficial *m/f* de registro (*BR*) or registo (*PT*), escrivão/vã *m/f*.

registration [rɛdʒɪs'treɪʃən] *n* (*act*) registro (*BR*), registo (*PT*); (*AUT: also:* ~ **number**) número da placa.

registry ['rɛdʒɪstrɪ] *n* registro (*BR*), registo (*PT*), cartório.

registry office (*BRIT*) *n* registro (*BR*) or registo (*PT*) civil, cartório; **to get married in a ~** casar-se no civil.

regret [rɪ'grɛt] *n* desgosto, pesar *m*; (*remorse*) remorso ♦ *vt* (*deplore*) lamentar; (*repent of*) arrepender-se de; **to ~ that** ... lamentar que ... + *sub*; **we ~ to inform you that** ... lamentamos informá-lo de que ....

regretfully [rɪ'grɛtfulɪ] *adv* com pesar, pesarosamente.

regrettable [rɪ'grɛtəbl] *adj* deplorável; (*loss*) lamentável.

regrettably [rɪ'grɛtəblɪ] *adv* lamentavelmente; **~, he was unable** ... infelizmente, ele não pôde ....

regroup [riː'gruːp] *vt* reagrupar ♦ *vi* reagrupar-se.

regt *abbr* = **regiment**.

regular ['rɛgjulə*] *adj* (*verb, service, shape*) regular; (*usual*) normal, habitual; (*soldier*) de linha; (*listener, reader*) assíduo; (*COMM: size*) médio ♦ *n* (*client etc*) habitual *m/f*.

regularity [rɛgju'lærɪtɪ] *n* regularidade *f*.

regularly ['rɛgjuləlɪ] *adv* regularmente.

regulate ['rɛgjuleɪt] *vt* regular; (*TECH*) ajustar.

regulation [rɛgju'leɪʃən] *n* (*rule*) regra, regulamento; (*adjustment*) ajuste *m* ♦ *cpd* regulamentar.

rehabilitation [riːhəbɪlɪ'teɪʃən] *n* reabilitação *f*.

rehash [riː'hæʃ] (*inf*) *vt* retocar.

rehearsal [rɪ'həːsəl] *n* ensaio; *see also* **dress**.

rehearse [rɪ'həːs] *vt, vi* ensaiar.

rehouse [riː'hauz] *vt* realojar.

reign [reɪn] *n* reinado; (*fig*) domínio ♦ *vi* reinar; (*fig*) imperar.

reigning ['reɪnɪŋ] *adj* (*monarch*) reinante; (*champion*) atual.

reimburse [riːɪm'bəːs] *vt* reembolsar.

reimbursement [riːɪm'bəːsmənt] *n* reembolso.

rein [reɪn] *n* (*for horse*) rédea; **to give ~ to** dar rédeas a, dar rédea larga a; **to give sb free ~** (*fig*) dar carta branca a alguém.

reincarnation [riːɪnkɑː'neɪʃən] *n* reencarnação *f*.

reindeer ['reɪndɪə*] *n inv* rena.

reinforce [riːɪn'fɔːs] *vt* reforçar.

reinforced [riːɪn'fɔːst] *adj* (*concrete*) armado.

reinforcement [riːɪn'fɔːsmənt] *n* (*action*) reforço; **~s** *npl* (*MIL*) reforços *mpl*.

reinstate [riːɪn'steɪt] *vt* (*worker*) readmitir; (*official*) reempossar.

reinstatement [riːɪn'steɪtmənt] *n* readmissão *f*.

reissue [riː'ɪʃuː] *vt* (*book*) reeditar; (*film*) relançar.

reiterate [riː'ɪtəreɪt] *vt* reiterar, repetir.

reject [*n* 'riːdʒɛkt, *vt* rɪ'dʒɛkt] *n* (*COMM*) artigo defeituoso ♦ *vt* rejeitar; (*COMM: goods*) refugar.

rejection [rɪ'dʒɛkʃən] *n* rejeição *f*.

rejoice [rɪ'dʒɔɪs] *vi*: **to ~ at** or **over** regozijar-se or alegrar-se de.

rejoinder [rɪ'dʒɔɪndə*] *n* (*retort*) réplica.

rejuvenate [rɪ'dʒuːvəneɪt] *vt* rejuvenescer.

rekindle [riː'kɪndl] *vt* reacender; (*fig*) despertar, reanimar.

relapse [rɪ'læps] *n* (*MED*) recaída; (*into crime*) reincidência.

relate [rɪ'leɪt] *vt* (*tell*) contar, relatar; (*connect*) relacionar ♦ *vi*: **to ~ to** relacionar-se com.

related [rɪ'leɪtɪd] *adj* (*connected*) afim, ligado; (*person*) aparentado.

relating [rɪ'leɪtɪŋ]: **~ to** *prep* relativo a, acerca de.

relation [rɪ'leɪʃən] *n* (*person*) parente *m/f*; (*link*) relação *f*; **diplomatic/international ~s**

relações diplomáticas/internacionais; **in ~ to** em relação a; **to bear no ~ to** não ter relação com.

relationship [rɪ'leɪʃənʃɪp] *n* relacionamento; (*personal ties*) relações *fpl*; (*also: family ~*) parentesco; (*affair*) caso.

relative ['rɛlətɪv] *n* parente *m/f* ♦ *adj* relativo; (*respective*) respectivo.

relatively ['rɛlətɪvlɪ] *adv* relativamente.

relax [rɪ'læks] *vi* (*rest*) descansar; (*unwind*) descontrair-se; (*calm down*) acalmar-se ♦ *vt* relaxar; (*mind, person*) descansar; **~!** (*calm down*) calma!; **to ~ one's grip** *or* **hold** afrouxar um pouco.

relaxation [riːlæk'seɪʃən] *n* (*rest*) descanso; (*ease*) relaxamento, relax *m*; (*amusement*) passatempo; (*entertainment*) diversão *f*.

relaxed [rɪ'lækst] *adj* relaxado; (*tranquil*) descontraído.

relaxing [rɪ'læksɪŋ] *adj* calmante, relaxante.

relay ['riːleɪ] *n* (*race*) (corrida de) revezamento ♦ *vt* (*message*) retransmitir.

release [rɪ'liːs] *n* (*from prison*) libertação *f*; (*from obligation*) liberação *f*; (*of shot*) disparo; (*of gas etc*) escape *m*; (*of film, book etc*) lançamento; (*device*) desengate *m* ♦ *vt* (*prisoner*) pôr em liberdade; (*book, film*) lançar; (*report, news*) publicar; (*gas etc*) soltar; (*free: from wreckage etc*) soltar; (*TECH: catch, spring etc*) desengatar, desapertar; (*let go*) soltar; **to ~ one's grip** *or* **hold** afrouxar; **to ~ the clutch** (*AUT*) desembrear.

relegate ['rɛləgeɪt] *vt* relegar, afastar; (*SPORT*) **to be ~d** descer.

relent [rɪ'lɛnt] *vi* abrandar-se; (*yield*) ceder.

relentless [rɪ'lɛntlɪs] *adj* implacável.

relevance ['rɛləvəns] *n* pertinência; (*importance*) relevância; **~ of sth to sth** relação de algo com algo.

relevant ['rɛləvənt] *adj* (*fact*) pertinente; (*apt*) apropriado; (*important*) relevante; **~ to** relacionado com.

reliability [rɪlaɪə'bɪlɪtɪ] *n* (*of person*) confiabilidade *f*, seriedade *f*; (*of method, machine*) segurança; (*of news*) fidedignidade *f*.

reliable [rɪ'laɪəbl] *adj* (*person, firm*) (digno) de confiança, confiável, sério; (*method, machine*) seguro; (*news*) fidedigno.

reliably [rɪ'laɪəblɪ] *adv*: **to be ~ informed that ...** saber de fonte segura que ....

reliance [rɪ'laɪəns] *n*: **~ (on)** (*trust*) confiança (em), esperança (em); (*dependence*) dependência (de).

reliant [rɪ'laɪənt] *adj*: **to be ~ on sth/sb** depender de algo/alguém.

relic ['rɛlɪk] *n* (*REL*) relíquia; (*of the past*) vestígio.

relief [rɪ'liːf] *n* (*from pain, anxiety*) alívio; (*help, supplies*) ajuda, socorro; (*of guard*) rendição *f*; (*ART, GEO*) relevo; **by way of light ~** como forma de diversão.

relief map *n* mapa *m* em relevo.

relief road (*BRIT*) *n* estrada alternativa.

relieve [rɪ'liːv] *vt* (*pain, patient*) aliviar; (*bring help to*) ajudar, socorrer; (*burden*) abrandar, mitigar; (*take over from: gen*) substituir, revezar; (: *guard*) render; **to ~ sb of sth** tirar algo de alguém; **to ~ sb of his command** exonerar alguém, destituir alguém de sua função; **to ~ o.s.** fazer as necessidades.

religion [rɪ'lɪdʒən] *n* religião *f*.

religious [rɪ'lɪdʒəs] *adj* religioso.

reline [riː'laɪn] *vt* (*brakes*) trocar o forro de.

relinquish [rɪ'lɪŋkwɪʃ] *vt* abandonar; (*plan, habit*) renunciar a.

relish ['rɛlɪʃ] *n* (*CULIN*) condimento, tempero; (*enjoyment*) entusiasmo ♦ *vt* (*food etc*) saborear; **to ~ doing** gostar de fazer.

relive [riː'lɪv] *vt* reviver.

reload [riː'ləud] *vt* recarregar.

relocate [riːləu'keɪt] *vt* deslocar ♦ *vi* deslocar-se; **to ~ in** instalar-se em.

reluctance [rɪ'lʌktəns] *n* relutância.

reluctant [rɪ'lʌktənt] *adj* relutante; **to be ~ to do sth** relutar em fazer algo.

reluctantly [rɪ'lʌktəntlɪ] *adv* relutantemente, de má vontade.

rely [rɪ'laɪ]: **to ~ on** *vt fus* confiar em, contar com; (*be dependent on*) depender de.

remain [rɪ'meɪn] *vi* (*stay*) ficar, permanecer; (*be left*) sobrar; (*continue*) continuar, manter-se; **to ~ silent** ficar calado; **I ~, yours faithfully** (*BRIT: in letters*) subscrevo-me, atenciosamente.

remainder [rɪ'meɪndə*] *n* resto, restante *m*.

remaining [rɪ'meɪnɪŋ] *adj* restante.

remains [rɪ'meɪnz] *npl* (*mortal*) restos *mpl*; (*leftovers*) sobras *fpl*.

remand [rɪ'mɑːnd] *n*: **on ~** sob prisão preventiva ♦ *vt*: **to ~ in custody** recolocar em prisão preventiva, manter sob custódia.

remand home (*BRIT*) *n* instituição *f* do juizado de menores, reformatório.

remark [rɪ'mɑːk] *n* observação *f*, comentário ♦ *vt* comentar ♦ *vi*: **to ~ on sth** comentar algo, fazer um comentário sobre algo.

remarkable [rɪ'mɑːkəbl] *adj* notável; (*outstanding*) extraordinário.

remarry [riː'mærɪ] *vi* casar-se de novo.

remedial [rɪ'miːdɪəl] *adj* (*tuition, classes*) de reforço.

remedy ['rɛmədɪ] *n*: **~ (for)** remédio (contra *or* a) ♦ *vt* remediar.

remember [rɪ'mɛmbə*] *vt* lembrar-se de, lembrar; (*memorize*) guardar; **I ~ seeing it, I ~ having seen it** eu me lembro de ter visto aquilo; **she ~ed to do it** ela se lembrou de fazer aquilo; **~ me to your wife** dê lembranças minhas à sua esposa.

remembrance [rɪ'mɛmbrəns] *n* (*memory*) memória; (*souvenir*) lembrança, recordação *f*.

remind [rɪ'maɪnd] *vt*: **to ~ sb to do sth** lembrar a alguém que tem de fazer algo; **to ~**

sb of sth lembrar algo a alguém; **she ~s me of her mother** ela me lembra a mãe dela; **that ~s me, ...** falando nisso, ...

reminder [rɪ'maɪndə*] n lembrete m; (souvenir) lembrança.

reminisce [rɛmɪ'nɪs] vi relembrar velhas histórias; **to ~ about sth** relembrar algo.

reminiscences [rɛmɪ'nɪsnsɪz] npl recordações fpl, lembranças fpl.

reminiscent [rɛmɪ'nɪsənt] adj: **to be ~ of sth** lembrar algo.

remiss [rɪ'mɪs] adj negligente, desleixado; **it was ~ of him** foi um descuido seu.

remission [rɪ'mɪʃən] n remissão f; (of sentence) diminuição f.

remit [rɪ'mɪt] vt (send: money) remeter, enviar, mandar.

remittance [rɪ'mɪtəns] n remessa.

remnant ['rɛmnənt] n resto; (of cloth) retalho; **~s** npl (COMM) retalhos mpl.

remonstrate ['rɛmənstreɪt] vi: **to ~ (with sb about sth)** reclamar (a alguém de algo).

remorse [rɪ'mɔːs] n remorso.

remorseful [rɪ'mɔːsful] adj arrependido.

remorseless [rɪ'mɔːslɪs] adj (fig) desapiedado, implacável.

remote [rɪ'məʊt] adj (distant) remoto, distante; (person) reservado, afastado; **there is a ~ possibility that ...** existe uma possibilidade remota de que ....

remote control n controle m remoto.

remote-controlled [-kən'trəʊld] adj (plane) telecomandado; (missile) teleguiado.

remotely [rɪ'məʊtlɪ] adv remotamente; (slightly) levemente.

remoteness [rɪ'məʊtnɪs] n afastamento, isolamento.

remould ['riːməʊld] (BRIT) n (tyre) pneu m recauchutado.

removable [rɪ'muːvəbl] adj (detachable) removível.

removal [rɪ'muːvəl] n (taking away) remoção f; (BRIT: from house) mudança; (from office: sacking) afastamento, demissão f; (MED) extração f.

removal man (irreg) n homem m da companhia de mudanças.

removal van (BRIT) n caminhão m (BR) or camião m (PT) de mudanças.

remove [rɪ'muːv] vt tirar, retirar; (employee) afastar, demitir; (name: from list) eliminar, remover; (doubt, abuse) afastar; (TECH) retirar, separar; (MED) extrair, extirpar; **first cousin once ~d** primo/a em segundo grau.

remover [rɪ'muːvə*] n (substance) removedor m; **~s** npl (BRIT: company) companhia de mudanças.

remunerate [rɪ'mjuːnəreɪt] vt remunerar.

remuneration [rɪmjuːnə'reɪʃən] n remuneração f.

rename [riː'neɪm] vt dar novo nome a.

rend [rɛnd] (pt, pp rent) vt rasgar, despedaçar.

render ['rɛndə*] vt (give: help) dar, prestar;

(: account) entregar; (make) fazer, tornar; (translate) traduzir; (fat: also: ~ down) clarificar; (wall) rebocar.

rendering ['rɛndərɪŋ] n (MUS etc) interpretação f.

rendezvous ['rɒndɪvuː] n encontro; (place) ponto de encontro ♦ vi encontrar-se; **to ~ with sb** encontrar-se com alguém.

renegade ['rɛnɪgeɪd] n renegado/a.

renew [rɪ'njuː] vt renovar; (resume) retomar, recomeçar; (loan etc) prorrogar; (negotiations, acquaintance) reatar.

renewable [rɪ'njuːəbl] adj renovável.

renewal [rɪ'njuːəl] n renovação f; (resumption) retomada; (of loan) prorrogação f.

renounce [rɪ'naʊns] vt renunciar a; (disown) repudiar, rejeitar.

renovate ['rɛnəveɪt] vt renovar; (house, room) reformar.

renovation [rɛnə'veɪʃən] n renovação f; (of house etc) reforma.

renown [rɪ'naʊn] n renome m.

renowned [rɪ'naʊnd] adj renomado, famoso.

rent [rɛnt] pt, pp of **rend** ♦ n aluguel m (BR), aluguer m (PT) ♦ vt (also: ~ out) alugar.

rental ['rɛntəl] n (for television, car) aluguel m (BR), aluguer m (PT).

renunciation [rɪnʌnsɪ'eɪʃən] n renúncia.

reopen [riː'əʊpən] vt reabrir.

reopening [riː'əʊpənɪŋ] n reabertura.

reorder [riː'ɔːdə*] vt encomendar novamente; (rearrange) reorganizar.

reorganize [riː'ɔːgənaɪz] vt reorganizar.

Rep. (US) abbr (POL) = representative; republican.

rep [rɛp] n abbr (COMM) = representative; (THEATRE) = repertory.

repaid [riː'peɪd] pt, pp of **repay**.

repair [rɪ'pɛə*] n reparação f, conserto; (patch) remendo ♦ vt consertar; **beyond ~** irreparável; **in good/bad ~** em bom/mau estado; **under ~** no conserto.

repair kit n (tool box) caixa de ferramentas.

repair man (irreg) n consertador m.

repair shop n oficina de reparos.

repartee [rɛpɑː'tiː] n resposta arguta e engenhosa; (skill) presteza em replicar.

repast [rɪ'pɑːst] n (formal) repasto.

repatriate [riː'pætrɪeɪt] vt repatriar.

repay [riː'peɪ] (irreg) vt (money) reembolsar, restituir; (person) pagar de volta; (debt) saldar, liquidar; (sb's efforts) corresponder, retribuir.

repayment [riː'peɪmənt] n reembolso, retribuição f; (of debt) pagamento; (of mortgage etc) prestação f.

repeal [rɪ'piːl] n (of law) revogação f; (of sentence) anulação f ♦ vt revogar; anular.

repeat [rɪ'piːt] n (RADIO, TV) repetição f ♦ vt repetir; (COMM: order) renovar ♦ vi repetir-se.

repeatedly [rɪ'piːtɪdlɪ] adv repetidamente.

repel [rɪ'pɛl] vt repelir.

repellent [rɪ'pɛlənt] adj repelente ♦ n: **insect ~** repelente m de insetos.

repent [rɪ'pɛnt] *vi*: **to ~ (of)** arrepender-se (de).

repentance [rɪ'pɛntəns] *n* arrependimento.

repercussion [riːpə'kʌʃən] *n* (*consequence*) repercussão *f*; **to have ~s** repercutir.

repertoire ['rɛpətwɑː*] *n* repertório.

repertory ['rɛpətərɪ] *n* (*also*: **~ theatre**) teatro de repertório.

repertory company *n* companhia teatral.

repetition [rɛpɪ'tɪʃən] *n* repetição *f*.

repetitious [rɛpɪ'tɪʃəs] *adj* (*speech*) repetitivo.

repetitive [rɪ'pɛtɪtɪv] *adj* repetitivo.

replace [rɪ'pleɪs] *vt* (*put back*) repor, devolver; (*take the place of*) substituir; (*TEL*): **"~ the receiver"** "desligue".

replacement [rɪ'pleɪsmənt] *n* (*substitution*) substituição *f*; (*putting back*) reposição *f*; (*person*) substituto/a.

replacement part *n* peça sobressalente.

replay ['riːpleɪ] *n* (*of match*) partida decisiva; (*TV*: *also*: *action* **~**) replay *m*.

replenish [rɪ'plɛnɪʃ] *vt* (*glass*) reencher; (*stock etc*) completar, prover; (*with fuel*) reabastecer.

replete [rɪ'pliːt] *adj* repleto; (*well-fed*) cheio, empanturrado.

replica ['rɛplɪkə] *n* réplica, cópia, reprodução *f*.

reply [rɪ'plaɪ] *n* resposta ♦ *vi* responder; **in ~ (to)** em resposta (a); **there's no ~** (*TEL*) ninguém atende.

reply coupon *n* cartão-resposta *m*.

report [rɪ'pɔːt] *n* relatório; (*PRESS etc*) reportagem *f*; (*also*: *school* **~**) boletim *m* escolar; (*of gun*) estampido, detonação *f* ♦ *vt* informar sobre; (*PRESS etc*) fazer uma reportagem sobre; (*bring to notice*: *occurrence*) comunicar, anunciar; (: *person*) denunciar ♦ *vi* (*make a report*): **to ~ (on)** apresentar um relatório (sobre); (*for newspaper*) fazer uma reportagem (sobre); (*present o.s.*): **to ~ (to sb)** apresentar-se (a alguém); **it is ~ed that** dizem que; **it is ~ed from Berlin that** há notícias de Berlim de que.

report card (*US, SCOTTISH*) *n* boletim *m* escolar.

reportedly [rɪ'pɔːtɪdlɪ] *adv*: **she is ~ living in Spain** dizem que ela mora na Espanha.

reported speech [rɪ'pɔːtɪd-] *n* (*LING*) discurso indireto.

reporter [rɪ'pɔːtə*] *n* (*PRESS*) jornalista *m/f*, repórter *m/f*; (*RADIO, TV*) repórter.

repose [rɪ'pəuz] *n*: **in ~** em repouso.

repossess [riːpə'zɛs] *vt* retomar.

reprehensible [rɛprɪ'hɛnsɪbl] *adj* repreensível, censurável, condenável.

represent [rɛprɪ'zɛnt] *vt* representar; (*fig*) falar em nome de; (*COMM*) ser representante de; (*explain*): **to ~ to sb that** explicar a alguém que.

representation [rɛprɪzɛn'teɪʃən] *n* representa-

ção *f*; (*petition*) petição *f*; **~s** *npl* (*protest*) reclamação *f*, protesto.

representative [rɛprɪ'zɛntətɪv] *n* representante *m/f*; (*US*: *POL*) deputado/a ♦ *adj*: **~ (of)** representativo (de).

repress [rɪ'prɛs] *vt* reprimir, subjugar.

repression [rɪ'prɛʃən] *n* repressão *f*.

repressive [rɪ'prɛsɪv] *adj* repressivo.

reprieve [rɪ'priːv] *n* (*LAW*) suspensão *f* temporária; (*fig*) alívio ♦ *vt* suspender temporariamente; aliviar.

reprimand ['rɛprɪmɑːnd] *n* reprimenda ♦ *vt* repreender, censurar.

reprint [*n* 'riːprɪnt, *vt* riː'prɪnt] *n* reimpressão *f* ♦ *vt* reimprimir.

reprisal [rɪ'praɪzl] *n* represália; **to take ~s** fazer *or* exercer represálias.

reproach [rɪ'prəutʃ] *n* repreensão *f*, censura ♦ *vt*: **to ~ sb with sth** repreender alguém por algo; **beyond ~** irrepreensível, impecável.

reproachful [rɪ'prəutʃful] *adj* repreensivo, acusatório.

reproduce [riːprə'djuːs] *vt* reproduzir ♦ *vi* reproduzir-se.

reproduction [riːprə'dʌkʃən] *n* reprodução *f*.

reproductive [riːprə'dʌktɪv] *adj* reprodutivo.

reproof [rɪ'pruːf] *n* reprovação *f*, repreensão *f*.

reprove [rɪ'pruːv] *vt* (*action*) reprovar; **to ~ sb for sth** repreender alguém por algo.

reproving [rɪ'pruːvɪŋ] *adj* (*look*) de reprovação; (*tone*) de censura.

reptile ['rɛptaɪl] *n* réptil *m*.

Repub. (*US*) *abbr* (*POL*) = **republican**.

republic [rɪ'pʌblɪk] *n* república.

republican [rɪ'pʌblɪkən] *adj*, *n* republicano/a.

repudiate [rɪ'pjuːdɪeɪt] *vt* (*accusation*) rejeitar, negar; (*friend*) repudiar; (*obligation*) desconhecer.

repugnant [rɪ'pʌgnənt] *adj* repugnante, repulsivo.

repulse [rɪ'pʌls] *vt* repelir.

repulsion [rɪ'pʌlʃən] *n* repulsa; (*PHYS*) repulsão *f*.

repulsive [rɪ'pʌlsɪv] *adj* repulsivo.

reputable ['rɛpjutəbl] *adj* (*make etc*) bem conceituado, de confiança; (*person*) honrado, respeitável.

reputation [rɛpju'teɪʃən] *n* reputação *f*; **to have a ~ for** ter fama por; **he has a ~ for being cruel** ele tem fama de ser cruel.

repute [rɪ'pjuːt] *n* reputação *f*, renome *m*.

reputed [rɪ'pjuːtɪd] *adj* suposto, pretenso; **he is ~ to be rich** dizem que ele é rico.

reputedly [rɪ'pjuːtɪdlɪ] *adv* segundo se diz, supostamente.

request [rɪ'kwɛst] *n* pedido; (*formal*) petição *f* ♦ *vt*: **to ~ sth of** *or* **from sb** pedir algo a alguém; (*formally*) solicitar algo a alguém; **on ~** a pedido; **at the ~ of** a pedido de; **"you are ~ed not to smoke"** "pede-se *or* favor não fumar".

request stop (*BRIT*) *n* (*for bus*) parada não

NB: European Portuguese adds the following consonants to certain words: **b** (sú(b)dito, su(b)til); **c** (a(c)ção, a(c)cionista, a(c)to); **m** (inde(m)ne); **p** (ado(p)ção, ado(p)tar); *for further details see p. xiii.*

obrigatória.

requiem ['rɛkwɪəm] n réquiem m.

require [rɪ'kwaɪə*] vt (need: subj: person) precisar de, necessitar; (: thing, situation) requerer, exigir; (want) pedir; (order): **to ~ sb to do sth/sth of sb** exigir que alguém faça algo/algo de alguém; **if ~d** se for necessário; **what qualifications are ~d?** quais são as qualificações necessárias?; **~d by law** exigido por lei.

required [rɪ'kwaɪəd] adj (necessary) necessário; (desired) desejado.

requirement [rɪ'kwaɪəmənt] n requisito; (need) necessidade f.

requisite ['rɛkwɪzɪt] n requisito ♦ adj necessário, indispensável; **toilet ~s** artigos de toalete pessoal.

requisition [rɛkwɪ'zɪʃən] n: **~ (for)** requerimento (para) ♦ vt (MIL) requisitar, confiscar.

reroute [riː'ruːt] vt (train etc) desviar.

resale [riː'seɪl] n revenda.

resale price maintenance n manutenção f de preços de revenda.

rescind [rɪ'sɪnd] vt (contract) rescindir; (law) revogar; (verdict) anular.

rescue ['rɛskjuː] n salvamento, resgate m ♦ vt (survivors, wounded etc) resgatar; (save, fig) salvar; **to come to sb's ~** ir ao socorro de alguém.

rescue party n grupo or expedição f de resgate.

rescuer ['rɛskjuə*] n (in disaster etc) resgatador(a) m/f; (fig) salvador(a) m/f.

research [rɪ'səːtʃ] n pesquisa ♦ vt pesquisar ♦ vi: **to ~ (into sth)** pesquisar (algo), fazer pesquisas (sobre algo); **a piece of ~** uma pesquisa; **~ and development** pesquisa e desenvolvimento.

researcher [rɪ'səːtʃə*] n pesquisador(a) m/f.

research work n trabalho de pesquisa.

resell [riː'sɛl] (irreg) vt revender.

resemblance [rɪ'zɛmbləns] n semelhança; **to bear a strong ~ to** ser muito parecido com.

resemble [rɪ'zɛmbl] vt parecer-se com.

resent [rɪ'zɛnt] vt (thing) ressentir-se de; (person) estar ressentido com.

resentful [rɪ'zɛntful] adj ressentido.

resentment [rɪ'zɛntmənt] n ressentimento.

reservation [rɛzə'veɪʃən] n (booking, doubt, protected area) reserva; (BRIT: AUT: also: central ~) canteiro divisor; **to make a ~** fazer reserva; **with ~s** (doubts) com reservas.

reservation desk (US) n (in hotel) recepção f.

reserve [rɪ'zəːv] n (restraint, protected area) reserva; (SPORT) suplente m/f, reserva m/f (BR) ♦ vt (seats etc) reservar; **~s** npl (MIL) (tropas fpl da) reserva; **in ~** de reserva.

reserve currency n moeda de reserva.

reserved [rɪ'zəːvd] adj reservado.

reserve price (BRIT) n preço mínimo de venda.

reserve team (BRIT) n time m reserva.

reservist [rɪ'zəːvɪst] n reservista m.

reservoir ['rɛzəvwɑː*] n (large) reservatório,

represa; (small) depósito.

reset [riː'sɛt] (irreg) vt reajustar; (COMPUT) dar reset em, restabelecer.

reshape [riː'ʃeɪp] vt (policy) reformar, remodelar.

reshuffle [riː'ʃʌfl] n see **cabinet**.

reside [rɪ'zaɪd] vi residir.

residence ['rɛzɪdəns] n residência; (formal: home) domicílio; **to take up ~** instalar-se; **in ~** (monarch) em residência; (doctor) residente.

residence permit (BRIT) n autorização f de residência.

resident ['rɛzɪdənt] n (of house, area) morador(a) m/f; (in hotel) hóspede m/f ♦ adj (population) permanente; (doctor) interno, residente.

residential [rɛzɪ'dɛnʃəl] adj residencial.

residue ['rɛzɪdjuː] n resto; (COMM) montante m líquido; (CHEM, PHYS) resíduo.

resign [rɪ'zaɪn] vt (one's post) renunciar a, demitir-se de ♦ vi: **to ~ (from)** demitir-se (de); **to ~ o.s. to** (endure) resignar-se a.

resignation [rɛzɪg'neɪʃən] n demissão f; (state of mind) resignação f; **to tender one's ~** pedir demissão.

resigned [rɪ'zaɪnd] adj resignado.

resilience [rɪ'zɪlɪəns] n (of material) elasticidade f; (of person) resistência.

resilient [rɪ'zɪlɪənt] adj (person) resistente.

resin ['rɛzɪn] n resina.

resist [rɪ'zɪst] vt resistir a.

resistance [rɪ'zɪstəns] n resistência.

resistant [rɪ'zɪstənt] adj: **~ (to)** resistente (a).

resold [riː'səuld] pt, pp of **resell**.

resolute ['rɛzəluːt] adj resoluto, firme.

resolution [rɛzə'luːʃən] n resolução f; **to make a ~** tomar uma resolução.

resolve [rɪ'zɔlv] n resolução f; (purpose) intenção f ♦ vt resolver; **to ~ to do** resolver-se a fazer.

resolved [rɪ'zɔlvd] adj decidido.

resonance ['rɛzənəns] n ressonância.

resonant ['rɛzənənt] adj ressonante.

resort [rɪ'zɔːt] n (town) local m turístico, estação f de veraneio; (recourse) recurso ♦ vi: **~ to** recorrer a; **seaside/winter sports ~** balneário/estação de inverno; **in the last ~** em último caso, em última instância.

resound [rɪ'zaund] vi ressoar, retumbar; **the room ~ed with shouts** os gritos ressoaram no quarto.

resounding [rɪ'zaundɪŋ] adj retumbante.

resource [rɪ'sɔːs] n recurso; **~s** npl recursos mpl; **natural ~s** recursos naturais.

resourceful [rɪ'sɔːsful] adj desembaraçado, engenhoso, expedito.

resourcefulness [rɪ'sɔːsfəlnɪs] n desembaraço, engenho.

respect [rɪs'pɛkt] n respeito ♦ vt respeitar; **~s** npl: **to pay one's ~s to sb** fazer visita de cortesia a alguém; **to pay one's last ~s to sb** prestar a última homenagem a alguém; **to have or show ~ for sb/sth** ter or mostrar respeito por alguém/algo; **out of ~ for** por

respeito a; **with ~ to** com respeito a; **in ~ of** a respeito de; **in this ~** neste respeito; **in some ~s** em alguns pontos; **with all due ~, I** ... com todo respeito, eu ....
respectability [rɪspɛktə'bɪlɪtɪ] n respeitabilidade f.
respectable [rɪs'pɛktəbl] adj respeitável; (large) considerável; (quite good: result, player) razoável.
respectful [rɪs'pɛktful] adj respeitoso.
respective [rɪs'pɛktɪv] adj respectivo.
respectively [rɪs'pɛktɪvlɪ] adv respectivamente.
respiration [rɛspɪ'reɪʃən] n respiração f.
respiratory [rɛs'pɪrətərɪ] adj respiratório.
respite ['rɛspaɪt] n pausa, folga; (LAW) adiamento, suspensão f.
resplendent [rɪs'plɛndənt] adj resplandecente.
respond [rɪs'pɒnd] vi (answer) responder; (react) reagir.
respondent [rɪs'pɒndənt] n (in survey) respondedor(a) m/f; (LAW) réu/ré m/f.
response [rɪs'pɒns] n (answer) resposta; (reaction) reação f; **in ~ to** em resposta a.
responsibility [rɪspɒnsɪ'bɪlɪtɪ] n responsabilidade f; **to take ~ for sth/sb** assumir a responsabilidade por algo/alguém.
responsible [rɪs'pɒnsɪbl] adj (character) sério, responsável; (job) de responsabilidade; (liable): **~ (for)** responsável (por); **to be ~ to sb (for sth)** ser responsável diante de alguém (por algo); **to hold sb ~ (for sth)** responsabilizar alguém (por algo).
responsibly [rɪs'pɒnsɪblɪ] adv com responsabilidade.
responsive [rɪs'pɒnsɪv] adj sensível.
rest [rɛst] n descanso, repouso; (MUS) pausa; (break) intervalo; (support) apoio; (remainder) resto ♦ vi descansar; (be supported): **to ~ on** apoiar-se em ♦ vt (lean): **to ~ sth on/against** apoiar algo em or sobre/contra; **the ~ of them** os outros; **to set sb's mind at ~** tranqüilizar alguém; **it ~s with him to do it** cabe a ele fazê-lo; **~ assured that ...** tenha certeza de que ....
restart [riː'stɑːt] vt (engine) arrancar de novo; (work) reiniciar, recomeçar.
restaurant ['rɛstərɒŋ] n restaurante m.
restaurant car (BRIT) n vagão-restaurante m.
rest cure n repouso forçado (para tratamento de saúde).
restful ['rɛstful] adj sossegado, tranqüilo, repousante.
rest home n asilo, casa de repouso.
restitution [rɛstɪ'tjuːʃən] n: **to make ~ to sb for sth** restituir or indenizar alguém de algo.
restive ['rɛstɪv] adj inquieto, impaciente; (horse) rebelão/ona, teimoso.
restless ['rɛstlɪs] adj desassossegado, irrequieto; **to get ~** impacientar-se.
restlessly ['rɛstlɪslɪ] adv inquietamente.
restock [riː'stɒk] vt reabastecer.

restoration [rɛstə'reɪʃən] n restauração f.
restorative [rɪ'stɒrətɪv] adj reconstituinte ♦ n reconstituinte m.
restore [rɪ'stɔː*] vt (building) restaurar; (sth stolen) restituir; (peace, health) restabelecer.
restorer [rɪ'stɔːrə*] n (ART etc) restaurador(a) m/f.
restrain [rɪs'treɪn] vt (feeling) reprimir, refrear; (person): **to ~ (from doing)** impedir (de fazer).
restrained [rɪs'treɪnd] adj (style) moderado, comedido.
restraint [rɪs'treɪnt] n (restriction) restrição f; (moderation) moderação f, comedimento; (of style) sobriedade f; **wage ~** restrição salarial.
restrict [rɪs'trɪkt] vt restringir, limitar.
restricted area [rɪ'strɪktɪd-] n (AUT) zona com limite de velocidade.
restriction [rɪs'trɪkʃən] n restrição f, limitação f.
restrictive [rɪs'trɪktɪv] adj restritivo.
restrictive practices npl (INDUSTRY) práticas fpl restritivas.
rest room (US) n banheiro (BR), lavabo (PT).
restructure [riː'strʌktʃə*] vt reestruturar.
result [rɪ'zʌlt] n resultado ♦ vi: **to ~ (from)** resultar (de); **to ~ in** resultar em; **as a ~ of** como resultado or conseqüência de.
resultant [rɪ'zʌltənt] adj resultante.
resume [rɪ'zjuːm] vt (work, journey) retomar, recomeçar; (sum up) resumir ♦ vi (work etc) recomeçar.
résumé ['reɪzjuːmeɪ] n (summary) resumo; (US: curriculum vitae) curriculum vitae m, currículo.
resumption [rɪ'zʌmpʃən] n retomada.
resurgence [rɪ'sɜːdʒəns] n ressurgimento.
resurrection [rɛzə'rɛkʃən] n ressurreição f.
resuscitate [rɪ'sʌsɪteɪt] vt (MED) ressuscitar, reanimar.
resuscitation [rɪsʌsɪ'teɪʃən] n ressuscitação f.
retail ['riːteɪl] n varejo (BR), venda a retalho (PT) ♦ cpd no varejo (BR), a retalho (PT) ♦ vt vender no varejo (BR) or a retalho (PT) ♦ vi: **to ~ at $10** ser vendido no varejo (BR) or a retalho (PT) por $10.
retailer ['riːteɪlə*] n varejista m/f (BR), retalhista m/f (PT).
retail outlet n ponto de venda.
retail price n preço no varejo (BR) or de venda a retalho (PT).
retail price index n ≈ índice m de preços ao consumidor.
retain [rɪ'teɪn] vt (keep) reter, conservar; (employ) contratar.
retainer [rɪ'teɪnə*] n (servant) empregado; (fee) adiantamento.
retaliate [rɪ'tælɪeɪt] vi: **to ~ (against)** revidar (contra).
retaliation [rɪtælɪ'eɪʃən] n represálias fpl,

NB: European Portuguese adds the following consonants to certain words: **b** (sú(b)dito, su(b)til); **c** (a(c)ção, a(c)cionista, a(c)to); **m** (inde(m)ne); **p** (ado(p)ção, ado(p)tar); for further details see p. xiii.

vingança; **in ~ for** em retaliação por.
retaliatory [rɪ'tælɪətərɪ] *adj* retaliativo, retalia-
tório.
retarded [rɪ'tɑːdɪd] *adj* retardado.
retch [rɛtʃ] *vi* fazer esforço para vomitar.
retentive [rɪ'tɛntɪv] *adj* (*memory*) retentivo,
fiel.
rethink ['riː'θɪŋk] (*irreg*) *vt* reconsiderar, repensar.
reticence ['rɛtɪsns] *n* reserva.
reticent ['rɛtɪsnt] *adj* reservado.
retina ['rɛtɪnə] *n* retina.
retinue ['rɛtɪnjuː] *n* séquito, comitiva.
retire [rɪ'taɪə*] *vi* (*give up work*) aposentar-se;
(*withdraw*) retirar-se; (*go to bed*) deitar-se.
retired [rɪ'taɪəd] *adj* (*person*) aposentado (*BR*),
reformado (*PT*).
retiree [rɪtaɪə'riː] (*US*) *n* aposentado/a (*BR*),
reformado/a (*PT*).
retirement [rɪ'taɪəmənt] *n* (*state*, *act*) aposentadoria (*BR*), reforma (*PT*).
retirement age *n* idade *f* de aposentadoria
(*BR*) *or* de reforma (*PT*).
retiring [rɪ'taɪərɪŋ] *adj* (*leaving*) de saída;
(*shy*) acanhado, retraído.
retort [rɪ'tɔːt] *n* (*reply*) réplica; (*container*)
retorta ♦ *vi* replicar, retrucar.
retrace [riː'treɪs] *vt*: **to ~ one's steps** voltar
sobre (os) seus passos, refazer o mesmo caminho.
retract [rɪ'trækt] *vt* (*statement*) retirar, retratar; (*claws*) encolher; (*undercarriage*, *aer-*
ial) recolher ♦ *vi* retratar-se.
retractable [rɪ'træktəbl] *adj* retrátil.
retrain [riː'treɪn] *vt* reciclar ♦ *vi* ser reciclado.
retraining [riː'treɪnɪŋ] *n* readaptação *f*
profissional, reciclagem *f*.
retread [*n* 'riːtrɛd, *vt* riː'trɛd] *vt* (*AUT*: *tyre*)
recauchutar ♦ *n* pneu *m* recauchutado.
retreat [rɪ'triːt] *n* (*place*) retiro; (*act*) retirada
♦ *vi* retirar-se; (*flood*) retroceder; **to beat a**
hasty ~ bater em retirada.
retrial [riː'traɪəl] *n* revisão *f* do processo.
retribution [rɛtrɪ'bjuːʃən] *n* desforra, revide
m, vingança.
retrieval [rɪ'triːvəl] *n* recuperação *f*.
retrieve [rɪ'triːv] *vt* (*sth lost*) reaver, recuperar; (*situation*, *honour*) salvar; (*error*, *loss*)
reparar; (*COMPUT*) recuperar.
retriever [rɪ'triːvə*] *n* cão *m* de busca, perdigueiro.
retroactive [rɛtrəʊ'æktɪv] *adj* retroativo.
retrograde ['rɛtrəgreɪd] *adj* retrógrado.
retrospect ['rɛtrəspɛkt] *n*: **in ~** retrospectivamente, em retrospecto.
retrospective [rɛtrə'spɛktɪv] *adj* (*law*) re-
trospectivo, retroativo ♦ *n* (*ART*) retrospectiva.
return [rɪ'tɜːn] *n* (*going or coming back*) regresso, volta; (*of sth stolen etc*) devolução *f*;
(*recompense*) recompensa; (*FINANCE*: *from*
land, *shares*) rendimento; (*report*) relatório ♦
cpd (*journey*) de volta; (*BRIT*: *ticket*) de ida
e volta; (*match*) de revanche ♦ *vi* (*person*

etc: *come or go back*) voltar, regressar;
(*symptoms etc*) voltar ♦ *vt* devolver;
(*favour*, *love etc*) retribuir; (*verdict*) proferir, anunciar; (*POL*: *candidate*) ele-
ger; **~s** *npl* (*COMM*) receita; (: **~ed goods**)
mercadorias *fpl* devolvidas; **in ~ (for)**
em troca (de); **many happy ~s (of the day)!**
parabéns!; **by ~ (of post)** por volta do
correio.
returnable [rɪ'tɜːnəbl] *adj* (*bottle etc*) restituí-
vel.
return key *n* (*COMPUT*) tecla de retorno.
reunion [riː'juːnɪən] *n* reunião *f*.
reunite [riːjuː'naɪt] *vt* reunir; (*reconcile*) reconciliar.
rev [rɛv] *n* *abbr* (*AUT*: = *revolution*) revolução
f ♦ *vt* (*also*: **~ up**) aumentar a velocidade de
♦ *vi* acelerar.
revaluation [riːvælju'eɪʃən] *n* reavaliação *f*.
revamp ['riː'væmp] *vt* dar um jeito em.
rev counter (*BRIT*) *n* tacômetro.
Rev(d). *abbr* = **reverend**.
reveal [rɪ'viːl] *vt* revelar.
revealing [rɪ'viːlɪŋ] *adj* revelador(a).
reveille [rɪ'vælɪ] *n* (*MIL*) toque *m* de alvorada.
revel ['rɛvl] *vi*: **to ~ in sth/in doing sth**
deleitar-se com algo/em fazer algo.
revelation [rɛvə'leɪʃən] *n* revelação *f*.
reveller ['rɛvlə*] *n* farrista *m/f*, folião/liã *m/f*.
revelry ['rɛvəlrɪ] *n* festança, folia.
revenge [rɪ'vɛndʒ] *n* vingança, desforra; (*in*
sport) revanche *f* ♦ *vt* vingar; **to take ~ on**
vingar-se de.
revengeful [rɪ'vɛndʒful] *adj* vingativo.
revenue ['rɛvənjuː] *n* receita, renda; (*on*
investment) rendimento.
reverberate [rɪ'vɜːbəreɪt] *vi* (*sound*) ressoar,
repercutir, ecoar; (*light*) reverberar.
reverberation [rɪvɜːbə'reɪʃən] *n* repercussão *f*.
revere [rɪ'vɪə*] *vt* reverenciar, venerar.
reverence ['rɛvərəns] *n* reverência.
reverend ['rɛvrənd] *adj* reverendo; **the R~**
John Smith o reverendo John Smith.
reverent ['rɛvərənt] *adj* reverente.
reverie ['rɛvərɪ] *n* devaneio, sonho.
reversal [rɪ'vɜːsl] *n* (*of order*) reversão *f*; (*of*
direction) mudança em sentido contrário; (*of*
decision) revogação *f*; (*of opinion*) reviravolta.
reverse [rɪ'vɜːs] *n* (*opposite*) contrário; (*back:*
of cloth) avesso; (: *of coin*) reverso; (: *of pa-*
per) dorso; (*AUT*: *also*: **~ gear**) marcha à ré
(*BR*), marcha atrás (*PT*) ♦ *adj* (*order*)
inverso, oposto; (*direction*) contrário ♦ *vt*
(*turn over*) virar do lado do avesso; (*invert*)
inverter; (*change*) mudar (totalmente) de;
(*LAW*: *judgment*) revogar ♦ *vi* (*BRIT*: *AUT*)
dar (marcha à) ré (*BR*), fazer marcha atrás
(*PT*); **to go into ~** dar ré (*BR*), fazer marcha
atrás (*PT*); **in ~ order** na ordem inversa.
reversed charge call [rɪ'vɜːst-] (*BRIT*) *n*
(*TEL*) ligação *f* a cobrar.
reverse video *n* vídeo reverso.
reversible [rɪ'vɜːsəbl] *adj* reversível.
reversing lights [rɪ'vɜːsɪŋ-] *npl* luzes *fpl* de ré

(*BR*), luzes *fpl* de marcha atrás (*PT*).
reversion [rɪ'vəːʃən] *n* volta.
revert [rɪ'vəːt] *vi*: **to ~ to** voltar a.
review [rɪ'vjuː] *n* (*magazine*, *MIL*) revista; (*of book*, *film*) crítica, resenha; (*examination*) recapitulação *f*, exame *m* ♦ *vt* rever, examinar; (*MIL*) passar em revista; (*book*, *film*) fazer a crítica *or* resenha de; **to come under ~** ser estudado.
reviewer [rɪ'vjuːə*] *n* crítico/a.
revile [rɪ'vaɪl] *vt* ultrajar, injuriar, vilipendiar.
revise [rɪ'vaɪz] *vt* (*manuscript*) corrigir; (*opinion*) alterar, modificar; (*study: subject*) recapitular; (*look over*) revisar, rever; **~d edition** edição *f* revista.
revision [rɪ'vɪʒən] *n* correção *f*, modificação *f*, revisão *f*; (*revised version*) revisão *f*.
revitalize [riː'vaɪtəlaɪz] *vt* revitalizar, revivificar.
revival [rɪ'vaɪvəl] *n* (*recovery*) restabelecimento; (*of interest*) renascença, renascimento; (*THEATRE*) reestréia; (*of faith*) despertar *m*.
revive [rɪ'vaɪv] *vt* (*person*) reanimar, ressuscitar; (*custom*) restabelecer, restaurar; (*hope, courage*) despertar; (*play*) reapresentar ♦ *vi* (*person*) voltar a si, recuperar os sentidos; (*hope, activity*) renascer.
revoke [rɪ'vəuk] *vt* revogar; (*decision, promise*) voltar atrás com.
revolt [rɪ'vəult] *n* revolta, rebelião *f*, insurreição *f* ♦ *vi* revoltar-se ♦ *vt* causar aversão a, repugnar.
revolting [rɪ'vəultɪŋ] *adj* revoltante, repulsivo.
revolution [rɛvə'luːʃən] *n* revolução *f*.
revolutionary [rɛvə'luːʃənərɪ] *adj*, *n* revolucionário/a.
revolutionize [rɛvə'luːʃənaɪz] *vt* revolucionar.
revolve [rɪ'vɒlv] *vi* girar.
revolver [rɪ'vɒlvə*] *n* revólver *m*.
revolving [rɪ'vɒlvɪŋ] *adj* (*chair etc*) giratório.
revolving credit *n* crédito rotativo.
revolving door *n* porta giratória.
revue [rɪ'vjuː] *n* (*THEATRE*) revista.
revulsion [rɪ'vʌlʃən] *n* aversão *f*, repugnância.
reward [rɪ'wɔːd] *n* recompensa ♦ *vt*: **to ~ (for)** recompensar *or* premiar (por).
rewarding [rɪ'wɔːdɪŋ] *adj* (*fig*) gratificante, compensador(a).
rewind [riː'waɪnd] (*irreg*) *vt* (*watch*) dar corda em; (*tape*) voltar para trás.
rewire [riː'waɪə*] *vt* (*house*) renovar a instalação elétrica de.
reword [riː'wɔːd] *vt* reformular, exprimir em outras palavras.
rewound [riː'waund] *pt*, *pp of* **rewind**.
rewrite [riː'raɪt] (*irreg*) *vt* reescrever, escrever de novo.
Reykjavik ['reɪkjəviːk] *n* Reikiavik.
RFD (*US*) *abbr* (*POST*) = **rural free delivery**.
Rh *abbr* (= *rhesus*) Rh.
rhapsody ['ræpsədɪ] *n* (*MUS*) rapsódia; (*fig*)

elocução *f* exagerada *or* empolada.
rhesus factor ['riːsəs-] *n* (*MED*) fator *m* Rh.
rhetoric ['rɛtərɪk] *n* retórica.
rhetorical [rɪ'tɔrɪkl] *adj* retórico.
rheumatic [ruː'mætɪk] *adj* reumático.
rheumatism ['ruːmətɪzəm] *n* reumatismo.
rheumatoid arthritis ['ruːmətɔɪd-] *n* artrite *f* reumatóide.
Rhine [raɪn] *n*: **the ~** o (rio) Reno.
rhinestone ['raɪnstəun] *n* diamante *m* postiço.
rhinoceros [raɪ'nɔsərəs] *n* rinoceronte *m*.
Rhodes [rəudz] *n* (ilha de) Rodes.
Rhodesia [rəu'diːʒə] *n* Rodésia.
Rhodesian [rəu'diːʒən] *adj*, *n* rodésio/a.
rhododendron [rəudə'dɛndrən] *n* rododendro.
Rhone [rəun] *n*: **the ~** o (rio) Ródano.
rhubarb ['ruːbɑːb] *n* ruibarbo.
rhyme [raɪm] *n* rima; (*verse*) verso(s) *m*(*pl*) rimado(s), poesia ♦ *vi*: **to ~ (with)** rimar (com); **without ~ or reason** sem pé nem cabeça.
rhythm ['rɪðm] *n* ritmo, cadência.
rhythmic(al) ['rɪðmɪk(l)] *adj* rítmico, compassado.
rhythmically ['rɪðmɪklɪ] *adv* ritmicamente.
RI *n* *abbr* (*BRIT*) = **religious instruction** ♦ *abbr* (*US*: *POST*) = **Rhode Island**.
rib [rɪb] *n* (*ANAT*) costela ♦ *vt* (*mock*) zombar de, encarnar em.
ribald ['rɪbəld] *adj* vulgarmente engraçado, irreverente.
ribbed [rɪbd] *adj* (*knitting*) em ponto de meia.
ribbon ['rɪbən] *n* fita; (*strip*) faixa, tira; **in ~s** (*torn*) em tirinhas, esfarrapado.
rice [raɪs] *n* arroz *m*.
ricefield ['raɪsfiːld] *n* arrozal *m*.
rice pudding *n* arroz *m* doce.
rich [rɪtʃ] *adj* rico; (*banquet*) suntuoso, opulento; (*soil*) fértil; (*food*) suculento, forte; (: *sweet*) rico; **the ~** *npl* os ricos; **~es** *npl* riquezas *fpl*; **to be ~ in sth** ser rico em algo.
richly ['rɪtʃlɪ] *adv* (*decorated*) suntuosamente; (*deserved*) tanto.
richness ['rɪtʃnɪs] *n* riqueza, opulência; (*of soil etc*) fertilidade *f*.
rickets ['rɪkɪts] *n* raquitismo.
rickety ['rɪkɪtɪ] *adj* sem firmeza, vacilante.
rickshaw ['rɪkʃɔː] *n* jinriquixá *m*.
ricochet ['rɪkəʃeɪ] *n* ricochete *m* ♦ *vi* ricochetear.
rid [rɪd] (*pt*, *pp* **rid**) *vt*: **to ~ sb of sth** livrar alguém de algo; **to get ~ of** livrar-se *or* desembaraçar-se de.
riddance ['rɪdns] *n*: **good ~!** bons ventos o levem!
ridden ['rɪdn] *pp of* **ride**.
riddle ['rɪdl] *n* (*conundrum*) adivinhação *f*; (*mystery*) enigma *m*, charada ♦ *vt*: **to be ~d with** estar cheio *or* crivado de.
ride [raɪd] (*pt* **rode**, *pp* **ridden**) *n* (*gen*) passeio; (*on horse*) passeio a cavalo; (*distance covered*) percurso, trajeto ♦ *vi* (*as*

NB: European Portuguese adds the following consonants to certain words: **b** (sú(b)dito, su(b)til); **c** (a(c)ção, a(c)cionista, a(c)to); **m** (inde(m)ne); **p** (ado(p)ção, ado(p)tar); *for further details see p. xiii.*

sport) montar; *(go somewhere: on horse, bicycle)* ir (a cavalo, de bicicleta); *(journey: on bicycle, motor cycle, bus)* viajar ♦ *vt (a horse)* montar a; *(distance)* percorrer; **to ~ a bicycle** andar de bicicleta; **can you ~ a bike?** você sabe andar de bicicleta?; **to ~ at anchor** *(NAUT)* estar ancorado; **horse/car ~** passeio a cavalo/de carro; **to go for a ~** dar um passeio *or* uma volta (de carro *or* de bicicleta *etc*); **to take sb for a ~** *(fig)* enganar alguém.
   ride out *vt*: **to ~ out the storm** *(fig)* superar as dificuldades.
rider ['raɪdə*] *n (on horse: male)* cavaleiro; (: *female)* amazona; *(on bicycle)* ciclista *m/f*; *(on motorcycle)* motociclista *m/f*; *(in document)* cláusula adicional.
ridge [rɪdʒ] *n (of hill)* cume *m*, topo; *(of roof)* cumeeira; *(wrinkle)* ruga.
ridicule ['rɪdɪkjuːl] *n* escárnio, zombaria, mofa ♦ *vt* ridicularizar, zombar de; **to hold sb/sth up to ~** ridicularizar alguém/algo.
ridiculous [rɪ'dɪkjuləs] *adj* ridículo.
riding ['raɪdɪŋ] *n* equitação *f*.
   riding school *n* escola de equitação.
rife [raɪf] *adj*: **to be ~** ser comum; **to be ~ with** estar repleto de, abundar em.
riffraff ['rɪfræf] *n* plebe *f*, ralé *f*, povinho.
rifle ['raɪfl] *n* rifle *m*, fuzil *m* ♦ *vt* saquear.
   rifle through *vt fus* vasculhar.
   rifle range *n* campo de tiro; *(at fair)* tiro ao alvo.
rift [rɪft] *n (fig: disagreement: between friends)* desentendimento; (: *in party)* rompimento, divergência.
rig [rɪg] *n (also: oil ~)* torre *f* de perfuração ♦ *vt (election etc)* adulterar *or* falsificar os resultados de.
   rig out *(BRIT) vt* ataviar, vestir.
   rig up *vt* instalar, montar, improvisar.
rigging ['rɪgɪŋ] *n (NAUT)* cordame *m*.
right [raɪt] *adj (true, correct)* certo, correto; *(suitable)* adequado, conveniente; *(just)* justo; *(morally good)* bom; *(not left)* direito ♦ *n (title, claim)* direito; *(not left)* direita ♦ *adv (correctly)* bem, corretamente; *(not on the left)* à direita; *(to the ~)* para a direita ♦ *vt* endireitar ♦ *excl* bom!; **all ~!** tudo bem!, está bem!; *(enough)* chega!, basta!; **the ~ time** *(precise)* a hora exata; *(not wrong)* a hora certa; **to be ~** *(person)* ter razão; (: *in guess etc)* acertar; *(answer)* estar certo; **to get sth ~** acertar em algo; **let's get it ~ this time!** vamos acertar desta vez; **you did the ~ thing** você fez a coisa certa; **to put a mistake ~** *(BRIT)* consertar um erro; **~ now** agora mesmo; **~ before/after** logo antes/depois; **~ against the wall** rente à parede; **~ in the middle** bem no meio; **~ away** imediatamente, logo, já; **to go ~ to the end of sth** ir até o finalzinho de algo; **by ~s** por direito; **on the ~** à direita; **to be in the ~** ter razão; **film ~s** direitos de adaptação para o cinema; **~ of way** *(AUT)* preferência.
   right angle *n* ângulo reto.

righteous ['raɪtʃəs] *adj* justo, honrado; *(anger)* justificado.
righteousness ['raɪtʃəsnɪs] *n* justiça.
rightful ['raɪtful] *adj (heir)* legítimo.
rightfully ['raɪtfəlɪ] *adv* legitimamente.
right-hand *adj* à direita.
right-handed [-'hændɪd] *adj (person)* destro.
right-hand man *(irreg) n* braço direito.
right-hand side *n* lado direito.
rightly ['raɪtlɪ] *adv* corretamente, devidamente; *(with reason)* com razão; **if I remember ~** *(BRIT)* se me lembro bem, se não me engano.
right-minded *adj* sensato, ajuizado.
rights issue *n (STOCK EXCHANGE)* emissão *f* de bônus de subscrição.
right wing *n (POL)* direita; *(SPORT)* ponta direita; *(MIL)* ala direita ♦ *adj*: **right-wing** de direita.
right-winger *n (POL)* direitista *m/f*; *(SPORT)* ponta-direita *m*.
rigid ['rɪdʒɪd] *adj* rígido; *(principle)* inflexível.
rigidity [rɪ'dʒɪdɪtɪ] *n* rigidez *f*, inflexibilidade *f*.
rigidly ['rɪdʒɪdlɪ] *adv* rigidamente; *(behave)* inflexivelmente.
rigmarole ['rɪgmərəul] *n (process)* processo; *(story)* ladainha.
rigor ['rɪgə*] *(US) n* = **rigour**.
rigor mortis [-'mɔːtɪs] *n* rigidez *f* cadavérica.
rigorous ['rɪgərəs] *adj* rigoroso.
rigorously ['rɪgərəslɪ] *adv* rigorosamente.
rigour ['rɪgə*] *(US rigor) n* rigor *m*.
rig-out *(BRIT: inf) n* roupa, traje *m*.
rile [raɪl] *vt* irritar, aborrecer.
rim [rɪm] *n* borda, beira, orla; *(of spectacles, wheel)* aro.
rimless ['rɪmlɪs] *adj (spectacles)* sem aro.
rind [raɪnd] *n (of bacon)* couro, pele *f*; *(of lemon etc)* casca; *(of cheese)* crosta, casca.
ring [rɪŋ] *(pt rang, pp rung) n (of metal)* aro; *(on finger)* anel *m*; *(also: wedding ~)* aliança; *(of people, objects)* círculo, grupo; *(of spies)* grupo; *(for boxing)* ringue *m*; *(of circus)* pista, picadeiro; *(bull~)* picadeiro, arena; *(sound: of small bell)* toque *m*; (: *of large bell)* badalada, repique *m*; *(telephone call)* chamada (telefônica), ligada ♦ *vi (on telephone)* telefonar; *(bell)* tocar; *(also: ~ out: voice, words)* soar; *(ears)* zumbir ♦ *vt (BRIT: TEL: also: ~ up)* telefonar a, ligar para; *(bell etc)* badalar; *(doorbell)* tocar; **to give sb a ~** *(TEL)* dar uma ligada *or* ligar para alguém; **that has the ~ of truth about it** isso tem jeito de ser verdade; **the name doesn't ~ a bell (with me)** o nome não me diz nada.
   ring back *(BRIT) vi (TEL)* telefonar *or* ligar de volta ♦ *vt* telefonar *or* ligar de volta para.
   ring off *(BRIT) vi (TEL)* desligar.
ring binder *n* fichário *(pasta)*.
ring finger *n* dedo anelar.
ringing ['rɪŋɪŋ] *n (of large bell)* repicar *m*; *(of doorbell)* tocar *m*; *(in ears)* zumbido.
ringing tone *(BRIT) n (TEL)* sinal *m* de chamada.

ringleader ['rɪŋliːdə*] n (of gang) cabeça m/f, cérebro.

ringlets ['rɪŋlɪts] npl caracóis mpl, argolinhas fpl.

ring road (BRIT) n estrada periférica or perimetral.

rink [rɪŋk] n (also: ice ~) pista de patinação, rinque m; (for roller skating) rinque.

rinse [rɪns] n enxaguada ♦ vt enxaguar.

Rio (de Janeiro) ['riːəu(dədʒə'nɪərəu)] n o Rio (de Janeiro).

riot ['raɪət] n distúrbio, motim m, desordem f ♦ vi provocar distúrbios, amotinar-se; **a ~ of colours** uma orgia de cores; **to run ~** desenfrear-se.

rioter ['raɪətə*] n desordeiro/a, amotinador(a) m/f.

riotous ['raɪətəs] adj (crowd) desordeiro; (party) tumultuado, barulhento; (uncontrolled) desenfreado.

riotously ['raɪətəslɪ] adv: ~ **funny** hilariante.

riot police n polícia anti-motim.

RIP abbr (= rest in peace) RIP.

rip [rɪp] n rasgão m; (opening) abertura ♦ vt rasgar ♦ vi rasgar-se.

rip up vt rasgar.

ripcord ['rɪpkɔːd] n corda de abertura (de pára-quedas).

ripe [raɪp] adj (fruit) maduro; (ready) pronto.

ripen ['raɪpən] vt, vi amadurecer.

ripeness ['raɪpnɪs] n maturidade f, amadurecimento.

rip-off (inf) n: **this is a ~** isso é roubo.

riposte [rɪ'pɔst] n riposta.

ripple ['rɪpl] n ondulação f, encrespação f; (sound) murmúrio ♦ vi encrespar-se ♦ vt ondular.

rise [raɪz] (pt rose, pp risen) n (slope) elevação f, ladeira; (hill) colina, rampa; (increase: in wages: BRIT) aumento; (: in prices, temperature) subida; (fig: to power etc) ascensão f ♦ vi (gen) levantar-se, erguer-se; (prices, waters) subir; (river) encher; (sun) nascer; (wind, person: from bed etc) levantar(-se); (also: ~ up: rebel) sublevar-se; (in rank) ascender, subir; **to give ~ to** ocasionar, dar origem a; **to ~ to the occasion** mostrar-se à altura da situação.

rising ['raɪzɪŋ] adj (increasing: prices) em alta; (: number) crescente, cada vez maior; (: unemployment) crescente; (tide) montante; (sun, moon) nascente ♦ n (uprising) insurreição f.

rising damp n umidade f que sobe.

risk [rɪsk] n risco, perigo ♦ vt arriscar; (dare) atrever-se a; **to take** or **run the ~ of doing** correr o risco de fazer; **at ~** em perigo; **at one's own ~** por sua própria conta e risco; **a fire/health/security ~** um risco de incêndio/à saúde/à segurança; **I'll ~ it** eu vou me arriscar.

risk capital n capital m de risco.

risky ['rɪskɪ] adj arriscado.

risqué ['riːskeɪ] adj (joke) picante.

rissole ['rɪsəul] n rissole m.

rite [raɪt] n rito; **funeral ~s** exéquias, cerimônia fúnebre; **last ~s** últimos sacramentos.

ritual ['rɪtjuəl] adj ritual ♦ n ritual m, rito.

rival ['raɪvl] adj, n rival m/f; (in business) concorrente m/f ♦ vt rivalizar or competir com; **to ~ sb/sth in** rivalizar com alguém/algo em.

rivalry ['raɪvlrɪ] n rivalidade f; (between companies) concorrência.

river ['rɪvə*] n rio ♦ cpd (port, traffic) fluvial; **up/down ~** rio acima/abaixo.

riverbank ['rɪvəbæŋk] n margem f (do rio).

riverbed ['rɪvəbed] n leito (do rio).

riverside ['rɪvəsaɪd] n beira, orla (do rio).

rivet ['rɪvɪt] n rebite m, cravo ♦ vt rebitar; (fig) cravar.

riveting ['rɪvɪtɪŋ] adj (fig) fascinante.

Riviera [rɪvɪ'ɛərə] n: **the (French) ~** a Costa Azul (francesa), a Riviera francesa.

Riyadh [rɪ'jɑːd] n Riad.

RN n abbr (BRIT) = **Royal Navy**; (US) = **registered nurse**.

RNA n abbr (= ribonucleic acid) ARN m.

RNLI (BRIT) n abbr (= Royal National Lifeboat Institution) ≈ Salvamar.

RNZAF n abbr = **Royal New Zealand Air Force**.

RNZN n abbr = **Royal New Zealand Navy**.

road [rəud] n via; (motorway etc) estrada (de rodagem); (in town) rua; (fig) caminho; **main ~** estrada principal; **major ~** via preferencial; **minor ~** via secundária; **it takes four hours by ~** leva quatro horas de carro; **"~ up"** (BRIT) "obras".

roadblock ['rəudblɔk] n barricada.

road haulage n transportes mpl rodoviários.

roadhog ['rəudhɔg] n dono da estrada.

road map n mapa m rodoviário.

road safety n segurança do trânsito.

roadside ['rəudsaɪd] n beira da estrada ♦ cpd à beira da estrada; **by the ~** à beira da estrada.

roadsign ['rəudsaɪn] n placa de sinalização.

roadsweeper ['rəudswiːpə*] (BRIT) n (person) gari m/f (BR), varredor(a) m/f (PT).

road transport n transportes mpl rodoviários.

road user n usuário/a da via pública.

roadway ['rəudweɪ] n pista, estrada.

roadworks ['rəudwɜːks] npl obras fpl (na estrada).

roadworthy ['rəudwɜːðɪ] adj (car) em bom estado de conservação e segurança.

roam [rəum] vi vagar, perambular, errar ♦ vt vagar or vadiar por.

roar [rɔː*] n (of animal) rugido, urro; (of crowd) bramido; (of vehicle, storm) estrondo; (of laughter) barulho ♦ vi rugir, bramar, bradar; **to ~ with laughter** dar garga-

---

NB: European Portuguese adds the following consonants to certain words: **b** (sú(b)dito, su(b)til); **c** (a(c)ção, a(c)cionista, a(c)to); **m** (inde(m)ne); **p** (ado(p)ção, ado(p)tar); for further details see p. xiii.

lhadas.

roaring ['rɔːrɪŋ] adj: **a ~ fire** labaredas; **a ~ success** um sucesso estrondoso; **to do a ~ trade** fazer um bom negócio.

roast [rəust] n carne f assada, assado ♦ vt (meat) assar; (coffee) torrar.

roast beef n rosbife m.

rob [rɔb] vt roubar; (bank) assaltar; **to ~ sb of sth** roubar algo de alguém; (fig: deprive) despojar alguém de algo.

robber ['rɔbə*] n ladrão/ladra m/f.

robbery ['rɔbərɪ] n roubo.

robe [rəub] n (for ceremony etc) toga, beca; (also: bath ~) roupão m (de banho) ♦ vt revestir.

robin ['rɔbɪn] n pisco-de-peito-ruivo (BR), pintarroxo (PT).

robot ['rəubɔt] n robô m.

robotics [rə'bɔtɪks] n robótica.

robust [rəu'bʌst] adj robusto, forte.

rock [rɔk] n (gen) rocha; (boulder) penhasco, rochedo; (BRIT: sweet) pirulito ♦ vt (swing gently: cradle) balançar, oscilar; (: child) embalar, acalentar; (shake) sacudir ♦ vi balançar-se; (child) embalar-se; (shake) sacudir-se; **on the ~s** (drink) com gelo; (marriage etc) arruinado, em dificuldades; **to ~ the boat** (fig) criar confusão.

rock and roll n rock-and-roll m.

rock-bottom adj (fig) mínimo, ínfimo ♦ n: **to hit** or **reach ~** (prices) chegar ao nível mais baixo; (person) chegar ao fundo do poço.

rock climber n alpinista m/f.

rock climbing n alpinismo.

rockery ['rɔkərɪ] n jardim de plantas rasteiras entre pedras.

rocket ['rɔkɪt] n foguete m ♦ vi (prices) disparar.

rocket launcher [-'lɔːntʃə*] n dispositivo lança-foguetes.

rock face n rochedo a pique.

rock fall n queda de pedras.

rocking chair ['rɔkɪŋ-] n cadeira de balanço.

rocking horse ['rɔkɪŋ-] n cavalo de balanço.

rocky ['rɔkɪ] adj rochoso; (unsteady: table) bambo, instável.

Rocky Mountains npl: **the ~** as Montanhas Rochosas.

rod [rɔd] n vara, varinha; (TECH) haste f; (also: fishing ~) vara de pescar.

rode [rəud] pt of **ride**.

rodent ['rəudnt] n roedor m.

rodeo ['rəudɪəu] n rodeio.

roe [rəu] n (of fish): **hard/soft ~** ova/esperma m de peixe.

roe (deer) n inv corça, cerva.

rogue [rəug] n velhaco, maroto.

roguish ['rəugɪʃ] adj travesso, brincalhão/lhona.

role [rəul] n papel m.

roll [rəul] n rolo; (of banknotes) maço; (also: bread ~) pãozinho; (register) rol m, lista; (sound: of drums etc) rufar m; (movement: of ship) jogo ♦ vt rolar; (also: ~ up: string) enrolar; (: sleeves) arregaçar; (cigarettes)

enrolar; (also: ~ out: pastry) esticar, alisar ♦ vi rolar; (drum) rufar; (in walking) gingar; (ship) balançar, jogar; **cheese ~** sanduíche de queijo (num pãozinho).

roll about vi ficar rolando.

roll around vi ficar rolando.

roll by vi (time) passar.

roll in vi (mail, cash) chegar em grande quantidade.

roll over vi dar uma volta.

roll up vi (inf: arrive) pintar, chegar, aparecer ♦ vt (carpet) enrolar; (sleeves) arregaçar; **to ~ o.s. up into a ball** enrolar-se.

roll call n chamada, toque m de chamada.

rolled gold [rəuld-] n plaquê m.

roller ['rəulə*] n rolo; (wheel) roda, roldana.

roller blind (BRIT) n estore m.

roller coaster n montanha-russa.

roller skates npl patins mpl de roda.

rollicking ['rɔlɪkɪŋ] adj alegre, brincalhão/lhona, divertido.

rolling ['rəulɪŋ] adj (landscape) ondulado.

rolling mill n laminador m.

rolling pin n rolo de pastel.

rolling stock n (RAIL) material m rodante.

roll-on-roll-off (BRIT) adj (ferry) para veículos.

roly-poly ['rəulɪ'pəulɪ] (BRIT) n (CULIN) bolo de rolo.

ROM [rɔm] n abbr (COMPUT: = read-only memory) ROM m.

Roman ['rəumən] adj, n romano/a.

Roman Catholic adj, n católico/a (romano/a).

romance [rə'mæns] n (love affair) aventura amorosa, romance m; (book etc) história de amor; (charm) romantismo.

Romania [ruː'meɪnɪə] n Romênia.

Romanian [ruː'meɪnɪən] adj romeno ♦ n romeno/a; (LING) romeno.

Roman numeral n número romano.

romantic [rə'mæntɪk] adj romântico.

romanticism [rə'mæntɪsɪzəm] n romantismo.

Romany ['rəumənɪ] adj cigano ♦ n cigano/a; (LING) romani m.

romp [rɔmp] n brincadeira, travessura ♦ vi (also: ~ about) brincar ruidosamente; **to ~ home** (horse) ganhar fácil.

rompers ['rɔmpəz] npl macacão m de bebê.

rondo ['rɔndəu] n (MUS) rondó.

roof [ruːf, pl ruːfs or ruːvz] n (of house) telhado; (of car) capota, teto; (of tunnel, cave) teto ♦ vt telhar, cobrir com telhas; **the ~ of the mouth** o céu da boca.

roof garden n jardim m em terraço.

roofing ['ruːfɪŋ] n cobertura.

roof rack n (AUT) bagageiro.

rook [ruk] n (bird) gralha; (CHESS) torre f.

room [ruːm] n (in house) quarto, aposento; (also: bed~) quarto, dormitório; (in school etc) sala; (space) espaço, lugar m; **~s** npl (lodging) alojamento; "**~s to let**" (BRIT), "**~s for rent**" (US) "alugam-se quartos or apartamentos"; **single ~** quarto individual;

double ~ quarto duplo *or* de casal *or* para duas pessoas; **is there** ~ **for this?** tem lugar para isto aqui?; **to make** ~ **for sb** dar lugar a alguém; **there is** ~ **for improvement** isso podia estar melhor.

rooming house ['ruːmɪŋ-] (*US: irreg*) *n* casa de cômodos.

roommate ['ruːmmeɪt] *n* companheiro/a de quarto.

room service *n* serviço de quarto.

room temperature *n* temperatura ambiente.

roomy ['ruːmɪ] *adj* espaçoso; (*garment*) folgado.

roost [ruːst] *n* poleiro ♦ *vi* empoleirar-se, pernoitar.

rooster ['ruːstə*] *n* galo.

root [ruːt] *n* (*BOT, MATH*) raiz *f*; (*fig: of problem*) origem *f* ♦ *vi* (*plant, belief*) enraizar; arraigar; **to take** ~ (*plant*) enraizar; (*idea*) criar raízes.

root about *vi* (*fig*): **to** ~ **about in** (*drawer*) vasculhar; (*house*) esquadrinhar.

root for (*inf*) *vt fus* torcer por.

root out *vt* desarraigar, extirpar.

rope [rəup] *n* corda; (*NAUT*) cabo ♦ *vt* (*climbers, box*) atar *or* amarrar com uma corda; (*horse, cow*) laçar; **to know the** ~**s** (*fig*) estar por dentro (do assunto).

rope in *vt* (*fig*): **to** ~ **sb in** persuadir alguém a tomar parte.

rope ladder *n* escada de corda.

rosary ['rəuzərɪ] *n* rosário.

rose [rəuz] *pt of* **rise** ♦ *n* rosa; (*also:* ~*bush*) roseira; (*on watering can*) crivo ♦ *adj* rosado, cor de rosa *inv*.

rosé ['rəuzeɪ] *n* rosado, rosé *m*.

rosebed ['rəuzbɛd] *n* roseiral *m*.

rosebud ['rəuzbʌd] *n* botão *m* de rosa.

rosebush ['rəuzbuʃ] *n* roseira.

rosemary ['rəuzmərɪ] *n* alecrim *m*.

rosette [rəu'zɛt] *n* rosácea, roseta.

ROSPA ['rɔspə] (*BRIT*) *n abbr* = **Royal Society for the Prevention of Accidents.**

roster ['rɔstə*] *n*: **duty** ~ lista de tarefas, escala de serviço.

rostrum ['rɔstrəm] *n* tribuna.

rosy ['rəuzɪ] *adj* rosado, rosáceo; **a** ~ **future** um futuro promissor.

rot [rɔt] *n* (*decay*) putrefação *f*, podridão *f*; (*fig: pej*) decadência ♦ *vt, vi* apodrecer; **to stop the** ~ (*BRIT: fig*) acabar com a onda de fracassos; **dry** ~ apodrecimento seco (*de madeira*); **wet** ~ putrefação fungosa.

rota ['rəutə] *n* lista de tarefas, escala de serviço; **on a** ~ **basis** em rodízio.

rotary ['rəutərɪ] *adj* rotativo.

rotate [rəu'teɪt] *vt* (*revolve*) fazer girar, dar voltas em; (*change round: crops*) alternar; (*: jobs*) alternar, revezar ♦ *vi* (*revolve*) girar, dar voltas.

rotating [rəu'teɪtɪŋ] *adj* (*movement*) rotativo.

rotation [rəu'teɪʃən] *n* rotação *f*; **in** ~ por

turnos.

rote [rəut] *n*: **by** ~ de cor.

rotor ['rəutə*] *n* rotor *m*.

rotten ['rɔtn] *adj* (*decayed*) podre; (*wood*) carcomido; (*fig*) corrupto; (*inf: bad*) péssimo; **to feel** ~ (*ill*) sentir-se podre.

rotting ['rɔtɪŋ] *adj* podre.

rotund [rəu'tʌnd] *adj* rotundo; (*person*) rechonchudo.

rouble ['ruːbl] (*US* **ruble**) *n* rublo.

rouge [ruːʒ] *n* rouge *m*, blush *m*, carmim *m*.

rough [rʌf] *adj* (*skin, surface*) áspero; (*terrain*) acidentado; (*road*) desigual; (*voice*) áspero, rouco; (*person, manner: coarse*) grosseiro, grosso; (*: violent*) violento; (*weather*) tempestuoso; (*treatment*) brutal, mau/má; (*cloth*) grosseiro; (*plan*) preliminar; (*guess*) aproximado ♦ *n* (*person*) grosseirão *m*; (*GOLF*): **in the** ~ na grama crescida; **the sea is** ~ **today** o mar está agitado hoje; **to have a** ~ **time (of it)** passar maus bocados; ~ **estimate** estimativa aproximada; **to** ~ **it** passar aperto; **to play** ~ jogar bruto; **to sleep** ~ (*BRIT*) dormir na rua; **to feel** ~ (*BRIT*) passar mal.

rough out *vt* (*draft*) rascunhar.

roughage ['rʌfɪdʒ] *n* fibras *fpl*.

rough-and-ready *adj* improvisado, feito às pressas.

rough-and-tumble *n* luta, confusão *f*.

roughcast ['rʌfkɑːst] *n* reboco.

rough copy *n* rascunho.

rough draft *n* rascunho.

roughen ['rʌfən] *vt* (*surface*) tornar áspero.

rough justice *n* justiça sumária.

roughly ['rʌflɪ] *adv* (*handle*) bruscamente; (*make*) toscamente; (*approximately*) aproximadamente.

roughness ['rʌfnɪs] *n* aspereza; (*rudeness*) grosseria.

roughshod ['rʌfʃɔd] *adv*: **to ride** ~ **over** (*person*) tratar a pontapés; (*objection*) passar por cima de.

rough work *n* (*at school etc*) rascunho.

roulette [ruː'lɛt] *n* roleta.

Roumania *etc* [ruː'meɪnɪə] *n* = **Romania** *etc*.

round [raund] *adj* redondo ♦ *n* círculo; (*BRIT: of toast*) rodela; (*of drinks*) rodada; (*of policeman*) ronda; (*of milkman*) trajeto; (*of doctor*) visitas *fpl*; (*game: of cards, in competition*) partida; (*stage of competition*) rodada, turno; (*of ammunition*) cartucho; (*BOXING*) rounde *m*, assalto; (*of talks*) ciclo ♦ *vt* (*corner*) virar, dobrar; (*bend*) fazer; (*cape*) dobrar ♦ *prep* ao/em redor de, em/à volta de ♦ *adv*: **right** ~, **all** ~ por todos os lados; **the long way** ~ o caminho mais comprido; **all the year** ~ durante todo o ano; **in** ~ **figures** em números redondos; **it's just** ~ **the corner** está logo depois de virar a esquina; (*fig*) está pertinho; **to ask sb** ~ convidar alguém (para sua casa); **I'll be** ~ **at 6**

o'clock estarei aí às 6 horas; **to go** ~ dar a volta; **to go** ~ **to sb's (house)** dar um pulinho na casa de alguém; **to go** ~ **an obstacle** contornar um obstáculo; **to go** ~ **the back** passar por detrás; **to go** ~ **a house** visitar uma casa; **enough to go** ~ suficiente para todos; **she arrived** ~ **(about) noon** (BRIT) ela chegou por volta do meio-dia; ~ **the clock** ininterrupto; **to go the** ~**s** (story) divulgar-se; **the daily** ~ (fig) o cotidiano; **a** ~ **of applause** uma salva de palmas; **a** ~ **of drinks** uma rodada de bebidas; ~ **of sandwiches** (BRIT) sanduíche m (BR), sandes f inv (PT).

round off vt (speech etc) terminar, completar.

round up vt (cattle) encurralar; (people) reunir; (prices) arredondar.

roundabout ['raundəbaut] n (BRIT: AUT) rotatória; (at fair) carrossel m ♦ adj (route, means) indireto.

rounded ['raundıd] adj arredondado; (style) expressivo.

rounders ['raundəz] npl (game) ≈ beisebol m.

roundly ['raundlı] adv (fig) energicamente, totalmente.

round-shouldered [-'ʃəuldəd] adj encurvado.

roundsman ['raundzmən] (BRIT: irreg) n entregador m a domicílio.

round trip n viagem f de ida e volta.

roundup ['raundʌp] n rodeio; (of criminals) batida; **a** ~ **of the latest news** um resumo das últimas notícias.

rouse [rauz] vt (wake up) despertar, acordar; (stir up) suscitar.

rousing ['rauzıŋ] adj emocionante, vibrante.

rout [raut] n (MIL) derrota; (flight) fuga, debandada ♦ vt derrotar.

route [ru:t] n caminho, rota; (of bus) trajeto; (of shipping) rumo, rota; "**all** ~**s**" (AUT) "todas as direções"; **the best** ~ **to London** o melhor caminho para Londres; **en** ~ **for** a caminho de; **en** ~ **from** ... **to** a caminho de ... para.

route map n (BRIT: for journey) mapa m rodoviário; (for trains etc) mapa da rede.

routine [ru:'ti:n] adj (work) rotineiro; (procedure) de rotina ♦ n rotina; (THEATRE) número; **daily** ~ cotidiano.

roving ['rəuvıŋ] adj (wandering) errante.

roving reporter n correspondente m/f.

row¹ [rəu] n (line) fila, fileira; (KNITTING) carreira, fileira ♦ vi, vt remar; **two days in a** ~ dois dias a fio.

row² [rau] n (noise, racket) barulho, balbúrdia; (dispute) discussão f, briga; (fuss) confusão f, bagunça; (scolding) repreensão f ♦ vi brigar; **to have a** ~ ter uma briga.

rowboat ['rəubəut] (US) n barco a remo.

rowdiness ['raudınıs] n barulheira; (fighting) brigas fpl.

rowdy ['raudı] adj (person: noisy) barulhento; (: quarrelsome) brigão/ona; (occasion) tumultuado ♦ n encrenqueiro, criador m de caso.

rowdyism ['raudıızəm] n violência.

rowing ['rəuıŋ] n remo.

rowing boat (BRIT) n barco a remo.

rowlock ['rɔlək] (BRIT) n toleteira, forqueta.

royal ['rɔıəl] adj real.

Royal Air Force (BRIT) n força aérea britânica.

royal blue adj azul vivo inv.

royalist ['rɔıəlıst] adj, n monarquista m/f (BR), monárquico/a (PT).

Royal Navy (BRIT) n marinha de guerra britânica.

royalty ['rɔıəltı] n (persons) família real, realeza; (payment: to author) direitos mpl autorais; (: to inventor) direitos mpl de exploração de patente.

RP (BRIT) n abbr (= received pronunciation) norma de pronúncia.

rpm abbr (= revolutions per minute) rpm.

RR (US) abbr = **railroad**.

R&R (US) n abbr (MIL) = **rest and recreation**.

RSA (BRIT) n abbr = **Royal Society of Arts**; **Royal Scottish Academy**.

RSPB (BRIT) n abbr = **Royal Society for the Protection of Birds**.

RSPCA (BRIT) n abbr = **Royal Society for the Prevention of Cruelty to Animals**.

RSVP abbr (= répondez s'il vous plaît) ER.

Rt Hon. (BRIT) abbr (= Right Honourable) título honorífico de conselheiro do estado ou juiz.

Rt Rev. abbr (= Right Reverend) reverendíssimo.

rub [rʌb] vt esfregar; (hard) friccionar ♦ n esfregadela; (hard) fricção f; (touch) roçar m; **to** ~ **sb up** (BRIT) or ~ **sb** (US) **the wrong way** irritar alguém.

rub down vt (person) esfregar; (horse) almofaçar.

rub in vt (ointment) esfregar.

rub off vi sair esfregando; **to** ~ **off on** transmitir-se para, influir sobre.

rub out vt apagar ♦ vi apagar-se.

rubber ['rʌbə*] n borracha; (BRIT: eraser) borracha.

rubber band n elástico, tira elástica.

rubber plant n (tree) seringueira; (plant) figueira.

rubber ring n (for swimming) bóia.

rubber stamp n carimbo ♦ vt: **to rubberstamp** (fig) aprovar sem questionar.

rubbery ['rʌbərı] adj elástico.

rubbish ['rʌbıʃ] n (from household) lixo; (fig: pej) porcarias fpl; (nonsense) disparates mpl, asneiras fpl ♦ vt (BRIT: inf) desprezar; **what you've just said is** ~ você acabou de dizer uma besteira; ~! que nada!, nado disso!

rubbish bin (BRIT) n lata de lixo.

rubbish dump n (in town) depósito (de lixo).

rubbishy ['rʌbıʃı] (BRIT: inf) adj micha, chinfrim.

rubble ['rʌbl] n escombros mpl.

ruble ['ru:bl] (US) n = **rouble**.

ruby ['ru:bı] n rubi m.

RUC (*BRIT*) *n abbr* = **Royal Ulster Constabulary**.

rucksack ['rʌksæk] *n* mochila.

ructions ['rʌkʃənz] *npl* confusão *f*, tumulto.

rudder ['rʌdə*] *n* leme *m*.

ruddy ['rʌdɪ] *adj* (*face*) corado, avermelhado; (*inf: damned*) maldito, desgraçado.

rude [ruːd] *adj* (*impolite: person*) grosso, mal-educado; (: *word, manners*) grosseiro; (*sudden*) brusco; (*shocking*) obsceno, chocante; **to be ~ to sb** ser grosso com alguém.

rudely ['ruːdlɪ] *adv* grosseiramente.

rudeness ['ruːdnɪs] *n* falta de educação.

rudiment ['ruːdɪmənt] *n* rudimento; **~s** *npl* primeiras noções *fpl*.

rudimentary [ruːdɪ'mɛntərɪ] *adj* rudimentar.

rue [ruː] *vt* arrepender-se de.

rueful ['ruːful] *adj* arrependido.

ruff [rʌf] *n* rufo.

ruffian ['rʌfɪən] *n* brigão *m*, desordeiro.

ruffle ['rʌfl] *vt* (*hair*) despentear, desmanchar; (*clothes*) enrugar, amarrotar; (*fig: person*) perturbar, irritar.

rug [rʌg] *n* tapete *m*; (*BRIT: for knees*) manta (de viagem).

rugby ['rʌgbɪ] *n* (*also:* ~ *football*) rúgbi *m* (*BR*), râguebi *m* (*PT*).

rugged ['rʌgɪd] *adj* (*landscape*) acidentado, irregular; (*features*) marcado; (*character*) severo, austero; (*determination*) teimoso.

rugger ['rʌgə*] (*BRIT: inf*) *n* rúgbi *m* (*BR*), râguebi *m* (*PT*).

ruin ['ruːɪn] *n* ruína ♦ *vt* arruinar; (*spoil*) estragar; **~s** *npl* ruínas *fpl*; **in ~s** em ruínas.

ruination [ruːɪ'neɪʃən] *n* ruína.

ruinous ['ruːɪnəs] *adj* desastroso.

rule [ruːl] *n* (*norm*) regra; (*government*) governo, domínio; (*ruler*) régua ♦ *vt* (*country, person*) governar; (*decide*) decidir; (*draw: lines*) traçar ♦ *vi* (*monarch*) reger; (*government*) governar; (*LAW*) decretar; **to ~ in favour of/against** decidir oficialmente a favor de/contra; **to ~ that** (*umpire, judge*) decidir que; **under British ~** sob domínio britânico; **it's against the ~s** não é permitido; **by ~ of thumb** empiricamente; **as a ~** por via de regra, geralmente.

rule out *vt* excluir.

ruled [ruːld] *adj* (*paper*) pautado.

ruler ['ruːlə*] *n* (*sovereign*) soberano/a; (*for measuring*) régua.

ruling ['ruːlɪŋ] *adj* (*party*) dominante; (*class*) dirigente ♦ *n* (*LAW*) parecer *m*, decisão *f*.

rum [rʌm] *n* rum *m* ♦ *adj* (*BRIT: inf*) esquisito.

Rumania *etc* [ruː'meɪnɪə] *n* = **Romania** *etc*.

rumble ['rʌmbl] *n* ruído surdo, barulho; (*of thunder*) estrondo, ribombo ♦ *vi* ribombar, ressoar; (*stomach*) roncar; (*pipe*) fazer barulho.

rumbunctious [rʌm'bʌŋkʃəs] (*US*) = **rumbustious**.

rumbustious [rʌm'bʌstʃəs] (*BRIT*) *adj*

(*person*) enérgico.

rummage ['rʌmɪdʒ] *vi* remexer, dar busca; **to ~ in** (*drawer*) vasculhar.

rumour ['ruːmə*] (*US* **rumor**) *n* rumor *m*, boato ♦ *vt*: **it is ~ed that ...** corre o boato de que ....

rump [rʌmp] *n* (*of animal*) anca, garupa; (*also:* ~ **steak**) alcatra.

rumple ['rʌmpl] *vt* (*hair*) despentear; (*clothes*) amarrotar.

rumpus ['rʌmpəs] (*inf*) *n* barulho, confusão *f*, zorra; (*quarrel*) bate-boca *m*; **to kick up a ~** fazer um escândalo.

run [rʌn] (*pt* **ran**, *pp* **run**) *n* (*race etc*) corrida; (*outing*) passeio (de carro); (*distance travelled*) trajeto, percurso; (*series*) série *f*; (*THEATRE*) temporada; (*SKI*) pista; (*in stockings*) fio puxado ♦ *vt* (*operate: business*) dirigir; (: *competition, course*) organizar; (: *hotel, house*) administrar; (*water*) deixar correr; (*bath*) encher; (*COMPUT: program*) rodar; (*pass: hand, finger*): **to ~ sth over** passar algo em ♦ *vi* correr; (*pass: road etc*) passar; (*work: machine*) funcionar; (*bus, train: operate*) circular; (: *travel*) ir; (*continue: play*) continuar em cartaz; (: *contract*) ser válido; (*slide: drawer*) deslizar; (*flow: river, bath*) fluir, correr; (*colours, washing*) desbotar; (*in election*) candidatar-se, **to go for a ~** fazer cooper; (*in car*) dar uma volta (de carro); **to break into a ~** pôr-se a correr; **a ~ of luck** um período de sorte; **to have the ~ of sb's house** ter a casa de alguém à sua disposição; **there was a ~ on** (*meat, tickets*) houve muita procura de; **in the long ~** no final das contas, mais cedo ou mais tarde; **on the ~** em fuga, fugindo; **to ~ for the bus** correr até o ônibus; **we'll have to ~ for it** vamos ter que correr atrás; **I'll ~ you to the station** vou te levar à estação; **to ~ a risk** correr um risco; **to ~ errands** fazer recados; **to make a ~ for it** fugir, dar no pé; **the train ~s between Gatwick and Victoria** o trem faz o percurso entre Gatwick e Victoria; **the bus ~s every 20 minutes** o ônibus passa a cada 20 minutos; **it's very cheap to ~** (*car, machine*) é muito econômico; **to ~ on petrol** (*BRIT*) or **gas** (*US*)/**on diesel/off batteries** funcionar a gasolina/a óleo diesel/a pilhas; **to ~ for president** candidatar-se à presidência, ser presidenciável; **their losses ran into millions** suas perdas se elevaram a milhões; **to be ~ off one's feet** (*BRIT*) não ter descanso, não parar um minuto; **my salary won't ~ to a car** meu salário não é suficiente para comprar um carro.

run about *vi* (*children*) correr por todos os lados.

run across *vt fus* (*find*) encontrar por acaso, topar com, dar com.

run away *vi* fugir.

NB: European Portuguese adds the following consonants to certain words: **b** (sú(b)dito, su(b)til); **c** (a(c)ção, a(c)cionista, a(c)to); **m** (inde(m)ne); **p** (ado(p)ção, ado(p)tar); *for further details see p. xiii.*

run down vi (clock) parar ♦ vt (AUT) atropelar; (BRIT: reduce: production) reduzir; (: factory) reduzir a produção de; (criticize) falar mal de, criticar; **to be ~ down** estar enfraquecido or exausto.

run in (BRIT) vt (car) rodar.

run into vt fus (meet: person) dar com, topar com; (: trouble) esbarrar em; (collide with) bater em; **to ~ into debt** endividar-se.

run off vt (water) deixar correr ♦ vi fugir.

run out vi (person) sair correndo; (liquid) escorrer, esgotar-se; (lease) caducar, vencer; (money) acabar.

run out of vt fus ficar sem; **I've ~ out of petrol** (BRIT) or **gas** (US) estou sem gasolina.

run over vt (AUT) atropelar ♦ vt fus (revise) recapitular.

run through vt fus (instructions) examinar, recapitular.

run up vt (debt) acumular ♦ vi: **to ~ up against** (difficulties) esbarrar em.

runaway ['rʌnəweɪ] adj (horse) desembestado; (truck) desgovernado; (person) fugitivo; (inflation) galopante.

rundown ['rʌndaun] (BRIT) n (of industry etc) redução f progressiva.

rung [rʌŋ] pp of **ring** ♦ n (of ladder) degrau m.

run-in (inf) n briga, bate-boca m.

runner ['rʌnə*] n (in race: person) corredor(a) m/f; (: horse) corredor m; (on sledge) patim m, lâmina; (on curtain) anel m; (wheel) roldana, roda; (for drawer etc) corrediça; (carpet: in hall etc) passadeira.

runner bean (BRIT) n (BOT) vagem f (BR), feijão m verde (PT).

runner-up n segundo/a colocado/a.

running ['rʌnɪŋ] n (sport, race) corrida; (of business) direção f; (of event) organização f; (of machine etc) funcionamento ♦ adj (water) corrente; (commentary) contínuo, seguido; **6 days ~** 6 dias seguidos or consecutivos; **to be in/out of the ~ for sth** disputar algo/estar fora da disputa por algo.

running costs npl (of business) despesas fpl operacionais; (of car) custos mpl de manutenção.

running head n (TYP, WORD PROCESSING) título corrido.

running mate (US) n (POL) companheiro/a de chapa.

runny ['rʌnɪ] adj (sauce, paint) aguado; (ice cream) derretido, mole; **to have a ~ nose** estar com coriza, estar com o nariz escorrendo.

run-off n (in contest, election) segundo turno; (extra race etc) corrida decisiva.

run-of-the-mill adj comum, normal.

runt [rʌnt] (also: pej) n nanico, anão/anã m/f.

run-through n ensaio.

run-up (BRIT) n: **~ to sth** período que antecede algo; **during** or **in the ~ to** nas vésperas de.

runway ['rʌnweɪ] n (AVIAT) pista (de decolagem or de pouso).

rupee [ruː'piː] n rupia.

rupture ['rʌptʃə*] n (MED) hérnia ♦ vt: **to ~ o.s.** provocar-se uma hérnia.

rural ['ruərl] adj rural, campestre.

ruse [ruːz] n ardil m, manha.

rush [rʌʃ] n ímpeto, investida; (hurry) pressa; (COMM) grande procura or demanda; (BOT) junco; (current) corrente f forte, torrente f ♦ vt apressar; (work) fazer depressa; (attack: town etc) assaltar; (BRIT: inf: charge) cobrar ♦ vi apressar-se, precipitar-se; **don't ~ me!** não me apresse!; **is there any ~ for this?** isso é urgente?; **to ~ sth off** (do quickly) fazer algo às pressas; (send) enviar depressa; **we've had a ~ of orders** recebimos uma enxurrada de pedidos; **to be in a ~** estar com pressa; **to do sth in a ~** fazer algo às pressas; **to be in a ~ to do sth** ter urgência em fazer algo.

rush through vt fus (work) fazer às pressas ♦ vt (COMM: order) executar com toda a urgência.

rush hour n rush m (BR), hora de ponta (PT).

rush job n trabalho urgente.

rush matting n tapete m de palha.

rusk [rʌsk] n rosca.

Russia ['rʌʃə] n Rússia.

Russian ['rʌʃən] adj russo ♦ n russo/a; (LING) russo.

rust [rʌst] n ferrugem f ♦ vi enferrujar.

rustic ['rʌstɪk] adj rústico, camponês/esa ♦ n (pej) caipira m/f.

rustle ['rʌsl] vi sussurrar ♦ vt (paper) farfalhar; (US: cattle) roubar, afanar.

rustproof ['rʌstpruːf] adj inoxidável, à prova de ferrugem.

rustproofing ['rʌstpruːfɪŋ] n tratamento contra ferrugem.

rusty ['rʌstɪ] adj enferrujado.

rut [rʌt] n sulco; (ZOOL) cio; **to be in a ~** ser escravo da rotina.

rutabaga [ruːtə'beɪɡə] (US) n rutabaga.

ruthless ['ruːθlɪs] adj implacável, sem piedade.

ruthlessness ['ruːθlɪsnɪs] n crueldade f, desumanidade f, insensibilidade f.

RV abbr (= revised version) tradução inglesa da Bíblia de 1885 ♦ n abbr (US) = **recreational vehicle**.

rye [raɪ] n centeio.

rye bread n pão m de centeio.

S

S, s [ɛs] n (letter) S, s m; (US: SCH: = satisfactory) satisfatório; **S for Sugar** S de Sandra.

S abbr (= south) S; (= saint) S, Sto, Sta.

SA *n abbr* = **South Africa; South America.**
Sabbath ['sæbəθ] *n (Christian)* domingo; *(Jewish)* sábado.
sabbatical [sə'bætɪkl] *adj*: ~ **year** ano sabático *or* de licença.
sabotage ['sæbətɑːʒ] *n* sabotagem *f* ♦ *vt* sabotar.
saccharin(e) ['sækərɪn] *n* sacarina.
sachet ['sæʃeɪ] *n* sachê *m*.
sack [sæk] *n (bag)* saco, saca ♦ *vt (dismiss)* despedir; *(plunder)* saquear; **to get the** ~ ser demitido; **to give sb the** ~ pôr alguém no olho da rua, despedir alguém.
sackful ['sækful] *n*: **a** ~ **of** um saco de.
sacking ['sækɪŋ] *n (dismissal)* demissão *f*; *(material)* aniagem *f*.
sacrament ['sækrəmənt] *n* sacramento.
sacred ['seɪkrɪd] *adj* sagrado.
sacrifice ['sækrɪfaɪs] *n* sacrifício ♦ *vt* sacrificar; **to make** ~**s (for sb)** fazer um sacrifício (por alguém).
sacrilege ['sækrɪlɪdʒ] *n* sacrilégio.
sacrosanct ['sækrəusæŋkt] *adj* sacrossanto.
sad [sæd] *adj (unhappy)* triste; *(deplorable)* deplorável, triste.
sadden ['sædn] *vt* entristecer.
saddle ['sædl] *n* sela; *(of cycle)* selim *m* ♦ *vt (horse)* selar; **to** ~ **sb with sth** *(inf: task, bill)* pôr algo nas costas de alguém; *(: responsibility)* sobrecarregar alguém com algo.
saddlebag ['sædlbæg] *n* alforje *m*.
sadism ['seɪdɪzm] *n* sadismo.
sadist ['seɪdɪst] *n* sádico/a.
sadistic [sə'dɪstɪk] *adj* sádico.
sadly ['sædlɪ] *adv* tristemente; *(regrettably)* infelizmente; ~ **lacking (in)** muito carente (de).
sadness ['sædnɪs] *n* tristeza.
sae *(BRIT)* *abbr* (= *stamped addressed envelope)* envelope selado e sobrescritado.
safari [sə'fɑːrɪ] *n* safári *m*.
safari park *n parque com animais selvagens*.
safe [seɪf] *adj (out of danger)* fora de perigo; *(not dangerous)* seguro; *(unharmed)* ileso, incólume; *(trustworthy)* digno de confiança ♦ *n* cofre *m*, caixa-forte *f*; ~ **and sound** são e salvo; **(just) to be on the** ~ **side** por via das dúvidas; **to play** ~ não correr riscos; **it is** ~ **to say that** ... posso afirmar que ...; ~ **journey!** boa viagem!
safe-breaker *(BRIT)* *n* arrombador *m* de cofres.
safe-conduct *n* salvo-conduto.
safe-cracker *n* arrombador *m* de cofres.
safe-deposit *n (vault)* cofre *m* de segurança; *(box)* caixa-forte *f*.
safeguard ['seɪfgɑːd] *n* salvaguarda, proteção *f* ♦ *vt* proteger, defender.
safekeeping [seɪf'kiːpɪŋ] *n* custódia, proteção.
safely ['seɪflɪ] *adv* com segurança, a salvo; *(without mishap)* sem perigo; **I can** ~ **say** ...

posso seguramente dizer ....
safety ['seɪftɪ] *n* segurança.
safety belt *n* cinto de segurança.
safety curtain *n* cortina de ferro.
safety net *n* rede *f* de segurança.
safety pin *n* alfinete *m* de segurança.
safety valve *n* válvula de segurança.
saffron ['sæfrən] *n* açafrão *m*.
sag [sæg] *vi* afrouxar.
saga ['sɑːgə] *n* saga; *(fig)* novela.
sage [seɪdʒ] *n (herb)* salva; *(man)* sábio.
Sagittarius [sædʒɪ'tɛərɪəs] *n* Sagitário.
sago ['seɪgəu] *n* sagu *m*.
Sahara [sə'hɑːrə] *n*: **the** ~ **(Desert)** o Saara.
said [sed] *pt, pp of* **say**.
sail [seɪl] *n (on boat)* vela; *(trip)*: **to go for a** ~ dar um passeio de barco a vela ♦ *vt (boat)* governar ♦ *vi (travel: ship)* navegar, velejar; *(: passenger)* ir de barco; *(set off)* zarpar; **to set** ~ zarpar; **they** ~**ed into Rio de Janeiro** entraram no porto do Rio de Janeiro.
sail through *vt fus (fig)* fazer com facilidade ♦ *vi* fazer de letra, fazer com um pé nas costas.
sailboat ['seɪlbəut] *(US)* *n* barco a vela.
sailing ['seɪlɪŋ] *n (SPORT)* navegação *f* a vela, vela; **to go** ~ ir velejar.
sailing boat *n* barco a vela.
sailing ship *n* veleiro.
sailor ['seɪlə*] *n* marinheiro, marujo.
saint [seɪnt] *n* santo/a; **S**~ **John** São João.
saintly ['seɪntlɪ] *adj* santo, santificado.
sake [seɪk] *n*: **for the** ~ **of** por (causa de), em consideração a; **for my** ~ por mim; **arguing for arguing's** ~ brigar por brigar; **for the** ~ **of argument** por exemplo; **for heaven's** ~! pelo amor de Deus!
salad ['sæləd] *n* salada.
salad bowl *n* saladeira.
salad cream *(BRIT)* *n* maionese *f*.
salad dressing *n* tempero *or* molho da salada.
salad oil *n* azeite *m* de mesa.
salami [sə'lɑːmɪ] *n* salame *m*.
salaried ['sælərɪd] *adj (staff)* assalariado.
salary ['sælərɪ] *n* salário.
salary scale *n* escala salarial.
sale [seɪl] *n* venda; *(at reduced prices)* liquidação *f*, saldo; **"for** ~**"** "vende-se"; **on** ~ à venda; **on** ~ **or return** em consignação; ~ **and lease back** *venda com cláusula de aluguel ao vendedor do item vendido.*
saleroom ['seɪlrum] *n* sala de vendas.
sales assistant *(BRIT)* *n* vendedor(a) *m/f*.
sales clerk *(US)* *n* vendedor(a) *m/f*.
sales conference *n* conferência de vendas.
sales drive *n* campanha de vendas.
sales force *n* equipe *m* de vendas.
salesman ['seɪlzmən] *(irreg)* *n* vendedor *m*; *(representative)* vendedor *m* viajante.
sales manager *n* gerente *m/f* de vendas.
salesmanship ['seɪlzmənʃɪp] *n* arte *f* de

---

*NB: European Portuguese adds the following consonants to certain words: **b** (sú(b)dito, su(b)til); **c** (a(c)ção, a(c)cionista, a(c)to); **m** (inde(m)ne); **p** (ado(p)ção, ado(p)tar); for further details see p. xiii.*

vender.

salesmen ['seɪlzmɛn] *npl of* **salesman**.

sales tax (*US*) *n* ≈ ICM *m* (*BR*), ≈ IVA *m* (*PT*).

saleswoman ['seɪlzwumən] (*irreg*) *n* vendedora; (*representative*) vendedora viajante.

salient ['seɪlɪənt] *adj* saliente.

saline ['seɪlaɪn] *adj* salino.

saliva [sə'laɪvə] *n* saliva.

sallow ['sæləu] *adj* amarelado.

sally forth ['sælɪ-] *vi* partir, pôr-se em marcha.

sally out ['sælɪ-] *vi* partir, pôr-se em marcha.

salmon ['sæmən] *n inv* salmão *m*.

saloon [sə'luːn] *n* (*US*) bar *m*, botequim *m*; (*AUT*) sedã *m*; (*ship's lounge*) salão *m*.

Salop ['sæləp] (*BRIT*) *n abbr* = **Shropshire**.

SALT [sɔːlt] *n abbr* (= *Strategic Arms Limitation Talks/Treaty*) SALT *m*.

salt [sɔːlt] *n* sal *m* ♦ *vt* salgar ♦ *cpd* de sal; (*CULIN*) salgado; **an old** ~ um lobo-do-mar.
   salt away *vt* pôr de lado.

salt cellar *n* saleiro.

salt-free *adj* sem sal.

saltwater ['sɔːltwɔːtə*] *adj* de água salgada.

salty ['sɔːltɪ] *adj* salgado.

salubrious [sə'luːbrɪəs] *adj* salubre, sadio.

salutary ['sæljutərɪ] *adj* salutar.

salute [sə'luːt] *n* (*tribute*) saudação *f*; (*of guns*) salva; (*MIL*) continência ♦ *vt* saudar; (*guns*) receber com salvas; (*MIL*) fazer continência a.

salvage ['sælvɪdʒ] *n* (*saving*) salvamento, recuperação *f*; (*things saved*) salvados *mpl* ♦ *vt* salvar.

salvage vessel *n* navio de salvamento.

salvation [sæl'veɪʃən] *n* salvação *f*.

Salvation Army *n* Exército da Salvação.

salve [sælv] *n* (*cream etc*) ungüento, pomada.

salver ['sælvə*] *n* bandeja, salva.

salvo ['sælvəu] *n* salva.

Samaritan [sə'mærɪtən] *n*: **the** ~**s** (*organization*) os Samaritanos.

same [seɪm] *adj* mesmo ♦ *pron*: **the** ~ o mesmo/a mesma; **the** ~ **book as** o mesmo livro que; **at the** ~ **time** ao mesmo tempo; **on the** ~ **day** no mesmo dia; **all** *or* **just the** ~ apesar de tudo, mesmo assim; **it's all the** ~ dá no mesmo, tanto faz; **they're one and the** ~ (*people*) são os mesmos; (*things*) são idênticos; **to do the** ~ (**as sb**) fazer o mesmo (que alguém); **the** ~ **to you!** igualmente!; ~ **here!** eu também!; **the** ~ **again!** (*in bar etc*) mais um ... por favor!

sample ['sɑːmpl] *n* amostra ♦ *vt* (*food, wine*) provar, experimentar; **to take a** ~ tirar uma amostra; **free** ~ amostra grátis.

sanatoria [sænə'tɔːrɪə] *npl of* **sanatorium**.

sanatorium [sænə'tɔːrɪəm] (*pl* **sanatoria**) *n* sanatório.

sanctify ['sæŋktɪfaɪ] *vt* santificar.

sanctimonious [sæŋktɪ'məunɪəs] *adj* santarrão/rona, sacripanta.

sanction ['sæŋkʃən] *n* sanção *f* ♦ *vt* sancionar, ratificar; **to impose economic** ~**s on** *or*

against impor sanções econômicas a.

sanctity ['sæŋktɪtɪ] *n* santidade *f*, divindade *f*; (*inviolability*) inviolabilidade *f*.

sanctuary ['sæŋktjuərɪ] *n* (*holy place*) santuário; (*refuge*) refúgio, asilo; (*for animals*) reserva.

sand [sænd] *n* areia ♦ *vt* arear, jogar areia em; (*also*: ~ **down**: *wood etc*) lixar; ~**s** *npl* praia.

sandal ['sændl] *n* sandália; (*wood*) sândalo.

sandbag ['sændbæg] *n* saco de areia.

sandbank ['sændbæŋk] *n* banco de areia.

sandblast ['sændblɑːst] *vt* limpar com jato de areia.

sandbox ['sændbɒks] (*US*) *n* (*for children*) caixa de areia.

sandcastle ['sændkɑːsl] *n* castelo de areia.

sand dune *n* duna (de areia).

sandpaper ['sændpeɪpə*] *n* lixa.

sandpit ['sændpɪt] (*BRIT*) *n* (*for children*) caixa de areia.

sandstone ['sændstəun] *n* arenito, grés *m*.

sandstorm ['sændstɔːm] *n* tempestade *f* de areia.

sandwich ['sændwɪtʃ] *n* sanduíche *m* (*BR*), sandes *f inv* (*PT*) ♦ *vt* (*also*: ~ **in**) intercalar; ~**ed between** encaixado entre; **cheese/ham** ~ sanduíche (*BR*) *or* sandes (*PT*) de queijo/presunto.

sandwich board *n* cartaz *m* ambulante.

sandwich course (*BRIT*) *n* curso profissionalizante de teoria e prática alternadas.

sandy ['sændɪ] *adj* arenoso; (*colour*) vermelho amarelado.

sane [seɪn] *adj* são/sã do juízo; (*sensible*) ajuizado, sensato.

sang [sæŋ] *pt of* **sing**.

sanguine ['sæŋgwɪn] *adj* otimista.

sanitaria [sænɪ'tɛərɪə] (*US*) *npl of* **sanitarium**.

sanitarium [sænɪ'tɛərɪəm] (*US*: *pl* **sanitaria**) *n* = **sanatorium**.

sanitary ['sænɪtərɪ] *adj* (*system, arrangements*) sanitário; (*clean*) higiênico.

sanitary towel (*US* **sanitary napkin**) *n* toalha higiênica *or* absorvente.

sanitation [sænɪ'teɪʃən] *n* (*in house*) instalações *fpl* sanitárias; (*in town*) saneamento.

sanitation department (*US*) *n* comissão *f* de limpeza urbana.

sanity ['sænɪtɪ] *n* sanidade *f*, equilíbrio mental; (*common sense*) juízo, sensatez *f*.

sank [sæŋk] *pt of* **sink**.

San Marino ['sænmə'riːnəu] *n* San Marino (*no article*).

Santa Claus [sæntə'klɔːz] *n* Papai Noel *m*.

Santiago [sæntɪ'ɑːgəu] *n* (*also*: ~ **de Chile**) Santiago (do Chile).

sap [sæp] *n* (*of plants*) seiva ♦ *vt* (*strength*) esgotar, minar.

sapling ['sæplɪŋ] *n* árvore *f* nova.

sapphire ['sæfaɪə*] *n* safira.

sarcasm ['sɑːkæzm] *n* sarcasmo.

sarcastic [sɑː'kæstɪk] *adj* sarcástico.

sarcophagi [sɑː'kɔfəgaɪ] *npl of* **sarcophagus**.

sarcophagus [sɑː'kɔfəgəs] (*pl* **sarcophagi**) *n* sarcófago.

sardine [sɑː'diːn] *n* sardinha.

Sardinia [sɑː'dɪnɪə] *n* Sardenha.

Sardinian [sɑː'dɪnɪən] *adj* sardo ♦ *n* sardo/a; (*LING*) sardo.

sardonic [sɑː'dɔnɪk] *adj* sardônico.

sari ['sɑːrɪ] *n* sári *m*.

sartorial [sɑː'tɔːrɪəl] *adj* indumentário.

SAS (*BRIT*) *n abbr* (*MIL*) = **Special Air Service**.

SASE (*US*) *n abbr* (= *self-addressed stamped envelope*) envelope selado e sobrescritado.

sash [sæʃ] *n* faixa, banda; (*belt*) cinto.

sash window *n* janela de guilhotina.

SAT (*US*) *n abbr* = **Scholastic Aptitude Test**.

Sat. *abbr* = (*Saturday*) sáb.

sat [sæt] *pt, pp of* **sit**.

Satan ['seɪtn] *n* Satanás *m*, Satã *m*.

satanic [sə'tænɪk] *adj* satânico, diabólico.

satchel ['sætʃl] *n* sacola.

sated ['seɪtɪd] *adj* saciado, farto.

satellite ['sætəlaɪt] *n* satélite *m*.

satiate ['seɪʃɪeɪt] *vt* saciar.

satin ['sætɪn] *n* cetim *m* ♦ *adj* acetinado; **with a ~ finish** acetinado.

satire ['sætaɪə*] *n* sátira.

satirical [sə'tɪrɪkl] *adj* satírico.

satirist ['sætɪrɪst] *n* (*writer*) satirista *m/f*; (*cartoonist*) chargista *m/f*.

satirize ['sætɪraɪz] *vt* satirizar.

satisfaction [sætɪs'fækʃən] *n* satisfação *f*; **has it been done to your ~?** você está satisfeito?

satisfactory [sætɪs'fæktərɪ] *adj* satisfatório.

satisfy ['sætɪsfaɪ] *vt* satisfazer; (*convince*) convencer, persuadir; **to ~ the requirements** satisfazer as exigências; **to ~ sb (that)** convencer alguém (de que); **to ~ o.s. of sth** convencer-se de algo.

satisfying ['sætɪsfaɪɪŋ] *adj* satisfatório.

saturate ['sætʃəreɪt] *vt*: **to ~ (with)** saturar *or* embeber (de).

saturation [sætʃə'reɪʃən] *n* saturação *f*.

Saturday ['sætədɪ] *n* sábado; *see also* **Tuesday**.

sauce [sɔːs] *n* molho; (*sweet*) calda; (*fig: cheek*) atrevimento.

saucepan ['sɔːspən] *n* panela (*BR*), caçarola (*PT*).

saucer ['sɔːsə*] *n* pires *m inv*.

saucy ['sɔːsɪ] *adj* atrevido, descarado; (*flirtatious*) flertivo, provocante.

Saudi Arabia ['saudɪ-] *n* Arábia Saudita.

Saudi (Arabian) ['saudɪ-] *adj, n* saudita *m/f*.

sauna ['sɔːnə] *n* sauna.

saunter ['sɔːntə*] *vi* caminhar devagar, perambular.

sausage ['sɔsɪdʒ] *n* salsicha, lingüiça; (*cold meat*) frios *mpl*.

sausage roll *n* folheado de salsicha.

sauté ['səuteɪ] *adj* (*CULIN: potatoes*) sauté; (: *onions*) frito rapidamente ♦ *vt* fritar levemente.

savage ['sævɪdʒ] *adj* (*cruel, fierce*) cruel, feroz; (*primitive*) selvagem ♦ *n* selvagem *m/f* ♦ *vt* (*attack*) atacar ferozmente.

savagery ['sævɪdʒrɪ] *n* selvageria, ferocidade *f*.

save [seɪv] *vt* (*rescue*) salvar, resgatar; (*money*) poupar, economizar; (*time*) ganhar; (*put by: food*) guardar; (*SPORT*) impedir; (*avoid: trouble*) evitar; (*COMPUT*) salvar ♦ *vi* (*also: ~ up*) poupar ♦ *n* (*SPORT*) salvamento ♦ *prep* salvo, exceto; **it will ~ me an hour** vou ganhar uma hora; **to ~ face** salvar as aparências; **God ~ the Queen!** Deus salve a Rainha!

saving ['seɪvɪŋ] *n* (*on price etc*) economia ♦ *adj*: **the ~ grace of** o único mérito de; **~s** *npl* economias *fpl*; **to make ~s** economizar.

savings account *n* (caderneta de) poupança.

savings bank *n* caixa econômica, caderneta de poupança.

saviour ['seɪvjə*] (*US* **savior**) *n* salvador(a) *m/f*.

savour ['seɪvə*] (*US* **savor**) *n* sabor *m* ♦ *vt* saborear.

savo(u)ry ['seɪvərɪ] *adj* saboroso; (*dish: not sweet*) salgado.

savvy ['sævɪ] (*inf*) *n* juízo.

saw [sɔː] (*pt* **~ed**, *pp* **~ed** *or* **sawn**) *pt of* **see** ♦ *n* (*tool*) serra ♦ *vt* serrar; **to ~ sth up** serrar algo em pedaços.

sawdust ['sɔːdʌst] *n* serragem *f*, pó *m* de serra.

sawed-off shotgun [sɔːd-] (*US*) *n* = **sawn-off shotgun**.

sawmill ['sɔːmɪl] *n* serraria.

sawn [sɔːn] *pp of* **saw**.

sawn-off shotgun (*BRIT*) *n* espingarda de cano serrado.

saxophone ['sæksəfəun] *n* saxofone *m*.

say [seɪ] (*pt, pp* **said**) *n*: **to have one's ~** exprimir sua opinião, vender seu peixe (*inf*) ♦ *vt* dizer, falar; **to have a** *or* **some ~ in sth** opinar sobre algo, ter que ver com algo; **~ after me ...** repita comigo ...; **to ~ yes/no** dizer (que) sim/não; **she said (that) I was to give you this** ela disse que eu deveria te dar isso; **my watch ~s 3 o'clock** meu relógio marca 3 horas; **shall we ~ Tuesday?** marcamos para terça?; **I should ~ it's worth about £100** acho que vale mais ou menos £100; **that doesn't ~ much for him** aquilo não o favorece; **when all is said and done** afinal das contas; **there is something** *or* **a lot to be said for it** isto tem muitas vantagens; **that is to ~** ou seja; **to ~ nothing of ...** por não falar em ...; **~ that ...** vamos supor que ...; **that goes without ~ing** é óbvio, nem é preciso dizer.

saying ['seɪɪŋ] *n* ditado, provérbio.

NB: *European Portuguese adds the following consonants to certain words:* **b** (sú(b)dito, su(b)til); **c** (a(c)ção, a(c)cionista, a(c)to); **m** (inde(m)ne); **p** (ado(p)ção, ado(p)tar); *for further details see p. xiii.*

SBA (US) n abbr (= Small Business Administration) órgão de auxílio às pequenas empresas.

SC (US) n abbr = **supreme court** ♦ abbr (POST) = **South Carolina**.

s/c abbr = **self-contained**.

scab [skæb] n casca, crosta (de ferida); (pej) fura-greve m/f inv.

scabby ['skæbɪ] adj cheio de casca or cicatrizes.

scaffold ['skæfəuld] n (for execution) cadafalso, patíbulo.

scaffolding ['skæfəuldɪŋ] n andaime m.

scald [skɔːld] n escaldadura ♦ vt escaldar, queimar.

scalding ['skɔːldɪŋ] adj (also: ~ hot) escaldante.

scale [skeɪl] n (gen, MUS) escala; (of fish) escama; (of salaries, fees etc) tabela; (of map, also size, extent) escala ♦ vt (mountain) escalar; (fish) escamar; ~s npl balança; **pay** ~ tabela de salários; **on a large** ~ em grande escala; ~ **of charges** tarifa, lista de preços; **to draw sth to** ~ desenhar algo em escala; **small-**~ **model** modelo reduzido.

scale down vt reduzir.

scale drawing n desenho em escala.

scale model n maquete f em escala.

scallion ['skæljən] n cebola.

scallop ['skɔləp] n (ZOOL) vieira, venera; (SEWING) barra, arremate m.

scalp [skælp] n couro cabeludo ♦ vt escalpar.

scalpel ['skælpl] n bisturi m.

scalper ['skælpə*] (US: inf) n (of tickets) cambista m/f.

scamp [skæmp] n moleque m.

scamper ['skæmpə*] vi: **to** ~ **away**, ~ **off** sair correndo.

scampi ['skæmpɪ] npl camarões mpl fritos.

scan [skæn] vt (examine) esquadrinhar, perscrutar; (glance at quickly) passar uma vista de olhos por; (TV, RADAR) explorar ♦ n (MED) exame m.

scandal ['skændl] n escândalo; (gossip) fofocas fpl.

scandalize ['skændəlaɪz] vt escandalizar.

scandalous ['skændələs] adj escandaloso; (libellous) difamatório, calunioso.

Scandinavia [skændɪ'neɪvɪə] n Escandinávia.

Scandinavian [skændɪ'neɪvɪən] adj, n escandinavo/a.

scanner ['skænə*] n (RADAR, MED) antena.

scant [skænt] adj escasso, insuficiente.

scantily ['skæntɪlɪ] adv: ~ **clad** or **dressed** precariamente vestido.

scanty ['skæntɪ] adj escasso.

scapegoat ['skeɪpgəut] n bode m expiatório.

scar [skɑː] n cicatriz f ♦ vt marcar (com uma cicatriz).

scarce [skɛəs] adj escasso, raro.

scarcely ['skɛəslɪ] adv mal, quase não; ~ **anybody** quase ninguém; **I can** ~ **believe it** mal posso acreditar.

scarcity ['skɛəsɪtɪ] n escassez f.

scarcity value n valor m de escassez.

scare [skɛə*] n susto; (panic) pânico ♦ vt assustar; **to** ~ **sb stiff** deixar alguém morrendo de medo; **bomb** ~ alarme de bomba.

scare away vt espantar.

scare off vt espantar.

scarecrow ['skɛəkrəu] n espantalho.

scared [skɛəd] adj: **to be** ~ estar assustado or com medo.

scaremonger ['skɛəmʌŋgə*] n alarmista m/f.

scarf [skɑːf] (pl **scarves**) n (long) cachecol m; (square) lenço (de cabeça).

scarlet ['skɑːlɪt] adj escarlate.

scarlet fever n escarlatina.

scarves [skɑːvz] npl of **scarf**.

scary ['skɛərɪ] (inf) adj assustador(a).

scathing ['skeɪðɪŋ] adj mordaz, severo; **to be** ~ **about sth** fazer uma crítica mordaz sobre algo.

scatter ['skætə*] vt (spread) espalhar; (put to flight) dispersar ♦ vi espalhar-se.

scatterbrained ['skætəbreɪnd] adj desmiolado, avoado; (forgetful) esquecido.

scattered ['skætəd] adj espalhado.

scatty ['skætɪ] (BRIT: inf) adj maluquinho.

scavenge ['skævəndʒ] vi (person): **to** ~ (**for**) filar; **to** ~ **for food** (hyenas etc) procurar comida.

scavenger ['skævəndʒə*] n (person) filante m/ f; (ZOOL) animal m (or ave f) que se alimenta de carniça.

SCE n abbr = **Scottish Certificate of Education**.

scenario [sɪ'nɑːrɪəu] n cenário.

scene [siːn] n (THEATRE, fig) cena; (of crime, accident) cenário; (sight, view) vista, panorama m; (fuss) escândalo; **behind the** ~s nos bastidores; **to make a** ~ (inf: fuss) fazer um escândalo; **to appear on the** ~ entrar em cena; **the political** ~ o panorama político.

scenery ['siːnərɪ] n (THEATRE) cenário; (landscape) paisagem f.

scenic ['siːnɪk] adj (picturesque) pitoresco.

scent [sɛnt] n perfume m; (smell) aroma; (fig: track) pista, rastro; (sense of smell) olfato ♦ vt perfumar; **to put** or **throw sb off the** ~ despistar alguém.

scepter ['sɛptə*] (US) n = **sceptre**.

sceptic ['skɛptɪk] (US **skeptic**) n cético/a.

sceptical ['skɛptɪkl] (US **skeptical**) adj cético.

scepticism ['skɛptɪsɪzm] (US **skepticism**) n ceticismo.

sceptre ['sɛptə*] (US **scepter**) n cetro.

schedule ['ʃɛdjuːl, (US) 'skɛdjuːl] n (of trains) horário; (of events) programa m; (plan) plano; (list) lista ♦ vt (timetable) planejar; (visit) marcar (a hora de); **as** ~d como previsto; **the meeting is** ~d **for 7.00** a reunião está programada para as 7.00h; **on** ~ na hora, sem atraso; **to be ahead of/behind** ~ estar adiantado/atrasado; **we are working to a very tight** ~ nosso horário está muito apertado; **everything went according to** ~

tudo correu como planejado.

scheduled ['ʃɛdjuːld, (US) 'skɛdjuːld] adj (date, time) marcado; (visit, event) programado; (train, bus, flight) de linha.

schematic [skɪ'mætɪk] adj esquemático.

scheme [skiːm] n (plan) plano, esquema m; (method) método; (plot) conspiração f; (trick) ardil m; (arrangement) disposição f ♦ vi conspirar.

scheming ['skiːmɪŋ] adj intrigante ♦ n intrigas fpl.

schism ['skɪzəm] n cisma m.

schizophrenia [skɪtsəu'friːnɪə] n esquizofrenia.

schizophrenic [skɪtsə'frɛnɪk] adj esquizofrênico.

scholar ['skɔlə*] n (pupil) aluno/a, estudante m/f; (learned person) sábio/a, erudito/a.

scholarly ['skɔləlɪ] adj erudito, douto.

scholarship ['skɔləʃɪp] n erudição f; (grant) bolsa de estudos.

school [skuːl] n escola; (in university) faculdade f; (secondary ~) colégio; (of fish) cardume m ♦ cpd escolar ♦ vt (animal) adestrar, treinar.

school age n idade f escolar.

schoolbook ['skuːlbuk] n livro escolar.

schoolboy ['skuːlbɔɪ] n aluno.

schoolchild ['skuːltʃaɪld] (irreg) n aluno/a.

schooldays ['skuːldeɪz] npl anos mpl escolares.

schoolgirl ['skuːlgɜːl] n aluna.

schooling ['skuːlɪŋ] n educação f, ensino.

school-leaving age [-'liːvɪŋ-] n idade f em que se termina a escola.

schoolmaster ['skuːlmɑːstə*] n professor m.

schoolmistress ['skuːlmɪstrɪs] n professora.

school report (BRIT) n boletim m escolar.

schoolroom ['skuːlrum] n sala de aula.

schoolteacher ['skuːltiːtʃə*] n professor(a) m/f.

schooner ['skuːnə*] n (ship) escuna; (glass) caneca, canecão m.

sciatica [saɪ'ætɪkə] n ciática.

science ['saɪəns] n ciência.

science fiction n ficção f científica.

scientific [saɪən'tɪfɪk] adj científico.

scientist ['saɪəntɪst] n cientista m/f.

sci-fi ['saɪfaɪ] (inf) n abbr = **science fiction**.

Scillies ['sɪlɪz] npl: **the** ~ as ilhas Scilly.

Scilly Isles ['sɪlɪ'aɪlz] npl: **the** ~ as ilhas Scilly.

scintillating ['sɪntɪleɪtɪŋ] adj (wit etc) brilhante.

scissors ['sɪzəz] npl tesoura; **a pair of** ~ uma tesoura.

sclerosis [sklɪ'rəusɪs] n esclerose f.

scoff [skɔf] vt (BRIT: inf: eat) engolir ♦ vi: **to** ~ **(at)** (mock) zombar (de).

scold [skəuld] vt ralhar.

scolding ['skəuldɪŋ] n repreensão f.

scone [skɔn] n bolinho.

scoop [skuːp] n colherona; (for flour etc) pá f;

(PRESS) furo (jornalístico).

scoop out vt escavar.

scoop up vt recolher.

scooter ['skuːtə*] n (motor cycle) moto f, lambreta; (toy) patinete m.

scope [skəup] n (of plan, undertaking) âmbito; (reach) alcance m; (of person) competência; (opportunity) oportunidade f; **within the** ~ **of** dentro dos limites de; **there is plenty of** ~ **for improvement** (BRIT) poderia ser muito melhor.

scorch [skɔːtʃ] vt (clothes) chamuscar; (earth, grass) secar, queimar.

scorched earth policy [skɔːtʃt-] n tática da terra arrasada.

scorcher ['skɔːtʃə*] (inf) n (hot day) dia m muito quente.

scorching ['skɔːtʃɪŋ] adj ardente.

score [skɔː*] n (points etc) escore m, contagem f; (MUS) partitura; (reckoning) conta; (twenty) vintena ♦ vt (goal, point) fazer; (mark) marcar, entalhar ♦ vi (FOOTBALL) marcar or fazer um gol; (keep score) marcar o escore; **on that** ~ a esse respeito, por esse motivo; **to have an old** ~ **to settle with sb** (fig) ter umas contas a ajustar com alguém; ~**s of** (fig) um monte de; **to keep (the)** ~ marcar os pontos; **to** ~ **6 out of 10** conseguir um escore de 6 num total de 10.

score out vt riscar.

scoreboard ['skɔːbɔːd] n marcador m, placar m.

scorecard ['skɔːkɑːd] n (SPORT) cartão m de marcação.

scorer ['skɔːrə*] n marcador(a) m/f.

scorn [skɔːn] n desprezo ♦ vt desprezar, rejeitar.

scornful ['skɔːnful] adj desdenhoso, zombador(a).

Scorpio ['skɔːpɪəu] n Escorpião m.

scorpion ['skɔːpɪən] n escorpião m.

Scot [skɔt] n escocês/esa m/f.

Scotch [skɔtʃ] n uísque m (BR) or whisky m (PT) escocês.

scotch [skɔtʃ] vt (rumour) desmentir; (plan) estragar.

Scotch tape ® n fita adesiva, durex m ® (BR).

scot-free adj: **to get off** ~ (unpunished) sair impune; (unhurt) sair ileso.

Scotland ['skɔtlənd] n Escócia.

Scots [skɔts] adj escocês/esa.

Scotsman ['skɔtsmən] (irreg) n escocês m.

Scotswoman ['skɔtswumən] (irreg) n escocesa.

Scottish ['skɔtɪʃ] adj escocês/esa.

scoundrel ['skaundrəl] n canalha m/f, patife m.

scour ['skauə*] vt (clean) limpar, esfregar; (search) esquadrinhar, procurar em.

scourer ['skaurə*] n esponja de aço, bombril m ® (BR).

NB: European Portuguese adds the following consonants to certain words: **b** (sú(b)dito, su(b)til); **c** (a(c)ção, a(c)cionista, a(c)to); **m** (inde(m)ne); **p** (ado(p)ção, ado(p)tar; for further details see p. xiii.

scourge [skə:dʒ] *n* açoite *m*, flagelo.
scout [skaut] *n* (*also*: *boy* ~) escoteiro; (*MIL*) explorador *m*, batedor *m*.
  scout around *vi* explorar.
scowl [skaul] *vi* franzir a testa; **to ~ at sb** olhar alguém carrancudamente.
scrabble ['skræbl] *vi*: **to ~ about** *or* **around for sth** tatear procurando algo ♦ *n*: **S~** ® mexe-mexe *m*.
scraggy ['skrægɪ] *adj* magricela, descarnado.
scram [skræm] (*inf*) *vi* dar o fora, safar-se.
scramble ['skræmbl] *n* (*climb*) escalada (difícil); (*struggle*) luta ♦ *vi*: **to ~ out** *or* **through** conseguir sair com dificuldade; **to ~ for** lutar por.
scrambled eggs ['skræmbld-] *npl* ovos *mpl* mexidos.
scrap [skræp] *n* (*bit*) pedacinho; (*fight*) rixa, luta; (*also*: ~ *iron*) ferro velho, sucata ♦ *vt* sucatar, jogar no ferro velho; (*discard*) descartar ♦ *vi* brigar; ~**s** *npl* (*waste*) sobras *fpl*, restos *mpl*; **to sell sth for** ~ vender algo como sucata.
scrapbook ['skræpbuk] *n* álbum *m* de recortes.
scrap dealer *n* ferro-velho *m*, sucateiro/a.
scrape [skreɪp] *n* (*fig*) aperto, enrascada ♦ *vt* raspar; (*skin etc*) arranhar; (~ *against*) roçar.
  scrape through *vi* (*in exam*) passar raspando.
scraper ['skreɪpə*] *n* raspador *m*.
scrap heap *n* (*fig*): **on the** ~ rejeitado, jogado fora.
scrap merchant (*BRIT*) *n* sucateiro/a.
scrap metal *n* sucata, ferro-velho.
scrap paper *n* papel *m* de rascunho.
scrappy ['skræpɪ] *adj* (*speech*) incoerente, desconexo; (*bitty*) fragmentário.
scrap yard *n* ferro-velho.
scratch [skrætʃ] *n* arranhão *m*; (*from claw*) arranhadura ♦ *adj*: ~ **team** time improvisado, escrete ♦ *vt* (*record*) marcar, riscar; (*with claw, nail*) arranhar, unhar; (*COMPUT*) apagar ♦ *vi* coçar(-se); **to start from** ~ partir do zero; **to be up to** ~ estar à altura (das circunstâncias).
scratchpad ['skrætʃpæd] (*US*) *n* bloco de rascunho.
scrawl [skrɔ:l] *n* garrancho, garatujas *fpl* ♦ *vi* garatujar, rabiscar.
scrawny ['skrɔ:nɪ] *adj* magricela.
scream [skri:m] *n* grito ♦ *vi* gritar; **it was a** ~ (*inf*) foi engraçadíssimo; **to ~ at sb** gritar com alguém.
scree [skri:] *n* seixos *mpl*.
screech [skri:tʃ] *vi* guinchar ♦ *n* guincho.
screen [skri:n] *n* (*CINEMA, TV*) tela (*BR*), écran *m* (*PT*); (*movable*) biombo; (*wall*) tapume *m*; (*also*: *wind*~) pára-brisa *m*; (*fig*) cortina ♦ *vt* (*conceal*) esconder, tapar; (*from the wind etc*) proteger; (*film*) projetar; (*candidates etc, MED*) examinar.
screen editing [-'edɪtɪŋ] *n* (*COMPUT*) edição *f* na tela.

screening ['skri:nɪŋ] *n* (*MED*) exame *m* médico; (*of film*) exibição *f*; (*for security*) controle *m*.
screen memory *n* (*COMPUT*) memória da tela.
screenplay ['skri:npleɪ] *n* roteiro.
screen test *n* teste *m* de cinema.
screw [skru:] *n* parafuso; (*propeller*) hélice *f* ♦ *vt* aparafusar; (*also*: ~ *in*) apertar, atarraxar; (*inf!: have sex with*) comer (*!*), trepar com (*!*); **to ~ sth to the wall** pregar algo na parede; **to have one's head** ~**ed on** (*fig*) ter juízo.
  screw up *vt* (*paper, material*) amassar; (*inf: ruin*) estragar; **to ~ up one's face** contrair as feições.
screwdriver ['skru:draɪvə*] *n* chave *f* de fenda *or* de parafuso.
screwy ['skru:ɪ] (*inf*) *adj* maluco, estranho.
scribble ['skrɪbl] *n* garrancho ♦ *vt* escrevinhar, rabiscar; **to ~ sth down** anotar algo apressadamente.
scribe [skraɪb] *n* escriba *m/f*.
script [skrɪpt] *n* (*CINEMA etc*) roteiro, script *m*; (*writing*) escrita, caligrafia.
scripted ['skrɪptɪd] *adj* (*RADIO, TV*) com script.
Scripture ['skrɪptʃə*] *n* Sagrada Escritura.
scriptwriter ['skrɪptraɪtə*] *n* roteirista *m/f*.
scroll [skrəul] *n* rolo de pergaminho ♦ *vt* (*COMPUT*) passar na tela.
scrotum ['skrəutəm] *n* escroto.
scrounge [skraundʒ] (*inf*) *vt*: **to ~ sth off** *or* **from sb** filar algo de alguém ♦ *vi*: **to ~ on sb** viver às custas de alguém.
scrounger ['skraundʒə*] (*inf*) *n* filão/lona *m/f*.
scrub [skrʌb] *n* (*clean*) esfregação *f*, limpeza; (*land*) mato, cerrado ♦ *vt* esfregar; (*reject*) cancelar, eliminar.
scrubbing brush ['skrʌbɪŋ-] *n* escova de esfrega.
scruff [skrʌf] *n*: **by the** ~ **of the neck** pelo cangote.
scruffy ['skrʌfɪ] *adj* desmazelado.
scrum(mage) ['skrʌm(ɪdʒ)] *n* rolo.
scruple ['skru:pl] *n* escrúpulo; **to have no** ~**s about doing sth** não ter escrúpulos em fazer algo.
scrupulous ['skru:pjuləs] *adj* escrupuloso.
scrupulously ['skru:pjuləslɪ] *adv* escrupulosamente.
scrutinize ['skru:tɪnaɪz] *vt* examinar minuciosamente; (*votes*) escrutinar.
scrutiny ['skru:tɪnɪ] *n* escrutínio, exame *m* cuidadoso; **under the** ~ **of** vigiado por.
scuba ['sku:bə] *n* equipamento de mergulho.
scuba diving *n* mergulho.
scuff [skʌf] *vt* desgastar.
scuffle ['skʌfl] *n* tumulto.
scull [skʌl] *n* ginga.
scullery ['skʌlərɪ] *n* copa.
sculptor ['skʌlptə*] *n* escultor(a) *m/f*.
sculpture ['skʌlptʃə*] *n* escultura.
scum [skʌm] *n* (*on liquid*) espuma; (*pej: people*) ralé *f*, gentinha; (*fig*) escória.
scupper ['skʌpə*] *vt* (*BRIT: ship*) afundar;

(fig: plans) estragar.
scurrilous ['skʌrɪləs] *adj* calunioso.
scurry off ['skʌrɪ-] *vi* sair correndo, dar no pé.
scurvy ['skə:vɪ] *n* escorbuto.
scuttle ['skʌtl] *n (also: coal ~)* balde *m* para carvão ♦ *vt (ship)* afundar voluntariamente, fazer ir a pique ♦ *vi (scamper)*: **to ~ away, ~ off** sair em disparada.
scythe [saɪð] *n* segadeira, foice *f* grande.
SD *(US) abbr (POST)* = **South Dakota**.
SDI *n abbr* (= *Strategic Defense Initiative*) IDE *f*.
SDLP *(BRIT) n abbr (POL)* = **Social Democratic and Labour Party**.
sea [si:] *n* mar *m* ♦ *cpd* do mar, marino; **on the ~** *(boat)* no mar; *(town)* junto ao mar; **by** *or* **beside the ~** *(holiday)* na praia; *(village)* à beira-mar; **to go by ~** viajar por mar; **out to** *(or* **at***) ~* em alto mar; **heavy** *or* **rough ~(s)** mar agitado; **a ~ of faces** *(fig)* uma grande quantidade de pessoas; **to be all at ~** *(fig)* estar confuso *or* desorientado.
sea anemone *n* anêmona-do-mar *f*.
sea bed *n* fundo do mar.
sea bird *n* ave *f* marinha.
seaboard ['si:bɔ:d] *n* costa, litoral *m*.
sea breeze *n* brisa marítima, viração *f*.
seafarer ['si:fɛərə*] *n* marinheiro, homem *m* do mar.
seafaring ['si:fɛərɪŋ] *adj (life)* de marinheiro; **~ people** povo navegante.
seafood ['si:fu:d] *n* mariscos *mpl*.
sea front *n* orla marítima.
seagoing ['si:gəʊɪŋ] *adj (ship)* de longo curso.
seagull ['si:gʌl] *n* gaivota.
seal [si:l] *n (animal)* foca; *(stamp)* selo ♦ *vt (close)* fechar; (: *with* ~) selar; *(decide: sb's fate)* decidir; (: *bargain*) fechar; **~ of approval** aprovação *f*.
seal off *vt (close)* fechar; *(cordon off)* isolar.
sea level *n* nível *m* do mar.
sealing wax ['si:lɪŋ-] *n* lacre *m*.
sea lion *n* leão-marinho *m*.
sealskin ['si:lskɪn] *n* pele *f* de foca.
seam [si:m] *n* costura; *(of metal)* junta, junção *f*; *(of coal)* veio, filão *m*; **the hall was bursting at the ~s** a sala estava apinhada de gente.
seaman ['si:mən] *(irreg) n* marinheiro.
seamanship ['si:mənʃɪp] *n* náutica.
seamen ['si:mɛn] *npl of* **seaman**.
seamless ['si:mlɪs] *adj* sem costura.
seamstress ['sɛmstrɪs] *n* costureira.
seamy ['si:mɪ] *adj* sórdido.
seance ['seɪɔns] *n* sessão *f* espírita.
seaplane ['si:pleɪn] *n* hidroavião *m*.
seaport ['si:pɔ:t] *n* porto de mar.
search [sə:tʃ] *n (for person, thing)* busca, procura; *(of drawer, pockets)* revista; *(inspection)* exame *m*, investigação *f* ♦ *vt*

(look in) procurar em; *(examine)* examinar; *(person, place)* revistar ♦ *vi*: **to ~ for** procurar; **in ~ of** à procura de; **"~ and replace"** *(COMPUT)* "procura e substituição".
search through *vt fus* dar busca em.
searching ['sə:tʃɪŋ] *adj* penetrante, perscrutador(a); *(study)* minucioso.
searchlight ['sə:tʃlaɪt] *n* holofote *m*.
search party *n* equipe *f* de salvamento.
search warrant *n* mandado de busca.
searing ['sɪərɪŋ] *adj (heat)* ardente; *(pain)* agudo.
seashore ['si:ʃɔ:*] *n* praia, beira-mar *f*, litoral *m*; **on the ~** na praia.
seasick ['si:sɪk] *adj* enjoado, mareado; **to be** *or* **get ~** enjoar.
seaside ['si:saɪd] *n* praia.
seaside resort *n* balneário.
season ['si:zn] *n (of year)* estação *f*; *(sporting etc)* temporada ♦ *vt (food)* temperar; **to be in/out of ~** *(fruit)* estar na época/fora de época; **the busy ~** *(shops)* a época de muito movimento; *(hotels)* a temporada de férias; **the open ~** *(HUNTING)* a temporada de caça.
seasonal ['si:zənəl] *adj* sazonal.
seasoned ['si:znd] *adj (wood)* tratado; *(fig: worker, troops)* calejado; **a ~ campaigner** um combatente experiente.
seasoning ['si:zənɪŋ] *n* tempero.
season ticket *n* bilhete *m* de temporada.
seat [si:t] *n (in bus, train: place)* assento; *(chair)* cadeira; *(POL)* lugar *m*, cadeira; *(of bicycle)* selim *m*; *(buttocks)* traseiro, nádegas *fpl*; *(of government)* sede *f*; *(of trousers)* fundilhos *mpl* ♦ *vt* sentar; *(have room for)* ter capacidade para; **to be ~ed** estar sentado; **are there any ~s left?** há algum lugar vago?; **to take one's ~** sentar-se; **please be ~ed** sentem-se.
seat belt *n* cinto de segurança.
seating ['si:tɪŋ] *n* lugares *mnpl* sentados ♦ *cpd*: **~ arrangements** distribuição *f* dos lugares sentados.
seating capacity *n* lotação *f*.
seating room *n* lugares *mpl* sentados.
SEATO ['si:təʊ] *n abbr* (= *Southeast Asia Treaty Organization*) OTSA *f*.
sea urchin *n* ouriço-do-mar *m*.
sea water *n* água do mar.
seaweed ['si:wi:d] *n* alga marinha.
seaworthy ['si:wə:ðɪ] *adj* em condições de navegar, resistente.
SEC *(US) n abbr* (= *Securities and Exchange Commission*) órgão que supervisiona o funcionamento da Bolsa de Valores.
sec. *abbr* (= *second*) seg.
secateurs [sɛkə'tə:z] *npl* tesoura para podar plantas.
secede [sɪ'si:d] *vi* separar-se.
secluded [sɪ'klu:dɪd] *adj* retirado; *(place)* afastado.

NB: *European Portuguese adds the following consonants to certain words:* **b** (sú(b)dito, su(b)til); **c** (a(c)ção, a(c)cionista, a(c)to); **m** (inde(m)ne); **p** (ado(p)ção, ado(p)tar); *for further details see p. xiii.*

seclusion [sɪ'kluːʒən] *n* reclusão *f*, isolamento.

second¹ ['sɛkənd] *adj* segundo ♦ *adv* (*in race etc*) em segundo lugar ♦ *n* segundo; (*AUT: also*: ~ *gear*) segunda; (*COMM*) artigo defeituoso ♦ *vt* (*motion*) apoiar, secundar; **Charles the S~** Carlos II; **just a ~!** (só) um minuto *or* minutinho!; ~ **floor** (*BRIT*) segundo andar; (*US*) primeiro andar; **to ask for a ~ opinion** (*MED*) querer uma segunda opinião; **to have ~ thoughts (about doing sth)** pensar duas vezes (antes de fazer algo); **on ~ thoughts** (*BRIT*) *or* **thought** (*US*) pensando bem.

second² [sɪ'kɔnd] *vt* (*employee*) transferir temporariamente.

secondary ['sɛkəndərɪ] *adj* secundário.

secondary picket *n* piquete *m* secundário.

secondary school *n* escola secundária, colégio.

second-best *n* segunda opção *f*.

second-class *adj* de segunda classe ♦ *adv*: **to send sth ~** remeter algo em segunda classe; **to travel ~** viajar em segunda classe; ~ **citizen** cidadão/dã da segunda classe.

second cousin *n* primo/a em segundo grau.

seconder ['sɛkəndə*] *n* pessoa que secunda uma moção.

secondhand [sɛkənd'hænd] *adj* de (*BR*) *or* em (*PT*) segunda mão, usado ♦ *adv* de (*BR*) *or* em (*PT*) segunda mão; **to hear sth ~** ouvir algo de fonte indireta.

second hand *n* (*on clock*) ponteiro de segundos.

second-in-command *n* suplente *m/f*.

secondly ['sɛkəndlɪ] *adv* em segundo lugar.

secondment [sɪ'kɔndmənt] *n* substituição *f* temporária.

second-rate *adj* de segunda categoria.

secrecy ['siːkrəsɪ] *n* sigilo; **in ~** sob sigilo, sigilosamente.

secret ['siːkrɪt] *adj* secreto ♦ *n* segredo; **in ~** em segredo; **to keep sth ~ from sb** esconder algo de alguém; **keep it ~** não diz nada a ninguém; **to make no ~ of sth** não esconder algo de ninguém.

secret agent *n* agente *m/f* secreto/a.

secretarial [sɛkrɪ'tɛərɪəl] *adj* de secretário/a, secretarial.

secretariat [sɛkrɪ'tɛərɪət] *n* secretaria, secretariado.

secretary ['sɛkrətərɪ] *n* secretário/a; **S~ of State** (*POL: BRIT*) Ministro/a de Estado; **Foreign S~** (: *US*) Ministro das Relações Exteriores.

secrete [sɪ'kriːt] *vt* (*ANAT, BIO, MED*) secretar; (*hide*) esconder.

secretion [sɪ'kriːʃən] *n* secreção *f*.

secretive ['siːkrətɪv] *adj* sigiloso, reservado, secretório.

secretly ['siːkrətlɪ] *adv* secretamente.

sect [sɛkt] *n* seita.

sectarian [sɛk'tɛərɪən] *adj* sectário.

section ['sɛkʃən] *n* seção *f*; (*part*) parte *f*, porção *f*; (*of document*) parágrafo, artigo; (*of opinion*) setor *m* ♦ *vt* secionar; **the business** *etc* ~ (*PRESS*) a seção de negócios *etc*.

sectional ['sɛkʃənəl] *adj* (*drawing*) transversal, secional.

sector ['sɛktə*] *n* setor *m*.

secular ['sɛkjulə*] *adj* secular, leigo.

secure [sɪ'kjuə*] *adj* (*free from anxiety*) seguro; (*firmly fixed*) firme, rígido; (*in safe place*) a salvo, em segurança ♦ *vt* (*fix*) prender; (*get*) conseguir, obter; (*COMM: loan*) garantir; **to make sth ~** firmar algo, segurar algo; **to ~ sth for sb** arranjar algo para alguém.

secured creditor [sɪ'kjuəd-] *n* credor *m* com garantia.

security [sɪ'kjurɪtɪ] *n* segurança; (*for loan*) fiança, garantia; (: *object*) penhor *m*; **securities** *npl* (*STOCK EXCHANGE*) títulos *mpl*, valores *mpl*; **to increase** *or* **tighten ~** aumentar a segurança.

security forces *npl* forças *fpl* de segurança.

security guard *n* (guarda *m/f* de) segurança *m/f*.

security risk *n* risco à segurança.

secy *abbr* (= *secretary*) secr.

sedan [sɪ'dæn] (*US*) *n* (*AUT*) sedã *m*.

sedate [sɪ'deɪt] *adj* (*calm*) sossegado, tranqüilo; (*formal*) sério, ponderado ♦ *vt* sedar, tratar com calmantes.

sedation [sɪ'deɪʃən] *n* (*MED*) sedação *f*; **to be under ~** estar sob o efeito de sedativos.

sedative ['sɛdɪtɪv] *n* calmante *m*, sedativo.

sedentary ['sɛdntrɪ] *adj* sedentário.

sediment ['sɛdɪmənt] *n* sedimento.

sedition [sɪ'dɪʃən] *n* sedição *f*.

seduce [sɪ'djuːs] *vt* seduzir.

seduction [sɪ'dʌkʃən] *n* sedução *f*.

seductive [sɪ'dʌktɪv] *adj* sedutor(a).

see [siː] (*pt* **saw**, *pp* **seen**) *vt* ver; (*make out*) enxergar; (*understand*) entender; (*accompany*): **to ~ sb to the door** acompanhar *or* levar alguém até a porta ♦ *vi* ver ♦ *n* sé *f*, sede *f*; **to ~ that** (*ensure*) assegurar que; **there was nobody to be ~n** não havia ninguém; **let me ~** deixa eu ver; **to go and ~ sb** ir visitar alguém; ~ **for yourself** veja você mesmo, confira; **I don't know what she ~s in him** não sei o que ela vê nele; **as far as I can ~** que eu saiba; ~ **you!** até logo! (*BR*), adeus! (*PT*); ~ **you soon/later/tomorrow!** até logo/mais tarde/amanhã!

see about *vt fus* tratar de.

see off *vt* despedir-se de.

see through *vt fus* enxergar através de ♦ *vt* levar a cabo.

see to *vt fus* providenciar.

seed [siːd] *n* semente *f*; (*fig*) germe *m*; (*TENNIS*) pré-selecionado/a; **to go to ~** produzir sementes; (*fig*) deteriorar-se.

seedless ['siːdlɪs] *adj* sem caroços.

seedling ['siːdlɪŋ] *n* planta brotada da semente, muda.

seedy ['siːdɪ] *adj* (*shabby*) gasto, surrado; (*person*) maltrapilho.

seeing ['siːɪŋ] *conj*: ~ **(that)** visto (que), considerando (que).

seek [siːk] (*pt*, *pp* **sought**) *vt* procurar; (*post*) solicitar; **to ~ advice/help from sb** pedir um conselho a alguém/procurar ajuda de alguém.

seek out *vt* (*person*) procurar.

seem [siːm] *vi* parecer; **it ~s (that) ...** parece que ...; **what ~s to be the trouble?** qual é o problema?; **I did what ~ed best** fiz o que me pareceu melhor.

seemingly ['siːmıŋlı] *adv* aparentemente, pelo que aparenta.

seen [siːn] *pp of* **see.**

seep [siːp] *vi* filtrar-se, penetrar.

seer [sıə*] *n* vidente *m/f*, profeta *m/f*.

seersucker ['sıəsʌkə*] *n* tecido listrado de algodão.

seesaw ['siːsɔː] *n* gangorra, balanço.

seethe [siːð] *vi* ferver; **to ~ with anger** estar danado (da vida).

see-through *adj* transparente.

segment ['sɛgmənt] *n* segmento.

segregate ['sɛgrıgeıt] *vt* segregar.

segregation [sɛgrı'geıʃən] *n* segregação *f.*

Seine [seın] *n*: **the ~** o Sena.

seismic ['saızmık] *adj* sísmico.

seize [siːz] *vt* (*grasp*) agarrar, pegar; (*take possession of*) apoderar-se de, confiscar; (: *territory*) tomar posse de; (*opportunity*) aproveitar.

seize up *vi* (*TECH*) gripar.

seize (up)on *vt fus* valer-se de.

seizure ['siːʒə*] *n* (*MED*) ataque *m*, acesso; (*LAW*) confisco, embargo.

seldom ['sɛldəm] *adv* raramente.

select [sı'lɛkt] *adj* seleto, escolhido; (*hotel, restaurant*) fino ♦ *vt* escolher, selecionar; (*SPORT*) selecionar, escalar; **a ~ few** uns poucos escolhidos.

selection [sı'lɛkʃən] *n* seleção *f*, escolha; (*COMM*) sortimento.

selection committee *n* comissão *f* de seleção.

selective [sı'lɛktıv] *adj* seletivo.

selector [sı'lɛktə*] *n* (*person*) selecionador(a) *m/f*, seletor(a) *m/f*; (*TECH*) selecionador *m*.

self [sɛlf] (*pl* **selves**) *pron see* **herself; himself; itself; myself; oneself; ourselves; themselves; yourself** ♦ *n*: **the ~** o eu ♦ *prefix* auto....

self-addressed [-ə'drɛst] *adj*: **~ envelope** envelope *m* endereçado ao remetente.

self-adhesive *adj* auto-adesivo.

self-appointed [-ə'pɔıntıd] *adj* auto-nomeado.

self-assertive *adj* autoritário.

self-assurance *n* autoconfiança.

self-assured [-ə'ʃuəd] *adj* seguro de si.

self-catering (*BRIT*) *adj* (*flat*) com cozinha; (*holiday*) em casa alugada.

self-centred [-'sɛntəd] (*US* **self-centered**) *adj* egocêntrico.

self-cleaning *adj* de limpeza automática.

self-coloured (*US* **self-colored**) *adj* de cor natural; (*of one colour*) de uma só cor.

self-confessed [-kən'fɛst] *adj* assumido.

self-confidence *n* autoconfiança, confiança em si.

self-conscious *adj* inibido, constrangido.

self-contained [-kən'teınd] *adj* (*gen*) independente; (*flat*) completo, autônomo.

self-control *n* autocontrole *m*, autodomínio.

self-defeating [-dı'fiːtıŋ] *adj* contraprodu- cente.

self-defence (*US* **self-defense**) *n* legítima defesa, autodefesa.

self-discipline *n* autodisciplina.

self-employed [-ım'plɔıd] *adj* autônomo.

self-esteem *n* amor m próprio.

self-evident *adj* patente.

self-explanatory *adj* que se explica por si mesmo.

self-governing *adj* autônomo.

self-help *n* iniciativa própria, esforço pessoal.

self-importance *n* presunção *f.*

self-important *adj* presunçoso, que se dá muita importância.

self-indulgent *adj* que se permite excessos.

self-inflicted [-ın'flıktıd] *adj* infligido a si mesmo.

self-interest *n* egoísmo.

selfish ['sɛlfıʃ] *adj* egoísta.

selfishness ['sɛlfıʃnıs] *n* egoísmo.

selfless ['sɛlflıs] *adj* desinteressado.

selflessly ['sɛlflıslı] *adv* desinteressadamente.

self-made man (*irreg*) *n* homem *m* que se fez por conta própria.

self-pity *n* pena de si mesmo.

self-portrait *n* auto-retrato.

self-possessed [-pə'zɛst] *adj* calmo, senhor(a) de si.

self-preservation *n* auto-preservação *f.*

self-raising [-'reızıŋ] (*BRIT*) *adj*: **~ flour** farinha de trigo com fermento acrescentado.

self-reliant *adj* seguro de si, independente.

self-respect *n* amor *m* próprio.

self-respecting [-rıs'pɛktıŋ] *adj* que se respeita.

self-righteous *adj* farisaico, santarrão/rona.

self-rising (*US*) *adj*: **~ flour** farinha de trigo com fermento acrescentado.

self-sacrifice *n* abnegação *f*, altruísmo.

self-same *adj* mesmo.

self-satisfied [-'sætısfaıd] *adj* satisfeito consigo mesmo.

self-sealing *adj* (*envelope*) auto-adesivo.

self-service *adj* de auto-serviço ♦ *n* auto- serviço.

self-styled [-staıld] *adj* pretenso.

self-sufficient *adj* auto-suficiente.

self-supporting [-sə'pɔːtıŋ] *adj* financeira- mente independente.

self-taught *adj* autodidata.

self-test *n* (*COMPUT*) auto-teste *m.*

sell [sɛl] (*pt*, *pp* **sold**) *vt* vender ♦ *vi* vender- se; **to ~ at** *or* **for £10** vender a *or* por 10 li- bras; **to ~ sb an idea** (*fig*) convencer alguém de uma idéia.

NB: *European Portuguese adds the following consonants to certain words:* **b** (sú(b)dito, su(b)til); **c** (a(c)ção, a(c)cionista, a(c)to); **m** (inde(m)ne); **p** (ado(p)ção, ado(p)tar); *for further details see p. xiii.*

sell off *vt* liquidar.

sell out *vi* vender todo o estoque ♦ *vt*: **the tickets are all sold out** todos os ingressos já foram vendidos; **to ~ out (to)** (*COMM*) vender o negócio (a); (*fig*) vender-se (a).

sell up *vi* vender o negócio.

sell-by date *n* vencimento.

seller ['sɛlə*] *n* vendedor(a) *m/f*; **~'s market** mercado de vendedor.

selling price ['sɛlɪŋ-] *n* preço de venda.

sellotape ['sɛləʊteɪp] ® *n* fita adesiva, durex *m* ® (*BR*).

sellout ['sɛlaut] *n* traição *f*; (*of tickets*): **it was a ~** foi um sucesso de bilheteria.

selves [sɛlvz] *npl of* **self**.

semantic [sə'mæntɪk] *adj* semântico.

semantics [sə'mæntɪks] *n* semântica.

semaphore ['sɛməfɔ:*] *n* semáforo.

semblance ['sɛmbləns] *n* aparência.

semen ['si:mən] *n* sêmen *m*.

semester [sə'mɛstə*] *n* semestre *m*.

semi ['sɛmɪ] (*BRIT*: *inf*) *n* (casa) geminada.

semi... [sɛmɪ] *prefix* semi..., meio....

semibreve ['sɛmɪbri:v] (*BRIT*) *n* semibreve *f*.

semicircle ['sɛmɪsɔ:kl] *n* semicírculo.

semicircular [sɛmɪ'sɔ:kjulə*] *adj* semicircular.

semi-colon *n* ponto e vírgula.

semiconductor [sɛmɪkən'dʌktə*] *n* semicondutor *m*.

semi-conscious *adj* semiconsciente.

semi-detached (house) (*BRIT*: *irreg*) *n* (casa) geminada.

semi-final *n* semifinal *f*.

seminar ['sɛmɪnɑ:*] *n* seminário.

seminary ['sɛmɪnərɪ] *n* (*for priests*) seminário.

semiprecious [sɛmɪ'prɛʃəs] *adj* semiprecioso.

semiquaver ['sɛmɪkweɪvə*] (*BRIT*) *n* semicolcheia.

semiskilled [sɛmɪ'skɪld] *adj*: **~ worker** operário/a semi-especializado/a.

semitone ['sɛmɪtəun] *n* (*MUS*) semitom *m*.

semolina [sɛmə'li:nə] *n* sêmola, semolina.

SEN (*BRIT*) *n abbr* = **State Enrolled Nurse**.

Sen. *abbr* = **Senator**; **Senior**.

sen. *abbr* = **senator**; **senior**.

senate ['sɛnɪt] *n* senado.

senator ['sɛnətə*] *n* senador(a) *m/f*.

send [sɛnd] (*pt*, *pp* **sent**) *vt* mandar, enviar; (*dispatch*) expedir, remeter; (*telegram*) passar; **to ~ by post** (*BRIT*) *or* **mail** (*US*) mandar pelo correio; **to ~ sb for sth** mandar alguém buscar algo; **to ~ word that ...** mandar dizer que ...; **she ~s (you) her love** ela lhe envia lembranças; **to ~ sb to Coventry** (*BRIT*) colocar alguém em ostracismo; **to ~ sb to sleep** dar sono a alguém; **to ~ sb into fits of laughter** dar um ataque de riso a alguém; **to ~ sth flying** derrubar algo.

send away *vt* (*letter*, *goods*) expedir, mandar.

send away for *vt fus* encomendar, pedir pelo correio.

send back *vt* devolver, mandar de volta.

send for *vt fus* mandar buscar; (*by post*) pedir pelo correio, encomendar.

send in *vt* (*report*, *application*) entregar.

send off *vt* (*goods*) despachar, expedir; (*BRIT*: *SPORT*: *player*) expulsar.

send on *vt* (*BRIT*: *letter*) remeter; (*luggage etc*: *in advance*) mandar com antecedência.

send out *vt* (*invitation*) distribuir; (*signal*) emitir.

send round *vt* (*letter*, *document*) circular.

send up *vt* (*person*, *price*) fazer subir; (*parody*) parodiar.

sender ['sɛndə*] *n* remetente *m/f*.

send-off *n*: **a good ~** uma boa despedida.

Senegal [sɛnɪ'gɔ:l] *n* Senegal *m*.

Senegalese [sɛnɪgə'li:z] *adj*, *n inv* senegalês/esa *m/f*.

senile ['si:naɪl] *adj* senil.

senility [sɪ'nɪlɪtɪ] *n* senilidade *f*.

senior ['si:nɪə*] *adj* (*older*) mais velho *or* idoso; (: *on staff*) mais antigo; (*of higher rank*) superior ♦ *n* o/a mais velho/a; (*on staff*) o/a mais antigo/a; **P. Jones ~** P. Jones Sênior.

senior citizen *n* idoso/a.

senior high school (*US*) *n* ≈ colégio.

seniority [si:nɪ'ɔrɪtɪ] *n* antiguidade *f*.

sensation [sɛn'seɪʃən] *n* sensação *f*; **to cause a ~** causar sensação.

sensational [sɛn'seɪʃənəl] *adj* sensacional.

sensationalism [sɛn'seɪʃənəlɪzəm] *n* sensacionalismo.

sense [sɛns] *n* sentido; (*feeling*) sensação *f*; (*good ~*) bom senso ♦ *vt* sentir, perceber; **~s** *npl* juízo; **it makes ~** faz sentido; **~ of humour** senso de humor; **there is no ~ in (doing) that** não há sentido em (fazer) isso; **to come to one's ~s** (*regain consciousness*) recobrar os sentidos; (*become reasonable*) recobrar o juízo; **to take leave of one's ~s** enlouquecer.

senseless ['sɛnslɪs] *adj* insensato, estúpido; (*unconscious*) sem sentidos, inconsciente.

sensibility [sɛnsɪ'bɪlɪtɪ] *n* sensibilidade *f*; **sensibilities** *npl* suscetibilidade *f*.

sensible ['sɛnsɪbl] *adj* sensato, de bom senso; (*reasonable*) lógico, razoável; (*shoes etc*) prático.

sensitive ['sɛnsɪtɪv] *adj* sensível; (*touchy*) suscetível.

sensitivity [sɛnsɪ'tɪvɪtɪ] *n* sensibilidade *f*; (*touchiness*) suscetibilidade *f*.

sensual ['sɛnsjuəl] *adj* sensual.

sensuous ['sɛnsjuəs] *adj* sensual.

sent [sɛnt] *pt*, *pp of* **send**.

sentence ['sɛntəns] *n* (*LING*) frase *f*, oração *f*; (*LAW*: *verdict*) sentença; (: *punishment*) pena ♦ *vt*: **to ~ sb to death/to 5 years** condenar alguém à morte/a 5 anos de prisão; **to pass ~ on sb** sentenciar alguém.

sentiment ['sɛntɪmənt] *n* sentimento; (*opinion*) opinião *f*.

sentimental [sɛntɪ'mɛntl] *adj* sentimental.

sentimentality [sɛntɪmɛn'tælɪtɪ] *n* sentimentalismo.

sentry ['sɛntrɪ] *n* sentinela *f*.

sentry duty *n*: **to be on ~** estar de guarda.

Seoul [səul] *n* Seul.
separable ['sɛprəbl] *adj* separável.
separate [*adj* 'sɛprɪt, *vt, vi* 'sɛpəreɪt] *adj* separado; (*distinct*) diferente ♦ *vt* separar; (*part*) dividir ♦ *vi* separar-se; ~ **from** separado de; **under** ~ **cover** (*COMM*) em separado; **to** ~ **into** dividir em.
separated ['sɛpəreɪtɪd] *adj* (*from spouse*) separado.
separately ['sɛprɪtlɪ] *adv* separadamente.
separates ['sɛprɪts] *npl* (*clothes*) roupas *fpl* que fazem jogo.
separation [sɛpə'reɪʃən] *n* separação *f*.
Sept. *abbr* (= *September*) set.
September [sɛp'tɛmbə*] *n* setembro; *see also* **July**.
septic ['sɛptɪk] *adj* sético; (*wound*) infeccionado.
septicaemia [sɛptɪ'siːmɪə] (*US* **septicemia**) *n* septicemia.
septic tank *n* fossa sética.
sequel ['siːkwl] *n* conseqüência, resultado; (*of story*) continuação *f*.
sequence ['siːkwəns] *n* série *f*, seqüência; (*CINEMA*) série; **in** ~ em seqüência.
sequential [sɪ'kwɛnʃəl] *adj*: ~ **access** (*COMPUT*) acesso seqüencial.
sequin ['siːkwɪn] *n* lantejoula, paetê *m*.
Serbo-Croat ['səːbəu'krəuæt] *n* (*LING*) serbo-croata *m*.
serenade [sɛrə'neɪd] *n* serenata ♦ *vt* fazer serenata para.
serene [sɪ'riːn] *adj* sereno, tranqüilo.
serenity [sə'rɛnɪtɪ] *n* serenidade *f*, tranqüilidade *f*.
sergeant ['sɑːdʒənt] *n* sargento.
sergeant major *n* sargento-ajudante *m*.
serial ['sɪərɪəl] *n* (*TV*) seriado; (*in newspaper*) história em folhetim ♦ *adj* (*COMPUT*: *interface, printer*) serial; (: *access*) seqüencial.
serialize ['sɪərɪəlaɪz] *vt* (*book*) publicar em folhetim; (*TV*) seriar.
serial number *n* número de série.
series ['sɪəriːz] *n inv* série *f*.
serious ['sɪərɪəs] *adj* sério; (*grave*) grave; **are you** ~ **(about it)?** você está falando sério?
seriously ['sɪərɪəslɪ] *adv* a sério, com seriedade; (*gravely*) gravemente; **to take sth/sb** ~ levar algo/alguém a sério.
seriousness ['sɪərɪəsnɪs] *n* seriedade *f*; gravidade *f*.
sermon ['səːmən] *n* sermão *m* .
serrated [sɪ'reɪtɪd] *adj* serrado, dentado.
serum ['sɪərəm] *n* soro.
servant ['səːvənt] *n* empregado/a *m/f*; (*fig*) servidor(a) *m/f*.
serve [səːv] *vt* servir; (*customer*) atender; (*subj: train*) passar por; (*treat*) tratar; (*apprenticeship*) fazer; (*prison term*) cumprir ♦ *vi* (*TENNIS etc*) sacar; (*be useful*): **to** ~ **as/ for/to do** servir como/para/para fazer ♦ *n* (*TENNIS*) saque *m*; **are you being** ~**d?** você

já foi atendido?; **to** ~ **on a committee/jury** fazer parte de um comitê/júri; **it** ~**s him right** é bem feito por ele; **it** ~**s my purpose** isso me serve.
serve out *vt* (*food*) servir.
serve up *vt* (*food*) servir.
service ['səːvɪs] *n* serviço; (*REL*) culto; (*AUT*) revisão *f*; (*also: dinner* ~) aparelho de jantar ♦ *vt* (*car, washing machine*) fazer a revisão de, revisar; (: *repair*) consertar; **the S**~**s** *npl* as Forças Armadas; **to be of** ~ **to sb, to do sb a** ~ ser útil a alguém.
serviceable ['səːvɪsəbl] *adj* aproveitável, prático, durável.
service area *n* (*on motorway*) posto de gasolina com bar, restaurante etc.
service charge (*BRIT*) *n* serviço.
service industries *npl* setor *m* de serviços.
serviceman ['səːvɪsmæn] (*irreg*) *n* militar *m*.
service station *n* posto de gasolina (*BR*), estação *f* de serviço (*PT*).
serviette [səːvɪ'ɛt] *n* guardanapo.
servile ['səːvaɪl] *adj* servil.
session ['sɛʃən] *n* (*sitting*) sessão *f*; (*SCH*) ano letivo; **to be in** ~ estar reunido em sessão.
set [sɛt] (*pt, pp* **set**) *n* (*of tools, glasses*) jogo; (*RADIO, TV*) aparelho; (*of utensils*) bateria de cozinha; (*of cutlery*) talher *m*; (*of books*) coleção *f*; (*group of people*) grupo; (*TENNIS, CINEMA*) set *m*; (*THEATRE*) cenário; (*HAIRDRESSING*) penteado; (*MATH*) conjunto ♦ *adj* (*fixed*) marcado, fixo; (*ready*) pronto; (*resolved*) decidido, estabelecido ♦ *vt* (*place*) pôr, colocar; (*fix*) fixar; (: *a time*) marcar; (*adjust*) ajustar; (*decide: rules etc*) estabelecer, decidir; (*record*) estabelecer; (*homework*) passar; (*TYP*) compor ♦ *vi* (*sun*) pôr-se; (*jam, jelly, concrete*) endurecer, solidificar-se; **to be** ~ **on doing sth** estar decidido a fazer algo; **to be all** ~ **to do** estar todo pronto para fazer; **to be (dead)** ~ **against** estar (completamente) contra; **he's** ~ **in his ways** ele tem opiniões fixas; **to** ~ **to music** musicar, pôr música em; **to** ~ **on fire** botar fogo em, incendiar; **to** ~ **free** libertar; **to** ~ **sth going** pôr algo em movimento; **to** ~ **sail** zarpar, alçar velas; ~ **phrase** frase *f* feita; **a** ~ **of false teeth** uma dentadura; **a** ~ **of dining-room furniture** um conjunto de salade jantar; **a film** ~ **in Rome** um filme ambientado em Roma.
set about *vt fus* (*task*) começar com; **to** ~ **about doing sth** começar a fazer algo.
set aside *vt* deixar de lado.
set back *vt* (*in time*): **to** ~ **back (by)** atrasar (por); (*place*): **a house** ~ **back from the road** uma casa afastada da estrada.
set in *vi* (*infection*) manifestar-se; (*complications*) surgir; **the rain has** ~ **in for the day** vai chover o dia inteiro.
set off *vi* partir, ir indo ♦ *vt* (*bomb*) fazer explodir; (*cause to start*) colocar em funcio-

---

NB: *European Portuguese adds the following consonants to certain words:* **b** (sú(b)dito, su(b)til); **c** (a(c)ção, a(c)cionista, a(c)to); **m** (inde(m)ne); **p** (ado(p)ção, ado(p)tar); *for further details see p. xiii.*

namento; (*show up well*) ressaltar.

set out *vi*: to ~ **out to do sth** pretender fazer algo ♦ *vt* (*arrange*) colocar, dispor; (*state*) expor, explicar; **to ~ out (from)** sair (de).

set up *vt* (*organization, record*) fundar, estabelecer; **to ~ up shop** (*fig*) estabelecer-se.

setback ['sɛtbæk] *n* (*hitch*) revés *m*, contratempo; (*in health*) piora.

set menu *n* refeição *f* a preço fixo.

set square *n* esquadro.

settee [sɛ'tiː] *n* sofá *m*.

setting ['sɛtɪŋ] *n* (*frame*) moldura; (*placing*) colocação *f*; (*of sun*) pôr(-do-sol) *m*; (*of jewel*) engaste *m*; (*location*) cenário.

setting lotion *n* loção *f* fixadora.

settle ['sɛtl] *vt* (*argument, matter*) resolver, esclarecer; (*accounts*) ajustar, liquidar; (*land*) colonizar; (*MED: calm*) acalmar, tranqüilizar ♦ *vi* (*dust etc*) assentar; (*weather*) firmar, melhorar; (*also*: ~ *down*) instalar-se, estabilizar-se; **to ~ to sth** concentrar-se em algo; **to ~ for sth** concordar em aceitar algo; **to ~ on sth** optar por algo; **that's ~d then** está resolvido então; **to ~ one's stomach** acomodar o estômago.

settle in *vi* instalar-se.

settle up *vi*: to ~ **up with sb** ajustar as contas com alguém.

settlement ['sɛtlmənt] *n* (*payment*) liquidação *f*; (*agreement*) acordo, convênio; (*village etc*) povoado, povoação *f*; **in ~ of our account** (*COMM*) em liquidação da nossa conta.

settler ['sɛtlə*] *n* colono/a, colonizador(a) *m/f*.

setup ['sɛtʌp] *n* (*arrangement*) organização *f*; (*situation*) situação *f*.

seven ['sɛvn] *num* sete; *see also* **five**.

seventeen ['sɛvn'tiːn] *num* dezessete; *see also* **five**.

seventh ['sɛvnθ] *num* sétimo; *see also* **fifth**.

seventy ['sɛvntɪ] *num* setenta; *see also* **fifty**.

sever ['sɛvə*] *vt* cortar; (*relations*) romper.

several ['sɛvərl] *adj, pron* vários/as; ~ **of us** vários de nós; ~ **times** várias vezes.

severance ['sɛvərəns] *n* (*of relations*) rompimento.

severance pay *n* indenização *f* pela demissão.

severe [sɪ'vɪə*] *adj* severo; (*serious*) grave; (*hard*) duro; (*pain*) intenso; (*plain*) austero.

severely [sɪ'vɪəlɪ] *adv* severamente; (*wounded, ill*) gravemente.

severity [sɪ'vɛrɪtɪ] *n* severidade *f*; austeridade *f*; intensidade *f*.

sew [səu] (*pt* ~**ed**, *pp* **sewn**) *vt, vi* coser, costurar.

sew up *vt* coser, costurar; **it's all sewn up** (*fig*) está no papo.

sewage ['suːɪdʒ] *n* detritos *mpl*.

sewer ['suːə*] *n* (*cano do*) esgoto, bueiro.

sewing ['səuɪŋ] *n* costura.

sewing machine *n* máquina de costura.

sewn [səun] *pp of* **sew**.

sex [sɛks] *n* sexo; **to have ~ with sb** fazer sexo com alguém.

sex act *n* ato sexual.

sexism ['sɛksɪzm] *n* sexismo.

sexist ['sɛksɪst] *adj* sexista.

sextet [sɛks'tɛt] *n* sexteto.

sexual ['sɛksjuəl] *adj* sexual; ~ **assault** atentado ao pudor; ~ **intercourse** relações *fpl* sexuais.

sexy ['sɛksɪ] *adj* sexy.

Seychelles [seɪ'ʃɛl(z)] *npl*: **the ~** Seychelles (*no article*).

SF *n abbr* = **science fiction**.

SG (*US*) *n abbr* = **Surgeon General**.

Sgt *abbr* (= *sergeant*) sarg.

shabbiness ['ʃæbɪnɪs] *n* (*of clothes*) pobreza; (*of building*) mau estado de conservação.

shabby ['ʃæbɪ] *adj* (*person*) esfarrapado, maltrapilho; (*clothes*) usado, surrado.

shack [ʃæk] *n* choupana, barraca.

shackles ['ʃæklz] *npl* algemas *fpl*, grilhões *mpl*.

shade [ʃeɪd] *n* sombra; (*for lamp*) quebra-luz *m*; (*for eyes*) viseira; (*of colour*) tom *m*, tonalidade *f*; (*US: window* ~) estore *m* ♦ *vt* sombrear, dar sombra a; ~**s** *npl* (*US: sunglasses*) óculos *mpl* escuros; **in the** ~ à sombra; **a** ~ **smaller** um pouquinho menor.

shadow ['ʃædəu] *n* sombra ♦ *vt* (*follow*) seguir de perto (sem ser visto); **without** *or* **beyond a** ~ **of doubt** sem sombra de dúvida.

shadow cabinet (*BRIT*) *n* (*POL*) *gabinete paralelo formado pelo partido da oposição*.

shadowy ['ʃædəuɪ] *adj* escuro; (*dim*) vago, indistinto.

shady ['ʃeɪdɪ] *adj* sombreado, à sombra; (*fig: dishonest*) suspeito, duvidoso; (: *deal*) desonesto.

shaft [ʃɑːft] *n* (*of arrow, spear*) haste *f*; (*column*) fuste *m*; (*AUT, TECH*) eixo, manivela; (*of mine, of lift*) poço; (*of light*) raio.

shaggy ['ʃægɪ] *adj* peludo, felpudo.

shake [ʃeɪk] (*pt* **shook**, *pp* **shaken**) *vt* sacudir; (*building, confidence*) abalar; (*surprise*) surpreender ♦ *vi* tremer ♦ *n* (*movement*) sacudidela; (*violent*) safanão *m*; **to ~ hands with sb** apertar a mão de alguém; **to ~ one's head** (*in refusal etc*) dizer não com a cabeça; (*in dismay*) sacudir a cabeça.

shake off *vt* sacudir; (*fig*) livrar-se de.

shake up *vt* sacudir.

shake-up *n* reorganização *f*.

shakily ['ʃeɪkɪlɪ] *adv* (*reply*) de voz trêmula; (*walk*) vacilante; (*write*) de mão trêmula.

shaky ['ʃeɪkɪ] *adj* (*hand, voice*) trêmulo; (*person: in shock*) abalado; (: *old*) frágil; (*chair*) bambo; (*knowledge*) duvidoso.

shale [ʃeɪl] *n* argila xistosa.

shall [ʃæl] (*conditional* **should**) *aux vb*: **I ~ go** irei.

shallot [ʃə'lɔt] (*BRIT*) *n* cebolinha.

shallow ['ʃæləu] *adj* raso; (*fig*) superficial.

sham [ʃæm] *n* fraude *f*, fingimento ♦ *adj* falso, simulado ♦ *vt* fingir, simular.

shambles ['ʃæmblz] *n* confusão *f*; **the economy is (in) a complete** ~ a economia está completamente desorganizada.

shame [ʃeɪm] *n* vergonha; (*pity*) pena ♦ *vt* envergonhar; **it is a** ~ **(that/to do)** é (uma) pena (que/fazer); **what a** ~**!** que pena!; **to put sb/sth to** ~ deixar alguém/algo envergonhado.

shamefaced ['ʃeɪmfeɪst] *adj* envergonhado.

shameful ['ʃeɪmful] *adj* vergonhoso.

shameless ['ʃeɪmlɪs] *adj* sem vergonha, descarado; (*immodest*) cínico, impudico.

shampoo [ʃæm'puː] *n* xampu *m* (*BR*), champô *m* (*PT*) ♦ *vt* lavar o cabelo (com xampu); ~ **and set** lavagem *f* e penteado.

shamrock ['ʃæmrɔk] *n* trevo.

shandy ['ʃændɪ] *n* mistura de cerveja com refresco gaseificado.

shan't [ʃɑːnt] = **shall not**.

shanty town ['ʃæntɪ-] *n* favela.

SHAPE [ʃeɪp] *n abbr* (= *Supreme Headquarters Allied Powers, Europe*) QG das forças aliadas na Europa.

shape [ʃeɪp] *n* forma ♦ *vt* formar, modelar; (*clay, stone*) dar forma a; (*sb's ideas*) moldar; (*sb's life, course of events*) determinar ♦ *vi* (*also*: ~ *up*) (*events*) desenrolar-se; (*person*) tomar jeito; **to take** ~ tomar forma; **in the** ~ **of a heart** em forma de coração; **I can't bear gardening in any** ~ **or form** não suporto jardinagem de forma alguma; **to get o.s. into** ~ ficar em forma.

-shaped [ʃeɪpt] *suffix*: **heart**~ em forma de coração.

shapeless ['ʃeɪplɪs] *adj* informe, sem forma definida.

shapely ['ʃeɪplɪ] *adj* escultural.

share [ʃɛə*] *n* (*part*) parte *f*; (*contribution*) cota; (*COMM*) ação *f* ♦ *vt* dividir; (*have in common*) compartilhar; **to** ~ **out (among** *or* **between)** distribuir (entre); **to** ~ **in** participar de; **to have a** ~ **in the profits** ter uma participação nos lucros.

share capital *n* capital *m* em ações.

share certificate *n* cautela de ação.

shareholder ['ʃɛəhəʊldə*] *n* acionista *m/f*.

share index *n* índice *m* da Bolsa de Valores.

share issue *n* emissão *f* de ações.

shark [ʃɑːk] *n* tubarão *m*.

sharp [ʃɑːp] *adj* (*razor, knife*) afiado; (*point*) pontiagudo; (*outline*) definido, bem marcado; (*pain*) agudo; (*curve, bend*) fechado; (*MUS*) desafinado; (*contrast*) marcado; (*voice*) agudo; (*person: quick-witted*) perspicaz; (*dishonest*) desonesto ♦ *n* (*MUS*) sustenido ♦ *adv*: **at 2 o'clock** ~ às 2 (horas) em ponto; **turn** ~ **left** vira logo à esquerda; **to be** ~ **with sb** ser brusco com alguém; **look** ~**!** rápido!

sharpen ['ʃɑːpən] *vt* afiar; (*pencil*) apontar, fazer a ponta de; (*fig*) aguçar.

sharpener ['ʃɑːpnə*] *n* (*also*: *pencil* ~) apontador *m* (*BR*), apara-lápis *m inv* (*PT*).

sharp-eyed [-aɪd] *adj* de vista aguda.

sharply ['ʃɑːplɪ] *adv* (*abruptly*) bruscamente; (*clearly*) claramente; (*harshly*) severamente.

sharp-tempered *adj* irascível.

sharp-witted [-'wɪtɪd] *adj* perspicaz, observador(a).

shatter ['ʃætə*] *vt* despedaçar, estilhaçar; (*fig: ruin*) destruir, acabar com; (: *upset*) arrasar ♦ *vi* despedaçar-se, estilhaçar-se.

shattered ['ʃætəd] *adj* (*overwhelmed*) arrasado; (*exhausted*) exausto.

shatterproof ['ʃætəpruːf] *adj* inestilhaçável.

shave [ʃeɪv] *vt* barbear, fazer a barba de ♦ *vi* fazer a barba, barbear-se ♦ *n*: **to have a** ~ fazer a barba.

shaven ['ʃeɪvn] *adj* (*head*) raspado.

shaver ['ʃeɪvə*] *n* barbeador *m*; **electric** ~ barbeador elétrico.

shaving ['ʃeɪvɪŋ] *n* (*action*) barbeação *f*; ~**s** *npl* (*of wood*) aparas *fpl*.

shaving brush *n* pincel *m* de barba.

shaving cream *n* creme *m* de barbear.

shaving soap *n* sabão *m* de barba.

shawl [ʃɔːl] *n* xale *m*.

she [ʃiː] *pron* ela; **there** ~ **is** lá está ela; ~-**elephant** *etc* elefante *etc* fêmea.

sheaf [ʃiːf] (*pl* **sheaves**) *n* (*of corn*) gavela; (*of arrows*) feixe *m*; (*of papers*) maço.

shear [ʃɪə*] (*pt* ~**ed**, *pp* ~**ed** *or* **shorn**) *vt* (*sheep*) tosquiar, tosar.

shear off *vt* cercear.

shears [ʃɪəz] *npl* (*for hedge*) tesoura de jardim.

sheath [ʃiːθ] *n* bainha; (*contraceptive*) camisa-de-vênus *f*, camisinha.

sheathe [ʃiːð] *vt* embainhar.

sheath knife (*irreg*) *n* faca com bainha.

sheaves [ʃiːvz] *npl of* **sheaf**.

shed [ʃed] (*pt, pp* **shed**) *n* alpendre *m*, galpão *m*; (*INDUSTRY, RAIL*) galpão *m* ♦ *vt* (*skin*) mudar; (*leaves, fur*) perder; (*tears*) derramar; **to** ~ **light on** (*problem, mystery*) esclarecer.

she'd [ʃiːd] = **she had**; **she would**.

sheen [ʃiːn] *n* brilho.

sheep [ʃiːp] *n inv* ovelha.

sheepdog ['ʃiːpdɔg] *n* cão *m* pastor.

sheep farmer *n* criador(a) *m/f* de ovelhas.

sheepish ['ʃiːpɪʃ] *adj* tímido, acanhado.

sheepskin ['ʃiːpskɪn] *n* pele *f* de carneiro, pelego.

sheepskin jacket *n* casaco de pele de carneiro.

sheer [ʃɪə*] *adj* (*utter*) puro, completo; (*steep*) íngreme, empinado; (*almost transparent*) fino, translúcido ♦ *adv* a pique; **by** ~ **chance** totalmente por acaso.

sheet [ʃiːt] *n* (*on bed*) lençol *m*; (*of paper*) folha; (*of glass, metal*) lâmina, chapa.

sheet feed *n* (*on printer*) alimentação *f* de papel (em folhas soltas).

sheet lightning *n* relâmpago difuso.

---

*NB: European Portuguese adds the following consonants to certain words: **b** (sú(b)dito, su(b)til); **c** (a(c)ção, a(c)cionista, a(c)to); **m** (inde(m)ne); **p** (ado(p)ção, ado(p)tar); for further details see p. xiii.*

sheet metal *n* metal *m* em chapa.
sheet music *n* música.
sheik(h) [ʃeɪk] *n* xeque *m*.
shelf [ʃelf] (*pl* **shelves**) *n* prateleira; **set of shelves** estante *f*.
shelf life *n* (*COMM*) validade *f* (de produtos perecíveis).
shell [ʃel] *n* (*on beach*) concha; (*of egg, nut etc*) casca; (*explosive*) obus *m*; (*of building*) armação *f*, esqueleto ♦ *vt* (*peas*) descascar; (*MIL*) bombardear.
  shell out (*inf*) *vi*: **to ~ out (for)** pagar.
she'll [ʃiːl] = **she will**; **she shall**.
shellfish [ʃelfɪʃ] *n inv* crustáceo, molusco; (*pl: as food*) frutos *mpl* do mar, mariscos *mpl*.
shelter [ʃeltə*] *n* abrigo, refúgio ♦ *vt* (*aid*) amparar, proteger; (*give lodging to*) abrigar; (*hide*) esconder ♦ *vi* abrigar-se, refugiar-se; **to take ~ from** abrigar-se de.
sheltered [ʃeltəd] *adj* (*life*) protegido; (*spot*) abrigado, protegido.
shelve [ʃelv] *vt* (*fig*) pôr de lado, engavetar.
shelves [ʃelvz] *npl of* **shelf**.
shelving [ʃelvɪŋ] *n* (*shelves*) prateleiras *fpl*.
shepherd [ʃepəd] *n* pastor *m* ♦ *vt* (*guide*) guiar, conduzir.
shepherdess [ʃepədɪs] *n* pastora.
shepherd's pie *n* empadão *m* de carne e batata.
sherbet [ʃɜːbət] *n* (*BRIT: powder*) pó doce e efervescente; (*US: water ice*) sorvete de frutas à base de água.
sheriff [ʃerɪf] *n* xerife *m*.
sherry [ʃerɪ] *n* (vinho de) Xerez *m*.
she's [ʃiːz] = **she is**; **she has**.
Shetland [ʃetlənd] *n* (*also:* **the ~s**, **the ~ Isles or Islands**) as ilhas Shetland.
shield [ʃiːld] *n* escudo; (*TECH*) blindagem *f* ♦ *vt*: **to ~ (from)** proteger contra.
shift [ʃɪft] *n* (*change*) mudança; (*of place*) transferência; (*of workers*) turno ♦ *vt* transferir; (*remove*) tirar ♦ *vi* mudar; (*change place*) mudar de lugar; **the wind has ~ed to the south** o vento virou para o sul; **a ~ in demand** (*COMM*) um deslocamento de demanda.
shift key *n* (*on typewriter*) tecla para maiúsculas.
shiftless [ʃɪftlɪs] *adj* indolente.
shift work *n* trabalho em turnos; **to do ~** trabalhar em turnos.
shifty [ʃɪftɪ] *adj* esperto, trapaceiro; (*eyes*) velhaco, maroto.
shilling [ʃɪlɪŋ] (*BRIT*) *n* xelim *m* (= *12 old pence; 20 in a pound*).
shilly-shally [ʃɪlɪʃælɪ] *vi* vacilar.
shimmer [ʃɪmə*] *n* reflexo trêmulo ♦ *vi* cintilar, tremeluzir.
shin [ʃɪn] *n* canela (da perna) ♦ *vi*: **to ~ up/down a tree** subir em/descer de uma árvore com mãos e pernas.
shindig [ʃɪndɪg] (*inf*) *n* arrasta-pé *m*.
shine [ʃaɪn] (*pt, pp* **shone**) *n* brilho, lustre *m* ♦ *vi* brilhar ♦ *vt* (*shoes*) lustrar; **to ~ a**

torch on sth apontar uma lanterna para algo.
shingle [ʃɪŋgl] *n* (*on beach*) pedrinhas *fpl*, seixinhos *mpl*; (*on roof*) telha.
shingles [ʃɪŋglz] *n* (*MED*) herpes-zoster *m*.
shining [ʃaɪnɪŋ] *adj* brilhante.
shiny [ʃaɪnɪ] *adj* brilhante, lustroso.
ship [ʃɪp] *n* barco; (*large*) navio ♦ *vt* (*goods*) embarcar; (*send*) transportar *or* mandar (por via marítima); **on board ~** a bordo.
shipbuilder [ʃɪpbɪldə*] *n* construtor *m* naval.
shipbuilding [ʃɪpbɪldɪŋ] *n* construção *f* naval.
ship canal *n* canal *m* de navegação.
ship chandler [-ˈtʃændlə*] *n* fornecedor *m* de provisões para navios.
shipment [ʃɪpmənt] *n* (*act*) embarque *m*; (*goods*) carregamento.
shipowner [ʃɪpəunə*] *n* armador(a) *m/f*.
shipper [ʃɪpə*] *n* exportador(a) *m/f*, expedidor(a) *m/f*.
shipping [ʃɪpɪŋ] *n* (*ships*) navios *mpl*; (*traffic*) navegação *f*.
shipping agent *n* agente *m/f* marítimo/a.
shipping company *n* companhia de navegação.
shipping lane *n* rota de navegação.
shipping line *n* companhia de navegação.
shipshape [ʃɪpʃeɪp] *adj* em ordem.
shipwreck [ʃɪprek] *n* naufrágio ♦ *vt*: **to be ~ed** naufragar.
shipyard [ʃɪpjaːd] *n* estaleiro.
shire [ʃaɪə*] (*BRIT*) *n* condado.
shirk [ʃɜːk] *vt* (*work*) esquivar-se de; (*obligations*) não cumprir, faltar a.
shirt [ʃɜːt] *n* camisa, blusa; **in ~ sleeves** em manga de camisa.
shirty [ʃɜːtɪ] (*BRIT: inf*) *adj* chateado, sem graça.
shit [ʃɪt] (*inf!*) *excl* merda (!).
shiver [ʃɪvə*] *n* tremor *m*, arrepio ♦ *vi* tremer, estremecer, tiritar.
shoal [ʃəul] *n* (*of fish*) cardume *m*.
shock [ʃɔk] *n* (*impact*) choque *m*; (*ELEC*) descarga; (*emotional*) comoção *f*, abalo; (*start*) susto, sobressalto; (*MED*) trauma *m* ♦ *vt* dar um susto em, chocar; (*offend*) escandalizar; **suffering from ~** (*MED*) traumatizado; **it gave us a ~** ficamos chocados; **it came as a ~ to hear that ...** ficamos atônitos ao saber que ....
shock absorber [-əbˈzɔːbə*] *n* amortecedor *m*.
shocking [ʃɔkɪŋ] *adj* (*awful*) chocante, lamentável; (*improper*) escandaloso; (*very bad*) péssimo.
shockproof [ʃɔkpruːf] *adj* à prova de choque.
shock therapy *n* terapia de choque.
shock treatment *n* terapia de choque.
shod [ʃɔd] *pt, pp of* **shoe** ♦ *adj* calçado.
shoddy [ʃɔdɪ] *adj* ordinário, de má qualidade.
shoe [ʃuː] (*pt, pp* **shod**) *n* sapato; (*for horse*) ferradura; (*also: brake ~*) sapata ♦ *vt* (*horse*) ferrar.
shoebrush [ʃuːbrʌʃ] *n* escova de sapato.
shoehorn [ʃuːhɔːn] *n* calçadeira.

shoelace ['ʃuːleɪs] *n* cadarço, cordão *m* (de sapato).
shoemaker ['ʃuːmeɪkə*] *n* sapateiro/a.
shoe polish *n* graxa de sapato.
shoe rack *n* porta-sapatos *m inv*.
shoeshop ['ʃuːʃɔp] *n* sapataria.
shoestring ['ʃuːstrɪŋ] *n*: **on a ~** (*fig*) com muito pouco dinheiro.
shoetree ['ʃuːtriː] *n* fôrma de sapato.
shone [ʃɔn] *pt, pp of* **shine.**
shoo [ʃuː] *excl* xô! ◊ *vt* (*also*: **~ away**, **~ off**) enxotar.
shook [ʃuk] *pt of* **shake.**
shoot [ʃuːt] (*pt, pp* **shot**) *n* (*on branch, seedling*) rebento, broto ◊ *vt* disparar; (*kill*) matar à bala, balear; (*wound*) ferir à bala, balear; (*execute*) fuzilar; (*film*) filmar, rodar ◊ *vi* (*with gun, bow*): **to ~ (at)** atirar (em); (*FOOTBALL*) chutar; **to ~ past sb** passar disparado por alguém; **to ~ in/out** entrar correndo/sair disparado.
shoot down *vt* (*plane*) derrubar, abater.
shoot up *vi* (*fig*) subir vertiginosamente.
shooting ['ʃuːtɪŋ] *n* (*shots*) tiros *mpl*, tiroteio; (*HUNTING*) caçada (com espingarda); (*attack*) tiroteio; (: *murder*) assassinato; (*CINEMA*) filmagens *fpl*.
shooting range *n* estande *m*.
shooting star *n* estrela cadente.
shop [ʃɔp] *n* loja; (*workshop*) oficina ◊ *vi* (*also*: **go ~ping**) ir fazer compras; **to talk ~** (*fig*) falar de negócios.
shop around *vi* comparar preços; (*fig*) estudar todas as possibilidades.
shop assistant (*BRIT*) *n* vendedor(a) *m/f*.
shop floor (*BRIT*) *n* operários *mpl*.
shopkeeper ['ʃɔpkiːpə*] *n* lojista *m/f*.
shoplift ['ʃɔplɪft] *vi* furtar (em lojas).
shoplifter ['ʃɔplɪftə*] *n* larápio/a de loja.
shoplifting ['ʃɔplɪftɪŋ] *n* furto (em lojas).
shopper ['ʃɔpə*] *n* comprador(a) *m/f*.
shopping ['ʃɔpɪŋ] *n* (*goods*) compras *fpl*.
shopping bag *n* bolsa (de compras).
shopping centre (*US* **shopping center**) *n* shopping (center) *m*.
shop-soiled (*BRIT*) *adj* manuseado.
shop steward *n* (*INDUSTRY*) representante *m/f* sindical.
shop window *n* vitrine *f* (*BR*), montra (*PT*).
shopworn ['ʃɔpwɔːn] (*US*) *adj* manuseado.
shore [ʃɔː*] *n* (*of sea*) costa, praia; (*of lake*) margem *f* ◊ *vt*: **to ~ (up)** reforçar, escorar; **on ~** em terra.
shore leave *n* (*NAUT*) licença para desembarcar.
shorn [ʃɔːn] *pp of* **shear.**
short [ʃɔːt] *adj* (*not long*) curto; (*in time*) breve, de curta duração; (*person*) baixo; (*curt*) seco, brusco; (*insufficient*) insuficiente, em falta ◊ *n* (*also*: **~ film**) curta-metragem *m*; **~s** *npl* (*also*: *a pair of* **~s**) um calção (*BR*), um short (*BR*), uns calções (*PT*); **to be ~ of**

sth estar em falta de algo; **to be in ~ supply** estar em falta; **I'm 3 ~** estão me faltando três; **in ~** em resumo; **~ of doing** a não ser fazer; **everything ~ of** tudo a não ser; **a ~ time ago** pouco tempo atrás; **in the ~ term** a curto prazo; **I'm ~ of time** tenho pouco tempo; **it is ~ for** é a abreviatura de; **to cut ~** (*speech, visit*) encurtar; (*person*) interromper; **to fall ~** ser deficiente; **to fall ~ of** não ser à altura de; **to run ~ of sth** ficar sem algo; **to stop ~** parar de repente; **to stop ~ of** chegar quase a.
shortage ['ʃɔːtɪdʒ] *n* escassez *f*, falta.
shortbread ['ʃɔːtbrɛd] *n* biscoito amanteigado.
short-change *vt*: **to ~ sb** roubar alguém no troco.
short-circuit *n* curto-circuito ◊ *vt* provocar um curto-circuito ◊ *vi* entrar em curto-circuito.
shortcoming ['ʃɔːtkʌmɪŋ] *n* defeito, imperfeição *f*, falha.
short(crust) pastry ['ʃɔːt(krʌst)-] (*BRIT*) *n* massa amanteigada.
shortcut ['ʃɔːtkʌt] *n* atalho.
shorten ['ʃɔːtən] *vt* encurtar; (*visit*) abreviar.
shortening ['ʃɔːtnɪŋ] *n* (*CULIN*) gordura.
shortfall ['ʃɔːtfɔːl] *n* déficit *m*.
shorthand ['ʃɔːthænd] (*BRIT*) *n* estenografia.
shorthand notebook (*BRIT*) *n* bloco para estenografia.
shorthand typist (*BRIT*) *n* estenodatilógrafo/a.
short list (*BRIT*) *n* (*for job*) lista dos candidatos escolhidos.
short-lived [-lɪvd] *adj* de curta duração.
shortly ['ʃɔːtlɪ] *adv* em breve, dentro em pouco.
shortness ['ʃɔːtnɪs] *n* (*of distance*) curteza; (*of time*) brevidade *f*; (*manner*) maneira brusca, secura.
short-sighted (*BRIT*) *adj* míope; (*fig*) imprevidente.
short-staffed [-stɑːft] *adj* com falta de pessoal.
short story *n* conto.
short-tempered *adj* irritadiço.
short-term *adj* (*effect*) a curto prazo.
short time *n*: **to work ~**, **to be on ~** trabalhar em regime de semana reduzida.
short wave *n* (*RADIO*) onda curta.
shot [ʃɔt] *pt, pp of* **shoot** ◊ *n* (*sound*) tiro, disparo; (*pellets*) chumbo; (*person*) atirador(a) *m/f*; (*try*) tentativa; (*injection*) injeção *f*; (*PHOT*) fotografia; **to fire a ~ at sb/sth** atirar em alguém/algo; **to have a ~ at (doing) sth** tentar fazer algo; **like a ~** disparado; (*very readily*) na hora; **to get ~ of sb/sth** (*inf*) livrar-se de alguém/algo; **a big ~** (*inf*) um mandachuva, um figurão.
shotgun ['ʃɔtgʌn] *n* espingarda.
should [ʃud] *aux vb*: **I ~ go now** devo ir embora agora; **he ~ be there now** ele já

deve ter chegado; **I ~ go if I were you** se eu fosse você eu iria; **I ~ like to** eu gostaria de; **~ he phone ...** caso ele telefone ....

shoulder ['ʃəuldə*] n ombro; (*BRIT: of road*): **hard ~** acostamento (*BR*), berma (*PT*) ♦ vt (*fig*) arcar com; **to look over one's ~** olhar para trás; **to rub ~s with sb** (*fig*) andar com alguém; **to give sb the cold ~** (*fig*) desprezar alguém, dar uma fria em alguém (*inf*).

shoulder bag n sacola a tiracolo.

shoulder blade n omoplata m.

shoulder strap n alça.

shouldn't ['ʃudnt] = **should not**.

shout [ʃaut] n grito ♦ vt gritar ♦ vi gritar, berrar; **to give sb a ~** chamar alguém.

shout down vt fazer calar com gritos.

shouting n gritaria, berreiro.

shove [ʃʌv] n empurrão m ♦ vt empurrar; (*inf: put*): **to ~ sth in** botar algo em; **he ~d me out of the way** ele me empurrou para o lado.

shove off vi (*NAUT*) zarpar, partir; (*fig: inf*) dar o fora.

shovel ['ʃʌvl] n pá f; (*mechanical*) escavadeira ♦ vt cavar com pá.

show [ʃəu] (*pt ~ed, pp shown*) n (*of emotion*) demonstração f; (*semblance*) aparência; (*exhibition*) exibição f; (*THEATRE*) espetáculo, representação f; (*CINEMA*) sessão f ♦ vt mostrar; (*courage etc*) demonstrar, dar prova de; (*exhibit*) exibir, expor; (*film*) exibir ♦ vi mostrar-se; (*appear*) aparecer; **it doesn't ~** não parece; **I've nothing to ~ for it** não consegui nada; **to ~ sb to his seat/to the door** levar alguém ao seu lugar/até a porta; **to ~ a profit/loss** (*COMM*) apresentar lucros/prejuízo; **it just goes to ~ (that)** ... isso só mostra (que) ...; **to ask for a ~ of hands** pedir uma votação pelo levantamento das mãos; **to be on ~** estar em exposição; **it's just for ~** isso é só para fazer efeito, isso é só pra bonito (*inf*); **who's running the ~ here?** (*inf*) quem é que manda aqui?

show in vt mandar entrar.

show off vi (*pej*) mostrar-se, exibir-se ♦ vt (*display*) exibir, mostrar; (*pej*) fazer ostentação de.

show out vt levar até a porta.

show up vi (*stand out*) destacar-se; (*inf: turn up*) aparecer, pintar ♦ vt descobrir; (*unmask*) desmascarar.

show business n o mundo do espetáculo.

showcase ['ʃəukeɪs] n vitrina.

showdown ['ʃəudaun] n confrontação f.

shower ['ʃauə*] n (*rain*) pancada de chuva; (*of stones etc*) chuva, enxurrada; (*also: ~ bath*) chuveiro ♦ vi tomar banho (de chuveiro) ♦ vt: **to ~ sb with** (*gifts etc*) cumular alguém de; **to have or take a ~** tomar banho (de chuveiro).

shower cap n touca de banho.

showerproof ['ʃauəpru:f] adj impermeável.

showery ['ʃauərɪ] adj (*weather*) chuvoso.

showground ['ʃəugraund] n recinto da feira.

showing ['ʃəuɪŋ] n (*of film*) projeção f, exibição f.

show jumping [-'dʒʌmpɪŋ] n hipismo.

showman ['ʃəumən] (*irreg*) n artista m/f; (*fig*) pessoa expansiva.

showmanship ['ʃəumənʃɪp] n senso teatral.

showmen ['ʃəumɛn] npl of **showman**.

shown [ʃəun] pp of **show**.

show-off (*inf*) n (*person*) exibicionista m/f, faroleiro/a.

showpiece ['ʃəupiːs] n (*of exhibition etc*) obra mais importante; **that hospital is a ~** aquele é um hospital modelo.

showroom ['ʃəurum] n sala de exposição.

showy ['ʃəuɪ] adj vistoso, chamativo.

shrank [ʃræŋk] pt of **shrink**.

shrapnel ['ʃræpnl] n estilhaços mpl.

shred [ʃrɛd] n (*gen pl*) tira, pedaço ♦ vt rasgar em tiras, retalhar; (*CULIN*) desfiar, picar; (*documents*) fragmentar; **not a ~ of evidence** prova alguma.

shredder ['ʃrɛdə*] n (*for documents*) fragmentadora.

shrew [ʃru:] n (*ZOOL*) musaranho; (*pej: woman*) megera.

shrewd [ʃru:d] adj astuto, perspicaz, sutil.

shrewdness ['ʃru:dnɪs] n astúcia.

shriek [ʃri:k] n grito ♦ vt, vi gritar, berrar.

shrift [ʃrɪft] n: **to give sb short ~** dar uma resposta a alguém sem maiores explicações.

shrill [ʃrɪl] adj agudo, estridente.

shrimp [ʃrɪmp] n camarão m.

shrine [ʃraɪn] n santuário, relicário.

shrink [ʃrɪŋk] (*pt shrank, pp shrunk*) vi encolher; (*be reduced*) reduzir-se ♦ vt fazer encolher ♦ n (*inf: pej*) psicanalista m/f; **to ~ from doing sth** não se atrever a fazer algo.

shrinkage ['ʃrɪŋkɪdʒ] n encolhimento, redução f.

shrink-wrap vt embalar a vácuo.

shrivel ['ʃrɪvl] vt (*also: ~ up: dry*) secar; (: *crease*) enrugar ♦ vi secar-se, enrugar-se, murchar.

shroud [ʃraud] n mortalha ♦ vt: **~ed in mystery** envolto em mistério.

Shrove Tuesday [ʃrəuv-] n terça-feira gorda.

shrub [ʃrʌb] n arbusto.

shrubbery ['ʃrʌbərɪ] n arbustos mpl.

shrug [ʃrʌg] n encolhimento dos ombros ♦ vt, vi: **to ~ (one's shoulders)** encolher os ombros, dar de ombros (*BR*).

shrug off vt negar a importância de.

shrunk [ʃrʌŋk] pp of **shrink**.

shrunken ['ʃrʌŋkn] adj encolhido.

shudder ['ʃʌdə*] n estremecimento, tremor m ♦ vi estremecer, tremer de medo.

shuffle ['ʃʌfl] vt (*cards*) embaralhar; **to ~ (one's feet)** arrastar os pés.

shun [ʃʌn] vt evitar, afastar-se de.

shunt [ʃʌnt] vt (*RAIL*) manobrar, desviar ♦ vi: **to ~ (to and fro)** ir e vir.

shunting ['ʃʌntɪŋ] n (*RAIL*) manobras fpl.

shunting yard n pátio de manobras.

shush [ʃuʃ] excl psiu!

shut [ʃʌt] (*pt, pp shut*) vt fechar ♦ vi

fechar(-se).
shut down vt fechar; (machine) parar ♦ vi fechar.
shut off vt (supply etc) cortar, interromper.
shut out vt (person, cold) impedir que entre; (noise) abafar; (memory) reprimir.
shut up vi (inf: keep quiet) calar-se, calar a boca ♦ vt (close) fechar; (silence) calar.
shutdown ['ʃʌtdaun] n paralização f.
shutter ['ʃʌtə*] n veneziana; (PHOT) obturador m.
shuttle ['ʃʌtl] n (in weaving) lançadeira; (plane: also: ~ service) ponte f aérea ♦ vi (vehicle, person) ir e vir ♦ vt (passengers) transportar de ida e volta.
shuttlecock ['ʃʌtlkɔk] n peteca.
shy [ʃaɪ] adj tímido ♦ vi: **to ~ away from doing sth** (fig) não se atrever a fazer algo.
shyness ['ʃaɪnɪs] n timidez f.
Siam [saɪ'æm] n Sião m.
Siamese [saɪə'miːz] adj: **~ cat** gato siamês; **~ twins** irmãos mpl siameses/irmãs fpl siamesas.
Siberia [saɪ'bɪərɪə] n Sibéria f.
siblings ['sɪblɪŋz] npl (formal) irmãos mpl.
Sicilian [sɪ'sɪlɪən] adj, n siciliano/a.
Sicily ['sɪsɪlɪ] n Sicília f.
sick [sɪk] adj (ill) doente; (nauseated) enjoado; (humour) negro; (vomiting): **to be ~** vomitar; **to feel ~** estar enjoado; **to fall ~** ficar doente; **to be (off) ~** estar ausente por motivo de doença; **to be ~ of** (fig) estar cheio or farto de; **he makes me ~** (fig: inf) ele me enche o saco.
sick bay n enfermaria.
sicken ['sɪkən] vt dar náuseas a ♦ vi: **to be ~ing for sth** (cold, flu etc) estar no começo de algo.
sickening ['sɪkənɪŋ] adj (fig) repugnante.
sickle ['sɪkl] n foice f.
sick leave n licença por doença.
sickly ['sɪklɪ] adj doentio; (causing nausea) nauseante.
sickness ['sɪknɪs] n doença, indisposição f; (vomiting) náusea, enjôo.
sickness benefit n auxílio-enfermidade m, auxílio-doença m.
sick pay n salário pago em período de doença.
sickroom ['sɪkruːm] n enfermaria.
side [saɪd] n (gen) lado; (of body) flanco; (of lake) margem f; (aspect) aspecto; (team) time m (BR), equipa (PT); (of hill) declive m; (page) página; (of meat) costela ♦ cpd (door, entrance) lateral ♦ vi: **to ~ with sb** tomar o partido de alguém; **by the ~ of** ao lado de; **~ by ~** lado a lado, juntos; **on this/that or the other ~** do lado de cá/do lado de lá; **they are on our ~** (in game) fazem parte do nosso time; (in discussion) concordam com nós; **from ~ to ~** para lá e para cá; **from all ~s** de todos os lados; **to take ~s with** pôr-se ao lado de.

sideboard ['saɪdbɔːd] n aparador m; **~s** npl (BRIT) suíças fpl, costeletas fpl.
sideburns ['saɪdbɜːnz] npl suíças fpl, costeletas fpl.
sidecar ['saɪdkɑː*] n sidecar m.
side dish n guarnição f.
side drum n (MUS) caixa clara.
side effect n efeito colateral.
sidekick ['saɪdkɪk] (inf) n camarada m/f.
sidelight ['saɪdlaɪt] n (AUT) luz f lateral.
sideline ['saɪdlaɪn] n (SPORT) linha lateral; (fig) linha adicional de produtos; (: job) emprego suplementar.
sidelong ['saɪdlɔŋ] adj de soslaio.
side plate n pequeno prato.
side road n rua lateral.
sidesaddle ['saɪdsædl] adv de silhão.
side show n (stall) barraca.
sidestep ['saɪdstɛp] vt evitar ♦ vi (BOXING etc) dar um passo para o lado.
sidetrack ['saɪdtræk] vt (fig) desviar (do seu propósito).
sidewalk ['saɪdwɔːk] n (US) n calçada.
sideways ['saɪdweɪz] adv de lado.
siding ['saɪdɪŋ] n (RAIL) desvio, ramal m.
sidle ['saɪdl] vi: **to ~ up (to)** aproximar-se furtivamente (de).
siege [siːdʒ] n sítio, assédio; **to lay ~ to** assediar.
siege economy n economia de guerra.
Sierra Leone [sɪ'ɛrəlɪ'əun] n Serra Leoa (no article).
sieve [sɪv] n peneira ♦ vt peneirar.
sift [sɪft] vt peneirar; (fig: information) esquadrinhar, analisar minuciosamente ♦ vi (fig): **to ~ through** examinar minuciosamente.
sigh [saɪ] n suspiro ♦ vi suspirar.
sight [saɪt] n (faculty) vista, visão f; (spectacle) espetáculo; (on gun) mira ♦ vt avistar; **in ~** à vista; **out of ~** longe dos olhos; **at ~** (COMM) à vista; **at first ~** à primeira vista; **I know her by ~** conheço-a de vista; **to catch ~ of sb/sth** avistar alguém/algo; **to lose ~ of sb/sth** perder alguém/algo de vista; **to set one's ~s on sth** visar algo.
sighted ['saɪtɪd] adj que enxerga; **partially ~** com vista parcial.
sightseeing ['saɪtsiːɪŋ] n turismo; **to go ~** fazer turismo, passear.
sightseer ['saɪtsiːə*] n turista m/f.
sign [saɪn] n (with hand) sinal m, aceno; (indication) indício; (trace) vestígio; (notice) letreiro, tabuleta; (also: road ~) placa; (of zodiac, LING) signo ♦ vt assinar; **as a ~ of** como sinal de; **it's a good/bad ~** é um bom/mau sinal; **plus/minus ~** sinal de mais/menos; **there's no ~ of a change of mind** não há sinal or indícios de uma mudança de atitude; **he was showing ~s of improvement** ele estava começando a melhorar; **to ~ one's name** assinar.
sign away vt (rights etc) abrir mão de.

NB: European Portuguese adds the following consonants to certain words: **b** (sú(b)dito, su(b)til); **c** (a(c)ção, a(c)cionista, a(c)to); **m** (inde(m)ne); **p** (ado(p)ção, ado(p)tar); for further details see p. xiii.

sign off vi (RADIO, TV) terminar a transmissão.

sign on vi (MIL) alistar-se; (as unemployed) cadastrar-se para receber auxílio-desemprego; (enrol): **to ~ on for a course** matricular-se num curso ♦ vt (MIL) alistar; (employee) efetivar.

sign out vi assinar o registro na partida.

sign over vt: **to ~ sth over to sb** assinar a transferência de algo para alguém.

sign up vi (MIL) alistar-se ♦ vt alistar.

signal ['sɪɡnl] n sinal m, aviso; (US: TEL) ruído discal ♦ vi (AUT) sinalizar, dar sinal ♦ vt (person) fazer sinais para; (message) transmitir; **to ~ a left/right turn** (AUT) dar sinal para esquerda/direita; **to ~ to sb (to do sth)** fazer sinais para alguém (fazer algo).

signal box n (RAIL) cabine f de sinaleiro.

signalman ['sɪɡnlmən] (irreg) n sinaleiro.

signatory ['sɪɡnətərɪ] n signatário/a.

signature ['sɪɡnətʃə*] n assinatura.

signature tune n tema m (de abertura).

signet ring ['sɪɡnət-] n anel m com o sinete or a chancela.

significance [sɪɡ'nɪfɪkəns] n significado; (importance) importância; **that is of no ~** isto não tem importância alguma.

significant [sɪɡ'nɪfɪkənt] adj significativo, importante.

significantly [sɪɡ'nɪfɪkəntlɪ] adv (improve, increase) significativamente; (smile) sugestivamente; **and, ~, ...** e, significativamente, ...

signify ['sɪɡnɪfaɪ] vt significar.

sign language n mímica, linguagem f através de sinais.

signpost ['saɪnpəʊst] n indicador m; (traffic) placa de sinalização.

silage ['saɪlɪdʒ] n (fodder) silagem f; (method) ensilagem f.

silence ['saɪləns] n silêncio ♦ vt silenciar, impor silêncio a; (guns) silenciar.

silencer ['saɪlənsə*] n (on gun) silenciador m; (AUT) silencioso.

silent ['saɪlənt] adj silencioso; (not speaking) calado; (film) mudo; **to keep** or **remain ~** manter-se em silêncio.

silently ['saɪləntlɪ] adv silenciosamente.

silent partner n (COMM) sócio/a comanditário/a.

silhouette [sɪluːˈɛt] n silhueta ♦ vt: **~d against** em silhueta contra.

silicon ['sɪlɪkən] n silício.

silicon chip n placa or chip m de silício.

silicone ['sɪlɪkəun] n silicone m.

silk [sɪlk] n seda ♦ cpd de seda.

silky ['sɪlkɪ] adj sedoso.

sill [sɪl] n (also: window ~) parapeito, peitoril m; (AUT) soleira.

silly ['sɪlɪ] adj (person) bobo, idiota, imbecil; (idea) absurdo, ridículo; **to do something ~** fazer uma besteira.

silo ['saɪləu] n silo.

silt [sɪlt] n sedimento, aluvião m.

silver ['sɪlvə*] n prata; (money) moedas fpl;

(also: ~ware) prataria ♦ cpd de prata.

silver foil n papel m de prata.

silver paper (BRIT) n papel m de prata.

silver-plated [-'pleɪtɪd] adj prateado, banhado a prata.

silversmith ['sɪlvəsmɪθ] n prateiro/a.

silverware ['sɪlvəwɛə*] n prataria.

silver wedding (anniversary) n bodas fpl de prata.

silvery ['sɪlvərɪ] adj prateado.

similar ['sɪmɪlə*] adj: **~ to** parecido com, semelhante a.

similarity [sɪmɪ'lærɪtɪ] n semelhança.

similarly ['sɪmɪləlɪ] adv da mesma maneira.

simmer ['sɪmə*] vi cozer em fogo lento, ferver lentamente.

simmer down (inf) vi (fig) acalmar-se.

simper ['sɪmpə*] vi sorrir afetadamente.

simpering ['sɪmpərɪŋ] adj idiota.

simple ['sɪmpl] adj simples inv; (foolish) ingênuo; **the ~ truth** a pura verdade.

simple interest n juros mpl simples.

simple-minded adj simplório.

simpleton ['sɪmpltən] n simplório/a, pateta m/ f.

simplicity [sɪm'plɪsɪtɪ] n simplicidade f.

simplification [sɪmplɪfɪ'keɪʃən] n simplificação f.

simplify ['sɪmplɪfaɪ] vt simplificar.

simply ['sɪmplɪ] adv simplesmente.

simulate ['sɪmjuleɪt] vt simular.

simulation [sɪmju'leɪʃən] n simulação f.

simultaneous [sɪməl'teɪnɪəs] adj simultâneo.

simultaneously [sɪməl'teɪnɪəslɪ] adv simultaneamente.

sin [sɪn] n pecado ♦ vi pecar.

Sinai ['saɪneɪaɪ] n Sinai m.

since [sɪns] adv desde então, depois ♦ prep desde ♦ conj (time) desde que; (because) porque, visto que, já que; **~ then** desde então; **~ Monday** desde segunda-feira; **(ever) ~ I arrived** desde que eu cheguei.

sincere [sɪn'sɪə*] adj sincero.

sincerely [sɪn'sɪəlɪ] adv sinceramente; **Yours ~** (at end of letter) atenciosamente.

sincerity [sɪn'sɛrɪtɪ] n sinceridade f.

sine [saɪn] n (MATH) seno.

sinew ['sɪnjuː] n tendão m.

sinful ['sɪnful] adj (thought) pecaminoso; (person) pecador(a).

sing [sɪŋ] (pt **sang**, pp **sung**) vt, vi cantar.

Singapore [sɪŋɡə'pɔː*] n Cingapura (no article).

singe [sɪndʒ] vt chamuscar.

singer ['sɪŋə*] n cantor(a) m/f.

Singhalese [sɪŋə'liːz] adj = **Sinhalese**.

singing ['sɪŋɪŋ] n (gen) canto; (songs) canções fpl; (in the ears) zumbido.

single ['sɪŋɡl] adj único, só; (unmarried) solteiro; (not double) simples inv ♦ n (also: **~ ticket**) passagem f de ida; (record) compacto; **~s** npl (TENNIS) simples f inv; (US: **~ people**) solteiros mpl; **not a ~ one was left** não sobrou nenhum; **every ~ day** todo santo dia.

single out vt (choose) escolher; (point out) distinguir.
single bed n cama de solteiro.
single-breasted [-'brɛstɪd] adj não trespassado.
single file n: **in** ~ em fila indiana.
single-handed [-'hændɪd] adv sem ajuda, sozinho.
single-minded adj determinado.
single parent n pai m solteiro/mãe f solteira.
single room n quarto individual.
singlet ['sɪŋglɪt] n camiseta.
singly ['sɪŋglɪ] adv separadamente.
singsong ['sɪŋsɔŋ] adj (tone) cantado ♦ n (songs): **to have a** ~ cantar.
singular ['sɪŋgjulə*] adj (odd) esquisito; (LING) singular ♦ n (LING) singular m; **in the feminine** ~ no feminino singular.
singularly ['sɪŋgjulǝlɪ] adv particularmente.
Sinhalese [sɪnhǝ'liːz] adj cingalês/esa.
sinister ['sɪnɪstǝ*] adj sinistro.
sink [sɪŋk] (pt **sank**, pp **sunk**) n pia ♦ vt (ship) afundar; (foundations) escavar; (piles etc): **to** ~ **sth** enterrar algo ♦ vi afundar-se, ir a pique; (share prices) cair; **he sank into a chair/the mud** ele afundou na cadeira/na lama; **a** ~**ing feeling** um vazio no estômago.
sink in vi (fig) penetrar, entranhar-se; **it took a long time to** ~ **in** demorou muito para ser entendido.
sinking fund ['sɪŋkɪŋ-] n fundo de amortização.
sink unit n pia.
sinner ['sɪnǝ*] n pecador(a) m/f.
Sino- ['saɪnǝu] prefix sino-.
sinuous ['sɪnjuǝs] adj sinuoso.
sinus ['saɪnǝs] n (ANAT) seio (nasal).
sinusitis [saɪnǝ'saɪtǝs] n sinusite f.
sip [sɪp] n gole m ♦ vt sorver, bebericar.
siphon ['saɪfǝn] n sifão m ♦ vt (also: ~ **off**) extrair com sifão; (fig: funds) desviar.
sir [sǝ*] n senhor m; **S**~ **John Smith** Sir John Smith; **yes** ~ sim, senhor; **Dear S**~ (in letter) (Prezado) Senhor.
siren ['saɪǝrn] n sirena.
sirloin ['sǝːlɔɪn] n lombo de vaca.
sirloin steak n filé m de alcatra.
sisal ['saɪsǝl] n sisal m.
sissy ['sɪsɪ] (inf) n fresco.
sister ['sɪstǝ*] n irmã f; (nurse) enfermeira-chefe f; (nun) freira ♦ cpd: ~ **organization** organização f congênere; ~ **ship** navio gêmeo.
sister-in-law (pl **sisters-in-law**) n cunhada.
sit [sɪt] (pt, pp **sat**) vi sentar-se; (be sitting) estar sentado; (assembly) reunir-se; (for painter) posar; (dress) cair ♦ vt (exam) prestar; **to** ~ **on a committee** ser membro de um comitê; **to** ~ **tight** não se mexer; (fig) esperar.
sit about vi ficar sentado não fazendo nada.
sit around vi ficar sentado não fazendo

nada.
sit back vi acomodar-se num assento.
sit down vi sentar-se; **to be** ~**ting down** estar sentado.
sit in vi: **to** ~ **in on a discussion** assistir a uma discussão.
sit up vi endireitar-se; (not go to bed) aguardar acordado, velar.
sitcom ['sɪtkɔm] n abbr (TV: = situation comedy) comédia de costumes.
sit-down adj: ~ **strike** greve f de braços cruzados; **a** ~ **meal** uma refeição servida à mesa.
site [saɪt] n local m, sítio; (also: building ~) lote m (de terreno) ♦ vt situar, localizar.
sit-in n (demonstration) ocupação de um local como forma de protesto, manifestação f pacífica.
siting ['saɪtɪŋ] n (location) localização f.
sitter ['sɪtǝ*] n (for painter) modelo; (also: baby~) baby-sitter m/f.
sitting ['sɪtɪŋ] n (of assembly etc) sessão f; (in canteen) turno.
sitting member n (POL) parlamentar m/f.
sitting room n sala de estar.
sitting tenant (BRIT) n inquilino/a.
situate ['sɪtjueɪt] vt situar.
situated ['sɪtjueɪtɪd] adj situado.
situation [sɪtju'eɪʃǝn] n situação f; "~**s vacant/wanted**" (BRIT) "empregos oferecem-se/procurados".
situation comedy n (THEATRE, TV) comédia de costumes.
six [sɪks] num seis; see also **five**.
sixteen ['sɪks'tiːn] num dezesseis; see also **five**.
sixth [sɪksθ] num sexto; **the upper/lower** ~ (BRIT: SCH) os dois últimos anos do colégio; see also **fifth**.
sixty ['sɪkstɪ] num sessenta; see also **fifty**.
size [saɪz] n (gen) tamanho; (extent) extensão f; (of clothing) tamanho, medida; (of shoes) número; (glue) goma; **I take** ~ **14** (of dress) ≈ meu tamanho é 44; **the small/large** ~ (of soap powder etc) o tamanho pequeno/grande; **what** ~ **do you take in shoes?** que número você calça?; **it's the** ~ **of** ... é do tamanho de ....
size up vt avaliar, formar uma opinião sobre.
sizeable ['saɪzǝbl] adj considerável, importante.
sizzle ['sɪzl] vi chiar.
SK (CANADA) abbr = **Saskatchewan**.
skate [skeɪt] (pl ~**s**) n patim m; (fish: pl: inv) arraia ♦ vi patinar.
skate around vt fus (problem) evitar.
skate over vt fus (problem) evitar.
skateboard ['skeɪtbɔːd] n skate m, patim-tábua m.
skater ['skeɪtǝ*] n patinador(a) m/f.
skating ['skeɪtɪŋ] n patinação f.

NB: European Portuguese adds the following consonants to certain words: **b** (sú(b)dito, su(b)til); **c** (a(c)ção, a(c)cionista, a(c)to); **m** (inde(m)ne); **p** (ado(p)ção, ado(p)tar); *for further details see p. xiii.*

skating rink *n* rinque *m* de patinação.
skeleton ['skɛlɪtn] *n* esqueleto; (*TECH*) armação *f*; (*outline*) esquema *m*, esboço.
skeleton key *n* chave *f* mestra.
skeleton staff *n* pessoal *m* reduzido (ao mínimo).
skeptic *etc* ['skɛptɪk] (*US*) = **sceptic** *etc*.
sketch [skɛtʃ] *n* (*drawing*) desenho; (*outline*) esboço, croqui *m*; (*THEATRE*) quadro, esquete *m* ♦ *vt* desenhar, esboçar.
sketch book *n* caderno de rascunho.
sketch pad *n* bloco de desenho.
sketchy ['skɛtʃɪ] *adj* incompleto, superficial.
skew [skjuː] (*BRIT*) *n*: **on the** ~ fora de esquadria.
skewer ['skjuːə*] *n* espetinho.
ski [skiː] *n* esqui *m* ♦ *vi* esquiar.
ski boot *n* bota de esquiar.
skid [skɪd] *n* derrapagem *f* ♦ *vi* derrapar, deslizar.
skid mark *n* marca de derrapagem.
skier ['skiːə*] *n* esquiador(a) *m/f*.
skiing ['skiːɪŋ] *n* esqui *m*; **to go** ~ ir esquiar.
ski instructor *n* instrutor(a) *m/f* de esqui.
ski jump *n* pista para saltos de esqui; (*event*) salto de esqui.
skilful ['skɪlful] (*US* **skillful**) *adj* habilidoso, jeitoso.
skilfully ['skɪlfəlɪ] (*US* **skillfully**) *adv* habilmente.
ski lift *n* ski lift *m*.
skill [skɪl] *n* habilidade *f*, perícia; (*technique*) técnica.
skilled [skɪld] *adj* hábil, perito; (*worker*) especializado, qualificado.
skillet ['skɪlɪt] *n* frigideira.
skillful *etc* ['skɪlful] (*US*) = **skilful** *etc*.
skim [skɪm] *vt* (*milk*) desnatar; (*glide over*) roçar ♦ *vi*: **to** ~ **through** (*book*) folhear.
skimmed milk [skɪmd-] *n* leite *m* desnatado.
skimp [skɪmp] *vt* (*work*) atamancar; (*cloth etc*) economizar, regatear.
skimpy ['skɪmpɪ] *adj* (*meagre*) escasso, insuficiente; (*skirt*) sumário.
skin [skɪn] *n* (*gen*) pele *f*; (*of fruit, vegetable*) casca; (*on pudding, paint*) película ♦ *vt* (*fruit etc*) descascar; (*animal*) tirar a pele de; **wet** *or* **soaked to the** ~ encharcado, molhado como um pinto.
skin-deep *adj* superficial.
skin diver *n* mergulhador(a) *m/f*.
skin diving *n* caça-submarina.
skinflint ['skɪnflɪnt] *n* pão-duro *m*.
skin graft *n* enxerto de pele.
skinny ['skɪnɪ] *adj* magro, descarnado.
skin test *n* cutirreação *f*.
skintight ['skɪn'taɪt] *adj* (*dress etc*) justo, grudado (no corpo).
skip [skɪp] *n* salto, pulo; (*container*) balde *m* ♦ *vi* saltar; (*with rope*) pular corda ♦ *vt* (*pass over*) omitir, saltar; **to** ~ **school** (*esp US*) matar aula.
ski pants *npl* calça (*BR*) *or* calças *fpl* (*PT*) de esquiar.
ski pole *n* vara de esqui.

skipper ['skɪpə*] *n* (*NAUT, SPORT*) capitão *m* ♦ *vt* capitanear.
skipping rope ['skɪpɪŋ-] (*BRIT*) *n* corda (de pular).
ski resort *n* estação *f* de esqui.
skirmish ['skəːmɪʃ] *n* escaramuça.
skirt [skəːt] *n* saia ♦ *vt* (*surround*) rodear; (*go round*) orlar, circundar.
skirting board ['skəːtɪŋ-] (*BRIT*) *n* rodapé *m*.
ski run *n* pista de esqui.
ski suit *n* traje *m* de esqui.
skit [skɪt] *n* paródia, sátira.
ski tow *n* ski lift *m*.
skittle ['skɪtl] *n* pau *m*; ~**s** *n* (*game*) (jogo de) boliche *m* (*BR*), jogo da bola (*PT*).
skive [skaɪv] (*BRIT: inf*) *vi* evitar trabalhar.
skulk [skʌlk] *vi* esconder-se.
skull [skʌl] *n* caveira; (*ANAT*) crânio.
skullcap ['skʌlkæp] *n* solidéu *m*; (*worn by Pope*) barrete *m*.
skunk [skʌŋk] *n* gambá *m*; (*fig: person*) cafajeste *m/f*, pessoa vil.
sky [skaɪ] *n* céu *m*; **to praise sb to the skies** pôr alguém nas nuvens.
sky-blue *adj* azul-celeste *inv*.
sky-high *adv* muito alto ♦ *adj*: **prices are** ~ os preços dispararam.
skylark ['skaɪlɑːk] *n* (*bird*) cotovia.
skylight ['skaɪlaɪt] *n* clarabóia, escotilha.
skyline ['skaɪlaɪn] *n* (*horizon*) linha do horizonte; (*of city*) silhueta.
skyscraper ['skaɪskreɪpə*] *n* arranha-céu *m*.
slab [slæb] *n* (*stone*) bloco; (*flat*) laje *f*; (*of cake*) fatia grossa.
slack [slæk] *adj* (*loose*) frouxo; (*slow*) lerdo; (*careless*) descuidado, desmazelado; (*COMM: market*) inativo, frouxo; (: *demand*) fraco ♦ *n* (*in rope*) brando; ~**s** *npl* calça (*BR*), calças *fpl* (*PT*); **business is** ~ os negócios vão mal.
slacken ['slækən] *vi* (*also*: ~ **off**) afrouxar-se ♦ *vt* afrouxar; (*speed*) diminuir.
slag [slæg] *n* escória, escombros *mpl*.
slag heap *n* monte *m* de escória *or* de escombros.
slain [sleɪn] *pp of* **slay**.
slake [sleɪk] *vt* (*one's thirst*) matar.
slalom ['slɑːləm] *n* slalom *m*.
slam [slæm] *vt* (*door*) bater *or* fechar (com violência); (*throw*) atirar violentamente; (*criticize*) malhar, criticar ♦ *vi* fechar-se (com violência).
slander ['slɑːndə*] *n* calúnia, difamação *f* ♦ *vt* caluniar, difamar.
slanderous ['slɑːndərəs] *adj* calunioso, difamatório.
slang [slæŋ] *n* gíria; (*jargon*) jargão *m*.
slant [slɑːnt] *n* declive *m*, inclinação *f*; (*fig*) ponto de vista.
slanted ['slɑːntɪd] *adj* tendencioso.
slanting ['slɑːntɪŋ] *adj* inclinado, de esguelha.
slap [slæp] *n* tapa *m* *or* *f* ♦ *vt* dar um(a) tapa em ♦ *adv* (*directly*) diretamente, exatamente.
slapdash ['slæpdæʃ] *adj* impetuoso, descuidado.
slapstick ['slæpstɪk] *n* (*comedy*) (comédia-)

pastelão *m*.
slap-up (*BRIT*) *adj*: **a ~ meal** uma refeição suntuosa.
slash [slæʃ] *vt* cortar, talhar; (*fig*: *prices*) cortar.
slat [slæt] *n* (*of wood*) ripa.
slate [sleɪt] *n* ardósia ♦ *vt* (*fig*: *criticize*) criticar duramente, arrasar.
slaughter ['slɔːtə*] *n* (*of animals*) matança; (*of people*) carnificina ♦ *vt* (*animals*) abater; (*people*) matar, massacrar.
slaughterhouse ['slɔːtəhaus] (*irreg*) *n* matadouro.
Slav [slɑːv] *adj*, *n* eslavo/a.
slave [sleɪv] *n* escravo ♦ *vi* (*also*: ~ *away*) trabalhar como escravo; **to ~ (away) at sth/at doing sth** trabalhar feito condenado em algo/ fazendo algo.
slave labour *n* trabalho escravo.
slaver ['slævə*] *vi* (*dribble*) babar.
slavery ['sleɪvərɪ] *n* escravidão *f*.
Slavic ['slɑːvɪk] *adj* eslavo.
slavish ['sleɪvɪʃ] *adj* servil.
Slavonic [slə'vɔnɪk] *adj* eslavo.
slay [sleɪ] (*pt* **slew**, *pp* **slain**) *vt* (*literary*) matar.
SLD (*BRIT*) *n abbr* (*POL*) = **Social and Liberal Democratic Party.**
sleazy ['sliːzɪ] *adj* (*fig*: *place*) sórdido.
sled [slɛd] (*US*) *n* trenó *m*.
sledge [slɛdʒ] (*BRIT*) *n* trenó *m*.
sledgehammer ['slɛdʒhæmə*] *n* marreta, malho.
sleek [sliːk] *adj* (*gen*) macio, lustroso; (*car*, *boat*) aerodinâmico.
sleep [sliːp] (*pt*, *pp* **slept**) *n* sono ♦ *vi* dormir ♦ *vt*: **we can ~ 4** podemos acomodar 4 pessoas; **to go to ~** dormir, adormecer; **to have a good night's ~** ter uma boa noite de sono; **to put to ~** (*patient*) fazer dormir; (*animal*: *euphemism*: *kill*) sacrificar; **to ~ lightly** ter sono leve; **to ~ with sb** (*euphemism*) dormir com alguém.
   sleep in *vi* (*oversleep*) dormir demais; (*lie in*) dormir até tarde.
sleeper ['sliːpə*] *n* (*person*) dorminhoco/a; (*RAIL*: *on track*) dormente *m*; (: *train*) vagão-leitos *m* (*BR*), carruagem-camas *f* (*PT*).
sleepily ['sliːpɪlɪ] *adv* sonolentamente.
sleeping ['sliːpɪŋ] *adj* adormecido, que dorme.
sleeping bag *n* saco de dormir.
sleeping car *n* vagão-leitos *m* (*BR*), carruagem-camas *f* (*PT*).
sleeping partner (*BRIT*) *n* (*COMM*) sócio comanditário.
sleeping pill *n* pílula para dormir.
sleepless ['sliːplɪs] *adj*: **a ~ night** uma noite em claro.
sleeplessness ['sliːplɪsnɪs] *n* insônia.
sleepwalker ['sliːpwɔːkə*] *n* sonâmbulo.
sleepy ['sliːpɪ] *adj* sonolento; **to be** *or* **feel ~** estar com sono.

sleet [sliːt] *n* chuva com neve *or* granizo.
sleeve [sliːv] *n* manga; (*of record*) capa.
sleeveless ['sliːvlɪs] *adj* (*garment*) sem manga.
sleigh [sleɪ] *n* trenó *m*.
sleight [slaɪt] *n*: **~ of hand** prestidigitação *f*.
slender ['slɛndə*] *adj* magro, delgado; (*means*) escasso, insuficiente.
slept [slɛpt] *pt*, *pp of* **sleep.**
sleuth [sluːθ] (*inf*) *n* detetive *m*.
slew [sluː] *pt of* **slay** ♦ *vi* (*also*: ~ *round*) virar.
slice [slaɪs] *n* (*of meat*, *bread*) fatia; (*of lemon*) rodela; (*of fish*) posta; (*utensil*) pá *f or* espátula de bolo ♦ *vt* cortar em fatias; **~d bread** pão *m* em fatias.
slick [slɪk] *adj* (*skilful*) jeitoso, ágil, engenhoso; (*quick*) rápido; (*astute*) astuto ♦ *n* (*also*: *oil* ~) mancha de óleo.
slid [slɪd] *pt*, *pp of* **slide.**
slide [slaɪd] (*pt*, *pp* **slid**) *n* (*in playground*) escorregador *m*; (*PHOT*) slide *m*; (*BRIT*: *also*: *hair* ~) passador *m*; (*microscope* ~) lâmina; (*in prices*) queda, baixa ♦ *vt* deslizar ♦ *vi* (*slip*) escorregar; (*glide*) deslizar; **to let things ~** (*fig*) deixar tudo ir por água abaixo.
slide projector *n* (*PHOT*) projetor *m* de slides.
slide rule *n* régua de cálculo.
sliding ['slaɪdɪŋ] *adj* (*door*) corrediço; ~ **roof** (*AUT*) teto deslizante.
sliding scale *n* escala móvel.
slight [slaɪt] *adj* (*slim*) fraco, franzino; (*frail*) delicado; (*pain etc*) leve; (*trifling*) insignificante; (*small*) pequeno ♦ *n* desfeita, desconsideração *f* ♦ *vt* (*offend*) desdenhar, menosprezar; **not in the ~est** em absoluto, de maneira alguma; **the ~est** o/a menor; **a ~ improvement** uma pequena melhora.
slightly ['slaɪtlɪ] *adv* ligeiramente, um pouco; ~ **built** magrinho.
slim [slɪm] *adj* magro, esbelto ♦ *vi* emagrecer.
slime [slaɪm] *n* lodo, limo, lama.
slimming ['slɪmɪŋ] *n* emagrecimento ♦ *adj* (*diet*, *pills*) para emagrecer.
slimy ['slaɪmɪ] *adj* pegajoso; (*covered with mud*) lodoso; (*fig*) falso.
sling [slɪŋ] (*pt*, *pp* **slung**) *n* (*MED*) tipóia; (*weapon*) estilingue *m*, funda ♦ *vt* atirar, arremessar, lançar; **to have one's arm in a ~** estar com o braço na tipóia.
slink [slɪŋk] (*pt*, *pp* **slunk**) *vi*: **to ~ away** *or* **off** escapulir.
slip [slɪp] *n* (*slide*) tropeção *m*; (*fall*) escorregão *m*; (*mistake*) erro, lapso; (*underskirt*) combinação *f*; (*of paper*) tira ♦ *vt* (*slide*) deslizar ♦ *vi* (*slide*) deslizar; (*lose balance*) escorregar; (*decline*) decair; **to let a chance ~ by** deixar passar uma oportunidade; **to ~ sth on/off** enfiar/tirar algo; **it ~ped from her hand** escorregou da mão dela; **to give sb**

the ~ esgueirar-se de alguém; **a ~ of the tongue** um lapso da língua; *see also* **Freudian.**

slip away *vi* escapulir.

slip in *vt* meter ♦ *vi* meter-se.

slip out *vi* (*go out*) sair (um momento).

slip-on *adj* sem fecho ou botões; ~ **shoes** mocassins *mpl.*

slipped disc [slɪpt-] *n* disco deslocado.

slipper ['slɪpə*] *n* chinelo.

slippery ['slɪpərɪ] *adj* escorregadio.

slip road (*BRIT*) *n* (*to motorway*) entrada para a rodovia.

slipshod ['slɪpʃɒd] *adj* descuidoso, desmazelado.

slip-up *n* (*error*) equívoco, mancada; (*by neglect*) descuido.

slipway ['slɪpweɪ] *n* carreira.

slit [slɪt] (*pt, pp* **slit**) *n* fenda; (*cut*) corte *m* ♦ *vt* rachar, cortar, fender; **to ~ sb's throat** cortar o pescoço de alguém.

slither ['slɪðə*] *vi* escorregar, deslizar.

sliver ['slɪvə*] *n* (*of glass, wood*) lasca; (*of cheese, sausage*) fatia fina.

slob [slɒb] (*inf*) *n* (*in manners*) porco/a; (*in appearance*) maltrapilho/a.

slog [slɒg] *vi* mourejar ♦ *n*: **it was a ~** deu um trabalho louco.

slogan ['sləʊgən] *n* lema *m*, slogan *m*.

slop [slɒp] *vi* (*also:* ~ **over**) transbordar, derramar ♦ *vt* transbordar, entornar.

slope [sləʊp] *n* (*up*) ladeira, rampa; (*down*) declive *m*; (*side of mountain*) encosta, vertente *f* ♦ *vi*: **to ~ down** estar em declive; **to ~ up** inclinar-se.

sloping ['sləʊpɪŋ] *adj* inclinado, em declive.

sloppy ['slɒpɪ] *adj* (*work*) descuidado; (*appearance*) relaxado; (*film etc*) piegas *inv.*

slosh [slɒʃ] (*inf*) *vi*: **to ~ about** *or* **around** (*children*) patinhar; (*liquid*) esparrinhar.

sloshed [slɒʃt] (*inf*) *adj* (*drunk*) com a cara cheia.

slot [slɒt] *n* (*in machine*) fenda; (*opening*) abertura; (*fig: in timetable, RADIO, TV*) horário ♦ *vt*: **to ~ into** encaixar em ♦ *vi*: **to ~ into** encaixar-se em.

sloth [sləʊθ] *n* (*vice, ZOOL*) preguiça.

slot machine *n* (*for gambling*) caça-níqueis *m inv*; (*BRIT: vending machine*) distribuidora automática.

slot meter (*BRIT*) *n* contador *m* (*de eletricidade ou gás*) operado por moedas.

slouch [slaʊtʃ] *vi* ter má postura.

slouch about *vi* vadiar.

slouch around *vi* vadiar.

slovenly ['slʌvənlɪ] *adj* (*dirty*) desalinhado, sujo; (*careless*) desmazelado.

slow [sləʊ] *adj* lento, vagaroso; (*watch*): **to be ~** atrasar ♦ *adv* lentamente, devagar ♦ *vi* (*also:* ~ **down**, ~ **up**) ir mais devagar; **"~"** (*road sign*) "devagar"; **at a ~ speed** devagar; **to be ~ to act/decide** ser lento nas ações/decisões, vacilar; **my watch is 20 minutes ~** meu relógio está atrasado vinte minutos; **business is ~** os negócios vão mal;

to go ~ (*driver*) dirigir devagar; (*in industrial dispute*) fazer uma greve tartaruga; **the ~ lane** a faixa da direita; **bake for 2 hours in a ~ oven** asse durante 2 horas em fogo brando.

slow-acting *adj* de ação lenta.

slowdown (*US*) *n* greve *f* de trabalho lento, operação *f* tartaruga.

slowly ['sləʊlɪ] *adv* lentamente, devagar.

slow motion *n*: **in ~** em câmara lenta.

slowness ['sləʊnɪs] *n* lentidão *f.*

sludge [slʌdʒ] *n* lama, lodo.

slug [slʌg] *n* lesma; (*bullet*) bala.

sluggish ['slʌgɪʃ] *adj* (*slow*) lerdo; (*lazy*) preguiçoso; (*business*) lento.

sluice [sluːs] *n* (*gate*) comporta, eclusa; (*channel*) canal *m* ♦ *vt*: **to ~ down** *or* **out** lavar com jorro d'água.

slum [slʌm] *n* (*area*) favela; (*house*) cortiço, barraco.

slumber ['slʌmbə*] *n* sono.

slump [slʌmp] *n* (*economic*) depressão *f*; (*in prices*) baixa, queda ♦ *vi* baixar repentinamente; **he was ~ed over the wheel** estava caído sobre a direção.

slung [slʌŋ] *pt, pp of* **sling.**

slunk [slʌŋk] *pt, pp of* **slink.**

slur [slə:*] *n* calúnia ♦ *vt* difamar, caluniar; (*word*) pronunciar indistintamente; **to cast a ~ on sb** manchar a reputação de alguém.

slurred [slə:d] *adj* (*pronunciation*) indistinto, ininteligível.

slush [slʌʃ] *n* neve *f* meio derretida.

slush fund *n* verba para suborno.

slushy ['slʌʃɪ] *adj* (*snow*) meio derretido; (*street*) lamacento; (*BRIT: fig*) piegas *inv.*

slut [slʌt] *n* mulher *f* desmazelada; (*whore*) prostituta.

sly [slaɪ] *adj* (*clever*) astuto; (*nasty*) malicioso, velhaco; **on the ~** às escondidas.

smack [smæk] *n* (*slap*) palmada; (*blow*) tabefe *m* ♦ *vt* dar uma palmada (*or* um tabefe) em ♦ *vi*: **to ~ of** cheirar a, saber a ♦ *adv* (*inf*): **it fell ~ in the middle** caiu exatamente no meio.

smacker ['smækə*] (*inf*) *n* (*kiss*) beijoca; (*BRIT: pound note*) libra; (*US: dollar bill*) dólar *m.*

small [smɔːl] *adj* pequeno; (*short*) baixo; (*letter*) minúsculo ♦ *n*: **the ~ of the back** os rins; **to get** *or* **grow ~er** diminuir; **to make ~er** diminuir; **a ~ shopkeeper** um pequeno comerciante.

small ads (*BRIT*) *npl* classificados *mpl.*

small arms *npl* armas *fpl* leves.

small change *n* trocado.

smallholder ['smɔːlhəʊldə*] (*BRIT*) *n* pequeno/a proprietário/a.

smallholding ['smɔːlhəʊldɪŋ] (*BRIT*) *n* minifúndio.

small hours *npl*: **in the ~** na madrugada, lá pelas tantas (*inf*).

smallish ['smɔːlɪʃ] *adj* de pequeno porte.

small-minded *adj* mesquinho.

smallpox ['smɔːlpɒks] *n* varíola.

small print *n* tipo miúdo.
small-scale *adj* (*model, map*) reduzido; (*business, farming*) de pequeno porte.
small talk *n* conversa fiada.
small-time *adj* (*farmer etc*) pequeno; **a** ~ **thief** um ladrão de galinha.
smart [smɑːt] *adj* elegante; (*clever*) inteligente, astuto; (*quick*) vivo, esperto ♦ *vi* arder, coçar; **the** ~ **set** a alta sociedade; **to look** ~ estar elegante; **my eyes are** ~**ing** meus olhos estão ardendo.
smarten up ['smɑːtən-] *vi* arrumar-se ♦ *vt* arrumar.
smash [smæʃ] *n* (*also:* ~*-up*) colisão *f*, choque *m*; (*sound*) estrondo ♦ *vt* (*break*) escangalhar, despedaçar; (*SPORT: record*) quebrar ♦ *vi* (*break*) despedaçar-se; (*against wall etc*) espatifar-se.
smash up *vt* destruir.
smash hit *n* sucesso absoluto.
smashing ['smæʃɪŋ] (*inf*) *adj* excelente.
smattering ['smætərɪŋ] *n*: **a** ~ **of** um conhecimento superficial de.
smear [smɪə*] *n* mancha, nódoa; (*MED*) esfregaço; (*insult*) difamação *f* ♦ *vt* untar, lambuzar; (*fig*) caluniar, difamar; **his hands were** ~**ed with oil/ink** as mãos dele estavam manchadas de óleo/tinta.
smear campaign *n* campanha de desmoralização.
smear test (*BRIT*) *n* (*MED*) esfregaço.
smell [smɛl] (*pt, pp* **smelt** *or* ~**ed**) *n* cheiro; (*sense*) olfato ♦ *vt* cheirar ♦ *vi* (*food etc*) cheirar; (*pej*) cheirar mal; **it** ~**s of garlic** cheira a alho; **it** ~**s good** cheira bem, tem um bom cheiro.
smelly ['smɛlɪ] *adj* fedorento, malcheiroso.
smelt [smɛlt] *pt, pp of* **smell** ♦ *vt* (*ore*) fundir.
smile [smaɪl] *n* sorriso ♦ *vi* sorrir.
smiling ['smaɪlɪŋ] *adj* sorridente, risonho.
smirk [smɜːk] *n* sorriso falso *or* afetado.
smith [smɪθ] *n* ferreiro.
smithy ['smɪðɪ] *n* forja, oficina de ferreiro.
smitten ['smɪtn] *adj*: ~ **with** (*charmed by*) encantado por; (*grief etc*) tomado por.
smock [smɔk] *n* guarda-pó *m*; (*children's*) avental *m*.
smog [smɔg] *n* nevoeiro com fumaça, poluição *f*.
smoke [sməuk] *n* fumaça (*BR*), fumo (*PT*) ♦ *vi* fumar; (*chimney*) fumegar ♦ *vt* (*cigarettes*) fumar; **to have a** ~ fumar; **do you** ~**?** você fuma?; **to go up in** ~ (*house etc*) queimar num incêndio; (*fig*) não dar em nada.
smoked [sməukt] *adj* (*bacon*) defumado; (*glass*) fumée.
smokeless fuel ['sməuklɪs-] *n* combustível *m* não poluente.
smokeless zone ['sməuklɪs-] (*BRIT*) *n* zona onde não é permitido o uso de combustíveis poluentes.
smoker ['sməukə*] *n* (*person*) fumante *m/f*;

(*RAIL*) vagão *m* para fumantes.
smoke screen *n* cortina de fumaça.
smoke shop
smoking ['sməukɪŋ] *n*: "**no** ~" (*sign*) "proibido fumar"; **he's given up** ~ ele deixou de fumar.
smoking compartment (*US* **smoking car**) *n* vagão *m* para fumantes.
smoky ['sməukɪ] *adj* fumegante; (*room*) cheio de fumaça (*BR*) *or* fumo (*PT*).
smolder ['sməuldə*] (*US*) *vi* = **smoulder**.
smooth [smuːð] *adj* liso, macio; (*sea*) tranqüilo, calmo; (*flat*) plano; (*flavour, movement*) suave; (*person*) culto, refinado; (: *pej*) meloso; (*flight, landing*) tranqüilo; (*cigarette*) suave ♦ *vt* alisar; (*also:* ~ **out:** *difficulties*) aplainar.
smooth over *vt*: **to** ~ **things over** (*fig*) arranjar as coisas.
smoothly ['smuːðlɪ] *adv* (*easily*) facilmente, sem problemas; **everything went** ~ tudo correu muito bem.
smother ['smʌðə*] *vt* sufocar; (*repress*) reprimir.
smoulder ['sməuldə*] (*US* **smolder**) *vi* arder sem chamas.
smudge [smʌdʒ] *n* mancha ♦ *vt* manchar, sujar.
smug [smʌg] *adj* metido, convencido.
smuggle ['smʌgl] *vt* contrabandear; **to** ~ **in/ out** (*goods etc*) fazer entrar/sair de contrabando.
smuggler ['smʌglə*] *n* contrabandista *m/f*.
smuggling ['smʌglɪŋ] *n* contrabando.
smut [smʌt] *n* (*of soot*) marca de fuligem; (*mark*) mancha; (*in conversation etc*) obscenidades *fpl*.
smutty ['smʌtɪ] *adj* (*fig*) obsceno, indecente.
snack [snæk] *n* lanche *m* (*BR*), merenda (*PT*); **to have a** ~ fazer um lanche.
snack bar *n* lanchonete *f* (*BR*), snackbar *m* (*PT*).
snag [snæg] *n* dificuldade *f*, obstáculo.
snail [sneɪl] *n* caracol *m*; (*water* ~) caramujo.
snake [sneɪk] *n* cobra.
snap [snæp] *n* (*sound*) estalo; (*of whip*) estalido; (*click*) clique *m*; (*photograph*) foto *f* ♦ *adj* repentino ♦ *vt* (*fingers, whip*) estalar; (*break*) quebrar; (*photograph*) tirar uma foto de ♦ *vi* (*break*) quebrar; (*fig: person*) retrucar asperamente; (*sound*) estalar; **to** ~ **shut** fechar com um estalo; **to** ~ **at sb** (*subj: person*) retrucar bruscamente a alguém; (: *dog*) tentar morder alguém; **to** ~ **one's fingers** estalar os dedos; **a cold** ~ uma onda de frio.
snap off *vt* (*break*) partir.
snap up *vt* arrebatar, comprar rapidamente.
snap fastener *n* colchete *m* de mola.
snappy ['snæpɪ] *adj* rápido; (*slogan*) vigoroso; **he's a** ~ **dresser** ele está sempre chique;

NB: *European Portuguese adds the following consonants to certain words:* **b** (sú(b)dito, su(b)til); **c** (a(c)ção, a(c)cionista, a(c)to); **m** (inde(m)ne); **p** (ado(p)ção, ado(p)tar); *for further details see p. xiii.*

make it ~! vai rápido!

snapshot ['snæpʃɔt] *n* foto *f* (instantânea).

snare [snɛə*] *n* armadilha, laço ♦ *vt* apanhar no laço *or* na armadilha.

snarl [snɑːl] *n* grunhido ♦ *vi* grunhir ♦ *vt*: **to get ~ed up** (*wool, plans*) ficar embaralhado; (*traffic*) ficar engarrafado.

snatch [snætʃ] *n* (*fig*) roubo; (*small amount*): ~**es of** pedacinhos *mpl* de ♦ *vt* (~ *away*) arrebatar; (*grasp*) agarrar ♦ *vi*: **don't ~!** não tome as coisas dos outros!; **to ~ a sandwich** fazer um lanche rapidinho; **to ~ some sleep** dormir um pouco.

snatch up *vt* agarrar.

sneak [sniːk] *vi*: **to ~ in/out** entrar/sair furtivamente ♦ *vt*: **to ~ a look at sth** olhar disfarçadamente para algo.

sneakers ['sniːkəz] *npl* tênis *m* (*BR*), sapatos *mpl* de treino (*PT*).

sneaking ['sniːkɪŋ] *adj*: **to have a ~ suspicion that** ... ter uma vaga suspeita de que ....

sneaky ['sniːkɪ] *adj* sorrateiro.

sneer [snɪə*] *n* sorriso de desprezo ♦ *vi* rir-se com desdém; **to ~ at** zombar de, desprezar.

sneeze [sniːz] *n* espirro ♦ *vi* espirrar.

snide [snaɪd] *adj* sarcástico.

sniff [snɪf] *n* (*of dog*) farejada; (*of person*) fungadela ♦ *vi* fungar ♦ *vt* fungar, farejar; (*glue, drug*) cheirar.

sniff at *vt fus*: **it's not to be ~ed at** isso não deve ser desprezado.

snigger ['snɪgə*] *n* riso dissimulado ♦ *vi* rir-se com dissimulação.

snip [snɪp] *n* tesourada; (*piece*) pedaço, retalho; (*bargain*) pechincha ♦ *vt* cortar com tesoura.

sniper ['snaɪpə*] *n* franco-atirador(a) *m/f*.

snippet ['snɪpɪt] *n* pedacinho.

snivelling ['snɪvlɪŋ] *adj* (*whimpering*) chorão/rona, lamuriento.

snob [snɔb] *n* esnobe *m/f*.

snobbery ['snɔbərɪ] *n* esnobismo.

snobbish ['snɔbɪʃ] *adj* esnobe.

snooker ['snuːkə*] *n* sinuca.

snoop [snuːp] *vi*: **to ~ about** bisbilhotar.

snooper ['snuːpə*] *n* bisbilhoteiro/a, xereta *m/f*.

snooty ['snuːtɪ] *adj* arrogante.

snooze [snuːz] *n* soneca ♦ *vi* tirar uma soneca, dormitar.

snore [snɔː*] *vi* roncar ♦ *n* ronco.

snoring ['snɔːrɪŋ] *n* roncadura, roncaria.

snorkel ['snɔːkl] *n* tubo snorkel.

snort [snɔːt] *n* bufo, bufido ♦ *vi* bufar ♦ *vt* (*drugs*) cheirar.

snot [snɔt] *n* (*inf*) ranho.

snotty ['snɔtɪ] *adj* ranhoso; (*fig*) altivo, arrogante.

snout [snaʊt] *n* focinho.

snow [snəʊ] *n* neve *f* ♦ *vi* nevar ♦ *vt*: **to be ~ed under with work** estar atolado *or* sobrecarregado de trabalho.

snowball ['snəʊbɔːl] *n* bola de neve ♦ *vi* acumular-se.

snowbound ['snəʊbaʊnd] *adj* bloqueado pela neve.

snow-capped [-kæpt] *adj* coberto de neve.

snowdrift ['snəʊdrɪft] *n* monte *m* de neve (formado pelo vento).

snowdrop ['snəʊdrɔp] *n* campainha branca.

snowfall ['snəʊfɔːl] *n* nevada.

snowflake ['snəʊfleɪk] *n* floco de neve.

snowman ['snəʊmæn] (*irreg*) *n* boneco de neve.

snowplough ['snəʊplaʊ] (*US* **snowplow**) *n* máquina limpa-neve, removedor *m* de neve.

snowshoe ['snəʊʃuː] *n* raquete *f* de neve.

snowstorm ['snəʊstɔːm] *n* nevasca, tempestade *f* de neve.

Snow White *n* Branca de Neve.

snowy ['snəʊɪ] *adj* nevoso.

SNP (*BRIT*) *n abbr* (*POL*) = **Scottish National Party**.

snub [snʌb] *vt* desdenhar, menosprezar ♦ *n* repulsa.

snub-nosed [-'nəʊzd] *adj* de nariz arrebitado.

snuff [snʌf] *n* rapé *m* ♦ *vt* (*also*: ~ *out*: *candle*) apagar.

snug [snʌg] *adj* (*sheltered*) abrigado, protegido; (*fitted*) justo, cômodo.

snuggle ['snʌgl] *vi*: **to ~ up to sb** aconchegar-se *or* aninhar-se a alguém.

snugly ['snʌglɪ] *adv* (*fit*) perfeitamente.

SO *abbr* (*BANKING*) = **standing order**.

so [səʊ] *adv* (*degree*) tão; (*manner: thus*) assim, deste modo ♦ *conj* conseqüentemente, portanto; ~ **as to do** para fazer; ~ **that** (*purpose*) para que, a fim de que; (*result*) de modo que; ~ **that's the reason!** então, esta é a razão!; ~ **do I** eu também; ~ **it is!**, ~ **it does!** é verdade!; **if** ~ se for assim, se assim é; **I hope** ~ espero que sim; **10 or** ~ 10 mais ou menos; **quite** ~! exatamente!; **even** ~ mesmo assim; ~ **far** até aqui; ~ **long!** tchau!; ~ **many** tantos; ~ **much** tanto; **she didn't** ~ **much** as **send me a birthday card** ela nem me mandou um cartão no meu aniversário; ~ **to speak** por assim dizer; ~ **(what)?** (*inf*) e daí?

soak [səʊk] *vt* (*drench*) embeber, ensopar; (*put in water*) pôr de molho ♦ *vi* estar de molho, impregnar-se.

soak in *vi* infiltrar.

soak up *vt* absorver.

soaking ['səʊkɪŋ] *adj* (*also*: ~ *wet*) encharcado.

so and so *n* fulano/a.

soap [səʊp] *n* sabão *m*.

soapflakes ['səʊpfleɪks] *npl* flocos *mpl* de sabão.

soap opera *n* novela.

soap powder *n* sabão *m* em pó.

soapsuds ['səʊpsʌdz] *n* água de sabão.

soapy ['səʊpɪ] *adj* ensaboado.

soar [sɔː*] *vi* (*on wings*) elevar-se em vôo; (*building etc*) levantar-se; (*price*) disparar; (*morale, spirits*) renascer.

soaring ['sɔːrɪŋ] *adj* (*flight*) a grande altura; (*prices, inflation*) disparado.

sob [sɔb] *n* soluço ♦ *vi* soluçar.

s.o.b. (US: inf!) n abbr (= son of a bitch) filho da puta (!).

sober ['səubə*] adj (serious) sério; (sensible) sensato; (moderate) moderado; (not drunk) sóbrio; (colour, style) discreto.
sober up vi tornar-se sóbrio.

sobriety [sə'braɪətɪ] n sobriedade f.

Soc. abbr = **society**.

so-called [-kɔːld] adj chamado.

soccer ['sɔkə*] n futebol m.

soccer pitch n campo de futebol.

soccer player n jogador m de futebol.

sociable ['səuʃəbl] adj sociável.

social ['səuʃl] adj social; (sociable) sociável ♦ n reunião f social.

social climber n arrivista m/f.

social club n clube m.

Social Democrat n democrata-social m/f.

social insurance (US) n seguro social.

socialism ['səuʃəlɪzəm] n socialismo.

socialist ['səuʃəlɪst] adj, n socialista m/f.

socialite ['səuʃəlaɪt] n socialite m/f, colunável m/f.

socialize ['səuʃəlaɪz] vi socializar.

socially ['səuʃəlɪ] adv socialmente.

social science n ciências fpl sociais.

social security n previdência social; **Department of S~ S~** (BRIT) ≈ Instituto Nacional de Assistência Médica e Previdência Social.

social welfare n bem-estar m social.

social work n assistência social, serviço social.

social worker n assistente m/f social.

society [sə'saɪətɪ] n sociedade f; (club) associação f; (also: high ~) alta sociedade ♦ cpd (party, column) da alta sociedade.

socio-economic ['səusɪəu-] adj sócio-econômico.

sociological [səusɪə'lɔdʒɪkl] adj sociológico.

sociologist [səusɪ'ɔlədʒɪst] n sociólogo/a.

sociology [səusɪ'ɔlədʒɪ] n sociologia.

sock [sɔk] n meia (BR), peúga (PT) ♦ vt (inf: hit) socar, dar um soco em; **to pull one's ~s up** (fig) tomar jeito.

socket ['sɔkɪt] n (ELEC) tomada.

sod [sɔd] n (of earth) gramado, torrão m; (BRIT: inf!) imbecil m/f ♦ vt: ~ **it!** (inf!) droga!

soda ['səudə] n (CHEM) soda; (also: ~ water) água com gás; (US: also: ~ pop) soda.

sodden ['sɔdn] adj encharcado.

sodium ['səudɪəm] n sódio.

sodium chloride n cloreto de sódio.

sofa ['səufə] n sofá m.

Sofia ['səufɪə] n Sófia.

soft [sɔft] adj (gen) macio; (spongy) mole; (gentle, not loud) suave; (kind) meigo, bondoso; (weak) fraco; (stupid) idiota.

soft-boiled egg [-bɔɪld-] n ovo quente.

soft currency n moeda fraca.

soft drink n refrigerante m.

soft drugs n drogas fpl leves.

soften ['sɔfn] vt amolecer, amaciar, enternecer ♦ vi abrandar-se, enternecer-se, suavizar-se.

softener ['sɔfnər] n amaciante m.

soft fruit (BRIT) n bagas fpl.

soft furnishings npl cortinas fpl e estofados mpl.

soft-hearted adj bondoso, caridoso.

softly ['sɔftlɪ] adv suavemente; (gently) delicadamente.

softness ['sɔftnɪs] n suavidade f, maciez f.

soft sell n venda de forma não agressiva.

soft toy n brinquedo de pelúcia.

software ['sɔftweə*] n software m.

software package n soft m, pacote m.

SOGAT ['səugæt] (BRIT) n abbr (= Society of Graphical and Allied Trades) sindicato dos impressores.

soggy ['sɔgɪ] adj ensopado, encharcado.

soil [sɔɪl] n (earth) terra, solo ♦ vt sujar, manchar.

soiled [sɔɪld] adj sujo.

sojourn ['sɔdʒɔːn] n (formal) estada f.

solace ['sɔlɪs] n consolo.

solar ['səulə*] adj solar.

solaria [sə'leərɪə] npl of **solarium**.

solarium [sə'leərɪəm] (pl **solaria**) n solário.

solar plexus [-'plɛksəs] n plexo solar.

sold [səuld] pt, pp of **sell**.

solder ['səuldə*] vt soldar ♦ n solda.

soldier ['səuldʒə*] n soldado; (army man) militar m; **toy ~** soldado de chumbo.
soldier on vi agüentar firme (inf), perseverar.

sold out adj (COMM) esgotado.

sole [səul] (pl ~s) n (of foot, of shoe) sola; (pl: inv: fish) solha, linguado ♦ adj único; **the ~ reason** a única razão.

solely ['səullɪ] adv somente, unicamente; **I will hold you ~ responsible** vou apontar-lhe como o único responsável.

solemn ['sɔləm] adj solene.

sole trader n (COMM) comerciante m/f independente.

solicit [sə'lɪsɪt] vt (request) solicitar ♦ vi (prostitute) aliciar fregueses.

solicitor [sə'lɪsɪtə*] n (for wills etc) tabelião/lioa m/f; (in court) ≈ advogado/a.

solid ['sɔlɪd] adj (not hollow) sólido; (gold etc) maciço; (person) sério; (line) contínuo; (vote) unânime ♦ n sólido; **we waited 2 ~ hours** esperamos por 2 horas a fio; **to be on ~ ground** estar em terra firme; (fig) ter base.

solidarity [sɔlɪ'dærɪtɪ] n solidariedade f.

solidify [sə'lɪdɪfaɪ] vi solidificar-se.

solidity [sə'lɪdɪtɪ] n solidez f.

solid-state adj de estado sólido.

soliloquy [sə'lɪləkwɪ] n monólogo.

solitaire [sɔlɪ'tɛə*] n (gem) solitário; (game) solitário, jogo de paciência.

solitary ['sɔlɪtərɪ] adj solitário, só; (isolated)

NB: *European Portuguese adds the following consonants to certain words:* **b** (sú(b)dito, su(b)til); **c** (a(c)ção, a(c)cionista, a(c)to); **m** (inde(m)ne); **p** (ado(p)ção, ado(p)tar); *for further details see p. xiii.*

isolado, retirado; (only) único.
solitary confinement n (LAW) prisão f celular, solitária.
solitude ['sɔlɪtjuːd] n solidão f.
solo ['səuləu] n solo.
soloist ['səuləuist] n solista m/f.
Solomon Islands ['sɔləmən-] npl: **the** ~ as ilhas Salomão.
solstice ['sɔlstɪs] n solstício.
soluble ['sɔljubl] adj solúvel.
solution [sə'luːʃən] n solução f.
solve [sɔlv] vt resolver, solucionar.
solvency ['sɔlvənsɪ] n (COMM) solvência.
solvent ['sɔlvənt] adj (COMM) solvente ♦ n (CHEM) solvente m.
solvent abuse n abuso de solventes alucinógenos.
Som. (BRIT) abbr = **Somerset.**
Somali [sə'mɑːlɪ] adj, n somaliano/a.
Somalia [sə'mɑːlɪə] n Somália.
sombre ['sɔmbə*] (US **somber**) adj sombrio, lúgubre.
some [sʌm] adj (a few) alguns/algumas; (certain) algum(a); (a certain number or amount) see phrases below; (unspecified) um pouco de ♦ pron alguns/algumas; (a bit) um pouco ♦ adv: ~ **10 people** umas 10 pessoas; ~ **children came** algumas crianças vieram; ~ **people say that ...** algumas pessoas dizem que ...; **have** ~ **tea** tome um pouco de chá; **there's** ~ **milk in the fridge** há leite na geladeira; ~ **(of it) was left** ficou um pouco; **could I have** ~ **of that cheese?** pode me dar um pouco daquele queijo?; **I've got** ~ (books etc) tenho alguns; (milk, money etc) tenho um pouco; **would you like** ~? você quer um pouco?; **after** ~ **time** depois de algum tempo; **at** ~ **length** com certa extensão; **in** ~ **form or other** de uma forma ou de outra.
somebody ['sʌmbədɪ] pron alguém; ~ **or other** um ou outro.
someday ['sʌmdeɪ] adv algum dia.
somehow ['sʌmhau] adv de alguma maneira; (for some reason) por uma razão ou outra.
someone ['sʌmwʌn] pron alguém.
someplace ['sʌmpleɪs] (US) adv (be) em algum lugar; (go) para algum lugar; ~ **else** (be) em outro lugar; (go) para outro lugar.
somersault ['sʌməsɔːlt] n (deliberate) salto mortal; (accidental) cambalhota ♦ vi dar um salto mortal or uma cambalhota.
something ['sʌmθɪŋ] pron alguma coisa, algo (BR); ~ **to do** alguma coisa para fazer; ~ **else** (in addition) alguma coisa a mais; (~ different) outra coisa; **he's** ~ **like me** ele é um pouco como eu; **it's** ~ **of a problem** é de certo modo um problema.
sometime ['sʌmtaɪm] adv (in future) algum dia, em outra oportunidade; (in past): ~ **last month** durante o mês passado; **I'll finish it** ~ vou terminar uma hora dessas.
sometimes ['sʌmtaɪmz] adv às vezes, de vez em quando.
somewhat ['sʌmwɔt] adv um tanto.
somewhere ['sʌmwɛə*] adv (be) em algum

lugar; (go) para algum lugar; ~ **else** (be) em outro lugar; (go) para outro lugar.
son [sʌn] n filho.
sonar ['səunɑː*] n sonar m.
sonata [sə'nɑːtə] n sonata.
song [sɔŋ] n canção f.
songbook ['sɔŋbuk] n cancioneiro.
songwriter ['sɔŋraɪtə*] n compositor(a) m/f de canções.
sonic ['sɔnɪk] adj (boom) sônico.
son-in-law ['sʌnɪnlɔː] (pl **sons-in-law**) n genro.
sonnet ['sɔnɪt] n soneto.
sonny ['sʌnɪ] (inf) n meu filho.
soon [suːn] adv logo, brevemente; (early) cedo; ~ **afterwards** pouco depois; **very/quite** ~ logo/daqui a pouco; **how** ~ **can you be ready?** quando você estará pronto?; **it's too** ~ **to tell** é muito cedo para dizer; **see you** ~! até logo!; see also **as.**
sooner ['suːnə*] adv (time) antes, mais cedo; (preference): **I would** ~ **do that** preferia fazer isso; ~ **or later** mais cedo ou mais tarde; **no** ~ **said than done** dito e feito; **the** ~ **the better** quanto mais cedo melhor; **no** ~ **had we left than he ...** mal partimos, ele ....
soot [sut] n fuligem f.
soothe [suːð] vt acalmar, sossegar; (pain) aliviar, suavizar.
soothing ['suːðɪŋ] adj calmante.
SOP n abbr = **standard operating procedure.**
sop [sɔp] n paliativo.
sophisticated [sə'fɪstɪkeɪtɪd] adj sofisticado.
sophistication [səfɪstɪ'keɪʃən] n sofisticação f.
sophomore ['sɔfəmɔː*] (US) n segundanista m/f.
soporific [sɔpə'rɪfɪk] adj soporífico.
sopping ['sɔpɪŋ] adj: ~ **wet** encharcado.
soppy ['sɔpɪ] (pej) adj piegas inv.
soprano [sə'prɑːnəu] n soprano m/f.
sorbet ['sɔːbeɪ] n sorvete de frutas à base de água.
sorcerer ['sɔːsərə*] n feiticeiro.
sordid ['sɔːdɪd] adj (dirty) imundo, sórdido; (wretched) miserável.
sore [sɔː*] adj (painful) dolorido; (offended) magoado, ofendido ♦ n chaga, ferida; **it's a** ~ **point** é um ponto delicado; **my eyes are** ~, **I've got** ~ **eyes** meus olhos estão doloridos.
sorely ['sɔːlɪ] adv: **I am** ~ **tempted** estou muito tentado.
sore throat n dor f de garganta.
sorrel ['sɔrəl] n azeda.
sorrow ['sɔrəu] n tristeza, mágoa, dor f.
sorrowful ['sɔrəuful] adj triste, aflito, magoado.
sorry ['sɔrɪ] adj (regretful) arrependido; (condition, sight) lamentável; ~! desculpe!, perdão!, sinto muito!; **to feel** ~ **for sb** sentir pena de alguém; **I feel** ~ **for him** estou com pena dele; **I'm** ~ **to hear that ...** lamento saber que ...; **to be** ~ **about sth** arrepender-se de algo.
sort [sɔːt] n tipo; (brand: of coffee etc) marca ♦ vt (also: ~ **out**: papers) classificar; (:

problems) solucionar, resolver; **what ~ do you want?** que tipo você quer?; **what ~ of car?** que tipo de carro?; **I'll do nothing of the ~!** não farei nada do gênero!; **it's ~ of awkward** *(inf)* é meio difícil.

sortie ['sɔːtɪ] *n* surtida.

sorting office ['sɔːtɪŋ-] *n* departamento de distribuição.

SOS *n abbr* (= *save our souls*) S.O.S. *m*.

so-so *adv* mais ou menos, regular.

soufflé ['suːfleɪ] *n* suflê *m*.

sought [sɔːt] *pt*, *pp of* **seek**.

sought-after *adj* desejado.

soul [səul] *n* alma; **I didn't see a ~** não vi uma alma; **God rest his ~** que a sua alma descanse em paz; **the poor ~ had nowhere to sleep** o pobre coitado não tinha onde dormir.

soul-destroying [-dɪs'trɔɪɪŋ] *adj* desalentador(a).

soulful ['səulful] *adj* emocional, sentimental.

soulless ['səullɪs] *adj* desalmado.

soul mate *n* companheiro/a ideal.

soul-searching *n*: **after much ~** depois de muita ponderação.

sound [saund] *adj (healthy)* saudável, sadio; *(safe, not damaged)* sólido, completo; *(secure)* seguro; *(reliable)* confiável; *(sensible)* sensato; *(argument, policy)* válido; *(move)* acertado ♦ *adv:* **~ asleep** dormindo profundamente ♦ *n (noise)* som *m*, ruído, barulho; *(GEO)* estreito, braço (de mar) ♦ *vt (alarm)* soar, tocar; *(also: ~ out: opinions)* sondar ♦ *vi* soar, tocar; *(fig: seem)* parecer; **to be of ~ mind** estar em juízo perfeito; **I don't like the ~ of it** eu não estou gostando disso; **to ~ like** parecer; **it ~s as if ...** parece que ....

sound off *(inf)* *vi:* **to ~ off (about)** pontificar (sobre).

sound barrier *n* barreira do som.

sound effects *npl* efeitos *mpl* sonoros.

sound engineer *n* engenheiro/a de som.

sounding ['saundɪŋ] *n (NAUT etc)* sondagem *f*.

sounding board *n (MUS)* caixa de ressonância; *(fig):* **to use sb as a ~ for one's ideas** testar suas idéias em alguém.

soundly ['saundlɪ] *adv (sleep)* profundamente; *(beat)* completamente.

soundproof ['saundpruːf] *adj* à prova de som ♦ *vt* insonorizar.

soundtrack ['saundtræk] *n (of film)* trilha sonora.

sound wave *n* onda sonora.

soup [suːp] *n (thick)* sopa; *(thin)* caldo; **in the ~** *(fig)* numa encrenca.

soup kitchen *n* local onde se distribui comida aos pobres.

soup plate *n* prato fundo (para sopa).

soupspoon ['suːpspuːn] *n* colher *f* de sopa.

sour ['sauə*] *adj* azedo, ácido; *(milk)* talhado; *(fig)* mal-humorado, rabugento; **to go** *or* **turn ~** *(milk, wine)* azedar; *(fig: relationship,*

plan) azedar, dar errado.

source [sɔːs] *n* fonte *f*; **I have it from a reliable ~ that ...** uma fonte confiável me assegura que ....

south [sauθ] *n* sul *m* ♦ *adj* do sul, meridional ♦ *adv* ao *or* para o sul; **(to the) ~ of** ao sul de; **the S~ of France** o Sul da França; **to travel ~** viajar para o sul.

South Africa *n* África do Sul.

South African *adj*, *n* sul-africano/a.

South America *n* América do Sul.

South American *adj*, *n* sul-americano/a.

southbound ['sauθbaund] *adj* em direção ao sul.

south-east *n* sudeste *m* ♦ *adj* do sudeste.

South-East Asia *n* o Sudeste da Ásia.

southerly ['sʌðəlɪ] *adj* meridional; *(from the south)* do sul.

southern ['sʌðən] *adj* meridional, do sul, sulista; **the ~ hemisphere** o Hemisfério Sul.

South Pole *n* Pólo Sul.

South Sea Islands *npl:* **the ~** as ilhas dos Mares do Sul.

South Seas *npl:* **the ~** os Mares do Sul.

southward(s) ['sauθwəd(z)] *adv* para o sul.

south-west *n* sudoeste *m*.

souvenir [suːvə'nɪə*] *n* lembrança.

sovereign ['sɔvrɪn] *adj*, *n* soberano/a.

sovereignty ['sɔvrɪntɪ] *n* soberania.

soviet ['səuvɪət] *adj* soviético.

Soviet Union *n:* **the ~** a União Soviética.

sow[1] [sau] *n* porca.

sow[2] [səu] *(pt ~ed, pp sown) vt (gen)* semear; *(spread)* disseminar, espalhar.

sown [səun] *pp of* **sow**[2].

soy [sɔɪ] *(US) n* = **soya**.

soya ['sɔɪə] *(BRIT) n* soja; **~ bean** semente *f* de soja; **~ sauce** molho de soja.

spa [spɑː] *n (town)* estância hidro-mineral; *(US: also: health ~)* estância balnear.

space [speɪs] *n (gen)* espaço; *(room)* lugar *m* ♦ *vt (also: ~ out)* espaçar; **in a confined ~** num espaço confinado; **in a short ~ of time** num curto espaço de tempo; **(with)in the ~ of an hour** dentro do espaço de uma hora; **to clear a ~ for sth** abrir espaço para algo.

space bar *n* tecla de espacejamento.

spacecraft ['speɪskrɑːft] *n inv* nave *f* espacial.

spaceman ['speɪsmæn] *(irreg) n* astronauta *m*, cosmonauta *m*.

spaceship ['speɪsʃɪp] *n* nave *f* espacial.

space shuttle *n* ônibus *m* espacial.

spacesuit ['speɪssuːt] *n* traje *m* espacial.

spacewoman ['speɪswumən] *(irreg) n* astronauta, cosmonauta.

spacing ['speɪsɪŋ] *n* espacejamento, espaçamento; **single/double ~** espacejamento simples/duplo.

spacious ['speɪʃəs] *adj* espaçoso.

spade [speɪd] *n (tool)* pá *f*; **~s** *npl (CARDS)* espadas *fpl*.

spadework ['speɪdwəːk] *n (fig)* trabalho preli-

minar.
spaghetti [spə'gɛtɪ] *n* espaguete *m*.
Spain [speɪn] *n* Espanha.
span [spæn] *n* (*also*: *wing*~) envergadura; (*of hand*) palma; (*of arch*) vão *m*; (*in time*) lapso, espaço ♦ *vt* estender-se sobre, atravessar; (*fig*) abarcar.
Spaniard ['spænjəd] *n* espanhol(a) *m/f*.
spaniel ['spænjəl] *n* spaniel *m*.
Spanish ['spænɪʃ] *adj* espanhol(a) ♦ *n* (*LING*) espanhol *m*, castelhano; **the** ~ *npl* os espanhóis; ~ **omelette** omelete *m* à espanhola.
spank [spæŋk] *vt* bater, dar palmadas.
spanner ['spænə*] *n* chave *f* inglesa.
spar [spɑ:*] *n* mastro, verga ♦ *vi* (*BOXING*) treinar.
spare [spɛə*] *adj* (*free*) vago, desocupado; (*surplus*) de sobra, a mais; (*available*) disponível, de reserva ♦ *n* (*part*) peça sobressalente ♦ *vt* (*do without*) dispensar, passar sem; (*afford to give*) dispor de, ter de sobra; (*refrain from hurting*) perdoar, poupar; (*be grudging with*) dar frugalmente; **there are 2 going** ~ (*BRIT*) há 2 sobrando; **to** ~ **no expense** não poupar despesas; **can you** ~ **(me) £10?** pode me ceder £10?; **can you** ~ **the time?** você tem tempo?; **there is no time to** ~ não há tempo a perder; **I've a few minutes to** ~ tenho alguns minutos de sobra.
spare part *n* peça sobressalente.
spare room *n* quarto de hóspedes.
spare time *n* tempo livre.
spare tyre *n* estepe *m*.
spare wheel *n* estepe *m*.
sparing ['spɛərɪŋ] *adj*: **to be** ~ **with** ser econômico com.
sparingly ['spɛərɪŋlɪ] *adv* escassamente.
spark [spɑ:k] *n* chispa, faísca; (*fig*) centelha.
spark(ing) plug ['spɑ:k(ɪŋ)-] *n* vela (de ignição).
sparkle ['spɑ:kl] *n* cintilação *f*, brilho ♦ *vi* cintilar; (*shine*) brilhar, faiscar.
sparkling ['spɑ:klɪŋ] *adj* cintilante; (*wine*) espumante.
sparrow ['spærəu] *n* pardal *m*.
sparse [spɑ:s] *adj* escasso; (*hair*) ralo.
spartan ['spɑ:tən] *adj* (*fig*) espartano.
spasm ['spæzəm] *n* (*MED*) espasmo; (*fig*) acesso, ataque *m*.
spasmodic [spæz'mɒdɪk] *adj* espasmódico.
spastic ['spæstɪk] *n* espástico/a.
spat [spæt] *pt*, *pp of* **spit** ♦ *n* (*US*) bate-boca *m*.
spate [speɪt] *n* série *f*; **in** ~ (*river*) em cheia.
spatial ['speɪʃəl] *adj* espacial.
spatter ['spætə*] *n* borrifo ♦ *vt* borrifar, salpicar ♦ *vi* borrifar.
spatula ['spætjulə] *n* espátula.
spawn [spɔ:n] *vi* desovar, procriar ♦ *vt* gerar; (*pej*: *create*) gerar, criar ♦ *n* ovas *fpl*.
SPCA (*US*) *n abbr* = **Society for the Prevention of Cruelty to Animals**.
SPCC (*US*) *n abbr* = **Society for the Prevention of Cruelty to Children**.
speak [spi:k] (*pt* **spoke**, *pp* **spoken**) *vt* (*language*) falar; (*truth*) dizer ♦ *vi* falar;

(*make a speech*) discursar; **to** ~ **to sb/of** *or* **about sth** falar com alguém/de *or* sobre algo; ~ **up!** fale alto!; ~**ing!** (*on phone*) é ele/ela mesmo!; **to** ~ **one's mind** desabafar; **he has no money to** ~ **of** ele quase não tem dinheiro.
speak for *vt fus*: **to** ~ **for sb** falar por alguém; **that picture is already spoken for** aquele quadro já está vendido.
speaker ['spi:kə*] *n* (*in public*) orador(a) *m/f*; (*also*: *loud*~) alto-falante *m*; (*POL*): **the S**~ o Presidente da Câmara; **are you a Welsh** ~? você fala galês?
speaking ['spi:kɪŋ] *adj* falante; **Italian-**~ **people** pessoas de língua italiana.
spear [spɪə*] *n* lança; (*for fishing*) arpão *m* ♦ *vt* lancear, arpoar.
spearhead ['spɪəhɛd] *n* ponta-de-lança ♦ *vt* (*attack*) encabeçar.
spearmint ['spɪəmɪnt] *n* hortelã *f*.
spec [spɛk] (*BRIT*: *inf*) *n*: **to buy sth on** ~ comprar algo por acaso.
special ['spɛʃl] *adj* especial; (*edition etc*) extra ♦ *n* (*train*) trem *m* especial; **take** ~ **care** tome muito cuidado; **nothing** ~ nada especial; **today's** ~ (*at restaurant*) especialidade do dia, prato do dia.
special delivery *n*: **by** ~ por entrega rápida.
specialist ['spɛʃəlɪst] *n* especialista *m/f*; **heart** ~ especialista em doenças do coração.
speciality [spɛʃɪ'ælɪtɪ] (*BRIT*) *n* especialidade *f*.
specialize ['spɛʃəlaɪz] *vi*: **to** ~ (**in**) especializar-se (em).
specially ['spɛʃəlɪ] *adv* especialmente.
special offer *n* oferta especial.
specialty ['spɛʃəltɪ] (*US*) *n* = **speciality**.
species ['spi:ʃi:z] *n inv* espécie *f*.
specific [spə'sɪfɪk] *adj* específico.
specifically [spə'sɪfɪklɪ] *adv* especificamente.
specification [spɛsɪfɪ'keɪʃən] *n* especificação *f*; ~**s** *npl* (*of car, machine*) ficha técnica; (*of building*) especificações *fpl*.
specify ['spɛsɪfaɪ] *vt*, *vi* especificar, pormenorizar; **unless otherwise specified** salvo indicação em contrário.
specimen ['spɛsɪmən] *n* espécime *m*, amostra; (*fig*) exemplar *m*.
specimen copy *n* exemplar *m* de amostra.
specimen signature *n* modelo de assinatura.
speck [spɛk] *n* mancha, pinta; (*particle*) grão *m*.
speckled ['spɛkld] *adj* manchado.
specs [spɛks] (*inf*) *npl* óculos *mpl*.
spectacle ['spɛktəkl] *n* espetáculo; ~**s** *npl* óculos *mpl*.
spectacle case *n* estojo de óculos.
spectacular [spɛk'tækjulə*] *adj* espetacular ♦ *n* (*CINEMA etc*) superprodução *f*.
spectator [spɛk'teɪtə*] *n* espectador(a) *m/f*.
specter ['spɛktə*] (*US*) *n* = **spectre**.
spectra ['spɛktrə] *npl of* **spectrum**.
spectre ['spɛktə*] (*US* **specter**) *n* espectro, aparição *f*.
spectrum ['spɛktrəm] (*pl* **spectra**) *n* espectro.
speculate ['spɛkjuleɪt] *vi* especular; (*try to*

guess): **to ~ about** especular sobre.
speculation [spɛkju'leɪʃən] *n* especulação *f*.
speculative ['spɛkjulətɪv] *adj* especulativo.
speculator ['spɛkjuleɪtə*] *n* especulador(a) *m/f*.
sped [spɛd] *pt, pp of* **speed**.
speech [spiːtʃ] *n* (*faculty, language*) fala; (*formal talk*) discurso.
speech day (*BRIT*) *n* (*SCH*) dia *m* de distribuição de prêmios.
speech impediment *n* defeito *m* de articulação.
speechless ['spiːtʃlɪs] *adj* estupefato, emudecido.
speech therapy *n* ortofonia.
speed [spiːd] (*pt, pp* **sped**) *n* velocidade *f*, rapidez *f*; (*haste*) pressa; (*promptness*) prontidão *f*; (*gear*) marcha ♦ *vi* (*in car*) correr; **the years sped by** os anos voaram; **at full** *or* **top ~** a toda a velocidade; **at a ~ of 70 km/h** a uma velocidade de 70 km/h; **shorthand/typing ~** velocidade de estenografia/datilografia; **at ~** em alta velocidade; **a five-~ gearbox** uma caixa de mudanças com cinco marchas.
  speed up (*pt, pp* **~ed up**) *vi* acelerar ♦ *vt* acelerar.
speedboat ['spiːdbəut] *n* lancha.
speedily ['spiːdɪlɪ] *adv* depressa, rapidamente.
speeding ['spiːdɪŋ] *n* (*AUT*) excesso de velocidade.
speed limit *n* limite *m* de velocidade, velocidade *f* máxima.
speedometer [spɪ'dɔmɪtə*] *n* velocímetro.
speed trap *n* área de fiscalização contra motoristas que dirigem em alta velocidade.
speedway ['spiːdweɪ] *n* (*SPORT*) pista de corrida, rodovia de alta velocidade; (: *also*: ~ *racing*) corrida de motocicleta.
speedy ['spiːdɪ] *adj* (*fast*) veloz, rápido; (*prompt*) pronto, imediato.
speleologist [spiːlɪ'ɔlədʒɪst] *n* espeleologista *m/f*.
spell [spɛl] (*pt, pp* **~ed** *or* **spelt**) *n* (*also*: *magic* ~) encanto, feitiço; (*period of time*) período, temporada ♦ *vt* (*also*: ~ *out*) soletrar; (*fig*) pressagiar, ser sinal de; **to cast a ~ on sb** enfeitiçar alguém; **he can't ~** não sabe escrever bem, comete erros de ortografia; **how do you ~ your name?** como você escreve o seu nome?; **can you ~ it for me?** pode soletrar isso para mim?
spellbound ['spɛlbaund] *adj* enfeitiçado, fascinado.
spelling ['spɛlɪŋ] *n* ortografia.
spelling mistake *n* erro ortográfico.
spelt [spɛlt] *pt, pp of* **spell**.
spend [spɛnd] (*pt, pp* **spent**) *vt* (*money*) gastar; (*time*) passar; **to ~ time/money on sth** gastar tempo/dinheiro em algo.
spending ['spɛndɪŋ] *n* gastos *mpl*; **government ~** gastos públicos.

spending money *n* dinheiro para pequenas despesas.
spending power *n* poder *m* aquisitivo.
spendthrift ['spɛndθrɪft] *n* esbanjador(a) *m/f*, perdulário/a.
spent [spɛnt] *pt, pp of* **spend** ♦ *adj* gasto.
sperm [spəːm] *n* esperma.
sperm whale *n* cachalote *m*.
spew [spjuː] *vt* vomitar, lançar.
sphere [sfɪə*] *n* esfera.
spherical ['sfɛrɪkl] *adj* esférico.
sphinx [sfɪŋks] *n* esfinge *f*.
spice [spaɪs] *n* especiaria ♦ *vt* condimentar.
spick-and-span [spɪk-] *adj* tudo arrumado.
spicy ['spaɪsɪ] *adj* condimentado; (*fig*) picante.
spider ['spaɪdə*] *n* aranha; **~'s web** teia de aranha.
spiel [spiːl] *n* lengalenga.
spike [spaɪk] *n* (*point*) ponta, espigão *m*; (*BOT*) espiga; **~s** *npl* (*SPORT*) ferrões *mpl*.
spike heel (*US*) *n* salto alto e fino.
spiky ['spaɪkɪ] *adj* espinhoso.
spill [spɪl] (*pt, pp* **spilt** *or* **~ed**) *vt* entornar, derramar; (*blood*) derramar ♦ *vi* derramar-se; **to ~ the beans** (*inf*) dar com a língua nos dentes.
  spill out *vi* (*come out*) sair; (*fall out*) cair.
  spill over *vi* transbordar.
spin [spɪn] (*pt, pp* **spun**) *n* (*revolution of wheel*) volta, rotação *f*; (*AVIAT*) parafuso; (*trip in car*) volta *or* passeio de carro ♦ *vt* (*wool etc*) fiar, tecer; (*wheel*) girar; (*clothes*) torcer ♦ *vi* girar, rodar; **the car spun out of control** o carro se desgovernou.
  spin out *vt* prolongar, alargar.
spinach ['spɪnɪtʃ] *n* espinafre *m*.
spinal ['spaɪnl] *adj* espinhal.
spinal column *n* coluna vertebral.
spinal cord *n* espinha dorsal.
spindly ['spɪndlɪ] *adj* alto e magro, espigado.
spin-dry *vt* torcer (na máquina).
spin-dryer (*BRIT*) *n* secadora.
spine [spaɪn] *n* espinha dorsal; (*thorn*) espinho.
spine-chilling [-'tʃɪlɪŋ] *adj* arrepiante.
spineless ['spaɪnlɪs] *adj* (*fig*) fraco, covarde.
spinner ['spɪnə*] *n* (*of thread*) fiandeiro/a.
spinning ['spɪnɪŋ] *n* (*of thread, art*) fiação *f*.
spinning top *n* pião *m*.
spinning wheel *n* roca de fiar.
spin-off *n* subproduto.
spinster ['spɪnstə*] *n* solteira; (*pej*) solteirona.
spiral ['spaɪərl] *n* espiral *f* ♦ *adj* em espiral, helicoidal ♦ *vi* (*prices*) disparar; **the inflationary ~** a espiral inflacionária.
spiral staircase *n* escada em caracol.
spire ['spaɪə*] *n* flecha, agulha.
spirit ['spɪrɪt] *n* espírito; (*soul*) alma; (*ghost*) fantasma *m*; (*humour*) humor *m*; (*courage*) coragem *f*, ânimo; **~s** *npl* (*drink*) álcool *m*; **in good ~s** alegre, de bom humor; **Holy S~** Espírito Santo; **community/public ~** espírito

---

NB: European Portuguese adds the following consonants to certain words: **b** (sú(b)dito, su(b)til); **c** (a(c)ção, a(c)cionista, a(c)to); **m** (inde(m)ne); **p** (ado(p)ção, ado(p)tar); *for further details see p. xiii.*

comunitário/público.

spirit duplicator n duplicador m a álcool.

spirited ['spɪrɪtɪd] adj animado, espirituoso.

spirit level n nível m de bolha.

spiritual ['spɪrɪtjuəl] adj espiritual ♦ n (also: Negro ~) canto religioso dos negros.

spiritualism ['spɪrɪtjuəlɪzəm] n espiritualismo.

spit [spɪt] (pt, pp **spat**) n (for roasting) espeto; (GEOG) restinga; (spittle) cuspe m, cusparada; (saliva) saliva ♦ vi cuspir; (sound) escarrar.

spite [spaɪt] n rancor m, ressentimento ♦ vt contrariar; **in ~ of** apesar de, a despeito de.

spiteful ['spaɪtful] adj maldoso, malévolo.

spitting ['spɪtɪŋ] n: "~ prohibited" "proibido cuspir" ♦ adj: **to be the ~ image** of sb ser a imagem escarrada de alguém.

spittle ['spɪtl] n cuspe m.

spiv [spɪv] (BRIT: inf) n negocista m.

splash [splæʃ] n (sound) borrifo, respingo; (of colour) mancha ♦ vt: **to ~ (with)** salpicar (de) ♦ vi (also: ~ about) borrifar, respingar ♦ excl pluft.

splashdown ['splæʃdaun] n amerissagem f.

spleen [spliːn] n (ANAT) baço.

splendid ['splendɪd] adj esplêndido.

splendour ['splendə*] (US **splendor**) n esplendor m; (of achievement) pompa, glória.

splice [splaɪs] vt juntar.

splint [splɪnt] n tala.

splinter ['splɪntə*] n (of wood) lasca; (in finger) farpa ♦ vi lascar-se, estilhaçar-se, despedaçar-se.

splinter group n grupo dissidente.

split [splɪt] (pt, pp **split**) n fenda, brecha; (fig) rompimento; (POL) divisão f ♦ vt partir, fender; (party) dividir; (work, profits) rachar, repartir ♦ vi (divide) dividir-se, repartir-se; **the ~s** npl: **to do the ~s** abrir or fazer espaguete; **to ~ sth down the middle** partir algo ao meio; (fig) dividir algo (pela metade).

split up vi (couple) separar-se, acabar; (meeting) terminar.

split-level adj em vários níveis.

split peas npl ervilhas secas fpl.

split personality n dupla personalidade f.

split second n fração f de segundo.

splitting ['splɪtɪŋ] adj (headache) lancinante.

splutter ['splʌtə*] vi crepitar; (person) balbuciar, gaguejar.

spoil [spɔɪl] (pt, pp **spoilt** or ~**ed**) vt (damage) danificar; (mar) estragar, arruinar; (child) mimar; (ballot paper) violar ♦ vi: **to be ~ing for a fight** estar querendo comprar uma briga.

spoils [spɔɪlz] npl desojo, saque m.

spoilsport ['spɔɪlspɔːt] n desmancha-prazeres m/f inv.

spoilt [spɔɪlt] pt, pp of **spoil** ♦ adj (child) mimado; (ballot paper) violado.

spoke [spəuk] pt of **speak** ♦ n (of wheel) raio.

spoken ['spəukn] pp of **speak**.

spokesman ['spəuksmən] (irreg) n porta-voz m.

spokeswoman ['spəukswumən] (irreg) n porta-voz f.

sponge [spʌndʒ] n esponja; (cake) pão-de-ló m ♦ vt (wash) lavar com esponja ♦ vi: **to ~ on sb** viver às custas de alguém.

sponge bag (BRIT) n bolsa de toalete.

sponge cake n pão-de-ló m.

sponger ['spʌndʒə*] (pej) n parasito/a.

spongy ['spʌndʒɪ] adj esponjoso.

sponsor ['spɔnsə*] n (RADIO, TV) patrocinador(a) m/f; (for membership) padrinho/madrinha; (COMM) fiador(a) m/f, financiador(a) m/f ♦ vt patrocinar; apadrinhar; fiar; (idea etc) promover; **I ~ed him at 3p a mile** eu o patrocinei à razão de 3p por milha.

sponsorship ['spɔnsəʃɪp] n patrocínio.

spontaneity [spɔntə'neɪɪtɪ] n espontaneidade f.

spontaneous [spɔn'teɪnɪəs] adj espontâneo.

spooky ['spuːkɪ] adj arrepiante.

spool [spuːl] n carretel m; (of sewing machine) bobina, novelo.

spoon [spuːn] n colher f.

spoon-feed ['spuːnfiːd] (irreg) vt dar de comer com colher; (fig) dar tudo mastigado a.

spoonful ['spuːnful] n colherada.

sporadic [spə'rædɪk] adj esporádico.

sport [spɔːt] n esporte m (BR), desporto (PT); (person) bom/boa perdedor(a) m/f; **indoor/outdoor ~s** esportes de salão/ao ar livre; **to say sth in ~** dizer algo de brincadeira.

sporting ['spɔːtɪŋ] adj esportivo (BR), desportivo (PT).

sport jacket (US) n = **sports jacket**.

sports car n carro esporte (BR), carro de sport (PT).

sports ground n campo de esportes (BR) or de desportos (PT).

sports jacket n casaco esportivo (BR) or desportivo (PT).

sportsman ['spɔːtsmən] (irreg) n esportista m (BR), desportista m (PT).

sportsmanship ['spɔːtsmənʃɪp] n espírito esportivo (BR) or desportivo (PT).

sportsmen ['spɔːtsmen] npl of **sportsman**.

sports page n página de esportes.

sportswear ['spɔːtsweə*] n roupa esportiva (BR) or desportiva (PT) or esporte.

sportswoman ['spɔːtswumən] (irreg) n esportista (BR), desportista (PT).

sporty ['spɔːtɪ] adj esportivo (BR), desportivo (PT).

spot [spɔt] n (place) lugar m, local m; (dot: on pattern) mancha, ponto; (pimple) espinha; (freckle) sarda, pinta; (small amount): **a ~ of** um pouquinho de ♦ vt (notice) notar; **on the ~** (at once) na hora; (there) ali mesmo; (in difficulty) em apuros.

spot check n fiscalização f de surpresa.

spotless ['spɔtlɪs] adj sem mancha, imaculado.

spotlight ['spɔtlaɪt] n holofote m, refletor m.

spot-on (BRIT: inf) adj acertado em cheio.

spot price n preço à vista.

spotted ['spɔtɪd] adj (pattern) com bolinhas.

spotty ['spɔtɪ] adj (face) manchado.

spouse [spauz] *n* cônjuge *m/f*.

spout [spaut] *n* (*of jug*) bico; (*pipe*) cano ♦ *vi* jorrar.

sprain [spreɪn] *n* distensão *f*, torcedura ♦ *vt*: **to ~ one's ankle** torcer o tornozelo.

sprang [spræŋ] *pt of* **spring**.

sprawl [sprɔːl] *vi* esparramar-se ♦ *n*: **urban ~** crescimento urbano; **to send sb ~ing** jogar alguém no chão.

spray [spreɪ] *n* (*of sea*) borrifo; (*container*) spray *m*, atomizador *m*; (*of paint*) pistola borrifadora; (*of flowers*) ramalhete *m* ♦ *vt* pulverizar; (*crops*) borrifar, regar ♦ *cpd* (*deodorant etc*) em spray.

spread [sprɛd] (*pt*, *pp* **spread**) *n* extensão *f*; (*distribution*) expansão *f*, difusão *f*; (*PRESS*, *TYP*: *two pages*) chapada; (*CULIN*) pasta ♦ *vt* espalhar; (*butter*) untar, passar; (*wings*, *sails*) abrir, desdobrar; (*scatter*) disseminar; (*payments*) espaçar ♦ *vi* espalhar-se, alastrar-se, difundir-se.

spread-eagled [-'iːgld] *adj*: **to be** *or* **lie ~** estar estirado.

spreadsheet ['sprɛdʃiːt] *n* (*COMPUT*) planilha.

spree [spriː] *n*: **to go on a ~** cair na farra.

sprig [sprɪg] *n* raminho.

sprightly ['spraɪtlɪ] *adj* vivo, desembaraçado.

spring [sprɪŋ] (*pt* **sprang**, *pp* **sprung**) *n* (*leap*) salto, pulo; (*coiled metal*) mola; (*bounciness*) elasticidade *f*; (*season*) primavera; (*of water*) fonte *f* ♦ *vi* pular, saltar ♦ *vt*: **to ~ a leak** (*pipe etc*) furar; **he sprang the news on me** ele me pegou de surpresa com a notícia; **in ~, in the ~** na primavera; **to ~ from** provir de; **to ~ into action** partir para ação; **to walk with a ~ in one's step** andar espevitado.

    spring up *vi* nascer *or* aparecer de repente.

springboard ['sprɪŋbɔːd] *n* trampolim *m*.

spring-clean *n* (*also*: ~*ing*) limpeza total, faxina (geral).

spring onion (*BRIT*) *n* cebolinha.

springtime ['sprɪŋtaɪm] *n* primavera.

springy ['sprɪŋɪ] *adj* elástico, flexível.

sprinkle ['sprɪŋkl] *vt* (*pour*) salpicar, borrifar; **to ~ water on,** **~ with water** borrifar *or* salpicar de água; **~d with** (*fig*) salpicado *or* polvilhado de.

sprinkler ['sprɪŋklə*] *n* (*for lawn etc*) regador *m*; (*to put out fire*) sprinkler *m*.

sprinkling ['sprɪŋklɪŋ] *n* (*of water*) borrifo; (*of salt*) pitada; (*of sugar*) bocado.

sprint [sprɪnt] *n* corrida de pequena distância ♦ *vi* correr a toda velocidade.

sprinter ['sprɪntə*] *n* corredor(a) *m/f*.

sprite [spraɪt] *n* duende *m*, elfo.

sprocket ['sprɔkɪt] *n* (*on printer etc*) dente *m* (de roda).

sprout [spraut] *vi* brotar, germinar.

sprouts [sprauts] *npl* (*also*: **Brussels ~**) couves-de-Bruxelas *fpl*.

spruce [spruːs] *n* (*BOT*) abeto ♦ *adj* arrumado,

limpo, elegante.

    spruce up *vt* arrumar; **to ~ o.s. up** arrumar-se.

sprung [sprʌŋ] *pp of* **spring**.

spry [spraɪ] *adj* vivo, ativo, ágil.

SPUC *n abbr* = **Society for the Protection of Unborn Children**.

spud [spʌd] (*inf*) *n* batata.

spun [spʌn] *pt*, *pp of* **spin**.

spur [spə:*] *n* espora; (*fig*) estímulo ♦ *vt* (*also*: ~ *on*) incitar, estimular; **on the ~ of the moment** de improviso, de repente.

spurious ['spjuərɪəs] *adj* espúrio, falso.

spurn [spə:n] *vt* desdenhar, desprezar.

spurt [spə:t] *n* (*of energy*) acesso; (*of water*) jorro ♦ *vi* (*water*) jorrar; **to put in** *or* **on a ~** (*runner*) dar uma arrancada; (*fig*: *in work etc*) dar uma virada.

sputter ['spʌtə*] *vi* crepitar; (*person*) balbuciar, gaguejar.

spy [spaɪ] *n* espião/espiã *m/f* ♦ *vi*: **to ~ on** espiar, espionar ♦ *vt* (*see*) enxergar, avistar ♦ *cpd* (*film*, *story*) de espionagem.

spying ['spaɪɪŋ] *n* espionagem *f*.

Sq. *abbr* (*in address*) = **square**.

sq. *abbr* (*MATH etc*) = **square**.

squabble ['skwɔbl] *n* briga, bate-boca *m* ♦ *vi* brigar, discutir.

squad [skwɔd] *n* (*MIL*, *POLICE*) pelotão *m*, esquadra; (*FOOTBALL*) seleção *f*; **flying ~** (*POLICE*) polícia de prontidão.

squad car (*BRIT*) *n* (*POLICE*) radiopatrulha.

squadron ['skwɔdrən] *n* (*MIL*) esquadrão *m*; (*AVIAT*) esquadrilha; (*NAUT*) esquadra.

squalid ['skwɔlɪd] *adj* sórdido.

squall [skwɔːl] *n* (*storm*) tempestade *f*; (*wind*) pé *m* (de vento), rajada.

squalor ['skwɔlə*] *n* sordidez *f*.

squander ['skwɔndə*] *vt* (*money*) esbanjar, dissipar; (*chances*) desperdiçar.

square [skwɛə*] *n* quadrado; (*in town*) praça; (*MATH*: *instrument*) esquadro ♦ *adj* quadrado; (*inf*: *ideas*, *tastes*) careta, antiquado ♦ *vt* (*arrange*) ajustar, acertar; (*MATH*) elevar ao quadrado ♦ *vi* (*agree*) ajustar-se; **all ~** igual, quite; **a ~ meal** uma refeição substancial; **2 metres ~** um quadrado de dois metros de lado; **1 ~ metre** um metro quadrado; **we're back to ~ one** voltamos à estaca zero.

    square up (*BRIT*) *vi* (*settle*) ajustar; **to ~ up with sb** acertar as contas com alguém.

square bracket *n* (*TYP*) colchete *m*.

squarely ['skwɛəlɪ] *adv* em forma quadrada; (*fully*) em cheio.

square root *n* raiz *f* quadrada.

squash [skwɔʃ] *n* (*BRIT*: *drink*): **lemon/ orange ~** suco (*BR*) *or* sumo (*PT*) de limão/ laranja; (*SPORT*) squash *m*; (*vegetable*) abóbora ♦ *vt* esmagar; **to ~ together** apinhar.

squat [skwɔt] *adj* agachado; (*short*) atarracado ♦ *vi* agachar-se, acocorar-se; (*on property etc*) ocupar ilegalmente.

NB: European Portuguese adds the following consonants to certain words: **b** (sú(b)dito, su(b)til); **c** (a(c)ção, a(c)cionista, a(c)to); **m** (inde(m)ne); **p** (ado(p)ção, ado(p)tar); *for further details see p. xiii.*

squatter ['skwɔtə*] n posseiro/a.
squawk [skwɔːk] vi grasnar.
squeak [skwiːk] n grunhido, chiado; (of shoe) rangido; (of mouse) guincho ♦ vi grunhir, chiar; ranger; guinchar.
squeal [skwiːl] vi guinchar, gritar agudamente; (inf: inform) delatar.
squeamish ['skwiːmɪʃ] adj melindroso, delicado.
squeeze [skwiːz] n aperto, compressão f; (of hand) apertão m; (in bus etc) apinhamento; (also: credit ~) arrocho (ao crédito) ♦ vt comprimir, socar; (hand, arm) apertar ♦ vi: **to ~ past/under sth** espremer-se para passar algo/para passar por baixo de algo; **a ~ of lemon** umas gotas de limão.
squeeze out vt espremer; (fig) extorquir.
squelch [skwɛltʃ] vi fazer ruído de passos na lama.
squib [skwɪb] n busca-pé m.
squid [skwɪd] (pl inv or ~s) n lula.
squiggle ['skwɪgl] n garatuja.
squint [skwɪnt] vi olhar or ser vesgo ♦ n (MED) estrabismo; **to ~ at sth** olhar algo de soslaio or de esguelha.
squire ['skwaɪə*] (BRIT) n proprietário rural.
squirm [skwəːm] vi retorcer-se.
squirrel ['skwɪrəl] n esquilo.
squirt [skwəːt] vi jorrar, esguichar.
Sr abbr = senior; (REL) = sister.
SRC (BRIT) n abbr = Students' Representative Council.
Sri Lanka [srɪ'læŋkə] n Sri Lanka m.
SRN (BRIT) n abbr = State Registered Nurse.
SRO (US) abbr = standing room only.
SS abbr = steamship.
SSA (US) abbr = Social Security Administration.
SST (US) abbr = supersonic transport.
ST (US) abbr = Standard Time.
St abbr (= saint) S.; = street.
stab [stæb] n (with knife etc) punhalada; (of pain) pontada; (inf: try): **to have a ~ at (doing) sth** tentar (fazer) algo ♦ vt apunhalar; **to ~ sb to death** matar alguém a facadas, esfaquear alguém.
stabbing ['stæbɪŋ] n: **there's been a ~** houve um esfaqueamento ♦ adj (pain) cortante.
stability [stə'bɪlɪtɪ] n estabilidade f.
stabilization [steɪbəlaɪ'zeɪʃən] n estabilização f.
stabilize ['steɪbəlaɪz] vt estabilizar ♦ vi estabilizar-se.
stabilizer ['steɪbəlaɪzə*] n estabilizador m.
stable ['steɪbl] adj estável ♦ n estábulo, cavalariça; **riding ~s** clube m de equitação.
staccato [stə'kɑːtəu] adv destacado, staccato ♦ adj (MUS) destacado, staccato; (noise) interrupto; (voice) quebrado.
stack [stæk] n montão m, pilha ♦ vt amontoar, empilhar; **there's ~s of time** (BRIT: inf) tem tempo de sobra.
stadium ['steɪdɪəm] n estádio.
staff [stɑːf] n (work force) pessoal m, quadro; (BRIT: SCH: also: teaching ~) corpo docente;

(stick) cajado, bastão m ♦ vt prover de pessoal; **the office is ~ed by women** o escritório está composto de mulheres.
staffroom ['stɑːfruːm] n sala dos professores.
Staffs (BRIT) abbr = Staffordshire.
stag [stæg] n veado, cervo.
stage [steɪdʒ] n (in theatre) palco, cena; (point) etapa, fase f; (platform) plataforma, estrado; (profession): **the ~** o palco, o teatro ♦ vt (play) pôr em cena, representar; (demonstration) montar, organizar; (fig: perform: recovery etc) realizar; **in ~s** por etapas; **to go through a difficult ~** passar por uma fase difícil; **in the early/final ~s** na fase inicial/final.
stagecoach ['steɪdʒkəutʃ] n diligência.
stage door n entrada dos artistas.
stage fright n medo da platéia.
stagehand ['steɪdʒhænd] n ajudante m/f de teatro.
stage-manage vt (fig) orquestrar.
stage manager n diretor(a) m/f de cena.
stagger ['stægə*] vi cambalear ♦ vt (amaze) surpreender, chocar; (hours, holidays) escalonar.
staggering ['stægərɪŋ] adj (amazing) surpreendente, chocante.
stagnant ['stægnənt] adj estagnado.
stagnate [stæg'neɪt] vi estagnar.
stagnation [stæg'neɪʃən] n estagnação f.
stag party n despedida de solteiro.
staid [steɪd] adj sério, sóbrio.
stain [steɪn] n mancha; (colouring) tinta, tintura ♦ vt manchar; (wood) tingir.
stained glass window [steɪnd-] n janela com vitral.
stainless ['steɪnlɪs] adj (steel) inoxidável.
stain remover n tira-manchas m.
stair [stɛə*] n (step) degrau m; **~s** npl escada.
staircase ['stɛəkeɪs] n escadaria, escada.
stairway ['stɛəweɪ] n escadaria, escada.
stairwell ['stɛəwel] n caixa de escada.
stake [steɪk] n estaca, poste m; (BETTING) aposta ♦ vt apostar; **to be at ~** estar em jogo; **to have a ~ in sth** ter interesse em algo; **to ~ a claim to sth** reivindicar algo.
stalactite ['stæləktaɪt] n estalactite f.
stalagmite ['stæləgmaɪt] n estalagmite f.
stale [steɪl] adj (bread) amanhecido; (food) passado, estragado.
stalemate ['steɪlmeɪt] n empate m; (fig) impasse m, beco sem saída.
stalk [stɔːk] n caule m, talo, haste f ♦ vt caçar de tocaia; **to ~ off** andar com arrogância.
stall [stɔːl] n (in market) barraca; (in stable) baia ♦ vt (AUT) fazer morrer ♦ vi (AUT) morrer; (fig) esquivar-se, ganhar tempo; **~s** npl (BRIT: in cinema, theatre) platéia; **a newspaper/flower ~** uma banca de jornais/ uma barraca de flores.
stallholder ['stɔːlhəuldə*] n feirante m/f.
stallion ['stæljən] n garanhão m.
stalwart ['stɔːlwət] adj (in build) robusto; (in spirit) leal, firme ♦ n partidário leal.
stamen ['steɪmən] n estame m.

stamina ['stæmɪnə] n resistência.
stammer ['stæmə*] n gagueira ♦ vi gaguejar, balbuciar.
stamp [stæmp] n selo; (mark, also fig) marca, impressão f; (on document) timbre m, sinete m ♦ vi (also: ~ one's foot) bater com o pé ♦ vt (letter) selar; (with rubber ~) carimbar; ~ed addressed envelope envelope m selado e sobrescritado.
stamp out vt (fire) apagar com os pés; (crime) eliminar; (opposition) esmagar.
stamp album n álbum m de selos.
stamp collecting [-kə'lektɪŋ] n filatelia.
stamp duty (BRIT) n imposto de selo.
stampede [stæm'piːd] n debandada, estouro (da boiada).
stamp machine n máquina de selos.
stance [stæns] n postura, posição f.
stand [stænd] (pt, pp stood) n (position) posição f, postura; (for taxis) ponto; (also: hall ~) pedestal m; (also: music ~) estante f; (SPORT) tribuna, palanque m; (also: news ~) banca de jornais ♦ vi (be) estar, encontrar-se; (be on foot) estar em pé; (rise) levantar-se; (remain) ficar em pé ♦ vt (place) pôr, colocar; (tolerate, withstand) agüentar, suportar; (cost) pagar; to make a ~ resistir; (fig) ater-se a um princípio; to take a ~ on an issue tomar posição definida sobre um assunto; to ~ for parliament (BRIT) apresentar-se como candidato ao parlamento; to ~ guard or watch (MIL) montar guarda; it ~s to reason é lógico; as things ~ como as coisas estão; to ~ sb a drink/meal pagar uma bebida/refeição para alguém; I can't ~ him não o agüento; to ~ still ficar parado.
stand aside vi pôr-se de lado.
stand by vi (be ready) estar a postos ♦ vt fus (opinion) aferrar-se a.
stand down vi (withdraw) retirar-se; (MIL) deixar o serviço.
stand for vt fus (defend) apoiar; (signify) significar; (tolerate) tolerar, permitir.
stand in for vt fus substituir.
stand out vi (be prominent) destacar-se.
stand up vi (rise) levantar-se.
stand up for vt fus defender.
stand up to vt fus enfrentar.
stand-alone adj (COMPUT) autônomo, stand-alone.
standard ['stændəd] n padrão m, critério; (flag) estandarte m; (level) nível m ♦ adj (size etc) padronizado, regular, normal; ~s npl (morals) valores mpl morais; to be or come up to ~ alcançar os padrões exigidos; to apply a double ~ ter dois pesos e duas medidas; ~ of living padrão de vida; the gold ~ (COMM) o padrão ouro.
standardization [stændədaɪ'zeɪʃən] n padronização f.
standardize ['stændədaɪz] vt padronizar.
standard lamp (BRIT) n abajur m de pé.

standard time n hora legal or oficial.
stand-by adj de reserva; (ticket, passenger) stand-by ♦ n: to be on ~ estar de sobreaviso or de prontidão.
stand-in n suplente m/f; (CINEMA) dublê m/f.
standing ['stændɪŋ] adj (upright) ereto vertical; (on foot) em pé; (permanent) permanente ♦ n posição f, reputação f; of 6 months' ~ de 6 meses de duração; of many years' ~ de muitos anos; he was given a ~ ovation ele foi ovacionado; it's a ~ joke é uma piada famosa; a man of some ~ um homem de posição.
standing order n (at bank) instrução f permanente; ~s npl (MIL) regulamento geral.
standing room n lugar m em pé.
stand-offish [-'ɔfɪʃ] adj incomunicativo, reservado.
standpat ['stændpæt] (US) adj inflexível, conservador(a).
standpipe ['stændpaɪp] n tubo de subida.
standpoint ['stændpɔɪnt] n ponto de vista.
standstill ['stændstɪl] n: at a ~ paralisado, parado; to come to a ~ (car) parar; (factory, traffic) ficar paralisado.
stank [stæŋk] pt of **stink**.
stanza ['stænzə] n estância, estrofe f.
staple ['steɪpl] n (for papers) grampo; (chief product) produto básico ♦ adj (food etc) básico ♦ vt grampear.
stapler ['steɪplə*] n grampeador m.
star [stɑː*] n estrela; (celebrity) astro/estrela ♦ vi: to ~ in ser a estrela em, estrelar ♦ vt (CINEMA) ser estrelado por; 4-~ hotel hotel 4 estrelas; 2-~ petrol gasolina simples (BR) or normal (PT); 4-~ petrol (BRIT) (gasolina) azul (BR) or súper (PT).
star attraction n atração f principal.
starboard ['stɑːbəd] n estibordo; to ~ a estibordo.
starch [stɑːtʃ] n (in food) amido, fécula; (for clothes) goma.
starched ['stɑːtʃt] adj (collar) engomado.
starchy ['stɑːtʃɪ] adj amiláceo.
stardom ['stɑːdəm] n estrelato.
stare [stɛə*] n olhar m fixo ♦ vi: to ~ at olhar fixamente, fitar.
starfish ['stɑːfɪʃ] n inv estrela-do-mar f.
stark [stɑːk] adj (bleak) severo, áspero; (colour) sóbrio; (reality, truth, simplicity) cru; (contrast) gritante ♦ adv: ~ naked completamente nu, em pêlo.
starlet ['stɑːlɪt] n (CINEMA) vedete f.
starlight ['stɑːlaɪt] n: by ~ à luz das estrelas.
starling ['stɑːlɪŋ] n estorninho.
starlit ['stɑːlɪt] adj iluminado pelas estrelas.
starry ['stɑːrɪ] adj estrelado.
starry-eyed (innocent) deslumbrado.
star-studded [-'stʌdɪd] adj: a ~ cast um elenco cheio de estrelas.
start [stɑːt] n (beginning) princípio, começo; (departure) partida; (sudden movement) so-

NB: European Portuguese adds the following consonants to certain words: **b** (sú(b)dito, su(b)til); **c** (a(c)ção, a(c)cionista, a(c)to); **m** (inde(m)ne); **p** (ado(p)ção, ado(p)tar); for further details see p. xiii.

bressalto, susto; (*advantage*) vantagem *f* ♦ *vt* começar, iniciar; (*cause*) causar; (*found*) fundar; (*engine*) ligar; (*fire*) provocar ♦ *vi* (*begin*) começar, iniciar; (*with fright*) sobressaltar-se, assustar-se; (*train etc*) sair; **to ~ doing sth** começar a fazer algo; **at the ~** no início; **for a ~** para início de conversa; **to make an early ~** sair *or* começar cedo; **to ~ (off) with ...** (*firstly*) para começar ...; (*at the beginning*) no início ...; **to give sb a ~** dar um susto em alguém.

start off *vi* começar, principiar; (*leave*) sair, pôr-se a caminho.

start over (*US*) *vi* começar de novo.

start up *vi* começar; (*car*) pegar, pôr-se em marcha ♦ *vt* começar; (*car*) ligar.

starter ['stɑːtə*] *n* (*AUT*) arranque *m*; (*SPORT*: *official*) juiz(a) *m/f* da partida; (: *runner*) corredor(a) *m/f*; (*BRIT*: *CULIN*) entrada.

starting handle ['stɑːtɪŋ-] (*BRIT*) *n* manivela de arranque.

starting point ['stɑːtɪŋ-] *n* ponto de partida.

starting price ['stɑːtɪŋ-] *n* preço inicial.

startle ['stɑːtl] *vt* assustar, aterrar.

startling ['stɑːtlɪŋ] *adj* surpreendente.

star turn (*BRIT*) *n* rei *m*/rainha *f* do show.

starvation [stɑːˈveɪʃən] *n* fome *f*; (*MED*) inanição *f*.

starve ['stɑːv] *vi* passar fome; (*to death*) morrer de fome ♦ *vt* fazer passar fome; (*fig*): **to ~ (of)** privar (*of* de); **I'm starving** estou morrendo de fome.

starving ['stɑːvɪŋ] *adj* faminto, esfomeado.

state [steɪt] *n* estado; (*pomp*): **in ~** com grande pompa ♦ *vt* (*say, declare*) afirmar, declarar; (*a case*) expor, apresentar; **the S~s** *npl* os Estados Unidos; **to be in a ~** estar agitado; **~ of emergency** estado de emergência; **~ of mind** estado de espírito; **the ~ of the art** a última palavra; **to lie in ~** estar exposto em câmara ardente.

State Department (*US*) *n* Departamento de Estado, ≈ Ministério das Relações Exteriores.

state education (*BRIT*) *n* educação *f* pública.

stateless ['steɪtlɪs] *adj* desnacionalizado.

stately ['steɪtlɪ] *adj* majestoso, imponente.

statement ['steɪtmənt] *n* afirmação *f*; (*LAW*) depoimento *m*; (*ECON*) balanço; **official ~** comunicado oficial; **~ of account** extrato de conta, extrato bancário.

state-owned [-əʊnd] *adj* estatal.

state secret *n* segredo de estado.

statesman ['steɪtsmən] (*irreg*) *n* estadista *m*.

statesmanship ['steɪtsmənʃɪp] *n* arte *f* de governar.

statesmen ['steɪtsmɛn] *npl of* **statesman**.

static ['stætɪk] *n* (*RADIO*) interferência; (*also*: **~ electricity**) (eletricidade *f*) estática ♦ *adj* estático.

station ['steɪʃən] *n* estação *f*; (*place*) posto, lugar *m*; (*POLICE*) delegacia; (*RADIO*) emissora; (*rank*) posição *f* social ♦ *vt* colocar; **to be ~ed in** (*MIL*) estar estacionado em.

stationary ['steɪʃnərɪ] *adj* estacionário.

stationer's (shop) ['steɪʃənəz-] *n* papelaria.

stationery ['steɪʃnərɪ] *n* artigos *mpl* de papelaria; (*writing paper*) papel *m* de carta.

station master *n* (*RAIL*) chefe *m* da estação.

station wagon (*US*) *n* perua (*BR*), canadiana (*PT*).

statistic [stəˈtɪstɪk] *n* estatística; **~s** *n* (*science*) estatística.

statistical [stəˈtɪstɪkl] *adj* estatístico.

statue ['stætjuː] *n* estátua.

statuesque [stætjuˈɛsk] *adj* escultural.

statuette [stætjuˈɛt] *n* estatueta.

stature ['stætʃə*] *n* estatura, altura; (*fig*) estatura, envergadura.

status ['steɪtəs] *n* posição *f*, categoria; (*reputation*) reputação *f*, status *m*; (*ADMIN*: *also*: **marital ~**) estado civil.

status quo [-kwəʊ] *n*: **the ~** o status quo.

status symbol *n* símbolo de prestígio.

statute ['stætjuːt] *n* estatuto, lei *f*; **~s** *npl* (*of club etc*) estatuto.

statute book *n* ≈ Código.

statutory ['stætjʊtərɪ] *adj* (*according to statutes*) estatutário; (*holiday etc*) regulamentar.

staunch [stɔːntʃ] *adj* firme, constante ♦ *vt* estancar.

stave [steɪv] *n* (*MUS*) pauta.

stave off *vt* (*attack*) repelir; (*threat*) evitar, protelar.

stay [steɪ] *n* (*period of time*) estadia, estada; (*LAW*): **~ of execution** adiamento de execução ♦ *vi* (*remain*) ficar; (*as guest*) hospedar-se; (*spend some time*) demorar-se; **to ~ put** não se mexer; **to ~ the night** pernoitar.

stay behind *vi* ficar atrás.

stay in *vi* (*at home*) ficar em casa.

stay on *vi* ficar.

stay out *vi* (*of house*) ficar fora de casa; (*strikers*) continuar em greve.

stay up *vi* (*at night*) velar, ficar acordado.

staying power ['steɪɪŋ-] *n* resistência, raça.

STD *n abbr* (*BRIT*: = *subscriber trunk dialling*) DDD *f*; (= *sexually transmitted disease*) DST *f*.

stead [stɛd] (*BRIT*) *n*: **in sb's ~** em lugar de alguém; **to stand sb in good ~** prestar bons serviços a alguém.

steadfast ['stɛdfɑːst] *adj* firme, estável, resoluto.

steadily ['stɛdɪlɪ] *adv* (*firmly*) firmemente; (*unceasingly*) sem parar, constantemente; (*drive*) a uma velocidade constante.

steady ['stɛdɪ] *adj* (*constant*) constante, fixo; (*unswerving*) firme; (*regular*) regular; (*person, character*) sensato, equilibrado; (*diligent*) diligente; (*boyfriend, job etc*) firme, estável; (*calm*) calmo, sereno ♦ *vt* (*hold*) manter firme; (*stabilize*) estabilizar; (*nerves*) acalmar; **to ~ o.s. on** *or* **against sth** firmar-se em algo.

steak [steɪk] *n* filé *m*; (*beef*) bife *m*.

steakhouse ['steɪkhaʊs] (*irreg*) *n* ≈ churrascaria.

steal [stiːl] (*pt* **stole**, *pp* **stolen**) *vt*, *vi* roubar.

steal away *vi* sair às escondidas.

steal off *vi* sair às escondidas.

stealth [stɛlθ] *n*: **by ~** furtivamente, às escondidas.

stealthy ['stɛlθɪ] *adj* furtivo.

steam [stiːm] *n* vapor *m* ♦ *vt* (*CULIN*) cozinhar no vapor ♦ *vi* fumegar; (*ship*): **to ~ along** avançar *or* mover-se (a vapor); **under one's own ~** (*fig*) por esforço próprio; **to run out of ~** (*fig: person*) perder o pique; **to let off ~** (*fig: inf*) desabafar.

steam up *vi* (*window*) embaçar; **to get ~ed up about sth** irritar-se com algo.

steam engine *n* máquina a vapor.

steamer ['stiːmə*] *n* vapor *m*, navio (a vapor).

steam iron *n* ferro a vapor.

steamroller ['stiːmrəʊlə*] *n* rolo compressor (a vapor).

steamy ['stiːmɪ] *adj* vaporoso; (*room*) cheio de vapor, úmido (*PT*: hu-).

steed [stiːd] *n* (*literary*) corcel *m*.

steel [stiːl] *n* aço ♦ *cpd* de aço.

steel band *n* banda de percussão do Caribe.

steel industry *n* indústria siderúrgica.

steel mill *n* (usina) siderúrgica.

steelworks ['stiːlwɜːks] *n* (usina) siderúrgica.

steely ['stiːlɪ] *adj* (*determination*) inflexível; (*gaze, eyes*) duro, frio; **~-grey** cor de aço *inv*.

steep [stiːp] *adj* íngreme, escarpado; (*stair*) empinado; (*price*) exorbitante ♦ *vt* ensopar, embeber, impregnar.

steeple ['stiːpl] *n* campanário, torre *f*.

steeplechase ['stiːpltʃeɪs] *n* corrida de obstáculos.

steeplejack ['stiːpldʒæk] *n* consertador *m* de torres *or* de chaminés altas.

steeply ['stiːplɪ] *adv* escarpadamente, a pique.

steer [stɪə*] *n* boi *m* ♦ *vt* guiar, dirigir, pilotar ♦ *vi* conduzir; **to ~ clear of sb/sth** (*fig*) evitar alguém/algo.

steering ['stɪərɪŋ] *n* (*AUT*) direção *f*.

steering column *n* (*AUT*) coluna da direção.

steering committee *n* comitê *m* dirigente.

steering wheel *n* volante *m*.

stellar ['stɛlə*] *adj* estelar.

stem [stɛm] *n* (*of plant*) caule *m*, haste *f*; (*of glass*) pé *m*; (*of pipe*) tubo ♦ *vt* deter, reter; (*blood*) estancar.

stem from *vt fus* originar-se de.

stench [stɛntʃ] *n* fedor *m*.

stencil ['stɛnsl] *n* (*typed*) estêncil *m*; (*lettering*) gabarito de letra ♦ *vt* imprimir com estêncil.

stenographer [stɛ'nɔɡrəfə*] (*US*) *n* estenógrafo/a.

stenography [stɛ'nɔɡrəfɪ] (*US*) *n* estenografia.

step [stɛp] *n* passo; (*stair*) degrau *m*; (*action*) medida, providência ♦ *vi*: **to ~ forward** avançar, dar um passo em frente; **~s** *npl* (*BRIT*) escada portátil *or* de abrir; **to ~ on** pisar, calcar; **~ by ~** passo a passo; **to be in ~ (with)** (*fig*) manter a paridade (com);

to be out of ~ (with) (*fig*) estar em disparidade (com); **to take ~s** tomar providências.

step down *vi* (*fig*) retirar-se.

step in *vi* (*fig*) intervir.

step off *vt fus* descer de.

step over *vt fus* passar por cima de.

step up *vt* (*increase*) aumentar; (*intensify*) intensificar.

stepbrother ['stɛpbrʌðə*] *n* meio-irmão *m*.

stepchild ['stɛptʃaɪld] (*irreg*) *n* enteado/a.

stepdaughter ['stɛpdɔːtə*] *n* enteada.

stepfather ['stɛpfɑːðə*] *n* padrasto.

stepladder ['stɛplædə*] (*BRIT*) *n* escada portátil *or* de abrir.

stepmother ['stɛpmʌðə*] *n* madrasta.

stepping stone ['stɛpɪŋ-] *n* pedra utilizada em passarelas; (*fig*) trampolim *m*.

stepsister ['stɛpsɪstə*] *n* meia-irmã *f*.

stepson ['stɛpsʌn] *n* enteado.

stereo ['stɛrɪəʊ] *n* estéreo; (*record player*) (aparelho de) som *m* ♦ *adj* (*also*: ~phonic) estereofônico; **in ~** em estéreo.

stereotype ['stɪərɪətaɪp] *n* estereótipo ♦ *vt* estereotipar.

sterile ['stɛraɪl] *adj* estéril.

sterility [stɛ'rɪlɪtɪ] *n* esterilidade *f*.

sterilization [stɛrɪlaɪ'zeɪʃən] *n* esterilização *f*.

sterilize ['stɛrɪlaɪz] *vt* esterilizar.

sterling ['stɜːlɪŋ] *adj* esterlino; (*silver*) de lei; (*fig*) genuíno, puro ♦ *n* (*currency*) libra esterlina; **a pound ~** uma libra esterlina.

sterling area *n* zona esterlina.

stern [stɜːn] *adj* severo, austero ♦ *n* (*NAUT*) popa, ré *f*.

sternum ['stɜːnəm] *n* esterno.

steroid ['stɪərɔɪd] *n* esteróide *m*.

stethoscope ['stɛθəskəʊp] *n* estetoscópio.

stevedore ['stiːvədɔː*] *n* estivador *m*.

stew [stjuː] *n* guisado, ensopado ♦ *vt, vi* guisar, ensopar; (*fruit*) cozinhar; **~ed tea** chá muito forte; **~ed fruit** compota de frutas.

steward ['stjuːəd] *n* (*AVIAT*) comissário de bordo; (*also*: *shop* ~) delegado/a sindical.

stewardess ['stjuːədɪs] *n* aeromoça (*BR*), hospedeira de bordo (*PT*).

stewing steak ['stjuːɪŋ-] (*US* **stew meat**) *n* carne *f* para ensopado.

St. Ex. *abbr* = **stock exchange**.

stg *abbr* = **sterling**.

stick [stɪk] (*pt, pp* **stuck**) *n* pau *m*; (*as weapon*) cacete *m*; (*walking* ~) bengala, cajado ♦ *vt* (*glue*) colar; (*thrust*): **to ~ sth into** cravar *or* enfiar algo em; (*inf: put*) meter; (*tolerate*) agüentar, suportar ♦ *vi* colar-se, aderir-se; (*get jammed*) emperrar; (*in mind etc*) gravar-se; **to get hold of the wrong end of the ~** (*BRIT: fig*) confundir-se; **to ~ to** (*promise, principles*) manter.

stick around (*inf*) *vi* ficar.

stick out *vi* estar saliente, projetar-se ♦ *vt*: **to ~ it out** (*inf*) agüentar firme.

stick up *vi* estar saliente, projetar-se.

NB: *European Portuguese adds the following consonants to certain words:* **b** (sú(b)dito, su(b)til); **c** (a(c)ção, a(c)cionista, a(c)to); **m** (inde(m)ne); **p** (ado(p)ção, ado(p)tar); *for further details see p. xiii.*

stick up for vt fus defender.
sticker ['stɪkə*] n adesivo.
sticking plaster ['stɪkɪŋ-] n esparadrapo.
stickleback ['stɪklbæk] n espinhela.
stickler ['stɪklə*] n: **to be a ~ for** insistir em, exigir.
stick-on adj adesivo.
stick-up (inf) n assalto a mão armada.
sticky ['stɪkɪ] adj pegajoso; (label) adesivo; (fig) espinhoso.
stiff [stɪf] adj rígido; (strong) forte; (hard) duro; (difficult) difícil; (door) empenado; **to be or feel ~** (person) ter dores musculares; **to have a ~ neck** estar com torcicolo; **~ upper lip** (BRIT: fig) fleuma britânica.
stiffen ['stɪfən] vt endurecer; (limb) entumecer ♦ vi enrijecer-se; (grow stronger) fortalecer-se.
stiffness ['stɪfnɪs] n rigidez f.
stifle ['staɪfl] vt sufocar, abafar.
stifling ['staɪflɪŋ] adj (heat) sufocante, abafado.
stigma ['stɪgmə] (pl ~ta) n (BOT, MED, REL) estigma m; (pl: ~s: fig) estigma m.
stigmata [stɪg'mɑːtə] npl of **stigma**.
stile [staɪl] n degraus para passar por uma cerca ou muro.
stiletto [stɪ'lɛtəu] (BRIT) n (also: ~ heel) salto alto e fino.
still [stɪl] adj (motionless) imóvel; (calm) quieto; (BRIT: orange drink etc) sem gás ♦ adv (up to this time) ainda; (even) ainda; (nonetheless) entretanto, contudo ♦ n (CINEMA) still m; **to stand ~** ficar parado; **keep ~!** não se mexa!; **he ~ hasn't arrived** ele ainda não chegou.
stillborn ['stɪlbɔːn] adj nascido morto, natimorto.
still life n natureza morta.
stilt [stɪlt] n perna de pau; (pile) estaca, suporte m.
stilted ['stɪltɪd] adj afetado.
stimulant ['stɪmjulənt] n estimulante m.
stimulate ['stɪmjuleɪt] vt estimular.
stimulating ['stɪmjuleɪtɪŋ] adj estimulante.
stimulation [stɪmju'leɪʃən] n estimulação f.
stimuli ['stɪmjulaɪ] npl of **stimulus**.
stimulus ['stɪmjuləs] (pl **stimuli**) n estímulo, incentivo.
sting [stɪŋ] (pt, pp **stung**) n (wound) picada; (pain) ardência; (of insect) ferrão m; (inf: confidence trick) conto-do-vigário ♦ vt picar ♦ vi arder.
stingy ['stɪndʒɪ] adj pão-duro, sovina.
stink [stɪŋk] (pt **stank**, pp **stunk**) n fedor m, catinga ♦ vi feder, cheirar mal.
stinker ['stɪŋkə*] (inf) n (problem, person) osso duro de roer.
stinking ['stɪŋkɪŋ] adj fedorento, fétido; **~ rich** ricaço.
stint [stɪnt] n tarefa, parte f ♦ vi: **to ~ on** ser parco com; **to do one's ~** fazer a sua parte.
stipend ['staɪpɛnd] n (of vicar etc) estipêndio, remuneração f.
stipendiary [staɪ'pɛndɪərɪ] adj: **~ magistrate**

juiz/juíza m/f estipendiário/a.
stipulate ['stɪpjuleɪt] vt estipular.
stipulation [stɪpju'leɪʃən] n estipulação f, cláusula.
stir [stəː*] n (fig: agitation) comoção f, rebuliço ♦ vt (tea etc) mexer; (fig: emotions) comover ♦ vi mover-se, remexer-se; **to give sth a ~** mexer algo; **to cause a ~** causar sensação or um rebuliço.
stir up vt excitar; (trouble) provocar.
stirring ['stəːrɪŋ] adj comovedor(a).
stirrup ['stɪrəp] n estribo.
stitch [stɪtʃ] n (SEWING, KNITTING, MED) ponto; (pain) pontada ♦ vt costurar; (MED) dar pontos em, suturar.
stoat [stəut] n arminho.
stock [stɔk] n (COMM: reserves) estoque m, provisão f; (: selection) sortimento; (AGR) gado; (CULIN) caldo; (fig: lineage) estirpe f, linhagem f; (FINANCE) valores mpl, títulos mpl; (: shares) ações fpl; (RAIL: also: rolling ~) material m circulante ♦ adj (fig: reply etc) de sempre, costumeiro; (: greeting) habitual ♦ vt (have in ~) ter em estoque, estocar; (sell) vender; **well-~ed** bem sortido; **in ~** em estoque; **out of ~** esgotado; **to take ~** (fig) fazer um balanço; **~s and shares** valores e títulos mobiliários; **government ~** títulos do governo, fundos públicos.
stock up vi: **to ~ up with** abastecer-se de.
stockade [stɔ'keɪd] n estacada.
stockbroker ['stɔkbrəukə*] n corretor(a) m/f de valores or da Bolsa.
stock control n (COMM) controle m de estoque.
stock cube (BRIT) n (CULIN) cubo de caldo.
stock exchange n Bolsa de Valores.
stockholder ['stɔkhəuldə*] (US) n acionista m/f.
Stockholm ['stɔkhəum] n Estocolmo.
stocking ['stɔkɪŋ] n meia.
stock-in-trade n (tool) instrumento de trabalho; (fig) arma.
stockist ['stɔkɪst] (BRIT) n estoquista m/f.
stock market n Bolsa, mercado de valores.
stock phrase n frase f feita.
stockpile ['stɔkpaɪl] n reservas fpl, estocagem f ♦ vt acumular reservas de, estocar.
stockroom ['stɔkruːm] n almoxarifado.
stocktaking ['stɔkteɪkɪŋ] (BRIT) n (COMM) inventário.
stocky ['stɔkɪ] adj (strong) robusto; (short) atarracado.
stodgy ['stɔdʒɪ] adj pesado.
stoic ['stəuɪk] n estóico/a.
stoical ['stəuɪkəl] adj estóico.
stoke [stəuk] vt atiçar, alimentar.
stoker ['stəukə*] n (RAIL, NAUT etc) foguista m.
stole [stəul] pt of **steal** ♦ n estola.
stolen ['stəuln] pp of **steal**.
stomach ['stʌmək] n (ANAT) estômago; (belly) barriga, ventre m ♦ vt suportar, tolerar.
stomach ache n dor f de estômago.
stomach pump n bomba gástrica.

stomach ulcer *n* úlcera gástrica.
stomp [stɔmp] *vi*: **to ~ in/out** entrar/sair como um furacão.
stone [stəun] *n* pedra; (*in fruit*) caroço; (*BRIT: weight*) = *6.348kg*; *14 pounds* ♦ *cpd* de pedra ♦ *vt* apedrejar; **within a ~'s throw of the station** pertinho da estação.
Stone Age *n*: **the ~** a Idade da Pedra.
stone-cold *adj* gelado.
stoned [stəund] (*inf*) *adj* (*on drugs*) doidão/dona, baratinado.
stone-deaf *adj* surdo como uma porta.
stonemason ['stəunmeɪsn] *n* pedreiro/a.
stonework ['stəunwɔːk] *n* cantaria.
stony ['stəunɪ] *adj* pedregoso; (*glance*) glacial.
stood [stud] *pt, pp of* **stand**.
stool [stuːl] *n* tamborete *m*, banco.
stoop [stuːp] *vi* (*also:* **have a ~**) ser corcunda; (*bend*) debruçar-se, curvar-se; (*fig*): **to ~ to sth/doing sth** rebaixar-se para algo/fazer algo.
stop [stɔp] *n* parada, interrupção *f*; (*for bus etc*) parada (*BR*), ponto (*BR*), paragem *f* (*PT*); (*in punctuation*) ponto ♦ *vt* parar, deter; (*break off*) interromper; (*also: put a ~ to*) terminar, pôr fim a ♦ *vi* parar, deter-se; (*end*) acabar; **to ~ doing sth** deixar de fazer algo; **to ~ sb (from) doing sth** impedir alguém de fazer algo; **to ~ dead** parar de repente; **~ it!** para com isso!
stop by *vi* dar uma passada.
stop off *vi* fazer pausa.
stop up *vt* (*hole*) tapar.
stopcock ['stɔpkɔk] *n* torneira de passagem.
stopgap ['stɔpgæp] *n* (*person*) tapa-buraco *m/f*; (*also:* **~ measure**) paliativo.
stoplights ['stɔplaɪts] *npl* (*AUT*) luzes *fpl* do freio (*BR*), faróis *mpl* de stop (*PT*).
stopover ['stɔpəuvə*] *n* escala.
stoppage ['stɔpɪdʒ] *n* (*strike*) greve *f*; (*temporary stop*) paralisação *f*; (*of pay*) suspensão *f*; (*blockage*) obstrução *f*.
stopper ['stɔpə*] *n* tampa, rolha.
stop press *n* notícia de última hora.
stopwatch ['stɔpwɔtʃ] *n* cronômetro.
storage ['stɔːrɪdʒ] *n* armazenagem *f*.
storage heater (*BRIT*) *n* tipo de aquecimento que armazena calor durante a noite, emitindo-o durante o dia.
store [stɔː*] *n* (*stock*) suprimento; (*depot, large shop*) armazém *m*; (*reserve*) estoque *m*; (*US: shop*) loja ♦ *vt* armazenar; (*keep*) guardar; **~s** *npl* víveres *mpl*, provisões *fpl*; **who knows what is in ~ for us?** quem sabe o que nos espera?; **to set great/little ~ by sth** dar grande/pouca importância a algo.
store up *vt* acumular.
storehouse ['stɔːhaus] (*irreg*) *n* depósito, armazém *m*.
storekeeper ['stɔːkiːpə*] (*US*) *n* lojista *m/f*.
storeroom ['stɔːruːm] *n* depósito, almoxarifado.

storey ['stɔːrɪ] (*US* **story**) *n* andar *m*.
stork [stɔːk] *n* cegonha.
storm [stɔːm] *n* tempestade *f*; (*wind*) borrasca, vendaval *m*; (*fig*) tumulto ♦ *vi* (*fig*) enfurecer-se ♦ *vt* tomar de assalto, assaltar.
storm cloud *n* nuvem *f* de tempestade.
storm door *n* porta adicional.
stormy ['stɔːmɪ] *adj* tempestuoso.
story ['stɔːrɪ] *n* história, estória; (*PRESS*) matéria; (*plot*) enredo; (*lie*) mentira; (*US*) = **storey**.
storybook ['stɔːrɪbuk] *n* livro de contos.
storyteller ['stɔːrɪtelə*] *n* contador(a) *m/f* de estórias.
stout [staut] *adj* (*strong*) sólido, forte; (*fat*) gordo, corpulento ♦ *n* cerveja preta.
stove [stəuv] *n* (*for cooking*) fogão *m*; (*for heating*) estufa, fogareiro; **gas/electric ~** (*cooker*) fogão a gás/elétrico.
stow [stəu] *vt* guardar; (*NAUT*) estivar.
stowaway ['stəuəweɪ] *n* passageiro/a clandestino/a.
straddle ['strædl] *vt* cavalgar.
strafe [strɑːf] *vt* metralhar.
straggle ['strægl] *vi* (*wander*) vagar, perambular; (*lag behind*) ficar para trás.
straggler ['stræglə*] *n* pessoa que fica para trás.
straggling ['stræglɪŋ] *adj* (*hair*) rebelde, emaranhado.
straggly ['stræglɪ] *adj* (*hair*) rebelde, emaranhado.
straight [streɪt] *adj* reto; (*frank*) franco, direto; (*simple*) simples *inv*; (*THEATRE: part, play*) sério; (*inf: conventional*) quadrado, careta (*inf*); (: *heterosexual*) heterossexual ♦ *adv* reto; (*drink*) puro ♦ *n*: **the ~** (*SPORT*) a reta; **to put or get ~** pôr em ordem, dar um jeito em; **let's get this ~** (*explaining*) então, vamos fazer assim; (*warning*) eu quero que isso fique bem claro; **10 ~ wins** 10 vitórias consecutivas; **to go ~ home** ir direto para casa; **~ away, ~ off** (*at once*) imediatamente; **~ off, ~ out** sem mais nem menos.
straighten ['streɪtən] *vt* (*also:* **~ out**) endireitar; **to ~ things out** arrumar as coisas.
straight-faced [-feɪst] *adj* impassível ♦ *adv* com cara séria.
straightforward [streɪt'fɔːwəd] *adj* (*simple*) simples *inv*, direto; (*honest*) honesto, franco.
strain [streɪn] *n* tensão *f*; (*TECH*) esforço; (*MED*) distensão *f*, luxação *f*; (*breed*) raça, estirpe *f*; (*of virus*) classe *f* ♦ *vt* (*back etc*) forçar, torcer, distender; (*tire*) extenuar; (*stretch*) puxar, estirar; (*filter*) filtrar ♦ *vi* esforçar-se; **~s** *npl* (*MUS*) acordes *mpl*; **he's been under a lot of ~** ele tem estado sob muita tensão.
strained [streɪnd] *adj* (*muscle*) distendido; (*laugh*) forçado; (*relations*) tenso.
strainer ['streɪnə*] *n* (*for tea, coffee*) coador *m*; (*sieve*) peneira.

NB: European Portuguese adds the following consonants to certain words: **b** (sú(b)dito, su(b)til); **c** (a(c)ção, a(c)cionista, a(c)to); **m** (inde(m)ne); **p** (ado(p)ção, ado(p)tar); *for further details see p. xiii.*

strait [streɪt] n (GEO) estreito; **to be in dire ~s** (fig) estar em apuros.

straitjacket ['streɪtdʒækɪt] n camisa-de-força.

strait-laced [-'leɪst] adj puritano, austero.

strand [strænd] n (of thread) fio ♦ vt (boat) encalhar.

stranded ['strændɪd] adj desamparado.

strange [streɪndʒ] adj (not known) desconhecido; (odd) estranho, esquisito.

strangely ['streɪndʒlɪ] adv estranhamente.

stranger ['streɪndʒə*] n desconhecido/a; (from another area) forasteiro/a.

strangle ['stræŋgl] vt estrangular; (sobs etc) sufocar.

stranglehold ['stræŋglhəʊld] n (fig) domínio total.

strangulation [stræŋgju'leɪʃən] n estrangulação f.

strap [stræp] n correia; (of slip, dress) alça ♦ vt prender com correia.

straphanging ['stræphæŋɪŋ] n viajar m em pé (no metrô etc).

strapless ['stræplɪs] adj (bra, dress) sem alças.

strapping ['stræpɪŋ] adj corpulento, robusto, forte.

Strasbourg ['stræzbɔːg] n Estrasburgo.

strata ['strɑːtə] npl of stratum.

stratagem ['strætɪdʒəm] n estratagema m.

strategic [strə'tiːdʒɪk] adj estratégico.

strategist ['strætɪdʒɪst] n estrategista m/f.

strategy ['strætɪdʒɪ] n estratégia.

stratosphere ['strætəsfɪə*] n estratosfera.

stratum ['strɑːtəm] (pl **strata**) n estrato, camada.

straw [strɔː] n palha; (drinking ~) canudo; **that's the last ~!** essa foi a última gota!

strawberry ['strɔːbərɪ] n morango; (plant) morangueiro.

stray [streɪ] adj (animal) extraviado; (bullet) perdido ♦ vi extraviar-se, perder-se.

streak [striːk] n listra, traço; (fig: of madness etc) sinal m ♦ vt listrar ♦ vi: **to ~ past** passar como um raio; **to have ~s in one's hair** fazer mechas no cabelo; **a winning/losing ~** uma fase de sorte/azar.

streaky ['striːkɪ] adj listrado.

streaky bacon (BRIT) n toicinho or bacon m em fatias (entremeado com gordura).

stream [striːm] n riacho, córrego; (current) fluxo, corrente f; (of people) fluxo ♦ vt (SCH) classificar ♦ vi correr, fluir; **to ~ in/out** (people) entrar/sair em massa; **against the ~** contra a corrente; **on ~** (power plant etc) em funcionamento.

streamer ['striːmə*] n serpentina; (pennant) flâmula.

stream feed n (on photocopier etc) alimentação f contínua.

streamline ['striːmlaɪn] vt aerodinamizar; (fig) agilizar.

streamlined ['striːmlaɪnd] adj aerodinâmico.

street [striːt] n rua; **the back ~s** as ruelas; **to be on the ~s** (homeless) estar desabrigado; (as prostitute) fazer a vida.

streetcar ['striːtkɑː*] (US) n bonde m (BR), eléctrico (PT).

street lamp n poste m de iluminação.

street lighting n iluminação f pública.

street map n mapa m.

street market n feira.

street plan n mapa m.

streetwise ['striːtwaɪz] (inf) adj malandro.

strength [streŋθ] n força; (of girder, knot etc) firmeza, resistência; (of chemical solution) concentração f; (of wine) teor m alcoólico; **on the ~ of** com base em; **at full ~** completo; **below ~** desfalcado.

strengthen ['streŋθən] vt fortalecer, intensificar.

strenuous ['strenjuəs] adj (tough) árduo, estrênuo; (energetic) enérgico; (determined) tenaz.

stress [stres] n (force, pressure) pressão f; (mental strain) tensão f, stress m; (accent) acento; (emphasis) ênfase f; (TECH) tensão ♦ vt realçar, dar ênfase a; **to lay great ~ on sth** dar muita ênfase a algo; **to be under ~** estar com estresse.

stressful ['stresful] adj (job) desgastante.

stretch [stretʃ] n (of sand etc) trecho, extensão f; (of time) período ♦ vi esticar-se; (extend): **to ~ to** or **as far as** estender-se até; (be enough: money, food): **to ~ to** dar para ♦ vt estirar, esticar; (make demands of) exigir o máximo de; **at a ~** sem parar; **to ~ one's legs** esticar as pernas.

stretch out vi esticar-se ♦ vt (arm etc) esticar; (spread) estirar.

stretcher ['stretʃə*] n maca, padiola.

stretcher-bearer n padioleiro.

stretch marks npl estrias fpl.

strewn [struːn] adj: **~ with** coberto or cheio de.

stricken ['strɪkən] adj (wounded) ferido; (devastated) arrasado; (ill) acometido; **~ with grief, grief-~** tomado pela dor.

strict [strɪkt] adj (person) severo, rigoroso; (precise) exato, estrito; **in ~ confidence** muito confidencialmente.

strictly ['strɪktlɪ] adv (exactly) estritamente; (severely) severamente; (definitively) rigorosamente; **~ confidential** estritamente confidencial; **~ speaking** a rigor; **~ between ourselves ...** cá entre nós ....

strictness ['strɪktnɪs] n rigor m, severidade f.

stridden ['strɪdn] pp of stride.

stride [straɪd] (pt **strode**, pp **stridden**) n passo largo ♦ vi andar a passos largos; **to take in one's ~** (fig: changes etc) não se perturbar com.

strident ['straɪdnt] adj estridente; (colour) berrante.

strife [straɪf] n conflito.

strike [straɪk] (pt, pp **struck**) n greve f; (of oil etc) descoberta; (attack) ataque m ♦ vt bater em; (oil etc) descobrir; (obstacle) esbarrar em; (deal) fechar, acertar ♦ vi estar em greve; (attack) atacar; (clock) bater, dar (as horas); **to go on** or **come out on ~** entrar em greve; **to call a ~** convocar uma greve; **to ~ a match** acender um fósforo; **to ~ a balance** (*fig*) encontrar um equilíbrio; **the clock struck nine** o relógio bateu nove horas.

strike back *vi* (*MIL*) contra-atacar; (*fig*) revidar.

strike down *vt* derrubar.

strike off *vt* (*from list*) tirar, cortar; (*doctor*) suspender.

strike out *vt* cancelar, rasurar.

strike up *vt* (*MUS*) começar a tocar; (*conversation, friendship*) travar.

strikebreaker ['straɪkbreɪkə*] *n* fura-greve *m/f* *inv*.

striker ['straɪkə*] *n* grevista *m/f*; (*SPORT*) atacante *m/f*.

striking ['straɪkɪŋ] *adj* impressionante; (*colour*) chamativo.

string [strɪŋ] (*pt, pp* **strung**) *n* (*cord*) barbante *m* (*BR*), cordel *m* (*PT*); (*MUS*) corda; (*series*) série *f*; (*of people, cars*) fila (*BR*), bicha (*PT*); (*COMPUT*) string *m* ♦ *vt*: **to ~ out** esticar; **the ~s** *npl* (*MUS*) os instrumentos de corda; **to ~ together** (*words*) unir; (*ideas*) concatenar; **to get a job by pulling ~s** (*fig*) usar pistolão; **with no ~s attached** (*fig*) sem condições.

string bean *n* vagem *f*.

string(ed) instrument [strɪŋ(d)-] *n* (*MUS*) instrumento de corda.

stringent ['strɪndʒənt] *adj* rigoroso.

string quartet *n* quarteto de cordas.

strip [strɪp] *n* tira; (*of land*) faixa; (*of metal*) lâmina, tira; (*SPORT*) cores *fpl* ♦ *vt* despir; (*fig*): **to ~ sb of sth** despojar alguém de algo; (*also*: ~ **down** : *machine*) desmontar ♦ *vi* despir-se.

strip cartoon *n* história em quadrinhos (*BR*), banda desenhada (*PT*).

stripe [straɪp] *n* listra; (*MIL*) galão *m*.

striped [straɪpt] *adj* listrado, com listras.

strip light (*BRIT*) *n* lâmpada fluorescente.

stripper ['strɪpə*] *n* artista *m/f* de striptease.

striptease ['strɪptiːz] *n* striptease *m*.

strive [straɪv] (*pt* **strove**, *pp* **striven**) *vi*: **to ~ to do sth** esforçar-se por *or* batalhar para fazer algo.

striven ['strɪvn] *pp of* **strive**.

strode [strəud] *pt of* **stride**.

stroke [strəuk] *n* (*blow*) golpe *m*; (*MED*) derrame *m* cerebral; (*caress*) carícia; (*of pen*) traço; (*SWIMMING*: *style*) nado; (: *movement*) braçada; (*of piston*) curso ♦ *vt* acariciar, afagar; **at a ~** de repente, de golpe; **on the ~ of 5** às cinco em ponto; **a ~ of luck** um golpe de sorte; **a 2-~ engine** um motor de dois tempos.

stroll [strəul] *n* volta, passeio ♦ *vi* passear, dar uma volta; **to go for a ~** dar uma volta.

stroller ['strəulə*] (*US*) *n* carrinho (de criança).

strong [strɔŋ] *adj* forte; (*object, material*) só-

lido; (*chemical*) concentrado ♦ *adv*: **to be going ~** (*company*) estar prosperando; (*person*) estar com boa saúde; **they are 50 ~** são 50.

strong-arm *adj* (*tactics, methods*) repressivo, violento.

strongbox ['strɔŋbɔks] *n* cofre-forte *m*.

strong drink *n* bebida alcoólica.

stronghold ['strɔŋhəuld] *n* fortaleza; (*fig*) baluarte *m*.

strong language *n* palavrões *mpl*.

strongly ['strɔŋlɪ] *adv* fortemente, vigorosamente; (*believe*) firmemente; **I feel ~ about it** tenho uma opinião firme sobre isso.

strongman ['strɔŋmæn] (*irreg*) *n* homem *m* forte.

strongroom ['strɔŋruːm] *n* casa-forte *f*.

strove [strəuv] *pt of* **strive**.

struck [strʌk] *pt, pp of* **strike**.

structural ['strʌktʃərəl] *adj* estrutural.

structurally ['strʌktʃrəlɪ] *adv* estruturalmente.

structure ['strʌktʃə*] *n* estrutura; (*building*) construção *f*.

struggle ['strʌgl] *n* luta, contenda ♦ *vi* lutar, batalhar; **to have a ~ to do sth** ter que batalhar para fazer algo.

strum [strʌm] *vt* (*guitar*) dedilhar.

strung [strʌŋ] *pt, pp of* **string**.

strut [strʌt] *n* escora, suporte *m* ♦ *vi* pavonear-se, empertigar-se.

strychnine ['strɪkniːn] *n* estricnina.

stub [stʌb] *n* (*of ticket etc*) canhoto; (*of cigarette*) toco, ponta; **to ~ one's toe (on sth)** dar uma topada (em algo).

stub out *vt* apagar.

stubble ['stʌbl] *n* restolho; (*on chin*) barba por fazer.

stubborn ['stʌbən] *adj* teimoso, cabeçudo, obstinado.

stubby ['stʌbɪ] *adj* atarracado.

stucco ['stʌkəu] *n* estuque.

stuck [stʌk] *pt, pp of* **stick** ♦ *adj* (*jammed*) emperrado; **to get ~** emperrar.

stuck-up *adj* convencido, metido, esnobe.

stud [stʌd] *n* (*shirt ~*) botão *m*; (*of boot*) cravo; (*of horses*) haras *m*; (*also*: ~ *horse*) garanhão *m* ♦ *vt* (*fig*): **~ded with** salpicado de.

student ['stjuːdənt] *n* estudante *m/f* ♦ *cpd* estudantil; **law/medical ~** estudante de direito/medicina.

student driver (*US*) *n* aprendiz *m/f*.

students' union (*BRIT*) *n* (*association*) união *f* dos estudantes; (*building*) centro estudantil.

studied ['stʌdɪd] *adj* estudado, calculado.

studio ['stjuːdɪəu] *n* estúdio; (*sculptor's*) ateliê *m*.

studio flat (*US* **studio apartment**) *n* (apartamento) conjugado.

studious ['stjuːdɪəs] *adj* estudioso, aplicado; (*studied*) calculado.

studiously ['stjuːdɪəslɪ] *adv* (*carefully*) com esmero.

***NB**: European Portuguese adds the following consonants to certain words:* **b** *(sú(b)dito, su(b)til);* **c** *(a(c)ção, a(c)cionista, a(c)to);* **m** *(inde(m)ne);* **p** *(ado(p)ção, ado(p)tar); for further details see p. xiii.*

study ['stʌdɪ] n estudo; (*room*) gabinete m ♦ vt estudar; (*examine*) examinar, investigar ♦ vi estudar; **to make a ~ of sth** estudar algo; **to ~ for an exam** estudar para um exame.

stuff [stʌf] n (*inf: substance*) troço; (: *things*) troços mpl, coisas fpl ♦ vt encher; (*CULIN*) rechear; (*animals*) empalhar; **my nose is ~ed up** meu nariz está entupido; **get ~ed!** (*inf!*) vai tomar banho!; **~ed toy** brinquedo de pelúcia.

stuffing ['stʌfɪŋ] n recheio.

stuffy ['stʌfɪ] adj (*room*) abafado, mal ventilado; (*person*) rabujento, melindroso.

stumble ['stʌmbl] vi tropeçar.
   stumble across vt fus (*fig*) topar com.

stumbling block ['stʌmblɪŋ-] n pedra no caminho.

stump [stʌmp] n (*of tree*) toco; (*of limb*) coto ♦ vt: **to be ~ed** ficar perplexo.

stun [stʌn] vt aturdir, pasmar.

stung [stʌŋ] pt, pp of **sting**.

stunk [stʌŋk] pp of **stink**.

stunning ['stʌnɪŋ] adj (*fig*) atordoante.

stunt [stʌnt] n façanha sensacional; (*AVIAT*) vôo acrobático; (*publicity ~*) truque m publicitário ♦ vt tolher.

stunted ['stʌntɪd] adj atrofiado, retardado.

stuntman ['stʌntmæn] (*irreg*) n dublê m.

stupefaction [stju:pɪ'fækʃən] n estupefação f, assombro.

stupefy ['stju:pɪfaɪ] vt deixar estupefato.

stupendous [stju:'pɛndəs] adj assombroso, prodigioso, monumental.

stupid ['stju:pɪd] adj estúpido, idiota.

stupidity [stju:'pɪdɪtɪ] n estupidez f.

stupidly ['stju:pɪdlɪ] adv estupidamente.

stupor ['stju:pə*] n estupor m.

sturdy ['stə:dɪ] adj robusto.

sturgeon ['stə:dʒən] n inv esturjão m.

stutter ['stʌtə*] n gagueira, gaguez f ♦ vi gaguejar.

sty [staɪ] n (*for pigs*) chiqueiro.

stye [staɪ] n (*MED*) terçol m.

style [staɪl] n estilo; (*allure*) charme m; **in the latest ~** na última moda; **hair ~** penteado.

styli ['staɪlaɪ] npl of **stylus**.

stylish ['staɪlɪʃ] adj elegante, chique.

stylist ['staɪlɪst] n (*hair ~*) cabeleireiro/a; (*literary*) estilista m/f.

stylized ['staɪlaɪzd] adj estilizado.

stylus ['staɪləs] (*pl* **styli** *or* **~es**) n (*of record player*) agulha.

suave [swɑːv] adj suave, melífluo.

sub [sʌb] n abbr = **submarine**; **subscription**.

sub... [sʌb] prefix sub....

subcommittee ['sʌbkəmɪtɪ] n subcomissão f.

subconscious [sʌb'kɔnʃəs] adj do subconsciente ♦ n subconsciente m.

subcontinent [sʌb'kɔntɪnənt] n: **the (Indian) ~** o subcontinente (da Índia).

subcontract [n sʌb'kɔntrækt, vt sʌbkən'trækt] n subcontrato ♦ vt subcontratar.

subcontractor [sʌbkən'træktə*] n subempreiteiro/a.

subdivide [sʌbdɪ'vaɪd] vt subdividir.

subdivision [sʌbdɪ'vɪʒən] n subdivisão f.

subdue [səb'dju:] vt subjugar; (*passions*) dominar.

subdued [səb'dju:d] adj (*light*) tênue; (*person*) desanimado.

subeditor ['sʌb'edɪtə*] (*BRIT*) n subeditor(a) m/f.

subject [n 'sʌbdʒɪkt, vt səb'dʒɛkt] n (*of king*) súdito/a; (*theme*) assunto; (*SCH*) matéria ♦ vt: **to ~ sb to sth** submeter alguém a algo ♦ adj: **to be ~ to** (*law*) estar sujeito a; **~ to confirmation in writing** sujeito a confirmação por escrito; **to change the ~** mudar de assunto.

subjection [səb'dʒɛkʃən] n submissão f, dependência.

subjective [səb'dʒɛktɪv] adj subjetivo.

subject matter n assunto; (*content*) conteúdo.

sub judice [-'dju:dɪsɪ] adj (*LAW*) sob apreciação judicial, sub judice.

subjugate ['sʌbdʒugeɪt] vt subjugar, submeter.

subjunctive [səb'dʒʌŋktɪv] adj, n subjuntivo.

sublet [sʌb'let] vt sublocar.

sublime [sə'blaɪm] adj sublime.

subliminal [sʌb'lɪmɪnl] adj subliminar.

submachine gun ['sʌbmə'ʃiːn-] n metralhadora de mão.

submarine ['sʌbməriːn] n submarino.

submerge [səb'mə:dʒ] vt submergir; (*flood*) inundar ♦ vi submergir-se.

submersion [səb'mə:ʃən] n submersão f, imersão f.

submission [səb'mɪʃən] n submissão f; (*to committee*) petição f.

submissive [səb'mɪsɪv] adj submisso.

submit [səb'mɪt] vt submeter ♦ vi submeter-se.

subnormal [sʌb'nɔːməl] adj anormal, subnormal; (*backward*) atrasado.

subordinate [sə'bɔːdɪnət] adj, n subordinado/a.

subpoena [səb'piːnə] n (*LAW*) intimação f, citação f judicial ♦ vt intimar a comparecer judicialmente, citar.

subroutine [sʌbruː'tiːn] n (*COMPUT*) subrotina.

subscribe [səb'skraɪb] vi subscrever; **to ~ to** (*opinion*) concordar com; (*fund*) contribuir para; (*newspaper*) assinar.

subscriber [səb'skraɪbə*] n (*to periodical, telephone*) assinante m/f.

subscript ['sʌbskrɪpt] n (*TYP*) subscrito.

subscription [səb'skrɪpʃən] n subscrição f; (*to magazine etc*) assinatura; (*to club*) cota, mensalidade f; **to take out a ~ to** fazer uma assinatura de.

subsequent ['sʌbsɪkwənt] adj subseqüente, posterior; **~ to** posterior a.

subsequently ['sʌbsɪkwəntlɪ] adv posteriormente, depois.

subside [səb'saɪd] vi baixar; (*flood*) descer; (*wind*) acalmar-se.

subsidence [səb'saɪdns] n baixa.

subsidiary [səb'sɪdɪərɪ] adj subsidiário; (*BRIT*:

SCH: subject) suplementar ♦ *n* subsidiária.
subsidize ['sʌbsɪdaɪz] *vt* subsidiar.
subsidy ['sʌbsɪdɪ] *n* subsídio.
subsist [səb'sɪst] *vi*: **to ~ on sth** subsistir de algo.
subsistence [səb'sɪstəns] *n* subsistência; (*allowance*) subsídio, ajuda de custo.
subsistence allowance *n* diária.
subsistence level *n* nível *m* de subsistência.
subsistence wage *n* salário de fome.
substance ['sʌbstəns] *n* substância; (*fig*) essência; **a man of ~** um homem de recursos; **to lack ~** não ter substância.
substandard [sʌb'stændəd] *adj* (*goods*) de qualidade inferior; (*housing*) inferior ao padrão.
substantial [səb'stænʃl] *adj* substancial, essencial; (*fig*) importante.
substantially [səb'stænʃəlɪ] *adv* substancialmente.
substantiate [səb'stænʃɪeɪt] *vt* comprovar, justificar.
substitute ['sʌbstɪtjuːt] *n* substituto/a; (*person*) suplente *m/f* ♦ *vt*: **to ~ A for B** substituir B por A.
substitute teacher (*US*) *n* professor(a) *m/f* suplente.
substitution [sʌbstɪ'tjuːʃən] *n* substituição *f*, troca.
subterfuge ['sʌbtəfjuːdʒ] *n* subterfúgio.
subterranean [sʌbtə'reɪnɪən] *adj* subterrâneo.
subtitle ['sʌbtaɪtl] *n* (*CINEMA*) legenda.
subtle ['sʌtl] *adj* sutil.
subtlety ['sʌtltɪ] *n* sutileza.
subtly ['sʌtlɪ] *adv* sutilmente.
subtotal [sʌb'təutl] *n* total *m* parcial, subtotal *m*.
subtract [səb'trækt] *vt* subtrair, deduzir.
subtraction [səb'trækʃən] *n* subtração *f*.
subtropical [sʌb'trɒpɪkl] *adj* subtropical.
suburb ['sʌbəːb] *n* subúrbio.
suburban [sə'bəːbən] *adj* suburbano; (*train etc*) de subúrbio.
suburbia [sə'bəːbɪə] *n* os subúrbios.
subvention [səb'venʃən] *n* subvenção *f*, subsídio.
subversion [səb'vəːʃən] *n* subversão *f*.
subversive [səb'vəːsɪv] *adj* subversivo.
subway ['sʌbweɪ] *n* (*BRIT*) passagem *f* subterrânea; (*US*) metrô *m* (*BR*), metro(-politano) (*PT*).
sub-zero *adj* abaixo de zero.
succeed [sək'siːd] *vi* (*person*) ser bem sucedido, ter êxito; (*plan*) sair bem ♦ *vt* suceder a; **to ~ in doing** conseguir fazer.
succeeding [sək'siːdɪŋ] *adj* (*following*) sucessivo, posterior.
success [sək'ses] *n* sucesso, êxito; (*gain*) triunfo.
successful [sək'sesful] *adj* (*venture*) bem sucedido; **to be ~ (in doing)** conseguir (fazer).
successfully [sək'sesfulɪ] *adv* com sucesso,

com êxito.
succession [sək'seʃən] *n* (*series*) sucessão *f*, série *f*; (*descendants*) descendência; **in ~** em sucessão; **3 years in ~** três anos consecutivos.
successive [sək'sesɪv] *adj* sucessivo; **on 3 ~ days** em 3 dias consecutivos.
successor [sək'sesə*] *n* sucessor(a) *m/f*.
succinct [sək'sɪŋkt] *adj* sucinto.
succulent ['sʌkjulənt] *adj* suculento ♦ *n* (*BOT*): **~s** suculentos *mpl*.
succumb [sə'kʌm] *vi* sucumbir.
such [sʌtʃ] *adj* tal, semelhante; (*of that kind*: *sg*): **~ a book** um livro parecido, tal livro; (: *pl*): **~ books** tais livros; (*so much*): **~ courage** tanta coragem ♦ *adv* tão; **~ a long trip** uma viagem tão longa; **~ good books** livros tão bons; **~ a lot of** tanto; **making ~ a noise that** fazendo tanto barulho que; **~ a long time ago** há tanto tempo atrás; **~ as** (*like*) tal como; **a noise ~ as to** um ruído tal que; **~ books as I have** os poucos livros que eu tenho; **I said no ~ thing** eu não disse tal coisa; **as ~** como tal; **until ~ time as** até que.
such-and-such *adj* tal e qual.
suchlike ['sʌtʃlaɪk] (*inf*) *pron*: **and ~** e coisas assim.
suck [sʌk] *vt* chupar; (*breast*) mamar; (*subj*: *pump, machine*) sugar.
sucker ['sʌkə*] *n* (*BOT*) rebento; (*ZOOL*) ventosa; (*inf*) trouxa *m/f*, otário/a.
suckle ['sʌkl] *vt* amamentar.
sucrose ['suːkrəuz] *n* sucrose *f*.
suction ['sʌkʃən] *n* sucção *f*.
suction pump *n* bomba de sucção.
Sudan [su'dɑːn] *n* Sudão *m*.
Sudanese [suːdə'niːz] *adj*, *n inv* sudanês/esa *m/f*.
sudden ['sʌdn] *adj* (*rapid*) repentino, súbito; (*unexpected*) imprevisto; **all of a ~** de repente; (*unexpectedly*) inesperadamente.
suddenly ['sʌdnlɪ] *adv* de repente; (*unexpectedly*) inesperadamente.
suds [sʌdz] *npl* água de sabão.
sue [suː] *vt* processar ♦ *vi*: **to ~ (for)** processar (por), promover ação (por); **to ~ for divorce** requerer divórcio; **to ~ sb for damages** intentar uma ação de perdas e danos contra alguém.
suede [sweɪd] *n* camurça ♦ *cpd* de camurça.
suet ['suɪt] *n* sebo.
Suez Canal ['suːɪz-] *n* Canal *m* de Suez.
Suff. (*BRIT*) *abbr* = **Suffolk.**
suffer ['sʌfə*] *vt* sofrer; (*bear*) agüentar, suportar ♦ *vi* sofrer, padecer; **to ~ from** (*illness*) sofrer de, estar com; **to ~ from the effects of alcohol** sofrer os efeitos do álcool.
sufferance ['sʌfrəns] *n*: **he was only there on ~** ele estava lá por tolerância.
sufferer ['sʌfərə*] *n* sofredor(a) *m/f*; (*MED*) doente *m/f*, paciente *m/f*.

NB: European Portuguese adds the following consonants to certain words: **b** (sú(b)dito, su(b)til); **c** (a(c)ção, a(c)cionista, a(c)to); **m** (inde(m)ne); **p** (ado(p)ção, ado(p)tar); *for further details see p. xiii.*

suffering ['sʌfərɪŋ] n sofrimento; (pain) dor f.
suffice [sə'faɪs] vi bastar, ser suficiente.
sufficient [sə'fɪʃənt] adj suficiente, bastante.
sufficiently [sə'fɪʃəntlɪ] adv suficientemente.
suffix ['sʌfɪks] n sufixo.
suffocate ['sʌfəkeɪt] vt sufocar, asfixiar ♦ vi sufocar(-se), asfixiar(-se).
suffocation [sʌfə'keɪʃən] n sufocação f; (MED) asfixia.
suffrage ['sʌfrɪdʒ] n sufrágio; (vote) direito de voto.
suffuse [sə'fjuːz] vt banhar; ~d with light/joy banhado de luz/alegria.
sugar ['ʃugə*] n açúcar m ♦ vt pôr açúcar em, açucarar.
sugar beet n beterraba (sacarina).
sugar bowl n açucareiro.
sugar cane n cana-de-açúcar f.
sugar-coated [-'kəʊtɪd] adj cristalizado.
sugar lump n torrão m de açúcar.
sugar refinery n refinaria de açúcar.
sugary ['ʃugərɪ] adj açucarado.
suggest [sə'dʒɛst] vt sugerir; (advise) aconselhar; **what do you ~ I do?** o que você sugere que eu faça?
suggestion [sə'dʒɛstʃən] n sugestão f.
suggestive [sə'dʒɛstɪv] adj sugestivo; (pej) indecente.
suicidal [suɪ'saɪdl] adj suicida.
suicide ['suɪsaɪd] n suicídio; (person) suicida m/f; **to commit ~** suicidar-se.
suicide attempt n tentativa de suicídio.
suicide bid n tentativa de suicídio.
suit [suːt] n (man's) terno (BR), fato (PT); (woman's) conjunto; (LAW) processo; (CARDS) naipe m ♦ vt (gen) convir a; (clothes) ficar bem a; (adapt): **to ~ sth to** adaptar or acomodar algo a; **to be ~ed to sth** ser apto para algo; **they are well ~ed** fazem um bom par; **to bring a ~ against sb** mover um processo contra alguém; **to follow ~** (fig) seguir o exemplo.
suitable ['suːtəbl] adj conveniente; (apt) apropriado; **would tomorrow be ~?** amanhã lhe convém?
suitably ['suːtəblɪ] adv convenientemente, apropriadamente.
suitcase ['suːtkeɪs] n mala.
suite [swiːt] n (of rooms) conjunto de salas; (MUS) suite f; (furniture): **bedroom/dining room ~** conjunto de quarto/de sala de jantar; **a three-piece ~** um conjunto estofado (sofá e duas poltronas).
suitor ['suːtə*] n pretendente m.
sulfate ['sʌlfeɪt] (US) n = **sulphate**.
sulfur etc ['sʌlfə*] (US) = **sulphur** etc.
sulk [sʌlk] vi ficar emburrado, fazer beicinho or biquinho (inf).
sulky ['sʌlkɪ] adj emburrado.
sullen ['sʌlən] adj rabugento, teimoso.
sulphate ['sʌlfeɪt] (US **sulfate**) n sulfato; see also **copper sulphate**.
sulphur ['sʌlfə*] (US **sulfur**) n enxofre m.
sulphuric [sʌl'fjuərɪk] (US **sulfuric**) adj: **~ acid** ácido sulfúrico.

sultan ['sʌltən] n sultão m.
sultana [sʌl'tɑːnə] n (fruit) passa branca.
sultry ['sʌltrɪ] adj (weather) abafado, mormacento; (seductive) sedutor(a).
sum [sʌm] n soma; (SCH etc) cálculo.
sum up vt sumariar, fazer um resumo de; (evaluate) avaliar ♦ vi resumir.
Sumatra [su'mɑːtrə] n Sumatra.
summarize ['sʌməraɪz] vt resumir.
summary ['sʌmərɪ] n resumo ♦ adj (justice) sumário.
summer ['sʌmə*] n verão m ♦ cpd de verão; **in (the) ~** no verão.
summer camp (US) n colônia de férias.
summerhouse ['sʌməhaus] (irreg) n (in garden) pavilhão m.
summertime ['sʌmətaɪm] n (season) verão m.
summer time n (by clock) horário de verão.
summery ['sʌmərɪ] adj estival, de verão.
summing-up ['sʌmɪŋ-] n resumo, recapitulação f.
summit ['sʌmɪt] n topo, cume m; (also: ~ conference) (conferência de) cúpula.
summon ['sʌmən] vt (person) mandar chamar; (meeting) convocar; **to ~ a witness** citar uma testemunha.
summon up vt (forces) concentrar; (courage) criar.
summons ['sʌmənz] n citação f, intimação f ♦ vt citar, intimar; **to serve a ~ on sb** entregar uma citação a alguém.
sump [sʌmp] (BRIT) n (AUT) cárter m.
sumptuous ['sʌmptjuəs] adj suntuoso.
Sun. abbr (= Sunday) dom.
sun [sʌn] n sol m; **in the ~** ao sol; **everything under the ~** cada coisa.
sunbathe ['sʌnbeɪð] vi tomar sol.
sunbeam ['sʌnbiːm] n raio de sol.
sunbed ['sʌnbed] n espreguiçadeira; (with sunlamp) cama para bronzeamento artificial.
sunburn ['sʌnbəːn] n queimadura do sol.
sunburned ['sʌnbəːnd] adj queimado.
sunburnt ['sʌnbəːnt] adj queimado.
sun cream n creme m solar.
sundae ['sʌndeɪ] n sorvete m (BR) or gelado (PT) com frutas e nozes.
Sunday ['sʌndɪ] n domingo; see also **Tuesday**.
Sunday school n escola dominical.
sundial ['sʌndaɪəl] n relógio de sol.
sundown ['sʌndaun] n pôr m do sol.
sundries ['sʌndrɪz] npl gêneros mpl diversos.
sundry ['sʌndrɪ] adj vários, diversos; **all and ~** todos.
sunflower ['sʌnflauə*] n girassol m.
sung [sʌŋ] pp of **sing**.
sunglasses ['sʌnglɑːsɪz] npl óculos mpl de sol.
sunk [sʌŋk] pp of **sink**.
sunken ['sʌŋkn] adj (ship) afundado; (eyes, cheeks) cavado; (bath) enterrado.
sunlamp ['sʌnlæmp] n lâmpada ultravioleta.
sunlight ['sʌnlaɪt] n (luz f do) sol m.
sunlit ['sʌnlɪt] adj ensolarado, iluminado pelo sol.
sunny ['sʌnɪ] adj cheio de sol; (day) ensolarado, de sol; (fig) alegre; **it's ~** faz sol.

sunrise ['sʌnraɪz] *n* nascer *m* do sol.

sun roof *n* (*AUT*) teto solar.

sunset ['sʌnsɛt] *n* pôr *m* do sol.

sunshade ['sʌnʃeɪd] *n* (*over table*) pára-sol *m*; (*on beach*) barraca.

sunshine ['sʌnʃaɪn] *n* (luz *f* do) sol *m*.

sunspot ['sʌnspɔt] *n* mancha solar.

sunstroke ['sʌnstrəuk] *n* insolação *f*.

suntan ['sʌntæn] *n* bronzeado.

suntanned ['sʌntænd] *adj* bronzeado, moreno.

suntan oil *n* óleo de bronzear, bronzeador *m*.

suntrap ['sʌntræp] *n* lugar *m* muito ensolarado.

super ['su:pə*] (*inf*) *adj* bacana (*BR*), muito giro (*PT*).

superannuation [su:pərænju'eɪʃən] *n* pensão *f* de aposentadoria.

superb [su:'pə:b] *adj* excelente.

supercilious [su:pə'sɪlɪəs] *adj* (*disdainful*) arrogante, desdenhoso; (*haughty*) altivo.

superficial [su:pə'fɪʃəl] *adj* superficial.

superficially [su:pə'fɪʃəlɪ] *adv* superficialmente.

superfluous [su'pə:fluəs] *adj* supérfluo, desnecessário.

superhuman [su:pə'hju:mən] *adj* sobre-humano.

superimpose [su:pərɪm'pəuz] *vt* sobrepor.

superintend [su:pərɪn'tɛnd] *vt* superintender, dirigir.

superintendent [su:pərɪn'tɛndənt] *n* superintendente *m/f*; (*POLICE*) chefe *m/f* de polícia.

superior [su'pɪərɪə*] *adj* superior; (*smug*) desdenhoso ♦ *n* superior *m*; **Mother S~** (*REL*) Madre Superiora.

superiority [supɪərɪ'ɔrɪtɪ] *n* superioridade *f*.

superlative [su'pə:lətɪv] *adj*, *n* superlativo.

superman ['su:pəmæn] (*irreg*) *n* super-homem *m*.

supermarket ['su:pəma:kɪt] *n* supermercado.

supernatural [su:pə'nætʃərəl] *adj* sobrenatural.

superpower ['su:pəpauə*] *n* (*POL*) superpotência.

supersede [su:pə'si:d] *vt* suplantar.

supersonic [su:pə'sɔnɪk] *adj* supersônico.

superstition [su:pə'stɪʃən] *n* superstição *f*.

superstitious [su:pə'stɪʃəs] *adj* supersticioso.

superstore ['su:pəstɔ:*] (*BRIT*) *n* hipermercado.

supertanker ['su:pətæŋkə*] *n* superpetroleiro.

supertax ['su:pətæks] *n* sobretaxa.

supervise ['su:pəvaɪz] *vt* supervisar, supervisionar.

supervision [su:pə'vɪʒən] *n* supervisão *f*; **under medical ~** a critério médico.

supervisor ['su:pəvaɪzə*] *n* supervisor(a) *m/f*; (*academic*) orientador(a) *m/f*.

supervisory [su:pə'vaɪzərɪ] *adj* fiscalizador(a).

supine ['su:paɪn] *adj* em supinação.

supper ['sʌpə*] *n* jantar *m*; **to have ~** jantar.

supplant [sə'plɑ:nt] *vt* suplantar.

supple ['sʌpl] *adj* flexível.

supplement [*n* 'sʌplɪmənt, *vt* sʌplɪ'mɛnt] *n* suplemento ♦ *vt* suprir, completar.

supplementary [sʌplɪ'mɛntərɪ] *adj* suplementar.

supplementary benefit (*BRIT*) *n* auxílio suplementar pago aos de renda baixa.

supplier [sə'plaɪə*] *n* abastecedor(a) *m/f*, fornecedor(a) *m/f*; (*stockist*) distribuidor(a) *m/f*.

supply [sə'plaɪ] *vt* (*provide*) abastecer, fornecer; (*need*) suprir a; (*equip*): **to ~ (with)** suprir (de) ♦ *n* fornecimento, provisão *f*; (*supplying*) abastecimento ♦ *adj* (*teacher etc*) suplente; **supplies** *npl* (*food*) víveres *mpl*; (*MIL*) apetrechos *mpl*; **office supplies** material *m* de escritório; **to be in short ~** estar escasso; **the electricity/water/gas ~** o abastecimento de força/água/gás; **~ and demand** oferta e procura.

supply teacher (*BRIT*) *n* professor(a) *m/f* suplente.

support [sə'pɔ:t] *n* (*moral, financial etc*) apoio; (*TECH*) suporte *m* ♦ *vt* apoiar; (*financially*) manter; (*uphold*) sustentar; (*SPORT: team*) torcer por; **to ~ o.s.** (*financially*) ganhar a vida.

supporter [sə'pɔ:tə*] *n* (*POL etc*) partidário/a; (*SPORT*) torcedor(a) *m/f*.

supporting [sə'pɔ:tɪŋ] *adj* (*THEATRE etc: role*) secundário; (: *actor*) coadjuvante.

suppose [sə'pəuz] *vt, vi* (*gen*) supor; (*imagine*) imaginar; **to be ~d to do sth** dever fazer algo; **he's ~d to be an expert** dizem que ele é um perito; **I don't ~ she'll come** eu acho que ela não virá.

supposedly [sə'pəuzɪdlɪ] *adv* supostamente, pretensamente.

supposing [sə'pəuzɪŋ] *conj* caso, supondo-se que; **always ~ he comes** caso ele venha.

supposition [sʌpə'zɪʃən] *n* suposição *f*.

suppository [sə'pɔzɪtərɪ] *n* supositório.

suppress [sə'prɛs] *vt* (*publication*) suprimir; (*feelings, revolt*) reprimir; (*yawn*) conter; (*scandal*) abafar, encobrir.

suppression [sə'prɛʃən] *n* repressão *f*.

suppressor [sə'prɛsə*] *n* (*ELEC etc*) supressor *m*.

supremacy [su'prɛməsɪ] *n* supremacia.

supreme [su'pri:m] *adj* supremo.

Supreme Court (*US*) *n* Corte *f* Suprema.

Supt. *abbr* (*POLICE*) = **superintendent**.

surcharge ['sə:tʃa:dʒ] *n* sobrecarga; (*extra tax*) sobretaxa.

sure [ʃuə*] *adj* (*gen*) seguro; (*definite*) certo; (*aim*) certeiro ♦ *adv* (*inf: esp US*): **that ~ is pretty** é bonito mesmo; **~!** (*of course*) claro que sim!; **~ enough** efetivamente; **I'm not ~ how/why/when** não tenho certeza como/por que/quando; **to be ~ of sth** ter certeza de alguma coisa; **to be ~ of o.s.** estar segu-

NB: European Portuguese adds the following consonants to certain words: **b** (sú(b)dito, su(b)til); **c** (a(c)ção, a(c)cionista, a(c)to); **m** (inde(m)ne); **p** (ado(p)ção, ado(p)tar); *for further details see p. xiii.*

ro de si; **to make ~ of** assegurar-se de, verificar.

sure-footed [-'futɪd] *adj* de andar seguro.

surely ['ʃuəlɪ] *adv* (*certainly*) certamente; **~ you don't mean that!** não acredito que você queira dizer isso.

surety ['ʃuərətɪ] *n* garantia, fiança; (*person*) fiador(a) *m/f*; **to go** *or* **stand ~ for sb** afiançar alguém, prestar fiança por alguém.

surf [sɔːf] *n* (*foam*) espuma; (*waves*) ondas *fpl*, arrebentação *f* ♦ *vi* fazer surfe, pegar onda (*inf*).

surface ['sɔːfɪs] *n* superfície *f* ♦ *vt* (*road*) revestir ♦ *vi* vir à superfície *or* à tona; **on the ~** (*fig*) à primeira vista.

surface area *n* área da superfície.

surface mail *n* correio comum.

surfboard ['sɔːfbɔːd] *n* prancha de surfe.

surfeit ['sɔːfɪt] *n*: **a ~ of** um excesso de.

surfer ['sɔːfə*] *n* surfista *m/f*.

surfing ['sɔːfɪŋ] *n* surfe *m*; **to go ~** fazer surfe, pegar onda (*inf*).

surge [sɔːdʒ] *n* onda; (*ELEC*) surto ♦ *vi* (*sea*) encapelar-se; (*feeling*) crescer de repente; **to ~ forward** avançar em tropel.

surgeon ['sɔːdʒən] *n* cirurgião/giã *m/f*.

Surgeon General (*US*) *n* diretor(a) *m/f* nacional de saúde.

surgery ['sɔːdʒərɪ] *n* cirurgia; (*BRIT*: *room*) consultório; **to undergo ~** operar-se.

surgery hours (*BRIT*) *npl* horas *fpl* de consulta.

surgical ['sɔːdʒɪkl] *adj* cirúrgico.

surgical spirit (*BRIT*) *n* álcool *m*.

surly ['sɔːlɪ] *adj* malcriado, rude.

surmise [sɔ'maɪz] *vt* conjeturar.

surmount [sɔ'maunt] *vt* superar, sobrepujar, vencer.

surname ['sɔːneɪm] *n* sobrenome *m* (*BR*), apelido (*PT*).

surpass [sɔː'pɑːs] *vt* superar, exceder, ultrapassar.

surplus ['sɔːpləs] *n* excedente *m*; (*COMM*) superávit *m* ♦ *adj* excedente, de sobra; **~ to my requirements** que me sobram; **~ stock** estoque *m* excedente.

surprise [sə'praɪz] *n* surpresa; (*astonishment*) assombro ♦ *vt* surpreender; **to take by ~** (*person*) pegar de surpresa; (*MIL*: *town*, *fort*) atacar de surpresa.

surprising [sə'praɪzɪŋ] *adj* surpreendente; (*unexpected*) inesperado.

surprisingly [sə'praɪzɪŋlɪ] *adv* (*easy*, *helpful*) surpreendentemente; **(somewhat) ~, he agreed** para surpresa de todos, ele concordou.

surrealism [sə'rɪəlɪzm] *n* surrealismo.

surrealist [sə'rɪəlɪst] *adj*, *n* surrealista *m/f*.

surrender [sə'rɛndə*] *n* rendição *f*, entrega ♦ *vi* render-se, entregar-se ♦ *vt* (*claim*, *right*) renunciar a.

surrender value *n* valor *m* de resgate.

surreptitious [sʌrəp'tɪʃəs] *adj* clandestino, furtivo.

surrogate ['sʌrəgɪt] *n* (*BRIT*: *substitute*) substituto ♦ *adj* substituto.

surrogate mother *n* mãe *f* portadora.

surround [sə'raund] *vt* circundar, rodear; (*MIL etc*) cercar.

surrounding [sə'raundɪŋ] *adj* circundante, adjacente.

surroundings [sə'raundɪŋz] *npl* arredores *mpl*, cercanias *fpl*.

surtax ['sɔːtæks] *n* sobretaxa.

surveillance [sɔː'veɪləns] *n* vigilância.

survey [*n* 'sɔːveɪ, *vt* sɔː'veɪ] *n* (*inspection*) inspeção *f*, vistoria; (*inquiry*) pesquisa, levantamento *f*; (*of land*) levantamento ♦ *vt* inspecionar, vistoriar; (*look at*) observar, contemplar; (*make inquiries about*) pesquisar, fazer um levantamento de; (*land*) fazer o levantamento de.

surveying [sɔː'veɪɪŋ] *n* agrimensura.

surveyor [sɔː'veɪə*] *n* (*of land*) agrimensor(a) *m/f*; (*of building*) inspetor(a) *m/f*.

survival [sə'vaɪvl] *n* sobrevivência ♦ *cpd* (*course*, *kit*) de sobrevivência.

survive [sə'vaɪv] *vi* sobreviver; (*custom etc*) perdurar ♦ *vt* sobreviver a.

survivor [sə'vaɪvə*] *n* sobrevivente *m/f*.

susceptible [sə'sɛptəbl] *adj*: **~ (to)** suscetível *or* sensível a.

suspect [*adj*, *n* 'sʌspɛkt, *vt* səs'pɛkt] *adj*, *n* suspeito/a ♦ *vt* suspeitar, desconfiar.

suspend [səs'pɛnd] *vt* suspender.

suspended sentence [səs'pɛndɪd-] *n* condenação *f* condicional.

suspender belt [səs'pɛndə*-] (*BRIT*) *n* cinta-liga.

suspenders [səs'pɛndəz] *npl* (*BRIT*) ligas *fpl*; (*US*) suspensórios *mpl*.

suspense [səs'pɛns] *n* incerteza, ansiedade *f*; (*in film etc*) suspense *m*.

suspense account *n* conta provisória.

suspension [səs'pɛnʃən] *n* (*gen*, *AUT*) suspensão *f*; (*of driving licence*) cassação *f*.

suspension bridge *n* ponte *f* pênsil.

suspicion [səs'pɪʃən] *n* suspeita; (*trace*) traço, vestígio; **to be under ~** estar sob suspeita; **arrested on ~ of murder** preso sob suspeita de homicídio.

suspicious [səs'pɪʃəs] *adj* (*suspecting*) suspeitoso; (*causing suspicion*) suspeito; **to be ~ of** *or* **about sb/sth** desconfiar de alguém/algo.

suss out [sʌs-] (*BRIT*: *inf*) *vt* (*discover*) descobrir; (*understand*) sacar.

sustain [səs'teɪn] *vt* sustentar, manter; (*suffer*) sofrer, agüentar.

sustained [səs'teɪnd] *adj* (*effort*) contínuo.

sustenance ['sʌstɪnəns] *n* sustento.

suture ['suːtʃə*] *n* sutura.

SW *abbr* (= *short wave*) OC.

swab [swɔb] *n* (*MED*) mecha de algodão ♦ *vt* (*NAUT*: *also*: **~ down**) lambazar.

swagger ['swægə*] *vi* andar com ar de superioridade.

swallow ['swɔləu] *n* (*bird*) andorinha; (*of food etc*) bocado; (*of drink*) trago ♦ *vt* engolir, tragar.

swallow up vt (savings etc) consumir.
swam [swæm] pt of **swim**.
swamp [swɔmp] n pântano, brejo ♦ vt atolar, inundar.
swampy ['swɔmpɪ] adj pantanoso.
swan [swɔn] n cisne m.
swank [swæŋk] (inf) vi esnobar.
swan song n (fig) canto do cisne.
swap [swɔp] n troca, permuta ♦ vt: to ~ (for) trocar (por).
swarm [swɔːm] n (of bees) enxame m; (gen) multidão f ♦ vi (bees) enxamear; (gen) formigar, aglomerar-se.
swarthy ['swɔːðɪ] adj moreno.
swashbuckling ['swɔʃbʌklɪŋ] adj (film) de capa e espada.
swastika ['swɔstɪkə] n suástica.
swat [swɔt] vt esmagar, bater ♦ n (BRIT: also: fly ~) pá f para matar mosca.
swathe [sweɪð] vt: to ~ in (bandages, blankets) enfaixar em, envolver em.
swatter ['swɔtə*] n (also: fly ~) pá f para matar mosca.
sway [sweɪ] vi balançar-se, oscilar ♦ vt (influence) influenciar ♦ n (rule, power) domínio (sobre); to hold ~ over sb dominar alguém.
Swaziland ['swɑːzɪlænd] n Suazilândia.
swear [swɛə*] (pt swore, pp sworn) vi (by oath) jurar; (curse) xingar ♦ vt: to ~ an oath prestar juramento; to ~ to sth afirmar algo sob juramento.
swear in vt (witness) ajuramentar; (president) empossar.
swearword ['swɛəwɔːd] n palavrão m.
sweat [swɛt] n suor m ♦ vi suar.
sweatband ['swɛtbænd] n (SPORT) tira elástica (para o cabelo).
sweater ['swɛtə*] n suéter m or f (BR), camisola (PT).
sweatshirt ['swɛtʃɜːt] n moletom m.
sweatshop ['swɛtʃɔp] n oficina onde os trabalhadores são explorados.
sweaty ['swɛtɪ] adj suado.
Swede [swiːd] n sueco/a.
swede [swiːd] n tipo de nabo.
Sweden ['swiːdən] n Suécia.
Swedish ['swiːdɪʃ] adj sueco ♦ n (LING) sueco.
sweep [swiːp] (pt, pp swept) n (act) varredura; (of arm) movimento circular; (range) extensão f, alcance m; (also: chimney ~) limpador m de chaminés ♦ vt varrer; (fashion, craze) espalhar-se por; (disease) arrasar ♦ vi varrer; (person) passar majestosamente.
sweep away vt varrer; (rub out) apagar.
sweep past vi passar rapidamente; (brush by) roçar.
sweep up vt, vi varrer.
sweeping ['swiːpɪŋ] adj (gesture) abarcador(a); (reform) radical; (statement) generalizado.

sweepstake ['swiːpsteɪk] n sweepstake m.
sweet [swiːt] n (candy) bala (BR), rebuçado (PT); (pudding) sobremesa ♦ adj doce; (sugary) açucarado; (fresh) fresco; (kind) meigo; (cute) bonitinho ♦ adv: to smell ~ ter bom cheiro; to taste ~ estar doce; ~ and sour agridoce.
sweetbread ['swiːtbrɛd] n moleja.
sweetcorn ['swiːtkɔːn] n milho.
sweeten ['swiːtən] vt adoçar; (add sugar to) pôr açúcar em.
sweetener ['swiːtnə*] n (CULIN) adoçante m.
sweetheart ['swiːthɑːt] n namorado/a; (as address) amor m.
sweetly ['swiːtlɪ] adv docemente; (gently) suavemente.
sweetness ['swiːtnɪs] n doçura.
sweet pea n ervilha-de-cheiro f.
sweet potato (irreg) n batata doce.
sweetshop ['swiːtʃɔp] n confeitaria.
swell [swɛl] (pt ~ed, pp swollen or ~ed) n (of sea) vaga, onda ♦ adj (inf: excellent) bacana ♦ vt engrossar ♦ vi engrossar; (MED) inchar(-se).
swelling ['swɛlɪŋ] n (MED) inchação f.
sweltering ['swɛltərɪŋ] adj sufocante, mormacento.
swept [swɛpt] pt, pp of **sweep**.
swerve [swɜːv] vi dar uma guinada, desviar-se.
swift [swɪft] n (bird) andorinhão m ♦ adj rápido, veloz.
swiftly ['swɪftlɪ] adv rapidamente, velozmente.
swiftness ['swɪftnɪs] n rapidez f, ligeireza.
swig [swɪg] (inf) n (drink) trago, gole m.
swill [swɪl] n lavagem f ♦ vt (also: ~ out, ~ down) lavar, limpar com água.
swim [swɪm] (pt swam, pp swum) n: to go for a ~ ir nadar ♦ vi nadar; (fig): my head/the room is ~ming estou com a cabeça zonza/sinto o quarto rodar ♦ vt atravessar a nado; (distance) percorrer (a nado); to go ~ming ir nadar; to ~ a length nadar uma volta.
swimmer ['swɪmə*] n nadador(a) m/f.
swimming ['swɪmɪŋ] n natação f.
swimming baths (BRIT) npl piscina.
swimming cap n touca de natação.
swimming costume (BRIT) n (woman's) maiô m (BR), fato de banho (PT); (man's) calção m de banho (BR), calções mpl de banho (PT).
swimming pool n piscina.
swimming trunks npl sunga (BR), calções mpl de banho (PT).
swimsuit ['swɪmsuːt] n (woman's) maiô m (BR), fato de banho (PT); (man's) calção m de banho (BR), calções mpl de banho (PT).
swindle ['swɪndl] n fraude f ♦ vt defraudar.
swindler ['swɪndlə*] n vigarista m/f.
swine [swaɪn] n inv porcos mpl; (inf) canalha m, calhorda m.

NB: European Portuguese adds the following consonants to certain words: **b** (sú(b)dito, su(b)til); **c** (a(c)ção, a(c)cionista, a(c)to); **m** (inde(m)ne); **p** (ado(p)ção, ado(p)tar); for further details see p. xiii.

swing [swɪŋ] (*pt, pp* **swung**) *n* (*in playground*) balanço; (*movement*) balanceio, oscilação *f*; (*change of direction*) virada; (*rhythm*) ritmo ♦ *vt* balançar; (*also:* ~ *round*) girar, rodar ♦ *vi* balançar(-se), oscilar; (*also:* ~ *round*) voltar-se bruscamente; **a** ~ **to the left** (*POL*) uma guinada para a esquerda; **to be in full** ~ estar em plena atividade; **to get into the** ~ **of things** familiarizar-se com tudo; **the road** ~**s south** a estrada vira em direção ao sul.
swing bridge *n* ponte *f* giratória.
swing door (*BRIT*) *n* porta de vaivém.
swingeing ['swɪndʒɪŋ] (*BRIT*) *adj* esmagador(a).
swinging ['swɪŋɪŋ] *adj* rítmico; (*person*) badalativo; ~ **door** (*US*) porta de vaivém.
swipe [swaɪp] *n* pancada violenta ♦ *vt* (*hit*) bater com violência; (*inf: steal*) afanar, roubar.
swirl [swəːl] *vi* redemoinhar ♦ *n* redemoinho.
swish [swɪʃ] *adj* (*BRIT: inf: smart*) chique ♦ *n* (*of whip*) silvo; (*of skirt, grass*) ruge-ruge *m*.
Swiss [swɪs] *adj, n inv* suíço/a.
Swiss roll *n* bolo de rolo, rocambole *m* doce.
switch [swɪtʃ] *n* (*for light, radio etc*) interruptor *m*; (*change*) mudança ♦ *vt* (*change*) trocar.
switch off *vt* apagar; (*engine*) desligar; (*BRIT: gas, water*) fechar.
switch on *vt* acender; (*engine, machine*) ligar; (*BRIT: gas, water*) abrir.
switchback ['swɪtʃbæk] (*BRIT*) *n* montanharussa.
switchblade ['swɪtʃbleɪd] *n* (*also:* ~ *knife*) canivete *m* de mola.
switchboard ['swɪtʃbɔːd] *n* (*TEL*) mesa telefônica.
switchboard operator *n* (*TEL*) telefonista *m/f*.
Switzerland ['swɪtsələnd] *n* Suíça.
swivel ['swɪvl] *vi* (*also:* ~ *round*) girar (sobre um eixo), fazer pião.
swollen ['swəulən] *pp of* **swell** ♦ *adj* inchado.
swoon [swuːn] *vi* desmaiar.
swoop [swuːp] *n* (*by police etc*) batida; (*of bird*) vôo picado ♦ *vi* (*also:* ~ *down*) precipitar-se, cair.
swop [swɔp] *n, vt* = **swap**.
sword [sɔːd] *n* espada.
swordfish ['sɔːdfɪʃ] *n inv* peixe-espada *m*.
swore [swɔː*] *pt of* **swear**.
sworn [swɔːn] *pp of* **swear**.
swot [swɔt] *vi* queimar as pestanas.
swum [swʌm] *pp of* **swim**.
swung [swʌŋ] *pt, pp of* **swing**.
sycamore ['sɪkəmɔː*] *n* sicômoro.
sycophant ['sɪkəfænt] *n* bajulador(a) *m/f*.
sycophantic [sɪkə'fæntɪk] *adj* (*person*) bajulador(a); (*behaviour*) bajulatório.
Sydney ['sɪdnɪ] *n* Sydney.
syllable ['sɪləbl] *n* sílaba.
syllabus ['sɪləbəs] *n* programa *m* de estudos; **on the** ~ no roteiro.
symbol ['sɪmbl] *n* símbolo.
symbolic(al) [sɪm'bɔlɪk(l)] *adj* simbólico.

symbolism ['sɪmbəlɪzəm] *n* simbolismo.
symbolize ['sɪmbəlaɪz] *vt* simbolizar.
symmetrical [sɪ'metrɪkl] *adj* simétrico.
symmetry ['sɪmɪtrɪ] *n* simetria.
sympathetic [sɪmpə'θetɪk] *adj* (*showing pity*) compassivo; (*understanding*) compreensivo; ~ **towards** favorável a.
sympathetically [sɪmpə'θetɪklɪ] *adv* (*with pity*) com compaixão; (*understandingly*) compreensivamente.
sympathize ['sɪmpəθaɪz] *vi:* **to** ~ **with sb** compadecer-se de alguém; **to** ~ **with** (*sb's feelings*) compreender.
sympathizer ['sɪmpəθaɪzə*] *n* (*POL*) simpatizante *m/f*.
sympathy ['sɪmpəθɪ] *n* (*pity*) compaixão *f*; **in** ~ **with** em acordo com; (*strike*) em solidariedade com; **with our deepest** ~ com nossos mais profundos pêsames.
symphonic [sɪm'fɔnɪk] *adj* sinfônico.
symphony ['sɪmfənɪ] *n* sinfonia.
symphony orchestra *n* orquestra sinfônica.
symposium [sɪm'pəuzɪəm] *n* simpósio.
symptom ['sɪmptəm] *n* sintoma *m*; (*sign*) indício.
symptomatic [sɪmptə'mætɪk] *adj* sintomático.
synagogue ['sɪnəgɔg] *n* sinagoga.
synchromesh ['sɪŋkrəumeʃ] *n* (*AUT*) engrenagem *f* sincronizada.
synchronize ['sɪŋkrənaɪz] *vt* sincronizar ♦ *vi:* **to** ~ **with** sincronizar-se com.
syncopated ['sɪŋkəpeɪtɪd] *adj* sincopado.
syndicate ['sɪndɪkɪt] *n* sindicato; (*of newspapers*) cadeia.
syndrome ['sɪndrəum] *n* síndrome *f*.
synonym ['sɪnənɪm] *n* sinônimo.
synonymous [sɪ'nɔnɪməs] *adj:* ~ (**with**) sinônimo (de).
synopses [sɪ'nɔpsiːz] *npl of* **synopsis**.
synopsis [sɪ'nɔpsɪs] *n* (*pl* **synopses**) *n* sinopse *f*, resumo.
syntax ['sɪntæks] *n* sintaxe *f*.
syntheses ['sɪnθəsiːz] *npl of* **synthesis**.
synthesis ['sɪnθəsɪs] *n* (*pl* **syntheses**) *n* síntese *f*.
synthesizer ['sɪnθəsaɪzə*] *n* (*MUS*) sintetizador *m*.
synthetic [sɪn'θetɪk] *adj* sintético ♦ *n:* ~**s** matérias *fpl* sintéticas.
syphilis ['sɪfɪlɪs] *n* sífilis *f*.
syphon ['saɪfən] = **siphon**.
Syria ['sɪrɪə] *n* Síria.
Syrian ['sɪrɪən] *adj, n* sírio/a.
syringe [sɪ'rɪndʒ] *n* seringa.
syrup ['sɪrəp] *n* xarope *m*; (*BRIT: also: golden* ~) melaço.
syrupy ['sɪrəpɪ] *adj* xaroposo.
system ['sɪstəm] *n* sistema *m*; (*method*) método; (*ANAT*) organismo.
systematic [sɪstə'mætɪk] *adj* sistemático.
system disk *n* (*COMPUT*) disco sistema.
systems analyst *n* analista *m/f* de sistemas.

T

T, t [tiː] *n* (*letter*) T, t *m*; **T for Tommy** T de Tereza.
TA (*BRIT*) *n abbr* = **Territorial Army**.
ta [tɑː] (*BRIT*: *inf*) *excl* obrigado/a.
tab [tæb] *n abbr* = **tabulator** ♦ *n* lingüeta, aba; (*label*) etiqueta; **to keep ~s on** (*fig*) vigiar.
tabby ['tæbɪ] *n* (*also*: ~ **cat**) gato malhado *or* listrado.
table ['teɪbl] *n* mesa; (*of statistics etc*) quadro, tabela ♦ *vt* (*motion etc*) apresentar; **to lay** *or* **set the ~** pôr a mesa; **to clear the ~** tirar a mesa; **league ~** (*BRIT*: *FOOTBALL*) classificação *f* dos times; **~ of contents** índice *m* das matérias.
tablecloth ['teɪblklɔθ] *n* toalha de mesa.
table d'hôte [tɑːbl'dəut] *n* refeição *f* comercial.
table lamp *n* abajur *m* (*BR*), candeeiro (*PT*).
tableland ['teɪbllænd] *n* planalto.
tablemat ['teɪblmæt] *n* descanso.
table salt *n* sal *m* fino.
tablespoon ['teɪblspuːn] *n* colher *f* de sopa; (*also*: ~**ful**: *as measurement*) colherada.
tablet ['tæblɪt] *n* (*MED*) comprimido; (: *for sucking*) pastilha; (*for writing*) bloco; (*of stone*) lápide *f*; **~ of soap** (*BRIT*) sabonete *m*.
table tennis *n* pingue-pongue *m*, tênis *m* de mesa.
table wine *n* vinho de mesa.
tabloid ['tæblɔɪd] *n* (*newspaper*) tablóide *m*; **the ~s** os jornais populares.
taboo [tə'buː] *n* tabu *m* ♦ *adj* tabu.
tabulate ['tæbjuleɪt] *vt* (*data, figures*) dispor em forma de tabela.
tabulator ['tæbjuleɪtə*] *n* tabulador *m*.
tachograph ['tækəgrɑːf] *n* tacógrafo.
tachometer [tæ'kɔmɪtə*] *n* tacômetro.
tacit ['tæsɪt] *adj* tácito, implícito.
taciturn ['tæsɪtəːn] *adj* taciturno.
tack [tæk] *n* (*nail*) tachinha, percevejo; (*BRIT*: *stitch*) alinhavo; (*NAUT*) amura ♦ *vt* prender com tachinha; alinhavar ♦ *vi* virar de bordo; **to change ~** virar de bordo; (*fig*) mudar de tática; **to ~ sth on to (the end of) sth** anexar algo a algo.
tackle ['tækl] *n* (*gear*) equipamento; (*also*: *fishing* ~) apetrechos *mpl*; (*for lifting*) guincho; (*FOOTBALL*) ato de tirar a bola de adversário ♦ *vt* (*difficulty*) atacar; (*grapple with*) atracar-se com; (*FOOTBALL*) tirar a bola de.
tacky ['tækɪ] *adj* pegajoso, grudento; (*inf*:

tasteless) cafona.
tact [tækt] *n* tato, diplomacia.
tactful ['tæktful] *adj* com tato, diplomático; **to be ~** ser diplomata.
tactfully ['tæktfulɪ] *adv* discretamente, com tato.
tactical ['tæktɪkl] *adj* tático.
tactics ['tæktɪks] *n, npl* tática.
tactless ['tæktlɪs] *adj* sem tato, sem diplomacia.
tactlessly ['tæktlɪslɪ] *adv* indiscretamente.
tadpole ['tædpəul] *n* girino.
taffy ['tæfɪ] (*US*) *n* puxa-puxa *m* (*BR*), caramelo (*PT*).
tag [tæg] *n* (*label*) etiqueta; **price/name ~** etiqueta de preço/com o nome.
tag along *vi* seguir.
Tahiti [tɑː'hiːtɪ] *n* Taiti (*no article*).
tail [teɪl] *n* rabo; (*of bird, comet etc*) cauda; (*of shirt, coat*) aba ♦ *vt* (*follow*) seguir bem de perto; **to turn ~** dar no pé; *see also* **head**.
tail away *vi* (*in size, quality etc*) diminuir gradualmente.
tail off *vi* (*in size, quality etc*) diminuir gradualmente.
tailback ['teɪlbæk] (*BRIT*) *n* fila (de carros).
tail coat *n* fraque *m*.
tail end *n* cauda, parte *f* final.
tailgate ['teɪlgeɪt] *n* (*AUT*) porta traseira.
tailor ['teɪlə*] *n* alfaiate *m* ♦ *vt*: **to ~ sth (to)** adaptar algo (a); **~'s (shop)** alfaiataria.
tailoring ['teɪlərɪŋ] *n* (*cut*) feitio.
tailor-made *adj* feito sob medida; (*fig*) especial.
tailwind ['teɪlwɪnd] *n* vento de popa *or* de cauda.
taint [teɪnt] *vt* (*meat, food*) estragar; (*fig*: *reputation*) manchar.
tainted ['teɪntɪd] *adj* (*food*) estragado, passado; (*water, air*) poluído; (*fig*) manchado.
Taiwan ['taɪ'wɑːn] *n* Taiuan (*no article*).
take [teɪk] (*pt* **took**, *pp* **taken**) *vt* (*gen*) tomar; (*grab*) pegar (em); (*gain*: *prize*) ganhar; (*require*: *effort, courage*) requerer, exigir; (*tolerate*) agüentar; (*accompany, bring, carry*) levar; (*exam*) prestar; (*hold*: *passengers etc*): **it ~s 50 people** cabem 50 pessoas ♦ *vi* (*dye, fire*) pegar ♦ *n* (*CINEMA*) tomada; **to ~ sth from** (*drawer etc*) tirar algo de; (*person*) pegar algo de; **I ~ it that** ... suponho que ...; **I took him for a doctor** eu o tomei por médico; **to ~ sb's hand** pegar a mão de alguém; **to ~ for a walk** levar a passeio; **to be taken ill** adoecer, ficar doente; **to ~ it upon o.s. to do sth** assumir a responsabilidade de fazer algo; **~ the first (street) on the left** pega a primeira (rua) à esquerda; **it won't ~ long** não vai demorar muito; **I was quite taken with it/her** gostei muito daquilo/dela.
take after *vt fus* parecer-se com.
take apart *vt* desmontar.

NB: European Portuguese adds the following consonants to certain words: **b** (sú(b)dito, su(b)til); **c** (a(c)ção, a(c)cionista, a(c)to); **m** (inde(m)ne); **p** (ado(p)ção, ado(p)tar); *for further details see p. xiii.*

take away vt (extract) tirar; (carry off) levar; (subtract) subtrair ♦ vi: **to ~ away from** diminuir.

take back vt (return) devolver; (one's words) retirar.

take down vt (building) demolir; (dismantle) desmontar; (letter etc) tomar por escrito.

take in vt (deceive) enganar; (understand) compreender; (include) abranger; (lodger) receber; (orphan, stray dog) acolher; (dress etc) apertar.

take off vi (AVIAT) decolar ♦ vt (remove) tirar; (imitate) imitar.

take on vt (work) empreender; (employee) empregar; (opponent) desafiar.

take out vt tirar; (extract) extrair; (licence) tirar; **to ~ sth out of** tirar algo de; **don't ~ it out on me!** não descarregue em cima de mim!

take over vt (business) tomar posse de ♦ vi: **to ~ over from sb** suceder a alguém.

take to vt fus (person) simpatizar com; (activity) afeiçoar-se a; **to ~ to doing sth** criar o hábito de fazer algo.

take up vt (dress) encurtar; (story) continuar; (occupy: time, space) ocupar; (engage in: hobby etc) dedicar-se a; (accept: offer, challenge) aceitar; (absorb: liquids) absorver ♦ vi: **to ~ up with sb** fazer amizade com alguém.

takeaway ['teɪkəweɪ] (BRIT) adj (food) para levar.

take-home pay n salário líquido.

taken ['teɪkən] pp of **take**.

takeoff ['teɪkɒf] n (AVIAT) decolagem f.

takeout ['teɪkaut] (US) adj (food) para levar.

takeover ['teɪkəuvə*] n (COMM) aquisição f de controle.

takeover bid n oferta pública de aquisição de controle.

takings ['teɪkɪŋz] npl (COMM) receita, renda.

talc [tælk] n (also: ~um powder) talco.

tale [teɪl] n (story) conto; (account) narrativa; **to tell ~s** (fig: lie) dizer mentiras; (: sneak) dedurar.

talent ['tælənt] n talento.

talented ['tæləntɪd] adj talentoso.

talent scout n caçador(a) m/f de talentos.

talk [tɔːk] n conversa, fala; (gossip) mexerico, fofocas fpl; (conversation) conversa, conversação f ♦ vi (speak) falar; (chatter) bater papo, conversar; **~s** npl (POL etc) negociações fpl; **to give a ~** dar uma palestra; **to ~ about** falar sobre; **~ing of films, have you seen ...?** por falar em filmes, você viu ...?; **to ~ sb into doing sth** convencer alguém a fazer algo; **to ~ sb out of doing sth** dissuadir alguém de fazer algo.

talk over vt discutir.

talkative ['tɔːkətɪv] adj loquaz, tagarela.

talker ['tɔːkə*] n falador(a) m/f.

talking point ['tɔːkɪŋ-] n assunto para discussão.

talking-to ['tɔːkɪŋ-] n: **to give sb a good ~**

passar um sabão em alguém.

talk show n (TV, RADIO) programa m de entrevistas.

tall [tɔːl] adj alto; (tree) grande; **to be 6 feet ~** medir 6 pés, ter 6 pés de altura; **how ~ are you?** qual é a sua altura?

tallboy ['tɔːlbɔɪ] (BRIT) n cômoda alta.

tallness ['tɔːlnɪs] n altura.

tall story n estória inverossímil.

tally ['tælɪ] n conta ♦ vi: **to ~ (with)** conferir (com); **to keep a ~ of sth** fazer um registro de algo.

talon ['tælən] n garra.

tambourine [tæmbə'riːn] n tamborim m, pandeiro.

tame [teɪm] adj (mild) manso; (tamed) domesticado; (fig: story, style) sem graça, insípido.

tamper ['tæmpə*] vi: **to ~ with** mexer em.

tampon ['tæmpən] n tampão m higiénico.

tan [tæn] n (also: sun~) bronzeado ♦ vt bronzear ♦ vi bronzear-se ♦ adj (colour) bronzeado, marrom claro; **to get a ~** bronzear-se.

tandem ['tændəm] n tandem m.

tang [tæŋ] n sabor m forte.

tangent ['tændʒənt] n (MATH) tangente f; **to go off at a ~** (fig) sair pela tangente.

tangerine [tændʒə'riːn] n tangerina, mexerica.

tangible ['tændʒəbl] adj tangível; **~ assets** ativos mpl tangíveis.

tangle ['tæŋgl] n emaranhado ♦ vt emaranhar; **to get in(to) a ~** meter-se num rolo.

tango ['tæŋgəu] n tango.

tank [tæŋk] n (water ~) depósito, tanque m; (for fish) aquário; (MIL) tanque m.

tankard ['tæŋkəd] n canecão m.

tanker ['tæŋkə*] n (ship) navio-tanque m; (: for oil) petroleiro; (truck) caminhão-tanque m.

tanned [tænd] adj (skin) moreno, bronzeado.

tannin ['tænɪn] n tanino.

tanning ['tænɪŋ] n (of leather) curtimento.

tannoy ['tænɔɪ] ® (BRIT) n alto-falante m; **over the ~** nos alto-falantes.

tantalizing ['tæntəlaɪzɪŋ] adj tentador(a).

tantamount ['tæntəmaunt] adj: **~ to** equivalente a.

tantrum ['tæntrəm] n chilique m, acesso (de raiva); **to throw a ~** ter um chilique or acesso.

Tanzania [tænzə'nɪə] n Tanzânia.

Tanzanian [tænzə'nɪən] adj, n tanzaniano/a.

tap [tæp] n (on sink etc) torneira; (gentle blow) palmadinha; (gas ~) chave f ♦ vt dar palmadinha em, bater de leve; (resources) utilizar, explorar; (telephone) grampear; **on ~** (beer) de barril; (resources) disponível.

tap-dancing n sapateado.

tape [teɪp] n fita; (also: magnetic ~) fita magnética; (sticky ~) fita adesiva ♦ vt (record) gravar (em fita); **on ~** (song etc) em fita.

tape deck n gravador m, toca-fitas m inv.

tape measure n fita métrica, trena.

taper ['teɪpə*] *n* círio ♦ *vi* afilar-se, estreitar-se.

tape-record *vt* gravar (em fita).

tape recorder *n* gravador *m*.

tape recording *n* gravação *f* (em fita).

tapered ['teɪpəd] *adj* afilado.

tapering ['teɪpərɪŋ] *adj* afilado.

tapestry ['tæpɪstrɪ] *n* (*object*) tapete *m* de parede; (*art*) tapeçaria.

tapeworm ['teɪpwəːm] *n* solitária.

tapioca [tæpɪ'əukə] *n* tapioca.

tappet ['tæpɪt] *n* (*AUT*) tucho (*BR*), ponteiro de válvula (*PT*).

tar [tɑː] *n* alcatrão *m*; (*on road*) piche *m*; **low-/middle-~ cigarettes** cigarros com baixo/médio teor de alcatrão.

tarantula [tə'ræntjulə] *n* tarântula.

tardy ['tɑːdɪ] *adj* tardio.

target ['tɑːgɪt] *n* alvo; (*fig: objective*) objetivo; **to be on ~** (*project*) progredir segundo as previsões.

target practice *n* exercício de tiro ao alvo.

tariff ['tærɪf] *n* tarifa.

tariff barrier *n* barreira alfandegária.

tarmac ['tɑːmæk] *n* (*BRIT: on road*) macadame *m*; (*AVIAT*) pista ♦ *vt* (*BRIT*) asfaltar.

tarnish ['tɑːnɪʃ] *vt* empanar o brilho de.

tarpaulin [tɑː'pɔːlɪn] *n* lona alcatroada.

tarragon ['tærəgən] *n* estragão *m*.

tart [tɑːt] *n* (*CULIN*) torta; (*BRIT: inf: pej: woman*) piranha ♦ *adj* (*flavour*) ácido, azedo.

tart up (*inf*) *vt* arrumar, dar um jeito em; **to ~ o.s. up** arrumar-se; (*pej*) empetecar-se.

tartan ['tɑːtn] *n* pano escocês axadrezado, tartan *m* ♦ *adj* axadrezado.

tartar ['tɑːtə*] *n* (*on teeth*) tártaro.

tartar(e) sauce ['tɑːtə*-] *n* molho tártaro.

task [tɑːsk] *n* tarefa; **to take to ~** repreender.

task force *n* (*MIL*, *POLICE*) força-tarefa.

taskmaster ['tɑːskmɑːstə*] *n*: **he's a hard ~** ele é muito exigente.

Tasmania [tæz'meɪnɪə] *n* Tasmânia *f*.

tassel ['tæsl] *n* borla, pendão *m*.

taste [teɪst] *n* gosto; (*also: after~*) gosto residual; (*sip*) golinho; (*fig: glimpse, idea*) amostra, idéia ♦ *vt* experimentar ♦ *vi*: **to ~ of or like** (*fish etc*) ter gosto de, saber a; **you can ~ the garlic (in it)** sente-se o gosto de alho; **can I have a ~ of this wine?** posso provar o vinho?; **to have a ~ for** sentir predileção por; **in good/bad ~** de bom/mau gosto.

taste bud *n* papila gustativa.

tasteful ['teɪstful] *adj* de bom gosto.

tastefully ['teɪstfulɪ] *adv* com bom gosto.

tasteless ['teɪstlɪs] *adj* (*food*) insípido, insosso; (*remark*) de mau gosto.

tasty ['teɪstɪ] *adj* saboroso, delicioso.

tattered ['tætəd] *adj* esfarrapado.

tatters ['tætəz] *npl*: **in ~** esfarrapado.

tattoo [tə'tuː] *n* tatuagem *f*; (*spectacle*) espetáculo militar ♦ *vt* tatuar.

tatty ['tætɪ] (*BRIT: inf*) *adj* (*worn*) surrado; (*dirty*) enxovalhado.

taught [tɔːt] *pt, pp of* **teach**.

taunt [tɔːnt] *n* zombaria, escárnio ♦ *vt* zombar de, mofar de.

Taurus ['tɔːrəs] *n* Touro.

taut [tɔːt] *adj* esticado, retesado.

tavern ['tævən] *n* taverna.

tawdry ['tɔːdrɪ] *adj* de mau gosto, espalhafatoso, berrante.

tawny ['tɔːnɪ] *adj* moreno, trigueiro.

tax [tæks] *n* imposto ♦ *vt* tributar; (*fig: test*) sobrecarregar; (: *patience*) esgotar; **before/after ~** antes/depois de impostos; **free of ~** isento de impostos.

taxable ['tæksəbl] *adj* (*income*) tributável.

tax allowance *n* abatimento da renda.

taxation [tæk'seɪʃən] *n* tributação *f*; **system of ~** sistema fiscal.

tax avoidance *n* evasão *f* de impostos.

tax collector *n* cobrador(a) *m/f* de impostos.

tax disc (*BRIT*) *n* (*AUT*) ≈ plaqueta.

tax evasion *n* sonegação *f* fiscal.

tax exemption *n* isenção *f* de impostos.

tax exile *n* pessoa que se expatria para evitar impostos excessivos.

tax-free *adj* isento de impostos.

tax haven *n* refúgio fiscal.

taxi ['tæksɪ] *n* táxi *m* ♦ *vi* (*AVIAT*) taxiar.

taxidermist ['tæksɪdəːmɪst] *n* taxidermista *m/f*.

taxi driver *n* motorista *m/f* de táxi.

taximeter ['tæksɪmiːtə*] *n* taxímetro.

tax inspector (*BRIT*) *n* fiscal *m/f* de imposto de renda.

taxi rank (*BRIT*) *n* ponto de táxi.

taxi stand *n* ponto de táxi.

tax payer *n* contribuinte *m/f*.

tax rebate *n* devolução *f* de imposto de renda.

tax relief *n* isenção *f* de imposto.

tax return *n* declaração *f* de rendimentos.

tax year *n* ano fiscal, exercício.

TB *abbr of* **tuberculosis**.

TD (*US*) *n* *abbr* = **Treasury Department**; (*FOOTBALL*) = **touchdown**.

tea [tiː] *n* chá *m*; (*snack*) lanche *m*; **high ~** (*BRIT*) jantar-lanche *m*.

tea bag *n* saquinho (*BR*) *or* carteira (*PT*) de chá.

tea break (*BRIT*) *n* pausa (para o chá).

teacake ['tiːkeɪk] (*BRIT*) *n* pãozinho doce.

teach [tiːtʃ] (*pt, pp* **taught**) *vt*: **to ~ sb sth, ~ sth to sb** ensinar algo a alguém ♦ *vi* ensinar; (*be a teacher*) lecionar (*PT*: -cc-); **it taught him a lesson** (*fig*) isto lhe serviu de lição.

teacher ['tiːtʃə*] *n* professor(a) *m/f*.

teacher training college *n* faculdade *f* de formação de professores.

teaching ['tiːtʃɪŋ] *n* ensino; (*as profession*) magistério.

teaching aids *npl* recursos *mpl* de ensino.

teaching hospital (*BRIT*) *n* hospital *m* esco-

NB: *European Portuguese adds the following consonants to certain words:* **b** (sú(b)dito, su(b)til); **c** (a(c)ção, a(c)cionista, a(c)to); **m** (inde(m)ne); **p** (ado(p)ção, ado(p)tar); *for further details see p. xiii.*

la.

teaching staff (*BRIT*) *n* corpo docente.

tea cosy *n* coberta do bule, abafador *m*.

teacup ['ti:kʌp] *n* xícara (*BR*) *or* chávena (*PT*) de chá.

teak [ti:k] *n* (madeira de) teca ♦ *cpd* de teca.

tea leaves *npl* folhas *fpl* de chá.

team [ti:m] *n* (*SPORT*) time *m* (*BR*), equipa (*PT*); (*group*) equipe *f* (*BR*), equipa (*PT*); (*of animals*) parelha.

team up *vi*: **to ~ up (with)** agrupar-se (com).

team games *npl* jogos *mpl* de equipe.

teamwork ['ti:mwɔːk] *n* trabalho de equipe.

tea party *n* chá *m* (*reunião*).

teapot ['ti:pɔt] *n* bule *m* de chá.

tear¹ [tɪə*] *n* lágrima; **in ~s** chorando, em lágrimas; **to burst into ~s** romper em lágrimas.

tear² [tɛə*] (*pt* **tore**, *pp* **torn**) *n* rasgão *m* ♦ *vt* rasgar ♦ *vi* rasgar-se; **to ~ to pieces** *or* **to bits** *or* **to shreds** despedaçar, estraçalhar; (*fig*) arrasar com.

tear along *vi* (*rush*) precipitar-se.

tear apart *vt* rasgar; (*fig*) arrasar.

tear away *vt*: **to ~ o.s. away (from sth)** desgrudar-se (de algo).

tear out *vt* (*sheet of paper, cheque*) arrancar.

tear up *vt* rasgar.

tearaway ['tɛərəweɪ] (*inf*) *n* bagunceiro/a.

teardrop ['tɪədrɔp] *n* lágrima.

tearful ['tɪəful] *adj* choroso.

tear gas *n* gás *m* lacrimogênio.

tearoom ['ti:ru:m] *n* salão *m* de chá.

tease [ti:z] *n* implicante *m/f* ♦ *vt* implicar com.

tea set *n* aparelho de chá.

teashop ['ti:ʃɔp] *n* salão *m* de chá.

teaspoon ['ti:spu:n] *n* colher *f* de chá; (*also*: **~ful**: *as measurement*) (conteúdo de) colher de chá.

tea strainer *n* coador *m* (de chá).

teat [ti:t] *n* (*of bottle*) bico (de mamadeira).

teatime ['ti:taɪm] *n* hora do chá.

tea towel (*BRIT*) *n* pano de prato.

tea urn *n* samovar *m*.

tech [tɛk] (*inf*) *n* *abbr* = **technology; technical college.**

technical ['tɛknɪkl] *adj* técnico.

technical college (*BRIT*) *n* escola técnica.

technicality [tɛknɪ'kælɪtɪ] *n* detalhe *m* técnico; (*quality*) tecnicidade *f*; **on a legal ~** devido a uma particularidade jurídica.

technically ['tɛknɪklɪ] *adv* tecnicamente.

technician [tɛk'nɪʃn] *n* técnico/a.

technique [tɛk'ni:k] *n* técnica.

technocrat ['tɛknəkræt] *n* tecnocrata *m/f*.

technological [tɛknə'lɔdʒɪkl] *adj* tecnológico.

technologist [tɛk'nɔlədʒɪst] *n* tecnólogo/a.

technology [tɛk'nɔlədʒɪ] *n* tecnologia.

teddy (bear) ['tɛdɪ-] *n* ursinho de pelúcia.

tedious ['ti:dɪəs] *adj* maçante, chato.

tedium ['ti:dɪəm] *n* tédio.

tee [ti:] *n* (*GOLF*) tee *m*.

teem [ti:m] *vi* abundar, pulular; **to ~ with** abundar em; **it is ~ing (with rain)** está chovendo a cântaros.

teenage ['ti:neɪdʒ] *adj* (*fashions etc*) de *or* para adolescentes.

teenager ['ti:neɪdʒə*] *n* adolescente *m/f*, jovem *m/f*.

teens [ti:nz] *npl*: **to be in one's ~** estar entre os 13 e 19 anos, estar na adolescência.

tee-shirt *n* = **T-shirt**.

teeter ['ti:tə*] *vi* balançar-se.

teeth [ti:θ] *npl of* **tooth**.

teethe [ti:ð] *vi* começar a ter dentes.

teething ring ['ti:ðɪŋ-] *n* mastigador *m* para a dentição.

teething troubles ['ti:ðɪŋ-] *npl* (*fig*) dificuldades *fpl* iniciais.

teetotal ['ti:'təutl] *adj* (*person*) abstêmio.

teetotaller ['ti:'təutlə*] (*US* **teetotaler**) *n* abstêmio/a.

TEFL ['tɛfl] *n abbr* = **Teaching of English as a Foreign Language.**

Teheran [tɛə'rɑ:n] *n* Teerá (*BR*), Teerão (*PT*).

tel. *abbr* (= *telephone*) tel.

Tel Aviv ['tɛlə'vi:v] *n* Telavive.

telecast ['tɛlɪkɑ:st] (*irreg*: *like* **cast**) *vt* televisionar, transmitir por televisão.

telecommunications [tɛlɪkəmju:nɪ'keɪʃənz] *n* telecomunicações *fpl*.

telegram ['tɛlɪgræm] *n* telegrama *m*.

telegraph ['tɛlɪgrɑ:f] *n* telégrafo.

telegraphic [tɛlɪ'græfɪk] *adj* telegráfico.

telegraph pole *n* poste *m* telegráfico.

telegraph wire *n* fio telegráfico.

telepathic [tɛlɪ'pæθɪk] *adj* telepático.

telepathy [tə'lɛpəθɪ] *n* telepatia.

telephone ['tɛlɪfəun] *n* telefone *m* ♦ *vt* (*person*) telefonar para; (*message*) telefonar; **to be on the ~** (*BRIT*), **to have a ~** (*subscriber*) ter telefone; **to be on the ~** (*be speaking*) estar falando no telefone.

telephone booth (*BRIT* **telephone box**) *n* cabine *f* telefônica.

telephone call *n* telefonema *m*.

telephone directory *n* lista telefônica, catálogo (*BR*).

telephone exchange *n* estação *f* telefônica.

telephone kiosk (*BRIT*) *n* cabine *f* telefônica.

telephone number *n* (número de) telefone *m*.

telephone operator *n* telefonista *m/f*.

telephone tapping [-'tæpɪŋ] *n* escuta telefônica.

telephonist [tə'lɛfənɪst] (*BRIT*) *n* telefonista *m/f*.

telephoto ['tɛlɪfəutəu] *adj*: **~ lens** teleobjetivo.

teleprinter ['tɛlɪprɪntə*] *n* teletipo.

Teleprompter ['tɛlɪprɔmptə*] ® (*US*) *n* ponto mecânico.

telescope ['tɛlɪskəup] *n* telescópio ♦ *vt*, *vi* abrir (*or* fechar) como um telescópio.

telescopic [tɛlɪ'skɔpɪk] *adj* telescópico.

Teletex ['tɛlətɛks] ® *n* (*TEL*) videotexto.

televiewer ['tɛlɪvju:ə*] *n* telespectador(a) *m/f*.

televise ['tɛlɪvaɪz] vt televisar, televisionar.
television ['tɛlɪvɪʒən] n televisão f.
television licence (BRIT) n licença para utilizar um televisor.
television programme n programa m de televisão.
television set n (aparelho de) televisão f, televisor m.
telex ['tɛlɛks] n telex m ♦ vt (message) enviar por telex, telexar; (person) mandar um telex para ♦ vi enviar um telex.
tell [tɛl] (pt, pp told) vt dizer; (relate: story) contar; (distinguish): **to ~ sth from** distinguir algo de ♦ vi (have effect) ter efeito; (talk): **to ~ (of)** falar (de or em); **to ~ sb to do sth** dizer para alguém fazer algo; (order) mandar alguém fazer algo; **to ~ sb about sth** falar a alguém de algo; (what happened) contar algo a alguém; **to ~ the time** (know how to) dizer as horas; (clock) marcar as horas; **can you ~ me the time?** pode me dizer a hora?; **(I) ~ you what ...** escuta ...; **I can't ~ them apart** não consigo diferenciar um do outro; **to ~ the difference** sentir a diferença; **how can you ~?** como você sabe?
tell off vt repreender, dar uma bronca em.
tell on vt fus (inform against) delatar, dedurar.
teller ['tɛlə*] n (in bank) caixa m/f.
telling ['tɛlɪŋ] adj (remark, detail) revelador(a).
telltale ['tɛlteɪl] adj (sign) denunciador(a), revelador(a).
telly ['tɛlɪ] (BRIT: inf) n abbr = **television**.
temerity [tə'mɛrɪtɪ] n temeridade f.
temp [tɛmp] (BRIT: inf) abbr (= temporary) n temporário/a ♦ vi trabalhar como temporário/a.
temper ['tɛmpə*] n (nature) temperamento; (mood) humor m; (bad ~) mau gênio; (fit of anger) cólera; (of child) birra ♦ vt (moderate) moderar; **to be in a ~** estar de mau humor; **to lose one's ~** perder a paciência or a calma, ficar zangado; **to keep one's ~** controlar-se.
temperament ['tɛmprəmənt] n (nature) temperamento.
temperamental [tɛmprə'mɛntl] adj temperamental.
temperance ['tɛmpərəns] n moderação f; (in drinking) sobriedade f.
temperate ['tɛmprət] adj moderado; (climate) temperado.
temperature ['tɛmprətʃə*] n temperatura; **to have or run a ~** ter febre.
temperature chart n (MED) tabela de temperatura.
tempered ['tɛmpəd] adj (steel) temperado.
tempest ['tɛmpɪst] n tempestade f.
tempestuous [tɛm'pɛstjuəs] adj (relationship) tempestuoso.

tempi ['tɛmpiː] npl of **tempo**.
template ['tɛmplɪt] n molde m.
temple ['tɛmpl] n (building) templo; (ANAT) têmpora.
templet ['tɛmplɪt] n = **template**.
tempo ['tɛmpəu] (pl ~s or **tempi**) n tempo; (fig: of life etc) ritmo.
temporal ['tɛmpərəl] adj temporal.
temporarily ['tɛmpərərɪlɪ] adv temporariamente; (closed) provisoriamente.
temporary ['tɛmpərərɪ] adj temporário; (passing) transitório; (worker) provisório; **~ secretary** secretária temporária; **~ teacher** professor suplente.
temporize ['tɛmpəraɪz] vi temporizar.
tempt [tɛmpt] vt tentar; **to ~ sb into doing sth** tentar or induzir alguém a fazer algo; **to be ~ed to do sth** ser tentado a fazer algo.
temptation [tɛmp'teɪʃən] n tentação f.
tempting ['tɛmptɪŋ] adj tentador(a).
ten [tɛn] num dez ♦ n: **~s of thousands** milhares mpl e milhares; see also **five**.
tenable ['tɛnəbl] adj sustentável.
tenacious [tə'neɪʃəs] adj tenaz.
tenacity [tə'næsɪtɪ] n tenacidade f.
tenancy ['tɛnənsɪ] n aluguel m; (of house) locação f.
tenant ['tɛnənt] n inquilino/a, locatário/a.
tend [tɛnd] vt (sick etc) cuidar de; (machine) vigiar ♦ vi: **to ~ to do sth** tender a fazer algo.
tendency ['tɛndənsɪ] n tendência.
tender ['tɛndə*] adj macio, tenro; (delicate) delicado; (gentle) terno; (sore) sensível, dolorido; (affectionate) carinhoso, afetuoso ♦ n (COMM: offer) oferta, proposta; (money): **legal ~** moeda corrente or legal ♦ vt oferecer; **to ~ one's resignation** pedir demissão; **to put in a ~ (for)** apresentar uma proposta (para); **to put work out to ~** (BRIT) abrir concorrência para uma obra.
tenderize ['tɛndəraɪz] vt (CULIN) amaciar.
tenderly ['tɛndəlɪ] adv afetuosamente.
tenderness ['tɛndənɪs] n ternura; (of meat) maciez f.
tendon ['tɛndən] n tendão m.
tenement ['tɛnəmənt] n conjunto habitacional.
Tenerife [tɛnə'riːf] n Tenerife (no article).
tenet ['tɛnət] n princípio.
tenner ['tɛnə*] (BRIT: inf) n nota de dez libras.
tennis ['tɛnɪs] n tênis m ♦ cpd (match, racket etc) de tênis.
tennis ball n bola de tênis.
tennis court n quadra de tênis.
tennis elbow n (MED) sinovite f do cotovelo.
tennis shoes npl tênis m.
tenor ['tɛnə*] n (MUS) tenor m; (of speech etc) teor m.
tenpin bowling ['tɛnpɪn-] (BRIT) n boliche m com 10 paus.
tense [tɛns] adj tenso; (stretched) estirado, esticado; (stiff) rígido, teso ♦ n (LING) tempo

---

NB: European Portuguese adds the following consonants to certain words: **b** (sú(b)dito, su(b)til); **c** (a(c)ção, a(c)cionista, a(c)to); **m** (inde(m)ne); **p** (ado(p)ção, ado(p)tar); *for further details see p. xiii.*

♦ *vt* (*tighten*: *muscles*) retesar.
tenseness ['tɛnsnɪs] *n* tensão *f*.
tension ['tɛnʃən] *n* tensão *f*.
tent [tɛnt] *n* tenda, barraca.
tentacle ['tɛntəkl] *n* tentáculo.
tentative ['tɛntətɪv] *adj* (*conclusion*) provisório, tentativo; (*person*) hesitante, indeciso.
tenterhooks ['tɛntəhuks] *npl*: **on ~ em**
suspense.
tenth [tɛnθ] *num* décimo; *see also* **fifth**.
tent peg *n* estaca.
tent pole *n* pau *m*.
tenuous ['tɛnjuəs] *adj* tênue.
tenure ['tɛnjuə*] *n* (*of property*) posse *f*; (*of job*) estabilidade *f*.
tepid ['tɛpɪd] *adj* tépido, morno.
term [tɜːm] *n* (*COMM*) prazo; (*word*) termo; (*period*) período; (*SCH*) trimestre *m*; (*LAW*) sessão *f* ♦ *vt* denominar; **~s** *npl* (*conditions*) condições *fpl*; (*COMM*) cláusulas *fpl*, termos *mpl*; **in ~s of** ... em função de ...; **~ of imprisonment** pena de prisão; **his ~ of office** seu mandato; **in the short/long ~** a curto/longo prazo; **to be on good ~s with sb** dar-se bem com alguém; **to come to ~s with** (*person*) chegar a um acordo com; (*problem*) adaptar-se a.
terminal ['tɜːmɪnl] *adj* terminal ♦ *n* (*ELEC*) borne *m*; (*BRIT*: *also*: *air ~*) terminal *m*; (*for oil, ore etc, also*: *COMPUT*) terminal *m*; (*BRIT*: *also*: *coach ~*) estação *f* rodoviária.
terminate ['tɜːmɪneɪt] *vt* terminar, pôr fim a ♦ *vi*: **to ~ in** acabar em.
termination [tɜːmɪ'neɪʃən] *n* término; (*of contract*) rescisão *f*; **~ of pregnancy** (*MED*) interrupção da gravidez.
termini ['tɜːmɪnaɪ] *npl of* **terminus**.
terminology [tɜːmɪ'nɔlədʒɪ] *n* terminologia.
terminus ['tɜːmɪnəs] (*pl* **termini**) *n* término, terminal *m*.
termite ['tɜːmaɪt] *n* cupim *m*.
Ter(r). *abbr* = **terrace**.
terrace ['tɛrəs] *n* terraço; (*BRIT*: *row of houses*) lance *m* de casas; **the ~s** *npl* (*BRIT*: *SPORT*) a arquibancada (*BR*), a geral (*PT*).
terraced ['tɛrəst] *adj* (*house*) ladeado por outras casas; (*garden*) em dois níveis.
terracotta ['tɛrə'kɔtə] *n* terracota.
terrain [tɛ'reɪn] *n* terreno.
terrible ['tɛrɪbl] *adj* terrível, horroroso; (*weather, job*) horrível.
terribly ['tɛrɪblɪ] *adv* terrivelmente; (*very badly*) pessimamente.
terrier ['tɛrɪə*] *n* terrier *m*.
terrific [tə'rɪfɪk] *adj* terrível, magnífico; (*wonderful*) maravilhoso, sensacional.
terrify ['tɛrɪfaɪ] *vt* apavorar.
territorial [tɛrɪ'tɔːrɪəl] *adj* territorial.
territorial waters *npl* águas *fpl* territoriais.
territory ['tɛrɪtərɪ] *n* território.
terror ['tɛrə*] *n* terror *m*.
terrorism ['tɛrərɪzəm] *n* terrorismo.
terrorist ['tɛrərɪst] *n* terrorista *m/f*.
terrorize ['tɛrəraɪz] *vt* aterrorizar.
terse [tɜːs] *adj* (*style*) conciso, sucinto; (*reply*)

brusco.
tertiary ['tɜːʃərɪ] *adj* terciário; **~ education** (*BRIT*) ensino superior.
Terylene ['tɛrɪliːn] ® (*BRIT*) *n* tergal *m* ®.
TESL ['tɛsl] *n* *abbr* = **Teaching of English as a Second Language**.
test [tɛst] *n* (*trial, check*) prova, ensaio; (: *of goods in factory*) controle *m*; (*of courage etc, CHEM*) prova; (*MED*) exame *m*; (*exam*) teste *m*, prova; (*also: driving ~*) exame de motorista ♦ *vt* testar, pôr à prova; **to put sth to the ~** pôr algo à prova.
testament ['tɛstəmənt] *n* testamento; **the Old/New T~** o Velho/Novo Testamento.
test ban *n* (*also: nuclear ~*) proibição *f* de testes nucleares.
test case *n* (*LAW, fig*) caso exemplar.
test flight *n* teste *m* de vôo.
testicle ['tɛstɪkl] *n* testículo.
testify ['tɛstɪfaɪ] *vi* (*LAW*) depor, testemunhar; **to ~ to sth** (*LAW*) atestar algo; (*gen*) testemunhar algo.
testimonial [tɛstɪ'məunɪəl] *n* (*reference*) carta de recomendação; (*gift*) obséquio, tributo.
testimony ['tɛstɪmənɪ] *n* (*LAW*) testemunho, depoimento.
testing ['tɛstɪŋ] *adj* (*situation, period*) difícil.
testing ground *n* campo de provas.
test match *n* (*CRICKET, RUGBY*) jogo internacional.
test paper *n* (*SCH*) prova escrita.
test pilot *n* piloto de prova.
test tube *n* proveta, tubo de ensaio.
test-tube baby *n* bebê *m* de proveta.
testy ['tɛstɪ] *adj* rabugento, irritável.
tetanus ['tɛtənəs] *n* tétano.
tetchy ['tɛtʃɪ] *adj* irritável.
tether ['tɛðə*] *vt* amarrar ♦ *n*: **at the end of one's ~** a ponto de perder a paciência *or* as estribeiras.
text [tɛkst] *n* texto.
textbook ['tɛkstbuk] *n* livro didático; (*SCH*) livro escolar.
textiles ['tɛkstaɪlz] *npl* têxteis *mpl*.
texture ['tɛkstʃə*] *n* textura.
TGIF (*inf*) *abbr* = **thank God it's Friday**.
TGWU (*BRIT*) *n* *abbr* (= *Transport and General Workers' Union*) sindicato dos transportadores.
Thai [taɪ] *adj* tailandês/esa ♦ *n* tailandês/esa *m/f*; (*LING*) tailandês *m*.
Thailand ['taɪlænd] *n* Tailândia.
thalidomide [θə'lɪdəmaɪd] ® *n* talidomida ®.
Thames [tɛmz] *n*: **the ~** o Tâmisa (*BR*), o Tamisa (*PT*).
than [ðæn, ðən] *conj* do que; (*with numerals*): **more ~ 10/once** mais de 10/uma vez; **I have more/less ~ you** tenho mais/menos do que você; **she has more apples ~ pears** ela tem mais maçãs do que peras; **it is better to phone ~ to write** é melhor telefonar do que escrever; **no sooner did he leave ~ the phone rang** ele acabou de sair quando o telefone tocou.
thank [θæŋk] *vt* agradecer; **~ you (very**

much) muito obrigado/a; ~ **heavens**, ~ **God** graças a Deus; **to ~ sb for sth** agradecer a alguém (por) algo; **to say ~ you** agradecer.

thankful ['θæŋkful] adj: ~ **(for)** agradecido (por); ~ **that** (relieved) aliviado que.

thankfully ['θæŋkfəlɪ] adv (gratefully) agradecidamente; (fortunately) felizmente.

thankless ['θæŋklɪs] adj ingrato.

thanks [θæŋks] npl agradecimentos mpl; (to God etc) graças fpl ♦ excl obrigado/a!; ~ **to** graças a.

Thanksgiving (Day) ['θæŋksgɪvɪŋ-] n Dia m de Ação de Graças.

that [ðæt, ðət] (pl **those**) conj que ♦ adj esse/essa; (more remote) aquele/aquela ♦ pron esse/essa, aquele/aquela; (neuter) isso, aquilo; (relative) que, quem, o qual/a qual etc; (with time): **on the day ~ he came** no dia em que ele veio ♦ adv: ~ **high** dessa altura, até essa altura; **it's about ~ high** é mais ou menos dessa altura; ~ **one** esse/essa; **what's ~?** o que é isso?; **who's ~?** quem é?; **is ~ you?** é você?; ~**'s what he said** foi isso o que ele disse; ~ **is ...** isto é ...; **all ~** tudo isso; **I can't work ~ much** não posso trabalhar tanto; **at** or **with ~, she ...** e assim, ela ..., aí, ela ... (inf); **do it like ~** faz assim; **not ~ I know of** que eu saiba, não.

thatched [θætʃt] adj (roof) de sapê; ~ **cottage** chalé m com telhado de sapê or de colmo.

thaw [θɔ:] n degelo ♦ vi (ice) derreter-se; (food) descongelar-se ♦ vt (food) descongelar; **it's ~ing** (weather) degela.

the [ðiː, ðə] def art (sg) o/a; (pl) os/as; (in titles): **Richard ~ Second** Ricardo II ♦ adv: ~ **sooner ~ better** quanto mais cedo, melhor; ~ **more he works ~ more he earns** quanto mais ele trabalha, mais ele ganha; ~ **rich and ~ poor** os ricos e os pobres; **do you know ~ Smiths?** você conhece os Smith?

theatre ['θɪətə*] (US **theater**) n teatro.

theatre-goer ['θɪətəgəuə*] n freqüentador(a) m/f de teatro.

theatrical [θɪ'ætrɪkl] adj teatral; ~ **company** companhia de teatro.

theft [θeft] n roubo.

their [ðeə*] adj seu/sua, deles/delas.

theirs [ðeəz] pron (o) seu/(a) sua; **a friend of** ~ um amigo seu/deles; **it's** ~ é deles.

them [ðɛm, ðəm] pron (direct) os/as; (indirect) lhes; (stressed, after prep) a eles/a elas; **I see** ~ eu os vejo; **give** ~ **the book** dê o livro a eles; **give me some of** ~ me dê alguns deles.

theme [θiːm] n tema m.

theme song n tema m musical.

themselves [ðəm'sɛlvz] pron (subject) eles mesmos/elas mesmas; (complement) se; (after prep) si (mesmos/as).

then [ðɛn] adv (at that time) então; (next) em seguida; (later) logo, depois; (and also) além

disso ♦ conj (therefore) então, nesse caso, portanto ♦ adj: **the** ~ **president** o então presidente; **by** ~ (past) até então; (future) até lá; **from** ~ **on** a partir de então; **before** ~ antes (disso); **until** ~ até lá; **and** ~ **what?** e então?, e daí?; **what do you want me to do** ~? o que você quer que eu faça depois?; (in that case) então, o que você quer que eu faça?

theologian [θɪə'ləudʒən] n teólogo/a.

theological [θɪə'lɔdʒɪkl] adj teológico.

theology [θɪ'ɔlədʒɪ] n teologia.

theorem ['θɪərəm] n teorema m.

theoretical [θɪə'rɛtɪkl] adj teórico.

theoretically [θɪə'rɛtɪklɪ] adv teoricamente.

theorize ['θɪəraɪz] vi teorizar, elaborar uma teoria.

theory ['θɪərɪ] n teoria; **in** ~ em teoria, teoricamente.

therapeutic(al) [θɛrə'pjuːtɪk(l)] adj terapêutico.

therapist ['θɛrəpɪst] n terapeuta m/f.

therapy ['θɛrəpɪ] n terapia.

there [ðeə*] adv aí, ali, lá; ~, ~! calma!; **it's** ~ está aí; **he went** ~ ele foi lá; ~ **is,** ~ **are** há, tem; ~ **he is** lá está ele; **on/in** ~ lá or aí encima/dentro; **back** ~ lá atrás; **down** ~ lá embaixo; **over** ~ ali; **through** ~ por aí; **to go** ~ **and back** ir e voltar.

thereabouts ['ðeərəbauts] adv por aí.

thereafter [ðeər'ɑːftə*] adv depois disso.

thereby ['ðeəbaɪ] adv assim, deste modo.

therefore ['ðeəfɔː] adv portanto.

there's [ðeəz] = **there is; there has.**

thereupon [ðeərə'pɔn] adv (at that point) após o que; (formal: on that subject) a respeito.

thermal ['θəːml] adj térmico; ~ **paper/printer** papel térmico/impressora térmica.

thermodynamics [θəːmədaɪ'næmɪks] n termodinâmica.

thermometer [θə'mɔmɪtə*] n termômetro.

thermonuclear [θəːməu'njuːklɪə*] adj termonuclear.

Thermos ['θəːməs] ® n (also: ~ **flask**) garrafa térmica (BR), termo (PT).

thermostat ['θəːməustæt] n termostato.

thesaurus [θɪ'sɔːrəs] n tesouro, dicionário de sinônimos.

these [ðiːz] pl adj, pron estes/estas.

theses ['θiːsiːz] npl of **thesis.**

thesis ['θiːsɪs] (pl **theses**) n tese f.

they [ðeɪ] pl pron eles/elas; ~ **say that ...** (it is said that) diz-se que ..., dizem que ....

they'd [ðeɪd] = **they had; they would.**

they'll [ðeɪl] = **they shall; they will.**

they're [ðeɪə*] = **they are.**

they've [ðeɪv] = **they have.**

thick [θɪk] adj espesso, grosso; (dense) denso, compacto; (stupid) burro ♦ n: **in the** ~ **of the battle** em plena batalha; **it's 20 cm** ~ tem 20 cm de espessura.

NB: European Portuguese adds the following consonants to certain words: **b** (sú(b)dito, su(b)til); **c** (a(c)ção, a(c)cionista, a(c)to); **m** (inde(m)ne); **p** (ado(p)ção, ado(p)tar); for further details see p. xiii.

thicken ['θιkən] *vi* espessar-se ♦ *vt* (*sauce etc*) engrossar.

thicket ['θιkιt] *n* matagal *m*.

thickly ['θιklι] *adv* (*spread*) numa camada espessa; (*cut*) em fatias grossas.

thickness ['θιknιs] *n* espessura, grossura.

thickset [θιk'sɛt] *adj* troncudo.

thick-skinned [-'skιnd] *adj* (*fig*) insensível, indiferente.

thief [θi:f] (*pl* **thieves**) *n* ladrão/ladra *m/f*.

thieves [θi:vz] *npl of* **thief**.

thieving ['θi:vιŋ] *n* roubo, furto.

thigh [θαι] *n* coxa.

thighbone ['θαιbəun] *n* fêmur *m*.

thimble ['θιmbl] *n* dedal *m*.

thin [θιn] *adj* magro; (*watery*) aguado; (*light*) tênue; (*hair, crowd*) escasso, ralo; (*fog*) pouco denso ♦ *vt* (*also*: ~ *down*: *sauce, paint*) diluir ♦ *vi* (*fog*) rarefazer-se; (*also*: ~ *out*: *crowd*) dispersar; **his hair is** ~ o cabelo dele está caindo.

thing [θιŋ] *n* coisa; (*object*) negócio; (*matter*) assunto, negócio; (*mania*) mania; **~s** *npl* (*belongings*) pertences *mpl*; **the best** ~ **would be to** ... o melhor seria ...; **how are ~s?** como vai?, tudo bem?; **first** ~ **(in the morning)** de manhã, antes de mais nada; **last** ~ **(at night)**, he ... logo antes de dormir, ele ...; **the** ~ **is** ... é que ..., o negócio é o seguinte ...; **for one** ~ primeiro; **she's got a** ~ **about** ... ela detesta ...; **poor** ~**!** coitadinho/a!

think [θιŋk] (*pt, pp* **thought**) *vi* pensar ♦ *vt* pensar, achar; (*imagine*) imaginar; **what did you** ~ **of them?** o que você achou deles?; **to** ~ **about sth/sb** pensar em algo/alguém; **I'll** ~ **about it** vou pensar sobre isso; **to** ~ **of doing sth** pensar em fazer algo; **I** ~ **so/not** acho que sim/não; **to** ~ **well of sb** fazer bom juízo de alguém; ~ **again!** pensa bem!; **to** ~ **aloud** pensar em voz alta.

   think out *vt* (*plan*) arquitetar; (*solution*) descobrir.

   think over *vt* refletir sobre, meditar sobre; **I'd like to** ~ **things over** eu gostaria de pensar sobre isso com cuidado.

   think through *vt* considerar todos os aspectos de.

   think up *vt* inventar, bolar.

thinking ['θιŋkιŋ] *n*: **to my (way of)** ~ na minha opinião.

think tank *n* comissão *f* de peritos.

thinly ['θιnlι] *adv* (*cut*) em fatias finas; (*spread*) numa camada fina.

thinness ['θιnnιs] *n* magreza.

third [θə:d] *adj* terceiro ♦ *n* terceiro/a; (*fraction*) terço; (*SCH: degree*) terceira categoria; *see also* **fifth**.

third-degree burns *npl* queimaduras *fpl* de terceiro grau.

thirdly ['θə:dlι] *adv* em terceiro lugar.

third party insurance *n* seguro contra terceiros.

third-rate *adj* medíocre.

Third World *n*: **the** ~ o Terceiro Mundo.

thirst [θə:st] *n* sede *f*.

thirsty ['θə:stι] *adj* (*person*) sedento, com sede; **to be** ~ estar com sede.

thirteen ['θə:'ti:n] *num* treze; *see also* **five**.

thirteenth [θə:'ti:nθ] *num* décimo terceiro; *see also* **fifth**.

thirtieth ['θə:tιəθ] *num* trigésimo; *see also* **fifth**.

thirty ['θə:tι] *num* trinta; *see also* **fifty**.

this [ðιs] (*pl* **these**) *adj* este/esta ♦ *pron* este/esta; (*neuter*) isto ♦ *adv*: ~ **high** dessa altura; **who is** ~**?** quem é esse?; **what is** ~**?** o que é isso?; ~ **is Mr Brown** (*in photo, introduction*) este é o Sr Brown; (*on phone*) aqui é o Sr Brown; ~ **is what he said** foi isto o que ele disse; ~ **time** desta vez; ~ **time last year** nessa época do ano passado; ~ **way** (*in this direction*) por aqui; (*in this fashion*) assim, desta maneira; **they were talking of** ~ **and that** estavam falando disso e daquilo.

thistle ['θιsl] *n* cardo.

thong [θɔŋ] *n* correia, tira de couro.

thorn [θɔ:n] *n* espinho.

thorny ['θɔ:nι] *adj* espinhoso.

thorough ['θʌrə] *adj* (*search*) minucioso; (*knowledge, research*) profundo; (*work*) meticuloso; (*cleaning*) completo.

thoroughbred ['θʌrəbrɛd] *adj* (*horse*) de puro sangue.

thoroughfare ['θʌrəfɛə*] *n* via, passagem *f*; **"no** ~**"** "passagem proibida".

thoroughly ['θʌrəlι] *adv* minuciosamente, profundamente, a fundo; **he** ~ **agreed** concordou completamente.

thoroughness ['θʌrənιs] *n* (*of person*) meticulosidade *f*; (*of search etc*) minuciosidade *f*.

those [ðəuz] *pl pron*, *adj* esses/essas; (*more remote*) aqueles/aquelas.

though [ðəu] *conj* embora, se bem que ♦ *adv* no entanto; **even** ~ mesmo que; **it's not easy,** ~ se bem que não é fácil.

thought [θɔ:t] *pt, pp of* **think** ♦ *n* pensamento; (*opinion*) opinião *f*; (*intention*) intenção *f*; **after much** ~ depois de muito pensar; **I've just had a** ~ acabei de pensar em alguma coisa; **to give sth some** ~ pensar sobre algo.

thoughtful ['θɔ:tful] *adj* pensativo; (*considerate*) atencioso.

thoughtfully ['θɔ:tfəlι] *adv* pensativamente; atenciosamente.

thoughtless ['θɔ:tlιs] *adj* descuidado, desatento.

thoughtlessly ['θɔ:tlιslι] *adv* desconsideradamente.

thousand ['θauzənd] *num* mil; **two** ~ dois mil; ~**s (of)** milhares *mpl* (de).

thousandth ['θauzənθ] *adj* milésimo.

thrash [θræʃ] *vt* surrar, malhar; (*defeat*) derrotar.

   thrash about *vi* debater-se.

   thrash out *vt* discutir exaustivamente.

thrashing ['θræʃιŋ] *n*: **to give sb a** ~ dar uma surra em alguém.

thread [θrɛd] *n* fio, linha; (*of screw*) rosca ♦

vt (*needle*) enfiar; **to ~ one's way between** passar por.

threadbare ['θrɛdbɛə*] *adj* surrado, puído.

threat [θrɛt] *n* ameaça; **to be under ~ of** estar sob ameaça de.

threaten ['θrɛtən] *vi* ameaçar ♦ *vt*: **to ~ sb with sth/to do** ameaçar alguém com algo/de fazer.

threatening ['θrɛtnɪŋ] *adj* ameaçador(a).

three [θriː] *num* três; *see also* **five**.

three-dimensional *adj* tridimensional, em três dimensões.

threefold ['θriːfəuld] *adv*: **to increase ~** triplicar.

three-piece suit *n* terno (3 peças) (*BR*), fato de 3 peças (*PT*).

three-piece suite *n* conjunto de sofá e duas poltronas.

three-ply *adj* (*wool*) triple, com três fios; (*wood*) com três espessuras.

three-quarters *npl* três quartos *mpl*; **~ full** cheio até os três quartos.

three-wheeler *n* (*car*) carro de três rodas.

thresh [θrɛʃ] *vt* (*AGR*) debulhar.

threshing machine ['θrɛʃɪŋ-] *n* debulhadora.

threshold ['θrɛʃhəuld] *n* limiar *m*; **to be on the ~ of** (*fig*) estar no limiar de.

threshold agreement *n* (*ECON*) acordo sobre a indexação de salários.

threw [θruː] *pt of* **throw**.

thrift [θrɪft] *n* economia, poupança.

thrifty ['θrɪftɪ] *adj* econômico, frugal.

thrill [θrɪl] *n* (*excitement*) emoção *f*; (*shudder*) estremecimento ♦ *vi* vibrar ♦ *vt* emocionar, vibrar; **to be ~ed** (*with gift etc*) estar emocionado.

thriller ['θrɪlə*] *n* romance *m* (*or* filme *m*) de suspense.

thrilling ['θrɪlɪŋ] *adj* (*book, play etc*) excitante; (*news, discovery*) emocionante.

thrive [θraɪv] (*pt* **~d** *or* **throve**, *pp* **~d** *or* **thriven**) *vi* (*grow*) vicejar; (*do well*) prosperar, florescer.

thriven ['θrɪvn] *pp of* **thrive**.

thriving ['θraɪvɪŋ] *adj* próspero, florescente.

throat [θrəut] *n* garganta; **to have a sore ~** estar com dor de garganta.

throb [θrɔb] *n* (*of heart*) batida; (*of engine*) vibração *f*; (*of pain*) latejo ♦ *vi* (*heart*) bater, palpitar; (*pain*) dar pontadas; (*engine*) vibrar; **my head is ~bing** minha cabeça está latejando.

throes [θrəuz] *npl*: **in the ~ of** no meio de.

thrombosis [θrɔm'bəusɪs] *n* trombose *f*.

throne [θrəun] *n* trono.

throng [θrɔŋ] *n* multidão *f* ♦ *vt* apinhar, apinhar-se em.

throttle ['θrɔtl] *n* (*AUT*) acelerador *m* ♦ *vt* estrangular.

through [θruː] *prep* por, através de; (*time*) durante; (*by means of*) por meio de, por intermédio de; (*owing to*) devido a ♦ *adj*

(*ticket, train*) direto ♦ *adv* através; **(from) Monday ~ Friday** (*US*) de segunda a sexta; **to let sb ~** deixar alguém passar; **to put sb ~ to sb** (*TEL*) ligar alguém com alguém; **to be ~** (*TEL*) estar na linha; (*have finished*) acabar; **"no ~ traffic"** (*US*) "trânsito proibido"; **"no ~ way"** "rua sem saída"; **I'm halfway ~ the book** estou na metade do livro.

throughout [θruː'aut] *prep* (*place*) por todo/a o/a; (*time*) durante todo/a o/a ♦ *adv* por *or* em todas as partes.

throughput ['θruːput] *n* (*of goods, materials*) quantidade *f* tratada; (*COMPUT*) capacidade *f* de processamento.

throve [θrəuv] *pt of* **thrive**.

throw [θrəu] (*pt* **threw**, *pp* **thrown**) *n* arremesso, tiro; (*SPORT*) lançamento ♦ *vt* jogar, atirar; (*SPORT*) lançar; (*rider*) derrubar; (*fig*) desconcertar; (*pot*) afeiçoar; **to ~ a party** dar uma festa.

throw about *vt* (*litter etc*) esparramar.

throw around *vt* (*litter etc*) esparramar.

throw away *vt* (*dispose of*) jogar fora; (*waste*) desperdiçar.

throw in *vt* (*SPORT*) pôr em jogo.

throw off *vt* desfazer-se de.

throw out *vt* (*person*) expulsar; (*things*) jogar fora; (*reject*) rejeitar.

throw together *vt* (*clothes, meal etc*) arranjar às pressas.

throw up *vi* vomitar, botar para fora.

throwaway ['θrəuəweɪ] *adj* descartável.

throwback ['θrəubæk] *n*: **it's a ~ to** é um retrocesso a.

throw-in *n* (*SPORT*) lance *m*.

thru [θruː] (*US*) *prep*, *adj*, *adv* = **through**.

thrush [θrʌʃ] *n* (*ZOOL*) tordo; (*MED*) monília.

thrust [θrʌst] (*pt*, *pp* **thrust**) *n* impulso; (*TECH*) empuxo ♦ *vt* empurrar; (*push in*) enfiar, meter.

thrusting ['θrʌstɪŋ] *adj* dinâmico.

thud [θʌd] *n* baque *m*, som *m* surdo.

thug [θʌg] *n* (*criminal*) criminoso/a; (*pej*) facínora *m/f*.

thumb [θʌm] *n* (*ANAT*) polegar *m*; (*inf*) dedão *m* ♦ *vt* (*book*) folhear; **to ~ a lift** pegar carona (*BR*), arranjar uma boléia (*PT*); **to give sb/sth the ~s up** (*approve*) dar luz verde a alguém/algo.

thumb index *n* índice *m* de dedo.

thumbnail ['θʌmneɪl] *n* unha do polegar.

thumbnail sketch *n* descrição *f* resumida.

thumbtack ['θʌmtæk] (*US*) *n* percevejo, tachinha.

thump [θʌmp] *n* murro, pancada; (*sound*) baque *m* ♦ *vt* dar um murro em ♦ *vi* bater.

thunder ['θʌndə*] *n* trovão *m*; (*sudden noise*) trovoada; (*of applause etc*) estrondo ♦ *vi* trovejar; (*train etc*): **to ~ past** passar como um raio.

thunderbolt ['θʌndəbəult] *n* raio.

thunderclap ['θʌndəklæp] *n* estampido do tro-

NB: European Portuguese adds the following consonants to certain words: **b** (sú(b)dito, su(b)til); **c** (a(c)ção, a(c)cionista, a(c)to); **m** (inde(m)ne); **p** (ado(p)ção, ado(p)tar); *for further details see p. xiii.*

vão.

thunderous ['θʌndərəs] *adj* estrondoso.

thunderstorm ['θʌndəstɔːm] *n* tempestade *f* com trovoada, temporal *m*.

thunderstruck ['θʌndəstrʌk] *adj* estupefato.

thundery ['θʌndərɪ] *adj* tempestuoso.

Thur(s). *abbr* (= *Thursday*) qui, 5ª.

Thursday ['θəːzdɪ] *n* quinta-feira; *see also* **Tuesday**.

thus [ðʌs] *adv* assim, desta maneira.

thwart [θwɔːt] *vt* frustrar.

thyme [taɪm] *n* tomilho.

thyroid ['θaɪrɔɪd] *n* tireóide *f*.

tiara [tɪ'ɑːrə] *n* tiara, diadema *m*.

Tibet [tɪ'bɛt] *n* Tibete *m*.

Tibetan [tɪ'bɛtən] *adj* tibetano ♦ *n* tibetano/a; (*LING*) tibetano.

tibia ['tɪbɪə] *n* tíbia.

tic [tɪk] *n* tique *m*.

tick [tɪk] *n* (*sound: of clock*) tique-taque *m*; (*mark*) tique *m*, marca; (*ZOOL*) carrapato; (*BRIT: inf*): **in a ~** num instante; (: *credit*): **to buy sth on ~** comprar algo a crédito ♦ *vi* fazer tique-taque ♦ *vt* marcar, ticar; **to put a ~ against sth** marcar or ticar algo.

tick off *vt* assinalar, ticar; (*person*) dar uma bronca em.

tick over (*BRIT*) *vi* (*engine*) funcionar em marcha lenta; (*fig*) ir indo.

ticker tape ['tɪkə*-] *n* fita de teleimpressor; (*US: in celebrations*) chuva de papel.

ticket ['tɪkɪt] *n* (*for bus, plane*) passagem *f*, bilhete *m*; (*for cinema*) entrada, ingresso; (*in shop: on goods*) etiqueta; (: *receipt*) ficha, nota fiscal; (*for library*) cartão *m*; (*US: POL*) chapa; **to get a (parking) ~** (*AUT*) ganhar uma multa (por estacionamento ilegal).

ticket agency *n* agência de ingressos teatrais.

ticket collector *n* revisor(a) *m/f*.

ticket holder *n* portador(a) *m/f* de um bilhete or ingresso.

ticket inspector *n* revisor(a) *m/f*.

ticket office *n* bilheteria (*BR*), bilheteira (*PT*).

tickle ['tɪkl] *n* cócegas *fpl* ♦ *vt* fazer cócegas em; (*captivate*) encantar; (*make laugh*) fazer rir.

ticklish ['tɪklɪʃ] *adj* (*person*) coceguento; (*which tickles: blanket etc*) que pica, que faz cócegas; (: *cough*) irritante; **to be ~** (*person*) ter cócegas.

tidal ['taɪdl] *adj* de maré.

tidal wave *n* macaréu *m*, onda gigantesca.

tidbit ['tɪdbɪt] (*esp US*) *n* = **titbit**.

tiddlywinks ['tɪdlɪwɪŋks] *n* jogo de fichas.

tide [taɪd] *n* maré *f*; (*fig: of events*) marcha, curso ♦ *vt*: **to ~ sb over** dar para alguém agüentar; **high/low ~** maré alta/baixa; **the ~ of public opinion** a corrente da opinião pública.

tidily ['taɪdɪlɪ] *adv* com capricho.

tidiness ['taɪdɪnɪs] *n* (*good order*) ordem *f*; (*neatness*) asseio, limpeza.

tidy ['taɪdɪ] *adj* (*room*) arrumado; (*dress, work*) limpo; (*person*) bem arrumado;

(*mind*) metódico ♦ *vt* (*also*: **~ up**) pôr em ordem, arrumar; **to ~ o.s. up** arrumar-se.

tie [taɪ] *n* (*string etc*) fita, corda; (*BRIT: also: neck~*) gravata; (*fig: link*) vínculo, laço; (*SPORT: draw*) empate *m*; (*US: RAIL*) dormente *m* ♦ *vt* amarrar, atar ♦ *vi* (*SPORT*) empatar; **to ~ in a bow** dar um laço em; **to ~ a knot in sth** dar um nó em algo; **family ~s** laços de família; **"black/white ~"** "smoking/traje a rigor".

tie down *vt* amarrar; (*fig*): **to ~ sb down to** obrigar alguém a.

tie in *vi*: **to ~ in (with)** combinar com.

tie on (*BRIT*) *vt* (*label etc*) prender (com barbante).

tie up *vt* (*parcel*) embrulhar; (*dog*) prender; (*boat*) amarrar; (*arrangements*) concluir; **to be ~d up** (*busy*) estar ocupado.

tie-break(er) *n* (*TENNIS*) tie-break *m*; (*in quiz etc*) decisão *f* de empate.

tie-on (*BRIT*) *adj* (*label*) para atar.

tie-pin (*BRIT*) *n* alfinete *m* de gravata.

tier [tɪə*] *n* fileira; (*of cake*) camada.

Tierra del Fuego [tɪ'ɛrədɛl'fweɪgəu] *n* Terra do Fogo.

tie tack (*US*) *n* alfinete *m* de gravata.

tie-up (*US*) *n* engarrafamento.

tiff [tɪf] *n* briga; (*lover's ~*) arrufo.

tiger ['taɪgə*] *n* tigre *m*.

tight [taɪt] *adj* (*rope*) esticado, firme; (*money*) escasso; (*clothes*) justo; (*budget, programme*) apertado; (*control*) rigoroso; (*inf: drunk*) bêbado ♦ *adv* (*squeeze*) bem forte; (*shut*) hermeticamente; **to be packed ~** (*suitcase*) estar abarrotado; (*people*) estar apinhado; **everybody hold ~!** segurem firme!

tighten ['taɪtən] *vt* (*rope*) esticar; (*screw, security*) apertar ♦ *vi* apertar-se; esticar-se.

tight-fisted [-'fɪstɪd] *adj* pão-duro.

tightly ['taɪtlɪ] *adv* (*grasp*) firmemente.

tight-rope *n* corda (bamba).

tight-rope walker *n* funâmbulo/a.

tights [taɪts] (*BRIT*) *npl* collant *m*.

tigress ['taɪgrɪs] *n* tigre fêmea.

tilde ['tɪldə] *n* til *m*.

tile [taɪl] *n* (*on roof*) telha; (*on floor*) ladrilho; (*on wall*) azulejo, ladrilho ♦ *vt* (*floor*) ladrilhar; (*wall, bathroom*) azulejar.

tiled [taɪld] *adj* ladrilhado; (*roof*) de telhas.

till [tɪl] *n* caixa (registradora) ♦ *vt* (*land*) cultivar ♦ *prep, conj* = **until**.

tiller ['tɪlə*] *n* (*NAUT*) cana do leme.

tilt [tɪlt] *vt* inclinar ♦ *vi* inclinar-se ♦ *n* (*slope*) inclinação *f*; (**at) full ~** a toda velocidade.

timber ['tɪmbə*] *n* (*material*) madeira; (*trees*) mata, floresta.

time [taɪm] *n* tempo; (*epoch: often pl*) época; (*by clock*) hora; (*moment*) momento; (*occasion*) vez *f*; (*MUS*) compasso ♦ *vt* calcular or medir o tempo de; (*race*) cronometrar; (*remark etc*) escolher o momento para; **a long ~** muito tempo; **3 at a ~** três de uma vez; **for the ~ being** por enquanto; **from ~ to ~** de vez em quando; **~ after ~, ~ and again**

repetidamente; **in** ~ (*soon enough*) a tempo; (*after some time*) com o tempo; (*MUS*) no compasso; **in a week's** ~ dentro de uma semana; **in no** ~ num abrir e fechar de olhos; **on** ~ na hora; **to be 30 minutes behind/ahead of** ~ estar atrasado/adiantado de 30 minutos; **by the** ~ he arrived até ele chegar; **5** ~**s 5 is 25** 5 vezes 5 são 25; **what** ~ **is it?** que horas são?; **what** ~ **do you make it?** que horas você tem?; **to have a good** ~ divertir-se; **we had a hard** ~ foi difícil para nós; **he'll do it in his own (good)** ~ (*without being hurried*) ele vai fazer isso quando tiver tempo; **he'll do it in** (*BRIT*) *or* **on** (*US*) **his own** ~ (*out of working hours*) ele vai fazer isso fora do expediente; **to be behind the** ~**s** estar antiquado.

time-and-motion study n estudo de tempos e movimentos.

time bomb n bomba-relógio f.

time clock n relógio de ponto.

time-consuming [-kən'sju:mɪŋ] adj que exige muito tempo.

time difference n fuso horário.

time-honoured [-'ɔnəd] (*US* **time-honored**) adj consagrado pelo tempo.

timekeeper ['taɪmki:pə*] n (*SPORT*) cronometrista m/f.

time lag (*BRIT*) n defasagem f; (*in travel*) fuso horário.

timeless ['taɪmlɪs] adj eterno.

time limit n limite m de tempo; (*COMM*) prazo.

timely ['taɪmlɪ] adj oportuno.

time off n tempo livre.

timer ['taɪmə*] n (*in kitchen*) cronômetro; (*switch*) timer m.

time-saving adj que economiza tempo.

time scale n prazos mpl.

time-sharing [-'ʃɛərɪŋ] n (*COMPUT*) tempo compartilhado.

time sheet n folha de ponto.

time signal n tope m, sinal m horário.

time switch (*BRIT*) n interruptor m horário.

timetable ['taɪmteɪbl] n horário; (*of project*) cronograma m.

time zone n fuso horário.

timid ['tɪmɪd] adj tímido.

timidity [tɪ'mɪdɪtɪ] n timidez f.

timing ['taɪmɪŋ] n escolha do momento; (*SPORT*) cronometragem f; **the** ~ **of his resignation** o momento que escolheu para se demitir.

timing device n (*on bomb*) dispositivo de retardamento.

Timor ['ti:mɔ:*] n Timor (*no article*).

timpani ['tɪmpənɪ] npl tímbales mpl.

tin [tɪn] n estanho; (*also:* ~ **plate**) folha-de-flandres f; (*BRIT: can*) lata; (: *for baking*) fôrma.

tin foil n papel m de estanho.

tinge [tɪndʒ] n matiz m, toque m ♦ vt: ~**d with** tingido de.

tingle ['tɪŋgl] n comichão f ♦ vi formigar.

tinker ['tɪŋkə*] n funileiro/a; (*gipsy*) cigano/a.

tinker with vt mexer com.

tinkle ['tɪŋkl] vi tilintar, tinir ♦ n (*inf*): **to give sb a** ~ dar uma ligada para alguém.

tin mine n mina de estanho.

tinned [tɪnd] (*BRIT*) adj (*food*) em lata, em conserva.

tinny ['tɪnɪ] adj metálico.

tin opener (*BRIT*) n abridor m de latas (*BR*), abre-latas m inv (*PT*).

tinsel ['tɪnsl] n ouropel m.

tint [tɪnt] n matiz m; (*for hair*) tintura, tinta ♦ vt (*hair*) pintar.

tinted ['tɪntɪd] adj (*hair*) pintado; (*spectacles, glass*) fumê inv.

tiny ['taɪnɪ] adj pequenininho, minúsculo.

tip [tɪp] n (*end*) ponta; (*gratuity*) gorjeta; (*BRIT: for rubbish*) depósito; (*advice*) dica ♦ vt (*waiter*) dar uma gorjeta a; (*tilt*) inclinar; (*winner*) apostar em; (*overturn: also:* ~ **over**) virar, emborcar; (*empty: also:* ~ **out**) esvaziar, entornar; **he** ~**ped out the contents of the box** esvaziou a caixa.

tip off vt avisar.

tip-off n (*hint*) aviso, dica.

tipped [tɪpt] adj (*BRIT: cigarette*) com filtro; **steel-**~ com ponta de aço.

Tipp-Ex ['tɪpɛks] ® (*BRIT*) n líquido corretor.

tipple ['tɪpl] (*BRIT*) vt bebericar ♦ n: **to have a** ~ beber um gole.

tipsy ['tɪpsɪ] adj embriagado, tocado, alto, alegre.

tiptoe ['tɪptəu] n: **on** ~ na ponta dos pés.

tiptop ['tɪp'tɔp] adj: **in** ~ **condition** em perfeitas condições.

tire ['taɪə*] n (*US*) = **tyre** ♦ vt cansar ♦ vi cansar-se; (*become bored*) chatear-se.

tire out vt esgotar, exaurir.

tired ['taɪəd] adj cansado; **to be** ~ **of sth** estar farto or cheio de algo.

tiredness ['taɪədnɪs] n cansaço.

tireless ['taɪəlɪs] adj incansável.

tiresome ['taɪəsəm] adj enfadonho, chato.

tiring ['taɪərɪŋ] adj cansativo.

tissue ['tɪʃu:] n tecido; (*paper handkerchief*) lenço de papel.

tissue paper n papel m de seda.

tit [tɪt] n (*bird*) passarinho; (*inf: breast*) teta; **to give** ~ **for tat** pagar na mesma moeda.

titanium [tɪ'teɪnɪəm] n titânio.

titbit ['tɪtbɪt] n (*food*) guloseima; (*news*) boato, rumor m.

titillate ['tɪtɪleɪt] vt titilar, excitar.

titivate ['tɪtɪveɪt] vt arrumar.

title ['taɪtl] n título; (*LAW: right*): ~ **(to)** direito (a).

title deed n (*LAW*) título de propriedade.

title page n página de rosto.

title role n papel m principal.

titter ['tɪtə*] vi rir-se com riso sufocado.

NB: European Portuguese adds the following consonants to certain words: **b** (sú(b)dito, su(b)til); **c** (a(c)ção, a(c)cionista, a(c)to); **m** (inde(m)ne); **p** (ado(p)ção, ado(p)tar); *for further details see p. xiii.*

tittle-tattle ['tɪtltætl] n fofocas fpl (BR), mexericos mpl (PT).

titular ['tɪtjulə*] adj (in name only) nominal, titular.

tizzy ['tɪzɪ] n: **to be in a ~** estar muito nervoso.

T-junction n bifurcação f em T.

TM n abbr = **trademark; transcendental meditation.**

TN (US) abbr (POST) = **Tennessee.**

TNT n abbr (= trinitrotoluene) Tnt m, trotil m.

to [tuː, tə] prep a, para; (towards) para; (of time) até ♦ with vb (purpose, result) para; (simple infin): **~ go/eat** ir/comer; (following another vb): **to want/try ~ do** querer/tentar fazer; **to give sth ~ sb** dar algo a alguém; **give it ~ me** me dá isso; **the key ~ the front door** a chave da porta da frente; **it belongs ~ him** pertence a ele, é dele; **the main thing is ~ ...** o principal é ...; **to go ~ France/school** ir à França/ao colégio; **8 apples ~ the kilo** 8 maçãs por quilo; **a quarter ~ 5** quinze para as 5 (BR), 5 menos um quarto (PT); **pull/push the door ~** puxar/empurrar a porta; **to go ~ and fro** ir de um lado para outro; **he did it ~ help you** ele fez isso para ajudar você; **I don't want ~** eu não quero; **I have things ~ do** eu tenho coisas para fazer; **ready ~ go** pronto para ir.

toad [təud] n sapo.

toadstool ['təudstuːl] n chapéu-de-cobra m, cogumelo venenoso.

toady ['təudɪ] vi ser bajulador(a), puxar saco (inf).

toast [təust] n (CULIN) torradas fpl; (drink, speech) brinde m ♦ vt (CULIN) torrar; (drink to) brindar; **a piece** or **slice of ~** uma torrada.

toaster ['təustə*] n torradeira.

toastmaster ['təustmɑːstə*] n mestre m de cerimônias.

toast rack n porta-torradas m inv.

tobacco [tə'bækəu] n tabaco, fumo (BR).

tobacconist [tə'bækənɪst] n vendedor(a) m/f de tabaco; **~'s (shop)** tabacaria, charutaria (BR).

Tobago [tə'beɪgəu] n see **Trinidad.**

toboggan [tə'bɔgən] n tobogã m.

today [tə'deɪ] adv, n (also: fig) hoje m; **what day is it ~?** que dia é hoje?; **what date is it ~?** qual é a data de hoje?; **~ is the 4th of March** hoje é dia 4 de março; **a week ago ~** há uma semana atrás; **a fortnight ~** daqui a quinze dias; **~'s paper** o jornal de hoje.

toddler ['tɔdlə*] n criança que começa a andar.

toddy ['tɔdɪ] n ponche m quente.

to-do n (fuss) rebuliço, alvoroço.

toe [təu] n dedo do pé; (of shoe) bico ♦ vt: **to ~ the line** (fig) conformar-se, cumprir as obrigações; **big ~** dedão m do pé; **little ~** dedo mindinho do pé.

toehold ['təuhəuld] n apoio.

toenail ['təuneɪl] n unha do pé.

toffee ['tɔfɪ] n puxa-puxa m (BR), caramelo (PT).

toffee apple (BRIT) n maçã f do amor.

toga ['təugə] n toga.

together [tə'geðə*] adv juntos; (at same time) ao mesmo tempo; **~ with** junto com.

togetherness [tə'geðənɪs] n companheirismo, camaradagem f.

toggle switch ['tɔgl-] n (COMPUT) (interruptor m) teimoso.

Togo ['təugəu] n Togo.

togs [tɔgz] (inf) npl (clothes) roupa.

toil [tɔɪl] n faina, labuta ♦ vi labutar, trabalhar arduamente.

toilet ['tɔɪlət] n (BRIT: lavatory) banheiro (BR), casa de banho (PT) ♦ cpd (bag, soap etc) de toalete; **to go to the ~** ir ao banheiro.

toilet bag (BRIT) n bolsa de toucador.

toilet bowl n vaso sanitário.

toilet paper n papel m higiênico.

toiletries ['tɔɪlɪtrɪz] npl artigos mpl de toalete; (make-up etc) artigos de toucador.

toilet roll n rolo de papel higiênico.

toilet water n água de colônia.

to-ing and fro-ing ['tuːɪŋən'frəuɪŋ] (BRIT) n vaivém m.

token ['təukən] n (sign) sinal m, símbolo, prova; (souvenir) lembrança; (voucher) cupom m, vale m ♦ cpd (fee, strike) simbólico; **by the same ~** (fig) pela mesma razão; **book/record ~** (BRIT) vale para comprar livros/discos.

Tokyo ['təukjəu] n Tóquio.

told [təuld] pt, pp of **tell.**

tolerable ['tɔlərəbl] adj (bearable) suportável; (fairly good) passável.

tolerably ['tɔlərəblɪ] adv: **~ good** razoável.

tolerance ['tɔlərəns] n (also: TECH) tolerância.

tolerant ['tɔlərənt] adj: **~ of** tolerante com.

tolerate ['tɔləreɪt] vt suportar; (MED, TECH) tolerar.

toleration [tɔlə'reɪʃən] n tolerância.

toll [təul] n (of casualties) número de baixas; (tax, charge) pedágio (BR), portagem f (PT) ♦ vi (bell) dobrar, tanger.

tollbridge ['təulbrɪdʒ] n ponte f de pedágio (BR) or de portagem (PT).

tomato [tə'mɑːtəu] (pl ~es) n tomate m.

tomb [tuːm] n tumba.

tombola [tɔm'bəulə] n tômbola.

tomboy ['tɔmbɔɪ] n menina moleque.

tombstone ['tuːmstəun] n lápide f.

tomcat ['tɔmkæt] n gato.

tomorrow [tə'mɔrəu] adv, n (also fig) amanhã m; **the day after ~** depois de amanhã; **~ morning** amanhã de manhã.

ton [tʌn] n tonelada (BRIT: = 1016 kg; US = 907 kg; metric = 1000 kg); (NAUT: also: register ~) tonelagem f de registro; **~s of** (inf) um monte de.

tonal ['təunl] adj tonal.

tone [təun] n tom m; (BRIT: TEL) sinal m ♦ vi harmonizar.

tone down vt (colour, criticism) suavizar; (sound) baixar; (MUS) entoar.

tone up vt (muscles) tonificar.
tone-deaf adj que não tem ouvido.
toner ['təunə*] n (for photocopier) tinta.
Tonga ['tɔŋgə] n Tonga (no article).
tongs [tɔŋz] npl (for coal) tenaz f; (for hair) pinças fpl.
tongue [tʌŋ] n língua; ~ **in cheek** ironicamente.
tongue-tied [-taɪd] adj (fig) calado.
tongue-twister [-'twɪstə*] n trava-língua m.
tonic ['tɔnɪk] n (MED) tônico; (MUS) tônica; (also: ~ water) (água) tônica.
tonight [tə'naɪt] adv, n esta noite, hoje à noite; (I'll) **see you ~!** até a noite!
tonnage ['tʌnɪdʒ] n (NAUT) tonelagem f.
tonne [tʌn] n (BRIT) n (metric ton) tonelada.
tonsil ['tɔnsəl] n amígdala; **to have one's ~s out** tirar as amígdalas.
tonsillitis [tɔnsɪ'laɪtɪs] n amigdalite f; **to have ~** estar com uma amigdalite.
too [tuː] adv (excessively) demais; (very) muito; (also) também; ~ **much** adv demais ♦ adj demasiado; ~ **many** adj muitos/as, demasiados/as; ~ **sweet** doce demais; **I went ~** eu fui também.
took [tuk] pt of **take**.
tool [tuːl] n ferramenta; (fig: person) joguete m ♦ vt trabalhar.
tool box n caixa de ferramentas.
tool kit n jogo de ferramentas.
toot [tuːt] n (of horn) buzinada; (of whistle) apito ♦ vi (with car horn) buzinar; (whistle) apitar.
tooth [tuːθ] (pl **teeth**) n (ANAT, TECH) dente m; (molar) molar m; **to have a ~ out** (BRIT) or **pulled** (US) arrancar um dente; **to brush one's teeth** escovar os dentes; **by the skin of one's teeth** (fig) por um triz.
toothache ['tuːθeɪk] n dor f de dente; **to have ~** estar com dor de dente.
toothbrush ['tuːθbrʌʃ] n escova de dentes.
toothpaste ['tuːθpeɪst] n pasta de dentes, creme m dental.
toothpick ['tuːθpɪk] n palito.
tooth powder n pó m dentifrício.
top [tɔp] n (of mountain) cume m, cimo; (of head) cocuruto; (of cupboard, table) superfície f, topo; (of box, jar, bottle) tampa; (of list etc) cabeça m; (toy) pião m; (DRESS: blouse etc) top m, blusa; (: of pyjamas) paletó m ♦ adj mais alto, máximo; (in rank) principal, superior; (best) melhor ♦ vt (exceed) exceder; (be first in) estar à cabeça de; **the ~ of the milk** (BRIT) a nata do leite; **at the ~ of the stairs/page/street** no alto da escada/no alto da página/no começo da rua; **on ~ of** sobre, em cima de; **from ~ to toe** (BRIT) da cabeça aos pés; **at the ~ of the list** à cabeça da lista; **at the ~ of one's voice** aos gritos; **at ~ speed** a toda velocidade; **a ~ surgeon** um dos melhores cirurgiões; **over the ~** (inf: behaviour etc) extravagante.

top up (US **top off**) vt completar.
topaz ['təupæz] n topázio.
topcoat ['tɔpkəut] n sobretudo.
topflight ['tɔpflaɪt] adj de primeira categoria.
top floor n último andar m.
top hat n cartola.
top-heavy adj (object) desequilibrado.
topic ['tɔpɪk] n tópico, assunto.
topical ['tɔpɪkl] adj atual.
topless ['tɔplɪs] adj (bather etc) topless inv, sem a parte superior do biquíni.
top-level adj (talks) de alto nível.
topmost ['tɔpməust] adj o mais alto.
topography [tə'pɔgrəfɪ] n topografia.
topping ['tɔpɪŋ] n (CULIN) cobertura.
topple ['tɔpl] vt derrubar, desabar ♦ vi cair para frente, ruir.
top-ranking [-'ræŋkɪŋ] adj de alto escalão.
TOPS [tɔps] (BRIT) n abbr (= Training Opportunities Scheme) programa de formação profissional.
top-secret adj ultra-secreto, supersecreto.
top-security (BRIT) adj de alta segurança.
topsy-turvy ['tɔpsɪ'təːvɪ] adj, adv de pernas para o ar, confuso, às avessas.
top-up n: **would you like a ~?** você quer mais?
torch [tɔːtʃ] n tocha, archote m; (BRIT: electric ~) lanterna.
tore [tɔː*] pt of **tear**.
torment [n 'tɔːment, vt tɔː'ment] n tormento, suplício ♦ vt atormentar; (fig: annoy) chatear, aborrecer.
torn [tɔːn] pp of **tear** ♦ adj: ~ **between** (fig) dividido entre.
tornado [tɔː'neɪdəu] (pl ~es) n tornado.
torpedo [tɔː'piːdəu] (pl ~es) n torpedo ♦ vt torpedear.
torpedo boat n torpedeiro.
torpor ['tɔːpə*] n torpor m.
torque [tɔːk] n momento de torção.
torrent ['tɔrənt] n torrente f.
torrential [tɔ'renʃl] adj torrencial.
torrid ['tɔrɪd] adj tórrido; (fig) abrasador(a).
torso ['tɔːsəu] n torso.
tortoise ['tɔːtəs] n tartaruga.
tortoiseshell ['tɔːtəʃel] cpd de tartaruga.
tortuous ['tɔːtjuəs] adj tortuoso.
torture ['tɔːtʃə*] n tortura ♦ vt torturar; (fig) atormentar.
torturer ['tɔːtʃərə*] n torturador(a) m/f.
Tory ['tɔːrɪ] (BRIT) adj, n (POL) conservador(a) m/f.
toss [tɔs] vt atirar, arremessar; (head) lançar para trás ♦ n (of head) meneio; (of coin) lançamento ♦ vi: **to ~ and turn in bed** virar de um lado para o outro na cama; **to ~ a coin** tirar cara ou coroa; **to ~ up for sth** (BRIT) jogar cara ou coroa por algo; **to win/lose the ~** ganhar/perder no cara ou coroa; (SPORT) ganhar/perder o sorteio.

NB: European Portuguese adds the following consonants to certain words: **b** (sú(b)dito, su(b)til); **c** (a(c)ção, a(c)cionista, a(c)to); **m** (inde(m)ne); **p** (ado(p)ção, ado(p)tar); for further details see p. xiii.

tot [tɔt] n (BRIT: drink) copinho, golinho; (child) criancinha.
tot up (BRIT) vt (figures) somar, adicionar.
total ['təutl] adj total ♦ n total m, soma ♦ vt (add up) somar; (amount to) montar a; **in ~ em total.**
totalitarian [təutælɪ'tɛərɪən] adj totalitário.
totality [təu'tælɪtɪ] n totalidade f.
totally ['təutəlɪ] adv totalmente.
tote bag [təut-] n sacola.
totem pole ['təutəm-] n mastro totêmico.
totter ['tɔtə*] vi cambalear; (object, government) vacilar.
touch [tʌtʃ] n toque m; (sense) tato; (contact) contato; (FOOTBALL): **in ~** fora do campo ♦ vt tocar (em); (emotionally) comover; **the personal ~** o toque pessoal; **to put the finishing ~es to sth** dar os últimos retoques em algo; **a ~ of** (fig) uma pitada de, um pouquinho de; **to get in ~ with sb** entrar em contato com alguém; **to lose ~** (friends) perder o contato; **to be out of ~ with events** não estar a par dos acontecimentos; **no artist in the country can ~ him** nenhum artista no país se compara a ele.
touch on vt fus (topic) tocar em, fazer menção de.
touch up vt (paint) retocar.
touch-and-go adj arriscado; **it was ~ whether we did it** por pouco fizemos aquilo.
touchdown ['tʌtʃdaun] n aterrissagem f (BR), aterragem f (PT); (on sea) amerissagem f (BR), amaragem f (PT); (US: FOOTBALL) touchdown m (colocação da bola no chão atrás da linha de gol).
touched [tʌtʃt] adj comovido; (inf) tocado, muito louco.
touching ['tʌtʃɪŋ] adj comovedor(a).
touchline ['tʌtʃlaɪn] n (SPORT) linha de fundo.
touch-type vi datilografar sem olhar para as teclas.
touchy ['tʌtʃɪ] adj (person) suscetível, sensitivo.
tough [tʌf] adj duro; (difficult) difícil; (resistant) resistente; (person) tenaz, obstinado; (exam, experience) brabo ♦ n (gangster etc) bandido, capanga m; **~ luck!** azar!; **they got ~ with the workers** começaram a falar grosso com os trabalhadores.
toughen ['tʌfən] vt endurecer.
toughness ['tʌfnɪs] n dureza; (difficulty) dificuldade f; (resistance) resistência; (of person) tenacidade f.
toupee ['tu:peɪ] n peruca.
tour ['tuə*] n viagem f, excursão f; (also: package ~) excursão organizada; (of town, museum) visita; (by artist) turnê f ♦ vt excursionar por; **to go on a ~ of** (museum, region) visitar; **to go on ~** fazer turnê.
touring ['tuərɪŋ] n viagens fpl turísticas, turismo.
tourism ['tuərɪzm] n turismo.
tourist ['tuərɪst] n turista m/f ♦ cpd turístico; **the ~ trade** o turismo.
tourist office n agência de turismo.

tournament ['tuənəmənt] n torneio.
tourniquet ['tuənɪkeɪ] n (MED) torniquete m.
tour operator (BRIT) n empresa de viagens.
tousled ['tauzld] adj (hair) despenteado.
tout [taut] vi: **to ~ for** angariar clientes para ♦ vt (BRIT): **to ~ sth (around)** tentar vender algo ♦ n (BRIT: ticket ~) cambista m/f.
tow [təu] n: **to give sb a ~** (AUT) rebocar alguém ♦ vt rebocar; **"on ~"** (BRIT), **"in ~"** (US) (AUT) "rebocado"; **with her husband in ~** com o marido a tiracolo.
toward(s) [tə'wɔ:d(z)] prep em direção a; (of attitude) para com; (of purpose) para; **~ noon/the end of the year** perto do meio-dia/ do fim do ano; **to feel friendly ~ sb** sentir amizade em relação a alguém.
towel ['tauəl] n toalha; (also: tea ~) pano; **to throw in the ~** (fig) dar-se por vencido.
towelling ['tauəlɪŋ] n (fabric) tecido para toalhas.
towel rail (US **towel rack**) n toalheiro.
tower ['tauə*] n torre f ♦ vi (building, mountain) elevar-se; **to ~ above or over sb/sth** dominar alguém/algo.
tower block (BRIT) n prédio alto, espigão m, cortiço (BR).
towering ['tauərɪŋ] adj elevado, eminente.
towline ['təulaɪn] n cabo de reboque.
town [taun] n cidade f; **to go to ~** ir à cidade; (fig) fazer com entusiasmo, mandar brasa (BR); **in the ~** na cidade; **to be out of ~** (person) estar fora da cidade.
town centre n centro (da cidade).
town clerk n administrador(a) m/f municipal.
town council n câmara municipal.
town hall n prefeitura (BR), concelho (PT).
town plan n mapa m da cidade.
town planner n urbanista m/f.
town planning n urbanismo.
townspeople ['taunzpi:pl] npl habitantes mpl da cidade.
towpath ['təupɑ:θ] n caminho de sirga.
towrope ['təurəup] n cabo de reboque.
tow truck (US) n reboque m (BR), pronto socorro (PT).
toxic ['tɔksɪk] adj tóxico.
toxin ['tɔksɪn] n toxina.
toy [tɔɪ] n brinquedo ♦ cpd de brinquedo.
toy with vt fus jogar com; (idea) andar com.
toyshop ['tɔɪʃɔp] n loja de brinquedos.
trace [treɪs] n traço, rasto ♦ vt (through paper) decalcar; (draw) traçar, esboçar; (follow) seguir a pista de; (locate) encontrar; **without ~** (disappear) sem deixar vestígios; **there was no ~ of it** não havia nenhum vestígio disso.
trace element n elemento traço.
trachea [trə'kɪə] n (ANAT) traquéia.
tracing paper ['treɪsɪŋ-] papel m de decalque.
track [træk] n (mark) pegada, vestígio; (path: gen) caminho, vereda; (: of bullet etc) trajetória; (: of suspect, animal) pista, rasto; (RAIL) trilhos (BR), carris mpl (PT); (on tape) trilha; (SPORT) pista; (on record) faixa

◆ *vt* seguir a pista de; **to keep** ~ **of** não perder de vista; *(fig)* manter-se informado sobre; **to be on the right** ~ *(fig)* estar no caminho certo.

track down *vt (prey)* seguir a pista de; *(sth lost)* procurar e encontrar.

tracked [trækt] *adj* com lagarta.

tracker dog ['trækə-] *(BRIT)* n cão *m* policial.

track events *npl (SPORT)* corridas *fpl*.

tracking station ['trækɪŋ-] *n (SPACE)* estação *f* de rastreamento.

track record *n*: **to have a good** ~ *(fig)* ter uma boa folha de serviço.

track suit *n* roupa de jogging.

tract [trækt] *n (GEO)* região *f*; *(pamphlet)* folheto; **respiratory** ~ *(ANAT)* aparelho respiratório.

traction ['trækʃən] *n* tração *f*.

tractor ['træktə*] *n* trator *m*.

tractor feed *n (on printer)* alimentação *f* a trator.

trade [treɪd] *n* comércio; *(skill, job)* ofício ◆ *vi* negociar, comerciar; **to** ~ **with/in** comerciar com/em; **foreign** ~ comércio exterior; **Department of T**~ **and Industry** *(BRIT)* Ministério de Indústria e Comércio.

trade in *vt (old car etc)* dar como parte do pagamento.

trade barrier *n* barreira comercial.

trade deficit *n* déficit *m* na balança comercial.

Trade Descriptions Act *(BRIT) n lei contra a publicidade mentirosa.*

trade discount *n* desconto de revendedor.

trade fair *n* feira industrial.

trade-in *n* venda.

trade-in price *n valor de um objeto usado que se desconta do preço do outro novo.*

trademark ['treɪdmɑːk] *n* marca de fábrica *or* comércio.

trade mission *n* missão *f* comercial.

trade name *n (of product)* marca registrada; *(of company)* razão *f* social.

trader ['treɪdə*] *n* comerciante *m/f*.

trade secret *n* segredo do ofício.

tradesman ['treɪdzmən] *(irreg)* n *(shopkeeper)* lojista *m*.

trade union *n* sindicato.

trade unionism [-'juːnjənɪzəm] *n* sindicalismo.

trade unionist [-'juːnjənɪst] *n* sindicalista *m/f*.

trade wind *n* vento alísio.

trading ['treɪdɪŋ] *n* comércio.

trading estate *(BRIT)* n parque *m* industrial.

trading stamp *n* selo de bonificação.

tradition [trə'dɪʃən] *n* tradição *f*.

traditional [trə'dɪʃənl] *adj* tradicional.

traffic ['træfɪk] *n* trânsito; *(air* ~ *etc)* tráfego; *(illegal)* tráfico ◆ *vi*: **to** ~ **in** *(pej: liquor, drugs)* traficar com, fazer tráfico com.

traffic circle *(US)* n rotatória.

traffic island *n* refúgio de segurança (para pedestres).

traffic jam *n* engarrafamento, congestionamento.

traffic lights *npl* sinal *m* luminoso.

trafficker ['træfɪkə*] *n* traficante *m/f*.

traffic offence *(BRIT)* n infração *f* de trânsito.

traffic sign *n* placa de sinalização.

traffic violation *(US)* n infração *f*.

traffic warden *n* guarda *m/f* de trânsito.

tragedy ['trædʒədɪ] *n* tragédia.

tragic ['trædʒɪk] *adj* trágico.

trail [treɪl] *n (tracks)* rasto, pista; *(path)* caminho, trilha; *(wake)* esteira ◆ *vt (drag)* arrastar; *(follow)* seguir a pista de; *(follow closely)* vigiar ◆ *vi* arrastar-se; **to be on sb's** ~ estar no encalço de alguém.

trail away *vi (sound, voice)* ir-se perdendo; *(interest)* diminuir.

trail behind *vi* atrasar-se.

trail off *vi (sound, voice)* ir-se perdendo; *(interest)* diminuir.

trailer ['treɪlə*] *n (AUT)* reboque *m*; *(US: caravan)* trailer *m (BR)*, rulote *f (PT)*; *(CINEMA)* trailer.

trailer truck *(US)* n caminhão-reboque *m*.

train [treɪn] *n* trem *m (BR)*, comboio *(PT)*; *(of dress)* cauda; *(series)* seqüência, série *f*; *(followers)* séquito, comitiva ◆ *vt (professionals etc)* formar; *(teach skills to)* instruir; *(SPORT)* treinar; *(dog)* adestrar, amestrar; *(point: gun etc)*: **to** ~ **on** apontar para ◆ *vi (SPORT)* treinar; *(be educated)* ser treinado; **to lose one's** ~ **of thought** perder o fio; **to go by** ~ ir de trem; **to** ~ **sb to do sth** treinar alguém para fazer algo.

train attendant *(US)* n revisor(a) *m/f*.

trained [treɪnd] *adj (worker)* especializado; *(teacher)* formado; *(animal)* adestrado.

trainee [treɪ'niː] *n* estagiário/a; *(in trade)* aprendiz *m/f*.

trainer ['treɪnə*] *n*; *(SPORT)* treinador(a) *m/f*; *(of animals)* adestrador(a) *m/f*; **~s** *npl (shoes)* tênis *m*.

training ['treɪnɪŋ] *n* instrução *f*; *(SPORT)* treinamento; *(professional)* formação.

training college *n (for teachers)* Escola Normal.

training course *n* curso de formação profissional.

training shoes *npl* tênis *m*.

traipse [treɪps] *vi* arrastar os pés.

trait [treɪt] *n* traço.

traitor ['treɪtə*] *n* traidor(a) *m/f*.

trajectory [trə'dʒɛktərɪ] *n* trajetória.

tram [træm] *(BRIT)* n *(also:* ~*car)* bonde *m (BR)*, eléctrico *(PT)*.

tramline ['træmlaɪn] *n* trilho para bondes.

tramp [træmp] *n (person)* vagabundo/a ◆ *vi* caminhar pesadamente ◆ *vt (walk through; town, streets)* percorrer, andar por.

trample ['træmpl] *vt*: **to** ~ **(underfoot)** calcar aos pés.

NB: *European Portuguese adds the following consonants to certain words:* **b** (sú(b)dito, su(b)til); **c** (a(c)ção, a(c)cionista, a(c)to); **m** (inde(m)ne); **p** (ado(p)ção, ado(p)tar); *for further details see p. xiii.*

trampoline ['træmpəli:n] n trampolim m.
trance [trɑ:ns] n estupor m; (MED) transe m hipnótico; **to go into a** ~ cair em transe.
tranquil ['træŋkwɪl] adj tranqüilo.
tranquillity [træŋ'kwɪlɪtɪ] n tranqüilidade f.
tranquillizer ['træŋkwɪlaɪzə*] n (MED) tranqüilizante m.
transact [træn'zækt] vt (business) negociar.
transaction [træn'zækʃən] n transação f, negócio; ~s npl (minutes) ata; **cash** ~ transação à vista.
transatlantic [trænzət'læntɪk] adj transatlântico.
transcend [træn'sɛnd] vt transcender, exceder; (excel over) ultrapassar.
transcendental [trænsɛn'dɛntl] adj: ~ **meditation** meditação f transcendental.
transcribe [træn'skraɪb] vt transcrever.
transcript ['trænskrɪpt] n cópia, traslado.
transcription [træn'skrɪpʃən] n transcrição f.
transept ['trænsɛpt] n transepto.
transfer [n 'trænsfə*, vt træns'fə:*] n transferência; (picture, design) decalcomania ♦ vt transferir, trasladar; **to** ~ **the charges** (BRIT: TEL) ligar a cobrar; **by bank** ~ por transferência bancária.
transferable [træns'fə:rəbl] adj transferível; **not** ~ intransferível.
transfix [træns'fɪks] vt trespassar; (fig): ~**ed with fear** paralisado de medo.
transform [træns'fɔ:m] vt transformar.
transformation [trænsfə'meɪʃən] n transformação f.
transformer [træns'fɔ:mə*] n (ELEC) transformador m.
transfusion [træns'fju:ʒən] n transfusão f.
transgress [træns'grɛs] vt transgredir.
transient ['trænzɪənt] adj transitório.
transistor [træn'zɪstə*] n (ELEC: also: ~ radio) transistor m.
transit ['trænzɪt] n: **in** ~ em trânsito, de passagem.
transit camp n campo de trânsito.
transition [træn'zɪʃən] n transição f.
transitional [træn'zɪʃənl] adj de transição, transicional.
transitive ['trænzɪtɪv] adj (LING) transitivo.
transit lounge n salão m de trânsito.
transitory ['trænzɪtərɪ] adj transitório.
translate [trænz'leɪt] vt: **to** ~ (**from/into**) traduzir (do/para o).
translation [trænz'leɪʃən] n tradução f.
translator [trænz'leɪtə*] n tradutor(a) m/f.
translucent [trænz'lu:snt] adj translúcido.
transmission [trænz'mɪʃən] n transmissão f.
transmit [trænz'mɪt] vt transmitir.
transmitter [trænz'mɪtə*] n transmissor m; (station) emissora.
transparency [træns'pɛərnsɪ] (BRIT) n (PHOT) transparência, diapositivo.
transparent [træns'pærnt] adj transparente.
transpire [træns'paɪə*] vi (happen) ocorrer, acontecer; (become known): **it finally** ~**d that** ... no final soube-se que ....
transplant [vt træns'plɑ:nt, n 'trænsplɑ:nt] vt

transplantar ♦ n (MED) transplante m; **to have a heart** ~ ter um transplante de coração.
transport [n 'trænspɔ:t, vt træns'pɔ:t] n transporte m ♦ vt transportar; (carry) acarretar; **public** ~ transportes coletivos; **Department of T**~ (BRIT) ministérioda dos Transportes.
transportation [trænspɔ:'teɪʃən] n transporte m; **Department of T**~ (US) ministério da Infra-estrutura.
transport café (BRIT) n lanchonete f de estrada.
transpose [træns'pəuz] vt transpor.
transship [træns'ʃɪp] vt baldear.
transverse ['trænzvɔ:s] adj transversal.
transvestite [trænz'vɛstaɪt] n travesti m/f.
trap [træp] n (snare, trick) armadilha, cilada; (carriage) aranha, charrete f ♦ vt pegar em armadilha; (immobilize) bloquear; (jam) emperrar; **to set** or **lay a** ~ (**for sb**) montar uma armadilha (para alguém); **to shut one's** ~ (inf) calar a boca; **to** ~ **one's finger in the door** prender o dedo na porta.
trap door n alçapão m.
trapeze [trə'pi:z] n trapézio.
trapper ['træpə*] n caçador m de peles.
trappings ['træpɪŋz] npl adornos mpl, enfeites mpl.
trash [træʃ] n (pej: goods) refugo, escória; (: nonsense) besteiras fpl; (US: rubbish) lixo.
trash can (US) n lata de lixo.
trauma ['trɔ:mə] n trauma m.
traumatic [trɔ:'mætɪk] adj traumático.
travel ['trævl] n viagem f ♦ vi viajar; (move) deslocar-se ♦ vt (distance) percorrer.
travel agency n agência de viagens.
travel agent n agente m/f de viagens.
travel brochure n prospecto turístico.
traveller ['trævələ*] (US **traveler**) n viajante m/f; (COMM) caixeiro/a viajante.
traveller's cheque (US **traveler's check**) n cheque m de viagem.
travelling ['trævəlɪŋ] (US **traveling**) n as viagens, viajar m ♦ adj (circus, exhibition) itinerante; (salesman) viajante ♦ cpd (bag, clock, expenses) de viagem.
travel(l)ing salesman (irreg) n caixeiro viajante.
travelogue ['trævəlɔg] n (book) livro de viagem; (film) documentário de viagem.
travel sickness n enjôo.
traverse ['trævəs] vt atravessar.
travesty ['trævəstɪ] n paródia.
trawler ['trɔ:lə*] n traineira.
tray [treɪ] n bandeja; (on desk) cesta.
treacherous ['trɛtʃərəs] adj traiçoeiro; **road conditions are** ~ as estradas estão perigosas.
treachery ['trɛtʃərɪ] n traição f.
treacle ['tri:kl] n melado.
tread [trɛd] (pt **trod**, pp **trodden**) n (step) passo, pisada; (sound) passada; (of tyre) banda de rodagem ♦ vi pisar.
tread on vt fus pisar (em).
treadle ['trɛdl] n pedal m.

treas. *abbr* = **treasurer.**
treason ['triːzn] *n* traição *f.*
treasure ['trɛʒə*] *n* tesouro ♦ *vt* (*value*) apreciar, estimar.
treasure hunt *n* caça ao tesouro.
treasurer ['trɛʒərə*] *n* tesoureiro/a.
treasury ['trɛʒərɪ] *n* tesouraria; **the T~** (*BRIT: POL*) *or* **T~ Department** (*US: POL*) ≈ o Tesouro Nacional.
treasury bill *n* letra do Tesouro (Nacional).
treat [triːt] *n* (*present*) regalo, deleite *m*; (*pleasure*) prazer *m* ♦ *vt* tratar; **to ~ sb to sth** convidar alguém para algo; **to give sb a ~** dar um prazer a alguém; **to ~ sth as a joke** não levar algo a sério.
treatise ['triːtɪz] *n* tratado.
treatment ['triːtmənt] *n* tratamento; **to have ~ for sth** (*MED*) fazer tratamento para algo.
treaty ['triːtɪ] *n* tratado, acordo.
treble ['trɛbl] *adj* tríplice ♦ *n* (*MUS*) soprano ♦ *vt* triplicar ♦ *vi* triplicar(-se).
treble clef *n* clave *f* de sol.
tree [triː] *n* árvore *f.*
tree-lined *adj* ladeado de árvores.
treetop ['triːtɔp] *n* copa (de árvore).
tree trunk *n* tronco de árvore.
trek [trɛk] *n* (*long journey*) jornada; (*walk*) caminhada; (*as holiday*) excursão *f* (a pé) ♦ *vi* (*as holiday*) caminhar.
trellis ['trɛlɪs] *n* grade *f* de ripas, latada.
tremble ['trɛmbl] *vi* tremer.
trembling ['trɛmblɪŋ] *n* tremor *m* ♦ *adj* trêmulo, trepidante.
tremendous [trɪ'mɛndəs] *adj* tremendo; (*enormous*) enorme; (*excellent*) sensacional, fantástico.
tremendously [trɪ'mɛndəslɪ] *adv* (*well, clever etc*) extraordinariamente; (*very much*) muitíssimo; (*very well*) muito bem.
tremor ['trɛmə*] *n* tremor *m*; (*also: earth ~*) tremor de terra.
trench [trɛntʃ] *n* trincheira.
trench coat *n* capa (de chuva).
trench warfare *n* guerra de trincheiras.
trend [trɛnd] *n* (*tendency*) tendência; (*of events*) curso; (*fashion*) modismo, tendência; **~ towards/away from doing** tendência a/ contra fazer; **to set the ~** dar o tom; **to set a ~** lançar uma moda.
trendy ['trɛndɪ] *adj* (*idea*) de acordo com a tendência atual; (*clothes*) da última moda.
trepidation [trɛpɪ'deɪʃən] *n* trepidação *f*; (*fear*) apreensão *f.*
trespass ['trɛspəs] *vi*: **to ~ on** invadir; "**no ~ing**" "entrada proibida".
trespasser ['trɛspəsə*] *n* intruso/a; "**~s will be prosecuted**" "aqueles que invadirem esta área serão punidos".
tress [trɛs] *n* trança.
trestle ['trɛsl] *n* cavalete *m.*
trestle table *n* mesa de cavaletes.
trial ['traɪəl] *n* (*LAW*) processo; (*test: of*

machine etc) prova, teste *m*; (*hardship*) provação *f*; **~s** *npl* (*SPORT*) eliminatórias *fpl*; **horse ~s** provas *fpl* de equitação; **by ~ and error** por tentativas; **~ by jury** julgamento por júri; **to be sent for ~** ser levado a julgamento; **to be on ~** ser julgado.
trial balance *n* (*COMM*) balancete *m.*
trial basis *n*: **on a ~** em experiência.
trial run *n* ensaio.
triangle ['traɪæŋgl] *n* (*MATH, MUS*) triângulo.
triangular [traɪ'æŋgjulə*] *adj* triangular.
tribal ['traɪbəl] *adj* tribal.
tribe [traɪb] *n* tribo *f.*
tribesman ['traɪbzmən] (*irreg*) *n* membro da tribo.
tribulation [trɪbju'leɪʃən] *n* tribulação *f*, aflição *f.*
tribunal [traɪ'bjuːnl] *n* tribunal *m.*
tributary ['trɪbjuːtərɪ] *n* (*river*) afluente *m.*
tribute ['trɪbjuːt] *n* homenagem *f*; (*payment*) tributo; **to pay ~** to prestar homenagem a, homenagear.
trice [traɪs] *n*: **in a ~** num instante.
trick [trɪk] *n* truque *m*; (*deceit*) fraude *f*, trapaça; (*joke*) peça, brincadeira; (*CARDS*) vaza ♦ *vt* enganar; **to play a ~ on sb** pregar uma peça em alguém; **to ~ sb into doing sth** induzir alguém a fazer algo pela astúcia; **to ~ sb out of sth** obter algo de alguém pela astúcia; **it's a ~ of the light** é uma ilusão de ótica; **that should do the ~** (*inf*) isso deveria dar resultado.
trickery ['trɪkərɪ] *n* trapaça, astúcia.
trickle ['trɪkl] *n* (*of water etc*) fio (de água) ♦ *vi* gotejar, pingar; **to ~ in/out** (*people*) ir entrando/saindo aos poucos.
trick question *n* pergunta capciosa.
trickster ['trɪkstə*] *n* vigarista *m/f.*
tricky ['trɪkɪ] *adj* difícil, complicado.
tricycle ['traɪsɪkl] *n* triciclo.
trifle ['traɪfl] *n* bagatela; (*CULIN*) tipo de bolo com fruta e creme ♦ *adv*: **a ~ long** um pouquinho longo ♦ *vi*: **to ~ with** brincar com.
trifling ['traɪflɪŋ] *adj* insignificante.
trigger ['trɪgə*] *n* (*of gun*) gatilho.
trigger off *vt* desencadear.
trigonometry [trɪgə'nɔmətrɪ] *n* trigonometria.
trilby ['trɪlbɪ] (*BRIT*) *n* (*also: ~ hat*) chapéu *m* de feltro.
trill [trɪl] *n* (*of bird, MUS*) trinado, trilo.
trilogy ['trɪlədʒɪ] *n* trilogia.
trim [trɪm] *adj* (*elegant*) elegante; (*house*) arrumado; (*garden*) bem cuidado; (*figure*) esbelto ♦ *n* (*haircut etc*) aparada; (*on car*) estofamento; (*embellishment*) acabamento, remate *m* ♦ *vt* (*cut*) aparar, cortar; (*decorate*) enfeitar; (*NAUT: sail*) ajustar; **to keep in (good) ~** manter em bom estado.
trimmings ['trɪmɪŋz] *npl* decoração *f*; (*extras: gen CULIN*) acompanhamentos *mpl.*
Trinidad and Tobago ['trɪnɪdæd-] *n* Trinidad e Tobago (*no article*).

NB: European Portuguese adds the following consonants to certain words: **b** (sú(b)dito, su(b)til); **c** (a(c)ção, a(c)cionista, a(c)to); **m** (inde(m)ne); **p** (ado(p)ção, ado(p)tar); *for further details see p. xiii.*

Trinity ['trɪnɪtɪ] n: **the** ~ a Trindade.
trinket ['trɪŋkɪt] n bugiganga; (piece of jewellery) berloque m, bijuteria.
trio ['triːəu] n trio.
trip [trɪp] n viagem f; (excursion) excursão f; (stumble) tropeção m ♦ vi (also: ~ up) tropeçar; (go lightly) andar com passos ligeiros ♦ vt fazer tropeçar; **on a** ~ de viagem.
   trip up vi tropeçar ♦ vt passar uma rasteira em.
tripartite [traɪ'pɑːtaɪt] adj (in three parts) tripartido; (POL) tripartidário.
tripe [traɪp] n (CULIN) bucho, tripa; (pej: rubbish) bobagem f.
triple ['trɪpl] adj triplo, tríplice ♦ adv: ~ **the distance/the speed** três vezes a distância/a velocidade.
triplets ['trɪplɪts] npl trigêmeos/as m/fpl.
triplicate ['trɪplɪkət] n: **in** ~ em triplicata, em três vias.
tripod ['traɪpɔd] n tripé m.
Tripoli ['trɪpəlɪ] n Trípoli.
tripper ['trɪpə*] (BRIT) n excursionista m/f.
tripwire ['trɪpwaɪə*] n fio de disparo.
trite [traɪt] adj gasto, banal.
triumph ['traɪʌmf] n triunfo ♦ vi: **to** ~ **(over)** triunfar (sobre).
triumphal [traɪ'ʌmfl] adj triunfal.
triumphant [traɪ'ʌmfənt] adj triunfante.
trivia ['trɪvɪə] npl trivialidades fpl.
trivial ['trɪvɪəl] adj insignificante; (commonplace) trivial.
triviality [trɪvɪ'ælɪtɪ] n trivialidade f.
trivialize ['trɪvɪəlaɪz] vt banalizar, trivializar.
trod [trɔd] pt of **tread**.
trodden ['trɔdn] pp of **tread**.
trolley ['trɔlɪ] n carrinho.
trolley bus n ônibus m elétrico (BR), trólei m (PT).
trollop ['trɔləp] n rameira.
trombone [trɔm'bəun] n trombone m.
troop [truːp] n bando, grupo ♦ vi: **to** ~ **in/out** entrar/sair em bando; ~**s** npl (MIL) tropas fpl; (: men) homens mpl; ~**ing the colour** (BRIT: ceremony) a saudação da bandeira.
troop carrier n (plane) avião m de transporte de tropas; (NAUT: also: troopship) navio-transporte m.
trooper ['truːpə*] n (MIL) soldado de cavalaria; (US: policeman) ≈ policial m militar, PM m.
troopship ['truːpʃɪp] n navio-transporte m.
trophy ['trəufɪ] n troféu m.
tropic ['trɔpɪk] n trópico; **in the** ~**s** nos trópicos; **T**~ **of Cancer/Capricorn** Trópico de Câncer/Capricórnio.
tropical ['trɔpɪkl] adj tropical.
trot [trɔt] n trote m ♦ vi trotar; **on the** ~ (fig: inf) a fio.
   trot out vt (excuse, reason) apresentar, dar; (names, facts) recitar.
trouble ['trʌbl] n problema(s) m(pl), dificuldade(s) f(pl); (worry) preocupação f; (bother, effort) incômodo, trabalho; (POL) distúrbios mpl; (MED): **stomach** ~ etc problemas mpl

gástricos etc ♦ vt perturbar; (worry) preocupar, incomodar ♦ vi: **to** ~ **to do sth** incomodar-se or preocupar-se de fazer algo; ~**s** npl (POL etc) distúrbios mpl; **to be in** ~ (in difficulty) estar num aperto; (for doing sth wrong) estar numa encrenca; **to go to the** ~ **of doing sth** dar-se ao trabalho de fazer algo; **to have** ~ **doing sth** ter dificuldade em fazer algo; **it's no** ~! não tem problema!; **please don't** ~ **yourself** por favor, não se dê trabalho!; **the** ~ **is** ... o problema é ...; **what's the** ~? qual é o problema?
troubled ['trʌbld] adj (person) preocupado; (epoch, life) agitado.
trouble-free adj sem problemas.
troublemaker ['trʌblmeɪkə*] n criador(a)-de-casos m/f; (child) encrenqueiro/a.
troubleshooter ['trʌblʃuːtə*] n (in conflict) conciliador(a) m/f; (solver of problems) solucionador(a) m/f de problemas.
troublesome ['trʌblsəm] adj incômodo, importuno.
trouble spot n área de conflito.
trough [trɔf] n (also: drinking ~) bebedouro, cocho; (also: feeding ~) gamela; (channel) canal m; ~ **of low pressure** (METEOROLOGY) cavado de baixa pressão.
trounce [trauns] vt (defeat) dar uma surra or um banho em.
troupe [truːp] n companhia teatral.
trouser press n passadeira de calças.
trousers ['trauzəz] npl calça (BR), calças fpl (PT).
trouser suit (BRIT) n terninho (BR), conjunto de calças casaco (PT).
trousseau ['truːsəu] (pl ~x or ~s) n enxoval m.
trousseaux ['truːsəuz] npl of **trousseau**.
trout [traut] n inv truta.
trowel ['trauəl] n colher f de jardineiro or de pedreiro.
truancy ['truənsɪ] n evasão f escolar.
truant ['truənt] (BRIT) n: **to play** ~ matar aula (BR), fazer gazeta (PT).
truce [truːs] n trégua, armistício.
truck [trʌk] n caminhão m (BR), camião m (PT); (RAIL) vagão m.
truck driver n caminhoneiro/a (BR), camionista m/f (PT).
trucker ['trʌkə*] (esp US) n caminhoneiro (BR), camionista m/f (PT).
truck farm (US) n horta.
trucking ['trʌkɪŋ] (esp US) n transporte m rodoviário.
trucking company (US) n transportadora.
truck stop (US) n bar m de estrada.
truculent ['trʌkjulənt] adj agressivo.
trudge [trʌdʒ] vi andar com dificuldade, arrastar-se.
true [truː] adj verdadeiro; (accurate) exato; (genuine) autêntico; (faithful) fiel, leal; (wall) aprumado; (beam) nivelado; (wheel) alinhado; **to come** ~ realizar-se, tornar-se realidade; ~ **to life** realista, fiel à realidade; **it's** ~ é verdade.

truffle ['trʌfl] *n* trufa.
truly ['truːlɪ] *adv* (*really*) realmente; (*truthfully*) verdadeiramente; (*faithfully*) fielmente; **yours** ~ (*in letter*) atenciosamente.
trump [trʌmp] *n* trunfo; **to turn** *or* **come up** ~**s** (*fig*) salvar a pátria.
trump card *n* (*also: fig*) trunfo.
trumped-up [trʌmpt-] *adj* inventado, forjado.
trumpet ['trʌmpɪt] *n* trombeta.
truncated [trʌŋ'keɪtɪd] *adj* truncado.
truncheon ['trʌntʃən] *n* cassetete *m*.
trundle ['trʌndl] *vt, vi*: **to** ~ **along** rolar *or* rodar fazendo ruído.
trunk [trʌŋk] *n* (*of tree, person*) tronco; (*of elephant*) tromba; (*case*) baú *m*; (*US: AUT*) mala (*BR*), porta-bagagens *m* (*PT*); ~**s** *npl* (*also: swimming* ~**s**) sunga (*BR*), calções *mpl* de banho (*PT*).
trunk call (*BRIT*) *n* (*TEL*) ligação *f* interurbana.
trunk road (*BRIT*) *n* ≈ rodovia nacional.
truss [trʌs] *n* (*MED*) funda ♦ *vt*: **to** ~ (**up**) atar, amarrar.
trust [trʌst] *n* confiança; (*COMM*) truste *m*; (*LAW*) fideicomisso ♦ *vt* (*rely on*) confiar em; (*entrust*): **to** ~ **sth to sb** confiar algo a alguém; (*hope*): **to** ~ (**that**) esperar que; **to take sth on** ~ aceitar algo sem verificação prévia; **in** ~ (*LAW*) em fideicomisso.
trust company *n* companhia fiduciária.
trusted ['trʌstɪd] *adj* de confiança.
trustee [trʌs'tiː] *n* (*LAW*) fideicomissário/a, depositário/a; (*of school etc*) administrador(a) *m/f*.
trustful ['trʌstful] *adj* confiante.
trust fund *n* fundo de fideicomisso.
trusting ['trʌstɪŋ] *adj* confiante.
trustworthy ['trʌstwəːðɪ] *adj* digno de confiança.
trusty ['trʌstɪ] *adj* fidedigno, fiel.
truth [truːθ, *pl* truːðz] *n* verdade *f*.
truthful ['truːθful] *adj* (*person*) sincero, honesto; (*account*) verídico.
truthfully ['truːθfulɪ] *adv* sinceramente.
truthfulness ['truːθfulnɪs] *n* veracidade *f*.
try [traɪ] *n* tentativa; (*RUGBY*) ensaio ♦ *vt* (*LAW*) julgar; (*test: sth new*) provar, pôr à prova; (*attempt*) tentar; (*food etc*) experimentar; (*strain*) cansar ♦ *vi* tentar; **to** ~ **to do sth** tentar fazer algo; **to** ~ **one's (very) best** *or* **one's (very) hardest** fazer (todo) o possível; **to give sth a** ~ tentar algo.
try on *vt* (*clothes*) experimentar, provar; **to** ~ **it on with sb** (*fig: test sb's patience*) testar a paciência de alguém; (: *try to trick*) tentar engambelar alguém.
try out *vt* experimentar, provar.
trying ['traɪɪŋ] *adj* penoso, árduo.
tsar [zɑː] *n* czar *m*.
T-shirt *n* camiseta (*BR*), T-shirt *f* (*PT*).
T-square *n* régua em T.

TT *adj abbr* (*BRIT: inf*) = **teetotal** ♦ *abbr* (*US: POST*) = **Trust Territory**.
tub [tʌb] *n* tina; (*bath*) banheira.
tuba ['tjuːbə] *n* tuba.
tubby ['tʌbɪ] *adj* gorducho.
tube [tjuːb] *n* tubo; (*BRIT: underground*) metrô *m* (*BR*), metro(-politano) (*PT*); (*for tyre*) câmara-de-ar *f*.
tubeless ['tjuːblɪs] *adj* sem câmara.
tuber ['tjuːbə*] *n* (*BOT*) tubérculo.
tuberculosis [tjubəːkju'ləusɪs] *n* tuberculose *f*.
tube station (*BRIT*) *n* estação *f* de metrô.
tubing ['tjuːbɪŋ] *n* tubulação *f*, encanamento; **a piece of** ~ um pedaço de tubo.
tubular ['tjuːbjulə*] *adj* tubular; (*furniture*) tubiforme.
TUC (*BRIT*) *n abbr* (= *Trades Union Congress*) ≈ CUT *f*.
tuck [tʌk] *n* (*SEWING*) prega, dobra ♦ *vt* (*put*) enfiar, meter.
tuck away *vt* esconder.
tuck in *vt* enfiar a beirada de; (*child*) aconchegar ♦ *vi* (*eat*) comer com apetite.
tuck up *vt* (*child*) aconchegar.
tuck shop *n* loja de balas.
Tue(s). *abbr* (= *Tuesday*) ter, 3ª.
Tuesday ['tjuːzdɪ] *n* terça-feira; **(the date) today is** ~ **23rd March** hoje é terça-feira, 23 de março; **on** ~ na terça(-feira); **on** ~**s** nas terças(-feiras); **every** ~ todas as terças(-feiras); **every other** ~ terça-feira sim, terça-feira não; **last/next** ~ na terça-feira passada/na terça-feira que vem; ~ **next** na terça-feira que vem; **the following** ~ na terça-feira seguinte; **a week on** ~ sem ser essa terça, a outra; **the** ~ **before last** na terça-feira retrasada; **the** ~ **after next** sem ser essa terça, a outra; ~ **morning/lunchtime/afternoon/evening** na terça-feira de manhã/ao meio-dia/à tarde/à noite; ~ **night** na terça-feira à noite; ~**'s newspaper** o jornal de terça-feira.
tuft [tʌft] *n* penacho; (*of grass etc*) tufo.
tug [tʌg] *n* (*ship*) rebocador *m* ♦ *vt* puxar.
tug-of-war *n* cabo-de-guerra *m*; (*fig*) disputa.
tuition [tjuː'ɪʃən] *n* ensino; (*private* ~) aulas *fpl* particulares; (*US: fees*) taxas *fpl* escolares.
tulip ['tjuːlɪp] *n* tulipa.
tumble ['tʌmbl] *n* (*fall*) queda ♦ *vi* cair, tombar ♦ *vt* derrubar; **to** ~ **to sth** (*inf*) sacar algo.
tumbledown ['tʌmbldaun] *adj* em ruínas.
tumble dryer (*BRIT*) *n* máquina de secar roupa.
tumbler ['tʌmblə*] *n* copo.
tummy ['tʌmɪ] (*inf*) *n* (*belly*) barriga; (*stomach*) estômago.
tumour ['tjuːmə*] (*US* **tumor**) *n* tumor *m*.
tumult ['tjuːmʌlt] *n* tumulto.
tumultuous [tjuː'mʌltjuəs] *adj* tumultuado.
tuna ['tjuːnə] *n inv* (*also:* ~ *fish*) atum *m*.

NB: *European Portuguese adds the following consonants to certain words:* **b** (sú(b)dito, su(b)til); **c** (a(c)ção, a(c)cionista, a(c)to); **m** (inde(m)ne); **p** (ado(p)ção, ado(p)tar); *for further details see p. xiii.*

tune [tjuːn] *n* melodia ♦ *vt* (*MUS*) afinar; (*RADIO, TV*) sintonizar; (*AUT*) regular; **to be in/ out of** ~ (*instrument*) estar afinado/ desafinado; (*singer*) cantar afinado/desafinar; **to be in/out of** ~ **with** (*fig*) harmonizar-se com/destoar de; **she was robbed to the** ~ **of £10,000** ela foi roubada em mais de £10,000.

tune in *vi* (*RADIO, TV*): **to** ~ **in(to)** sintonizar (com).

tune up *vi* (*musician*) afinar (seu instrumento).

tuneful ['tjuːnful] *adj* melodioso.

tuner ['tjuːnə*] *n* (*radio set*) sintonizador *m*; **piano** ~ afinador(a) *m/f* de pianos.

tuner amplifier *n* sintonizador *m* amplificador.

tungsten ['tʌŋstən] *n* tungstênio.

tunic ['tjuːnɪk] *n* túnica.

tuning ['tjuːnɪŋ] *n* (*of radio*) sintonia; (*MUS*) afinação *f*; (*of car*) regulagem *f*.

tuning fork *n* diapasão *m*.

Tunis ['tjuːnɪs] *n* Túnis.

Tunisia [tjuːˈnɪzɪə] *n* Tunísia.

Tunisian [tjuːˈnɪzɪən] *adj*, *n* tunisiano/a.

tunnel ['tʌnl] *n* túnel *m*; (*in mine*) galeria ♦ *vi* abrir um túnel (*or* uma galeria).

tunny ['tʌnɪ] *n* atum *m*.

turban ['tɜːbən] *n* turbante *m*.

turbid ['tɜːbɪd] *adj* turvo.

turbine ['tɜːbaɪn] *n* turbina.

turbojet [tɜːbəʊˈdʒɛt] *n* turbojato (*PT*: -ct-).

turboprop [tɜːbəʊˈprɔp] *n* (*engine*) turboélice *m*.

turbot ['tɜːbət] *n inv* rodovalho.

turbulence ['tɜːbjʊləns] *n* (*AVIAT*) turbulência.

turbulent ['tɜːbjʊlənt] *adj* turbulento.

tureen [təˈriːn] *n* terrina.

turf [tɜːf] *n* torrão *m* ♦ *vt* relvar, gramar; **the** T~ o turfe.

turf out (*inf*) *vt* (*thing*) jogar fora; (*person*) pôr no olho da rua.

turf accountant (*BRIT*) *n* corretor *m* de apostas.

turgid ['tɜːdʒɪd] *adj* (*speech*) pomposo.

Turk [tɜːk] *n* turco/a.

Turkey ['tɜːkɪ] *n* Turquia.

turkey ['tɜːkɪ] *n* peru(a) *m/f*.

Turkish ['tɜːkɪʃ] *adj* turco/a ♦ *n* (*LING*) turco.

Turkish bath *n* banho turco.

Turkish delight *n* lokum *m*.

turmeric ['tɜːmərɪk] *n* açafrão-da-terra *m*.

turmoil ['tɜːmɔɪl] *n* tumulto, distúrbio, agitação *f*.

turn [tɜːn] *n* volta, turno; (*in road*) curva; (*go*) vez *f*, turno; (*tendency*: *of mind, events*) propensão *f*, tendência; (*THEATRE*) número; (*MED*) choque *m* ♦ *vt* dar volta a, fazer girar; (*collar*) virar; (*steak*) virar; (*milk*) azedar; (*shape*: *wood*) tornear; (*change*): **to** ~ **sth into** converter algo em ♦ *vi* virar; (*person*: *look back*) voltar-se; (*reverse direction*) mudar de direção; (*milk*) azedar; (*change*) mudar; (*become*) tornar-se, virar; **to** ~ **into** converter-se em; **a good** ~ um favor; **it gave me quite a** ~ me deu um susto

enorme; **"no left** ~**"** (*AUT*) "proibido virar à esquerda"; **it's your** ~ é a sua vez; **in** ~ por sua vez; **to take** ~**s (at)** revezar (em); **at the** ~ **of the year/century** no final do ano/ século; **to take a** ~ **for the worse** (*situation, patient*) piorar; **to** ~ **left** (*AUT*) virar à esquerda; **she has no one to** ~ **to** ela não tem a quem recorrer.

turn about *vi* dar meia-volta.

turn away *vi* virar a cabeça ♦ *vt* (*reject*: *person*) rejeitar; (: *business*) recusar.

turn back *vi* voltar atrás.

turn down *vt* (*refuse*) recusar; (*reduce*) baixar; (*fold*) dobrar, virar para baixo.

turn in *vi* (*inf*: *go to bed*) ir dormir ♦ *vt* (*fold*) dobrar para dentro.

turn off *vi* (*from road*) virar, sair do caminho ♦ *vt* (*light, radio etc*) apagar; (*engine*) desligar.

turn on *vt* (*light*) acender; (*engine, radio*) ligar.

turn out *vt* (*light, gas*) apagar; (*produce*) produzir ♦ *vi* (*troops*) ser mobilizado; **to** ~ **out to be ...** revelar-se (ser) ..., resultar (ser) ...., vir a ser ....

turn over *vi* (*person*) virar-se ♦ *vt* (*object*) virar.

turn round *vi* voltar-se, virar-se ♦ *vt* girar.

turn up *vi* (*person*) aparecer, pintar; (*lost object*) aparecer ♦ *vt* (*collar*) subir; (*volume, radio etc*) aumentar.

turnabout ['tɜːnəbaʊt] *n* reviravolta.

turnaround ['tɜːnəraʊnd] *n* reviravolta.

turncoat ['tɜːnkəʊt] *n* vira-casaca *m/f*.

turned-up [tɜːnd-] *adj* (*nose*) arrebitado.

turning ['tɜːnɪŋ] *n* (*in road*) via lateral; **the first** ~ **on the right** a primeira à direita.

turning circle (*BRIT*) *n* raio de viragem.

turning point *n* (*fig*) momento decisivo, virada.

turning radius (*US*) *n* raio de viragem.

turnip ['tɜːnɪp] *n* nabo.

turnout ['tɜːnaʊt] *n* assistência; (*in election*) afluência às urnas.

turnover ['tɜːnəʊvə*] *n* (*COMM*: *amount of money*) volume *m* de negócios; (: *of goods*) movimento; (*CULIN*) espécie de pastel; **there is a rapid** ~ **in staff** há uma alta rotatividade no quadro de pessoal.

turnpike ['tɜːnpaɪk] (*US*) *n* estrada *or* rodovia com pedágio (*BR*) *or* portagem (*PT*).

turnstile ['tɜːnstaɪl] *n* borboleta (*BR*), torniquete *m* (*PT*).

turntable ['tɜːnteɪbl] *n* (*on record player*) prato.

turn-up (*BRIT*) *n* (*on trousers*) volta, dobra.

turpentine ['tɜːpəntaɪn] *n* (*also*: *turps*) aguarrás *f*.

turquoise ['tɜːkwɔɪz] *n* (*stone*) turquesa ♦ *adj* azul-turquesa *inv*.

turret ['tʌrɪt] *n* torrinha.

turtle ['tɜːtl] *n* tartaruga, cágado.

turtleneck (sweater) ['tɜːtlnɛk-] *n* pulôver *m* (*BR*) *or* camisola (*PT*) de gola alta.

tusk [tʌsk] *n* defesa (de elefante).

tussle ['tʌsl] *n* (*fight*) luta; (*scuffle*) contenda, rixa.

tutor ['tjuːtə*] *n* professor(a) *m/f*.

tutorial [tjuː'tɔːrɪəl] *n* (*SCH*) seminário.

tuxedo [tʌk'siːdəu] (*US*) *n* smoking *m*.

TV *n abbr* (= *television*) TV *f*.

twaddle ['twɔdl] *n* bobagens *fpl*, disparates *mpl*.

twang [twæŋ] *n* (*of instrument*) dedilhado; (*of voice*) timbre *m* nasal *or* fanhoso ♦ *vi* vibrar ♦ *vt* (*guitar*) dedilhar.

tweak [twiːk] *vt* (*nose, ear*) beliscar; (*hair*) puxar.

tweed [twiːd] *n* tweed *m*, pano grosso de lã.

tweezers ['twiːzəz] *npl* pinça (pequena).

twelfth [twɛlfθ] *num* décimo segundo; *see also* **fifth**.

Twelfth Night *n* noite *f* de Reis, Epifania.

twelve [twɛlv] *num* doze; **at ~ (o'clock)** (*midday*) ao meio-dia; (*midnight*) à meia-noite; *see also* **five**.

twentieth ['twɛntɪɪθ] *num* vigésimo; *see also* **fifth**.

twenty ['twɛntɪ] *num* vinte; *see also* **five**.

twerp [twəːp] (*inf*) *n* imbecil *m/f*.

twice [twaɪs] *adv* duas vezes; **~ as much** duas vezes mais; **~ a week** duas vezes por semana; **she is ~ your age** ela tem duas vezes a sua idade.

twiddle ['twɪdl] *vt, vi*: **to ~ (with)** sth mexer em algo; **to ~ one's thumbs** (*fig*) chupar o dedo.

twig [twɪg] *n* graveto, varinha ♦ *vt, vi* (*inf*) sacar.

twilight ['twaɪlaɪt] *n* crepúsculo, meia-luz *f*; **in the ~** na penumbra.

twill [twɪl] *n* sarja.

twin [twɪn] *adj, n* gêmeo/a ♦ *vt* irmanar.

twin(-bedded) room [-'bɛdɪd-] *n* quarto com duas camas.

twin beds *npl* camas *fpl* separadas.

twin-carburettor *adj* de dois carburadores.

twine [twaɪn] *n* barbante *m* (*BR*), cordel *m* (*PT*) ♦ *vi* (*plant*) enroscar-se, enrolar-se.

twin-engined [-'ɛndʒɪnd] *adj* bimotor; **~ aircraft** (avião *m*) bimotor *m*.

twinge [twɪndʒ] *n* (*of pain*) pontada; (*of conscience*) remorso.

twinkle ['twɪŋkl] *n* cintilação *f* ♦ *vi* cintilar; (*eyes*) pestanejar.

twin town *n* cidade *f* irmã.

twirl [twəːl] *n* giro, volta ♦ *vt* fazer girar ♦ *vi* girar rapidamente.

twist [twɪst] *n* (*action*) torção *f*; (*in road, coil*) curva; (*in wire, flex*) virada; (*in story*) mudança imprevista ♦ *vt* torcer, retorcer; (*weave*) entrelaçar; (*roll around*) enrolar; (*fig*) deformar ♦ *vi* serpentear; **to ~ one's ankle/wrist** torcer o tornozelo/pulso.

twisted ['twɪstɪd] *adj* (*wire, rope, ankle*) torcido; (*fig: mind, logic*) deturpado.

twit [twɪt] (*inf*) *n* idiota *m/f*, bobo/a.

twitch [twɪtʃ] *n* puxão *m*; (*nervous*) tique *m* nervoso ♦ *vi* contrair-se.

two [tuː] *num* dois; **~ by ~, in ~s** de dois em dois; **to put ~ and ~ together** (*fig*) tirar conclusões; *see also* **five**.

two-door *adj* (*AUT*) de duas portas.

two-faced [-feɪst] (*pej*) *adj* (*person*) falso.

twofold ['tuːfəuld] *adv*: **to increase ~** duplicar ♦ *adj* (*increase*) em cem por cento; (*reply*) duplo.

two-piece *n* (*also*: **~ suit**) traje *m* de duas peças; (*also*: **~ swimsuit**) maiô *m* de duas peças, biquíni *m*.

two-seater [-'siːtə*] *n* (*plane*) avião *m* de dois lugares; (*car*) carro de dois lugares.

twosome ['tuːsəm] *n* (*people*) casal *m*.

two-stroke *n* (*also*: **~ engine**) motor *m* de dois tempos ♦ *adj* de dois tempos.

two-tone *adj* em dois tons.

two-way *adj*: **~ radio** rádio emissor-receptor; **~ traffic** trânsito em mão dupla.

TX (*US*) *abbr* (*POST*) = **Texas**.

tycoon [taɪ'kuːn] *n*: **(business) ~** magnata *m*.

type [taɪp] *n* (*category*) tipo, espécie *f*; (*model*) modelo; (*TYP*) tipo, letra *f* ♦ *vt* (*letter etc*) datilografar, bater (à máquina); **what ~ do you want?** que tipo você quer?; **in bold/italic ~** em negrito/itálico.

typecast ['taɪpkɑːst] *adj* que representa sempre o mesmo papel.

typeface ['taɪpfeɪs] *n* tipo, letra.

typescript ['taɪpskrɪpt] *n* texto datilografado.

typeset ['taɪpsɛt] (*irreg*) *vt* compor (*para imprimir*).

typesetter ['taɪpsɛtə*] *n* compositor(a) *m/f*.

typewriter ['taɪpraɪtə*] *n* máquina de escrever.

typewritten ['taɪprɪtn] *adj* datilografado.

typhoid ['taɪfɔɪd] *n* febre *f* tifóide.

typhoon [taɪ'fuːn] *n* tufão *m*.

typhus ['taɪfəs] *n* tifo.

typical ['tɪpɪkl] *adj* típico.

typify ['tɪpɪfaɪ] *vt* tipificar, simbolizar.

typing ['taɪpɪŋ] *n* datilografia.

typing error *n* erro de datilografia.

typing pool *n* seção *f* de datilografia.

typist ['taɪpɪst] *n* datilógrafo/a *m/f*.

typo ['taɪpəu] (*inf*) *n abbr* (= *typographical error*) erro tipográfico.

typography [taɪ'pɔgrəfɪ] *n* tipografia.

tyranny ['tɪrənɪ] *n* tirania.

tyrant ['taɪərənt] *n* tirano/a.

tyre ['taɪə*] (*US* **tire**) *n* pneu *m*.

tyre pressure *n* pressão *f* dos pneus.

Tyrrhenian Sea [tɪ'riːnɪən-] *n*: **the ~** o mar Tirreno.

tzar [zɑː*] *n* = **tsar**.

NB: *European Portuguese adds the following consonants to certain words:* **b** (sú(b)dito, su(b)til); **c** (a(c)ção, a(c)cionista, a(c)to); **m** (inde(m)ne); **p** (ado(p)ção, ado(p)tar); *for further details see p. xiii.*

U

U, u [ju:] *n* (*letter*) U, u *m*; **U for Uncle** U de Úrsula.

U (*BRIT*) *n abbr* (*CINEMA*: = *universal*) ≈ livre.

UAW (*US*) *n abbr* (= *United Automobile Workers*) *sindicato dos trabalhadores na indústria automobilística*.

UB40 (*BRIT*) *n abbr* (= *unemployment benefit form 40*) *carteira que comprova que o portador recebe o auxílio-desemprego*.

U-bend *n* (*in pipe*) curva em U.

ubiquitous [ju:'bɪkwɪtəs] *adj* ubíquo, onipresente.

UCCA ['ʌkə] (*BRIT*) *n abbr* = **Universities Central Council on Admissions.**

UDA (*BRIT*) *n abbr* = **Ulster Defence Association.**

UDC (*BRIT*) *n abbr* = **Urban District Council.**

udder ['ʌdə*] *n* ubre *f*.

UDI (*BRIT*) *n abbr* (*POL*) = **unilateral declaration of independence.**

UDR (*BRIT*) *n abbr* = **Ulster Defence Regiment.**

UEFA [ju:'eɪfə] *n abbr* (= *Union of European Football Associations*) UEFA *f*.

UFO ['ju:fəu] *n abbr* (= *unidentified flying object*) óvni *m*.

Uganda [ju:'gændə] *n* Uganda (*no article*).

Ugandan [ju:'gændən] *adj, n* ugandense *m/f*.

ugh [ə:h] *excl* uh!

ugliness ['ʌglɪnɪs] *n* feiúra.

ugly ['ʌglɪ] *adj* feio; (*dangerous*) perigoso.

UHF (= *ultra-high frequency*) UHF, frequência ultra-alta.

UHT *adj abbr* (= *ultra-heat treated*): ~ **milk** leite *m* longa-vida.

UK *n abbr* = **United Kingdom.**

ulcer ['ʌlsə*] *n* úlcera; **mouth** ~ afta.

Ulster ['ʌlstə*] *n* Ulster *m*, Irlanda do Norte.

ulterior [ʌl'tɪərɪə*] *adj* ulterior; ~ **motive** segundas intenções *fpl*.

ultimata [ʌltɪ'meɪtə] *npl of* **ultimatum.**

ultimate ['ʌltɪmət] *adj* último, final; (*authority*) máximo ♦ *n*: **the** ~ **in luxury** o máximo em luxo.

ultimately ['ʌltɪmətlɪ] *adv* (*in the end*) no final, por último; (*fundamentally*) no fundo.

ultimatum [ʌltɪ'meɪtəm] (*pl* ~**s** *or* **ultimata**) *n* ultimato.

ultrasonic [ʌltrə'sɔnɪk] *adj* ultra-sônico.

ultrasound ['ʌltrəsaund] *n* (*MED*) ultra-som *m*.

ultraviolet [ʌltrə'vaɪəlɪt] *adj* ultravioleta.

umbilical cord [ʌmbɪ'laɪkl-] *n* cordão *m* umbilical.

umbrage ['ʌmbrɪdʒ] *n*: **to take** ~ ofender-se.

umbrella [ʌm'brɛlə] *n* guarda-chuva *m*; (*fig*):

under the ~ **of** sob a égide de.

umpire ['ʌmpaɪə*] *n* árbitro ♦ *vt* arbitrar.

umpteen [ʌmp'ti:n] *adj* inúmeros/as.

umpteenth [ʌmp'ti:nθ] *adj*: **for the** ~ **time** pela enésima vez.

UMW *n abbr* (= *United Mineworkers of America*) sindicato dos mineiros.

UN *n abbr* (= *United Nations*) ONU *f*.

unabashed [ʌnə'bæʃt] *adj* imperturbado.

unabated [ʌnə'beɪtɪd] *adj* sem diminuir.

unable [ʌn'eɪbl] *adj*: **to be** ~ **to do sth** não poder fazer algo; (*be incapable*) ser incapaz de fazer algo.

unabridged [ʌnə'brɪdʒd] *adj* integral.

unacceptable [ʌnək'sɛptəbl] *adj* (*behaviour*) insuportável; (*price, proposal*) inaceitável.

unaccompanied [ʌnə'kʌmpənɪd] *adj* desacompanhado; (*singing, song*) sem acompanhamento.

unaccountably [ʌnə'kauntəblɪ] *adv* inexplicavelmente.

unaccounted [ʌnə'kauntɪd] *adj*: **two passengers are** ~ **for** dois passageiros estão desaparecidos.

unaccustomed [ʌnə'kʌstəmd] *adj* desacostumado; **to be** ~ **to** não estar acostumado a.

unacquainted [ʌnə'kweɪntɪd] *adj*: **to be** ~ **with** (*person*) não conhecer; (*facts etc*) não estar familiarizado com.

unadulterated [ʌnə'dʌltəreɪtɪd] *adj* puro, natural.

unaffected [ʌnə'fɛktɪd] *adj* (*person, behaviour*) natural, simples *inv*; (*emotionally*): **to be** ~ **by** não se comover com.

unafraid [ʌnə'freɪd] *adj*: **to be** ~ não ter medo.

unaided [ʌn'eɪdɪd] *adj* sem ajuda, por si só.

unanimity [ju:nə'nɪmɪtɪ] *n* unanimidade *f*.

unanimous [ju:'nænɪməs] *adj* unânime.

unanimously [ju:'nænɪməslɪ] *adv* unanimemente.

unanswered [ʌn'ɑ:nsəd] *adj* sem resposta.

unappetizing [ʌn'æpɪtaɪzɪŋ] *adj* pouco apetitoso.

unappreciative [ʌnə'pri:ʃɪətɪv] *adj* (*ungrateful*) ingrato.

unarmed [ʌn'ɑ:md] *adj* (*without a weapon*) desarmado; (*defenceless*) indefeso.

unashamed [ʌnə'ʃeɪmd] *adj* (*open*) desembaraçado; (*impudent*) descarado.

unassisted [ʌnə'sɪstɪd] *adj, adv* sem ajuda.

unassuming [ʌnə'sju:mɪŋ] *adj* modesto, despretencioso.

unattached [ʌnə'tætʃt] *adj* (*person*) livre; (*part etc*) solto, separado.

unattended [ʌnə'tɛndɪd] *adj* (*car, luggage*) sem vigilância, abandonado.

unattractive [ʌnə'træktɪv] *adj* sem atrativos, pouco atraente.

unauthorized [ʌn'ɔ:θəraɪzd] *adj* não autorizado, sem autorização.

unavailable [ʌnə'veɪləbl] *adj* (*article, room, book*) indisponível; (*person*) não disponível.

unavoidable [ʌnə'vɔɪdəbl] *adj* inevitável.

unavoidably [ʌnə'vɔɪdəblɪ] *adv* inevitavelmente.

unaware [ʌnə'wɛə*] *adj*: **to be ~ of** ignorar, não perceber.

unawares [ʌnə'wɛəz] *adv* improvisadamente, de surpresa.

unbalanced [ʌn'bælənst] *adj* desequilibrado.

unbearable [ʌn'bɛərəbl] *adj* insuportável.

unbeatable [ʌn'biːtəbl] *adj (team)* invencível; *(price)* sem igual.

unbeaten [ʌn'biːtn] *adj* invicto; *(record)* não batido.

unbecoming [ʌnbɪ'kʌmɪŋ] *adj (unseemly: language, behaviour)* inconveniente; *(unflattering: garment)* que não fica bem.

unbeknown(st) [ʌnbɪ'nəun(st)] *adv*: **~ to me** sem eu saber.

unbelief [ʌnbɪ'liːf] *n* incredulidade *f*.

unbelievable [ʌnbɪ'liːvəbl] *adj* inacreditável, incrível.

unbelievingly [ʌnbɪ'liːvɪŋlɪ] *adv* incredulamente.

unbend [ʌn'bɛnd] *(irreg) vi* relaxar-se ♦ *vt (wire)* desentortar.

unbending [ʌn'bɛndɪŋ] *adj* inflexível.

unbent [ʌn'bɛnt] *pt, pp of* **unbend**.

unbias(s)ed [ʌn'baɪəst] *adj* imparcial.

unblemished [ʌn'blɛmɪʃt] *adj* imaculado.

unblock [ʌn'blɔk] *vt (pipe)* desentupir.

unborn [ʌn'bɔːn] *adj* por nascer.

unbounded [ʌn'baundɪd] *adj* ilimitado, infinito, imenso.

unbreakable [ʌn'breɪkəbl] *adj* inquebrável.

unbridled [ʌn'braɪdld] *adj (fig)* desenfreado.

unbroken [ʌn'brəukən] *adj (seal)* intacto; *(line)* contínuo; *(series)* ininterrupto; *(record)* mantido; *(spirit)* indômito.

unbuckle [ʌn'bʌkl] *vt* desafivelar.

unburden [ʌn'bəːdn] *vt*: **to ~ o.s.** desabafar.

unbutton [ʌn'bʌtn] *vt* desabotoar.

uncalled-for [ʌn'kɔːld-] *adj* desnecessário, gratuito.

uncanny [ʌn'kænɪ] *adj (strange)* estranho; *(mysterious)* sobrenatural.

unceasing [ʌn'siːsɪŋ] *adj* ininterrupto.

unceremonious [ʌnsɛrɪ'məunɪəs] *adj (abrupt)* incerimonioso.

uncertain [ʌn'səːtn] *adj* incerto; *(character)* indeciso; **we were ~ whether ...** não tínhamos certeza se ...; **in no ~ terms** em termos precisos.

uncertainty [ʌn'səːtntɪ] *n* incerteza.

unchallenged [ʌn'tʃælənʤd] *adj* incontestado; **to go ~** não ser contestado.

unchanged [ʌn'tʃeɪnʤd] *adj* sem mudar, inalterado.

uncharitable [ʌn'tʃærɪtəbl] *adj* sem caridade.

uncharted [ʌn'tʃɑːtɪd] *adj* inexplorado.

unchecked [ʌn'tʃɛkt] *adj* desenfreado.

uncivilized [ʌn'sɪvəlaɪzd] *adj* incivilizado, primitivo.

uncle ['ʌŋkl] *n* tio.

unclear [ʌn'klɪə*] *adj (not obvious)* pouco evidente; *(confused)* confuso; *(indistinct)* indistinto; **I'm still ~ about what I'm supposed to do** ainda não sei exatamente o que devo fazer.

uncoil [ʌn'kɔɪl] *vt* desenrolar ♦ *vi* desenrolar-se.

uncomfortable [ʌn'kʌmfətəbl] *adj* incômodo; *(uneasy)* pouco à vontade; *(situation)* desagradável.

uncomfortably [ʌn'kʌmftəblɪ] *adv* desconfortavelmente; *(uneasily)* sem graça; *(unpleasantly)* desagradavelmente.

uncommitted [ʌnkə'mɪtɪd] *adj* não comprometido.

uncommon [ʌn'kɔmən] *adj* raro, incomum, excepcional.

uncommunicative [ʌnkə'mjuːnɪkətɪv] *adj* reservado.

uncomplicated [ʌn'kɔmplɪkeɪtɪd] *adj* descomplicado, simples *inv*.

uncompromising [ʌn'kɔmprəmaɪzɪŋ] *adj* intransigente, inflexível.

unconcerned [ʌnkən'səːnd] *adj* indiferente, despreocupado; **to be ~ (about)** não estar preocupado (com).

unconditional [ʌnkən'dɪʃənl] *adj* incondicional.

uncongenial [ʌnkən'ʤiːnɪəl] *adj* desagradável.

unconnected [ʌnkə'nɛktɪd] *adj* não relacionado.

unconscious [ʌn'kɔnʃəs] *adj* sem sentidos, desacordado; *(unaware)* inconsciente ♦ *n*: **the ~** o inconsciente; **to knock sb ~** pôr alguém nocaute, nocautear alguém.

unconsciously [ʌn'kɔnʃəslɪ] *adv* inconscientemente.

unconstitutional [ʌnkɔnstɪ'tjuːʃənl] *adj* inconstitucional.

uncontested [ʌnkən'tɛstɪd] *adj* incontestado.

uncontrollable [ʌnkən'trəuləbl] *adj (temper)* ingovernável; *(laughter)* incontrolável.

uncontrolled [ʌnkən'trəuld] *adj* descontrolado.

unconventional [ʌnkən'vɛnʃənl] *adj (person)* inconvencional; *(approach)* heterodoxo.

unconvinced [ʌnkən'vɪnst] *adj*: **to be ~** não estar convencido.

unconvincing [ʌnkən'vɪnsɪŋ] *adj* pouco convincente.

uncork [ʌn'kɔːk] *vt* desarrolhar.

uncorroborated [ʌnkə'rɔbəreɪtɪd] *adj* não confirmado.

uncouth [ʌn'kuːθ] *adj* rude, grosseiro, inculto.

uncover [ʌn'kʌvə*] *vt* descobrir; *(take lid off)* destapar, destampar.

unctuous ['ʌŋktjuəs] *adj* untuoso, pegajoso.

undamaged [ʌn'dæmɪʤd] *adj (goods)* intacto; *(fig: reputation)* incólume.

undaunted [ʌn'dɔːntɪd] *adj* impávido, inabalável.

undecided [ʌndɪ'saɪdɪd] *adj (character)* inde-

NB: *European Portuguese adds the following consonants to certain words:* **b** (sú(b)dito, su(b)til); **c** (a(c)ção, a(c)cionista, a(c)to); **m** (inde(m)ne); **p** (ado(p)ção, ado(p)tar); *for further details see p. xiii.*

ciso; *(question)* não respondido, pendente.

undelivered [ʌndɪ'lɪvəd] *adj* não entregue.

undeniable [ʌndɪ'naɪəbl] *adj* inegável.

under ['ʌndə*] *prep* embaixo de *(BR)*, debaixo de *(PT)*; *(fig)* sob; *(less than)* menos de, inferior a; *(according to)* segundo, de acordo com ♦ *adv* embaixo; *(movement)* por baixo; **from ~ sth** de embaixo de algo; **~ there** ali embaixo; **in ~ 2 hours** em menos de 2 horas; **~ anaesthetic** sob anestesia; **~ discussion** em discussão; **~ the circumstances** nas circunstâncias; **~ repair** em conserto.

under... [ʌndə*] *prefix* sub-.

under-age *adj* menor de idade.

underarm ['ʌndərɑːm] *adv* com a mão por baixo ♦ *adj (throw)* com a mão por baixo; *(deodorant)* para as axilas.

undercapitalized [ʌndə'kæpɪtəlaɪzd] *adj* subcapitalizado.

undercarriage ['ʌndəkærɪdʒ] *(BRIT)* n *(AVIAT)* trem *m* de aterrissagem.

undercharge [ʌndə'tʃɑːdʒ] *vt* não cobrar o suficiente.

underclothes ['ʌndəkləuðz] *npl* roupa de baixo, roupa íntima.

undercoat ['ʌndəkəut] n *(paint)* primeira mão *f*.

undercover ['ʌndəkʌvə*] *adj* secreto, clandestino.

undercurrent ['ʌndəkʌrənt] n corrente *f* submarina; *(fig)* tendência.

undercut [ʌndə'kʌt] *(irreg)* *vt* vender por menos que.

underdeveloped [ʌndədɪ'vɛləpt] *adj* subdesenvolvido.

underdog ['ʌndədɒg] n o mais fraco.

underdone [ʌndə'dʌn] *adj (CULIN)* mal passado.

under-employment n subemprego.

underestimate [ʌndər'estɪmeɪt] *vt* subestimar.

underexposed [ʌndərɪk'spəuzd] *adj (PHOT)* sem exposição suficiente.

underfed [ʌndə'fɛd] *adj* subnutrido.

underfoot [ʌndə'fut] *adv* sob os pés.

undergo [ʌndə'gəu] *(irreg)* *vt* sofrer; *(treatment)* receber; **the car is ~ing repairs** o carro está sendo consertado.

undergraduate [ʌndə'grædjuət] n universitário/a ♦ *cpd:* **~ courses** profissões *fpl* universitárias.

underground ['ʌndəgraund] n *(BRIT)* metrô *m* *(BR)*, metro(-politano) *(PT)*; *(POL)* organização *f* clandestina ♦ *adj* subterrâneo; *(fig)* clandestino.

undergrowth ['ʌndəgrəuθ] n vegetação *f* rasteira.

underhand(ed) [ʌndə'hænd(ɪd)] *adj (fig)* esperto.

underinsured [ʌndərɪn'ʃuəd] *adj* segurado abaixo do valor corrente.

underlie [ʌndə'laɪ] *(irreg)* *vt (fig)* ser a base de.

underline [ʌndə'laɪn] *vt* sublinhar.

underling ['ʌndəlɪŋ] *(pej)* n subalterno/a.

underlying [ʌndə'laɪɪŋ] *adj:* **the ~ cause** a causa subjacente.

undermanning [ʌndə'mænɪŋ] n falta de mão-de-obra.

undermentioned [ʌndə'mɛnʃənd] *adj* abaixo mencionado.

undermine [ʌndə'maɪn] *vt* minar, solapar.

underneath [ʌndə'niːθ] *adv* embaixo, debaixo, por baixo ♦ *prep* embaixo de *(BR)*, debaixo de *(PT)*.

undernourished [ʌndə'nʌrɪʃt] *adj* subnutrido.

underpaid [ʌndə'peɪd] *adj* mal pago.

underpants ['ʌndəpænts] *(BRIT)* *npl* cueca *(BR)*, cuecas *fpl (PT)*.

underpass ['ʌndəpɑːs] *(BRIT)* n passagem *f* inferior.

underpin [ʌndə'pɪn] *vt (argument, case)* sustentar.

underplay [ʌndə'pleɪ] *(BRIT)* *vt* minimizar.

underpopulated [ʌndə'pɒpjuleɪtɪd] *adj* de população reduzida.

underprice [ʌndə'praɪs] *vt* vender abaixo do preço.

underprivileged [ʌndə'prɪvɪlɪdʒd] *adj* menos favorecido.

underrate [ʌndə'reɪt] *vt* depreciar, subestimar.

underscore [ʌndə'skɔː*] *vt* sublinhar.

underseal [ʌndə'siːl] *(BRIT)* *vt* fazer bronzina em.

undersecretary [ʌndə'sɛkrətərɪ] n subsecretário/a.

undersell [ʌndə'sɛl] *(irreg)* *vt (competitors)* vender por preço mais baixo que.

undershirt ['ʌndəʃɜːt] *(US)* n camiseta.

undershorts ['ʌndəʃɔːts] *(US)* *npl* cueca *(BR)*, cuecas *fpl (PT)*.

underside ['ʌndəsaɪd] n parte *f* inferior.

undersigned ['ʌndəsaɪnd] *adj, n* abaixo assinado/a.

underskirt ['ʌndəskɜːt] *(BRIT)* n anágua.

understaffed [ʌndə'stɑːft] *adj* com falta de pessoal.

understand [ʌndə'stænd] *(irreg)* *vt* entender, compreender; *(assume)* subentender; **I ~ that ...** *(I hear)* ouço dizer que ...; *(I sympathize)* eu compreendo que ...; **to make o.s. understood** fazer-se entender.

understandable [ʌndə'stændəbl] *adj* compreensível.

understanding [ʌndə'stændɪŋ] *adj* compreensivo ♦ n compreensão *f*, entendimento; *(agreement)* acordo; **to come to an ~** chegar a um acordo; **on the ~ that ...** sob condição que ..., contanto que ....

understate [ʌndə'steɪt] *vt* minimizar.

understatement [ʌndə'steɪtmənt] n subestimação *f*; *(euphemism)* eufemismo.

understood [ʌndə'stud] *pt, pp of* **understand** ♦ *adj* entendido; *(implied)* subentendido, implícito.

understudy ['ʌndəstʌdɪ] n ator *m* substituto/ atriz *f* substituta.

undertake [ʌndə'teɪk] *(irreg)* *vt (job, project)* empreender; *(task, duty)* incumbir-se de, encarregar-se de; **to** ~ **to do sth** comprometer-se a fazer algo.

undertaker ['ʌndəteɪkə*] n agente m/f funerário/a.

undertaking [ʌndə'teɪkɪŋ] n empreendimento; (*promise*) promessa.

undertone ['ʌndətəʊn] n (*of criticism etc*) sugestão f; (*low voice*): **in an** ~ em meia voz.

undertook [ʌndə'tʊk] pt of **undertake**.

undervalue [ʌndə'vælju:] vt subestimar.

underwater [ʌndə'wɔːtə*] adv sob a água ♦ adj subaquático.

underwear ['ʌndəwɛə*] n roupa de baixo.

underweight [ʌndə'weɪt] adj de peso inferior ao normal; (*person*) magro.

underwent [ʌndə'went] pt of **undergo**.

underworld ['ʌndəwɜːld] n (*of crime*) submundo.

underwrite [ʌndə'raɪt] (*irreg*) vt (*COMM*) subscrever.

underwriter ['ʌndəraɪtə*] n (*INSURANCE*) subscritor(a) m/f (que faz resseguro).

underwritten [ʌndə'rɪtn] pp of **underwrite**.

underwrote [ʌndə'rəʊt] pt of **underwrite**.

undeserving [ʌndɪ'zɜːvɪŋ] adj: **to be** ~ **of** não merecer.

undesirable [ʌndɪ'zaɪərəbl] adj indesejável.

undeveloped [ʌndɪ'veləpt] adj (*land, resources*) não desenvolvido.

undid [ʌn'dɪd] pt of **undo**.

undies ['ʌndɪz] (*inf*) npl roupa de baixo, roupa íntima.

undignified [ʌn'dɪgnɪfaɪd] adj sem dignidade, indecoroso.

undiluted [ʌndaɪ'luːtɪd] adj não diluído, puro; (*pleasure*) puro.

undiplomatic [ʌndɪplə'mætɪk] adj pouco diplomático, inábil.

undischarged [ʌndɪs'tʃɑːdʒd] adj: ~ **bankrupt** falido/a não reabilitado/a.

undisciplined [ʌn'dɪsɪplɪnd] adj indisciplinado.

undisguised [ʌndɪs'gaɪzd] adj (*dislike etc*) patente.

undisputed [ʌndɪ'spjuːtɪd] adj incontestável, evidente.

undistinguished [ʌndɪs'tɪŋgwɪʃt] adj medíocre, regular.

undisturbed [ʌndɪs'tɜːbd] adj (*sleep*) tranqüilo; **to leave sth** ~ não mexer em algo.

undivided [ʌndɪ'vaɪdɪd] adj: **can I have your** ~ **attention?** quero a sua total atenção.

undo [ʌn'duː] (*irreg*) vt desfazer.

undoing [ʌn'duːɪŋ] n ruína, desgraça.

undone [ʌn'dʌn] pp of **undo** ♦ adj: **to come** ~ desfazer-se.

undoubted [ʌn'daʊtɪd] adj indubitável.

undoubtedly [ʌn'daʊtɪdlɪ] adv sem dúvida, indubitavelmente.

undress [ʌn'dres] vi despir-se, tirar a roupa ♦ vt despir, tirar a roupa de.

undrinkable [ʌn'drɪŋkəbl] adj (*unpalatable*) intragável; (*poisonous*) impotável.

undue [ʌn'djuː] adj indevido, excessivo.

undulating ['ʌndjuleɪtɪŋ] adj ondulante.

unduly [ʌn'djuːlɪ] adv indevidamente, impropriamente.

undying [ʌn'daɪɪŋ] adj eterno.

unearned [ʌn'ɜːnd] adj (*praise, respect*) imerecido; ~ **income** rendimento não ganho com o trabalho individual.

unearth [ʌn'ɜːθ] vt desenterrar.

unearthly [ʌn'ɜːθlɪ] adj sobrenatural; **at an** ~ **hour of the night** na calada da noite.

uneasy [ʌn'iːzɪ] adj inquieto, desassossegado; (*worried*) preocupado; **to feel** ~ **about doing sth** estar apreensivo quanto a fazer algo.

uneconomic(al) [ʌniːkə'nɒmɪk(l)] adj antieconômico; (*unprofitable*) não rentável.

uneducated [ʌn'edjukeɪtɪd] adj inculto, sem instrução, não escolarizado.

unemployed [ʌnɪm'plɔɪd] adj desempregado ♦ npl: **the** ~ os desempregados.

unemployment [ʌnɪm'plɔɪmənt] n desemprego.

unemployment benefit (*US* **unemployment compensation**) n auxílio-desemprego.

unending [ʌn'endɪŋ] adj interminável.

unenthusiastic [ʌnɪnθuːzɪ'æstɪk] adj sem entusiasmo.

unenviable [ʌn'envɪəbl] adj nada invejável.

unequal [ʌn'iːkwəl] adj desigual.

unequalled [ʌn'iːkwɔld] (*US* **unequaled**) adj inigualável, sem igual.

unequivocal [ʌnə'kwɪvəkl] adj (*answer*) inequívoco; (*person*) categórico.

unerring [ʌn'ɜːrɪŋ] adj infalível.

UNESCO [juː'neskəʊ] n abbr (= *United Nations Educational, Scientific and Cultural Organization*) UNESCO f.

unethical [ʌn'eθɪkl] adj (*methods*) imoral; (*professional behaviour*) contrário à ética.

uneven [ʌn'iːvn] adj desigual; (*road etc*) irregular, acidentado.

uneventful [ʌnɪ'ventful] adj tranqüilo, rotineiro.

unexceptional [ʌnɪk'sepʃənl] adj regular, corriqueiro.

unexciting [ʌnɪk'saɪtɪŋ] adj monótono.

unexpected [ʌnɪk'spektɪd] adj inesperado.

unexpectedly [ʌnɪk'spektɪdlɪ] adv inesperadamente.

unexplained [ʌnɪk'spleɪnd] adj inexplicado.

unexploded [ʌnɪk'spləʊdɪd] adj não explodido.

unfailing [ʌn'feɪlɪŋ] adj inexaurível.

unfair [ʌn'fɛə*] adj: ~ **(to)** injusto (com); **it's** ~ **that ...** não é justo que ....

unfair dismissal n demissão f injusta or infundada.

unfairly [ʌn'fɛəlɪ] adv injustamente.

unfaithful [ʌn'feɪθful] adj infiel.

unfamiliar [ʌnfə'mɪlɪə*] adj pouco familiar, desconhecido; **to be** ~ **with sth** não estar familiarizado com algo.

unfashionable [ʌn'fæʃnəbl] adj fora da moda.

NB: European Portuguese adds the following consonants to certain words: **b** (sú(b)dito, su(b)til); **c** (a(c)ção, a(c)cionista, a(c)to); **m** (inde(m)ne); **p** (ado(p)ção, ado(p)tar); *for further details see p. xiii.*

unfasten [ʌn'fɑːsn] *vt* desatar.
unfathomable [ʌn'fæðəməbl] *adj* insondável.
unfavourable [ʌn'feɪvərəbl] (*US* **unfavorable**) *adj* desfavorável.
unfavo(u)rably [ʌn'feɪvrəblɪ] *adv*: **to look ~ upon** não ser favorável a.
unfeeling [ʌn'fiːlɪŋ] *adj* insensível.
unfinished [ʌn'fɪnɪʃt] *adj* incompleto, inacabado.
unfit [ʌn'fɪt] *adj* (*physically*) sem preparo físico; (*incompetent*) incompetente, incapaz; **~ for work** inapto para trabalhar.
unflagging [ʌn'flægɪŋ] *adj* incansável.
unflappable [ʌn'flæpəbl] *adj* imperturbável, sereno.
unflattering [ʌn'flætərɪŋ] *adj* (*dress, hairstyle*) que não fica bem; (*remark*) pouco elogioso.
unflinching [ʌn'flɪntʃɪŋ] *adj* destemido, intrépido.
unfold [ʌn'fəʊld] *vt* desdobrar; (*fig*) revelar ♦ *vi* (*story, situation*) desdobrar-se.
unforeseeable [ʌnfɔː'siːəbl] *adj* imprevisível.
unforeseen [ʌnfɔː'siːn] *adj* imprevisto.
unforgettable [ʌnfə'getəbl] *adj* inesquecível.
unforgivable [ʌnfə'gɪvəbl] *adj* imperdoável.
unformatted [ʌn'fɔːmætɪd] *adj* (*disk, text*) não formatado.
unfortunate [ʌn'fɔːtʃənət] *adj* infeliz; (*event, remark*) inoportuno.
unfortunately [ʌn'fɔːtʃənətlɪ] *adv* infelizmente.
unfounded [ʌn'faundɪd] *adj* infundado.
unfriendly [ʌn'frendlɪ] *adj* antipático.
unfulfilled [ʌnful'fɪld] *adj* (*ambition, prophecy*) não realizado; (*desire*) não satisfeito; (*promise, terms of contract*) não cumprido; (*person*) que não se realizou.
unfurl [ʌn'fɜːl] *vt* desfraldar.
unfurnished [ʌn'fɜːnɪʃt] *adj* desmobiliado, sem mobília.
ungainly [ʌn'geɪnlɪ] *adj* desalinhado.
ungodly [ʌn'gɒdlɪ] *adj* ímpio; **at an ~ hour** às altas horas da madrugada.
ungrateful [ʌn'greɪtful] *adj* mal-agradecido, ingrato.
unguarded [ʌn'gɑːdɪd] *adj*: **~ moment** momento de inatenção.
unhappily [ʌn'hæpəlɪ] *adv* tristemente; (*unfortunately*) infelizmente.
unhappiness [ʌn'hæpɪnɪs] *n* tristeza.
unhappy [ʌn'hæpɪ] *adj* (*sad*) triste; (*unfortunate*) desventurado; (*childhood*) infeliz; **~ with** (*arrangements etc*) descontente com, insatisfeito com.
unharmed [ʌn'hɑːmd] *adj* ileso.
unhealthy [ʌn'hɛlθɪ] *adj* insalubre; (*person*) doentio.
unheard-of [ʌn'hɜːd-] *adj* (*extraordinary*) inaudito, insólito; (*unknown*) desconhecido.
unhelpful [ʌn'helpful] *adj* (*person*) imprestável; (*advice*) inútil.
unhesitating [ʌn'hezɪteɪtɪŋ] *adj* (*loyalty*) firme; (*reply*) imediato.
unhook [ʌn'huk] *vt* desenganchar; (*from*

wall) despendurar; (*dress*) abrir, soltar.
unhurt [ʌn'hɜːt] *adj* ileso.
unhygienic [ʌnhaɪ'dʒiːnɪk] *adj* anti-higiênico.
UNICEF ['juːnɪsef] *n abbr* (= *United Nations International Children's Emergency Fund*) Unicef *m*.
unicorn ['juːnɪkɔːn] *n* licorne *m*, unicórnio.
unidentified [ʌnaɪ'dentɪfaɪd] *adj* não-identificado.
uniform ['juːnɪfɔːm] *n* uniforme *m* ♦ *adj* uniforme.
uniformity [juːnɪ'fɔːmɪtɪ] *n* uniformidade *f*.
unify ['juːnɪfaɪ] *vt* unificar, unir.
unilateral [juːnɪ'lætərəl] *adj* unilateral.
unimaginable [ʌnɪ'mædʒɪnəbl] *adj* inimaginável, inconcebível.
unimaginative [ʌnɪ'mædʒɪnətɪv] *adj* sem imaginação.
unimpaired [ʌnɪm'peəd] *adj* inalterado.
unimportant [ʌnɪm'pɔːtənt] *adj* sem importância.
unimpressed [ʌnɪm'prest] *adj* indiferente.
uninhabited [ʌnɪn'hæbɪtɪd] *adj* inabitado.
uninhibited [ʌnɪn'hɪbɪtɪd] *adj* sem inibições.
uninjured [ʌn'ɪndʒəd] *adj* ileso.
uninspired [ʌnɪn'spaɪəd] *adj* insípido.
unintelligent [ʌnɪn'telɪdʒənt] *adj* ininteligente.
unintentional [ʌnɪn'tenʃənəl] *adj* involuntário, não intencional.
unintentionally [ʌnɪn'tenʃənəlɪ] *adv* sem querer.
uninvited [ʌnɪn'vaɪtɪd] *adj* (*guest*) não convidado.
uninviting [ʌnɪn'vaɪtɪŋ] *adj* (*place*) pouco convidativo; (*food*) pouco apetitoso.
union ['juːnjən] *n* união *f*; (*also: trade ~*) sindicato (de trabalhadores) ♦ *cpd* sindical.
unionize ['juːnjənaɪz] *vt* sindicalizar.
Union Jack *n* bandeira britânica.
Union of Soviet Socialist Republics *n* União *f* das Repúblicas Socialistas Soviéticas.
union shop *n* empresa onde todos os trabalhadores têm que filiar-se ao sindicato.
unique [juː'niːk] *adj* único, sem igual.
unisex ['juːnɪseks] *adj* unissex *inv*.
unison ['juːnɪsn] *n*: **in ~** em harmonia, em uníssono.
unit ['juːnɪt] *n* unidade *f*; (*team, squad*) grupo; **sink ~** pia de cozinha; **production ~** unidade de produção.
unit cost *n* custo unitário.
unite [juː'naɪt] *vt* unir ♦ *vi* unir-se.
united [juː'naɪtɪd] *adj* unido.
United Arab Emirates *npl* Emirados *mpl* Árabes Unidos.
United Kingdom *n* Reino Unido.
United Nations (Organization) *n* (Organização *f* das) Nações *fpl* Unidas.
United States (of America) *n* Estados Unidos *mpl* (da América).
unit price *n* preço unitário.
unit trust (*BRIT*) *n* (*COMM*) fundo de investimento.
unity ['juːnɪtɪ] *n* unidade *f*.
Univ. *abbr* = **university**.

universal [ju:nɪ'və:sl] adj universal.
universe ['ju:nɪvə:s] n universo.
university [ju:nɪ'və:sɪtɪ] n universidade f, faculdade f ♦ cpd universitário.
unjust [ʌn'dʒʌst] adj injusto.
unjustifiable [ʌndʒʌstɪ'faɪəbl] adj injustificável.
unjustified [ʌn'dʒʌstɪfaɪd] adj injustificado; (text) não alinhado.
unkempt [ʌn'kɛmpt] adj desleixado, descuidado; (hair) despenteado.
unkind [ʌn'kaɪnd] adj maldoso; (comment etc) cruel.
unkindly [ʌn'kaɪndlɪ] adv (treat, speak) maldosamente.
unknown [ʌn'nəun] adj desconhecido; ~ to me sem eu saber; ~ quantity (MATH, fig) incógnita.
unladen [ʌn'leɪdn] adj (ship, weight) sem carga.
unlawful [ʌn'lɔ:ful] adj ilegal.
unleash [ʌn'li:ʃ] vt soltar; (fig) desencadear.
unleavened [ʌn'lɛvənd] adj sem fermento.
unless [ʌn'lɛs] conj a menos que, a não ser que; ~ he comes a menos que ele venha; ~ otherwise stated salvo indicação contrária; ~ I am mistaken se não me engano.
unlicensed [ʌn'laɪsnst] (BRIT) adj sem licença para a venda de bebidas alcoólicas.
unlike [ʌn'laɪk] adj diferente ♦ prep diferentemente de, ao contrário de.
unlikelihood [ʌn'laɪklɪhud] n improbabilidade f.
unlikely [ʌn'laɪklɪ] adj (result, event) improvável; (explanation) inverossímil.
unlimited [ʌn'lɪmɪtɪd] adj ilimitado.
unlisted [ʌn'lɪstɪd] adj (STOCK EXCHANGE) não cotado na Bolsa de Valores; (US: TEL): an ~ number um número que não consta na lista telefônica.
unlit [ʌn'lɪt] adj (room) sem luz.
unload [ʌn'ləud] vt descarregar.
unlock [ʌn'lɔk] vt destrancar.
unlucky [ʌn'lʌkɪ] adj infeliz; (object, number) de mau agouro; **to be** ~ ser azarado, ter azar.
unmanageable [ʌn'mænɪdʒəbl] adj (unwieldy: tool) de difícil manuseio, difícil de manejar; (: situation) difícil de controlar.
unmanned [ʌn'mænd] adj não tripulado, sem tripulação.
unmarked [ʌn'mɑːkt] adj (unstained) sem marca; ~ **police car** carro policial sem identificação.
unmarried [ʌn'mærɪd] adj solteiro.
unmask [ʌn'mɑːsk] vt desmascarar.
unmatched [ʌn'mætʃt] adj sem igual, inigualável.
unmentionable [ʌn'mɛnʃnəbl] adj (topic) que não se deve mencionar; (word) que não se diz.
unmerciful [ʌn'mə:sɪful] adj impiedoso.

unmistakable [ʌnmɪs'teɪkəbl] adj inconfundível.
unmitigated [ʌn'mɪtɪgeɪtɪd] adj não mitigado, absoluto.
unnamed [ʌn'neɪmd] adj (nameless) sem nome; (anonymous) anônimo.
unnatural [ʌn'nætʃrəl] adj antinatural, artificial; (manner) afetado; (habit) depravado.
unnecessary [ʌn'nɛsəsərɪ] adj desnecessário, inútil.
unnerve [ʌn'nə:v] vt amedrontar.
unnoticed [ʌn'nəutɪst] adj: **to go** ~ passar despercebido.
UNO ['ju:nəu] n abbr (= United Nations Organization) ONU f.
unobservant [ʌnəb'zə:vənt] adj desatento.
unobtainable [ʌnəb'teɪnəbl] adj inalcançável.
unobtrusive [ʌnəb'tru:sɪv] adj discreto.
unoccupied [ʌn'ɔkjupaɪd] adj (seat etc) desocupado, livre; (house) desocupado, vazio.
unofficial [ʌnə'fɪʃl] adj não-oficial, informal; (strike) desautorizado.
unopened [ʌn'əupənd] adj por abrir.
unopposed [ʌnə'pəuzd] adj incontestado, sem oposição.
unorthodox [ʌn'ɔ:θədɔks] adj pouco ortodoxo, heterodoxo.
unpack [ʌn'pæk] vi desfazer as malas, desembrulhar.
unpaid [ʌn'peɪd] adj (bill) a pagar, não pago; (holiday) não pago, sem salário; (work, worker) não remunerado.
unpalatable [ʌn'pælətəbl] adj (truth) desagradável.
unparalleled [ʌn'pærəleld] adj (unequalled) sem paralelo; (unique) único, incomparável.
unpatriotic [ʌnpætrɪ'ɔtɪk] adj (person) antipatriota; (speech, attitude) antipatriótico.
unplanned [ʌn'plænd] adj (visit) imprevisto; (baby) não previsto.
unpleasant [ʌn'plɛznt] adj (disagreeable) desagradável; (person, manner) antipático.
unplug [ʌn'plʌg] vt desligar.
unpolluted [ʌnpə'lu:tɪd] adj impoluído.
unpopular [ʌn'pɔpjulə*] adj impopular.
unprecedented [ʌn'prɛsɪdəntɪd] adj sem precedentes.
unpredictable [ʌnprɪ'dɪktəbl] adj imprevisível.
unprejudiced [ʌn'prɛdʒudɪst] adj (not biased) imparcial; (having no prejudices) sem preconceitos.
unprepared [ʌnprɪ'pɛəd] adj (person) despreparado; (speech) improvisado.
unprepossessing [ʌnpri:pə'zɛsɪŋ] adj pouco atraente.
unpretentious [ʌnprɪ'tɛnʃəs] adj despretensioso.
unprincipled [ʌn'prɪnsɪpld] adj sem princípios.
unproductive [ʌnprə'dʌktɪv] adj improdutivo.

NB: European Portuguese adds the following consonants to certain words: **b** (sú(b)dito, su(b)til); **c** (a(c)ção, a(c)cionista, a(c)to); **m** (inde(m)ne); **p** (ado(p)ção, ado(p)tar); for further details see p. xiii.

unprofessional [ʌnprə'fɛʃənl] *adj* (*conduct*) pouco profissional.

unprofitable [ʌn'prɔfitəbl] *adj* não lucrativo.

unprovoked [ʌnprə'vəukt] *adj* sem provocação.

unpunished [ʌn'pʌnɪʃt] *adj* ímpune.

unqualified [ʌn'kwɔlifaɪd] *adj* (*teacher*) não qualificado, inabilitado; (*success*) irrestrito, absoluto.

unquestionably [ʌn'kwɛstʃənəblɪ] *adv* indubitavelmente.

unquestioning [ʌn'kwɛstʃənɪŋ] *adj* (*obedience*, *acceptance*) incondicional, total.

unravel [ʌn'rævl] *vt* desemaranhar.

unreal [ʌn'rɪəl] *adj* irreal, ilusório.

unrealistic [ʌnrɪə'lɪstɪk] *adj* pouco realista.

unreasonable [ʌn'riːznəbl] *adj* desproposidado; (*demand*) absurdo, injusto.

unrecognizable [ʌnrɛkəg'naɪzəbl] *adj* irreconhecível.

unrecognized [ʌn'rɛkəgnaɪzd] *adj* (*talent*, *genius*) não reconhecido.

unrecorded [ʌnrə'kɔːdɪd] *adj* não registrado.

unrefined [ʌnrə'faɪnd] *adj* (*sugar*, *petroleum*) não refinado.

unrehearsed [ʌnrɪ'həːst] *adj* improvisado.

unrelated [ʌnrɪ'leɪtɪd] *adj* sem relação; (*family*) sem parentesco.

unrelenting [ʌnrɪ'lɛntɪŋ] *adj* implacável.

unreliable [ʌnrɪ'laɪəbl] *adj* (*person*) indigno de confiança; (*machine*) incerto, perigoso.

unrelieved [ʌnrɪ'liːvd] *adj* (*monotony*) invariável.

unremitting [ʌnrɪ'mɪtɪŋ] *adj* constante, incessante.

unrepeatable [ʌnrɪ'piːtəbl] *adj* (*offer*) irrepetível.

unrepentant [ʌnrɪ'pɛntənt] *adj* convicto, impenitente.

unrepresentative [ʌnrɛprɪ'zɛntətɪv] *adj* pouco representativo *or* característico.

unreserved [ʌnrɪ'zəːvd] *adj* (*seat*) não reservado; (*approval*, *admiration*) total, integral.

unresponsive [ʌnrɪs'pɔnsɪv] *adj* indiferente, impassível.

unrest [ʌn'rɛst] *n* inquietação *f*, desassossego; (*POL*) distúrbios *mpl*.

unrestricted [ʌnrɪ'strɪktɪd] *adj* irrestrito, ilimitado.

unrewarded [ʌnrɪ'wɔːdɪd] *adj* sem sucesso.

unripe [ʌn'raɪp] *adj* verde, imaturo.

unrivalled [ʌn'raɪvəld] (*US* **unrivaled**) *adj* sem igual, incomparável.

unroll [ʌn'rəul] *vt* desenrolar.

unruffled [ʌn'rʌfld] *adj* (*person*) sereno, imperturbável; (*hair*) liso.

unruly [ʌn'ruːlɪ] *adj* indisciplinado.

unsafe [ʌn'seɪf] *adj* perigoso; ~ **to eat/drink** não comestível/potável.

unsaid [ʌn'sɛd] *adj*: **to leave sth** ~ deixar algo sem dizer.

unsaleable [ʌn'seɪləbl] (*US* **unsalable**) *adj* invendável, invendível.

unsatisfactory [ʌnsætɪs'fæktərɪ] *adj* insatisfa-

tório.

unsatisfied [ʌn'sætɪsfaɪd] *adj* descontente.

unsavoury [ʌn'seɪvərɪ] (*US* **unsavory**) *adj* (*fig*) repugnante, vil.

unscathed [ʌn'skeɪðd] *adj* ileso.

unscientific [ʌnsaɪən'tɪfɪk] *adj* não científico.

unscrew [ʌn'skruː] *vt* desparafusar.

unscrupulous [ʌn'skruːpjuləs] *adj* inescrupuloso, imoral.

unsecured [ʌnsə'kjuəd] *adj*: ~ **creditor** credor(a) *m/f* quirografário/a.

unseemly [ʌn'siːmlɪ] *adj* inconveniente.

unseen [ʌn'siːn] *adj* (*person*) despercebido; (*danger*) escondido.

unselfish [ʌn'sɛlfɪʃ] *adj* desinteressado.

unsettled [ʌn'sɛtld] *adj* (*uncertain*) incerto, duvidoso; (*weather*) variável, instável; (*person*) inquieto.

unsettling [ʌn'sɛtlɪŋ] *adj* inquietador(a), inquietante.

unshak(e)able [ʌn'ʃeɪkəbl] *adj* inabalável.

unshaven [ʌn'ʃeɪvn] *adj* com a barba por fazer.

unsightly [ʌn'saɪtlɪ] *adj* feio, disforme.

unskilled [ʌn'skɪld] *adj*: ~ **worker** operário/a não-especializado/a.

unsociable [ʌn'səuʃəbl] *adj* anti-social.

unsocial [ʌn'səuʃl] *adj* (*hours*) fora do horário normal.

unsold [ʌn'səuld] *adj* não vendido.

unsolicited [ʌnsə'lɪsɪtɪd] *adj* não solicitado, espontâneo.

unsophisticated [ʌnsə'fɪstɪkeɪtɪd] *adj* simples *inv*, natural.

unsound [ʌn'saund] *adj* (*health*) mau; (*floor*, *foundations*) em mau estado; (*policy*, *advice*) infundado.

unspeakable [ʌn'spiːkəbl] *adj* indizível; (*bad*) inqualificável.

unspoken [ʌn'spəukən] *adj* (*agreement*, *approval*) tácito.

unsteady [ʌn'stɛdɪ] *adj* instável.

unstinting [ʌn'stɪntɪŋ] *adj* (*support*) irrestrito, total; (*generosity*) ilimitado.

unstuck [ʌn'stʌk] *adj*: **to come** ~ despregar-se; (*fig*) fracassar.

unsubstantiated [ʌnsəb'stænʃɪeɪtɪd] *adj* (*rumour*) que não foi confirmado; (*accusation*) sem provas.

unsuccessful [ʌnsək'sɛsful] *adj* (*attempt*) frustrado, vão/vã; (*writer*, *proposal*) sem êxito; **to be** ~ (*in attempting sth*) ser mal sucedido, não conseguir; (*application*) ser recusado.

unsuccessfully [ʌnsək'sɛsfulɪ] *adv* em vão, debalde.

unsuitable [ʌn'suːtəbl] *adj* inadequado, inconveniente.

unsuited [ʌn'suːtɪd] *adj*: **to be** ~ **for** *or* **to** ser inadequado *or* impróprio para.

unsupported [ʌnsə'pɔːtɪd] *adj* (*claim*) não verificado; (*theory*) não sustentado.

unsure [ʌn'ʃuə*] *adj* inseguro, incerto; **to be** ~ **of o.s.** não ser seguro de si.

unsuspecting [ʌnsə'spɛktɪŋ] *adj* confiante,

insuspeitado.

unsweetened [ʌn'swiːtənd] *adj* não adoçado, sem açúcar.

unswerving [ʌn'swɜːvɪŋ] *adj* inabalável, firme, resoluto.

unsympathetic [ʌnsɪmpə'θetɪk] *adj* insensível; (*unpleasant*) antipático; ~ **to** indiferente a.

untangle [ʌn'tæŋgl] *vt* desemaranhar, desenredar.

untapped [ʌn'tæpt] *adj* (*resources*) inexplorado.

untaxed [ʌn'tækst] *adj* (*goods*) isento de impostos; (*income*) não tributado.

unthinkable [ʌn'θɪŋkəbl] *adj* impensável, inconcebível, incalculável.

untidy [ʌn'taɪdɪ] *adj* (*room*) desarrumado, desleixado; (*appearance*) desmazelado, desalinhado.

untie [ʌn'taɪ] *vt* desatar, desfazer; (*dog, prisoner*) soltar.

until [ən'tɪl] *prep* até ♦ *conj* até que; ~ **he comes** até que ele venha; ~ **now** até agora; ~ **then** até então; **from morning** ~ **night** de manhã à noite.

untimely [ʌn'taɪmlɪ] *adj* inoportuno, intempestivo; (*death*) prematuro.

untold [ʌn'təuld] *adj* (*story*) inédito; (*suffering*) incalculável; (*wealth*) inestimável.

untouched [ʌn'tʌtʃt] *adj* (*not used*) intacto; (*safe: person*) ileso; ~ **by** indiferente a.

untoward [ʌntə'wɔːd] *adj* desfavorável, inconveniente.

untrammelled [ʌn'træmld] *adj* sem entraves.

untranslatable [ʌntræns'leɪtəbl] *adj* impossível de traduzir, intraduzível.

untrue [ʌn'truː] *adj* falso.

untrustworthy [ʌn'trʌstwɜːðɪ] *adj* indigno de confiança.

unusable [ʌn'juːzəbl] *adj* inutilizável, imprestável.

unused¹ [ʌn'juːzd] *adj* novo, sem uso.

unused² [ʌn'juːst] *adj*: **to be** ~ **to sth/to doing sth** não estar acostumado com algo/a fazer algo.

unusual [ʌn'juːʒuəl] *adj* incomum, extraordinário, insólito.

unusually [ʌn'juːʒəlɪ] *adv* extraordinariamente.

unveil [ʌn'veɪl] *vt* (*statue*) desvelar, descobrir.

unwanted [ʌn'wɒntɪd] *adj* não desejado, indesejável.

unwarranted [ʌn'wɔrəntɪd] *adj* injustificado.

unwary [ʌn'wɛərɪ] *adj* imprudente.

unwavering [ʌn'weɪvərɪŋ] *adj* firme, inabalável.

unwelcome [ʌn'wɛlkəm] *adj* (*at a bad time*) inoportuno, indesejável; (*unpleasant*) desagradável; **to feel** ~ não se sentir à vontade.

unwell [ʌn'wɛl] *adj*: **to be** ~ estar doente; **to feel** ~ estar indisposto.

unwieldy [ʌn'wiːldɪ] *adj* difícil de manejar,

pesado.

unwilling [ʌn'wɪlɪŋ] *adj*: **to be** ~ **to do sth** relutar em fazer algo, não querer fazer algo.

unwillingly [ʌn'wɪlɪŋlɪ] *adv* de má vontade.

unwind [ʌn'waɪnd] (*irreg*) *vt* desenrolar ♦ *vi* (*relax*) relaxar-se.

unwise [ʌn'waɪz] *adj* imprudente.

unwitting [ʌn'wɪtɪŋ] *adj* inconsciente, involuntário.

unworkable [ʌn'wɜːkəbl] *adj* (*plan etc*) inviável, inexequível.

unworthy [ʌn'wɜːðɪ] *adj* indigno.

unwound [ʌn'waund] *pt*, *pp* of **unwind**.

unwrap [ʌn'ræp] *vt* desembrulhar.

unwritten [ʌn'rɪtən] *adj* (*agreement*) tácito.

unzip [ʌn'zɪp] *vt* abrir (o fecho ecler de).

up [ʌp] *prep*: **to go/be** ~ **sth** subir algo/estar em cima de algo ♦ *adv* em cima, para cima ♦ *vi* (*inf*): **she** ~**ped and left** ela foi embora ♦ *vt* (*inf: price etc*) aumentar; ~ **there** lá em cima; ~ **above** em cima; ~ **to** até; **"this side** ~**"** "este lado para cima"; **to be** ~ (*out of bed*) estar levantado; **prices are** ~ **by 10%** os preços aumentaram em 10%; **when the year was** ~ no fim do ano; **time's** ~ o tempo acabou; **it is** ~ **to you** você é quem sabe, você decide; **what is he** ~ **to?** o que ele está querendo?, o que ele está tramando?; **he is not** ~ **to it** ele não é capaz de fazê-lo; **he's well** ~ **in** *or* **on** ... (*BRIT: knowledgeable*) ele entende de ...; ~ **with Celtic!** pra frente, Celtic!; **what's** ~**?** (*inf*) o que é que é?, o que é que houve?; **what's** ~ **with him?** (*inf*) qual é o problema com ele?

up-and-coming *adj* promissor(a).

upbeat ['ʌpbiːt] *adj* (*MUS*) movimentado; (*optimistic*) otimista.

upbraid [ʌp'breɪd] *vt* repreender, censurar.

upbringing ['ʌpbrɪŋɪŋ] *n* educação *f*, criação *f*.

update [ʌp'deɪt] *vt* atualizar, pôr em dia; (*contract etc*) atualizar.

upend [ʌp'ɛnd] *vt* colocar em pé.

upgrade [ʌp'greɪd] *vt* (*person*) promover; (*job*) revalorizar; (*property, equipment*) atualizar; (*COMPUT*) fazer um upgrade de.

upheaval [ʌp'hiːvl] *n* transtorno; (*unrest*) convulsão *f*.

upheld [ʌp'hɛld] *pt*, *pp* of **uphold**.

uphill [ʌp'hɪl] *adj* ladeira acima; (*fig: task*) trabalhoso, árduo ♦ *adv*: **to go** ~ ir morro acima.

uphold [ʌp'həuld] (*irreg*) *vt* suster, sustentar.

upholstery [ʌp'həulstərɪ] *n* estofamento.

upkeep ['ʌpkiːp] *n* manutenção *f*.

up-market *adj* (*product*) requintado.

upon [ə'pɒn] *prep* sobre.

upper ['ʌpəʳ] *adj* superior, de cima ♦ *n* (*of shoe*) gáspea, parte *f* superior.

upper class *n*: **the** ~ a classe alta ♦ *adj*: **upper-class** da classe alta.

uppermost ['ʌpəməust] *adj* mais elevado;

NB: European Portuguese adds the following consonants to certain words: **b** (sú(b)dito, su(b)til); **c** (a(c)ção, a(c)cionista, a(c)to); **m** (inde(m)ne); **p** (ado(p)ção, ado(p)tar); *for further details see p. xiii.*

what was ~ in my mind o que me preocupava mais.

Upper Volta [-'vɔltə] n Alto Volta m.

upright ['ʌpraɪt] adj vertical; (fig) honrado, honesto ♦ n viga vertical.

uprising ['ʌpraɪzɪŋ] n revolta, rebelião f, sublevação f.

uproar ['ʌprɔː*] n tumulto, algazarra.

uproot [ʌp'ruːt] vt desarraigar, arrancar.

ups [ʌps] npl: ~ **and downs** (fig) altos e baixos mpl.

upset [n 'ʌpsɛt, vt, adj ʌp'sɛt] (irreg: like **set**) n (to plan etc) revés m, reviravolta; (MED) indisposição f ♦ vt (glass etc) virar; (spill) derramar; (plan) perturbar; (person: annoy) aborrecer, perturbar; (: sadden) afligir ♦ adj aborrecido, contrariado; (sad) aflito; (stomach) indisposto.

upset price (US, SCOTTISH) n preço mínimo.

upsetting [ʌp'sɛtɪŋ] adj desconcertante.

upshot ['ʌpʃɔt] n resultado, conclusão f.

upside down ['ʌpsaɪd-] adv de cabeça para baixo.

upstairs [ʌp'stɛəz] adv em cima, lá em cima ♦ adj (room) de cima ♦ n andar m de cima.

upstart ['ʌpstɑːt] n novo-rico, pessoa sem classe.

upstream [ʌp'striːm] adv rio acima.

upsurge ['ʌpsəːdʒ] n (of enthusiasm etc) explosão f.

uptake ['ʌpteɪk] n: **he is quick on the** ~ ele vê longe; **he is slow on the** ~ ele tem raciocínio lento.

uptight [ʌp'taɪt] (inf) adj nervoso.

up-to-date adj moderno, atualizado; **to be** ~ **with the facts** estar a par dos fatos.

upturn ['ʌptəːn] n (in luck) virada; (in economy) retomada.

upturned ['ʌptəːnd] adj (nose) arrebitado.

upward ['ʌpwəd] adj ascendente, para cima.

upward(s) ['ʌpwəd(z)] adv para cima.

URA (US) n abbr = **Urban Renewal Administration**.

Ural Mountains ['juərəl-] npl: **the** ~ (also: the Urals) as montanhas Urais, os Urais.

uranium [juə'reɪnɪəm] n urânio.

Uranus [juə'reɪnəs] n Urano.

urban ['əːbən] adj urbano, da cidade.

urbane [əː'beɪn] adj gentil, urbano.

urbanization [əːbənaɪ'zeɪʃən] n urbanização f.

urchin ['əːtʃɪn] n moleque m, criança maltrapilha.

urge [əːdʒ] n (force) impulso; (desire) desejo ♦ vt: **to** ~ **sb to do sth** incitar alguém a fazer algo.

urge on vt animar, encorajar.

urgency ['əːdʒənsɪ] n urgência; (of tone) insistência.

urgent ['əːdʒənt] adj urgente; (tone, plea) insistente.

urgently ['əːdʒəntlɪ] adv urgentemente.

urinal ['juərɪnl] (BRIT) n urinol m, mictório.

urinate ['juərɪneɪt] vi urinar, mijar.

urine ['juərɪn] n urina.

urn [əːn] n urna; (also: tea ~) samovar m.

Uruguay ['juərəgwaɪ] n Uruguai m.

Uruguayan [juərə'gwaɪən] adj, n uruguaio/a.

US n abbr (= United States) EUA mpl.

us [ʌs] pron nos; (after prep) nós.

USA n abbr (= United States (of America)) EUA mpl; (MIL) = **United States Army**.

usable ['juːzəbl] adj usável, utilizável.

USAF n abbr = **United States Air Force**.

usage ['juːsɪdʒ] n uso, costume m.

USCG n abbr = **United States Coast Guard**.

USDA n abbr = **United States Department of Agriculture**.

USDAW ['ʌzdɔː] (BRIT) n abbr (= Union of Shop, Distributive and Allied Workers) sindicato dos varejistas e distribuidores.

USDI n abbr = **United States Department of the Interior**.

use [n juːs, vt juːz] n uso, emprego; (usefulness) utilidade f ♦ vt usar, utilizar, empregar; **she** ~**d to do it** ela costumava fazê-lo; **in** ~ em uso; **out of** ~ fora de uso; **ready for** ~ pronto para ser usado; **to be of** ~ ser útil; **it's no** ~ (pointless) é inútil; (not useful) não serve; **to have** ~ **of** ter uso de; **to make** ~ **of** fazer uso de.

use up vt esgotar, consumir.

used¹ [juːzd] adj (car) usado.

used² [juːst] adj: **to be** ~ **to** estar acostumado a; **to get** ~ **to** acostumar-se a.

useful ['juːsful] adj útil; **to come in** ~ ser útil.

usefulness ['juːsfəlnɪs] n utilidade f.

useless ['juːslɪs] adj inútil.

user ['juːzə*] n usuário/a (BR), utente m/f (PT).

user-friendly adj de fácil utilização, user-friendly.

USES n abbr = **United States Employment Service**.

usher ['ʌʃə*] n (in cinema) lanterninha m (BR), arrumador m (PT); (LAW) oficial m de justiça ♦ vt: **to** ~ **sb in** fazer alguém entrar.

usherette [ʌʃə'rɛt] n (in cinema) lanterninha (BR), arrumadora (PT).

USIA n abbr = **United States Information Agency**.

USM n abbr = **United States Mail; United States Mint**.

USN n abbr = **United States Navy**.

USPHS n abbr = **United States Public Health Service**.

USPO n abbr = **United States Post Office**.

USS n abbr = **United States Ship; United States Steamer**.

USSR n abbr (= Union of Soviet Socialist Republics) URSS f.

usu. abbr = **usually**.

usual ['juːʒuəl] adj usual, habitual; **as** ~ como de hábito, como sempre.

usually ['juːʒuəlɪ] adv normalmente.

usurer ['juːʒərə*] n usurário/a.

usurp [juː'zəːp] vt usurpar.

UT (US) abbr (POST) = **Utah**.

utensil [juː'tɛnsl] n utensílio.

uterus ['juːtərəs] n útero.

utilitarian [juːtɪlɪ'tɛərɪən] adj utilitário.

utility [ju:'tɪlɪtɪ] n utilidade f.
utility room n copa.
utilization [ju:tɪlaɪ'zeɪʃən] n utilização f.
utilize ['ju:tɪlaɪz] vt utilizar.
utmost ['ʌtməust] adj maior ♦ n: **to do one's** ~ fazer todo o possível; **of the** ~ **importance** da maior importância.
utter ['ʌtə*] adj completo, total ♦ vt proferir, pronunciar.
utterance ['ʌtərəns] n declaração f.
utterly ['ʌtəlɪ] adv completamente, totalmente.
U-turn n retorno; (fig) reviravolta.

V

V, v [vi:] n (letter) V, v m; **V for Victor** V de Vera.
v abbr = **verse**; (= vide: see) vide; (= versus) x; (= volt) v.
VA (US) abbr (POST) = **Virginia**.
vac [væk] (BRIT: inf) n abbr = **vacation**.
vacancy ['veɪkənsɪ] n (BRIT: job) vaga; (room) quarto livre; **"no vacancies"** "cheio".
vacant ['veɪkənt] adj (house) vazio; (post) vago; (seat etc) desocupado, livre; (expression) distraído.
vacant lot n terreno vago; (uncultivated) terreno baldio.
vacate [və'keɪt] vt (house) desocupar; (job) deixar; (throne) renunciar a.
vacation [və'keɪʃən] (esp US) n férias fpl; **to take a** ~ tirar férias; **on** ~ de férias.
vacation course n curso de férias.
vacationer [və'keɪʃənə*] (US) n veranista m/f.
vaccinate ['væksɪneɪt] vt vacinar.
vaccination [væksɪ'neɪʃən] n vacinação f.
vaccine ['væksi:n] n vacina.
vacuum ['vækjum] n vácuo m.
vacuum bottle (US) n garrafa térmica (BR), termo (PT).
vacuum cleaner n aspirador m de pó.
vacuum flask (BRIT) n garrafa térmica (BR), termo (PT).
vacuum-packed adj embalado a vácuo.
vagabond ['vægəbɒnd] n vagabundo/a.
vagary ['veɪgərɪ] n extravagância, capricho.
vagina [və'dʒaɪnə] n vagina.
vagrancy ['veɪgrənsɪ] n vadiagem f.
vagrant ['veɪgrənt] n vagabundo/a, vadio/a.
vague [veɪg] adj vago; (blurred: memory) fraco; (person) que divaga; **I haven't the** ~**st idea** não tenho a mínima idéia.
vaguely ['veɪglɪ] adv vagamente.
vain [veɪn] adj (conceited) vaidoso; (useless)

vão/vã, inútil; **in** ~ em vão.
valance ['væləns] n sanefa.
vale [veɪl] n vale m.
valedictory [vælɪ'dɪktərɪ] adj de despedida.
valentine ['væləntaɪn] n (also: ~ card) cartão m do Dia dos Namorados; **V**~**'s Day** Dia m dos Namorados.
valet ['vælɪt] n (of lord) criado pessoal; (in hotel) camareiro.
valet parking n estacionamento por manobrista.
valet service n (for clothes) lavagem f a seco; (for car) limpeza completa.
valiant ['vælɪənt] adj valente.
valid ['vælɪd] adj válido.
validate ['vælɪdeɪt] vt (contract, document) validar, legitimar; (argument, claim) confirmar, corroborar.
validity [və'lɪdɪtɪ] n validade f.
valise [və'li:z] n maleta.
valley ['vælɪ] n vale m.
valour ['vælə*] (US valor) n valor m, valentia.
valuable ['væljuəbl] adj (jewel) de valor; (time) valioso.
valuables ['væljuəblz] npl objetos mpl de valor.
valuation [vælju'eɪʃən] n avaliação f.
value ['vælju:] n valor m; (importance) importância ♦ vt (fix price of) avaliar; (esteem) valorizar, estimar; (cherish) apreciar; **you get good** ~ **(for money) in that shop** o seu dinheiro rende mais naquela loja; **to lose (in)** ~ desvalorizar-se; **to gain (in)** ~ valorizar-se; **to be of great** ~ **to sb** (fig) ser de grande utilidade para alguém; **to be** ~**d at $8** ser avaliado em $8.
value added tax [-'ædɪd-] (BRIT) n imposto sobre a circulação de mercadorias (BR), imposto sobre valor acrescentado (PT).
valued ['vælju:d] adj (appreciated) valorizado.
valuer ['væljuə*] n avaliador(a) m/f.
valve [vælv] n válvula; (in radio) lâmpada.
vampire ['væmpaɪə*] n vampiro/a.
van [væn] n (AUT) camionete f (BR), camioneta (PT).
V and A (BRIT) n abbr = **Victoria and Albert Museum**.
vandal ['vændl] n vândalo/a.
vandalism ['vændəlɪzəm] n vandalismo.
vandalize ['vændəlaɪz] vt destruir, depredar.
vanguard ['vænɡɑːd] n vanguarda.
vanilla [və'nɪlə] n baunilha ♦ cpd (ice cream) de baunilha.
vanish ['vænɪʃ] vi desaparecer, sumir.
vanity ['vænɪtɪ] n vaidade f.
vanity case n bolsa de maquilagem.
vantage point ['vɑːntɪdʒ-] n posição f estratégica.
vapor etc ['veɪpə*] (US) n = **vapour** etc.
vaporize ['veɪpəraɪz] vt vaporizar ♦ vi vaporizar-se.
vapour ['veɪpə*] (US vapor) n vapor m.

NB: European Portuguese adds the following consonants to certain words: **b** (sú(b)dito, su(b)til); **c** (a(c)ção, a(c)cionista, a(c)to); **m** (inde(m)ne); **p** (ado(p)ção, ado(p)tar); for further details see p. xiii.

vapo(u)r trail *n* (*AVIAT*) esteira de vapor.
variable ['vɛərɪəbl] *adj* variável ♦ *n* variável *f*.
variance ['vɛərɪəns] *n*: **to be at ~ (with)** estar em desacordo (com).
variant ['vɛərɪənt] *n* variante *f*.
variation [vɛərɪ'eɪʃən] *n* variação *f*; (*variant*) variante *f*; (*in opinion*) mudança.
varicose veins ['værɪkəʊs-] *npl* varizes *fpl*.
varied ['vɛərɪd] *adj* variado.
variety [və'raɪətɪ] *n* variedade *f*, diversidade *f*; (*quantity*): **a wide ~ of** uma grande variedade de; **for a ~ of reasons** por várias *or* diversas razões.
variety show *n* espetáculo de variedades.
various ['vɛərɪəs] *adj* vários/as, diversos/as; (*several*) vários/as; **at ~ times** (*different*) em horas variadas; (*several*) várias vezes.
varnish ['vɑːnɪʃ] *n* verniz *m*; (*nail ~*) esmalte *m* ♦ *vt* envernizar; (*nails*) pintar (com esmalte).
vary ['vɛərɪ] *vt* variar; (*change*) mudar ♦ *vi* variar; (*deviate*) desviar-se; **to ~ with** *or* **according to** variar de acordo com.
varying ['vɛərɪɪŋ] *adj* variado.
vase [vɑːz] *n* vaso.
vasectomy [væ'sɛktəmɪ] *n* vasectomia.
vaseline ['væsɪliːn] ® *n* vaselina ®.
vast [vɑːst] *adj* vasto, enorme; (*success*) imenso.
vastly ['vɑːstlɪ] *adv* (*underestimate etc*) enormemente; (*different*) completamente.
vastness ['vɑːstnɪs] *n* imensidão *f*.
VAT [væt] (*BRIT*) *n abbr* (= *value added tax*) ≈ ICM *m* (*BR*), IVA *m* (*PT*).
vat [væt] *n* tina, cuba.
Vatican ['vætɪkən] *n*: **the ~** o Vaticano.
vault [vɔːlt] *n* (*of roof*) abóbada; (*tomb*) sepulcro; (*in bank*) caixa-forte *f*; (*jump*) salto ♦ *vt* (*also*: *~ over*) saltar (por cima de).
vaunted ['vɔːntɪd] *adj*: **much-~** tão alardeado.
VC *n abbr* = **vice-chairman**; (*BRIT*: = *Victoria Cross*) *distinção militar*.
VCR *n abbr* = **video cassette recorder**.
VD *n abbr* = **venereal disease**.
VDU *n abbr* = **visual display unit**.
veal [viːl] *n* carne *f* de vitela.
veer [vɪə*] *vi* virar.
veg. [vɛdʒ] (*BRIT*: *inf*) *n abbr* = **vegetable(s)**.
vegetable ['vɛdʒtəbl] *n* (*BOT*) vegetal *m*; (*edible plant*) legume *m*, hortaliça ♦ *adj* vegetal; **~s** *npl* (*cooked*) verduras *fpl*.
vegetable garden *n* horta.
vegetarian [vɛdʒɪ'tɛərɪən] *adj, n* vegetariano/a.
vegetate ['vɛdʒɪteɪt] *vi* vegetar.
vegetation [vɛdʒɪ'teɪʃən] *n* vegetação *f*.
vehemence ['viːɪməns] *n* veemência, violência.
vehement ['viːɪmənt] *adj* veemente; (*impassioned*) apaixonado.
vehicle ['viːɪkl] *n* veículo.
vehicular [vɪ'hɪkjulə*] *adj*: **"no ~ traffic"** "proibido trânsito de veículos automotores".
veil [veɪl] *n* véu *m* ♦ *vt* velar; **under a ~ of secrecy** (*fig*) sob um manto de sigilo.

veiled [veɪld] *adj* velado.
vein [veɪn] *n* veia; (*of ore etc*) filão *m*; (*on leaf*) nervura; (*fig*: *mood*) tom *m*.
vellum ['vɛləm] *n* papel *m* velino.
velocity [vɪ'lɒsɪtɪ] *n* velocidade *f*.
velvet ['vɛlvɪt] *n* veludo ♦ *adj* aveludado.
vendetta [vɛn'dɛtə] *n* vendeta.
vending machine ['vɛndɪŋ-] *n* vendedor *m* automático.
vendor ['vɛndə*] *n* vendedor(a) *m/f*; **street ~** camelô *m*.
veneer [və'nɪə*] *n* capa exterior, folheado; (*wood*) compensado; (*fig*) aparência.
venerable ['vɛnərəbl] *adj* venerável.
venereal [vɪ'nɪərɪəl] *adj*: **~ disease** doença venérea.
Venetian blind [vɪ'niːʃən-] *n* persiana.
Venezuela [vɛnɛ'zweɪlə] *n* Venezuela.
Venezuelan [vɛnɛ'zweɪlən] *adj, n* venezuelano/a.
vengeance ['vɛndʒəns] *n* vingança; **with a ~** (*fig*) para valer.
vengeful ['vɛndʒful] *adj* vingativo.
Venice ['vɛnɪs] *n* Veneza.
venison ['vɛnɪsn] *n* carne *f* de veado.
venom ['vɛnəm] *n* veneno.
venomous ['vɛnəməs] *adj* venenoso.
vent [vɛnt] *n* (*opening, in jacket*) abertura; (*air-hole*) respiradouro; (*in wall*) abertura para ventilação ♦ *vt* (*fig*: *feelings*) desabafar, descarregar.
ventilate ['vɛntɪleɪt] *vt* ventilar.
ventilation [vɛntɪ'leɪʃən] *n* ventilação *f*.
ventilation shaft *n* poço de ventilação.
ventilator ['vɛntɪleɪtə*] *n* ventilador *m*.
ventriloquist [vɛn'trɪləkwɪst] *n* ventríloquo.
venture ['vɛntʃə*] *n* empreendimento ♦ *vt* aventurar; (*opinion*) arriscar ♦ *vi* arriscar-se, ousar; **a business ~** um empreendimento comercial; **to ~ to do sth** aventurar-se *or* arriscar-se a fazer algo.
venture capital *n* capital *m* de especulação.
venue ['vɛnjuː] *n* local *m*; (*meeting place*) ponto de encontro; (*theatre etc*) espaço.
Venus ['viːnəs] *n* (*planet*) Vênus *f*.
veracity [və'ræsɪtɪ] *n* veracidade *f*.
veranda(h) [və'rændə] *n* varanda.
verb [vɜːb] *n* verbo.
verbal ['vɜːbəl] *adj* verbal.
verbally ['vɜːbəlɪ] *adv* verbalmente.
verbatim [vɜː'beɪtɪm] *adj, adv* palavra por palavra.
verbose [vɜː'bəus] *adj* prolixo.
verdict ['vɜːdɪkt] *n* veredicto, decisão *f*; (*fig*) opinião *f*, parecer *m*; **~ of guilty/not guilty** veredicto de culpado/não culpado.
verge [vɜːdʒ] *n* beira, margem *f*; (*on road*) acostamento (*BR*), berma (*PT*); **to be on the ~ of doing sth** estar a ponto *or* à beira de fazer algo.
verge on *vt fus* beirar em.
verger ['vɜːdʒə*] *n* (*REL*) sacristão *m*.
verification [vɛrɪfɪ'keɪʃən] *n* verificação *f*.
verify ['vɛrɪfaɪ] *vt* verificar.
veritable ['vɛrɪtəbl] *adj* verdadeiro.

vermin ['vɜːmɪn] *npl* (*animals*) bichos *mpl*; (*insects*, *fig*) insetos *mpl* nocivos.

vermouth ['vɜːməθ] *n* vermute *m*.

vernacular [və'nækjulə*] *n* vernáculo; **in the** ~ na língua corrente.

versatile ['vɜːsətaɪl] *adj* (*person*) versátil; (*machine*, *tool etc*) polivalente; (*mind*) ágil, flexível.

verse [vɜːs] *n* verso, poesia; (*stanza*) estrofe *f*; (*in bible*) versículo; **in** ~ em verso.

versed [vɜːst] *adj*: **(well-)**~ **in** versado em.

version ['vɜːʃən] *n* versão *f*.

versus ['vɜːsəs] *prep* contra, versus.

vertebra ['vɜːtɪbrə] (*pl* ~**e**) *n* vértebra.

vertebrae ['vɜːtɪbriː] *npl of* **vertebra**.

vertebrate ['vɜːtɪbrɪt] *n* vertebrado.

vertical ['vɜːtɪkl] *adj* vertical ♦ *n* vertical *f*.

vertically ['vɜːtɪklɪ] *adv* verticalmente.

vertigo ['vɜːtɪgəu] *n* vertigem *f*; **to suffer from** ~ ter vertigens.

verve [vɜːv] *n* garra, pique *m*.

very ['vɛrɪ] *adv* muito ♦ *adj*: **the** ~ **book which** o mesmo livro que; **the** ~ **thought (of it)** ... só de pensar (nisso) ...; **at the** ~ **end** bem no final; **the** ~ **last** o último (de todos), bem o último; **at the** ~ **least** no mínimo; ~ **much** muitíssimo; ~ **little** muito pouco, pouquíssimo.

vespers ['vɛspəz] *npl* vésperas *fpl*.

vessel ['vɛsl] *n* (*ANAT*) vaso; (*NAUT*) navio, barco; (*container*) vaso, vasilha.

vest [vɛst] *n* (*BRIT*) camiseta (*BR*), camisola interior (*PT*); (*US*: *waistcoat*) colete *m* ♦ *vt*: **to** ~ **sb with sth, to** ~ **sth in sb** investir alguém de algo, conferir algo a alguém.

vested interest ['vɛstɪd-] *n*: **to have a** ~ **in doing** ter um interesse em fazer; ~**s** *npl* (*COMM*) direitos *mpl* adquiridos.

vestibule ['vɛstɪbjuːl] *n* vestíbulo.

vestige ['vɛstɪdʒ] *n* vestígio.

vestry ['vɛstrɪ] *n* sacristia.

Vesuvius [vɪ'suːvɪəs] *n* Vesúvio.

vet [vɛt] *n* *abbr* (= *veterinary surgeon*) veterinário/a ♦ *vt* examinar.

veteran ['vɛtərn] *n* veterano/a; (*also*: *war* ~) veterano de guerra ♦ *adj*: **she's a** ~ **campaigner for** ... ela é uma veterana nas campanhas de ....

veteran car *n* carro antigo.

veterinarian [vɛtrɪ'nɛərɪən] (*US*) *n* veterinário/a.

veterinary ['vɛtrɪnərɪ] *adj* veterinário.

veterinary surgeon (*BRIT*) *n* veterinário/a.

veto ['viːtəu] (*pl* ~**es**) *n* veto ♦ *vt* vetar; **to put a** ~ **on** opor seu veto a.

vex [vɛks] *vt* (*irritate*) irritar, apoquentar; (*make impatient*) impacientar.

vexed [vɛkst] *adj* (*question*) controvertido, discutido.

VFD (*US*) *n* *abbr* = **voluntary fire department**.

VG (*BRIT*) *n* *abbr* (*SCH*) = **very good**.

VHF *abbr* (= *very high frequency*) VHF, fre-

qüência muito alta.

VI (*US*) *abbr* (*POST*) = **Virgin Islands**.

via ['vaɪə] *prep* por, via.

viability [vaɪə'bɪlɪtɪ] *n* viabilidade *f*.

viable ['vaɪəbl] *adj* viável.

viaduct ['vaɪədʌkt] *n* viaduto.

vibrant ['vaɪbrənt] *adj* (*sound*, *colour*) vibrante.

vibrate [vaɪ'breɪt] *vi* vibrar.

vibration [vaɪ'breɪʃən] *n* vibração *f*.

vicar ['vɪkə*] *n* vigário.

vicarage ['vɪkərɪdʒ] *n* vicariato.

vicarious [vɪ'kɛərɪəs] *adj* (*pleasure*, *existence*) indireto.

vice [vaɪs] *n* (*evil*) vício; (*TECH*) torno mecânico.

vice- [vaɪs] *prefix* vice-.

vice-chairman (*irreg*) *n* vice-presidente *m/f*.

vice-chancellor (*BRIT*) *n* reitor(a) *m/f*.

vice-president *n* vice-presidente *m/f*.

vice squad *n* delegacia de costumes.

vice versa ['vaɪsɪ'vɜːsə] *adv* vice-versa.

vicinity [vɪ'sɪnɪtɪ] *n* (*area*) vizinhança; (*nearness*) proximidade *f*.

vicious ['vɪʃəs] *adj* (*violent*) violento; (*depraved*) depravado, vicioso; (*cruel*) cruel; (*bitter*) rancoroso; **a** ~ **circle** um círculo vicioso.

viciousness ['vɪʃəsnɪs] *n* violência; depravação *f*; crueldade *f*; rancor *m*.

vicissitudes [vɪ'sɪsɪtjuːdz] *npl* vicissitudes *fpl*.

victim ['vɪktɪm] *n* vítima *f*.

victimization [vɪktɪmaɪ'zeɪʃən] *n* perseguição *f*; (*in strike*) represálias *fpl*.

victimize ['vɪktɪmaɪz] *vt* (*strikers etc*) fazer represália contra.

victor ['vɪktə*] *n* vencedor(a) *m/f*.

Victorian [vɪk'tɔːrɪən] *adj* vitoriano.

victorious [vɪk'tɔːrɪəs] *adj* vitorioso.

victory ['vɪktərɪ] *n* vitória; **to win a** ~ **over sb** conseguir uma vitória sobre alguém.

video ['vɪdɪəu] *n* (~ *film*) vídeo; (*pop* ~) videoclipe *m*; (*also*: ~ *cassette*) videocassete *m*; (*also*: ~ *cassette recorder*) videocassete *m* ♦ *cpd* de vídeo.

video cassette *n* videocassete *m*.

video cassette recorder *n* videocassete *m*.

video recording *n* gravação *f* em vídeo.

video tape *n* videoteipe *m*; (*cassette*) videocassete *m*.

vie [vaɪ] *vi*: **to** ~ **with** competir com.

Vienna [vɪ'ɛnə] *n* Viena.

Viet Nam ['vjɛt'næm] *n* = **Vietnam**.

Vietnam ['vjɛt'næm] *n* Vietnã *m* (*BR*), Vietname *m* (*PT*).

Vietnamese [vjɛtnə'miːz] *adj* vietnamita ♦ *n* *inv* vietnamita *m/f*; (*LING*) vietnamita *m*.

view [vjuː] *n* vista, perspectiva; (*landscape*) paisagem *f*; (*opinion*) opinião *f*, parecer *m* ♦ *vt* (*look at*) olhar; (*examine*) examinar; **on** ~ (*in museum etc*) em exposição; **in full** ~ **(of)** à plena vista (de); **an overall** ~ **of the**

NB: *European Portuguese adds the following consonants to certain words:* **b** (sú(b)dito, su(b)til); **c** (a(c)ção, a(c)cionista, a(c)to); **m** (inde(m)ne); **p** (ado(p)ção, ado(p)tar); *for further details see p. xiii.*

situation uma visão geral da situação; **in my ~** na minha opinião; **in ~ of the fact that** em vista do fato de que; **with a ~ to doing sth** com a intenção de fazer algo.

viewdata ['vju:deɪtə] (*BRIT*) *n* teletexto, videotexto.

viewer ['vju:ə*] *n* (*small projector*) visor *m*; (*TV*) telespectador(a) *m/f.*

viewfinder ['vju:faɪndə*] *n* visor *m.*

viewpoint ['vju:pɔɪnt] *n* ponto de vista.

vigil ['vɪdʒɪl] *n* vigília; **to keep ~** velar.

vigilance ['vɪdʒɪləns] *n* vigilância.

vigilance committee *n* comitê *m* de vigilância.

vigilant ['vɪdʒɪlənt] *adj* vigilante.

vigor ['vɪgə*] (*US*) *n* = **vigour.**

vigorous ['vɪgərəs] *adj* enérgico, vigoroso.

vigour ['vɪgə*] (*US* **vigor**) *n* energia, vigor *m.*

vile [vaɪl] *adj* (*action*) vil, infame; (*smell*) repugnante, repulsivo; (*temper*) violento.

vilify ['vɪlɪfaɪ] *vt* vilipendiar.

villa ['vɪlə] *n* (*country house*) casa de campo; (*suburban house*) vila, quinta.

village ['vɪlɪdʒ] *n* aldeia, povoado.

villager ['vɪlɪdʒə*] *n* aldeão/aldeã *m/f.*

villain ['vɪlən] *n* (*scoundrel*) patife *m*; (*criminal*) marginal *m/f*; (*in novel etc*) vilão *m.*

VIN (*US*) *n* *abbr* = **vehicle identification number.**

vindicate ['vɪndɪkeɪt] *vt* vingar, desagravar.

vindication [vɪndɪ'keɪʃən] *n*: **in ~ of** em defesa de.

vindictive [vɪn'dɪktɪv] *adj* vingativo.

vine [vaɪn] *n* vinha, videira; (*climbing plant*) planta trepadeira.

vinegar ['vɪnɪgə*] *n* vinagre *m.*

vine grower *n* vinhateiro/a, viticultor(a) *m/f.*

vine-growing *adj* vitícola ♦ *n* viticultura.

vineyard ['vɪnjɑːd] *n* vinha, vinhedo.

vintage ['vɪntɪdʒ] *n* vindima; (*year*) safra, colheita; **the 1970 ~** a safra de 1970.

vintage car *n* carro antigo.

vintage wine *n* vinho velho.

vinyl ['vaɪnl] *n* vinil *m.*

viola [vɪ'əulə] *n* viola.

violate ['vaɪəleɪt] *vt* violar.

violation [vaɪə'leɪʃən] *n* violação *f*; **in ~ of** (*rule, law*) em violação de.

violence ['vaɪələns] *n* violência.

violent ['vaɪələnt] *adj* violento; (*intense*) intenso; **a ~ dislike of sb/sth** uma forte aversão a alguém/algo.

violently ['vaɪələntlɪ] *adv* violentemente; (*ill, angry*) extremamente.

violet ['vaɪələt] *adj* violeta ♦ *n* (*plant*) violeta.

violin [vaɪə'lɪn] *n* violino.

violinist [vaɪə'lɪnɪst] *n* violinista *m/f.*

VIP *n* *abbr* (= *very important person*) VIP *m/f.*

viper ['vaɪpə*] *n* víbora.

virgin ['vɜːdʒɪn] *n* virgem *m/f* ♦ *adj* virgem; **the Blessed V~** a Virgem Santíssima.

virginity [vɜː'dʒɪnɪtɪ] *n* virgindade *f.*

Virgo ['vɜːgəu] *n* Virgem *f.*

virile ['vɪraɪl] *adj* viril.

virility [vɪ'rɪlɪtɪ] *n* virilidade *f.*

virtual ['vɜːtjuəl] *adj* (*COMPUT, PHYSICS*) virtual; (*in effect*): **it's a ~ impossibility** é praticamente impossível; **the ~ leader** o líder na prática.

virtually ['vɜːtjuəlɪ] *adv* (*almost*) praticamente.

virtue ['vɜːtjuː] *n* virtude *f*; (*advantage*) vantagem *f*; **by ~ of** em virtude de.

virtuoso [vɜːtju'əuzəu] *n* virtuoso/a.

virtuous ['vɜːtjuəs] *adj* virtuoso.

virulent ['vɪrulənt] *adj* virulento.

virus ['vaɪərəs] *n* vírus *m.*

visa ['viːzə] *n* visto.

vis-à-vis [viːzə'viː] *prep* com relação a.

viscount ['vaɪkaunt] *n* visconde *m.*

viscous ['vɪskəs] *adj* viscoso.

vise [vaɪs] (*US*) *n* (*TECH*) = **vice.**

visibility [vɪzɪ'bɪlɪtɪ] *n* visibilidade *f.*

visible ['vɪzəbl] *adj* visível; **~ exports/imports** exportações *fpl*/importações *fpl* visíveis.

visibly ['vɪzəblɪ] *adv* visivelmente.

vision ['vɪʒən] *n* (*sight*) vista, visão *f*; (*foresight, in dream*) visão *f.*

visionary ['vɪʒənərɪ] *n* visionário/a.

visit ['vɪzɪt] *n* visita ♦ *vt* (*person*) visitar, fazer uma visita a; (*place*) ir a, ir conhecer; **on a private/official ~** em visita particular/oficial.

visiting ['vɪzɪtɪŋ] *adj* (*speaker, team*) visitante.

visiting card *n* cartão *m* de visita.

visiting hours *npl* horário de visita.

visiting professor *n* professor(a) *m/f* de outra faculdade.

visitor ['vɪzɪtə*] *n* visitante *m/f*; (*to one's house*) visita; (*tourist*) turista *m/f*; (*tripper*) excursionista *m/f.*

visitors' book *n* livro de visitas.

visor ['vaɪzə*] *n* viseira.

VISTA ['vɪstə] *n* *abbr* (= *Volunteers in Service to America*) programa de assistência às regiões pobres.

vista ['vɪstə] *n* vista, perspectiva.

visual ['vɪzjuəl] *adj* visual.

visual aid *n* meio visual (de ensino).

visual display unit *n* terminal *m* de vídeo.

visualize ['vɪzjuəlaɪz] *vt* visualizar; (*foresee*) prever.

visually ['vɪzjuəlɪ] *adv* visualmente; **~ handicapped** deficiente visual.

vital ['vaɪtl] *adj* (*essential*) essencial, indispensável; (*important*) de importância vital; (*crucial*) crucial; (*of life*) vital; **of ~ importance** de importância vital.

vitality [vaɪ'tælɪtɪ] *n* energia, vitalidade *f.*

vitally ['vaɪtəlɪ] *adv*: **~ important** de importância vital.

vital statistics *npl* (*of population*) estatística demográfica; (*inf*: *woman's*) medidas *fpl.*

vitamin ['vɪtəmɪn] *n* vitamina.

vitiate ['vɪʃɪeɪt] *vt* viciar.

vitreous ['vɪtrɪəs] *adj* vítreo.

vitriolic [vɪtrɪ'ɔlɪk] *adj* (*fig*) mordaz.

viva ['vaɪvə] *n* (*also*: **~ voce**) exame *m* oral.

vivacious [vɪ'veɪʃəs] *adj* vivaz, animado.

vivacity [vɪ'væsɪtɪ] n vivacidade f.
vivid ['vɪvɪd] adj (account) vívido; (light) claro, brilhante; (imagination) vivo.
vividly ['vɪvɪdlɪ] adv (describe) vividamente; (remember) distintamente.
vivisection [vɪvɪ'sɛkʃən] n vivissecção f.
vixen ['vɪksn] n raposa; (pej: woman) megera.
viz abbr (= videlicet: namely) a saber.
VLF abbr = **very low frequency**.
V-neck n decote m em V.
VOA n abbr (= Voice of America) voz f da América, emissora que transmite para o estrangeiro.
vocabulary [vəu'kæbjulərɪ] n vocabulário.
vocal ['vəukl] adj vocal; (noisy) clamoroso.
vocal cords npl cordas fpl vocais.
vocalist ['vəukəlɪst] n vocalista m/f, cantor(a) m/f.
vocals ['vəuklz] npl vozes fpl.
vocation [vəu'keɪʃən] n vocação f.
vocational [vəu'keɪʃənl] adj vocacional; ~ **guidance/training** orientação f vocacional/ensino profissionalizante.
vociferous [və'sɪfərəs] adj vociferante.
vodka ['vɔdkə] n vodca.
vogue [vəug] n voga, moda; **to be in** ~ estar na moda.
voice [vɔɪs] n voz f ♦ vt (opinion) expressar; **in a low/loud** ~ em voz baixa/alta; **to give** ~ **to** dar voz a.
void [vɔɪd] n vazio; (hole) oco ♦ adj (null) nulo; ~ **of** destituido de.
voile [vɔɪl] n voile m.
vol. abbr (= volume) vol.
volatile ['vɔlətaɪl] adj volátil.
volcanic [vɔl'kænɪk] adj vulcânico.
volcano [vɔl'keɪnəu] (pl ~**es**) n vulcão m.
volition [və'lɪʃən] n: **of one's own** ~ de livre vontade.
volley ['vɔlɪ] n (of gunfire) descarga, salva; (of stones etc) chuva; (TENNIS etc) voleio.
volleyball ['vɔlɪbɔːl] n voleibol m, vôlei m (BR).
volt [vəult] n volt m.
voltage ['vəultɪdʒ] n voltagem f; **high/low** ~ alta/baixa tensão.
voluble ['vɔljubl] adj tagarela, loquaz.
volume ['vɔljuːm] n volume m; (of tank) capacidade f; ~ **one/two** tomo um/dois; **his expression spoke** ~**s** sua expressão disse tudo.
volume control n (RADIO, TV) controle m de volume.
volume discount n (COMM) desconto de volume.
voluminous [və'luːmɪnəs] adj volumoso.
voluntarily ['vɔləntrɪlɪ] adv livremente, voluntariamente.
voluntary ['vɔləntərɪ] adj voluntário, intencional; (unpaid) (a título) gratuito.
voluntary liquidation n (COMM) liquidação f requerida pela empresa.

voluntary redundancy (BRIT) n demissão f voluntária.
volunteer [vɔlən'tɪə*] n voluntário/a ♦ vi (MIL) alistar-se voluntariamente; **to** ~ **to do** oferecer-se voluntariamente para fazer.
voluptuous [və'lʌptjuəs] adj voluptuoso.
vomit ['vɔmɪt] n vômito ♦ vt, vi vomitar.
vote [vəut] n voto; (votes cast) votação f; (right to ~) direito de votar; (franchise) título de eleitor ♦ vt (chairman) eleger ♦ vi votar; **to put sth to the** ~, **to take a** ~ **on sth** votar algo, submeter algo à votação; **to** ~ **for sb** votar em alguém; **to** ~ **for/against a proposal** votar a favor de/contra uma proposta; **to** ~ **to do sth** votar a favor de fazer algo; ~ **of censure** voto de censura; ~ **of confidence** voto de confiança; ~ **of thanks** agradecimento.
voter ['vəutə*] n votante m/f, eleitor(a) m/f.
voting ['vəutɪŋ] n votação f.
voting paper (BRIT) n cédula eleitoral.
voting right n direito de voto.
vouch for [vautʃ-] vt fus garantir, responder por.
voucher ['vautʃə*] n (for meal, petrol) vale m; (receipt) comprovante m.
vow [vau] n voto ♦ vi fazer votos; **to take** or **make a** ~ **to do sth** fazer voto de fazer algo.
vowel ['vauəl] n vogal f.
voyage ['vɔɪdʒ] n (journey) viagem f; (crossing) travessia.
VP n abbr = **vice-president**.
vs abbr (= versus) x.
VSO (BRIT) n abbr = **Voluntary Service Overseas**.
VT (US) abbr (POST) = **Vermont**.
vulgar ['vʌlgə*] adj (rude) grosseiro, ordinário; (in bad taste) vulgar, baixo.
vulgarity [vʌl'gærɪtɪ] n grosseria, vulgaridade f.
vulnerability [vʌlnərə'bɪlɪtɪ] n vulnerabilidade f.
vulnerable ['vʌlnərəbl] adj vulnerável.
vulture ['vʌltʃə*] n abutre m, urubu m.

W

W, w ['dʌbljuː] n (letter) W, w m; **W for William** W de William.
W abbr (= west) o; (ELEC: = watt) W.
WA (US) abbr (POST) = **Washington**.
wad [wɔd] n (of cotton wool) chumaço; (of paper) bola; (of banknotes etc) maço.
wadding ['wɔdɪŋ] n enchimento.
waddle ['wɔdl] vi andar gingando or bambo-

---

*NB: European Portuguese adds the following consonants to certain words: **b** (sú(b)dito, su(b)til); **c** (a(c)ção, a(c)cionista, a(c)to); **m** (inde(m)ne); **p** (ado(p)ção, ado(p)tar); for further details see p. xiii.*

leando.

wade [weɪd] vi: **to ~ through** andar em; (fig: a book) ler com dificuldade ♦ vt vadear, atravessar (a vau).

wafer ['weɪfə*] n (biscuit) bolacha; (REL) hóstia; (COMPUT) pastilha.

wafer-thin adj fininho, finíssimo.

waffle ['wɔfl] n (CULIN) waffle m; (inf) lengalenga ♦ vi lengalengar.

waffle iron n fôrma para fazer waffles.

waft [wɔft] vt levar ♦ vi flutuar.

wag [wæg] vt sacudir, menear ♦ vi acenar, abanar; **the dog ~ged its tail** o cachorro abanou o rabo.

wage [weɪdʒ] n (also: ~s) salário, ordenado ♦ vt: **to ~ war** empreender or fazer guerra; **a day's ~s** uma diária.

wage claim n reivindicação f salarial.

wage differential n desnível m salarial, diferença de salário.

wage earner ['weɪdʒ'ə:nə*] n assalariado/a.

wage freeze n congelamento de salários.

wage packet (BRIT) n envelope m de pagamento.

wager ['weɪdʒə*] n aposta, parada ♦ vt apostar.

waggle ['wægl] vt sacudir, agitar.

wag(g)on ['wægən] n (horse-drawn) carroça; (BRIT: RAIL) vagão m.

wail [weɪl] n lamento, gemido ♦ vi lamentar-se, gemer.

waist [weɪst] n cintura.

waistcoat ['weɪskəut] (BRIT) n colete m.

waistline ['weɪstlaɪn] n cintura.

wait [weɪt] n espera ♦ vi esperar; **to lie in ~ for** aguardar em emboscada; **I can't ~ to** (fig) estou morrendo de vontade de; **to ~ for** esperar, aguardar; **to keep sb ~ing** deixar alguém esperando; **~ a minute!** espera aí!; **"repairs while you ~"** "conserta-se na hora".

wait behind vi ficar para trás.

wait on vt fus servir.

wait up vi esperar, não ir dormir; **don't ~ up for me** vá dormir, não espere por mim.

waiter ['weɪtə*] n garçom m (BR), empregado (PT).

waiting ['weɪtɪŋ] n: **"no ~"** (BRIT: AUT) "proibido estacionar".

waiting list ['weɪtɪŋ-] n lista de espera.

waiting room n sala de espera.

waitress ['weɪtrɪs] n garçonete f (BR), empregada (PT).

waive [weɪv] vt renunciar a.

waiver ['weɪvə*] n desistência.

wake [weɪk] (pt **woke**, pp **woken**) vt, vi (also: ~ **up**) acordar ♦ n (for dead person) velório; (NAUT) esteira; **to ~ up to sth** (fig) abrir os olhos or acordar para algo; **in the ~ of** (fig) na esteira de; **to follow in sb's ~** (fig) seguir a esteira or o exemplo de alguém.

waken ['weɪkən] vt, vi = **wake**.

Wales [weɪlz] n País m de Gales.

walk [wɔk] n passeio; (hike) excursão f a pé,

caminhada; (gait) passo, modo de andar; (in park etc) alameda, passeio ♦ vi andar; (for pleasure, exercise) passear ♦ vt (distance) percorrer a pé, andar; (dog) levar para passear; **it's 10 minutes' ~ from here** daqui são 10 minutos a pé; **to go for a ~** (ir) dar uma volta; **I'll ~ you home** you andar com você até a sua casa; **people from all ~s of life** pessoas de todos os níveis.

walk out vi (go out) sair; (strike) entrar em greve; **to ~ out on sb** abandonar alguém.

walker ['wɔkə*] n (person) caminhante m/f.

walkie-talkie ['wɔkɪ'tɔkɪ] n transmissor-receptor m portátil, walkie-talkie m.

walking ['wɔkɪŋ] n o andar; **it's within ~ distance** dá para ir a pé.

walking holiday n férias fpl fazendo excursões a pé.

walking shoes npl sapatos mpl para andar.

walking stick n bengala.

walk-on adj (THEATRE: part) de figurante.

walkout ['wɔkaut] n (of workers) greve f branca.

walkover ['wɔkəuvə*] (inf) n barbada.

walkway ['wɔkweɪ] n passeio, passadiço.

wall [wɔl] n parede f; (exterior) muro; (city ~ etc) muralha; **to go to the ~** (fig: firm etc) falir, quebrar.

wall in vt (garden etc) cercar com muros.

wall cupboard n armário de parede.

walled [wɔld] adj (city) cercado por muralhas; (garden) murado, cercado.

wallet ['wɔlɪt] n carteira.

wallflower ['wɔlflauə*] n goivo-amarelo; **to be a ~** (fig) tomar chá de cadeira.

wall hanging n tapete m.

wallop ['wɔləp] (BRIT: inf) vt surrar, espancar.

wallow ['wɔləu] vi chafurdar, deitar e rolar; **to ~ in one's own grief** regozijar-se na própria dor.

wallpaper ['wɔlpeɪpə*] n papel m de parede.

wall-to-wall adj: **~ carpeting** carpete m.

wally ['wɔlɪ] (inf) n mané m, boboca m.

walnut ['wɔlnʌt] n noz f; (tree) nogueira.

walrus ['wɔlrəs] (pl ~ or ~**es**) n morsa, vaca marinha.

waltz [wɔlts] n valsa ♦ vi valsar.

wan [wɔn] adj pálido.

wand [wɔnd] n (also: magic ~) varinha de condão.

wander ['wɔndə*] vi (person) vagar, perambular; (thoughts) divagar; (get lost) extraviar-se ♦ vt percorrer.

wanderer ['wɔndərə*] n vagabundo/a.

wandering ['wɔndərɪŋ] adj errante; (thoughts) distraído; (tribe) nômade; (minstrel, actor) itinerante.

wane [weɪn] vi diminuir; (moon) minguar.

wangle ['wæŋgl] (inf) vt: **to ~ sth** conseguir algo através de pistolão.

want [wɔnt] vt (wish for) querer; (demand) exigir; (need) precisar de, necessitar de; (lack) carecer de ♦ n (poverty) pobreza, miséria;

~s npl (needs) necessidades fpl; **for ~ of** por falta de; **to ~ to do** querer fazer; **to ~ sb to do sth** querer que alguém faça algo; **you're ~ed on the phone** estão querendo falar com você no telefone; **"cook ~ed"** "precisa-se cozinheiro".

want ads (US) npl classificados mpl.

wanting ['wɔntɪŋ] adj falto, deficiente; **to be found ~** não estar à altura da situação; **to be ~ in** carecer de.

wanton ['wɔntən] adj (destruction) gratuito, irresponsável; (licentious) libertino, lascivo.

war [wɔː*] n guerra; **to make ~** fazer guerra; **to go to ~** entrar na guerra; **~ of attrition** guerra de atrição.

warble ['wɔːbl] n gorjeio ♦ vi gorjear.

war cry n grito de guerra.

ward [wɔːd] n (in hospital) ala; (POL) distrito eleitoral; (LAW: child) tutelado/a, pupilo/a.

ward off vt desviar, aparar; (attack) repelir.

warden ['wɔːdn] n (BRIT: of institution) diretor(a) m/f; (of park, game reserve) administrador(a) m/f; (BRIT: also: traffic ~) guarda m/f.

warder ['wɔːdə*] (BRIT) n carcereiro/a.

wardrobe ['wɔːdrəub] n (cupboard) armário; (clothes) guarda-roupa m.

warehouse ['wɛəhaus] (irreg) n armazém m, depósito.

wares [wɛəz] npl mercadorias fpl.

warfare ['wɔːfɛə*] n guerra, combate m.

war game n jogo de estrategia militar.

warhead ['wɔːhed] n ogiva.

warily ['wɛərɪlɪ] adv cautelosamente, com precaução.

warlike ['wɔːlaɪk] adj guerreiro, bélico.

warm [wɔːm] adj (clothes, day) quente; (thanks, welcome) caloroso, cordial; (supporter) entusiasmado; **it's ~** está quente; **I'm ~** estou com calor; **to keep sth ~** manter algo aquecido.

warm up vi (person, room) aquecer, esquentar; (athlete) fazer aquecimento; (discussion) esquentar-se ♦ vt esquentar.

warm-blooded [-'blʌdɪd] adj de sangue quente.

war memorial n monumento aos mortos.

warm-hearted [-'hɑːtɪd] adj afetuoso.

warmly ['wɔːmlɪ] adv calorosamente, afetuosamente.

warmonger ['wɔːmʌŋgə*] n belicista m/f.

warmongering ['wɔːmʌŋgərɪŋ] n belicismo.

warmth [wɔːmθ] n calor m.

warm-up n (SPORT) aquecimento.

warn [wɔːn] vt prevenir, avisar; **to ~ sb against sth** prevenir alguém contra algo; **to ~ sb not to do sth** or **against doing sth** prevenir alguém de não fazer algo.

warning ['wɔːnɪŋ] n advertência, aviso; **without (any) ~** (suddenly) de improviso, inopinadamente; (without notice) sem aviso pré-

vio, sem avisar; **gale ~** (METEOROLOGY) aviso de vendaval.

warning light n luz f de advertência.

warning triangle n (AUT) triângulo de advertência.

warp [wɔːp] n (TEXTILES) urdidura ♦ vt deformar ♦ vi empenar, deformar-se.

warpath ['wɔːpɑːθ] n: **to be on the ~** (fig) estar disposto a brigar.

warped [wɔːpt] adj (wood) empenado; (fig: sense of humour) pervertido, deformado.

warrant ['wɔrnt] n (guarantee) garantia; (LAW: to arrest) mandado de prisão; (: to search) mandado de busca ♦ vt (justify) justificar.

warrant officer n (MIL) subtenente m; (NAUT) suboficial m.

warranty ['wɔrəntɪ] n garantia; **under ~** (COMM) sob garantia.

warren ['wɔrən] n (of rabbits) lura; (house) coelheira.

warring ['wɔːrɪŋ] adj (nations) em guerra; (interests etc) antagônico.

warrior ['wɔrɪə*] n guerreiro/a.

Warsaw ['wɔːsɔː] n Varsóvia.

warship ['wɔːʃɪp] n navio de guerra.

wart [wɔːt] n verruga.

wartime ['wɔːtaɪm] n: **in ~** em tempo de guerra.

wary ['wɛərɪ] adj cauteloso, precavido; **to be ~ about** or **of doing sth** hesitar em fazer algo.

was [wɔz] pt of **be**.

wash [wɔʃ] vt lavar; (sweep, carry: sea etc) levar, arrastar; (: ashore) lançar ♦ vi lavar-se ♦ n (clothes etc) lavagem f; (of ship) esteira; **to have a ~** lavar-se; **to give sth a ~** lavar algo; **he was ~ed overboard** foi arrastado do navio pelas águas.

wash away vt (stain) tirar ao lavar; (subj: river etc) levar, arrastar.

wash down vt lavar; (food) regar.

wash off vt tirar lavando ♦ vi sair ao lavar.

wash up vi lavar a louça; (US) lavar-se.

washable ['wɔʃəbl] adj lavável.

washbasin ['wɔʃbeɪsn] n pia (BR), lavatório (PT).

washbowl ['wɔʃbəul] (US) n = **washbasin**.

washcloth ['wɔʃklɔθ] (US) n pano para lavar o rosto.

washer ['wɔʃə*] n (TECH) arruela, anilha.

wash-hand basin (BRIT) n pia (BR), lavatório (PT).

washing ['wɔʃɪŋ] (BRIT) n (dirty) roupa suja; (clean) roupa lavada.

washing line (BRIT) n corda de estender roupa, varal m.

washing machine n máquina de lavar roupa, lavadora.

washing powder (BRIT) n sabão m em pó.

Washington ['wɔʃɪŋtən] n (city, state) Washington.

NB: European Portuguese adds the following consonants to certain words: **b** (sú(b)dito, su(b)til); **c** (a(c)ção, a(c)cionista, a(c)to); **m** (inde(m)ne); **p** (ado(p)ção, ado(p)tar); for further details see p. xiii.

washing-up n: **to do the** ~ lavar a louça.
washing-up liquid (BRIT) n detergente m.
wash-out (inf) n fracasso, fiasco.
washroom ['wɔʃruːm] n banheiro (BR), casa de banho (PT).
wasn't ['wɔznt] = **was not**.
WASP [wɔsp] (US: inf) n abbr (= White Anglo-Saxon Protestant) apelido, muitas vezes pejorativo, dado aos membros da classe dominante nos EUA.
Wasp [wɔsp] (US: inf) = **WASP**.
wasp [wɔsp] n vespa.
waspish ['wɔspɪʃ] adj irritadiço.
wastage ['weɪstɪdʒ] n desgaste m, desperdício; (loss) perda; **natural** ~ desgaste natural.
waste [weɪst] n desperdício, esbanjamento; (wastage) desperdício; (of time) perda; (food) sobras fpl; (rubbish) lixo ♦ adj (material) de refugo; (left over) de sobra; (land) baldio ♦ vt (squander) esbanjar, desperdiçar; (time, opportunity) perder; ~s npl ermos mpl; **it's a** ~ **of money** é jogar dinheiro fora; **to go to** ~ ser desperdiçado; **to lay** ~ (destroy) devastar.
waste away vi definhar.
wastebin ['weɪstbɪn] (BRIT) n lata de lixo.
waste disposal (unit) (BRIT) n triturador m de lixo.
wasteful ['weɪstful] adj esbanjador(a); (process) anti-econômico.
waste ground (BRIT) n terreno baldio.
wasteland ['weɪstlənd] n terra inculta; (in town) terreno baldio.
wastepaper basket ['weɪstpeɪpə*-] n cesta de papéis.
waste pipe n cano de esgoto.
waste products (INDUSTRY) n resíduos mpl.
watch [wɔtʃ] n (clock) relógio; (act of ~ing) vigia; (guard: MIL) sentinela; (NAUT: spell of duty) quarto ♦ vt (look at) observar, olhar; (programme, match) assistir a; (television) ver; (spy on, guard) vigiar; (be careful of) tomar cuidado com ♦ vi ver, olhar; (keep guard) montar guarda; **to keep a close** ~ **on sb/sth** vigiar alguém/algo, ficar de olho em alguém/algo; ~ **what you're doing** presta atenção no que você está fazendo.
watch out vi ter cuidado.
watchband ['wɔtʃbænd] (US) n pulseira de relógio.
watchdog ['wɔtʃdɔg] n cão m de guarda; (fig) vigia m/f.
watchful ['wɔtʃful] adj vigilante, atento.
watchmaker ['wɔtʃmeɪkə*] n relojoeiro/a.
watchman ['wɔtʃmən] (irreg) n vigia m; (also: **night** ~) guarda m noturno; (: in factory) vigia m noturno.
watch stem (US) n botão m de corda.
watch strap n pulseira de relógio.
watchword ['wɔtʃwɔːd] n lema m, divisa.
water ['wɔːtə*] n água ♦ vt (plant) regar ♦ vi (eyes) lacrimejar; **a drink of** ~ um copo d'água; **in British** ~s nas águas territoriais britânicas; **to pass** ~ urinar; **to make sb's**

mouth ~ dar água na boca de alguém.
water down vt (milk) aguar; (fig) diluir.
water closet (BRIT) n privada.
watercolour ['wɔːtəkʌlə*] (US **watercolor**) n aquarela.
water-cooled [-kuːld] adj refrigerado a água.
watercress ['wɔːtəkrɛs] n agrião m.
waterfall ['wɔːtəfɔːl] n cascata, cachoeira.
waterfront ['wɔːtəfrʌnt] n (seafront) orla marítima; (docks) zona portuária.
water heater n aquecedor m de água, boiler m.
water hole n bebedouro, poço.
water ice (BRIT) n sorvete de frutas à base de água.
watering can ['wɔːtərɪŋ-] n regador m.
water level n nível m d'água.
water lily n nenúfar m.
waterline ['wɔːtəlaɪn] n (NAUT) linha d'água.
waterlogged ['wɔːtəlɔgd] adj alagado.
water main n adutora.
watermark ['wɔːtəmɑːk] n (on paper) filigrana.
watermelon ['wɔːtəmɛlən] n melancia.
water polo n pólo aquático.
waterproof ['wɔːtəpruːf] adj impermeável; (watch) à prova d'água.
water-repellent adj hidrófugo.
watershed ['wɔːtəʃɛd] n (GEO) linha divisória das águas; (fig) momento crítico.
water-skiing n esqui m aquático.
water softener n abrandador m de água.
water tank n depósito d'água.
watertight ['wɔːtətaɪt] adj hermético, à prova d'água.
water vapour n vapor m de água.
waterway ['wɔːtəweɪ] n hidrovia.
waterworks ['wɔːtəwɔːks] npl usina hidráulica.
watery ['wɔːtərɪ] adj (colour) pálido; (coffee) aguado; (eyes) húmido.
watt [wɔt] n watt m.
wattage ['wɔtɪdʒ] n wattagem f.
wattle ['wɔtl] n caniçada.
wave [weɪv] n (gen, RADIO) onda; (of hand) aceno, sinal m; (in hair) onda, ondulação f ♦ vi acenar com a mão; (flag) tremular, flutuar ♦ vt (handkerchief) acenar com; (weapon) brandir; (hair) ondular; **to** ~ **goodbye to sb** despedir-se de alguém com um aceno; **short/medium/long** ~ (RADIO) ondas curtas/médias/longas; **the new** ~ (CINEMA, MUS) a nova onda.
wave aside vt (fig: suggestion, objection) rejeitar; (: doubts) pôr de lado; (person): **to** ~ **sb aside** fazer sinal para alguém pôr-se de lado.
wave away vt (fig: suggestion, objection) rejeitar; (: doubts) pôr de lado; (person): **to** ~ **sb away** fazer sinal para alguém pôr-se de lado.
waveband ['weɪvbænd] n faixa de onda.
wavelength ['weɪvlɛŋθ] n comprimento de onda.
waver ['weɪvə*] vi vacilar.

wavy ['weɪvɪ] adj ondulado, ondulante.
wax [wæks] n cera ♦ vt encerar ♦ vi (moon) crescer.
waxworks ['wækswɔːks] npl museu m de cera.
way [weɪ] n caminho; (distance) percurso; (direction) direção f, sentido; (manner) maneira, modo; (habit) costume m; (condition) estado; **which ~?** — **this ~** por onde? — por aqui; **to crawl one's ~ to ...** arrastar-se até ...; **to lie one's ~ out of it** mentir para livrar-se de apuros; **on the ~ (to)** a caminho (de); **to be on one's ~** estar a caminho; **to be in the ~** atrapalhar; **to keep out of sb's ~** evitar alguém; **it's a long ~ away** é muito longe; **the village is rather out of the ~** o lugarejo é um pouco fora de mão; **to go out of one's ~ to do sth** (fig) dar-se ao trabalho de fazer algo; **to lose one's ~** perder-se; **to be under ~** (work, project) estar em andamento; **to make ~ (for sb/sth)** abrir caminho (para alguém/algo); **to get one's own ~** conseguir o que quer; **to put sth the right ~ up** (BRIT) colocar algo na posição certa; **to be the wrong ~ round** estar às avessas; **he's in a bad ~** ele vai muito mal; **in a ~** de certo modo, até certo ponto; **in some ~s** a certos respeitos; **by the ~** a propósito; **"~ in"** (BRIT) "entrada"; **"~ out"** (BRIT) "saída"; **the ~ back** o caminho de volta; **"give ~"** (AUT) "dê a preferência"; **in the ~ of** em matéria de; **by ~ of** (through) por, via; (as a sort of) à guisa de; **no ~!** (inf) de jeito nenhum!
waybill ['weɪbɪl] n (COMM) conhecimento.
waylay [weɪ'leɪ] (irreg) vt armar uma cilada para; (fig): **I got waylaid** alguém me deteve.
wayside ['weɪsaɪd] n beira da estrada; **to fall by the ~** (fig) desistir; (morally) corromper-se.
way station (US) n (RAIL) apeadeiro; (fig) etapa.
wayward ['weɪwəd] adj (wilful) voluntarioso, teimoso; (capricious) caprichoso; (naughty) travesso.
WC ['dʌblju'siː] (BRIT) n abbr = **water closet**.
WCC n abbr = **World Council of Churches**.
we [wiː] pron nós.
weak [wiːk] adj fraco, débil; (tea) aguado, ralo; **to grow ~(er)** enfraquecer, ficar cada vez mais fraco.
weaken ['wiːkən] vi enfraquecer(-se); (give way) ceder ♦ vt enfraquecer; (lessen) diminuir.
weak-kneed [-niːd] adj (fig) covarde.
weakling ['wiːklɪŋ] n pessoa fraca or delicada.
weakly ['wiːklɪ] adj fraco ♦ adv fracamente.
weakness ['wiːknɪs] n fraqueza; (fault) ponto fraco.
wealth [welθ] n (money, resources) riqueza; (of details) abundância.
wealth tax n imposto sobre fortunas.
wealthy ['welθɪ] adj rico, abastado.

wean [wiːn] vt desmamar.
weapon ['wepən] n arma.
wear [weə*] (pt wore, pp worn) n (use) uso; (deterioration through use) desgaste m; (clothing): **baby/sports ~** roupa infantil/de esporte ♦ vt (clothes) usar; (shoes) usar, calçar; (put on) vestir; (damage: through use) desgastar; (beard etc) ter ♦ vi (last) durar; (rub etc through) gastar-se; **~ and tear** desgaste m; **to ~ a hole in sth** fazer um buraco em algo pelo uso.
wear away vt gastar ♦ vi desgastar-se.
wear down vt gastar; (strength) esgotar.
wear off vi (pain etc) passar.
wear on vi alongar-se.
wear out vt desgastar; (person, strength) esgotar.
wearable ['weərəbl] adj que se pode usar.
wearily ['wɪərɪlɪ] adv de maneira cansada.
weariness ['wɪərɪnɪs] n cansaço, fadiga; (boredom) aborrecimento.
wearisome ['wɪərɪsəm] adj (tiring) cansativo; (boring) fastidioso.
weary ['wɪərɪ] adj (tired) cansado; (dispirited) deprimido ♦ vt aborrecer ♦ vi: **to ~ of** cansar-se de.
weasel ['wiːzl] n (ZOOL) doninha.
weather ['weðə*] n tempo ♦ vt (storm, crisis) resistir a; **what's the ~ like?** como está o tempo?; **under the ~** (fig: ill) doente.
weather-beaten adj curtido.
weather cock n cata-vento.
weather forecast n previsão f do tempo.
weatherman ['weðəmæn] (irreg) n meteorologista m.
weatherproof ['weðəpruːf] adj (garment) impermeável; (building) à prova de intempérie.
weather report n boletim m meteorológico.
weather vane [-veɪn] n cata-vento.
weave [wiːv] (pt wove, pp woven) vt (cloth) tecer; (fig) compor, criar ♦ vi (fig: pt, pp ~d: move in and out) ziguezaguear.
weaver ['wiːvə*] n tecelão/loa m/f.
weaving ['wiːvɪŋ] n tecelagem f.
web [web] n (of spider) teia; (on foot) membrana; (network) rede f.
webbed [webd] adj (foot) palmípede.
webbing ['webɪŋ] n (on chair) tira de tecido forte.
wed [wed] (pt, pp ~ded) vt casar ♦ vi casar-se ♦ n: **the newly-~s** os recém-casados.
Wed. abbr (= Wednesday) qua., 4ª.
we'd [wiːd] = **we had**; **we would**.
wedded ['wedɪd] pt, pp of **wed**.
wedding ['wedɪŋ] n casamento, núpcias fpl.
wedding anniversary n aniversário de casamento; **silver/golden ~** bodas fpl de prata/de ouro.
wedding day n dia m de casamento.
wedding dress n vestido de noiva.
wedding night n noite f de núpcias.

NB: European Portuguese adds the following consonants to certain words: **b** (sú(b)dito, su(b)til); **c** (a(c)ção, a(c)cionista, a(c)to); **m** (inde(m)ne); **p** (ado(p)ção, ado(p)tar); for further details see p. xiii.

wedding present n presente m de casamento.

wedding ring n anel m or aliança de casamento.

wedge [wedʒ] n (of wood etc) cunha, calço; (of cake) fatia ♦ vt (pack tightly) socar, apertar; (door) pôr calço em.

wedge-heeled shoes [-hiːld-] npl sapatos mpl tipo Annabella.

wedlock ['wedlɔk] n matrimônio, casamento.

Wednesday ['wednzdɪ] n quarta-feira; see also **Tuesday**.

wee [wiː] (SCOTTISH) adj pequeno, pequenino.

weed [wiːd] n erva daninha ♦ vt capinar.

weed-killer n herbicida m.

weedy ['wiːdɪ] adj (man) fraquinho.

week [wiːk] n semana; **once/twice a** ~ uma vez/duas vezes por semana; **in two** ~s' **time** daqui a duas semanas; **Tuesday** ~, **a** ~ **on Tuesday** sem ser essa terça-feira, a outra; **every other** ~ uma semana sim, uma semana não.

weekday ['wiːkdeɪ] n dia m de semana; (COMM) dia útil; **on** ~s durante a semana.

weekend ['wiːkɛnd] n fim m de semana.

weekend case n maleta.

weekly ['wiːklɪ] adv semanalmente ♦ adj semanal ♦ n semanário.

weep [wiːp] (pt, pp **wept**) vi (person) chorar; (MED: wound) supurar.

weeping willow ['wiːpɪŋ-] n salgueiro chorão.

weft [weft] n (TEXTILES) trama.

weigh [weɪ] vt, vi pesar; **to** ~ **anchor** levantar ferro; **to** ~ **the pros and cons** pesar os prós e contras.

weigh down vt sobrecarregar; (fig: with worry) deprimir, acabrunhar.

weigh out vt (goods) pesar.

weigh up vt ponderar, avaliar.

weighbridge ['weɪbrɪdʒ] n báscula automática.

weighing machine ['weɪɪŋ-] n balança.

weight [weɪt] n peso ♦ vt carregar com peso; (fig: statistic) ponderar; **to lose/put on** ~ emagrecer/engordar; **sold by** ~ vendido por peso; ~s **and measures** pesos e medidas.

weighting ['weɪtɪŋ] n: ~ **allowance** indenização f de residência.

weightlessness ['weɪtlɪsnɪs] n ausência de peso.

weightlifter ['weɪtlɪftə*] n levantador m de pesos.

weighty ['weɪtɪ] adj pesado, importante.

weir [wɪə*] n represa, açude m.

weird [wɪəd] adj esquisito, estranho.

welcome ['welkəm] adj bem-vindo ♦ n acolhimento, recepção f ♦ vt (be glad of) acolher; **you're** ~ (after thanks) de nada; **to make sb** ~ dar bom acolhimento a alguém; **you're** ~ **to try** pode tentar se quiser.

welcoming ['welkəmɪŋ] adj acolhedor(a); (speech) de boas-vindas.

weld [weld] n solda ♦ vt soldar, unir.

welder ['weldə*] n (person) soldador(a) m/f.

welding ['weldɪŋ] n soldagem f, solda.

welfare ['welfɛə*] n bem-estar m; (social aid) assistência social.

welfare state n país auto-financiador da sua assistência social.

welfare work n trabalho social.

well [wel] n poço; (pool) nascente f ♦ adv bem ♦ adj: **to be** ~ estar bem (de saúde) ♦ excl bem!, então!; **as** ~ também; **as** ~ **as** assim como; ~ **done!** muito bem!; **get** ~ **soon!** melhoras!; **to do** ~ ir or sair-se bem; **to think** ~ **of sb** ter um bom conceito a respeito de alguém; **I don't feel** ~ não estou me sentindo bem; **you might as** ~ **tell me** é melhor você me contar logo; ~, **as I was saying** ... bem, como eu estava dizendo ....

well up vi brotar, manar.

we'll [wiːl] = **we will**; **we shall**.

well-behaved [-bɪ'heɪvd] adj bem educado, bem comportado.

well-being n bem-estar m.

well-bred adj bem educado.

well-built adj (person) robusto; (house) bem construído.

well-chosen adj bem escolhido.

well-deserved [-dɪ'zɜːvd] adj bem merecido.

well-developed [-dɪ'veləpt] adj bem desenvolvido.

well-disposed adj: ~ **to(wards)** favorável a.

well-dressed [-drest] adj bem vestido.

well-earned adj (rest) bem merecido.

well-groomed [-gruːmd] adj bem tratado.

well-heeled [-hiːld] (inf) adj (wealthy) rico.

well-informed adj bem informado, versado.

wellingtons ['welɪŋtənz] n (also: wellington boots) botas de borracha até os joelhos.

well-kept adj (house, hands etc) bem tratado; (secret) bem guardado.

well-known adj conhecido; **it's a** ~ **fact that** ... é sabido que ....

well-mannered [-'mænəd] adj bem educado.

well-meaning adj bem intencionado.

well-nigh [-naɪ] adv: ~ **impossible** praticamente impossível.

well-off adj próspero, rico.

well-read adj lido, versado.

well-spoken adj (person) bem-falante.

well-stocked [-stɔkt] adj bem abastecido.

well-timed [-taɪmd] adj oportuno.

well-to-do adj abastado.

well-wisher [-'wɪʃə*] n simpatizante m/f; (admirer) admirador(a) m/f.

Welsh [welʃ] adj galês/galesa ♦ n (LING) galês m; **the** ~ npl os galeses.

Welshman ['welʃmən] (irreg) n galês m.

Welsh rarebit n torradas com queijo derretido.

Welshwoman ['welʃwumən] (irreg) n galesa.

welter ['weltə*] n tumulto.

went [went] pt of **go**.

wept [wept] pt, pp of **weep**.

were [wɜː*] pt of **be**.

we're [wɪə*] = **we are**.

weren't [wɜːnt] = **were not**.

werewolf ['wɪəwulf] (*irreg*) *n* lobisomem *m*.

west [wɛst] *n* oeste *m* ♦ *adj* ocidental, do oeste ♦ *adv* para o oeste *or* ao oeste; **the W~** o Oeste, o Ocidente.

westbound ['wɛstbaund] *adj* em direção ao oeste.

West Country *n*: **the ~** o sudoeste da Inglaterra.

westerly ['wɛstəlɪ] *adj* (*situation*) ocidental; (*wind*) oeste.

western ['wɛstən] *adj* ocidental ♦ *n* (*CINEMA*) western *m*, bangue-bangue (*BR*: *inf*).

westernized ['wɛstənaɪzd] *adj* ocidentalizado.

West German *adj*, *n* alemão/ã *m/f* ocidental.

West Germany *n* Alemanha Ocidental.

West Indian *adj*, *n* antilhano/a.

West Indies [-'ɪndɪz] *npl* Antilhas *fpl*.

westward(s) ['wɛstwəd(z)] *adv* para o oeste.

wet [wɛt] (*pt*, *pp* **wet** *or* **~ted**) *adj* molhado; (*damp*) úmido; (**~** *through*) encharcado; (*rainy*) chuvoso ♦ *vt* molhar; **to ~ one's pants** *or* **o.s.** fazer xixi na calça; **to get ~** molhar-se; "**~ paint**" "tinta fresca".

wet blanket *n* (*fig*) desmancha-prazeres *m/f inv*.

wetness ['wɛtnɪs] *n* umidade *f*.

wet suit *n* roupa de mergulho.

we've [wiːv] = **we have**.

whack [wæk] *vt* bater.

whacked [wækt] (*inf*) *adj* morto, esgotado.

whale [weɪl] *n* (*ZOOL*) baleia.

whaler ['weɪlə*] *n* baleeiro.

wharf [wɔːf] (*pl* **wharves**) *n* cais *m inv*.

wharves [wɔːvz] *npl of* **wharf**.

what [wɔt] *excl* quê!, como! ♦ *adj* que ♦ *pron* (*interrogative*) que, o que; (*relative*, *indirect*: *object*, *subject*) o que; **~ are you doing?** o que é que você está fazendo?; **~'s happened?** o que aconteceu?; **~'s in there?** o que é que tem lá dentro?; **for ~ reason?** por que razão?; **I saw ~ you did** eu vi o que você fez; **I don't know ~ to do** não sei o que fazer; **~ a mess!** que bagunça!; **~ is it called?** como se chama?; **~ about doing ...** que tal fazer ...; **~ about me?** e eu?; **~ is his address?** qual é o endereço dele?; **~ I want is a cup of tea** (o que eu) quero é uma xícara de chá; **~ will it cost?** quanto vai custar?

whatever [wɔt'ɛvə*] *adj*: **~ book you choose** qualquer livro que você escolha ♦ *pron*: **do ~ is necessary** faça tudo o que for preciso; **~ happens** aconteça o que acontecer; **no reason ~** *or* **whatsoever** nenhuma razão seja qual for *or* em absoluto; **nothing ~** nada em absoluto.

wheat [wiːt] *n* trigo.

wheatgerm ['wiːtdʒəːm] *n* germe *m* de trigo.

wheatmeal ['wiːtmiːl] *n* farinha de trigo.

wheedle ['wiːdl] *vt*: **to ~ sth out of sb** conseguir algo de alguém por meio de agrados.

wheel [wiːl] *n* roda; (*AUT*: *also*: *steering ~*)

volante *m*; (*NAUT*) roda do leme ♦ *vt* (*pram etc*) empurrar ♦ *vi* (*also*: **~** *round*) girar, dar voltas, virar-se.

wheelbarrow ['wiːlbærəu] *n* carrinho de mão.

wheelbase ['wiːlbeɪs] *n* distância entre os eixos.

wheelchair ['wiːltʃɛə*] *n* cadeira de rodas.

wheel clamp *n* (*AUT*) grampo com que se imobiliza carros estacionados ilegalmente.

wheeler-dealer ['wiːlə*-] *n* negocista *m/f*.

wheelhouse ['wiːlhaus] (*irreg*) *n* casa do leme.

wheeling ['wiːlɪŋ] *n*: **~ and dealing** negociatas *fpl*.

wheeze [wiːz] *n* respiração *f* difícil, chiado ♦ *vi* respirar ruidosamente.

when [wɛn] *adv* quando ♦ *conj* quando; (*whereas*) ao passo que; **on the day ~ I met him** no dia em que o conheci.

whenever [wɛn'ɛvə*] *conj* quando, quando quer que; (*every time that*) sempre que ♦ *adv* quando você quiser.

where [wɛə*] *adv* onde ♦ *conj* onde, aonde; **this is ~** aqui é onde; **~ are you from?** de onde você é?

whereabouts ['wɛərəbauts] *adv* (por) onde ♦ *n*: **nobody knows his ~** ninguém sabe o seu paradeiro.

whereas [wɛər'æz] *conj* uma vez que, ao passo que.

whereby [wɛə'baɪ] *adv* (*formal*) pelo qual (*or* pela qual *etc*).

whereupon [wɛərə'pɔn] *adv* depois do que.

wherever [wɛər'ɛvə*] *adv* onde quer que; (*interrogative*) onde?; **sit ~ you like** sente-se onde quiser.

wherewithal ['wɛəwɪðɔːl] *n* recursos *mpl*, meios *mpl*.

whet [wɛt] *vt* afiar; (*appetite*) abrir.

whether ['wɛðə*] *conj* se; **I don't know ~ to accept or not** não sei se aceito ou não; **~ you go or not** quer você vá quer não.

whey [weɪ] *n* soro (de leite).

which [wɪtʃ] *adj* (*interrogative*) que, qual ♦ *pron* (*interrogative*) qual; (*relative*: *subject*, *object*) que, o que, o qual, *etc*; **~ one of you?** qual de vocês?; **~ do you want?** qual você quer?; **~ picture do you want?** que quadro você quer?; **I don't mind ~** não me importa qual; **the apple ~ is on the table** a maçã que está sobre a mesa; **the chair on ~ you are sitting** a cadeira na qual você está sentado; **he said he knew, ~ is true** ele disse que sabia, o que é verdade; **in ~ case** em cujo caso; **after ~** depois do que; **by ~ time** momento em que.

whichever [wɪtʃ'ɛvə*] *adj*: **take ~ book you prefer** pegue o livro que preferir; **~ book you take** qualquer livro que você pegue.

whiff [wɪf] *n* baforada, cheiro; **to catch a ~ of sth** tomar o cheiro de algo.

while [waɪl] *n* tempo, momento ♦ *conj*

NB: *European Portuguese adds the following consonants to certain words*: **b** (sú(b)dito, su(b)til); **c** (a(c)ção, a(c)cionista, a(c)to); **m** (inde(m)ne); **p** (ado(p)ção, ado(p)tar); *for further details see p. xiii.*

enquanto; *(although)* embora; **for a ~ du-rante algum tempo; in a ~** daqui a pouco; **all the ~** todo o tempo; **we'll make it worth your ~** faremos com que valha a pena para você.

whilst [waɪlst] *conj* = **while**.

whim [wɪm] *n* capricho, veneta.

whimper ['wɪmpə*] *n (weeping)* choradeira; *(moan)* lamúria ♦ *vi* choramingar, soluçar.

whimsical ['wɪmzɪkl] *adj (person)* caprichoso, de veneta; *(look)* excêntrico.

whine [waɪn] *n (of pain)* gemido; *(of engine)* zunido ♦ *vi* gemer, zunir; *(dog)* ganir.

whip [wɪp] *n* açoite *m*; *(for riding)* chicote *m*; *(BRIT: POL)* líder *m/f* da bancada ♦ *vt* chico-tear; *(snatch)* apanhar de repente; *(cream)* bater.

whip up *vt (cream)* bater; *(inf: meal)* arrumar; *(stir up: feeling)* atiçar; *(: support)* angariar.

whiplash ['wɪplæʃ] *n (MED: also: ~ injury)* golpe *m* de chicote, chicotinho.

whipped cream [wɪpt-] *n* (creme *m*) chantilly *m*.

whipping boy ['wɪpɪŋ-] *n (fig)* bode *m* expiatório.

whip-round *n* coleta, vaquinha.

whirl [wə:l] *n* remoinho ♦ *vt* fazer rodar, rodo-piar ♦ *vi* girar; *(leaves, water etc)* redemoi-nhar.

whirlpool ['wə:lpu:l] *n* remoinho.

whirlwind ['wə:lwɪnd] *n* furacão *m*, remoinho.

whirr [wə:*] *vi* zumbir.

whisk [wɪsk] *n (CULIN)* batedeira ♦ *vt* bater; **to ~ sth away from sb** arrebatar algo de alguém; **to ~ sb away** *or* **off** levar rapida-mente alguém.

whiskers ['wɪskəz] *npl (of animal)* bigodes *mpl*; *(of man)* suíças *fpl*.

whisky ['wɪskɪ] *(IRISH, US* **whiskey**) *n* uísque *m (BRIT)*, whisky *m (PT)*.

whisper ['wɪspə*] *n* sussurro, murmúrio; *(ru-mour)* rumor *m* ♦ *vt, vi* sussurrar; **to ~ sth to sb** sussurrar algo para alguém.

whispering ['wɪspərɪŋ] *n* sussurros *mpl*.

whist [wɪst] *(BRIT)* *n* uíste *m (BR)*, whist *m (PT)*.

whistle ['wɪsl] *n (sound)* assobio; *(object)* api-to ♦ *vt, vi* assobiar.

whistle-stop *adj:* **to make a ~ tour** *(POL)* fazer uma viagem eleitoral.

Whit [wɪt] *n* Pentecostes *m*.

white [waɪt] *adj* branco; *(pale)* pálido ♦ *n* branco; *(of egg)* clara; **the ~s** *npl (washing)* a roupa branca; **tennis ~s** traje *m* de tênis; **to turn** *or* **go ~** *(person)* ficar branco *or* páli-do; *(hair)* ficar grisalho.

whitebait ['waɪtbeɪt] *n* filhote *m* de arenque.

white coffee *(BRIT)* *n* café *m* com leite.

white-collar worker *n* empregado/a de escritório.

white elephant *n (fig)* elefante *m* branco.

white goods *n* eletrodomésticos *mpl*.

white-hot *adj (metal)* incandescente.

white lie *n* mentira inofensiva *or* social.

whiteness ['waɪtnɪs] *n* brancura.

white noise *n* ruído branco.

whiteout ['waɪtaut] *n* resplendor *m* branco.

white paper *n (POL)* livro branco.

whitewash ['waɪtwɔʃ] *n (paint)* cal *f* ♦ *vt* caiar; *(fig)* encobrir.

whiting ['waɪtɪŋ] *n inv* pescada-marlonga.

Whit Monday *n* segunda-feira de Pente-costes.

Whitsun ['wɪtsn] *n* Pentecostes *m*.

whittle ['wɪtl] *vt* aparar; **to ~ away, ~ down** reduzir gradualmente, corroer.

whizz [wɪz] *vi* zunir; **to ~ past** *or* **by** passar a toda velocidade.

whizz kid *(inf)* *n* prodígio.

WHO *n abbr* (= *World Health Organization)* OMS *f*.

who [hu:] *pron (relative)* que, o qual *etc*, quem; *(interrogative)* quem?

whodunit [hu:'dʌnɪt] *(inf)* *n* romance *m (or* filme *m)* policial.

whoever [hu:'ɛvə*] *pron:* **~ finds it** quem quer que *or* seja quem for que o encontre; **ask ~ you like** pergunte a quem quiser; **~ he marries** não importa com quem se case; **~ told you that?** quem te disse isso pelo amor de Deus?

whole [həul] *adj (complete)* todo, inteiro; *(not broken)* intacto ♦ *n (total)* total *m*; *(sum)* conjunto; **the ~ lot (of it)** tudo; **the ~ lot (of them)** todos/as; **the ~ of the time** o tempo todo; **the ~ of the town** toda a cidade, a ci-dade inteira; **~ villages were destroyed** lu-garejos inteiros foram destruídos; **on the ~, as a ~** como um todo, no conjunto.

wholehearted [həul'ha:tɪd] *adj* sincero, irres-trito.

wholemeal ['həulmi:l] *(BRIT)* *adj (flour, bread)* integral.

whole note *(US)* *n* semibreve *f*.

wholesale ['həulseɪl] *n* venda por atacado ♦ *adj* por atacado; *(destruction)* em grande escala.

wholesaler ['həulseɪlə*] *n* atacadista *m/f*.

wholesome ['həulsəm] *adj* saudável, sadio.

wholewheat ['həulwi:t] *adj (flour, bread)* integral.

wholly ['həulɪ] *adv* totalmente, completa-mente.

whom [hu:m] *pron* que, o qual, quem; *(interrogative)* quem?; **those to ~ I spoke** aqueles com os quais eu falei.

whooping cough ['hu:pɪŋ-] *n* coqueluche *f*.

whoosh [wuʃ] *n* chio.

whopper ['wɔpə*] *(inf)* *n (lie)* lorota; *(large thing)*: **it was a ~** era enorme.

whopping ['wɔpɪŋ] *(inf)* *adj (big)* imenso.

whore [hɔ:*] *(pej)* *n* puta.

whose [hu:z] *adj:* **~ book is this?** de quem é este livro? ♦ *pron:* **~ is this?** de quem é isto?; **I know ~ it is** eu sei de quem é; **~ pen have you taken?** de quem é a caneta que você pegou?, você pegou a caneta de quem?; **the man ~ son you rescued** o ho-mem cujo filho você salvou; **the girl ~ sister**

you were speaking to a menina com cuja irmã você estava falando.
Who's Who n Quem é quem (registro de notabilidades).
why [waɪ] adv por que (BR), porque (PT); (at end of sentence) por quê (BR) porquê (PT) ♦ excl ora essa!, bem!; **tell me** ~ diga-me por quê; **the reason** ~ a razão por que.
whyever [waɪ'ɛvə*] adv mas por que.
WI n abbr (BRIT: = Women's Institute) associação de mulheres ♦ abbr (GEO) = **West Indies**; (US: POST) = **Wisconsin**.
wick [wɪk] n mecha, pavio.
wicked ['wɪkɪd] adj malvado; (mischievous) malicioso; (inf: terrible: prices, waste) terrível.
wicker ['wɪkə*] n (also: ~work) (trabalho de) vime m.
wicket ['wɪkɪt] n (CRICKET) arco.
wicket keeper n (CRICKET) guarda-meta m (no críquete).
wide [waɪd] adj largo; (broad) extenso, amplo; (region, knowledge) vasto; (choice) variado ♦ adv: **to open** ~ abrir totalmente; **to shoot** ~ atirar longe do alvo; **it is 4 metres** ~ tem 4 metros de largura.
wide-angle lens n lente f grande angular.
wide-awake adj bem acordado; (fig) vivo, esperto.
wide-eyed [-aɪd] adj de olhos arregalados; (fig) ingênuo.
widely ['waɪdlɪ] adv (different) extremamente; **it is** ~ **believed that ...** há uma convicção generalizada de que ...; **to be** ~ **read** ser muito lido.
widen ['waɪdən] vt alargar.
wideness ['waɪdnɪs] n largura; (breadth) extensão f.
wide open adj (eyes) arregalado; (door) escancarado.
wide-ranging [-'reɪndʒɪŋ] adj (survey, report) abrangente; (interests) diversos.
widespread ['waɪdspred] adj (belief etc) difundido, comum.
widow ['wɪdəu] n viúva.
widowed ['wɪdəud] adj viúvo.
widower ['wɪdəuə*] n viúvo.
width [wɪdθ] n largura; **it's 7 metres in** ~ tem 7 metros de largura.
widthways ['wɪdθweɪz] adv transversalmente.
wield [wiːld] vt (sword) brandir, empunhar; (power) exercer.
wife [waɪf] (pl **wives**) n mulher f, esposa.
wig [wɪg] n peruca.
wigging ['wɪgɪŋ] (BRIT: inf) n sabão m, descompostura.
wiggle ['wɪgl] vt menear, agitar ♦ vi menear, agitar-se.
wiggly ['wɪglɪ] adj (line) ondulado.
wild [waɪld] adj (animal) selvagem; (plant) silvestre; (rough) violento, furioso; (idea) disparatado, extravagante; (person) louco,

insensato; (enthusiastic): **to be** ~ **about** ser louco por ♦ n: **the** ~ a natureza; **~s** npl regiões fpl selvagens, terras fpl virgens.
wild card n (COMPUT) carácter m de substituição.
wildcat ['waɪldkæt] n gato selvagem; (US: lynx) lince m.
wildcat strike n greve espontánea e não autorizada pelo sindicato.
wilderness ['wɪldənɪs] n ermo; (in Brazil) sertão m.
wildfire ['waɪldfaɪə*] n: **to spread like** ~ espalhar-se rapidamente.
wild-goose chase n (fig) busca inútil.
wildlife ['waɪldlaɪf] n animais (e plantas) selvagens.
wildly ['waɪldlɪ] adv (roughly) violentamente; (foolishly) loucamente; (rashly) desenfreadamente.
wiles [waɪlz] npl artimanhas fpl, estratagemas mpl.
wilful ['wɪlful] (US **willful**) adj (person) teimoso, voluntarioso; (action) deliberado, intencional; (crime) premeditado.
will [wɪl] (conditional **would**) aux vb: **he** ~ **come** ele virá; ♦ vt (pt, pp ~**ed**): **to** ~ **sb to do sth** desejar que alguém faça algo ♦ n vontade f; (testament) testamento; **you won't lose it,** ~ **you?** não vai perder isto, tá?; **that** ~ **be the postman** deve ser o carteiro; ~ **you sit down** queira sentar-se; **the car won't start** o carro não quer pegar; **he** ~**ed himself to go on** reuniu grande força de vontade para continuar; **to do sth of one's own free** ~ fazer algo de livre vontade; **against one's** ~ a contragosto.
willful ['wɪlful] (US) adj = **wilful**.
willing ['wɪlɪŋ] adj (with goodwill) disposto, pronto; (submissive) complacente ♦ n: **to show** ~ mostrar boa vontade; **he's** ~ **to do it** ele é disposto a fazê-lo.
willingly ['wɪlɪŋlɪ] adv de bom grado, de boa vontade.
willingness ['wɪlɪŋnɪs] n boa vontade f, disposição f.
will-o'-the-wisp n fogo-fátuo; (fig) quimera.
willow ['wɪləu] n salgueiro.
will power n força de vontade.
willy-nilly ['wɪlɪ'nɪlɪ] adv quer queira ou não.
wilt [wɪlt] vi murchar, definhar.
Wilts [wɪlts] (BRIT) abbr = **Wiltshire**.
wily ['waɪlɪ] adj esperto, astuto.
wimp [wɪmp] (inf) n banana m.
win [wɪn] (pt, pp **won**) n (in sports etc) vitória ♦ vt ganhar, vencer; (obtain) conseguir, obter ♦ vi ganhar.
win over vt conquistar.
win round (BRIT) vt conquistar.
wince [wɪns] vi encolher-se, estremecer ♦ n estremecimento.
winch [wɪntʃ] n guincho.
Winchester disk ['wɪntʃestə*-] n (COMPUT)

NB: European Portuguese adds the following consonants to certain words: **b** (sú(b)dito, su(b)til); **c** (a(c)ção, a(c)cionista, a(c)to); **m** (inde(m)ne); **p** (ado(p)ção, ado(p)tar); for further details see p. xiii.

(disco) Winchester m.

wind¹ [wɪnd] n vento; (MED) gases mpl, flatulência; (breath) fôlego ♦ vt (take breath away from) deixar sem fôlego; **the ~(s)** (MUS) instrumentos mpl de sopro; **into** or **against the** ~ contra o vento; **to get** ~ **of** sth (fig) ter notícia de algo, tomar conhecimento de algo; **to break** ~ soltar gases intestinais.

wind² [waɪnd] (pt, pp **wound**) vt enrolar, bobinar; (wrap) envolver; (clock, toy) dar corda a ♦ vi (road, river) serpentear.

wind down vt (car window) abaixar, abrir; (fig: production, business) diminuir gradativamente.

wind up vt (clock) dar corda em; (debate) rematar, concluir.

windbreak ['wɪndbreɪk] n quebra-ventos m.

windbreaker ['wɪndbreɪkə*] (US) n anoraque m.

windcheater ['wɪndtʃiːtə*] (BRIT) n anoraque m.

winder ['waɪndə*] (BRIT) n (on watch) botão m de corda.

windfall ['wɪndfɔːl] n golpe m de sorte.

winding ['waɪndɪŋ] adj (road) sinuoso, tortuoso; (staircase) de caracol, em espiral.

wind instrument n (MUS) instrumento de sopro.

windmill ['wɪndmɪl] n moinho de vento.

window ['wɪndəu] n janela; (in shop etc) vitrine f (BR), montra (PT).

window box n jardineira (no peitoril da janela).

window cleaner n (person) limpador(a) m/f de janelas.

window dressing n decoração f de vitrines.

window envelope n envelope m de janela.

window frame n caixilho da janela.

window ledge n peitoril m da janela.

window pane n vidraça, vidro.

window-shopping n: **to go** ~ ir ver vitrines.

windowsill ['wɪndəusɪl] n peitoril m, soleira.

windpipe ['wɪndpaɪp] n traquéia.

windscreen ['wɪndskriːn] (BRIT) n pára-brisa m.

windscreen washer (BRIT) n lavador m de pára-brisa.

windscreen wiper [-'waɪpə*] (BRIT) n limpador m de pára-brisa.

windshield etc ['wɪndʃiːld] (US) n = **windscreen** etc.

windswept ['wɪndswept] adj varrido pelo vento.

wind tunnel n túnel m aerodinâmico.

windy ['wɪndɪ] adj com muito vento, batido pelo vento; **it's** ~ está ventando (BR), faz vento (PT).

wine [waɪn] n vinho ♦ vt: **to** ~ **and dine sb** levar alguém para jantar.

wine cellar n adega.

wine glass n cálice m (de vinho).

wine list n lista de vinhos.

wine merchant n negociante m/f de vinhos.

wine tasting [-'teɪstɪŋ] n degustação f de vinhos.

wine waiter n garção m dos vinhos

wing [wɪŋ] n asa; (of building) ala; (AUT) aleta, pára-lamas m inv; ~s npl (THEATRE) bastidores mpl.

winger ['wɪŋə*] n (SPORT) ponta, extremo.

wing mirror (BRIT) n espelho lateral.

wing nut n porca borboleta.

wingspan ['wɪŋspæn] n envergadura.

wingspread ['wɪŋspred] n envergadura.

wink [wɪŋk] n piscadela ♦ vi piscar o olho; (light etc) piscar.

winkle ['wɪŋkl] n búzio.

winner ['wɪnə*] n vencedor(a) m/f.

winning ['wɪnɪŋ] adj (team) vencedor(a); (goal) decisivo; (manner) sedutor(a).

winning post n meta de chegada.

winnings ['wɪnɪŋz] npl ganhos mpl.

winsome ['wɪnsəm] adj encantador(a), cativante.

winter ['wɪntə*] n inverno ♦ vi hibernar.

winter sports npl esportes mpl (BR) or desportos mpl (PT) de inverno.

wintry ['wɪntrɪ] adj glacial, invernal.

wipe [waɪp] n: **to give sth a** ~ limpar algo com um pano ♦ vt limpar; **to** ~ **one's nose** limpar o nariz.

wipe off vt remover esfregando.

wipe out vt (debt) liquidar; (memory) apagar; (destroy) exterminar.

wipe up vt (liquid) limpar; (dishes) enxugar.

wire ['waɪə*] n arame m; (ELEC) fio (elétrico); (TEL) telegrama m ♦ vt (house) instalar a rede elétrica em; (also: ~ up) conectar; (TEL) telegrafar para.

wire brush n escova de aço.

wire cutters [-'kʌtəz] npl alicate m corta-arame.

wireless ['waɪəlɪs] (BRIT) n rádio.

wire netting n rede f de arame.

wire-tapping [-'tæpɪŋ] n escuta telefônica.

wiring ['waɪərɪŋ] n instalação f elétrica.

wiry ['waɪərɪ] adj nervoso.

wisdom ['wɪzdəm] n sabedoria, sagacidade f; (good sense) bom senso; (care) prudência.

wisdom tooth (irreg) n dente m do siso.

wise [waɪz] adj sábio; (sensible) sensato; (careful) prudente; **I'm none the** ~**r** eu não entendi nada.

wise up (inf) vi: **to** ~ **up to** abrir os olhos para.

...wise [waɪz] suffix: **time**~ com relação ao tempo.

wisecrack ['waɪzkræk] n piada.

wish [wɪʃ] n (desire) desejo ♦ vt desejar; (want) querer; **best** ~**es** (on birthday etc) parabéns mpl, felicidades fpl; **with best** ~**es** (in letter) cumprimentos; **give her my best** ~**es** dá um abraço para ela; **to** ~ **sb goodbye** despedir-se de alguém; **he** ~**ed me well** me desejou boa sorte; **to** ~ **to do/sb to do sth** querer fazer/que alguém faça algo; **to** ~ **for** desejar; **to** ~ **sth on sb** desejar algo a alguém.

wishful ['wɪʃful] adj: **it's** ~ **thinking** é doce ilusão.

wishy-washy ['wɪʃɪ'wɔʃɪ] (inf) adj (person) sem caráter; (ideas, thinking) aguado.

wisp [wɪsp] n mecha, tufo; (of smoke) fio.

wistful ['wɪstful] adj melancólico, saudoso.

wit [wɪt] n (wittiness) presença de espírito, engenho; (intelligence) entendimento; (person) espirituoso/a; **to be at one's** ~**s' end** (fig) não saber para onde se virar; **to have one's** ~**s about one** ter uma presença de espírito; **to** ~ a saber.

witch [wɪtʃ] n bruxa.

witchcraft ['wɪtʃkrɑːft] n bruxaria.

witch doctor n médico feiticeiro, pajé m (BR).

witch-hunt n caça às bruxas.

with [wɪð, wɪθ] prep com; **red** ~ **anger** vermelho de raiva; **the man** ~ **the grey hat** o homem do chapéu cinza; **to tremble** ~ **fear** tremer de medo; **to stay overnight** ~ **friends** dormir na casa de amigos; **to be** ~ **it** (fig: aware) estar a par da situação; **I am** ~ **you** (I understand) compreendo.

withdraw [wɪð'drɔː] (irreg) vt tirar, remover ♦ vi retirar-se; (go back on promise) voltar atrás; **to** ~ **money (from the bank)** retirar dinheiro (do banco); **to** ~ **into o.s.** introverter-se.

withdrawal [wɪð'drɔːəl] n retirada.

withdrawal symptoms npl síndrome f de abstinência; **to have** ~ ter uma reação.

withdrawn [wɪð'drɔːn] pp of **withdraw** ♦ adj (person) reservado, introvertido.

wither ['wɪðə*] vi murchar.

withered ['wɪðəd] adj murcho.

withhold [wɪð'həuld] (irreg) vt (money) reter; (decision) adiar; (permission) negar; (information) esconder.

within [wɪð'ɪn] prep dentro de ♦ adv dentro; ~ **reach** ao alcance da mão; ~ **sight** à vista; ~ **the week** antes do fim da semana; ~ **an hour from now** daqui a uma hora; **to be** ~ **the law** estar dentro da lei.

without [wɪð'aut] prep sem; ~ **anybody knowing** sem ninguém saber; **to go** or **do** ~ **sth** passar sem algo.

withstand [wɪð'stænd] (irreg) vt resistir a.

witness ['wɪtnɪs] n (person) testemunha; (evidence) testemunho ♦ vt (event) testemunhar, presenciar; (document) legalizar; **to bear** ~ **to sth** testemunhar algo; ~ **for the prosecution/defence** testemunha para acusação/defesa; **to** ~ **to sth/having seen sth** testemunhar algo/ter visto algo.

witness box (US **witness stand**) n banco das testemunhas.

witticism ['wɪtɪsɪzm] n observação f espirituosa, chiste m.

witty ['wɪtɪ] adj espirituoso, engenhoso.

wives [waɪvz] npl of **wife**.

wizard ['wɪzəd] n feiticeiro, mago.

wizened ['wɪznd] adj encarquilhado.

wk abbr = **week**.

Wm. abbr = **William**.

WO n abbr = **warrant officer**.

wobble ['wɔbl] vi oscilar; (chair) balançar.

wobbly ['wɔblɪ] adj (table) balançante, bambo.

woe [wəu] n dor f, mágoa.

woke [wəuk] pt of **wake**.

woken ['wəukən] pp of **wake**.

wolf [wulf] (pl **wolves**) n lobo.

wolves [wulvz] npl of **wolf**.

woman ['wumən] (pl **women**) n mulher f ♦ cpd: ~ **doctor** médica; ~ **teacher** professora; **young** ~ mulher jovem; **women's page** (PRESS) página da mulher.

womanize ['wumənaɪz] vi paquerar as mulheres.

womanly ['wumənlɪ] adj feminino.

womb [wuːm] n (ANAT) matriz f, útero.

women ['wɪmɪn] npl of **woman**.

Women's (Liberation) Movement n (also: women's lib) Movimento pela Libertação da Mulher.

won [wʌn] pt, pp of **win**.

wonder ['wʌndə*] n maravilha, prodígio; (feeling) espanto ♦ vi: **to** ~ **whether** perguntar-se a si mesmo se; **to** ~ **at** admirar-se de; **to** ~ **about** pensar sobre or em; **it's no** ~ **that** não é de admirar que.

wonderful ['wʌndəful] adj maravilhoso.

wonderfully ['wʌndəfulɪ] adv maravilhosamente.

wonky ['wɔŋkɪ] (BRIT) adj errado, torto.

won't [wəunt] = **will not**.

woo [wuː] vt (woman) namorar, cortejar.

wood [wud] n (timber) madeira; (forest) floresta, bosque m; (firewood) lenha ♦ cpd de madeira.

wood carving n escultura em madeira, entalhe m.

wooded ['wudɪd] adj arborizado.

wooden ['wudən] adj de madeira; (fig) inexpressivo.

woodland ['wudlənd] n floresta, bosque m.

woodpecker ['wudpekə*] n pica-pau m.

wood pigeon n pombo torcaz.

woodwind ['wudwɪnd] n (MUS) instrumentos mpl de sopro de madeira.

woodwork ['wudwəːk] n carpintaria.

woodworm ['wudwəːm] n carcoma, caruncho.

woof [wuf] n (of dog) latido ♦ vi latir; ~, ~! au-au!

wool [wul] n lã f; **to pull the** ~ **over sb's eyes** (fig) enganar alguém, vender a alguém gato por lebre.

woollen ['wulən] (US **woolen**) adj de lã.

woollens ['wulənz] (US **woolens**) npl artigos mpl de lã.

woolly ['wulɪ] (US **wooly**) adj lanoso; (fig: ideas) confuso.

NB: European Portuguese adds the following consonants to certain words: **b** (sú(b)dito, su(b)til); **c** (a(c)ção, a(c)cionista, a(c)to); **m** (inde(m)ne); **p** (ado(p)ção, ado(p)tar); *for further details see p. xiii.*

word [wəːd] *n* palavra; (*news*) notícia; (*message*) aviso ♦ *vt* (*express*) expressar; (*document*) redigir; **in other ~s** em outras palavras, ou seja; **to break/keep one's ~** faltar à palavra/cumprir a promessa; **~ for ~** ao pé da letra; **what's the ~ for "pen" in Portuguese?** como se fala "pen" em português?; **to put sth into ~s** expressar algo; **to have a ~ with sb** falar com alguém; **to have ~s with sb** discutir com alguém; **I'll take your ~ for it** acredito em você; **to send ~ that ...** mandar dizer que ...; **to leave ~ that ...** deixar recado dizendo que ....

wording ['wəːdɪŋ] *n* fraseio.

word-perfect *adj*: **he was ~ in his speech** *etc*, **his speech** *etc* **was ~** ele sabia o discurso de cor.

word processing *n* processamento de textos.

word processor [-'prəusɛsə*] *n* processador *m* de textos.

wordwrap ['wəːdræp] *n* (*COMPUT*) marginação *f* automática.

wordy ['wəːdɪ] *adj* prolixo, verboso.

wore [wɔː*] *pt of* **wear**.

work [wəːk] *n* trabalho; (*job*) emprego, trabalho; (*ART, LITERATURE*) obra ♦ *vi* trabalhar; (*mechanism*) funcionar; (*medicine*) surtir efeito, ser eficaz; (*plan*) dar certo ♦ *vt* (*wood etc*) talhar; (*mine etc*) explorar; (*machine*) fazer trabalhar, manejar; **~s** *n* (*BRIT*: *factory*) fábrica, usina ♦ *npl* (*of clock, machine*) mecanismo; **road ~s** obras *fpl* (na estrada); **to go to ~** ir trabalhar; **to set to ~**, **to start ~** começar a trabalhar; **to be at ~ (on sth)** estar trabalhando (em algo); **to be out of ~** estar desempregado; **to ~ hard** trabalhar muito; **to ~ loose** (*part*) soltar-se; (*knot*) afrouxar-se.

work on *vt fus* trabalhar em, dedicar-se a; (*principle*) basear-se em.

work out *vi* (*plans etc*) dar certo, surtir efeito ♦ *vt* (*problem*) resolver; (*plan*) elaborar, formular; **it ~s out at £100** monta *or* soma a 100 libras.

workable ['wəːkəbl] *adj* (*solution*) viável.

workaholic [wəːkə'hɔlɪk] *n* burro de carga.

workbench ['wəːkbɛntʃ] *n* banco, bancada.

worked up [wəːkt-] *adj*: **to get ~** ficar exaltado.

worker ['wəːkə*] *n* trabalhador(a) *m/f*, operário/a; **office ~** empregado/a de escritório.

work force *n* força de trabalho.

work-in (*BRIT*) *n* ocupação *f* de fábrica *etc* (*sem paralisação da produção*).

working ['wəːkɪŋ] *adj* (*day, tools etc, conditions*) de trabalha; (*wife*) que trabalha; (*population, partner*) ativo; **in ~ order** em bom estado de funcionamento; **a ~ knowledge of English** um conhecimento prático do inglês.

working capital *n* (*COMM*) capital *m* de giro.

working class ['wəːkɪŋ-] *n* proletariado, classe *f* operária ♦ *adj*: **working-class** do proletariado, da classe operária.

working man (*irreg*) *n* trabalhador *m*.

working model *n* modelo articulado.

working party (*BRIT*) *n* grupo de trabalho.

working week *n* semana de trabalho.

work-in-progress *n* (*COMM*) produção *f* em curso.

workload ['wəːkləud] *n* carga de trabalho.

workman ['wəːkmən] (*irreg*) *n* operário, trabalhador *m*.

workmanship ['wəːkmənʃɪp] *n* (*art*) acabamento; (*skill*) habilidade *f*.

workmate ['wəːkmeɪt] *n* colega *m/f* de trabalho.

workout ['wəːkaut] *n* treinamento, treino.

work permit *n* permissão *f* de trabalho.

works council *n* comissão *f* de operários.

work sheet *n* registro das horas de trabalho; (*COMPUT*) folha de trabalho.

workshop ['wəːkʃɔp] *n* oficina.

work station *n* estação *f* de trabalho.

work study *n* estudo de trabalho.

work-to-rule (*BRIT*) *n* paralisação *f* de trabalho extraordinário.

world [wəːld] *n* mundo ♦ *cpd* mundial; **to think the ~ of sb** (*fig*) ter alguém em alto conceito; **all over the ~** no mundo inteiro; **what in the ~ is he doing?** o que é que ele está fazendo, pelo amor de Deus?; **to do sb a ~ of good** fazer muito bem a alguém; **W~ War One/Two** Primeira/Segunda Guerra Mundial; **out of this ~** sensacional.

World Cup *n*: **the ~** (*FOOTBALL*) a Copa do Mundo.

world-famous *adj* de fama mundial.

worldly ['wəːldlɪ] *adj* mundano.

world-wide *adj* mundial, universal ♦ *adv* no mundo inteiro.

worm [wəːm] *n* verme *m*; (*earth~*) minhoca, lombriga.

worn [wɔːn] *pp of* **wear** ♦ *adj* usado.

worn-out *adj* (*object*) gasto; (*person*) esgotado, exausto.

worried ['wʌrɪd] *adj* preocupado; **to be ~ about sth** estar preocupado com algo.

worrier ['wʌrɪə*] *n*: **he's a ~** ele se preocupa com tudo.

worry ['wʌrɪ] *n* preocupação *f* ♦ *vt* preocupar, inquietar ♦ *vi* preocupar-se, afligir-se; **to ~ about** *or* **over sth/sb** preocupar-se com algo/ alguém.

worrying ['wʌrɪɪŋ] *adj* inquietante, preocupante.

worse [wəːs] *adj, adv* pior ♦ *n* o pior; **a change for the ~** uma mudança para pior, uma piora; **to get ~** piorar; **he's none the ~ for it** não lhe fez mal; **so much the ~ for you!** pior para você!

worsen ['wəːsən] *vt, vi* piorar.

worse off *adj* com menos dinheiro; (*fig*): **you'll be ~ this way** assim você ficará pior que nunca.

worship ['wəːʃɪp] *n* culto; (*act*) adoração *f* ♦ *vt* adorar, venerar; **Your W~** (*BRIT*: *to mayor*) vossa Excelência; (: *to judge*) senhor Juiz.

worshipper ['wəːʃɪpə*] *n* devoto/a, venerador(a) *m/f*.

worst [wɔːst] *adj* (o/a) pior ♦ *adv* pior ♦ *n* o pior; **at** ~ na pior das hipóteses; **if the** ~ **comes to the** ~ se o pior acontecer.

worsted ['wɔːstɪd] *n*: (**wool**) ~ lã *f* penteada.

worth [wɔːθ] *n* valor *m*, mérito ♦ *adj*: **to be** ~ valer; **it's** ~ **it** vale a pena; **how much is it** ~? quanto vale?; **50 pence** ~ **of apples** maçãs no valor de 50 pence.

worthless ['wɔːθlɪs] *adj* sem valor; (*useless*) inútil.

worthwhile [wɔːθ'waɪl] *adj* (*activity*) que vale a pena; (*cause*) de mérito, louvável; **a** ~ **book** um livro que vale a pena ler.

worthy ['wɔːðɪ] *adj* (*person*) merecedor(a), respeitável; (*motive*) justo; ~ **of** digno de.

would [wud] *aux vb*: **she** ~ **come** ela viria; **he** ~ **have come** ele teria vindo; ~ **you like a biscuit?** você quer um biscoito?; **he** ~ **go on Mondays** costumava ir às segundas-feiras; ~ **you close the door, please?** quer fechar a porta por favor?; **you WOULD say that,** ~**n't you?** é lógico que você vai dizer isso; **she** ~**n't leave** ele não queria sair.

would-be (*pej*) *adj* aspirante, que pretende ser.

wound¹ [waund] *pt, pp of* **wind**.

wound² [wuːnd] *n* ferida ♦ *vt* ferir.

wove [wəuv] *pt of* **weave**.

woven ['wəuvən] *pp of* **weave**.

WP *n* *abbr* = **word processing**; **word processor** ♦ *abbr* (*BRIT*: *inf*) = **weather permitting**.

WPC (*BRIT*) *n* *abbr* = **woman police constable**.

wpm *abbr* (= *words per minute*) palavras por minuto.

WRAC (*BRIT*) *n* *abbr* = **Women's Royal Army Corps**.

WRAF (*BRIT*) *n* *abbr* = **Women's Royal Air Force**.

wrangle ['ræŋgl] *n* briga ♦ *vi* brigar.

wrap [ræp] *n* (*stole*) xale *m*; (*cape*) capa ♦ *vt* (*also*: ~ *up*) embrulhar; **under** ~**s** (*fig*: *plan, scheme*) em sigilo.

wrapper ['ræpə*] *n* envoltório, invólucro; (*BRIT*: *of book*) capa.

wrapping paper ['ræpɪŋ-] *n* papel *m* de embrulho.

wrath [rɔθ] *n* cólera, ira.

wreak [riːk] *vt* (*destruction*) causar; **to** ~ **havoc** causar estragos; **to** ~ **vengeance on** vingar-se em, tirar vingança de.

wreath [riːθ, *pl* riːðz] *n* (*funeral* ~) coroa; (*of flowers*) grinalda.

wreathe [riːð] *vt* trançar, cingir.

wreck [rɛk] *n* naufrágio; (*ship*) restos *mpl* do naufrágio; (*pej*: *person*) ruína, caco ♦ *vt* destruir, danificar; (*fig*) arruinar, arrasar.

wreckage ['rɛkɪdʒ] *n* restos *mpl*; (*of building*) escombros *mpl*.

wrecker ['rɛkə*] *n* (*US*) (*breakdown van*) rebo-

que *m* (*BR*), pronto socorro (*PT*).

WREN [rɛn] (*BRIT*) *n* *abbr* membro do WRNS.

wren [rɛn] *n* (*ZOOL*) carriça.

wrench [rɛntʃ] *n* (*TECH*) chave *f* inglesa; (*tug*) puxão *m*; (*fig*) separação *f* penosa ♦ *vt* arrancar; **to** ~ **sth from sb** arrancar algo de alguém.

wrest [rɛst] *vt*: **to** ~ **sth from sb** extorquir algo de *or* a alguém.

wrestle ['rɛsl] *vi*: **to** ~ (**with sb**) lutar (com *or* contra alguém); **to** ~ **with** (*fig*) lutar com.

wrestler ['rɛslə*] *n* lutador *m*.

wrestling ['rɛslɪŋ] *n* luta (livre).

wrestling match *n* partida de luta romana.

wretch [rɛtʃ] *n* desgraçado/a; **little** ~! (*often humorous*) seu desgraçado!

wretched ['rɛtʃɪd] *adj* desventurado, infeliz; (*inf*) maldito.

wriggle ['rɪgl] *n* contorção *f* ♦ *vi* retorcer-se, contorcer-se.

wring [rɪŋ] (*pt, pp* **wrung**) *vt* torcer, espremer; (*wet clothes*) torcer; (*fig*): **to** ~ **sth out of sb** arrancar algo de alguém.

wringer ['rɪŋə*] *n* máquina de espremer roupa.

wringing ['rɪŋɪŋ] *adj* (*also*: ~ *wet*) encharcado, ensopado.

wrinkle ['rɪŋkl] *n* (*on skin*) ruga; (*on paper*) prega ♦ *vt* franzir, preguear ♦ *vi* enrugar-se; (*cloth etc*) franzir-se.

wrinkled ['rɪŋkld] *adj* (*fabric, paper*) franzido, pregueado; (*surface, skin*) enrugado.

wrinkly ['rɪŋklɪ] *adj* (*fabric, paper*) franzido, pregueado; (*surface, skin*) enrugado.

wrist [rɪst] *n* pulso.

wristband ['rɪstbænd] (*BRIT*) *n* (*of shirt*) punho; (*of watch*) pulseira.

wrist watch *n* relógio *m* de pulso.

writ [rɪt] *n* mandado judicial; **to issue a** ~ **against sb, serve a** ~ **on sb** demandar judicialmente alguém.

write [raɪt] (*pt* **wrote**, *pp* **written**) *vt, vi* escrever; **to** ~ **sb a letter** escrever uma carta para alguém.

write away *vi*: **to** ~ **away for** (*information*) escrever pedindo; (*goods*) encomendar pelo correio.

write down *vt* escrever; (*note*) anotar.

write off *vt* (*debt*) cancelar; (*capital*) reduzir; (*smash up*: *car*) destroçar.

write out *vt* escrever por extenso; (*fair copy*) passar a limpo.

write up *vt* redigir.

write-off *n* perda total; **the car is a** ~ o carro virou sucata *or* está destroçado.

write-protect *vt* (*COMPUT*) proteger de escrita *or* contra gravação.

writer ['raɪtə*] *n* escritor(a) *m/f*.

write-up *n* crítica.

writhe [raɪð] *vi* contorcer-se.

writing ['raɪtɪŋ] *n* escrita; (*hand-*~) caligrafia,

NB: European Portuguese adds the following consonants to certain words: **b** (sú(b)dito, su(b)til); **c** (a(c)ção, a(c)cionista, a(c)to); **m** (inde(m)ne); **p** (ado(p)ção, ado(p)tar); *for further details see p. xiii.*

letra; (of author) obra; **in** ~ por escrito; **to put sth in** ~ pôr algo no papel; **in my own** ~ do próprio punho.

writing case n pasta com material de escrita.

writing desk n escrivaninha.

writing paper n papel m para escrever.

written ['rɪtn] pp of **write**.

WRNS (BRIT) n abbr = **Women's Royal Naval Service**.

wrong [rɔŋ] adj (bad) errado, mau; (unfair) injusto; (incorrect) errado, equivocado; (not suitable) impróprio, inconveniente ♦ adv mal, errado ♦ n mal m; (injustice) injustiça ♦ vt ser injusto com; (hurt) ofender; **to be** ~ estar errado; **you are** ~ **to do it** você se engana ao fazê-lo; **it's** ~ **to steal, stealing is** ~ é errado roubar; **you are** ~ **about that, you've got it** ~ você está enganado sobre isso; **to be in the** ~ não ter razão; **what's** ~? o que é que há?; **there's nothing** ~ não há nada de errado, não tem problema; **what's** ~ **with the car?** qual é o problema com o carro?; **to go** ~ (person) desencaminhar-se; (plan) dar errado; (machine) sofrer uma avaria.

wrongful ['rɔŋful] adj injusto; ~ **dismissal** demissão f injusta.

wrongly ['rɔŋlɪ] adv (treat) injustamente; (answer, do) errado.

wrong number n (TEL): **you have the** ~ o número está errado.

wrong side n (of cloth) avesso.

wrote [rəut] pt of **write**.

wrought [rɔːt] adj: ~ **iron** ferro forjado.

wrung [rʌŋ] pt, pp of **wring**.

WRVS (BRIT) n abbr (= Women's Royal Voluntary Service) instituição de caridade.

wry [raɪ] adj (smile) irônico; **to make a** ~ **face** fazer uma careta.

wt. abbr = **weight**.

WV (US) abbr (POST) = **West Virginia**.

WY (US) abbr (POST) = **Wyoming**.

WYSIWYG ['wɪzɪwɪg] abbr (COMPUT: = what you see is what you get) o documento sairá na impressora exatamente como aparece na tela.

X

X, x [ɛks] n (letter) X, x m; (BRIT: CINEMA: old) (proibido para menores de) 18 anos; **X for Xmas** X de Xavier; **if you have** ~ **dollars a year ...** se você tem x dólares por ano ....

Xerox ['zɪərɔks] ® n (also: ~ machine) xerox m ®; (photocopy) xerox m ®♦ vt xerocar, tirar um xerox de.

XL abbr = **extra large**.

Xmas ['ɛksməs] n abbr = **Christmas**.

X-rated [-'reɪtɪd] (US) adj (film) proibido para menores de 18 anos.

X-ray [ɛks'reɪ] n radiografia ♦ vt radiografar, tirar uma chapa de; ~**s** npl raios mpl X; **to have an** ~ tirar or bater um raio x.

xylophone ['zaɪləfəun] n xilofone m.

Y

Y, y [waɪ] n (letter) Y, y m; **Y for Yellow** (BRIT) or **Yoke** (US) Y de Yolanda.

yacht [jɔt] n iate m; (smaller) veleiro.

yachting ['jɔtɪŋ] n (sport) iatismo.

yachtsman ['jɔtsmən] (irreg) n iatista m.

yam [jæm] n inhame m.

Yank [jæŋk] (pej) n ianque m/f.

yank [jæŋk] vt arrancar.

Yankee ['jæŋkɪ] (pej) n ianque m/f.

yap [jæp] vi (dog) ganir.

yard [jɑːd] n pátio, quintal m; (US: garden) jardim m; (measure) jarda (= 914 mm; 3 feet); **builder's** ~ depósito de material de construção.

yardstick ['jɑːdstɪk] n (fig) critério, padrão m.

yarn [jɑːn] n fio; (tale) história inverossímil.

yawn [jɔːn] n bocejo ♦ vi bocejar.

yawning ['jɔːnɪŋ] adj (gap) enorme.

yd abbr = **yard(s)**.

yeah [jɛə] (inf) adv é.

year [jɪə*] n ano; **to be 8** ~**s old** ter 8 anos; **every** ~ todos os anos, todo ano; **this** ~ este ano; **a** or **per** ~ por ano; ~ **in,** ~ **out** entra ano, sai ano; **an eight-**~**-old child** uma criança de oito anos (de idade).

yearbook ['jɪəbuk] n anuário, almanaque m.

yearly ['jɪəlɪ] adj anual ♦ adv anualmente; **twice** ~ duas vezes por ano.

yearn [jɜːn] vi: **to** ~ **to do/for sth** ansiar fazer/por algo.

yearning ['jɜːnɪŋ] n ânsia, desejo ardente.

yeast [jiːst] n levedura, fermento.

yell [jɛl] n grito, berro ♦ vi gritar, berrar.

yellow ['jɛləu] adj, n amarelo.

yellow fever n febre f amarela.

yellowish ['jɛləuɪʃ] adj amarelado.

Yellow Sea n: **the** ~ o mar Amarelo.

yelp [jɛlp] n latido ♦ vi latir.

Yemen ['jɛmən] n Iêmen m (BR), Iémene m (PT).

yen [jɛn] n (currency) iene m; (craving): ~ **for/to do** desejo de/de fazer.

yeoman ['jəumən] (irreg) n: **Y**~ **of the Guard** membro da guarda real.

yes [jɛs] adv, n sim m; **do you speak English?** — ~ **I do** você fala inglês? — falo (sim); **does the plane leave at six?** — ~ o avião sai às seis? — é; **to say** ~ **to sth/sb** (ap-

prove) dar o sim a algo/alguém.

yesterday ['jɛstədɪ] *adv, n* ontem *m*; **the day before** ~ anteontem; ~ **morning/evening** ontem de manhã/à noite; **all day** ~ ontem o dia inteiro.

yet [jɛt] *adv* ainda ♦ *conj* porém, no entanto; **it is not finished** ~ ainda não está acabado; **must you go just** ~**?** você já tem que ir?; **the best** ~ o melhor até agora; **as** ~ até agora, ainda; **a few days** ~ mais alguns dias; ~ **again** mais uma vez.

yew [ju:] *n* teixo.

YHA (*BRIT*) *n abbr* = **Youth Hostels Association.**

Yiddish ['jɪdɪʃ] *n* (i)ídiche *m*.

yield [ji:ld] *n* produção *f*; (*AGR*) colheita; (*COMM*) rendimento ♦ *vt* (*gen*) produzir; (*profit*) render; (*surrender*) ceder ♦ *vi* (*give way*) render-se, ceder; (*US*: *AUT*) ceder; **a** ~ **of 5%** um rendimento de 5%.

YMCA *n abbr* (= *Young Men's Christian Association*) ≈ ACM *f*.

yob(bo) ['jɔb(əu)] (*BRIT*: *inf*) *n* bagunçeiro.

yodel ['jəudl] *vi* cantar tirolesa.

yoga ['jəugə] *n* ioga.

yog(h)ourt ['jəugət] *n* iogurte *m*.

yog(h)urt ['jəugət] *n* = **yog(h)ourt.**

yoke [jəuk] *n* canga, cangalha; (*pair of oxen*) junta; (*on shoulders*) balancim *m*; (*fig*) jugo ♦ *vt* (*also*: ~ *together*) unir, ligar.

yolk [jəuk] *n* gema (do ovo).

yonder ['jɔndə*] *adv* além, acolá.

Yorks [jɔ:ks] (*BRIT*) *abbr* = **Yorkshire.**

you [ju:] *pron* (*subject*) tu, você; (: *pl*) vós, vocês; (*direct object*) te, o/a; (: *pl*) vos, os/as; (*indirect object*) te, lhe; (: *pl*) vos, lhes; (*after prep*) ti, você; (: *pl*) vós, vocês; (*polite form*) o senhor/a senhora; (: *pl*) os senhores/as senhoras; (*one*): ~ **never know** nunca se sabe; **with** ~ contigo, com você; convosco, com vocês; com o senhor *etc*; **apples do** ~ **good** as maçãs fazem bem à saúde; **if I were** ~ se eu fosse você.

you'd [ju:d] = **you had; you would.**

you'll [ju:l] = **you will; you shall.**

young [jʌŋ] *adj* jovem ♦ *npl* (*of animal*) filhotes *mpl*, crias *fpl*; (*people*): **the** ~ a juventude, os jovens; **a** ~ **man** um jovem; **a** ~ **lady** (*unmarried*) uma jovem, uma moça; (*married*) uma jovem senhora; **my** ~**er brother** o meu irmão mais novo; **the** ~**er generation** a geração mais jovem.

youngish ['jʌŋɪʃ] *adj* bem novo.

youngster ['jʌŋstə*] *n* jovem *m/f*, moço/a.

your [jɔ:*] *adj* teu/tua, seu/sua; (*pl*) vosso, seu/sua; (*formal*) do senhor/da senhora.

you're [juə*] = **you are.**

yours [jɔ:z] *pron* teu/tua, seu/sua; (*pl*) vosso, seu/sua; (*formal*) do senhor/da senhora; ~ **is blue** o teu/a tua é azul; **is it** ~**?** é teu *etc*?; ~ **sincerely** *or* **faithfully** atenciosamente; **a friend of** ~ um amigo seu.

yourself [jɔ:'sɛlf] *pron* (*subject*) tu mesmo, você mesmo; (*direct/indirect object*) te, se; (*after prep*) ti mesmo, si mesmo; (*formal*) o senhor mesmo/a senhora mesma; **you** ~ **told me** você mesmo me falou; **(all) by** ~ sozinho/a.

yourselves [jɔ:'sɛlvz] *pron* (*subject*) vós mesmos, vocês mesmos; (*direct/indirect object*) vos, se; (*formal*) os senhores mesmos/as senhoras mesmas.

youth [ju:θ, *pl* ju:ðz] *n* mocidade *f*, juventude *f*; (*young man*) jovem *m*; **in my** ~ na minha juventude.

youth club *n* associação *f* de juventude.

youthful ['ju:θful] *adj* juvenil.

youthfulness ['ju:θfəlnəs] *n* juventude *f*.

youth hostel *n* albergue *m* da juventude.

you've [ju:v] = **you have.**

yowl [jaul] *n* uivo ♦ *vi* uivar.

YTS (*BRIT*) *n abbr* (= *Youth Training Scheme*) *programa de ensino profissionalizante.*

Yugoslav ['ju:gəusla:v] *adj, n* iugoslavo/a.

Yugoslavia [ju:gəu'sla:vɪə] *n* Iugoslávia.

Yugoslavian [ju:gəu'sla:vɪən] *adj* iugoslavo.

Yule [ju:l]: ~ **log** n acha de Natal.

Yuletide ['ju:ltaɪd] *n* época natalina *or* do Natal.

yuppie ['jʌpɪ] *n* yuppie *m/f*.

YWCA *n abbr* (= *Young Women's Christian Association*) ≈ ACM *f*.

Z

Z, z [zɛd, (*US*) zi:] *n* (*letter*) Z, z *m*; **Z for Zebra** Z de Zebra.

Zaire [zɑ:'i:ə*] *n* Zaire *m*.

Zambia ['zæmbɪə] *n* Zâmbia.

Zambian ['zæmbɪən] *adj, n* zambiano/a.

zany ['zeɪnɪ] *adj* tolo, bobo.

zap [zæp] *vt* (*COMPUT*) apagar.

zeal [zi:l] *n* zelo, fervor *m*.

zealot ['zɛlət] *n* fanático/a.

zealous ['zɛləs] *adj* zeloso, entusiasta.

zebra ['zi:brə] *n* zebra.

zebra crossing (*BRIT*) *n* faixa (para pedestres) (*BR*), passadeira (*PT*).

zenith ['zɛnɪθ] *n* (*ASTRONOMY*) zênite *m*; (*fig*) apogeu *m*.

zero ['zɪərəu] *n* zero ♦ *vi*: **to** ~ **in on** fazer mira em; **5° below** ~ 5 graus abaixo de zero.

zero hour *n* hora zero.

zero-rated [-'reɪtɪd] (*BRIT*) *adj* isento de IVA.

zest [zɛst] *n* vivacidade *f*, entusiasmo *m*; (*of lemon etc*) zesto.

zigzag ['zɪgzæg] *n* ziguezague *m* ♦ *vi* ziguezag-

NB: European Portuguese adds the following consonants to certain words: **b** (sú(b)dito, su(b)til); **c** (a(c)ção, a(c)cionista, a(c)to); **m** (inde(m)ne); **p** (ado(p)ção, ado(p)tar); *for further details see p. xiii.*

guear.

Zimbabwe [zɪm'bɑːbwɪ] *n* Zimbábue *m* (*BR*), Zimbabwe *m* (*PT*).

Zimbabwean [zɪm'bɑːbwɪən] *adj*, *n* zimbabuano/a (*BR*), zimbabweano/a (*PT*).

zinc [zɪŋk] *n* zinco.

Zionism ['zaɪənɪzm] *n* sionismo.

Zionist ['zaɪənɪst] *adj*, *n* sionista *m/f*.

zip [zɪp] *n* (*also*: ~ *fastener*, ~*per*) fecho ecler (*BR*) *or* éclair (*PT*); (*energy*) vigor *m* ♦ *vt* (*also*: ~ *up*) fechar o fecho ecler de, subir o fecho ecler de.

zip code (*US*) *n* código postal.

zither ['zɪðə*] *n* citara.

zodiac ['zəudɪæk] *n* zodíaco.

zombie ['zɔmbɪ] *n* (*fig*): **like a** ~ como um zumbi.

zone [zəun] *n* zona.

zoo [zuː] *n* (jardim *m*) zoológico.

zoological [zuə'lɔdʒɪkl] *adj* zoológico.

zoologist [zuː'ɔlədʒɪst] *n* zoólogo/a.

zoology [zuː'ɔlədʒɪ] *n* zoologia.

zoom [zuːm] *vi*: **to** ~ **past** passar zunindo; **to** ~ **in (on sb/sth)** (*PHOT*, *CINEMA*) fechar a câmera (em alguém/algo).

zoom lens *n* zoom *m*, zum *m*.

zucchini [zuː'kiːnɪ] (*US*) *n inv* abobrinha.

Zulu ['zuːluː] *adj*, *n* zulu *m/f*.

Zurich ['zjuərɪk] *n* Zurique.

PORTUGUÊS-INGLÊS
PORTUGUESE-ENGLISH

A

A, a [a] (*pl* **as**) *m* A, a; **A de Antônio** A for Andrew (*BRIT*) *ou* Able (*US*).

a [a] *art def* the ♦ *pron* her; (*você*) you; (*coisa*) it ♦ *prep* (*direção*) to; (*tempo*) at; (*com vb*): **começou ~ nevar** it started to snow; (*com infin*: = *gerúndio*): **~ correr** running; (*col: usado como substantivo*): **qual é ~ dele?** where's he at?; (*usos pronominais*) *V* o; **à direita/esquerda** on the right/left; **ao lado de** beside, at the side of; **~ que horas?** at what time?; **às 5 horas** at 5 o'clock; **à noite** at night; **aos 15 anos** at 15 years of age; **ao vê-lo** when I saw him; **~ cavalo/pé** on horseback/foot; **~ negócios** on business; (*maneira*): **à força** by force; **~ mão/tinta** by hand/in ink; **dia ~ dia** day by day; **pouco ~ pouco** little by little; **aos poucos** gradually; **~ Cr$2000 o quilo** Cr$2000 a kilo.

à [a] = **a + a**.

(a) *abr* (= *assinado*) signed.

AAB *abr f* (= *Aliança Anticomunista Brasileira*) *terrorist group*.

aba ['aba] *f* (*de chapéu*) brim; (*de casaco*) tail; (*de montanha*) foot.

abacate [aba'katʃi] *m* avocado (pear).

abacaxi [abaka'ʃi] (*BR*) *m* pineapple; (*col: problema*) pain.

abade/abadessa [a'badʒi/aba'desa] *m/f* abbot/abbess.

Abadi [aba'dʒi] *abr f* = **Associação Brasileira das Administradoras de Imóveis.**

abadia [aba'dʒia] *f* abbey.

abafadiço/a [abafa'dʒisu/a] *adj* stifling; (*ar*) stuffy.

abafado/a [aba'fadu/a] *adj* (*ar*) stuffy; (*tempo*) humid, close; (*ocupado*) extremely busy; (*angustiado*) anxious.

abafamento [abafa'mẽtu] *m* fug; (*sufocação*) suffocation.

abafar [aba'fa*] *vt* to suffocate; (*ocultar*) to suppress; (*som*) to muffle; (*encobrir*) to cover up; (*col*) to pilfer ♦ *vi* (*col: fazer sucesso*) to steal the show.

abagunçado/a [abagũ'sadu/a] *adj* messy.

abagunçar [abagũ'sa*] *vt* to make a mess of, mess up.

abaixar [abaj'ʃa*] *vt* to lower; (*preço*) to reduce; (*luz, som*) to turn down; **~-se** *vr* to stoop.

abaixo [a'bajʃu] *adv* down ♦ *prep*: **~ de** below; **~ o governo!** down with the government!; **morro ~** downhill; **rio ~** downstream; **mais ~** further down; **~ e acima** up and down; **~ assinado** undersigned.

abaixo-assinado [-asi'nadu] (*pl* **~s**) *m* (*documento*) petition.

abajur [aba'ʒu*] (*BR*) *m* (*cúpula*) lampshade; (*luminária*) table lamp.

abalado/a [aba'ladu/a] *adj* unstable, unsteady; (*fig*) shaken.

abalar [aba'la*] *vt* to shake; (*fig: comover*) to affect ♦ *vi* to shake; **~-se** *vr* to be moved.

abalizado/a [abali'zadu/a] *adj* eminent, distinguished; (*opinião*) reliable.

abalo [a'balu] *m* (*comoção*) shock; (*ação*) shaking; **~ sísmico** earth tremor.

abalroar [abawro'a*] *vt* to collide with, run into.

abanar [aba'na*] *vt* to shake; (*rabo*) to wag; (*com leque*) to fan.

abandalhar [abáda'ʎa*] *vt* to debase.

abandonar [abádo'na*] *vt* (*deixar*) to leave, desert; (*repudiar*) to reject; (*renunciar*) to abandon, give up; (*descuidar*) to neglect; **~-se** *vr*: **~-se a** to abandon o.s. to.

abandono [abã'donu] *m* (*ato*) desertion; (*estado*) neglect.

abarcar [abax'ka*] *vt* (*abranger*) to comprise; (*conter*) to enclose.

abarque [a'baxki] *etc vb V* **abarcar.**

abarrotado/a [abaxo'tadu/a] *adj* crammed full; (*lugar*) crowded, crammed.

abarrotar [abaxo'ta*] *vt*: **~ de** to cram with.

abastado/a [abaʃ'tadu/a] *adj* wealthy.

abastança [abaʃ'tãsa] *f* abundance, surfeit.

abastardar [abaʃtax'da*] *vt* to corrupt.

abastecer [abaʃte'se*] *vt* to supply; (*motor*) to fuel; (*AUTO*) to fill up; (*AER*) to refuel; **~-se** *vr*: **~-se de** to stock up with.

abastecimento [abaʃtesi'mẽtu] *m* supply; (*comestíveis*) provisions *pl*; (*ato*) supplying; (*de carro, avião*) refuelling (*BRIT*), refueling (*US*); **~s** *mpl* supplies.

abater [aba'te*] *vt* (*derrubar*) to knock down; (*gado*) to slaughter; (*preço*) to reduce, lower; (*debilitar*) to weaken; (*desalentar*) to dishearten.

abatido/a [aba'tʃidu/a] *adj* depressed, downcast; (*fisionomia*) haggard.

NB: *European Portuguese adds the following consonants to certain words:* **b** (sú(b)dito, su(b)til); **c** (a(c)ção, a(c)cionista, a(c)to); **m** (inde(m)ne); **p** (ado(p)ção, ado(p)tar); *for further details see p. xiii.*

abatimento [abatʃi'mẽtu] *m* (*fraqueza*) weakness; (*de preço*) reduction; (*prostração*) depression; **fazer um** ~ to give a discount.

abaulado/a [abaw'ladu/a] *adj* convex; (*estrada*) cambered.

abaular-se [abaw'laxsi] *vr* to bulge.

ABBC *abr f* = **Associação Brasileira dos Bancos Comerciais.**

ABBR *abr f* (= *Associação Brasileira Beneficente de Reabilitação*) charity for the disabled.

abcesso [ab'sɛsu] *m* tumour (*BRIT*), tumor (*US*); (*de dentes*) abscess.

abdicação [abdʒika'sãw] (*pl* **-ões**) *f* abdication.

abdicar [abdʒi'ka*] *vt*, *vi* to abdicate.

abdômen [ab'domẽ] *m* abdomen.

á-bê-cê [abe'se] *m* alphabet; (*fig*) rudiments *pl*.

abecedário [abese'darju] *m* alphabet, ABC.

Abeenras *abr f* = **Associação Brasileira das Empresas de Engenharia, Reparos e Atividades Subaquáticas.**

abeirar [abej'ra*] *vt* to bring near; ~**-se** *vr*: ~**-se de** to draw near to.

abelha [a'beʎa] *f* bee.

abelha-mestra (*pl* **abelhas-mestras**) *f* queen bee.

abelhudo/a [abe'ʎudu/a] *adj* nosy.

abençoar [abẽ'swa*] *vt* to bless.

abendiçoar [abẽdʒi'swa*] *vt* to bless.

aberração [abexa'sãw] (*pl* **-ões**) *f* aberration.

aberta [a'bɛxta] *f* opening; (*clareira*) glade; (*intervalo*) break.

aberto/a [a'bɛxtu/a] *pp de* **abrir** ♦ *adj* open; (*céu*) clear; (*sinal*) green; (*torneira*) on; (*desprotegido*) exposed; (*liberal*) open-minded.

abertura [abex'tura] *f* opening; (*FOTO*) aperture; (*ranhura*) gap, crevice; (*POL*) liberalization.

abestalhado/a [abeʃta'ʎadu/a] *adj* stupid.

ABH *abr f* = **Associação Brasileira da Indústria de Hóteis.**

ABI *abr f* = **Associação Brasileira de Imprensa.**

Abifarma *abr f* = **Associação Brasileira da Industria Farmacêutica.**

abilolado/a [abilo'ladu/a] *adj* crazy.

abismado/a [abiʒ'madu/a] *adj* astonished.

abismo [a'biʒmu] *m* abyss, chasm; (*fig*) depths *pl*.

abjeção [abʒe'sãw] (*PT*: **-cç-**) *f* baseness.

abjeto/a [ab'ʒetu/a] (*PT*: **-ct-**) *adj* abject, contemptible.

abjudicar [abʒudʒi'ka*] *vt* to seize.

ABL *abr f* = **Academia Brasileira de Letras.**

ABMU *abr f* = **Associação Brasileira de Mulheres Universitárias.**

abnegação [abnega'sãw] *f* self-denial.

abnegado/a [abne'gadu/a] *adj* self-sacrificing.

abnegar [abne'ga*] *vt* to renounce.

abóbada [a'bobada] *f* vault; (*telhado*) arched roof.

abobalhado/a [aboba'ʎadu/a] *adj* stupid.

abóbora [a'bobora] *f* pumpkin.

abobrinha [abo'briɲa] *f* courgette (*BRIT*), zucchini (*US*).

abocanhar [aboka'ɲa*] *vt* (*apanhar com a boca*) to seize with the mouth; (*morder*) to bite.

abolição [aboli'sãw] *f* abolition.

abolir [abo'li*] *vt* to abolish.

abominação [abomina'sãw] (*pl* **-ões**) *f* abomination.

abominar [abomi'na*] *vt* to loathe, detest.

abominável [abomi'navew] (*pl* **-eis**) *adj* abominable.

abonar [abo'na*] *vt* to guarantee.

abono [a'bɔnu] *m* guarantee; (*JUR*) bail; (*louvor*) praise; ~ **de família** child benefit.

abordagem [abox'daʒẽ] (*pl* **-ns**) *f* approach.

abordar [abox'da*] *vt* (*NÁUT*) to board; (*pessoa*) to approach; (*assunto*) to broach, tackle.

aborígene [abo'riʒeni] *adj* native, aboriginal ♦ *m/f* native, aborigine.

aborrecer [aboxe'se*] *vt* (*chatear*) to annoy; (*maçar*) to bore; ~**-se** *vr* to get upset; to get bored.

aborrecido/a [aboxe'sidu/a] *adj* boring; (*chateado*) annoyed.

aborrecimento [aboxesi'mẽtu] *m* boredom; (*chateação*) annoyance.

abortar [abox'ta*] *vi* to miscarry ♦ *vt* to abort.

aborto [a'boxtu] *m* (*MED*) miscarriage; (*forçado*) abortion; **fazer um** ~ to have an abortion.

abotoadura [abotwa'dura] *f* cufflink.

abotoar [abo'twa*] *vt* to button up ♦ *vi* (*BOT*) to bud.

abr. *abr* (= *abril*) Apr.

abraçar [abra'sa*] *vt* to hug; (*causa*) to embrace; ~**-se** *vr* to embrace; **ele abraçou-se a mim** he embraced me.

abraço [a'brasu] *m* embrace, hug; **com um** ~ (*em carta*) with best wishes.

abrandar [abrã'da*] *vt* to reduce; (*suavizar*) to soften ♦ *vi* to diminish; (*acalmar*) to calm down.

abranger [abrã'ʒe*] *vt* to include, comprise; (*alcançar*) to reach.

abranjo [a'brãʒu] *etc vb* V **abranger.**

abrasar [abra'za*] *vt* to burn; (*desbastar*) to erode ♦ *vi* to be on fire.

abrasileirado/a [abrazilej'radu/a] *adj* Brazilianized.

ABRATES *abr f* = **Associação Brasileira de Tradutores.**

ABRATT *abr f* = **Associação Brasileira dos Transportadores Exclusivos de Turismo.**

abre-garrafas ['abri-] (*PT*) *m inv* bottle opener.

abre-latas ['abri-] (*PT*) *m inv* tin (*BRIT*) *ou* can opener.

abreugrafia [abrewgra'fia] *f* X-ray.

abreviação [abrevja'sãw] (pl -ões) f abbreviation; (de texto) abridgement.

abreviar [abre'vja*] vt to abbreviate; (encurtar) to shorten; (texto) to abridge.

abreviatura [abrevja'tura] f abbreviation.

abridor [abri'do*] (BR) m opener; ~ **(de lata)** tin (BRIT) ou can opener; ~ **de garrafa** bottle opener.

abrigar [abri'ga*] vt to shelter; (proteger) to protect; ~**-se** vr to take shelter.

abrigo [a'brigu] m shelter, cover; ~ **anti-aéreo** air-raid shelter; ~ **anti-nuclear** fall-out shelter.

abril [a'briw] (PT: **A~**) m April; V tb **julho**.

abrilhantar [abriʎã'ta*] vt to enhance.

abrir [a'bri*] vt to open; (fechadura) to unlock; (vestuário) to unfasten; (torneiras) to turn on; (buraco, exceção) to make; (processo) to start ♦ vi to open; (sinal) to go green; (tempo) to clear up; ~**-se** vr: ~**-se com alguém** to confide in sb, open up to sb.

ab-rogação [abxoga'sãw] (pl ~**ões**) f repeal, annulment.

ab-rogar [abxo'ga*] vt to repeal, annul.

abrolho [a'broʎu] m thorn.

abrupto/a [a'bruptu/a] adj abrupt; (repentino) sudden.

abrutalhado/a [abruta'ʎadu/a] adj (pessoa) coarse; (sapatos) heavy.

absenteísta [absẽte'iʃta] m/f absentee.

absentismo [absẽ'tʃiʒmu] m absenteeism.

abside [ab'sidʒi] f apse; (relicário) shrine.

absolutamente [absoluta'mẽtʃi] adv absolutely; (de jeito nenhum) absolutely not, not at all.

absolutismo [absolu'tʃiʒmu] m absolutism.

absolutista [absolu'tʃiʃta] adj, m/f absolutist.

absoluto/a [abso'lutu/a] adj absolute; **em** ~ absolutely not, not at all.

absolver [absow've*] vt to absolve; (JUR) to acquit.

absolvição [absowvi'sãw] (pl -ões) f absolution; (JUR) acquittal.

absorção [absox'sãw] f absorption.

absorto/a [ab'soxtu/a] pp de **absorver** ♦ adj absorbed, engrossed.

absorvente [absox'vẽtʃi] adj (papel etc) absorbent; (livro etc) absorbing.

absorver [absox've*] vt to absorb; ~**-se em** to concentrate on.

abstêmio/a [abʃ'temju/a] adj abstemious; (álcool) teetotal ♦ m/f abstainer, teetotaller (BRIT), teetotaler (US).

abstenção [abʃtẽ'sãw] (pl -ões) f abstention.

abstencionista [abʃtẽsjo'niʃta] adj abstaining ♦ m/f abstainer.

abstenções [abʃtẽ'sõjʃ] fpl de **abstenção**.

abster-se [ab'ʃtexsi] (irreg: como **ter**) vr: ~ **de** to abstain ou refrain from.

abstinência [abʃtʃi'nẽsja] f abstinence;

(jejum) fasting.

abstinha [abʃ'tʃiɲa] etc vb V **abster-se**.

abstive [abʃ'tʃivi] etc vb V **abster-se**.

abstração [abʃtra'sãw] (PT: **-cç-**) f abstraction; (concentração) concentration.

abstrair [abʃtra'i*] vt to abstract; (omitir) to omit; (separar) to separate.

abstrato/a [abʃ'tratu/a] (PT: **-ct-**) adj abstract.

absurdo/a [abi'suxdu/a] adj absurd ♦ m nonsense.

abulia [abu'lia] f apathy.

abundância [abũ'dãsja] f abundance.

abundante [abũ'dãtʃi] adj abundant.

abundar [abũ'da*] vi to abound.

aburguesado/a [abuxge'zadu/a] adj middleclass, bourgeois.

abusar [abu'za*] vi (exceder-se) to go too far; ~ **de** to abuse.

abuso [a'buzu] m abuse; (JUR) indecent assault; ~ **de confiança** breach of trust.

abutre [a'butri] m vulture.

AC abr = **Acre**.

a.C. abr (= antes de Cristo) B.C.

a/c abr (= aos cuidados de) c/o.

acabado/a [aka'badu/a] adj finished; (esgotado) worn out; (envelhecido) aged.

acabamento [akaba'mẽtu] m finish.

acabar [aka'ba*] vt (terminar) to finish, complete; (levar a cabo) to accomplish; (aperfeiçoar) to complete; (consumir) to use up; (rematar) to finish off ♦ vi to finish, end, come to an end; ~**-se** vr (terminar) to be over; (prazo) to expire; (esgotar-se) to run out; ~ **com** to put an end to; (destruir) to do away with; (namorado) to finish with; ~ **de chegar** to have just arrived; ~ **por** to end (up) by; **acabou-se!** that's enough!, it's all over!; **ele acabou cedendo** he eventually gave in, he ended up giving in; ... **que não acaba mais** no end of ...; **quando acaba** (no final) in the end.

acabrunhado/a [akabru'ɲadu/a] adj (abatido) depressed; (envergonhado) embarrassed.

acabrunhar [akabru'ɲa*] vt (entristecer) to distress; (envergonhar) to embarrass.

acácia [a'kasja] f acacia.

academia [akade'mia] f academy; ~ **(de ginástica)** gym.

acadêmico/a [aka'demiku/a] adj, m/f academic.

açafrão [asa'frãw] m saffron.

acalcanhar [akawka'ɲa*] vt (sapato) to put out of shape.

acalentar [akalẽ'ta*] vt to rock to sleep; (esperanças) to cherish.

acalmar [akaw'ma*] vt to calm ♦ vi (vento etc) to abate; ~**-se** vr to calm down.

acalorado/a [akalo'radu/a] adj heated.

acalorar [akalo'ra*] vt to heat; (fig) to inflame; ~**-se** vr (fig) to get heated.

NB: *European Portuguese adds the following consonants to certain words:* **b** (sú(b)dito, su(b)til); **c** (a(c)ção, a(c)cionista, a(c)to); **m** (inde(m)ne); **p** (ado(p)ção, ado(p)tar); *for further details see p. xiii.*

acamado/a [aka'madu/a] *adj* bedridden.

açambarcar [asãbax'ka*] *vt* to appropriate; (*mercado*) to corner.

acampamento [akãpa'mẽtu] *m* camping; (*MIL*) camp, encampment; **levantar** ~ to raise camp.

acampar [akã'pa*] *vi* to camp.

acanhado/a [aka'ɲadu/a] *adj* shy.

acanhamento [akaɲa'mẽtu] *m* shyness.

acanhar-se [aka'ɲaxsi] *vr* to be shy.

ação [a'sãw] (*pl* **-ões**) *f* action; (*ato*) act, deed; (*MIL*) battle; (*enredo*) plot; (*JUR*) lawsuit; (*COM*) share; ~ **bonificada** (*COM*) bonus share; ~ **de graças** thanksgiving; ~ **integralizada/diferida** (*COM*) fully paid-in/deferred share; ~ **ordinária/preferencial** (*COM*) ordinary/preference share.

acarajé [akara'ʒɛ] *m* (*CULIN*) beans fried in palm oil.

acareação [akarja'sãw] (*pl* **-ões**) *f* confrontation.

acarear [aka'rja*] *vt* to confront.

acariciar [akari'sja*] *vt* to caress; (*fig*) to cherish.

acarinhar [akari'ɲa*] *vt* to caress; (*fig*) to treat with tenderness.

acarretar [akaxe'ta*] *vt* to result in, bring about.

acasalamento [akazala'mẽtu] *m* mating.

acasalar [akaza'la*] *vt* to mate; ~-**se** *vr* to mate.

acaso [a'kazu] *m* chance, accident; **ao** ~ at random; **por** ~ by chance.

acastanhado/a [akaʃta'ɲadu/a] *adj* brownish; (*cabelo*) auburn.

acatamento [akata'mẽtu] *m* respect; (*deferência*) deference.

acatar [aka'ta*] *vt* (*respeitar*) to respect; (*honrar*) to honour (*BRIT*), honor (*US*); (*lei*) to obey.

acautelar [akawte'la*] *vt* to warn; ~-**se** *vr* to be cautious; ~-**se contra** to guard against.

ACC *abr m* = **adiantamento de contratos de câmbio.**

acção [a'sãw] (*PT*) *f* = **ação.**

accionar *etc* [asjo'na*] (*PT*) = **acionar** *etc*.

acebolado/a [asebo'ladu/a] *adj* (*CULIN*) flavoured (*BRIT*) *ou* flavored (*US*) with onion.

aceder [ase'de*] *vi*: ~ **a** to agree to, accede to.

aceitação [asejta'sãw] *f* acceptance; (*aprovação*) approval.

aceitar [asej'ta*] *vt* to accept; **você aceita uma bebida?** would you like a drink?

aceitável [asej'tavew] (*pl* **-eis**) *adj* acceptable.

aceite [a'sejtʃi] (*PT*) *pp de* **aceitar** ♦ *adj* accepted ♦ *m* acceptance.

aceito/a [a'sejtu/a] *pp de* **aceitar** ♦ *adj* accepted.

aceleração [aselera'sãw] *f* acceleration; (*pressa*) haste.

acelerado/a [asele'radu/a] *adj* (*rápido*) quick; (*apressado*) hasty.

acelerador [aselera'do*] *m* accelerator.

acelerar [asele'ra*] *vt*, *vi* to accelerate; ~ **o passo** to go faster.

acenar [ase'na*] *vi* (*com a mão*) to wave; (*com a cabeça*) to nod; ~ **com** (*oferecer*) to offer, promise.

acendedor [asẽde'do*] *m* lighter.

acender [asẽ'de*] *vt* (*cigarro, fogo*) to light; (*luz*) to switch on; (*fig*) to excite, inflame.

aceno [a'sɛnu] *m* sign, gesture; (*com a mão*) wave; (*com a cabeça*) nod.

acento [a'sẽtu] *m* accent; (*de intensidade*) stress; ~ **agudo/circunflexo** acute/circumflex accent.

acentuação [asẽtwa'sãw] *f* accentuation; (*ênfase*) stress.

acentuado/a [asẽ'twadu/a] *adj* (*sílaba*) stressed; (*saliente*) conspicuous.

acentuar [asẽ'twa*] *vt* (*marcar com acento*) to accent; (*salientar*) to stress, emphasize; (*realçar*) to enhance.

acepção [asep'sãw] (*pl* **-ões**) *f* (*de uma palavra*) sense.

acepipe [ase'pipi] *m* tit-bit, delicacy; ~**s** *mpl* (*PT*) hors d'œuvres.

acerca [a'sexka]: ~ **de** *prep* about, concerning.

acercar-se [asex'kaxsi] *vr*: ~ **de** to approach, draw near to.

acérrimo/a [a'seximu/a] *adj* (*muito acre*) very bitter; (*defensor*) staunch.

acertado/a [asex'tadu/a] *adj* (*certo*) right, correct; (*sensato*) sensible.

acertar [asex'ta*] *vt* (*ajustar*) to put right; (*relógio*) to set; (*alvo*) to hit; (*acordo*) to reach; (*pergunta*) to get right ♦ *vi* to get it right, be right; ~ **com** to hit upon; ~ **o caminho** to find the right way.

acervo [a'sexvu] *m* heap; (*JUR*) estate; (*de museu etc*) collection; **um** ~ **de** vast quantities of.

aceso/a [a'sezu/a] *pp de* **acender** ♦ *adj* (*luz, gás, TV*) on; (*fogo*) alight; (*excitado*) excited; (*furioso*) furious.

acessar [ase'sa*] *vt* (*COMPUT*) to access.

acessível [ase'sivew] (*pl* **-eis**) *adj* accessible; (*pessoa*) approachable; (*preço*) reasonable, affordable.

acesso [a'sɛsu] *m* access; (*MED*) fit, attack; **um** ~ **de cólera** a fit of anger; **de fácil** ~ easy to get to; **múltiplo** ~ (*COMPUT*) multiple access; **tempo de** ~ (*COMPUT*) access time.

acessório/a [ase'sɔrju/a] *adj* accessory ♦ *m* accessory.

ACET (*BR*) *abr f* = **Agência Central dos Teatros.**

acetona [ase'tɔna] *f* nail varnish remover; (*QUÍM*) acetone.

achacar [aʃa'ka*] (*col*) *vt* (*dinheiro*) to extort.

achado/a [a'ʃadu/a] *adj*: **não se dar por** ~ to play dumb ♦ *m* find, discovery; (*pechincha*) bargain; (*sorte*) godsend.

achaque [a'ʃaki] *m* ailment.

achar [a'ʃa*] *vt* (*descobrir*) to find; (*pensar*)

to think; **~-se** *vr* (*considerar-se*) to think (that) one is; (*encontrar-se*) to be; **~ de fazer** (*resolver*) to decide to do; **o que é que você acha disso?** what do you think of it?; **acho que ...** I think (that) ...; **acho que sim** I think so; **~ algo bom/estranho** *etc* to find sth good/strange *etc*; **~ ruim** to be cross.

achatar [aʃa'ta*] *vt* to squash, flatten; (*fig*) to talk round, convince.

achegar-se [aʃe'gaxsi] *vr*: **~ a** *ou* **de** to approach, get closer to.

acidentado/a [asidē'tadu/a] *adj* (*terreno*) rough; (*estrada*) bumpy; (*viagem*) eventful; (*vida*) chequered (*BRIT*), checkered (*US*) ♦ *m/f* injured person.

acidental [asidē'taw] (*pl* **-ais**) *adj* accidental.

acidente [asi'dētʃi] *m* accident; (*acaso*) chance; **por ~** by accident.

acidez [asi'deʒ] *f* acidity.

ácido/a ['asidu/a] *adj* acid; (*azedo*) sour ♦ *m* acid; **~ sulfúrico** sulphuric (*BRIT*) *ou* sulfuric (*US*) acid.

acima [a'sima] *adv* above; (*para cima*) up ♦ *prep*: **~ de** above; (*além de*) beyond; **mais ~** higher up; **rio ~** up river; **passar rua ~** to go up the street; **~ de 1000** more than 1000.

acinte [a'sītʃi] *m* provocation ♦ *adv* deliberately, on purpose.

acintosamente [asītoza'mētʃi] *adv* on purpose.

acinzentado/a [asīzē'tadu/a] *adj* greyish (*BRIT*), grayish (*US*).

acionado/a [asjo'nadu/a] *m/f* (*JUR*) defendant; **~s** *mpl* gestures.

acionar [asjo'na*] *vt* to set in motion; (*máquina*) to operate; (*JUR*) to sue.

acionista [asjo'niʃta] *m/f* shareholder; **~ majoritário/minoritário** majority/minority shareholder.

acirrado/a [asi'xadu/a] *adj* (*luta*, *competição*) tough.

acirrar [asi'xa*] *vt* to incite, stir up.

aclamação [aklama'sãw] *f* acclamation; (*ovação*) applause.

aclamar [akla'ma*] *vt* to acclaim; (*aplaudir*) to applaud.

aclarado/a [akla'radu/a] *adj* clear.

aclarar [akla'ra*] *vt* to explain, clarify ♦ *vi* to clear up; **~-se** *vr* to become clear.

aclimatação [aklimata'sãw] *f* acclimatization.

aclimatar [aklima'ta*] *vt* to acclimatize (*BRIT*), acclimate (*US*); **~-se** *vr* to become acclimatized *ou* acclimated.

aclive [a'klivi] *m* slope, incline.

ACM *abr f* (= *Associação Cristã de Moços*) YMCA.

aço ['asu] *m* (*metal*) steel; **~ inox** stainless steel.

acocorar-se [akoko'raxsi] *vr* to squat, crouch.

acode [a'kɔdʒi] *etc vb V* **acudir**.

ações [a'sõjʃ] *fpl de* **ação**.

acoitar [akoj'ta*] *vt* to shelter, give refuge to.

açoitar [asoj'ta*] *vt* to whip, lash.

açoite [a'sojtʃi] *m* whip, lash.

acolá [ako'la] *adv* over there.

acolchoado/a [akow'ʃwadu/a] *adj* quilted ♦ *m* quilt.

acolchoar [akow'ʃwa*] *vt* (*costurar*) to quilt; (*forrar*) to pad; (*estofar*) to upholster.

acolhedor(a) [akoʎe'do*(a)] *adj* welcoming; (*hospitaleiro*) hospitable.

acolher [ako'ʎe*] *vt* to welcome; (*abrigar*) to shelter; (*aceitar*) to accept; **~-se** *vr* to shelter.

acolhida [ako'ʎida] *f* (*recepção*) reception, welcome; (*refúgio*) refuge.

acolhimento [akoʎi'mētu] *m* (*recepção*) reception, welcome; (*refúgio*) refuge.

acometer [akome'te*] *vt* (*atacar*) to attack; (*suj: doença*) to take hold of.

acomodação [akomoda'sãw] (*pl* **-ões**) *f* accommodation; (*arranjo*) arrangement; (*adaptação*) adaptation.

acomodar [akomo'da*] *vt* (*alojar*) to accommodate; (*arrumar*) to arrange; (*tornar cômodo*) to make comfortable; (*adaptar*) to adapt.

acompanhamento [akõpaɲa'mētu] *m* attendance; (*cortejo*) procession; (*MÚS*) accompaniment; (*CULIN*) side dish.

acompanhante [akõpa'ɲãtʃi] *m/f* companion; (*MÚS*) accompanist.

acompanhar [akõpa'ɲa*] *vt* to accompany, go along with; (*MÚS*) to accompany; (*assistir*) to watch; (*eventos*) to keep up with; **~ alguém até a porta** to show sb to the door.

aconchegado/a [akõʃe'gadu/a] *adj* snug, cosy (*BRIT*), cozy (*US*).

aconchegante [akõʃe'gãtʃi] *adj* cosy (*BRIT*), cozy (*US*).

aconchegar [akõʃe'ga*] *vt* to bring near; **~-se** *vr* (*acomodar-se*) to make o.s. comfortable; **~-se com** to snuggle up to.

aconchego [akõ'ʃegu] *m* cuddle.

acondicionamento [akõdʒisjona'mētu] *m* packaging.

acondicionar [akõdʒisjo'na*] *vt* to condition; (*empacotar*) to pack; (*embrulhar*) to wrap (up).

aconselhar [akõse'ʎa*] *vt* to advise; (*recomendar*) to recommend; **~-se** *vr*: **~-se com** to consult; **~ alguém a fazer** to advise sb to do.

aconselhável [akõse'ʎavew] (*pl* **-eis**) *adj* advisable.

acontecer [akõte'se*] *vi* to happen.

acontecimento [akõtesi'mētu] *m* event.

acoplador [akopla'do*] *m*: **~ acústico** (*COMPUT*) acoustic coupler.

acordar [akox'da*] *vt* (*despertar*) to wake

NB: European Portuguese adds the following consonants to certain words: **b** (sú(b)dito, su(b)til); **c** (a(c)ção, a(c)cionista, a(c)to); **m** (inde(m)ne); **p** (ado(p)ção, ado(p)tar); *for further details see p. xiii.*

(up); (*concordar*) to agree (on) ♦ *vi* (*despertar*) to wake up.

acorde [a'kɔrdʒi] *m* chord.

acordeão [akox'dʒiãw] (*pl* -ões) *m* accordion.

acordeonista [akoxdʒjo'niʃta] *m/f* accordionist.

acordo [a'koxdu] *m* agreement; **de** ~ agreed; **de** ~ **com** (*pessoa*) in agreement with; (*conforme*) in accordance with; **estar de** ~ to agree; ~ **de cavalheiros** gentlemen's agreement.

Açores [a'soriʃ] *mpl*: **os** ~ the Azores.

açoriano/a [aso'rjanu/a] *adj*, *m/f* Azorean.

acorrentar [akoxẽ'ta*] *vt* to chain (up).

acorrer [ako'xe*] *vi*: ~ **a alguém** to come to sb's aid.

acossar [ako'sa*] *vt* (*perseguir*) to pursue; (*atormentar*) to harass.

acostamento [akoʃta'mẽtu] *m* hard shoulder (*BRIT*), berm (*US*).

acostar [akoʃ'ta*] *vt* to lean against; (*NÁUT*) to bring alongside; ~**-se** *vr* to lean back.

acostumado/a [akoʃtu'madu/a] *adj* (*habitual*) usual, customary; **estar** ~ to be used to it; **estar** ~ **a algo** to be used to sth.

acostumar [akoʃtu'ma*] *vt* to accustom; ~**-se** *vr*: ~**-se a** to get used to.

acotovelar [akotove'la*] *vt* to jostle; ~**-se** *vr* to jostle.

açougue [a'sogi] *m* butcher's (shop).

açougueiro [aso'gejru] *m* butcher.

acovardado/a [akovax'dadu/a] *adj* intimidated.

acovardar-se [akovax'daxsi] *vr* (*desanimar*) to lose courage; (*amedrontar-se*) to flinch, cower.

acre ['akri] *adj* (*amargo*) bitter; (*ríspido*) harsh; (*aroma*) acrid, strong.

acreano/a [a'krjanu/a] *adj* from Acre ♦ *m/f* native *ou* inhabitant of Acre.

acreditado/a [akredʒi'tadu/a] *adj* accredited.

acreditar [akredʒi'ta*] *vt* to believe; (*COM*) to credit; (*afiançar*) to guarantee ♦ *vi*: ~ **em** to believe in; (*ter confiança em*) to have faith in; "**acredite na sinalização**" "follow traffic signs".

acreditável [akredʒi'tavew] (*pl* -eis) *adj* credible.

acre-doce *adj* (*CULIN*) sweet and sour.

acrescentar [akresẽ'ta*] *vt* to add.

acrescer [akre'se*] *vt* (*aumentar*) to increase; (*juntar*) to add ♦ *vi* to increase; **acresce que** ... add to that the fact that ....

acréscimo [a'krεsimu] *m* addition; (*aumento*) increase; (*elevação*) rise.

acriançado/a [akrjã'sadu/a] *adj* childish.

acrílico [a'kriliku] *m* acrylic.

acrimônia [akri'monja] *f* acrimony.

acrobacia [akroba'sia] *f* acrobatics *pl*; ~**s** *fpl* aéreas aerobatics *pl*.

acrobata [akro'bata] *m/f* acrobat.

activo/a *etc* [a'tivu/a] (*PT*) = **ativo** *etc*.

acto ['atu] (*PT*) *m* = **ato**.

actor [a'to*] (*PT*) *m* = **ator**.

actriz [a'triʒ] (*PT*) *f* = **atriz**.

actual *etc* [a'twaw] (*PT*) = **atual** *etc*.

actuar *etc* [a'twa*] (*PT*) = **atuar** *etc*.

acuar [a'kwa*] *vt* to corner.

açúcar [a'suka*] *m* sugar; ~ **mascavo** brown sugar.

açucarado/a [asuka'radu/a] *adj* sugary.

açucarar [asuka'ra*] *vt* to sugar; (*adoçar*) to sweeten.

açucareiro [asuka'rejru] *m* (*vaso*) sugar bowl.

açude [a'sudʒi] *m* dam.

acudir [aku'dʒi*] *vi* (*ir em socorro*) to go to help; (*responder*) to reply, respond; ~ **a** to come to the aid of.

acuidade [akwi'dadʒi] *f* perceptiveness.

açular [asu'la*] *vt* (*incitar*) to incite; ~ **um cachorro contra alguém** to set a dog on sb.

acumulação [akumula'sãw] (*pl* -ões) *f* accumulation; (*montão*) heap.

acumulado/a [akumu'ladu/a] *adj* (*COM*: *juros*, *despesas*) accrued.

acumular [akumu'la*] *vt* to accumulate; (*reunir*) to collect; (*amontoar*) to pile up; (*funções*) to combine.

acúmulo [a'kumulu] *m* accumulation.

acusação [akuza'sãw] (*pl* -ões) *f* accusation, charge; (*ato*) accusation; (*JUR*) prosecution.

acusado/a [aku'zadu/a] *m/f* accused.

acusar [aku'za*] *vt* to accuse; (*revelar*) to reveal; (*culpar*) to blame; ~ **o recebimento de** to acknowledge receipt of.

acústica [a'kuʃtʃika] *f* (*ciência*) acoustics *sg*; (*de uma sala*) acoustics *pl*.

acústico/a [a'kuʃtʃiku/a] *adj* acoustic.

adaga [a'daga] *f* dagger.

adágio [a'daʒu] *m* adage; (*MÚS*) adagio.

adaptabilidade [adaptabili'dadʒi] *f* adaptability.

adaptação [adapta'sãw] (*pl* -ões) *f* adaptation.

adaptado/a [adap'tadu/a] *adj* (*criança*) well-adjusted.

adaptar [adap'ta*] *vt* (*modificar*) to adapt; (*acomodar*) to fit; ~**-se** *vr*: ~**-se a** to adapt to.

ADECIF (*BR*) *abr f* = **Associação de Diretores de Empresas de Créditos, Investimentos e Financiamento**.

adega [a'dεga] *f* cellar.

adelgaçado/a [adewga'sadu/a] *adj* thin; (*aguçado*) pointed.

ademais [adʒi'majʃ] *adv* (*além disso*) besides, moreover.

ADEMI (*BR*) *abr f* = **Associação de Dirigentes de Empresa do Mercado Imobiliário**.

adentro [a'dẽtru] *adv* inside, in; **mata** ~ into the woods.

adepto/a [a'dεptu/a] *m/f* follower; (*PT*: *de time*) supporter.

adequado/a [ade'kwadu/a] *adj* appropriate.

adequar [ade'kwa*] *vt* to adapt, make suitable.

adereçar [adere'sa*] *vt* to adorn, decorate; ~-

se *vr* to dress up.
adereço [ade'resu] *m* adornment; **~s** *mpl* (*TEATRO*) stage props.
aderência [ade'rēsja] *f* adherence.
aderente [ade'rētʃi] *adj* adherent, sticking ♦ *m/f* (*partidário*) supporter.
aderir [ade'ri*] *vi* to adhere; (*colar*) to stick; (*a uma moda etc*) to join in.
adesão [ade'zāw] *f* adhesion; (*patrocínio*) support.
adesivo/a [ade'zivu/a] *adj* adhesive, sticky ♦ *m* adhesive tape; (*MED*) sticking plaster.
adestrado/a [adeʃ'tradu/a] *adj* skilful (*BRIT*), skillful (*US*), skilled.
adestrador(a) [adeʃtra'do*(a)] *m/f* trainer.
adestramento [adeʃtra'mētu] *m* training.
adestrar [adeʃ'tra*] *vt* to train, instruct; (*cavalo*) to break in.
- adeus [a'dewʃ] *excl* goodbye!; **dizer ~** to say goodbye, bid farewell.
adiamento [adʒja'mētu] *m* postponement; (*de uma sessão*) adjournment.
adiantado/a [adʒjā'tadu/a] *adj* advanced; (*relógio*) fast; **chegar ~** to arrive ahead of time; **pagar ~** to pay in advance.
adiantamento [adʒjāta'mētu] *m* progress; (*dinheiro*) advance payment.
adiantar [adʒjā'ta*] *vt* (*dinheiro, salário*) to advance, pay in advance; (*relógio*) to put forward; (*trabalho*) to advance; (*dizer*) to say in advance ♦ *vi* (*relógio*) to be fast; (*conselho, violência etc*) to be of use; **~-se** *vr* to advance, get ahead; **não adianta reclamar/insistir** there's no point *ou* it's no use complaining/insisting; **~-se a alguém** to get ahead of sb; **~-se para** to go/come up to.
adiante [a'dʒjātʃi] *adv* (*na frente*) in front; (*para a frente*) forward; **mais ~** further on; (*no futuro*) later on.
adiar [a'dʒja*] *vt* to postpone, put off; (*sessão*) to adjourn.
adição [adʒi'sāw] (*pl* **-ões**) *f* addition; (*MAT*) sum.
adicionar [adʒisjo'na*] *vt* to add.
adições [adʒi'sōjʃ] *fpl de* **adição**.
adido/a [a'dʒidu/a] *m/f* attaché.
adiro [a'diru] *etc vb V* **aderir**.
Adis-Abeba [adʒiza'bɛba] *n* Addis Ababa.
adivinhação [adʒiviɲa'sāw] *f* (*destino*) fortune-telling; (*conjetura*) guessing, guesswork.
adivinhar [adʒivi'ɲa*] *vt, vi* to guess; (*ler a sorte*) to foretell; **~ o pensamento de alguém** to read sb's mind.
adivinho/a [adʒi'viɲu/a] *m/f* fortune-teller.
adjacente [adʒa'sētʃi] *adj* adjacent.
adjetivo [adʒe'tʃivu] *m* adjective.
adjudicação [adʒudʒika'sāw] (*pl* **-ões**) *f* grant; (*de contratos*) award; (*JUR*) decision.
adjudicar [adʒudʒi'ka*] *vt* to award, grant.

adjunto/a [ad'ʒūtu/a] *adj* joined, attached ♦ *m/f* assistant.
administração [adʒiminiʃtra'sāw] (*pl* **-ões**) *f* administration; (*direção*) management; (*comissão*) board; **~ de empresas** business administration, management; **~ fiduciária** trusteeship.
administrador(a) [adʒiminiʃtra'do*(a)] *m/f* administrator; (*diretor*) director; (*gerente*) manager.
administrar [adʒiminiʃ'tra*] *vt* to administer, manage; (*governar*) to govern; (*remédio*) to administer.
admiração [adʒimira'sāw] *f* (*assombro*) wonder; (*estima*) admiration; *V tb* **ponto**.
admirado/a [adʒimi'radu/a] *adj* astonished, surprised.
admirador(a) [adʒimira'do*(a)] *adj* admiring.
admirar [adʒimi'ra*] *vt* to admire; **~-se** *vr*: **~-se de** to be astonished *ou* surprised at; **não me admiro!** I'm not surprised; **não é de se ~** it's not surprising.
admirável [adʒimi'ravew] (*pl* **-eis**) *adj* (*assombroso*) amazing.
admissão [adʒimi'sāw] (*pl* **-ões**) *f* admission; (*consentimento para entrar*) admittance; (*de escola*) intake.
admitir [adʒimi'tʃi*] *vt* (*aceitar*) to admit; (*permitir*) to allow; (*funcionário*) to take on.
admoestação [admweʃta'sāw] (*pl* **-ões**) *f* admonition; (*repreensão*) reprimand.
admoestar [admweʃ'ta*] *vt* to admonish.
adoção [ado'sāw] *f* adoption.
adoçar [ado'sa*] *vt* to sweeten.
adocicado/a [adosi'kadu/a] *adj* slightly sweet.
adoecer [adoe'se*] *vi* to fall ill ♦ *vt* to make ill; **~ de** *ou* **com** to fall ill with.
adoidado/a [adoj'dadu/a] *adj* crazy ♦ *adv* (*col*) like mad *ou* crazy.
adolescente [adole'sētʃi] *adj, m/f* adolescent.
adoptar *etc* [ado'ta*] (*PT*) = **adotar** *etc*.
adoração [adora'sāw] *f* adoration; (*veneração*) worship.
adorar [ado'ra*] *vt* to adore; (*venerar*) to worship; (*col: gostar muito de*) to love.
adorável [ado'ravew] (*pl* **-eis**) *adj* adorable.
adormecer [adoxme'se*] *vi* to fall asleep; (*entorpecer-se*) to go numb.
adormecido/a [adoxme'sidu/a] *adj* sleeping; (*dormente*) numb ♦ *m/f* sleeper.
adornar [adox'na*] *vt* to adorn, decorate.
adorno [a'doxnu] *m* adornment.
adotar [ado'ta*] *vt* to adopt.
adotivo/a [ado'tʃivu/a] *adj* (*filho*) adopted.
adquirir [adʒiki'ri*] *vt* to acquire; (*obter*) to obtain.
adrede [a'dredʒi] *adv* on purpose, deliberately.
Adriático/a [a'drjatʃiku/a] *adj*: **o (mar) ~** the Adriatic.
adro ['adru] *m* (church) forecourt; (*em volta*

NB: *European Portuguese adds the following consonants to certain words:* **b** (sú(b)dito, su(b)til); **c** (a(c)ção, a(c)cionista, a(c)to); **m** (inde(m)ne); **p** (ado(p)ção, ado(p)tar); *for further details see p. xiii.*

da igreja) churchyard.

aduana [a'dwana] *f* customs *pl*, customs house.

aduaneiro/a [adwa'nejru/a] *adj* customs *atr* ♦ *m* customs officer.

adubação [aduba'sãw] *f* fertilizing.

adubar [adu'ba*] *vt* to manure; (*fertilizer*) to fertilize.

adubo [a'dubu] *m* (*fertilizante*) fertilizer.

adulação [adula'sãw] *f* flattery.

adulador(a) [adula'do*(a)] *adj* flattering ♦ *m/f* flatterer.

adular [adu'la*] *vt* to flatter.

adulteração [aduwtera'sãw] *f* adulteration; (*de contas*) falsification.

adulterador(a) [aduwtera'do*(a)] *m/f* adulterator.

adulterar [aduwte'ra*] *vt* (*vinho*) to adulterate; (*contas*) to falsify ♦ *vi* to commit adultery.

adultério [aduw'tɛrju] *m* adultery.

adúltero/a [a'duwteru/a] *m/f* adulterer/ adulteress.

adulto/a [a'duwtu/a] *adj, m/f* adult.

adunco/a [a'dũku/a] *adj* (*nariz*) hook.

adveio [ad'veju] *etc vb V* **advir**.

adventício/a [advẽ'tʃisju/a] *adj* (*casual*) accidental; (*estrangeiro*) foreign ♦ *m/f* (*estrangeiro*) foreigner.

advento [ad'vẽtu] *m* advent; **o A~** Advent.

advérbio [ad'vexbju] *m* adverb.

adversário [adʒivex'sarju/a] *m* adversary, opponent, enemy.

adversidade [adʒivexsi'dadʒi] *f* adversity, misfortune.

adverso/a [adʒi'vɛxsu/a] *adj* adverse, unfavourable; (*oposto*): **~ a** opposed to.

advertência [adʒivex'tẽsja] *f* warning; (*repreensão*) (gentle) reprimand.

advertido/a [adʒivex'tʃidu/a] *adj* prudent; (*informado*) well advised.

advertir [adʒivex'tʃi*] *vt* to warn; (*repreender*) to reprimand; (*chamar a atenção a*) to draw attention to.

advier [ad'vje*] *etc vb V* **advir**.

advindo/a [ad'vĩdu/a] *adj*: **~ de** resulting from.

advir [ad'vi*] (*irreg: como* **vir**) *vi*: **~ de** to result from.

advocacia [adʒivoka'sia] *f* legal profession, law.

advogado/a [adʒivo'gadu/a] *m/f* lawyer.

advogar [adʒivo'ga*] *vt* (*promover*) to advocate; (*JUR*) to plead ♦ *vi* to practise (*BRIT*) *ou* practice (*US*) law.

aéreo/a [a'ɛrju/a] *adj* air *atr*; (*pessoa*) vague.

aerobarco [aero'baxku] *m* hovercraft.

aeroclube [aero'klubi] *m* flying club.

aerodinâmica [aerodʒi'namika] *f* aerodynamics *sg*.

aerodinâmico/a [aerodʒi'namiku/a] *adj* aerodynamic.

aerodrómo [aero'drɔmu] *m* airfield.

aeroespacial [aeroiʃpa'sjaw] (*pl* **-ais**) *adj* aero-

space *atr*.

aerofagia [aerofa'ʒia] *f* (*MED*) hyperventilation.

aerofoto [aero'fɔtu] *f* aerial photograph.

aeromoço/a [aero'mosu/a] (*BR*) *m/f* steward/ air hostess.

aeromodelismo [aeromode'liʒmu] *m* aeromodelling.

aeronauta [aero'nawta] *m/f* airman/woman.

aeronáutica [aero'nawtʃika] *f* air force; (*ciência*) aeronautics *sg*; **Departamento de A~ Civil** ≈ Civil Aviation Authority.

aeronave [aero'navi] *f* aircraft.

aeroporto [aero'poxtu] *m* airport.

aerossol [aero'sɔw] (*pl* **-óis**) *m* aerosol.

afã [a'fã] *m* (*entusiasmo*) enthusiasm; (*diligência*) diligence; (*ânsia*) eagerness; (*esforço*) effort; (*faina*) task, job; **no seu ~ de agradar** in his eagerness to please.

afabilidade [afabili'dadʒi] *f* friendliness, kindness.

afaço [a'fasu] *etc vb V* **afazer**.

afagar [afa'ga*] *vt* (*acariciar*) to caress; (*cabelo*) to stroke.

afamado/a [afa'madu/a] *adj* renowned, celebrated.

afanar [afa'na*] (*col*) *vt* to nick, pinch.

afanoso/a [afa'nozu/ɔza] *adj* laborious; (*meticuloso*) painstaking.

afasia [afa'zia] *f* aphasia.

afastado/a [afaʃ'tadu/a] *adj* (*distante*) remote; (*isolado*) secluded; (*pernas*) apart; (*amigo*) distant; **manter-se ~** to keep to o.s.

afastamento [afaʃta'mẽtu] *m* removal; (*distância*) distance; (*de emprego solicitado*) rejection; (*de pessoal*) lay-off, sacking.

afastar [afaʃ'ta*] *vt* to remove; (*amigo*) to distance; (*separar*) to separate; (*idéia*) to put out of one's mind; (*pessoal*) to lay off; **~-se** *vr* (*ir-se embora*) to move away, go away; (*de amigo*) to distance o.s.; (*de cargo*) to step down; **~-se do assunto** to stray from the subject; **~ os olhos de** to take one's eyes off.

afável [a'favew] (*pl* **-eis**) *adj* friendly, genial.

afazer [afa'ze*] (*irreg: como* **fazer**) *vt* to accustom; **~-se** *vr*: **~-se a** to get used to.

afazeres [afa'zeriʃ] *mpl* business *sg*; (*dever*) duties, tasks; **~ domésticos** household chores.

afectar *etc* [afek'ta*] (*PT*) = **afetar** *etc*.

afegã [afe'gã] *f de* **afegão**.

Afeganistão [afeganiʃ'tãw] *m*: **o ~** Afghanistan.

afegão/gã [afe'gãw/'gã] (*pl* **-ões/~s**) *adj, m/f* Afghan.

afeição [afej'sãw] *f* (*amor*) affection, fondness; (*dedicação*) devotion.

afeiçoado/a [afej'swadu/a] *adj* (*amoroso*) fond; (*devotado*) devoted ♦ *m/f* friend.

afeiçoar-se [afej'swaxsi] *vr*: **~ a** (*tomar gosto por*) to take a liking to.

afeito/a [a'fejtu/a] *pp de* **afazer** ♦ *adj:* ~ a accustomed to, used to.

afeminado/a [afemi'nadu/a] *adj* effeminate.

aferidor [aferi'do*] *m (de pesos e medidas)* inspector; *(verificador)* checker; *(instrumento)* gauge *(BRIT)*, gage *(US)*.

aferir [afe'ri*] *vt (verificar)* to check, inspect; *(comparar)* to compare; *(conhecimentos, resultados)* to assess.

aferrado/a [afe'xadu/a] *adj* obstinate, stubborn.

aferrar [afe'xa*] *vt (prender)* to secure; *(NÁUT)* to anchor; *(agarrar)* to grasp; ~-se *vr:* ~-se a to cling to.

aferrolhar [afexo'ʎa*] *vt* to bolt; *(pessoa)* to imprison; *(coisas)* to hoard.

aferventar [afexvẽ'ta*] *vt* to bring to the *(BRIT)* ou a *(US)* boil.

afetação [afeta'sãw] *f* affectation.

afetado/a [afe'tadu/a] *adj* pretentious, affected.

afetar [afe'ta*] *vt* to affect; *(fingir)* to feign.

afetividade [afetʃivi'dadʒi] *f* affection.

afetivo/a [afe'tʃivu/a] *adj* affectionate; *(problema)* emotional.

afeto [a'fɛtu] *m* affection.

afetuoso/a [afe'twozu/ɔza] *adj* affectionate, tender.

afez [a'fɛʒ] *etc vb V* **afazer**.

AFI *abr m (= Alfabeto Fonético Internacional)* IPA.

afiado/a [a'fjadu/a] *adj* sharp; *(pessoa)* well-trained.

afiançar [afjã'sa*] *vt (JUR)* to stand bail for; *(garantir)* to guarantee.

afiar [a'fja*] *vt* to sharpen.

aficionado/a [afisjo'nadu/a] *m/f* enthusiast.

afigurar-se [afigu'raxsi] *vr* to seem, appear; **afigura-se-me que** it seems to me that.

afilado/a [afi'ladu/a] *adj (nariz)* thin.

afilhado/a [afi'ʎadu/a] *m/f* godson/ goddaughter.

afiliação [afilja'sãw] *(pl -ões) f* affiliation.

afiliada [afi'ljada] *f* affiliate, affiliated company.

afiliado/a [afi'ljadu/a] *adj* affiliated.

afiliar [afi'lja*] *vt* to affiliate; ~-se *vr:* ~-se a to join.

afim [a'fĩ] *(pl -ns) adj (semelhante)* similar; *(consangüíneo)* related ♦ *m/f* relative, relation; **estar** ~ **de (fazer) algo/alguém** *V* **fim**.

afinação [afina'sãw] *f (MÚS)* tuning.

afinado/a [afi'nadu/a] *adj* in tune.

afinal [afi'naw] *adv* at last, finally; ~ **(de contas)** after all.

afinar [afi'na*] *vt (MÚS)* to tune ♦ *vi (adelgaçar)* to taper.

afinco [a'fĩku] *m* tenacity, persistence; **com** ~ tenaciously.

afinidade [afini'dadʒi] *f* affinity.

afins [a'fĩʃ] *m/fpl de* **afim**.

afirmação [afixma'sãw] *(pl -ões) f* affirmation; *(declaração)* statement.

afirmar [afix'ma*] *vt, vi* to affirm, assert; *(declarar)* to declare.

afirmativo/a [afixma'tʃivu/a] *adj* affirmative.

afiro [a'firu] *etc vb V* **aferir**.

afivelar [afive'la*] *vt* to buckle.

afixar [afik'sa*] *vt (cartazes)* to stick, post.

afiz [a'fiʒ] *etc vb V* **afazer**.

afizer [afi'ze*] *etc vb V* **afazer**.

aflição [afli'sãw] *f (sofrimento)* affliction; *(ansiedade)* anxiety; *(angústia)* anguish.

afligir [afli'ʒi*] *vt* to distress; *(atormentar)* to torment; *(inquietar)* to worry; ~-se *vr:* ~-se com to worry about.

aflijo [a'fliʒu] *etc vb V* **afligir**.

aflito/a [a'flitu/a] *pp de* **afligir** ♦ *adj* distressed, anxious.

aflorar [aflo'ra*] *vi* to emerge, appear.

afluência [a'flwẽsja] *f* affluence; *(corrente copiosa)* great flow; *(de pessoas)* crowd.

afluente [a'flwẽtʃi] *adj* copious; *(rico)* affluent ♦ *m* tributary.

afluir [a'flwi*] *vi* to flow; *(pessoas)* to congregate.

afobação [afoba'sãw] *f* fluster; *(ansiedade)* panic.

afobado/a [afo'badu/a] *adj* flustered; *(ansioso)* panicky, nervous.

afobamento [afoba'mẽtu] *m* fluster; *(ansiedade)* panic.

afobar [afo'ba*] *vt* to fluster; *(deixar ansioso)* to make nervous ou panicky ♦ *vi* to get flustered; *(ficar ansioso)* to panic, get nervous; ~-se *vr* to get flustered.

afofar [afo'fa*] *vt* to fluff.

afogado/a [afo'gadu/a] *adj* drowned.

afogador [afoga'do*] *(BR) m (AUTO)* choke.

afogar [afo'ga*] *vt* to drown ♦ *vi (AUTO)* to flood; ~-se *vr* to drown, be drowned.

afoito/a [a'fojtu/a] *adj* bold, daring.

afonia [afo'nia] *f* voice loss.

afônico/a [a'foniku/a] *adj:* **estou** ~ I've lost my voice.

afora [a'fɔra] *prep* except for, apart from ♦ *adv:* **rua** ~ down the street; **pelo mundo** ~ throughout the world; **porta** ~ out into the street.

aforismo [afo'riʒmu] *m* aphorism.

aforrar [afo'xa*] *vt (roupa)* to line; *(poupar)* to save; *(liberar)* to free.

afortunado/a [afoxtu'nadu/a] *adj* fortunate, lucky.

afrescalhado/a [afreʃka'ʎadu/a] *(col) adj* effeminate, camp.

afresco [a'freʃku] *m* fresco.

África ['afrika] *f:* **a** ~ Africa; **a** ~ **do Sul** South Africa.

africano/a [afri'kanu/a] *adj, m/f* African.

NB: *European Portuguese adds the following consonants to certain words:* **b** (sú(b)dito, su(b)til); **c** (a(c)ção, a(c)cionista, a(c)to); **m** (inde(m)ne); **p** (ado(p)ção, ado(p)tar); *for further details see p. xiii.*

AFRMM (BR) abr m (= Adicional ao Frete para Renovação da Marinha Mercante) tax on goods imported by sea.

afro-brasileiro/a ['afru-] (pl ~s) adj Afro-Brazilian.

afrodisíaco [afrodʒi'ziaku] m aphrodisiac.

afronta [a'frõta] f insult, affront.

afrontado/a [afrõ'tadu/a] adj (ofendido) offended; (com má digestão) too full.

afrontar [afrõ'ta*] vt to insult; (ofender) to offend.

afrouxar [afro'ʃa*] vt (desapertar) to slacken; (soltar) to loosen ♦ vi (soltar-se) to come loose.

afta ['afta] f (mouth) ulcer.

afugentar [afuʒẽ'ta*] vt to drive away, put to flight.

afundar [afũ'da*] vt (submergir) to sink; (cavidade) to deepen; ~-se vr to sink; (col: num exame) to do badly.

agá [a'ga] m aitch, h.

agachar-se [aga'ʃaxsi] vr (acaçapar-se) to crouch, squat; (curvar-se) to stoop; (fig) to cringe.

agarração [agaxa'sãw] (col) f necking.

agarrado/a [aga'xadu/a] adj: ~ a (preso) stuck to; (a uma pessoa) very attached to.

agarramento [agaxa'mẽtu] m (a uma pessoa) close attachment; (col: agarração) necking.

agarrar [aga'xa*] vt to seize, grasp; ~-se vr: ~-se a to cling to, hold on to.

agasalhado/a [agaza'ʎadu/a] adj warmly dressed, wrapped up.

agasalhar [agaza'ʎa*] vt to dress warmly, wrap up; ~-se vr to wrap o.s. up.

agasalho [aga'zaʎu] m (casaco) coat; (suéter) sweater.

ágeis ['aʒejʃ] adj pl de **ágil**.

agência [a'ʒẽsja] f agency; (escritório) office; (de banco etc) branch; ~ de correio (BR) post office; ~ de viagens travel agency; ~ publicitária advertising agency.

agenciar [aʒẽ'sja*] vt (negociar) to negotiate; (obter) to procure; (ser agente de) to act as an agent for.

agenda [a'ʒẽda] f diary.

agente [a'ʒẽtʃi] m/f agent; (de polícia) policeman/woman; ~ de seguros (insurance) underwriter.

agigantado/a [aʒigã'tadu/a] adj gigantic.

ágil ['aʒiw] (pl -eis) adj agile.

agilidade [aʒili'dadʒi] f agility.

agilizar [aʒili'za*] vt: ~ algo (dar andamento a) to get sth moving; (acelerar) to speed sth up.

ágio ['aʒju] m premium.

agiota [a'ʒjɔta] m/f moneylender.

agir [a'ʒi*] vi to act; ~ bem/mal to do right/wrong.

agitação [aʒita'sãw] (pl -ões) f agitation; (perturbação) disturbance; (inquietação) restlessness.

agitado/a [aʒi'tadu/a] adj agitated, disturbed;

(inquieto) restless.

agitar [aʒi'ta*] vt to agitate, disturb; (sacudir) to shake; (cauda) to wag; (mexer) to stir; (os braços) to swing, wave; ~-se vr to get upset; (mar) to get rough.

aglomeração [aglomera'sãw] (pl -ões) f gathering; (multidão) crowd.

aglomerado [aglome'radu] m: ~ urbano city.

aglomerar [aglome'ra*] vt to heap up, pile up; ~-se vr (multidão) to crowd together.

AGO abr f (= assembléia geral ordinária) AGM.

ago. abr (= agosto) Aug.

agonia [ago'nia] f agony, anguish; (ânsia da morte) death throes pl; (indecisão) indecision.

agoniado/a [ago'njadu/a] adj anguished.

agonizante [agoni'zãtʃi] adj dying ♦ m/f dying person.

agonizar [agoni'za*] vi to be dying; (afligir-se) to agonize.

agora [a'gɔra] adv now; (hoje em dia) now, nowadays; **e ~?** now what?; ~ **mesmo** right now; (há pouco) a moment ago; **a partir de** ~, **de** ~ **em diante** from now on; **até** ~ so far, up to now; **por** ~ for now; ~ **que** now that; **eu lhe disse ontem;** ~, **se ele esquecer ...** I told him yesterday; but if he forgets ....

agorinha [ago'riɲa] adv just now.

agosto [a'goʃtu] (PT: **A~**) m August; V tb **julho**.

agourar [ago'ra*] vt to predict, foretell ♦ vi to augur ill.

agouro [a'goru] m omen; (mau ~) bad omen.

agraciar [agra'sja*] vt (condecorar) to decorate.

agradabilíssimo/a [agradabi'lisimu/a] adj superl de **agradável**.

agradar [agra'da*] vt (deleitar) to please; (fazer agrados a) to be nice to ♦ vi (ser agradável) to be pleasing; (satisfazer: show, piada etc) to go down well.

agradável [agra'davew] (pl -eis) adj pleasant.

agradecer [agrade'se*] vt: ~ **algo a alguém**, ~ **a alguém por algo** to thank sb for sth.

agradecido/a [agrade'sidu/a] adj grateful; **mal** ~ ungrateful.

agradecimento [agradesi'mẽtu] m gratitude; ~s mpl thanks.

agrado [a'gradu] m: **fazer um** ~ **a alguém** (afagar) to be affectionate with sb; (ser agradável) to be nice to sb.

agrário/a [a'grarju/a] adj agrarian; **reforma agrária** land reform.

agravação [agrava'sãw] (PT) f aggravation; (piora) worsening.

agravamento [agrava'mẽtu] (BR) m aggravation.

agravante [agra'vãtʃi] adj aggravating ♦ f aggravating circumstance.

agravar [agra'va*] vt to aggravate, make worse; ~-se vr (piorar) to get worse.

agravo [a'gravu] *m* (*JUR*) appeal.
agredir [agre'dʒi*] *vt* to attack; (*insultar*) to insult.
agregado/a [agre'gadu/a] *m/f* (*lavrador*) tenant farmer; (*BR*) lodger ♦ *m* aggregate, sum total.
agregar [agre'ga*] *vt* (*juntar*) to collect; (*acrescentar*) to add.
agressão [agre'sãw] (*pl* **-ões**) *f* aggression; (*ataque*) attack; (*assalto*) assault.
agressividade [agresivi'dadʒi] *f* aggressiveness.
agressivo/a [agre'sivu/a] *adj* aggressive.
agressões [agre'sójʃ] *fpl de* **agressão**.
agressor(a) [agre'so*(a)] *m/f* aggressor.
agreste [a'grɛʃtʃi] *adj* rural, rustic; (*terreno*) wild, uncultivated.
agrião [a'grjãw] *m* watercress.
agrícola [a'grikola] *adj* agricultural.
agricultável [agrikuw'tavew] (*pl* **-eis**) *adj* arable.
agricultor [agrikuw'to*] *m* farmer.
agricultura [agrikuw'tura] *f* agriculture, farming.
agrido [a'gridu] *etc vb* V **agredir**.
agridoce [agri'dosi] *adj* bittersweet.
agronomia [agrono'mia] *f* agronomy.
agrônomo/a [a'gronomu/a] *m/f* agronomist.
agropecuária [agrope'kwarja] *f* farming, agriculture.
agropecuário/a [agrope'kwarju/a] *adj* farming *atr*, agricultural.
agrotóxico [agro'tɔksiku] *m* pesticide.
agrupamento [agrupa'mẽtu] *m* grouping.
agrupar [agru'pa*] *vt* to group; **~-se** *vr* to group together.
agrura [a'grura] *f* bitterness.
água ['agwa] *f* water; **~s** *fpl* (*mar*) waters; (*chuvas*) rain *sg*; (*maré*) tides; **~ abaixo/acima** downstream/upstream; **até debaixo da ~** (*fig*) one thousand per cent; **dar ~ na boca** (*comida*) to be mouthwatering; **estar na ~** (*bêbado*) to be drunk; **fazer ~** (*NÁUT*) to leak; **ir nas ~s de alguém** (*fig*) to follow in sb's footsteps; **~ benta** holy water; **~ corrente** running water; **~ doce** fresh water; **~ dura/leve** hard/soft water; **~ mineral** mineral water; **~ oxigenada** peroxide; **~ salgada** salt water; **~ sanitária** household bleach; **jogar ~ na fervura** (*fig*) to put a damper on things; **mudar como da ~ para o vinho** to change radically; **desta ~ não beberei!** that won't happen to me!; **~s passadas não movem moinhos** it's all water under the bridge.
aguaceiro [agwa'sejru] *m* (*chuva*) heavy shower, downpour; (*com vento*) squall.
água-com-açúcar *adj inv* schmalzy, mushy.
água-de-coco *f* coconut water.
água-de-colônia (*pl* **águas-de-colônia**) *f* eau-de-cologne.
aguado/a [a'gwadu/a] *adj* watery.
água-furtada [-fux'tada] (*pl* **águas-furtadas**) *f* garret, attic.
água-marinha (*pl* **águas-marinhas**) *f* aquamarine.
aguar [a'gwa*] *vt* to water ♦ *vi:* **~ por** (*salivar*) to drool over.
aguardar [agwax'da*] *vt* to wait for, await; (*contar com*) to expect ♦ *vi* to wait.
aguardente [agwax'dẽtʃi] *m* spirit.
aguarrás [agwa'xajʃ] *f* turpentine.
água-viva (*pl* **águas-vivas**) *f* jellyfish.
aguçado/a [agu'sadu/a] *adj* pointed; (*espírito*, *sentidos*) acute.
aguçar [agu'sa*] *vt* (*afiar*) to sharpen; (*estimular*) to excite; **~ a vista** to keep one's eyes peeled.
agudeza [agu'deza] *f* sharpness; (*perspicácia*) perspicacity; (*de som*) shrillness.
agudo/a [a'gudu/a] *adj* sharp; (*som*) shrill; (*intenso*) acute.
agüentar [agwẽ'ta*] *vt* (*muro etc*) to hold up; (*dor, injustiças*) to stand, put up with; (*peso*) to withstand, stand; (*resistir a*) to stand up to ♦ *vi* to last, hold out; (*resistir a peso*) to hold; **~-se** *vr* (*manter-se*) to remain, hold on; **~ com** to hold, withstand; **~ fazer algo** to manage to do sth; **não ~ de** not to be able to stand; **~ firme** to hold out.
aguerrido/a [age'xidu/a] *adj* warlike, bellicose; (*corajoso*) courageous.
águia ['agja] *f* eagle; (*fig*) genius.
agulha [a'guʎa] *f* (*de coser, tricó*) needle; (*NÁUT*) compass; (*estrada de ferro*) points *pl* (*BRIT*), switch (*US*); **trabalho de ~** needlework.
agulheta [agu'ʎeta] *f* (*bico*) nozzle.
ah [a] *excl* oh!
AI *abr f* = **Anistia Internacional** ♦ *abr m* (*BR*) = **Ato Institucional**; **AI-5** *measure passed in 1968 suspending congress and banning opposition politicians.*
ai [aj] *excl* (*suspiro*) oh!; (*de dor*) ouch! ♦ *m* (*suspiro*) sigh; (*gemido*) groan; **~ de mim** poor me!
aí [a'i] *adv* there; (*então*) then; **por ~** (*em lugar indeterminado*) somewhere over there, thereabouts; **espera ~!** wait!, hang on a minute!; **está ~!** (*col*) right!; **~ é que 'tá!** (*col*) that's just the point; **e por ~ afora** *ou* **vai** and so on; **já não está ~ quem falou** (*col*) I stand corrected; **e ~?** and then what?; **e ~ (como vai)?** (*col*) how are things with you?
aiatolá [ajato'la] *m* ayatollah.
aidético/a [aj'dɛtʃiku/a] *adj* suffering from AIDS ♦ *m/f* person with AIDS.
AIDS ['ajdʒs] *f* AIDS.
ainda [a'ĩda] *adv* still; (*mesmo*) even; **~ ago-**

NB: European Portuguese adds the following consonants to certain words: **b** (sú(b)dito, su(b)til); **c** (a(c)ção, a(c)cionista, a(c)to); **m** (inde(m)ne); **p** (ado(p)ção, ado(p)tar); *for further details see p. xiii.*

ra just now; ~ **assim** even so, nevertheless; ~ **bem** just as well; ~ **por cima** on top of all that, in addition; ~ **não** not yet; ~ **que** even if; **maior** ~ even bigger.
aipim [aj'pĩ] *m* cassava.
aipo ['ajpu] *m* celery.
airado/a [aj'radu/a] *adj* (*frívolo*) frivolous; (*leviano*) dissolute.
airoso/a [aj'rozu/ɔza] *adj* graceful, elegant.
ajantarado [aʒãta'radu] *m* lunch and dinner combined.
ajardinar [aʒaxdʒi'na*] *vt* to make into a garden.
ajeitar [aʒej'ta*] *vt* (*adaptar*) to fit, adjust; (*arranjar*) to arrange, fix; ~-**se** *vr* to adapt; **aos poucos as coisas se ajeitam** things will gradually sort themselves out.
ajo ['aʒu] *etc vb* V **agir**.
ajoelhado/a [aʒwe'ʎadu/a] *adj* kneeling.
ajoelhar [aʒwe'ʎa*] *vi* to kneel (down); ~-**se** *vr* to kneel down.
ajuda [a'ʒuda] *f* help, aid; (*subsídio*) grant, subsidy; **sem** ~ unaided; **dar** ~ **a alguém** to lend *ou* give sb a hand; ~ **de custo** allowance.
ajudante [aʒu'dãtʃi] *m* assistant, helper; (*MIL*) adjutant.
ajudar [aʒu'da*] *vt* to help.
ajuizado/a [aʒwi'zadu/a] *adj* (*sensato*) sensible; (*sábio*) wise; (*prudente*) discreet.
ajuizar [aʒwi'za*] *vt* to judge; (*calcular*) to calculate.
ajuntamento [aʒũta'mẽtu] *m* gathering.
ajuntar [aʒũ'ta*] *vt* (*unir*) to join, add; (*documentos*) to attach; (*reunir*) to gather.
ajustagem [aʒuʃ'taʒẽ] (*BR*: *pl* -**ns**) *f* (*TEC*) adjustment.
ajustamento [aʒuʃta'mẽtu] *m* adjustment; (*de contas*) settlement.
ajustagens [aʒuʃ'taʒẽʃ] *fpl de* **ajustagem**.
ajustar [aʒuʃ'ta*] *vt* (*regular*) to adjust; (*conta, disputa*) to settle; (*acomodar*) to fit; (*roupa*) to take in; (*contratar*) to contract; (*estipular*) to stipulate; (*preço*) to agree on; ~-**se** *vr*: ~-**se a** to conform to; (*adaptar-se*) to adapt to.
ajustável [aʒuʃ'tavew] (*pl* -**eis**) *adj* adjustable; (*aplicável*) applicable.
ajuste [a'ʒuʃtʃi] *m* (*acordo*) agreement; (*de contas*) settlement; (*adaptação*) adjustment; ~ **final** (*COM*) settlement of account.
AL *abr* = **Alagoas** ♦ *abr f* (*BR*: = *Aliança Liberal*) *former political party*.
Al. *abr* = **Alameda**.
ala ['ala] *f* (*fileira*) row; (*passagem*) aisle; (*de edifício, exército, ave*) wing.
Alá [a'la] *m* Allah.
ALADI *abr f* = **Associação Latino-Americana de Desenvolvimento e Intercâmbio**.
alagação [alaga'sãw] *f* flooding.
alagadiço/a [alaga'dʒisu/a] *adj* swampy, marshy ♦ *m* swamp, marsh.
alagamento [alaga'mẽtu] *m* flooding;

(*arrasamento*) destruction.
alagar [ala'ga*] *vt*, *vi* to flood.
alagoano/a [ala'gwanu/a] *adj* from Alagoas ♦ *m/f* native *ou* inhabitant of Alagoas.
alambique [alã'biki] *m* still.
alameda [ala'meda] *f* (*avenida*) avenue; (*arvoredo*) grove.
álamo ['alamu] *m* poplar.
alanhar [ala'ɲa*] *vt* to slash; (*peixe*) to gut.
alar [a'la*] *vt* to haul, heave.
alaranjado/a [alarã'ʒadu/a] *adj* orangy.
alarde [a'laxdʒi] *m* (*ostentação*) ostentation; (*jactância*) boasting; **fazer** ~ **de** to boast about.
alardear [alax'dʒja*] *vt* to show off; (*gabar-se de*) to boast of ♦ *vi* to boast; ~-**se** *vr* to boast; ~ **fazer** to boast of doing; ~(-**se**) **de valente** to boast of being strong.
alargamento [alaxga'mẽtu] *m* enlargement.
alargar [alax'ga*] *vt* (*ampliar*) to extend; (*fazer mais largo*) to widen, broaden; (*afrouxar*) to loosen, slacken.
alarido [ala'ridu] *m* (*clamor*) outcry; (*tumulto*) uproar.
alarma [a'laxma] *f* alarm; (*susto*) panic; (*tumulto*) tumult; (*vozearia*) outcry; **dar o sinal de** ~ to raise the alarm; ~ **de roubo** burglar alarm.
alarmante [alax'mãtʃi] *adj* alarming.
alarmar [alax'ma*] *vt* to alarm; ~-**se** *vr* to be alarmed.
alarme [a'laxmi] *m* = **alarma**.
alarmista [alax'miʃta] *adj*, *m/f* alarmist.
Alasca [a'laʃka] *m*: **o** ~ Alaska.
alastrado/a [alaʃ'tradu/a] *adj*: ~ **de** strewn with.
alastrar [alaʃ'tra*] *vt* (*espalhar*) to scatter; (*disseminar*) to spread; (*lastrar*) to ballast; ~-**se** *vr* (*epidemia, rumor*) to spread.
alavanca [ala'vãka] *f* lever; (*pé-de-cabra*) crowbar; ~ **de mudanças** gear lever.
albanês/esa [awba'neʃ/eza] *adj*, *m/f* Albanian ♦ *m* (*LING*) Albanian.
Albânia [aw'banja] *f*: **a** ~ Albania.
albergar [awbex'ga*] *vt* (*hospedar*) to provide lodging for; (*abrigar*) to shelter.
albergue [aw'bexgi] *m* (*estalagem*) inn; (*refúgio*) hospice, shelter; ~ **noturno** hotel; ~ **para jovens** youth hostel.
albino/a [aw'binu/a] *adj*, *m/f* albino.
albufeira [awbu'fejra] *f* lagoon.
álbum ['awbũ] (*pl* -**ns**) *m* album; ~ **de recortes** scrapbook.
alça ['awsa] *f* strap; (*asa*) handle; (*de fusil*) sight.
alcácer [aw'kase*] *m* fortress.
alcachofra [awka'ʃofra] *f* artichoke.
alcaçuz [awka'suʒ] *m* liquorice.
alçada [aw'sada] *f* (*jurisdição*) jurisdiction; (*competência*) competence; **isso não é da minha** ~ that is beyond my control.
alcagüete [awka'gwetʃi] *m/f* informer.
álcali ['awkali] *m* alkali.

alcalino/a [awka'linu/a] *adj* alkaline.

alcançar [awkã'sa*] *vt* to reach; (*estender*) to hand, pass; (*obter*) to obtain, get; (*atingir*) to attain; (*compreender*) to understand ♦ *vi* to reach; **~-se** *vr* (*fazer um desfalque*) to embezzle funds; (*desfalcar*): **~ uma firma em $1 milhão** to embezzle $1 million from a firm.

alcançável [awkã'savew] (*pl* **-eis**) *adj* (*acessível*) reachable; (*atingível*) attainable.

alcance [aw'kãsi] *m* reach; (*competência*) power, competence; (*compreensão*) understanding; (*de tiro, visão*) range; (*desfalque*) embezzlement; **ao ~ de** within reach/range of; **ao ~ da voz** within earshot; **de grande ~** of great consequence; **fora do ~ da mão** out of reach; **fora do ~ de alguém** beyond sb's grasp.

alcantilado/a [awkãtʃi'ladu/a] *adj* (*íngreme*) steep; (*penhascoso*) craggy.

alçapão [awsa'pãw] (*pl* **-ões**) *m* trapdoor; (*arapuca*) trap.

alcaparra [awka'paxa] *f* caper.

alçapões [awsa'põjʃ] *mpl de* **alçapão**.

alçaprema [awsa'prɛma] *f* (*alavanca*) crowbar.

alçar [aw'sa*] *vt* to lift (up); (*voz*) to raise; **~ vôo** to take off.

alcaravia [awkara'via] *f*: **sementes de ~** caraway seeds.

alcatéia [awka'tɛja] *f* (*de lobos*) pack; (*de ladrões*) gang.

alcatra [aw'katra] *f* rump (steak).

alcatrão [awka'trãw] *m* tar.

álcool ['awkɔw] *m* alcohol.

alcoólatra [aw'kɔlatra] *m/f* alcoholic.

alcoólico/a [aw'kɔliku/a] *adj, m/f* alcoholic.

alcoolismo [awko'liʒmu] *m* alcoholism.

Alcorão [awko'rãw] *m* Koran.

alcova [aw'kova] *f* bedroom.

alcoviteiro/a [awkovi'tejru/a] *m/f* pimp/procuress.

alcunha [aw'kuɲa] *f* nickname.

aldeão/eã [aw'dʒãw/jã] (*pl* **-ões/~s**) *m/f* villager.

aldeia [aw'deja] *f* village.

aldeões [aw'dʒjõjʃ] *mpl de* **aldeão**.

aldraba [aw'draba] *f* (*PT: tranqueta*) latch; (*de bater*) door knocker.

aleatório/a [alea'tɔrju/a] *adj* random.

alecrim [ale'krĩ] *m* rosemary.

alegação [alega'sãw] (*pl* **-ões**) *f* allegation.

alegado [ale'gadu] *m* (*JUR*) plea.

alegar [ale'ga*] *vt* to allege; (*JUR*) to plead.

alegoria [alego'ria] *f* allegory.

alegórico/a [ale'gɔriku/a] *adj* allegorical; *V tb* **carro**.

alegrar [ale'gra*] *vt* (*tornar feliz*) to cheer (up), gladden; (*ambiente*) to brighten up; (*animar*) to liven (up); **~-se** *vr* to cheer up.

alegre [a'lɛgri] *adj* (*jovial*) cheerful; (*contente*) happy, glad; (*cores*) bright; (*embriagado*) merry, tight.

alegria [ale'gria] *f* joy, happiness.

aleguei [ale'gej] *etc vb V* **alegar**.

aléia [a'lɛja] *f* (tree-lined) avenue; (*passagem*) alley.

aleijado/a [alej'ʒadu/a] *adj* crippled, disabled ♦ *m/f* cripple.

aleijão [alej'ʒãw] (*pl* **-ões**) *m* deformity.

aleijar [alej'ʒa*] *vt* (*mutilar*) to maim.

aleijões [alej'ʒõjʃ] *mpl de* **aleijão**.

aleitamento [alejta'mẽtu] *m* breast feeding.

aleitar [alej'ta*] *vt, vi* to breast-feed.

além [a'lẽj] *adv* (*lá ao longe*) over there; (*mais adiante*) further on ♦ *m*: **o ~** the hereafter ♦ *prep*: **~ de** beyond; (*no outro lado de*) on the other side of; (*para mais de*) over; (*ademais de*) apart from, besides; **~ disso** moreover; **mais ~** further.

alemã [ale'mã] *f de* **alemão**.

alemães [ale'mãjʃ] *mpl de* **alemão**.

Alemanha [ale'mãɲa] *f*: **a ~** Germany; **a ~ Ocidental/Oriental** West/East Germany.

alemão/mã [ale'mãw/'mã] (*pl* **-ães/~s**) *adj, m/f* German ♦ *m* (*LING*) German.

alentado/a [alẽ'tadu/a] *adj* (*valente*) valiant; (*grande*) great; (*volumoso*) substantial.

alentador(a) [alẽta'do*(a)] *adj* encouraging.

alentar [alẽ'ta*] *vt* to encourage; **~-se** *vr* to cheer up.

alentejano/a [alẽte'ʒanu/a] *adj* from Alentejo ♦ *m/f* native ou inhabitant of Alentejo.

alento [a'lẽtu] *m* (*fôlego*) breath; (*ânimo*) courage; **dar ~** to encourage; **tomar ~** to draw breath.

alergia [alex'ʒia] *f*: **~ (a)** allergy (to); (*fig*) aversion (to).

alérgico/a [a'lɛxʒiku/a] *adj*: **~ (a)** allergic (to).

alerta [a'lɛxta] *adj* alert ♦ *adv* on the alert ♦ *m* alert.

alertar [alex'ta*] *vt* to alert; **~-se** *vr* to be alerted.

Alf. *abr* = **Alferes**.

alfabético/a [awfa'bɛtʃiku/a] *adj* alphabetical.

alfabetização [awfabetʃiza'sãw] *f* literacy.

alfabetizado/a [awfabetʃi'zadu/a] *adj* literate.

alfabetizar [awfabetʃi'za*] *vt* to teach to read and write; **~-se** *vr* to learn to read and write.

alfabeto [awfa'bɛtu] *m* alphabet.

alface [aw'fasi] *f* lettuce.

alfaia [aw'faja] *f* (*móveis*) furniture; (*utensílio*) utensil; (*enfeite*) ornament.

alfaiataria [awfajata'ria] *f* tailor's shop.

alfaiate [awfa'jatʃi] *m* tailor.

alfândega [aw'fãdʒiga] *f* customs *pl*, customs house.

alfandegário/a [awfãde'garju/a] *adj* customs *atr* ♦ *m/f* customs officer.

---

*NB: European Portuguese adds the following consonants to certain words: **b** (sú(b)dito, su(b)til); **c** (a(c)ção, a(c)cionista, a(c)to); **m** (inde(m)ne); **p** (ado(p)ção, ado(p)tar); for further details see p. xiii.*

alfanumérico/a [awfanu'meriku/a] adj alphanumeric.

alfavaca [awfa'vaka] f basil.

alfazema [awfa'zɛma] f lavender.

alfena [aw'fɛna] f privet.

alfinetada [awfine'tada] f prick; (dor aguda) stabbing pain; (fig) dig.

alfinetar [awfine'ta*] vt to prick (with a pin); (marcar costura) to pin; (fig) to needle.

alfinete [awfi'netʃi] m pin; ~ **de chapéu** hat pin; ~ **de fralda** nappy (BRIT) ou diaper (US) pin; ~ **de segurança** safety pin.

alfineteira [awfine'tejra] f pin cushion; (caixa) pin box.

alga ['awga] f seaweed; (BOT) alga.

algarismo [awga'riʒmu] m numeral, digit; ~ **arábico/romano** Arabic/Roman numeral.

Algarve [aw'gaxvi] m: o ~ the Algarve.

algarvio/a [awgax'viu/a] adj from the Algarve ♦ m/f native ou inhabitant of the Algarve.

algazarra [awga'zaxa] f uproar, racket.

álgebra ['awʒebra] f algebra.

algemar [awʒe'ma*] vt to handcuff.

algemas [aw'ʒemaʃ] fpl handcuffs.

algibeira [awʒi'bejra] f pocket.

algo ['awgu] adv somewhat, rather ♦ pron something; (qualquer coisa) anything.

algodão [awgo'dãw] m cotton; ~(-doce) candy floss; ~ (hidrófilo) cotton wool (BRIT), absorbent cotton (US).

algodoeiro/a [awgo'dwejru/a] adj (indústria) cotton atr ♦ m cotton plant.

algoritmo [awgo'xitʃimu] m algorithm.

algoz [aw'gos] m beast, cruel person.

alguém [aw'gẽj] pron someone, somebody; (em frases interrogativas ou negativas) anyone, anybody; **ser** ~ **na vida** to be somebody in life.

algum(a) [aw'gũ/'guma] adj some; (em frases interrogativas ou negativas) any ♦ pron one; (no plural) some; (negativa): **de modo** ~ in no way; **coisa** ~a nothing; ~ **dia** one day; ~ **tempo** for a while; ~**a coisa** something; ~**a vez** sometime.

algures [aw'guriʃ] adv somewhere.

alheio/a [a'ʎeju/a] adj (de outrem) someone else's; (estranho) alien; (estrangeiro) foreign; (impróprio) inappropriate; ~ **a** foreign to; (desatento) unaware of; ~ **de** (afastado) removed from, far from; (ignorante) unaware of.

alho ['aʎu] m garlic; **confundir** ~**s com bugalhos** to get things mixed up.

alho-poró [-po'rɔ] (pl **alhos-porós**) m leek.

ali [a'li] adv there; **até** ~ up to there; **por** ~ around there, somewhere there; (direção) that way; ~ **por** (tempo) round about; **de** ~ **por diante** from then on; ~ **dentro** in there.

aliado/a [a'ljadu/a] adj allied ♦ m/f ally.

aliança [a'ljãsa] f alliance; (anel) wedding ring.

aliar [a'lja*] vt to ally; ~**-se** vr to make an alliance.

aliás [a'ljajʃ] adv (a propósito) as a matter of fact; (ou seja) rather, that is; (contudo) nevertheless; (diga-se de passagem) incidentally.

álibi ['alibi] m alibi.

alicate [ali'katʃi] m pliers pl; ~ **de unhas** nail clippers pl.

alicerçar [alisex'sa*] vt (argumento etc) to base; (consolidar) to consolidate.

alicerce [ali'sexsi] m (de edifício) foundation; (fig: base) basis.

aliciar [ali'sja*] vt (seduzir) to entice; (atrair) to attract.

alienação [aljena'sãw] f alienation; (de bens) transfer (of property); ~ **mental** insanity.

alienado/a [alje'nadu/a] adj alienated; (demente) insane; (bens) transferred ♦ m/f lunatic.

alienar [alje'na*] vt (bens) to transfer; (afastar) to alienate; ~**-se** vr to become alienated.

alienígena [alje'niʒena] adj, m/f alien.

alijar [ali'ʒa*] vt to jettison; (livrar-se de) to get rid of; ~**-se** vr: ~**-se de** to free o.s. of.

alimentação [alimẽta'sãw] f (alimentos) food; (ação) feeding; (nutrição) nourishment; (ELET) supply.

alimentar [alimẽ'ta*] vt to feed; (fig) to nurture ♦ adj (produto) food atr; (hábitos) eating atr; ~**-se** vr: ~**-se de** to feed on.

alimentício/a [alimẽ'tʃisju/a] adj nourishing; **gêneros** ~**s** foodstuffs.

alimento [ali'mẽtu] m food; (nutrição) nourishment.

alínea [a'linja] f opening line of a paragraph; (subdivisão de artigo) sub-heading.

alinhado/a [ali'nadu/a] adj (elegante) elegant; (texto) aligned; ~ **à esquerda/direita** (texto) ranged left/right.

alinhamento [alina'mẽtu] m alignment; ~ **da margem** justification.

alinhar [ali'na*] vt to align; ~**-se** vr (enfileirar-se) to form a line.

alinhavar [alina'va*] vt (COSTURA) to tack.

alinhavo [ali'navu] m tacking.

alinho [a'linu] m (alinhamento) alignment; (elegância) neatness.

alíquota [a'likwota] f bracket, percentage.

alisar [ali'za*] vt (tornar liso) to smooth; (cabelo) to straighten; (cariciar) to stroke.

alistamento [aliʃta'mẽtu] m enlistment.

alistar [aliʃ'ta*] vt (MIL) to recruit; ~**-se** vr to enlist.

aliteração [alitera'sãw] f alliteration.

aliviado/a [ali'vjadu/a] adj (pessoa) relieved; (: folgado) free; (carga) lightened; (dor) relieved.

aliviar [ali'vja*] vt to relieve; (carga etc) to lighten ♦ vi (diminuir) to diminish; (acalmar) to give relief; ~**-se** vr: ~**-se de** to unburden o.s. of.

alívio [a'livju] m relief.

Alm. abr = **Almirante**.

alma ['awma] *f* soul; *(entusiasmo)* enthusiasm; *(caráter)* character; **eu daria a ~ para fazer** I would give anything to do; **sua ~, sua palma** don't say I didn't warn you.

almanaque [awma'naki] *m* almanac; **cultura de ~** superficial knowledge.

almejar [awme'ʒa*] *vt* to long for, yearn for.

almirantado [awmirã'tadu] *m* admiralty.

almirante [awmi'rãtʃi] *m* admiral.

almoçado/a [awmo'sadu/a] *adj*: **ele está ~** he's had lunch.

almoçar [awmo'sa*] *vi* to have lunch ♦ *vt*: **~ peixe** to have fish for lunch.

almoço [aw'mosu] *m* lunch; **pequeno ~** *(PT)* breakfast.

almofada [awmo'fada] *f* cushion; *(PT: travesseiro)* pillow.

almofadado/a [awmofa'dadu/a] *adj* cushioned.

almofadinha [awmofa'dʒiɲa] *f* pin cushion.

almôndega [aw'mõdega] *f* meat ball.

almotolia [awmoto'lia] *f* oilcan.

almoxarifado [awmoʃari'fadu] *m* storeroom.

almoxarife [awmoʃa'rifi] *m* storekeeper.

ALN *(BR) abr f* (= *Ação Libertadora Nacional*) *former group opposed to junta.*

alô [a'lo] *(BR) excl (TEL)* hullo.

alocação [aloka'sãw] *(pl* **-ões)** *f* allocation.

alocar [alo'ka*] *vt* to allocate.

aloirado/a [aloj'radu/a] *adj* = **alourado/a.**

alojamento [aloʒa'mẽtu] *m* accommodation *(BRIT)*, accommodations *(US)*; *(habitação)* housing; *(MIL)* billet.

alojar [alo'ʒa*] *vt* to lodge; *(MIL)* to billet; **~-se** *vr* to stay.

alongamento [alõga'mẽtu] *m* lengthening; *(prazo)* extension; *(ginástica)* stretching.

alongar [alõ'ga*] *vt (fazer longo)* to lengthen; *(prazo)* to extend; *(prolongar)* to prolong; *(braço)* to stretch out; **~-se** *vr (sobre um assunto)* to dwell.

aloprado/a [alo'pradu/a] *(col) adj* nutty.

alourado/a [alo'radu/a] *adj* blondish.

alpaca [aw'paka] *f* alpaca.

alpendre [aw'pẽdri] *m* *(telheiro)* shed; *(pórtico)* porch.

alpercata [awpex'kata] *f* sandal.

Alpes ['awpiʃ] *mpl*: **os ~** the Alps.

alpinismo [awpi'niʒmu] *m* mountaineering, climbing.

alpinista [awpi'niʃta] *m/f* mountaineer, climber.

alq. *abr* = **alqueires.**

alquebrar [awke'bra*] *vt* to bend; *(enfraquecer)* to weaken ♦ *vi (curvar)* to stoop, be bent double.

alqueire [aw'kejri] *m* = *4.84 hectares (in São Paulo = 2.42 hectares).*

alqueive [aw'kejvi] *m* fallow land.

alquimia [awki'mia] *f* alchemy.

alquimista [awki'miʃta] *m/f* alchemist.

Alsácia [aw'sasja] *f*: **a ~** Alsace.

alta ['awta] *f (de preços)* rise; *(de hospital)* discharge; *(na bolsa)* high; **estar em ~** to be on the up; **pessoa da ~** high-class *ou* high-society person.

alta-fidelidade *f* hi-fi, high fidelity.

altaneiro/a [awta'nejru/a] *adj (soberbo)* proud.

altar [aw'ta*] *m* altar.

altar-mor [-mɔ*] *(pl* **altares-mores)** *m* high altar.

alta-roda *f* high society.

alta-tensão *f* high tension.

altear [aw'tʃja*] *vt* to raise; *(reputação)* to enhance ♦ *vi* to spread out; **~-se** *vr (reputação)* to be enhanced.

alteração [awtera'sãw] *(pl* **-ões)** *f (mudança)* alteration; *(desordem)* disturbance; *(falsificação)* falsification.

alterado/a [awte'radu/a] *adj (de mau humor)* bad-tempered, irritated.

alterar [awte'ra*] *vt (mudar)* to alter; *(falsificar)* to falsify; **~-se** *vr (mudar-se)* to become altered; *(enfurecer-se)* to get angry, lose one's temper.

alternado/a [awtex'nadu/a] *adj* alternate.

altercar [awtex'ka*] *vi* to have an altercation ♦ *vt* to argue for, advocate.

alter ego [awter-] *m* alter ego.

alternância [awtex'nãsja] *f (AGR)* crop rotation.

alternar [awtex'na*] *vt*, *vi* to alternate; **~-se** *vr* to alternate; *(por turnos)* to take turns.

alternativa [awtexna'tʃiva] *f* alternative.

alternativo/a [awtexna'tʃivu/a] *adj* alternative; *(ELET)* alternating.

alteroso/a [awte'rozu/ɔza] *adj* towering; *(majestoso)* majestic.

alteza [aw'teza] *f* highness.

altissonante [awtʃiso'nãtʃi] *adj* high-sounding.

altista [aw'tʃiʃta] *m/f (BOLSA)* bull ♦ *adj (tendência)* bullish; **mercado ~** bull market.

altitude [awtʃi'tudʒi] *f* altitude.

altivez [awtʃi'veʒ] *f (arrogância)* haughtiness; *(nobreza)* loftiness.

altivo/a [aw'tʃivu/a] *adj (arrogante)* haughty; *(elevado)* lofty.

alto/a ['awtu/a] *adj* high; *(de grande estatura)* tall; *(som)* high, sharp; *(importância, luxo)* great; *(GEO)* upper ♦ *adv (falar)* loudly, loud; *(voar)* high ♦ *excl* halt! ♦ *m (topo)* top, summit; **~ lá!** just a minute!; **do ~** from above; **por ~** superficially; **estar ~** *(bêbado)* to be tipsy; **alta fidelidade** high fidelity, hi-fi; **alta noite** dead of night; **~s e baixos** ups and downs.

alto-astral *(col) m* good vibes *pl*; **estar de ~** to be on good form.

alto-falante *(pl* **~s)** *m* loudspeaker.

altruísmo [awtru'iʒmu] *m* altruism.

altruísta [awtru'iʃta] *adj* altruistic.

NB: European Portuguese adds the following consonants to certain words: **b** *(sú(b)dito, su(b)til);* **c** *(a(c)ção, a(c)cionista, a(c)to);* **m** *(inde(m)ne);* **p** *(ado(p)ção, ado(p)tar); for further details see p. xiii.*

altruístico/a [awtru'iʃtʃiku/a] *adj* altruistic.

altura [aw'tura] *f* height; (*momento*) point, juncture; (*altitude*) altitude; (*de um som*) pitch; (*lugar*) whereabouts; **em que ~ da Rio Branco fica a livraria?** whereabouts in Rio Branco is the bookshop?; **na ~ do banco** near the bank; **nesta ~** at this juncture; **estar à ~ de** (*ser capaz de*) to be up to; **pôr alguém nas ~s** (*fig*) to praise sb to the skies; **ter 1.80 metros de ~** to be 1.80 metres (*BRIT*) *ou* meters (*US*) tall.

alucinação [alusina'sãw] (*pl* **-ões**) *f* hallucination.

alucinado/a [alusi'nadu/a] *adj* (*maluco*) crazy; **~ por** crazy about.

alucinante [alusi'nãtʃi] *adj* crazy; **o tráfego no Rio é ~** the traffic in Rio drives you crazy.

aludir [alu'dʒi*] *vi*: **~ a** to allude to, hint at.

alugar [alu'ga*] *vt* (*tomar de aluguel*) to rent, hire; (*dar de aluguel*) to let, rent out; **~-se** *vr* to let.

aluguei [alu'gej] *etc vb V* **alugar**.

aluguel [alu'gew] (*pl* **-éis**) (*BR*) *m* rent; (*ação*) renting; **~ de carro** car hire (*BRIT*) *ou* rental (*US*).

aluguer [alu'gɛ*] (*PT*) *m* = **aluguel**.

aluir [a'lwi*] *vt* (*abalar*) to shake; (*derrubar*) to demolish; (*arruinar*) to ruin ♦ *vi* to collapse; (*ameaçar ruína*) to crumble.

alumiar [alu'mja*] *vt* to light (up) ♦ *vi* to give light.

alumínio [alu'minju] *m* aluminium (*BRIT*), aluminum (*US*).

alunissagem [aluni'saʒẽ] (*pl* **-ns**) *f* moon landing.

alunissar [aluni'sa*] *vi* to land on the moon.

aluno/a [a'lunu/a] *m/f* pupil, student; **~ excepcional** pupil with learning difficulties; **~ externo** day pupil; **~ interno** boarder.

alusão [alu'zãw] (*pl* **-ões**) *f* allusion, reference.

alusivo/a [alu'zivu/a] *adj* allusive.

alusões [alu'zõjʃ] *fpl de* **alusão**.

alvará [awva'ra] *m* permit.

alvejante [awve'ʒãtʃi] *m* bleach.

alvejar [awve'ʒa*] *vt* (*tomar como alvo*) to aim at; (*branquear*) to whiten, bleach ♦ *vi* to whiten.

alvenaria [awvena'ria] *f* masonry, brickwork; **de ~** brick *atr*, brick-built.

alvéolo [aw'vɛolu] *m* cavity; (*de dentes*) socket.

alvitrar [awvi'tra*] *vt* to propose, suggest.

alvitre [aw'vitri] *m* opinion.

alvo/a ['awvu/a] *adj* white ♦ *m* target; **acertar no ~** *ou* **atingir o ~** to hit the mark; **ser ~ de críticas** *etc* to be the object of criticism *etc*.

alvorada [awvo'rada] *f* dawn.

alvorecer [awvore'se*] *vi* to dawn.

alvoroçar [awvoro'sa*] *vt* (*agitar*) to stir up; (*entusiasmar*) to excite; **~-se** *vr* to get agitated.

alvoroço [awvo'rosu] *m* (*agitação*) commo-

tion; (*entusiasmo*) enthusiasm.

alvura [aw'vura] *f* (*brancura*) whiteness; (*pureza*) purity.

AM *abr* = **Amazonas**; (*RÁDIO*: = amplitude modulada*) AM.

Amã [a'mã] *n* Amman.

amabilidade [amabili'dadʒi] *f* kindness; (*simpatia*) friendliness.

amabilíssimo/a [amabi'lisimu/a] *adj superl de* **amável**.

amaciante [ama'sjatʃi] *m*: **~ (de roupa)** (fabric) conditioner.

amaciar [ama'sja*] *vt* (*tornar macio*) to soften; (*carro*) to run in.

ama-de-leite ['ama-] (*pl* **amas-de-leite**) *f* wet-nurse.

amado/a [a'madu/a] *m/f* beloved, sweetheart.

amador/a [ama'do*(a)] *adj*, *m/f* amateur.

amadorismo [amado'riʒmu] *m* amateur status.

amadorístico/a [amado'riʃtʃiku/a] *adj* amateurish.

amadurecer [amadure'se*] *vt*, *vi* (*frutos*) to ripen; (*fig*) to mature.

âmago ['amagu] *m* (*centro*) heart, core; (*medula*) pith; (*essência*) essence.

amainar [amaj'na*] *vi* (*tempestade*) to abate; (*cólera*) to calm down.

amaldiçoar [amawdʒi'swa*] *vt* to curse, swear at.

amálgama [a'mawgama] *f* amalgam.

amalgamar [amawga'ma*] *vt* to amalgamate; (*combinar*) to fuse (*BRIT*), fuze (*US*), blend.

amalucado/a [amalu'kadu/a] *adj* crazy, whacky.

amamentação [amamẽta'sãw] *f* breast-feeding.

amamentar [amamẽ'ta*] *vt* to breast-feed.

AMAN (*BR*) *abr f* = **Academia Militar das Agulhas Negras**.

amanhã [ama'ɲã] *adv*, *m* tomorrow; **~ de manhã** tomorrow morning; **~ de tarde** tomorrow afternoon; **~ à noite** tomorrow night; **depois de ~** the day after tomorrow.

amanhecer [amaɲe'se*] *vi* (*alvorecer*) to dawn; (*encontrar-se pela manhã*): **amanhecemos em Paris** we were in Paris at daybreak ♦ *m* dawn; **ao ~** at daybreak.

amansar [amã'sa*] *vt* (*animais*) to tame; (*cavalos*) to break in; (*aplacar*) to placate ♦ *vi* to grow tame.

amante [a'mãtʃi] *m/f* lover.

amanteigado/a [amãtej'gadu/a] *adj V* **biscoito**.

amapaense [amapa'ẽsi] *adj* from Amapá ♦ *m/f* native *ou* inhabitant of Amapá.

amar [a'ma*] *vt* to love.

amarelado/a [amare'ladu/a] *adj* yellowish; (*pele*) sallow.

amarelar [amare'la*] *vt*, *vi* to yellow.

amarelinha [amare'liɲa] *f* (*jogo*) hopscotch.

amarelo/a [ama'rɛlu/a] *adj* yellow ♦ *m* yellow.

amarfanhar [amaxfa'ɲa*] *vt* to screw up.

amargar [amax'ga*] *vt* to make bitter; (*fig*) to embitter; (*sofrer*) to suffer; **ser de** ~ to be murder.

amargo/a [a'maxgu/a] *adj* bitter.

amargura [amax'gura] *f* bitterness; (*fig*: *sofrimento*) sadness, suffering.

amargurado/a [amaxgu'radu/a] *adj* sad.

amargurar [amaxgu'ra*] *vt* to embitter, sadden; (*sofrer*) to endure.

amarração [amaxa'sãw] *f*: **ser uma** ~ (*col*) to be great.

amarrado/a [ama'xadu/a] *adj* (*cara*) scowling, angry; (*col*: *casado etc*) spoken for.

amarrar [ama'xa*] *vt* to tie (up); (*NÁUT*) to moor; ~**-se** *vr*: ~**se em** to like very much; ~ **a cara** to frown, scowl.

amarronzado/a [amaxõ'zadu/a] *adj* brownish.

amarrotar [amaxo'ta*] *vt* to crease.

ama-seca ['ama-] (*pl* **amas-secas**) *f* nanny.

amassado/a [ama'sadu/a] *adj* (*roupa*) creased; (*papel*) screwed up; (*carro*) smashed in.

amassar [ama'sa*] *vt* (*pão*) to knead; (*mistu-rar*) to mix; (*papel*) to screw up; (*roupa*) to crease; (*carro*) to dent.

amável [a'mavew] (*pl* **-eis**) *adj* (*afável*) kind.

amazona [ama'zɔna] *f* horsewoman.

Amazonas [ama'zɔnaʃ] *m*: **o** ~ the Amazon.

amazonense [amazo'nẽsi] *adj* from Amazonas ♦ *m/f* native *ou* inhabitant of Amazonas.

Amazônia [ama'zonja] *f*: **a** ~ the Amazon region.

amazônico/a [ama'zoniku/a] *adj* Amazonian.

âmbar ['ãba*] *m* amber.

ambição [ambi'sãw] (*pl* **-ões**) *f* ambition.

ambicionar [ãbisjo'na*] *vt* (*ter ambição de*) to aspire to; (*desejar*) to crave for.

ambicioso/a [ãbi'sjozu/ɔza] *adj* ambitious.

ambições [ãbi'sõjʃ] *fpl de* **ambição**.

ambidestro/a [ãbi'deʃtru/a] *adj* ambidextrous.

ambiental [ãbjẽ'taw] (*pl* **-ais**) *adj* environmental.

ambientalista [ãbjẽta'liʃta] *m/f* environmentalist.

ambientar [ãbjẽ'ta*] *vt* (*filme etc*) to set; (*adaptar*) to fit in; ~**-se** *vr* to fit in.

ambiente [ã'bjẽtʃi] *m* atmosphere; (*meio*, COMPUT) environment; (*de uma casa*) ambience ♦ *adj* surrounding; **meio** ~ environment; **temperatura** ~ room temperature.

ambigüidade [ambigwi'dadʃi] *f* ambiguity.

ambíguo/a [ã'bigwu/a] *adj* ambiguous.

âmbito ['ãbitu] *m* (*extensão*) extent; (*campo de ação*) scope, range; **no** ~ **nacional/internacional** at (the) national/international level.

ambivalência [ãbiva'lẽsja] *f* ambivalence.

ambivalente [ãbiva'lẽtʃi] *adj* ambivalent.

ambos/as ['ãbuʃ/aʃ] *adj pl* both; ~ **nós** both of us; ~ **os lados** both sides.

ambrosia [ãbro'zia] *f eggs and milk cooked in sugar*.

ambulância [ãbu'lãsja] *f* ambulance.

ambulante [ãbu'lãtʃi] *adj* walking; (*errante*) wandering; (*biblioteca*) mobile.

ambulatório [ãbula'tɔrju] *m* outpatient department.

ameaça [ame'asa] *f* threat.

ameaçador(a) [ameasa'do*(a)] *adj* threatening, menacing.

ameaçar [amea'sa*] *vt* to threaten.

ameba [a'mɛba] *f* amoeba (*BRIT*), ameba (*US*).

amedrontador(a) [amedrõta'do*(a)] *adj* intimidating, frightening.

amedrontar [amedrõ'ta*] *vt* to scare, intimidate; ~**-se** *vr* to be frightened.

ameia [a'meja] *f* battlement.

ameixa [a'mejʃa] *f* plum; (*passa*) prune.

amélia [a'mɛlja] (*col*) *f* long-suffering wife (*ou* girlfriend).

amém [a'mẽj] *excl* amen; **dizer** ~ **a** (*fig*) to agree to.

amêndoa [a'mẽdwa] *f* almond.

amendoado/a [amẽ'dwadu/a] *adj* (*olhos*) almond-shaped.

amendoeira [amẽ'dwejra] *f* almond tree.

amendoim [amẽdo'ĩ] (*pl* **-ns**) *m* peanut.

amenidade [ameni'dadʒi] *f* wellbeing; ~**s** *fpl* small talk *sg*.

amenizar [ameni'za*] *vt* (*abrandar*) to soften; (*tornar agradável*) to make pleasant; (*facilitar*) to ease; (*briga*) to settle.

ameno/a [a'mɛnu/a] *adj* (*agradável*) pleasant; (*clima*) mild, gentle.

América [a'mɛrika] *f*: **a** ~ America; **a** ~ **do Norte/do Sul** North/South America; **a** ~ **Central/Latina** Central/Latin America.

americanizado/a [amerikani'zadu/a] *adj* Americanized.

americano/a [ameri'kanu/a] *adj*, *m/f* American.

amesquinhar [ameʃki'ɲa*] *vt* to belittle; ~**-se** *vr* (*humilhar-se*) to belittle o.s.; (*tornar-se avarento*) to become stingy.

amestrar [ameʃ'tra*] *vt* to train.

ametista [ame'tʃiʃta] *f* amethyst.

amianto [a'mjãtu] *m* asbestos.

amicíssimo/a [ami'sisimu/a] *adj superl de* **amigo/a**.

amido [a'midu] *m* starch.

amigar-se [ami'gaxsi] *vr*: ~ (**com**) to become friends (with).

amigável [ami'gavew] (*pl* **-eis**) *adj* amicable.

amígdala [a'migdala] *f* tonsil.

amigdalite [amigda'litʃi] *f* tonsillitis.

amigo/a [a'migu/a] *adj* friendly ♦ *m/f* friend; **ser** ~ **de** to be friends with; ~ **do peito** bosom friend.

amigo/a-da-onça (*pl* **amigos/as-da-onça**) *m/f* false friend.

NB: European Portuguese adds the following consonants to certain words: **b** (sú(b)dito, su(b)til); **c** (a(c)ção, a(c)cionista, a(c)to); **m** (inde(m)ne); **p** (ado(p)ção, ado(p)tar); *for further details see p. xiii.*

amistoso/a [amiʃ'tozu/ɔza] *adj* friendly, cordial ♦ *m* (*jogo*) friendly.
AMIU (*BR*) *abr f* (= *Assistência Médica Infantil de Urgencia*) *emergency paediatric* (*BRIT*) *ou pediatric* (*US*) *service*.
amiudar [amju'da*] *vt, vi* to repeat; ~ **as visitas** to make frequent visits.
amiúde [a'mjudʒi] *adv* often, frequently.
amizade [ami'zadʒi] *f* (*relação*) friendship; (*simpatia*) friendliness; **fazer** ~**s** to make friends; ~ **colorida** casual relationship.
amnésia [am'nɛzja] *f* amnesia.
amnistia [amniʃ'tia] (*PT*) *f* = **anistia**.
amofinar [amofi'na*] *vt* to trouble; ~**-se** *vr* to fret (over).
amolação [amola'sãw] (*pl* **-ões**) *f* bother, annoyance; (*desgosto*) upset.
amolador(a) [amola'do*(a)] *m/f* knife sharpener.
amolante [amo'lãtʃi] (*BR*) *adj* bothersome.
amolar [amo'la*] *vt* (*afiar*) to sharpen; (*aborrecer*) to annoy, bother ♦ *vi* to be annoying; ~**-se** *vr* (*aborrecer-se*) to get annoyed.
amoldar [amow'da*] *vt* to mould (*BRIT*), mold (*US*); ~**-se** *vr*: ~**-se a** (*conformar-se*) to conform to; (*acostumar-se*) to get used to.
amolecimento [amolesi'mẽtu] *m* softening.
amolecer [amole'se*] *vt* to soften; (*abrandar-se*) to relent ♦ *vi* to soften.
amônia [a'monja] *f* ammonia.
amoníaco [amo'niaku] *m* ammonia.
amontoado [amõ'twadu/a] *m* mass; (*de coisas*) pile.
amontoar [amõ'twa*] *vt* to pile up, accumulate; ~ **riquezas** to amass a fortune.
amor [a'mo*] *m* love; **por** ~ **de** for the sake of; **fazer** ~ to make love; **ela é um** ~ **(de pessoa)** she's a lovely person; ~ **próprio** self-esteem; (*orgulho*) conceit.
amora [a'mɔra] *f* mulberry; ~ **silvestre** (*PT*) blackberry.
amoral [amo'raw] (*pl* **-ais**) *adj* amoral.
amora-preta (*pl* **amoras-pretas**) *f* blackberry.
amordaçar [amorda'sa*] *vt* to gag.
amoreco [amo'rɛku] *m*: **ela é um** ~ she's a lovely person.
amorenado/a [amore'nadu/a] *adj* darkish.
amorfo/a [a'mɔxfu/a] *adj* (*objeto*) amorphous; (*pessoa*) dull.
amornar [amox'na*] *vt* to warm.
amoroso/a [amo'rozu/ɔza] *adj* loving, affectionate.
amor-perfeito (*pl* **amores-perfeitos**) *m* pansy.
amortecedor [amoxtese'do*] *m* shock absorber.
amortecer [amoxte'se*] *vt* to deaden ♦ *vi* to weaken, fade.
amortecido/a [amoxte'sidu/a] *adj* deadened; (*enfraquecido*) weak.
amortização [amoxtʃiza'sãw] *f* payment in in-

stalments (*BRIT*) *ou* installments (*US*); (*COM*) amortization.
amortizar [amoxtʃi'za*] *vt* to pay in instalments (*BRIT*) *ou* installments (*US*).
amostra [a'mɔʃtra] *f* sample.
amostragem [amoʃ'traʒẽ] *f* sampling.
amotinado/a [amotʃi'nadu/a] *adj* mutinous, rebellious.
amotinar [amotʃi'na*] *vi* to rebel, mutiny; ~**-se** *vr* to rebel, mutiny.
amparar [ãpa'ra*] *vt* to support; (*ajudar*) to assist; ~**-se** *vr*: ~**-se em/contra** (*apoiar-se*) to lean on/against.
amparo [ã'paru] *m* (*apoio*) support; (*auxílio*) help, assistance.
ampère [ã'pɛri] (*BR*) *m* ampere, amp.
ampliação [amplja'sãw] (*pl* **-ões**) *f* (*aumento*) enlargement; (*extensão*) extension.
ampliar [ã'plja*] *vt* to enlarge; (*conhecimento*) to broaden.
amplidão [ãpli'dãw] *f* vastness.
amplificação [ãplifika'sãw] (*pl* **-ões**) *f* (*aumento*) enlargement; (*de som*) amplification.
amplificador [ãplifika'do*] *m* amplifier.
amplificar [ãplifi'ka*] *vt* to amplify.
amplitude [ãpli'tudʒi] *f* (*TEC*) amplitude; (*espaço*) spaciousness; (*fig: extensão*) extent.
amplo/a ['ãplu/a] *adj* (*sala*) spacious; (*conhecimento, sentido*) broad; (*possibilidade*) ample.
ampola [ã'pola] *f* ampoule (*BRIT*), ampule (*US*).
amputação [ãputa'sãw] (*pl* **-ões**) *f* amputation.
amputar [ãpu'ta*] *vt* to amputate.
Amsterdã [amiʃtex'dã] *n* Amsterdam.
amuado/a [a'mwadu/a] *adj* sulky.
amuar [a'mwa*] *vi* to sulk.
amuleto [amu'letu] *m* charm.
amuo [a'muu] *m* sulkiness.
anã [a'nã] *f de* **anão**.
anacrônico/a [ana'kroniku/a] *adj* anachronistic.
anacronismo [anakro'niʒmu] *m* anachronism.
anagrama [ana'grama] *m* anagram.
anágua [a'nagwa] *f* petticoat.
ANAI *abr f* = **Associação Nacional de Apoio ao Índio**.
anais [a'najʃ] *mpl* annals.
analfabetismo [anawfabe'tʃiʒmu] *m* illiteracy.
analfabeto/a [anawfa'bɛtu/a] *adj, m/f* illiterate.
analgésico/a [anaw'ʒɛziku/a] *adj* analgesic ♦ *m* painkiller.
analisar [anali'za*] *vt* to analyse.
análise [a'nalizi] *f* analysis.
analista [ana'liʃta] *m/f* analyst; ~ **de sistemas** systems analyst.
analítico/a [ana'litʃiku/a] *adj* analytical.
analogia [analo'ʒia] *f* analogy.
análogo/a [a'nalogu/a] *adj* analogous.
ananás [ana'naʃ] (*pl* **ananases**) *m* (*BR*) va-

riety of pineapple; (*PT*) pineapple.

anão/anã [a'nãw/a'nã] (*pl* -**ões/~s**) *m/f* dwarf.

anarquia [anax'kia] *f* anarchy; (*fig*) chaos.

anárquico/a [a'naxkiku/a] *adj* anarchic.

anarquista [anax'kiʃta] *m/f* anarchist.

anarquizar [anaxki'za*] *vt* (*povo*) to incite to anarchy; (*desordenar*) to mess up; (*ridicularizar*) to ridicule.

anátema [a'natema] *m* anathema.

anatomia [anato'mia] *f* anatomy.

anatômico/a [ana'tomiku/a] *adj* anatomical.

anavalhar [anava'ʎa*] *vt* to slash.

Anbid (*BR*) *abr f* = **Associação Nacional de Bancos de Investimentos e Desenvolvimento.**

anca ['ãka] *f* (*de pessoa*) hip; (*de animal*) rump.

Ancara [ã'kara] *n* Ankara.

ancestrais [ãseʃ'trajʃ] *mpl* ancestors.

anchova [ã'ʃova] *f* anchovy.

ancião/anciã [ã'sjãw/ã'sjã] (*pl* -**ões/~s**) *adj* old ♦ *m/f* old man/woman; (*de uma tribo*) elder.

ancinho [ã'siɲu] *m* rake.

anciões [a'sjõjʃ] *mpl de* **ancião.**

âncora ['ãkora] *f* anchor.

ancoradouro [ãkora'doru] *m* anchorage.

ancorar [ãko'ra*] *vt*, *vi* to anchor.

andada [ã'dada] *f* walk; **dar uma ~** to go for a walk.

andaime [ã'dajmi] *m* (*ARQ*) scaffolding.

Andaluzia [ãdalu'zia] *f*: **a ~** Andalucia.

andamento [ãda'mẽtu] *m* (*progresso*) progress; (*rumo*) course; (*MÚS*) tempo; **em ~** in progress; **dar ~ a algo** to set sth in motion.

andanças [ã'dãsaʃ] *fpl* wanderings.

andar [ã'da*] *vi* (*ir a pé*) to walk; (*a cavalo*) to ride; (*máquina*) to work; (*progredir*) to go, progress ♦ *m* (*modo de caminhar*) gait; (*pavimento*) floor, storey (*BRIT*), story (*US*); **andal** hurry up!; **~ com alguém** to have an affair with sb; **~ de trem/avião/bicicleta** to travel by train/fly/ride a bike; **ela anda triste** she's been sad lately.

andarilho/a [ãda'riʎu/a] *m/f* good walker.

ANDC (*BR*) *abr f* = **Associação Nacional de Defesa do Consumidor.**

Andes ['ãdʒiʃ] *mpl*: **os ~** the Andes.

Andima (*BR*) *abr f* = **Associação Nacional das Instituições de Mercado Aberto.**

andorinha [ãdo'riɲa] *f* (*pássaro*) swallow.

Andorra [ã'dɔxa] *f* Andorra.

andrógino/a [ã'drɔʒinu/a] *adj* androgynous.

anedota [ane'dɔta] *f* anecdote.

anedótico/a [ane'dɔtʃiku/a] *adj* anecdotal.

anel [a'nɛw] (*pl* -**éis**) *m* ring; (*elo*) link; (*de cabelo*) curl; **~ de casamento** wedding ring.

anelado/a [ane'ladu/a] *adj* curly.

anemia [ane'mia] *f* anaemia (*BRIT*), anemia

(*US*).

anêmico/a [a'nemiku/a] *adj* anaemic (*BRIT*), anemic (*US*).

anestesia [aneʃte'zia] *f* anaesthesia (*BRIT*), anesthesia (*US*); (*anestésico*) anaesthetic (*BRIT*), anesthetic (*US*).

anestesiar [aneʃte'zja*] *vt* to anaesthetize (*BRIT*), anesthetize (*US*).

anestésico [aneʃ'tɛziku] *m* (*MED*) anaesthetic (*BRIT*), anesthetic (*US*).

anestesista [aneʃte'ziʃta] *m/f* anaesthetist (*BRIT*), anesthetist (*US*).

anexação [aneksa'sãw] (*pl* -**ões**) *f* annexation; (*de documento*) enclosure.

anexar [anek'sa*] *vt* to annex; (*juntar*) to attach; (*documento*) to enclose.

anexo/a [a'nɛksu/a] *adj* attached ♦ *m* annexe; (*de igreja*) hall; (*em carta*) enclosure; **segue em ~** please find enclosed.

Anfavea (*BR*) *abr f* = **Associação Nacional dos Fabricantes de Veículos Automotores.**

anfetamina [ãfeta'mina] *f* amphetamine.

anfíbio/a [ã'fibju/a] *adj* amphibious ♦ *m* amphibian.

anfiteatro [ãfi'tʃjatru] *m* amphitheatre (*BRIT*), amphitheater (*US*); (*no teatro*) dress circle.

anfitrião/anfitriã [ãfi'trjãw/'trjã] (*pl* -**ões/~s**) *m/f* host/hostess.

angariar [ãga'rja*] *vt* (*fundos*, *donativos*) to raise; (*adeptos*) to attract; (*reputação*, *simpatia*) to gain; **~ votos** to canvass (for votes).

angelical [ãʒeli'kaw] (*pl* -**ais**) *adj* angelic.

angina [ã'ʒina] *f*: **~ do peito** angina (pectoris).

anglicano/a [ãgli'kanu/a] *adj*, *m/f* Anglican.

anglicismo [ãgli'siʒmu] *m* Anglicism.

anglo-saxão/-saxôni(c)a [ãglosak'sãw/ sak'soni(k)a] (*pl* -**ões/~s**) *m/f* Anglo-Saxon.

anglo-saxônico/a [ãglosak'soniku/a] *adj* Anglo-Saxon.

Angola [ã'gɔla] *f* Angola.

angolano/a [ãgo'lanu/a] *adj*, *m/f* Angolan.

angolense [ãgo'lẽsi] *adj*, *m/f* Angolan.

angorá [ãgo'ra] *adj* angora.

angra ['ãgra] *f* inlet, cove.

angu [ã'gu] *m* corn-meal purée.

angular [ãgu'la*] *adj* angular.

ângulo ['ãgulu] *m* angle; (*canto*) corner; (*fig*) angle, point of view.

angústia [ã'guʃtʃja] *f* anguish, distress.

angustiado/a [ãguʃ'tʃjadu/a] *adj* distressed.

angustiante [ãguʃ'tʃjãtʃi] *adj* distressing; (*momentos*) anxious, nerve-racking.

angustiar [ãguʃ'tʃja*] *vt* to distress.

anil [a'niw] *m* (*cor*) indigo.

animação [anima'sãw] *f* (*vivacidade*) liveliness; (*movimento*) bustle; (*entusiasmo*) enthusiasm.

animado/a [ani'madu/a] *adj* (*vivo*) lively;

NB: European Portuguese adds the following consonants to certain words: b (sú(b)dito, su(b)til); c (a(c)ção, a(c)cionista, a(c)to); m (inde(m)ne); p (ado(p)ção, ado(p)tar); for further details see p. xiii.

(*alegre*) cheerful; ~ **com** enthusiastic about.

animador(a) [anima'do*(a)] *adj* encouraging ♦ *m/f* (*BR*: *TV*) presenter.

animal [ani'maw] (*pl* **-ais**) *adj*, *m* animal; ~ **de estimação** pet (animal).

animalesco/a [anima'leʃku/a] *adj* bestial, brutish.

animar [ani'ma*] *vt* (*dar vida*) to liven up; (*encorajar*) to encourage; ~**-se** *vr* (*alegrar-se*) to cheer up; (*festa etc*) to liven up; ~**-se a** to bring o.s. to.

ânimo ['animu] *m* (*coragem*) courage; ~**!** cheer up!; **perder o** ~ to lose heart; **recobrar o** ~ to pluck up courage; (*alegrar-se*) to cheer up.

animosidade [animozi'dadʒi] *f* animosity.

aninhar [ani'ɲa*] *vt* to nestle; ~**-se** *vr* to nestle.

aniquilação [anikila'sãw] *f* annihilation.

aniquilar [aniki'la*] *vt* to annihilate; (*destruir*) to destroy; (*prostrar*) to shatter; ~**-se** *vr* to be annihilated; (*moralmente*) to be shattered.

anis [a'niʃ] *m* aniseed.

anistia [aniʃ'tʃia] *f* amnesty.

aniversariante [anivexsa'rjãtʃi] *m/f* birthday boy/girl.

aniversário [anivex'sarju] *m* anniversary; (*de nascimento*) birthday; (: *festa*) birthday party; ~ **de casamento** wedding anniversary.

anjo ['ãʒu] *m* angel; ~ **da guarda** guardian angel.

ANL (*BR*) *abr f* (= *Aliança Nacional Libertadora*) 1930's left-wing movement.

ano ['anu] *m* year; **Feliz A~ Novo!** Happy New Year!; **o** ~ **passado** last year; **o** ~ **que vem** next year; **por** ~ per annum; **fazer** ~**s** to have a birthday; **ele faz** ~**s hoje** it's his birthday today; **ter dez** ~**s** to be ten (years old); ~ **bissexto** leap year; ~ **civil** calendar year; ~ **corrente** current year; ~ **financeiro** financial year; ~ **letivo** academic year; (*da escola*) school year.

ano-bom *m* New Year.

anões [a'nõjʃ] *mpl de* **anão**.

anoitecer [anojte'se*] *vi* to grow dark ♦ *m* nightfall; **ao** ~ at nightfall.

anomalia [anoma'lia] *f* anomaly.

anômalo/a [a'nomalu/a] *adj* anomalous.

anonimato [anoni'matu] *m* anonymity.

anônimo/a [a'nonimu/a] *adj* anonymous; (*COM*): **sociedade anônima** limited company (*BRIT*), stock company (*US*).

anoraque [ano'raki] *m* anorak.

anorexia [ano'rɛksja] *f* anorexia.

anoréxico/a [ano'rɛksiku/a] *adj* anorexic.

anormal [anox'maw] (*pl* **-ais**) *adj* abnormal; (*incomum*) unusual; (*excepcional*) handicapped.

anormalidade [anoxmali'dadʒi] *f* abnormality.

anotação [anota'sãw] (*pl* **-ões**) *f* (*comentário*) annotation; (*nota*) note.

anotar [ano'ta*] *vt* (*tomar nota*) to note down;

(*esclarecer*) to annotate.

anseio [ã'seju] *etc vb* V **ansiar**.

ânsia ['ãsja] *f* (*ansiedade*) anxiety; (*desejo*): ~ **(de)** longing (for); **ter** ~**s (de vômito)** to feel sick.

ansiado/a [ã'sjadu/a] *adj* longed for.

ansiar [ã'sja*] *vi*: ~ **por** (*desejar*) to yearn for; ~ **por fazer** to long to do.

ansiedade [ãsje'dadʒi] *f* anxiety; (*desejo*) eagerness.

ansioso/a [ã'sjozu/ɔza] *adj* anxious; (*desejoso*) eager.

antagônico/a [ãta'goniku/a] *adj* antagonistic; (*rival*) opposing.

antagonismo [ãtago'niʒmu] *m* (*hostilidade*) antagonism; (*oposição*) opposition.

antagonista [ãtago'niʃta] *m/f* antagonist; (*adversário*) opponent.

antártico/a [ã'taxtʃiku/a] *adj* antarctic ♦ *m*: **o A~** the Antarctic.

ante ['ãtʃi] *prep* (*na presença de*) before; (*em vista de*) in view of, faced with.

antebraço [ãtʃi'brasu] *m* forearm.

antecedência [ãtese'dẽsja] *f*: **com** ~ in advance; **3 dias de** ~ three days' notice.

antecedente [ãtese'dẽtʃi] *adj* (*anterior*) preceding ♦ *m* antecedent; ~**s** *mpl* record *sg*, background *sg*; ~**s criminais** criminal record *sg ou* past *sg*.

anteceder [ãtese'de*] *vt* to precede.

antecessor(a) [ãtese'so*(a)] *m/f* predecessor.

antecipação [ãtesipa'sãw] *f* anticipation; **com um mês de** ~ a month in advance; ~ **de pagamento** advance payment.

antecipadamente [ãtesipada'mẽtʃi] *adv* in advance, beforehand; **pagar** ~ to pay in advance.

antecipado/a [ãtesi'padu/a] *adj* (*pagamento*) (in) advance.

antecipar [ãtesi'pa*] *vt* to anticipate, forestall; (*adiantar*) to bring forward; ~**-se** *vr* (*adiantar-se*) to be previous.

antegozar [ãtego'za*] *vt* to anticipate.

antemão [ãte'mãw]: **de** ~ *adv* beforehand.

antena [ã'tɛna] *f* (*BIO*) antenna, feeler; (*RADIO*, *TV*) aerial; ~ **direcional** directional aerial; ~ **parabólica** satellite dish.

anteontem [ãtʃi'õtẽ] *adv* the day before yesterday.

anteparo [ãte'paru] *m* (*proteção*) screen.

antepassado [ãtʃipa'sadu] *m* ancestor.

antepor [ãte'po*] (*irreg*: *como* **pôr**) *vt* (*pôr antes*) to put before; ~**-se** *vr* to anticipate.

anteprojeto [ãtepro'ʒetu] (*PT*: **-ect-**) *m* outline, draft; ~ **de lei** draft bill.

antepunha [ãte'puɲa] *etc vb* V **antepor**.

antepus [ãte'puʃ] *etc vb* V **antepor**.

antepuser [ãtepu'ze*] *etc vb* V **antepor**.

anterior [ãte'rjo*] *adj* (*prévio*) previous; (*antigo*) former; (*de posição*) front.

antes ['ãtʃiʃ] *adv* before; (*antigamente*) formerly; (*ao contrário*) rather; **o quanto** ~ as soon as possible; ~ **de** before; ~ **de partir**

before leaving; ~ **do tempo** ahead of time; ~ **de tudo** above all; ~ **que** before.

ante-sala *f* ante-room.

antever [ãte've*] (*irreg: como* **ver**) *vt* to anticipate, foresee.

antevisto/a [ãte'viʃtu/a] *pp de* **antever**.

anti- [ãtʃi] *prefixo* anti-.

antiácido/a [ã'tʃjasidu/a] *adj* antacid ♦ *m* antacid.

antiaéreo/a [ãtʃja'ɛrju/a] *adj* anti-aircraft.

antiamericano/a [ãtʃjameri'kanu/a] *adj* anti-American.

antibiótico/a [ãtʃi'bjɔtʃiku/a] *adj* antibiotic ♦ *m* antibiotic.

anticaspa [ãtʃi'kaʃpa] *adj inv* anti-dandruff.

anticiclone [ãtʃisi'kloni] *m* anticyclone.

anticlímax [ãtʃi'klimaks] *m* anticlimax.

anticoncepcional [ãtʃikõsepsjo'naw] (*pl* **-ais**) *adj, m* contraceptive.

anticongelante [ãtʃikõʒe'lãtʃi] *m* antifreeze.

anticonstitucional [ãtʃikõʃtʃitusjo'naw] (*pl* **-ais**) *adj* unconstitutional.

anticorpo [ãtʃi'koxpu] *m* antibody.

antidemocrático/a [ãtʃidemo'kratʃiku/a] *adj* undemocratic.

antidepressivo/a [ãtʃidepre'sivu/a] *adj* anti-depressant ♦ *m* anti-depressant.

antiderrapante [ãtʃidexa'pãtʃi] *adj* (*pneu*) non-skid.

antídoto [ã'tʃidotu] *m* antidote.

antiestético/a [ãtʃjeʃ'tɛtʃiku/a] *adj* tasteless.

antiético/a [ã'tʃjetʃiku/a] *adj* unethical.

antigamente [ãtʃiga'mẽtʃi] *adv* formerly; (*no passado*) in the past.

antigo/a [ã'tʃigu/a] *adj* old; (*histórico*) ancient; (*de estilo*) antique; (*chefe etc*) former; **ele é muito ~ na firma** he's been with the firm for many years; **os ~s** (*gregos etc*) the ancients.

Antígua [ã'tʃigwa] *f* Antigua.

antiguidade [ãtʃigi'dadʒi] *f* antiquity, ancient times *pl*; (*de emprego*) seniority; **~s** *fpl* (*monumentos*) ancient monuments; (*artigos*) antiques.

anti-higiênico/a *adj* unhygienic.

anti-histamínico/a [-iʃta'miniku/a] *adj* anti-histamine ♦ *m* antihistamine.

anti-horário/a *adj* anticlockwise.

antilhano/a [ãtʃi'ʎanu/a] *adj, m/f* West Indian.

Antilhas [ã'tʃiʎaʃ] *fpl*: **as ~** the West Indies.

antílope [ã'tʃilopi] *m* antelope.

antipatia [ãtʃipa'tʃia] *f* antipathy, dislike.

antipático/a [ãtʃi'patʃiku/a] *adj* unpleasant, unfriendly.

antipatizar [ãtʃipatʃi'za*] *vi*: **~ com alguém** to dislike sb.

antipatriótico/a [ãtʃipa'trjɔtʃiku/a] *adj* unpatriotic.

antipoluente [ãtʃipo'lwẽtʃi] *adj* non-pollutant.

antiquado/a [ãtʃi'kwadu/a] *adj* antiquated;

(*fora de moda*) out of date, old-fashioned.

antiquário/a [ãtʃi'kwarju/a] *m/f* antique dealer ♦ *m* (*loja*) antique shop.

antiquíssimo/a [ãtʃi'kisimu/a] *adj superl de* **antigo/a**.

anti-semita *adj* anti-Semitic.

anti-semitismo [-semi'tʃiʒmu] *m* anti-Semitism.

anti-séptico/a *adj* antiseptic ♦ *m* antiseptic.

anti-social (*pl* **-ais**) *adj* antisocial.

antítese [ã'tʃitezi] *f* antithesis.

antitruste [ãtʃi'truʃtʃi] *adj V* **legislação**.

antolhos [ã'tɔʎuʃ] *mpl* (*pala*) eye-shade *sg*; (*de cavalo*) blinkers.

antologia [ãtolo'ʒia] *f* anthology.

antônimo [ã'tonimu] *m* antonym.

antro ['ãtru] *m* cave, cavern; (*de animal*) lair; (*de ladrões*) den.

antropofagia [ãtropofa'ʒia] *f* cannibalism.

antropófago/a [ãtro'pofagu/a] *m/f* cannibal.

antropologia [ãtropolo'ʒia] *f* anthropology.

antropólogo/a [ãtro'pɔlogu/a] *m/f* anthropologist.

ANTTUR (*BR*) *abr f* = **Associação Nacional de Transportadores de Turismo e Agências de Viagens**.

anual [a'nwaw] (*pl* **-ais**) *adj* annual, yearly.

anuário [a'nwarju] *m* yearbook.

anuidade [anwi'dadʒi] *f* annuity.

anuir [a'nwi*] *vi*: **~ a** to agree to; **~ com** to comply with.

anulação [anula'sãw] (*pl* **-ões**) *f* cancellation; (*de contrato, casamento*) annulment.

anular [anu'la*] *vt* to cancel; (*contrato, casamento*) to annul; (*efeito*) to cancel out ♦ *m* ring finger.

anunciante [anũ'sjãtʃi] *m* (*COM*) advertiser.

anunciar [anũ'sja*] *vt* to announce; (*COM: produto*) to advertise.

anúncio [a'nũsju] *m* announcement; (*COM*) advertisement, advert; (*cartaz*) notice; **~ luminoso** neon sign; **~s classificados** small *ou* classified ads.

ânus ['anuʃ] *m inv* anus.

anverso [ã'vɛxsu] *m* (*de moeda*) obverse.

anzol [ã'zɔw] (*pl* **-óis**) *m* fish-hook.

ao [aw] = **a** + **o**; *V* **a**.

aonde [a'õdʒi] *adv* where; **~ quer que** wherever.

aos [awʃ] = **a** + **os**; *V* **a**.

AP *abr* = **Amapá**.

Ap. *abr* = **apartamento**.

apadrinhar [apadri'na*] *vt* (*ser padrinho*) to act as godfather to; (: *de noivo*) to be best man to; (*proteger*) to protect; (*patrocinar*) to support.

apagado/a [apa'gadu/a] *adj* (*fogo*) out; (*luz elétrica*) off; (*indistinto*) faint; (*pessoa*) dull.

apagar [apa'ga*] *vt* (*fogo*) to put out; (*luz elétrica*) to switch off; (*vela*) to blow out; (*com*

NB: European Portuguese adds the following consonants to certain words: **b** (sú(b)dito, su(b)til); **c** (a(c)ção, a(c)cionista, a(c)to); **m** (inde(m)ne); **p** (ado(p)ção, ado(p)tar); *for further details see p. xiii.*

borracha) to rub out, erase; (*quadro-negro*) to clean; (*COMPUT*) to delete, erase; **~-se** *vr* to go out; (*desmaiar*) to pass out; (*col: dormir*) to nod off.

apaguei [apa'gej] *etc vb* V **apagar**.

apaixonado/a [apajʃo'nadu/a] *adj* (*pessoa*) in love; (*discurso*) impassioned; **ele está ~ por ela** he is in love with her; **ele é ~ por tênis** he's mad about tennis.

apaixonar-se [apajʃo'naxsi] *vr*: **~ por** to fall in love with.

apaixonante [apajʃo'nãtʃi] *adj* captivating.

Apalaches [apa'laʃiʃ] *mpl*: **os ~** the Appalachians.

apalermado/a [apalex'madu/a] *adj* silly.

apalpadela [apawpa'dɛla] *f* touch.

apalpar [apaw'pa*] *vt* to touch, feel; (*MED*) to examine.

apanhado [apa'ɲadu] *m* (*de flores*) bunch; (*resumo*) summary; (*pregas*) gathering.

apanhar [apa'ɲa*] *vt* to catch; (*algo à mão, do chão*) to pick up; (*ir buscar, surra, táxi*) to get; (*colher*) to pick; (*agarrar*) to grab; (*sol*) to take ♦ *vi* (*ser espancado*) to get a beating; (*em jogo*) to take a beating; **~ chuva** to get soaked.

apaniguado/a [apani'gwadu/a] *m/f* (*protegido*) protégé(e).

apapagaiado/a [apapaga'jadu/a] *adj* loud, garish.

apara [a'para] *f* (*de madeira*) shaving; (*de papel*) clipping.

aparador [apara'do*] *m* sideboard.

aparafusar [aparafu'za*] *vt* to screw.

apara-lápis [apara'lapiʃ] (*PT*) *m* pencil sharpener.

aparar [apa'ra*] *vt* (*cabelo*) to trim; (*lápis*) to sharpen; (*o que é atirado ou cai*) to catch; (*pancada*) to parry; (*madeira*) to plane.

aparato [apa'ratu] *m* pomp; (*coleção*) array.

aparatoso/a [apara'tozu/ɔza] *adj* grand.

aparecer [apare'se*] *vi* to appear; (*apresentar-se*) to turn up; (*ser publicado*) to be published; **~ em casa de alguém** to drop in on sb, call on sb.

aparecimento [aparesi'mẽtu] *m* appearance; (*publicação*) publication.

aparelhado/a [apare'ʎadu/a] *adj* (*preparado*) ready, prepared; (*madeira*) planed.

aparelhagem [apare'ʎaʒẽ] *f* equipment; (*carpintaria*) finishing; (*NÁUT*) rigging.

aparelhar [apare'ʎa*] *vt* (*preparar*) to prepare, get ready; (*NÁUT*) to rig; **~-se** *vr* to get ready.

aparelho [apa'reʎu] *m* apparatus; (*equipamento*) equipment; (*PESCA*) tackle, gear; (*máquina*) machine; (*BR: fone*) telephone; (*POL*) hide-out; **~ de barbear** electric shaver; **~ de chá** tea set; **~ de rádio/TV** radio/TV set; **~ digestivo** digestive system; **~ doméstico** domestic appliance; **~ fonador** vocal tract; **~ sanitário** bathroom suite.

aparência [apa'rẽsja] *f* appearance; (*aspecto*)

aspect; **na ~** apparently; **sob a ~ de** under the guise of; **manter as ~s** to keep up appearances; **salvar as ~s** to save face; **as ~s enganam** appearances are deceptive.

aparentado/a [aparẽ'tadu/a] *adj* related; **bem ~** well connected.

aparentar [aparẽ'ta*] *vt* (*fingir*) to feign; (*parecer*) to give the appearance of.

aparente [apa'rẽtʃi] *adj* apparent; (*concreto, madeira*) exposed.

aparição [apari'sãw] (*pl* **-ões**) *f* (*visão*) apparition; (*fantasma*) ghost.

aparo [a'paru] (*PT*) *m* (*de caneta*) (pen) nib.

apartamento [apaxta'mẽtu] *m* apartment, flat (*BRIT*).

apartar [apax'ta*] *vt* to separate; **~-se** *vr* to separate.

aparte [a'paxtʃi] *m* aside.

apartheid [apax'tajdʒi] *m* apartheid.

aparvalhado/a [apaxva'ʎadu/a] *adj* idiotic.

apatetado/a [apate'tadu/a] *adj* sluggish.

apatia [apa'tʃia] *f* apathy.

apático/a [a'patʃiku/a] *adj* apathetic.

apátrida [a'patrida] *m/f* stateless person.

apavorado/a [apavo'radu/a] *adj* terrified.

apavoramento [apavora'mẽtu] *m* terror.

apavorante [apavo'rãtʃi] *adj* terrifying.

apavorar [apavo'ra*] *vt* to terrify ♦ *vi* to be terrifying; **~-se** *vr* to be terrified.

apaziguar [apazi'gwa*] *vt* to appease; **~-se** *vr* to calm down.

apear-se [a'pjaxsi] *vr*: **~ de** (*cavalo*) to dismount from.

apedrejar [apedre'ʒa*] *vt* to stone.

apegado/a [ape'gadu/a] *adj* attached.

apegar-se [ape'gaxsi] *vr*: **~ a** (*afeiçoar-se*) to become attached to.

apego [a'pegu] *m* (*afeição*) attachment.

apeguei [ape'gej] *etc vb* V **apegar**.

apelação [apela'sãw] (*pl* **-ões**) *f* appeal.

apelante [ape'lãtʃi] *m/f* appellant.

apelar [ape'la*] *vi* to appeal; **~ da sentença** (*JUR*) to appeal against the sentence; **~ para** to appeal to; **~ para a ignorância/violência** to resort to abuse/violence.

apelidar [apeli'da*] *vt* (*BR*) to nickname; (*PT*) to give a surname to; **~-se** *vr*: **~-se de** to go by the name of; **Eduardo, apelidado de Dudu** Eduardo, nicknamed Dudu.

apelido [ape'lidu] *m* (*PT: nome de família*) surname; (*BR: alcunha*) nickname; **feio é ~!** (*col*) ugly is not the word for it!

apelo [a'pelu] *m* appeal.

apenas [a'penaʃ] *adv* only.

apêndice [a'pẽdʒisi] *m* appendix; (*anexo*) supplement.

apendicite [apẽdʒi'sitʃi] *f* appendicitis.

Apeninos [ape'ninuʃ] *mpl*: **os ~** the Apennines.

apenso/a [a'pẽsu/a] *adj* attached.

apequenar [apeke'na*] *vt* to belittle.

aperceber-se [apexse'bexsi] *vr*: **~ de** to notice, see.

aperfeiçoamento [apexfejswa'mētu] *m* (*perfeição*) perfection; (*melhoramento*) improvement.

aperfeiçoar [apexfej'swa*] *vt* to perfect; (*melhorar*) to improve; ~-se *vr* to improve o.s.

aperitivo [aperi'tʃivu] *m* aperitif.

aperreação [apexja'sãw] *f* annoyance.

aperreado/a [ape'xjadu/a] *adj* fed up.

aperrear [ape'xja*] *vt* to annoy.

apertado/a [apex'tadu/a] *adj* tight; (*estreito*) narrow; (*sem dinheiro*) hard-up; (*vida*) hard.

apertar [apex'ta*] *vt* (*agarrar*) to hold tight; (*roupa*) to take in; (*cinto*) to tighten; (*esponja*) to squeeze; (*botão*) to press; (*despesas*) to limit; (*vigilância*) to step up; (*coração*) to break; (*fig: pessoa*) to put pressure on ♦ *vi* (*sapatos*) to pinch; (*chuva, frio*) to get worse; (*estrada*) to narrow; ~-se *vr* (*com roupa*) to corset o.s.; (*reduzir despesas*) to cut down (on expenses); (*ter problemas financeiros*) to feel the pinch; ~ **em** (*insistir*) to insist on, press; ~ **a mão de alguém** (*cumprimentar*) to shake hands with sb.

aperto [a'pextu] *m* (*pressão*) pressure; (*situação difícil*) spot of bother, jam; **um ~ de mãos** a handshake.

apesar [ape'za*] *prep*: ~ **de** in spite of, despite; ~ **disso** nevertheless; ~ **de que** in spite of the fact that, even though.

apetecer [apete'se*] *vi* (*comida*) to be appetizing; **esse prato não me apetece** I don't fancy that dish.

apetecível [apete'sivew] (*pl* -**eis**) *adj* tempting.

apetite [ape'tʃitʃi] *m* appetite; (*desejo*) desire; (*fig: ânimo*) go; **abrir o** ~ to get up an appetite; **bom** ~! enjoy your meal!

apetitoso/a [apeti'tozu/ɔza] *adj* appetizing.

apetrechar [apetre'ʃa*] *vt* to fit out, equip.

apetrechos [ape'treʃuʃ] *mpl* gear *sg*; (*de pesca*) tackle *sg*.

ápice ['apisi] *m* (*cume*) summit, top; (*vértice*) apex; **num** ~ (*PT*) in a trice.

apicultura [apikuw'tura] *f* beekeeping, apiculture.

apiedar-se [apje'daxsi] *vr*: ~ **de** (*ter piedade*) to pity; (*compadecer-se*) to take pity on.

apimentado/a [apimē'tadu/a] *adj* peppery.

apimentar [apimē'ta*] *vt* to pepper.

apinhado/a [api'ɲadu/a] *adj* crowded.

apinhar [api'ɲa*] *vt* to crowd, pack; ~-se *vr* (*aglomerar-se*) to crowd together; ~-se **de** (*gente*) to be filled *ou* packed with.

apitar [api'ta*] *vi* to whistle; (*col*): **ele não apita em nada em casa** he doesn't have a say in anything at home ♦ *vt* (*jogo*) to referee.

apito [a'pitu] *m* whistle.

aplacar [apla'ka*] *vt* to placate ♦ *vi* to calm down; ~-se *vr* to calm down.

aplainar [aplaj'na*] *vt* (*madeira*) to plane; (*nivelar*) to level out.

aplanar [apla'na*] *vt* (*alisar*) to smooth; (*nivelar*) to level; (*dificuldades*) to smooth over.

aplaudir [aplaw'dʒi*] *vt* to applaud.

aplauso [a'plawzu] *m* applause; (*apoio*) support; (*elogio*) praise; (*aprovação*) approval; ~**s** applause *sg*.

aplicação [aplika'sãw] (*pl* -**ões**) *f* application; (*esforço*) effort; (*COSTURA*) appliqué; (*da lei*) enforcement; (*de dinheiro*) investment; (*de aluno*) diligence; **pacote de aplicações** (*COMPUT*) applications package.

aplicado/a [apli'kadu/a] *adj* hard-working.

aplicar [apli'ka*] *vt* to apply; (*dinheiro*) to invest; (*lei*) to enforce; ~-se *vr*: ~-se **a** to devote o.s. to, apply o.s. to.

aplicativo/a [aplika'tʃivu/a] *adj*: **pacote/software** ~ applications package/software ♦ *m* (*COMPUT*) applications program.

aplicável [apli'kavew] (*pl* -**eis**) *adj* applicable.

aplique [a'pliki] *m* (*luz*) wall light; (*peruca*) hairpiece.

apliquei [apli'kej] *etc vb V* **aplicar**.

apocalipse [apoka'lipsi] *f* apocalypse.

apócrifo/a [a'pɔkrifu/a] *adj* apocryphal.

apoderar-se [apode'raxsi] *vr*: ~ **de** to seize, take possession of.

apodrecer [apodre'se*] *vt* to rot; (*dente*) to decay ♦ *vi* to rot, decay.

apodrecimento [apodresi'mētu] *m* rottenness, decay; (*de dentes*) decay.

apogeu [apo'ʒew] *m* (*ASTRONOMIA*) apogee; (*fig*) height, peak.

apoiar [apo'ja*] *vt* to support; (*basear*) to base; (*moção*) to second; ~-se *vr*: ~-se **em** to rest on.

apoio [a'poju] *m* support; (*financeiro*) backing; ~ **moral** moral support.

apólice [a'pɔlisi] *f* (*certificado*) policy, certificate; (*ação*) share, bond; ~ **de seguro** insurance policy.

apologia [apolo'ʒia] *f* (*elogio*) eulogy; (*defesa*) defence (*BRIT*), defense (*US*).

apologista [apolo'ʒiʃta] *m/f* apologist.

apontador [apõta'do*] *m* pencil sharpener.

apontamento [apõta'mētu] *m* (*nota*) note.

apontar [apõ'ta*] *vt* (*fusil*) to aim; (*erro*) to point out; (*com o dedo*) to point at *ou* to; (*razão*) to put forward; (*nomes*) to name ♦ *vi* (*aparecer*) to begin to appear; (*brotar*) to sprout; (*com o dedo*) to point; ~! take aim!; ~ **para** to point to; (*com arma*) to aim at.

apoplético/a [apo'plɛtʃiku/a] *adj* apoplectic.

apoquentar [apokē'ta*] *vt* to annoy, pester; ~-se *vr* to get annoyed.

aporrinhação [apoxiɲa'sãw] *f* annoyance.

NB: *European Portuguese adds the following consonants to certain words:* **b** (sú(b)dito, su(b)til); **c** (a(c)ção, a(c)cionista, a(c)to); **m** (inde(m)ne); **p** (ado(p)ção, ado(p)tar); *for further details see p. xiii.*

aporrinhar [apoxi'ɲa*] vt to pester, annoy.

aportar [apox'ta*] vi to dock.

aportuguesado/a [apoxtuge'zadu/a] adj made Portuguese.

após [a'pɔjʃ] prep after.

aposentado/a [apozẽ'tadu/a] adj retired ♦ m/f retired person, pensioner; **ficar** ~ to be retired.

aposentadoria [apozẽtado'ria] f retirement; (dinheiro) pension.

aposentar [apozẽ'ta*] vt to retire; ~-se vr to retire.

aposento [apo'zẽtu] m room.

após-guerra m post-war period; **a Alemanha do** ~ post-war Germany.

apossar-se [apo'saxsi] vr: ~ **de** to take possession of, seize.

aposta [a'pɔʃta] f bet.

apostar [apoʃ'ta*] vt to bet ♦ vi: ~ **em** to bet on.

a posteriori [apoʃte'rjɔri] adv afterwards.

apostila [apoʃ'tʃila] f students' notes pl, study aid.

apóstolo [a'pɔʃtolu] m apostle.

apóstrofo [a'pɔʃtrofu] m apostrophe.

apoteose [apote'ɔzi] f apotheosis.

aprazar [apra'za*] vt to allow.

aprazer [apra'ze*] vi to be pleasing; ~ **a alguém** to please sb; **ele faz o que lhe apraz** he does as he pleases; **aprazia-lhe escrever cartas** he liked to write letters.

aprazível [apra'zivew] (pl -eis) adj pleasant.

apreçar [apre'sa*] vt to value, price.

apreciação [apresja'sãw] f appreciation.

apreciar [apre'sja*] vt to appreciate; (gostar de) to enjoy.

apreciativo/a [apresja'tʃivu/a] adj appreciative.

apreciável [apre'sjavew] (pl -eis) adj appreciable.

apreço [a'presu] m (estima) esteem, regard; (consideração) consideration; **em** ~ in question.

apreender [aprjẽ'de*] vt to apprehend; (tomar) to seize; (entender) to grasp.

apreensão [aprjẽ'sãw] (pl -ões) f (percepção) perception; (tomada) seizure, arrest; (receio) apprehension.

apreensivo/a [aprjẽ'sivu/a] adj apprehensive.

apreensões [aprjẽ'sõjʃ] fpl de **apreensão**.

apregoar [apre'gwa*] vt to proclaim, announce; (mercadorias) to cry.

aprender [aprẽ'de*] vt, vi to learn; ~ **a ler** to learn to read; ~ **de cor** to learn by heart.

aprendiz [aprẽ'dʒiʒ] m apprentice; (condutor) learner.

aprendizado [aprẽdʒi'zadu] m (num ofício) apprenticeship; (numa profissão) training; (escolar) learning.

aprendizagem [aprẽdʒi'zaʒẽ] f (num ofício) apprenticeship; (numa profissão) training; (escolar) learning.

apresentação [aprezẽta'sãw] (pl -ões) f pres-

entation; (de peça, filme) performance; (de pessoas) introduction; (porte pessoal) appearance; ~ **de contas** (COM) rendering of accounts.

apresentador(a) [aprezẽta'do*(a)] m/f presenter.

apresentar [aprezẽ'ta*] vt to present; (pessoas) to introduce; (entregar) to hand; (trabalho, documento) to submit; (queixa) to lodge; ~-se vr (identificar-se) to introduce o.s.; (problema) to present itself; (à polícia etc) to report; **quero** ~-lhe may I introduce you to.

apresentável [aprezẽ'tavew] (pl -eis) adj presentable.

apressado/a [apre'sadu/a] adj hurried, hasty; **estar** ~ to be in a hurry.

apressar [apre'sa*] vt to hurry, hasten; ~-se vr to hurry (up).

aprestar [apreʃ'ta*] vt (aparelhar) to equip, fit out; (aprontar) to get ready; ~-se vr to get ready.

aprestos [a'preʃtuʃ] mpl (preparativos) preparations.

aprimorado/a [aprimo'radu/a] adj (trabalho) polished; (pessoa) elegant.

aprimorar [aprimo'ra*] vt to improve; ~-se vr (no vestir) to make o.s. look nice.

a priori [a'prjɔri] adv beforehand.

aprisionamento [aprizjona'mẽtu] m imprisonment.

aprisionar [aprizjo'na*] vt (cativar) to capture; (encarcerar) to imprison.

aprofundar [aprofũ'da*] vt to deepen, make deeper; ~-se vr: ~-se **em** to go deeper into.

aprontar [aprõ'ta*] vt to get ready, prepare; (briga) to pick ♦ vi (col) to play up; ~-se vr to get ready; ~ **alguma** (col) to be up to something.

apropriação [aproprja'sãw] (pl -ões) f appropriation; (tomada) seizure; ~ **de custos** (COM) cost appropriation.

apropriado/a [apro'prjadu/a] adj appropriate, suitable.

apropriar [apro'prja*] vt to appropriate; ~-se vr: ~-se **de** to seize, take possession of.

aprovação [aprova'sãw] f approval; (louvor) praise; (num exame) pass.

aprovado/a [apro'vadu/a] adj approved; **ser** ~ **num exame** to pass an exam; **o índice de** ~**s** the pass rate.

aprovar [apro'va*] vt to approve of; (aluno) to pass ♦ vi to make the grade, come up to scratch.

aproveitador(a) [aprovejta'do*(a)] m/f opportunist.

aproveitamento [aprovejta'mẽtu] m use, utilization; (nos estudos) progress.

aproveitar [aprovej'ta*] vt (tirar proveito de) to take advantage of; (utilizar) to use; (não desperdiçar) to make the most of; (oportunidade) to take; (fazer bom uso de) to make good use of ♦ vi to make the most of it;

(PT) to be of use; **não aproveita** it's no use; **aproveite!** enjoy yourself!, have a good time!

aproveitável [aprovej'tavew] *(pl* **-eis)** *adj* usable.

aprovisionamento [aprovizjona'mẽtu] *m* supply, provision.

aprovisionar [aprovizjo'na*] *vt* to supply; *(estocar)* to stock.

aproximação [aprosima'sãw] *(pl* **-ões)** *f* *(estimativa)* approximation; *(chegada)* approach; *(proximidade)* nearness, closeness.

aproximado/a [aprosi'madu/a] *adj (cálculo)* approximate; *(perto)* nearby.

aproximar [aprosi'ma*] *vt* to bring near; *(aliar)* to bring together; **~-se** *vr:* **~-se de** *(acercar-se)* to approach.

aprumado/a [apru'madu/a] *adj* vertical; *(altivo)* upright; *(elegante)* well-dressed.

aprumo [a'prumu] *m* vertical position; *(elegância)* elegance; *(altivez)* haughtiness.

aptidão [aptʃi'dãw] *f* aptitude, ability; *(jeito)* knack; **~ física** physical fitness.

aptitude [aptʃi'tudʒi] *f* aptitude, ability; *(jeito)* knack.

apto/a ['aptu/a] *adj* apt; *(capaz)* capable.

apto. *abr* = **apartamento.**

APU *(PT)* *abr f* (= *Aliança Povo Unido)* political party.

apunhalar [apuɲa'la*] *vt* to stab.

apuração [apura'sãw] *f (de votos)* counting; *(descoberta)* ascertainment; *(averiguação)* investigation; **~ de contas** *(COM)* settlement of accounts; **~ de custos** *(COM)* costing.

apurado/a [apu'radu/a] *adj* refined.

apurar [apu'ra*] *vt (aperfeiçoar)* to perfect; *(descobrir)* to find out; *(averiguar)* to investigate; *(dinheiro)* to raise, get; *(votos)* to count; **~-se** *vr (no trajar)* to dress up.

apuro [a'puru] *m (elegância)* refinement, elegance; *(dificuldade)* difficulty; **estar em ~s** to be in trouble.

aquarela [akwa'rɛla] *f* watercolour *(BRIT)*, watercolor *(US)*.

aquário [a'kwarju] *m* aquarium; **A~** *(ASTRO-LOGIA)* Aquarius.

aquartelar [akwaxte'la*] *vt (MIL)* to billet, quarter.

aquático/a [a'kwatʃiku/a] *adj* aquatic, water *atr.*

aquecedor(a) [akese'do*(a)] *adj* warming ♦ *m* heater.

aquecer [ake'se*] *vt* to heat ♦ *vi* to heat up; **~-se** *vr* to heat up.

aquecido/a [ake'sidu/a] *adj* heated.

aquecimento [akesi'mẽtu] *m* heating; *(da economia)* acceleration; **~ central** central heating.

aqueduto [ake'dutu] *m* aqueduct.

aquele/ela [a'keli/ɛla] *adj (sg)* that; *(pl)* those

♦ *pron (sg)* that one; *(pl)* those; **sem mais aquela** *(inesperadamente)* all of a sudden; *(sem cerimônia)* without so much as a "by your leave"; **foi aquela confusão** it was a real mess.

àquele/ela [a'keli/ɛla] = **a** + **aquele/ela.**

aquém [a'kẽj] *adv* on this side; **~ de** on this side of.

aqui [a'ki] *adv* here; **eis ~** here is/are; **~ mesmo** right here; **até ~** up to here; **por ~** hereabouts; *(nesta direção)* this way; **por ~ e por ali** here and there; **estou por ~!** *(col)* I've had it up to here!; *V tb* **daqui.**

aquiescência [akje'sẽsja] *f* consent.

aquiescer [akje'se*] *vi:* **~ (a)** to consent (to).

aquietar [akje'ta*] *vt* to calm, quieten; **~-se** *vr* to calm down.

aquilatar [akila'ta*] *vt (metais)* to value; *(avaliar)* to evaluate.

aquilo [a'kilu] *pron* that; **~ que** what.

àquilo [a'kilu] = **a** + **aquilo.**

aquisição [akizi'sãw] *(pl* **-ões)** *f* acquisition.

aquisitivo/a [akizi'tʃivu/a] *adj V* **poder.**

ar [a*] *m* air; *(aspecto)* look; *(brisa)* breeze; *(PT: AUTO)* choke; **~es** *mpl* airs; *(clima)* climate *sg*; **ao ~ livre** in the open air; **ir ao/ sair do ~** *(TV, RÁDIO)* to go on/off the air; **no ~** *(TV, RÁDIO)* on air; *(fig: planos)* up in the air; **dar-se ~es** to put on airs; **ir pelos ~es** *(explodir)* to blow up; **tomar ~** to get some air; **~ condicionado** *(aparelho)* air conditioner; *(sistema)* air conditioning.

árabe ['arabi] *adj, m/f* Arab ♦ *m (LING)* Arabic.

Arábia [a'rabja] *f:* **a ~ Saudita** Saudi Arabia.

arado [a'radu] *m* plough *(BRIT)*, plow *(US)*.

aragem [a'raʒẽ] *(pl* **-ns)** *f* breeze.

arame [a'rami] *m* wire; **~ farpado** barbed wire.

aranha [a'raɲa] *f* spider.

aranha-caranguejeira [-karãge'ʒejra] *(pl* **aranhas-caranguejeiras)** *f* bird-eating spider.

arar [a'ra*] *vt* to plough *(BRIT)*, plow *(US)*.

arapuca [ara'puka] *f* trap; *(truque)* trick.

araque [a'raki] *m:* **de ~** *(col)* phony, bogus.

arara [a'rara] *f* parrot; **estar/ficar uma ~** *(fig)* to be/get angry.

arbitragem [axbi'traʒẽ] *f* arbitration; *(ESPORTE)* refereeing.

arbitrar [axbi'tra*] *vt* to arbitrate; *(ESPORTE)* to referee; *(adjudicar)* to award.

arbitrariedade [axbitrarje'dadʒi] *f* arbitrariness; *(ato)* arbitrary act.

arbitrário/a [axbi'trarju/a] *adj* arbitrary.

arbítrio [ax'bitrju] *m* decision; **ao ~ de** at the discretion of.

árbitro ['axbitru] *m (juiz)* arbiter; *(JUR)* arbitrator; *(FUTEBOL)* referee; *(TÊNIS)* umpire.

arborizado/a [axbori'zadu/a] *adj* green, wooded; *(rua)* tree-lined.

NB: *European Portuguese adds the following consonants to certain words:* **b** (sú(b)dito, su(b)til); **c** (a(c)ção, a(c)cionista, a(c)to); **m** (inde(m)ne); **p** (ado(p)ção, ado(p)tar); *for further details see p. xiii.*

arborizar [axbori'za*] *vt* to plant with trees.

arbusto [ax'buʃtu] *m* shrub, bush.

arca ['axka] *f* chest, trunk; ~ **de Noé** Noah's Ark.

arcabouço [axka'bosu] *m* outline(s).

arcada [ax'kada] *f* (*série de arcos*) arcade; (*arco*) arch, span; ~ **dentária** dental ridge.

arcaico/a [ax'kajku/a] *adj* archaic; (*antiquado*) antiquated.

arcanjo [ax'kãʒu] *m* archangel.

arcar [ax'ka*] *vt*: ~ **com** (*responsabilidades*) to shoulder; (*despesas*) to handle; (*conseqüencias*) to take.

arcebispo [arse'biʃpu] *m* archbishop.

arco ['axku] *m* (*ARQ*) arch; (*MIL*, *MÚS*) bow; (*ELET*, *MAT*) arc; (*de barril*) hoop.

arco-da-velha *m*: **coisa/história do** ~ amazing thing/story.

arco-íris *m inv* rainbow.

ardente [ax'dẽtʃi] *adj* burning; (*intenso*) fervent; (*apaixonado*) ardent.

arder [ax'de*] *vi* to burn; (*pele*, *olhos*) to sting; ~ **de febre** to burn up with fever; ~ **de raiva** to seethe (with rage).

ardido/a [ax'dʒidu/a] *adj* (*picante*) hot.

ardil [ax'dʒiw] (*pl* -**is**) *m* trick, ruse.

ardiloso/a [axdʒi'lozu/ɔza] *adj* cunning.

ardis [ax'dʒiʃ] *mpl de* **ardil**.

ardor [ax'do*] *m* (*paixão*) ardour (*BRIT*), ardor (*US*), passion.

ardoroso/a [axdo'rozu/ɔza] *adj* ardent.

ardósia [ax'dɔzja] *f* slate.

árduo/a ['axdwu/a] *adj* arduous; (*difícil*) hard, difficult.

área ['arja] *f* area; (*ESPORTE*) penalty area; (*fig*) field; ~ **(de serviço)** balcony (*for hanging washing etc*).

arear [a'rja*] *vt* to polish.

areia [a'reja] *f* sand; ~ **movediça** quicksand.

arejado/a [are'ʒadu/a] *adj* aired, ventilated.

arejar [are'ʒa*] *vt* to air ♦ *vi* to get some air; (*descansar*) to have a breather; ~-**se** *vr* to get some air; to have a break.

ARENA (*BR*) *abr f* (= *Aliança Renovadora Nacional*) *former political party*.

arena [a'rɛna] *f* arena; (*de circo*) ring.

arenito [are'nitu] *m* sandstone.

arenoso/a [are'nozu/ɔza] *adj* sandy.

arenque [a'rẽki] *m* herring.

aresta [a'rɛʃta] *f* edge.

arfar [ax'fa*] *vi* (*ofegar*) to pant, gasp for breath; (*NÁUT*) to pitch.

argamassa [axga'masa] *f* mortar.

argamassar [axgama'sa*] *vt* to cement.

Argel [ax'ʒew] *n* Algiers.

Argélia [ax'ʒɛlja] *f*: **a** ~ Algeria.

argelino/a [axʒe'linu/a] *adj*, *m/f* Algerian.

Argentina [axʒẽ'tʃina] *f*: **a** ~ Argentina.

argentino/a [axʒẽ'tʃinu/a] *adj*, *m/f* Argentinian.

argila [ax'ʒila] *f* clay.

argiloso/a [axʒi'lozu/ɔza] *adj* (*terreno*) clay.

argola [ax'gɔla] *f* ring; ~**s** *fpl* (*brincos*) hooped

earrings; ~ **(de porta)** door-knocker.

argúcia [ax'gusja] *f* (*sutileza*) subtlety; (*agudeza*) astuteness.

argüição [axgwi'sãw] (*pl* -**ões**) *f* oral test.

argüir [ax'gwi*] *vt* (*examinar*) to test, examine.

argumentação [axgumẽta'sãw] *f* argumentation.

argumentador(a) [axgumẽta'do*(a)] *adj* argumentative ♦ *m/f* arguer.

argumentar [axgumẽ'ta*] *vt*, *vi* to argue.

argumento [axgu'mẽtu] *m* argument; (*de obra*) theme.

arguto/a [ax'gutu/a] *adj* (*sutil*) subtle; (*astuto*) shrewd.

ária ['arja] *f* aria.

ariano/a [a'rjanu/a] *adj*, *m/f* Aryan; (*do signo Áries*) Arian.

aridez [ari'deʒ] *f* (*secura*) dryness; (*esterilidade*) barrenness; (*falta de interesse*) dullness.

árido/a ['aridu/a] *adj* (*seco*) arid, dry; (*estéril*) barren; (*maçante*) dull, boring.

Áries ['ariʃ] *f* Aries.

arisco/a [a'riʃku/a] *adj* unsociable.

aristocracia [ariʃtokra'sia] *f* aristocracy.

aristocrata [ariʃto'krata] *m/f* aristocrat.

aristocrático/a [ariʃto'kratʃiku/a] *adj* aristocratic.

aritmética [aritʃ'mɛtʃika] *f* arithmetic.

aritmético/a [aritʃ'mɛtʃiku/a] *adj* arithmetical.

arma ['axma] *f* weapon; ~**s** *fpl* (*nucleares etc*) arms; (*brasão*) coat *sg* of arms; **de** ~**s e bagagem** with all one's belongings; **depor as** ~**s** to lay down arms; **passar pelas** ~**s** to shoot, execute; ~ **branca** cold steel; ~ **convencional/nuclear** conventional/nuclear weapon; ~ **de fogo** firearm.

armação [axma'sãw] (*pl* -**ões**) *f* (*armadura*) frame; (*PESCA*) tackle; (*NÁUT*) rigging; (*de óculos*) frames *pl*.

armada [ax'mada] *f* navy.

armadilha [axma'dʒiʎa] *f* trap.

armado/a [ax'madu/a] *adj* armed; ~ **até os dentes** armed to the teeth.

armador [axma'do*] *m* (*NÁUT*) shipowner; (*operário*) frame-layer.

armadura [axma'dura] *f* armour (*BRIT*), armor (*US*); (*ELET*) armature; (*CONSTR*) framework.

armamento [axma'mẽtu] *m* (*armas*) armaments *pl*, weapons *pl*; (*NÁUT*) equipment; (*ato*) arming.

armar [ax'ma*] *vt* to arm; (*montar*) to assemble; (*barraca*) to pitch; (*um aparelho*) to set up; (*armadilha*) to set; (*maquinar*) to hatch; (*NÁUT*) to fit out; ~-**se** *vr* to arm o.s.; ~ **uma briga com** to pick a quarrel with; ~ **uma confusão** to cause chaos.

armarinho [axma'riɲu] *m* haberdashery (*BRIT*), notions *pl* (*US*).

armário [ax'marju] *m* cupboard; (*de roupa*) wardrobe.

armazém [axma'zẽj] (pl -ns) m (depósito) warehouse; (loja) grocery store.

armazenagem [axmaze'naʒẽ] f storage.

armazenamento [axmazena'mẽtu] m storage.

armazenar [axmaze'na*] vt to store; (provisões) to stock; (COMPUT) to store.

armazéns [axma'zẽjʃ] mpl de **armazém**.

armeiro [ax'mejru] m gunsmith.

Armênia [ax'menja] f: **a** ~ Armenia.

arminho [ax'miɲu] m ermine.

armistício [axmiʃ'tʃisju] m armistice.

aro ['aru] m (argola) ring; (de óculos, roda) rim; (de porta) frame.

aroma [a'rɔma] f (de comida, café) aroma; (de perfume) fragrance.

aromático/a [aro'matʃiku/a] adj (comida) aromatic; (perfume) fragrant.

arpão [ax'pãw] (pl -ões) m harpoon.

arpejo [ax'peʒu] m arpeggio.

arpoar [ax'pwa*] vt to harpoon.

arpões [ax'põjʃ] mpl de **arpão**.

arqueado/a [ax'kjadu/a] adj arched.

arquear [ax'kja*] vt to arch; ~-**se** vr to bend, arch; (entortar-se) to warp.

arquei [ax'kej] etc vb V **arcar**.

arqueiro/a [ax'kejru/a] m/f archer; (goleiro) goalkeeper.

arquejar [axke'ʒa*] vi to pant, wheeze.

arquejo [ax'keʒu] m panting, gasping.

arqueologia [axkjolo'ʒia] f archaeology (BRIT), archeology (US).

arqueológico/a [axkjo'lɔʒiku/a] adj archaeological (BRIT), archeological (US).

arqueólogo/a [ax'kjɔlogu/a] m/f archaeologist (BRIT), archeologist (US).

arquétipo [ax'kɛtʃipu] m archetype.

arquibancada [axkibã'kada] f terrace.

arquipélago [axki'pɛlagu] m archipelago.

arquitetar [axkite'ta*] (PT: -ect-) vt to think up.

arquiteto/a [axki'tɛtu/a] (PT: -ect-) m/f architect.

arquitetônico/a [axkite'toniku/a] (PT: -ect-) adj architectural.

arquitetura [axkite'tura] (PT: -ect-) f architecture.

arquivamento [axkiva'mẽtu] m filing; (de projeto) shelving.

arquivar [axki'va*] vt to file; (suspender) to shelve.

arquivista [axki'viʃta] m/f archivist.

arquivo [ax'kivu] m file; (lugar) archive; (de empresa) files pl; (móvel) filing cabinet; (COMPUT) file; **abrir/fechar um** ~ (COMPUT) to open/close a file; **nome do** ~ (COMPUT) file name; ~ **ativo** (COMPUT) active file.

arrabaldes [axa'bawdʒiʃ] mpl suburbs.

arraia [a'xaja] f (peixe) ray.

arraial [axa'jaw] (pl -ais) m (povoação) village; (PT: festa) fair.

arraia-miúda f masses pl.

arraigado/a [axaj'gadu/a] adj deep-rooted; (fig) ingrained.

arraigar [axaj'ga*] vi to root; ~-**se** vr (enraizar-se) to take root; (estabelecer-se) to settle.

arrancada [axã'kada] f (puxão) pull, jerk; (partida) start; (investida) charge; (de atleta) burst of speed.

arrancar [axã'ka*] vt to pull out; (botão etc) to pull off; (arrebatar) to snatch (away); (fig: confissão) to extract; (: aplausos) to get ♦ vi to start (off); ~-**se** vr (partir) to leave; (fugir) to run off.

arranco [a'xãku] m (puxão) pull, jerk; (partida) sudden start.

arranha-céu [a'xaɲa-] (pl ~s) m skyscraper.

arranhadura [axaɲa'dura] f scratch.

arranhão [axa'ɲãw] (pl -ões) m scratch.

arranhar [axa'ɲa*] vt to scratch; ~ (n)**uma língua** to know a smattering of a language.

arranhões [axa'ɲõjʃ] mpl de **arranhão**.

arranjador(a) [axãʒa'do*(a)] m/f (MÚS) arranger.

arranjar [axã'ʒa*] vt to arrange; (emprego etc) to get, find; (doença) to get, catch; (namorado) to find; (questão) to settle; ~-**se** vr (virar-se) to manage; (conseguir emprego) to get a job; ~-**se sem** to do without.

arranjo [a'xãʒu] m arrangement; (negociata) shady deal; (col: caso) affair.

arranque [a'xãki] m V **motor**.

arranquei [axã'kej] etc vb V **arrancar**.

arrasador(a) [axaza'do*(a)] adj devastating.

arrasar [axa'za*] vt to devastate; (demolir) to demolish; (estragar) to ruin; (verbalmente) to lambast; ~-**se** vr to be devastated; (destruir-se) to destroy o.s.; (arruinar-se) to lose everything; (nos exames) to do terribly.

arrastado/a [axaʃ'tadu/a] adj (rasteiro) crawling; (demorado) dragging; (voz) drawling.

arrastão [axaʃ'tãw] (pl -ões) m tug, jerk; (rede) dragnet.

arrasta-pé [a'xaʃta-] (pl ~s) (col) m knees-up, shindig.

arrastar [axaʃ'ta*] vt to drag; (atrair) to draw ♦ vi to trail; ~-**se** vr (rastejar) to crawl; (andar a custo) to drag o.s.; (tempo) to drag; (processo) to drag on.

arrasto [a'xaʃtu] m (ação) dragging; (rede) trawl-net; (TEC) drag.

arrazoado/a [axa'zwadu/a] adj (argumento) reasoned ♦ m (JUR) defence (BRIT), defense (US).

arrazoar [axa'zwa*] vi (discutir) to argue.

arrear [a'xja*] vt (cavalo etc) to bridle.

arrebanhar [axeba'ɲa*] vt (gado) to herd; (juntar) to gather.

arrebatado/a [axeba'tadu/a] adj (impetuoso) rash, impetuous; (enlevado) entranced.

NB: *European Portuguese adds the following consonants to certain words:* **b** *(sú(b)dito, su(b)til);* **c** *(a(c)ção, a(c)cionista, a(c)to);* **m** *(inde(m)ne);* **p** *(ado(p)ção, ado(p)tar); for further details see p. xiii.*

arrebatador(a) [axebata'do*(a)] *adj* enchanting.

arrebatamento [axebata'mẽtu] *m* (*impetuosidade*) impetuosity; (*enlevo*) ecstasy.

arrebatar [axeba'ta*] *vt* (*arrancar*) to snatch (away); (*levar*) to carry off; (*enlevar*) to entrance; (*enfurecer*) to enrage; **~-se** *vr* (*entusiasmar-se*) to be entranced.

arrebentação [axebẽta'sãw] *f* (*na praia*) surf.

arrebentado/a [axebẽ'tadu/a] *adj* (*quebrado*) broken; (*vaso etc*) smashed; (*estafado*) worn out.

arrebentar [axebẽ'ta*] *vi* to smash; (*porta*) to break down; (*corda*) to snap, break ♦ *vi* to smash; to snap, break; (*guerra*) to break out; (*bomba*) to explode; (*ondas*) to break.

arrebitado/a [axebi'tadu/a] *adj* turned-up; (*nariz*) snub.

arrebitar [axebi'ta*] *vt* to turn up.

arrecadação [axekada'sãw] *f* (*de impostos etc*) collection; (*impostos arrecadados*) tax revenue, taxes *pl*.

arrecadar [axeka'da*] *vt* (*impostos etc*) to collect.

arrecife [axe'sifi] *m* reef.

arredar [axe'da*] *vt* to move away, move back; **~-se** *vr* to move away; **não ~ pé** not to budge, to stand one's ground.

arredio/a [axe'dʒiu/a] *adj* (*pessoa*) withdrawn.

arredondado/a [axedõ'dadu/a] *adj* round, rounded.

arredondar [axedõ'da*] *vt* to round (off); (*conta*) to round up.

arredores [axe'dɔriʃ] *mpl* suburbs; (*cercanias*) outskirts.

arrefecer [axefe'se*] *vt* to cool; (*febre*) to lower; (*desanimar*) to discourage ♦ *vi* to cool (off); to get discouraged.

arrefecimento [axefesi'mẽtu] *m* cooling.

ar-refrigerado (*pl* **ares-refrigerados**) *m* (*aparelho*) air conditioner; (*sistema*) air conditioning.

arregaçar [axega'sa*] *vt* to roll up.

arregalado/a [axega'ladu/a] *adj* (*olhos*) wide; **com os olhos ~s** pop-eyed.

arregalar [axega'la*] *vt*: **~ os olhos** to stare in amazement.

arreganhar [axega'ɲa*] *vt* (*dentes*) to bare; (*lábios*) to draw back.

arreios [a'xejuʃ] *mpl* harness *sg*.

arrematar [axema'ta*] *vt* (*dizer concluindo*) to conclude; (*comprar*) to buy by auction; (*vender*) to sell by auction; (*COSTURA*) to finish off.

arremate [axe'matʃi] *m* (*COSTURA*) finishing off; (*conclusão*) conclusion; (*FUTEBOL*) finishing.

arremedar [axeme'da*] *vt* to mimic.

arremedo [axe'medu] *m* mimicry.

arremessar [axeme'sa*] *vt* to throw, hurl; **~-se** *vr* to hurl o.s.

arremesso [axe'mesu] *m* (*lançamento*) throw; **~ de peso** shot-put.

arremeter [axeme'te*] *vi* to lunge; **~ contra** (*acometer*) to attack, assail.

arremetida [axeme'tʃida] *f* attack, onslaught.

arrendador(a) [axẽda'do*(a)] *m/f* landlord/landlady.

arrendamento [axẽda'mẽtu] *m* (*ação*) leasing; (*contrato*) lease.

arrendar [axẽ'da*] *vt* to lease.

arrendatário/a [axẽda'tarju/a] *m/f* tenant.

arrepender-se [axepẽ'dexsi] *vr* to repent; (*mudar de opinião*) to change one's mind; **~ de** to regret, be sorry for.

arrependido/a [axepẽ'dʒidu/a] *adj* (*pessoa*) sorry.

arrependimento [axepẽdʒi'mẽtu] *m* regret; (*REL, de crime*) repentance.

arrepiado/a [axe'pjadu/a] *adj* (*cabelo*) standing on end; (*pele, pessoa*) goose-pimply; (*horrorizado*) horrified.

arrepiar [axe'pja*] *vt* (*amedrontar*) to horrify; (*cabelo etc*) to cause to stand on end; **~-se** *vr* (*sentir calafrios*) to shiver; (*cabelo*) to stand on end; **isso me arrepia** it gives me goose flesh; **(ser) de ~ os cabelos** (to be) hair-raising.

arrepio [axe'piu] *m* shiver; (*de frio*) chill; **isso me dá ~s** it gives me the creeps.

arresto [a'xɛʃtu] *m* (*JUR*) seizure, confiscation.

arrevesado/a [axeve'zadu/a] *adj* (*obscuro*) obscure; (*intricado*) intricate.

arrevesar [axeve'za*] *vt* (*complicar*) to complicate.

arriado/a [a'xjadu/a] *adj* (*exausto*) exhausted; (*por doença*) very weak.

arriar [a'xja*] *vt* (*baixar*) to lower; (*depor*) to lay down ♦ *vi* (*cair*) to drop; (*vergar*) to sag; (*desistir*) to give up; (*fig*) to collapse; (*AUTO: bateria*) to go flat.

arribação [axiba'sãw] (*BR: pl* **-ões**) *f* (*de aves*) migration.

arribar [axi'ba*] *vi* (*recuperar-se*) to recuperate.

arrimo [a'ximu] *m* support; **~ de família** breadwinner.

arriscado/a [axiʃ'kadu/a] *adj* risky; (*audacioso*) daring.

arriscar [axiʃ'ka*] *vt* to risk; (*pôr em perigo*) to endanger, jeopardize; **~-se** *vr* to take a risk; **~-se a fazer** to risk doing.

arrisquei [axiʃ'kej] *etc vb V* **arriscar**.

arrivista [axi'viʃta] *m/f* upstart; (*oportunista*) opportunist.

arroba [a'xoba] *f* = 15 kg.

arrochado/a [axo'ʃadu/a] *adj* (*vestido*) skin-tight; (*fig*) tough.

arrochar [axo'ʃa*] *vt* (*apertar*) to tighten up ♦ *vi* (*ser exigente*) to be demanding.

arrocho [a'xoʃu] *m* squeeze; (*fig*) predicament; **~ salarial/ao crédito** wage/credit squeeze.

arrogância [axo'gãsja] *f* arrogance, haughtiness.

arrogante [axo'gãtʃi] *adj* arrogant, haughty.

arrogar-se [axo'gaxsi] *vr* (*direitos, privilégios*) to claim.

arroio [a'xɔju] *m* stream.

arrojado/a [axo'ʒadu/a] *adj* (*design*) bold; (*temerário*) rash; (*ousado*) daring.

arrojar [axo'ʒa*] *vt* (*lançar*) to hurl.

arrojo [a'xoʒu] *m* (*ousadia*) boldness.

arrolamento [axola'mẽtu] *m* list.

arrolar [axo'la*] *vt* to list.

arrolhar [axo'ʎa*] *vt* to cork.

arromba [a'xõba] *f*: **de ~** great.

arrombar [axõ'ba*] *vt* (*porta*) to break down; (*cofre*) to crack.

arrotar [axo'ta*] *vi* to belch ♦ *vt* (*alardear*) to boast of.

arroto [a'xotu] *m* burp.

arroubo [a'xobu] *m* ecstasy, rapture.

arroz [a'xoʒ] *m* rice; **~ doce** rice pudding.

arrozal [axo'zaw] (*pl* **-ais**) *m* rice field.

arruaça [a'xwasa] *f* street riot.

arruaceiro/a [axwa'sejru/a] *m/f* rioter.

arruela [a'xwɛla] *f* (*TEC*) washer.

arruinar [axwi'na*] *vt* to ruin; (*destruir*) to destroy; **~-se** *vr* to be ruined; (*perder a saúde*) to ruin one's health.

arrulhar [axu'ʎa*] *vi* (*pombos*) to coo.

arrulho [a'xuʎu] *m* cooing.

arrumação [axuma'sãw] *f* (*arranjo*) arrangement; (*de um quarto etc*) tidying up; (*de malas*) packing.

arrumadeira [axuma'dejra] *f* cleaning lady; (*num hotel*) chambermaid.

arrumar [axu'ma*] *vt* (*pôr em ordem*) to put in order, arrange; (*quarto etc*) to tidy up; (*malas*) to pack; (*emprego*) to get; (*vestir*) to dress up; (*desculpa*) to make up, find; (*vida*) to sort out; **~-se** *vr* (*aprontar-se*) to get dressed, get ready; (*na vida*) to sort o.s. out; (*virar-se*) to manage.

arsenal [axse'naw] (*pl* **-ais**) *m* (*MIL*) arsenal; **~ de Marinha** naval dockyard.

arsênio [ax'senju] *m* arsenic.

arte ['axtʃi] *f* art; (*habilidade*) skill; (*ofício*) trade, craft; **fazer ~** (*fig*) to get up to mischief.

artefato [axtʃi'fatu] (*PT*: **-act-**) *m* (*manufactured*) article; **~s de couro** leather goods, leatherware *sg*.

arteiro/a [ax'tejru/a] *adj* (*criança*) mischievous.

artéria [ax'tɛrja] *f* (*ANAT*) artery.

arterial [axte'rjaw] (*pl* **-ais**) *adj* V **pressão**.

arteriosclerose [axterjoʃkle'rɔzi] *f* hardening of the arteries, arteriosclerosis.

artesã [axte'zã] *f de* **artesão**.

artesanal [axteza'naw] (*pl* **-ais**) *adj* craft.

artesanato [axteza'natu] *m* craftwork; **artigos de ~** craft items.

artesão/sã [axte'zãw/zã] (*pl* **~s/~s**) *m/f* artisan, craftsman/woman.

ártico/a ['axtʃiku/a] *adj* Arctic ♦ *m*: **o A~** the Arctic.

articulação [axtʃikula'sãw] (*pl* **-ões**) *f* articulation; (*MED*) joint.

articulado/a [axtʃiku'ladu/a] *adj* articulated, jointed.

articular [axtʃiku'la*] *vt* (*pronunciar*) to articulate; (*ligar*) to join together.

artífice [ax'tʃifisi] *m/f* craftsman/woman; (*inventor*) inventor.

artificial [axtʃifi'sjaw] (*pl* **-ais**) *adj* artificial; (*pessoa*) affected.

artifício [axtʃi'fisju] *m* stratagem, trick.

artificioso/a [axtʃifi'sjozu/ɔza] *adj* (*hábil*) skilful (*BRIT*), skillful (*US*); (*astucioso*) artful.

artigo [ax'tʃigu] *m* article; (*COM*) item; **~s** *mpl* goods; **~ definido/indefinido** (*LING*) definite/indefinite article; **~ de fundo** leading article, editorial; **~s de toucador** toiletries.

artilharia [axtʃiʎa'ria] *f* artillery.

artilheiro [axtʃi'ʎejru] *m* gunner, artilleryman; (*FUTEBOL*) striker.

artimanha [axtʃi'maɲa] *f* (*ardil*) stratagem; (*astúcia*) cunning.

artista [ax'tʃiʃta] *m/f* artist.

artístico/a [ax'tʃiʃtʃiku/a] *adj* artistic.

artrite [ax'tritʃi] *f* (*MED*) arthritis.

arvorar [axvo'ra*] *vt* (*bandeira*) to hoist; (*elevar*): **~ alguém em** to promote *ou* elevate sb to; **~-se** *vr*: **~-se em** to set o.s. up as.

árvore ['axvori] *f* tree; (*TEC*) shaft; **~ de Natal** Christmas tree.

arvoredo [axvo'redu] *m* grove.

as [aʃ] *art def* V **a**.

ás [ajʃ] *m* ace.

às [ajʃ] = **a** + **as**.

asa ['aza] *f* wing; (*de xícara etc*) handle; **dar ~s à imaginação** to give free rein to one's imagination.

asa-delta *f* hang-glider.

asbesto [aʒ'bɛʃtu] *m* asbestos.

ascendência [asẽ'dẽsja] *f* (*antepassados*) ancestry; (*domínio*) ascendency, sway.

ascendente [asẽ'dẽtʃi] *adj* rising, upward.

ascender [asẽ'de*] *vi* (*subir*) to rise, ascend.

ascensão [asẽ'sãw] (*pl* **-ões**) *f* ascent; (*fig*) rise; **dia da A~** Ascension Day.

ascensor [asẽ'so*] *m* elevator (*US*), lift (*BRIT*).

ascensorista [asẽso'riʃta] *m/f* lift operator.

asceta [a'sɛta] *m/f* ascetic.

asco ['aʃku] *m* loathing, revulsion; **dar ~** to be revolting *ou* disgusting.

asfaltar [aʃfaw'ta*] *vt* to asphalt.

asfalto [aʃ'fawtu] *m* asphalt.

asfixia [aʃfik'sia] *f* asphyxia, suffocation.

asfixiar [aʃfik'sja*] *vt* to asphyxiate, suffocate.

Ásia ['azja] *f*: **a ~** Asia.

asiático/a [a'zjatʃiku/a] *adj, m/f* Asian.

asilar [azi'la*] *vt* to give refuge to; **~-se** *vr* to

NB: European Portuguese adds the following consonants to certain words: **b** (sú(b)dito, su(b)til); **c** (a(c)ção, a(c)cionista, a(c)to); **m** (inde(m)ne); **p** (ado(p)ção, ado(p)tar); *for further details see p. xiii.*

take refuge.
asilo [a'zilu] *m* (*refúgio*) refuge; (*estabelecimento*) home; ~ **político** political asylum.
asma ['aʒma] *f* asthma.
asmático/a [aʒ'matʃiku/a] *adj*, *m/f* asthmatic.
asneira [aʒ'nejra] *f* (*tolice*) stupidity; (*ato*, *dito*) stupid thing.
asno ['aʒnu] *m* donkey; (*fig*) ass.
aspas ['aʃpaʃ] *fpl* inverted commas; **entre** ~ in inverted commas.
aspargo [aʃ'paxgu] *m* asparagus.
aspecto [aʃ'pɛktu] *m* (*de uma questão*) aspect; (*aparência*) look, appearance; (*característica*) feature; (*ponto de vista*) point of view; **ter bom** ~ to look good; **tomar um** ~ to take on an aspect.
aspereza [aʃpe'reza] *f* roughness; (*severidade*) harshness; (*rudeza*) rudeness.
aspergir [aʃpex'ʒi*] *vt* to sprinkle.
áspero/a ['aʃperu/a] *adj* rough; (*severo*) harsh; (*rude*) rude.
asperso/a [aʃ'pɛxsu/a] *pp de* **aspergir** ♦ *adj* scattered.
aspiração [aʃpira'sãw] (*pl* -ões) *f* aspiration; (*inalação*) inhalation.
aspirador [aʃpira'do*] *m*: ~ (**de pó**) vacuum cleaner; **passar o** ~ (**em**) to vacuum.
aspirante [aʃpi'rãtʃi] *adj* aspiring ♦ *m/f* candidate; (*MIL*) cadet; (*NÁUT*) midshipman.
aspirar [aʃpi'ra*] *vt* to breathe in; (*bombear*) to suck up; (*LING*) to aspirate ♦ *vi* to breathe; (*soprar*) to blow; (*desejar*): ~ **a algo** to aspire to sth.
aspirina [aʃpi'rina] *f* aspirin.
aspirjo [aʃ'pixʒu] *etc vb* V **aspergir**.
asqueroso/a [aʃke'rozu/ɔza] *adj* disgusting, revolting.
assadeira [asa'dejra] *f* roasting tin.
assado/a [a'sadu/a] *adj* roasted; (*CULIN*) roast ♦ *m* roast; **carne assada** roast beef.
assadura [asa'dura] *f* rash; (*em bebê*) nappy rash.
assalariado/a [asala'rjadu/a] *adj* salaried ♦ *m/f* wage-earner.
assaltante [asaw'tãtʃi] *m/f* assailant; (*de banco*) robber; (*de casa*) burglar; (*na rua*) mugger.
assaltar [asaw'ta*] *vt* (*atacar*) to attack; (*casa*) to break into; (*banco*) to rob; (*pessoa na rua*) to mug.
assalto [a'sawtu] *m* (*ataque*) attack, raid; (*a um banco etc*) raid, robbery; (*BOXE*) round; (*a uma casa*) burglary, break-in; (*a uma pessoa na rua*) mugging.
assanhado/a [asa'ɲadu/a] *adj* excited; (*criança*) excitable; (*desavergonhado*) brazen; (*namorador*) amorous.
assanhar [asa'ɲa*] *vt* to excite; ~**-se** *vr* to get excited.
assar [a'sa*] *vt* to roast; (*na grelha*) to grill.
assassinar [asasi'na*] *vt* to murder, kill; (*POL*) to assassinate.
assassinato [asasi'natu] *m* murder, killing;

(*POL*) assassination.
assassínio [asa'sinju] *m* murder, killing; (*POL*) assassination.
assassino/a [asa'sinu/a] *m/f* murderer; (*POL*) assassin.
assaz [a'saʒ] *adv* (*suficientemente*) sufficiently; (*muito*) rather.
asseado/a [a'sjadu/a] *adj* clean.
assediar [ase'dʒja*] *vt* (*sitiar*) to besiege; (*importunar*) to pester.
assédio [a'sɛdʒu] *m* siege; (*insistência*) insistence.
assegurar [asegu'ra*] *vt* (*tornar seguro*) to secure; (*garantir*) to ensure; (*afirmar*) to assure; ~**-se** *vr*: ~**-se de** to make sure of.
asseio [a'seju] *m* cleanliness.
assembléia [asẽ'bleja] *f* assembly; (*reunião*) meeting; ~ **geral** (*ordinária*) annual general meeting; ~ **geral extraordinária** extraordinary general meeting.
assemelhar [aseme'ʎa*] *vt* to liken; ~**-se** *vr* (*ser parecido*) to be alike; ~**-se a** to resemble, look like.
assenhorear-se [aseɲo'rjaxsi] *vr*: ~ **de** to take possession of.
assentado/a [asẽ'tadu/a] *adj* (*firme*) fixed, secure; (*combinado*) agreed; (*ajuizado*) sensible.
assentamento [asẽta'mẽtu] *m* registration; (*nota*) entry, record.
assentar [asẽ'ta*] *vt* (*fazer sentar*) to seat; (*colocar*) to place; (*tijolos*) to lay; (*estabelecer*) to establish; (*decidir*) to decide upon; (*determinar*) to fix, settle; (*soco*) to land ♦ *vi* (*pó etc*) to settle; ~**-se** *vr* to sit down; ~ **com** to go with; ~ **em** *ou* **a** (*roupa*) to suit.
assente [a'sẽtʃi] *pp de* **assentar** ♦ *adj* agreed, decided.
assentimento [asẽtʃi'mẽtu] *m* assent, agreement.
assentir [asẽ'tʃi*] *vi* to agree; ~ (**em**) to consent *ou* agree (to); ~ (**a**) to accede (to).
assento [a'sẽtu] *m* seat; (*base*) base; **tomar** ~ (*sentar*) to take a seat; (*pó*) to settle.
assertiva [asex'tʃiva] *f* assertion.
assessor(a) [ase'so*(a)] *m/f* adviser; (*POL*) aide; (*assistente*) assistant.
assessoramento [asesora'mẽtu] *m* assistance.
assessorar [aseso'ra*] *vt* to advise.
assessoria [aseso'ria] *f* advisory body.
assestar [aseʃ'ta*] *vt* to aim, point.
asseveração [asevera'sãw] (*pl* -ões) *f* assertion.
asseverar [aseve'ra*] *vt* to affirm, assert.
assexuado/a [asek'swadu/a] *adj* asexual.
assiduidade [asidwi'dadʒi] *f* (*às aulas, etc*) regular attendance; (*diligência*) assiduity.
assíduo/a [a'sidwu/a] *adj* (*aluno*) who attends regularly; (*diligente*) assiduous; (*constante*) constant; **ser** ~ **num lugar** to be a regular visitor to a place.
assim [a'si] *adv* (*deste modo*) like this, in this way, thus; (*portanto*) therefore; (*igualmente*)

likewise; ~ ~ so-so; ~ **mesmo** in any case; **e** ~ **por diante** and so on; ~ **como** as well as; **como** ~**?** how do you mean?; ~ **que** (*logo que*) as soon as; **nem tanto** ~ not as much as that.

assimétrico/a [asi'mɛtriku/a] *adj* asymmetrical.

assimilação [asimila'sãw] *f* assimilation.

assimilar [asimi'la*] *vt* to assimilate; (*apreender*) to take in; (*assemelhar*) to compare.

assinalado/a [asina'ladu/a] *adj* (*marcado*) marked; (*notável*) notable; (*célebre*) eminent.

assinalar [asina'la*] *vt* (*marcar*) to mark; (*distinguir*) to distinguish; (*especificar*) to point out.

assin. *abr* = **assinatura**.

assinante [asi'nãtʃi] *m/f* (*de jornal etc*) subscriber.

assinar [asi'na*] *vt* to sign.

assinatura [asina'tura] *f* (*nome*) signature; (*de jornal etc*) subscription; (*TEATRO*) season ticket; **fazer a** ~ **de** (*revista etc*) to take out a subscription to.

assinto [a'sĩtu] *etc vb* V **assentir**.

assistência [asiʃ'tésja] *f* (*presença*) presence; (*público*) audience; (*auxílio*) aid, assistance; ~ **médica** medical aid; ~ **social** social work; (*serviços*) social services *pl*; ~ **técnica** technical back-up.

assistente [asiʃ'tẽtʃi] *adj* assistant ♦ *m/f* (*pessoa presente*) spectator, onlooker; (*ajudante*) assistant; ~ **social** social worker.

assistir [asiʃ'tʃi*] *vt*, *vi*: ~ (**a**) (*auxiliar*) to assist; (*MED*) to attend to; (*TV*, *filme*, *jogo*) to watch; (*reunião*) to attend; ~ **a** (*caber*) to fall to.

assoalho [aso'aʎu] *m* (wooden) floor.

assoar [aso'a*] *vt*: ~ **o nariz** to blow one's nose; ~**-se** *vr* (*PT*) to blow one's nose.

assoberbado/a [asobex'badu/a] *adj* (*pessoa*: *de serviço*) snowed under with work.

assoberbar [asobex'ba*] *vt* (*de serviço*) to overload.

assobiar [aso'bja*] *vi* to whistle.

assobio [aso'biu] *m* whistle; (*instrumento*) whistle; (*de vapor*) hiss.

associação [asosja'sãw] (*pl* **-ões**) *f* association; (*organização*) society; (*parceria*) partnership; ~ **de moradores** residents' association.

associado/a [aso'sjadu/a] *adj* associate ♦ *m/f* associate, member; (*COM*) associate; (*sócio*) partner.

associar [aso'sja*] *vt* to associate; ~**-se** *vr* (*COM*) to form a partnership; ~**-se a** to associate with.

assolador(a) [asola'do*(a)] *adj* devastating.

assolar [aso'la*] *vt* to devastate.

assomar [aso'ma*] *vi* (*aparecer*) to appear; ~ **a** (*subir*) to climb to the top of.

assombração [asõbra'sãw] (*pl* **-ões**) *f* (*fantasma*) ghost.

assombrado/a [asõ'bradu/a] *adj* astonished, amazed.

assombrar [asõ'bra*] *vt* to astonish, amaze; ~**-se** *vr* to be amazed.

assombro [a'sõbru] *m* amazement, astonishment; (*maravilha*) marvel.

assombroso/a [asõ'brozu/ɔza] *adj* (*espantoso*) astonishing, amazing.

assoprar [aso'pra*] *vi* to blow ♦ *vt* to blow; (*velas*) to blow out.

assoviar [aso'vja*] *vt* = **assobiar**.

assovio [aso'viu] *m* = **assobio**.

assumir [asu'mi*] *vt* to assume, take on; (*reconhecer*) to accept, admit ♦ *vi* to take office.

Assunção [asũ'sãw] *n* (*no Paraguai*) Asunción.

assuntar [asũ'ta*] *vt* (*prestar atenção*) to pay attention to; (*verificar*) to find out ♦ *vi* (*meditar*) to cogitate.

assunto [a'sũtu] *m* (*tema*) subject, matter; (*enredo*) plot.

assustadiço/a [asuʃta'dʒisu/a] *adj* timorous.

assustador(a) [asuʃta'do*(a)] *adj* (*alarmante*) startling; (*amedrontador*) frightening.

assustar [asuʃ'ta*] *vt* to frighten, scare, startle; ~**-se** *vr* to be frightened.

asteca [aʃ'tɛka] *adj*, *m/f* Aztec.

asterisco [aʃte'riʃku] *m* asterisk.

astigmatismo [aʃtʃigma'tʃiʒmu] *m* astigmatism.

astral [aʃ'traw] (*pl* **-ais**) *m* state of mind.

astro ['aʃtru] *m* star.

astrologia [aʃtrolo'ʒia] *f* astrology.

astrólogo/a [aʃ'trɔlogu/a] *m/f* astrologer.

astronauta [aʃtro'nawta] *m/f* astronaut.

astronave [aʃtro'navi] *f* spaceship.

astronomia [aʃtrono'mia] *f* astronomy.

astronômico/a [aʃtro'nomiku/a] *adj* (*preço*) astronomical.

astrônomo/a [aʃ'tronomu/a] *m/f* astronomer.

astúcia [aʃ'tusja] *f* cunning.

astuto/a [aʃ'tutu/a] *adj* astute; (*esperto*) cunning.

ata ['ata] *f* (*de reunião*) minutes *pl*.

atacadista [ataka'dʒiʃta] *adj* wholesale ♦ *m/f* wholesaler.

atacado/a [ata'kadu/a] *adj* (*col*: *pessoa*) in a bad mood ♦ *m*: **por** ~ wholesale.

atacante [ata'kãtʃi] *adj* attacking ♦ *m/f* attacker, assailant ♦ *m* (*FUTEBOL*) forward.

atacar [ata'ka*] *vt* to attack; (*problema etc*) to tackle.

atado/a [a'tadu/a] *adj* (*desajeitado*) clumsy, awkward; (*perplexo*) puzzled.

atadura [ata'dura] *f* bandage.

atalaia [ata'laja] *f* lookout post.

atalhar [ata'ʎa*] *vt* (*impedir*) to prevent;

NB: *European Portuguese adds the following consonants to certain words:* **b** (sú(b)dito, su(b)til); **c** (a(c)ção, a(c)cionista, a(c)to); **m** (inde(m)ne); **p** (ado(p)ção, ado(p)tar); *for further details see p. xiii.*

(abreviar) to shorten ♦ *vi (tomar um atalho)* to take a short cut.

atalho [a'taʎu] *m (caminho)* short cut.

atapetar [atape'ta*] *vt* to carpet.

ataque [a'taki] *m* attack; **ter um ~ (de raiva)** to have a fit; **ter um ~ de riso** to burst out laughing; **~ aéreo** air raid.

ataquei [ata'kej] *etc vb V* **atacar.**

atar [a'ta*] *vt* to tie (up), fasten; **não ~ nem desatar** *(pessoa)* to waver; *(negócio)* to be in the air.

atarantado/a [atarã'tadu/a] *adj (pessoa)* flustered, in a flap.

atarantar [atarã'ta*] *vt* to fluster.

atarefado/a [atare'fadu/a] *adj* busy.

atarracado/a [ataxa'kadu/a] *adj* stocky.

atarraxar [ataxa'ʃa*] *vt* to screw.

ataúde [ata'udʒi] *m* coffin.

ataviar [ata'vja*] *vt* to adorn, decorate; **~-se** *vr* to get dressed up.

atavio [ata'viu] *m* adornment.

atazanar [ataza'na*] *vt* to pester.

até [a'tɛ] *prep (PT: + a)*: *(lugar)* up to, as far as; *(tempo etc)* until, till ♦ *adv (tb: ~ mesmo)* even; **~ agora** up to now; **~ certo ponto** to a certain extent; **~ em cima** to the top; **~ já** see you soon; **~ logo** bye!; **~ onde** as far as; **~ que** until; **~ que enfim!** at last!

atear [ate'a*] *vt (fogo)* to kindle; *(fig)* to incite, inflame; **~-se** *vr (fogo)* to blaze; *(paixões)* to flare up; **~ fogo a** to set light to.

atéia [a'tɛja] *f de* **ateu.**

ateísmo [ate'iʒmu] *m* atheism.

ateliê [ate'lje] *m* studio.

atemorizador(a) [atemoriza'do*(a)] *adj* frightening.

atemorizar [atemori'za*] *vt* to frighten; *(intimidar)* to intimidate.

Atenas [a'tenaʃ] *n* Athens.

atenção [atẽ'sãw] *(pl* **-ões)** *f* attention; *(cortesia)* courtesy; *(bondade)* kindness; **~!** be careful!; **chamar a ~** to attract attention; **chamar a ~ de alguém** to tell sb off.

atencioso/a [atẽ'sjozu/ɔza] *adj* considerate.

atenções [atẽ'sõjʃ] *fpl de* **atenção.**

atender [atẽ'de*] *vt:* **~ (a)** to attend to; *(receber)* to receive; *(em loja)* to serve; *(deferir)* to grant; *(telefone etc)* to answer; *(paciente)* to see ♦ *vi (ao telefone, porta)* to answer; *(dar atenção)* to pay attention.

atendimento [atẽdʒi'mẽtu] *m* service; *(recepção)* reception; answering; **horário de ~** opening hours; *(em consultório)* surgery *(BRIT)* ou office *(US)* hours.

atenho [a'teɲu] *etc vb V* **ater-se.**

atentado [atẽ'tadu] *m (ataque)* attack; *(crime)* crime; *(contra a vida de alguém)* attempt on sb's life; **~ ao pudor** indecent exposure.

atentar [atẽ'ta*] *vt (empreender)* to undertake ♦ *vi* to make an attempt; **~ a** ou **em** ou **para** to pay attention to; **~ contra a vida de alguém** to make an attempt on sb's life; **~**

contra a moral to offend against morality.

atento/a [a'tẽtu/a] *adj* attentive; *(exame)* careful; **estar ~ a** to be aware ou mindful of.

atenuação [atenwa'sãw] *(pl* **-ões)** *f* reduction, lessening.

atenuante [ate'nwãtʃi] *adj* extenuating ♦ *m* extenuating circumstance.

atenuar [ate'nwa*] *vt (diminuir)* to reduce, lessen.

aterrador(a) [atexa'do*(a)] *adj* terrifying.

aterragem [ate'xaʒej] *(PT: pl* **-ns)** *f (AER)* landing.

aterrar [ate'xa*] *vt (cobrir com terra)* to cover with earth; *(praia)* to reclaim ♦ *vi (PT: AER)* to land.

aterrissagem [atexi'saʒẽ] *(BR: pl* **-ns)** *f (AER)* landing.

aterrissar [atexi'sa*] *(BR) vi (AER)* to land.

aterrizar [atexi'za*] *vi =* **aterrissar.**

aterro [a'texu] *m* landfill.

aterrorizado/a [atexori'zadu/a] *adj* terrified.

aterrorizador(a) [atexoriza'do*(a)] *adj* terrifying.

aterrorizante [atexori'zãtʃi] *adj* terrifying.

aterrorizar [atexori'za*] *vt* to terrorize.

ater-se [a'texsi] *(irreg: como* **ter)** *vr:* **~ a** *(prender-se)* to get caught up in; *(limitar-se)* to restrict o.s. to.

atestado/a [ateʃ'tadu/a] *adj* certified ♦ *m* certificate; *(prova)* proof; *(JUR)* testimony.

atestar [ateʃ'ta*] *vt (certificar)* to certify; *(testemunhar)* to bear witness to; *(provar)* to prove.

ateu/atéia [a'tew/a'tɛja] *adj, m/f* atheist.

ateve [a'tevi] *etc vb V* **ater-se.**

atiçador [atʃisa'do*] *m (utensílio)* poker.

atiçar [atʃi'sa*] *vt (fogo)* to poke; *(incitar)* to incite; *(provocar)* to provoke; *(sentimento)* to induce.

atilado/a [atʃi'ladu/a] *adj (esperto)* clever.

atinado/a [atʃi'nadu/a] *adj (sensato)* wise, sensible.

atinar [atʃi'na*] *vt (acertar)* to guess correctly ♦ *vi:* **~ com** *(solução)* to find; **~ em** to notice; **~ a fazer algo** to succeed in doing sth.

atingir [atʃi'ʒi*] *vt (acertar)* to reach; *(acertar)* to hit; *(afetar)* to affect; *(objetivo)* to achieve; *(compreender)* to grasp.

atingível [atʃi'ʒivew] *(pl* **-eis)** *adj* attainable.

atinha [a'tʃiɲa] *etc vb V* **ater-se.**

atinjo [a'tʃiʒu] *etc vb V* **atingir.**

atípico/a [a'tʃipiku/a] *adj* atypical, untypical.

atirador(a) [atʃira'do*(a)] *m/f* marksman/woman; **~ de tocaia** sniper.

atirar [atʃi'ra*] *vt (lançar)* to throw, fling, hurl ♦ *vi (arma)* to shoot; **~-se** *vr:* **~-se a** *(lançar-se a)* to hurl o.s. at; **~ (em)** to shoot (at).

atitude [atʃi'tudʒi] *f* attitude; *(postura)* posture; **tomar uma ~** *(reagir)* to do something about it.

ativa [a'tʃiva] *f (MIL)* active service.

ativar [atʃi'va*] vt to activate; (apressar) to hasten.

ative [a'tʃivi] etc vb V **ater-se**.

atividade [atʃivi'dadʒi] f activity.

ativo/a [a'tʃivu/a] adj active ♦ m (COM) assets pl.

atlântico/a [at'lãtʃiku/a] adj Atlantic ♦ m: o A~ the Atlantic.

atlas ['atlaʃ] m inv atlas.

atleta [at'leta] m/f athlete.

atlético/a [at'lɛtʃiku/a] adj athletic.

atletismo [atle'tʃiʒmu] m athletics sg.

atmosfera [atmoʃ'fɛra] f atmosphere.

ato ['atu] m act; (ação) action; (cerimônia) ceremony; (TEATRO) act; **em ~ contínuo** straight after; **no ~** on the spot; **no mesmo ~** at the same time; **~ falho** Freudian slip; **~ público** public ceremony.

à-toa adj (insignificante) insignificant; (simples) simple, easy ♦ adv V **toa**.

atoalhado/a [atoa'ʎadu/a] adj: **(tecido) ~** towelling.

atolado/a [ato'ladu/a] adj (tb fig) bogged down.

atolar [ato'la*] vt to bog down; **~-se** vr to get bogged down.

atoleiro [ato'lejru] m bog, quagmire; (fig) quandary, fix.

atômico/a [a'tomiku/a] adj atomic.

atomizador [atomiza'do*] m atomizer.

átomo ['atomu] m atom.

atônito/a [a'tonitu/a] adj astonished, amazed.

ator [a'to*] m actor.

atordoado/a [atox'dwadu/a] adj dazed.

atordoador(a) [atoxdwa'do*(a)] adj stunning.

atordoamento [atoxdwa'mẽtu] m daze.

atordoar [atox'dwa*] vt to daze, stun.

atormentar [atoxmẽ'ta*] vt to torment; (importunar) to plague.

atracação [ataka'sãw] (pl -ões) f (NÁUT) mooring; (briga) fight; (col: agarração) necking.

atração [atra'sãw] (pl -ões) f attraction.

atracar [atra'ka*] vt, vi (NÁUT) to moor; **~-se** vr to grapple; (col: abraçar-se) to neck.

atrações [atra'sõjʃ] fpl de **atração**.

atractivo/a [atra'tivu/a] (PT) adj = **atrativo**.

atraente [atra'ẽtʃi] adj attractive.

atraiçoar [atraj'swa*] vt to betray.

atrair [atra'i*] vt to attract; (fascinar) to fascinate.

atrapalhação [atrapaʎa'sãw] f (confusão) confusion.

atrapalhar [atrapa'ʎa*] vt (confundir) to confuse; (perturbar) to disturb; (dificultar) to hinder ♦ vi to disturb; to be a hindrance; **~-se** vr to get confused.

atrás [a'trajʃ] adv behind; (no fundo) at the back; **~ de** behind; (no tempo) after; (em busca de) after; **um ~ de outro** one after

the other; **dois meses ~** two months ago; **não ficar ~** (fig) not to be far behind.

atrasado/a [atra'zadu/a] adj late; (país etc) backward; (relógio etc) slow; (pagamento) overdue; (costumes, pessoa) antiquated; (número de revista) back; **estar ~ nos pagamentos** to be in arrears.

atrasados [atra'zaduʃ] mpl (COM) arrears.

atrasar [atra'za*] vt to delay; (progresso, desenvolvimento) to hold back; (relógio) to put back; (pagamento) to be late with ♦ vi (relógio etc) to be slow; (avião, pessoa) to be late; **~-se** vr (chegar tarde) to be late; (num trabalho) to fall behind; (num pagamento) to get into arrears.

atraso [a'trazu] m delay; (de país etc) backwardness; **~s** mpl (COM) arrears; **chegar com ~** to arrive late; **com 20 minutos de ~** 20 minutes late; **com um ~ de 6 meses** (COM: pagamento) six months in arrears; **um ~ de vida** a hindrance.

atrativo/a [atra'tʃivu/a] adj attractive ♦ m attraction, appeal; (incentivo) incentive; **~s** mpl charms.

atravancar [atravã'ka*] vt to block, obstruct; (encher) to fill up.

através [atra'vɛʃ] adv across; **~ de** (de lado a lado) across; (pelo centro de) through; (por meio de) through.

atravessado/a [atrave'sadu/a] adj (na garganta) stuck; **estar com alguém ~ na garganta** to be peeved with sb.

atravessar [atrave'sa*] vt (cruzar) to cross; (pôr ao través) to put ou lay across; (traspassar) to pass through; (crise etc) to go through.

atrelar [atre'la*] vt (cão) to put on a leash; (cavalo) to harness; (duas viaturas) to couple up.

atrever-se [atre'vexsi] vr: **~ a** to dare to.

atrevido/a [atre'vidu/a] adj (petulante) cheeky, impudent; (corajoso) bold.

atrevimento [atrevi'mẽtu] m (ousadia) boldness; (insolência) cheek, insolence.

atribuição [atribwi'sãw] (pl -ões) f attribution; **atribuições** fpl rights, powers.

atribuir [atri'bwi*] vt: **~ algo a** to attribute sth to; (prêmios, regalias) to confer sth on.

atribulação [atribula'sãw] (pl -ões) f tribulation.

atribular [atribu'la*] vt to trouble, distress; **~-se** vr to be distressed.

atributo [atri'butu] m attribute.

átrio ['atrju] m hall; (pátio) courtyard.

atrito [a'tritu] m (fricção) friction; (desentendimento) disagreement.

atriz [a'triʒ] f actress.

atrocidade [atrosi'dadʒi] f atrocity.

atrofia [atro'fia] f atrophy.

atrofiar [atro'fja*] vt to atrophy; **~-se** vr to

atrophy.

atropeladamente [atropelada'mẽtʃi] *adv* haphazardly.

atropelamento [atropela'mẽtu] *m* (*de pedestre*) running over.

atropelar [atrope'la*] *vt* to knock down, run over; (*empurrar*) to jostle.

atropelo [atro'pelu] *m* bustle, scramble; (*confusão*) confusion.

atroz [a'trɔʒ] *adj* (*cruel*) merciless; (*crime*) heinous; (*dor, lembrança, feiúra*) terrible, awful.

attaché [ata'ʃe] *m* attaché.

atuação [atwa'sãw] (*pl* -ões) *f* acting; (*de ator etc*) performance.

atuado/a [a'twadu/a] *adj* (*pessoa*) in a bad mood.

atual [a'twaw] (*pl* -ais) *adj* current; (*pessoa, carro*) modern.

atualidade [atwali'dadʒi] *f* present (time); ~s *fpl* news *sg*.

atualização [atwaliza'sãw] (*pl* -ões) *f* updating.

atualizado/a [atwali'zadu/a] *adj* up-to-date.

atualizar [atwali'za*] *vt* to update; ~-se *vr* to bring o.s. up to date.

atualmente [atwaw'mẽtʃi] *adv* at present, currently; (*hoje em dia*) nowadays.

atuante [a'twãtʃi] *adj* active.

atuar [a'twa*] *vi* to act; ~ **para** to contribute to; ~ **sobre** to influence.

atulhar [atu'ʎa*] *vt* (*encher*) to cram full; (*meter*) to stuff, cram.

atum [a'tũ] (*pl* -ns) *m* tuna (fish).

aturar [atu'ra*] *vt* (*suportar*) to endure, put up with.

aturdido/a [atux'dʒidu/a] *adj* stunned; (*com barulho*) deafened; (*com confusão, movimento*) bewildered.

aturdimento [atuxdʒi'mẽtu] *m* bewilderment.

aturdir [atux'dʒi*] *vt* to stun; (*suj: barulho*) to deafen; (: *confusão, movimento*) to bewilder.

atxim [a'tʃĩ] *excl* achoo!

audácia [aw'dasja] *f* boldness; (*insolência*) insolence; **que** ~! what a cheek!

audacioso/a [awda'sjozu/ɔza] *adj* daring; (*insolente*) insolent.

audaz [aw'daʒ] *adj* daring; (*insolente*) insolent.

audição [awdʒi'sãw] (*pl* -ões) *f* audition; (*concerto*) recital.

audiência [aw'dʒjẽsja] *f* audience; (*de tribunal*) session, hearing.

audiovisual [awdʒjovi'zwaw] (*pl* -ais) *adj* audiovisual.

auditar [awdʒi'ta*] *vt* (*COM*) to audit.

auditivo/a [awdʒi'tʃivu/a] *adj* hearing *atr*, auditory.

auditor(a) [awdʒi'to*(a)] *m/f* (*COM*) auditor; (*juiz*) judge; (*ouvinte*) listener.

auditoria [awdʒito'ria] *f* auditing; **fazer a** ~ **de** to audit.

auditório [awdʒi'tɔrju] *m* (*ouvintes*) audience; (*recinto*) auditorium; **programa de** ~ program(me) recorded before a live audience.

audível [aw'dʒivew] (*pl* -eis) *adj* audible.

auferir [awfe'ri*] *vt* (*lucro*) to derive.

auge ['awʒi] *m* height, peak.

augurar [awgu'ra*] *vt* to augur; (*felicidades*) to wish.

augúrio [aw'gurju] *m* omen.

aula ['awla] *f* (*PT*: *sala*) classroom; (*lição*) lesson, class; **dar** ~ to teach.

aumentar [awmẽ'ta*] *vt* to increase; (*salários, preços*) to raise; (*sala, casa*) to expand, extend; (*suj: lente*) to magnify; (*acrescentar*) to add ♦ *vi* to increase; (*preço, salário*) to rise, go up; ~ **de peso** (*pessoa*) to put on weight.

aumento [aw'mẽtu] *m* increase; (*de preços*) rise; (*ampliação*) enlargement; (*crescimento*) growth.

áureo/a ['awrju/a] *adj* golden.

auréola [aw'reola] *f* halo.

aurora [aw'rɔra] *f* dawn.

auscultar [awʃkuw'ta*] *vt* (*opinião pública*) to sound out; (*paciente*): ~ **alguém** to sound sb's chest.

ausência [aw'zẽsja] *f* absence.

ausentar-se [awzẽ'taxsi] *vr* (*ir-se*) to go away; (*afastar-se*) to stay away.

ausente [aw'zẽtʃi] *adj* absent ♦ *m/f* missing person.

auspiciar [awʃpi'sja*] *vt* to augur.

auspício [aw'ʃpisju] *m*: **sob os** ~**s de** under the auspices of.

auspicioso/a [awʃpi'sjozu/ɔza] *adj* auspicious.

austeridade [awʃteri'dadʒi] *f* austerity.

austero/a [awʃ'tɛru/a] *adj* austere.

austral [awʃ'traw] (*pl* -ais) *adj* southern.

Austrália [awʃ'tralja] *f*: **a** ~ Australia.

australiano/a [awʃtra'ljanu/a] *adj, m/f* Australian.

Áustria ['awʃtrja] *f*: **a** ~ Austria.

austríaco/a [awʃ'triaku/a] *adj, m/f* Austrian.

autarquia [awtax'kia] *f* quango (*BRIT*), nongovernmental organization.

autárquico/a [aw'taxkiku/a] *adj* nongovernmental.

autenticar [awtẽtʃi'ka*] *vt* to authenticate; (*COM, JUR*) to certify.

autenticidade [awtẽtʃisi'dadʒi] *f* authenticity.

autêntico/a [aw'tẽtʃiku/a] *adj* authentic; (*pessoa*) genuine; (*verdadeiro*) true, real.

autismo [aw'tʃiʒmu] *m* autism.

autista [aw'tʃiʃta] *adj* autistic ♦ *m/f* autistic person.

auto ['awtu] *m* (*automóvel*) car; ~**s** *mpl* (*JUR*: *processo*) legal proceedings; (*documentos*) legal papers.

auto-adesivo/a *adj* self-adhesive.

auto-afirmação *f* self-assertion.

autobiografia [awtobjogra'fia] *f* autobiography.

autobiográfico/a [awtobjo'grafiku/a] *adj* autobiographical.

autocarro [awto'kaxu] (*PT*) *m* bus.
autocontrole [awtokõ'troli] *m* self-control.
autocrata [awto'krata] *adj* autocratic.
autóctone [aw'tɔktoni] *adj* indigenous ♦ *m/f* native.
autodefesa [awtode'feza] *f* self-defence (*BRIT*), self-defense (*US*).
autodestruição [awtodeʃ'trwisãw] *f* self-destruction.
autodeterminação [awtodetexmina'sãw] *f* self-determination.
autodidata [awtodʒi'data] *adj* self-taught ♦ *m/f* autodidact.
autodisciplina [awtodʒisi'plina] *f* self-discipline.
autodomínio [awtodo'minju] *m* self-control.
autódromo [aw'tɔdromu] *m* race track.
auto-escola *f* driving school.
auto-estrada *f* motorway (*BRIT*), expressway (*US*).
autografar [awtogra'fa*] *vt* to autograph.
autógrafo [aw'tɔgrafu] *m* autograph.
automação [awtoma'sãw] *f* automation; ~ **de escritórios** office automation.
automático/a [awto'matʃiku/a] *adj* automatic.
automatização [awtomatʃiza'sãw] *f* = **automação**.
automatizar [awtomatʃi'za*] *vt* to automate.
autômato [aw'tomatu] *m* automaton.
automedicar-se [awtomedʒi'kaxsi] *vr* to treat o.s.
automobilismo [awtomobi'liʒmu] *m* motoring; (*ESPORTE*) motor car racing.
automóvel [awto'mɔvew] (*pl* -**eis**) *m* motor car (*BRIT*), automobile (*US*).
autonomia [awtono'mia] *f* autonomy.
autônomo/a [aw'tonomu/a] *adj* autonomous; (*trabalhador*) self-employed ♦ *m/f* self-employed person.
autopeça [awto'pɛsa] *f* car spare.
autópsia [aw'tɔpsja] *f* autopsy, post-mortem.
autor(a) [aw'to*(a)] *m/f* author(ess); (*de um crime*) perpetrator; (*JUR*) plaintiff.
autoral [awto'raw] (*pl* -**ais**) *adj* V **direito**.
auto-retrato *m* self-portrait.
autoridade [awtori'dadʒi] *f* authority.
autoritário/a [awtori'tarju/a] *adj* authoritarian.
autoritarismo [awtorita'riʒmu] *m* authoritarianism.
autorização [awtoriza'sãw] (*pl* -**ões**) *f* permission, authorization; **dar** ~ **a alguém para** to give sb permission to, authorize sb to.
autorizar [awtori'za*] *vt* to authorize.
auto-serviço *m* self-service.
auto-suficiente *adj* self-sufficient.
auto-sugestão *f* autosuggestion.
autuar [aw'twa*] *vt* to sue.
auxiliar [awsi'lja*] *adj* auxiliary ♦ *m/f* assistant ♦ *vt* to help, assist.

auxílio [aw'silju] *m* help, assistance, aid.
auxílio-doença (*pl* **auxílios-doença**) *m* sickness benefit.
Av *abr* (= *avenida*) Ave.
avacalhado/a [avaka'ʎadu/a] *adj* sloppy.
avacalhar [avaka'ʎa*] (*col*) *vt* to screw up.
aval [a'vaw] (*pl* -**ais**) *m* guarantee; (*COM*) surety.
avalancha [ava'lãʃa] *f* avalanche.
avalanche [ava'lãʃi] *f* = **avalancha**.
avaliação [avalja'sãw] (*pl* -**ões**) *f* valuation; (*apreciação*) assessment, evaluation.
avaliador(a) [avalja'do*(a)] *m/f*: ~ **de danos** loss adjuster.
avaliar [ava'lja*] *vt* to value; (*apreciar*) to assess, evaluate; (*imaginar*) to imagine; ~ **algo em $100** to value sth at $100.
avalista [ava'liʃta] *m/f* guarantor.
avalizar [avali'za*] *vt* to guarantee.
avançada [avã'sada] *f* advance.
avançado/a [avã'sadu/a] *adj* advanced; (*idéias, pessoa*) progressive.
avançar [avã'sa*] *vt* to move forward ♦ *vi* to advance.
avanço [a'vãsu] *m* advancement; (*progresso*) progress; (*melhora*) improvement, advance.
avantajado/a [avãta'ʒadu/a] *adj* (*corpulento*) stout.
avante [a'vãtʃi] *adv* forward.
avarento/a [ava'rẽtu/a] *adj* mean ♦ *m/f* miser.
avareza [ava'reza] *f* meanness.
avaria [ava'ria] *f* damage; (*TEC*) breakdown.
avariado/a [ava'rjadu/a] *adj* damaged; (*máquina*) out of order; (*carro*) broken down.
avariar [ava'rja*] *vt* to damage ♦ *vi* to suffer damage; (*TEC*) to break down.
avaro/a [a'varu/a] *adj* mean ♦ *m/f* miser.
ave ['avi] *f* bird; ~ **de rapina** bird of prey.
aveia [a'veja] *f* oats pl.
aveio [a'veju] *etc vb* V **avir-se**.
avelã [ave'lã] *f* hazelnut.
aveludado/a [avelu'dadu/a] *adj* velvety; (*voz*) smooth.
avenho [a'veɲu] *etc vb* V **avir-se**.
avenida [ave'nida] *f* avenue.
avental [avẽ'taw] (*pl* -**ais**) *m* apron; (*vestido*) pinafore dress.
aventar [avẽ'ta*] *vt* (*idéia etc*) to put forward.
aventura [avẽ'tura] *f* adventure; (*proeza*) exploit.
aventurar [avẽtu'ra*] *vt* (*ousar*) to risk, venture; ~**-se** *vr*: ~**-se a** to dare to.
aventureiro/a [avẽtu'rejru/a] *adj* adventurous ♦ *m/f* adventurer.
averiguação [averigwa'sãw] (*pl* -**ões**) *f* investigation, inquiry; (*verificação*) verification.
averiguar [averi'gwa*] *vt* (*inquirir*) to investigate, ascertain; (*verificar*) to verify.
avermelhado/a [avexme'ʎadu/a] *adj* reddish.
aversão [avex'sãw] (*pl* -**ões**) *f* aversion.

NB: European Portuguese adds the following consonants to certain words: **b** (sú(b)dito, su(b)til); **c** (a(c)ção, a(c)cionista, a(c)to); **m** (inde(m)ne); **p** (ado(p)ção, ado(p)tar); *for further details see p. xiii.*

averso/a [a'vɛxsu/a] *adj*: ~ **a** averse to.

aversões [avex'sõjʃ] *fpl de* **aversão**.

avesso/a [a'vesu/a] *adj* (*lado*) opposite, reverse ♦ *m* wrong side, reverse; **ao** ~ inside out; **às avessas** (*inverso*) upside down; (*oposto*) the wrong way round; **virar pelo** ~ to turn inside out.

avestruz [aveʃ'truʒ] *m* ostrich.

aviação [avja'sãw] *f* aviation, flying.

aviado/a [a'vjadu/a] *adj* (*executado*) ready; (*apressado*) hurried.

aviador(a) [avja'do*(a)] *m/f* aviator, airman/woman.

aviamento [avja'mẽtu] *m* (*COSTURA*) haberdashery (*BRIT*), notions *pl* (*US*); (*de receita médica*) filling; (*COM*) goodwill.

avião [a'vjãw] (*pl* **-ões**) *m* aeroplane; ~ **a jato** jet.

aviar [a'vja*] *vt* (*receita médica*) to make up.

avicultor(a) [avikuw'to*(a)] *m/f* poultry farmer.

avicultura [avikuw'tura] *f* poultry farming.

avidez [avi'deʒ] *f* (*cobiça*) greediness; (*desejo*) eagerness.

ávido/a ['avidu/a] *adj* (*cobiçoso*) greedy; (*desejoso*) eager.

aviltamento [aviwta'mẽtu] *m* debasement.

aviltar [aviw'ta*] *vt* to debase; ~**-se** *vr* to demean o.s.

avim [a'vĩ] *etc vb V* **avir-se**.

avinagrado/a [avina'gradu/a] *adj* vinegary.

aviões [a'vjõjʃ] *mpl de* **avião**.

avir-se [a'vixsi] (*irreg*: *como* **vir**) *vr* (*conciliar-se*) to reach an understanding.

avisar [avi'za*] *vt* (*advertir*) to warn; (*informar*) to tell, let know; **ele avisou que chega amanhã** he said he's arriving tomorrow.

aviso [a'vizu] *m* (*comunicação*) notice; (*advertência*) warning; ~ **prévio** notice.

avistar [aviʃ'ta*] *vt* to catch sight of; ~**-se** *vr*: ~**-se com** (*ter entrevista*) to have an interview with.

avitaminose [avitami'nɔzi] *f* vitamin deficiency.

avivar [avi'va*] *vt* (*intensificar*) to intensify, heighten; (*memória*) to bring back.

avizinhar-se [avizi'ɲaxsi] *vr* (*aproximar-se*) to approach, come near.

avo ['avu] *m*: **um doze** ~**s** one twelfth.

avô/avó [a'vo/a'vɔ] *m/f* grandfather/mother; **avós** *mpl* grandparents.

avoado/a [avo'adu/a] *adj* (*pessoa*) absent-minded.

avolumar [avolu'ma*] *vt* (*aumentar*: *em volume*) to swell; (: *em número*) to accumulate; (*ocupar espaço*) to fill; ~**-se** *vr* to increase; to swell.

avulso/a [a'vuwsu/a] *adj* separate, detached ♦ *m* single copy.

avultado/a [avuw'tadu/a] *adj* large, bulky.

avultar [avuw'ta*] *vt* to enlarge, expand ♦ *vi* (*sobressair*) to stand out; (*aumentar*) to increase.

axila [ak'sila] *f* armpit.

axioma [a'sjɔma] *m* axiom.

azáfama [a'zafama] *f* bustle; (*pressa*) hurry.

azaléia [aza'lɛja] *f* azalea.

azar [a'za*] *m* bad luck; ~**!** too bad, bad luck!; **estar com** ~ to be unlucky; **ter** ~ to be unlucky.

azarado/a [aza'radu/a] *adj* unlucky.

azarento/a [aza'rẽtu/a] *adj* unlucky.

azedar [aze'da*] *vt* to turn sour; (*pessoa*) to put in a bad mood ♦ *vi* to turn sour; (*leite*) to go off.

azedo/a [a'zedu/a] *adj* (*sabor*) sour; (*leite*) off; (*fig*) grumpy, bad-tempered.

azedume [aze'dumi] *m* (*sabor*) sourness; (*fig*) grumpiness.

azeitar [azej'ta*] *vt* (*untar*) to grease; (*lubrificar*) to oil.

azeite [a'zejtʃi] *m* oil; (*de oliva*) olive oil.

azeitona [azej'tɔna] *f* olive.

Azerbaijão [azexbaj'ʒãw] *m*: **o** ~ Azerbaijan.

azeviche [aze'viʃi] *m* (*cor*) jet black.

azevinho [aze'viɲu] *m* holly.

azia [a'zia] *f* heartburn.

aziago/a [a'zjagu/a] *adj* (*de mau agouro*) ominous.

azinhaga [azi'ɲaga] *f* (*country*) lane.

azinhavre [azi'ɲavri] *m* verdigris.

azo ['azu] *m* (*oportunidade*) opportunity; (*pretexto*) pretext; **dar** ~ **a** to give occasion to.

azougue [a'zogi] *m* quicksilver; (*QUÍM*) mercury; (*fig*: *pessoa*: *inquieta*) livewire; (: *esperta*) sharp person.

azucrinar [azukri'na*] *vt* to bother, pester.

azul [a'zuw] (*pl* **-uis**) *adj* blue; **tudo** ~ (*fig*) everything's rosy.

azular [azu'la*] *vi* to flee.

azulejar [azule'ʒa*] *vt* to tile.

azulejo [azu'leʒu] *m* (glazed) tile.

azul-marinho *adj inv* navy blue.

azul-turquesa *adj inv* turquoise.

B

B, b [be] (*pl* **bs**) *m* B, b; **B de Beatriz** B for Benjamin (*BRIT*) *ou* Baker (*US*).

baba ['baba] *f* saliva, dribble.

babá [ba'ba] *f* nanny.

babaca [ba'baka] (*col*) *adj* stupid ♦ *m/f* idiot.

baba-de-moça (*pl* **babas-de-moça**) *f* sweet made with sugar, coconut milk and eggs.

babado [ba'badu] *m* frill; (*col*) piece of gossip.

babador [baba'do*] *m* bib.

babaquice [baba'kisi] *f* stupidity; (*ato*, *dito*)

stupid thing.

babar [ba'ba*] vt to dribble on ♦ vi to dribble; ~-se vr to dribble; ~(-se) por to drool over.

babeiro [ba'bejru] (PT) m bib.

babel [ba'bɛw] (pl -éis) f (fig) muddle.

baby-sitter ['bejbisite*] (pl ~s) m/f baby-sitter.

bacalhau [baka'ʎaw] m (dried) cod.

bacalhoada [bakaʎo'ada] f salt cod stew.

bacana [ba'kana] (col) adj great.

bacanal [baka'naw] (pl -ais) m orgy.

bacharel [baʃa'rɛw] (pl -éis) m bachelor, graduate.

bacharelado [baʃare'ladu] m bachelor's degree.

bacharelar-se [baʃare'laxsi] vr to graduate.

bacia [ba'sia] f basin; (sanitária) bowl; (ANAT) pelvis.

background [bɛk'grãwdʒi] (pl ~s) m background.

backup [ba'kapi] (pl ~s) m (COMPUT) backup; **tirar um ~ de** to back up.

baço/a ['basu/a] adj dull; (metal) tarnished ♦ m (ANAT) spleen.

bacon ['bejkõ] m bacon.

bactéria [bak'tɛrja] f germ, bacterium; ~s fpl bacteria.

badalado/a [bada'ladu/a] (col) adj talked about, famous.

badalar [bada'la*] vt (sino) to ring ♦ vi to ring; (col) to go out and about.

badalativo/a [badala'tʃivu/a] (col) adj fun-loving.

badalo [ba'dalu] m clapper.

badejo [ba'deʒu] m sea bass.

baderna [ba'dɛxna] f commotion.

badulaque [badu'laki] m trinket; ~s mpl junk sg.

bafafá [bafa'fa] (col) m kerfuffle.

bafejar [bafe'ʒa*] vt (aquecer com o bafo) to blow; (fortuna) to smile upon.

bafejo [ba'feʒu] m (sopro) whiff; ~ da sorte stroke of luck.

bafio [ba'fiu] m musty smell.

bafo ['bafu] m (hálito) (bad) breath; **isso é ~ dele** (col) he's just making it up.

bafômetro [ba'fometru] m Breathalyser ®.

baforada [bafo'rada] f (fumaça) puff.

bagaço [ba'gasu] m (de frutos) pulp; (PT: cachaça) brandy; **estar/ficar um ~** (fig: pessoa) to be/get run down.

bagageiro [baga'ʒejru] m (AUTO) roofrack; (PT) porter.

bagagem [ba'gaʒẽ] f luggage; (fig) baggage; **recebimento de ~** (AER) baggage reclaim.

bagatela [baga'tɛla] f trinket; (fig) trifle.

Bagdá [bagi'da] n Baghdad.

bago ['bagu] m (fruto) berry; (uva) grape; (de chumbo) pellet; (col!) ball (!).

bagulho [ba'guʎu] m (objeto) piece of junk;

(pessoa): **ser um ~** to be as ugly as sin.

bagunça [ba'gũsa] f (confusão) mess, shambles sg.

bagunçado/a [bagũ'sadu/a] adj in a mess.

bagunçar [bagũ'sa*] vt to mess up.

bagunceiro/a [bagũ'sejru/a] adj messy.

Bahamas [ba'amaʃ] fpl: **as ~** the Bahamas.

baia ['baja] f bail.

baía [ba'ia] f bay.

baiano/a [ba'janu/a] adj, m/f Bahian.

baila ['bajla] f: **trazer/vir à ~** to bring/come up.

bailado [baj'ladu] m dance; (balé) ballet.

bailar [baj'la*] vt, vi to dance.

bailarino/a [bajla'rinu/a] m/f ballet dancer.

baile ['bajli] m dance; (formal) ball; **dar um ~ em alguém** to pull sb's leg; **~ à fantasia** fancy-dress ball.

bainha [ba'iɲa] f (de arma) sheath; (de costura) hem.

baioneta [bajo'neta] f bayonet; **~ calada** fixed bayonet.

bairrista [baj'xiʃta] adj loyal to one's neighbo(u)rhood ♦ m/f proud local.

bairro ['bajxu] m district.

baita ['bajta] adj huge; (gripe) bad.

baixa ['bajʃa] f decrease; (de preço) reduction, fall; (diminuição) drop; (BOLSA) low; (em combate) casualty; (do serviço) discharge; **dar ou ter ~** to be discharged.

baixada [baj'ʃada] f lowland.

baixa-mar f low tide.

baixar [baj'ʃa*] vt to lower; (bandeira) to take down; (ordem) to issue; (lei) to pass; (COMPUT) to download ♦ vi to go (ou come) down; (temperatura, preço) to drop, fall; (col: aparecer) to show up; **~ ao hospital** to go into hospital.

baixaria [bajʃa'ria] f vulgarity; (ação) cheap trick.

baixela [baj'ʃɛla] f serving set.

baixeza [baj'ʃeza] f meanness, baseness.

baixinho [baj'ʃiɲu] adv (em voz baixa) softly, quietly; (em segredo) secretly.

baixio [baj'ʃiu] m sandbank, sandbar.

baixista [baj'ʃiʃta] adj, m/f (COM) bear atr.

baixo/a ['bajʃu/a] adj low; (pessoa) short, small; (rio) shallow; (linguagem) common; (cabeça, olhos) lowered; (som) quiet; (atitude) mean, base; (metal) base ♦ adv low; (em posição baixa) low down; (falar) softly ♦ m (MÚS) bass; **em ~** below; (em casa) downstairs; **para ~** down, downwards; (em casa) downstairs; **por ~ de** under, underneath; **altos e ~s** ups and downs; **estar por ~** to be down on one's luck.

baixo-astral (col) m bad vibes pl; **estar num ~** to be at a low ebb.

baixote/a [baj'ʃɔtʃi/ta] adj shortish.

bajulador(a) [baʒula'do*(a)] adj obsequious.

NB: European Portuguese adds the following consonants to certain words: **b** (sú(b)dito, su(b)til); **c** (a(c)ção, a(c)cionista, a(c)to); **m** (inde(m)ne); **p** (ado(p)ção, ado(p)tar); for further details see p. xiii.

bajular [baʒu'la*] vt to fawn over.
bala ['bala] f bullet; (BR: doce) sweet; **estar em ponto de** ~ (fig) to be in tip-top condition; **estar/ficar uma** ~ (fig) to be/get furious.
balada [ba'lada] f ballad.
balaio [ba'laju] m straw basket.
balança [ba'lãsa] f scales pl; **B**~ (ASTROLOGIA) Libra; ~ **comercial** balance of trade; ~ **de pagamentos** balance of payments.
balançar [balã'sa*] vt (fazer oscilar) to swing; (pesar) to weigh (up) ♦ vi (oscilar) to swing; (carro, avião) to shake; (navio) to roll; (em cadeira) to rock; ~-**se** vr to swing.
balancear [balã'sja*] vt to balance.
balancete [balã'setʃi] m (COM) trial balance.
balanço [ba'lãsu] m (movimento) swinging; (brinquedo) swing; (de navio) rolling; (de carro, avião) shaking; (COM: registro) balance (sheet); (: verificação) audit; **fazer um** ~ **de** (fig) to take stock of.
balangandã [balãgã'dã] m bauble.
balão [ba'lãw] (pl -**ões**) m balloon; (em história em quadrinhos) speech bubble; (AUTO) turning area; ~ **de oxigênio** oxygen tank.
balão-de-ensaio (pl balões-de-ensaio) m: **soltar um** ~ (fig) to put out feelers.
balar [ba'la*] vi to bleat.
balaustrada [balawʃ'trada] f balustrade.
balaústre [bala'uʃtri] m bannister.
balbuciar [bawbu'sja*] vt, vi to babble.
balbucio [bawbu'siu] m babbling.
balbúrdia [baw'buxdʒja] f uproar, bedlam.
balcão [baw'kãw] (pl -**ões**) m balcony; (de loja) counter; (TEATRO) circle.
balconista [bawko'niʃta] m/f shop assistant.
baldado/a [baw'dadu/a] adj unsuccessful, fruitless.
baldar [baw'da*] vt to frustrate, foil.
balde ['bawdʒi] m bucket, pail.
baldeação [bawdʒja'sãw] (pl -**ões**) f transfer; **fazer** ~ to change.
baldio/a [baw'dʒiu/a] adj fallow, uncultivated; (terreno) ~ (a piece of) waste ground.
balé [ba'lɛ] m ballet.
baleeira [bale'ejra] f whaler.
baleia [ba'leja] f whale.
baleiro/a [ba'lejru/a] m/f confectioner.
balido [ba'lidu] m bleating; (um só) bleat.
balística [ba'liʃtʃika] f ballistics sg.
balístico/a [ba'liʃtʃiku/a] adj ballistic.
baliza [ba'liza] f (estaca) post; (bóia) buoy; (luminosa) beacon; (ESPORTE) goal.
balizar [bali'za*] vt to mark out.
balneário [baw'njarju] m bathing resort.
balões [ba'lõjʃ] mpl de **balão**.
balofo/a [ba'lofu/a] adj (fofo) fluffy; (gordo) plump, tubby.
baloiço [ba'lojsu] (PT) m (de criança) swing; (ação) swinging.
balouçar [balo'sa*] (PT) vt, vi to swing, sway.
balouço [ba'losu] (PT) m = **baloiço**.
balsa ['bawsa] f raft; (barca) ferry.

bálsamo ['bawsamu] m balm.
báltico/a ['bawtʃiku/a] adj Baltic ♦ m: **o B**~ the Baltic.
baluarte [ba'lwaxtʃi] m rampart, bulwark; (fig) supporter.
balzaquiana [bawza'kjana] f woman in her thirties.
bamba ['bãba] adj, m/f expert.
bambear [bã'bja*] vt to loosen ♦ vi to work loose; (pessoa) to grow weak.
bambo/a ['bãbu/a] adj slack, loose; (pernas) limp, wobbly.
bambolê [bãbo'le] m hula hoop.
bamboleante [bãbo'ljãtʃi] adj swaying; (sem firmeza) wobbly.
bambolear [bãbo'lja*] vt to swing ♦ vi (pessoa) to sway, totter; (coisa) to wobble.
bambu [bã'bu] m bamboo.
banal [ba'naw] (pl -**ais**) adj banal.
banalidade [banali'dadʒi] f banality.
banana [ba'nana] f banana ♦ m/f (col) wimp; **dar uma** ~ ≈ to stick two fingers up.
bananada [bana'nada] f banana paste.
bananeira [bana'nejra] f banana tree.
bananosa [bana'nɔza] (col) f: **estar numa** ~ to be in a fix.
banca ['bãka] f (de trabalho) bench; (escritório) office; (em jogo) bank; ~ (**de jornais**) newsstand; **botar** ~ (col) to show off; **botar** ~ **em** ou **para cima de** (col) to lay down the law to; ~ **examinadora** examining body, examination board.
bancada [bã'kada] f (banco, POL) bench; (de cozinha) work surface.
bancar [bã'ka*] vt (financiar) to finance; ~ **o idiota** etc to play the fool etc; ~ **que** to pretend that.
bancário/a [bã'karju/a] adj bank atr ♦ m/f bank employee.
bancarrota [bãka'xota] f bankruptcy; **ir à** ~ to go bankrupt.
banco ['bãku] m (assento) bench; (COM) bank; (de cozinha) stool; ~ **de areia** sandbank; ~ **de dados** (COMPUT) database.
banda ['bãda] f band; (lado) side; (cinto) sash; **de** ~ sideways; **pôr de** ~ to put aside; **nestas** ~**s** in these parts; ~ **de percussão** steel band; ~ **desenhada** (PT) cartoon.
bandear-se [bãde'axsi] vr: ~ **para** ou **a** to go over to.
bandeira [bã'dejra] f flag; (estandarte, fig) banner; (de porta) fanlight; ~ **a meio pau** flag at half mast; **dar uma** ~ **em alguém** (col) to give sb the brush-off; **levar uma** ~ to get the brush-off; **dar** ~ (col) to give o.s. away.
bandeirante [bãdej'rãtʃi] m pioneer ♦ f girl guide.
bandeirinha [bãdej'riɲa] m (ESPORTE) linesman.
bandeja [bã'deʒa] f tray; **dar algo de** ~ **a alguém** (col) to give sb sth on a plate.
bandido [bã'dʒidu/a] m bandit ♦ m/f (fig)

rascal.

bando ['bãdu] *m* band; (*grupo*) group; (*de malfeitores*) gang; (*de ovelhas*) flock; (*de gado*) herd; **um ~ de livros** a pile of books.

bandô [bã'do] *m* pelmet.

bandoleiro [bãdo'lejru] *m* robber, bandit.

bandolim [bãdo'lĩ] (*pl* **-ns**) *m* mandolin.

bangalô [bãga'lo] *m* bungalow.

Bangcoc [bãŋ'kɔki] *n* Bangkok.

Bangladesh [bãgla'dɛʃ] *m* Bangladesh.

bangue-bangue [bãgi'bãgi] *m*: **(filme de)** ~ western.

banguela [bã'gɛla] *adj* toothless.

banha ['baɲa] *f* fat; (*de porco*) lard.

banhar [ba'ɲa*] *vt* (*molhar*) to wet; (*mergulhar*) to dip; (*lavar*) to wash, bathe; **~-se** *vr* (*no mar*) to bathe.

banheira [ba'ɲejra] *f* bath.

banheiro [ba'ɲejru] *m* bathroom; (*PT*) lifeguard.

banhista [ba'ɲiʃta] *m/f* bather; (*salva-vidas*) lifeguard.

banho ['baɲu] *m* (*TEC*: *na banheira*) bath; (*mergulho*) dip; **dar um ~ de cerveja** *etc* **em alguém** to spill beer *etc* all over sb; **tomar ~** to have a bath; (*de chuveiro*) to have a shower; **tomar um ~ de** (*fig*) to have a heavy dose of; **vai tomar ~!** (*col*) get lost!; **~ de chuveiro** shower; **~ de espuma** bubble bath; **tomar ~ de mar** to have a swim (in the sea); **~ de sol** sunbathing.

banho-maria (*pl* **banhos-marias** *ou* **banhos-maria**) *m* (*CULIN*) bain-marie.

banimento [bani'mẽtu] *m* banishment.

banir [ba'ni*] *vt* to banish.

banjo ['bãʒu] *m* banjo.

banquei [bã'kej] *etc vb V* **bancar**.

banqueiro/a [bã'kejru/a] *m/f* banker.

banqueta [bã'keta] *f* stool.

banquete [bã'ketʃi] *m* banquet; (*fig*) feast.

banquetear [bãke'tʃja*] *vt* to feast; **~-se** *vr*: **~-se com** to feast on.

banqueteiro/a [bãke'tejru/a] *m/f* caterer.

banzé [bã'zɛ] (*col*) *m* kerfuffle.

baptismo *etc* [ba'tiʒmu] (*PT*) = **batismo** *etc*.

baptizar [bati'za*] *etc* (*PT*) = **batizar** *etc*.

baque ['baki] *m* thud, thump; (*contratempo*) setback; (*queda*) fall; **levar um ~** to be hard hit.

baquear [ba'kja*] *vi* to topple over.

bar [ba*] *m* bar.

barafunda [bara'fũda] *f* confusion; (*de coisas*) hotch-potch.

barafustar [barafuʃ'ta*] *vi*: **~ por** to burst through.

baralhada [bara'ʎada] *f* muddle.

baralhar [bara'ʎa*] *vt* (*fig*) to mix up, confuse.

baralho [ba'raʎu] *m* pack of cards.

barão [ba'rãw] (*pl* **-ões**) *m* baron.

barata [ba'rata] *f* cockroach; **entregue às ~s**

(*pessoa*) gone to the dogs; (*plano*) gone out the window.

baratear [bara'tʃja*] *vt* to cut the price of; (*menosprezar*) to belittle.

barateiro/a [bara'tejru/a] *adj* cheap.

baratinado/a [baratʃi'nadu/a] (*col*) *adj* in a flap; (*transtornado*) shaken up.

baratinar [baratʃi'na*] (*col*) *vt* to drive crazy; (*transtornar*) to shake up.

barato/a [ba'ratu/a] *adj* cheap ♦ *adv* cheaply ♦ *m* (*col*): **a festa foi um ~** the party was great.

barba ['baxba] *f* beard; **~s** *fpl* whiskers; **nas ~s de** (*fig*) under the nose of; **fazer a ~** to shave; **pôr as ~s de molho** to take precautions.

barbada [bax'bada] (*col*) *f* cinch, piece of cake; (*TURFE*) favourite.

barbado/a [bax'badu/a] *adj* bearded.

Barbados [bax'baduʃ] *m* Barbados.

barbante [bax'bãtʃi] (*BR*) *m* string.

barbaramente [baxbara'mẽtʃi] *adv* (*muito*) a lot.

barbaridade [baxbari'dadʒi] *f* barbarity, cruelty; (*disparate*) nonsense; **que ~!** good heavens!

barbárie [bax'barie] *f* barbarism.

barbarismo [baxba'riʒmu] *m* barbarism.

bárbaro/a ['baxbaru/a] *adj* barbaric; (*dor, calor*) terrible; (*maravilhoso*) great.

barbatana [baxba'tana] *f* fin.

barbeador [baxbja'do*] *m* razor; (*elétrico*) shaver.

barbear [bax'bja*] *vt* to shave; **~-se** *vr* to shave.

barbearia [baxbja'ria] *f* barber's (shop).

barbeiragem [baxbej'raʒẽ] *f* bad driving; **fazer uma ~** to drive badly; (*fig*) to bungle it.

barbeiro [bax'bejru] *m* barber; (*loja*) barber's; (*motorista*) bad driver, Sunday driver.

barbitúrico [baxbi'turiku] *m* barbiturate.

barbudo/a [bax'budu/a] *adj* bearded.

barca ['baxka] *f* barge; (*de travessia*) ferry.

barcaça [bax'kasa] *f* barge.

barco ['baxku] *m* boat; **estar no mesmo ~** (*fig*) to be in the same boat; **deixar o ~ correr** (*fig*) to let things take their course; **tocar o ~ para a frente** (*fig*) to struggle on; **~ a motor** motorboat; **~ a remo** rowing boat; **~ a vela** sailing boat.

Barein [ba'rẽj] *m*: **o ~** Bahrain.

barganha [bax'gaɲa] *f* bargain.

barganhar [baxga'ɲa*] *vt*, *vi* to negotiate.

barítono [ba'ritonu] *m* baritone.

barlavento [baxla'vẽtu] *m* (*NÁUT*) windward; **a ~** to windward.

barman [bax'mã] (*pl* **-men**) *m* barman.

barnabé [baxna'bɛ] (*col*) *m* petty civil servant.

NB: *European Portuguese adds the following consonants to certain words:* **b** (sú(b)dito, su(b)til); **c** (a(c)ção, a(c)cionista, a(c)to); **m** (inde(m)ne); **p** (ado(p)ção, ado(p)tar); *for further details see p. xiii.*

barões [ba'rōjʃ] *mpl de* **barão.**
barômetro [ba'romɛtru] *m* barometer.
baronesa [baro'neza] *f* baroness.
barqueiro [bax'kejru] *m* boatman.
barra ['baxa] *f* bar; *(faixa)* strip; *(traço)* stroke; *(alavanca)* lever; *(col: situação)* scene; **agüentar** *ou* **segurar a** ~ to hold out; **forçar a** ~ *(col)* to force the issue; **ser uma** ~ *(pessoa, entrevista)* to be tough; ~ **de direção** steering column; ~ **fixa** high bar; ~**s paralelas** parallel bars.
barraca [ba'xaka] *f (tenda)* tent; *(de feira)* stall; *(de madeira)* hut; *(de praia)* sunshade.
barracão [baxa'kãw] *(pl* -ões*) m (de madeira)* shed.
barraco [ba'xaku] *m* shack, shanty.
barracões [baxa'kõjʃ] *mpl de* **barracão.**
barragem [ba'xaʒẽ] *(pl* -ns*) f (represa)* dam; *(impedimento)* barrier.
barranco [ba'xãku] *m* ravine, gully; *(de rio)* bank.
barra-pesada *adj inv (lugar)* rough; *(pessoa)* shady; *(difícil)* difficult ♦ *m/f (pl:* **barras-pesadas**) shady character.
barrar [ba'xa*] *vt* to bar.
barreira [ba'xejra] *f* barrier; *(cerca)* fence; *(ESPORTE)* hurdle; **pôr** ~**s a** to put obstacles in the way of; ~ **do som** sound barrier.
barrento/a [ba'xẽtu/a] *adj* muddy.
barrete [ba'xetʃi] *(PT) m* cap.
barricada [baxi'kada] *f* barricade.
barriga [ba'xiga] *f* belly; **estar de** ~ to be pregnant; **falar** *ou* **chorar de** ~ **cheia** to complain for no reason; **fazer** ~ to bulge; ~ **da perna** calf.
barrigudo/a [baxi'gudu/a] *adj* paunchy, pot-bellied.
barril [ba'xiw] *(pl* -is*) m* barrel, cask.
barro ['baxu] *m* clay; *(lama)* mud.
barroco/a [ba'xoku/a] *adj* baroque; *(ornamentado)* extravagant.
barrote [ba'xɔtʃi] *m* beam.
barulhada [baru'ʎada] *f* racket, din.
barulhento/a [baru'ʎẽtu/a] *adj* noisy.
barulho [ba'ruʎu] *m (ruído)* noise; *(tumulto)* din.
base ['bazi] *f* base; *(fig)* basis; **sem** ~ groundless; **com** ~ **em** based on; **na** ~ **de** *(por meio de)* by means of.
baseado/a [ba'zjadu/a] *adj* well-founded ♦ *m (col)* joint.
basear [ba'zja*] *vt* to base; ~**-se** *vr:* ~**-se em** to be based on.
básico/a ['baziku/a] *adj* basic.
basquete [baʃ'kɛtʃi] *m* = **basquetebol.**
basquetebol [baʃkete'bɔw] *m* basketball.
basta ['baʃta] *m:* **dar um** ~ **em** to call a halt to.
bastante [baʃ'tãtʃi] *adj (suficiente)* enough; *(muito)* quite a lot (of) ♦ *adv (suficientemente)* enough; *(muito)* a lot.
bastão [baʃ'tãw] *(pl* -ões*) m* stick.
bastar [baʃ'ta*] *vi* to be enough, be sufficient;

~**-se** *vr* to be self-sufficient; **basta!** (that's) enough!; ~ **para** to be enough to.
bastardo/a [baʃ'taxdu/a] *adj, m/f* bastard.
bastidor [baʃtʃi'do*] *m* frame; ~**es** *mpl (TEATRO)* wings; **nos** ~**es** *(fig)* behind the scenes.
basto/a ['baʃtu/a] *adj (espesso)* thick; *(denso)* dense.
bastões [baʃ'tõjʃ] *mpl de* **bastão.**
bata ['bata] *f (de mulher)* smock; *(de médico)* overall.
batalha [ba'taʎa] *f* battle.
batalhador(a) [bataʎa'do*(a)] *adj* struggling ♦ *m/f* fighter.
batalhão [bata'ʎãw] *(pl* -ões*) m* battalion.
batalhar [bata'ʎa*] *vi* to battle, fight; *(esforçar-se)* to make an effort, try hard ♦ *vt (emprego)* to go after.
batalhões [bata'ʎõjʃ] *mpl de* **batalhão.**
batata [ba'tata] *f* potato; ~ **doce** sweet potato; ~ **frita** chips *pl (BRIT)*, French fries *pl; (de pacote)* crisps *pl (BRIT)*, (potato) chips *pl (US)*.
bate-boca ['batʃi-] *(pl* ~**s**) *m* row, quarrel.
bate-bola ['batʃi-] *(pl* ~**s**) *m* kick around.
batedeira [bate'dejra] *f* beater; *(elétrica)* mixer; *(de manteiga)* churn.
batedor [bate'do*] *m* beater; *(polícia)* escort; *(CRIQUETE)* batsman; ~ **de carteiras** pickpocket.
bátega ['batega] *f* downpour.
batelada [bate'lada] *f:* **uma** ~ **de** a whole bunch of.
batente [ba'tẽtʃi] *m* doorpost; *(col)* job; **no** ~ at work.
bate-papo ['batʃi-] *(pl* ~**s**) *(BR) m* chat.
bater [ba'te*] *vt* to beat; *(golpear)* to hit; *(horas)* to strike; *(o pé)* to stamp; *(foto)* to take; *(datilografar)* to type; *(porta)* to slam; *(asas)* to flap; *(recorde)* to break; *(roupa: usar muito)* to wear all the time ♦ *vi (porta)* to slam; *(sino)* to ring; *(janela)* to bang; *(coração)* to beat; *(sol)* to beat down; ~**-se** *vr:* ~**-se para fazer/por** to fight to do/for; ~ **(à porta)** to knock at the door; ~ **à máquina** to type; ~ **em** to hit; *(lugar)* to arrive in; *(assunto)* to harp on; ~ **com o carro** *ou* ~ **o carro** to crash one's car; ~ **com a cabeça** to bang one's head; ~ **com o pé (em)** to kick; **ele não bate bem** *(col)* he is a bit crazy; ~ **a carteira de alguém** *(col)* to nick sb's wallet.
bateria [bate'ria] *f* battery; *(MÚS)* drums *pl;* ~ **de cozinha** kitchen utensils *pl.*
baterista [bate'riʃta] *m/f* drummer.
batida [ba'tʃida] *f* beat; *(da porta)* slam; *(à porta)* knock; *(da polícia)* raid; *(AUTO)* crash; *(bebida)* cocktail of cachaça, *fruit and sugar;* **dar uma** ~ **em** *(polícia)* to raid; *(colidir com)* to bump into; **dar uma** ~ **com o carro** to crash one's car; **dar uma** ~ **no carro de alguém** to crash into sb's car.
batido/a [ba'tʃidu/a] *adj* beaten; *(roupa)* worn; *(assunto)* hackneyed ♦ *m:* ~ **de leite** *(PT)* milkshake.

batina [ba'tʃina] *f* (*REL*) cassock.
batismal [batʃiʒ'maw] (*pl* **-ais**) *adj* V **pia**.
batismo [ba'tʃiʒmu] *m* baptism, christening.
batizado [batʃi'zadu] *m* christening.
batizar [batʃi'za*] *vt* to baptize, christen; (*vinho*) to dilute.
batom [ba'tõ] (*pl* **-ns**) *m* lipstick.
batucada [batu'kada] *f* dance percussion group.
batucar [batu'ka*] *vt, vi* to drum.
batuque [ba'tuki] *m* drumming.
batuta [ba'tuta] *f* baton ♦ *adj* (*col*) clever.
baú [ba'u] *m* trunk.
baunilha [baw'niʎa] *f* vanilla.
bazar [ba'za*] *m* bazaar; (*loja*) shop.
bazófia [ba'zɔfja] *f* boasting, bragging.
BB *abr m* = **Banco do Brasil**.
BBF *abr f* = **Bolsa Brasileira de Futuros**.
BC *abr m* = **Banco Central do Brasil**.
BCG *abr m* (= *Bacilo Calmette-Guerin*) BCG.
bê-á-bá [bea'ba] *m* ABC.
beatitude [beatʃi'tudʒi] *f* bliss.
beato/a [be'atu/a] *adj* blessed; (*devoto*) overpious.
bêbado/a ['bebadu/a] *adj, m/f* drunk.
bebê [be'be] *m* baby.
bebedeira [bebe'dejra] *f* drunkenness; **tomar uma** ~ to get drunk.
bêbedo/a ['bebedu/a] *adj, m/f* = **bêbado**.
bebedor(a) [bebe'do*(a)] *m/f* drinker; (*ébrio*) drunkard.
bebedouro [bebe'douru] *m* drinking fountain.
beber [be'be*] *vt* to drink; (*absorver*) to drink up, soak up ♦ *vi* to drink.
bebericar [beberi'ka*] *vt, vi* to sip.
bebida [be'bida] *f* drink.
beca ['bɛka] *f* gown.
beça ['bɛsa] (*col*) *f*: **à** ~ (*com vb*) a lot; (*com n*) a lot of; (*com adj*) really.
beco ['bɛku] *m* alley, lane; ~ **sem saída** cul-de-sac; (*fig*) dead end.
bedelho [be'deʎu] *m* kid; **meter o** ~ **em** to poke one's nose into.
bege ['bɛʒi] *adj inv* beige.
beicinho [bej'siɲu] *m*: **fazer** ~ to sulk.
beiço ['bejsu] *m* lip; **fazer** ~ to pout.
beiçudo/a [bej'sudu/a] *adj* thick-lipped.
beija-flor [bejʒa-'flɔ*] (*pl* **~es**) *m* hummingbird.
beijar [bej'ʒa*] *vt* to kiss; **~-se** *vr* to kiss (one another).
beijo ['bejʒu] *m* kiss; **dar ~s em alguém** to kiss sb.
beijoca [bej'ʒɔka] *f* kiss.
beijocar [bejʒo'ka*] *vt*: ~ **alguém** to kiss sb.
beira ['bejra] *f* (*borda*) edge; (*de rio*) bank; (*orla*) border; **à** ~ **de** on the edge of; (*ao lado de*) beside, by; (*fig*) on the verge of; ~ **do telhado** eaves *pl*.
beirada [bej'rada] *f* edge.

beira-mar *f* seaside.
beirar [bej'ra*] *vt* (*ficar à beira de*) to be at the edge of; (*caminhar à beira de*) to skirt; (*desespero*) to be on the verge of; (*idade*) to approach, near ♦ *vi*: ~ **com** to border on; ~ **por** (*idade*) to approach.
Beirute [bej'rutʃi] *n* Beirut.
beisebol [bejsi'bɔw] *m* baseball.
belas-artes *fpl* fine arts.
beldade [bew'dadʒi] *f* beauty.
beleléu [bele'lɛw] (*col*) *m*: **ir para o** ~ to go wrong.
belenense [bele'nēsi] *adj* from Belém ♦ *m/f* native *ou* inhabitant of Belém.
beleza [be'leza] *f* beauty; **que ~!** how lovely!; **ser uma** ~ to be lovely; **concurso de** ~ beauty contest.
belga ['bewga] *adj, m/f* Belgian.
Bélgica ['bewʒika] *f*: **a** ~ Belgium.
Belgrado [bew'gradu] *n* Belgrade.
beliche [be'liʃi] *m* bunk.
bélico/a ['beliku/a] *adj* war *atr*.
belicoso/a [beli'kozu/ɔza] *adj* warlike.
beligerante [beliʒe'rãtʃi] *adj* belligerent.
beliscão [beliʃ'kãw] (*pl* **-ões**) *m* pinch.
beliscar [beliʃ'ka*] *vt* to pinch, nip; (*comida*) to nibble.
beliscões [beliʃ'kõjʃ] *mpl* de **beliscão**.
Belize [be'lizi] *m* Belize.
belo/a ['bɛlu/a] *adj* beautiful.
belo-horizontino/a [-orizõ'tʃinu/a] *adj* from Belo Horizonte ♦ *m/f* person from Belo Horizonte.
bel-prazer [bɛw-] *m*: **a seu** ~ at one's own convenience.
beltrano [bew'tranu] *m* so-and-so.
belvedere [bewve'deri] *m* lookout point.
bem [bẽj] *adv* well; (*muito*) very; (*bastante*) quite; (*cheirar*) good, nice ♦ *m* (*ventura, utilidade*) good; (*amado*) love; **o** ~ **comum** the common good; **bens** *mpl* property *sg*; **bens de consumo** consumer goods; ~ **ali** right there; **não é** ~ **assim** it's not quite like that; **está** ~ OK; **fazer** ~ **a** to be good for; **fazer** ~ **em fazer** to do well to do; **ficar** ~ to look good; **ficar** ~ **em** (*roupa*) to suit; **tudo ~?** how's it going?; **tudo** ~ (*como resposta*) fine; ~ **como** as well as; **se** ~ **que** though; **por** ~ **ou por mal** for better or worse; **nem** ~ as soon as, no sooner; **de** ~ **com alguém** on good terms with sb; **para o** ~ **de** for the good of; ~ **feito!** (*col*) it serves you right!; ~ **que eu falei** I told you so; **muito** ~! well done!; ~ **de família** family home; **bens móveis/imóveis** moveable property/real estate; **bens de capital** capital goods.
bem-agradecido/a *adj* grateful.
bem-apessoado/a [-ape'swadu/a] *adj* smart, well-groomed.
bem-arrumado/a [-axu'madu/a] *adj* well-

NB: European Portuguese adds the following consonants to certain words: **b** (sú(b)dito, su(b)til); **c** (a(c)ção, a(c)cionista, a(c)to); **m** (inde(m)ne); **p** (ado(p)ção, ado(p)tar); *for further details see p. xiii.*

dressed.
bem-casado/a [-ka'zadu/a] *adj* happily married.
bem-comportado/a [-kôpox'tadu/a] *adj* well-behaved.
bem-conceituado/a *adj* highly regarded.
bem-disposto/a *adj* well, in good form.
bem-educado/a *adj* well-mannered.
bem-estar *m* well-being.
bem-humorado/a [-umo'radu/a] *adj* good-tempered.
bem-intencionado/a *adj* well-intentioned.
bem-me-quer (*pl* ~es) *m* daisy.
bem-passado/a *adj* (*CULIN*) well-done.
bem-sucedido/a *adj* successful.
bem-vindo/a *adj* welcome.
bem-visto/a *adj* well thought of.
bênção ['bẽsãw] (*pl* ~s) *f* blessing.
bendigo [bẽ'dʒigu] *etc vb V* **bendizer**.
bendisse [bẽ'dʒisi] *etc vb V* **bendizer**.
bendito/a [bẽ'dʒitu/a] *pp de* **bendizer** ♦ *adj* blessed.
bendizer [bẽdʒi'ze*] (*irreg: como* **dizer**) *vt* (*louvar*) to praise; (*abençoar*) to bless.
beneficência [benefi'sẽsja] *f* (*bondade*) kindness; (*caridade*) charity; **obra de** ~ charity.
beneficente [benefi'sẽtʃi] *adj* (*organização*) charitable; (*feira*) charity *atr*.
beneficiado/a [benefi'sjadu/a] *m/f* beneficiary.
beneficiar [benefi'sja*] *vt* (*favorecer*) to benefit; (*melhorar*) to improve; ~-se *vr* to benefit.
benefício [bene'fisju] *m* (*proveito*) benefit, profit; (*favor*) favour (*BRIT*), favor (*US*); **em** ~ **de** in aid of; **em** ~ **próprio** for one's own benefit.
benéfico/a [be'nɛfiku/a] *adj* (*benigno*) beneficial; (*generoso*) generous.
Benelux [bene'luks] *m* Benelux.
benemérito/a [bene'mɛritu/a] *adj* (*digno*) worthy.
beneplácito [bene'plasitu] *m* consent, approval.
benevolência [benevo'lẽsja] *f* benevolence, kindness.
benévolo/a [be'nɛvolu/a] *adj* benevolent, kind.
Benfam [bẽ'fami] *abr f* = **Sociedade Brasileira de Bem-Estar da Família**.
benfazejo/a [bẽfa'zeʒu/a] *adj* benevolent.
benfeitor(a) [bẽfej'to*(a)] *m/f* benefactor/benefactress.
benfeitoria [bẽfejto'ria] *f* improvement.
bengala [bẽ'gala] *f* walking stick.
benigno/a [be'nignu/a] *adj* (*bondoso*) kind; (*agradável*) pleasant; (*MED*) benign.
Benin [be'nĩ] *m*: **o** ~ Benin.
benquisto/a [bẽ'kiʃtu/a] *adj* well-loved, well-liked.
bens [bẽjʃ] *mpl de* **bem**.
bento/a ['bẽtu/a] *pp de* **benzer** ♦ *adj* blessed; (*água*) holy.
benzedeiro/a [bẽze'dejru/a] *m/f* sorcerer/sorceress.

benzer [bẽ'ze*] *vt* to bless; ~-se *vr* to cross o.s.
berçário [bex'sarju] *m* nursery.
berço ['bexsu] *m* (*com balanço*) cradle; (*cama*) cot; (*origem*) birthplace; **nascer em** ~ **de ouro** (*fig*) to be born with a silver spoon in one's mouth; **ter** ~ to be from a good family.
berimbau [berĩ'baw] *m percussion instrument*.
berinjela [berĩ'ʒela] *f* aubergine (*BRIT*), eggplant (*US*).
Berlim [bex'lĩ] *n* Berlin.
berlinda [bex'lĩda] *f*: **estar na** ~ to be in the firing-line.
berma ['bexma] (*PT*) *f* hard shoulder (*BRIT*), berm (*US*).
bermuda [bex'muda] *f* Bermuda shorts *pl*.
Bermudas [bex'mudaʃ] *fpl*: **as** ~ Bermuda *sg*.
Berna ['bexna] *n* Berne.
berrante [be'xãtʃi] *adj* flashy, gaudy.
berrar [be'xa*] *vi* to bellow; (*criança*) to bawl.
berreiro [be'xejru] *m* yelling; **abrir o** ~ to burst out crying.
berro ['bexu] *m* yell.
besouro [be'zoru] *m* beetle.
besta ['beʃta] *adj* (*tolo*) stupid; (*convencido*) full of oneself; (*pretensioso*) pretentious ♦ *f* (*animal*) beast; (*pessoa*) fool; ~ **de carga** beast of burden; **ficar** ~ (*col: surpreso*) to be amazed; **fazer alguém de** ~ (*col*) to make a fool of sb.
bestar [beʃ'ta*] *vi* to laze around.
besteira [beʃ'tejra] *f* (*tolice*) foolishness; (*insignificância*) small thing; **dizer** ~s to talk nonsense; **fazer uma** ~ to do something silly.
bestial [beʃ'tʃjaw] (*pl* -ais) *adj* bestial; (*repugnante*) repulsive.
bestialidade [beʃtʃjali'dadʒi] *f* bestiality.
bestificar [beʃtʃifi'ka*] *vt* to astonish, dumbfound.
best-seller ['bɛst'sɛle*] (*pl* ~s) *m* best seller.
besuntar [bezũ'ta*] *vt* to smear, daub.
betão [be'tãw] (*PT*) *m* concrete.
beterraba [bete'xaba] *f* beetroot.
betoneira [beto'nejra] *f* cement mixer.
betume [be'tumi] *m* asphalt.
bexiga [be'ʃiga] *f* (*órgão*) bladder.
bezerro/a [be'zexu/a] *m/f* calf.
bianual [bja'nwaw] (*pl* -ais) *adj* biannual, twice yearly.
bibelô [bibe'lo] *m* ornament.
Bíblia ['biblja] *f* Bible.
bíblico/a ['bibliku/a] *adj* biblical.
bibliografia [bibljogra'fia] *f* bibliography.
biblioteca [bibljo'tɛka] *f* library; (*estante*) bookcase.
bibliotecário/a [bibljote'karju/a] *m/f* librarian.
biblioteconomia [bibljotekono'mia] *f* librarianship.
bica ['bika] *f* tap; (*PT*) black coffee, expresso; **suar em** ~s to drip with sweat.
bicada [bi'kada] *f* peck.
bicama [bi'kama] *f* pull-out bed.

bicar [bi'ka*] vt to peck.

bicarbonato [bikaxbo'natu] m bicarbonate.

bíceps ['biseps] m inv biceps.

bicha ['biʃa] f (lombriga) worm; (PT: fila) queue; (BR: col, pej: homossexual) queer.

bichado/a [bi'ʃadu/a] adj eaten away.

bicheiro [bi'ʃejru] m (illegal) bookie.

bicho ['biʃu] m animal; (inseto) insect, bug; (col: pessoa: intratável) pain (in the neck); (: feio): **ela é um ~ (feio)** she's as ugly as sin; **virar ~** (col) to get mad; **ver que ~ dá** (col) to see what happens; **que ~ te mordeu?** what's got into you?

bicho-da-seda (pl **bichos-da-seda**) m silk worm.

bicho-de-sete-cabeças m: **fazer um ~** to make a mountain out of a molehill.

bicho-do-mato (pl **bichos-do-mato**) m extremely shy person.

bicho-papão [-pa'pãw] (pl **bichos-papões**) m bogeyman.

bicicleta [bisi'klɛta] f bicycle; (col) bike; **andar de ~** to cycle.

bico ['biku] m (de ave) beak; (ponta) point; (de chaleira) spout; (boca) mouth; (de pena) nib; (do peito) nipple; (de gás) jet; (col: emprego) job; (chupeta) dummy; **calar o ~** to shut up; **não abrir o ~** not to say a word; **fazer ~** to sulk.

bicudo/a [bi'kudu/a] adj pointed; (difícil) tricky.

BID abr m = **Banco Interamericano de Desenvolvimento**.

bidê [bi'de] m bidet.

bidimensional [bidʒimẽsjo'naw] (pl **-ais**) adj two-dimensional.

bidirecional [bidʒiresjo'naw] (pl **-ais**) adj bidirectional.

biela ['bjɛla] f con(necting) rod.

bienal [bje'naw] (pl **-ais**) adj biennial ♦ f (biennial) art exhibition.

bife ['bifi] m (beef) steak; **~ a cavalo** steak with fried eggs; **~ à milanesa** beef escalope; **~ de panela** beef stew.

bifocal [bifo'kaw] (pl **-ais**) adj bifocal.

bifurcação [bifuxka'sãw] (pl **-ões**) f fork.

bifurcar-se [bifux'kaxsi] vr to fork, divide.

bigamia [biga'mia] f bigamy.

bígamo/a ['bigamu/a] adj bigamous ♦ m/f bigamist.

bigode [bi'gɔdʒi] m moustache.

bigodudo/a [bigo'dudu/a] adj with a big moustache.

bigorna [bi'gɔxna] f anvil.

bijuteria [biʒute'ria] f (costume) jewellery (BRIT) ou jewelry (US).

bilateral [bilate'raw] (pl **-ais**) adj bilateral.

bilhão [bi'ʎãw] (pl **-ões**) m billion.

bilhar [bi'ʎa*] m (jogo) billiards sg.

bilhete [bi'ʎetʃi] m ticket; (cartinha) note; ~

de ida single (BRIT) ou one-way ticket; **~ de ida e volta** return (BRIT) ou round-trip (US) ticket; **o ~ azul** (fig) the sack.

bilheteira [biʎe'tejra] (PT) f = **bilheteria**; V tb **bilheteiro**.

bilheteiro/a [biʎe'tejru/a] m/f ticket seller.

bilheteria [biʎete'ria] f ticket office; (TEATRO) box office; **sucesso de ~** box-office success.

bilhões [bi'ʎõjʃ] mpl de **bilhão**.

bilíngüe [bi'līgwi] adj bilingual.

bilionário/a [biljo'narju/a] adj, m/f billionaire.

bilioso/a [bi'ljozu/ɔza] adj bilious, liverish; (fig) bad-tempered.

bílis ['biliʃ] m bile.

bimensal [bimẽ'saw] (pl **-ais**) adj twice-monthly.

bimestral [bimeʃ'traw] (pl **-ais**) adj two-monthly.

bimotor [bimo'to*] adj twin-engined.

binário/a [bi'narju/a] adj binary.

bingo ['bīgu] m bingo.

binóculo [bi'nɔkulu] m binoculars pl; (para teatro) opera glasses pl.

biodegradável [bjodegra'davew] (pl **-eis**) adj biodegradable.

biografia [bjogra'fia] f biography.

biográfico/a [bjo'grafiku/a] adj biographical.

biógrafo/a ['bjɔgrafu/a] m/f biographer.

biologia [bjolo'ʒia] f biology.

biológico/a [bjo'lɔʒiku/a] adj biological.

biólogo/a ['bjɔlogu/a] m/f biologist.

biombo ['bjõbu] m (tapume) screen.

biônico/a ['bjoniku/a] adj bionic; (POL: senador) non-elected.

biópsia ['bjɔpsja] f biopsy.

bioquímica [bjo'kimika] f biochemistry.

bipartidarismo [bipaxtʃida'riʒmu] m two-party system.

bipartidário/a [bipaxtʃi'darju/a] adj two-party atr, bipartite.

biquíni [bi'kini] m bikini.

BIRD abr m = **Banco Internacional de Reconstrução e Desenvolvimento**.

birita [bi'rita] (col) f drink.

birmanês/esa [bixma'neʃ/eza] adj, m/f Burmese ♦ m (LING) Burmese.

Birmânia [bix'manja] f: **a ~** Burma.

birô [bi'ro] m (COMPUT) bureau.

birra ['bixa] f (teima) wilfulness (BRIT), willfulness (US), obstinacy; (aversão) aversion; **fazer ~** to have a tantrum; **ter ~ com** to dislike.

birrento/a [bi'xẽtu/a] adj stubborn, obstinate.

biruta [bi'ruta] adj crazy ♦ f windsock.

bis [biʃ] excl encore!

bisar [bi'za*] vt (suj: público) to ask for an encore of; (: artista) to do an encore of.

bisavô/ó [biza'vo/ɔ] m/f great-grandfather/great-grandmother.

bisavós [biza'vɔʃ] mpl great-grandparents.

NB: European Portuguese adds the following consonants to certain words: **b** (sú(b)dito, su(b)til); **c** (a(c)ção, a(c)cionista, a(c)to); **m** (inde(m)ne); **p** (ado(p)ção, ado(p)tar); for further details see p. xiii.

bisbilhotar [biʒbiʎo'ta*] *vt* to pry into ♦ *vi* to snoop.
bisbilhoteiro/a [biʒbiʎo'tejru/a] *adj* prying ♦ *m/f* snoop.
bisbilhotice [biʒbiʎo'tʃisi] *f* prying.
Biscaia [biʃ'kaja] *f*: **o golfo de** ~ the Bay of Biscay.
biscate [biʃ'katʃi] *m* odd job.
biscateiro/a [biʃka'tejru/a] *m/f* odd-job person.
biscoito [biʃ'kojtu] *m* biscuit (*BRIT*), cookie (*US*); ~ **amanteigado** shortbread.
bisnaga [biʒ'naga] *f* (*tubo*) tube; (*pão*) French stick.
bisneto/a [biʒ'nɛtu/a] *m/f* great-grandson/great-granddaughter; ~**s** *mpl* great-grandchildren.
bisonho/a [bi'zɔɲu/a] *adj* inexperienced ♦ *m/f* newcomer.
bispado [biʃ'padu] *m* bishopric.
bispo ['biʃpu] *m* bishop.
bissemanal [bisema'naw] (*pl* -**ais**) *adj* twice-weekly.
bissexto/a [bi'seʃtu/a] *adj* **V** **ano.**
bissexual [bisek'swaw] (*pl* -**ais**) *adj*, *m/f* bisexual.
bisturi [biʃtu'ri] *m* scalpel.
bit ['bitʃi] *m* (*COMPUT*) bit.
bitola [bi'tɔla] *f* gauge (*BRIT*), gage (*US*); (*padrão*) pattern; (*estalão*) standard.
bitolado/a [bito'ladu/a] *adj* narrow-minded.
bizarro/a [bi'zaxu/a] *adj* bizarre.
blablablá [blabla'bla] (*col*) *m* chitchat.
black-tie ['blɛktaj] *m* evening dress.
blasé [bla'zɛ] *adj* blasé.
blasfemar [blaʃfe'ma*] *vt* to curse ♦ *vi* to blaspheme, curse.
blasfêmia [blaʃ'femja] *f* blasphemy; (*ultraje*) swearing.
blasfemo/a [blaʃ'femu/a] *adj* blasphemous ♦ *m/f* blasphemer.
blazer ['blejze*] (*pl* ~**s**) *m* blazer.
blecaute [ble'kawtʃi] *m* power cut.
blefar [ble'fa*] *vi* to bluff.
blefe ['blɛfi] *m* bluff.
blindado/a [bli'dadu/a] *adj* armoured (*BRIT*), armored (*US*).
blindagem [bli'daʒẽ] *f* armo(u)r(-plating).
blitz [blits] *f* police raid; (*na estrada*) police spot-check.
bloco ['blɔku] *m* block; (*POL*) bloc; (*de escrever*) writing pad; **voto em** ~ block vote; ~ **de carnaval** carnival troupe; ~ **de cilindros** cylinder block.
bloquear [blo'kja*] *vt* to blockade; (*obstruir*) to block.
bloqueio [blo'keju] *m* (*MIL*) blockade; (*obstrução*) blockage; (*PSICO*) mental block.
blusa ['bluza] *f* (*de mulher*) blouse; (*de homem*) shirt; ~ **de lã** jumper.
blusão [blu'zãw] (*pl* -**ões**) *m* jacket.
BMeF (*BR*) *abr f* = **Bolsa Mercantil e de Futuros.**
BMSP *abr f* = **Bolsa de Mercadorias de São**

Paulo.
BNDES *abr m* (= *Banco Nacional de Desenvolvimento Econômico e Social*) Brazilian development bank.
BNH (*BR*) *abr m* (= *Banco Nacional da Habitação*) home-funding bank.
boa ['boa] *adj f de* **bom** ♦ *f* boa constrictor.
boa-gente *adj inv* nice.
boa-pinta (*pl* **boas-pintas**) *adj* handsome.
boa-praça (*pl* **boas-praças**) *adj* nice.
boate ['bwatʃi] *f* nightclub.
boateiro/a [bwa'tejru/a] *adj* gossipy ♦ *m/f* gossip.
boato ['bwatu] *m* rumour (*BRIT*), rumor (*US*).
boa-vida (*pl* **boas-vidas**) *m/f* loafer.
bobagem [bo'baʒẽ] (*pl* -**ns**) *f* silliness, nonsense; (*dito*, *ato*) silly thing; **deixe de bobagens!** stop being silly!
bobeada [bo'bjada] *f* slip-up.
bobear [bo'bja*] *vi* to miss out.
bobice [bo'bisi] *f* silliness, nonsense; (*dito*, *ato*) silly thing.
bobina [bo'bina] *f* reel, bobbin; (*ELET*) coil; (*FOTO*) spool; (*de papel*) roll.
bobo/a ['bobu/a] *adj* silly, daft ♦ *m/f* fool ♦ *m* (*de corte*) jester; **fazer-se de** ~ to act the fool.
bobó [bo'bɔ] *m* beans, palm oil and manioc.
boboca [bo'bɔka] *adj* silly ♦ *m/f* fool.
boca ['boka] *f* mouth; (*entrada*) entrance; (*de fogão*) ring; **de** ~ orally; **de** ~ **aberta** open-mouthed, amazed; **bater** ~ to argue; **botar a** ~ **no mundo** (*berrar*) to scream; (*revelar*) to spill the beans; **falar da** ~ **para fora** to say one thing and mean another; **ser boa** ~ to eat anything; **vira essa** ~ **para lá!** don't tempt providence!; ~ **da noite** nightfall.
boca-de-fumo (*pl* **bocas-de-fumo**) *f* drug den.
boca-de-sino *adj inv* bell-bottomed.
bocadinho [boka'dʒiɲu] *m*: **um** ~ (*pouco tempo*) a little while; (*pouquinho*) a little bit.
bocado [bo'kadu] *m* (*quantidade na boca*) mouthful, bite; (*pedaço*) piece, bit; **um** ~ **de tempo** quite some time.
bocal [bo'kaw] (*pl* -**ais**) *m* (*de vaso*) mouth; (*MÚS*, *de aparelho*) mouthpiece; (*de cano*) nozzle.
boçal [bo'saw] (*pl* -**ais**) *adj* ignorant; (*grosseiro*) uncouth.
boçalidade [bosali'dadʒi] *f* coarseness; (*ignorância*) ignorance.
boca-livre (*pl* **bocas-livres**) *f* free meal.
bocejar [bose'ʒa*] *vi* to yawn.
bocejo [bo'seʒu] *m* yawn.
bochecha [bo'ʃeʃa] *f* cheek.
bochechar [boʃe'ʃa*] *vi* to rinse one's mouth.
bochecho [bo'ʃeʃu] *m* mouthwash.
bochechudo/a [boʃe'ʃudu/a] *adj* puffy-cheeked.
boda ['boda] *f* wedding; ~**s** *fpl* wedding anniversary *sg*; ~**s de prata/ouro** silver/golden wedding *sg*.

bode ['bɔdʒɪ] *m* goat; ~ **expiatório** scapegoat; **vai dar** ~ (*col*) there'll be trouble.

bodega [bo'dɛga] *f* piece of rubbish.

bodum [bo'dũ] *m* stink.

boêmio/a [bo'emju/a] *adj, m/f* Bohemian.

bofetada [bofe'tada] *f* slap.

bofetão [bofe'tãw] (*pl* **-ões**) *m* punch.

Bogotá [bogo'ta] *n* Bogota.

boi [boj] *m* ox; **pegar o** ~ **pelos chifres** (*fig*) to take the bull by the horns.

bói [bɔj] *m* office boy.

bóia ['bɔja] *f* buoy; (*col*) grub; (*de braço*) armband, water wing.

boiada [bo'jada] *f* herd of cattle.

bóia-fria (*pl* **bóias-frias**) *m/f* (*itinerante*) farm labourer (*BRIT*) *ou* laborer (*US*).

boiar [bo'ja*] *vt* to float ♦ *vi* to float; (*col*) to be lost; ~ **em** (*inglês etc*) to be hopeless at.

boicotar [bojko'ta*] *vt* to boycott.

boicote [boj'kɔtʃi] *m* boycott.

boiler ['bɔjla*] (*pl* **~s**) *m* boiler.

boina ['bojna] *f* beret.

bojo ['boʒu] *m* (*saliência*) bulge.

bojudo/a [bo'ʒudu/a] *adj* bulging; (*arredondado*) rounded.

bola ['bɔla] *f* ball; (*confusão*) confusion; **dar** ~ **(para)** (*col*) to care (about); (*dar atenção*) to pay attention (to); **dar** ~ **para** (*flertar*) to flirt with; **não dar** ~ **para alguém** to ignore sb; **ela não dá a menor** ~ **(para isso)** she couldn't care less (about it); **pisar na** ~ (*fig*) to make a mistake; **ser bom de** ~ to be good at football; **não ser certo da** ~ (*col*) not to be right in the head; **ser uma** ~ (*pessoa: gordo*) to be fat; (: *engraçado*) to be a real character; ~ **de futebol** football; ~ **de gude** marble; ~ **de neve** snowball.

bolacha [bo'laʃa] *f* biscuit (*BRIT*), cookie (*US*); (*col*: *bofetada*) wallop; (*para chope*) beermat.

bolada [bo'lada] *f* (*dinheiro*) lump sum.

bolar [bo'la*] *vt* to think up; **bem bolado** clever.

bole ['bɔli] *etc vb V* **bulir**.

boleia [bo'leja] *f* driver's seat; **dar uma** ~ (*PT*) to give a lift.

boletim [bole'tʃĩ] (*pl* **-ns**) *m* report; (*publicação*) newsletter; (*EDUC*) report; ~ **meteorológico** weather forecast.

bolha ['boʎa] *f* (*na pele*) blister; (*de ar, sabão*) bubble ♦ *m/f* (*col*) fool.

boliche [bo'liʃi] *m* (*jogo*) bowling, skittles *sg*.

bolinar [boli'na*] *vt*: ~ **alguém** (*col*) to feel sb up.

bolinho [bo'liɲu] *m*: ~ **de carne** meat ball; ~ **de arroz/bacalhau** rice/dry cod cake.

Bolívia [bo'livja] *f*: **a** ~ Bolivia.

boliviano/a [boli'vjanu/a] *adj, m/f* Bolivian.

bolo ['bolu] *m* cake; **dar o** ~ **em alguém** to stand sb up; **vai dar** ~ (*col*) there's going to

be trouble; **um** ~ **de gente/papéis** a bundle of people/papers.

bolor [bo'lo*] *m* mould (*BRIT*), mold (*US*); (*nas plantas*) mildew; (*bafio*) mustiness.

bolorento/a [bolo'rẽtu/a] *adj* mouldy (*BRIT*), moldy (*US*).

bolota [bo'lɔta] *f* acorn.

bolsa ['bowsa] *f* bag; (*COM*: *tb*: ~ **de valores**) stock exchange; ~ **(de estudos)** scholarship; ~ **de mercadorias** commodities market.

bolsista [bow'siʃta] *m/f* scholarship holder.

bolso ['bowsu] *m* pocket; **dicionário de** ~ pocket dictionary.

bom/boa [bõ/'boa] *adj* good; (*bondoso*) nice, kind; (*de saúde*) well; (*tempo*) fine; **um** ~ **quarto de hora** a good quarter of an hour; **essa é boa!** that's a good one!; **numa boa** (*col*) well; **metido numa boa** in a tight spot; **estar numa boa** (*col*) to be doing fine; ~, ... right, ...; **está** ~? OK?; **tudo** ~? how's it going?; **ficar** ~ (*trabalho*) to turn out well; (*de saúde*) to get better; **acho** ~ **você não fazer** I think it's better if you don't do; ~ **dia** good morning; **dar** ~ **dia em alguém** to say good morning to sb.

bomba ['bõba] *f* (*MIL*) bomb; (*TEC*) pump; (*CULIN*) éclair; (*fig*) bombshell; ~ **atômica/de fumaça/relógio** atomic/smoke/time bomb; ~ **de gasolina** petrol (*BRIT*) *ou* gas (*US*) pump; ~ **de incêndio** fire extinguisher; **levar** ~ (*em exame*) to fail.

bombada [bõ'bada] *f* (*prejuízo*) loss.

Bombaim [bõba'ĩ] *n* Bombay.

bombardear [bõbax'dʒja*] *vt* to bomb, bombard; (*fig*) to bombard.

bombardeio [bõbax'deju] *m* bombing, bombardment.

bomba-relógio (*pl* **bombas-relógio**) *f* time bomb.

bombástico/a [bõ'baʃtʃiku/a] *adj* pompous.

bombear [bõ'bja*] *vt* to pump.

bombeiro [bõ'bejru] *m* fireman; (*BR*: *encanador*) plumber; **o corpo de** ~**s** fire brigade.

bombom [bõ'bõ] (*pl* **-ns**) *m* chocolate.

bombordo [bõ'bɔxdu] *m* (*NÁUT*) port.

bonachão/chona [bona'ʃãw/'ʃɔna] (*pl* **-ões/~s**) *adj* simple and kind-hearted.

bonança [bo'nãsa] *f* fair weather; (*fig*) calm.

bondade [bõ'dadʒi] *f* goodness, kindness; **tenha a** ~ **de vir** would you please come.

bonde ['bõdʒi] (*BR*) *m* tram.

bondoso/a [bõ'dozu/ɔza] *adj* kind, good.

boné [bo'nɛ] *m* cap.

boneca [bo'nɛka] *f* doll.

boneco [bo'neku] *m* dummy.

bonificação [bonifika'sãw] (*pl* **-ões**) *f* bonus.

bonina [bo'nina] (*PT*) *f* daisy.

boníssimo/a [bo'nisimu/a] *adj superl de* **bom/boa**.

NB: European Portuguese adds the following consonants to certain words: **b** (sú(b)dito, su(b)til); **c** (a(c)ção, a(c)cionista, a(c)to); **m** (inde(m)ne); **p** (ado(p)ção, ado(p)tar); *for further details see p. xiii.*

bonitão/tona [boni'tãw/'tɔna] (pl -ões/~s) adj very attractive.

bonito/a [bo'nitu/a] adj (belo) pretty; (gesto, dia) nice ♦ m (peixe) tunny; **fazer um** ~ to do a good deed.

bonitões [boni'tõjʃ] mpl de **bonitão**.

bonitona [boni'tɔna] f de **bonitão**.

bônus ['bonuʃ] m inv bonus.

boquiaberto/a [bokja'bɛxtu/a] adj dumbfounded, astonished.

borboleta [boxbo'leta] f butterfly; (BR: roleta) turnstile.

borboletear [boxbole'tʃja*] vi to flutter, flit.

borbotão [boxbo'tãw] (pl -ões) m gush, spurt; **sair aos borbotões** to gush out.

borbulhante [boxbu'ʎãtʃi] adj bubbling.

borbulhar [boxbu'ʎa*] vi to bubble; (jorrar) to gush out.

borco ['boxku] m: **de** ~ (coisa) upside down; (pessoa) face down.

borda ['bɔxda] f edge; (do rio) bank; **à** ~ **de** on the edge of.

bordado [box'dadu] m embroidery.

bordão [box'dãw] (pl -ões) m staff; (MÚS) bass string; (arrimo) support; (frase) catchphrase.

bordar [box'da*] vt to embroider.

bordejar [boxde'ʒa*] vi (NÁUT) to tack.

bordel [box'dɛw] (pl -éis) m brothel.

bordo ['bɔxdu] m (ao bordejar) tack; (de navio) side; **a** ~ on board.

bordoada [box'dwada] f blow.

bordões [box'dõjʃ] mpl de **bordão**.

borla ['bɔxla] f tassel.

borocoxô [boroko'ʃo] adj dispirited.

borra ['boxa] f dregs pl.

borracha [bo'xaʃa] f rubber.

borracheiro [boxa'ʃejru] m tyre (BRIT) ou tire (US) specialist.

borracho/a [bo'xaʃu/a] adj drunk ♦ m/f drunk(ard).

borrador [boxa'do*] m (COM) day book.

borrão [bo'xãw] (pl -ões) m (rascunho) rough draft; (mancha) blot.

borrar [bo'xa*] vt to blot; (riscar) to cross out; (pintar) to daub; (sujar) to dirty.

borrasca [bo'xaʃka] f storm; (no mar) squall.

borrifar [boxi'fa*] vt to sprinkle.

borrifo [bo'xifu] m spray.

borrões [bo'xõjʃ] mpl de **borrão**.

bosque ['bɔʃki] m wood, forest.

bossa ['bɔsa] f (charme) charm; (inchaço) swelling; (no crânio) bump; (corcova) hump; **ter** ~ **para** to have an aptitude for.

bosta ['bɔʃta] f dung; (de humanos) excrement.

bota ['bɔta] f boot; ~s **de borracha** wellingtons; **bater as** ~s (col) to kick the bucket.

bota-fora (pl ~s) f (despedida) send-off.

botânica [bo'tanika] f botany; V tb **botânico**.

botânico/a [bo'taniku/a] adj botanical ♦ m/f botanist.

botão [bo'tãw] (pl -ões) m button; (flor) bud; **dizer com os seus botões** (fig) to say to o.s.

botar [bo'ta*] vt to put; (PT: lançar) to throw; (roupa, sapatos) to put on; (mesa) to set; (defeito) to find; (ovos) to lay; ~ **para quebrar** (col) to go for broke, go all out; ~ **em dia** to get up to date.

bote ['bɔtʃi] m (barco) boat; (com arma) thrust; (salto) spring; (de cobra) strike.

boteco [bo'tɛku] (col) m bar.

botequim [botʃi'kĩ] (pl -ns) m bar.

boticário/a [botʃi'karju/a] m/f pharmacist, chemist (BRIT).

botija [bo'tʃiʒa] f (earthenware) jug.

botina [bo'tʃina] f ankle boot.

botoeira [bo'twejra] f buttonhole.

botões [bo'tõjʃ] mpl de **botão**.

Botsuana [bot'swana] f: **a** ~ Botswana.

Bovespa [bo'vɛʃpa] abr f = **Bolsa de Valores do Estado de São Paulo**.

bovino/a [bo'vinu/a] adj bovine.

boxe ['bɔksi] m boxing.

boxeador [boksja'do*] m boxer.

boy [bɔj] m = **bói**.

brabo/a ['brabu/a] adj (feroz) fierce; (zangado) angry; (ruim) bad; (calor) unbearable; (gripe) bad.

braça ['brasa] f (NÁUT) fathom.

braçada [bra'sada] f armful; (NATAÇÃO) stroke.

braçadeira [brasa'dejra] f armband; (de cortina) tie-back; (metálica) bracket; (ESPORTE) sweatband.

braçal [bra'saw] (pl -ais) adj manual.

bracejar [brase'ʒa*] vi to wave one's arms about.

bracelete [brase'letʃi] m bracelet.

braço ['brasu] m arm; (trabalhador) hand; ~ **direito** (fig) right-hand man; **a** ~s **com** struggling with; **de** ~s **cruzados** with arms folded; (fig) without lifting a finger; **de** ~ **dado** arm-in-arm; **cruzar os** ~s (fig) to down tools; **não dar o** ~ **a torcer** (fig) not to give in; **meter o** ~ **em** (col) to clobber; **receber de** ~s **abertos** (fig) to welcome with open arms.

bradar [bra'da*] vt, vi to shout, yell.

brado ['bradu] m shout, yell.

braguilha [bra'giʎa] f flies pl.

braile ['brajli] m braille.

bramido [bra'midu] m roar.

bramir [bra'mi*] vi to roar.

branco/a ['brãku/a] adj white ♦ m/f white man/woman ♦ m (espaço) blank; **em** ~ blank; **noite em** ~ sleepless night; **deu um** ~ **nele** he drew a blank.

brancura [brã'kura] f whiteness.

brandir [brã'dʒi*] vt to brandish.

brando/a ['brãdu/a] adj gentle; (mole) soft.

brandura [brã'dura] f gentleness; (moleza) softness.

branquear [brã'kja*] vt to whiten; (alvejar) to bleach ♦ vi to turn white.

brasa ['braza] *f* hot coal; **em ~** red-hot; **pisar em ~** to be on tenterhooks; **mandar ~** (*col*) to go for it; **puxar a ~ para a sua sardinha** (*col*) to look out for o.s.

brasão [bra'zãw] (*pl* **-ões**) *m* coat of arms.

braseiro [bra'zejru] *m* brazier.

Brasil [bra'ziw] *m*: **o ~** Brazil.

brasileirismo [brazilej'riʒmu] *m* Brazilianism.

brasileiro/a [brazi'lejru/a] *adj, m/f* Brazilian.

Brasília [bra'zilja] *n* Brasília.

brasilianista [brazilja'niʃta] *m/f* Brazilianist.

brasiliense [brazi'ljẽsi] *adj* from Brasília ♦ *m/f* person from Brasília.

brasões [bra'zõjʃ] *mpl de* **brasão**.

bravata [bra'vata] *f* bravado, boasting.

bravatear [brava'tʃja*] *vi* to boast, brag.

bravio/a [bra'viu/a] *adj* (*selvagem*) wild, untamed; (*feroz*) ferocious.

bravo/a ['bravu/a] *adj* (*corajoso*) brave; (*furioso*) angry; (*mar*) rough, stormy ♦ *m* brave man; **~!** bravo!

bravura [bra'vura] *f* courage, bravery.

breca ['brɛka] *f*: **ser levado da ~** to be very naughty.

brecar [bre'ka*] *vt* (*carro*) to stop; (*reprimir*) to curb ♦ *vi* to brake.

brecha ['brɛʃa] *f* breach; (*abertura*) opening; (*dano*) damage; (*meio de escapar*) loophole; (*col*) chance.

brega ['brɛga] (*col*) *adj* tacky.

brejeiro/a [bre'ʒejru/a] *adj* impish.

brejo ['breʒu] *m* marsh, swamp; **ir para o ~** (*fig*) to go down the drain.

brenha ['brɛɲa] *f* (*mata*) dense wood.

breque ['brɛki] *m* (*freio*) brake.

breu [brew] *m* tar, pitch; **escuro como ~** pitch black.

breve ['brɛvi] *adj* short; (*conciso, rápido*) brief ♦ *adv* soon; **em ~** soon, shortly; **até ~** see you soon.

brevê [bre've] *m* pilot's licence (*BRIT*) *ou* license (*US*).

brevidade [brevi'dadʒi] *f* brevity, shortness.

bridge ['bridʒi] *m* bridge.

briga ['briga] *f* (*luta*) fight; (*verbal*) quarrel.

brigada [bri'gada] *f* brigade.

brigadeiro [briga'dejru] *m* brigadier; (*doce*) chocolate truffle.

brigão/ona [bri'gãw/ɔna] (*pl* **-ões/~s**) *adj* quarrelsome ♦ *m/f* troublemaker.

brigar [bri'ga*] *vi* (*lutar*) to fight; (*altercar*) to quarrel.

brigões [bri'gõjʃ] *mpl de* **brigão**.

brigona [bri'gɔna] *f de* **brigão**.

briguei [bri'gej] *etc vb V* **brigar**.

brilhante [bri'ʎãtʃi] *adj* brilliant ♦ *m* diamond.

brilhar [bri'ʎa*] *vi* to shine.

brilho ['briʎu] *m* (*luz viva*) brilliance; (*esplendor*) splendour (*BRIT*), splendor (*US*); (*nos sapatos*) shine; (*de metais, olhos*) gleam.

brincadeira [brĩka'dejra] *f* (*divertimento*) fun; (*gracejo*) joke; (*de criança*) game; **deixe de ~s!** stop fooling!; **de ~** for fun; **fora de ~** joking apart; **não é ~** it's no joke.

brincalhão/ona [brĩka'ʎãw/ɔna] (*pl* **-ões/~s**) *adj* playful ♦ *m/f* joker, teaser.

brincar [brĩ'ka*] *vi* to play; (*gracejar*) to joke; **estou brincando** I'm only kidding; **~ de soldados** to play (at) soldiers; **~ com alguém** (*mexer com*) to tease sb.

brinco ['brĩku] *m* (*jóia*) earring; **estar um ~** to be spotless.

brindar [brĩ'da*] *vt* (*beber*) to drink to; (*presentear*) to give a present to.

brinde ['brĩdʒi] *m* (*saudação*) toast; (*presente*) free gift.

brinquedo [brĩ'kedu] *m* toy.

brinquei [brĩ'kej] *etc vb V* **brincar**.

brio ['briu] *m* self-respect, dignity.

brioso/a ['brjozu/ɔza] *adj* self-respecting.

brisa ['briza] *f* breeze.

britânico/a [bri'taniku/a] *adj* British ♦ *m/f* Briton.

broca ['brɔka] *f* drill.

broche ['brɔʃi] *m* brooch.

brochura [bro'ʃura] *f* (*livro*) paperback; (*folheto*) brochure, pamphlet.

brócolis ['brɔkoliʃ] *mpl* broccoli *sg*.

brócolos ['brɔkoluʃ] (*PT*) *mpl* = **brócolis**.

bronca ['brõka] (*col*) *f* telling off; **dar uma ~ em** to tell off; **levar uma ~** to get told off.

bronco/a ['brõku/a] *adj* (*rude*) coarse; (*burro*) thick.

bronquear [brõ'kja*] (*col*) *vi* to get angry; **~ com** to tell off.

bronquite [brõ'kitʃi] *f* bronchitis.

bronze ['brõzi] *m* bronze.

bronzeado/a [brõ'zjadu/a] *adj* (*da cor do bronze*) bronze; (*pelo sol*) suntanned ♦ *m* suntan.

bronzear [brõ'zja*] *vt* to tan; **~-se** *vr* to tan.

brotar [bro'ta*] *vt* to produce ♦ *vi* (*manar*) to flow; (*BOT*) to sprout; (*nascer*) to spring up.

brotinho [bro'tʃiɲu/a] *m/f* teenager.

broto ['brotu] *m* bud; (*fig*) youngster.

broxa ['brɔʃa] *f* (*large*) paint brush.

bruços ['brusuʃ]: **de ~** *adv* face down.

bruma ['bruma] *f* mist, haze.

brumoso/a [bru'mozu/ɔza] *adj* misty, hazy.

brunido/a [bru'nidu/a] *adj* polished.

brunir [bru'ni*] *vt* to polish.

brusco/a ['bruʃku/a] *adj* brusque; (*súbito*) sudden.

brutal [bru'taw] (*pl* **-ais**) *adj* brutal.

brutalidade [brutali'dadʒi] *f* brutality.

brutamontes [bruta'mõtʃiʃ] *m inv* (*corpulento*) hulk; (*bruto*) brute.

bruto/a ['brutu/a] *adj* brutish; (*grosseiro*)

NB: European Portuguese adds the following consonants to certain words: **b** (sú(b)dito, su(b)til); **c** (a(c)ção, a(c)cionista, a(c)to); **m** (inde(m)ne); **p** (ado(p)ção, ado(p)tar); *for further details see p. xiii.*

coarse; (*móvel*) heavy; (*diamante*) uncut; (*petróleo*) crude; (*peso*, *COM*) gross; (*aggressivo*) aggressive ♦ *m* brute; **em** ~ raw, unworked; **um** ~ **resfriado** an awful cold.

bruxa ['bruʃa] *f* witch; (*velha feia*) hag.

bruxaria [bruʃa'ria] *f* witchcraft.

Bruxelas [bru'ʃelaʃ] *n* Brussels.

bruxo ['bruʃu] *m* wizard.

bruxulear [bruʃu'lja*] *vi* to flicker.

BTN (*BR*) *abr m* (= *Bónus do Tesouro Nacional*) *government bond used to quote prices*.

Bucareste [buka'rɛʃtʃi] *n* Bucharest.

bucha ['buʃa] *f* (*para parafuso*) rawlplug ®; (*para buracos*) bung; **acertar na** ~ (*fig*) to hit the nail on the head.

bucho ['buʃu] (*col*) *m* gut; **ela é um** ~ **(feio)** she's as ugly as sin.

buço ['busu] *m* down.

Budapest [buda'pɛʃtʃi] *n* Budapest.

budismo [bu'dʒiʒmu] *m* Buddhism.

budista [bu'dʒiʃta] *adj*, *m/f* Buddhist.

bueiro [bu'ejru] *m* storm drain.

Buenos Aires ['bwɛnuz'ajriʃ] *n* Buenos Aires.

búfalo ['bufalu] *m* buffalo.

bufante [bu'fãtʃi] *adj* puffed, full.

bufar [bu'fa*] *vi* to puff, pant; (*com raiva*) to snort; (*reclamar*) to moan, grumble.

bufê [bu'fe] *m* (*móvel*) sideboard; (*comida*) buffet; (*serviço*) catering service.

buffer ['bafe*] (*pl* ~**s**) *m* (*COMPUT*) buffer.

bugiganga [buʒi'gãga] *f* trinket; ~**s** *fpl* knicknacks.

bujão [bu'ʒãw] (*pl* -**ões**) *m* (*TEC*) cap; ~ **de gás** gas cylinder.

bula ['bula] *f* (*REL*) papal bull; (*MED*) directions *pl* for use.

bulbo ['buwbu] *m* bulb.

buldôzer [buw'doze*] (*pl* ~**es**) *m* bulldozer.

bule ['buli] *m* (*de chá*) tea pot; (*de café*) coffeepot.

Bulgária [buw'garja] *f*: **a** ~ Bulgaria.

búlgaro/a ['buwgaru/a] *adj*, *m/f* Bulgarian ♦ *m* (*LING*) Bulgarian.

bulha ['buʎa] *f* row.

bulhufas [bu'ʎufaʃ] (*col*) *pron* nothing.

bulício [bu'lisju] *m* (*agitação*) bustle; (*sussurro*) rustling.

buliçoso/a [buli'sozu/ɔza] *adj* (*vivo*) lively; (*agitado*) restless.

bulir [bu'li*] *vt* to move ♦ *vi* to move, stir; ~ **com** to tease; ~ **em** to touch, meddle with.

bumbum [bũ'bũ] (*pl* -**ns**) (*col*) *m* bottom.

bunda ['bũda] (*col*) *f* bottom, backside.

buquê [bu'ke] *m* bouquet.

buraco [bu'raku] *m* hole; (*de agulha*) eye; (*jogo*) rummy; **ser um** ~ (*difícil*) to be tough; ~ **da fechadura** keyhole.

burburinho [buxbu'riɲu] *m* hubbub; (*murmúrio*) murmur.

burguês/guesa [bux'geʃ/'geza] *adj* middle-class, bourgeois.

burguesia [buxge'zia] *f* middle class,

bourgeoisie.

buril [bu'riw] (*pl* -**is**) *m* chisel.

burilar [buri'la*] *vt* to chisel.

buris [bu'riʃ] *mpl de* **buril**.

Burkina [bux'kina] *m*: **o** ~ Burkina Faso.

burla ['buxla] *f* trick, fraud; (*zombaria*) mockery.

burlar [bux'la*] *vt* (*enganar*) to cheat; (*defraudar*) to swindle; (*a lei, impostos*) to evade.

burlesco/a [bux'leʃku/a] *adj* burlesque.

burocracia [burokra'sia] *f* bureaucracy; (*excessiva*) red tape.

burocrata [buro'krata] *m/f* bureaucrat.

burocrático/a [buro'kratʃiku/a] *adj* bureaucratic.

burrice [bu'xisi] *f* stupidity.

burro/a ['buxu/a] *adj* stupid; (*pouco inteligente*) dim, thick ♦ *m/f* (*ZOOL*) donkey; (*pessoa*) fool, idiot; **pra** ~ (*col*) a lot; (*com adj*) really; **dar com os** ~**s** **n'água** (*fig*) to come a cropper; ~ **de carga** (*fig*) hard worker.

Burundi [burũ'dʒi] *m*: **o** ~ Burundi.

busca ['buʃka] *f* search; **em** ~ **de** in search of; **dar** ~ **a** to search for.

busca-pé [buʃka'pɛ] (*pl* ~**s**) *m* banger.

buscar [buʃ'ka*] *vt* to fetch; (*procurar*) to look *ou* search for; **ir** ~ to fetch, go for; **mandar** ~ to send for.

busquei [buʃ'kej] *etc vb V* **buscar**.

bússola ['busola] *f* compass.

bustiê [buʃtʃi'e*] *m* boob tube.

busto ['buʃtu] *m* bust.

butique [bu'tʃiki] *m* boutique.

buzina [bu'zina] *f* horn.

buzinada [buzi'nada] *f* toot, hoot.

buzinar [buzi'na*] *vi* to sound one's horn, toot the horn ♦ *vt* to hoot; ~ **nos ouvidos de alguém** (*fig*) to hassle sb; ~ **algo nos ouvidos de alguém** (*fig*) to drum sth into sb.

búzio ['buzju] *m* (*concha*) conch.

BVRJ *abr f* = **Bolsa de Valores do Rio de Janeiro**.

C

C [se] (*pl* **cs**) *m* C, c; **C de Carlos** C for Charlie.

c/ *abr* = **com**.

Ca *abr* (= *companhia*) Co.

cá [ka] *adv* here; **de** ~ on this side; **para** ~ here, over here; **para lá e para** ~ back and forth; **de lá para** ~ since then; **de um ano para** ~ in the last year; ~ **entre nós** just between us.

caatinga [ka'tʃĩga] (*BR*) *f* scrub(-land).

cabal [ka'baw] (*pl* **-ais**) *adj* (*completo*) complete; (*exato*) exact.

cabala [ka'bala] *f* (*maquinação*) conspiracy, intrigue.

cabalar [kaba'la*] *vt* (*votos etc*) to canvass (for) ♦ *vi* to canvass.

cabana [ka'bana] *f* hut.

cabaré [kaba'rɛ] *m* (*boate*) night club.

cabeça [ka'besa] *f* head; (*inteligência*) brain; (*de uma lista*) top ♦ *m/f* (*de uma revolta*) leader; (*de uma organização*) brains *sg*; **cinqüenta ~s de gado** fifty head of cattle; **de ~** out of one's head, off the top of one's head; (*calcular*) in one's head; **de ~ para baixo** upside down; **por ~ per** person, per head; **deu-lhe na ~ de** he took it into his head to; **esquentar a ~** (*col*) to lose one's cool; **não estar com a ~ para fazer** not to feel like doing; **fazer a ~ de alguém** (*col*) to talk sb into it; **levar na ~** (*col*) to come a cropper; **meter na ~** to get into one's head; **tirar algo da ~** to put sth out of one's mind; **perder a ~** to lose one's head; **quebrar a ~** to rack one's brains; **subir à ~** (*sucesso etc*) to go to sb's head; **com a ~ no ar** absent-minded; **~ fria** cool-headedness.

cabeçada [kabe'sada] *f* (*pancada com cabeça*) butt; (*FUTEBOL*) header; (*asneira*) blunder; **dar uma ~ (em)** to bang one's head (on); **dar uma ~** (*fazer asneira*) to make a blunder; **dar uma ~ na bola** (*FUTEBOL*) to head the ball.

cabeça-de-casal (*pl* **cabeças-de-casal**) *m* dominant partner.

cabeça-de-porco (*pl* **cabeças-de-porco**) (*col*) *f* tenement building.

cabeça-de-vento (*pl* **cabeças-de-vento**) *m/f* scatterbrain.

cabeçalho [kabe'saʎu] *m* (*de livro*) title page; (*de página, capítulo*) heading.

cabecear [kabe'sja*] *vt* (*FUTEBOL*) to head ♦ *vi* to nod; to play a header.

cabeceira [kabe'sejra] *f* (*de cama*) head; (*de mesa*) end; **leitura de ~** bedtime reading.

cabeçudo/a [kabe'sudu/a] *adj* big-headed; (*teimoso*) pigheaded.

cabedal [kabe'daw] (*pl* **-ais**) *m* wealth.

cabeleira [kabe'lejra] *f* head of hair; (*postiça*) wig.

cabeleireiro/a [kabelej'rejru/a] *m/f* hairdresser.

cabelo [ka'belu] *m* hair; **~ liso/crespo/pixaim** straight/curly/frizzy hair; **~ à escovinha** crew cut; **cortar/fazer o ~** to have one's hair cut/done; **ter ~ na venta** to be short-tempered.

cabeludo/a [kabe'ludu/a] *adj* hairy; (*difícil*) complicated; (*obsceno*) obscene.

caber [ka'be*] *vi*: **~ (em)** (*poder entrar*) to fit,

go; (*roupa*) to fit; (*ser compatível*) to be appropriate (in); **~ a** (*em partilha*) to fall to; **cabe a alguém fazer** it is up to sb to do; **~ por** to fit through; **não cabe aqui fazer comentários** this is not the time or place to comment; **acho que cabe exigir um explicação** I think it is reasonable to demand an explanation; **são fatos que cabe apurar** they are facts which should be investigated; **tua dúvida cabe perfeitamente** your doubt is perfectly in order; **não ~ em si de** to be beside o.s. with.

cabide [ka'bidʒi] *m* (*coat*) hanger; (*móvel*) hat stand; (*fixo à parede*) coat rack; **~ de empregos** person who has several jobs.

cabideiro [kabi'dejru] *m* hatstand; (*na parede*) coat rack; (*para sapatos*) rack.

cabimento [kabi'mẽtu] *m* suitability; **ter ~** to be fitting *ou* appropriate; **não ter ~** to be inconceivable.

cabine [ka'bini] *f* cabin; (*em loja*) fitting room; **~ do piloto** (*AER*) cockpit; **~ telefônica** telephone booth.

cabisbaixo/a [kabiʒ'bajʃu/a] *adj* (*deprimido*) dispirited, crestfallen; (*com a cabeça para baixo*) head down.

cabível [ka'bivew] (*pl* **-eis**) *adj* conceivable.

cabo ['kabu] *m* (*extremidade*) end; (*de faca, vassoura etc*) handle; (*corda*) rope; (*elétrico etc*) cable; (*GEO*) cape; (*MIL*) corporal; **ao ~ de** at the end of; **de ~ a rabo** from beginning to end; **levar a ~** to carry out; **dar ~ de** to do away with; **~ eleitoral** canvasser.

caboclo/a [ka'boklu/a] (*BR*) *adj* copper-coloured (*BRIT*), copper-colored (*US*) ♦ *m/f* mestizo.

cabotino/a [kabo'tʃinu/a] *adj* ostentatious ♦ *m/f* show-off.

Cabo Verde *m* Cape Verde.

cabo-verdiano/a [-vex'dʒjanu/a] *adj*, *m/f* Cape Verdean.

cabra ['kabra] *f* goat ♦ *m* (*BR*: *sujeito*) guy; (: *capanga*) hired gun.

cabra-cega *f* blind man's buff.

cabra-macho (*pl* **cabras-machos**) *m* tough guy.

cabreiro/a [ka'brejru/a] (*col*) *adj* suspicious.

cabresto [kab'reʃtu] *m* (*de cavalos*) halter.

cabrito [ka'britu] *m* kid.

cabrocha [ka'brɔʃa] *f* mulatto girl.

caça ['kasa] *f* hunting; (*busca*) hunt; (*animal*) quarry, game ♦ *m* (*AER*) fighter (plane); **à ~ de** in pursuit of.

caçada [ka'sada] *f* (*jornada de caçadores*) hunting trip.

caçador(a) [kasa'do*(a)] *m/f* hunter.

caçamba [ka'sãba] *f* (*balde*) bucket.

caça-minas *m inv* minesweeper.

caça-níqueis *m inv* slot machine.

cação [ka'sãw] (*pl* **-ões**) *m* shark.

NB: *European Portuguese adds the following consonants to certain words:* **b** (sú(b)dito, su(b)til); **c** (a(c)ção, a(c)cionista, a(c)to); **m** (inde(m)ne); **p** (ado(p)ção, ado(p)tar); *for further details see p. xiii.*

caçapa [ka'sapa] *f* pocket.

caçar [ka'sa*] *vt* to hunt; (*com espingarda*) to shoot; (*procurar*) to seek ♦ *vi* to hunt, go hunting.

cacareco [kaka'rɛku] *m* piece of junk; **~s** *mpl* junk *sg*.

cacarejar [kakare'ʒa*] *vi* (*galinhas etc*) to cluck.

cacarejo [kaka'reʒu] *m* clucking.

caçarola [kasa'rɔla] *f* (sauce)pan.

cacau [ka'kaw] *m* cocoa; (*BOT*) cacao.

cacaueiro [kaka'wejru] *m* cocoa tree.

cacetada [kase'tada] *f* blow (with a stick).

cacete [ka'setʃi] *adj* tiresome, boring ♦ *m/f* bore ♦ *m* club, stick; **está quente pra ~** (*col!*) it's bloody hot (!).

caceteação [kasetʃja'sãw] *f* annoyance.

cacetear [kase'tʃja*] *vt* to annoy.

Cacex [ka'sɛks] *abr f* (= *Carteira do Comércio Exterior*) *part of Banco do Brasil which helps to finance foreign trade*.

cachaça [ka'ʃasa] *f* (white) rum.

cachaceiro/a [kaʃa'sejru/a] *adj* drunk ♦ *m/f* drunkard.

cachaço [ka'ʃasu] *m* neck.

cachê [ka'ʃe] *m* fee.

cachecol [kaʃe'kɔw] (*pl* **-óis**) *m* scarf.

cachepô [kaʃe'po] *m* plant pot.

cachimbo [ka'ʃĩbu] *m* pipe.

cacho ['kaʃu] *m* bunch; (*de cabelo*) curl, lock; (*longo*) ringlet; (*col: caso*) affair.

cachoeira [kaʃ'wejra] *f* waterfall.

cachorra [ka'ʃoxa] *f* bitch; (*PT*) (female) puppy; **estar com a ~** (*col*) to be in a foul mood.

cachorrada [kaʃo'xada] *f* pack of dogs; (*sujeira*) dirty trick.

cachorrinho/a [kaʃo'xiɲu/a] *m/f* puppy ♦ *m* (*nado*) doggy paddle.

cachorro [ka'ʃoxu] *m* dog; (*PT*) puppy; (*filhote de animal*) cub; (*patife*) rascal; **soltar os ~s em cima de alguém** (*fig*) to lash out at sb; **estar matando ~ a grito** (*col*) to be scraping the barrel.

cachorro-quente (*pl* **cachorros-quentes**) *m* hot dog.

cacilda [ka'siwda] *excl* wow!, crikey!

cacique [ka'siki] *m* (Indian) chief; (*mandachuva*) local boss.

caco ['kaku] *m* bit, fragment; (*pessoa velha*) old relic; **chegamos ~s humanos** we arrived dead on our feet.

caçoada [ka'swada] *f* jibe.

caçoar [ka'swa*] *vt* to mock, make fun of ♦ *vi* to mock.

cações [ka'sõjʃ] *mpl de* **cação**.

cacoete [ka'kwetʃi] *m* twitch.

cacto ['kaktu] *m* cactus.

caçula [ka'sula] *m/f* youngest child.

cada ['kada] *adj inv* each; (*todo*) every; **$10 ~** $10 each; **~ um** each one; **~ semana** each week; **a ~ 3 horas** every 3 hours; **em ~ 3 crianças, uma já teve sarampo** out of every

3 children, one has already had measles; **~ vez mais** more and more; **~ vez mais barato** cheaper and cheaper; **tem ~ museu em Londres!** there are so many different museums in London; **tem ~ um!** it takes all sorts!

cadafalso [kada'fawsu] *m* (*forca*) gallows.

cadarço [ka'daxsu] *m* shoelace.

cadastrar [kadaʃ'tra*] *vt* (*COMPUT*: *banco de dados*) to set up.

cadastro [ka'daʃtru] *m* (*registro*) register; (*ato*) registration; (*de criminosos*) criminal record; (*de banco etc*) client records *pl*; (*de imóveis*) land registry; **~ bancário** (*de pessoa*) credit rating.

cadáver [ka'dave*] *m* corpse, dead body; **só passando por cima do meu ~** over my dead body; **ao chegar ao hospital, o motorista já era ~** the driver was dead on arrival at hospital.

cadavérico/a [kada'vɛriku/a] *adj* (*exame*) post-mortem; (*pessoa*) emaciated.

CADE (*BR*) *abr m* = **Conselho Administrativo de Defesa Econômica**.

cadê [ka'de] (*col*) *adv*: **~ ...?** where's/where are ...?, what's happened to ...?

cadeado [ka'dʒjadu] *m* padlock.

cadeia [ka'deja] *f* chain; (*prisão*) prison; (*rede*) network.

cadeira [ka'dejra] *f* (*móvel*) chair; (*disciplina*) subject; (*TEATRO*) stall; (*função*) post; **~s** *fpl* (*ANAT*) hips; **~ cativa** private seat; **~ de balanço** rocking chair; **~ de rodas** wheelchair; **falar de ~** (*fig*) to speak with authority.

cadeirudo/a [kadej'rudu/a] *adj* big-hipped.

cadela [ka'dɛla] *f* (*cão*) bitch.

cadência [ka'dẽsja] *f* cadence; (*ritmo*) rhythm.

cadenciado/a [kadẽ'sjadu/a] *adj* rhythmic; (*pausado*) slow.

cadente [ka'dẽtʃi] *adj* (*estrela*) falling.

caderneta [kadex'neta] *f* notebook; **~ de poupança** savings account.

caderno [ka'dɛxnu] *m* exercise book; (*de notas*) notebook; (*de jornal*) section.

cadete [ka'detʃi] *m* cadet.

cadinho [ka'dʒiɲu] *m* crucible; (*fig*) melting pot.

caducar [kadu'ka*] *vi* (*documentos*) to lapse, expire; (*pessoa*) to become senile.

caduco/a [ka'duku/a] *adj* (*nulo*) invalid, expired; (*senil*) senile; (*BOT*) deciduous.

caduquice [kadu'kisi] *f* senility.

cães [kãjʃ] *mpl de* **cão**.

cafajeste [kafa'ʒɛʃtʃi] (*col*) *adj* roguish; (*vulgar*) vulgar, coarse ♦ *m/f* rogue; rough customer.

café [ka'fɛ] *m* coffee; (*estabelecimento*) café; **~ com leite** white coffee (*BRIT*), coffee with cream (*US*); **~ preto** black coffee; **~ da manhã** (*BR*) breakfast; **é ~ pequeno** it's child's play.

café-com-leite *adj inv* coffee-coloured (*BRIT*),

coffee-colored (US).
cafeeiro/a [kafe'ejru/a] adj coffee atr ♦ m coffee plant.
cafeicultor [kafejkuw'to*] m coffee-grower.
cafeicultura [kafejkuw'tura] f coffee-growing.
cafeína [kafe'ina] f caffein(e).
cafetã [kafe'tã] m caftan.
cafetão [kafe'tãw] (pl -ões) m pimp.
cafeteira [kafe'tejra] f (vaso) coffee pot; (máquina) percolator.
cafetina [kafe'tʃina] f madam.
cafetões [kafe'tõjʃ] mpl de **cafetão**.
cafezal [kafe'zaw] (pl -ais) m coffee plantation.
cafezinho [kafe'ziɲu] m small black coffee.
cafona [ka'fɔna] adj tacky ♦ m/f tacky person.
cafonice [kafo'nisi] f tackiness; (coisa) tacky thing.
cafundó-do-judas [kafũ'dɔ-] m: no ~ out in the sticks.
cafuné [kafu'nɛ] m: fazer ~ em alguém to stroke sb's hair.
cagaço [ka'gasu] (col!) m shits pl (!).
cagada [ka'gada] (col!) f shit (!); (coisa malfeita) cock-up (!).
cágado ['kagadu] m turtle; a passos de ~ (fig) at a snail's pace.
caganeira [kaga'nejra] (col) f runs pl.
cagão/gona [ka'gãw/'gɔna] (pl -ões/~s) (col) m/f: ser ~ to be a chicken.
cagar [ka'ga*] (col!) vi to (have a) shit (!) ♦ vt: ~ regras to tell others what to do; ~-se vr: ~-se de medo to be shit scared (!); ~ (para) not to give a shit (about) (!).
cagões [ka'gõjʃ] mpl de **cagão**.
cagona [ka'gɔna] f de **cagão**.
cagüetar [kagwe'ta*] vt to inform on.
cagüete [ka'gwetʃi] m informer.
caiaque [ka'jaki] m kayak.
caiar [kaj'a*] vt to whitewash.
caiba ['kajba] etc vb V **caber**.
cãibra ['kãjbra] f (MED) cramp.
caibro ['kajbru] m joist.
caída [ka'ida] f = **queda**.
caído/a [ka'idu/a] adj (deprimido) dejected; (derrubado) fallen; (pendente) droopy; ~ por (apaixonado) in love with.
câimbra ['kãjbra] f = **cãibra**.
caimento [kaj'mẽtu] m hang, fall.
caipira [kaj'pira] adj countrified; (sem traquejo social) provincial ♦ m/f yokel.
caipirinha [kajpi'riɲa] f cocktail of cachaça, lemon and sugar.
cair [ka'i*] vi to fall; (ser vítima de logro) to be taken in; ~ bem/mal (col: pessoa) to look good/bad; ~ em si to come to one's senses; ~ de quatro to land on all fours; estou caindo de sono I'm really sleepy; ~ para trás (fig) to be taken aback; ao ~ da noite at nightfall; o Natal

caiu num domingo Christmas fell on a Sunday; **essa comida me caiu mal** that food did not agree with me.
Cairo ['kajru] m: o ~ Cairo.
cais [kajʃ] m (NÁUT) quay; (PT: FERRO) platform.
caixa ['kajʃa] f box; (cofre) safe; (de uma loja) cashdesk ♦ m/f (pessoa) cashier; **de alta/baixa** ~ (col) well-off/poor; **fazer a** ~ (COM) to cash up; **pequena** ~ petty cash; ~ **acústica** loudspeaker; ~ **de correio** letter box; ~ **de mudanças** (BR) ou **de velocidades** (PT) gear box; ~ **econômica** savings bank; ~ **postal** P.O. box; ~ **registradora** cash register.
caixa-alta (pl **caixas-altas**) (col) adj rich ♦ m/f fat cat.
caixa-d'água (pl **caixas-d'água**) f water tank.
caixa-forte (pl **caixas-fortes**) f vault.
caixão [kaj'ʃãw] (pl -ões) m (ataúde) coffin; (caixa grande) large box.
caixa-preta (pl **caixas-pretas**) f (AER) black box.
caixeiro/a [kaj'ʃejru/a] m/f shop assistant; (entregador) delivery man/woman.
caixeiro/a-viajante (pl **caixeiros/as-viajantes**) m/f commercial traveller (BRIT) ou traveler (US).
caixilho [kaj'ʃiʎu] m (moldura) frame.
caixões [kaj'ʃõjʃ] mpl de **caixão**.
caixote [kaj'ʃɔtʃi] m packing case; ~ **do lixo** (PT) dustbin (BRIT), garbage can (US).
caju [ka'ʒu] m cashew fruit.
cajueiro [ka'ʒwejru] m cashew tree.
cal [kaw] f lime; (na água) chalk; (para caiar) whitewash.
calabouço [kala'bosu] m dungeon.
calada [ka'lada] f: **na** ~ **da noite** at dead of night.
calado/a [ka'ladu/a] adj quiet.
calafetar [kalafe'ta*] vt to stop up.
calafrio [kala'friu] m shiver; **ter** ~**s** to shiver.
calamar [kala'ma*] m squid.
calamidade [kalami'dadʒi] f calamity, disaster.
calamitoso/a [kalami'tozu/ɔza] adj disastrous.
calão [ka'lãw] m: (baixo) ~ (BR) bad language; (PT) slang.
calar [ka'la*] vt (não dizer) to keep quiet about; (impor silêncio a) to silence ♦ vi to go quiet; (manter-se calado) to keep quiet; ~-se vr to go quiet; to keep quiet; ~ em (penetrar) to mark; **cala a boca!** shut up!
calça ['kawsa] f (tb: ~s) trousers pl (BRIT), pants pl (US).
calçada [kaw'sada] f (PT: rua) roadway; (BR: passeio) pavement (BRIT), sidewalk (US).
calçadão [kawsa'dãw] (pl -ões) m pedestrian precinct (BRIT).
calçadeira [kawsa'dejra] f shoe-horn.

NB: European Portuguese adds the following consonants to certain words: **b** (sú(b)dito, su(b)til); **c** (a(c)ção, a(c)cionista, a(c)to); **m** (inde(m)ne); **p** (ado(p)ção, ado(p)tar); for further details see p. xiii.

calçado/a [kaw'sadu/a] *adj* (*rua*) paved ♦ *m* shoe; ~s *mpl* footwear *sg.*

calçadões [kawsa'dõjʃ] *mpl de* **calçadão.**

calçamento [kawsa'mẽtu] *m* paving.

calcanhar [kawka'ɲa*] *m* (*ANAT*) heel.

calcanhar-de-aquiles [-dʒia'kiliʃ] *m* Achilles' heel.

calção [kaw'sãw] (*pl* -**ões**) *m* shorts *pl*; ~ **de banho** swimming trunks *pl.*

calcar [kaw'ka*] *vt* (*pisar em*) to tread on; (*espezinhar*) to trample (on); (*comprimir*) to press; (*reprimir*) to repress.

calçar [kaw'sa*] *vt* (*sapatos, luvas*) to put on; (*pavimentar*) to pave; (*pôr calço*) to wedge; ~-**se** *vr* to put on one's shoes; **o sapato calça bem?** does the shoe fit?; **ela calça (número) 28** she takes size 28 (in shoes).

calcário/a [kaw'karju/a] *adj* (*água*) hard ♦ *m* limestone.

calceiro/a [kaw'sejru/a] *m/f* shoe-maker.

calcinha [kaw'siɲa] *f* panties *pl.*

cálcio ['kawsju] *m* calcium.

calço ['kawsu] *m* (*cunha*) wedge.

calções [kaw'sõjʃ] *mpl de* **calção.**

calculadora [kawkula'dora] *f* calculator.

calcular [kawku'la*] *vt* to calculate; (*imaginar*) to imagine ♦ *vi* to make calculations; ~ **que** to reckon that.

calculável [kawku'lavew] (*pl* -**eis**) *adj* calculable.

calculista [kawku'liʃta] *adj* calculating ♦ *m/f* opportunist.

cálculo ['kawkulu] *m* calculation; (*MAT*) calculus; (*MED*) stone.

calda ['kawda] *f* (*de doce*) syrup; ~**s** *fpl* hot springs.

caldeira [kaw'dejra] *f* (*TEC*) boiler.

caldeirada [kawdej'rada] (*PT*) *f* (*guisado*) fish stew.

caldeirão [kawdej'rãw] (*pl* -**ões**) *m* cauldron.

caldo ['kawdu] *m* (*sopa*) broth; (*de fruta*) juice; ~ **de carne/galinha** beef/chicken stock; ~ **verde** potato and cabbage broth.

calefação [kalefa'sãw] *f* heating.

caleidoscópio [kalejdo'ʃkɔpju] *m* kaleidoscope.

calejado/a [kale'ʒadu/a] *adj* calloused; (*fig: experiente*) experienced; (: *endurecido*) callous.

calejar [kale'ʒa*] *vt* (*mãos*) to callous; (*pessoa*) to harden; ~-**se** *vr* (*mãos*) to get calluses; (*insensibilizar-se*) to become callous; (*tornar-se experiente*) to get experience.

calendário [kalẽ'darju] *m* calendar.

calha ['kaʎa] *f* (*sulco*) channel; (*para água*) gutter.

calhamaço [kaʎa'masu] *m* tome.

calhambeque [kaʎã'bɛki] (*col*) *m* old banger.

calhar [ka'ʎa*] *vi*: **calhou viajarmos no mesmo avião** we happened to travel on the same plane; **calhou que** it so happened that; **ele calhou de chegar** he happened to arrive;

~ **a** (*cair bem*) to suit; **vir a** ~ to come at the right time; **se** ~ (*PT*) perhaps, maybe.

calhau [ka'ʎaw] *m* stone, pebble.

calibrado/a [kali'bradu/a] *adj* (*meio bêbado*) tipsy.

calibrar [kali'bra*] *vt* to gauge (*BRIT*), gage (*US*), calibrate.

calibre [ka'libri] *m* (*de cano*) bore, calibre (*BRIT*), caliber (*US*); (*fig*) calibre.

cálice ['kalisi] *m* (*copinho*) wine glass; (*REL*) chalice.

calidez [kali'deʒ] *f* warmth.

cálido/a ['kalidu/a] *adj* warm.

caligrafia [kaligra'fia] *f* (*arte*) calligraphy; (*letra*) handwriting.

calista [ka'liʃta] *m/f* chiropodist (*BRIT*), podiatrist (*US*).

calma ['kawma] *f* calm; **conservar/perder a** ~ to keep/lose one's temper; ~! take it easy!

calmante [kaw'mãtʃi] *adj* soothing ♦ *m* (*MED*) tranquillizer.

calmo/a ['kawmu/a] *adj* calm, tranquil.

calo ['kalu] *m* callus; (*no pé*) corn; **pisar nos** ~**s de alguém** (*fig*) to hit a (raw) nerve.

calombo [ka'lõbu] *m* lump; (*na estrada*) bump.

calor [ka'lo*] *m* heat; (*agradável*) warmth; (*fig*) warmth; **está** *ou* **faz** ~ it is hot; **estar com** ~ to be hot.

calorento/a [kalo'rẽtu/a] *adj* (*pessoa*) sensitive to heat; (*lugar*) hot.

caloria [calo'ria] *f* calorie.

caloroso/a [kalo'rozu/ɔza] *adj* warm; (*entusiástico*) enthusiastic; (*protesto*) fervent.

calota [ka'lɔta] *f* (*AUTO*) hubcap.

calote [ka'lɔtʃi] (*col*) *m* (*dívida*) bad debt; **dar o** ~ to welsh (on one's debts).

caloteiro/a [kalo'tejru/a] (*col*) *adj* unreliable ♦ *m/f* bad payer.

calouro/a [ka'loru/a] *m/f* (*EDUC*) fresher; (: *US*) freshman; (*noviço*) novice.

calúnia [ka'lunja] *f* slander.

caluniador(a) [kalunja'do*(a)] *adj* slanderous ♦ *m/f* slanderer.

caluniar [kalu'nja*] *vt* to slander.

calunioso/a [kalu'njozu/ɔza] *adj* slanderous.

calvície [kaw'visi] *f* baldness.

calvo/a ['kawvu/a] *adj* bald.

cama ['kama] *f* bed; ~ **de casal** double bed; ~ **de solteiro** single bed; **de** ~ (*doente*) ill (in bed); **ficar de** ~ to take to one's bed.

cama-beliche (*pl* **camas-beliches**) *f* bunk bed.

camada [ka'mada] *f* layer; (*de tinta*) coat.

camafeu [kama'few] *m* cameo.

câmara ['kamara] *f* chamber; (*FOTO*) camera; ~ **municipal** (*BR*) town council; (*PT*) town hall; **em** ~ **lenta** in slow motion.

câmara-ardente *f*: **estar exposto em** ~ to lie in state.

camarada [kama'rada] *adj* friendly, nice; (*preço*) good ♦ *m/f* comrade; (*sujeito*) guy/woman.

camaradagem [kamara'daʒẽ] *f* comradeship, camaraderie; **por** ~ out of friendliness.

câmara-de-ar (*pl* **câmaras-de-ar**) *f* inner tube.

camarão [kama'rãw] (*pl* **-ões**) *m* shrimp; (*graúdo*) prawn.

camareiro/a [kama'rejru/a] *m/f* cleaner/ chambermaid.

camarilha [kama'riʎa] *f* clique.

camarim [kama'rĩ] (*pl* **-ns**) *m* (*TEATRO*) dressing room.

Camarões [kama'rõjʃ] *m*: **o** ~ Cameroon.

camarões [kama'rõjʃ] *mpl de* **camarão**.

camarote [kama'rɔtʃi] *m* (*NÁUT*) cabin; (*TEATRO*) box.

cambada [kã'bada] *f* bunch, gang.

cambaio/a [kã'baju/a] *adj* (*mesa*) wobbly, rickety.

cambalacho [kãba'laʃu] *m* scam.

cambaleante [kãba'ljãtʃi] *adj* unsteady (on one's feet).

cambalear [kãba'lja*] *vi* to stagger, reel.

cambalhota [kãba'ʎɔta] *f* somersault.

cambar [kã'ba*] *vi* to lean.

cambial [kã'bjaw] (*pl* **-ais**) *adj* exchange *atr*.

cambiante [kã'bjãtʃi] *adj* changing, variable ♦ *m* (*cor*) shade.

cambiar [kã'bja*] *vt* to change; (*trocar*) to exchange.

câmbio ['kãbju] *m* (*dinheiro etc*) exchange; (*preço de câmbio*) rate of exchange; ~ **livre** free trade; ~ **negro** black market; ~ **oficial/paralelo** official/black market.

cambista [kã'biʃta] *m* (*de dinheiro*) money changer; (*BR: de ingressos*) (ticket-)tout.

Camboja [kã'bɔja] *m*: **o** ~ Cambodia.

cambojano/a [kãbo'ʒanu/a] *adj*, *m/f* Cambodian.

camburão [kãbu'rãw] (*pl* **-ões**) *m* police van.

camélia [ka'mɛlja] *f* camelia.

camelo [ka'melu] *m* camel; (*fig*) dunce.

camelô [kame'lo] *m* street pedlar.

camião [ka'mjãw] (*pl* **-ões**) (*PT*) *m* lorry (*BRIT*), truck (*US*).

caminhada [kami'ɲada] *f* walk.

caminhante [kami'ɲãtʃi] *m/f* walker.

caminhão [kami'ɲãw] (*pl* **-ões**) (*BR*) *m* lorry (*BRIT*), truck (*US*).

caminhar [kami'ɲa*] *vi* (*ir a pé*) to walk; (*processo*) to get under way; (*negócios*) to go, progress.

caminho [ka'miɲu] *m* way; (*vereda*) road, path; ~ **de ferro** (*PT*) railway (*BRIT*), railroad (*US*); **a meio** ~ halfway (there); **ser meio** ~ **andado** (*fig*) to be halfway there; **a** ~ on the way, en route; **cortar** ~ to take a short cut; **ir pelo mesmo** ~ to go the same way; **pôr-se a** ~ to set off.

caminhões [kami'ɲõjʃ] *mpl de* **caminhão**.

caminhoneiro/a [kamiɲo'nejru/a] *m/f* lorry

driver (*BRIT*), truck driver (*US*).

caminhonete [kamiɲo'nɛtʃi] *m* (*AUTO*) van.

camiões [ka'mjõjʃ] *mpl de* **camião**.

camioneta [kamjo'neta] (*PT*) *f* (*para passageiros*) coach; (*comercial*) van.

camionista [kamjo'niʃta] (*PT*) *m/f* lorry driver (*BRIT*), truck driver (*US*).

camisa [ka'miza] *f* shirt; ~ **de dormir** nightshirt; ~ **esporte/pólo/social** sports/polo/dress shirt; **mudar de** ~ (*ESPORTE*) to change sides.

camisa-de-força (*pl* **camisas-de-força**) *f* straitjacket.

camisa-de-vênus (*pl* **camisas-de-vênus**) *f* condom.

camiseta [kami'zɛta] (*BR*) *f* T-shirt; (*interior*) vest.

camisinha [kami'ziɲa] (*col*) *f* condom.

camisola [kami'zɔla] *f* (*BR*) nightdress; (*PT*: *pulôver*) sweater; ~ **interior** (*PT*) vest.

camomila [kamo'mila] *f* camomile.

campa ['kãpa] *f* (*de sepultura*) gravestone.

campainha [kãpa'iɲa] *f* bell.

campal [kã'paw] (*pl* **-ais**) *adj*: **batalha** ~ pitched battle; **missa** ~ open-air mass.

campanário [kãpa'narju] *m* (*torre*) church tower, steeple.

campanha [kã'paɲa] *f* (*MIL etc*) campaign; (*planície*) plain.

campeão/peã [kã'pjãw/'pjã] (*pl* **-ões/~s**) *m/f* champion.

campeonato [kãpjo'natu] *m* championship.

campestre [kã'pɛʃtri] *adj* rural, rustic.

campina [kã'pina] *f* prairie, grassland.

camping ['kãpĩ] (*BR*: *pl* ~**s**) *m* camping; (*lugar*) campsite.

campismo [kã'piʒmu] (*PT*) *m* camping; **parque de** ~ campsite.

campista [kã'piʃta] *m/f* camper.

campo [kãpu] *m* field; (*fora da cidade*) countryside; (*ESPORTE*) ground; (*acampamento*) camp; (*âmbito*) field; (*TÊNIS*) court.

camponês/esa [kãpo'neʃ/eza] *m/f* countryman/woman; (*agricultor*) farmer.

campus ['kãpuʃ] *m inv* campus.

camuflagem [kamu'flaʒẽ] *f* camouflage.

camuflar [kamu'fla*] *vt* to camouflage.

camundongo [kamũ'dõgu] (*BR*) *m* mouse.

camurça [ka'muxsa] *f* suede.

CAN (*BR*) *abr m* = **Correio Aéreo Nacional**.

cana ['kana] *f* cane; (*col*: *cadeia*) nick; (*de açúcar*) sugar cane; **ir em** ~ to be put behind bars.

Canadá [kana'da] *m*: **o** ~ Canada.

canadense [kana'dẽsi] *adj*, *m/f* Canadian.

canal [ka'naw] (*pl* **-ais**) *m* channel; (*de navegação*) canal; (*ANAT*) duct.

canalha [ka'naʎa] *f* rabble, mob ♦ *m/f* wretch, scoundrel.

canalização [kanaliza'sãw] *f* (*de água*) plumb-

NB: *European Portuguese adds the following consonants to certain words:* **b** (sú(b)dito, su(b)til); **c** (a(c)ção, a(c)cionista, a(c)to); **m** (inde(m)ne); **p** (ado(p)ção, ado(p)tar); *for further details see p. xiii.*

ing; (de gás) piping.
canalizador(a) [kanaliza'do*(a)] (PT) m/f plumber.
canalizar [kanali'za*] vt (água, esforços) to channel; (colocar canos) to lay pipes in.
canapé [kana'pɛ] m sofa.
canapé [kana'pɛ] m (CULIN) canapé.
canário [ka'narju] m canary.
canastra [ka'naʃtra] f (big) basket; (jogo) canasta.
canastrão/trona [kanaʃ'trãw/'trɔna] (pl -ões/ ~s) m/f ham actor/actress.
canavial [kana'vjaw] (pl -ais) m cane field.
canavieiro/a [kana'vjejru/a] adj sugar cane atr.
canção [kã'sãw] (pl -ões) f song; ~ de ninar lullaby.
cancela [kã'sɛla] f gate.
cancelamento [kãsela'mẽtu] m cancellation.
cancelar [kãse'la*] vt to cancel; (invalidar) to annul; (riscar) to cross out.
câncer ['kãse*] m cancer; C~ (ASTROLOGIA) Cancer.
canceriano/a [kãse'rjanu/a] adj, m/f Cancerian.
cancerígeno/a [kãse'riʒenu/a] adj carcinogenic.
cancerologista [kãserolo'ʒiʃta] m/f cancer specialist, oncologist.
canceroso/a [kãse'rozu/ɔza] adj (célula) cancerous ♦ m/f cancer sufferer.
canções [kã'sõjʃ] fpl de canção.
cancro ['kãkru] (PT) m cancer.
candango/a [kã'dãgu/a] m/f person from Brasília.
candeeiro [kãdʒi'ejru] m (BR) oil-lamp (ou gas-lamp); (PT) lamp.
candelabro [kãde'labru] m (castiçal) candlestick; (lustre) chandelier.
candente [kã'dẽtʃi] adj white hot; (fig) inflamed.
candidatar-se [kãdʒida'taxsi] vr: ~ a (vaga) to apply for; (presidência) to stand for.
candidato/a [kãdʒi'datu/a] m/f candidate; (a cargo) applicant.
candidatura [kãdʒida'tura] f candidature; (a cargo) application.
cândido/a ['kãdʒidu/a] adj (ingênuo) naive; (inocente) innocent.
candomblé [kãdõ'blɛ] m candomblé (Afro-Brazilian religion); (local) candomblé shrine.
candura [kã'dura] f (simplicidade) simplicity; (inocência) innocence.
caneca [ka'nɛka] f mug.
caneco [ka'nɛku] m tankard; pintar os ~s (col) to play up.
canela [ka'nɛla] f (especiaria) cinnamon; (ANAT) shin.
canelada [kane'lada] f kick in the shins; dei uma ~ na mesa I hit my shins on the table.
caneta [ka'neta] f pen; ~ esferográfica ballpoint pen; ~ pilot felt-tip pen; ~ seletora (COMPUT) light pen.

caneta-tinteiro (pl canetas-tinteiro) f fountain pen.
canga ['kãga] f beach wrap.
cangaceiro [kãga'sejru] (BR) m bandit.
cangote [kã'gotʃi] m (back of the) neck.
canguru [kãgu'ru] m kangaroo.
cânhamo ['kaɲamu] m hemp.
canhão [ka'ɲãw] (pl -ões) m (MIL) cannon; (GEO) canyon.
canhestro/a [ka'ɲeʃtru/a] adj awkward.
canhões [ka'ɲõjʃ] mpl de canhão.
canhoto/a [ka'ɲotu/a] adj left-handed ♦ m/f left-handed person ♦ m (de cheque) stub.
canibal [kani'baw] (pl -ais) m/f cannibal.
canibalismo [kaniba'liʒmu] m cannibalism.
caniço/a [ka'nisu/a] adj (col) skinny ♦ m reed.
canícula [ka'nikula] f searing heat.
canil [ka'niw] (pl -is) m kennel.
caninha [ka'niɲa] (col) f rum.
canino/a [ka'ninu/a] adj canine; (fome) terrible ♦ m canine.
canis [ka'niʃ] mpl de canil.
canivete [kani'vetʃi] m penknife; nem que chovam ~s whatever happens, come what may.
canja ['kãʒa] f (sopa) chicken broth; (col) cinch, pushover.
canjica [kã'ʒika] f maize porridge.
cano ['kanu] m pipe; (tubo) tube; (de arma de fogo) barrel; (de bota) top; ~ de esgoto sewer; entrar pelo ~ (col) to come off badly.
canoa [ka'noa] f canoe.
canoagem [ka'nwaʒẽ] f canoeing.
canoeiro/a [ka'nwejru/a] m/f canoeist.
canoísta [kano'iʃta] m/f canoeist.
canonizar [kanoni'za*] vt to canonize.
cansaço [kã'sasu] m tiredness.
cansado/a [kã'sadu/a] adj tired.
cansar [kã'sa*] vt (fatigar) to tire; (entediar) to bore ♦ vi (ficar cansado) to get tired; ~-se vr to get tired.
cansativo/a [kãsa'tʃivu/a] adj tiring; (tedioso) tedious.
canseira [kã'sejra] f (cansaço) weariness; (trabalho árduo) toil; dar ~ em alguém to wear sb out.
cantada [kã'tada] (col) f sweet talk; dar uma ~ em to sweet-talk.
cantado/a [kã'tadu/a] adj (missa) sung; (sotaque) sing-song.
cantar [kã'ta*] vt to sing; (respostas etc) to sing out; (col: seduzir) to sweet-talk ♦ vi to sing ♦ m song.
cantarolar [kãtaro'la*] vt to hum.
canteiro [kã'tejru] m stonemason; (de flores) flower bed; (de obra) site office.
cantiga [kã'tʃiga] f ballad; ~ de ninar lullaby.
cantil [kã'tʃiw] (pl -is) m canteen, flask.
cantina [kã'tʃina] f canteen.
cantis [kã'tʃiʃ] mpl de cantil.
canto ['kãtu] m corner; (lugar) place; (canção) song.
cantor(a) [kã'to*(a)] m/f singer.

cantoria [kãto'ria] *f* singing.

canudo [ka'nudu] *m* tube; *(para beber)* straw.

cão [kãw] *(pl* cães) *m* dog; *(pessoa)* rascal; ser *ou* estar um ~ de ruim *(col)* to be awful.

caolho/a [ka'oʎu/a] *adj* cross-eyed.

caos ['kaoʃ] *m* chaos.

caótico/a [ka'ɔtʃiku/a] *adj* chaotic.

capa ['kapa] *f (roupa)* cape; *(cobertura)* cover; livro de ~ dura/mole hardback/paperback (book).

capacete [kapa'setʃi] *m* helmet.

capacho [ka'paʃu] *m* door mat; *(fig)* toady.

capacidade [kapasi'dadʒi] *f* capacity; *(aptidão)* ability, competence; ser uma ~ *(pessoa)* to be brilliant; ~ ociosa *(COM)* idle capacity.

capacíssimo/a [kapa'sisimu/a] *adj superl de* capaz.

capacitar [kapasi'ta*] *vt*: ~ alguém a fazer/para algo to prepare sb to do/for sth; ~-se *vr*: ~-se de/de que to convince o.s. of/that.

capar [ka'pa*] *vt* to castrate, geld.

capataz [kapa'taʒ] *m* foreman.

capaz [ka'paʒ] *adj* able, capable; ser ~ de to be able to] *(ou* capable of); sou ~ de ... *(talvez)* I might ...; é ~ de chover hoje it might rain today.

capcioso/a [kap'sjozu/ɔza] *adj (pergunta)* trick; *(pessoa)* tricky.

capela [ka'pɛla] *f* chapel.

capelão [kape'lãw] *(pl* -ães) *m (REL)* chaplain.

Capemi [kape'mi] *(BR) abr f (= Caixa de Pecúlios, Pensões e Montepios dos Militares) military pension fund.*

capenga [ka'pẽga] *adj* lame ♦ *m/f* cripple.

capengar [kapẽ'ga*] *vi* to limp.

Capes *(BR) abr f (EDUC:* = *Coordenação de Aperfeiçoamento de Pessoal de Nível Superior) grant-awarding body.*

capeta [ka'peta] *m* devil; ele é um ~ he's a little devil.

capilar [kapi'la*] *adj* hair *atr.*

capim [ka'pĩ] *m* grass.

capinar [kapi'na*] *vt* to weed ♦ *vi* to weed; *(col)* to clear off.

capitães [kapi'tãjʃ] *mpl de* capitão.

capital [kapi'taw] *(pl* -ais) *adj, m* capital ♦ *f (cidade)* capital; ~ circulante *(COM)* circulating capital; ~ de giro *(COM)* working capital; ~ investido *(COM)* investment capital; ~ (em) ações *(COM)* share capital; ~ imobilizado *ou* fixo *(COM)* fixed capital; ~ integralizado *(COM)* paid-up capital; ~ próprio *ou* social *(COM)* equity capital; ~ de risco *(COM)* venture capital.

capitalismo [kapita'liʒmu] *m* capitalism.

capitalista [kapita'liʃta] *m/f* capitalist.

capitalizar [kapitali'za*] *vt (tirar proveito de)* to capitalize on; *(COM)* to capitalize.

capitanear [kapita'nja*] *vt* to command, head.

capitania [kapita'nia] *f:* ~ do porto port authority.

capitão [kapi'tãw] *(pl* -ães) *m* captain.

capitulação [kapitula'sãw] *f* capitulation, surrender.

capitular [kapitu'la*] *vt (falhas, causas)* to list; *(descrever)* to characterize; *(rendição)* to fix the terms of ♦ *vi* to capitulate; ~ alguém de algo to brand sb (as) sth.

capítulo [ka'pitulu] *m* chapter; *(de novela)* episode.

capô [ka'po] *m (AUTO)* bonnet *(BRIT),* hood *(US).*

capoeira [ka'pwejra] *f (PT)* hencoop; *(mata)* brushwood; *(jogo)* capoeira *(foot-fighting dance).*

capota [ka'pɔta] *f (AUTO)* hood, top.

capotar [kapo'ta*] *vi* to overturn.

capote [ka'pɔtʃi] *m* overcoat.

caprichar [kapri'ʃa*] *vi:* ~ em to take trouble over.

capricho [ka'priʃu] *m* whim, caprice; *(teimosia)* obstinacy; *(apuro)* care.

caprichoso/a [kapri'ʃozu/ɔza] *adj* capricious; *(com apuro)* meticulous.

Capricórnio [kapri'kɔxnju] *m* Capricorn.

capricorniano/a [kaprikox'njanu/a] *adj, m/f* Capricorn.

cápsula ['kapsula] *f* capsule.

captar [kap'ta*] *vt (atrair)* to win; *(RÁDIO)* to pick up; *(águas)* to collect, dam up; *(compreender)* to catch.

captura [kap'tura] *f* capture.

capturar [kaptu'ra*] *vt* to capture, seize.

capuz [ka'puʒ] *m* hood.

caquético/a [ka'kɛtʃiku/a] *adj* doddery.

caqui [ka'ki] *m* persimmon.

cáqui ['kaki] *adj* khaki.

cara ['kara] *f (de pessoa)* face; *(aspecto)* appearance ♦ *m (col)* guy; *(coragem)* courage, heart; ~ ou coroa? heads or tails?; de ~ straightaway; está na ~ it's obvious; dar de ~ com to bump into; estar com boa ~ to look well; *(comida)* to look good; não vou com a ~ dele *(col)* I'm not very keen on him; meter a ~ *(col)* to put one's back into it; ser a ~ de *(col)* to be the spitting image of; ter ~ de to look (like).

carabina [kara'bina] *f* rifle.

Caracas [ka'rakaʃ] *n* Caracas.

caracol [kara'kɔw] *(pl* -óis) *m* snail; *(de cabelo)* curl; *V tb* escada.

caracteres [karak'teriʃ] *mpl de* caráter.

característica [karakte'riʃtʃika] *f* characteristic, feature.

característico/a [karakte'riʃtʃiku/a] *adj* characteristic.

caracterização [karakteriza'sãw] *f* characterization; *(de ator)* make-up.

caracterizar [karakteri'za*] *vt* to characterize,

typify; (ator) to make up; ~-se vr to be characterized; (ator) to get in character.

cara-de-pau (pl **caras-de-pau**) adj brazen ♦ m/f: **ele é ~** he's very forward.

caraíba [kara'iba] adj Caribbean.

caramanchão [karamã'ʃãw] (pl **-ões**) m summerhouse.

caramba [ka'rãba] excl blimey (BRIT), gee (US); **quente pra ~** (col) really hot.

carambola [karã'bɔla] f carambole (fruit).

caramelo [kara'mɛlu] m caramel; (bala) toffee.

cara-metade (pl **caras-metades**) f better half.

caranguejo [karã'geʒu] m crab.

carão [ka'rãw] (pl **-ões**) m telling-off; **passar/levar um ~** to give/get a telling-off.

carapuça [kara'pusa] f cap; **enfiar a ~** to take the hint personally.

caratê [kara'te] m karate.

caráter [ka'rate*] (pl **caracteres**) m character; **de ~ social** of a social nature; **a ~** in character; **uma pessoa de ~** a person of hono(u)r.

caravana [kara'vana] f caravan.

carboidrato [kaxboi'dratu] m carbohydrate.

carbônico/a [kax'boniku/a] adj carbon atr.

carbonizar [kaxboni'za*] vt to carbonize; (queimar) to char.

carbono [kax'bɔnu] m carbon.

carburador [kaxbura'do*] m carburettor (BRIT), carburator (US).

carcaça [kax'kasa] f (esqueleto) carcass; (armação) frame; (de navio) hull.

carcamano/a [kaxka'manu/a] m/f Italian-Brazilian.

cárcere ['kaxseri] m prison.

carcereiro/a [kaxse'rejru/a] m/f jailer, warder.

carcomido/a [kaxko'midu/a] adj worm-eaten; (rosto) pock-marked, pitted.

cardápio [kax'dapju] (BR) m menu.

cardeal [kax'dʒjaw] (pl **-ais**) adj, m cardinal.

cardíaco/a [kax'dʒiaku/a] adj cardiac ♦ m/f person with a heart condition; **ataque ~** heart attack; **parada cardíaca** cardiac arrest.

cardigã [kaxdʒi'gã] m cardigan.

cardinal [kaxdʒi'naw] (pl **-ais**) adj cardinal.

cardiológico/a [kaxdʒjo'lɔʒiku/a] adj heart atr.

cardiologista [kaxdʒjolo'ʒiʃta] m/f heart specialist, cardiologist.

cardume [kax'dumi] m (peixes) shoal.

careca [ka'rɛka] adj bald ♦ f baldness; **estar ~ de fazer/saber** (col) to be used to doing/know full well.

carecer [kare'se*] vi: **~ de** (ter falta) to lack; (precisar) to need.

careiro/a [ka'rejru/a] adj expensive.

carência [ka'rẽsja] f (falta) lack, shortage; (necessidade) need; (privação) deprivation.

carente [ka'rẽtʃi] adj wanting; (pessoa) needy, deprived; (de carinho) in need of affection.

carestia [kareʃ'tʃia] f high cost; (preços altos)

high prices pl; (escassez) scarcity.

careta [ka'reta] adj (col) straight, square ♦ f grimace; **fazer uma ~** to pull a face.

carga ['kaxga] f load; (de um navio) cargo; (ato de carregar) loading; (ELET) charge; (fig: peso) burden; (MIL) attack, charge; **dar ~ em** (COMPUT) to boot (up); **voltar à ~** to insist; **~ d'água** heavy downpour; **~ horária** workload; **~ aérea** air cargo.

cargo ['kaxgu] m (responsabilidade) responsibility; (função) post; **a ~ de** in charge of; **ter a ~** to be in charge of; **tomar a ~** to take charge of; **~ honorífico** honorary post; **~ de confiança** position of trust; **~ público** public office.

cargueiro [kax'gejru] m cargo ship.

cariar [ka'rja*] vt, vi to decay.

Caribe [ka'ribi] m: **o ~** the Caribbean (Sea).

caricatura [karika'tura] f caricature.

caricatural [karikatu'raw] (pl **-ais**) adj (fig) grotesque.

caricaturar [karikatu'ra*] vt to caricature.

caricaturista [karikatu'riʃta] m/f caricaturist.

carícia [ka'risja] f caress.

caridade [kari'dadʒi] f charity; **obra de ~** charity.

caridoso/a [kari'dozu/ɔza] adj charitable.

cárie ['kari] f tooth decay; (MED) caries.

carimbar [karĩ'ba*] vt to stamp; (no correio) to postmark.

carimbo [ka'rĩbu] m stamp; (postal) postmark.

carinho [ka'riɲu] m affection, fondness; (carícia) caress; **fazer ~** to caress; **com ~** affectionately; (com cuidado) with care.

carinhoso/a [kari'ɲozu/ɔza] adj affectionate.

carioca [ka'rjɔka] adj of Rio de Janeiro ♦ m/f native of Rio de Janeiro ♦ m (PT: café) type of weak coffee.

carisma [ka'riʒma] m charisma.

carismático/a [kariʒ'matʃiku/a] adj charismatic.

caritativo/a [karita'tʃivu/a] adj charitable.

carnal [kax'naw] (pl **-ais**) adj carnal; **primo ~** first cousin.

carnaval [kaxna'vaw] (pl **-ais**) m carnival; (fig) mess; **conhecer alguém de outros carnavais** (col) to know sb from way back.

carnavalesco/a [kaxnava'leʃku/a] adj (festa) carnival atr; (pessoa) keen on carnival; (fig) grotesque ♦ m/f carnival organizer.

carne ['kaxni] f flesh; (CULIN) meat; **em ~ e osso** in the flesh; **ser de ~ e osso** to be human; **~ assada** roast beef.

carnê [kax'ne] m (para compras) payment book.

carneiro [kax'nejru] m sheep; (macho) ram; **perna/costeleta de ~** leg of lamb/lamb chop.

carniça [kax'nisa] f carrion; **pular ~** to play leapfrog.

carnificina [kaxnifi'sina] f slaughter.

carnívoro/a [kax'nivoru/a] adj carnivorous ♦ m carnivore.

carnudo/a [kax'nudu/a] *adj* plump, fleshy; (*col*) beefy; (*lábios*) thick; (*fruta*) fleshy.

caro/a ['karu/a] *adj* dear, expensive; (*estimado*) dear; **sair** ~ to work out expensive; **cobrar/pagar** ~ to charge a lot/ pay dearly.

carochinha [karo'ʃiɲa] *f V* **conto**.

caroço [ka'rosu] *m* (*de frutos*) stone; (*endurecimento*) lump.

carões [ka'rõjʃ] *mpl de* **carão**.

carola [ka'rɔla] (*col*) *m/f* pious person.

carona [ka'rɔna] *f* lift; **viajar de** ~ to hitchhike; **pegar uma** ~ to get a lift.

carpete [kax'petʃi] *m* (fitted) carpet.

carpintaria [kaxpita'ria] *f* carpentry.

carpinteiro [kaxpĩ'tejru] *m* carpenter; (*TEATRO*) stagehand.

carranca [ka'xãka] *f* frown, scowl.

carrancudo/a [kaxã'kudu/a] *adj* (*soturno*) sullen; (*semblante*) scowling.

carrapato [kaxa'patu] *m* (*inseto*) tick; (*pessoa*) hanger-on.

carrapicho [kaxa'piʃu] *m* (*do cabelo*) bun.

carrasco [ka'xaʃku] *m* executioner; (*fig*) tyrant.

carrear [ka'xja*] *vt* (*transportar*) to transport; (*arrastar*) to carry; (*acarretar*) to bring on.

carreata [kaxe'ata] *f* motorcade.

carregado/a [kaxe'gadu/a] *adj* loaded, laden; (*semblante*) sullen; (*céu*) dark; (*ambiente*) tense.

carregador [kaxega'do*] *m* porter.

carregamento [kaxega'mẽtu] *m* (*ação*) loading; (*carga*) load, cargo.

carregar [kaxe'ga*] *vt* to load; (*levar*) to carry; (*bateria*) to charge; (*PT: apertar*) to press; (*levar para longe*) to take away ♦ *vi*: ~ **em** (*pôr em demasia*) to overdo, put too much; (*pôr enfase*) to bring out.

carreira [ka'xejra] *f* (*ação de correr*) run, running; (*profissão*) career; (*TURFE*) race; (*NÁUT*) slipway; (*fileira*) row; **às** ~**s** in a hurry; **dar uma** ~ to go quickly; **fazer** ~ to make a career; **arrepiar** ~ to abandon one's career.

carreirista [kaxej'riʃta] *adj, m/f* careerist.

carreta [ka'xeta] *f* cart.

carreteiro [kaxe'tejru] *m* cart driver.

carretel [kaxe'tɛw] (*pl* -**éis**) *m* spool, reel.

carreto [ka'xetu] *m* freight.

carril [ka'xiw] (*pl* -**is**) (*PT*) *m* (*FERRO*) rail.

carrilhão [kaxi'ʎãw] (*pl* -**ões**) *m* chime.

carrinho [ka'xiɲu] *m* (*para bagagem, compras*) trolley; (*brinquedo*) toy car; ~ (**de criança**) pram; ~ **de mão** wheelbarrow; ~ **de chá** tea trolley.

carris [ka'xiʃ] *mpl de* **carril**.

carro ['kaxo] *m* (*automóvel*) car; (*de bois*) cart; (*de mão*) handcart, barrow; (*de máquina de escrever*) carriage; **pôr o** ~ **adiante**

dos bois (*fig*) to put the cart before the horse; ~ **alegórico** float; ~ **de corrida** racing car; ~ **de passeio** saloon car; ~ **de praça** cab; ~ **de bombeiro** fire engine; ~ **esporte** sports car.

carroça [ka'xɔsa] *f* cart, waggon.

carroçeria [kaxose'ria] *f* (*AUTO*) bodywork.

carro-chefe (*pl* **carros-chefes**) *m* (*de desfile*) main float; (*fig*) flagship, centrepiece (*BRIT*), centerpiece (*US*).

carrocinha [kaxo'siɲa] *f* wagon.

carro-forte (*pl* **carros-fortes**) *m* security van.

carrossel [kaxo'sɛw] (*pl* -**éis**) *m* merry-go-round.

carruagem [ka'xwaʒẽ] (*pl* -**ns**) *f* carriage, coach.

carta ['kaxta] *f* letter; (*de jogar*) card; (*mapa*) chart; ~ **aberta** open letter; ~ **aérea** airmail letter; ~ **registrada** registered letter; ~ **de apresentação** letter of introduction; ~ **de crédito/intenção** letter of credit/intent; ~ **de condução** (*PT*) driving licence (*BRIT*), driver's license (*US*); **dar as** ~**s** to deal; **dar/ter** ~ **branca** to give/have carte blanche; **pôr as** ~**s na mesa** (*fig*) to put one's cards on the table; ~ **magna** charter; ~ **patente** patent.

carta-bomba (*pl* **cartas-bomba**) *f* letter bomb.

cartada [kax'tada] *f* (*fig*) move.

cartão [kax'tãw] (*pl* -**ões**) *m* card; (*PT: material*) cardboard; ~ **de visita** (calling) card; ~ **de crédito** credit card; ~ **comercial** business card.

cartão-postal (*pl* **cartões-postais**) *m* postcard.

cartaz [kax'taʒ] *m* poster, bill (*US*); **ter** ~ (*ser famoso*) to be well-known; (*ter popularidade*) to be popular; (**estar**) **em** ~ (*TEATRO, CINEMA*) (to be) showing.

cartear [kax'tʃja*] *vt* to play ♦ *vi* to play cards.

carteira [kax'tejra] *f* (*móvel*) desk; (*para dinheiro*) wallet; (*de ações*) portfolio; ~ **de identidade** identity card; ~ **de motorista** driving licence (*BRIT*), driver's license (*US*).

carteiro [kax'tejru] *m* postman (*BRIT*), mailman (*US*).

cartel [kax'tɛw] (*pl* -**éis**) *m* cartel.

cartilagem [kaxtʃi'laʒẽ] (*pl* -**ns**) *f* (*ANAT*) cartilage.

cartões [kax'tõjʃ] *mpl de* **cartão**.

cartografia [kaxtogra'fia] *f* cartography.

cartola [kax'tɔla] *f* top hat.

cartolina [kaxto'lina] *f* card.

cartomante [kaxto'mãtʃi] *m/f* fortune-teller.

cartório [kax'tɔrju] *m* registry office.

cartucho [kax'tuʃu] *m* cartridge; (*saco de papel*) packet.

cartum [kax'tũ] (*pl* -**ns**) *m* cartoon.

cartunista [kaxtu'niʃta] *m/f* cartoonist.

NB: European Portuguese adds the following consonants to certain words: **b** (sú(b)dito, su(b)til); **c** (a(c)ção, a(c)cionista, a(c)to); **m** (inde(m)ne); **p** (ado(p)ção, ado(p)tar); *for further details see p. xiii.*

cartuns [kax'tũʃ] *mpl de* **cartum**.
caruncho [ka'rũʃu] *m* (*inseto*) woodworm.
carvalho [kax'vaʎu] *m* oak.
carvão [kax'vãw] (*pl* -ões) *m* coal; (*de madeira*) charcoal.
carvoeiro [kaxvo'ejru] *m* coal merchant.
carvões [kax'võjʃ] *mpl de* **carvão**.
casa ['kaza] *f* house; (*lar*) home; (*COM*) firm; (*MAT*: *decimal*) place; ~ **de botão** buttonhole; ~ **de câmbio** exchange bureau; ~ **de pensão** boarding house; ~ **de saúde** hospital; ~ **da moeda** mint; ~ **de banho** (*PT*) bathroom; **em/para** ~ (at) home/home; ~ **e comida** board and lodging; **ser de** ~ to be like one of the family; **ter dez anos de** ~ (*numa firma*) to have ten years' service behind one; ~ **de campo** country house; ~ **de cômodos** tenement; ~ **de máquinas** engine room; ~ **popular** ≈ council house.
casaca [ka'zaka] *f* tails *pl*; **virar a** ~ to become a turncoat.
casacão [kaza'kãw] (*pl* -ões) *m* overcoat.
casaco [ka'zaku] *m* coat; (*paletó*) jacket; ~ **de peles** fur coat.
casacões [kaza'kõjʃ] *mpl de* **casacão**.
casa-forte (*pl* **casas-fortes**) *f* vault.
casa-grande (*pl* **casas-grandes**) *f* plantation owner's house.
casal [ka'zaw] (*pl* -ais) *m* couple.
casamenteiro/a [kazamẽ'tejru/a] *adj* wedding *atr*.
casamento [kaza'mẽtu] *m* marriage; (*boda*) wedding; (*fig*) combination.
casar [ka'za*] *vt* to marry; (*combinar*) to match (up); ~**-se** *vr* to get married; (*harmonizar-se*) to combine well.
casarão [kaza'rãw] (*pl* -ões) *m* mansion.
casca ['kaʃka] *f* (*de árvore*) bark; (*de banana*) skin; (*de ferida*) scab; (*de laranja*) peel; (*de nozes, ovos*) shell; (*de milho etc*) husk; (*de pão*) crust.
casca-grossa (*pl* **cascas-grossas**) *adj* coarse, uneducated.
cascalho [kaʃ'kaʎu] *m* gravel; (*na praia*) shingle.
cascão [kaʃ'kãw] *m* crust; (*sujeira*) grime.
cascata [kaʃ'kata] *f* waterfall; (*col*: *mentira*) tall story.
cascateiro/a [kaʃka'tejru/a] (*col*) *adj* bigmouthed ♦ *m/f* storyteller.
cascavel [kaʃka'vɛw] (*pl* -éis) *m* (*serpente*) rattlesnake.
casco ['kaʃku] *m* (*crânio*) skull; (*de animal*) hoof; (*de navio*) hull; (*para bebidas*) empty bottle; (*de tartaruga*) shell.
cascudo [kaʃ'kudu] *m* rap on the head.
casebre [ka'zɛbri] *m* hovel, shack.
caseiro/a [ka'zejru/a] *adj* (*produtos*) homemade; (*pessoa, vida*) domestic ♦ *m/f* housekeeper.
caserna [ka'zɛxna] *f* barracks *pl*.
casmurro/a [kaʒ'muxu/a] *adj* introverted.
caso ['kazu] *m* case; (*tb*: ~ *amoroso*) affair;

(*estória*) story ♦ *conj* in case, if; **de** ~ **pensado** deliberately; **no** ~ **de** in case (of); **em todo** ~ in any case; **neste** ~ in that case; ~ **necessário** if necessary; **criar** ~ to cause trouble; **fazer pouco** ~ **de** to belittle; **não fazer** ~ **de** to ignore; **vir ao** ~ to be relevant; ~ **de emergência** emergency.
casório [ka'zɔrju] (*col*) *m* wedding.
caspa ['kaʃpa] *f* dandruff.
casquinha [kaʃ'kiɲa] *f* (*de sorvete*) cone; (*pele*) skin.
cassação [kasa'sãw] *f* withholding; (*de políticos*) banning.
cassar [ka'sa*] *vt* (*direitos, licença*) to cancel, withhold; (*políticos*) to ban.
cassete [ka'sɛtʃi] *m* cassette.
cassetete [kase'tɛtʃi] *m* truncheon (*BRIT*), nightstick (*US*).
cassino [ka'sinu] *m* casino.
casta ['kaʃta] *f* caste; (*estirpe*) lineage.
castanha [kaʃ'taɲa] *f* chestnut; ~ **de caju** cashew nut.
castanha-do-pará [-pa'ra] (*pl* **castanhas-do-pará**) *f* Brazil nut.
castanho/a [kaʃ'taɲu/a] *adj* brown.
castanheiro [kaʃta'ɲejru] *m* chestnut tree.
castanholas [kaʃta'ɲɔlaʃ] *fpl* castanets.
castelo [kaʃ'tɛlu] *m* castle; **fazer** ~**s no ar** (*fig*) to build castles in the air.
castiçal [kaʃtʃi'saw] (*pl* -ais) *m* candlestick.
castiço/a [kaʃ'tʃisu/a] *adj* pure; (*de boa casta*) of good stock, pedigree *atr*.
castidade [kaʃtʃi'dadʒi] *f* chastity.
castigar [kaʃtʃi'ga*] *vt* to punish; (*aperfeiçoar*) to perfect; (*col*: *tocar*) to play.
castigo [kaʃ'tʃigu] *m* punishment; (*fig*: *mortificação*) pain; **estar/ficar de** ~ (*criança*) to be getting punished/be punished.
casto/a ['kaʃtu/a] *adj* chaste.
castor [kaʃ'to*] *m* beaver.
castrar [kaʃ'tra*] *vt* to castrate.
casual [ka'zwaw] (*pl* -ais) *adj* chance *atr*, accidental; (*fortuito*) fortuitous.
casualidade [kazwali'dadʒi] *f* chance; (*acidente*) accident; **por** ~ by chance, accidentally.
casulo [ka'zulu] *m* (*de sementes*) pod; (*de insetos*) cocoon.
cata ['kata] *f*: **à** ~ **de** in search of.
cataclismo [kata'kliʒmu] *m* cataclysm.
catacumbas [kata'kũbaʃ] *fpl* catacombs.
catalizador(a) [kataliza'do*(a)] *adj* catalytic ♦ *m* catalyst.
catalogar [katalo'ga*] *vt* to catalogue (*BRIT*), catalog (*US*).
catálogo [ka'talogu] *m* catalogue (*BRIT*), catalog (*US*); ~ **(telefônico)** telephone directory.
Catalunha [kata'luɲa] *f*: **a** ~ Catalónia.
catapora [kata'pora] (*BR*) *f* chickenpox.
Catar [ka'ta*] *m*: **o** ~ Qatar.
catar [ka'ta*] *vt* to pick (up); (*procurar*) to look for, search for; (*arroz*) to clean; (*re-*

colher) to collect, gather.
catarata [kata'rata] *f* waterfall; (*MED*) cataract.
catarro [ka'taxu] *m* catarrh.
catártico/a [ka'taxtʃiku/a] *adj* cathartic.
catástrofe [ka'taʃtrɔfi] *f* catastrophe.
catastrófico/a [kataʃ'trɔfiku/a] *adj* catastrophic.
catatau [kata'tau] *m*: **um ~ de** a lot of.
cata-vento *m* weathercock.
catecismo [kate'siʒmu] *m* catechism.
cátedra ['katedra] *f* chair.
catedral [kate'draw] (*pl* **-ais**) *f* cathedral.
catedrático/a [kate'dratʃiku/a] *m/f* professor.
categoria [katego'ria] *f* category; (*social*) rank; (*qualidade*) quality; **de alta ~** first-rate.
categórico/a [kate'gɔriku/a] *adj* categorical.
categorizar [kategori'za*] *vt* to categorize.
catequizar [kateki'za*] *vt* to talk round; (*REL*) to catechize.
catinga [ka'tʃĩga] *f* stench, stink.
catinguento/a [katʃĩ'gẽtu/a] *adj* smelly.
catiripapo [katʃiri'papu] *m* punch.
cativante [katʃi'vãtʃi] *adj* captivating; (*atraente*) charming.
cativar [katʃi'va*] *vt* (*escravizar*) to enslave; (*fascinar*) to captivate; (*atrair*) to charm.
cativeiro [katʃi'vejru] *m* captivity; (*escravidão*) slavery; (*cadeia*) prison.
cativo/a [ka'tʃivu/a] *m/f* (*escravo*) slave; (*prisioneiro*) prisoner.
catolicismo [katoli'siʒmu] *m* catholicism.
católico/a [ka'tɔliku/a] *adj*, *m/f* catholic.
catorze [ka'toxzi] *num* fourteen; *V tb* **cinco**.
catucar [katu'ka*] *vt* = **cutucar**.
caturrice [katu'xisi] *f* obstinacy.
caução [kaw'sãw] (*pl* **-ões**) *f* security, guarantee; (*JUR*) bail; **prestar ~** to give bail; **sob ~** on bail.
caucionante [kawsjo'nãtʃi] *m/f* guarantor.
caucionar [kawsjo'na*] *vt* to guarantee, stand surety for; (*JUR*) to stand bail for.
cauções [kaw'sõjʃ] *fpl de* **caução**.
cauda ['kawda] *f* tail; (*de vestido*) train.
caudal [kaw'daw] (*pl* **-ais**) *m* torrent.
caudaloso/a [kawda'lozu/ɔza] *adj* torrential.
caudilho [kaw'dʒiʎu] *m* leader, chief.
caule ['kauli] *m* stalk, stem.
causa ['kawza] *f* cause; (*motivo*) motive, reason; (*JUR*) lawsuit, case; **por ~ de** because of; **em ~** in question.
causador(a) [kawza'do*(a)] *adj* which caused ♦ *m* cause.
causar [kaw'za*] *vt* to cause, bring about.
cáustico/a ['kawʃtʃiku/a] *adj* caustic.
cautela [kaw'tɛla] *f* caution; (*senha*) ticket; (*título*) share certificate; **~ (de penhor)** pawn ticket.
cautelar [kawte'la*] *adj* precautionary.

cauteloso/a [kawte'lozu/ɔza] *adj* cautious, wary.
cauterizar [kawteri'za*] *vt* to cauterize.
cava ['kava] *f* (*de manga*) armhole.
cavação [kava'sãw] (*col*) *f* wheeling and dealing.
cavaco [ka'vaku] *m*: **~s do ofício** occupational hazards.
cavado/a [ka'vadu/a] *adj* (*olhos*) sunken; (*roupa*) low-cut.
cavador(a) [kava'do*(a)] *adj* go-getting ♦ *m/f* go-getter.
cavala [ka'vala] *f* mackerel.
cavalar [kava'la*] *adj* enormous, huge.
cavalaria [kavala'ria] *f* (*MIL*) cavalry; (*instituição medieval*) chivalry.
cavalariça [kavala'risa] *f* stable.
cavaleiro [kava'lejru] *m* rider, horseman; (*medieval*) knight.
cavalete [kava'letʃi] *m* stand; (*FOTO*) tripod; (*de pintor*) easel; (*de mesa*) trestle; (*do violino*) bridge.
cavalgar [kavaw'ga*] *vt* to ride ♦ *vi*: **~ em** to ride on; **~ (sobre)** to jump over.
cavalheiresco/a [kavaʎej'reʃku/a] *adj* courteous, gallant, gentlemanly.
cavalheiro/a [kava'ʎejru/a] *adj* courteous, gallant ♦ *m* gentleman; (*DANÇA*) partner.
cavalinho-de-pau [kava'liɲu-] (*pl* **cavalinhos-de-pau**) *m* rocking horse.
cavalo [ka'valu] *m* horse; (*XADREZ*) knight; (*pessoa*): **ser um ~** to be rude; **a ~** on horseback; **50 ~s(-vapor), 50 ~s (de força)** 50 horsepower; **quantos ~s tem esse carro?** how many horsepower is that car?; **fazer de algo um ~ de batalha** to make a mountain out of a molehill about sth; **tirar o ~ da chuva** (*fig*) to drop the idea; **~ de corrida** racehorse.
cavalo-marinho (*pl* **cavalos-marinhos**) *m* seahorse.
cavanhaque [kava'ɲaki] *m* goatee (beard).
cavaquinho [kava'kiɲu] *m* small guitar.
cavar [ka'va*] *vt* to dig; (*decote*) to lower; (*esforçar-se para obter*) to try to get ♦ *vi* to dig; (*animal*) to burrow; (*esforçar-se*) to try hard; (*fig*) to delve; **~ a vida** to earn one's living.
cave ['kavi] (*PT*) *f* wine-cellar.
caveira [ka'vejra] *f* skull; **fazer a ~ de alguém** (*col*) to blacken sb's name.
caverna [ka'vɛxna] *f* cavern.
cavernoso/a [kavex'nozu/ɔza] *adj* (*voz*) booming; (*pessoa*) horrible.
caviar [ka'vja*] *m* caviar.
cavidade [kavi'dadʒi] *f* cavity.
cavilha [ka'viʎa] *f* (*de madeira*) peg, dowel; (*de metal*) bolt.
cavo/a ['kavu/a] *adj* (*côncavo*) concave.
caxias [ka'ʃiaʃ] *adj inv* overdisciplined ♦ *m/f*

inv stickler for discipline.

caxumba [ka'ʃuba] *f* mumps *sg*.

CBA *abr f* = **Confederação Brasileira de Automobilismo.**

CBAt *abr f* = **Confederação Brasileira de Atletismo.**

CBD *abr f* = **Confederação Brasileira de Desportos.**

CBF *abr f* = **Confederação Brasileira de Futebol.**

CBT *abr m* = **Código Brasileiro de Telecomunicações.**

CBTU *abr f* = **Companhia Brasileira de Trens Urbanos.**

CCT (*BR*) *abr m* = **Conselho Científico e Tecnológico.**

c/c *abr* (= *conta corrente*) c/a.

CDB *abr m* = **Certificado de Depósito Bancário.**

CDC (*BR*) *abr m* = **Conselho de Desenvolvimento Comercial.**

CDDPH (*BR*) *abr m* = **Conselho de Defesa dos Direitos da Pessoa Humana.**

CDI (*BR*) *abr m* = **Certificado de Depósito Interbancário;** = **Conselho de Desenvolvimento Industrial.**

cê [se] (*col*) *pron* = **você.**

cear [sja*] *vt* to have for supper ♦ *vi* to dine.

cearense [sea'rẽsi] *adj* from Ceará ♦ *m/f* person from Ceará.

cebola [se'bola] *f* onion.

cebolinha [sebo'liɲa] *f* spring onion.

Cebrae (*BR*) *abr f* = **Centro de Apoio à Pequena e Média Empresa.**

Cebrap *abr m* = **Centro Brasileiro de Análise e Planejamento.**

cecear [se'sja*] *vi* to lisp.

cê-cedilha (*pl* **cês-cedilhas**) *m* c cedilla.

ceceio [se'seju] *m* lisp.

cê-dê-efe [-'ɛfi] (*col*: *pl* ~**s**) *m/f* swot.

ceder [se'de*] *vt* to give up; (*dar*) to hand over; (*emprestar*) to lend ♦ *vi* to give in, yield; (*porta, calça etc*) to give (way); ~ **a** to give in to.

cedilha [se'dʒiʎa] *f* cedilla.

cedo ['sedu] *adv* early; (*em breve*) soon; **mais ~ ou mais tarde** sooner or later; **o mais ~ possível** as soon as possible.

cedro ['sɛdru] *m* cedar.

cédula ['sɛdula] *f* (*moeda-papel*) banknote; (*eleitoral*) ballot paper.

CEE *abr f* (= *Comunidade Econômica Européia*) EEC.

CEF (*BR*) *abr f* (= *Caixa Econômica Federal*) federal bank.

cegar [se'ga*] *vt* to blind; (*ofuscar*) to dazzle; (*tesoura*) to blunt ♦ *vi* (*ofuscar*) to be dazzling.

cego/a ['sɛgu/a] *adj* blind; (*total*) complete, total; (*tesoura*) blunt ♦ *m/f* blind man/woman; **às cegas** blindly; **ser ~ por alguém** to be mad about sb.

cegonha [se'goɲa] *f* stork.

cegueira [se'gejra] *f* blindness.

CEI (*BR*) *abr f* (= *Comissão Especial de Inquérito*) commission of inquiry.

ceia ['seja] *f* supper.

ceifa ['sejfa] *f* harvest; (*fig*) destruction.

ceifar [sej'fa*] *vt* to reap, harvest; (*vidas*) to destroy.

cela ['sɛla] *f* cell.

celebração [selebra'sãw] (*pl* **-ões**) *f* celebration.

celebrar [sele'bra*] *vt* to celebrate; (*exaltar*) to praise; (*acordo*) to seal.

célebre ['sɛlebri] *adj* famous, well-known.

celebridade [selebri'dadʒi] *f* celebrity.

celebrizar [selebri'za*] *vt* to make famous; ~**se** *vr* to become famous.

celeiro [se'lejru] *m* granary; (*depósito*) barn.

célere ['sɛleri] *adj* swift, quick.

celeste [se'lɛʃtʃi] *adj* celestial, heavenly.

celeuma [se'lewma] *f* pandemonium, uproar.

celibatário/a [seliba'tarju/a] *adj* unmarried, single ♦ *m/f* bachelor/spinster.

celibato [seli'batu] *m* celibacy.

celofane [selo'fani] *m* cellophane.

celta ['sɛwta] *adj* Celtic ♦ *m/f* Celt.

célula ['sɛlula] *f* (*BIO, ELET*) cell.

celular [selu'la*] *adj* cellular.

celulite [selu'litʃi] *f* cellulite.

celulose [selu'lɔzi] *f* cellulose.

cem [sẽ] *num* hundred; **ser ~ por cento** (*fig*) to be great; *V tb* **cinqüenta.**

cemitério [semi'tɛrju] *m* cemetery, graveyard.

cena ['sɛna] *f* scene; (*palco*) stage; **em ~** on the stage; **levar à ~** to stage; **fazer uma ~** to make a scene.

cenário [se'narju] *m* (*TEATRO*) scenery; (*CINEMA*) scenario; (*de um acontecimento*) scene, setting; (*panorama*) view.

cenho ['sɛɲu] *m* face.

cênico/a ['seniku/a] *adj* (*TEATRO*) stage *atr*; (*CINEMA*) set *atr*.

cenografia [senogra'fia] *f* set design.

cenógrafo/a [se'nɔgrafu/a] *m/f* (*TEATRO*) set designer.

cenoura [se'nora] *f* carrot.

censo ['sẽsu] *m* census.

censor(a) [sẽ'so*(a)] *m/f* censor.

censura [sẽ'sura] *f* (*POL etc*) censorship; (*reprovação*) censure, criticism; (*repreensão*) reprimand.

censurar [sẽsu'ra*] *vt* (*reprovar*) to censure; (*filme, livro etc*) to censor.

censurável [sẽsu'ravew] (*pl* **-eis**) *adj* reprehensible.

centavo [sẽ'tavu] *m* cent; **estar sem um ~** to be penniless.

centeio [sẽ'teju] *m* rye.

centelha [sẽ'teʎa] *f* spark; (*fig*) flash.

centena [sẽ'tɛna] *f* hundred; **às ~s** in hundreds.

centenário/a [sẽte'narju/a] *adj* centenary ♦ *m/f* centenarian ♦ *m* centenary, centennial.

centésimo/a [sẽ'tɛzimu/a] *adj* hundredth ♦ *m*

hundredth (part).

centígrado [sē'tʃigradu] *m* centigrade.

centilitro [sētʃi'litru] *m* centilitre (*BRIT*), centiliter (*US*).

centímetro [sē'tʃimetru] *m* centimetre (*BRIT*), centimeter (*US*).

cento ['sētu] *m*: ~ **e um** one hundred and one; **por** ~ per cent.

centopeia [sēto'peja] *f* centipede.

central [sē'traw] (*pl* -**ais**) *adj* central ♦ *f* (*de polícia etc*) head office; ~ **elétrica** (electric) power station; ~ **telefônica** telephone exchange.

centralização [sētraliza'sãw] *f* centralization.

centralizar [sētrali'za*] *vt* to centralize; ~-**se** *vr* to be centralized.

centrar [sē'tra*] *vt* to centre (*BRIT*), center (*US*).

centro ['sētru] *m* centre (*BRIT*), center (*US*); (*de uma cidade*) town centre; ~ **das atenções** centre of attention; ~ **de custo/lucro** (*COM*) cost/profit centre; ~ **de mesa** centrepiece (*BRIT*), centerpiece (*US*).

centroavante [sētroa'vātʃi] *m* (*FUTEBOL*) centre forward.

CEP ['sɛpi] (*BR*) *abr m* (= *Código de Endereçamento Postal*) postcode (*BRIT*), zip code (*US*).

cepo ['sepu] *m* (*toco*) stump; (*toro*) log.

céptico/a *etc* ['septiku/a] (*PT*) = **cético** *etc*.

ceptro ['setru] (*PT*) *m* = **cetro**.

cera ['sera] *f* wax; **fazer** ~ (*fig*) to dawdle, waste time.

cerâmica [se'ramika] *f* pottery; (*arte*) ceramics *sg*.

cerâmico/a [se'ramiku/a] *adj* ceramic.

ceramista [sera'miʃta] *m/f* potter.

cerca ['sexka] *f* (*de madeira, arame*) fence ♦ *prep*: ~ **de** (*aproximadamente*) around, about; ~ **viva** hedge.

cercado/a [sex'kadu/a] *adj* surrounded; (*com cerca*) fenced in ♦ *m* enclosure; (*para animais*) pen; (*para crianças*) playpen.

cercanias [sexka'niaʃ] *fpl* (*arredores*) outskirts; (*vizinhança*) neighbourhood *sg* (*BRIT*), neighborhood *sg* (*US*).

cercar [sex'ka*] *vt* to enclose; (*pôr cerca em*) to fence in; (*rodear*) to surround; (*assediar*) to besiege.

cercear [sex'sja*] *vt* (*liberdade*) to curtail, restrict.

cerco ['sexku] *m* encirclement; (*MIL*) siege; **pôr** ~ **a** to besiege.

cereal [se'rjaw] (*pl* -**ais**) *m* cereal.

cerebral [sere'braw] (*pl* -**ais**) *adj* cerebral, brain *atr*.

cérebro ['serebru] *m* brain; (*fig*) intelligence, brains *pl*.

cereja [se'reʒa] *f* cherry.

cerejeira [sere'ʒejra] *f* cherry tree.

cerimônia [seri'monja] *f* ceremony; **de** ~ formal; **sem** ~ informal; **fazer** ~ to stand on ceremony; ~ **de posse** swearing-in ceremony, investiture.

cerimonial [serimo'njaw] (*pl* -**ais**) *adj, m* ceremonial.

cerimonioso/a [serimo'njozu/ɔza] *adj* ceremonious.

ceroulas [se'rolaʃ] *fpl* long johns.

cerração [sexa'sãw] *f* (*nevoeiro*) fog.

cerrado/a [se'xadu/a] *adj* shut, closed; (*punho*) clenched; (*denso*) dense, thick ♦ *m* (*vegetação*) scrub(land).

cerrar [se'xa*] *vt* to close, shut; ~-**se** *vr* to close, shut.

certame [sex'tami] *m* (*concurso*) contest, competition.

certeiro/a [sex'tejru/a] *adj* (*tiro*) accurate, well-aimed; (*acertado*) correct.

certeza [sex'teza] *f* certainty; **com** ~ certainly, surely; (*provavelmente*) probably; **ter** ~ **de** to be certain of; **ter** ~ **de que** to be sure that; **tem** ~? are you sure?

certidão [sextʃi'dãw] (*pl* -**ões**) *f* certificate.

certificado [sextʃifi'kadu] *m* (*garantia*) certificate.

certificar [sextʃifi'ka*] *vt* to certify; (*assegurar*) to assure; ~-**se** *vr*: ~-**se de** to make sure of.

certo/a ['sextu/a] *adj* certain, sure; (*exato, direito*) right; (*um, algum*) a certain ♦ *adv* correctly; **na certa** certainly; **ao** ~ for certain; **dar** ~ to work; **está** ~ okay, all right.

cerveja [sex'veʒa] *f* beer.

cervejaria [sexveʒa'ria] *f* (*fábrica*) brewery; (*bar*) bar, public house.

cervical [sexvi'kaw] (*pl* -**ais**) *adj* cervical.

cérvice [sex'visi] *f* cervix.

cervo ['sexvu] *m* deer.

cerzir [sex'zi*] *vt* to darn.

cesariana [seza'rjana] *f* Caesarian (*BRIT*), Cesarian (*US*).

cessão [se'sãw] (*pl* -**ões**) *f* (*cedência*) surrender; (*transferência*) transfer.

cessação [sesa'sãw] *f* halting, ceasing.

cessar [se'sa*] *vi* to cease, stop; **sem** ~ continually.

cessar-fogo *m inv* cease-fire.

cessões [se'sõjʃ] *fpl de* **cessão**.

cesta ['seʃta] *f* basket.

cesto ['seʃtu] *m* basket; (*com tampa*) hamper.

ceticismo [setʃi'siʒmu] *m* scepticism (*BRIT*), skepticism (*US*).

cético/a ['setʃiku/a] *adj* sceptical (*BRIT*), skeptical (*US*) ♦ *m/f* sceptic (*BRIT*), skeptic (*US*).

cetim [se'tʃĩ] *m* satin.

cetro ['setru] *m* sceptre (*BRIT*), scepter (*US*).

céu [sɛw] *m* sky; (*REL*) heaven; (*da boca*) roof; **cair do** ~ (*fig*) to come at the right time; **mover** ~**s e terra** (*fig*) to move heaven

NB: *European Portuguese adds the following consonants to certain words:* **b** (sú(b)dito, su(b)til); **c** (a(c)ção, a(c)cionista, a(c)to); **m** (inde(m)ne); **p** (ado(p)ção, ado(p)tar); *for further details see p. xiii.*

and earth.

cevada [se'vada] *f* barley.

cevar [se'va*] *vt* (*engordar*) to fatten; (*alimentar*) to feed; (*engodar*) to bait.

CGC (*BR*) *abr m* (= *Cadastro Geral de Contribuintes*) roll of tax payers.

CGT (*BR*) *abr f* (= *Central Geral dos Trabalhadores*) trade union.

chá [ʃa] *m* tea; (*reunião*) tea party; **dar um ~ de sumiço** (*col*) to disappear; **tomar ~ de cadeira** (*fig*) to be a wallflower.

chacal [ʃa'kaw] (*pl* **-ais**) *m* jackal.

chácara ['ʃakara] *f* (*granja*) farm; (*casa de campo*) country house.

chacina [ʃa'sina] *f* slaughter.

chacinar [ʃasi'na*] *vt* (*matar*) to slaughter.

chacoalhar [ʃakwa'ʎa*] *vt* to shake; (*col: amolar*) to bug ♦ *vi* to shake about; to be annoying.

chacota [ʃa'kɔta] *f* (*zombaria*) mockery.

chacrinha [ʃa'kriɲa] (*col*) *f* get-together.

Chade ['ʃadʒi] *m*: **o ~** Chad.

chã-de-dentro [ʃã-] (*pl* **chãs-de-dentro**) *f* round of beef.

chá-de-panela *m* ≈ hen night, ≈ wedding shower (*us*).

chafariz [ʃafa'riʒ] *m* fountain.

chafurdar [ʃafux'da*] *vi*: **~ em** to wallow in; **~-se** *vr*: **~-se em** to wallow in.

chaga ['ʃaga] *f* (*MED*) wound; (*fig*) disease.

chalé [ʃa'lɛ] *m* chalet.

chaleira [ʃa'lejra] *f* kettle; (*bajulador*) crawler, toady.

chaleirar [ʃalej'ra*] *vt* to crawl to.

chama ['ʃama] *f* flame; **em ~s** on fire.

chamada [ʃa'mada] *f* call; (*MIL*) roll call; (*EDUC*) register; (*no jornal*) headline; **dar uma ~ em alguém** (*repreender*) to tell sb off.

chamar [ʃa'ma*] *vt* to call; (*convidar*) to invite; (*atenção*) to attract ♦ *vi* to call; (*telefone*) to ring; **~-se** *vr* to be called; **chamo-me João** my name is John; **~ alguém de idiota/Dudu** to call sb an idiot/Dudu; **mandar ~** to summon, send for.

chamariz [ʃama'riʒ] *m* decoy; (*fig*) lure.

chamativo/a [ʃama'tʃivu/a] *adj* showy, flashy.

chamego [ʃa'megu] *m* cuddle.

chaminé [ʃami'nɛ] *f* chimney; (*de navio*) funnel.

champanha [ʃã'paɲa] *m ou f* champagne.

champanhe [ʃã'paɲi] *m ou f* = **champanha**.

champu [ʃã'pu] (*PT*) *m* shampoo.

chamuscar [ʃamuʃ'ka*] *vt* to scorch, singe; **~-se** *vr* to scorch o.s.

chance ['ʃãsi] *f* chance.

chancela [ʃã'sɛla] *f* seal, official stamp.

chancelaria [ʃãsela'ria] *f* chancellery.

chanceler [ʃãse'le*] *m* chancellor.

chanchada [ʃã'ʃada] *f* second-rate film (*ou* play).

chantagear [ʃãta'ʒja*] *vt* to blackmail.

chantagem [ʃã'taʒẽ] *f* blackmail.

chantagista [ʃãta'ʒiʃta] *m/f* blackmailer.

chão [ʃãw] (*pl* **~s**) *m* ground; (*terra*) soil; (*piso*) floor.

chapa ['ʃapa] *f* (*placa*) plate; (*eleitoral*) list ♦ *m/f* (*col*) mate, friend; **~ de matrícula** (*PT: AUTO*) number (*BRIT*) *ou* license (*US*) plate; **bife na ~** grilled steak; **oi, meu ~!** hi, mate!

chapa-branca (*pl* **chapas-brancas**) *m* civil service car.

chapelaria [ʃapela'ria] *f* (*loja*) hatshop.

chapeleira [ʃape'lejra] *f* hat box; *V tb* **chapeleiro**.

chapeleiro/a [ʃape'lejru/a] *m/f* milliner.

chapéu [ʃa'pɛw] *m* hat.

chapéu-coco (*pl* **chapéus-cocos**) *m* bowler hat.

chapinha [ʃa'piɲa] *f*: **~ (de garrafa)** (bottle) top.

chapinhar [ʃapi'ɲa*] *vi* to splash.

charada [ʃa'rada] *f* (*quebra-cabeça*) puzzle.

charco ['ʃaxku] *m* marsh, bog.

charge ['ʃaxʒi] *f* (*political*) cartoon.

chargista [ʃax'ʒiʃta] *m/f* (*political*) cartoonist.

charlatão [ʃaxla'tãw] (*pl* **-ães**) *m* charlatan; (*curandeiro*) quack.

charme ['ʃaxmi] *m* charm; **fazer ~** to be nice, use one's charm.

charmoso/a [ʃax'mozu/ɔza] *adj* charming.

charneca [ʃax'nɛka] *f* moor, heath.

charrete [ʃa'xetʃi] *f* cart.

charter ['tʃaxte*] *adj inv* charter ♦ *m* (*pl*: **~s**) charter flight.

charuto [ʃa'rutu] *m* cigar.

chassis [ʃa'si] *m* (*AUTO, ELET*) chassis.

chata ['ʃata] *f* (*embarcação*) barge; *V tb* **chato**.

chateação [ʃatʃja'sãw] (*pl* **-ões**) *f* bother, upset; (*maçada*) bore.

chatear [ʃa'tʃja*] *vt* (*aborrecer*) to bother, upset; (*importunar*) to pester; (*entediar*) to bore; (*irritar*) to annoy ♦ *vi* to be upsetting; to be boring; to be annoying; **~-se** *vr* to get upset; to get bored; to get annoyed.

chatice [ʃa'tʃisi] (*PT*) *f* nuisance.

chato/a ['ʃatu/a] *adj* (*plano*) flat, level; (*pé*) flat; (*tedioso*) boring; (*irritante*) annoying; (*que fica mal*) bad, rude ♦ *m/f* bore; (*quem irrita*) pain.

chatura [ʃa'tura] (*col*) *f* pain (in the neck).

chauvinismo [ʃawvi'niʒmu] *m* chauvinism.

chauvinista [ʃawvi'niʃta] *adj* chauvinistic ♦ *m/f* chauvinist.

chavão [ʃa'vãw] (*pl* **-ões**) *m* cliché.

chave ['ʃavi] *f* key; (*ELET*) switch; (*TIP*) curly bracket; **~ de porcas** spanner; **~ inglesa** (monkey) wrench; **~ de fenda** screwdriver.

-chave *sufixo* key *atr*.

chaveiro [ʃa'vejru] *m* (*utensílio*) key ring; (*pessoa*) locksmith.

chávena ['ʃavena] (*PT*) *f* cup.

checar [ʃe'ka*] *vt* to check.

check-up [tʃe'kapi] (*pl* **~s**) *m* check-up.

chefatura [ʃefa'tura] *f*: **~ de polícia** police

headquarters *sg.*

chefe [ˈʃɛfi] *m/f* head, chief; *(patrão)* boss; ~ **de turma** foreman; ~ **de estação** stationmaster.

chefia [ʃeˈfia] *f (liderança)* leadership; *(direção)* management; *(repartição)* headquarters *sg;* **estar com a** ~ **de** to be in charge of.

chefiar [ʃeˈfjaˆ] *vt* to lead.

chega [ˈʃega] *(col) m:* **dar um** ~ **em alguém** to tell sb off ♦ *prep* even.

chegada [ʃeˈgada] *f* arrival; **dar uma** ~ to drop by.

chegado/a [ʃeˈgadu/a] *adj (próximo)* near; *(íntimo)* close; **ser** ~ **a** *(bebidas, comidas)* to be keen on.

chegar [ʃeˈgaˆ] *vt (aproximar)* to bring near ♦ *vi* to arrive; *(ser suficiente)* to be enough; ~-**se** *vr:* ~-**se a** to approach; **chega!** that's enough!; ~ **a** *(atingir)* to reach; *(conseguir)* to manage to; ~ **algo para cá/para lá** to bring sth closer/move sth over; **chega (mais) para cá/para lá!** come closer!/move over!; **vou chegando** I'm leaving.

cheia [ˈʃeja] *f* flood.

cheio/a [ˈʃeju/a] *adj* full; *(repleto)* full up; *(col: farto)* fed up; ~ **de si** self-important; ~ **de dedos** all fingers and thumbs; *(inibido)* awkward; ~ **de frescura** *(col)* fussy; ~ **da nota** *(col)* rich, loaded; **acertar em** ~ to be exactly right, hit the nail on the head; **estar** ~ **de algo** *(col)* to be fed up with sth.

cheirar [ʃejˈraˆ] *vt, vi* to smell; ~ **a** to smell of; **isto não me cheira bem** there's something fishy about this.

cheiro [ˈʃejru] *m* smell; **ter** ~ **de** to smell of.

cheiroso/a [ʃejˈrozu/ɔza] *adj:* **ser** *ou* **estar** ~ to smell nice.

cheiro-verde *m* bunch of parsley and spring onion.

cheque [ˈʃɛki] *m* cheque *(BRIT)*, check *(US)*; *(XADREZ)* check; ~ **cruzado** crossed cheque; ~ **em branco** blank cheque; ~ **sem fundos** uncovered cheque, rubber cheque *(col)*; ~ **voador** rubber cheque.

chequei [ʃɛˈkej] *etc vb V* **checar.**

cheque-mate *m* checkmate.

cherne [ˈʃɛxni] *m* grouper.

chiado [ˈʃjadu] *m* squeak(ing); *(de vapor)* hiss(ing).

chiar [ʃjaˆ] *vi* to squeak; *(porta)* to creak; *(vapor)* to hiss; *(fritura)* to sizzle; *(col: reclamar)* to grumble.

chibata [ʃiˈbata] *f (vara)* cane.

chiclete [ʃiˈklɛtʃi] *m* chewing gum; ~ **de bola** bubble gum.

chicória [ʃiˈkɔrja] *f* chicory.

chicote [ʃiˈkɔtʃi] *m* whip.

chicotear [ʃikoˈtʃjaˆ] *vt* to whip, lash.

chifrada [ʃiˈfrada] *f (golpe)* butt; **dar uma** ~

to cheat.

chifrar [ʃiˈfraˆ] *vt* to two-time.

chifre [ˈʃifri] *m (corno)* horn; **pôr** ~ **em alguém** *(col)* to be unfaithful to sb, cheat on sb.

chifrudo/a [ʃiˈfrudu/a] *(col) adj* cuckolded.

Chile [ˈʃili] *m:* **o** ~ Chile.

chileno/a [ʃiˈlɛnu/a] *adj, m/f* Chilean.

chilique [ʃiˈliki] *(col) m* fit.

chilrear [ʃiwˈxjaˆ] *vi* to chirp, twitter.

chilreio [ʃiwˈxeju] *m* chirping.

chimarrão [ʃimaˈxãw] *(pl* -**ões**) *m maté tea without sugar taken from a pipe-like cup.*

chimpanzé [ʃĩpãˈzɛ] *m* chimpanzee.

China [ˈʃina] *f:* **a** ~ China.

china [ˈʃina] *m/f* Chinese.

chinelo [ʃiˈnɛlu] *m* slipper; **botar no** ~ *(fig)* to put to shame.

chinês/esa [ʃiˈneʃ/eza] *adj, m/f* Chinese ♦ *m (LING)* Chinese.

chinfrim [ʃĩˈfrĩ] *(pl* -**ns**) *adj* cheap and cheerful.

chio [ˈʃiu] *m* squeak; *(de rodas)* screech.

chip [ˈʃipi] *m (COMPUT)* chip.

Chipre [ˈʃipri] *f* Cyprus.

chique [ˈʃiki] *adj* stylish, chic.

chiqueiro [ʃiˈkejru] *m* pigsty.

chispa [ˈʃiʃpa] *f* spark.

chispada [ʃiʃˈpada] *(BR) f* dash.

chispar [ʃiʃˈpaˆ] *vi (correr)* to dash.

chita [ˈʃita] *f* printed cotton, calico.

choça [ˈʃɔsa] *f* shack, hut.

chocalhar [ʃokaˈʎaˆ] *vt, vi* to rattle.

chocalho [ʃoˈkaʎu] *m (MÚS, brinquedo)* rattle; *(para animais)* bell.

chocante [ʃoˈkãtʃi] *adj* shocking; *(col)* amazing.

chocar [ʃoˈkaˆ] *vt (incubar)* to hatch, incubate; *(ofender)* to shock, offend ♦ *vi* to shock; ~-**se** *vr* to crash, collide; to be shocked.

chocho/a [ˈʃoʃu/a] *adj* hollow, empty; *(fraco)* weak; *(sem graça)* dull.

chocolate [ʃokoˈlatʃi] *m* chocolate.

chofer [ʃoˈfeˆ] *m* driver.

chofre [ˈʃofri] *m:* **de** ~ all of a sudden.

chongas [ˈʃõgaʃ] *(col) pron* nothing, bugger all *(col)*.

chopada [ʃoˈpada] *f* drinking session.

chope [ˈʃopi] *m* draught beer.

choque [ˈʃɔki] *etc vb V* **chocar** ♦ *m (abalo)* shock; *(colisão)* collision; *(MED, ELET)* shock; *(impacto)* impact; *(conflito)* clash, conflict; ~ **cultural** culture shock.

choradeira [ʃoraˈdejra] *f* fit of crying.

chorado/a [ʃoˈradu/a] *adj (canto)* sad; *(gol)* hard-won.

choramingar [ʃoramĩˈgaˆ] *vi* to whine, whimper.

choramingas [ʃoraˈmĩgaʃ] *m/f inv* crybaby.

NB: *European Portuguese adds the following consonants to certain words:* **b** (sú(b)dito, su(b)til); **c** (a(c)ção, a(c)cionista, a(c)to); **m** (inde(m)ne); **p** (ado(p)ção, ado(p)tar); *for further details see p. xiii.*

choramingo [ʃora'mĩgu] m whine, whimper.

chorão/rona [ʃo'ráw/rɔna] (pl -ões/~s) adj tearful ♦ m/f crybaby ♦ m (BOT) weeping willow.

chorar [ʃo'ra*] vt, vi to weep, cry.

chorinho [ʃo'riɲu] m type of Brazilian music.

choro ['ʃoru] m crying; (MÚS) type of Brazilian music.

choroso/a [ʃo'rozu/ɔza] adj tearful.

choupana [ʃo'pana] f shack, hut.

chouriço [ʃo'risu] m (BR) black pudding; (PT) spicy sausage.

chove-não-molha [ʃovináw'mɔʎa] (col) m shilly-shallying.

chover [ʃo've*] vi to rain; ~ a cântaros to rain cats and dogs; **choveram cartas** letters poured in.

chuchu [ʃu'ʃu] m chayote (vegetable); **ele fala/está quente pra** ~ (col) he talks a lot/ it's really hot.

chucrute [ʃu'krutʃi] m sauerkraut.

chué [ʃu'ɛ] (col) adj lousy.

chulé [ʃu'lɛ] m foot odour (BRIT) ou odor (US).

chulear [ʃu'lja*] vt to hem.

chulo/a ['ʃulu/a] adj vulgar.

chumaço [ʃu'masu] m (de papel, notas) wad; (material) wadding.

chumbado/a [ʃũ'badu/a] (col) adj (cansado) dog-tired; (doente) laid out.

chumbar [ʃũ'ba*] vt to fill with lead; (soldar) to solder; (atirar em) to fire at ♦ vi (PT: reprovar) to fail.

chumbo ['ʃũbu] m lead; (de caça) gunshot; (PT: de dente) filling; **esta mala está um** ~ this case weighs a ton.

chupado/a [ʃu'padu/a] (col) adj (cara, pessoa) drawn.

chupar [ʃu'pa*] vt to suck; (absorver) to absorb.

chupeta [ʃu'peta] f (para criança) dummy (BRIT), pacifier (US).

churrascaria [ʃuxaʃka'ria] f barbecue restaurant.

churrasco [ʃu'xaʃku] m barbecue.

churrasqueira [ʃuxaʃ'kejra] f barbecue.

churrasquinho [ʃuxaʃ'kiɲu] m kebab.

chutar [ʃu'ta*] vt to kick; (col: adivinhar) to guess at; (: dar o fora em) to dump ♦ vi to kick; to guess; (col: mentir) to lie.

chute ['ʃutʃi] m kick; (para o gol) shot; (col: mentira) lie; **dar o** ~ **em alguém** (col) to give sb the boot.

chuteira [ʃu'tejra] f football boot; **pendurar as** ~**s** (col) to retire.

chuva ['ʃuva] f rain; **tomar** ~ to get caught in the rain; **estar na** ~ (fig) to be drunk; ~ **de pedra** hailstorm.

chuvarada [ʃuva'rada] f torrential rain.

chuveirada [ʃuvej'rada] f shower.

chuveiro [ʃu'vejru] m shower.

chuviscar [ʃuviʃ'ka*] vi to drizzle.

chuvisco [ʃu'viʃku] m drizzle.

chuvoso/a [ʃu'vozu/ɔza] adj rainy.

CIA abr f (= Central Intelligence Agency) CIA.

Cia. abr (= companhia) Co.

cibernética [sibex'nɛtʃika] f cybernetics sg.

CIC (BR) abr m = **Cartão de Identificação do Contribuinte**.

cica ['sika] f sharpness.

cicatriz [sika'triʒ] f scar.

cicatrização [sikatriza'sãw] f scarring.

cicatrizar [sikatri'za*] vt (rosto) to scar; (ferida) to heal; (fig) to cure, heal ♦ vi to heal; to scar.

cicerone [sise'rɔni] m tourist guide.

ciciar [si'sja*] vi to whisper; (rumorejar) to murmur.

cíclico/a ['sikliku/a] adj cyclical.

ciclismo [si'kliʒmu] m cycling.

ciclista [si'kliʃta] m/f cyclist.

ciclo ['siklu] m cycle; ~ **básico** foundation year.

ciclone [si'klɔni] m cyclone.

ciclovia [siklo'via] f cycle path.

cidadã [sida'dã] f de **cidadão**.

cidadania [sidada'nia] f citizenship.

cidadão/cidadã [sida'dãw/sida'dã] (pl ~**s**/~**s**) m/f citizen.

cidade [si'dadʒi] f town; (grande) city.

cidadela [sida'dɛla] f citadel.

cidra ['sidra] f citron.

CIE (BR) abr m = **Centro de Informações do Exército**.

ciência ['sjẽsja] f science; (erudição) knowledge; ~**s humanas/socias** business studies/ social sciences.

ciente ['sjẽtʃi] adj aware.

científico/a [sjẽ'tʃifiku/a] adj scientific.

cientista [sjẽ'tʃiʃta] m/f scientist.

CIEP (BR) abr m (= Centro Integrado de Educação Popular) combined school and community centre.

cifra ['sifra] f (escrita secreta) cipher; (algarismo) number, figure; (total) sum.

cifrão [si'frãw] (pl -ões) m money sign.

cifrar [si'fra*] vt to write in code.

cifrões [si'frõjʃ] mpl de **cifrão**.

cigano/a [si'ganu/a] adj, m/f gypsy.

cigarra [si'gaxa] f cicada; (ELET) buzzer.

cigarreira [siga'xejra] f (estojo) cigarette case.

cigarrilha [siga'xiʎa] f cheroot.

cigarro [si'gaxu] m cigarette.

cilada [si'lada] f (emboscada) ambush; (armadilha) trap; (embuste) trick.

cilíndrico/a [si'lĩdriku/a] adj cylindrical.

cilindro [si'lĩdru] m cylinder; (rolo) roller.

cílio ['silju] m eyelash.

cima ['sima] f: **de** ~ **para baixo** from top to bottom; **para** ~ up; **em** ~ **de** on, on top of; **por** ~ **de** over; **de** ~ from above; **lá em** ~ up there; (em casa) upstairs; **ainda por** ~ on top of that; **estar por** ~ to be better off; **dar em** ~ **de alguém** (col) to be after sb; **tudo em** ~? (col) how's it going?

cimeira [si'mejra] (PT) f summit.

cimentar [simẽ'ta*] vt to cement.

cimento [si'mẽtu] *m* cement; (*chão*) concrete floor; (*fig*) foundation; ~ **armado** reinforced concrete.

cimo ['simu] *m* top, summit.

cinco ['sĩku] *num* five; **somos** ~ there are five of us; **ela tem** ~ **anos** she is five (years old); **aos** ~ **anos (de idade)** at the age of five; **são** ~ **horas** it's five o'clock; **às** ~ **(horas)** at five (o'clock); **hoje é dia** ~ **de julho** today is the fifth of July; **no dia** ~ **de julho** on the fifth of July, on July the fifth; **eles moram no número** ~/**na Barata Ribeiro número** ~ they live at number five/number five Barata Ribeiro Street; ~ **e um quarto/meio** five and a quarter/half.

Cindacta [sĩ'dakta] (*BR*) *abr m* = **Centro Integrado de Defesa Aérea e Controle de Tráfego Aéreo.**

cindir [sĩ'dʒi*] *vt* to split; (*cortar*) to cut.

cineasta [sine'aʃta] *m/f* film maker.

cinegrafista [sinegra'fiʃta] *m/f* cameraman/woman.

cinema [si'nɛma] *f* cinema.

cinematográfico/a [sinemato'grafiku/a] *adj* cinematographic.

Cingapura [sĩga'pura] *f* Singapore.

cingir [sin'ʒi*] *vt* (*pór à cintura*) to fasten round one's waist; (*prender em volta*) to tie round; (*cercar*) to encircle, ring; (*coroa, espada*) to put on; ~**-se** *vr*: ~**-se a** (*restringir-se*) to restrict o.s. to.

cínico/a ['siniku/a] *adj* cynical ♦ *m/f* cynic.

cinismo [si'niʒmu] *m* cynicism.

cinjo ['sĩʒu] *etc vb V* **cingir.**

cinqüenta [sĩ'kwẽta] *num* fifty; **umas** ~ **pessoas** about fifty people; **ele tem uns** ~ **anos** he's about fifty; **ele está na casa dos** ~ **anos** he's in his fifties; **nos anos** ~ in the fifties; **ir a** ~ (*AUTO*) to do fifty (km/h).

cinqüentão/tona [sĩkwẽ'tãw/'tɔna] (*pl* -**tões/**~**s**) *m/f* person in his/her fifties ♦ *adj* in his/her fifties.

cinta ['sĩta] *f* (*faixa*) sash; (*de mulher*) girdle.

cintado/a [sĩ'tadu/a] *adj* gathered at the waist.

cintilante [sĩtʃi'lãtʃi] *adj* sparkling.

cintilar [sĩtʃi'la*] *vi* to sparkle, glitter.

cinto ['sĩtu] *m* belt; ~ **de segurança** safety belt; (*AUTO*) seatbelt.

cintura [sĩ'tura] *f* waist; (*linha*) waistline.

cinturão [sĩtu'rãw] (*pl* -**ões**) *m* belt; ~ **verde** green belt.

cinza ['sĩza] *adj inv* grey (*BRIT*), gray (*US*) ♦ *f* ash, ashes *pl*.

cinzeiro [sĩ'zejru] *m* ashtray.

cinzel [sĩ'zɛw] (*pl* -**éis**) *m* chisel.

cinzelar [sĩze'la*] *vt* to chisel; (*gravar*) to carve, engrave.

cinzento/a [sĩ'zẽtu/a] *adj* grey (*BRIT*), gray (*US*).

cio [siu] *m* mating season; **no** ~ on heat, in season.

cioso/a ['sjozu/ɔza] *adj* conscientious.

CIP (*BR*) *abr m* = **Conselho Interministerial de Preços.**

cipreste [si'prɛʃtʃi] *m* cypress (tree).

cipriota [si'prjɔta] *adj, m/f* Cypriot.

circense [six'sẽsi] *adj* circus *atr.*

circo ['sixku] *m* circus.

circuito [six'kwitu] *m* circuit.

circulação [sixkula'sãw] *f* circulation.

circular [sixku'la*] *adj* circular, round ♦ *f* (*carta*) circular ♦ *vi* to circulate; (*girar, andar*) to go round ♦ *vt* to circulate; (*estar em volta de*) to surround; (*percorrer em roda*) to go round.

círculo ['sixkulu] *m* circle.

circunavegar [sixkunave'ga*] *vt* to circumnavigate, sail round.

circuncidar [sixkũsi'da*] *vt* to circumcise.

circuncisão [sixkũsi'zãw] *f* circumcision.

circundante [sixkũ'dãtʃi] *adj* surrounding.

circundar [sixkũ'da*] *vt* to surround.

circunferência [sixkũfe'rẽsja] *f* circumference.

circunflexo/a [sixkũ'flɛksu/a] *adj* circumflex ♦ *m* circumflex.

circunlóquio [sixkũ'lɔkju] *m* circumlocution.

circunscrever [sixkũʃkre've*] *vt* to circumscribe, limit; (*epidemia*) to contain; (*abranger*) to cover; ~**-se** *vr* to be limited.

circunscrição [sixkũʃkri'sãw] (*pl* -**ões**) *f* district; ~ **eleitoral** constituency.

circunscrito/a [sixkũʃ'kritu/a] *pp de* **circunscrever.**

circunspecção [sixkũʃpe'sãw] *f* seriousness.

circunspeto/a [sixkũ'ʃpetu/a] *adj* serious.

circunstância [sixkũ'ʃtãsja] *f* circumstance; ~**s atenuantes** mitigating circumstances.

circunstanciado/a [sixkũʃtã'sjadu/a] *adj* detailed.

circunstancial [sixkũʃtã'sjaw] (*pl* -**ais**) *adj* circumstantial.

circunstante [sixkũ'ʃtãtʃi] *m/f* onlooker, bystander; ~**s** *mpl* audience *sg.*

cirrose [si'xɔzi] *f* cirrhosis.

cirurgia [sirux'ʒia] *f* surgery; ~ **plástica/estética** plastic/cosmetic surgery.

cirurgião/cirurgiã [sirux'ʒjãw/sirux'ʒjã] (*pl* -**ões/**~**s**) *m/f* surgeon.

cirúrgico/a [si'ruxʒiku/a] *adj* surgical.

cirurgiões [sirux'ʒjõjʃ] *mpl de* **cirurgião.**

cirzo ['sixzu] *etc vb V* **cerzir.**

cisão [si'zãw] (*pl* -**ões**) *f* (*divisão*) split, division; (*desacordo*) disagreement.

cisco ['siʃku] *m* speck.

cisma ['siʒma] *m* schism ♦ *f* (*mania*) silly idea; (*suspeita*) suspicion; (*antipatia*) dislike; (*devaneio*) dream.

cismado/a [siʒ'madu/a] *adj* with fixed ideas.

cismar [siʒ'ma*] *vi* (*pensar*): ~ **em** to brood over; (*antipatizar*): ~ **com** to take a dislike

---

NB: *European Portuguese adds the following consonants to certain words:* **b** (sú(b)dito, su(b)til); **c** (a(c)ção, a(c)cionista, a(c)to); **m** (inde(m)ne); **p** (ado(p)ção, ado(p)tar); *for further details see p. xiii.*

to ♦ *vt*: ~ **que** to be convinced that; ~ **de** *ou* **em fazer** (*meter na cabeça*) to get into one's head to do; (*insistir*) to insist on doing.

cisne ['siʒni] *m* swan.

cisões [si'zõjʃ] *fpl de* **cisão**.

cisterna [siʃ'tɛxna] *f* cistern, tank.

cistite [siʃ'tʃitʃi] *f* cystitis.

citação [sita'sãw] (*pl* -ões) *f* quotation; (*JUR*) summons *sg*.

citadino/a [sita'dʒinu/a] *adj* town *atr*.

citar [si'ta*] *vt* to quote; (*JUR*) to summon.

cítrico/a ['sitriku/a] *adj* (*fruta*) citrus; (*ácido*) citric.

ciumada [sju'mada] *f* fit of jealousy.

ciúme ['sjumi] *m* jealousy; **ter ~s de** to be jealous of.

ciumeira [sju'mejra] (*col*) *f* = **ciumada**.

ciumento/a [sju'mẽtu/a] *adj* jealous.

cívico/a ['siviku/a] *adj* civic.

civil [si'viw] (*pl* -is) *adj* civil ♦ *m/f* civilian.

civilidade [sivili'dadʒi] *f* politeness.

civilização [siviliza'sãw] (*pl* -ões) *f* civilization.

civilizador(a) [siviliza'do*(a)] *adj* civilizing.

civilizar [sivili'za*] *vt* to civilize.

civis [si'viʃ] *pl de* **civil**.

civismo [si'viʒmu] *m* public spirit.

clamar [kla'ma*] *vt* to clamour (*BRIT*) *ou* clamor (*US*) for ♦ *vi* to cry out, clamo(u)r.

clamor [kla'mo*] *m* outcry, uproar.

clamoroso/a [klamo'rozu/ɔza] *adj* noisy.

clandestino/a [klãdeʃ'tʃinu/a] *adj* clandestine; (*ilegal*) underground.

clara ['klara] *f* egg white.

carabóia [klara'bɔja] *f* skylight.

clarão [kla'rãw] (*pl* -ões) *m* (*cintilação*) flash; (*claridade*) gleam.

clarear [kla'rja*] *vi* (*dia*) to dawn; (*tempo*) to clear up, brighten up ♦ *vt* to clarify.

clareira [kla'rejra] *f* (*na mata*) clearing.

clareza [kla'reza] *f* clarity.

claridade [klari'dadʒi] *f* (*luz*) brightness.

clarim [kla'rĩ] (*pl* -ns) *m* bugle.

clarinete [klari'netʃi] *m* clarinet.

clarinetista [klarine'tʃiʃta] *m/f* clarinet player.

clarins [kla'rĩʃ] *mpl de* **clarim**.

clarividente [klarivi'dẽtʃi] *adj* (*prudente*) far-sighted, prudent.

claro/a ['klaru/a] *adj* clear; (*luminoso*) bright; (*cor*) light; (*evidente*) clear, evident ♦ *m* (*na escrita*) space; (*clareira*) clearing ♦ *adv* clearly; ~! of course!; ~ **que sim!/não!** of course!/of course not!; **às claras** openly; (*publicamente*) publicly; **dia** ~ daylight; **passar a noite em** ~ not to sleep a wink all night; ~ **como água** crystal clear.

clarões [kla'rõjʃ] *mpl de* **clarão**.

classe ['klasi] *f* class; ~ **média/operária** middle/working class.

clássico/a ['klasiku/a] *adj* classical; (*fig*) classic; (*habitual*) usual ♦ *m* classic.

classificação [klasifika'sãw] (*pl* -ões) *f* classification; (*ESPORTE*) place, placing.

classificado/a [klasifi'kadu/a] *adj* (*em exame*)

successful; (*anúncio*) classified; (*ESPORTE*) placed, qualified ♦ *m* (*anúncio*) classified ad.

classificar [klasifi'ka*] *vt* to classify; ~**-se** *vr*: ~**-se de algo** to call o.s. sth, describe o.s. as sth.

classificatório/a [klasifika'tɔrju/a] *adj* qualifying.

classudo/a [kla'sudu/a] (*col*) *adj* classy.

claudicar [klawdʒi'ka*] *vi* (*mancar*) to limp; (*errar*) to err.

claustro ['klawʃtru] *m* cloister.

claustrofobia [klawʃtrofo'bia] *f* claustrophobia.

claustrofóbico/a [klawʃtro'fɔbiku/a] *adj* claustrophobic.

cláusula ['klawzula] *f* clause.

clausura [klaw'zura] *f* (*recinto*) enclosure; (*vida*) cloistered existence.

clave ['klavi] *f* (*MÚS*) clef.

clavícula [kla'vikula] *f* collar bone.

clemência [kle'mẽsja] *f* mercy.

clemente [kle'mẽtʃi] *adj* merciful.

cleptomaníaco/a [kleptoma'niaku/a] *m/f* kleptomaniac.

clérigo ['klɛrigu] *m* clergyman.

clero ['klɛru] *m* clergy.

clichê [kli'ʃe] *m* (*FOTO*) plate; (*chavão*) cliché.

cliente ['kljẽtʃi] *m* client; (*de loja*) customer; (*de médico*) patient.

clientela [kljẽ'tɛla] *f* clientele; (*de loja*) customers *pl*; (*de médico*) patients *pl*.

clima ['klima] *m* climate.

climático/a [kli'matʃiku/a] *adj* climatic.

clímax ['klimaks] *m inv* climax.

clínica ['klinika] *f* clinic; ~ **geral** general practice; *V tb* **clínico**.

clinicar [klini'ka*] *vi* to have a practice.

clínico/a ['kliniku/a] *adj* clinical ♦ *m/f* doctor; ~ **geral** general practitioner, GP.

clipe ['klipi] *m* clip; (*para papéis*) paper clip.

clitóris [kli'tɔriʃ] *m inv* clitoris.

clone ['klɔni] *m* clone.

clorar [klo'ra*] *vt* to chlorinate.

cloro ['klɔru] *m* chlorine.

clorofórmio [kloro'fɔxmju] *m* chloroform.

close ['klɔzi] *m* close-up.

clube ['klubi] *m* club.

CMB *abr f* (= *Casa da Moeda do Brasil*) Brazilian National Mint.

CMN (*BR*) *abr m* = **Conselho Monetário Nacional**.

CNA *abr m* (= *Congresso Nacional Africano*) ANC; (*BR*) = **Conselho Nacional do Álcool**.

CNB (*BR*) *abr m* = **Conselho Nacional da Borracha**.

CNBB *abr f* = **Confederação Nacional dos Bispos do Brasil**.

CNBV (*BR*) *abr f* = **Comissão Nacional da Bolsa de Valores**.

CND (*BR*) *abr m* = **Conselho Nacional de Desportos**.

CNDC (*BR*) *abr m* = **Conselho Nacional de Defesa ao Consumidor**.

CNDM (*BR*) *abr m* = **Conselho Nacional dos Direitos da Mulher.**

CNDU (*BR*) *abr m* = **Conselho Nacional de Desenvolvimento Urbano.**

CNEN (*BR*) *abr f* (= *Comissão Nacional de Energia Nuclear*) ≈ AEA (*BRIT*), ≈ AEC (*US*).

CNPq (*BR*) *abr m* (= *Conselho Nacional de Desenvolvimento Científico*) *organization supporting higher education.*

CNS (*BR*) *abr m* = **Conselho Nacional de Saúde.**

CNT (*BR*) *abr m* = **Conselho Nacional de Transportes.**

CNV (*BR*) *abr m* = **Cadastro Nacional de Veículos.**

coabitar [koabi'ta*] *vi* to live together, cohabit.

coação [koa'sãw] (*PT*: **-cç-**) *f* coercion.

coadjuvante [koadʒu'vãtʃi] *adj* supporting ♦ *m/f* (*num crime*) accomplice; (*TEATRO, CINEMA*) co-star.

coadjuvar [koadʒu'va*] *vt* to aid; (*TEATRO, CINEMA*) to support.

coador [koa'do*] *m* strainer; (*de café*) filter bag; (*para legumes*) colander.

coadunar [koadu'na*] *vt* to combine; **~-se** *vr* to combine.

coagir [koa'ʒi*] *vt* to coerce, compel.

coagular [koagu'la*] *vt, vi* to coagulate; (*sangue*) to clot; **~-se** *vr* to congeal.

coágulo [ko'agulu] *m* clot.

coajo [ko'aʒu] *etc vb V* **coagir.**

coalhada [koa'ʎada] *f* live yoghurt.

coalhado/a [koa'ʎadu/a] *adj* curdled; **~ de gente** packed.

coalhar [koa'ʎa*] *vt, vi* (*leite*) to curdle; **~-se** *vr* to curdle.

coalizão [koali'zãw] (*pl* **-ões**) *f* coalition.

coar [ko'a*] *vt* (*líquido*) to strain.

co-autor(a) [ko-] *m/f* (*de livro*) co-author; (*de crime*) accomplice.

coaxar [koa'ʃa*] *vi* to croak ♦ *m* croaking.

COB *abr m* = **Comité Olímpico Brasileiro.**

cobaia [ko'baja] *f* guinea pig.

cobalto [ko'bawtu] *m* cobalt.

coberta [ko'bɛxta] *f* cover, covering; (*NÁUT*) deck.

coberto/a [ko'bɛxtu/a] *pp de* **cobrir** ♦ *adj* covered.

cobertor [kobɛx'to*] *m* blanket.

cobertura [kobɛx'tura] *f* covering; (*telhado*) roof; (*apartamento*) penthouse; (*TV, RÁDIO, JORNALISMO*) coverage; (*SEGUROS*) cover.

cobiça [ko'bisa] *f* greed.

cobiçar [kobi'sa*] *vt* to covet.

cobiçoso/a [kobi'sozu/ɔza] *adj* covetous.

cobra ['kɔbra] *f* snake ♦ *m/f* (*col*) expert ♦ *adj* (*col*) expert; **dizer ~s e lagartos de alguém** to say bad things about sb.

cobrador(a) [kobra'do*(a)] *m/f* collector; (*em*

transporte) conductor; **~ de impostos** tax collector.

cobrança [ko'brãsa] *f* collection; (*ato de cobrar*) charging; **~ de pênalti/falta** penalty/free kick.

cobrar [ko'bra*] *vt* to collect; (*preço*) to charge; (*pênalti*) to take; **~ o prometido** to remind sb of what they promised; **~ uma falta** (*FUTEBOL*) to take a free kick.

cobre ['kɔbri] *m* copper; **~s** *mpl* money *sg.*

cobrir [ko'bri*] *vt* to cover; **~-se** *vr* to cover o.s.

coca ['kɔka] *f* (*arbusto*) coca bush.

coça ['kɔsa] (*col*) *f* wallop.

cocada [ko'kada] *f* coconut sweet.

cocaína [koka'ina] *f* cocaine.

coçar [ko'sa*] *vt* to scratch ♦ *vi* (*comichar*) to itch; **~-se** *vr* to scratch o.s.; **não ter tempo nem para se ~** to have no time to breathe.

cócegas ['kɔsegaʃ] *fpl*: **fazer ~ em** to tickle; **tenho ~ nos pés** my feet tickle; **sentir ~ to** be ticklish; **estar em ~ para fazer** to be itching to do.

coceira [ko'sejra] *f* itch; (*qualidade*) itchiness.

cocheira [ko'ʃejra] *f* stable.

cochichar [koʃi'ʃa*] *vi* to whisper.

cochicho [ko'ʃiʃu] *m* whispering.

cochilada [koʃi'lada] *f* snooze; **dar uma ~** to have a snooze.

cochilar [koʃi'la*] *vi* to snooze, doze.

cochilo [ko'ʃilu] *m* nap.

coco ['koku] *m* coconut.

cocô [ko'ko] (*col*) *m* pooh.

cócoras ['kɔkoraʃ] *fpl*: **de ~** squatting; **ficar de ~** to squat (down).

cocoricar [kokori'ka*] *vi* to crow.

cocuruto [koku'rutu] *m* top.

côdea ['kodʒa] *f* crust.

codeína [kode'ina] *f* codeine.

Codici [kodʒi'si] (*BR*) *abr f* = **Comissão de Defesa dos Direitos do Cidadão.**

codificador [kodʒifika'do*] *m* (*COMPUT*) encoder.

codificar [kodʒifi'ka*] *vt* (*leis*) to codify; (*mensagem*) to encode, code.

código ['kɔdʒigu] *m* code; **~ de barras** bar code; **~ de ética profissional** code of practice.

codinome [kodʒi'nɔmi] *m* code name.

codorna [ko'dɔxna] *f* quail.

co-editar [ko-] *vt* to co-publish.

coeficiente [koefi'sjētʃi] *m* (*MAT*) coefficient; (*fig*) factor.

coelho [ko'eʎu] *m* rabbit; **matar dois ~s de uma cajadada só** (*fig*) to kill two birds with one stone.

coentro [ko'ētru] *m* coriander.

coerção [koex'sãw] *f* coercion.

coerência [koe'rēsja] *f* coherence; (*conseqüência*) consistency.

NB: *European Portuguese adds the following consonants to certain words:* **b** (sú(b)dito, su(b)til); **c** (a(c)ção, a(c)cionista, a(c)to); **m** (inde(m)ne); **p** (ado(p)ção, ado(p)tar); *for further details see p. xiii.*

coerente [koe'rɛ̃tʃi] *adj* coherent; *(consequente)* consistent.

coesão [koe'zãw] *f* cohesion.

coeso/a ['kwɛzu/a] *adj* cohesive.

coexistência [koezif'tẽsja] *f* coexistence.

coexistir [koezif'tʃi*] *vi* to coexist.

Cofie *(BR) abr f* = **Comissão de Fusão e Incorporação de Empresas.**

cofre ['kɔfri] *m* safe; *(caixa)* strongbox; **os ~s públicos** public funds.

cogitação [koʒita'sãw] *f* contemplation; **estar fora de ~** to be out of the question.

cogitar [koʒi'ta*] *vt, vi* to contemplate.

cognominar [kognomi'na*] *vt* to nickname.

cogumelo [kogu'mɛlu] *m* mushroom; **~ venenoso** toadstool.

COHAB *(BR) abr f* = **Companhia de Habitação Popular.**

coibição [koibi'sãw] *(pl -ões) f* restraint, restriction.

coibir [koi'bi*] *vt* to restrain; **~ de** to restrain from; **~-se** *vr*: **~-se de** to abstain from.

coice ['kojsi] *m* kick; *(de arma)* recoil; **dar ~s em** to kick; *(fig)* to be aggressive with.

coincidência [koĩsi'dẽsja] *f* coincidence.

coincidir [koĩsi'dʒi*] *vi* to coincide; *(concordar)* to agree.

coisa ['kojza] *f* thing; *(assunto)* matter; **~s** *fpl* things; *(col: órgãos genitais)* privates; **~ de** about; **ser uma ~** *(col)* to be really something; *(ruim)* to be terrible; **que ~!** gosh!; **não dizer ~ com ~** not to make any sense; **deu uma ~ nele** something strange got into him.

coisíssima [koj'zisima] *f*: **~ nenhuma** *(nada)* nothing; *(de modo algum)* not at all.

coitado/a [koj'tadu/a] *adj* poor, wretched; **~!** poor thing!; **~ do João** poor John.

coito ['kojtu] *m* intercourse, coitus.

cola ['kɔla] *f* glue; *(BR: cópia)* crib.

colaboração [kolabora'sãw] *(pl -ões) f* collaboration; *(num jornal etc)* contribution.

colaborador(a) [kolabora'do*(a)] *m/f* collaborator; *(em jornal)* contributor.

colaborar [kolabo'ra*] *vi* to collaborate; *(ajudar)* to help; *(escrever artigos etc)* to contribute.

colagem [ko'laʒẽ] *f* collage.

colante [ko'lãtʃi] *adj (roupa)* skin-tight.

colapso [ko'lapsu] *m* collapse; **~ cardíaco** heart failure.

colar [ko'la*] *vt* to stick, glue; *(BR: copiar)* to crib ♦ *vi* to stick; to cheat; *(col: ser acreditado)* to stand up, stick ♦ *m* necklace; **~ grau** to graduate .

colarinho [kola'riɲu] *m* collar; *(col: na cerveja)* head.

colarinho-branco *(pl colarinhos-brancos) m* white-collar worker.

colateral [kolate'raw] *(pl -ais) adj V* efeito.

colcha ['kowʃa] *f* bedspread.

colchão [kow'ʃãw] *(pl -ões) m* mattress.

colcheia [kow'ʃeja] *f (MÚS)* quaver.

colchete [kow'ʃetʃi] *m* clasp, fastening; *(parêntese)* square bracket; **~ de gancho** hook and eye; **~ de pressão** press stud.

colchões [kow'ʃõjʃ] *mpl de* **colchão.**

colchonete [kowʃo'netʃi] *m* (portable) mattress.

coleção [kole'sãw] *(PT:* **-cç-:** *pl* **-ões)** *f* collection.

colecionador(a) [kolesjona'do*(a)] *(PT:* **-cc-)** *m/f* collector.

colecionar [kolesjo'na*] *(PT:* **-cc-)** *vt* to collect.

coleções [kole'sõjʃ] *fpl de* **coleção.**

colectar *etc* [kolek'ta*] *(PT)* = **coletar** *etc.*

colega [ko'lɛga] *m/f (de trabalho)* colleague; *(de escola)* classmate; *(amigo)* friend.

colegial [kole'ʒjaw] *(pl* **-ais)** *adj* school *atr* ♦ *m/f* schoolboy/girl.

colégio [ko'lɛʒu] *m* school; **~ eleitoral** electoral college.

coleguismo [kole'ʒiʒmu] *m* loyalty to one's colleagues.

coleira [ko'lejra] *f* collar.

cólera ['kɔlera] *f (ira)* anger; *(fúria)* rage ♦ *m ou f (MED)* cholera.

colérico/a [ko'lɛriku/a] *adj (irado)* angry; *(furioso)* furious ♦ *m/f (MED)* cholera patient.

colesterol [kolɛʃte'rɔw] *m* cholesterol.

coleta [ko'lɛta] *f* collection; *(imposto)* levy.

coletânea [kole'tanja] *f* collection.

coletar [kole'ta*] *vt* to tax; *(arrecadar)* to collect.

colete [ko'letʃi] *m* waistcoat *(BRIT)*, vest *(US)*; **~ salva-vidas** life jacket *(BRIT)*, life preserver *(US)*.

coletividade [koletʃivi'dadʒi] *f* community.

coletivo/a [kole'tʃivu/a] *adj* collective; *(transportes)* public ♦ *m* bus.

coletor(a) [kole'to*(a)] *m/f* collector.

coletoria [koleto'ria] *f* tax office.

colheita [ko'ʎejta] *f* harvest; *(produto)* crop.

colher [ko'ʎe*] *vt (recolher)* to gather, pick; *(dados)* to gather ♦ *f* spoon; **~ de chá/sopa** teaspoon/tablespoon; **dar uma ~ de chá a alguém** *(fig)* to do sb a favo(u)r; **de ~** *(col)* on a silver platter.

colherada [koʎe'rada] *f* spoonful.

colibri [koli'bri] *m* hummingbird.

cólica ['kɔlika] *f* colic.

colidir [koli'dʒi*] *vi*: **~ com** to collide with, crash into.

coligação [koliga'sãw] *(pl -ões) f* coalition.

coligar [koli'ga*] *vt* to bring together, unit; **~-se** *vr* to join forces.

coligir [koli'ʒi*] *vt* to collect.

colina [ko'lina] *f* hill.

colírio [ko'lirju] *m* eyewash.

colisão [koli'zãw] *(pl -ões) f* collision.

colis postaux [ko'li pos'to] *mpl* small packets.

colite [ko'litʃi] *f* colitis.

collant [ko'lã] *(pl* **~s)** *m* tights *pl (BRIT)*, pantihose *(US)*; *(blusa)* leotard.

colmeia [kow'meja] f beehive.

colo ['kɔlu] m neck; (regaço) lap; **no ~ on** one's lap, in one's arms.

colocação [koloka'sãw] (pl -ões) f placing; (emprego) job, position; (de pneus, tapete etc) fitting; (de uma questão, idéia) positing; (opinião) position.

colocar [kolo'ka*] vt to put, place; (empregar) to find a job for, place; (COM) to market; (pneus, tapetes) to fit; (questão, idéia) to put forward, state; **~-se** vr to place o.s.; **coloque-se no meu lugar** put yourself in my position.

Colômbia [ko'lôbja] f: **a ~** Colombia.

colombiano/a [kolô'bjanu/a] adj, m/f Colombian.

cólon ['kɔlô] m colon.

colônia [ko'lonja] f colony; (perfume) cologne.

colonial [kolo'njaw] (pl -ais) adj colonial.

colonialismo [kolonja'liʒmu] m colonialism.

colonização [koloniza'sãw] f colonization.

colonizador(a) [koloniza'do*(a)] adj colonizing ♦ m/f colonist, settler.

colonizar [koloni'za*] vt to colonize.

colono [ko'lɔnu/a] m/f settler; (cultivador) tenant farmer.

coloquei [kolo'kej] etc vb V **colocar**.

coloquial [kolo'kjaw] (pl -ais) adj colloquial.

colóquio [ko'lɔkju] m conversation; (congresso) conference.

coloração [kolora'sãw] f colouration (BRIT), coloration (US).

colorido/a [kolo'ridu/a] adj colourful (BRIT), colorful (US) ♦ m colouring (BRIT), coloring (US).

colorir [kolo'ri*] vt to colour (BRIT), color (US).

colossal [kolo'saw] (pl -ais) adj colossal.

colosso [ko'losu] m (pessoa) giant; (coisa) extraordinary thing.

coluna [ko'luna] f column; (pilar) pillar; **~ dorsal** ou **vertebral** spine.

colunável [kolu'navew] (pl -eis) adj famous ♦ m/f celebrity.

colunista [kolu'niʃta] m/f columnist.

com [kõ] prep with; **estar ~ fome** to be hungry; **~ cuidado** carefully; **estar ~ dinheiro/câncer** to have some money on one/ have cancer; **"não ultrapasse ~ faixa contínua"** "do not overtake when centre line is unbroken".

coma ['kɔma] f coma.

comadre [ko'madri] f (urinol) bedpan; **minha ~** the godmother of my child (ou the mother of my godchild).

comandante [komã'dãtʃi] m commander; (MIL) commandant; (NÁUT) captain.

comandar [komã'da*] vt to command.

comando [ko'mãdu] m command.

combate [kõ'batʃi] m combat, fight; (fig) battle.

combatente [kõba'tẽtʃi] m/f combatant.

combater [kõba'te*] vt to fight, combat; (opor-se a) to oppose ♦ vi to fight; **~-se** vr to fight.

combinação [kõbina'sãw] (pl -ões) f combination; (QUÍM) compound; (acordo) arrangement; (plano) scheme; (roupa) slip.

combinar [kõbi'na*] vt to combine; (jantar etc) to arrange; (fuga etc) to plan ♦ vi (roupas etc) to go together; **~-se** vr to combine; (pessoas) to get on well together; (temperamentos) to go well together; **~ com** (harmonizar-se) to go with; **~ de fazer** to arrange to do; **combinado!** agreed!

comboio [kõ'boju] m (PT) train; (de navios) convoy.

combustão [kõbuʃ'tãw] (pl -ões) f combustion.

combustível [kõbuʃ'tʃivew] m fuel.

combustões [kõbuʃ'tõjʃ] fpl de **combustão**.

começar [kome'sa*] (irreg) vt, vi to begin, start; **~ a fazer** to begin ou start to do.

começo [ko'mesu] etc vb V **comedir-se** ♦ m beginning, start.

comédia [ko'mɛdʒja] f comedy.

comediante [kome'dʒjãtʃi] m/f (comic) actor/ actress.

comedido/a [kome'dʒidu/a] adj moderate; (prudente) prudent.

comedir-se [kome'dʒixsi] vr to control o.s.

comedorias [komedo'riaʃ] fpl food.

comemoração [komemora'sãw] (pl -ões) f commemoration.

comemorar [komemo'ra*] vt to commemorate; (celebrar: sucesso etc) to celebrate.

comemorativo/a [komemora'tʃivu/a] adj commemorative.

comensal [komẽ'saw] (pl -ais) m/f diner.

comentar [komẽ'ta*] vt to comment on; (maliciosamente) to make comments about.

comentário [komẽ'tarju] m comment, remark; (análise) commentary; **sem ~** no comment.

comentarista [komẽta'riʃta] m/f commentator.

comer [ko'me*] vt to eat; (damas, xadrez) to take, capture; (dinheiro) to eat up; (corroer) to eat away ♦ vi to eat; **~-se** vr: **~-se (de)** to be consumed (with); **dar de ~ a** to feed; **~ por quatro** (fig) to eat like a horse; **~ fogo** (col) to go through hell.

comercial [komex'sjaw] (pl -ais) adj commercial; (relativo ao negócio) business atr ♦ m commercial.

comercialização [komexsjaliza'sãw] f marketing.

comercializar [komexsjali'za*] vt to market.

comercializável [komexsjali'zavew] (pl -eis) adj marketable.

comerciante [komex'sjãtʃi] m/f trader.

comerciar [komex'sja*] vi to trade, do business.

comerciário/a [komɛx'sjarju/a] *m/f* employee in business.

comércio [ko'mɛxsju] *m* commerce; (*tráfico*) trade; (*negócio*) business; (*lojas*) shops *pl*; **de fechar o ~** (*col*) really stunning.

comes ['kɔmiʃ] *mpl*: **~ e bebes** food and drink.

comestíveis [komeʃ'tʃíveis] *mpl* foodstuffs, food *sg*.

comestível [komeʃ'tʃivew] (*pl* -**eis**) *adj* edible.

cometa [ko'meta] *m* comet.

cometer [kome'te*] *vt* to commit.

cometimento [kometʃi'mētu] *m* undertaking, commitment.

comichão [komi'ʃãw] *f* itch, itching.

comichar [komi'ʃa*] *vt*, *vi* to itch.

comício [ko'misju] *m* (*POL*) rally, meeting; (*assembléia*) assembly.

comicidade [komisi'dadʒi] *f* comic quality.

cômico/a ['komiku/a] *adj* comic(al) ♦ *m* comedian; (*de teatro*) actor.

comida [ko'mida] *f* (*alimento*) food; (*refeição*) meal; **~ caseira** home cooking.

comigo [ko'migu] *pron* with me; (*reflexivo*) with myself.

comilança [komi'lãsa] *f* overeating.

comilão/lona [komi'lãw/lɔna] (*pl* -**ões/~s**) *adj* greedy ♦ *m/f* glutton.

cominho [ko'miɲu] *m* cumin.

comiserar [komize'ra*] *vt* to move to pity; **~-se** *vr*: **~-se (de)** to sympathize (with).

comissão [komi'sãw] (*pl* -**ões**) *f* commission; (*comitê*) committee.

comissário [komi'sarju] *m* commissioner; (*COM*) agent; **~ de bordo** (*AER*) steward; (*NÁUT*) purser.

comissionar [komisjo'na*] *vt* to commission.

comissões [komi'sõjʃ] *fpl de* **comissão**.

comitê [komi'te] *m* committee.

comitiva [komi'tʃiva] *f* entourage.

como ['kɔmu] *adv* as; (*assim como*) like; (*de que maneira*) how ♦ *conj* (*porque*) as, since; (*da mesma maneira que*) as; **~?** pardon?; **~ assim?** how do you mean?; **~!** what!; **~ não!** of course!; **~ se** as if; **~ quer que** however; **seja ~ for** be that as it may; **assim ~** as well as; **~ quiser** as you wish; **e ~!** and how.

comoção [komo'sãw] (*pl* -**ões**) *f* (*abalo*) distress; (*revolta*) commotion.

cômoda ['komoda] *f* chest of drawers (*BRIT*), bureau (*US*).

comodidade [komodʒi'dadʒi] *f* (*conforto*) comfort; (*conveniência*) convenience.

comodismo [komo'dʒiʒmu] *m* complacency.

comodista [komo'dʒiʃta] *adj* complacent.

cômodo/a ['komodu/a] *adj* (*confortável*) comfortable; (*conveniente*) convenient ♦ *m* (*aposento*) room.

comovedor(a) [komove'do*(a)] *adj* moving, touching.

comovente [komo'vētʃi] *adj* moving, touch-

ing.

comover [komo've*] *vt* to move ♦ *vi* to be moving; **~-se** *vr* to be moved.

comovido/a [komo'vidu/a] *adj* moved.

compacto/a [kõ'paktu/a] *adj* (*pequeno*) compact; (*espesso*) thick; (*sólido*) solid ♦ *m* (*disco*) single.

compadecer-se [kõpade'sexsi] *vr*: **~-se de** to be sorry for, pity.

compadecido/a [kõpade'sidu/a] *adj* sympathetic.

compadecimento [kõpadesi'mētu] *m* sympathy; (*piedade*) pity.

compadre [kõ'padri] *m* (*col*: *companheiro*) buddy, pal, crony; **meu ~** the godfather of my child (*ou* the father of my godchild).

compaixão [kõpaj'ʃãw] *m* (*piedade*) compassion, pity; (*misericórdia*) mercy.

companheirão/rona [kõpaɲej'rãw/'rɔna] (*pl* -**ões/~s**) *m/f* good friend.

companheirismo [kõpaɲej'riʒmu] *m* companionship.

companheiro/a [kõpa'ɲejru/a] *m/f* companion; (*colega*) friend; (*col*) buddy, mate; **~ de viagem** fellow traveller (*BRIT*) *ou* traveler (*US*), travelling (*BRIT*) *ou* traveling (*US*) companion.

companheirões [kõpaɲej'rõjʃ] *mpl de* **companheirão**.

companheirona [kõpaɲej'rɔna] *f de* **companheirão**.

companhia [kõpa'ɲia] *f* (*COM*) company, firm; (*convivência*) company; **fazer ~ a alguém** to keep sb company; **em ~ de** accompanied by; **dama de ~** companion.

comparação [kõpara'sãw] (*pl* -**ões**) *f* comparison.

comparar [kõpa'ra*] *vt* to compare; **~-se** *vr*: **~-se com** to bear comparison with; **~ a** to liken to; **~ com** to compare with.

comparativo/a [kõpara'tʃivu/a] *adj* comparative.

comparável [kõpa'ravew] (*pl* -**eis**) *adj* comparable.

comparecer [kõpare'se*] *vi* to appear, make an appearance; **~ a uma reunião** to attend a meeting.

comparecimento [kõparesi'mētu] *m* (*presença*) attendance.

comparsa [kõ'paxsa] *m/f* (*TEATRO*) extra; (*cúmplice*) accomplice.

compartilhar [kõpaxtʃi'ʎa*] *vt* (*partilhar*) to share; **~ de** (*participar de*) to share in, participate in; **~ com alguém** to share with sb.

compartimentar [kõpaxtʃimē'ta*] *vt* to compartmentalize.

compartimento [kõpaxtʃi'mētu] *m* compartment; (*aposento*) room.

compartir [kõpax'tʃi*] *vt* (*dividir*) to share out ♦ *vi*: **~ de** to share in.

compassado/a [kõpa'sadu/a] *adj* (*medido*) measured; (*moderado*) moderate;

(cadenciado) regular; (pausado) slow.

compassivo/a [kõpa'sivu/a] adj compassionate.

compasso [kõ'pasu] m (instrumento) a pair of compasses; (MÚS) time; (ritmo) beat; **dentro do ~** in time with the music; **fora do ~** out of time.

compatibilidade [kõpatʃibili'dadʒi] f compatibility.

compatível [kõpa'tʃivew] (pl -eis) adj compatible; **~ com o IBM-PC** IBM compatible.

compatriota [kõpa'trjɔta] m/f fellow countryman/woman, compatriot.

compelir [kõpe'li*] vt to force, compel.

compêndio [kõ'pēdʒju] m (sumário) compendium; (livro de texto) text book.

compenetração [kõpenetra'sãw] (pl -ões) f conviction.

compenetrar [kõpene'tra*] vt to convince; **~-se** vr to be convinced.

compensação [kõpēsa'sãw] (pl -ões) f compensation; (de cheques) clearance; **em ~** on the other hand.

compensado [kõpē'sadu] m hardboard.

compensador(a) [kõpēsa'do*(a)] adj compensatory.

compensar [kõpē'sa*] vt (reparar o dano) to make up for, compensate for; (equilibrar) to offset, counterbalance; (cheque) to clear.

competência [kõpe'tēsja] f competence, ability; **isto é de minha ~** this is my responsibility.

competente [kõpe'tētʃi] adj (capaz) competent, able; (apropriado) appropriate.

competição [kõpetʃi'sãw] (pl -ões) f competition.

competidor(a) [kõpetʃi'do*(a)] m/f competitor.

competir [kõpe'tʃi*] vi to compete; **~ a alguém** (ser da competência de) to be sb's responsibility; (caber) to be up to sb; **~ com** to compete with.

competitividade [kõpetʃitʃivi'dadʒi] f competitiveness.

competitivo/a [kõpetʃi'tʃivu/a] adj competitive.

compilação [kõpila'sãw] (pl -ões) f compilation.

compilar [kõpi'la*] vt to compile.

compilo [kõ'pilu] etc vb V **compelir**.

compito [kõ'pitu] etc vb V **competir**.

complacência [kõpla'sēsja] f complaisance.

complacente [kõpla'sētʃi] adj obliging.

compleição [kõplej'sãw] (pl -ões) f build.

complementar [kõplemē'ta*] adj complementary ♦ vt to supplement.

complemento [kõple'mētu] m complement.

completamente [kõpleta'mētʃi] adv completely, quite.

completar [kõple'ta*] vt to complete; (tanque,

água) to fill up, top up; **~ dez anos** to be ten.

completo/a [kõ'pletu/a] adj complete; (cheio) full (up); **por ~** completely.

complexado/a [kõplek'sadu/a] adj hung-up; **estar/ficar ~** to have/get a complex.

complexidade [kõpleksi'dadʒi] f complexity.

complexo/a [kõ'pleksu/a] adj complex ♦ m complex; **~ de Édipo** Oedipus complex.

complicação [kõplika'sãw] (pl -ões) f complication.

complicado/a [kõpli'kadu/a] adj complicated.

complicar [kõpli'ka*] vt to complicate; **~-se** vr to become complicated; (enredo) to thicken.

complô [kõ'plo] m plot, conspiracy.

compõe [kõ'põj] etc vb V **compor**.

compomos [kõ'pomoʃ] etc vb V **compor**.

componho [kõ'poɲu] etc vb V **compor**.

componente [kõpo'nētʃi] adj, m component.

compor [kõ'po*] (irreg: como **pôr**) vt to compose; (discurso, livro) to write; (arranjar) to arrange; (TIP) to set ♦ vi to compose; **~-se** vr (controlar-se) to compose o.s.; **~-se de** to be made up of, be composed of.

comporta [kõ'pɔxta] f floodgate; (de canal) lock.

comportamento [kõpoxta'mētu] m behaviour (BRIT), behavior (US); (conduta) conduct; **mau ~** misbehavio(u)r.

comportar [kõpox'ta*] vt (suportar) to put up with, bear; (conter) to hold; **~-se** vr (portar-se) to behave; **~-se mal** to misbehave, behave badly.

compôs [kõ'poʃ] vb V **compor**.

composição [kõpozi'sãw] (pl -ões) f composition; (TIP) typesetting; (conciliação) compromise.

compositor(a) [kõpozi'to*(a)] m/f composer; (TIP) typesetter.

composto/a [kõ'poʃtu/'pɔʃta] pp de **compor** ♦ adj (sério) serious; (de muitos elementos) composite, compound ♦ m compound; **~ de** made up of, composed of.

compostura [kõpoʃ'tura] f composure.

compota [kõ'pɔta] f fruit in syrup; **~ de laranja** oranges in syrup.

compra ['kõpra] f purchase; **fazer ~s** to go shopping.

comprador(a) [kõpra'do*(a)] m/f buyer, purchaser.

comprar [kõ'pra*] vt to buy; (subornar) to bribe; **~ briga** to look for trouble; **~ a briga de alguém** to fight sb's battle for him.

comprazer-se [kõpra'zexsi] vr: **~ com/em fazer** to take pleasure in/in doing.

compreender [kõprjen'de*] vt (entender) to understand; (constar de) to be comprised of, consist of; (abranger) to cover.

---

*NB: European Portuguese adds the following consonants to certain words: **b** (sú(b)dito, su(b)til); **c** (a(c)ção, a(c)cionista, a(c)to); **m** (inde(m)ne); **p** (ado(p)ção, ado(p)tar); for further details see p. xiii.*

compreensão [kõprjē'sãw] *f* understanding, comprehension.

compreensível [kõprjē'sivew] (*pl* **-eis**) *adj* understandable, comprehensible.

compreensivo/a [kõprjē'sivu/a] *adj* understanding.

compressa [kõ'prɛsa] *f* compress.

compressão [kõpre'sãw] (*pl* **-ões**) *f* compression.

compressor(a) [kõpre'so*(a)] *adj V* **rolo**.

comprido/a [kõ'pridu/a] *adj* long; (*alto*) tall; **ao** ~ lengthways.

comprimento [kõpri'mētu] *m* length.

comprimido/a [kõpri'midu/a] *adj* compressed ♦ *m* (*pílula*) pill; (*pastilha*) tablet.

comprimir [kõpri'mi*] *vt* to compress; (*apertar*) to squeeze.

comprometedor(a) [kõpromete'do*(a)] *adj* compromising.

comprometer [kõprome'te*] *vt* to compromise; (*envolver*) to involve; (*arriscar*) to jeopardize; (*empenhar*) to pledge; ~**-se** *vr* to commit o.s.; ~**-se a** to undertake to, promise to; ~**-se com alguém** to make a commitment to sb.

comprometido/a [kõprome'tʃidu/a] *adj* (*ocupado*) busy; (*noivo etc*) spoken for.

compromisso [kõpro'misu] *m* (*promessa*) promise; (*obrigação*) commitment; (*hora marcada*) appointment, engagement; (*acordo*) agreement; **sem** ~ without obligation.

comprovação [kõprova'sãw] (*pl* **-ões**) *f* proof, evidence; (*ADMIN*) receipts *pl*.

comprovante [kõpro'vãtʃi] *adj* of proof ♦ *m* receipt, voucher.

comprovar [kõpro'va*] *vt* to prove; (*confirmar*) to confirm.

compulsão [kõpuw'sãw] (*pl* **-ões**) *f* compulsion.

compulsivo/a [kõpuw'sivu/a] *adj* compulsive.

compulsões [kõpuw'sõjʃ] *fpl de* **compulsão**.

compulsório/a [kõpuw'sɔrju/a] *adj* compulsory.

compunção [kõpũ'sãw] *f* compunction.

compungir [kõpũ'ʒi*] *vt* to pain ♦ *vi* to be painful.

compunha [kõ'puɲa] *etc vb V* **compor**.

compus [kõ'puʃ] *etc vb V* **compor**.

compuser [kõpu'ze*] *etc vb V* **compor**.

computação [kõputa'sãw] *f* computation; (*ciência, curso*) computer science, computing.

computador [kõputa'do*] *m* computer.

computadorizar [kõputadori'za*] *vt* to computerize.

computar [kõpu'ta*] *vt* to compute; (*calcular*) to calculate; (*contar*) to count.

cômputo ['kõputu] *m* computation.

comum [ko'mũ] (*pl* **-ns**) *adj* (*pessoa*) ordinary, common; (*habitual*) usual ♦ *m* the usual thing; **o** ~ **é partirmos às 8** we usually set off at 8; **fora do** ~ unusual; **temos muito**

em ~ we have a lot in common.

comuna [ko'muna] (*col*) *m/f* communist.

comungar [komũ'ga*] *vi* to take communion.

comunhão [komu'ɲãw] (*pl* **-ões**) *f* communion; (*REL*) Holy Communion; ~ **de bens** joint ownership.

comunicação [komunika'sãw] (*pl* **-ões**) *f* communication; (*mensagem*) message; (*curso*) media studies *sg*; (*acesso*) access.

comunicado [komuni'kadu] *m* notice; (*oficial*) communiqué.

comunicar [komuni'ka*] *vt* to communicate; (*unir*) to join ♦ *vi* to communicate; ~**-se** *vr* to communicate; ~ **algo a alguém** to inform sb of sth; ~**-se com** (*entrar em contato*) to get in touch with.

comunicativo/a [comunika'tʃivu/a] *adj* communicative; (*riso*) infectious.

comunidade [komuni'dadʒi] *f* community; **C**~ **Econômica Européia** European (Economic) Community.

comunismo [komu'niʒmu] *m* communism.

comunista [komu'niʃta] *adj, m/f* communist.

comunitário/a [komuni'tarju/a] *adj* community *atr*.

comuns [ko'mũʃ] *pl de* **comum**.

comutador [komuta'do*] *m* switch.

comutar [komu'ta*] *vt* (*JUR*) to commute; (*trocar*) to exchange.

concatenar [kõkate'na*] *vt* (*idéias*) to string together.

côncavo/a ['kõkavu/a] *adj* concave; (*cavado*) hollow ♦ *m* hollow.

conceber [kõse'be*] *vt* to conceive; (*imaginar*) to conceive of, imagine; (*entender*) to understand ♦ *vi* to become pregnant.

concebível [kõse'bivew] (*pl* **-eis**) *adj* conceivable.

conceder [kõse'de*] *vt* (*permitir*) to allow; (*outorgar*) to grant, accord; (*admitir*) to concede; (*dar*) to give ♦ *vi*: ~ **em** to agree to.

conceito [kõ'sejtu] *m* (*idéia*) concept, idea; (*fama*) reputation; (*opinião*) opinion.

conceituado/a [kõsej'twadu/a] *adj* well thought of, highly regarded.

conceituar [kõsej'twa*] *vt* to conceptualize.

concentração [kõsẽtra'sãw] (*pl* **-ões**) *f* concentration; (*ESPORTE*) training camp.

concentrado/a [kõsẽ'tradu/a] *adj* concentrated ♦ *m* concentrate.

concentrar [kõsẽ'tra*] *vt* to concentrate; (*atenção*) to focus; (*reunir*) to bring together; (*molho*) to thicken; ~**-se** *vr* to concentrate; ~**-se em** to concentrate on.

concepção [kõsep'sãw] (*pl* **-ões**) *f* (*geração*) conception; (*noção*) idea, concept; (*opinião*) opinion.

concernente [kõsex'nẽtʃi] *adj*: ~ **a** concerning.

concernir [kõsex'ni*] *vi*: ~ **a** to concern.

concertar [kõsex'ta*] *vt* (*endireitar*) to adjust; (*conciliar*) to reconcile.

concerto [kő'sextu] *m* concert.

concessão [kőse'sãw] (*pl* **-ões**) *f* concession; (*permissão*) permission.

concessionária [kősesjo'narja] *f* dealer, dealership.

concessionário [kősesjo'narju] *m* concessionaire.

concessões [kőse'sõjʃ] *fpl de* **concessão**.

concha ['kőʃa] *f* (*moluscos*) shell; (*para líquidos*) ladle.

conchavo [kő'ʃavu] *m* conspiracy.

conciliação [kősilja'sãw] (*pl* **-ões**) *f* reconciliation.

conciliador(a) [kősilja'do*(a)] *adj* conciliatory ♦ *m/f* conciliator.

conciliar [kősi'lja*] *vt* to reconcile; ~ **o sono** to get to sleep.

conciliatório/a [kősilja'tɔrju/a] *adj* conciliatory.

conciliável [kősi'ljavew] (*pl* **-eis**) *adj* reconcilable.

concílio [kő'silju] *m* (*REL*) council.

concisão [kősi'zãw] *f* concision, conciseness.

conciso/a [kő'sizu/a] *adj* brief, concise.

concitar [kősi'ta*] *vt* (*estimular*) to stir up, arouse; (*incitar*) to incite.

conclamar [kőkla'ma*] *vt* to shout; (*aclamar*) to acclaim; (*convocar*) to call together.

Conclat [kő'klatʃi] (*BR*) *abr f* (= *Conferência Nacional da Classe Trabalhadora*) trade union.

conclave [kő'klavi] *m* conclave.

concludente [kőklu'dẽtʃi] *adj* conclusive.

concluir [kő'klwi*] *vt* (*terminar*) to end, conclude ♦ *vi* (*deduzir*) to conclude.

conclusão [kőklu'zãw] (*pl* **-ões**) *f* (*término*) end; (*dedução*) conclusion; **chegar a uma** ~ to come to a conclusion; ~, **ele não veio** (*col*) the upshot is, he didn't come.

conclusivo/a [kőklu'zivu/a] *adj* conclusive.

conclusões [kőklu'zõjʃ] *fpl de* **conclusão**.

concomitante [kőkomi'tãtʃi] *adj* concomitant.

concordância [kőkox'dãsja] *f* agreement.

concordante [kőkox'dãtʃi] *adj* (*fatos*) concordant.

concordar [kőkox'da*] *vi*, *vt* to agree; **não concordo!** I disagree!; ~ **com** to agree with; ~ **em** to agree to.

concordata [kőkox'data] *f* liquidation agreement.

concórdia [kő'kɔxdʒja] *f* (*acordo*) agreement; (*paz*) peace.

concorrência [kőko'xẽsja] *f* competition; (*a um cargo*) application.

concorrente [kőko'xẽtʃi] *m/f* (*competidor*) contestant; (*candidato*) candidate.

concorrer [kőko'xe*] *vi* (*competir*) to compete; ~ **a** (*candidatar-se*) to apply for; ~ **para** (*contribuir*) to contribute to.

concorrido/a [kőko'xidu/a] *adj* popular.

concretização [kőkretʃiza'sãw] *f* realization.

concretizar [kőkretʃi'za*] *vt* to make real; ~**se** *vr* (*sonho*) to come true; (*ambições*) to be realized.

concreto/a [kő'krɛtu/a] *adj* concrete; (*verdadeiro*) real; (*sólido*) solid ♦ *m* concrete; ~ **armado** reinforced concrete.

concupiscência [kőkupi'sẽsja] *f* greed; (*lascívia*) lust.

concurso [kő'kuxsu] *m* contest; (*exame*) competition; ~ **público** open competition.

concussão [kőku'sãw] *f* concussion; (*desfalque*) embezzlement.

condado [kő'dadu] *m* county.

condão [kő'dãw] *m V* **varinha**.

conde ['kődʒi] *m* count.

condecoração [kődekora'sãw] (*pl* **-ões**) *f* decoration.

condecorar [kődeko'ra*] *vt* to decorate.

condenação [kődena'sãw] (*pl* **-ões**) *f* condemnation; (*JUR*) conviction.

condenar [kőde'na*] *vt* to condemn; (*JUR*: *sentenciar*) to sentence; (: *declarar culpado*) to convict.

condenável [kőde'navew] (*pl* **-eis**) *adj* reprehensible.

condensação [kődẽsa'sãw] *f* condensation.

condensar [kődẽ'sa*] *vt* to condense; ~**se** *vr* to condense.

condescendência [kődesẽ'dẽsja] *f* acquiescence.

condescendente [kődesẽ'dẽtʃi] *adj* condescending.

condescender [kődesẽ'de*] *vi* to acquiesce; ~ **a** *ou* **em** to condescend to, deign to.

condessa [kő'desa] *f* countess.

condição [kődʒi'sãw] (*pl* **-ões**) *f* condition; (*social*) status; (*qualidade*) capacity; **com a** ~ **de que** on condition that, provided that; **ter** ~ *ou* **condições para fazer** to be able to do; **em condições de fazer** (*pessoa*) able to do; (*carro etc*) in condition to do; **em sua** ~ **de líder** in his capacity as leader.

condicionado/a [kődʒisjo'nadu/a] *adj* conditioned; *V tb* **ar**.

condicional [kődʒisjo'naw] (*pl* **-ais**) *adj* conditional.

condicionamento [kődʒisjona'mẽtu] *m* conditioning.

condições [kődʒi'sõjʃ] *fpl de* **condição**.

condigno/a [kő'dʒignu/a] *adj* (*apropriado*) fitting; (*merecido*) deserved.

condigo [kő'dʒigu] *etc vb V* **condizer**.

condimentar [kődʒimẽ'ta*] *vt* to season.

condimento [kődʒi'mẽtu] *m* seasoning.

condisse [kő'dʒisi] *etc vb V* **condizer**.

condito [kő'dʒitu] *pp de* **condizer**.

condizente [kődʒi'zẽtʃi] *adj*: ~ **com** in keeping with.

condizer [kődʒi'ze*] (*irreg: como* **dizer**) *vi*: ~

NB: European Portuguese adds the following consonants to certain words: **b** (sú(b)dito, su(b)til); **c** (a(c)ção, a(c)cionista, a(c)to); **m** (inde(m)ne); **p** (ado(p)ção, ado(p)tar); *for further details see p. xiii.*

com to match.
condoer-se [kŏdo'exsi] *vr*: ~ **de** to pity.
condolência [kŏdo'lẽsja] *f* condolence.
condomínio [kŏdo'minju] *m* condominium; (*contribuição*) service charge.
condução [kŏdu'sãw] *f* (*ato de conduzir*) driving; (*transporte*) transport; (*ônibus*) bus; (*FÍS*) conduction.
conducente [kŏdu'sẽtʃi] *adj*: ~ **a** conducive to.
conduta [kŏ'duta] *f* conduct; **má** ~ misconduct.
conduto [kŏ'dutu] *m* (*tubo*) tube; (*cano*) pipe; (*canal*) channel.
condutor(a) [kŏdu'to*(a)] *m/f* (*de veículo*) driver ♦ *m* (*ELET*) conductor.
conduzir [kŏdu'zi*] *vt* (*PT*: *veículo*) to drive; (*levar*) to lead; (*negócio*) to manage; (*FÍS*) to conduct ♦ *vi* (*PT*) to drive; ~-**se** *vr* to behave; ~ **a** to lead to.
cone ['kɔni] *m* cone.
conectar [konek'ta*] *vt* to connect.
cônego ['konegu] *m* (*REL*) canon.
conexão [konek'sãw] (*pl* -**ões**) *f* connection.
conexo/a [ko'nɛksu/a] *adj* connected.
conexões [konek'sõjʃ] *fpl de* **conexão**.
confabular [kŏfabu'la*] *vi* to talk; ~ **com** to talk to.
confecção [kŏfek'sãw] (*pl* -**ões**) *f* (*feitura*) making; (*de um boletim*) production; (*roupa*) ready-to-wear clothes *pl*; (*negócio*) *business selling ready-to-wear clothes*.
confeccionar [kŏfeksjo'na*] *vt* (*fazer*) to make; (*fabricar*) to manufacture.
confeccionista [kŏfeksjo'niʃta] *m/f maker of ready-to-wear clothes*.
confecções [kŏfek'sõjʃ] *fpl de* **confecção**.
confederação [kŏfedera'sãw] (*pl* -**ões**) *f* confederation; (*liga*) league.
confederar [kŏfede'ra*] *vt* to unite; ~-**se** *vr* to form an alliance.
confeitar [kŏfej'ta*] *vt* (*bolo*) to ice.
confeitaria [kŏfejta'ria] *f* patisserie.
confeiteiro/a [kŏfej'tejru/a] *m/f* confectioner.
conferência [kŏfe'rẽsja] *f* conference; (*discurso*) lecture; **fazer uma** ~ to give a lecture.
conferencista [kŏfere'siʃta] *m/f* (*que fala*) speaker.
conferente [kŏfe'rẽtʃi] *m/f* (*verificador*) checker.
conferir [kŏfe'ri*] *vt* (*verificar*) to check; (*comparar*) to compare; (*outorgar*) to grant; (*título*) to confer ♦ *vi* (*estar certo*) to tally; **confira!** see for yourself, check it out (*col*).
confessar [kŏfe'sa*] *vt*, *vi* to confess; ~-**se** *vr* to confess; ~ **alguém** (*REL*) to hear sb's confession; ~-**se culpado** (*JUR*) to plead guilty.
confessionário [kŏfesjo'narju] *m* confessional.
confessor [kŏfe'so*] *m* confessor.
confete [kŏ'fɛtʃi] *m* confetti; **jogar** ~ (*col*) to be flattering.
confiabilidade [kŏfjabili'dadʒi] *f* reliability.

confiado/a [kŏ'fjadu/a] (*col*) *adj* cheeky.
confiança [kŏ'fjãsa] *f* confidence; (*fé*) trust; (*familiaridade*) familiarity; **de** ~ reliable; **digno de** ~ trustworthy; **ter** ~ **em alguém** to trust sb; **dar** ~ **a alguém** (*no tratamento*) to be on informal terms with sb.
confiante [kŏ'fjãtʃi] *adj* confident; ~ **em** confident of.
confiar [kŏ'fja*] *vt* to entrust; (*segredo*) to confide ♦ *vi*: ~ **em** to trust; (*ter fé*) to have faith in.
confiável [kŏ'fjavew] (*pl* -**eis**) *adj* reliable.
confidência [kŏfi'dẽsja] *f* secret; **em** ~ in confidence.
confidencial [kŏfidẽ'sjaw] (*pl* -**ais**) *adj* confidential.
confidenciar [kŏfidẽ'sja*] *vt* to tell in confidence.
confidente [kŏfi'dẽtʃi] *m/f* confidant/confidante.
configuração [kŏfigura'sãw] (*pl* -**ões**) *f* configuration; (*forma*) shape, form.
configurar [kŏfigu'ra*] *vt* to shape, form; (*representar*) to represent; (*COMPUT*) to configure.
confinamento [kŏfina'mẽtu] *m* confinement.
confinar [kŏfi'na*] *vt* (*limitar*) to limit; (*enclausurar*) to confine ♦ *vi*: ~ **com** to border on; ~-**se** *vr*: ~-**se a** to confine o.s. to.
confins [kŏ'fiʃ] *mpl* limits, boundaries; **nos** ~ **de judas** (*col*) out in the sticks.
confirmação [kŏfixma'sãw] (*pl* -**ões**) *f* confirmation.
confirmar [kŏfix'ma*] *vt* to confirm; ~-**se** *vr* (*REL*) to be confirmed; (*realizar-se*) to come true.
confiro [kŏ'firu] *etc vb V* **conferir**.
confiscar [kŏfiʃ'ka*] *vt* to confiscate, seize.
confisco [kŏ'fiʃku] *m* confiscation.
confissão [kŏfi'sãw] (*pl* -**ões**) *f* confession.
conflagração [kŏflagra'sãw] (*pl* -**ões**) *f* conflagration.
conflagrar [kŏfla'gra*] *vt* to inflame, set alight; (*fig*) to plunge into turmoil.
conflitante [kŏfli'tãtʃi] *adj* conflicting.
conflito [kŏ'flitu] *m* conflict; **entrar em** ~ (**com**) to clash (with).
confluente [kŏ'flwẽtʃi] *m* tributary.
conformação [kŏfoxma'sãw] (*pl* -**ões**) *f* (*resignação*) resignation; (*forma*) form.
conformado/a [kŏfox'madu/a] *adj* resigned.
conformar [kŏfox'ma*] *vt* (*formar*) to form; ~-**se** *vr*: ~-**se com** to resign o.s. to; (*acomodar-se*) to conform to; ~ **com** to conform to.
conforme [kŏ'fɔxmi] *prep* according to ♦ *conj* (*logo que*) as soon as; (*como*) as, according to what; (*à medida que*) as; (*dependendo de*) depending on; **você vai?** — ~ are you going? — it depends.
conformidade [kŏfoxmi'dadʒi] *f* agreement; **em** ~ **com** in accordance with.
conformismo [kŏfox'miʒmu] *m* conformity.

conformista [kõfox'miʃta] *m/f* conformist.
confortante [kõfox'tãtʃi] *adj* comforting.
confortar [kõfox'ta*] *vt* (*consolar*) to comfort, console.
confortável [kõfox'tavew] (*pl* **-eis**) *adj* comfortable.
conforto [kõ'foxtu] *m* comfort.
confraria [kõfra'ria] *f* fraternity.
confraternizar [kõfratexni'za*] *vi* to fraternize.
confrontação [kõfrõta'sãw] (*pl* **-ões**) *f* (*acareação*) confrontation; (*comparação*) comparison.
confrontar [kõfrõ'ta*] *vt* (*acarear*) to confront; (*comparar*) to compare; **~-se** *vr* to face each other.
confronto [kõ'frõtu] *m* confrontation; (*comparação*) comparison.
confundir [kõfũ'dʒi*] *vt* to confuse; **~-se** *vr* to get mixed up, get confused.
confusão [kõfu'zãw] (*pl* **-ões**) *f* confusion; (*tumulto*) uproar; (*problemas*) trouble; (*barafunda*) chaos; **isso vai dar tanta ~** this will cause so much trouble; **fazer ~** (*confundir-se*) to get mixed up *ou* confused.
confuso/a [kõ'fuzu/a] *adj* confused; (*problema*) confusing; **está tudo muito ~ aqui hoje** it's all very chaotic in here today.
confusões [kõfu'zõjʃ] *fpl de* **confusão**.
congelado/a [kõʒe'ladu/a] *adj* frozen.
congelador [kõʒela'do*] *m* freezer, deep freeze.
congelamento [kõʒela'mẽtu] *m* freezing; (*ECON*) freeze.
congelar [kõʒe'la*] *vt* to freeze; **~-se** *vr* to freeze.
congênere [kõ'ʒeneri] *adj* similar.
congênito/a [kõ'ʒenitu/a] *adj* congenital.
congestão [kõʒeʃ'tãw] *f* congestion.
congestionado/a [kõʒeʃtʃio'nadu/a] *adj* (*trânsito*) congested; (*olhos*) bloodshot; (*rosto*) flushed.
congestionamento [kõʒeʃtʃjona'mẽtu] *m* congestion; **um ~ (de tráfego)** a traffic jam.
congestionar [kõʒeʃtʃjo'na*] *vt* to congest; **~-se** *vr* (*rosto*) to go red.
conglomeração [kõglomera'sãw] (*pl* **-ões**) *f* conglomeration.
conglomerado [kõglome'radu] *m* conglomerate.
conglomerar [kõglome'ra*] *vt* to heap together; **~-se** *vr* (*unir-se*) to join together, group together.
Congo ['kõgu] *m*: **o ~** the Congo.
congratular [kõgratu'la*] *vt*: **~ alguém por** to congratulate sb on.
congregação [kõgrega'sãw] (*pl* **-ões**) *f* (*REL*) congregation; (*reunião*) gathering.
congregar [kõgre'ga*] *vt* to bring together; **~-se** *vr* to congregate.

congressista [kõgre'siʃta] *m/f* congressman/woman.
congresso [kõ'grɛsu] *m* congress, conference.
conhaque [ko'ɲaki] *m* cognac, brandy.
conhecedor(a) [koɲese'do*(a)] *adj* knowing ♦ *m/f* connoisseur, expert.
conhecer [koɲe'se*] *vt* to know; (*travar conhecimento com*) to meet; (*descobrir*) to discover; **~-se** *vr* (*travar conhecimento*) to meet; (*ter conhecimento*) to know each other; **~ alguém de nome/vista** to know sb by name/sight; **quero ~ sua casa** I'd like to see your house; **você conhece Paris?** have you ever been to Paris?
conhecido/a [koɲe'sidu/a] *adj* known; (*célebre*) well-known ♦ *m/f* acquaintance.
conhecimento [koɲesi'mẽtu] *m* knowledge; (*idéia*) idea; (*conhecido*) acquaintance; (*COM*) bill of lading; **~s** *mpl* knowledge *sg*; **levar ao ~ de alguém** to bring to sb's notice; **ter ~ de** to know; **tomar ~ de** to learn about; **não tomar ~ de** (*não dar atenção a*) to take no notice of; **é de ~ geral** it is common knowledge; **~ aéreo** air waybill.
cônico/a ['koniku/a] *adj* conical.
conivência [koni'vẽsja] *f* connivance.
conivente [koni'vẽtʃi] *adj* conniving; **ser ~ em** to connive in.
conjetura [kõʒe'tura] (*PT*: **-ct-**) *f* conjecture, supposition; **fazer ~ (sobre)** to guess (at).
conjeturar [kõʒetu'ra*] (*PT*: **-ct-**) *vt* to guess at ♦ *vi* to conjecture.
conjugação [kõʒuga'sãw] (*pl* **-ões**) *f* conjugation.
conjugado [kõʒu'gadu] *m* bed-sitter.
conjugal [kõʒu'gaw] (*pl* **-ais**) *adj* conjugal; **vida ~** married life.
conjugar [kõʒu'ga*] *vt* (*verbo*) to conjugate; (*unir*) to join; **~-se** *vr* to join together.
cônjuge ['kõʒuʒi] *m* spouse.
conjunção [kõʒũ'sãw] (*pl* **-ões**) *f* (*união*) union; (*LING*) conjunction.
conjuntivite [kõʒũtʃi'vitʃi] *f* conjunctivitis.
conjuntivo [kõʒũ'tʃivu] (*PT*) *m* (*LING*) subjunctive.
conjunto/a [kõ'ʒũtu/a] *adj* joint ♦ *m* (*totalidade*) whole; (*coleção*) collection; (*músicos*) group; (*roupa*) outfit; **em ~** together.
conjuntura [kõʒũ'tura] *f* situation.
conluio [kõ'luju] *m* collusion.
conosco [ko'noʃku] *pron* with us.
conotação [konota'sãw] (*pl* **-ões**) *f* connotation.
conotar [kono'ta*] *vt* to connote.
conquanto [kõ'kwantu] *conj* although, though.
conquista [kõ'kiʃta] *f* conquest; (*da ciência*) achievement.
conquistador(a) [kõkiʃta'do*(a)] *adj* conquering ♦ *m* conqueror; (*namorador*) ladies' man.

NB: *European Portuguese adds the following consonants to certain words:* **b** (sú(b)dito, su(b)til); **c** (a(c)ção, a(c)cionista, a(c)to); **m** (inde(m)ne); **p** (ado(p)ção, ado(p)tar); *for further details see p. xiii.*

conquistar [kõkiʃ'ta*] vt (subjugar) to conquer; (alcançar) to achieve; (ganhar) to win, gain; (pessoa) to win over.

consagração [kõsagra'sãw] (pl -ões) f (REL) consecration; (aclamação) acclaim; (exaltação) praise; (dedicação) dedication; (de uma expressão) establishment.

consagrado/a [kõsa'gradu/a] adj (estabelecido) established.

consagrar [kõsa'gra*] vt (REL) to consecrate; (aclamar) to acclaim; (dedicar) to dedicate; (tempo) to devote; (expressão) to establish; (exaltar) to glorify; ~-se vr: ~-se a to devote o.s. to.

consangüíneo/a [kõsã'gwinju/a] adj related by blood ♦ m/f blood relation.

consciência [kõ'sjẽsja] f (moral) conscience; (percepção) awareness; (senso de responsabilidade) conscientiousness; **estar com a ~ limpa/pesada** to have a clear/guilty conscience; **ter ~ de** to be conscious of.

conscencioso/a [kõsjẽ'sjozu/ɔza] adj conscientious.

consciente [kõ'sjẽtʃi] adj conscious.

conscientizar [kõsjẽtʃi'za*] vt: ~ **alguém** (politicamente) to raise sb's awareness; ~-se vr to become more aware; ~-se de to be aware of; ~ **alguém de algo** to make sb aware of sth.

cônscio/a ['kõsju/a] adj aware.

conscrição [kõʃkri'sãw] f conscription.

consecução [kõseku'sãw] f attainment.

consecutivo/a [kõseku'tʃivu/a] adj consecutive.

conseguinte [kõse'gĩtʃi] adj: **por ~** consequently.

conseguir [kõse'gi*] vt (obter) to get, obtain; ~ **fazer** to manage to do, succeed in doing; **não consigo abrir a porta** I can't open the door.

conselheiro/a [kõse'ʎejru/a] m/f (que aconselha) counsellor (BRIT), counselor (US), adviser; (POL) councillor.

conselho [kõ'seʎu] m piece of advice; (corporação) council; ~s mpl advice sg; ~ **de guerra** court martial; **C~ de ministros** (POL) Cabinet; **C~ de Diretoria** board of directors.

consenso [kõ'sẽsu] m consensus, agreement.

consensual [kõsẽ'swaw] (pl -ais) adj agreed.

consentimento [kõsẽtʃi'mẽtu] m consent, permission.

consentir [kõsẽ'tʃi*] vt (admitir) to allow, permit; (aprovar) to agree to ♦ vi: ~ **em** to agree to.

conseqüência [kõse'kwẽsja] f consequence; **por ~** consequently; **em ~ de** as a consequence of.

conseqüente [kõse'kwẽtʃi] adj consequent; (coerente) consistent.

consertar [kõsex'ta*] vt to mend, repair; (remediar) to put right.

conserto [kõ'sextu] m repair.

conserva [kõ'sexva] f pickle; **em ~** pickled; **fábrica de ~s** cannery.

conservação [kõsexva'sãw] f conservation; (de vida, alimentos) preservation.

conservacionista [kõsexvasjo'niʃta] adj, m/f conservationist.

conservado/a [kõsex'vadu/a] adj (pessoa) well-preserved.

conservador(a) [kõsexva'do*(a)] adj conservative ♦ m/f (POL) conservative.

conservadorismo [kõsexvado'riʒmu] m conservatism.

conservante [kõsex'vãtʃi] m preservative.

conservar [kõsex'va*] vt (preservar) to preserve, maintain; (reter, manter) to keep, retain; ~-se vr to keep; **"conserve-se à direita"** "keep right".

conservatório [kõsexva'tɔrju] m conservatory.

consideração [kõsidera'sãw] (pl -ões) f consideration; (estima) respect, esteem; (reflexão) thought; **levar em ~** to take into account.

considerado/a [kõside'radu/a] adj respected, well thought of.

considerar [kõside'ra*] vt to consider; (prezar) to respect ♦ vi to consider; ~-se vr to consider o.s.

considerável [kõside'ravew] (pl -eis) adj considerable.

consignação [kõsigna'sãw] (pl -ões) f consignment; (registro) recording; (de verbas) assignment.

consignar [kõsig'na*] vt (mercadorias) to send, dispatch; (registrar) to record; (verba etc) to assign.

consigo [kõ'sigu] pron (m) with him; (f) with her; (pl) with them; (com você) with you ♦ vb V **conseguir**.

consinto [kõ'sĩtu] etc vb V **consentir**.

consistência [kõsiʃ'tẽsja] f consistency.

consistente [kõsiʃ'tẽtʃi] adj (sólido) solid; (espesso) thick.

consistir [kõsiʃ'tʃi*] vi: ~ **em** to be made up of, consist of.

consoante [kõso'ãtʃi] f consonant ♦ prep according to ♦ conj as; ~ **prometera** as he had promised.

consolação [kõsola'sãw] (pl -ões) f consolation.

consolador(a) [kõsola'do*(a)] adj consoling.

consolar [kõso'la*] vt to console; ~-se vr to console o.s.

console [kõ'sɔli] f (COMPUT) console.

consolidar [kõsoli'da*] vt to consolidate; (fratura) to mend, knit ♦ vi to become solid; to mend, knit together.

consolo [kõ'solu] m consolation.

consome [kõ'somi] etc vb V **consumir**.

consomê [kõso'me] m consommé.

consonância [kõso'nãsja] f (harmonia) harmony; (concordância) agreement.

consorciar [kõsox'sja*] vt to join; (combinar) to combine ♦ vi: ~ **a** to unite with.

consórcio [kõ'sɔxsju] *m* (*união*) partnership; (*COM*) consortium.

consorte [kõ'sɔxtʃi] *m/f* consort.

conspícuo/a [kõ'ʃpikwu/a] *adj* conspicuous.

conspiração [kõʃpira'sãw] (*pl* -ões) *f* plot, conspiracy.

conspirador(a) [kõʃpira'do*(a)] *m/f* plotter, conspirator.

conspirar [kõʃpi'ra*] *vt* to plot ♦ *vi* to plot, conspire.

constância [kõʃ'tãsja] *f* constancy; (*estabilidade*) steadiness.

constante [kõʃ'tãtʃi] *adj* constant; (*estável*) steady ♦ *f* constant.

constar [kõʃ'ta*] *vi* to be in; **consta que** it says that; ~ **de** to consist of; **não me constava que ...** I was not aware that ...; **ao que me consta** as far as I know.

constatação [kõʃtata'sãw] (*pl* -ões) *f* observation.

constatar [kõʃta'ta*] *vt* (*estabelecer*) to establish; (*notar*) to notice; (*evidenciar*) to show up; (*óbito*) to certify; **pudemos ~ que** we could see that.

constelação [kõʃtela'sãw] (*pl* -ões) *f* constellation; (*grupo*) cluster.

constelado/a [kõʃte'ladu/a] *adj* (*estrelado*) starry.

consternação [kõʃtexna'sãw] *f* (*desalento*) depression; (*desolação*) distress.

consternado/a [kõʃtex'nadu/a] *adj* (*desalentado*) depressed; (*desolado*) distressed.

consternar [kõʃtex'na*] *vt* (*desolar*) to distress; (*desalentar*) to depress; ~**-se** *vr* to be distressed; to be depressed.

constipação [kõʃtʃipa'sãw] (*pl* -ões) *f* constipation; (*PT*) cold.

constipado/a [kõʃtʃi'padu/a] *adj*: **estar ~** to be constipated; (*PT*) to have a cold.

constipar-se [kõʃtʃi'paxsi] (*PT*) *vr* to catch a cold.

constitucional [kõʃtʃitusjo'naw] (*pl* -ais) *adj* constitutional.

constituição [kõʃtʃitwi'sãw] (*pl* -ões) *f* constitution.

constituinte [kõʃtʃi'twĩtʃi] *adj* constituent ♦ *m/f* (*deputado*) member ♦ *f*: **a C~** the Constituent Assembly.

constituir [kõʃtʃi'twi*] *vt* (*representar*) to constitute; (*formar*) to form; (*estabelecer*) to establish, set up; (*nomear*) to appoint; ~**-se** *vr*: ~**-se em** to set o.s. up as; (*representar*) to constitute.

constrangedor(a) [kõʃtrãʒe'do*(a)] *adj* restricting; (*que acanha*) embarrassing.

constranger [kõʃtrã'ʒe*] *vt* to constrain; (*acanhar*) to embarrass; ~**-se** *vr* (*acanhar-se*) to feel embarrassed.

constrangimento [kõʃtrãʒi'mẽtu] *m* constraint; (*acanhamento*) embarrassment.

constranjo [kõʃ'trãʒu] *etc vb* V **constranger**.

construção [kõʃtru'sãw] (*pl* -ões) *f* building, construction.

construir [kõʃ'trwi*] *vt* to build, construct.

construtivo/a [kõʃtru'tʃivu/a] *adj* constructive.

construtor(a) [kõʃtru'to*(a)] *adj* building *atr*, construction *atr* ♦ *m/f* builder ♦ *f* building contractor.

cônsul ['kõsuw] (*pl* ~es) *m* consul.

consulado [kõsu'ladu] *m* consulate.

consulesa [kõsu'leza] *f* lady consul; (*esposa*) consul's wife.

consulta [kõ'suwta] *f* consultation; **livro de ~** reference book; **horário de ~** surgery hours *pl* (*BRIT*), office hours *pl* (*US*).

consultar [kõsuw'ta*] *vt* to consult; ~ **alguém sobre** to ask sb's opinion about.

consultivo/a [kõsuw'tʃivu/a] *adj* advisory.

consultor(a) [kõsuw'to*(a)] *m/f* adviser, consultant.

consultoria [kõsuwto'ria] *f* consultancy.

consultório [kõsuw'tɔrju] *m* surgery.

consumação [kõsuma'sãw] (*pl* -ões) *f* consummation; (*em restaurante etc*) minimum order.

consumado/a [kõsu'madu/a] *adj* consummate; *V tb* **fato**.

consumar [kõsu'ma*] *vt* to consummate; ~**-se** *vr* to be consummated.

consumidor(a) [kõsumi'do*(a)] *adj* consumer *atr* ♦ *m/f* consumer.

consumir [kõsu'mi*] *vt* to consume; (*devorar*) to eat away; (*gastar*) to use up; ~**-se** *vr* to waste away.

consumismo [kõsu'miʒmu] *m* consumerism

consumista [kõsu'miʃta] *adj*, *m/f* consumerist.

consumo [kõ'sumu] *m* consumption; **artigos de ~** consumer goods.

conta ['kõta] *f* (*cálculo*) count; (*em restaurante*) bill; (*fatura*) invoice; (*bancária*) account; (*de colar*) bead; (*responsabilidade*) responsibility; ~**s** *fpl* (*COM*) accounts; **à ~ de** to the account of; **ajustar ~s com** (*fig*) to settle an account with; **fazer de ~ que** to pretend that; **levar** *ou* **ter em ~** to take into account; **por ~ própria** of one's own accord; **trabalhar por ~ própria** to work for oneself; **prestar ~s de** to account for; **não é da sua ~** it's none of your business; **tomar ~ de** (*criança etc*) to look after; (*encarregar-se de*) to take care of; (*dominar*) to take hold of; **afinal de ~s** after all; **dar-se ~ de** to realize; (*notar*) to notice; **isso fica por sua ~** this is for you to deal with; **dar ~ de** (*notar*) to notice; (*prestar ~s de*) to account for; (*de tarefa*) to handle, cope with; **ficar por ~** (*furioso*) to get mad; **ser a ~** to be just enough; **dar ~ do recado** (*col*) to deliver the goods; ~ **bancária** bank account; ~

NB: *European Portuguese adds the following consonants to certain words*: **b** (sú(b)dito, su(b)til); **c** (a(c)ção, a(c)cionista, a(c)to); **m** (inde(m)ne); **p** (ado(p)ção, ado(p)tar); *for further details see p. xiii.*

conjunta joint account; ~ **corrente** current account.

contábil [kõ'tabiw] (pl -eis) adj accounting atr.

contabilidade [kõtabili'dadʒi] f book-keeping, accountancy; (departamento) accounts department; ~ **de custos** cost accounting.

contabilista [kõtabi'liʃta] (PT) m/f accountant.

contabilizar [kõtabili'za*] vt to write up, book; **valor contabilizado** (COM) book value.

contacto etc [kõ'tatu] (PT) = **contato** etc.

contado/a [kõ'tadu/a] adj: **dinheiro de ~** (PT) cash payment; **estamos com dinheiro ~ para só três meses** we've got just enough money for three months.

contador(a) [kõta'do*(a)] m/f (COM) accountant ♦ m (TEC: medidor) meter; ~ **de estórias** story-teller.

contadoria [kõtado'ria] f audit department.

contagem [kõ'taʒẽ] (pl -ns) f (de números) counting; (escore) score; **abrir a ~** (FUTEBOL) to open the scoring.

contagiante [kõta'ʒjãtʃi] adj contagious.

contagiar [kõta'ʒja*] vt to infect; ~-**se** vr to become infected.

contágio [kõ'taʒju] m infection.

contagioso/a [kõta'ʒozu/ɔza] adj contagious.

conta-gotas m inv dropper.

contaminação [kõtamina'sãw] f contamination.

contaminar [kõtami'na*] vt to contaminate.

contanto que [kõ'tãtu ki] conj provided that.

conta-quilômetros (PT) m inv speedometer.

contar [kõ'ta*] vt to count; (narrar) to tell; (pretender) to intend; (imaginar) to think ♦ vi to count; ~ **com** to count on; (esperar) to expect; **ela contava que a fossem ajudar** she expected them to help her; ~ **em fazer** to count on doing, expect to do.

contatar [kõta'ta*] vt to contact.

contato [kõ'tatu] m contact; **entrar em ~ com** to get in touch with, contact.

contêiner [kõ'tejne*] m container.

contemplação [kõtẽpla'sãw] f contemplation.

contemplar [kõtẽ'pla*] vt to contemplate; (olhar) to gaze at ♦ vi to meditate; ~-**se** vr to look at o.s.

contemplativo/a [kõtẽpla'tʃivu/a] adj (pessoa) thoughtful; (vida, literatura) contemplative.

contemporâneo/a [kõtẽpo'ranju/a] adj, m/f contemporary.

contemporizar [kõtẽpori'za*] vt (situação) to ease ♦ vi to ease the situation.

contenção [kõtẽ'sãw] (pl -ões) f restriction, containment; ~ **de despesas** cutbacks pl.

contencioso/a [kõtẽ'sjozu/ɔza] adj contentious.

contenções [kõtẽ'sõjʃ] fpl de **contenção**.

contenda [kõ'tẽda] f quarrel, dispute.

contenho [kõ'teɲu] etc vb V **conter**.

contentamento [kõtẽta'mẽtu] m (felicidade) happiness; (satisfação) contentment.

contentar [kõtẽ'ta*] vt (dar prazer) to please; (dar satisfação) to content; ~-**se** vr to be satisfied.

contente [kõ'tẽtʃi] adj (alegre) happy; (satisfeito) pleased, satisfied.

contento [kõ'tẽtu] m: **a ~** satisfactorily.

conter [kõ'te*] (irreg: como **ter**) vt (encerrar) to contain, hold; (refrear) to restrain, hold back; (gastos) to curb; ~-**se** vr to restrain o.s.

conterrâneo/a [kõte'xanju/a] adj fellow ♦ m/f compatriot, fellow countryman/woman.

contestação [kõteʃta'sãw] (pl -ões) f challenge; (negação) denial.

contestar [kõteʃ'ta*] vt (contrariar) to dispute, contest, question; (impugnar) to challenge.

contestável [kõteʃ'tavew] (pl -eis) adj questionable.

conteúdo [kõte'udu] m contents pl; (de um texto) content.

conteve [kõ'tevi] etc vb V **conter**.

contexto [kõ'teʃtu] m context.

contido/a [kõ'tʃidu/a] pp de **conter** ♦ adj contained; (raiva) repressed.

contigo [kõ'tʃigu] pron with you.

contigüidade [kõtʃigwi'dadʒi] f proximity.

contíguo/a [kõ'tʃigwu/a] adj: ~ **a** next to.

continência [kõtʃi'nẽsja] f (militar) salute; **fazer ~ a** to salute.

continental [kõtʃinẽ'taw] (pl -ais) adj continental.

continente [kõtʃi'nẽtʃi] m continent.

contingência [kõtʃĩ'ʒẽsja] f contingency.

contingente [kõtʃĩ'ʒẽtʃi] adj uncertain ♦ m (MIL) contingent; (COM) contingency, reserve.

continuação [kõtʃĩnwa'sãw] f continuation.

continuar [kõtʃĩ'nwa*] vt to continue ♦ vi to continue, go on; ~ **falando** ou **a falar** to go on talking, continue talking ou to talk; **continue!** carry on!; **ela continua doente** she is still sick.

continuidade [kõtʃĩnwi'dadʒi] f continuity.

contínuo/a [kõ'tʃĩnwu/a] adj (persistente) continual; (sem interrupção) continuous ♦ m office boy.

contista [kõ'tʃiʃta] m/f story writer.

contive [kõ'tʃivi] etc vb V **conter**.

contiver [kõtʃi've*] etc vb V **conter**.

conto ['kõtu] m story, tale; (PT: dinheiro) 1000 escudos; ~ **da carochinha** ou **de fadas** fairy tale.

conto-do-vigário (pl **contos-do-vigário**) m confidence trick.

contorção [kõtox'sãw] (pl -ões) f contortion; (dos músculos) twitch.

contorcer [kõtox'se*] vt to twist; ~-**se** vr to writhe.

contorções [kõtox'sõjʃ] fpl de **contorção**.

contornar [kõtox'na*] vt (rodear) to go round; (ladear) to skirt; (fig: problema) to get round.

contornável [kõtox'navew] (*pl* -**eis**) *adj* avoidable.

contorno [kõ'toxnu] *m* outline; (*da terra*) contour; (*da cara*) profile.

contra ['kõtra] *prep* against ♦ *m*: **os prós e os ~s** the pros and cons; **dar o ~ (a)** to be opposed (to); **ser do ~** to be against it.

contra-almirante *m* rear-admiral.

contra-argumento *m* counter-argument.

contra-atacar *vt* to counterattack.

contra-ataque *m* counterattack.

contrabaixo [kõtra'bajʃu] *m* double bass.

contrabalançar [kõtrabalã'sa*] *vt* to counterbalance; (*compensar*) to compensate.

contrabandear [kõtrabã'dʒja*] *vt*, *vi* to smuggle.

contrabandista [kõtrabã'dʒiʃta] *m/f* smuggler.

contrabando [kõtra'bãdu] *m* smuggling; (*artigos*) contraband.

contrabarra [kõtra'baxa] *f* (*COMPUT*) backslash.

contração [kõtra'sãw] (*pl* -**ões**) *f* contraction.

contracapa [kõtra'kapa] *f* inside cover.

contracenar [kõtrase'na*] *vi*: ~ **com** to act alongside, star with.

contraceptivo/a [kõtrasep'tʃivu/a] *adj* contraceptive ♦ *m* contraceptive.

contracheque [kõtra'ʃɛki] *m* pay slip (*BRIT*), check stub (*US*).

contrações [kõtra'sõjʃ] *fpl de* **contração**.

contradição [kõtradʒi'sãw] (*pl* -**ões**) *f* contradiction.

contradigo [kõtra'dʒigu] *etc vb V* **contradizer**.

contradisse [kõtra'dʒisi] *etc vb V* **contradizer**.

contradito [kõtra'dʒitu] *pp de* **contradizer**.

contraditório/a [kõtradʒi'tɔrju/a] *adj* contradictory.

contradizer [kõtradʒi'ze*] (*irreg: como* **dizer**) *vt* to contradict; ~-**se** *vr* (*pessoa*) to contradict o.s.; (*atitudes*) to be contradictory.

contrafazer [kõtrafa'ze*] (*irreg: como* **fazer**) *vt* to forge, counterfeit; (*pessoa*) to imitate, take off.

contrafeito/a [kõtra'fejtu/a] *pp de* **contrafazer** ♦ *adj* constrained.

contrafez [kõtra'feʒ] *etc vb V* **contrafazer**.

contrafilé [kõtrafi'lɛ] *m* rump steak.

contrafiz [kõtra'fiʒ] *etc vb V* **contrafazer**.

contrafizer [kõtrafi'ze*] *etc vb V* **contrafazer**.

contragosto [kõtra'goʃtu] *m*: **a** ~ against one's will, unwillingly.

contraído/a [kõtra'idu/a] *adj* (*tímido*) timid, shy.

contra-indicação (*pl* -**ões**) *f* contra-indication.

contra-indicado/a *adj* inadvisable.

contrair [kõtra'i*] *vt* to contract; (*doença*) to contract, catch; (*hábito*) to form; ~-**se** *vr* to contract; ~ **matrimônio** to get married.

contralto [kõ'trawtu] *m* contralto.

contramão [kõtra'mãw] *adj* one-way ♦ *f*: **na** ~ the wrong way down a one-way street.

contramestre/tra [kõtra'mɛʃtri/tra] *m/f* (*em fábrica*) supervisor ♦ *m* (*NÁUT*) boatswain.

Contran [kõ'trã] (*BR*) *abr m* = **Conselho Nacional de Trânsito**.

contra-ofensiva *f* counteroffensive.

contra-oferta *f* counteroffer.

contraparente/a [kõtrapa'rẽtʃi/ta] *m/f* distant relative; (*afim*) in-law.

contrapartida [kõtrapax'tʃida] *f* (*COM*) counterentry; (*fig*) compensation; **em** ~ **a** in the face of.

contrapesar [kõtrape'za*] *vt* to counterbalance; (*fig*) to compensate for.

contrapeso [kõtra'pezu] *m* counterbalance; (*TEC*) counterweight; (*COM*) makeweight.

contrapor [kõtra'po*] (*irreg: como* **pôr**) *vt* (*comparar*) to compare; ~ **algo a algo** to set sth against sth; ~-**se** *vr*: ~-**se a** to be in opposition to; (*atitude*) to go against.

contraproducente [kõtraprodu'sẽtʃi] *adj* counterproductive, self-defeating.

contrapunha [kõtra'puɲa] *etc vb V* **contrapor**.

contrapus [kõtra'puʃ] *etc vb V* **contrapor**.

contrapuser [kõtrapu'ze*] *etc vb V* **contrapor**.

contra-regra (*pl* ~**s**) *m/f* stage manager.

contra-revolução (*pl* -**ões**) *f* counter-revolution.

contrariar [kõtra'rja*] *vt* (*contradizer*) to contradict; (*aborrecer*) to annoy.

contrariedade [kõtrarje'dadʒi] *f* (*aborrecimento*) annoyance, vexation.

contrário/a [kõ'trarju/a] *adj* (*oposto*) opposite; (*pessoa*) opposed; (*desfavorável*) unfavourable (*BRIT*), unfavorable (*US*), adverse ♦ *m* opposite; **do** ~ otherwise; **pelo** *ou* **ao** ~ on the contrary; **ao** ~ (*do outro lado*) the other way round; **muito pelo** ~ on the contrary, quite the opposite.

contra-senso *f* nonsense.

contrastante [kõtraʃ'tãtʃi] *adj* contrasting.

contrastar [kõtraʃ'ta*] *vt* to contrast.

contraste [kõ'traʃtʃi] *m* contrast.

contratante [kõtra'tãtʃi] *adj* contracting ♦ *m/f* contractor.

contratação [kõtrata'sãw] *f* (*de pessoal*) employment.

contratar [kõtra'ta*] *vt* (*serviços*) to contract; (*empregar*) to employ, take on.

contratempo [kõtra'tẽpu] *m* (*imprevisto*) setback; (*aborrecimento*) upset; (*dificuldade*) difficulty.

contrato [kõ'tratu] *m* contract; (*acordo*) agreement.

contratual [kõtra'twaw] (*pl* -**ais**) *adj* contractual.

contravapor [kõtrava'po*] (*col*) *m* rebuff.

contravenção [kõtravẽ'sãw] (*pl* -**ões**) *f* con-

NB: *European Portuguese adds the following consonants to certain words:* **b** *(sú(b)dito, su(b)til);* **c** *(a(c)ção, a(c)cionista, a(c)to);* **m** *(inde(m)ne);* **p** *(ado(p)ção, ado(p)tar); for further details see p. xiii.*

travention, violation.

contraventor(a) [kõtravẽ'to*(a)] m/f offender.

contribuição [kõtribwi'sãw] (pl -ões) f contribution; (imposto) tax.

contribuinte [kõtri'bwĩtʃi] m/f contributor; (que paga impostos) taxpayer.

contribuir [kõtri'bwi*] vt to contribute ♦ vi to contribute; (pagar impostos) to pay taxes.

contrição [kõtri'sãw] f contrition.

contrito/a [kõ'tritu/a] adj contrite.

controlar [kõtro'la*] vt to control; ~-se vr to control o.s.

controlável [kõtro'lavew] (pl -eis) adj controllable.

controle [kõ'troli] m control; ~ remoto remote control; ~ de crédito (COM) credit control; ~ de qualidade (COM) quality control.

controvérsia [kõtro'vɛxsja] f controversy; (discussão) debate.

controverso/a [kõtro'vɛxsu/a] adj controversial.

contudo [kõ'tudu] conj nevertheless, however.

contumácia [kõtu'masja] f obstinacy; (JUR) contempt of court.

contumaz [kõtu'majʒ] adj obstinate, stubborn ♦ m/f (JUR) defaulter.

contundente [kõtũ'dẽtʃi] adj bruising; (argumento) cutting; **instrumento** ~ blunt instrument.

contundir [kõtũ'dʒi*] vt to bruise; ~-se vr to bruise o.s.

conturbação [kõtuxba'sãw] (pl -ões) f disturbance, unrest; (motim) riot.

conturbado/a [kõtux'badu/a] adj disturbed.

conturbar [kõtux'ba*] vt to disturb; (amotinar) to stir up.

contusão [kõtu'zãw] (pl -ões) f bruise.

contuso/a [kõ'tuzu/a] adj bruised.

contusões [kõtu'zõjʃ] fpl de **contusão**.

convalescença [kõvale'sẽsa] f convalescence.

convalescer [kõvale'se*] vi to convalesce.

conveio [kõ'veju] etc vb V **convir**.

convenção [kõvẽ'sãw] (pl -ões) f convention; (acordo) agreement.

convencer [kõvẽ'se*] vt to convince; (persuadir) to persuade; ~-se vr: ~-se de to be convinced about.

convencido/a [kõvẽ'sidu/a] adj (convicto) convinced; (col: imodesto) conceited, smug.

convencimento [kõvẽsi'mẽtu] m (convicção) conviction; (col: imodéstia) conceit, smugness.

convencional [kõvẽsjo'naw] (pl -ais) adj conventional.

convenções [kõvẽ'sõjʃ] fpl de **convenção**.

convenha [kõ'veɲa] etc vb V **convir**.

conveniência [kõve'njẽsja] f convenience.

convencionar [kõvẽsjo'na*] vt to agree on; ~-se vr: ~-se em to agree to.

conveniente [kõve'njẽtʃi] adj convenient, suitable; (vantajoso) advantageous.

convênio [kõ'venju] m (reunião) convention; (acordo) agreement.

convento [kõ'vẽtu] m convent.

convergir [kõvex'ʒi*] vi to converge.

conversa [kõ'vɛxsa] f conversation; ~ fiada idle chat; (promessa falsa) hot air; ir na ~ de alguém (col) to be taken in by sb; ~ vai, ~ vem in the course of conversation; ele não tem muita ~ he hasn't got a lot to say for himself.

conversação [kõvexsa'sãw] (pl -ões) f (ato) conversation.

conversadeira [kõvexsa'dejra] f de **conversador**.

conversado/a [kõvex'sadu/a] adj (assunto) talked about; (pessoa) talkative, chatty; **estamos ~s** we've said all we had to say.

conversador/deira [kõvexsa'do*/'dejra] adj talkative, chatty.

conversa-fiada (pl **conversas-fiadas**) m/f: **ser um** ~ to be all talk.

conversão [kõvex'sãw] (pl -ões) f conversion.

conversar [kõvex'sa*] vi to talk.

conversibilidade [kõvexsibili'dadʒi] f convertibility.

conversível [kõvex'sivew] (pl -eis) adj convertible ♦ m (AUTO) convertible.

conversões [kõvex'sõjʃ] fpl de **conversão**.

converter [kõvex'te*] vt to convert; ~-se vr to be converted.

convertido/a [kõvex'tʃidu/a] adj converted ♦ m/f convert.

convés [kõ'vɛʃ] (pl -eses) m (NÁUT) deck.

convexo/a [kõ'vɛksu/a] adj convex.

convicção [kõvik'sãw] (pl -ões) f conviction; (certeza) certainty.

convicto/a [kõ'viktu/a] adj (convencido) convinced; (réu) convicted; (patriota etc) staunch.

convidado/a [kõvi'dadu/a] adj invited ♦ m/f guest.

convidar [kõvi'da*] vt to invite; ~-se vr to invite o.s.

convidativo/a [kõvida'tʃivu/a] adj inviting.

convier [kõ'vje*] etc vb V **convir**.

convincente [kõvĩ'sẽtʃi] adj convincing.

convir [kõ'vi*] (irreg: como **vir**) vi (ser conveniente) to suit, be convenient; (ficar bem) to be appropriate; **convém fazer isso o mais rápido possível** we must do this as soon as possible; **você há de** ~ **que** ... you must agree that ....

convirjo [kõ'vixʒu] etc vb V **convergir**.

convite [kõ'vitʃi] m invitation.

conviva [kõ'viva] m/f guest.

convivência [kõvi'vẽsja] f living together; (familiaridade) familiarity, intimacy.

conviver [kõvi've*] vi (viver em comum) to live together; (ter familiaridade) to be on familiar terms.

convívio [kõ'vivju] m (viver em comum) living together; (familiaridade) familiarity.

convocar [kõvo'ka*] vt to summon, call upon; (reunião, eleições) to call; (para o serviço militar) to call up.

convosco [kõ'voʃku] *adv* with you.

convulsão [kõvuw'sãw] (*pl* **-ões**) *f* convulsion; (*fig*) upheaval.

convulsionar [kõvuwsjo'na*] *vt* (*abalar*) to shake; (*excitar*) to stir up.

convulsivo/a [kõvuw'sivu/a] *adj* convulsive.

convulsões [kõvuw'sõjʃ] *fpl de* **convulsão**.

cooper ['kupe*] *m* jogging, running; **fazer** ~ to go jogging *ou* running.

cooperação [koopera'sãw] *f* cooperation.

cooperante [koope'rãtʃi] *adj* cooperative, helpful.

cooperar [koope'ra*] *vi* to cooperate.

cooperativa [koopera'tʃiva] *f* (*COM*) cooperative.

cooperativo/a [koopera'tʃivu/a] *adj* cooperative.

coordenação [kooxdena'sãw] *f* co-ordination.

coordenada [kooxde'nada] *f* coordinate.

coordenar [kooxde'na*] *vt* to co-ordinate.

copa ['kɔpa] *f* (*de árvore*) top; (*dum chapéu*) crown; (*compartimento*) pantry; (*torneio*) cup; ~**s** *fpl* (*CARTAS*) hearts.

copeira [ko'pejra] *f* kitchen maid.

Copenhague [kope'ɲagi] *n* Copenhagen.

cópia ['kɔpja] *f* copy; **tirar** ~ **de** to copy.

copiadora [kopja'dora] *f* (*máquina*) duplicating machine.

copiar [ko'pja*] *vt* to copy.

copidesque [kopi'dɛʃki] *m* copy editing ♦ *m/f* copy editor.

co-piloto [kopi'lotu] *m* co-pilot.

copioso/a [ko'pjozu/ɔza] *adj* abundant, numerous; (*refeição*) large; (*provas*) ample.

copirraite [kopi'xajtʃi] *m* copyright.

copo ['kɔpu] *m* glass; **ser um bom** ~ (*col*) to be a good drinker.

copyright [kopi'xajtʃi] *m* = **copirraite**.

coque ['kɔki] *m* (*penteado*) bun.

coqueiro [ko'kejru] *m* (*BOT*) coconut palm.

coqueluche [koke'luʃi] *f* (*MED*) whooping cough; (*mania*) rage.

coquete [ko'kɛtʃi] *adj* coquettish.

coquetel [koke'tɛw] (*pl* **-éis**) *m* cocktail; (*festa*) cocktail party.

cor¹ [kɔ*] *m*: **de** ~ by heart.

cor² [ko*] *f* colour (*BRIT*), color (*US*); **de** ~ colo(u)red.

coração [kora'sãw] (*pl* **-ões**) *m* heart; **de bom** ~ kind-hearted; (*de todo o* ~ wholeheartedly.

corado/a [ko'radu/a] *adj* ruddy.

coragem [ko'raʒẽ] *f* courage; (*atrevimento*) nerve.

corais [ko'rajʃ] *mpl de* **coral**.

corajoso/a [kora'ʒozu/ɔza] *adj* courageous.

coral [ko'raw] (*pl* **-ais**) *adj* choral ♦ *m* (*MÚS*) choir; (*ZOOL*) coral.

corante [ko'rãtʃi] *adj*, *m* colouring (*BRIT*), coloring (*US*).

corar [ko'ra*] *vt* (*pintar*) to paint; (*roupa*) to

bleach (in the sun) ♦ *vi* (*ruborizar-se*) to blush; (*tornar-se branco*) to bleach.

corbelha [kox'bɛʎa] *f* basket.

corcova [kox'kɔva] *f* hump.

corcunda [kox'kũda] *adj* hunchbacked ♦ *m/f* hump; (*pessoa*) hunchback.

corda ['kɔxda] *f* (*cabo*) rope, line; (*MÚS*) string; (*varal*) clothes line; (*de relógio*) spring; **dar** ~ **em** to wind up; **roer a** ~ to go back on one's word; ~**s vocais** vocal chords; **estar com toda a** ~ (*pessoa*) to be really wound up; **dar** ~ **a alguém** (*deixar falar*) to set sb off; (*flertar*) to flirt with sb.

cordão [kox'dãw] (*pl* **-ões**) *m* string, twine; (*jóia*) chain; (*no carnaval*) group; (*ELET*) lead; (*fileira*) row; ~ **de sapato** shoestring; ~ **umbilical** umbilical cord.

cordeiro [kox'dejru] *m* lamb; (*fig*) sheep.

cordel [kox'dɛw] (*PT*: *pl* **-éis**) *m* string; **literatura de** ~ pamphlet literature.

cor-de-rosa *adj inv* pink.

cordial [kox'dʒjaw] (*pl* **-ais**) *adj* cordial ♦ *m* (*bebida*) cordial.

cordialidade [koxdʒjali'dadʒi] *f* warmth, cordiality.

cordilheira [koxdʒi'ʎejra] *f* chain of mountains.

cordões [kox'dõjʃ] *mpl de* **cordão**.

coreano/a [ko'rjanu/a] *adj* Korean ♦ *m/f* Korean ♦ *m* (*LING*) Korean.

Coréia [ko'rɛja] *f*: **a** ~ **do Norte/Sul** North/South Korea.

coreografia [korjogra'fia] *f* choreography.

coreógrafo/a [ko'rjɔgrafu/a] *m/f* choreographer.

coreto [ko'retu] *m* bandstand; **bagunçar o** ~ **(de alguém)** (*col*) to spoil things (for sb).

corisco [ko'riʃku] *m* (*faísca*) flash.

corista [ko'riʃta] *m/f* chorister ♦ *f* (*TEATRO*) chorus girl.

coriza [ko'riza] *f* runny nose.

corja ['kɔxʒa] *f* (*PT*: *canalha*) rabble; (*bando*) gang.

córnea ['kɔxnja] *f* cornea.

córner ['kɔxne*] *m* (*FUTEBOL*) corner.

corneta [kox'neta] *f* cornet; (*MIL*) bugle.

corneteiro [koxne'tejru] *m* bugler.

cornetim [koxne'tʃĩ] *m* (*MÚS*) french horn.

coro ['koru] *m* chorus; (*conjunto de cantores*) choir; **em** ~ in chorus.

coroa [ko'roa] *f* crown; (*de flores*) garland ♦ *m/f* (*BR*: *col*) old timer.

coroação [korwa'sãw] (*pl* **-ões**) *f* coronation.

coroar [koro'a*] *vt* to crown; (*premiar*) to reward.

coronel [koro'nɛw] (*pl* **-éis**) *m* colonel; (*político*) local political boss.

coronha [ko'roɲa] *f* (*de um fuzil*) butt; (*de um revólver*) handle.

corpete [kox'petʃi] *m* bodice.

NB: *European Portuguese adds the following consonants to certain words:* **b** (sú(b)dito, su(b)til); **c** (a(c)ção, a(c)cionista, a(c)to); **m** (inde(m)ne); **p** (ado(p)ção, ado(p)tar); *for further details see p. xiii.*

corpo ['koxpu] *m* body; *(aparência física)* figure; (: *de homem)* build; *(de vestido)* bodice; *(MIL)* corps *sg*; **de ~ e alma** *(fig)* wholeheartedly; **lutar ~ a ~** to fight hand to hand; **fazer ~ mole** to get out of it; **tirar o ~ fora** *(col)* to duck out; **~ diplomático** diplomatic corps *sg*; **~ discente** student body; **~ docente** teaching staff *(BRIT)*, faculty *(US)*; **~ estranho** *(MED)* foreign body.

corporal [koxpo'raw] *(pl* **-ais)** *adj* physical.

corpulência [koxpu'lẽsja] *f* stoutness.

corpulento/a [koxpu'lẽtu/a] *adj* stout.

correção [koxe'sãw] *(PT:* **-çç-:** *pl* **-ões)** *f* correction; *(exatidão)* correctness; **casa de ~ reformatory; **~ salarial/monetária** wage/ monetary correction.

corre-corre [kɔxi'kɔxi] *(pl* **~s)** *m* rush.

correcto/a *etc* [ko'xektu/a] *(PT)* = **correto** *etc*.

corrediço/a [koxe'dʒisu/a] *adj* sliding.

corredor(a) [koxe'do*(a)] *m/f* runner ♦ *m (passagem)* corridor, passageway; *(em avião etc)* aisle; *(cavalo)* racehorse.

córrego ['kɔxegu] *m* stream, brook.

correia [ko'xeja] *f* strap; *(de máquina)* belt; *(para cachorro)* leash.

correio [ko'xeju] *m* mail, post; *(local)* post office; *(carteiro)* postman *(BRIT)*, mailman *(US)*; **~ aéreo** air mail; **pôr no ~** to post; **pelo ~** by post; **~ eletrônico** electronic mail.

correlação [koxela'sãw] *(pl* **-ões)** *f* correlation.

correlacionar [koxelasjo'na*] *vt* to correlate.

correlações [koxela'sõjʃ] *fpl de* **correlação**.

correligionário/a [koxeliʒjo'narju/a] *m/f (POL)* fellow party member.

corrente [ko'xẽtʃi] *adj (atual)* current; *(águas)* running; *(fluente)* flowing; *(comum)* usual, common ♦ *f* current; *(cadeia, jóia)* chain; **~ de ar** draught *(BRIT)*, draft *(US)*.

correnteza [koxẽ'teza] *f (de ar)* draught *(BRIT)*, draft *(US)*; *(de rio)* current.

correr [ko'xe*] *vt* to run; *(viajar por)* to travel across; *(cortina)* to draw; *(expulsar)* to drive out ♦ *vi* to run; *(em carro)* to drive fast, speed; *(líquido)* to flow, run; *(o tempo)* to elapse; *(boato)* to go round; *(atuar com rapidez)* to rush; **está tudo correndo bem** everything is going well; **as despesas correrão por minha conta** I will handle the expenses.

correria [koxe'ria] *f* rush.

correspondência [koxeʃpõ'dẽsja] *f* correspondence.

correspondente [koxeʃpõ'dẽtʃi] *adj* corresponding ♦ *m* correspondent.

corresponder [koxeʃpõ'de*] *vi:* **~ a** to correspond to; *(ser igual)* to match (up to); *(retribuir)* to reciprocate; **~-se** *vr:* **~-se com** to correspond with.

corretagem [koxe'taʒẽ] *f* brokerage.

corretivo/a [koxe'tʃivu/a] *adj* corrective ♦ *m* punishment.

correto/a [ko'xetu/a] *adj* correct; *(conduta)* right; *(pessoa)* straight.

corretor(a) [koxe'to*(a)] *m/f* broker ♦ *m (para datilografia)* correction strip; **~ de fundos** *ou* **de bolsa** stockbroker; **~ de imóveis** estate agent *(BRIT)*, realtor *(US)*.

corrida [ko'xida] *f (ato de correr)* running; *(certame)* race; *(de taxi)* fare; **~ de cavalos** horse race; **~ armamentista** arms race.

corrido/a [ko'xidu/a] *adj (rápido)* quick; *(expulso)* driven out ♦ *adv* quickly.

corrigir [koxi'ʒi*] *vt* to correct; *(defeito, injustiça)* to put right.

corrimão [koxi'mãw] *(pl* **~s)** *m* handrail.

corriqueiro/a [koxi'kejru/a] *adj* common; *(problema)* trivial.

corroa [ko'xoa] *etc vb V* **corroer**.

corroboração [koxobora'sãw] *(pl* **-ões)** *f* confirmation.

corroborar [koxobo'ra*] *vt* to corroborate, confirm.

corroer [koxo'e*] *(irreg) vt (metais)* to corrode; *(fig)* to eat away; **~-se** *vr* to corrode; to be eaten away.

corromper [koxõ'pe*] *vt* to corrupt; *(subornar)* to bribe; **~-se** *vr* to be corrupted.

corrosão [koxo'zãw] *f (de metais)* corrosion; *(fig)* erosion.

corrosivo/a [koxo'zivu/a] *adj* corrosive.

corrupção [koxup'sãw] *f* corruption.

corrupto/a [ko'xuptu/a] *adj* corrupt.

Córsega ['kɔxsega] *f:* **a ~** Corsica.

cortada [kox'tada] *f (ESPORTE)* smash; **dar uma ~ em alguém** *(fig)* to cut sb short.

cortado [kox'tadu] *m (aperto)* tight spot; **trazer alguém num ~** to keep sb under one's thumb.

cortadura [koxta'dura] *f (corte)* cut; *(entre montes)* gap.

cortante [kox'tãtʃi] *adj* cutting.

cortar [kox'ta*] *vt* to cut; *(eliminar)* to cut out; *(água, telefone etc)* to cut off; *(efeito)* to stop; *(AUTO)* to cut up ♦ *vi* to cut; *(encurtar caminho)* to take a short cut; **~-se** *vr* to cut o.s.; **~ o cabelo** *(no cabeleireiro)* to have one's hair cut; **~ a palavra de alguém** to interrupt sb.

corte¹ ['kɔxtʃi] *m* cut; *(gume)* cutting edge; *(de luz)* cut-out; **~ de cabelo** haircut; **esta tesoura está sem ~** these scissors are blunt.

corte² ['kɔxtʃi] *f (de um monarca)* court; *(de uma pessoa)* retinue; **~s** *fpl (PT)* parliament *sg*.

cortejar [koxte'ʒa*] *vt* to court.

cortejo [kox'teʒu] *m (procissão)* procession.

cortês [kox'teʃ] *(pl* **-eses)** *adj* polite.

cortesão/tesã [koxte'zãw/te'zã] *(pl* **~s/~s)** *adj* courtly ♦ *m/f* courtier/courtesan.

cortesia [koxte'zia] *f* politeness; *(de empresa)* free offer.

cortiça [kox'tʃisa] *f (matéria)* cork.

cortiço [kox'tʃisu] *m (habitação)* slum tenement.

cortina [kox'tʃina] *f* curtain; **~ de rolo** roller blind; **~ de voile** net curtain.

cortisona [koxtʃi'zɔna] f cortisone.

coruja [ko'ruʒa] adj: **pai/mãe** ~ proud father/mother ♦ f owl; **sessão** ~ late show.

coruscar [koruʃ'ka*] vi to sparkle, glitter.

corvo ['koxvu] m crow.

cós [kɔʃ] m inv waistband; (cintura) waist.

cosca ['kɔʃka] f: **fazer** ~ to tickle.

coser [ko'ze*] vt, vi to sew, stitch.

cosmético/a [kɔʒ'mɛtʃiku/a] adj cosmetic ♦ m cosmetic.

cósmico/a ['kɔʒmiku/a] adj cosmic.

cosmo ['kɔʒmu] m cosmos.

cosmonauta [kɔʒmo'nawta] m/f cosmonaut.

cosmopolita [kɔʒmopo'lita] adj cosmopolitan.

cospe ['kɔʃpi] etc vb V **cuspir**.

costa ['kɔʃta] f coast; ~s fpl back sg; **dar as** ~s **a** to turn one's back on; **ter** ~s **largas** (fig) to be thick-skinned; **ter** ~s **quentes** (fig) to have powerful backing, have friends in high places.

costado [koʃ'tadu] m back; **de quatro** ~s through and through.

Costa do Marfim f: **a** ~ the Ivory Coast.

Costa Rica f: **a** ~ Costa Rica.

costarriquenho/a [koʃtaxi'keɲu/a] adj, m/f Costa Rican.

costear [koʃ'tʃja*] vt (rodear) to go round; (gado) to round up; (NÁUT) to follow ♦ vi to follow the coast.

costela [koʃ'tɛla] f rib.

costeleta [koʃte'leta] f chop, cutlet; ~s fpl (suíças) side-whiskers.

costumar [koʃtu'ma*] vt (habituar) to accustom ♦ vi: **ele costuma chegar às 6.00** he usually arrives at 6.00; **costumava dizer ... he** used to say ....

costume [koʃ'tumi] m custom, habit; (traje) costume; ~s mpl behaviour sg (BRIT), behavior sg (US), conduct sg; (de um povo) customs; **de** ~ usual; **como de** ~ as usual; **ter o** ~ **de fazer** to have a habit of doing.

costumeiro/a [koʃtu'mejru/a] adj usual, habitual.

costura [koʃ'tura] f sewing, needlework; (sutura) seam; **sem** ~ seamless.

costurar [koʃtu'ra*] vt, vi to sew.

costureira [koʃtu'rejra] f dressmaker; (móvel) sewing box.

cota ['kɔta] f (quinhão) quota, share; (GEO) height.

cotação [kota'sãw] (pl -ões) f (de preços) list, quotation; (na bolsa) price; (consideração) esteem; ~ **bancária** bank rate.

cotado/a [ko'tadu/a] adj (ação) quoted; (bem-conceituado) well thought of; (num concurso) fancied.

cotar [ko'ta*] vt (ações) to quote; ~ **algo em** to value sth at.

cotejar [kote'ʒa*] vt to compare.

cotejo [ko'teʒu] m comparison.

cotidiano/a [kotʃi'dʒjanu/a] adj daily, everyday ♦ m: **o** ~ daily life.

cotoco [ko'toku] m (do corpo) stump; (de uma vela etc) stub.

cotonete [koto'netʃi] m cotton bud.

cotovelada [kotove'lada] f (pancada) shove; (cutucada) nudge.

cotovelo [koto'velu] m (ANAT) elbow; (curva) bend; **falar pelos** ~s to talk non-stop.

coube ['kobi] etc vb V **caber**.

couraça [ko'rasa] f (para o peito) breastplate; (de navio etc) armour-plate (BRIT), armor-plate (US); (de animal) plating, shell.

couraçado [kora'sadu] (PT) m battleship.

couro ['koru] m leather; (de um animal) hide; ~ **cabeludo** scalp.

couve ['kovi] f spring greens pl.

couve-de-bruxelas (pl **couves-de-bruxelas**) f Brussels sprout.

couve-flor (pl **couves-flores**) f cauliflower.

couvert [ku'vɛx] m cover charge.

cova ['kɔva] f (escavação) pit; (caverna) cavern; (sepultura) grave.

covarde [ko'vaxdʒi] adj cowardly ♦ m/f coward.

covardia [kovax'dʒia] f cowardice.

coveiro [ko'vejru] m gravedigger.

covil [ko'viw] (pl -is) m den, lair.

covinha [ko'viɲa] f dimple.

covis [ko'viʃ] mpl de **covil**.

coxa ['koʃa] f thigh.

coxear [ko'ʃja*] vi to limp, hobble.

coxia [ko'ʃia] f (passagem) aisle, gangway.

coxo/a ['koʃu/a] adj lame.

cozer [ko'ze*] vt, vi to cook.

cozido [ko'zidu] m stew.

cozinha [ko'ziɲa] f (compartimento) kitchen; (arte) cookery; (modo de cozinhar) cuisine.

cozinhar [kozi'ɲa*] vt to cook; (remanchar) to put off ♦ vi to cook.

cozinheiro/a [kozi'ɲejru/a] m/f cook.

CP abr = **Caminhos de Ferro Portugueses** ♦ abr m (BR: = certificado de privatização) share in state company.

CPF (BR) abr m (= Cadastro de Pessoa Física) identification number.

CPI (BR) abr f = **Comissão Parlamentar de Inquérito**.

CPJ (BR) abr m (= Cadastro de Pessoa Jurídica) register of companies.

Cr$ abr = **cruzeiro**.

crachá [kra'ʃa] m badge.

crânio ['kranju] m skull; **ser um** ~ (col) to be a whizz kid.

craque ['kraki] m/f ace, expert ♦ m (jogador de futebol) soccer star.

crasso/a ['krasu/a] adj crass.

cratera [kra'tɛra] f crater.

cravar [kra'va*] vt (prego etc) to drive (in); (pedras) to set; (com os olhos) to stare at;

NB: European Portuguese adds the following consonants to certain words: **b** (sú(b)dito, su(b)til); **c** (a(c)ção, a(c)cionista, a(c)to); **m** (inde(m)ne); **p** (ado(p)ção, ado(p)tar); for further details see p. xiii.

~-se *vr* to penetrate.
cravejar [krave'ʒa*] *vt* (*com cravos*) to nail; (*pedras*) to set; ~ **alguém de balas** to spray sb with bullets.
cravo ['kravu] *m* (*flor*) carnation; (*MÚS*) harpsichord; (*especiaria*) clove; (*na pele*) blackhead; (*prego*) nail.
creche ['krɛʃi] *f* crèche.
Creci [krɛ'si] (*BR*) *abr m* (= *Conselho Regional dos Corretores de Imóveis*) *regulatory body of estate agents*.
credenciais [kredẽ'sjajʃ] *fpl* credentials.
credenciar [kredẽ'sja*] *vt* to accredit; (*habilitar*) to qualify.
crediário [kre'dʒjarju] *m* credit plan.
credibilidade [kredʒibili'dadʒi] *f* credibility.
creditar [kredʒi'ta*] *vt* to guarantee; ~ **algo a alguém** (*quantia*) to credit sb with sth; (*garantir*) to assure sb of sth; ~ **alguém em** to credit sb with; ~ **uma quantia numa conta** to deposit an amount into an account.
crédito ['krɛdʒitu] *m* credit; **a** ~ on credit; **digno de** ~ reliable.
credo ['krɛdu] *m* creed; ~! (*PT*) heavens!
credor(a) [kre'do*(a)] *adj* worthy, deserving; (*COM*: *saldo*) credit *atr* ♦ *m/f* creditor.
credulidade [kreduli'dadʒi] *f* credulity.
crédulo/a ['krɛdulu/a] *adj* credulous.
creio ['kreju] *etc vb V* **crer**.
cremação [krema'sãw] (*pl* -**ões**) *f* cremation.
cremalheira [krema'ʎejra] *f* ratchet.
cremar [kre'ma*] *vt* to cremate.
crematório [krema'tɔrju] *m* crematorium.
creme ['krɛmi] *adj inv* cream-coloured (*BRIT*), cream-colored (*US*) ♦ *m* cream; (*CULIN*: *doce*) custard; ~ **dental** toothpaste; ~ **de leite** single cream.
cremoso/a [kre'mozu/ɔza] *adj* creamy.
crença ['krẽsa] *f* belief.
crendice [krẽ'dʒisi] *f* superstition.
crente ['krẽtʃi] *adj* believing ♦ *m/f* believer; (*protestante*) Protestant; **estar** ~ **que** to think (that).
creosoto [kreo'zotu] *m* creosote.
crepitação [krepita'sãw] *f* crackling.
crepitante [krepi'tãtʃi] *adj* crackling.
crepitar [krepi'ta*] *vi* to crackle.
crepom [kre'põ] *adj V* **papel**.
crepuscular [krepuʃku'la*] *adj* twilight *atr*.
crepúsculo [kre'puʃkulu] *m* dusk, twilight.
crer [kre*] *vt*, *vi* to believe; ~-**se** *vr* to believe o.s. to be; ~ **em** to believe in; ~ **que** to think (that); **creio que sim** I think so.
crescendo [kre'sẽdu[*m* crescendo.
crescente [kre'sẽtʃi] *adj* growing; (*forma*) crescent ♦ *m* crescent.
crescer [kre'se*] *vi* to grow; (*CULIN*: *massa*) to rise.
crescido/a [kre'sidu/a] *adj* (*pessoa*) grown up.
crescimento [kresi'mẽtu] *m* growth.
crespo/a ['krɛʃpu/a] *adj* (*cabelo*) curly.
cretinice [kretʃi'nisi] *f* stupidity; (*ato*, *dito*) stupid thing.

cretino [kre'tʃinu] *m* cretin, imbecile.
cria ['kria] *f* (*animal*) baby animal, young.
criação [krja'sãw] (*pl* -**ões**) *f* creation; (*de animais*) raising, breeding; (*educação*) upbringing; (*animais domésticos*) livestock; **filho de** ~ adopted child.
criado/a ['krjadu/a] *m/f* servant.
criado-mudo (*pl* **criados-mudos**) *m* bedside table.
criador(a) [krja'do*(a)] *m/f* creator; ~ **de gado** cattle breeder.
criança ['krjãsa] *adj* childish; **ela é muito** ~ **para entender certas coisas** she's too young to understand certain things ♦ *f* child.
criançada [krjã'sada] *f*: **a** ~ the kids.
criancice [krjã'sisi] *f* (*ato*, *dito*) childish thing; (*qualidade*) childishness.
criar [krja*] *vt* to create; (*crianças*) to bring up; (*animais*) to raise, breed; (*amamentar*) to suckle, nurse; (*planta*) to grow; ~-**se** *vr*: ~-**se** (**com**) to grow up (with); ~ **fama/coragem** to achieve notoriety/pluck up courage; ~ **caso** to make trouble.
criatividade [kriatʃivi'dadʒi] *f* creativity.
criativo/a [kria'tʃivu/a] *adj* creative.
criatura [kria'tura] *f* creature; (*indivíduo*) individual.
crime ['krimi] *m* crime.
criminal [krimi'naw] (*pl* -**ais**) *adj* criminal.
criminalidade [kriminali'dadʒi] *f* crime.
criminoso/a [krimi'nozu/ɔza] *adj*, *m/f* criminal.
crina ['krina] *f* mane.
crioulo/a ['krjolu/a] *adj* creole ♦ *m/f* creole; (*BR*: *negro*) black (person).
críquete ['krikɛtʃi] *m* cricket.
crisálida [kri'zalida] *f* chrysalis.
crisântemo [kri'zãtemu] *m* chrysanthemum.
crise ['krizi] *f* crisis; (*escassez*) shortage; (*MED*) attack, fit; ~ **de choro** fit of hysterical crying.
crisma ['kriʒma] *f* (*REL*) confirmation.
crismar [kriʒ'ma*] *vt* (*REL*) to confirm; ~-**se** *vr* (*REL*) to be confirmed.
crista ['kriʃta] *f* (*de serra*, *onda*) crest; (*de galo*) cock's comb; **estar na** ~ **da onda** (*fig*) to enjoy a prominent position.
cristal [kriʃ'taw] (*pl* -**ais**) *m* crystal; (*vidro*) glass; **cristais** *mpl* glassware *sg*.
cristalino/a [kriʃta'linu/a] *adj* crystal-clear.
cristalizar [kriʃtali'za*] *vi* to crystallize.
cristandade [kriʃtã'dadʒi] *f* Christianity.
cristão/tã [kriʃ'tãw/'tã] (*pl* ~**s/**~**s**) *adj*, *m/f* Christian.
cristianismo [kriʃtʃja'niʒmu] *m* Christianity.
Cristo ['kriʃtu] *m* Christ.
critério [kri'tɛrju] *m* (*norma*) criterion; (*juízo*) discretion, judgement; **deixo isso a seu** ~ I'll leave that to your discretion.
criterioso/a [krite'rjozu/ɔza] *adj* thoughtful, careful.
crítica ['kritʃika] *f* criticism; (*artigo*) critique; (*conjunto de críticos*) critics *pl*; *V tb* **crítico**.

criticar [kritʃi'ka*] *vt* to criticize; (*um livro*) to review.
crítico/a ['kritʃiku/a] *adj* critical ♦ *m/f* critic.
critiquei [kritʃi'kej] *etc vb V* **criticar**.
crivar [kri'va*] *vt* (*com balas etc*) to riddle; (*de perguntas, de insultos*) to bombard.
crível ['krivew] (*pl* -eis) *adj* credible.
crivo ['krivu] *m* sieve; (*fig*) scrutiny.
crocante [kro'kãtʃi] *adj* crunchy.
crochê [kro'ʃe] *m* crochet.
crocodilo [kroko'dʒilu] *m* crocodile.
cromo ['krɔmu] *m* chrome.
cromossomo [kromo'sɔmu] *m* chromosome.
crônica ['kronika] *f* chronicle; (*coluna de jornal*) newspaper column; (*texto jornalístico*) feature; (*conto*) short story.
crônico/a ['kroniku/a] *adj* chronic.
cronista [kro'niʃta] *m/f* (*de jornal*) columnist; (*historiógrafo*) chronicler; (*contista*) short story writer.
cronologia [kronolo'ʒia] *f* chronology.
cronológico/a [krono'lɔʒiku/a] *adj* chronological.
cronometrar [kronome'tra*] *vt* to time.
cronômetro [kro'nometru] *m* stopwatch.
croquete [kro'ketʃi] *m* croquette.
croqui [kro'ki] *m* sketch.
crosta ['krɔʃta] *f* crust; (*MED*) scab.
cru(a) [kru/'krua] *adj* raw; (*não refinado*) crude; (*ignorante*) not very good; (*realidade*) harsh, stark.
crucial [kru'sjaw] (*pl* -ais) *adj* crucial.
crucificação [krusifika'sãw] (*pl* -ões) *f* crucifixion.
crucificar [krusifi'ka*] *vt* to crucify.
crucifixo [krusi'fiksu] *m* crucifix.
crudelíssimo/a [krude'lisimu/a] *adj superl de* **cruel**.
cruel [kru'ɛw] (*pl* -éis) *adj* cruel.
crueldade [kruew'dadʒi] *f* cruelty.
cruento/a [kru'ẽtu/a] *adj* bloody.
crupe ['krupi] *m* (*MED*) croup.
crustáceos [kruʃ'tasjuʃ] *mpl* crustaceans.
cruz [kruʒ] *f* cross; (*infortúnio*) undoing; ~ **gamada** swastika; **C~ Vermelha** Red Cross; **estar entre a ~ e a caldeirinha** (*fig*) to be between the devil and the deep (*BRIT*), be between a rock and a hard place (*US*).
cruzada [kru'zada] *f* crusade.
cruzado/a [kru'zadu/a] *adj* crossed ♦ *m* crusader; (*moeda*) cruzado.
cruzador [kruza'do*] *m* (*navio*) cruiser.
cruzamento [kruza'mẽtu] *m* (*de estradas*) crossroads; (*mestiçagem*) cross.
cruzar [kru'za*] *vt* to cross ♦ *vi* (*NÁUT*) to cruise; ~-**se** *vr* to cross; (*pessoas*) to pass by each other; ~ **com** to meet.
cruzeiro [kru'zejru] *m* (*cruz*) (monumental) cross; (*moeda*) cruzeiro; (*viagem de navio*) cruise.

cu [ku] (*col!*) *m* arse (*!*); **vai tomar no ~ fuck off** (*!*).
CSN (*BR*) *abr m* = **Conselho de Segurança Nacional**.
CTB *abr f* = **Companhia Telefônica Brasileira**.
Cuba ['kuba] *f* Cuba.
cubano/a [ku'banu/a] *adj*, *m/f* Cuban.
cúbico/a ['kubiku/a] *adj* cubic.
cubículo [ku'bikulu] *m* cubicle.
cubismo [ku'biʒmu] *m* cubism.
cubo ['kubu] *m* cube; (*de roda*) hub.
cubro ['kubru] *etc vb V* **cobrir**.
cuca ['kuka] (*col*) *f* head; **fundir a ~** (*quebrar a cabeça*) to rack one's brain; (*baratinar*) to boggle the mind; (*perturbar*) to drive crazy.
cuca-fresca (*pl* **cucas-frescas**) (*col*) *m/f* cool guy/girl.
cuco ['kuku] *m* cuckoo.
cucuia [ku'kuja] *f*: **ir para a ~** (*col*) to go down the drain.
cu-de-ferro (*pl* **cus-de-ferro**) (*col*) *m/f* swot.
cueca ['kweka] (*BR*) *f* underpants *pl*; ~**s** (*PT*: *para homens*) underpants *pl*; (: *para mulheres*) panties *pl*.
cueiro [ku'ejru] *m* wrap.
cuíca ['kwika] *f kind of musical instrument*.
cuidado [kwi'dadu] *m* care; **aos** ~**s de** in the care of; **ter** ~ to be careful; ~**!** watch out!, be careful!; **tomar** ~ **(de)** to be careful (of); ~ **para não se cortar** be careful you don't cut yourself.
cuidadoso/a [kwida'dozu/ɔza] *adj* careful.
cuidar [kwi'da*] *vi*: ~ **de** to take care of, look after; ~-**se** *vr* to look after o.s.
cujo/a ['kuʒu/a] *pron* (*de quem*) whose; (*de que*) of which.
culatra [ku'latra] *f* (*de arma*) breech.
culinária [kuli'narja] *f* cookery.
culinário/a [kuli'narju/a] *adj* culinary.
culminância [kuwmi'nãsja] *f* culmination.
culminante [kuwmi'nãtʃi] *adj V* **ponto**.
culminar [kuwmi'na*] *vi*: ~ **(com)** to culminate (in).
culote [ku'lɔtʃi] *m* (*calça*) jodhpurs *pl*; (*gordura*) flab on the thighs.
culpa ['kuwpa] *f* fault; (*JUR*) guilt; **ter** ~ **de** to be to blame for; **por** ~ **de** because of; **pôr a** ~ **em** to put the blame on; **sentimento de** ~ guilty conscience.
culpabilidade [kuwpabili'dadʒi] *f* guilt.
culpado/a [kuw'padu/a] *adj* guilty ♦ *m/f* culprit.
culpar [kuw'pa*] *vt* to blame; (*acusar*) to accuse; ~-**se** *vr* to take the blame.
culpável [kuw'pavew] (*pl* -eis) *adj* guilty.
cultivar [kuwtʃi'va*] *vt* to cultivate; (*plantas*) to grow.
cultivável [kuwtʃi'vavew] (*pl* -eis) *adj* cultivable.
cultivo [kuw'tʃivu] *m* cultivation.

NB: European Portuguese adds the following consonants to certain words: **b** (sú(b)dito, su(b)til); **c** (a(c)ção, a(c)cionista, a(c)to); **m** (inde(m)ne); **p** (ado(p)ção, ado(p)tar); *for further details see p. xiii.*

culto/a ['kuwtu/a] *adj* cultured ♦ *m* (*homenagem*) worship; (*religião*) cult.

cultura [kuw'tura] *f* culture; (*da terra*) cultivation.

cultural [kuwtu'raw] (*pl* **-ais**) *adj* cultural.

cumbuca [kũ'buka] *f* pot.

cume ['kumi] *m* top, summit; (*fig*) climax.

cúmplice ['kũplisi] *m/f* accomplice.

cumplicidade [kũplisi'dadʒi] *f* complicity.

cumpridor(a) [kũpri'do*(a)] *adj* punctilious, responsible.

cumprimentar [kũprimẽ'ta*] *vt* (*saudar*) to greet; (*dar parabéns*) to congratulate; ~**-se** *vr* to greet one another.

cumprimento [kũpri'mẽtu] *m* (*realização*) fulfilment; (*saudação*) greeting; (*elogio*) compliment; ~**s** *mpl* best wishes; ~ **de uma lei/ordem** compliance with a law/an order.

cumprir [kũ'pri*] *vt* (*desempenhar*) to carry out; (*promessa*) to keep (*lei*) to obey ♦ *vi* (*convir*) to be necessary; ~**-se** *vr* to be fulfilled; ~ **a palavra** to keep one's word; **fazer** ~ to enforce; ~ **pena** to serve a sentence.

cumulativo/a [kumula'tʃivu/a] *adj* cumulative.

cúmulo ['kumulu] *m* height; **é o** ~! that's the limit!

cunha ['kuɲa] *f* wedge.

cunhado/a [ku'ɲadu/a] *m/f* brother-in-law/sister-in-law.

cunhar [ku'ɲa*] *vt* (*moedas*) to mint; (*palavras*) to coin.

cunho ['kuɲu] *m* (*marca*) hallmark; (*caráter*) nature.

cupê [ku'pe] *m* coupé.

cupim [ku'pĩ] (*pl* **-ns**) *m* termite.

cupincha [ku'pĩʃa] *m/f* mate, friend.

cupins [ku'pĩʃ] *mpl de* **cupim**.

cupom [ku'põ] (*pl* **-ns**) *m* coupon.

cúpula ['kupula] *f* (*ARQ*) dome; (*de abajur*) shade; (*de partido etc*) leadership; (**reunião de**) ~ summit (meeting).

cura ['kura] *f* (*ato de curar*) cure; (*tratamento*) treatment; (*de carnes etc*) curing, preservation ♦ *m* priest.

curador(a) [kura'do*(a)] *m/f* (*de menores, órfãos*) guardian; (*de instituição*) trustee.

curandeiro [kurã'dejru] *m* (*feiticeiro*) healer, medicine man; (*charlatão*) quack.

curar [ku'ra*] *vt* (*doença*) to cure; (*ferida*) to treat; (*carne etc*) to cure, preserve; ~**-se** *vr* to get well.

curativo [kura'tʃivu] *m* dressing.

curável [ku'ravew] (*pl* **-eis**) *adj* curable.

curetagem [kure'taʒẽ] *f* curettage.

curinga [ku'rĩga] *m* wild card.

curingão [kurĩ'gãw] (*pl* **-ões**) *m* joker.

curiosidade [kurjozi'dadʒi] *f* curiosity; (*objeto raro*) curio.

curioso/a [ku'rjozu/ɔza] *adj* curious ♦ *m/f* snooper, inquisitive person; ~**s** *mpl* (*espectadores*) onlookers; **o** ~ **é** ... the strange thing is ....

curitibano/a [kuritʃi'banu/a] *adj* from Curitiba ♦ *m/f* person from Curitiba.

curral [ku'xaw] (*pl* **-ais**) *m* pen, enclosure.

currar [ku'xa*] (*col*) *vt* to rape.

currículo [ku'xikulu] *m* curriculum; (*curriculum*) curriculum vitae, CV.

curriculum vitae [ku'xikulũ 'vite] *m* curriculum vitae.

cursar [kux'sa*] *vt* (*aulas, escola*) to attend; (*cursos*) to follow; **ele está cursando História** he's studying *ou* doing history.

cursivo [kux'sivu] *m* (*TIP*) script.

curso ['kuxsu] *m* course; (*direção*) direction; **em** ~ (*ano etc*) current; (*processo*) in progress; (*dinheiro*) in circulation; ~ **primário/secundário/superior** primary school/secondary school/degree course; ~ **normal** teacher-training course.

cursor [kux'so*] *m* (*COMPUT*) cursor.

curta ['kuxta] *m* (*CINEMA*) short.

curta-metragem (*pl* **curtas-metragens**) *m* short film.

curtição [kuxtʃi'sãw] *f* (*col*) fun; (*de couro*) tanning.

curtido/a [kux'tʃidu/a] *adj* (*fig*) hardened.

curtir [kux'tʃi*] *vt* (*couro*) to tan; (*tornar rijo*) to toughen up; (*padecer*) to suffer, endure; (*col*) to enjoy.

curto/a ['kuxtu/a] *adj* short; (*inteligência*) limited ♦ *m* (*ELET*) short (circuit).

curto-circuito (*pl* **curtos-circuitos**) *m* short circuit.

curva ['kuxva] *f* curve; (*de estrada, rio*) bend; ~ **fechada** hairpin bend.

curvar [kux'va*] *vt* to bend, curve; (*submeter*) to put down; ~**-se** *vr* (*abaixar-se*) to stoop; ~**-se a** (*submeter-se*) to submit to.

curvatura [kuxva'tura] *f* curvature.

curvo/a ['kuxvu/a] *adj* curved; (*estrada*) winding.

cuscuz [kuʃ'kuʒ] *m* couscous.

cusparada [kuʃpa'rada] *f* spit; **dar uma** ~ to spit.

cuspe ['kuʃpi] *m* spit, spittle.

cuspido/a [kuʃ'pidu/a] *adj* covered in spittle; **ele é o pai** ~ **e escarrado** (*col*) he's the spitting image of his father.

cuspir [kuʃ'pi*] *vt, vi* to spit; ~ **no prato em que se come** to bite the hand that feeds one.

custa ['kuʃta] *f*: **à** ~ **de** at the expense of; ~**s** *fpl* (*JUR*) costs.

custar [kuʃ'ta*] *vi* to cost; (*ser difícil*) to be difficult; (*demorar*) to take a long time; ~ **caro** to be expensive; ~ **a fazer** (*ter dificuldade*) to have trouble doing; (*demorar*) to take a long time to do; **não custa nada perguntar** there's no harm in asking.

custear [kuʃ'tʃja*] *vt* to bear the cost of.

custeio [kuʃ'teju] *m* funding; (*relação de custos*) costing.

custo ['kuʃtu] *m* cost; **a** ~ with difficulty; **a todo** ~ at all costs; ~**/benefício** (*COM*) cost/benefit.

custódia [kuʃ'tɔdʒja] *f* custody.
CUT (*BR*) *abr f* (= *Central Única de Trabalhadores*) trade union.
cutelaria [kutela'ria] *f* knife-making.
cutelo [ku'tɛlu] *m* cleaver.
cutícula [ku'tʃikula] *f* cuticle.
cútis ['kutʃiʃ] *f inv* (*pele*) skin; (*tez*) complexion.
cutucada [kutu'kada] *f* nudge; (*com o dedo*) prod.
cutucar [kutu'ka*] *vt* (*com o dedo*) to prod, poke; (*com o cotovelo*) to nudge.
CVV (*BR*) *abr m* (= *Centro de Valorização da Vida*) Samaritan organization.
Cz$ *abr* = **cruzado.**

D

D, d [de] (*pl* **ds**) D, d ♦ *abr* = **Dom; Dona;** (= *direito*) r; (= *deve*) d; **D de dado** D for David (*BRIT*) *ou* dog (*US*).
d/ *abr* = **dia.**
da [da] = **de** + **a.**
dá [da] *vb* V **dar.**
dádiva ['dadʒiva] *f* (*donativo*) donation; (*oferta*) gift.
DAC (*BR*) *abr m* = **Departamento de Aviação Civil.**
dactilografar *etc* [datilogra'fa*] (*PT*) = **datilografar** *etc*.
dadaísmo [dada'iʒmu] *m* Dadaism.
dadivoso/a [dadʒi'vozu/ɔza] *adj* generous.
dado/a ['dadu/a] *adj* given; (*sociável*) sociable ♦ *m* (*em jogo*) die; (*fato*) fact; (*COMPUT*) piece of data; **~s** *mpl* (*em jogo*) dice; (*fatos, COMPUT*) data *sg*; **ser ~ a algo** to be prone *ou* given to sth; **em ~ momento** at a given moment; **~ que** (*suposto que*) supposing that; (*uma vez que*) given that.
daí [da'ji] *adv* (= **de** + **aí**) (*desse lugar*) from there; (*desse momento*) from then; (*col: num relato*) then; **~ a um mês** a month later; **~ por ou em diante** from then on; **e ~?** (*col*) so what?
dali [da'li] *adv* (= **de** + **ali**) from there.
dália ['dalja] *f* dahlia.
daltônico/a [daw'toniku/a] *adj* colour-blind (*BRIT*), color-blind (*US*).
daltonismo [dawto'niʒmu] *m* colour (*BRIT*) *ou* color (*US*) blindness.
dama ['dama] *f* lady; (*XADREZ, CARTAS*) queen; **~s** *fpl* draughts (*BRIT*), checkers (*US*); **~ de honra** bridesmaid.

Damasco [da'maʃku] *n* Damascus.
damasco [da'maʃku] *m* (*fruta*) apricot; (*tecido*) damask.
danação [dana'sãw] *f* damnation; (*travessura*) mischief, naughtiness.
danado/a [da'nadu/a] *adj* (*condenado*) damned; (*zangado*) furious, angry; (*menino*) mischievous, naughty; **cão ~** mad dog; **ela está com uma fome/dor danada** she's really hungry/got a terrible pain; **uma gripe danada/um susto ~** a really bad case of flu/a hell of a fright; **ele é ~ de bom** (*col*) he's really good; **ser ~ em algo** to be really good at sth.
danar-se [dã'naxsi] *vr* (*enfurecer-se*) to get furious; **dane-se!** (*col*) damn it!; **danou-se!** (*col*) oh, gosh!
dança ['dãsa] *f* dance; **entrar na ~** to get involved.
dançar [dã'sa*] *vi* to dance; (*col: pessoa: sair-se mal*) to lose out; (: *em exame*) to fail; (: *coisa*) to go by the board.
dançarino/a [dãsa'rinu/a] *m/f* dancer.
danceteria [dãsete'ria] *f* disco(theque).
dancing ['dãsĩŋ] *m* dance hall.
danificar [danifi'ka*] *vt* (*objeto*) to damage.
daninho/a [da'niɲu/a] *adj* harmful; (*gênio*) nasty.
dano ['danu] *m* (*tb*: **~s**) damage; (*moral*) harm; (*a uma pessoa*) injury.
danoso/a [da'nozu/ɔza] *adj* (*a uma pessoa*) harmful; (*a uma coisa*) damaging.
dantes ['dãtʃiʃ] *adv* before, formerly.
Danúbio [da'nubju] *m*: **o ~** the Danube.
daquela [da'kɛla] = **de** + **aquela**; V **aquele.**
daquele [da'keli] = **de** + **aquele**; V **aquele.**
daqui [da'ki] *adv* (= **de** + **aqui**) (*deste lugar*) from here; **~ a pouco** soon, in a little while; **~ a uma semana** a week from now, in a week's time; **~ em diante** from now on.
daquilo [da'kilu] = **de** + **aquilo**; V **aquilo.**
dar [da*] *vt* (*ger*) to give; (*flor, leite, fruta*) to produce; (*cheiro*) to give off; (*notícias no jornal*) to publish; (*cartas*) to deal; (*problemas*) to cause; (*matemática, francês etc*) to teach ♦ *vi* to give; (*impess: ser possível*) to be possible; (*ser suficiente*): **~ para/para fazer** to be enough for/to do; **~-se** *vr* (*acontecer*) to happen; (*sair-se*) to get on; **~ algo por acabado** *etc* to consider sth finished *etc*; **(não) dá tempo para fazer** there's (no) time to do; **dez libras dão ou dá 100 francs** ten pounds is equivalent to 100 francs; **a sala dele dá duas da minha** his lounge is twice as big as mine; **ter roupa** *etc* **para ~ e vender** to have loads of clothes *etc*; **~ de beber/comer a** to give a drink to/feed; **~ (a alguém)** (*col: sexualmente*) to go all the way (with sb); **~ com** (*coisa*) to find; (*pessoa*) to meet; **~ de** *ou* **para fazer**

(começar) to take to doing; ~ **em** *(bater)* to hit; *(resultar)* to lead to; *(lugar)* to come to; **não deu em nada** it came to nothing; **o que deu nela?** what got into her?; **ele dá para médico/para tomar conta de crianças** he'll make a good doctor/he's good at looking after children; **dá para você vir amanhã?** — **não, amanhã não vai** ~ can you come tomorrow? — no, tomorrow I can't; **dá para trocar dinheiro aqui?** is it possible to change money here?; ~ **por** to notice; ~**-se bem/mal** *(sair-se)* to get on well/badly; ~**-se bem (com alguém)** to get on well (with sb); ~**-se ao luxo/trabalho de fazer algo** to allow o.s. the luxury of doing sth/take the trouble to do sth; ~**-se com alguém** *(ter amizade)* to be acquainted with sb; ~**-se por** to consider o.s.; ~**-se por vencido** to give up; **não me dou bem com o clima** the climate doesn't agree with me; **pouco se me dá** I don't care.

Dardanelos [daxda'nɛluʃ] *mpl:* **os** ~ the Dardanelles.

dardo ['daxdu] *m* dart; *(grande)* spear.

das [daʃ] = **de** + **as**; *V* **de.**

data ['data] *f* date; *(época)* time; **de longa** ~ of long standing.

datação [data'sãw] *f* dating.

datar [da'ta*] *vt* to date ♦ *vi:* ~ **de** to date from.

datilografar [datʃilogra'fa*] *vt* to type.

datilografia [datʃilogra'fia] *f* typing.

datilógrafo/a [datʃi'lɔgrafu/a] *m/f* typist *(BRIT)*, stenographer *(US)*.

dativo/a [da'tʃivu/a] *adj* dative ♦ *m* dative.

d.C. *abr (= depois de Cristo)* AD.

DDD *abr f (= discagem direta a distância)* STD *(BRIT)*, ≈ direct dialling.

DDI *abr f (= discagem direta internacional)* IDD.

de [dʒi] *prep* of; *(movimento, procedência)* from; **venho** ~ **São Paulo** I come from São Paulo; **a casa** ~ **João** John's house; **um romance** ~ a novel by; **o infeliz do homem** the poor man; **um vestido** ~ **seda** a silk dress; ~ **manhã** in the morning; ~ **dia** by day; **vestido** ~ **branco** dressed in white; **um homem** ~ **cabelo comprido** a man with long hair; ~ **dois em dois dias** every other day; ~ **trem** by train.

dê [de] *etc vb V* **dar.**

deão [dʒi'ãw] *(pl* ~**s)** *m* dean.

debaixo [de'bajʃu] *adv* below, underneath ♦ *prep:* ~ **de** under, beneath.

debalde [de'bawdʒi] *adv* in vain.

debandada [debã'dada] *f* stampede; **em** ~ in confusion.

debandar [debã'da*] *vt* to put to flight ♦ *vi* to disperse.

debate [de'batʃi] *m (discussão)* discussion, debate; *(disputa)* argument.

debater [deba'te*] *vt* to debate; *(discutir)* to discuss; ~**-se** *vr* to struggle.

débeis ['debejʃ] *pl de* **débil.**

debelar [debe'la*] *vt* to put down, suppress; *(crise)* to overcome; *(doença)* to cure.

debênture [de'bẽturi] *f (COM)* debenture.

debicar [debi'ka*] *vt (caçoar)* to make fun of.

débil ['debiw] *(pl -eis) adj (pessoa)* weak, feeble; *(PSICO)* retarded ♦ *m:* ~ **mental** mentally handicapped person; *(col: ofensivo)* moron.

debilidade [debili'dadʒi] *f* weakness; ~ **mental** mental handicap.

debilitação [debilita'sãw] *f* weakening.

debilitante [debili'tãtʃi] *adj* debilitating.

debilitar [debili'ta*] *vt* to weaken; ~**-se** *vr* to become weak, weaken.

debilóide [debi'lɔjdʒi] *(col) m/f* idiot ♦ *adj* idiotic.

debique [de'biki] *m* mockery, ridicule.

debitar [debi'ta*] *vt* to debit; ~ **a conta de alguém em $40** to debit sb's account by $40; ~ **$40 à ou na conta de alguém** to debit $40 to sb's account.

débito ['debitu] *m* debit.

debochado/a [debo'ʃadu/a] *adj (pessoa)* sardonic; *(jeito, tom)* mocking ♦ *m/f* sardonic person.

debochar [debo'ʃa*] *vt* to mock ♦ *vi:* ~ **de** to mock.

deboche [de'bɔʃi] *m* gibe.

debruar [de'brwa*] *vt (roupa)* to edge; *(desenho)* to adorn.

debruçar [debru'sa*] *vt* to bend over; ~**-se** *vr* to bend over; *(inclinar-se)* to lean over; ~**-se na janela** to lean out of the window.

debrum [de'brũ] *m* edging.

debulha [de'buʎa] *f (de trigo)* threshing.

debulhar [debu'ʎa*] *vt (grão)* to thresh; *(descascar)* to shell; ~**-se** *vr:* ~**-se em lágrimas** to burst into tears.

debutante [debu'tãtʃi] *f* débutante.

debutar [debu'ta*] *vi* to appear for the first time, make one's début.

década ['dɛkada] *f* decade.

decadência [deka'dẽsja] *f* decadence.

decadente [deka'dẽtʃi] *adj* decadent.

decair [deka'i*] *vi* to decline; *(restaurante etc)* to go downhill; *(pressão, velocidade)* to drop; *(planta)* to wilt.

decalcar [dekaw'ka*] *vt* to trace; *(fig)* to copy.

decalque [de'kawki] *m* tracing.

decano [de'kanu] *m* oldest member.

decantar [dekã'ta*] *vt (líquido)* to decant; *(purificar)* to purify.

decapitar [dekapi'ta*] *vt* to behead, decapitate.

decatlo [de'katlu] *m* decathlon.

decência [de'sẽsja] *f* decency.

decênio [de'senju] *m* decade.

decente [de'sẽtʃi] *adj* decent; *(apropriado)* proper; *(honrado)* honourable *(BRIT)*, honorable *(US)*; *(trabalho)* neat, presentable.

decentemente [desẽtʃi'mẽtʃi] *adv (com decoro)* decently; *(apropriadamente)* properly; *(honradamente)* honourably *(BRIT)*, honor-

ably (*US*).
decepar [dese'pa*] *vt* to cut off, chop off.
decepção [desep'sãw] (*pl* -**ões**) *f* disappointment; (*desilusão*) disillusionment.
decepcionar [desepsjo'na*] *vt* to disappoint, let down; (*desiludir*) to disillusion; ~-**se** *vr* to be disappointed; to be disillusioned; **o filme decepcionou** the film was disappointing.
decepções [desep'sõjʃ] *fpl de* **decepção**.
decerto [dʒi'sɛxtu] *adv* certainly.
decidido/a [desi'dʒidu/a] *adj* (*pessoa*) determined; (*questão*) resolved.
decidir [desi'dʒi*] *vt* (*determinar*) to decide; (*solucionar*) to resolve; ~-**se** *vr*: ~-**se a** to make up one's mind to; ~-**se por** to decide on, go for.
decíduo/a [de'sidwu/a] *adj* (*BOT*) deciduous.
decifrar [desi'fra*] *vt* to decipher; (*futuro*) to foretell; (*compreender*) to understand.
decifrável (*pl* -**eis**) *adj* decipherable.
decimal [desi'maw] (*pl* -**ais**) *adj* decimal ♦ *m* (*número*) decimal.
décimo/a ['dɛsimu/a] *adj* tenth ♦ *m* tenth; *V tb* **quinto**.
decisão [desi'zãw] (*pl* -**ões**) *f* decision; (*capacidade de decidir*) decisiveness, resolution.
decisivo/a [desi'zivu/a] *adj* (*fator*) decisive; (*jogo*) deciding.
decisões [desi'zõjʃ] *fpl de* **decisão**.
declamação [deklama'sãw] *f* (*de poema*) recitation; (*pej*) ranting.
declamar [dekla'ma*] *vt* (*poemas*) to recite ♦ *vi* (*pej*) to rant.
declaração [deklara'sãw] (*pl* -**ões**) *f* declaration; (*depoimento*) statement; (*revelação*) revelation; ~ **de amor** proposal; ~ **de imposto de renda** income tax return; ~ **juramentada** affidavit.
declarado/a [dekla'radu/a] *adj* (*intenção*) declared; (*opinião*) professed; (*inimigo*) sworn; (*alcoólatra*) self-confessed; (*cristão etc*) avowed.
declarante [dekla'rãtʃi] *m/f* (*JUR*) witness.
declarar [dekla'ra*] *vt* to declare; (*confessar*) to confess.
Dec-lei [dek-] *abr m* = **decreto-lei**.
declinação [deklina'sãw] (*pl* -**ões**) *f* (*LING*) declension.
declinar [dekli'na*] *vt* (*recusar*) to decline, refuse; (*nomes*) to give; (*LING*) to decline ♦ *vi* (*sol*) to go down; (*terreno*) to slope down.
declínio [de'klinju] *m* decline.
declive [de'klivi] *m* slope, incline.
decô [de'ko] *adj inv* Art-Deco.
decodificador [dekodʒifika'do*] *m* (*COMPUT*) decoder.
decodificar [dekodʒifi'ka*] *vt* to decode.
decolagem [deko'laʒẽ] (*pl* -**ns**) *f* (*AER*) take-off.
decolar [deko'la*] *vi* (*AER*) to take off.

decompor [dekõ'po*] (*irreg: como* **pôr**) *vt* (*analisar*) to analyse; (*apodrecer*) to rot; (*rosto*) to contort; ~-**se** *vr* to rot, decompose.
decomposição [dekõpozi'sãw] (*pl* -**ões**) *f* (*apodrecimento*) decomposition; (*análise*) dissection; (*do rosto*) contortion.
decomposto [dekõ'poʃtu] *pp de* **decompor**.
decompunha [dekõ'puɲa] *etc vb V* **decompor**.
decompus [dekõ'puʃ] *etc vb V* **decompor**.
decompuser [dekõpu'ze*] *etc vb V* **decompor**.
decoração [dekora'sãw] *f* decoration; (*TEATRO*) scenery.
decorar [deko'ra*] *vt* to decorate; (*aprender*) to learn by heart.
decorativo/a [dekora'tʃivu/a] *adj* decorative.
decoro [de'koru] *m* (*decência*) decency; (*dignidade*) decorum.
decoroso/a [deko'rozu/ɔza] *adj* decent, respectable.
decorrência [deko'xẽsja] *f* consequence, result; **em ~ de** as a result of.
decorrente [deko'xẽtʃi] *adj*: ~ **de** resulting from.
decorrer [deko'xe*] *vi* (*tempo*) to pass; (*acontecer*) to take place, happen ♦ *m*: **no ~ de** in the course of; ~ **de** to result from.
decotado/a [deko'tadu/a] *adj* (*roupa*) low-cut.
decote [de'kɔtʃi] *m* (*vestido*) low neckline.
decrépito/a [de'krɛpitu/a] *adj* decrepit.
decrescente [dekre'sẽtʃi] *adj* decreasing, diminishing.
decrescer [dekre'se*] *vi* to decrease, diminish.
decréscimo [de'krɛsimu] *m* decrease, decline.
decretação [dekreta'sãw] (*pl* -**ões**) *f* announcement; (*de estado de sítio*) declaration.
decretar [dekre'ta*] *vt* to decree, order; (*estado de sítio*) to declare; (*anunciar*) to announce; (*determinar*) to determine.
decreto [de'krɛtu] *m* decree, order; **nem por ~** not for love nor money.
decreto-lei (*pl* **decretos-leis**) *m* act, law.
decúbito [de'kubitu] *m*: **em ~** recumbent.
decurso [de'kuxsu] *m* (*tempo*) course; **no ~ de** in the course of, during.
dedal [de'daw] (*pl* -**ais**) *m* thimble.
dedão [de'dãw] (*pl* -**ões**) *m* thumb; (*do pé*) big toe.
dedetização [dedetʃiza'sãw] *f* spraying with insecticide.
dedetizar [dedetʃi'za*] *vt* to spray with insecticide.
dedicação [dedʒika'sãw] *f* dedication; (*devotamento*) devotion.
dedicado/a [dedʒi'kadu/a] *adj* (*tb: COMPUT*) dedicated.
dedicar [dedʒi'ka*] *vt* (*poema*) to dedicate; (*tempo, atenção*) to devote; ~-**se** *vr*: ~-**se a** to devote o.s. to.

NB: *European Portuguese adds the following consonants to certain words*: **b** (sú(b)dito, su(b)til); **c** (a(c)ção, a(c)cionista, a(c)to); **m** (inde(m)ne); **p** (ado(p)ção, ado(p)tar); *for further details see p. xiii.*

dedicatória [dedʒika'tɔrja] f (de obra) dedication.

dedilhar [dedʒi'ʎa*] vt (MÚS: no braço) to finger; (: nas cordas) to pluck.

dedo ['dedu] m finger; (do pé) toe; **dois ~s (de)** a little bit (of); **escolher a ~** to handpick; **~ anular** ring finger; **~ indicador** index finger; **~ mínimo** ou **mindinho** little finger; **~ polegar** thumb.

dedo-duro (pl **dedos-duros**) (col) m (criminoso) grass; (criança) sneak, tell-tale.

dedões [de'dõjʃ] mpl de **dedão**.

dedução [dedu'sãw] (pl **-ões**) f deduction.

dedurar [dedu'ra*] (col) vt: **~ alguém** (criminoso) to grass on sb; (colega etc) to drop sb in it.

dedutivo/a [dedu'tʃivu/a] adj deductive.

deduzir [dedu'zi*] vt to deduct; (concluir): **~ (de)** to deduce, infer (from) ♦ vi (concluir) to deduce, infer.

defasado/a [defa'zadu/a] adj: **~ (de)** out of step (with).

defasagem [defa'zaʒẽ] (pl **-ns**) f discrepancy.

defecar [defe'ka*] vi to defecate.

defecção [defek'sãw] (pl **-ões**) f defection; (deserção) desertion.

defectivo/a [defek'tʃivu/a] adj faulty, defective; (LING) defective.

defeito [de'fejtu] m defect, flaw; **pôr ~s em** to find fault with; **com ~** broken, out of order; **para ninguém botar ~** (col) perfect.

defeituoso/a [defej'twozu/ɔza] adj defective, faulty.

defender [defẽ'de*] vt (ger, JUR) to defend; (proteger) to protect; **~-se** vr to stand up for o.s.; (numa língua) to get by; **~-se de** (de ataque) to defend o.s. against; (do frio etc) to protect o.s. against.

defensável [defẽ'savew] (pl **-eis**) adj defensible.

defensiva [defẽ'siva] f defensive; **estar** ou **ficar na ~** to be on the defensive.

defensor(a) [defẽ'so*(a)] m/f defender; (JUR) defending counsel.

deferência [defe'rẽsja] f (condescendência) deference; (respeito) respect.

deferente [defe'rẽtʃi] adj deferential.

deferimento [deferi'mẽtu] m (concessão) granting; (de prêmio, condecoração) awarding; (aceitação) acceptance.

deferir [defe'ri*] vt (pedido, petição) to grant; (prêmio, condecoração) to award ♦ vi: **~ a** (pedido, petição) to grant; (sugestão) to accept.

defesa [de'feza] f defence (BRIT), defense (US); (JUR) counsel for the defence ♦ m (PT: FUTEBOL) back.

deficiência [defi'sjẽsja] f deficiency.

deficiente [defi'sjẽtʃi] adj (imperfeito) defective; (carente): **~ (em)** deficient (in).

déficit ['dɛfisitʃi] (pl **~s**) m deficit.

deficitário/a [defisi'tarju/a] adj: **empresa/conta deficitária** company/account in deficit.

definhar [defi'ɲa*] vt to debilitate ♦ vi

(consumir-se) to waste away; (BOT) to wither.

definição [defini'sãw] (pl **-ões**) f definition.

definir [defi'ni*] vt to define; **~-se** vr (decidir-se) to make a decision; (explicar-se) to make one's position clear; **~-se contra/a favor de algo** to come out against/in favo(u)r of sth; **~-se como** to describe o.s. as.

definitivamente [definitʃiva'mẽtʃi] adv (finalmente) definitively; (permanentemente) for good; (sem dúvida) definitely.

definitivo/a [defini'tʃivu/a] adj (final) final, definitive; (permanente) permanent; (resposta, data) definite.

definível [defi'nivew] (pl **-eis**) adj definable.

defira [defi'ra] etc vb V **deferir**.

defiro [de'firu] etc vb V **deferir**.

deflação [defla'sãw] f deflation.

deflacionar [deflasjo'na*] vt to deflate.

deflacionário/a [deflasjo'narju/a] adj deflationary.

deflagração [deflagra'sãw] (pl **-ões**) f explosion; (fig) outbreak.

deflagrar [defla'gra*] vi to explode; (fig) to break out ♦ vt to set off; (fig) to trigger.

deflorar [deflo'ra*] vt to deflower.

deformação [defoxma'sãw] (pl **-ões**) f loss of shape; (de corpo) deformation; (de imagem, pensamento) distortion.

deformar [defox'ma*] vt to put out of shape; (corpo) to deform; (imagem, pensamento) to distort; **~-se** vr to lose shape; to be deformed; to become distorted.

deformidade [defoxmi'dadʒi] f deformity.

defraudação [defrawda'sãw] (pl **-ões**) f fraud; (de dinheiro) embezzlement.

defraudar [defraw'da*] vt (dinheiro) to embezzle; (uma pessoa) to defraud; **~ alguém de algo** to cheat sb of sth.

defrontar [defrõ'ta*] vt to face ♦ vi: **~ com** to face; (dar com) to come face to face with; **~-se** vr to face each other.

defronte [de'frõtʃi] adv opposite ♦ prep: **~ de** opposite.

defumado/a [defu'madu/a] adj smoked.

defumar [defu'ma*] vt (presunto) to smoke; (perfumar) to perfume.

defunto/a [de'fũtu/a] adj dead ♦ m/f dead person.

degelar [deʒe'la*] vt to thaw; (geladeira) to defrost ♦ vi to thaw out; to defrost.

degelo [de'ʒelu] m thaw.

degeneração [deʒenera'sãw] f (processo) degeneration; (estado) degeneracy.

degenerar [deʒene'ra*] vi: **~ (em)** to degenerate (into); **~-se** vr to become degenerate.

deglutir [deglu'tʃi*] vt, vi to swallow.

degolação [degola'sãw] (pl **-ões**) f beheading, decapitation.

degolar [dego'la*] vt to decapitate.

degradação [degrada'sãw] f degradation.

degradante [degra'dãtʃi] adj degrading.

degradar [degra'da*] vt to degrade, debase;

~-se *vr* to demean o.s.
dégradé [degra'de] *adj inv* (*cor*) shaded off.
degrau [de'graw] *m* step; (*de escada de mão*) rung.
degredar [degre'da*] *vt* to exile.
degredo [de'gredu] *m* exile.
degringolar [degrĩgo'la*] *vi* (*cair*) to tumble down; (*fig*) to collapse; (*: deteriorar-se*) to deteriorate; (*desorganizar-se*) to get messed up.
degustação [deguʃta'sãw] (*pl* **-ões**) *f* tasting, sampling; (*saborear*) savouring (*BRIT*), savoring (*US*).
degustar [deguʃ'ta*] *vt* (*provar*) to taste; (*saborear*) to savour (*BRIT*), savor (*US*).
dei [dej] *etc vb V* **dar.**
deificar [dejfi'ka*] *vt* to deify.
deitada [dej'tada] (*col*) *f*: **dar uma ~** to have a lie-down.
deitado/a [dej'tadu/a] *adj* (*estendido*) lying down; (*na cama*) in bed.
deitar [dej'ta*] *vt* to lay down; (*na cama*) to put to bed; (*colocar*) to put, place; (*lançar*) to cast; (*PT: líquido*) to pour; **~-se** *vr* to lie down; to go to bed; **~ sangue** (*PT*) to bleed; **~ abaixo** to knock down, flatten; **~ a fazer algo** to start doing sth; **~ uma carta** (*PT*) to post a letter; **~ fora** (*PT*) to throw away *ou* out; **~ e rolar** (*col*) to do as one likes.
deixa [dej'ʃa] *f* clue, hint; (*TEATRO*) cue; (*chance*) chance.
deixar [dej'ʃa*] *vt* to leave; (*abandonar*) to abandon; (*permitir*) to let, allow ♦ *vi*: **~ de** (*parar*) to stop; (*não fazer*) to fail to; **não posso ~ de ir** I must go; **não posso ~ de rir** I can't help laughing; **~ cair** to drop; **~ alguém louco** to drive sb crazy *ou* mad; **~ alguém cansado/nervoso** *etc* to make sb tired/nervous *etc*; **~ a desejar** to leave something to be desired; **deixa disso!** (*col*) come off it!; **deixa para lá!** (*col*) forget it!
dela ['dɛla] = **de** + **ela**; *V* **ela.**
delação [dela'sãw] (*pl* **-ões**) *f* (*de pessoa: denúncia*) accusation; (*: traição*) betrayal; (*de abusos*) disclosure.
delatar [dela'ta*] *vt* (*pessoa*) to inform on; (*abusos*) to reveal; (*à polícia*) to report.
delator(a) [dela'to*(a)] *m/f* informer.
délavé [dela've] *adj inv* (*jeans*) faded.
dele ['deli] = **de** + **ele**; *V* **ele.**
delegação [delega'sãw] (*pl* **-ões**) *f* delegation.
delegacia [delega'sia] *f* office; **~ de polícia** police station.
delegado/a [dele'gadu/a] *m/f* delegate, representative; **~ de polícia** police chief.
delegar [dele'ga*] *vt* to delegate.
deleitar [delej'ta*] *vt* to delight; **~-se** *vr*: **~-se com** to delight in.
deleite [de'lejtʃi] *m* delight.
deleitoso/a [delej'tozu/ɔza] *adj* delightful.

deletar [dele'ta*] *vt* (*COMPUT*) to delete.
deletério/a [dele'tɛrju/a] *adj* harmful.
delével [de'lɛvew] (*pl* **-eis**) *adj* erasable.
delgado/a [dew'gadu/a] *adj* thin; (*esbelto*) slim, slender; (*fino*) fine.
Délhi ['dɛli] *n*: **(Nova) ~** (New) Delhi.
deliberação [delibera'sãw] (*pl* **-ões**) *f* deliberation; (*decisão*) decision.
deliberar [delibe'ra*] *vt* to decide, resolve ♦ *vi* to deliberate.
deliberativo/a [delibera'tʃivu/a] *adj* (*conselho*) deliberative.
delicadeza [delika'deza] *f* delicacy; (*cortesia*) kindness.
delicado/a [deli'kadu/a] *adj* delicate; (*frágil*) fragile; (*cortês*) polite; (*sensível*) sensitive.
delícia [de'lisja] *f* delight; (*prazer*) pleasure; **esse bolo é uma ~** this cake is delicious; **que ~!** how lovely!
deliciar [deli'sja*] *vt* to delight; **~-se** *vr*: **~-se com algo** to take delight in sth.
delicioso/a [deli'sjozu/ɔza] *adj* lovely; (*comida, bebida*) delicious.
delimitação [delimita'sãw] *f* delimitation.
delimitar [delimi'ta*] *vt* to delimit.
delineador [delinja'do*] *m* (*de olhos*) eyeliner.
delinear [deli'nja*] *vt* to outline.
delinqüência [delĩ'kwẽsja] *f* delinquency.
delinqüente [delĩ'kwẽtʃi] *adj, m/f* delinquent, criminal.
delinqüir [delĩ'kwi*] *vi* to commit an offence (*BRIT*) *ou* offense (*US*).
delir [de'li*] *vt* to erase.
delirante [deli'rãtʃi] *adj* delirious; (*show, atuação*) thrilling.
delirar [deli'ra*] *vi* (*com febre*) to be delirious; (*de ódio, prazer*) to go mad, go wild.
delírio [de'lirju] *m* (*MED*) delirium; (*êxtase*) ecstasy; (*excitação*) excitement.
delirium tremens [de'liriũ 'trɛmẽs] *m* delirium tremens.
delito [de'litu] *m* (*crime*) crime; (*pecado*) offence (*BRIT*), offense (*US*).
delonga [de'lõga] *f* delay; **sem mais ~s** without more ado.
delongar [delõ'ga*] *vt* to delay; **~-se** *vr* (*conversa*) to wear on; **~-se em** to dwell on.
delta ['dɛwta] *f* delta.
demagogia [demago'ʒia] *f* demagogy.
demagógico/a [dema'gɔʒiku/a] *adj* demagogic.
demagogo [dema'gogu] *m* demagogue.
demais [dʒi'majʃ] *adv* (*em demasia*) too much; (*muitíssimo*) a lot, very much ♦ *pron*: **os/as ~** the rest (of them); **já é ~!** this is too much!; **é bom ~** it's really good; **foi ~** (*col: bacana*) it was great.
demanda [de'mãda] *f* (*JUR*) lawsuit; (*disputa*) claim; (*requisição*) request; (*ECON*) demand; **em ~ de** in search of.

NB: European Portuguese adds the following consonants to certain words: **b** (sú(b)dito, su(b)til), **c** (a(c)ção, a(c)cionista, a(c)to); **m** (inde(m)ne); **p** (ado(p)ção, ado(p)tar); *for further details see p. xiii.*

demandar [demã'da*] *vt* (*JUR*) to sue; (*exigir*, *reclamar*) to demand; (*porto*) to head for.

demão [de'mãw] (*pl* ~s) *f* (*de tinta*) coat, layer.

demarcação [demaxka'sãw] *f* demarcation.

demarcar [demax'ka*] *vt* (*delimitar*) to demarcate; (*fixar*) to mark out.

demarcatório/a [demaxka'tɔrju/a] *adj* V **linha**.

demasia [dema'zia] *f* excess, surplus; (*imoderação*) lack of moderation; **em** ~ (*dinheiro*, *comida etc*) too much; (*cartas*, *problemas etc*) too many.

demasiadamente [demazjada'mẽtʃi] *adv* too much; (*com adj*) too.

demasiado/a [dema'zjadu/a] *adj* too much; (*pl*) too many ♦ *adv* too much; (*com adj*) too.

demência [de'mẽsja] *f* dementia.

demente [de'mẽtʃi] *adj* insane, demented.

demérito/a [de'mɛritu/a] *adj* unworthy ♦ *m* demerit.

demissão [demi'sãw] (*pl* -ões) *f* dismissal; **pedido de** ~ resignation; **pedir** ~ to resign.

demissionário/a [demisjo'narju/a] *adj* resigning, outgoing.

demissões [demi'sõjʃ] *fpl de* **demissão**.

demitir [demi'tʃi*] *vt* to dismiss; (*col*) to sack, fire; ~-**se** *vr* to resign.

democracia [demokra'sia] *f* democracy.

democrata [demo'krata] *m/f* democrat.

democrático/a [demo'kratʃiku/a] *adj* democratic.

democratização [demokratʃiza'sãw] *f* democratization.

democratizar [demokratʃi'za*] *vt* to democratize.

démodé [demo'de] *adj inv* old-fashioned.

demografia [demogra'fia] *f* demography.

demográfico/a [demo'grafiku/a] *adj* demographic.

demolição [demoli'sãw] (*pl* -ões) *f* demolition.

demolir [demo'li*] *vt* to demolish, knock down; (*fig*) to destroy.

demoníaco/a [demo'niaku/a] *adj* devilish.

demônio [de'monju] *m* devil, demon; (*col*: *criança*) brat.

demonstração [demõʃtra'sãw] (*pl* -ões) *f* (*lição prática*) demonstration; (*de amizade*) show, display; (*prova*) proof; ~ **de contas** (*COM*) statement of account; ~ **de lucros e perdas** (*COM*) profit and loss statement.

demonstrar [demõʃ'tra*] *vt* (*mostrar*) to demonstrate; (*provar*) to prove; (*amizade etc*) to show.

demonstrativo/a [demõʃtra'tʃivu/a] *adj* demonstrative.

demonstrável [demõ'ʃtravew] (*pl* -eis) *adj* demonstrable.

demora [de'mɔra] *f* delay; (*parada*) stop; **sem** ~ at once, without delay; **qual é a** ~ **disso?** how long will this take?

demorado/a [demo'radu/a] *adj* slow.

demorar [demo'ra*] *vt* to delay, slow down ♦

vi (*permanecer*) to stay; (*tardar a vir*) to be late; (*conserto*) to take (a long) time; ~-**se** *vr* to stay for a long time, linger; ~ **a chegar** to be a long time coming; **vai** ~ **muito?** will it take long?; **não vou** ~ I won't be long.

demover [demo've*] *vt*: ~ **alguém de algo** to talk sb out of sth; ~-**se** *vr*: ~-**se de algo** to be talked out of sth.

Denatran [dena'trã] (*BR*) *abr m* (= *Departamento Nacional de Trânsito*) ≈ Ministry of Transport.

dendê [dẽ'de] *m* (*CULIN*: *óleo*) palm oil; (*BOT*) oil palm.

denegrir [dene'gri*] *vt* to blacken; (*difamar*) to denigrate.

dengo [dẽgu] *m* coyness; (*choro*) whimpering.

dengoso/a [dẽ'gozu/ɔza] *adj* coy; (*criança*: *choraminguento*): **ser** ~ to be a crybaby.

dengue [dẽgi] *m* (*MED*) dengue.

denigro [de'nigru] *etc vb* V **denegrir**.

denodado/a [deno'dadu/a] *adj* brave, daring.

denominação [denomina'sãw] (*pl* -ões) *f* (*REL*) denomination; (*título*) name; (*ato*) naming.

denominador [denomina'do*] *m*: ~ **comum** (*MAT*, *fig*) common denominator.

denominar [denomi'na*] *vt*: ~ **algo/alguém** ... to call sth/sb ...; ~-**se** *vr* to be called; (*a si mesmo*) to call o.s.

denotar [deno'ta*] *vt* (*indicar*) to show, indicate; (*significar*) to signify.

densidade [dẽsi'dadʒi] *f* density; **disco de alta** ~ (*COMPUT*) high-density disk; **disco de** ~ **simples/dupla** (*COMPUT*) single-/double-density disk.

denso/a [dẽsu/a] *adj* (*cerrado*) dense; (*espesso*) thick; (*compacto*) compact.

dentada [dẽ'tada] *f* bite.

dentado/a [dẽ'tadu/a] *adj* serrated.

dentadura [dẽta'dura] *f* teeth *pl*, set of teeth; (*artificial*) dentures *pl*.

dental [dẽ'taw] (*pl* -ais) *adj* dental.

dentário/a [dẽ'tarju/a] *adj* dental.

dente ['dẽtʃi] *m* tooth; (*de animal*) fang; (*de elefante*) tusk; (*de alho*) clove; **falar entre os** ~**s** to mutter, mumble; ~ **de leite/do siso** milk/wisdom tooth; ~ **postiço** false tooth.

dente-de-leão (*pl* **dentes-de-leão**) *m* dandelion.

Dentel [dẽ'tɛw] (*BR*) *abr m* = **Departamento Nacional de Telecomunicações**.

dentição [dẽtʃi'sãw] *f* (*formação dos dentes*) teething; (*dentes*) teeth *pl*; **primeira** ~ milk teeth; **segunda** ~ second teeth.

dentifrício [dẽtʃi'frisju] *m* toothpaste.

dentina [dẽ'tʃina] *f* dentine.

dentista [dẽ'tʃiʃta] *m/f* dentist.

dentre ['dẽtri] *prep* (from) among.

dentro ['dẽtru] *adv* inside; **aí** ~ in there ♦ *prep*: ~ **de** inside; (*tempo*) (with)in; ~ **pouco** *ou* **em breve** soon, before long; **de** ~ **para fora** inside out; **dar uma** ~ (*col*) to get it right; **por** ~ on the inside; **estar por** ~ (*col*:

fig) to be in the know; **estar por ~ de algo** (*col*: *fig*) to know the ins and outs of sth.

dentuça [dē'tusa] *f* buck teeth *pl*; V *tb* **dentuço.**

dentuço/a [dē'tusu/a] *adj* buck-toothed ♦ *m/f* buck-toothed person; **ser ~** to have buck teeth.

denúncia [de'nũsja] *f* denunciation; (*acusação*) accusation; (*de roubo*) report.

denunciar [denũ'sja*] *vt* to denounce, inform against; (*revelar*) to reveal.

deparar [depa'ra*] *vt* (*revelar*) to reveal; (*fazer aparecer*) to present ♦ *vi*: **~ com** to come across, meet; **~-se** *vr*: **~-se com** to come across, meet.

departamental [depaxtamē'taw] (*pl* -**ais**) *adj* departmental.

departamento [depaxta'mētu] *m* department; **D~ de Marcas e Patentes** Patent Office.

depauperar [depawpe'ra*] *vt*: **~ algo/alguém** to bleed sth/sb dry.

depenar [depe'na*] *vt* to pluck; (*col*: *roubar*) to clean out.

dependência [depē'dēsja] *f* dependence; (*edificação*) annexe (*BRIT*), annex (*US*); (*colonial*) dependency; (*cômodo*) room.

dependente [depē'dētʃi] *m/f* dependant.

depender [depē'de*] *vi*: **~ de** to depend on.

dependurar [depēdu'ra*] *vi* to hang.

depilação [depila'sãw] (*pl* -**ões**) *f* depilation.

depilador(a) [depila'do*(a)] *m/f* beauty therapist.

depilar [depi'la*] *vt* to wax; **~ as pernas** (*mandar fazer*) to have one's legs done; (*fazer sozinho*) to do one's legs.

depilatório [depila'tɔrju] *m* hair-remover.

deplorar [deplo'ra*] *vt* (*lamentar*) to regret; (*morte*, *perda*) to lament.

deplorável [deplo'ravew] (*pl* -**eis**) *adj* deplorable; (*lamentável*) regrettable.

depoente [de'pwētʃi] *m/f* witness.

depoimento [depoj'mētu] *m* testimony, evidence; (*na polícia*) statement.

depois [de'pojʃ] *adv* afterwards ♦ *prep*: **~ de** after; **~ de comer** after eating; **~ que** after.

depor [de'po*] (*irreg*: *como* **pôr**) *vt* (*pôr*) to place; (*indicar*) to indicate; (*rei*) to depose; (*governo*) to overthrow ♦ *vi* (*JUR*) to testify, give evidence; (*na polícia*) to give a statement; **esses fatos depõem contra/a favor dele** these facts speak against him/in his favo(u)r.

deportação [depoxta'sãw] (*pl* -**ões**) *f* deportation.

deportar [depox'ta*] *vt* to deport.

deposição [depozi'sãw] (*pl* -**ões**) *f* deposition; (*governo*) overthrow.

depositante [depozi'tātʃi] *m/f* depositor ♦ *adj* depositing.

depositar [depozi'ta*] *vt* to deposit; (*voto*) to cast; (*colocar*) to place; **~-se** *vr* (*líquido*) to form a deposit; **~ confiança em** to place one's confidence in.

depositário/a [depozi'tarju/a] *m/f* trustee; (*fig*) confidant(e).

depósito [de'pɔzitu] *m* deposit; (*armazém*) warehouse, depot; (*de lixo*) dump; (*reservatório*) tank; **~ a prazo fixo** fixed-term deposit; **~ de bagagens** left-luggage office.

depravação [deprava'sãw] *f* depravity, corruption.

depravado/a [depra'vadu/a] *adj* depraved ♦ *m/f* degenerate.

depravar [depra'va*] *vt* to deprave, corrupt; (*estragar*) to ruin; **~-se** *vr* to become depraved.

deprecar [depre'ka*] *vt* to beg for, pray for ♦ *vi* to plead.

depreciação [depresja'sãw] *f* depreciation.

depreciador(a) [depresja'do*(a)] *adj* deprecatory.

depreciar [depre'sja*] *vt* (*desvalorizar*) to devalue; (*COM*) to write down; (*menosprezar*) to belittle; **~-se** *vr* to depreciate, lose value; (*menosprezar-se*) to belittle o.s.

depredação [depreda'sãw] *f* depredation.

depredador(a) [depreda'do*(a)] *adj* destructive ♦ *m/f* vandal.

depredar [depre'da*] *vt* to wreck.

depreender [deprjē'de*] *vt*: **~ algo/que ... (de algo)** to gather sth/that ... (from sth).

depressa [dʒi'presa] *adv* fast, quickly; **vamos ~** let's get a move on!

depressão [depre'sãw] (*pl* -**ões**) *f* (*ger*) depression.

depressivo/a [depre'sivu/a] *adj* depressive.

depressões [depre'sõjʃ] *fpl de* **depressão.**

deprimente [depri'mētʃi] *adj* depressing.

deprimido/a [depri'midu/a] *adj* depressed, low.

deprimir [depri'mi*] *vt* to depress; **~-se** *vr* to get depressed.

depuração [depura'sãw] *f* purification.

depurar [depu'ra*] *vt* to purify; (*COMPUT*: *programa*) to debug.

deputado/a [depu'tadu/a] *m/f* deputy; (*agente*) agent; (*POL*) ≈ Member of Parliament (*BRIT*), Representative (*US*).

deputar [depu'ta*] *vt* to delegate.

deque ['dɛki] *m* deck.

DER (*BR*) *abr m* (= *Departamento de Estradas de Rodagem*) state highways dept.

der [de*] *etc vb* V **dar.**

deriva [de'riva] *f* drift; **ir à ~** to drift; **ficar à ~** to be adrift.

derivação [deriva'sãw] (*pl* -**ões**) *f* derivation.

derivar [deri'va*] *vt* (*desviar*) to divert; (*LING*) to derive ♦ *vi* (*ir à deriva*) to drift; **~-se** *vr* (*palavra*) to be derived; (*ir à deriva*) to drift; (*provir*): **~(-se) (de)** to derive *ou* be derived (from).

dermatologia [dexmatolo'ʒia] *f* dermatology.
dermatologista [dexmatolo'ʒiʃta] *m/f* dermatologist.
dernier cri [dex'nje 'kri] *m* last word.
derradeiro/a [dexa'dejru/a] *adj* last, final.
derramamento [dexama'mētu] *m* spilling; (*de sangue, lágrimas*) shedding.
derramar [dexa'ma*] *vt* (*sem querer*) to spill; (*entornar*) to pour; (*sangue, lágrimas*) to shed; ~**-se** *vr* to pour out.
derrame [de'xami] *m* haemorrhage (*BRIT*), hemorrhage (*US*).
derrapagem [dexa'paʒē] (*pl* **-ns**) *f* skid; (*ação*) skidding.
derrapar [dexa'pa*] *vi* to skid.
derredor [dexe'do*] *adv, prep*: **em** ~ **(de)** around.
derreter [dexe'te*] *vt* to melt; ~**-se** *vr* to melt; (*coisa congelada*) to thaw; (*enternecer-se*) to be touched; ~ **alguém** to win sb's heart; ~**-se por alguém** to fall for sb.
derretido/a [dexe'tʃidu/a] *adj* melted; (*enternecido*) touched; (*apaixonado*) smitten; **estar** ~ **por alguém** to be crazy about sb.
derrocada [dexo'kada] *f* downfall; (*ruína*) collapse.
derrogação [dexoga'sãw] (*pl* **-ões**) *f* amendment.
derrota [de'xɔta] *f* defeat, rout; (*NÁUT*) route.
derrotar [dexo'ta*] *vt* (*vencer*) to defeat; (*em jogo*) to beat.
derrubar [dexu'ba*] *vt* to knock down; (*governo*) to bring down; (*suj: doença*) to lay low; (*col: prejudicar*) to put down.
desabafar [dʒizaba'fa*] *vt* (*sentimentos*) to give vent to ♦ *vi*: ~ **(com)** to unburden o.s. (to); ~**-se** *vr*: ~**-se (com)** to unburden o.s. (to).
desabafo [dʒiza'bafu] *m* confession.
desabalado/a [dʒizaba'ladu/a] *adj*: **correr/sair** ~ to run headlong/rush out.
desabamento [dʒizaba'mētu] *m* collapse.
desabar [dʒiza'ba*] *vi* (*edifício, ponte*) to collapse; (*chuva*) to pour down; (*tempestade*) to break.
desabilitar [dʒizabili'ta*] *vt*: ~ **alguém a** *ou* **para (fazer) algo** to bar sb from (doing) sth.
desabitado/a [dʒizabi'tadu/a] *adj* uninhabited.
desabituar [dʒizabi'twa*] *vt*: ~ **alguém de (fazer) algo** to get sb out of the habit of (doing) sth; ~**-se** *vr*: ~**-se de (fazer) algo** to get out of the habit of (doing) sth.
desabonar [dʒizabo'na*] *vt* to discredit; ~**-se** *vr* to be discredited.
desabotoar [dʒizabo'twa*] *vt* to unbutton.
desabrido/a [dʒiza'bridu/a] *adj* rude, brusque.
desabrigado/a [dʒizabri'gadu/a] *adj* (*sem casa*) homeless; (*exposto*) exposed.
desabrigar [dʒizabri'ga*] *vt* to make homeless.
desabrochar [dʒizabro'ʃa*] *vi* (*flores, fig*) to blossom ♦ *m* blossoming.
desabusado/a [dʒizabu'zadu/a] *adj* (*sem pre-*

conceitos) unprejudiced; (*atrevido*) impudent.
desacatar [dʒizaka'ta*] *vt* (*desrespeitar*) to have *ou* show no respect for; (*afrontar*) to defy; (*desprezar*) to scorn ♦ *vi* (*col*) to be amazing.
desacato [dʒiza'katu] *m* (*falta de respeito*) disrespect; (*desprezo*) disregard; (*col*): **ele é um** ~ he's amazing.
desaceleração [dʒizaselera'sãw] *f* (*tb: ECON*) slowing down.
desacelerar [dʒizasele'ra*] *vt* to slow down.
desacerto [dʒiza'sextu] *m* mistake, blunder.
desacomodar [dʒizakomo'da*] *vt* to move out.
desacompanhado/a [dʒizakõpa'ɲadu/a] *adj* on one's own, alone.
desaconselhar [dʒizakõse'ʎa*] *vt*: ~ **algo (a alguém)** to advise (sb) against sth.
desaconselhável [dʒizakõse'ʎavew] (*pl* **-eis**) *adj* inadvisable.
desacordado/a [dʒizakox'dadu/a] *adj* unconscious.
desacordo [dʒiza'koxdu] *m* (*falta de acordo*) disagreement; (*desarmonia*) discord.
desacostumado/a [dʒizakoʃtumadu/a] *adj* unaccustomed.
desacostumar [dʒizakoʃtu'ma*] *vt*: ~ **alguém de algo** to get sb out of the habit of sth; ~**-se** *vr*: ~**-se de algo** to give sth up.
desacreditado/a [dʒizakredʒi'tadu/a] *adj* discredited.
desacreditar [dʒizakredʒi'ta*] *vt* to discredit; ~**-se** *vr* to lose one's reputation.
desafeto [dʒiza'fɛtu] *m* coldness.
desafiador(a) [dʒizafja'do*(a)] *adj* challenging; (*pessoa*) defiant ♦ *m/f* challenger.
desafiar [dʒiza'fja*] *vt* (*propor combate*) to challenge; (*afrontar*) to defy.
desafinação [dʒizafina'sãw] *f* dissonance.
desafinado/a [dʒizafi'nadu/a] *adj* out of tune.
desafinar [dʒizafi'na*] *vt* to put out of tune ♦ *vi* to play out of tune; (*cantor*) to sing out of tune.
desafio [dʒiza'fiu] *m* challenge; (*PT: ESPORTE*) match, game.
desafivelar [dʒizafive'la*] *vt* to unbuckle.
desafogado/a [dʒizafo'gadu/a] *adj* (*desimpedido*) clear; (*desembaraçado*) free.
desafogar [dʒizafo'ga*] *vt* (*libertar*) to free; (*desapertar*) to relieve; (*desabafar*) to give vent to; ~**-se** *vr* (*desapertar-se*) to free o.s.; (*desabafar-se*) to unburden o.s.
desafogo [dʒiza'fogu] *m* (*alívio*) relief; (*folga*) leisure.
desaforado/a [dʒizafo'radu/a] *adj* rude, insolent.
desaforo [dʒiza'foru] *m* insolence, abuse.
desafortunado/a [dʒizafoxtu'nadu/a] *adj* unfortunate, unlucky.
desafronta [dʒiza'frõta] *f* (*satisfação*) redress; (*vingança*) revenge.
desagasalhado/a [dʒizagaza'ʎadu/a] *adj*

scantily clad.

desagradar [dʒizagra'da*] *vt* to displease ♦ *vi*: ~ **a alguém** to displease sb.

desagradável [dʒizagra'davew] (*pl* -eis) *adj* unpleasant.

desagrado [dʒiza'gradu] *m* displeasure.

desagravar [dʒizagra'va*] *vt* (*insulta*) to make amends for; (*pessoa*) to make amends to; ~-**se** *vr* to avenge o.s.

desagravo [dʒiza'gravu] *m* amends *pl*.

desagregação [dʒizagrega'sãw] *f* (*separação*) separation; (*dissolução*) disintegration.

desagregar [dʒizagre'ga*] *vt* (*desunir*) to break up, split; (*separar*) to separate; ~-**se** *vr* to break up, split; to separate.

desaguar [dʒiza'gwa*] *vt* to drain ♦ *vi*: ~ (**em**) to flow *ou* empty (into).

desairoso/a [dʒizaj'rozu/ɔza] *adj* inelegant.

desajeitado/a [dʒizaʒej'tadu/a] *adj* clumsy, awkward.

desajuizado/a [dʒizaʒwi'zadu/a] *adj* foolish, unwise.

desajustado/a [dʒizaʒuʃ'tadu/a] *adj* (*PSICO*) maladjusted; (*peças*) in need of adjustment ♦ *m/f* maladjusted person.

desajustamento [dʒizaʒuʃta'mẽtu] *m* (*PSICO*) maladjustment.

desajustar [dʒizaʒuʃ'ta*] *vt* (*peças*) to mess up.

desajuste [dʒiza'ʒuʃtʃi] *m* (*PSICO*) maladjustment; (*mecânico*) problem.

desalentado/a [dʒizalẽ'tadu/a] *adj* disheartened.

desalentar [dʒizalẽ'ta*] *vt* to discourage; (*deprimir*) to depress.

desalento [dʒiza'lẽtu] *m* discouragement.

desalinhado/a [dʒizali'ɲadu/a] *adj* untidy.

desalinho [dʒiza'liɲu] *m* untidiness.

desalmado/a [dʒizaw'madu/a] *adj* cruel, inhuman.

desalojar [dʒizalo'ʒa*] *vt* (*expulsar*) to oust; ~-**se** *vr* to move out.

desamarrar [dʒizama'xa*] *vt* to untie ♦ *vi* (*NÁUT*) to cast off.

desamarrotar [dʒizamaxo'ta*] *vt* to smooth out.

desamassar [dʒizama'sa*] *vt* (*papel*) to smooth out; (*chapéu etc*) to straighten out; (*carro*) to beat out.

desambientado/a [dʒizãbjẽ'tadu/a] *adj* unsettled.

desamor [dʒiza'mo*] *m* dislike.

desamparado/a [dʒizãpa'radu/a] *adj* (*abandonado*) abandoned; (*sem apoio*) helpless.

desamparar [dʒizãpa'ra*] *vt* to abandon.

desamparo [dʒizã'paru] *m* helplessness.

desandar [dʒizã'da*] *vi* (*maionese, clara*) to separate; ~ **a fazer** to begin to do; ~ **a correr** to break into a run; ~ **a chorar** to

burst into tears.

desanimação [dʒizanima'sãw] *f* dejection.

desanimado/a [dʒizani'madu/a] *adj* (*pessoa*) fed up, dispirited; (*festa*) dull; **ser** ~ (*pessoa*) to be apathetic.

desanimar [dʒizani'ma*] *vt* (*abater*) to dishearten; (*desencorajar*): ~ (**de fazer**) to discourage (from doing) ♦ *vi* to lose heart; (*ser desanimador*) to be discouraging; ~ **de fazer algo** to lose the will to do sth; (*desistir*) to give up doing sth.

desânimo [dʒi'zanimu] *m* dejection.

desanuviado/a [dʒizanu'vjadu/a] *adj* cloudless, clear.

desanuviar [dʒizanu'vja*] *vt* (*céu*) to clear; ~-**se** *vr* to clear; (*fig*) to stop; ~ **alguém** to put sb's mind at rest.

desapaixonado/a [dʒizapajʃo'nadu/a] *adj* dispassionate.

desaparafusar [dʒizaparafu'za*] *vt* to unscrew.

desaparecer [dʒizapare'se*] *vi* to disappear, vanish.

desaparecido/a [dʒizapare'sidu/a] *adj* lost, missing ♦ *m/f* missing person.

desaparecimento [dʒizaparesi'mẽtu] *m* disappearance; (*falecimento*) death.

desapegado/a [dʒizape'gadu/a] *adj* indifferent, detached.

desapegar [dʒizape'ga*] *vt* to detach; ~-**se** *vr*: ~-**se de** to go off.

desapego [dʒiza'pegu] *m* indifference, detachment.

desapercebido/a [dʒizapexse'bidu/a] *adj* unnoticed.

desapertar [dʒizapex'ta*] *vt* (*afrouxar*) to loosen; (*livrar*) to free.

desapiedado/a [dʒizapje'dadu/a] *adj* pitiless, ruthless.

desapontador(a) [dʒizapõta'do*(a)] *adj* disappointing.

desapontamento [dʒizapõta'mẽtu] *m* disappointment.

desapontar [dʒizapõ'ta*] *vt* to disappoint.

desapossar [dʒizapo'sa*] *vt*: ~ **alguém de algo** to take sth away from sb; ~-**se** *vr*: ~-**se de algo** to give sth up.

desaprender [dʒizaprẽ'de*] *vt* to forget ♦ *vi*: ~ **a fazer** to forget how to do.

desapropriação [dʒizaproprja'sãw] *f* (*de bens*) expropriation; (*de pessoa*) dispossession.

desapropriar [dʒizapro'prja*] *vt* (*bens*) to expropriate; (*pessoa*) to dispossess.

desaprovação [dʒizaprova'sãw] *f* disapproval.

desaprovar [dʒizapro'va*] *vt* (*reprovar*) to disapprove of; (*censurar*) to object to.

desaproveitado/a [dʒizaprovej'tadu/a] *adj* wasted; (*terras*) undeveloped.

desaquecimento [dʒizakesi'mẽtu] *m* (*ECON*) cooling.

NB: *European Portuguese adds the following consonants to certain words:* **b** (sú(b)dito, su(b)til); **c** (a(c)ção, a(c)cionista, a(c)to); **m** (inde(m)ne); **p** (ado(p)ção, ado(p)tar); *for further details see p. xiii.*

desarmamento [dʒizaxma'mẽtu] *m* disarmament.

desarmar [dʒizax'ma*] *vt* to disarm; (*desmontar*) to dismantle; (*bomba*) to defuse.

desarmonia [dʒizaxmo'nia] *f* discord.

desarraigar [dʒizaxaj'ga*] *vt* to uproot.

desarranjado/a [dʒizaxã'ʒadu/a] *adj* (*intestino*) upset; (*TEC*) out of order; **estar** ~ (*pessoa*) to have diarrhoea (*BRIT*) *ou* diarrhea (*US*).

desarranjar [dʒizaxã'ʒa*] *vt* (*transtornar*) to upset, disturb; (*desordenar*) to mess up.

desarranjo [dʒiza'xãʒu] *m* (*desordem*) disorder; (*enguiço*) breakdown; (*diarréia*) diarrhoea (*BRIT*), diarrhea (*US*).

desarregaçar [dʒizaxega'sa*] *vt* (*mangas*) to roll down.

desarrumado/a [dʒizaxu'madu/a] *adj* untidy, messy.

desarrumar [dʒizaxu'ma*] *vt* to mess up; (*mala*) to unpack.

desarticulado/a [dʒizaxtʃiku'ladu/a] *adj* dislocated.

desarticular [dʒizaxtʃiku'la*] *vt* (*osso*) to dislocate.

desarvorado/a [dʒizaxvo'radu/a] *adj* disoriented, at a loss.

desassociar [dʒizaso'sja*] *vt* to disassociate; ~-**se** *vr*: ~-**se de algo** to disassociate o.s. from sth.

desassossego [dʒizaso'segu] *m* (*inquietação*) disquiet; (*perturbação*) restlessness.

desastrado/a [dʒizaʃ'tradu/a] *adj* clumsy.

desastre [dʒi'zaʃtri] *m* disaster; (*acidente*) accident; (*de avião*) crash.

desastroso/a [dʒizaʃ'trozu/ɔza] *adj* disastrous.

desatar [dʒiza'ta*] *vt* (*nó*) to undo, untie ♦ *vi*: ~ **a fazer** to begin to do; ~ **a chorar** to burst into tears; ~ **a rir** to burst out laughing.

desatarraxar [dʒizataxa'ʃa*] *vt* to unscrew.

desatencioso/a [dʒizatẽ'sjozu/ɔza] *adj* inattentive; (*descortês*) impolite.

desatender [dʒizatẽ'de*] *vt* (*não fazer caso de*) to pay no attention to, ignore ♦ *vi*: ~ **a** to ignore.

desatento/a [dʒiza'tẽtu/a] *adj* inattentive.

desatinado/a [dʒizatʃi'nadu/a] *adj* crazy, wild ♦ *m/f* lunatic.

desatinar [dʒizatʃi'na*] *vi* to behave foolishly.

desatino [dʒiza'tʃinu] *m* (*loucura*) madness; (*ato*) folly.

desativar [dʒizatʃi'va*] *vt* (*firma, usina*) to shut down; (*veículos*) to withdraw from service; (*bomba*) to deactivate, defuse.

desatracar [dʒizatra'ka*] *vt* (*navio*) to unmoor; (*brigões*) to separate ♦ *vi* (*navio*) to cast off.

desatravancar [dʒizatravã'ka*] *vt* to clear.

desatrelar [dʒizatre'la*] *vt* to unhitch.

desatualizado/a [dʒizatwali'zadu/a] *adj* out of date; (*pessoa*) out of touch.

desautorizar [dʒizawtori'za*] *vt* (*prática*) to disallow; (*desacreditar*) to discredit; ~ **alguém** (*tirar a autoridade de*) to undermine sb's authority.

desavença [dʒiza'vẽsa] *f* (*briga*) quarrel; (*discórdia*) disagreement; **em** ~ at loggerheads.

desavergonhado/a [dʒizavexgo'ɲadu/a] *adj* insolent, impudent, shameless.

desavir-se [dʒiza'vixsi] (*irreg: como* **vir**) *vr*: ~ (**com alguém em algo**) to quarrel *ou* disagree (with sb about sth).

desavisado/a [dʒizavi'zadu/a] *adj* careless.

desbancar [dʒiʒbã'ka*] *vt*: ~ **alguém (em algo)** to outdo sb (in sth).

desbaratar [dʒiʒbara'ta*] *vt* to ruin; (*desperdiçar*) to waste, squander; (*vencer*) to crush; (*pôr em desordem*) to mess up.

desbarrigado/a [dʒiʒbaxi'gadu/a] *adj* flat-bellied.

desbastar [dʒiʒbaʃ'ta*] *vt* (*cabelo, plantas*) to thin (out); (*vegetação*) to trim.

desbocado/a [dʒiʒbo'kadu/a] *adj* (*pessoa*) foul-mouthed, crude.

desbotar [dʒiʒbo'ta*] *vt* to discolour (*BRIT*), discolor (*US*) ♦ *vi* to fade.

desbragadamente [dʒiʒbragada'mẽtʃi] *adv* (*beber*) to excess; (*mentir*) blatantly.

desbravador(a) [dʒiʒbrava'do*(a)] *m/f* explorer.

desbravar [dʒiʒbra'va*] *vt* (*terras desconhecidas*) to explore.

desbundante [dʒiʒbũ'dãtʃi] (*col*) *adj* fantastic.

desbundar [dʒiʒbũ'da*] (*col*) *vt* to knock out ♦ *vi* to flip, freak out.

desbunde [dʒiʒ'bũdʒi] (*col*) *m* knockout.

desburocratizar [dʒiʒburokratʃi'za*] *vt*: ~ **algo** to remove the bureaucracy from sth.

descabelar [dʒiʃkabe'la*] *vt*: ~ **alguém** to mess up sb's hair; ~-**se** *vr* to get one's hair messed up.

descabido/a [dʒiʃka'bidu/a] *adj* (*impróprio*) improper; (*inoportuno*) inappropriate.

descadeirado/a [dʒiʃkadej'radu/a] *adj* (*cansado*) weary; **ficar** ~ (*com dor*) to get backache.

descalabro [dʒiʃka'labru] *m* disaster.

descalçar [dʒiʃkaw'sa*] *vt* (*sapatos*) to take off; ~-**se** *vr* to take off one's shoes.

descalço/a [dʒiʃ'kawsu/a] *adj* barefoot.

descambar [dʒiʃkã'ba*] *vi*: ~ (**de algo**) **para algo** to sink *ou* deteriorate (from sth) to sth; ~ **para** *ou* **em** to degenerate into.

descampado [dʒiʃkã'padu] *m* open country.

descansado/a [dʒiʃkã'sadu/a] *adj* (*tranqüilo*) calm, quiet; (*vagaroso*) slow; **fique** ~ don't worry; **pode ficar** ~ **que** ... you can rest assured that ....

descansar [dʒiʃkã'sa*] *vt* to rest; (*apoiar*) to lean ♦ *vi* to rest.

descanso [dʒiʃ'kãsu] *m* (*repouso*) rest; (*folga*) break; (*para prato*) mat; **sem** ~ without a break.

descapitalização [dʒiʃkapitaliza'sãw] *f* (*COM*)

decapitalization.

descarado/a [dʒiʃka'radu/a] *adj* cheeky, impudent.

descaramento [dʒiʃkara'mētu] *m* cheek, impudence.

descarga [dʒiʃ'kaxga] *f* unloading; (*vaso sanitário*) flushing; (*MIL*) volley; (*ELET*) discharge; **dar a** ~ to flush the toilet.

descarnado/a [dʒiʃkax'nadu/a] *adj* scrawny, skinny.

descaroçar [dʒiʃkaro'sa*] *vt* (*semente*) to seed; (*fruto*) to stone, core; (*algodão*) to gin.

descarregadouro [dʒiʃkaxega'doru] *m* wharf.

descarregamento [dʒiʃkaxega'mētu] *m* (*de carga*) unloading; (*ELET*) discharge.

descarregar [dʒiʃkaxe'ga*] *vt* (*carga*) to unload; (*ELET*) to discharge; (*aliviar*) to relieve; (*raiva*) to vent, give vent to; (*arma*) to fire ♦ *vi* to unload; (*bateria*) to run out; ~ **a raiva em alguém** to take it out on sb.

descarrilhamento [dʒiʃkaxiʎa'mētu] *m* derailment.

descarrilhar [dʒiʃkaxi'ʎa*] *vt* to derail ♦ *vi* to run off the rails; (*fig*) to go off the rails.

descartar [dʒiʃkax'ta*] *vt* to discard; ~**-se** *vr*: ~**-se de** to get rid of.

descartável [dʒiʃkax'tavew] (*pl* **-eis**) disposable.

descascador [dʒiʃkaʃka'do*] *m* peeler.

descascar [dʒiʃkaʃ'ka*] *vt* (*fruta*) to peel; (*ervilhas*) to shell ♦ *vi* (*depois do sol*) to peel; **o feijão descascou** the skin came off the beans; **a cobra descascou** the snake shed its skin.

descaso [dʒiʃ'kazu] *m* disregard.

descendência [desẽ'dẽsja] *f* descendants *pl*, offspring *pl*.

descendente [desẽ'dẽtʃi] *adj* descending, going down ♦ *m/f* descendant.

descender [desẽ'de*] *vi*: ~ **de** to descend from.

descentralização [dʒisẽtraliza'sãw] *f* decentralization.

descentralizar [dʒisẽtrali'za*] *vt* to decentralize.

descer [de'se*] *vt* (*escada*) to go (*ou* come) down; (*bagagem*) to take down ♦ *vi* (*saltar*) to get off; (*baixar*) to go (*ou* come) down; ~ **a pormenores** to get down to details.

descida [de'sida] *f* descent; (*declive*) slope; (*abaixamento*) fall, drop.

desclassificação [dʒiʃklasifika'sãw] *f* disqualification.

desclassificar [dʒiʃklasifi'ka*] *vt* (*eliminar*) to disqualify; (*desacreditar*) to discredit.

descoberta [dʒiʃko'bɛxta] *f* discovery; (*invenção*) invention.

descoberto/a [dʒiʃko'bɛxtu/a] *pp de* **descobrir** ♦ *adj* (*nu*) bare, naked; (*exposto*) exposed; (*COM: conta*) overdrawn; (: *saldo, compra*) uncovered ♦ *m* overdraft; **a** ~ openly; **pôr** *ou* **sacar a** ~ (*conta*) to overdraw.

descobridor(a) [dʒiʃkobri'do*(a)] *m/f* discoverer; (*explorador*) explorer.

descobrimento [dʒiʃkobri'mētu] *m* discovery.

descobrir [dʒiʃko'bri*] *vt* to discover; (*tirar a cobertura de*) to uncover; (*panela*) to take the lid off; (*averiguar*) to find out; (*enigma*) to solve.

descolar [dʒiʃko'la*] *vt* to unstick; (*col: arranjar*) to get hold of; (: *dar*) to give ♦ *vi*: **a criança não descola da mãe** the child won't leave its mother's side.

descoloração [dʒiʃkolora'sãw] *f* discolouration (*BRIT*), discoloration (*US*).

descolorante [dʒiʃkolo'rãtʃi] *adj* bleaching ♦ *m* bleach.

descolorar [dʒiʃkolo'ra*] *vt, vi* = **descorar**.

descolorir [dʒiʃkolo'ri*] *vt* to discolour (*BRIT*), discolor (*US*); (*cabelo*) to bleach ♦ *vi* to fade.

descomedimento [dʒiʃkomedʒi'mētu] *m* lack of moderation.

descompassado/a [dʒiʃkõpa'sadu/a] *adj* (*exagerado*) out of all proportion; (*ritmo*) out of step.

descompor (*irreg: como* **pôr**) *vt* to disarrange; (*insultar*) to abuse; (*repreender*) to scold, tell off; (*fisionomia*) to distort, twist; ~**-se** *vr* (*desordinar-se*) to fall into disarray; (*fisionomia*) to be twisted; (*desarrumar-se*) to expose o.s.

descomposto/a [dʒiʃkõ'poʃtu/'poʃta] *pp de* **descompor** ♦ *adj* (*desalinhado*) dishevelled; (*fisionomia*) twisted.

descompostura [dʒiʃkõpoʃ'tura] *f* (*repreensão*) dressing-down; (*insulto*) abuse; **passar uma** ~ **em alguém** (*repreender*) to give sb a dressing-down; (*insultar*) to hurl abuse at sb.

descompressão [dʒiʃkõpre'sãw] *f* decompression.

descomprometido/a [dʒiʃkõprome'tʃidu/a] *adj* (*sem namorado*) free.

descomunal [dʒiʃkomu'naw] (*pl* **-ais**) *adj* (*fora do comum*) extraordinary; (*colossal*) huge, enormous.

desconcentrar [dʒiʃkõsẽ'tra*] *vt* to distract; ~**-se** *vr* to lose one's concentration.

desconcertado/a [dʒiʃkõsex'tadu/a] *adj* disconcerted.

desconcertante [dʒiʃkõsex'tãtʃi] *adj* disconcerting.

desconcertar [dʒiʃkõsex'ta*] *vt* (*atrapalhar*) to confuse, baffle; ~**-se** *vr* to get upset.

desconexo/a [dʒiʃko'nɛksu/a] *adj* (*desunido*) disconnected, unrelated; (*incoerente*) incoherent.

desconfiado/a [dʒiʃkõ'fjadu/a] *adj* suspicious, distrustful ♦ *m/f* suspicious person.

desconfiança [dʒiʃkõ'fjãsa] *f* suspicion, dis-

NB: *European Portuguese adds the following consonants to certain words:* **b** (sú(b)dito, su(b)til); **c** (a(c)ção, a(c)cionista, a(c)to); **m** (inde(m)ne); **p** (ado(p)ção, ado(p)tar); *for further details see p. xiii.*

trust.

desconfiar [dʒiʃkõ'fja*] vi to be suspicious; ~ **de alguém** (não ter confiança em) to distrust sb; (suspeitar) to suspect sb; ~ **que** ... to have the feeling that ....

desconforme [dʒiʃkõ'fɔxmi] adj disagreeing, at variance.

desconfortável [dʒiʃkõfox'tavew] (pl -eis) adj uncomfortable.

desconforto [dʒiʃkõ'foxtu] m discomfort.

descongelar [dʒiʃkõʒe'la*] vt (degelar) to thaw out; ~**-se** vr (derreter-se) to melt.

descongestionante [dʒiʃkõʒeʃtʃjo'nãtʃi] adj, m decongestant.

descongestionar [dʒiʃkõʃeʃtʃjo'na*] vt (cabeça, trânsito) to clear; (rua, cidade) to relieve congestion in.

desconhecer [dʒiʃkoɲe'se*] vt (ignorar) not to know; (não reconhecer) not to recognise; (um benefício) not to acknowledge; (não admitir) not to accept.

desconhecido/a [dʒiʃkoɲe'sidu/a] adj unknown ♦ m/f stranger.

desconhecimento [dʒiʃkoɲesi'mẽtu] m ignorance.

desconjuntado/a [dʒiʃkõʒũ'tadu/a] adj disjointed; (ossos) dislocated.

desconjuntar [dʒiʃkõʒũ'ta*] vt (ossos) to dislocate; ~**-se** vr to come apart.

desconsideração [dʒiʃkõsidera'sãw] f: ~ **(de algo)** disregard (for sth).

desconsiderar [dʒiʃkõside'ra*] vt: ~ **alguém** to show a lack of consideration for sb; ~ **algo** to fail to take sth into consideration.

desconsolado/a [dʒiʃkõso'ladu/a] adj miserable, disconsolate.

desconsolador(a) [dʒiʃkõsola'do*(a)] adj distressing.

desconsolar [dʒiʃkõso'la*] vt to sadden, depress; ~**-se** vr to despair.

descontar [dʒiʃkõ'ta*] vt (abater) to deduct; (não levar em conta) to discount; (não fazer caso de) to make light of.

descontentamento [dʒiʃkõtẽta'mẽtu] m discontent; (desprazer) displeasure.

descontentar [dʒiʃkõtẽ'ta*] vt to displease.

descontente [dʒiʃkõ'tẽtʃi] adj discontented, dissatisfied.

descontínuo/a [dʒiʃkõ'tʃinwu/a] adj broken.

desconto [dʒiʃ'kõtu] m discount; **com** ~ at a discount; **dar um** ~ (fig) to make allowances.

descontração [dʒiʃkõtra'sãw] f casualness.

descontraído/a [dʒiʃkõtra'idu/a] adj casual, relaxed.

descontrair [dʒiʃkõtra'i*] vt to relax; ~**-se** vr to relax.

descontrolar-se [dʒiʃkõtro'laxsi] vr (situação) to get out of control; (pessoa) to lose one's self-control.

descontrole [dʒiʃkõ'troli] m lack of control.

desconversar [dʒiʃkõvex'sa*] vi to change the subject.

descorar [dʒiʃko'ra*] vt to discolour (BRIT), discolor (US) ♦ vi to pale, fade.

descortês/esa [dʒiʃkox'teʃ/teza] adj rude, impolite.

descortesia [dʒiʃkoxte'zia] f rudeness, impoliteness.

descortinar [dʒiʃkoxtʃi'na*] vt (retrato) to unveil; (avistar) to catch sight of; (notar) to notice.

descoser [dʒiʃko'ze*] vt (descosturar) to unstitch; (rasgar) to rip apart; ~**-se** vr to come apart at the seams.

descosturar [dʒiʃkoʃtu'ra*] (BR) vt to unstitch; (rasgar) to pull apart; ~**-se** vr to come apart at the seams.

descrédito [dʒiʃ'krɛdʒitu] m discredit.

descrença [dʒiʃ'krẽsa] f disbelief, incredulity.

descrente [dʒiʃ'krẽtʃi] adj sceptical (BRIT), skeptical (US) ♦ m/f sceptic (BRIT), skeptic (US).

descrer [dʒiʃ'kre*] (irreg: como **crer**) vt to disbelieve ♦ vi: ~ **de** not to believe in.

descrever [dʒiʃkre've*] vt to describe.

descrição [dʒiʃkri'sãw] (pl -ões) f description.

descritivo/a [dʒiʃkri'tʃivu/a] adj descriptive.

descrito/a [dʒiʃ'kritu/a] pp de **descrever**.

descubro [dʒiʃ'kubru] etc vb V **descobrir**.

descuidado/a [dʒiʃkwi'dadu/a] adj careless.

descuidar [dʒiʃkwi'da*] vt to neglect ♦ vi: ~ **de** to neglect, disregard.

descuido [dʒiʃ'kwidu] m (falta de cuidado) carelessness; (negligência) neglect; (erro) oversight, slip; **por** ~ inadvertently.

desculpa [dʒiʃ'kuwpa] f (pretexto, escusa) excuse; (perdão) pardon; **pedir ~s a alguém por** ou **de algo** to apologise to sb for sth.

desculpar [dʒiʃkuw'pa*] vt (justificar) to excuse; (perdoar) to pardon, forgive; ~**-se** vr to apologize; ~ **algo a alguém** to forgive sb for sth; **desculpe!** (I'm) sorry, I beg your pardon.

desculpável [dʒiʃkuw'pavew] (pl -eis) adj excusable.

desde ['deʒdʒi] prep (tempo) from, since; (lugar) from ♦ conj: ~ **que** since; ~ **então** from that time, ever since; ~ **há muito** for a long time (now); ~ **já** (de agora) from now; (imediatamente) at once, right now; ~ ... **a** ... from ... to ....

desdém [deʒ'dẽ] m scorn, disdain.

desdenhar [deʒde'na*] vt to scorn, disdain.

desdenhoso/a [deʒdeɲozu/ɔza] adj disdainful, scornful.

desdentado/a [deʒdẽ'tadu/a] adj toothless.

desdigo [dʒiʒ'dʒigu] etc vb V **desdizer**.

desdisse [dʒiʒ'dʒisi] etc vb V **desdizer**.

desdita [dʒiʒ'dʒita] f (desventura) misfortune; (infelicidade) unhappiness.

desdizer [dʒiʒdʒi'ze*] (irreg: como **dizer**) vt to contradict; ~**-se** vr to go back on one's word.

desdobramento [dʒiʒdobra'mẽtu] m (de aventura, crise) ramification; (de obra etc) spin-off; (COM: de conta) breakdown.

desdobrar [dʒiʒdo'bra*] vt (abrir) to unfold; (esforços) to increase, redouble; (tropas) to deploy; (COM: conta) to break down; (bandeira) to unfurl; (dividir em grupos) to split up; ~-**se** vr to unfold; (empenhar-se) to work hard, make a big effort.

deseducar [dʒizedu'ka*] vt: ~ **alguém** to neglect sb's education.

desejar [dese'ʒa*] vt to want, desire; ~ **ardentemente** to long for; **que deseja?** what would you like?; ~ **algo a alguém** to wish sb sth.

desejável [dese'ʒavew] (pl -eis) adj desirable.

desejo [de'zeʒu] m wish, desire.

desejoso/a [deze'ʒozu/ɔza] adj: ~ **de algo** wishing for sth; ~ **de fazer** keen to do.

deselegância [dʒizele'gãsja] f lack of elegance.

deselegante [dʒizele'gãtʃi] adj inelegant.

desemaranhar [dʒizimara'ɲa*] vt to disentangle.

desembainhar [dʒizēbaj'ɲa*] vt (espada) to draw.

desembalar [dʒizēba'la*] vt to unwrap.

desembaraçado/a [dʒizēbara'sadu/a] adj (livre) free, clear; (desinibido) uninhibited, free and easy; (expedito) efficient; (cabelo) untangled.

desembaraçar [dʒizēbara'sa*] vt (livrar) to free; (COM: navio, remessa) to clear; (cabelo) to untangle; ~-**se** vr (desinibir-se) to lose one's inhibitions; (tornar-se expedito) to show initiative; ~-**se de** to get rid of.

desembaraço [dʒizēba'rasu] m liveliness; (facilidade) ease; (confiança) self-assurance; ~ **alfandegário** customs clearance.

desembarcar [dʒizēbax'ka*] vt (carga) to unload; (passageiros) to let off ♦ vi to disembark.

desembargador(a) [dʒizēbaxga'do*(a)] m/f High Court judge.

desembarque [dʒizē'baxki] m landing, disembarkation; "~" (no aeroporto) "arrivals".

desembestado/a [dʒizēbeʃ'tadu/a] adj: **sair** ~ to rush off ou out.

desembocadura [dʒizēboka'dura] f mouth.

desembocar [dʒizēbo'ka*] vi: ~ **em** (rio) to flow into; (rua) to lead into.

desembolsar [dʒizēbow'sa*] vt to spend.

desembolso [dʒizē'bowsu] m expenditure.

desembrulhar [dʒizēbru'ʎa*] vt to unwrap.

desembuchar [dʒizēbu'ʃa*] (col) vt to get off one's chest ♦ vi to get things off one's chest.

desempacotar [dʒizēpako'ta*] vt to unpack.

desempatar [dʒizēpa'ta*] vt to decide ♦ vi to decide the match (ou race etc).

desempate [dʒizē'patʃi] m: **partida de** ~ (jogo) play-off, decider.

desempenar [dʒizēpe'na*] vt (endireitar) to straighten; ~-**se** vr to stand up straight.

desempenhar [dʒizēpe'ɲa*] vt (cumprir) to carry out, fulfil (BRIT), fulfill (US); (papel) to play.

desempenho [dʒizē'peɲu] m performance; (de obrigações etc) fulfilment (BRIT), fulfillment (US).

desemperrar [dʒizēpe'xa*] vt, vi to loosen.

desempregado/a [dʒizēpre'gadu/a] adj unemployed ♦ m/f unemployed person.

desempregar-se [dʒizēpre'gaxsi] vr to lose one's job.

desemprego [dʒizē'pregu] m unemployment.

desencadear [dʒizēka'dʒja*] vt to unleash; (despertar) to provoke, trigger off ♦ vi (chuva) to pour; ~-**se** vr to break loose; (tempestade) to break.

desencaixado/a [dʒizēkaj'ʃadu/a] adj misplaced.

desencaixar [dʒizēkaj'ʃa*] vt to put out of joint; (deslocar) to dislodge, gouge out; ~-**se** vr to become dislodged.

desencaixotar [dʒizēkajʃo'ta*] vt to unpack.

desencalhar [dʒizēka'ʎa*] vt (navio) to refloat ♦ vi to be refloated; (col: moça) to find a husband.

desencaminhar [dʒizēkami'ɲa*] vt to lead astray; (dinheiro) to embezzle; ~-**se** vr to go astray.

desencantar [dʒizēkã'ta*] vt to disenchant; (desiludir) to disillusion.

desencardir [dʒizēkax'dʒi*] vt to clean.

desencargo [dʒizē'kaxgu] m fulfilment (BRIT), fulfillment (US); **para** ~ **de consciência** to clear one's conscience.

desencarregar-se [dʒizēkaxe'gaxsi] vr (de obrigação) to discharge o.s.

desencavar [dʒizēka'va*] vt to unearth.

desencontrar [dʒizēkõ'tra*] vt to keep apart; ~-**se** vr (não se encontrar) to miss each other; (perder-se um do outro) to lose each other; ~-**se de** to miss; to get separated from.

desencontro [dʒizē'kõtru] m failure to meet.

desencorajar [dʒizēkora'ʒa*] vt to discourage.

desencostar [dʒizēkoʃ'ta*] vt to move away; ~-**se** vr: ~-**se de** to move away from.

desenfastiar [dʒizēfaʃ'tʃja*] vt to amuse; ~-**se** vr to amuse o.s.

desenferrujar [dʒizēfexu'za*] vt (metal) to clean the rust off; (pernas) to stretch; (língua) to brush up.

desenfreado/a [dʒizē'frjadu/a] adj wild.

desenganado/a [dʒizēga'nadu/a] adj (sem cura) incurable; (desiludido) disillusioned.

desenganar [dʒizēga'na*] vt: ~ **alguém** to disillusion sb; (de falsas crenças) to open sb's eyes; (doente) to give up hope of curing; ~-**se** vr to become disillusioned; (sair de erro) to realize the truth.

desengano [dʒizē'ganu] m disillusionment; (desapontamento) disappointment.

NB: European Portuguese adds the following consonants to certain words: **b** (sú(b)dito, su(b)til); **c** (a(c)ção, a(c)cionista, a(c)to); **m** (inde(m)ne); **p** (ado(p)ção, ado(p)tar); *for further details see p. xiii.*

desengarrafar [dʒizēgaxa'fa*] *vt* (*trânsito*) to unblock; (*vinho*) to pour out.

desengatar [dʒizēga'ta*] *vt* to unhitch; (*FERRO*) to uncouple.

desengonçado/a [dʒizēgō'sadu/a] *adj* (*malseguro*) rickety; (*pessoa*) ungainly.

desengrenado/a [dʒizēgre'nadu/a] *adj* (*AUTO*) out of gear, in neutral.

desengrenar [dʒizēgre'na*] *vt* to disengage; (*carro*) to put in neutral.

desengrossar [dʒizēgro'sa*] *vt* to thin.

desenhar [deze'ɲa*] *vt* to draw; (*TEC*) to design; ~-se *vr* (*destacar-se*) to stand out; (*figurar-se*) to take shape.

desenhista [deze'ɲiʃta] *m/f* (*TEC*) designer.

desenho [de'zɛɲu] *m* drawing; (*modelo*) design; (*esboço*) sketch; (*plano*) plan; ~ **animado** cartoon; ~ **industrial** industrial design.

desenlace [dʒizē'lasi] *m* outcome.

desenredar [dʒizēxe'da*] *vt* to disentangle; (*mistério*) to unravel; (*questão*) to sort out, resolve; (*dúvida*) to clear up; (*explicação*) to clarify; ~-se *vr*: ~-se **de algo** to extricate o.s. from sth; ~ **alguém de algo** to extricate sb from sth.

desenrolar [dʒizēxo'la*] *vt* to unroll; (*narrativa*) to develop; ~-se *vr* to unfold.

desentender [dʒizētē'de*] *vt* (*não entender*) to misunderstand; ~-se *vr*: ~-se **com** to have a disagreement with.

desentendido/a [dʒizētē'dʒidu/a] *adj*: **fazer-se de** ~ to pretend not to understand.

desentendimento [dʒizētēdʒi'mētu] *m* misunderstanding.

desenterrar [dʒizēte'xa*] *vt* (*cadáver*) to exhume; (*tesouro*) to dig up; (*descobrir*) to bring to light.

desentoado/a [dʒizē'twadu/a] *adj* (*desafinado*) out of tune.

desentranhar [dʒizētra'ɲa*] *vt* to disembowel; (*raiz*) to draw out; (*lembranças*) to dredge up; (*mistério*) to fathom.

desentrosado/a [dʒizētro'zadu/a] *adj* unintegrated.

desentupir [dʒizētu'pi*] *vt* to unblock.

desenvolto/a [dʒizē'vowtu/a] *adj* (*desembaraçado*) self-assured, confident; (*desinibido*) uninhibited.

desenvoltura [dʒizēvow'tura] *f* (*desembaraço*) self-confidence.

desenvolver [dʒizēvow've*] *vt* to develop; ~-se *vr* to develop.

desenvolvido/a [dʒizēvow'vidu/a] *adj* developed.

desenvolvimento [dʒizēvowvi'mētu] *m* development; (*crescimento*) growth; **país em** ~ developing country.

desenxabido/a [dʒizēʃa'bidu/a] *adj* dull.

desequilibrado/a [dʒizekili'bradu/a] *adj* unbalanced.

desequilibrar [dʒizekili'bra*] *vt* (*pessoa*) to throw off balance; (*objeto*) to tip over; (*fig*) to unbalance; ~-se *vr* to lose one's balance;

to tip over.

desequilíbrio [dʒizeki'librju] *m* imbalance.

deserção [dezex'sãw] *f* desertion.

desertar [desex'ta*] *vt* to desert, abandon ♦ *vi* to desert.

deserto/a [de'zɛxtu/a] *adj* deserted ♦ *m* desert.

desertor(a) [dezex'to*(a)] *m/f* deserter.

desesperado/a [dʒizeʃpe'radu/a] *adj* desperate; (*furioso*) furious.

desesperador(a) [dʒizeʃpera'do*(a)] *adj* desperate; (*enfurecedor*) maddening.

desesperança [dʒizeʃpe'rãsa] *f* despair.

desesperançar [dʒizeʃperã'sa*] *vt*: ~ **alguém** to make sb despair.

desesperar [dʒizeʃpe'ra*] *vt* to drive to despair; (*enfurecer*) to infuriate; ~-se *vr* to despair; (*enfurecer-se*) to become infuriated.

desespero [dʒizeʃ'peru] *m* despair, desperation; (*raiva*) fury; **levar ao** ~ to drive to despair.

desestabilizar [dʒizeʃtabili'za*] *vt* to destabilize.

desestimulador(a) [dʒizeʃtʃimula'do*(a)] *adj* discouraging.

desestimular [dʒizeʃtʃimu'la*] *vt* to discourage.

desfaçatez [dʒiʃfasa'teʒ] *f* impudence, cheek.

desfalcar [dʒiʃfaw'ka*] *vt* (*aparelho de jantar*) to spoil; (*dinheiro*) to embezzle; (*reduzir*): ~ **(de)** to reduce (by); ~ **uma firma em $400** to embezzle $400 from a firm.

desfalecer [dʒiʃfale'se*] *vt* (*enfraquecer*) to weaken ♦ *vi* (*enfraquecer*) to weaken; (*desmaiar*) to faint.

desfalecimento [dʒiʃfalesi'mētu] *m* (*enfraquecimento*) weakening; (*desmaio*) faint.

desfalque [dʒiʃ'fawki] *m* (*de dinheiro*) embezzlement; (*diminuição*) reduction.

desfavor [dʒiʃfa'vo*] *m* disfavour (*BRIT*), disfavor (*US*).

desfavorável [dʒiʃfavo'ravew] (*pl* **-eis**) *adj* unfavourable (*BRIT*), unfavorable (*US*).

desfavorecer [dʒiʃfavore'se*] *vt* to discriminate against.

desfazer [dʒiʃfa'ze*] (*irreg*: *como* **fazer**) *vt* (*costura*) to undo; (*dúvidas*) to dispel; (*agravo*) to redress; (*grupo*) to break up; (*contrato*) to dissolve; (*noivado*) to break off ♦ *vi*: ~ **de alguém** to belittle sb; ~-se *vr* (*desaparecer*) to vanish; (*tecido*) to come to pieces; (*grupo*) to break up; (*vaso*) to break; ~-se **de** (*livrar-se*) to get rid of; ~-se **em lágrimas/gentilezas** to burst into tears/go out of one's way to please.

desfechar [dʒiʃfe'ʃa*] *vt* (*disparar*) to fire; (*setas*) to shoot; (*golpe*) to deal; (*insultos*) to hurl.

desfecho [dʒiʃ'feʃu] *m* ending, outcome.

desfeita [dʒiʃ'fejta] *f* affront, insult.

desfeito/a [dʒiʃ'fejtu/a] *pp de* **desfazer** ♦ *adj* (*desmanchado*) undone; (*cama*) unmade; (*contrato*) broken.

desferir [dʒiʃfe'ri*] vt (golpe) to strike; (sons) to emit; (lançar) to throw.

desfiar [dʒiʃ'fja*] vt (tecido) to unravel; (galinha) to strip; ~-**se** vr to become frayed; ~ **o rosário** to say one's rosary.

desfiguração* [dʒiʃfigura'sãw] f distortion.

desfigurar [dʒiʃfigu'ra*] vt (pessoa, cidade) to disfigure; (texto) to mutilate; ~-**se** vr to be disfigured.

desfiladeiro [dʒiʃfila'dejru] m (de montanha) pass.

desfilar [dʒiʃfi'la*] vi to parade.

desfile [dʒiʃ'fili] m parade, procession.

desflorestamento [dʒiʃfloreʃta'mẽtu] m deforestation.

desflorestar [dʒiʃfloreʃ'ta*] vt to clear of forest.

desforra [dʒiʃ'fɔxa] f (vingança) revenge; (reparação) redress; **tirar** ~ to get even.

desfraldar [dʒiʃfraw'da*] vt to unfurl.

desfranzir [dʒiʃfrã'zi*] vt to smooth out.

desfrutar [dʒiʃfru'ta*] vt to enjoy ♦ vi: ~ **de** to enjoy; ~ **de bom conceito** to have a good reputation, be well thought of.

desfrute [dʒiʃ'frutʃi] m (deleite) enjoyment; (desplante): **ter o** ~ **de fazer algo** to have the nerve to do sth.

desgarrado/a [dʒiʒga'xadu/a] adj stray; (navio) off course.

desgarrar-se [dʒiʒga'xaxsi] vr: ~ **de** to stray from.

desgastante [dʒiʒgaʃ'tãtʃi] adj (fig) stressful.

desgastar [dʒiʒgaʃ'ta*] vt to wear away, erode; (pessoa) to wear out, get down; ~-**se** vr to be worn away; (pessoa) to get worn out.

desgaste [dʒiʒ'gaʃtʃi] m wear and tear; (mental) stress.

desgostar [dʒiʒgoʃ'ta*] vt to upset ♦ vi: ~ **de** to dislike; ~-**se** vr: ~-**se de** to lose one's liking for; ~-**se com** to take offence at.

desgosto [dʒiʒ'goʃtu] m (desprazer) displeasure; (pesar) sorrow, unhappiness.

desgostoso/a [dʒiʒgoʃ'tozu/ɔza] adj sad, sorrowful.

desgraça [dʒiʒ'grasa] f (desventura) misfortune; (miséria) misery; (desfavor) disgrace.

desgraçado/a [dʒiʒgra'sadu/a] adj poor; (col: admirável) amazing ♦ m/f wretch; **estou com uma gripe desgraçada** (col) I've got a hell of a cold.

desgraçar [dʒiʒgra'sa*] vt to disgrace.

desgraceira [dʒiʒgra'sejra] f series of misfortunes.

desgravar [dʒiʒgra'va*] vt (música) to wipe, rub off.

desgrenhado/a [dʒiʒgre'ɲadu/a] adj dishevelled, tousled.

desgrenhar [dʒiʒgre'ɲa*] vt to tousle; ~-**se** vr to get tousled.

desgrudar [dʒiʒgru'da*] vt to unstick ♦ vi: ~ **de** to tear o.s. away from; ~ **algo de algo** to take sth off sth.

desguarnecer [dʒiʒgwaxne'se*] vt to strip.

desguiar [dʒiʒ'gja*] (col) vi to go away.

desidratação [dʒizidrata'sãw] f dehydration.

desidratante [dʒizidra'tãtʃi] adj dehydrating.

desidratar [dʒizidra'ta*] vt to dehydrate.

design [dʒi'zãjn] m design.

designação [dezigna'sãw] (pl -**ões**) f designation; (nomeação) appointment.

designar [dezig'na*] vt to designate; (nomear) to name, appoint; (dia, data) to fix.

designer [dʒi'zajne*] (pl ~**s**) m/f designer.

desígnio [de'zignju] m (propósito) purpose; (intenção) intention.

desigual [dezi'gwaw] (pl -**ais**) adj unequal; (terreno) uneven.

desigualdade [dʒizigwaw'dadʒi] f inequality.

desiludir [dʒizilu'dʒi*] vt (desenganar) to disillusion; (causar decepção a) to disappoint; ~-**se** vr to lose one's illusions.

desilusão [dʒizilu'zãw] f disillusionment, disenchantment.

desimpedido/a [dʒizĩpe'dʒidu/a] adj free.

desimpedir [dʒizĩpe'dʒi*] vt (desobstruir) to unblock; (trânsito) to ease.

desinchar [dʒizin'ʃa*] vt (MED) to get rid of the swelling on ♦ vi: **meu pé desinchou** the swelling in my foot went down.

desincumbir-se [dʒizĩkũ'bixsi] vr: ~ **de algo** to carry sth out.

desinfeccionar [dʒizĩfeksjo'na*] vt to disinfect.

desinfetante [dʒizĩfe'tãtʃi] (PT: -**ct**-) adj, m disinfectant.

desinfetar [dʒizĩfe'ta*] (PT: -**ct**-) vt to disinfect.

desinflamar [dʒizĩfla'ma*] vt to remove ou get rid of the inflammation on; ~-**se** vr to become less inflamed.

desinibido/a [dʒizini'bidu/a] adj uninhibited.

desinibir [dʒizini'bi*] vt to make less inhibited; ~-**se** vr to lose one's inhibitions.

desintegração [dʒizĩtegra'sãw] f disintegration, break-up.

desintegrar [dʒizĩte'gra*] vt to separate; ~-**se** vr to disintegrate, fall to pieces.

desinteressado/a [dʒizĩtere'sadu/a] adj disinterested.

desinteressar [dʒizĩtere'sa*] vt: ~ **alguém de algo** to make sb lose interest in sth; ~-**se** vr to lose interest.

desinteresse [dʒizĩte'resi] m (falta de interesse) lack of interest.

desintoxicar [dʒizĩtoksi'ka*] vt to detoxify.

desistência [deziʃ'tẽsja] f giving up; (cancelamento) cancellation.

desistir [deziʃ'tʃi*] vi to give up; ~ **de fumar**

to stop smoking; **ele ia, mas no final desistiu** he was going, but in the end he gave up the idea *ou* he decided not to.

desjejum [dʒiʒe'ʒũ] *m* breakfast.

deslanchar [dʒiʒlã'ʃa*] *vi* (*carro*) to move off; (*projeto*) to get off the ground, take off.

deslavado/a [dʒiʒla'vadu/a] *adj* (*pessoa, atitude*) shameless; (*mentira*) blatant.

desleal [dʒiʒle'aw] (*pl* -ais) *adj* disloyal.

deslealdade [dʒiʒleaw'dadʒi] *f* disloyalty.

desleixado/a [dʒiʒlej'ʃadu/a] *adj* sloppy.

desleixo [dʒiʒ'lejʃu] *m* sloppiness.

desligado/a [dʒiʒli'gadu/a] *adj* (*eletricidade*) off; (*pessoa*) absent-minded; **estar ~** to be miles away.

desligar [dʒiʒli'ga*] *vt* (*TEC*) to disconnect; (*luz, TV, motor*) to switch off; (*telefone*) to hang up; **~-se** *vr*: **~-se de algo** (*afastar-se*) to leave sth; (*problemas etc*) to turn one's back on sth; **não desligue** (*TEL*) hold the line.

deslizante [dʒiʒli'zãtʃi] *adj* slippery.

deslizar [dʒiʒli'za*] *vi* to slide; (*por acidente*) to slip; (*passar de leve*) to glide.

deslize [dʒiʒ'lizi] *m* (*lapso*) lapse; (*escorregadela*) slip.

deslocado/a [dʒiʒlo'kadu/a] *adj* (*membro*) dislocated; (*desambientado*) out of place.

deslocamento [dʒiʒloka'mẽtu] *m* moving; (*de membro*) dislocation; (*de funcionário*) transfer.

deslocar [dʒiʒlo'ka*] *vt* (*mover*) to move; (*articulação*) to dislocate; (*funcionário*) to transfer; **~-se** *vr* (*mover-se*) to move; (*membro*) to be dislocated; **eu me desloquei até lá à toa** I went all the way there for nothing.

deslumbrado/a [dʒiʒlũ'bradu/a] *adj* (*ofuscado*) dazzled; (*maravilhado*) amazed ♦ *m/f* impressionable person.

deslumbramento [dʒiʒlũbra'mẽtu] *m* dazzle; (*fascinação*) fascination.

deslumbrante [dʒiʒlũ'brãtʃi] *adj* (*ofuscante*) dazzling; (*casa, festa*) amazing.

deslumbrar [dʒiʒlũ'bra*] *vt* (*ofuscar*) to dazzle; (*maravilhar*) to amaze; (*fascinar*) to fascinate ♦ *vi* (*ofuscar*) to be dazzling; (*maravilhar*) to be amazing; **~-se** *vr*: **~-se com** to be fascinated by.

deslustrar [dʒiʒluʃ'tra*] *vt* to tarnish.

desmaiado/a [dʒiʒma'jadu/a] *adj* (*sem sentidos*) unconscious; (*cor*) pale.

desmaiar [dʒiʒma'ja*] *vi* to faint.

desmaio [dʒiʒ'maju] *m* faint.

desmamar [dʒiʒma'ma*] *vt* to wean.

desmancha-prazeres [dʒiʒ'manʃa-] *m/f inv* kill-joy, spoilsport.

desmanchar [dʒiʒman'ʃa*] *vt* (*costura*) to undo; (*contrato*) to break; (*noivado*) to break off; (*penteado*) to mess up; **~-se** *vr* (*costura*) to come undone.

desmantelar [dʒiʒmãte'la*] *vt* (*demolir*) to demolish; (*desmontar*) to dismantle, take apart.

desmarcar [dʒiʒmax'ka*] *vt* (*compromisso*) to cancel.

desmascarar [dʒiʒmaʃka'ra*] *vt* to unmask.

desmatamento [dʒiʒmata'mẽtu] *m* deforestation.

desmatar [dʒiʒma'ta*] *vt* to clear the forest from.

desmazelado/a [dʒiʒmaze'ladu/a] *adj* slovenly, untidy.

desmazelar-se [dʒiʒmaze'laxsi] *vr* to get untidy.

desmedido/a [dʒiʒme'dʒidu/a] *adj* excessive.

desmembramento [dʒiʒmẽbra'mẽtu] *m* dismemberment.

desmembrar [dʒiʒmẽ'bra*] *vt* to dismember.

desmemoriado/a [dʒiʒmemo'rjadu/a] *adj* forgetful.

desmentido [dʒiʒmẽ'tʃidu] *m* (*negação*) denial; (*contradição*) contradiction.

desmentir [dʒiʒmẽ'tʃi*] *vt* (*contradizer*) to contradict; (*negar*) to deny.

desmerecer [dʒiʒmere'se*] *vt* (*não merecer*) not to deserve; (*desfazer de*) to belittle.

desmesurado/a [dʒiʒmezu'radu/a] *adj* immense, enormous.

desmilingüido/a [dʒiʒmilĩ'gwidu/a] (*col*) *adj* spent.

desmiolado/a [dʒiʒmjo'ladu/a] *adj* brainless; (*esquecido*) forgetful.

desmistificar [dʒiʒmiʃtʃifi'ka*] *vt* to demystify; **~ alguém** to remove the mystery surrounding sb.

desmitificar [dʒiʒmitʃifi'ka*] *vt*: **~ algo/ alguém** to dispel the myth(s) surrounding sth/sb.

desmontar [dʒiʒmõ'ta*] *vt* (*máquina*) to take to pieces ♦ *vi* (*do cavalo*) to dismount, get off.

desmoralização [dʒiʒmoraliza'sãw] *f* demoralization.

desmoralizante [dʒiʒmorali'zãtʃi] *adj* demoralizing.

desmoralizar [dʒiʒmorali'za*] *vt* to demoralize.

desmoronamento [dʒiʒmorona'mẽtu] *m* collapse.

desmoronar [dʒiʒmoro'na*] *vt* to knock down ♦ *vi* to collapse.

desmotivado/a [dʒiʒmotʃi'vadu/a] *adj* despondent.

desmunhecar [dʒiʒmuɲe'ka*] (*col*) *vi* (*declarar-se homossexual*) to come out; (*fazer gestos efeminados*) to be camp.

desnatar [dʒiʒna'ta*] *vt* to skim.

desnaturado/a [dʒiʒnatu'radu/a] *adj* inhumane ♦ *m/f* monster.

desnecessário/a [dʒiʒnese'sarju/a] *adj* unnecessary.

desnível [dʒiʒ'nivew] *m* unevenness; (*fig*) difference.

desnorteado/a [dʒiʒnox'tʃjadu/a] *adj* (*perturbado*) bewildered, confused; (*desori-

entado) off course.

desnortear [dʒiʒnox'tʃja*] *vt (desorientar)* to throw off course; *(perturbar)* to bewilder; **~-se** *vr* to lose one's way; *(perturbar-se)* to become confused.

desnudar [dʒiʒnu'da*] *vt* to strip; *(revelar)* to expose; **~-se** *vr* to undress.

desnutrição [dʒiʒnutri'sãw] *f* malnutrition.

desnutrido/a [dʒiʒnu'tridu/a] *adj* malnourished.

desobedecer [dʒizobede'se*] *vt* to disobey.

desobediência [dʒizobe'dʒjẽsja] *f* disobedience.

disobediente [dʒizobe'dʒjẽtʃi] *adj* disobedient.

desobrigar [dʒizobri'ga*] *vt*: **~ (de)** to free (from); **~ de fazer algo** to free from doing sth.

desobstruir [dʒizobiʃ'trwi*] *vt* to unblock.

desocupação [dʒizokupa'sãw] *f (de casa)* vacating; *(falta de ocupação)* leisure; *(desemprego)* unemployment.

desocupado/a [dʒizoku'padu/a] *adj (casa)* empty, vacant; *(disponível)* free; *(sem trabalho)* unemployed.

desocupar [dʒizoku'pa*] *vt (casa)* to vacate; *(liberar)* to free.

desodorante [dʒizodo'rãtʃi] *(PT:* **-dorizante)** *m* deodorant.

desodorizar [dʒizodori'za*] *vt* to deodorize.

desolação [dezola'sãw] *f (consternação)* grief; *(de um lugar)* desolation.

desolado/a [dezo'ladu/a] *adj (consternado)* distressed; *(lugar)* desolate.

desolar [dezo'la*] *vt (consternar)* to distress; *(lugar)* to devastate.

desonestidade [dezoneʃtʃi'dadʒi] *f* dishonesty.

desonesto/a [dezo'nɛʃtu/a] *adj* dishonest.

desonra [dʒi'zõxa] *f* dishonour *(BRIT)*, dishonor *(US)*; *(descrédito)* disgrace.

desonrar [dʒizõ'xa*] *vt (infamar)* to disgrace; *(mulher)* to seduce; **~-se** *vr* to disgrace o.s.

desonroso/a [dʒizõ'xozu/oza] *adj* dishonourable *(BRIT)*, dishonorable *(US)*.

desopilar [dʒizopi'la*] *vt (MED)* to flush out; *(mente)* to clear.

desoprimir [dʒizopri'mi*] *vt* to relieve; **~-se** *vr* to be relieved.

desordeiro/a [dʒizox'dejru/a] *adj* troublemaking ♦ *m/f* troublemaker, hooligan.

desordem [dʒi'zoxdẽ] *f* disorder, confusion; **em ~** *(casa)* untidy.

desordenar [dʒizoxde'na*] *vt (tirar da ordem)* to put out of order; *(desarrumar)* to mess up.

desorganização [dʒizoxganiza'sãw] *f* disorganization.

desorganizar [dʒizoxgani'za*] *vt* to disorganize; *(dissolver)* to break up; **~-se** *vr* to become disorganized; to break up.

desorientação [dʒizorjẽta'sãw] *f* bewilder-

ment, confusion.

desorientar [dʒizorjẽ'ta*] *vt (desnortear)* to throw off course; *(perturbar)* to confuse; *(desvairar)* to unhinge; **~-se** *vr (perder-se)* to lose one's way; *(perturbar-se)* to get confused; *(desvairar-se)* to go mad.

desossar [dʒizo'sa*] *vt (galinha)* to bone.

desovar [dʒizo'va*] *vt* to lay; *(peixe)* to spawn.

despachado/a [dʒiʃpa'ʃadu/a] *adj (pessoa)* efficient.

despachante [dʒiʃpa'ʃãtʃi] *m/f (de mercadorias)* forwarding agent; *(de documentos)* agent *(who handles official bureaucracy)*.

despachar [dʒiʃpa'ʃa*] *vt (expedir)* to dispatch, send off; *(atender, resolver)* to deal with; *(despedir)* to sack ♦ *vi (funcionário)* to work; **~-se** *vr* to hurry (up).

despacho [dʒiʃ'paʃu] *m* dispatch; *(de negócios)* handling; *(nota em requerimento)* ruling; *(reunião)* consultation; *(macumba)* witchcraft.

desparafusar [dʒiʃparafu'sa*] *vt* to unscrew.

despeço [dʒiʃ'pesu] *etc vb V* **despedir**.

despedaçar [dʒiʃpeda'sa*] *vt (quebrar)* to smash; *(rasgar)* to tear apart; **~-se** *vr* to smash; *(rasgar-se)* to tear.

despedida [dʒiʃpe'dʒida] *f (adeus)* farewell; *(de trabalhador)* dismissal.

despedir [dʒiʃpe'dʒi*] *vt (de emprego)* to dismiss, sack; **~-se** *vr*: **~-se (de)** to say goodbye (to).

despeitado/a [dʒiʃpej'tadu/a] *adj* spiteful; *(ressentido)* resentful.

despeito [dʒiʃ'pejtu] *m* spite; **a ~ de** in spite of, despite.

despejar [dʒiʃpe'ʒa*] *vt (água)* to pour; *(esvaziar)* to empty; *(inquilino)* to evict.

despejo [dʒiʃ'peʒu] *m (de casa)* eviction; **quarto de ~** junk room.

despencar [dʒiʃpẽ'ka*] *vi* to fall down, tumble down.

despender [dʒiʃpẽ'de*] *vt (dinheiro)* to spend; *(energia)* to expend.

despenhadeiro [dʒiʃpeɲa'dejro] *m* cliff, precipice.

despensa [dʒiʃ'pẽsa] *f* larder.

despentear [dʒiʃpẽ'tʃja*] *vt (cabelo: sem querer)* to mess up; *(: de propósito)* to let down; **~-se** *vr* to mess one's hair up; to let one's hair down.

despercebido/a [dʒiʃpexse'bidu/a] *adj* unnoticed.

desperdiçar [dʒiʃpexdʒi'sa*] *vt* to waste; *(dinheiro)* to squander.

desperdício [dʒiʃpex'dʒisju] *m* waste.

despersonalizar [dʒiʃpexsonali'za*] *vt* to depersonalize.

despersuadir [dʒiʃpexswa'dʒi*] *vt*: **~ alguém de fazer algo** to dissuade sb from doing sth.

NB: *European Portuguese adds the following consonants to certain words:* **b** *(sú(b)dito, su(b)til);* **c** *(a(c)ção, a(c)cionista, a(c)to);* **m** *(inde(m)ne);* **p** *(ado(p)ção, ado(p)tar); for further details see p. xiii.*

despertador [dʒiʃpexta'do*] *m* (*tb: relogio* ~) alarm clock.

despertar [dʒiʃpex'ta*] *vt* (*pessoa*) to wake; (*suspeitas, interesse*) to arouse; (*reminiscências*) to revive; (*apetite*) to whet ♦ *vi* to wake up, awake ♦ *m* awakening.

desperto/a [dʒiʃ'pextu/a] *adj* awake.

despesa [dʒiʃ'peza] *f* expense; ~**s** *fpl* expenses, costs; ~**s antecipadas** prepayments; ~**s gerais** (*COM*) overheads; ~**s mercantis** sales and marketing expenses; ~**s não-operacionais** non-operating expenses *ou* costs; ~**s operacionais** operating expenses *ou* costs; ~**s tributárias** (*de uma empresa*) corporation tax.

despido/a [dʒiʃ'pidu/a] *adj* (*nu*) naked, bare; (*livre*) free.

despir [dʒiʃ'pi*] *vt* (*roupa*) to take off; (*pessoa*) to undress; (*despojar*) to strip; ~**se** *vr* to undress.

despistar [dʒiʃpiʃ'ta*] *vt* to throw off the scent.

desplante [dʒiʃ'plătʃi] *m* (*fig*) nerve.

despojado/a [dʒiʃpo'ʒadu/a] *adj* (*pessoa*) unambitious; (*lugar*) spartan, basic.

despojar [dʒiʃpo'ʒa*] *vt* (*casas*) to loot, sack; (*pessoas*) to rob; ~ **alguém de algo** to strip sb of sth.

despojo [dʒiʃ'poʒu] *m* loot, booty; ~**s** *mpl*: ~**s mortais** mortal remains.

despoluir [dʒiʃpo'lwi*] *vt* to clean up.

despontar [dʒiʃpõ'ta*] *vi* to emerge; (*sol*) to come out; (: *ao amanhecer*) to come up; **ao** ~ **do dia** at daybreak.

desporto [dʒiʃ'poxtu] (*PT*) *m* sport.

déspota ['dɛʃpota] *m/f* despot.

despotismo [deʃpo'tʃiʒmu] *m* despotism.

despovoado/a [dʒiʃpo'vwadu/a] *adj* uninhabited ♦ *m* wilderness.

despovoar [dʒiʃpo'vwa*] *vt* to depopulate.

desprazer [dʒiʃpra'ze*] *m* displeasure.

desprecavido/a [dʒiʃpreka'vidu/a] *adj* unprepared, careless.

despregar [dʒiʃpre'ga*] *vt* to take off, detach; ~**se** *vr* to come off; ~ **os olhos de algo** to take one's eyes off sth.

desprender [dʒiʃprẽ'de*] *vt* (*soltar*) to loosen; (*desatar*) to unfasten; (*emitir*) to emit; ~**se** *vr* (*botão*) to come off; (*cheiro*) to be given off; ~**se dos braços de alguém** to extricate o.s. from sb's arms.

desprendido/a [dʒiʃprẽ'dʒidu/a] *adj* (*abnegado*) disinterested.

despreocupado/a [dʒiʃprɛoku'padu/a] *adj* carefree, unconcerned; **com a notícia ele ficou mais** ~ after hearing the news he was less concerned *ou* worried.

despreocupar [dʒiʃpreoku'pa*] *vt*: ~ **alguém (de algo)** to set sb's mind at rest (about sth); ~**se** *vr*: ~**se (de algo)** to stop worrying (about sth).

despreparado/a [dʒiʃprepa'radu/a] *adj* unprepared.

despretensioso/a [dʒiʃpretẽ'sjozu/ɔza] *adj* unpretentious, modest.

desprestigiar [dʒiʃpreʃtʃi'ʒja*] *vt* to discredit; ~**se** *vr* to lose prestige.

desprevenido/a [dʒiʃpreve'nidu/a] *adj* unprepared, unready; **apanhar** ~ to catch unawares.

desprezar [dʒiʃpre'za*] *vt* (*desdenhar*) to despise, disdain; (*não dar importância a*) to disregard, ignore.

desprezível [dʒiʃpre'zivew] (*pl* -**eis**) *adj* despicable.

desprezo [dʒiʃ'prezu] *m* scorn, contempt; **dar ao** ~ to ignore.

desproporção [dʒiʃpropox'sãw] *f* disproportion.

desproporcionado/a [dʒiʃpropoxsjo'nadu/a] *adj* disproportionate; (*desigual*) unequal.

desproporcional [dʒiʃpropoxsjo'naw] *adj* disproportionate.

despropositado/a [dʒiʃpropozi'tadu/a] *adj* (*absurdo*) preposterous.

despropósito [dʒiʃpro'pɔzitu] *m* nonsense.

desproteger [dʒiʃprote'ʒe*] *vt* to leave unprotected.

desprover [dʒiʃpro've*] *vt*: ~ **alguém (de algo)** to deprive sb (of sth).

desprovido/a [dʒiʃpro'vidu/a] *adj* deprived; ~ **de** without.

despudorado/a [dʒiʃpudo'radu/a] *adj* shameless.

desqualificar [dʒiʃkwalifi'ka*] *vt* (*ESPORTE etc*) to disqualify; (*tornar indiguo*) to disgrace, lower.

desquitar-se [dʒiʃki'taxsi] *vr* to get a legal separation.

desquite [dʒiʃ'kitʃi] *m* legal separation.

desregrado/a [dʒiʒxe'gradu/a] *adj* (*desordenado*) disorderly, unruly; (*devasso*) immoderate.

desregrar-se [dʒiʒxe'graxsi] *vr* to run riot.

desregular [dʒiʒxegu'la*] *vt* (*mercado*) to deregulate.

desrespeitar [dʒiʒxeʃpej'ta*] *vt* to have no respect for.

desrespeito [dʒiʒxe'ʃpejtu] *m* disrespect.

desrespeitoso/a [dʒiʒxeʃpej'tozu/ɔza] *adj* disrespectful.

desse ['desi] *etc vb* **V** **dar** ♦ = **de** + **esse**.

destacado/a [dʒiʃta'kadu/a] *adj* outstanding; (*separado*) detached.

destacamento [dʒiʃtaka'mẽtu] *m* (*MIL*) detachment.

destacar [dʒiʃta'ka*] *vt* (*MIL*) to detail; (*separar*) to detach; (*fazer sobressair*) to highlight; (*enfatizar*) to emphasize ♦ *vi* to stand out; ~**se** *vr* to stand out; (*pessoa*) to be outstanding.

destampar [dʒiʃtã'pa*] *vt* to take the lid off.

destapar [dʒiʃta'pa*] *vt* to uncover.

destaque [dʒiʃ'taki] *m* distinction; (*pessoa, coisa*) highlight; (*do noticiário*) main point; **pessoa de** ~ distinguished person.

deste ['deʃtʃi] *etc* = **de** + **este;** *V* **este.**

destemido/a [deʃte'midu/a] *adj* fearless, intrepid.

destemperar [dʒiʃtẽpe'ra*] *vt* (*diluir*) to dilute, weaken ♦ *vi* (*perder a cabeça*) to go mad.

desterrar [dʒiʃte'xa*] *vt* (*exilar*) to exile; (*fig*) to banish.

desterro [dʒiʃ'texu] *m* exile.

destilação [deʃtʃila'sãw] *f* distillation.

destilar [deʃtʃi'la*] *vt* to distil (*BRIT*), distill (*US*).

destilaria [deʃtʃila'ria] *f* distillery.

destinação [deʃtʃina'sãw] (*pl* **-ões**) *f* destination.

destinar [deʃ'tʃina*] *vt* to destine; **~-se** *vr*: **~-se a** to be intended for, be addressed to; **~ dinheiro para** to set aside money for.

destinatário/a [deʃtʃina'tarju/a] *m/f* addressee.

destino [deʃ'tʃinu] *m* destiny, fate; (*lugar*) destination; **com ~ a** a bound for; **sem ~** *adj* aimless ♦ *adv* aimlessly.

destituição [deʃtʃitwi'sãw] (*pl* **-ões**) *f* (*demissão*) dismissal.

destituir [deʃtʃi'twi*] *vt* (*demitir*) to dismiss; **~ de** (*privar de*) to deprive of; (*demitir de*) to dismiss from.

destoante [dʒiʃto'ãtʃi] *adj* (*som*) discordant; (*opiniões*) diverging.

destoar [dʒiʃto'a*] *vi* (*som*) to jar; **~ (de)** (*não condizer*) to be out of keeping (with); (*traje, cor*) to clash (with); (*pessoa: discordar*) to disagree (with).

destorcer [dʒiʃtox'se*] *vt* to straighten out.

destrambelhado/a [dʒiʃtrãbe'ʎadu/a] *adj* scatterbrained.

destrancar [dʒiʃtrã'ka*] *vt* to unlock.

destratar [dʒiʃtra'ta*] *vt* to abuse, insult.

destravar [dʒiʃtra'va*] *vt* (*veículo*) to take the brake off; (*fechadura*) to unlatch.

destreza [deʃ'treza] *f* (*habilidade*) skill; (*agilidade*) dexterity.

destrinchar [dʒiʃtrĩ'ʃa*] *vt* (*desenredar*) to unravel; (*esmiuçar*) to treat in detail; (*problema*) to solve, resolve.

destro/a ['dɛʃtru/a] *adj* (*hábil*) skilful (*BRIT*), skillful (*US*); (*ágil*) agile; (*não canhoto*) right-handed.

destrocar [dʒiʃtro'ka*] *vt* to give back, return.

destroçar [dʒiʃtro'sa*] *vt* (*destruir*) to destroy; (*quebrar*) to smash, break; (*devastar*) to ruin, wreck.

destroços [dʒiʃ'trɔsuʃ] *mpl* wreckage *sg*.

destróier [dʒiʃ'troje*] *m* destroyer.

destronar [dʒiʃtro'na*] *vt* to depose.

destroncar [dʒiʃtrõ'ka*] *vt* to dislocate.

destruição [dʒiʃtrwi'sãw] *f* destruction.

destruidor(a) [dʒiʃtrwi'do*(a)] *adj* destructive.

destruir [dʒiʃ'trwi*] *vt* to destroy.

desumano/a [dʒizu'manu/a] *adj* inhuman; (*bárbaro*) cruel.

desunião [dʒizun'jãw] *f* disunity; (*separação*) separation.

desunir [dʒizu'ni*] *vt* (*separar*) to separate; (*TEC*) to disconnect; (*fig: desavir*) to cause a rift between.

desusado/a [dʒizu'zadu/a] *adj* (*não usado*) disused; (*incomum*) unusual.

desuso [dʒi'zuzu] *m* disuse; **em ~** outdated.

desvairado/a [dʒizvaj'radu/a] *adj* (*louco*) crazy, demented; (*desorientado*) bewildered.

desvairar [dʒizvaj'ra*] *vt* to drive mad.

desvalido/a [dʒizva'lidu/a] *adj* (*desamparado*) helpless; (*miserável*) destitute.

desvalorização [dʒizvaloriza'sãw] (*pl* **-ões**) *f* devaluation.

desvalorizar [dʒizvalori'za*] *vt* to devalue; **~-se** *vr* (*pessoa*) to undervalue o.s.; (*carro*) to depreciate; (*moeda*) to lose value.

desvanecer [dʒizvane'se*] *vt* (*envaidecer*) to make proud; (*sentimentos*) to dispel; **~-se** *vr* (*envaidecer-se*) to feel proud; (*sentimentos*) to vanish.

desvanecido/a [dʒizvane'sidu/a] *adj* proud.

desvantagem [dʒizvã'taʒẽ] (*pl* **-ns**) *f* disadvantage.

desvantajoso/a [dʒizvãta'ʒozu/ɔza] *adj* disadvantageous.

desvão [dʒiʒ'vãw] (*pl* **-s**) *m* loft.

desvario [dʒizva'riu] *m* madness, folly.

desvelar [dʒizve'la*] *vt* (*noiva, estátua*) to unveil; (*corpo, trama*) to uncover; (*segredo*) to reveal; (*problema*) to clarify; **~-se** *vr* (*pessoa*) to go to a lot of trouble.

desvelo [dʒiʒ'velu] *m* (*cuidado*) care; (*dedicação*) devotion.

desvencilhar [dʒizvẽsi'ʎa*] *vt* to free, extricate; **~-se** *vr* to free o.s., extricate o.s.

desvendar [dʒizvẽ'da*] *vt* (*tirar a venda*) to remove the blindfold from; (*revelar*) to disclose; (*mistério*) to solve.

desventura [dʒizvẽ'tura] *f* (*infortúnio*) misfortune; (*infelicidade*) unhappiness.

desventurado/a [dʒizvẽtu'radu/a] *adj* (*desafortunado*) unfortunate; (*infeliz*) unhappy ♦ *m/f* wretch.

desviar [dʒiʒ'vja*] *vt* to divert; (*golpe*) to deflect; (*dinheiro*) to embezzle; **~-se** *vr* (*afastar-se*) to turn away; **~-se de** (*evitar*) to avoid; **~-se do assunto** to digress; **~ os olhos** to look away; **desviei o carro para a direita** I pulled the car over to the right; **tentei desviá-lo do assunto** I tried to get *ou* steer him off the subject.

desvincular [dʒizvĩku'la*] *vt*: **~ algo de algo** to divest sth of sth; **~-se** *vr*: **~-se de algo** to disassociate o.s. from sth.

desvio [dʒiʒ'viu] *m* diversion, detour; (*curva*) bend; (*fig*) deviation; (*de dinheiro*) embezzle-

---

NB: *European Portuguese adds the following consonants to certain words:* **b** (sú(b)dito, su(b)til); **c** (a(c)ção, a(c)cionista, a(c)to); **m** (inde(m)ne); **p** (ado(p)ção, ado(p)tar); *for further details see p. xiii.*

ment; (de mercadorias) misappropriation; (FERRO) siding; (da coluna vertebral) dislocation.

desvirar [dʒiʒvi'ra*] vt to turn back.

desvirginar [dʒiʒvixʒi'na*] vt to deflower.

desvirtuar [dʒiʒvix'twa*] vt (fatos) to misrepresent.

detalhadamente [detaʎada'mētʃi] adv in detail.

detalhado/a [deta'ʎadu/a] adj detailed.

detalhar [deta'ʎa*] vt to (give in) detail.

detalhe [de'taʎi] m detail; **entrar em** ~ to go into detail.

detalhista [deta'ʎiʃta] adj painstaking, meticulous.

detectar [detek'ta*] vt to detect.

detective [detek'tivə] (PT) m = **detetive**.

detector [detek'to*] m detector.

detenção [detē'sãw] (pl -ões) f detention.

détente [de'tātʃi] f détente.

detento/a [de'tētu/a] m/f detainee.

detentor(a) [detē'to*(a)] m/f (de título, recorde) holder.

deter [de'te*] (irreg: como **ter**) vt (fazer parar) to stop; (prender) to arrest, detain; (documento) to keep; (reter) to keep; (conter: riso) to contain; ~-se vr (parar) to stop; (ficar) to stay; (conter-se) to restrain o.s.; ~-se em minúcias etc to get bogged down in details etc.

detergente [detex'ʒētʃi] m detergent.

deterioração [deterjora'sãw] f deterioration.

deteriorar [deterjo'ra*] vt to spoil, damage; ~-se vr to deteriorate; (relações) to worsen.

determinação [detexmina'sãw] f (firmeza) determination; (decisão) decision; (ordem) order; **por ~ de** by order of.

determinado/a [detexmi'nadu/a] adj (resoluto) determined; (certo) certain, given.

determinar [detexmi'na*] vt (fixar, precisar) to determine; (decretar) to order; (resolver) to decide (on); (causar) to cause; (fronteiras) to mark out.

detestar [deteʃ'ta*] vt to hate, detest.

detestável [deteʃ'tavew] (pl -eis) adj horrible, hateful.

detetive [dete'tʃivi] m detective.

detidamente [detʃida'mētʃi] adv carefully, thoroughly.

detido/a [de'tʃidu/a] adj (preso) under arrest; (minucioso) thorough.

detonação [detona'sãw] (pl -ões) f explosion.

detonar [deto'na*] vi to detonate, go off ♦ vt to detonate.

Detran [de'trã] (BR) abr m (= Departamento de Trânsito) state traffic department.

detrás [de'trajʃ] adv behind ♦ prep: ~ **de** behind; **por** ~ (from) behind.

detrimento [detri'mētu] m: **em** ~ **de** to the detriment of.

detrito [de'tritu] m debris sg; (de comida) remains pl; (resíduo) dregs pl.

deturpação [detuxpa'sãw] f corruption; (de palavras) distortion.

deturpar [detux'pa*] vt to corrupt; (desfigurar) to disfigure; **você deturpou minhas palavras** you twisted my words.

deu [dew] vb V **dar**.

deus(a) [dewʃ(sa)] m/f god/goddess; **D~ me livre!** God forbid!; **graças a D~** thank goodness; **se D~ quiser** God willing; **meu D~!** good Lord!; **D~ e o mundo** everybody.

deus-dará [-da'ra] adv: **viver ao** ~ to live from hand to mouth; **estar ao** ~ (casa) to be unattended.

deus-nos-acuda [-a'kuda] m commotion.

devagar [dʒiva'ga*] adv slowly ♦ adj inv (col): **ele é um cara tão** ~ he's such an old fogey.

devagarinho [dʒivaga'riɲu] adv nice and slowly.

devanear [deva'nja*] vt to imagine, dream of ♦ vi to daydream; (divagar) to wander, digress.

devaneio [deva'neju] m daydream.

devassa [de'vasa] f investigation, inquiry.

devassado/a [deva'sadu/a] adj (casa) exposed.

devassidão [devasi'dãw] f debauchery.

devasso/a [de'vasu/a] adj dissolute.

devastar [devaʃ'ta*] vt (destruir) to devastate; (arruinar) to ruin.

deve ['dɛvi] m (débito) debit; (coluna) debit column.

devedor(a) [deve'do*(a)] adj (pessoa) in debt ♦ m/f debtor; **saldo** ~ debit balance.

dever [de've*] m duty ♦ vt to owe ♦ vi (suposição): **deve (de) estar doente** he must be ill; (obrigação): **devo partir às oito** I must go at eight; **você devia ir ao médico** you should go to the doctor; **ele devia ter vindo** he should have come; **que devo fazer?** what shall I do?

deveras [dʒi'vɛraʃ] adv really, truly.

devidamente [devida'mētʃi] adv properly; (preencher formulário etc) duly.

devido/a [de'vidu/a] adj (maneira) proper; (respeito) due; ~ **a** due to, owing to; **no** ~ **tempo** in due course.

devoção [devo'sãw] f devotion.

devolução [devolu'sãw] f devolution; (restituição) return; (reembolso) refund; ~ **de impostos** tax rebate.

devolver [devow've*] vt to give back, return; (COM) to refund.

devorar [devo'ra*] vt to devour; (destruir) to destroy.

devotar [devo'ta*] vt to devote; ~-se vr: ~-se **a** to devote o.s. to.

devoto/a [de'vɔtu/a] adj devout ♦ m/f devotee.

dez [dɛʒ] num ten; V tb **cinco**.

dez. abr (= dezembro) Dec.

dezanove [deza'nɔvə] (PT) num = **dezenove**.

dezasseis [deza'sejʃ] (PT) num = **dezesseis**.

dezassete [deza'setə] (PT) num = **dezessete**.

dezembro [de'zēbru] (PT: **D-**) m December; V tb **julho**.

dezena [de'zena] *f*: **uma ~ ten.**

dezenove [deze'nɔvi] *num* nineteen; *V tb* **cinco.**

dezesseis [deze'sejʃ] *num* sixteen; *V tb* **cinco.**

dezessete [dezi'setʃi] *num* seventeen; *V tb* **cinco.**

dezoito [dʒi'zojtu] *num* eighteen; *V tb* **cinco.**

DF (*BR*) *abr* = **Distrito Federal.**

dia ['dʒia] *m* day; (*claridade*) daylight; **~ a ~** day by day; **~ de anos** (*PT*) birthday; **~ de folga** day off; **~ santo** holy day; **~ útil** weekday; **estar** *ou* **andar em ~** (*com*) to be up to date (with); **de ~** in the daytime, by day; **mais ~ menos ~** sooner or later; **todo ~, todos os ~s** every day; **o ~ inteiro** all day (long); **~ sim, ~ não** every other day; **de dois em dois ~s** every two days; **no ~ seguinte** the next day; **~ após ~** day after day; **do ~ para a noite** (*fig*) overnight; **bom ~** good morning; **um ~ desses** one of these days; **~s a fio** days on end; **~ cheio/morto** busy/quiet *ou* slow day; **todo santo ~** (*col*) every single day, day after day; **recebo por ~** I'm paid by the day; **um bebê de ~s** a newborn baby; **ele está com os ~s contados** his days are numbered.

dia-a-dia *m* daily life, everyday life.

diabete(s) [dʒia'betʃi(ʃ)] *f* diabetes.

diabético/a [dʒia'betʃiku/a] *adj, m/f* diabetic.

diabo ['dʒiabu] *m* devil; **que ~!** (*col*) damn it!; **por que ~ ...?** why the devil ...?; **o ~ é que ...** (*col*) the darnedest thing is that ...; **o ~ do eletricista não apareceu** (*col*) the damned electricity man didn't turn up; **estar um calor do ~** (*col*) it's damned *ou* bloody (*!*) hot; **deu um trabalho dos ~s** (*col*) it was a hell of a job; **quente pra ~** (*col*) damned hot; **dizer o ~ de alguém** to slag sb off.

diabólico/a [dʒia'bɔliku/a] *adj* diabolical.

diabrete [dʒia'bretʃi] *m* imp.

diabrura [dʒia'brura] *f* prank; **~s** *fpl* mischief *sg*.

diacho ['dʒiaʃu] (*col*) *excl* hell!

diadema [dʒia'dema] *m* diadem; (*jóia*) tiara.

diáfano/a ['dʒiafanu/a] *adj* (*tecido*) diaphanous; (*águas*) clear.

diafragma [dʒia'fragma] *m* diaphragm; (*anticoncepcional*) diaphragm, cap.

diagnosticar [dʒiagnoʃtʃi'ka*] *vt* to diagnose.

diagnóstico [dʒiag'nɔʃtʃiku] *m* diagnosis.

diagonal [dʒiago'naw] (*pl -ais*) *adj, f* diagonal.

diagrama [dʒia'grama] *m* diagram.

diagramador(a) [dʒiagrama'do*(a)] *m/f* designer.

diagramar [dʒiagra'ma*] *vt* to design.

dialecto [dja'lɛktu] (*PT*) *m* = **dialeto.**

dialética [dʒia'lɛtʃika] *f* dialectics *sg*.

dialeto [dʒia'letu] *m* dialect.

dialogar [dʒialo'ga*] *vi*: **~ (com alguém)** to

talk (to sb); (*POL*) to have *ou* hold talks (with sb).

diálogo ['dʒjalogu] *m* dialogue; (*conversa*) talk, conversation.

diamante [dʒja'mãtʃi] *m* diamond.

diâmetro ['dʒjametru] *m* diameter.

diante ['dʒjãtʃi] *prep*: **~ de** before; (*na frente de*) in front of; (*problemas etc*) in the face of; **e assim por ~** and so on; **para ~** forward.

dianteira [dʒjã'tejra] *f* front, vanguard; **tomar a ~** to get ahead.

dianteiro/a [dʒjã'tejru/a] *adj* front.

diapasão [dʒjapa'zãw] (*pl -ões*) *m* (*afinador*) tuning fork; (*tom*) pitch; (*extensão de voz ou instrumento*) range.

diapositivo [dʒjapozi'tʃivu] *m* (*FOTO*) slide.

diária ['dʒjarja] *f* (*de hotel*) daily rate.

diário/a ['dʒjarju/a] *adj* daily ♦ *m* diary; (*jornal*) (daily) newspaper; (*COM*) daybook; **~ de bordo** log book.

diarista [dʒja'riʃta] *m/f* casual worker, worker paid by the day; (*em casa*) cleaner.

diarréia [dʒja'xɛja] *f* diarrhoea (*BRIT*), diarrhea (*US*).

dica ['dʒika] (*col*) *f* hint.

dicção [dʒik'sãw] *f* diction.

dicionário [dʒisjo'narju] *m* dictionary.

dicionarista [dʒisjona'riʃta] *m/f* lexicographer.

dicotomia [dʒikoto'mia] *f* dichotomy.

didata [dʒi'data] (*PT*: **-ct-**) *m/f* teacher.

didática [dʒi'datʃika] (*PT*: **-ct-**) *f* education, teaching.

didático/a [dʒi'datʃiku/a] (*PT*: **-ct-**) *adj* (*livro*) educational; (*método*) teaching; (*modo*) didactic.

diesel ['dʒizew] *m*: **motor a ~** diesel engine.

dieta ['dʒjeta] *f* diet; **fazer ~** to go on a diet.

dietético/a [dʒje'tɛtʃiku/a] *adj* dietetic.

dietista [dʒje'tʃiʃta] *m/f* dietician.

difamação [dʒjifama'sãw] *f* (*falada*) slander; (*escrita*) libel.

difamador(a) [dʒjifama'do*(a)] *adj* defamatory ♦ *m/f* slanderer.

difamar [dʒjifa'ma*] *vt* to slander; (*por escrito*) to libel.

difamatório/a [dʒjifama'tɔrju/a] *adj* defamatory.

diferença [dʒjife'rẽsa] *f* difference; **ela tem uma ~ comigo** she's got something against me.

diferenciação [dʒjiferẽsja'sãw] *f* (*tb*: *MAT*) differentiation.

diferenciar [dʒjiferẽ'sja*] *vt* to differentiate.

diferente [dʒjife'rẽtʃi] *adj* different; **estar ~ com alguém** to be at odds with sb.

diferimento [dʒjiferi'mẽtu] *m* deferment.

diferir [dʒjife'ri*] (*irreg*) *vi*: **~ (de)** to differ (from) ♦ *vt* (*adiar*) to defer.

difícil [dʒi'fisiw] (*pl -eis*) *adj* (*trabalho, vida*) difficult, hard; (*problema, situação*) difficult;

NB: *European Portuguese adds the following consonants to certain words:* **b** (sú(b)dito, su(b)til); **c** (a(c)ção, a(c)cionista, a(c)to); **m** (inde(m)ne); **p** (ado(p)ção, ado(p)tar); *for further details see p. xiii.*

(*pessoa*: *intratável*) difficult; (: *exigente*) hard to please; (*improvável*) unlikely; **o ~ é ... the difficult thing is ...; acho ~ ela aceitar nossa proposta** I think it's unlikely she will accept our proposal; **falar ~** to use big words; **bancar o ~** to play hard to get.

dificílimo/a [dʒifi'silimu/a] *adj superl* de **difícil**.

dificilmente [dʒifisiw'mētʃi] *adv* with difficulty; (*mal*) hardly; (*raramente*) hardly ever; **~ ele poderá ...** it won't be easy for him to ....

dificuldade [dʒifikuw'dadʒi] *f* difficulty; (*aperto*) trouble; **em ~s** in trouble.

dificultar [dʒifikuw'ta*] *vt* to make difficult; (*complicar*) to complicate.

difteria [dʒifte'ria] *f* diphtheria.

difundir [dʒifū'dʒi*] *vt* (*luz*) to diffuse; (*espalhar*) to spread; (*notícia*) to spread, circulate; (*idéias*) to disseminate.

difusão [dʒifu'zãw] *f* (*de luz*) diffusion; (*espalhamento*) spreading; (*de notícias*) circulation; (*de idéias*) dissemination.

difuso/a [dʒi'fuzu/a] *adj* diffuse.

diga ['dʒiga] *etc vb* V **dizer**.

digerir [dʒiʒe'ri*] *vt, vi* to digest.

digestão [dʒiʒeʃ'tãw] *f* digestion.

digital [dʒiʒi'taw] (*pl* -**ais**) *adj* digital; **impressão ~** fingerprint.

digitar [dʒiʒi'ta*] *vt* (*COMPUT*: *dados*) to key (in).

dígito ['dʒiʒitu] *m* digit.

digladiar [dʒigla'dʒja*] *vi* to fight, fence; **~-se** *vr*: **~ (com alguém)** to do battle (with sb).

dignar-se [dʒig'naxsi] *vr*: **~ de** to deign to, condescend to.

dignidade [dʒigni'dadʒi] *f* dignity.

dignificar [dʒignifi'ka*] *vt* to dignify.

digno/a ['dʒignu/a] *adj* (*merecedor*) worthy; (*nobre*) dignified.

digo ['dʒigu] *etc vb* V **dizer**.

digressão [dʒigre'sãw] (*pl* -**ões**) *f* digression.

dilaceração [dʒilasera'sãw] (*pl* -**ões**) *f* laceration.

dilacerante [dʒilase'rãtʃi] *adj* (*dor*) excruciating; (*cruel*) cruel.

dilacerar [dʒilase'ra*] *vt* to tear to pieces, lacerate; **~-se** *vr* to tear one another to pieces.

dilapidação [dʒilapida'sãw] *f* (*de casas etc*) demolition; (*de dinheiro*) squandering.

dilapidar [dʒilapi'da*] *vt* (*fortuna*) to squander; (*casa*) to demolish.

dilatação [dʒilata'sãw] *f* dilation.

dilatar [dʒila'ta*] *vt* to dilate, expand; (*prolongar*) to prolong; (*retardar*) to delay.

dilatório/a [dʒila'tɔrju/a] *adj* dilatory.

dilema [dʒi'lema] *m* dilemma.

diletante [dʒile'tãtʃi] *adj, m/f* amateur; (*pej*) dilettante.

diletantismo [dʒiletã'tʃiʒmu] *m* amateurism; (*pej*) dilettantism.

diligência [dʒili'ʒēsja] *f* diligence; (*pesquisa*) inquiry; (*veículo*) stagecoach.

diligenciar [dʒiliʒē'sja*] *vt* to strive for; **~ (por) fazer** to strive to do.

diligente [dʒili'ʒētʃi] *adj* hardworking, industrious.

diluição [dʒilwi'sãw] *f* dilution.

diluir [dʒi'lwi*] *vt* to dilute.

dilúvio [dʒi'luvju] *m* flood.

dimensão [dʒimē'sãw] (*pl* -**ões**) *f* dimension; **dimensões** *fpl* measurements.

dimensionar [dʒimēsjo'na*] *vt*: **~ algo** to calculate the size of sth; (*fig*) to assess the extent of sth.

diminuição [dʒiminwi'sãw] *f* reduction.

diminuir [dʒimi'nwi*] *vt* to reduce; (*som*) to turn down; (*interesse*) to lessen ♦ *vi* to lessen, diminish; (*preço*) to go down; (*dor*) to wear off; (*barulho*) to die down.

diminutivo/a [dʒiminu'tʃivu/a] *adj* diminutive ♦ *m* diminutive.

diminuto/a [dʒimi'nutu/a] *adj* minute, tiny.

Dinamarca [dʒina'maxka] *f* Denmark.

dinamarquês/quesa [dʒinamax'keʃ/'keza] *adj* Danish ♦ *m/f* Dane ♦ *m* (*LING*) Danish.

dinâmico/a [dʒi'namiku/a] *adj* dynamic.

dinamismo [dʒina'miʒmu] *m* (*fig*) energy, drive.

dinamitar [dʒinami'ta*] *vt* to blow up.

dinamite [dʒina'mitʃi] *f* dynamite.

dínamo ['dʒinamu] *m* dynamo.

dinastia [dʒinaʃ'tʃia] *f* dynasty.

dinda ['dʒīda] (*col*) *f* godmother.

dinheirão [dʒiɲej'rãw] *m*: **um ~** loads *pl* of money.

dinheiro [dʒi'ɲejru] *m* money; **~ à vista** ready cash; **sem ~** penniless; **em ~** in cash; **~ em caixa** ready cash; **~ em espécie** cash; **~ vivo** hard cash.

dinossauro [dʒino'sawru] *m* dinosaur.

diocese [dʒjo'sezi] *f* diocese.

dióxido ['dʒjɔksidu] *m* dioxide; **~ de carbono** carbon dioxide.

DIP (*BR*) *abr m* = **Departamento de Imprensa e Propaganda**.

diploma [dʒip'lɔma] *m* diploma.

diplomacia [dʒiploma'sia] *f* diplomacy; (*fig*) tact.

diplomando/a [dʒiplo'mādu/a] *m/f* diploma candidate.

diplomar [dʒiplo'ma*] *vt* to graduate; **~-se** *vr*: **~-se (em algo)** to get one's diploma (in sth).

diplomata [dʒiplo'mata] *m/f* diplomat.

diplomático/a [dʒiplo'matʃiku/a] *adj* diplomatic; (*discreto*) tactful.

dique ['dʒiki] *m* dam; (*GEO*) dike.

direção [dʒire'sãw] (*PT*: **-cç-**: *pl* -**ões**) *f* direction; (*endereço*) address; (*AUTO*) steering; (*administração*) management; (*comando*) leadership; (*diretoria*) board of directors; **em ~ a** towards.

directo/a [di'rektu/a] *etc* (*PT*) = **direto** *etc*.

direi [dʒi'rej] *etc vb* V **dizer**.

direita [dʒi'rejta] *f* (*mão*) right hand; (*lado*) right-hand side; (*POL*) right wing; **à ~** on the right; **"mantenha-se à ~"** "keep right".

direitinho [dʒirej'tʃiɲu] *adv* properly, just right; (*diretamente*) directly.

direitista [dʒirej'tʃiʃta] *adj* right-wing ♦ *m/f* right-winger.

direito/a [dʒi'rejtu/a] *adj* (*lado*) right-hand; (*mão*) right; (*honesto*) honest; (*devido*) proper; (*justo*) right, just ♦ *m* (*prerrogativa*) right; (*JUR*) law; (*de tecido*) right side ♦ *adv* (*em linha reta*) straight; (*bem*) right; (*de maneira certa*) properly; **~s** *mpl* rights; (*alfandegários*) duty *sg*; **~ civil** civil law; **~s autorais** copyright *sg*; **~s civis** civil rights; **~s de importação** import duty; **~s humanos** human rights; **livre de ~s** duty-free; **ter ~ a** to have a right to, be entitled to; **minha roupa está direita?/meu cabelo está ~?** are my clothes/is my hair all right?

diretas [dʒi'rɛtaʃ] *fpl* (*POL*) direct elections.

direto/a [dʒi'rɛtu/a] *adj* direct ♦ *adv* straight; **transmissão direta** (*TV*) live broadcast; **ir ~ ao assunto** to get straight to the point.

diretor(a) [dʒire'to*(a)] *adj* directing, guiding ♦ *m/f* (*COM*, *de cinema*) director; (*de jornal*) editor; (*de escola*) head teacher.

diretor(a)-gerente *m/f* managing director.

diretoria [dʒireto'ria] *f* (*cargo*) directorship; (: *em escola*) headship; (*direção: COM*) management; (*sala*) boardroom.

diretório [dʒire'tɔrju] *m* directorate; (*COMPUT*) directory; **~ acadêmico** students' union.

diretriz [dʒire'triʒ] *f* directive.

dirigente [dʒiri'ʒētʃi] *adj* (*classe*) ruling ♦ *m/f* (*de país*, *partido*) leader; (*diretor*) director; (*gerente*) manager.

dirigir [dʒiri'ʒi*] *vt* to direct; (*COM*) to manage, run; (*veículo*) to drive; (*atenção*) to turn ♦ *vi* to drive; **~-se** *vr*: **~-se a** (*falar com*) to speak to, address; (*ir*, *recorrer*) to go to; (*esforços*) to be directed towards.

dirimir [dʒiri'mi*] *vt* (*dúvida*, *contenda*) to settle, clear up.

discagem [dʒiʃ'kaʒē] *f* (*TEL*) dialling; **~ direta** direct dialling.

discar [dʒiʃ'ka*] *vt* to dial.

discente [dʒi'sētʃi] *adj* **V corpo**.

discernimento [dʒisexni'mētu] *m* discernment.

discernir [dʒisex'ni*] *vt* (*perceber*) to discern, perceive; (*diferenciar*) to discriminate, distinguish.

discernível [dʒisex'nivew] (*pl* **-eis**) *adj* discernible.

disciplina [dʒisi'plina] *f* discipline.

disciplinador(a) [dʒisiplina'do*(a)] *adj* disciplinary.

disciplinar [dʒisipli'na*] *vt* to discipline; **~-se** *vr* to discipline o.s.

discípulo/a [dʒi'sipulu/a] *m/f* disciple; (*aluno*) pupil.

disc-jóquei [dʒiʃk-] *m/f* disc jockey, DJ.

disco ['dʒiʃku] *m* disc; (*COMPUT*) disk; (*MÚS*) record; (*de telefone*) dial; **~ laser** (*máquina*) compact disc player, CD player; (*disco*) compact disc, CD; **~ flexível/rígido** (*COMPUT*) floppy/hard disk; **~ mestre** (*COMPUT*) master disk; **~ do sistema** system disk; **~ voador** flying saucer; **mudar o ~** (*col*) to change the subject.

discordância [dʒiʃkox'dasja] *f* disagreement; (*de opiniões*) difference.

discordante [dʒiʃkox'dãtʃi] *adj* divergent, conflicting.

discordar [dʒiʃkox'da*] *vi*: **~ de alguém em algo** to disagree with sb on sth.

discórdia [dʒiʃ'kɔxdʒja] *f* discord, strife.

discorrer [dʒiʃko'xe*] *vi*: **~ (sobre)** (*falar*) to talk (about).

discoteca [dʒiʃko'tɛka] *f* (*boate*) discotheque, disco (*col*); (*coleção de discos*) record library.

discotecário/a [dʒiʃkote'karju/a] *m/f* disc jockey, DJ.

discrepância [dʒiʃkre'pãsja] *f* discrepancy; (*desacordo*) disagreement.

discrepante [dʒiʃkre'pãtʃi] *adj* conflicting.

discrepar [dʒiʃkre'pa*] *vi*: **~ de** to differ from.

discreto/a [dʒiʃ'krɛtu/a] *adj* discreet; (*modesto*) modest; (*prudente*) shrewd; (*roupa*) plain, sober.

discrição [dʒiʃkri'sãw] *f* discretion, good sense.

discricionário/a [dʒiʃkrisjo'narju/a] *adj* discretionary.

discriminação [dʒiʃkrimina'sãw] *f* discrimination; (*especificação*) differentiation; **~ racial** racial discrimination.

discriminar [dʒiʃkrimi'na*] *vt* to distinguish ♦ *vi*: **~ entre** to discriminate between.

discriminatório/a [dʒiʃkrimina'tɔrju/a] *adj* discriminatory.

discursar [dʒiʃkux'sa*] *vi* (*em público*) to make a speech; (*falar*) to speak.

discurso [dʒiʃ'kuxsu] *m* speech; (*LING*) discourse.

discussão [dʒiʃku'sãw] (*pl* **-ões**) *f* (*debate*) discussion, debate; (*contenda*) argument.

discutir [dʒiʃku'tʃi*] *vt* to discuss ♦ *vi*: **~ (sobre algo)** (*debater*) to talk (about sth); (*contender*) to argue (about sth).

discutível [dʒiʃku'tʃivew] (*pl* **-eis**) *adj* debatable.

disenteria [dʒizēte'ria] *f* dysentery.

disfarçar [dʒiʃfax'sa*] *vt* to disguise ♦ *vi* to pretend; **~-se** *vr*: **~-se em** *ou* **de algo** to disguise o.s. as sth.

disfarce [dʒiʃ'faxsi] *m* disguise; (*máscara*) mask.

NB: European Portuguese adds the following consonants to certain words: **b** (sú(b)dito, su(b)til); **c** (a(c)ção, a(c)cionista, a(c)to); **m** (inde(m)ne); **p** (ado(p)ção, ado(p)tar); *for further details see p. xiii.*

disfasia [dʒiʃfa'zia] *f* (*MED*) speech defect.

disforme [dʒiʃ'fɔxmi] *adj* deformed, hideous.

disfunção [dʒiʃfũ'sãw] (*pl* -ões) *f* (*MED*) dysfunction.

dislético/a [dʒiʒ'lɛtʃiku/a] *adj*, *m/f* dyslexic.

dislexia [dʒiʒlek'sia] *f* dyslexia.

disléxico/a [dʒiʒ'lɛksiku/a] *adj*, *m/f* dyslexic.

díspar ['dʒiʃpa*] *adj* dissimilar.

disparada [dʒiʃpa'rada] *f*: **dar uma** ~ to surge ahead; **em** ~ at full tilt.

disparado/a [dʒiʃpa'radu/a] *adj* very fast ♦ *adv* by a long way.

disparar [dʒiʃpa'ra*] *vt* to shoot, fire ♦ *vi* to fire; (*arma*) to go off; (*correr*) to shoot off, bolt.

disparatado/a [dʒiʃpara'tadu/a] *adj* silly, absurd.

disparate [dʒiʃpa'ratʃi] *m* nonsense, rubbish; (*ação*) blunder.

disparidade [dʒiʃpari'dadʒi] *f* disparity.

dispêndio [dʒiʃ'pẽdʒu] *m* expenditure.

dispendioso/a [dʒiʃpẽ'dʒiozu/ɔza] *adj* costly, expensive.

dispensa [dʒiʃ'pẽsa] *f* exemption; (*REL*) dispensation.

dispensar [dʒiʃpẽ'sa*] *vt* (*desobrigar*) to excuse; (*prescindir de*) to do without; (*conferir*) to grant.

dispensário [dʒiʃpẽ'sarju] *m* dispensary.

dispensável [dʒiʃpẽ'savew] (*pl* -eis) *adj* expendable.

dispepsia [dʒiʃpep'sia] *f* dyspepsia.

dispersão [dʒiʃpex'sãw] *f* dispersal.

dispersar [dʒiʃpex'sa*] *vt*, *vi* to disperse.

dispersivo/a [dʒiʃpex'sivu/a] *adj* (*pessoa*) scatterbrained.

disperso/a [dʒiʃ'pexsu/a] *adj* scattered.

displicência [dʒiʃpli'sensja] (*BR*) *f* (*descuido*) negligence, carelessness.

displicente [dʒiʃpli'sẽtʃi] *adj* careless.

dispo ['dʒiʃpu] *etc vb* V **despir**.

disponibilidade [dʒiʃponibili'dadʒi] *f* availability; (*finanças*) liquid *ou* available assets *pl*; ~ **de caixa** cash in hand.

disponível [dʒiʃpo'nivew] (*pl* -eis) *adj* available.

dispor [dʒiʃ'po*] (*irreg*: *como* **pôr**) *vt* (*arranjar*) to arrange; (*colocar em ordem*) to put in order ♦ *vi*: ~ **de** (*usar*) to have the use of; (*ter*) to have, own; (*pessoas*) to have at one's disposal; ~**-se** *vr*: ~**-se a** (*estar pronto a*) to be prepared to, be willing to; (*decidir*) to decide to; ~ **sobre** to talk about; **não disponho de tempo para** ... I can't afford the time to ...; **disponha!** feel free!

disposição [dʒiʃpozi'sãw] (*pl* -ões) *f* arrangement; (*humor*) disposition; (*inclinação*) inclination; **à sua** ~ at your disposal.

dispositivo [dʒiʃpozi'tʃivu] *m* (*mecanismo*) gadget, device; (*determinação de lei*) provision; (*conjunto de meios*): ~ **de segurança** security operation; ~ **intra-uterino** intra-uterine device.

disposto/a [dʒiʃ'poftu/'pɔʃta] *pp* *de* **dispor** ♦ *adj* (*arranjado*) arranged; **estar** ~ **a** to be willing to; **estar bem** ~ to look well; **sentir-se** ~ **a fazer algo** to feel like doing sth.

disputa [dʒiʃ'puta] *f* (*contenda*) dispute, argument; (*competição*) contest.

disputar [dʒiʃpu'ta*] *vt* to dispute; (*lutar por*) to fight over; (*concorrer a*) to compete for ♦ *vi* (*discutir*) to quarrel, argue; (*competir*) to compete; ~ **uma corrida** to run a race.

disquete [dʒiʃ'ketʃi] *m* (*COMPUT*) floppy disk, diskette.

dissabor [dʒisa'bo*] *m* (*desgosto*) sorrow; (*aborrecimento*) annoyance.

disse ['dʒisi] *etc vb* V **dizer**.

dissecar [dʒise'ka*] *vt* to dissect.

disseminação [dʒisemina'sãw] *f* (*de pólen etc*) spread(ing); (*de idéias*) dissemination.

disseminar [dʒisemi'na*] *vt* to disseminate; (*espalhar*) to spread.

dissensão [dʒisẽ'sãw] *f* dissension, discord.

dissentir [dʒisẽ'tʃi*] *vi*: ~ **de alguém (em algo)** to be in disagreement with sb (over sth); ~ **de algo** (*não combinar*) to be at variance with sth.

disse-que-disse *m* gossip, tittle-tattle.

dissertação [dʒisexta'sãw] (*pl* -ões) *f* dissertation; (*discurso*) lecture.

dissertar [dʒisex'ta*] *vi* to speak.

dissidência [dʒisi'dẽsja] *f* (*divergência*) dissension; (*dissidentes*) dissidents *pl*: (*cisão*) split, difference of opinion.

dissidente [dʒisi'dẽtʃi] *adj*, *m/f* dissident.

dissídio [dʒi'sidʒu] *m* (*JUR*): ~ **coletivo/individual** collective/individual dispute.

dissimilar [dʒisimi'la*] *adj* dissimilar.

dissimulação [dʒisimula'sãw] *f* (*fingimento*) pretence (*BRIT*), pretense (*US*); (*disfarce*) disguise.

dissimular [dʒisimu'la*] *vt* (*ocultar*) to hide; (*fingir*) to feign ♦ *vi* to dissemble.

dissinto [dʒi'sĩtu] *etc vb* V **dissentir**.

dissipação [dʒisipa'sãw] *f* waste, squandering.

dissipar [dʒisi'pa*] *vt* (*dispersar*) to disperse, dispel; (*malgastar*) to squander, waste; ~**-se** *vr* to vanish.

disso ['dʒisu] = **de** + **isso**.

dissociar [dʒiso'sja*] *vt*: ~ **algo (de/em algo)** to separate sth (from sth)/break sth up (into sth); ~**-se** *vr*: ~**-se de algo** to dissociate o.s. from sth.

dissolução [dʒisolu'sãw] *f* (*dissolvência*) dissolving; (*libertinagem*) debauchery; (*de casamento*) dissolution.

dissoluto/a [dʒiso'lutu/a] *adj* dissolute, debauched.

dissolver [dʒisow've*] *vt* to dissolve; (*dispersar*) to disperse; (*motim*) to break up.

dissonância [dʒiso'nãsja] *f* dissonance; (*discordância*) discord.

dissonante [dʒiso'nãtʃi] *adj* (*som*) dissonant, discordant; (*fig*) discordant.

dissuadir [dʒiswa'dʒi*] *vt* to dissuade; ~

alguém de fazer algo to talk sb out of doing sth, dissuade sb from doing sth.

dissuasão [dʒiswa'zãw] f dissuasion.

dissuasivo/a [dʒiswa'zivu/a] adj dissuasive.

distância [dʒiʃ'tãsja] f distance; **a grande ~** far away; **a 3 quilômetros de ~** 3 kilometres (BRIT) ou kilometers (US) away.

distanciamento [dʒiʃtãsja'mẽtu] m distancing.

distanciar [dʒiʃtã'sja*] vt (afastar) to distance, set apart; (colocar por intervalos) to space out; **~-se** vr to move away; (fig) to distance o.s.

distante [dʒiʃ'tãtʃi] adj distant, far-off; (fig) aloof.

distar [dʒiʃ'ta*] vi to be far away; **o aeroporto dista 10 quilômetros da cidade** the airport is 10 km away from the city.

distender [dʒiʃtẽ'de*] vt (estender) to expand; (estirar) to stretch; (dilatar) to distend; (músculo) to pull; **~-se** vr (estender-se) to expand; (dilatar-se) to distend.

distinção [dʒiʃtʃĩ'sãw] (pl -ões) f distinction; **fazer ~** to make a distinction.

distinguir [dʒiʃtʃĩ'gi*] vt (diferenciar) to distinguish, differentiate; (avistar, ouvir) to make out; (enobrecer) to distinguish; **~-se** vr to stand out; **~ algo de algo/entre** to distinguish sth from sth/between.

distintivo/a [dʒiʃtʃĩ'tʃivu/a] adj distinctive ♦ m (insígnia) badge; (emblema) emblem.

distinto/a [dʒiʃ'tʃĩtu/a] adj (diferente) different; (eminente) distinguished; (claro) distinct; (refinado) refined.

disto ['dʒiʃtu] = **de** + **isto**.

distorção [dʒiʃtox'sãw] (pl -ões) f distortion.

distorcer [dʒiʃtox'se*] vt to distort.

distorções [dʒiʃtox'sõjʃ] fpl de **distorção**.

distração [dʒiʃtra'sãw] (PT: -cç-: pl -ões) f (alheamento) absent-mindedness; (divertimento) pastime; (descuido) oversight.

distraído/a [dʒiʃtra'idu/a] adj absent-minded; (não atento) inattentive.

distrair [dʒiʃtra'i*] vt (tornar desatento) to distract; (divertir) to amuse; **~-se** vr to amuse o.s.

distribuição [dʒiʃtribwi'sãw] f distribution; (de cartas) delivery.

distribuidor(a) [dʒiʃtribwi'do*(a)] m/f distributor ♦ m (AUTO) distributor ♦ f (COM) distribution company, distributor.

distribuir [dʒiʃtri'bwi*] vt to distribute; (repartir) to share out; (cartas) to deliver.

distrito [dʒiʃ'tritu] m district; (delegacia) police station; **~ eleitoral** constituency; **~ federal** federal area.

distúrbio [dʒiʃ'tuxbju] m disturbance; **~s** mpl (POL) riots.

ditado [dʒi'tadu] m dictation; (provérbio) saying.

ditador [dʒita'do*] m dictator.

ditadura [dʒita'dura] f dictatorship.

ditame [dʒi'tami] m (da consciência) dictate; (regra) rule.

ditar [dʒi'ta*] vt to dictate; (impor) to impose.

ditatorial [dʒitato'rjaw] (pl -ais) adj dictatorial.

dito/a ['dʒitu/a] pp de **dizer** ♦ m: **~ espirituoso** witticism; **~ e feito** no sooner said than done.

dito-cujo (pl **ditos-cujos**) (col) m said person.

ditongo [dʒi'tõgu] m diphthong.

ditoso/a [dʒi'tozu/ɔza] adj (feliz) happy; (venturoso) lucky.

DIU abr m (= dispositivo intra-uterino) IUD.

diurético/a [dʒju'rɛtʃiku/a] adj diuretic ♦ m diuretic.

diurno/a ['dʒjuxnu/a] adj daytime atr.

divã [dʒi'vã] m couch, divan.

divagação [dʒivaga'sãw] (pl -ões) f (andança) wandering; (digressão) digression; (devaneio) rambling.

divagar [dʒiva'ga*] vi (vaguear) to wander; (falar sem nexo) to ramble (on); **~ do assunto** to wander off the subject, digress.

divergência [dʒivex'ʒẽsja] f divergence; (desacordo) disagreement.

divergente [dʒivex'ʒẽtʃi] adj divergent.

divergir [dʒivex'ʒi*] (irreg) vi to diverge; **~ (de alguém)** to disagree (with sb).

diversão [dʒivex'sãw] (pl -ões) f (divertimento) amusement; (passatempo) pastime.

diversidade [dʒivexsi'dadʒi] f diversity.

diversificação [dʒivexsifika'sãw] f diversification.

diversificar [dʒivexsifi'ka*] vt to diversify ♦ vi to vary.

diverso/a [dʒi'vexsu/a] adj (diferente) different; (pl) various.

diversões [dʒivex'sõjʃ] fpl de **diversão**.

diversos/as [dʒi'vexsuʃ/aʃ] adj several ♦ mpl (na contabilidade) sundries.

divertido/a [dʒivex'tʃidu/a] adj amusing, funny.

divertimento [dʒivextʃi'mẽtu] m amusement, entertainment.

divertir [dʒivex'tʃi*] vt to amuse, entertain; **~-se** vr to enjoy o.s., have a good time.

dívida ['dʒivida] f debt; (obrigação) indebtedness; **contrair ~s** to run into debt; **~ externa** foreign debt.

dividendo [dʒivi'dẽdu] m dividend.

dividido/a [dʒivi'dʒidu/a] adj divided; **sentir-se ~ entre duas coisas** to feel torn between two things.

dividir [dʒivi'dʒi*] vt to divide; (despesas, lucro, comida etc) to share; (separar) to separate ♦ vi (MAT) to divide; **~-se** vr to divide, split up; **as opiniões se dividem** opinions are divided; **ele tem que se ~ entre**

a família e o trabalho he has to divide his time between the family and work; ~ **21 por 7** to divide 21 by 7; ~ **algo em 3 partes** to divide sth into 3 parts; ~ **algo pela metade** to divide sth in half *ou* in two.

divindade [dʒivĩ'dadʒi] *f* divinity.

divino/a [dʒi'vinu/a] *adj* divine; (*col*) gorgeous ♦ *m* Holy Ghost.

divirjo [dʒi'vixʒu] *etc vb* V **divergir.**

divisa [dʒi'viza] *f* (*emblema*) emblem; (*frase*) slogan; (*fronteira*) border; (*MIL*) stripe; ~**s** *fpl* foreign exchange *sg*, foreign currency *sg*.

divisão [dʒivi'zãw] (*pl* -**ões**) *f* division; (*discórdia*) split; (*partilha*) sharing.

divisar [dʒivi'za*] *vt* (*avistar*) to see, make out.

divisível [dʒivi'zivew] (*pl* -**eis**) *adj* divisible.

divisões [dʒivi'zõjʃ] *fpl de* **divisão.**

divisória [dʒivi'zɔrja] *f* partition.

divisório/a [dʒivi'zɔrju/a] *adj* (*linha*) dividing.

divorciado/a [dʒivox'sjadu/a] *adj* divorced ♦ *m/f* divorcé(e).

divorciar [dʒivox'sja*] *vt* to divorce; ~**-se** *vr* to get divorced.

divórcio [dʒi'vɔxsju] *m* divorce.

divulgação [dʒivuwga'sãw] *f* (*de notícias*) spread; (*de segredo*) divulging; (*de produto*) marketing.

divulgar [dʒivuw'ga*] *vt* (*notícias*) to spread; (*segredo*) to divulge; (*produto*) to market; (*tornar conhecido*) to publish; ~**-se** *vr* to leak out.

dizer [dʒi'ze*] *vt* to say ♦ *m* saying; ~**-se** *vr* to claim to be; **diz-se** *ou* **dizem que** ... it is said that ...; **diga-se de passagem** by the way; ~ **algo a alguém** (*informar, avisar*) to tell sb sth; (*falar*) to say sth to sb; ~ **a alguém que** ... to tell sb that ...; **o que você diz da minha sugestão?** what do you think of my suggestion?; ~ **para alguém fazer** to tell sb to do; **o filme não me disse nada** (*não interessou*) the film left me cold; **o nome não me diz nada** (*não significa*) the name means nothing to me; ~ **bem com** to go well with; **querer** ~ to mean; **quer** ~ that is to say; **nem é preciso** ~ that goes without saying; **não** ~ **coisa com coisa** to make no sense; **digo** (*ou seja*) I mean; **diga!** what is it?; **não diga!** you don't say!; **digamos** let's say; **bem que eu te disse, eu não disse?** I told you so; **ele tem dificuldade em acordar às sete, que dirá às cinco** he finds it difficult to wake at seven, let alone *ou* never mind five; **por assim** ~ so to speak; **até** ~ **chega** as much as possible.

dizimar [dʒizi'ma*] *vt* to decimate; (*herança*) to fritter away.

Djibuti [dʒibu'tʃi] *m*: **o** ~ Djibouti.

DNER (*BR*) *abr m* (= *Departamento Nacional de Estradas de Rodagem*) national highways department.

DNOCS (*BR*) *abr m* = **Departamento Nacional de Obras contra as Secas.**

DNPM (*BR*) *abr m* = **Departamento Nacional de Produção Mineral.**

do [du] = **de** + **o.**

dó [dɔ] *m* (*lástima*) pity; (*MÚS*) do; **ter** ~ **de** to feel sorry for.

doação [doa'sãw] (*pl* -**ões**) *f* donation, gift.

doador(a) [doa'do*(a)] *m/f* donor.

doar [do'a*] *vt* to donate, give.

dobra ['dɔbra] *f* fold; (*prega*) pleat; (*de calças*) turn-up.

dobradiça [dobra'dʒisa] *f* hinge.

dobradiço/a [dobra'dʒisu/a] *adj* flexible.

dobradinha [dobra'dʒiɲa] *f* (*CULIN*) tripe stew; (*col*: *dupla*) pair, partnership.

dobrar [do'bra*] *vt* (*duplicar*) to double; (*papel*) to fold; (*joelho*) to bend; (*esquina*) to turn, go round; (*fazer ceder*): ~ **alguém** to bring sb round ♦ *vi* (*duplicar-se*) to double; (*sino*) to toll; (*vergar*) to bend; ~**-se** *vr* to double (up).

dobro ['dobru] *m* double.

DOC (*BR*) *abr f* = **Diretoria de Obras de Cooperação.**

doca ['dɔka] *f* (*NÁUT*) dock.

doce ['dosi] *adj* sweet; (*terno*) gentle ♦ *m* sweet; **ele é um** ~ he's a sweetie; **fazer** ~ (*col*) to play hard to get.

doce-de-coco (*pl* **doces-de-coco**) *m* (*pessoa*) sweetie.

doceiro/a [do'sejru/a] *m/f* sweet-seller.

docemente [dose'mẽtʃi] *adv* gently.

docência [do'sẽsja] *f* teaching.

docente [do'sẽtʃi] *adj* teaching; **o corpo** ~ teaching staff.

dócil ['dɔsiw] *adj* docile.

documentação [dokumẽta'sãw] *f* documentation; (*documentos*) papers *pl*.

documentar [dokumẽ'ta*] *vt* to document.

documentário/a [dokumẽ'tarju/a] *adj* documentary ♦ *m* documentary.

documento [doku'mẽtu] *m* document; **não é** ~ (*col*) it doesn't mean a thing.

doçura [do'sura] *f* sweetness; (*brandura*) gentleness.

Dodecaneso [dodeka'nezu] *m*: **o** ~ the Dodecanese.

dodói [do'dɔj] (*col*) *m*: **você tem** ~**?** does it hurt? ♦ *adj inv* ill, under the weather.

doença [do'ẽsa] *f* illness.

doente [do'ẽtʃi] *adj* ill, sick ♦ *m/f* sick person; (*cliente*) patient.

doentio/a [doẽ'tʃiu/a] *adj* (*pessoa*) sickly; (*clima*) unhealthy; (*curiosidade*) morbid.

doer [do'e*] *vi* to hurt, ache; ~ **a alguém** (*pesar*) to grieve sb; **dói ver tanta pobreza** it's sad to see so much poverty.

dogma ['dɔgma] *m* dogma.

dogmático/a [dog'matʃiku/a] *adj* dogmatic.

DOI (*BR*) *abr m* (= *Destacamento de Operações Internas*) military secret police.

Doi-Codi ['dɔi-'kɔdʒi] (*BR*) *abr m* (= *Departamento de Operações e Informações — Centro de Operação e Defesa Interna*) secret police

HQ during the military dictatorship.

doidão/dona [doj'dãw/'dɔna] *(pl -ões/-s) adj:* **(ser)** ~ (to be) completely crazy; **(estar)** ~ (to be) high.

doideira [doj'dejra] *f* madness, foolishness.

doidice [doj'dʒisi] *f* madness, foolishness.

doidivanas [dojdʒi'vanaʃ] *m/f inv* hothead.

doido/a ['dojdu/a] *adj* mad, crazy; ~ **por** mad/crazy about ♦ *m/f* madman/woman; ~ **de pedras** *or* **varrido** *(col)* raving loony.

doído/a [do'idu/a] *adj* sore, painful; *(moralmente)* hurt; *(que causa dor)* painful.

doidões [doj'dõjʃ] *adj pl de* **doidão**.

doidona [doj'dɔna] *f de* **doidão**.

doirar [doj'ra*] *vt =* **dourar**.

dois [dojʃ] *num* two; **conversa a** ~ tête-à-tête; *V tb* **cinco**.

dólar ['dɔla*] *m* dollar; ~ **oficial/paralelo** dollar at the official/black-market rate; ~-**turismo** dollar at the special tourist rate.

doleiro/a [do'lejru/a] *m/f* (black market) dollar dealer.

dolo ['dɔlu] *m* fraud.

dolorido/a [dolo'ridu/a] *adj* painful, sore; *(fig)* sorrowful.

dolorosa [dolo'rɔza] *f* bill.

doloroso/a [dolo'rozu/ɔza] *adj* painful.

dom [dõ] *m* gift; *(aptidão)* knack; **o** ~ **da palavra** the gift of the gab.

dom. *abr* (= *domingo*) Sun.

domador(a) [domado*(a)] *m/f* tamer.

domar [do'ma*] *vt* to tame.

doméstica [do'mɛʃtʃika] *f* maid.

domesticado/a [domeʃtʃi'kadu/a] *adj* domesticated; *(manso)* tame.

domesticar [domeʃtʃi'ka*] *vt* to domesticate; *(povo)* to tame.

doméstico/a [do'mɛʃtʃiku/a] *adj* domestic; *(vida)* home *atr*.

domiciliar [domisi'lja*] *adj* home *atr*.

domicílio [domi'silju] *m* home, residence; **vendas/entrega a** ~ home sales/delivery; "**entregamos a** ~" "we deliver".

dominação [domina'sãw] *f* domination.

dominador(a) [domina'do*(a)] *adj (pessoa)* domineering; *(olhar)* imposing ♦ *m/f* ruler.

dominante [domi'nãtʃi] *adj* dominant; *(predominante)* predominant.

dominar [domi'na*] *vt* to dominate; *(reprimir)* to overcome ♦ *vi* to dominate, prevail; ~-**se** *vr* to control o.s.

domingo [do'mĩgu] *m* Sunday; *V tb* **terça-feira**.

domingueiro/a [domĩ'gejru/a] *adj* Sunday *atr*; *V tb* **traje**.

Dominica [domi'nika] *f* Dominica.

dominicano/a [domini'kanu/a] *adj, m/f* Dominican; **República Dominicana** Dominican Republic.

domínio [do'minju] *m (poder)* power;

(dominação) control; *(território)* domain; *(esfera)* sphere; ~ **próprio** self-control.

dom-juan [-'jwã] *m* ladies' man, Don Juan.

domo ['dɔmu] *m* dome.

dona ['dɔna] *f (proprietária)* owner; *(col: mulher)* lady; ~ **de casa** housewife; **D**~ **Luísa** *etc* corresponde ao uso de Mrs *ou* Miss seguido do sobrenome da mulher em inglês.

donatário/a [dona'tarju/a] *m/f* recipient.

donde ['dõdə] *(PT) adv* from where; *(daí)* thus; ~ **vem?** where do you come from?

dondoca [dõ'dɔka] *(col) f* society lady, lady of leisure.

dono ['donu] *m (proprietário)* owner.

donzela [dõ'zɛla] *f (mulher)* maiden.

dopar [do'pa*] *vt* to drug; ~-**se** *vr (atleta)* to take drugs.

DOPS *(BR) abr m* (= *Departamento de Ordem Política e Social) internal security agency.*

dor [do*] *f* ache; *(aguda)* pain; *(fig)* grief, sorrow; ~ **de cabeça** headache; ~ **de dentes** toothache; ~ **de estômago** stomach ache.

doravante [dora'vãtʃi] *adv* henceforth.

dor-de-cotovelo *(col) m* jealousy; **estar com** ~ to be jealous.

dormência [dox'mẽsja] *f* numbness.

dormente [dox'mẽtʃi] *adj* numb ♦ *m (FERRO)* sleeper.

dormida [dox'mida] *f* sleep; *(lugar)* place to sleep; **dar uma** ~ to have a sleep.

dormideira [doxmi'dejra] *f* drowsiness.

dorminhoco/a [doxmi'ɲoku/a] *adj* dozy ♦ *m/f* sleepyhead.

dormir [dox'mi*] *vi* to sleep; ~ **como uma pedra** *ou* **a sono solto** to sleep like a log *ou* soundly; **hora de** ~ bedtime; ~ **no ponto** *(fig)* to miss the boat; ~ **fora** to spend the night away.

dormitar [doxmi'ta*] *vi* to doze.

dormitório [doxmi'tɔrju] *m* bedroom; *(coletivo)* dormitory.

dorsal [dox'saw] *(pl -ais) adj V* **coluna**.

dorso ['doxsu] *m* back.

dos [duʃ] = **de** + **os**.

dosagem [do'zaʒẽ] *m* dosage.

dosar [do'za*] *vt (medicamento)* to judge the correct dosage of; *(graduar)* to give in small doses; **você tem que** ~ **bem o que diz para ele** you have to be careful what you say to him.

dose ['dɔzi] *f* dose; ~ **cavalar** huge dose; ~ **excessiva** overdose; **é** ~ **para leão** *or* **cavalo** *(col)* it's too much.

dossiê [do'sje] *m* dossier, file.

dotação [dota'sãw] *(pl -ões) f* endowment, allocation.

dotado/a [do'tadu/a] *adj* gifted; ~ **de** endowed with.

dotar [do'ta*] *vt (filha)* to give a dowry to; ~

---

alguém de algo to endow sb with sth.
dote ['dɔtʃi] m dowry; (fig) gift.
DOU abr m (= Diário Oficial da União) official journal of Brazilian government.
dou [do] vb V **dar**.
dourado/a [do'radu/a] adj golden; (com camada de ouro) gilt, gilded ♦ m gilt; (cor) golden colour (BRIT) ou color (US).
dourar [do'ra*] vt to gild.
douto/a ['dotu/a] adj learned.
doutor(a) [do'to*(a)] m/f doctor; **D~** (forma de tratamento) Sir; **D~ Eduardo** etc corresponde ao uso de Mr com o sobrenome do homem em inglês.
doutorado [doto'radu] m doctorate.
doutrina [do'trina] f doctrine.
doze ['dozi] num twelve; V tb **cinco**.
DP (BR) abr f = **delegacia policial**.
DPF (BR) abr m = **Departamento de Polícia Federal**.
DPNRE (BR) abr m = **Departamento de Parques Nacionais e Reservas Equivalentes**.
Dr. abr (= Doutor) Dr.
Dra. abr (= Doutora) Dr.
dracma ['drakma] f drachma.
draga ['draga] f dredger.
dragagem [dra'gaʒē] f dredging.
dragão [dra'gãw] (pl -ões) m dragon; (MIL) dragoon.
dragar [dra'ga*] vt to dredge.
drágea [dra'ʒja] f pastille.
dragões [dra'gõjʃ] mpl de **dragão**.
drama ['drama] m (teatro) drama; (peça) play; **fazer ~** (col) to make a scene; **ser um ~** (col) to be an ordeal.
dramalhão [drama'ʎãw] (pl -ões) m melodrama.
dramático/a [dra'matʃiku/a] adj dramatic.
dramatização [dramatʃiza'sãw] (pl -ões) f dramatization.
dramatizar [dramatʃi'za*] vt, vi (tb fig) to dramatize.
dramaturgo/a [drama'tuxgu/a] m/f playwright, dramatist.
drapeado/a [dra'pjadu/a] adj draped ♦ m hang.
drástico/a ['draʃtʃiku/a] adj drastic.
drenagem [dre'naʒē] f drainage.
drenar [dre'na*] vt to drain.
dreno ['drenu] m drain.
driblar [dri'bla*] vt (FUTEBOL) to dribble round; (fig) to get round ♦ vi to dribble.
drinque ['drĩki] m drink.
drive ['drajvi] m (COMPUT) (disk) drive.
droga ['drɔga] f drug; (fig) rubbish ♦ excl: ~! damn!, blast!; **ser uma ~** (col: filme, caneta etc) to be a dead loss; (obrigação, atividade) to be a drag.
drogado/a [dro'gadu/a] m/f drug addict.
drogar [dro'ga*] vt to drug; **~-se** vr to take drugs.
drogaria [droga'ria] f chemist's shop (BRIT), drugstore (US).

dromedário [drome'darju] m dromedary.
duas ['duaʃ] f de **dois**.
duas-peças m inv two-piece.
dúbio/a ['dubju/a] adj dubious; (vago) uncertain.
dublagem [du'blaʒē] f (de filme) dubbing.
dublar [du'bla*] vt to dub.
dublê [du'ble] m/f double.
ducentésimo/a [dusē'tɛzimu/a] num two-hundredth.
ducha ['duʃa] f shower; (MED) douche.
ducto ['duktu] m duct.
duelo ['dwɛlu] m duel.
duende ['dwēdʒi] m elf, sprite.
dueto ['dwetu] m duet.
dulcíssimo/a [duw'sisimu/a] adj superl de **doce**.
dumping ['dãpĩ] m (ECON) dumping.
duna ['duna] f dune.
duodécimo/a [dwo'dɛsimu/a] num twelfth.
duodeno [dwo'dɛnu] m duodenum.
dupla ['dupla] f pair; (ESPORTE): **~ masculina/feminina/mista** men's/women's/mixed doubles.
dúplex ['dupleks] adj inv two-storey (BRIT), two-story (US) ♦ m inv luxury maisonette, duplex.
duplicação [duplika'sãw] f (repetição) duplication; (aumento) doubling.
duplicar [dupli'ka*] vt (repetir) to duplicate ♦ vi (dobrar) to double.
duplicata [dupli'kata] f (cópia) duplicate; (título) trade note, bill.
duplicidade [duplisi'dadʒi] f (fig) duplicity.
duplo/a ['duplu/a] adj double ♦ m double.
duque ['duki] m duke.
duquesa [du'keza] f duchess.
durabilidade [durabili'dadʒi] f durability.
duração [dura'sãw] f duration; **de pouca ~** short-lived.
duradouro/a [dura'doru/a] adj lasting.
durante [du'ratʃi] prep during; **~ uma hora** for an hour.
durão/rona [du'rãw/'rɔna] (col: pl -ões/~s) adj strict, tough.
durar [du'ra*] vi to last.
durável [du'ravew] (pl -eis) adj lasting.
durex [du'rɛks] adj V **fita**.
dureza [du'reza] f hard°ness; (severidade) harshness; (col: falta de dinheiro) lack of funds.
durmo ['duxmu] etc vb V **dormir**.
duro/a ['duru/a] adj hard; (som) harsh; (resistente) tough; (sentença, palavras) harsh, tough; (inverno) hard, harsh; (fig: difícil) hard, tough; **ser ~ com alguém** to be hard on sb; **estar ~** (col) to be broke; **dar um ~** (col: trabalhar) to work hard; **dar um ~ em alguém** (col) to come down hard on sb; **~ de roer** (fig) hard to take; **no ~** (col) really; **a praia estava dura de gente** the beach was packed.
durões [du'rõjʃ] adj pl de **durão**.
durona [du'rɔna] f de **durão**.

DUT (*BR*) *abr m* (= *documento único de trânsito*) *vehicle licensing document.*

dúvida ['duvida] *f* doubt; **sem** ~ undoubtedly, without a doubt.

duvidar [duvi'da*] *vt* to doubt ♦ *vi* to have one's doubts; ~ **de alguém/algo** to doubt sb/sth; ~ **que** ... to doubt that ...; **duvido!** I doubt it!; **duvido que você consiga correr a maratona** I bet you don't manage to run the marathon.

duvidoso/a [duvi'dozu/ɔza] *adj* (*incerto*) doubtful; (*suspeito*) dubious.

duzentos/as [du'zētuʃ/aʃ] *num* two hundred.

dúzia ['duzja] *f* dozen; **meia** ~ half a dozen.

dz. *abr* = **dúzia.**

E

E, e [ε] *m* (*pl* **es**) E, e ♦ *abr* (= *esquerda*) L.; (= *este*) E; (= *editor*) Ed.; **E de Eliane** E for Edward (*BRIT*) *ou* Easy (*US*).

e [i] *conj* and; ~ **a bagagem?** what about the luggage?

é [ε] *vb* V **ser.**

EAPAC (*BR*) *abr f* (= *Escola de Aperfeiçoamento e Preparação Civil*) *civil service training school.*

ébano ['ɛbanu] *m* ebony.

EBN *abr f* = **Empresa Brasileira de Notícias.**

ébrio/a ['ɛbrju/a] *adj* drunk ♦ *m/f* drunkard.

EBTU *abr f* = **Empresa Brasileira de Transportes Urbanos.**

ebulição [ebuli'sãw] *f* boiling; (*fig*) ferment.

ebuliente [ebu'ljētʃi] *adj* boiling.

ECEME (*BR*) *abr f* (= *Escola de Comando e Estado-Maior do Exército*) *officer training school.*

eclesiástico/a [ekle'zjastʃiku/a] *adj* ecclesiastical, church *atr* ♦ *m* clergyman.

eclético/a [e'klɛtʃiku/a] *adj* eclectic.

eclipsar [eklip'sa*] *vt* (*tb fig*) to eclipse.

eclipse [e'klipsi] *m* eclipse.

eclodir [eklo'dʒi*] *vi* (*aparecer*) to emerge; (*revolução*) to break out; (*flor*) to open.

eclusa [e'kluza] *f* (*de canal*) lock; (*comporta*) floodgate.

eco ['ɛku] *m* echo; **ter** ~ to catch on.

ecoar [e'kwa*] *vt* to echo ♦ *vi* (*ressoar*) to echo; (*fig: repercutir*) to have repercussions.

ecologia [ekolo'ʒia] *f* ecology.

ecológico/a [eko'lɔʒiku/a] *adj* ecological.

ecologista [ekolo'ʒiʃta] *m/f* ecologist.

economia [ekono'mia] *f* economy; (*ciência*)

economics *sg*; ~**s** *fpl* savings; **fazer** ~ **(de)** to economize (with).

econômico/a [eko'nomiku/a] *adj* (*barato*) cheap; (*que consome pouco*) economical; (*pessoa*) thrifty; (*COM*) economic.

economista [ekono'miʃta] *m/f* economist.

economizar [ekonomi'za*] *vt* (*gastar com economia*) to economize on; (*poupar*) to save (up) ♦ *vi* to economize; to save up.

écran ['ɛkrã] (*PT*) *m* screen.

ECT *abr f* = **Empresa Brasileira de Correios e Telégrafos.**

ecumênico/a [eku'meniku/a] *adj* ecumenical.

eczema [eg'zema] *m* eczema.

Ed. *abr* = **edifício.**

ed. *abr* = **edição.**

éden ['ɛdē] *m* (*tb fig*) paradise.

edição [edʒi'sãw] (*pl* -**ões**) *f* (*publicação*) publication; (*conjunto de exemplares*) edition; (*TV*, *CINEMA*) editing; ~ **atualizada/revista** updated/revised edition; ~ **extra** special edition; ~ **de imagem** video editing.

edicto [e'ditu] (*PT*) *m* = **edito.**

edificação [edʒifika'sãw] *f* construction, building; (*fig: moral*) edification.

edificante [edʒifi'kãtʃi] *adj* edifying.

edificar [edʒifi'ka*] *vt* (*construir*) to build; (*fig*) to edify ♦ *vi* to be edifying.

edifício [edʒi'fisju] *m* building; ~ **garagem** multistorey car park (*BRIT*), multistory parking lot (*US*).

Edimburgo [edʒĩ'buxgu] *n* Edinburgh.

Édipo ['edʒipu] *m* V **complexo.**

edital [edʒi'taw] (*pl* -**ais**) *m* announcement.

editar [edʒi'ta*] *vt* to publish; (*COMPUT etc*) to edit.

edito [e'dʒitu] *m* edict, decree.

editor(a) [edʒi'to*(a)] *adj* publishing *atr* ♦ *m/f* publisher; (*redator*) editor ♦ *f* publishing company; **casa** ~**a** publishing house; ~ **de imagem** video editor; ~ **de texto** (*COMPUT*) text editor.

editoração [edʒitora'sãw] *f*: ~ **eletrônica** desktop publishing.

editoria [edʒito'ria] *f* section; ~ **de esportes** (*em jornal*) sports desk.

editorial [edʒitor'jaw] (*pl* -**ais**) *adj* publishing *atr* ♦ *m* editorial.

edredão [ədrə'dãw] (*pl* -**ões**) (*PT*) *m* = **edredom.**

edredom [edre'dõ] (*pl* -**ns**) *m* eiderdown.

educação [eduka'sãw] *f* (*ensino*) education; (*criação*) upbringing; (*de animais*) training; (*maneiras*) good manners *pl*; **é falta de** ~ **falar com a boca cheia** it's rude to talk with your mouth full.

educacional [edukasjo'naw] (*pl* -**ais**) *adj* education *atr*.

educado/a [edu'kadu/a] *adj* (*bem-educado*) polite.

NB: European Portuguese adds the following consonants to certain words: **b** (sú(b)dito, su(b)til); **c** (a(c)ção, a(c)cionista, a(c)to); **m** (inde(m)ne); **p** (ado(p)ção, ado(p)tar); *for further details see p. xiii.*

educador(a) [eduka'do*(a)] m/f educator.
educandário [edukã'darju] m educational establishment.
educar [edu'ka*] vt (instruir) to educate; (criar) to bring up; (animal) to train.
educativo/a [eduka'tʃivu/a] adj educational.
efectivamente [efektʃiva'mɛtə] (PT) adv = **efetivamente**.
efectivo/a etc [efek'tivu/a] (PT) adj = **efetivo** etc.
efectuar [efek'twa*] (PT) vt = **efetuar**.
efeito [e'fejtu] m effect; **fazer** ~ to work; **levar a** ~ to put into effect; **com** ~ indeed; **para todos os** ~**s** to all intents and purposes; ~ **colateral** side effect; ~ **estufa** greenhouse effect.
efêmero/a [e'femeru/a] adj ephemeral, short-lived.
efeminado [efemi'nadu] adj effeminate ♦ m effeminate man.
efervescência [efexve'sɛsja] f effervescence; (fig) ferment.
efervescente [efexve'sɛtʃi] adj fizzy.
efervescer [efexve'se*] vi to fizz; (fig) to hum.
efetivamente [efetʃiva'mɛtʃi] adv effectively; (realmente) really, in fact.
efetivar [efetʃi'va*] vt (mudanças, cortes) to bring into effect; (professor, estagiário) to take on permanently.
efetividade [efetʃivi'dadʒi] f effectiveness; (realidade) reality.
efetivo/a [efe'tʃivu/a] adj effective; (real) actual, real; (cargo, funcionário) permanent ♦ m (COM) liquid assets pl.
efetuar [efe'twa*] vt to carry out; (soma) to do, perform.
eficácia [efi'kasja] f (de pessoa) efficiency; (de tratamento) effectiveness.
eficacíssimo/a [efika'sisimu/a] adj superl de **eficaz**.
eficaz [efi'kaʒ] adj (pessoa) efficient; (tratamento) effective.
eficiência [efi'sjɛsja] f efficiency.
eficiente [efi'sjɛtʃi] adj efficient, competent.
efígie [e'fiʒi] f effigy.
efusão [efu'zãw] (pl -ões) f effusion.
efusivo/a [efu'zivu/a] adj effusive.
efusões [efu'zõjʃ] fpl de **efusão**.
Egeu [e'ʒew] m: **o (mar)** ~ the Aegean (Sea).
EGF (BR) abr m = **empréstimo do governo federal**.
égide ['ɛʒidʒi] f: **sob a** ~ **de** under the aegis (BRIT) ou egis (US) of.
egípcio/a [e'ʒipsju/a] adj, m/f Egyptian.
Egito [e'ʒitu] (PT: -pt-) m: **o** ~ Egypt.
ego ['ɛgu] m ego.
egocêntrico/a [ego'sɛtriku/a] adj self-centred (BRIT), self-centered (US), egocentric.
egoísmo [ego'iʒmu] m selfishness, egoism.
egoísta [ego'iʃta] adj selfish, egoistic ♦ m/f egoist ♦ m earplug.
egolatria [egola'tria] f self-admiration.
egotismo [ego'tʃiʒmu] m egotism.

egotista [ego'tʃiʃta] m/f egotist ♦ adj egotistical.
egrégio/a [e'greʒju/a] adj distinguished.
egresso [e'grɛsu] m (preso) ex-prisoner; (frade) former monk; (universidade) graduate.
égua ['ɛgwa] f mare.
ei [ej] excl hey!
ei-lo etc = **eis** + **o**; V **eis**.
eira ['ejra] (PT) f threshing floor; **sem** ~ **nem beira** down and out.
eis [ejʃ] adv (sg) here is; (pl) here are; ~ **aí** there is; there are.
eivado/a [ej'vadu/a] adj (fig) full.
eixo ['ejʃu] m (de rodas) axle; (MAT) axis; (de máquina) shaft; ~ **de transmissão** drive shaft; **entrar nos** ~**s** (pessoa) to get back on the straight and narrow; (situação) to get back to normal; **pôr algo/alguém nos** ~**s** to set sth/sb straight; **sair dos** ~**s** to step out of line; **o** ~ **Rio-São Paulo** the Rio-São Paulo area.
ejacular [eʒaku'la*] vt (sêmen) to ejaculate; (líquido) to spurt ♦ vi to ejaculate.
ejetar [eʒe'ta*] vt to eject.
ela ['ɛla] pron (pessoa) she; (coisa) it; (com prep: pessoa) her; (: coisa) it; ~**s** fpl they; (com prep) them; ~**s por** ~**s** (col) tit for tat; **aí é que são** ~**s** (col) that's just the point.
elã [e'lã] m enthusiasm, drive.
elaboração [elabora'sãw] (pl -ões) f (de uma teoria) working out; (preparo) preparation.
elaborador(a) [elabora'do*(a)] m/f maker.
elaborar [elabo'ra*] vt (preparar) to prepare; (fazer) to make.
elasticidade [elaʃtʃisi'dadʒi] f elasticity; (flexibilidade) suppleness.
elástico/a [e'laʃtʃiku/a] adj elastic; (flexível) flexible; (colchão) springy ♦ m elastic band.
ele ['eli] pron he; (coisa) it; (com prep: pessoa) him; (: coisa) it; ~**s** mpl they; (com prep) them.
electri... etc [elektri...] (PT) = **eletri...** etc.
eléctrico/a [e'lɛktriku/a] (PT) adj = **elétrico** ♦ m tram (BRIT), streetcar (US).
electro... etc [elektru...] (PT) = **eletro...** etc.
eléctrodo [e'lɛktrodu] (PT) m = **eletrodo**.
elefante/ta [ele'fãtʃi/ta] m/f elephant; (col: pessoa gorda) fatso, fatty; ~ **branco** (fig) white elephant.
elefantino/a [elefã'tʃinu/a] adj elephantine.
elegância [ele'gãsja] f elegance.
elegante [ele'gãtʃi] adj elegant; (da moda) fashionable.
eleger [ele'ʒe*] vt (por votação) to elect; (escolher) to choose.
elegia [ele'ʒia] f elegy.
elegibilidade [eleʒibili'dadʒi] f eligibility.
elegível [ele'ʒivew] (pl -eis) adj eligible.
eleição [elej'sãw] (pl -ões) f (por votação) election; (escolha) choice.
eleito/a [e'lejtu/a] pp de **eleger** ♦ adj (por

votação) elected; (*escolhido*) chosen.
eleitor(a) [elej'to*(a)] *m/f* voter.
eleitorado [elejto'radu] *m* electorate; **conhecer o seu** ~ (*fig: col*) to know what one is up against.
eleitoral [elejto'raw] (*pl* **-ais**) *adj* electoral.
elejo [ele'ʒu] *etc vb* V **eleger**.
elementar [elemẽ'ta*] *adj* (*simples*) elementary; (*fundamental*) basic, fundamental.
elemento [ele'mẽtu] *m* element; (*parte*) component; (*ambiente*) element; (*recurso*) means; (*informação*) grounds *pl*; ~**s** *mpl* rudiments; **ele é mau** ~ he's a bad lot.
elenco [e'lẽku] *m* list; (*de atores*) cast.
elepê [eli'pe] *m* LP, album.
eletivo/a [ele'tʃivu/a] *adj* elective.
eletricidade [eletrisi'dadʒi] *f* electricity.
eletricista [eletri'siʃta] *m/f* electrician.
elétrico/a [e'letriku/a] *adj* electric; (*fig*: *agitado*) worked up.
eletrificar [eletrifi'ka*] *vt* to electrify.
eletrizar [eletri'za*] *vt* to electrify; (*fig*) to thrill.
eletro [e'lɛtru] *m* (*MED*) ECG.
eletro... [eletru] *prefixo* electro....
Eletrobrás [eletro'braʃ] *abr f* Brazilian state electricity company.
eletrocutar [eletroku'ta*] *vt* to electrocute.
eletrodo [ele'trodu] *m* electrode.
eletrodomésticos [eletrodo'mɛʃtʃikuʃ] (*BR*) *mpl* (electrical) household appliances.
eletrônica [ele'tronika] *f* electronics *sg*.
eletrônico/a [ele'troniku/a] *adj* electronic.
elevação [eleva'sãw] (*pl* **-ões**) *f* (*ARQ*) elevation; (*aumento*) rise; (*ato*) raising; (*altura*) height; (*promoção*) elevation, promotion; (*ponto elevado*) bump.
elevado/a [ele'vadu/a] *adj* high; (*pensamento, estilo*) elevated ♦ *m* (*via*) elevated road.
elevador [eleva'do*] *m* lift (*BRIT*), elevator (*US*); ~ **de serviço** service lift.
elevar [ele'va*] *vt* (*levantar*) to lift up; (*voz, preço*) to raise; (*exaltar*) to exalt; (*promover*) to elevate, promote; ~**-se** *vr* to rise.
eliminação [elimina'sãw] *f* elimination.
eliminar [elimi'na*] *vt* to remove, eliminate; (*suprimir*) to delete; (*possibilidade*) to eliminate, rule out; (*MED, banir*) to expel; (*ESPORTE*) to eliminate.
eliminatória [elimina'tɔrja] *f* (*ESPORTE*) heat, preliminary round; (*exame*) test.
eliminatório/a [elimina'tɔrju/a] *adj* eliminatory.
elipse [e'lipsi] *f* ellipse; (*LING*) ellipsis.
elite [e'litʃi] *f* elite.
elitismo [eli'tʃiʒmu] *m* elitism.
elitista [eli'tʃiʃta] *adj*, *m/f* elitist.
elitizar [elitʃi'za*] *vt* (*arte, ensino*) to make elitist.

elixir [elik'si*] *m* elixir.
elo ['elu] *m* link.
elocução [eloku'sãw] *f* elocution.
elogiar [elo'ʒja*] *vt* to praise; ~ **alguém por algo** to compliment sb on sth.
elogio [elo'ʒiu] *m* praise; (*cumprimento*) compliment.
elogioso/a [elo'ʒozu/ɔza] *adj* complimentary.
eloqüência [elo'kwẽsja] *f* eloquence.
eloqüente [elo'kwẽtʃi] *adj* eloquent; (*persuasivo*) persuasive.
El Salvador [ew-] *n* El Salvador.
elucidação [elusida'sãw] *f* elucidation.
elucidar [elusi'da*] *vt* to elucidate, clarify.
elucidativo/a [elusida'tʃivu/a] *adj* elucidatory.
elucubração [elukubra'sãw] (*pl* **-ões**) *f* cogitation, musing.
em [ẽ] *prep* in; (*sobre*) on; **no bolso** in the pocket; **na mesa** on the table; **no Brasil** in Brazil; ~ **casa** at home; ~ **São Paulo** in São Paulo; **nessa altura** at that time; ~ **breve** soon; **nessa ocasião** on that occasion; **tudo aconteceu** ~ **6 dias** it all happened in *or* within six days; **fui lá na vizinha** I went to my neighbour's; **estou na vizinha** I'm at my neighbour's; **ir de porta** ~ **porta** to go from door to door; **reduzir/aumentar** ~ **20%** to reduce/increase by 20%.
Emaer [ema'e*] (*BR*) *abr m* = **Estado-Maior da Aeronáutica**.
emagrecer [imagre'se*] *vt* to make thin ♦ *vi* to grow thin; (*mediante regime*) to slim.
emagrecimento [imagresi'mẽtu] *m* (*mediante regime*) slimming.
emanar [ema'na*] *vi*: ~ **de** to come from, emanate from.
emancipação [imãsipa'sãw] (*pl* **-ões**) *f* emancipation; (*atingir a maioridade*) coming of age.
emancipar [imãsi'pa*] *vt* to emancipate; ~**-se** *vr* (*atingir a maioridade*) to come of age.
emaranhado/a [imara'ɲadu/a] *adj* tangled ♦ *m* tangle.
emaranhar [imara'ɲa*] *vt* to tangle; (*complicar*) to complicate; ~**-se** *vr* to get entangled; (*fig*) to get mixed up.
emassar [ema'sa*] *vt* (*parede*) to plaster; (*janela*) to putty.
Emater [ema'te*] (*BR*) *abr f* (= *Empresa de Assistência Técnica e Extensão Rural*) company giving aid to farmers.
embaçado/a [ẽba'sadu/a] *adj* (*vidro*) steamed up.
embaçar [ẽba'sa*] *vt* to steam up.
embaciado/a [ẽba'sjadu/a] *adj* dull; (*vidro*) misted; (*janela*) steamed up; (*olhos*) misty.
embaciar [ẽba'sja*] *vt* (*vidro*) to steam up; (*olhos*) to cloud ♦ *vi* to steam up; (*olhos*) grow misty.
embainhar [ẽbaj'ɲa*] *vt* (*espada*) to put

NB: *European Portuguese adds the following consonants to certain words:* **b** (sú(b)dito, su(b)til); **c** (a(c)ção, a(c)cionista, a(c)to); **m** (inde(m)ne); **p** (ado(p)ção, ado(p)tar); *for further details see p. xiii.*

away, sheathe; (calça etc) to hem.
embaixada [ēbaj'ʃada] f embassy.
embaixador(a) [ēbajʃa'do*(a)] m/f ambassador.
embaixatriz [ēbajʃa'triʒ] f ambassador; (mulher de embaixador) ambassador's wife.
embaixo [ē'bajʃu] adv below, underneath ♦ prep: ~ **de** under, underneath; **(lá)** ~ (em andar inferior) downstairs.
embalado/a [ēba'ladu/a] adj (acelerado) fast; (drogado) high; **ir** ~ to race (along).
embalagem [ēba'laʒē] f packing; (de produto: caixa etc) packaging.
embalar [ēba'la*] vt to pack; (balançar) to rock.
embalo [ē'balu] m (balanço) rocking; (impulso) rush; (col: com drogas) high; **aproveitar o** ~ to take the opportunity.
embalsamar [ēbawsa'ma*] vt (perfumar) to perfume; (cadáver) to embalm.
embananado/a [ēbana'nadu/a] (col) adj (confuso) muddled; (em dificuldades) in trouble.
embananamento [ēbanana'mētu] (col) m muddle; (bananosa) jam.
embananar [ēbana'na*] (col) vt (tornar confuso) to muddle up; (complicar) to complicate; (meter em dificuldades) to get into trouble; ~-**se** vr to get tied up in knots.
embaraçar [ēbara'sa*] vt (impedir) to hinder; (complicar) to complicate; (encabular) to embarrass; (confundir) to confuse; (obstruir) to block; ~-**se** vr to become embarrassed.
embaraço [ēba'rasu] m (estorvo) hindrance; (cábula) embarrassment.
embaraçoso/a [ēbara'sozu/ɔza] adj embarrassing.
embarafustar [ēbarafuʃ'ta*] vi: ~ **por** to burst ou barge into.
embaralhar [ēbara'ʎa*] vt (confundir) to muddle up; (cartas) to shuffle; ~-**se** vr to get mixed up.
embarcação [ēbaxka'sāw] (pl -ões) f vessel.
embarcadiço [ēbaxka'dʒisu] m seafarer.
embarcadouro [ēbaxka'doru] m wharf.
embarcar [ēbax'ka*] vt to embark, put on board; (mercadorias) to ship, stow ♦ vi to go on board, embark; ~ **em algo** (fig: col) to fall for sth.
embargar [ēbax'ga*] vt (JUR) to seize; (pôr obstáculos a) to hinder; (reprimir: voz) to keep down; (impedir) to forbid.
embargo [ē'baxgu] m (de navio) embargo; (JUR) seizure; (impedimento) impediment; **sem** ~ nevertheless.
embarque [ē'baxkɪ] m (de pessoas) boarding, embarkation; (de mercadorias) shipment.
embasamento [ēbaza'mētu] m (ARQ) foundation; (de coluna) base; (fig) basis.
embasbacado/a [ēbaʒba'kadu/a] adj gaping, open-mouthed.
embasbacar [ēbaʒba'ka*] vt to leave open-mouthed; ~-**se** vr to be taken aback, be dumbfounded.

embate [ē'batʃi] m clash; (choque) shock.
embatucar [ēbatu'ka*] vt to dumbfound ♦ vi to be speechless.
embebedar [ēbebe'da*] vt to make drunk ♦ vi: **o vinho embebeda** wine makes you drunk; ~-**se** vr to get drunk.
embeber [ēbe'be*] vt to soak up, absorb; ~-**se** vr: ~-**se em** to become absorbed in.
embelezador(a) [ēbeleza'do*(a)] adj cosmetic.
embelezar [ēbele'za*] vt to make beautiful; (casa) to brighten up; ~-**se** vr to make o.s. beautiful.
embevecer [ēbeve'se*] vt to captivate; ~-**se** vr to be captivated.
embicar [ēbi'ka*] vi (NÁUT) to enter port, dock; (fig): ~ **para** to head for; ~ **com alguém** to quarrel with sb.
embirrar [ēbi'xa*] vi to sulk; ~ **em** to insist on; ~ **com** to dislike.
emblema [ē'blema] m emblem; (na roupa) badge.
embocadura [ēboka'dura] f (de rio) mouth; (MÚS) mouthpiece; (de freio) bit.
emboço [ē'bosu] m roughcast, render.
embolar [ēbo'la*] vt (confundir) to confuse ♦ vi: ~ **com** to grapple with; ~-**se** vr: ~-**se (com)** to grapple (with).
êmbolo ['ēbolu] m piston.
embolorar [ēbolo'ra*] vi to go musty.
embolsar [ēbow'sa*] vt to pocket; (herança etc) to come by; (indenizar) to refund.
embonecar [ēbone'ka*] vt to doll up; ~-**se** vr to doll o.s. up, get dolled up.
embora [ē'bɔra] conj though, although ♦ excl even so, what of it?; **ir(-se)** ~ to go away.
emborcar [ēbox'ka*] vt to turn upside down.
emboscada [ēboʃ'kada] f ambush.
embotar [ēbo'ta*] vt (lâmina) to blunt; (fig) to deaden, dull.
embrabecer [ēbrabe'se*] vi = **embravecer**.
Embraer [ēbrãe*] abr f (= Empresa Brasileira de Aeronáutica SA) aerospace company.
embranquecer [ēbrãke'se*] vt, vi to turn white.
Embratur [ēbra'tu*] abr f (= Empresa Brasileira de Turismo) state tourist board.
embravecer [ēbrave'se*] vr to get furious; ~-**se** vr to get furious.
embreagem [ēb'rjaʒē] (pl -ns) f (AUTO) clutch.
embrear [ē'brja*] vt (AUTO) to disengage ♦ vi to let in the clutch.
embrenhar [ēbre'ɲa*] vt to penetrate; ~-**se** vr: ~-**se (em/por)** to make one's way (into/through).
embriagante [ēbrja'gātʃi] adj intoxicating.
embriagar [ēbrja'ga*] vt to make drunk, intoxicate; ~-**se** vr to get drunk.
embriaguez [ēbrja'geʒ] f drunkenness; (fig) rapture; ~ **no volante** drunk(en) driving.
embrião [e'brjãw] (pl -ões) m embryo.
embrionário/a [ēbrjo'narju/a] adj (tb fig) embryonic.

embromação [ēbroma'sãw] (pl -ões) f stalling; (trapaça) con.

embromador(a) [ēbroma'do*(a)] adj (remanchador) slow; (trapaçeiro) dishonest, bent ♦ m/f (remanchador) staller; (trapaçeiro) con merchant.

embromar [ēbro'ma*] vt to put off, string along; (enganar) to con, cheat ♦ vi (prometer e não cumprir) to make empty promises, be all talk (and no action); (protelar) to stall; (falar em rodeios) to beat about the bush.

embrulhada [ēbru'ʎada] f muddle, mess.

embrulhar [ēbru'ʎa*] vt (pacote) to wrap; (enrolar) to roll up; (confundir) to muddle up; (enganar) to cheat; (estômago) to upset; ~-se vr to get into a muddle; **ao contar a estória, ele embrulhou tudo** when he told the story he got everything mixed up.

embrulho [ē'bruʎu] m (pacote) package, parcel; (confusão) mix-up.

embrutecer [ēbrute'se*] vt to brutalize ♦ vi to have a brutalizing effect; ~-se vr to be brutalized.

emburrar [ēbu'xa*] vi to sulk.

embuste [ē'buʃtʃi] m (engano) deception; (ardil) trick.

embusteiro/a [ēbuʃ'tejru/a] adj deceitful ♦ m/f cheat; (mentiroso) liar; (impostor) impostor.

embutido/a [ēbu'tʃidu/a] adj (armário) built-in, fitted.

embutir [ēbu'tʃi*] vt to build in; (marfim etc) to inlay.

emenda [e'mēda] f correction; (JUR) amendment; (de uma pessoa) improvement; (ligação) join; (sambladura) joint; (COSTURA) seam.

emendar [emē'da*] vt (corrigir) to correct; (reparar) to mend; (injustiças) to make amends for; (JUR) to amend; (ajuntar) to put together; ~-se vr to mend one's ways.

ementa [e'mēta] (PT) f menu.

emergência [imex'ʒēsja] f (nascimento) emergence; (crise) emergency.

emergente [imex'ʒētʃi] adj emerging.

emergir [imex'ʒi*] vi to emerge, appear; (submarino) to surface.

EMFA (BR) abr m = **Estado-maior das Forças Armadas**.

emigração [emigra'sãw] (pl -ões) f emigration; (de aves) migration.

emigrado/a [emi'gradu/a] adj emigrant.

emigrante [emi'grãtʃi] m/f emigrant.

emigrar [emi'gra*] vi to emigrate; (aves) to migrate.

eminência [emi'nēsja] f eminence; (altura) height.

eminente [emi'nētʃi] adj eminent, distinguished; (GEO) high.

Emirados Árabes Unidos [emi'raduʃ-] mpl:

os ~ the United Arab Emirates.

emirjo [e'mixʒu] etc vb V **emergir**.

emissão [emi'sãw] (pl -ões) f emission; (RÁDIO) broadcast; (de moeda, ações) issue.

emissário/a [emi'sarju/a] m/f emissary ♦ m outlet.

emissões [emi'sõjʃ] fpl de **emissão**.

emissor(a) [emi'so*(a)] adj (de moeda-papel) issuing ♦ m (RÁDIO) transmitter ♦ f (estação) broadcasting station; (empresa) broadcasting company.

emitente [emi'tētʃi] adj (COM) issuing ♦ m/f (COM) issuer.

emitir [emi'tʃi*] vt (som) to give out; (cheiro) to give off; (moeda, ações) to issue; (RÁDIO) to broadcast; (opinião) to express ♦ vi (emitir moeda) to print money.

emoção [emo'sãw] (pl -ões) f emotion; (excitação) excitement.

emocional [imosjo'naw] (pl -ais) adj emotional.

emocionante [imosjo'nãtʃi] adj (comovente) moving; (excitante) exciting.

emocionar [imosjo'na*] vt (comover) to move; (perturbar) to upset; (excitar) to excite, thrill ♦ vi to be exciting; (comover) to be moving; ~-se vr to get emotional.

emoções [emo'sõjʃ] fpl de **emoção**.

emoldurar [emowdu'ra*] vt to frame.

emotividade [emotʃivi'dadʒi] f emotions pl.

emotivo/a [emo'tʃivu/a] adj emotional.

empacar [ēpa'ka*] vi (cavalo) to baulk; (fig: negócios etc) to grind to a halt; (orador) to dry up; ~ **numa palavra** to get stuck on a word.

empachado/a [ēpa'ʃadu/a] adj full up.

empacotar [ēpako'ta*] vt to pack, wrap up ♦ vi (col: morrer) to pop one's clogs.

empada [ē'pada] f pie.

empadão [ēpa'dãw] (pl -ões) m pie.

empalhar [ēpa'ʎa*] vt (animal) to stuff; (louça, fruta) to pack with straw.

empalidecer [ēpalide'se*] vt, vi to turn pale.

empanar [ēpa'na*] vt (fig) to tarnish; (CULIN) to batter.

empanturrar [ēpātu'xa*] vt: ~ **alguém de algo** to stuff sb full of sth; ~-se vr to gorge o.s., stuff o.s. (col).

empanzinado/a [ēpãzi'nadu/a] adj full.

empapar [ēpa'pa*] vt to soak; ~-se vr to get soaked.

empapuçado/a [ēpapu'sadu/a] adj (olhos) puffy; (blusa) full.

emparedar [ēpare'da*] vt to wall in; (pessoa) to shut up.

emparelhar [ēpare'ʎa*] vt to pair; (equiparar) to match ♦ vi: ~ **com** to be equal to.

empastado/a [ēpaʃ'tadu/a] adj (cabelo) plastered down.

empastar [ēpaʃ'ta*] vt: ~ **algo de algo** to

NB: *European Portuguese adds the following consonants to certain words:* **b** (sú(b)dito, su(b)til); **c** (a(c)ção, a(c)cionista, a(c)to); **m** (inde(m)ne); **p** (ado(p)ção, ado(p)tar); *for further details see p. xiii.*

plaster sth with sth.

empatar [ẽpa'ta*] *vt* (*embaraçar*) to hinder; (*dinheiro*) to tie up; (*no jogo*) to draw; (*corredores*) to tie; (*tempo*) to take up ♦ *vi* (*no jogo*): ~ **(com)** to draw (with).

empate [ẽ'patʃi] *m* (*no jogo*) draw; (*numa corrida etc*) tie; (*XADREZ*) stalemate; (*em negociações*) deadlock.

empatia [ẽpa'tʃia] *f* empathy.

empavonar-se [ẽpavo'naxsi] *vr* to strut.

empecilho [ẽpe'siʎu] *m* obstacle; (*col*) snag.

empedernido/a [ẽpedex'nidu/a] *adj* hard-hearted.

empedrar [ẽpe'dra*] *vt* to pave.

empenar [ẽpe'na*] *vt*, *vi* (*curvar*) to warp.

empenhar [ẽpe'ɲa*] *vt* (*objeto*) to pawn; (*palavra*) to pledge; (*empregar*) to exert; (*compelir*) to oblige; ~**-se** *vr*: ~**-se em fazer** to strive to do, do one's utmost to do.

empenho [ẽ'peɲu] *m* (*de um objeto*) pawning; (*palavra*) pledge; (*insistência*): ~ **(em)** commitment (to); **ele pôs todo seu ~ neste projeto** he committed himself wholeheartedly to this project .

emperiquitar-se [ẽperiki'taxsi] *vr* to get done up to the nines.

emperrar [ẽpe'xa*] *vt* (*máquina*) to jam; (*porta, junta*) to make stiff; (*fazer calar*) to cut short ♦ *vi* (*máquina*) to jam; (*gaveta, porta*) to stick; (*junta*) to go stiff; (*calar*) to go quiet.

empertigado/a [ẽpextʃi'gadu/a] *adj* upright.

empertigar-se [ẽpextʃi'gaxsi] *vr* to stand up straight.

empestar [ẽpeʃ'ta*] *vt* (*infetar*) to infect; (*tornar desagradável*) to pollute, stink out (*col*).

empetecar [ẽpete'ka*] *vt* to doll up; ~**-se** *vr* to doll o.s. up.

empilhar [ẽpi'ʎa*] *vt* to pile up.

empinado/a [ẽpi'nadu/a] *adj* (*direito*) upright; (*cavalo*) rearing; (*colina*) steep.

empinar [ẽpi'na*] *vt* to raise, uplift; (*ressaltar*) to thrust out; (*papagaio*) to fly; (*copo*) to empty.

empipocar [ẽpipo'ka*] *vi* to come out in spots.

empírico/a [ẽ'piriku/a] *adj* empirical.

empistolado/a [ẽpiʃto'ladu/a] *adj* with contacts.

emplacar [ẽpla'ka*] *vt* (*col: anos, sucessos*) to notch up; (*carro*) to put number (*BRIT*) *ou* license (*US*) plates on; ~ **o ano 2000** to make it to the year 2000.

emplastrar [ẽplaʃ'tra*] *vt* to put in plaster.

emplastro [ẽ'plaʃtru] *m* (*MED*) plaster.

empobrecer [ẽpobre'se*] *vt* to impoverish ♦ *vi* to become poor.

empobrecimento [ẽpobresi'mẽtu] *m* impoverishment.

empoeirar [ẽpoej'ra*] *vt* to cover in dust.

empola [ẽ'pola] *f* (*na pele*) blister; (*de água*) bubble.

empolado/a [ẽpo'ladu/a] *adj* covered with

blisters; (*estilo*) pompous, bombastic.

empolgação [ẽpowga'sãw] *f* excitement; (*entusiasmo*) enthusiasm.

empolgante [ẽpow'gãtʃi] *adj* exciting.

empolgar [ẽpow'ga*] *vt* to stimulate, fill with enthusiasm; (*prender a atenção de*): ~ **alguém** to keep sb riveted.

emporcalhar [ẽpoxka'ʎa*] *vt* to dirty; ~**-se** *vr* to get dirty.

empório [ẽ'pɔrju] *m* (*mercado*) market; (*armazém*) department store.

empossar [ẽpo'sa*] *vt* to appoint.

empreendedor(a) [ẽprjẽde'do*(a)] *adj* enterprising ♦ *m/f* entrepreneur.

empreender [ẽprjẽ'de*] *vt* to undertake.

empreendimento [ẽprjẽdʒi'mẽtu] *m* undertaking.

empregada [ẽpre'gada] *f* (*BR*: *doméstica*) maid; (*PT*: *de restaurante*) waitress; *V tb* **empregado**.

empregado/a [ẽpre'gadu/a] *m/f* employee; (*em escritório*) clerk ♦ *m* (*PT*: *de restaurante*) waiter.

empregador(a) [ẽprega'do*(a)] *m/f* employer.

empregar [ẽpre'ga*] *vt* (*pessoa*) to employ; (*coisa*) to use; ~**-se** *vr* to get a job.

empregatício/a [ẽprega'tʃisju/a] *adj* **V vínculo**.

emprego [ẽ'pregu] *m* (*ocupação*) job; (*uso*) use.

empreguismo [ẽpre'giʒmu] *m* patronage, nepotism.

empreitada [ẽprej'tada] *f* (*COM*) contract job; (*tarefa*) enterprise, venture.

empreiteira [ẽprej'tejra] *f* (*firma*) contractor.

empreiteiro [ẽprej'tejru] *m* contractor.

empresa [ẽ'preza] *f* undertaking; (*COM*) enterprise, firm.

empresariado [ẽpreza'rjadu] *m* business community.

empresarial [ẽpreza'rjaw] (*pl*: **-ais**) *adj* business *atr*.

empresário/a [ẽpre'zarju/a] *m/f* businessman/woman; (*de cantor, boxeador etc*) manager; ~ **teatral** impresario.

emprestado/a [ẽpreʃ'tadu/a] *adj* on loan; **pedir** ~ to borrow.

emprestar [ẽpreʃ'ta*] *vt* to lend.

empréstimo [ẽ'preʃtʃimu] *m* loan.

emproado/a [ẽpro'adu/a] *adj* arrogant.

empulhação [ẽpuʎa'sãw] (*pl* **-ões**) *f* (*ato*) trickery; (*embuste*) con.

empulhar [ẽpu'ʎa*] *vt* to trick, con.

empunhar [ẽpu'ɲa*] *vt* to grasp, seize.

empurrão [ẽpu'xãw] (*pl* **-ões**) *m* push, shove; **aos empurrões** jostling.

empurrar [ẽpu'xa*] *vt* to push.

empurrões [ẽpu'xõjʃ] *mpl de* **empurrão**.

emudecer [emude'se*] *vt* to silence ♦ *vi* to fall silent, go quiet.

emular [emu'la*] *vt* to emulate.

enaltecer [enawte'se*] *vt* (*fig*) to elevate.

enamorado/a [enamo'radu/a] *adj* (*encantar*)

enchanted; (apaixonado) in love.

ENAP (BR) abr f (= **Escola Nacional de Administração Pública**) civil service training school.

encabeçar [ĕkabe'sa*] vt to head.

encabulação [ĕkabula'sãw] f (vergonha) embarrassment; (acanhamento) shyness.

encabulado/a [ĕkabu'ladu/a] adj shy.

encabular [ĕkabu'la*] vt to embarrass ♦ vi (fato, situação) to be embarrassing; (pessoa) to get embarrassed; **não se encabule!** don't be shy!

encaçapar [ĕkasa'pa*] vt (bola) to sink; (col: surrar) to bash.

encadeamento [ĕkadʒja'mĕtu] m (série) chain; (conexão) link.

encadear [ĕka'dʒja*] vt to chain together, link together.

encadernação [ĕkadexna'sãw] (pl -ões) f (de livro) binding.

encadernado/a [ĕkadex'nadu/a] adj bound; (de capa dura) hardback.

encadernador(a) [ĕkadexna'do*(a)] m/f bookbinder.

encadernar [ĕkadex'na*] vt to bind.

encafuar [ĕka'fwa*] vt to hide; **~-se** vr to hide.

encaixar [ĕkaj'ʃa*] vt (colocar) to fit in; (inserir) to insert ♦ vi to fit.

encaixe [ĕ'kajʃi] m (ato) fitting; (ranhura) groove; (buraco) socket.

encaixotar [ĕkajʃo'ta*] vt to pack into boxes.

encalacrar [ĕkala'kra*] vt: ~ **alguém** to get sb into trouble; **~-se** vr to get into debt.

encalço [ĕ'kawsu] m pursuit; **ir no ~ de** to pursue.

encalhado/a [ĕka'ʎadu/a] adj stranded; (mercadoria) unsaleable; (col: solteiro) unmarried.

encalhar [ĕka'ʎa*] vi (embarcação) to run aground; (fig: processo) to grind to a halt; (: mercadoria) to be returned, not to sell; (col: ficar solteiro) to be left on the shelf.

encalorado/a [ĕkalo'radu/a] adj hot.

encaminhar [ĕkami'ɲa*] vt (dirigir) to direct; (no bom caminho) to put on the right path; (processo) to set in motion; **~-se** vr: **~-se para/a** to set out for/to; **eu encaminhei-os para a seção devida** I referred them to the appropriate department; **~ uma petição a alguém** to refer an application to sb; **foi minha mãe quem me encaminhou para as letras** it was my mother who steered me towards literature; **as coisas se encaminham bem no momento** things are going well at the moment.

encampar [ĕkã'pa*] vt (empresa) to expropriate; (opinião, medida) to adopt.

encanador [ĕkana'do*] (BR) m plumber.

encanamento [ĕkana'mĕtu] (BR) m plumbing.

encanar [ĕka'na*] vt to channel; (BR: col: prender) to throw in jail.

encanecido/a [ĕkane'sidu/a] adj grey (BRIT), gray (US); (cabelo) white.

encantado/a [ĕkã'tadu/a] adj (contente) delighted; (castelo etc) enchanted; (fascinado): ~ **(por alguém/algo)** to be smitten (with sb/sth).

encantador(a) [ĕkãta'do*(a)] adj delightful, charming ♦ m/f enchanter/enchantress.

encantamento [ĕkãta'mĕtu] m (magia) spell; (fascinação) charm.

encantar [ĕkã'ta*] vt (enfeitiçar) to bewitch; (cativar) to charm; (deliciar) to delight.

encanto [ĕ'kãtu] m (delícia) delight; (fascinação) charm.

encapar [ĕka'pa*] vt (cobrir) to cover; (envolver) to wrap; (livro) to cover.

encapelar [ĕkape'la*] vt (mar) to swell ♦ vi (mar) to turn rough.

encapetado/a [ĕkape'tadu/a] adj (criança) mischievous.

encapotar [ĕkapo'ta*] vt to wrap up; **~-se** vr to wrap o.s. up.

encaracolar [ĕkarako'la*] vt, vi to curl; **~-se** vr to curl up.

encarangar [ĕkarã'ga*] vt to cripple ♦ vi (pessoa) to be crippled; (reumatismo) to be crippling.

encarapinhado/a [ĕkarapi'ɲadu/a] adj (cabelo) frizzy.

encarapitar [ĕkarapi'ta*] vt to perch; **~-se** vr: **~-se em algo** to climb on top of sth; (num cargo etc) to get o.s. fixed up in sth.

encarar [ĕka'ra*] vt to face; (olhar) to look at; (considerar) to consider.

encarcerar [ĕkaxse'ra*] vt to imprison.

encardido/a [ĕkax'dʒidu/a] adj (roupa, casa) grimy; (pele) sallow.

encardir [ĕkax'dʒi*] vt to make grimy ♦ vi to get grimy.

encarecer [ĕkare'se*] vt (subir o preço) to raise the price of; (louvar) to praise; (exagerar) to exaggerate ♦ vi to go up in price, get dearer.

encarecidamente [ĕkaresida'mĕtʃi] adv insistently.

encarecimento [ĕkaresi'mĕtu] m (preço) increase.

encargo [ĕ'kaxgu] m (responsabilidade) responsibility; (ocupação) job, assignment; (oneroso) burden; **dar a alguém o ~ de fazer** to give sb the job of doing sth.

encarnação [ĕkaxna'sãw] (pl -ões) f incarnation.

encarnado/a [ĕkax'nadu/a] adj red, scarlet.

encarnar [ĕkax'na*] vt to embody, personify; (TEATRO) to play ♦ vi to be embodied; **~-se** vr to be embodied; **~ em alguém** (col) to pick on sb.

encarneirado/a [ẽkaxnej'radu/a] *adj* (*mar*) choppy.

encaroçar [ẽkaro'sa*] *vi* (*molho*) to go lumpy; (*pele*) to come up in bumps.

encarquilhado/a [ẽkaxki'ʎadu/a] *adj* (*fruta*) wizened; (*rosto*) wrinkled.

encarregado/a [ẽkaxe'gadu/a] *adj*: ~ **de** in charge of ♦ *m/f* person in charge ♦ *m* (*de operários*) foreman; ~ **de negócios** chargé d'affaires.

encarregar [ẽkaxe'ga*] *vt*: ~ **alguém de algo** to put sb in charge of sth; ~**-se** *vr*: ~**-se de fazer** to undertake to do.

encarreirar [ẽkaxej'ra*] *vt* to guide; (*negócios*) to run; (*moralmente*): ~ **alguém** to put sb on the right track.

encarrilhar [ẽkaxi'ʎa*] *vt* to put back on the rails; (*fig*) to put on the right track.

encartar [ẽkax'ta*] *vt* to insert.

encarte [ẽ'kaxtʃi] *m* insert.

encasacar-se [ẽkaza'kaxsi] *vr* to put on one's coat.

encasquetar [ẽkaʃke'ta*] *vt*: ~ **uma idéia** to get an idea into one's head.

encatarrado/a [ẽkata'xadu/a] *adj* congested.

encenação [ẽsena'sãw] (*pl* **-ões**) *f* (*de peça*) staging, putting on; (*produção*) production; (*fingimento*) playacting; (*atitude fingida*) put-on, put-up job (*col*); **fazer** ~ (*col*) to put it on.

encenador(a) [ẽsena'do*(a)] *m/f* (*TEATRO*) director.

encenar [ẽse'na*] *vt* (*TEATRO*: *pôr em cena*) to stage, put on; (: *produzir*) to produce; (*fingir*) to put on.

enceradeira [ẽsera'dejra] *f* floor-polisher.

encerar [ẽse'ra*] *vt* to wax.

encerramento [ẽsexa'mẽtu] *m* (*término*) close, end.

encerrar [ẽse'xa*] *vt* (*confinar*) to shut in, lock up; (*conter*) to contain; (*concluir*) to close.

encestar [ẽseʃ'ta*] *vt* (*BASQUETE*) to put in the basket ♦ *vi* to score a basket.

encetar [ẽse'ta*] *vt* to start, begin.

encharcar [ẽʃax'ka*] *vt* (*alagar*) to flood; (*ensopar*) to soak, drench; ~**-se** *vr* to get soaked *ou* drenched; ~**-se de algo** (*beber muito*) to drink gallons of sth.

encheção [ẽʃe'sãw] (*col*) *f* annoyance.

enchente [ẽ'ʃẽtʃi] *f* flood.

encher [ẽ'ʃe*] *vt* to fill (up); (*balão*) to blow up; (*tempo*) to fill, take up ♦ *vi* (*col*) to be annoying; ~**-se** *vr* to fill up; ~**-se (de)** (*col*) to get fed up (with); ~ **de** *ou* **com** to fill up with; ~ **o saco de alguém** (*col*) to bug sb, piss sb off (!); **ela enche o filho de presentes** she showers her son with presents.

enchimento [ẽʃi'mẽtu] *m* filling.

enchova [ẽ'ʃova] *f* anchovy.

enciclopédia [ẽsiklo'pɛdʒja] *f* encyclopedia, encyclopaedia (*BRIT*).

enciumar [ẽsju'ma*] *vt* to make jealous; ~**-se** *vr* to get jealous.

enclausurar [ẽklawzu'ra*] *vt* to shut away; ~**-se** *vr* to shut o.s. away.

encoberto/a [ẽko'bɛxtu/a] *pp de* **encobrir** ♦ *adj* (*escondido*) concealed; (*tempo*) overcast.

encobrir [ẽko'bri*] *vt* to conceal, hide.

encolerizar [ẽkoleri'za*] *vt* to irritate, annoy; ~**-se** *vr* to get angry.

encolher [ẽko'ʎe*] *vt* (*pernas*) to draw up; (*os ombros*) to shrug; (*roupa*) to shrink ♦ *vi* to shrink; ~**-se** *vr* (*de frio*) to huddle; (*para dar lugar*) to hunch up.

encomenda [ẽko'mẽda] *f* order; **feito de** ~ made to order, custom-made; **vir de** ~ (*fig*) to come just at the right time.

encomendar [ẽkomẽ'da*] *vt* to order; ~ **algo a alguém** to order sth from sb.

encompridar [ẽkõpri'da*] *vt* to lengthen.

encontrão [ẽkõ'trãw] (*pl* **-ões**) *m* (*esbarrão*) collision, impact; (*empurrão*) shove; **dar um** ~ **em** to bump into; **ir aos encontrões pela multidão** to jostle one's way through the crowd.

encontrar [ẽkõ'tra*] *vt* (*achar*) to find; (*inesperadamente*) to come across, meet; (*dar com*) to bump into ♦ *vi*: ~ **com** to bump into; ~**-se** *vr* (*achar-se*) to be; (*ter encontro*): ~**-se (com alguém)** to meet (sb).

encontro [ẽ'kõtru] *m* (*de pessoas*) meeting; (*MIL*) encounter; ~ **marcado** appointment; **ir/vir ao** ~ **de** to go/come and meet; **ir** *ou* **vir ao** ~ **de** (*aspirações*) to meet, fulfil (*BRIT*), fulfill (*US*); **ir de** ~ **a** to go against, run contrary to; **meu carro foi de** ~ **ao muro** my car ran into the wall.

encontrões [ẽkõ'trõjʃ] *mpl de* **encontrão**.

encorajamento [ẽkoraʒa'mẽtu] *m* encouragement.

encorajar [ẽkora'ʒa*] *vt* to encourage.

encorpado/a [ẽkox'padu/a] *adj* stout; (*vinho*) full-bodied; (*tecido*) closely-woven; (*papel*) thick.

encorpar [ẽkox'pa*] *vt* (*ampliar*) to expand ♦ *vi* (*criança*) to fill out.

encosta [ẽ'kɔʃta] *f* slope.

encostar [ẽkoʃ'ta*] *vt* (*cabeça*) to put down; (*carro*) to park; (*pôr de lado*) to put to one side; (*pôr junto*) to put side by side; (*porta*) to leave ajar ♦ *vi* to pull in; ~**-se** *vr*: ~**-se em** to lean against; (*deitar-se*) to lie down on; ~ **em** to lean against; ~ **a mão em** (*bater*) to hit; **ele está sempre se encostando nos outros** he's always depending on others.

encosto [ẽ'kɔʃtu] *m* (*arrimo*) support; (*de cadeira*) back.

encouraçado/a [ẽkora'sadu/a] *adj* armoured (*BRIT*), armored (*US*) ♦ *m* (*NÁUT*) battleship.

encravado/a [ẽkra'vadu/a] *adj* (*unha*) ingrowing.

encravar [ẽkra'va*] *vt*: ~ **algo em algo** to stick sth into sth; (*diamante num anel*) to mount sth in sth.

encrenca [ẽ'krẽka] (*col*) *f* (*problema*) fix,

jam; (*briga*) fight; **meter-se numa** ~ to get into trouble.

encrenar [ẽkrẽ'ka*] (*col*) *vt* (*situação*) to complicate; (*pessoa*) to get into trouble ♦ *vi* (*complicar-se*) to get complicated; (*carro*) to break down; ~**se** *vr* to get complicated; to get into trouble; ~ (**com alguém**) to fall out (with sb).

encrenqueiro/a [ẽkrẽ'kejru/a] (*col*) *m/f* troublemaker ♦ *adj* troublemaking.

encrespado/a [ẽkreʃ'padu/a] *adj* (*cabelo*) curly; (*mar*) choppy; (*água*) rippling.

encrespar [ẽkreʃ'pa*] *vt* (*o cabelo*) to curl; ~**-se** *vr* (*o cabelo*) to curl; (*água*) to ripple; (*o mar*) to get choppy.

encruar [ẽkru'a*] *vi* (*negócio*) to grind to a halt.

encruzilhada [ẽkruzi'ʎada] *f* crossroads *sg*.

encucação [ẽkuka'sãw] (*pl* **-ões**) *f* fixation.

encucado/a [ẽku'kadu/a] (*col*) *adj*: ~ (**com**) hung up (about).

encucar [ẽku'ka*] (*col*) *vt*: ~ **alguém** to give sb a hang-up ♦ *vi*: ~ **com** *ou* **em algo/alguém** to be hung up about sth/sb.

encurralar [ẽkura'la*] *vt* (*gado, pessoas*) to herd; (*cercar*) to corner.

encurtar [ẽkux'ta*] *vt* to shorten.

endêmico/a [ẽ'demiku/a] *adj* endemic.

endemoninhado/a [ẽdemoni'ɲadu/a] *adj* (*pessoa*) possessed; (*espíritu*) demoniac; (*fig: criança*) naughty.

endentar [ẽdẽ'ta*] *vt* to engage.

endereçamento [ẽderesa'mẽtu] *m* (*tb: COMPUT*) addressing; (*endereço*) address.

endereçar [ẽdere'sa*] *vt* (*carta*) to address; (*encaminhar*) to direct.

endereço [ẽde'resu] *m* address; ~ **absoluto/relativo** (*COMPUT*) absolute/relative address.

endeusar [ẽdew'za*] *vt* to deify; (*amado*) to worship.

endiabrado/a [ẽdʒja'bradu/a] *adj* devilish; (*travesso*) mischievous.

endinheirado/a [ẽdʒiɲej'radu/a] *adj* rich, wealthy, well-off.

endireitar [ẽdʒirej'ta*] *vt* (*objeto*) to straighten; (*retificar*) to put right; (*fig*) to straighten out; ~**-se** *vr* to straighten up.

endividado/a [ẽdʒivi'dadu/a] *adj* in debt.

endividamento [ẽdʒivida'mẽtu] *m* debt.

endividar [ẽdʒivi'da*] *vt* to put into debt; ~**-se** *vr* to run into debt.

endócrino/a [ẽ'dɔkrinu/a] *adj* V **glândula**.

endoidecer [ẽdojde'se*] *vt* to madden ♦ *vi* to go mad.

endoscopia [ẽdoʃko'pia] *f* (*MED*) endoscopy.

endossante [ẽdo'sãtʃi] *m/f* endorser.

endossar [ẽdo'sa*] *vt* to endorse.

endossável [ẽdo'savew] (*pl* **-eis**) *adj* endorsable.

endosso [ẽ'dosu] *m* endorsement.

endurecer [ẽdure'se*] *vt, vi* to harden.

endurecido/a [ẽdure'sidu/a] *adj* hardened.

endurecimento [ẽduresi'mẽtu] *m* hardening.

ENE *abr* (= *és-nordeste*) ENE.

enegrecer [enegre'se*] *vt* to darken; (*fig: nome*) to blacken ♦ *vi* to darken.

enema [e'nema] *m* enema.

energético/a [enex'ʒetʃiku/a] *adj* energy *atr* ♦ *m* energy source.

energia [enex'ʒia] *f* (*vigor*) energy, drive; (*TEC*) power, energy.

enérgico/a [e'nexʒiku/a] *adj* energetic, vigorous; **ele é** ~ **com os filhos** he is hard on his children.

enervação [enexva'sãw] *f* annoyance, irritation.

enervante [enex'vãtʃi] *adj* annoying.

enervar [enex'va*] *vt* to annoy, irritate ♦ *vi* to be irritating; ~**-se** *vr* to get annoyed.

enevoado/a [ene'vwadu/a] *adj* misty, hazy.

enfadar [ẽfa'da*] *vt* (*entediar*) to bore; (*incomodar*) to annoy; ~**-se** *vr*: ~**-se de** to get tired of; ~**-se com** (*aborrecer-se*) to get fed up with.

enfado [ẽ'fadu] *m* annoyance.

enfadonho/a [ẽfa'doɲu/a] *adj* (*cansativo*) tiresome; (*aborrecido*) boring.

enfaixar [ẽfaj'ʃa*] *vt* (*perna*) to bandage, bind; (*bebê*) to wrap up.

enfarte [ẽ'faxtʃi] *m* (*MED*) coronary.

ênfase ['ẽfazi] *f* emphasis, stress.

enfastiado/a [ẽfaʃ'tʃiadu/a] *adj* bored.

enfastiar [ẽfaʃ'tʃia*] *vt* (*cansar*) to weary; (*aborrecer*) to bore; ~**-se** *vr*: ~**-se de** *ou* **com** (*cansar-se*) to get tired of; (*aborrecer-se*) to get bored with.

enfático/a [ẽ'fatʃiku/a] *adj* emphatic.

enfatizar [ẽfatʃi'za*] *vt* to emphasize.

enfear [ẽfe'a*] *vt* (*pessoa etc*) to make ugly; (*deturpar*) to distort ♦ *vi* to become ugly.

enfeitar [ẽfej'ta*] *vt* to decorate; ~**-se** *vr* to dress up.

enfeitiçante [ẽfejtʃi'sãtʃi] *adj* enchanting, charming.

enfeite [ẽ'fejtʃi] *m* decoration.

enfeitiçar [ẽfejtʃi'sa*] *vt* to bewitch, cast a spell on.

enfermagem [ẽfex'maʒẽ] *f* nursing.

enfermaria [ẽfexma'ria] *f* ward.

enfermeiro/a [ẽfex'mejru/a] *m/f* nurse.

enfermidade [ẽfexmi'dadʒi] *f* illness.

enfermo/a [ẽ'fexmu/a] *adj* ill, sick ♦ *m/f* sick person, patient.

enferrujar [ẽfexu'ʒa*] *vt* to rust, corrode ♦ *vi* to go rusty.

enfezado/a [ẽfe'zadu/a] *adj* (*irritadiço*) irritable; (*irritado*) angry, mad.

enfezar [ẽfe'za*] *vt* (*irritar*) to make angry; ~**-se** *vr* to become angry.

enfiada [ẽ'fjada] *f* (*de pérolas*) string; (*fila*)

NB: European Portuguese adds the following consonants to certain words: **b** (sú(b)dito, su(b)til); **c** (a(c)ção, a(c)cionista, a(c)to); **m** (inde(m)ne); **p** (ado(p)ção, ado(p)tar); *for further details see p. xiii.*

row.

enfiar [ẽ'fja*] *vt* (*meter*) to put; (*agulha*) to thread; (*pérolas*) to string together; (*vestir*) to slip on; **~-se** *vr*: **~-se em** to slip into.

enfileirar [ẽfilej'ra*] *vt* to line up.

enfim [ẽ'fĩ] *adv* finally, at last; (*em suma*) in short; **até que ~!** at last!

enfocar [ẽfo'ka*] *vt* (*assunto*) to tackle.

enfoque [ẽ'fɔki] *m* approach.

enforcamento [ẽfoxka'mẽtu] *m* hanging.

enforcar [ẽfox'ka*] *vt* to hang; (*trabalho*, *aulas*) to skip; **~-se** *vr* to hang o.s.; **~ a sexta-feira** to take the Friday off.

enfraquecer [ẽfrake'se*] *vt* to weaken ♦ *vi* to grow weak.

enfraquecimento [ẽfrakesi'mẽtu] *m* weakening.

enfrentar [ẽfrẽ'ta*] *vt* (*encarar*) to face; (*confrontar*) to confront; (*problemas*) to face up to.

enfronhado/a [ẽfro'ɲadu/a] *adj*: **estar bem ~ num assunto** to be well versed in a subject.

enfronhar [ẽfro'ɲa*] *vi*: **~ alguém em algo** to instruct sb in sth; **~-se** *vr*: **~-se em algo** to learn about sth, become well versed in sth.

enfumaçado/a [ẽfuma'sadu/a] *adj* full of smoke, smoky.

enfumaçar [ẽfuma'sa*] *vt* to fill with smoke.

enfurecer [ẽfure'se*] *vt* to infuriate; **~-se** *vr* to get furious.

enfurnar [ẽfux'na*] *vt* to hide away; (*meter*) to stow away; **~-se** *vr* to hide (o.s.) away.

eng⁴ *abr* (=*engenheira*) Eng.

engaiolar [ẽgajo'la*] (*col*) *vt* to jail.

engajamento [ẽgaʒa'mẽtu] *m* (*empenho*, POL) commitment; (*de trabalhadores*) hiring; (MIL) enlistment.

engajar [ẽga'ʒa*] *vt* (*trabalhadores*) to take on, hire; **~-se** *vr* to take up employment; (MIL) to enlist; **~-se em algo** to get involved in sth; (POL) to be committed to sth.

engalfinhar-se [ẽgawfi'ɲaxsi] *vr* (*atacar-se*) to fight; (*discutir*) to argue.

engambelar [ẽgãbe'la*] *vt* to con, trick.

enganado/a [ẽga'nadu/a] *adj* (*errado*) mistaken; (*traído*) deceived.

enganador(a) [ẽgana'do*(a)] *adj* (*mentiroso*) deceitful; (*artificioso*) fake; (*conselho*) misleading; (*aspecto*) deceptive.

enganar [ẽga'na*] *vt* to deceive; (*desonrar*) to seduce; (*cônjuge*) to be unfaithful to; (*fome*) to stave off; **~-se** *vr* (*cair em erro*) to be wrong, be mistaken; (*iludir-se*) to deceive o.s.; **as aparências enganam** appearances are deceptive.

enganchar [ẽgã'ʃa*] *vt*: **~ algo (em algo)** to hook sth up (to sth).

engano [ẽ'gãnu] *m* (*error*) mistake; (*ilusão*) deception; (*logro*) trick; **é ~** (TEL) I've (*ou* you've) got the wrong number.

engarrafado/a [ẽgaxa'fadu/a] *adj* bottled; (*trânsito*) blocked.

engarrafamento [ẽgaxafa'mẽtu] *m* bottling;

(*de trânsito*) traffic jam.

engarrafar [ẽgaxa'fa*] *vt* to bottle; (*trânsito*) to block.

engasgar [ẽgaʒ'ga*] *vt* to choke ♦ *vi* to choke; (*carro*) to backfire; **~-se** *vr* to choke.

engasgo [ẽ'gaʒgu] *m* choking.

engastar [ẽgaʃ'ta*] *vt* (*jóias*) to set, mount.

engaste [ẽ'gaʃtʃi] *m* setting, mounting.

engatar [ẽga'ta*] *vt* (*vagões*) to couple, hitch up; (AUTO) to put into gear.

engatilhar [ẽgatʃi'ʎa*] *vt* (*revólver*) to cock; (*fig: resposta etc*) to prepare.

engatinhar [ẽgatʃi'ɲa*] *vi* to crawl; (*fig*) to be feeling one's way.

engavetamento [ẽgaveta'mẽtu] *m* (*de carros*) pile-up.

engavetar [ẽgave'ta*] *vt* (*fig: projeto*) to shelve; **~-se** *vr* to crash into one another; **~-se em algo** to crash into (the back of) sth.

engelhar [ẽʒe'ʎa*] *vt*, *vi* (*pele*) to wrinkle.

engendrar [ẽʒẽ'dra*] *vt* to dream up.

engenharia [ẽʒeɲa'ria] *f* engineering.

engenheiro/a [ẽʒe'ɲejru/a] *m/f* engineer.

engenho [ẽ'ʒeɲu] *m* (*talento*) talent; (*destreza*) skill; (*máquina*) machine; (*moenda*) mill; (*fazenda*) sugar plantation.

engenhoso/a [ẽʃe'ɲozu/ɔza] *adj* clever, ingenious.

engessar [ẽʒe'sa*] *vt* (*perna*) to put in plaster; (*parede*) to plaster.

englobar [ẽglo'ba*] *vt* to include.

eng° *abr* (= *engenheiro*) Eng.

engodar [ẽgo'da*] *vt* to lure, entice.

engodo [ẽ'godu] *m* (*para peixe*) bait; (*para pessoas*) lure, enticement.

engolir [ẽgo'li*] *vt* (*tb fig*) to swallow; **até hoje não engoli o que ele me fez** I still haven't forgiven him for what he did to me.

engomar [ẽgo'ma*] *vt* to starch; (*passar*) to iron.

engonço [ẽ'gõsu] *m* hinge.

engordar [ẽgox'da*] *vt* to fatten ♦ *vi* to put on weight; **o açúcar engorda** sugar is fattening.

engordurado/a [ẽgoxdu'radu/a] *adj* (*comida*) fatty; (*mãos*) greasy.

engordurar [ẽgoxdu'ra*] *vt* to cover with grease.

engraçado/a [ẽgra'sadu/a] *adj* funny, amusing.

engraçar-se [ẽgra'saxsi] (*col*) *vr*: **~ com alguém** to take advantage of sb.

engradado [ẽgra'dadu] *m* crate.

engrandecer [ẽgrãde'se*] *vt* to elevate ♦ *vi* to grow; **~-se** *vr* to become great.

engravatar-se [ẽgrava'taxsi] *vr* to put on a tie; (*vestir-se bem*) to dress smartly.

engravidar [ẽgravi'da*] *vt*: **~ alguém** to get sb pregnant; (MED) to impregnate sb ♦ *vi* to get pregnant.

engraxador [ẽgraʃa'do*] (PT) *m* shoe shiner.

engraxar [ẽgra'ʃa*] *vt* to polish.

engraxate [ẽgra'ʃatʃi] *m* shoe shiner.

engrenagem [ẽgre'naʒẽ] (*pl* **-ns**) *f* (AUTO)

gear.

engrenar [ẽgre'na*] *vt* (*AUTO*) to put into gear; (*fig: conversa*) to strike up ♦ *vi:* ~ **com alguém** to get on with sb.

engrolado/a [ẽgro'ladu/a] *adj* (*voz*) slurred.

engrossar [ẽgro'sa*] *vt* (*sopa*) to thicken; (*aumentar*) to swell; (*voz*) to raise ♦ *vi* to thicken; to swell; to rise; (*col: pessoa, conversa*) to turn nasty.

engrupir [ẽgru'pi*] (*col*) *vt* to con, trick.

enguia [ẽ'gia] *f* eel.

enguiçar [ẽgi'sa*] *vi* (*máquina*) to break down ♦ *vt* to cause to break down.

enguiço [ẽ'gisu] *m* (*empecilho*) snag; (*desarranjo*) breakdown.

engulho [ẽ'guʎu] *m* nausea.

enigma [e'nigima] *m* enigma; (*mistério*) mystery.

enigmático/a [enigi'matʃiku/a] *adj* enigmatic.

enjaular [ẽʒaw'la*] *vt* (*fera*) to cage, cage up; (*prender: pessoa*) to imprison.

enjeitado/a [ẽʒej'tadu/a] *m/f* foundling, waif.

enjeitar [ẽʒej'ta*] *vt* (*rejeitar*) to reject; (*abandonar*) to abandon; (*condenar*) to condemn.

enjoado/a [ẽ'ʒwadu/a] *adj* sick; (*enfastiado*) bored; (*enfadonho*) boring; (*mal-humorado*) in a bad mood.

enjoar [ẽ'ʒwa*] *vt* to make sick; (*enfastiar*) to bore ♦ *vi* (*pessoa*) to be sick; (*remédio, comida*) to cause nausea; ~**-se** *vr:* ~**se de** to get sick of; **eu enjôo com o cheiro de fritura** the smell of frying makes me sick; **eu enjoei de ir ao cinema** I'm sick of going to the cinema.

enjoativo/a [ẽʒwa'tʃivu/a] *adj* (*comida*) revolting; (*tedioso*) boring.

enjôo [ẽ'ʒou] *m* sickness; (*em carro*) travel sickness; (*em navio*) seasickness; (*aborrecimento*) boredom; **que ~!** what a bore!

enlaçar [ẽla'sa*] *vt* (*atar*) to tie, bind; (*abraçar*) to hug; (*unir*) to link, join; (*bois*) to hitch; (*cingir*) to wind around; ~**-se** *vr* to be linked.

enlace [ẽ'lasi] *m* link, connection; (*casamento*) marriage, union.

enlamear [ẽla'mja*] *vt* to cover in mud; (*reputação*) to besmirch.

enlatado/a [ẽla'tadu/a] *adj* tinned (*BRIT*), canned ♦ *m* (*pej: filme*) foreign import; ~**s** *mpl* tinned (*BRIT*) *ou* canned foods.

enlatar [ẽla'ta*] *vt* (*comida*) to can.

enlevar [ẽle'va*] *vt* (*extasiar*) to enrapture; (*absorver*) to absorb.

enlevo [ẽ'levu] *m* (*êxtase*) rapture; (*deleite*) delight.

enlouquecer [ẽloke'se*] *vt* to drive mad ♦ *vi* to go mad.

enluarado/a [ẽlua'radu/a] *adj* moonlit.

enlutado/a [ẽlu'tadu/a] *adj* in mourning.

enlutar-se [ẽlu'taxsi] *vr* to go into mourning.

enobrecer [enobre'se*] *vt* to ennoble ♦ *vi* to be ennobling.

enojar [eno'ja*] *vt* to disgust, sicken.

enorme [e'nɔxmi] *adj* enormous, huge.

enormidade [enoxmi'dadʒi] *f* enormity; **uma ~ (de)** (*col*) a hell of a lot (of).

enovelar [enove'la*] *vt* to wind into a ball; (*enrolar*) to roll up.

enquadrar [ẽkwa'dra*] *vt* to fit; (*gravura*) to frame ♦ *vi:* ~ **com** (*condizer*) to fit *ou* tie in with.

enquanto [ẽ'kwãtu] *conj* while; (*considerado como*) as; ~ **isso** meanwhile; **por** ~ for the time being; ~ **ele não vem** until he comes; ~ **que** whereas.

enquête [ã'kɛtʒi] *f* survey.

enrabichar-se [ẽxabi'ʃaxsi] *vr:* ~ **por alguém** to fall for sb.

enraivecer [ẽxajve'se*] *vt* to enrage.

enraizar [ẽxaj'za*] *vi* to take root; ~**-se** *vr* (*pessoa*) to settle down.

enrascada [ẽxaʃ'kada] *f* tight spot, predicament; **meter-se numa** ~ to get into a spot of bother.

enrascar [ẽxaʃ'ka*] *vt* to embroil; ~**-se** *vr* to get embroiled.

enredar [ẽxe'da*] *vt* (*emaranhar*) to entangle; (*complicar*) to complicate; ~**-se** *vr* to get entangled.

enredo [ẽ'xedu] *m* (*de uma obra*) plot; (*intriga*) intrigue; **ele faz tanto** ~ (*fig*) he makes such a fuss.

enregelado/a [ẽxeʒe'ladu/a] *adj* (*pessoa, mão*) frozen; (*muito frio*) freezing.

enrijecer [ẽxiʒe'se*] *vt* to stiffen; ~**-se** *vr* to stiffen; (*fortalecer*) to get stronger.

enriquecer [ẽxike'se*] *vt* to make rich; (*fig*) to enrich ♦ *vi* to get rich; ~**-se** *vr* to get rich.

enriquecimento [ẽxikesi'mẽtu] *m* enrichment.

enrolado/a [ẽxo'ladu/a] (*col*) *adj* complicated.

enrolar [ẽxo'la*] *vt* to roll up; (*agasalhar*) to wrap up; (*col: enganar*) to con ♦ *vi* (*col*) to waffle; ~**-se** *vr* to roll up; (*agasalhar-se*) to wrap up; (*col: confundir-se*) to get mixed *ou* muddled up.

enroscar [ẽxoʃ'ka*] *vt* (*torcer*) to twist, wind (round); ~**-se** *vr* to coil up.

enrouquecer [ẽxoke'se*] *vt* to make hoarse ♦ *vi* to go hoarse.

enrubescer [ẽxube'se*] *vt* to redden, colour (*BRIT*), color (*US*) ♦ *vi* (*por vergonha*) to blush, go red.

enrugar [ẽxu'ga*] *vt* (*pele*) to wrinkle; (*testa*) to furrow; (*tecido*) to crease ♦ *vi* (*pele, mãos*) to go wrinkly; (*pessoa*) to get wrinkles.

enrustido/a [ẽxuʃ'tʃido/a] (*col*) *adj* withdrawn.

ensaboar [ẽsa'bwa*] *vt* to wash with soap; ~-

NB: European Portuguese adds the following consonants to certain words: **b** (sú(b)dito, su(b)til); **c** (a(c)ção, a(c)cionista, a(c)to); **m** (inde(m)ne); **p** (ado(p)ção, ado(p)tar); *for further details see p. xiii.*

se vr to soap o.s.

ensaiar [ẽsa'ja*] vt (provar) to test, try out; (treinar) to practise (BRIT), practice (US); (TEATRO) to rehearse.

ensaio [ẽ'saju] m (prova) test; (tentativa) attempt; (treino) practice; (TEATRO) rehearsal; (literário) essay.

ensaísta [ẽsaj'iʃta] m/f essayist.

ensangüentado/a [ẽsãgwẽ'tadu/a] adj bloody.

ensangüentar [ẽsãgwẽ'ta*] vt to stain with blood.

enseada [ẽ'sjada] f inlet, cove; (baía) bay.

ensebado/a [ẽse'badu/a] adj greasy; (sujo) soiled.

ensejar [ẽse'ʒa*] vt: ~ algo (a alguém) to provide (sb with) an opportunity for sth.

ensejo [ẽ'seʒu] m chance, opportunity.

ensimesmado/a [ẽsimeʒ'madu/a] adj lost in thought.

ensimesmar-se [ẽsimeʒ'maxsi] vr to be lost in thought; ~ em to be lost in.

ensinamento [ẽsina'mẽtu] m teaching; (exemplo) lesson.

ensinar [ẽsi'na*] vt, vi to teach; ~ alguém a patinar to teach sb to skate; ~ algo a alguém to teach sb sth; ~ o caminho a alguém to show sb the way; você quer ~ o padre a rezar missa? are you trying to teach your grandmother to suck eggs?

ensino [ẽ'sinu] m teaching, tuition; (educação) education.

ensolarado/a [ẽsola'radu/a] adj sunny.

ensombrecido/a [ẽsõbre'sidu/a] adj darkened.

ensopado/a [ẽso'padu/a] adj soaked ♦ m stew.

ensopar [ẽso'pa*] vt to soak, drench.

ensurdecedor(a) [ẽsuxdese'do*(a)] adj deafening.

ensurdecer [ẽsuxde'se*] vt to deafen ♦ vi to go deaf.

entabular [ẽtabu'la*] vt (negociação) to start, open; (empreender) to undertake; (assunto) to broach; (conversa) to strike up.

entalado/a [ẽta'ladu/a] adj (apertado) wedged, jammed; (enrascado) embroiled, involved; (engasgado) choking.

entalar [ẽta'la*] vt (encravar) to wedge, jam; (fig) to put in a fix; ela me entalou de comida she stuffed me full of food.

entalhador(a) [ẽtaʎa'do*(a)] m/f woodcarver.

entalhar [ẽta'ʎa*] vt to carve.

entalhe [ẽ'taʎi] m groove, notch.

entalho [ẽ'taʎu] m woodcarving.

entanto [ẽ'tãtu]: no ~ adv yet, however.

então [ẽ'tãw] adv then; até ~ up to that time; desde ~ ever since; e ~? well then?; para ~ so that; pois ~ in that case; ~, você vai ou não? so, are you going or not?

entardecer [ẽtaxde'se*] vi to get late ♦ m sunset.

ente ['ẽtʃi] m being.

enteado/a [ẽ'tʃjadu/a] m/f stepson/stepdaughter.

entediante [ẽte'dʒjãtʃi] adj boring, tedious.

entediar [ẽte'dʒja*] vt to bore; ~-se vr to get bored.

entendedor(a) [ẽtẽde'do*(a)] adj knowledgeable ♦ m: a bom ~ meia palavra basta a word to the wise is enough.

entender [ẽtẽ'de*] vt (compreender) to understand; (pensar) to think; (ouvir) to hear; ~-se vr (compreender-se) to understand one another; dar a ~ to imply; no meu ~ in my opinion; ~ de música to know about music; ~ de fazer to decide to do; ~-se por to be meant by; ~-se com alguém to get along with sb; (dialogar) to sort things out with sb.

entendido/a [ẽtẽ'dʒidu/a] adj (col) gay; (conhecedor): ~ em good at ♦ m expert; (col) homosexual, gay; bem ~ that is.

entendimento [ẽtẽdʒi'mẽtu] m (compreensão) understanding; (opinião) opinion; (combinação) agreement.

enternecedor(a) [ẽtexnese'do*(a)] adj touching.

enternecer [ẽtexne'se*] vt to move, touch; ~-se vr to be moved.

enterrar [ẽte'xa*] vt to bury; (faca) to plunge; (lever à ruina) to ruin; (assunto) to close; ~ o chapéu na cabeça to put one's hat on.

enterro [ẽ'texu] m burial; (funeral) funeral.

entidade [ẽtʃi'dadʒi] f (ser) being; (corporação) body; (coisa que existe) entity.

entoação [ẽtoa'sãw] f singing.

entoar [ẽ'twa*] vt (cantar) to chant.

entonação [ẽtona'sãw] (pl -ões) f intonation.

entontecer [ẽtõte'se*] vt to make dizzy; (enlouquecer) to drive mad ♦ vi to become ou get dizzy; to go mad; o vinho entontece wine makes you dizzy.

entornar [ẽtox'na*] vt to spill; (fig: copo) to drink ♦ vi to drink a lot.

entorpecente [ẽtoxpe'sẽtʃi] m narcotic.

entorpecer [ẽtoxpe'se*] vt (paralisar) to numb, stupefy; (retardar) to slow down.

entorpecimento [ẽtoxpesi'mẽtu] m numbness; (torpor) lethargy.

entorse [ẽ'tɔxsi] f sprain.

entortar [ẽtox'ta*] vt (curvar) to bend; (empenar) to warp; ~ os olhos to squint.

entourage [ãtu'raʒi] m entourage.

entrada [ẽ'trada] f (ato) entry; (lugar) entrance; (TEC) inlet; (de casa) doorway; (começo) beginning; (bilhete) ticket; (CULIN) starter, entrée; (COMPUT) input; (pagamento inicial) down payment; (corredor de casa) hall; (no cabelo) receding hairline; ~ gratuita admission free; "~ proibida" "no entry", "no admittance"; meia ~ half-price ticket; dar ~ a (requerimento) to submit; (processo) to institute; dar uma ~ to go in; ~ de serviço service entrance.

entrado/a [ẽ'tradu/a] adj: ~ em anos (PT) elderly.

entra-e-sai ['ẽtrai'saj] m comings and goings

pl.

entranhado/a [ĕtra'ɲadu/a] *adj* deep-rooted.

entranhar-se [ĕtra'ɲaxsi] *vr* to penetrate.

entranhas [ĕ'traɲaʃ] *fpl* bowels, entrails; *(sentimentos)* feelings; *(centro)* heart *sg.*

entrar [ĕ'tra*] *vi* to go *ou* come in, enter; *(conseguir* ~) to get in; **deixar** ~ to let in; ~ **com** *(COMPUT: dados etc)* to enter; **eu entrei com £10** I contributed £10; ~ **de férias/licença** to start one's holiday *(BRIT) ou* vacation *(US)*/leave; ~ **em** *(casa etc)* to go *ou* come into, enter; *(assunto)* to get onto; *(comida, bebida)* to start in on; *(universidade)* to enter; ~ **em detalhes** to go into details; ~ **em vigor** to come into force; **ele entra às 9 no trabalho** he starts work at 9.00; **o que entra nesta receita?** what goes into this recipe?; ~ **para um clube** to join a club; **quando a primavera entra** when spring comes; ~ **bem** *(col)* to get into trouble.

entravar [ĕtra'va*] *vt* to obstruct, impede.

entrave [ĕ'travi] *m* *(fig)* impediment.

entre ['ĕtri] *prep (dois)* between; *(mais de dois)* among(st); ~ **si** amongst themselves.

entreaberto/a [ĕtrja'bɛxtu/a] *pp de* **entreabrir** ♦ *adj* half-open; *(porta)* ajar.

entreabrir [ĕtrja'bri*] *vt* to half open; **~-se** *vr (flores)* to open up.

entrechocar-se [ĕtriʃo'kaxsi] *vr* to collide, crash; *(fig)* to clash.

entrecortado/a [ĕtrikox'tadu/a] *adj* intermittent; **região entrecortada de estradas** region intersected by roads.

entrecosto [ĕtri'koʃtu] *m* *(CULIN)* entrecôte.

entrega [ĕ'trɛga] *f (de mercadorias)* delivery; *(a alguém)* handing over; *(rendição)* surrender; **caminhão/serviço de** ~ delivery van/service; **pronta** ~ speedy delivery; ~ **rápida** special delivery; ~ **a domicílio** home delivery.

entregar [ĕtre'ga*] *vt (dar)* to hand over; *(mercadorias)* to deliver; *(denunciar)* to hand over; *(confiar)* to entrust; *(devolver)* to return; **~-se** *vr (render-se)* to give o.s. up; *(dedicar-se)* to devote o.s.; **~-se à dor/bebida** to be overcome by grief/take to drink; **~-se a um homem** to sleep with a man; ~ **os pontos** to give up, throw in the towel.

entregue [ĕ'trɛgi] *pp de* **entregar.**

entrelaçar [ĕtrila'sa*] *vt* to entwine.

entrelinha [ĕtre'liɲa] *f* line spacing; **ler nas ~s** to read between the lines.

entremear [ĕtri'mja*] *vt* to intermingle.

entremostrar [ĕtrimoʃ'tra*] *vt* to give a glimpse of.

entreolhar-se [ĕtrio'ʎaxsi] *vr* to exchange glances.

entrepernas [ĕtri'pɛxnaʃ] *adv* between one's legs.

entrepor [ĕtripo*] *(irreg: como* **pôr)** *vt* to in-

sert; **~-se** *vr:* **~-se entre** to come between.

entressafra [ĕtri'safra] *f* time between harvests; *(fig)*: **as ~s de algo** the periods without sth.

entretanto [ĕtri'tãtu] *conj* however.

entretenimento [ĕtriteni'mĕtu] *m* entertainment; *(distração)* pastime.

entretela [ĕtri'tɛla] *f (COSTURA)* interlining, buckram.

entreter [ĕtri'te*] *(irreg: como* **ter)** *vt (divertir)* to entertain, amuse; *(ocupar)* to occupy; *(manter)* to keep up; *(esperanças)* to cherish; **~-se** *vr (divertir-se)* to amuse o.s.; *(ocupar-se)* to occupy o.s.

entrever [ĕtre'va*] *vt* to paralyse, cripple.

entrever [ĕtri'vc*] *(irreg: como* **ver)** *vt* to glimpse, catch a glimpse of.

entrevista [ĕtre'viʃta] *f* interview; ~ **coletiva** *(à imprensa)* press conference.

entrevistador(a) [ĕtreviʃta'do*(a)] *m/f* interviewer.

entrevistar [ĕtreviʃ'ta*] *vt* to interview; **~-se** *vr* to have an interview.

entrevisto/a [ĕtre'viʃtu/a] *pp de* **entrever.**

entristecedor(a) [ĕtriʃtese'do*(a)] *adj* saddening, sad.

entristecer [ĕtriʃte'se*] *vt* to sadden, grieve ♦ *vi* to feel sad; **~-se** *vr* to feel sad.

entroncamento [ĕtrõka'mĕtu] *m* junction.

entrosado/a [ĕtro'zadu/a] *adj (fig)* integrated.

entrosamento [ĕtroza'mĕtu] *m* *(fig)* integration.

entrosar [ĕtro'za*] *vt (rodas)* to mesh; *(peças)* to fit; *(fig)* to integrate ♦ *vi* to mesh; to fit; ~ **com** *(fig)* to fit in with; ~ **em** *(adaptar-se)* to settle into.

entrudo [ĕ'trudu] *(PT)* *m* carnival; *(REL)* Shrovetide.

entulhar [ĕtu'ʎa*] *vt* to cram full; *(suj: multidão)* to pack.

entulho [ĕ'tuʎu] *m* rubble, debris *sg.*

entupido/a [ĕtu'pidu/a] *adj* blocked; **estar** ~ *(col: congestionado)* to have a blocked-up nose; *(de comida)* to be fit to burst, be full up.

entupimento [ĕtupi'mĕtu] *m* blockage.

entupir [ĕtu'pi*] *vt* to block, clog; **~-se** *vr* to become blocked; *(de comida)* to stuff o.s.

entupitivo/a [ĕtupi'tʃivu/a] *adj* filling.

enturmar-se [ĕtux'maxsi] *vr:* ~ **(com)** to make friends (with).

entusiasmar [ĕtuzjaʒ'ma*] *vt* to fill with enthusiasm; *(animar)* to excite; **~-se** *vr* to get excited.

entusiasmo [ĕtu'zjaʒmu] *m* enthusiasm; *(júbilo)* excitement.

entusiasta [ĕtu'zjaʃta] *adj* enthusiastic ♦ *m/f* enthusiast.

entusiástico/a [ĕtu'zjaʃtʃiku/a] *adj* enthusiastic.

NB: European Portuguese adds the following consonants to certain words: **b** (sú(b)dito, su(b)til); **c** (a(c)ção, a(c)cionista, a(c)to); **m** (inde(m)ne); **p** (ado(p)ção, ado(p)tar); *for further details see p. xiii.*

enumeração [enumera'sãw] (pl -ões) f enumeration; (numeração) numbering.

enumerar [enume'ra*] vt to enumerate; (com números) to number.

enunciar [enū'sja*] vt to express, state.

envaidecer [ēvajde'se*] vt to make conceited; ~-se vr to become conceited.

envelhecer [ēveʎe'se*] vt to age ♦ vi to grow old, age.

envelhecimento [ēveʎesi'mētu] m aging.

envelope [ēve'lɔpi] m envelope.

envenenado/a [ēvene'nadu/a] adj poisoned; (col: festa, roupa) wild, great; (: carro) souped up.

envenenamento [ēvenena'mētu] m poisoning; ~ do sangue blood poisoning.

envenenar [ēvene'na*] vt to poison; (fig) to corrupt; (: declaração, palavras) to distort, twist; (tornar amargo) to sour; (col: carro) to soup up ♦ vi to be poisonous; ~-se vr to poison o.s.

enverdecer [ēvexde'se*] vt to turn green.

enveredar [ēvere'da*] vi: ~ por um caminho to follow a road; ~ para to head for.

envergadura [ēvexga'dura] f (asas, velas) spread; (avião) wingspan; (fig) scope; de grande ~ large-scale.

envergar [ēvex'ga*] vt (arquear) to bend; (vestir) to wear.

envergonhado/a [ēvexgo'ɲadu/a] adj ashamed; (tímido) shy.

envergonhar [ēvexgo'ɲa*] vt to shame; (degradar) to disgrace; ~-se vr to be ashamed.

envernizar [ēvexni'za*] vt to varnish.

enviado/a [ē'vjadu/a] m/f envoy, messenger.

enviar [ē'vja*] vt to send.

envidar [ēvi'da*] vt: ~ esforços (para fazer algo) to endeavour (BRIT) ou endeavor (US) (to do sth).

envidraçado/a [ēvidra'sadu/a] adj V varanda.

envidraçar [ēvidra'sa*] vt to glaze.

enviesado/a [ēvje'zadu/a] adj slanting.

envilecer [ēvile'se*] vt to debase, degrade.

envio [ē'viu] m sending; (expedição) dispatch; (remessa) remittance; (de mercadorias) consignment.

enviuvar [ēvju'va*] vi to be widowed.

envolto/a [ē'vowtu/a] pp de envolver.

envoltório [ēvow'tɔrju] m cover.

envolvente [ēvow'vētʃi] adj compelling.

envolver [ēvow've*] vt (embrulhar) to wrap (up); (cobrir) to cover; (comprometer, acarretar) to involve; (nos braços) to embrace; ~-se vr (intrometer-se) to become involved; (cobrir-se) to wrap o.s. up.

envolvimento [ēvowvi'mētu] m involvement.

enxada [ē'ʃada] f hoe.

enxadrista [ēʃa'driʃta] m/f chess player.

enxaguada [ēʃa'gwada] f rinse.

enxaguar [ēʃa'gwa*] vt to rinse.

enxame [ē'ʃami] m swarm.

enxaqueca [ēʃa'keka] f migraine.

enxergão [ēʃex'gãw] (pl -ões) m (straw) mattress.

enxergar [ēʃex'ga*] vt (avistar) to catch sight of; (divisar) to make out; (notar) to observe, see; ~-se vr: ele não se enxerga he doesn't know his place.

enxergões [ēʃex'gõjʃ] mpl de enxergão.

enxerido/a [ēʃe'ridu/a] adj nosy, interfering.

enxertar [ēʃex'ta*] vt to graft; (fig) to incorporate.

enxerto [ē'ʃextu] m graft.

enxó [ē'ʃɔ] m adze.

enxofre [ē'ʃofri] m sulphur (BRIT), sulfur (US).

enxota-moscas [ē'ʃota-] (PT) m fly swatter.

enxotar [ēʃo'ta*] vt (expulsar) to drive out.

enxoval [ēʃo'vaw] (pl -ais) m (de noiva) trousseau; (de recém-nascido) layette.

enxovalhar [ēʃova'ʎa*] vt (sujar) to soil; (amarrotar) to crumple; (reputação) to blacken; (insultar) to insult; ~-se vr to disgrace o.s.

enxugador [ēʃuga'do*] m clothes drier.

enxugar [ēʃu'ga*] vt to dry; (fig: texto) to tidy up; ~ as lágrimas to dry one's eyes.

enxurrada [ēʃu'xada] f (de água) torrent; (fig) spate.

enxuto/a [ē'ʃutu/a] adj dry; (corpo) shapely; (bonito) good-looking.

enzima [ē'zima] f enzyme.

epicentro [epi'sētru] m epicentre (BRIT), epicenter (US).

épico/a ['ɛpiku/a] adj epic ♦ m epic poet.

epidemia [epide'mia] f epidemic.

epidêmico/a [epi'demiku/a] adj epidemic.

Epifania [epifa'nia] f Epiphany.

epilepsia [epile'psia] f epilepsy.

epiléptico/a [epi'lɛptʃiku/a] adj, m/f epileptic.

epílogo [e'pilogu] m epilogue.

episcopado [epiʃko'padu] m bishopric.

episódio [epi'zɔdʒu] m episode.

epístola [e'piʃtola] f epistle; (carta) letter.

epitáfio [epi'tafju] m epitaph.

epítome [e'pitomi] m summary; (fig) epitome.

época ['ɛpoka] f time, period; (da história) age, epoch; ~ da colheita harvest time; naquela ~ at that time; fazer ~ to be epoch-making; fazer segunda ~ to resit one's exams.

epopéia [epo'pɛja] f epic.

equação [ekwa'sãw] (pl -ões) f equation.

equacionar [ekwasjo'na*] vt to set out.

equações [ekwa'sõjʃ] fpl de equação.

Equador [ekwa'do*] m: o ~ Ecuador.

equador [ekwa'do*] m equator.

equânime [e'kwanimi] adj fair; (caráter) unbiased, neutral.

equatorial [ekwato'rjaw] (pl -ais) adj equatorial.

equatoriano/a [ekwato'rjanu/a] adj, m/f Ecuadorian.

eqüestre [e'kwɛʃtri] adj equestrian.

eqüidade [ekwi'dadʒi] f equity.

eqüidistante [ekwidʒiʃ'tātʃi] adj equidistant.

eqüilátero/a [ekwi'lateru/a] adj equilateral.

equilibrado/a [ekili'bradu/a] *adj* balanced; (*pessoa*) level-headed.

equilibrar [ekili'bra*] *vt* to balance; ~-**se** *vr* to balance.

equilíbrio [eki'librju] *m* balance; **perder o** ~ to lose one's balance.

eqüino/a [e'kwinu/a] *adj* equine.

equipa [e'kipa] (*PT*) *f* team.

equipamento [ekipa'mẽtu] *m* equipment, kit.

equipar [eki'pa*] *vt* (*navio*) to fit out; (*prover*) to equip.

equiparação [ekipara'sãw] (*pl* -ões) *f* comparison.

equiparar [ekipara*] *vt* (*comparar*) to equate; ~-**se** *vr*: ~-**se a** to equal.

equiparável [ekipa'ravew] (*pl* -eis) *adj* comparable, equitable.

equipe [e'kipi] (*BR*) *f* team.

equitação [ekita'sãw] *f* (*ato*) riding; (*arte*) horsemanship.

eqüitativo/a [ekwita'tʃivu/a] *adj* fair, equitable.

equivalência [ekiva'lẽsja] *f* equivalence.

equivalente [ekiva'lẽtʃi] *adj*, *m* equivalent.

equivaler [ekiva'le*] *vi*: ~ **a** to be the same as, equal.

equivocado/a [ekivo'kadu/a] *adj* mistaken, wrong.

equivocar-se [ekivo'kaxsi] *vr* to make a mistake, be wrong.

equívoco/a [e'kivoku/a] *adj* ambiguous ♦ *m* (*engano*) mistake.

ER *abr* (= *espera resposta*) RSVP.

era ['era] *etc vb V* **ser** ♦ *f* era, age.

erário [e'rarju] *m* exchequer.

ereção [ere'sãw] (*PT*: -cç-: *pl* -ões) (*tb*: *FISIOL*) erection.

erecto/a [e'rɛktu/a] (*PT*) *adj* = **ereto**.

eremita [ere'mita] *m/f* hermit.

eremitério [eremi'tɛrju] *m* hermitage.

ereto/a [e'rɛtu/a] *adj* upright, erect.

erguer [ex'ge*] *vt* (*levantar*) to raise, lift; (*edificar*) to build, erect; ~-**se** *vr* to rise; (*pessoa*) to stand up.

eriçado/a [eri'sadu/a] *adj* bristling; (*cabelos*) (standing) on end.

eriçar [eri'sa*] *vt*: ~ **o cabelo de alguém** to make sb's hair stand on end; ~-**se** *vr* to bristle; (*cabelos*) to stand on end.

erigir [eri'ʒi*] (*irreg*) *vt* to erect.

ermo/a ['exmu/a] *adj* (*solitário*) lonely; (*desabitado*) uninhabited ♦ *m* wilderness.

erógeno/a [e'rɔʒenu/a] *adj* erogenous.

erosão [ero'zãw] *f* erosion.

erótico/a [e'rɔtʃiku/a] *adj* erotic.

erotismo [ero'tʃiʒmu] *m* eroticism.

erradicar [exadʒi'ka*] *vt* to eradicate.

errado/a [e'xadu/a] *adj* wrong; **dar** ~ to go wrong.

errante [e'xãtʃi] *adj* wandering.

errar [e'xa*] *vt* (*o alvo*) to miss; (*a conta*) to get wrong ♦ *vi* (*vaguear*) to wander, roam; (*enganar-se*) to be wrong, make a mistake; ~ **o caminho** to lose one's way.

errata [e'xata] *f* errata.

erro ['exu] *m* mistake; **salvo** ~ unless I am mistaken; ~ **de imprensa** misprint; ~ **de programa** (*COMPUT*) bug; ~ **de pronúncia** mispronunciation.

errôneo/a [e'xonju/a] *adj* wrong, mistaken; (*falso*) false, untrue.

erudição [erudʒi'sãw] *f* erudition, learning.

erudito/a [eru'dʒitu/a] *adj* learned, scholarly ♦ *m* scholar.

erupção [erup'sãw] (*pl* -ões) *f* eruption; (*na pele*) rash; (*fig*) outbreak.

erva ['exva] *f* herb; ~ **daninha** weed; (*col*: *dinheiro*) dosh; (: *maconha*) dope.

erva-cidreira [-si'drejra] (*pl* **ervas-cidreiras**) *f* lemon verbena.

erva-doce (*pl* **ervas-doces**) *f* fennel.

erva-mate [(*pl* **ervas-mates**) *f* matte.

ervilha [ex'viʎa] *f* pea.

ES (*BR*) *abr* = **Espírito Santo**.

ESAO [e'saw] (*BR*) *abr f* (= *Escola Superior de Aperfeiçoamento de Oficiais*) officer training school.

esbaforido/a [iʒbafo'ridu/a] *adj* breathless, panting.

esbaldar-se [iʒbaw'daxsi] *vr* to have a great time, really enjoy o.s.

esbandalhado/a [iʒbãda'ʎadu/a] *adj* (*pessoa*) scruffy; (*casa*, *jardim*) untidy.

esbanjador(a) [iʒbãʒa'do*(a)] *adj* extravagant, spendthrift ♦ *m/f* spendthrift.

esbanjamento [iʒbãʒa'mẽtu] *m* (*ato*) squandering; (*qualidade*) extravagance.

esbanjar [iʒbã'ʒa*] *vt* to squander, waste; **estar esbanjando saúde** to be bursting with health.

esbarrão [iʒba'xãw] (*pl* -ões) *m* collision.

esbarrar [iʒba'xa*] *vi*: ~ **em** to bump into; (*obstáculo*, *problema*) to come up against.

esbarrões [iʒba'xõjʃ] *mpl de* **esbarrão**.

esbeltez [iʒbew'teʒ] *f* slenderness.

esbelto/a [iʒ'bɛwtu/a] *adj* svelte.

esboçar [iʒbo'sa*] *vt* to sketch; (*delinear*) to outline; (*plano*) to draw up; ~ **um sorriso** to give a little smile.

esboço [iʒ'bosu] *m* (*desenho*) sketch; (*primeira versão*) draft; (*fig*: *resumo*) outline.

esbodegado/a [iʒbode'gadu/a] *adj* tatty; (*cansado*) worn out.

esbodegar [iʒbode'ga*] (*col*) *vt* to ruin.

esbofar [iʒbo'fa*] *vt* to tire out; ~-**se** *vr* to be worn out.

esbofetear [iʒbofe'tʃja*] *vt* to slap, hit.

esbórnia [iʒ'bɔxnja] *f* orgy.

esborrachar [iʒboxa'ʃa*] *vt* to squash; (*esbofetear*) to hit; ~-**se** *vr* to go sprawling.

NB: European Portuguese adds the following consonants to certain words: **b** (sú(b)dito, su(b)til); **c** (a(c)ção, a(c)cionista, a(c)to); **m** (inde(m)ne); **p** (ado(p)ção, ado(p)tar); *for further details see p. xiii.*

esbranquiçado/a [iʒbrãki'sadu/a] *adj* whitish; (*lábios*) pale.

esbravejar [iʒbrave'ʒa*] *vt, vi* to shout.

esbregue [iʒ'brɛgi] (*col*) *m* (*descompostura*) telling-off, dressing-down (*BRIT*); (*rolo*) punch-up, brawl.

esburacado/a [iʒbura'kadu/a] *adj* full of holes, holey; (*rua*) full of potholes.

esburacar [iʒbura'ka*] *vt* to make holes (*ou* a hole) in.

esbugalhado/a [iʒbuga'ʎadu/a] *adj* V olho.

esbugalhar-se [iʒbuga'ʎaxsi] *vr* to goggle, boggle.

esc (*PT*) *abr* = **escudo**.

escabeche [iʃka'beʃi] *m* (*CULIN*) marinade, *sauce of spiced vinegar and onion.*

escabroso/a [iʃka'brozu/ɔza] *adj* (*difícil*) tough; (*indecoroso*) indecent.

escada [iʃ'kada] *f* (*dentro da casa*) staircase, stairs *pl*; (*fora da casa*) steps *pl*; (*de mão*) ladder; ~ **em caracol** spiral staircase; ~ **de incêndio** fire escape; ~ **rolante** escalator.

escadaria [iʃkada'ria] *f* staircase.

escafandrista [iʃkafã'driʃta] *m/f* deep-sea diver.

escafandro [iʃka'fãdru] *m* diving suit.

escafeder-se [iʃkafe'dexsi] (*col*) *vi* to sneak off.

escala [iʃ'kala] *f* scale; (*NÁUT*) port of call; (*parada*) stop; **fazer** ~ **em** to call at; **sem** ~ non-stop; ~ **móvel** sliding scale.

escalação [iʃkala'sãw] *f* climbing; (*designação*) selection.

escalada [iʃka'lada] *f* (*de guerra*) escalation.

escalafobético/a [iʃkalafo'bɛtʃiku/a] (*col*) *adj* weird, strange.

escalão [eʃka'lãw] (*pl* **-ões**) *m* step; (*MIL*) echelon; **o primeiro** ~ **do governo** the highest level of government.

escalar [iʃka'la*] *vt* (*montanha*) to climb; (*muro*) to scale; (*designar*) to select.

escalavrar [iʃkala'vra*] *vt* (*pele*) to graze; (*parede*) to damage.

escaldado/a [iʃkaw'dadu/a] *adj* (*fig*) cautious, wary.

escaldar [iʃkaw'da*] *vt* to scald; (*CULIN*) to blanch; **~-se** *vr* to scald o.s.

escaler [iʃka'lɛ*] *m* launch.

escalfar [iʃkaw'fa*] (*PT*) *vt* (*ovos*) to poach.

escalões [eʃka'lõjʃ] *mpl de* **escalão**.

escalonamento [iʃkalona'mẽtu] *m* (*COM*: *de dívida*) scheduling.

escalonar [iʃkalo'na*] *vt* (*argumentos*, *opiniões*) to set out; (*dívida*) to spread, schedule.

escalope [iʃka'lɔpi] *m* escalope (*BRIT*), cutlet (*US*).

escama [iʃ'kama] *f* (*de peixe*) scale; (*de pele*) flake.

escamar [iʃka'ma*] *vt* to scale.

escamotear [iʃkamo'tʃja*] *vt* (*furtar*) to pilfer, pinch (*BRIT*); (*empalmar*) to make disappear (by sleight of hand).

escancarado/a [iʃkãka'radu/a] *adj* wide open.

escancarar [iʃkãka'ra*] *vt* to open wide.

escandalizar [iʃkãdali'za*] *vt* to shock; **~-se** *vr* to be shocked; (*ofender-se*) to be offended.

escândalo [iʃ'kãdalu] *m* scandal; (*indignação*) outrage; **fazer** *ou* **dar um** ~ to make a scene.

escandaloso/a [iʃkãdalozu/ɔza] *adj* shocking, scandalous.

Escandinávia [iʃkãdʒi'navja] *f*: **a** ~ Scandinavia.

escandinavo/a [iʃkãdʒi'navu/a] *adj*, *m/f* Scandinavian.

escangalhar [iʃkãga'ʎa*] *vt* to break, smash (up); (*a saúde*) to ruin; **~-se** *vr*: **~-se de rir** to split one's sides laughing.

escaninho [iʃka'niɲu] *m* (*na secretária*) pigeonhole.

escanteio [iʃkã'teju] *m* (*FUTEBOL*) corner.

escapada [iʃka'pada] *f* escape; (*ato leviano*) escapade.

escapar [iʃka'pa*] *vi*: ~ **a** *ou* **de** to escape from; (*fugir*) to run away from; **~-se** *vr* to run away, flee; **deixar** ~ (*uma oportunidade*) to miss; (*palavras*) to blurt out; ~ **da morte/de uma incumbência** to escape death/get out of a task; **ele escapou de ser atropelado** he escaped being run over; **o vaso escapou-lhe das mãos** the vase slipped out of his hands; **nada lhe escapa** (*passar despercebido*) nothing escapes him, he doesn't miss a thing; **o nome me escapa no momento** the name escapes me for the moment; **não está bom, mas escapa** it's not good, but it'll do; ~ **de boa** (*col*) to have a close shave.

escapatória [iʃkapa'tɔrja] *f* (*saída*) way out; (*desculpa*) excuse.

escape [iʃ'kapi] *m* (*de gás*) leak; (*AUTO*) exhaust.

escapismo [iʃka'piʒmu] *m* escapism.

escapulida [iʃkapu'lida] *f* escape.

escapulir [iʃkapu'li*] *vi*: ~ **(de)** to get away (from); (*suj: coisa*) to slip (from).

escarafunchar [iʃkarafũ'ʃa*] *vt*: ~ **algo** (*remexer em*) to rummage in sth; (*com as unhas*) to scratch at sth; (*investigar*) to pore over sth.

escaramuça [iʃkara'musa] *f* skirmish.

escaravelho [iʃkara'veʎu] *m* beetle.

escarcéu [iʃkax'sɛw] *m* (*fig*): **fazer um** ~ to make a scene.

escarlate [iʃkax'latʃi] *adj* scarlet.

escarlatina [iʃkaxla'tʃina] *f* scarlet fever.

escarnecer [iʃkaxne'se*] *vt* to mock, make fun of ◆ *vi*: ~ **de** to mock, make fun of.

escárnio [iʃ'kaxnju] *m* mockery; (*desprezo*) derision.

escarpa [iʃ'kaxpa] *f* steep slope.

escarpado/a [iʃkax'padu/a] *adj* steep.

escarrado/a [iʃka'xadu/a] *adj* (*fig*): **ela é o pai** ~ she's the spitting image of her father.

escarrapachar-se [iʃkaxapa'ʃaxsi] *vr* to sprawl.

escarrar [iʃka'xa*] vt to spit, cough up ♦ vi to spit.

escarro [iʃ'kaxu] m phlegm, spit.

escasseamento [iʃkasja'mẽtu] m (COM) shortage.

escassear [iʃka'sja*] vt to skimp on ♦ vi to become scarce.

escassez [iʃka'seʒ] f (falta) shortage.

escasso/a [iʃ'kasu/a] adj scarce.

escavação [iʃkava'sãw] (pl -ões) f digging, excavation.

escavadeira [iʃkava'dejra] f digger.

escavar [iʃka'va*] vt to excavate.

esclarecedor(a) [iʃklarese'do*(a)] adj explanatory; (que alarga o conhecimento) informative.

esclarecer [iʃklare'se*] vt (situação) to explain; (mistério) to clear up, explain; ~-se vr: ~-se (sobre algo) to find out (about sth); ~ alguém sobre algo to explain to sb about sth.

esclarecido/a [iʃklare'sidu/a] adj (pessoa) enlightened.

esclarecimento [iʃklaresi'mẽtu] m explanation; (informação) information.

esclerosado/a [iʃklero'zadu/a] (col) adj (pessoa) batty, nutty.

esclerótica [iʃkle'rɔtʃika] f white of the eye.

escoadouro [iʃkoa'doru] m drain; (cano) drainpipe.

escoar [iʃko'a*] vt to drain off ♦ vi to drain away; ~-se vr to seep out.

escocês/esa [iʃko'seʃ/seza] adj Scottish ♦ m/f Scot, Scotsman/woman.

Escócia [iʃ'kɔsja] f Scotland.

escoicear [iʃkoj'sja*] vt to kick; (fig) to illtreat ♦ vi to kick.

escol [iʃ'kɔw] m best; de ~ of excellence.

escola [iʃ'kɔla] f school; ~ naval naval college; ~ primária/secundária primary (BRIT) ou elementary (US)/secondary (BRIT) ou high (US) school; ~ particular/pública private/state (BRIT) ou public (US) school; ~ superior college; fazer ~ to win converts.

escolado/a [iʃko'ladu/a] adj (esperto) shrewd; (experiente) experienced.

escolar [iʃko'la*] adj school atr ♦ m/f schoolboy/girl; ~es mpl schoolchildren.

escolaridade [iʃkolari'dadʒi] f schooling.

escolarização [iʃkolariza'sãw] f education, schooling.

escolarizar [iʃkolari'za*] vt to educate (in school).

escolha [iʃ'koʎa] f choice.

escolher [iʃko'ʎe*] vt to choose, select.

escolho [iʃ'koʎu] m (recife) reef; (rocha) rock.

escolta [iʃ'kɔwta] f escort.

escoltar [iʃkow'ta*] vt to escort.

escombros [iʃ'kõbruʃ] mpl ruins, debris sg.

esconde-esconde [iʃkõdʒiʃ'kõdʒi] m hide-and-seek.

esconder [iʃkõ'de*] vt to hide, conceal; ~-se vr to hide; brincar de ~ to play hide-and-seek.

esconderijo [iʃkõde'riʒu] m hiding place; (de bandidos) hideout.

escondidas [iʃkõ'dʒidaʃ] fpl: às ~ secretly.

esconjurar [iʃkõʒu'ra*] vt (o Demônio) to exorcize; (afastar) to keep off; (amaldiçoar) to curse; ~-se vr (lamentar-se) to complain.

escopo [iʃ'kopu] m aim, purpose.

escora [iʃ'kɔra] f prop, support; (cilada) ambush.

escorar [iʃko'ra*] vt to prop (up); (amparar) to support; (esperar de espreita) to lie in wait for ♦ vi to lie in wait; ~-se vr: ~-se em (fundamentar-se) to go by; (amparar-se) to live off.

escorbuto [iʃkox'butu] m scurvy.

escore [iʃ'kɔri] m score.

escória [iʃ'kɔrja] f (de metal) dross; a ~ da humanidade the scum of the earth.

escoriação [iʃkorja'sãw] (pl -ões) f abrasion, scratch.

escorpiano/a [iʃkox'pjanu/a] adj, m/f (ASTROLOGIA) Scorpio.

escorpião [iʃkoxpi'ãw] (pl -ões) m scorpion; E~ (ASTROLOGIA) Scorpio.

escorraçar [iʃkoxa'sa*] vt (tratar mal) to illtreat; (expulsar) to throw out; ~ alguém de casa ou para fora de casa to throw sb out of the house.

escorrega [iʃko'xɛga] f slide.

escorregadela [iʃkoxega'dɛla] f slip.

escorregadi(ç)o/a [iʃkoxega'dʒi(s)u/a] adj slippery.

escorregador [iʃkoxega'do*] m slide.

escorregão [iʃkoxe'gãw] (pl -ões) m slip; (fig) slip, slip-up.

escorregar [iʃkoxe'ga*] vi to slip; (errar) to slip up.

escorregões [iʃkoxe'gõjʃ] mpl de escorregão.

escorrer [iʃko'xe*] vt (fazer correr) to drain (off); (verter) to pour out ♦ vi (pingar) to drip; (correr em fio) to trickle.

escoteiro [iʃko'tejru] m scout.

escotilha [iʃko'tʃiʎa] f hatch, hatchway.

escova [iʃ'kova] f brush; (penteado) blow-dry; ~ de dentes toothbrush; fazer ~ no cabelo to blow-dry one's hair; (por outra pessoa) to have a blow-dry.

escovar [iʃko'va*] vt to brush.

escovinha [iʃko'viɲa] f V cabelo.

escrachado/a [iʃkra'ʃadu/a] (col) adj (desleixado) scruffy; estar ou ser ~ (ter ficha na polícia) to have a criminal record.

escravatura [iʃkrava'tura] f (tráfico) slave trade; (escravidão) slavery.

escravidão [iʃkravi'dãw] f slavery.

NB: European Portuguese adds the following consonants to certain words: **b** (sú(b)dito, su(b)til); **c** (a(c)ção, a(c)cionista, a(c)to); **m** (inde(m)ne); **p** (ado(p)ção, ado(p)tar); for further details see p. xiii.

escravização [iʃkraviza'sãw] f enslavement.

escravizar [iʃkravi'za*] vt to enslave; (cativar) to captivate.

escravo/a [iʃ'kravu/a] adj captive ♦ m/f slave; **ele é um ~ do amigo/trabalho** he's a slave to his friend/work.

escrete [iʃ'krɛtʃi] m team.

escrevente [iʃkre'vẽtʃi] m/f clerk.

escrever [iʃkre've*] vt, vi to write; **~-se** vr to write to each other; **~ à máquina** to type.

escrevinhador(a) [iʃkreviɲa'do*(a)] (col) m/f hack (writer).

escrevinhar [iʃkrevi'ɲa*] vt to scribble.

escrita [eʃ'krita] f writing; (pessoal) handwriting; **pôr a ~ em dia** to bring one's correspondence up to date.

escrito/a [eʃ'kritu/a] pp de **escrever** ♦ adj written ♦ m piece of writing; **~ à mão** handwritten; **dar por ~** to put in writing; **ela é o pai ~** she's the spitting image of her father.

escritor(a) [iʃkri'to*(a)] m/f writer; (autor) author.

escritório [iʃkri'tɔrju] m office; (em casa) study.

escritura [iʃkri'tura] f (JUR) deed; (ato na compra de imóveis) ≈ exchange of contracts; **as Sagradas E~s** the Scriptures.

escrituração [iʃkritura'sãw] f book-keeping; (de transações, quantias) entering, recording; **~ por partidas simples/dobradas** (COM) single-entry/double-entry book-keeping.

escriturar [iʃkritu'ra*] vt (contas) to register, enter up; (documento) to draw up.

escriturário/a [iʃkritu'rarju/a] m/f clerk.

escrivã [iʃkri'vã] f de **escrivão**.

escrivaninha [iʃkriva'niɲa] f writing desk.

escrivão/vã [iʃkri'vãw/vã] (pl -ões/~s) m/f registrar, recorder.

escroque [iʃ'krɔki] m swindler, conman.

escroto/a [iʃ'krotu/a] m scrotum ♦ adj (col!: pessoa) vile, gross; (: filme etc) crappy (!), shitty (!).

escrúpulo [iʃ'krupulu] m scruple; (cuidado) care; **sem ~** unscrupulous.

escrupuloso/a [iʃkrupu'lozu/ɔza] adj scrupulous; (cuidadoso) careful.

escrutinar [iʃkrutʃina*] vi to act as a scrutineer.

escrutínio [iʃkru'tʃinju] m (votação) poll; (apuração de votos) counting; (exame atento) scrutiny; **~ secreto** secret ballot.

escudar [iʃku'da*] vt to shield; **~-se** vr to shield o.s.; (apoiar-se): **~-se em algo** to rely on sth.

escudeiro [iʃku'dejru] m squire.

escudo [iʃ'kudu] m shield; (moeda) escudo.

esculachado/a [iʃkula'ʃadu/a] (col) adj sloppy.

esculachar [iʃkula'ʃa*] (col) vt (bagunçar) to mess up; (espancar) to beat up; (criticar) to get at; (repreender) to tick off.

esculacho [iʃku'laʃu] (col) m mess; (repreensão) telling-off.

esculhambação [iʃkuʎãba'sãw] (pl -ões) (col!) f mess; (repreensão) telling-off, bollocking (!).

esculhambado/a [iʃkuʎã'badu/a] (col!) adj (descuidado) shabby, slovenly; (estragado) messed up, knackered.

esculhambar [iʃkuʎã'ba*] (col!) vt to mess up, fuck up (!); **~ alguém** (criticar) to give sb stick; (descompor) to give sb a bollocking (!).

esculpir [iʃkuw'pi*] vt to carve, sculpt; (gravar) to engrave.

escultor(a) [iʃkuw'to*(a)] m/f sculptor.

escultura [iʃkuw'tura] f sculpture.

escultural [iʃkuwtu'raw] (pl -ais) adj sculptural; (corpo) statuesque.

escuma [iʃ'kuma] (PT) f foam; (em cerveja) froth.

escumadeira [iʃkuma'dejra] f skimmer.

escuna [iʃ'kuna] f (NÁUT) schooner.

escuras [iʃ'kuraʃ] fpl: **às ~** in the dark.

escurecer [iʃkure'se*] vt to darken ♦ vi to get dark; **ao ~** at dusk.

escurecimento [iʃkuresi'mẽtu] m darkening.

escuridão [iʃkuri'dãw] f (trevas) dark.

escuro/a [iʃ'kuru/a] adj (sombrio) dark; (dia) overcast; (pessoa) swarthy; (negócios) shady ♦ m darkness.

escusa [iʃ'kuza] f excuse.

escusado/a [iʃku'zadu/a] adj unnecessary; **é ~ fazer isso** there's no need to do that.

escusar [iʃku'za*] vt (desculpar) to excuse, forgive; (justificar) to vindicate; (dispensar) to exempt; (não precisar de) not to need; **~-se** vr (desculpar-se) to apologise; **~-se de fazer** to refuse to do; **escuso-me de dar maiores explicações** I need not explain further.

escuta [iʃ'kuta] f listening; **à ~** listening out; **ficar na ~** to stand by; **~ eletrônica/telefônica** bugging/phone tapping.

escutar [iʃku'ta*] vt to listen to; (sem prestar atenção) to hear ♦ vi to listen; to hear; **escuta! listen!**; **ele não escuta bem** he is hard of hearing; **o médico escutou o paciente** the doctor listened to the patient's chest.

esdrúxulo/a [iʒ'druʃulu/a] adj weird, odd.

esfacelar [iʃfase'la*] vt (destruir) to destroy.

esfaimado/a [iʃfaj'madu/a] adj famished, ravenous.

esfalfar [iʃfaw'fa*] vt to tire out, exhaust; **~-se** vr to tire o.s. out.

esfaquear [iʃfaki'a*] vt to stab.

esfarelar [iʃfare'la*] vt to crumble; **~-se** vr to crumble.

esfarrapado/a [iʃfaxa'padu/a] adj ragged, in tatters.

esfarrapar [iʃfaxa'pa*] vt to tear to pieces.

esfera [iʃ'fɛra] f (tb fig) sphere; (globo) globe; (TIP, COMPUT) golfball; **máquina de ~** golfball typewriter.

esférico/a [iʃ'fɛriku/a] adj spherical.

esferográfico/a [iʃfero'grafiku/a] adj: **caneta esferográfica** ballpoint pen.

esfiapar [iʃfja'pa*] *vt* to fray; **~-se** *vr* to fray.

esfinge [iʃ'fiʒi] *f* sphinx.

esfogueado/a [iʃfo'gjadu/a] *adj* impatient.

esfolar [iʃfo'la*] *vt* to skin; (*arranhar*) to graze; (*cobrar demais a*) to overcharge, fleece.

esfomeado/a [iʃfo'mjadu/a] *adj* famished, starving.

esforçado/a [iʃfox'sadu/a] *adj* committed, dedicated.

esforçar-se [iʃfox'saxsi] *vr*: **~ para** to try hard to, strive to.

esforço [iʃ'foxsu] *m* effort; **fazer ~** to try hard, make an effort.

esfregação [iʃfrega'sãw] *f* rubbing; (*col*) necking, petting.

esfregaço [iʃfre'gasu] *m* smear.

esfregar [iʃfre'ga*] *vt* to rub; (*com água*) to scrub.

esfriamento [iʃfrja'mẽtu] *m* cooling.

esfriar [iʃ'frja*] *vt* to cool, chill ♦ *vi* to get cold; (*fig*) to cool off.

esfumaçar [iʃfuma'sa*] *vt* to fill with smoke.

esfumar [iʃfu'ma*] *vt* to disperse; **~-se** *vr* to fade away.

esfuziante [iʃfu'zjãtʃi] *adj* (*pessoa*) bubbly; (*alegria*) irrepressible.

ESG (*BR*) *abr f* (= *Escola Superior de Guerra*) military training school.

esganado/a [iʒga'nadu/a] *adj* (*sufocado*) choked; (*voraz*) greedy; (*avaro*) grasping.

esganar [iʒga'na*] *vt* to strangle, choke.

esganiçado/a [iʒgani'sadu/a] *adj* (*voz*) shrill.

esgaravatar [iʒgarava'ta*] *vt* (*fig*) to delve into.

esgarçar [iʒgax'sa*] *vt*, *vi* to tear; (*com o uso*) to wear into a hole.

esgazeado/a [iʒga'zjadu/a] *adj* (*olhos*, *olhar*) crazed.

esgoelar [iʒgoe'la*] *vt* to yell; (*estrangular*) to choke; **~-se** *vr* to yell, scream.

esgotado/a [iʒgo'tadu/a] *adj* (*exausto*) exhausted; (*consumido*) used up; (*livros*) out of print; **os ingressos estão ~s** the tickets are sold out.

esgotamento [iʒgota'mẽtu] *m* exhaustion.

esgotar [iʒgo'ta*] *vt* (*vazar*) to drain, empty; (*recursos*) to use up; (*pessoa*, *assunto*) to exhaust; **~-se** *vr* (*cansar-se*) to become exhausted; (*mercadorias*, *edição*) to be sold out; (*recursos*) to run out.

esgoto [iʒ'gotu] *m* drain; (*público*) sewer.

esgrima [iʒ'grima] *f* (*ESPORTE*) fencing.

esgrimir [iʒgri'mi*] *vi* to fence.

esgrouvinhado/a [iʒgrovi'ɲadu/a] *adj* dishevelled.

esgueirar-se [iʒgej'raxsi] *vr* to slip away, sneak off.

esguelha [iʒ'geʎa] *f* slant; **olhar alguém de ~** to look at sb out of the corner of one's eye.

esguichar [iʒgi'ʃa*] *vt* to squirt ♦ *vi* to squirt out.

esguicho [iʒ'giʃu] *m* (*jacto*) jet; (*de mangueira etc*) spout.

esguio/a [eʒ'giu/a] *adj* slender.

eslavo/a [iʃ'lavu/a] *adj* Slavic ♦ *m/f* Slav.

emaecer [iʒmaje'se*] *vi* to fade.

esmagador(a) [iʒmagado*(a)] *adj* crushing; (*provas*) irrefutable; (*maioria*) overwhelming.

esmagar [iʒma'ga*] *vt* to crush.

esmaltado/a [iʒmaw'tadu/a] *adj* enamelled (*BRIT*), enameled (*US*).

esmalte [iʒ'mawtʃi] *m* enamel; (*de unhas*) nail polish.

esmerado/a [iʒme'radu/a] *adj* careful, neat; (*bem acabado*) polished.

esmeralda [iʒme'rawda] *f* emerald.

esmerar-se [iʒme'raxsi] *vr* to take great care.

esmero [iʒ'mɛru] *m* (great) care.

esmigalhar [iʒmiga'ʎa*] *vt* to crumble; (*despedaçar*) to shatter; (*esmagar*) to crush; **~-se** *vr* (*pão etc*) to crumble; (*vaso*) to smash, shatter.

esmirrado/a [iʒmi'xadu/a] *adj* (*roupa*) skimpy, tight.

esmiuçar [iʒmju'sa*] *vt* (*pão*) to crumble; (*examinar*) to examine in detail.

esmo ['eʒmu] *m*: **a ~** at random; **andar a ~** to walk aimlessly; **falar a ~** to prattle.

esmola [iʒ'mɔla] *f* alms *pl*; (*col*: *surra*) thrashing; **pedir ~s** to beg.

esmolar [iʒmo'la*] *vt*, *vi*: **~ (algo a alguém)** to beg (sth from sb).

esmorecer [iʒmore'se*] *vt* to discourage ♦ *vi* (*desanimar-se*) to lose heart.

esmorecimento [iʒmoresi'mẽtu] *m* dismay, discouragement; (*enfraquecimento*) weakening.

esmurrar [iʒmu'xa*] *vt* to punch.

Esni [eʒ'ni] (*BR*) *abr f* (= *Escola Nacional de Informações*) training school for intelligence services.

esnobação [iʒnoba'sãw] *f* snobbishness.

esnobar [iʒno'ba*] *vi* to be snobbish ♦ *vt*: **~ alguém** to give sb the cold shoulder.

esnobe [iʒ'nɔbi] *adj* snobbish; (*col*) stuck-up ♦ *m/f* snob.

esnobismo [iʒno'biʒmu] *m* snobbery.

esôfago [e'zofagu] *m* oesophagus (*BRIT*), esophagus (*US*).

esotérico/a [ezo'tɛriku/a] *adj* esoteric.

espaçado/a [iʃpa'sadu/a] *adj* spaced out.

espaçar [iʃpa'sa*] *vt* to space out; **~ visitas/saídas** etc to visit/go out etc less often.

espacejamento [iʃpaseʃa'mẽtu] *m* (*TIP*) spacing; **~ proporcional** proportional spacing.

espacial [iʃpa'sjaw] (*pl* **-ais**) *adj* spatial, space *atr*; **nave ~** spaceship.

---

*NB: European Portuguese adds the following consonants to certain words: **b** (sú(b)dito, su(b)til); **c** (a(c)ção, a(c)cionista, a(c)to); **m** (inde(m)ne); **p** (ado(p)ção, ado(p)tar) etc often. for further details see p. xiii.*

espaço [iʃ'pasu] *m* space; *(tempo)* period; ~ **para 3 pessoas** room for 3 people; **a ~s** from time to time; **sujeito a ~** *(em avião)* standby.

espaçoso/a [iʃpa'sozu/ɔza] *adj* spacious, roomy.

espada [iʃ'pada] *f* sword; **~s** *fpl* (CARTAS) spades; **estar entre a ~ e a parede** to be between the devil and the deep blue sea.

espadachim [iʃpada'ʃĩ] *(pl* **-ns**) *m* swordsman.

espadarte [iʃpa'daxtʃi] *m* swordfish.

espádua [iʃ'padwa] *f* shoulder blade.

espairecer [iʃpajre'se*] *vt* to amuse, entertain ♦ *vi* to relax; **~-se** *vr* to relax.

espairecimento [iʃpajresi'mẽtu] *m* recreation.

espaldar [iʃpaw'da*] *m* (chair) back.

espalha-brasas [iʃpaʎa'-] *m/f inv* troublemaker.

espalhafato [iʃpaʎa'fatu] *m* din, commotion.

espalhafatoso/a [iʃpaʎafa'tozu/ɔza] *adj* *(pessoa)* loud, rowdy; *(roupa)* loud, garish.

espalhar [iʃpa'ʎa*] *vt* to scatter; *(boato, medo)* to spread; *(luz)* to shed; **~-se** *vr* *(fogo, boato)* to spread; *(refestelar-se)* to lounge.

espanador [iʃpana'do*] *m* duster.

espanar [iʃpa'na*] *vt* to dust.

espancamento [iʃpãka'mẽtu] *m* beating.

espancar [iʃpã'ka*] *vt* to beat up.

espandongado/a [iʃpãdõ'gadu/a] *adj* *(no vestir)* scruffy; *(estragado)* tatty.

Espanha [iʃ'paɲa] *f*: **a ~** Spain.

espanhol(a) [iʃpa'ɲow/ola] *(pl* **-óis/~s**) *adj* Spanish ♦ *m/f* Spaniard ♦ *m* (LING) Spanish; **os espanhóis** the Spanish.

espantado/a [iʃpã'tadu/a] *adj* astonished; *(cor)* loud, garish.

espantalho [iʃpã'taʎu] *m* scarecrow.

espantar [iʃpã'ta*] *vt* *(causar medo a)* to frighten; *(admirar)* to amaze, astonish; *(afugentar)* to frighten away ♦ *vi* to be amazing; **~-se** *vr* *(admirar-se)* to be amazed; *(assustar-se)* to be frightened.

espanto [iʃ'pãtu] *m* *(medo)* fright, fear; *(admiração)* amazement.

espantoso/a [iʃpã'tozu/ɔza] *adj* amazing.

esparadrapo [iʃpara'drapu] *m* (sticking) plaster (BRIT), bandaid ® (US).

espargir [iʃpax'ʒi*] *vt* *(líquido)* to sprinkle; *(flores)* to scatter; *(luz)* to shed.

esparramar [iʃpaxa'ma*] *vt* *(líquido)* to splash; *(espalhar)* to scatter.

esparso/a [iʃ'paxsu/a] *adj* scattered; *(solto)* loose.

espartano/a [iʃpax'tanu/a] *adj* *(fig)* spartan.

espartilho [iʃpax'tʃiʎu] *m* corset.

espasmo [iʃ'paʒmu] *m* spasm, convulsion.

espasmódico/a [iʃpaʒ'mɔdʒiku/a] *adj* spasmodic.

espatifar [iʃpatʃi'fa*] *vt* to smash; **~-se** *vr* to smash; *(avião)* to crash.

espavorir [iʃpavo'ri*] *vt* to terrify.

EsPCEx (BR) *abr f* = **Escola Preparatória de Cadetes do Exército.**

especial [iʃpe'sjaw] *(pl* **-ais**) *adj* special; **em ~** especially.

especialidade [iʃpesjali'dadʒi] *f* speciality (BRIT), specialty (US); *(ramo de atividades)* specialization.

especialista [iʃpesja'liʃta] *m/f* specialist; *(perito)* expert.

especialização [iʃpesjaliza'sãw] *(pl* **-ões**) *f* specialization.

especializado/a [iʃpesjali'zadu/a] *adj* specialized; *(operário, mão de obra)* skilled.

especializar-se [iʃpesjali'zaxsi] *vr*: **~ (em)** to specialize (in).

especiaria [iʃpesja'ria] *f* spice.

espécie [iʃ'pɛsi] *f* (BIO) species; *(tipo)* sort, kind; **causar ~** to be surprising; **pagar em ~** to pay in cash.

especificação [iʃpesifika'sãw] *(pl* **-ões**) *f* specification.

especificar [iʃpesifi'ka*] *vt* to specify.

específico/a [iʃpe'sifiku/a] *adj* specific.

espécime [iʃ'pɛsimi] *m* specimen.

espécimen [iʃ'pɛsimẽ] *(pl* **~s**) *m* = **espécime.**

espectáculo *etc* [iʃpek'takulu] (PT) *m* = **espetáculo** *etc*.

espectador(a) [iʃpekta'do*(a)] *m/f* *(testemunha)* onlooker; *(TV)* viewer; *(ESPORTE)* spectator; *(TEATRO)* member of the audience; **~es** *mpl* audience *sg*.

espectro [iʃ'pɛktru] *m* spectre (BRIT), specter (US); *(FÍS)* spectrum; *(pessoa)* gaunt figure.

especulação [iʃpekula'sãw] *(pl* **-ões**) *f* speculation.

especulador(a) [iʃpekula'do*(a)] *adj* speculating ♦ *m/f* *(na Bolsa etc)* speculator; *(explorador)* opportunist.

especular [iʃpeku'la*] *vi*: **~ (sobre)** to speculate (on).

especulativo/a [iʃpekula'tʃivu/a] *adj* speculative.

espelhar [iʃpe'ʎa*] *vt* to mirror; **~-se** *vr* to be mirrored; **seus olhos espelham malícia, espelha-se malícia nos seus olhos** there is malice in his eyes.

espelho [iʃ'peʎu] *m* mirror; *(fig)* model; **~ retrovisor** (AUTO) rearview mirror.

espelunca [iʃpe'lũka] *(col)* *f* *(bar)* dive; *(casa)* dump, hole.

espera [iʃ'pɛra] *f* *(demora)* wait; *(expectativa)* expectation; **à ~ de** waiting for; **à minha ~** waiting for me.

espera-marido *(pl* **-s**) *m* (CULIN) sweet made with burnt sugar and eggs.

esperança [iʃpe'rãsa] *f* *(confiança)* hope; *(expectativa)* expectation; **dar ~s a alguém** to get sb's hopes up; **que ~!** *(col)* no chance!

esperançar [iʃperã'sa*] *vt*: **~ alguém** to give sb hope.

esperançoso/a [iʃperã'sozu/ɔza] *adj* hopeful.

esperar [iʃpe'ra*] *vt* *(aguardar)* to wait for; *(contar com, bebê)* to expect; *(desejar)* to

hope for ◆ *vi* to wait; (*desejar*) to hope;
(*contar com*) to expect; **espero que sim/não**
I hope so/not; **fazer alguém** ~ to keep sb
waiting; **espera aí!** hold on!; (*col: não vem*)
come off it!

esperável [iʃpe'ravew] (*pl* -**eis**) *adj* expected,
probable.

esperma [iʃ'pɛxma] *f* sperm.

espernear [iʃpex'nja*] *vi* to kick out;
(*protestar*) to protest.

espertalhão/lhona [iʃpexta'ʎãw/ʎɔna] (*pl*
-**ões/~s**) *m/f* shrewd operator ◆ *adj* crafty,
shrewd.

esperteza [iʃpex'teza] *f* cleverness; (*astúcia*)
cunning.

esperto/a [iʃ'pɛxtu/a] *adj* clever; (*esperta-
lhão*) crafty; (*col: bacana*) great.

espesso/a [iʃ'pesu/a] *adj* thick.

espessura [iʃpe'sura] *f* thickness.

espetacular [iʃpetaku'la*] *adj* spectacular.

espetáculo [iʃpe'takulu] *m* (*TEATRO*) show;
(*vista*) sight; (*cena ridícula*) spectacle; **dar**
~ to make a spectacle of o.s.; **ela/a casa é
um** ~ (*col*) she/the house is fabulous.

espetada [iʃpe'tada] *f* prick.

espetar [iʃpe'ta*] *vt* (*carne*) to put on a spit;
(*cravar*) to stick; **~-se** *vr* to prick o.s.; ~
algo em algo to pin sth to sth.

espetinho [iʃpe'tʃiɲu] *m* skewer.

espeto [iʃ'petu] *m* spit; (*pau*) pointed stick;
(*fig: pessoa magra*) beanpole; **ser um** ~ (*ser
difícil*) to be awkward.

espevitado/a [iʃpevi'tadu/a] *adj* (*fig: vivo*)
lively.

espezinhar [iʃpezi'ɲa*] *vt* to trample (on);
(*humilhar*) to treat like dirt.

espia [iʃ'pia] *m/f* spy.

espiã [iʃ'pjã] *f de* **espião**.

espiada [iʃ'pjada] *f*: **dar uma** ~ to have a
look.

espião/piã [iʃ'pjãw/'pjã] (*pl* -**ões/~s**) *m/f* spy.

espiar [iʃ'pja*] *vt* (*espionar*) to spy on; (*uma
ocasião*) to watch out for; (*olhar*) to watch ◆
vi to spy; (*olhar*) to peer.

espicaçar [iʃpika'sa*] *vt* to trouble, torment.

espichar [iʃpi'ʃa*] *vt* (*couro*) to stretch out;
(*pescoço, pernas*) to stretch ◆ *vi* (*col:
crescer*) to shoot up; **~-se** *vr* to stretch out.

espiga [iʃ'piga] *f* (*de milho*) ear.

espigado/a [iʃpigadu/a] *adj* (*milho*) fully-
grown; (*ereto*) upright.

espigueiro [iʃpi'gejru] *m* granary.

espinafração [iʃpinafra'sãw] (*pl* -**ões**) (*col*) *f*
telling-off.

espinafrar [iʃpina'fra*] (*col*) *vt*: ~ **alguém**
(*repreender*) to give sb a telling-off;
(*criticar*) to get at sb; (*ridicularizar*) to jeer
at sb.

espinafre [iʃpi'nafri] *m* spinach.

espingarda [iʃpĩ'gaxda] *f* shotgun, rifle; ~ **de**

ar comprimido air rifle.

espinha [iʃ'piɲa] *f* (*de peixe*) bone; (*na pele*)
spot, pimple; (*coluna vertebral*) spine.

espinhar [iʃpi'na*] *vt* (*picar*) to prick;
(*irritar*) to irritate, annoy.

espinheiro [iʃpi'ɲejro] *m* bramble bush.

espinhento/a [iʃpi'ɲĕtu/a] *adj* spotty, pimply.

espinho [iʃ'piɲu] *m* thorn; (*de animal*) spine;
(*fig: dificuldade*) snag.

espinhoso/a [iʃpi'ɲozu/ɔza] *adj* (*planta*)
prickly, thorny; (*fig: difícil*) difficult; (:
problema) thorny.

espinotear [iʃpino'tʃja*] *vi* (*cavalo*) to buck;
(*pessoa*) to leap about.

espiões [iʃ'pjõjʃ] *mpl de* **espião**.

espionagem [iʃpio'naʒĕ] *f* spying, espionage.

espionar [iʃpjo'na*] *vt* to spy on ◆ *vi* to spy,
snoop.

espiral [iʃpi'raw] (*pl* -**ais**) *adj, f* spiral.

espírita [iʃ'pirita] *adj, m/f* spiritualist.

espiritismo [iʃpiri'tʃiʒmu] *m* spiritualism.

espírito [iʃ'piritu] *m* spirit; (*pensamento*)
mind; ~ **de porco** wet blanket; ~ **esportivo**
sense of humour (*BRIT*) *ou* humor (*US*); ~
forte/fraco (*fig: pessoa*) freethinker/sheep;
E~ Santo Holy Spirit.

espiritual [iʃpiri'twaw] (*pl* -**ais**) *adj* spiritual.

espirituoso/a [iʃpiri'twozu/ɔza] *adj* witty.

espirrar [iʃpi'xa*] *vi* to sneeze; (*jorrar*) to
spurt out ◆ *vt* (*água*) to spurt.

espirro [iʃ'pixu] *m* sneeze.

esplanada [iʃpla'nada] *f* esplanade.

esplêndido/a [iʃ'plĕdʒidu/a] *adj* splendid.

esplendor [iʃplĕ'do*] *m* splendour (*BRIT*),
splendor (*US*).

espocar [iʃpo'ka*] *vi* to explode.

espoleta [iʃpo'leta] *f* (*de arma*) fuse.

espoliar [iʃpo'lja*] *vt* to plunder.

espólio [iʃ'pɔlju] *m* (*herança*) estate,
property; (*roubado*) booty, spoils *pl*.

esponja [iʃ'põʒa] *f* sponge; (*de pó de arroz*)
puff; (*parasita*) sponger; (*col: ébrio*) boozer.

esponjoso/a [iʃpõ'ʒozu/ɔza] *adj* spongy.

espontaneidade [iʃpõtanei'dadʒi] *f* spontaneity.

espontâneo/a [iʃpõ'tanju/a] *adj* spontaneous;
(*pessoa: natural*) straightforward.

espora [iʃ'pɔra] *f* spur.

esporádico/a [iʃpo'radʒiku/a] *adj* sporadic.

esporão [iʃpo'rãw] (*pl* -**ões**) *m* (*de galo*) spur.

esporear [iʃpo'rja*] *vt* (*picar*) to spur on; (*fig*)
to incite.

esporões [iʃpo'rõjʃ] *mpl de* **esporão**.

esporte [iʃ'pɔxtʃi] (*BR*) *m* sport.

esportista [iʃpox'tʃiʃta] *adj* sporting ◆ *m/f*
sportsman/woman.

esportiva [iʃpox'tʃiva] *f* sense of humour
(*BRIT*) *ou* humor (*US*); **perder a** ~ to lose
one's sense of humo(u)r.

esportivo/a [iʃpox'tʃivu/a] *adj* sporting.

NB: *European Portuguese adds the following consonants to certain words*: **b** (sú(b)dito, su(b)til); **c** (a(c)ção,
a(c)cionista, a(c)to); **m** (inde(m)ne); **p** (ado(p)ção, ado(p)tar); *for further details see p. xiii.*

esposa [iʃ'poza] f wife.
esposar [iʃpo'za*] vt to marry; (causa) to defend.
esposo [iʃ'pozu] m husband.
espoucar [iʃpo'ka*] vt = **espocar**.
espraiar [iʃpra'ja*] vt, vi to spread; (dilatar) to expand; **~-se** vr (mar) to wash across the beach; (rio) to spread out; (fig: epidemia) to spread.
espreguiçadeira [iʃpregisa'dejra] f deck chair; (com lugar para as pernas) lounger.
espreguiçar-se [iʃpregi'saxsi] vr to stretch.
espreita [iʃ'prejta] f: **ficar à ~** to keep watch.
espreitar [iʃprej'ta*] vt (espiar) to spy on; (observar) to observe, watch.
espremedor [iʃpreme'do*] m squeezer.
espremer [iʃpre'me*] vt (fruta) to squeeze; (roupa molhada) to wring out; (pessoas) to squash; **~-se** vr (multidão) to be squashed together; (uma pessoa) to squash up.
espuma [iʃ'puma] f foam; (de cerveja) froth, head; (de sabão) lather; (de ondas) surf; **colchão de ~** foam mattress; **~ de borracha** foam rubber.
espumante [iʃpu'mãtʃi] adj frothy, foamy; (vinho) sparkling.
espumar [iʃpu'ma*] vi to foam; (fera, cachorro) to foam at the mouth.
espúrio/a [iʃ'purju/a] adj spurious, bogus.
esputinique [iʃputʃi'niki] m satellite, sputnik.
esq. abr (= esquerdo/a) l.; = **esquina**.
esquadra [iʃ'kwadra] f (NÁUT) fleet; (PT: da polícia) police station.
esquadrão [iʃkwa'drãw] (pl -ões) m squadron.
esquadrilha [iʃkwa'driʎa] f squadron.
esquadrinhar [iʃkwadri'ɲa*] vt (casa, área) to search, scour; (fatos) to scrutinize.
esquadro [iʃ'kwadru] m set square.
esquadrões [iʃkwa'drõjʃ] mpl de **esquadrão**.
esqualidez [iʃkwali'deʒ] f squalor.
esquálido/a [iʃ'kwalidu/a] adj squalid, filthy.
esquartejar [iʃkwaxte'ʒa*] vt to quarter.
esquecer [iʃke'se*] vt, vi to forget; **~-se** vr: **~-se de** to forget; **~-se de fazer algo** to forget to do sth; **~-se (de) que ...** to forget that ....
esquecido/a [iʃke'sidu/a] adj forgotten; (pessoa) forgetful.
esquecimento [iʃkesi'mẽtu] m (falta de memória) forgetfulness; (olvido) oblivion; **cair no ~** to fall into oblivion.
esquelético/a [iʃke'lɛtʃiku/a] adj (ANAT) skeletal; (pessoa) scrawny.
esqueleto [iʃke'letu] m skeleton; (arcabouço) framework; **ser um ~** (fig: pessoa) to be just skin and bone.
esquema [iʃ'kema] m (resumo) outline; (plano) scheme; (diagrama) diagram, plan; **~ de segurança** security operation.
esquemático/a [iʃke'matʃiku/a] adj schematic.
esquematizar [iʃkematʃi'za*] vt to represent schematically; (planejar) to plan.

esquentado/a [iʃkẽ'tadu/a] adj (fig: irritado) annoyed; (: irritadiço) irritable.
esquentar [iʃkẽ'ta*] vt to heat (up), warm (up); (fig: irritar) to annoy ♦ vi to warm up; (casaco) to be warm; **~-se** vr to get annoyed; **~ a cabeça** (col) to get worked up; **não esquenta!** don't worry!
esquerda [iʃ'kexda] f (tb: POL) left; **à ~** on the left; **dobrar à ~** to turn left; **políticos de ~** left-wing politicians; **a ~ festiva** the trendy left.
esquerdista [iʃkex'dʒiʃta] adj left-wing ♦ m/f left-winger.
esquerdo/a [iʃ'kexdu/a] adj left.
esquete [iʃ'kɛtʃi] m (TEATRO, TV) sketch.
esqui [iʃ'ki] m (patim) ski; (esporte) skiing; **~ aquático** water skiing; **fazer ~** to go skiing.
esquiador(a) [iʃkja'do*(a)] m/f skier.
esquiar [iʃ'kja*] vi to ski.
esquilo [iʃ'kilu] m squirrel.
esquina [iʃ'kina] f corner; **fazer ~ com** to join.
esquisitão/ona [iʃkizi'tãw/ɔna] (pl -ões/~s) adj odd, peculiar.
esquisitice [iʃkizi'tʃisi] f oddity, peculiarity; (ato, dito) strange thing.
esquisito/a [iʃki'zitu/a] adj strange, odd.
esquisitões [iʃkizi'tõjʃ] mpl de **esquisitão**.
esquisitona [iʃkizi'tɔna] f de **esquisitão**.
esquiva [iʃ'kiva] f dodge.
esquivar-se [iʃki'vaxsi] vr: **~ de** to escape from, get away from; (deveres) to get out of.
esquivo/a [iʃ'kivu/a] adj aloof, standoffish.
esquizofrenia [iʃkizofre'nia] f schizophrenia.
esquizofrênico/a [iʃkizo'freniku/a] adj, m/f schizophrenic.
esqº abr = **esquerdo**.
essa ['ɛsa] pron: **~ é/foi boa** that is/was a good one; **~ não, sem ~** come off it!; **vamos nessa** let's go!; **ainda mais ~!** that's all I need!; **corta ~!** cut it out!; **gostei dessa** I like that; **estou nessa** count me in, I'm game; **por ~s e outras** for these and other reasons; **~ de fazer ...** this business of doing ....
esse ['esi] adj (sg) that; (pl) those; (BR: este: sg) this; (: pl) these ♦ pron (sg) that one; (pl) those; (BR: este: sg) this one; (: pl) these.
essência [e'sẽsja] f essence.
essencial [esẽ'sjaw] (pl -ais) adj essential; (principal) main ♦ m: **o ~** the main thing.
Est. abr (= Estação) Stn.; (= Estrada) ≈ Rd.
esta ['ɛʃta] f de **este**.
estabanado/a [iʃtaba'nadu/a] adj clumsy.
estabelecer [iʃtabele'se*] vt to establish; (fundar) to set up; **~-se** vr to establish o.s., set o.s. up; **estabeleceu-se que ...** it was established that ...; **o governo estabeleceu que ...** the government decided that ....
estabelecimento [iʃtabelesi'mẽtu] m establishment; (casa comercial) business.

estabilidade [iʃtabili'dadʒi] f stability.
estabilização [iʃtabiliza'sáw] f stabilization.
estabilizar [iʃtabili'za*] vt to stabilize; **~-se** vr to stabilize.
estábulo [iʃ'tabulu] m cow-shed.
estaca [iʃ'taka] f post, stake; (de barraca) peg; **voltar à ~ zero** to go back to square one.
estacada [iʃta'kada] f (defensiva) stockade; (fileira de estacas) fencing.
estação [iʃta'sáw] (pl **-ões**) f station; (do ano) season; **~ de águas** spa; **~ balneária** seaside resort; **~ emissora** broadcasting station.
estacar [iʃta'ka*] vt to prop up ♦ vi to stop short, halt.
estacionamento [iʃtasjona'mẽtu] m (ato) parking; (lugar) car park (BRIT), parking lot (US).
estacionar [iʃtasjo'na*] vt to park ♦ vi to park; (não mover) to remain stationary.
estacionário/a [iʃtasjo'narju/a] adj (veículo) stationary; (COM) slack.
estações [iʃta'sõjʃ] fpl de **estação**.
estada [iʃ'tada] f stay.
estadia [iʃta'dʒia] f = **estada**.
estádio [iʃ'tadʒu] m stadium.
estadista [iʃta'dʒiʃta] m/f statesman/woman.
estado [i'ʃtadu] m state; **E~s Unidos (da América)** United States (of America), USA; **~ civil** marital status; **~ de espírito** state of mind; **~ de saúde** condition; **~ maior** staff; **em bom ~** in good condition; **estar em ~ interessante** to be expecting; **estar em ~ de fazer** to be in a position to do.
estadual [iʃta'dwaw] (pl **-ais**) adj state atr.
estadunidense [iʃtaduni'dẽsi] adj (North) American, US atr.
estafa [iʃ'tafa] f fatigue; (esgotamento) nervous exhaustion.
estafante [iʃta'fãtʃi] adj exhausting.
estafar [iʃta'fa*] vt to tire out, fatigue; **~-se** vr to tire o.s. out.
estafermo [iʃta'fexmu] (PT) m scarecrow; (col) nincompoop.
estagiar [iʃta'ʒja*] vi to work as a trainee, do a traineeship.
estagiário/a [iʃta'ʒjarju/a] m/f probationer, trainee; (professor) student teacher; (médico) junior doctor.
estágio [iʃ'taʒu] m (aprendizado) traineeship; (fase) stage.
estagnação [iʃtagna'sáw] f stagnation.
estagnado/a [iʃtag'nadu/a] adj stagnant.
estagnar [iʃtag'na*] vt to make stagnant; (país) to bring to a standstill ♦ vi to stagnate; **~-se** vr to stagnate.
estalagem [iʃta'laʒẽ] (pl **-ns**) f inn.
estalar [iʃta'la*] vt (quebrar) to break; (os dedos) to snap ♦ vi (fender-se) to split, crack; (crepitar) to crackle; **estou estalando**

de dor de cabeça I've got a splitting headache.
estaleiro [iʃta'lejru] m shipyard.
estalido [iʃta'lidu] m pop.
estalo [iʃ'talu] m (do chicote) crack; (dos dedos) snap; (dos lábios) smack; (de foguete) bang; **~ de trovão** thunderclap; **de ~ suddenly**; **me deu um ~** it clicked, the penny dropped.
estampa [iʃ'tãpa] f (figura impressa) print; (ilustração) picture; **ter uma bela ~** (fig) to be beautiful.
estampado/a [iʃtã'padu/a] adj printed ♦ m (tecido) print; (num tecido) pattern; **sua angústia estava estampada no rosto** his anxiety was written on his face.
estampar [iʃtã'pa*] vt (imprimir) to print; (marcar) to stamp.
estamparia [iʃtãpa'ria] f (oficina) printshop; (tecido, figura) print.
estampido [iʃtã'pidu] m bang.
estancar [iʃtã'ka*] vt (sangue, água) to staunch; (fazer cessar) to stop; **~-se** vr (parar) to stop.
estância [iʃ'tãsja] f (fazenda) ranch, farm; (versos) stanza; **~ hidromineral** spa resort.
estandardizar [iʃtãdaxdʒi'za*] vt to standardize.
estandarte [iʃtã'daxtʃi] m standard, banner.
estande [iʃ'tãdʒi] m stand.
estanho [iʃ'taɲu] m (metal) tin.
estanque [iʃ'tãki] adj watertight.
estante [iʃ'tãtʃi] f (armário) bookcase; (suporte) stand.
estapafúrdio/a [iʃtapa'fuxdʒu/a] adj outlandish, odd.
estar [iʃ'ta*] vi to be; (em casa) to be in; (no telefone): **a Lúcia está? - não, ela não está** is Lúcia there? — no, she's not here; **a Maria não está** Maria's not in; **~ fora** (de casa) to be out; (de viagem) to be away; **~ fazendo** (BR) ou **a fazer** (PT) to be doing; **~ bem** (de saúde) to be all right; (de aparência) to look all right; (financeiramente) to be well off; **está bem, 'tá** (col) OK; **~ bem com** to be on good terms with; **~ calor/frio** (o tempo) to be hot/cold; **~ com fome/sede/medo** to be hungry/thirsty/afraid; **~ doente** to be ill; **você está muito elegante hoje** you look very smart today; **~ sentado** to be sitting down; **ela estava de chapéu** she had a hat on, she was wearing a hat; **~ de férias/licença** to be on holiday (BRIT) ou vacation (US)/leave; **o preço está em 3 milhões** the price is 3 million; **~ na hora de fazer** to be time to do; **estou na minha** (col) I'm doing my own thing; **ele está para chegar a qualquer momento** he'll be here any minute; **não ~ para conversas** not to be in the mood for talking; **~ para fazer** to be about to do; **não estou**

---

*NB: European Portuguese adds the following consonants to certain words: **b** (sú(b)dito, su(b)til); **c** (a(c)ção, a(c)cionista, a(c)to); **m** (inde(m)ne); **p** (ado(p)ção, ado(p)tar); for further details see p. xiii.*

para ninguém I'm not available to see anyone; **~ por algo** to be in favour (BRIT) ou favor (US) of sth; **~ por fazer** to be still to be done.

estardalhaço [iʃtaxda'ʎasu] m fuss; (ostentação) ostentation.

estarrecer [iʃtaxe'se*] vt to petrify ♦ vi to be petrified.

estas ['ɛʃtaʃ] adj, pron fpl de **este**.

estatal [iʃta'taw] (pl -ais) adj nationalized, state-owned ♦ f state-owned company.

estatelado/a [iʃtate'ladu/a] adj (cair) sprawling.

estatelar [iʃtate'la*] vt to send sprawling; (estarrecer) to stun; **~-se** vr (cair) to go sprawling.

estática [iʃ'tatʃika] f (TEC) static.

estático/a [iʃ'tatʃiku/a] adj static.

estatística [iʃta'tʃiʃtʃika] f statistic; (ciência) statistics sg.

estatístico/a [iʃta'tʃiʃtʃiku/a] adj statistical.

estatização [iʃtatʃiza'sãw] (pl -ões) f nationalization.

estatizar [iʃtatʃi'za*] vt to nationalize.

estátua [iʃ'tatwa] f statue.

estatueta [iʃta'tweta] f statuette.

estatura [iʃta'tura] f stature.

estatuto [iʃta'tutu] m (JUR) statute; (de cidade) bye-law; (de associação) rule; **~s sociais** ou **da empresa** (COM) articles of association.

estável [iʃ'tavew] (pl -eis) adj stable.

este ['ɛʃtʃi] m east ♦ adj inv (região) eastern; (vento, direção) easterly.

este/ta ['eʃtʃi/'ɛʃta] adj (sg) this; (pl) these ♦ pron this one; (pl) these; (a quem/que se referiu por último) the latter; **esta noite** (noite passada) last night; (noite de hoje) tonight.

esteio [iʃ'teju] m prop, support; (NÁUT) stay.

esteira [iʃ'tejra] f mat; (de navio) wake; (rumo) path.

esteja [iʃ'teʒa] etc vb V **estar**.

estelionato [iʃteljo'natu] m fraud.

estêncil [iʃ'tẽsiw] (pl -eis) m stencil.

estender [iʃtẽ'de*] vt to extend; (mapa) to spread out; (pernas) to stretch; (massa) to roll out; (conversa) to draw out; (corda) to pull tight; (roupa molhada) to hang out; **~-se** vr (no chão) to lie down; (fila, terreno) to stretch, extend; **~-se sobre algo** to dwell on sth, expand on sth; **esta lei estende-se a todos** this law applies to all; **o conferencista estendeu-se demais** the speaker went on too long; **~ a mão** to hold out one's hand; **~ uma cadeira para alguém** to offer sb a chair; **~ uma crítica a todos** to extend a criticism to everyone.

estenodatilógrafo/a [iʃtenodatʃi'lɔgrafu/a] m/f shorthand typist (BRIT), stenographer (US).

estenografar [iʃtenogra'fa*] vt to write in shorthand.

estenografia [iʃtenogra'fia] f shorthand.

estepe [iʃ'tɛpi] m spare wheel.

esterco [iʃ'texku] m manure, dung.

estéreis [iʃ'tɛrejʃ] adj pl de **estéril**.

estereo... [iʃterju-] prefix stereo....

estereofônico/a [iʃterjo'foniku/a] adj stereo(phonic).

estereotipado/a [iʃterjotʃi'padu/a] adj stereotypical.

estereotipar [iʃterjotʃi'pa*] vt to stereotype.

estereótipo [iʃte'rjɔtʃipu] m stereotype.

estéril [iʃ'tɛriw] (pl -eis) adj sterile; (terra) infertile; (fig) futile.

esterilidade [iʃterili'dadʒi] f sterility; (de terra) infertility; (escassez) dearth.

esterilização [iʃteriliza'sãw] f sterilization.

esterilizar [iʃterili'za*] vt to sterilize.

esterlino/a [iʃtex'linu/a] adj sterling ♦ m sterling; **libra esterlina** pound sterling.

esteróide [iʃte'rɔjdʒi] m steroid.

esteta [iʃ'tɛta] m/f aesthete (BRIT), esthete (US).

estética [iʃ'tɛtʃika] f aesthetics sg (BRIT), esthetics sg (US).

esteticista [iʃtetʃi'siʃta] m/f beautician.

estético/a [iʃ'tɛtʃiku/a] adj aesthetic (BRIT), esthetic (US).

estetoscópio [iʃteto'skɔpju] m stethoscope.

esteve [iʃ'tevi] vb V **estar**.

estiagem [iʃ'tʃjaʒẽ] (pl -ns) f (depois da chuva) calm after the storm; (falta de chuva) dry spell.

estiar [iʃ'tʃja*] vi (não chover) to stop raining; (o tempo) to clear up.

estibordo [iʃtʃi'bɔxdu] m starboard.

esticada [iʃtʃi'kada] f: **dar uma ~** (esticar-se) to stretch, have a stretch; **dar uma ~ numa boate** (col) to go on to a nightclub.

esticar [iʃtʃi'ka*] vt (uma corda) to stretch, tighten; (a perna) to stretch; **~-se** vr to stretch out; **~ as canelas** (col) to pop one's clogs, kick the bucket; **depois da festa esticamos numa boate** (col) after the party we went on to a nightclub.

estigma [iʃ'tʃigima] m (marca) mark, scar; (fig) stigma.

estigmatizar [iʃtʃigimatʃi'za*] vt to brand; **~ alguém de algo** to brand sb (as) sth.

estilhaçar [iʃtʃiʎa'sa*] vt to splinter; (despedaçar) to shatter; **~-se** vr to shatter.

estilhaço [iʃtʃi'ʎasu] m fragment, chip, splinter.

estilista [iʃtʃi'liʃta] m/f stylist; (de moda) designer.

estilística [iʃtʃi'liʃtʃika] f stylistics sg.

estilístico/a [iʃtʃi'liʃtʃiku/a] adj stylistic.

estilizar [iʃtʃili'za*] vt to stylize.

estilo [iʃ'tʃilu] m style; (TEC) stylus; **~ de vida** way of life; **móveis de ~** stylish furniture; **o vestido não é do meu ~** ou **não faz o meu ~** the dress isn't my style.

estima [iʃ'tʃima] f esteem; (afeto) affection.

estimação [iʃtʃima'sãw] f: **... de ~** favourite (BRIT) ..., favorite (US) ....

estimado/a [iʃtʃi'madu/a] *adj* respected; *(em cartas)*: **E~ Senhor** Dear Sir.

estimar [iʃtʃi'ma*] *vt* *(apreciar)* to appreciate; *(avaliar)* to value; *(ter estima a)* to have a high regard for; *(calcular aproximadamente)* to estimate; **~-se** *vr*: **eles se estimam muito** they have a high regard for one another; **estima-se o número de ouvintes em 3 milhões** the number of listeners is estimated to be 3 million; **~ em** *(avaliar)* to value at; *(população)* to estimate to be; **estimo que você tenha exito** I wish you success.

estimativa [iʃtʃima'tʃiva] *f* estimate; **fazer uma ~ de algo** to estimate sth; **~ de custo** estimate, costing.

estimável [iʃtʃi'mavew] *(pl* -**eis***) adj (digno de estima)* decent; **prejuízo ~ em 3 milhões** loss estimated at 3 million.

estimulação [iʃtʃimula'sãw] *f* stimulation.

estimulante [iʃtʃimu'lãtʃi] *adj* stimulating ♦ *m* stimulant.

estimular [iʃtʃimu'la*] *vt* to stimulate; *(incentivar)* to encourage; **~ alguém a fazer algo** to encourage sb to do sth.

estímulo [iʃ'tʃimulu] *m* stimulus; *(ânimo)* encouragement; **falta de ~** lack of incentive; **ele não tem ~ para nada no momento** he has got no incentive to do anything at the moment.

estio [iʃ'tʃiu] *m* summer.

estipêndio [iʃtʃi'pẽdʒu] *m* pay.

estipulação [iʃtʃipula'sãw] *(pl* -**ões***) f* stipulation, condition.

estipular [iʃtʃipu'la*] *vt* to stipulate.

estirar [iʃtʃi'ra*] *vt* to stretch (out); **~-se** *vr* to stretch.

estirpe [iʃ'tʃixpi] *f* stock, lineage.

estivador(a) [iʃtʃiva'do*(a)] *m/f* docker.

estive [iʃ'tʃivi] *etc vb V* **estar**.

estocada [iʃto'kada] *f* stab, thrust.

estocado/a [iʃto'kadu/a] *adj (COM)* in stock.

estocagem [iʃto'kaʒẽ] *f (estocar)* stockpiling; *(estoque)* stock.

estocar [iʃto'ka*] *vt* to stock.

Estocolmo [iʃto'kɔwmu] *n* Stockholm.

estofador(a) [iʃtofa'do*(a)] *m/f* upholsterer.

estofar [iʃto'fa*] *vt* to upholster; *(acolchoar)* to pad, stuff.

estofo [iʃ'tofu] *m (tecido)* material; *(para acolchoar)* padding, stuffing.

estóico/a [iʃ'tɔjku/a] *adj* stoic(al) ♦ *m/f* stoic.

estojo [iʃ'toʒu] *m* case; **~ de ferramentas** tool kit; **~ de óculos** glasses case; **~ de tintas** paintbox; **~ de unhas** manicure set.

estola [iʃ'tɔla] *f* stole.

estólido/a [iʃ'tɔlidu/a] *adj* stupid.

estômago [iʃ'tomagu] *m* stomach; **ter ~ para (fazer) algo** to be up to (doing) sth; **estar com o ~ embrulhado** to have an upset stomach; **forrar o ~** to have a little bite to eat.

Estônia [iʃ'tonja] *f*: **a ~** Estonia.

estoniano/a [iʃto'njanu/a] *adj*, *m/f* Estonian.

estonteante [iʃtõ'tʃjãtʃi] *adj* stunning.

estontear [iʃtõ'tʃja*] *vt* to stun, daze.

estoque [iʃ'tɔki] *m (COM)* stock; **em ~** in stock.

estore [iʃ'tɔri] *m* blind.

estória [iʃ'tɔrja] *f* story.

estorninho [iʃtox'niɲu] *m* starling.

estorricar [iʃtoxi'ka*] *vt, vi* = **esturricar**.

estorvar [iʃtox'va*] *vt* to hinder, obstruct; *(fig: importunar)* to bother, disturb; **~ alguém de fazer** to prevent sb from doing.

estorvo [iʃ'toxvu] *m* hindrance, obstacle; *(amolação)* bother, nuisance.

estourado/a [iʃto'radu/a] *adj (temperamental)* explosive; *(col: cansado)* knackered, worn out.

estoura-peito [iʃtora'-] *(col: pl* ~**s***) m* strong cigarette.

estourar [iʃto'ra*] *vi* to explode; *(pneu)* to burst; *(escândalo)* to blow up; *(guerra)* to break out; *(BR: chegar)* to turn up, arrive; **~ (com alguém)** *(zangar-se)* to blow up (at sb); **estou estourando de dor de cabeça** I've got a splitting headache; **eu devo chegar às 9.00, estourando, 9 e meia** I should get there at 9 o'clock, or 9.30 at the latest.

estouro [iʃ'toru] *m* explosion; **ser um ~** *(col)* to be great; **dar o ~** *(fig: zangar-se)* to blow up, blow one's top.

estouvado/a [iʃto'vadu/a] *adj* rash, foolhardy.

estrábico/a [iʃ'trabiku/a] *adj* cross-eyed.

estrabismo [iʃtra'biʒmu] *m* squint.

estraçalhar [iʃtrasa'ʎa*] *vt (livro, objeto)* to pull to pieces; *(pessoa)* to tear to pieces; **~-se** *vr* to mutilate one another.

estrada [iʃ'trada] *f* road; **~ de contorno** ring road *(BRIT)*, beltway *(US)*; **~ de ferro** *(BR)* railway *(BRIT)*, railroad *(US)*; **~ de rodagem** *(BR)* (trunk) road; **~ de terra** dirt road; **~ principal** main road *(BRIT)*, state highway *(US)*; **~ secundária** minor road.

estrado [iʃ'tradu] *m (tablado)* platform; *(de cama)* base.

estragado/a [iʃtra'gadu/a] *adj* ruined, wrecked; *(saúde)* ruined; *(fruta)* rotten; *(muito mimado)* spoiled, spoilt *(BRIT)*.

estraga-prazeres [iʃtraga-] *m/f inv* spoilsport.

estragão [iʃtra'gãw] *m* tarragon.

estragar [iʃtra'ga*] *vt* to spoil; *(arruinar)* to ruin, wreck; *(desperdiçar)* to waste; *(saúde)* to damage; *(mimar)* to spoil.

estrago [iʃ'tragu] *m (destruição)* destruction; *(desperdício)* waste; *(dano)* damage; **os ~s da guerra** the ravages of war.

estrangeiro/a [iʃtrã'ʒejru/a] *adj* foreign ♦ *m/f* foreigner; **no ~** abroad.

NB: European Portuguese adds the following consonants to certain words: **b** (sú(b)dito, su(b)til); **c** (a(c)ção, a(c)cionista, a(c)to); **m** (inde(m)ne); **p** (ado(p)ção, ado(p)tar); *for further details see p. xiii.*

estrangulação [iʃtrãgula'sãw] *f* strangulation.

estrangulador [iʃtrãgula'do*] *m* strangler.

estrangular [iʃtrãgu'la*] *vt* to strangle; **esta suéter está me estrangulando** this sweater is too tight for me.

estranhar [iʃtra'ɲa*] *vt* (*surpreender-se de*) to be surprised at; (*achar estranho*): ~ **algo** to find sth strange; **estranhei o clima** the climate did not agree with me; **minha filha estranhou a visita/a cama nova** my daughter was shy with the visitor/found it hard to get used to the new bed; **não é de se** ~ it's not surprising; **você não quer um chocolate? — estou te estranhando** you don't want a chocolate? — that's not like you.

estranho/a [iʃ'traɲu/a] *adj* strange, odd; (*influências*) outside ♦ *m/f* (*desconhecido*) stranger; (*de fora*) outsider; **o nome não me é** ~ the name rings a bell.

Estrasburgo [iʃtraʒ'buxgu] *n* Strasbourg.

estratagema [iʃtrata'ʒɛma] *m* (*MIL*) stratagem; (*ardil*) trick.

estratégia [iʃtra'tɛʒa] *f* strategy.

estratégico/a [iʃtra'tɛʒiku/a] *adj* strategic.

estratificar-se [iʃtratʃifi'kaxsi] *vr* (*fig*: idéias, opiniões*) to become entrenched.

estrato [iʃ'tratu] *m* layer, stratum.

estratosfera [iʃtratoʃ'fɛra] *f* stratosphere.

estreante [iʃ'trjãtʃi] *adj* new ♦ *m/f* newcomer.

estrear [iʃ'trja*] *vt* (*vestido*) to wear for the first time; (*peça de teatro*) to perform for the first time; (*veículo*) to use for the first time; (*filme*) to show for the first time, première; (*iniciar*): ~ **uma carreira** to embark on or begin a career ♦ *vi* (*ator, jogador*) to make one's first appearance; (*filme, peça*) to open.

estrebaria [iʃtreba'ria] *f* stable.

estrebuchar [iʃtrebu'ʃa*] *vi* to struggle; (*ao morrer*) to shake (in death throes).

estréia [iʃ'treja] *f* (*de artista*) debut; (*de uma peça*) first night; (*de um filme*) première, opening; **é a** ~ **do meu carro** it's the first time I've used my car.

estreitamento [iʃtrejta'mẽtu] *m* (*diminuição*) narrowing; (*aperto*) tightening; (*de relações*) strengthening.

estreitar [iʃtrej'ta*] *vt* (*reduzir*) to narrow; (*roupa*) to take in; (*abraçar*) to hug; (*laços de amizade*) to strengthen ♦ *vi* (*estrada*) to narrow; **~-se** *vr* (*laços de amizade*) to deepen.

estreiteza [iʃtrej'teza] *f* narrowness; (*de regulamento*) strictness; ~ **de pontos de vista** narrowmindedness.

estreito/a [iʃ'trejtu/a] *adj* narrow; (*saia*) straight; (*vínculo, relação*) close; (*medida*) strict ♦ *m* strait; **ter convivência estreita com alguém** to live at close quarters with sb.

estrela [iʃ'trela] *f* star; ~ **cadente** shooting star; ~ **de cinema** film (*BRIT*) *ou* movie (*US*) star; **ter boa** ~ to be lucky.

estrelado/a [iʃtre'ladu/a] *adj* (*céu*) starry; (*PT*: ovo*) fried; **um filme** ~ **por Marilyn**

Monroe a film starring Marilyn Monroe.

estrela-do-mar   (*pl* **estrelas-do-mar**)   *f* starfish.

estrelar [iʃtre'la*] *vt* (*PT*: ovos) to fry; **~-se** *vr* (*céu*) to fill with stars; ~ **um filme/uma peça** to star in a film/play.

estrelato [iʃtre'latu] *m*: **o** ~ stardom.

estrelinha [iʃtre'liɲa] *f* (*fogo de artifício*) sparkler.

estrelismo [iʃtre'liʒmu] *m* star quality.

estremadura [iʃtrema'dura] *f* frontier.

estremecer [iʃtreme'se*] *vt* (*sacudir*) to shake; (*amizade*) to strain; (*fazer tremer*): ~ **alguém** to make sb shudder ♦ *vi* (*vibrar*) to shake; (*tremer*) to tremble; (*horrorizar-se*) to shudder; (*amizade*) to be strained; **ela estremeceu de susto, o susto estremeceu-a** the fright made her jump.

estremecido/a [iʃtreme'sidu/a] *adj* (*sacudido*) shaken; (*sobressaltado*) startled; (*amizade*) strained.

estremecimento [iʃtremesi'mẽtu] *m* (*sacudida*) shaking, trembling; (*tremor*) tremor; (*abalo numa amizade*) tension.

estremunhado/a [iʃtremu'ɲadu/a] *adj* half-asleep.

estrepar-se [iʃtre'paxsi] *vr* (*fig*) to come unstuck.

estrepe [iʃ'trɛpi] (*col*) *m* (*mulher*) dog.

estrépito [iʃ'trɛpitu] *m* din, racket; **com** ~ with a lot of noise, noisily; **fazer** ~ to make a din.

estrepitoso/a [iʃtrepitozu/ɔza] *adj* noisy, rowdy; (*fig*) sensational.

estressante [iʃtre'sãtʃi] *adj* stressful.

estressar [iʃtre'sa*] *vt* to stress.

estresse [iʃ'trɛsi] *m* stress.

estria [iʃ'tria] *f* groove; (*na pele*) stretch mark.

estribar [iʃtri'ba*] *vt* to base; **~-se** *vr*: **~-se em** to be based on.

estribeira [iʃtri'bejra] *f*: **perder as** ~**s** (*col*) to fly off the handle, lose one's temper.

estribilho [iʃtri'biʎu] *m* (*MÚS*) chorus.

estribo [iʃ'tribu] *m* (*de cavalo*) stirrup; (*degrau*) step; (*fig*: apoio) support.

estricnina [iʃtrik'nina] *f* strychnine.

estridente [iʃtri'dẽtʃi] *adj* shrill, piercing.

estrilar [iʃtri'la*] (*col*) *vi* (*zangar-se*) to get mad; (*reclamar*) to moan.

estrilo [iʃ'trilu] *m*: **dar um** ~ to blow one's top.

estripulia [iʃtripu'lia] *f* prank.

estrito/a [iʃ'tritu/a] *adj* (*rigoroso*) strict; (*restrito*) restricted; **no sentido** ~ **da palavra** in the strict sense of the word.

estrofe [iʃ'trɔfi] *f* stanza.

estrogonofe [iʃtrogo'nɔfi] *m* (*CULIN*) stroganoff.

estropiado/a [iʃtrõ'padu/a] *adj* worn out; (*pessoa*) exhausted.

estrondar [iʃtrõ'da*] *vi* to boom; (*fig*) to resound.

estrondo [iʃ'trõdu] *m* (*de trovão*) rumble; (*de armas*) din; ~ **sônico** sonic boom.

estrondoso/a [iʃtrõ'dozu/ɔza] *adj* (*ovação*) tumultuous, thunderous; (*sucesso*) resounding; (*notícia*) sensational.

estropiar [iʃtro'pja*] *vt* (*aleijar*) to maim, cripple; (*fatigar*) to wear out, exhaust; (*texto*) to mutilate; (*pronunciar mal*) to mispronounce.

estrumar [iʃtru'ma*] *vt* to spread manure on.

estrume [iʃ'trumi] *m* manure.

estrutura [iʃtru'tura] *f* structure; (*armação*) framework; (*de edifício*) fabric.

estrutural [iʃtrutu'raw] (*pl* -**ais**) *adj* structural.

estruturalismo [iʃtrutura'liʒmu] *m* structuralism.

estruturar [iʃtrutu'ra*] *vt* to structure.

estuário [iʃtu'arju] *m* estuary.

estudado/a [iʃtu'dadu/a] *adj* (*fig*) studied, affected.

estudantada [iʃtudã'tada] *f* students *pl*.

estudante [iʃtu'dãtʃi] *m/f* student.

estudantil [iʃtudã'tʃiw] (*pl* -**is**) *adj* student *atr*.

estudar [iʃtu'da*] *vt*, *vi* to study.

estúdio [iʃ'tudʒu] *m* studio.

estudioso/a [iʃtudʒozu/ɔza] *adj* studious ♦ *m/f* student.

estudo [iʃ'tudu] *m* study; ~ **de caso** case study; ~ **de viabilidade** feasibility study.

estufa [iʃ'tufa] *f* (*fogão*) stove; (*de plantas*) greenhouse; (*de fogão*) plate warmer; **este quarto é uma** ~ this room is like an oven.

estufado/a [iʃtu'fadu] (*PT*) *m* stew.

estufar [iʃtu'fa*] *vt* (*peito*) to puff up; (*almofada*) to stuff.

estulto/a [iʃ'tuwtu/a] *adj* foolish, silly.

estupefação [iʃtupefa'sãw] (*PT*: -**çç**-) *f* amazement, astonishment.

estupefato/a [iʃtupe'fatu/a] (*PT*: -**ct**-) *adj* dumbfounded; **ele me olhou** ~ he looked at me in astonishment.

estupendo/a [iʃtu'pẽdu/a] *adj* wonderful; (*col*) fantastic, terrific.

estupidamente [iʃtupida'mẽtʃi] *adv* stupidly; **uma cerveja** ~ **gelada** (*col*) an ice-cold beer.

estupidez [iʃtupi'deʒ] *f* stupidity; (*ato, dito*) stupid thing; (*grosseria*) rudeness; **que** ~! what a stupid thing to do! (*ou* to say!).

estúpido/a [iʃ'tupidu/a] *adj* stupid; (*grosseiro*) rude, churlish ♦ *m/f* idiot; (*grosseiro*) oaf; **calor** ~ incredible heat.

estupor [iʃtu'po*] *m* stupor; (*fig: pessoa de mau caráter*) bad lot; (: *pessoa feia*) fright.

estuporado/a [iʃtupo'radu/a] *adj* (*estragado*) ruined; (*cansado*) tired out; (*ferido*) seriously injured.

estuporar-se [iʃtupo'raxsi] (*col*) *vr* (*num acidente*) to be seriously injured.

estuprador [iʃtupra'do*] *m* rapist.

estuprar [iʃtu'pra*] *vt* to rape.

estupro [iʃ'tupru] *m* rape.

estuque [iʃ'tuki] *m* stucco; (*massa*) plaster.

esturricado/a [iʃtuxi'kadu/a] *adj* (*seco*) shrivelled, dried out; (*roupa*) skimpy, tight.

esturricar [iʃtuxi'ka*] *vt*, *vi* to shrivel, dry out.

esvaecer-se [iʒvaje'sexsi] *vr* to fade away, vanish.

esvair-se [iʒva'jixsi] *vr* to vanish, disappear; ~ **em sangue** to lose a lot of blood.

esvaziamento [iʒvazja'mẽtu] *m* emptying.

esvaziar [iʒva'zja*] *vt* to empty; ~-**se** *vr* to empty.

esverdeado/a [iʒvex'dʒjado/a] *adj* greenish.

esvoaçante [iʒvwa'sãtʃi] *adj* billowing.

esvoaçar [iʒvoa'sa*] *vi* to flutter.

ETA ['ɛta] *abr m* (= *Euskadi Ta Askatasuna*) ETA.

eta ['ɛta] (*col*) *excl*: ~ **filme chato!** what a boring film!; ~ **ferro!** gosh!

etapa [e'tapa] *f* (*fase*) stage; **por** ~**s** in stages.

etário/a [e'tarju/a] *adj* age *atr*.

etc. *abr* (= *et cetera*) etc.

éter ['ɛte*] *m* ether.

eternidade [etexni'dadʒi] *f* eternity.

eternizar [etexni'za*] *vt* (*fazer eterno*) to make eternal; (*nome, pessoa*) to immortalize; (*discussão, processo*) to drag out; ~-**se** *vr* to be immortalized; to drag on.

eterno/a [e'texnu/a] *adj* eternal.

ética ['ɛtʃika] *f* ethics *pl*.

ético/a ['ɛtʃiku/a] *adj* ethical.

etimologia [etʃimolo'ʒia] *f* etymology.

etíope [e'tʃiopi] *adj*, *m/f* Ethiopian.

Etiópia [e'tʃjɔpja] *f*: **a** ~ Ethiopia.

etiqueta [etʃi'keta] *f* (*maneiras*) etiquette; (*rótulo*) label; (*que se amarra*) tag; (*em roupa*) label; ~ **adesiva** adhesive *ou* stick-on label.

etiquetar [etʃike'ta*] *vt* to label.

étnico/a ['ɛtʃniku/a] *adj* ethnic.

etnocêntrico/a [etʃno'sẽtriku/a] *adj* ethnocentric.

etnografia [etʃnogra'fia] *f* ethnography.

etnologia [etʃnolo'ʒia] *f* ethnology.

etos ['ɛtuʃ] *m inv* ethos.

eu [ew] *pron* I ♦ *m* self; **sou** ~ it's me; ~ **mesmo** I myself; ~, **hein?** I don't know ... (how strange!).

EUA *abr mpl* (= *Estados Unidos da América*) USA; **nos** ~ in the USA.

eucalipto [ewka'liptu] *m* eucalyptus.

eucaristia [ewkari'tʃia] *f* Holy Communion.

eufemismo [ewfe'miʒmu] *m* euphemism.

eufonia [ewfo'nia] *f* euphony.

euforia [ewfo'ria] *f* euphoria.

eunuco [ew'nuku] *m* eunuch.

Europa [ew'rɔpa] *f*: **a** ~ Europe.

européia [euro'peja] *f de* **europeu**.

europeizar [ewropeji'za*] *vt* to Europeanize; ~-**se** *vr* to become Europeanized.

NB: European Portuguese adds the following consonants to certain words: **b** (sú(b)dito, su(b)til); **c** (a(c)ção, a(c)cionista, a(c)to); **m** (inde(m)ne); **p** (ado(p)ção, ado(p)tar); *for further details see p. xiii.*

europeu/péia [ewro'peu/'pɛja] *adj, m/f* European.

eutanásia [ewta'nazja] *f* euthanasia.

evacuação [evakwa'sãw] (*pl* -ões) *f* evacuation.

evacuar [eva'kwa*] *vt* to evacuate; (*sair de*) to leave; (*MED*) to discharge ♦ *vi* to defecate.

evadir [eva'dʒi*] *vt* to evade; (*col*) to dodge; ~-se *vr* to escape.

evanescente [evane'sẽtʃi] *adj* fading, vanishing.

evangelho [evã'ʒeʎu] *m* gospel.

evangélico/a [evã'ʒeliku/a] *adj* evangelical.

evaporação [evapora'sãw] *f* evaporation.

evaporar [evapo'ra*] *vt, vi* to evaporate; ~-se *vr* to evaporate; (*desaparecer*) to vanish.

evasão [eva'zãw] (*pl* -ões) *f* escape, flight; (*fig*) evasion; ~ **de impostos** tax avoidance.

evasê [eva'ze] *adj* (*saia*) flared.

evasiva [eva'ziva] *f* excuse.

evasivo/a [eva'zivu/a] *adj* evasive.

evasões [eva'zõjʃ] *fpl de* **evasão**.

evento [e'vẽtu] *m* (*acontecimento*) event; (*eventualidade*) eventuality.

eventual [evẽ'tuaw] (*pl* -ais) *adj* fortuitous, accidental.

eventualidade [evẽtwali'dadʒi] *f* eventuality.

evicção [evik'sãw] (*pl* -ões) *f* (*JUR*) eviction.

evidência [evi'dẽsja] *f* evidence, proof.

evidenciar [evidẽ'sja*] *vt* (*comprovar*) to prove; (*mostrar*) to show; ~-se *vr* to be evident, be obvious.

evidente [evi'dẽtʃi] *adj* obvious, evident.

evitar [evi'ta*] *vt* to avoid; ~ **de fazer algo** to avoid doing sth.

evitável [evi'tavew] (*pl* -eis) *adj* avoidable.

evocação [evoka'sãw] (*pl* -ões) *f* evocation; (*de espíritos*) invocation.

evocar [evo'ka*] *vt* to evoke; (*espíritos*) to invoke.

evolução [evolu'sãw] (*pl* -ões) *f* (*desenvolvimento*) development; (*MIL*) manoeuvre (*BRIT*), maneuver (*US*); (*movimento*) movement; (*BIO*) evolution.

evoluído/a [evo'lwidu/a] *adj* advanced; (*pessoa*) broad-minded.

evoluir [evo'lwi*] *vi* to evolve; ~ **para** to evolve into; **ela não evoluiu com os tempos** she hasn't moved with the times.

ex- [eʃ-, eʒ-] *prefixo* ex-, former.

Ex.ª *abr* = **Excelência**.

exacerbação [ezasexba'sãw] *f* worsening; (*exasperação*) irritation.

exacerbante [ezasex'bãtʃi] *adj* exacerbating.

exacerbar [ezasex'ba*] *vt* (*irritar*) to irritate, annoy; (*agravar*) to aggravate, worsen; (*revolta, indignação*) to deepen.

exacto/a *etc* [e'zatu/a] (*PT*) = **exato** *etc*.

exagerado/a [ezaʒe'radu/a] *adj* (*relato*) exaggerated; (*maquilagem etc*) overdone; (*pessoa*): **ele é** ~ (*na maneira de falar*) he exaggerates; (*nos gestos*) he overdoes it *ou* things.

exagerar [ezaʒe'ra*] *vt* to exaggerate ♦ *vi* to exaggerate; (*agir com exagero*) to overdo it.

exagero [eza'ʒeru] *m* exaggeration.

exalação [ezala'sãw] (*pl* -ões) *f* fume.

exalar [eza'la*] *vt* (*odor*) to give off.

exaltação [ezawta'sãw] *f* (*de virtudes etc*) exaltation; (*excitamento*) excitement; (*irritação*) annoyance.

exaltado/a [ezaw'tadu/a] *adj* (*fanático*) fanatical; (*apaixonado*) overexcited.

exaltar [ezaw'ta*] *vt* (*elevar: pessoa, virtude*) to exalt; (*louvar*) to praise; (*excitar*) to excite; (*irritar*) to annoy; ~-se *vr* (*irritar-se*) to get worked up; (*arrebatar-se*) to get carried away.

exame [e'zami] *m* (*EDUC*) examination, exam; (*MED etc*) examination; **fazer um** ~ (*EDUC*) to take an exam; (*MED*) to have an examination; ~ **de direção** driving test; ~ **de sangue** blood test; ~ **médico** medical (examination); (~) **vestibular** university entrance exam.

examinador(a) [ezamina'do*(a)] *m/f* examiner ♦ *adj* examining.

examinando/a [ezami'nãdu/a] *m/f* (exam) candidate.

examinar [ezami'na*] *vt* to examine.

exangue [e'zãgi] *adj* (*sem sangue*) bloodless.

exasperação [ezaʃpera'sãw] *f* exasperation.

exasperador(a) [ezaʃpera'do*(a)] *adj* exasperating.

exasperante [ezaʃpe'rãtʃi] *adj* exasperating.

exasperar [ezaʃpe'ra*] *vt* to exasperate; ~-se *vr* to get exasperated.

exatidão [ezatʃi'dãw] *f* (*precisão*) accuracy; (*perfeição*) correctness.

exato/a [e'zatu/a] *adj* (*certo*) right, correct; (*preciso*) exact; ~! exactly!

exaurir [ezaw'ri*] *vt* to exhaust, drain; ~-se *vr* to become exhausted.

exaustão [ezaw'ʃtãw] *f* exhaustion.

exaustar [ezaw'ʃta*] *vt* to exhaust, drain; ~-se *vr* to become exhausted.

exaustivo/a [ezaw'ʃtʃivu/a] *adj* (*tratado*) exhaustive; (*trabalho*) exhausting.

exausto/a [e'zawʃtu/a] *pp de* **exaurir** ♦ *adj* exhausted.

exaustor [ezaw'ʃto*] *m* extractor fan.

exceção [ese'sãw] (*pl* -ões) *f* exception; **com** ~ **de** with the exception of; **abrir** ~ to make an exception.

excedente [ese'dẽtʃi] *adj* excess; (*COM*) surplus ♦ *m* (*COM*) surplus; (**aluno**) ~ pupil *who cannot be given a place because the school is full.*

exceder [ese'de*] *vt* to exceed; (*superar*) to surpass; ~-se *vr* (*cometer excessos*) to go too far; (*cansar-se*) to overdo things; ~ **em peso/brilho** to outweigh/outshine.

excelência [ese'lẽsja] *f* excellence; **por** ~ par excellence; **Vossa E**~ Your Excellency.

excelente [ese'lẽtʃi] *adj* excellent.

excelentíssimo/a [eselẽ'tʃisimu/a] *adj superl de* **excelente**; (*tratamento*) honourable

(*BRIT*), honorable (*US*).

excelso/a [e'sɛwsu/a] *adj* (*sublime*) sublime; (*excelente*) excellent.

excentricidade [esẽtrisi'dadʒi] *f* eccentricity.

excêntrico/a [e'sẽtriku/a] *adj, m/f* eccentric.

excepção [ese'sãw] (*PT*) *f* = **exceção**.

excepcional [esepsjo'naw] (*pl* **-ais**) *adj* (*extraordinário*) exceptional; (*especial*) special; (*MED*) handicapped.

excepcionalidade [esepsjonali'dadʒi] *f* exceptional nature.

excepto *etc* [e'sɛtu] (*PT*) = **exceto** *etc.*

excerto [e'sɛxtu] *m* fragment, excerpt.

excessivo/a [ese'sivu/a] *adj* excessive.

excesso [e'sɛsu] *m* excess; (*COM*) surplus; **em ~** in excess; **~ de peso** excess weight; **~ de velocidade** excessive speed.

exceto [e'sɛtu] *prep* except (for), apart from.

excetuar [ese'twa*] *vt* to except, make an exception of; **todos, excetuando você** everyone except you.

excitação [esita'sãw] *f* excitement.

excitado/a [esi'tadu/a] *adj* excited; (*estimulado*) aroused.

excitante [esi'tãtʃi] *adj* exciting.

excitar [esi'ta*] *vt* to excite; (*estimular*) to arouse; **~-se** *vr* to get excited.

excitável [esi'tavew] (*pl* **-eis**) *adj* excitable.

exclamação [iʃklama'sãw] (*pl* **-ões**) *f* exclamation.

exclamar [iʃkla'ma*] *vi* to exclaim.

exclamativo/a [iʃklama'tʃivu/a] *adj* exclamatory; *V tb* **ponto**.

excluir [iʃ'klwi*] *vt* to exclude; (*deixar fora*) to leave out; (*eliminar*) to rule out; (*ser incompatível com*) to preclude.

exclusão [iʃklu'zãw] *f* exclusion.

exclusividade [iʃkluzivi'dadʒi] *f* exclusiveness; (*COM*) exclusive rights *pl*; **com ~ no "Globo"** only in the "Globo".

exclusivo/a [iʃklu'zivu/a] *adj* exclusive; **para uso ~** de for the sole use of.

excluso/a [iʃ'kluzu/a] *adj* excluded.

excomungar [iʃkomũ'ga*] *vt* to excommunicate.

excremento [iʃkre'mẽtu] *m* excrement.

excruciante [iʃkru'sjãtʃi] *adj* excruciating.

excursão [iʃkux'sãw] (*pl* **-ões**) *f* trip, outing; (*em grupo*) excursion; **~ a pé** hike.

excursionar [iʃkuxsjo'na*] *vi* to go on a trip; **~ pela Europa** *etc* to tour Europe *etc.*

excursionista [iʃkuxsjo'niʃta] *m/f* tourist; (*para o dia*) day-tripper; (*a pé*) hiker.

excursões [iʃkux'sõjʃ] *fpl de* **excursão**.

execrável [eze'kravew] (*pl* **-eis**) *adj* execrable, deplorable.

execução [ezeku'sãw] (*pl* **-ões**) *f* execution; (*de música*) performance; **~ de hipoteca** (*COM*) foreclosure.

executante [ezeku'tãtʃi] *m/f* player, performer.

executar [ezeku'ta*] *vt* to execute; (*MÚS*) to perform; (*plano*) to carry out; (*papel teatral*) to play; **~ uma hipoteca** (*COM*) to foreclose on a mortgage.

executivo/a [ezeku'tʃivu/a] *adj, m/f* executive.

executor(a) [ezeku'to*(a)] *m/f* executioner.

exemplar [ezẽ'pla*] *adj* exemplary ♦ *m* model, example; (*BIO*) specimen; (*livro*) copy; (*peça*) piece.

exemplificar [ezẽplifi'ka*] *vt* to exemplify.

exemplo [e'zẽplu] *m* example; **por ~** for example; **dar o ~** to set an example; **servir de ~ a alguém** to be an example to sb; **a ~ de** just like; **a ~ do que** just as; **ela é um ~ de bondade** she's a model of kindness.

exéquias [e'zɛkjaʃ] *fpl* funeral rites.

exeqüível [eze'kwivew] (*pl* **-eis**) *adj* feasible.

exercer [ezex'se*] *vt* to exercise; (*influência, pressão*) to exert; (*função*) to perform; (*profissão*) to practise (*BRIT*), practice (*US*); (*obrigações*) to carry out.

exercício [ezex'sisju] *m* (*ginástica*, *EDUC*) exercise; (*de medicina*) practice; (*de direitos*) exercising; (*MIL*) drill; (*COM*) financial year; **em ~** (*funcionário*) in office; (*professor etc*) in service; **em pleno ~ de suas faculdades mentais** in full command of one's mental faculties; **~ anterior/corrente** (*COM*) previous/current (financial) year.

exercitar [ezexsi'ta*] *vt* (*profissão*) to practise (*BRIT*), practice (*US*); (*direitos, músculos*) to exercise; (*adestrar*) to train.

exército [e'zɛxsitu] *m* army.

exibição [ezibi'sãw] (*pl* **-ões**) *f* show, display; (*de filme*) showing.

exibicionismo [ezibisjo'niʒmu] *m* flamboyance; (*PSICO*) exhibitionism.

exibicionista [ezibisjo'niʃta] *adj* flamboyant; (*PSICO*) exhibitionist ♦ *m/f* flamboyant character; exhibitionist.

exibições [ezibi'sõjʃ] *fpl de* **exibição**.

exibido/a [ezi'bidu/a] *adj* (*exibicionista*) flamboyant ♦ *m/f* show-off.

exibidor(a) [ezibi'do*(a)] *m/f* exhibitor; (*CINEMA*) cinema owner.

exibir [ezi'bi*] *vt* to show, display; (*alardear*) to show off; (*filme*) to show, screen; **~-se** *vr* to show off; (*indecentemente*) to expose o.s.

exigência [ezi'ʒẽsja] *f* demand; (*o necessário*) requirement.

exigente [ezi'ʒẽtʃi] *adj* demanding; **ser ~ com alguém** to be hard on sb.

exigibilidades [eziʒibili'dadʒiʃ] *fpl* (*COM*) liabilities.

exigir [ezi'ʒi*] *vt* to demand; **~ que alguém faça algo** to demand that sb do sth; **o médico exigiu-lhe repouso absoluto** the doctor ordered him to have complete rest.

exigível [ezi'ʒivew] (*pl* **-eis**) *adj* (*COM*:

passivo): ~ **a curto/longo prazo** current/ long-term liabilities *pl*.

exíguo/a [e'zigwu/a] *adj* (*diminuto*) small; (*escasso*) scanty.

exilado/a [ezi'ladu/a] *adj* exiled ♦ *m/f* exile.

exilar [ezi'la*] *vt* to exile; (*pessoa indesejável*) to deport; ~-**se** *vr* to go into exile.

exílio [e'zilju] *m* exile; (*forçado*) deportation.

exímio/a [e'zimju/a] *adj* (*eminente*) famous, distinguished; (*excelente*) excellent.

eximir [ezi'mi*] *vt*: ~ **de** to exempt from; (*obrigação*) to free from; (*culpa*) to clear of; ~-**se** *vr*: ~-**se de** to avoid, shun.

existência [ezi'tēsja] *f* existence; (*vida*) life.

existencial [ezitē'sjaw] (*pl* -**ais**) *adj* existential.

existencialismo [ezitēsja'liʒmu] *m* existentialism.

existencialista [ezitēsja'liʃta] *adj*, *m/f* existentialist.

existente [ezi'tētʃi] *adj* extant; (*vivente*) living.

existir [ezi'tʃi*] *vi* to exist; **existe/existem** ... (*há*) there is/are ...; **ela não existe** (*col*) she's incredible.

êxito ['ezitu] *m* (*resultado*) result; (*sucesso*) success; (*música*, *filme etc*) hit; **ter** ~ (**em**) to succeed (in), be successful (in); **não ter** ~ (**em**) to fail (in), be unsuccessful (in).

Exmo(s)/a(s) *abr* (= *Excelentíssimo(s)/a(s)*) Dear.

êxodo ['ezodu] *m* exodus.

exoneração [ezonera'sãw] (*pl* -**ões**) *f* dismissal.

exonerar [ezone'ra*] *vt* (*demitir*) to dismiss; ~ **de uma obrigação** to free from an obligation.

exorbitante [ezoxbi'tātʃi] *adj* (*preço*) exorbitant; (*pretensões*) extravagant; (*exigências*) excessive.

exorcismo [ezox'siʒmu] *m* exorcism.

exorcista [ezox'siʃta] *m/f* exorcist.

exorcizar [ezoxsi'za*] *vt* to exorcise.

exortação [ɛzoxta'sãw] (*pl* -**ões**) *f* exhortation.

exortar [ezox'ta*] *vt*: ~ **alguém a fazer algo** to urge sb to do sth.

exortativo/a [ezoxta'tʃivu/a] *adj* (*tom*) encouraging.

exótico/a [e'zɔtʃiku/a] *adj* exotic.

exotismo [ezo'tʃiʒmu] *m* exoticism, exotic nature.

expandir [iʃpã'dʒi*] *vt* to expand; (*espalhar*) to spread; ~-**se** *vr* (*dilatar-se*) to expand; ~-**se com alguém** to be frank with sb.

expansão [iʃpã'sãw] *f* expansion, spread; (*de alegria*) effusiveness.

expansividade [iʃpãsivi'dadʒi] *f* outgoing nature.

expansivo/a [iʃpã'sivu/a] *adj* (*pessoa*) outgoing.

expatriação [iʃpatrja'sãw] *f* expatriation.

expatriado/a [iʃpa'trjadu/a] *adj*, *m/f* expatriate.

expatriar [iʃpa'trja*] *vt* to expatriate.

expeça [iʃ'pɛsa] *etc vb V* **expedir**.

expectativa [iʃpekta'tʃiva] *f* (*esperança*) expectation; **na** ~ **de** in expectation of; **estar na** ~ to be expectant; (*em suspense*) to be in suspense; ~ **de vida** life expectancy.

expectorante [iʃpekto'rãtʃi] *adj*, *m* expectorant.

expectorar [iʃpekto'ra*] *vt* to cough up ♦ *vi* to expectorate.

expedição [iʃpedʒi'sãw] (*pl* -**ões**) *f* (*viagem*) expedition; (*de mercadorias*) despatch; (*por navio*) shipment; (*de passaporte etc*) issue.

expediência [iʃpe'dʒjēsja] *f* (*desembaraço*) efficiency.

expediente [iʃpe'dʒjētʃi] *m* means; (*serviço*) working day; (*correspondência*) correspondence ♦ *adj* expedient; ~ **bancário** banking hours *pl*; ~ **do escritório** office hours *pl*; **meio** ~ part-time working; **só trabalho meio** ~ I only work part-time; **viver de** ~**s** to live on one's wits; **ser** *ou* **ter** ~ (*pessoa*) to be resourceful, have initiative.

expedir [iʃpe'dʒi*] *vt* (*enviar*) to send, despatch; (*bilhete*, *passaporte*, *decreto*) to issue.

expedito/a [iʃpe'dʒitu/a] *adj* prompt, speedy; (*pessoa*) efficient.

expelir [iʃpe'li*] *vt* (*expulsar*) to expel; (*sangue*) to spit.

experiência [iʃpe'rjēsja] *f* (*prática*) experience; (*prova*) experiment, test; **em** ~ on trial.

experienciar [iʃperjē'sja*] *vt* to experience.

experiente [iʃpe'rjētʃi] *adj* experienced.

experimentação [iʃperimēta'sãw] *f* experimentation.

experimentado/a [iʃperimē'tadu/a] *adj* (*experiente*) experienced; (*testado*) tried; (*provado*) tested.

experimental [iʃperimē'taw] (*pl* -**ais**) *adj* experimental.

experimentar [iʃperimē'ta*] *vt* (*comida*) to taste; (*vestido*) to try on; (*pôr à prova*) to try out, test; (*conhecer pela experiência*) to experience; (*sofrer*) to suffer, undergo; ~ **fazer algo** to try doing sth, have a go at doing sth.

experimento [iʃperi'mētu] *m* (*científico*) experiment.

expiar [iʃ'pja*] *vt* to atone for.

expiatório/a [iʃpja'tɔrju/a] *adj V* **bode**.

expilo [iʃ'pilu] *etc vb V* **expelir**.

expiraçao [iʃpira'sãw] (*pl* -**ões**) *f* (*de ar*) exhalation; (*termo*) expiry.

expirar [iʃpi'ra*] *vt* (*ar*) to exhale, breathe out ♦ *vi* (*morrer*) to die; (*terminar*) to end.

explanação [iʃplana'sãw] (*pl* -**ões**) *f* explanation.

explanar [iʃpla'na*] *vt* to explain.

explicação [iʃplika'sãw] (*pl* -**ões**) *f* explanation; (*PT*: *lição*) private lesson.

explicar [iʃpli'ka*] *vt*, *vi* to explain; ~-**se** *vr* to explain o.s.; **isto não se explica** this does not make sense.

explicável [iʃpli'kavew] (pl -eis) adj explicable, explainable.

explícito/a [iʃ'plisitu/a] adj explicit, clear.

explodir [iʃplo'dʒi*] vi to explode, blow up ♦ vt (bomba) to explode.

exploração [iʃplora'sãw] f (de um país) exploration; (abuso) exploitation; (de uma mina) running.

explorador(a) [iʃplora'do*(a)] adj exploitative ♦ m/f (descobridor) explorer; (de outros) exploiter.

explorar [iʃplo'ra*] vt (região) to explore; (mina) to work, run; (ferida) to probe; (trabalhadores etc) to exploit.

explosão [iʃplo'zãw] (pl -ões) f explosion, blast; (fig) outburst.

explosivo/a [iʃplo'zivu/a] adj explosive; (pessoa) hot-headed ♦ m explosive.

explosões [iʃplo'sõjʃ] fpl de explosão.

Expoagro [eʃpu'agru] abr f = Exposição Agropecuária Internacional do Rio de Janeiro.

expor [iʃ'po*] (irreg: como pôr) vt to expose; (a vida) to risk; (teoria) to explain; (revelar) to reveal; (mercadorias) to display; (quadros) to exhibit; ~-se vr to expose o.s.; ~(-se) a algo to expose (o.s.) to sth; seu rosto expõe sinais de cansaço his face shows signs of tiredness.

exportação [iʃpoxta'sãw] f (ato) export(ing); (mercadorias) exports pl.

exportador(a) [iʃpoxta'do*(a)] adj exporting ♦ m/f exporter.

exportar [iʃpox'ta*] vt to export.

expôs [iʃ'poʃ] etc vb V expor.

exposição [iʃposi'sãw] (pl -ões) f (exibição) exhibition; (explicação) explanation; (declaração) statement; (narração) account; (FOTO) exposure.

expositor(a) [iʃpozi'to*(a)] m/f exhibitor.

exposto/a [iʃ'poʃtu/'poʃta] pp de expor ♦ adj (lugar) exposed; (quadro, mercadoria) on show ou display ♦ m: o acima ~ the above; estar ~ a algo to be open ou exposed to sth.

expressão [iʃpre'sãw] (pl -ões) f expression.

expressar [iʃpre'sa*] vt to express; ~-se vr to express o.s.

expressividade [iʃpresivi'dadʒi] f expressiveness.

expressivo/a [iʃpre'sivu/a] adj expressive; (pessoa) demonstrative.

expresso/a [iʃ'presu/a] pp de exprimir ♦ adj (manifesto) definite, clear; (trem, ordem, carta) express ♦ m express.

expressões [iʃpre'sõjʃ] fpl de expressão.

exprimir [iʃpri'mi*] vt to express; ~-se vr to express o.s.

expropriar [iʃpro'prja*] vt to expropriate.

expugnar [iʃpugi'na*] vt to take by storm.

expulsado/a [iʃpuw'sadu/a] pp de expulsar.

expulsão [iʃpul'sãw] (pl -ões) f expulsion; (ESPORTE) sending off.

expulsar [iʃpuw'sa*] vt to expel; (de uma festa, clube etc) to throw out; (inimigo) to drive out; (estrangeiro) to expel, deport; (jogador) to send off.

expulso/a [iʃ'puwsu/a] pp de expulsar.

expulsões [iʃpul'sõjʃ] fpl de expulsão.

expunha [iʃ'puɲa] etc vb V expor.

expus [iʃ'puʃ] etc vb V expor.

expuser [iʃpu'ze*] etc vb V expor.

expurgar [iʃpux'ga*] vt to expurgate.

êxtase ['eʃtazi] m ecstasy; (transe) trance; **estar em** ~ to be in a trance.

extasiado/a [iʃta'zjadu/a] adj entranced.

extensão [iʃtẽ'sãw] (pl -ões) f (ger, TEL) extension; (de uma empresa) expansion; (terreno) expanse; (tempo) length, duration; (de conhecimentos) extent.

extensivo/a [iʃtẽ'sivu/a] adj extensive; **ser** ~ **a** to extend to.

extenso/a [iʃ'tẽsu/a] adj (amplo) extensive, wide; (comprido) long; (conhecimentos) extensive; (artigo) full, comprehensive; **por** ~ in full.

extensões [iʃtẽ'sõjʃ] fpl de extensão.

extenuado/a [iʃte'nwadu/a] adj (esgotado) worn out.

extenuante [iʃte'nwãtʃi] adj exhausting; (debilitante) debilitating.

extenuar [iʃte'nwa*] vt to exhaust; (debilitar) to weaken.

exterior [iʃte'rjo*] adj (de fora) outside, exterior; (aparência) outward; (comércio) foreign ♦ m (da casa) outside; (aspecto) outward appearance; **do** ~ (do estrangeiro) from abroad; **no** ~ abroad.

exteriorizar [iʃterjori'za*] vt to show, manifest.

exteriormente [iʃterjox'mẽtʃi] adv on the outside.

exterminação [iʃtexmina'sãw] f extermination.

exterminar [iʃtexmi'na*] vt (inimigo) to wipe out, exterminate; (acabar com) to do away with.

extermínio [iʃtex'minju] m extermination, wiping out.

externato [iʃtex'natu] m day school.

externo/a [iʃ'texnu/a] adj external; (aparente) outward; **"para uso** ~**"** "external use only".

extinção [iʃtʃĩ'sãw] f extinction.

extinguir [iʃtʃĩ'gi*] vt (fogo) to put out, extinguish; (um povo) to wipe out; ~-se vr (fogo, luz) to go out; (BIO) to become extinct.

extinto/a [iʃ'tʃĩtu/a] adj (fogo) extinguished; (língua) dead; (animal, vulcão) extinct; (associação etc) defunct; (pessoa) dead.

extintor [iʃtʃĩ'to*] m (fire) extinguisher.

NB: European Portuguese adds the following consonants to certain words: **b** (sú(b)dito, su(b)til); **c** (a(c)ção, a(c)cionista, a(c)to); **m** (inde(m)ne); **p** (ado(p)ção, ado(p)tar); for further details see p. xiii.

extirpar [iʃtix'pa*] *vt* (*desarraigar*) to uproot; (*corrupção*) to eradicate; (*tumor*) to remove.
extorquir [iʃtox'ki*] *vt* to extort.
extorsão [iʃtox'sãw] *f* extortion.
extorsivo/a [iʃtox'sivu/a] *adj* extortionate.
extra ['ɛʃtra] *adj* extra ♦ *m/f* extra person; (*TEATRO*) extra; *V* **tb hora**.
extração [iʃtra'sãw] (*PT*: **-cç-**: *pl* **-ões**) *f* extraction; (*de loteria*) draw.
extraconjugal [eʃtrakõʒu'gaw] (*pl* **-ais**) *adj* extramarital.
extracto [iʃ'tratu] (*PT*) *m* = **extrato**.
extracurricular [eʃtrakuxiku'la*] *adj* extracurricular.
extradição [eʃtradʒi'sãw] *f* extradition.
extraditar [eʃtradʒi'ta*] *vt* to extradite.
extrafino/a [eʃtra'finu/a] *adj* extra high-quality.
extrair [iʃtra'ji*] *vt* to extract, take out.
extra-oficial (*pl* **-ciais**) *adj* unofficial.
extraordinário/a [iʃtraoxdʒi'narju/a] *adj* extraordinary; (*despesa*) extra; (*reunião*) special; **nada de ~** nothing out of the ordinary.
extrapolar [iʃtrapo'la*] *vt* to extrapolate.
extraterrestre [eʃtrate'xɛʃtri] *adj* extraterrestrial.
extrato [iʃ'tratu] *m* extract; (*resumo*) summary; **~ (bancário)** (bank) statement.
extravagância [iʃtrava'gãsja] *f* extravagance.
extravagante [iʃtrava'gãtʃi] *adj* extravagant; (*roupa*) outlandish; (*conduta*) wild.
extravasar [iʃtrava'za*] *vi* to overflow.
extraviado/a [iʃtra'vjadu/a] *adj* lost, missing.
extraviar [iʃtra'vja*] *vt* (*perder*) to mislay; (*pessoa*) to lead astray; (*dinheiro*) to embezzle; **~-se** *vr* to get lost.
extravio [iʃtra'viu] *m* (*perda*) loss; (*roubo*) embezzlement; (*fig*) deviation.
extremado/a [iʃtre'madu/a] *adj* extreme.
extremar-se [iʃtre'maxsi] *vt* to do one's utmost, make every effort; (*distinguir-se*) to distinguish o.s.; **~ em gentilezas** to show extreme kindness.
extrema-unção [iʃtremaũ'sãw] (*pl* **extrema-unções**) *f* (*REL*) extreme unction.
extremidade [iʃtremi'dadʒi] *f* extremity; (*do dedo*) tip; (*ponta*) end; (*beira*) edge.
extremo/a [iʃ'tremu/a] *adj* extreme ♦ *m* extreme; **~s** *mpl* (*carinho*) doting *sg*; (*descomedimento*) extremes; **ao ~** extremely; **de um ~ a outro** from one extreme to another; **o E~ Oriente** the Far East.
extremoso/a [iʃtre'mozu/ɔza] *adj* doting.
extroversão [eʃtrovex'sãw] *f* extroversion.
extroverso/a [eʃtro'vexsu/a] *adj* extrovert.
extroverter-se [eʃtrovex'texsi] *vr* to be outgoing.
extrovertido/a [eʃtrovex'tʃidu/a] *adj* extrovert, outgoing ♦ *m/f* extrovert.
exu [e'ʃu] *m* devil (*in voodoo rituals*).
exuberância [ezube'rãsja] *f* exuberance.

exuberante [ezube'rãtʃi] *adj* exuberant.
exultação [ezuwta'sãw] *f* joy, exultation.
exultante [ezuw'tãtʃi] *adj* jubilant, exultant.
exultar [ezuw'ta*] *vi* to rejoice.
exumar [ezu'ma*] *vt* (*corpo*) to exhume; (*fig*) to dig up.
ex-voto *m* votive offering.

F

F, f ['ɛfi] (*pl* **fs**) *m* F, f; **F de Francisco** F for Frederick (*BRIT*) *ou* Fox (*US*).
f *abr* = **folha**.
F-1 *abr* = **Fórmula Um**.
fá [fa] *m* (*MÚS*) F.
fã [fã] (*col*) *m/f* fan.
FAB ['fabi] *abr f* = **Força Aérea Brasileira**.
fábrica ['fabrika] *f* factory; **~ de cerveja** brewery; **~ de conservas** cannery; **~ de papel** paper mill; **a preço de ~** wholesale.
fabricação [fabrika'sãw] *f* manufacture; **de ~ caseira/própria** home-made/own-make; **~ em série** mass production.
fabricante [fabri'kãtʃi] *m/f* manufacturer.
fabricar [fabri'ka*] *vt* to manufacture, make; (*inventar*) to fabricate.
fabrico [fa'briku] *m* production.
fabril [fa'briw] (*pl* **-is**) *adj* *V* **industria**.
fábula ['fabula] *f* fable; (*conto*) tale; (*BR: grande quantia*) fortune.
fabuloso/a [fabu'lozu/ɔza] *adj* fabulous.
faca ['faka] *f* knife; **é uma ~ de dois gumes** (*fig*) it's a two-edged sword; **entrar na ~** (*col*) to be operated on, go under the knife; **ter a ~ e o queijo na mão** (*fig*) to have things in hand.
facada [fa'kada] *f* stab, cut; **dar uma ~ em alguém** to stab sb; (*fig: col*) to touch sb for money.
façanha [fa'saɲa] *f* exploit, deed.
facão [fa'kãw] (*pl* **-ões**) *m* carving knife; (*para cortar o mato*) machete.
facção [fak'sãw] (*pl* **-ões**) *f* faction.
faccioso/a [fak'sjozu/ɔza] *adj* factious.
facções [fak'sõjʃ] *fpl* **de facção**.
face ['fasi] *f* (*rosto, de moeda*) face; (*bochecha*) cheek; **em ~ de** in view of; **fazer ~ a** to face up to; **~ a ~** face to face; **disquete de ~ simples/dupla** (*COMPUT*) single-/double-sided disk.
faceiro/a [fa'sejru/a] *adj* (*elegante*) smart; (*alegre*) cheerful.
fáceis ['fasejʃ] *adj pl de* **fácil**.
faceta [fa'seta] *f* (*tb fig*) facet.
fachada [fa'ʃada] *f* (*tb fig*) façade, front; (*col: rosto*) face, mug (*col*).

facho ['faʃu] *m* beam.

facial [fa'sjaw] (*pl* **-ais**) *adj* facial.

fácil ['fasiw] (*pl* **-eis**) *adj* easy; (*temperamento, pessoa*) easy-going; (*mulher*) easy ♦ *adv* easily.

facilidade [fasili'dadʒi] *f* ease; (*jeito*) facility; **~s** *fpl* facilities; **ter ~ para algo** to have a talent *ou* a facility for sth; **com ~** easily.

facílimo/a [fa'silimu/a] *adj superl de* **fácil**.

facilitação [fasilita'sãw] *f* facilitation; (*fornecimento*) provision.

facilitar [fasili'ta*] *vt* to facilitate, make easy; (*fornecer*) to provide ♦ *vi* (*agir sem cautela*) to be careless.

facínora [fa'sinora] *m* criminal.

fã-clube [fã'klubi] (*pl* **fãs-clubes**) *m* fan club.

faço ['fasu] *etc vb V* **fazer**.

facões [fa'kõjʃ] *fpl de* **facão**.

fac-símile [fak-] (*pl* **~s**) *m* (*cópia*) facsimile; (*carta*) fax; (*máquina*) fax (machine); **enviar por ~** to fax.

factício/a [fak'tʃisju/a] *adj* unnatural.

facto ['faktu] (*PT*) *m* = **fato**.

factor [fak'to*] (*PT*) *m* = **fator**.

factótum [fak'tɔtu] *m* factotum.

factual [fak'twaw] (*pl* **-ais**) *adj* factual.

factura *etc* [fak'tura] (*PT*) = **fatura** *etc*.

faculdade [fakuw'dadʒi] *f* faculty; (*poder*) power; (*BR*: *escola*) university, college; (*corpo docente*) teaching staff (*BRIT*), faculty (*US*); **fazer ~** to go to university *ou* college.

facultar [fakuw'ta*] *vt* (*permitir*) to allow; (*conceder*) to grant.

facultativo/a [fakuwta'tʃivu/a] *adj* optional ♦ *m/f* doctor.

fada ['fada] *f* fairy.

fadado/a [fa'dadu/a] *adj* fated, destined, doomed.

fada-madrinha (*pl* **fadas-madrinhas**) *f* fairy godmother.

fadiga [fa'dʒiga] *f* fatigue.

fadista [fa'dʒiʃta] (*PT*) *m/f* "fado" singer ♦ *m* ruffian.

fado ['fadu] *m* fate; (*canção*) traditional song of Portugal.

Faferj [fa'fexʒi] *abr f* = **Federação das Associações das Favelas do Estado do Rio de Janeiro.**

fagueiro/a [fa'gejru/a] *adj* (*contente*) happy; (*agradável*) pleasant.

fagulha [fa'guʎa] *f* spark.

fahrenheit [farẽ'ajtʃi] *adj inv* Fahrenheit.

faia ['faja] *f* beech (tree).

faina ['fajna] *f* toil, work; (*tarefa*)· task, job.

fair-play ['fexplej] *m* fair play.

faisão [faj'zãw] (*pl* **-ães** *ou* **-ões**) *m* pheasant.

faísca [fa'iʃka] *f* spark; (*brilho*) flash.

faiscante [faj'ʃkãtʃi] *adj* flashing; (*fogo*) flickering.

faiscar [fajʃ'ka*] *vi* to sparkle; (*brilhar*) to

flash.

faisões [faj'zõjʃ] *mpl de* **faisão**.

faixa ['fajʃa] *f* (*cinto*) belt; (*tira*) strip; (*área*) zone; (*AUTO*: *pista*) lane; (*BR*: *para pedestres*) zebra crossing (*BRIT*), crosswalk (*US*); (*MED*) bandage; (*num disco*) track; (*JUDÔ*) belt; **~ etária** age group.

faixa-título *f* (*MÚS*) title track.

fajuto/a [fa'ʒutu/a] (*col*) *adj* (*pão*) rough; (*falso*: *nota*) fake.

fala ['fala] *f* speech; **chamar às ~s** to call to account; **sem ~** speechless; **perder a ~** to be struck dumb.

falação [fala'sãw] (*pl* **-ões**) *f* (*ato*) talk; (*discurso*) speech.

falácia [fa'lasja] *f* fallacy.

falações [fala'sõjʃ] *fpl de* **falação**.

faladeira [fala'dejra] *f de* **falador**.

falado/a [fa'ladu/a] *adj* (*caso etc*) talked about, much discussed; (*famoso*) well-known; (*de má fama*) notorious; (*CINEMA*) talking.

falador/deira [fala'do*/dejra] *adj* talkative ♦ *m/f* chatterbox.

falante [fa'lãtʃi] *adj* talkative.

falar [fa'la*] *vt* (*língua*) to speak; (*besteira etc*) to talk; (*dizer*) to say; (*verdade, mentira*) to tell ♦ *vi* to speak, talk; (*discursar*) to speak; **~-se** *vr* to talk to one another; **~ algo a alguém** to tell sb sth; **~ que** to say that; **~ de** *ou* **em algo** to talk about sth; **~ com alguém** to talk to sb; **por ~ em** speaking of; **por ~ nisso** by the way; **sem ~ em** not to mention; **~ alto** to talk loudly; **~ alto com alguém** (*fig*) to give sb a good talking-to; **sua consciência falou mais alto** his conscience got the better of him; **falou!, 'tá falado!** (*col*) OK!; **falando sério ...** but seriously ...; **~ sozinho** to talk to o.s.; **ele está falando da boca para fora** (*col*) he's just saying that, he doesn't mean it; **ele falou por ~** he was just saying that; **dar que ~** to cause a stir; **~ para dentro** to talk into one's beard; **~ pelos cotovelos** to talk one's head off; **eles não se falam** (*estão de mal*) they are not speaking to one another; **nem se fala!** definitely not!

falatório [fala'torju] *m* (*ruído de vozes*) voices *pl*, talking; (*falar demorado*) diatribe; (*maledicência*) rumour (*BRIT*), rumor (*US*).

falaz [fa'laʒ] *adj* deceptive, misleading; (*falso*) false.

falcão [faw'kãw] (*pl* **-ões**) *m* falcon.

falcatrua [fawka'trua] *f* fraud.

falcões [faw'kõjʃ] *mpl de* **falcão**.

falecer [fale'se*] *vi* to die.

falecido/a [fale'sidu/a] *adj* dead, late ♦ *m/f* deceased.

falecimento [falesi'mẽtu] *m* death.

falência [fa'lẽsja] *f* bankruptcy; **abrir ~** to declare o.s. bankrupt; **ir à ~** to go bankrupt;

NB: European Portuguese adds the following consonants to certain words: **b** (sú(b)dito, su(b)til); **c** (a(c)ção, a(c)cionista, a(c)to); **m** (inde(m)ne); **p** (ado(p)ção, ado(p)tar); *for further details see p. xiii.*

levar à ~ to bankrupt.

falésia [fa'lɛzja] f cliff.

falha ['faʎa] f (defeito, GEO etc) fault; (lacuna) omission; (de caráter) flaw.

falhar [fa'ʎa*] vi to fail; (não acertar) to miss; (errar) to be wrong; **o motor está falhando** the engine is missing.

falho/a ['faʎu/a] adj faulty; (deficiente) wanting.

fálico/a ['faliku/a] adj phallic.

falido/a [fa'lidu/a] adj, m/f bankrupt.

falir [fa'li*] vi to fail; (COM) to go bankrupt.

falível [fa'livew] (pl -eis) adj fallible.

falo ['falu] m phallus.

falsário/a [faw'sarju/a] m/f forger.

falsear [faw'sja*] vt to forge, falsify; (verdade) to twist; **~ o pé** to put a foot wrong.

falseta [faw'scta] (col) f dirty trick.

falsete [faw'setʃi] m falsetto.

falsidade [fawsi'dadʒi] f falsehood; (fingimento) pretence (BRIT), pretense (US); (mentira) lie.

falsificação [fawsifika'sãw] (pl -ões) f (ato) falsification; (efeito) forgery; (falsa interpretação) misrepresentation.

falsificador(a) [fawsifika'do*(a)] m/f forger.

falsificar [fawsifi'ka*] vt to forge, falsify; (adulterar) to adulterate; (desvirtuar) to misrepresent.

falsificações [fawsifika'sõjʃ] fpl de **falsificação**.

falso/a ['fawsu/a] adj false; (fraudulento) dishonest; (errôneo) wrong; (jóia, moeda, quadro) fake; (pessoa: insincero) two-faced; **pisar em ~** to miss one's step, put a foot wrong.

falta ['fawta] f (carência) lack; (ausência) absence; (defeito, culpa) fault; (FUTEBOL) foul; **por ou na ~ de** for lack of; **sem ~** without fail; **cometer/cobrar uma ~** (FUTEBOL) to commit a foul/take a free kick; **estar em ~ com alguém** to feel guilty about sb; **fazer ~** to be lacking, be needed; **ela faz ~** she is missed; **este livro não vai te fazer ~?** won't you need this book?; **sentir ~ de alguém/algo** to miss sb/sth; **ter ~ de** to lack, be in need of; **~ de água** water shortage; **~ de ânimo** lack of enthusiasm; **~ de educação ou modos** rudeness; **~ de tato** tactlessness.

faltar [faw'ta*] vi (escassear) to be lacking, be wanting; (pessoa) to be absent; (falhar) to fail; **~ ao trabalho** to be absent from work; **~ à palavra** to break one's word; **falta pouco para ...** it won't be long until ...; **falta uma semana para nossas férias** it's only a week until our holidays; **faltam 10 minutos para as 3** it's ten minutes to three; **faltam 3 páginas (para eu acabar)** there are 3 pages to go (before I finish); **faltam chegar duas pessoas** two people are still to come; **falta fazermos mais algumas coisas** there are still a few things for us to do; **só faltava essa!** that's all I (ou we etc) needed!; **nada me**

falta I have all I need.

falto/a ['fawtu/a] adj lacking, deficient.

faltoso/a [faw'tozu/ɔza] adj (culpado) at fault; (que costuma faltar) frequently absent.

fama ['fama] f (renome) fame; (reputação) reputation; **ter ~ de (ser) generoso** to be said to be generous; **de ~** famous; **de má ~** notorious, of ill repute.

Famerj [fa'mɛxʒi] abr f = **Federação das Associações de Moradores do Estado do Rio de Janeiro.**

famigerado/a [famiʒe'radu/a] adj (malfeitor) notorious; (autor etc) famous.

família [fa'milja] f family; (COMPUT) font ♦ adj inv (col: pessoa) decent; (: festa) proper; **de boa ~** from a good family; **estar em ~** to be one of the family, be among friends; **isso é de ~** this runs in the family, this is a family trait.

familiar [fami'lja*] adj (da família) family atr; (conhecido) familiar ♦ m/f relation, relative.

familiaridade [familjari'dadʒi] f familiarity; (sem-cerimônia) informality.

familiarização [familjariza'sãw] f familiarization.

familiarizar [familjari'za*] vt to familiarize; **~-se** vr: **~-se com algo** to familiarize o.s. with sth.

faminto/a [fa'mĩtu/a] adj hungry; (fig): **~ de** eager for.

famoso/a [fa'mozu/ɔza] adj famous.

fanático/a [fa'natʃiku/a] adj fanatical ♦ m/f fanatic.

fanatismo [fana'tʃiʒmu] m fanaticism.

fanfarrão/rona [fãfa'xãw/'xɔna] (pl -ões/~s) adj boastful ♦ m/f braggart.

fanhoso/a [fa'ɲozu/ɔza] adj (pessoa) with a nasal voice; (voz) nasal; **falar ou ser ~** to talk through one's nose.

faniquito [fani'kitu] (col) m fit of nerves.

fantasia [fãta'zia] f fantasy; (imaginação) imagination; (capricho) fancy; (traje) fancy dress; **jóia (de) ~** (piece of) costume jewellery (BRIT) ou jewelry (US).

fantasiar [fãta'zja*] vt to imagine ♦ vi to daydream; **~-se** vr to dress up (in fancy dress).

fantasioso/a [fãta'zjozu/ɔza] adj imaginative.

fantasista [fãta'ziʃta] adj imaginative.

fantasma [fã'taʒma] m ghost; (alucinação) illusion; **ela está um ~** she's like a ghost.

fantasmagórico/a [fãtaʒma'gɔriku/a] adj ghostly.

fantástico/a [fã'taʃtʃiku/a] adj fantastic; (ilusório) imaginary; (incrível) unbelievable.

fantoche [fã'tɔʃi] m (tb fig) puppet.

fanzoca [fã'zɔka] (col) m/f great fan.

faqueiro [fa'kejru] m (jogo de talheres) set of cutlery; (pessoa) cutler.

faquir [fa'ki*] m fakir.

faraó [fara'ɔ] m pharaoh.

faraônico/a [fara'oniku/a] adj (fig: obra) large-scale.

farda ['faxda] f uniform.

fardar [fax'da*] *vt* to dress in uniform.

fardo ['faxdu] *m* bundle; (*carga*) load; (*fig*) burden.

farei [fa'rej] *etc vb* V **fazer**.

farejar [fare'ʒa*] *vt* to smell (out), sniff (out); ♦ *vi* to sniff.

farelo [fa'rɛlu] *m* (*de pão*) crumb; (*de madeira*) sawdust; ~ **de trigo** bran.

farfalhante [faxfa'ʌãtʃi] *adj* rustling.

farfalhar [faxfa'ʌa*] *vi* to rustle.

farfalhudo/a [faxfa'ʌudu/a] *adj* ostentatious.

farináceo/a [fari'nasju/a] *adj* (*alimento*) starchy; (*molho etc*) floury.

farináceos [fari'nasjuʃ] *mpl* (*alimentos*) starchy foods.

faringe [fa'rĩʒi] *f* pharynx.

faringite [farĩ'ʒitʃi] *f* pharyngitis.

farinha [fa'riɲa] *f*: ~ **(de mesa)** (manioc) flour; ~ **de arroz** rice flour; ~ **de osso** bonemeal; ~ **de rosca** breadcrumbs *pl*; ~ **de trigo** plain flour.

farmacêutico/a [faxma'sewtʃiku/a] *adj* pharmaceutical ♦ *m/f* pharmacist, chemist (*BRIT*).

farmácia [fax'masja] *f* pharmacy, chemist's (shop) (*BRIT*); (*ciência*) pharmacy.

farnel [fax'nɛw] (*pl* **-éis**) *m* (*provisões*) provisions *pl*; (*saco*) food parcel.

faro ['faru] *m* sense of smell; (*fig*) flair.

faroeste [fa'rwɛʃtʃi] *m* (*filme*) western; (*região*) wild west.

farofa [fa'rɔfa] *f* (*CULIN*) side dish based on manioc flour.

farofeiro/a [faro'fejru/a] *m/f* picnicker (*who comes to the beach from far away*).

farol [fa'rɔw] (*pl* **-óis**) *m* lighthouse; (*AUTO*) headlight; (*col*) bragging; ~ **alto/baixo** (*AUTO*) full (*BRIT*) *ou* high (*US*) beam/dipped (*BRIT*) *ou* dimmed (*US*) beam; **contar** ~ (*col*) to brag.

faroleiro [faro'lejru] *m* lighthouse keeper; (*col*) braggart.

farolete [faro'letʃi] *m* (*AUTO*: *dianteiro*) sidelight; (*tb*: ~ *traseiro*) tail-light.

farpa ['faxpa] *f* barb; (*estilha*) splinter.

farpado/a [fax'padu/a] *adj* barbed; V *tb* **arame**.

farra ['faxa] *f* binge, spree; **cair na** ~ to go on the razzle; **só de** *ou* **por** ~ just for the fun of it.

farrapo [fa'xapu] *m* rag; **ela parecia um** ~ she looked like a tramp; **esta blusa está um** ~ this blouse is a sight.

farrear [fa'xja*] *vi* to go on a spree.

farripas [fa'xipaʃ] *fpl* wisps of hair.

farrista [fa'xiʃta] *m/f* raver ♦ *adj* gallivanting.

farsa ['faxsa] *f* farce.

farsante [fax'sãtʃi] *m/f* joker; (*pessoa sem palavra*) smooth operator.

farta ['faxta] *f*: **comer à** ~ to eat one's fill.

fartar [fax'ta*] *vt* to satiate, fill up; ~**-se** *vr* to gorge o.s.; ~**-se de** (*cansar-se*) to get fed up with; **me fartei (de comer)** I'm full up.

farto/a ['faxtu/a] *adj* full, satiated; (*abundante*) plentiful; (*aborrecido*) fed up; **cabeleira farta** full head of hair, shock of hair.

fartum [fax'tũ] (*pl* **-ns**) *m* stench.

fartura [fax'tura] *f* abundance, plenty.

fascículo [fa'sikulu] *m* (*de publicação*) instalment (*BRIT*), installment (*US*).

fascinação [fasina'sãw] *f* fascination; **ter** ~ **por alguém** to be infatuated with sb.

fascinante [fasi'nãtʃi] *adj* fascinating.

fascinar [fasi'na*] *vt* to fascinate; (*encantar*) to charm.

fascínio [fa'sinju] *m* fascination.

fascismo [fa'siʒmu] *m* fascism.

fascista [fa'siʃta] *adj*, *m/f* fascist.

fase ['fazi] *f* phase; (*etapa*) stage.

fastidioso/a [faʃtʃi'dʒjozu/ɔza] *adj* tedious; (*enfadonho*) annoying.

fastígio [faʃ'tʃiʒju] *m* (*fig*) height.

fastio [faʃ'tʃiu] *m* lack of appetite; (*tédio*) boredom.

fatal [fa'taw] (*pl* **-ais**) *adj* (*mortal*) fatal; (*inevitável*) fateful.

fatalidade [fatali'dadʒi] *f* (*destino*) fate; (*desgraça*) disaster.

fatalista [fata'liʃta] *adj* fatalistic ♦ *m/f* fatalist.

fatalmente [fataw'mẽtʃi] *adv* (*de modo fatal*) fatally; (*certamente*) inevitably, doubtlessly.

fatia [fa'tʃia] *f* slice.

fatídico/a [fa'tʃidʒiku/a] *adj* fateful.

fatigante [fatʃi'gãtʃi] *adj* tiring; (*aborrecido*) tiresome.

fatigar [fatʃi'ga*] *vt* to tire; (*aborrecer*) to bore; ~**-se** *vr* to get tired.

fato ['fatu] *m* fact; (*acontecimento*) event; (*PT*: *traje*) suit; ~ **de banho** (*PT*) swimming costume (*BRIT*), bathing suit (*US*); ~ **consumado** fait accompli; **de** ~ in fact, really; **o** ~ **é que** ... the fact remains that ...; **chegar às vias de** ~ to come to blows.

fator [fa'to*] *m* factor; ~ **Rh** (*MED*) Rh *ou* rhesus (*BRIT*) factor.

fátuo/a ['fatwu/a] *adj* (*vão*) fatuous.

fatura [fa'tura] *f* bill, invoice.

faturamento [fatura'mẽtu] *m* (*COM*: *volume de negócios*) turnover; (*faturar*) invoicing.

faturar [fatu'ra*] *vt* to invoice; (*dinheiro*) to make; (*col*: *gol*) to score, notch up ♦ *vi* (*col*: *ganhar dinheiro*): ~ **(alto)** to rake it in; ~ **algo a alguém** to invoice sb for sth.

fauna ['fawna] *f* fauna.

fausto/a ['fawʃtu/a] *adj* lucky ♦ *m* luxury.

fava ['fava] *f* (broad) bean; **mandar alguém às** ~**s** to send sb packing.

favela [fa'vɛla] *f* slum, shanty town.

favelado/a [fave'ladu/a] *m/f* slum-dweller.

NB: European Portuguese adds the following consonants to certain words: **b** (sú(b)dito, su(b)til); **c** (a(c)ção, a(c)cionista, a(c)to); **m** (inde(m)ne); **p** (ado(p)ção, ado(p)tar); *for further details see p. xiii.*

favo ['favu] *m* honeycomb.

favor [fa'vo*] *m* favour (*BRIT*), favor (*US*); **a ~ de** in favo(u)r of; **em ~ de** on behalf of; **por ~** please; **fazer um ~ para alguém** to do sb a favo(u)r; **faça** *ou* **faz o ~ de ...** would you be so good as to ..., kindly ...; **faça-me o ~!** (*col*) do me a favo(u)r!; **ter a seu ~** to have to one's credit.

favorável [favo'ravew] (*pl* -**eis**) *adj*: **~ (a)** favourable (*BRIT*) *ou* favorable (*US*) (to).

favorecer [favore'se*] *vt* to favour (*BRIT*), favor (*US*); (*beneficiar*) to benefit; (*suj: vestido*) to suit; (: *retrato*) to flatter.

favoritismo [favori'tʃizmu] *m* favouritism (*BRIT*), favoritism (*US*).

favorito/a [favo'ritu/a] *adj*, *m/f* favourite (*BRIT*), favorite (*US*).

faxina [fa'ʃina] *f* (*limpeza*) cleaning (up); **fazer ~** to clean up.

faxineiro/a [faʃi'nejru/a] *m/f* (*pessoa*) cleaner.

faz-de-conta [fajʒ-] *m*: **o ~** make-believe.

fazedor(a) [faze'do*(a)] *m/f* maker.

fazenda [fa'zēda] *f* farm; (*de café*) plantation; (*de gado*) ranch; (*pano*) cloth, fabric; (*ECON*) treasury, exchequer.

fazendeiro [fazē'dejru] *m* farmer; (*de café*) plantation-owner; (*de gado*) rancher, ranch-owner.

fazer [fa'ze*] *vt* to make; (*executar*) to do; (*pergunta*) to ask; (*construir*) to build; (*poema*) to write ♦ *vi* (*portar-se*) to act, behave; **~-se** *vr* (*tornar-se*) to become; (*ter êxito*) to make it; **~-se de algo** to pretend to be sth; **ele faz anos hoje** it's his birthday today; **fiz 30 anos ontem** I was 30 yesterday; **~ com que alguém faça algo** to make sb do sth; **~ que** (*fingir*) to pretend that; **~ bem/mal** to do the right/wrong thing; **faz um ano** a year ago; **faz dois anos que ele se formou** it's two years since he graduated; **faz três meses que ele está aqui** he's been here for three months; **não faz mal** never mind; **tanto faz** it's all the same; **não fiz por mal** I didn't mean any harm, I didn't mean it; **isso vai me dar que ~** this will be a tough job; **~ por onde** to work for it.

faz-tudo [fajʒ-] *m/f inv* jack-of-all-trades.

FBI *abr m* (= *Federal Bureau of Investigation*) FBI.

FC *abr m* (= *Futebol Clube*) FC.

FDLP *abr f* (= *Frente Democrática para a Libertação da Palestina*) PFLP.

fé [fε] *f* faith; (*crença*) belief; (*confiança*) trust; **de boa/má ~** in good/bad faith; **dar ~ de** to bear witness to; **fazer ~ em** to have faith in; **~ em Deus e pé na tábua** go for it.

fealdade [feaw'dadʒi] *f* ugliness.

FEB ['fεbi] *abr f* (= *Força Expedicionária Brasileira*) force sent out in World War II.

FEBEM [fe'bẽ] (*BR*) *abr f* (= *Fundação Estadual do Bem-Estar do Menor*) reform school.

febrão [fe'brãw] (*pl* -**ões**) *m* raging fever.

febre ['fεbri] *f* fever; (*fig*) excitement; **~ amarela** yellow fever; **~ de poder** *etc* hunger for power *etc*; **~ do feno** hay fever.

febril [fe'briw] (*pl* -**is**) *adj* feverish.

febrões [fe'brõjʃ] *mpl de* **febrão**.

fecal [fe'kaw] (*pl* -**ais**) *adj* V **matéria**.

fechada [fe'ʃada] *f*: **dar uma ~ em alguém** (*AUTO*) to cut sb up; **levar uma ~** to be cut up.

fechado/a [fe'ʃadu/a] *adj* shut, closed; (*pessoa*) reserved; (*sinal*) red; (*luz, torneira*) off; (*tempo*) overcast; (*cara*) stern; **noite fechada** well into the night.

fechadura [feʃa'dura] *f* (*de porta*) lock.

fechamento [feʃa'mẽtu] *m* closure.

fechar [fe'ʃa*] *vt* to close, shut; (*concluir*) to finish, conclude; (*luz, torneira*) to turn off; (*rua*) to close off; (*ferida*) to close up; (*bar, loja*) to close down; (*negócio*) to close, make; (*AUTO*) to cut up ♦ *vi* to close (up), shut; (*ferida*) to heal; (*sinal*) to turn red; (*bar, empresa*) to close down; (*tempo*) to cloud over; **~-se** *vr* to close, shut; (*pessoa*) to withdraw; **~-se no quarto** *etc* to shut o.s. away in one's room *etc*; **~ à chave** to lock; **~ a cara** to look annoyed; **ser de ~ o comércio** (*col*) to be a real show-stopper.

fecho ['feʃu] *m* fastening; (*trinco*) latch; (*término*) close, closing; **~ ecler** zip fastener (*BRIT*), zipper (*US*).

fécula ['fεkula] *f* starch.

fecundação [fekūda'sãw] *f* fertilization.

fecundar [fekū'da*] *vt* to fertilize, make fertile.

fecundidade [fekūdʒi'dadʒi] *f* fertility.

fecundo/a [fe'kūdu/a] *adj* fertile; (*produtivo*) fruitful; (*fig*) prolific.

fedelho/a [fe'deʎu/a] *m/f* kid.

feder [fe'de*] *vi* to stink; **não ~ nem cheirar** (*fig*) to be wishy-washy.

federação [federa'sãw] (*pl* -**ões**) *f* federation.

federal [fede'raw] (*pl* -**ais**) *adj* federal; (*col: grande*) huge.

federativo/a [federa'tʃivu/a] *adj* federal.

fedor [fe'do*] *m* stench.

fedorento/a [fedo'rētu/a] *adj* stinking.

FEEM (*BR*) *abr f* (= *Fundação Estadual de Educação do Menor*) children's home.

Feema [fe'εma] (*BR*) *abr f* (= *Fundação Estadual de Engenharia do Meio Ambiente*) environmental protection agency.

feérico/a [fe'εriku/a] *adj* magical.

feição [fej'sãw] (*pl* -**ões**) *f* form, shape; (*caráter*) nature; (*modo*) manner; **feições** *fpl* (*face*) features; **à ~ de** in the manner of.

feijão [fej'ʒãw] (*pl* -**ões**) *m* bean(s) (*pl*); (*preto*) black bean(s) (*pl*).

feijão-fradinho [-fra'dʒiɲu] (*pl* **feijões-fradinhos**) *m* black-eyed bean(s) (*pl*).

feijão-mulatinho [-mula'tʃiɲu] (*pl* **feijões-mulatinhos**) *m* red kidney bean(s) (*pl*).

feijão-preto (*pl* **feijões-pretos**) *m* black bean(s) (*pl*).

feijão-soja (*pl* **feijões-sojas**) *m* soya bean(s)

(pl) *(BRIT)*, soybean(s) *(pl)* *(US)*.

feijão-tropeiro [-tro'pejru] *(pl* **feijões-tropeiros)** *m (CULIN)* bean stew.

feijoada [fej'ʒwada] *f (CULIN)* meat, rice and black beans.

feijões [fej'ʒõjʃ] *mpl de* **feijão**.

feijoeiro [fej'ʒwejru] *m* bean plant.

feio/a ['feju/a] *adj* ugly; *(situação)* grim; *(atitude)* bad; *(tempo)* horrible ♦ *adv (perder)* badly; **olhar** ~ to give a filthy look; **fazer** ~ to make a bad impression; **ficar** ~ *(dar má impressão)* to look bad; *(situação)* to turn nasty; **quem ama o** ~, **bonito lhe parece** love is blind.

feioso/a [fe'jozu/ɔza] *adj* plain.

feira ['fejra] *f* fair; *(mercado)* market; **fazer a** ~ to go to market; ~ **livre** market.

feirante [fej'rãtʃi] *m/f* market trader, stallholder.

feita ['fejta] *f*: **certa** ~ once, on one occasion; **de uma** ~ once and for all.

feitiçaria [fejtʃisa'ria] *f* witchcraft, magic.

feiticeira [fejtʃi'sejra] *f* witch.

feiticeiro/a [fejtʃi'sejru/a] *adj* bewitching, enchanting ♦ *m* wizard.

feitiço [fej'tʃisu] *m* charm, spell; **virou o** ~ **contra o feiticeiro** *(fig)* the tables were turned.

feitio [fej'tʃiu] *m* shape, pattern; *(caráter)* nature, manner; *(TEC)* workmanship.

feito/a ['fejtu/a] *pp de* **fazer** ♦ *adj (terminado)* finished, ready ♦ *m* act, deed; *(façanha)* feat ♦ *conj* like; ~ **a mão** hand-made; **homem** ~ grown man; **que é** ~ **dela?** what has become of her?; **bem** ~ **(por você)!** (it) serves you right!; **dito e** ~ no sooner said than done; **estar** ~ *(pessoa: ter dinheiro etc)* to have it made.

feitor(a) [fej'to*(a)] *m/f* administrator; *(capataz)* supervisor.

feitura [fej'tura] *f* work.

feiúra [fe'jura] *f* ugliness.

feixe ['fejʃi] *m* bundle, bunch; *(TEC)* beam.

fel [few] *m* bile, gall; *(fig)* bitterness; **esse remédio é um** ~ that medicine is really bitter.

felicidade [felisi'dadʒi] *f* happiness; *(sorte)* good luck; *(êxito)* success; ~**s** *fpl* congratulations.

felicíssimo/a [feli'sisimu/a] *adj superl de* **feliz**.

felicitações [felisita'sõjʃ] *fpl* congratulations, best wishes.

felicitar [felisi'ta*] *vt* to congratulate.

felino/a [fe'linu/a] *adj* feline; *(fig: traiçoeiro)* treacherous ♦ *m* feline.

feliz [fe'liʒ] *adj* happy; *(afortunado)* fortunate; *(idéia, sugestão)* timely; *(próspero)* successful; *(expressão)* fortunate; ~ **aniversário/ Natal!** happy birthday/Christmas!; **dar-se por** ~ to think o.s. lucky.

felizardo/a [feli'zaxdu/a] *m/f* lucky devil.

felizmente [feliʒ'mẽtʃi] *adv* fortunately.

felonia [felo'nia] *f (traição)* treachery.

felpa ['fewpa] *f (de animais)* down; *(de tecido)* nap.

felpudo/a [few'pudu/a] *adj* fuzzy, downy.

feltro ['fewtru] *m* felt.

fêmea ['femja] *f (BIO, BOT)* female.

feminil [femi'niw] *(pl* **-is)** *adj* feminine.

feminilidade [feminili'dadʒi] *f* femininity.

feminino/a [femi'ninu/a] *adj* feminine; *(sexo)* female; *(equipe, roupas)* women's ♦ *m (LING)* feminine.

feminis [femi'niʃ] *adj pl de* **feminil**.

feminismo [femi'niʒmu] *m* feminism.

feminista [femi'niʃta] *adj*, *m/f* feminist.

fêmur ['femu*] *m (ANAT)* femur.

fenda ['fẽda] *f* slit, crack; *(GEO)* fissure.

fender [fẽ'de*] *vt*, *vi* to split, crack.

fenecer [fene'se*] *vi* to die; *(terminar)* to come to an end.

feno ['fenu] *m* hay.

fenomenal [fenome'naw] *(pl* **-ais)** *adj* phenomenal; *(espantoso)* amazing; *(pessoa)* brilliant.

fenômeno [fe'nomenu] *m* phenomenon.

fera ['fera] *f* wild animal; *(fig: pessoa cruel)* beast; *(: pessoa severa)* hothead; **ser** ~ **em algo** to be brilliant at sth; **ficar uma** ~ **(com alguém)** *(fig)* to get mad (with sb).

féretro ['feretru] *m* coffin.

feriado [fe'rjadu] *m* holiday *(BRIT)*, vacation *(US)*; ~ **bancário** bank *(BRIT)* ou public holiday.

férias ['fɛrjaʃ] *fpl* holidays, vacation *sg*; **de** ~ on holiday; **tirar** ~ to have ou take a holiday.

ferida [fe'rida] *f* wound, injury; **tocar na** ~ *(fig)* to hit home; *V tb* **ferido**.

ferido/a [fe'ridu/a] *adj* injured; *(em batalha)* wounded; *(magoado)* hurt ♦ *m/f* casualty.

ferimento [feri'mẽtu] *m* injury; *(em batalha)* wound.

ferino/a [fe'rinu/a] *adj (cruel)* cruel; *(crítica, ironia)* biting.

ferir [fe'ri*] *vt* to injure, wound; *(ofender)* to offend.

fermentar [fexmẽ'ta*] *vt* to ferment; *(fig)* to excite ♦ *vi* to ferment.

fermento [fex'mẽtu] *m* yeast; ~ **em pó** baking powder.

ferocidade [ferosi'dadʒi] *f* fierceness, ferocity.

ferocíssimo/a [fero'sisimu/a] *adj superl de* **feroz**.

feroz [fe'roʒ] *adj* fierce, ferocious; *(cruel)* cruel.

ferrado/a [fe'xadu/a] *adj (cavalgadura)* shod; *(col: sem saída)* done for; ~ **no sono** sound asleep.

ferradura [fexa'dura] *f* horseshoe.

ferragem [fe'xaʒẽ] *(pl* **-ns)** *f (peças)* hardware; *(guarnição)* metalwork.

NB: European Portuguese adds the following consonants to certain words: **b** (sú(b)dito, su(b)til); **c** (a(c)ção, a(c)cionista, a(c)to); **m** (inde(m)ne); **p** (ado(p)ção, ado(p)tar); *for further details see p. xiii.*

ferramenta [fexa'mēta] *f* tool; *(caixa de* ~s) tool kit.

ferrão [fe'xãw] *(pl* **-ões)** *m* goad; *(de inseto)* sting.

ferrar [fe'xa*] *vt* to spike; *(cavalo)* to shoe; *(gado)* to brand; ~**-se** *vr (col)* to come to grief.

ferreiro [fe'xejru] *m* blacksmith.

ferrenho/a [fe'xeɲu/a] *adj (vontade)* iron; *(marxista etc)* staunch.

férreo/a ['fɛxju/a] *adj* iron *atr: (QUÍM)* ferrous; *(vontade)* iron; *(disciplina)* strict.

ferrete [fe'xetʃi] *m* branding iron; *(fig)* stigma.

ferro ['fexu] *m* iron; ~**s** *mpl* shackles, chains; ~ **batido** wrought iron; ~ **de passar** iron; ~ **fundido** cast iron; ~ **ondulado** corrugated iron; **a** ~ **e fogo** at all costs; **ninguém é/não sou de** ~ *(fig)* we're all/I'm only human.

ferrões [fe'xõjʃ] *mpl de* **ferrão**.

ferrolho [fe'xoʎu] *m (trinco)* bolt.

ferro-velho *(pl* **ferros-velhos)** *m (pessoa)* scrap metal dealer; *(lugar)* scrap metal yard; *(sucata)* scrap metal.

ferrovia [fexo'via] *f* railway *(BRIT)*, railroad *(US)*.

ferroviário/a [fexo'vjarju/a] *adj* railway *atr (BRIT)*, railroad *atr (US)* ♦ *m/f* railway *ou* railroad worker.

ferrugem [fe'xuʒē] *f* rust; *(BOT)* blight.

fértil ['fɛxtʃiw] *(pl* **-eis)** *adj* fertile.

fertilidade [fextʃili'dadʒi] *f* fertility; *(abundância)* fruitfulness.

fertilizante [fextʃili'zãtʃi] *adj* fertilizing ♦ *m* fertilizer.

fertilizar [fextʃili'za*] *vt* to fertilize.

fervente [fex'vētʃi] *adj* boiling.

ferver [fex've*] *vt, vi* to boil; ~ **de raiva/ indignação** to seethe with rage/indignation; ~ **em fogo baixo** *(CULIN)* to simmer.

fervilhar [fexvi'ʎa*] *vi (ferver)* to simmer; *(com excitação)* to hum; *(pulular)*: ~ **de** to swarm with.

fervor [fex'vo*] *m* fervour *(BRIT)*, fervor *(US)*.

fervoroso/a [fexvo'rozu/ɔza] *adj* zealous, fervent.

fervura [fex'vura] *f* boiling.

festa ['fɛʃta] *f (reunião)* party; *(conjunto de ceremônias)* festival; ~**s** caresses; **boas** ~**s** Merry Christmas and a Happy New Year; **dia de** ~ public holiday; **fazer** ~ **a alguém** to make a fuss of sb; **fazer** ~**(s) em alguém** to caress sb; **fazer a** ~ *(fig)* to have a ball, have a whale of a time; ~ **caipira** hoedown; ~ **de arromba** *(col)* big party; ~ **de embalo** *(col)* wild party.

festança [feʃ'tãsa] *f* big party.

festeiro/a [feʃ'tejru/a] *adj* party-going.

festejar [feʃte'ʒa*] *vt (celebrar)* to celebrate; *(acolher)* to welcome, greet.

festejo [feʃ'teʒu] *m (festividade)* festivity; *(ato)* celebration.

festim [feʃ'tʃĩ] *(pl* **-ns)** *m* feast.

festival [feʃtʃi'vaw] *(pl* **-ais)** *m* festival.

festividade [feʃtʃivi'dadʒi] *f* festivity.

festivo/a [feʃ'tʃivu/a] *adj* festive.

fetiche [fe'tʃiʃi] *m* fetish.

fetichismo [fetʃi'ʃiʒmu] *m* fetishism.

fetichista [fetʃi'ʃiʃta] *adj* fetishistic ♦ *m/f* fetishist.

fétido/a ['fɛtʃidu/a] *adj* foul.

feto ['fetu] *m (MED)* foetus *(BRIT)*, fetus *(US)*; *(BOT)* fern.

feudal [few'daw] *(pl* **-ais)** *adj* feudal.

feudalismo [fewda'liʒmu] *m* feudalism.

fev. *abr* = **fevereiro**.

fevereiro [feve'rejru] *(PT:* **F-)** *m* February; *V tb* **julho**.

fez [feʒ] *vb V* **fazer**.

fezes ['feziʃ] *fpl* faeces *(BRIT)*, feces *(US)*.

FGTS *(BR) abr m (= Fundo de Garantia por Tempo de Serviço) pension fund.*

FGV *(BR) abr f (= Fundação Getúlio Vargas) economic research agency.*

fiação [fja'sãw] *(pl* **-ões)** *f* spinning; *(fábrica)* textile mill; *(ELET)* wiring; **fazer a** ~ **da casa** to rewire the house.

fiada ['fjada] *f (fileira)* row, line.

fiado/a ['fjadu/a] *adj (a crédito)* on credit; **comprar/vender** ~ to buy/sell on credit.

fiador(a) [fja'do*(a)] *m/f (JUR)* guarantor; *(COM)* backer.

fiambre ['fjãbri] *m* cold meat; *(presunto)* ham.

fiança ['fjãsa] *f* surety, guarantee; *(JUR)* bail; **prestar** ~ **por** to stand bail for; **sob** ~ on bail.

fiapo ['fjapu] *m* thread.

fiar ['fja*] *vt (algodão etc)* to spin; *(confiar)* to entrust; *(vender a crédito)* to sell on credit; ~**-se** *vr:* ~**-se em** to trust.

fiasco ['fjaʃku] *m* fiasco.

FIBGE *abr f* = **Fundação do Instituto Brasileiro de Geografia e Estatística.**

fibra ['fibra] *f* fibre *(BRIT)*, fiber *(US)*; *(fig)*: **pessoa de** ~ person of character; ~ **ótica** optical fibre *ou* fiber.

ficar [fi'ka*] *vi (permanecer)* to stay; *(sobrar)* to be left; *(tornar-se)* to become; *(estar situado)* to be; *(durar)* to last; *(ser adiado)* to be postponed; ~ **cego/surdo/louco** to go blind/deaf/mad; **fiquei contente ao saber a notícia** I was happy when I heard the news; ~ **perguntando/olhando** *etc* to keep asking/ looking *etc*; ~ **com algo** *(guardar)* to keep sth; ~ **com raiva/medo** to get angry/ frightened; ~ **de fazer algo** *(combinar)* to arrange to do sth; *(prometer)* to promise to do sth; ~ **por fazer** to be still to be done; ~ **bom** *(de saúde)* to get better; *(trabalho, foto etc)* to turn out well; ~ **bem** *(roupa, comportamento)* to look good; **esta saia não fica bem para você** that skirt doesn't suit you; ~ **para trás** to be left behind; **ficou por isso mesmo** nothing came of it; ~ **sem algo** to be left without sth, run out of sth; ~ **de**

bem/mal com alguém (col) to make up/fall out with sb; ~ **de pé** to stand up.

ficção [fik'sãw] f fiction.

ficcionista [fiksjo'niʃta] m/f author, fiction writer.

ficha ['fiʃa] f (tb: ~ de telefone) token; (tb: ~ de jogo) chip; (de fichário) (index) card; (fig) record; (PT: ELET) plug; (em loja, lanchonete) ticket; **dar a ~ de alguém** (fig: col) to give the low-down on sb; **ter ~ na polícia** to have a criminal record; **ter ~ limpa** (col) to have a clean record; ~ **de identidade** means sg of identification, ID.

fichar [fi'ʃa*] vt to file, index.

fichário [fi'ʃarju] m (móvel) filing cabinet; (caixa) card index; (caderno) file.

ficheiro [fi'ʃejru] (PT) m = **fichário**.

fictício/a [fik'tʃisju/a] adj fictitious.

FIDA (BR) abr m = **Fundo Internacional para o Desenvolvimento Agrícola**.

fidalgo [fi'dawgu] m nobleman.

fidedigno/a [fide'dʒignu/a] adj trustworthy.

fidelidade [fideli'dadʒi] f (lealdade) fidelity, loyalty; (exatidão) accuracy.

fidelíssimo/a [fide'lisimu/a] adj superl de **fiel**.

fiduciário/a [fidu'sjarju/a] adj (companhia) trust atr ♦ m/f trustee.

fiéis [fjejʃ] adj pl de **fiel** ♦ mpl: **os** ~ the faithful.

fiel [fjew] (pl -**éis**) adj (leal) faithful, loyal; (tradução) accurate; (que não falha) reliable.

Fiesp [fi'ɛʃpi] abr f = **Federação das Indústrias do Estado de São Paulo**.

FIFA ['fifa] abr f (= Fédération Internationale de Football Association) FIFA.

figa ['figa] f talisman; **fazer uma** ~ to make a figa, ≈ cross one's fingers; **de uma** ~ (col) damned.

figada [fi'gada] f fig jelly.

fígado ['figadu] m liver; **de maus** ~**s** bad-tempered, vindictive.

figo ['figu] m fig.

figueira [fi'gejra] f fig tree.

figura [fi'gura] f figure; (forma) form, shape; (GRAMÁTICA) figure of speech; (aspecto) appearance; (CARTAS) face card; (ilustração) picture; (col: pessoa) character; **fazer** ~ to cut a figure; **fazer má** ~ to make a bad impression; **mudar de** ~ to take on a new aspect; **ser uma** ~ **difícil** (col) to be difficult to get hold of; **ele é uma** ~ (col) he's a real character .

figura-chave (pl **figuras-chave**) f key figure.

figurado/a [figu'radu/a] adj figurative.

figurante [figu'rãtʃi] m/f (CINEMA) extra.

figurão [figu'rãw] (pl -**ões**) m big shot.

figurar [figu'ra*] vi (ator) to appear; (fazer parte): ~ (**entre/em**) to figure ou appear (among/in) ♦ vt (imaginar) to imagine; **ela**

figura ter menos de 30 anos she looks younger than 30.

figurinha [figu'riɲa] f sticker; ~ **difícil** (col) person who is difficult to get hold of.

figurinista [figuri'niʃta] m/f fashion designer.

figurino [figu'rinu] m fashion plate; (revista) fashion magazine; (CINEMA, TEATRO) costume design; (exemplo) example; **como manda o** ~ as it should be.

figurões [figu'rõjʃ] mpl de **figurão**.

Fiji [fi'ʒi] m Fiji.

fila ['fila] f row, line; (BR: fileira de pessoas) queue (BRIT), line (US); (num teatro, cinema) row ♦ m (cão) Brazilian mastiff; **em** ~ in a row; **fazer** ~ to form a line, queue; ~ **indiana** single file.

Filadélfia [fila'dewfja] f Philadelphia.

filamento [fila'mẽtu] m filament.

filante [fi'lãtʃi] m/f sponger ♦ adj sponging.

filantropia [filãtro'pia] f philanthropy.

filantrópico/a [filã'trɔpiku/a] adj philanthropic.

filantropo [filã'tropu] m philanthropist.

filão [fi'lãw] (pl -**ões**) m (JORNALISMO) lead.

filar [fi'la*] vt (agarrar) to seize; (col: pedir/ obter gratuitamente) to scrounge.

filarmônica [filax'monika] f philharmonic.

filarmônico/a [filax'moniku/a] adj philharmonic.

filatelia [filate'lia] f philately.

filé [fi'lɛ] m (bife) steak; (peixe) fillet; ~ **mignon** filet mignon.

fileira [fi'lejra] f file, row, line; ~**s** fpl military service sg.

filete [fi'letʃi] m fillet; (de parafuso) thread.

filharada [fiʎa'rada] f herd of children.

filhinho/a [fi'ʎiɲu/a] m/f little son/daughter; ~ **de mamãe** mummy's boy; ~ **de papai** rich kid.

filho/a ['fiʎu/a] m/f son/daughter; ~**s** mpl children; (de animais) young; **minha filha/ meu** ~ (col) dear, darling; **ter um** ~ to have a child; (fig: col) to have kittens, have a fit; **ele também é** ~ **de Deus** he is just as good as anyone else; ~ **adotivo** adoptive child; ~ **da mãe** (col!) bastard(!); ~ **da puta** (col!) wanker(!), bastard(!); ~ **de criação** foster child; ~ **ilegítimo/natural** illegitimate/ natural child; ~ **único** only child; ~ **único de mãe viúva** (fig) one in a million.

filhote [fi'ʎɔtʃi] m (de leão, urso etc) cub; (cachorro) pup(py).

filiação [filja'sãw] (pl -**ões**) f affiliation.

filial [fi'ljaw] (pl -**ais**) f (sucursal) branch ♦ adj filial; **gerente de** ~ branch manager.

filigrana [fili'grana] f filigree.

Filipinas [fili'pinaʃ] fpl: **as** ~ the Philippines.

filipino/a [fili'pinu/a] adj, m/f Filipino ♦ m (LING) Filipino.

filmagem [fiw'maʒẽ] f filming.

---

filmar [fiw'ma*] vt, vi to film.

filme ['fiwmi] m film (BRIT), movie (US); ~ **(de) bangue-bangue** ou **faroeste** western; ~ **(de) curta/longa metragem** short/feature film; ~ **de época** period film; ~ **de capa e espada** swashbuckling film.

filmoteca [fiwmo'tɛka] f (lugar) film library; (coleção) film collection.

filó [fi'lɔ] m tulle.

filões [fi'lõjʃ] mpl de **filão**.

filologia [filolo'ʒia] f philology.

filólogo/a [fi'lɔlogu/a] m/f philologist.

filosofar [filozo'fa*] vi to philosophize.

filosofia [filozo'fia] f philosophy.

filosófico/a [filo'zɔfiku/a] adj philosophical.

filósofo/a [fi'lɔzofu/a] m/f philosopher.

filtrar [fiw'tra*] vt to filter; ~**-se** vr (líquidos) to filter; (infiltrar-se) to infiltrate.

filtro ['fiwtru] m (TEC) filter.

fim [fĩ] (pl **-ns**) m end; (motivo) aim, purpose; (de história, filme) ending; **a ~ de** in order to; **por ~** finally; **ter por ~** to aim at; **no ~ das contas** after all; **levar ao ~** to carry through; **pôr** ou **dar ~ a** to put an end to; **ter ~** to come to an end; **sem ~** endless; ~ **de semana** weekend; ~ **de mundo** (fig) hole; **ele mora no ~ do mundo** he lives miles from anywhere; **é o ~ (do mundo** ou **da picada)** (fig) it's the pits; **estar a ~ de (fazer) algo** to feel like (doing) sth, fancy (doing) sth; **estar a ~ de alguém** (col) to fancy sb.

finado/a [fi'nadu/a] adj, m/f deceased.

final [fi'naw] (pl **-ais**) adj final, last ♦ m end; (MÚS) finale ♦ f (ESPORTE) final.

finalista [fina'liʃta] m/f finalist.

finalização [finaliza'sãw] (pl **-ões**) f conclusion.

finalizar [finali'za*] vt to finish, conclude ♦ vi (FUTEBOL) to finish; ~**-se** vr to end.

Finam [fĩ'nã] abr m (= Fundo de Investimento da Amazônia) regional development fund.

Finame [fi'nami] (BR) abr m = **Agência Especial de Financiamento Industrial**.

finanças [fi'nãsaʃ] fpl finance sg.

financeiro/a [finã'sejru/a] adj financial ♦ m/f financier.

financiamento [finãsja'mētu] m financing.

financiar [finã'sja*] vt to finance.

financista [finã'siʃta] m/f financier.

finar-se [fi'naxsi] vr (consumir-se) to waste away; (morrer) to die.

fincar [fĩ'ka*] vt (cravar) to drive in; (fixar) to fix; (apoiar) to lean.

findar [fĩ'da*] vt, vi to end, finish.

findo/a ['fĩdu/a] adj (ano) past; (assunto) closed.

fineza [fi'neza] f fineness; (gentileza) kindness.

fingido/a [fĩ'ʒidu/a] adj pretend; (pessoa) two-faced, insincere ♦ m/f hypocrite.

fingimento [fĩʒi'mētu] m pretence (BRIT), pretense (US).

fingir [fĩ'ʒi*] vt (simular) to feign ♦ vi to pre-

tend; ~**-se** vr: ~**-se de** to pretend to be; ~ **fazer/que** to pretend to do/that.

finito/a [fi'nitu/a] adj finite.

finlandês/esa [fĩlã'deʃ/eza] adj Finnish ♦ m/f Finn ♦ m (LING) Finnish.

Finlândia [fĩ'lãdʒia] f: **a ~** Finland.

fino/a ['finu/a] adj fine; (delgado) slender; (educado) polite; (som, voz) shrill; (elegante) refined, posh (col) ♦ adv: **falar ~** to talk in a high voice; **ser o ~** (col) to be the business; **tirar um ~ em alguém** to almost drive into sb.

Finor [fi'no*] (BR) abr m (= Fundo de Investimento do Nordeste) regional development fund.

finório/a [fi'nɔrju/a] adj crafty, sly.

fins [fĩʃ] mpl de **fim**.

Finsocial [fĩso'sjaw] (BR) abr m = **Fundo de Investimento Social**.

finura [fi'nura] f fineness; (elegância) finesse.

fio ['fiu] m thread; (BOT) fibre (BRIT), fiber (US); (ELET) wire; (TEL) line; (de líquido) trickle; (gume) edge; (encadeamento) series; **horas/dias a ~** hours/days on end; **de ~ a pavio** from beginning to end; **por um ~** (fig: escapar) by the skin of one's teeth; **bater um ~** (col) to make a call; **estar por um ~** to be on one's last legs; **perder o ~ (da meada)** (fig) to lose one's thread; **retomar o ~ perdido** (fig) to take up the thread again; ~ **condutor** (fig) connecting thread.

fiorde ['fjoxdʒi] m fjord.

Firjan [fix'ʒã] abr f = **Federação das Indústrias do Rio de Janeiro**.

firma ['fixma] f (assinatura) signature; (COM) firm, company.

firmamento [fixma'mētu] m firmament.

firmar [fix'ma*] vt (tornar firme) to secure, make firm; (assinar) to sign; (estabelecer) to establish; (basear) to base ♦ vi (tempo) to settle; ~**-se** vr: ~**-se em** (basear-se) to rest on, be based on.

firme ['fixmi] adj firm; (estável) stable; (sólido) solid; (tempo) settled ♦ adv firmly; **agüentar ~** to hang on; **pisar ~** to stride out.

firmeza [fix'meza] f firmness; (estabilidade) stability; (solidez) solidity.

FISA ['fiza] abr f (= Federação Internacional de Automobilismo Esportivo) FISA.

fiscal [fiʃ'kaw] (pl **-ais**) m/f supervisor; (aduaneiro) customs officer; (de impostos) tax inspector.

fiscalização [fiʃkaliza'sãw] (pl **-ões**) f inspection.

fiscalizar [fiʃkali'za*] vt (supervisionar) to supervise; (examinar) to inspect, check.

fisco ['fiʃku] m: **o ~** ≈ the Inland Revenue (BRIT), ≈ the Internal Revenue Service (US).

Fiset [fi'sɛtʃi] (BR) abr m = **Fundo de Investimentos Setoriais**.

fisgada [fiʒ'gada] f stabbing pain.

fisgar [fiʒ'ga*] vt to catch.

física ['fizika] f physics sg; ~ **nuclear** nuclear

physics; *V tb* **físico.**

físico/a ['fiziku/a] *adj* physical ♦ *m/f*
(*cientista*) physicist ♦ *m* (*corpo*) physique.

fisiologia [fizjolo'ʒia] *f* physiology.

fisionomia [fizjono'mia] *f* (*rosto*) face; (*ar*)
expression, look; (*aspecto de algo*) physiog-
nomy; (*conjunto de caracteres*) make-up.

fisionomista [fizjono'miʃta] *m/f* person with a
good memory for faces.

fisioterapeuta [fizjotera'pewta] *m/f* physiotherapist.

fisioterapia [fizjotera'pia] *f* physiotherapy.

fissura [fi'sura] *f* crack; (*col*: *ansia*) craving.

fissurado/a [fisu'radu/a] *adj* cracked; **estar ~
em** (*col*) to be wild about.

fissurar [fisu'ra*] *vt* to crack.

fita ['fita] *f* (*tira*) strip, band; (*de seda,
algodão*) ribbon, tape; (*filme*) film; (*para
máquina de escrever*) ribbon; (*magnética,
adesiva*) tape; **~ durex** ® adhesive tape,
sellotape ® (*BRIT*), scotchtape ® (*US*); **~ isolante** insulating tape; **~ métrica** tape
measure; **fazer ~** (*col*) to put on an act; **isso
é ~ dela** (*col*) it's just an act.

fitar [fi'ta*] *vt* (*com os olhos*) to stare at, gaze
at; **~-se** *vr* to stare at each other.

fiteiro/a [fi'tejru/a] *adj* melodramatic.

fito/a ['fitu/a] *adj* fixed ♦ *m* aim, intention.

fivela [fi'vɛla] *f* buckle.

fixação [fiksa'sãw] (*pl* **-ões**) *f* fixation.

fixador [fiksa'do*] *m* (*de cabelo*) hair gel; (:
líquido) setting lotion (*BRIT*).

fixar [fik'sa*] *vt* (*estabelecer*: *hora, lugar*) to
fix; (: *data, regras*) to set; (*colar, prender*)
to stick; (*atenção*) to concentrate; **~-se** *vr*:
~-se em (*assunto*) to concentrate on;
(*detalhe*) to fix on; (*apegar-se a*) to be
attached to; **~ os olhos em** to stare at; **~
residência** to set up house, settle down; **~
algo na memória** to fix sth in one's mind.

fixo/a ['fiksu/a] *adj* fixed; (*firme*) firm;
(*permanente*) permanent; (*cor*) fast.

fiz [fiʒ] *etc vb V* **fazer.**

flacidez [flasi'deʒ] *f* softness, flabbiness.

flácido/a ['flasidu/a] *adj* flabby.

Fla-Flu [fla-] *m* local derby (*football match
between rivals Flamengo and Fluminense*).

flagelado/a [flaʒe'ladu/a] *m/f*: **os ~s** the
afflicted, the victims.

flagrante [fla'grãtʃi] *adj* flagrant; **apanhar
em ~** (**delito**) to catch red-handed *ou* in the
act.

flagrar [fla'gra*] *vt* to catch.

flambar [flã'ba*] *vt* (*CULIN*) to flambé.

flamejante [flame'ʒãtʃi] *adj* flaming.

flamejar [flame'ʒa*] *vi* to blaze.

flamengo/a [fla'mẽgu/a] *adj* Flemish ♦ *m*
(*LING*) Flemish.

flamingo [fla'mĩgu] *m* flamingo.

flâmula ['flamula] *f* pennant.

flanco ['flãku] *m* flank.

Flandres ['flãdriʃ] *f* Flanders.

flanela [fla'nɛla] *f* flannel.

flanquear [flã'kja*] *vt* to flank; (*MIL*) to out-
flank.

flash [flaʃ] *m* (*FOTO*) flash.

flash-back [flaʃ'baki] (*pl* **~s**) *m* flashback.

flatulência [flatu'lẽsja] *f* flatulence.

flauta ['flawta] *f* flute; **ele leva tudo na ~**
(*col*) he doesn't take anything seriously; **~
doce** (*MÚS*) recorder.

flautista [flaw'tʃiʃta] *m/f* flautist.

flecha ['flɛʃa] *f* arrow.

flechada [fle'ʃada] *f* (*golpe*) shot; (*ferimento*)
arrow wound.

flertar [flex'ta*] *vi*: **~ (com alguém)** to flirt
(with sb).

flerte ['flextʃi] *m* flirtation.

fleu(g)ma ['flewma] *f* phlegm.

flexão [flek'sãw] (*pl* **-ões**) *f* flexing; (*exercício*)
press-up; (*LING*) inflection.

flexibilidade [fleksibili'dadʒi] *f* flexibility.

flexionar [fleksjo'na*] *vt*, *vi* (*LING*) to inflect.

flexível [flek'sivew] (*pl* **-eis**) *adj* flexible.

flexões [flek'sõjʃ] *fpl de* **flexão.**

fliperama [flipe'rama] *m* pinball machine.

floco ['flɔku] *m* flake; **~ de milho** cornflake;
~ de neve snowflake; **sorvete de ~s**
chocolate chip ice-cream.

flor [flo*] *f* flower; (*o melhor*) cream, pick;
em ~ in bloom; **a fina ~** the elite; **a ~ de**
on the surface of; **ele não é ~ que se cheire**
(*col*) he's a bad lot.

flora ['flɔra] *f* flora.

floreado/a [flo'rjadu/a] *adj* (*jardim*) full of
flowers; (*relevo*) ornate; (*estilo*) florid.

floreio [flo'reju] *m* clever turn of phrase.

florescente [flore'sẽtʃi] *adj* (*BOT*) in flower;
(*próspero*) flourishing.

florescer [flore'se*] *vi* (*BOT*) to flower;
(*prosperar*) to flourish.

floresta [flo'rɛʃta] *f* forest.

florestal [floreʃ'taw] (*pl* **-ais**) *adj* forest *atr*.

florianopolitano/a [florjanopoli'tanu/a] *adj*
from Florianópolis ♦ *m/f* native of Florianópolis.

Flórida ['flɔrida] *f*: **a ~** Florida.

florido/a [flo'ridu/a] *adj* (*jardim*) in flower;
(*mesa*) decorated with flowers.

florir [flo'ri*] *vi* to flower.

flotilha [flo'tʃiʎa] *f* flotilla.

flozô [flo'zo] (*col*) *m*: **ficar de ~** to lounge
around; **viver de ~** to lead a life of leisure.

Flu [flu] *abr m* = **Fluminense Futebol Clube.**

fluência [flu'ẽsja] *f* fluency.

fluente [flu'ẽtʃi] *adj* fluent.

fluidez [flui'deʒ] *f* fluidity.

fluido/a ['flwidu/a] *adj* fluid ♦ *m* fluid.

fluir [flwi*] *vi* to flow.

fluminense [flumi'nẽsi] *adj* from the state of

NB: *European Portuguese adds the following consonants to certain words:* **b** (sú(b)dito, su(b)til); **c** (a(c)ção,
a(c)cionista, a(c)to); **m** (inde(m)ne); **p** (ado(p)ção, ado(p)tar); *for further details see p. xiii.*

Rio de Janeiro ♦ *m/f* native *ou* inhabitant of the state of Rio de Janeiro.

fluorescente [flwore'sĕtʃi] *adj* fluorescent.

flutuação [flutwa'sãw] (*pl* **-ões**) *f* fluctuation.

flutuante [flu'twãtʃi] *adj* floating; (*bandeira*) fluttering; (*fig*: *vacilante*) hesitant, wavering; (*COM*: *câmbio*) floating.

flutuar [flu'twa*] *vi* to float; (*bandeira*) to flutter; (*fig*: *vacilar*) to waver.

fluvial [flu'vjaw] (*pl* **-ais**) *adj* river *atr*.

fluxo ['fluksu] *m* (*corrente*) flow; (*ELET*) flux; ~ **de caixa** (*COM*) cash flow.

fluxograma [flukso'grama] *m* flow chart.

FM *abr* (*RÁDIO*: *freqüencia modulada*) FM ♦ *f* (*pl* **~s**) FM (radio) station.

FMI *abr m* (= *Fundo Monetário Internacional*) IMF.

FMS *abr f* = **Federação Mundial dos Sindicatos**.

FN (*BR*) *abr m* = **Fuzileiro Naval**.

FND (*BR*) *abr m* = **Fundo Nacional de Desenvolvimento**.

fobia [fo'bia] *f* phobia.

foca ['fɔka] *f* (*animal*) seal ♦ *m/f* (*col*: *jornalista*) cub reporter.

focalização [fokaliza'sãw] *f* focusing.

focalizar [fokali'za*] *vt* to focus (on).

focinho [fo'siɲu] *m* snout; (*col*: *cara*) face, clock (*col*).

foco ['fɔku] *m* focus; (*MED*, *fig*) seat, centre (*BRIT*), center (*US*); **fora de** ~ out of focus.

fofo/a ['fofu/a] *adj* soft; (*col*: *pessoa*) cute.

fofoca [fo'fɔka] *f* piece of gossip; ~**s** *fpl* gossip *sg*; **fazer** ~ to gossip.

fofocar [fofo'ka*] *vi* to gossip.

fofoqueiro/a [fofo'kejru/a] *adj* gossipy ♦ *m/f* gossip.

fofura [fo'fura] (*col*) *f* cutie.

fogão [fo'gãw] (*pl* **-ões**) *m* stove, cooker.

fogareiro [foga'rejru] *m* stove.

foge ['fɔʒi] *etc vb V* **fugir**.

fogo ['fogu] *m* fire; (*fig*) ardour (*BRIT*), ardor (*US*); **você tem** ~? have you got a light?; ~**s de artifício** fireworks; **a** ~ **lento** on a low flame; **à prova de** ~ fireproof; **abrir** ~ to open fire; **brincar com** ~ (*fig*) to play with fire; **cessar** ~ (*MIL*) to cease fire; **estar com** ~ (*col*: *pessoa*) to be randy; **estar de** ~ (*col*: *bêbado*) to be drunk; **pegar** ~ to catch fire; (*estar com febre*) to burn up; **pôr** ~ **a** to set fire to; **ser bom para o** ~ (*fig*) to be useless; **ser** ~ (**na roupa**) (*col*: *pessoa*) to be a pain; (: *trabalho etc*) to be murder; (: *ser incrível*) to be amazing.

fogões [fo'gõjʃ] *mpl de* **fogão**.

fogo-fátuo (*pl* **fogos-fátuos**) *m* will-o'-the-wisp.

fogoso/a [fo'gozu/ɔza] *adj* fiery; (*libidinoso*) lustful.

fogueira [fo'gejra] *f* bonfire.

foguete [fo'getʃi] *m* rocket; (*pessoa*) live wire; **soltar os** ~**s antes da festa** (*fig*) to jump the gun.

foi [foj] *vb V* **ir**, **ser**.

foice ['fɔjsi] *f* scythe.

folclore [fowk'lɔri] *m* folklore.

folclórico/a [fowk'lɔriku/a] *adj* folkloric.

fole ['fɔli] *m* bellows *sg*.

fôlego ['folegu] *m* breath; (*folga*) breathing space; **perder o** ~ to get out of breath; **tomar** ~ to pause for breath.

folga ['fɔwga] *f* (*descanso*) rest, break; (*espaço livre*) clearance; (*ócio*) inactivity; (*col*: *atrevimento*) cheek; **dia de** ~ day off; **que** ~**!** what a cheek!

folgado/a [fow'gadu/a] *adj* (*roupa*) loose; (*vida*) leisurely; (*col*: *atrevido*) cheeky; (: *boa vida*) easy-living ♦ *m/f* (*col*: *atrevido*) cheeky devil; (: *boa vida*) loafer.

folgar [fow'ga*] *vt* to loosen, slacken ♦ *vi* (*descansar*) to rest, relax; (*divertir-se*) to have fun, amuse o.s.; ~ **em saber que ...** to be pleased to hear that ....

folgazão/zona [fowga'zãw/'zɔna] (*pl* **-ões/~s**) *adj* (*pessoa*) fun-loving; (*gênio*) lively.

folha ['foʎa] *f* leaf; (*de papel, de metal*) sheet; (*página*) page; (*de faca*) blade; (*jornal*) paper; **novo em** ~ brand new; ~ **de estanho** tinfoil (*BRIT*), aluminum foil (*US*); ~ **de pagamento** payroll; ~ **de rosto** imprint page; ~**s soltas** (*COMPUT*) single sheets, cut sheets.

folhagem [fo'ʎaʒẽ] *f* foliage.

folha-seca (*pl* **folhas-secas**) *f* (*FUTEBOL*) swerving shot.

folheado/a [fo'ʎjadu/a] *adj* veneered; ~ **a ouro** gold-plated.

folhear [fo'ʎja*] *vt* to leaf through.

folheto [fo'ʎetu] *m* booklet, pamphlet.

folhinha [fo'ʎiɲa] *f* tear-off calendar.

folhudo/a [fo'ʎudu/a] *adj* leafy.

folia [fo'lia] *f* revelry, merriment.

folião/liona [fo'ʎjãw/'ʎjɔna] (*pl* **-ões/~s**) *m/f* reveller (*in carnival*).

folículo [fo'likulu] *m* follicle.

foliões [fo'ʎõjʃ] *mpl de* **folião**.

foliona [fo'ʎjɔna] *f de* **folião**.

fome ['fɔmi] *f* hunger; (*escassez*) famine; (*fig*: *avidez*) longing; **passar** ~ to go hungry; **estar com** *ou* **ter** ~ to be hungry; **varado de** ~ starving, ravenous.

fomentar [fomẽ'ta*] *vt* to instigate, promote; (*discórdia*) to sow, cause.

fomento [fo'mẽtu] *m* (*MED*) fomentation; (*estímulo*) promotion; (*de discórdia, ódio etc*) stirring up.

fominha [fo'miɲa] (*col*) *adj* stingy ♦ *m/f* skinflint.

fonador(a) [fona'do*(a)] *adj V* **aparelho**.

fone ['fɔni] *m* telephone, phone; (*peça do telefone*) receiver.

fonema [fo'nema] *m* (*LING*) phoneme.

fonética [fo'netʃika] *f* phonetics *sg*.

fonético/a [fo'netʃiku/a] *adj* phonetic.

fonfom [fõ'fõ] (*pl* **-ns**) *m* toot.

fonologia [fonolo'ʒia] *f* phonology.

fonte ['fõtʃi] f (nascente) spring; (chafariz) fountain; (origem) source; (ANAT) temple; **de ~ limpa** from a reliable source; **retido/ tributado na ~** (COM) deducted/taxed at source.

footing ['futʃiŋ] m jogging.

for [fo*] etc vb V **ir**; **ser**.

fora ['fɔra] etc vb V **ir**; **ser** ♦ adv out, outside ♦ prep (além de) apart from ♦ m: **dar o ~** (bateria, radio) to give out; (pessoa) to leave, be off; **dar um ~** to slip up; **dar um ~ em alguém** (namorado) to chuck sb, dump sb; (esnobar) to snub sb; **levar um ~** (de namorado) to be given the boot; (ser esnobado) to get the brush-off; **~ de** outside; **~ de si** beside o.s.; **estar ~** (viajando) to be away; **estar ~** (**de casa**) to be out; **lá ~** outside; (no exterior) abroad; **jantar ~** to eat out; **com os braços de ~** with bare arms; **ser de ~** to be from out of town; **ficar de ~** not to join in; **lá para ~** outside; **ir para ~** (viajar) to go out of town; **com a cabeça para ~ da janela** with one's head sticking out of the window; **costurar/cozinhar para ~** to do sewing/cooking for other people; **por ~** on the outside; **cobrar por ~** to charge extra; **~ de dúvida** beyond doubt; **~ de propósito** irrelevant.

fora-de-lei m/f inv outlaw.

foragido/a [fora'ʒidu/a] adj, m/f (fugitivo) fugitive.

foragir-se [fora'ʒixsi] vr to go into hiding.

forasteiro/a [foraʃ'tejru/a] adj (estranho) alien ♦ m/f outsider, stranger; (de outro país) foreigner.

forca ['foxka] f gallows sg.

força ['foxsa] f (energia física) strength; (TEC, ELET) power; (esforço) effort; (coerção) force; **à ~** by force; **à ~ de** by dint of; **com ~** hard; **por ~** of necessity; **dar (uma) ~ a** to back up, encourage; **fazer ~** to try (hard); **como vai essa ~?** (col) how's it going?; **F~ Aérea** Air Force; **~ de trabalho** workforce; **~ maior** (COM) act of God.

forcado [fox'kadu] m pitchfork.

forçado/a [fox'sadu/a] adj forced; (afetado) false.

forçar [fox'sa*] vt to force; (olhos, voz) to strain; **~-se** vr: **~-se a** to force o.s. to.

força-tarefa (pl **forças-tarefa**) f task force.

forcejar [foxse'ʒa*] vi (esforçar-se) to strive; (lutar) to struggle.

fórceps ['fɔxsipʃ] m inv forceps pl.

forçoso/a [fox'sozu/ɔza] adj (necessário) necessary; (obrigatório) obligatory.

forja ['fɔxʒa] f forge.

forjar [fox'ʒa*] vt to forge; (pretexto) to make up.

forma ['fɔxma] f form; (de um objeto) shape; (físico) figure; (maneira) way; (MED)

fitness; **desta ~** in this way; **de (tal) ~ que** in such a way that; **de qualquer ~** anyway; **da mesma ~** likewise; **de outra ~** otherwise; **de ~ alguma** in no way whatsoever; **em ~ de pêra/comprimido** pear-shaped/in tablet form; **estar fora de/em ~** (pessoa) to be unfit/fit; **manter a ~** to keep fit; **~ de pagamento** means of payment.

fôrma ['foxma] f (CULIN) cake tin; (molde) mould (BRIT), mold (US); (para sapatos) last.

formação [foxma'sãw] (pl **-ões**) f formation; (antecedentes) background; (caráter) make-up; (profissional) training.

formado/a [fox'madu/a] adj (modelado) formed; ♦ m/f graduate; **ser ~ de** to consist of; **ser ~ em** to be a graduate in.

formal [fox'maw] (pl **-ais**) adj formal.

formalidade [foxmali'dadʒi] f formality.

formalizar [foxmali'za*] vt to formalize.

formando/a [fox'mãdu/a] m/f graduating student, graduand.

formão [fox'mãw] (pl **-ões**) m chisel.

formar [fox'ma*] vt to form; (constituir) to constitute, make up; (educar) to train, educate; (soldados) to form up ♦ vi to form up; **~-se** vr (tomar forma) to form; (EDUC) to graduate.

formatar [foxma'ta*] vt (COMPUT) to format.

formato [fox'matu] m format; (de papel) size.

formatura [foxma'tura] f (MIL) formation; (EDUC) graduation.

fórmica ['fɔxmika] ® f formica ®.

formidável [foxmi'davew] (pl **-eis**) adj tremendous, great.

formiga [fox'miga] f ant.

formigar [foxmi'ga*] vi (ser abundante) to abound; (sentir comichão) to itch; **~ de algo** to swarm with sth.

formigueiro [foxmi'gejru] m ants' nest; (multidão) throng, swarm.

formões [fox'mõjʃ] mpl de **formão**.

Formosa [fox'mɔza] f Taiwan.

formoso/a [fox'mozu/ɔza] adj (belo) beautiful; (esplêndido) superb.

formosura [foxmo'zura] f beauty.

fórmula ['fɔxmula] f formula.

formulação [foxmula'sãw] (pl **-ões**) f formulation.

formular [foxmu'la*] vt to formulate; (queixas) to voice; **~ votos** to express one's hopes/wishes.

formulário [foxmu'larju] m form; **~s mpl contínuos** (COMPUT) continuous stationery sg.

fornalha [fox'naʎa] f furnace; (fig: lugar quente) oven.

fornecedor(a) [foxnese'do*(a)] m/f supplier ♦ f (empresa) supplier ♦ adj supply atr.

fornecer [foxne'se*] vt to supply, provide; **~ algo a alguém** to supply sb with sth.

fornecimento [foxnesi'mẽtu] m supply.

NB: European Portuguese adds the following consonants to certain words: **b** (sú(b)dito, su(b)til), **c** (a(c)ção, a(c)cionista, a(c)to); **m** (inde(m)ne); **p** (ado(p)ção, ado(p)tar); for further details see p. xiii.

fornicar [foxni'ka*] *vi* to fornicate.

forno ['foxnu] *m* (*CULIN*) oven; (*TEC*) furnace; (*para cerâmica*) kiln; **alto** ~ blast furnace; **cozinheiro/a de** ~ **e fogão** expert cook.

foro ['foru] *m* forum; (*JUR*) Court of Justice; ~**s** *mpl* privileges; **de** ~ **íntimo** personal, private.

forra ['foxa] *f*: **ir à** ~ (*col*) to get one's own back.

forragem [fo'xaʒē] *f* fodder.

forrar [fo'xa*] *vt* (*cobrir*) to cover; (*: interior*) to line; (*de papel*) to paper.

forro ['foxu] *m* (*cobertura*) covering; (*interior*) lining; **com** ~ **de pele** fur-lined.

forró [fo'xɔ] (*col*) *m* shindig, dance.

fortalecer [foxtale'se*] *vt* to strengthen.

fortalecimento [foxtalesi'mētu] *m* strengthening.

fortaleza [foxta'leza] *f* (*forte*) fortress; (*força*) strength; (*moral*) fortitude; **ser uma** ~ to be as strong as an ox.

fortalezense [foxtale'zēsi] *adj* from Fortaleza. ♦ *m/f* native *ou* inhabitant of Fortaleza.

forte ['fɔxtʃi] *adj* strong; (*pancada*) hard; (*chuva*) heavy; (*som*) loud; (*dor*) sharp, strong; (*filme*) powerful; (*pessoa: musculoso*) muscular ♦ *adv* strongly; (*som*) loud(ly) ♦ *m* (*fortaleza*) fort; (*talento*) strength; **ser** ~ **em algo** (*versado*) to be good at sth *ou* strong in sth.

fortificação [foxtʃifika'sāw] (*pl* -**ões**) *f* fortification; (*fortaleza*) fortress.

fortificante [foxtʃifi'kãtʃi] *adj* fortifying ♦ *m* fortifier.

fortificar [foxtʃifi'ka*] *vt* to fortify; ~**-se** *vr* to build o.s. up.

fortuitamente [foxtwita'mētʃi] *adv* (*imprevisívelmente*) by chance, unexpectedly; (*ocasionalmente*) casually.

fortuito/a [fox'twitu/a] *adj* accidental.

fortuna [fox'tuna] *f* fortune; (*sorte*) (good) luck; (*riqueza*) fortune, wealth; **custar uma** ~ to cost a fortune.

fosco/a ['foʃku/a] *adj* (*sem brilho*) dull; (*opaco*) opaque.

fosfato [foʃ'fatu] *m* phosphate.

fosforescente [foʃfore'sētʃi] *adj* phosphorescent.

fósforo ['fɔʃforu] *m* match; (*QUÍM*) phosphorus.

fossa ['fɔsa] *f* pit; (*col*) blues *pl*; **estar/ficar na** ~ (*col*) to be/get down in the dumps *ou* depressed; **tirar alguém da** ~ (*col*) to cheer sb up; ~ **séptica** cesspit, septic tank.

fosse ['fosi] *etc vb V* **ir**; **ser**.

fóssil ['fɔsiw] (*pl* **fósseis**) *m* fossil.

fosso ['fosu] *m* trench, ditch; (*de uma fortaleza*) moat.

foto ['fɔtu] *f* photo.

fotocópia [foto'kɔpja] *f* photocopy.

fotocopiadora [fotokopja'dora] *f* photocopier.

fotocopiar [fotoko'pja*] *vt* to photocopy.

fotogênico/a [foto'ʒeniku/a] *adj* photogenic.

fotografar [fotogra'fa*] *vt* to photograph.

fotografia [fotogra'fia] *f* photography; (*uma foto*) photograph.

fotográfico/a [foto'grafiku/a] *adj* photographic; *V tb* **máquina**.

fotógrafo/a [fo'tɔgrafu/a] *m/f* photographer.

fotonovela [fotono'vɛla] *f* photo story.

fotossíntese [foto'sĩtezi] *f* (*BIOL*) photosynthesis.

foxtrote [foks'trɔtʃi] *m* foxtrot.

foyer [fua'je] *m* foyer.

foz [fɔʒ] *f* river mouth.

FP-25 *abr fpl* (= *Forças Populares do 25 de Abril*) Portuguese terrorist group.

fração [fra'sāw] (*pl* -**ões**) *f* fraction.

fracassar [fraka'sa*] *vi* to fail.

fracasso [fra'kasu] *m* failure.

fracção [fra'sāw] (*PT*) *f* = **fração**.

fracionar [frasjo'na*] *vt* to break up; ~**-se** *vr* to break up, fragment.

fraco/a ['fraku/a] *adj* weak; (*sol, som*) faint ♦ *m* weakness; **estar** ~ **em algo** to be poor at sth; **ter um** ~ **por algo** to have a weakness for sth.

frações [fra'sõjʃ] *fpl de* **fração**.

fractura *etc* [fra'tura] (*PT*) *f* = **fratura** *etc*.

frade ['fradʒi] *m* (*REL*) friar; (*: monge*) monk.

fraga ['fraga] *f* crag, rock.

fragata [fra'gata] *f* (*NÁUT*) frigate.

frágil ['fraʒiw] (*pl* -**eis**) *adj* (*débil*) fragile; (*quebradiço*) breakable; (*pessoa*) frail; (*saúde*) delicate, poor.

fragilidade [fraʒili'dadʒi] *f* fragility; (*de uma pessoa*) frailty.

fragílimo/a [fra'ʒilimu/a] *adj superl de* **frágil**.

fragmentar [fragmē'ta*] *vt* to break up; ~**-se** *vr* to break up.

fragmento [frag'mētu] *m* fragment.

fragrância [fra'grãsja] *f* fragrance, perfume.

fragrante [fra'grãtʃi] *adj* fragrant.

frajola [fra'ʒɔla] (*col*) *adj* smart.

fralda ['frawda] *f* (*da camisa*) shirt tail; (*para bebê*) nappy (*BRIT*), diaper (*US*); (*de montanha*) foot; **mal saído das** ~**s** (*fig*) still wet behind the ears.

framboesa [frã'beza] *f* raspberry.

França ['frãsa] *f* France.

francamente [frãka'mētʃi] *adv* (*abertamente*) frankly; (*realmente*) really.

francês/esa [frã'seʃ/eza] *adj* French ♦ *m/f* Frenchman/woman ♦ *m* (*LING*) French.

franco/a ['frãku/a] *adj* (*sincero*) frank; (*isento de pagamento*) free; (*óbvio*) clear ♦ *m* franc; **entrada franca** free admission.

frangalho [frã'gaʎu] *m* (*trapo*) rag, tatter; (*pessoa*) wreck; **em** ~**s** in tatters.

frango ['frãgu] *m* chicken; (*FUTEBOL*) easy goal.

franja ['frãʒa] *f* fringe (*BRIT*), bangs *pl* (*US*).

franquear [frã'kja*] *vt* (*caminho*) to clear; (*isentar de imposto*) to exempt from duties; (*carta*) to frank; ~ **algo a alguém** (*facultar*) to make sth available to sb.

franqueza [frã'keza] *f* frankness.

franquia [frã'kia] *f* (*COM*) franchise; (*isenção*) exemption; ~ **de bagagem** baggage allowance; ~ **diplomática** diplomatic immunity; ~ **postal** freepost.

franzido [frã'zidu] *m* pleat.

franzino/a [frã'zinu/a] *adj* skinny.

franzir [frã'zi*] *vt* (*preguear*) to pleat; (*enrugar*) to wrinkle, crease; (*lábios*) to curl; ~ **as sobrancelhas** to frown.

fraque ['fraki] *m* morning suit.

fraquejar [frake'ʒa*] *vi* to grow weak; (*vontade*) to weaken.

fraqueza [fra'keza] *f* weakness.

frasco ['fraʃku] *m* (*de remédio, perfume*) bottle.

frase ['frazi] *f* sentence; ~ **feita** set phrase.

fraseado [fra'zjadu] *m* wording.

frasqueira [fraʃ'kejra] *f* vanity case.

fraternal [fratex'naw] (*pl* -**ais**) *adj* fraternal.

fraternidade [fratexni'dadʒi] *f* fraternity.

fraternizar [fratexni'za*] *vt* to bring together ♦ *vi* to fraternize.

fraterno/a [fra'texnu/a] *adj* fraternal.

fratura [fra'tura] *f* fracture, break.

fraturar [fratu'ra*] *vt* to fracture.

fraudar [fraw'da*] *vt* to defraud; (*expectativa, esperanças*) to dash.

fraude ['frawdʒi] *f* fraud.

fraudulento/a [frawdu'lẽtu/a] *adj* fraudulent.

freada [fre'ada] (*BR*) *f* burst on the brake; **dar uma** ~ to slam on the brakes.

frear [fre'a*] (*BR*) *vt* (*conter*) to curb, restrain; (*veículo*) to stop ♦ *vi* (*veículo*) to brake.

freelance [fri'lãs] *m/f* freelancer.

freezer ['frize*] *m* freezer.

frege ['freʒi] *m* mess.

freguês/guesa [fre'geʃ/'geza] *m/f* (*cliente*) customer; (*PT*) parishioner.

freguesia [frege'zia] *f* customers *pl*; (*PT*) parish.

frei [frej] *m* friar, monk; (*título*) Brother.

freio ['freju] *m* (*BR*: *veículo*) brake; (*cavalo*) bridle; (*bocado do freio*) bit; (*fig*) check; ~ **de mão** handbrake.

freira ['frejra] *f* nun.

freixo ['frejʃu] *m* (*BOT*) ash.

Frelimo [fre'limo] *abr f* (= *Frente de Libertação de Moçambique*) Frelimo.

fremente [fre'mẽtʃi] *adj* (*fig*) rousing.

fremir [fre'mi*] *vi* (*bramar*) to roar; (*tremer*) to tremble.

frêmito ['fremitu] *m* (*fig*: *de alegria etc*) wave.

frenesi [frene'zi] *m* frenzy.

frenético/a [fre'nɛtʃiku/a] *adj* frantic, frenzied.

frente ['frẽtʃi] *f* (*de objeto, POL, MIL*) front; (*rosto*) face; (*fachada*) façade; ~ **a** ~ face to face; **à** ~ **de** at the front of; **de** ~ **para** facing; **em** ~ **de** in front of; (*defronte a*) opposite; **para a** ~ ahead, forward; **de trás para** ~ from back to front; **porta da** ~ front door; **apartamento de** ~ apartment at the front; **seguir em** ~ to continue ahead; **a casa em** ~ the house opposite; **na minha** (*ou sua etc*) ~ in front of me (*ou you etc*); **sair da** ~ to get out of the way; **sai da minha** ~! get out of my sight!; **pela** ~ ahead; **pra** ~ (*col*) fashionable, trendy; **fazer** ~ **a algo** to face sth; **ir para a** ~ (*progredir*) to progress; **levar à** ~ to carry through; ~ **de combate** (*MIL*) front; ~ **de trabalho** area of employment; ~ **fria/quente** (*METEOROLOGIA*) cold/warm front.

freqüência [fre'kwẽsja] *f* frequency; **com** ~ often, frequently.

freqüentador(a) [frekwẽta'do*(a)] *m/f* regular visitor; (*de restaurante etc*) regular customer.

freqüentar [frekwẽ'ta*] *vt* to frequent; ~ **a casa de alguém** to go to sb's house a lot; ~ **um curso** to attend a course.

freqüente [fre'kwẽtʃi] *adj* frequent.

fresca ['freʃka] *f* cool breeze.

frescão [freʃ'kãw] (*pl* -**ões**) *m* air-conditioned coach.

fresco/a ['freʃku/a] *adj* fresh; (*vento, tempo*) cool; (*col: efeminado*) camp; (: *afetado*) pretentious; (: *cheio de luxo*) fussy ♦ *m* (*ar*) fresh air; (*ARTE*) fresco.

frescobol [freʃko'bɔw] *m* (kind of) racketball (*played mainly on the beach*).

frescões [freʃ'kõjʃ] *mpl* **de frescão**.

frescor [freʃ'ko*] *m* freshness.

frescura [freʃ'kura] *f* freshness; (*frialdade*) coolness; (*col: luxo*) fussiness; (: *afetaçuo*) pretentiousness; **que** ~! how fussy!; how pretentious!

fresta ['freʃta] *f* gap, slit.

fretar [fre'ta*] *vt* (*avião, navio*) to charter; (*caminhão*) to hire.

frete ['fretʃi] *m* (*carregamento*) freight, cargo; (*tarifa*) freightage; **a** ~ for hire.

freudiano/a [frɔj'dʒjanu/a] *adj* Freudian.

frevo ['frevu] *m* improvised Carnival dance.

fria ['fria] *f*: **dar uma** ~ **em alguém** to give sb the cold shoulder; **estar/entrar numa** ~ (*col*) to be in/get into a mess; **levar uma** ~ **de alguém** to get the cold shoulder from sb.

friagem ['frjaʒẽ] *f* cold weather.

frialdade [frjaw'dadʒi] *f* coldness; (*indiferença*) indifference, coolness.

fricção [frik'sãw] *f* friction; (*ato*) rubbing; (*MED*) massage.

friccionar [friksjo'na*] *vt* to rub.

fricote [fri'kɔtʃi] (*col*) *m* finickiness.

fricoteiro/a [fiko'tejru/a] (*col*) *adj* finicky ♦ *m/f* fusspot.

frieira ['frjejra] *f* chilblain.

NB: *European Portuguese adds the following consonants to certain words:* **b** (sú(b)dito, su(b)til); **c** (a(c)ção, a(c)cionista, a(c)to); **m** (inde(m)ne); **p** (ado(p)ção, ado(p)tar); *for further details see p. xiii.*

frieza ['frjeza] f coldness; (indiferença) coolness.
frigideira [friʒi'dejra] f frying pan.
frigidez [friʒi'deʒ] f frigidity.
frígido/a ['friʒidu/a] adj frigid.
frigir [fri'ʒi*] vt to fry.
frigorífico [frigo'rifiku] m refrigerator; (congelador) freezer.
frincha ['frĩʃa] f chink, slit.
frio/a ['friu/a] adj cold; (col) forged ♦ m coldness; ~s mpl cold meats; **estou com** ~ I'm cold; **faz** ou **está** ~ it's cold.
friorento/a [frjo'rētu/a] adj (pessoa) sensitive to the cold; (lugar) chilly.
frisar [fri'za*] vt (encrespar) to curl; (salientar) to emphasize.
Frísia ['frizja] f: **a** ~ Frisia.
friso ['frizu] m border; (na parede) frieze; (ARQ) moulding (BRIT), molding (US).
fritada [fri'tada] f fry-up; **dar uma** ~ **em algo** to fry sth.
fritar [fri'ta*] vt to fry.
fritas ['fritas] fpl chips (BRIT), French fries (US).
frito/a ['fritu/a] adj fried; (col): **estar** ~ to be done for.
fritura [fri'tura] f fried food.
frivolidade [frivoli'dadʒi] f frivolity.
frívolo/a ['frivolu/a] adj frivolous.
fronha ['froɲa] f pillowcase.
front [frõ] (pl ~s) m (MIL, fig) front.
fronte ['frõtʃi] f (ANAT) forehead, brow.
fronteira [frõ'tejra] f frontier, border.
fronteiriço/a [frõtej'risu/a] adj frontier atr.
fronteiro/a [frõ'tejru/a] adj front.
frontispício [frõtʃiʃ'pisju] m (de edifício) main façade; (de livro) frontispiece; (rosto) face.
frota ['frɔta] f fleet.
frouxo/a ['froʃu/a] adj loose; (corda) slack; (fraco) weak; (indolente) lax; (col: condescendente) soft.
frufru [fru'fru] m (enfeite) ruff.
frugal [fru'gaw] (pl -ais) adj frugal.
fruição [frwi'sãw] f enjoyment.
fruir ['frwi*] vt to enjoy ♦ vi: ~ **de algo** to enjoy sth.
frustração [fruʃtra'sãw] f frustration.
frustrado/a [fruʃ'tradu/a] adj frustrated; (planos) thwarted.
frustrante [fruʃ'trãtʃi] adj frustrating.
frustrar [fruʃ'tra*] vt to frustrate.
fruta ['fruta] f fruit.
fruta-de-conde (pl **frutas-de-conde**) f sweetsop.
fruta-pão (pl **frutas-pães** ou **frutas-pão**) f breadfruit.
fruteira [fru'tejra] f fruit bowl.
frutífero/a [fru'tʃiferu/a] adj (proveitoso) fruitful; (árvore) fruit-bearing.
fruto ['frutu] m (BOT) fruit; (resultado) result, product; **dar** ~ to bear fruit.
fubá [fu'ba] m corn meal.
fubeca [fu'bɛka] (col) f thrashing.

fubica [fu'bika] (col) f heap, jalopy.
fuçar [fu'sa*] vi: ~ **em algo** (remexer) to rummage in sth; (meter-se) to meddle in sth.
fuças ['fusaʃ] (col) fpl face sg, chops.
fuga ['fuga] f flight, escape; (de gás etc) leak; (da prisão) escape; (de namorados) elopement; (MÚS) fugue.
fugacíssimo/a [fuga'sisimu/a] adj superl de fugaz.
fugaz [fu'gaʒ] adj fleeting.
fugida [fu'ʒida] f sortie; **dar uma** ~ ou **fugidinha** to pop out for a moment.
fugir [fu'ʒi*] vi to flee, escape; (prisioneiro) to escape; (criança: de casa) to run away; (namorados) to elope; ~ **a algo** to avoid sth.
fugitivo/a [fuʒi'tʃivu/a] adj, m/f fugitive.
fui [fuj] vb V **ir**; **ser**.
fulano/a [fu'lanu/a] m/f so-and-so; ~ **de tal** what's-his-name/what's-her-name; ~, **beltrano e sicrano** Tom, Dick and Harry.
fulcro ['fuwkru] m fulcrum.
fuleiro/a [fu'lejru/a] adj tacky.
fúlgido/a ['fuwʒidu/a] adj brilliant.
fulgir [fuw'ʒi*] vi to shine.
fulgor [fuw'go*] m brilliance.
fuligem [fu'liʒē] f soot.
fulminante [fuwmi'nãtʃi] adj (devastador) devastating; (palavras) scathing.
fulminar [fuwmi'na*] vt (ferir, matar) to strike down; (petrificar) to stop dead; (aniquilar) to annihilate ♦ vi to flash with lightning; **fulminado por um raio** struck by lightning.
fulo/a ['fulu/a] adj: **estar** ou **ficar** ~ **de raiva** to be furious.
fumaça [fu'masa] (BR) f (de fogo) smoke; (de gás) fumes pl; **500 e lá vai** ~ (col) 500 and then some.
fumador(a) [fuma'do*(a)] (PT) m/f smoker.
fumante [fu'mãtʃi] m/f smoker.
fumar [fu'ma*] vt, vi to smoke.
fumê [fu'me] adj inv (vidro) smoked.
fumo ['fumu] m (PT: de fogo) smoke; (: de gás) fumes pl; (BR: tabaco) tobacco; (fumar) smoking; (BR: col: maconha) dope; ~ **louro** Virginia tobacco; **puxar** ~ (col) to smoke dope.
FUNABEM [funa'bē] (BR) abr f (= Fundação Nacional do Bem-Estar do Menor) children's home.
Funai [fu'naj] (BR) abr f = **Fundação Nacional do Índio**.
Funarte [fu'naxtʃi] (BR) abr f = **Fundaçao Nacional de Arte**.
função [fũ'sãw] (pl -ões) f function; (ofício) duty; (papel) role; (espetáculo) performance.
Funcep [fũ'sɛpi] (BR) abr f = (Fundação Centro de Formação do Servidor Público) civil service training centre.
funcho ['fũʃu] m (BOT) fennel.
funcional [fũsjo'naw] (pl -ais) adj functional.
funcionalismo [fũsjona'liʒmu] m: ~ **público** civil service.

funcionamento [fũsjona'mẽtu] m functioning, working; **pôr em** ~ to set going, start.

funcionar [fũsjo'na*] vi to function; (máquina) to work, run; (dar bom resultado) to work.

funcionário/a [fũsjo'narju/a] m/f official; ~ (público) civil servant.

funções [fũ'sõjʃ] fpl de **função**.

fundação [fũda'sãw] (pl -ões) f foundation.

fundador(a) [fũda'do*(a)] m/f founder ♦ adj founding.

fundamental [fũdamẽ'taw] (pl -ais) adj fundamental, basic.

fundamentar [fũdamẽ'ta*] vt (argumento) to substantiate; (basear): ~ (em) to base (on).

fundamento [fũda'mẽtu] m (fig) foundation, basis; (motivo) motive; **sem** ~ groundless.

fundar [fũ'da*] vt to establish, found; (basear) to base; ~**-se** vr: ~**-se em** to be based on.

fundear [fũ'dʒja*] vi to anchor.

fundição [fũdʒi'sãw] (pl -ões) f fusing; (fábrica) foundry.

fundilho [fũ'dʒiʎu] m (da calça) seat.

fundir [fũ'dʒi*] vt to fuse; (metal) to smelt, melt down; (COM: empresas) to merge; (em molde) to cast; ~**-se** vr (derreter-se) to melt; (juntar-se) to merge, fuse; (COM) to merge; ~ **a cuca** to crack up.

fundo/a ['fũdu/a] adj deep; (fig) profound; (col: ignorante) ignorant; (: despreparado) hopeless ♦ m (do mar, jardim) bottom; (profundidade) depth; (base) basis; (da loja, casa, do papel) back; (de quadro) background; (de dinheiro) fund ♦ adv deeply; ~**s** mpl (COM) funds; (da casa etc) back sg; **a** ~ thoroughly; **ao** ~ in the background; **ir ao** ~ (navio) to sink, go down; **no** ~ (de caixa etc) at the bottom; (de casa etc) at the back; (de quadro) in the background; (fig) basically, at bottom; **sem** ~ (poço) bottomless; **dar** ~**s para** (casa etc) to back on to; ~ **de contingência** contingency fund; ~ **de investimento** investment fund; **F**~ **Monetário Internacional** International Monetary Fund.

fundura [fũ'dura] f depth; (col) ignorance.

fúnebre ['funebri] adj funeral atr, funereal; (fig: triste) gloomy, lugubrious.

funeral [fune'raw] (pl -ais) m funeral.

funerário/a [fune'rarju/a] adj funeral atr; **casa funerária** undertakers pl.

funesto/a [fu'nɛʃtu/a] adj (fatal) fatal; (infausto) disastrous; (notícia) fateful.

fungar [fũ'ga*] vt, vi to sniff.

fungo ['fũgu] m (BOT) fungus.

funil [fu'niw] (pl -is) m funnel.

Funrural [fũxu'raw] (BR) abr m = **Fundo de Assistência e Previdência ao Trabalhador Rural**.

Funtevê [fũte've] abr f = **Fundação Centro-Brasileira de TV Educativa**.

fura-bolo ['fura-] (pl **fura-bolos**) (col) m index finger.

furacão [fura'kãw] (pl -ões) m hurricane; **entrar/sair como um** ~ to stomp in/out.

furado/a [fu'radu/a] adj perforated; (pneu) flat; (orelha) pierced; (col: programa) crummy.

furão/rona [fu'rãw/'rɔna] (pl -ões/~s) m ferret ♦ m/f (col) go-getter ♦ adj (col) hardworking, dynamic.

furar [fu'ra*] vt (perfurar) to bore, perforate; (penetrar) to penetrate; (frustrar) to foil; (fila) to jump ♦ vi (col: programa) to fall through; ~ **uma greve** to break a strike.

furdúncio [fux'dũsju] (col) m commotion.

furgão [fux'gãw] (pl -ões) m van.

furgoneta [fuxgo'neta] (PT) f van.

fúria ['furja] f fury, rage; **estar uma** ~ to be furious.

furibundo/a [furi'bũdu/a] adj furious.

furioso/a [fu'rjozu/ɔza] adj furious.

furo ['furu] m hole; (num pneu) puncture; ~ **jornalístico** scoop; **dar um** ~ (col) to make a blunder; **estar muitos** ~**s acima de algo** (fig) to be a cut above sth, be a lot better than sth.

furões [fu'rõjʃ] mpl de **furão**.

furona [fu'rɔna] f de **furão**.

furor [fu'ro*] m fury, rage; **causar** ~ to cause a furore; **fazer** ~ to be all the rage.

furta-cor ['fuxta-] (pl **furta-cores**) adj iridescent ♦ m iridescence.

furtar [fux'ta*] vt, vi to steal; ~**-se** vr: ~**-se a** to avoid, evade.

furtivo/a [fux'tʃivu/a] adj furtive, stealthy.

furto ['fuxtu] m theft.

furúnculo [fu'rũkulu] m (MED) boil.

fusão [fu'zãw] (pl -ões) f fusion; (COM) merger; (derretimento) melting; (união) union.

fusca ['fuʃka] (col) m (VW) beetle.

fusco/a ['fuʃku/a] adj dark, dusky.

fuselagem [fuze'laʒẽ] (pl -ns) f fuselage.

fusível [fu'zivew] (pl -eis) m (ELET) fuse.

fuso ['fuzu] m (TEC) spindle; ~ **horário** time zone.

fusões [fu'zõjʃ] fpl de **fusão**.

fustão [fuʃ'tãw] m corduroy.

fustigar [fuʃtʃi'ga*] vt (açoitar) to flog, whip; (suj: vento) to lash; (maltratar) to lash out at.

futebol [futʃi'bɔw] m football; ~ **de salão** five-a-side football; ~ **totó** table football; **fazer um** ~ **de algo** (col) to get sth all mixed up.

fútil ['futʃiw] (pl -eis) adj (pessoa) superficial, shallow; (insignificante) trivial.

futilidade [futʃili'dadʒi] f (de pessoa) shallowness; (insignificância) triviality; (coisa fútil) trivial thing.

futurismo [futu'riʒmu] m futurism.

NB: European Portuguese adds the following consonants to certain words: **b** (sú(b)dito, su(b)til); **c** (a(c)ção, a(c)cionista, a(c)to); **m** (inde(m)ne); **p** (ado(p)ção, ado(p)tar); for further details see p. xiii.

futuro/a [fu'turu/a] *adj* future ♦ *m* future; **no** ~ in the future; **num** ~ **próximo** in the near future.

fuxicar [fuʃi'ka*] *vi* to gossip.

fuxico [fu'ʃiku] *m* piece of gossip.

fuxiqueiro/a [fuʃi'kejru/a] *m/f* gossip ♦ *adj* gossipy.

fuzil [fu'ziw] (*pl* -**is**) *m* rifle.

fuzilamento [fuzila'mētu] *m* shooting.

fuzilante [fuzi'lātʃi] *adj* (*olhos*) blazing.

fuzilar [fuzi'la*] *vt* to shoot ♦ *vi* (*olhos*) to blaze; (*pessoa*)to fume.

fuzileiro/a [fuzi'lejru/a] *m/f*: ~ **naval** (*MIL*) marine.

fuzis [fu'ziʃ] *mpl de* **fuzil**.

fuzuê [fu'zwe] *m* commotion.

G

G, g [ʒe] (*pl* **gs**) *m* G, g; **G de Gomes** G for George.

g. *abr* (= *grama*) gr.; (= *grau*) deg.

Gabão [ga'bãw] *m*: **o** ~ Gabon.

gabar [ga'ba*] *vt* to praise; ~-**se** *vr*: ~-**se de** to boast about.

gabardine [gabax'dʒini] *f* gabardine.

gabaritado/a [gabari'tadu/a] *adj* (*pessoa*) well-qualified.

gabarito [gaba'ritu] *m* (*fig*): **ter** ~ **para** to have the ability to; **de** ~ (of) high calibre *atr* (*BRIT*) *ou* caliber *atr* (*US*).

gabinete [gabi'netʃi] *m* (*COM*) office; (*escritório*) study; (*POL*) cabinet.

gado ['gadu] *m* livestock; (*bovino*) cattle; ~ **leiteiro** dairy cattle; ~ **suíno** pigs *pl*.

gaélico/a [ga'ɛliku/a] *adj* Gaelic ♦ *m* (*LING*) Gaelic.

gafanhoto [gafa'ɲotu] *m* grasshopper.

gafe ['gafi] *f* gaffe, faux pas; **dar** *ou* **cometer uma** ~ to make a faux pas.

gafieira [ga'fjejra] (*col*) *f* (*lugar*) dive; (*baile*) knees-up.

gagá [ga'ga] *adj* senile.

gago/a ['gagu/a] *adj* stuttering ♦ *m/f* stutterer.

gagueira [ga'gejra] *f* stutter.

gaguejar [gage'ʒa*] *vi* to stammer, stutter ♦ *vt* (*resposta*) to stammer.

gaiato/a [ga'jatu/a] *adj* funny.

gaiola [ga'jɔla] *f* (*para pássaro*) cage; (*cadeia*) jail ♦ *m* (*barco*) riverboat.

gaita ['gajta] *f* harmonica; (*col*: *dinheiro*) cash, dough; **cheio/a da** ~ (*col*) loaded; **solta a** ~! (*col*) hand over your cash!; ~ **de foles** bagpipes *pl*.

gaivota [gaj'vɔta] *f* seagull.

gajo ['gaʒu] (*PT*: *col*) *m* guy, fellow.

gala ['gala] *f*: **traje de** ~ full dress; **festa de** ~ gala.

galã [ga'lã] *m* (*ator*) leading man; (*fig*) ladies' man.

galalau [gala'law] *m* giant.

galante [ga'lātʃi] *adj* (*gracioso*) graceful; (*gentil*) gallant.

galanteador [galātʃja'do*] *m* suitor, admirer.

galantear [galã'tʃja*] *vt* to court, woo.

galanteio [galã'teju] *m* wooing.

galantina [galã'tʃina] *f* (*CULIN*): ~ **de galinha** chicken in aspic.

galão [ga'lãw] (*pl* -**ões**) *m* (*MIL*) stripe; (*medida*) gallon; (*PT*: *café*) white coffee; (*passamanaria*) braid.

Galápagos [ga'lapaguʃ]: (**as**) **Ilhas** ~ (the) Galapagos Islands.

galardão [galax'dãw] (*pl* -**ões**) *m* reward.

galardoar [galax'dwa*] *vt*: ~ **alguém (com algo)** to reward sb (with sth).

galardões [galax'dõjʃ] *mpl de* **galardão**.

galáxia [ga'laksja] *m* galaxy.

galé [ga'lɛ] *f* (*NÁUT*) galley ♦ *m* galley slave.

galego/a [ga'legu/a] *adj* Galician ♦ *m/f* Galician; (*col*, *pej*) Portuguese ♦ *m* (*LING*) Galician.

galera [ga'lɛra] *f* (*NÁUT*) galley; (*col*: *pessoas*, *público*) crowd.

galeria [gale'ria] *f* gallery; (*TEATRO*) circle; (*para águas pluviais*) storm drain.

Gales ['galiʃ] *m*: **País de** ~ Wales.

galês/esa [ga'leʃ/eza] *adj* Welsh ♦ *m/f* Welshman/woman ♦ *m* (*LING*) Welsh; **os galeses** *mpl* the Welsh.

galeto [ga'letu] *m* spring chicken.

galgar [gaw'ga*] *vt* (*saltar*) to leap over; (*subir*) to climb up.

galgo ['gawgu] *m* greyhound.

galhardia [gaʎax'dʒia] *f* (*elegância*) elegance; (*bravura*, *gentileza*) gallantry; **com** ~ gallantly.

galhardo/a [ga'ʎaxdu/a] *adj* (*elegante*) elegant; (*bravo*, *gentil*) gallant.

galheteiro [gaʎe'tejru] *m* cruet stand.

galho ['gaʎu] *m* (*de árvore*) branch; (*col*: *bico*) part-time job; (: *problema*): **dar o** ~ to cause trouble; **quebrar um** *ou* **o** ~ to sort it out.

galicismo [gali'siʒmu] *m* Gallicism.

galináceos [gali'nasjuʃ] *mpl* poultry *sg*.

galinha [ga'liɲa] *f* hen; (*CULIN*; *fig*: *covarde*) chicken; (*fig*: *puta*) slut; **a** ~ **do vizinho é sempre mais gorda** (*fig*) the grass is always greener (on the other side of the fence); **matar a** ~ **dos ovos de ouro** (*fig*) to kill the goose that lays the golden egg.

galinha-d'angola [-dã'gɔla] (*pl* **galinhas-d'angolas**) *f* guinea fowl.

galinha-morta (*pl* **galinhas-mortas**) (*col*) *f* (*pechincha*) bargain; (*coisa fácil*) piece of cake ♦ *m/f* (*pessoa*) weakling.

galinheiro [gali'ɲejru] *m* (*lugar*) hen-house.

galo ['galu] *m* cock, rooster; (*inchação*) bump;

missa do ~ midnight mass; **ouvir cantar o ~ e não saber onde** (*fig*) to jump to conclusions; ~ **de briga** fighting cock; (*fig: pessoa*) troublemaker.

galocha [ga'lɔʃa] *f* (*bota*) Wellington (boot).

galões [ga'lõjʃ] *mpl* **de galão**.

galopante [galo'pãtʃi] *adj* (*fig:* *inflação*) galloping; (: *doença*) rampant.

galopar [galo'pa*] *vi* to gallop.

galope [ga'lɔpi] *m* gallop.

galpão [gaw'pãw] (*pl* **-ões**) *m* shed.

galvanizar [gawvani'za*] *vt* to galvanize.

gama ['gama] *f* (*MÚS*) scale; (*fig*) range; (*ZOOL*) doe.

gamado/a [ga'madu/a] (*col*) *adj*: **ser** *ou* **estar ~ por** to be crazy about.

gamão [ga'mãw] *m* backgammon.

gamar [ga'ma*] (*col*) *vi*: ~ **(por)** to fall in love (with).

gambá [gã'ba] *m* (*ZOO*) opossum; **bêbado/a como um** ~ (*col*) pissed as a newt.

Gâmbia ['gãbja] *m*: **o** ~ (the) Gambia.

gambito [gã'bitu] *m* (*XADREZ etc*) gambit; (*col: perna*) pin.

gamo ['gamu] *m* (fallow) deer.

Gana ['gana] *m* Ghana.

gana ['gana] *f* (*desejo*) craving, desire; (*ódio*) hate; **ter** ~**s de (fazer) algo** to feel like (doing) sth; **ter** ~ **de alguém** to hate sb.

ganância [ga'nãsja] *f* greed.

ganancioso/a [ganã'sjozu/ɔza] *adj* greedy.

gancho ['gãʃu] *m* hook; (*de calça*) crotch.

gandaia [gã'daja] *f* (*vadiagem*) idling; (*farra*) living it up; **viver na** ~ to lead the life of Riley; **cair na** ~ to live it up.

Ganges ['gãʒiʃ] *m*: **o** ~ the Ganges.

gânglio ['gãglju] *m* (*MED*) ganglion.

gangorra [gã'goxa] *f* seesaw.

gangrena [gã'grena] *f* gangrene.

gangrenar [gãgre'na*] *vi* to go gangrenous.

gângster ['gãʃte*] *m* gangster.

gangue ['gãgi] (*col*) *f* gang.

ganhador(a) [gaɲa'do*(a)] *adj* winning ♦ *m/f* winner.

ganha-pão ['gaɲa-] (*pl* **-ães**) *m* living, livelihood.

ganhar [ga'ɲa*] *vt* to win; (*salário*) to earn; (*adquirir*) to get; (*lugar*) to reach; (*lucrar*) to gain ♦ *vi* (*vencer*) to win; ~ **de alguém** (*num jogo*) to beat sb; ~ **a alguém em algo** to outdo sb in sth; ~ **tempo** to gain time; **sair ganhando** to come out better off, come off better; **ganhei o dia** (*fig*) it made my day.

ganho/a ['gaɲu/a] *pp de* **ganhar** ♦ *m* (*lucro*) profit, gain; ~**s** *mpl* (*ao jogo*) winnings; ~ **de capital** (*COM*) capital gain.

ganido [ga'nidu] *m* (*de cão*) yelp; (*de pessoa*) squeal.

ganir [ga'ni*] *vi* (*cão*) to yelp; (*pessoa*) to

squeal ♦ *vt* (*gemido, gritos*) to let out.

ganso/a ['gãsu/a] *m/f* gander/goose.

garagem [ga'raʒẽ] (*pl* **-ns**) *f* garage.

garagista [gara'ʒiʃta] *m/f* garage owner.

garanhão [gara'ɲãw] (*pl* **-ões**) *m* stallion; (*col: homem*) stud.

garantia [garã'tʃia] *f* guarantee; (*de dívida*) surety; **estar na** ~ (*compra*) to be under guarantee; **empréstimo sem** ~ (*COM*) unsecured loan.

garantir [garã'tʃi*] *vt* to guarantee; ~**-se** *vr*: ~**-se contra algo** to defend o.s. against sth; ~ **algo (a alguém)** (*prometer*) to promise (sb) sth; ~ **que ...** to maintain that ...; ~ **a alguém que ...** to assure sb that ...; ~ **alguém contra algo** to defend sb against sth.

garatujar [garatu'ʒa*] *vt* to scribble, scrawl.

garbo ['gaxbu] *m* (*elegância*) elegance; (*distinção*) distinction.

garboso/a [gax'bozu/ɔza] *adj* (*elegante*) elegant; (*distinto*) distinguished.

garça ['gaxsa] *f* heron.

garçom [gax'sõ] (*BR: pl* **-ns**) *m* waiter.

garçonete [gaxso'netʃi] (*BR*) *f* waitress.

garçonnière [gaxso'njɛ*] *f* love nest.

garçons [gax'sõʃ] *mpl* **de garçom**.

garfada [gax'fada] *f* forkful.

garfo ['gaxfu] *m* fork; **ser um bom** ~ (*fig*) to enjoy one's food.

gargalhada [gaxga'ʎada] *f* burst of laughter; **rir às** ~**s** to roar with laughter; **dar** *ou* **soltar uma** ~ to burst out laughing; ~ **homérica** guffaw.

gargalo [gax'galu] *m* (*tb fig*) bottleneck.

garganta [gax'gãta] *f* (*ANAT*) throat; (*GEO*) gorge, ravine ♦ *m/f* (*col*) braggart, loudmouth ♦ *adj* (*col*) loudmouth(ed); **limpar a** ~ to clear one's throat; **molhar a** ~ (*col*) to wet one's whistle; **aquilo não me passou pela** ~ (*fig*) that stuck in my craw.

gargantilha [gaxgã'tʃiʎa] *f* choker.

gargarejar [gaxgare'ʒa*] *vi* to gargle.

gargarejo [gaxga'reʒu] *m* (*ato*) gargling; (*líquido*) gargle.

gari ['gari] *m/f* (*na rua*) roadsweeper (*BRIT*), streetsweeper (*US*); (*lixeiro*) dustman (*BRIT*), garbage man (*US*).

garimpar [garĩ'pa*] *vi* to prospect.

garimpeiro [garĩ'pejru] *m* prospector.

garoa [ga'roa] *f* drizzle.

garoar [ga'rwa*] *vi* to drizzle.

garota [ga'rota] (*BR: col*) *f* (*cerveja*) beer; *V tb* **garoto**.

garotada [garo'tada] *f*: **a** ~ the kids *pl*.

garota-de-programa (*pl* **garotas-de-programa**) (*col*) *f* good-time girl.

garoto/a [ga'rotu/a] *m/f* boy/girl; (*namorado*) boyfriend/girlfriend; (*PT: café*) coffee with milk.

garoto/a-propaganda (*pl* **garotos/as-**

NB: European Portuguese adds the following consonants to certain words: **b** (sú(b)dito, su(b)til); **c** (a(c)ção, a(c)cionista, a(c)to); **m** (inde(m)ne); **p** (ado(p)ção, ado(p)tar); *for further details see p. xiii.*

propaganda) *m/f* publicity boy/girl.
garoupa [ga'ropa] *f* (*peixe*) grouper.
garra ['gaxa] *f* claw; (*de ave*) talon; (*fig*: *entusiasmo*) enthusiasm, drive; ~**s** *fpl* (*fig*) clutches.
garrafa [ga'xafa] *f* bottle; ~ **térmica** (*BR*) Thermos flask ®.
garrafada [gaxa'fada] *f*: **dar uma** ~ **em alguém** to hit sb with a bottle.
garrafão [gaxa'fãw] (*pl* -ões) *m* flagon.
garrancho [ga'xãʃu] *m* scrawl.
garrido/a [ga'xidu/a] *adj* (*elegante*) smart; (*alegre*) lively; (*vistoso*) showy; (*gracioso*) pretty.
garrote [ga'xɔtʃi] *m* (*MED*) tourniquet; (*tortura*) garrote.
garupa [ga'rupa] *f* (*de cavalo*) hindquarters *pl*; (*de moto*) back seat; **andar na** ~ (*de moto*) to ride pillion.
gás [gajʃ] *m* gas; **gases** *mpl* (*do intestino*) wind *sg*; ~ **lacrimogêneo** tear gas; ~ **natural** natural gas.
gaseificar [gazejfi'ka*] *vt* to vapourize (*BRIT*), vaporize (*US*); ~**-se** *vr* to vapo(u)rize.
gasoduto [gazo'dutu] *m* gas pipeline.
gasóleo [ga'zɔlju] *m* diesel oil.
gasolina [gazo'lina] *f* petrol (*BRIT*), gas(oline) (*US*).
gasômetro [ga'zometru] *m* gasometer.
gasosa [ga'zɔza] *f* fizzy drink, soda pop (*US*).
gasoso/a [ga'zozu/ɔza] *adj* (*QUÍM*) gaseous; (*água*) sparkling; (*bebida*) fizzy.
gáspea ['gaʃpja] *f* (*de sapato*) upper.
gastador/deira [gaʃta'do*/'dejra] *adj*, *m/f* spendthrift.
gastar [gaʃ'ta*] *vt* (*dinheiro, tempo*) to spend; (*gasolina, electricidade*) to use; (*roupa, sapato*) to wear out; (*salto, piso etc*) to wear down; (*saúde*) to damage; (*desperdiçar*) to waste ♦ *vi* to spend; to wear out; to wear down; ~**-se** *vr* to wear out; to wear down.
gasto/a ['gaʃtu/a] *pp de* **gastar** ♦ *adj* (*dinheiro, tempo, energias*) spent; (*frase*) trite; (*sapato etc, fig*: *pessoa*) worn out; (*salto, piso*) worn down ♦ *m* (*despesa*) expense; ~**s** *mpl* expenses, expenditure *sg*; ~**s públicos** public spending *sg*; **dar para o** ~ (*col*) to do, be OK.
gastrenterite [gaʃtrête'ritʃi] *f* (*MED*) gastroenteritis.
gástrico/a ['gaʃtriku/a] *adj* gastric.
gastrite [gaʃ'tritʃi] *f* (*MED*) gastritis.
gastronomia [gaʃtrono'mia] *f* gastronomy.
gastronômico/a [gaʃtro'nomiku/a] *adj* gastronomic.
gata ['gata] *f* (she-)cat; (*col*: *mulher*) sexy lady; **andar de** ~**s** (*PT*) to go on all fours; ~ **borralheira** Cinderella; (*mulher*) stay-at-home.
gatão [ga'tãw] (*col*: *pl* -ões) *m* (*homem*) hunk.
gatilho [ga'tʃiʎu] *m* trigger.
gatinha [ga'tʃiɲa] (*col*) *f* (*mulher*) sexy lady.

gatinhas [ga'tʃiɲaʃ] *fpl*: **andar de** ~ (*BR*) to go on all fours.
gato ['gatu] *m* cat; (*col*: *homem*) dish, hunk; **ter um** ~ (*col*) to have kittens; ~ **escaldado tem medo de água fria** once bitten, twice shy; ~ **montês** wild cat.
gatões [ga'tójʃ] *mpl de* **gatão**.
gatos-pingados *mpl* stalwarts.
gato-sapato *m*: **fazer alguém de** ~ to walk all over sb, treat sb as a doormat.
GATT *abr m* (= *Acordo Geral sobre Tarifas Aduaneiras e Comércio*) GATT.
gatuno/a [ga'tunu/a] *adj* thieving ♦ *m/f* thief.
gaúcho/a [ga'uʃu/a] *adj* from Rio Grande do Sul ♦ *m/f* native of Rio Grande do Sul.
gaveta [ga'veta] *f* drawer.
gavetão [gave'tãw] (*pl* -ões) *m* big drawer.
gavião [ga'vjãw] (*pl* -ões) *m* hawk.
Gaza ['gaza] *f*: **a faixa de** ~ the Gaza Strip.
gaza ['gaza] *f* gauze.
gaze ['gazi] *f* = **gaza**.
gazela [ga'zɛla] *f* gazelle.
gazeta [ga'zeta] *f* (*jornal*) newspaper, gazette; **fazer** ~ to play truant.
gazua [ga'zua] *f* skeleton key.
GB *abr* (= *Guanabara*) former state, now Rio de Janeiro.
geada ['ʒjada] *f* frost.
geladeira [ʒela'dejra] (*BR*) *f* refrigerator, ice-box (*US*).
gelado/a [ʒe'ladu/a] *adj* frozen ♦ *m* (*PT*: *sorvete*) ice cream.
gelar [ʒe'la*] *vt* to freeze; (*vinho etc*) to chill ♦ *vi* to freeze.
gelatina [ʒela'tʃina] *f* gelatine; (*sobremesa*) jelly (*BRIT*), jello (*US*).
gelatinoso/a [ʒelatʃi'nozu/ɔza] *adj* gooey.
geléia [ʒe'lɛja] *f* jam.
geleira [ʒe'lejra] *f* (*GEO*) glacier.
gélido/a ['ʒɛlidu/a] *adj* chill, icy.
gelo ['ʒelu] *adj inv* light grey (*BRIT*) or gray (*US*) ♦ *m* ice; (*cor*) light grey (*BRIT*) or gray (*US*); **quebrar o** ~ (*fig*) to break the ice; **hoje está um** ~ it's freezing today; **dar o** ~ **em alguém** (*col*) to give sb the cold shoulder.
gelo-seco *m* dry ice.
gema ['ʒema] *f* (*de ovo*) yolk; (*pedra preciosa*) gem; **ser da** ~ to be genuine; **ela é paulista da** ~ she's a real Paulista.
gemada [ʒe'mada] *f* eggnog.
gêmeo/a ['ʒemju/a] *adj*, *m/f* twin; **G~s** *mpl* (*ASTROLOGIA*) Gemini *sg*.
gemer [ʒe'me*] *vt* (*canção*) to croon ♦ *vi* (*de dor*) to groan, moan; (*lamentar-se*) to wail, howl; (*animal*) to whine; (*vento*) to howl.
gemido [ʒe'midu] *m* groan, moan; (*lamento*) wail; (*de animal*) whine.
gen. *abr* (= *general*) Gen.
gene ['ʒɛni] *m* gene.
genealogia [ʒenjalo'ʒia] *f* genealogy.
genealógico/a [ʒenja'lɔʒiku/a] *adj* genealogical; **árvore genealógica** family tree.
Genebra [ʒe'nɛbra] *n* Geneva.

genebra [ʒe'nɛbra] (*PT*) *f* gin.
general [ʒene'raw] (*pl* **-ais**) *m* (*MIL*) general.
generalidade [ʒenerali'dadʒi] *f* generality; (*maioria*) majority; **~s** *fpl* basics, principles.
generalização [ʒeneraliza'sãw] (*pl* **-ões**) *f* generalization.
generalizar [ʒenerali'za*] *vt* (*propagar*) to propagate ♦ *vi* to generalize; **~-se** *vr* to become general, spread.
genérico/a [ʒe'nɛriku/a] *adj* generic.
gênero ['ʒeneru] *m* (*espécie*) type, kind; (*LITERATURA*) genre; (*BIO*) genus; (*GRAMÁTICA*) gender; **~s** *mpl* goods; **~s alimentícios** foodstuffs; **~s de primeira necessidade** essentials; **~ de vida** way of life; **~ humano** humankind, human race; **essa roupa/ele não faz o meu ~** this outfit is not my style/he is not my type.
generosidade [ʒenerozi'dadʒi] *f* generosity.
generoso/a [ʒene'rozu/ɔza] *adj* generous.
gênese ['ʒenezi] *f* origin, beginning; **G~** (*REL*) Genesis.
genética [ʒe'nɛtʃika] *f* genetics *sg*.
genético/a [ʒe'nɛtʃiku/a] *adj* genetic.
gengibre [ʒẽ'ʒibri] *m* ginger.
gengiva [ʒẽ'ʒiva] *f* (*ANAT*) gum.
genial [ʒe'njaw] (*pl* **-ais**) *adj* inspired; (*idéia*) brilliant; (*col*) terrific, fantastic.
gênio ['ʒenju] *m* (*temperamento*) nature; (*irascibilidade*) temper; (*talento, pessoa*) genius; **de bom ~** good-natured; **de mau ~** bad-tempered; **um cientista de ~** a scientific genius, a genius at science.
genioso/a [ʒe'njozu/ɔza] *adj* bad-tempered.
genital [ʒeni'taw] (*pl* **-ais**) *adj* genital.
genitivo [ʒeni'tʃivu] *m* (*LING*) genitive.
genitora [ʒeni'tora] *f* mother.
genocídio [ʒeno'sidʒiu] *m* genocide.
genro ['ʒẽxu] *m* son-in-law.
gentalha [ʒẽ'taʎa] *f* rabble.
gente ['ʒẽtʃi] *f* (*pessoas*) people *pl*; (*col*) folks *pl*; (*família*) folks *pl*, family; **a ~** (*nós: suj*) we; (: *obj*) us; **vai com a ~** come with us; **a casa da ~** our house; **toda a ~** everybody; **ficar ~** to grow up; **ser ~** (*ser alguém*) to be somebody; **também ser ~** (*col*) to be as good as anyone else; **ser ~ boa** *ou* **fina** (*col*) to be a nice person; **a ~ bem** the upper crust; **~ grande** grown-ups *pl*; **tem ~ batendo à porta** there's somebody knocking at the door; **oi/tchau, ~!** hi/bye, folks!; **~!** (*exprime admiração, surpresa*) gosh!
gentil [ʒẽ'tʃiw] (*pl* **-is**) *adj* kind.
gentileza [ʒẽtʃi'leza] *f* kindness; **por ~** if you please; **tenha a ~ de fazer ...?** would you be so kind as to do ...?
gentinha [ʒẽ'tʃiɲa] *f* rabble.
gentio/a [ʒẽ'tʃiu/a] *adj, m/f* heathen.
gentis [ʒe'tʃiʃ] *adj pl de* **gentil**.
genuflexão [ʒenuflek'sãw] (*pl* **-ões**) *f* (*REL*) genuflection.

genuíno/a [ʒe'nwinu/a] *adj* genuine.
geofísica [ʒeo'fizika] *f* geophysics *sg*.
geografia [ʒeogra'fia] *f* geography.
geográfico/a [ʒeo'grafiku/a] *adj* geographical.
geógrafo/a [ʒe'ɔgrafu/a] *m/f* geographer.
geologia [ʒeolo'ʒia] *f* geology.
geólogo/a [ʒe'ɔlogu/a] *m/f* geologist.
geometria [ʒeome'tria] *f* geometry.
geométrico/a [ʒeo'mɛtriku/a] *adj* geometrical.
geopolítico/a [ʒeopo'litʃiku/a] *adj* geopolitical.
Geórgia ['ʒɔxʒa] *f*: **a ~** Georgia.
georgiano/a [ʒox'ʒanu/a] *adj, m/f* Georgian.
geração [ʒera'sãw] (*pl* **-ões**) *f* (*tb*: *COMPUT*) generation; **linguagem de quarta ~** (*COMPUT*) fourth-generation language.
gerador(a) [ʒera'do*(a)] *adj*: **~ de algo** causing sth ♦ *m/f* (*produtor*) creator ♦ *m* (*TEC*) generator.
geral [ʒe'raw] (*pl* **-ais**) *adj* general ♦ *f* (*TEATRO*) gallery; (*revisão*) general overhaul; **dar uma ~ em algo** (*col*) to have a blitz on sth; **em ~** in general, generally; **de um modo ~** on the whole.
geralmente [ʒeraw'mẽtʃi] *adv* generally, usually.
gerânio [ʒe'ranju] *m* geranium.
gerar [ʒe'ra*] *vt* (*produzir*) to produce; (*filhos*) to beget; (*causar: ódios etc*) to engender, cause; (*eletricidade*) to generate.
gerativo/a [ʒera'tʃivu/a] *adj* generative.
gerência [ʒe'rẽsja] *f* management.
gerenciador [ʒerẽsja'do*] *m*: **~ de banco de dados** (*COMPUT*) database manager.
gerencial [ʒerẽ'sjaw] (*pl* **-ais**) *adj* management *atr*.
gerenciar [ʒerẽ'sja*] *vt, vi* to manage.
gerente [ʒe'rẽtʃi] *adj* managing ♦ *m/f* manager.
gergelim [ʒexʒe'lĩ] *m* (*BOT*) sesame.
geriatria [ʒerja'tria] *f* geriatrics *sg*.
geriátrico/a [ʒe'rjatriku/a] *adj* geriatric.
geringonça [ʒerĩ'gõsa] *f* contraption.
gerir [ʒe'ri*] *vt* to manage, run.
germânico/a [ʒex'maniku/a] *adj* Germanic.
germe ['ʒɛxmi] *m* (*embrião*) embryo; (*micróbio*) germ; (*fig*) origin; **o ~ de uma idéia** the germ of an idea.
germicida [ʒexmi'sida] *adj* germicidal ♦ *m* germicide.
germinação [ʒexmina'sãw] *f* germination.
germinar [ʒexmi'na*] *vi* (*semente*) to germinate; (*fig*) to develop.
gerontologia [ʒerõtolo'ʒia] *f* gerontology.
gerúndio [ʒe'rũdʒiu] *m* (*LING*) gerund.
gesso ['ʒesu] *m* plaster (of Paris).
gestação [ʒeʃta'sãw] *f* gestation.
gestante [ʒeʃ'tãtʃi] *f* pregnant woman.

NB: *European Portuguese adds the following consonants to certain words:* **b** (sú(b)dito, su(b)til); **c** (a(c)ção, a(c)cionista, a(c)to); **m** (inde(m)ne); **p** (ado(p)ção, ado(p)tar); *for further details see p. xiii.*

gestão [ʒeʃ'tãw] f management.
gesticular [ʒeʃtʃiku'la*] vi to make gestures, gesture ♦ vt: ~ **um adeus** to wave goodbye.
gesto ['ʒɛʃtu] m gesture; **fazer ~s** to gesture.
gibi [ʒi'bi] (col) m comic; **não estar no ~** (fig) to be incredible ou amazing.
Gibraltar [ʒibraw'ta*[f Gibraltar.
gigante/a [ʒi'gãtʃi] adj gigantic, huge ♦ m giant.
gigantesco/a [ʒigã'teʃku/a] adj gigantic.
gigolô [ʒigo'lo] m gigolo.
gilete [ʒi'letʃi] (BR) f (lâmina) razor blade; (col) bisexual, bi.
gim [ʒĩ] (pl -ns) m gin.
ginásio [ʒi'nazju] m (para ginástica) gymnasium; (escola) secondary (BRIT) ou high (US) school.
ginasta [ʒi'naʃta] m/f gymnast.
ginástica [ʒi'naʃtʃika] f (competitiva) gymnastics sg; (para fortalecer o corpo) keep-fit.
ginecologia [ʒinekolo'ʒia] f gynaecology (BRIT), gynecology (US).
ginecologista [ʒinekolo'ʒiʃta] m/f gynaecologist (BRIT), gynecologist (US).
ginete [ʒi'netʃi] m thoroughbred.
gingar [ʒĩ'ga*] vi to sway.
ginja ['ʒiʒa] (PT) f morello cherry.
ginjinha [ʒĩ'ʒiɲa] (PT) f cherry brandy.
gins [ʒĩʃ] mpl de **gim**.
gira ['ʒira] adj crazy.
gira-discos (PT) m inv record-player.
girafa [ʒi'rafa] f giraffe; (col: pessoa) giant.
girar [ʒi'ra*] vt to turn, rotate; (como pião) to spin ♦ vi to go round; to spin; (vaguear) to wander; **ele não gira bem** (col) he's not all there.
girassol [ʒira'sɔw] (pl -óis) m sunflower.
giratório/a [ʒira'tɔrju/a] adj revolving; (cadeira) swivel atr.
gíria ['ʒirja] f (calão) slang; (jargão) jargon.
giro ['ʒiru] etc vb V **gerir** ♦ m turn; **dar um ~** to go for a wander; (em veículo) to go for a spin; **que ~!** (PT) terrific!
giz [ʒiʒ] m chalk.
glacê [gla'se] m icing.
glacial [gla'sjaw] (pl -ais) adj icy.
gladiador [gladʒia'do*] m gladiator.
glamouroso/a [glamu'rozu/ɔza] adj glamorous.
glândula ['glãdula] f gland; ~ **endócrina** endocrine (gland).
glandular [glãdu'la*] adj glandular.
gleba ['glɛba] f field.
glicerina [glise'rina] f glycerine.
glicose [gli'kɔzi] f glucose.
global [glo'baw] (pl -ais) adj (da terra) global; (total) overall; **quantia ~** lump sum.
globo ['globu] m globe; ~ **ocular** eyeball.
globular [globu'la*] adj (forma) rounded.
glóbulo ['glɔbulu] m (tb: ~ **sanguíneo**) corpuscle.
glória ['glɔrja] f glory.
gloriar-se [glo'rjaxsi] vr: ~ **de** to boast of.

glorificar [glorifi'ka*] vt to glorify.
glorioso/a [glo'rjozu/ɔza] adj glorious.
glosa ['glɔza] f comment.
glosar [glo'za*] vt to comment on; (conta) to cancel.
glossário [glo'sarju] m glossary.
glote ['glɔtʃi] f (ANAT) glottis.
gluglu [glu'glu] m (de peru) gobble-gobble; (de água) glug-glug.
glutão/tona [glu'tãw/tɔna] (pl -ões/~s) adj greedy ♦ m/f glutton.
glúten ['glutẽ] (pl ~s) m gluten.
glutões [glu'tõjʃ] mpl de **glutão**.
glutona [glu'tɔna] f de **glutão**.
gnomo ['gnomu] m gnome.
GO abr = **Goiás**.
Goa ['goa] n Goa.
godê [go'de] adj (saia) flared.
goela ['gwɛla] f throat.
goela-de-pato (pl **goelas-de-pato**) f (CULIN) pasta strand.
gogó [go'gɔ] (col) m Adam's apple.
goiaba [go'jaba] f guava.
goiabada [goja'bada] f guava jelly.
goiabeira [goja'bejra] f guava tree.
goian(i)ense [goja'n(j)ẽsi] adj from Goiânia ♦ m/f native of Goiânia.
goiano/a [go'janu/a] adj from Goiás ♦ m/f native of Goiás.
gol [gow] (pl ~s) m goal; **marcar um ~** to score a goal.
gola ['gɔla] f collar; ~ **rulê** polo neck.
golaço [go'lasu] m (FUTEBOL) great goal.
Golan [go'lã] m: **as colinas de ~** the Golan heights.
gole ['gɔli] m gulp, swallow; (pequeno) sip; **de um só ~** at one gulp; **dar um ~** to have a sip.
goleada [go'ljada] f (FUTEBOL) convincing win.
golear [go'lja*] vt to thrash ♦ vi to win convincingly.
goleiro [go'lejru] (BR) m goalkeeper.
golfada [gow'fada] f (jacto) spurt.
golfar [gow'fa*] vt (vomitar) to spit up; (lançar) to throw out ♦ vi (sair) to spurt out; (bebê) to bring up some milk.
golfe ['gowfi] m golf; **campo de ~** golf course.
golfinho [gow'fiɲu] m (ZOOL) dolphin.
golfista [gow'fiʃta] m/f golfer.
golfo ['gowfu] m gulf.
golinho [go'liɲu] m sip; **beber algo aos ~s** to sip sth.
golo ['golu] (PT) m = **gol**.
golpe ['gowpi] m (tb moral) blow; (de mão) smack; (de punho) punch; (manobra) ploy; **de um só ~** at a stroke; **dar um ~ em alguém** (golpear) to hit sb; (fig: trapacear) to trick sb; **o ~ é fazer ...** the clever thing is to do ...; **dar o ~ do baú** (fig) to marry for money; ~ **baixo** (fig, col) dirty trick; ~ **(de estado)** coup (d'état); ~ **de mestre** masterstroke; ~ **de vento** gust of wind; ~ **de vista** (olhar) glance; (de motorista) eye

for distances; ~ **mortal** death blow.
golpear [gow'pja*] *vt* (*tb fig*) to hit; (*com navalha*) to stab; (*com o punho*) to punch.
golpista [gow'piʃta] *adj* tricky.
golquíper [gow'kipe*] *m* goalkeeper.
goma ['gɔma] *f* (*cola*) gum, glue; (*de roupa*) starch; ~ **de mascar** chewing gum.
gomo ['gomu] *m* (*de laranja*) slice.
gôndola ['gõdola] *f* (*NÁUT*) gondola; (*em supermercado*) rack.
gondoleiro [gõdo'lejru] *m* gondolier.
gongo ['gõgu] *m* (*MÚS*) gong; (*sineta*) bell.
gonorréia [gono'xɛja] *f* (*MED*) gonorrhea.
gonzo ['gõzu] *m* hinge.
gorar [go'ra*] *vt* to frustrate, thwart ♦ *vi* (*plano*) to fail, go wrong.
gordo/a ['goxdu/a] *adj* (*pessoa*) fat; (*gordurento*) greasy; (*carne*) fatty; (*fig: quantia*) considerable, ample ♦ *m/f* fat man/woman; **nunca vi mais** ~ (*col*) I've never seen him (*ou* her, them *etc*) before in my life.
gorducho/a [gox'duʃu/a] *adj* plump, tubby ♦ *m/f* plump person.
gordura [gox'dura] *f* fat; (*derretida*) grease; (*obesidade*) fatness.
gordurento/a [goxdu'rẽtu/a] *adj* (*ensebado*) greasy; (*gordo*) fatty.
gorduroso/a [goxdu'rozu/ɔza] *adj* (*pele*) greasy, oily; (*comida*) fatty, greasy; (*mãos*) greasy.
gorgolejar [goxgole'ʒa*] *vi* to gurgle.
gorila [go'rila] *m* gorilla.
gorjear [gox'ʒja*] *vi* to chirp, twitter.
gorjeio [gox'ʒeju] *m* twittering, chirping.
gorjeta [gox'ʒeta] *f* tip, gratuity.
gororoba [goro'rɔba] (*col*) *f* (*comida*) grub; (*comida ruim*) muck.
gorro ['goxu] *m* cap; (*de lã*) hat.
gosma ['gɔʒma] *f* spittle; (*fig*) slime.
gosmento/a [goʒ'mẽtu/a] *adj* slimy.
gostar [goʃ'ta*] *vi*: ~ **de** to like; (*férias, viagem etc*) to enjoy; ~**-se** *vr* to like each other; ~ **de fazer algo** to like *ou* enjoy doing sth; **eu** ~**ia de ir** I would like to go; **gosto de sua companhia** I enjoy your company; **gosto de nadar** I like *ou* enjoy swimming; **gostei muito de falar com você** it was very nice talking to you; ~ **mais de ...** to prefer ..., to like ... better.
gosto ['goʃtu] *m* taste; (*prazer*) pleasure; **falta de** ~ lack of taste; **a seu** ~ to your liking; **com** ~ willingly; (*vestir-se*) tastefully; (*comer*) heartily; **de bom/mau** ~ in good/bad taste; **para o meu** ~ for my liking; **ter** ~ **de** to taste of; **tenho muito** ~ **em ...** it gives me a lot of pleasure to ...; **tomar** ~ **por** to take a liking to.
gostosão/sona [goʃto'zaw/'zɔna] (*col*: *pl* -**ões/**~**s**) *m/f* stunner.
gostoso/a [goʃ'tozu/ɔza] *adj* (*comida*) tasty;

(*ambiente*) pleasant; (*cheiro*) lovely; (*risada*) good; (*col: pessoa*) gorgeous ♦ *m/f* (*col*) cracker; **é** ~ **viajar** it's really nice to travel.
gostosões [goʃto'zõjʃ] *mpl de* **gostosão**.
gostosona [goʃto'zɔna] *f de* **gostosão**.
gostosura [goʃto'zura] *f*: **ser uma** ~ (*comida*) to be delicious; (*bebê, jogo etc*) to be lovely.
gota ['gota] *f* drop; (*de suor*) bead; (*MED*) gout; ~ **a** ~ drop by drop; **ser a** ~ **d'água** *ou* **a última** ~ (*fig*) to be the last straw; **ser uma** ~ **d'água no oceano** (*fig*) to be a drop in the ocean.
goteira [go'tejra] *f* (*cano*) gutter; (*buraco*) leak.
gotejante [gote'ʒãtʃi] *adj* dripping.
gotejar [gote'ʒa*] *vt* to drip ♦ *vi* to drip; (*telhado*) to leak.
gótico/a ['gɔtʃiku/a] *adj* Gothic.
gotícula [go'tʃikula] *f* droplet.
gourmet [gux'me] (*pl* ~**s**) *m/f* gourmet.
governador(a) [govexnado*(a)] *m/f* governor.
governamental [govexnamẽ'taw] (*pl* -**ais**) *adj* government *atr*.
governanta [govex'nãta] *f* (*de casa*) housekeeper; (*de criança*) governess.
governante [govex'nãtʃi] *adj* ruling ♦ *m/f* ruler ♦ *f* governess.
governar [govex'na*] *vt* (*POL*) to govern, rule; (*barco*) to steer.
governista [govex'niʃta] *adj* pro-government ♦ *m/f* government supporter.
governo [go'vexnu] *m* government; (*controle*) control; (*NÁUT*) steering; **para o seu** ~ (*col*) for the record, for your information.
gozação [goza'sãw] (*pl* -**ões**) *f* (*desfrute*) enjoyment; (*zombaria*) teasing; (*uma* ~) joke.
gozada [go'zada] *f*: **dar uma** ~ **em alguém** to pull sb's leg.
gozado/a [go'zadu/a] *adj* funny; (*estranho*) strange, odd.
gozador(a) [goza'do*(a)] *adj* (*caçoador*) comical; (*boa-vida*) happy-go-lucky ♦ *m/f* joker; loafer.
gozar [go'za*] *vt* to enjoy; (*col: rir de*) to make fun of ♦ *vi* to enjoy o.s.; (*ao fazer sexo*) to have an orgasm; ~ **de** to enjoy; to make fun of.
gozo ['gozu] *m* (*prazer*) pleasure; (*uso*) enjoyment, use; (*orgasmo*) orgasm; **estar em pleno** ~ **de suas faculdades mentais** to be in full possession of one's faculties; **ser um** ~ (*ser engraçado*) to be a laugh.
G/P *abr* (*COM*) = **ganhos e perdas**.
gr. *abr* = **grátis**; (= *grau*) deg.; (= *gross*) gr.
Grã-Bretanha [grã-bre'taɲa] *f* Great Britain.
graça ['grasa] *f* (*REL*) grace; (*charme*) charm; (*gracejo*) joke; (*JUR*) pardon; **de** ~ (*grátis*) for nothing; (*sem motivo*) for no reason; **sem** ~ dull, boring; **fazer** *ou* **ter** ~ to be funny;

NB: *European Portuguese adds the following consonants to certain words:* **b** (sú(b)dito, su(b)til); **c** (a(c)ção, a(c)cionista, a(c)to); **m** (inde(m)ne); **p** (ado(p)ção, ado(p)tar); *for further details see p. xiii.*

ficar sem ~ to be embarrassed; **~s a** thanks to; **não tem** ~ **fazer** (é *chato*) it's no fun to do; (*não é certo*) it's not right to do; **deixa de** ~ don't be cheeky; **não sei que** ~ **você vê nele/nisso** I don't know what you see in him/it; **ser uma** ~ to be lovely.

gracejar [grase'ʒa*] *vi* to joke.

gracejo [gra'seʒu] *m* joke.

gracinha [gra'siɲa] *f*: **ser uma** ~ to be sweet *ou* cute; **que ~!** how sweet!

gracioso/a [gra'sjozu/ɔza] *adj* (*pessoa*) charming; (*gestos*) gracious.

gradação [grada'sãw] (*pl* **-ões**) *f* gradation.

gradativo/a [grada'tʃivu/a] *adj* gradual.

grade ['gradʒi] *f* (*no chão*) grating; (*grelha*) grill; (*na janela*) bars *pl*; (*col*: *cadeia*) prison.

gradear [gra'dʒja*] *vt* (*janela*) to put bars up at; (*jardim*) to fence off.

grado/a ['gradu/a] *adj* (*importante*) important ♦ *m*: **de bom/mau** ~ willingly/unwillingly.

graduação [gradwa'sãw] (*pl* **-ões**) *f* gradation; (*classificação*) grading; (*EDUC*) graduation; (*MIL*) rank; **curso de** ~ degree course.

graduado/a [gra'dwadu/a] *adj* (*dividido em graus*) graduated; (*diplomado*) graduate; (*eminente*) highly thought of.

gradual [gra'dwaw] (*pl* **-ais**) *adj* gradual.

graduando/a [gra'dwandu/a] *m/f* graduating student, graduand.

graduar [gra'dwa*] *vt* (*termômetro*) to graduate; (*classificar*) to grade; (*luz, fogo*) to regulate; **~-se** *vr* to graduate; ~ **alguém em algo** (*EDUC*) to confer a degree in sth on sb; ~ **alguém em coronel** *etc* (*MIL*) to make sb a colonel *etc*.

graduável [gra'dwavew] (*pl* **-eis**) *adj* adjustable.

grafia [gra'fia] *f* (*escrita*) writing; (*ortografia*) spelling.

gráfica ['grafika] *f* (*arte*) graphics *sg*; (*estabelecimento*) printer's; (*seção: de jornal etc*) production department; *V tb* **gráfico**.

gráfico/a ['grafiku/a] *adj* graphic ♦ *m/f* printer ♦ *m* (*MAT*) graph; (*diagrama*) diagram, chart; **~s** *mpl* (*COMPUT*) graphics; ~ **de barras** bar chart.

grã-finagem [grãfi'naʒẽ] *f*: **a** ~ the upper crust.

grã-finismo [grãfi'niʒmu] *m* (*qualidade*) poshness; (*ato*) thing which posh people do; **o** ~ (*pessoas*) the upper crust.

grã-fino/a [grã-] *adj* posh ♦ *m/f* nob, toff.

grafite [gra'fitʃi] *f* (*lápis*) lead; (*pichação*) (piece of) graffiti.

grafologia [grafolo'ʒia] *f* graphology.

grama ['grama] *m* (*peso*) gramme ♦ *f* (*BR*: *capim*) grass.

gramado [gra'madu] (*BR*) *m* lawn; (*FUTEBOL*) pitch.

gramar [gra'ma*] *vt* to plant *ou* sow with grass; (*PT*: *col*) to be fond of ♦ *vi* (*PT*: *col*) to cry out.

gramática [gra'matʃika] *f* grammar; *V tb* **gramático**.

gramatical [gramatʃi'kaw] (*pl* **-ais**) *adj* grammatical.

gramático/a [gra'matʃiku/a] *adj* grammatical ♦ *m/f* grammarian.

gramofone [gramo'fɔni] *m* gramophone.

grampeador [grãpja'do*] *m* stapler.

grampear [grã'pja*] *vt* to staple; (*BR*: *TEL*) to tap; (*col*: *prender*) to nick.

grampo ['grãpu] *m* staple; (*no cabelo*) hairgrip; (*de carpinteiro*) clamp; (*de chapéu*) hatpin.

grana ['grana] (*col*) *f* cash.

Granada [gra'nada] *f* Grenada.

granada [gra'nada] *f* (*MIL*) shell; (*pedra*) garnet; ~ **de mão** hand grenade.

grandalhão/lhona [grãda'ʎãw/'ʎɔna] (*pl* **-ões/~s**) *adj* enormous.

grandão/dona [grã'dãw/'dɔna] (*pl* **-ões/~s**) *adj* huge.

grande ['grãdʒi] *adj* big, large; (*alto*) tall; (*notável, intenso*) great; (*longo*) long; (*adulto*) grown-up; **mulher** ~ big woman; ~ **mulher** great woman; **a G~ Londres** Greater London.

grandessíssimo/a [grãdʒi'sisimu/a] *adj superl de* **grande**.

grandeza [grã'deza] *f* (*tamanho*) size; (*fig*) greatness; (*ostentação*) grandeur; **ter mania de** ~ to have delusions of grandeur.

grandiloqüente [grãdʒilo'kwẽtʃi] *adj* grandiloquent.

grandiosidade [grãdʒiozi'dadʒi] *f* grandeur, magnificence.

grandioso/a [grã'dʒjozu/ɔza] *adj* magnificent, grand.

grandíssimo/a [grã'dʒisimu/a] *adj superl de* **grande**.

grandões [grã'dõjʃ] *mpl de* **grandão**.

grandona [grã'dɔna] *f de* **grandão**.

granel [gra'nɛw] *m*: **a** ~ (*COM*) in bulk; **compra a** ~ bulk buying.

granfa ['grãfa] (*col*) *adj* posh ♦ *m/f* nob, toff.

granito [gra'nitu] *m* (*GEO*) granite.

granizo [gra'nizu] *m* hail; **chover** ~ to hail; **chuva de** ~ hail.

granja ['grãʒa] *f* farm; (*de galinhas*) chicken farm.

granjear [grã'ʒja*] *vt* (*simpatia, amigos*) to win, gain; (*bens, fortuna*) to procure; ~ **algo a** *ou* **para alguém** to win sb sth.

granulado/a [granu'ladu/a] *adj* grainy; (*açúcar*) granulated.

grânulo ['granulu] *m* granule.

grão ['grãw] (*pl* **~s**) *m* grain; (*semente*) seed; (*de café*) bean.

grão-de-bico (*pl* **grãos-de-bico**) *m* chick pea.

grapefruit [greip'frutʃi] (*pl* **~s**) *m* grapefruit.

grasnar [graʒ'na*] *vi* (*corvo*) to caw; (*pato*) to quack; (*rã*) to croak.

gratidão [gratʃi'dãw] *f* gratitude.

gratificação [gratʃifika'sãw] (*pl* **-ões**) *f*

(gorjeta) gratuity, tip; *(bônus)* bonus; *(recompensa)* reward.

gratificado/a [gratʃifi'kadu/a] *adj* *(grato)* grateful.

gratificante [gratʃifi'kãtʃi] *adj* rewarding.

gratificar [gratʃifi'ka*] *vt* *(dar gorjeta a)* to tip; *(dar bônus a)* to give a bonus to; *(recompensar)* to reward.

gratinado/a [gratʃi'nadu/a] *adj* *(CULIN)* au gratin ♦ *m* *(prato)* gratin; *(crosta)* crust.

grátis ['gratʃiʃ] *adj* free.

grato/a ['gratu/a] *adj* *(agradecido)* grateful; *(agradável)* pleasant; **ficar ~ a alguém por** to be grateful to sb for.

gratuidade [gratwi'dadʒi] *f* gratuity.

gratuito/a [gra'twitu/a] *adj* *(grátis)* free; *(infundado)* gratuitous.

grau [graw] *m* degree; *(nível)* level; *(EDUC)* class; **a temperatura é de 38 ~s** the temperature is 38 degrees; **primo/a em segundo ~** second cousin; **em alto ~** to a high degree; **primeiro/segundo ~** *(EDUC)* primary/secondary level; **ensino de primeiro/segundo ~** primary *(BRIT)* ou elementary *(US)*/secondary education; **estar no 1°/2° ~** *(EDUC)* to be at primary/secondary *(BRIT)* ou high *(US)* school.

graúdo/a [gra'udu/a] *adj* *(grande)* big; *(pessoa: influente)* important ♦ *m/f* bigwig.

gravação [grava'sãw] *f* *(em madeira)* carving; *(em disco, fita)* recording.

gravador(a) [grava'do*(a)] *m* tape recorder ♦ *m/f* engraver ♦ *f* *(empresa)* record company.

gravame [gra'vami] *m* *(imposto)* duty; *(JUR)* lien.

gravar [gra'va*] *vt* *(madeira)* to carve; *(metal, pedra)* to engrave; *(na memória)* to memorize; *(disco, fita)* to record; **~ algo/alguém com impostos** to mark sth up/burden sb with taxes; **aquele dia ficou gravado na minha mente/memória** that day remained fixed in my mind/memory.

gravata [gra'vata] *f* tie; **dar ou aplicar uma ~ em alguém** to get sb in a stranglehold; **~ borboleta** bow tie.

grave ['gravi] *adj* *(situação, falta)* serious, grave; *(doença)* serious; *(tom)* deep; *(LING)* grave.

gravemente [grave'mẽtʃi] *adv* *(doente, ferido)* seriously.

graveto [gra'vetu] *m* piece of kindling.

grávida ['gravida] *adj* pregnant.

gravidade [gravi'dadʒi] *f* *(FÍS)* gravity; *(de doença, situação)* seriousness.

gravidez [gravi'deʒ] *f* pregnancy; **~ tubária** ectopic pregnancy.

gravitação [gravita'sãw] *f* gravitation.

gravura [gra'vura] *f* *(em madeira)* engraving; *(estampa)* print.

graxa ['graʃa] *f* *(para sapatos)* polish; *(lu-*

brificante) grease.

Grécia ['grɛsja] *f*: **a ~** Greece.

grega ['grega] *f* *(galão)* braid; *V tb* **grego**.

gregário/a [gre'garju/a] *adj* gregarious.

grego/a ['gregu/a] *adj, m/f* Greek ♦ *m* *(LING)* Greek.

grei [grej] *f* flock.

grelar [gre'la*] *vt* to stare at.

grelha ['grɛʎa] *f* grill; *(de fornalha)* grate; **bife na ~** grilled steak.

grelhado/a [gre'ʎadu/a] *adj* grilled ♦ *m* *(prato)* grill.

grelhar [gre'ʎa*] *vt* to grill.

grêmio ['gremju] *m* *(associação)* guild; *(clube)* club.

grená [gre'na] *adj, m* dark red.

greta ['greta] *f* crack.

gretado/a [gre'tadu/a] *adj* cracked.

greve ['grɛvi] *f* strike; **fazer ~** to go on strike; **~ de fome** hunger strike; **~ branca** go-slow.

grevista [gre'viʃta] *m/f* striker.

grifado/a [gri'fadu/a] *adj* in italics.

grifar [gri'fa*] *vt* to italicize; *(sublinhar)* to underline; *(fig)* to emphasize.

griffe ['grifi] *m* designer label.

grifo ['grifu] *m* italics *pl*.

grilado/a [gri'ladu/a] *(col)* *adj* full of hangups; **estar ~ com algo** to be hung-up about sth.

grilar [gri'la*] *(col)* *vt*: **~ alguém** to get sb worked up; **~-se** *vr* to get worked up.

grilhão [gri'ʎãw] *(pl -ões)* *m* chain; **grilhões** *mpl* *(fig)* fetters.

grilo ['grilu] *m* cricket; *(AUTO)* squeak; *(col: de pessoa)* hang-up; **qual é o ~?** what's the matter?; **dar ~** *(col)* to cause problems; **se der ~** *(impess)* if there's a problem; **não tem ~!** *(col)* (there's) no problem!

grimpar [grĩ'pa*] *vi* to climb.

grinalda [gri'nawda] *f* garland.

gringada [grĩ'gada] *f* *(grupo)* bunch of foreigners; *(gringos)* foreigners *pl*.

gringo/a ['grĩgu/a] *(col: pej)* *m/f* foreigner.

gripado/a [gri'padu/a] *adj*: **estar/ficar ~** to have/get a cold.

gripar-se [gri'paxsi] *vr* to catch flu.

gripe ['gripi] *f* flu, influenza.

grisalho/a [gri'zaʎu/a] *adj* *(cabelo)* grey *(BRIT)*, gray *(US)*.

grita ['grita] *f* uproar.

gritante [gri'tãtʃi] *adj* glaring, gross, blatant; *(cor)* loud, garish.

gritar [gri'ta*] *vt* to shout, yell ♦ *vi* to shout; *(de dor, medo)* to scream; *(protestar)* to speak out; **~ com alguém** to shout at sb.

gritaria [grita'ria] *f* shouting, din.

grito ['gritu] *m* shout; *(de medo)* scream; *(de dor)* cry; *(de animal)* call; **dar um ~** to cry out; **falar/protestar aos ~s** to shout/shout protests; **no ~** *(col)* by force.

NB: *European Portuguese adds the following consonants to certain words:* **b** *(sú(b)dito, su(b)til)*; **c** *(a(c)ção, a(c)cionista, a(c)to)*; **m** *(inde(m)ne)*; **p** *(ado(p)ção, ado(p)tar); for further details see p. xiii.*

Groenlândia [grwē'lādʒja] *f*: **a** ~ Greenland.
grogue ['grɔgi] *adj* groggy.
groom [grũ] (*pl* ~**s**) *m* groom.
grosa ['grɔza] *f* gross.
groselha [gro'zeʎa] *f* (red)currant.
grosseiro/a [gro'sejru/a] *adj* (*pessoa, comentário*) rude; (*piada*) crude; (*modos*) coarse; (*tecido*) coarse, rough; (*móvel*) roughly-made.
grosseria [grose'ria] *f* rudeness; (*ato, dito*) rude thing; **fazer uma** ~ to be rude; **dizer uma** ~ to be rude, say something rude.
grosso/a ['grosu/'grɔsa] *adj* (*tamanho, consistência*) thick; (*áspero*) rough; (*voz*) deep; (*col: pessoa, piada*) rude ♦ *m*: **o** ~ **de** the bulk of ♦ *adv*: **falar** ~ to talk in a deep voice; **falar** ~ **com alguém** (*fig*) to get tough with sb; **a** ~ **modo** roughly.
grossura [gro'sura] *f* thickness.
grotão [gro'tãw] (*pl* -**ões**) *m* gorge.
grotesco/a [gro'teʃku/a] *adj* grotesque.
grotões [gro'tõjʃ] *mpl de* grotão.
grua ['grua] *f* (*MEC*) crane.
grudado/a [gru'dadu/a] *adj* (*fig*): **ser** ~ **com** *ou* **em alguém** to be very attached to sb.
grudar [gru'da*] *vt* to glue, stick ♦ *vi* to stick.
grude ['grudʒi] *f* glue; (*col: comida*) grub; (*ligação entre pessoas*): **ficar numa** ~ to cling to sb.
grudento/a [gru'dētu/a] *adj* sticky.
gruja ['gruʒa] (*col*) *f* tip.
grunhido [gru'ɲidu] *m* grunt.
grunhir [gru'ɲi*] *vi* (*porco*) to grunt; (*tigre*) to growl; (*resmungar*) to grumble.
grupo ['grupu] *m* group; (*TEC*) unit, set; ~ **sanguíneo** blood group.
gruta ['gruta] *f* grotto.
guache ['gwaʃi] *m* gouache.
guapo/a ['gwapu/a] *adj* beautiful.
guaraná [gwara'na] *m* guarana; (*bebida*) soft drink flavoured with guarana.
guarani [gwara'ni] *adj*, *m/f* Guarani ♦ *m* (*LING*) Guarani; (*moeda*) guarani.
guarda ['gwaxda] *f* (*polícia*) policewoman; (*vigilância*) guarding; (*de objeto*) safekeeping; ♦ *m* (*MIL*) guard; (*polícia*) policeman; **estar de** ~ to be on guard; **pôr-se em** ~ to be on one's guard; **a velha** ~ the old guard; **a G~ Civil** the Civil Guard.
guarda-chuva (*pl* ~**s**) *m* umbrella.
guarda-civil (*pl* **guardas-civis**) *m* civil guard.
guarda-costas *m inv* (*NÁUT*) coastguard boat; (*capanga*) bodyguard.
guardador(a) [gwaxda'do*(a)] *m/f* car attendant.
guardados [gwax'daduʃ] *mpl* keepsakes, valuables.
guarda-florestal (*pl* **guardas-florestais**) *m/f* forest ranger.
guarda-fogo (*pl* ~**s**) *m* fireguard.
guarda-louça [gwaxda-'losa] (*pl* ~**s**) *m* sideboard.
guarda-marinha (*pl* **guardas-marinha(s)**) *m* naval ensign.
guarda-mor [-mɔ*] (*pl* **guardas-mores**) *m* inspector of customs.
guardamoria [gwaxdamo'ria] *f* customs authorities *pl*.
guarda-móveis *m inv* furniture storage warehouse.
guardanapo [gwaxda'napu] *m* napkin.
guarda-noturno (*pl* **guardas-noturnos**) *m* night watchman.
guardar [gwax'da*] *vt* (*pôr em algum lugar*) to put away; (*zelar por*) to guard; (*conservar; segredo*) to keep; (*vigiar*) to watch over; (*gravar na memória*) to remember; ~**-se** *vr* (*defender-se*) to protect o.s.; ~**-se de** (*acautelar-se*) to guard against; ~ **silêncio** to keep quiet; ~ **o lugar para alguém** to keep sb's seat; **vou** ~ **este resto de bolo para ele** I'll keep this last piece of cake for him.
guarda-redes (*PT*) *m inv* goalkeeper.
guarda-roupa (*pl* ~**s**) *m* wardrobe.
guarda-sol (*pl* -**óis**) *m* sunshade, parasol.
guardião/diã [gwax'dʒjãw/'dʒjã] (*pl* -**ães** *ou* -**ões/**~**s**) *m/f* guardian.
guarida [gwa'rida] *f* refuge.
guarita [gwa'rita] *f* (*casinha*) sentry box; (*torre*) watch tower.
guarnecer [gwaxne'se*] *vt* (*MIL: fronteira*) to garrison; (*comida*) to garnish; (*NÁUT: tripular*) to crew; ~ **alguém (de algo)** to equip sb (with sth); ~ **a despensa** *etc* (**de algo**) to stock the pantry *etc* (with sth).
guarnição [gwaxni'sãw] (*pl* -**ões**) *f* (*MIL*) garrison; (*NÁUT*) crew; (*CULIN*) garnish.
Guatemala [gwate'mala] *f*: **a** ~ Guatemala.
guatemalteco/a [gwatemaw'tɛku/a] *adj*, *m/f* Guatemalan.
gude ['gudʒi] *m*: **bola de** ~ marble; (*jogo*) marbles *pl*.
gueixa ['gejʃa] *f* geisha.
guelra ['gɛwxa] *f* (*de peixe*) gill.
guerra ['gɛxa] *f* war; **em** ~ at war; **declarar** ~ **(a alguém)** to declare war (on sb); **estar em pé de** ~ **(com)** (*países, facções*) to be at war (with); (*vizinhos, casal*) to be at loggerheads (with); **fazer** ~ to wage war; ~ **atômica** *ou* **nuclear** nuclear war; ~ **civil** civil war; ~ **de nervos** war of nerves; ~ **fria** cold war; ~ **mundial** world war; ~ **santa** holy war.
guerrear [ge'xja*] *vi* to wage war.
guerreiro/a [ge'xejru/a] *adj* (*espírito*) fighting; (*belicoso*) warlike ♦ *m* warrior.
guerrilha [ge'xiʎa] *f* (*luta*) guerrilla warfare; (*tropa*) guerrilla band.
guerrilhar [gexi'ʎa*] *vi* to engage in guerilla warfare.
guerrilheiro/a [gexi'ʎejru/a] *adj* guerrilla *atr* ♦ *m/f* guerrilla.
gueto ['getu] *m* ghetto.
guia ['gia] *f* (*orientação*) guidance; (*COM*) permit, bill of lading; (*formulário*) advice slip ♦ *m* (*livro*) guide(book) ♦ *m/f* (*pessoa*) guide; **para que lhe sirva de** ~ as a guide.

Guiana ['gjana] f: **a** ~ Guyana; **a** ~ **Francesa** French Guyana.

guiar [gja*] vt (orientar) to guide; (AUTO) to drive; (cavalos) to steer ♦ vi (AUTO) to drive; ~-**se** vr: ~-**se por** to go by.

guichê [gi'ʃe] m ticket window; (em banco, repartição) window, counter.

guidão [gi'dãw] (pl -ões) m = **guidom**.

guidom [gi'dõ] (pl -ns) m handlebar.

guilder [giw'de*] m guilder.

guilhotina [giʎo'tʃina] f guillotine.

guimba ['gĩba] (col) f (cigarette) butt.

guinada [gi'nada] f (NÁUT) lurch; (virada) swerve; **dar uma** ~ (com o carro) to swerve; (fig: governo etc) to do a U-turn.

guinchar [gĩ'ʃa*] vt (carro) to tow.

guincho ['gĩʃu] m (de animal, rodas) squeal; (de pessoa) shriek.

guindar [gĩ'da*] vt to hoist, lift; (fig): ~ **alguém a** to promote sb to.

guindaste [gĩ'daʃtʃi] m hoist, crane.

Guiné [gi'nɛ] f: **a** ~ Guinea.

Guiné-Bissau [-bi'saw] f: **a** ~ Guinea-Bissau.

guisa ['giza] f: **à** ~ **de** like, by way of.

guisado [gi'zadu] m stew.

guisar [gi'za*] vt to stew.

guitarra [gi'taxa] f (electric) guitar.

guitarrista [gita'xiʃta] m/f guitarist; (col) forger (of money).

guizo ['gizu] m bell.

gula ['gula] f gluttony, greed.

gulodice [gulo'dʒisi] f greed.

guloseima [gulo'zejma] f delicacy, titbit.

guloso/a [gu'lozu/ɔza] adj greedy.

gume ['gumi] m cutting edge; (fig) sharpness.

guri(a) [gu'ri(a)] m/f ♦ f (namorada) girlfriend.

gurizote [guri'zɔtʃi] m lad.

guru [gu'ru] m/f guru.

gustação [guʃta'sãw] f tasting.

gutural [gutu'raw] (pl -ais) adj guttural.

H

NB: initial H is usually silent in Portuguese.

H, h [a'ga] (pl **hs**) m H, h; **H de Henrique** H for Harry (BRIT) ou How (US).

há [a] vb V **haver**.

hã [ã] excl: ~! aha!

habeas-corpus ['abjas-'kɔxpus] m habeas corpus.

hábil ['abiw] (pl -eis) adj (competente) competent, capable; (com as mãos) clever; (astucioso, esperto) clever, shrewd; (sutil)

diplomatic; (JUR) qualified; **em tempo** ~ in reasonable time.

habilidade [abili'dadʒi] f (aptidão, competência) skill, ability; (astúcia, esperteza) shrewdness; (tato) discretion; (JUR) qualification; **ele não teve a menor** ~ **com ela** (tato) he wasn't at all tactful with her; **ela não tem a menor** ~ **com crianças** (jeito) she's hopeless with children; **ter** ~ **manual** to be good with one's hands.

habilidoso/a [abili'dozu/ɔza] adj skilful (BRIT), skillful (US), clever.

habilitação [abilita'sãw] (pl -ões) f (aptidão) competence; (ato) qualification; (JUR) attestation; **habilitações** fpl (conhecimentos) qualifications pl.

habilitado/a [abili'tadu/a] adj qualified; (manualmente) skilled.

habilitar [abili'ta*] vt (tornar apto) to enable; (dar direito a) to qualify, entitle; (preparar) to prepare; (JUR) to qualify.

habitação [abita'sãw] (pl -ões) f dwelling, residence; (POL: alojamento) housing.

habitacional [abitasjo'naw] (pl -ais) adj housing atr.

habitações [abita'sõjʃ] fpl de **habitação**.

habitante [abi'tãtʃi] m/f inhabitant.

habitar [abi'ta*] vt (viver em) to live in; (povoar) to inhabit ♦ vi to live.

hábitat ['abitatʃi] m habitat.

habitável [abi'tavew] (pl -eis) adj (in)habitable.

hábito ['abitu] m habit; (social) custom; (REL: traje) habit; **adquirir/perder o** ~ **de (fazer) algo** to get into/out of the habit of (doing) sth; **ter o** ~ **de (fazer) algo** to be in the habit of (doing) sth; **por força do** ~ by force of habit.

habituação [abitwa'sãw] f acclimatization (BRIT), acclimatation (US), adjustment.

habituado/a [abi'twadu/a] adj: ~ **a (fazer) algo** used to (doing) sth.

habitual [abi'twaw] (pl -ais) adj usual.

habituar [abi'twa*] vt: ~ **alguém a** to get sb used to, accustom sb to; ~-**se** vr: ~-**se a** to get used to.

habitué [abi'twe] m habitué.

hacker ['ake*] (pl ~**s**) m (COMPUT) hacker.

hadoque [a'dɔki] m haddock.

Haia ['aja] n the Hague.

Haiti [aj'tʃi] m: **o** ~ Haiti.

haitiano/a [aj'tʃjanu/a] adj, m/f Haitian.

haja ['aʒa] etc vb V **haver**.

hálito ['alitu] m breath; **mau** ~ bad breath.

halitose [ali'tɔzi] f halitosis.

hall [xɔw] (pl ~**s**) m hall; (de teatro, hotel) foyer; ~ **de entrada** entrance hall.

halo ['alu] m halo.

haltere [aw'tɛri] m dumbbell.

halterofilismo [awterofi'liʒmu] m weight

*NB: European Portuguese adds the following consonants to certain words: **b** (sú(b)dito, su(b)til); **c** (a(c)ção, a(c)cionista, a(c)to); **m** (inde(m)ne); **p** (ado(p)ção, ado(p)tar); for further details see p. xiii.*

lifting.
halterofilista [awterofi'liʃta] *m/f* weight lifter.
hambúrguer [ã'buxge*] *m* hamburger.
handicap [ãdʒi'kapi] *m* handicap.
hangar [ã'ga*] *m* hangar.
hão [ãw] *vb* V **haver**.
haras ['araʃ] *m inv* stud.
hardware ['xadwe*] *m* (*COMPUT*) hardware.
harém [a'rɛ̃] (*pl* **-ns**) *m* harem.
harmonia [axmo'nia] *f* harmony.
harmônica [ax'monika] *f* concertina.
harmonioso/a [axmo'njozu/ɔza] *adj* harmonious.
harmonizar [axmoni'za*] *vt* (*MÚS*) to harmonize; (*conciliar*): ~ **algo** (**com algo**) to reconcile sth with sth; **~-se** *vr*: **~(-se)** (**com algo**) (*idéias etc*) to coincide (with sth); (*pessoas*) to be in agreement (with sth); (*música*) to fit in (with sth); (*tapete*) to match (sth).
harpa ['axpa] *f* harp.
harpista [ax'piʃta] *m/f* harpist.
hasta ['aʃta] *f*: ~ **pública** auction.
haste ['aʃtʃi] *f* (*de bandeira*) flagpole; (*TEC*) shaft, rod; (*BOT*) stem.
hastear [aʃ'tʃja*] *vt* to raise, hoist.
Havaí [avaj'i] *m*: **o** ~ Hawaii.
havaiano/a [avaj'anu/a] *adj*, *m/f* Hawaiian ♦ *m* (*LING*) Hawaiian.
Havana [a'vana] *n* Havana.
havana [a'vana] *adj inv* light brown ♦ *m* (*charuto*) Havana cigar.
haver [a've*] *vb impess*: **há** (*sg*) there is; (*pl*) there are ♦ *vb aux*: **ele havia saído** he had left ♦ *m* (*COM*) credit; **~-se** *vr*: **~-se com alguém** to sort things out with sb; **~es** *mpl* property *sg*, possessions; (*riqueza*) wealth *sg*; **havia** (*sg*) there was; (*pl*) there were; **haja o que houver** come what may; **o que é que há?** what's the matter?; **o que é que houve?** what happened, what was that?; **não há como ...** there's no way to ...; **não há de quê** you're welcome, don't mention it; **o que há de novo?** what's new?; **o que há com ela?** what's up with her?; **há séculos/cinco dias que não o vejo** I haven't seen him for ages/five days; **há um ano que ela chegou** it's a year since she arrived; **há cinco dias (atrás)** five days ago; **você há de ver** you'll see; **quem ~ia de dizer que ...** who would have thought that ....
haxixe [a'ʃiʃi] *m* hashish.
hebraico/a [e'brajku/a] *adj*, *m/f* Hebrew ♦ *m* (*LING*) Hebrew.
hebreu/bréia [e'brew/'brɛja] *adj*, *m/f* Hebrew.
Hébridas ['ɛbridaʃ] *fpl*: **as (ilhas)** ~ the Hebrides.
hecatombe [eka'tõbi] *f* (*fig*) massacre.
hectare [ek'tari] *m* hectare.
hectograma [ekto'grama] *m* hectogram.
hectolitro [ekto'litru] *m* hectolitre (*BRIT*), hectoliter (*US*).
hediondo/a [e'dʒjõdu/a] *adj* (*repulsivo*) vile,

revolting; (*crime*) heinous; (*horrendo*) hideous.
hedonista [edo'niʃta] *adj* hedonistic ♦ *m/f* hedonist.
hegemonia [eʒemo'nia] *f* hegemony.
hei [ej] *vb* V **haver**.
hein [ẽj] *excl* eh?; (*exprimindo indignação*) hmm.
hélice ['ɛlisi] *f* propeller.
helicóptero [eli'kɔpteru] *m* helicopter.
hélio ['ɛlju] *m* helium.
heliporto [eli'poxtu] *m* heliport.
Helsinque [ew'sĩki] *n* Helsinki.
hem [ẽj] *excl* = **hein**.
hematologia [ematolo'ʒia] *f* haematology (*BRIT*), hematology (*US*).
hematoma [ema'tɔma] *m* bruise.
hemisférico/a [emiʃ'fɛriku/a] *adj* hemispherical.
hemisfério [emiʃ'fɛrju] *m* hemisphere.
hemofilia [emofi'lia] *f* haemophilia (*BRIT*), hemophilia (*US*).
hemofílico/a [emo'filiku/a] *adj*, *m/f* haemophiliac (*BRIT*), hemophiliac (*US*).
hemoglobina [emoglo'bina] *f* haemoglobin (*BRIT*), hemoglobin (*US*).
hemograma [emo'grama] *m* blood count.
hemorragia [emoxa'ʒia] *f* haemorrhage (*BRIT*), hemorrhage (*US*); ~ **nasal** nosebleed.
hemorróidas [emo'xɔjdaʃ] *fpl* haemorrhoids (*BRIT*), hemorrhoids (*US*), piles.
hena ['ɛna] *f* henna.
henê [e'ne] *m* henna.
hepatite [epa'tʃitʃi] *f* hepatitis.
heptágono [ep'tagonu] *m* heptagon.
hera ['ɛra] *f* ivy.
heráldica [e'rawdʒika] *f* heraldry.
herança [e'rãsa] *f* inheritance; (*fig*) heritage.
herbáceo/a [ex'basju/a] *adj* herbaceous.
herbicida [exbi'sida] *m* weed-killer, herbicide.
herbívoro/a [ex'bivoru/a] *adj* herbivorous ♦ *m/f* herbivore.
herdade [ex'dadʒi] (*PT*) *f* large farm.
herdar [ex'da*] *vt*: ~ **algo (de)** to inherit sth (from); ~ **a** to bequeath to.
herdeiro/a [ex'dejru/a] *m/f* heir(ess).
hereditário/a [eredʒi'tarju/a] *adj* hereditary.
herege [e'reʒi] *m/f* heretic.
heresia [ere'zia] *f* heresy.
herético/a [e'rɛtʃiku/a] *adj* heretical.
hermafrodita [exmafro'dʒita] *m/f* hermaphrodite.
hermético/a [ex'mɛtʃiku/a] *adj* airtight; (*fig*) obscure, impenetrable.
hérnia ['ɛxnja] *f* hernia; ~ **de hiato** hiatus hernia.
herói [e'rɔj] *m* hero.
heróico/a [e'rɔjku/a] *adj* heroic.
heroína [ero'ina] *f* heroine; (*droga*) heroin.
heroismo [ero'iʒmu] *m* heroism.
herpes ['expiʃ] *m inv* herpes *sg*.
herpes-zoster [-'zɔʃte*] *m* (*MED*) shingles *sg*.
hertz ['extzi] *m inv* hertz.

hesitação [ezita'sãw] *f (pl -ões)* hesitation.
hesitante [ezi'tãtʃi] *adj* hesitant.
hesitar [ezi'ta*] *vi* to hesitate; ~ **em (fazer) algo** to hesitate in (doing) sth.
heterodoxo/a [etero'dɔksu/a] *adj* unorthodox.
heterogêneo/a [etero'ʒenju/a] *adj* heterogeneous.
heterônimo [ete'ronimu] *m* pen name, nom de plume.
heterossexual [eterosek'swaw] *(pl -ais) adj, m/f* heterosexual.
heterossexualidade [eterosekswali'dadʒi] *f* heterosexuality.
hexagonal [eksago'naw] *(pl -ais) adj* hexagonal.
hexágono [ek'sagonu] *m* hexagon.
hiato ['jatu] *m* hiatus.
hibernação [ibexna'sãw] *f* hibernation.
hibernar [ibex'na*] *vi* to hibernate.
hibisco [i'biʃku] *m (BOT)* hibiscus.
híbrido/a ['ibridu/a] *adj* hybrid.
hidramático/a [idra'matʃiku/a] *adj (mudança)* hydraulic; *(carro)* with hydraulic transmission.
hidratante [idra'tãtʃi] *adj* moisturizing ♦ *m* moisturizer.
hidratar [idra'ta*] *vt* to hydrate; *(pele)* to moisturize.
hidrato [i'dratu] *m:* ~ **de carbono** carbohydrate.
hidráulica [i'drawlika] *f* hydraulics *sg.*
hidráulico/a [i'drawliku/a] *adj* hydraulic; **força hidráulica** hydraulic power.
hidrelétrica [idre'lɛtrika] *(PT: -ct-) f (usina)* hydroelectric power station; *(empresa)* hydroelectric power company.
hidreletricidade [idreletrisi'dadʒi] *(PT: -ct-) f* hydroelectric power.
hidrelétrico/a [idre'lɛtriku/a] *(PT: -ct-) adj* hydroelectric.
hidro... [idru] *prefixo* hydro..., water... *atr.*
hidroavião [idrua'vjãw] *(pl -ões) m* seaplane.
hidrocarboneto [idrokaxbo'netu] *m* hydrocarbon.
hidrófilo/a [i'drɔfilu/a] *adj* absorbent; **algodão** ~ cotton wool *(BRIT)*, absorbent cotton *(US).*
hidrofobia [idrofo'bia] *f* rabies *sg.*
hidrogênio [idro'ʒenju] *m* hydrogen.
hidroterapia [idrotera'pia] *f* hydrotherapy.
hidrovia [idro'via] *f* waterway.
hiena ['jena] *f* hyena.
hierarquia [jerax'kia] *f* hierarchy.
hierárquico/a [je'raxkiku/a] *adj* hierarchical.
hierarquizar [jeraxki'za*] *vt* to place in a hierarchy.
hieroglífico/a [jero'glifiku/a] *adj* hieroglyphic.
hieróglifo [je'rɔglifu] *m* hieroglyph(ic).
hífen ['ifẽ] *(pl ~s) m* hyphen.
higiene [i'ʒjeni] *f* hygiene; ~ **mental** (mental) rest.

higiênico/a [i'ʒjeniku/a] *adj* hygienic; *(pessoa)* clean; **papel** ~ toilet paper.
hilariante [ila'rjãtʃi] *adj* hilarious.
Himalaia [ima'laja] *m:* **o** ~ the Himalayas *pl.*
hímen ['imẽ] *(pl ~s) m (ANAT)* hymen.
hindi [ĩ'dʒi] *m (LING)* Hindi.
hindu [ĩ'du] *adj, m/f* Hindu; *(indiano)* Indian.
hinduismo [ĩ'dwiʒmu] *m* Hinduism.
hino ['inu] *m* hymn; ~ **nacional** national anthem.
hinterlândia [ĩtex'lãdʒja] *f* hinterland.
hiper... [ipe*] *prefixo* hyper...; *(col)* really.
hipérbole [i'pexboli] *f* hyperbole.
hipermercado [ipexmex'kadu] *m* hypermarket.
hipersensível [ipexsẽ'sivew] *(pl -eis) adj* hypersensitive.
hipertensão [ipextẽ'sãw] *f* high blood pressure.
hípico/a ['ipiku/a] *adj* riding *atr;* **clube** ~ riding club.
hipismo [i'piʒmu] *m (turfe)* horse racing; *(esporte)* (horse) riding.
hipnose [ip'nɔzi] *f* hypnosis.
hipnótico/a [ip'nɔtʃiku/a] *adj* hypnotic; *(substância)* sleep-inducing ♦ *m* sleeping drug.
hipnotismo [ipno'tʃiʒmu] *m* hypnotism.
hipnotizador(a) [ipnotʃizado*(a)] *m/f* hypnotist.
hipnotizar [ipnotʃi'za*] *vt* to hypnotize.
hipocondríaco/a [ipokõ'driaku/a] *adj, m/f* hypochondriac.
hipocrisia [ipokri'sia] *f* hypocrisy.
hipodérmico/a [ipo'dexmiku/a] *adj* hypodermic.
hipócrita [i'pɔkrita] *adj* hypocritical ♦ *m/f* hypocrite.
hipódromo [i'pɔdromu] *m* racecourse.
hipopótamo [ipo'pɔtamu] *m* hippopotamus.
hipoteca [ipo'tɛka] *f* mortgage.
hipotecar [ipote'ka*] *vt* to mortgage.
hipotecário/a [ipote'karju/a] *adj* mortgage *atr;* **credor/devedor** ~ mortgagee/mortgager.
hipotermia [ipotex'mia] *f* hypothermia.
hipótese [i'pɔtezi] *f* hypothesis; **na** ~ **de** in the event of; **em** ~ **alguma** under no circumstances; **na melhor/pior das** ~**s** at best/worst.
hipotético/a [ipo'tɛtʃiku/a] *adj* hypothetical.
hirsuto/a [ix'sutu/a] *adj (cabeludo)* hairy, hirsute; *(barba)* spiky; *(fig: ríspido)* harsh.
hirto/a ['ixtu/a] *adj* stiff, rigid; **ficar** ~ *(pessoa)* to stand stock still.
hispânico/a [iʃ'paniku/a] *adj* Hispanic.
hispanista [iʃpa'niʃta] *m/f* Hispanist.
hispano-americano/a [iʃ'pano-] *adj* Spanish American.
histamina [iʃta'mina] *f* histamine.
histerectomia [iʃterekto'mia] *f* hysterectomy.
histeria [iʃte'ria] *f* hysteria; ~ **coletiva** mass

hysteria.

histérico/a [iʃ'tɛriku/a] *adj* hysterical.

histerismo [iʃte'riʒmu] *m* hysteria.

história [iʃ'tɔrja] *f* (*estudo, ciência*) history; (*conto*) story; ~s *fpl* (*chateação*) bother *sg*, fuss *sg*; **a mesma ~ de sempre** the same old story; **isso é outra ~** that's a different matter; **é tudo ~ dela** she's making it all up; **deixe de ~!** come off it!; **que ~ é essa?** what's going on?; **essa ~ de ...** (*col*: *troço*) this business of ...; **~ antiga/natural** ancient/natural history; **~ da carochinha** nursery story; **~ do arco-da-velha** apocryphal story; **~ em quadrinhos** comic strip.

historiador(a) [iʃtorja'do*(a)] *m/f* historian.

historiar [iʃto'rja*] *vt* to recount.

histórico/a [iʃ'tɔriku/a] *adj* (*personagem, pesquisa etc*) historical; (*fig*: *notável*) historic ♦ *m* history.

historieta [iʃto'rjeta] *f* anecdote, very short story.

histrionismo [iʃtrjo'niʒmu] *m* histrionics *pl*.

hobby ['xɔbi] (*pl* -**bies**) *m* hobby.

hodierno/a [o'dʒjɛxnu/a] *adj* today's, present.

hoje ['oʒi] *adv* today; (*atualmente*) now(adays); **~ à noite** tonight; **de ~ a uma semana** in a week's time; **de ~ em diante** from now on; **~ em dia** nowadays; **~ faz uma semana** a week ago today; **ainda ~** (before the end of) today; **de ~ para amanhã** in one day; **por ~ é só** that's all for today.

Holanda [o'lãda] *f*: **a ~** Holland.

holandês/esa [olã'deʃ/eza] *adj* Dutch ♦ *m/f* Dutchman/woman ♦ *m* (*LING*) Dutch.

holding ['xowdiŋ] (*pl* ~**s**) *m* holding company.

holocausto [olo'kawʃtu] *m* holocaust.

holofote [olo'fɔtʃi] *m* searchlight; (*em campo de futebol etc*) floodlight.

holograma [olo'grama] *m* hologram.

homem ['omē] (*pl* -**ns**) *m* man; (*a humanidade*) mankind; **uma conversa de ~ para ~** a man-to-man talk; **ser o ~ da casa** (*fig*) to wear the trousers; **ser outro ~** (*fig*) to be a changed man; **~ da lei** lawyer; **~ da rua** man in the street; **~ de ação** man of action; **~ de bem** honest man; **~ de empresa** *ou* **negócios** businessman; **~ de estado** statesman; **~ de letras** man of letters; **~ de palavra** man of his word; **~ de peso** influential man; **~ de recursos** man of means; **~ público** public servant.

homem-feito (*pl* **homens-feitos**) *m* grown man.

homem-rã (*pl* **homens-rã(s)**) *m* frogman.

homem-sanduíche (*pl* **homens-sanduíche**) *m* sandwich board man.

homenageado/a [omena'ʒjadu/a] *adj* honoured (*BRIT*), honored (*US*) ♦ *m/f* person hono(u)red.

homenageante [omena'ʒjãtʃi] *adj* respectful.

homenagear [omena'ʒja*] *vt* (*pessoa*) to pay

tribute to, honour (*BRIT*), honor (*US*).

homenagem [ome'naʒē] *f* tribute; (*REL*) homage; **prestar ~ a alguém** to pay tribute to sb; **em ~ a** in honour (*BRIT*) *ou* honor (*US*) of.

homenzarrão [omēza'xãw] (*pl* -**ões**) *m* hulk (of a man).

homenzinho [omē'ziɲu] *m* little man; (*jovem*) young man.

homens ['omēʃ] *mpl de* **homem**.

homeopata [omjo'pata] *m/f* homoeopath(ic doctor) (*BRIT*), homeopath(ic doctor) (*US*).

homeopatia [omjopa'tʃia] *f* homoeopathy (*BRIT*), homeopathy (*US*).

homeopático/a [omjo'patʃiku/a] *adj* homoeopathic (*BRIT*), homeopathic (*US*); (*fig*): **em doses homeopáticas** in tiny quantities.

homérico/a [o'mɛriku/a] *adj* (*fig*) phenomenal.

homicida [omi'sida] *adj* (*pessoa*) homicidal ♦ *m/f* murderer.

homicídio [omi'sidʒju] *m* murder; **~ involuntário** manslaughter.

homiziado/a [omi'zjadu/a] *adj* in hiding ♦ *m/f* fugitive.

homiziar [omi'zja*] *vt* (*esconder*) to hide; **~-se** *vr* to hide.

homogeneidade [omoʒenej'dadʒi] *f* homogeneity.

homogeneizado/a [omoʒenej'zadu/a] *adj* V **leite**.

homogêneo/a [omo'ʒenju/a] *adj* homogeneous; (*CULIN*) blended.

homologar [omolo'ga*] *vt* to ratify.

homólogo/a [o'mɔlogu/a] *adj* homologous; (*fig*) equivalent ♦ *m/f* opposite number.

homônimo [o'monimu] *m* (*de pessoa*) namesake; (*LING*) homonym.

homossexual [omosek'swal] (*pl* -**ais**) *adj, m/f* homosexual.

homossexualismo [omosekswa'liʒmu] *m* homosexuality.

Honduras [õ'duraʃ] *f* Honduras.

hondurenho/a [õdu'reɲu/a] *adj, m/f* Honduran.

honestidade [oneʃtʃi'dadʒi] *f* honesty; (*decência*) decency; (*justeza*) fairness.

honesto/a [o'nɛʃtu/a] *adj* honest; (*decente*) decent; (*justo*) fair, just.

Hong Kong [oŋ'koŋ] *f* Hong Kong.

honorário/a [ono'rarju/a] *adj* honorary.

honorários [ono'rarjuʃ] *mpl* fees.

honorífico/a [ono'rifiku/a] *adj* honorific.

honra ['õxa] *f* honour (*BRIT*), honor (*US*); ~**s** *fpl* **fúnebres** funeral rites; **convidado de ~** guest of hono(u)r; **em ~ de** in hono(u)r of; **por ~ da firma** (*por obrigação*) out of a sense of duty; (*para salvar as aparências*) to save face; **fazer as ~s da casa** to do the hono(u)rs, attend to the guests.

honradez [õxa'deʒ] *f* honesty; (*de pessoa*) integrity.

honrado/a [õ'xadu/a] *adj* honest; (*respeitado*)

honourable (*BRIT*), honorable (*US*).
honrar [õ'xa*] *vt* to honour (*BRIT*), honor (*US*); ~-**se** *vr*: ~-**se em fazer** to be hono(u)red to do.
honraria [õxa'ria] *f* honour (*BRIT*), honor (*US*).
honroso/a [õ'xozu/ɔza] *adj* honourable (*BRIT*), honorable (*US*).
hóquei ['ɔkej] *m* hockey; ~ **sobre gelo** ice hockey.
hora ['ɔra] *f* (*60 minutos*) hour; (*momento*) time; **a que** ~**s**? (at) what time?; **que** ~**s são**? what time is it?; **são duas** ~**s** it's two o'clock; **você tem as** ~**s**? have you got the time?; **isso são** ~**s**? what time do you call this?; **dar as** ~**s** (*relógio*) to strike the hour; **fazer** ~ to kill time; **fazer** ~ **com alguém** (*col*) to tease sb; **marcar** ~ to make an appointment; **perder a** ~ to be late; **não vejo a** ~ **de** ... I can't wait to ...; **às altas** ~**s da noite** *ou* **da madrugada** in the small hours; **de** ~ **em** ~ every hour; **em boa/má** ~ at the right/wrong time; **chegar em cima da** ~ to arrive just in time *ou* on the dot; **fora de** ~ at the wrong moment; **na** ~ (*no ato, em seguida*) on the spot; (*em boa hora*) at the right moment; (*na hora H*) at the moment of truth; **na** ~ **H** (*no momento certo*) in the nick of time; (*na hora crítica*) at the moment of truth, when it comes (*ou* came) to it; **está na** ~ **de** ... it's time to ...; **bem na** ~ just in time; **chegar na** ~ to be on time; **de última** ~ *adj* last-minute ♦ *adv* at the last minute; ~ **de dormir** bedtime; **meia** ~ half an hour; ~ **local** local time; ~**s extras** overtime *sg*; **trabalhei 2** ~**s extras** I worked 2 hours overtime; **você recebe por** ~ **extra?** do you get paid overtime?; ~**s vagas** spare time *sg*.
horário/a [o'rarju/a] *adj*: **100 km** ~**s** 100 km an hour ♦ *m* (*tabela*) timetable; (*hora*) time; ~ **de expediente** working hours *pl*; (*de um escritório*) office hours *pl*; ~ **de verão** summer time; ~ **integral** full time; ~ **nobre** (*TV*) prime time.
horda ['ɔxda] *f* horde.
horista [o'rifta] *adj* paid by the hour ♦ *m/f* hourly-paid worker.
horizontal [orizõ'taw] (*pl* -**ais**) *adj* horizontal ♦ *f*: **estar na** ~ (*col*) to be lying down.
horizonte [ori'zõtfi] *m* horizon.
hormonal [oxmo'naw] (*pl* -**ais**) *adj* hormonal.
hormônio [ox'monju] *m* hormone.
horóscopo [o'rɔʃkopu] *m* horoscope.
horrendo/a [o'xēdu/a] *adj* horrendous, frightful.
horripilante [oxipi'lätʃi] *adj* horrifying, hairraising.
horripilar [oxipi'la*] *vt* to horrify; ~-**se** *vr* to be horrified.
horrível [o'xivew] (*pl* -**eis**) *adj* awful, horrible.

horror [o'xo*] *m* horror; **que** ~! how awful!; **ser um** ~ to be awful; **ter** ~ **a algo** to hate sth; **um** ~ **de** (*porção*) a lot of; **dizer/fazer** ~**es** to say/do terrible things; ~**es de** (*muitos*) loads of; **ele está faturando** ~**es** he's raking it in, he's making a fortune.
horrorizar [oxori'za*] *vt* to horrify, frighten ♦ *vi*: **cenas de** ~ horrifying scenes; ~-**se** *vr* to be horrified.
horroroso/a [oxo'rozu/ɔza] *adj* horrible, ghastly.
horta ['ɔxta] *f* vegetable garden.
hortaliças [oxta'lisaʃ] *fpl* vegetables.
hortelã [oxte'lã] *f* mint; ~ **pimenta** peppermint.
hortelão/loa [oxte'lãw/loa] (*pl* ~**s** *ou* -**ões**/~**s**) (*PT*) *m/f* (market) gardener.
hortênsia [ox'tẽsja] *f* hydrangea.
horticultor(a) [oxtʃikuw'to*(a)] *m/f* market gardener (*BRIT*), truck farmer (*US*).
horticultura [oxtʃikuw'tura] *f* horticulture.
hortifrutigranjeiros [oxtʃifrutʃigrã'ʒejruʃ] *mpl* fruit and vegetables.
hortigranjeiros [oxtʃigrã'ʒejruʃ] *mpl* garden vegetables.
horto ['oxtu] *m* market garden (*BRIT*), truck farm (*US*).
hospedagem [oʃpe'daʒẽ] *f* lodging.
hospedar [oʃpe'da*] *vt* to put up, lodge; ~-**se** *vr* to stay, lodge.
hospedaria [oʃpeda'ria] *f* inn.
hóspede ['oʃpedʒi] *m* (*amigo*) guest; (*estranho*) lodger.
hospedeira [oʃpe'dejra] *f* landlady; (*PT: de bordo*) stewardess, air hostess (*BRIT*).
hospedeiro/a [oʃpe'dejru/a] *adj* hospitable ♦ *m* (*dono*) landlord.
hospício [oʃ'pisju] *m* mental hospital.
hospital [oʃpi'taw] (*pl* -**ais**) *m* hospital.
hospitalar [oʃpita'la*] *adj* hospital *atr*.
hospitaleiro/a [oʃpita'lejru/a] *adj* hospitable.
hospitalidade [oʃpitali'dadʒi] *f* hospitality.
hospitalização [oʃpitaliza'sãw] (*pl* -**ões**) *f* hospitalization.
hospitalizar [oʃpitali'za*] *vt* to hospitalize, take to hospital.
hostess ['ɔʃtes] (*pl* -**es**) *f* hostess.
hóstia ['ɔʃtʃia] *f* Host, wafer.
hostil [oʃ'tʃiw] (*pl* -**is**) *adj* hostile.
hostilidade [oʃtʃili'dadʒi] *f* hostility.
hostilizar [oʃtʃili'za*] *vt* to antagonize; (*MIL*) to wage war on.
hostis [oʃ'tʃiʃ] *pl de* **hostil**.
hotel [o'tɛw] (*pl* -**éis**) *m* hotel; ~ **de alta rotatividade** *motel for sexual encounters*.
hotelaria [otela'ria] *f* (*curso*) hotel management; (*conjunto de hotéis*) hotels *pl*.
hoteleiro/a [ote'lejru/a] *adj* hotel *atr* ♦ *m/f* hotelier; **rede hoteleira** hotel chain.
houve ['ovi] *etc vb* V **haver**.

NB: *European Portuguese adds the following consonants to certain words: **b** (sú(b)dito, su(b)til); **c** (a(c)ção, a(c)cionista, a(c)to); **m** (inde(m)ne); **p** (ado(p)ção, ado(p)tar); for further details see p. xiii.*

h(s). *abr* (= *hora*(*s*)) o'clock.
humanidade [umani'dadʒi] *f* (*os homens*) man(kind); (*compaixão*) humanity; ~s *fpl* (*EDUC*) humanities.
hui [wi] *excl* (*de dor*) ow!; (*de susto, surpresa*) ah!; (*de repugnância*) ugh!
hum [ũ] *excl* hmm.
humanismo [uma'niʒmu] *m* humanism.
humanista [uma'niʃta] *adj, m/f* humanist.
humanitário/a [umani'tarju/a] *adj* humanitarian; (*benfeitor*) humane ♦ *m/f* humanitarian.
humanizar [umani'za*] *vt* to humanize; ~**-se** *vr* to become more human.
humano/a [u'manu/a] *adj* human; (*bondoso*) humane.
humanos [u'manuʃ] *mpl* humans.
húmido/a (*PT*) *adj* = **úmido**.
humildade [umiw'dadʒi] *f* humility; (*pobreza*) humbleness.
humilde [u'miwdʒi] *adj* humble; (*pobre*) poor.
humildes [u'miwdʒiʃ] *m/fpl*: **os** (*ou* **as**) ~ the poor.
humilhação [umiʎa'sãw] *f* humiliation.
humilhante [umi'ʎãtʃi] *adj* humiliating.
humilhar [umi'ʎa*] *vt* to humiliate ♦ *vi* to be humiliating; ~**-se** *vr* to humble o.s.
humor [u'mo*] *m* (*disposição*) mood, temper; (*graça*) humour (*BRIT*), humor (*US*); **de bom/mau** ~ in a good/bad mood.
humorismo [umo'riʒmu] *m* humour (*BRIT*), humor (*US*).
humorista [umo'riʃta] *m/f* (*escritor*) humorist; (*na TV, no palco*) comedian.
humorístico/a [umo'riʃtʃiku/a] *adj* humorous.
húmus ['umuʃ] *m inv* humus.
húngaro/a ['ũgaru/a] *adj, m/f* Hungarian.
Hungria [ũ'gria] *f*: **a** ~ Hungary.
hurra ['uxa] *m* cheer ♦ *excl* hurrah!
Hz *abr* (= *hertz*) Hz.

I

I, i [i:] (*pl* **is**) *m* I, i; **I de Irene** I for Isaac (*BRIT*) *ou* Item (*US*).
ia ['ia] *etc vb* V **ir**.
IAB *abr m* = **Instituto dos Advogados do Brasil; Instituto dos Arquitetos do Brasil.**
ialorixá [jalori'ʃa] *f* macumba priestess.
IAPAS (*BR*) *abr m* = **Instituto de Administração da Previdência e Assistência Social.**
iate ['jatʃi] *m* yacht; ~ **clube** yacht club.
iatista [ja'tʃiʃta] *m/f* yachtsman/woman.
iatismo [ja'tʃiʒmu] *m* yachting.
IBAM *abr m* = **Instituto Brasileiro de Administração Municipal.**
IBDF *abr m* = **Instituto Brasileiro de Des-**

envolvimento Florestal.
ibérico/a [i'beriku/a] *adj, m/f* Iberian.
ibero/a [i'bɛru/a] *adj, m/f* Iberian.
ibero-americano/a [iberu-] *adj, m/f* Ibero-American.
IBGE *abr m* = **Instituto Brasileiro de Geografia e Estatística.**
IBMC *abr m* = **Instituto Brasileiro do Mercado de Capitais.**
Ibope [i'bɔpi] *abr m* = **Instituto Brasileiro de Opinião Pública e Estatística; dar i~** (*TV*) to get high ratings; (*fig: ser popular*) to be popular.
IBV *abr m* = **Índice da Bolsa de Valores (do Rio de Janeiro).**
içar [i'sa*] *vt* to hoist, raise.
iceberg [ajs'bexgi] (*pl* ~s) *m* iceberg.
ICM (*BR*) *abr m* (= *Imposto sobre Circulação de Mercadorias*) ≈ VAT.
ICM/S (*BR*) *abr m* (*Imposto sobre Circulação de Mercadorias e Serviços*) ≈ VAT.
icone ['ikoni] *m* icon.
iconoclasta [ikono'klaʃta] *adj* iconoclastic ♦ *m/f* iconoclast.
icterícia [ikte'risja] *f* jaundice.
ida ['ida] *f* going, departure; ~ **e volta** round trip, return; **a** (**viagem de**) ~ the outward journey; **na** ~ on the way there; ~**s e vindas** comings and goings; **comprei só a** ~ I only bought a single *ou* one-way (*US*) (ticket).
idade [i'dadʒi] *f* age; **ter cinco anos de** ~ to be five (years old); **de meia** ~ middle-aged; **qual é a** ~ **dele?** how old is he?; **na minha** ~ at my age; **ser menor/maior de** ~ to be under/of age; **pessoa de** ~ elderly person; **estar na** ~ **de trabalhar** to be (of) working age; **já não estou mais em** ~ **de fazer** I'm past doing; ~ **atômica** atomic age; ~ **da pedra** Stone Age; **I~ Média** Middle Ages *pl*.
ideação [idea'sãw] (*pl* -**ões**) *f* conception.
ideal [ide'jaw] (*pl* -**ais**) *adj, m* ideal.
idealismo [idea'liʒmu] *m* idealism.
idealista [idea'liʃta] *m/f* idealist ♦ *adj* idealistic.
idealização [idealiza'sãw] (*pl* -**ões**) *f* idealization; (*planejamento*) creation.
idealizar [ideali'za*] *vt* to idealize; (*planejar*) to devise, create.
idear [ide'a*] *vt* (*imaginar*) to imagine, think up; (*idealizar*) to create.
ideário [i'dʒarju] *m* ideas *pl*, thinking.
idéia [i'dɛja] *f* idea; (*mente*) mind; **mudar de** ~ to change one's mind; **não ter a mínima** ~ to have no idea; **não faço** ~ I can't imagine; **estar com** ~ **de fazer** to plan to do; **fazer uma** ~ **errada de algo** to get the wrong idea about sth; ~ **fixa** obsession; ~ **genial** brilliant idea.
idem ['idẽ] *pron* ditto.
idêntico/a [i'dẽtʃiku/a] *adj* identical.
identidade [idẽtʃi'dadʒi] *f* identity; **carteira de** ~ identity (*BRIT*) *ou* identification (*US*) card.
identificação [idẽtʃiʃifika'sãw] *f* identification.

identificar [idẽtʃifi'ka*] vt to identify; ~-se vr: ~-se com to identify with.
ideologia [ideolo'ʒia] f ideology.
ideológico/a [ideo'lɔʒiku/a] adj ideological.
ideólogo/a [ide'ɔlogu/a] m/f ideologue.
ídiche ['idiʃi] m = **iídiche**.
idílico/a [i'dʒiliku/a] adj idyllic.
idílio [i'dʒilju] m idyll.
idioma [i'dʒɔma] m language.
idiomático/a [idʒɔ'matʃiku/a] adj idiomatic.
idiossincrasia [idʒosĩkra'zia] f character.
idiota [i'dʒɔta] adj idiotic ♦ m/f idiot.
idiotice [idʒo'tʃisi] f idiocy.
ido/a ['idu/a] adj past.
idólatra [i'dɔlatra] adj idolatrous ♦ m/f idolater/tress.
idolatrar [idola'tra*] vt to idolize.
idolatria [idola'tria] f idolatry.
ídolo ['idolu] m idol.
idoneidade [idonej'dadʒi] f suitability; (competência) competence; ~ **moral** moral probity.
idôneo/a [i'donju/a] adj (adequado) suitable, fit; (pessoa) able, capable.
idos ['iduʃ] mpl bygone days.
idoso/a [i'dozu/ɔza] adj elderly, old.
Iemanjá [jemã'ʒa] f Iemanjá (Afro-Brazilian sea goddess).
lêmen ['jemẽ] m: **o** ~ **(do Sul)** (South) Yemen.
iemenita [jeme'nita] adj, m/f Yemeni.
iene ['jɛni] m yen.
iglu [i'glu] m igloo.
IGC (BR) abr m = **Imposto sobre Ganhos de Capital**.
ignaro/a [igi'naru/a] adj ignorant.
ignição [igni'sãw] (pl -ões) f ignition.
ignóbil [ig'nɔbiw] (pl -eis) adj ignoble.
ignomínia [igno'minja] f disgrace, ignominy.
ignominioso/a [ignomi'njozu/ɔza] adj ignominious.
ignorado/a [igno'radu/a] adj unknown.
ignorância [igno'rãsja] f ignorance; **apelar para a** ~ (col) to lose one's rag.
ignorante [igno'rãtʃi] adj ignorant, uneducated ♦ m/f ignoramus.
ignorar [igno'ra*] vt not to know; (não dar atenção a) to ignore.
ignoto/a [ig'nɔtu/a] adj (formal) unknown.
IGP (BR) abr m = **Índice Geral de Preços**.
igreja [i'greʒa] f church.
igual [i'gwaw] (pl -ais) adj equal; (superfície) even ♦ m/f equal; **em partes iguais** in equal parts; **ser** ~ **a** to be the same; **ser** ~ **a** to be the same as, be like; ~ **se** ... as if ...; **por** ~ equally; **sem** ~ unequalled, without equal; **de** ~ **para** ~ on equal terms; **tratar alguém de** ~ **para** ~ to treat sb as an equal; **nunca vi coisa** ~ I've never seen anything like it.
igualar [igwa'la*] vt (ser igual a) to equal; (fa-

zer igual) to make equal; (nivelar) to level ♦ vi: ~ **a** ou **com** to be equal to, be the same as; (ficar no mesmo nível) to be level with; ~-se vr: ~-se **a alguém** to be sb's equal; ~ **algo com** ou **a algo** to equal sth to sth; ~ **algo com algo** (terreno etc) to level sth with sth.
igualdade [igwaw'dadʒi] f (paridade) equality; (uniformidade) evenness, uniformity.
igualitário/a [igwali'tarju/a] adj egalitarian.
igualmente [igwaw'mẽtʃi] adv equally; (também) likewise, also; ~! (saudação) the same to you!
iguana [i'gwana] f iguana.
iguaria [igwa'ria] f (CULIN) delicacy.
ih [i:] excl (de admiração, surpresa) cor (BRIT), gee (US); (de perigo próximo) ooh.
iídiche ['jidiʃi] m (LING) Yiddish.
ilação [ila'sãw] (pl -ões) f inference, deduction.
I.L. Ano (BR) abr (COM) = **Índice de Lucratividade no Ano**.
ilegal [ile'gaw] (pl -ais) adj illegal.
ilegalidade [ilegali'dadʒi] f illegality.
ilegítimo/a [ile'ʒitʃimu/a] adj illegitimate; (ilegal) unlawful.
ilegível [ile'ʒivew] (pl -eis) adj illegible.
ileso/a [i'lɛzu/a] adj unhurt; **sair** ~ to escape unhurt.
iletrado/a [ile'tradu/a] adj, m/f illiterate.
ilha ['iʎa] f island.
ilhar [i'ʎa*] vt to cut off, isolate.
ilharga [i'ʎaxga] f (ANAT) side.
ilhéu/ilhoa [i'ʎew/i'ʎoa] m/f islander.
ilhós [i'ʎɔʃ] (pl ilhoses) m eyelet.
ilhota [i'ʎɔta] f small island.
ilícito/a [i'lisitu/a] adj illicit.
ilimitado/a [ilimi'tadu/a] adj unlimited.
ilógico/a [i'lɔʒiku/a] adj illogical; (absurdo) absurd.
iludir [ilu'dʒi*] vt to delude; (enganar) to deceive; (a lei) to evade; ~-se vr to delude o.s.
iluminação [ilumina'sãw] (pl -ões) f lighting; (fig) enlightenment.
iluminado/a [ilumi'nadu/a] adj illuminated, lit; (estádio) floodlit; (fig) enlightened.
iluminante [ilumi'nãtʃi] adj bright.
iluminar [ilumi'na*] vt to light up; (estádio etc) to floodlight; (fig) to enlighten.
ilusão [ilu'zãw] (pl -ões) f illusion; (quimera) delusion; ~ **de ótica** optical illusion; **viver de ilusões** to live in a dream-world.
ilusionista [iluzjo'niʃta] m/f conjurer; (que escapa) escapologist.
ilusões [ilu'zõjʃ] f pl de **ilusão**.
ilusório/a [ilu'zɔrju/a] adj (enganoso) deceptive.
ilustração [iluʃtra'sãw] (pl -ões) f (figura, exemplo) illustration; (saber) learning.
ilustrado/a [iluʃ'tradu/a] adj (com gravuras)

illustrated; (*instruído*) learned.

ilustrador(a) [iluʃtra'do*(a)] *m/f* illustrator.

ilustrar [iluʃ'tra*] *vt* (*com gravuras*) to illustrate; (*instruir*) to instruct; (*exemplificar*) to illustrate; **~-se** *vr* (*distinguir-se*) to excel; (*instruir-se*) to inform o.s.

ilustrativo/a [iluʃtra'tʃivu/a] *adj* illustrative.

ilustre [i'luʃtri] *adj* famous, illustrious; **um ~ desconhecido** a complete stranger.

ilustríssimo/a [iluʃ'trisimu/a] *adj superl de* **ilustre**; (*tratamento*): **~ senhor** dear Sir.

ímã ['imã] *m* magnet.

imaculado/a [imaku'ladu/a] *adj* immaculate.

imagem [i'maʒē] (*pl* **-ns**) *f* image; (*semelhança*) likeness; (*TV*) picture; **imagens** *fpl* (*LITERATURA*) imagery *sg*; **ela é a ~ do pai** she's the image of her father.

imaginação [imaʒina'sãw] (*pl* **-ões**) *f* imagination.

imaginar [imaʒi'na*] *vt* to imagine; (*supor*) to suppose; **~-se** *vr* to imagine o.s.; **imagine só!** just imagine!; **obrigado — imagina!** thank you — don't worry about it!

imaginário/a [imaʒi'narju/a] *adj* imaginary.

imaginativo/a [imaʒina'tʃivu/a] *adj* imaginative.

imaginável [imaʒi'navew] (*pl* **-eis**) *adj* imaginable.

imaginoso/a [imaʒi'nozu/ɔza] *adj* (*pessoa*) imaginative.

íman ['imã] (*PT*) *m* = **ímã**.

imanente [ima'nētʃi] *adj*: **~ (a)** inherent (in).

imantar [imã'ta*] *vt* to magnetize.

imaturidade [imaturi'dadʒi] *f* immaturity.

imaturo/a [ima'turu/a] *adj* immature.

imbatível [iba'tʃivew] (*pl* **-eis**) *adj* invincible.

imbecil [ĩbe'siw] (*pl* **-is**) *adj* stupid ♦ *m/f* imbecile, half-wit.

imbecilidade [ĩbesili'dadʒi] *f* stupidity.

imbecis [ĩbe'siʃ] *pl de* **imbecil**.

imberbe [ĩ'bɛxbi] *adj* (*sem barba*) beardless; (*jovem*) youthful.

imbricar [ĩbri'ka*] *vt* to overlap; **~-se** *vr* to overlap.

imbuir [ĩ'bwi*] *vt*: **~ alguém de** (*sentimentos*) to imbue sb with.

IME (*BR*) *abr m* = **Instituto Militar de Engenharia**.

imediações [imedʒa'sõjʃ] *fpl* vicinity *sg*, neighbourhood *sg* (*BRIT*), neighborhood *sg* (*US*).

imediatamente [imedʒata'mētʃi] *adv* immediately, right away.

imediato/a [ime'dʒatu/a] *adj* immediate; (*seguinte*) next ♦ *m* second-in-command; **~ a** next to; **de ~** straight away.

imemorial [imemo'rjaw] (*pl* **-ais**) *adj* immemorial.

imensidade [imẽsi'dadʒi] *f* immensity.

imensidão [imẽsi'dãw] *f* hugeness, enormity.

imenso/a [i'mẽsu/a] *adj* immense, huge; (*ódio, amor*) great.

imensurável [imẽsu'ravew] (*pl* **-eis**) *adj* immeasurable.

imerecido/a [imere'sidu/a] *adj* undeserved.

imergir [imex'ʒi*] *vt* to immerse; (*fig*) to plunge ♦ *vi* to be immersed; to plunge.

imersão [imex'sãw] (*pl* **-ões**) *f* immersion.

imerso/a [i'mɛxsu/a] *adj* (*tb fig*) immersed.

imersões [imex'sõjʃ] *fpl de* **imersão**.

imigração [imigra'sãw] (*pl* **-ões**) *f* immigration.

imigrante [imi'grãtʃi] *adj*, *m/f* immigrant.

imigrar [imi'gra*] *vi* to immigrate.

iminência [imi'nẽsja] *f* imminence.

iminente [imi'nẽtʃi] *adj* imminent.

imiscuir-se [imiʃ'kwixsi] *vr* to meddle, interfere.

imitação [imita'sãw] (*pl* **-ões**) *f* imitation, copy; **jóia de ~** imitation jewel.

imitador(a) [imita'do*(a)] *adj* imitative ♦ *m/f* imitator.

imitar [imi'ta*] *vt* to imitate; (*assinatura*) to copy.

imobiliária [imobi'ljarja] *f* estate agent's (*BRIT*), real estate broker's (*US*).

imobiliário/a [imobi'ljarju/a] *adj* property *atr*, real estate *atr*.

imobilidade [imobili'dadʒi] *f* immobility.

imobilizar [imobili'za*] *vt* to immobilize; (*fig*: *economia, progresso*) to bring to a standstill; (*COM*: *capital*) to tie up.

imoderação [imodera'sãw] *f* lack of moderation.

imoderado/a [imode'radu/a] *adj* immoderate.

imodéstia [imo'dɛʃtʃja] *f* immodesty.

imodesto/a [imo'dɛʃtu/a] *adj* immodest.

imódico/a [i'mɔdʒiku/a] *adj* exorbitant.

imolar [imo'la*] *vt* (*sacrificar*) to sacrifice; (*prejudicar*) to harm.

imoral [imo'raw] (*pl* **-ais**) *adj* immoral.

imoralidade [imorali'dadʒi] *f* immorality.

imortal [imox'taw] (*pl* **-ais**) *adj* immortal ♦ *m/f* (*membro da ABL*) member of the Brazilian Academy of Letters.

imortalidade [imoxtali'dadʒi] *f* immortality.

imortalizar [imoxtali'za*] *vt* to immortalize.

imóvel [i'mɔvew] (*pl* **-eis**) *adj* (*parado*) motionless, still; (*não movediço*) immovable ♦ *m* property; (*edifício*) building; **imóveis** *mpl* real estate *sg*, property *sg*.

impaciência [ĩpa'sjẽsja] *f* impatience.

impacientar-se [ĩpasjē'taxsi] *vr* to lose one's patience.

impaciente [ĩpa'sjẽtʃi] *adj* impatient; (*inquieto*) anxious.

impacto [ĩ'paktu] (*PT*: **-cte**) *m* impact.

impagável [ĩpa'gavew] (*pl* **-eis**) *adj* (*fig*) priceless.

impaludismo [ĩpalu'dʒiʒmu] *m* malaria.

ímpar ['ĩpa*] *adj* (*números*) odd; (*sem igual*) unique, unequalled.

imparcial [ĩpax'sjaw] (*pl* **-ais**) *adj* fair, impartial.

imparcialidade [ĩpaxsjali'dadʒi] *f* impartiality.

impasse [ĩ'pasi] *m* impasse, deadlock.

impassível [ĩpa'sivew] (*pl* -**eis**) *adj* impassive.

impávido/a [ĩ'pavidu/a] *adj* (*formal*) fearless, intrepid.

impecável [ĩpe'kavew] (*pl* -**eis**) *adj* perfect, impeccable.

impeço [ĩ'pɛsu] *etc vb* V **impedir**.

impedido/a [ĩpe'dʒidu/a] *adj* hindered; (*estrada*) blocked; (*FUTEBOL*) offside; (*PT: TEL*) engaged (*BRIT*), busy (*US*).

impedimento [ĩpedʒi'mɛtu] *m* impediment; (*FUTEBOL*) offside; (*POL*) impeachment.

impedir [ĩpe'dʒi*] *vt* to obstruct; (*estrada*, *passagem*, *tráfego*) to block; (*movimento*, *execução*, *progresso*) to impede; ~ **alguém de fazer** to prevent sb from doing; (*proibir*) to forbid sb from doing; ~ **(que aconteça) algo** to prevent sth (happening).

impelir [ĩpe'li*] *vt* to drive (on); (*obrigar*) to force; (*incitar*) to incite.

impenetrável [ĩpene'travew] (*pl* -**eis**) *adj* impenetrable.

impenitência [ĩpeni'tẽsja] *f* unrepentance.

impenitente [ĩpeni'tẽtʃi] *adj* unrepentant.

impensado/a [ĩpẽ'sadu/a] *adj* (*imprevidente*) thoughtless; (*não calculado*) unpremeditated; (*imprevisto*) unforeseen.

impensável [ĩpẽ'savew] (*pl* -**eis**) *adj* unthinkable.

imperador [ĩpera'do*] *m* emperor.

imperar [ĩpe'ra*] *vi* to reign, rule; (*fig: prevalecer*) to prevail.

imperativo/a [ĩpera'tʃivu/a] *adj* (*tb LING*) imperative ♦ *m* absolute necessity; imperative.

imperatriz [ĩpera'triʒ] *f* empress.

imperceptível [ĩpexsep'tʃivew] (*pl* -**eis**) *adj* imperceptible.

imperdível [ĩpex'dʒivew] (*pl* -**eis**) *adj* (*questão*) impossible to lose; (*filme*) unmissable.

imperdoável [ĩpex'dwavew] (*pl* -**eis**) *adj* unforgivable, inexcusable.

imperecível [ĩpere'sivew] (*pl* -**eis**) *adj* imperishable.

imperfeição [ĩmpexfej'sãw] (*pl* -**ões**) *f* imperfection; (*falha*) flaw.

imperfeito/a [ĩpex'fejtu/a] *adj* imperfect ♦ *m* (*LING*) imperfect.

imperial [ĩpe'rjaw] (*pl* -**ais**) *adj* imperial.

imperialismo [ĩperja'liʒmu] *m* imperialism.

imperícia [ĩpe'risja] *f* (*inabilidade*) inability; (*inexperiência*) inexperience.

imperialista [ĩperja'liʃta] *adj*, *m/f* imperialist.

império [ĩ'pɛrju] *m* empire.

imperioso/a [ĩpe'rjozu/ɔza] *adj* (*dominador*) domineering; (*necessidade*) pressing, urgent; (*tom*, *olhar*) imperious.

impermeabilidade [ĩpexmjabili'dadʒi] *f* imperviousness.

impermeabilizar [ĩpexmjabili'za*] *vt* to waterproof.

impermeável [ĩpex'mjavew] (*pl* -**eis**) *adj* impervious; (*à água*) waterproof ♦ *m* raincoat; ~ **a** (*tb fig*) impervious to.

impertinência [ĩpextʃi'nẽsja] *f* impertinence; (*irrelevância*) irrelevance.

impertinente [ĩpextʃi'nẽtʃi] *adj* (*alheio*) irrelevant; (*insolente*) impertinent.

imperturbável [ĩpextux'bavew] (*pl* -**eis**) *adj* imperturbable; (*impassível*) impassive.

impessoal [ĩpe'swaw] (*pl* -**ais**) *adj* impersonal.

impetigo [ĩpe'tʃigo] *m* impetigo.

ímpeto ['ĩpetu] *m* (*TEC*: *força*) impetus; (*movimento súbito*) start; (*de cólera*) fit; (*de emoção*) surge; (*de chamas*) fury; **agir com** ~ to act on impulse; **levantar-se num** ~ to get up with a start; **senti um** ~ **de sair correndo** I felt an urge to run away.

impetrante [ĩpe'trãtʃi] *m/f* (*JUR*) petitioner.

impetrar [ĩpe'tra*] *vt* (*JUR*): ~ **algo** to petition for sth.

impetuosidade [ĩpetwozi'dadʒi] *f* impetuosity.

impetuoso/a [ĩpe'twozu/ɔza] *adj* (*pessoa*) headstrong, impetuous; (*ato*) rash, hasty; (*rio*) fast-moving.

impiedade [ĩpje'dadʒi] *f* irreverence; (*crueldade*) cruelty.

impiedoso/a [ĩpje'dozu/ɔza] *adj* merciless, cruel.

impilo [ĩ'pilu] *etc vb* V **impelir**.

impingir [ĩpĩ'ʒi*] *vt*: ~ **algo a alguém** (*mentiras*, *mercadorias*) to palm sth off on sb; ~ **algo em alguém** (*bofetada*, *pontapé etc*) to land sth on sb.

implacável [ĩpla'kavew] (*pl* -**eis**) *adj* (*pessoa*) unforgiving; (*destino*, *doença*, *perseguição*) relentless.

implantação [ĩplãta'sãw] (*pl* -**ões**) *f* introduction; (*MED*) implant.

implantar [ĩplã'ta*] *vt* to introduce; (*MED*) to implant.

implante [ĩ'plãtʃi] *m* (*MED*) implant.

implausível [ĩplaw'zivew] (*pl* -**eis**) *adj* implausible.

implementação [ĩplemẽta'sãw] (*pl* -**ões**) *f* implementation.

implementar [ĩplemẽ'ta*] *vt* to implement.

implemento [ĩple'mẽtu] *m* implement.

implicação [ĩplika'sãw] (*pl* -**ões**) *f* implication; (*envolvimento*) involvement.

implicância [ĩpli'kãsja] *f* (*ato de chatear*) teasing; (*antipatia*) horribleness; **estar de** ~ **com alguém** to pick on sb, have it in for sb.

implicante [ĩpli'kãtʃi] *adj* horrible ♦ *m/f* stirrer.

implicar [ĩpli'ka*] *vt* (*envolver*) to implicate; (*pressupor*) to imply; ~**-se** *vr* (*envolver-se*) to get involved; ~ **com alguém** (*antipatizar*) to be horrible to sb; (*chatear*) to tease sb, pick on sb; ~ **(em) algo** to involve sth.

implícito/a [ĩ'plisitu/a] *adj* implicit.

NB: *European Portuguese adds the following consonants to certain words:* **b** (sú(b)dito, su(b)til); **c** (a(c)ção, a(c)cionista, a(c)to); **m** (inde(m)ne); **p** (ado(p)ção, ado(p)tar); *for further details see p. xiii.*

impliquei [ĩpli'kej] *etc vb V* **implicar**.
implodir [ĩplo'dʒi*] *vi* to implode.
imploração [ĩplora'sãw] *f* begging.
implorar [ĩplo'ra*] *vt*: ~ **(algo a alguém)** to beg *ou* implore (sb for sth).
impõe [ĩ'põj] *etc vb V* **impor**.
impoluto/a [ĩpo'lutu/a] *adj* immaculate; (*pessoa*) beyond reproach.
impomos [ĩ'pomoʃ] *vb V* **impor**.
imponderado/a [ĩpõde'radu/a] *adj* rash.
imponderável [ĩpõde'ravew] (*pl* **-eis**) *adj* imponderable.
imponência [ĩpo'nẽsja] *f* impressiveness.
imponente [ĩpo'nẽtʃi] *adj* impressive, imposing.
imponho [ĩ'poɲu] *etc vb V* **impor**.
impontual [ĩpõ'twaw] (*pl* **-ais**) *adj* unpunctual.
impopular [ĩpopu'la*] *adj* unpopular.
impopularidade [ĩpopulari'dadʒi] *f* unpopularity.
impor [ĩ'po*] (*irreg: como* **pôr**) *vt* to impose; (*respeito*) to command; ~**-se** *vr* to assert o.s.; ~ **algo a alguém** to impose sth on sb.
importação [ĩpoxta'sãw] (*pl* **-ões**) *f* (*ato*) importing; (*mercadoria*) import.
importador(a) [ĩpoxta'do*(a)] *adj* import *atr* ♦ *m/f* importer ♦ *f* (*empresa*) import company; (*loja*) shop selling imported goods.
importância [ĩpox'tãsja] *f* importance; (*de dinheiro*) sum, amount; **não tem** ~ it doesn't matter, never mind; **ter** ~ to be important; **dar** ~ **a algo/alguém** to attach importance to sth/show consideration for sb; **sem** ~ unimportant; **não dê** ~ **ao que ele disse** take no notice of what he said; **de certa** ~ of some importance.
importante [ĩpox'tãtʃi] *adj* important; (*arrogante*) self-important ♦ *m*: **o (mais)** ~ the (most) important thing.
importar [ĩpox'ta*] *vt* (*COM*) to import; (*trazer*) to bring in; (*causar: prejuízos etc*) to cause; (*implicar*) to imply, involve ♦ *vi* to matter, be important; ~**-se** *vr*: ~**-se com algo** to mind sth; **não me importo** I don't care; **não** *ou* **pouco importa!** it doesn't matter!; ~ **em** (*preço*) to add up to, amount to; (*resultar*) to lead to; **eu pouco me importo que ela venha ou não** I don't care whether she comes or not.
importe [ĩ'pɔxtʃi] *m* (*soma*) amount; (*custo*) cost.
importunação [ĩpoxtuna'sãw] (*pl* **-ões**) annoyance.
importunar [ĩpoxtu'na*] *vt* to bother, annoy.
importuno/a [ĩpox'tunu/a] *adj* (*maçante*) annoying; (*inoportuno*) inopportune ♦ *m/f* nuisance.
impôs [ĩ'poʃ] *vb V* **impor**.
imposição [ĩpozi'sãw] (*pl* **-ões**) *f* imposition.
impossibilidade [ĩposibili'dadʒi] *f* impossibility.
impossibilitado/a [ĩposibili'tadu/a] *adj*: ~ **de fazer** unable to do.

impossibilitar [ĩposibili'ta*] *vt*: ~ **algo** to make sth impossible; ~ **alguém de fazer**, ~ **a alguém fazer** to prevent sb doing; ~ **algo a alguém**, ~ **alguém para algo** to make sth impossible for sb.
impossível [ĩpo'sivew] (*pl* **-eis**) *adj* impossible; (*insuportável: pessoa*) insufferable; (*incrível*) incredible.
impostação [ĩpoʃta'sãw] *f* (*da voz*) diction, delivery.
impostar [ĩpoʃ'ta*] *vt* (*voz*) to throw.
imposto/a [ĩ'poʃtu/'pɔʃta] *pp de* **impor** ♦ *m* tax; **antes/depois de** ~**s** before/after tax; ~ **de renda** (*BR*) income tax; ~ **predial** rates *pl*; ~ **sobre ganhos de capital** capital transfer tax (*BRIT*), inheritance tax (*US*); ~ **sobre os lucros** profits tax; ~ **sobre transferência de capital** capital transfer tax; **I~ sobre Circulação de Mercadorias (e Serviços)** (*BR*), ~ **sobre valor agregado** (*PT*) value added tax (*BRIT*), sales tax (*US*).
impostor [ĩpoʃ'to*] *m* impostor.
impostura [ĩpoʃ'tura] *f* deception.
impotência [ĩpo'tẽʃja] *f* impotence.
impotente [ĩpo'tẽtʃi] *adj* powerless; (*MED*) impotent.
impraticabilidade [ĩpratʃikabili'dadʒi] *f* impracticability.
impraticável [ĩpratʃi'kavew] (*pl* **-eis**) *adj* impracticable; (*rua, rio etc*) impassable.
imprecisão [ĩpresi'zãw] (*pl* **-ões**) *f* inaccuracy.
impreciso/a [ĩpre'sizu/a] *adj* vague; (*falto de rigor*) inaccurate.
imprecisões [ĩpresi'zõjʃ] *fpl de* **imprecisão**.
impregnar [ĩpreg'na*] *vt* to impregnate; ~ **algo de** to impregnate sth with; (*fig: mente etc*) to fill sth with.
imprensa [ĩ'prẽsa] *f* (*a arte*) printing; (*máquina, jornais*) press; ~ **marrom** tabloid press, gutter press.
imprensar [ĩprẽ'sa*] *vt* (*no prelo*) to stamp; (*apertar*) to squash; (*fig*): ~ **alguém (contra a parede)** to press sb.
imprescindível [ĩpresĩ'dʒivew] (*pl* **-eis**) *adj* essential, indispensable.
impressão [ĩpre'sãw] (*pl* **-ões**) *f* impression; (*de livros*) printing; (*marca*) imprint; **causar boa** ~ to make a good impression; **ficar com/ter a** ~ **(de) que** to get/have the impression that; **ter má** ~ **de algo** to have a bad impression of sth; ~ **digital** fingerprint.
impressionante [ĩpresjo'nãtʃi] *adj* impressive; (*abalador*) amazing.
impressionar [ĩpresjo'na*] *vt* to impress; (*abalar*) to affect ♦ *vi* to be impressive; to make an impression; ~**-se** *vr*: ~**-se (com algo)** (*comover-se*) to be moved (by sth).
impressionável [ĩpresjo'navew] (*pl* **-eis**) *adj* impressionable.
impressionismo [ĩpresjo'niʒmu] *m* impressionism.
impressionista [ĩpresjo'niʃta] *adj, m/f* impressionist.

impresso/a [ĩ'prɛsu/a] *pp de* **imprimir** ♦ *adj* printed ♦ *m (para preencher)* form; *(folheto)* leaflet; ~**s** *mpl* printed matter *sg*.

impressões [impre'sõjʃ] *fpl de* **impressão**.

impressor [ĩpre'so*] *m* printer.

impressora [ĩpre'sora] *f* printing machine; *(COMPUT)* printer; ~ **a laser** laser printer; ~ **de linha** line printer; ~ **margarida** daisy-wheel printer; ~ **matricial** dot-matrix printer.

imprestável [ĩpreʃ'tavew] *(pl -eis) adj (inútil)* useless; *(pessoa)* unhelpful.

impreterível [ĩprete'rivew] *(pl -eis) adj (compromisso)* essential; *(prazo)* final.

imprevidente [ĩprevi'dētʃi] *adj* short-sighted.

imprevisão [ĩprevi'zãw] *f* lack of foresight, short-sightedness.

imprevisível [ĩprevi'zivew] *(pl -eis) adj* unforeseeable.

imprevisto/a [ĩpre'viʃtu/a] *adj* unexpected, unforeseen ♦ *m:* **um** ~ something unexpected.

imprimir [ĩpri'mi*] *vt* to print; *(marca)* to stamp; *(infundir)* to instil *(US);* *(COMPUT)* to print out; ~**-se** *vr* to be stamped, be impressed; ~**-se na memória** to impress o.s. on the memory; ~ **algo a algo** to stamp sth on sth.

improbabilidade [ĩprobabili'dadʒi] *f* improbability.

improcedente [ĩprose'dētʃi] *adj* groundless, unjustified.

improdutivo/a [ĩprodu'tʃivu/a] *adj* unproductive.

improfícuo/a [impro'fikwu/a] *adj* useless, futile.

impropério [ĩpro'pɛrju] *m* insult; **dizer** ~**s** to swear.

impropriedade [ĩproprje'dadʒi] *f* inappropriateness; *(moral)* impropriety.

impróprio/a [ĩ'prɔprju/a] *adj (inadequado)* inappropriate; *(indecente)* improper; **filme** ~ **para menores de 18 anos** X-certificate *ou* X-rated film.

improrrogável [ĩproxo'gavew] *(pl -eis) adj* non-extendible.

improvável [ĩpro'vavew] *(pl -eis) adj* unlikely.

improvidência [ĩprovi'dēsja] *f* lack of foresight.

improvidente [ĩprovi'dētʃi] *adj* lacking foresight.

improvisado/a [ĩprovi'zadu/a] *adj* improvised, impromptu.

improvisação [ĩproviza'sãw] *(pl -ões) f* improvisation.

improvisar [ĩprovi'za*] *vt, vi* to improvise; *(TEATRO)* to ad-lib.

improviso [ĩpro'vizu] *m* impromptu talk; **de** ~ *(de repente)* suddenly; *(sem preparação)* without preparation; **falar de** ~ to talk off the cuff.

imprudência [ĩpru'dēsja] *f* rashness; *(descui-*

do) carelessness.

imprudente [ĩpru'dētʃi] *adj (irrefletido)* rash; *(motorista)* careless.

impudico/a [ĩpu'dʒiku/a] *adj* shameless.

impugnar [ĩpug'na*] *vt (refutar)* to refute; *(opor-se a)* to oppose.

impulsionar [ĩpuwsjo'na*] *vt (impelir)* to drive, impel; *(fig: estimular)* to urge.

impulsividade [ĩpuwsivi'dadʒi] *f* impulsiveness.

impulsivo/a [ĩpuw'sivu/a] *adj* impulsive.

impulso [ĩ'puwsu] *m* impulse; *(fig: estímulo)* urge, impulse; **tomar** ~ *(fig: empresa, negócio)* to take off; **compra por** ~ *(ato)* impulse buying.

impune [ĩ'puni] *adj* unpunished.

impunemente [ĩpune'mētʃi] *adv* with impunity.

impunha [ĩ'puɲa] *etc vb V* **impor**.

impunidade [ĩpuni'dadʒi] *f* impunity.

impureza [ĩpu'reza] *f* impurity.

impuro/a [ĩ'puru/a] *adj* impure.

impus [ĩ'puʃ] *etc vb V* **impor**.

impuser [ĩpu'ze*] *etc vb V* **impor**.

imputação [imputa'sãw] *(pl -ões) f* accusation.

imputar [ĩpu'ta*] *vt:* ~ **algo a** *(atribuir)* to attribute sth to; ~ **algo a alguém** to blame sb for sth.

imputável [ĩpu'tavew] *(pl -eis) adj* attributable.

imundice [imũ'dʒisi] *f* = **imundície**.

imundície [imũ'dʒisji] *f* filth.

imundo/a [i'mũdu/a] *adj* filthy; *(obsceno)* dirty.

imune [i'muni] *adj:* ~ **a** immune to.

imunidade [imuni'dadʒi] *f* immunity.

imunizar [imuni'za*] *vt:* ~ **alguém (contra algo)** *(MED)* to immunize sb (against sth); *(fig)* to protect sb (from sth).

imutável [imu'tavew] *(pl -eis) adj* fixed, unalterable, unchanging.

inabalável [inaba'lavew] *(pl -eis) adj* unshakeable.

inábil [i'nabiw] *(pl -eis) adj (incapaz)* incapable; *(desajeitado)* clumsy.

inabilidade [inabili'dadʒi] *f (incompetência)* incompetence; *(falta de destreza)* clumsiness.

inabilidoso/a [inabili'dozu/ɔza] *adj* clumsy, awkward.

inabilitação [inabilita'sãw] *(pl -ões) f* disqualification.

inabilitar [inabili'ta*] *vt (incapacitar)* to incapacitate; *(em exame)* to disqualify.

inabitado/a [inabi'tadu/a] *adj* uninhabited.

inabitável [inabi'tavew] *(pl -eis) adj* uninhabitable.

inacabado/a [inaka'badu/a] *adj* unfinished.

inacabável [inaka'bavew] *(pl -eis) adj* interminable, unending.

---

inação [ina'sãw] (PT: **-cç-**) f (inércia) inactivity; (irresolução) indecision.

inaceitável [inasej'tavew] (pl **-eis**) adj unacceptable.

Inacen [ina'sẽ] (BR) abr m = **Instituto Nacional de Artes Cênicas.**

inacessível [inase'sivew] (pl **-eis**) adj inaccessible.

inacreditável [inakredʒi'tavew] (pl **-eis**) adj unbelievable, incredible.

inactivo/a etc [ina'tivu/a] (PT) = **inativo/a** etc.

inadaptado/a [inadap'tadu/a] adj maladjusted.

inadequação [inadekwa'sãw] (pl **-ões**) f inadequacy; (impropriedade) unsuitability.

inadequado/a [inade'kwadu/a] adj inadequate; (impróprio) unsuitable.

inadiável [ina'dʒavew] (pl **-eis**) adj pressing.

inadimplência [inadʒĩ'plẽsja] f (JUR) breach of contract, default.

inadimplente [inadʒĩ'plẽtʃi] adj (JUR) in breach of contract, at fault.

inadimplir [inadʒĩ'pli*] vt, vi: ~ **(algo)** to default (on sth).

inadmissível [inadʒimi'sivew] (pl **-eis**) adj inadmissible.

inadquirível [inadʒiki'rivew] (pl **-eis**) adj unobtainable.

inadvertência [inadʒivex'tẽsja] f oversight; **por** ~ by mistake.

inadvertido/a [inadʒivex'tʃidu/a] adj inadvertent.

inalação [inala'sãw] (pl **-ões**) f inhalation.

inalar [ina'la*] vt to inhale, breathe in.

inalcançável [inawkã'savew] (pl **-eis**) adj out of reach; (sucesso, ambição) unattainable.

inalterado/a [inawte'radu/a] adj unchanged; (sereno) unperturbed.

inalterável [inawte'ravew] (pl **-eis**) adj unchangeable; (impassível) imperturbable.

Inamps [i'nãps] (BR) abr m = **Instituto Nacional de Assistência Médica e Previdência Social.**

inanição [inani'sãw] (pl **-ões**) f starvation.

inanimado/a [inani'madu/a] adj inanimate.

inapetência [inape'tẽsja] f loss of appetite.

inapetente [inape'tẽtʃi] adj off one's food.

inaplicado/a [inapli'kadu/a] adj (aluno) idle, lazy.

inaplicável [inapli'kavew] (pl **-eis**) adj inapplicable.

inapreciável [inapre'sjavew] (pl **-eis**) adj invaluable.

inaproveitável [inaprovej'tavew] (pl **-eis**) adj useless.

inaptidão [inaptʃi'dãw] (pl **-ões**) f inability.

inapto/a [i'naptu/a] adj (incapaz) unfit, incapable; (inadequado) unsuited.

inarticulado/a [inaxtʃiku'ladu/a] adj inarticulate.

inatacável [inata'kavew] (pl **-eis**) adj unassailable.

inatenção [inatẽ'sãw] f inattention.

inatingido/a [inatʃĩ'ʒidu/a] adj unconquered.

inatingível [inatʃĩ'ʒivew] (pl **-eis**) adj unattainable.

inatividade [inatʃivi'dadʒi] f inactivity; (aposentadoria) redundancy (BRIT), dismissal (US); (MIL: reforma) retirement (on health grounds).

inativo/a [ina'tʃivu/a] adj inactive; (aposentado, reformado) retired.

inato/a [i'natu/a] adj innate, inborn.

inaudito/a [inaw'dʒitu/a] adj unheard-of.

inaudível [inaw'dʒivew] (pl **-eis**) adj inaudible.

inauguração [inawgura'sãw] (pl **-ões**) f inauguration; (de exposição) opening; (de estátua) unveiling.

inaugural [inawgu'raw] (pl **-ais**) adj inaugural.

inaugurar [inawgu'ra*] vt to inaugurate; (exposição) to open; (estátua) to unveil.

inca ['ĩka] adj, m/f Inca.

incabível [ĩka'bivew] (pl **-eis**) adj unacceptable.

incalculável [ĩkawku'lavew] (pl **-eis**) adj incalculable.

incandescente [ĩkãde'sẽtʃi] adj incandescent.

incansável [ĩkã'savew] (pl **-eis**) adj tireless, untiring.

incapacidade [ĩkapasi'dadʒi] f incapacity; (incompetência) incompetence; ~ **de fazer** inability to do.

incapacitado/a [ĩkapasi'tadu/a] adj (inválido) disabled, handicapped ♦ m/f handicapped person; **estar** ~ **de fazer** to be unable to do.

incapacitar [ĩkapasi'ta*] vt: ~ **alguém (para)** to make sb unable (to).

incapaz [ĩka'pajʒ] adj, m/f incompetent; ~ **de fazer** incapable of doing; ~ **para** unfit for.

incauto/a [ĩ'kawtu/a] adj (imprudente) rash.

incendiar [ĩsẽ'dʒja*] vt to set fire to; (fig) to inflame; ~**-se** vr to catch fire.

incendiário/a [ĩsẽ'dʒjarju/a] adj incendiary; (fig) inflammatory ♦ m/f arsonist; (agitador) agitator.

incêndio [ĩ'sẽdʒju] m fire; ~ **criminoso** ou **premeditado** arson.

incenso [ĩ'sẽsu] m incense.

incentivador(a) [ĩsẽtʃiva'do*(a)] adj stimulating, encouraging.

incentivar [ĩsẽtʃi'va*] vt to stimulate, encourage.

incentivo [ĩsẽ'tʃivu] m incentive; ~ **fiscal** tax incentive.

incerteza [ĩsex'teza] f uncertainty.

incerto/a [ĩ'sextu/a] adj uncertain.

incessante [ĩse'sãtʃi] adj incessant.

incesto [ĩ'sɛʃtu] m incest.

incestuoso/a [ĩseʃ'twozu/ɔza] adj incestuous.

inchação [ĩʃa'sãw] (pl **-ões**) f swelling.

inchado/a [ĩ'ʃadu/a] adj swollen; (fig) conceited.

inchar [ĩ'ʃa*] vt to swell ♦ vi to swell; ~**-se** vr to swell (up); (fig) to become conceited.

incidência [ĩsi'dẽsja] f incidence, ocurrence.

incidente [ĩsi'dẽtʃi] m incident.

incidir [ĩsi'dʒi*] *vi*: ~ **em erro** to go wrong; ~ **em** *ou* **sobre algo** (*luz*) to fall on sth; (*influir*) to affect sth; (*imposto*) to be payable on sth.
incinerar [ĩsine'ra*] *vt* to burn.
incipiente [ĩsi'pjẽtʃi] *adj* incipient.
incisão [ĩsi'zãw] (*pl* -**ões**) *f* cut; (*MED*) incision.
incisivo/a [ĩsi'zivu/a] *adj* cutting, sharp; (*fig*) incisive ♦ *m* incisor.
incisões [ĩsi'zõjʃ] *fpl de* **incisão**.
incitação [ĩsita'sãw] (*pl* -**ões**) *f* incitement.
incitamento [ĩsita'mẽtu] *m* incitement.
incitar [ĩsi'ta*] *vt* to incite; (*pessoa, animal*) to drive on; (*instigar*) to rouse; ~ **alguém a (fazer) algo** to urge sb on to (do) sth, incite sb to (do) sth.
incivil [ĩsi'viw] (*pl* -**is**) *adj* rude, ill-mannered.
incivilidade [ĩsivili'dadʒi] *f* rudeness.
incivilizado/a [ĩsivili'zadu/a] *adj* uncivilized.
incivis [ĩsi'viʃ] *adj pl de* **incivil**.
inclemência [ĩkle'mẽsja] *f* harshness, rigour (*BRIT*), rigor (*US*); (*tempo*) inclemency.
inclemente [ĩkle'mẽtʃi] *adj* severe, harsh; (*tempo*) inclement.
inclinação [ĩklina'sãw] (*pl* -**ões**) *f* (*tb fig*) inclination; (*da terra*) slope; (*simpatia*) liking; ~ **da cabeça** nod.
inclinado/a [ĩkli'nadu/a] *adj* (*terreno, estrada*) sloping; (*corpo, torre*) leaning; **estar** ~/**pouco** ~ **a** to be inclined/loath to.
inclinar [ĩkli'na*] *vt* (*objeto*) to tilt; (*cabeça*) to nod ♦ *vi* (*terra*) to slope; (*objeto*) to tilt; ~-**se** *vr* (*objeto*) to tilt; (*dobrar o corpo*) to bow, stoop; ~ **para** (*propensão*) to lean towards; ~-**se sobre algo** to lean over sth; ~(-**se**) **para trás** to lean back.
ínclito/a ['ĩklitu/a] *adj* illustrious, renowned.
incluir [ĩ'klwi*] *vt* to include; (*em carta*) to enclose; ~-**se** *vr* to be included; **tudo incluído** (*COM*) all in.
inclusão [ĩklu'zãw] *f* inclusion.
inclusive [ĩklu'zivi] *prep* including ♦ *adv* inclusive; (*até mesmo*) even; **de segunda à sexta** ~ from Monday to Friday inclusive; **e** ~ **falou que** ... and furthermore he said that ....
incluso/a [ĩ'kluzu/a] *adj* included; (*em carta*) enclosed.
incobrável [ĩko'bravew] (*pl* -**eis**) *adj* (*COM*): **dívida** ~ bad debt.
incoercível [ĩkoex'sivew] (*pl* -**eis**) *adj* uncontrollable.
incoerência [ĩkoe'rẽsja] *f* incoherence; (*contradição*) inconsistency.
incoerente [ĩkoe'rẽtʃi] *adj* incoherent; (*contraditório*) inconsistent.
incógnita [ĩ'kɔgnita] *f* (*MAT*) unknown; (*fato incógnito*) mystery.
incógnito/a [ĩ'kɔgnitu/a] *adj* unknown ♦ *adv*

incognito.
incolor [ĩko'lo*] *adj* colourless (*BRIT*), colorless (*US*).
incólume [ĩ'kɔlumi] *adj* safe and sound; (*ileso*) unharmed.
incomensurável [ĩkomẽsu'ravew] (*pl* -**eis**) *adj* immense.
incomodada [ĩkomo'dada] *adj* (*menstruada*) having one's period.
incomodar [ĩkomo'da*] *vt* (*importunar*) to bother, trouble; (*aborrecer*) to annoy ♦ *vi* to be bothersome; ~-**se** *vr* to bother, put o.s. out; ~-**se com algo** to be bothered by sth, mind sth; **não se incomode!** don't worry!; **você se incomoda se eu abrir a janela?** do you mind if I open the window?
incômodo/a [ĩ'komodu/a] *adj* (*desconfortável*) uncomfortable; (*incomodativo*) troublesome; (*inoportuno*) inconvenient ♦ *m* (*menstruação*) period; (*maçada*) nuisance, trouble; (*amolação*) inconvenience.
incomparável [ĩkõpa'ravew] (*pl* -**eis**) *adj* incomparable.
incompatibilidade [ĩkõpatʃibili'dadʒi] *f* incompatibility.
incompatibilizar [ĩkõpatʃibili'za*] *vt*: ~ **alguém (com alguém)** to alienate sb (from sb); ~-**se** *vr*: ~-**se (com alguém)** to alienate o.s. (from sb).
incompatível [ĩkõpa'tʃivew] (*pl* -**eis**) *adj* incompatible.
incompetência [ĩkõpe'tẽsja] *f* incompetence.
incompetente [ĩkõpe'tẽtʃi] *adj*, *m/f* incompetent.
incompleto/a [ĩkõ'plɛtu/a] *adj* incomplete, unfinished.
incompreendido/a [ĩkõprjẽ'dʒidu/a] *adj* misunderstood.
incompreensão [ĩkõprjẽ'sãw] *f* incomprehension.
incompreensível [ĩkõprjẽ'sivew] (*pl* -**eis**) *adj* incomprehensible.
incompreensivo/a [ĩkõprjẽ'sivu/a] *adj* uncomprehending.
incomum [ĩko'mũ] *adj* uncommon.
incomunicável [ĩkomuni'kavew] (*pl* -**eis**) *adj* cut off; (*privado de comunicação, fig*) incommunicado; (*preso*) in solitary confinement.
inconcebível [ĩkõse'bivew] (*pl* -**eis**) *adj* inconceivable; (*incrível*) incredible.
inconciliável [ĩkõsi'ljavew] (*pl* -**eis**) *adj* irreconcilable.
inconcludente [ĩkõklu'dẽtʃi] *adj* inconclusive.
inconcluso/a [ĩkõ'kluzu/a] *adj* unfinished.
incondicional [ĩkõdʒisjo'naw] (*pl* -**ais**) *adj* unconditional; (*apoio*) wholehearted; (*partidário*) staunch; (*amizade, fã*) loyal.
inconfesso/a [ĩkõ'fɛsu/a] *adj* closet *atr*.
inconfidência [ĩkõfi'dẽsja] *f* disloyalty; (*JUR*)

NB: *European Portuguese adds the following consonants to certain words:* **b** (sú(b)dito, su(b)til); **c** (a(c)ção, a(c)cionista, a(c)to); **m** (inde(m)ne); **p** (ado(p)ção, ado(p)tar); *for further details see p. xiii.*

treason.

inconfidente [ĩkõfi'dētʃi] *adj* disloyal ♦ *m* conspirator.

inconformado/a [ĩkõfox'madu/a] *adj* bitter; ~ **com** unreconciled to.

inconfundível [ĩkõfũ'dʒivew] (*pl* -eis) *adj* unmistakeable.

incongruência [ĩkõ'grwẽsja] *f*: **ser uma** ~ to be incongruous.

incongruente [ĩkõ'grwētʃi] *adj* incongruous.

incôngruo/a [ĩ'kõgrwu/a] *adj* incongruous.

inconsciência [ĩkõ'sjẽsja] *f* (*MED*) unconsciousness; (*irreflexão*) thoughtlessness.

inconsciente [ĩkõ'sjẽtʃi] *adj* (*MED*, *PSICO*) unconscious; (*involuntário*) unwitting; (*irresponsável*) irresponsible ♦ *m* (*PSICO*) unconscious ♦ *m/f* (*irresponsável*) irresponsible person.

inconseqüência [ĩkõse'kwẽsja] *f* (*irresponsabilidade*) irresponsibility; (*incoerência*) inconsistency.

inconseqüente [ĩkõse'kwẽtʃi] *adj* (*incoerente*) inconsistent; (*contraditório*) illogical; (*irresponsável*) irresponsible.

inconsistência [ĩkõsiʃ'tẽsja] *f* inconsistency; (*falta de solidez*) runny consistency.

inconsistente [ĩkõsiʃ'tẽtʃi] *adj* inconsistent; (*sem solidez*) runny.

inconsolável [ĩkõso'lavew] (*pl* -eis) *adj* inconsolable.

inconstância [ĩkõʃ'tãsja] *f* fickleness; (*do tempo*) changeability.

inconstante [ĩkõʃ'tãtʃi] *adj* fickle; (*tempo*) changeable.

inconstitucional [ĩkõʃtʃitusjo'naw] (*pl* -ais) *adj* unconstitutional.

incontável [ĩkõ'tavew] (*pl* -eis) *adj* countless.

incontestável [ĩkõteʃ'tavew] (*pl* -eis) *adj* undeniable.

incontinência [ĩkõtʃi'nẽsja] *f* (*MED*) incontinence; (*sensual*) licentiousness.

incontinente [ĩkõtʃi'nẽtʃi] *adj* (*MED*) incontinent; (*sensual*) licentious.

incontinenti [ĩkõtʃi'nẽtʃi] *adv* immediately.

incontrolável [ĩkõtro'lavew] (*pl* -eis) *adj* uncontrollable.

incontroverso/a [ĩkõtro'vɛxsu/a] *adj* incontrovertible.

inconveniência [ĩkõve'njẽsja] *f* (*inadequação*) inconvenience; (*impropriedade*) inappropriateness; (*descortesia*) impoliteness; (*ato*, *dito*) indiscretion.

inconveniente [ĩkõve'njẽtʃi] *adj* (*incômodo*) inconvenient; (*inoportuno*) awkward; (*grosseiro*) rude; (*importuno*) annoying ♦ *m* (*desvantagem*) disadvantage; (*obstáculo*) difficulty, problem.

Incor [ĩ'ko*] *abr m* (= *Instituto do Coração*) hospital in São Paulo.

incorporação [ĩkoxpora'sãw] (*pl* -ões) *f* (*tb*: *COM*) incorporation; (*no espiritismo*) embodiment, incorporation.

incorporado/a [ĩkoxpo'radu/a] *adj* (*TEC*)

built-in.

incorporar [ĩkoxpo'ra*] *vt* to incorporate; (*juntar*) to add; (*COM*) to merge; ~**-se** *vr* (*espírito*) to be embodied; ~ **-se a** *ou* **em** to join.

incorreção [ĩkoxe'sãw] (*PT*: -cç-; *pl* -ões) *f* (*erro*) inaccuracy.

incorrecto/a [ĩko'xɛktu/a] (*PT*) *adj* = **incorreto/a**.

incorrer [ĩko'xe*] *vi*: ~ **em** to incur.

incorreto/a [ĩko'xɛtu/a] *adj* incorrect; (*desonesto*) dishonest.

incorrigível [ĩkoxi'ʒivew] (*pl* -eis) *adj* incorrigible.

incorruptível [ĩkoxup'tʃivew] (*pl* -eis) *adj* incorruptible.

incorrupto/a [ĩko'xuptu/a] *adj* incorrupt.

INCRA ['ĩkra] (*BR*) *abr m* = **Instituto Nacional de Colonização e Reforma Agrária**.

incredulidade [ĩkreduli'dadʒi] *f* incredulity; (*ceticismo*) scepticism (*BRIT*), skepticism (*US*).

incrédulo/a [ĩ'kredulu/a] *adj* incredulous; (*cético*) sceptical (*BRIT*), skeptical (*US*) ♦ *m/f* sceptic (*BRIT*), skeptic (*US*).

incrementado/a [ĩkremẽ'tadu/a] *adj* (*indústria*) well-developed; (*col*: *festa*) lively; (: *roupa*) trendy; (: *carro*) expensive.

incrementar [ĩkremẽ'ta*] *vt* (*desenvolver*) to develop; (*aumentar*) to increase; (*col*: *festa*, *roupa*) to liven up.

incremento [ĩkre'mẽtu] *m* (*desenvolvimento*) growth; (*aumento*) increase.

incriminação [ĩkrimina'sãw] *f* criminalization.

incriminar [ĩkrimi'na*] *vt* to criminalize; ~ **alguém de algo** to accuse sb of sth.

incrível [ĩ'krivew] (*pl* -eis) *adj* incredible.

incrustar [ĩkruʃ'ta*] *vt* to encrust; (*móveis etc*) to inlay.

incubadora [ĩkuba'dora] *f* incubator.

incubar [ĩku'ba*] *vt* (*ovos*, *doença*) to incubate; (*plano*) to hatch ♦ *vi* (*ovos*) to incubate.

inculpar [ĩkuw'pa*] *vt*: ~ **alguém de algo** (*culpar*) to blame sb for sth; (*acusar*) to accuse sb of sth; ~**-se** *vr*: ~**-se de algo** to blame o.s. for sth.

inculto/a [ĩ'kuwtu/a] *adj* (*pessoa*) uncultured, uneducated; (*terreno*) uncultivated.

incumbência [ĩkũ'bẽsja] *f* task, duty; **não é da minha** ~ it is not part of my duty.

incumbir [ĩkũ'bi*] *vt*: ~ **alguém de algo** *ou* **algo a alguém** to put sb in charge of sth ♦ *vi*: ~ **a alguém** to be sb's duty; ~**-se** *vr*: ~**-se de** to undertake, take charge of.

incurável [ĩku'ravew] (*pl* -eis) *adj* incurable.

incúria [ĩ'kurja] *f* carelessness.

incursão [ĩkux'sãw] (*pl* -ões) *f* (*invasão*) raid, attack; (*penetração*) foray.

incursionar [ĩkuxsjo'na*] *vi*: ~ **por algo** to make forays into sth.

incursões [ĩkux'sõjʃ] *fpl de* **incursão**.

incutir [ĩku'tʃi*] *vt*: ~ **algo (em** *ou* **a alguém)**

to instil (*BRIT*) *ou* instill (*US*) *ou* inspire sth (in sb).

inda ['ĩda] *adv*= **ainda**.

indagação [ĩdaga'sãw] (*pl* -**ões**) *f* (*investigação*) investigation; (*pergunta*) inquiry, question.

indagar [ĩda'ga*] *vt* (*investigar*) to investigate, inquire into ♦ *vi* to inquire; ~-**se** *vr*: ~-**se a si mesmo** to ask o.s.; ~ **algo de alguém** to ask sb about sth; ~ **(de alguém) sobre** *ou* **de algo** to inquire (of sb) about sth.

indébito/a [ĩ'dɛbitu/a] *adj* undue; (*queixa*) unfounded.

indecência [ĩde'sẽsja] *f* indecency; (*ato*, *dito*) vulgar thing.

indecente [ĩde'sẽtʃi] *adj* indecent, improper; (*obsceno*) rude, vulgar.

indecifrável [ĩdesi'fravew] (*pl* -**eis**) *adj* undecipherable; (*pessoa*) inscrutable.

indecisão [ĩdesi'zãw] *f* indecision.

indeciso/a [ĩde'sizu/a] *adj* (*irresoluto*) undecided, hesitant; (*indistinto*) vague; (*por decidir*) undecided.

indeclinável [ĩdekli'navew] (*pl* -**eis**) *adj* indeclinable.

indecoroso/a [ĩdeko'rozu/ɔza] *adj* indecent, improper.

indefensável [ĩdefẽ'savew] (*pl* -**eis**) *adj* indefensible.

indeferido/a [ĩdefe'ridu/a] *adj* refused, rejected.

indeferir [ĩdefe'ri*] *vt* (*desatender*) to reject; (*requerimento*) to turn down.

indefeso/a [ĩde'fezu/a] *adj* undefended; (*fraco*) defenceless.

indefinição [ĩdefini'sãw] (*pl* -**ões**) *f* (*de pessoa*) vague stance.

indefinido/a [ĩdefi'nidu/a] *adj* indefinite; (*vago*) vague, undefined; **por tempo** ~ indefinitely.

indefinível [ĩdefi'nivew] (*pl* -**eis**) *adj* indefinable.

indefiro [ĩde'firu] *etc vb V* **indeferir**.

indelével [ĩde'lɛvew] (*pl* -**eis**) *adj* indelible.

indelicadeza [ĩdelika'deza] *f* impoliteness; (*ação*, *dito*) rude thing.

indelicado/a [ĩdeli'kadu/a] *adj* impolite, rude.

indene [ĩ'dɛni] (*PT*: -**mn**-) *adj* (*pessoa*) unharmed; (*objeto*) undamaged.

indenização [ĩdeniza'sãw] (*PT*: -**mn**-; *pl* -**ões**) *f* compensation; (*COM*) indemnity; (*de demissão*) redundancy (*BRIT*) *ou* severance (*US*) payment.

indenizar [ĩdeni'za*] (*PT*: -**mn**-) *vt*: ~ **alguém por** *ou* **de algo** (*compensar*) to compensate sb for sth; (*por gastos*) to reimburse sb for sth.

independência [ĩdepẽ'dẽsja] *f* independence.

independente [ĩdepẽ'dẽtʃi] *adj* independent; (*auto-suficiente*) self-sufficient; **quarto** ~

room with private entrance.

independer [ĩdepẽ'de*] *vi*: ~ **de algo** not to depend on sth.

indescritível [ĩdeʃkri'tʃivew] (*pl* -**eis**) *adj* indescribable.

indesculpável [ĩdʒiʃkuw'pavew] (*pl* -**eis**) *adj* inexcusable.

indesejável [ĩdeze'ʒavew] (*pl* -**eis**) *adj* undesirable.

indestrutível [ĩdʒiʃtru'tʃivew] (*pl* -**eis**) *adj* indestructible.

indeterminado/a [ĩdetexmi'nadu/a] *adj* indeterminate.

indevassável [ĩdeva'savew] (*pl* -**eis**) *adj* impenetrable.

indevido/a [ĩde'vidu/a] *adj* (*imerecido*) unjust; (*impróprio*) inappropriate.

índex ['ĩdeks] (*pl* **índices**) *m* = **índice**.

indexar [ĩdek'sa*] *vt* to index.

Índia ['ĩdʒa] *f*: **a** ~ India; **as** ~**s Ocidentais** the West Indies.

indiano/a [ĩ'dʒanu/a] *adj*, *m/f* Indian.

indicação [ĩdʒika'sãw] (*pl* -**ões**) *f* indication; (*de termômetro*) reading; (*para um cargo*, *prêmio*) nomination; (*recomendação*) recommendation; (*de um caminho*) directions *pl*.

indicado/a [ĩdʒi'kadu/a] *adj* (*apropriado*) appropriate.

indicador(a) [ĩdʒika'do*(a)] *m* indicator; (*TEC*) gauge; (*dedo*) index finger; (*ponteiro*) pointer ♦ *adj*: ~ **de** indicative of; ~ **econômico** economic indicator.

indicar [ĩdʒi'ka*] *vt* (*mostrar*) to indicate; (*apontar*) to point to; (*temperatura*) to register; (*recomendar*) to recommend; (*para um cargo*) to nominate; (*determinar*) to determine; ~ **o caminho a alguém** to give sb directions; **ao que tudo indica** ... by the looks of things ....

indicativo/a [ĩdʒika'tʃivu/a] *adj* (*tb*: *LING*) indicative.

índice ['ĩdʒisi] *m* (*de livro*) index; (*dedo*) index finger; (*taxa*) rate; ~ **do custo de vida** cost of living index; ~ **de audiência** (*TV*) rating.

índices ['ĩdʒisiʃ] *mpl de* **índex**.

indiciado/a [ĩdʒi'sjadu/a] *m/f* defendant.

indiciar [ĩdʒi'sja*] *vt* (*acusar*) to charge; (*submeter a inquérito*) to investigate.

indício [ĩ'dʒisju] *m* (*sinal*) sign; (*vestígio*) trace; (*JUR*) clue.

indiferença [ĩdʒife'rẽsa] *f* indifference.

indiferente [ĩdʒife'rẽtʃi] *adj*: ~ **(a)** indifferent (to); **isso me é** ~ it's all the same to me.

indígena [ĩ'dʒiʒena] *adj*, *m/f* native; (*índio*) Indian.

indigência [ĩdʒi'ʒẽsja] *f* poverty; (*fig*) lack, need.

indigente [ĩdʒi'ʒẽtʃi] *adj* destitute, indigent.

NB: *European Portuguese adds the following consonants to certain words:* **b** (sú(b)dito, su(b)til); **c** (a(c)ção, a(c)cionista, a(c)to); **m** (inde(m)ne); **p** (ado(p)ção, ado(p)tar); *for further details see p. xiii.*

indigestão [ĭdʒiʒeʃ'tãw] *f* indigestion.

indigesto/a [ĭdʒi'ʒeʃtu/a] *adj* indigestible; (*fig*: *aborrecido*) dull, boring; (: *obscuro*) turgid.

indignação [ĭdʒigna'sãw] *f* indignation.

indignado/a [ĭdʒig'nadu/a] *adj* indignant.

indignar [ĭdʒig'na*] *vt* to anger, incense; ~-se *vr* to get angry; ~-se com to get indignant about.

indignidade [ĭdʒigni'dadʒi] *f* indignity; (*ultraje*) outrage.

indigno/a [ĭ'dʒignu/a] *adj* (*não merecedor*) unworthy; (*desprezível*) disgraceful, despicable.

índio/a ['ĭdʒju/a] *adj, m/f* (*da América*) Indian.

indiquei [ĭdʒi'kej] *etc vb V* indicar.

indireta [ĭdʒi'rɛta] (*PT*: **-ct-**) *f* insinuation; **dar uma** ~ to drop a hint.

indireto/a [ĭdʒi'rɛtu/a] (*PT*: **-ct-**) *adj* indirect; (*olhar*) sidelong; (*procedimento*) roundabout.

indisciplina [ĭdʒisi'plina] *f* indiscipline.

indisciplinado/a [ĭdʒisipli'nadu/a] *adj* undisciplined.

indiscreto/a [ĭdʒiʃ'krɛtu/a] *adj* indiscreet.

indiscrição [ĭdʒiʃkri'sãw] (*pl* **-ões**) *f* indiscretion.

indiscriminado/a [ĭdʒiʃkrimi'nadu/a] *adj* indiscriminate.

indiscutível [ĭdʒiʃku'tʃivew] (*pl* **-eis**) *adj* indisputable.

indispensável [ĭdʒiʃpē'savew] (*pl* **-eis**) *adj* essential, vital ♦ *m* essentials *pl*.

indispõe [ĭdʒiʃ'põj] *etc vb V* indispor.

indispomos [ĭdʒiʃ'pomoʃ] *etc vb V* indispor.

indisponho [ĭdʒiʃ'poɲu] *etc vb V* indispor.

indisponível [ĭdʒiʃpo'nivew] (*pl* **-eis**) *adj* unavailable.

indispor [ĭdʒiʃ'po*] (*irreg*: *como* pôr) *vt* (*de saúde*) to make ill; (*aborrecer*) to upset; ~-se *vr*: ~-se com um amigo to fall out with a friend; ~-se com *ou* contra alguém (*governo etc*) to turn against sb; ~ alguém com *ou* contra alguém to turn sb against sb.

indisposição [ĭdʒiʃpozi'sãw] (*pl* **-ões**) *f* illness.

indisposto/a [ĭdʒiʃ'poʃtu/'poʃta] *pp de* indispor ♦ *adj* (*doente*) unwell, poorly.

indispunha [ĭdʒiʃ'puɲa] *etc vb V* indispor.

indispus [ĭdʒiʃ'puʃ] *etc vb V* indispor.

indispuser [ĭdʒiʃpu'ze*] *etc vb V* indispor.

indisputável [ĭdʒiʃpu'tavew] (*pl* **-eis**) *adj* indisputable.

indissolúvel [ĭdʒiso'luvew] (*pl* **-eis**) *adj* (*material*) insoluble; (*contrato*) indissoluble.

indistinguível [ĭdʒiʃtʃĩ'givew] (*pl* **-eis**) *adj* indistinguishable.

indistinto/a [ĭdʒiʃ'tʃĩtu/a] *adj* indistinct.

individual [ĭdʒivi'dwaw] (*pl* **-ais**) *adj* individual.

individualidade [ĭdʒividwali'dadʒi] *f* individuality.

individualismo [ĭdʒividwa'liʒmu] *m* individualism.

individualista [ĭdʒividwa'liʃta] *adj* in-

dividualist(ic) ♦ *m/f* individualist.

individualizar [ĭdʒividwali'za*] *vt* to individualize.

indivíduo [ĭdʒi'vidwu] *m* individual; (*col*: *sujeito*) person.

indivisível [ĭdʒivi'zivew] (*pl* **-eis**) *adj* indivisible.

indiviso/a [ĭdʒi'vizu/a] *adj* undivided; (*propriedade*) joint.

indizível [ĭdʒi'zivew] (*pl* **-eis**) *adj* unspeakable; (*indescritível*) indescribable.

Ind. Lucr. (*BR*) *abr* (*COM*) = **Índice de Lucratividade**.

indóceis [ĭ'dɔsejʃ] *adj pl de* indócil.

Indochina [ĭdo'ʃina] *f*: **a** ~ Indochina.

indócil [ĭ'dɔsiw] (*pl* **-eis**) *adj* (*rebelde*) unruly, wayward; (*impaciente*) restless.

indo-europeu/péia [ĭdu-] *adj* Indo-European.

índole ['ĭdoli] *f* (*temperamento*) nature; (*tipo*) sort, type.

indolência [ĭdo'lẽsja] *f* laziness, indolence; (*apatia*) apathy.

indolente [ĭdo'lẽtʃi] *adj* indolent; (*apático*) apathetic.

indolor [ĭdo'lo*] *adj* painless.

indomável [ĭdo'mavew] (*pl* **-eis**) *adj* (*animal*) untameable; (*coragem*) indomitable; (*criança*) unmanageable; (*paixão*) consuming.

indômito/a [ĭ'domitu/a] *adj* untamed, wild.

Indonésia [ĭdo'nɛzja] *f*: **a** ~ Indonesia.

indonésio/a [ĭdo'nɛzju/a] *adj, m/f* Indonesian.

indoor [ĭ'do*] *adj inv* (*ESPORTE*) indoor.

indubitável [ĭdubi'tavew] (*pl* **-eis**) *adj* indubitable.

indução [ĭdu'sãw] (*pl* **-ões**) *f* induction; (*persuasão*) inducement.

indulgência [ĭduw'ʒẽsja] *f* indulgence; (*tolerância*) leniency; (*JUR*) clemency.

indulgente [ĭduw'ʒẽtʃi] *adj* (*juiz, atitude*) lenient; (*olhar*) indulgent.

indultar [ĭduw'ta*] *vt* (*JUR*) to reprieve.

indulto [ĭ'duwtu] *m* (*JUR*) reprieve.

indumentária [ĭdumẽ'tarja] *f* costume.

indústria [ĭ'duʃtrja] *f* industry; "~ brasileira" "made in Brazil"; ~ automobilística car industry; ~ de consumo *ou* de ponta *ou* leve light industry; ~ de base key industry; ~ pesada heavy industry; ~ de transformação process industry; ~ fabril manufacturing industry.

industrial [ĭduʃ'trjaw] (*pl* **-ais**) *adj* industrial ♦ *m/f* industrialist.

industrialização [ĭduʃtrjaliza'sãw] *f* industrialization.

industrializado/a [ĭduʃtrjali'zadu/a] *adj* (*país*) industrialized; (*produto*) manufactured; (*gêneros*) processed; (*pão*) sliced.

industrializar [ĭduʃtrjali'za*] *vt* (*país*) to industrialize; (*aproveitar*) to process; ~-se *vr* to become industrialized.

industriar [ĭduʃ'trja*] *vt* (*orientar*) to instruct; (*amestrar*) to train.

industrioso/a [ĭduʃ'trjozu/ɔza] *adj* (*traba-*

lhador) hard-working, industrious; (*hábil*) clever, skilful (*BRIT*), skillful (*US*).

indutivo/a [idu'tʃivu/a] *adj* inductive.

induzir [idu'zi*] *vt* to induce; ~ **alguém a fazer** to persuade sb to do; ~ **alguém em erro** to mislead sb; ~ **(algo de algo)** to infer (sth from sth).

inebriante [ine'brjãtʃi] *adj* intoxicating.

inebriar [ine'brja*] *vt* (*fig*) to intoxicate; ~**-se** *vr* to be intoxicated.

inédito/a [i'nɛdʒitu/a] *adj* (*livro*) unpublished; (*incomum*) unheard-of, rare.

inefável [ine'favew] (*pl* **-eis**) *adj* indescribable.

ineficácia [inefi'kasja] *f* (*de remédio, medida*) ineffectiveness; (*de empregado, máquina*) inefficiency.

ineficaz [inefi'kaj3] *adj* (*remédio, medida*) ineffective; (*empregado, máquina*) inefficient.

ineficiência [inefi'sjẽsja] *f* inefficiency.

ineficiente [inefi'sjẽtʃi] *adj* inefficient.

inegável [ine'gavew] (*pl* **-eis**) *adj* undeniable.

inelutável [inelu'tavew] (*pl* **-eis**) *adj* inescapable.

inépcia [i'nɛpsja] *f* ineptitude.

inepto/a [i'nɛptu/a] *adj* inept, incompetent.

inequívoco/a [ine'kivoku/a] *adj* (*evidente*) clear; (*inconfundível*) unmistakeable.

inércia [i'nɛxsja] *f* (*torpor*) lassitude, lethargy; (*FIS*) inertia.

inerente [ine'rẽtʃi] *adj* inherent.

inerme [i'nɛxmi] *adj* (*formal: não armado*) unarmed; (*indefeso*) defenceless (*BRIT*), defenseless (*US*).

inerte [i'nɛxtʃi] *adj* lethargic; (*FIS*) inert.

INES (*BR*) *abr m* = **Instituto Nacional de Educação dos Surdos.**

inescrupuloso/a [ineʃkrupu'lozu/ɔza] *adj* unscrupulous.

inescrutável [ineʃkru'tavew] (*pl* **-eis**) *adj* inscrutable.

inescusável [ineʃku'zavew] (*pl* **-eis**) *adj* (*indesculpável*) inexcusable; (*indispensável*) essential.

inesgotável [ine3go'tavew] (*pl* **-eis**) *adj* inexhaustible; (*superabundante*) boundless, abundant.

inesperado/a [ineʃpe'radu/a] *adj* unexpected, unforeseen ♦ *m:* **o** ~ the unexpected.

inesquecível [ineʃke'sivew] (*pl* **-eis**) *adj* unforgettable.

inestimável [ineʃtʃi'mavew] (*pl* **-eis**) *adj* invaluable.

inevitável [inevi'tavew] (*pl* **-eis**) *adj* inevitable.

inexatidão [inezatʃi'dãw] (*PT:* **-ct-**; *pl* **-ões**) *f* inaccuracy.

inexato/a [ine'zatu/a] (*PT:* **-ct-**) *adj* inaccurate.

inexaurível [inezaw'rivew] (*pl* **-eis**) *adj* inexhaustible.

inexcedível [inese'dʒivew] (*pl* **-eis**) *adj* unsurpassed.

inexeqüível [ineze'kwivew] (*pl* **-eis**) *adj* impracticable, unworkable.

inexistência [ineziʃ'tẽsja] *f* lack.

inexistente [ineziʃ'tẽtʃi] *adj* non-existent.

inexistir [ineziʃ'tʃi*] *vi* not to exist.

inexorável [inezo'ravew] (*pl* **-eis**) *adj* implacable.

inexperiência [ineʃpe'rjẽsja] *f* inexperience, lack of experience.

inexperiente [ineʃpe'rjẽtʃi] *adj* inexperienced; (*ingênuo*) naive.

inexplicável [ineʃpli'kavew] (*pl* **-eis**) *adj* inexplicable.

inexplorado/a [ineʃplo'radu/a] *adj* unexplored.

inexpressivo/a [ineʃpre'sivu/a] *adj* expressionless.

inexpugnável [ineʃpug'navew] (*pl* **-eis**) *adj* (*fortaleza*) impregnable; (*invencível*) invincible.

inextinto/a [ineʃ'tʃĩtu/a] *adj* unextinguished.

inextricável [ineʃtri'kavew] (*pl* **-eis**) *adj* inextricable.

infalível [ifa'livew] (*pl* **-eis**) *adj* infallible; (*sucesso*) guaranteed.

infame [ĩ'fami] *adj* (*pessoa, procedimento*) mean, nasty; (*comida, trabalho*) awful.

infâmia [ĩ'famja] *f* (*desonra*) disgrace; (*vileza*) villainy; (*dito*) nasty thing.

infância [ĩ'fãsja] *f* childhood; **primeira** ~ infancy, early childhood.

infantaria [ĩfãta'ria] *f* infantry.

infante/a [ĩ'fãtʃi/a] *m/f* (*filho dos reis*) prince/ princess ♦ *m* (*soldado*) foot soldier.

infanticídio [ĩfãtʃi'sidʒu] *m* infanticide.

infantil [ĩfã'tʃiw] (*pl* **-is**) *adj* (*ingênuo*) childlike; (*pueril*) childish; (*para crianças*) children's.

infantilidade [ĩfãtʃili'dadʒi] *f* childishness; (*dito, ação*) childish thing.

infantis [ĩfã'tʃiʃ] *adj pl de* **infantil**.

infanto-juvenil [ĩfãto-] (*pl* **-is**) *adj* children's.

infarto [ĩ'faxtu] *m* heart attack.

infatigável [ĩfatʃi'gavew] (*pl* **-eis**) *adj* untiring.

infausto/a [ĩ'fawʃtu/a] *adj* unlucky.

infecção [ĩfek'sãw] (*pl* **-ões**) *f* infection; (*contaminação*) contamination.

infeccionar [ĩfeksjo'na*] *vt* (*ferida*) to infect; (*contaminar*) to contaminate.

infeccioso/a [ĩfek'sjozu/ɔza] *adj* infectious.

infecções [ĩfek'sõjʃ] *fpl de* **infecção**.

infectar [ĩfek'ta*] (*PT*) *vt* = **infetar**.

infelicidade [ĩfelisi'dadʒi] *f* unhappiness; (*desgraça*) misfortune.

infelicíssimo/a [ĩfeli'sisimu/a] *adj superl de* **infeliz**.

infeliz [ĩfe'li3] *adj* (*triste*) unhappy; (*infausto*) unfortunate; (*ação, medida*) unfortunate; (*sugestão, idéia*) inappropriate ♦ *m/f* unhappy

---

NB: *European Portuguese adds the following consonants to certain words:* **b** (sú(b)dito, su(b)til); **c** (a(c)ção, a(c)cionista, a(c)to); **m** (inde(m)ne); **p** (ado(p)ção, ado(p)tar); *for further details see p. xiii.*

person; **como um** ~ (col) like there's no tomorrow.

infelizmente [ĩfeliʒ'mẽtʃi] adv unfortunately.

infenso/a [ĩ'fẽsu/a] adj adverse.

inferior [ĩfe'rjo*] adj: ~ **(a)** (em valor, qualidade) inferior (to); (mais baixo) lower (than) ♦ m/f inferior, subordinate.

inferioridade [ĩferjori'dadʒi] f inferiority.

inferiorizar [ĩferjori'za*] vt to put down; ~-se vr to become inferior.

inferir [ĩfe'ri*] vt to infer, deduce.

infernal [ĩfex'naw] (pl -ais) adj infernal; (col: excepcional) amazing.

inferninho [ĩfex'niɲu] m club.

infernizar [ĩfexni'za*] vt: ~ **a vida de alguém** to make sb's life hell.

inferno [ĩ'fexnu] m hell; **é um** ~ (fig) it's hell; **vá pro** ~! (col) piss off!

infértil [ĩ'fextʃiw] (pl -eis) adj infertile.

infertilidade [ĩfextʃili'dadʒi] f infertility.

infestar [ĩfeʃ'ta*] vt to infest.

infetar [ĩfe'ta*] vt to infect, contaminate.

infidelidade [ĩfideli'dadʒi] f infidelity, unfaithfulness; (REL) disbelief; ~ **conjugal** marital infidelity.

infidelíssimo/a [ĩfide'lisimu/a] adj superl de **infiel**.

infiel [ĩ'fjew] (pl -éis) adj (desleal) disloyal; (marido) unfaithful; (texto) inaccurate ♦ m/f (REL) non-believer.

infiltração [ĩfiwtra'sãw] (pl -ões) f infiltration.

infiltrar [ĩfiw'tra*] vt to permeate; ~-se vr (água, luz, odor) to permeate; ~-se em algo (pessoas) to infiltrate sth.

ínfimo/a ['ĩfimu/a] adj lowest; (qualidade) poorest.

infindável [ĩfi'davew] (pl -eis) adj unending, constant.

infinidade [ĩfini'dadʒi] f infinity; **uma** ~ **de** countless.

infinitesimal [ĩfinitezi'maw] (pl -ais) adj infinitesimal.

infinitivo/a [ĩfini'tʃivu/a] adj (LING) infinitive ♦ m infinitive.

infinito/a [ĩfi'nitu/a] adj infinite ♦ m infinity.

infiro [ĩ'firu] etc vb V **inferir**.

inflação [ĩfla'sãw] f inflation.

inflacionar [ĩflasjo'na*] vt (ECON) to inflate.

inflacionário/a [ĩflasjo'narju/a] adj inflationary.

inflacionista [ĩflasjo'niʃta] adj, m/f inflationist.

inflamação [ĩflama'sãw] (pl -ões) f (MED) inflammation; (de madeira etc) combustion.

inflamado/a [ĩfla'madu/a] adj (MED) inflamed; (discurso) heated.

inflamar [ĩfla'ma*] vt (madeira, pólvora) to set fire to; (MED, fig) to inflame; ~-se vr to catch fire; (fig) to get worked up; ~-se de algo to be consumed with sth.

inflamatório/a [ĩflama'tɔrju/a] adj inflammatory.

inflamável [ĩfla'mavew] (pl -eis) adj inflammable.

inflar [ĩ'fla*] vt to inflate, blow up; ~-se vr to swell (up); ~ **algo de algo** to inflate sth ou fill sth up with sth.

inflexibilidade [ĩfleksibili'dadʒi] f inflexibility.

inflexível [ĩflek'sivew] (pl -eis) adj stiff, rigid; (fig) unyielding.

infligir [ĩfli'ʒi*] vt: ~ **algo (a alguém)** to inflict sth (upon sb).

influência [ĩ'flwẽsja] f influence; **sob a** ~ **de** under the influence of.

influenciar [ĩflwẽ'sja*] vt to influence ♦ vi: ~ **em algo** to influence sth, have an influence on sth; ~-se vr: ~-se por to be influenced by.

influenciável [ĩflwẽ'sjavew] (pl -eis) adj open to influence.

influente [ĩ'flwẽtʃi] adj influential.

influir [ĩ'flwi*] vi (importar) to matter, be important; ~ **em** ou **sobre** to influence, have an influence on.

influxo [ĩ'fluksu] m influx; (maré-cheia) high tide.

informação [ĩfoxma'sãw] (pl -ões) f (piece of) information; (notícia) news; (MIL) intelligence; (JUR) inquiry; (COMPUT) piece of data; (instrução) instruction; **informações** fpl information sg; **Informações** (TEL) directory enquiries (BRIT), information (US); **pedir informações sobre** to ask about, inquire about; **serviço de** ~ intelligence service.

informado/a [ĩfox'madu/a] adj informed.

informal [ĩfox'maw] (pl -ais) adj informal.

informalidade [ĩfoxmali'dadʒi] f informality.

informante [ĩfox'mãtʃi] m informant; (JUR) informer.

informar [ĩfox'ma*] vt: ~ **alguém (de/sobre algo)** to inform sb (of/about sth) ♦ vi to inform, be informative; ~ **de** to report on; ~-se vr: ~-se de to find out about, inquire about; ~ **algo a alguém** to tell sb sth.

informática [ĩfox'matʃika] f (ciência) computer science; (ramo) computing, computers pl.

informativo/a [ĩfoxma'tʃivu/a] adj informative.

informatização [ĩfoxmatʃiza'sãw] f computerization.

informatizar [ĩfoxmatʃi'za*] vt to computerize.

informe [ĩ'fɔxmi] m (piece of) information; (MIL) briefing; ~**s** mpl information sg.

infortúnio [ĩfox'tunju] m misfortune.

infração [ĩfra'sãw] (PT: -cç-; pl -ões) f breach, infringement; (FUTEBOL) foul; ~ **de trânsito** traffic offence (BRIT) ou violation (US).

infractor(a) [ĩfra'to*(a)] (PT) m/f = **infrator(a)**.

infra-estrutura [ĩfra-] f infrastructure.

infrator(a) [ĩfra'to*(a)] m/f offender.

infravermelho/a [ĩfravex'meʎu/a] adj infrared.

infreqüente [ĩfre'kwẽtʃi] adj infrequent.

infringir [ĩfrĩ'ʒi*] vt to infringe, contravene.

infrutífero/a [ĩfru'tʃiferu/a] adj fruitless.

infundado/a [ĩfũ'dadu/a] adj groundless, unfounded.

infundir [ĩfũ'dʒi*] vt to infuse; (terror) to strike; (incutir) to instil (BRIT), instill (US).
infusão [ĩfu'zãw] (pl -ões) f infusion.
ingenuidade [ĩʒenwi'dadʒi] f ingenuousness.
ingênuo/a [ĩ'ʒenwu/a] adj ingenuous, naïve; (comentário) harmless ♦ m/f naïve person.
ingerência [ĩʒe'rẽsja] f interference.
ingerir [ĩʒe'ri*] vt to ingest; (engolir) to swallow; ~-se vr: ~-se em algo to interfere in sth.
Inglaterra [ĩgla'tɛxa] f: a ~ England.
inglês/esa [ĩ'gleʃ/eza] adj English ♦ m/f Englishman/woman ♦ m (LING) English; os ingleses mpl the English; (só) para ~ ver (col) (just) for show.
inglesar [ĩgle'za*] vt to Anglicize; ~-se vr to become Anglicized.
inglório/a [ĩ'glɔrju/a] adj inglorious.
ingovernável [ĩgovex'navew] (pl -eis) adj ungovernable.
ingratidão [ĩgratʒi'dãw] f ingratitude.
ingrato/a [ĩ'gratu/a] adj ungrateful.
ingrediente [ĩgre'dʒjẽtʃi] m ingredient.
íngreme ['ĩgremi] adj steep.
ingressar [ĩgre'sa*] vi: ~ em to enter, go into; (um clube) to join.
ingresso [ĩ'gresu] m (entrada) entry; (admissão) admission; (bilhete) ticket.
inhaca [i'ɲaka] (col) f (fedor) stink.
inhame [i'ɲami] m yam.
inibição [inibi'sãw] (pl -ões) f inhibition.
inibido/a [ini'bidu/a] adj inhibited.
inibidor(a) [inibi'do*(a)] adj inhibiting.
inibir [ini'bi*] vt: ~ alguém (de fazer) to inhibit sb (from doing); ~-se vr: ~-se (de fazer) to be inhibited (from doing).
iniciação [inisja'sãw] (pl -ões) f initiation.
iniciado/a [ini'sjadu/a] m/f initiate.
iniciador(a) [inisja'do*(a)] adj initiating ♦ m/f initiator.
inicial [ini'sjaw] (pl -ais) adj initial, first ♦ f initial.
inicializar [inisjali'za*] vt (COMPUT) to initialize.
iniciar [ini'sja*] vt, vi (começar) to begin, start; ~ alguém em algo (arte, seita) to initiate sb into sth.
iniciativa [inisja'tʃiva] f initiative; tomar a ~ to take the initiative; por ~ própria on one's own initiative, off one's own bat (BRIT); ~ privada (ECON) private enterprise; não ter ~ to lack initiative.
início [i'nisju] m beginning, start; no ~ at the start.
inigualável [inigwa'lavew] (pl -eis) adj unequalled.
inimaginável [inimaʒi'navew] (pl -eis) adj unimaginable.
inimigo/a [ini'migu/a] adj, m/f enemy.
inimizade [inimi'zadʒi] f enmity, hatred.

inimizar [inimi'za*] vt: ~ alguém com alguém to set sb against sb; ~-se vr: ~-se com to fall out with.
ininteligível [inĩteli'ʒivew] (pl -eis) adj unintelligible.
ininterrupto/a [inĩte'xuptu/a] adj continuous; (esforço) unstinting; (vôo) non-stop; (serviço) 24-hour.
iniqüidade [inikwi'dadʒi] f iniquity.
iníquo/a [i'nikwu/a] adj iniquitous.
injeção [inʒe'sãw] (PT: -cç-; pl -ões) f injection.
injetado/a [iʒe'tadu/a] (PT: -ct-) adj (olhos) bloodshot.
injetar [iʒe'ta*] (PT: -ct-) vt to inject.
injunção [iʒũ'sãw] (pl -ões) f (ordem) order; (pressão) pressure.
injúria [ĩ'ʒurja] f (insulto) insult.
injuriar [ĩʒu'rja*] vt to insult.
injurioso/a [ĩʒu'rjozu/ɔza] adj insulting; (ofensivo) offensive.
injustiça [ĩʒuʃ'tʃisa] f injustice.
injustiçado/a [ĩʒuʃtʃi'sadu/a] adj wronged ♦ m/f victim of injustice.
injustificável [ĩʒuʃtʃifi'kavew] (pl -eis) adj unjustifiable.
injusto/a [ĩ'ʒuʃtu/a] adj unfair, unjust.
INM (BR) abr m = Instituto Nacional de Meteorologia.
inobservado/a [inobizex'vadu/a] adj unobserved; (nunca visto) never witnessed.
inobservância [inobizex'vãsja] f nonobservance.
inobservante [inobizex'vãtʃi/a] adj inobservant.
inocência [ino'sẽsja] f innocence.
inocentar [inosẽ'ta*] vt: ~ alguém (de algo) to clear sb (of sth).
inocente [ino'sẽtʃi] adj innocent ♦ m/f innocent man/woman; os ~s the innocent.
inoculação [inokula'sãw] (pl -ões) f inoculation.
inocular [inoku'la*] vt to inoculate.
inócuo/a [i'nɔkwu/a] adj harmless.
inodoro/a [ino'dɔru/a] adj odourless (BRIT), odorless (US).
inofensivo/a [inofẽ'sivu/a] adj harmless, inoffensive.
inolvidável [inowvi'davew] (pl -eis) adj unforgettable.
inoperante [inope'rãtʃi] adj inoperative.
inopinado/a [inopi'nadu/a] adj unexpected.
inoportuno/a [inopox'tunu/a] adj inconvenient, inopportune.
inorgânico/a [inox'ganiku/a] adj inorganic.
inóspito/a [i'nɔʃpitu/a] adj inhospitable.
inovação [inova'sãw] (pl -ões) f innovation.
inovar [ino'va*] vt to innovate.
inoxidável [inoksi'davew] (pl -eis) adj: aço ~ stainless steel.
INPC (BR) abr m (= Índice Nacional de Pre-

---

*NB: European Portuguese adds the following consonants to certain words: **b** (sú(b)dito, su(b)til); **c** (a(c)ção, a(c)cionista, a(c)to); **m** (inde(m)ne); **p** (ado(p)ção, ado(p)tar); for further details see p. xiii.*

ços ao Consumidor) RPI.

INPS (*br*) *abr m* (= *Instituto Nacional de Previdência Social*) ≈ DSS (*BRIT*), ≈ Welfare Dept (*US*).

inqualificável [ĩkwalifi'kavew] (*pl* -**eis**) *adj* incalculable; (*vil*) unacceptable.

inquebrantável [ĩkebrã'tavew] (*pl* -**eis**) *adj* unbreakable; (*fig*) unshakeable.

inquestionável [ĩkeʃtʃjo'navew] (*pl* -**eis**) *adj* unquestionable.

inquérito [ĩ'kɛritu] *m* inquiry; (*JUR*) inquest.

inquietação [ĩkjeta'sãw] *f* (*preocupação*) anxiety, uneasiness; (*agitação*) restlessness.

inquietador(a) [ĩkjeta'do*(a)] *adj* worrying, disturbing.

inquietante [ĩkje'tãtʃi] *adj* worrying, disturbing.

inquietar [ĩkje'ta*] *vt* to worry, disturb; ~-**se** *vr* to worry, bother.

inquieto/a [ĩ'kjɛtu/a] *adj* (*ansioso*) anxious, worried; (*agitado*) restless.

inquietude [ĩkje'tudʒi] *f* (*preocupação*) anxiety, uneasiness; (*agitação*) restlessness.

inquilino/a [ĩki'linu/a] *m/f* tenant.

inquirição [ĩkiri'sãw] (*pl* -**ões**) *f* investigation; (*JUR*) cross-examination.

inquirir [ĩki'ri*] *vt* (*investigar*) to investigate; (*perguntar*) to question; (*JUR*) to cross-examine ♦ *vi* to enquire.

inquisição [ĩkizi'sãw] (*pl* -**ões**) *f*: **a I~** the Inquisition.

inquisitivo/a [ĩkizi'tʃivu/a] *adj* inquisitive.

insaciável [ĩsa'sjavew] (*pl* -**eis**) *adj* insatiable.

insalubre [ĩsa'lubri] *adj* unhealthy.

insanidade [ĩsani'dadʒi] *f* madness, insanity.

insano/a [ĩ'sanu/a] *adj* insane; (*fig*: *trabalho*) exhaustive.

insatisfação [ĩsatʃiʃfa'sãw] *f* dissatisfaction.

insatisfatório/a [ĩsatʃiʃfa'tɔrju/a] *adj* unsatisfactory.

insatisfeito/a [ĩsatʃiʃ'fejtu/a] *adj* dissatisfied, unhappy.

inscrever [ĩʃkre've*] *vt* (*gravar*) to inscribe; (*aluno*) to enrol (*BRIT*), enroll (*US*); (*em registro*) to register; ~-**se** *vr* to enrol(l); to register.

inscrição [ĩʃkri'sãw] (*pl* -**ões**) *f* (*legenda*) inscription; (*EDUC*) enrolment (*BRIT*), enrollment (*US*); (*em lista etc*) registration.

inscrito/a [ĩ'ʃkritu/a] *pp de* **inscrever**.

insecto *etc* [ĩ'sɛktu] (*PT*) = **inseto** *etc*.

insegurança [ĩsegu'rãsa] *f* insecurity.

inseguro/a [ĩse'guru/a] *adj* insecure.

inseminação [ĩsemina'sãw] *f*: ~ **artificial** artificial insemination.

inseminar [ĩsemi'na*] *vt* to inseminate.

insensatez [ĩsẽsa'teʒ] *f* folly, madness.

insensato/a [ĩsẽ'satu/a] *adj* unreasonable, foolish.

insensibilidade [ĩsẽsibili'dadʒi] *f* insensitivity; (*dormência*) numbness.

insensível [ĩsẽ'sivew] (*pl* -**eis**) *adj* insensitive; (*dormente*) numb.

inseparável [ĩsepa'ravew] (*pl* -**eis**) *adj* inseparable.

inserção [ĩsex'sãw] (*pl* -**ões**) *f* insertion; (*COMPUT*) entry.

inserir [ĩse'ri*] *vt* to insert, put in; (*COMPUT*: *dados*) to enter; ~-**se** *vr*: ~-**se em** to become part of.

inseticida [ĩsetʃi'sida] *m* insecticide.

inseto [ĩ'sɛtu] *m* insect.

insidioso/a [ĩsi'dʒjozu/ɔza] *adj* insidious.

insigne [ĩ'signi] *adj* distinguished, eminent.

insígnia [ĩ'signia] *f* (*sinal distintivo*) badge; (*emblema*) emblem.

insignificância [ĩsignifi'kãsja] *f* insignificance.

insignificante [ĩsignifi'kãtʃi] *adj* insignificant.

insinceridade [ĩsĩseri'dadʒi] *f* insincerity.

insincero/a [ĩsĩ'sɛru/a] *adj* insincere.

insinuação [ĩsinwa'sãw] (*pl* -**ões**) *f* insinuation; (*sugestão*) hint.

insinuante [ĩsi'nwãtʃi] *adj* ingratiating.

insinuar [ĩsi'nwa*] *vt* to insinuate, imply ♦ *vi* to make insinuations; ~-**se** *vr*: ~-**se por** *ou* **entre** to slip through; ~-**se na confiança de alguém** to worm one's way into sb's confidence.

insípido/a [ĩ'sipidu/a] *adj* insipid; (*fig*) dull.

insiro [ĩ'siru] *etc vb V* **inserir**.

insistência [ĩsiʃ'tẽsja] *f*: ~ (**em**) insistence (on); (*obstinação*) persistence (in).

insistente [ĩsiʃ'tẽtʃi] *adj* (*pessoa*) insistent; (*apelo*) urgent.

insistir [ĩsiʃ'tʃi*] *vi*: ~ (**em**) (*exigir*) to insist (on); (*perseverar*) to persist (in); ~ **por algo** to stand up for sth; ~ **sobre algo** to dwell on sth; ~ (**para**) **que alguém faça** to insist that sb do *ou* on sb doing; ~ (**em**) **que** to insist that.

insociável [ĩso'sjavew] (*pl* -**eis**) *adj* unsociable, antisocial.

insofismável [ĩsofiʒ'mavew] (*pl* -**eis**) *adj* simple.

insofrido/a [ĩso'fridu/a] *adj* impatient, restless.

insolação [ĩsola'sãw] *f* sunstroke; **pegar uma** ~ to get sunstroke.

insolência [ĩso'lẽsja] *f* insolence.

insolente [ĩso'lẽtʃi] *adj* insolent.

insólito/a [ĩ'sɔlitu/a] *adj* unusual.

insolúvel [ĩso'luvew] (*pl* -**eis**) *adj* insoluble.

insolvência [ĩsow'vẽsja] *f* insolvency.

insolvente [ĩsow'vẽtʃi] *adj* insolvent.

insondável [ĩsõ'davew] (*pl* -**eis**) *adj* unfathomable.

insone [ĩ'sɔni] *adj* (*pessoa*) insomniac; (*noite*) sleepless.

insônia [ĩ'sonja] *f* insomnia.

insosso/a [ĩ'sosu/a] *adj* unsalted; (*sem sabor*) tasteless; (*pessoa*) uninteresting, dull.

inspeção [ĩʃpe'sãw] (*PT*: -**çç**-; *pl* -**ões**) *f* inspection, check; (*departamento*) inspectorate.

inspecionar [ĩʃpesjo'na*] (*PT*: -**cc**-) *vt* to inspect.

inspeções [ĩʃpe'sõjʃ] *fpl de* **inspeção**.

inspetor(a) [iʃpe'to*(a)] (*PT*: -ct-) *m/f* inspector.

inspetoria [iʃpeto'ria] (*PT*: -ct-) *f* inspectorate.

inspiração [iʃpira'sãw] (*pl* -ões) *f* inspiration; (*nos pulmões*) inhalation.

inspirador(a) [iʃpira'do*(a)] *adj* inspiring.

inspirar [iʃpi'ra*] *vt* to inspire; (*MED*) to inhale; ~-**se** *vr* to be inspired; **ele não me inspira confiança** he does not inspire me with confidence.

instabilidade [iʃtabili'dadʒi] *f* instability.

instalação [iʃtala'sãw] (*pl* -ões) *f* installation; ~ **elétrica** electrics *pl*, electrical system; ~ **hidráulica** waterworks *sg*.

instalar [iʃta'la*] *vt* (*equipamento*) to install; (*estabelecer*) to set up; (*alojar*) to accommodate, put up; (*num cargo*) to place, install; ~-**se** *vr* (*numa cadeira*) to install o.s.; (*alojar-se*) to settle in; (*num cargo*) to take up office.

instância [iʃ'tãsja] *f* (*insistência*) persistence; (*súplica*) entreaty; (*legislativa*) authority; (*JUR*): **tribunal de primeira** ~ ≈ magistrate's court (*BRIT*), ≈ district court (*US*); **em última** ~ as a last resort.

instantâneo/a [iʃtã'tanju/a] *adj* instant, instantaneous; (*café*) instant ♦ *m* (*FOTO*) snapshot.

instante [iʃ'tãtʃi] *m* moment ♦ *adj* urgent; **nesse** ~ just a moment ago; **num** ~ in an instant, quickly; **a cada** ~ (at) any moment; **só um** ~! just a moment!

instar [iʃ'ta*] *vt* to urge ♦ *vi* to insist; ~ **com alguém para que faça algo** to urge sb to do sth.

instauração [iʃtawra'sãw] *f* establishment; (*de processo, inquérito*) institution.

instaurar [iʃtaw'ra*] *vt* to establish, set up; (*processo, inquérito*) to institute.

instável [iʃ'tavew] (*pl* -eis) *adj* unstable; (*tempo*) unsettled; (*mesa*) unsteady.

instigação [iʃtʃiga'sãw] *f* instigation; **por** ~ **de alguém** at sb's instigation.

instigar [iʃtʃi'ga*] *vt* (*incitar*) to urge; (*provocar*) to provoke; ~ **alguém contra alguém** to set sb against sb.

instilar [iʃtʃi'la*] *vt*: ~ **algo em algo** (*veneno*) to inject sth into sth; ~ **algo em alguém** (*fig*: *ódio etc*) to instil (*BRIT*) *ou* instill (*US*) sth in sb.

instintivo/a [iʃtʃĩ'tʃivu/a] *adj* instinctive.

instinto [iʃ'tʃĩtu] *m* instinct; **por** ~ instinctively; ~ **de conservação** survival instinct.

institucional [iʃtʃitusjo'naw] (*pl* -ais) *adj* institutional.

instituição [iʃtʃitwi'sãw] (*pl* -ões) *f* institution.

instituir [iʃtʃi'twi*] *vt* to institute; (*fundar*) to establish, found; (*prazo*) to set.

instituto [iʃtʃi'tutu] *m* (*escola*) institute; (*instituição*) institution; ~ **de beleza** beauty salon; **I~ de Pesos e Medidas** ≈ British Standards Institution.

instrução [iʃtru'sãw] (*PT*: -cç-; *pl* -ões) *f* education; (*erudição*) learning; (*diretriz*) instruction; (*MIL*) training; **instruções** *fpl* (*para o uso*) instructions (for use); **manual de instruções** instruction manual.

instructor(a) [iʃtru'to*(a)] (*PT*) *m/f* = **instrutor(a)**.

instruído/a [iʃ'trwidu/a] *adj* educated.

instruir [iʃ'trwi*] *vt* to instruct; (*MIL*) to train; (*JUR*: *processo*) to prepare; ~-**se** *vr*: ~-**se em algo** to learn sth; ~ **alguém de** *ou* **sobre algo** to inform sb about sth.

instrumentação [iʃtrumẽta'sãw] *f* (*MÚS*) instrumentation.

instrumental [iʃtrumẽ'taw] (*pl* -ais) *adj* instrumental ♦ *m* instruments *pl*.

instrumentar [iʃtrumẽ'ta*] *vt* (*MÚS*) to score.

instrumentista [iʃtrumẽ'tʃiʃta] *m/f* instrumentalist.

instrumento [iʃtru'mẽtu] *m* instrument; (*ferramenta*) implement; (*JUR*) deed, document; ~ **de cordas/percussão/sopro** stringed/percussion/wind instrument; ~ **de trabalho** tool.

instrutivo/a [iʃtru'tʃivu/a] *adj* instructive.

instrutor(a) [iʃtru'to*(a)] *m/f* instructor; (*ESPORTE*) coach.

insubordinação [isuboxdʒina'sãw] *f* rebellion; (*MIL*) insubordination.

insubordinado/a [isuboxdʒi'nadu/a] *adj* unruly; (*MIL*) insubordinate.

insubordinar-se [isuboxdʒi'naxsi] *vr* to rebel; (*NÁUT*) to mutiny.

insubstituível [isubiʃtʃi'twivew] (*pl* -eis) *adj* irreplaceable.

insucesso [isu'sesu] *m* failure.

insuficiência [isufi'sjẽsja] *f* inadequacy; (*carência*) shortage; (*MED*) deficiency; ~ **cardíaca** heart failure.

insuficiente [isufi'sjẽtʃi] *adj* (*não bastante*) insufficient; (*EDUC*: *nota*) ≈ fail; (*pessoa*) incompetent.

insuflar [isu'fla*] *vt* to blow up, inflate; (*ar*) to blow; (*fig*): ~ **algo (em** *ou* **a alguém)** to instil (*BRIT*) *ou* instill (*US*) sth (in sb).

insular [isu'la*] *vt* (*TEC*) to insulate ♦ *adj* insular.

insulina [isu'lina] *f* insulin.

insultar [isuw'ta*] *vt* to insult.

insulto [i'suwtu] *m* insult.

insultuoso/a [isuw'twozu/ɔza] *adj* insulting.

insumo [i'sumu] *m* raw materials *pl*; (*ECON*) input.

insuperável [isupe'ravew] (*pl* -eis) *adj* (*dificuldade*) insuperable; (*qualidade*) unsurpassable.

insuportável [isupox'tavew] (*pl* -eis) *adj* unbearable.

NB: European Portuguese adds the following consonants to certain words: **b** (sú(b)dito, su(b)til); **c** (a(c)ção, a(c)cionista, a(c)to); **m** (inde(m)ne); **p** (ado(p)ção, ado(p)tar); *for further details see p. xiii.*

insurgente [ĩsux'ʒẽtʃi] *adj* rebellious ♦ *m/f* rebel.

insurgir-se [ĩsux'ʒixsi] *vr* to rebel, revolt.

insurreição [ĩsuxej'sãw] (*pl* **-ões**) *f* rebellion, insurrection.

insurreto/a [ĩsu'xɛtu/a] *adj* rebellious ♦ *m/f* insurgent.

insuspeito/a [ĩsuʃ'pejtu/a] *adj* unsuspected; (*imparcial*) impartial.

insustentável [ĩsuʃtẽ'tavew] (*pl* **-eis**) *adj* untenable.

intacto/a [ĩ'tatu/a] (*PT*) *adj* = **intato/a**.

intangível [ĩtã'ʒivew] (*pl* **-eis**) *adj* intangible.

intato/a [ĩ'tatu/a] *adj* intact; (*ileso*) unharmed; (*fig*) pure.

íntegra ['ĩtegra] *f* full text; **na** ~ in full.

integração [ĩtegra'sãw] *f* integration.

integral [ĩte'graw] (*pl* **-ais**) *adj* whole ♦ *f* (*MAT*) integral; **arroz** ~ brown rice; **pão** ~ wholemeal (*BRIT*) *ou* wholewheat (*US*) bread.

integralismo [ĩtegra'liʒmu] *m Brazilian fascism*.

integralmente [ĩtegraw'mẽtʃi] *adv* in full, fully.

integrante [ĩte'grãtʃi] *adj* integral ♦ *m/f* member.

integrar [ĩte'gra*] *vt* to unite, combine; (*completar*) to form, make up; (*MAT*, *raças*) to integrate; **~-se** *vr* to become complete; **~-se em** *ou* **a algo** (*juntar-se*) to join sth; (*adaptar-se*) to integrate into sth.

integridade [ĩtegri'dadʒi] *f* (*totalidade*) entirety; (*fig*: *de pessoa*) integrity.

íntegro/a ['ĩtegru/a] *adj* entire; (*honesto*) upright, honest.

inteiramente [ĩtejra'mẽtʃi] *adv* completely.

inteirar [ĩtej'ra*] *vt* (*completar*) to complete; **~-se** *vr*: **~-se de** to find out about; ~ **alguém de** to inform sb of.

inteireza [ĩtej'reza] *f* entirety; (*moral*) integrity.

inteiriçado/a [ĩtejri'sadu/a] *adj* stiff.

inteiriço/a [ĩtej'risu/a] *adj* (*pedaço de pano*) single; (*vestido*) one-piece.

inteiro/a [ĩ'tejru/a] *adj* (*todo*) whole, entire; (*ileso*) unharmed; (*não quebrado*) undamaged; (*completo*, *ilimitado*) complete; (*vestido*) one-piece; (*fig*: *caráter*) upright.

intelecto [ĩte'lɛktu] *m* intellect.

intelectual [ĩtelek'twaw] (*pl* **-ais**) *adj*, *m/f* intellectual.

intelectualidade [ĩtelektwali'dadʒi] *f* (*qualidade*) intellect; (*pessoas*) intellectuals *pl*.

inteligência [ĩteli'ʒẽsja] *f* intelligence; (*interpretação*) interpretation; (*pessoa*) intellect, thinker; ~ **artificial** artificial intelligence.

inteligente [ĩteli'ʒẽtʃi] *adj* (*pessoa*) intelligent, clever; (*decisão*, *romance*, *filme etc*) clever.

inteligível [ĩteli'ʒivew] (*pl* **-eis**) *adj* intelligible.

intempérie [ĩtẽ'pɛri] *f* bad weather.

intempestivo/a [ĩtẽpeʃ'tʃivu/a] *adj* ill-timed.

intenção [ĩtẽ'sãw] (*pl* **-ões**) *f* intention; **segundas intenções** ulterior motives; **ter a** ~

de to intend to; **com boa** ~ with good intent; **com má** ~ maliciously; (*JUR*) with malice aforethought.

intencionado/a [ĩtẽsjo'nadu/a] *adj*: **bem** ~ well-meaning; **mal** ~ ill-intentioned.

intencional [ĩtẽsjo'naw] (*pl* **-ais**) *adj* intentional, deliberate.

intencionar [ĩtẽsjo'na*] *vt*: ~ **fazer** to intend to do.

intenções [ĩtẽ'sõjʃ] *fpl de* **intenção**.

intendência [ĩtẽ'dẽsja] (*PT*) *f* management, administration.

intendente [ĩtẽ'dẽtʃi] *m/f* manager; (*MIL*) quartermaster.

intensidade [ĩtẽsi'dadʒi] *f* intensity.

intensificação [ĩtẽsifika'sãw] *f* intensification.

intensificar [ĩtẽsifi'ka*] *vt* to intensify; **~-se** *vr* to intensify.

intensivo/a [ĩtẽ'sivu/a] *adj* intensive.

intenso/a [ĩ'tẽsu/a] *adj* intense; (*emoção*) deep; (*impressão*) vivid; (*trabalho*) intensive; (*vida social*) full.

intentar [ĩtẽ'ta*] *vt* (*obra*) to plan; (*assalto*) to commit; (*tentar*) to attempt; ~ **fazer** to intend to do; ~ **uma ação contra** (*JUR*) to sue.

intento [ĩ'tẽtu] *m* aim, purpose.

intentona [ĩtẽ'tona] *f* (*POL*) plot, conspiracy.

interação [ĩtera'sãw] (*PT*: **-cç-**) *f* interaction.

interagir [ĩtera'ʒi*] *vi*: ~ (**com**) to interact (with).

interamericano/a [ĩter-] *adj* inter-American.

interativo/a [ĩtera'tʃivu/a] *adj* (*COMPUT*) interactive.

intercalar [ĩtexka'la*] *vt* to insert; (*COMPUT*: *arquivos*) to merge.

intercâmbio [ĩtex'kãbju] *m* exchange.

interceder [ĩtexse'de*] *vi*: ~ **por** to intercede on behalf of.

interceptar [ĩtexsep'ta*] *vt* to intercept; (*fazer parar*) to stop; (*ligação telefônica*) to cut off; (*ser obstáculo a*) to hinder.

intercessão [ĩtexse'sãw] (*pl* **-ões**) *f* intercession.

interconexão [ĩtexkonek'sãw] (*pl* **-ões**) *f* interconnection.

intercontinental [ĩtexkõtʃinẽ'taw] (*pl* **-ais**) *adj* intercontinental.

intercostal [ĩtexkoʃ'taw] (*pl* **-ais**) *adj* (*MED*) intercostal.

interdependência [ĩtexdepẽ'dẽsja] *f* interdependence.

interdição [ĩtexdʒi'sãw] (*pl* **-ões**) *f* (*de estrada*, *porta*) closure; (*JUR*) injunction; ~ **de direitos civis** removal of civil rights.

interdisciplinar [ĩtexdʒisipli'na*] *adj* interdisciplinary.

interditado/a [ĩtexdʒi'tadu/a] *adj* closed, sealed off.

interditar [ĩtexdʒi'ta*] *vt* (*importação etc*) to ban; (*estrada*, *praia*) to close off; (*cinema etc*) to close down; (*JUR*) to interdict.

interdito/a [ĩtex'dʒitu/a] *adj* (*JUR*) interdicted

◆ *m* (*JUR*: *interdição*) injunction.

interessado/a [ītere'sadu/a] *adj* interested; (*amizade*) based on self-interest ◆ *m/f* interested party.

interessante [ītere'sātʃi] *adj* interesting; **estar em estado** ~ to be expecting *ou* pregnant.

interessar [ītere'sa*] *vt* to interest, be of interest to ◆ *vi* to be interesting; ~**-se** *vr*: ~**-se em** *ou* **por** to take an interest in, be interested in; **a quem possa** ~ to whom it may concern.

interesse [īte'resi] *m* interest; (*próprio*) self-interest; (*proveito*) advantage; **no** ~ **de** for the sake of; **por** ~ (**próprio**) for one's own ends.

interesseiro/a [ītere'sejru/a] *adj* self-seeking.

interestadual [ītereʃta'dwaw] (*pl* **-ais**) *adj* interstate.

interface [ītex'fasi] *f* (*COMPUT*) interface.

interferência [ītexfe'rēsja] *f* interference.

interferir [ītexfe'ri*] *vi*: ~ **em** to interfere in; (*rádio*) to jam.

interfone [ītex'fɔni] *m* intercom.

ínterim ['ĩterĩ] *m* interim; **nesse** ~ in the meantime.

interino/a [īte'rinu/a] *adj* temporary, interim.

interior [īte'rjo*] *adj* inner, inside; (*vida*) inner; (*COM*) domestic, internal ◆ *m* inside, interior; (*coração*) heart; (*do país*): **no** ~ inland, in the country; **Ministério do I**~ Home Office (*BRIT*), Department of the Interior (*US*); **Ministro do I**~ Home Secretary (*BRIT*), Secretary of the Interior (*US*); **na parte** ~ inside.

interiorizar [īterjori'za*] *vt* to internalize.

interjeição [ītexʒej'sãw] (*pl* **-ões**) *f* interjection.

interligar [ītexli'ga*] *vt* to interconnect; ~**-se** *vr* to be interconnected.

interlocutor(a) [ītexloku'to*(a)] *m/f* speaker; **meu** ~ the person I was speaking to.

interlúdio [ītex'ludʒu] *m* interlude.

intermediário/a [ītexme'dʒjarju/a] *adj* intermediary ◆ *m/f* (*COM*) middleman; (*mediador*) intermediary, mediator.

intermédio [ītex'mɛdʒu] *m*: **por** ~ **de** through.

interministerial [ītexminiʃte'rjaw] (*pl* **-ais**) *adj* interministerial.

interminável [ītexmi'navew] (*pl* **-eis**) *adj* endless.

intermissão [ītexmi'sãw] (*pl* **-ões**) *f* interval.

intermitente [ītexmi'tētʃi] *adj* intermittent.

internação [ītexna'sãw] (*pl* **-ões**) *f* internment; (*de aluno*) sending to boarding school.

internacional [ītexnasjo'naw] (*pl* **-ais**) *adj* international.

internacionalismo [ītexnasjona'liʒmu] *m* internationalism.

internacionalizar [ītexnasjonali'za*] *vt* to internationalize; ~**-se** *vr* to become international.

internações [ītexna'sõjʃ] *fpl de* **internação**.

internar [ītex'na*] *vt* (*aluno*) to put into boarding school; (*doente*) to take into hospital; (*MIL*, *POL*) to intern.

internato [ītex'natu] *m* boarding school.

interno/a [ī'tɛxnu/a] *adj* internal, interior; (*do país*) internal, domestic; (*aluno*) boarding ◆ *m/f* (*aluno*) boarder; (*MED*: *estudante*) houseman (*BRIT*), intern (*US*); **de uso** ~ (*MED*) for internal use.

interpelação [ītexpela'sãw] (*pl* **-ões**) *f* questioning; (*JUR*) summons *sg*.

interpelar [ītexpe'la*] *vt*: ~ **alguém sobre algo** to question sb about sth; (*pedir explicações*) to challenge sb about sth.

interplanetário/a [ītexplane'tarju/a] *adj* interplanetary.

interpõe [ītex'põj] *etc vb V* **interpor**.

interpolar [ītexpo'la*] *vt* to interpolate.

interpor [ītex'po*] (*irreg: como* **pôr**) *vt* to put in, interpose; ~**-se** *vr* to intervene; ~**-se a algo** (*contrapor-se*) to militate against sth; ~ **A** (**a B**) (*argumentos etc*) to counter (B) with A.

interposto/a [ītex'poʃtu/'pɔʃta] *pp de* **interpor**.

interpretação [ītexpreta'sãw] (*pl* **-ões**) *f* interpretation; (*TEATRO*) performance; **má** ~ misinterpretation.

interpretar [ītexpre'ta*] *vt* to interpret; (*um papel*) to play; ~ **mal** to misinterpret.

intérprete [ī'tɛxpretʃi] *m/f* (*LING*) interpreter; (*TEATRO*) performer, artist.

interpunha [ītex'puɲa] *etc vb V* **interpor**.

interpus [ītex'puʃ] *etc vb V* **interpor**.

interpuser [ītexpu'ze*] *etc vb V* **interpor**.

inter-racial [ītex-] (*pl* **-ais**) *adj* interracial.

interrogação [ītexoga'sãw] (*pl* **-ões**) *f* questioning, interrogation; **ponto de** ~ question mark.

interrogador(a) [ītexoga'do*(a)] *m/f* interrogator.

interrogar [ītexo'ga*] *vt* to question, interrogate; (*JUR*) to cross-examine.

interrogativo/a [ītexoga'tʃivu/a] *adj* interrogative.

interrogatório [ītexoga'tɔrju] *m* cross-examination.

interromper [ītexõ'pe*] *vt* to interrupt; (*parar*) to stop; (*ELET*) to cut off.

interrupção [ītexup'sãw] (*pl* **-ões**) *f* interruption; (*intervalo*) break.

interruptor [ītexup'to*] *m* (*ELET*) switch.

interseção [ītexse'sãw] (*PT*: **-cç-**; *pl* **-ões**) *f* intersection.

interstício [ītexʃ'tʃisju] *m* gap.

interurbano/a [īterux'banu/a] *adj* (*TEL*) long-distance ◆ *m* long-distance *ou* trunk call.

---

*NB: European Portuguese adds the following consonants to certain words: **b** (sú(b)dito, su(b)til); **c** (a(c)ção, a(c)cionista, a(c)to); **m** (inde(m)ne); **p** (ado(p)ção, ado(p)tar); for further details see p. xiii.*

intervalado/a [ĩtexva'ladu/a] *adj* spaced out.
intervalo [ĩtex'valu] *m* interval; *(descanso)* break; **a ~s** every now and then.
interveio [ĩtex'veju] *etc vb* V **intervir**.
intervenção [ĩtexvẽ'sãw] *(pl -ões)* f intervention; **~ cirúrgica** *(MED)* operation.
interventor(a) [ĩtexvẽ'to*(a)] *m/f* inspector; *(POL)* caretaker governor.
intervir [ĩtex'vi*] *(irreg: como* **vir)** *vi* to intervene; *(sobrevir)* to come up.
intestinal [ĩteʃtʃi'naw] *(pl -ais) adj* intestinal.
intestino [ĩteʃ'tʃinu] *m* intestine; **~ delgado/ grosso** small/large intestine; **~ solto** loose bowels *pl*, diarrhoea *(BRIT)*, diarrhea *(US)*.
inti [ĩ'tʃi] *m* inti *(Peruvian currency)*.
intimação [ĩtʃima'sãw] *(pl -ões)* f *(ordem)* order; *(JUR)* summons.
intimar [ĩtʃi'ma*] *vt* *(JUR)* to summon; **~ alguém a fazer** *ou* **a alguém que faça** to order sb to do.
intimidação [ĩtʃimida'sãw] f intimidation.
intimidade [ĩtʃimi'dadʒi] f intimacy; *(vida privada)* private life; *(familiaridade)* familiarity; **ter ~ com alguém** to be close to sb; **ela é pessoa de minha ~** she's a close friend of mine.
intimidar [ĩtʃimi'da*] *vt* to intimidate; **~-se** *vr* to be intimidated.
íntimo/a ['ĩtʃimu/a] *adj* intimate; *(senti-mentos)* innermost; *(amigo)* close; *(vida)* private ♦ *m/f* close friend; **no ~** at heart; **festa íntima** small gathering.
intitular [ĩtʃitu'la*] *vt* *(livro)* to title; **~-se** *vr* to be called; *(livro)* to be entitled; *(a si mesmo)* to call oneself; **~ algo de algo** to call sth sth.
intocável [ĩto'kavew] *(pl -eis) adj* untouchable.
intolerância [ĩtole'rásja] f intolerance.
intolerante [ĩtole'rãtʃi] *adj* intolerant.
intolerável [ĩtole'ravew] *(pl -eis) adj* intolerable, unbearable.
intoxicação [ĩtoksika'sãw] f poisoning; **~ alimentar** food poisoning.
intoxicar [ĩtoksi'ka*] *vt* to poison.
intraduzível [ĩtradu'zivew] *(pl -eis) adj* untranslateable.
intragável [ĩtra'gavew] *(pl -eis) adj* unpalatable; *(pessoa)* unbearable.
intranqüilidade [ĩtrãkwili'dadʒi] f disquiet.
intranqüilo/a [ĩtrã'kwilu/a] *adj* *(aflito)* worried; *(desassossegado)* restless.
intransferível [ĩtrãʃfe'rivew] *(pl -eis) adj* non-transferable.
intransigência [ĩtrãsi'ʒẽsja] f intransigence.
intransigente [ĩtrãsi'ʒẽtʃi] *adj* uncompromising; *(fig: rígido)* strict.
intransitável [ĩtrãsi'tavew] *(pl -eis) adj* impassable.
intransitivo/a [ĩtrãsi'tʃivu/a] *adj* intransitive.
intransponível [ĩtrãʃpo'nivew] *(pl -eis) adj* *(rio)* impossible to cross; *(problema)* insurmountable.
intratável [ĩtra'tavew] *(pl -eis) adj* *(pessoa)*

contrary, awkward; *(doença)* untreatable; *(problema)* insurmountable.
intra-uterino/a ['ĩtra-] *adj:* **dispositivo ~** intra-uterine device.
intravenoso/a [ĩtrave'nozu/ɔza] *adj* intravenous.
intrepidez [ĩtrepi'deʒ] f courage, bravery.
intrépido/a [ĩ'trepidu/a] *adj* daring, intrepid.
intriga [ĩ'triga] f intrigue; *(enredo)* plot; *(fofoca)* piece of gossip; **~ amorosa** *(PT)* love affair; **~s** *(fofocas)* gossip *sg*.
intrigante [ĩtri'gãtʃi] *m/f* troublemaker ♦ *adj* intriguing.
intrigar [ĩtri'ga*] *vt* to intrigue ♦ *vi* to be intriguing.
intrincado/a [ĩtrĩ'kadu/a] *adj* intricate.
intrínseco/a [ĩ'trĩseku/a] *adj* intrinsic.
introdução [ĩtrodu'sãw] *(pl -ões)* f introduction.
introdutório/a [ĩtrodu'tɔrju/a] *adj* introductory.
introduzir [ĩtrodu'zi*] *vt* to introduce; *(prego)* to insert.
intróito [ĩ'trɔjtu] *m* beginning; *(REL)* introit.
intrometer-se [ĩtrome'texsi] *vr* to interfere, meddle.
intrometido/a [ĩtrome'tʃidu/a] *adj* interfering; *(col)* nosey ♦ *m/f* busybody.
intromissão [ĩtromi'sãw] *(pl -ões)* f interference, meddling.
introspecção [ĩtroʃpek'sãw] f introspection.
introspectivo/a [ĩtroʃpek'tʃivu/a] *adj* introspective.
introversão [ĩtrovex'sãw] f introversion.
introvertido/a [ĩtrovex'tʃidu/a] *adj* introverted ♦ *m/f* introvert.
intrujão/jona [ĩtru'ʒãw/'ʒona] *(pl -ões/~s)* *m/ f* swindler.
intrujar [ĩtru'ʒa*] *vt* to trick, swindle.
intrujões [ĩtru'ʒõjʃ] *mpl de* **intrujão**.
intrujona [ĩtru'ʒona] *f de* **intrujão**.
intruso/a [ĩ'truzu/a] *m/f* intruder.
intuição [ĩtwi'sãw] *(pl -ões)* f intuition; *(pressentimento)* feeling; **por ~** by intuition, intuitively.
intuir [ĩ'twi*] *vt, vi* to intuit.
intuitivo/a [ĩtwi'tʃivu/a] *adj* intuitive.
intuito [ĩ'tuito] *m* *(intento)* intention; *(fim)* aim, purpose.
intumescência [ĩtume'sẽsja] f swelling.
intumescer-se [ĩtume'sexsi] *vr* to swell (up).
intumescido/a [ĩtume'sidu/a] *adj* swollen.
inumano/a [inu'manu/a] *adj* inhuman.
inumerável [inume'ravew] *(pl -eis) adj* countless, innumerable.
inúmero/a [i'numeru/a] *adj* countless, innumerable.
inundação [inũda'sãw] *(pl -ões)* f *(enchente)* flood; *(ato)* flooding.
inundar [inũ'da*] *vt* to flood; *(fig)* to inundate ♦ *vi* *(rio)* to flood.
inusitado/a [inuzi'tadu/a] *adj* unusual.
inútil [i'nutʃiw] *(pl -eis) adj* useless; *(esforço)*

futile; *(desnecessário)* pointless ◆ *m/f* good-for-nothing; **ser** ~ to be of no use, be no good.

inutilidade [inutʃili'dadʒi] *f* uselessness.

inutilizar [inutʃili'za*] *vt* to make useless, render useless; *(incapacitar)* to put out of action; *(danificar)* to ruin; *(esforços)* to thwart; ~**-se** *vr (pessoa)* to become incapacitated.

inutilizável [inutʃili'zavew] *(pl -eis) adj* unusable.

inutilmente [inutʃiw'mẽtʃi] *adv* in vain.

invadir [ĩva'dʒi*] *vt* to invade; *(suj: água)* to overrun; (: *sentimento)* to overtake.

invalidação [ĩvalida'sãw] *f* invalidation.

invalidar [ĩvali'da*] *vt* to invalidate; *(pessoa)* to make an invalid.

invalidez [ĩvali'deʒ] *f* disability.

inválido/a [ĩ'validu/a] *adj, m/f* invalid; ~ **de guerra** wounded war veteran.

invariável [ĩva'rjavew] *(pl -eis) adj* invariable.

invasão [ĩva'zãw] *(pl -ões) f* invasion.

invasor(a) [ĩva'zo*(a)] *adj* invading ◆ *m/f* invader.

inveja [ĩ'vɛʒa] *f* envy.

invejar [ĩve'ʒa*] *vt* to envy; *(cobiçar: bens)* to covet ◆ *vi* to be envious.

invejável [ĩve'ʒavew] *(pl -eis) adj* enviable.

invejoso/a [ĩve'ʒozu/ɔza] *adj* envious ◆ *m/f* envious person.

invenção [ĩvẽ'sãw] *(pl -ões) f* invention.

invencível [ĩvẽ'sivew] *(pl -eis) adj* invincible.

invenções [ĩvẽ'sõjʃ] *fpl de* **invenção.**

inventar [ĩvẽ'ta*] *vt* to invent; *(história, desculpa)* to make up; *(nome)* to think up ◆ *vi* to make things up; ~ **de fazer** to take it into one's head to do.

inventariação [ĩvẽtarja'sãw] *(pl -ões) f (COM)* stocktaking.

inventariar [ĩvẽta'rja*] *vt*: ~ **algo** to make an inventory of sth.

inventário [ĩvẽ'tarju] *m* inventory.

inventiva [ĩvẽ'tʃiva] *f* inventiveness.

inventivo/a [ĩvẽ'tʃivu/a] *adj* inventive.

inventor(a) [ĩvẽ'to*(a)] *m/f* inventor.

inverdade [ĩvex'dadʒi] *f* untruth.

inverificável [ĩverifi'kavew] *(pl -eis) adj* impossible to verify.

invernada [ĩvex'nada] *f* winter pasture.

invernar [ĩvex'na*] *vi* to spend the winter.

inverno [ĩ'vɛxnu] *m* winter.

inverossímil [ĩvero'simiw] *(PT:* **-osí-**; *pl* **-eis)** *adj (improvável)* unlikely, improbable; *(inacreditável)* implausible.

inversão [ĩvex'sãw] *(pl -ões) f* reversal, inversion.

inverso/a [ĩ'vɛxsu/a] *adj* inverse; *(oposto)* opposite; *(ordem)* reverse ◆ *m* opposite, reverse; **ao** ~ **de** contrary to.

inversões [ĩvex'sõjʃ] *fpl de* **inversão.**

invertebrado/a [ĩvexte'bradu/a] *adj* invertebrate ◆ *m* invertebrate.

inverter [ĩvex'te*] *vt (mudar)* to alter; *(ordem)* to invert, reverse; *(colocar às avessas)* to turn upside down, invert; ~ **a marcha** *(AUTO)* to reverse.

invés [ĩ'vɛʃ] *m*: **ao** ~ **de** instead of.

investida [ĩveʃ'tʃida] *f* attack; *(tentativa)* attempt.

investidura [ĩveʃtʃi'dura] *f* investiture.

investigação [ĩveʃtʃiga'sãw] *(pl -ões) f* investigation; *(pesquisa)* research.

investigar [ĩveʃtʃi'ga*] *vt* to investigate; *(examinar)* to examine; *(pesquisar)* to research into.

investimento [ĩveʃtʃi'mẽtu] *m* investment.

investir [ĩveʃ'tʃi*] *vt (dinheiro)* to invest ◆ *vi* to invest; ~ **contra** *ou* **para alguém** *(atacar)* to attack sb; ~ **alguém no cargo de presidente** to install sb in the presidency; ~ **para algo** *(atirar-se)* to rush towards sth.

inveterado/a [ĩvete'radu/a] *adj (mentiroso)* inveterate; *(criminoso)* hardened; *(hábito)* deep-rooted.

inviabilidade [ĩvjabili'dadʒi] *f* impracticality.

inviabilizar [ĩvjabili'za*] *vt*: ~ **algo** to make sth impracticable.

inviável [ĩ'vjavew] *(pl -eis) adj* impracticable.

invicto/a [ĩ'viktu/a] *adj* unconquered; *(invencível)* unbeatable.

inviolabilidade [ĩvjolabili'dadʒi] *f* inviolability; *(JUR)* immunity.

inviolável [ĩvjo'lavew] *(pl -eis) adj* inviolable; *(JUR)* immune.

invisível [ĩvi'zivew] *(pl -eis) adj* invisible.

invisto [ĩ'viʃtu] *etc vb V* **investir.**

invocado/a [ĩvo'kadu/a] *adj*: **estar/ficar** ~ **com alguém** to dislike/take a dislike to sb.

invocar [ĩvo'ka*] *vt* to invoke; *(col: irritar)* to provoke; (: *impressionar)* to have a profound effect on ◆ *vi*: ~ **com alguém** *(col: antipatizar)* to take a dislike to sb.

invólucro [ĩ'vɔlukru] *m (cobertura)* covering; *(envoltório)* wrapping; *(caixa)* box.

involuntário/a [ĩvolũ'tarju/a] *adj (movimento)* involuntary; *(ofensa)* unintentional.

invulnerável [ĩvuwne'ravew] *(pl -eis) adj* invulnerable.

iodo ['jodu] *m* iodine.

IOF *(BR) abr m* = **Imposto sobre Operações Financeiras.**

ioga ['jɔga] *f* yoga.

iogurte [jo'guxtʃi] *m* yogurt.

ioiô [jo'jo] *m* yoyo.

íon ['ĩõ] *(pl* ~**s)** *m* ion.

iônico/a ['joniku/a] *adj* ionic.

IPC *(BR) abr m* (= *Índice de Preços ao Consumidor)* RPI.

IPEA *(BR) abr m* = **Instituto de Planejamento Econômico Social.**

NB: European Portuguese adds the following consonants to certain words: **b** (sú(b)dito, su(b)til); **c** (a(c)ção, a(c)cionista, a(c)to); **m** (inde(m)ne); **p** (ado(p)ção, ado(p)tar); *for further details see p. xiii.*

ipecacuanha [ipɛka'kwaɲa] *f* ipecac.

IPI *(BR) abr m* = **Imposto sobre Produtos In-dustrializados.**

IPM *(BR) abr m* = **Inquérito Policial-Militar.**

IPT *(BR) abr m* = **Instituto de Pesquisas Tecnológicas.**

IPTU *(BR) abr m* (= *Imposto Predial e Terri-torial Urbano*) ≈ rates *pl (BRIT)*, ≈ property tax *(US)*.

IPVA *(BR) abr m* (= *Imposto Sobre Veículos Automóveis*) road *(BRIT) ou* motor-vehicle *(US)* tax.

IR *(BR) abr m* = **Imposto de Renda.**

ir [i*] *vi* to go; (+ *infin*): **vou fazer** I will do, I am going to do; (+ *gerúndio*): ~ **fazendo** to keep on doing; ~-**se** *vr* to go away, leave; **vamos!** let's go!; **vamos lá!** let's get started!; **já vou!** I'm coming!; ~ **bem** *(negócio)* to go well; *(pessoa: de saúde)* to be well; (: *na escola etc*) to get on well; ~ **a cavalo/a pé** to ride/walk; ~ **atrás de alguém** *(seguir)* to follow sb; *(confiar)* to take sb's word for it; ~ **com alguém** *(fig: simpatizar)* to like sb; **eu vou de cerveja** *(col)* I'll have a beer; **vamos nessa!** *(col: vamos embora)* let's go!; (: *vamos tentar*) let's go for it!; **já vai para dez anos que ele morreu** it's getting on for ten years since he died; **vai por mim** *(col)* take my word for it, believe you me; **vá lá!** go on!; **vá lá que seja** all right then; **vai daí que ela tem** ... that's why she has ...; **vamos que** ... *(suponhamos)* let's suppose (that) ...; **e vão 3** *(MAT)* carry 3; **lá se foram meus planos** that was the end of my plans.

IRA *abr m* (= *Irish Republican Army*) IRA.

ira ['ira] *f* anger, rage.

Irã [i'rã] *m*: **o** ~ Iran.

irado/a [i'radu/a] *adj* angry, irate.

iraniano/a [ira'njanu/a] *adj*, *m/f* Iranian.

Irão [i'rãw] *(PT) m* = **Irã.**

Iraque [i'raki] *m*: **o** ~ Iraq.

iraquiano/a [ira'kjanu/a] *adj*, *m/f* Iraqi.

irascibilidade [irasibili'dadʒi] *f* irritability.

irascível [ira'sivew] *(pl* -**eis)** *adj* irritable, short-tempered.

ir-e-vir *(pl* **ires-e-vires)** *m* coming and going.

íris ['irif] *f inv* iris.

Irlanda [ix'lãda] *f*: **a** ~ Ireland; **a** ~ **do Norte** Northern Ireland.

irlandês/esa [ixlã'deʃ/eza] *adj* Irish ♦ *m/f* Irishman/woman ♦ *m (LING)* Irish.

irmã [ix'mã] *f* sister ♦ *adj (empresa etc)* sister; **almas** ~**s** kindred souls; ~ **Paula** *(fig)* good Samaritan; ~ **gêmea/de criação** twin-/half-sister.

irmanar [ixma'na*] *vt* to join together, unite.

irmandade [ixmã'dadʒi] *f* brotherhood; *(con-fraternidade)* fraternity; *(associação)* broth-erhood.

irmão [ix'mãw] *(pl* ~**s)** *m* brother; *(fig: similar)* twin; *(col: companheiro)* mate; ~ **de criação** half-brother; ~ **gêmeo** twin

brother; ~**s siameses** Siamese twins.

ironia [iro'nia] *f* irony; *(sarcasmo)* sarcasm; **com** ~ ironically; *(com sarcasmo)* sarcastic-ally; **por** ~ **do destino** by a quirk of fate.

irônico/a [i'roniku/a] *adj* ironic(al); *(sar-cástico)* sarcastic.

ironizar [ironi'za*] *vt* to be ironic about ♦ *vi* to be ironic.

IRPF *(BR) abr m* (= *Imposto de Renda Pessoa Física)* personal income tax.

IRPJ *(BR) abr m* (= *Imposto de Renda Pessoa Jurídica)* corporation tax.

irra! ['ixa] *(PT) excl* damn!

irracional [ixasjo'naw] *(pl* -**ais)** *adj* irrational.

irracionalidade [ixasjonali'dadʒi] *f* irra-tionality.

irradiação [ixadʒja'sãw] *(pl* -**ões)** *f (de luz)* radiation; *(espalhamento)* spread; *(RÁDIO)* broadcasting; *(MED)* radiation treatment.

irradiar [ixa'dʒja*] *vt (luz)* to radiate; *(espalhar)* to spread; *(RÁDIO)* to broadcast, transmit; *(simpatia)* to radiate, exude ♦ *vi* to radiate; *(RÁDIO)* to be on the air; ~-**se** *vr* to spread; to be transmitted.

irreais [ixe'ajʃ] *adj pl de* **irreal.**

irreajustável [ixeaʒuʃ'tavew] *(pl* -**eis)** *adj* fixed.

irreal [ixe'aw] *(pl* -**ais)** *adj* unreal.

irrealizado/a [ixeali'zadu/a] *adj (pessoa)* un-fulfilled; *(sonhos)* unrealized.

irrealizável [ixeali'zavew] *(pl* -**eis)** *adj* un-realizable.

irreconciliável [ixekõsi'ljavew] *(pl* -**eis)** *adj* irreconcilable.

irreconhecível [ixekõɲe'sivew] *(pl* -**eis)** *adj* unrecognizable.

irrecorrível [ixeko'xivew] *(pl* -**eis)** *adj (JUR)* unappealable.

irrecuperável [ixekupe'ravew] *(pl* -**eis)** *adj* irretrievable.

irrecusável [ixeku'zavew] *(pl* -**eis)** *adj (in-contestável)* irrefutable; *(convite)* which cannot be turned down.

irrefletido/a [ixefle'tʃidu/a] *adj* rash; **de ma-neira irrefletida** rashly.

irrefreável [ixe'frjavew] *(pl* -**eis)** *adj* uncon-trollable.

irrefutável [ixefu'tavew] *(pl* -**eis)** *adj* irrefut-able.

irregular [ixegu'la*] *adj* irregular; *(vida)* un-conventional; *(feições)* unusual; *(aluno, gênio)* erratic.

irregularidade [ixegulari'dadʒi] *f* irregularity.

irrelevância [ixele'vãsja] *f* irrelevance.

irrelevante [ixele'vãtʃi] *adj* irrelevant.

irremediável [ixeme'dʒjavew] *(pl* -**eis)** *adj* irremediable; *(sem remédio)* incurable.

irreparável [ixepa'ravew] *(pl* -**eis)** *adj* irrepar-able.

irrepreensível [ixeprjẽ'sivew] *(pl* -**eis)** *adj* irreproachable, impeccable.

irreprimível [ixepri'mivew] *(pl* -**eis)** *adj* irrepressible.

irrequietação [ixekjeta'sãw] *f* restlessness.
irrequieto/a [ixe'kjɛtu/a] *adj* restless.
irresgatável [ixeʒga'tavew] *(pl -eis) adj (COM)* irredeemable.
irrevogável [ixevo'gavew] *(pl -eis) adj* irrevocable.
irresistível [ixeziʃ'tʃivew] *(pl -eis) adj* irresistible; *(desejo)* overwhelming.
irresoluto/a [ixezo'lutu/a] *adj (pessoa)* irresolute, indecisive; *(problema)* unresolved.
irresponsabilidade [ixeʃpõsabili'dadʒi] *f* irresponsibility.
irresponsável [ixeʃpõ'savew] *(pl -eis) adj* irresponsible.
irrestrito/a [ixeʃ'tritu/a] *adj* unrestricted.
irreverente [ixeve'rẽtʃi] *adj* irreverent.
irreversível [ixevex'sivew] *(pl -eis) adj* irreversible.
irrigação [ixiga'sãw] *f* irrigation.
irrigar [ixi'ga*] *vt* to irrigate.
irrisório/a [ixi'zɔrju/a] *adj* derisory, ludicrous; *(quantia)* derisory, paltry.
irritabilidade [ixitabili'dadʒi] *f* irritability.
irritação [ixita'sãw] *(pl -ões) f* irritation.
irritadiço/a [ixita'dʒisu/a] *adj* irritable.
irritante [ixi'tãtʃi] *adj* irritating, annoying.
irritar [ixi'ta*] *vt* to irritate, annoy; *(MED)* to irritate; ~**-se** *vr* to get angry, get annoyed.
irritável [ixi'tavew] *(pl -eis) adj* irritable.
irromper [ixõ'pe*] *vi*: ~ **(em)** to burst in(to); *(epidemia)* to break out; *(surgir)* to emerge; *(lágrimas)* to well; *(voz)* to be heard.
irrupção [ixup'sãw] *(pl -ões) f* invasion; *(de idéias)* emergence; *(de doença)* outbreak.
isca ['iʃka] *f (PESCA)* bait; *(fig)* lure, bait.
iscambau [iʃkã'baw] *(col) m:* **e o** ~ and what not.
isenção [izẽ'sãw] *(pl -ões) f* exemption; ~ **de impostos** tax exemption.
isentar [izẽ'ta*] *vt (dispensar)* to exempt; *(livrar)* to free.
isento/a [i'zẽtu/a] *adj (dispensado)* exempt; *(livre)* free; ~ **de taxas** duty-free; ~ **de impostos** tax-free.
Islã [iʒ'lã] *m* Islam.
islâmico/a [iʒ'lamiku/a] *adj* Islamic.
islamismo [iʒla'miʒmu] *m* Islam.
islamita [iʒla'mita] *adj, m/f* Muslim.
islandês/esa [iʒlã'deʃ/eza] *adj* Icelandic ♦ *m/f* Icelander ♦ *m (LING)* Icelandic.
Islândia [iʒ'lãdʒa] *f:* **a** ~ Iceland.
isolado/a [izo'ladu/a] *adj (separado)* isolated; *(solitário)* lonely; *(ELET)* insulated.
isolamento [izola'mẽtu] *m* isolation; *(MED)* isolation ward; *(ELET)* insulation; ~ **acústico** soundproofing.
isolante [izo'lãtʃi] *adj (ELET)* insulating.
isolar [izo'la*] *vt* to isolate; *(ELET)* to insulate ♦ *vi (afastar mau agouro)* to touch wood *(BRIT)*, knock on wood *(US)*; ~**-se** *vr* to

isolate o.s., cut o.s. off.
isonomia [izono'mia] *f* equality.
isopor [izo'po*] ® *m* polystyrene.
isqueiro [iʃ'kejru] *m* (cigarette) lighter.
Israel [iʒxa'ew] *m* Israel.
israelense [iʒxae'lẽsi] *adj, m/f* Israeli.
israelita [iʒxae'lita] *adj, m/f* Israelite.
ISS *(BR) abr m* = **Imposto Sobre Serviços**.
isso ['isu] *pron* that; *(col: isto)* this; ~ **mesmo** exactly; **por** ~ therefore, so; **por** ~ **mesmo** for that very reason; **só** ~**?** is that all?; ~**!** that's it!; **é** ~, **é** ~ **aí** *(col) (você tem razão)* that's right; *(é tudo)* that's it, that's all; **é** ~ **mesmo** exactly, that's right; **não seja por** ~ that's no big deal; **eu não tenho nada com** ~ it's got nothing to do with me; **que é** ~**?** *(exprime indignação)* what's going on?, what's all this?; ~ **de fazer** ... this business of doing ....
Istambul [iʃta'buw] *n* Istanbul.
istmo ['iʃtʃimu] *m* isthmus.
isto ['iʃtu] *pron* this; ~ **é** that is, namely.
ITA *(BR) abr m* = **Instituto Tecnológico da Aeronáutica**.
Itália [i'talja] *f:* **a** ~ Italy.
italiano/a [ita'ljanu/a] *adj, m/f* Italian ♦ *m (LING)* Italian.
itálico [i'taliku] *m* italics *pl*.
Itamarati [itamara'tʃi] *m:* **o** ~ the Brazilian Foreign Ministry.
item ['itẽ] *(pl -ns) m* item.
iterar [ite'ra*] *vt* to repeat.
itinerante [itʃine'rãtʃi] *adj, m/f* itinerant.
itinerário [itʃine'rarju] *m (plano)* itinerary; *(caminho)* route.
Iugoslávia [jugoʒ'lavja] *f:* **a** ~ Yugoslavia.
iugoslavo/a [jugoʒ'lavu/a] *adj, m/f* Yugoslav(ian).

J

J, j ['ʒɔta] *(pl js) m* J, j; **J de José** J for Jack *(BRIT) ou* Jig *(US)*.
já [ʒa] *adv* already; *(em perguntas)* yet; *(agora)* now; *(imediatamente)* right now, at once; *(agora mesmo)* right away ♦ *conj* on the other hand; **até** ~ bye; **desde** ~ from now on; **desde** ~ **lhe agradeço** thanking you in anticipation; **é para** ~ it won't be a minute; ~ **esteve na Inglaterra?** have you ever been to England?; ~ **não** no longer; **ele** ~ **não vem mais aqui** he doesn't come here any more; ~ **que** as, since; ~ **se vê** of

course; ~ **vou** I'm coming; ~ **até** even; ~,
~ **right away**; ~ **era** (col) it's been and
gone; **você** ~ **viu o filme?** — ~ have you
seen the film? — yes.
jabaculê [ʒabaku'le] (col) m backhander.
jabota [ʒa'bɔta] f giant tortoise.
jabuti [ʒabu'tʃi] m giant tortoise.
jabuticaba [ʒabutʃi'kaba] f jaboticaba (type of
berry).
jaca ['ʒaka] f jack fruit.
jacarandá [ʒakarã'da] m jacaranda.
jacaré [ʒaka'rɛ] m alligator; **fazer** ou **pegar** ~
to body-surf.
Jacarta [ʒa'kaxta] n Jakarta.
jacente [ʒa'sẽtʃi] adj lying; (herança) un-
claimed.
jacinto [ʒa'sĩtu] m hyacinth.
jactância [ʒak'tãsja] f boasting.
jactar-se [ʒak'taxsi] vr: ~ **de** to boast about.
jacto ['ʒaktu] (PT) m = **jato**.
jade ['ʒadʒi] m jade.
jaez [ʒa'eʒ] m harness; (fig: categoria) sort.
jaguar [ʒa'gwa*] m jaguar.
jaguatirica [ʒagwatʃi'rika] f leopard cat.
jagunço [ʒa'gũsu] m hired gun(man).
jaleco [ʒa'lɛku] m jacket.
jamais [ʒa'majʃ] adv never; (com palavra
negativa) ever; **ninguém** ~ **o tratou assim**
nobody ever treated him like that.
Jamaica [ʒa'majka] f: **a** ~ Jamaica.
jamaicano/a [ʒamaj'kanu/a] adj, m/f Jamaican.
jamanta [ʒa'mãta] f juggernaut (BRIT), truck-
trailer (US).
jamegão [ʒame'gãw] (pl **-ões**) (col) m
signature.
jan. abr = **janeiro**.
janeiro [ʒa'nejru] (PT: **J-**) m January; V tb julho.
janela [ʒa'nɛla] f window; **(~) basculante**
louvre (BRIT) ou louver (US) window.
janelão [ʒane'lãw] (pl **-ões**) m picture window.
jangada [ʒã'gada] f raft.
jangadeiro [ʒãga'dejru] m jangada fisherman.
janota [ʒa'nɔta] adj foppish ♦ m dandy.
janta ['ʒãta] (col) f dinner.
jantar [ʒã'ta*] m dinner ♦ vt to have for dinner
♦ vi to have dinner; ~ **americano** buffet
dinner; ~ **dançante** dinner dance.
jantarado [ʒãta'radu] m tea.
Japão [ʒa'pãw] m: **o** ~ Japan.
japona [ʒa'pɔna] f (casaco) three-quarter
length coat ♦ m/f (col) Japanese.
japonês/esa [ʒapo'neʃ/eza] adj, m/f Japanese
♦ m (LING) Japanese.
jaqueira [ʒa'kejra] f jack tree.
jaqueta [ʒa'keta] f jacket.
jaquetão [ʒake'tãw] (pl **-ões**) m double-
breasted coat.
jararaca [ʒara'raka] f (cobra) jararaca
(snake); (fig: mulher) shrew.
jarda ['ʒaxda] f yard.
jardim [ʒax'dʒĩ] (pl **-ns**) m garden; ~ **zoológi-**

co zoo.
jardim-de-infância (pl **jardins-de-infância**) m
kindergarten.
jardim-de-inverno (pl **jardins-de-inverno**) m
conservatory.
jardinagem [ʒaxdʒi'naʒẽ] f gardening.
jardinar [ʒaxdʒi'na*] vt to cultivate ♦ vi to
garden.
jardineira [ʒaxdʒi'nejra] f (móvel) flower-
stand; (caixa) trough; (ônibus) open bus;
(calça) dungarees pl; (vestido) pinafore
dress (BRIT), jumper (US); V tb **jardineiro**.
jardineiro/a [ʒaxdʒi'nejru/a] m/f gardener.
jardins [ʒax'dʒĩʃ] mpl de **jardim**.
jargão [ʒax'gãw] m jargon.
jarra ['ʒaxa] f pot.
jarro ['ʒaxu] m jug.
jasmim [ʒaʒ'mĩ] m jasmine.
jato ['ʒatu] m jet; (de luz) flash; (de ar) blast;
a ~ at top speed.
jaula ['ʒawla] f cage.
Java ['ʒava] f Java.
javali [ʒava'li] m wild boar.
jazer [ʒa'ze*] vi to lie.
jazida [ʒa'zida] f deposit.
jazigo [ʒa'zigu] m grave; (monumento) tomb;
~ **de família** family tomb.
jazz [dʒɛz] m jazz.
jazzista [dʒa'ziʃta] m/f (músico) jazz artist;
(fã) jazz fan.
jazzístico/a [dʒa'ziʃtʃiku/a] adj jazzy.
JB abr m = **Jornal do Brasil**.
JEC (BR) abr f = **Juventude Estudantil
Católica**.
jeca ['ʒɛka] m/f Brazilian hillbilly ♦ adj rustic;
(cafona) tacky.
jeca-tatu (pl **jecas-tatus**) m/f Brazilian
hillbilly.
jeitão [ʒej'tãw] (col: pl **-ões**) m (aspecto)
look; (modo de ser) style, way.
jeitinho [ʒej'tʃiɲu] m knack.
jeito ['ʒejtu] m (maneira) way; (aspecto)
appearance; (aptidão, habilidade) skill,
knack; (modos pessoais) manner; **falta de** ~
clumsiness; **ter** ~ **de** to look like; **ter** ou **levar** ~ **para** to have a gift for, be good at;
não ter ~ (pessoa) to be awkward;
(situação) to be hopeless; **dar um** ~ **em algo**
(pé) to twist sth; (quarto, casa, papéis) to
tidy sth up; (consertar) to fix sth; **dar um** ~
em alguém to sort sb out; **dar um** ~ to find
a way; **tomar** ~ to pull one's socks up; **o** ~
é ... the thing to do is ...; **é o** ~ it's the
best way; **ao** ~ **de** in the style of; **com** ~
tactfully; **daquele** ~ (in) that way; (col: em
desordem, mal) anyhow; **de qualquer** ~ anyway; **de** ~ **nenhum!** no way!; **ficar sem** ~
to feel awkward.
jeitões [ʒej'tõjʃ] mpl de **jeitão**.
jeitoso/a [ʒej'tozu/ɔza] adj (hábil) skilful
(BRIT), skillful (US); (elegante) handsome;
(apropriado) suitable.
jejuar [ʒe'ʒwa*] vi to fast.

jejum [ʒeˈʒũ] (pl -ns) m fast; **em** ~ fasting.
Jeová [ʒeoˈva] m: **testemunha de** ~ Jehovah's witness.
jequice [ʒeˈkisi] f country ways pl; (cafonice) tackiness.
jerico [ʒeˈriku] m donkey; **idéia de** ~ stupid idea.
jérsei [ˈʒɛxsej] m jersey.
Jerusalém [ʒeruzaˈlɛ̃] n Jerusalem.
jesuíta [ʒeˈzwita] m Jesuit.
Jesus [ʒeˈzuʃ] m Jesus ♦ excl heavens!
jetom [ʒeˈtõ] (pl -ns) m (ficha) token; (remuneração) fee.
jibóia [ʒiˈbɔja] f boa (constrictor).
jiboiar [ʒiboˈjaˈ] vi to let one's dinner go down.
jiló [ʒiˈlɔ] m kind of vegetable.
jingle [ˈdʒĩgew] m jingle.
jipe [ˈʒipi] m jeep.
jirau [ʒiˈraw] m (na cozinha) rack; (palanque) platform.
jiu-jitsu [ʒuˈʒitsu] m jiu-jitsu.
joalheiro/a [ʒoaˈʎejru/a] m/f jeweller (BRIT), jeweler (US).
joalheria [ʒoaʎeˈria] f jeweller's (shop) (BRIT), jewelry store (US).
joanete [ʒwaˈnetʃi] m bunion.
joaninha [ʒwaˈniɲa] f ladybird (BRIT), ladybug (US).
joão-ninguém m nonentity.
JOC (BR) abr f = **Juventude Operária Católica**.
joça [ˈʒɔsa] (col) f thing, contraption.
jocoso/a [ʒoˈkozu/ɔza] adj jocular, humorous.
joelhada [ʒoeˈʎada] f: **dar uma** ~ **em alguém** to knee sb.
joelheira [ʒoeˈʎejra] f (ESPORTE) kneepad.
joelho [ʒoˈeʎu] m knee; **de** ~**s** kneeling; **ficar de** ~**s** to kneel down.
jogada [ʒoˈgada] f (num jogo) move; (lanço) throw; (negócio) scheme; (col: modo de agir) move; **a** ~ **é a seguinte** (col) this is the situation; **morar na** ~ (col) to catch on.
jogado/a [ʒoˈgadu/a] adj (prostrado) flat out; (abandonado) abandoned.
jogador(a) [ʒogaˈdoˈ(a)] m/f player; (de jogo de azar) gambler; ~ **de futebol** footballer.
jogão [ʒoˈgãw] (pl -ões) m great game.
jogar [ʒoˈgaˈ] vt to play; (em jogo de azar) to gamble; (atirar) to throw; (indiretas) to drop ♦ vi to play; (em jogo de azar) to gamble; (barco) to pitch; ~**-se** vr to throw o.s.; ~ **fora** to throw away; ~ **na Bolsa** to play the markets; ~ **no bicho** to play the numbers game; ~ **com** (combinar) to match.
jogatina [ʒogaˈtʃina] f gambling.
jogging [ˈʒɔgĩŋ] m jogging; (roupa) track suit; **fazer** ~ to go jogging, jog.
jogo [ˈʒogu] m game; (jogar) play; (de azar) gambling; (conjunto) set; (artimanha) trick; **abrir o** ~ (fig) to lay one's cards on the table, come clean; **esconder o** ~ to play one's cards close to one's chest; **estar em** ~ (fig) to be at stake; **fazer o** ~ **de alguém** to play sb's game, go along with sb; **ter** ~ **de cintura** (fig) to be flexible; ~ **de armar** construction set; ~ **de cartas** card game; ~ **de damas** draughts sg (BRIT), checkers sg (US); ~ **de luz** lighting effects pl; ~ **de salão** indoor game; ~ **do bicho** (illegal) numbers game; **J**~**s Olímpicos** Olympic Games; ~ **limpo/sujo** fair play/dirty tricks pl; **o** ~ **político** political manoeuvring (BRIT) ou maneuvering (US).
jogo-da-velha m noughts and crosses.
jogões [ʒoˈgójʃ] mpl de **jogão**.
joguei [ʒoˈgej] etc vb V **jogar**.
joguete [ʒoˈgetʃi] m plaything; **fazer alguém de** ~ to toy with sb.
jóia [ˈʒɔja] f jewel; (taxa) entry fee ♦ adj (col) great; **tudo** ~? (col) how's things?
jóquei [ˈʒɔkej] m (clube) jockey club; (cavaleiro) jockey.
jóquei-clube (pl **jóqueis-clubes**) m jockey club.
Jordânia [ʒoxˈdanja] f: **a** ~ Jordan.
jordaniano/a [ʒoxdaˈnjanu/a] adj, m/f Jordanian.
Jordão [ʒoxˈdãw] m: **o (rio)** ~ the Jordan (River).
jornada [ʒoxˈnada] f (viagem) journey; (percurso diário) day's journey; ~ **de trabalho** working day.
jornal [ʒoxˈnaw] (pl -ais) m newspaper; (TV, RÁDIO) news.
jornaleiro/a [ʒoxnaˈlejru/a] m/f newsagent (BRIT), newsdealer (US).
jornalismo [ʒoxnaˈliʒmu] m journalism.
jornalista [ʒoxnaˈliʃta] m/f journalist.
jornalístico/a [ʒoxnaˈliʃtʃiku/a] adj journalistic.
jorrante [ʒoˈxãtʃi] adj gushing.
jorrar [ʒoˈxaˈ] vi to gush, spurt out.
jorro [ˈʒoxu] m jet; (de sangue) spurt; (fig) stream, flood.
jovem [ˈʒɔvẽ] (pl -ns) adj young; (aspecto) youthful; (música) youth atr ♦ m/f young person, youngster.
jovial [ʒoˈvjaw] (pl -ais) adj jovial, cheerful.
jovialidade [ʒovjaliˈdadʒi] f joviality.
JPCCC (BR) abr f = **Justiça de Pequenas Causas Cíveis e Criminais**.
Jr abr = **Júnior**.
JT (BR) abr m = **Jornal da Tarde**.
juba [ˈʒuba] f (de leão) mane; (col: cabelo) mop.
jubilação [ʒubilaˈsãw] f (aposentadoria) retirement; (de estudante) sending down.
jubilar [ʒubiˈlaˈ] vt (aposentar) to retire, pension off; (aluno) to send down.
jubileu [ʒubiˈlew] m jubilee; ~ **de prata** silver

NB: European Portuguese adds the following consonants to certain words: **b** (sú(b)dito, su(b)til); **c** (a(c)ção, a(c)cionista, a(c)to); **m** (inde(m)ne); **p** (ado(p)ção, ado(p)tar); for further details see p. xiii.

jubilee.
júbilo ['ʒubilu] *m* rejoicing; **com** ~ jubilantly.
jubiloso/a [ʒubi'lozu/ɔza] *adj* jubilant.
JUC (*BR*) *abr f* = **Juventude Universitária Católica.**
judaico/a [ʒu'dajku/a] *adj* Jewish.
judaísmo [ʒuda'iʒmu] *m* Judaism.
judas ['ʒudaʃ] *m* (*fig*) Judas; (*boneco*) effigy; **onde J~ perdeu as botas** (*col*) at the back of beyond.
judeu/judia [ʒu'dew/ʒu'dʒia] *adj* Jewish ♦ *m/f* Jew.
judiação [ʒudʒja'sãw] *f* ill-treatment.
judiar [ʒu'dʒja*] *vi*: ~ **de alguém/algo** to ill-treat sb/sth.
judiaria [ʒudʒja'ria] *f* ill-treatment; **que** ~! how cruel!
judicatura [ʒudʒika'tura] *f* (*cargo*) office of judge; (*magistratura*) judicature.
judicial [ʒudʒi'sjaw] (*pl* **-ais**) *adj* judicial.
judiciário/a [ʒudʒi'sjarju/a] *adj* judicial; **o (poder)** ~ the judiciary.
judicioso/a [ʒudʒi'sjozu/ɔza] *adj* judicious, wise.
judô [ʒu'do] *m* judo.
jugo ['ʒugu] *m* yoke.
juiz/íza [ʒwiʒ/'iza] *m/f* judge; (*em jogos*) referee; ~ **de menores** juvenile judge; ~ **de paz** justice of the peace.
juizado [ʒwi'zado] *m* court; **J~ de Menores** Juvenile Court; **J~ de Pequenas Causas** small claims court.
juízo ['ʒwizu] *m* judgement; (*parecer*) opinion; (*siso*) common sense; (*foro*) court; **J~ Final** Day of Judgement, doomsday; **perder o** ~ to lose one's mind; **não ter** ~ to be foolish; **tomar ou criar** ~ to come to one's senses; **chamar/levar a** ~ to summon/take to court; ~! behave yourself!
jujuba [ʒu'ʒuba] *f* (*BOT*) jujube; (*bala*) jujube sweet.
jul. *abr* = **julho.**
julgador(a) [ʒuwga'do*(a)] *adj* judging ♦ *m/f* judge.
julgamento [ʒuwga'mẽtu] *m* judgement; (*audiência*) trial; (*sentença*) sentence.
julgar [ʒuw'ga*] *vt* to judge; (*achar*) to think; (*JUR: sentenciar*) to sentence; ~**-se** *vr*: ~**-se algo** to consider o.s. sth, think of o.s. as sth.
julho ['ʒuʎu] (*PT*: **J-**) *m* July; **dia primeiro de** ~ the first of July (*BRIT*), July first (*US*); **dia dois/onze de** ~ the second/eleventh of July (*BRIT*), July second/eleventh (*US*); **ele chegou no dia cinco de** ~ he arrived on 5th July *ou* July 5th; **em** ~ in July; **no começo/fim de** ~ at the beginning/end of July; **em meados de** ~ in mid July; **todo ano em** ~ every July; **em** ~ **do ano que vem/do ano passado** next/last July.
jumento/a [ʒu'mẽtu/a] *m/f* donkey.
jun. *abr* = **junho.**
junção [ʒũ'sãw] (*pl* **-ões**) *f* (*ato*) joining; (*junta*) join.

junco ['ʒũku] *m* reed, rush.
junções [ʒũ'sõjʃ] *fpl de* **junção.**
junho ['ʒuɲu] (*PT*: **J-**) *m* June; *V tb* **julho.**
junino/a [ʒu'ninu/a] *adj* June; **festa junina** St John's day party.
júnior ['ʒunjo*] (*pl* **juniores**) *adj* younger ♦ *m/f* (*ESPORTE*) junior; **Eduardo Autran J~** Eduardo Autran Junior.
junta ['ʒũta] *f* (*comissão*) board, committee; (*POL*) junta; (*articulação, juntura*) joint; ~ **comercial** board of trade; ~ **médica** medical team.
juntar [ʒũ'ta*] *vt* (*por junto*) to join; (*reunir*) to bring together; (*aglomerar*) to gather together; (*recolher*) to collect up; (*acrescentar*) to add; (*dinheiro*) to save up ♦ *vi* to gather; ~**-se** *vr* to gather; (*associar-se*) to join up; ~**-se a alguém** to join sb; ~**-se com alguém** to (go and) live with sb.
junto/a ['ʒũtu/a] *adj* joined; (*chegado*) near; **ir** ~**s** to go together; ~ **a/de** near/next to; **segue** ~ (*COM*) please find enclosed.
juntura [ʒũ'tura] *f* join; (*articulação*) joint.
Júpiter ['ʒupite*] *m* Jupiter.
jura ['ʒura] *f* vow.
jurado/a [ʒu'radu/a] *adj* sworn ♦ *m/f* juror.
juramentado/a [ʒuramẽ'tadu/a] *adj* accredited, legally certified.
juramento [ʒura'mẽtu] *m* oath.
jurar [ʒu'ra*] *vt, vi* to swear; **jura?** really?
júri ['ʒuri] *m* jury.
jurídico/a [ʒu'ridʒiku/a] *adj* legal.
jurisconsulto/a [ʒuriʃkõ'suwtu/a] *m/f* legal advisor.
jurisdição [ʒuriʃdʒi'sãw] *f* jurisdiction.
jurisprudência [ʒuriʃpru'dẽsja] *f* jurisprudence.
jurista [ʒu'riʃta] *m/f* jurist.
juros ['ʒuruʃ] *mpl* (*ECON*) interest *sg*; **a/sem** ~ at interest/interest-free; **render** ~ to yield *ou* bear interest; ~ **fixos/variáveis** fixed/variable interest; ~ **simples/compostos** simple/compound interest.
jururu [ʒuru'ru] *adj* melancholy, wistful.
jus [ʒuʃ] *m*: **fazer** ~ **a algo** to live up to sth.
jusante [ʒu'zãtʃi] *f*: **a** ~ **(de)** downstream (from).
justamente [ʒuʃta'mẽtʃi] *adv* (*com justiça*) fairly, justly; (*precisamente*) exactly.
justapor [ʒuʃta'po*] (*irreg: como* **pôr**) *vt* to juxtapose; ~**-se** *vr* to be juxtaposed; ~ **algo a algo** to juxtapose sth with sth.
justaposição [ʒuʃtapozi'sãw] (*pl* **-ões**) *f* juxtaposition.
justaposto [ʒuʃta'poʃtu] *pp de* **justapor.**
justapunha [ʒuʃta'puɲa] *etc vb V* **justapor.**
justapus [ʒuʃta'puʃ] *etc vb V* **justapor.**
justapuser [ʒuʃtapu'ze*] *etc vb V* **justapor.**
justeza [ʒuʃ'teza] *f* fairness; (*precisão*) precision.
justiça [ʒuʃ'tʃisa] *f* justice; (*poder judiciário*) judiciary; (*eqüidade*) fairness; (*tribunal*) court; **com** ~ justly, fairly; **ir à** ~ to go to

court; **fazer ~ a** to do justice to; **J~ Eleitoral** Electoral Court; **J~ do Trabalho** industrial tribunal (*BRIT*), labor relations board (*US*).

justiceiro/a [ʒuʃtʃi'sejru/a] *adj* righteous; (*inflexível*) inflexible.

justificação [ʒuʃtʃifika'sãw] (*pl* **-ões**) *f* justification.

justificar [ʒuʃtʃifi'ka*] *vt* to justify; **~-se** *vr* to justify o.s.

justificativa [ʒuʃtʃifika'tʃiva] *f* (*JUR*) justification.

justificável [ʒuʃtʃifi'kavew] (*pl* **-eis**) *adj* justifiable.

justo/a ['ʒuʃtu/a] *adj* just, fair; (*legítimo*: *queixa*) legitimate, justified; (*exato*) exact; (*apertado*) tight ♦ *adv* just.

juta ['ʒuta] *f* jute.

juvenil [ʒuve'niw] (*pl* **-is**) *adj* (*ar*) youthful; (*roupa*) young; (*livro*) for young people; (*ESPORTE*: *equipe*, *campeonato*) youth *atr*, junior ♦ *m* (*ESPORTE*) junior championship.

juventude [ʒuvẽ'tudʒi] *f* youth; (*jovialidade*) youthfulness; (*jovens*) young people *pl*, youth.

K

K, k [ka] (*pl* **ks**) *m* K, k; **K de Kátia** K for king.

kanga ['kãga] *f* beach wrap.

karaokê [karao'ke] *m* karaoke; (*lugar*) karaoke bar.

kart ['kaxtʃi] (*pl* **~s**) *m* go-kart.

ketchup [ke'tʃupi] *m* ketchup.

kg *abr* (= *quilograma*) kg.

KGB *abr f* KGB.

kHz *abr* (= *quilohertz*) kHz.

kibutz [ki'butz] *m inv* kibbutz.

kilt ['kiwtʃi] (*pl* **~s**) *m* kilt.

kirsch [kixʃ] *m* kirsch.

kit ['kitʃi] (*pl* **~s**) *m* kit; **~ de sobrevivência** survival kit.

kitchenette [kitʃe'netʃi] *f* studio flat.

kitsch [kitʃ] *adj inv*, *m* kitsch.

kl *abr* (= *quilolitro*) kl.

km *abr* (= *quilômetro*) km.

km/h *abr* (= *quilômetros por hora*) km/h.

know-how ['now'haw] *m* know-how.

Kremlin [krẽ'li] *m*: **a ~** the Kremlin.

Kuweit [ku'wejtʃi] *m*: **a ~** Kuwait.

kW *abr* (= *quilowatt*) kW.

kwh *abr* (= *quilowatt-hora*) kwh.

L

L, L ['eli] (*pl* **ls**) *m* L, l; **L de Lúcia** L for Lucy (*BRIT*) *ou* Love (*US*).

L *abr* = **Largo**.

-la [la] *pron* her; (*você*) you; (*coisa*) it.

lá [la] *adv* there ♦ *m* (*MÚS*) A; **~ fora** outside; **~ em baixo** down there; **por ~** (*direção*) that way; (*situação*) over there; **até ~** (*no espaço*) there; (*no tempo*) until then; **~ pelas tantas** in the small hours; **para ~ de** (*mais do que*) more than; **diga ~ ...** come on and say ...; **sei ~!** don't ask me!; **ela sabe ~** she's got no idea; **ele pode ~ pagar um aluguel tão caro** there's no way he can pay such a high rent; **o apartamento não é ~ essas coisas** the apartment is nothing special; **estar mais para ~ do que para cá** (*de cansaço*) to be dead on one's feet; (*prestes a morrer*) to be at death's door.

lã [lã] *f* wool; **de ~** woollen (*BRIT*), woolen (*US*); **de pura ~** pure wool; **~ de camelo** camel hair.

labareda [laba'reda] *f* flame; (*fig*) ardour (*BRIT*), ardor (*US*).

labia ['labja] *f* (*astúcia*) cunning; **ter ~** to have the gift of the gab.

labial [la'bjaw] (*pl* **-ais**) *adj* lip *atr*; (*LING*) labial ♦ *f* (*LING*) labial.

lábio ['labju] *m* lip; **~ leporino** hare lip.

labirinto [labi'rĩtu] *m* labyrinth, maze.

labor [la'bo*] *m* work, labour (*BRIT*), labor (*US*).

laborar [labo'ra*] *vi*: **~ em erro** to labour (*BRIT*) *ou* labor (*US*) under a misconception.

laboratório [labora'tɔrju] *m* laboratory.

laborioso/a [labo'rjozu/ɔza] *adj* (*diligente*) hard-working; (*árduo*) laborious.

LABRE *abr f* = **Liga de Amadores Brasileiros de Radio Emissão**.

labuta [la'buta] *f* toil, drudgery.

labutar [labu'ta*] *vi* to toil; (*esforçar-se*) to struggle, strive.

laca ['laka] *f* lacquer.

laçada [la'sada] *f* (*nó*) slipknot; (*no tricô*) loop.

laçar [la'sa*] *vt* to bind, tie; (*boi*) to rope.

laçarote [lasa'rɔtʃi] *m* big bow.

laço ['lasu] *m* bow; (*de gravata*) knot; (*armadilha*) snare; (*fig*) bond, tie; **dar um ~** to tie a bow; **~s de família** family ties.

lacônico/a [la'koniku/a] *adj* laconic.

lacraia [la'kraja] *f* centipede.

NB: European Portuguese adds the following consonants to certain words: **b** (sú(b)dito, su(b)til), **c** (a(c)ção, a(c)cionista, a(c)to); **m** (inde(m)ne); **p** (ado(p)ção, ado(p)tar); *for further details see p. xiii.*

lacrar [la'kra*] *vt* to seal (with wax).

lacre ['lakri] *m* sealing wax.

lacrimal [lakri'maw] (*pl* -**ais**) *adj* (*canal*) tear *atr*.

lacrimejante [lakrime'ʒatʃi] *adj* weeping.

lacrimejar [lakrime'ʒa*] *vi* (*olhos*) to water; (*chorar*) to weep.

lacrimogêneo/a [lakrimo'ʒenju/a] *adj* tear-jerking; *V tb* **gás**.

lacrimoso/a [lakri'mozu/ɔza] *adj* tearful.

lactação [lakta'sãw] *f* lactation; (*amamentação*) breastfeeding.

lácteo/a ['laktju/a] *adj* milk *atr*; **Via Láctea** Milky Way.

lacticínio [laktʃi'sinju] *m* dairy product.

lactose [lak'tɔzi] *f* lactose.

lacuna [la'kuna] *f* gap; (*omissão*) omission; (*espaço em branco*) blank.

ladainha [lada'iɲa] *f* litany; (*fig*) rigmarole.

ladear [la'dʒja*] *vt* to flank; (*problema*) to get round; **o rio ladeia a estrada** the river runs by the side of the road.

ladeira [la'dejra] *f* slope.

ladino/a [la'dʒinu/a] *adj* cunning, crafty.

lado ['ladu] *m* side; (*MIL*) flank; (*rumo*) direction; **ao ~** (*perto*) close by; **a casa ao ~** the house next door; **ao ~ de** beside; **de ~** sideways; **deixar de ~** to set aside; (*fig*) to leave out; **de um ~ para outro** back and forth; **do ~ de dentro/fora** on the inside/outside; **do ~ de cá/lá** on this/that side; **no outro ~ da rua** across the road; **ela foi para aqueles ~s** she went that way; **por um ~ ... por outro ~** on the one hand ... on the other hand; **por todos os ~s** all around; **~ a ~** side by side; **o meu ~** (*col: interesses*) my interests.

ladra [ˈladra] *f* thief, robber; (*picareta*) crook.

ladrão/ona [la'drãw/ɔna] (*pl* -**ões/~s**) *adj* thieving ♦ *m/f* thief, robber; (*picareta*) crook ♦ *m* (*tubo*) overflow pipe; **pega ~!** stop thief!

ladrar [la'dra*] *vi* to bark.

ladrilhar [ladri'ʎa*] *vt*, *vi* to tile.

ladrilheiro/a [ladri'ʎejru/a] *m/f* tiler.

ladrilho [la'driʎu] *m* tile; (*chão*) tiled floor, tiles *pl*.

ladro ['ladru] *m* (*latido*) bark; (*ladrão*) thief.

ladroagem [la'drwaʒẽ] (*pl* -**ns**) *f* robbery.

ladroeira [la'drwejra] *f* robbery.

ladrões [la'drõjʃ] *mpl de* **ladrão**.

ladrona [la'drɔna] *f de* **ladrão**.

lagarta [la'gaxta] *f* caterpillar.

lagartixa [lagax'tʃiʃa] *f* gecko.

lagarto [la'gaxtu] *m* lizard; (*carne*) silverside.

lago ['lagu] *m* lake; (*de jardim*) pond; (*de sangue*) pool.

lagoa [la'goa] *f* pool, pond; (*lago*) lake.

lagosta [la'goʃta] *f* lobster.

lagostim [lagoʃ'tʃĩ] (*pl* -**ns**) *m* crayfish.

lágrima ['lagrima] *f* tear; **~s de crocodilo** crocodile tears; **chorar ~s de sangue** to cry bitterly.

laguna [la'guna] *f* lagoon.

laia ['laja] *f* kind, sort, type.

laico/a ['lajku/a] *adj* (*pessoa*) lay; (*ensino etc*) secular.

laivos ['lajvuʃ] *mpl* hints, traces.

laje ['laʒi] *f* paving stone, flagstone.

lajedo [la'ʒedu] *m* rock.

lajear [la'ʒja*] *vt* to pave.

lajota [la'ʒota] *f* paving stone.

lama ['lama] *f* mud; **tirar alguém da ~** (*fig*) to rescue sb from poverty.

lamaçal [lama'saw] (*pl* -**ais**) *m* quagmire; (*pântano*) bog, marsh.

lamaceiro [lama'sejru] *m* = **lamaçal**.

lamacento/a [lama'sẽtu/a] *adj* muddy.

lambança [lãˈbãsa] *f* mess.

lambão/bona [lãˈbãw/ˈbɔna] (*pl* -**ões/~s**) *adj* (*guloso*) greedy; (*no trabalho*) sloppy; (*ao comer*) messy; (*tolo*) idiotic.

lamber [lãˈbe*] *vt* to lick; **de ~ os beiços** (*comida*) delicious.

lambida [lãˈbida] *f* lick; **dar uma ~ em algo** to lick sth.

lambido/a [lãˈbidu/a] *adj* (*cara*) without make-up; (*cabelo*) plastered down.

lambiscar [lãbiʃ'ka*] *vt*, *vi* to nibble, pick at.

lambisgóia [lãbiʒ'gɔja] *f* haggard person.

lambões [lãˈbõjʃ] *mpl de* **lambão**.

lambona [lãˈbɔna] *f de* **lambão**.

lambreta [lãˈbreta] *f* scooter.

lambri(s) [lãˈbri(ʃ)] *m*(*pl*) panelling *sg* (*BRIT*), paneling *sg* (*US*).

lambuja [lãˈbuʒa] *f* start, advantage.

lambujem [lãˈbuʒẽ] (*pl* -**ns**) *f* start, advantage.

lambuzar [lãbu'za*] *vt* to smear.

lambuzeira [lãbu'zejra] *f* sticky mess.

lamentação [lamẽta'sãw] (*pl* -**ões**) *f* lamentation.

lamentar [lamẽ'ta*] *vt* to lament; (*sentir*) to regret; **~-se** *vr*: **~-se (de algo)** to lament (sth); **~ (que)** to be sorry (that).

lamentável [lamẽ'tavew] (*pl* -**eis**) *adj* regrettable; (*deplorável*) deplorable.

lamentavelmente [lamẽtavew'mẽtʃi] *adv* regrettably.

lamento [la'mẽtu] *m* lament; (*gemido*) moan.

lamentoso/a [lamẽ'tozu/ɔza] *adj* (*voz*, *som*) sorrowful; (*lamentável*) lamentable.

lâmina ['lamina] *f* (*chapa*) sheet; (*placa*) plate; (*de faca*) blade; (*de persiana*) slat.

laminado/a [lami'nadu/a] *adj* laminated ♦ *m* laminate.

laminar [lami'na*] *vt* to laminate.

lâmpada ['lãpada] *f* lamp; (*tb*: **~ elétrica**) light bulb; **~ de mesa** table lamp; **~ fluorescente** fluorescent light.

lamparina [lãpa'rina] *f* lamp.

lampejante [lãpe'ʒatʃi] *adj* flashing, glittering.

lampejar [lãpe'ʒa*] *vi* to glisten, flash ♦ *vt* to give off.

lampejo [lãˈpeʒu] *m* flash.

lampião [lãˈpjãw] (*pl* -**ões**) *m* lantern; (*de rua*) street lamp.

lamúria [la'murja] *f* whining, lamentation.

lamuriante [lamu'rjãtʃi] *adj* whining.

lamuriar-se [lamu'rjaxsi] *vr:* ~ **de algo** to moan about sth.

lança ['lãsa] *f* lance, spear.

lançadeira [lãsa'dejra] *f* shuttle.

lançador(a) [lãsa'do*(a)] *m/f* (ESPORTE) thrower; (*em leilão*) bidder; (COM) company which (ou *person who*) *launches a product.*

lançamento [lãsa'mẽtu] *m* throwing; (COM: *em livro*) entry; (NÁUT, COM: *de produto, campanha*) launch; (: *de disco, filme*) release; **novo** ~ (*livro*) new title; (*filme, disco*) new release; (*produto*) new product; ~ **do dardo** (ESPORTE) javelin; ~ **do disco** (ESPORTE) discus; ~ **do martelo** (ESPORTE) hammer.

lança-perfume (*pl* ~**s**) *m* ether spray (*used as a drug in carnival*).

lançar [lã'sa*] *vt* to throw; (NÁUT, COM) to launch; (*disco, filme*) to release; (*em livro comercial*) to enter; (*em leilão*) to bid; (*imposto*) to assess; ~**-se** *vr* to throw o.s.; ~ **ações no mercado** to float shares on the market; ~ **mão de algo** to make use of sth.

lance ['lãsi] *m* (*arremesso*) throw; (*incidente*) incident; (*história*) story; (*situação*) position; (*fato*) fact; (ESPORTE: *jogada*) shot; (*em leilão*) bid; (*de escada*) flight; (*de casas*) row; (*episódio*) moment; (*de muro, estrada*) stretch.

lancha ['lãʃa] *f* launch; (*col: sapato, pé*) clodhopper; ~ **torpedeira** torpedo boat.

lanchar [lã'ʃa*] *vi* to have a snack ♦ *vt* to have as a snack.

lanche ['lãʃi] *m* snack.

lanchonete [lãʃo'netʃi] (BR) *f* snack bar.

lancinante [lãsi'nãtʃi] *adj* (*dor*) stabbing; (*grito*) piercing.

langanho [lã'gaɲu] *m* rake.

languidez [lãgi'deʒ] *f* languor, listlessness.

lânguido/a ['lãgidu/a] *adj* languid, listless.

lanhar [la'ɲa*] *vt* to slash, gash; (*peixe*) to gut; ~**-se** *vr* to cut o.s.

lanho ['laɲu] *m* slash, gash.

lanígero/a [la'niʒeru/a] *adj* (*gado*) woolproducing; (*planta*) downy.

lanolina [lano'lina] *f* lanolin.

lantejoula [lãte'ʒola] *f* sequin.

lanterna [lã'texna] *f* lantern; (*portátil*) torch (BRIT), flashlight (US).

lanternagem [lãtex'naʒẽ] (*pl* -**ns**) *f* (AUTO) panel-beating; (*oficina*) bodyshop.

lanterneiro/a [lãtex'nejru/a] *m/f* panel-beater.

lanterninha [lãtex'niɲa] (BR) *m/f* usher(ette).

lanugem [la'nuʒẽ] *f* down, fluff.

Laos ['lawʃ] *m:* **o** ~ Laos.

lapão/pona [la'pãw/'pɔna] (*pl* -**ões**/~**s**) *adj, m/f* Lapp.

lapela [la'pɛla] *f* lapel.

lapidador(a) [lapida'do*(a)] *m/f* cutter.

lapidar [lapi'da*] *vt* (*jóias*) to cut; (*fig*) to polish, refine ♦ *adj* (*fig*) masterful.

lápide ['lapidʒi] *f* (*tumular*) tombstone; (*comemorativa*) memorial stone.

lápis ['lapiʃ] *m inv* pencil; **escrever a** ~ to write in pencil; ~ **de cor** coloured (BRIT) ou colored (US) pencil, crayon; ~ **de olho** eyebrow pencil.

lapiseira [lapi'zejra] *f* propelling (BRIT) ou mechanical (US) pencil; (*caixa*) pencil case.

lápis-lazúli [-la'zuli] *m* lapis-lazuli.

lapões [la'põjʃ] *mpl de* **lapão**.

lapona [la'pɔna] *f de* **lapão**.

Lapônia [la'ponja] *f:* **a** ~ Lappland.

lapso ['lapsu] *m* lapse; (*de tempo*) interval; (*erro*) slip.

laquê [la'ke] *m* lacquer.

laquear [la'kja*] *vt* to lacquer.

lar [la*] *m* home.

laranja [la'rãʒa] *adj inv* orange ♦ *f* orange ♦ *m* (*cor*) orange.

laranjada [larã'ʒada] *f* orangeade.

laranjal [larã'ʒaw] (*pl* -**ais**) *m* orange grove.

laranjeira [larã'ʒejra] *f* orange tree.

larápio [la'rapju] *m* thief.

lardo ['laxdu] *m* bacon.

lareira [la'rejra] *f* hearth, fireside.

larga ['laxga] *f:* **à** ~ lavishly; **dar** ~**s a** to give free rein to; **viver à** ~ to lead a lavish life.

largada [lax'gada] *f* start; **dar a** ~ to start; (*fig*) to make a start.

largado/a [lax'gadu/a] *adj* spurned; (*no vestir*) scruffy.

largar [lax'ga*] *vt* (*soltar*) to let go of, release; (*deixar*) to leave; (*deixar cair*) to drop; (*risada*) to let out; (*velas*) to unfurl; (*piada*) to tell; (*pôr em liberdade*) to let go ♦ *vi* (NÁUT) to set sail; ~**-se** *vr* (*desprender-se*) to free o.s.; (*ir-se*) to go off; (*pôr-se*) to proceed; **ele não a larga** ou **não larga dela um instante** he won't leave her alone for a moment; **me larga!** leave me alone!; ~ **a mão em alguém** to wallop sb; ~ **de fazer** to stop doing; **largue de besteira** stop being stupid.

largo/a ['laxgu/a] *adj* wide, broad; (*amplo*) extensive; (*roupa*) loose, baggy; (*conversa*) long ♦ *m* (*praça*) square; (*alto-mar*) open sea; **ao** ~ at a distance, far off; **fazer-se ao** ~ to put out to sea; **passar de** ~ **sobre um assunto** to gloss over a subject; **passar ao** ~ **de algo** (*fig*) to sidestep sth.

larguei [lax'gej] *etc vb V* **largar**.

largueza [lax'geza] *f* largesse.

largura [lax'gura] *f* width, breadth.

laringe [la'rĩʒi] *f* larynx.

laringite [larĩ'ʒitʃi] *f* laryngitis.

larva ['laxva] *f* larva, grub.

lasanha [la'zaɲa] *f* lasagna.

lasca ['laʃka] *f* (*de madeira, metal*) splinter;

NB: *European Portuguese adds the following consonants to certain words:* **b** (sú(b)dito, su(b)til); **c** (a(c)ção, a(c)cionista, a(c)to); **m** (inde(m)ne); **p** (ado(p)ção, ado(p)tar); *for further details see p. xiii.*

(de pedra) chip; *(fatia)* slice.

lascado/a [laʃ'kadu/a] *(col)* *adj* in a hurry *ou* rush.

lascar [laʃ'ka*] *vt* to chip; *(pergunta)* to throw in; *(tapa)* to let go ♦ *vi* to chip; **ser** *ou* **estar de ~** to be horrible.

lascívia [la'sivja] *f* lewdness.

lascivo/a [la'sivu/a] *adj* lewd; *(movimentos)* sensual.

laser ['lejze*] *m* laser; **raio ~** laser beam.

lassidão [lasi'dãw] *f* lassitude, weariness.

lassitude [lasi'tudʒi] *f* lassitude, weariness.

lasso/a [ˈlasu/a] *adj* lax; *(cansado)* weary.

lástima ['laʃtʃima] *f* pity, compassion; *(infortúnio)* misfortune; **é uma ~ (que)** it's a shame (that).

lastimar [laʃtʃi'ma*] *vt* to lament; **~-se** *vr* to complain, be sorry for o.s.

lastimável [laʃtʃi'mavew] *(pl -eis)* *adj* lamentable.

lastimoso/a [laʃtʃi'mozu/ɔza] *adj* *(lamentável)* pitiful; *(plangente)* mournful.

lastro ['laʃtru] *m* ballast.

lata ['lata] *f* tin, can; *(material)* tin-plate; **~ de lixo** rubbish bin *(BRIT)*, garbage can *(US)*; **~ velha** *(col: carro)* old banger *(BRIT)* *ou* clunker *(US)*.

latada [la'tada] *f* trellis.

latão [la'tãw] *m* brass.

lataria [lata'ria] *f* *(AUTO)* bodywork; *(enlatados)* canned food.

látego ['lategu] *m* whip.

latejante [late'ʒãtʃi] *adj* throbbing.

latejar [late'ʒa*] *vi* to throb.

latejo [la'teʒu] *m* throbbing, beat.

latente [la'tẽtʃi] *adj* latent, hidden.

lateral [late'raw] *(pl -ais)* *adj* side, lateral ♦ *f* *(FUTEBOL)* sideline ♦ *m* *(FUTEBOL)* throw-in.

látex ['lateks] *m inv* latex.

laticínio [latʃi'sinju] *m* = **lacticínio**.

latido [la'tʃidu] *m* bark(ing), yelp(ing).

latifundiário/a [latʃifū'dʒjarju/a] *adj* landowning ♦ *m/f* landowner.

latifúndio [latʃi'fũdʒju] *m* large estate.

latim [la'tʃĩ] *m* *(LING)* Latin; **gastar o seu ~** to waste one's breath.

latino/a [la'tʃinu/a] *adj* Latin.

latino-americano/a *adj*, *m/f* Latin-American.

latir [la'tʃi*] *vi* to bark, yelp.

latitude [latʃi'tudʒi] *f* latitude; *(largura)* breadth; *(fig)* scope.

lato/a ['latu/a] *adj* broad.

latrina [la'trina] *f* latrine.

latrocínio [latro'sinju] *m* armed robbery.

lauda ['lawda] *f* page.

laudatório/a [lawda'tɔrju/a] *adj* laudatory.

laudo ['lawdu] *m* *(JUR)* decision; *(resultados)* findings *pl*; *(peça escrita)* report.

laureado/a [lawre'adu/a] *adj* honoured *(BRIT)*, honored *(US)* ♦ *m* laureate.

laurear [law'rja*] *vt* to honour *(BRIT)*, honor *(US)*.

laurel [law'rɛw] *(pl -éis)* *m* laurel wreath; *(fig)*

prize, reward.

lauto/a ['lawtu/a] *adj* sumptuous; *(abundante)* lavish, abundant.

lava ['lava] *f* lava.

lavabo [la'vabu] *m* toilet.

lavadeira [lava'dejra] *f* washerwoman.

lavadora [lava'dora] *f* washing machine.

lavadouro [lava'doru] *m* washing place.

lavagem [la'vaʒẽ] *f* washing; **~ a seco** dry cleaning; **~ cerebral** brainwashing; **dar uma ~ em alguém** *(col: ESPORTE)* to thrash sb.

lavanda [la'vãda] *f* *(BOT)* lavender; *(colônia)* lavender water; *(para lavar os dedos)* fingerbowl.

lavanderia [lavãde'ria] *f* laundry; *(aposento)* laundry room.

lavar [la'va*] *vt* to wash; *(culpa)* to wash away; **~ a seco** to dry clean; **~ a égua** *(col: ESPORTE)* to win hands down; **~ as mãos de algo** *(fig)* to wash one's hands of sth.

lavatório [lava'tɔrju] *m* washbasin; *(aposento)* toilet.

lavoura [la'vora] *f* tilling; *(agricultura)* farming; *(terreno)* plantation.

lavra ['lavra] *f* ploughing *(BRIT)*, plowing *(US)*; *(de minerais)* mining; *(mina)* mine; **ser da ~ de** to be the work of.

lavradio/a [lavra'dʒiu/a] *adj* workable, arable ♦ *m* farming.

lavrador(a) [lavra'do*(a)] *m/f* farmhand, farm labourer.

lavrar [la'vra*] *vt* to work; *(esculpir)* to carve; *(redigir)* to draw up.

laxante [la'ʃãtʃi] *adj*, *m* laxative.

laxativo/a [laʃa'tʃivu/a] *adj* laxative ♦ *m* laxative.

lazer [la'ze*] *m* leisure.

LBA *abr f* (= *Legião Brasileira de Assistência*) *charity*.

LBC *(BR)* *abr f* = **Letra do Banco Central**.

leal [le'aw] *(pl -ais)* *adj* loyal.

lealdade [leaw'dadʒi] *f* loyalty.

leão [le'ãw] *(pl -ões)* *m* lion; **L~** *(ASTROLOGIA)* Leo; **o L~** *(BR: fisco)* ≈ the Inland Revenue *(BRIT)*, the IRS *(US)*.

leão-de-chácara *(pl* **leões-de-chácara)** *m* bouncer.

lebre ['lɛbri] *f* hare.

lecionar [lesjo'na*] *(PT: -cc-)* *vt*, *vi* to teach.

lecitina [lesi'tʃina] *f* lecithin.

lectivo/a [lek'tivu/a] *(PT)* *adj* = **letivo/a**.

legação [lega'sãw] *(pl -ões)* *f* legation.

legado [le'gadu] *m* envoy, legate; *(herança)* legacy, bequest.

legal [le'gaw] *(pl -ais)* *adj* legal, lawful; *(col)* fine; *(: pessoa)* nice ♦ *adv* *(col)* well; **(tá) ~!** OK!

legalidade [legali'dadʒi] *f* legality, lawfulness.

legalização [legaliza'sãw] *f* legalization; *(de documento)* authentication.

legalizar [legali'za*] *vt* to legalize; *(documento)* to authenticate.

legar [le'ga*] *vt* to bequeath, leave.

legatário/a [lega'tarju/a] *m/f* legatee.
legenda [le'ʒẽda] *f* inscription; (*texto explicativo*) caption; (*CINEMA*) subtitle; (*POL*) party.
legendário/a [leʒẽ'darju/a] *adj* legendary.
legião [le'ʒjãw] (*pl* -ões) *f* legion; **a L~** Estrangeira the Foreign Legion.
legionário/a [leʒjo'narju/a] *adj* legionary ♦ *m* legionary.
legislação [leʒiʒla'sãw] *f* legislation; **~ antitruste** (*COM*) antitrust legislation.
legislador(a) [leʒiʒla'do*(a)] *m/f* legislator.
legislar [leʒiʒ'la*] *vi* to legislate ♦ *vt* to pass.
legislativo/a [leʒiʒla'tʃivu/a] *adj* legislative ♦ *m* legislature.
legislatura [leʒiʒla'tura] *f* legislature; (*período*) term of office.
legista [le'ʒiʃta] *adj*: **médico ~** expert in medical law ♦ *m/f* legal expert; (*médico*) expert in medical law.
legitimar [leʒitʃi'ma*] *vt* to legitimize; (*justificar*) to legitimate; (*filho*) to adopt legally.
legitimidade [leʒitʃimi'dadʒi] *f* legitimacy.
legítimo/a [le'ʒitʃimu/a] *adj* legitimate; (*justo*) rightful; (*autêntico*) genuine; **legítima defesa** self-defence (*BRIT*), self-defense (*US*).
legível [le'ʒivew] (*pl* -eis) *adj* legible, readable; **~ por máquina** machine readable.
légua ['lɛgwa] *f* league.
legume [le'gumi] *m* vegetable.
lei [lej] *f* law; (*regra*) rule; (*metal*) standard; **prata de ~** sterling silver; **ditar a ~** to lay down the law; **~ marcial** martial law.
leiaute [lej'awtʃi] *m* layout.
leigo/a ['lejgu/a] *adj* (*REL*) lay, secular ♦ *m* layman; **ser ~ em algo** (*fig*) to be no expert at sth, be unversed in sth.
leilão [lej'lãw] (*pl* -ões) *m* auction; **vender em ~** to sell by auction, auction off.
leiloamento [lejlwa'mẽtu] *m* auctioning.
leiloar [lej'lwa*] *vt* to auction.
leiloeiro/a [lej'lwejru/a] *m/f* auctioneer.
leilões [lej'lõjʃ] *mpl de* **leilão**.
leio ['leju] *etc vb V* **ler**.
leitão/toa [lej'tãw/'toa] (*pl* -ões/~s) *m/f* suckling (*BRIT*) *ou* suckling (*US*) pig.
leite ['lejtʃi] *m* milk; **~ em pó** powdered milk; **~ desnatado** *ou* **magro** skimmed milk; **~ de magnésia** milk of magnesia; **~ condensado/evaporado/homogeneizado** condensed/evaporated/homogenized milk; **~ de vaca** cow's milk.
leite-de-onça *m* milk with cachaça.
leiteira [lej'tejra] *f* (*para ferver*) milk pan; (*para servir*) milk jug.
leiteiro/a [lej'tejru/a] *adj* (*vaca, gado*) dairy; (*trem*) milk *atr* ♦ *m/f* milkman/woman.
leiteria [lejte'ria] *f* dairy.
leito ['lejtu] *m* bed.

leitoa [lej'toa] *f de* **leitão**.
leitões [lej'tõjʃ] *mpl de* **leitão**.
leitor(a) [lej'to*(a)] *m/f* reader; (*professor*) lector.
leitoso/a [lej'tozu/ɔza] *adj* milky.
leitura [lej'tura] *f* reading; (*livro etc*) reading matter; **pessoa de muita ~** well-read person; **~ dinâmica** speed reading.
lelé [le'lɛ] (*col*) *adj* nuts, crazy; **~ da cuca** out of one's mind.
lema ['lɛma] *m* motto; (*POL*) slogan.
lembrança [lẽ'brãsa] *f* recollection, memory; (*presente*) souvenir; **~s** *fpl*: **~s a sua mãe!** regards to your mother!
lembrar [lẽ'bra*] *vt*, *vi* to remember; **~-se** *vr*: **~(-se) de** to remember; **~(-se) (de) que** to remember that; **~ algo a alguém**, **~ alguém de algo** to remind sb of sth; **~ alguém de que**, **~ a alguém que** to remind sb that; **esta rua lembra a rua onde eu ...** this street reminds me of the street where I ...; **ele lembra meu irmão** he reminds me of my brother, he is like my brother.
lembrete [lẽ'bretʃi] *m* reminder.
leme ['lɛmi] *m* rudder; (*NÁUT*) helm; (*fig*) control.
lenço ['lẽsu] *m* handkerchief; (*de pescoço*) scarf; (*de cabeça*) headscarf; **~ de papel** tissue.
lençol [lẽ'sɔw] (*pl* -óis) *m* sheet; **estar em maus lençóis** to be in a fix; **~ de água** water table.
lenda ['lẽda] *f* legend; (*fig: mentira*) lie.
lendário/a [lẽ'darju/a] *adj* legendary.
lengalenga [lẽga'lẽga] *f* rigmarole.
lenha ['lɛɲa] *f* firewood; **fazer ~** (*de carro*) to have a race; **meter a ~ em alguém** (*col: surrar*) to give sb a beating; (: *criticar*) to run sb down; **ser uma ~** (*col*) to be tough; **botar ~ no fogo** (*fig*) to fan the flames, make things worse.
lenhador [lɛɲa'do*] *m* woodcutter.
lenho ['lɛɲu] *m* (*tora*) log; (*material*) timber.
Leningrado [leni'gradu] *n* Leningrad.
leninista [leni'niʃta] *adj*, *m/f* Leninist.
lenitivo/a [leni'tʃivu/a] *adj* soothing ♦ *m* palliative; (*fig: alívio*) relief.
lenocínio [leno'sinju] *m* living off immoral earnings.
lente ['lẽtʃi] *f* lens *sg*; **~ de aumento** magnifying glass; **~s de contato** contact lenses.
lentidão [lẽtʃi'dãw] *f* slowness.
lentilha [lẽ'tʃiʎa] *f* lentil.
lento/a ['lẽtu/a] *adj* slow.
leoa [le'oa] *f* lioness.
leões [le'õjʃ] *mpl de* **leão**.
leopardo [ljo'paxdu] *m* leopard.
lépido/a ['lɛpidu/a] *adj* (*alegre*) sprightly, bright; (*ágil*) nimble, agile.

NB: European Portuguese adds the following consonants to certain words: **b** (sú(b)dito, su(b)til); **c** (a(c)ção, a(c)cionista, a(c)to); **m** (inde(m)ne); **p** (ado(p)ção, ado(p)tar); *for further details see p. xiii.*

leporino/a [lepo'rinu/a] *adj V* **lábio.**
lepra ['lɛpra] *f* leprosy.
leprosário [lepro'zarju] *m* leprosy hospital.
leproso/a [le'prozu/ɔza] *adj* leprous ♦ *m/f* leper.
leque ['lɛki] *m* fan; (*fig*) array.
ler [le*] *vt, vi* to read; ~ **a sorte de alguém** to tell sb's fortune; ~ **nas entrelinhas** (*fig*) to read between the lines.
lerdeza [lex'deza] *f* sluggishness.
lerdo/a ['lɛxdu/a] *adj* slow, sluggish.
lero-lero [lɛru'lɛru] (*col*) *m* chit-chat, idle talk.
lés [lɛʃ] (*PT*) *m*: **de ~ a ~** from one end to the other.
lesão [le'zãw] (*pl* **-ões**) *f* harm, injury; (*JUR*) violation; (*MED*) lesion; ~ **corporal** (*JUR*) bodily harm.
lesar [le'za*] *vt* to harm, damage; (*direitos*) to violate; ~ **alguém** (*financeiramente*) to leave sb short; ~ **o fisco** to withhold one's taxes.
lesbianismo [leʒbja'niʒmu] *m* lesbianism.
lésbica ['lɛʒbika] *f* lesbian.
lesco-lesco [lɛʃku'lɛʃku] (*col*) *m* daily grind; **estar no ~** to be on the go *ou* hard at it.
leseira [le'zejra] *f* lethargy.
lesionar [lezjo'na*] *vt* to injure.
lesivo/a [le'zivu/a] *adj* harmful.
lesma ['leʒma] *f* slug; (*fig*: *pessoa*) slowcoach.
lesões [le'zõjʃ] *fpl de* **lesão.**
Lesoto [le'zotu] *m*: **o ~** Lesotho.
lesse ['lesi] *etc vb V* **ler.**
leste ['lɛʃtʃi] *m* east.
letal [le'taw] (*pl* **-ais**) *adj* lethal.
letargia [letax'ʒia] *f* lethargy.
letárgico/a [le'taxʒiku/a] *adj* lethargic.
letivo/a [le'tʃivu/a] *adj* school *atr*; **ano ~** academic year.
Letônia [le'tonja] *f*: **a ~** Latvia.
letra ['letra] *f* letter; (*caligrafia*) handwriting; (*de canção*) lyrics *pl*; **L~s** *fpl* (*curso*) language and literature; **à ~** literally; **seguir à ~** to follow to the letter; **ao pé da ~** literally, word for word; **fazer** *ou* **tirar algo de ~** (*col*) to be able to do sth standing on one's head; ~ **de câmbio** (*COM*) bill of exchange; ~ **de fôrma** block letter; ~ **de imprensa** print; ~ **de médico** (*fig*) scrawl; ~ **maiúscula/minúscula** capital/small letter.
letrado/a [le'tradu/a] *adj* learned, erudite ♦ *m/f* scholar; **ser ~ em algo** to be well-versed in sth.
letreiro [le'trejru] *m* sign, notice; (*inscrição*) inscription; (*CINEMA*) subtitle; ~ **luminoso** neon sign.
leu [lew] *etc vb V* **ler.**
léu [lɛw] *m*: **ao ~** (*à toa*) aimlessly; (*à mostra*) uncovered.
leucemia [lewse'mia] *f* leukaemia (*BRIT*), leukemia (*US*).
leva ['lɛva] *f* (*de pessoas*) group.
levadiço/a [leva'dʒisu/a] *adj V* **ponte.**
levado/a [le'vadu/a] *adj* mischievous; (*criança*) naughty; ~ **da breca** naughty.

leva-e-traz [-'traʒ] *m/f inv* gossip, stirrer.
levantador(a) [levãta'do*(a)] *adj* lifting ♦ *m/f*: ~ **de pesos** weightlifter.
levantamento [levãta'mẽtu] *m* lifting, raising; (*revolta*) uprising, rebellion; (*arrolamento*) survey; ~ **de pesos** weightlifting.
levantar [levã'ta*] *vt* to lift, raise; (*voz, capital*) to raise; (*apanhar*) to pick up; (*suscitar*) to arouse; (*ambiente*) to brighten up ♦ *vi* to stand up; (*da cama*) to get up; (*dar vida*) to brighten; ~**-se** *vr* to stand up; (*da cama*) to get up; (*rebelar-se*) to rebel; ~ **vôo** to take off; ~ **a mão** to raise *ou* put up one's hand.
levante [le'vãtʃi] *m* east; (*revolta*) revolt.
levar [le'va*] *vt* to take; (*portar*) to carry; (*tempo*) to pass, spend; (*roupa*) to wear; (*lidar com*) to handle; (*induzir*) to lead; (*filme*) to show; (*peça teatral*) to do, put on ♦ *vi* to get a beating; ~ **a** to lead to; ~ **a mal** to take amiss; ~ **a cabo** to carry out; ~ **adiante** to go ahead with; ~ **uma vida feliz** to lead a happy life; ~ **a melhor/pior** to get a good/raw deal; ~ **pancadas/um susto/uma bronca** to get hit/a fright/told off; ~ **a educação a todos** to bring education to all; **deixar-se ~ por** to be carried along by.
leve ['lɛvi] *adj* light; (*insignificante*) slight; **de ~** lightly, softly.
levedo [le'vedu] *m* yeast.
levedura [leve'dura] *f* = **levedo.**
leveza [le'veza] *f* lightness.
levezinho [leve'ziɲu] *adj*: **de ~** very lightly.
leviandade [levjã'dadʒi] *f* frivolity.
leviano/a [le'vjanu/a] *adj* frivolous.
levitação [levita'sãw] *f* levitation.
levitar [levi'ta*] *vi* to levitate.
lexical [leksi'kaw] (*pl* **-ais**) *adj* lexical.
léxico/a ['lɛksiku/a] *adj* lexical ♦ *m* lexicon.
lexicografia [leksikogra'fia] *f* lexicography.
lexicógrafo/a [leksi'kɔgrafu/a] *m/f* lexicographer.
leziria [le'zirja] (*PT*) *f* marshland.
LFT (*BR*) *abr f* = **Letra Financeira do Tesouro.**
lha(s) [ʎa(ʃ)] = **lhe** + **a(s).**
lhama ['ʎama] *m* llama.
lhaneza [ʎa'neza] *f* amiability.
lhano/a ['ʎanu/a] *adj* amiable.
lhe [ʎi] *pron* to him (*a ele*) to her; (*a ela*) to her; (*a você*) to you.
lhes [ʎiʃ] *pron pl* (*a eles/elas*) to them; (*a vocês*) to you.
lho(s) [ʎu(ʃ)] = **lhe** + **o(s).**
lhufas ['ʎufaʃ] (*col*) *pron* nothing, bugger all (!).
li [li] *etc vb V* **ler.**
lia ['lia] *f* dregs *pl*, sediment.
liame ['ljami] *m* tie, bond.
libanês/esa [liba'neʃ/eza] *adj* Lebanese.
Líbano ['libanu] *m*: **o ~** (the) Lebanon.
libelo [li'bɛlu] *m* satire, lampoon; (*JUR*) formal indictment.
libélula [li'bɛlula] *f* dragonfly.

liberação [libera'sãw] *f* liberation.
liberal [libe'raw] (*pl* **-ais**) *adj*, *m/f* liberal.
liberalidade [liberali'dadʒi] *f* liberality.
liberalismo [libera'liʒmu] *m* liberalism.
liberalização [liberaliza'sãw] *f* liberalization.
liberalizante [liberali'zãtʃi] *adj* liberalizing.
liberalizar [liberali'za*] *vt* to liberalize.
liberar [libe'ra*] *vt* to release; (*libertar*) to free; (*COMPUT*: *dados*) to output.
liberdade [libex'dadʒi] *f* freedom; **~s** *fpl* (*direitos*) liberties; **tomar ~s com alguém** to take liberties with sb; **pôr alguém em ~** to set sb free; **estar em ~** to be free; **tomar a ~ de fazer** to take the liberty of doing; **~ condicional** probation; **~ de expressão** freedom of expression; **~ de cultos** freedom of worship; **~ de palavra** freedom of speech; **~ de pensamento** freedom of thought; **~ de imprensa** press freedom; **~ sob palavra** parole.
Libéria [li'bɛrja] *f*: **a ~** Liberia.
líbero ['liberu] *m* (*FUTEBOL*) sweeper.
libérrimo/a [li'beximu/a] *adj superl de* **livre**.
libertação [libexta'sãw] *f* release.
libertador(a) [libexta'do*(a)] *m/f* liberator.
libertar [libex'ta*] *vt* to free.
libertinagem [libextʃi'naʒẽ] *f* licentiousness, loose living.
libertino/a [libex'tʃinu/a] *adj* loose-living ♦ *m/f* libertine.
liberto/a [li'bɛxtu/a] *pp de* **libertar**.
Líbia ['libja] *f*: **a ~** Libya.
líbio/a ['libju/a] *adj*, *m/f* Libyan.
libidinoso/a [libidʒi'nozu/ɔza] *adj* lecherous, lustful.
libido [li'bidu] *f* libido.
libra ['libra] *f* pound; **~ esterlina** pound sterling; **L~** (*ASTROLOGIA*) Libra.
librar [li'bra*] *vt* to support.
libreto [li'bretu] *m* libretto.
libriano/a [li'brjanu/a] *adj*, *m/f* Libran.
lição [li'sãw] (*pl* **-ões**) *f* lesson; **que isto lhe sirva de ~** let this be a lesson to you.
licença [li'sẽsa] *f* licence (*BRIT*), license (*US*); (*permissão*) permission; (*do trabalho*, *MIL*) leave; **estar de ~** to be on leave; **com ~** excuse me; **dá ~?** may I?; **tirar ~** to go on leave; **sob ~** under licence; **~ poética** poetic licence.
licença-prêmio (*pl* **licenças-prêmio**) *f* long paid leave.
licenciado/a [lisẽ'sjadu/a] *m/f* graduate.
licenciar [lisẽ'sja*] *vt* to license; **~-se** *vr* (*EDUC*) to graduate; (*ficar de licença*) to take leave; **~ alguém** to give sb leave.
licenciatura [lisẽsja'tura] *f* (*título*) degree; (*curso*) degree course.
licencioso/a [lisẽ'sjozu/ɔza] *adj* licentious.
liceu [li'sew] (*PT*) *m* secondary (*BRIT*) *ou* high (*US*) school.

licitação [lisita'sãw] (*pl* **-ões**) *f* auction; (*concorrência*) tender; **abrir ~** to put out to tender.
licitante [lisi'tãtʃi] *m/f* bidder.
licitar [lisi'ta*] *vt* (*pôr em leilão*) to put up for auction ♦ *vi* to bid.
lícito/a ['lisitu/a] *adj* (*JUR*) lawful; (*justo*) fair, just; (*permissível*) permissible.
lições [li'sõjʃ] *fpl de* **lição**.
licor [li'ko*] *m* liqueur.
licoroso/a [liko'rozu/ɔza] *adj* (*vinho*) fortified.
lida ['lida] *f* toil; (*col*: *leitura*): **dar uma ~ em** to have a read of.
lidar [li'da*] *vi*: **~ com** (*ocupar-se*) to deal with; (*combater*) to struggle against; **~ em algo** to work in sth.
lide ['lidʒi] *f* (*trabalho*) work, chores *pl*; (*luta*) fight; (*JUR*) case.
líder ['lide*] *m/f* leader.
liderança [lide'rãsa] *f* leadership; (*ESPORTE*) lead.
liderar [lide'ra*] *vt* to lead.
lido/a ['lidu/a] *pp de* **ler** ♦ *adj* (*pessoa*) well-read.
lifting ['liftĩŋ] (*pl* **~s**) *m* face lift.
liga ['liga] *f* league; (*de meias*) garter, suspender; (*metal*) alloy.
ligação [liga'sãw] (*pl* **-ões**) *f* connection; (*fig*: *de amizade*) bond; (*TEL*) call; (*relação amorosa*) liaison; **fazer uma ~ para alguém** to call sb; **não consigo completar a ~** (*TEL*) I can't get through; **caiu a ~** (*TEL*) I (*ou* he *etc*) was cut off.
ligada [li'gada] *f* (*TEL*) ring, call; **dar uma ~ para alguém** (*col*) to give sb a ring.
ligado/a [li'gadu/a] *adj* (*TEC*) connected; (*luz*, *rádio etc*) on; (*metal*) alloy; **estar ~ (em)** (*col*: *absorto*) to be wrapped up (in); (: *em droga*) to be hooked (on); (*afetivamente*) to be attached (to).
ligadura [liga'dura] *f* bandage; (*MÚS*) ligature.
ligamento [liga'mẽtu] *m* ligament.
ligar [li'ga*] *vt* to tie, bind; (*unir*) to join, connect; (*luz*, *TV*) to switch on; (*afetivamente*) to bind together; (*carro*) to start (up) ♦ *vi* (*telefonar*) to ring; **~-se *vr* to join; **~-se com alguém** to join with sb; **~-se a algo** to be connected with sth; **~ para alguém** to ring sb up; **~ para fora** to ring out; **~ para ou a algo** (*dar atenção*) to take notice of sth; (*dar importância*) to care about sth; **eu nem ligo** it doesn't bother me; **não ligo a mínima (para)** I couldn't care less (about).
ligeireza [liʒej'reza] *f* lightness; (*rapidez*) swiftness; (*agilidade*) nimbleness.
ligeiro/a [li'ʒejru/a] *adj* light; (*ferimento*) slight; (*referência*) passing; (*conhecimentos*) scant; (*rápido*) quick, swift; (*ágil*) nimble ♦ *adv* swiftly, nimbly.
liguei [li'gej] *etc vb V* **ligar**.

NB: *European Portuguese adds the following consonants to certain words*: **b** (sú(b)dito, su(b)til); **c** (a(c)ção, a(c)cionista, a(c)to); **m** (inde(m)ne); **p** (ado(p)ção, ado(p)tar); *for further details see p. xiii.*

lilás [li'laʃ] *adj, m* lilac.
lima ['lima] *f* (*laranja*) type of (very sweet) orange; (*ferramenta*) file; ~ **de unhas** nail file.
limão [li'mãw] (*pl* -ões) *m* lime.
limão(-galego) (*pl* **limões(-galegos)**) *m* lemon.
limar [li'ma*] *vt* to file.
limbo ['lĩbu] *m*: **estar no** ~ to be in limbo.
limeira [li'mejra] *f* lime tree.
limiar [li'mja*] *m* threshold.
liminar [limi'na*] *f* (*JUR*) preliminary verdict.
limitação [limita'sãw] (*pl* -ões) *f* limitation, restriction.
limitado/a [limi'tadu/a] *adj* limited; **ele é meio** *ou* **bem** ~ he's not very bright.
limitar [limi'ta*] *vt* to limit, restrict; ~**-se** *vr*: ~**-se a** to limit o.s. to; ~**(-se) com** to border on; **ele limitava-se a dizer ...** he did nothing more than say ....
limite [li'mitʃi] *m* (*de terreno etc*) limit, boundary; (*fig*) limit; **passar dos** ~**s** to go too far; ~ **de crédito** credit limit; ~ **de idade** age limit.
limo ['limu] *m* (*BOT*) water weed; (*lodo*) slime.
limoeiro [li'mwejru] *m* lemon tree.
limões [li'mõjʃ] *mpl de* **limão**.
limonada [limo'nada] *f* lemonade (*BRIT*), lemon soda (*US*).
limpa ['lĩpa] (*col*) *f* clean; (*roubo*): **fazer uma** ~ **em** to clean out.
limpação [lĩpa'sãw] *f* cleaning.
limpador [lĩpa'do*] *m*: ~ **de pára-brisas** windscreen wiper (*BRIT*), windshield wiper (*US*).
limpa-pés *m inv* shoe scraper.
limpar [lĩ'pa*] *vt* to clean; (*lágrimas, suor*) to wipe away; (*polir*) to shine, polish; (*fig*) to clean up; (*arroz, peixe*) to clean; (*roubar*) to rob.
limpa-trilhos *m inv* cowcatcher.
limpeza [lĩ'peza] *f* cleanliness; (*esmero*) neatness; (*ato*) cleaning; (*fig*) clean-up; (*roubo*): **fazer uma** ~ **em** to clean out; ~ **de pele** facial; ~ **pública** rubbish (*BRIT*) *ou* garbage (*US*) collection, sanitation.
límpido/a ['lĩpidu/a] *adj* limpid.
limpo/a ['lĩpu/a] *pp de* **limpar** ♦ *adj* clean; (*céu, consciência*) clear; (*COM*) net, clear; (*fig*) pure; (*col: pronto*) ready; **passar a** ~ to make a fair copy; **tirar a** ~ to find out the truth about, clear up; **estar** ~ **com alguém** (*col*) to be in with sb.
limusine [limu'zini] *f* limousine.
lince ['lĩsi] *m* lynx; **ter olhos de** ~ to have eyes like a hawk.
linchar [lĩ'ʃa*] *vt* to lynch.
lindeza [lĩ'deza] *f* beauty.
lindo/a ['lĩdu/a] *adj* lovely; ~ **de morrer** (*col*) stunning.
linear [li'nja*] *adj* linear.
linfático/a [lĩ'fatʃiku/a] *adj* lymphatic.
lingerie [lĩʒe'ri] *m* lingerie.
lingote [lĩ'gotʃi] *m* ingot.
língua ['lĩgwa] *f* tongue; (*linguagem*) lan-

guage; **botar a** ~ **para fora** to stick out one's tongue; **dar com a** ~ **nos dentes** to let the cat out of the bag; **dobrar a** ~ to bite one's tongue; **estar na ponta da** ~ to be on the tip of one's tongue; **ficar de** ~ **de fora** (*exausto*) to be pooped; **pagar pela** ~ to live to regret one's words; **saber algo na ponta da** ~ to know sth inside out; **ter uma** ~ **comprida** (*fig*) to have a big mouth; **em** ~ **da gente** (*col*) in plain English; ~ **franca** lingua franca; ~ **materna** mother tongue.
linguado [lĩ'gwadu] *m* (*peixe*) sole.
linguagem [lĩ'gwaʒẽ] (*pl* -**ns**) *f* (*tb*: *COMPUT*) language; (*falada*) speech; ~ **de alto nível** (*COMPUT*) high-level language; ~ **de máquina** (*COMPUT*) machine language; ~ **de montagem** (*COMPUT*) assembly language; ~ **de programação** (*COMPUT*) programming language.
linguajar [lĩgwa'ʒa*] *m* speech, language.
linguarudo/a [lĩgwa'rudu/a] *adj* gossiping ♦ *m/f* gossip.
lingüeta [lĩ'gweta] *f* (*fechadura*) bolt; (*balança*) pointer.
lingüiça [lĩ'gwisa] *f* sausage; **encher** ~ (*col*) to waffle on.
lingüista [lĩ'gwiʃta] *m/f* linguist.
lingüística [lĩ'gwiʃtʃika] *f* linguistics *sg*.
lingüístico/a [lĩ'gwiʃtʃiku/a] *adj* linguistic.
linha ['liɲa] *f* line; (*para costura*) thread; (*barbante*) string, cord; (*fila*) row; ~**s** *fpl* (*carta*) letter *sg*; **as** ~**s gerais de um projeto** the outlines of a project; **em** ~ in line, in a row; (*COMPUT*) on line; **fora de** ~ (*COMPUT*) off line; **andar na** ~ (*fig*) to toe the line; **sair da** ~ (*fig*) to step out of line; **comportar-se com muita** ~ to behave very correctly; **manter/perder a** ~ to keep/lose one's cool; **o telefone não deu** ~ the line was dead; ~ **aérea** airline; ~ **de ataque** (*FUTEBOL*) forward line, forwards *pl*; ~ **de conduta** course of action; ~ **de crédito** (*COM*) credit line; ~ **de fogo** firing line; ~ **demarcatória** demarcation line; ~ **de mira** sights *pl*; ~ **de montagem** assembly line; ~ **de partido** party line; ~ **de saque** (*TÊNIS*) baseline; ~ **férrea** railway (*BRIT*), railroad (*US*).
linhaça [li'ɲasa] *f* linseed.
linha-dura (*pl* **linhas-duras**) *m/f* hardliner.
linhagem [li'ɲaʒẽ] *f* lineage.
linho ['liɲu] *m* linen; (*planta*) flax.
linóleo [li'nɔlju] *m* linoleum.
lipoaspiração [lipuaʃpira'sãw] *f* liposuction.
liquefazer [likefa'ze*] (*irreg: como* **fazer**) *vt* to liquefy.
líquen ['likẽ] *m* lichen.
liquidação [likida'sãw] (*pl* -ões) *f* liquidation; (*em loja*) (clearance) sale; (*de conta*) settlement; **em** ~ on sale; **entrar em** ~ to go into liquidation.
liquidante [liki'dãtʃi] *m/f* liquidator.
liquidar [liki'da*] *vt* to liquidate; (*conta*) to settle; (*mercadoria*) to sell off; (*assunto*) to

lay to rest ♦ *vi* (*loja*) to have a sale; ~-**se** *vr* (*destruir-se*) to be destroyed; ~ **(com)** **alguém** (*fig*: *arrasar*) to destroy sb; (: *matar*) to do away with sb.

liquidez [likiˈdeʒ] *f* (*COM*) liquidity.

liqüidificador [likwidʒifikaˈdo*] *m* liquidizer.

liqüidificar [likwidʒifiˈka*] *vt* to liquidize.

líquido/a [ˈlikidu/a] *adj* liquid, fluid; (*COM*) net ♦ *m* liquid.

lira [ˈlira] *f* lyre; (*moeda*) lira.

lírica [ˈlirika] *f* (*MÚS*) lyrics *pl*; (*poesia*) lyric poetry.

lírico/a [ˈliriku/a] *adj* lyric(al).

lírio [ˈlirju] *m* lily.

lírio-do-vale (*pl* **lírios-do-vale**) *m* lily of the valley.

lirismo [liˈriʒmu] *m* lyricism.

Lisboa [liʒˈboa] *n* Lisbon.

lisboeta [liʒˈbweta] *adj* Lisbon *atr* ♦ *m/f* inhabitant *ou* native of Lisbon.

liso/a [ˈlizu/a] *adj* smooth; (*tecido*) plain; (*cabelo*) straight; (*col*: *sem dinheiro*) broke; **estar ~, leso e louco** (*col*) to be flat broke.

lisonja [liˈzõʒa] *f* flattery.

lisonjeador(a) [lizõʒjaˈdo*(a)] *adj* flattering ♦ *m/f* flatterer.

lisonjear [lizõˈʒja*] *vt* to flatter.

lisonjeiro/a [lizõˈʒejru/a] *adj* flattering.

lista [ˈliʃta] *f* list; (*listra*) stripe; (*PT*: *menu*) menu; ~ **civil** civil list; ~ **negra** black list; ~ **telefônica** telephone directory.

listado/a [liʃˈtadu/a] *adj* = **listrado/a**.

listagem [liʃˈtaʒẽ] (*pl* **-ns**) *f* (*COMPUT*) listing.

listar [liʃˈta*] *vt* (*COMPUT*) to list.

listra [ˈliʃtra] *f* stripe.

listrado/a [liʃˈtradu/a] *adj* striped.

literal [liteˈraw] (*pl* **-ais**) *adj* literal.

literário/a [liteˈrarju/a] *adj* literary.

literato [liteˈratu] *m* man of letters.

literatura [literaˈtura] *f* literature.

litigante [litʃiˈgãtʃi] *m/f* (*JUR*) litigant.

litigar [litʃiˈga*] *vt* to contend ♦ *vi* to go to law.

litígio [liˈtʃiʒju] *m* (*JUR*) lawsuit; (*contenda*) dispute.

litigioso/a [litʃiˈʒozu/ɔza] *adj* (*JUR*) disputed.

litografia [litograˈfia] *f* (*processo*) lithography; (*gravura*) lithograph.

litogravura [litograˈvura] *f* lithograph.

litoral [litoˈraw] (*pl* **-ais**) *adj* coastal ♦ *m* coast, seaboard.

litorâneo/a [litoˈranju/a] *adj* coastal.

litro [ˈlitru] *m* litre (*BRIT*), liter (*US*).

Lituânia [liˈtwanja] *f*: **a ~** Lithuania.

liturgia [lituxˈʒia] *f* liturgy.

litúrgico/a [liˈtuxʒiku/a] *adj* liturgical.

lívido/a [ˈlividu/a] *adj* livid.

living [ˈlivĩ] (*pl* **~s**) *m* living room.

livramento [livraˈmẽtu] *m* release; ~ **condicional** parole.

livrar [liˈvra*] *vt* to release, liberate; (*salvar*)

to save; ~-**se** *vr* to escape; ~-**se de** to get rid of; (*compromisso*) to get out of; **Deus me livre!** Heaven forbid!

livraria [livraˈria] *f* bookshop (*BRIT*), bookstore (*US*).

livre [ˈlivri] *adj* free; (*lugar*) unoccupied; (*desimpedido*) clear, open; ~ **de impostos** tax-free; **estar ~ de algo** to be free of sth; **de ~ e espontânea vontade** of one's own free will.

livre-arbítrio *m* free will.

livreiro/a [livˈrejru/a] *m/f* bookseller.

livresco/a [liˈvreʃku/a] *adj* book *atr*; (*pessoa*) bookish.

livrete [liˈvretʃi] *m* booklet.

livro [ˈlivru] *m* book; ~ **brochado** paperback; ~ **caixa** (*COM*) cash book; ~ **de bolso** pocket-sized book; ~ **de cabeceira** favo(u)rite book; ~ **de cheques** cheque book (*BRIT*), check book (*US*); ~ **de consulta** reference book; ~ **de cozinha** cookery book (*BRIT*), cookbook (*US*); ~ **de mercadorias** stock book; ~ **de registro** catalogue (*BRIT*), catalog (*US*); ~ **de texto** *ou* **didático** text book; ~ **encadernado** *ou* **de capa dura** hardback.

lixa [ˈliʃa] *f* sandpaper; (*de unhas*) nail-file; (*peixe*) dogfish.

lixadeira [liʃaˈdejra] *f* sander.

lixar [liˈʃa*] *vt* to sand; ~-**se** *vr* (*col*): **estou me lixando com isso** I couldn't care less about it.

lixeira [liˈʃejra] *f* dustbin (*BRIT*), garbage can (*US*).

lixeiro [liˈʃejru] *m* dustman (*BRIT*), garbage man (*US*).

lixo [ˈliʃu] *m* rubbish, garbage (*US*); **ser um ~** (*col*) to be rubbish; ~ **atômico** nuclear waste.

Lj. *abr* = **loja.**

lj. *abr* = **loja.**

-lo [lu] *pron* him; (*você*) you; (*coisa*) it.

lobby [ˈlɔbi] (*pl* **-ies**) *m* (*POL*) lobby.

lobinho [loˈbiɲu] *m* (*ZOOL*) wolf cub; (*escoteiro*) cub.

lóbi [ˈlɔbi] *m* = **lobby.**

lobisomem [lobiˈsomẽ] (*pl* **-ns**) *m* werewolf.

lobista [loˈbiʃta] *m/f* lobbyist.

lobo [ˈlobu] *m* wolf.

lobo-do-mar (*pl* **lobos-do-mar**) *m* old salt.

lobo-marinho (*pl* **lobos-marinhos**) *m* sea lion.

lobrigar [lobriˈga*] *vt* to glimpse.

lóbulo [ˈlɔbulu] *m* lobe.

locação [lokaˈsãw] (*pl* **-ões**) *f* lease; (*de vídeo etc*) rental.

locador(a) [lokaˈdo*(a)] *m/f* (*de casa*) landlord; (*de carro, filme*) rental agent ♦ *f* rental company; ~**a de vídeo** video rental shop.

local [loˈkaw] (*pl* **-ais**) *adj* local ♦ *m* site, place

♦ *f* (*notícia*) story.
localidade [lokali'dadʒi] *f* (*lugar*) locality; (*povoação*) town.
localização [lokaliza'sãw] (*pl* **-ões**) *f* location.
localizar [lokali'za*] *vt* to locate; (*situar*) to place; **~-se** *vr* (*estabelecer-se*) to be located; (*orientar-se*) to get one's bearings.
loção [lo'sãw] (*pl* **-ões**) *f* lotion; **~ após-barba** aftershave (lotion).
locatário/a [loka'tarju/a] *m/f* (*de casa*) tenant; (*de carro, filme*) hirer.
locaute [lo'kawtʃi] *m* lockout.
loções [lo'sõjʃ] *fpl de* **loção**.
locomoção [lokomo'sãw] (*pl* **-ões**) *f* locomotion.
locomotiva [lokomo'tʃiva] *f* railway (*BRIT*) *ou* railroad (*US*) engine, locomotive.
locomover-se [lokomo'vexsi] *vr* to move around.
locução [loku'sãw] (*pl* **-ões**) *f* (*LING*) phrase; (*dicção*) diction.
locutor(a) [loku'to*(a)] *m/f* (*TV*, *RÁDIO*) announcer.
lodacento/a [loda'sẽtu/a] *adj* muddy.
lodo ['lodu] *m* mud, slime.
lodoso/a [lo'dozu/ɔza] *adj* muddy.
logaritmo [loga'ritʃimo] *m* logarithm.
lógica ['lɔʒika] *f* logic.
lógico/a ['lɔʒiku/a] *adj* logical; (**é**) **~!** of course!
logística [lo'ʒiʃtʃika] *f* logistics *sg*.
logo ['lɔgu] *adv* (*imediatamente*) right away, at once; (*em breve*) soon; (*justamente*) just, right; (*mais tarde*) later; **~**, **~** straightaway, without delay; **~ mais** later; **~ no começo** right at the start; **~ que, tão ~** as soon as; **até ~!** bye!; **~ antes/depois** just before/ shortly afterwards; **~ de saída** *ou* **de cara** straightaway, right away.
logopedia [logope'dʒia] *f* speech therapy.
logopedista [logope'dʒiʃta] *m/f* speech therapist.
logotipo [logo'tʃipu] *m* logo.
logradouro [logra'doru] *m* public area.
lograr [lo'gra*] *vt* (*alcançar*) to achieve; (*obter*) to get, obtain; (*enganar*) to cheat; **~ fazer** to manage to do.
logro ['logru] *m* fraud.
loiro/a ['lojru/a] *adj* = **louro/a**.
loja ['lɔʒa] *f* shop; (*maçônica*) lodge; **~ de antiguidades** antique shop; **~ de brinquedos** toy shop; **~ de departamentos** department store; **~ de ferragens** ironmonger's (*BRIT*), hardware store; **~ de produtos naturais** health food shop.
lojista [lo'ʒiʃta] *m/f* shopkeeper.
lomba ['lõba] *f* ridge; (*ladeira*) slope.
lombada [lõ'bada] *f* (*de animal*) back; (*de livro*) spine; (*na estrada*) ramp.
lombar [lõ'ba*] *adj* lumbar.
lombeira [lõ'bejra] *f* listlessness.
lombinho [lõ'biɲu] *m* (*carne*) tenderloin.
lombo ['lõbu] *m* back; (*carne*) loin.

lombriga [lõ'briga] *f* ringworm.
lona ['lɔna] *f* canvas; **estar na última ~** (*col*) to be broke.
Londres ['lõdriʃ] *n* London.
londrino/a [lõ'drinu/a] *adj* London *atr* ♦ *m/f* Londoner.
longa-metragem (*pl* **longas-metragens**) *m*: (**filme de**) **~** feature (film).
longe ['lõʒi] *adv* far, far away ♦ *adj* distant; **ao ~** in the distance; **de ~** from far away; (*sem dúvida*) by a long way; **~ dos olhos, ~ do coração** out of sight, out of mind; **~ de** a long way *ou* far from; **~ disso** far from it; **ir ~ demais** (*fig*) to go too far; **essa sua mania vem de ~** he's had this habit for a long time; **ver ~** (*fig*) to have vision.
longevidade [lõʒevi'dadʒi] *f* longevity.
longínquo/a [lõ'ʒĩkwu/a] *adj* distant, remote.
longíquo/a [lõ'ʒĩkwu/a] *adj* = **longínquo/a**.
longitude [lõʒi'tudʒi] *f* (*GEO*) longitude.
longitudinal [lõʒitudʒi'naw] (*pl* **-ais**) *adj* longitudinal.
longo/a ['lõgu/a] *adj* long ♦ *m* (*vestido*) long dress, evening dress; **ao ~ de** along, alongside.
lontra ['lõtra] *f* otter.
loquacidade [lokwasi'dadʒi] *f* loquacity.
loquaz [lo'kwaʒ] *adj* talkative.
lorde ['lɔxdʒi] *m* lord.
lorota [lo'rɔta] (*col*) *f* fib.
losango [lo'zãgu] *m* lozenge, diamond.
lotação [lota'sãw] *f* capacity; (*vinho*) blending; (*de funcionários*) complement; (*BR*: *ônibus*) bus; **~ completa** *ou* **esgotada** (*TEATRO*) sold out.
lotado/a [lo'tadu/a] *adj* (*TEATRO*) full; (*ônibus*) full up; (*bar, praia*) packed, crowded.
lotar [lo'ta*] *vt* to fill, pack; (*funcionário*) to place ♦ *vi* to fill up.
lote ['lɔtʃi] *m* (*porção*) portion, share; (*em leilão*) lot; (*terreno*) plot; (*de ações*) parcel, batch.
loteamento [lotʃja'mẽtu] *m* division into lots.
lotear [lo'tʃja*] *vt* to divide into lots.
loteca [lo'tɛka] (*col*) *f* pools *pl* (*BRIT*), lottery (*US*).
loteria [lote'ria] *f* lottery; **ganhar na ~** to win the lottery; **~ esportiva** football pools *pl* (*BRIT*), lottery (*US*).
loto¹ ['lɔtu] *m* lotus.
loto² ['lɔtu] *m* bingo.
lótus ['lɔtuʃ] *m inv* lotus.
louça ['losa] *f* china; (*conjunto*) crockery; (*tb*: **~ sanitária**) bathroom suite; **de ~** china *atr*; **~ de barro** earthenware; **~ de jantar** dinner service; **lavar a ~** to do the washing up (*BRIT*) *ou* the dishes.
louçaria [losa'ria] *f* china; (*loja*) china shop.
louco/a ['loku/a] *adj* crazy, mad; (*sucesso*) runaway; (*frio*) freezing ♦ *m/f* lunatic; **~ varrido** raving mad; **~ de fome/raiva** ravenous/hopping mad; **~ por** crazy about; **deixar alguém ~** to drive sb crazy; **ser uma**

coisa de ~ (*col*) to be really something; **estar/ficar** ~ **da vida (com)** to be/get mad (at); ~ **de pedra** (*col*) stark staring mad; **deu uma louca nele e ...** ~ something strange came over him and ...; **cada** ~ **com sua mania** whatever turns you on.

loucura [lo'kura] *f* madness; (*ato*) crazy thing; **ser** ~ **(fazer)** to be crazy (to do); **ser uma** ~ to be crazy; (*col: ser muito bom*) to be fantastic; **ter** ~ **por** to be crazy about.

louquice [lo'kisi] *f* madness; (*ato, dito*) crazy thing.

louro/a ['loru/a] *adj* blond, fair ♦ *m* laurel; (*CULIN*) bay leaf; (*cor*) blondness; (*papagaio*) parrot; ~**s** *mpl* (*fig*) laurels.

lousa ['loza] *f* flagstone; (*tumular*) gravestone; (*quadro-negro*) blackboard.

louva-a-deus ['lova-] *m inv* praying mantis.

louvação [lova'sãw] (*pl* **-ões**) *f* praise.

louvar [lo'va*] *vt, vi:* ~ **(a) Deus** to praise God.

louvável [lo'vavew] (*pl* **-eis**) *adj* praiseworthy.

louvor [lo'vo*] *m* praise.

LP *abr m* LP.

lpm *abr* (= *linhas por minuto*) lpm.

Ltda. *abr* (= *Limitada*) Ltd.

lua ['lua] *f* moon; **estar** *ou* **viver no mundo da** ~ to have one's head in the clouds; **estar de** ~ (*col*) to be in a mood; **ser de** ~ (*col*) to be moody; ~ **cheia/nova** full/new moon.

lua-de-mel *f* honeymoon.

Luanda ['lwãda] *n* Luanda.

luar ['lwa*] *m* moonlight; **banhado de** ~ moonlit.

luarento/a [lwa'rẽtu/a] *adj* moonlit.

lubrificação [lubrifika'sãw] (*pl* **-ões**) *f* lubrication.

lubrificante [lubrifi'kãtfi] *m* lubricant ♦ *adj* lubricating.

lubrificar [lubrifi'ka*] *vt* to lubricate.

lucidez [lusi'deʒ] *f* lucidity, clarity.

lúcido/a ['lusidu/a] *adj* lucid.

lúcio ['lusju] *m* (*peixe*) pike.

lucrar [lu'kra*] *vt* (*tirar proveito*) to profit from *ou* by; (*dinheiro*) to make; (*gozar*) to enjoy ♦ *vi* to make a profit; ~ **com** *ou* **em** to profit by.

lucratividade [lukratʃivi'dadʒi] *f* profitability.

lucrativo/a [lukra'tʃivu/a] *adj* lucrative, profitable.

lucro ['lukru] *m* gain; (*COM*) profit; ~ **bruto/líquido** (*COM*) gross/net profit; **participação nos** ~**s** (*COM*) profit-sharing; ~**s e perdas** (*COM*) profit and loss.

lucubração [lukubra'sãw] (*pl* **-ões**) *f* meditation, pondering.

ludibriar [ludʒi'brja*] *vt* (*enganar*) to dupe, deceive; (*escarnecer*) to mock, deride.

lúdico/a ['ludʒiku/a] *adj* playful.

lufada [lu'fada] *f* gust (of wind).

lugar [lu'ga*] *m* place; (*espaço*) space, room; (*para sentar*) seat; (*emprego*) job; (*ocasião*) opportunity; **em** ~ **de** instead of; **dar** ~ **a** (*causar*) to give rise to; ~ **comum** commonplace; **em primeiro** ~ in the first place; **em algum/nenhum/outro/todo** ~ somewhere/nowhere/somewhere else, elsewhere/everywhere; **ter** ~ (*acontecer*) to take place; **ponha-se em meu** ~ put yourself in my position; **ponha-se no seu** ~ don't get ideas above your station; **ele foi no meu** ~ he went instead of me *ou* in my place; **tirar o primeiro** ~ to come first; **conhecer o seu** ~ to know one's place; ~ **de nascimento** place of birth.

lugarejo [luga'reʒu] *m* village.

lúgubre ['lugubri] *adj* mournful; (*escuro*) gloomy.

lula ['lula] *f* squid.

lumbago [lũ'bagu] *m* lumbago.

lume ['lumi] *m* fire; (*luz*) light.

luminária [lumi'narja] *f* lamp; ~**s** *fpl* illuminations.

luminosidade [luminozi'dadʒi] *f* brightness.

luminoso/a [lumi'nozu/ɔza] *adj* luminous, bright; (*fig: raciocínio*) clear; (: *idéia, talento*) brilliant; (*letreiro*) illuminated.

lunar [lu'na*] *adj* lunar ♦ *m* (*na pele*) mole.

lunático/a [lu'natʃiku/a] *adj* mad.

luneta [lu'neta] *f* eye-glass; (*telescópio*) telescope.

lupa ['lupa] *f* magnifying glass.

lúpulo ['lupulu] *m* (*BOT*) hop.

lusco-fusco ['luʃku-] *m* twilight.

lusitano/a [luzi'tanu/a] *adj* Portuguese, Lusitanian.

luso/a ['luzu/a] *adj* Portuguese.

luso-brasileiro/a (*pl* ~**s**) *adj* Luso-Brazilian.

lustra-móveis ['luʃtra-] *m inv* furniture polish.

lustrar [luʃ'tra*] *vt* to polish, clean.

lustre ['luʃtri] *m* gloss, sheen; (*fig*) lustre (*BRIT*), luster (*US*); (*luminária*) chandelier.

lustroso/a [luʃ'trozu/ɔza] *adj* shiny.

luta ['luta] *f* fight, struggle; ~ **armada** armed combat; ~ **de boxe** boxing; ~ **de classes** class struggle; ~ **livre** wrestling; **foi uma** ~ **convencê-lo** it was a struggle to convince him.

lutador(a) [luta'do*(a)] *m/f* fighter; (*atleta*) wrestler.

lutar [lu'ta*] *vi* to fight, struggle; (*luta livre*) to wrestle ♦ *vt* (*caratê, judô*) to do; ~ **contra/por algo** to fight against/for sth; ~ **para fazer algo** to fight *ou* struggle to do sth; ~ **com** (*dificuldades*) to struggle against; (*competir*) to fight with.

luto ['lutu] *m* mourning; (*tristeza*) grief; **de** ~ in mourning; **pôr** ~ to go into mourning.

luva ['luva] *f* glove; ~**s** *fpl* (*pagamento*) pay-

NB: European Portuguese adds the following consonants to certain words: **b** (sú(b)dito, su(b)til); **c** (a(c)ção, a(c)cionista, a(c)to); **m** (inde(m)ne); **p** (ado(p)ção, ado(p)tar); *for further details see p. xiii.*

ment *sg*; (*ao locador*) fee *sg*; **caber como uma** ~ to fit like a glove.

luxação [luʃa'sãw] (*pl* -**ões**) *f* dislocation.

luxar [lu'ʃa*] *vi* to show off.

Luxemburgo [luʃẽ'buxgu] *m*: **o** ~ Luxembourg.

luxento/a [lu'ʃẽtu/a] *adj* fussy, finnicky.

luxo ['luʃu] *m* luxury; **de** ~ luxury *atr*; **dar-se ao** ~ **de** to allow o.s. to; **poder dar-se ao** ~ **de** to be able to afford to; **cheio de** ~ (*col*) prissy, finnicky; **deixe de** ~ (*col*) don't come it; **fazer** ~ (*col*) to play hard to get; **com** ~ luxurious(ly); (*vestir-se*) fancily.

luxuosidade [luʃwozi'dadʒi] *f* luxuriousness.

luxuoso/a [lu'ʃwozu/ɔza] *adj* luxurious.

luxúria [lu'ʃurja] *f* lust.

luxuriante [luʃu'rjãtʃi] *adj* lush.

luz [luʒ] *f* light; (*eletricidade*) electricity; **à** ~ **de** by the light of; (*fig*) in the light of; **a meia** ~ with subdued lighting; **dar à** ~ (**um filho**) to give birth (to a son); **deu-me uma** ~ I had an idea; ~ **artificial/natural** artificial/natural light; ~ **de vela** candlelight; **pessoa de muita** ~ enlightened person.

luzidio/a [luzi'dʒiu/a] *adj* shining, glossy.

luzir [lu'zi*] *vi* to shine, gleam; (*fig*) to be successful.

Lx.a *abr* = **Lisboa**.

lycra ['lajkra] ® *f* lycra ®.

M

M, m ['emi] (*pl* **ms**) *m* M, m; **M de Maria** M for Mike.

MA *abr* = **Maranhão**.

ma [ma] *pron* = **me** + **a**.

má [ma] *adj f de* **mau**.

maca ['maka] *f* stretcher.

maçã [ma'sã] *f* apple; ~ **do rosto** cheekbone.

macabro/a [ma'kabru/a] *adj* macabre.

macaca [ma'kaka] *f* she-monkey; **estar com a** ~ (*col*) to be in a foul mood.

macacada [maka'kada] *f* (*turma*): **a** ~ the gang.

macacão [maka'kãw] (*pl* -**ões**) *m* (*de trabalhador*) overalls *pl* (*BRIT*), coveralls *pl* (*US*); (*da moda*) jump-suit.

macaco [ma'kaku] *m* monkey; (*MEC*) jack; (**fato**) ~ (*PT*) overalls *pl* (*BRIT*), coveralls *pl* (*US*); (*pessoa feia*) ugly mug; (*tb*: ~ **de imitação**) copycat; ~ **velho** (*fig*) old hand; ~**s me mordam** (*col*) blow me down.

macacões [maka'kõjʃ] *mpl de* **macacão**.

maçada [ma'sada] *f* bore.

macadame [maka'dami] *m* asphalt, tarmac (*BRIT*).

maçador(a) [masa'do*(a)] (*PT*) *adj* boring.

macambúzio/a [makã'buzju/a] *adj* sullen.

maçaneta [masa'neta] *f* knob.

maçante [ma'sãtʃi] (*BR*) *adj* boring.

macaquear [maka'kja*] *vt* to ape.

macaquice [maka'kisi] *f*: **fazer** ~**s** to clown around.

maçar [ma'sa*] *vt* to bore.

maçarico [masa'riku] *m* (*tubo*) blowpipe; (*ave*) curlew.

maçaroca [masa'rɔka] *f* wad.

macarrão [maka'xãw] *m* pasta; (*em forma de canudo*) spaghetti.

macarronada [makaxo'nada] *f* pasta with cheese and tomato sauce.

macarrônico/a [maka'xoniku/a] *adj* (*francês etc*) broken, halting.

Macau [ma'kaw] *n* Macao.

maceioense [masej'wẽsi] *adj* from Maceió ♦ *m/f* person from Maceió.

macerado/a [mase'radu/a] *adj* (*rosto*) haggard.

macerar [mase'ra*] *vt* (*amolecer*) to soften; (*fig*: *mortificar*) to mortify; (: *rosto*) to make haggard.

macérrimo/a [ma'sɛximu/a] *adj superl de* **magro**.

macete [ma'setʃi] *m* mallet; (*col*) trick; **dar o** ~ **a alguém** (*col*) to show sb the way.

maceteado/a [mase'tʃjadu/a] (*col*) *adj* (*plano*) clever; (*casa*) well-designed.

machadada [maʃa'dada] *f* blow with an axe (*BRIT*) *ou* ax (*US*).

machado [ma'ʃadu] *m* axe (*BRIT*), ax (*US*).

machão/ona [ma'ʃãw/ɔna] (*pl* -**ões/~s**) *adj* tough; (*mulher*) butch ♦ *m* macho man; (*valentão*) tough guy.

machê [ma'ʃe] *adj*: **papel** ~ papier-mâché.

machete [ma'ʃetʃi] *m* machete.

machismo [ma'ʃiʒmu] *m* male chauvinism, machismo; (*col*) toughness.

machista [ma'ʃiʃta] *adj* chauvinistic, macho ♦ *m* male chauvinist.

macho ['maʃu] *adj* male; (*fig*) virile, manly; (*valentão*) tough ♦ *m* male; (*TEC*) tap.

machões [ma'ʃõjʃ] *mpl de* **machão**.

machona [ma'ʃɔna] *f* butch woman; (*col*: *ofensivo*: *lésbica*) dyke.

machucado/a [maʃu'kadu/a] *adj* hurt; (*pé*, *braço*) bad ♦ *m* injury; (*lugar*) sore patch.

machucar [maʃu'ka*] *vt* to hurt; (*produzir contusão*) to bruise ♦ *vi* to hurt; ~**-se** *vr* to hurt o.s.; (*col*: *estrepar-se*) to come a cropper, mess up.

maciço/a [ma'sisu/a] *adj* solid; (*espesso*) thick; (*quantidade*) massive ♦ *m* (*GEO*) massif; **ouro** ~ solid gold; **uma dose maciça** a massive dose.

macieira [ma'sjejra] *f* apple tree.

maciez [ma'sjeʒ] *f* softness.

macilento/a [masi'lẽtu/a] *adj* gaunt, haggard.

macio/a [ma'siu/a] *adj* soft; (*liso*) smooth.

maciota [ma'sjɔta] *f*: **na** ~ without problems.

maço ['masu] *m* (*de folhas, notas*) bundle; (*de cigarros*) packet.

maçom [ma'sõ] (*pl* **-ns**) *m* freemason.

maçonaria [masona'ria] *f* freemasonry.

maconha [ma'kɔɲa] *f* dope; **cigarro de ~** joint.

maconhado/a [mako'ɲadu/a] *adj* stoned.

maconheiro/a [mako'ɲejru/a] *m/f* (*viciado*) dope fiend; (*vendedor*) dope peddler.

maçônico/a [ma'soniku/a] *adj* masonic; **loja maçônica** masonic lodge.

maçons [ma'sõʃ] *mpl de* **maçom**.

má-criação (*pl* **-ões**) *f* rudeness; (*ato, dito*) rude thing.

macrobiótica [makro'bjɔtʃika] *f* (*dieta*) macrobiotic diet.

macrobiótico/a [makro'bjɔtʃiku/a] *adj* macrobiotic.

macroeconomia [makroekono'mia] *f* macroeconomics.

mácula ['makula] *f* stain, blemish.

macumba [ma'kũba] *f* voodoo; (*despacho*) voodoo offering.

macumbeiro/a [makũ'bejru/a] *adj* voodoo ♦ *m/f* follower of macumba.

madama [ma'dama] *f* = **madame**.

madame [ma'dami] *f* (*senhora*) lady; (*col: dona-de-casa*) lady of the house; (: *esposa*) missus; (: *de bordel*) madame.

Madeira [ma'dejra] *f*: **a ~** Madeira.

madeira [ma'dejra] *f* wood ♦ *m* Madeira (wine); **~ compensada** plywood; **de ~** wooden; **~ de lei** hardwood; **bater na ~** (*fig*) to touch (*BRIT*) *ou* knock on (*US*) wood.

madeira-branca (*pl* **madeiras-brancas**) *f* softwood.

madeiramento [madejra'mẽtu] *m* woodwork.

madeirense [madej'rẽsi] *adj, m/f* Madeiran.

madeiro [ma'dejru] *m* (*lenho*) log; (*viga*) beam.

madeixa [ma'dejʃa] *f* (*de cabelo*) lock; **~s** *fpl* locks.

madona [ma'dɔna] *f* madonna.

madrasta [ma'draʃta] *f* stepmother; (*fig*) heartless mother.

madre ['madri] *f* (*freira*) nun; (*superiora*) mother superior.

madrepérola [madre'pɛrola] *f* mother of pearl.

madressilva [madre'siwva] *f* honeysuckle.

Madri [ma'dri] *n* Madrid.

Madrid [ma'drid] (*PT*) *n* Madrid.

madrinha [ma'driɲa] *f* godmother; (*fig: patrocinadora*) patron.

madrugada [madru'gada] *f* (early) morning; (*alvorada*) dawn, daybreak; **duas horas da ~** two in the morning.

madrugador(a) [madruga'do*(a)] *m/f* early riser; (*fig*) early bird ♦ *adj* early-rising.

madrugar [madru'ga*] *vi* to get up early;

(*aparecer cedo*) to be early.

madurar [madu'ra*] *vt, vi* (*fruta*) to ripen; (*fig*) to mature.

madureza [madu'reza] *f* (*de pessoa*) maturity.

maduro/a [ma'duro/a] *adj* (*fruta*) ripe; (*fig*) mature; (: *prudente*) prudent.

mãe [mãj] *f* mother; **~ adotiva/de criação** adoptive/foster mother; **~ de família** wife and mother.

mãe-benta (*pl* **mães-bentas**) *f* (*CULIN*) coconut cookie.

mãe-de-santo (*pl* **mães-de-santo**) *f* voodoo priestess.

MAer (*BR*) *abr m* = **Ministério da Aeronáutica**.

maestria [majʃ'tria] *f* mastery; **com ~** in a masterly way.

maestro/trina [ma'ɛʃtru/'trina] *m/f* conductor.

má-fé *f* bad faith, malicious intent.

máfia ['mafja] *f* mafia.

mafioso/a [ma'fjozu/ɔza] *adj* gangsterish ♦ *m* mobster.

mafuá [ma'fwa] *m* fair; (*bagunça*) mess.

magarefe [maga'rɛfi] (*PT*) *m* butcher; slaughterer.

magazine [maga'zini] *m* magazine; (*loja*) department store.

magia [ma'ʒia] *f* magic; **~ negra** black magic.

mágica ['maʒika] *f* magic; (*truque*) magic trick; *V tb* **mágico**.

mágico/a ['maʒiku/a] *adj* magic ♦ *m/f* magician.

magistério [maʒiʃ'tɛrju] *m* (*ensino*) teaching; (*profissão*) teaching profession; (*professorado*) teachers *pl*.

magistrado [maʒiʃ'tradu] *m* magistrate.

magistral [maʒiʃ'traw] (*pl* **-ais**) *adj* magisterial; (*fig*) masterly.

magistratura [maʒiʃtra'tura] *f* magistracy.

magnanimidade [magnanimi'dadʒi] *f* magnanimity.

magnânimo/a [mag'nanimu/a] *adj* magnanimous.

magnata [mag'nata] *m* magnate, tycoon.

magnésia [mag'nɛzja] *f* magnesia.

magnésio [mag'nɛzju] *m* magnesium.

magnético/a [mag'nɛtʃiku/a] *adj* magnetic.

magnetismo [magne'tʃizmu] *m* magnetism.

magnetizar [magnetʃi'za*] *vt* to magnetize; (*fascinar*) to mesmerize.

magnificência [magnifi'sẽsja] *f* magnificence, splendour (*BRIT*), splendor (*US*).

magnífico/a [mag'nifiku/a] *adj* splendid, magnificent.

magnitude [magni'tudʒi] *f* magnitude.

magno/a ['magnu/a] *adj* (*grande*) great; (*importante*) important.

magnólia [mag'nɔlja] *f* magnolia.

mago ['magu] *m* magician; **os reis ~s** the Three Wise Men, the Three Kings.

NB: European Portuguese adds the following consonants to certain words: **b** (sú(b)dito, su(b)til); **c** (a(c)ção, a(c)cionista, a(c)to); **m** (inde(m)ne); **p** (ado(p)ção, ado(p)tar); *for further details see p. xiii.*

mágoa ['magwa] *f* (*tristeza*) sorrow, grief; (*fig: desagrado*) hurt.

magoado/a [ma'gwadu/a] *adj* hurt.

magoar [ma'gwa*] *vt*, *vi* to hurt; ~**-se** *vr*: ~**se com algo** to be hurt by sth.

MAgr (*BR*) *abr m* = **Ministério da Agricultura**.

magreza [ma'greza] *f* slimness; (*de carne*) leanness; (*fig*) meagreness (*BRIT*), meagerness (*US*).

magricela [magri'sɛla] *adj* skinny.

magrinho/a [ma'griɲu/a] *adj* thin, skinny.

magro/a ['magru/a] *adj* (*pessoa*) slim; (*carne*) lean; (*fig: parco*) meagre (*BRIT*), meager (*US*); (*leite*) skimmed; **ser ~ como um palito** to be like a beanpole.

mai. *abr* = **maio**.

mainframe [mẽj'frejm] *m* mainframe.

maio ['maju] (*PT*: **M-**) *m* May; *V tb* **julho**.

maiô [ma'jo] (*BR*) *m* swimsuit.

maionese [majo'nezi] *f* mayonnaise.

maior [ma'jɔ*] *adj* (*compar: de tamanho*) bigger; (: *de importância*) greater; (*superl: de tamanho*) biggest; (: *de importância*) greatest ♦ *m/f* adult; **tive a ~ discussão com ela** I had a real argument with her; **foi o ~ barato** (*col*) it was really great; **tenho a ~ para te contar, não te conto a ~** the best is yet to come; **~ de idade** of age, adult; **~ de 21 anos** over 21; **ser de ~** (*col*) to be of age *ou* grown up; **ser ~ e vacinado** (*col*) to be one's own master.

maioral [majo'raw] (*pl* **-ais**) *m* boss; **o ~** the greatest.

Maiorca [maj'ɔxka] *f* Majorca.

maioria [majo'ria] *f* majority; **a ~ de** most of; **~ absoluta** absolute majority.

maioridade [majori'dadʒi] *f* adulthood; **atingir a ~** to come of age.

mais [majʃ] *adv*, *adj*, *pron* more ♦ *conj* plus, and ♦ *m*: **o ~** the rest; **~ um livro** another book; **~ cerveja** more beer; **ela é quem tem ~ livros** she has the most books; **~ alguma coisa?** anything else?; **nada/ninguém ~** nothing/no-one else; **~ alto/interessante** higher/more interesting; **o ~ alto** the highest; **correr/durar ~** to run faster/last longer; **~ de** more than; **~ dois** two more; **~ ou menos** more or less; **~ uma vez** once more; **não ~** no longer, not anymore; **nunca ~** never again; **a ~** too much; **um dia a ~** one more day; **cada vez ~** more and more; **não estudo ~** I don't study any more *ou* any longer; **por ~ que** however much; **quanto ~ ganha, ~ gasta** the more he earns, the more he spends; **e no ~, tudo bem?** how are you otherwise?; **até ~!** bye!; **~ adiante** further on; **logo ~** a bit later; **de ~ a ~** besides, anyhow; **~ a tempo** sooner; **~ cedo ou ~ tarde**, **~ dia menos dia** sooner or later; **~ essa!** not that too!; **no ~ tardar** at the latest; **para ~ de** over; **não tem nada de ~ você fazer ...** there's nothing wrong with you

doing ...; **sem ~ nem menos** out of the blue; **nem ~ nem menos** nothing more, nothing less; **que lugar ~ feio!** what a horrible place!

maisena [maj'zena] *f* cornflower.

mais-valia (*pl* **~s**) *f* surplus value.

maître ['metrə] *m* head waiter.

maiúscula [ma'juʃkula] *f* capital letter.

majestade [maʒeʃ'tadʒi] *f* majesty; **Sua/Vossa M~** His (*ou* Her)/Your Majesty.

majestoso/a [maʒeʃ'tozu/ɔza] *adj* majestic.

major [ma'ʒɔ*] *m* (*MIL*) major.

majoritário/a [maʒori'tarju/a] *adj* majority *atr*.

mal [maw] (*pl* **~es**) *m* harm; (*MED*) illness ♦ *adv* badly; (*quase não*) hardly ♦ *conj* hardly; **~ desliguei o fone, a campainha tocou** I had hardly put the phone down when the doorbell rang; **o bem e o ~** good and bad; **o ~ é que** ... the bad thing is that ...; **falar ~ de alguém** to speak ill of sb, run sb down; **desejar ~ a alguém** to wish sb ill; **fazer ~ a alguém** to harm sb; (*deflorar*) to deflower sb; **fazer ~ à saúde de alguém** to damage sb's health; **fazer ~ em fazer** to be wrong to do; **não faz ~** never mind; **não fiz por ~** I meant no harm, I didn't mean it; **levar algo a ~** to take offence (*BRIT*) *ou* offense (*US*) at sth; **querer ~ a alguém** to bear sb ill; **estar ~** (*doente*) to be ill; **passar ~** to be sick; **estar ~ da vida** to be in a bad way; **viver ~ com alguém** not to get on with sb; **~ e porcamente** in a slapdash way; **estar de ~ com alguém** not to be speaking to sb; **dos ~es o menor** the lesser of two evils.

mal- [mal-] *prefixo* badly.

mala ['mala] *f* suitcase; (*BR: AUTO*) boot, trunk (*US*); **~s** *fpl* luggage *sg*; **fazer as ~s** to pack; **~ aérea** air courier; **~ de mão** piece of hand luggage; **~ direta** (*COM*) direct mail; **~ postal** mail bag.

malabarismo [malaba'riʒmu] *m* juggling; (*fig*) shrewd manoeuvre (*BRIT*) *ou* maneuver (*US*).

malabarista [malaba'riʃta] *m/f* juggler; (*fig*) smooth operator.

mal-acabado/a *adj* badly finished; (*pessoa*) deformed.

mal-acostumado/a *adj* maladjusted.

mal-afamado/a *adj* notorious, of ill repute.

malagradecido/a [malagrade'sidu/a] *adj* ungrateful.

malagueta [mala'geta] *f* chilli pepper.

malaio/a [ma'laju/a] *adj*, *m/f* Malay ♦ *m* (*LING*) Malay.

Malaísia [mala'izja] *f*: **a ~** Malaysia.

malaísio/a [mala'izju/a] *adj*, *m/f* Malaysian.

mal-ajambrado/a [-aʒã'bradu/a] *adj* scruffy.

mal-amada *adj* unloved ♦ *f* single woman.

malandragem [malã'draʒẽ] *f* (*patifaria*) double-dealing; (*preguiça*) idleness; (*esperteza*) cunning.

malandrear [malã'drja*] *vi* to loaf.

malandrice [malã'drisi] *f* = **malandragem**.

malandro/a [ma'lãdru/a] *adj* (*patife*) double-dealing; (*preguiçoso*) idle; (*esperto*) wily, cunning ♦ *m/f* (*patife*) crook; (*preguiçoso*) idler, layabout; (*esperto*) streetwise person.
mal-apanhado/a *adj* unpleasant-looking.
mal-apessoado/a [-ape'swadu/a] *adj* unpleasant-looking.
malária [ma'larja] *f* malaria.
mal-arrumado/a [-axu'madu/a] *adj* untidy.
mal-assombrado/a *adj* haunted.
Malavi [mala'vi] *m*: **o** ~ Malawi.
mal-avisado/a [-avi'zadu/a] *adj* rash.
malbaratar [mawbara'ta*] *vt* (*dinheiro*) to squander, waste.
malcasado/a [mawka'zadu/a] *adj* unhappily married; (*com pessoa inferior*) married to sb below one's class.
malcheiroso/a [mawʃej'rozu/ɔza] *adj* evil-smelling.
malcomportado/a [mawkõpox'tadu/a] *adj* badly behaved.
malconceituado/a [mawkõsej'twadu/a] *adj* badly thought of.
malcriado/a [maw'krjadu/a] *adj* rude ♦ *m/f* slob.
maldade [maw'dadʒi] *f* cruelty; (*malícia*) malice; **é uma** ~ it is cruel.
maldição [mawdʒi'sãw] (*pl* -**ões**) *f* curse.
maldigo [maw'dʒigu] *etc vb* V **maldizer**.
maldisposto/a [mawdʒiʃ'poʃtu/'pɔʃta] *adj* indisposed.
maldisse [maw'dʒisi] *etc vb* V **maldizer**.
maldito/a [maw'dʒitu/a] *pp de* **maldizer** ♦ *adj* damned.
Maldivas [maw'dʒivaʃ] *fpl*: **as (ilhas)** ~ the Maldives.
maldiz [maw'dʒiʒ] *etc vb* V **maldizer**.
maldizente [mawdʒi'zẽtʃi] *m/f* slanderer.
maldizer [mawdʒi'ze*] (*irreg: como* **dizer**) *vt* to curse.
maldoso/a [maw'dozu/ɔza] *adj* wicked; (*malicioso*) malicious.
maldotado/a [mawdo'tadu/a] *adj* untalented.
maleável [ma'ljavew] (*pl* -**eis**) *adj* malleable.
maledicência [maledʒi'sẽsja] *f* slander.
maledicente [maledʒi'sẽtʃi] *m/f* slanderer.
mal-educado/a *adj* rude ♦ *m/f* slob.
malefício [male'fisju] *m* harm.
maléfico/a [ma'lɛfiku/a] *adj* (*pessoa*) malicious; (*prejudicial*) harmful, injurious.
mal-empregado/a *adj* wasted.
mal-encarado/a *adj* shady, shifty.
mal-entendido/a *adj* misunderstood ♦ *m* misunderstanding.
mal-estar *m* (*indisposição*) indisposition, discomfort; (*embaraço*) uneasiness.
maleta [ma'leta] *f* small suitcase, grip.
malevolência [malevo'lẽsja] *f* malice, spite.
malevolente [malevo'lẽtʃi] *adj* malicious.
malévolo/a [ma'lɛvolu/a] *adj* malicious, spite-

ful.
malfadado/a [mawfa'dadu/a] *adj* unlucky; (*viagem*) fateful.
malfeito/a [mal'fejtu/a] *adj* (*roupa*) poorly made; (*corpo*) misshapen; (*fig*: *injusto*) wrong, unjust.
malfeitor/a [mawfej'to*(a)] *m/f* wrong-doer.
malgastar [mawgaʃ'ta*] *vt* to waste.
malgasto/a [maw'gaʃtu/a] *adj* wasted.
malgrado [maw'gradu] *prep* despite.
malha ['maʎa] *f* (*de rede*) mesh; (*tecido*) jersey; (*suéter*) sweater; (*de ginástica*) leotard; **fazer** ~ (*PT*) to knit; **artigos de** ~ knitwear; ~ **perdida** ladder, run; **vestido de** ~ jersey dress.
mal-habituado/a *adj* maladjusted.
malhado/a [ma'ʎadu/a] *adj* spotted, mottled, dappled; (*roque*) heavy.
malhar [ma'ʎa*] *vt* (*bater*) to beat; (*cereais*) to thresh; (*col*: *criticar*) to knock, run down ♦ *vi* (*col*: *fazer ginástica*) to work out.
malharia [maʎa'ria] *f* (*fábrica*) mill; (*artigos de malha*) knitted goods *pl*.
malho ['maʎu] *m* (*maço*) mallet; (*grande*) sledgehammer.
mal-humorado/a [-umo'radu/a] *adj* grumpy, sullen.
Mali [ma'li] *m*: **o** ~ Mali.
malícia [ma'lisja] *f* malice; (*astúcia*) slyness; (*esperteza*) cleverness; **pôr** ~ **em algo** to give sth a double meaning.
maliciar [mali'sja*] *vt* (*ação*) to see malice in; (*palavras*) to misconstrue.
malicioso/a [mali'sjozu/ɔza] *adj* malicious; (*astuto*) sly; (*esperto*) clever; (*quem interpreta erradamente*) dirty-minded.
malignidade [maligni'dadʒi] *f* malice, spite; (*MED*) malignancy.
maligno/a [ma'lignu/a] *adj* (*maléfico*) evil, malicious; (*danoso*) harmful; (*MED*) malignant.
má-língua (*pl* **más-línguas**) *f* backbiting ♦ *m/f* backbiter.
mal-intencionado/a *adj* malicious.
malmequer [mawme'ke*] *m* marigold.
maloca [ma'lɔka] *f* (*casa*) communal hut; (*aldeia*) (Indian) village; (*esconderijo*) bolt-hole.
malocar [malo'ka*] (*col*) *vt* to hide.
malogrado/a [malo'gradu/a] *adj* (*plano*) abortive, frustrated; (*sem êxito*) unsuccessful.
malograr [malo'gra*] *vt* (*planos*) to spoil, upset; (*frustrar*) to thwart, frustrate ♦ *vi*, ~-**se** *vr* (*planos*) to fall through; (*fracassar*) to fail.
malogro [ma'logru] *m* failure.
malote [ma'lɔtʃi] *m* pouch; (*serviço*) express courier.
mal-passado/a *adj* underdone; (*bife*) rare.
malproporcionado/a [mawpropoxsjo'nadu/a]

---

adj ill-proportioned.

malquerença [mawke'rẽsa] *f* ill will, enmity.

malquisto/a [maw'kiʃtu/a] *adj* disliked.

malsão/sã [maw'sãw/'sã] (*pl* ~**s**) *adj* (*insalubre*) unhealthy; (*nocivo*) harmful.

malsucedido/a [mawsuse'dʒidu/a] *adj* unsuccessful.

Malta ['mawta] *f* Malta.

malta ['mawta] (*PT*) *f* gang, mob.

malte ['mawtʃi] *m* malt.

maltrapilho/a [mawtra'piʎu/a] *adj* in rags, ragged ♦ *m/f* ragamuffin.

maltratar [mawtra'ta*] *vt* to ill-treat; (*com palavras*) to abuse; (*estragar*) to ruin, damage.

maluco/a [ma'luku/a] *adj* crazy, daft ♦ *m/f* madman/woman.

maluquice [malu'kisi] *f* madness; (*ato, dito*) crazy thing.

malvadez [mawva'deʒ] *f* = **malvadeza**.

malvadeza [mawva'deza] *f* wickedness; (*ato*) wicked thing.

malvado/a [maw'vadu/a] *adj* wicked.

malversação [mawvexsa'sãw] *f* (*de dinheiro*) embezzlement; (*má administração*) mismanagement.

malversar [mawvex'sa*] *vt* (*dinheiro*) to embezzle, misappropriate; (*administrar mal*) to mismanage.

Malvinas [maw'vinaʃ] *fpl*: **as (ilhas)** ~ the Falklands, the Falkland Islands.

MAM (*BR*) *abr m* = **Museu de Arte Moderna** (*no Rio*).

mama ['mama] *f* breast.

mamada [ma'mada] *f* feeding.

mamadeira [mama'dejra] (*BR*) *f* feeding bottle.

mamãe [ma'mãj] *f* mum, mummy.

mamão [ma'mãw] (*pl* -**ões**) *m* papaya.

mamar [ma'ma*] *vt* to suck; (*dinheiro*) to extort, get; (*empresa*) to milk (dry) ♦ *vi* (*bebê*) to be breastfed; ~ **numa empresa** to get a rake-off from a company; **dar de** ~ **a um bebê** to (breast)feed a baby.

mamata [ma'mata] *f* (*negociata*) racket; (*boa vida*) cushy number.

mambembe [mã'bẽbi] *m/f* amateur thespian ♦ *adj* shoddy, second-rate.

mameluco/a [mame'luku/a] *m/f* half-breed (*of Indian and white*).

mamífero [ma'miferu] *m* mammal.

mamilo [ma'milu] *m* nipple.

mamoeiro [ma'mwejru] *m* papaya tree.

mamões [ma'mõjʃ] *mpl de* **mamão**.

mana ['mana] *f* sister.

manada [ma'nada] *f* herd, drove.

manancial [manã'sjaw] (*pl* -**ais**) *m* spring; (*fig: fonte*) source; (: *abundância*) wealth.

manar [ma'na*] *vt, vi* to pour.

manauense [manaw'ẽsi] *adj* from Manaus ♦ *m/f* person from Manaus.

mancada [mã'kada] *f* (*erro*) mistake; (*gafe*) blunder; **dar uma** ~ to make a blunder.

mancar [mã'ka*] *vt* to cripple ♦ *vi* to limp; ~**-se** *vr* (*col*) to get the message, take the hint.

manceba [mã'seba] *f* young woman; (*concubina*) concubine.

mancebo [mã'sebu] *m* young man, youth.

Mancha ['mãʃa] *f*: **o canal da** ~ the English Channel.

mancha ['mãʃa] *f* (*nódoa*) stain; (*na pele*) mark, spot; (*em pintura*) blotch; **sem** ~**s** (*reputação*) spotless.

manchado/a [mã'ʃadu/a] *adj* (*sujo*) soiled; (*malhado*) mottled, spotted.

manchar [mã'ʃa*] *vt* to stain, mark; (*reputação*) to soil.

manchete [mã'ʃetʃi] *f* headline; **virar** ~ to make *ou* hit (*col*) the headlines.

manco/a ['mãku/a] *adj* crippled, lame ♦ *m/f* cripple.

mancomunar [mãkomu'na*] *vt* to contrive; ~**-se** *vr*: ~**-se (com)** to conspire (with).

mandachuva [mãda'ʃuva] *m* (*figurão*) big shot; (*chefe*) boss.

mandado [mã'dadu] *m* (*ordem*) order; (*JUR*) writ, injunction; ~ **de arresto** repossession order; ~ **de prisão/busca** warrant for sb's arrest/search warrant; ~ **de segurança** injunction.

mandamento [mãda'mẽtu] *m* order, command; (*REL*) commandment.

mandante [mã'dãtʃi] *m/f* instigator; (*dirigente*) person in charge; (*COM*) principal.

mandão/dona [mã'dãw/'dɔna] (*pl* -**ões**/~**s**) *adj* bossy, domineering ♦ *m/f* bossy person.

mandar [mã'da*] *vt* (*ordenar*) to order; (*enviar*) to send ♦ *vi* to be in charge; ~**-se** *vr* (*col: partir*) to make tracks, get going; (*fugir*) to take off; ~ **buscar** *ou* **chamar** to send for; ~ **dizer** to send word; ~ **embora** to send away; ~ **fazer um vestido** to have a dress made; ~ **que alguém faça**, ~ **alguém fazer** to tell sb to do; ~ **alguém passear** (*fig*) to send sb packing; ~ **alguém para o inferno** to tell sb to go to hell; **o que é que você manda?** (*col*) what can I do for you?; ~ **em alguém** to boss sb around; **mandal** (*col*) fire away!; ~ **ver** (*col*) to go to town; **a mão,** ~ **um soco (em alguém)** to hit (sb); **aqui quem manda sou eu** I give the orders around here.

mandarim [mãda'rĩ] *m* (*LING*) Mandarin; (*fig*) mandarin.

mandatário/a [mãda'tarju/a] *m/f* (*delegado*) delegate; (*representante*) representative, agent.

mandato [mã'datu] *m* (*autorização*) mandate; (*ordem*) order; (*POL*) term of office.

mandíbula [mã'dʒibula] *f* jaw.

mandinga [mã'dʒĩga] *f* witchcraft.

mandioca [mã'dʒjɔka] *f* cassava, manioc.

mando ['mãdu] *m* (*comando*) command; (*poder*) power; **a** ~ **de** by order of.

mandões [mã'dõjʃ] *mpl de* **mandão**.

mandona [mã'dɔna] *f de* **mandão**.

mandrião/driona [mã'drjãw/'drjɔna] (*pl -ões/* ~**s**) (*PT*) *adj* lazy ♦ *m/f* idler, lazybones *sg*.

mandriar [mã'drja*] *vi* to idle, loaf about.

mandriões [mã'drjõjʃ] *mpl de* **mandrião**.

mandriona [mã'drjɔna] *f de* **mandrião**.

maneira [ma'nejra] *f* (*modo*) way; (*estilo*) style, manner; ~**s** *fpl* manners; **à** ~ **de** like; **de** ~ **que** so that; **de** ~ **alguma** *ou* **nenhuma** not at all; **desta** ~ in this way; **de qualquer** ~ anyway; **não houve** ~ **de convencê-lo** it was impossible to convince him.

maneirar [manej'ra*] (*col*) *vt* to sort out, fix ♦ *vi* to sort things out; **maneira!** take it easy!

maneiro/a [ma'nejru/a] *adj* (*ferramenta*, *roupa*) manageable; (*trabalho*) easy; (*pessoa*) capable; (*col*: *bacana*) great, brilliant.

manejar [mane'ʒa*] *vt* (*instrumento*) to handle; (*máquina*) to work.

manejável [mane'ʒavew] (*pl -eis*) *adj* manageable.

manejo [ma'neʒu] *m* handling.

manequim [mane'kĩ] (*pl -ns*) *m* (*boneco*) dummy ♦ *m/f* model.

maneta [ma'neta] *adj* one-handed ♦ *m/f* one-handed person.

manga ['mãga] *f* sleeve; (*fruta*) mango; (*filtro*) filter; **em** ~**s de camisa** in (one's) shirt sleeves.

manganês [mãga'neʃ] *m* manganese.

mangue ['mãgi] *m* mangrove swamp; (*planta*) mangrove; (*col*: *zona*) red-light district.

mangueira [mã'gejra] *f* hose(pipe); (*árvore*) mango tree.

manguinha [mã'giɲa] *f*: **botar as** ~**s de fora** (*col*) to let one's hair down.

manha ['maɲa] *f* (*malícia*) guile, craftiness; (*destreza*) skill; (*ardil*) trick; (*birra*) tantrum; **fazer** ~ to have a tantrum.

manhã [ma'ɲã] *f* morning; **de** *ou* **pela** ~ in the morning; **amanhã/hoje de** ~ tomorrow/ this morning; **de** ~ **cedo** early in the morning; **4 hs da** ~ 4 o'clock in the morning.

manhãzinha [maɲã'ziɲa] *f*: **de** ~ early in the morning.

manhoso/a [ma'ɲozu/ɔza] *adj* (*ardiloso*) crafty, sly; (*criança*) whining.

mania [ma'nia] *f* (*MED*) mania; (*obsessão*) craze; **ela é cheia de** ~**s** she's very compulsive; **estar com** ~ **de ...** to have a thing about ...; ~ **de grandeza** delusions *pl* of grandeur; ~ **de perseguição** persecution complex.

maníaco/a [ma'niaku/a] *adj* manic ♦ *m/f* maniac.

maníaco-depressivo (*pl* ~**s**) *adj*, *m/f* manic depressive.

manicômio [mani'komju] *m* asylum, mental hospital.

manicura [mani'kura] *f* (*tratamento*) manicure; (*pessoa*) manicurist.

manicure [mani'kuri] *f* = **manicura**.

manifestação [manifeʃta'sãw] (*pl -ões*) *f* demonstration, display; (*expressão*) expression, declaration; (*política*) demonstration.

manifestante [manifeʃ'tãtʃi] *m/f* demonstrator.

manifestar [manifeʃ'ta*] *vt* (*revelar*) to show, display; (*declarar*) to express, declare; ~-**se** *vr* to manifest o.s.; (*pronunciar-se*) to express an opinion.

manifesto/a [mani'fɛʃtu/a] *adj* obvious, clear ♦ *m* manifesto.

manilha [ma'niʎa] *f* (ceramic) drain-pipe.

manipulação [manipula'sãw] *f* handling; (*fig*) manipulation.

manipular [manipu'la*] *vt* to manipulate; (*manejar*) to handle.

manivela [mani'vɛla] *f* (*ferramenta*) crank.

manjado/a [mã'ʒadu/a] (*col*) *adj* well-known.

manjar [mã'ʒa*] *m* (*iguaria*) delicacy, titbit ♦ *vt* (*col*: *conhecer*) to know; (: *entender*) to grasp; (: *observar*) to check out ♦ *vi* (*col*) to catch on; ~ **de algo** to know about sth; **manjou?** (*col*) get it?, see?

manjar-branco *m* blancmange.

manjedoura [mãʒe'dora] *f* manger, crib.

manjericão [mãʒeri'kãw] *m* basil.

mano ['manu] *m* brother.

manobra [ma'nɔbra] *f* (*de carro*, *barco*) manoeuvre (*BRIT*), maneuver (*US*); (*de mecanismo*) operation; (*de trens*) shunting; (*fig*) move; (: *artimanha*) manoeuvre *ou* maneuver, trick; ~**s** *mpl* (*MIL*) manoeuvres *ou* maneuvers.

manobrar [mano'bra*] *vt* to manoeuvre (*BRIT*), maneuver (*US*); (*mecanismo*) to operate, work; (*governar*) to take charge of; (*manipular*) to manipulate ♦ *vi* to manoeuvre *ou* maneuver; (*tomar medidas*) to make moves.

manobreiro/a [mano'brejru/a] *m/f* operator.

manobrista [mano'briʃta] *m/f* parking attendant.

manquejar [mãke'ʒa*] *vi* to limp.

mansão [mã'sãw] (*pl -ões*) *f* mansion.

mansidão [mãsi'dãw] *f* gentleness, meekness; (*do mar*) calmness; (*de animal*) tameness.

mansinho [mã'siɲu] *adv*: **de** ~ (*devagar*) slowly; (*de leve*) gently; (*sorrateiramente*): **sair/entrar de** ~ to creep out/in.

manso/a [mã'su/a] *adj* (*brando*) gentle; (*mar*) calm; (*animal*) tame.

mansões [mã'sõjʃ] *fpl de* **mansão**.

manta ['mãta] *f* (*cobertor*) blanket; (*xale*) shawl; (*agasalho*) cloak; (*de viajar*) travelling rug.

manteiga [mã'tejga] *f* butter; ~ **derretida** (*fig*,

NB: *European Portuguese adds the following consonants to certain words:* **b** (sú(b)dito, su(b)til); **c** (a(c)ção, a(c)cionista, a(c)to); **m** (inde(m)ne); **p** (ado(p)ção, ado(p)tar); *for further details see p. xiii.*

col) cry baby; ~ **de cacau** cocoa butter.
manteigueira [mãtej'gejra] *f* butter dish.
mantém [mã'tɛ̃] *etc vb V* **manter.**
mantenedor(a) [mãtene'do*(a)] *m/f* (*da família*) breadwinner; (*de opinião, princípio*) holder; (*de ordem, ESPORTE*) retainer.
manter [mã'te*] (*irreg: como* **ter**) *vt* to maintain; (*num lugar*) to keep; (*uma família*) to support; (*a palavra*) to keep; (*princípios*) to abide by; ~-**se** *vr* (*sustentar-se*) to support o.s.; (*permanecer*) to remain; ~-**se firme** to stand firm.
mantilha [mã'tʃiʎa] *f* mantilla; (*véu*) veil.
mantimento [mãtʃi'mētu] *m* maintenance; ~**s** *mpl* provisions.
mantinha [mã'tʃiɲa] *etc vb V* **manter.**
mantive [mã'tʃivi] *etc vb V* **manter.**
mantiver [mãtʃi've*] *etc vb V* **manter.**
manto ['mãtu] *m* cloak; (*de cerimônia*) robe.
mantô [mã'to] *m* coat.
manual [ma'nwaw] (*pl* -**ais**) *adj* manual ♦ *m* handbook; (*compêndio*) manual; **ter habilidade** ~ to be good with one's hands.
manufatura [manufa'tura] (*PT*: -**ct**-) *f* manufacture.
manufaturados [manufatu'raduʃ] (*PT*: -**ct**-) *mpl* manufactured products.
manufaturar [manufatu'ra*] (*PT*: -**ct**-) *vt* to manufacture.
manuscrever [manuʃkre've*] *vt* to write by hand.
manuscrito/a [manuʃ'kritu/a] *adj* handwritten ♦ *m* manuscript.
manusear [manu'zja*] *vt* (*manejar*) to handle; (*livro*) to leaf through.
manuseio [manu'zeju] *m* handling.
manutenção [manutē'sãw] *f* maintenance; (*da casa*) upkeep.
mão [mãw] (*pl* ~**s**) *f* hand; (*de animal*) paw; (*demão*) coat; (*de direção*) flow of traffic; **à** ~ by hand; (*perto*) at hand; **feito à** ~ handmade; **de** ~**s dadas** hand in hand; **de ou em primeira** ~ first-hand; **de segunda** ~ second-hand; **em** ~ by hand; **fora de** ~ out of the way; **abrir** ~ **de algo** (*fig*) to give sth up; **agüentar a** ~ (*col: suportar*) to hold out; (: *esperar*) to hang on; **dar a** ~ **à palmatória** to admit one's mistake; **dar a** ~ **a alguém** to hold sb's hand; (*cumprimentar*) to shake hands with sb; **dar uma** ~ **a alguém** to give sb a hand, help sb out; **ficar na** ~ (*col*) to be stood up; **forçar a** ~ to go overboard; **lançar** ~ **de algo** to have recourse to sth; **largar algo de** ~ to give sth up; **uma** ~ **lava a outra** (*fig*) one good turn deserves another; **meter a** ~ **em alguém** to hit sb; **meter** *ou* **passar a** ~ **em algo** (*col*) to nick sth; **passar a** ~ **pela cabeça de alguém** (*fig*) to let sb off; **pôr a** ~ **no fogo por alguém** (*fig*) to vouch for sb; **pôr** ~**s à obra** to set to work; **ser uma** ~ **na roda** (*fig*) to be a great help; **ter** ~ **leve** (*bater facilmente*) to be violent; (*ser ladrão*) to be light-fingered; **ter a** ~ **pe-**

sada to be heavy-handed; **ter uma boa** ~ **para** to be good at; **vir com as** ~**s abanando** (*fig*) to come back empty-handed; ~ **única/ dupla** one-way/two-way traffic; **esta rua dá** ~ **para o centro** this street goes to the centre (*BRIT*) *ou* center (*US*); **rua de duas** ~**s** two-way street; ~**s ao alto!** hands up!; **de** ~ **beijada** (*fig*) for nothing.
mão-aberta (*pl* **mãos-abertas**) *adj* generous ♦ *m/f* generous person.
mão-cheia *f*: **de** ~ first-rate.
mão-de-obra *f* (*trabalho*) workmanship; (*trabalhadores*) labour (*BRIT*), labor (*US*); (*coisa difícil*) tricky thing; ~ **especializada** skilled labo(u)r.
maoísta [maw'iʃta] *adj, m/f* Maoist.
mão-leve (*pl* **mãos-leves**) *m/f* pilferer.
mãozinha [mãw'ziɲa] *f*: **dar uma** ~ **a alguém** to give sb a hand, help sb out.
mapa ['mapa] *m* map; (*gráfico*) chart; **não estar no** ~ (*fig, col*) to be extraordinary; **sair do** ~ (*col*) to disappear.
mapa-múndi [-'mũdʒi] (*pl* **mapas-múndi**) *m* world map.
Maputo [ma'putu] *n* Maputo.
maquete [ma'kɛtʃi] *f* model.
maquiador(a) [makja'do*(a)] *m/f* make-up artist.
maquiagem [ma'kjaʒẽ] *f* = **maquilagem.**
maquiar [ma'kja*] *vt* to make up; (*fig*) to touch up; ~-**se** *vr* to make o.s. up, put on make-up.
maquiavélico/a [makja'vɛliku/a] *adj* Machiavellian.
maquilagem [maki'laʒẽ] (*PT*: -**lha**-) *f* make-up; (*ato*) making up.
maquilar [makila*] (*PT*: -**lha**-) *vt* to make up; ~-**se** *vr* to put on one's make-up.
máquina ['makina] *f* machine; (*de trem*) engine; (*de relógio*) movement; (*fig*) machinery; ~ **a vapor** steam engine; ~**s agrícolas** agricultural machinery; ~ **de calcular** calculator; ~ **de costura** sewing machine; ~ **fotográfica** *ou* **de filmar** camera; ~ **de escrever** typewriter; ~ **de lavar (roupa)** washing-machine; ~ **de lavar pratos** dishwasher; ~ **de tricotar** knitting machine; **costurar/escrever à** ~ to machine-sew/type; **escrito à** ~ typewritten; **preencher um formulário à** ~ to fill in a form on the typewriter.
maquinação [makina'sãw] (*pl* -**ões**) *f* machination, plot.
maquinal [maki'naw] (*pl* -**ais**) *adj* mechanical, automatic.
maquinar [maki'na*] *vt* to plot ♦ *vi* to conspire.
maquinaria [makina'ria] *f* machinery.
maquinismo [maki'niʒmu] *m* mechanism; (*máquinas*) machinery; (*TEATRO*) stage machinery.
maquinista [maki'niʃta] *m* (*FERRO*) engine driver; (*NÁUT*) engineer.

mar [ma*] *m* sea; **por** ~ by sea; **cair no** ~ to fall overboard; **fazer-se ao** ~ to set sail; ~ **aberto** open sea; **pleno** ~, ~ **alto** high sea; **um** ~ **de** (*fig*) a sea of; ~ **de rosas** calm sea; (*fig*) bed of roses; **nem tanto ao** ~ **nem tanto à terra** (*fig*) somewhere in between; **o** ~ **Cáspio** the Caspian Sea; **o** ~ **Morto** the Dead Sea; **o** ~ **Negro** the Black Sea; **o** ~ **Vermelho** the Red Sea.

maraca [ma'raka] *f* maraca.

maracujá [maraku'ʒa] *m* passion fruit; **pé de** ~ passion flower.

maracujazeiro [marakuʒa'zejru] *m* passion-fruit plant.

maracutaia [maraku'taja] *f* dirty trick.

marafa [ma'rafa] (*col*) *f* loose living.

marafona [mara'fɔna] (*col*) *f* whore.

marajá [mara'ʒa] *m* maharaja; (*BR*: *POL*) civil service fat-cat.

maranhense [mara'ɲẽsi] *adj* from Maranhão ♦ *m/f* person from Maranhão.

marasmo [ma'raʒmu] *m* (*inatividade*) stagnation; (*apatia*) apathy.

maratona [mara'tona] *f* marathon.

maratonista [marato'niʃta] *m/f* marathon runner.

maravilha [mara'viʎa] *f* marvel, wonder; **às mil** ~**s** wonderfully.

maravilhar [maravi'ʎa*] *vt* to amaze, astonish ♦ *vi* to be amazing; ~**-se** *vr*: ~**-se de** to be astonished at, be amazed at.

maravilhoso/a [maravi'ʎozu/ɔza] *adj* marvellous (*BRIT*), marvelous (*US*), wonderful.

marca ['maxka] *f* mark; (*COM*) make, brand; (*carimbo*) stamp; (*da prata*) hallmark; (*fig*: *categoria*) calibre (*BRIT*), caliber (*US*); **de maior** (*fig*) of the first order; ~ **de fábrica** trademark; ~ **registrada** registered trademark.

marcador [maxka'do*] *m* marker; (*de livro*) bookmark; (*ESPORTE*: *quadro*) scoreboard; (: *jogador*) scorer.

marcante [max'kãtʃi] *adj* outstanding.

marcapasso [maxka'pasu] *m* (*MED*) pacemaker.

marcar [max'ka*] *vt* to mark; (*hora*, *data*) to fix, set; (*PT*: *discar*) to dial; (*animal*) to brand; (*delimitar*) to demarcate; (*observar*) to keep an eye on; (*gol*, *ponto*) to score; (*FUTEBOL*: *jogador*) to mark; (*produzir impressão em*) to leave one's mark on ♦ *vi* (*impressionar*) to make one's mark; ~ **uma consulta**, ~ **hora** to make an appointment; ~ **um encontro** to arrange to meet; ~ **uma reunião/um jantar para sexta-feira** to

arrange a meeting/a dinner for Friday; ~ **época** to make history; ~ **o ponto** to punch the clock; **ter hora marcada com alguém** to have an appointment with sb; ~ **o tempo de algo** to time sth.

marcenaria [maxsena'ria] *f* joinery; (*oficina*) joiner's.

marceneiro [maxse'nejru] *m* cabinet-maker, joiner.

marcha ['maxʃa] *f* march; (*ato*) marching; (*de acontecimentos*) course; (*passo*) pace; (*AUTO*) gear; (*progresso*) progress; ~ **à ré** (*BR*), ~ **atrás** (*PT*) reverse (gear); **primeira** (~) first (gear); **pôr-se em** ~ to set off.

marchar [max'ʃa*] *vi* (*ir*) to go; (*andar a pé*) to walk; (*MIL*) to march.

marcha-rancho (*pl* **marchas-rancho**) *f* carnival march.

marchetar [maxʃe'ta*] *vt* to inlay.

marcial [max'sjaw] (*pl* **-ais**) *adj* martial; **lei** ~ martial law; **corte** ~ court martial.

marciano/a [max'sjanu/a] *adj*, *m* Martian.

marco ['maxku] *m* landmark; (*de janela*) frame; (*fig*) frontier; (*moeda*) mark.

março ['maxsu] (*PT*: **M-**) *m* March; *V tb* **julho**.

maré [ma'rɛ] *f* tide; (*fig*: *oportunidade*) chance; ~ **alta/baixa** high/low tide; **estar de boa** ~ *ou* **de** ~ **alta** to be in a good mood; **remar contra a** ~ (*fig*) to swim against the tide.

marear [ma'rja*] *vt* to make seasick; (*oxidar*) to dull, stain ♦ *vi* to be seasick.

marechal [mare'ʃaw] (*pl* **-ais**) *m* marshal.

marejar [mare'ʒa*] *vt* to wet ♦ *vi* to get wet.

maremoto [mare'mɔtu] *m* tidal wave.

maresia [mare'zia] *f* smell of the sea, sea air.

marfim [max'fĩ] *m* ivory.

margarida [maxga'rida] *f* daisy; (*COMPUT*) daisy-wheel.

margarina [maxga'rina] *f* margarine.

margear [max'ʒja*] *vt* to border.

margem ['maxʒẽ] (*pl* **-ns**) *f* (*borda*) edge; (*de rio*) bank; (*litoral*) shore; (*de impresso*) margin; (*fig*: *tempo*) time; (: *lugar*) space; (: *oportunidade*) chance; **à** ~ **de** alongside; **dar** ~ **a alguém** to give sb a chance; ~ **de erro** margin of error; ~ **de lucro** profit margin.

marginal [maxʒi'naw] (*pl* **-ais**) *adj* marginal ♦ *m/f* delinquent.

marginalidade [maxʒinali'dadʒi] *f* delinquency.

marginalizar [maxʒinali'za*] *vt* to marginalize.

maria-fumaça [ma'ria-] (*pl* **marias-fumaças**) *f* steam train.

maria-sem-vergonha [ma'ria-] (*pl* **marias-sem-vergonha**) *f* (*BOT*) busy lizzie.

maria-vai-com-as-outras [ma'ria-] *m/f inv* sheep, follower.

maricas [ma'rikaʃ] (*PT*: *col*) *m inv* queer, poof.

NB: European Portuguese adds the following consonants to certain words: **b** (sú(b)dito, su(b)til); **c** (a(c)ção, a(c)cionista, a(c)to); **m** (inde(m)ne); **p** (ado(p)ção, ado(p)tar); *for further details see p. xiii.*

marido [ma'ridu] *m* husband.
marimbondo [mari'bõdu] *m* hornet.
marina [ma'rina] *f* marina.
marinha [ma'riɲa] *f* (*tb*: ~ *de guerra*) navy; (*pintura*) seascape; ~ **mercante** merchant navy.
marinheiro [mari'ɲejru] *m* seaman, sailor; ~ **de primeira viagem** (*fig*) beginner.
marinho/a [ma'riɲu/a] *adj* sea, marine.
marionete [marjo'netʃi] *f* puppet.
mariposa [mari'poza] *f* moth.
marisco [ma'riʃku] *m* shellfish.
marital [mari'taw] (*pl* -**ais**) *adj* marital.
maritalmente [maritaw'mẽtʃi] *adv*: **viver** ~ **(com alguém)** to live (with sb) as man and wife.
marítimo/a [ma'ritʃimu/a] *adj* sea, maritime; **pesca marítima** sea fishing.
marketing ['maxketʃiŋ] *m* marketing.
marmanjo [max'mãʒu] *m* grown man.
marmelada [maxme'lada] *f* quince jam; (*col*) double-dealing.
marmelo [max'mɛlu] *m* quince.
marmita [max'mita] *f* (*vasilha*) pot.
mármore ['maxmori] *m* marble.
marmóreo/a [max'mɔrju/a] *adj* marble; (*fig*) cold.
marola [ma'rɔla] *f* wave, roller.
maroto/a [ma'rotu/a] *m/f* rogue, rascal; (*criança*) naughty boy/girl ♦ *adj* roguish; (*criança*) naughty.
marquei [max'kej] *etc vb V* **marcar**.
marquês/quesa [max'keʃ/'keza] *m/f* marquis/marchioness.
marquise [max'kizi] *f* awning, canopy.
marra ['maxa] *f*: **na** ~ (*à força*) forcibly; (*a qualquer preço*) whatever the cost.
marreco [ma'xɛku] *m* duck.
Marrocos [ma'xɔkuʃ] *m*: **o** ~ Morocco.
marrom [ma'xõ] (*pl* -**ns**) *adj*, *m* brown.
marroquino/a [maxo'kinu/a] *adj*, *m/f* Moroccan.
Marte ['maxtʃi] *m* Mars.
martelada [maxte'lada] *f* (*pancada*) blow (with a hammer); (*ruído*) hammering sound.
martelar [maxte'la*] *vt* to hammer; (*amolar*) to bother ♦ *vi* to hammer; (*insistir*): ~ **(em algo)** to keep *ou* harp on (about sth).
martelo [max'tɛlu] *m* hammer.
martíni [max'tʃini] ® *m* martini ®.
Martinica [maxtʃi'nika] *f*: **a** ~ Martinique.
mártir ['maxtʃi*] *m/f* martyr.
martírio [max'tʃirju] *m* martyrdom; (*fig*) torment.
martirizante [maxtʃiri'zãtʃi] *adj* agonizing.
martirizar [maxtʃiri'za*] *vt* to martyr; (*atormentar*) to afflict; ~-**se** *vr* to agonize.
marujo [ma'ruʒu] *m* sailor.
marulhar [maru'ʎa*] *vi* (*mar*) to surge; (*ondas*) to lap; (*produzir ruído*) to roar.
marulho [ma'ruʎu] *m* (*do mar*) surge; (*das ondas*) lapping.
marxismo [max'ksiʒmu] *m* Marxism.

marxista [max'ksiʃta] *adj*, *m/f* Marxist.
marzipã [maxzi'pã] *m* marzipan.
mas [ma(j)ʃ] *conj* but ♦ *pron* = **me** + **as**.
mascar [maʃ'ka*] *vt* to chew.
máscara ['maʃkara] *f* mask; (*para limpeza de pele*) face-pack; **sob a** ~ **de** under the guise of; **tirar a** ~ **de alguém** (*fig*) to unmask sb; **baile de** ~**s** masked ball; ~ **de oxigênio** oxygen mask.
mascarado/a [maʃka'radu/a] *adj* masked; (*convencido*) conceited.
mascarar [maʃka'ra*] *vt* to mask; (*disfarçar*) to disguise; (*encobrir*) to cover up.
mascate [maʃ'katʃi] *m* peddler, hawker (*BRIT*).
mascavo [maʃ'kavu] *adj V* **açúcar**.
mascote [maʃ'kɔtʃi] *f* mascot.
masculinidade [maʃkulini'dadʒi] *f* masculinity.
masculino/a [maʃku'linu/a] *adj* masculine; (*BIO*) male ♦ *m* (*LING*) masculine; **roupa masculina** men's clothes *pl*.
másculo/a ['maʃkulu/a] *adj* masculine; (*viril*) manly.
masmorra [maʒ'mɔxa] *f* dungeon; (*fig*) black hole.
masoquismo [mazo'kiʒmu] *m* masochism.
masoquista [mazo'kiʃta] *m/f* masochist ♦ *adj* masochistic.
MASP *abr m* = **Museu de Arte de São Paulo**.
massa ['masa] *f* (*física*) mass; (*de tomate*) paste; (*CULIN: de pão*) dough; (: *macarrão etc*) pasta; (*fig*) mass; **as** ~**s** the masses; **em** ~ en masse; ~ **de vidraceiro** putty; **estar com as mãos na** ~ (*fig*) to be about *ou* at it.
massacrante [masa'krãtʃi] *adj* annoying.
massacrar [masa'kra*] *vt* to massacre; (*fig: chatear*) to annoy; (: *torturar*) to tear apart.
massacre [ma'sakri] *f* massacre; (*fig*) annoyance.
massagear [masa'ʒja*] *vt* to massage ♦ *vi* to do massage.
massagem [ma'saʒẽ] (*pl* -**ns**) *f* massage.
massagista [masa'ʒiʃta] *m/f* masseur/masseuse.
massificar [masifi'ka*] *vt* to influence (through mass communication).
massudo/a [ma'sudu/a] *adj* bulky; (*espesso*) thick; (*com aspecto de massa*) doughy.
mastectomia [maʃtekto'mia] *f* mastectomy.
mastigado/a [maʃtʃi'gadu/a] *adj* (*fig*) well-planned.
mastigar [maʃtʃi'ga*] *vt* to chew; (*pronunciar mal*) to mumble, mutter; (*fig: refletir*) to mull over.
mastim [maʃ'tʃĩ] (*pl* -**ns**) *m* watchdog.
mastodonte [maʃto'dõtʃi] *m* (*fig: pessoa gorda*) hulk, lump.
mastro ['maʃtru] *m* (*NÁUT*) mast; (*para bandeira*) flagpole.
masturbação [maʃtuxba'sãw] *f* masturbation.
masturbar [maʃtux'ba*] *vt* to masturbate; ^

se *vr* to masturbate.
mata ['mata] *f* forest, wood; ~ **virgem** virgin forest.
mata-bicho *m* tot of brandy, snifter.
mata-borrão *m* blotting paper.
matacão [mata'kãw] (*pl* -**ões**) *m* lump; (*pedra*) boulder.
matado/a [ma'tadu/a] *adj* (*trabalho*) badly done.
matador(a) [mata'do*(a)] *m/f* killer ♦ *m* (*em tourada*) matador.
matadouro [mata'doru] *m* slaughterhouse.
matagal [mata'gaw] (*pl* -**ais**) *m* bush; (*brenha*) thicket, undergrowth.
mata-moscas *m inv* fly-killer.
mata-mosquito (*pl* ~**s**) *m* mosquito exterminator.
matança [ma'tãsa] *f* massacre; (*de reses*) slaughter(ing).
mata-piolho (*pl* ~**s**) (*col*) *m* thumb.
matar [ma'ta*] *vt* to kill; (*sede*) to quench; (*fome*) to satisfy; (*aula*) to skip; (*trabalho*: *não aparecer*) to skive off; (: *fazer rápido*) to dash off; (*tempo*) to kill; (*adivinhar*) to guess, get ♦ *vi* to kill; ~-**se** *vr* to kill o.s.; (*esfalfar-se*) to wear o.s. out; **um calor/uma dor de** ~ stifling heat/excruciating pain; ~ **saudades** to catch up.
mata-rato (*pl* ~**s**) *m* (*veneno*) rat poison; (*cigarro*) throat-scraper.
mate ['matʃi] *adj* matt ♦ *m* (*chá*) maté tea; (*xeque*~) checkmate.
matelassê [matela'se] *adj* quilted ♦ *m* quilting.
matemática [mate'matʃika] *f* mathematics *sg*, maths *sg* (*BRIT*), math (*US*); *V tb* **matemático**.
matemático/a [mate'matʃiku/a] *adj* mathematical ♦ *m/f* mathematician.
matéria [ma'terja] *f* matter; (*TEC*) material; (*EDUC*: *assunto*) subject; (*tema*) topic; (*jornalística*) story, article; **em ~ de** on the subject of; ~ **fecal** faeces *pl* (*BRIT*), feces *pl* (*US*); ~ **plástica** plastic.
material [mate'rjaw] (*pl* -**ais**) *adj* material; (*físico*) physical ♦ *m* material; (*TEC*) equipment; (*col*: *corpo*) body; ~ **humano** manpower; ~ **bélico** armaments *pl*; ~ **de construção** building materials *pl*; ~ **de limpeza** cleaning materials *pl*; ~ **escolar** school materials *pl*.
materialismo [materja'liʒmu] *m* materialism.
materialista [materja'liʃta] *adj* materialistic ♦ *m/f* materialist.
materializar [materjali'za*] *vt* to materialize; ~-**se** *vr* to materialize.
matéria-prima (*pl* **matérias-primas**) *f* raw material.
maternal [matex'naw] (*pl* -**ais**) *adj* motherly, maternal; **escola** ~ nursery (school).
maternidade [matexni'dadʒi] *f* motherhood,

maternity; (*hospital*) maternity hospital.
materno/a [ma'texnu/a] *adj* motherly, maternal; (*língua*) native; (*avó*) maternal.
matilha [ma'tʃiʎa] *f* (*cães*) pack; (*fig*: *corja*) rabble.
matina [ma'tʃina] *f* morning.
matinal [matʃi'naw] (*pl* -**ais**) *adj* morning.
matinê [matʃi'ne] *f* matinée.
matiz [ma'tʃiʒ] *m* (*de cor*) shade; (*fig*: *de ironia*) tinge; (*cor política*) colouring (*BRIT*), coloring (*US*).
matizar [matʃi'za*] *vt* (*colorir*) to tinge, colour (*BRIT*), color (*US*); (*combinar cores*) to blend; ~ **algo de algo** (*fig*) to tinge sth with sth.
mato ['matu] *m* scrubland, bush; (*plantas agrestes*) scrub; (*o campo*) country; **ser** ~ (*col*) to be there for the taking; **estar num** ~ **sem cachorro** (*col*) to be up the creek without a paddle.
mato-grossano/a [-gro'sanu/a] *adj, m/f* = **mato-grossense**.
mato-grossense [-gro'sẽsi] *adj* from Mato Grosso ♦ *m/f* person from Mato Grosso.
matraca [ma'traka] *f* rattle; (*pessoa*) chatterbox; **falar como uma** ~ to talk nineteen to the dozen (*BRIT*) *ou* a blue streak (*US*).
matraquear [matra'kja*] *vi* to rattle, clatter; (*tagarelar*) to chatter, rabbit on.
matreiro/a [ma'trejru/a] *adj* cunning, crafty.
matriarca [ma'trjaxka] *f* matriarch.
matriarcal [matrjax'kaw] (*pl* -**ais**) *adj* matriarchal.
matrícula [ma'trikula] *f* (*lista*) register; (*inscrição*) registration; (*pagamento*) enrolment (*BRIT*) *ou* enrollment (*US*) fee; (*PT*: *AUTO*) registration number (*BRIT*), license number (*US*); **fazer a** ~ to enrol (*BRIT*), enroll (*US*).
matricular [matriku'la*] *vt*, ~-**se** *vr* to enrol (*BRIT*), enroll (*US*), register.
matrimonial [matrimo'njaw] (*pl* -**ais**) *adj* marriage *atr*, matrimonial.
matrimônio [matri'monju] *m* marriage; **contrair** ~ (**com alguém**) to be joined in marriage (with sb).
matriz [ma'triʒ] *f* (*MED*) womb; (*fonte*) source; (*molde*) mould (*BRIT*), mold (*US*); (*COM*) head office; (*col*) wife; **igreja** ~ mother church.
matrona [ma'trona] *f* matron.
maturação [matura'sãw] *f* maturing; (*de fruto*) ripening.
maturidade [maturi'dadʒi] *f* maturity.
matusquela [matuʃ'kela] (*col*) *m/f* lunatic.
matutar [matu'ta*] *vt* (*planejar*) to plan ♦ *vi*: ~ **em** *ou* **sobre algo** to turn sth over in one's mind.
matutino/a [matu'tʃinu/a] *adj* morning ♦ *m* morning paper.
matuto/a [ma'tutu/a] *adj, m/f* (*caipira*) rustic; (*provinciano*) provincial.

NB: *European Portuguese adds the following consonants to certain words:* **b** (sú(b)dito, su(b)til); **c** (a(c)ção, a(c)cionista, a(c)to); **m** (inde(m)ne); **p** (ado(p)ção, ado(p)tar); *for further details see p. xiii.*

mau/má [maw/ma] *adj* bad; *(malvado)* evil, wicked ♦ *m* bad; *(REL)* evil; **os ~s** bad people; *(num filme)* the baddies.

mau-caráter *(pl* **maus-carateres)** *m* bad lot ♦ *adj* shady.

mau-olhado [-o'ʎadu] *m* evil eye.

Maurício [maw'risju] *m* Mauritius.

Mauritânia [mawri'tanja] *f*: **a ~** Mauritania.

mausoléu [mawzo'lɛw] *m* mausoleum.

maus-tratos *mpl* ill-treatment *sg.*

mavioso/a [ma'vjozu/ɔza] *adj* tender, soft; *(som)* sweet.

máx. *abr* (= *máximo)* max.

máxi ['maksi] *adj inv* (*saia)* maxi.

maxidesvalorização [maksidʒiʒvaloriza'sãw] *(pl* **-ões)** *f* large-scale devaluation.

maxila [mak'sila] *f* jawbone.

maxilar [maksi'la*] *m* jawbone ♦ *adj* jaw *atr.*

máxima ['masima] *f* maxim, saying.

máxime ['maksimɛ] *adv* especially.

maximizar [masimi'za*] *vt* to maximize; *(superestimar)* to play up.

máximo/a ['masimu/a] *adj (maior que todos)* greatest; *(o maior possível)* maximum ♦ *m* maximum; *(o cúmulo)* peak; *(temperature)* high; **o ~ cuidado** the greatest of care; **no ~** at most; **ao ~** to the utmost; **chegar ao ~** *(fig)* to reach a peak; **ele acha-a o ~** *(col)* he thinks she is the greatest.

maxixe [ma'ʃiʃi] *m* gherkin; *(BR: dança)* 19th-century dance.

mazela [ma'zɛla] *f* *(ferida)* sore spot; *(doença)* illness; *(fig)* blemish.

MCE *abr m* = **Mercado Comum Europeu.**

MCom *(BR)* *abr m* = **Ministério das Comunicações.**

MCT *(BR)* *abr m* = **Ministério de Ciência e Tecnologia.**

MD *(BR)* *abr m* = **Ministério da Desburocratização.**

MDB *abr m* *(old)* = **Movimento Democrático Brasileiro.**

me [mi] *pron (direto)* me; *(indireto)* (to) me; *(reflexivo)* (to) myself.

meada ['mjada] *f* skein, hank.

meado ['mjadu] *m* middle; **em ~s** *ou* **no(s) ~(s) de julho/do ano** in mid-July/in the middle of the year.

meandro ['mjãdru] *m* meander; **os ~s** *(fig)* the ins and outs.

MEC *(BR)* *abr m* = **Ministério de Educação e Cultura.**

Meca ['mɛka] *n* Mecca.

mecânica [me'kanika] *f* *(ciência)* mechanics *sg;* *(mecanismo)* mechanism; *V tb* **mecânico.**

mecânico/a [me'kaniku/a] *adj* mechanical ♦ *m/f* mechanic; **broca mecânica** power drill.

mecanismo [meka'niʒmu] *m* mechanism.

mecanização [mekaniza'sãw] *f* mechanization.

mecanizar [mekani'za*] *vt* to mechanize.

mecenas [me'sɛnaʃ] *m inv* patron.

mecha ['mɛʃa] *f* *(de vela)* wick; *(cabelo)* tuft;

(tingida) highlight; *(MED)* swab; **fazer ~ no cabelo** to put highlights in one's hair, to highlight one's hair.

mechado/a [me'ʃadu/a] *adj* highlighted.

meço ['mɛsu] *etc vb* **V medir.**

méd. *abr* (= *médio)* av.

medalha [me'daʎa] *f* medal.

medalhão [meda'ʎãw] *(pl* **-ões)** *m* medallion; *(fig: figurão)* big name; *(jóia)* locket.

média ['mɛdʒa] *f* average; *(café)* coffee with milk; **em ~** on average; **fazer ~** to ingratiate o.s.

mediação [medʒja'sãw] *f* mediation; **por ~ de** through.

mediador(a) [medʒja'do*(a)] *m/f* mediator.

mediano/a [me'dʒjanu/a] *adj* medium, average; *(medíocre)* mediocre.

mediante [me'dʒjãtʃi] *prep* by (means of), through; *(a troco de)* in return for.

mediar [me'dʒja*] *vt* to mediate (for) ♦ *vi (ser mediador)* to mediate; **a distância que medeia entre** the distance between.

medicação [medʒika'sãw] *(pl* **-ões)** *f* treatment; *(medicamentos)* medication.

medicamento [medʒika'mētu] *m* medicine.

medição [medʒi'sãw] *(pl* **-ões)** *f* measurement.

medicar [medʒi'ka*] *vt* to treat ♦ *vi* to practise *(BRIT)* ou practice *(US)* medicine; **~-se** *vr* to take medicine, doctor o.s. up.

medicina [medʒi'sina] *f* medicine; **~ legal** forensic medicine.

medicinal [medʒisi'naw] *(pl* **-ais)** *adj* medicinal.

médico/a ['mɛdʒiku/a] *adj* medical ♦ *m/f* doctor; **receita médica** prescription.

médico-cirurgião/médica-cirurgiã *(pl* **médicos-cirurgiões/médicas-cirurgiãs)** *m/f* surgeon.

medições [medʒi'sõjʃ] *fpl de* **medição.**

médico-hospitalar *(pl* **-es)** *adj* hospital and medical.

médico-legal *(pl* **-ais)** *adj* forensic.

médico-legista *(pl* **médicos-legistas)** *m* forensic expert *(BRIT)*, medical examiner *(US)*.

medida [me'dʒida] *f* measure; *(providência)* step; *(medição)* measurement; *(moderação)* prudence; **à ~ que** while, as; **tomar ~s** to take steps; **tomar as ~s de** to measure; **feito sob ~** made to measure; **software sob ~** bespoke software; **ir além da ~** to go too far; **encher as ~s** *(satisfazer)* to fit the bill; **encher as ~s de alguém** *(chatear)* to get on sb's wick; **na ~ em que** in so far as; **tirar as ~s de alguém** to take sb's measurements; **~ de emergência/urgência** emergency/urgent measure.

medidor [medʒi'do*] *m*: **~ de pressão** pressure gauge; **~ de gás** gas meter.

medieval [medʒje'vaw] *(pl* **-ais)** *adj* medieval.

médio/a ['mɛdʒju/a] *adj (dedo, classe)* middle; *(tamanho, estatura)* medium; *(mediano)* average; **a ~ prazo** in the medium term;

ensino ~ secondary education; **o brasileiro** ~ the average Brazilian.

medíocre [me'dʒiokri] adj mediocre.

mediocridade [medʒiokri'dadʒi] f mediocrity.

mediocrizar [medʒiokri'za*] vt to make mediocre.

medir [me'dʒi*] vt to measure; (atos, palavras) to weigh; (avaliar: conseqüências, distâncias) to weigh up ♦ vi to measure; **~-se** vr to measure o.s.; **~-se (com alguém)** (comparar-se) to be on a par (with sb); **quanto você mede?** — **meço 1.60 m** how tall are you? — I'm 1.60 m (tall); **a saia mede 80 cm de comprimento** the skirt is 80 cm long; **meça suas palavras!** watch your language!; ~ **alguém dos pés à cabeça** (fig) to eye sb up; **não ter mãos a** ~ (fig) to have one's hands full.

meditação [medʒita'sãw] (pl -ões) f meditation.

meditar [medʒi'ta*] vi to meditate; ~ **sobre algo** to ponder (on) sth.

meditativo/a [medʒita'tʃivu/a] adj thoughtful, reflective.

mediterrâneo/a [medʒite'xanju/a] adj Mediterranean ♦ m: **o M~** the Mediterranean.

médium ['mɛdʒjũ] (pl -ns) m (pessoa) medium.

mediunidade [medʒjuni'dadʒi] f second sight.

médiuns ['mɛdʒjũʃ] mpl de **médium**.

medo ['medu] m fear; **com** ~ afraid; **ter** ~ **de** to be afraid of; **ficar com** ~ to get frightened; **meter** ~ to be frightening; **meter** ~ **em alguém** to frighten sb; **com** ~ **que** for fear that; **ter um** ~ **que se péla** (fig) to be frightened out of one's wits.

medonho/a [me'doɲu/a] adj terrible, awful.

medrar [me'dra*] vi to thrive, flourish; (col: ter medo) to get frightened.

medroso/a [me'drozu/ɔza] adj (com medo) frightened; (tímido) timid.

medula [me'dula] f marrow.

megabyte [mega'bajtʃi] m megabyte.

megalomania [megaloma'nia] f megalomania.

megalomaníaco/a [megaloma'niaku/a] adj, m/f megalomaniac.

megaton [mega'tõ] m megaton.

megera [me'ʒera] f shrew; (mãe) cruel mother.

meia ['meja] f stocking; (curta) sock; (meia-entrada) half-price ticket ♦ num six; **(ponto de)** ~ stocking stitch.

meia-calça (pl **meias-calças**) f tights pl, panty hose (US).

meia-direita (pl **meias-direitas**) f (FUTEBOL) inside right ♦ m (jogador) inside right.

meia-entrada (pl **meias-entradas**) f half-price ticket.

meia-esquerda (pl **meias-esquerdas**) f (FUTEBOL) inside left ♦ m (jogador) inside left.

meia-estação f: **roupa de** ~ spring ou autumn clothing.

meia-idade f middle age; **pessoa de** ~ middle-aged person.

meia-lua f half moon; (formato) semicircle.

meia-luz f half light.

meia-noite f midnight.

meia-tigela f: **de** ~ two-bit.

meia-volta (pl **meias-voltas**) f (tb: MIL) about-turn (BRIT), about-face (US).

meigo/a ['mejgu/a] adj sweet.

meiguice [mej'gisi] f sweetness.

meio/a ['meju/a] adj half ♦ adv a bit, rather ♦ m (centro) middle; (social, profissional) milieu; (tb: ~ ambiente) environment; (recurso) means pl; (maneira) way; ~s mpl means pl; **cortar ao** ~ to cut in half; **no** ~ **(de)** in the middle (of); **o quarto do** ~ the middle room, the room in the middle; **dividir algo** ~ **a** ~ to divide sth in half ou fifty-fifty; **em** ~ **a** amid; **deixar algo pelo** ~ to leave sth half-finished; **por** ~ **de** through; **por todos os** ~s by all available means; **não há** ~ **de chover/de ela chegar cedo** there is no way it's going to rain/she will arrive early; ~ **quilo** half a kilo; **um mês e** ~ one and a half months; **embolar o** ~ **de campo** (fig) to foul things up; **nos** ~s **financeiros** in financial circles; ~ **de transporte** means of transport; **~s de comunicação (de massa)** (mass) media pl; **~s de produção** means pl of production.

meio-de-campo (pl **meios-de-campo**) m (FUTEBOL) centre (BRIT) ou center (US) forward; (: posição) midfield.

meio-dia m midday, noon.

meio-feriado (pl **meios-feriados**) m half-day holiday.

meio-fio m kerb (BRIT), curb (US).

meio-termo (pl **meios-termos**) m (fig) compromise.

meio-tom (pl **meios-tons**) m (MÚS) semitone; (nuança) half-tone.

mel [mɛw] m honey.

melaço [me'lasu] m molasses pl.

melado/a [me'ladu/a] adj (pegajoso) sticky ♦ m (melaço: US) molasses; (: BRIT) treacle.

melancia [melã'sia] f watermelon.

melancieira [melã'sjejra] f watermelon plant.

melancolia [melãko'lia] f melancholy, sadness.

melancólico/a [melã'kɔliku/a] adj sad, melancholy.

Melanésia [mela'nɛzja] f: **a** ~ Melanesia.

melão [me'lãw] (pl -ões) m melon.

melar [me'la*] vt to dirty ♦ vi (gorar) to flop; **~-se** vr to get messy.

meleca [me'lɛka] (col) f snot; (uma ~) bogey; **tirar** ~ to pick one's nose; **que ~!** (col) what crap!

NB: European Portuguese adds the following consonants to certain words: **b** (sú(b)dito, su(b)til); **c** (a(c)ção, a(c)cionista, a(c)to); **m** (inde(m)ne); **p** (ado(p)ção, ado(p)tar); *for further details see p. xiii.*

meleira [me'lejra] *f* sticky mess.

melena [me'lena] *f* long hair.

melhor [me'ʎɔ*] *adj, adv (compar)* better; *(superl)* best; ~ **que nunca** better than ever; **quanto mais** ~ the more the better; **seria** ~ **começarmos** we had better begin; **tanto** ~ so much the better; ~ **ainda** even better; **bem** ~ much better; **o** ~ **é ...** the best thing is ...; **levar a** ~ to come off best; **ou** ~ ... *(ou antes)* or rather ...; **fiz o** ~ **que pude** I did the best I could; **no** ~ **da festa** *(fig: no melhor momento)* all the best *(ou* were) in full swing; (: *inesperadamente*) all of a sudden.

melhora [me'ʎɔra] *f* improvement; ~**s!** get well soon!

melhorada [meʎo'rada] *(col) f*: **dar uma** ~ to get better.

melhoramento [meʎora'mẽtu] *m* improvement.

melhorar [meʎo'ra*] *vt* to improve, make better; *(doente)* to make better ♦ *vi* to improve, get better; *(doente)* to get better; ~ **de vida** to improve one's circumstances; ~ **no emprego** to get better at one's job.

meliante [me'ljãtʃi] *m* scoundrel; *(vagabundo)* tramp.

melindrar [melĩ'dra*] *vt* to offend, hurt; ~**-se** *vr* to take offence *(BRIT) ou* offense *(US)*, be hurt.

melindre [me'lĩdri] *m* sensitivity.

melindroso/a [melĩ'drozu/ɔza] *adj (sensível)* sensitive, touchy; *(problema, situação)* tricky; *(operação)* delicate.

melodia [melo'dʒia] *f* melody; *(composição)* tune.

melódico/a [me'lɔdʒiku/a] *adj* melodic.

melodrama [melo'drama] *m* melodrama.

melodramático/a [melodra'matʃiku/a] *adj* melodramatic.

meloeiro [me'lwejru] *m* melon plant.

melões [me'lõjʃ] *mpl de* **melão**.

meloso/a [me'lozu/ɔza] *adj* sweet; *(voz)* mellifluous; *(fig: pessoa)* sweet-talking.

melro ['mɛwxu] *m* blackbird.

membrana [mẽ'brana] *f* membrane.

membro ['mẽbru] *m* member; *(ANAT: braço, perna)* limb.

membrudo/a [mẽ'brudu/a] *adj* big; *(fig)* robust.

memento [me'mẽtu] *m* reminder; *(caderneta)* jotter.

memorando [memo'rãdu] *m (aviso)* note; *(COM: comunicação)* memorandum.

memorável [memo'ravew] *(pl* -**eis**) *adj* memorable.

memória [me'mɔrja] *f* memory; ~**s** *fpl (de autor)* memoirs; **de** ~ by heart; **em** ~ **de** in memory of; ~ **fraca** bad memory; **falta de** ~ loss of memory; **digno de** ~ memorable; **vir à** ~ to come to mind; **varrer da** ~ *(fig)* to wipe sth from one's memory; ~ **RAM** RAM memory; ~ **não-volátil** non-volatile memory.

memorial [memo'rjaw] *(pl* -**ais**) *m* memorial; *(JUR)* brief.

memorizar [memori'za*] *vt* to memorize.

menção [mẽ'sãw] *(pl* -**ões**) *f* mention, reference; ~ **honrosa** honours *(BRIT)*, honors *(US)*, distinction; **fazer** ~ **de algo** to mention sth; **fazer** ~ **de sair** to make as if to leave, begin to leave.

mencionar [mẽsjo'na*] *vt* to mention; **para não** ~ ... not to mention ...; **sem** ~ ... let alone ....

menções [mẽ'sõjʃ] *fpl de* **menção**.

mendicância [mẽdʒi'kãsja] *f* begging.

mendicante [mẽdʒi'kãtʃi] *adj* mendicant ♦ *m/f* beggar.

mendigar [mẽdʒi'ga*] *vt* to beg for ♦ *vi* to beg.

mendigo/a [mẽ'dʒigu/a] *m/f* beggar.

menear [me'nja*] *vt (corpo, cabeça)* to shake; *(quadris)* to swing; ~ **a cabeça de modo afirmativo** to nod (one's head).

meneio [me'neju] *m (balanço)* swaying.

meninada [meni'nada] *f* kids *pl*.

meningite [menĩ'ʒitʃi] *f* meningitis.

meninice [meni'nisi] *f (infância)* childhood; *(modos de criança)* childishness; *(ato, dito)* childish thing.

menino/a [me'ninu/a] *m/f* boy/girl; *(olhos)*: **menina do olho** pupil; **ser a menina dos olhos de alguém** *(fig)* to be the apple of sb's eye; **seu sorriso de** ~ his boyish smile.

meninote/a [meni'nɔtʃi/ta] *m/f* boy/girl.

menopausa [meno'pawza] *f* menopause.

menor [me'nɔ*] *adj (mais pequeno: compar)* smaller; (: *superl*) smallest; *(mais jovem: compar)* younger; (: *superl*) youngest; *(o mínimo)* the least, slightest; *(tb:* ~ **de idade)** under age ♦ *m/f* juvenile, young person; *(JUR)* minor; ~ **abandonado** abandoned child; **proibido para** ~**es** over 18s only; *(filme)* X-certificate *(BRIT)*, X-rated *(US)*; **um** ~ **de 10 anos** a child of ten; **não tenho a** ~ **idéia** I haven't the slightest idea.

menoridade [menori'dadʒi] *f* under-age status.

menos ['menuʃ] *adj (compar: sg)* less; (: *pl*) fewer; *(superl: sg)* least; (: *pl*) fewest ♦ *adv (compar)* less; *(superl)* least ♦ *prep* except ♦ *conj* minus, less ♦ *m*: **o** ~ the least; **a** *ou* **de** ~ *(faltando)* missing; **ele me deu £1 a** *ou* **de** ~ he gave me £1 too little; **a** ~ **que** unless; **ao** *ou* **pelo** ~ at least; **mais ou** ~ more or less; ~ **de** *(ou* **que)** less than; ~ **cansativo** less tiring; **trabalhar** ~ to work less; **quanto** ~ **você** ... the less you ...; **muito** ~ ... much less ..., let alone ...; **nem ao** ~ not even, not as much as; **quando** ~ **se espera** when you least expect it; **tudo** ~ **isso!** anything but that!; **não é para** ~ it's no wonder; **isso é o de** ~ that's nothing.

menosprezar [menuʃpre'za*] *vt (subestimar)* to underrate; *(desprezar)* to despise, scorn.

menosprezível [menuʃpre'zivew] *(pl* -**eis**) *adj* despicable.

menosprezo [menuʃ'prezu] *m* contempt, disdain.

mensageiro/a [mẽsa'ʒejru/a] *adj* messenger *atr* ◊ *m/f* messenger.

mensagem [mẽ'saʒẽ] (*pl* **-ns**) *f* message; ~ **de erro** (*COMPUT*) error message.

mensal [mẽ'saw] (*pl* **-ais**) *adj* monthly; **ele ganha £1000 mensais** he earns £1000 a month.

mensalidade [mẽsali'dadʒi] *f* monthly payment.

mensalmente [mẽsaw'mẽtʃi] *adv* monthly.

menstruação [mẽʃtrwa'sãw] *f* period, menstruation.

menstruada [mẽʃ'trwada] *adj* having one's period; (*MED*) menstruating.

menstrual [mẽʃ'trwaw] (*pl* **-ais**) *adj* menstrual.

menstruar [mẽʃ'trwa*] *vi* to menstruate, have a period.

mênstruo ['mẽʃtru] *m* period, menstruation.

menta ['mẽta] *f* mint.

mental [mẽ'taw] (*pl* **-ais**) *adj* mental.

mentalidade [mẽtali'dadʒi] *f* mentality.

mentalizar [mẽtali'za*] *vt* (*plano*) to conceive; ~ **alguém de algo** to make sb realize sth.

mente ['mẽtʃi] *f* mind; **de boa** ~ willingly; **ter em** ~ to bear in mind.

mentecapto/a [mẽtʃi'kaptu/a] *adj* mad, crazy ◊ *m/f* fool, idiot.

mentir [mẽ'tʃi*] *vi* to lie; **minto!** (I) tell a lie!

mentira [mẽ'tʃira] *f* lie; (*ato*) lying; **parece** ~ **que** it seems incredible that; **de** ~ not for real; ~**!** (*acusação*) that's a lie!, you're lying; (*de surpresa*) you don't say!, no!

mentiroso/a [mẽtʃi'rozu/ɔza] *adj* lying; (*enganoso*) deceitful; (*falso*) deceptive ◊ *m/f* liar.

mentol [mẽ'tɔw] (*pl* **-óis**) *m* menthol.

mentolado/a [mẽto'ladu/a] *adj* mentholated.

mentor [mẽ'to*] *m* mentor.

menu [me'nu] *m* (*tb: COMPUT*) menu.

mercadinho [mexka'dʒiɲu] *m* local market.

mercado [mex'kadu] *m* market; **M~ Comum** Common Market; ~ **negro** *ou* **paralelo** black market; ~ **externo/interno** foreign/domestic *ou* home market; ~ **das pulgas** flea market; ~ **de capitais** capital market; ~ **de trabalho** labo(u)r market; ~ **à vista** spot market.

mercadologia [mexkadolo'ʒia] *f* marketing.

mercador [mexka'do*] *m* merchant, trader.

mercadoria [mexkado'ria] *f* commodity; ~**s** *fpl* goods.

mercante [mex'kãtʃi] *adj* merchant *atr*.

mercantil [mexkã'tʃiw] (*pl* **-is**) *adj* mercantile, commercial.

mercê [mex'se] *f* (*favor*) favour (*BRIT*), favor (*US*); (*perdão*) mercy; **à** ~ **de** at the mercy of.

mercearia [mexsja'ria] *f* grocer's (shop) (*BRIT*), grocery store.

merceeiro [mex'sjejru] *m* grocer.

mercenário/a [mexse'narju/a] *adj* mercenary ◊ *m* mercenary.

mercerizado/a [mexseri'zadu/a] *adj* mercerized.

mercúrio [mex'kurju] *m* mercury; **M~** Mercury.

merda ['mɛxda] (*col!*) *f* shit (*!*) ◊ *m/f* (*pessoa*) jerk; **a** ~ **do carro** the bloody (*BRIT*) *ou* goddamn (*US*) car (*!*); **mandar alguém à** ~ to tell sb to piss off (*!*); **estar numa** ~ to be fucked up (*!*); ~ **nenhuma** fuck all (*!*); **ser uma** ~ (*viagem, filme*) to be crap (*!*).

merecedor(a) [merese'do*(a)] *adj* deserving.

merecer [mere'se*] *vt* to deserve; (*consideração*) to merit; (*valer*) to be worth ◊ *vi* to be worthy.

merecido/a [mere'sidu/a] *adj* deserved; (*castigo, prêmio*) just.

merecimento [meresi'mẽtu] *m* desert; (*valor, talento*) merit.

merenda [me'rẽda] *f* packed lunch; ~ **escolar** free school meal.

merendar [merẽ'da*] *vi* to have school dinner.

merendeira [merẽ'dejra] *f* (*maleta*) lunch-box; (*funcionária*) dinner-lady.

merengue [me'rẽgi] *m* meringue.

meretrício [mere'trisju] *m* prostitution.

meretriz [mere'triʒ] *f* prostitute.

mergulhador(a) [mexguʎa'do*(a)] *adj* diving ◊ *m/f* diver.

mergulhar [mexgu'ʎa*] *vi* (*para nadar*) to dive; (*penetrar*) to plunge ◊ *vt*: ~ **algo em algo** (*num líquido*) to dip sth into sth; (*na terra etc*) to plunge sth into sth; ~ **no trabalho/na floresta** to immerse o.s. in one's work/go deep into the forest.

mergulho [mex'guʎu] *m* dip(ping), immersion; (*em natação*) dive; (*vôo*) nose-dive; **dar um** ~ (*na praia*) to go for a dip.

meridiano [meri'dʒjanu] *m* meridian.

meridional [meridʒjo'naw] (*pl* **-ais**) *adj* southern.

mérito ['mɛritu] *m* merit.

meritório/a [meri'tɔrju/a] *adj* meritorious.

merluza [mex'luza] *f* hake.

mero/a ['mɛru/a] *adj* mere.

mertiolate [mextʃjo'latʃi] *m* antiseptic.

mês [meʃ] *m* month; **pago por** ~ paid by the month; **duas vezes por** ~ twice a month; ~ **corrente** this month; **o** ~ **que vem** next month.

mesa ['meza] *f* table; (*de trabalho*) desk; (*comitê*) board; (*numa reunião*) panel; **pôr/tirar a** ~ to lay/clear the table; **à** ~ at the table; **por baixo da** ~ (*tb fig*) under the table; ~ **de bilhar** billiard table; ~ **de centro** coffee table; ~ **de cozinha/jantar** kitchen/dining table; ~ **de jogo** card table; ~ **de toalete** dressing table; ~ **telefônica**

NB: European Portuguese adds the following consonants to certain words: **b** (sú(b)dito, su(b)til); **c** (a(c)ção, a(c)cionista, a(c)to); **m** (inde(m)ne); **p** (ado(p)ção, ado(p)tar); *for further details see p. xiii.*

switchboard.

mesada [me'zada] *f* monthly allowance; *(de criança)* pocket-money.

mesa-de-cabeceira *(pl* **mesas-de-cabeceira)** *f* bedside table.

mesa-redonda *(pl* **mesas-redondas)** *f* discussion panel.

mescla ['mɛʃkla] *f* mixture, blend.

mesclar [meʃ'kla*] *vt* to mix (up); *(cores)* to blend.

meseta [me'zeta] *f* plateau, tableland.

mesmice [meʒ'misi] *f* sameness.

mesmo/a ['meʒmu/a] *adj* same; *(enfático)* very ♦ *adv (exatamente)* right; *(até)* even; *(realmente)* really ♦ *m/f:* **o ~/a mesma** the same (one); **o ~** *(a mesma coisa)* the same (thing); **eu ~** I myself; **este ~ homem** this very man; **ele ~ o fez** he did it himself; **o Rei ~** the King himself; **continuar na mesma** to be just the same; **dá no ~** *ou* **na mesma** it's all the same; **aqui/agora/hoje ~** right here/right now/this very day; **~ que** even if; **é ~** it's true; **é ~?** really?; **(é) isso ~!** exactly!, that's right!; **por isso ~** that's why; **~ assim** even so; **nem ~** not even; **~ quando** even when; **só ~** only; **por si ~** by one's self; *(referindo-se a pessoa já mencionada):* **..., e estive com o ~ ontem** ..., and I was with him yesterday; **ficar na mesma** *(não entender)* to be none the wiser; **isto para mim é o ~** it's all the same to me; **o ~, por favor!** *(num bar etc)* the same again, please.

mesquinharia [meʃkiɲa'ria] *f* meanness; *(ato, dito)* mean thing.

mesquinho/a [meʃ'kiɲu/a] *adj* mean.

mesquita [meʃ'kita] *f* mosque.

messias [me'siaʃ] *m* Messiah.

mestiçar-se [meʃtʃi'saxsi] *vr:* **~ (com)** to interbreed (with).

mestiço/a [meʃ'tʃisu/a] *adj* half-caste, of mixed race; *(animal)* crossbred ♦ *m/f* half-caste; *(animal)* half-breed.

mestrado [meʃ'trado] *m* master's degree; **fazer/tirar o ~** to do/get one's master's (degree).

mestre/a ['mɛʃtri/a] *adj (chave, viga)* master; *(linha, estrada)* main; *(qualidade)* masterly ♦ *m/f* master/mistress; *(professor)* teacher; **de ~** masterly; **obra mestra** masterpiece; **ele é ~ em mentir** he's an expert liar.

mestre-cuca *(pl* **mestres-cucas)** *(col) m* chef.

mestre-de-cerimônias *(pl* **mestres-de-cerimônias)** *m* master of ceremonies, MC.

mestre-de-obras *(pl* **mestres-de-obras)** *m* foreman.

mestria [meʃ'tria] *f* mastery; *(habilidade)* expertise; **com ~** to perfection.

mesura [me'zura] *f* *(cumprimento)* bow; *(cortesia)* courtesy; **cheio de ~s** cap in hand.

meta ['mɛta] *f* *(em corrida)* finishing post; *(re-gata)* finishing line; *(gol)* goal; *(objetivo)* aim, goal.

metabolismo [metabo'liʒmu] *m* metabolism.

metade [me'tadʒi] *f* half; *(meio)* middle; **~ de uma laranja** half an orange; **pela ~** halfway through.

metafísica [meta'fizika] *f* metaphysics *sg.*

metafísico/a [meta'fiziku/a] *adj* metaphysical.

metáfora [me'tafora] *f* metaphor.

metafórico/a [meta'fɔriku/a] *adj* metaphorical.

metal [me'taw] *(pl* **-ais)** *m* metal; **metais** *mpl* *(MÚS)* brass *sg.*

metálico/a [me'taliku/a] *adj* *(som)* metallic; *(de metal)* metal.

metalinguagem [metali'gwaʒẽ] *(pl* **-ns)** *f* metalanguage.

metalizado/a [metali'zadu/a] *adj* metallic.

metalurgia [metalux'ʒia] *f* metallurgy.

metalúrgica [meta'luxʒika] *f* metal works; *V tb* **metalúrgico.**

metalúrgico/a [meta'luxʒiku/a] *adj* metallurgical ♦ *m/f* metalworker.

metamorfose [metamox'fɔzi] *f* metamorphosis.

metamorfosear [metamoxfo'zja*] *vt:* **~ alguém em algo** to transform sb into sth.

metano [me'tanu] *m* methane.

meteórico/a [mete'ɔriku/a] *adj* meteoric.

meteorito [meteo'ritu] *m* meteorite.

meteoro [me'tjɔru] *m* meteor.

meteorologia [meteorolo'ʒia] *f* meteorology.

meteorológico/a [meteoro'lɔʒiku/a] *adj* meteorological.

meteorologista [meteorolo'ʒiʃta] *m/f* meteorologist; *(TV, RÁDIO)* weather forecaster.

meter [me'te*] *vt* *(colocar)* to put; *(envolver)* to involve; *(introduzir)* to introduce; **~-se** *vr* *(esconder-se)* to hide; *(retirar-se)* to closet o.s.; **~ na cabeça** to take it into one's head; **~-se na cama** to get into bed; **~-se com** *(provocar)* to pick a quarrel with; *(associar-se)* to get involved with; **~-se a médico** to set o.s. up as a doctor; **~-se a fazer** to decide to have a go at doing; **~-se em** to get involved in; *(intrometer-se)* to interfere in; **~-se onde não é chamado** to poke one's nose in(to other people's business); **meta-se com a sua vida** mind your own business.

meticulosidade [metʃikulozi'dadʒi] *f* meticulousness.

meticuloso/a [metʃiku'lozu/ɔza] *adj* meticulous.

metido/a [me'tʃidu/a] *adj* *(envolvido)* involved; *(intrometido)* meddling; **~ (a besta)** snobbish.

metódico/a [me'tɔdʒiku/a] *adj* methodical.

metodismo [meto'dʒiʒmu] *m* *(REL)* Methodism.

metodista [meto'dʒiʃta] *adj, m/f* Methodist.

método ['metodu] *m* method.

metodologia [metodolo'ʒia] *f* methodology.

metragem [me'traʒẽ] *f* length (in metres

(*BRIT*) *ou* meters (*US*)); (*CINEMA*) footage, length; **filme de longa/curta** ~ feature *ou* full-length/short film.

metralhadora [metraʎa'dora] *f* sub-machine gun.

metralhar [metra'ʎa*] *vt* (*ferir*, *matar*) to shoot; (*fazer fogo contra*) to spray with machine-gun fire.

métrica ['mɛtrika] *f* (*em poesia*) metre (*BRIT*), meter (*US*).

métrico/a ['mɛtriku/a] *adj* metric; **fita métrica** tape measure.

metro ['mɛtru] *m* metre (*BRIT*), meter (*US*); (*PT*: *metropolitano*) underground (*BRIT*), subway (*US*); ~ **quadrado/cúbico** square/cubic metre.

metrô [me'tro] (*BR*) *m* underground (*BRIT*), subway (*US*).

metrópole [me'trɔpoli] *f* metropolis; (*capital*) capital.

metropolitano/a [metropoli'tanu/a] *adj* metropolitan ♦ *m* (*PT*) underground (*BRIT*), subway (*US*).

metroviário/a [metro'vjarju/a] *adj* underground *atr* (*BRIT*), subway *atr* (*US*) ♦ *m/f* underground (*BRIT*) *ou* subway (*US*) worker.

meu/minha [mew/'miɲa] *adj* my ♦ *pron* mine; **um amigo** ~ a friend of mine; **este livro é** ~ this book is mine; **os** ~**s** *mpl* (*minha família*) my family *ou* folks (*col*); **estou na minha** I'm doing my own thing.

MEx (*BR*) *abr m* = **Ministério do Exército**.

mexer [me'ʃe*] *vt* (*mover*) to move; (*cabeça*: *dizendo sim*) to nod; (: *dizendo não*) to shake; (*misturar*) to stir; (*ovos*) to scramble ♦ *vi* (*mover*) to move; ~**-se** *vr* to move; (*apressar-se*) to get a move on; ~ **em algo** to touch sth; ~ **com algo** (*trabalhar*) to work with sth; (*comerciar*) to deal in sth; ~ **com alguém** (*provocar*) to tease sb; (*comover*) to have a profound effect on sb, get to sb (*col*); **mexa-se!** get going!, move yourself!

mexerica [meʃe'rika] *f* tangerine.

mexericar [meʃeri'ka*] *vi* to gossip.

mexerico [meʃe'riku] *m* piece of gossip; ~**s** *mpl* gossip *sg*.

mexeriqueiro/a [meʃeri'kejru/a] *adj* gossiping ♦ *m/f* gossip, busybody.

mexicano/a [meʃi'kanu/a] *adj*, *m/f* Mexican.

México ['mɛʃiku] *m*: **o** ~ Mexico; **a Cidade do** ~ Mexico City.

mexida [me'ʃida] *f* mess, disorder.

mexido/a [me'ʃidu/a] *adj* (*papéis*) mixed up; (*ovos*) scrambled.

mexilhão [meʃi'ʎãw] (*pl* **-ões**) *m* mussel.

mezanino [meza'ninu] *m* mezzanine (floor).

MF (*BR*) *abr m* = **Ministério da Fazenda**.

MG (*BR*) *abr* = **Minas Gerais**.

mg *abr* (= *miligrama*) mg.

mi [mi] *m* (*MÚS*) E.

miado ['mjadu] *m* miaow.

miar [mja*] *vi* to miaow; (*vento*) to whistle.

miasma ['mjaʒma] *m* (*fig*) decay.

miau [mjaw] *m* miaow.

MIC (*BR*) *abr m* = **Ministério de Indústria e Comércio**.

miçanga [mi'sãga] *f* beads *pl*.

micção [mik'sãw] *f* urination.

mico ['miku] *m* capuchin monkey.

micose [mi'kɔzi] *f* mycosis.

micrão [mi'krãw] (*pl* **-ões**) *m* (*COMPUT*) super-micro.

micro ['mikru] *m* (*COMPUT*) micro.

micro- [mikru] *prefixo* micro-.

micróbio [mi'krɔbju] *m* germ, microbe.

microcirurgia [mikrosirux'ʒia] *f* microsurgery.

microcomputador [mikrokõputa'do*] *m* microcomputer.

microcosmo [mikro'kɔʒmu] *m* microcosm.

microempresa [mikroẽ'preza] *f* small business.

micrões [mi'krõjʃ] *mpl de* **micrão**.

microfilme [mikro'fiwmi] *m* microfilm.

microfone [mikro'fɔni] *m* microphone.

microinformática [mikroĩfox'matʃika] *f* micro-computing.

Micronésia [mikro'nɛzja] *f*: **a** ~ Micronesia.

microonda [mikro'õda] *f* microwave.

microondas [mikro'õdaʃ] *m inv* (*tb*: *forno de* ~) microwave (oven).

microônibus [mikro'onibuʃ] *m inv* minibus.

microplaqueta [mikropla'keta] *f* microchip; ~ **de silicone** silicon chip.

microprocessador [mikroprosesa'do*] *m* microprocessor.

microrganismo [mikroxga'niʒmu] *m* micro-organism.

microscópico/a [mikro'ʃkɔpiku/a] *adj* microscopic.

microscópio [mikro'ʃkɔpju] *m* microscope.

mídi ['midʒi] *adj inv* midi.

mídia ['midʒja] *f* media *pl*.

migalha [mi'gaʎa] *f* crumb; ~**s** *fpl* scraps.

migração [migra'sãw] (*pl* **-ões**) *f* migration.

migrar [mi'gra*] *vi* to migrate.

migratório/a [migra'tɔrju/a] *adj* migratory; **aves migratórias** birds of passage.

miguel [mi'gew] (*pl* **-eis**) (*col*) *m* (*banheiro*) loo (*BRIT*), john (*US*).

mijada [mi'ʒada] (*col*) *f* pee; **dar uma** ~ to have a pee.

mijar [mi'ʒa*] (*col*) *vi* to pee; ~**-se** *vr* to wet o.s.

mijo ['miʒu] (*col*) *m* pee, piss (*!*).

mil [miw] *num* thousand; **dois** ~ two thousand; **estar a** ~ (*col*) to be buzzing.

milagre [mi'lagri] *m* miracle; **por** ~ miraculously.

milagroso/a [mila'grozu/ɔza] *adj* miraculous.

milenar [mile'na*] *adj* thousand-year-old; (*fig*)

ancient.

milênio [mi'lenju] *m* millennium.

milésimo/a [mi'lɛzimu/a] *num* thousandth.

mil-folhas *f inv* (*massa*) millefeuille pastry; (*doce*) cream slice.

milha ['miʎa] *f* mile; (*col: mil cruzeiros*): **dez ~s** ten grand; **~ marítima** nautical mile.

milhão [mi'ʎãw] (*pl -ões*) *m* million; **um ~ de vezes** hundreds of times; **adorei milhões!** (*col*) I loved it!

milhar [mi'ʎa*] *m* thousand; **turistas aos ~es** tourists in their thousands.

milharal [miʎa'raw] (*pl -ais*) *m* maize (*BRIT*) *ou* corn (*US*) field.

milho ['miʎu] *m* maize (*BRIT*), corn (*US*).

milhões [mi'ʎõjs] *mpl de* **milhão**.

miliardário/a [miljax'darju/a] *adj, m/f* billionaire.

milícia [mi'lisja] *f* (*MIL*) militia; (: *vida*) military life; (: *força*) military force.

milico [mi'liku] (*col*) *m* military type.

miligrama [mili'grama] *m* milligram.

mililitro [mili'litru] *m* millilitre (*BRIT*), milliliter (*US*).

milímetro [mi'limetru] *m* millimetre (*BRIT*), millimeter (*US*).

milionário/a [miljo'narju/a] *adj, m/f* millionaire.

militância [mili'tãsja] *f* militancy.

militante [mili'tãtʃi] *adj, m/f* militant.

militar [mili'ta*] *adj* military ♦ *m* soldier ♦ *vi* to fight; **~ em** (*MIL: regimento*) to serve in; (*POL: partido*) to belong to, be active in; (*profissão*) to work in.

militarismo [milita'riʒmu] *m* militarism.

militarista [milita'riʃta] *adj, m/f* militarist.

militarizar [militari'za*] *vt* to militarize.

mil-réis *m inv former unit of currency in Brazil and Portugal*.

mim [mĩ] *pron* me; (*reflexivo*) myself; **de ~ para ~** to myself.

mimado/a [mi'madu/a] *adj* spoiled, spoilt (*BRIT*).

mimar [mi'ma*] *vt* to pamper, spoil.

mimeógrafo [mime'ɔgrafu] *m* duplicating machine.

mimetismo [mime'tʃiʒmu] *m* (*BIO*) mimicry.

mímica ['mimika] *f* mime; (*jogo*) charades; *V tb* **mímico**.

mímico/a ['mimiku/a] *m/f* mime artist.

mimo ['mimu] *m* (*presente*) gift; (*pessoa, coisa encantadora*) delight; (*carinho*) tenderness; (*gentileza*) kindness; **cheio de ~s** (*criança*) spoiled, spoilt (*BRIT*).

mimoso/a [mi'mozu/ɔza] *adj* (*delicado*) delicate; (*carinhoso*) tender, loving, sweet; (*encantador*) delightful.

MIN (*BR*) *abr m* = **Ministério do Interior**.

min. *abr* (= *mínimo*) min.

mina ['mina] *f* mine; (*fig: de riquezas*) gold mine; (: *de informações*) mine of information; (*col: garota*) girl; **~ de carvão** coal mine; **~ de ouro** (*tb fig*) gold mine.

minar [mi'na*] *vt* to mine; (*fig*) to undermine.

minarete [mina'retʃi] *m* minaret.

Minc (*BR*) *abr m* = **Ministério da Cultura**.

mindinho [mĩ'dʒiɲu] *m* (*tb: dedo ~*) little finger.

mineiro/a [mi'nejru/a] *adj* mining; (*de Minas Gerais*) from Minas Gerais ♦ *m/f* miner; (*de Minas Gerais*) person from Minas Gerais.

mineração [minera'sãw] *f* mining.

mineral [mine'raw] (*pl -ais*) *adj, m* mineral.

mineralogia [mineralo'ʒia] *f* mineralogy.

minerar [mine'ra*] *vt, vi* to mine.

minério [mi'nɛrju] *m* ore; **~ de ferro** iron ore.

mingau [mĩ'gaw] *m* porridge; (*fig*) slop; **~ de aveia** porridge.

míngua ['mĩgwa] *f* lack; **à ~ de** for want of; **viver à ~** to live in poverty.

minguado/a [mĩ'gwadu/a] *adj* scant; (*criança*) stunted; **~ de algo** short of sth.

minguante [mĩ'gwãtʃi] *adj* waning; (**quarto**) **~** (*ASTRONOMIA*) last quarter.

minguar [mĩ'gwa*] *vi* (*diminuir*) to decrease, dwindle; (*faltar*) to run short.

minha ['miɲa] *f de* **meu**.

minhoca [mi'ɲɔka] *f* (earth)worm; (*col: bobagem*) daft idea; **~ da terra** (*fig: caipira*) country person.

míni ['mini] *adj inv* mini ♦ *m* minicomputer.

mini- [mini-] *prefixo* mini-.

miniatura [minja'tura] *adj, f* miniature.

mínima ['minima] *f* (*temperatura*) low; (*MÚS*) minim.

minicomputador [minikõputa'do*] *m* minicomputer.

minimalista [minima'liʃta] *adj* (*fig*) stark.

minimizar [minimi'za*] *vt* to minimize; (*subestimar*) to play down.

mínimo/a ['minimu/a] *adj* minimum ♦ *m* minimum; (*tb: dedo ~*) little finger; **não dou *ou* ligo a mínima para isso** I couldn't care less about it; **a mínima importância/idéia** the slightest importance/idea; **o ~ que podem fazer** the least they can do; **no ~** at least; **no ~ às 11 horas** at 11.00 at the earliest.

minissaia [mini'saja] *f* miniskirt.

ministerial [miniʃte'rjaw] (*pl -ais*) *adj* ministerial.

ministeriável [miniʃte'rjavew] (*pl -eis*) *adj* eligible to be a minister.

ministério [mini'ʃterju] *m* ministry; **M~ das Relações Exteriores** Foreign Office (*BRIT*), State Department (*US*); **~ da Fazenda** Treasury (*BRIT*), Treasury Department (*US*); **M~ da Marinha/Educação/Saúde** Admiralty/Ministry of Education/Health; **~ do Trabalho** Department of Employment (*BRIT*) *ou* Labor (*US*); **~ público** public prosecution service; **M~ do Interior** Home Office (*BRIT*), Department of the Interior (*US*).

ministrar [miniʃ'tra*] *vt* (*dar*) to supply; (*remédio*) to administer; (*aulas*) to give ♦ *vi* to serve as a minister.

ministro/a [mi'niʃtru/a] *m/f* minister; ~ **da Fazenda** Chancellor of the Exchequer (*BRIT*), Head of the Treasury Department (*US*); ~ **das Relações Exteriores** Foreign Secretary (*BRIT*), Head of the State Department (*US*); ~ **do Interior** Home Secretary (*BRIT*); ~ **sem pasta** minister without portfolio.

minorar [mino'ra*] *vt* to lessen, reduce.

Minorca [mi'nɔxka] *f* Menorca.

minoritário/a [minori'tarju/a] *adj* minority *atr*.

minto ['mĩtu] *etc vb* V **mentir**.

minoria [mino'ria] *f* minority.

minúcia [mi'nusja] *f* detail.

minucioso/a [minu'sjozu/ɔza] *adj* (*indivíduo*, *busca*) thorough; (*explicação*) detailed.

minúsculo/a [mi'nuʃkulu/a] *adj* minute, tiny; **letra minúscula** small letter.

minuta [mi'nuta] *f* (*rascunho*) rough draft; (*CULIN*) dish cooked to order; ~ **de contrato** draft contract.

minutar [minu'ta*] *vt* to draft.

minuto [mi'nutu] *m* minute.

miolo ['mjolu] *m* inside; (*polpa*) pulp; (*de maçã*) core; ~**s** *mpl* (*cérebro*, *inteligência*) brains.

míope ['miopi] *adj* short-sighted ♦ *m/f* myopic.

miopia [mjo'pia] *f* short-sightedness.

miosótis [mjo'zɔtʃiʃ] *m inv* (*BOT*) forget-me-not.

mira ['mira] *f* (*de fuzil*) sight; (*pontaria*) aim; (*fig*) aim, purpose; **à ~ de** on the lookout for; **ter em ~** to have one's eye on.

mirabolante [mirabo'lãtʃi] *adj* (*roupa*) showy, loud; (*plano*) ambitious; (*surpreendente*) amazing.

mirada [mi'rada] *f* look.

miradouro [mira'doru] *m* viewpoint, belvedere.

miragem [mi'raʒẽ] (*pl* **-ns**) *f* mirage.

miramar [mira'ma*] *m* sea view.

mirante [mi'rãtʃi] *m* viewpoint, belvedere.

mirar [mi'ra*] *vt* to look at; (*observar*) to watch; (*apontar para*) to aim at ♦ *vi*: ~ **em** to aim at; ~**-se** *vr* to look at o.s.; ~ **para** to look onto.

miríade [mi'riadʒi] *f* myriad.

mirim [mi'rĩ] (*pl* **-ns**) *adj* little.

mirrado/a [mi'xadu/a] *adj* (*planta*) withered; (*pessoa*) haggard.

mirrar-se [mi'xaxsi] *vr* (*planta*) to wither, dry up; (*pessoa*) to waste away.

misantropo/a [mizã'tropu/a] *m/f* misanthrope ♦ *adj* misanthropic.

miscelânea [mise'lanja] *f* miscellany; (*confusão*) muddle.

miscigenação [misiʒena'sãw] *f* interbreeding.

mise-en-plis [mizã'pli] *m* shampoo and set.

miserável [mize'ravew] (*pl* **-eis**) *adj* (*digno de compaixão*) wretched; (*pobre*) impoverished;

(*avaro*) stingy, mean; (*insignificante*) paltry; (*lugar*) squalid; (*infame*) despicable ♦ *m* (*indigente*) wretch; (*coitado*) poor thing; (*pessoa infame*) rotter.

miserê [mize're] (*col*) *m* poverty, pennilessness.

miséria [mi'zɛrja] *f* (*estado lastimável*) misery; (*pobreza*) poverty; (*avareza*) stinginess; **ganhar/custar uma** ~ to earn/cost a pittance; **chorar** ~ to complain that one is hard up; **fazer** ~**s** (*col*) to do wonders; **ser uma** ~ (*col*) to be awful.

misericórdia [mizeri'kɔxdʒja] *f* (*compaixão*) pity, compassion; (*graça*) mercy.

misógino/a [mi'zɔʒinu/a] *adj* misogynistic ♦ *m* misogynist.

missa ['misa] *f* (*REL*) mass; **não saber da** ~ **a metade** (*col*) not to know the half of it.

missal [mi'saw] (*pl* **-ais**) *m* missal.

missão [mi'sãw] (*pl* **-ões**) *f* mission; (*dever*) duty; (*incumbência*) job.

misse ['misi] *f* beauty queen.

míssil ['misiw] (*pl* **-eis**) *m* missile; ~ **balístico/guiado** ballistic/guided missile; ~ **de curto/médio/longo alcance** short-/medium-/long-range missile.

missionário/a [misjo'narju/a] *m/f* missionary.

missiva [mi'siva] *f* missive.

missões [mi'sõjʃ] *fpl de* **missão**.

mister [miʃ'te*] *m* (*ocupação*) occupation; (*trabalho*) job; **ser** ~ to be necessary; **ter-se** ~ **de algo** to need sth; **não há** ~ **de** there's no need for.

mistério [miʃ'tɛrju] *m* mystery; **fazer** ~ **de algo** to make a mystery of sth; **não ter** ~ to be straightforward.

misterioso/a [miʃte'rjozu/ɔza] *adj* mysterious.

misticismo [miʃtʃi'siʒmu] *m* mysticism.

místico/a ['miʃtʃiku/a] *adj*, *m/f* mystic.

mistificar [miʃtʃifi'ka*] *vt*, *vi* to fool.

misto/a ['miʃtu/a] *adj* mixed; (*confuso*) mixed up; (*escola*) mixed ♦ *m* mixture.

misto-quente *m* toasted cheese and ham sandwich.

mistura [miʃ'tura] *f* mixture; (*ato*) mixing.

misturada [miʃtu'rada] *f* jumble.

misturar [miʃtu'ra*] *vt* to mix; (*confundir*) to mix up; ~**-se** *vr*: ~**-se com** to mix in with, mingle with.

mítico/a ['mitʃiku/a] *adj* mythical.

mitificar [mitʃifi'ka*] *vt* to mythicize; (*mulher*, *estrela*) to idolize.

mitigar [mitʃi'ga*] *vt* (*raiva*) to temper; (*dor*) to relieve; (*sede*) to lessen.

mito ['mitu] *m* myth.

mitologia [mitolo'ʒia] *f* mythology.

mitológico/a [mito'lɔʒiku/a] *adj* mythological.

miudezas [mju'dezaʃ] *fpl* minutiae; (*bugigangas*) odds and ends; (*objetos pequenos*) trinkets.

NB: European Portuguese adds the following consonants to certain words: **b** (sú(b)dito, su(b)til); **c** (a(c)ção, a(c)cionista, a(c)to); **m** (inde(m)ne); **p** (ado(p)ção, ado(p)tar); *for further details see p. xiii.*

miúdo/a ['mjudu/a] *adj* (*pequeno*) tiny, minute ♦ *m/f* (*PT: criança*) youngster, kid; ~**s** *mpl* (*dinheiro*) change *sg*; (*de aves*) giblets; **dinheiro** ~ small change; **trocar em** ~**s** (*fig*) to spell it out.

mixa ['miʃa] (*col*) *adj* (*insignificante*) measly; (*de má qualidade*) crummy; (*festa*) dull.

mixagem [mik'saʒẽ] *f* mixing.

mixar¹ [mi'ʃa*] *vt* to mess up ♦ *vi* (*gorar*) to go down the drain; (*acabar*) to finish.

mixar² [mik'sa*] *vt* (*sons*) to mix.

mixaria [miʃa'ria] (*col*) *f* (*coisa sem valor*) trifle; (*insignificância*) trivial matter.

mixórdia [mi'ʃɔxdʒia] *f* mess, jumble.

MJ *abr m* = **Ministério da Justiça**.

MM *abr m* = **Ministério da Marinha**.

mm *abr* (= *milímetro*) mm.

MME (*BR*) *abr m* = **Ministério de Minas e Energia**.

mnemônico/a [mne'moniku/a] *adj* mnemonic.

mo [mu] *pron* = **me** + **o**.

mó [mɔ] *f* (*de moinho*) millstone; (*para afiar*) grindstone.

moa ['moa] *etc vb V* **moer**.

moagem ['mwaʒẽ] *f* grinding.

móbil ['mɔbiw] (*pl* -**eis**) *adj* = **móvel**.

mobilar [mobi'la*] (*PT*) *vt* to furnish.

móbile ['mɔbili] *m* mobile.

mobília [mo'bilja] *f* furniture.

mobiliar [mobi'lja*] (*BR*) *vt* to furnish.

mobiliária [mobi'ljarja] *f* furniture shop.

mobiliário [mobi'ljarju] *m* furnishings *pl*.

mobilidade [mobili'dadʒi] *f* mobility; (*fig: de espírito*) changeability.

mobilização [mobiliza'sãw] *f* mobilization.

mobilizar [mobili'za*] *vt* to mobilize; (*movimentar*) to move.

Mobral [mo'braw] *abr m* = **Movimento Brasileiro de Alfabetização**.

moça ['mosa] *f* girl, young woman.

moçada [mo'sada] *f* (*moços*) boys *pl*; (*moças*) girls *pl*.

moçambicano/a [mosãbi'kanu/a] *adj*, *m/f* Mozambican.

Moçambique [mosã'biki] *m* Mozambique.

moção [mo'sãw] (*pl* -**ões**) *f* motion.

mocassim [moka'sĩ] (*pl* -**ns**) *m* mocassin; (*sapato esporte*) slip-on.

mochila [mo'ʃila] *f* rucksack.

mocidade [mosi'dadʒi] *f* youth; (*os moços*) young people.

mocinho/a [mo'siɲu/a] *m/f* little boy/girl ♦ *m* (*herói*) hero, good guy.

moço/a ['mosu/a] *adj* young ♦ *m* young man, lad; ~ **de bordo** ordinary seaman; ~ **de cavalariça** groom.

moções [mo'sõjʃ] *fpl de* **moção**.

mocorongo/a [moko'rõgu/a] (*col*) *m/f* country bumpkin.

moda ['mɔda] *f* fashion; **estar na** ~ to be in fashion, be all the rage; **fora da** ~ old-fashioned; **sair da** *ou* **cair de** ~ to go out of fashion; **a última** ~ the latest fashion; **à** ~

brasileira in the Brazilian way; **ele faz tudo à sua** ~ he does everything his own way; **fazer** ~ to make up stories.

modalidade [modali'dadʒi] *f* kind; (*ESPORTE*) event.

modelagem [mode'laʒẽ] *f* modelling; ~ **do corpo** bodybuilding.

modelar [mode'la*] *vt* to model; (*assinalar os contornos de*) to shape, highlight; ~(-**se**) **a algo** to model (o.s.) on sth.

modelista [mode'liʃta] *m/f* designer.

modelo [mo'delu] *m* model; (*criação de estilista*) design.

moderação [modera'sãw] (*pl* -**ões**) *f* moderation.

moderado/a [mode'radu/a] *adj* moderate; (*clima*) mild.

moderar [mode'ra*] *vt* to moderate; (*violência*) to control, restrain; (*velocidade*) to reduce; (*voz*) to lower; (*gastos*) to cut down; ~-**se** *vr* to control o.s.

modernidade [modexni'dadʒi] *f* modernity.

modernismo [modex'niʒmu] *m* modernism.

modernização [modexniza'sãw] (*pl* -**ões**) *f* modernization.

modernizar [modexni'za*] *vt* to modernize; ~-**se** *vr* to modernize.

moderno/a [mo'dɛxnu/a] *adj* modern; (*atual*) present-day.

modernoso/a [modex'nozu/ɔza] *adj* new-fangled.

módess ['mɔdeʃ] ® (*col*) *m inv* sanitary towel (*BRIT*) *ou* napkin (*US*).

modéstia [mo'dɛʃtʃja] *f* modesty.

modesto/a [mo'dɛʃtu/a] *adj* modest; (*simples*) simple, plain; (*vida*) frugal.

módico/a ['mɔdʒiku/a] *adj* moderate; (*preço*) reasonable; (*bens*) scant.

modificação [modʒifika'sãw] (*pl* -**ões**) *f* modification.

modificar [modʒifi'ka*] *vt* to modify, alter.

modinha [mo'dʒiɲa] *f* popular song, tune.

modismo [mo'dʒiʒmu] *m* idiom.

modista [mo'dʒiʃta] *f* dressmaker.

modo ['mɔdu] *m* (*maneira*) way, manner; (*método*) way; (*LING*) mood; (*MÚS*) mode; ~**s** *mpl* manners; ~ **de pensar** way of thinking; **de (tal)** ~ **que** so (that); **de** ~ **nenhum** in no way; **de qualquer** ~ anyway, anyhow; **tenha** ~**s!** behave yourself!; **de** ~ **geral** in general; ~ **de andar** way of walking, walk; ~ **de escrever** style of writing; ~ **de emprego** instructions *pl* for use; ~ **de ser** way (of being), manner; ~ **de vida** way of life.

modorra [mo'doxa] *f* (*sonolência*) drowsiness; (*letargia*) lethargy.

modulação [modula'sãw] (*pl* -**ões**) *f* modulation; ~ **de freqüência** frequency modulation.

modular [modu'la*] *vt* to modulate ♦ *adj* modular.

módulo ['mɔdulu] *m* module; ~ **lunar** lunar module.

moeda ['mwɛda] *f* (*uma*) coin; (*dinheiro*)

currency; **uma** ~ **de 10p** a 10p piece; ~ **corrente** currency; **pagar na mesma** ~ to give tit for tat; **Casa da M**~ the Mint (*BRIT*), the (US) Mint; ~ **falsa** forged money; ~ **forte** hard currency.

moedor [moe'do*] *m* (*de café*) grinder; (*de carne*) mincer.

moenda ['mwēda] *f* grinding equipment.

moer [mwe*] *vt* (*café*) to grind; (*cana*) to crush; (*bater*) to beat; (*cansar*) to tire out.

mofado/a [mo'fadu/a] *adj* mouldy (*BRIT*), moldy (*US*).

mofar [mo'fa*] *vi* to go mouldy (*BRIT*) *ou* moldy (*US*); (*na prisão*) to rot; (*ficar esperando*) to hang around; (*zombar*) to mock, scoff ♦ *vt* to cover in mo(u)ld.

mofo ['mofu] *m* (*BOT*) mould (*BRIT*), mold (*US*); **cheiro de** ~ musty smell.

mogno ['mɔgnu] *m* mahogany.

mói [mɔj] *etc vb* **V moer.**

moía [mo'ia] *etc vb* **V moer.**

moído/a [mo'idu/a] *pp de* **moer** ♦ *adj* (*café*) ground; (*carne*) minced; (*cansado*) tired out; (*corpo*) aching.

moinho ['mwiɲu] *m* mill; (*de café*) grinder; ~ **de vento** windmill.

moisés [moj'zɛʃ] *m inv* carry-cot.

moita ['mɔjta] *f* thicket; ~! mum's the word!; **na** ~ (*fig*) on the quiet; **ficar na** ~ (*fazer segredo*) to keep quiet, not say a word; (*ficar na expectativa*) to stand by.

mola ['mɔla] *f* (*TEC*) spring; (*fig*) motive, motivation.

molambo [mo'lãbu] *m* rag.

molar [mo'la*] *m* molar (tooth).

moldar [mow'da*] *vt* to mould (*BRIT*), mold (*US*); (*metal*) to cast; (*fig*) to mo(u)ld, shape.

Moldávia [mow'davja] *f*: **a** ~ Moldavia.

molde ['mɔwdʒi] *m* mould (*BRIT*), mold (*US*); (*de papel*) pattern; (*fig*) model; ~ **de vestido** dress pattern.

moldura [mow'dura] *f* (*de pintura*) frame; (*ornato*) moulding (*BRIT*), molding (*US*).

moldurar [mowdu'ra*] *vt* to frame.

mole ['mɔli] *adj* (*macio, fofo*) soft; (*sem energia*) listless; (*carnes*) flabby; (*col: fácil*) easy; (*pessoa: sentimental*) soft; (*lento*) slow; (*preguiçoso*) sluggish ♦ *adv* (*facilmente*) easily; (*lentamente*) slowly.

moleca [mo'lɛka] *f* urchin; (*menina*) youngster.

molecada [mole'kada] *f* urchins *pl*.

molecagem [mole'kaʒē] (*pl* **-ns**) *f* (*de criança*) piece of mischief; (*sujeira*) dirty trick; (*brincadeira*) joke.

molécula [mo'lɛkula] *f* molecule.

molecular [moleku'la*] *adj* molecular.

molejo [mo'leʒu] *m* (*de carro*) suspension; (*col: de pessoa*) wiggle.

moleque [mo'lɛki] *m* (*de rua*) urchin; (*menino*) youngster; (*pessoa sem palavra*) unreliable person; (*canalha*) scoundrel ♦ *adj* (*levado*) mischievous; (*brincalhão*) funny.

molestar [moleʃ'ta*] *vt* (*ofender*) to upset; (*enfadar*) to annoy; (*importunar*) to bother.

moléstia [mo'lɛʃtʃja] *f* illness.

molesto/a [mo'lɛʃtu/a] *adj* tiresome; (*prejudicial*) unhealthy.

moletom [mole'tõ] (*pl* **-ns**) *m* (*de lã*) fleece; (*de algodão*) sweatshirt material; **blusa de** ~ sweatshirt.

moleza [mo'leza] *f* softness; (*falta de energia*) listlessness; (*falta de força*) weakness; **ser** (**uma**) ~ (*col*) to be easy; **na** ~ without exerting oneself.

molhada [mo'ʎada] *f* soaking.

molhado/a [mo'ʎadu/a] *adj* wet, damp.

molhar [mo'ʎa*] *vt* to wet; (*de leve*) to moisten, dampen; (*mergulhar*) to dip; **~-se** *vr* to get wet; (*col: urinar*) to wet o.s.

molhe ['moʎi] (*PT*) *m* jetty; (*cais*) wharf, quay.

molheira [mo'ʎejra] *f* sauce boat; (*para carne*) gravy boat.

molho¹ ['mɔʎu] *m* (*de chaves*) bunch; (*de trigo*) sheaf.

molho² ['moʎu] *m* (*CULIN*) sauce; (: *de salada*) dressing; (: *de carne*) gravy; **pôr de** ~ to soak; **estar/deixar de** ~ (*roupa etc*) to be/leave to soak; **estar/ficar de** ~ (*fig*) to be/ stay in bed; ~ **branco** white sauce; ~ **inglês** Worcester sauce.

molinete [moli'netʃi] *m* reel; (*caniço*) fishing rod.

molóide [mo'lɔjdʒi] (*col*) *adj* slow ♦ *m/f* lazybones.

molusco [mo'luʃku] *m* mollusc (*BRIT*), mollusk (*US*).

momentâneo/a [momē'tanju/a] *adj* momentary.

momento [mo'mētu] *m* moment; (*TEC*) momentum; **a todo** ~ constantly; **de um** ~ **para outro** suddenly; **no** ~ **em que** just as; **no/neste** ~ at the/this moment; **a qualquer** ~ at any moment.

Mônaco ['monaku] *m* Monaco.

monarca [mo'naxka] *m/f* monarch, ruler.

monarquia [monax'kia] *f* monarchy.

monarquista [monax'kiʃta] *adj*, *m/f* monarchist.

monastério [monaʃ'tɛrju] *m* monastery.

monástico/a [mo'naʃtʃiku/a] *adj* monastic.

monção [mõ'sãw] (*pl* **-ões**) *f* monsoon.

mondar [mõ'da*] (*PT*) *vt* (*ervas daninhas*) to pull up; (*árvores*) to prune; (*fig*) to weed out.

monetário/a [mone'tarju/a] *adj* monetary; **correção monetária** currency adjustment.

monetarismo [moneta'riʒmu] *m* monetarism.

monetarista [moneta'riʃta] *adj*, *m/f* monetar-

NB: *European Portuguese adds the following consonants to certain words:* **b** (sú(b)dito, su(b)til); **c** (a(c)ção, a(c)cionista, a(c)to); **m** (inde(m)ne); **p** (ado(p)ção, ado(p)tar); *for further details see p. xiii.*

ist.

monge ['mõʒi] *m* monk.

mongol [mõ'gow] (*pl* **-óis**) *adj, m/f* Mongol, Mongolian.

Mongólia [mõ'gɔlja] *f:* **a ~** Mongolia.

mongolismo [mõgo'liʒmu] *m* (*MED*) mongolism.

mongolóide [mõgo'lɔjdʒi] *adj, m/f* mongol.

monitor [moni'to*] *m* monitor; **~ (de vídeo)** (*COMPUT*) monitor, VDU.

monitorar [monito'ra*] *vt* to monitor.

monitorizar [monitori'za*] *vt* = **monitorar**.

monja ['mõʒa] *f* nun.

monocromo/a [mono'krɔmu/a] *adj* monochrome.

monóculo [mo'nɔkulu] *m* monocle.

monocultura [monokuw'tura] *f* monoculture.

monogamia [monoga'mia] *f* monogamy.

monógamo/a [mo'nɔgamu/a] *adj* monogamous.

monograma [mono'grama] *m* monogram.

monologar [monolo'ga*] *vi* to talk to o.s.; (*TEATRO*) to speak a monologue ♦ *vt* to say to o.s.

monólogo [mo'nɔlogu] *m* monologue.

monoplano [mono'planu] *m* monoplane.

monopólio [mono'pɔlju] *m* monopoly.

monopolizar [monopoli'za*] *vt* to monopolize.

monossilábico/a [monosi'labiku/a] *adj* monosyllabic.

monossílabo [mono'silabu] *m* monosyllable; **responder por ~s** to reply in monosyllables.

monotonia [monoto'nia] *f* monotony.

monótono/a [mo'nɔtonu/a] *adj* monotonous.

monotrilho [mono'triʎu] *m* monorail.

monóxido [mo'nɔksidu] *m:* **~ de carbono** carbon monoxide.

monsenhor [mõse'ɲo*] *m* monsignor.

monstro/a ['mõʃtru/a] *adj inv* giant ♦ *m* (*tb fig*) monster; **~ sagrado** superstar.

monstruosidade [mõʃtrwozi'dadʒi] *f* monstrosity.

monstruoso/a [mõ'ʃtrwozu/ɔza] *adj* monstrous; (*enorme*) gigantic, huge.

monta ['mõta] *f:* **de pouca ~** trivial, of little account.

montador(a) [mõta'do*(a)] *m/f* (*CINEMA*) editor.

montagem [mõ'taʒẽ] (*pl* **-ns**) *f* assembly; (*ARQ*) erection; (*CINEMA*) editing; (*TEATRO*) production.

montanha [mõ'taɲa] *f* mountain.

montanha-russa *f* roller coaster.

montanhês/esa [mõta'ɲeʃ/eza] *adj* mountain *atr* ♦ *m/f* highlander.

montanhismo [mõta'ɲiʒmu] *m* mountaineering.

montanhista [mõta'ɲiʃta] *m/f* mountaineer ♦ *adj* mountaineering.

montanhoso/a [mõta'ɲozu/ɔza] *adj* mountainous.

montante [mõ'tãtʃi] *m* amount, sum ♦ *adj* (*maré*) rising; **a ~** upstream.

montão [mõ'tãw] (*pl* **-ões**) *m* heap, pile.

montar [mõ'ta*] *vt* (*subir a*) to mount, get on; (*colocar em*) to put on; (*cavalgar*) to ride; (*peças*) to assemble, put together; (*loja, máquina*) to set up; (*casa*) to put up; (*peça teatral*) to put on ♦ *vi* to ride; **~ a** *ou* **em** (*animal*) to get on; (*cavalgar*) to ride; (*despesa*) to come to.

montaria [mõta'ria] *f* (*cavalgadura*) mount.

monte ['mõtʃi] *m* hill; (*pilha*) heap, pile; **um ~ de** (*muitos*) a lot of, lots of; **gente aos ~s** loads of people.

montepio [mõtʃi'piu] *m* (*pensão*) pension; (*fundo*) trust fund.

montês [mõ'teʃ] *adj:* **cabra ~** mountain goat.

Montevidéu [mõtʃivi'dɛw] *n* Montevideo.

montoeira [mõ'twejra] *f* stack.

montões [mõ'tõjʃ] *mpl de* **montão**.

montra ['mõtra] (*PT*) *f* shop window.

monumental [monumẽ'taw] (*pl* **-ais**) *adj* monumental; (*fig*) magnificent, splendid.

monumento [monu'mẽtu] *m* monument.

moqueca [mo'kɛka] *f* fish or seafood simmered in pepper and oil; **~ de camarão** prawn moqueca.

morada [mo'rada] *f* home, residence; (*PT:* **endereço**) address.

moradia [mora'dʒia] *f* home, dwelling.

morador(a) [mora'do*(a)] *m/f* (*de casa, bairro*) resident; (*de casa alugada*) tenant.

moral [mo'raw] (*pl* **-ais**) *adj* moral ♦ *f* (*ética*) ethics *pl;* (*conclusão*) moral; (*ânimo*) morale ♦ *m* (*de pessoa*) sense of morality; (*ânimo*) morale; **levantar a ~** to raise morale; **estar de ~ baixa** to be demoralized; **~ da história** moral of the story.

moralidade [morali'dadʒi] *f* morality.

moralista [mora'liʃta] *adj* moralistic ♦ *m/f* moralist.

moralizar [morali'za*] *vi* to moralize ♦ *vt* to preach at.

morango [mo'rãgu] *m* strawberry.

morangueiro [morã'gejru] *m* strawberry plant.

morar [mo'ra*] *vi* to live, reside; (*col: entender*) to catch on; **~ em algo** (*col*) to grasp sth; **morou?** got it?, see?

moratória [mora'tɔrja] *f* moratorium.

morbidez [moxbi'deʒ] *f* morbidness.

mórbido/a ['mɔxbidu/a] *adj* morbid.

morcego [mox'segu] *m* (*BIO*) bat.

morcela [mox'sela] (*PT*) *f* black pudding (*BRIT*), blood sausage (*US*).

mordaça [mox'dasa] *f* (*de animal*) muzzle; (*fig*) gag.

mordaz [mox'daʒ] *adj* scathing.

morder [mox'de*] *vt* to bite; (*corroer*) to corrode; **~-se** *vr* to bite o.s.; **~ a língua** to bite one's tongue; **~-se de inveja** to be green with envy.

mordida [mox'dʒida] *f* bite.

mordomia [moxdo'mia] *f* (*de executivos*) perk; (*col: regalia*) luxury, comfort.

mordomo [mox'dɔmu] *m* butler.
morenaço/a [more'nasu/a] *m/f* dark beauty.
moreno/a [mo'renu/a] *adj* dark(-skinned); (*de cabelos*) dark(-haired); (*de tomar sol*) brown ♦ *m/f* dark person; **ela é loura ou morena?** is she a blonde or a brunette?
morfina [mox'fina] *f* morphine.
morfologia [moxfolo'ʒia] *f* morphology.
morgada [mox'gada] *f* heiress.
morgado [mox'gadu] (*PT*) *m* (*herdeiro*) heir; (*filho mais velho*) eldest son; (*propriedade*) entailed estate.
moribundo/a [mori'būdu/a] *adj* dying.
morigerado/a [moriʒe'radu/a] *adj* upright.
moringa [mo'rĩga] *f* water-cooler.
mormacento/a [moxma'sẽtu/a] *adj* sultry.
mormaço [mox'masu] *m* sultry weather.
mormente [mox'mẽtʃi] *adv* chiefly, especially.
mórmon ['mɔxmõ] *m/f* Mormon.
morno/a ['mɔxnu/'mɔxna] *adj* lukewarm, tepid.
morosidade [morozi'dadʒi] *f* slowness.
moroso/a [mo'rozu/ɔza] *adj* slow, sluggish.
morrer [mo'xe*] *vi* to die; (*luz, cor*) to fade; (*fogo*) to die down; (*AUTO*) to stall; ~ **de rir** to kill o.s. laughing; **estou morrendo de fome/inveja/medo/saudades** I'm starving/green with envy/scared stiff/really missing you (*ou* him, home *etc*); ~ **de amores por alguém** to be mad about sb; **estou morrendo de vontade de fazer** I'm dying to do; ~ **atropelado/afogado** to be knocked down and killed/drown; **lindo de** ~ (*col*) stunning; ~ **em** (*col: pagar*) to fork out.
morrinha [mo'xiɲa] *f* (*fedor*) stench ♦ *m/f* (*col: chato*) pain (in the neck) ♦ *adj* (*col*) boring.
morro ['moxu] *m* hill; (*favela*) shanty-town, slum.
mortadela [moxta'dɛla] *f* salami.
mortal [mox'taw] (*pl* -**ais**) *adj* mortal; (*letal, insuportável*) deadly; (*pecado*) deadly ♦ *m* mortal; **restos mortais** mortal remains.
mortalha [mox'taʎa] *f* shroud.
mortalidade [moxtali'dadʒi] *f* mortality; ~ **infantil** infant mortality.
mortandade [moxta'dadʒi] *f* slaughter.
morte ['mɔxtʃi] *f* death; **pena de** ~ death penalty; **ser de** ~ (*fig*) to be impossible; **estar às portas da** ~ to be at death's door; **pensar na** ~ **da bezerra** (*fig*) to be miles away.
morteiro [mox'tejru] *m* mortar.
mortiço/a [mox'tʃisu/a] *adj* (*olhar*) dull; (*desanimado*) lifeless; (*luz*) dimming.
mortífero/a [mox'tʃiferu/a] *adj* deadly, lethal.
mortificar [moxtʃifi'ka*] *vt* (*torturar*) to torture; (*afligir*) to annoy, torment.
morto/a ['moxtu/'mɔxta] *pp de* **matar**; **morrer** ♦ *adj* (*cor*) dull; (*exausto*) exhausted; (*inexpressivo*) lifeless ♦ *m/f* dead man/woman;

cem/os ~**s** a hundred/the dead; **estar** ~ to be dead; **ser** ~ to be killed; **estar** ~ **de inveja** to be green with envy; **estar** ~ **de vontade de** to be dying to; ~ **de medo/cansaço** scared stiff/dead tired; **nem** ~! not on your life!, no way!; ~ **da silva** (*col*) dead as a doornail.
mos [muʃ] *pron* = **me** + **os**.
mosaico [mo'zajku] *m* mosaic.
mosca ['moʃka] *f* fly; **estar às** ~**s** (*bar etc*) to be deserted.
mosca-morta (*pl* **moscas-mortas**) (*col*) *m/f* (*pessoa*) stiff.
Moscou [moʃ'ku] (*BR*) *n* Moscow.
Moscovo [moʃ'kovu] (*PT*) *n* Moscow.
mosquitada [moʃki'tada] *f* load of mosquitos.
mosquiteiro [moʃki'tejru] *m* mosquito net.
mosquito [moʃ'kitu] *m* mosquito.
mossa ['mɔsa] *f* dent; (*fig*) impression.
mostarda [moʃ'taxda] *f* mustard.
mosteiro [moʃ'tejru] *m* monastery; (*de monjas*) convent.
mosto ['moʃtu] *m* (*do vinho*) must.
mostra ['mɔʃtra] *f* (*exibição*) display; (*sinal*) sign, indication; **dar** ~**s de** to show signs of.
mostrador [moʃtra'do*] *m* (*de relógio*) face, dial.
mostrar [moʃ'tra*] *vt* to show; (*mercadorias*) to display; (*provar*) to demonstrate, prove; ~**-se** *vr* to show o.s. to be; (*exibir-se*) to show off.
mostruário [moʃ'trwarju] *m* display case.
mote ['mɔtʃi] *m* motto.
motel [mo'tɛw] (*pl* -**éis**) *m* motel.
motejar [mote'ʒa*] *vi*: ~ **de** (*zombar*) to jeer at, make fun of.
motejo [mo'teʒu] *m* mockery, derision.
motilidade [motʃili'dadʒi] *f* mobility.
motim [mo'tʃĩ] (*pl* -**ns**) *m* riot, revolt; (*militar*) mutiny.
motivação [motʃiva'sãw] (*pl* -**ões**) *f* motivation.
motivado/a [motʃi'vadu/a] *adj* (*causado*) caused; (*pessoa*) motivated.
motivar [motʃi'va*] *vt* (*causar*) to cause, bring about; (*estimular*) to motivate.
motivo [mo'tʃivu] *m* (*causa*): ~ (**de** *ou* **para**) cause (of), reason (for); (*fim*) motive; (*ARTE, MÚS*) motif; **ser** ~ **de riso** *etc* to be a cause of laughter *etc*; **dar** ~ **de algo a alguém** to give sb cause for sth; **por** ~ **de** because of, owing to; **sem** ~ for no reason.
moto ['mɔtu] *f* motorbike ♦ *m* (*lema*) motto; **de** ~ **próprio** of one's own accord.
motoca [mo'tɔka] (*col*) *f* motorbike, bike.
motocicleta [motosi'kleta] *f* motorcycle, motorbike.
motociclismo [motosi'kliʒmu] *m* motorcycling.
motociclista [motosi'kliʃta] *m/f* motorcyclist.

*NB: European Portuguese adds the following consonants to certain words: **b** (sú(b)dito, su(b)til); **c** (a(c)ção, a(c)cionista, a(c)to); **m** (inde(m)ne); **p** (ado(p)ção, ado(p)tar); for further details see p. xiii.*

motociclo [moto'siklu] (*PT*) *m* = **motocicleta**.
motoneta [moto'neta] *f* (motor-)scooter.
motoniveladora [motonivela'dora] *f* bull-dozer.
motoqueiro/a [moto'kejru/a] (*col*) *m/f* biker, motorcyclist.
motor/motriz [mo'to*/mo'triʒ] *adj* (*TEC*) driving; (*ANAT*) motor ♦ *m* motor; (*de carro, avião*) engine; ~ **de arranque** starter (motor); ~ **de explosão** internal combustion engine; ~ **de popa** outboard motor; ~ **diesel** diesel engine; **com** ~ motorized.
motorista [moto'riʃta] *m/f* driver.
motorizado/a [motori'zadu/a] *adj* motorized; (*col: com carro*) motorized, driving.
motorizar [motori'za*] *vt* to motorize; ~-**se** *vr* to get a car.
motorneiro/a [motox'nejru/a] *m/f* tram (*BRIT*) *ou* streetcar (*US*) driver.
motoserra [moto'sexa] *f* chain-saw.
motriz [mo'triʒ] *f de* **motor**; **força** ~ driving force.
mouco/a ['moku/a] *adj* deaf, hard of hearing; **fazer ouvido** ~ to pretend not to hear.
movediço/a [move'dʒisu/a] *adj* easily moved; (*instável*) unsteady; *V tb* **areia**.
móvel ['mɔvew] (*pl* -**eis**) *adj* movable ♦ *m* (*peça de mobília*) piece of furniture; **móveis** *mpl* furniture *sg*; **bens móveis** personal property; **móveis e utensílios** (*COM*) fixtures and fittings.
mover [mo've*] *vt* to move; (*cabeça*) to shake; (*mecanismo: acionar*) to drive; (*campanha*) to set in motion; ~-**se** *vr* to move; ~ **uma ação** to start a lawsuit; ~ **alguém a fazer** to move sb to do.
movido/a [mo'vidu/a] *adj* moved; (*impelido*) powered; (*causado*) caused; ~ **a álcool** alcohol-powered.
movimentação [movimēta'sãw] (*pl* -**ões**) *f* movement; (*na rua*) bustle.
movimentado/a [movimē'tadu/a] *adj* (*rua, lugar*) busy; (*pessoa*) active; (*show, música*) up-tempo.
movimentar [movimē'ta*] *vt* to move; (*animar*) to liven up.
movimento [movi'mētu] *m* movement; (*TEC*) motion; (*na rua*) activity, bustle; **de muito** ~ (*loja, rua etc*) busy; **pôr algo em** ~ to set sth in motion.
movível [mo'vivew] (*pl* -**eis**) *adj* movable.
MPAS (*BR*) *abr m* = **Ministério da Previdência e Assistência Social**.
MPB *abr f* = **Música Popular Brasileira**.
MPlan (*BR*) *abr m* = **Ministério do Planejamento**.
MRE (*BR*) *abr m* = **Ministério das Relações Exteriores**.
MS (*BR*) *abr* = **Mato Grosso do Sul** ♦ *abr m* = **Ministério da Saúde**.
MT (*BR*) *abr* = **Mato Grosso** ♦ *abr m* = **Ministério dos Transportes**.
MTb (*BR*) *abr m* = **Ministério do Trabalho**.

muamba ['mwãba] (*col*) *f* (*contrabando*) contraband; (*objetos roubados*) loot.
muambeiro/a [mwã'bejru/a] *m/f* smuggler; (*de objetos roubados*) fence.
muar [mwa*] *m/f* mule.
muco ['muku] *m* mucus.
mucosa [mu'kɔza] *f* (*ANAT*) mucous membrane.
muçulmano/a [musuw'manu/a] *adj, m/f* Moslem.
muda ['muda] *f* (*planta*) seedling; (*vestuário*) outfit; ~ **de roupa** change of clothes.
mudança [mu'dãsa] *f* change; (*de casa*) move; (*AUTO*) gear.
mudar [mu'da*] *vt* to change; (*deslocar*) to move ♦ *vi* to change; (*ave*) to moult (*BRIT*), molt (*US*); ~-**se** *vr* (*de casa*) to move (away); ~ **de roupa/de assunto** to change clothes/the subject; ~ **de casa** to move (house); ~ **de idéia** to change one's mind.
mudez [mu'deʒ] *f* muteness; (*silêncio*) silence.
mudo/a ['mudu/a] *adj* dumb; (*calado, CINEMA*) silent; (*telefone*) dead ♦ *m/f* mute.
mugido [mu'ʒidu] *m* moo.
mugir [mu'ʒi*] *vi* (*vaca*) to moo, low.
mugunzá [mugũ'za] *m* = **munguzá**.
muito/a ['mwĩtu/a] *adj* a lot of; (*em frase negativa ou interrogativa: sg*) much, (: *pl*) many ♦ *pron* a lot; (*em frase negativa ou interrogativa: sg*) much; (: *pl*) many ♦ *adv* a lot; (+ *adj*) very; (+ *compar*): ~ **melhor** much *ou* far *ou* a lot better; ~ **admirado** much admired; ~ **tempo** a long time; ~ **depois** long after; **há** ~ a long time ago; **não demorou** ~ it didn't take long; **muitas vezes** often; **por** ~ **que** however much; **quando** ~ at most; **ter** ~ **de alguém** (*parecer-se com*) to look a lot like sb; **ele faz** ~ **erro** he makes a lot of mistakes.
mula ['mula] *f* mule.
mulato/a [mu'latu/a] *adj, m/f* mulatto.
muleta [mu'leta] *f* crutch; (*fig*) support.
mulher [mu'ʎe*] *f* woman; (*esposa*) wife; ~ **da vida** prostitute.
mulheraço [muʎe'rasu] *m* fantastic woman.
mulherão [muʎe'rãw] (*pl* -**ões**) *m* = **mulheraço**.
mulherengo [muʎe'rẽgu] *m* womanizer ♦ *adj* womanizing.
mulherio [muʎe'riu] *m* women *pl*.
multa ['muwta] *f* fine; **levar uma** ~ to get fined.
multar [muw'ta*] *vt* to fine; ~ **alguém em $1000** to fine sb $1000.
multi- [muwtʃi-] *prefixo* multi-.
multicolor [muwtʃiko'lo*] *adj* multicoloured (*BRIT*), multicolored (*US*).
multidão [muwtʃi'dãw] (*pl* -**ões**) *f* crowd; **uma** ~ **de** (*muitos*) lots of.
multiforme [muwtʃi'fɔxme] *adj* manifold, multifarious.
multilateral [muwtʃilate'raw] (*pl* -**ais**) *adj* multilateral.

multimilionário/a [muwtʃimiljo'narju/a] *adj*, *m/f* multimillionaire.

multinacional [muwtʃinasjo'naw] (*pl* -**ais**) *adj*, *f* multinational.

multiplicação [muwtʃiplika'sãw] *f* multiplication.

multiplicar [muwtʃipli'ka*] *vt* (*MAT*) to multiply; (*aumentar*) to increase.

multiplicidade [muwtʃiplisi'dadʒi] *f* multiplicity.

múltiplo/a ['muwtʃiplu/a] *adj* multiple ♦ *m* multiple; **múltipla escolha** multiple choice.

multirracial [muwtʃixa'sjaw] (*pl* -**ais**) *adj* multiracial.

multiusuário/a [muwtʃiju'zwarju/a] *adj* (*COMPUT*) multiuser.

múmia ['mumja] *f* mummy; (*fig*) plodder.

mundano/a [mũ'danu/a] *adj* worldly.

mundial [mũ'dʒjaw] (*pl* -**ais**) *adj* worldwide; (*guerra*, *recorde*) world ♦ *m* (*campeonato*) world championship; **o ~ de futebol** the World Cup.

mundo ['mũdu] *m* world; **todo o ~** everybody; **um ~ de** lots of, a great many; **correr ~** to see the world; **vir ao ~** to come into the world; **como este ~ é pequeno!** (what a) small world!; **desde que o ~ é ~** since time immemorial; **~s e fundos** (*quantia altíssima*) the earth; **prometer ~s e fundos** to promise the earth; **tinha meio ~ no comício** there were loads of people at the rally; **com esta notícia meu ~ veio abaixo** the news shattered my world; **abarcar o ~ com as pernas** (*fig*) to take on too much; **Novo/Velho/Terceiro M~** New/Old/Third World.

munguzá [mũgu'za] *m* corn meal.

munheca [mu'ɲeka] *f* wrist.

munição [muni'sãw] (*pl* -**ões**) *f* (*de armas*) ammunition; (*chumbo*) shot; (*MIL*) munitions *pl*, supplies *pl*.

municipal [munisi'paw] (*pl* -**ais**) *adj* municipal.

municipalidade [munisipali'dadʒi] *f* local authority.

município [muni'sipju] *m* local authority; (*cidade*) town; (*condado*) county.

munições [muni'sõjʃ] *fpl de* **munição**.

munir [mu'ni*] *vt*: **~ de** to provide with, supply with; **~-se** *vr*: **~-se de** (*provisões*) to equip o.s. with; (*paciência*) to arm o.s. with.

mural [mu'raw] (*pl* -**ais**) *adj*, *m* mural.

muralha [mu'raʎa] *f* (*de fortaleza*) rampart; (*muro*) wall.

murchar [mux'ʃa*] *vt* (*BOT*) to wither; (*sentimentos*) to dull; (*pessoa*) to sadden ♦ *vi* (*BOT*) to wither, wilt; (*fig*) to fade; (: *pessoa*) to grow sad.

murcho/a ['muxʃu/a] *adj* (*planta*) wilting; (*esvaziado*) shrunken; (*fig*) languid, resigned.

murmuração [muxmura'sãw] *f* muttering;

(*maledicência*) gossiping.

murmurante [muxmu'rãtʃi] *adj* murmuring.

murmurar [muxmu'ra*] *vi* (*segredar*) to murmur, whisper; (*queixar-se*) to mutter, grumble; (*água*) to ripple; (*folhagem*) to rustle ♦ *vt* to murmur.

murmurinho [muxmu'riɲu] *m* (*de vozes*) murmuring; (*som confuso*) noise; (*de folhas*) rustling; (*de água*) trickling.

murmúrio [mux'murju] *m* murmuring, whispering; (*queixa*) grumbling; (*de água*) rippling; (*de folhagem*) rustling.

muro ['muru] *m* wall.

murro ['muxu] *m* punch, sock; **dar um ~ em alguém** to punch sb; **levar um ~ de alguém** to be punched by sb; **dar ~ em ponta de faca** (*fig*) to bash one's head against a brick wall.

musa ['muza] *f* muse.

musculação [muʃkula'sãw] *f* body-building.

muscular [muʃku'la*] *adj* muscular.

musculatura [muʃkula'tura] *f* musculature.

músculo ['muʃkulu] *m* muscle.

musculoso/a [muʃku'lozu/oza] *adj* muscular.

museu [mu'zew] *m* museum; (*de pintura*) gallery.

musgo ['muʒgu] *m* moss.

musgoso/a [muʒ'gozu/oza] *adj* mossy.

música ['muzika] *f* music; (*canção*) song; **dançar conforme a ~** (*fig*) to play the game; **~ de câmara** chamber music; **~ de fundo** background music; **~ erudita** classical music; **~ folclórica** folk music; *V tb* **músico**.

musicado/a [muzi'kadu/a] *adj* set to music.

musical [muzi'kaw] (*pl* -**ais**) *adj*, *m* musical; **fundo ~** background music.

musicalidade [muzikali'dadʒi] *f* musicality.

músico/a ['muziku/a] *adj* musical ♦ *m/f* musician.

musse ['musi] *f* mousse.

musselina [muse'lina] *f* muslin.

mutação [muta'sãw] (*pl* -**ões**) *f* change, alteration; (*BIO*) mutation.

mutável [mu'tavew] (*pl* -**eis**) *adj* changeable.

mutilação [mutʃila'sãw] *f* mutilation; (*de texto*) cutting.

mutilado/a [mutʃi'ladu/a] *adj* mutilated; (*pessoa*) maimed ♦ *m/f* cripple.

mutilar [mutʃi'la*] *vt* to mutilate; (*pessoa*) to maim; (*texto*) to cut; (*árvore*) to strip.

mutirão [mutʃi'rãw] (*pl* -**ões**) *m* collective effort.

mútua ['mutwa] *f* loan company.

mutuante [mu'twãtʃi] *m/f* lender.

mutuário/a [mu'twarju/a] *m/f* borrower.

mútuo/a ['mutwu/a] *adj* mutual.

muxiba [mu'ʃiba] *f* (*pelancas*) wrinkled flesh; (*carne para cães*) dogmeat; (*seios*) drooping breasts *pl*.

muxoxo [mu'ʃoʃu] *m* tutting; **fazer ~** to tut.

NB: *European Portuguese adds the following consonants to certain words:* **b** (sú(b)dito, su(b)til); **c** (a(c)ção, a(c)cionista, a(c)to); **m** (inde(m)ne); **p** (ado(p)ção, ado(p)tar); *for further details see p. xiii.*

MVR (BR) abr m = **Maior Valor de Referência**.

N

N, n ['eni] (pl **ns**) m N, n; **N de Nair** N for Nelly (BRIT) ou Nan (US).

N abr (= norte) N.

n. abr (= nascido) b; (= nome) name.

ñ abr = **não.**

na [na] = **em + a.**

-na [na] pron her; (coisa) it.

nabo ['nabu] m turnip.

nac. abr (= nacional) nat.

nação [na'sãw] (pl **-ões**) f nation; **as Nações Unidas** the United Nations.

nácar ['naka*] m mother-of-pearl; (cor) pink.

nacional [nasjo'naw] (pl **-ais**) adj national; (carro, vinho etc) domestic, home-produced.

nacionalidade [nasjonali'dadʒi] f nationality.

nacionalismo [nasjona'liʒmu] m nationalism.

nacionalista [nasjona'liʃta] adj, m/f nationalist.

nacionalização [nasjonaliza'sãw] (pl **-ões**) f nationalization.

nacionalizar [nasjonali'za*] vt to nationalize.

naco ['naku] m piece, chunk.

nações [na'sõjʃ] fpl de **nação.**

nada ['nada] pron nothing ◆ m nothingness; (pessoa) nonentity ◆ adv at all; **não dizer ~** to say nothing, not to say anything; **antes de mais ~** first of all; **não é ~ difícil** it's not at all hard, it's not hard at all; **~ mais** nothing else; **quase ~** hardly anything; **~ de novo** nothing new; **~ feito** nothing doing; **~ mau** not bad (at all); **obrigado — de ~** thank you — not at all ou don't mention it; **(que) ~!, ~ disso!** nonsense!, not at all!, **não foi ~** it was nothing; **por ~ nesse mundo** (not) for love nor money; **ele fez o que você pediu? — fez ~!** did he do as you asked? — no, he did not!; **não ser de ~** (col) to be a dead loss; **é uma coisinha de ~** it's nothing; **de ~** (à-toa) trifling; **discutimos por um ~** we argued over nothing.

nadada [na'dada] f swim; **dar uma ~** to go for a swim.

nadadeira [nada'dejra] f (de peixe) fin; (de golfinho, foca, mergulhador) flipper.

nadador(a) [nada'do*(a)] adj swimming ◆ m/f swimmer.

nadar [na'da*] vi to swim; **~ em** to be dripping with; **estar** ou **ficar nadando** (fig) to be out of it, be out of one's depth; **ele está nadando em dinheiro** he's rolling in money.

nádegas ['nadegaʃ] fpl buttocks.

nadinha [na'dʒiɲa] pron absolutely nothing.

nado ['nadu] m: **~ livre** freestyle; **~ borboleta** butterfly (stroke); **~ de peito** breaststroke; **~ de cachorrinho** doggy paddle; **~ de costas** backstroke; **a ~** swimming; **atravessar a ~** to swim across.

naftalina [nafta'lina] f naphthaline.

náilon ['najilõ] m nylon.

naipe ['najpi] m (cartas) suit; (fig: categoria) order.

Nairobi [naj'rɔbi] n Nairobi.

namoradeira [namora'dejra] adj flirtatious ◆ f flirt.

namorado/a [namo'radu/a] m/f boyfriend/girlfriend.

namorador(a) [namora'do*(a)] adj flirtatious ◆ m ladies' man.

namorar [namo'ra*] vt (ser namorado de) to be going out with; (cobiçar) to covet; (fitar) to stare longingly at ◆ vi (casal) to go out together; (homem, mulher) to have a boyfriend (ou girlfriend).

namoricar [namori'ka*] vt to flirt with ◆ vi to flirt.

namoro [na'moru] m relationship.

nanar [na'na*] (col) vi to sleep, kip.

nanico/a [na'niku/a] adj tiny.

nanquim [nã'kĩ] m Indian ink.

não [nãw] adv not; (resposta) no ◆ m no; **~ sei** I don't know; **~ muito** not much; **~ só ... mas também** not only ... but also; **agora ~** not now; **~ tem de quê** don't mention it; **~ é?** isn't it?, won't you? (etc, segundo o verbo precedente); **eles são brasileiros, ~ é?** they're Brazilian, aren't they?

não- [nãw-] prefixo non-.

não-agressão f: **pacto de ~** non-aggression treaty.

não-alinhado/a adj non-aligned.

não-conformista adj, m/f non-conformist.

não-intervenção f non-intervention.

napa ['napa] f napa leather.

naquela(s) [na'kɛla(ʃ)] = **em + aquela(s).**

naquele(s) [na'keli(ʃ)] = **em + aquele(s).**

naquilo [na'kilu] = **em + aquilo.**

narcisismo [naxsi'ziʒmu] m narcissism.

narcisista [naxsi'ziʃta] adj narcissistic.

narciso [nax'sizu] m (BOT) narcissus; (pessoa) narcissist; **~ dos prados** daffodil.

narcótico/a [nax'kɔtʃiku/a] adj narcotic ◆ m narcotic.

narcotizar [naxkotʃi'za*] vt to drug; (fig) to bore.

narigudo/a [nari'gudu/a] adj with a big nose; **ser ~** to have a big nose.

narina [na'rina] f nostril.

nariz [na'riʒ] m nose; **~ adunco/arrebitado** hook/snub nose; **meter o ~ em** to poke one's nose into; **torcer o ~ para** to turn one's nose up at; **ser dono/a do seu ~** to know one's own mind; **dar com o ~ na porta** (fig) to find (the) doors closed to one.

narração [naxa'sãw] (pl **-ões**) f narration; (re-

lato) account.

narrador(a) [naxa'do*(a)] *m/f* narrator.

narrar [na'xa*] *vt* to narrate, recount.

narrativa [naxa'tʃiva] *f* narrative; (*história*) story.

narrativo/a [naxa'tʃivu/a] *adj* narrative.

nas [naʃ] = **em** + **as**.

-nas [naʃ] *pron* them.

NASA ['naza] *abr f* NASA.

nasal [na'zaw] (*pl* -**ais**) *adj* nasal.

nasalado/a [naza'ladu/a] *adj* nasalized, nasal.

nasalização [nazaliza'sãw] *f* nasalization.

nascença [na'sẽsa] *f* birth; **de** ~ by birth; **ele é surdo de** ~ he was born deaf.

nascente [na'sẽtʃi] *adj* nascent ♦ *m* East, Orient ♦ *f* (*fonte*) spring.

nascer [na'se*] *vi* to be born; (*plantas*) to sprout; (*o sol*) to rise; (*ave*) to hatch; (*dente*) to come through; (*fig: ter origem*) to come into being ♦ *m*: ~ **do sol** sunrise; ~ **de** (*descender*) to be born of; (*fig: originar-se*) to be born out of; ~ **de novo** (*fig*) to have a narrow escape, escape with one's life; **não nasci ontem** I wasn't born yesterday; ~ **em berço de ouro** to be born with a silver spoon in one's mouth; **ele nasceu para médico** *etc* he's a born doctor *etc*; **não nasci para fazer isto** I wasn't cut out to do this.

nascido/a [na'sidu/a] *adj* born; **bem** ~ from a good family.

nascimento [nasi'mẽtu] *m* birth; (*fig*) origin; (*estirpe*) descent.

Nassau [na'saw] *n* Nassau.

nata ['nata] *f* (*CULIN*) cream; (*elite*) élite.

natação [nata'sãw] *f* swimming.

natais [na'tajʃ] *adj pl de* **natal**.

Natal [na'taw] *m* Christmas; **Feliz** ~! Merry Christmas!

natal [na'taw] (*pl* -**ais**) *adj* (*relativo ao nascimento*) natal; (*país*) native; **cidade** ~ home town; **terra** ~ birthplace.

natalício/a [nata'lisju/a] *adj*: **aniversário** ~ birthday ♦ *m* birthday.

natalidade [natali'dadʒi] *f*: (**índice de)** ~ birth rate.

natalino/a [nata'linu/a] *adj* Christmas *atr*.

natividade [natʃivi'dadʒi] *f* nativity.

nativo/a [na'tʃivu/a] *adj*, *m/f* native.

NATO ['natu] *abr f* NATO.

nato/a ['natu/a] *adj* born.

natural [natu'raw] (*pl* -**ais**) *adj* natural; (*nativo*) native ♦ *m/f* (*nativo*) native; **de tamanho** ~ full-scale; **ao** ~ (*CULIN*) fresh, uncooked.

naturalidade [naturali'dadʒi] *f* naturalness; **falar com** ~ to talk openly; **agir com a maior** ~ to act as if nothing had happened; **de** ~ **paulista** *etc* born in São Paulo *etc*.

naturalismo [natura'liʒmu] *m* naturalism.

naturalista [natura'liʃta] *adj*, *m/f* naturalist.

naturalização [naturaliza'sãw] *f* naturalization.

naturalizado/a [naturali'zadu/a] *adj* naturalized ♦ *m/f* naturalized citizen.

naturalizar [naturali'za*] *vt* to naturalize; ~-**se** *vr* to become naturalized.

naturalmente [naturaw'mẽtʃi] *adv* naturally; ~! of course!

natureza [natu'reza] *f* nature; (*espécie*) kind, type; ~ **morta** still life; **por** ~ by nature.

naturismo [natu'riʒmu] *m* naturism.

naturista [natu'riʃta] *adj*, *m/f* naturist.

nau [naw] *f* (*literário*) ship.

naufragar [nawfra'ga*] *vi* (*navio*) to be wrecked; (*marinheiro*) to be shipwrecked; (*fig: malograr-se*) to fail.

naufrágio [naw'fraʒu] *m* shipwreck; (*fig*) failure.

náufrago/a ['nawfragu/a] *m/f* castaway.

náusea ['nawzea] *f* nausea; **dar** ~**s a alguém** to make sb feel sick; **sentir** ~**s** to feel sick.

nauseabundo/a [nawzja'bũdu/a] *adj* nauseating, sickening.

nauseante [naw'zjãtʃi] *adj* nauseating, sickening.

nausear [naw'zja*] *vt* to nauseate, sicken ♦ *vi* to feel sick.

náutica ['nawtʃika] *f* seamanship.

náutico/a ['nawtʃiku/a] *adj* nautical.

naval [na'vaw] (*pl* -**ais**) *adj* naval; **construção** ~ shipbuilding.

navalha [na'vaʎa] *f* (*de barba*) razor; (*faca*) knife.

navalhada [nava'ʎada] *f* cut (*with a razor*).

navalhar [nava'ʎa*] *vt* to cut *ou* slash with a razor.

nave ['navi] *f* (*de igreja*) nave; ~ **espacial** spaceship.

navegação [navega'sãw] *f* navigation, sailing; ~ **aérea** air traffic; ~ **costeira** coastal shipping; ~ **fluvial** river traffic; **companhia de** ~ shipping line.

navegador(a) [navega'do*(a)] *m/f* navigator.

navegante [nave'gãtʃi] *m* navigator, seafarer.

navegar [nave'ga*] *vt* to navigate; (*mares*) to sail ♦ *vi* to sail; (*dirigir o rumo*) to navigate.

navegável [nave'gavew] (*pl* -**eis**) *adj* navigable.

navio [na'viu] *m* ship; ~ **aeródromo** aircraft carrier; ~ **cargueiro** cargo ship, freighter; ~ **de carreira** liner; ~ **de guerra** warship; ~ **escola** training ship; ~ **fábrica** factory ship; ~ **mercante** merchant ship; ~ **petroleiro** oil tanker; ~ **tanque** tanker; **ficar a ver** ~**s** to be left high and dry.

Nazaré [naza'rɛ] *n* Nazareth.

nazi [na'zi] (*PT*) *adj*, *m/f* = **nazista**.

nazismo [na'ziʒmu] *m* Nazism.

nazista [na'ziʃta] (*BR*) *adj*, *m/f* Nazi.

NB *abr* (= *note bem*) NB.

n/c *abr* (= *nossa carta*) our letter; (= *nossa*

conta) our account; (= *nossa casa*) our firm.

N da R *abr* = **nota da redação.**

N do A *abr* = **nota do autor.**

N do E *abr* = **nota do editor.**

N do T *abr* = **nota do tradutor.**

NE *abr* (= *nordeste*) NE.

neblina [ne'blina] *f* fog, mist.

nebulosa [nebu'lɔza] *f* (*ASTRONOMIA*) nebula.

nebulosidade [nebulozi'dadʒi] *f* cloud.

nebuloso/a [nebu'lozu/ɔza] *adj* foggy, misty; (*céu*) cloudy; (*fig*) vague.

neca ['nɛka] (*col*) *pron* nothing ♦ *excl* nope.

necessaire [nese'se*] *m* toilet bag.

necessário/a [nese'sarju/a] *adj* necessary ♦ *m*: **o** ~ the necessities *pl*; **se for** ~ if necessary.

necessidade [nesesi'dadʒi] *f* need, necessity; (*o que se necessita*) need; (*pobreza*) poverty, need; **ter** ~ **de** to need; **não há** ~ **de algo/ de fazer algo** there is no need for sth/to do sth; **em caso de** ~ if need be; **gêneros de primeira** ~ basic foodstuffs; **passar por muitas** ~**s** to suffer many deprivations; **fazer suas** ~**s** (*col*) to go to the toilet.

necessitado/a [nesesi'tadu/a] *adj* needy, poor ♦ *m/f* person in need; **os** ~**s** the needy *pl*; ~ **de** in need of.

necessitar [nesesi'ta*] *vt* to need, require ♦ *vi* to be in need; ~ **de** to need.

necrológio [nekro'lɔʒu] *m* obituary.

necrópole [ne'krɔpoli] *f* cemetery.

necrose [ne'krɔzi] *f* necrosis.

necrotério [nekro'tɛrju] *m* mortuary, morgue (*US*).

néctar ['nɛkta*] *m* nectar.

nectarina [nekta'rina] *f* nectarine.

nédio/a ['nɛdʒu/a] *adj* (*luzidio*) glossy, sleek; (*rechonchudo*) plump.

neerlandês/esa [neexlã'deʃ/eza] *adj* Dutch ♦ *m/f* Dutchman/woman.

Neerlândia [neex'lãdʒa] *f* the Netherlands *pl*.

nefando/a [ne'fãdu/a] *adj* atrocious, heinous.

nefasto/a [ne'faʃtu/a] *adj* (*de mau agouro*) ominous; (*trágico*) tragic.

negaça [ne'gasa] *f* lure, bait; (*engano*) deception; (*recusa*) refusal; (*desmentido*) denial.

negação [nega'sãw] (*pl* **-ões**) *f* negation; (*recusa*) refusal; (*desmentido*) denial; **ele é uma** ~ **em matéria de cozinha** he's hopeless at cooking.

negacear [nega'sja*] *vt* (*atrair*) to entice; (*enganar*) to deceive; (*recusar*) to refuse ♦ *vi* (*cavalo*) to balk; (*HIPISMO*) to refuse.

negações [nega'sõjʃ] *fpl de* **negação.**

negar [ne'ga*] *vt* (*desmentir*) to deny; (*recusar*) to refuse; (*não permitir*) to deny; ~**-se** *vr*: ~**-se a** to refuse to.

negativa [nega'tʃiva] *f* (*LING*) negative; (*recusa*) denial.

negativo/a [nega'tʃivu/a] *adj* negative ♦ *m* (*TEC*, *FOTO*) negative ♦ *excl* (*col*) nope!

negável [ne'gavew] *adj* (*pl* **-eis**) deniable.

negligé [negli'ge] *m* negligee.

negligência [negli'ʒẽsja] *f* negligence, carelessness.

negligenciar [negliʒẽ'sja*] *vt* to neglect.

negligente [negli'ʒẽtʃi] *adj* negligent, careless.

nego/a ['negu/a] (*col*) *m/f* (*negro*) black; (*camarada*): **tudo bem, (meu)** ~**?** how are you, mate?; (*querido*): **tchau, (meu)** ~ bye, dear *ou* darling.

negociação [negosja'sãw] (*pl* **-ões**) *f* negotiation; (*transação*) transaction.

negociador(a) [negosja'do*(a)] *adj* negotiating ♦ *m/f* negotiator.

negociante [nego'sjãtʃi] *m/f* businessman/woman; (*comerciante*) merchant.

negociar [nego'sja*] *vt* (*POL etc*) to negotiate; (*COM*) to trade ♦ *vi*: ~ **(com)** to trade *ou* deal (in); to negotiate (with).

negociata [nego'sjata] *f* crooked deal; ~**s** wheeling and dealing *sg*.

negociável [nego'sjavew] (*pl* **-eis**) *adj* negotiable.

negócio [ne'gɔsju] *m* (*COM*) business; (*transação*) deal; (*questão*) matter; (*col*: *troço*) thing; (*assunto*) affair, business; **homem de** ~**s** businessman; **a** ~**s** on business; **fazer um bom** ~ (*pessoa*) to get a good deal; (*loja etc*) to do good business; **fechar um** ~ to make a deal; ~ **fechado!** it's a deal!; **isso não é** ~ it's not worth it; **a casa dela é um** ~ (*col*) her house is really something; **tenho um** ~ **para te contar** I've got something to tell you; **aconteceu um** ~ **estranho comigo** something strange happened to me; **mas que** ~ **é esse?** (*col*) what's the big idea?; **meu** ~ **é outro** (*col*) this isn't my thing; **o** ~ **é o seguinte ...** (*col*) the thing is ....

negocista [nego'siʃta] *m/f* wheeler-dealer ♦ *adj* crooked.

negridão [negri'dãw] *f* blackness.

negrito [ne'gritu] *m* (*TIP*) bold (face).

negritude [negri'tudʒi] *f* (*POL etc*) black awareness.

negro/a ['negru/a] *adj* black; (*raça*) Negro; (*fig*: *lúgubre*) black, gloomy ♦ *m/f* black man/woman; Negro/Negress; **a situação está negra** the situation is bad; **humor** ~ black humo(u)r; **magia negra** black magic.

negrume [ne'grumi] *m* black, darkness.

negrura [ne'grura] *f* blackness.

neguei [ne'gej] *etc vb V* **negar.**

nela(s) ['nɛla(ʃ)] = **em** + **ela(s).**

nele(s) ['neli(ʃ)] = **em** + **ele(s).**

nem [nẽj] *conj* nor, neither; ~ **(sequer)** not even; ~ **que** even if; ~ **bem** hardly; ~ **um só** not a single one; ~ **estuda** ~ **trabalha** he neither studies nor works; ~ **eu** nor me; **sem** ~ without even; ~ **todos** not all; ~ **tanto** not so much; ~ **sempre** not always; ~ **por isso** nonetheless; **ele fala português que** ~ **brasileiro** he speaks Portuguese like a Brazilian; ~ **vem (que não tem)** (*col*) don't give me that.

nenê [ne'ne] *m/f* baby.

neném [ne'nẽj] (pl -ns) m/f = **nenê.**

nenhum(a) [ne'nũ/'ɲuma] adj no, not any ♦ pron (nem um só) none, not one; (de dois) neither; ~ **professor** no teacher; **não vi professor** ~ I didn't see any teachers; ~ **dos professores** none of the teachers; ~ **dos dois** neither of them; ~ **lugar** nowhere; **ele não fez** ~ **comentário** he didn't make any comments, he made no comments; **não vou a** ~ **lugar** I'm not going anywhere; **estar a** ~ (col) to be flat broke.

neofascismo [neofa'siʒmu] m neofascism.

neolatino/a [neola'tʃinu/a] adj: **línguas neolatinas** Romance languages.

neolítico/a [neo'litʃiku/a] adj neolithic.

neologismo [neolo'ʒiʒmu] m neologism.

néon ['nɛõ] m neon.

neônio [ne'onju] m = **néon.**

neo-realismo ['neo-] m new realism.

neozelandês/esa [neozelã'deʃ/deza] adj New Zealand atr ♦ m/f New Zealander.

Nepal [ne'paw] m: **o** ~ Nepal.

nepotismo [nepo'tʃiʒmu] m nepotism.

nervo ['nexvu] m (ANAT) nerve; (fig) energy, strength; (em carne) sinew; **ser** ou **estar uma pilha de** ~**s** to be a bundle of nerves.

nervosismo [nexvo'ziʒmu] m (nervosidade) nervousness; (irritabilidade) irritability.

nervoso/a [nex'vozu/ɔza] adj nervous; (irritável) touchy, on edge; (exaltado) worked up; **isso/ele me deixa** ~ he gets on my nerves; **sistema** ~ nervous system.

nervudo/a [ner'vudu/a] (PT) adj (robusto) robust.

nervura [nex'vura] f rib; (BOT) vein.

néscio/a ['nɛsju/a] adj (idiota) stupid; (insensato) foolish.

nesga ['neʒga] f (COSTURA) flare, gore; (porção: de comida) portion; (: de mesa, terra) corner, patch.

nessa(s) ['nɛsa(ʃ)] = **em** + **essa(s).**

nesse(s) ['nesi(ʃ)] = **em** + **esse(s).**

nesta(s) ['nɛʃta(ʃ)] = **em** + **esta(s).**

neste(s) ['neʃtʃi(ʃ)] = **em** + **este(s).**

neto/a ['nɛtu/a] m/f grandson/daughter; ~**s** mpl grandchildren.

neuralgia [newraw'ʒia] f neuralgia.

neurastênico/a [newraʃ'teniku/a] adj (PSICO) neurasthenic; (col: irritadiço) irritable.

neurite [new'ritʃi] f (MED) neuritis.

neurocirurgião/giã [newrosirux3jãw/3jã] (pl -ões/~s) m/f neurosurgeon.

neurologia [newrolo'ʒia] f neurology.

neurológico/a [newro'lɔʒiku/a] adj neurological.

neurologista [newrolo'ʒiʃta] m/f neurologist.

neurose [new'rɔzi] f neurosis.

neurótico/a [new'rɔtʃiku/a] adj, m/f neurotic.

neutralidade [newtrali'dadʒi] f neutrality.

neutralização [newtraliza'sãw] f neutraliza-

tion.

neutralizar [newtrali'za*] vt to neutralize; (anular) to counteract.

neutrão [new'trãw] (PT; pl -ões) m = **nêutron.**

neutro/a ['newtru/a] adj neuter.

neutrões [new'trõjs] mpl de **neutrão.**

nêutron ['newtrõ] (pl ~s) m neutron; **bomba de** ~**s** neutron bomb.

nevada [ne'vada] f snowfall.

nevado/a [ne'vadu/a] adj snow-covered; (branco) snow-white.

nevar [ne'va*] vi to snow.

nevasca [ne'vaʃka] f snowstorm.

neve ['nɛvi] f snow; **clara em** ~ (CULIN) beaten egg-white.

névoa ['nɛvoa] f fog.

nevoeiro [nevo'ejru] m thick fog.

nevralgia [nevraw'ʒia] f neuralgia.

nexo ['nɛksu] m connection, link; **sem** ~ disconnected, incoherent.

nhenhenhém [ɲeɲe'ɲẽj] m (conversa fiado) idle talk; (reclamação) whinging.

nhoque ['ɲɔki] m (CULIN) gnocchi.

Nicarágua [nika'ragwa] f: **a** ~ Nicaragua.

nicaragüense [nikara'gwẽsi] adj, m/f Nicaraguan.

nicho ['niʃu] m niche.

Nicósia [ni'kɔzja] n Nicosia.

nicotina [niko'tʃina] f nicotine.

Níger ['niʒe*] m: **o** ~ Niger.

Nigéria [ni'ʒerja] f: **a** ~ Nigeria.

nigeriano/a [niʒe'rjanu/a] adj, m/f Nigerian.

niilista [nii'liʃta] adj nihilistic ♦ m/f nihilist.

Nilo ['nilu] m: **o** ~ the Nile.

nimbo ['nĩbu] m (nuvem) rain cloud; (GEO) halo.

ninar [ni'na*] vt to sing to sleep; ~**-se** vr: ~**se para algo** to ignore sth.

ninfeta [nĩ'feta] f nymphette.

ninfomaníaca [nĩfoma'niaka] f nymphomaniac.

ninguém [nĩ'gẽj] pron nobody, no-one; ~ **o conhece** no-one knows him; **não vi** ~ I saw no-one, I didn't see anybody; ~ **mais** nobody else.

ninhada [ni'ɲada] f brood.

ninharia [niɲa'ria] f trifle.

ninho ['niɲu] m (de aves) nest; (toca) lair; (lar) home; ~ **de rato** (col) mess, tip.

níquel ['nikew] m nickel; **estar sem um** ~ to be penniless.

niquelar [nike'la*] vt (TEC) to nickel-plate.

nirvana [nix'vana] f nirvana.

nisei [ni'zej] adj, m/f second-generation Japanese Brazilian.

nisso ['nisu] = **em** + **isso.**

nisto ['niʃtu] = **em** + **isto.**

nitidez [nitʃi'deʒ] f (clareza) clarity; (brilho) brightness; (imagem) sharpness.

nítido/a ['nitʃidu/a] adj clear, distinct;

NB: European Portuguese adds the following consonants to certain words: **b** (sú(b)dito, su(b)til); **c** (a(c)ção, a(c)cionista, a(c)to); **m** (inde(m)ne); **p** (ado(p)ção, ado(p)tar); for further details see p. xiii.

(brilhante) bright; *(imagem)* sharp, clear.
nitrato [ni'tratu] *m* nitrate.
nítrico/a ['nitriku/a] *adj*: **ácido ~** nitric acid.
nitrogênio [nitro'ʒenju] *m* nitrogen.
nitroglicerina [nitroglise'rina] *f* nitroglycerine.
nível ['nivew] *(pl -eis)* *m* level; *(fig: padrão)* level, standard; (: *ponto)* point, pitch; **~ de vida** standard of living; **~ do mar** sea level; **a ~ de** in terms of; **ao ~ de** level with.
nivelamento [nivela'mẽtu] *m* levelling *(BRIT)*, leveling *(US)*.
nivelar [nive'la*] *vt* *(terreno etc)* to level ♦ *vi*: **~ com** to be level with; **~-se** *vr*: **~-se com** to be equal to; **a morte nivela os homens** death is the great leveller *(BRIT)* *ou* leveler *(US)*.
NO *abr* (= *nordoeste*) NW.
no [nu] = **em + o**.
-no [nu] *pron* him; *(coisa)* it.
nº *abr* (= *número*) no.
n/o *abr* = **nossa ordem**.
nó *m* knot; *(de uma questão)* crux; **~ corredio** slipknot; **~ na garganta** lump in the throat; **~s dos dedos** knuckles; **dar um ~** to tie a knot.
nobilíssimo/a [nobi'lisimu/a] *adj superl de* **nobre**.
nobilitar [nobili'ta*] *vt* to ennoble.
nobre ['nɔbri] *adj* noble; *(bairro etc)* exclusive ♦ *m/f* noble; **horário ~** prime time.
nobreza [no'breza] *f* nobility.
noção [no'sãw] *(pl -ões)* *f* notion; **noções** *fpl* rudiments, basics; **~ vaga** inkling; **não ter a menor ~ de algo** not to have the slightest idea about sth.
nocaute [no'kawtʃi] *m* knockout; *(soco)* knockout blow ♦ *adv*: **pôr alguém ~** to knock sb out.
nocautear [nokaw'tʃja*] *vt* to knock out.
nocivo/a [no'sivu/a] *adj* harmful.
noções [no'sõjʃ] *fpl de* **noção**.
nocturno/a [no'tuxnu/a] *(PT)* *adj* = **noturno**.
nódoa ['nɔdwa] *f* spot; *(mancha)* stain.
nódulo ['nɔdulu] *m* nodule.
nogueira [no'gejra] *f* *(árvore)* walnut tree; *(madeira)* walnut.
noitada [noj'tada] *f* *(noite inteira)* whole night; *(noite de divertimento)* night out.
noite ['nojtʃi] *f* night; *(início da ~)* evening; **à ou de ~** at night, in the evening; **ontem/hoje/amanhã à ~** last night/tonight/tomorrow night; **boa ~** good evening; *(despedida)* good night; **da ~ para o dia** overnight; **tarde da ~** late at night; **passar a ~ em claro** to have a sleepless night; **a ~ carioca** Rio nightlife; **~ de estréia** opening night.
noitinha [noj'tʃiɲa] *f*: **à ~s** at nightfall.
noivado [noj'vadu] *m* engagement.
noivar [noj'va*] *vi*: **~ (com)** *(ficar noivo)* to get engaged (to); *(ser noivo)* to be engaged (to).
noivo/a ['nojvu/a] *m/f* *(prometido)* fiancé/fiancée; *(no casamento)* bridegroom/bride;

os ~s *mpl* *(prometidos)* the engaged couple; *(no casamento)* the bride and groom; *(recém-casados)* the newly-weds.
nojeira [no'ʒejra] *f* disgusting thing; *(trabalho)* filthy job.
nojento/a [no'ʒẽtu/a] *adj* disgusting.
nojo ['noʒu] *m* *(náusea)* nausea; *(repulsão)* disgust, loathing; **ela é um ~** she's horrible; **este trabalho está um ~** this work is messy.
no-la = **nos + a**.
no-lo = **nos + o**.
no-las = **nos + as**.
no-los = **nos + os**.
nômade ['nomadʒi] *adj* nomadic ♦ *m/f* nomad.
nome ['nɔmi] *m* name; *(fama)* fame; **de ~** by name; **escritor de ~** famous writer; **um restaurante de ~** a restaurant with a good reputation; **em ~ de** in the name of; **dar ~ aos bois** to call a spade a spade; **esse ~ não me é estranho** the name rings a bell; **~ comercial** trade name; **~ completo** full name; **~ de batismo** Christian name; **~ de família** family name; **~ de guerra** nickname; **~ feio** swearword; **~ próprio** *(LING)* proper name.
nomeação [nomja'sãw] *(pl -ões)* *f* nomination; *(para um cargo)* appointment.
nomeada [no'mjada] *f* fame.
nomeadamente [nomjada'mẽtʃi] *adv* namely.
nomear [no'mja*] *vt* to nominate; *(conferir um cargo)* to appoint; *(dar nome a)* to name.
nomenclatura [nomẽkla'tura] *f* nomenclature.
nominal [nomi'naw] *(pl -ais)* *adj* nominal.
nonagésimo/a [nona'ʒɛzimu/a] *num* ninetieth.
nono/a ['nonu/a] *num* ninth; *V tb* **quinto**.
nora ['nɔra] *f* daughter-in-law.
nordeste [nox'dɛʃtʃi] *m* northeast; **o N~** the Northeast.
nordestino/a [noxdeʃ'tʃinu/a] *adj* northeastern ♦ *m/f* Northeasterner.
nórdico/a ['nɔxdʒiku/a] *adj*, *m/f* Nordic.
norma ['nɔxma] *f* standard, norm; *(regra)* rule; **como ~** as a rule.
normal [nox'maw] *(pl -ais)* *adj* normal; *(habitual)* usual; **escola ~** ≈ teacher training college; **curso ~** primary *(BRIT)* *ou* elementary *(US)* school teacher training; **está um calor que não é ~** it's incredibly hot.
normalidade [noxmali'dadʒi] *f* normality.
normalista [noxma'liʃta] *m/f* trainee primary *(BRIT)* *ou* elementary *(US)* school teacher.
normalização [noxmaliza'sãw] *f* normalization.
normalizar [noxmali'za*] *vt* to bring back to normal; *(POL: relações etc)* to normalize; **~-se** *vr* to return to normal.
normativo/a [noxma'tʃivu/a] *adj* prescriptive.
noroeste [nor'weʃtʃi] *adj* northwest, northwestern ♦ *m* northwest.
norte ['nɔxtʃi] *adj* northern, north; *(vento, direção)* northerly ♦ *m* north; **ao ~ de** to the north of.
norte-africano/a *adj*, *m/f* North African.
norte-americano/a *adj*, *m/f* (North) American.

nortear [nox'tʃja*] vt to orientate; ~**-se** vr to orientate o.s.

norte-coreano/a adj, m/f North Korean.

norte-vietnamita adj, m/f North Vietnamese.

nortista [nox'tʃiʃta] adj northern ♦ m/f Northerner.

Noruega [nor'wega] f Norway.

norueguês/esa [norwe'geʃ/geza] adj, m/f Norwegian ♦ m (LING) Norwegian.

nos¹ [nuʃ] = **em** + **os**.

nos² [nuʃ] pron (direto) us; (indireto) us, to us, for us; (reflexivo) (to) ourselves; (recíproco) (to) each other.

-nos [nuʃ] pron them.

nós [nɔʃ] pron we; ~ **mesmos** we ourselves; **para** ~ for us; ~ **dois** we two, both of us; **cá entre** ~ between the two (ou three etc) of us.

nossa ['nɔsa] excl: ~! my goodness!

nosso/a ['nɔsu/a] adj our ♦ pron ours; **um amigo** ~ a friend of ours; **Nossa Senhora** (REL) Our Lady; **os** ~**s** (família) our family sg.

nostalgia [noʃtaw'ʒia] f nostalgia; (saudades da pátria etc) homesickness.

nostálgico/a [noʃ'tawʒiku/a] adj nostalgic.

nota ['nɔta] f note; (EDUC) mark; (conta) bill; (cédula) banknote; **digno de** ~ noteworthy; **cheio da** ~ (col) flush; **custar uma** ~ (**preta**) (col) to cost a bomb; **tomar** ~ to make a note; ~ **de venda** sales receipt; ~ **fiscal** receipt; (~) **promissória** promissory note.

notabilidade [notabili'dadʒi] f notability; (pessoa) notable.

notabilizar [notabili'za*] vt to make known; ~**-se** vr to become known.

notação [nota'sãw] (pl -**ões**) f notation.

notadamente [notada'mẽtʃi] adv especially.

notar [no'ta*] vt (reparar em) to notice, note; ~**-se** vr to be obvious; **é de** ~ **que** it is to be noted that; **fazer** ~ to call attention to.

notável [no'tavew] (pl -**eis**) adj notable, remarkable.

notícia [no'tʃisja] f (uma ~) piece of news; (TV etc) news item; ~**s** fpl news sg; **pedir** ~**s de** to inquire about; **ter** ~**s de** to hear from.

noticiar [notʃi'sja*] vt to announce, report.

noticiário [notʃi'sjarju] m (de jornal) news section; (CINEMA) newsreel; (RÁDIO etc) news bulletin.

noticiarista [notʃisja'riʃta] m/f news writer, reporter; (TV, RÁDIO) newsreader, newscaster.

noticioso/a [notʃi'sjozu/ɔza] adj news atr.

notificação [notʃifika'sãw] (pl -**ões**) f notification.

notificar [notʃifi'ka*] vt to notify, inform.

notívago/a [no'tʃivagu/a] adj nocturnal ♦ m/f sleepwalker; (pessoa que gosta da noite) night bird.

notoriedade [notorje'dadʒi] f renown, fame.

notório/a [no'tɔrju/a] adj well-known.

noturno/a [no'tuxnu/a] adj nocturnal, nightly; (trabalho) night atr ♦ m (trem) night train.

nouveau-riche [nuvo'xiʃi] (pl **nouveaux-riches**) m/f nouveau-riche.

nov. abr (= novembro) Nov.

nova ['nɔva] f piece of news; ~**s** fpl news sg.

novamente [nova'mẽtʃi] adv again.

novato/a [no'vatu/a] adj inexperienced, raw ♦ m/f (principiante) beginner, novice; (EDUC) fresher.

nove ['nɔvi] num nine; V tb **cinco**.

novecentos/as [nove'sẽtuʃ/aʃ] num nine hundred.

novela [no'vɛla] f short novel, novella; (RÁDIO TV) soap opera.

novelista [nove'liʃta] m/f novella writer.

novelo [no'velu] m ball of thread.

novembro [no'vẽbru] (PT: **N-**) m November; V tb **julho**.

novena [no'vena] f (REL) novena.

noventa [no'vẽta] num ninety; V tb **cinqüenta**.

noviciado [novi'sjadu] m (REL) novitiate.

noviço/a [no'visu/a] m/f (REL, fig) novice.

novidade [novi'dadʒi] f novelty; (notícia) piece of news; ~**s** fpl news sg; **sem** ~ without incident.

novidadeiro/a [novida'dejru/a] adj chatty ♦ m/f gossip.

novilho/a [no'viʎu/a] m/f young bull/heifer.

novo/a ['novu/'nɔva] adj new; (jovem) young; (adicional) further; **de** ~ again; ~ **em folha** brand new; **o que há de** ~? what's new?; ~ **rico** nouveau riche.

noz [nɔʒ] f walnut, nut; ~ **moscada** nutmeg.

nu(a) [nu/'nua] adj (corpo, pessoa) naked; (braço, arvore, sala, parede) bare ♦ m nude; ~ **em pêlo** stark naked; **a olho** ~ with the naked eye; **a verdade nua e crua** the stark truth ou reality; **pôr a** ~ (fig) to expose.

nuança [nu'ãsa] f nuance.

nubente [nu'bẽtʃi] adj, m/f betrothed.

nublado/a [nu'bladu/a] adj cloudy, overcast.

nublar [nu'bla*] vt to darken; ~**-se** vr to cloud over.

nuca ['nuka] f nape (of the neck).

nuclear [nu'klja*] adj nuclear; **energia/usina** ~ nuclear energy/power station.

núcleo ['nuklju] m nucleus sg; (centro) centre (BRIT), center (US).

nudez [nu'deʒ] f nakedness, nudity; (de paredes etc) bareness.

nudismo [nu'dʒiʒmu] m nudism.

nudista [nu'dʒiʃta] adj, m/f nudist.

nulidade [nuli'dadʒi] f nullity, invalidity; (pessoa) nonentity.

nulo/a ['nulu/a] adj (JUR) null, void; (nenhum) non-existent; (sem valor) worthless; (esforço) vain, useless; **ele é** ~ **em matemática** he's useless at maths (BRIT) ou math

(US).

num [nũ] = **em** + **um** ♦ adv (col: não) not.

numa(s) ['numa(ʃ)] = **em** + **uma(s)**.

numeração [numera'sãw] f (ato) numbering; (números) numbers pl; (de sapatos etc) sizes pl.

numerado/a [nume'radu/a] adj numbered; (em ordem numérica) in numerical order.

numeral [nume'raw] (pl -ais) m numeral ♦ adj numerical.

numerar [nume'ra*] vt to number.

numerário [nume'rarju] m cash, money.

numérico/a [nu'mɛriku/a] adj numerical.

número ['numeru] m number; (de jornal) issue; (TEATRO etc) act; (de sapatos, roupa) size; **sem** ~ countless; **um sem** ~ **de vezes** hundreds ou thousands of times; **amigo/ escritor** ~ **um** number one friend/writer; **fazer** ~ to make up the numbers; **ele é um** ~ (col) he's a riot; ~ **cardinal/ordinal** cardinal/ordinal number; ~ **de matrícula** registration (BRIT) ou license plate (US) number; ~ **primo** prime number.

numeroso/a [nume'rozu/ɔza] adj numerous.

nunca ['nũka] adv never; ~ **mais** never again; **como** ~ as never before; **quase** ~ hardly ever; **mais que** ~ more than ever.

nuns [nũʃ] = **em** + **uns**.

nupcial [nup'sjaw] adj (pl -ais) wedding atr.

núpcias ['nupsjaʃ] fpl nuptials, wedding sg.

nutrição [nutri'sãw] f nutrition.

nutricionista [nutrisjo'niʃta] m/f nutritionist.

nutrido/a [nu'tridu/a] adj (bem alimentado) well-nourished; (robusto) robust.

nutrimento [nutri'mẽtu] m nourishment.

nutrir [nu'tri*] vt (sentimento) to harbour (BRIT), harbor (US); (fig) to feed ♦ vi to be nourishing; ~ **(de)** to nourish (with), feed (on).

nutritivo/a [nutri'tʃivu/a] adj nourishing; **valor** ~ nutritional value.

nuvem ['nuvẽj] (pl -ns) f cloud; (de insetos) swarm; **cair das nuvens** (fig) to be astounded; **estar nas nuvens** to be daydreaming, be miles away; **pôr nas nuvens** to praise to the skies; **o aniversário passou em brancas nuvens** the birthday went by without any celebration.

O

O, o [ɔ] (pl os) m O, o; **O de Osvaldo** O for Oliver (BRIT) ou Oboe (US).

o [u] (pl os) art def the ♦ pron him; (coisa) it; (usos pronominais): ~ **que** the one (that); ~ **quê?** what?; **não entendi** ~ **que ele falou** I

didn't understand what he said; **meu carro é melhor do que** ~ **dele** my car is better then his; **dos dois carros, eu prefiro** ~ **verde/**~ **que tem 4 portas** of the two cars, I prefer the green one/the one which has 4 doors.

ó [ɔ] excl oh!; (olha) look!; ~ **Pedro** hey Pedro.

ô [o] excl oh!; ~ **Pedro** hey Pedro; ~ **de casa!** anyone at home?; ~ **criança difícil!** oh, what a difficult child!

OAB abr f = **Ordem dos Advogados do Brasil**.

oásis [o'asiʃ] m inv oasis.

oba ['oba] excl wow! great!; (saudação) hi!

obcecado/a [obise'kadu/a] adj obsessed.

obcecar [obise'ka*] vt to obsess.

obedecer [obede'se*] vi: ~ **a** to obey; **obedeça!** (a criança) do as you're told!

obediência [obe'dʒẽsja] f obedience.

obediente [obe'dʒẽtʃi] adj obedient.

obelisco [obe'liʃku] m obelisk.

obesidade [obezi'dadʒi] f obesity.

obeso/a [o'bɛzu/a] adj obese.

óbice ['ɔbisi] m obstacle.

óbito ['ɔbitu] m death; **atestado de** ~ death certificate.

obituário [obi'twarju] m obituary.

objeção [obʒe'sãw] (PT: **-cç-**; pl **-ões**) f objection; (obstáculo) obstacle; **fazer** ou **pôr objeções a** to object to.

objetar [obʒe'ta*] (PT: **-ct-**) vt to object ♦ vi: ~ **(a algo)** to object (to sth).

objetiva [obʒe'tʃiva] (PT: **-ct-**) f lens; **sem** ~ aimlessly.

objetivar [obʒetʃi'va*] (PT: **-ct-**) vt (visar) to aim at; ~ **fazer** to aim to do, set out to do.

objetividade [obʒetʃivi'dadʒi] (PT: **-ct-**) f objectivity.

objetivo/a [obʒe'tʃivu/a] (PT: **-ct-**) adj objective ♦ m objective, aim.

objeto [ob'ʒɛtu] (PT: **-ct-**) m object; ~ **de uso pessoal** personal effect.

oblíqua [o'blikwa] f oblique.

oblíquo/a [o'blikwu/a] adj oblique, slanting; (olhar) sidelong; (LING) oblique.

obliterar [oblite'ra*] vt to obliterate; (MED) to close off.

oblongo/a [ob'lõgu/a] adj oblong.

oboé [o'bwɛ] m oboe.

oboísta [o'bwiʃta] m/f oboe player.

obra ['ɔbra] f work; (ARQ) building, construction; (TEATRO) play; **em** ~**s** under repair; ~**s públicas** public works; **ser** ~ **de alguém** to be the work of sb; **ser** ~ **de algo** to be the result of sth; ~ **de arte** work of art; ~ **de caridade** charity; ~**s completas** complete works.

obra-mestra (pl **obras-mestras**) f masterpiece.

obra-prima (pl **obras-primas**) f masterpiece.

obreiro/a [o'brejru/a] adj working ♦ m/f worker.

obrigação [obriga'sãw] (pl **-ões**) f obligation,

duty; (*COM*) bond; **cumprir (com) suas obrigações** to fulfil(l) one's obligations; **dever obrigações a alguém** to owe sb favo(u)rs; ~ **ao portador** bearer bond.

obrigado/a [obri'gadu/a] *adj* (*compelido*) obliged, compelled ♦ *excl*: ~! thank you; (*recusa*) no, thank you.

obrigar [obri'ga*] *vt* to oblige, compel; ~**-se** *vr*: ~**-se a fazer algo** to undertake to do sth.

obrigatoriedade [obrigatorje'dadʒi] *f* compulsory nature.

obrigatório/a [obriga'tɔrju/a] *adj* compulsory, obligatory.

obscenidade [obiseni'dadʒi] *f* obscenity.

obsceno/a [obi'sɛnu/a] *adj* obscene.

obscurecer [obiʃkure'se*] *vt* to darken; (*entendimento, verdade etc*) to obscure; (*prestígio*) to dim ♦ *vi* to get dark.

obscuridade [obiʃkuri'dadʒi] *f* (*falta de luz*) darkness; (*fig*) obscurity.

obscuro/a [obi'ʃkuru/a] *adj* dark; (*fig*) obscure.

obsequiar [obse'kja*] *vt* (*presentear*) to give presents to; (*tratar com agrados*) to treat kindly.

obséquio [ob'sɛkju] *m* favour (*BRIT*), favor (*US*), kindness; **faça o ~ de ...** would you be kind enough to ....

obsequioso/a [obse'kjozu/ɔza] *adj* obliging, courteous.

observação [obisexva'sãw] (*pl* -**ões**) *f* observation; (*comentário*) remark, comment; (*de leis, regras*) observance.

observador(a) [obisexva'do*(a)] *adj* observant ♦ *m/f* observer.

observância [obisex'vãsja] *f* observance.

observar [obisex'va*] *vt* to observe; (*notar*) to notice; (*replicar*) to remark; ~ **algo a alguém** to point sth out to sb.

observatório [obisexva'tɔrju] *m* observatory.

obsessão [obise'sãw] (*pl* -**ões**) *f* obsession.

obsessivo/a [obise'sivu/a] *adj* obsessive.

obsessões [obise'sõjʃ] *fpl de* **obsessão**.

obsoleto/a [obiso'lɛtu/a] *adj* obsolete.

obstáculo [obi'ʃtakulu] *m* obstacle; (*dificuldade*) hindrance, drawback.

obstante [obi'ʃtãtʃi]: **não ~** *conj* nevertheless, however ♦ *prep* in spite of, notwithstanding.

obstar [obi'ʃta*] *vi*: ~ **a** to hinder; (*opor-se*) to oppose.

obstetra [obi'ʃtɛtra] *m/f* obstetrician.

obstetrícia [obiʃte'trisja] *f* obstetrics *sg*.

obstétrico/a [obi'ʃtɛtriku/a] *adj* obstetric.

obstinação [obiʃtʃina'sãw] *f* obstinacy.

obstinado/a [obiʃtʃi'nadu/a] *adj* obstinate, stubborn.

obstinar-se [obiʃtʃi'naxsi] *vr* to be obstinate; ~ **em** (*insistir em*) to persist in.

obstrução [obiʃtru'sãw] (*pl* -**ões**) *f* obstruc-

tion.

obstruir [obi'ʃtrwi*] *vt* to obstruct; (*impedir*) to impede.

obtêm [obi'tẽ] *etc vb V* **obter**.

obtemperar [obitẽpe'ra*] *vt* to reply respectfully ♦ *vi*: ~ **(a algo)** to demur (at sth).

obtenção [obitẽ'sãw] (*pl* -**ões**) *f* acquisition; (*consecução*) attainment.

obtenho [ob'teɲu] *etc vb V* **obter**.

obtenível [obite'nivew] (*pl* -**eis**) *adj* obtainable.

obter [obi'te*] (*irreg: como* **ter**) *vt* to obtain, get; (*alcançar*) to gain.

obturação [obitura'sãw] (*pl* -**ões**) *f* (*de dente*) filling.

obturador [obitura'do*] *m* (*FOTO*) shutter.

obturar [obitu'ra*] *vt* to stop up, plug; (*dente*) to fill.

obtuso/a [obi'tuzu/a] *adj* (*ger*) obtuse; (*fig: pessoa*) thick, slow, dull.

obviedade [obvje'dadʒi] *f* obviousness; (*coisa óbvia*) obvious fact.

óbvio/a ['ɔbvju/a] *adj* obvious; **(é)** ~! of course!; **é o ~ ululante** it's glaringly *ou* screamingly (*col*) obvious.

OC *abr* (= *onda curta*) SW.

ocasião [oka'zjãw] (*pl* -**ões**) *f* (*oportunidade*) opportunity, chance; (*momento, tempo*) occasion, time.

ocasional [okazjo'naw] (*pl* -**ais**) *adj* chance.

ocasionar [okazjo'na*] *vt* to cause, bring about.

ocaso [o'kazu] *m* (*do sol*) sunset; (*ocidente*) the west; (*decadência*) decline.

Oceania [osja'nia] *f*: **a ~** Oceania.

oceânico/a [o'sjaniku/a] *adj* ocean *atr*.

oceano [o'sjanu] *m* ocean; **O~ Atlântico/ Pacífico/Índico** Atlantic/Pacific/Indian Ocean.

oceanografia [osjanogra'fia] *f* oceanography.

ocidental [oside'taw] (*pl* -**ais**) *adj* western ♦ *m/f* westerner.

ocidente [osi'dẽtʃi] *m* west; **o O~** (*POL*) the West.

ócio ['ɔsju] *m* (*lazer*) leisure; (*inação*) idleness.

ociosidade [osjozi'dadʒi] *f* idleness.

ocioso/a [o'sjozu/ɔza] *adj* idle; (*vaga*) unfilled.

oco/a ['oku/a] *adj* hollow, empty; (*cabeça*) empty.

ocorrência [oko'xẽsja] *f* incident, event; (*circunstância*) circumstance.

ocorrer [oko'xe*] *vi* to happen, occur; (*vir ao pensamento*) to come to mind; ~ **a alguém** to happen to sb; (*vir ao pensamento*) to occur to sb.

ocre ['ɔkri] *adj* ochre (*BRIT*), ocher (*US*) ♦ *m* ochre.

octogenário/a [oktoʒe'narju/a] *adj* eighty-year-old ♦ *m/f* octogenarian.

octogonal [oktogo'naw] (*pl* -**ais**) *adj*

octagonal.

octógono [ok'tɔgonu] *m* octagon.

ocular [oku'la*] *adj* ocular; **testemunha** ~ eye witness.

oculista [oku'liʃta] *m/f* optician.

óculo ['ɔkulu] *m* spyglass; ~**s** *mpl* glasses, spectacles; ~**s de proteção** goggles.

ocultar [okuw'ta*] *vt* to hide, conceal.

ocultas [o'kuwtaʃ] *fpl*: **às** ~ in secret.

oculto/a [o'kuwtu/a] *adj* hidden; (*desconhecido*) unknown; (*secreto*) secret; (*sobrenatural*) occult.

ocupação [okupa'sãw] (*pl* -**ões**) *f* occupation.

ocupacional [okupasjo'naw] (*pl* -**ais**) *adj* occupational.

ocupações [okupa'sõjʃ] *fpl de* **ocupação**.

ocupado/a [oku'padu/a] *adj* (*pessoa*) busy; (*lugar*) taken, occupied; (*BR*: *telefone*) engaged (*BRIT*), busy (*US*); **sinal de** ~ (*BR*: *TEL*) engaged tone (*BRIT*), busy signal (*US*).

ocupar [oku'pa*] *vt* to occupy; (*tempo*) to take up; (*pessoa*) to keep busy; ~**-se** *vr* to keep o.s. occupied; ~**-se com** *ou* **de** *ou* **em algo** (*dedicar-se a*) to deal with sth; (*cuidar de*) to look after sth; (*passar seu tempo com*) to occupy o.s. with sth; **posso** ~ **esta mesa/ cadeira?** can I take this table/chair?

ode ['ɔdʒi] *f* ode.

odiar [o'dʒja*] *vt* to hate.

odiento/a [o'dʒjẽtu/a] *adj* hateful.

ódio ['ɔdʒju] *m* hate, hatred; **que** ~**!** (*col*) I'm (*ou* was) furious!

odioso/a [o'dʒjozu/ɔza] *adj* hateful.

odontologia [odõtolo'ʒia] *f* dentistry.

odor [o'do*] *m* smell.

OEA *abr f* (= *Organização dos Estados Americanos*) OAS.

oeste ['wɛʃtʃi] *m* west ♦ *adj inv* (*região*) western; (*direção*, *vento*) westerly; **ao** ~ **de** to the west of; **em direção ao** ~ westwards.

ofegante [ofe'gãtʃi] *adj* breathless, panting.

ofegar [ofe'ga*] *vi* to pant, puff.

ofender [ofẽ'de*] *vt* to offend; ~**-se** *vr* to take offence (*BRIT*) *ou* offense (*US*).

ofensa [o'fẽsa] *f* insult; (*à lei*, *moral*) offence (*BRIT*), offense (*US*).

ofensiva [ofẽ'siva] *f* (*MIL*) offensive; **tomar a** ~ to go on to the offensive.

ofensivo/a [ofẽ'sivu/a] *adj* offensive; (*agressivo*) aggressive; ~ **à moral** morally offensive.

oferecer [ofere'se*] *vt* to offer; (*presentear*) to give; (*jantar*) to give; (*propor*) to propose; (*dedicar*) to dedicate; ~**-se** *vr* (*pessoa*) to offer o.s., volunteer; (*oportunidade*) to present o.s., arise; ~**-se para fazer** to offer to do.

oferecido/a [ofere'sidu/a] *adj* (*intrometido*) pushy.

oferecimento [oferesi'mẽtu] *m* offer.

oferenda [ofe'rẽda] *f* (*REL*) offering.

oferta [o'fɛxta] *f* (*oferecimento*) offer; (*dádiva*) gift; (*COM*) bid; (*em loja*) special

offer; **a** ~ **e a demanda** (*ECON*) supply and demand; **em** ~ (*numa loja*) on special offer.

ofertar [ofex'ta*] *vt* to offer.

office-boy [ɔfis'bɔj] (*pl* ~**s**) *m* messenger.

oficial [ofi'sjaw] (*pl* -**ais**) *adj* official ♦ *m/f* official; (*MIL*) officer; ~ **de justiça** bailiff.

oficializar [ofisjali'za*] *vt* to make official.

oficiar [ofi'sja*] *vi* (*REL*) to officiate ♦ *vt*: ~ **(algo) a alguém** to report (sth) to sb.

oficina [ofi'sina] *f* workshop; ~ **mecânica** garage.

ofício [o'fisju] *m* (*profissão*) profession, trade; (*REL*) service; (*carta*) official letter; (*função*) function; (*encargo*) job, task; **bons** ~**s** good offices; ~ **de notas** notary public.

oficioso/a [ofi'sjozu/ɔza] *adj* (*não oficial*) unofficial.

ofsete [of'setʃi] *m* offset printing.

oftálmico/a [of'tawmiku/a] *adj* ophthalmic.

oftalmologia [oftawmolo'ʒia] *f* ophthalmology.

ofuscante [ofuʃ'kãtʃi] *adj* dazzling.

ofuscar [ofuʃ'ka*] *vt* (*obscurecer*) to blot out; (*deslumbrar*) to dazzle; (*entendimento*) to colour (*BRIT*), color (*US*); (*suplantar em brilho*) to outshine ♦ *vi* to be dazzling.

ogro ['ɔgru] *m* ogre.

ogum [o'gũ] *m* *Afro-Brazilian god of war*.

oh [ɔ] *excl* oh.

oi [ɔj] *excl* oh; (*saudação*) hi; (*resposta*) yes?

oitava-de-final (*pl* **oitavas-de-final**) *f* round before the quarter finals.

oitavo/a [oj'tavu/a] *adj* eighth ♦ *m* eighth; *V tb* **quinto**.

oitenta [oj'tẽta] *num* eighty; *V tb* **cinqüenta**.

oito ['ojtu] *num* eight; **ou** ~ **ou oitenta** all or nothing; *V tb* **cinco**.

oitocentos/as [ojtu'sẽtuʃ/aʃ] *num* eight hundred; **os O**~ the nineteenth century.

ojeriza [oʒe'riza] *f* dislike; **ter** ~ **a alguém** to dislike sb.

o.k. [o'ke] *excl*, *adv* OK, okay.

olá [o'la] *excl* hello!

olaria [ola'ria] *f* (*fábrica*: *de louças de barro*) pottery; (*de tijolos*) brickworks *sg*.

oleado [o'ljadu] *m* oil cloth.

oleiro/a [o'lejru/a] *m/f* potter; (*de tijolos*) brickmaker.

óleo ['ɔlju] *m* (*lubricante*) oil; **pintura a** ~ oil painting; ~ **combustível** fuel oil; ~ **de bronzear** suntan oil; ~ **de rícino** castor oil; ~ **diesel** diesel oil.

oleoduto [oljo'dutu] *m* (oil) pipeline.

oleoso/a [o'ljozu/ɔza] *adj* oily; (*gorduroso*) greasy.

olfato [ow'fatu] *m* sense of smell.

olhada [o'ʎada] *f* glance, look; **dar uma** ~ to have a look.

olhadela [oʎa'dɛla] *f* peep.

olhar [o'ʎa*] *vt* to look at; (*observar*) to watch; (*ponderar*) to consider; (*cuidar de*) to look after ♦ *vi* to look ♦ *m* look; ~**-se** *vr* to look at o.s.; (*duas pessoas*) to look at each other; **olha!** look!; ~ **fixamente** to stare at;

~ **para** to look at; ~ **por** to look after; ~ **alguém de frente** to look sb straight in the eye; **e olha lá** (col) and that's pushing it; **olha lá o que você vai me arranjar!** careful you don't make things worse for me!; ~ **fixo** stare.

olheiras [oʎej'raʃ] fpl dark rings under the eyes.

olho ['oʎu] m (ANAT, de agulha) eye; (vista) eyesight; (de queijo) hole; ~ **nele!** watch him!; ~ **vivo!** keep your eyes open!; **a** ~ (medir, calcular etc) by eye; **a** ~ **nu** with the naked eye; **a** ~**s vistos** visibly; **abrir os** ~**s de alguém** (fig) to open sb's eyes; **andar** ou **estar de** ~ **em algo** to have one's eyes on sth; **custar/pagar os** ~**s da cara** to cost/pay the earth; **ficar de** ~ to keep an eye out; **ficar de** ~ **em algo** to keep an eye on sth; **ficar de** ~ **comprido em algo** to look longingly at sth; **passar os** ~**s por algo** to scan over sth; **pôr alguém nos** ~**s da rua** to put sb on the street; (de emprego) to fire sb; **não pregar o** ~ not to sleep a wink; **ter bom** ~ **para** to have a good eye for; **ver com bons** ~**s** to approve of; ~ **clínico** sharp ou keen eye; ~ **de lince** sharp eye; **ter** ~ **de peixe morto** to be glassy-eyed; ~**s esbugalhados** goggle eyes; ~ **grande** (fig) envy; **estar de** ~ **grande em algo** to covet sth; **ter** ~ **grande** to be envious; ~ **mágico** (na porta) peephole, magic eye; ~ **roxo** black eye; ~ **por** ~ an eye for an eye; **num abrir e fechar de** ~**s** in a flash; **longe dos** ~**s, longe do coração** out of sight, out of mind; **ele tem o** ~ **maior que a barriga** his eyes are bigger than his belly.

oligarquia [oligax'kia] f oligarchy.

olimpíada [oli'piada] f: **as O**~**s** the Olympics.

olimpicamente [olĩpika'mẽtʃi] adj blissfully.

olímpico/a [o'lĩpiku/a] adj (jogos, chama) Olympic.

olival [oli'vaw] (pl **-ais**) m olive grove.

olivedo [oli'vedu] m = **olival**.

oliveira [oli'vejra] f olive tree.

olmeiro [ow'mejru] m = **olmo**.

olmo ['ɔwmu] m elm.

OLP abr f (= Organização para a Libertação da Palestina) PLO.

OM abr (= onda média) MW.

Omã [o'mã] m: **(o)** ~ Oman.

ombreira [õ'brejra] f (de porta) doorpost; (de roupa) shoulder pad.

ombro ['õbru] m shoulder; **encolher os** ~**s** ou **dar de** ~**s** to shrug one's shoulders; **chorar no** ~ **de alguém** to cry on sb's shoulder.

omeleta [ome'leta] (PT) f = **omelete**.

omelete [ome'letʃi] (BR) f omelette (BRIT), omelet (US).

omissão [omi'sãw] (pl **-ões**) f omission; (negligência) negligence; (ato de não se

manifestar) failure to appear.

omisso/a [o'misu/a] adj omitted; (negligente) negligent; (que não se manifesta) absent.

omissões [omi'sõjʃ] fpl de **omissão**.

omitir [omi'tʃi*] vt to omit; ~**-se** vr to fail to appear.

OMM abr f (= Organização Meteorológica Mundial) WMO.

omnipotente etc [omnipo'tẽtə] (PT) = **onipotente** etc.

omnipresente [omnipre'zẽtə] (PT) adj = **onipresente**.

omnisciente [omni'sjẽtə] (PT) adj = **onisciente**.

omnivoro/a [om'nivoru/a] (PT) adj = **onivoro**.

omoplata [omo'plata] f shoulder blade.

OMS abr f (= Organização Mundial da Saúde) WHO.

ON abr (COM: de ações) = **ordinária nominativa**.

onça ['õsa] f (peso) ounce; (animal) jaguar; **ser do tempo da** ~ to be as old as the hills; **ficar uma** ou **virar** ~ (col) to get furious; **estou numa** ~ **danada** (col) I'm flat broke.

onça-parda (pl **onças-pardas**) f puma.

onda ['õda] f wave; (moda) fashion; (confusão) commotion; ~ **sonora/luminosa** sound/light wave; ~ **curta/média/longa** short/medium/long wave; ~ **de calor** heat wave; **pegar** ~ to go surfing; **ir na** ~ (col) to follow the crowd; **ir na** ~ **de alguém** (col) to be taken in by sb; **estar na** ~ to be in fashion; **fazer** ~ (col) to make a fuss; **deixa de** ~**!** (col) cut the crap!; **isso é** ~ **dela** (col) that's just something she's made up; **tirar uma** ~ **de algo** to act like sth.

onde ['õdʒi] adv where ♦ conj where, in which; **de** ~ **você é?** where are you from?; **por** ~ through which; **por** ~**?** which way?; ~ **quer que** wherever; **não ter** ~ **cair morto** (fig) to have nothing to call one's own; **fazer por** ~ to work for it.

ondeado/a [õ'dʒjadu/a] adj wavy ♦ m (de cabelo) wave.

ondeante [õ'dʒjãtʃi] adj waving, undulating.

ondear [õ'dʒja*] vt to wave ♦ vi to wave; (água) to ripple; (serpear) to meander, wind.

ondulação [õdula'sãw] (pl **-ões**) f undulation.

ondulado/a [õdu'ladu/a] adj wavy.

ondulante [õdu'lãtʃi] adj wavy.

onerar [one'ra*] vt to burden; (COM) to charge.

oneroso/a [one'rozu/ɔza] adj onerous; (dispendioso) costly.

ônibus ['onibuʃ] (BR) m inv bus; **ponto de** ~ bus-stop.

onipotência [onipo'tẽsja] f omnipotence.

onipotente [onipo'tẽtʃi] adj omnipotent.

onipresente [onipre'zẽtʃi] adj omnipresent, ever-present.

NB: European Portuguese adds the following consonants to certain words: **b** (sú(b)dito, su(b)til); **c** (a(c)ção, a(c)cionista, a(c)to); **m** (inde(m)ne); **p** (ado(p)ção, ado(p)tar); for further details see p. xiii.

onírico/a [o'niriku/a] *adj* dreamlike.
onisciente [oni'sjẽtʃi] *adj* omniscient.
onívoro/a [o'nivoru/a] *adj* omnivorous.
onomástico/a [ono'maʃtʃiku/a] *adj*: **índice** ~ index of proper names; **dia** ~ name day.
onomatopéia [onomato'pɛja] *f* onomatopoeia.
ônix ['oniks] *m* onyx.
ontem ['ŏtẽ] *adv* yesterday; ~ **à noite** last night; ~ **à tarde/de manhã** yesterday afternoon/morning.
ONU ['onu] *abr f* (= *Organização das Nações Unidas*) UNO.
ônus ['onuʃ] *m inv* onus; (*obrigação*) obligation; (*COM*) charge; (*encargo desagradável*) burden; (*imposto*) tax burden.
onze ['ŏzi] *num* eleven; *V tb* **cinco**.
OP *abr* (*COM*: *ações*) = **ordinária ao portador**.
opa ['opa] *excl* (*de admiração*) wow!; (*de espanto*) oops!; (*saudação*) hi!
opacidade [opasi'dadʒi] *f* opaqueness; (*escuridão*) blackness.
opaco/a [o'paku/a] *adj* opaque; (*obscuro*) dark.
opala [o'pala] *f* opal; (*tecido*) fine muslin.
opalino/a [opa'linu/a] *adj* bluish white.
opção [op'sãw] (*pl* **-ões**) *f* option, choice; (*preferência*) first claim, right.
open ['opẽ] *m* = **open market**.
open market [-'maxkitʃ] *m* open market.
OPEP [o'pɛpı] *abr f* (= *Organização dos Países Exportadores de Petróleo*) OPEC.
ópera ['ɔpera] *f* opera; ~ **bufa** comic opera.
operação [opera'sãw] (*pl* **-ões**) *f* operation; (*COM*) transaction.
operacional [operasjo'naw] (*pl* **-ais**) *adj* operational; (*sistema, custos*) operating.
operações [opera'sõjʃ] *fpl de* **operação**.
operado/a [ope'radu/a] *adj* (*MED*) who has (*ou* have) had an operation ♦ *m/f* person who has had an operation.
operador(a) [opera'do*(a)] *m/f* operator; (*cirurgião*) surgeon; (*num cinema*) projectionist.
operante [ope'rãtʃi] *adj* effective.
operar [ope'ra*] *vt* to operate; (*produzir*) to effect, bring about; (*MED*) to operate on ♦ *vi* to operate; (*agir*) to act, function; ~**-se** *vr* (*suceder*) to take place; (*MED*) to have an operation.
operariado [opera'rjadu] *m*: **o** ~ the working class.
operário/a [ope'rarju/a] *adj* working ♦ *m/f* worker; **classe operária** working class.
opereta [ope'reta] *f* operetta.
opinar [opi'na*] *vt* (*julgar*) to think ♦ *vi* (*dar o seu parecer*) to give one's opinion.
opinião [opi'njãw] (*pl* **-ões**) *f* opinion; **na minha** ~ in my opinion; **ser de** *ou* **da** ~ **(de) que** to be of the opinion that; **ser da** ~ **de alguém** to think the same as sb, share sb's view; **mudar de** ~ to change one's mind; ~ **pública** public opinion.
ópio ['ɔpju] *m* opium.

opíparo/a [o'piparu/a] *adj* (*formal*) splendid, lavish.
opõe [o'põj] *etc vb V* **opor**.
opomos [o'pomoʃ] *vb V* **opor**.
oponente [opo'nẽtʃi] *adj* opposing ♦ *m/f* opponent.
opor [o'po*] (*irreg*: *como* **pôr**) *vt* to oppose; (*resistência*) to put up, offer; (*objeção, dificuldade*) to raise; ~**-se** *vr*: ~**-se a** (*fazer objeção*) to object to; (*resistir*) to oppose; ~ **algo a algo** (*colocar em contraste*) to contrast sth with sth.
oportunamente [opoxtuna'mẽtʃi] *adv* at an opportune moment.
oportunidade [opoxtuni'dadʒi] *f* opportunity; **na primeira** ~ at the first opportunity.
oportunismo [opoxtu'niʒmu] *m* opportunism.
oportunista [opoxtu'niʃta] *adj, m/f* opportunist.
oportuno/a [opox'tunu/a] *adj* (*momento*) opportune, right; (*oferta de ajuda*) well-timed; (*conveniente*) convenient, suitable.
opôs [o'poʃ] *vb V* **opor**.
oposição [opozi'sãw] *f* opposition; **em** ~ **a** against; **fazer** ~ **a** to oppose.
oposicionista [opozisjo'niʃta] *adj* opposition *atr* ♦ *m/f* member of the opposition.
oposto/a [o'poʃtu/'pɔʃta] *pp de* **opor** ♦ *adj* (*contrário*) opposite; (*em frente*) facing, opposite; (*opiniões*) opposing, opposite ♦ *m* opposite.
opressão [opre'sãw] (*pl* **-ões**) *f* oppression; (*sufocação*) feeling of suffocation, tightness in the chest.
opressivo/a [opre'sivu/a] *adj* oppressive.
opressões [opre'sõjʃ] *fpl de* **opressão**.
opressor(a) [opre'so*(a)] *m/f* oppressor.
oprimido/a [opri'midu/a] *adj* oppressed ♦ *m*: **os** ~**s** the oppressed.
oprimir [opri'mi*] *vt* to oppress; (*comprimir*) to press ♦ *vi* to be oppressive.
opróbrio [o'prɔbrju] *m* (*infâmia*) ignominy; (*formal: desonra*) shame.
optar [op'ta*] *vi* to choose; ~ **por** to opt for; ~ **por fazer** to opt to do; ~ **entre** to choose between.
optativo/a [opta'tʃivu/a] *adj* optional; (*LING*) optative.
óptico/a *etc* ['ɔtʃiku/a] (*PT*) = **ótico** *etc*.
óptimo/a *etc* ['ɔtʃimu/a] (*PT*) *adj* = **ótimo** *etc*.
opulência [opu'lẽsja] *f* opulence.
opulento/a [opu'lẽtu/a] *adj* opulent.
opunha [o'puɲa] *etc vb V* **opor**.
opus [o'puʃ] *etc vb V* **opor**.
opúsculo [o'puʃkulu] *m* (*livreto*) booklet; (*pequena obra*) pamphlet.
opuser [opu'ze*] *etc vb V* **opor**.
ora ['ɔra] *adv* now ♦ *conj* well; **por** ~ for the time being; ~ ..., ~ ... one moment ..., the next ...; ~ **sim**, ~ **não** first yes, then no; ~ **essa!** the very idea!, come off it!; ~ **bem** now then; ~ **viva!** hello there!; ~, **que besteira!** well, how stupid!; ~ **bolas!** (*col*)

for heaven's sake!

oração [ora'sãw] (*pl* **-ões**) *f* (*reza*) prayer; (*discurso*) speech; (*LING*) clause.

oráculo [o'rakulu] *m* oracle.

orador(a) [ora'do*(a)] *m/f* (*aquele que fala*) speaker.

oral [o'raw] (*pl* **-ais**) *adj* oral ♦ *f* oral (exam).

orangotango [orãgu'tãgu] *m* orang-utan.

orar [o'ra*] *vi* (*REL*) to pray.

oratória [ora'tɔrja] *f* public speaking, oratory.

oratório/a [ora'tɔrju/a] *adj* oratorical ♦ *m* (*MÚS*) oratorio; (*REL*) oratory.

orbe ['ɔxbi] *m* globe.

órbita ['ɔxbita] *f* orbit; (*do olho*) socket; **entrar/colocar em** ~ to go/put into orbit; **estar em** ~ to be in orbit.

orbital [oxbi'taw] (*pl* **-ais**) *adj* orbital.

Órcades ['ɔxkadʒiʃ] *fpl*: **as** ~ the Orkneys.

orçamentário/a [oxsamẽ'tarju/a] *adj* budget *atr.*

orçamento [oxsa'mẽtu] *m* (*do estado etc*) budget; (*avaliação*) estimate; ~ **sem compromisso** estimate with no obligation.

orçar [ox'sa*] *vt* to value, estimate ♦ *vi*: ~ **em** (*gastos etc*) to be valued at, be put at; ~ **a** to reach, go up to; **ele orça por 20 anos** he is around 20; **um projeto orçado em $100** a project valued at $100.

ordeiro/a [ox'dejru/a] *adj* orderly.

ordem ['ɔxdẽ] (*pl* **-ns**) *f* order; **às suas ordens** at your service; **um lucro da** ~ **de $60 milhões** a profit in the order of $60 million; **até nova** ~ until further notice; **de primeira** ~ first-rate; **estar em** ~ to be tidy; **pôr em** ~ to arrange, tidy; **tudo em** ~? (*col*) everything OK?; **por** ~ in order, in turn; **dar/receber ordens** to give/take orders; **dar uma** ~ **na casa** to tidy the house; ~ **alfabética/cronológica** alphabetical/chronological order; ~ **bancária** banker's order; ~ **de grandeza** order of magnitude; ~ **de pagamento** (*COM*) banker's draft; ~ **de prisão** (*JUR*) prison order; ~ **do dia** agenda; **O**~ **dos Advogados** Bar Association; ~ **público** public order, law and order; ~ **social** social order.

ordenação [oxdena'sãw] (*pl* **-ões**) *f* (*REL*) ordination; (*ordem*) order; (*arrumação*) tidiness, orderliness.

ordenado/a [oxde'nadu/a] *adj* (*posto em ordem*) in order; (*metódico*) orderly; (*REL*) ordained ♦ *m* salary, wages *pl*.

ordenança [oxde'nãsa] *m* (*MIL*) orderly ♦ *f* (*regulamento*) ordinance.

ordenar [oxde'na*] *vt* to arrange, put in order; (*determinar*) to order; (*REL*) to ordain; ~**-se** *vr* (*REL*) to be ordained; ~ **que alguém faça** to order sb to do; ~ **algo a alguém** to order sth of sb.

ordenhar [oxde'ɲa*] *vt* to milk.

ordens ['ɔxdẽʃ] *fpl de* **ordem.**

ordinariamente [oxdʒinarja'mẽte] *adv* ordinarily, usually.

ordinário/a [oxdʒi'narju/a] *adj* ordinary; (*comum*) usual; (*medíocre*) mediocre; (*grosseiro*) coarse, vulgar; (*de má qualidade*) inferior; (*sem caráter*) rough; **de** ~ usually.

orégano [o'rɛganu] *m* oregano.

orelha [o'reʎa] *f* (*ANAT*) ear; (*aba*) flap; **de** ~**s em pé** (*col*) on one's guard; **endividado até as** ~**s** up to one's ears in debt; ~**s de abano** flappy ears.

orelhada [ore'ʎada] (*col*) *f*: **de** ~ through the grapevine.

orelhão [ore'ʎãw] (*pl* **-ões**) *m* open telephone booth.

órfã ['ɔxfã] *f de* **órfão.**

orfanato [oxfa'natu] *m* orphanage.

órfão/fã ['ɔxfãw/fã] (*pl* ~**s**) *m/f* orphan ♦ *adj* orphan; ~ **de pai** with no father; ~ **de** (*fig*) starved of.

orfeão [ox'fjãw] (*pl* **-ões**) *m* choral society.

orgânico/a [ox'ganiku/a] *adj* organic.

organismo [oxga'niʒmu] *m* organism; (*entidade*) organization.

organista [oxga'niʃta] *m/f* organist.

organização [oxganiza'sãw] (*pl* **-ões**) *f* organization; ~ **de caridade** charity; ~ **de fachada** front; ~ **sem fins lucrativos** nonprofit-making organization.

organizador(a) [oxganiza'do*(a)] *m/f* organiser ♦ *adj* (*comitê*) organizing.

organizar [oxgani'za*] *vt* to organize.

organograma [oxgano'grama] *m* organization chart.

órgão ['ɔxgãw] (*pl* ~**s**) *m* organ; (*governamental etc*) institution, body; ~ **de imprensa** news publication.

orgasmo [ox'gaʒmu] *m* orgasm.

orgia [ox'ʒia] *f* orgy.

orgulhar [oxgu'ʎa*] *vt* to make proud; ~**-se** *vr*: ~**-se de** to be proud of.

orgulho [ox'guʎu] *m* pride; (*arrogância*) arrogance.

orgulhoso/a [oxgu'ʎozu/ɔza] *adj* proud; (*arrogante*) haughty.

orientação [orjẽta'sãw] *f* (*direção*) direction; (*de tese*) supervision; (*posição*) position; (*tendência*) tendency; ~ **educacional** training, guidance; ~ **vocacional** careers guidance.

orientador(a) [orjẽta'do*(a)] *m/f* advisor; (*de tese*) supervisor ♦ *adj* guiding; ~ **profissional** careers advisor.

oriental [orjẽ'taw] (*pl* **-ais**) *adj* eastern; (*do Extremo Oriente*) oriental ♦ *m/f* oriental.

orientar [orjẽ'ta*] *vt* (*situar*) to orientate; (*indicar o rumo*) to direct; (*aconselhar*) to guide; ~**-se** *vr* to get one's bearings; ~**-se**

por algo to follow sth.

oriente [o'rjĕtʃi] *m*: **o O~** the East; **Extremo O~** Far East; **O~ Médio/Próximo** Middle/ Near East.

orifício [ori'fisju] *m* hole, opening.

origem [o'riʒĕ] (*pl* **-ns**) *f* origin; (*ascendência*) lineage, descent; **lugar de ~** birthplace; **pessoa de ~ brasileira/humilde** person of Brazilian origin/of humble origins; **dar ~ a** to give rise to; **país de ~** country of origin; **ter ~** to originate.

original [oriʒi'naw] (*pl* **-ais**) *adj* original; (*estranho*) strange, odd ♦ *m* original; (*na datilografia*) top copy.

originalidade [oriʒinali'dadʒi] *f* originality; (*excentricidade*) eccentricity.

originar [oriʒi'na*] *vt* to give rise to, start; **~-se** *vr* to arise; **~-se de** to originate from.

originário/a [oriʒi'narju/a] *adj* (*natural*) native; **~ de** (*proveniente*) originating from; **um pássaro ~ do Brasil** a bird native to Brazil.

oriundo/a [o'rjũdu/a] *adj* (*procedente*) arising from; (*natural*) native of.

orixá [ori'ʃa] *m* Afro-Brazilian deity.

orla ['ɔxla] *f* (*borda*) edge, border; (*de roupa*) hem; (*faixa*) strip; **~ marítima** seafront.

orlar [ox'la*] *vt*: **~ algo de algo** to edge sth with sth.

ornamentação [oxnamĕta'sãw] *f* ornamentation.

ornamental [oxnamĕ'taw] (*pl* **-ais**) *adj* ornamental.

ornamentar [oxnamĕ'ta*] *vt* to decorate, adorn.

ornamento [oxna'mĕtu] *m* adornment, decoration.

ornar [ox'na*] *vt* to adorn, decorate.

ornato [ox'natu] *m* adornment, decoration.

ornitologia [oxnitolo'ʒia] *f* ornithology.

ornitologista [oxnitolo'ʒiʃta] *m/f* ornithologist.

orquestra [ox'keʃtra] *f* orchestra; **~ de câmara/sinfônica** chamber/symphony orchestra.

orquestração [oxkeʃtra'sãw] *f* (*MÚS*) orchestration; (*fig*) harmonization.

orquestrar [oxkeʃ'tra*] *vt* (*MÚS*) to orchestrate; (*fig*) to harmonize.

orquídea [ox'kidʒja] *f* orchid.

ortodoxia [oxtodok'sia] *f* orthodoxy.

ortodoxo/a [oxto'dɔksu/a] *adj* orthodox.

ortografia [oxtogra'fia] *f* spelling.

ortopedia [oxtope'dʒia] *f* orthopaedics *sg* (*BRIT*), orthopedics *sg* (*US*).

ortopédico/a [oxto'pɛdʒiku/a] *adj* orthopaedic (*BRIT*), orthopedic (*US*).

ortopedista [oxtope'dʒiʃta] *m/f* orthopaedic (*BRIT*) *ou* orthopedic (*US*) specialist.

orvalhar [ox'vaʎa*] *vt* to sprinkle with dew.

orvalho [ox'vaʎu] *m* dew.

os [uʃ] *art def V* **o**.

Osc. *abr* (= *oscilação*) *change in price from previous day.*

oscilação [osila'sãw] (*pl* **-ões**) *f* (*movimento*) oscillation; (*flutuação*) fluctuation; (*hesitação*) hesitation.

oscilante [osi'lãtʃi] *adj* oscillating; (*fig*: *hesitante*) hesitant.

oscilar [osi'la*] *vi* (*balançar-se*) to sway, swing; (*variar*) to fluctuate; (*hesitar*) to hesitate.

ossatura [osa'tura] *f* skeleton, frame.

ósseo/a ['ɔsju/a] *adj* bony; (*ANAT*: *medula etc*) bone *atr*.

osso ['osu] *m* bone; (*dificuldade*) predicament; **um ~ duro de roer** a hard nut to crack; **~s do ofício** occupational hazards.

ossudo/a [o'sudu/a] *adj* bony.

ostensivo/a [oʃtĕ'sivu/a] *adj* ostensible, apparent; (*com alarde*) ostentatious.

ostentação [oʃtĕta'sãw] (*pl* **-ões**) *f* ostentation; (*exibição*) display, show.

ostentar [oʃtĕ'ta*] *vt* to show; (*alardear*) to show off, flaunt.

ostentoso/a [oʃtĕ'tozu/ɔza] *adj* ostentatious, showy.

osteopata [oʃtʃjo'pata] *m/f* osteopath.

ostra ['oʃtra] *f* oyster.

ostracismo [oʃtra'siʒmu] *m* ostracism.

OTAN ['otã] *abr f* (= *Organização do Tratado do Atlântico Norte*) NATO.

otário [o'tarju] (*col*) *m* fool, idiot.

OTE (*BR*) *abr f* = **Obrigação do Tesouro Estadual.**

ótica ['ɔtʃika] *f* optics *sg*; (*loja*) optician's; (*fig*: *ponto de vista*) viewpoint; *V tb* **ótico.**

ótico/a ['ɔtʃiku/a] *adj* optical ♦ *m/f* optician.

otimismo [otʃi'miʒmu] *m* optimism.

otimista [otʃi'miʃta] *adj* optimistic ♦ *m/f* optimist.

otimizar [otʃimi'za*] *vt* to optimize.

ótimo/a ['ɔtʃimu/a] *adj* excellent, splendid ♦ *excl* great!, super!

OTN (*BR*) *abr f* = **Obrigação do Tesouro Nacional.**

otorrino [oto'xinu] *m/f* ear, nose and throat specialist.

ou [o] *conj* or; **~ este ~ aquele** either this one or that one; **~ seja** in other words.

OUA *abr f* (= *Organização da Unidade Africana*) OAU.

ouço ['osu] *etc vb V* **ouvir.**

ourela [o'rela] *f* edge, border.

ouriçado/a [ori'sadu/a] (*col*) *adj* excited.

ouriçar [ori'sa*] *vt* (*col*: *animar*) to liven up; (: *excitar*) to excite; **~-se** *vr* to bristle; (*col*) to get excited.

ouriço [o'risu] *m* (*europeu*) hedgehog; (*casca*) shell; (*col*: *animação*) riot.

ouriço-cacheiro [-ka'ʃejru] (*pl* **ouriços-cacheiros**) *m* coendu.

ouriço-do-mar (*pl* **ouriços-do-mar**) *m* sea urchin.

ourives [o'riviʃ] *m/f inv* (*fabricante*) goldsmith; (*vendedor*) jeweller (*BRIT*), jeweler (*US*).

ourivesaria [oriveza'ria] *f* (*arte*) goldsmith's art; (*loja*) jeweller's (shop) (*BRIT*), jewelry store (*US*).

ouro ['oru] *m* gold; ~**s** *mpl* (*CARTAS*) diamonds; **de** ~ golden; **nadar em** ~ to be rolling in money; **valer** ~**s** to be worth one's weight in gold.

ousadia [oza'dʒia] *f* daring; (*lance ousado*) daring move; **ter a** ~ **de fazer** to have the cheek to do.

ousado/a [o'zadu/a] *adj* daring, bold.

ousar [o'za*] *vt, vi* to dare.

out. *abr* (= *Outubro*) Oct.

outdoor [awt'dɔ*] (*pl* ~**s**) *m* billboard.

outeiro [o'tejru] *m* hill.

outonal [oto'naw] (*pl* **-ais**) *adj* autumnal.

outono [o'tɔnu] *m* autumn.

outorga [o'tɔxga] *f* granting, concession.

outorgante [otox'gãtʃi] *m/f* grantor.

outorgar [otox'ga*] *vt* to grant.

outrem [o'trẽ] *pron inv* (*sg*) somebody else; (*pl*) other people.

outro/a ['otru/a] *adj* (*sg*) another; (*pl*) other ◊ *pron* another (one); ~**s** others; **o** ~ the other one; **outra coisa** something else; ~ **qualquer** any other; **de** ~ **modo, de outra maneira** otherwise; ~ **tanto** the same again; **na casa dos** ~**s** in other people's houses; **outra vez** again; **no** ~ **dia** the next day; **ela está outra** (*mudada*) she's changed; **estar em outra** (*col*) to be into something else; **em** ~ **lugar** somewhere else; **não deu outra** (*col*) that's exactly what happened.

outrora [o'trɔra] *adv* formerly.

outrossim [otro'sĩ] *adv* likewise, moreover.

outubro [o'tubru] (*PT*: **O-**) *m* October; *V tb* **julho.**

ouvido [o'vidu] *m* (*ANAT*) ear; (*sentido*) hearing; **de** ~ by ear; **dar** ~**s a** to listen to; **entrar por um** ~ **e sair pelo outro** to go in one ear and out the other; **fazer** ~**s moucos** *ou* **de mercador** to turn a deaf ear, pretend not to hear; **ser todo** ~**s** to be all ears; **ter bom** ~ **para música** to have a good ear for music; **se isso chegar aos** ~**s dele, ...** if he gets to hear about it, ...

ouvinte [o'vĩtʃi] *m/f* listener; (*estudante*) auditor.

ouvir [o'vi*] *vt* to hear; (*com atenção*) to listen to; (*missa*) to attend ◊ *vi* to hear; to listen; (*levar descompostura*) to catch it; ~ **dizer que** ... to hear that ...; ~ **falar de** to hear of.

ova ['ɔva] *f* roe; **uma** ~**!** (*col*) my eye!, no way!

ovação [ova'sãw] (*pl* **-ões**) *f* ovation, acclaim.

ovacionar [ovasjo'na*] *vt* to acclaim; (*pessoa no palco*) to give a standing ovation to.

ovações [ova'sõjʃ] *fpl de* **ovação.**

oval [o'vaw] (*pl* **-ais**) *adj, f* oval.

ovalado/a [ova'ladu/a] *adj* oval.

ovário [o'varju] *m* ovary.

ovelha [o'veʎa] *f* sheep; ~ **negra** (*fig*) black sheep.

over ['ove*] *m* overnight market ◊ *adj* overnight.

overnight [ovex'najtʃi] *m, adj* = **over.**

óvni ['ɔvni] *m* UFO.

ovo ['ovu] *m* egg; ~**s cozidos duros** hard-boiled eggs; ~**s escaldados** (*PT*) *ou* **pochê** (*BR*) poached eggs; ~**s estrelados** *ou* **fritos** fried eggs; ~**s mexidos** scrambled eggs; ~**s quentes** soft-boiled eggs; ~**s de granja** free-range eggs; ~ **de Páscoa** Easter egg; **estar/ acordar de** ~ **virado** (*col*) to be/wake up in a bad mood; **pisar em** ~**s** (*fig*) to tread carefully; **ser um** ~ (*apartamento etc*) to be a shoebox.

ovulação [ovula'sãw] *f* ovulation.

óvulo ['ɔvulu] *m* egg, ovum.

oxalá [oʃa'la] *excl* let's hope ...; ~ **a situação melhore em breve** let's hope the situation improves soon.

oxidação [oksida'sãw] *f* (*QUÍM*) oxidation; (*ferrugem*) rusting.

oxidado/a [oksi'dadu/a] *adj* rusty; (*QUÍM*) oxidized.

oxidar [oksi'da*] *vt* to rust; (*QUÍM*) to oxidize; ~**-se** *vr* to rust, go rusty; to oxidize.

óxido ['ɔksidu] *m* oxide; ~ **de carbono** carbon monoxide.

oxigenado/a [oksiʒe'nadu/a] *adj* (*cabelo*) bleached; (*QUÍM*) oxygenated; **água oxigenada** peroxide; **uma loura oxigenada** a peroxide blonde.

oxigenar [oksiʒe'na*] *vt* to oxygenate; (*cabelo*) to bleach.

oxigênio [oksi'ʒenju] *m* oxygen.

oxum [o'ʃũ] *m Afro-Brazilian river god.*

ozônio [o'zonju] *m* ozone; **camada de** ~ ozone layer.

P

P, p [pe] (*pl* **ps**) *m* P, p; **P de Pedro** P for Peter.

P. *abr* (= *Praça*) Sq.; = **Padre.**

p. *abr* (= *página*) p.; (= *parte*) pt; = **por;** = **próximo.**

p/ *abr* = **para.**

PA *abr* = **Pará** ◊ *abr* (*COM*: *de ações*) = **preferencial, classe A.**

p.a. *abr* (= *por ano*) p.a.

pá [pa] *f* shovel; (*de remo, hélice*) blade; (*de moinho*) sail ♦ *m* (*PT*) pal, mate; ~ **de lixo** dustpan; ~ **mecânica** bulldozer; **uma** ~ **de lots of; da** ~ **virada** (*col*) wild.

paca ['paka] *f* (*ZOOL*) paca ♦ *m/f* fool ♦ *adj* stupid ♦ *adv* (*col*): **'tá quente** ~ it's bloody hot.

pacatez [paka'teʒ] *f* (*de pessoa*) quietness; (*de lugar, vida*) peacefulness.

pacato/a [pa'katu/a] *adj* (*pessoa*) quiet; (*lugar*) peaceful.

pachorra [pa'ʃoxa] *f* phlegm, impassiveness; **ter a** ~ **de fazer** to have the gall to do.

pachorrento/a [paʃo'xētu/a] *adj* slow, sluggish.

paciência [pa'sjēsja] *f* patience; (*CARTAS*) patience; **ter** ~ to be patient; ~! we'll (*ou* you'll *etc*) just have to put up with it!; **perder a** ~ to lose one's patience.

paciente [pa'sjētʃi] *adj, m/f* patient.

pacificação [pasifika'sãw] *f* pacification.

pacificador(a) [pasifika'do*(a)] *adj* calming ♦ *m/f* peacemaker.

pacificar [pasifi'ka*] *vt* to pacify, calm (down); ~**-se** *vr* to calm down.

pacífico/a [pa'sifiku/a] *adj* (*pessoa*) peaceloving; (*aceito sem discussão*) undisputed; (*sossegado*) peaceful; **(Oceano) P~** Pacific Ocean; **ponto** ~ undisputed point.

pacifismo [pasi'fiʒmu] *m* pacifism.

pacifista [pasi'fiʃta] *m/f* pacifist.

paço ['pasu] *m* palace; (*fig*) court.

paçoca [pa'sɔka] *f* (*doce*) peanut fudge; (*fig: misturada*) jumble, hotchpotch; (: *coisa amassada*) crumpled mess.

pacote [pa'kɔtʃi] *m* packet; (*embrulho*) parcel; (*ECON, COMPUT, TURISMO*) package.

pacto ['paktu] *m* pact; (*ajuste*) agreement; ~ **de não-agressão** non-aggression treaty; ~ **de sangue** blood pact; **P~ de Varsóvia** Warsaw Pact.

pactuar [pak'twa*] *vt* to agree on ♦ *vi* : ~ **(com)** to make a pact *ou* an agreement with.

padaria [pada'ria] *f* bakery, baker's (shop).

padecer [pade'se*] *vt* to suffer; (*suportar*) to put up with, endure ♦ *vi*: ~ **de** to suffer from.

padecimento [padesi'mētu] *m* suffering; (*dor*) pain.

padeiro [pa'dejru] *m* baker.

padiola [pa'dʒɔla] *f* stretcher.

padrão [pa'drãw] (*pl* **-ões**) *m* standard; (*medida*) gauge; (*desenho*) pattern; (*fig: modelo*) model; ~ **de vida** standard of living.

padrasto [pa'draʃtu] *m* stepfather.

padre ['padri] *m* priest; **O Santo P~** the Holy Father.

padrinho [pa'driɲu] *m* (*REL*) godfather; (*de noivo*) best man; (*fig*) sponsor; (*paraninfo*) guest of honour.

padroeiro/a [pa'drwejru/a] *m/f* patron; (*santo*) patron saint.

padrões [pa'drõjʃ] *mpl de* **padrão**.

padronização [padroniza'sãw] *f* standardization.

padronizado/a [padroni'zadu/a] *adj* standardized, standard.

padronizar [padroni'za*] *vt* to standardize.

pães [pãjʃ] *mpl de* **pão**.

paetê [pae'te] *m* sequin.

pág. *abr* (= *página*) p.

paga ['paga] *f* payment; (*salário*) pay; **em** ~ **de** in return for.

pagã [pa'gã] *f de* **pagão**.

pagador(a) [paga'do*(a)] *adj* paying ♦ *m/f* (*quem paga*) payer; (*de salário*) pay clerk; (*de banco*) teller.

pagadoria [pagado'ria] *f* payment office.

pagamento [paga'mētu] *m* payment; ~ **a prazo** *ou* **em prestações** payment in install(l)ments; ~ **à vista** cash payment; ~ **contra entrega** (*COM*) COD, cash on delivery.

pagão/gã [pa'gãw/gã] (*pl* ~**s**/~**s**) *adj, m/f* pagan.

pagar [pa'ga*] *vt* to pay; (*compras, pecados*) to pay for; (*o que devia*) to pay back; (*retribuir*) to repay ♦ *vi* to pay; ~ **por algo** (*tb fig*) to pay for sth; ~ **a prestações** to pay in install(l)ments; ~ **à vista** (*PT* **a pronto**) to pay on the spot, pay at the time of purchase; ~ **de contado** (*PT*) to pay cash; **a** ~ unpaid; ~ **caro** (*fig*) to pay a high price; ~ **a pena** to pay the penalty; ~ **na mesma moeda** (*fig*) to give tit for tat; ~ **para ver** (*fig*) to call sb's bluff, demand proof; **você me paga!** you'll pay for this!

página ['paʒina] *f* page; ~ **de rosto** frontispiece, title page; ~ **em branco** blank page.

paginação [paʒina'sãw] *f* pagination.

paginar [paʒi'na*] *vt* to paginate.

pago/a ['pagu/a] *pp de* **pagar** ♦ *adj* paid; (*fig*) even ♦ *m* pay.

pagode [pa'gɔdʒi] *m* pagoda; (*fig*) fun, high jinks *pl*; (*festa*) knees-up.

pagto. *abr* = **pagamento**.

paguei [pa'gej] *etc vb V* **pagar**.

pai [paj] *m* father; ~**s** *mpl* parents; ~ **adotivo** adoptive father; ~ **de família** family man; **um idiota de** ~ **e mãe** (*col*) a complete idiot.

pai-de-santo (*pl* **pais-de-santo**) *m* macumba priest.

pai-de-todos (*pl* **pais-de-todos**) (*col*) *m* middle finger.

pai-dos-burros (*pl* **pais-dos-burros**) (*col*) *m* dictionary.

painel [paj'nɛw] (*pl* **-éis**) *m* (*numa parede*) panel; (*quadro*) picture; (*AUTO*) dashboard; (*de avião*) instrument panel; (*reunião de especialistas*) panel (of experts).

paio ['paju] *m* pork sausage.

paiol [pa'jɔw] (*pl* **-óis**) *m* storeroom; (*celeiro*) barn; (*de pólvora*) powder magazine; ~ **de carvão** coal bunker.

pairar [paj'ra*] *vi* to hover; (*embarcação*) to lie to.

país [pa'jiʃ] *m* country; (*região*) land; ~

encantado fairyland; ~ **natal** native land.
paisagem [paj'zaʒẽ] (pl -**ns**) f scenery, landscape; (pintura) landscape.
paisano/a [paj'zanu/a] adj civilian ♦ m/f (não militar) civilian; (compatriota) fellow countryman; **à paisana** (soldado) in civvies; (policial) in plain clothes.
Países Baixos mpl: **os** ~ the Netherlands.
paixão [paj'ʃãw] (pl -ões) f passion.
paixonite [pajʃo'nitʃi] (col) f: ~ (**aguda**) crush, infatuation.
pajé [pa'ʒɛ] m medicine man.
pajear [pa'ʒja*] vt (cuidar) to look after; (paparicar) to mollycoddle.
pajem ['paʒẽ] (pl -**ns**) m (moço) page.
pala ['pala] f (de boné) peak; (em automóvel) sun visor; (de vestido) yoke; (de sapato) strap; (col: dica) tip.
palacete [pala'setʃi] m small palace.
palácio [pa'lasju] m palace; ~ **da justiça** courthouse; ~ **real** royal palace.
paladar [pala'da*] m taste; (ANAT) palate.
paladino [pala'dʒinu] m (medieval, fig) champion.
palafita [pala'fita] f (estacaria) stilts pl; (habitação) stilt house.
palanque [pa'lãki] m (estrado) stand.
palatável [pala'tavew] (pl -**eis**) adj palatable.
palato [pa'latu] m palate.
palavra [pa'lavra] f word; (fala) speech; (promessa) promise; (direito de falar) right to speak; ~! honestly!; **pessoa de/sem** ~ reliable/unreliable person; **em outras** ~**s** in other words; **em poucas** ~**s** briefly; **cumprir a/faltar com a** ~ to keep/break one's word; **dar a** ~ **a alguém** to give sb the chance to speak; **não dar uma** ~ not to say a word; **dirigir a** ~ **a** to address; **estar com a** ~ **na boca** to have the word on the tip of one's tongue; **pedir a** ~ to ask permission to speak; **ter** ~ (pessoa) to be reliable; **tirar a** ~ **da boca de alguém** to take the words right out of sb's mouth; **tomar a** ~ to take the floor; **a última** ~ (tb fig) the last word; ~ **de honra** word of honour; ~ **de ordem** watchword, formula; ~**s cruzadas** crossword (puzzle) sg.
palavra-chave (pl **palavras-chaves**) f key word.
palavrão [pala'vrãw] (pl -ões) m (obsceno) swearword.
palavreado [pala'vrjadu] m babble, gibberish; (loquacidade) smooth talk.
palavrões [pala'vrójʃ] mpl de **palavrão**.
palco ['palku] m (TEATRO) stage; (fig: local) scene.
paleontologia [paljõtolo'ʒia] f palaeontology (BRIT), paleontology (US).
palerma [pa'lɛrma] adj silly, stupid ♦ m/f fool.
Palestina [paleʃ'tʃina] f: **a** ~ Palestine.

palestino/a [paleʃ'tʃinu/a] adj, m/f Palestinian.
palestra [pa'lɛʃtra] f (conversa) chat, talk; (conferência) lecture, talk.
palestrar [paleʃ'tra*] vi to chat, talk.
paleta [pa'leta] f palette.
paletó [pale'tɔ] m jacket; **abotoar o** ~ (col) to kick the bucket.
palha ['paʎa] f straw; **chapéu de** ~ straw hat; **não mexer ou levantar uma** ~ (col) not to lift a finger.
palhaçada [paʎa'sada] f (ato, dito) joke; (cena) farce.
palhaço [pa'ʎasu] m clown.
palheiro [pa'ʎejru] m hayloft; (monte de feno) haystack.
palheta [pa'ʎeta] f (de veneziana) slat; (de turbina) blade; (de pintor) palette.
palhoça [pa'ʎɔsa] f thatched hut.
paliar [pa'lja*] vt (disfarçar) to disguise, gloss over; (atenuar) to mitigate, extenuate.
paliativo/a [palja'tʃivu/a] adj palliative.
paliçada [pali'sada] f fence; (militar) stockade; (para torneio) enclosure.
palidez [pali'deʒ] f paleness.
pálido/a ['palidu/a] adj pale.
pálio ['palju] m canopy.
palitar [pali'ta*] vt to pick ♦ vi to pick one's teeth.
paliteiro [pali'tejru] m toothpick holder.
palito [pa'litu] m stick; (para os dentes) toothpick; (pessoa) beanpole; (perna) pin.
palma ['pawma] f (folha) palm leaf; (da mão) palm; **bater** ~**s** to clap; **conhecer algo como a** ~ **da mão** to know sth like the back of one's hand; **trazer alguém nas** ~**s da mão** (fig) to pamper sb.
palmada [paw'mada] f slap.
palmatória [pawma'tɔrja] f: ~ **do mundo** self-righteous person; V tb **mão**.
palmeira [paw'mejra] f palm tree.
palmilha [paw'miʎa] f inner sole.
palmilhar [pawmi'ʎa*] vt, vi to walk.
palmito [paw'mitu] m palm heart.
palmo ['pawmu] m (hand) span; ~ **a** ~ inch by inch; **não enxerga um** ~ **adiante do nariz** he can't see further than the nose on his face.
palpável [paw'pavew] (pl -**eis**) adj tangible; (fig) obvious.
pálpebra ['pawpebra] f eyelid.
palpitação [pawpita'sãw] (pl -ões) f beating, throbbing; **palpitações** fpl palpitations.
palpitante [pawpi'tãtʃi] adj beating, throbbing; (fig: emocionante) thrilling; (: de interesse atual) sensational.
palpitar [pawpi'ta*] vi (coração) to beat; (comover-se) to shiver; (dar palpite) to stick one's oar in.
palpite [paw'pitʃi] m (intuição) hunch; (em

NB: European Portuguese adds the following consonants to certain words: **b** (sú(b)dito, su(b)til); **c** (a(c)ção, a(c)cionista, a(c)to); **m** (inde(m)ne); **p** (ado(p)ção, ado(p)tar); for further details see p. xiii.

jogo, turfe) tip; (*opinião*) opinion; **dar ~ to** give one's two cents' worth, stick one's oar in.

palpiteiro/a [pawpi'tejru/a] *adj* meddling ♦ *m/f* meddler.

palude [pa'ludʒi] *m* marsh, swamp.

paludismo [palu'dʒiʒmu] *m* malaria.

palustre [pa'luʃtri] *adj* (*terra*) marshy; (*aves*) marsh-dwelling.

pamonha [pa'moɲa] *m/f* nitwit ♦ *adj* idiotic.

pampa ['pãpa] *f* pampas; **às ~s** (+ *n*) (*col*) loads of; (+ *adj, adv*) really.

panaca [pa'naka] *m/f* fool ♦ *adj* stupid.

panacéia [pana'sɛja] *f* panacea.

Panamá [pana'ma] *m*: **o ~** Panama.

panamenho/a [pana'mɛɲu/a] *adj, m/f* Panamanian.

pan-americano/a [pan-] *adj* Pan-American.

pança ['pãsa] *f* belly, paunch.

pancada [pã'kada] *f* (*no corpo*) blow, hit; (*choque*) knock; (*relógio*) stroke ♦ *m/f* (*col*) loony ♦ *adj* crazy; **~ d'água** downpour; **dar uma ~ com a cabeça** to bang one's head; **dar ~ em alguém** to hit sb; **levar uma ~** to get hit.

pancadaria [pãkada'ria] *f* (*surra*) beating; (*tumulto*) fight.

pâncreas ['pãkrjaʃ] *m inv* pancreas.

pançudo/a [pã'sudu/a] *adj* fat, potbellied.

panda ['pãda] *f* panda.

pandarecos [pãda'rɛkuʃ] *mpl*: **em ~** in pieces; (*fig: exausto*) worn out; (: *moralmente*) devastated.

pândega ['pãdega] *f* merrymaking, good time.

pândego/a ['pãdegu/a] *adj* (*farrista*) merrymaking; (*engraçado*) jolly ♦ *m/f* (*farrista*) merrymaker; (*pessoa engraçada*) joker.

pandeiro [pã'dejru] *m* tambourine.

pandemônio [pãde'monju] *m* pandemonium.

pane ['pani] *f* breakdown.

panegírico [pane'ʒiriku] *m* panegyric.

panejar [pane'ʒa*] *vi* to flap.

panela [pa'nɛla] *f* (*de barro*) pot; (*de metal*) pan; (*de cozinhar*) saucepan; (*no dente*) large cavity, hole; **~ de pressão** pressure cooker.

panelinha [pane'liɲa] *f* clique.

panfletar [pãfle'ta*] *vi* to distribute pamphlets.

panfleto [pã'fletu] *m* pamphlet.

pangaré [pãga'rɛ] *m* (*cavalo*) nag.

pânico ['paniku] *m* panic; **em ~** panic-stricken; **entrar em ~** to panic.

panificação [panifika'sãw] *f* (*fabricação*) bread-making; (*padaria*) bakery.

panificadora [panifika'dora] *f* baker's.

pano ['panu] *m* cloth; (*TEATRO*) curtain; (*largura de tecido*) width; (*vela*) sheet, sail; **~ de chão** floorcloth; **~ de pratos** tea-towel; **~ de pó** duster; **~ de fundo** (*tb fig*) backdrop; **a todo o ~** at full speed; **por baixo do ~** (*fig*) under the counter; **dar ~ para mangas** (*fig*) to give food for thought; **pôr**

~s quentes em algo (*fig*) to dampen sth down.

panorama [pano'rama] *m* (*vista*) view; (*fig: observação*) survey.

panorâmica [pano'ramika] *f* (*exposição*) survey.

panorâmico/a [pano'ramiku/a] *adj* panoramic.

panqueca [pã'kɛka] *f* pancake.

pantalonas [pãta'lonaʃ] *fpl* baggy trousers.

pantanal [pãta'naw] (*pl* **-ais**) *m* swampland.

pântano ['pãtanu] *m* marsh, swamp.

pantanoso/a [pãta'nozu/ɔza] *adj* marshy, swampy.

panteão [pã'tjãw] (*pl* **-ões**) *m* pantheon.

pantera [pã'tɛra] *f* panther.

pantomima [pãto'mima] *f* pantomime.

pantufa [pã'tufa] *f* slipper.

pão [pãw] (*pl* **pães**) *m* bread; **o P~ de Açúcar** (*no Rio*) Sugarloaf Mountain; **~ de carne** meat loaf; **~ de centeio** rye bread; **~ de fôrma** sliced loaf; **~ caseiro** home-made bread; **~ francês** French bread; **~ integral** wholemeal (*BRIT*) *ou* wholewheat (*US*) bread; **~ preto** black bread; **~ torrado** toast; **ganhar o ~** to earn a living; **~ dormido** dayold bread; **dizer ~, ~, queijo, queijo** (*col*) to call a spade a spade, pull no punches; **comer o ~ que o diabo amassou** (*fig*) to have it tough; **tirar o ~ da boca de alguém** (*fig*) to take the food out of sb's mouth.

pão-de-ló [-lɔ] *m* sponge cake.

pão-durismo [-du'riʒmu] (*col*) *m* meanness, stinginess.

pão-duro (*pl* **pães-duros**) (*col*) *adj* mean, stingy ♦ *m/f* miser.

pãozinho [pãw'ziɲu] *m* roll.

papa ['papa] *m* Pope; (*fig*) spiritual leader ♦ *f* mush, pap; (*mingau*) porridge; **não ter ~s na língua** to be outspoken, not to mince one's words.

papada [pa'pada] *f* double chin.

papagaiada [papagaj'ada] (*col*) *f* showing off.

papagaio [papa'gaju] *m* parrot; (*pipa*) kite; (*COM*) accommodation bill; (*AUTO*) provisional licence (*BRIT*), student driver's license (*US*) ♦ *excl* (*col*) heavens!

papai [pa'paj] *m* dad, daddy; **P~ Noel** Santa Claus, Father Christmas; **o ~ aqui** (*col*) yours truly.

papal [pa'paw] (*pl* **-ais**) *adj* papal.

papa-moscas *f inv* (*BIO*) flycatcher.

papar [pa'pa*] (*col*) *vt, vi* (*comer*) to eat; (*extorquir*): **~ algo a alguém** to get sth out of sb.

paparicar [papari'ka*] *vt* to pamper.

paparicos [papa'rikuʃ] *mpl* (*mimos*) pampering *sg*.

papear [pa'pja*] *vi* to chat.

papel [pa'pɛw] (*pl* **-éis**) *m* paper; (*no teatro*) part, role; (*função*) role; **fazer o ~ de** to play the part of; **fazer ~ de idiota** *etc* to play the fool *etc*; **~ aéreo** airmail paper; **~ celofane** cling film; **~ crepom** crêpe paper;

~ **de embrulho** wrapping paper; ~ **de escrever/de alumínio** writing paper/tinfoil; ~ **higiênico** toilet paper; ~ **de parede** wallpaper; ~ **de seda/transparente** tissue paper/ tracing paper; ~ **laminado** *ou* **lustroso** coated paper; ~ **ofício** foolscap; ~ **pardo** brown paper; ~ **timbrado** headed paper; ~ **usado** waste paper; ~ **yes** ® tissue, kleenex ®; **ficar no** ~ *(fig)* to stay on the drawing board; **pôr no** ~ to put down on paper *ou* in writing; **de** ~ **passado** officially.

papelada [pape'lada] *f* pile of papers; *(burocracia)* paperwork, red tape.

papelão [pape'lãw] *m* cardboard; *(fig)* fiasco; **fazer um** ~ to make a fool of o.s.

papelaria [papela'ria] *f* stationer's (shop).

papel-carbono *m* carbon paper.

papeleta [pape'leta] *f* *(cartaz)* notice; *(papel avulso)* piece of paper; *(MED)* chart.

papel-moeda *(pl* **papéis-moeda(s))** *m* paper money, banknotes *pl*.

papel-pergaminho *m* parchment.

papelzinho [papew'ziɲu[*m* scrap of paper.

papiro [pa'piru] *m* papyrus.

papo ['papu] *m (de ave)* crop; *(col: de pessoa)* double chin; *(: conversa)* chat; *(: chute)* hot air; *(numa roupa)* tuck; **ele é um bom** ~ *(col)* he's a good talker; **bater** *ou* **levar um** ~ *(col)* to have a chat; **ficar de** ~ **para o ar** *(fig)* to laze around; ~ **firme** *(col: verdade)* gospel (truth); *(: pessoa)* straight talker; ~ **furado** *(col: promessa)* hot air; *(: conversa)* idle chat.

papo-de-anjo *(pl* **papos-de-anjo)** *m sweet made of egg yolks*.

papo-firme *(pl* **papos-firmes)** *(col)* adj reliable ♦ *m/f* reliable sort.

papo-furado *(pl* **papos-furados)** *(col)* adj unreliable ♦ *m/f*: **ele é um** ~ he never comes up with the goods.

papoula [pa'pola] *f* poppy.

páprica ['paprika] *f* paprika.

Papua Nova Guiné [pa'pua-] *f* Papua New Guinea.

papudo/a [pa'pudu/a] *adj* fat in the face, double-chinned.

paqueração [pakera'sãw] *(col: pl* **-ões)** *f* pick-up.

paquerador(a) [pakera'do*(a)] *(col)* adj flirtatious ♦ *m/f* flirt.

paquerar [pake'ra*] *(col)* *vi* to flirt ♦ *vt* to chat up.

paquete [pa'ketʃi] *m* steamship.

paquistanês/esa [pakiʃta'neʃ/eza] adj, *m/f* Pakistani.

Paquistão [pakiʃ'tãw] *m*: **o** ~ Pakistan.

par [pa*] *adj (igual)* equal; *(número)* even ♦ *m* pair; *(casal)* couple; *(pessoa na dança)* partner; ~ **a** ~ side by side, level; **ao** ~ *(COM)* at par; **sem** ~ incomparable; **abaixo**

de ~ *(COM, GOLFE)* below par; **estar/ficar a** ~ **de algo** to be/get up to date with sth.

para ['para] *prep* for; *(direção)* to, towards; **bom** ~ **comer** good to eat; ~ **não ser ouvido** so as not to be heard; ~ **que** so that, in order that; ~ **quê?** what for?, why?; **ir** ~ **São Paulo** to go to São Paulo; **ir** ~ **casa** to go home; ~ **com** *(atitude)* towards; **de lá** ~ **cá** since then; ~ **a semana** next week; **estar** ~ to be about to; **é** ~ **nós ficarmos aqui?** should we stay here?

parabenizar [parabeni'za*] *vt*: ~ **alguém por algo** to congratulate sb on sth.

parabéns [para'bẽjʃ] *mpl* congratulations; *(no aniversário)* happy birthday; **dar** ~ **a** to congratulate; **você está de** ~ you are to be congratulated.

parábola [par'rabola] *f* parable; *(MAT)* parabola.

pára-brisa ['para-] *(pl* ~**s)** *m* windscreen *(BRIT)*, windshield *(US)*.

pára-choque ['para-] *(pl* ~**s)** *m (AUTO)* bumper.

parada [pa'rada] *f* stop; *(COM)* stoppage; *(militar, colegial)* parade; *(col: coisa difícil)* ordeal; **ser uma** ~ *(col: pessoa: difícil)* to be awkward; *(: ser bonito)* to be gorgeous; **agüentar a** ~ *(col)* to stick it out; **topar a** ~ *(col)* to accept the challenge; **topar qualquer** ~ *(col)* to be game for anything; ~ **cardíaca** heart failure.

paradeiro [para'dejru] *m* whereabouts.

paradigma [para'dʒigma] *m* paradigm.

paradisíaco/a [paradʒi'ʒiaku/a] *adj (fig)* idyllic.

parado/a [pa'radu/a] *adj (pessoa: imóvel)* standing still; *(: sem vida)* lifeless; *(carro)* stationary; *(máquina)* out of action; *(olhar)* fixed; *(trabalhador, fábrica)* idle; **fiquei** ~ **uma hora no ponto de ônibus** I stood for an hour at the bus stop; **não fique aí** ~**!** don't just stand there!

paradoxal [paradok'saw] *(pl* **-ais)** *adj* paradoxical.

paradoxo [para'dɔksu] *m* paradox.

paraense [para'ẽsi] *adj* from Pará ♦ *m/f* person from Pará.

parafernália [parafex'nalja] *f (de uso pessoal)* personal items *pl*; *(equipamento)* equipment; *(tralha)* paraphernalia.

parafina [para'fina] *f* paraffin.

paráfrase [pa'rafrazi] *f* paraphrase.

parafrasear [parafra'zja*] *vt* to paraphrase.

parafusar [parafu'za*] *vt* to screw in ♦ *vi*: ~ *(meditar)* to ponder.

parafuso [para'fuzu] *m* screw; **entrar em** ~ *(col)* to get into a state; **ter um** ~ **de menos** *(col)* to have a screw loose.

paragem [pa'raʒẽ] *(pl* **-ns)** *f* stop; ~ **de eléctrico** *(PT)* tram *(BRIT)* *ou* streetcar *(US)* stop;

paragens *pl* (*lugares*) places, parts.
parágrafo [pa'ragrafu] *m* paragraph.
Paraguai [para'gwaj] *m*: **o** ~ Paraguay.
paraguaio/a [para'gwaju/a] *adj, m/f* Paraguayan.
paraíba [para'iba] (*col*) *m* (*operário*) labourer (*BRIT*), laborer (*US*) ♦ *f* (*mulher macho*) butch woman.
paraibano/a [paraj'banu/a] *adj* from Paraíba ♦ *m/f* person from Paraíba.
paraíso [para'izu] *m* paradise.
pára-lama ['para-] (*pl* ~**s**) *m* wing (*BRIT*), fender (*US*); (*de bicicleta*) mudguard.
paralelamente [paralela'mĕtʃi] *adv* in parallel; (*ao mesmo tempo*) at the same time.
paralela [para'lɛla] *f* parallel line; ~**s** *fpl* (*ESPORTE*) parallel bars.
paralelepípedo [paralele'pipedu] *m* paving stone.
paralelo/a [para'lɛlu/a] *adj* (*tb*: *COMPUT*) parallel ♦ *m* (*GEO, comparação*) parallel.
paralisação [paraliza'sãw] (*pl* **-ões**) *f* (*suspensão*) stoppage.
paralisar [parali'za*] *vt* to paralyse; (*trabalho*) to bring to a standstill; ~**-se** *vr* to become paralysed; (*fig*) to come to a standstill.
paralisia [parali'zia] *f* paralysis.
paralítico/a [para'litʃiku/a] *adj, m/f* paralytic.
paramédico/a [para'mɛdʒiku/a] *adj* paramedical.
paramentado/a [paramĕ'tadu/a] *adj* smart.
paramento [para'mĕtu] *m* (*adorno*) ornament; ~**s** *mpl* (*vestes*) vestments; (*de igreja*) hangings.
parâmetro [pa'rametru] *m* parameter.
paramilitar [paramili'ta*] *adj* paramilitary.
paranaense [parana'ẽsi] *adj* from Paraná ♦ *m/f* person from Paraná.
paraninfo [para'nifu] *m* patron; (*pessoa homenageada*) guest of honour (*BRIT*) ou honor (*US*).
paranóia [para'nɔja] *f* paranoia.
paranóico/a [para'nɔjku/a] *adj, m/f* paranoid.
paranormal [paranox'maw] (*pl* **-ais**) *adj* paranormal.
parapeito [para'pejtu] *m* (*muro*) wall, parapet; (*da janela*) windowsill.
paraplégico/a [para'plɛʒiku/a] *adj, m/f* paraplegic.
pára-quedas ['para-] *m inv* parachute; **saltar de** ~ to parachute.
pára-quedismo [parake'dʒiʒmu] *m* parachuting, sky-diving.
pára-quedista [parake'dʒiʃta] *m/f* parachutist ♦ *m* (*MIL*) paratrooper.
parar [pa'ra*] *vi* to stop; (*ficar*) to stay ♦ *vt* to stop; **fazer** ~ (*deter*) to stop; ~ **na cadeia** to end up in jail; ~ **de fazer** to stop doing.
pára-raios ['para-] *m inv* lightning conductor.
parasita [para'zita] *adj* parasitic ♦ *m* parasite.
parasitar [parazi'ta*] *vi* to sponge ♦ *vt*: ~ **alguém** to sponge off sb.

parasito [para'zitu] *m* parasite.
parceiro/a [pax'sejru/a] *adj* matching ♦ *m/f* partner.
parcela [pax'sɛla] *f* piece, bit; (*de pagamento*) instalment (*BRIT*), installment (*US*); (*de terra*) plot; (*do eleitorado etc*) section; (*MAT*) item.
parcelado/a [paxse'ladu/a] *adj* (*pagamento*) in instalments (*BRIT*) ou installments (*US*).
parcelar [paxse'la*] *vt* (*pagamento, dívida*) to schedule in instalments (*BRIT*) ou installments (*US*).
parceria [paxse'ria] *f* partnership.
parcial [pax'sjaw] (*pl* **-ais**) *adj* (*incompleto*) partial; (*feito por partes*) in parts; (*pessoa*) biased; (*POL*) partisan.
parcialidade [paxsjali'dadʒi] *f* bias, partiality; (*POL*) partisans *pl*.
parcimonioso/a [paxsimo'njozu/ɔza] *adj* parsimonious.
parco/a ['paxku/a] *adj* (*escasso*) scanty; (*econômico*) thrifty; (*refeição*) frugal.
pardal [pax'daw] (*pl* **-ais**) *m* sparrow.
pardieiro [pax'dʒjejru] *m* ruin, heap.
pardo/a ['paxdu/a] *adj* (*cinzento*) grey (*BRIT*), gray (*US*); (*castanho*) brown; (*mulato*) mulatto.
parecença [pare'sẽsa] *f* resemblance.
parecer [pare'se*] *m* (*opinião*) opinion ♦ *vi* (*ter a aparência de*) to look, seem; ~ (**com**) (*ter semelhança com*) to look like; ~**-se** *vr* to look alike, resemble each other; ~**-se com alguém** to look like sb; **ao que parece** apparently; **parece-me que** I think that, it seems to me that; **que lhe parece?** what do you think?; **parece que** it looks as if; ~ **de auditoria** (*COM*) auditors' report.
parecido/a [pare'sidu/a] *adj* alike, similar; ~ **com** like.
paredão [pare'dãw] (*pl* **-ões**) *m* (*de serra*) face.
parede [pa'redʒi] *f* wall; **imprensar** ou **pôr alguém contra a** ~ to put sb on the spot, buttonhole sb; ~ **divisória** partition wall.
paredões [pare'dõjʃ] *mpl de* **paredão**.
parelha [pa'reʎa] *f* (*de cavalos*) team; (*par*) pair.
parente/a [pa'rẽtʃi] *m/f* relative, relation; **ser** ~ **de alguém** to be related to sb.
parentela [parẽ'tɛla] *f* relations *pl*.
parentesco [parẽ'teʃku] *m* relationship; (*fig*) connection.
parêntese [pa'rẽtezi] *m* parenthesis; (*na escrita*) bracket; (*fig*: *digressão*) digression.
páreo ['parju] *m* race; (*fig*) competition; **ser um** ~ **duro** to be a hard nut to crack.
pareô [pa'rjo] *m* beach wrap.
pária ['parja] *m* pariah.
paridade [pari'dadʒi] *f* (*igualdade*) equality; (*de câmbio, remuneração*) parity; **abaixo/acima da** ~ below/above par.
parir [pa'ri*] *vt* to give birth to ♦ *vi* to give birth; (*mulher*) to have a baby.

Paris [pa'riʃ] *n* Paris.

parisiense [pari'zjẽsi] *adj*, *m/f* Parisian.

parlamentar [paxlamẽ'ta*] *adj* parliamentary ♦ *m/f* parliamentarian, MP ♦ *vi* to parley.

parlamentarismo [paxlamẽta'riʒmu] *m* parliamentary democracy.

parlamentarista [paxlamẽta'riʃta] *adj* in favo(u)r of parliamentary democracy ♦ *m/f* supporter of the parliamentary system.

parlamento [paxla'mẽtu] *m* parliament.

parmesão [paxme'zãw] *adj*: **(queijo)** ~ Parmesan (cheese).

pároco ['paroku] *m* parish priest.

paródia [pa'rɔdʒja] *f* parody.

parodiar [paro'dʒja*] *vt* (*fazer paródia de*) to parody; (*imitar*) to mimic, copy.

paróquia [pa'rɔkja] *f* (*REL*) parish; (*col: localidade*) neighbourhood (*BRIT*), neighborhood (*US*).

paroquial [paro'kjaw] (*pl* -ais) *adj* parochial.

paroquiano/a [paro'kjanu/a] *m/f* parishioner.

paroxismo [parok'siʒmu] *m* fit, attack; ~s *mpl* death throes.

parque ['paxki] *m* park; ~ **industrial** industrial estate; ~ **infantil** children's playground; ~ **nacional** national park.

parqueamento [paxkja'mẽtu] *m* parking.

parquear [pax'kja*] *vt* to park.

parreira [pa'xejra] *f* trellised vine.

parrudo/a [pa'xudu/a] *adj* muscular, well-built.

part. *abr* (= *particular*) priv.

parte ['paxtʃi] *f* part; (*quinhão*) share; (*lado*) side; (*ponto*) point; (*JUR*) party; (*papel*) role; ~ **interna** inside; **a maior** ~ **de** most of; **a maior** ~ **das vezes** most of the time; **à** ~ aside; (*separado*) separate; (*separadamente*) separately; (*além de*) apart from; **da** ~ **de alguém** on sb's part; **de** ~ **a** ~ each other; **em** ~ in part, partly; **em grande** ~ to a great extent; **em alguma/qualquer** ~ somewhere/anywhere; **em** ~ **alguma** nowhere; **por toda (a)** ~ everywhere; **por** ~s in parts; **por** ~ **da mãe** on one's mother's side; **pôr de** ~ to set aside; **tomar** ~ **em** to take part in; **dar** ~ **de alguém à polícia** to report sb to the police; **fazer** ~ **de algo** to be part of sth; **mandar alguém àquela** ~ (*col!*) to tell sb to go to hell.

parteira [pax'tejra] *f* midwife.

partição [paxtʃi'sãw] *f* splitting.

participação [paxtʃisipa'sãw] *f* participation; (*COM*) stake, share; (*comunicação*) announcement, notification.

participante [paxtʃisi'pãtʃi] *m/f* participant ♦ *adj* participating.

participar [paxtʃisi'pa*] *vt* to announce, notify of ♦ *vi*: ~ **de** *ou* **em** (*tomar parte*) to participate in, take part in; (*compartilhar*) to share in.

particípio [paxtʃi'sipju] *m* participle.

partícula [pax'tʃikula] *f* particle.

particular [paxtʃiku'la*] *adj* (*especial*) particular, special; (*privativo*, *pessoal*) private ♦ *m* particular; (*indivíduo*) individual; **em** ~ in private; ~**es** *mpl* details.

particularidade [paxtʃikulari'dadʒi] *f* peculiarity.

particularizar [paxtʃikulari'za*] *vt* (*especificar*) to specify; (*detalhar*) to give details of; ~**-se** *vr* to distinguish o.s.

particularmente [paxtʃikulax'mẽtʃi] *adv* privately; (*especialmente*) particularly.

partida [pax'tʃida] *f* (*saída*) departure; (*ESPORTE*) game, match; (*COM: quantidade*) lot; (: *remessa*) shipment; (*em corrida*) start; **dar** ~ **em** to start; **perder a** ~ to lose.

partidário/a [paxtʃi'darju/a] *adj* supporting ♦ *m/f* supporter, follower.

partido/a [pax'tʃidu/a] *adj* (*dividido*) divided; (*quebrado*) broken ♦ *m* (*POL*) party; (*em jogo*) handicap; **tirar** ~ **de** to profit from; **to-mar o** ~ **de** to side with.

partilha [pax'tʃiʎa] *f* share.

partilhar [paxtʃi'ʎa*] *vt* to share; (*distribuir*) to share out.

partir [pax'tʃi*] *vt* (*quebrar*) to break; (*dividir*) to divide, split ♦ *vi* (*pôr-se a caminho*) to set off, set out; (*ir-se embora*) to leave, depart; ~**-se** *vr* (*quebrar-se*) to break; ~ **de** (*começar*, *tomar por base*) to start from; (*originar*) to arise from; **a** ~ **de** (*starting*) from; **a** ~ **de agora** from now on, starting from now; ~ **ao meio** to split down the middle; **eu parto do princípio que ...** I am working on the principle that ...; ~ **para** (*col: recorrer a*) to resort to; ~ **para outra** (*col*) to change tack.

partitura [paxtʃi'tura] *f* score.

parto ['paxtu] *m* (child)birth; **estar em trabalho de** ~ to be in labour (*BRIT*) *ou* labor (*US*); ~ **induzido** induced labo(u)r; ~ **prematuro** premature birth.

parturiente [paxtu'rjẽtʃi] *f* woman about to give birth.

parvo/a ['paxvu/a] *adj* stupid, silly ♦ *m/f* fool, idiot.

parvoíce [pax'vwisi] *f* silliness, stupidity.

Pasart [pa'zaxtʃi] (*BR*) *abr m* = **Partido Socialista Agrário e Renovador Trabalhista**.

Páscoa ['paʃkwa] *f* Easter; (*dos judeus*) Passover; **a ilha da** ~ Easter Island.

Pasep [pa'zɛpi] (*BR*) *abr m* = **Programa de Formação do Patrimônio do Servidor Público**.

pasmaceira [paʒma'sejra] *f* (*apatia*) indolence.

pasmado/a [paʒ'madu/a] *adj* amazed, astonished.

pasmar [paʒ'ma*] *vt* to amaze, astonish; ~**-se** *vr*: ~**-se com** to be amazed at.

---

*NB: European Portuguese adds the following consonants to certain words: **b** (sú(b)dito, su(b)til); **c** (a(c)ção, a(c)cionista, a(c)to); **m** (inde(m)ne); **p** (ado(p)ção, ado(p)tar); for further details see p. xiii.*

pasmo/a ['paʒmu/a] *m* amazement ♦ *adj* astonished.
paspalhão/lhona [paʃpa'ʎãw/'ʎɔna] (*pl -ões/ ~s*) *adj* stupid ♦ *m/f* fool.
paspalho [paʃ'paʎu] *m* simpleton.
paspalhões [paʃpa'ʎõjʃ] *mpl de* **paspalhão**.
paspalhona [paʃpa'ʎɔna] *f de* **paspalhão**.
pasquim [paʃ'kĩ] (*pl -ns*) *m* (*jornal*) satirical newspaper.
passa ['pasa] *f* raisin.
passada [pa'sada] *f* (*passo*) step; **dar uma ~ em** to call in at.
passadeira [pasa'dejra] *f* (*tapete*) stair carpet; (*mulher*) ironing lady; (*PT: para peões*) zebra crossing (*BRIT*), crosswalk (*US*).
passadiço/a [pasa'dʒisu/a] *adj* passing ♦ *m* walkway; (*NÁUT*) bridge.
passado/a [pa'sadu/a] *adj* (*decorrido*) past; (*antiquado*) old-fashioned; (*fruta*) bad; (*peixe*) off ♦ *m* past; **o ano ~** last year; **bem/mal passada** (*carne*) well done/rare; **ficar ~** (*encabulado*) to be very embarrassed.
passageiro/a [pasa'ʒejru/a] *adj* (*transitório*) passing ♦ *m/f* passenger.
passagem [pa'saʒẽ] (*pl -ns*) *f* passage; (*preço de condução*) fare; (*bilhete*) ticket; **~ de nível** level (*BRIT*) ou grade (*US*) crossing; **~ de ida e volta** return ticket, round trip ticket (*US*); **~ subterrânea** underpass, subway (*BRIT*); **~ de pedestres** pedestrian crossing (*BRIT*), crosswalk (*US*); **de ~** in passing; **estar de ~** to be passing through.
passamanaria [pasamana'ria] *f* trimming.
passamento [pasa'mẽtu] *m* (*morte*) passing.
passaporte [pasa'pɔxtʃi] *m* passport.
passar [pa'sa*] *vt* to pass; (*ponte, rio*) to cross; (*exceder*) to go beyond, exceed; (*coar: farinha*) to sieve; (: *líquido*) to strain; (: *café*) to percolate; (*a ferro*) to iron; (*tarefa*) to set; (*telegrama*) to send; (*o tempo*) to spend; (*bife*) to cook; (*a outra pessoa*) to pass on; (*pomada*) to put on; (*contrabandear*) to smuggle ♦ *vi* to pass; (*na rua*) to go past; (*tempo*) to go by; (*dor*) to wear off; (*terminar*) to be over; (*ser razoável*) to pass, be passable; (*mudar*) to change; **~-se** *vr* (*acontecer*) to go on, happen; (*desertar*) to go over; (*tempo*) to go by; **~ bem** (*de saúde*) to be well; **como está passando?** how are you?; **~ a** (*questão*) to move on to; (*suj: propriedade*) to pass to; **~ a fazer** to start to do; **~ a ser** to become; **passava das dez horas** it was past ten o' clock; **ele passa dos 50 anos** he's over 50; **não ~ de** to be only; **~ na frente** to go ahead; **~ alguém para trás** to con sb; (*cônjuge*) to cheat on sb; **~ pela casa de** to call in on; **~ pela cabeça de** to occur to; **~ por algo** (*sofrer*) to go through sth; (*transitar: estrada*) to go along sth; (*ser considerado como*) to be thought of as sth; **~ por cima de algo** to overlook sth; **~ algo por algo** to put *ou* pass sth through sth; **~ sem** to do with-

out.
passarela [pasa'rɛla] *f* footbridge; (*para modelos*) catwalk.
pássaro ['pasaru] *m* bird.
passatempo [pasa'tẽpu] *m* pastime; **como ~** for fun.
passável [pa'savew] (*pl -eis*) *adj* passable, so-so, all right.
passe ['pasi] *m* (*licença*) pass; (*FUTEBOL*: *ato*) pass; (: *contrato*) contract; **~ de mágica** sleight of hand.
passear [pa'sja*] *vt* to take for a walk ♦ *vi* (*a pé*) to go for a walk; (*sair*) to go out; **~ a cavalo** (*ou de carro*) to go for a ride; **não moro aqui, estou passeando** I don't live here, I'm on holiday (*BRIT*) *ou* vacation (*US*); **mandar alguém ~** (*col*) to send sb packing.
passeata [pa'sjata] *f* (*marcha coletiva*) protest march; (*passeio*) stroll.
passeio [pa'seju] *m* walk; (*de carro*) drive, ride; (*excursão*) outing; (*calçada*) pavement (*BRIT*), sidewalk (*US*); **dar um ~** to go for a walk; (*de carro*) to go for a drive *ou* ride; **~ público** promenade.
passional [pasjo'naw] (*pl -ais*) *adj* passionate; **crime ~** crime of passion.
passista [pa'siʃta] *m/f* dancer (*in carnival parade*).
passível [pa'sivew] (*pl -eis*) *adj*: **~ de** (*dor etc*) susceptible to; (*pena, multa*) subject to.
passividade [pasivi'dadʒi] *f* passivity.
passivo/a [pa'sivu/a] *adj* passive ♦ *m* (*COM*) liabilities *pl*.
passo ['pasu] *m* step; (*medida*) pace; (*modo de andar*) walk; (*ruído dos passos*) footstep; (*sinal de pé*) footprint; **~ a ~** one step at a time; **a cada ~** constantly; **a um ~ de** (*fig*) on the verge of; **a dois ~s de** (*perto de*) a stone's throw away from; **ao ~ que** while; **apertar o ~** to hurry up; **ceder o ~ a** to give way to; **dar um ~** to take a step; **dar um mau ~** to slip up; **marcar ~** (*fig*) to mark time; **seguir os ~s de alguém** (*fig*) to follow in sb's footsteps; **~ de cágado** snail's pace.
pasta ['paʃta] *f* paste; (*de couro*) briefcase; (*de cartolina*) folder; (*de ministro*) portfolio; **~ dentifrícia** *ou* **de dentes** toothpaste; **~ de galinha** chicken pâté.
pastagem [paʃ'taʒẽ] (*pl -ns*) *f* pasture.
pastar [paʃ'ta*] *vt* to graze on ♦ *vi* to graze.
pastel [paʃ'tɛw] (*pl -éis*) *m* samosa; (*desenho*) pastel drawing ♦ *adj inv* (*cor*) pastel.
pastelão [paʃte'lãw] *m* (*comédia*) slapstick.
pastelaria [paʃtela'ria] *f* (*loja*) cake shop; (*comida*) pastry.
pasteurizado/a [paʃtewri'zadu/a] *adj* pasteurized.
pastiche [paʃ'tʃiʃi] *m* pastiche.
pastilha [paʃ'tʃiʎa] *f* (*MED*) tablet; (*doce*) pastille; (*COMPUT*) chip.
pastio [paʃ'tʃiu] *m* pasture; (*ato*) grazing.
pasto ['paʃtu] *m* (*erva*) grass; (*terreno*) pasture; **casa de ~** (*PT*) cheap restaurant,

diner.

pastor(a) [paʃ'to*(a)] *m/f* shepherd(ess) ♦ *m* (*REL*) clergyman, pastor.

pastoral [paʃto'raw] (*pl* **-ais**) *adj* pastoral.

pastorear [paʃto'rja*] *vt* (*gado*) to watch over.

pastoril [paʃto'riw] (*pl* **-is**) *adj* pastoral.

pastoso/a [paʃ'tozu/ɔza] *adj* pasty.

pata ['pata] *f* (*pé de animal*) foot, paw; (*ave*) duck; (*col: pé*) foot; **meter a** ~ to put one's foot in it.

pata-choca (*pl* **patas-chocas**) *f* lump.

patada [pa'tada] *f* kick; **dar uma** ~ to kick; (*fig: col*) to behave rudely; **levar uma** ~ (*fig*) to be treated rudely.

Patagônia [pata'gonja] *f*: **a** ~ Patagonia.

patamar [pata'ma*] *m* (*de escada*) landing; (*fig*) level.

patavina [pata'vina] *pron* nothing, (not) anything.

patê [pa'te] *m* pâté.

patente [pa'tẽtʃi] *adj* obvious, evident ♦ *f* (*COM*) patent; (*MIL: título*) commission; **altas ~s** high-ranking officers.

patentear [patẽ'tʃja*] *vt* to show, reveal; (*COM*) to patent; **~-se** *vr* to be shown, be evident.

paternal [patex'naw] (*pl* **-ais**) *adj* paternal.

paternalista [patexna'liʃta] *adj* paternalistic.

paternidade [patexni'dadʒi] *f* paternity.

paterno/a [pa'tɛxnu/a] *adj* fatherly, paternal; **casa paterna** family home.

pateta [pa'tɛta] *adj* stupid, daft ♦ *m/f* idiot.

patetice [pate'tʃisi] *f* stupidity; (*ato*, *dito*) daft thing.

patético/a [pa'tʃɛtʃiku/a] *adj* pathetic, moving.

patíbulo [pa'tʃibulu] *m* gallows *sg*.

patifaria [patʃifa'ria] *f* roguishness; (*ato*) nasty thing.

patife [pa'tʃifi] *m* scoundrel, rogue.

patim [pa'tʃĩ] (*pl* **-ns**) *m* skate; ~ **de rodas** roller skate.

patinação [patʃina'sãw] (*pl* **-ões**) *f* skating; (*lugar*) skating rink.

patinador(a) [patʃinado*(a)] *m/f* skater.

patinar [patʃi'na*] *vi* to skate; (*AUTO: derrapar*) to skid.

patinhar [patʃi'na*] *vi* (*como um pato*) to dabble; (*em lama*) to splash about, slosh.

patinete [patʃi'nɛtʃi] *f* skateboard.

patinho [pa'tʃiɲu] *m* duckling; (*carne*) leg of beef; (*urinol*) bedpan; **cair como um** ~ to be taken in.

patins [pa'tʃĩʃ] *mpl de* **patim**.

pátio ['patʃju] *m* (*de uma casa*) patio, backyard; (*espaço cercado de edifícios*) courtyard; (*de escola*) playground; (*MIL*) parade ground; ~ **de recreio** playground.

pato ['patu] *m* duck; (*macho*) drake; (*col: otário*) sucker; **pagar o** ~ (*col*) to carry the can.

patologia [patolo'ʒia] *f* pathology.

patológico/a [patolo'ʒʒiku/a] *adj* pathological.

patologista [patolo'ʒiʃta] *m/f* pathologist.

patota [pa'tɔta] *f* (*col*) gang.

patrão [pa'trãw] (*pl* **-ões**) *m* (*COM*) boss; (*dono de casa*) master; (*proprietário*) landlord; (*NÁUT*) skipper; (*col: tratamento*) sir.

pátria ['patrja] *f* homeland; **lutar pela** ~ to fight for one's country; **salvar a** ~ (*fig*) to save the day.

patriarca [pa'trjaxka] *m* patriarch.

patriarcal [patrjax'kaw] (*pl* **-ais**) *adj* patriarchal.

patrício/a [pa'trisju/a] *adj*, *m/f* patrician.

patrimonial [patrimo'njaw] (*pl* **-ais**) *adj* (*bens*) family *atr*; (*imposto*) wealth *atr*.

patrimônio [patri'monju] *m* (*herança*) inheritance; (*fig*) heritage; (*bens*) property; ~ **líquido** equity.

patriota [pa'trjɔta] *m/f* patriot.

patriótico/a [pa'trjɔtʃiku/a] *adj* patriotic.

patriotismo [patrjo'tʃiʒmu] *m* patriotism.

patroa [pa'troa] *f* (*mulher do patrão*) boss's wife; (*dona de casa*) lady of the house; (*proprietária*) landlady; (*col: esposa*) missus, wife; (: *tratamento*) madam.

patrocinador(a) [patrosina'do*(a)] *m/f* sponsor, backer ♦ *adj* sponsoring.

patrocinar [patrosi'na*] *vt* to sponsor; (*proteger*) to support.

patrocínio [patro'sinju] *m* sponsorship, backing; (*proteção*) support.

patrões [pa'trõjʃ] *mpl de* **patrão**.

patrono [pa'tronu] *m* patron; (*advogado*) counsel.

patrulha [pa'truʎa] *f* patrol.

patrulhar [patru'ʎa*] *vt*, *vi* to patrol.

pau [paw] *m* (*madeira*) wood; (*vara*) stick; (*col: briga*) punch-up; (: *cruzeiro*) cruzeiro; (*col!: pênis*) cock (!); **~s** *mpl* (*CARTAS*) clubs; ~ **a** ~ neck and neck; **a meio** ~ (*bandeira*) at half-mast; **o** ~ **comeu** (*col*) all hell broke loose; **estar/ficar** ~ **da vida** (*col*) to be/get mad; **ir ao** *ou* **levar** ~ (*em exame*) to fail; **meter o** ~ **em alguém** (*col: espancar*) to beat sb up; (: *criticar*) to run sb down; **mostrar a alguém com quantos ~s se faz uma canoa** (*fig*) to teach sb a lesson; **ser** ~ (*col: maçante*) to be a drag; **ser** ~ **para toda obra** to be a jack of all trades; **comida a dar com um** ~ tons of food; ~ **de bandeira** flagpole.

pau-a-pique *m* wattle and daub.

pau-d'água (*pl* **paus-d'água**) *m* drunkard.

pau-de-arara (*pl* **paus-de-arara**) *m* (*tortura*) upside-down torture ♦ *m/f* migrant (*from North-East*); (*pej*) North-Easterner.

pau-de-cabeleira (*pl* **paus-de-cabeleira**) *m* chaperon.

paulada [paw'lada] *f* blow (with a stick).

NB: *European Portuguese adds the following consonants to certain words:* **b** (sú(b)dito, su(b)til); **c** (a(c)ção, a(c)cionista, a(c)to); **m** (inde(m)ne); **p** (ado(p)ção, ado(p)tar); *for further details see p. xiii.*

paulatinamente [pawlatʃina'mētʃi] *adv* gradually.

paulatino/a [pawla'tʃinu/a] *adj* slow, gradual.

paulicéia [pawli'sɛja] *f*: **a P~** São Paulo.

paulificante [pawlifi'kātʃi] *adj* annoying.

paulificar [pawlifi'ka*] *vt* to annoy, bother.

paulista [paw'liʃta] *adj* from (the state of) São Paulo ♦ *m/f* person from São Paulo.

paulistano/a [pawliʃi'tanu/a] *adj* from (the city of) São Paulo ♦ *m/f* person from São Paulo.

pau-mandado (*pl* **paus-mandados**) *m* yes man.

paupérrimo/a [paw'pɛximu/a] *adj* poverty-stricken.

pausa ['pawza] *f* pause; (*intervalo*) break; (*descanso*) rest.

pausado/a [paw'zadu/a] *adj* (*lento*) slow; (*sem pressa*) leisurely; (*cadenciado*) measured ♦ *adv* (*falar*) in measured tones.

pauta ['pawta] *f* (*linha*) (guide)line; (*MÚS*) stave; (*lista*) list; (*folha*) ruled paper; (*de programa de TV*) running order; (*ordem do dia*) agenda; (*indicações*) guidelines *pl*; **sem ~** (*papel*) plain; **em ~** on the agenda.

pautado/a [paw'tadu/a] *adj* (*papel*) ruled.

pautar [paw'ta*] *vt* (*papel*) to rule; (*assuntos*) to put in order, list; (*conduta*) to regulate.

pauzinho [paw'ziɲu] *m*: **mexer os ~s** to pull strings.

pavão/voa [pa'vãw/'voa] (*pl* **-ões/~s**) *m/f* peacock/peahen.

pavê [pa've] *m* (*CULIN*) cream cake.

pavilhão [pavi'ʎãw] (*pl* **-ões**) *m* (*tenda*) tent; (*de madeira*) hut; (*no jardim*) summerhouse; (*em exposição*) pavilion; (*bandeira*) flag; **~ de isolamento** isolation ward.

pavimentação [pavimēta'sãw] *f* (*da rua*) paving; (*piso*) flooring.

pavimentar [pavimē'ta*] *vt* to pave.

pavimento [pavi'mētu] *m* (*chão, andar*) floor; (*da rua*) road surface.

pavio [pa'viu] *m* wick.

pavoa [pa'voa] *f de* **pavão**.

pavões [pa'võjʃ] *mpl de* **pavão**.

pavonear [pavo'nja*] *vt* (*ostentar*) to show off ♦ *vi* (*caminhar*) to strut; **~-se** *vr* to show off.

pavor [pa'vo*] *m* dread, terror; **ter ~ de** to be terrified of.

pavoroso/a [pavo'rozu/ɔza] *adj* dreadful, terrible.

paz [pajʒ] *f* peace; **fazer as ~es** to make up, be friends again; **estar em ~** to be at peace; **deixar alguém em ~** to leave sb alone; **ser de boa ~** to be easy-going.

PB *abr f* = **Paraíba** ♦ *abr* (*COM: de ações*) = **preferencial, classe B**.

PC *abr m* = **Partido Comunista**; = **personal computer**.

Pça. *abr* (= **Praça**) Sq.

PCB *abr m* = **Partido Comunista Brasileiro**.

PCBR *abr m* = **Partido Comunista Brasileiro Revolucionário**.

PCC *abr m* = **Partido Comunista Chinês**.

PC do B *abr m* = **Partido Comunista do Brasil**.

PCN (*BR*) *abr m* = **Partido Comunitário Nacional**.

PCUS *abr m* = **Partido Comunista da União Soviética**.

PDC (*BR*) *abr m* = **Partido Demócrata-Cristão**.

PDI (*BR*) *abr m* = **Partido Democrático Independente**.

PDS (*BR*) *abr m* = **Partido Democrático Social**.

PDT (*BR*) *abr m* = **Partido Democrático Trabalhista**.

PE *abr m* = **Pernambuco**.

pé [pɛ] *m* foot; (*da mesa*) leg; (*fig: base*) footing; (*de alface*) head; (*milho, café*) plant; **ir a ~** to walk, go on foot; **ao ~ de** near, by; **ao ~ da letra** literally; **ao ~ do ouvido** in secret; **~ ante ~** on tip-toe; **com um ~ nas costas** (*com facilidade*) standing on one's head; **estar de ~** (*festa etc*) to be on; **estar de ~ no chão** to be barefoot; **em ou de ~** standing (up); **em ~ de guerra/igualdade** on a war/an equal footing; **dar no ~** (*col*) to run away, take off; **pôr-se em ~**, **ficar de ~** to stand up; **arredar ~** to move; **bater o ~** (*fig*) to dig one's heels in; **não chegar aos ~s de** (*fig*) to be nowhere near as good as; **a água dá ~** (*NATAÇÃO*) you can touch the bottom; **ficar com o ~ atrás** to be suspicious; **ficar no ~ de alguém** to keep on at sb; **larga meu ~!** leave me alone!; **levantar-se ou acordar com o ~ direito/esquerdo** to wake up in a good mood/get out of bed on the wrong side; **meter os ~s pelas mãos** to mess up; **perder o ~** (*no mar*) to get out of one's depth; **pôr os ~s em** to set foot in; **não ter ~ nem cabeça** (*fig*) to make no sense; **ter os ~s na terra** (*fig*) to be down-to-earth, have one's feet firmly on the ground.

peão [pjãw] (*pl* **-ões**) *m* (*PT*) pedestrian; (*MIL*) foot soldier; (*XADREZ*) pawn; (*trabalhador*) farm labourer (*BRIT*) *ou* laborer (*US*).

peça ['pɛsa] *f* (*pedaço*) piece; (*AUTO*) part; (*aposento*) room; (*TEATRO*) play; (**serviço**) **pago por ~** piecework; **~ de reposição** spare part; **~ de roupa** garment; **pregar uma ~ em alguém** to play a trick on sb.

pecado [pe'kadu] *m* sin; **~ mortal** deadly sin.

pecador(a) [peka'do*(a)] *m/f* sinner, wrongdoer.

pecaminoso/a [pekami'nozu/ɔza] *adj* sinful.

pecar [pe'ka*] *vi* to sin; (*cometer falta*) to do wrong; **~ por excesso de zelo** to be over-zealous.

pechincha [pe'ʃiʃa] *f* (*vantagem*) godsend; (*coisa barata*) bargain.

pechinchar [peʃi'ʃa*] *vi* to bargain, haggle.

pechincheiro/a [peʃi'ʃejru/a] *m/f* bargain hunter.

peço ['pɛsu] *etc vb* **V** **pedir**.

peçonha [pe'sɔɲa] f poison.
pectina [pɛk'tʃina] f pectin.
pecuária [pe'kwarja] f cattle-raising.
pecuário/a [pe'kwarju/a] adj cattle atr.
pecuarista [pekwa'riʃta] m/f cattle farmer.
peculiar [peku'lja*] adj (especial) special, peculiar; (particular) particular.
peculiaridade [pekuljari'dadʒi] f peculiarity.
pecúlio [pe'kulju] m (acumulado) savings pl; (bens) wealth.
pecuniário/a [pecu'njarju/a] adj money atr, financial.
pedaço [pe'dasu] m piece; (fig: trecho) bit; **aos ~s** in pieces; **caindo aos ~s** (objeto, carro) tatty, broken-down; (casa) tumble-down; (pessoa) worn out.
pedágio [pe'daʒju] (BR) m (pagamento) toll; (posto) tollbooth.
pedagogia [pedago'ʒia] f pedagogy; (curso) education.
pedagógico/a [peda'gɔʒiku/a] adj educational, teaching atr.
pedagogo/a [peda'gogu/a] m/f educationalist.
pé-d'água (pl pés-d'água) m shower, down-pour.
pedal [pe'daw] (pl -ais) m pedal.
pedalada [peda'lada] f turn of the pedals; **dar uma ~** to pedal.
pedalar [peda'la*] vt, vi to pedal.
pedalinho [peda'liɲu] m pedalo (boat).
pedante [pe'dãtʃi] adj pretentious ♦ m/f pseud.
pedantismo [pedã'tʃiʒmu] m pretentiousness.
pé-de-atleta m athlete's foot.
pé-de-galinha (pl pés-de-galinha) m crow's foot.
pé-de-meia (pl pés-de-meia) m nest egg, savings pl.
pé-de-moleque (pl pés-de-moleque) m (doce) nut brittle; (calçamento) crazy paving.
pé-de-pato (pl pés-de-pato) m flipper.
pederneira [pedex'nejra] f flint.
pedestal [pedeʃ'taw] (pl -ais) m pedestal.
pedestre [pe'dɛʃtri] (BR) m pedestrian.
pé-de-vento (pl pés-de-vento) m gust of wind.
pediatra [pe'dʒjatra] m/f paediatrician (BRIT), pediatrician (US).
pediatria [pedʒja'tria] f paediatrics sg (BRIT), pediatrics sg (US).
pedicuro/a [pedʒi'kuru/a] m/f chiropodist (BRIT), podiatrist (US).
pedida [pe'dʒida] f: **boa ~** (col) good idea.
pedido [pe'dʒidu] m (solicitação) request; (COM) order; **a ~ de alguém** at sb's request; **~ de casamento** proposal (of marriage); **~ de demissão** resignation; **~ de desculpa** apology; **~ de informação** inquiry.
pedigree [pedʒi'gri] m pedigree.
pedinte [pe'dʒĩtʃi] m/f beggar ♦ adj begging.

pedir [pe'dʒi*] vt to ask for; (COM, comida) to order; (exigir) to demand ♦ vi to ask; (num restaurante) to order; **~ algo a alguém** to ask sb for sth; **~ a alguém que faça, ~ para alguém fazer** to ask sb to do; **~ desculpa** to apologize; **~ emprestado** to borrow; **~ $100 por algo** to ask $100 for sth; **~ alguém em casamento** ou **a mão de alguém** to ask for sb's hand in marriage, propose to sb.
pedra ['pɛdra] f stone; (rochedo) rock; (de granizo) hailstone; (de açúcar) lump; (quadro-negro) slate; **~ de amolar** grind-stone; **~ de gelo** ice cube; **~ preciosa** precious stone; **~ falsa** (MED) stone; **~ de toque** (fig) touchstone, benchmark; **doido de ~s** raving mad; **dormir como uma ~** to sleep like a log; **pôr uma ~ em cima de algo** (fig) to consider sth dead and buried; **ser de ~** (fig) to be hard-hearted; **ser uma ~ no sapato de alguém** (fig) to be a thorn in sb's side; **vir** ou **responder com quatro ~s na mão** (fig) to be aggressive; **uma ~ no caminho** (fig) a stumbling block, a hindrance.
pedrada [pe'drada] f blow with a stone; **dar ~s em** to throw stones at.
pedra-mármore f polished marble.
pedra-pomes [-pɔmiʃ] f pumice stone.
pedregal [pedre'gaw] (pl -ais) m stony ground.
pedregoso/a [pedre'gozu/ɔza] adj stony, rocky.
pedregulho [pedre'guʎu] m gravel.
pedreira [pe'drejra] f quarry.
pedreiro [pe'drejru] m stonemason.
pedúnculo [pe'dũkulu] m stalk.
pê-eme [pe'ɛmi] (pl pê-emes) f military police ♦ m/f military policeman/woman.
pé-frio (pl pés-frios) (col) m jinx.
pega [m 'pɛga, f 'pega] m (briga) quarrel ♦ f magpie; (PT: col: moça) bird; (: meretriz) tart.
pegada [pe'gada] f (de pé) footprint; (no futebol) save; **ir nas ~s de alguém** (fig) to follow in sb's footsteps.
pegado/a [pe'gadu/a] adj (colado) stuck; (unido) together; **a casa pegada** the house next door.
pega-gelo (pl pega-gelos) m ice tongs pl.
pegajoso/a [pega'ʒozu/ɔza] adj sticky.
pega-pra-capar (col) m inv scuffle.
pegar [pe'ga*] vt to catch; (selos) to stick (on); (segurar) to take hold of; (hábito, mania) to get into; (compreender) to take in; (trabalho) to take on; (estação de rádio) to pick up, get ♦ vi (aderir) to stick; (planta) to take; (moda) to catch on; (doença) to be catching; (motor) to start; (vacina) to take; (mentira) to stand up, stick; (fogueira) to catch; **~-se** vr (brigar) to have a fight, quarrel; **~ em** (começar) to start on; (segurar) to grab, pick up; **~ com** (casa) to be

next door to; ~ **a fazer** to start to do; **ir** ~ (*buscar*) to go and get; ~ **um emprego** to get a job; ~ **uma rua** to take a street; ~ **fogo a algo** to set fire to sth; ~ **3 anos de cadeia** to get 3 years in prison; ~ **alguém fazendo** to catch sb doing; **pega, ladrão!** stop thief!; ~ **no sono** to fall asleep; **ele pegou e disse ...** he upped and said ...; ~ **pegue e pague** cash and carry; ~ **bem/mal** (*col*) to go down well/badly.

pega-rapaz (*pl* ~**es**) *m* kiss curl.

pego/a ['pɛgu/a] *pp de* **pegar**.

peguei [pe'gej] *etc vb* V **pegar**.

peidar [pej'da*] (*col!*) *vi* to fart (*!*).

peido ['pejdu] (*col!*) *m* fart (*!*).

peitilho [pej'tʃiʎu] *m* shirt front.

peito ['pejtu] *m* (*ANAT*) chest; (*de ave, mulher*) breast; (*fig*) courage; **dar o** ~ **a um bebê** to breastfeed a baby; **largar o** ~ to be weaned; **meter os** ~**s** (*col*) to put one's heart into it; **no** ~ **(e na raça)** (*col*) whatever it takes; ~ **do pé** instep; **amigo do** ~ bosom pal, close friend.

peitoril [pejto'riw] (*pl* -**is**) *m* windowsill.

peitudo/a [pej'tudu/a] *adj* big-chested; (*valente*) feisty.

peixada [pej'ʃada] *f* cooked fish.

peixaria [pejʃa'ria] *f* fishmonger's.

peixe ['pejʃi] *m* fish; **P~s** *mpl* (*ASTROLOGIA*) Pisces *sg*; **como** ~ **fora d'água** like a fish out of water; **filho de** ~, **peixinho é** like father, like son; **não ter nada com o** ~ (*fig*) to have nothing to do with the matter; **vender seu** ~ (*ver seus interesses*) to feather one's nest; (*falar*) to say one's piece, have one's say.

peixeira [pej'ʃejra] *f* fishwife; (*faca*) fish knife.

peixeiro [pej'ʃejru] *m* fishmonger.

pejar-se [pe'ʒaxsi] *vr* to be ashamed.

pejo ['peʒu] *m* shame; **ter** ~ to be ashamed.

pejorativo/a [peʒora'tʃivu/a] *adj* pejorative.

pela ['pɛla] = **por** + **a**.

pelada [pe'lada] *f* football game.

pelado/a [pe'ladu/a] *adj* (*sem pele*) skinned; (*sem pêlo, cabelo*) shorn; (*nu*) naked, in the nude; (*sem dinheiro*) broke.

pelanca [pe'lãka] *f* fold of skin; (*de carne*) lump.

pelancudo/a [pelã'kudu/a] *adj* (*pessoa*) flabby.

pelar [pe'la*] *vt* (*tirar a pele*) to skin; (*tirar o pêlo*) to shear; (*col*) to fleece; ~**-se** *vr*: ~**-se por** to be crazy about, adore; ~**-se de medo** to be scared stiff.

pelas ['pɛlaʃ] = **por** + **as**.

pele ['peli] *f* (*de pessoa, fruto*) skin; (*couro*) leather; (*como agasalho*) fur (coat); (*de animal*) hide; **cair na** ~ **de alguém** (*col*) to pester sb; **arriscar/salvar a** ~ (*col*) to risk one's neck/save one's skin; **sentir algo na** ~ (*fig*) to feel sth at first hand; **estar na** ~ **de alguém** (*fig*) to be in sb's shoes; **ser** *ou* **estar** ~ **e osso** to be all skin and bone.

peleja [pe'leʒa] *f* (*luta*) fight; (*briga*) quarrel.

pelejar [pele'ʒa*] *vi* (*lutar*) to fight; (*discutir*) to quarrel; ~ **pela paz** to fight for peace; ~ **para fazer/para que alguém faça** to fight to do/to fight to get sb to do.

pelerine [pele'rini] *f* cape.

peleteiro/a [pele'tejru/a] *m/f* furrier.

peleteria [pelete'ria] *f* furrier's.

pele-vermelha (*pl* **peles-vermelhas**) *m/f* redskin.

pelica [pe'lika] *f* kid (leather).

pelicano [peli'kanu] *m* pelican.

película [pe'likula] *f* film; (*de pele*) film of skin.

pelintra [pe'lĩtra] (*PT*) *adj* shabby; (*pobre*) penniless.

pelo ['pelu] = **por** + **o**.

pêlo ['pelu] *m* hair; (*de animal*) fur, coat; **nu em** ~ stark naked; **montar em** ~ to ride bareback.

Peloponeso [pelopo'nɛzu] *m*: **o** ~ the Peloponnese.

pelos ['pɛluʃ] = **por** + **os**.

pelota [pe'lɔta] *f* ball; (*num molho*) lump; (*na pele*) bump; **dar** ~ **para** (*col*) to pay attention to.

pelotão [pelo'tãw] (*pl* -**ões**) *m* platoon, squad.

pelúcia [pe'lusja] *f* plush.

peludo/a [pe'ludu/a] *adj* hairy; (*animal*) furry.

pélvico/a ['pɛwviku/a] *adj* pelvic.

pélvis ['pɛwviʃ] *f inv* pelvis.

pena ['pena] *f* (*pluma*) feather; (*de caneta*) nib; (*escrita*) writing; (*JUR*) penalty, punishment; (*sofrimento*) suffering; (*piedade*) pity; **que** ~! what a shame!; **a duras** ~**s** with great difficulty; **sob** ~ **de** under penalty of; **cumprir** ~ to serve a term in jail; **dar** ~ to be upsetting; **é uma** ~ **que ...** it is a pity that ...; **ter** ~ **de** to feel sorry for; **valer a** ~ to be worthwhile; **não vale a** ~ it's not worth it; ~ **capital** capital punishment.

penacho [pe'naʃu] *m* plume; (*crista*) crest.

penal [pe'naw] (*pl* -**ais**) *adj* penal.

penalidade [penali'dadʒi] *f* (*JUR*) penalty; (*castigo*) punishment; **impor uma** ~ **a** to penalize.

penalizar [penali'za*] *vt* (*causar pena a*) to trouble; (*castigar*) to penalize.

pênalti ['penawtʃi] *m* (*FUTEBOL*) penalty; **cobrar um** ~ to take a penalty.

penar [pe'na*] *vt* to grieve ♦ *vi* to suffer.

penca ['pẽka] *f* bunch; **gente em** ~ lots of people.

pence ['pẽsi] *f* dart.

pendão [pẽ'dãw] (*pl* -**ões**) *m* pennant; (*fig*) banner; (*do milho*) blossom.

pendência [pẽ'dẽsja] *f* dispute, quarrel.

pendente [pẽ'dẽtʃi] *adj* (*pendurado*) hanging; (*por decidir*) pending; (*inclinado*) sloping ♦ *m* pendant; ~ **de** (*dependente*) dependent on.

pender [pẽ'de*] *vt* to hang ♦ *vi* to hang; (*estar para cair*) to sag, droop; ~ **de** (*depender de*) to depend on; (*estar pendurado*) to hang from; ~ **para** (*inclinar*) to lean towards; (*ter tendência para*) to tend towards; ~ **a** (*estar disposto a*) to be inclined to.

pendões [pẽ'dõjʃ] *mpl de* **pendão**.

pendor [pẽ'do*] *m* inclination, tendency.

pêndulo ['pẽdulu] *m* pendulum.

pendura [pẽ'dura] *f*: **estar na** ~ (*col*) to be broke.

pendurado/a [pẽdu'radu/a] *adj* hanging; (*col: compra*) on tick.

pendurar [pẽdu'ra*] *vt* to hang; (*conta*) to put on tick ♦ *vi*: ~ **de** to hang from; **não estou com dinheiro hoje, posso** ~? (*col*) I haven't got any money today, can I pay you later?

penduricalho [pẽduri'kaʎu] *m* pendant.

pendurucalho [pẽduru'kaʎu] *m* = **penduricalho**.

penedo [pe'nedu] *m* rock, boulder.

peneira [pe'nejra] *f* (*da cozinha*) sieve; (*do jardim*) riddle.

peneirar [penej'ra*] *vt* to sift, sieve ♦ *vi* (*chover*) to drizzle.

penetra [pe'nɛtra] (*col*) *m/f* gatecrasher; **entrar de** ~ to gatecrash.

penetração [penetra'sãw] *f* penetration; (*perspicácia*) insight, sharpness.

penetrante [pene'trãtʃi] *adj* (*olhar*) searching; (*ferida*) deep; (*frio*) biting; (*som, análise*) penetrating; piercing; (*dor, arma*) sharp; (*inteligência, idéias*) incisive.

penetrar [pene'tra*] *vt* to get into, penetrate; (*em segredo*) to steal into; (*compreender*) to understand ♦ *vi*: ~ **em** *ou* **por** *ou* **entre** to penetrate.

penha ['peɲa] *f* (*rocha*) rock; (*penhasco*) cliff.

penhasco [pe'ɲaʃku] *m* cliff, crag.

penhoar [pe'ɲwa*] *m* dressing gown.

penhor [pe'ɲo*] *m* pledge; **casa de** ~**es** pawnshop; **dar em** ~ to pawn.

penhora [pe'ɲɔra] *f* (*JUR*) seizure.

penhoradamente [peɲorada'mẽtʃi] *adv* gratefully.

penhorado/a [peɲo'radu/a] *adj* pawned.

penhorar [peɲo'ra*] *vt* (*dar em penhor*) to pledge, pawn; (*apreender*) to confiscate; (*fig*) to put under an obligation; **a ajuda do amigo penhorou-a bastante** she was very grateful for her friend's help.

pêni ['peni] *m* penny.

penicilina [penisi'lina] *f* penicillin.

penico [pe'niku] *m* (*col*) potty; **pedir** ~ (*col*) to chicken out.

Peninos [pe'ninuʃ] *mpl*: **os** ~ the Pennines.

península [pe'nĩsula] *f* peninsula.

peninsular [penĩsu'la*] *adj* peninsular.

pênis ['peniʃ] *m inv* penis.

penitência [peni'tẽsja] *f* (*contrição*) penitence; (*expiação*) penance.

penitenciar [penitẽ'sja*] *vt* to impose penance

on; (*crime etc*) to pay for; ~-**se** *vr* to castigate o.s.

penitenciária [penitẽ'sjarja] *f* prison; V *tb* **penitenciário**.

penitenciário/a [penitẽ'sjarju/a] *adj* prison *atr* ♦ *m/f* prisoner, inmate.

penitente [peni'tẽtʃi] *adj* repentant ♦ *m/f* penitent.

penosa [pe'noza] (*col*) *f* chicken.

penoso/a [pe'nozu/ɔza] *adj* (*assunto, tratamento*) painful; (*trabalho*) hard.

pensado/a [pẽ'sadu/a] *adj* deliberate, intentional.

pensador(a) [pẽsa'do*(a)] *m/f* thinker.

pensamento [pẽsa'mẽtu] *m* thought; (*ato*) thinking; (*mente*) thought, mind; (*opinião*) way of thinking; (*idéia*) idea.

pensante [pẽ'sãtʃi] *adj* thinking.

pensão [pẽ'sãw] (*pl* -**ões**) *f* (*pequeno hotel*) boarding house; (*comida*) board; ~ **completa** full board; ~ **de aposentadoria** (retirement) pension; ~ **alimentícia** alimony, maintenance; ~ **de invalidez** disability allowance.

pensar [pẽ'sa*] *vi* to think; (*imaginar*) to imagine ♦ *vt* to think about; (*ferimento*) to dress; ~ **em** to think of *ou* about; ~ **fazer** (*ter intenção*) to intend to do, be thinking of doing; ~ **sobre** (*meditar*) to ponder over; **pensando bem** on second thoughts; ~ **alto** to think out loud; ~ **melhor** to think better of it.

pensativo/a [pẽsa'tʃivu/a] *adj* thoughtful, pensive.

Pensilvânia [pẽsiw'vanja] *f*: **a** ~ Pennsylvania.

pensionato [pẽsjo'natu] *m* boarding school

pensionista [pẽsjo'niʃta] *m/f* pensioner; (*que mora em pensão*) boarder.

penso/a ['pẽsu/a] *adj* leaning ♦ *m* (*curativo*) dressing.

pensões [pẽ'sõjʃ] *fpl de* **pensão**.

pentágono [pẽ'tagonu] *m* pentagon; **o P**~ the Pentagon.

pentatlo [pẽ'tatlu] *m* pentathlon.

pente ['pẽtʃi] *m* comb.

penteadeira [pẽtʃja'dejra] *f* dressing table.

penteado/a [pẽ'tʃjadu/a] *adj* (*cabelo*) in place; (*pessoa*) groomed ♦ *m* hairdo, hairstyle.

pentear [pẽ'tʃja*] *vt* to comb; (*arranjar o cabelo*) to do, style; ~-**se** *vr* (*com um pente*) to comb one's hair; (*arranjar o cabelo*) to do one's hair.

Pentecostes [pẽtʃi'kɔʃtʃiʃ] *m* Whitsun.

pente-fino [pẽtʃi'finu] (*pl* **pentes-finos**) *m* fine-tooth comb.

penugem [pe'nuʒẽ] *f* (*de ave*) down; (*pêlo*) fluff.

penúltimo/a [pe'nuwtʃimu/a] *adj* last but one, penultimate.

penumbra [pe'nũbra] *f* (*ao cair da tarde*) twi-

NB: *European Portuguese adds the following consonants to certain words:* **b** (sú(b)dito, su(b)til); **c** (a(c)ção, a(c)cionista, a(c)to); **m** (inde(m)ne); **p** (ado(p)ção, ado(p)tar); *for further details see p. xiii.*

light, dusk; (sombra) shadow; (meia-luz) half-light.

penúria [pe'nurja] f poverty.

peões [pjõjʃ] mpl de **peão**.

pepino [pe'pinu] m cucumber.

pepita [pe'pita] f (de ouro) nugget.

pequena [pe'kena] f girl; (namorada) girlfriend.

pequenez [peke'neʒ] f smallness; (fig: mesquinhez) meanness; ~ **de sentimentos** pettiness.

pequenininho/a [pekeni'niɲu/a] adj tiny.

pequenino/a [peke'ninu/a] adj little.

pequeninos [peke'ninuʃ] mpl: **os** ~ the little children.

pequeno/a [pe'kenu/a] adj small; (mesquinho) petty ♦ m boy; **em** ~ **eu fazia ...** when I was small I used to do ....

pequeno-burguês/esa (pl -eses/~s) adj petty bourgeois.

pequerrucho/a [peke'xuʃu/a] adj tiny ♦ m thimble.

Pequim [pe'kĩ] n Pekin, Peking.

pequinês [peki'neʃ] m (cão) Pekinese.

pêra ['pera] f pear.

peralta [pe'rawta] adj naughty ♦ m/f (menino) naughty child.

perambular [perãbu'la*] vi to wander.

perante [pe'rãtʃi] prep before, in the presence of.

pé-rapado [-xa'padu] (pl **pés-rapados**) m nobody.

percalço [pex'kawsu] m (de uma tarefa) difficulty; (de profissão, matrimônio etc) pitfall.

per capita [pɛx'kapita] adv, adj per capita.

perceber [pexse'be*] vt (notar) to realize; (por meio dos sentidos) to perceive; (compreender) to understand; (ver) to see; (ouvir) to hear; (ver ao longe) to make out; (dinheiro: receber) to receive.

percentagem [pexsẽ'taʒẽ] f percentage.

percentual [pexsẽ'twaw] (pl -ais) adj percentage atr ♦ m percentage.

percepção [pexsep'sãw] f perception; (compreensão) understanding.

perceptível [pexsep'tʃivew] (pl -eis) adj perceptible, noticeable; (som) audible.

perceptividade [pexseptʃivi'dadʒi] f perceptiveness, perception.

perceptivo/a [pexsep'tʃivu/a] adj perceptive.

percevejo [pexse'veʒu] m (inseto) bug; (prego) drawing pin (BRIT), thumbtack (US).

perco ['pexku] etc vb V **perder**.

percorrer [pexko'xe*] vt (viajar por) to travel (across ou over); (passar por) to go through, traverse; (investigar) to search through.

percurso [pex'kuxsu] m (espaço percorrido) distance (covered); (trajeto) route; (viagem) journey; **fazer o** ~ **entre** to travel between.

percussão [pexku'sãw] f (MÚS) percussion.

percussionista [pexkusjo'niʃta] m/f percussionist, percussion player.

percutir [pexku'tʃi*] vt to strike ♦ vi to reverberate.

perda ['pexda] f loss; (desperdício) waste; ~ **de tempo** waste of time;' ~**s e danos** damages, losses.

perdão [pex'dãw] m pardon, forgiveness; ~**!** sorry!; **pedir** ~ **a alguém** to ask sb for forgiveness; ~ **da dívida** cancellation of the debt; ~ **da pena** (JUR) pardon.

perder [pex'de*] vt to lose; (tempo) to waste; (trem, show, oportunidade) to miss ♦ vi to lose; ~**-se** vr (extraviar-se) to get lost; (arruinar-se) to be ruined; (desaparecer) to disappear; (em reflexões) to be lost; (num discurso) to lose one's thread; ~**-se de alguém** to lose sb; ~ **algo de vista** to lose sight of sth; **a** ~ **de vista** (fig) as far as the eye can see; **pôr tudo a** ~ to risk losing everything; **saber** ~ to be a good loser.

perdição [pexdʒi'sãw] f perdition, ruin; (desonra) depravity; **ser uma** ~ (col) to be irresistible.

perdido/a [pex'dʒidu/a] adj lost; (pervertido) depraved; ~ **por** (apaixonado) desperately in love with; ~**s e achados** lost and found, lost property.

perdigão [pexdʒi'gãw] (pl -ões) m (macho) partridge.

perdigueiro [pexdʒi'gejru] m (cachorro) pointer, setter.

perdiz [pex'dʒiʒ] f partridge.

perdoar [pex'dwa*] vt (desculpar) to forgive; (pena) to lift; (dívida) to cancel; ~ (algo) a **alguém** to forgive sb (for sth).

perdoável [pex'dwavew] (pl -eis) adj forgivable.

perdulário/a [pexdu'larju/a] adj wasteful ♦ m/f spendthrift.

perdurar [pexdu'ra*] vi (durar muito) to last a long time; (continuar a existir) to still exist.

pereba [pe'rɛba] f (ferida pequena) scratch.

perecer [pere'se*] vi to perish; (morrer) to die; (acabar) to come to nothing.

perecível [pere'sivew] (pl -eis) adj perishable.

peregrinação [peregrina'sãw] (pl -ões) f (viagem) travels pl; (REL) pilgrimage.

peregrinar [peregri'na*] vi (viajar) to travel; (REL) to go on a pilgrimage.

peregrino/a [pere'grinu/a] adj (beleza) rare ♦ m/f pilgrim.

pereira [pe'rejra] f pear tree.

peremptório/a [perẽp'tɔrju/a] adj (final) final; (decisivo) decisive.

perene [pe'rɛni] adj (perpétuo) everlasting; (BOT) perennial.

perereca [pere'rɛka] f tree frog.

perfazer [pexfa'ze*] (irreg: como **fazer**) vt (completar o número de) to make up; (concluir) to complete.

perfeccionismo [pexfeksjo'niʒmu] m perfectionism.

perfeccionista [pexfeksjo'niʃta] adj, m/f perfectionist.

perfeição [pexfej'sãw] *f* perfection; **à** ~ **to** perfection.

perfeitamente [pexfejta'mẽtʃi] *adv* perfectly ✦ *excl* exactly!

perfeito/a [pex'fejtu/a] *adj* perfect; *(carro etc)* in perfect condition ✦ *m (LING)* perfect.

perfez [pex'feʒ] *vb V* **perfazer**.

perfídia [pex'fidʒja] *f* treachery.

pérfido/a ['pexfidu/a] *adj* treacherous.

perfil [pex'fiw] *(pl* -**is**) *m (do rosto, fig)* profile; *(silhueta)* silhouette, outline; *(ARQ)* (cross) section; **de** ~ in profile.

perfilar [perfi'la*] *vt (soldados)* to line up; *(aprumar)* to straighten up; ~**-se** *vr* to stand to attention.

perfilhar [pexfi'ʎa*] *vt (JUR)* to legally adopt; *(princípio, teoria)* to adopt.

perfis [pex'fiʃ] *mpl de* **perfil**.

perfiz [pex'fiʒ] *vb V* **perfazer**.

perfizer [pexfi'ze*] *etc vb V* **perfazer**.

performance [pex'fɔxmãs] *f* performance.

perfumado/a [pexfu'madu/a] *adj* sweet-smelling; *(pessoa)* wearing perfume.

perfumar [pexfu'ma*] *vt* to perfume; ~**-se** *vr* to put perfume on.

perfumaria [pexfuma'ria] *f* perfumery; *(col)* idle talk.

perfume [pex'fumi] *m* perfume; *(cheiro)* scent.

perfunctório/a [pexfũk'tɔrju/a] *adj* perfunctory.

perfurado/a [pexfu'radu/a] *adj (cartão)* punched.

perfurador [pexfura'do*] *m* punch.

perfurar [pexfu'ra*] *vt (o chão)* to drill a hole in; *(papel)* to punch (a hole in).

perfuratriz [pexfura'triʒ] *f* drill.

pergaminho [pexga'miɲu] *m* parchment; *(diploma)* diploma.

pérgula ['pexgula] *f* arbour *(BRIT)*, arbor *(US)*.

pergunta [pex'gũta] *f* question; **fazer uma** ~ **a alguém** to ask sb a question.

perguntador(a) [pexgũta'do*(a)] *adj* inquiring, inquisitive ✦ *m/f* questioner.

perguntar [pexgũ'ta*] *vt* to ask; *(interrogar)* to question ✦ *vi:* ~ **por alguém** to ask after sb; ~**-se** *vr* to wonder; ~ **algo a alguém** to ask sb sth.

perícia [pe'risja] *f (conhecimento)* expertise; *(destreza)* skill; *(exame)* investigation; ~ **(criminal)** criminal investigation; *(os peritos criminais)* criminal investigators *pl.*

pericial [peri'sjaw] *(pl* -**ais**) *adj* expert.

periclitante [perikli'tãtʃi] *adj (situação)* perilous; *(saúde)* shaky.

periclitar [perikli'ta*] *vi* to be in danger; *(negócio etc)* to be at risk.

periculosidade [perikulozi'dadʒi] *f* dangerousness; *(JUR)* risk factor.

peridural [peridu'raw] *(pl* -**ais**) *f (MED)* epidural.

periferia [perife'ria] *f* periphery; *(da cidade)* outskirts *pl.*

periférico/a [peri'fɛriku/a] *adj* peripheral ✦ *m (COMPUT)* peripheral; **estrada periférica** ring road.

perífrase [pe'rifrazi] *f* circumlocution.

perigar [peri'ga*] *vi* to be at risk; ~ **ser ... to** risk being ..., be in danger of being ....

perigo [pe'rigu] *m* danger; **correr** ~ to be in danger; **fora de** ~ safe, out of danger; **pôr em** ~ to endanger; **o carro dele é um** ~ his car is a deathtrap; **ser um** ~ *(col: pessoa)* to be a tease; **estar a** ~ *(col: sem dinheiro)* to be broke; (: *em situação difícil)* to be in a bad way.

perigoso/a [peri'gozu/ɔza] *adj* dangerous; *(arriscado)* risky.

perímetro [pe'rimetru] *m* perimeter; ~ **urbano** city limits *pl.*

periódico/a [pe'rjɔdʒiku/a] *adj* periodic; *(chuvas)* occasional; *(doença)* recurrent ✦ *m (revista)* magazine, periodical; *(jornal)* (news)paper.

período [pe'riodu] *m* period; *(estação)* season; ~ **letivo** term (time).

peripécia [peri'pɛsja] *f (aventura)* adventure; *(incidente)* turn of events.

periquito [peri'kitu] *m* parakeet.

periscópio [perif'kɔpju] *m* periscope.

perito/a [pe'ritu/a] *adj* expert; ~ **em** *(atividade)* expert at, clever at; *(matéria)* highly knowledgeable in ✦ *m/f* expert; *(quem faz perícia)* investigator; ~ **em matéria de** expert in.

peritonite [perito'nitʃi] *f* peritonitis.

perjurar [pexʒu'ra*] *vi* to commit perjury.

perjúrio [pex'ʒurju] *m* perjury.

perjuro/a [pex'ʒuru/a] *m/f* perjurer.

permanecer [pexmane'se*] *vi* to remain; *(num lugar)* to stay; *(continuar a ser)* to remain, keep; ~ **parado** to keep still.

permanência [pexma'nẽsja] *f* permanence; *(estada)* stay.

permanente [pexma'nẽtʃi] *adj (dor)* constant; *(cor)* fast; *(residência, pregas)* permanent ✦ *m (cartão)* pass ✦ *f* perm; **fazer uma** ~ to have a perm.

permeável [pex'mjavew] *(pl* -**eis**) *adj* permeable.

permeio [pex'meju]: **de** ~ *adv* in between.

permissão [pexmi'sãw] *f* permission, consent.

permissível [pexmi'sivew] *(pl* -**eis**) *adj* permissible.

permissivo/a [pexmi'sivu/a] *adj* permissive.

permitir [pexmi'tʃi*] *vt* to allow, permit; *(conceder)* to grant; ~ **a alguém fazer** to let sb do, allow sb to do.

permuta [pex'muta] *f* exchange; *(COM)* barter.

permutação [pexmuta'sãw] *(pl* -**ões**) *f (MAT)*

NB: *European Portuguese adds the following consonants to certain words:* **b** (sú(b)dito, su(b)til); **c** (a(c)ção, a(c)cionista, a(c)to); **m** (inde(m)ne); **p** (ado(p)ção, ado(p)tar); *for further details see p. xiii.*

permutation; (*troca*) exchange.

permutar [pexmu'ta*] *vt* to exchange; (*COM*) to barter.

perna ['pɛxna] *f* leg; **de ~(s) para o ar** upside down, topsy turvy; **em cima da ~** (*col*) sloppily, in a slapdash way; **bater ~s** (*col*) to wander; **passer a ~ em alguém** (*col*) to put one over on sb; **trocar as ~s** (*col*) to stagger; **~ de pau** wooden leg; **~ mecânica** artificial leg; **~s tortas** bow legs.

perna-de-pau (*pl* **pernas-de-pau**) *m/f* pegleg; (*FUTEBOL*) carthorse, bad player.

pernambucano/a [pɛxnãbu'kanu/a] *adj* from Pernambuco ♦ *m/f* person from Pernambuco.

perneira [pex'nejra] *f* (*de dançarina etc*) legwarmer.

perneta [pex'neta] *m/f* one-legged person.

pernicioso/a [pexni'sjozu/ɔza] *adj* pernicious; (*MED*) malignant.

pernil [pex'niw] (*pl* **-is**) *m* (*de animal*) haunch; (*CULIN*) leg.

pernilongo [pexni'lõgu] *m* mosquito.

pernis [pex'niʃ] *mpl de* **pernil**.

pernoitar [pexnoj'ta*] *vi* to spend the night.

pernóstico/a [pex'nɔʃtʃiku/a] *adj* pedantic ♦ *m/f* pedant.

pérola ['pɛrola] *f* pearl.

perpassar [pexpa'sa*] *vi* (*tempo*) to go by; **~ (por)** to pass by; **~ a mão em/por** to run one's hand through/over.

perpendicular [pexpẽdʒiku'la*] *adj*, *f* perpendicular; **ser ~ a** to be at right angles to.

perpetração [pexpetra'sãw] *f* perpetration.

perpetrar [pexpe'tra*] *vt* to perpetrate, commit.

perpetuar [pexpe'twa*] *vt* to perpetuate.

perpetuidade [pexpetwi'dadʒi] *f* eternity.

perpétuo/a [pex'petwu/a] *adj* perpetual; (*eterno*) eternal; **prisão perpétua** life imprisonment.

perplexidade [pexpleksi'dadʒi] *f* confusion, bewilderment.

perplexo/a [pex'plɛksu/a] *adj* (*confuso*) bewildered, puzzled; (*indeciso*) uncertain; **ficar ~** (*atônito*) to be taken aback.

perquirir [pexki'ri*] *vt* to probe, investigate.

persa ['pɛxsa] *adj*, *m/f* Persian.

perscrutar [pexʃkru'ta*] *vt* to scrutinize, examine.

perseguição [pexsegi'sãw] *f* pursuit; (*REL, POL*) persecution.

perseguidor(a) [pexsegi'do*(a)] *m/f* pursuer; (*REL, POL*) persecutor.

perseguir [pexse'gi*] *vt* (*seguir*) to pursue; (*correr atrás*) to chase (after); (*REL, POL*) to persecute; (*importunar*) to harass, pester.

perseverança [pexseve'rãsa] *f* (*insistência*) persistence; (*constância*) perseverance.

perseverante [pexseve'rãtʃi] *adj* persistent.

perseverar [pexseve'ra*] *vi* to persevere; **~ em** (*conservar-se firme*) to persevere in; **~ corajoso** to keep one's courage up; **~ em**

erro to persist in doing wrong.

Pérsia ['pexsja] *f*: **a ~** Persia.

persiana [pex'sjana] *f* blind.

Pérsico/a ['pexsiku/a] *adj*: **o golfo ~** the Persian Gulf.

persignar-se [pexsig'naxsi] *vr* to cross o.s.

persigo [pex'sigu] *etc vb* **V perseguir**.

persistência [pexsiʃ'tẽsja] *f* persistence.

persistente [pexsiʃ'tẽtʃi] *adj* persistent.

persistir [pexsiʃ'tʃi*] *vi* to persist; **~ em** to persist in; **~ calado** to keep quiet.

personagem [pexso'naʒẽ] (*pl* **-ns**) *m/f* famous person, celebrity; (*num livro, filme*) character.

personalidade [pexsonali'dadʒi] *f* personality; **~ dupla** dual personality.

personalizado/a [pexsonali'zadu/a] *adj* personalized; (*móveis etc*) custom-made.

personalizar [pexsonali'za*] *vt* to personalize; (*personificar*) to personify; (*nomear*) to name.

personificação [pexsonifika'sãw] *f* personification.

personificar [pexsonifi'ka*] *vt* to personify.

perspectiva [pexʃpek'tʃiva] *f* (*na pintura*) perspective; (*panorama*) view; (*probabilidade*) prospect; (*ponto de vista*) point of view; **em ~** in prospect.

perspicácia [pexʃpi'kasja] *f* insight, perceptiveness.

perspicaz [pexʃpi'kajʒ] *adj* (*que observa*) observant; (*sagaz*) shrewd.

persuadir [pexswa'dʒi*] *vt* to persuade; **~-se** *vr* to convince o.s., make up one's mind; **~ alguém de que/alguém a fazer** to persuade sb that/sb to do.

persuasão [pexswa'zãw] *f* persuasion; (*convicção*) conviction.

persuasivo/a [pexswa'zivu/a] *adj* persuasive.

pertencente [pextẽ'sẽtʃi] *adj* belonging; **~ a** (*pertinente*) pertaining to.

pertencer [pextẽ'se*] *vi*: **~ a** to belong to; (*referir-se*) to concern.

pertences [pex'tẽsiʃ] *mpl* (*de uma pessoa*) belongings.

pertinácia [pextʃi'nasja] *f* (*persistência*) persistence; (*obstinação*) obstinacy.

pertinaz [pextʃi'najʒ] *adj* (*persistente*) persistent; (*obstinado*) obstinate.

pertinência [pextʃi'nẽsja] *f* relevance.

pertinente [pextʃi'nẽtʃi] *adj* relevant; (*apropriado*) appropriate.

perto/a ['pextu/a] *adj* nearby ♦ *adv* near; **~ de** near to; (*em comparação com*) next to; **~ da casa** near *ou* close to the house; **~ de 100 cruzeiros** about 100 cruzeiros; **estar ~ de fazer** (*a ponto de*) to be close to doing; **de ~** closely; **conhecer de ~** to know very well; **ela não enxerga bem de ~** she can't see well close up.

perturbação [pextuxba'sãw] (*pl* **-ões**) *f* disturbance; (*desorientação*) perturbation; (*MED*) trouble; (*POL*) disturbance; **~ da**

ordem breach of the peace.
perturbador(a) [pextuxba'do*(a)] *adj (pessoa)* disruptive; *(notícia)* perturbing, disturbing.
perturbado/a [pextux'badu/a] *adj* perturbed; *(desvairado)* unbalanced.
perturbar [pextux'ba*] *vt* to disturb; *(abalar)* to upset, trouble; *(atrapalhar)* to put off; *(andamento, trânsito)* to disrupt; *(envergonhar)* to embarrass; *(alterar)* to affect; **não perturba!** do not disturb!; **~ a ordem** to cause a breach of the peace.
Peru [pe'ru] *m*: **o ~** Peru.
peru [pe'ru] *m* turkey; *(col!: pênis)* cock *(!)*.
perua [pe'rua] *f (carro)* estate (car) *(BRIT)*, station wagon *(US)*; *(ZOOL)* turkey.
peruada [pe'rwada] *(col) f (palpite)* tip.
peruano/a [pe'rwanu/a] *adj, m/f* Peruvian.
peruar [pe'rwa*] *vt (jogo)* to watch ♦ *vi* to hang around.
peruca [pe'ruka] *f* wig.
perversão [pexvex'sãw] *(pl -ões) f* perversion.
perversidade [pexvexsi'dadʒi] *f* perversity.
perverso/a [pex'vexsu/a] *adj* perverse; *(malvado)* wicked.
perversões [pexvex'sõjʃ] *fpl de* **perversão**.
perverter [pexvex'te*] *vt (corromper)* to corrupt, pervert; **~-se** *vr* to become corrupt.
pervertido/a [pexvex'tʃidu/a] *adj* perverted ♦ *m/f* pervert.
pesada [pe'zada] *f* weighing.
pesadelo [peza'delu] *m* nightmare.
pesado/a [pe'zadu/a] *adj* heavy; *(ambiente)* tense; *(trabalho)* hard; *(estilo)* dull, boring; *(andar)* slow; *(piada)* coarse; *(comida)* stodgy; *(ar)* sultry ♦ *adv* heavily; **pegar no ~** *(col)* to work hard; **da pesada** *(col: legal)* great; *(: barra-pesada)* rough, violent.
pesagem [pe'zaʒẽ] *f* weighing.
pêsames ['pesamiʃ] *mpl* condolences, sympathy *sg*.
pesar [pe'za*] *vt* to weigh; *(fig)* to weigh up ♦ *vi* to weigh; *(ser pesado)* to be heavy; *(influir)* to carry weight; *(causar mágoa)*: **~ a** to hurt, grieve ♦ *m* grief; **~ sobre** *(recair)* to fall upon; **em que pese a** despite; **apesar dos ~es** despite everything.
pesaroso/a [peza'rozu/ɔza] *adj (triste)* sorrowful, sad; *(arrependido)* regretful, sorry.
pesca ['peʃka] *f (ato)* fishing; *(os peixes)* catch; **ir à ~** to go fishing; **~ submarina** skin diving.
pescada [peʃ'kada] *f* whiting.
pescado [peʃ'kadu] *m* fish.
pescador(a) [peʃka'do*(a)] *m/f* fisherman/woman; **~ à linha** angler.
pescar [peʃ'ka*] *vt (peixe)* to catch; *(tentar apanhar)* to fish for; *(retirar como que pescando)* to fish out; *(um marido)* to catch, get ♦ *vi* to fish; *(BR: col)* to understand; **~ de algo** *(col)* to know about sth; **pescou?** got

it?, see?
pescoção [peʃko'sãw] *(pl -ões) m* slap.
pescoço [peʃ'kosu] *m* neck; **até o ~** *(endividado)* up to one's neck.
pescoções [peʃko'sõjʃ] *mpl de* **pescoção**.
pescoçudo/a [peʃko'sudu/a] *adj* bull-necked.
peso ['pezu] *m* weight; *(fig: ônus)* burden; *(importância)* importance; **pessoa/argumento de ~** important person/weighty argument; **de pouco ~** lightweight; **em ~** in full force; **~ atômico** atomic weight; **~ bruto/líquido** gross/net weight; **~ morto** dead weight; **ter dois ~s e duas medidas** *(fig)* to have double standards.
pespontar [peʃpõ'ta*] *vt* to backstitch.
pesponto [peʃ'põtu] *m* backstitch.
pesquei [peʃ'kej] *etc vb V* **pescar**.
pesqueiro/a [peʃ'kejru/a] *adj* fishing.
pesquisa [peʃ'kiza] *f* inquiry, investigation; *(científica)* research; **~ de campo** field work; **~ de mercado** market research; **~ e desenvolvimento** research and development.
pesquisador(a) [peʃkiza'do*(a)] *m/f* investigator; *(científico, de mercado)* researcher.
pesquisar [peʃki'za*] *vt, vi* to investigate; *(nas ciências etc)* to research.
pêssego ['pesegu] *m* peach.
pessegueiro [pese'gejru] *m* peach tree.
pessimismo [pesi'miʒmu] *m* pessimism.
pessimista [pesi'miʃta] *adj* pessimistic ♦ *m/f* pessimist.
péssimo/a ['pesimu/a] *adj* very bad, awful; **estar ~** *(pessoa)* to be in a bad way.
pessoa [pe'soa] *f* person; **~s** *fpl* people; **em ~** personally; **~ de bem** honest person; **~ física/jurídica** *(JUR)* individual/legal entity.
pessoal [pe'swaw] *(pl -ais) adj* personal ♦ *m* personnel *pl*, staff *pl*; *(col)* people *pl*, folks *pl*; **oi, ~!** *(col)* hi, everyone!, hi, folks!
pestana [peʃ'tana] *f* eyelash; **tirar uma ~** *(col)* to have a nap.
pestanejar [peʃtane'ʒa*] *vi* to blink; **sem ~** *(fig)* without batting an eyelid.
peste ['peʃtʃi] *f (epidemia)* epidemic; *(bubônica)* plague; *(fig)* pest, nuisance.
pesticida [peʃtʃi'sida] *m* pesticide.
pestífero/a [peʃ'tʃiferu/a] *adj (fig)* pernicious.
pestilência [peʃtʃi'lẽsja] *f* plague; *(epidemia)* epidemic; *(fedor)* stench.
pestilento/a [peʃtʃi'lẽtu/a] *adj* pestilential, plague *atr*; *(malcheiroso)* putrid.
pétala ['petala] *f* petal.
peteca [pe'tɛka] *f (kind of)* shuttlecock; **fazer alguém de ~** to make a fool of sb; **não deixar a ~ cair** *(col)* to keep the ball rolling.
peteleco [pete'lɛku] *m* flick; **dar um ~ em algo** to flick sth.
petição [petʃi'sãw] *(pl -ões) f (rogo)* request; *(documento)* petition; **em ~ de miséria** in a terrible state.

NB: *European Portuguese adds the following consonants to certain words:* **b** (sú(b)dito, su(b)til); **c** (a(c)ção, a(c)cionista, a(c)to); **m** (inde(m)ne); **p** (ado(p)ção, ado(p)tar); *for further details see p. xiii.*

peticionário/a [petʃisjo'narju/a] m/f petitioner; (JUR) plaintiff.

petições [petʃi'sõjʃ] fpl de **petição**.

petiscar [petʃiʃ'ka*] vt to nibble at, peck at ♦ vi to have a nibble.

petisco [pe'tʃiʃku] m savoury (BRIT), savory (US), titbit (BRIT), tidbit (US).

petit-pois [petʃi'pwa] m inv pea.

petiz [pe'tʃiʒ] (PT) m boy.

petrechos [pe'treʃuʃ] mpl equipment sg; (MIL) stores, equipment sg; (de cozinha) utensils.

petrificar [petrifi'ka*] vt to petrify; (empedernir) to harden; (assombrar) to stun; ~-se vr to be petrified; to be stunned; to become hard.

Petrobrás [petro'brajʃ] abr f Brazilian state oil company.

petrodólar [petro'dɔla*] m petrodollar.

petroleiro/a [petro'lejru/a] adj oil atr, petroleum atr ♦ m (navio) oil tanker.

petróleo [pe'trɔlju] m oil, petroleum; ~ **bruto** crude oil.

petrolífero/a [petro'liferu/a] adj oil-producing.

petroquímica [petro'kimika] f petrochemicals pl; (ciência) petrochemistry.

petroquímico/a [petro'kimiku/a] adj petrochemical.

petulância [petu'lãsja] f impudence.

petulante [petu'lãtʃi] adj impudent.

petúnia [pe'tunja] f petunia.

peúga ['pjuga] (PT) f sock.

pevide [pe'vidʒi] (PT) f (de melão) seed; (de maçã) pip.

p. ex. abr (= por exemplo) e.g.

pexote [pe'ʃotʃi] m/f (criança) little kid; (novato) beginner, novice.

PF (BR) abr f = **Polícia Federal**.

PFL (BR) abr m = **Partido da Frente Liberal**.

PH (BR) abr m = **Partido Humanitário**.

PI abr = **Piauí**.

pia ['pia] f wash basin; (da cozinha) sink; ~ **batismal** font.

piada ['pjada] f joke.

piadista [pja'dʒiʃta] m/f joker.

pianista [pja'niʃta] m/f pianist.

piano ['pjanu] m piano; ~ **de cauda** grand piano.

pião [pjãw] (pl -ões) m (brinquedo) top.

piar [pja*] vi (pinto) to cheep; (coruja) to hoot; **não** ~ not to say a word.

piauiense [pjaw'jẽsi] adj from Piauí ♦ m/f person from Piauí.

PIB abr m (= Produto Interno Bruto) GNP.

picada [pi'kada] f (de agulha etc) prick; (de abelha) sting; (de mosquito, cobra) bite; (de avião) dive; (de navalha) stab; (atalho) path, trail; (de droga) shot.

picadeiro [pika'dejru] m (circo) ring.

picadinho [pika'dʒiɲu] m stew.

picado/a [pi'kadu/a] adj (por agulha) pricked; (por abelha) stung; (por cobra, mosquito) bitten; (papel) shredded; (carne) minced; (legumes) chopped.

picante [pi'kãtʃi] adj (tempero) hot; (piada) risqué, blue; (comentário) saucy.

pica-pau ['pika-] (pl ~s) m woodpecker.

picar [pi'ka*] vt (com agulha) to prick; (suj: abelha) to sting; (: mosquito) to bite; (: pássaro) to peck; (um animal) to goad; (carne) to mince; (papel) to shred; (fruta) to chop up; (comichar) to prickle ♦ vi (a isca) to take the bait; (comichar) to prickle; (avião) to dive; ~-se vr to prick o.s.

picardia [pikax'dʒia] f (implicância) spitefulness; (esperteza) craftiness.

picaresco/a [pika'reʃku/a] adj comic, ridiculous.

picareta [pika'reta] f pickaxe (BRIT), pickax (US) ♦ m/f crook.

picaretagem [pikare'taʒẽ] (pl -ns) f con.

pícaro/a ['pikaru/a] adj crafty, cunning.

pichação [piʃa'sãw] (pl -ões) f (ato) spraying; (grafite) piece of graffiti.

pichar [pi'ʃa*] vt (dizeres, muro) to spray; (aplicar piche em) to cover with pitch; (col: espinafrar) to run down ♦ vi (col) to criticize.

piche ['piʃi] m pitch.

piclés ['pikliʃ] mpl pickles.

pico ['piku] m (cume) peak; (ponta aguda) sharp point; (PT: um pouco) a bit; **mil e** ~ just over a thousand; **meio-dia e** ~ just after midday.

picolé [piko'lɛ] m lolly.

picotar [piko'ta*] vt to perforate; (bilhete) to punch.

picote [pi'kɔtʃi] m perforation.

pictórico/a [pik'tɔriku/a] adj pictorial.

picuinha [pi'kwiɲa] f: **estar de** ~ **com alguém** to have it in for sb.

piedade [pje'dadʒi] f (devoção) piety; (compaixão) pity; **ter** ~ **de** to have pity on.

piedoso/a [pje'dozu/ɔza] adj (REL) pious; (compassivo) merciful.

piegas ['pjegaʃ] adj inv sentimental; (col) soppy ♦ m/f inv softy.

pieguice [pje'gisi] f sentimentality.

píer ['pie*] m pier.

pifa ['pifa] (col) m booze-up; **tomar um** ~ to get smashed.

pifado/a [pi'fadu/a] (col) adj (carro) broken down; (TV etc) broken.

pifar [pi'fa*] (col) vi (carro) to break down; (rádio) to go wrong; (plano, programa) to fall through.

pigarrear [piga'xja*] vi to clear one's throat.

pigarro [pi'gaxu] (col) m frog in the throat.

pigméia [pig'mɛja] f de **pigmeu**.

pigmentação [pigmẽta'sãw] f pigmentation, colouring (BRIT), coloring (US).

pigmento [pig'mẽtu] m pigment.

pigmeu/méia [pig'mew/'meja] adj, m/f pigmy.

pijama [pi'ʒama] m pyjamas pl.

pilantra [pi'lãtra] (col) m/f crook.

pilantragem [pilã'traʒẽ] f rip-off.

pilão [pi'lãw] (pl -ões) m crusher; (rural)

mortar.

pilar [pi'la*] *vt* to pound, crush ♦ *m* pillar.

pilastra [pi'laftra] *f* pilaster.

pileque [pi'lɛki] *m* booze-up; **tomar um ~** to get smashed *ou* plastered; **estar de ~** to be smashed *ou* plastered.

pilha ['piʎa] *f* (ELET) battery; (monte) pile, heap; (COMPUT) stack; **às ~s** in vast quantities; **estar uma ~ (de nervos)** to be a bundle of nerves.

pilhagem [pi'ʎaʒẽ] *f* (ato) pillage; (objetos) plunder, booty.

pilhar [pi'ʎa] *vt* (saquear) to plunder, pillage; (roubar) to rob; (surpreender) to catch.

pilhéria [pi'ʎɛrja] *f* joke.

pilheriar [piʎe'rja*] *vi* to joke, jest.

pilões [pi'lõjʃ] *mpl de* **pilão**.

pilotagem [pilo'taʒẽ] *f* flying; **escola de ~** flying school.

pilotar [pilo'ta*] *vt* (avião) to fly; (carro de corrida) to drive ♦ *vi* to fly.

pilotis [pilo'tʃiʃ] *mpl* stilts.

piloto [pi'lotu] *m* (de avião) pilot; (de navio) first mate; (motorista) (racing) driver; (bico de gás) pilot light ♦ *adj inv* (usina, plano) pilot; (peça) sample *atr*; **~ automático** automatic pilot; **~ de prova** test pilot.

pílula ['pilula] *f* pill; **a ~ (anticoncepcional)** the pill.

pimba ['pĩba] *excl* wham!

pimenta [pi'mẽta] *f* (CULIN) pepper; **~ de Caiena** cayenne pepper.

pimenta-do-reino *f* black pepper.

pimenta-malagueta (pl **pimentas-malagueta**) *f* chilli (BRIT) *ou* chili (US) pepper.

pimentão [pimẽ'tãw] *m* (BOT) pepper; **~ verde** green pepper.

pimenteira [pimẽ'tejra] *f* (BOT) pepper plant; (à mesa) pepper pot; (: moedor) pepper mill.

pimpão/pona [pĩ'pãw/'pɔna] (PT: pl **-ões/~s**) *adj* smart, flashy ♦ *m/f* show-off.

pimpolho [pĩ'poʎu] *m* (criança) youngster.

pimpona [pĩ'pɔna] *f de* **pimpão**.

PIN (BR) *abr m* = **Plano de Integração Nacional**.

pinacoteca [pinako'tɛka] *f* art gallery; (coleção de quadros) art collection.

pináculo [pi'nakulu] *m* (tb fig) pinnacle.

pinça ['pĩsa] *f* (de sobrancelhas) tweezers *pl*; (de casa) tongs *pl*; (MED) callipers *pl* (BRIT), calipers *pl* (US).

pinçar [pĩ'sa*] *vt* to pick up; (sobrancelhas) to pluck; (fig: exemplos, defeitos) to pick out.

píncaro ['pĩkaru] *m* summit, peak.

pincel [pĩ'sɛw] (pl **-éis**) *m* brush; (para pintar) paintbrush; **~ de barba** shaving brush.

pincelada [pĩse'lada] *f* (brush) stroke.

pincelar [pĩse'la*] *vt* to paint.

pincenê [pĩse'ne] *m* pince-nez.

pindaíba [pĩda'iba] *f*: **estar na ~** (col) to be broke.

pinel [pi'nɛw] (pl **-éis**) (col) *m/f*: **ser/ficar ~** to be/go crazy.

pinga ['pĩga] *f* (cachaça) rum; (PT: trago) drink.

pingado/a [pĩ'gadu/a] *adj*: **~ de** covered in drops of.

pingar [pĩ'ga*] *vi* to drip; (começar a chover) to start to rain.

pingente [pĩ'ʒẽtʃi] *m* pendant.

pingo ['pĩgu] *m* (gota) drop; (ortografia) dot; **~ de gente** (col) slip of a child; **um ~ de** (comida etc) a spot of; (educação etc) a scrap of.

pingue-pongue [pĩgi-'põgi] *m* ping-pong.

pingüim [pĩ'gwĩ] (pl **-ns**) *m* penguin.

pinguinho [pĩ'giɲu] *m* little drop; (pouquinho): **um ~** a tiny bit.

pingüins [pĩ'gwĩʃ] *mpl de* **pingüim**.

pinha ['piɲa] *f* pine cone.

pinheiral [piɲej'raw] (pl **-ais**) *m* pine wood.

pinheiro [pi'ɲejru] *m* pine (tree).

pinho ['piɲu] *m* pine.

pinicada [pini'kada] *f* (beliscão) pinch; (cutucada) poke; (de pássaro) peck.

pinicar [pini'ka*] *vt* (pele) to prickle; (com o bico) to peck; (beliscar) to pinch; (cutucar) to poke.

pinimba [pi'nĩba] (col) *f*: **estar de ~ com alguém** to have it in for sb.

pino ['pinu] *m* (peça) pin; (AUT: na porta) lock; **a ~** upright; **sol a ~** noon-day sun; **bater ~** (AUTO) to knock; (col) to be in a bad way.

pinóia [pi'nɔja] (col) *f* piece of trash; **que ~!** what a drag!

pinote [pi'nɔtʃi] *m* buck.

pinotear [pino'tʃja*] *vi* to buck.

pinta ['pĩta] *f* (mancha) spot; (col: aparência) appearance, looks *pl*; (: sujeito) guy; **dar na ~** (col) to give o.s. away; **ela tem ~ de (ser) inglesa** she looks English; **está com ~ de chover** it looks like rain.

pinta-braba [pĩta'braba] (pl **pintas-brabas**) *m/f* hoodlum, shady character.

pintado/a [pĩ'tadu/a] *adj* painted; (cabelo) dyed; (olhos, lábios) made up; **é o avô ~** he's the image of his grandfather; **não querer ver alguém nem ~** (col) to hate the sight of sb.

pintar [pĩ'ta*] *vt* to paint; (cabelo) to dye; (rosto) to make up; (descrever) to describe; (imaginar) to picture ♦ *vi* to paint; (col: aparecer) to appear, turn up; (: problemas, oportunidade) to crop up; **~-se** *vr* to make o.s. up; **~ (o sete)** to paint the town red.

pintarroxo [pĩta'xoʃu] *m* linnet; (PT) robin.

pinto ['pĩtu] *m* chick; (col!) prick (!); **como**

um ~ (molhado) like a drowned rat; **ser ~** to be a piece of cake.

pintor(a) [pĩ'to*(a)] *m/f* painter.

pintura [pĩ'tura] *f* painting; *(maquiagem)* make-up; **~ a óleo** oil painting.

pio/a ['piu/a] *adj (devoto)* pious; *(caridoso)* charitable ♦ *m* cheep, chirp; **não dar um ~** not to make a sound.

piões [pjõjʃ] *mpl de* **pião**.

piolho ['pjoʎu] *m* louse.

pioneiro/a [pjo'nejru/a] *adj* pioneering ♦ *m* pioneer.

piopio [pju'pju] *(col) m* birdie, dicky bird.

pior ['pjɔ*] *adj, adv (comparativo)* worse; *(superlativo)* worst ♦ *m*: **o ~** worst of all ♦ *f*: **estar na ~** *(col)* to be in a jam.

piora ['pjɔra] *f* worsening.

piorar [pjo'ra*] *vt* to make worse, worsen ♦ *vi* to get worse.

pipa ['pipa] *f* barrel, cask; *(de papel)* kite.

piparote [pipa'rɔtʃi] *m (com o dedo)* flick.

pipi [pi'pi] *m (col: urina)* pee; **fazer ~** to have a pee, pee.

pipilar [pipi'la*] *vi* to chirp.

pipoca [pi'pɔka] *f* popcorn; *(col: na pele)* blister; **~s!** blast!

pipocar [pipo'ka*] *vi* to go pop, pop; *(aparecer)* to spring up.

pipoqueiro/a [pipo'kejru/a] *m/f* popcorn seller.

pique ['piki] *m (corte)* nick; *(auge)* peak; *(grande disposição)* keenness, enthusiasm; **a ~** vertically, steeply; **a ~ de** on the verge of; **ir/pôr a ~** to sink; **perder o ~** to lose one's momentum; **estou no maior ~ no momento** I'm really in the mood *ou* keen at the moment.

piquei [pi'kej] *etc vb V* **picar**.

piquenique [piki'niki] *m* picnic; **fazer ~** to have a picnic.

piquete [pi'ketʃi] *m (MIL)* squad; *(em greve)* picket.

pira ['pira] *(col) f*: **dar o ~** to take off.

pirado/a [pi'radu/a] *(col) adj* crazy.

pirâmide [pi'ramidʒi] *f* pyramid.

piranha [pi'raɲa] *f* piranha (fish); *(col: mulher)* tart.

pirão [pi'rãw] *m* manioc meal.

pirar [pi'ra*] *(col) vi* to go mad; *(com drogas)* to get high; *(ir embora)* to take off.

pirata [pi'rata] *m* pirate; *(namorador)* ladykiller; *(vigarista)* crook ♦ *adj* pirate.

pirataria [pirata'ria] *f* piracy; *(patifaria)* crime.

pires ['piriʃ] *m inv* saucer.

pirilampo [piri'lãpu] *m* glow worm.

Pirineus [piri'newʃ] *mpl*: **os ~** the Pyrenees.

piriri [piri'ri] *(col) m (diarréia)* the runs *pl*.

pirotecnia [pirotek'nia] *f* pyrotechnics *sg*, art of making fireworks.

pirraça [pi'xasa] *f* spiteful thing; **fazer ~** to be spiteful.

pirracento/a [pixa'sẽtu/a] *adj* spiteful, bloody-minded.

pirralho/a [pi'xaʎu/a] *m/f* child.

pirueta [pi'rweta] *f* pirouette.

pirulito [piru'litu] *(BR) m* lollipop.

PISA *(BR) abr f* = **Papel de Imprensa SA**.

pisada [pi'zada] *f (passo)* footstep; *(rastro)* footprint.

pisar [pi'za*] *vt (andar por cima de)* to tread on; *(uvas)* to tread, press; *(esmagar, subjugar)* to crush; *(café)* to pound; *(assunto)* to harp on ♦ *vi (andar)* to step, tread; *(acelerar)* to put one's foot down; **~ em** *(grama, pé)* to step *ou* tread on; *(casa de alguém, pátria)* to set foot in; **"não pise na grama"** "do not walk on the grass''; **~ forte** to stomp; **pisa mais leve!** don't stamp your feet!

piscadela [piʃka'dɛla] *f (involuntária)* blink; *(sinal)* wink.

pisca-pisca [piʃka-'piʃka] *(pl ~s) m (AUTO)* indicator.

piscar [piʃ'ka*] *vt* to blink; *(dar sinal)* to wink; *(estrelas)* to twinkle ♦ *m*: **num ~ de olhos** in a flash.

piscicultor(a) [pisikuw'to*(a)] *m/f* fish farmer.

piscicultura [pisikuw'tura] *f* fish farming.

piscina [pi'sina] *f* swimming pool; *(para peixes)* fish pond.

piscoso/a [piʃ'kozu/ɔza] *adj* rich in fish.

piso ['pizu] *m* floor; **~ salarial** wage floor, lowest wage.

pisotear [pizo'tʃja*] *vt* to trample (on); *(fig)* to ride roughshod over.

pisquei [piʃ'kej] *etc vb V* **piscar**.

píssico/a ['pisiku/a] *adj* crazy, mad.

pista ['piʃta] *f (vestígio)* track, trail; *(indicação)* clue; *(de corridas)* track; *(AVIAT)* runway; *(de equitação)* ring; *(de estrada)* lane; *(de dança)* (dance) floor.

pistache [piʃ'taʃi] *m* pistachio (nut).

pistacho [piʃ'taʃu] *m* = **pistache**.

pistão [piʃ'tãw] *(pl -ões) m* = **pistom**.

pistola [piʃ'tɔla] *f (arma)* pistol; *(para tinta)* spray gun.

pistolão [piʃto'lãw] *(pl -ões) m* contact.

pistoleiro [piʃto'lejru] *m* gunman.

pistolões [piʃto'lõjʃ] *mpl de* **pistolão**.

pistom [piʃ'tõ] *(pl -ns) m* piston.

pitada [pi'tada] *f (porção)* pinch.

pitanga [pi'tãga] *f* Surinam cherry.

pitar [pi'ta*] *vt, vi* to smoke.

piteira [pi'tejra] *f* cigarette-holder.

pito ['pitu] *m (cachimbo)* pipe; *(col: repreensão)* telling-off; **sossegar o ~** to calm down.

pitonisa [pito'niza] *f* fortune-teller.

pitoresco/a [pito'reʃku/a] *adj* picturesque.

pituitário/a [pitwi'tarju/a] *adj (glândula)* pituitary.

pivete [pi'vetʃi] *m* child thief.

pivô [pi'vo] *m (TEC)* pivot; *(fig)* central figure, prime mover.

pixaim [piʃa'ĩ] *m* frizzy hair ♦ *adj* frizzy.

pixote [pi'ʃɔtʃi] *m/f* = **pexote**.

pizza ['pitsa] *f* pizza.
pizzaria [pitsa'ria] *f* pizzeria.
PJ (*BR*) *abr m* = **Partido da Juventude**.
PL (*BR*) *abr m* = **Partido Liberal**.
PLB *abr m* = **Partido Liberal Brasileiro**.
plá [pla] (*col*) *m* (*dica*) tip; (*papo*) chat.
placa ['plaka] *f* plate; (*AUTO*) number plate
(*BRIT*), license plate (*US*); (*comemorativa*)
plaque; (*COMPUT*) board; (*na pele*) blotch; ~
de sinalização roadsign; ~ **fria** false number
ou license plate.
placar [pla'ka*] *m* scoreboard; **abrir o** ~ to
open the scoring.
placebo [pla'sebu] *m* placebo.
placenta [pla'sēta] *f* placenta.
placidez [plasi'deʒ] *f* peacefulness, serenity.
plácido/a ['plasidu/a] *adj* (*sereno*) calm;
(*manso*) placid.
plagiador(a) [plaʒja'do*(a)] *m/f* = **plagiário/a**.
plagiário/a [pla'ʒjarju/a] *m/f* plagiarist.
plagiar [pla'ʒja*] *vt* to plagiarize.
plágio ['plaʒu] *m* plagiarism.
plaina ['plajna] *f* (*instrumento*) plane.
plana ['plana] *f*: **de primeira** ~ first-class.
planador [plana'do*] *m* glider.
planalto [pla'nawtu] *m* tableland, plateau.
planar [pla'na*] *vi* to glide.
planear [pla'nja*] (*PT*) *vt* = **planejar**.
planejador(a) [planeʒa'do*(a)] *m/f* planner.
planejamento [planeʒa'mētu] *m* planning;
(*ARQ*) design; ~ **familiar** family planning.
planejar [plane'ʒa*] (*BR*) *vt* to plan; (*edifício*)
to design.
planeta [pla'neta] *m* planet.
planetário/a [plane'tarju/a] *adj* planetary ♦ *m*
planetarium.
plangente [pla'ʒētʃi] *adj* plaintive, mournful.
planície [pla'nisi] *f* plain.
planificar [planifi'ka*] *vt* (*programar*) to plan
out; (*uma região*) to make a plan of.
planilha [pla'niʎa] *f* (*COMPUT*) spreadsheet.
plano/a ['planu/a] *adj* (*terreno*) flat, level;
(*liso*) smooth ♦ *m* plan; (*MAT*) plane; ~ **diretor** master plan; **em primeiro/em último** ~
in the foreground/background.
planta ['plāta] *f* (*BIO*) plant; (*de pé*) sole;
(*ARQ*) plan.
plantação [plāta'sãw] *f* (*ato*) planting;
(*terreno*) planted land; (*o que se plantou*)
crops *pl*.
plantado/a [plā'tadu/a] *adj*: **deixar alguém/
ficar** ~ **em algum lugar** (*col*) to leave sb/be
left standing somewhere.
plantão [plā'tāw] (*pl* **-ões**) *m* duty; (*noturno*)
night duty; (*plantonista*) person on duty;
(*MIL*: *serviço*) sentry duty; (: *pessoa*) sentry; **estar de** ~ to be on duty; **médico/
farmácia de** ~ duty doctor/pharmacy *ou*
chemist's (*BRIT*).
plantar [plā'ta*] *vt* to plant; (*semear*) to sow;

(*estaca*) to drive in; (*estabelecer*) to set up;
~**-se** *vr* to plant o.s.
plantio [plā'tʃiu] *m* planting; (*terreno*) planted
land.
plantões [plā'tõjʃ] *mpl de* **plantão**.
plantonista [plāto'niʃta] *m/f* person on duty.
planura [pla'nura] *f* plain.
plaquê [pla'ke] (*PT*) *m* gold plate.
plaqueta [pla'keta] *f* plaque; (*AUTO*) licensing
badge (*attached to number plate*); (*COMPUT*)
chip.
plasma ['plaʒma] *m* plasma.
plasmar [plaʒ'ma*] *vt* to mould (*BRIT*), mold
(*US*), shape.
plástica ['plaʃtʃika] *f* (*cirurgia*) piece of
plastic surgery; (*do corpo*) build; **fazer uma**
~ to have plastic surgery.
plástico/a ['plaʃtʃiku/a] *adj* plastic ♦ *m*
plastic.
plastificado/a [plaʃtʃifi'kadu/a] *adj* plastic-
coated.
plataforma [plata'fɔxma] *f* platform; ~ **de exploração de petróleo** oil rig; ~ **de lançamento** launch pad.
plátano ['platanu] *m* plane tree.
platéia [pla'teja] *f* (*TEATRO etc*) stalls *pl*
(*BRIT*), orchestra (*US*); (*espectadores*)
audience.
platina [pla'tʃina] *f* platinum.
platinado/a [platʃi'nadu/a] *adj* platinum *atr*;
loura platinada platinum blonde.
platinados [platʃi'naduʃ] *mpl* (*AUTO*) points.
platinar [platʃi'na*] *vt* (*cabelo*) to dye
platinum blonde.
platô [pla'to] *m* plateau.
platônico/a [pla'toniku/a] *adj* platonic.
plausibilidade [plawzibili'dadʒi] *f* plausibility.
plausível [plaw'zivew] (*pl* **-eis**) *adj* credible,
plausible.
playboy [plej'bɔi] (*pl* ~**s**) *m* playboy.
playground [plej'grãwdʒi] (*pl* ~**s**) *m* children's playground.
plebe ['plɛbi] *f* common people, populace.
plebeu/béia [ple'bew/'bɛja] *adj* plebeian ♦ *m/f*
pleb.
plebiscito [plebi'situ] *m* referendum,
plebiscite.
plectro ['plektru] *m* (*MÚS*) plectrum.
pleitear [plej'tʃja*] *vt* (*JUR*: *causa*) to plead;
(*contestar*) to contest; (*tentar conseguir*) to
go after; (*concorrer a*) to compete for.
pleito ['plejtu] *m* lawsuit, case; (*fig*) dispute;
~ (**eleitoral**) election.
plenamente [plena'mētʃi] *adv* fully,
completely.
plenário/a [ple'narju/a] *adj* plenary ♦ *m*
plenary session; (*local*) chamber.
plenipotência [plenipo'tēsja] *f* full powers *pl*.
plenipotenciário/a [plenipotē'sjarju/a] *adj*,
m/f plenipotentiary.

NB: *European Portuguese adds the following consonants to certain words*: **b** (sú(b)dito, su(b)til); **c** (a(c)ção,
a(c)cionista, a(c)to); **m** (inde(m)ne); **p** (ado(p)ção, ado(p)tar); *for further details see p. xiii.*

plenitude [pleni'tudʒi] *f* plenitude, fullness.

pleno/a ['plenu/a] *adj* full; (*completo*) complete; **em ~ dia** in broad daylight; **em plena rua/Londres** in the middle of the street/London; **em ~ inverno** in the middle *ou* depths of winter; **em ~ mar** out at sea; **ter plena certeza** to be completely sure; **~s poderes** full powers.

pleonasmo [pljo'naʒmu] *m* pleonasm.

pletora [ple'tɔra] *f* plethora.

pleurisia [plewri'zia] *f* pleurisy.

plinto ['plĩtu] *m* plinth.

plissado/a [pli'sadu/a] *adj* pleated.

pluma ['pluma] *f* feather.

plumagem [plu'maʒẽ] *f* plumage.

plural [plu'raw] (*pl* **-ais**) *adj, m* plural.

pluralismo [plura'liʒmu] *m* pluralism.

pluralista [plura'liʃta] *adj, m/f* pluralist.

Plutão [plu'tãw] *m* Pluto.

plutocrata [pluto'krata] *m/f* plutocrat.

plutônio [plu'tonju] *m* plutonium.

pluvial [plu'vjaw] (*pl* **-ais**) *adj* pluvial, rain *atr*.

PM (*BR*) *abr f, m* = **Polícia Militar**.

PMB *abr m* = **Partido Municipalista Brasileiro**.

PMC (*BR*) *abr m* = **Partido Municipalista Comunitário**.

PMDB *abr m* = **Partido do Movimento Democrático Brasileiro**.

PMN (*BR*) *abr m* = **Partido da Mobilização Nacional**.

PN *abr m* (*BR*) = **Partido Nacionalista** ♦ *abr f* (*COM: de ações*) = **preferencial nominativa**.

PNA (*BR*) *abr m* = **Plano Nacional de Álcool**.

PNB *abr m* (= *Produto Nacional Bruto*) GNP.

PNC (*BR*) *abr m* = **Partido Nacionalista Comunitário**.

PND (*BR*) *abr m* = **Plano Nacional de Desenvolvimento; Partido Nacionalista Democrático**.

pneu ['pnew] *m* tyre (*BRIT*), tire (*US*).

pneumático/a [pnew'matʃiku/a] *adj* pneumatic ♦ *m* tyre (*BRIT*), tire (*US*).

pneumonia [pnewmo'nia] *f* pneumonia.

PNR (*BR*) *abr m* = **Partido da Nova República**.

pó [pɔ] *m* (*partículas*) powder; (*sujeira*) dust; (*col: cocaína*) coke; **~ de arroz** face powder; **ouro/sabão em ~** gold dust/soap powder; **tirar o ~ (de algo)** to dust (sth).

pô [po] (*col*) *excl* (*dando ênfase*) blimey; (*mostrando desagrado*) damn it!

pobre ['pɔbri] *adj* poor ♦ *m/f* poor person; **os ~s** *mpl* the poor; **~ de espírito** simple, dull; **um Sinatra dos ~s** a poor man's Sinatra.

pobre-diabo (*pl* **pobres-diabos**) *m* poor devil.

pobretão/tona [pobre'tãw/'tɔna] (*pl* **-ões/~s**) *m/f* pauper.

pobreza [po'breza] *f* poverty; **~ de espírito** simplicity.

poça ['pɔsa] *f* puddle, pool; **~ de sangue** pool of blood.

poção [po'sãw] (*pl* **-ões**) *f* potion.

pocilga [po'siwga] *f* pigsty.

poço ['posu] *m* well; (*de mina, elevador*) shaft; **ser um ~ de ciência/bondade** (*fig*) to be a fount of knowledge/kindness; **~ de petróleo** oil well.

poções [po'sõjʃ] *fpl de* **poção**.

poda ['pɔda] *f* pruning.

podadeira [poda'dejra] *f* pruning knife.

podar [po'da*] *vt* to prune.

pôde ['podʒi] *etc vb V* **poder**.

pó-de-arroz *m* face powder.

poder [po'de*] *vi* (*ser capaz de*) to be able to, can; (*ter o direito de*) to be allowed to, may ♦ *m* power; (*autoridade*) authority; **pode ser** maybe; **pode ser que** it may be that; **ele poderá vir amanhã** he might come tomorrow; **até não mais ~** with all one's might; **~ com** (*ser superior a*) to be a match for; **não posso com ele** I cannot cope with him; **pudera!** no wonder!; **como é que pode?** (*col*) you're joking!; **pode entrar?** (*posso*) can I come in?; **a ~ de** by dint of; **em ~ de alguém** in sb's hands; **estar no ~** to be in power; **~ aquisitivo** purchasing power; **~ de fogo** fire power.

poderio [pode'riu] *m* might, power.

poderoso/a [pode'rozu/ɔza] *adj* mighty, powerful; (*COMPUT*) powerful.

pódio ['pɔdʒju] *m* podium.

podre ['podri] *adj* rotten, putrid; (*fig*) rotten, corrupt; **sentir-se ~** (*col: mal*) to feel grotty; **~ de rico/cansaço** filthy rich/dog tired.

podres ['podriʃ] *mpl* faults.

podridão [podri'dãw] *f* decay, rottenness; (*fig*) corruption.

põe [põj] *etc vb V* **pôr**.

poeira ['pwejra] *f* dust; **~ radioativa** fall-out.

poeirada [pwej'rada] *f* pile of dust.

poeirento/a [pwej'rẽtu/a] *adj* dusty.

poema ['pwema] *m* poem.

poente ['pwẽtʃi] *m* west; (*do sol*) setting.

poesia [poe'zia] *f* poetry; (*poema*) poem.

poeta ['pwɛta] *m* poet.

poética [po'wɛtʃika] *f* poetics *sg*.

poético/a ['pwɛtʃiku/a] *adj* poetic.

poetisa [pwe'tʃiza] *f* poetess.

poetizar [pwetʃi'za*] *vt* to set to poetry ♦ *vi* to write poetry.

pogrom [po'grõ] (*pl* **~s**) *m* pogrom.

pois [pojʃ] *adv* (*portanto*) so; (*PT: assentimento*) yes ♦ *conj* as, since, because; (*mas*) but; **~ bem** well then; **~ é** that's right; **~ não!** (*BR*) of course!; **~ não?** (*numa loja*) what can I do for you?; (*PT*) isn't it?, aren't you?, didn't they? *etc*; **~ sim!** certainly not!; **~ (então)** then.

polaco/a [po'laku/a] (*PT*) *adj* Polish ♦ *m/f* Pole ♦ *m* (*LING*) Polish.

polainas [po'lajnaʃ] *fpl* gaiters.

polar [po'la*] *adj* polar.

polaridade [polari'dadʒi] *f* polarity.

polarizar [polari'za*] *vt* to polarize.
polca ['pɔwka] *f* polka.
poldro/a ['powdru/a] *m/f* colt/filly.
polegada [pole'gada] *f* inch.
polegar [pole'ga*] *m* (*tb: dedo* ~) thumb.
poleiro [po'lejru] *m* perch.
polêmica [po'lemika] *f* controversy.
polêmico/a [po'lemiku/a] *adj* controversial.
polemista [pole'miʃta] *adj* argumentative ♦ *m/f* debater.
polemizar [polemi'za*] *vi* to debate, argue.
pólen ['pɔlẽ] *m* pollen.
polia [po'lia] *f* pulley.
poliamida [polja'mida] *f* polyamide.
polichinelo [poliʃi'nelu] *m* Mr Punch.
polícia [po'lisja] *f* police, police force ♦ *m/f* policeman/woman; **agente de** ~ police officer; ~ **aduaneira** border police; ~ **militar** military police; ~ **rodoviária** traffic police.
policial [poli'sjaw] (*pl* **-ais**) *adj* police *atr*; **novela** *ou* **romance** ~ detective novel ♦ *m/f* (*BR*) policeman/woman.
policial-militar (*pl* **policiais-militares**) *adj* military police *atr*.
policiamento [polisja'mẽtu] *m* policing.
policiar [poli'sja*] *vt* to police; (*instintos*, *modos*) to control, keep in check; ~**-se** *vr* to control o.s.
policlínica [poli'klinika] *f* general hospital.
policultura [polikuw'tura] *f* mixed farming.
polidez [poli'deʒ] *f* good manners *pl*, politeness.
polido/a [po'lidu/a] *adj* (*lustrado*) polished, shiny; (*cortês*) well-mannered, polite.
poliéster [po'ljɛʃte*] *m* polyester.
poliestireno [poljeʃtʃi'renu] *m* polystyrene.
polietileno [poljetʃi'lenu] *m* polyethylene.
poligamia [poliga'mia] *f* polygamy.
polígamo/a [po'ligamu/a] *adj* polygamous.
poliglota [poli'glɔta] *adj, m/f* polyglot.
polígono [po'ligonu] *m* polygon.
polimento [poli'mẽtu] *m* (*lustração*) polishing; (*finura*) refinement.
Polinésia [poli'nɛzja] *f*: **a** ~ Polynesia.
polinésio/a [poli'nɛzju/a] *adj, m/f* Polynesian.
polinização [poliniza'sãw] *f* pollination.
polinizar [polini'za*] *vt, vi* to pollinate.
pólio ['pɔlju] *f* polio.
poliomielite [poljomje'litʃi] *f* poliomyelitis.
pólipo ['pɔlipu] *m* polyp.
polir [po'li*] *vt* to polish.
polissílabo/a [poli'silabu/a] *adj* polysyllabic ♦ *m* polysyllable.
politécnica [poli'tɛknika] *f* (*EDUC*) polytechnic.
política [po'litʃika] *f* politics *sg*; (*programa*) policy; (*diplomacia*) tact; (*astúcia*) cunning; *V tb* **político**.
politicagem [politʃi'kaʒẽ] *f* politicking.
politicar [politʃi'ka*] *vi* to be involved in politics; (*discorrer*) to talk politics.

político/a [po'litʃiku/a] *adj* political; (*astuto*) crafty ♦ *m/f* politician.
politiqueiro/a [politʃi'kejru/a] *m/f* political wheeler-dealer ♦ *adj* politicking.
politizar [politʃi'za*] *vt* to politicize; (*trabalhadores*) to mobilize politically; ~**-se** *vr* to become politically aware.
pólo ['pɔlu] *m* pole; (*ESPORTE*) polo; ~ **aquático** water polo; ~ **petroquímico** petrochemical complex; **P**~ **Norte/Sul** North/South Pole.
polonês/esa [polo'neʃ/eza] *adj* Polish ♦ *m/f* Pole ♦ *m* (*LING*) Polish.
Polônia [po'lonja] *f*: **a** ~ Poland.
polpa ['powpa] *f* pulp.
polpudo/a [pow'pudu/a] *adj* (*fruta*) fleshy; (*negócio*) profitable, lucrative; (*quantia*) sizeable, considerable.
poltrão/trona [pow'trãw/'trɔna] (*pl* **-ões/~s**) *adj* cowardly ♦ *m/f* coward.
poltrona [pow'trɔna] *f* armchair; (*em teatro*, *cinema*) upholstered seat; *V tb* **poltrão**.
poluente [po'lwẽtʃi] *adj, m* pollutant.
poluição [polwi'sãw] *f* pollution.
poluidor(a) [polwi'do*(a)] *adj* pollutant.
poluir [po'lwi*] *vt* to pollute.
polvilhar [powvi'ʎa*] *vt* to sprinkle, powder.
polvilho [pow'viʎu] *m* powder; (*farinha*) manioc flour.
polvo ['powvu] *m* octopus.
pólvora ['pɔwvora] *f* gunpowder.
polvorosa [powvo'rɔza] (*col*) *f* uproar; **em** ~ (*apressado*) in a flap; (*desarrumado*) in a mess.
pomada [po'mada] *f* ointment.
pomar [po'ma*] *m* orchard.
pomba ['põba] *f* dove; ~**(s)!** for heaven's sake!
pombal [põ'baw] (*pl* **-ais**) *m* dovecote.
pombo ['põbu] *m* pigeon.
pombo-correio (*pl* **pombos-correios**) *m* carrier pigeon.
pomo ['pomu] *m*: ~ **de discórdia** bone of contention.
pomo-de-Adão [-a'dãw] *m* Adam's apple.
pomos ['pomoʃ] *vb V* **pôr**.
pompa ['põpa] *f* pomp.
Pompéia [põ'peja] *n* Pompeii.
pompom [põ'põ] (*pl* **-ns**) *m* pompom.
pomposo/a [põ'pozu/ɔza] *adj* ostentatious, pompous.
ponche ['põʃi] *m* punch.
poncheira [põ'ʃejra] *f* punchbowl.
poncho ['põʃu] *m* poncho, cape.
ponderação [põdera'sãw] *f* consideration, meditation; (*prudência*) prudence.
ponderado/a [põde'radu/a] *adj* prudent.
ponderar [põde'ra*] *vt* to consider, weigh up ♦ *vi* to meditate, muse; ~ **que** (*alegar*) to point out that.

NB: European Portuguese adds the following consonants to certain words: **b** (sú(b)dito, su(b)til); **c** (a(c)ção, a(c)cionista, a(c)to); **m** (inde(m)ne); **p** (ado(p)ção, ado(p)tar); *for further details see p. xiii.*

pônei ['ponej] *m* pony.
ponho ['poɲu] *etc vb V* **pôr**.
ponta ['pôta] *f* tip; (*de faca*) point; (*de sapato*) toe; (*extremidade*) end; (*TEATRO, CINEMA*) walk-on part; (*FUTEBOL*: posição) wing; (: *jogador*) winger; **uma ~ de** (*um pouco*) a touch of; **~ de cigarro** cigarette end; **~ do dedo** fingertip; **na ~ da língua** on the tip of one's tongue; **na(s) ~(s) dos pés** on tiptoe; **de ~ a ~** from one end to the other; (*do princípio ao fim*) from beginning to end; **~ de terra** point; **estar de ~ com alguém** to be at odds with sb; **agüentar as ~s** (*col*) to hold on.
ponta-cabeça *f*: **de ~** upside down; (*cair*) head first.
pontada [pô'tada] *f* (*dor*) twinge.
ponta-de-lança (*pl* **pontas-de-lança**) *m/f* (*fig*) spearhead.
ponta-direita (*pl* **pontas-direitas**) *m* (*FUTEBOL*) right winger.
ponta-esquerda (*pl* **pontas-esquerdas**) *m* (*FUTEBOL*) left winger.
pontal [pô'taw] (*pl* **-ais**) *m* (*de terra*) point, promontory.
pontão [pô'tãw] *m* pontoon.
pontapé [pôta'pɛ] *m* kick; **dar ~s em alguém** to kick sb.
pontaria [pôta'ria] *f* aim; **fazer ~** to take aim.
ponte ['pôtʃi] *f* bridge; **~ aérea** air shuttle, airlift; **~ de safena** (heart) bypass operation; **~ levadiça** drawbridge; **~ móvel** swing bridge; **~ suspensa** *ou* **pênsil** suspension bridge.
ponteado/a [pô'tʃjadu/a] *adj* stippled, dotted ♦ *m* stipple.
pontear [po'tʃja*] *vt* (*pontilhar*) to dot, stipple; (*dar pontos*) to sew, stitch.
ponteira [pô'tejra] *f* ferrule, tip.
ponteiro [pô'tejru] *m* (*indicador*) pointer; (*de relógio*) hand; (*MÚS*: *plectro*) plectrum.
pontiagudo/a [pôtʃja'gudu/a] *adj* sharp, pointed.
pontificado [pôtʃifi'kadu] *m* pontificate.
pontificar [pôtʃifi'ka*] *vi* to pontificate.
pontífice [pô'tʃifisi] *m* pontiff, Pope.
pontilhado/a [pôtʃi'ʎadu/a] *adj* dotted ♦ *m* dotted area.
pontilhar [pôtʃi'ʎa*] *vt* to dot, stipple.
pontinha [pô'tʃiɲa] *f*: **uma ~ de** a bit *ou* touch of.
ponto ['pôtu] *m* point; (*MED, COSTURA, TRICÔ*) stitch; (*pequeno sinal, do i*) dot; (*na pontuação*) full stop (*BRIT*), period (*US*); (*na pele*) spot; (*TEATRO*) prompter; (*de ônibus*) stop; (*de táxi*) rank (*BRIT*), stand (*US*); (*tb*: **~ cantado**) macumba chant; (*matéria escolar*) subject; (*boca-de-fumo*) drug den; **estar a ~ de fazer** to be on the point of doing; **ao ~** (*bife*) medium; **até certo ~** to a certain extent; **às cinco em ~** at five o'clock on the dot; **em ~ de bala** (*col*) all set; **assinar o ~** to sign in; (*fig*) to put in an appear-

ance; **dar ~s** (*MED*) to put in stitches; **não dar ~ sem nó** (*fig*) to look out for one's own interests; **entregar os ~s** (*fig*) to give up; **fazer ~ em** to hang out at; **pôr um ~ em algo** (*fig*) to put a stop to sth; **dois ~s** colon *sg*; **~ cardeal** cardinal point; **~ culminante** highest point; (*fig*) peak; **~ de admiração** (*PT*) exclamation mark; **~ de equilíbrio** (*COM*) break-even point; **~ de exclamação/interrogação** exclamation/question mark; **~ de meia/de tricô** stocking/plain stitch; **~ de mira** bead; **~ de partida** starting point; **~ de referência** point of reference; **~ de vista** point of view, viewpoint; **~ facultativo** optional day off; **~ final** (*fig*) end; (*de ônibus*) terminus; **~ fraco** weak point.
ponto-de-venda (*pl* **pontos-de-venda**) *m* (*COM*) point of sale, outlet.
ponto-e-vírgula (*pl* **ponto-e-vírgulas**) *m* semicolon.
pontuação [pôtwa'sãw] *f* punctuation.
pontual [pô'twaw] (*pl* **-ais**) *adj* punctual.
pontualidade [pôtwali'dadʒi] *f* punctuality.
pontuar [pô'twa*] *vt* to punctuate.
pontudo/a [pô'tudu/a] *adj* pointed.
poodle ['pudw] *m* poodle.
pool [puw] *m* pool.
popa ['popa] *f* stern, poop; **à ~** astern, aft.
popelina [pope'lina] *f* poplin.
população [popula'sãw] (*pl* **-ões**) *f* population.
populacional [populasjo'naw] (*pl* **-ais**) *adj* population *atr*.
populações [popula'sõjʃ] *fpl de* **população**.
popular [popu'la*] *adj* popular.
popularidade [populari'dadʒi] *f* popularity.
popularizar [populari'za*] *vt* to popularize, make popular; **~-se** *vr* to become popular.
populista [popu'liʃta] *adj* populist.
populoso/a [popu'lozu/za] *adj* populous.
pôquer ['poke*] *m* poker.
por [po*] *prep* (*a favor de*) for; (*por causa de*) out of, because of, from; (*meio, agente*) by; (*troca*) (in exchange) for; (*através de*) through; **~ hábito/natureza** out of habit/by nature; **soubemos disso ~ carta** we learnt about it by letter; **viemos pelo parque** we came through the park; **faço isso ~ ela** I do it for her; **~ volta das duas horas** at about two o'clock; **~ aqui** this way; **~ isso** therefore; **~ cento** per cent; **~ mais difícil que seja** however difficult it is; **pelo amor de Deus!** for heaven's sake!; **~ escrito** in writing; **~ fora/~ dentro** outside/inside; **~ exemplo** for example; **~ ano** yearly; **~ mês** monthly; **~ semana** weekly; **~ dia** daily; **~ si** by o.s.; **está ~ acontecer** it is about to happen, it is yet to happen; **está ~ fazer** it is still to be done; **~ que** (*BR*) why; **~ quê?** (*BR*) why?
pôr [po*] *vt* to put; (*roupas*) to put on; (*objeções, dúvidas*) to raise; (*ovos, mesa*) to lay; (*defeito*) to find ♦ *m*: **o ~ do sol** sunset; **~-se** *vr* (*sol*) to set; **~ furioso** to infuriate;

~ **de lado** to set aside; ~ **o dedo na ferida** (*fig*) to hit a raw nerve; **você põe açúcar?** do you take sugar?; **ponhamos que** ... let us suppose (that) ..., supposing ...; ~**-se de pé** to stand up; ~**-se a caminho** to set off; ~**-se a chorar** to start crying; **ponha-se no meu lugar** put yourself in my position.

porão [po'rãw] (*pl* **-ões**) *m* (*NÁUT*) hold; (*de casa*) basement; (: *armazém*) cellar.

porca ['pɔxka] *f* (*animal*) sow; (*TEC*) nut.

porcalhão/lhona [poxka'ʎãw/'ʎɔna] (*pl* **-ões/** ~**s**) *adj* filthy ♦ *m/f* pig.

porção [pox'sãw] (*pl* **-ões**) *f* portion, piece; **uma** ~ **de** a lot of.

porcaria [poxka'ria] *f* filth; (*dito sujo*) obscenity; (*coisa ruim*) piece of junk ♦ *excl* damn!; **o filme era uma** ~ the film was a load of rubbish.

porcelana [poxse'lana] *f* porcelain, china.

porcentagem [poxsẽ'taʒẽ] (*pl* **-ns**) *f* percentage.

porco/a ['poxku/'pɔxka] *adj* filthy ♦ *m* (*animal*) pig, hog (*US*); (*carne*) pork; ~ **chauvinista** male chauvinist pig.

porções [pox'sõjʃ] *fpl de* **porção**.

porco-espinho (*pl* **porcos-espinhos**) *m* porcupine.

porco-montês [-mõ'teʃ] (*pl* **porcos-monteses**) *m* wild boar.

porejar [pore'ʒa*] *vt* to exude ♦ *vi* to be exuded.

porém [po'rẽ] *conj* however.

porfia [pox'fia] *f* (*altercação*) dispute, wrangle; (*rivalidade*) rivalry.

pormenor [poxme'no*] *m* detail.

pormenorizar [poxmenori'za*] *vt* to detail.

pornô [pox'no] (*col*) *adj inv* porn ♦ *m* (*filme*) porn film.

pornochanchada [poxnoʃã'ʃada] *f* (*filme*) soft porn movie.

pornografia [poxnogra'fia] *f* pornography.

pornográfico/a [poxno'grafiku/a] *adj* pornographic.

poro ['pɔru] *m* pore.

porões [po'rõjs] *mpl de* **porão**.

pororoca [poro'rɔka] *f* bore.

poroso/a [po'rozu/ɔza] *adj* porous.

porquanto [pox'kwãtu] *conj* since, seeing that.

porque ['poxke] *conj* because; (*interrogativo*: *PT*) why.

porquê [pox'ke] *adv* why; ~? (*PT*) why? ♦ *m* reason, motive.

porquinho-da-índia [pox'kiɲu-] (*pl* **porquinhos-da-índia**) *m* guinea pig.

porra ['poxa] (*col!*) *f* come (!), spunk (!) ♦ *excl* fuck (!), fucking hell (!); **para quê** ~? what the fuck for? (!).

porrada [po'xada] *f* (*col*: *pancada*) beating; **uma** ~ **de** (*col!*) fucking loads of (!).

porra-louca (*pl* **porras-loucas**) (*col!*) *m/f*

fucking maniac (!) ♦ *adj* fucking crazy (!).

porre ['pɔxi] (*col*) *m* booze-up; **tomar um** ~ to get plastered; **estar de** ~ to be plastered; **ser um** ~ (*ser chato*) to be boring, be a drag.

porretada [poxe'tada] *f* clubbing.

porrete [po'xetʃi] *m* club.

porta ['pɔxta] *f* door; (*vão da* ~) doorway; (*de um jardim*) gate; (*COMPUT*) port; **a** ~**s fechadas** behind closed doors; **de** ~ **em** ~ from door to door; ~ **corrediça** sliding door; ~ **da rua/da frente/dos fundos** street/front/back door; ~ **de entrada** entrance door; ~ **de vaivém** swing door; ~ **giratória** revolving door; ~ **sanfonada** folding door.

porta-aviões *m inv* aircraft carrier.

porta-bandeira (*pl* ~**s**) *m/f* standard-bearer.

porta-chaves *m inv* key-holder.

portador(a) [pɔxta'do*(a)] *m/f* bearer; **ao** ~ (*COM*) payable to the bearer.

porta-espada (*pl* ~**s**) *m* sheath.

porta-estandarte (*pl* ~**s**) *m/f* standard-bearer.

porta-fólio [-'fɔlju] (*pl* ~**s**) *m* portfolio.

portagem [pox'taʒẽ] (*PT*: *pl* **-ns**) *f* toll.

porta-jóias *m inv* jewellery (*BRIT*) *ou* jewelry (*US*) box.

portal [pox'taw] (*pl* **-ais**) *m* doorway.

porta-lápis *m inv* pencil box.

portaló [pɔxta'lɔ] *m* (*NÁUT*) gangway.

porta-luvas *m inv* (*AUTO*) glove compartment.

porta-malas *m inv* (*AUTO*) boot (*BRIT*), trunk (*US*).

porta-moedas (*PT*) *m* purse.

porta-níqueis *m inv* purse.

portanto [pox'tãtu] *conj* so, therefore.

portão [pox'tãw] (*pl* **-ões**) *m* gate.

porta-partitura (*pl* ~**s**) *m* music stand.

portar [pox'ta*] *vt* to carry; ~**-se** *vr* to behave.

porta-retratos *m inv* photo frame.

porta-revistas *m inv* magazine rack.

portaria [pɔxta'ria] *f* (*de um edifício*) entrance hall; (*recepção*) reception desk; (*do governo*) edict, decree; **baixar uma** ~ to issue a decree.

porta-seios *m inv* bra, brassiere.

portátil [pox'tatʃiw] (*pl* **-eis**) *adj* portable.

porta-toalhas *m inv* towel rail.

porta-voz (*pl* ~**es**) *m/f* (*pessoa*) spokesman/woman.

porte ['pɔxtʃi] *m* (*transporte*) transport; (*custo*) freight charge, carriage; (*NÁUT*) tonnage, capacity; (*atitude*) bearing; ~ **pago** post paid; **de grande** ~ far-reaching, important; **empresa de** ~ **medio** medium-sized enterprise; **um autor do** ~ **de** ... an author of the calibre (*BRIT*) *ou* caliber (*US*) of ....

NB: European Portuguese adds the following consonants to certain words: **b** (sú(b)dito, su(b)til); **c** (a(c)ção, a(c)cionista, a(c)to); **m** (inde(m)ne); **p** (ado(p)ção, ado(p)tar); *for further details see p. xiii.*

porteiro/a [pox'tejru/a] *m/f* caretaker; ~ **eletrônico** entryphone.

portenho/a [pox'tɛɲu/a] *adj* from Buenos Aires ♦ *m/f* person from Buenos Aires.

portento [pox'tẽtu] *m* wonder, marvel.

portentoso/a [poxtẽ'tozu/ɔza] *adj* amazing, marvellous (*BRIT*), marvelous (*US*).

pórtico ['pɔxtʃiku] *m* porch, portico.

portinhola [poxtʃi'ɲɔla] *f* small door; (*de carruagem*) door.

porto ['poxtu] *m* (*do mar*) port, harbour (*BRIT*), harbor (*US*); (*vinho*) port; **o P~** Oporto; ~ **de escala** port of call; ~ **franco** freeport.

porto-alegrense [-ale'grẽsi] *adj* from Porto Alegre ♦ *m/f* person from Porto Alegre.

portões [pox'tõjʃ] *mpl de* **portão**.

Porto Rico *m* Puerto Rico.

porto-riquenho/a [poxtuxi'keɲu/a] *adj, m/f* Puertorican.

portuense [pox'twẽsi] *adj* from Oporto ♦ *m/f* person from Oporto.

portuga [pox'tuga] *m/f* (*pej*) Portuguese.

Portugal [poxtu'gaw] *m* Portugal.

português/guesa [portu'geʃ/'geza] *adj* Portuguese ♦ *m/f* Portuguese ♦ *m* (*LING*) Portuguese; ~ **de Portugal/do Brasil** European/Brazilian Portuguese.

portunhol [poxtu'ɲɔw] *m* *mixture of Spanish and Portuguese*.

porventura [poxvẽ'tura] *adj* by chance; **se** ~ **você ...** if you happen to ....

porvir [pox'vi*] *m* future.

pôs [poʃ] *vb V* **pôr**.

pós- [pɔjʃ-] *prefixo* post-.

posar [po'za*] *vi* (*FOTO*) to pose.

pós-datado/a [-da'tadu/a] *adj* post-dated.

pós-datar *vt* to postdate.

pose ['pozi] *f* pose.

pós-escrito *m* postscript.

pós-graduação *f* postgraduation; **curso de** ~ postgraduate course.

pós-graduado/a *adj, m/f* postgraduate.

pós-guerra *m* post-war period; **o Brasil do** ~ post-war Brazil.

posição [pozi'sãw] (*pl* **-ões**) *f* position; (*social*) standing, status; (*de esportista no mundo*) ranking; **tomar uma** ~ to take a stand.

posicionar [pozisjo'na*] *vt* to position; ~**-se** *vr* to position o.s.; (*tomar atitude*) to take a position.

positivo/a [pozi'tʃivu/a] *adj* positive ♦ *m* positive ♦ *excl* (*col*) yeah! sure!

posologia [pozolo'ʒia] *f* dosage.

pós-operatório/a [-opera'tɔrju/a] *adj* post-operative.

pospor [poʃ'po*] (*irreg: como* **pôr**) *vt* to put after; (*adiar*) to postpone.

possante [po'sãtʃi] *adj* powerful, strong; (*carro*) flashy.

posse ['pɔsi] *f* possession, ownership; (*investidura*) swearing in; ~**s** *fpl* possessions,

belongings; **tomar** ~ to take office; **tomar** ~ **de** to take possession of; **cerimônia de** ~ swearing in ceremony; **pessoa de** ~**s** person of means; **viver de acordo com suas** ~**s** to live according to one's means.

posseiro/a [po'sejru/a] *adj* leaseholding ♦ *m/f* leaseholder.

possessão [pose'sãw] *f* possession.

possessivo/a [pose'sivu/a] *adj* possessive.

possesso/a [po'sɛsu/a] *adj* possessed; (*furioso*) furious.

possibilidade [posibili'dadʒi] *f* possibility; (*oportunidade*) chance; ~**s** *fpl* means.

possibilitar [posibili'ta*] *vt* to make possible, permit.

possível [po'sivew] (*pl* **-eis**) *adj* possible; **fazer todo o** ~ to do one's best; **não é** ~**!** (*col*) you're joking!

posso ['posu] *etc vb V* **poder**.

possuidor(a) [poswi'do*(a)] *m/f* (*de casa, livro etc*) owner; (*de dinheiro, talento etc*) possessor; **ser** ~ **de** to be the owner/possessor of.

possuir [po'swi*] *vt* (*casa, livro etc*) to own; (*dinheiro, talento*) to possess; (*dominar*) to possess, grip; (*sexualmente*) to take, have.

posta ['pɔʃta] *f* (*pedaço*) piece, slice.

postal [poʃ'taw] (*pl* **-ais**) *adj* postal ♦ *m* postcard.

postar [poʃ'ta*] *vt* to place, post; ~**-se** *vr* to position o.s.

posta-restante (*pl* **postas-restantes**) *f* poste-restante (*BRIT*), general delivery (*US*).

poste ['pɔʃtʃi] *m* pole, post.

pôster ['poʃte*] *m* poster.

postergar [poʃtex'ga*] *vt* (*adiar*) to postpone; (*amigos*) to pass over; (*interesse pessoal*) to set *ou* put aside; (*lei, norma*) to disregard.

posteridade [poʃteri'dadʒi] *f* posterity.

posterior [poʃte'rjo*] *adj* (*mais tarde*) subsequent, later; (*traseiro*) rear, back ♦ *m* (*col*) posterior, bottom.

posteriormente [poʃterjox'mẽtʃi] *adv* later, subsequently.

postiço/a [poʃ'tʃisu/a] *adj* false, artificial; **dentes** ~**s** false teeth.

postigo [poʃ'tʃigu] *m* (*em porta*) peephole.

posto/a ['poʃtu/'poʃta] *pp de* **pôr** ♦ *m* post, position; (*emprego*) job; (*de diplomata: local*) posting; ~ **de comando** command post; ~ **de gasolina** service *ou* petrol station; ~ **que** although; **a** ~**s** at action stations; ~ **do corpo de bombeiros** fire station; ~ **de saúde** health centre *ou* center.

posto-chave (*pl* **postos-chaves**) *m* key position *ou* post.

postulado [poʃtu'ladu] *m* postulate, assumption.

postulante [poʃtu'lãtʃi] *m/f* petitioner; (*candidato*) candidate.

postular [poʃtu'la*] *vt* (*pedir*) to request; (*teoria*) to postulate.

póstumo/a ['pɔʃtumu/a] *adj* posthumous.

postura [po'ftura] *f* (*posição*) posture, position; (*aspecto físico*) appearance; (*fig*) posture.
posudo/a [po'zudu/a] *adj* poseurish.
potassa [po'tasa] *f* potash.
potássio [po'tasju] *m* potassium.
potável [po'tavew] (*pl* **-eis**) *adj* drinkable; **água** ~ drinking water.
pote ['pɔtʃi] *m* jug, pitcher; (*de geléia*) jar; (*de creme*) pot; **chover a** ~**s** (*PT*) to rain cats and dogs; **dinheiro aos** ~**s** (*fig*) pots of money.
potência [po'tẽsja] *f* power; (*força*) strength; (*nação*) power; (*virilidade*) potency.
potencial [potẽ'sjaw] (*pl* **-ais**) *adj* potential, latent ♦ *m* potential; **riquezas** *etc* **em** ~ potential wealth *etc*.
potentado [potẽ'tadu] *m* potentate.
potente [po'tẽtʃi] *adj* powerful, potent.
pot-pourri [popu'xi] *m* (*MÚS*) medley; (*fig*) pot-pourri.
potro/a ['potru/a] *m/f* (*cavalo*) colt/filly, foal.
pouca-vergonha (*pl* **poucas-vergonhas**) *f* (*ato*) shameful act, disgrace; (*falta de vergonha*) shamelessness.
pouco/a ['poku/a] *adj*, *pron* (*sg*) little; (*pl*) few ♦ *adv* not much, little ♦ *m*: **um** ~ a little; **há** ~ **(tempo)** a short time ago; **poucas vezes** rarely; ~ **a** ~ gradually, bit by bit; **por** ~ almost; **aos** ~**s** gradually; **fazer** ~ **de** (*desprezar*) to belittle; (*zombar*) to make light of; **nem um** ~ not at all; **dentro em** ~, **daqui a** ~ shortly; ~ **antes** a short while before; **ouvir poucas e boas** to hear some home truths.
pouco-caso *m* scorn.
poupador(a) [popa'do*(a)] *adj* thrifty.
poupança [po'pãsa] *f* thrift; (*economias*) savings *pl*; (*tb*: **caderneta de** ~) savings bank.
poupar [po'pa*] *vt* to save; (*vida*) to spare; ~ **alguém** (*de sofrimentos*) to spare sb; ~ **algo a alguém**, ~ **alguém de algo** (*trabalho etc*) to save sb sth; (*aborrecimentos*) to spare sb sth.
pouquinho [po'kiɲu] *m*: **um** ~ **(de)** a little.
pouquíssimo/a [po'kisimu/a] *adj*, *adv superl de pouco*.
pousada [po'zada] *f* (*hospedagem*) lodging; (*hospedaria*) inn.
pousar [po'za*] *vt* to place; (*mão*) to rest, place ♦ *vi* (*avião*, *pássaro*) to land; (*pernoitar*) to spend the night.
pouso ['pozu] *m* landing; (*lugar*) resting place.
povão [po'vãw] *m* ordinary people.
povaréu [pova'rɛw] *m* crowd of people.
povo ['povu] *m* people; (*raça*) people *pl*, race; (*plebe*) common people *pl*; (*multidão*) crowd.
povoação [povwa'sãw] (*pl* **-ões**) *f* (*aldeia*) village, settlement; (*habitantes*) population;

(*ato de povoar*) settlement, colonization.
povoado/a [po'vwadu/a] *adj* populated ♦ *m* village.
povoamento [povwa'mẽtu] *m* settlement.
povoar [po'vwa*] *vt* (*de habitantes*) to people, populate; (*de animais etc*) to stock.
poxa ['poʃa] *excl* gosh!
PP *abr* (*COM*: *de ações*) = **preferencial ao portador**.
PPB *abr m* = **Partido do Povo Brasileiro**.
PR (*BR*) *abr* = **Paraná** ♦ *abr f* = **Polícia Rodoviária**.
pra [pra] (*col*) *prep* = **para**; **para a**.
praça ['prasa] *f* (*largo*) square; (*mercado*) marketplace; (*soldado*) soldier; (*cidade*) town ♦ *m* (*MIL*) private; (*polícia*) constable; **sentar** ~ to enlist; ~ **de touros** bull ring; ~ **forte** stronghold.
praça-d'armas (*pl* **praças-d'armas**) *m* officers' mess.
pracinha [pra'siɲa] *m* GI.
prado ['pradu] *m* meadow, grassland; (*BR*: *hipódromo*) racecourse.
pra-frente (*col*) *adj inv* trendy.
prafrentex [prafrẽ'tɛks] (*col*) *adj inv* trendy.
Praga ['praga] *n* Prague.
praga ['praga] *f* (*maldição*) curse; (*coisa, pessoa importuna*) nuisance; (*desgraça*) misfortune; (*erva daninha*) weed; **rogar** ~ **a alguém** to curse sb.
pragmático/a [prag'matʃiku/a] *adj* (*prático*) pragmatic.
pragmatismo [pragma'tʃiʒmu] *m* pragmatism.
pragmatista [pragma'tʃiʃta] *adj*, *m/f* pragmatist.
praguejar [prage'ʒa*] *vt*, *vi* to curse.
praia ['praja] *f* beach, seashore.
pralina [pra'lina] *f* praline.
prancha ['prãʃa] *f* plank; (*NÁUT*) gangplank; (*de surfe*) board.
prancheta [prã'ʃeta] *f* (*mesa*) drawing board.
prantear [prã'tʃja*] *vt* to mourn ♦ *vi* to weep.
pranto ['prãtu] *m* weeping; **debulhar-se em** ~ to weep bitterly.
Prata ['prata] *f*: **o rio da** ~ the River Plate.
prata ['prata] *f* silver; (*col*: *cruzeiro*) ≈ quid (*BRIT*), ≈ buck (*US*); **de** ~ silver *atr*; ~ **de lei** sterling silver.
prataria [prata'ria] *f* silverware; (*pratos*) crockery.
pratarrão [prata'xãw] (*pl* **-ões**) *m* large plate.
prateado/a [pra'tʃjadu/a] *adj* silver-plated; (*brilhante*) silvery; (*cor*) silver ♦ *m* (*cor*) silver; (*de um objeto*) silver-plating; **papel** ~ silver paper.
pratear [pra'tʃja*] *vt* to silver-plate; (*fig*) to turn silver.
prateleira [prate'lejra] *f* shelf.
prática ['pratʃika] *f* (*ato de praticar*) practice; (*experiência*) experience, know-how; (*cos-*

NB: *European Portuguese adds the following consonants to certain words:* **b** (sú(b)dito, su(b)til); **c** (a(c)ção, a(c)cionista, a(c)to); **m** (inde(m)ne); **p** (ado(p)ção, ado(p)tar); *for further details see p. xiii.*

tume) habit, custom; **na ~** in practice; **pôr em ~** to put into practice; **aprender com a ~** to learn with practice; *V tb* **prático**.

praticagem [pratʃi'kaʒẽ] *f (NÁUT)* pilotage.

praticante [pratʃi'kãtʃi] *adj* practising *(BRIT)*, practicing *(US)* ♦ *m/f* apprentice; *(de esporte)* practitioner.

praticar [pratʃi'ka*] *vt* to practise *(BRIT)*, practice *(US)*; *(profissão, medicina)* to practise *ou* practice; *(roubo, operação)* to carry out.

praticável [pratʃi'kavew] *(pl* **-eis)** *adj* practical, feasible.

prático/a ['pratʃiku/a] *adj* practical ♦ *m/f* expert ♦ *m (NÁUT)* pilot.

prato ['pratu] *m (louça)* plate; *(comida)* dish; *(de uma refeição)* course; *(de toca-discos)* turntable; **~s** *mpl (MÚS)* cymbals; **~ raso/ fundo/de sobremesa** dinner/soup/dessert plate; **~ do dia** dish of the day; **cuspir no ~ em que comeu** *(fig)* to bite the hand that feeds one; **pôr algo em ~s limpos** to get to the bottom of sth; **~ de resistência** pièce de résistance.

praxe ['praksi] *f* custom, usage; **de ~** usually; **ser de ~** to be the norm.

prazenteiro/a [prazẽ'tejru/a] *adj* cheerful, pleasant.

prazer [pra'ze*] *m* pleasure ♦ *vi:* **~ a alguém** to please sb; **muito ~ em conhecê-lo** pleased to meet you.

prazeroso/a [praze'rozu/ɔza] *adj (pessoa)* pleased; *(viagem)* pleasurable.

prazo ['prazu] *m* term, period; *(vencimento)* expiry date, time limit; **a curto/médio/longo ~** in the short/medium/long term; **comprar a ~** to buy on hire purchase *(BRIT) ou* on the installment plan *(US)*; **último ~ ou ~ final** deadline.

pre- [pri-] *prefixo* pre-.

pré- [pre-] *prefixo* pre-.

preamar [prea'ma*] *(BR) f* high tide.

preâmbulo [pre'ãbulu] *m* preamble, introduction; **sem mais ~s** without further ado.

preaquecer [prjake'se*] *vt* to preheat.

pré-aviso *m* (prior) notice.

precário/a [pre'karju/a] *adj* precarious, insecure; *(escasso)* failing; *(estado de saúde)* delicate.

precatado/a [preka'tadu/a] *adj* cautious.

precatar-se [preka'taxsi] *vr* to take precautions; **~-se contra** to be wary of; **precate-se para o pior** prepare yourself for the worst.

precatória [preka'tɔrja] *f (JUR)* writ, prerogative order.

precaução [prekaw'sãw] *(pl* **-ões)** *f* precaution.

precaver-se [preka'vexsi] *vr:* **~ (contra *ou* de)** to be on one's guard (against); **~ para algo/ fazer algo** to prepare o.s for sth/be prepared to do sth.

precavido/a [preka'vidu/a] *adj* cautious.

prece ['presi] *f* prayer; *(súplica)* entreaty.

precedência [prese'dẽsja] *f* precedence; **ter ~ sobre** to take precedence over.

precedente [prese'dẽtʃi] *adj* preceding ♦ *m* precedent; **sem ~(s)** unprecedented.

preceder [prese'de*] *vt, vi* to precede; **~ a algo** to precede sth; *(ter primazia)* to take precedence over sth.

preceito [pre'sejtu] *m* precept, ruling.

preceituar [presej'twa*] *vt* to set down, prescribe.

preceptor [presep'to*] *m* mentor.

preciosidade [presjozi'dadʒi] *f (qualidade)* preciousness; *(coisa)* treasure.

preciosismo [presjo'ziʒmu] *m* preciosity.

precioso/a [pre'sjozu/ɔza] *adj* precious; *(de grande importância)* invaluable.

precipício [presi'pisju] *m* precipice; *(fig)* abyss.

precipitação [presipita'sãw] *f* haste; *(imprudência)* rashness.

precipitado/a [presipi'tadu/a] *adj* hasty; *(imprudente)* rash.

precipitar [presipi'ta*] *vt (atirar)* to hurl; *(acontecimentos)* to precipitate ♦ *vi (QUÍM)* to precipitate; **~-se** *vr (atirar-se)* to hurl o.s.; *(contra, para)* to rush; *(agir com precipitação)* to be rash, act rashly; **~ alguém/ ~-se em** *(situação)* to plunge sb/be plunged into; *(aventuras, perigos)* to sweep sb/be swept into.

precisado/a [presi'zadu/a] *adj* needy, in need.

precisamente [presiza'mẽtʃi] *adv* precisely.

precisão [presi'zãw] *f (exatidão)* precision, accuracy; **ter ~ de** to need.

precisar [presi'za*] *vt* to need; *(especificar)* to specify ♦ *vi* to be in need; **~-se** *vr:* **"precisa-se"** "needed"; **~ de** to need; *(uso impessoal):* **não precisa você se preocupar** you needn't worry; **precisa de um passaporte** a passport is necessary *ou* needed; **preciso ir** I have to go; **~ que alguém faça** to need sb to do.

preciso/a [pre'sizu/a] *adj (exato)* precise, accurate; *(necessário)* necessary; *(claro)* concise; **é ~ você ir** you must go.

preclaro/a [pre'klaru/a] *adj* famous, illustrious.

preço ['presu] *m* price; *(custo)* cost; *(valor)* value; **por qualquer ~** at any price; **a ~ de banana** *(BR) ou* **de chuva** *(PT)* dirt cheap; **não ter ~** *(fig)* to be priceless; **~ por atacado/a varejo** wholesale/retail price; **~ de custo** cost price; **~ de venda** sale price; **~ de fábrica/de revendedor** factory/trade price; **~ à vista** cash price; *(de commodities)* spot price; **~ pedido** asking price.

precoce [pre'kɔsi] *adj* precocious; *(antecipado)* early; *(calvície)* premature.

precocidade [prekosi'dadʒi] *f* precociousness.

preconcebido/a [prekõse'bidu/a] *adj* preconceived.

preconceito [prekõ'sejtu] *m* prejudice.

preconizar [prekoni'za*] *vt* to extol;

(*aconselhar*) to advocate.

precursor(a) [prɛkux'so*(a)] *m/f* (*predecessor*) precursor, forerunner; (*mensageiro*) herald.

predador [preda'do*] *m* predator.

pré-datado/a [-da'tadu/a] *adj* predated.

pré-datar *vt* to predate.

predatório/a [preda'tɔrju/a] *adj* predatory.

predecessor [predese'so*] *m* predecessor.

predestinado/a [predeʃtʃi'nadu/a] *adj* predestined.

predestinar [predeʃtʃi'na*] *vt* to predestine.

predeterminado/a [predetexmi'nadu/a] *adj* predetermined.

predeterminar [predetexmi'na*] *vt* to predetermine.

predial [pre'dʒjaw] (*pl* -**ais**) *adj* property *atr*, real-estate *atr*; **imposto** ~ domestic rates.

prédica ['prɛdʒika] *f* sermon.

predicado [predʒi'kadu] *m* predicate.

predição [predʒi'sãw] (*pl* -**ões**) *f* prediction, forecast.

predigo [pre'dʒigu] *etc vb* V **predizer.**

predileção [predʒile'sãw] (*PT:* -**cç**-: *pl* -**ões**) *f* preference, predilection.

predileto/a [predʒi'lɛtu/a] (*PT:* -**ct**-) *adj* favourite (*BRIT*), favorite (*US*).

prédio ['prɛdʒju] *m* building; ~ **de apartamentos** block of flats (*BRIT*), apartment house (*US*).

predispor [predʒiʃ'po*] (*irreg: como* **pôr**) *vt*: ~ **alguém contra** to prejudice sb against; ~- **se** *vr*: ~-**se a/para** to get o.s. in the mood to/for; **a natação me predispõe para o trabalho** swimming puts me in the mood for work; **a notícia os predispôs para futuros problemas** the news prepared them for future problems.

predisposição [predʒiʃpozi'sãw] *f* predisposition.

predisposto/a [predʒiʃ'poʃtu/'pɔʃta] *pp de* **predispor** ♦ *adj* predisposed.

predispunha [predʒiʃ'puɲa] *etc vb* V **predispor.**

predispus [predʒiʃ'puʃ] *etc vb* V **predispor.**

predispuser [predʒiʃpu'ze*] *etc vb* V **predispor.**

predizer [predʒi'ze*] (*irreg: como* **dizer**) *vt* to predict, forecast.

predominância [predomi'nãsja] *f* predominance, prevalence.

predominante [predomi'nãtʃi] *adj* predominant.

predominar [predomi'na*] *vi* to predominate, prevail.

predomínio [predo'minju] *m* predominance, supremacy.

pré-eleitoral (*pl* -**ais**) *adj* pre-election.

preeminência [preemi'nẽsja] *f* pre-eminence, superiority.

preeminente [prɛemi'nẽtʃi] *adj* pre-eminent,

superior.

preencher [preẽ'ʃe*] *vt* (*formulário*) to fill in (*BRIT*) ou out, complete; (*requisitos*) to fulfil (*BRIT*), fulfill (*US*), meet; (*espaço, vaga, tempo, cargo*) to fill; ~ **à máquina** (*formulário*) to complete on a typewriter.

preenchimento [preẽʃi'mẽtu] *m* completion; (*de requisitos*) meeting; (*de vaga*) filling.

pré-escolar *adj* pre-school.

preestabelecer [preeʃtabele'se*] *vt* to prearrange.

pré-estréia *f* preview.

preexistir [preeziʃ'tʃi*] *vi* to preexist; ~ **a algo** to exist before sth.

pré-fabricado/a [-fabri'kadu/a] *adj* prefabricated.

prefaciar [prefa'sja*] *vt* to preface.

prefácio [pre'fasju] *m* preface.

prefeito/a [pre'fejtu/a] *m/f* mayor.

prefeitura [prefej'tura] *f* town hall.

preferência [prefe'rẽsja] *f* preference; (*AUTO*) priority; **de** ~ preferably; **ter** ~ **por** to have a preference for.

preferencial [preferẽ'sjaw] (*pl* -**ais**) *adj* (*rua*) main; (*ação*) preference *atr* ♦ *f* main road (*with priority*).

preferido/a [prefe'ridu/a] *adj* favourite (*BRIT*), favorite (*US*).

preferir [prefe'ri*] *vt* to prefer; ~ **algo a algo** to prefer sth to sth.

preferível [prefe'rivew] (*pl* -**eis**) *adj*: ~ **(a)** preferable (to).

prefigurar [prefigu'ra*] *vt* to prefigure.

prefiro [pre'firu] *etc vb* V **preferir.**

prefixo [pre'fiksu] *m* (*LING*) prefix; (*TEL*) code.

prega ['prɛga] *f* pleat, fold.

pregado/a [pre'gadu/a] *adj* exhausted.

pregador [prega'do*] *m* preacher; (*de roupa*) peg.

pregão [pre'gãw] (*pl* -**ões**) *m* proclamation, cry; **o** ~ (*na Bolsa*) trading; (*em leilão*) bidding.

pregar¹ [prɛ'ga*] *vt* (*sermão*) to preach; (*anunciar*) to proclaim; (*idéias, virtude*) to advocate ♦ *vi* to preach.

pregar² [pre'ga*] *vt* (*com prego*) to nail; (*fixar*) to pin, fasten; (*cosendo*) to sew on ♦ *vi* to give out; ~ **uma peça** to play a trick; ~ **os olhos em** to fix one's eyes on; **não** ~ **olho** not to sleep a wink; ~ **mentiras em alguém** to fob sb off with lies; ~ **um susto em alguém** to give sb a fright.

prego ['prɛgu] *m* nail; (*col: casa de penhor*) pawn shop; **dar o** ~ (*pessoa, carro*) to give out; **pôr algo no** ~ to pawn sth; **não meter** ~ **sem estopa** (*fig*) to be out for one's own advantage.

pregões [pre'gõjʃ] *mpl de* **pregão.**

pré-gravado/a [-gra'vadu/a] *adj* prerecorded.

pregresso/a [pre'grɛsu/a] *adj* past, previous.

***NB:** European Portuguese adds the following consonants to certain words:* **b** (sú(b)dito, su(b)til); **c** (a(c)ção, a(c)cionista, a(c)to); **m** (inde(m)ne); **p** (ado(p)ção, ado(p)tar); *for further details see p. xiii.*

preguear [pre'gja*] *vt* to pleat, fold.

preguiça [pre'gisa] *f* laziness; *(animal)* sloth; **estar com ~** to feel lazy; **estou com ~ de cozinhar** I can't be bothered to cook.

preguiçar [prɛgi'sa*] *vi* to laze around.

preguiçoso/a [pregi'sozu/ɔza] *adj* lazy ♦ *m/f* lazybones.

pré-história *f* prehistory.

pré-histórico/a *adj* prehistoric.

preia ['prɛja] *f* prey.

preia-mar *(PT)* *f* high tide.

preito ['prejtu] *m* homage, tribute; **render ~ a** to pay homage to.

prejudicar [preʒudʒi'ka*] *vt* to damage; *(atrapalhar)* to hinder; **~-se** *vr* *(pessoa)* to do o.s. no favours *(BRIT)* *ou* favors *(US)*.

prejudicial [preʒudʒi'sjaw] *(pl* **-ais)** *adj* damaging; *(à saúde)* harmful.

prejuízo [pre'ʒwizu] *m* *(dano)* damage, harm; *(em dinheiro)* loss; **com ~** *(COM)* at a loss; **em ~ de** to the detriment of.

prejulgar [preʒuw'ga*] *vt* to prejudge.

prelado [pre'ladu] *m* prelate.

preleção [prele'sãw] *(PT:* **-cç-:** *pl* **-ões)** *f* lecture.

preliminar [prelimi'na*] *adj* preliminary ♦ *f* *(partida)* preliminary ♦ *m* preliminary.

prelo ['prɛlu] *m* (printing) press; **no ~** in the press.

prelúdio [pre'ludʒju] *m* prelude.

prematuro/a [prema'turu/a] *adj* premature.

premeditação [premedʒita'sãw] *f* premeditation.

premeditado/a [premedʒi'tadu/a] *adj* premeditated.

premeditar [premedʒi'ta*] *vt* to premeditate.

premência [pre'mẽsja] *f* urgency, pressing nature.

pré-menstrual *(pl* **-ais)** *adj* premenstrual.

premente [pre'mẽtʃi] *adj* pressing.

premer [pre'me*] *vt* to press.

premiado/a [pre'mjadu/a] *adj* prize-winning; *(bilhete)* winning ♦ *m/f* prize-winner.

premiar [pre'mja*] *vt* to award a prize to; *(recompensar)* to reward.

premiê [pre'mje] *m* *(POL)* premier.

premier [pre'mje] *m* = **premiê**.

prêmio ['premju] *m* prize; *(recompensa)* reward; *(SEGUROS)* premium; **Grande P~** Grand Prix; **~ de consolação** consolation prize.

premir [pre'mi*] *vt* = **premer**.

premissa [pre'misa] *f* premise.

pré-moldado/a [-mow'dadu/a] *adj* precast ♦ *m* breeze block.

premonição [premoni'sãw] *(pl* **-ões)** *f* premonition.

premonitório/a [premoni'tɔrju/a] *adj* premonitory.

pré-natal *(pl* **-ais)** *adj* antenatal *(BRIT)*, prenatal *(US)*.

prenda ['prẽda] *f* gift, present; *(em jogo)* forfeit; **~s** *fpl* talents; **~s domésticas** housework *sg*.

prendado/a [prẽ'dadu/a] *adj* gifted, talented; *(homem: em afazeres domésticos)* domesticated.

prendedor [prẽde'do*] *m* fastener; *(de cabelo, gravata)* clip; **~ de roupa** clothes peg; **~ de papéis** paper clip.

prender [prẽ'de*] *vt* *(pregar)* to fasten, fix; *(roupa, cabelo)* to clip; *(capturar)* to arrest; *(amarrar)* to tie; *(atenção)* to catch; *(afetivamente)* to tie, bind; *(reter: suj: doença, compromisso)* to keep; *(movimentos)* to restrict; **~-se** *vr* to get caught, stick; **~-se a alguém** *(por amizade)* to be attached to sb; *(casar-se)* to tie o.s. down to sb; **~-se a algo** *(detalhes, maus hábitos)* to get caught up in sth; **~-se com algo** to be connected with sth.

prenhe ['prɛɲi] *adj* pregnant.

prenhez [pre'ɲeʒ] *f* pregnancy.

prenome [pre'nɔmi] *m* first name, Christian name.

prensa ['prẽsa] *f* *(ger)* press.

prensar [prẽ'sa*] *vt* to press, compress; *(fruta)* to squeeze; *(uvas)* to press; **~ alguém contra a parede** to push sb up against the wall.

prenunciar [prenũ'sja*] *vt* to predict, foretell; **as nuvens prenunciam chuva** the clouds suggest rain.

prenúncio [pre'nũsju] *m* forewarning, sign.

preocupação [preokupa'sãw] *(pl* **-ões)** *f* *(idéia fixa)* preoccupation; *(inquietação)* worry, concern.

preocupante [preoku'pãtʃi] *adj* worrying.

preocupar [preoku'pa*] *vt* *(absorver)* to preoccupy; *(inquietar)* to worry; **~-se** *vr:* **~-se com** to worry about, be worried about.

preparação [prepara'sãw] *(pl* **-ões)** *f* preparation.

preparado [prepa'radu] *m* preparation.

preparar [prepa'ra*] *vt* to prepare; **~-se** *vr* to get ready; **~-se para algo/para fazer** to prepare for sth/to do.

preparativos [prepara'tʃivuʃ] *mpl* preparations, arrangements.

preparo [pre'paru] *m* preparation; *(instrução)* ability; **~ físico** physical fitness.

preponderância [prepõde'rãsja] *f* preponderance, predominance.

preponderante [prepõde'rãtʃi] *adj* predominant.

preponderar [prepõde'ra*] *vi:* **~ (sobre)** to prevail (over).

preposição [prepozi'sãw] *(pl* **-ões)** *f* preposition.

preposto/a [pre'poʃtu/'pɔʃta] *m/f* person in charge; *(representante)* representative.

prepotência [prepo'tẽsja] *f* superiority; *(despotismo)* absolutism.

prepotente [prepo'tẽtʃi] *adj* *(poderoso)* predominant; *(despótico)* despotic; *(atitude)* overbearing.

prerrogativa [prexoga'tʃiva] *f* prerogative, privilege.

presa ['preza] *f (na guerra)* spoils *pl*; *(vítima)* prey; *(dente de animal)* fang.

presbiteriano/a [preʒbite'rjanu/a] *adj, m/f* Presbyterian.

presbitério [preʒbi'tɛrju] *m* presbytery.

presciência [pre'sjẽsja] *f* foreknowledge, foresight.

presciente [pre'sjẽtʃi] *adj* far-sighted, prescient.

prescindir [presĩ'dʒi*] *vi*: ~ **de algo** to do without sth.

prescindível [presĩ'dʒivew] *(pl* **-eis)** *adj* dispensable.

prescrever [preʃkre've*] *vt* to prescribe; *(prazo)* to set ♦ *vi (JUR: crime, direito)* to lapse; *(cair em desuso)* to fall into disuse.

prescrição [preʃkri'sãw] *(pl* **-ões)** *f* order, rule; *(MED)* instruction; *(: de um remédio)* prescription; *(JUR)* lapse.

prescrito/a [preʃ'kritu/a] *pp de* **prescrever**.

presença [pre'zẽsa] *f* presence; *(freqüência)* attendance; ~ **de espírito** presence of mind; **ter boa** ~ to be presentable; **na** ~ **de** in the presence of.

presenciar [prezẽ'sja*] *vt* to be present at; *(testemunhar)* to witness.

presente [pre'zẽtʃi] *adj* present; *(fig: interessado)* attentive; *(: evidente)* clear, obvious ♦ *m* present ♦ *f (COM: carta)*: **a** ~ this letter; **os ~s** *mpl* those present; **ter algo** ~ to bear sth in mind; **dar/ganhar de** ~ to give/get as a present; ~ **de grego** undesirable gift, mixed blessing; **anexamos à** ~ **we** enclose herewith; **pela** ~ hereby.

presentear [prezẽ'tʃja*] *vt*: ~ **alguém (com algo)** to give sb (sth as) a present.

presentemente [prezẽtʃe'mẽtʃi] *adv* at present.

presepada [preze'pada] *f (fanfarrice)* boasting; *(atitude, espetáculo ridículo)* joke.

presépio [pre'zɛpju] *m* Nativity scene, crib.

preservação [prezexva'sãw] *f* preservation.

preservar [prezex'va*] *vt* to preserve, protect.

preservativo [prezexva'tʃivu] *m* preservative; *(anticoncepcional)* condom.

presidência [prezi'dẽsja] *f (de um país)* presidency; *(de uma assembléia)* chair, presidency; **assumir a** ~ *(POL)* to become president.

presidencial [prezidẽ'sjaw] *(pl* **-ais)** *adj* presidential.

presidencialismo [prezidẽsja'liʒmu] *m* presidential system.

presidenciável [prezidẽ'sjavew] *(pl* **-eis)** *adj* eligible for the presidency ♦ *m/f* presidential candidate.

presidente/a [prezi'dẽtʃi/ta] *m/f (de um país)* president; *(de uma assembléia, COM)* chair, president; **o P~ da República** the President (of Brazil).

presidiário/a [prezi'dʒjarju/a] *m/f* convict.

presídio [pre'zidʒju] *m* prison.

presidir [prezi'dʒi*] *vt, vi*: ~ **(a)** to preside over; *(reunião)* to chair; *(suj: leis, critérios)* to govern.

presilha [pre'ziʎa] *f* fastener; *(para o cabelo)* slide.

preso/a ['prezu/a] *adj (em prisão)* imprisoned; *(capturado)* under arrest, captured; *(atado)* bound, tied; *(moralmente)* bound ♦ *m/f* prisoner; **ficar** ~ **a detalhes** to get bogged down in detail(s); **ficar** ~ **em casa** *(com filhos pequenos etc)* to be stuck at home; **estar** ~ **a alguém** to be attached to sb; **você está** ~! you're under arrest!; **com a greve dos ônibus, fiquei** ~ **na cidade** with the bus strike I got stuck in town.

pressa ['prɛsa] *f* haste, hurry; *(rapidez)* speed; *(urgência)* urgency; **às** ~**s** hurriedly; **estar com** ~ to be in a hurry; **sem** ~ unhurriedly; **não tem** ~ there's no hurry; **ter** ~ **de** *ou* **em fazer** to be in a hurry to do.

pressagiar [presa'ʒja*] *vt* to foretell, presage.

presságio [pre'saʒu] *m* omen, sign; *(pressentimento)* premonition.

pressago/a [pre'sagu/a] *adj (comentário)* portentous.

pressão [pre'sãw] *(pl* **-ões)** *f* pressure; **(colchete de)** ~ press stud, popper; **fazer** ~ **(sobre alguém/algo)** to put pressure on (sb/sth); ~ **arterial** *ou* **sanguínea** blood pressure.

pressentimento [presẽtʃi'mẽtu] *m* premonition, presentiment.

pressentir [presẽ'tʃi*] *vt (pressagiar)* to foresee; *(suspeitar)* to sense; *(inimigo)* to preempt.

pressionar [presjo'na*] *vt (botão)* to press; *(coagir)* to pressure ♦ *vi* to press, put on pressure.

pressões [pre'sõjʃ] *fpl de* **pressão**.

pressupor [presu'po*] *(irreg: como* **pôr)** *vt* to presuppose.

pressuposto/a [presu'poʃtu/'pɔʃta] *pp de* **pressupor** ♦ *m (conjetura)* presupposition.

pressupunha [presu'puɲa] *etc vb* V **pressupor**.

pressupus [presu'puʃ] *etc vb* V **pressupor**.

pressupuser [presu'puze*] *etc vb* V **pressupor**.

pressurização [presuriza'sãw] *f* pressurization.

pressurizado/a [presuri'zadu/a] *adj* pressurized.

pressuroso/a [presu'rozu/ɔza] *adj (apressado)* hurried, in a hurry; *(zeloso)* keen, eager.

prestação [preʃta'sãw] *(pl* **-ões)** *f* instalment *(BRIT)*, installment *(US)*; *(por uma casa)* repayment; **à** ~, **a prestações** in instal(l)-ments; ~ **de contas/serviços** accounts/

services rendered.

prestamente [preʃta'mẽtʃi] *adv* promptly.

prestamista [preʃta'miʃta] *m/f* moneylender; (*comprador*) person paying hire purchase (*BRIT*) *ou* on the installment plan (*US*).

prestar [preʃ'ta*] *vt* (*cuidados*) to give; (*favores, serviços*) to do; (*contas*) to render; (*informações*) to supply; (*uma qualidade a algo*) to lend ♦ *vi*: ~ **a alguém para algo** to be of use to sb for sth; **~-se** *vr*: **~-se a** (*servir*) to be suitable for; (*admitir*) to lend o.s. to; (*dispor-se*) to be willing to; ~ **atenção** to pay attention; ~ **juramento** to take an oath; **isto não presta para nada** it's absolutely useless; **ele não presta** he's good for nothing; ~ **homenagem/culto a** to pay tribute to/worship.

prestativo/a [preʃta'tʃivu/a] *adj* helpful, obliging.

prestável [preʃ'tavew] (*pl* **-eis**) *adj* serviceable.

prestes ['preʃtʃiʃ] *adj inv* (*pronto*) ready; (*a ponto de*): ~ **a partir** about to leave.

presteza [preʃ'teza] *f* (*prontidão*) promptness; (*rapidez*) speed; **com** ~ promptly.

prestidigitação [preʃtʃidʒiʒita'sãw] *f* sleight of hand, conjuring, magic tricks *pl*.

prestidigitador [preʃtʃidʒiʒita'do*] *m* conjurer, magician.

prestigiar [preʃtʃi'ʒja*] *vt* to give prestige to.

prestígio [preʃ'tʃiʒu] *m* prestige.

prestigioso/a [preʃtʃi'ʒozu/ɔza] *adj* prestigious, eminent.

préstimo ['prɛʃtʃimu] *m* use, usefulness; **~s** *mpl* favours (*BRIT*), favors (*US*), services; **sem** ~ useless, worthless.

presto/a ['prɛʃtu/a] *adj* swift.

presumido/a [prezu'midu/a] *adj* vain, self-important.

presumir [prezu'mi*] *vt* to presume.

presunção [prezũ'sãw] (*pl* **-ões**) *f* (*suposição*) presumption; (*vaidade*) conceit, self-importance.

presunçoso/a [prezũ'sozu/ɔza] *adj* vain, self-important.

presunto [pre'zũtu] *m* ham; (*col: cadáver*) stiff.

pret-à-porter [prɛtapox'te] *adj inv* ready to wear.

pretendente [pretẽ'dẽtʃi] *m/f* claimant; (*candidato*) candidate, applicant ♦ *m* (*de uma mulher*) suitor.

pretender [pretẽ'de*] *vt* to claim; (*cargo, emprego*) to go for; ~ **fazer** to intend to do.

pretensamente [pretẽsa'mẽtʃi] *adv* supposedly.

pretensão [pretẽ'sãw] (*pl* **-ões**) *f* (*reivindicação*) claim; (*vaidade*) pretension; (*propósito*) aim; (*aspiração*) aspiration; **pretensões** *fpl* (*presunção*) pretentiousness.

pretensioso/a [pretẽ'sjozu/ɔza] *adj* pretentious.

pretenso/a [pre'tẽsu/a] *adj* alleged, supposed.

pretensões [pretẽ'sõjʃ] *fpl de* **pretensão**.

preterir [prete'ri*] *vt* (*desprezar*) to ignore; (*deixar de promover*) to pass over; (*ocupar cargo de*) to displace; (*ser usado em lugar de*) to displace; (*omitir*) to disregard.

pretérito/a [pre'tɛritu/a] *adj* past ♦ *m* (*LING*) preterite.

pretextar [preteʃ'ta*] *vt* to give as an excuse.

pretexto [pre'teʃtu] *m* pretext, excuse; **a** ~ **de** on the pretext of.

preto/a ['pretu/a] *adj* black; ♦ *m/f* black (man/woman); **pôr o** ~ **no branco** to put it down in writing.

preto-e-branco *adj inv* (*filme, TV*) black and white.

pretume [pre'tumi] *m* blackness.

prevalecente [prevale'sẽtʃi] *adj* prevalent.

prevalecer [prevale'se*] *vi* to prevail; **~-se** *vr*: **~-se de** (*aproveitar-se*) to take advantage of; ~ **sobre** to outweigh.

prevaricar [prevari'ka*] *vi* (*faltar ao dever*) to fail in one's duty; (*proceder mal*) to behave badly; (*cometer adultério*) to commit adultery.

prevê [pre've*] *etc vb* V **prever**.

prevejo [pre'veʒu] *etc vb* V **prever**.

prevenção [prevẽ'sãw] (*pl* **-ões**) *f* (*ato de evitar*) prevention; (*preconceito*) prejudice; (*cautela*) caution; **estar de** ~ **com** *ou* **contra alguém** to be biased against sb.

prevenido/a [preve'nidu/a] *adj* (*cauteloso*) cautious, wary; (*avisado*) forewarned; **estar** ~ (*com dinheiro*) to have cash on one.

prevenir [preve'ni*] *vt* (*evitar*) to prevent; (*avisar*) to warn; (*preparar*) to prepare; **~-se** *vr* (*acautelar-se*): **~-se contra** to be wary of; (*equipar-se*): **~-se de** to equip o.s. with; **~-se para** to prepare (o.s.) for.

preventivo/a [prevẽ'tʃivu/a] *adj* preventive.

prever [pre've*] (*irreg: como* **ver**) *vt* to predict, foresee; (*pressupor*) to presuppose.

pré-vestibular [preveʃtʃibu'la*] *adj* (*curso*) preparing for university entry ♦ *m* preparation for university entry.

previa [pre'via] *etc vb* V **prever**.

prévia ['prɛvja] *f* opinion poll.

previamente [prevja'mẽtʃi] *adv* previously.

previdência [previ'dẽsja] *f* (*previsão*) foresight; (*precaução*) precaution; ~ **social** social welfare; (*instituição*) welfare department, ≈ DSS (*BRIT*).

previdente [previ'dẽtʃi] *adj* with foresight; **ser** ~ to show foresight.

previno [pre'vinu] *etc vb* V **prevenir**.

prévio/a ['prɛvju/a] *adj* prior; (*preliminar*) preliminary.

previr [pre'vi*] *etc vb* V **prever**.

previsão [previ'zãw] (*pl* **-ões**) *f* (*antevisão*) foresight; (*prognóstico*) prediction, forecast; ~ **do tempo** weather forecast.

previsível [previ'zivew] (*pl* **-eis**) *adj* predictable.

previsões [previ'zõjʃ] *fpl de* **previsão**.

previsto/a [pre'viʃtu/a] *pp de* **prever** ♦ *adj* predicted; *(na lei etc)* prescribed.

prezado/a [pre'zadu/a] *adj* esteemed; *(numa carta)* dear.

prezar [pre'za*] *vt (amigos)* to value highly; *(autoridade)* to respect; *(gostar de)* to appreciate; **~-se** *vr (ter dignidade)* to have self-respect; **~-se de** *(orgulhar-se)* to pride o.s. on.

primado [pri'madu] *m (primazia)* primacy.

prima-dona *(pl ~s) f* leading lady.

primar [pri'ma*] *vi* to excel, stand out.

primário/a [pri'marju/a] *adj* primary; *(elementar)* basic, rudimentary; *(primitivo)* primitive ♦ *m (curso)* elementary education.

primata [pri'mata] *m* primate.

primavera [prima'vɛra] *f* spring; *(planta)* primrose.

primaveril [primave'riw] *(pl -is) adj* spring *atr*; *(pessoa)* youthful, young.

primaz [pri'majʒ] *m* primate.

primazia [prima'zia] *f* primacy; *(prioridade)* priority; *(superioridade)* superiority.

primeira [pri'mejra] *f (AUTO)* first gear.

primeira-dama *(pl* **primeiras-damas)** *f (POL)* first lady.

primeiranista [primejra'niʃta] *m/f* first-year (student).

primeiro/a [pri'mejru/a] *adj* first; *(funda-mental)* fundamental, prime ♦ *adv* first; **de primeira** *(pessoa, restaurante)* first-class; *(carne)* prime; **viajar de primeira** to travel first class; **à primeira vista** at first sight; **em ~ lugar** first of all; **de ~** first; **~s socorros** first aid *sg*; **primeira página** *(de jornal)* front page; **ele foi o ~ que disse isso** he was the first to say this.

primeiro-de-abril *(pl* **primeiros-de-abril)** *m* April fool.

primeiro-time *(col) adj inv* top-notch, first rate.

primitivo/a [primi'tʃivu/a] *adj* primitive; *(original)* original.

primo/a ['primu/a] *m/f* cousin; **~ irmão** first cousin; **~ em segundo grau** second cousin; **(número)** ~ prime number.

primogênito/a [primo'ʒenitu/a] *adj, m/f* first-born.

primor [pri'mo*] *m* excellence, perfection; *(beleza)* beauty; **com ~** to perfection; **é um ~** it's perfect.

primordial [primox'dʒjaw] *(pl -ais) adj (primitivo)* primordial, primeval; *(principal)* principal, fundamental.

primórdio [pri'mɔxdʒju] *m* origin.

primoroso/a [primo'rozu/za] *adj (excelente)* excellent; *(belo)* exquisite.

princesa [prĩ'seza] *f* princess.

principado [prĩsi'padu] *m* principality.

principal [prĩsi'paw] *(pl -ais) adj* principal;

(entrada, razão, rua) main ♦ *m (chefe)* head, principal; *(essencial, de dívida)* principal ♦ *f (LING)* main clause.

príncipe ['prĩsipi] *m* prince.

principiante [prĩsi'pjãtʃi] *m/f* beginner.

principiar [prĩsi'pja*] *vt, vi* to begin; **~ a fazer** to begin to do.

princípio [prĩ'sipju] *m (começo)* beginning, start; *(origem)* origin; *(legal, moral)* principle; **~s** *mpl (de matéria)* rudiments; **em ~** in principle; **no ~** in the beginning; **por ~** on principle; **do ~ ao fim** from beginning to end; **uma pessoa de ~s** a person of principle.

prior [prjo*] *m (sacerdote)* parish priest; *(de convento)* prior.

prioridade [prjori'dadʒi] *f* priority; **ter ~ sobre** to have priority over.

prioritário/a [prjori'tarju/a] *adj* priority *atr*.

prisão [pri'zãw] *(pl -ões) f (encarceramento)* imprisonment; *(cadeia)* prison, jail; *(detenção)* arrest; **ordem de ~** warrant for arrest; **~ perpétua** life imprisonment; **~ preventiva** protective custody; **~ de ventre** constipation.

prisioneiro/a [prizjo'nejru/a] *m/f* prisoner.

prisma ['priʒma] *m* prism; **sob esse ~** *(fig)* in this light, from this angle.

prisões [pri'zõjʃ] *fpl de* **prisão**.

privação [priva'sãw] *(pl -ões) f* deprivation; **privações** *fpl (penúria)* hardship *sg*.

privacidade [privasi'dadʒi] *f* privacy.

privações [priva'sõjʃ] *fpl de* **privação**.

privada [pri'vada] *f* toilet.

privado/a [pri'vadu/a] *adj (particular)* private; *(carente)* deprived.

privar [pri'va*] *vt:* **~ alguém de algo** to deprive sb of sth; **~-se** *vr:* **~-se de algo** to deprive o.s. of sth, go without sth.

privativo/a [priva'tʃivu/a] *adj (particular)* private; **~ de** peculiar to.

privatização [privatʃiza'sãw] *(pl -ões) f* privatization.

privatizar [privatʃi'za*] *vt* to privatize.

privilegiado/a [privile'ʒjadu/a] *adj* privileged; *(excepcional)* unique, exceptional.

privilegiar [privile'ʒja*] *vt* to privilege; *(favo-recer)* to favour (BRIT), favor (US).

privilégio [privi'lɛʒu] *m* privilege.

pro [pru] *(col)* = **para + o**.

pró [prɔ] *adv* for, in favour (BRIT) *ou* favor (US) ♦ *m* advantage; **os ~s e os contras** the pros and cons; **em ~ de** in favo(u)r of.

pró- [prɔ] *prefixo* pro-; **~soviético** pro-Soviet.

proa ['proa] *f* prow, bow.

probabilidade [probabili'dadʒi] *f* probability, likelihood; **~s** *fpl* odds; **segundo todas as ~s** in all probability.

probabilíssimo/a [probabi'lisimu/a] *adj superl de* **provável**.

NB: European Portuguese adds the following consonants to certain words: **b** (sú(b)dito, su(b)til); **c** (a(c)ção, a(c)cionista, a(c)to); **m** (inde(m)ne); **p** (ado(p)ção, ado(p)tar); *for further details see p. xiii.*

problema [prob'lɛma] *m* problem.
problemática [proble'matʃika] *f* problematics *sg*; (*problemas*) problems *pl*.
problemático/a [proble'matʃiku/a] *adj* problematic.
procedência [prose'dēsja] *f* (*origem*) origin, source; (*lugar de saída*) point of departure.
procedente [prose'dētʃi] *adj* (*oriundo*) derived, rising; (*lógico*) logical.
proceder [prose'de*] *vi* (*ir adiante*) to proceed; (*comportar-se*) to behave; (*agir*) to act; (*JUR*) to take legal action ♦ *m* conduct; ~ **a** to carry out; ~ **de** (*originar-se*) to originate from; (*descender*) to be descended from.
procedimento [prosedʒi'mẽtu] *m* (*comportamento*) conduct, behaviour (*BRIT*), behavior (*US*); (*processo*) procedure; (*JUR*) proceedings *pl*.
procela [pro'sɛla] *f* storm, tempest.
proceloso/a [prose'lozu/ɔza] *adj* stormy.
prócer ['prɔse*] *m* chief, leader.
processador [prosesa'do*] *m* processor; ~ **de texto** word processor.
processamento [prosesa'mẽtu] *m* (*de requerimentos*, *COMPUT*) processing; (*JUR*) prosecution; (*verificação*) verification; (*de depoimentos*) taking down; ~ **de dados** data processing; ~ **por lotes** batch processing; ~ **de texto** word processing.
processar [prose'sa*] *vt* (*JUR*) to take proceedings against, prosecute; (*verificar*) to check, verify; (*depoimentos*) to take down; (*requerimentos*, *COMPUT*) to process.
processo [pro'sɛsu] *m* process; (*procedimento*) procedure; (*JUR*) lawsuit, legal proceedings *pl*; (: *autos*) record; (*conjunto de documentos*) documents *pl*; (*de uma doença*) course, progress; **abrir um** ~ (**contra alguém**) to start legal proceedings (against sb); ~ **inflamatório** (*MED*) inflammation.
procissão [prosi'sãw] (*pl* **-ões**) *f* procession.
proclamação [proklama'sãw] (*pl* **-ões**) *f* proclamation.
proclamar [prokla'ma*] *vt* to proclaim.
proclamas [pro'klamaʃ] *mpl* banns.
procrastinar [prokraʃtʃi'na*] *vt* to put off ♦ *vi* to procrastinate.
procriação [prokrja'sãw] *f* procreation.
procriar [pro'krja*] *vt*, *vi* to procreate.
procura [pro'kura] *f* search; (*COM*) demand; **em** ~ **de** in search of.
procuração [prokura'sãw] (*pl* **-ões**) *f* power of attorney; (*documento*) letter of attorney; **por** ~ by proxy.
procurado/a [proku'radu/a] *adj* sought after, in demand.
procurador(a) [prokura'do*(a)] *m/f* (*advogado*) attorney; (*mandatário*) proxy; **P~ Geral da República** Attorney General.
procurar [proku'ra*] *vt* to look for, seek; (*emprego*) to apply for; (*ir visitar*) to call

on, go and see; (*contatar*) to get in touch with; ~ **fazer** to try to do.
prodigalizar [prodʒigali'za*] *vt* (*gastar excessivamente*) to squander; (*dar com profusão*) to lavish.
prodígio [pro'dʒiʒu] *m* prodigy.
prodigioso/a [prodʒi'ʒozu/ɔza] *adj* prodigious, marvellous (*BRIT*), marvelous (*US*).
pródigo/a ['prɔdʒigu/a] *adj* (*perdulário*) wasteful; (*generoso*) lavish; **filho** ~ prodigal son.
produção [produ'sãw] (*pl* **-ões**) *f* production; (*volume de produção*) output; (*produto*) product; ~ **em massa** *ou* **série** mass production.
produtividade [produtʃivi'dadʒi] *f* productivity.
produtivo/a [produ'tʃivu/a] *adj* productive; (*rendoso*) profitable.
produto [pro'dutu] *m* product; (*renda*) proceeds *pl*, profit; ~**s alimentícios** foodstuffs; ~**s agrícolas** agricultural produce *sg*; **ser** ~ **de** to be a product of; ~ **nacional bruto** gross national product; ~**s acabados/semi-acabados** finished/semi-finished products.
produtor(a) [produ'to*(a)] *adj* producing ♦ *m/f* producer.
produzido/a [produ'zidu/a] *adj* trendy.
produzir [produ'zi*] *vt* to produce; (*ocasionar*) to cause, bring about; (*render*) to produce, bring in ♦ *vi* to be productive; (*ECON*) to produce.
proeminência [proemi'nēsja] *f* prominence; (*protuberância*) protuberance; (*elevação de terreno*) elevation.
proeminente [proemi'nētʃi] *adj* prominent.
proeza [pro'eza] *f* achievement, feat.
profanação [profana'sãw] *f* sacrilege, profanation.
profanar [profa'na*] *vt* to desecrate, profane.
profano/a [pro'fanu/a] *adj* profane; (*secular*) secular ♦ *m/f* layman/woman.
profecia [profe'sia] *f* prophecy.
proferir [profe'ri*] *vt* to utter; (*sentença*) to pronounce; ~ **um discurso** to make a speech.
professar [profe'sa*] *vt* to profess; (*profissão*) to practise (*BRIT*), practice (*US*) ♦ *vi* (*REL*) to take religious vows.
professo/a [pro'fɛsu/a] *adj* (*católico etc*) confirmed; (*político etc*) seasoned.
professor(a) [profe'so*(a)] *m/f* teacher; (*universitário*) lecturer; ~ **titular** *ou* **catedrático** (university) professor; ~ **associado** reader.
professorado [profeso'radu] *m* (*professores*) teachers *pl*; (*magistério*) teaching profession.
profeta [pro'feta] *m* prophet.
profético/a [pro'fɛtʃiku/a] *adj* prophetic.
profetisa [profe'tʃiza] *f* prophetess.
profetizar [profetʃi'za*] *vt*, *vi* to prophesy, predict.
proficiência [profi'sjēsja] *f* proficiency, competence.

proficiente [profi'sjɛtʃi] *adj* proficient, competent.

profícuo/a [pro'fikwu/a] *adj* useful, advantageous.

profiro [pro'firu] *etc vb* V **proferir**.

profissão [profi'sãw] (*pl* **-ões**) *f* (*ofício*) profession; (*de fé*) declaration; ~ **liberal** liberal profession.

profissional [profisjo'naw] (*pl* **-ais**) *adj*, *m/f* professional.

profissionalizante [profisjonali'zãtʃi] *adj* (*ensino*) vocational.

profissionalizar [profisjonali'za*] *vt* to professionalize; ~**-se** *vr* to turn professional; (*atividade*) to become professional.

profissões [profi'sõjʃ] *fpl de* **profissão**.

profundas [pro'fũdaʃ] *fpl* depths.

profundidade [profũdʒi'dadʒi] *f* depth; (*fig*) profoundness, depth; **tem 4 metros de** ~ it is 4 metres *ou* meters deep.

profundo/a [pro'fũdu/a] *adj* deep; (*fig*) profound.

profusão [profu'zãw] *f* profusion, abundance.

profuso/a [pro'fuzu/a] *adj* (*abundante*) profuse, abundant.

progênie [pro'ʒeni] *f* (*ascendência*) lineage; (*prole*) offspring, progeny.

progenitor(a) [proʒeni'to*(a)] *m/f* ancestor; (*pai/mãe*) father/mother.

prognosticar [prognoʃtʃi'ka*] *vt* to predict, forecast ♦ *vi* (*MED*) to make a prognosis.

prognóstico [prog'noʃtʃiku] *m* prediction, forecast; (*MED*) prognosis.

programa [pro'grama] *m* programme (*BRIT*), program (*US*); (*COMPUT*) program; (*plano*) plan; (*diversão*) thing to do; (*de um curso*) syllabus; **fazer um** ~ to go out; ~ **de índio** (*col*) boring thing to do.

programação [programa'sãw] *f* planning; (*TV*, *RADIO*) programming; (*COMPUT*) programming; ~ **visual** graphic design.

programador(a) [programa'do*(a)] *m/f* programmer; ~ **visual** graphic designer.

programar [progra'ma*] *vt* to plan; (*COMPUT*) to program.

programável [progra'mavew] (*pl* **-eis**) *adj* programmable.

progredir [progre'dʒi*] *vi* to progress, make progress; (*avançar*) to move forward; (*infecção*) to progress.

progressão [progre'sãw] *f* progression.

progressista [progre'siʃta] *adj*, *m/f* progressive.

progressivo/a [progre'sivu/a] *adj* progressive; (*gradual*) gradual.

progresso [pro'gresu] *m* progress.

progrido [pro'gridu] *etc vb* V **progredir**.

proibição [proibi'sãw] (*pl* **-ões**) *f* prohibition, ban.

proibir [proi'bi*] *vt* to prohibit, forbid; (*livro*,

espetáculo*) to ban; " **é proibido fumar" "no smoking"; ~ **alguém de fazer**, ~ **que alguém faça** to forbid sb to do.

proibitivo/a [proibi'tʃivu/a] *adj* prohibitive.

projeção [proʒe'sãw] (*PT*: **-cç-**: *pl* **-ões**) *f* projection; (*arremesso*) throwing; (*proeminência*) prominence; **tempo de** ~ (*de filme*) running time.

projetar [proʒe'ta*] (*PT*: **-ct-**) *vt* to project; (*arremessar*) to throw; (*planejar*) to plan; (*ARQ*, *TEC*) to design; ~**-se** *vr* (*lançar-se*) to hurl o.s.; (*sombra etc*) to fall; (*delinear-se*) to jut out; ~ **fazer** to plan to do.

projétil [pro'ʒɛtʃiw] (*PT*: **-ct-**: *pl* **-eis**) *m* projectile, missile; (*MIL*) missile.

projetista [proʒe'tʃiʃta] (*PT*: **-ct-**) *m/f* designer ♦ *adj* design *atr*.

projeto [pro'ʒɛtu] (*PT*: **-ct-**) *m* (*empreendimento*) project; (*plano*, *ARQ*) plan; (*TEC*) design; (*de tese etc*) draft; ~ **de lei** bill; ~ **assistido por computador** computer-aided design.

projetor [proʒe'to*] (*PT*: **-ct-**) *m* (*CINEMA*) projector; (*holofote*) searchlight.

prol [prɔw] *m* advantage; **em** ~ **de** on behalf of, for the benefit of.

pró-labore [-la'bɔri] *m* remuneration, fee.

prolapso [pro'lapsu] *m* (*MED*) prolapse.

prole ['prɔli] *f* offspring, progeny.

proletariado [proleta'rjadu] *m* proletariat.

proletário/a [prole'tarju/a] *adj*, *m/f* proletarian.

proliferação [prolifera'sãw] *f* proliferation.

proliferar [prolife'ra*] *vi* to proliferate.

prolífico/a [pro'lifiku/a] *adj* prolific.

prolixo/a [pro'liksu/a] *adj* long-winded, tedious.

prólogo ['prɔlogu] *m* prologue.

prolongação [prolõga'sãw] *f* extension.

prolongado/a [prolõ'gadu/a] *adj* (*demorado*) prolonged; (*alongado*) extended.

prolongamento [prolõga'mẽtu] *m* extension.

prolongar [prolõ'ga*] *vt* (*tornar mais longo*) to extend, lengthen; (*adiar*) to prolong; (*vida*) to prolong; ~**-se** *vr* to extend; (*durar*) to last.

promessa [pro'mɛsa] *f* promise; (*compromisso*) pledge.

prometedor(a) [promete'do*(a)] *adj* promising.

prometer [prome'te*] *vt* to promise ♦ *vi* to promise; (*ter potencial*) to show promise; ~ **fazer/que** to promise to do/that.

prometido/a [prome'tʃidu/a] *adj* promised ♦ *m*: **o** ~ what one promised; **cumprir o** ~ to keep to one's promise.

promiscuidade [promiʃkwi'dadʒi] *f* (*sexual*) promiscuity; (*desordem*) untidiness.

promiscuir-se [promiʃ'kwixsi] *vr*: ~ (**com**) to mix (with).

---

*NB: European Portuguese adds the following consonants to certain words: **b** (sú(b)dito, su(b)til); **c** (a(c)ção, a(c)cionista, a(c)to); **m** (inde(m)ne); **p** (ado(p)ção, ado(p)tar); for further details see p. xiii.*

promíscuo/a [pro'miʃkwu/a] *adj* (*misturado*) disorderly, mixed up; (*comportamento sexual*) promiscuous.

promissor(a) [promi'so*(a)] *adj* promising.

promissório/a [promi'sɔrju/a] *adj*, *f*: **(nota) promissória** promissory note.

promoção [promo'sãw] (*pl* **-ões**) *f* promotion; **fazer ~ de alguém/algo** to promote sb/sth.

promontório [promõ'tɔrju] *m* headland, promontory.

promotor(a) [promo'to*(a)] *adj* promoting ♦ *m/f* promoter; (*JUR*) prosecutor; **~ público** public prosecutor.

promover [promo've*] *vt* (*dar impulso a*) to promote; (*causar*) to cause; (*elevar a cargo superior*) to promote; (*reunião, encontro*) to bring about.

promulgação [promuwga'sãw] *f* promulgation.

promulgar [promuw'ga*] *vt* (*lei etc*) to promulgate; (*tornar público*) to declare publicly.

pronome [pro'nɔmi] *m* pronoun.

pronta-entrega (*pl* **~s**) *f* immediate delivery department.

prontidão [prõtʃi'dãw] *f* (*estar preparado*) readiness; (*rapidez*) promptness, speed; **estar de ~** to be at the ready.

prontificar [prõtʃifi'ka*] *vt* to have ready; **~-se** *vr*: **~-se a fazer/para algo** to volunteer to do/for sth.

pronto/a [prõtu/a] *adj* ready; (*rápido*) quick, speedy; (*imediato*) prompt; (*col*: *sem dinheiro*) broke ♦ *adv* promptly; **de ~** promptly; **estar ~ a ...** to be prepared *ou* willing to ...; **(e) ~!** (and) that's that!

pronto-socorro (*pl* **prontos-socorros**) *m* emergency hospital; (*PT*: *reboque*) towtruck.

prontuário [prõ'twarju] *m* (*manual*) handbook; (*policial*) record.

pronúncia [pro'nũsja] *f* pronunciation; (*JUR*) indictment.

pronunciação [pronũsja'sãw] (*pl* **-ões**) *f* pronouncement; (*LING*) pronunciation.

pronunciamento [pronũsja'mẽtu] *m* proclamation, pronouncement.

pronunciar [pronũ'sja*] *vt* to pronounce; (*discurso*) to make, deliver; (*JUR*: *réu*) to indict; (: *sentença*) to pass; **~-se** *vr* (*expressar opinião*) to express one's opinion; **~ mal** to mispronounce.

propagação [propaga'sãw] *f* propagation; (*fig*: *difusão*) dissemination.

propaganda [propa'gãda] *f* (*POL*) propaganda; (*COM*) advertising; (: *uma ~*) advert, advertisement; **fazer ~ de** to advertise.

propagar [propa'ga*] *vt* to propagate; (*fig*: *difundir*) to disseminate.

propender [propẽ'de*] *vi* to lean; **~ para algo** (*fig*) to incline *ou* tend towards sth.

propensão [propẽ'sãw] (*pl* **-ões**) *f* inclination, tendency.

propenso/a [pro'pẽsu/a] *adj*: **~ a** inclined to, with a tendency to; **ser ~ a** to be inclined to,

have a tendency to.

propensões [propẽ'sõjʃ] *fpl de* **propensão**.

propiciar [propi'sja*] *vt* (*tornar favorável*) to favour (*BRIT*), favor (*US*); (*permitir*) to allow; (*proporcionar*) to provide.

propício/a [pro'pisju/a] *adj* (*favorável*) favourable (*BRIT*), favorable (*US*), propitious; (*apropriado*) appropriate.

propina [pro'pina] *f* (*gorjeta*) tip; (*PT*: *cota*) fee.

propor [pro'po*] (*irreg*: *como* **pôr**) *vt* to propose; (*oferecer*) to offer; (*um problema*) to pose; (*JUR*: *ação*) to start, move; **~-se** *vr*: **~-se (a) fazer** (*pretender*) to intend to do; (*visar*) to aim to do; (*dispor-se*) to decide to do; (*oferecer-se*) to offer to do; **~-se a** *ou* **para governador** *etc* to stand for governor *etc*.

proporção [propox'sãw] (*pl* **-ões**) *f* proportion; **proporções** *fpl* dimensions; **à ~ que** as.

proporcionado/a [propoxsjo'nadu/a] *adj* proportionate.

proporcional [propoxsjo'naw] (*pl* **-ais**) *adj* proportional.

proporcionar [propoxsjo'na*] *vt* (*dar*) to provide, give; (*adaptar*) to adjust, adapt.

proporções [propox'sõjʃ] *fpl de* **proporção**.

propôs [pro'poʃ] *vb* V **propor**.

proposição [propozi'sãw] (*pl* **-ões**) *f* proposition, proposal.

propositado/a [propozi'tadu/a] *adj* intentional.

proposital [propozi'taw] (*pl* **-ais**) *adj* intentional.

propósito [pro'pɔzitu] *m* (*intenção*) purpose; (*objetivo*) aim; **a ~** by the way; (*oportunamente*) at an opportune moment; **a ~ de** with regard to; **de ~** on purpose; **fora de ~** irrelevant; **com o ~ de** with the purpose of.

proposta [pro'pɔʃta] *f* proposal; (*oferecimento*) offer.

proposto/a [pro'poʃtu/'poʃta] *pp de* **propor**.

propriamente [proprja'mẽtʃi] *adv* properly, exactly; **~ falando** *ou* **dito** strictly speaking; **a Igreja ~ dita** the Church proper.

propriedade [proprje'dadʒi] *f* property; (*direito de proprietário*) ownership; (*o que é apropriado*) appropriateness, propriety; **~ imobiliária** real estate.

proprietário/a [proprje'tarju/a] *m/f* owner, proprietor; (*de casa alugada*) landlord/lady; (*de jornal*) publisher.

próprio/a ['prɔprju/a] *adj* (*possessivo*) own, of one's own; (*mesmo*) very, selfsame; (*hora, momento*) opportune, right; (*nome*) proper; (*característico*) characteristic; (*sentido*) proper, true; (*depois de pronome*) -self; **~ (para)** suitable (for); **eu ~** I myself; **ele ~** he himself; **mora em casa própria** he lives in a house of his own; **por si ~** of one's own accord; **o ~ homem** the very man; **ele é o ~ inglês** he's a typical Englishman; **é o ~** it's him himself.

propulsão [propuw'sãw] *f* propulsion; ~ **a jato** jet propulsion.

propulsor(a) [propuw'so*(a)] *adj* propelling ♦ *m* propellor.

propus [pro'puʃ] *etc vb* V **propor**.

propuser [propu'ze*] *etc vb* V **propor**.

prorrogação [proxoga'sãw] (*pl* **-ões**) *f* extension; (*COM*) deferment; (*JUR*) stay; (*FUTE-BOL*) extra time.

prorrogar [proxo'ga*] *vt* to extend, prolong.

prorrogável [proxo'gavel] (*pl* **-eis**) *adj* extendible.

prorromper [proxõ'pe*] *vi* (*águas, lágrimas*) to burst forth; (*vaias*) to break out; ~ **em choro/gargalhadas** to burst into tears/burst out laughing.

prosa ['prɔza] *f* prose; (*conversa*) chatter; (*fanfarrice*) boasting, bragging ♦ *adj* full of oneself; **ter boa** ~ to have the gift of the gab.

prosador(a) [proza'do*(a)] *m/f* prose writer.

prosaico/a [pro'zajku/a] *adj* prosaic.

proscênio [pro'senju] *m* proscenium.

proscrever [proʃkre've*] *vt* to prohibit, ban; (*expulsar*) to ban, exile; (*vícios, usos*) to do away with.

proscrição [proʃkri'sãw] (*pl* **-ões**) *f* proscription; (*proibição*) prohibition, ban; (*desterro*) exile; (*abolição*) abolition.

proscrito/a [proʃ'kritu/a] *pp de* **proscrever** ♦ *m/f* (*desterrado*) exile.

prosear [pro'zja*] *vi* to chat.

prosélito [pro'zɛlitu] *m* convert.

prosódia [pro'zɔdʒja] *f* prosody.

prosopopéia [prozopo'pɛja] *f* (*fig*) diatribe; (*col: pose*) pose.

prospecto [proʃ'pɛktu] *m* (*desdobrável*) leaflet; (*em forma de livro*) brochure.

prospector [proʃpek'to*] *m* prospector.

prosperar [proʃpe'ra*] *vi* to prosper, thrive.

prosperidade [proʃperi'dadʒi] *f* prosperity; (*bom êxito*) success.

próspero/a ['prɔʃperu/a] *adj* prosperous; (*bem sucedido*) successful; (*favorável*) favourable (*BRIT*), favorable (*US*).

prosseguimento [prosegi'mẽtu] *m* continuation.

prosseguir [prose'gi*] *vt* to continue ♦ *vi* to continue, go on; ~ **em** to continue (with).

prostituição [proʃtʃitwi'sãw] *f* prostitution.

próstata ['prɔʃtata] *f* prostate.

prostíbulo [proʃ'tʃibulu] *m* brothel.

prostituir [proʃtʃi'twi*] *vt* to prostitute; (*fig: desonrar*) to debase; ~**-se** *vr* (*tornar-se prostituta*) to become a prostitute; (*ser prostituta*) to be a prostitute; (*no trabalho*) to prostitute o.s.; (*corromper-se*) to be corrupted; (*desonrar-se*) to debase o.s.

prostituta [proʃti'tuta] *f* prostitute.

prostração [proʃtra'sãw] *f* (*cansaço*) exhaus-

tion; (*moral*) desolation.

prostrado/a [proʃ'tradu/a] *adj* prostrate.

prostrar [proʃ'tra*] *vt* (*derrubar*) to knock down, throw down; (*extenuar*) to tire out; (*abater*) to lay low; ~**-se** *vr* to prostrate o.s.

protagonista [protago'niʃta] *m/f* protagonist.

protagonizar [protagoni'za*] *vt* to play the lead role in; (*fig*) to be at the centre (*BRIT*) *ou* center (*US*) of.

proteção [prote'sãw] (*PT*: **-cç-**) *f* protection; (*amparo*) support, backing.

protecionismo [protesjo'niʒmu] (*PT*: **-cç-**) *m* protectionism.

protector(a) [protek'to*(a)] (*PT*) = **protetor**.

proteger [prote'ʒe*] *vt* to protect.

protegido/a [prote'ʒidu/a] *adj* protected ♦ *m/f* protégé(e).

proteína [prote'ina] *f* protein.

protejo [pro'teʒu] *etc vb* V **proteger**.

protelar [prote'la*] *vt* to postpone, put off.

PROTERRA (*BR*) *abr m* = **Programa de Redistribuição da Terra e de Estímulo Agro-Industrial do Norte e Nordeste**.

protestante [proteʃ'tãtʃi] *adj, m/f* Protestant.

protestantismo [proteʃtã'tʃiʒmu] *m* Protestantism.

protestar [proteʃ'ta*] *vt* to protest; (*declarar*) to declare, affirm ♦ *vi* to protest.

protesto [pro'tɛʃtu] *m* protest; (*declaração*) affirmation.

protetor(a) [prote'to*(a)] *adj* protective ♦ *m/f* protector.

protocolar [protoko'la*] *adj* protocol *atr* ♦ *vt* to record.

protocolo [proto'kɔlu] *m* protocol; (*recibo*) record slip.

protótipo [pro'tɔtʃipu] *m* prototype.

protuberância [protube'rãsja] *f* bump.

protuberante [protube'rãtʃi] *adj* sticking out.

prova ['prɔva] *f* proof; (*TEC: teste*) test, trial; (*EDUC: exame*) examination; (*sinal*) sign; (*de comida, bebida*) taste; (*de roupa*) fitting; (*ESPORTE*) competition; (*TIP*) proof; ~**(s)** (*JUR*) evidence *sg*; **à** ~ on trial; **à** ~ **de bala/fogo/água** bulletproof/fireproof/waterproof; **pôr à** ~ to put to the test; ~ **circunstancial/documental** (piece of) circumstantial/documentary evidence.

provação [prova'sãw] *f* (*sofrimento*) trial.

provado/a [pro'vadu/a] *adj* proven.

provar [pro'va*] *vt* to prove; (*comida*) to taste, try; (*roupa*) to try on ♦ *vi* to try.

provável [pro'vavew] (*pl* **-eis**) *adj* probable, likely; **é** ~ **que não venha** he probably won't come.

provê [pro've] *etc vb* V **prover**.

provedor(a) [prove'do*(a)] *m/f* provider.

proveio [pro'veju] *etc vb* V **provir**.

proveito [pro'vejtu] *m* (*vantagem*) advantage; (*ganho*) profit; **em** ~ **de** for the benefit of;

NB: European Portuguese adds the following consonants to certain words: **b** (sú(b)dito, su(b)til); **c** (a(c)ção, a(c)cionista, a(c)to); **m** (inde(m)ne); **p** (ado(p)ção, ado(p)tar); *for further details see p. xiii.*

fazer ~ de to make use of; **tirar ~ de** to benefit from.

proveitoso/a [provej'tozu/ɔza] *adj* profitable, advantageous; (*útil*) useful.

provejo [pro'veʒu] *etc vb* V **prover**.

proveniência [prove'njẽsja] *f* source, origin.

proveniente [prove'njẽtʃi] *adj:* ~ **de** originating from; (*que resulta de*) arising from.

proventos [pro'vẽtuʃ] *mpl* proceeds *pl.*

prover [pro've*] (*irreg: como* **ver**) *vt* (*fornecer*) to provide, supply; (*vaga*) to fill ♦ *vi:* ~ **a** to take care of, see to; **~-se** *vr:* **~-se de algo** to provide o.s. with sth; ~ **alguém de algo** to provide sb with sth; (*dotar*) to endow sb with sth.

provérbio [pro'vɛxbju] *m* proverb.

proveta [pro'veta] *f* test tube; **bebê de ~** test-tube baby.

provi [pro'vi] *etc vb* V **prover**.

provia [pro'via] *etc vb* V **prover**.

providência [provi'dẽsja] *f* providence; **~s** *fpl* measures, steps; **tomar ~s** to take steps.

providencial [providẽ'sjaw] (*pl* **-ais**) *adj* opportune.

providenciar [providẽ'sja*] *vt* (*prover*) to provide; (*tomar providências*) to arrange ♦ *vi* (*tomar providências*) to make arrangements, take steps; (*prover*) to make provision; ~ **para que** to see to it that.

providente [provi'dẽtʃi] *adj* provident; (*prudente*) prudent, careful.

provido/a [pro'vidu/a] *adj* (*fornecido*) supplied, provided; (*cheio*) full up, fully stocked.

provier [pro'vje*] *etc vb* V **provir**.

provim [pro'vĩ] *etc vb* V **provir**.

provimento [provi'mẽtu] *m* provision; **dar ~** (*JUR*) to grant a petition.

província [pro'vĩsja] *f* province.

provinciano/a [provĩ'sjanu/a] *adj* provincial.

provindo/a [pro'vĩdu/a] *pp de* **provir** ♦ *adj:* ~ **de** coming from, originating from.

provir¹ [pro'vi*] *etc vb* V **prover**.

provir² [pro'vi*] (*irreg: como* **vir**) *vi:* ~ **de** to come from, derive from.

provisão [provi'zãw] (*pl* **-ões**) *f* provision, supply; **provisões** *fpl* provisions.

provisoriamente [provizɔrja'mẽtʃi] *adv* provisionally.

provisório/a [provi'zɔrju/a] *adj* provisional, temporary.

provisto/a [pro'viʃtu/a] *pp de* **prover**.

provocação [provoka'sãw] (*pl* **-ões**) *f* provocation.

provocador(a) [provoka'do*(a)] *adj* provocative ♦ *m/f* provoker.

provocante [provo'kãtʃi] *adj* provocative.

provocar [provo'ka*] *vt* to provoke; (*ocasionar*) to cause; (*atrair*) to tempt, attract; (*estimular*) to rouse, stimulate ♦ *vi* to provoke, be provocative.

proximidade [prosimi'dadʒi] *f* proximity, nearness; (*iminência*) imminence; **~s** *fpl*

neighbourhood *sg* (*BRIT*), **neighborhood** *sg* (*US*), vicinity *sg.*

próximo/a ['prɔsimu/a] *adj* (*no espaço*) near, close; (*no tempo*) close; (*seguinte*) next; (*amigo, parente*) close; (*vizinho*) neighbouring (*BRIT*), neighboring (*US*) ♦ *adv* near ♦ *m* fellow man; ~ **a** *ou* **de** near to, close to; **futuro** ~ near future; **até a próxima!** see you again soon!

PRP (*BR*) *abr m* = **Partido Renovador Progressista**.

PRT (*BR*) *abr m* = **Partido Reformador Trabalhista**.

prudência [pru'dẽsja] *f* (*comedimento*) care, prudence; (*cautela*) care, caution.

prudente [pru'dẽtʃi] *adj* sensible, prudent; (*cauteloso*) cautious.

prumo ['prumu] *m* plumb line; (*NÁUT*) lead; **a** ~ perpendicularly, vertically.

prurido [pru'ridu] *m* itch.

Prússia ['prusja] *f:* **a** ~ Prussia.

PS (*BR*) *abr m* = **Partido Socialista**.

PSB *abr m* = **Partido Socialista Brasileiro**.

PSC (*BR*) *abr m* = **Partido Social Cristão**.

PSD (*BR*) *abr m* = **Partido Social Democrático**.

PSDB *abr m* = **Partido Social-Democrata Brasileiro**.

pseudônimo [psew'donimu] *m* pseudonym.

psicanálise [psika'nalizi] *f* psychoanalysis.

psicanalista [psikana'liʃta] *m/f* psychoanalyst.

psicanalítico/a [psikana'litʃiku/a] *adj* psychoanalytic(al).

psicodélico/a [psiko'dɛliku/a] *adj* psychedelic.

psicologia [psikolo'ʒia] *f* psychology.

psicológico/a [psiko'lɔʒiku/a] *adj* psychological.

psicólogo/a [psi'kɔlogu/a] *m/f* psychologist.

psicopata [psiko'pata] *m/f* psychopath.

psicose [psi'kɔzi] *f* psychosis; **estar com** ~ **de** to be obsessed with *ou* by.

psicossomático/a [psikoso'matʃiku/a] *adj* psychosomatic.

psicoterapeuta [psikotera'pewta] *m/f* psychotherapist.

psicoterapia [psikotera'pia] *f* psychotherapy.

psicótico/a [psi'kɔtʃiku/a] *adj* psychotic.

psique ['psiki] *f* psyche.

psiquiatra [psi'kjatra] *m/f* psychiatrist.

psiquiatria [psikja'tria] *f* psychiatry.

psiquiátrico/a [psi'kjatriku/a] *adj* psychiatric.

psíquico/a ['psikiku/a] *adj* psychological.

psiu [psiw] *excl* hey!

PST (*BR*) *abr m* = **Partido Social Trabalhista**.

PT (*BR*) *abr m* = **Partido dos Trabalhadores**.

PTN (*BR*) *abr m* = **Partido Tancredista Nacional**.

PTR (*BR*) *abr m* = **Partido Trabalhista Renovador**.

PUA (*BR*) *abr m* (= *Pacto de Unidade e Ação*) *workers' movement*.

pua ['pua] *f* (*de broca*) bit; **sentar a** ~ **em alguém** (*col*) to give sb a beating.

puberdade [pubex'dadʒi] *f* puberty.
púbere ['puberi] *adj* pubescent.
púbis ['pubiʃ] *m inv* pubis.
publicação [publika'sãw] *f* publication.
publicar [publi'ka*] *vt* (*editar*) to publish; (*divulgar*) to divulge; (*proclamar*) to announce.
publicidade [publisi'dadʒi] *f* publicity; (*COM*) advertising.
publicitário/a [publisi'tarju/a] *adj* publicity *atr*; (*COM*) advertising *atr* ◆ *m/f* (*COM*) advertising executive.
público/a ['publiku/a] *adj* public ◆ *m* public; (*CINEMA, TEATRO etc*) audience; **em ~** in public; **o grande ~** the general public.
PUC (*BR*) *abr f* = **Pontifícia Universidade Católica**.
púcaro ['pukaru] (*PT*) *m* jug, mug.
pude ['pudʒi] *etc vb V* **poder**.
pudera [pu'dɛra] *etc vb V* **poder**.
pudicícia [pudi'sisja] *f* modesty.
pudico/a [pu'dʒiku/a] *adj* bashful; (*pej*) prudish.
pudim [pu'dʒĩ] (*pl* **-ns**) *m* pudding; **~ de leite** crème caramel.
pudim-flã [pudĩ'flã] (*PT*) *m* crème caramel.
pudins [pu'dʒĩʃ] *mpl de* **pudim**.
pudor [pu'do*] *m* bashfulness, modesty; (*moral*) decency; **atentado ao ~** indecent assault.
puerícia [pwe'risja] *f* childhood.
puericultura [pwerikuw'tura] *f* child care.
pueril [pwe'riw] (*pl* **-is**) *adj* puerile.
puerilidade [pwerili'dadʒi] *f* childishness, foolishness.
pueris [pwe'riʃ] *adj pl de* **pueril**.
pufe ['pufi] *m* pouf(fe).
pugilismo [puʒi'liʒmu] *m* boxing.
pugilista [puʒi'liʃta] *m* boxer.
pugna ['pugna] *f* fight, struggle.
pugnar [pug'na*] *vi* to fight.
pugnaz [pug'najʒ] *adj* pugnacious.
puído/a ['pwidu/a] *adj* worn.
puir [pwi*] *vt* to wear thin.
pujança [pu'ʒãsa] *f* vigour (*BRIT*), vigor (*US*), strength; (*de vegetação*) lushness; **na ~ da vida** in the prime of life.
pujante [pu'ʒãtʃi] *adj* powerful; (*saúde*) robust.
pular [pu'la*] *vi* to jump; (*no Carnaval*) to celebrate ◆ *vt* (*muro*) to jump (over); (*páginas, trechos*) to skip; **~ de alegria** to jump for joy; **~ Carnaval** to celebrate Carnival; **~ corda** to skip.
pulga ['puwga] *f* flea; **estar/ficar com a ~ atrás da orelha** to smell a rat.
pulgão [puw'gãw] (*pl* **-ões**) *m* greenfly.
pulha ['puʎa] *m* rat, creep.
pulmão [puw'mãw] (*pl* **-ões**) *m* lung.
pulmonar [puwmo'na*] *adj* pulmonary, lung

atr.
pulo ['pulu] *etc vb V* **polir** ◆ *m* jump; **dar ~s** (**de contente**) to be delighted; **dar um ~ em** to stop off at; **aos ~s** by leaps and bounds; **a um ~ de** a stone's throw away from; **num ~** in a flash.
pulôver [pu'love*] (*BR*) *m* pullover.
púlpito ['puwpitu] *m* pulpit.
pulsação [puwsa'sãw] *f* pulsation, beating; (*MED*) pulse.
pulsar [puw'sa*] *vi* (*palpitar*) to pulsate, throb.
pulseira [puw'sejra] *f* bracelet; (*de sapato*) strap.
pulso ['puwsu] *m* (*ANAT*) wrist; (*MED*) pulse; (*fig*) vigour (*BRIT*), vigor (*US*), energy; **obra de ~** work of great importance; **homem de ~** energetic man; **tomar o ~ de alguém** to take sb's pulse; **tomar o ~ de algo** (*fig*) to look into sth, sound sth out; **a ~** by force.
pulular [pulu'la*] *vi* to abound; (*surgir*) to spring up; **~ de** to teem with; (*de turistas, mendigos*) to be crawling with.
pulverizador [puwveriza'do*] *m* (*para líquidos etc*) spray, spray gun.
pulverizar [puwveri'za*] *vt* to pulverize; (*líquido*) to spray; (*polvilhar*) to dust.
pum [pũ] *excl* bang! ◆ *m* (*col*) fart (*!*), trump.
pumba ['pũba] *excl* zoom!
punção [pũ'sãw] (*pl* **-ões**) *m* (*instrumento*) punch ◆ *f* (*MED*) puncture.
Pundjab [pũ'dʒabi] *m*: **o ~** the Punjab.
pundonor [pũdo'no*] *m* dignity, self-respect.
pungente [pũ'ʒẽtʃi] *adj* painful.
pungir [pũ'ʒi*] *vt* to afflict ◆ *vi* to be painful.
punguear [pũ'gja*] (*col*) *vt* (*bolso*) to pick; (*bolsa*) to snatch.
punguista [pũ'giʃta] *m* pickpocket.
punha ['puɲa] *etc vb V* **pôr**.
punhado [pu'ɲadu] *m* handful.
punhal [pu'ɲaw] (*pl* **-ais**) *m* dagger.
punhalada [puɲa'lada] *f* stab.
punho ['puɲu] *m* (*ANAT*) fist; (*de manga*) cuff; (*de espada*) hilt; **de (seu) próprio ~** in one's own hand(writing).
punição [puni'sãw] (*pl* **-ões**) *f* punishment.
punir [pu'ni*] *vt* to punish.
punitivo/a [puni'tʃivu/a] *adj* punitive.
punja ['pũʒa] *etc vb V* **pungir**.
pupila [pu'pila] *f* (*ANAT*) pupil; (*tutelada*) ward.
pupilo [pu'pilu] *m* (*tutelado*) ward; (*aluno*) pupil.
purê [pu're] *m* purée; **~ de batatas** mashed potatoes.
pureza [pu'reza] *f* purity.
purgação [puxga'sãw] (*pl* **-ões**) *f* purge; (*purificação*) purification.
purgante [pux'gãtʃi] *m* purgative; (*col: pessoa*) bore.
purgar [pux'ga*] *vt* to purge; (*purificar*) to

purify.
purgativo/a [puxga't∫ivu/a] *adj* purgative ♦ *m* purgative.
purgatório [puxga'tɔrju] *m* purgatory.
purificação [purifika'sãw] *f* purification.
purificar [purifi'ka*] *vt* to purify.
purista [pu'ri∫ta] *m/f* purist.
puritanismo [purita'niʒmu] *m* puritanism.
puritano/a [puri'tanu/a] *adj* (*atitude*) puritanical; (*seita*) puritan ♦ *m/f* puritan.
puro/a ['puru/a] *adj* pure; (*uísque*) neat; (*verdade*) plain; (*intenções*) honourable (*BRIT*), honorable (*US*); (*estilo*) clear; **isto é pura imaginação sua** it's pure imagination on your part, you're just imagining it; **~ e simples** pure and simple.
puro-sangue (*pl* **puros-sangues**) *adj*, *m* thoroughbred.
púrpura ['puxpura] *f* purple.
purpúreo/a [pux'purju/a] *adj* (*cor*) crimson.
purpurina [puxpu'rina] *f* metallic paint.
purulento/a [puru'létu] *adj* festering, suppurating.
pus¹ [pu∫] *m* pus, matter.
pus² [pu∫] *etc vb* V **pôr**.
puser [pu'ze*] *etc vb* V **pôr**.
pusilânime [puzi'lanimi] *adj* fainthearted; (*covarde*) cowardly.
pústula ['pu∫tula] *f* pustule; (*fig*) rotter.
puta ['puta] (*col!*) *f* whore; **~ vida!** fucking hell! (*!*); **mandar alguém para a ~ que (o) pariu** to tell sb to fuck off (*!*); *V tb* **puto**.
putativo/a [puta't∫ivu/a] *adj* supposed.
puto/a ['putu/a] (*col!*) *m/f* (*sem-vergonha*) bastard ♦ *adj* (*zangado*) furious; (*incrível*): **um ~ ...** a hell of a ...; **o ~ de ...** the bloody ....
putrefação [putrefa'sãw] *f* rotting, putrefaction.
putrefato/a [putre'fatu/a] *adj* rotten.
putrefazer [putrefa'ze*] (*irreg: como* **fazer**) *vt* to rot ♦ *vi* to putrefy, rot; **~-se** *vr* to putrefy, rot.
pútrido/a ['putridu/a] *adj* putrid, rotten.
puxa ['pu∫a] *excl* gosh; **~ vida!** gosh!
puxada [pu'∫ada] *f* pull; (*puxão*) tug; **dar uma ~** (*nos estudos*) to make an effort.
puxado/a [pu'∫adu/a] *adj* (*col: aluguel*) steep, high; (*: curso*) tough; (*: trabalho*) hard.
puxador [pu∫a'do*] *m* handle, knob.
puxão [pu'∫ãw] (*pl* **-ões**) *m* tug, jerk.
puxa-puxa (*pl* **~s**) *m* toffee.
puxar [pu'∫a*] *vt* to pull; (*sacar*) to pull out; (*assunto*) to bring up; (*conversa*) to strike up; (*briga*) to pick ♦ *vi*: **~ de uma perna** to limp; **~ a** to take after; **~ por** (*alunos, etc*) to push; **uma coisa puxa a outra** one thing leads to another; **os paulistas puxam pelo esse** the s is very pronounced in São Paulo.
puxa-saco (*pl* **~s**) *m* creep, crawler.
puxo ['pu∫u] *m* (*em parto*) push.
puxões [pu'∫õj∫] *mpl de* **puxão**.

Q

Q, q [ke] (*pl* **qs**) *m* Q, q; **Q de Quintela** Q for Queen.
q. *abr* (= *quartel*) *60 kg.*
QC *abr m* (= *Quartel-General*) HQ.
QI *abr m* (= *Quociente de Inteligência*) IQ.
ql. *abr* (= *quilate*) ct.
qtd. *abr* (= *quantidade*) qty.
qua. *abr* = (*quarta-feira*) Weds.
quadra ['kwadra] *f* (*quarteirão*) block; (*de tênis etc*) court; (*período*) time, period; (*jogos*) four; (*estrofe*) quatrain.
quadrado/a [kwa'dradu/a] *adj* square; (*col: antiquado*) square ♦ *m* square ♦ *m/f* (*col*) square.
quadragésimo/a [kwadra'ʒezimu/a] *num* fortieth; *V tb* **quinto**.
quadrangular [kwadrãgu'la*] *adj* quadrangular.
quadrângulo [kwa'drãgulu] *m* quadrangle.
quadrar [kwa'dra*] *vt* to square, make square ♦ *vi*: **~ a** (*ser conveniente*) to suit; **~ com** (*condizer*) to square with.
quadriculado/a [kwadriku'ladu/a] *adj* checkered; **papel ~** squared paper.
quadril [kwa'driw] (*pl* **-is**) *m* hip.
quadrilátero/a [kwadri'lateru/a] *adj* quadrilateral.
quadrilha [kwa'driʎa] *f* gang; (*dança*) square dance.
quadrimotor [kwadrimo'to*] *adj* four-engined ♦ *m* four-engined plane.
quadrinho [kwa'driɲu] *m* (*de tira*) frame; **história em ~s** (*BR*) cartoon.
quadris [kwa'dri∫] *mpl de* **quadril**.
quadro ['kwadru] *m* (*pintura*) painting; (*gravura, foto*) picture; (*lista*) list; (*tabela*) chart, table; (*TEC: painel*) panel; (*pessoal*) staff; (*time*) team; (*TEATRO, fig*) scene; (*fig: MED*) patient's condition; **~ de avisos** bulletin board; **~ de reserva** (*MIL*) reserve list; **~ clínico** clinical picture; **o ~ político** (*fig*) the political scene; **~ social** (*de um clube*) members *pl*; (*de uma empresa*) partners *pl*.
quadro-negro (*pl* **quadros-negros**) *m* blackboard.
quadrúpede [kwa'drupedʒi] *adj*, *m* quadruped ♦ *m/f* (*fig*) blockhead.
quadruplicar [kwadrupli'ka*] *vt*, *vi* to quadruple.
quádruplo/a ['kwadruplu/a] *adj*, *m* quadruple ♦ *m/f* (*quadrigêmeo*) quad.
qual [kwaw] (*pl* **-ais**) *pron* which ♦ *conj* as,

like ♦ *excl* what!; ~ **deles** which of them; ~ **é o problema/o seu nome?** what's the problem/your name?; **o** ~ which; (*pessoa: sujeito*) who; (*pessoa: objeto*) whom; **seja** ~ for whatever *ou* whichever it may be; **cada** ~ each one; ~ **é?** *ou* ~ **é a tua?** (*col*) what are you up to?; ~ **seja** such as; **tal** ~ just like; ~ **nada!** *ou* ~ **o quê!** no such thing!

qual. *abr* (= *qualidade*) qual.

qualidade [kwali'dadʒi] *f* quality; **na** ~ **de** in the capacity of; **produto de** ~ quality product; **Q**~ **Carta** (*COMPUT*) letter quality.

qualificação [kwalifika'sãw] (*pl* -**ões**) *f* qualification.

qualificado/a [kwalifi'kadu/a] *adj* qualified; **não** ~ unqualified.

qualificar [kwalifi'ka*] *vt* to qualify; (*avaliar*) to evaluate; ~**-se** *vr* to qualify; ~ **de** *ou* **como** to classify as, regard as.

qualificativo/a [kwalifika'tʃivu/a] *adj* qualifying ♦ *m* qualifier.

qualitativo/a [kwalita'tʃivu/a] *adj* qualitative.

qualquer [kwaw'ke*] (*pl* **quaisquer**) *adj* any ♦ *pron* any; ~ **pessoa** anyone, anybody; ~ **um dos dois** either; ~ **outro** any other; ~ **dia** any day; ~ **que seja** whichever it may be; **um disco** ~ any record at all, any record you like; **a** ~ **momento** at any moment; **a** ~ **preço** at any price; **de** ~ **jeito** *ou* **maneira** anyway; (*a* ~ *preço*) no matter what; (*sem cuidado*) anyhow; **um/uma** ~ (*pej*) any old person.

quando ['kwãdu] *adv* when ♦ *conj* when; (*interrogativo*) when?; (*ao passo que*) whilst; ~ **muito** at most; ~ **quer que** whenever; **de** ~ **em** ~, **de vez em** ~ now and then; **desde** ~**?** how long?, since when?; ~ **mais não seja** if for no other reason; ~ **de** on the occasion of; ~ **menos se esperava** when we (*ou* they, I *etc*) least expected (it).

quant. *abr* (= *quantidade*) quant.

quantia [kwã'tʃia] *f* sum, amount.

quantidade [kwãtʃi'dadʒi] *f* quantity, amount; **uma** ~ **de** a large amount of; **em** ~ in large amounts.

quantificar [kwãtʃifi'ka*] *vt* to quantify.

quantitativo/a [kwãtʃita'tʃivu/a] *adj* quantitative.

quanto/a ['kwãtu/a] *adj*, *pron* all that, as much as; (*interrogativo: sg*) how much?; (: *pl*) how many?; ~ **tempo?** how long?; ~ **custa?** how much does it cost?; ~ **a** as regards; ~ **a mim** as for me; ~ **antes** as soon as possible; ~ **mais** (*principalmente*) specially; (*muito menos*) let alone; ~ **mais cedo melhor** the sooner the better; ~ **mais trabalha, mais ganha** the more he works, the more he earns; ~ **mais, (tanto) melhor** the more, the better; **tanto** ~ **possível** as much as possible; **tanto/tantos** ... ~ ... as much/

as many ... as ...; **tão** ... ~ ... as ... as ...; **tudo** ~ everything that, as much as; **um tanto** ~ somewhat, rather; ~ **sofria!** how he suffered!; ~ **sofrimento!** what suffering!; **um Luís não sei dos** ~**s** a Luís something or other; **sei o** ~ **você se esforçou** I know how much you tried; **não saber a quantas anda** not to know how things stand; **a** ~ **está o jogo?** what's the score?; **a** ~ **está o dólar?** what's the rate for the dollar?

quão [kwãw] *adv* how.

quarenta [kwa'rẽta] *num* forty; *V tb* **cinqüenta.**

quarentão/ona [kwarẽ'tãw/'tɔna] (*pl* -**ões**/~**s**) *adj* in one's forties ♦ *m/f* man/woman in his/her forties.

quarentena [kwarẽ'tɛna] *f* quarantine.

quarentões [kwarẽ'tõjʃ] *mpl de* **quarentão.**

quarentona [kwarẽ'tɔna] *f de* **quarentão.**

quaresma [kwa'reʒma] *f* Lent.

quart. *abr* = **quarteirão.**

quarta ['kwaxta] *f* (*tb:* ~**-feira**) Wednesday; (*parte*) quarter; (*AUTO*) fourth (gear); (*MÚS*) fourth.

quarta-de-final (*pl* **quartas-de-final**) *f* quarter final.

quarta-feira ['kwaxta-'fejra] (*pl* **quartas-feiras**) *f* Wednesday; ~ **de cinzas** Ash Wednesday; *V tb* **terça-feira.**

quartanista [kwaxta'niʃta] *m/f* fourth-year.

quarteirão [kwaxtej'rãw] (*pl* -**ões**) *m* (*de casas*) block.

quartel [kwax'tɛw] (*pl* -**éis**) *m* barracks *sg*.

quartel-general (*pl* **quartéis-generais**) *m* headquarters *pl*.

quarteto [kwax'tetu] *m* (*MÚS*) quartet; ~ **de cordas** string quartet.

quarto/a ['kwaxtu/a] *num* fourth ♦ *m* (*quarta parte*) quarter; (*aposento*) room; (*MIL*) watch; (*anca*) haunch; ~ **de banho** bathroom; ~ **de dormir** bedroom; ~ **de casal** double bedroom; ~ **de solteiro** single room; ~ **crescente/minguante** (*ASTRO*) first/last quarter; **três** ~**s de hora** three quarters of an hour; **passar um mau** ~ **de hora** (*fig*) to have a rough time; *V tb* **quinto.**

quarto-e-sala (*pl* ~**s**) *m* two-room apartment.

quartzo ['kwaxtsu] *m* quartz.

quase ['kwazi] *adv* almost, nearly; ~ **nada** hardly anything; ~ **nunca** hardly ever; ~ **sempre** nearly always.

quaternário/a [kwatex'narju/a] *adj* quaternary.

quatorze [kwa'toxzi] *num* fourteen; *V tb* **cinco.**

quatro ['kwatru] *num* four; **estar/ficar de** ~ to be/get down on all fours; *V tb* **cinco.**

quatrocentos/as [kwatro'sẽtuʃ/aʃ] *num* four hundred.

NB: *European Portuguese adds the following consonants to certain words:* **b** (sú(b)dito, su(b)til); **c** (a(c)ção, a(c)cionista, a(c)to); **m** (inde(m)ne); **p** (ado(p)ção, ado(p)tar); *for further details see p. xiii.*

que [ki] *pron (sujeito)* who, that; (: *coisa*) which, that; (*complemento*) whom, that; (: *coisa*) which, that; (*interrogativo*) what? ♦ *conj* that; (*porque*) because; **ele não tem nada ~ fazer** he's got nothing to do; **~ nem** (*BR*) like; **~ pena!** what a pity!; **(do) ~** than; **mais do ~ pensa** more than you think; **não há nada ~ fazer** there's nothing to be done; **~ lindo!** how lovely!; **~ susto!** what a fright!; **espero ~ sim/não** I hope so/not; **dizer ~ sim/não** to say yes/no; *V tb* **tal**.

quê [ke] *m* something ♦ *pron* what; **~ !** what!; **não tem de ~** don't mention it; **para ~?** what for?; **por ~?** why?; **sem ~ nem por ~** for no good reason, all of a sudden.

Quebec [ke'bɛk] *n* Quebec.

quebra ['kɛbra] *f* break, rupture; (*falência*) bankruptcy; (*de energia elétrica*) cut; (*de disciplina*) breakdown; **de ~** in addition; **~ de página** (*COMPUT*) page break.

quebra-cabeça (*pl* **~s**) *m* puzzle, problem; (*jogo*) jigsaw puzzle.

quebrada [ke'brada] *f* (*vertente*) slope; (*barranco*) ravine, gully.

quebradiço/a [kebra'dʒisu/a] *adj* fragile, breakable.

quebrado/a [ke'bradu/a] *adj* broken; (*cansado*) exhausted; (*falido*) bankrupt; (*carro, máquina*) broken down; (*telefone*) out of order; (*col: pronto*) broke.

quebrados [ke'braduʃ] *mpl* loose change *sg*.

quebra-galho (*pl* **~s**) (*col*) *m* lifesaver.

quebra-gelos *m inv* (*NÁUT*) icebreaker.

quebra-mar (*pl* **~es**) *m* breakwater, sea wall.

quebra-molas *m inv* speed bump, sleeping policeman.

quebra-nozes *m inv* nutcrackers *pl* (*BRIT*), nutcracker (*US*).

quebrantar [kebrã'ta*] *vt* to break; (*entusiasmo, ânimo*) to dampen; (*debilitar*) to weaken, wear out; **~-se** *vr* (*tornar-se fraco*) to grow weak.

quebranto [ke'brãtu] *m* (*fraqueza*) weakness; (*mau-olhado*) blight, evil eye.

quebra-pau (*pl* **~s**) (*col*) *m* row.

quebra-quebra (*pl* **~s**) *m* riot.

quebrar [ke'bra*] *vt* to break; (*entusiasmo*) to dampen; (*espancar*) to beat; (*dobrar*) to bend ♦ *vi* to break; (*carro*) to break down; (*COM*) to go bankrupt; (*ficar sem dinheiro*) to go broke.

quebra-vento (*pl* **~s**) *m* (*AUTO*) fanlight.

quéchua ['kɛʃwa] *m* (*LING*) Quechua.

queda ['kɛda] *f* fall; (*fig: ruína*) downfall; **ter ~ para algo** to have a bent for sth; **ter uma ~ por alguém** to have a soft spot for sb; **~ de barreira** landslide.

queda-d'água (*pl* **quedas-d'água**) *f* waterfall.

queda-de-braço *f* arm wrestling.

quedê [ke'de] (*col*) *adv* where is/are?

queijada [kej'ʒada] *f* cheesecake.

queijadinha [kejʒa'dʒiɲa] *f* coconut sweet.

queijeira [kej'ʒejra] *f* cheese dish.

queijo ['kejʒu] *m* cheese; **~ prato** ≈ cheddar cheese; **~ ralado** grated cheese.

queijo-de-minas *m* white cheese (≈ *Cheshire*).

queijo-do-reino *m* ≈ Edam cheese.

queima ['kejma] *f* burning; (*COM*) clearance sale.

queimada [kej'mada] *f* burning (of forests).

queimado/a [kej'madu/a] *adj* burnt; (*de sol: machucado*) sunburnt; (: *bronzeado*) brown, tanned; (*plantas, folhas*) dried up; **cheiro/gosto de ~** smell of burning/burnt taste.

queimadura [kejma'dura] *f* burn; (*de sol*) sunburn; **~ de primeiro/terceiro grau** first-/third-degree burn.

queimar [kej'ma*] *vt* to burn; (*roupa*) to scorch; (*com líquido*) to scald; (*bronzear a pele*) to tan; (*planta, folha*) to wither; (*calorias*) to burn off ♦ *vi* to burn; (*estar quente*) to be burning hot; (*lâmpada, fusível*) to blow; **~-se** *vr* (*pessoa*) to burn o.s.; to tan; (*zangar-se*) to get angry.

queima-roupa ['kejma-] *f*: **à ~** point-blank, at point-blank range.

queira ['kejra] *etc vb V* **querer**.

queixa ['kejʃa] *f* complaint; (*lamentação*) lament; **fazer ~ de alguém** to complain about sb; **ter ~ de alguém** to have a problem with sb.

queixa-crime (*pl* **queixas-crime(s)**) *f* (*JUR*) citation.

queixada [kej'ʃada] *f* (*de animal*) jaw; (*queixo grande*) prominent chin.

queixar-se [kej'ʃaxsi] *vr* to complain; **~ de** to complain about; (*dores etc*) to complain of.

queixo ['kejʃu] *m* chin; (*maxilar*) jaw; **ficar de ~ caído** to be open-mouthed; **bater o ~** to shiver.

queixoso/a [kej'ʃozu/ɔza] *adj* complaining; (*magoado*) doleful ♦ *m/f* (*JUR*) plaintiff.

queixume [kej'ʃumi] *m* complaint; (*lamentação*) lament.

quem [kẽj] *pron* who; (*como objeto*) who(m); **~ quer que** whoever; **seja ~ for** whoever it may be; **de ~ é isto?** whose is this?; **~ é?** who is it?; **a pessoa com ~ trabalha** the person he works with; **para ~ você deu o livro?** who did you give the book to?; **convide ~ você quiser** invite whoever you want; **~ disse isso, se enganou** whoever said that was wrong; **~ fez isso fui eu** it was me who did it, the person who did it was me; **~ diria!** who would have thought (it)!; **~ me dera ser rico** if only I were rich; **~ me dera que isso não fosse verdade** I wish it weren't true; **~ sabe** (*talvez*) perhaps; **~ sou eu para negar?** who am I to deny it?

Quênia ['kenja] *m*: **o ~** Kenya.

queniano/a [ke'njanu/a] *adj, m/f* Kenyan.

quentão [kẽ'tãw] *m* ≈ mulled wine.

quente ['kẽtʃi] *adj* hot; (*roupa*) warm;

(*notícia*) reliable, solid; **o ~ agora é ...**
(*col*) the big thing now is ....
quentinha [kē'tʃiɲa] *f* heatproof carton (*for food*).
quentura [kē'tura] *f* heat, warmth.
quer [ke*] *vb V* **querer ∳** *conj* ~ ... ~ ...
whether ... or ...; **~ chova ~ não** whether it rains or not; **~ você queira, ~ não** whether you like it or not; **onde ~ que** wherever; **quando ~ que** whenever; **quem ~ que** whoever; **o que ~ que seja** whatever it is; **~ chova, ~ faça sol** come rain or shine.
querela [ke'rɛla] *f* dispute; (*JUR*) complaint, accusation.
querelado [kere'ladu] *m* (*JUR*) defendant.
querelador(a) [kerela'do*(a)] *m/f* (*JUR*) plaintiff.
querelante [kere'lãtʃi] *m/f* (*JUR*) plaintiff.
querelar [kere'la*] *vt* (*JUR*) to prosecute, sue **∳** *vi*: **~ contra** *ou* **de** (*queixar-se*) to lodge a complaint against.
querer [ke're*] *vt* to want; (*ter afeição*) to be fond of; (*amar*) to love **∳** *m* (*vontade*) wish; (*afeto*) affection; **~-se** *vr* to love one another; **~ bem a** to be fond of; **~ mal a** to dislike; **sem ~** unintentionally, by accident; **por ~** intentionally; **como queira** as you wish; **você quer fechar a janela?** will you shut the window?; **queira entrar/sentar** do come in/sit down; **~ que alguém faça** to want sb to do; **você vai ~ sair amanhã?** do you want to go out tomorrow?; **eu vou ~ uma cerveja** (*num bar etc*) I'd like a beer; **o forno não quer acender** the oven won't light; **~ dizer** (*significar*) to mean; (*pretender dizer*) to mean to say; **quer dizer** (*com outras palavras*) in other words; (*quero dizer*) I mean, that is to say; **está querendo chover** it feels like rain; **não ~ nada com** to want to have nothing to do with; **como quem não quer nada** casually.
querido/a [ke'ridu/a] *adj* dear **∳** *m/f* darling; **~ no grupo/por todos** prized in the group/by all; **o ator ~ das mulheres** the women's favo(u)rite actor; **Q~ João** Dear John.
quermesse [kex'mɛsi] *f* fête.
querosene [kero'zɛni] *m* kerosene oil.
querubim [keru'bĩ] (*pl* **-ns**) *m* cherubim.
quesito [ke'zitu] *m* (*questão*) query, question; (*requisito*) requirement.
questão [keʃ'tãw] (*pl* **-ões**) *f* (*pergunta*) question, inquiry; (*problema*) matter, question; (*JUR*) case; (*contenda*) dispute, quarrel; **fazer ~ (de)** to insist (on); **em ~** in question; **há ~ de um ano** about a year ago; **~ de tempo/de vida ou morte** question of time/ matter of life and death; **~ de ordem** point of order; **~ fechada** point of principle.
questionar [keʃtʃjo'na*] *vi* to question, argue **∳** *vt* to question, call into question.

questionário [keʃtʃjo'narju] *m* questionnaire.
questionável [keʃtʃjo'navew] (*pl* **-eis**) *adj* questionable.
questões [keʃ'tõjʃ] *fpl de* **questão**.
qui. *abr* (= *quinta-feira*) Thurs.
quiabo ['kjabu] *m* okra.
quibe ['kibi] *m* deep-fried mince with flour and mint.
quibebe [ki'bɛbi] *m* pumpkin purée.
quicar [ki'ka*] *vi* (*bola*) to bounce; (*col: pessoa*) to go mad **∳** *vt* to bounce.
quiche ['kiʃi] *f* quiche.
quieto/a ['kjɛtu/a] *adj* quiet; (*imóvel*) still; **fica ~!** be quiet!
quietude [kje'tudʒi] *f* calm, tranquillity.
quilate [ki'latʃi] *m* carat; (*fig*) calibre (*BRIT*), caliber (*US*).
quilha ['kiʎa] *f* (*NÁUT*) keel.
quilo ['kilu] *m* kilo.
quilobyte [kilo'bajtʃi] *m* kilobyte.
quilograma [kilo'grama] *m* kilogram.
quilohertz [kilo'hexts] *m* kilohertz.
quilometragem [kilome'traʒẽ] *f* number of kilometres *ou* kilometers travelled, ≈ mileage.
quilometrar [kilome'tra*] *vt* to measure in kilometres *ou* kilometers.
quilométrico/a [kilo'mɛtriku/a] *adj* (*distância*) in kilometres *ou* kilometers; (*fig: fila etc*) ≈ mile-long.
quilômetro [ki'lometru] *m* kilometre (*BRIT*), kilometer (*US*).
quilowatt [kilo'watʃi] *m* kilowatt.
quimbanda [kĩ'bãda] *m* (*ritual*) macumba ceremony; (*feiticeiro*) medicine man; (*local*) macumba site.
quimera [ki'mɛra] *f* chimera.
quimérico/a [ki'mɛriku/a] *adj* fantastic.
química ['kimika] *f* chemistry; *V tb* **químico**.
químico/a ['kimiku/a] *adj* chemical **∳** *m/f* chemist.
quimioterapia [kimjotera'pia] *f* chemotherapy.
quimono [ki'mɔnu] *m* kimono; (*penhoar*) robe.
quina ['kina] *f* (*canto*) corner; (*de mesa etc*) edge; **de ~** edgeways (*BRIT*), edgewise (*US*).
quindim [kĩ'dʒĩ] *m* sweet made of egg yolks, coconut and sugar.
quinhão [ki'ɲãw] (*pl* **-ões**) *m* share, portion.
quinhentista [kiɲē'tʃiʃta] *adj* sixteenth century *atr*.
quinhentos/as [ki'ɲētuʃ/aʃ] *num* five hundred; **isso são outros ~** (*col*) that's a different matter, that's a different kettle of fish.
quinhões [ki'ɲõjʃ] *mpl de* **quinhão**.
quinina [ki'nina] *f* quinine.
qüinquagésimo/a [kwĩkwa'ʒɛzimu/a] *num* fiftieth; *V tb* **quinto**.

NB: European Portuguese adds the following consonants to certain words: **b** (sú(b)dito, su(b)til); **c** (a(c)ção, a(c)cionista, a(c)to); **m** (inde(m)ne); **p** (ado(p)ção, ado(p)tar); *for further details see p. xiii.*

quinquilharias [kĩkiʎa'riaʃ] *fpl* odds and ends; (*miudezas*) knicknacks, trinkets.

quinta ['kĩta] *f* (*tb*: ~-*feira*) Thursday; (*propriedade*) estate; (*PT*) farm.

quinta-essência (*pl* ~s) *f* quintessence.

quinta-feira ['kĩta-'fejra] (*pl* **quintas-feiras**) *f* Thursday; *V tb* **terça-feira**.

quintal [kĩ'taw] (*pl* **-ais**) *m* back yard.

quintanista [kĩta'niʃta] *m/f* fifth-year.

quinteiro [kĩ'tejru] (*PT*) *m* farmer.

quinteto [kĩ'tetu] *m* quintet.

quinto/a ['kĩtu/a] *num* fifth; **ele tirou o ~ lugar** he came fifth; **eu fui o ~ a chegar** I was the fifth to arrive, I arrived fifth; (*numa corrida*) I came fifth.

quintuplo/a [kĩ'tuplu/a] *adj*, *m* quintuple ♦ *m/ f*: ~**s** (*crianças*) quins.

quinze ['kĩzı] *num* fifteen; **duas e ~** a quarter past (*BRIT*) *ou* after (*US*) two; **~ para as sete** a quarter to (*BRIT*) *ou* of (*US*) seven; *V tb* **cinco.**

quinzena [kĩ'zɛna] *f* two weeks, fortnight (*BRIT*); (*salário*) two weeks' wages.

quinzenal [kĩze'naw] (*pl* **-ais**) *adj* fortnightly.

quinzenalmente [kĩzenaw'mẽtʃi] *adv* fortnightly.

quiosque ['kjɔʃki] *m* kiosk; (*de jardim*) gazebo.

qüiproquó [kwipro'kwɔ] *m* misunderstanding, mix-up.

quiromante [kiro'mãtʃi] *m/f* palmist, fortune teller.

quis [kiʒ] *etc vb V* **querer**.

quiser [ki'ze*] *etc vb V* **querer**.

quisto ['kiʃtu] *m* cyst.

quitação [kita'sãw] (*pl* **-ões**) *f* (*remissão*) discharge, remission; (*pagamento*) settlement; (*recibo*) receipt.

quitanda [ki'tãda] *f* (*loja*) grocer's (shop) (*BRIT*), grocery store (*US*).

quitandeiro/a [kitã'dejru/a] *m/f* grocer; (*vendedor de hortaliças*) greengrocer (*BRIT*), produce dealer (*US*).

quitar [ki'ta*] *vt* (*dívida: pagar*) to pay off; (*: perdoar*) to cancel; (*devedor*) to release.

quite ['kitʃi] *adj* (*livre*) free; (*com um credor*) squared up; (*igualado*) even; **estar ~ (com alguém)** to be quits (with sb).

quitute [ki'tutʃi] *n* titbit (*BRIT*), tidbit (*US*).

quizumba [ki'zũba] (*col*) *f* punch-up, brawl.

quociente [kwo'sjẽtʃi] *m* quotient; **~ de inteligência** intelligence quotient.

quorum ['kwɔrũ] *m* quorum.

quota ['kwota] *f* quota; (*porção*) share, portion.

quotidiano/a [kwotʃi'dʒjanu/a] *adj* everyday.

q.v. *abr* (= *queira ver*) q.v.

R

R, r ['ɛxi] (*pl* **rs**) *m* R, r; **R de Roberto** R for Robert (*BRIT*) *ou* Roger (*US*).

R *abr* (= *rua*) St.

rã [xã] *f* frog.

rabada [xa'bada] *f* (*rabo*) tail; (*fig*) tail end; (*CULIN*) oxtail stew.

rabanada [xaba'nada] *f* (*CULIN*) cinnamon toast; (*golpe*) blow with the tail; **dar uma ~ em alguém** (*col*) to give sb the brush-off.

rabanete [xaba'netʃi] *m* radish.

rabear [xa'bja*] *vi* (*cão*) to wag one's tail; (*navio*) to wheel around; (*carro*) to skid round.

rabecão [xabe'kãw] (*pl* **-ões**) *m* mortuary wagon.

rabicho [xa'biʃu] *m* pony tail.

rabino [xa'binu] *m* rabbi.

rabiscar [xabiʃ'ka*] *vt* (*escrever*) to scribble; (*papel*) to scribble on ♦ *vi* to doodle; (*escrever mal*) to scribble.

rabisco [xa'biʃku] *m* scribble.

rabo ['xabu] *m* (*cauda*) tail; (*col!*) bum; **meter o ~ entre as pernas** (*fig*) to be left with one's tail between one's legs; **olhar alguém com o ~ do olho** to look at sb out of the corner of one's eye; **pegar em ~ de foguete** (*col*) to stick one's neck out; **ser ~ de foguete** (*col*) to be a minefield.

rabo-de-cavalo (*pl* **rabos-de-cavalo**) *m* ponytail.

rabo-de-saia (*pl* **rabos-de-saia**) (*col*) *m* woman; **não poder ver ~** to be a womanizer.

rabugento/a [xabu'ʒẽtu/a] *adj* grumpy.

rabugice [xabu'ʒisi] *f* grumpiness.

rabujar [xabu'ʒa*] *vi* to be grumpy; (*criança*) to have a tantrum.

raça ['xasa] *f* breed; (*grupo étnico*) race; **cão/ cavalo de ~** pedigree dog/thoroughbred horse; **(no peito e) na ~** (*col*) by sheer effort; **ter ~** to have guts; (*ter ascendência africana*) to be of African origin.

ração [xa'sãw] (*pl* **-ões**) *f* ration; (*para animal*) food; **~ de cachorro** dog food.

racha ['xaʃa] *f* (*fenda*) split; (*greta*) crack ♦ *m* (*col*) scrap.

rachadura [xaʃa'dura] *f* (*fenda*) crack.

rachar [xa'ʃa*] *vt* (*fender*) to crack; (*objeto, despesas*) to split; (*lenha*) to chop ♦ *vi* to split; (*cristal*) to crack; ~**-se** *vr* to split; to crack; **frio de ~** bitter cold; **sol de ~** scorching sun; **ou vai ou racha** it's make or break.

racial [xa'sjaw] (*pl* **-ais**) *adj* racial; **preconcei-**

to ~ racial prejudice.
raciocinar [xasjosi'na*] *vi* to reason.
raciocínio [xasjo'sinju] *m* reasoning.
racional [xasjo'naw] (*pl* -ais) *adj* rational.
racionalização [xasjonaliza'sãw] *f* rationalization.
racionalizar [xasjonali'za*] *vt* to rationalize.
racionamento [xasjona'mẽtu] *m* rationing.
racionar [xasjo'na*] *vt* (*distribuir*) to ration out; (*limitar a venda de*) to ration.
racismo [xa'siʒmu] *m* racism.
racista [xa'siʃta] *adj*, *m/f* racist.
raçoes [xa'sõjʃ] *fpl de* **ração**.
radar [xa'da*] *m* radar.
radiação [xadʒja'sãw] (*pl* -ões) *f* radiation; (*raio*) ray.
radiador [xadʒja'do*] *m* radiator.
radialista [xadʒja'liʃta] *m/f* radio announcer; (*na produção*) radio producer.
radiante [xa'dʒjãtʃi] *adj* radiant; (*de alegria*) overjoyed.
radical [xadʒi'kaw] (*pl* -ais) *adj* radical ♦ *m* radical; (*LING*) root.
radicalismo [xadʒika'liʒmu] *m* radicalism.
radicalizar [xadʒikali'za*] *vt* to radicalize; ~-se *vr* to become radical.
radicar-se [xadʒi'kaxsi] *vr* to take root; (*fixar residência*) to settle.
rádio ['xadʒju] *m* radio; (*QUÍM*) radium ♦ *f* radio station.
radioactivo/a *etc* [xadjua'tivu/a] (*PT*) *adj* = **radioativo** *etc*.
radioamador(a) [xadʒjuama'do*(a)] *m/f* radio ham.
radioatividade [xadʒjuatʃivi'dadʒi] *f* radioactivity.
radioativo/a [xadʒjua'tʃivu/a] *adj* radioactive.
radiodifusão [xadʒjodʒifu'zãw] *f* broadcasting.
radiodifusora [xadʒjodʒifu'zora] *f* radio station.
radioemissora [xadʒjuemi'sora] *f* radio station.
radiografar [xadʒjogra'fa*] *vt* (*MED*) to X-ray; (*notícia*) to radio.
radiografia [xadʒjogra'fia] *f* X-ray.
radiograma [xadʒjo'grama] *m* cablegram.
radiogravador [xadʒjograva'do*] *m* radio cassette.
radiojornal [xadʒjoʒox'naw] (*pl* -ais) *m* radio news *sg*.
radiologia [xadʒjolo'ʒia] *f* radiology.
radiologista [xadʒjolo'ʒiʃta] *m/f* radiologist.
radionovela [xadʒjono'vɛla] *f* radio serial.
radiopatrulha [xadʒjopa'truʎa] *f* radio patrol; (*viatura*) patrol car.
radiooperador(a) [xadʒjoopera'do*(a)] *m/f* radio operator.
radiorrepórter [xadʒjoxe'pɔxte*] *m/f* radio reporter.
radioso/a [xa'dʒjozu/ɔza] *adj* radiant, brilliant.

radiotáxi [xadʒjo'taksi] *m* radio taxi *ou* cab.
radioterapia [xadʒjotera'pia] *f* radiotherapy.
radiouvinte [xadʒjo'vitʃi] *m/f* (radio) listener.
ragu [xa'gu] *m* stew, ragoût.
raia ['xaja] *f* (*risca*) line; (*fronteira*) boundary; (*limite*) limit; (*de corrida*) lane; (*peixe*) ray; **chegar às ~s** to reach the limit.
raiado/a [xa'jadu/a] *adj* striped.
raiar [xa'ja*] *vi* (*brilhar*) to shine; (*madrugada*) to dawn; (*aparecer*) to appear.
rainha [xa'iɲa] *f* queen; **ela é a ~ da preguiça** (*col*) she's the world's worst for laziness.
rainha-mãe (*pl* **rainhas-mães**) *f* queen mother.
raio ['xaju] *m* (*de sol*) ray; (*de luz*) beam; (*de roda*) spoke; (*relâmpago*) flash of lightning; (*distância*) range; (*MAT*) radius; **~s X** X-rays; **~ de ação** range; **onde está o ~ da chave?** (*col*) where's the blasted key?
raiva ['xajva] *f* rage, fury; (*MED*) rabies *sg*; **ter ~ de** to hate; **estar/ficar com ~ (de)** to be/get angry (with); **tomar ~ de** to begin to hate; **estar morto de ~** to be furious; **que ~!** I am (*ou* was *etc*) furious!
raivoso/a [xaj'vozu/ɔza] *adj* furious; (*MED*) rabid, mad.
raiz [xa'iʒ] *f* root; (*origem*) source; **~ quadrada** square root; **criar raízes** to put down roots.
rajada [xa'ʒada] *f* (*vento*) gust; (*de tiros*) burst.
ralado/a [xa'ladu/a] *adj* grated; (*esfolado*) grazed.
ralador [xala'do*] *m* grater.
ralar [xa'la*] *vt* to grate; (*esfolar*) to graze.
ralé [xa'lɛ] *f* common people *pl*, rabble.
ralhar [xa'ʎa*] *vi* to scold; **~ com alguém** to tell sb off.
rali [xa'li] *m* rally.
ralo/a [xalu/a] *adj* (*cabelo*) thinning; (*tecido*) thin, flimsy; (*vegetação*) sparse; (*sopa*) thin, watery; (*café*) weak ♦ *m* (*de regador*) rose, nozzle; (*de pia, banheiro*) drain.
rama ['xama] *f* branches *pl*, foliage; **algodão em ~** raw cotton; **pela ~** superficially.
ramagem [xa'maʒẽ] *f* branches *pl*, foliage; (*num tecido*) floral pattern.
ramal [xa'maw] (*pl* -ais) *m* (*FERRO*) branch line; (*telefônico*) extension; (*AUTO*) branch (road).
ramalhete [xama'ʎetʃi] *m* bouquet, posy.
rameira [xa'mejra] *f* prostitute.
ramerrão [xame'xãw] (*pl* -ões) *m* routine, round.
ramificação [xamifika'sãw] (*pl* -ões) *f* (*tb: COMPUT*) branching; (*ramo*) branch.
ramificar-se [xamifi'kaxsi] *vr* to branch out.
ramo ['xamu] *m* branch; (*profissão, negócios*) line; (*de flores*) bunch; **Domingo de R~s** Palm Sunday; **um perito do ~** an expert in

NB: European Portuguese adds the following consonants to certain words: **b** (sú(b)dito, su(b)til), **c** (a(c)ção, a(c)cionista, a(c)to); **m** (inde(m)ne); **p** (ado(p)ção, ado(p)tar); *for further details see p. xiii.*

the field.

rampa ['xãpa] *f* ramp; (*ladeira*) slope.

rançar [xã'sa*] *vi* to go rancid.

rancheiro [xã'ʃejru] *m* cook.

rancho ['xãʃu] *m* (*grupo*) group, band; (*cabana*) hut; (*refeição*) meal.

rancor [xã'ko*] *m* (*ressentimento*) bitterness; (*ódio*) hatred.

rancoroso/a [xãko'rozu/ɔza] *adj* bitter, resentful; (*odiento*) hateful.

ranço ['xãsu] *m* rancidness; (*cheiro*) musty smell.

rançoso/a [xã'sozu/ɔza] *adj* rancid; (*cheiro*) musty.

randevu [xãde'vu] *m* brothel.

ranger [xã'ʒe*] *vi* to creak ♦ *vt*: ~ **os dentes** to grind one's teeth.

rangido [xã'ʒidu] *m* creak.

rango ['xãgu] (*col*) *m* grub.

Rangum [xã'gũ] *n* Rangoon.

ranheta [xa'ɲeta] *adj* sullen, surly.

ranhetice [xaɲe'tʃisi] *f* sullenness; (*ato*) surly thing.

ranho ['xaɲu] (*col*) *m* snot.

ranhura [xa'ɲura] *f* groove; (*para moeda*) slot.

ranjo ['xãʒu] *etc vb V* ranger.

ranzinza [xã'zĩza] *adj* surly, bolshy (*col*).

rapa ['xapa] *m* (*de comida*) remains *pl*; (*carro*) illegal trading patrol car; (*policial*) policeman concerned with illegal street trading.

rapadura [xapa'dura] *f* (*doce*) raw brown sugar.

rapagão [xapa'gãw] (*pl* **-ões**) *m* hunk.

rapapé [xapa'pɛ] *m* touch of the forelock; ~**s** *mpl* bowing and scraping; (*lisonja*) flattery *sg*; **fazer** ~**s a alguém** to bow and scrape to sb.

rapar [xa'pa*] *vt* to scrape; (*barbear*) to shave; (*o cabelo*) to crop; ~ **algo a alguém** (*roubar*) to steal sth from sb.

rapariga [xapa'riga] (*PT*) *f* girl.

rapaz [xa'pajʒ] *m* boy; (*col*) lad; **ô, ~, tudo bem?** hi, mate, how's it going?

rapaziada [xapa'zjada] *f* (*grupo*) lads *pl*.

rapazote [xapa'zɔtʃi] *m* little boy.

rapé [xa'pɛ] *m* snuff.

rapidez [xapi'deʒ] *f* speed, rapidity; **com** ~ quickly, fast.

rápido/a ['xapidu/a] *adj* quick, fast ♦ *adv* fast, quickly ♦ *m* (*trem*) express.

rapina [xa'pina] *f* robbery; *V tb* **ave**.

raposo/a [xa'pozu/ɔza] *m/f* fox/vixen; (*fig*) crafty person.

rapsódia [xap'sɔdʒja] *f* rhapsody.

raptado/a [xap'tadu/a] *m/f* kidnap victim.

raptar [xap'ta*] *vt* to kidnap.

rapto ['xaptu] *m* kidnapping.

raptor [xap'to*] *m* kidnapper.

raqueta [xa'keta] (*PT*) *f* = **raquete**.

raquetada [xake'tada] *f* stroke with a (*ou* the) racquet.

raquete [xa'ketʃi] *f* (*de tênis*) racquet; (*de pingue-pongue*) bat.

raquidiana [xaki'dʒjana] *f* (*anestesia*) epidural.

raquítico/a [xa'kitʃiku/a] *adj* (*MED*) suffering from rickets; (*franzino*) puny; (*vegetação*) poor.

raquitismo [xaki'tʃiʒmu] *m* (*MED*) rickets *sg*.

raramente [xara'mẽtʃi] *adv* rarely, seldom.

rarear [xa'rja*] *vt* to make rare; (*diminuir*) to thin out ♦ *vi* to become rare; (*cabelos*) to thin; (*casas etc*) to thin out.

rarefazer [xarefa'ze*] (*irreg: como* **fazer**) *vt*, *vi* to rarefy; (*nuvens*) to disperse, blow away; (*multidão*) to thin out.

rarefeito/a [xare'fejtu/a] *pp de* **rarefazer** ♦ *adj* rarefied; (*multidão, população*) sparse.

rarefez [xare'feʒ] *vb V* **rarefazer**.

rarefizer [xarefi'ze*] *etc vb V* **rarefazer**.

raridade [xari'dadʒi] *f* rarity.

raro/a ['xaru/a] *adj* rare ♦ *adv* rarely, seldom; **não** ~ often.

rasante [xa'zãtʃi] *adj* (*avião*) low-flying; (*vôo*) low.

rascunhar [xaʃku'ɲa*] *vt* to draft, make a rough copy of.

rascunho [xaʃ'kuɲu] *m* rough copy, draft.

rasgado/a [xaʒ'gadu/a] *adj* (*roupa*) torn, ripped; (*cumprimentos, elogio, gesto*) effusive.

rasgão [xaʒ'gãw] (*pl* **-ões**) *m* tear, rip.

rasgar [xaʒ'ga*] *vt* to tear, rip; (*destruir*) to tear up, rip up; ~**-se** *vr* to split.

rasgo ['xaʒgu] *m* (*rasgão*) tear, rip; (*risco*) stroke; (*ação*) feat; (*ímpeto*) burst; (*da imaginação*) flight.

rasgões [xaʒ'gõjʃ] *mpl de* **rasgão**.

rasguei [xaʒ'gej] *etc vb V* **rasgar**.

raso/a ['xazu/a] *adj* (*liso*) flat, level; (*sapato*) flat; (*não fundo*) shallow; (*baixo*) low; (*colher: como medida*) level ♦ *m*: **o** ~ the shallow water; **soldado** ~ private.

raspa ['xaʃpa] *f* (*de madeira*) shaving; (*de metal*) filing.

raspadeira [xaʃpa'dejra] *f* scraper.

raspão [xaʃ'pãw] (*pl* **-ões**) *m* scratch, graze; **tocar de** ~ to graze.

raspar [xaʃ'pa*] *vt* (*limpar, tocar*) to scrape; (*alisar*) to file; (*tocar de raspão*) to graze; (*arranhar*) to scratch; (*pêlos, cabeça*) to shave; (*apagar*) to rub out ♦ *vi*: ~ **em** to scrape; **passar raspando (num exame)** to scrape through (an exam).

raspões [xaʃ'põjʃ] *mpl de* **raspão**.

rasteira [xaʃ'tejra] *f* (*pernada*) trip; **dar uma** ~ **em alguém** to trip sb up.

rasteiro/a [xaʃ'tejru/a] *adj* (*que se arrasta*) crawling; (*planta*) creeping; (*a pouca altura*) low-lying; (*ordinário*) common.

rastejante [xaʃte'ʒãtʃi] *adj* trailing; (*arrastando-se*) creeping; (*voz*) slurred.

rastejar [xaʃte'ʒa*] *vi* to crawl; (*furtivamente*) to creep; (*fig: rebaixar-se*) to grovel ♦ *vt* (*fu-*

gitivo etc) to track.

rastilho [xaʃ'tʃiʎu] *m* (*de pólvora*) fuse.

rasto ['xaʃtu] *m* (*pegada*) track; (*de veículo*) trail; (*fig*) sign, trace; **de ~s** crawling; **andar de ~s** to crawl; **levar de ~s** to drag along.

rastrear [xaʃ'trja*] *vt* to track; (*investigar*) to scan ♦ *vi* to track.

rastro ['xaʃtru] *m* = **rasto**.

rasura [xa'zura] *f* deletion.

rasurar [xazu'ra*] *vt* to delete items from.

rata ['xata] *f* rat; (*pequena*) mouse; **dar uma ~** to slip up.

ratão [xa'tãw] (*pl* **-ões**) *m* rat.

rataplã [xata'plã] *m* drum roll.

ratazana [xata'zana] *f* rat.

ratear [xa'tʃja*] *vt* (*dividir*) to share ♦ *vi* (*motor*) to miss.

rateio [xa'teju] *m* (*de custos*) sharing, spreading.

ratificação [xatʃifika'sãw] *f* ratification.

ratificar [xatʃifi'ka*] *vt* to confirm, ratify.

rato ['xatu] *m* rat; (*~ pequeno*) mouse; **~ de biblioteca** bookworm; **~ de hotel/praia** hotel/beach thief.

ratoeira [xa'twejra] *f* rat trap; (*pequena*) mousetrap.

ratões [xa'tõjʃ] *mpl de* **ratão**.

ravina [xa'vina] *f* ravine.

ravióli [xa'vjɔli] *m* ravioli.

razão [xa'zãw] (*pl* **-ões**) *f* reason; (*bom senso*) common sense; (*raciocínio, argumento*) reasoning, argument; (*conta*) account; (*MAT*) ratio ♦ *m* (*COM*) ledger; **à ~ de** at the rate of; **com/sem ~** with good reason/for no reason; **em ~ de** on account of; **dar ~ a alguém** to support sb; **ter ~/não ter ~** to be right/be wrong; **ter toda ~ (em fazer)** to be quite right (to do); **estar coberto de ~** to be quite right; **a ~ pela qual** ... the reason why ...; **~ demais para você ficar aqui** all the more reason for you to stay here; **~ de Estado** reason of State.

razoável [xa'zwavew] (*pl* **-eis**) *adj* reasonable.

razões [xa'zõjʃ] *fpl de* **razão**.

r/c (*PT*) *abr* = **rés-do-chão**.

RDA *abr f* (*antes:* = *República Democrática Alemã*) GDR.

ré [xɛ] *f* (*AUTO*) reverse (gear); **dar (marcha à) ~** to reverse, back up; *V tb* **réu**.

reá [xɛ'a] *vb V* **reaver**.

reabastecer [xeabaʃte'se*] *vt* (*carro, avião*) to refuel; **~-se** *vr*: **~-se de** to replenish one's supply of.

reabastecimento [xeabaʃtesi'mētu] *m* (*de carro, avião*) refuelling; (*de uma cidade*) re-provisioning.

reaberto/a [xea'bextu/a] *pp de* **reabrir**.

reabertura [xeabex'tura] *f* reopening.

reabilitação [xeabilita'sãw] *f* rehabilitation; ~

motora physiotherapy.

reabilitar [xeabili'ta*] *vt* to rehabilitate; (*falido*) to discharge, rehabilitate.

reabrir [xea'bri*] *vt* to reopen.

reaça [xe'asa] (*col*) *m/f* reactionary.

reação [xea'sãw] (*PT*: **-cç-**: *pl* **-ões**) *f* reaction; **~ em cadeia** chain reaction.

reacender [xeasẽ'de*] *vt* to relight; (*fig*) to re-kindle.

reacionário/a [xeasjo'narju/a] *adj* reactionary.

reações [xea'sõjʃ] *fpl de* **reação**.

reactor [xea'to*] (*PT*) *m* = **reator**.

readaptar [xeadap'ta*] *vt* to readapt.

readmitir [xeadʒimi'tʃi*] *vt* to readmit; (*funcionário*) to reinstate.

readquirir [xeadʒiki'ri*] *vt* to reacquire.

reafirmar [xeafix'ma*] *vt* to reaffirm.

reagir [xea'ʒi*] *vi* to react; (*doente, time perdedor*) to fight back; **~ a** (*resistir*) to resist; (*protestar*) to rebel against.

reais [xe'ajʃ] *adj pl de* **real**.

reaja [xe'aʒa] *etc vb V* **reagir; reaver**.

reajustar [xeaʒuʃ'ta*] *vt* to readjust; (*MECÂNICA*) to regulate; (*salário, preço*) to adjust (*in line with inflation*).

reajuste [xea'ʒuʃtʃi] *m* adjustment; **~ salarial/de preços** wage/price adjustment (*in line with inflation*).

real [xe'aw] (*pl* **-ais**) *adj* real; (*relativo à realeza*) royal.

realçar [xeaw'sa*] *vt* to highlight.

realce [xe'awsi] *m* (*destaque*) emphasis; (*mais brilho*) highlight; **dar ~ a** to enhance.

realejo [xea'leʒu] *m* barrel organ.

realeza [xea'leza] *f* royalty.

realidade [xeali'dadʒi] *f* reality; **na ~** actually, in fact.

realimentação [xealimẽta'sãw] *f* (*ELET*) feedback.

realismo [xea'liʒmu] *m* realism.

realista [xea'liʃta] *adj* realistic ♦ *m/f* realist.

realização [xealiza'sãw] *f* fulfilment (*BRIT*), fulfillment (*US*), realization; (*de projeto*) execution, carrying out; (*transformação em dinheiro*) conversion into cash.

realizado/a [xeali'zadu/a] *adj* (*pessoa*) fulfilled.

realizador(a) [xealiza'do*(a)] *adj* (*pessoa*) enterprising.

realizar [xeali'za*] *vt* (*um objetivo*) to achieve; (*projeto*) to carry out; (*ambições, sonho*) to fulfil (*BRIT*), fulfill (*US*), realize; (*negócios*) to transact; (*converter em dinheiro*) to realize; (*perceber*) to realize; **~-se** *vr* (*acontecer*) to take place; (*ambições*) to be realized; (*sonhos*) to come true; (*pessoa*) to fulfil(l) o.s.; **o congresso será realizado em Lisboa** the conference will be held in Lisbon.

realizável [xeali'zavew] (*pl* **-eis**) *adj* realizable.

realmente [xeaw'mẽtʃi] *adv* really; (*de fato*)

NB: *European Portuguese adds the following consonants to certain words:* **b** (sú(b)dito, su(b)til); **c** (a(c)ção, a(c)cionista, a(c)to); **m** (inde(m)ne); **p** (ado(p)ção, ado(p)tar); *for further details see p. xiii.*

actually.

reanimar [xeani'ma*] vt to revive; (encorajar) to encourage; ~-se vr (pessoa) to cheer up.

reão [xe'ãw] vb V **reaver**.

reaparecer [xeapare'se*] vi to reappear.

reaprender [xeaprẽ'de*] vt to relearn.

reapresentar [xeaprezẽ'ta*] vt to represent; (espetáculo) to put on again.

reaproximação [xeaprosima'sãw] (pl -ões) f (entre pessoas, países) rapprochement.

reaproximar [xeaprosi'ma*] vt to bring back together; ~-se vr to be brought back together.

reaquecer [xeake'se*] vt to reheat.

reassumir [xeasu'mi*] vt, vi to take over again.

reatar [xea'ta*] vt (continuar) to resume, take up again; (nó) to retie.

reativar [xeatʃi'va*] vt to reactivate; (organização, lei) to revive.

reator [xea'to*] m reactor.

reavaliação [xeavalja'sãw] f revaluation.

reaver [xea've*] vt to recover, get back.

reavivar [xeavi'va*] vt (cor) to brighten up; (lembrança) to revive; (sofrimento, dor) to bring back.

rebaixa [xe'bajʃa] f reduction.

rebaixar [xebaj'ʃa*] vt (tornar mais baixo) to lower; (o preço de) to lower the price of; (humilhar) to put down, humiliate ♦ vi to drop; ~-se vr to demean o.s.

rebanho [xe'baɲu] m (de carneiros, fig) flock; (de gado, elefantes) herd.

rebarbar [xebax'ba*] vt (opor-se a) to oppose ♦ vi (reclamar) to complain.

rebarbativo/a [xebaxba'tʃivu/a] adj (pessoa) disagreeable, unpleasant.

rebate [xe'batʃi] m (sinal) alarm; (COM) discount; ~ **falso** false alarm.

rebater [xeba'te*] vt (um golpe) to ward off; (acusações, argumentos) to refute; (bola) to knock back; (à máquina) to retype.

rebelar [xebe'la*] vt to cause to rebel; ~-se vr to rebel.

rebelde [xe'bɛwdʒi] adj rebellious; (indisciplinado) unruly, wild ♦ m/f rebel.

rebeldia [xebew'dʒia] f rebelliousness; (fig: obstinação) stubbornness; (: oposição) defiance.

rebelião [xebe'ljãw] (pl -ões) f rebellion.

rebentar [xebẽ'ta*] vi (guerra) to break out; (louça) to smash; (corda) to snap; (represa) to burst; (ondas) to break ♦ vt (louça) to smash; (corda) to snap; (porta, ponte) to break down.

rebento [xe'bẽtu] m (filho) offspring.

rebite [xe'bitʃi] m (TEC) rivet.

reboar [xe'bwa*] vi to resound, echo.

rebobinar [xebobi'na*] vt (vídeo) to rewind.

rebocador [xeboka'do*] m (NÁUT) tug(boat).

rebocar [xebo'ka*] vt (paredes) to plaster; (veículo mal estacionado) to tow away; (dar reboque a) to tow.

reboco [xe'boku] m plaster.

rebolar [xebo'la*] vt to swing ♦ vi to sway; (fig) to work hard; ~-se vr to sway.

rebolo [xe'bolu] m (mó) grindstone; (cilindro) cylinder.

reboque [xe'bɔki] etc vb V **rebocar** ♦ m (ato) tow; (veículo) trailer; (cabo) towrope; (BR: de socorro) towtruck; **carro** ~ trailer; **a** ~ in tow.

rebordo [xe'boxdu] m rim, edge; ~ **da lareira** mantelpiece.

rebordosa [xebox'dɔza] f (situação difícil) difficult situation; (doença grave) serious illness; (reincidência de moléstia) recurrence; (pancadaria) commotion.

rebu [xe'bu] (col) m commotion, rumpus.

rebuçado [xebu'sadu] (PT) m sweet, candy (US).

rebuliço [xebu'lisu] m commotion, hubbub.

rebuscado/a [xebuʃ'kadu/a] adj affected.

recado [xe'kadu] m message; **mandar** ~ to send word; **menino de** ~**s** errand boy; **deixar** ~ to leave a message; **dar o** ~, **dar conta do** ~ (fig) to deliver the goods.

recaída [xeka'ida] f relapse.

recair [xeka'i*] vi (doente) to relapse; ~ **em erro** ou **falta** to go wrong again; **a culpa recaiu nela** she got the blame; **o acento recai na última sílaba** the accent falls on the last syllable.

recalcado/a [xekaw'kadu/a] adj repressed.

recalcar [xekaw'ka*] vt to repress.

recalcitrante [xekawsi'trãtʃi] adj recalcitrant.

recalque [xe'kawki] etc vb V **recalcar** ♦ m repression.

recamado/a [xeka'madu/a] adj embroidered.

recambiar [xekã'bja*] vt to send back.

recanto [xe'kãtu] m (lugar aprazível) corner, nook; (esconderijo) hiding place.

recapitulação [xekapitula'sãw] f (resumo) recapitulation; (rememorar) revision.

recapitular [xekapitu'la*] vt (resumir) to sum up, recapitulate; (fatos) to review; (matéria escolar) to revise.

recatado/a [xeka'tadu/a] adj (modesto) modest; (reservado) reserved.

recatar-se [xeka'taxsi] vr to become withdrawn; (ocultar-se) to hide.

recato [xe'katu] m (modéstia) modesty.

recauchutado/a [xekawʃu'tadu/a] adj (fig) revamped; (col: pessoa) having had cosmetic surgery; **pneu** ~ (AUTO) retread, remould (BRIT).

recauchutagem [xekawʃu'taʒẽ] (pl -ns) f (de pneu) retreading; (fig) face-lift.

recauchutar [xekawʃu'ta*] vt (pneu) to retread; (fig) to give a face-lift to.

recear [xe'sja*] vt to fear ♦ vi: ~ **por** to fear for; ~ **fazer/que** to be afraid to do/that.

recebedor(a) [xesebe'do*(a)] m/f receiver; (de impostos) collector.

receber [xese'be*] vt to receive; (ganhar) to earn, get; (hóspedes) to take in; (con-

vidados) to entertain; (*acolher bem*) to welcome ♦ *vi* (~ *convidados*) to entertain; (*ser pago*) to be paid; **a** ~ (*COM*) receivable.

recebimento [xesebi'mẽtu] (*BR*) *m* reception; (*de uma carta*) receipt; **acusar o** ~ **de** to acknowledge receipt of.

receio [xe'seju] *m* fear; **não tenha** ~ never fear; **ter** ~ **de que** to fear that.

receita [xe'sejta] *f* (*renda*) income; (*do Estado*) revenue; (*MED*) prescription; (*culinária*) recipe; ~ **pública** tax revenue; **R~ Federal** ≈ Inland Revenue (*BRIT*), ≈ IRS (*US*).

receitar [xesej'ta*] *vt* to prescribe ♦ *vi* to write prescriptions.

recém [xe'sẽ] *adv* recently, newly.

recém-casado/a *adj* newly-married; **os** ~**s** the newlyweds.

recém-chegado/a *m/f* newcomer.

recém-nascido/a *m/f* newborn child.

recém-publicado/a *adj* newly *ou* recently published.

recender [xesẽ'de*] *vt*: ~ **um cheiro** to give off a smell ♦ *vi* to smell; ~ **a** to smell of.

recenseamento [xesẽsja'mẽtu] *m* census.

recensear [xesẽ'sja*] *vt* to take a census of.

recente [xe'sẽtʃi] *adj* recent; (*novo*) new ♦ *adv* recently.

recentemente [xesẽtʃi'mẽtʃi] *adv* recently.

receoso/a [xe'sjozu/ɔza] *adj* (*medroso*) frightened, fearful; (*apreensivo*) afraid; **estar** ~ **de (fazer)** to be afraid of (doing).

recepção [xesep'sãw] (*pl* -**ões**) *f* reception; (*PT: de uma carta*) receipt; **acusar a** ~ **de** (*PT*) to acknowledge receipt of.

recepcionar [xesepsjo'na*] *vt* to receive.

recepcionista [xesepsjo'niʃta] *m/f* receptionist.

recepcões [xesep'sõjʃ] *fpl de* **recepção**.

receptáculo [xesep'takulu] *m* receptacle.

receptador(a) [xesepta'do*(a)] *m/f* fence, receiver of stolen goods.

receptar [xesep'ta*] *vt* to fence, receive.

receptivo/a [xesep'tʃivu/a] *adj* receptive; (*acolhedor*) welcoming.

receptor [xesep'to*] *m* (*TEC*) receiver.

recessão [xese'sãw] (*pl* -**ões**) *f* recession.

recesso [xe'sɛsu] *m* recess.

recessões [xese'sõjʃ] *fpl de* **recessão**.

rechaçar [xeʃa'sa*] *vt* (*ataque*) to repel; (*idéias, argumentos*) to oppose; (*oferta*) to turn down.

réchaud [xe'ʃo] *m* (*pl* ~**s**) plate-warmer.

recheado/a [xe'ʃjadu/a] *adj* (*ave, carne*) stuffed; (*empada, bolo*) filled; (*cheio*) full, crammed.

rechear [xe'ʃja*] *vt* to fill; (*ave, carne*) to stuff.

recheio [xe'ʃeju] *m* (*para carne assada*) stuffing; (*de empada, de bolo*) filling; (*o conteúdo*) contents *pl*.

rechonchudo/a [xeʃõ'ʃudu/a] *adj* chubby, plump.

recibo [xe'sibu] *m* receipt.

reciclagem [xesi'klaʒẽ] *f* (*de papel etc*) recycling; (*de professores, funcionários*) retraining.

reciclar [xesi'kla*] *vt* (*papel etc*) to recycle; (*professores, funcionários*) to retrain.

recidiva [xesi'dʒiva] *f* recurrence.

recife [xe'sifi] *m* reef.

recifense [xesi'fẽsi] *adj* from Recife ♦ *m/f* person from Recife.

recinto [xe'sĩtu] *m* (*espaço fechado*) enclosure; (*lugar*) area.

recipiente [xesi'pjẽtʃi] *m* container, receptacle.

recíproca [xe'siproka] *f* reverse.

reciprocar [xesipro'ka*] *vt* to reciprocate.

reciprocidade [xesiprosi'dadʒi] *f* reciprocity.

recíproco/a [xe'siproku/a] *adj* reciprocal.

récita ['xɛsita] *f* (*teatral*) performance.

recitação [xesita'sãw] (*pl* -**ões**) *f* recitation.

recital [xesi'taw] (*pl* -**ais**) *m* recital.

recitar [xesi'ta*] *vt* (*declamar*) to recite.

reclamação [xeklama'sãw] (*pl* -**ões**) *f* (*queixa*) complaint; (*JUR*) claim.

reclamante [xekla'mãtʃi] *m/f* claimant.

reclamar [xekla'ma*] *vt* (*exigir*) to demand; (*herança*) to claim ♦ *vi*: ~ **(de)** (*comida etc*) to complain (about); (*dores etc*) to complain (of); ~ **contra** to complain about.

reclame [xe'klami] *m* advertisement.

reclinado/a [xekli'nadu/a] *adj* (*inclinado*) leaning; (*recostado*) lying back.

reclinar [xekli'na*] *vt* to rest, lean; ~**-se** *vr* to lie back; (*deitar-se*) to lie down.

reclinável [xekli'navew] (*pl* -**eis**) *adj* (*cadeira*) reclinable.

reclusão [xeklu'zãw] *f* (*isolamento*) seclusion; (*encarceramento*) imprisonment.

recluso/a [xe'kluzu/a] *adj* reclusive ♦ *m/f* recluse; (*prisioneiro*) prisoner.

recobrar [xeko'bra*] *vt* to recover, get back; ~**-se** *vr* to recover.

recolher [xeko'ʎe*] *vt* to collect; (*coisas dispersas*) to collect up; (*gado, roupa do varal*) to bring in; (*juntar*) to gather together; (*abrigar*) to give shelter to; (*notas antigas*) to withdraw; (*encolher*) to draw in; ~**-se** *vr* (*ir para casa*) to go home; (*deitar-se*) to go to bed; (*ir para o quarto*) to retire; (*em meditações*) to meditate; ~ **alguém a algum lugar** to take sb somewhere.

recolhido/a [xeko'ʎidu/a] *adj* (*lugar*) secluded; (*retraído*) withdrawn.

recolhimento [xekoʎi'mẽtu] *m* (*vida retraída*) retirement; (*arrecadação*) collection; (*ato de levar*) taking.

recomeçar [xekome'sa*] *vt, vi* to restart; ~ **a fazer** to start to do again.

---

recomeço [xeko'mesu] *m* restart.

recomendação [xekoměda'sǎw] (*pl* -ões) *f* recommendation; **recomendações** *fpl* (*cumprimentos*) regards; **carta de** ~ letter of recommendation.

recomendar [xekomě'da*] *vt* to recommend; ~ **alguém a alguém** (*enviar cumprimentos*) to remember sb to sb, give sb's regards to sb; (*pedir favor*) to put in a word for sb with sb; ~ **algo a alguém** (*confiar*) to entrust sth to sb; ~ **que alguém faça** to recommend that sb do; (*lembrar, pedir*) to urge that sb do.

recomendável [xekomě'davew] (*pl* -eis) *adj* advisable.

recompensa [xekǒ'pěsa] *f* (*prêmio*) reward; (*indenização*) recompense.

recompensar [xekǒpě'sa*] *vt* (*premiar*) to reward; ~ **alguém de algo** (*indenizar*) to compensate sb for sth.

recompor [xekǒ'po*] (*irreg*: *como* **pôr**) *vt* (*reorganizar*) to reorganize; (*restabelecer*) to restore.

recôncavo [xe'kǒkavu] *m* (*enseada*) bay area.

reconciliação [xekǒsilja'sǎw] (*pl* -ões) *f* reconciliation.

reconciliar [xekǒsi'lja*] *vt* to reconcile; ~-se *vr* to become reconciled.

recondicionar [xekǒdʒisjo'na*] *vt* to recondition.

recôndito/a [xe'kǒdʒitu/a] *adj* (*escondido*) hidden; (*lugar*) secluded.

reconfortar [xekǒfox'ta*] *vt* to invigorate; ~-se *vr* to be invigorated.

reconhecer [xekoɲe'se*] *vt* to recognize; (*admitir*) to admit; (*MIL*) to reconnoitre (*BRIT*), reconnoiter (*US*); (*assinatura*) to witness.

reconhecido/a [xekoɲe'sidu/a] *adj* recognized; (*agradecido*) grateful, thankful.

reconhecimento [xekoɲesi'mětu] *m* recognition; (*admissão*) admission; (*gratidão*) gratitude; (*MIL*) reconnaissance; (*de assinatura*) witnessing.

reconhecível [xekoɲe'sivew] (*pl* -eis) *adj* recognizable.

reconquista [xekǒ'kiʃta] *f* reconquest.

reconsiderar [xekǒside'ra*] *vt, vi* to reconsider.

reconstituinte [xekǒʃtʃi'twĩtʃi] *m* tonic.

reconstituir [xekǒʃtʃi'twi*] *vt* to reconstitute; (*doente*) to build up; (*crime*) to piece together.

reconstrução [xekǒʃtru'sǎw] *f* reconstruction.

reconstruir [xekǒʃ'trwi*] *vt* to rebuild, reconstruct.

recontar [xekǒ'ta*] *vt* (*objetos, pessoas*) to recount; (*história*) to retell.

recordação [xekoxda'sǎw] (*pl* -ões) *f* (*reminiscência*) memory; (*objeto*) memento.

recordar [xekox'da*] *vt* (*relembrar*) to remember; (*parecer*) to look like; (*lição*) to revise; ~-se *vr*: ~-se de to remember; ~ **algo a alguém** to remind sb of sth.

recorde [xe'kɔxdʒi] *adj inv* record *atr* ♦ *m* record; **em tempo** ~ in record time; **bater um** ~ to break a record.

recordista [xekox'dʒiʃta] *m/f* record-breaker; (*quem detém o recorde*) record-holder ♦ *adj* record-breaking; ~ **mundial** world record-holder.

recorrer [xeko'xe*] *vi*: ~ **a** (*para socorro*) to turn to; (*valer-se de*) to resort to; ~ **da sentença/decisão** to appeal against the sentence/decision.

recortar [xekox'ta*] *vt* to cut out.

recorte [xe'kɔxtʃi] *m* (*ato*) cutting out; (*de jornal*) cutting, clipping.

recostar [xekoʃ'ta*] *vt* to lean, rest; ~-se *vr* to lean back; (*deitar-se*) to lie down.

recosto [xe'koʃtu] *m* back(rest).

recreação [xekrja'sǎw] *f* recreation.

recrear [xe'krja*] *vt* to entertain, amuse; ~-se *vr* to have fun.

recreativo/a [xekrja'tʃivu/a] *adj* recreational.

recreio [xe'kreju] *m* recreation; (*EDUC*) playtime; **viagem de** ~ trip, outing; **hora do** ~ break.

recriar [xe'krja*] *vt* to recreate.

recriminação [xekrimina'sǎw] (*pl* -ões) *f* recrimination.

recriminador(a) [xekrimina'do*(a)] *adj* reproving.

recriminar [xekrimi'na*] *vt* to reproach, reprove.

recrudescência [xekrude'sěsja] *f* = **recrudescimento**.

recrudescer [xekrude'se*] *vi* to grow worse, worsen.

recrudescimento [xekrudesi'mětu] *m* worsening.

recruta [xe'kruta] *m/f* recruit.

recrutamento [xekruta'mětu] *m* recruitment.

recrutar [xekru'ta*] *vt* to recruit.

rectângulo *etc* [xek'tǎgulu] (*PT*) = **retângulo** *etc*.

rectificar *etc* [xektifi'ka*] (*PT*) = **retificar** *etc*.

recto/a *etc* ['xɛkto/a] (*PT*) = **reto** *etc*.

récua ['xekwa] *f* (*de mulas*) pack, train; (*de cavalos*) drove.

recuado/a [xe'kwadu/a] *adj* (*prédio*) set back.

recuar [xe'kwa*] *vt, vi* to move back; (*exército*) to retreat; (*num intento*) to back out; (*num compromisso*) to backpedal; (*ciência*) to regress; ~ **de** (*lugar*) to move back from; (*intenções, planos*) to back out of; ~ **a** *ou* **para** (*no tempo*) to return *ou* regress to; (*numa decisão, opinião*) to back down to.

recuo [xe'kuu] *m* retreat; (*de ciência*) regression; (*de intento*) climbdown; (*de um prédio*) frontage.

recuperação [xekupera'sǎw] *f* recovery.

recuperar [xekupe'ra*] *vt* to recover; (*tempo perdido*) to make up for; (*reabilitar*) to rehabilitate; ~-se *vr* to recover; ~-se de to recover *ou* recuperate from.

recurso [xe'kuxsu] *m* (*meio*) resource; (*JUR*) appeal; ~**s** *mpl* (*financeiros*) resources; **em último** ~ as a last resort; **o** ~ **à violência** resorting to violence; **não há outro** ~ **contra a fome** there is no other solution to famine; ~**s próprios** (*COM*) own resources.

recusa [xe'kuza] *f* refusal; (*negação*) denial.

recusar [xeku'za*] *vt* to refuse; (*negar*) to deny; ~**-se** *vr*: ~**-se a** to refuse to; ~ **fazer** to refuse to do; ~ **algo a alguém** to refuse *ou* deny sb sth.

redação [xeda'sãw] (*PT*: **-cç-**: *pl* **-ões**) *f* (*ato*) writing; (*escolar*) composition, essay; (*redatores*) editorial staff; (*lugar*) editorial office.

redactor(a) *etc* [xeda'to*(a)] (*PT*) *m/f* = **redator(a)** *etc*.

redargüir [xedax'gwi*] *vi* to retort.

redator(a) [xeda'to*(a)] *m/f* journalist; (*editor*) editor; (*quem redige*) writer.

redator(a)-chefe *m/f* editor in chief.

rede ['xedʒi] *f* net; (*de salvamento*) safety net; (*de cabelos*) hairnet; (*de dormir*) hammock; (*cilada*) trap; (*FERRO, TEC, fig*) network; ~ **bancária** banking system; ~ **de esgotos** drainage system; **comunicar-se em** ~ (**com**) (*COMPUT*) to network (with); **operação em** ~ (*COMPUT*) networking.

rédea ['xedʒja] *f* rein; **dar** ~ **larga a** to give free rein to; **tomar as** ~**s** (*fig*) to take control, take over; **falar à** ~ **solta** to talk nineteen to the dozen.

redenção [xedẽ'sãw] *f* redemption.

redentor(a) [xedẽ'to*(a)] *adj* redeeming ◆ *m/f* redeemer.

redigir [xedʒi'ʒi*] *vt, vi* to write.

redime [xe'dʒimi] *etc vb V* **remir**.

redimir [xedʒi'mi*] *vt* (*livrar*) to free; (*REL*) to redeem.

redobrar [xedo'bra*] *vt* (*dobrar de novo*) to fold again; (*aumentar*) to increase; (*esforços*) to redouble; (*sinos*) to ring ◆ *vi* to increase; (*intensificar*) to intensify; to ring out.

redoma [xe'dɔma] *f* glass dome.

redondamente [xedõda'mẽtʃi] *adv* (*completamente*) completely.

redondeza [xedõ'deza] *f* roundness; ~**s** *fpl* (*arredores*) surroundings.

redondo/a [xe'dõdu/a] *adj* round; (*gordo*) plump.

redor [xe'do*] *m*: **ao** *ou* **em** ~ (**de**) around, round about.

redução [xedu'sãw] (*pl* **-ões**) *f* reduction; (*conversão: de moeda*) conversion.

redundância [xedũ'dãsja] *f* redundancy.

redundante [xedũ'dãtʃi] *adj* redundant.

redundar [xedũ'da*] *vi*: ~ **em** (*resultar em*) to result in.

reduto [xe'dutu] *m* stronghold; (*refúgio*)

haven.

reduzido/a [xedu'zidu/a] *adj* reduced; (*limitado*) limited; (*pequeno*) small; **ficar** ~ **a** to be reduced to.

reduzir [xedu'zi*] *vt* to reduce; (*converter: dinheiro*) to convert; (*abreviar*) to abridge; ~**-se** *vr*: ~**-se a** to be reduced to; (*fig*: *resumir-se em*) to come down to; "**reduza a velocidade**" "reduce speed now".

reedificar [xeedʒifi'ka*] *vt* to rebuild.

reeditar [xeedʒi'ta*] *vt* (*livro*) to republish; (*repetir*) to repeat.

reeducar [xeedu'ka*] *vt* to reeducate.

reeleger [xeele'ʒe*] *vt* to re-elect; ~**-se** *vr* to be re-elected.

reeleição [xeelej'sãw] *f* re-election.

reelejo [xee'leʒu] *etc vb V* **reeleger**.

reembolsar [xeẽbow'sa*] *vt* (*reaver*) to recover; (*restituir*) to reimburse; (*depósito*) to refund; ~ **alguem de algo** *ou* **algo a alguém** to reimburse sb for sth.

reembolso [xeẽ'bowsu] *m* refund, reimbursement; ~ **postal** cash on delivery.

reencarnação [xeẽkaxna'sãw] *f* reincarnation.

reencarnar [xeẽkax'na*] *vi* to be reincarnated.

reencontrar [xeẽkõ'tra*] *vt* to meet again; ~**-se** *vr*: ~**-se** (**com**) to meet up (with).

reencontro [xeẽ'kõtru] *m* reunion.

reentrância [xeẽ'trãsja] *f* recess.

reescalonamento [xeeʃkalona'mẽtu] *m* rescheduling.

reescalonar [xeeʃkalo'na*] *vt* (*dívida*) to reschedule.

reescrever [xeeʃkre've*] *vt* to rewrite.

reexaminar [xeezami'na*] *vt* to re-examine.

refaço [xe'fasu] *etc vb V* **refazer**.

refastelado/a [xefaʃte'ladu/a] *adj* stretched out.

refastelar-se [xefaʃte'laxsi] *vr* to stretch out, lounge.

refazer [xefa'ze*] (*irreg*: *como* **fazer**) *vt* (*trabalho*) to redo; (*consertar*) to repair, fix; (*forças*) to restore; (*finanças*) to recover; (*vida*) to rebuild; ~**-se** *vr* (*MED etc*) to recover; ~**-se de despesas** to recover one's expenses.

refeição [xefej'sãw] (*pl* **-ões**) *f* meal; **na hora da** ~ at mealtimes.

refeito/a [xe'fejtu/a] *pp de* **refazer**.

refeitório [xefej'tɔrju] *m* dining hall, refectory.

refém [xe'fẽ] (*pl* **-ns**) *m* hostage.

referência [xefe'rẽsja] *f* reference; **com** ~ **a** with reference to, about; **fazer** ~ **a** to make reference to, refer to; ~**s** *fpl* references.

referendar [xeferẽ'da*] *vt* to countersign, endorse; (*aprovar: tratado etc*) to ratify.

referendum [xefe'rẽdũ] *m* (*POL*) referendum.

referente [xefe'rẽtʃi] *adj*: ~ **a** concerning, regarding.

referido/a [xefe'ridu/a] *adj* aforesaid, already

---

*NB: European Portuguese adds the following consonants to certain words: **b** (sú(b)dito, su(b)til); **c** (a(c)ção, a(c)cionista, a(c)cto); **m** (inde(m)ne); **p** (ado(p)ção, ado(p)tar); for further details see p. xiii.*

mentioned.

referir [xefe'ri*] *vt* (*contar*) to relate, tell; **~-se** *vr*: **~-se a** to refer to.

REFESA (*BR*) *f* = **Rede Ferroviária SA.**

refestelar-se [xefeʃte'laxsi] *vr* = **refastelar-se.**

refez [xe'feʒ] *vb V* **refazer.**

refil [xe'fiw] (*pl* **-is**) *m* refill.

refiz [xe'fiʒ] *vb V* **refazer.**

refizer [xefi'ze*] *etc vb V* **refazer.**

refinado/a [xefi'nadu/a] *adj* refined.

refinamento [xefina'mẽtu] *m* refinement.

refinanciamento [xefinãsja'mẽtu] *m* refinancing.

refinanciar [xefinã'sja*] *vt* to refinance.

refinar [xefi'na*] *vt* to refine.

refinaria [xefina'ria] *f* refinery.

refiro [xe'firu] *etc vb V* **referir.**

refis [xe'fiʃ] *mpl de* **refil.**

refletido/a [xefle'tʃidu/a] (*PT*: **-ct-**) *adj* reflected; (*prudente*) thoughtful; (*ação*) prudent, shrewd.

refletir [xefle'tʃi*] (*PT*: **-ct-**) *vt* (*espelhar*) to reflect; (*som*) to echo; (*fig: revelar*) to reveal ♦ *vi*: **~ em** *ou* **sobre** (*pensar*) to consider, think about; **~-se** *vr* to be reflected; **~-se em** (*repercutir-se*) to have implications for.

refletor(a) [xefle'to*(a)] (*PT*: **-ct-**) *adj* reflecting ♦ *m* reflector.

reflexão [xeflek'sãw] (*pl* **-ões**) *f* reflection; (*meditação*) thought, reflection.

reflexivo/a [xeflek'sivu/a] *adj* reflexive.

reflexo/a [xe'fleksu/a] *adj* (*luz*) reflected; (*ação*) reflex ♦ *m* reflection; (*ANAT*) reflex; (*no cabelo*) streak.

reflexões [xeflek'sõjʃ] *fpl de* **reflexão.**

reflito [xe'flitu] *etc vb V* **refletir.**

refluxo [xe'fluksu] *m* ebb.

refogado/a [xefo'gadu/a] *adj* sautéed ♦ *m* (*molho*) sautéed seasonings; (*prato*) stew.

refogar [xefo'ga*] *vt* to sauté.

reforçado/a [xefox'sadu/a] *adj* reinforced; (*pessoa*) strong; (*café da manhã, jantar*) hearty.

reforçar [xefox'sa*] *vt* to reinforce; (*revigorar*) to invigorate.

reforço [xe'foxsu] *m* reinforcement.

reforma [xe'foxma] *f* reform; (*ARQ*) renovation; (*REL*) reformation; (*aposentadoria*) retirement; **fazer ~s em casa** to have building work done in the house; **o banheiro está em ~** the bathroom is being done up; **~ agrária** land reform; **~ ministerial** cabinet reshuffle.

reformado/a [xefox'madu/a] *adj* reformed; (*ARQ*) renovated; (*PT: MIL*) retired.

reformar [xefox'ma*] *vt* to reform; (*ARQ*) to renovate; (*aposentar*) to retire; (*sentença*) to commute; **~-se** *vr* (*militar*) to retire; (*criminoso*) to reform, mend one's ways.

reformatar [xefoxma'ta*] *vt* to reformat.

reformatório [xefoxma'tɔrju] *m* approved school, borstal.

refractário/a [xefra'tarju/a] (*PT*) *adj* =

refratário/a.

refrão [xe'frãw] (*pl* **-ãos** *ou* **-ães**) *m* (*cantado*) chorus, refrain; (*provérbio*) saying.

refratário/a [xefra'tarju/a] *adj* (*rebelde*) difficult, unmanageable; (*TEC*) heat-resistant; (*CULIN*) ovenproof; **ser ~ a** (*admoestações etc*) to be impervious to.

refrear [xefre'a*] *vt* (*cavalo*) to rein in; (*inimigo*) to contain, check; (*paixões, raiva*) to control; **~-se** *vr* to restrain o.s.; **~ a língua** to mind one's language.

refrega [xe'frega] *f* fight.

refrescante [xefreʃ'kãtʃi] *adj* refreshing.

refrescar [xefreʃ'ka*] *vt* (*ar, ambiente*) to cool; (*pessoa*) to refresh ♦ *vi* to cool down; **~-se** *vr* to refresh o.s.

refresco [xe'freʃku] *m* cool drink; **~s** *mpl* refreshments.

refrigeração [xefriʒera'sãw] *f* cooling; (*de alimentos*) refrigeration; (*de casa*) air conditioning.

refrigerado/a [xefriʒe'radu/a] *adj* cooled; (*casa*) air-conditioned; (*alimentos*) refrigerated; **~ a ar** air-cooled.

refrigerador [xefriʒera'do*] *m* refrigerator, fridge (*BRIT*).

refrigerante [xefriʒe'rãtʃi] *m* soft drink.

refrigerar [xefriʒe'ra*] *vt* to keep cool; (*com geladeira*) to refrigerate.

refrigério [xefri'ʒɛrju] *m* solace, consolation.

refugar [xefu'ga*] *vt* (*alimentos*) to reject; (*proposta, conselho*) to reject, dismiss ♦ *vi* (*cavalo*) to baulk, refuse.

refugiado/a [xefu'ʒjadu/a] *adj, m/f* refugee.

refugiar-se [xefu'ʒjaxsi] *vr* to take refuge; **~ na leitura** *etc* to seek solace in reading *etc*.

refúgio [xe'fuʒju] *m* refuge.

refugo [xe'fugu] *m* waste, rubbish, garbage (*US*); (*mercadoria*) reject.

refulgência [xefuw'ʒẽsja] *f* brilliance.

refulgir [xefuw'ʒi*] *vi* to shine out.

refutação [xefuta'sãw] (*pl* **-ões**) *f* refutation.

refutar [xefu'ta*] *vt* to refute.

reg *abr* = **regimento; regular.**

rego *abr* = **regulamento.**

rega ['xɛga] *f* watering; (*PT: irrigação*) irrigation.

regaço [xe'gasu] *m* (*colo*) lap.

regador [xega'do*] *m* watering can.

regalado/a [xega'ladu/a] (*PT*) *adj* (*encantado*) delighted; (*confortável*) comfortable ♦ *adv* comfortably.

regalar [xega'la*] (*PT*) *vt* (*causar prazer*) to delight; **~-se** *vr* (*divertir-se*) to enjoy o.s.; (*alegrar-se*) to be delighted; **~ alguém com algo** to give sb sth, present sb with sth.

regalia [xega'lia] *f* privilege.

regalo [xe'galu] *m* (*presente*) present; (*prazer*) pleasure, treat.

regar [xe'ga*] *vt* (*plantas, jardim*) to water; (*umedecer*) to sprinkle; **~ o jantar a vinho** to wash one's dinner down with wine.

regata [xe'gata] *f* regatta.

regatear [xɛga'tʃja*] *vt* (*o preço*) to haggle over, bargain for ♦ *vi* to haggle.

regateio [xega'teju] *m* haggling.

regato [xe'gatu] *m* brook, stream.

regência [xe'ʒẽsja] *f* regency; (*LING*) government; (*MÚS*) conducting.

regeneração [xeʒenera'sãw] *f* regeneration; (*de criminosos*) reform.

regenerar [xeʒene'ra*] *vt* to regenerate; (*criminoso*) to reform; **~-se** *vr* to regenerate; to reform.

regente [xe'ʒẽtʃi] *m* (*POL*) regent; (*de orquestra*) conductor; (*de banda*) leader.

reger [xe'ʒe*] *vt* to govern, rule; (*regular, LING*) to govern; (*orquestra*) to conduct; (*empresa*) to run ♦ *vi* (*governar*) to rule; (*maestro*) to conduct; **~** **uma cadeira** (*EDUC*) to hold a chair.

região [xe'ʒjãw] (*pl* **-ões**) *f* region; (*de uma cidade*) area.

regime [xe'ʒimi] *m* (*POL*) regime; (*dieta*) diet; (*maneira*) way; **meu ~ agora é levantar cedo** my routine now is to get up early; **fazer ~** to diet; **estar de ~** to be on a diet; **o ~ das prisões/dos hospitais** the prison/hospital system; **~ de vida** way of life.

regimento [xeʒi'mẽtu] *m* regiment; (*regras*) regulations *pl*, rules *pl*; **~ interno** (*de empresa*) company rules *pl*.

régio/a ['xɛʒju/a] *adj* (*real*) royal; (*digno do rei*) regal; (*suntuoso*) princely.

regiões [xe'ʒjõjʃ] *fpl de* **região**.

regional [xeʒjo'naw] (*pl* **-ais**) *adj* regional.

registrador(a) [xeʒiʃtra'do*(a)] (*PT:* **registador(a)**) *m/f* registrar, recorder; **(caixa) registradora** cash register, till.

registrar [xeʒiʃ'tra*] (*PT:* **registar**) *vt* to register; (*anotar*) to record; (*com máquina registradora*) to ring up.

registro [xe'ʒiʃtru] (*PT:* **registo**) *m* (*ato*) registration; (: *anotação*) recording; (*livro, LING*) register; (*histórico, COMPUT*) record; (*relógio*) meter; (*MÚS*) range; (*torneira*) stopcock; **~ civil** registry office.

rego ['xegu] *m* (*para água*) ditch; (*de arado*) furrow; (*col!*) crack.

regozijar [xegozi'ʒa*] *vt* to gladden; **~-se** *vr* to be delighted, rejoice.

regozijo [xego'ziʒu] *m* joy, delight.

regra ['xɛgra] *f* rule; **~s** *fpl* (*MED*) periods; **sair da ~** to step out of line; **em ~** as a rule, usually; **por via de ~** as a rule.

regrado/a [xe'gradu/a] *adj* (*sensato*) sensible.

regredir [xegre'dʒi*] *vi* to regress; (*doença*) to retreat.

regressão [xegre'sãw] *f* regression.

regressar [xegre'sa*] *vi* to come (*ou* go) back, return.

regressivo/a [xegre'sivu/a] *adj* regressive; **contagem regressiva** countdown.

regresso [xe'grɛsu] *m* return.

regrido [xe'gridu] *etc vb* **V regredir**.

régua ['xɛgwa] *f* ruler; **~ de calcular** slide rule.

regulador(a) [xegula'do*(a)] *adj* regulating ♦ *m* regulator.

regulagem [xegu'laʒẽ] *f* (*de motor, carro*) tuning.

regulamentação [xegulamẽta'sãw] *f* regulation; (*regras*) regulations *pl*.

regulamento [xegula'mẽtu] *m* rules *pl*, regulations *pl*.

regular [xegu'la*] *adj* regular; (*estatura*) average, medium; (*tamanho*) normal; (*razoável*) not bad ♦ *vt* to regulate; (*reger*) to govern; (*máquina*) to adjust; (*carro, motor*) to tune; (*relógio*) to put right ♦ *vi* to work, function; **~-se** *vr:* **~-se por** to be guided by; **ele não regula (bem)** he's not quite right in the head; **~ por** to be about; **~ com alguém** to be about the same age as sb.

regularidade [xegulari'dadʒi] *f* regularity.

regularizar [xegulari'za*] *vt* to regularize.

regurgitar [xeguxʒi'ta*] *vt, vi* to regurgitate.

rei [xej] *m* king; **ele é o ~ da bagunça** (*col*) he's the world's worst for untidiness; **ter o ~ na barriga** to be full of oneself; **Dia de R~s** Epiphany; **R~ Momo** carnival king.

reimprimir [xeĩpri'mi*] *vt* to reprint.

reinado [xej'nadu] *m* reign.

reinar [xej'na*] *vi* to reign; (*fig*) to reign, prevail.

reincidência [xeĩsi'dẽsja] *f* backsliding; (*de criminoso*) recidivism.

reincidir [xeĩsi'dʒi*] *vi* to relapse; (*criminoso*) to commit the offence (*BRIT*) *ou* offense (*US*) again; **~ em erro** to do wrong again.

reingressar [xeĩgre'sa*] *vi:* **~ (em)** to re-enter.

reiniciar [xejni'sja*] *vt* to restart.

reino ['xejnu] *m* kingdom; (*fig*) realm; **~ animal** animal kingdom; **o R~ Unido** the United Kingdom.

reintegrar [xeĩte'gra*] *vt* (*em emprego*) to reinstate; (*reconduzir*) to return, restore.

reiterar [xeite'ra*] *vt* to reiterate, repeat.

reitor(a) [xej'to*(a)] *m/f* (*de uma universidade*) vice-chancellor (*BRIT*), president (*US*) ♦ *m* (*PT: pároco*) rector.

reitoria [xejto'ria] *f* (*de universidade: cargo*) vice-chancellorship (*BRIT*), presidency (*US*); (*gabinete*) vice-chancellor's (*BRIT*) *ou* president's (*US*) office.

reivindicação [xejvĩdʒika'sãw] (*pl* **-ões**) *f* claim, demand.

reivindicar [xejvĩdʒi'ka*] *vt* to reclaim; (*aumento salarial, direitos*) to demand.

rejeição [xeʒej'sãw] (*pl* **-ões**) *f* rejection.

rejeitar [xeʒej'ta*] *vt* to reject; (*recusar*) to refuse.

NB: *European Portuguese adds the following consonants to certain words:* **b** (sú(b)dito, su(b)til), **c** (a(c)ção, a(c)cionista, a(c)to); **m** (inde(m)ne); **p** (ado(p)ção, ado(p)tar); *for further details see p. xiii.*

rejo ['xeju] *etc vb V* **reger.**

rejubilar [xeʒubi'la*] *vt* to fill with joy ♦ *vi* to rejoice; **~-se** *vr* to rejoice.

rejuvenescedor(a) [xeʒuvenese'do*(a)] *adj* rejuvenating.

rejuvenescer [xeʒuvene'se*] *vt* to rejuvenate ♦ *vi* to be rejuvenated; **~-se** *vr* to be rejuvenated.

relação [xela'sãw] (*pl* **-ões**) *f* relation; (*conexão*) connection, relationship; (*relacionamento*) relationship; (*MAT*) ratio; (*lista*) list; **com** *ou* **em ~ a** regarding, with reference to; **ter relações com alguém** to have intercourse with sb; **relações públicas** public relations.

relacionado/a [xelasjo'nadu/a] *adj* (*listado*) listed; (*ligado*) related, connected; **uma pessoa bem** *ou* **muito relacionada** a well-connected person.

relacionamento [xelasjona'mẽtu] *m* relationship.

relacionar [xelasjo'na*] *vt* (*listar*) to make a list of; **~-se** *vr* to be connected *ou* related; **~ algo com algo** to connect sth with sth, relate sth to sth; **~ alguém com alguém** to bring sb into contact with sb; **~-se com** (*ligar-se*) to be connected with, have to do with; (*conhecer*) to become acquainted with.

relaçoes [xela'sõjʃ] *fpl de* **relação.**

relações-públicas *m/f inv* PR person.

relâmpago [xe'lãpagu] *m* flash of lightning; **~s** lightning *sg* ♦ *adj* (*visita*) lightning *atr*; **passar como um ~** to flash past; **como um ~** like lightning, as quick as a flash.

relampejar [xelãpe'ʒa*] *vi* to flash; **relampejou** the lightning flashed.

relance [xe'lãsi] *m* glance; **olhar de ~** to glance at.

relapso/a [xe'lapsu/a] *adj* (*reincidente*) lapsed; (*negligente*) negligent.

relatar [xela'ta*] *vt* to give an account of.

relativo/a [xela'tʃivu/a] *adj* relative.

relato [xe'latu] *m* account.

relator(a) [xela'to*(a)] *m/f* storyteller.

relatório [xela'tɔrju] *m* report; **~ anual** (*COM*) annual report.

relaxado/a [xela'ʃadu/a] *adj* relaxed; (*desleixado*) slovenly, sloppy; (*relapso*) complacent.

relaxamento [xelaʃa'mẽtu] *m* relaxation; (*de moral, costumes*) debasement; (*desleixo*) slovenliness; (*de relapsos*) complacency.

relaxante [xela'ʃãtʃi] *adj* relaxing ♦ *m* tranquillizer.

relaxar [xela'ʃa*] *vt* to relax; (*moral, costumes*) to debase ♦ *vi* to relax; (*tornar-se negligente*): **~ (em)** to grow complacent in; **~ com** (*transigir*) to acquiesce in.

relaxe [xe'laʃi] *m* relaxation.

relegar [xele'ga*] *vt* to relegate.

relê [xe'le] *vb V* **reler.**

releio [xe'leju] *etc vb V* **reler.**

relembrar [xelẽ'bra*] *vt* to recall.

relento [xe'lẽtu] *m*: **ao ~** out of doors.

reler [xe'le*] (*irreg*: *como* **ler**) *vt* to reread.

reles ['xɛliʃ] *adj inv* (*gente*) common, vulgar; (*comportamento*) despicable; (*mero*) mere.

relevância [xele'vãsja] *f* relevance.

relevante [xele'vãtʃi] *adj* relevant.

relevar [xele'va*] *vt* (*tornar saliente*) to emphasize; (*atenuar*) to relieve; (*desculpar*) to pardon, forgive.

relevo [xe'levu] *m* relief; (*fig*) prominence, importance; **pôr em ~** to emphasize.

reli [xe'li] *vb V* **reler.**

relicário [xeli'karju] *m* reliquary, shrine.

relido/a [xe'lidu/a] *pp de* **reler.**

religião [xeli'ʒãw] (*pl* **-ões**) *f* religion.

religioso/a [xeli'ʒozu/ɔza] *adj* religious; (*casamento*) church ♦ *m/f* religious person; (*frade/freira*) monk/nun ♦ *m* (*casamento*) church wedding.

relinchar [xeli'ʃa*] *vi* to neigh.

relincho [xe'liʃu] *m* (*som*) neigh; (*ato*) neighing.

relíquia [xe'likja] *f* relic; **~ de família** family heirloom.

relógio [xe'lɔʒu] *m* clock; (*de gás*) meter; **~ de pé** grandfather clock; **~ de ponto** time clock; **~ de sol** sundial; **~ (de pulso)** (wrist)watch; **corrida contra o ~** race against the clock.

relojoaria [xeloʒwa'ria] *f* watchmaker's, watch shop.

relojoeiro/a [xelo'ʒwejru/a] *m/f* watchmaker.

relutância [xelu'tãsja] *f* reluctance.

relutante [xelu'tãtʃi] *adj* reluctant.

relutar [xelu'ta*] *vi*: **~ (em fazer)** to be reluctant (to do); **~ contra algo** to be reluctant to accept sth.

reluzente [xelu'zẽtʃi] *adj* brilliant, shining.

reluzir [xelu'zi*] *vi* to gleam, shine.

relva ['xɛwva] *f* grass; (*terreno gramado*) lawn.

relvado [xew'vadu] (*PT*) *m* lawn.

rem *abr* (= *remetente*) sender.

remador(a) [xema'do*(a)] *m/f* rower, oarsman/woman.

remanchar [xemã'ʃa*] *vi* to delay, take one's time.

remanescente [xemane'sẽtʃi] *adj* remaining ♦ *m* remainder; (*excesso*) surplus.

remanescer [xemane'se*] *vi* to remain.

remanso [xe'mãsu] *m* (*pausa*) pause, rest; (*sossego*) stillness, quiet; (*água*) backwater.

remar [xe'ma*] *vt* to row; (*canoa*) to paddle ♦ *vi* to row; **~ contra a maré** (*fig*) to swim against the tide.

remarcação [xemaxka'sãw] *f* (*de preços*) changing; (*de artigos*) repricing; (*artigos remarcados*) repriced goods *pl*.

remarcar [xemax'ka*] *vt* (*preços*) to adjust; (*artigos*) to reprice.

rematado/a [xema'tadu/a] *adj* (*concluído*) completed.

rematar [xema'ta*] *vt* to finish off.

remate [xe'matʃi] *m* (*fim*) end; (*acabamento*)

finishing touch; (ARQ) coping; (fig: cume) peak; (de piada) punch line.

remedeio [xeme'deju] etc vb V **remediar**.

remediado/a [xeme'dʒjadu/a] adj comfortably off.

remediar [xeme'dʒja*] vt (corrigir) to put right, remedy.

remediável [xeme'dʒjavew] (pl -eis) adj rectifiable.

remédio [xe'mɛdʒju] m (medicamento) medicine; (recurso, solução) remedy; (JUR) recourse; **não tem ~** there's no way; **que ~?** what else can one do?; **~ caseiro** home remedy.

remela [xe'mɛla] f (nos olhos) sleep.

remelento/a [xeme'lẽtu/a] adj bleary-eyed.

remelexo [xeme'leʃu] m (requebro) swaying.

rememorar [xememo'ra*] vt to remember.

rememorável [xememo'ravew] (pl -eis) adj memorable.

remendar [xemẽ'da*] vt to mend; (com pano) to patch.

remendo [xe'mẽdu] m repair; (de pano) patch.

remessa [xe'mɛsa] f (COM) shipment, dispatch; (de dinheiro) remittance.

remetente [xeme'tẽtʃi] m/f (de carta) sender; (COM) shipper.

remeter [xeme'te*] vt (expedir) to send, dispatch; (dinheiro) to remit; (entregar) to hand over; **~-se** vr: **~-se a** (referir-se) to refer to.

remexer [xeme'ʃe*] vt (papéis) to shuffle; (sacudir: braços, folhas) to shake; (revolver: areia, lama) to stir up ♦ vi: **~ em** to rummage through; **~-se** vr (mover-se) to move around; (rebolar-se) to sway.

reminiscência [xemini'sẽsja] f reminiscence.

remição [xemi'sãw] f redemption.

remir [xe'mi*] vt (coisa penhorada, REL) to redeem; (livrar) to free; (danos, perdas) to make good; **~-se** vr (pecador) to redeem o.s.

remissão [xemi'sãw] (pl -ões) f (COM, REL) redemption; (compensação) payment; (num livro) cross-reference.

remisso/a [xe'misu/a] adj remiss; **~ em fazer** (lento) slow to do.

remissões [xemi'sõjʃ] fpl de **remissão**.

remível [xe'mivew] (pl -eis) adj redeemable.

remo ['xɛmu] m oar; (de canoa) paddle; (ESPORTE) rowing.

remoa [xe'moa] etc vb V **remoer**.

remoção [xemo'sãw] f removal.

remoçar [xemo'sa*] vt to rejuvenate; ♦ vi to be rejuvenated.

remoer [xe'mwe*] vt (café) to regrind; (no pensamento) to turn over in one's mind; (amofinar) to eat away; **~-se** vr (amofinar-se) to be consumed ou eaten away.

remoinho [xemo'iɲu] m = **rodamoinho**.

remontar [xemõ'ta*] vt (elevar) to raise; (tornar a armar) to re-assemble ♦ vi (em cavalo) to remount; **~ ao passado** to return to the past; **~ ao século XV** etc to date back to the 15th century etc; **~ o vôo** to soar.

remoque [xe'mɔki] m gibe, taunt.

remorso [xe'mɔxsu] m remorse.

remoto/a [xe'mɔtu/a] adj remote, far off; (controle, COMPUT) remote.

remover [xemo've*] vt (mover) to move; (transferir) to transfer; (demitir) to dismiss; (retirar, afastar) to remove; (terra) to churn up.

remuneração [xemunera'sãw] (pl -ões) f remuneration; (salário) wage.

remunerador(a) [xemunera'do*(a)] adj remunerative; (recompensador) rewarding.

remunerar [xemune'ra*] vt to remunerate; (premiar) to reward.

rena ['xɛna] f reindeer.

renal [xe'naw] (pl -ais) adj renal, kidney atr.

Renamo [xe'namu] abr f = **Resistência Nacional Moçambicana**.

Renascença [xena'sẽsa] f: **a ~** the Renaissance.

renascer [xena'se*] vi to be reborn; (fig) to be revived.

renascimento [xenasi'mẽtu] m rebirth; (fig) revival; **o R~** the Renaissance.

Renavam (BR) abr m = **Registro Nacional de Veículos Automotores**.

renda ['xẽda] f income; (nacional) revenue; (de aplicação, locação) yield; (tecido) lace; **~ bruta/líquida** gross/net income; **imposto de ~** income tax; **~ per capita** per capita income.

rendado/a [xẽ'dadu/a] adj lace-trimmed; (com aspecto de renda) lacy ♦ m lacework.

rendeiro/a [xẽ'dejru/a] m/f lacemaker.

render [xẽ'de*] vt (lucro, dinheiro) to bring in, yield; (preço) to fetch; (homenagem) to pay; (graças) to give; (serviços) to render; (armas) to surrender; (guarda) to relieve; (causar) to bring ♦ vi (dar lucro) to pay; (trabalho) to be productive; (comida) to go a long way; (conversa, caso) to go on, last; **~-se** vr to surrender.

rendez-vous [xãde'vu] m inv = **randevu**.

rendição [xẽdʒi'sãw] f surrender.

rendido/a [xẽ'dʒidu/a] adj subdued.

rendimento [xẽdʒi'mẽtu] m (renda) income; (lucro) profit; (juro) yield, interest; (produtividade) productivity; (de máquina) efficiency; (de um produto) value for money; **~ por ação** (COM) earnings per share, earnings yield; **~ de capital** (COM) return on capital.

rendoso/a [xẽ'dozu/ɔza] adj profitable.

renegado/a [xene'gadu/a] adj, m/f renegade.

renegar [xene'ga*] vt (crença) to renounce;

(*detestar*) to hate; (*trair*) to betray; (*negar*) to deny; (*desprezar*) to reject.

renhido/a [xe'ɲidu/a] *adj* hard-fought; (*batalha*) bloody.

renitência [xeni'tẽsja] *f* obstinacy.

renitente [xeni'tẽtʃi] *adj* obstinate, stubborn.

Reno ['xenu] *m*: **o** ~ the Rhine.

renomado/a [xeno'madu/a] *adj* renowned.

renome [xe'nɔmi] *m* fame, renown; **de** ~ renowned.

renovação [xenova'sãw] (*pl* **-ões**) *f* renewal; (*ARQ*) renovation.

renovar [xeno'va*] *vt* to renew; (*ARQ*) to renovate; (*ensino, empresa*) to revamp ♦ *vi* to be renewed.

renque ['xẽki] *m* row.

rentabilidade [xẽtabili'dadʒi] *f* profitability.

rentável [xẽ'tavew] (*pl* **-eis**) *adj* profitable.

rente ['xẽtʃi] *adj* (*cabelo*) close-cropped; (*casa*) nearby ♦ *adv* close; (*muito curto*) very short; ~ **a** close by.

renúncia [xe'nũsja] *f* renunciation; (*de cargo*) resignation; ~ **a um direito** waiver (of a right).

renunciar [xenũ'sja*] *vt* to give up, renounce ♦ *vi* to resign; ~ **a algo** to give sth up; (*direito*) to surrender sth; (*fé, crença*) to renounce sth.

reorganizar [xeoxgani'za*] *vt* to reorganize.

reouve [xe'ovi] *etc vb V* **reaver**.

reouver [xeo've*] *etc vb V* **reaver**.

reparação [xepara'sãw] (*pl* **-ões**) *f* (*conserto*) mending, repairing; (*de mal, erros*) remedying; (*de prejuizos, ofensa*) making amends; (*fig*) amends *pl*, reparation.

reparar [xepa'ra*] *vt* (*consertar*) to repair; (*forças*) to restore; (*mal, erros*) to remedy; (*prejuizo, danos, ofensa*) to make amends for; (*notar*) to notice ♦ *vi*: ~ **em** to notice; **não repare em** pay no attention to; **repare em** (*olhe*) look at.

reparo [xe'paru] *m* (*conserto*) repair; (*crítica*) criticism; (*observação*) observation.

repartição [xepaxtʃi'sãw] (*pl* **-ões**) *f* (*ato*) distribution; (*seção*) department; (*escritório*) office; ~ (*pública*) government department.

repartir [xepax'tʃi*] *vt* (*distribuir*) to distribute; (*dividir entre vários*) to share out; (*dividir em várias porções*) to divide up; (*cabelo*) to part; ~**-se** *vr* (*dividir-se*) to divide.

repassar [xepa'sa*] *vt* (*ponte, fronteira*) to go over again; (*lição*) to revise, go over ♦ *vi* to go by again; **passar e** ~ to go back and forth.

repasto [xe'paʃtu] *m* (*refeição*) meal, repast; (*banquete*) feast.

repatriar [xepa'trja*] *vt* to repatriate; ~**-se** *vr* to go back home.

repelão [xepe'lãw] (*pl* **-ões**) *m* push, shove; **de** ~ brusquely.

repelente [xepe'lẽtʃi] *adj, m* repellent.

repelir [xepe'li*] *vt* to repel; (*curiosos*) to

drive away; (*idéias, atitudes*) to reject, repudiate; **seu estômago repele certos alimentos** his stomach cannot take certain foods.

repelões [xepe'lõjʃ] *fpl de* **repelão**.

repensar [xepẽ'sa*] *vi* to reconsider, rethink.

repente [xe'pẽtʃi] *m* outburst; **de** ~ suddenly; (*col: talvez*) maybe.

repentino/a [xepẽ'tʃinu/a] *adj* sudden.

repercussão [xepexku'sãw] (*pl* **-ões**) *f* repercussion.

repercutir [xepexku'tʃi*] *vt* (*som*) to echo ♦ *vi* (*som*) to reverberate, echo; (*fig*): ~ (**em**) to have repercussions (on).

repertório [xepex'tɔrju] *m* (*lista*) list; (*coleção*) collection; (*MÚS*) repertoire.

repetição [xepetʃi'sãw] (*pl* **-ões**) *f* repetition.

repetidamente [xepetʃida'mẽtʃi] *adj* repeatedly.

repetido/a [xepe'tʃidu/a] *adj* repeated; **repetidas vezes** repeatedly, again and again.

repetir [xepe'tʃi*] *vt* to repeat; (*vestido*) to wear again ♦ *vi* (*ao comer*) to have seconds; ~**-se** *vr* (*acontecer de novo*) to happen again; (*pessoa*) to repeat o.s.

repetitivo/a [xepetʃi'tʃivu/a] *adj* repetitive.

repicar [xepi'ka*] *vt* (*sinos*) to ring ♦ *vi* to ring (out).

repilo [xe'pilu] *etc vb V* **repelir**.

repimpado/a [xepĩ'padu/a] *adj* (*refestelado*) lolling; (*satisfeito*) full up.

repique [xe'piki] *etc vb V* **repicar** ♦ *m* (*de sinos*) peal; ~ **falso** false alarm.

repisar [xepi'za*] *vt* (*repetir*) to repeat; (*uvas*) to tread ♦ *vi*: ~ **em** (*assunto*) to keep on about, harp on.

repito [xe'pitu] *etc vb V* **repetir**.

replay [xe'plei] (*pl* ~**s**) *m* (*TV*) (action) replay.

repleto/a [xe'plɛtu/a] *adj* replete, full up.

réplica ['xɛplika] *f* (*cópia*) replica; (*contestação*) reply, retort.

replicar [xepli'ka*] *vt* to answer, reply to ♦ *vi* to reply, answer back.

repõe [xe'põj] *etc vb V* **repor**.

repolho [xe'poʎu] *m* cabbage.

repomos [xe'pomoʃ] *vb V* **repor**.

reponho [xe'poɲu] *etc vb V* **repor**.

repontar [xepõ'ta*] *vi* (*aparecer*) to appear.

repor [xe'po*] (*irreg: como* **pôr**) *vt* to put back, replace; (*restituir*) to return; ~**-se** *vr* (*pessoa*) to recover.

reportagem [xepox'taʒẽ] (*pl* **-ns**) *f* (*ato*) reporting; (*notícia*) report; (*repórteres*) reporters *pl*.

reportar [xepox'ta*] *vt*: ~ **a** (*o pensamento*) to take back to; (*atribuir*) to attribute to; ~**-se** *vr*: ~**-se a** to refer to; (*relacionar-se a*) to be connected with.

repórter [xe'pɔxte*] *m/f* reporter.

repôs [xe'poʃ] *vb V* **repor**.

reposição [xepozi'sãw] (*pl* **-ões**) *f* replacement; (*restituição*) return; ~ **salarial** wage adjustment.

repositório [xepozi'tɔrju] *m* repository.

reposto/a [xe'poʃtu/'pɔʃta] *pp de* **repor**.

repousar [xepo'za*] *vi* to rest.

repouso [xe'pozu] *m* rest.

repreender [xeprjẽ'de*] *vt* to reprimand.

repreensão [xeprjẽ'sãw] *(pl* -ões) *f* rebuke, reprimand.

repreensível [xeprjẽ'sivew] *(pl* -eis) *adj* reprehensible.

repreensões [xeprjẽ'sõjʃ] *fpl de* **repreensão**.

represa [xe'preza] *f* dam.

represália [xepre'zalja] *f* reprisal.

representação [xeprezẽta'sãw] *(pl* -ões) *f* representation; *(representantes)* representatives *pl*; *(TEATRO)* performance; *(atuação do ator)* acting.

representante [xeprezẽ'tãtʃi] *m/f* representative.

representativo/a [xeprezẽta'tʃivu/a] *adj* representative.

representar [xeprezẽ'ta*] *vt* to represent; *(TEATRO: papel)* to play; *(: encenar)* to put on ♦ *vi (ator)* to act; *(tb: JUR)* to make a complaint.

repressão [xepre'sãw] *(pl* -ões) *f* repression.

repressivo/a [xepre'sivu/a] *adj* repressive.

repressões [xepre'sõjʃ] *fpl de* **repressão**.

reprimido/a [xepri'midu/a] *adj* repressed.

reprimir [xepri'mi*] *vt* to repress; *(lágrimas)* to keep back.

reprise [xe'prizi] *f* reshowing.

réprobo/a ['xɛprobu/a] *adj, m/f* reprobate.

reprodução [xeprodu'sãw] *(pl* -ões) *f* reproduction.

reprodutor(a) [xeprodu'to*(a)] *adj* reproductive.

reproduzir [xeprodu'zi*] *vt* to reproduce; *(repetir)* to repeat; *~-se* *vr* to breed, multiply; *(repetir-se)* to be repeated.

reprovação [xeprova'sãw] *(pl* -ões) *f* disapproval; *(em exame)* failure.

reprovado/a [xepro'vadu/a] *m/f* failed candidate, failure; **taxa de ~s** failure rate.

reprovador(a) [xeprova'do*(a)] *adj (olhar)* disapproving, reproving.

reprovar [xepro'va*] *vt (condenar)* to disapprove of; *(aluno)* to fail.

réptil ['xɛptʃiw] *(pl* -eis) *m* reptile.

repto ['xɛptu] *m* challenge, provocation.

república [xe'publika] *f* republic; **~ de estudantes** students' house; **~ popular** people's republic.

republicano/a [xepubli'kanu/a] *adj, m/f* republican.

repudiar [xepu'dʒja*] *vt* to repudiate, reject; *(abandonar)* to disown.

repúdio [xe'pudʒju] *m* rejection, repudiation.

repugnância [xepug'nãsja] *f* repugnance; *(por comida etc)* disgust; *(aversão)* aversion; *(moral)* abhorrence.

repugnante [xepug'nãtʃi] *adj* repugnant, repulsive.

repugnar [xepug'na*] *vt* to oppose ♦ *vi* to be repulsive; *~* **a alguém** to disgust sb; *(moralmente)* to be repugnant to sb.

repulsão [xepuw'sãw] *(pl* -ões) *f* repulsion; *(rejeição)* rejection.

repulsa [xe'puwsa] *f (ato)* rejection; *(sentimento)* repugnance; *(física)* repulsion.

repulsivo/a [xepuw'sivu/a] *adj* repulsive.

repulsões [xepuw'sõjʃ] *fpl de* **repulsão**.

repunha [xe'puɲa] *etc vb* V **repor**.

repus [xe'puʃ] *etc vb* V **repor**.

repuser [xepu'ze*] *etc vb* V **repor**.

reputação [reputa'sãw] *(pl* -ões) *f* reputation.

reputado/a [xepu'tadu/a] *adj* renowned.

reputar [xepu'ta*] *vt* to consider, regard as.

repuxado/a [xepu'ʃadu/a] *adj (pele)* tight, firm; *(olhos)* slanted.

repuxar [xepu'ʃa*] *vt (puxar)* to tug; *(esticar)* to pull tight.

repuxo [xe'puʃu] *m (de água)* fountain; **agüentar o ~** *(col)* to bear up.

requebrado [xeke'bradu] *m (rebolado)* swing, sway.

requebrar [xeke'bra*] *vt* to wiggle, swing; *~-se* *vr* to wiggle, swing.

requeijão [xekej'ʒãw] *m* cheese spread.

requeira [xe'kejra] *etc vb* V **requerer**.

requentar [xekẽ'ta*] *vt* to reheat, warm up.

requer [xe'ke*] *vb* V **requerer**.

requerente [xeke'rẽtʃi] *m/f (JUR)* petitioner.

requerer [xeke're*] *vt (emprego)* to apply for; *(pedir)* to request, ask for; *(exigir)* to require; *(JUR)* to petition for.

requerimento [xekeri'mẽtu] *m* application; *(pedido)* request; *(petição)* petition.

réquiem ['xɛkjẽ] *(pl* -ns) *m* requiem.

requintado/a [xekĩ'tadu/a] *adj* refined, elegant.

requintar [xekĩ'ta*] *vt* to refine ♦ *vi*: *~* **em** to be refined in.

requinte [xe'kĩtʃi] *m* refinement, elegance; *(cúmulo)* height.

requisição [xekizi'sãw] *(pl* -ões) *f* request, demand.

requisitado/a [xekizi'tadu/a] *adj (requerido)* required; *(muito procurado)* sought after.

requisitar [xekizi'ta*] *vt* to make a request for; *(MIL)* to requisition.

requisito [xeki'zitu] *m* requirement.

rês [xeʃ] *f* head of cattle; **reses** *fpl* cattle, livestock *sg*.

rescindir [xesĩ'dʒi*] *vt (contrato)* to rescind.

rescrever [xeʃkre've*] *vt* = **reescrever**.

rés-do-chão [xɛʒ-] *(PT)* *m inv (andar térreo)* ground floor *(BRIT)*, first floor *(US)*.

resenha [xe'zɛɲa] *f (relatório)* report; *(resumo)* summary; *(de livro)* review; **fazer a ~ de** *(livro)* to review.

NB: *European Portuguese adds the following consonants to certain words:* **b** (sú(b)dito, su(b)til); **c** (a(c)ção, a(c)cionista, a(c)to); **m** (inde(m)ne); **p** (ado(p)ção, ado(p)tar); *for further details see p. xiii.*

reserva [xe'zɛxva] *f* reserve; *(para hotel, fig: ressalva)* reservation; *(discrição)* discretion ♦ *m/f (ESPORTE)* reserve; ~ **de mercado** *(COM)* protected market; ~ **de petróleo** oil reserve; ~ **natural** nature reserve; ~ **em dinheiro** cash reserve.

reservado/a [xezex'vadu/a] *adj* reserved; *(pej: retraído)* standoffish.

reservar [xezex'va*] *vt* to reserve; *(guardar de reserva)* to keep; *(forças)* to conserve; ~-**se** *vr* to save o.s.; ~-**se o direito de fazer** to reserve the right to do; **ele não sabe o que o futuro lhe reserva** he does not know what the future has in store for him.

reservatório [xezexva'tɔrju] *m* *(lago)* reservoir.

reservista [xezex'viʃta] *m/f (MIL)* member of the reserves.

resfolegar [xeʃfole'ga*] *vi* to pant.

resfriado/a [xeʃ'frjadu/a] *(BR) adj:* **estar** ~ to have a cold; **ficar** ~ to catch cold ♦ *m* cold, chill.

resfriar [xeʃ'frja*] *vt* to cool, chill ♦ *vi* *(pessoa)* to catch (a) cold; ~-**se** *vr* to catch (a) cold.

resgatar [xeʒga'ta*] *vt* *(prisioneiro)* to ransom; *(salvar)* to rescue; *(retomar)* to get back, recover; *(dívida)* to pay off; *(COM: ação, coisa penhorada)* to redeem.

resgatável [xeʒga'tavew] *(pl -eis) adj* redeemable.

resgate [xeʒ'gatʃi] *m* *(salvamento)* rescue; *(para livrar reféns)* ransom; *(COM: de ações, coisa penhorada)* redemption; *(retomada)* recovery.

resguardar [xeʒgwax'da*] *vt* to protect; ~-**se** *vr:* ~-**se de** to guard against.

resguardo [xeʒ'gwaxdu] *m* protection; *(cuidado)* care; *(convalescência):* **estar** *ou* **ficar de** ~ to take *ou* be taking things easy.

residência [xezi'dẽsja] *f* residence.

residencial [xezidẽ'sjaw] *(pl -ais) adj* *(zona, edifício)* residential; *(computador, telefone etc)* home *atr.*

residente [xezi'dẽtʃi] *adj, m/f* resident; ~ **na memória** *(COMPUT)* memory-resident.

residir [xezi'dʒi*] *vi* to live, reside; *(achar-se)* to reside.

resíduo [xe'zidwu] *m* residue.

resignação [xezigna'sãw] *(pl -ões) f* resignation.

resignadamente [xezignada'mẽtʃi] *adj* with resignation.

resignado/a [xezig'nadu/a] *adj* resigned.

resignar-se [xezig'naxsi] *vr:* ~ **com** to resign o.s. to.

resiliente [xezi'ljẽtʃi] *adj* resilient.

resina [xe'zina] *f* resin.

resistência [xeziʃ'tẽsja] *f* resistance; *(de atleta)* stamina; *(de material, objeto)* strength; *(moral)* morale.

resistente [xeziʃ'tẽtʃi] *adj* resistant; *(material, objeto)* hard-wearing, strong; ~ **a traças** mothproof.

resistir [xeziʃ'tʃi*] *vi* *(suporte)* to hold; *(pessoa)* to hold out; ~ **a** *(não ceder)* to resist; *(sobreviver)* to survive; ~ **ao uso** to wear well; ~ **(ao tempo)** to endure, stand the test of time.

resma ['xeʒma] *f* ream.

resmungar [xeʒmũ'ga*] *vt, vi* to mutter, mumble.

resmungo [xeʒ'mũgu] *m* grumbling.

resolução [xezolu'sãw] *(pl -ões) f* resolution; *(coragem)* courage; *(de um problema)* solution; **de alta** ~ **(gráfica)** *(COMPUT)* high-resolution.

resoluto/a [xezo'lutu/a] *adj* decisive; ~ **a fazer** resolved to do.

resolver [xezow've*] *vt* to sort out; *(problema)* to solve; *(questão)* to resolve; *(decidir)* to decide; ~-**se** *vr:* ~-**se (a fazer)** *(decidir)* to make up one's mind (to do), decide (to do); **chorar não resolve** crying doesn't help, it's no use crying; ~-**se por** to decide on.

resolvido/a [xezow'vidu/a] *adj* *(pessoa)* decisive.

respaldo [xeʃ'pawdu] *m* *(de cadeira)* backrest; *(fig)* support, backing.

respectivo/a [xeʃpek'tʃivu/a] *adj* respective.

respeitador(a) [xeʃpejta'do*(a)] *adj* respectful.

respeitante [xeʃpej'tãtʃi] *adj:* ~ **a** concerning, with regard to.

respeitar [xeʃpej'ta*] *vt* to respect.

respeitável [xeʃpej'tavew] *(pl -eis) adj* respectable; *(considerável)* considerable.

respeito [xeʃ'pejtu] *m:* ~ **(a** *ou* **por)** respect (for); ~**s** *mpl* regards; **a** ~ **de, com** ~ **a** as to, as regards; *(sobre)* about; **dizer** ~ **a** to concern; **faltar ao** ~ **a** to be rude to; **em** ~ **a** with respect to; **dar-se ao** ~ to command respect; **pessoa de** ~ respected person; **ela não me disse nada a seu** ~ she didn't tell me anything about you; **não sei nada a** ~ **(disso)** I know nothing about it.

respeitoso/a [xeʃpej'tozu/ɔza] *adj* respectful.

respingar [xeʃpĩ'ga*] *vt, vi* to splash, spatter.

respingo [xeʃ'pĩgu] *m* splash.

respiração [xeʃpira'sãw] *f* breathing; *(MED)* respiration.

respirador [xeʃpira'do*] *m* respirator.

respirar [xeʃpi'ra*] *vt* to breathe; *(revelar)* to reveal, show ♦ *vi* to breathe; *(descansar)* to have a respite.

respiratório/a [xeʃpira'tɔrju/a] *adj* respiratory.

respiro [xeʃ'piru] *m* breath; *(descanso)* respite; *(abertura)* vent.

resplandecente [xeʃplãde'sẽtʃi] *adj* resplendent.

resplandecer [xeʃplãde'se*] *vi* to gleam, shine (out).

resplendor [xeʃplẽ'do*] *m* brilliance; *(fig)* glory.

respondão/dona [xeʃpõ'dãw/'dɔna] (pl -ões/ ~s) adj cheeky, insolent.

responder [xeʃpõ'de*] vt to answer ♦ vi to answer; (ser respondão) to answer back; ~ **por** to be responsible for, answer for; (COM) to be liable for; ~ **a** (tratamento, agressão) to respond to; (processo, inquérito) to undergo.

respondões [xeʃpõ'dõjʃ] mpl de **respondão**.

respondona [xeʃpõ'dɔna] f de **respondão**.

responsabilidade [xeʃpõsabili'dadʒi] f responsibility; (JUR) liability.

responsabilizar [xeʃpõsabili'za*] vt: ~ **alguém (por algo)** to hold sb responsible (for sth); ~-se vr: ~-se por to take responsibility for.

responsável [xeʃpõ'savew] (pl -eis) adj: ~ (por) responsible (for) ♦ m person responsible ou in charge; ~ a answerable to, accountable to.

resposta [xeʃ'pɔʃta] f answer, reply.

resquício [xeʃ'kisju] m (vestígio) trace.

ressabiado/a [xesa'bjadu/a] adj (desconfiado) wary; (ressentido) resentful.

ressaca [xe'saka] f (refluxo) undertow; (mar bravo) rough sea; (fig: de quem bebeu) hangover; **estar de** ~ (mar) to be rough; (pessoa) to have a hangover.

ressaibo [xe'sajbu] m (mau sabor) unpleasant taste; (fig: indício) trace; (: ressentimento) ill feeling.

ressaltar [xesaw'ta*] vt to emphasize ♦ vi to stand out.

ressalva [xe'sawva] f (proteção) safeguard; (MIL) exemption certificate; (correção) correction; (restrição) reservation, proviso; (exceção) exception.

ressarcir [xesax'si*] vt (pagar) to compensate; (compensar) to compensate for; ~ **alguém de** to compensate sb for.

ressecado/a [xese'kadu/a] adj (terra, lábios) parched; (pele, planta) very dry.

ressecar [xese'ka*] vt, vi to dry up.

resseguro [xese'guru] m reinsurance.

ressentido/a [xesẽ'tʃidu/a] adj resentful.

ressentimento [xesẽtʃi'mẽtu] m resentment.

ressentir-se [xesẽ'tʃixsi] vr: ~ **de** (magoar-se) to resent, be hurt by; (sofrer) to suffer from, feel the effects of.

ressequido/a [xese'kidu/a] adj = **ressecado/a**.

ressinto [xe'sĩtu] etc vb V **ressentir-se**.

ressoar [xe'swa*] vi to resound; (ecoar) to echo.

ressonância [xeso'nãsja] f resonance; (eco) echo.

ressonante [xeso'nãtʃi] adj resonant.

ressurgimento [xesuxʒi'mẽtu] m resurgence, revival.

ressurreição [xesuxej'sãw] (pl -ões) f resurrection.

ressuscitar [xesusi'ta*] vt to revive, resuscitate; (costumes etc) to revive ♦ vi to revive.

restabelecer [xeʃtabele'se*] vt to re-establish; (ordem, forças) to restore; (doente) to restore to health; ~-se vr to recover, recuperate.

restabelecimento [xeʃtabelesi'mẽtu] m re-establishment; (da ordem) restoration; (MED) recovery.

restante [xeʃ'tãtʃi] m rest ♦ adj remaining.

restar [xeʃ'ta*] vi to remain, be left; (esperança, dúvida) to remain; **não lhe resta nada** he has nothing left; **resta-me fechar o negócio** I still have to close the deal; **não resta dúvida de que** there is no longer any doubt that.

restauração [xeʃtawra'sãw] (pl -ões) f restoration; (de doente) restoring to health; (de costumes, usos) revival.

restaurante [xeʃtaw'rãtʃi] m restaurant.

restaurar [xeʃtaw'ra*] vt to restore; (recuperar: doente) to restore to health; (de costumes, usos) to revive, restore.

réstia ['xɛʃtʃja] f (de cebolas) string; (luz) ray.

restinga [xeʃ'tʃĩga] f spit.

restituição [xeʃtʃitwi'sãw] (pl -ões) f restitution, return; (de dinheiro) repayment; (a cargo) reinstatement.

restituir [xeʃtʃi'twi*] vt to return; (dinheiro) to repay; (forças, saúde) to restore; (usos) to revive; (reempossar) to reinstate.

resto ['xɛʃtu] m rest; (MAT) remainder; ~s mpl remains; (de comida) scraps; ~s **mortais** mortal remains; **de** ~ apart from that.

restrição [xeʃtri'sãw] (pl -ões) f restriction.

restringir [xeʃtrĩ'ʒi*] vt to restrict; ~-se vr: ~-se a to be restricted to; (pessoa) to restrict o.s. to.

restrito/a [xeʃ'tritu/a] adj restricted.

resultado [xezuw'tadu] m result; **dar** ~ to work, be effective; ~ ... (col) the upshot being ....

resultante [xezuw'tãtʃi] adj resultant; ~ **de** resulting from.

resultar [xezuw'ta*] vi: ~ **(de/em)** to result (from/in) ♦ vi (vir a ser) to turn out to be.

resumido/a [xezu'midu/a] adj abbreviated, abridged; (curto) concise.

resumir [xezu'mi*] vt to summarize; (livro) to abridge; (reduzir) to reduce; (conter em resumo) to sum up; ~-se vr: ~-se a ou em to consist in ou of.

resumo [xe'zumu] m summary, résumé; **em** ~ in short, briefly.

resvalar [xeʒva'la*] vt to slide, slip.

resvés [xeʃ'vɛʃ] adj tight ♦ adv closely; ~ **a** right by; (na conta) just.

---

reta ['xɛta] *f* (*linha*) straight line; (*trecho de estrada*) straight; ~ **final** *ou* **de chegada** home straight; **na** ~ **final** (*tb fig*) on the home straight.

retaguarda [xeta'gwaxda] *f* rearguard; (*posição*) rear.

retalhar [xeta'ʎa*] *vt* to cut up; (*separar*) to divide; (*despedaçar*) to shred; (*ferir*) to slash.

retalho [xe'taʎu] *m* (*de pano*) scrap, remnant; **vender a** ~ (*PT*) to sell retail; **colcha de** ~**s** patchwork quilt.

retaliação [xetalja'sãw] (*pl* **-ões**) *f* retaliation.

retaliar [xeta'lja*] *vt* to repay ♦ *vi* to retaliate.

retangular [xetãgu'la*] *adj* rectangular.

retângulo [xe'tãgulu] *m* rectangle.

retardado/a [xetax'dadu/a] *adj* (*PSICO*) retarded.

retardar [xetax'da*] *vt* to hold up, delay; (*adiar*) to postpone.

retardatário/a [xetaxda'tarju/a] *m/f* latecomer.

retardo [xe'taxdu] *m* (*PSICO*) retardedness.

retenção [xetẽ'sãw] *f* retention.

reter [xe'te*] (*irreg*: *como* **ter**) *vt* (*guardar, manter*) to keep; (*deter*) to stop, detain; (*segurar*) to hold; (*ladrão, suspeito*) to detain, hold; (*na memória*) to retain; (*lágrimas, impulsos*) to hold back; (*impedir de sair*) to keep back; ~**-se** *vr* to restrain o.s.

retesado/a [xete'zadu/a] *adj* taut.

retesar [xete'za*] *vt* (*músculo*) to flex; (*corda*) to pull taut.

reteve [xe'tevi] *vb* V **reter**.

reticência [xetʃi'sẽsja] *f* reticence, reserve; ~**s** *fpl* suspension points.

reticente [xetʃi'sẽtʃi] *adj* reticent.

retidão [xetʃi'dãw] *f* (*integridade*) rectitude; (*de linha*) straightness.

retificar [xetʃifi'ka*] *vt* to rectify.

retinha [xe'tʃiɲa] *etc vb* V **reter**.

retinir [xetʃi'ni*] *vi* (*ferros*) to clink; (*campainha*) to ring, jingle; (*ressoar*) to resound.

retirada [xetʃi'rada] *f* (*MIL*) withdrawal, retreat; (*salário, saque*) withdrawal; **bater em** ~ to beat a retreat.

retirado/a [xetʃi'radu/a] *adj* (*vida*) solitary; (*lugar*) isolated.

retirante [xetʃi'rãtʃi] *m/f* migrant (*from the NE of Brazil*).

retirar [xetʃi'ra*] *vt* to withdraw; (*tirar*) to take out; (*afastar*) to take away, remove; (*fazer sair*) to get out; (*ganhar*) to make; ~**-se** *vr* to withdraw; (*de uma festa etc*) to leave; (*da política etc*) to retire; (*recolher-se*) to retire, withdraw; (*MIL*) to retreat.

retiro [xe'tʃiru] *m* retreat.

retitude [xetʃi'tudʒi] *f* rectitude.

retive [xe'tʃivi] *etc vb* V **reter**.

retiver [xetʃi've*] *etc vb* V **reter**.

reto/a ['xɛtu/a] *adj* straight; (*fig*: *justo*) fair; (: *honesto*) honest, upright ♦ *m* (*ANAT*) rectum.

retocar [xeto'ka*] *vt* (*pintura*) to touch up; (*texto*) to tidy up.

retomar [xeto'ma*] *vt* to take up again; (*reaver*) to get back.

retoque [xe'tɔki] *etc vb* V **retocar** ♦ *m* finishing touch.

retorcer [xetox'se*] *vt* to twist; ~**-se** *vr* to wriggle, writhe; ~**-se de dor** to writhe in pain.

retórica [xe'tɔrika] *f* rhetoric; (*pej*) affectation.

retórico/a [xe'tɔriku/a] *adj* rhetorical; (*pej*) affected.

retornar [xetox'na*] *vi* to return, go back.

retorno [xe'toxnu] *m* return; (*COM*) barter, exchange; (*em rodovia*) turning area; **dar** ~ to do a U-turn; ~ **sobre investimento** return on investment; ~ **(do carro)** (*COMPUT*) (carriage) return.

retorquir [xetox'ki*] *vi* to retort, reply ♦ *vt* to reply; **ela não retorquiu nada** she said nothing in reply.

retractação [xetrata'sãw] (*PT*) *f* = **retratação**.

retraído/a [xetra'idu/a] *adj* retracted; (*fig*) reserved, timid.

retraimento [xetraj'mẽtu] *m* withdrawal; (*contração*) contraction; (*fig*: *de pessoa*) timidity, shyness.

retrair [xetra'i*] *vt* to withdraw; (*contrair*) to contract; (*pessoa*) to make reserved; ~**-se** *vr* to withdraw; (*encolher-se*) to retract.

retrasado/a [xetra'zadu/a] *adj*: **a semana retrasada** the week before last.

retratação [xetrata'sãw] (*pl* **-ões**) *f* retraction.

retratar [xetra'ta*] *vt* to portray, depict; (*mostrar*) to show; (*dito*) to retract; ~**-se** *vr*: ~**-se (de algo)** to retract (sth).

retrátil [xe'tratʃiw] (*pl* **-eis**) *adj* retractable; **cinto de segurança** ~ inertia-reel seat belt.♦

retratista [xetra'tʃiʃta] *m/f* portraitist.

retrato [xe'tratu] *m* portrait; (*FOTO*) photo; (*fig*: *efígie*) likeness; (: *representação*) portrayal; **ela é o** ~ **da mãe** she's the image of her mother; **tirar um** ~ **(de alguém)** to take a photo (of sb); ~ **a meio corpo/de corpo inteiro** half/full-length portrait; ~ **falado** identikit picture.

retribuição [xetribwi'sãw] (*pl* **-ões**) *f* reward, recompense; (*pagamento*) remuneration; (*de hospitalidade, favor*) return, reciprocation.

retribuir [xetri'bwi*] *vt* (*recompensar*) to reward, recompense; (*pagar*) to remunerate; (*hospitalidade, favor, sentimento, visita*) to return.

retroactivo/a [xetroa'tivu/a] (*PT*) *adj* = **retroativo**.

retroagir [xetroa'ʒi*] *vi* (*lei*) to be retroactive; (*modificar o que está feito*) to change what has been done.

retroativo/a [xetroa'tʃivu/a] *adj* retroactive; (*pagamento*): ~ **(a)** backdated (to).

retroceder [xetrose'de*] *vi* to retreat, fall back; (*decair*) to decline; (*num intento*) to back down.

retrocesso [xetro'sɛsu] *m* retreat; *(ao passado)* return; *(decadência)* decline; *(tecla)* backspace (key); *(da economia)* slowdown.

retrógrado/a [xe'trɔgradu/a] *adj* retrograde; *(reacionário)* reactionary.

retroprojetor [xetroproʒe'to*] *m* overhead projector.

retrospectiva [xetroʃpek'tʃiva] *f* retrospective.

retrospectivamente [xetroʃpektʃiva'mētʃi] *adv* in retrospect.

retrospectivo/a [xetroʃpek'tʃivu/a] *adj* retrospective.

retrospecto [xetro'ʃpektu] *m* retrospective look; **em ~** in retrospect.

retrovisor [xetrovi'zo*] *adj, m*: **(espelho) ~** (rear-view) mirror.

retrucar [xetru'ka*] *vi* to retort, reply ♦ *vt* to retort.

retumbância [xetũ'bãsja] *f* resonance.

retumbante [xetũ'bãtʃi] *adj (tb fig)* resounding.

retumbar [xetũ'ba*] *vi* to resound, echo; *(ribombar)* to rumble, boom.

returco [xe'tuxku] *etc vb V* **retorquir**.

réu/ré [xɛw/xɛ] *m/f* defendant; *(culpado)* culprit, criminal; **~ de morte** condemned man.

reumático/a [xew'matʃiku/a] *adj* rheumatic.

reumatismo [xewma'tʃiʒmu] *m* rheumatism.

reumatologista [xewmatolo'ʒiʃta] *m/f* rheumatologist.

reunião [xeu'njãw] *(pl -ões) f* meeting; *(ato, reencontro)* reunion; *(festa)* get-together; party; **~ de cúpula** summit (meeting); **~ de diretoria** board meeting.

reunir [xeu'ni*] *vt (pessoas)* to bring together; *(partes)* to join, unite; *(qualidades)* to combine; **~-se** *vr* to meet; *(amigos)* to meet, get together; **~-se a** to join.

reutilizar [xeutʃili'za*] *vt* to re-use.

revalorizar [xevalori'za*] *vt (moeda)* to revalue.

revanche [xe'vãʃi] *f* revenge; *(ESPORTE)* return match.

revê [xe've] *etc vb V* **rever**.

reveillon [xeve'jõ] *m* New Year's Eve.

revejo [xe'veʒu] *etc vb V* **rever**.

revelação [xevela'sãw] *(pl -ões) f* revelation; *(FOTO)* development; *(novo cantor, ator etc)* promising newcomer.

revelar [xeve'la*] *vt* to reveal; *(mostrar)* to show; *(FOTO)* to develop; **~-se** *vr* to turn out to be; **ela se revelou nessa crise** she showed her true colo(u)rs in this crisis.

revelia [xeve'lia] *f* default; **à ~** by default; **à ~ de** without the knowledge *ou* consent of.

revendedor(a) [xevēde'do*(a)] *m/f* dealer.

revender [xevē'de*] *vt* to resell.

rever [xe've*] *(irreg: como* **ver)** *vt* to see again; *(examinar)* to check; *(revisar)* to check, revise; *(provas tipográficas)* to proofread.

reverberar [xevexbe'ra*] *vt (luz)* to reflect ♦ *vi* to be reflected.

reverdecer [xevexde'se*] *vt, vi* to turn green again.

reverência [xeve'rēsja] *f* reverence, respect; *(ato)* bow; *(: de mulher)* curtsey; **fazer uma ~** to bow; to curtsey.

reverenciar [xeverē'sja*] *vt* to revere, venerate; *(obedecer)* to obey.

reverendo/a [xeve'rēdu/a] *adj* venerable ♦ *m* priest, clergyman.

reverente [xeve'rētʃi] *adj* reverential.

reversão [xevex'sãw] *(pl -ões) f* reversion.

reversível [xevex'sivew] *(pl -eis) adj* reversible.

reverso [xe'vɛxsu] *m* reverse; **o ~ da medalha** *(fig)* the other side of the coin.

reversões [xevex'sõjʃ] *fpl de* **reversão**.

reverter [xevex'te*] *vt* to revert; *(a questão)* to return; **~ em benefício de** to benefit.

revertério [xevex'tɛrju] *m*: **dar o ~** *(col)* to go wrong.

revés [xe'vɛʃ] *m* reverse; *(infortúnio)* setback, mishap; **ao ~** *(roupa)* inside out; **de ~** *(olhar)* askance.

revestimento [xeveʃtʃi'mētu] *m (da parede)* covering; *(de sofá)* cover; *(de caixa)* lining.

revestir [xeveʃ'tʃi*] *vt (traje)* to put on; *(cobrir: paredes etc)* to cover; *(interior de uma caixa etc)* to line; **~-se** *vr*: **~-se de** *(poderes)* to assume, take on; *(paciência)* to arm o.s. with; *(coragem)* to take, pluck up; **~ alguém de poderes** *etc* to invest sb with powers *etc*.

revezamento [xeveza'mētu] *m* alternation.

revezar [xeve'za*] *vt* to alternate ♦ *vi* to take turns, alternate; **~-se** *vr* to take turns, alternate.

revi [xe'vi] *vb V* **rever**.

revia [xe'via] *etc vb V* **rever**.

revidar [xevi'da*] *vt (soco, insulto)* to return; *(retrucar)* to retort; *(crítica)* to rise to, respond to ♦ *vi* to hit back; *(retrucar)* to respond.

revide [xe'vidʒi] *m* response.

revigorar [xevigo'ra*] *vt* to reinvigorate ♦ *vi* to regain one's strength; **~-se** *vr* to regain one's strength.

revir [xe'vi*] *etc vb V* **rever**.

revirado/a [xevi'radu/a] *adj (casa)* untidy, upside-down.

revirar [xevi'ra*] *vt* to turn round; *(gaveta)* to turn out, go through; **~-se** *vr (na cama)* to toss and turn; **~ os olhos** to roll one's eyes.

reviravolta [xevira'vɔwta] *f* about-turn, U-turn; *(mudança da situação)* turn.

NB: European Portuguese adds the following consonants to certain words: **b** (sú(b)dito, su(b)til); **c** (a(c)ção, a(c)cionista, a(c)to); **m** (inde(m)ne); **p** (ado(p)ção, ado(p)tar); *for further details see p. xiii.*

revisão [xevi'zãw] (pl **-ões**) f revision; (de máquina) overhaul; (de carro) service; (JUR) appeal; ~ **de provas** proofreading.

revisar [xevi'za*] vt to revise; (prova tipográfica) to proofread.

revisões [xevi'zõjʃ] fpl de **revisão**.

revisor(a) [xevi'zo*(a)] m/f (FERRO) ticket inspector; (de provas) proofreader.

revista [xe'viʃta] f (busca) search; (MIL, exame) inspection; (publicação) magazine; (: profissional, erudita) journal; (TEATRO) revue; **passar ~ a** to review; (MIL) to inspect, review; ~ **em quadrinhos** comic; ~ **literária** literary review; ~ **para mulheres** women's magazine.

revistar [xeviʃ'ta*] vt to search; (tropa) to review; (examinar) to examine.

revisto [xe'viʃtu] etc vb V **revestir**.

revisto/a [xe'viʃtu/a] pp de **rever**.

revitalizar [xevitali'za*] vt to revitalize.

reviu [xe'viu] vb V **rever**.

reviver [xevi've*] vt to relive; (costumes, palavras) to revive ♦ vi to come back to life; (doente) to pick up.

revocar [xevo'ka*] vt (o passado) to evoke; (mandar voltar) to recall; ~ **alguém a/de** to bring sb back to/from.

revogação [xevoga'sãw] (pl **-ões**) f (de lei) repeal; (de ordem) reversal.

revogar [xevo'ga*] vt to revoke.

revolta [xe'vɔwta] f revolt; (fig: indignação) disgust.

revoltado/a [xevow'tadu/a] adj (indignado) disgusted; (amargo) bitter; (revoltoso) in revolt.

revoltante [xevow'tãtʃi] adj disgusting; (repugnante) revolting.

revoltar [xevow'ta*] vt to disgust; (insurgir) to incite to revolt ♦ vi to cause indignation; ~**se** vr to rebel, revolt; (indignar-se) to be disgusted.

revolto/a [xe'vowtu/a] pp de **revolver** ♦ adj (década) turbulent; (mundo) troubled; (cabelo) dishevelled; (mar) rough; (desarrumado) untidy.

revoltoso/a [xevow'tozu/ɔza] adj in revolt.

revolução [xevolu'sãw] (pl **-ões**) f revolution.

revolucionar [xevolusjo'na*] vt to revolutionize.

revolucionário/a [xevolusjo'narju/a] adj, m/f revolutionary.

revoluções [xevolu'sõjʃ] fpl de **revolução**.

revolver [xevow've*] vt (terra) to turn over, dig over; (gaveta) to rummage through; (olhos) to roll; (suj: vento) to blow around ♦ vi (girar) to revolve, rotate.

revólver [xe'vɔwve*] m revolver, gun.

reza ['xɛza] f prayer.

rezar [xe'za*] vt (missa, prece) to say ♦ vi to pray; ~ **(que)** (contar, dizer) to state (that).

RFA abr f (antes: República Federal Alemã) FRG.

RFFSA (BR) abr f = **Rede Ferroviária Federal SA**.

RG (BR) abr m (= Registro Geral) identity document.

rh abr: **factor** ~ Rh. ou rhesus (BRIT) factor; ~ **negativo/positivo** rhesus negative/positive.

riacho ['xjaʃu] m stream, brook.

ribalta [xi'bawta] f footlights pl; (fig) boards pl.

ribanceira [xibã'sejra] f (margem) steep river bank; (rampa) steep slope; (precipício) cliff.

ribeira [xi'bejra] f riverside; (riacho) river.

ribeirão [xibej'rãw] (BR: pl **-ões**) m stream.

ribeirinho/a [xibej'riɲu/a] adj riverside atr.

ribeiro [xi'bejru] m brook, stream.

ribeirões [xibej'rõjʃ] mpl de **ribeirão**.

ribombar [xibõ'ba*] vi (trovão) to rumble, boom; (ressoar) to resound.

ricaço [xi'kasu] m plutocrat, very rich man.

rícino ['xisinu] m castor-oil plant; **óleo de** ~ castor oil.

rico/a ['xiku/a] adj rich; (PT: lindo) beautiful; (: excelente) splendid ♦ m/f rich man/woman.

ricochetear [xikoʃe'tʃja*] vi to ricochet.

ricota [xi'kɔta] f cream cheese.

ridicularizar [xidʒikulari'za*] vt to ridicule.

ridículo/a [xi'dʒikulu/a] adj ridiculous.

rifa ['xifa] f raffle.

rifão [xi'fãw] (pl **-ões** ou **-ães**) m proverb, saying.

rifar [xi'fa*] vt to raffle; (col: abandonar) to dump.

rififi [xifi'fi] (col) m fight, brawl.

rifle ['xifli] m rifle.

rifões [xi'fõjʃ] mpl de **rifão**.

rigidez [xiʒi'deʒ] f rigidity, stiffness; (austeridade) severity, strictness; (inflexibilidade) inflexibility.

rígido/a [xi'ʒidu/a] adj rigid, stiff; (fig) strict.

rigor [xi'go*] m rigidity; (meticulosidade) rigour (BRIT), rigor (US); (severidade) harshness, severity; (exatidão) precision; **a** ~ strictly speaking; **vestido a** ~ in full evening dress; **ser de** ~ to be essential ou obligatory; **no** ~ **do inverno** in the depths of winter.

rigoroso/a [xigo'rozu/ɔza] adj rigorous, strict; (severo) strict; (exigente) demanding; (minucioso) precise, accurate; (inverno) hard, harsh.

rijo/a ['xiʒu/a] adj tough, hard; (severo) harsh, severe; (músculos, braços) firm.

rim [xĩ] (pl **-ns**) m kidney; **rins** mpl (parte inferior das costas) small sg of the back.

rima ['xima] f rhyme; (poema) verse, poem.

rimar [xi'ma*] vt, vi to rhyme; ~ **com** (condizer) to agree with, tally with.

rímel ['ximew] (®: pl **-eis**) m mascara.

rinçagem [xĩ'saʒẽ] (pl **-ns**) f rinse.

rinçar [xĩ'sa*] vt to rinse.

rinchar [xĩ'ʃa*] vi to neigh, whinny.

rincho ['xĩʃu] m neigh(ing).

ringue ['xĩgi] m ring.

rinha ['xiɲa] f cock-fight.

rinoceronte [xinose'rõtʃi] m rhinoceros.

rinque ['xĩki] *m* rink.
rins [xĩʃ] *mpl de* **rim**.
Rio ['xiu] *m*: **o ~ (de Janeiro)** Rio (de Janeiro).
rio ['xiu] *m* river.
ripa ['xipa] *f* lath, slat.
riqueza [xi'keza] *f* wealth, riches *pl*; (*qualidade*) richness; (*fartura*) abundance; (*fecundidade*) fertility.
rir [xi*] *vi* to laugh; **~ de** to laugh at; **morrer de ~** to laugh one's head off.
risada [xi'zada] *f* (*riso*) laughter; (*gargalhada*) guffaw.
risca ['xiʃka] *f* stroke; (*listra*) stripe; (*no cabelo*) parting; **à ~** to the letter, exactly.
riscar [xiʃ'ka*] *vt* (*papel*) to draw lines on; (*marcar*) to mark; (*apagar*) to cross out; (*desenhar*) to outline; (*fósforo*) to strike; (*expulsar*) *sócios*) to expel, throw out; (*eliminar*) to do away with; (*amigo*) to write off.
risco ['xiʃku] *m* (*marca*) mark, scratch; (*traço*) stroke; (*desenho*) drawing, sketch; (*perigo*) risk; **sob o ~ de** at the risk of; **correr o ~ de** to run the risk of; **correr ~s** to take risks; **pôr em ~** to put at risk, risk.
risível [xi'zivew] (*pl* **-eis**) *adj* laughable, ridiculous.
riso ['xizu] *m* laughter; **não ser motivo de ~** to be no laughing matter.
risonho/a [xi'zoɲu/a] *adj* laughing, smiling; (*contente*) cheerful; **estar muito ~** to be all smiles.
risoto [xi'zotu] *m* risotto.
rispidez [xiʃpi'deʒ] *f* brusqueness; (*aspereza*) harshness.
ríspido/a ['xiʃpidu/a] *adj* brusque; (*áspero*) harsh.
risquei [xiʃ'kej] *etc vb V* **riscar**.
rissole [xi'sɔli] *m* rissole.
riste ['xiʃtʃi] *m*: **em ~** (*dedo*) pointing; (*orelhas*) pointed.
rítmico/a ['xitʃmiku/a] *adj* rhythmic(al).
ritmo ['xitʃmu] *m* rhythm.
rito ['xitu] *m* rite; (*seita*) cult.
ritual [xi'twaw] (*pl* **-ais**) *adj*, *m* ritual.
rival [xi'vaw] (*pl* **-ais**) *adj*, *m/f* rival.
rivalidade [xivali'dadʒi] *f* rivalry.
rivalizar [xivali'za*] *vt* to rival ♦ *vi*: **~ com** to compete with, vie with.
rixa ['xiʃa] *f* quarrel, fight.
RJ *abr* = **Rio de Janeiro**.
RN *abr* = **Rio Grande do Norte**.
RNVA (*BR*) *abr m* = **Registro Nacional de Veículos Automotores**.
RO *abr* = **Rondônia**.
roa ['xoa] *etc vb V* **roer**.
robalo [xo'balu] *m* snook (*type of fish*).
robô [xo'bo] *m* robot.
robustecer [xobuʃte'se*] *vt* to strengthen ♦ *vi* to become stronger; **~-se** *vr* to become stronger.
robustez [xobuʃ'teʒ] *f* strength.
robusto/a [xo'buʃtu/a] *adj* strong, robust.
roça ['xɔsa] *f* plantation; (*no mato*) clearing; (*campo*) country.
roçado [xo'sadu] *m* clearing.
rocambole [xokã'bɔli] *m* roll.
roçar [xo'sa*] *vt* (*terreno*) to clear; (*tocar de leve*) to brush against ♦ *vi*: **~ em** *ou* **por** to brush against.
roceiro [xo'sejru/a] *m/f* (*lavrador*) peasant; (*caipira*) country bumpkin.
rocha ['xɔʃa] *f* rock; (*penedo*) crag.
rochedo [xo'ʃedu] *m* crag, cliff.
rock ['xɔki] *m* = **roque**.
rock-and-roll [-ã'xɔw] *m* rock and roll.
roda ['xɔda] *f* wheel; (*círculo, grupo de pessoas*) circle; (*de saia*) width, fullness; **~ dentada** cog(wheel); **alta ~** high society; **em** *ou* **à ~ de** round, around; **~ de direção** steering wheel; **~ do leme** ship's wheel, helm; **brincar de ~** to play in the round.
rodada [xo'dada] *f* (*de bebidas, ESPORTE*) · round.
roda-d'água (*pl* **rodas-d'água**) *f* water wheel.
rodado/a [xo'dadu/a] *adj* (*saia*) full, wide; **o carro tem 5000 km ~s** the car has 5000 km on the clock.
rodagem [xo'daʒẽ] (*pl* **-ns**) *f* V **estrada**.
roda-gigante (*pl* **rodas-gigantes**) *f* big wheel.
rodamoinho [xodamo'iɲu] *m* (*na água*) whirlpool; (*de vento*) whirlwind; (*no cabelo*) swirl.
Ródano ['xɔdanu] *m*: **o ~** the Rhône.
rodapé [xoda'pɛ] *m* skirting board (*BRIT*), baseboard (*US*); (*de página*) foot.
rodar [xo'da*] *vt* (*fazer girar*) to turn, spin; (*viajar por*) to tour, travel; (*percorrer de carro*) to drive round; (*a pé*) to walk round; (*quilômetros*) to do; (*filme*) to make; (*imprimir*) to print; (*COMPUT: programa*) to run ♦ *vi* (*girar*) to turn round; (*AUTO*) to drive around; (*col: ser reprovado*) to fail; (: *sair*) to make o.s. scarce; (: *ser excluído*) to be ruled out; **~ por** (*a pé*) to wander around; (*de carro*) to drive around.
roda-viva (*pl* **rodas-vivas**) *f* bustle, commotion; **estou numa ~ danada** I'm in a real flap.
rodear [xo'dʒja*] *vt* to go round; (*circundar*) to encircle, surround; (*pessoa*) to surround.
rodeio [xo'deju] *m* (*em discurso*) circumlocution; (*subterfúgio*) subterfuge; (*de gado*) round-up; **fazer ~s** to beat about the bush; **sem ~s** plainly, frankly.
rodela [xo'dɛla] *f* (*pedaço*) slice.
rodízio [xo'dʒizju] *m* rota; **à ~** (*em restaurante*) at discretion; **em ~** on a rota basis.
rodo ['xodu] *m* rake; (*para puxar água*) water

rake; **a ~** in abundance.
rododentro [xodo'détru] *m* rhododendron.
rodoferroviário/a [xodofexo'vjarju/a] *adj* road and rail *atr*.
rodopiar [xodo'pja*] *vi* to whirl around, swirl.
rodopio [xodo'piu] *m* spin.
rodovia [xodo'via] *f* highway, ≈ motorway (*BRIT*), ≈ interstate (*US*).
rodoviária [xodo'vjarja] *f* (*tb: estação ~*) bus station; *V tb* **rodoviário**.
rodoviário/a [xodo'vjarju/a] *adj* road *atr*; (*polícia*) traffic *atr* ♦ *m/f* roadworker.
roedor(a) [xwe'do*(a)] *adj* gnawing ♦ *m* rodent.
roer [xwe*] *vt* to gnaw, nibble; (*enferrujar*) to corrode; (*afligir*) to eat away; **ser duro de ~** to be a hard nut to crack.
rogado [xo'gadu] *adj*: **fazer-se de ~** to play hard to get.
rogar [xo'ga*] *vi* to ask, request; **~ a alguém que faça** to beg sb to do.
rogo ['xogu] *m* request; **a ~ de** at the request of.
rói [xɔj] *vb V* **roer**.
roía [xo'ia] *etc vb V* **roer**.
róis [xɔjʃ] *mpl de* **rol**.
rojão [xo'ʒãw] (*pl -ões*) *m* (*foguete*) rocket; (*fig: ritmo intenso*) hectic pace; **agüentar o ~** (*fig*) to stick it out.
rol [xɔw] (*pl* **róis**) *m* roll, list.
rolagem [xo'laʒẽ] *f* (*de uma dívida*) snowballing.
rolar [xo'la*] *vt* to roll; (*dívida*) to run up ♦ *vi* to roll; (*na cama*) to toss and turn; (*col: vinho etc*) to flow; (: *estender-se*) to roll on.
roldana [xow'dana] *f* pulley.
roleta [xo'leta] *f* roulette; (*borboleta*) turnstile.
roleta-paulista *f*: **fazer uma ~** (*AUTO*) to go through a red light.
roleta-russa *f* Russian roulette.
rolha ['xoʎa] *f* cork; (*fig*) gag (on free speech).
roliço/a [xo'lisu/a] *adj* (*pessoa*) plump, chubby; (*objeto*) round, cylindrical.
rolo ['xolu] *m* (*de papel etc*) roll; (*para nivelar o solo, para pintura*) roller; (*almofada*) bolster; (*para cabelo*) curler; (*col: briga*) brawl, fight; **~ compressor** steamroller; **~ de massa** *ou* **pastel** rolling pin.
Roma ['xoma] *n* Rome.
romã [xo'mã] *f* pomegranate.
romance [xo'mãsi] *m* (*livro*) novel; (*caso amoroso*) romance; (*fig: história*) complicated story; **~ policial** detective story; **fazer um ~ (de algo)** (*exagerar*) to dramatize (sth).
romanceado/a [xomã'sjadu/a] *adj* (*biografia*) in the style of a novel; (*exagerado*) exaggerated, fanciful.
romancear [xomã'sja*] *vt* (*biografia*) to write in the style of a novel; (*exagerar*) to exaggerate, embroider ♦ *vi* (*inventar histórias*) to tell tales.

romancista [xomã'siʃta] *m/f* novelist.
românico/a [xo'maniku/a] *adj* (*LING*) Romance; (*ARQ*) romanesque.
romano/a [xo'manu/a] *adj, m/f* Roman.
romântico/a [xo'mãtʃiku/a] *adj* romantic.
romantismo [xomã'tʃiʒmu] *m* romanticism; (*romance*) romance.
romaria [xoma'ria] *f* (*peregrinação*) pilgrimage; (*festa*) festival.
rombo ['xõbu] *m* (*buraco*) hole; (*MAT*) rhombus; (*fig: desfalque*) embezzlement; (: *prejuízo*) loss, shortfall.
rombudo/a [xõ'budu/a] *adj* very blunt.
romeiro/a [xo'mejru/a] *m/f* pilgrim.
Romênia [xo'menja] *f*: **a ~** Romania.
romeno/a [xo'menu/a] *adj, m/f* Rumanian ♦ *m* (*LING*) Rumanian.
romeu-e-julieta [xo'mewiʒu'ljeta] *m* (*CULIN*) guava jelly with cheese.
rompante [xõ'pãtʃi] *m* outburst.
romper [xõ'pe*] *vt* to break; (*rasgar*) to tear; (*relações*) to break off ♦ *vi* (*sol, manhã*) to break through; **~ com** to break with; **~ de** (*jorrar*) to well up from; **~ em pranto** *ou* **lágrimas** to burst into tears; **~ em soluços** to sob.
rompimento [xõpi'mẽtu] *m* (*ato*) breakage; (*fenda*) break; (*de relações*) breaking off.
roncar [xõ'ka*] *vi* to snore.
ronco ['xõku] *m* snore; (*de motor*) roar; (*de porco*) grunt.
ronda ['xõda] *f* patrol, beat; **fazer a ~** to do the rounds.
rondar [xõ'da*] *vt* to patrol, go the rounds of; (*espreitar*) to prowl, hang around; (*rodear*) to go round ♦ *vi* to prowl about, lurk; (*fazer a ronda*) to patrol, do the rounds; **a inflação ronda os 30% ao mês** inflation is in the region of 30% a month.
rondoniano/a [xõdo'njanu/a] *adj* from Rondônia ♦ *m/f* person from Rondônia.
ronquei [xõ'kej] *etc vb V* **roncar**.
ronqueira [xõ'kejra] *f* wheeze.
ronrom [xõ'xõ] *m* purring.
ronronar [xõxo'na*] *vi* to purr.
roque ['xɔki] *m* (*XADREZ*) rook, castle; (*MÚS*) rock.
roqueiro/a [xo'kejru/a] *m/f* rock musician.
roraimense [xoraj'mẽsi] *adj* from Roraima ♦ *m/f* person from Roraima.
rosa ['xoza] *f* rose ♦ *adj inv* pink; **a vida não é feita de ~s** life is not a bed of roses.
rosado/a [xo'zadu/a] *adj* rosy, pink.
rosa-dos-ventos *f inv* compass.
rosário [xo'zarju] *m* rosary.
rosa-shocking [-'ʃɔkĩ] *adj inv* shocking pink.
rosbife [xoʒ'bifi] *m* roast beef.
rosca ['xoʃka] *f* spiral, coil; (*de parafuso*) thread; (*pão*) ring-shaped loaf.
roseira [xo'zejra] *f* rosebush.
róseo/a ['xɔzju/a] *adj* rosy.
roseta [xo'zeta] *f* rosette.
rosetar [xoze'ta*] *vi* to loaf around.

rosnar [xoʒ'na*] *vi* (*cão*) to growl, snarl; (*murmurar*) to mutter, mumble.

rossio [xo'siu] (*PT*) *m* large square.

rosto ['xoʃtu] *m* (*cara*) face; (*frontispício*) title page.

rota ['xɔta] *f* route, course.

rotação [xota'sãw] (*pl* **-ões**) *f* rotation; **~ de estoques** turnover of stock.

rotativa [xota'tʃiva] *f* rotary printing press.

rotatividade [xotatʃivi'dadʒi] *f* rotation; **hotel de alta ~** hotel renting rooms by the hour, motel.

rotativo/a [xota'tʃivu/a] *adj* rotary.

roteirista [xotej'riʃta] *m/f* scriptwriter.

roteiro [xo'tejru] *m* (*itinerário*) itinerary; (*ordem*) schedule; (*guia*) guidebook; (*de filme*) script; (*de discussão, trabalho escrito*) list of topics; (*fig: norma*) norm.

rotina [xo'tʃina] *f* (*tb: COMPUT*) routine.

rotineiro/a [xotʃi'nejru/a] *adj* routine.

roto/a ['xotu/a] *adj* broken; (*rasgado*) torn; (*maltrapilho*) scruffy; **o ~ rindo do esfarrapado** the pot calling the kettle black.

rótula ['xɔtula] *f* (*ANAT*) kneecap.

rotular [xotu'la*] *vt* (*tb fig*) to label; **~ alguém/algo de** to label sb/sth as.

rótulo ['xɔtulu] *m* label, tag; (*fig*) label.

rotunda [xo'tũda] *f* (*ARQ*) rotunda.

rotundo/a [xo'tũdu/a] *adj* (*redondo*) round; (*gorducho*) rotund.

roubalheira [xoba'ʎejra] *f* (*roubo vultoso*) wholesale robbery; (*do Estado, de empresa*) embezzlement.

roubar [xo'ba*] *vt* to steal; (*loja, casa, pessoa*) to rob ♦ *vi* to steal; (*em jogo, no preço*) to cheat; **~ algo a alguém** to steal sth from sb.

roubo ['xobu] *m* theft, robbery; **$100 é ~** $100 is daylight robbery.

rouco/a ['xoku/a] *adj* hoarse.

round ['xãwdʒi] (*pl* **~s**) *m BOXE*) round.

roupa ['xopa] *f* clothes *pl*, clothing; **~ de baixo** underwear; **~ de cama** bedclothes *pl*, bed linen.

roupagem [xo'paʒẽ] (*pl* **-ns**) *f* clothes *pl*, apparel; (*fig*) appearance.

roupão [xo'pãw] (*pl* **-ões**) *m* dressing gown.

rouquidão [xoki'dãw] *f* hoarseness.

rouxinol [xoʃi'nɔw] (*pl* **-óis**) *m* nightingale.

roxo/a ['xoʃu/a] *adj* purple, violet; **~ por** (*col*) mad about; **~ de saudades** pining away.

royalty ['xɔjawtʃi] (*pl* **-ies**) *m* royalty.

RR *abr* = **Roraima**.

RS *abr* = **Rio Grande do Sul**.

rua ['xua] *f* street ♦ *excl*: **~!** get out!, clear off!; **botar alguém na ~** to put sb out on the street; **ir para a ~** to be out; (*ser despedido*) to get the sack; **viver na ~** to be out all the time; **estar na ~ da amargura** to be going through hell; **~ principal** main street; **~ sem saída** no through road, cul-de-sac.

Ruanda ['xwãda] *f* Rwanda.

rubéola [xu'bɛola] *f* (*MED*) German measles.

rubi [xu'bi] *m* ruby.

rublo ['xublu] *m* r(o)uble.

rubor [xu'bo*] *m* blush; (*fig*) shyness, bashfulness.

ruborizar [xubori'za*] *vt* to make blush; **~-se** *vr* to blush.

rubrica [xu'brika] *f* signed initials *pl*.

rubricar [xubri'ka*] *vt* to initial.

rubro/a ['xubru/a] *adj* ruby-red; (*faces*) rosy, ruddy.

rubro-negro/a *adj* of Flamengo FC.

ruço/a ['xusu/a] *adj* grey (*BRIT*), gray (*US*), dun; (*desbotado*) faded; (*col*) tough, tricky.

rude ['xudʒi] *adj* (*povo*) simple, primitive; (*ignorante*) simple; (*grosseiro*) rude.

rudeza [xu'deza] *f* simplicity; (*grosseria*) rudeness.

rudimentar [xudʒimẽ'ta*] *adj* rudimentary.

rudimento [xudʒi'mẽtu] *m* rudiment; **~s** *mpl* rudiments, first principles.

ruela ['xwɛla] *f* lane, alley.

rufar [xu'fa*] *vt* (*tambor*) to roll ♦ *m* roll.

rufião [xu'fjãw] (*pl* **-ães** *ou* **-ões**) *m* pimp.

ruflar [xuf'la*] *vt, vi* to rustle.

ruga ['xuga] *f* (*na pele*) wrinkle; (*na roupa*) crease.

rúgbi ['xugbi] *m* rugby.

ruge ['xuʒi] *m* rouge.

rugido [xu'ʒidu] *m* roar.

rugir [xu'ʒi*] *vi* to roar, bellow.

ruibarbo [xwi'baxbu] *m* rhubarb.

ruído ['xwidu] *m* noise, din; (*ELET, TEC*) noise.

ruidoso/a [xwi'dozu/ɔza] *adj* noisy.

ruim [xu'ĩ] (*pl* **-ns**) *adj* bad; (*defeituoso*) defective; **achar ~** (*col*) to get upset.

ruína ['xwina] *f* ruin; (*decadência*) downfall; **levar alguém à ~** to ruin sb, be sb's downfall.

ruindade [xwĩ'dadʒi] *f* wickedness, evil; (*ação*) bad thing.

ruins [xu'ĩʃ] *adj pl de* **ruim**.

ruir ['xwi*] *vi* to collapse, go to ruin.

ruivo/a ['xwivu/a] *adj* red-haired ♦ *m/f* redhead.

rujo ['xuju] *etc vb V* **rugir**.

rulê [xu'le] *adj*: **gola ~** roll-neck (collar).

rum [xũ] *m* rum.

rumar [xu'ma*] *vt* (*barco*) to steer ♦ *vi*: **~ para** to head for.

rumba ['xũba] *f* rumba.

ruminação [xumina'sãw] (*pl* **-ões**) *f* rumination.

ruminante [xumi'nãtʃi] *adj, m* ruminant.

ruminar [xumi'na*] *vt* to chew; (*fig*) to ponder ♦ *vi* (*tb fig*) to ruminate.

rumo ['xumu] *m* course, bearing; (*fig*) course; **~ a** bound for; **sem ~** adrift.

NB: *European Portuguese adds the following consonants to certain words:* **b** (sú(b)dito, su(b)til), **c** (a(c)ção, a(c)cionista, a(c)to); **m** (inde(m)ne); **p** (ado(p)ção, ado(p)tar); *for further details see p. xiii.*

rumor [xu'mo*] *m* (*ruído*) noise; (*notícia*) rumour (*BRIT*), rumor (*US*), report.

rumorejar [xumore'ʒa*] *vi* to murmur; (*folhas*) to rustle; (*água*) to ripple.

rupia [xu'pia] *f* rupee.

ruptura [xup'tura] *f* break, rupture.

rural [xu'raw] (*pl* **-ais**) *adj* rural.

rusga ['xuʒga] *f* (*briga*) quarrel, row.

rush [xʌʃ] *m* rush; (**a hora do**) ~ rush hour; **o** ~ **imobiliário** the rush to buy property.

Rússia ['xusja] *f*: **a** ~ Russia.

russo/a ['xusu/a] *adj*, *m/f* Russian ♦ *m* (*LING*) Russian.

rústico/a ['xuʃtʃiku/a] *adj* rustic; (*pessoa*) simple; (*utensílio*, *objeto*) rough; (*casa*) rustic-style; (*lugar*) countrified.

S

S, s ['ɛsi] (*pl* **ss**) *m* S, s; **S de Sandra** S for Sugar.

S. *abr* (= *Santo*; *Santa*; *São*) St.

SA *abr* (= *Sociedade Anônima*) Ltd., Inc. (*US*).

sã [sã] *f de* **são**.

Saara [sa'ara] *m*: **o** ~ the Sahara.

sáb. *abr* (= *sábado*) Sat.

sábado ['sabadu] *m* Saturday; (*dos judeus*) Sabbath; ~ **de aleluia** Easter Saturday; *V tb* **terça-feira**.

sabão [sa'bãw] (*pl* **-ões**) *m* soap; (*descompostura*): **passar um** ~ **em alguém/levar um** ~ to give sb a telling-off/get a telling-off; ~ **de coco** coconut soap; ~ **em pó** soap powder.

sabatina [saba'tʃina] *f* revision test.

sabedor(a) [sabe'do*(a)] *adj* informed.

sabedoria [sabedo'ria] *f* wisdom; (*erudição*) learning.

saber [sa'be*] *vt*, *vi* to know; (*descobrir*) to find out ♦ *m* knowledge; ~ **fazer** to know how to do, be able to do; ~ **de cor (e salteado)** to know off by heart; **ele sabe nadar?** can he swim?; **a** ~ namely; **sei lá** (*col*) I've got no idea, heaven knows; **sei** (*col*: *como resposta*) I see; **você é quem sabe, você que sabe** (*col*) it's up to you; **que eu saiba** as far as I know; **sabe de uma coisa?** (*col*) you know what?

Sabesp [sa'bɛʃpi] *abr m* = **Saneamento Básico do Estado de São Paulo**.

sabiá [sa'bja] *m/f* thrush.

sabichão/chona [sabi'ʃãw/'ʃona] (*pl* **-ões/~s**) *m/f* know-it-all, smart aleck.

sabido/a [sa'bidu/a] *adj* (*versado*) knowledgeable; (*esperto*) shrewd, clever.

sábio/a ['sabju/a] *adj* wise; (*erudito*) learned ♦

m/f wise person; (*erudito*) scholar.

sabões [sa'bõjʃ] *mpl de* **sabão**.

sabonete [sabo'netʃi] *m* toilet soap.

saboneteira [sabone'tejra] *f* soap dish.

sabor [sa'bo*] *m* taste, flavour (*BRIT*), flavor (*US*); **ao** ~ **de** at the mercy of.

saborear [sabo'rja*] *vt* to taste, savour (*BRIT*), savor (*US*); (*fig*) to relish.

saboroso/a [sabo'rozu/ɔza] *adj* tasty, delicious.

sabotador(a) [sabota'do*(a)] *m/f* saboteur.

sabotagem [sabo'taʒẽ] *f* sabotage.

sabotar [sabo'ta*] *vt* to sabotage.

saburrento/a [sabu'xẽtu/a] *adj* (*língua*) furry.

saca ['saka] *f* sack.

sacada [sa'kada] *f* balcony; *V tb* **sacado**.

sacado/a [sa'kadu/a] *m/f* (*COM*) drawee.

sacador(a) [saka'do*(a)] *m/f* (*COM*) drawer.

sacal [sa'kaw] (*col*: *pl* **-ais**) *adj* boring; **ser** ~ to be a pain.

sacana [sa'kana] (*col!*) *adj* (*canalha*) crooked; (*lascivo*) randy.

sacanagem [saka'naʒẽ] (*col*: *pl* **-ns**) *f* (*sujeira*) dirty trick; (*libidinagem*) screwing; **fazer uma** ~ **com alguém** (*sujeira*) to screw sb; **filme de** ~ blue movie.

sacanear [saka'nja*] (*col!*) *vt*: ~ **alguém** (*fazer sujeira*) to screw sb; (*amolar*) to take the piss out of sb (*!*).

sacar [sa'ka*] *vt* to take out, pull out; (*dinheiro*) to withdraw; (*arma*, *cheque*) to draw; (*ESPORTE*) to serve; (*col*: *entender*) to understand ♦ *vi* (*col*: *entender*) to understand; (: *mentir*) to tell fibs; (: *dar palpites*) to talk off the top of one's head; ~ **de um revólver** to pull a gun; ~ **sobre um devedor** to borrow money from sb.

saçaricar [sasari'ka*] *vi* to have fun, fool around.

sacarina [saka'rina] *f* saccharine (*BRIT*), saccharin (*US*).

saca-rolhas *m inv* corkscrew.

sacerdócio [sasex'dɔsju] *m* priesthood.

sacerdote [sasex'dɔtʃi] *m* priest.

sachê [sa'ʃe] *m* sachet.

saci [sa'si] *m* (*in Brazilian folklore*) one-legged black man who ambushes travellers.

saciar [sa'sja*] *vt* (*fome etc*) to satisfy; (*sede*) to quench.

saco ['saku] *m* bag; (*enseada*) inlet; (*col*: *testículos*) balls *pl* (*!*); ~! (*BR*: *col*) damn!; **que** ~! (*BR*: *col*) how boring!; **encher o** ~ **de alguém** (*BR*: *col*) to annoy sb, get on sb's nerves; **estar de** ~ **cheio (de)** to be fed up (with); **haja** ~! give me strength!; **puxar o** ~ **de alguém** (*col*) to suck up to sb; **ser um** ~ (*col*) to be a drag; **ter** ~ (*col*) to have patience; **ter o** ~ **de fazer algo** to be bothered to do sth; ~ **de água quente** hot water bottle; ~ **de café** coffee filter; ~ **de dormir** sleeping bag.

sacode [sa'kɔdʒi] *etc vb V* **sacudir**.

sacola [sa'kɔla] *f* bag.

sacolejar [sakolɛ'ʒa*] *vt*, *vi* to shake.

sacramentar [sakramẽ'ta*] *vt* (*documento etc*) to legalize.

sacramento [sakra'mẽtu] *m* sacrament.

sacrificar [sakrifi'ka*] *vt* to sacrifice; (*consagrar*) to dedicate; (*submeter*) to subject; (*animal*) to have put down; **~-se** *vr* to sacrifice o.s.

sacrifício [sakri'fisju] *m* sacrifice.

sacrilégio [sakri'lɛʒu] *m* sacrilege.

sacrílego/a [sa'krilegu/a] *adj* sacrilegious.

sacristão [sakri'ʃtáw] (*pl* **~s** *ou* **-ões**) *m* sacristan, sexton.

sacristia [sakriʃ'tʃia] *f* sacristy.

sacristões [sakriʃ'tõjʃ] *mpl de* **sacristão**.

sacro/a ['sakru/a] *adj* sacred; (*santo*) holy; (*música*) religious.

sacrossanto/a [sakro'sátu/a] *adj* sacrosanct.

sacudida [saku'dʒida] *f* shake.

sacudidela [sakudʒi'dela] *f* shake, jolt.

sacudido/a [saku'dʒidu/a] *adj* shaken; (*movimento*) rapid, quick; (*robusto*) sturdy.

sacudir [saku'dʒi*] *vt* to shake; **~-se** *vr* to shake.

sádico/a ['sadʒiku/a] *adj* sadistic ♦ *m/f* sadist.

sadio/a [sa'dʒiu/a] *adj* healthy.

sadismo [sa'dʒiʒmu] *m* sadism.

sadomasoquista [sadomazo'kiʃta] *adj* sadomasochistic ♦ *m/f* sadomasochist.

safadeza [safa'deza] *f* (*vileza*) meanness; (*imoralidade*) crudity; (*travessura*) mischief.

safado/a [sa'fadu/a] *adj* (*descarado*) shameless, barefaced; (*imoral*) dirty; (*travesso*) mischievous ♦ *m* rogue; (*imoral*) coarse person; **estar/ficar ~ (da vida) com** to be/get furious with.

safanão [safa'náw] (*pl* **-ões**) *m* (*puxão*) tug; (*tapa*) slap.

safári [sa'fari] *m* safari.

safira [sa'fira] *f* sapphire.

safo/a ['safu/a] *adj* (*livre*) clear; (*col: esperto*) quick, clever.

safra ['safra] *f* harvest; (*fig: de músicos etc*) crop.

saga ['saga] *f* saga.

sagacidade [sagasi'dadʒi] *f* sagacity, shrewdness.

sagaz [sa'gajʒ] *adj* sagacious, shrewd.

sagitariano/a [saʒita'rjanu/a] *adj*, *m/f* Sagittarian.

Sagitário [saʒi'tarju] *m* Sagittarius.

sagrado/a [sa'gradu/a] *adj* sacred, holy.

saguão [sa'gwáw] (*pl* **-ões**) *m* (*pátio*) yard, patio; (*entrada*) foyer, lobby; (*de estação*) entrance hall.

saia ['saja] *f* skirt; (*col: mulher*) woman; **viver agarrado às ~s de alguém** (*fig*) to be tied to sb's apron strings; **~ escocesa** kilt.

saibro ['sajbru] *m* gravel.

saia-calça (*pl* **saias-calças**) *f* culottes *pl*.

saiba ['sajba] *etc vb* V **saber**.

saída [sa'ida] *f* (*porta*) exit, way out; (*partida*) departure; (*ato: de pessoa*) going out; (*fig: solução*) way out; (*COMPUT: de programa*) exit; (: *de dados*) output; **de ~** (*primeiro*) first; (*de cara*) straight away; **estar de ~** to be on one's way out; **na ~ do cinema** on the way out of the cinema; **(não) ter boa ~** (*produto*) (not) to sell well; **uma mercadoria de muita ~** a commodity which sells well; **dar uma ~** to go out; **ter boas ~s** (*réplicas*) to be witty; **não tem ~** (*fig*) there is no escaping it; **~ de emergência** emergency exit.

saideira [saj'dejra] *f* last drink.

saidinha [saj'dʒinha] *f*: **dar uma ~** to pop out.

saiote [sa'jɔtʃi] *m* short skirt.

sair [sa'i*] *vi* to go (*ou* come) out; (*partir*) to leave; (*realizar-se*) to turn out; (*COMPUT*) to exit; **~-se** *vr*: **~-se bem/mal de** to be successful/unsuccessful in; **~-se com** (*dito*) to come out with; **~ caro/barato** to work out expensive/cheap; **~ ganhando/perdendo** to come out better/worse off; **~ a alguém** (*parecer-se*) to take after sb; **~ de** (*casa etc*) to leave; (*situação difícil*) to get out of; (*doença*) to come out of; **a notícia saiu na TV/no jornal** the news was on TV/in the paper.

sal [saw] (*pl* **sais**) *m* salt; **sem ~** (*comida*) salt-free; (*pessoa*) lacklustre (*BRIT*), lackluster (*US*); **~ de banho** bath salts *pl*; **~ de cozinha** cooking salt.

sala ['sala] *f* room; (*num edifício público*) hall; (*classe, turma*) class; **fazer ~ a alguém** to entertain sb; **~ de audiências** (*JUR*) courtroom; **~ (de aula)** classroom; **~ de conferências** conference room; **~ de embarque** departure lounge; **~ de espera** waiting room; **~ de espetáculo** concert hall; **~ (de estar)** living room, lounge; **~ de jantar** dining room; **~ de operação** (*MED*) operating theatre (*BRIT*) *ou* theater (*US*); **~ de parto** delivery room.

salada [sa'lada] *f* salad; (*fig*) confusion, jumble; **~ de frutas** fruit salad; **~ russa** (*CULIN*) Russian salad; (*fig*) hotchpotch.

saladeira [sala'dejra] *f* salad bowl.

sala-e-quarto *m* two-room flat *ou* apartment.

salafra [sa'lafra] (*col*) *m/f* rat.

salafrário [sala'frarju] (*col*) *m* crook.

salame [sa'lami] *m* (*CULIN*) salami.

salaminho [sala'miɲu] *m* pepperoni (sausage).

salão [sa'láw] (*pl* **-ões**) *m* large room, hall; (*exposição*) show; (*cabeleireiro*) hairdressing salon; **de ~** (*jogos*) indoor; (*anedota*) proper, acceptable; **~ de baile** dance studio; **~ de beleza** beauty salon.

salarial [sala'rjaw] (*pl* **-ais**) *adj* wage *atr*, pay *atr*.

NB: European Portuguese adds the following consonants to certain words: **b** (sú(b)dito, su(b)til); **c** (a(c)ção, a(c)cionista, a(c)to); **m** (inde(m)ne); **p** (ado(p)ção, ado(p)tar); *for further details see p. xiii.*

salário [sa'larju] *m* wages *pl*, salary; ~ **mínimo** minimum wage.

salário-família (*pl* **salários-família**) *m* family allowance.

saldar [saw'da*] *vt* (*contas*) to settle; (*dívida*) to pay off.

saldo ['sawdu] *m* balance; (*sobra*) surplus; (*fig*: *resultado*) result; ~ **anterior/credor/devedor** opening balance/credit balance/debit balance.

saleiro [sa'lejru] *m* salt cellar; (*moedor*) salt mill.

salgadinho [sawga'dʒiɲu] *m* savoury (*BRIT*), savory (*US*), snack.

salgado/a [saw'gadu/a] *adj* salty, salted; (*preço*) exorbitant.

salgar [saw'ga*] *vt* to salt.

salgueiro [saw'gejru] *m* willow; ~ **chorão** weeping willow.

saliência [sa'ljẽsja] *f* projection; (*assanhamento*) forwardness.

salientar [saljẽ'ta*] *vt* to point out; (*acentuar*) to stress, emphasise; ~-**se** *vr* (*pessoa*) to distinguish o.s.

saliente [sa'ljẽtʃi] *adj* jutting out, prominent; (*evidente*) clear, conspicuous; (*importante*) outstanding; (*assanhado*) forward.

salina [sa'lina] *f* salt bed; (*empresa*) salt company.

salino/a [sa'linu/a] *adj* saline.

salitre [sa'litri] *m* saltpetre (*BRIT*), saltpeter (*US*), nitre (*BRIT*), niter (*US*).

saliva [sa'liva] *f* saliva; **gastar** ~ (*col*) to waste one's breath.

salivar [sali'va*] *vi* to salivate.

salmão [saw'mãw] (*pl* -**ões**) *m* salmon ♦ *adj inv* salmon-pink.

salmo ['sawmu] *m* psalm.

salmões [saw'mõjʃ] *mpl de* **salmão**.

salmonela [sawmo'nɛla] *f* salmonella.

salmoura [saw'mora] *f* brine.

salobro/a [sa'lobru/a] *adj* salty, brackish.

salões [sa'lõjʃ] *mpl de* **salão**.

saloio [sa'lɔju] (*PT*) *m* (*camponês*) country bumpkin.

Salomão [salo'mãw]: (**as) ilhas** *fpl* **de** ~ (the) Solomon Islands.

salpicão [sawpi'kãw] (*pl* -**ões**) *m* (*paio*) pork sausage; (*prato*) fricassee.

salpicar [sawpi'ka*] *vt* to splash; (*polvilhar*, *fig*) to sprinkle.

salpicões [sawpi'kõjʃ] *mpl de* **salpicão**.

salsa ['sawsa] *f* parsley.

salsicha [saw'siʃa] *f* sausage.

salsichão [sawsi'ʃãw] (*pl* -**ões**) *m* sausage.

saltado/a [saw'tadu/a] *adj* (*saliente*) protruding.

saltar [saw'ta*] *vt* to jump (over), leap (over); (*omitir*) to skip ♦ *vi* to jump, leap; (*sangue*) to spurt out; (*de ônibus*, *cavalo*): ~ **de** to get off; ~ **à vista** *ou* **aos olhos** to be obvious.

salteado/a [saw'tʃjadu/a] *adj* broken up; (*CULIN*) sautéed.

salteador [sawtʃja'do*] *m* highwayman.

saltear [saw'tʃja*] *vt* (*trechos de um livro*) to skip; (*CULIN*) to sauté.

saltimbanco [sawtʃĩ'bãku] *m* travelling (*BRIT*) *ou* traveling (*US*) player.

saltitante [sawtʃi'tãtʃi] *adj*: ~ **de alegria** as pleased as punch.

saltitar [sawtʃi'ta*] *vi* (*pássaros*) to hop; (*fig*: *de um assunto a outro*) to skip.

salto ['sawtu] *m* jump, leap; (*de calçado*) heel; **dar um** ~ to jump, leap; **dar** ~**s de alegria** *ou* **de contente** to jump for joy; ~ **de vara** pole vault; ~ **em altura** high jump; ~ **em distância** long jump.

salto-mortal (*pl* **saltos-mortais**) *m* somersault.

salubre [sa'lubri] *adj* healthy, salubrious.

salutar [salu'ta*] *adj* salutary, beneficial.

salva ['sawva] *f* salvo; (*bandeja*) tray, salver; (*BOT*) sage; ~ **de palmas** round of applause; ~ **de tiros** round of gunfire.

salvação [sawva'sãw] *f* salvation; ~ **da pátria** *ou* **da lavoura** (*col*) lifesaver.

salvador [sawva'do*] *m* saviour (*BRIT*), savior (*US*).

salvados [saw'vaduʃ] *mpl* salvage *sg*; (*COM*) salvaged goods.

salvaguarda [sawva'gwaxda] *f* protection, safeguard.

salvaguardar [sawvagwax'da*] *vt* to safeguard.

salvamento [sawva'mẽtu] *m* rescue; (*de naufrágio*) salvage.

salvar [saw'va*] *vt* (*tb*: *COMPUT*) to save; (*resgatar*) to rescue; (*objetos*, *de ruína*) to salvage; (*honra*) to defend; ~-**se** *vr* to escape.

salva-vidas *m inv* (*bóia*) lifebuoy; (*pessoa*) lifeguard; **barco** ~ lifeboat.

salve ['sawvi] *excl* hooray (for)!

salvo/a ['sawvu/a] *adj* safe ♦ *prep* except, save; **a** ~ in safety; **pôr-se a** ~ to run to safety; **todos** ~ **ele** all except him.

salvo-conduto (*pl* ~**s** *ou* **salvos-condutos**) *m* safe-conduct.

samambaia [samã'baja] *f* fern.

samaritano [samari'tanu] *m*: **bom** ~ good Samaritan; (*pej*) do-gooder.

samba ['sãba] *m* samba; **cueca** ~ boxer shorts *pl*.

samba-canção (*pl* **sambas-canção**) *m* slow samba.

sambar [sã'ba*] *vi* to dance the samba.

sambista [sã'biʃta] *m/f* (*dançarino*) samba dancer; (*compositor*) samba composer.

sambódromo [sã'bɔdromu] *m* carnival parade ground.

Samoa [sa'moa] *m*: ~ **Ocidental** Western Samoa.

samovar [samo'va*] *m* tea urn.

sanar [sa'na*] *vt* to cure; (*remediar*) to remedy.

sanatório [sana'tɔrju] *m* sanatorium (*BRIT*),

sanitorium (US).
sanável [sa'navew] (pl -eis) adj curable; (remediável) remediable.
sanca ['sāka] f cornice, moulding (BRIT), molding (US).
sanção [sā'sāw] (pl -ões) f sanction.
sancionar [sansjo'na*] vt to sanction; (autorizar) to authorize.
sanções [sā'sōjʃ] fpl de sanção.
sândalo ['sādalu] m sandalwood.
sandália [sā'dalja] f sandal.
sandes ['sādəʃ] (PT) f inv sandwich.
sanduíche [sand'wiʃi] (BR) m sandwich; ~ **americano** ham and egg sandwich; ~ **misto** ham and cheese sandwich; ~ **natural** wholemeal sandwich.
saneamento [sanja'mētu] m sanitation; (de governo etc) clean-up.
sanear [sa'nja*] vt to clean up; (pântanos) to drain.
sanfona [sā'fɔna] f (MÚS) accordion; (TRICÔ) ribbing.
sanfonado/a [sāfo'nadu/a] adj (porta) folding; (suéter) ribbed.
sangrar [sā'gra*] vt, vi to bleed; ~ **alguém** (fig) to bleed sb dry.
sangrento/a [sā'grẽtu/a] adj bloody; (ensanguentado) bloodstained; (CULIN: carne) rare.
sangria [sā'gria] f bloodshed; (extorsão) extortion; (bebida) sangria.
sangue ['sāgi] m blood; ~ **pisado** bruise.
sangue-frio m cold-bloodedness.
sanguessuga [sāgi'suga] f leech.
sanguinário/a [sāgi'narju/a] adj bloodthirsty, cruel.
sanguíneo/a [sā'ginju/a] adj blood atr; **vaso** ~ blood vessel.
sanha ['saɲa] f rage, fury.
sanidade [sani'dadʒi] f (saúde) healthiness; (mental) sanity.
sanita [sa'nita] (PT) f toilet, lavatory.
sanitário/a [sani'tarju/a] adj sanitary; **vaso** ~ toilet, lavatory (bowl).
sanitários [sani'tarjuʃ] mpl toilets.
sanitarista [sanita'riʃta] m/f health worker.
Santiago [sā'tʃjagu] n: ~ **(do Chile)** Santiago (de Chile).
santidade [sātʃi'dadʒi] f holiness, sanctity; **Sua S~** His Holiness (the Pope).
santificar [sātʃifi'ka*] vt to sanctify, make holy.
santinho [sā'tʃiɲu] m (imagem) holy picture; (col: pessoa) saint.
santista [sā'tʃiʃta] adj from Santos ♦ m/f person from Santos.
santo/a ['sātu/a] adj holy, sacred; (pessoa) saintly; (remédio) effective ♦ m/f saint; **todo** ~ **dia** every single day; **ter** ~ **forte** (col) to have good backing.

santuário [sā'twarju] m shrine, sanctuary.
São [sāw] m Saint.
são/sã [sāw/sā] (pl ~s/~s) adj healthy; (conselho) sound; (atitude) wholesome; (mentalmente) sane; ~ **e salvo** safe and sound.
São Lourenço [-lo'rẽsu] m: **o (rio)** ~ the St. Lawrence river.
São Marinho m San Marino.
São Paulo [-'pawlu] n São Paulo.
são-tomense [-to'mẽsi] adj from São Tomé e Príncipe ♦ m/f native ou inhabitant of São Tomé e Príncipe.
sapata [sa'pata] m (do freio) shoe.
sapatão [sapa'tāw] (pl -ões) m big shoe; (col: lésbica) lesbian.
sapataria [sapata'ria] f shoe shop.
sapateado [sapa'tʃjadu] m tap dancing.
sapateador(a) [sapatʃja'do*(a)] m/f tap dancer.
sapatear [sapa'tʃja*] vi to tap one's feet; (dançar) to tap-dance.
sapateiro [sapa'tejru] m shoemaker; (vendedor) shoe salesman; (que conserta) shoe repairer; (loja) shoe repairer's.
sapatilha [sapa'tʃiʎa] f (de balé) shoe; (sapato) pump; (de atleta) running shoe.
sapato [sa'patu] m shoe.
sapatões [sapa'tōjʃ] mpl de sapatão.
sapé [sa'pɛ] m = **sapê**.
sapê [sa'pɛ] m thatch; **teto de** ~ thatched roof.
sapeca [sa'pɛka] adj flirtatious; (criança) cheeky.
sapecar [sapɛ'ka*] vt (tapa, pontapé) to land ♦ vi (flertar) to flirt.
sapiência [sa'pjēsja] f wisdom, learning.
sapiente [sa'pjẽtʃi] adj wise.
sapinho [sa'piɲu] m (MED) thrush.
sapo ['sapu] m toad; **engolir** ~**s** (fig) to sit back and take it.
saque ['saki] etc vb V **sacar** ♦ m (de dinheiro) withdrawal; (COM) draft, bill; (ESPORTE) serve; (pilhagem) plunder, pillage; (col: mentira) fib; ~ **a descoberto** (COM) overdraft.
saquear [sa'kja*] vt to pillage, plunder.
saracotear [sarako'tʃja*] vi to wiggle one's hips; (vaguear) to wander around ♦ vt to shake.
Saragoça [sara'gɔsa] n Zaragoza.
saraiva [sa'rajva] f hail.
saraivada [sarai'vada] f hailstorm; **uma** ~ **de** (fig) a hail of.
saraivar [sarai'va*] vi to hail; (fig) to spray.
sarampo [sa'rāpu] m measles sg.
sarapintado/a [sarapĩ'tadu/a] adj spotted, speckled.
sarar [sa'ra*] vt to cure; (ferida) to heal ♦ vi to recover, be cured.
sarau [sa'raw] m soirée.

NB: *European Portuguese adds the following consonants to certain words:* **b** (sú(b)dito, su(b)til); **c** (a(c)ção, a(c)cionista, a(c)to); **m** (inde(m)ne); **p** (ado(p)ção, ado(p)tar); *for further details see p. xiii.*

sarcasmo [sax'kaʒmu] *m* sarcasm.
sarcástico/a [sax'kaʃtʃiku/a] *adj* sarcastic.
sarda ['saxda] *f* freckle.
Sardenha [sax'deɲa] *f:* **a** ~ Sardinia.
sardento/a [sax'dẽtu/a] *adj* freckled, freckly.
sardinha [sax'dʒiɲa] *f* sardine; **como** ~ **em lata** (*apertado*) like sardines.
sardônico/a [sax'doniku/a] *adj* sardonic, sarcastic.
sargento [sax'ʒẽtu] *m* sergeant.
sári ['sari] *m* sari.
sarjeta [sax'ʒeta] *f* gutter.
sarna ['saxna] *f* scabies *sg*.
sarrafo [sa'xafu] *m*: **baixar o** ~ **em alguém** (*col*) to let sb have it.
sarro ['saxu] *m* (*de vinho, nos dentes*) tartar; (*na língua*) fur, coating; (*col*) laugh; **tirar um** ~ (*col*) to pet, neck.
Satã [sa'tã] *m* Satan, the Devil.
Satanás [sata'naʃ] *m* Satan, the Devil.
satânico/a [sa'taniku/a] *adj* satanic; (*fig*) devilish.
satélite [sa'tɛlitʃi] *adj* satellite *atr* ♦ *m* satellite.
sátira ['satʃira] *f* satire.
satírico/a [sa'tʃiriku/a] *adj* satirical.
satirizar [satʃiri'za*] *vt* to satirize.
satisfação [satʃiʃfa'sãw] (*pl* **-ões**) *f* satisfaction; (*recompensa*) reparation; **dar uma** ~ **a alguém** to give sb an explanation; **ela não dá satisfações a ninguém** she answers to no-one; **tomar satisfações de alguém** to ask sb for an explanation.
satisfaço [satʃiʃ'fasu] *etc vb* V **satisfazer**.
satisfações [satʃiʃfa'sõjʃ] *fpl* de **satisfação**.
satisfatório/a [satʃiʃfa'tɔrju/a] *adj* satisfactory.
satisfazer [satʃiʃfa'ze*] (*irreg: como* **fazer**) *vt* to satisfy; (*dívida*) to pay off ♦ *vi* (*ser satisfatório*) to be satisfactory; **~-se** *vr* to be satisfied; (*saciar-se*) to fill o.s. up; **~ a** to satisfy; **~ com** to fulfil (*BRIT*), fulfill (*US*).
satisfeito/a [satʃiʃ'fejtu/a] *pp* de **satisfazer** ♦ *adj* satisfied; (*alegre*) content; (*saciado*) full; **dar-se por** ~ **com algo** to be content with sth; **dar alguém por** ~ to make sb happy.
satisfez [satʃiʃ'feʒ] *vb* V **satisfazer**.
satisfiz [satʃiʃ'fiʒ] *etc vb* V **satisfazer**.
saturado/a [satu'radu/a] *adj* (*de comida*) full; (*aborrecido*) fed up; (*COM: mercado*) saturated.
saturar [satu'ra*] *vt* to saturate; (*de comida, aborrecimento*) to fill.
Saturno [sa'tuxnu] *m* Saturn.
saudação [sawda'sãw] (*pl* **-ões**) *f* greeting.
saudade [saw'dadʒi] *f* (*desejo ardente*) longing, yearning; (*lembrança nostálgica*) nostalgia; **deixar** ~s to be greatly missed; **matar as** ~s **de alguém/algo** to catch up with sb/cure one's nostalgia for sth; **ter** ~s **de** (*desejar*) to long for; (*sentir falta de*) to miss; ~s **(de casa** *ou* **da família** *ou* **da pátria)** homesickness *sg*.

saudar [saw'da*] *vt* (*cumprimentar*) to greet; (*dar as boas vindas*) to welcome; (*aclamar*) to acclaim.
saudável [saw'davew] (*pl* **-eis**) *adj* healthy; (*moralmente*) wholesome.
saúde [sa'udʒi] *f* health; (*brinde*) toast; ~! (*brindando*) cheers!; (*quando se espirra*) bless you!; **à sua** ~! your health!; **beber à** ~ **de** to drink to, toast; **estar bem/mal de** ~ to be well/ill; **não ter mais** ~ **para fazer** not to be up to doing; **vender** ~ to be bursting with health; ~ **pública** public health; (*órgão*) health service.
saudosismo [sawdo'ziʒmu] *m* nostalgia.
saudoso/a [saw'dozu/oza] *adj* (*nostálgico*) nostalgic; (*da família ou terra natal*) homesick; (*de uma pessoa*) longing; (*que causa saudades*) much-missed.
sauna ['sawna] *f* sauna; **fazer** ~ to have *ou* take a sauna.
saveiro [sa'vejru] *m* sailing boat.
saxofone [sakso'fɔni] *m* saxophone.
saxofonista [saksofo'niʃta] *m/f* saxophonist.
sazonado/a [sazo'nadu/a] *adj* ripe, mature.
sazonal [sazo'naw] (*pl* **-ais**) *adj* seasonal.
SBPC *abr f* = **Sociedade Brasileira para o Progresso da Ciência**.
SBT *abr m* (= *Sistema Brasileiro de Televisão*) television station.
SC *abr* = **Santa Catarina**.
SCDF (*BR*) *abr f* = **Sagrada Congregação para a Doutrina da Fé**.
SE *abr* = **Sergipe**.
se [si] *conj* if; (*em pergunta indireta*) whether ♦ *pron* oneself; (*m*) himself; (*f*) herself; (*coisa*) itself; (*você*) yourself; (*vocês*) yourselves; (*eles/elas*) themselves; (*reciprocamente*) each other; ~ **bem que** even though; **come-~ bem aqui** you can eat well here; **diz-~ que** ... it is said that ...; **sabe-~ que** ... it is known that ...; **vende(m)-~ jornais naquela loja** they sell newspapers in that shop.
sé [sɛ] *f* cathedral; **Santa S**~ Holy See.
sê [se] *vb* V **ser**.
Seade [se'adʒi] (*BR*) *abr m* = **Sistema Estadual de Análise de Dados**.
seara ['sjara] *f* (*campo de cereais*) wheat (*ou* corn) field; (*campo cultivado*) tilled field.
sebe ['sɛbi] (*PT*) *f* fence; ~ **viva** hedge.
sebento/a [se'bẽtu/a] *adj* greasy; (*sujo*) dirty, filthy.
sebo ['sebu] *m* fat, tallow; (*livraria*) second-hand bookshop.
seborréia [sebo'xɛja] *f* seborrhoea (*BRIT*), seborrhea (*US*).
seboso/a [se'bozu/ɔza] *adj* greasy; (*sujo*) dirty; (*col*) stuck-up.
seca ['sɛka] *f* (*estiagem*) drought.
secador [seka'do*] *m* drier; ~ **de cabelo/roupa** hairdrier/clothes drier.
secagem [se'kaʒẽ] *f* drying.
seção [se'sãw] (*pl* **-ões**) *f* section; (*em loja, re-*

partição) department; ~ **rítmica** rhythm section.

secar [se'ka*] *vt* to dry; *(planta)* to parch; *(rio)* to dry up ♦ *vi* to dry; *(plantas)* to wither; *(fonte)* to dry up.

secarrão/rrona [seka'xãw/'xɔna] *(pl -ões/~s) m/f* cold fish.

secção [sek'sãw] *(PT) f* = **seção.**

seccionar [seksjo'na*] *vt* to split up.

secessão [sese'sãw] *(pl -ões) f* secession.

seco/a ['seku/a] *adj* dry; *(árido)* arid; *(fruta, carne)* dried; *(ríspido)* curt, brusque; *(pancada, ruído)* dull; *(magro)* thin; *(pessoa: frio)* cold; (: *sério)* serious; **em** ~ *(barco)* aground; **estar** ~ **por algo/para fazer** *(col)* to be dying for sth/to do.

seções [se'sõjʃ] *fpl de* **seção.**

secreção [sekre'sãw] *(pl -ões) f* secretion.

secretaria [sekreta'ria] *f (local)* general office, secretary's office; *(ministério)* ministry.

secretária [sekre'tarja] *f (mesa)* writing desk; ~ **eletrônica** (telephone) answering machine; *V tb* **secretário.**

secretariar [sekreta'rja*] *vt* to work as a secretary to ♦ *vi* to work as a secretary.

secretário/a [sekre'tarju/a] *m/f* secretary; ~ **particular** private secretary; **S~ de Estado** Secretary of State.

secretário/a-geral *(pl* **secretários/as-gerais)** *m/f* secretary-general.

secreto/a [se'krɛtu/a] *adj* secret.

sectário/a [sek'tarju/a] *adj* sectarian ♦ *m/f* follower.

sectarismo [sekta'riʒmu] *m* sectarianism.

sector [sek'to*] *(PT) m* = **setor.**

secular [seku'la*] *adj (leigo)* secular, lay; *(muito antigo)* age-old.

secularizar [sekulari'za*] *vt* to secularize.

século ['sɛkulu] *m (cem anos)* century; *(época)* age; **há** ~**s** *(fig)* for ages; (: *atrás)* ages ago.

secundar [sekũ'da*] *vt (apoiar)* to support, back up; *(ajudar)* to help; *(pedido)* to follow up.

secundário/a [sekũ'darju/a] *adj* secondary.

secura [se'kura] *f* dryness; *(fig)* coldness; *(col: desejo)* keenness.

seda ['seda] *f* silk; **ser** *ou* **estar uma** ~ to be nice; **bicho da** ~ silkworm.

sedã [se'dã] *m (AUTO)* saloon (car) *(BRIT)*, sedan *(US)*.

sedativo/a [seda'tʃivu/a] *adj* sedative ♦ *m* sedative.

SEDE *(BR) abr m* = **Sistema Estadual de Empregos.**

sede¹ ['sɛdʒi] *f (de empresa, instituição)* headquarters *sg*; *(de governo)* seat; *(REL)* see, diocese; ~ **social** head office.

sede² ['sedʒi] *f* thirst; *(fig)*: ~ **(de)** craving (for); **estar com** *ou* **ter** ~ to be thirsty; **ma-**

tar a ~ to quench one's thirst.

sedentário/a [sedẽ'tarju/a] *adj* sedentary.

sedento/a [se'dẽtu/a] *adj* thirsty; *(fig)*: ~ **(de)** eager (for).

sediar [se'dʒja*] *vt* to base.

sedição [sedʒi'sãw] *f* sedition.

sedicioso/a [sedʒi'sjozu/ɔza] *adj* seditious.

sedimentar [sedʒimẽ'ta*] *vi* to silt up.

sedimento [sedʒi'mẽtu] *m* sediment.

sedoso/a [se'dozu/ɔza] *adj* silky.

sedução [sedu'sãw] *(pl -ões) f* seduction; *(atração)* allure, charm.

sedutor(a) [sedu'to*(a)] *adj* seductive; *(oferta etc)* tempting ♦ *m/f* seducer.

seduzir [sedu'zi*] *vt* to seduce; *(fascinar)* to fascinate; *(desencaminhar)* to lead astray.

Sefiti [sefi'tʃi] *(BR) abr m* = **Serviço de Fiscalização de Trânsito Interestadual e Internacional.**

seg. *abr (= segunda-feira)* Mon.

segmentar [segmẽ'ta*] *vt* to segment.

segmento [seg'mẽtu] *m* segment.

segredar [segre'da*] *vt, vi* to whisper.

segredo [se'gredu] *m* secret; *(sigilo)* secrecy; *(de fechadura)* combination; **em** ~ in secret; ~ **de estado** state secret.

segregação [segrega'sãw] *f* segregation.

segregar [segre'ga*] *vt* to segregate, separate.

seguidamente [segida'mẽtʃi] *adv (sem parar)* continuously; *(logo depois)* soon afterwards.

seguido/a [se'gidu/a] *adj* following; *(contínuo)* continuous, consecutive; ~ **de** *ou* **por** followed by; **três dias** ~**s** three days running; **horas seguidas** for hours on end; **em seguida** next; *(logo depois)* soon afterwards; *(imediatamente)* immediately, right away.

seguidor(a) [segi'do*(a)] *m/f* follower.

seguimento [segi'mẽtu] *m* continuation; **dar** ~ **a** to proceed with; **em** ~ **de** after.

seguinte [se'gĩtʃi] *adj* following, next; **(o negócio)** **é o** ~ *(col)* the thing is; **eu lhe disse o** ~ this is what I said to him; **pelo** ~ hereby.

seguir [se'gi*] *vt* to follow; *(continuar)* to continue ♦ *vi* to follow; *(continuar)* to continue, carry on; *(ir)* to go; ~**-se** *vr*: ~**-se (a)** to follow; **logo a** ~ next; ~**-se (de)** to result (from); **ao jantar seguiu-se uma reunião** the dinner was followed by a meeting.

segunda [se'gũda] *f (tb:* ~**-feira)** Monday; *(MÚS)* second; *(AUTO)* second (gear); **de** ~ second-rate.

segunda-feira *(pl* **segundas-feiras)** *f* Monday; *V tb* **terça-feira.**

segundanista [segũda'niʃta] *m/f* second year.

segundo/a [se'gũdu/a] *adj* second ♦ *prep* according to ♦ *conj* as, from what ♦ *adv* secondly ♦ *m* second; **de segunda mão** second-hand; **de segunda (classe)** second-class; ~ **ele disse** according to what he said; ~ **dizem** apparently; ~ **me consta** as far as I know; ~ **se afirma** according to what is said, from what is said; **segundas intenções** ulterior motives; ~ **tempo** (*FUTEBOL*) second half; *V tb* **quinto**.

segundo-time *adj inv* (*pessoa*) second-rate.

segurado/a [segu'radu/a] *adj*, *m/f* (*COM*) insured.

segurador(a) [segura'do*(a)] *m/f* insurer ♦ *f* insurance company.

seguramente [segura'mētʃi] *adv* (*com certeza*) certainly; (*muito provavelmente*) surely.

segurança [segu'rāsa] *f* security; (*ausência de perigo*) safety; (*confiança*) confidence; (*convicção*) assurance ♦ *m/f* security guard; **com** ~ assuredly; ~ **nacional** national security.

segurar [segu'ra*] *vt* to hold; (*amparar*) to hold up; (*COM: bens*) to insure ♦ *vi:* ~ **em** to hold; ~**-se** *vr* (*COM: fazer seguro*) to insure o.s.; ~**-se em** to hold on to.

seguro/a [se'guru/a] *adj* (*livre de perigo*) safe; (*livre de risco, firme*) secure; (*certo*) certain, assured; (*confiável*) reliable; (*de si mesmo*) secure, confident; (*tempo*) settled ♦ *adv* confidently ♦ *m* (*COM*) insurance; ~ **de si** self-assured; ~ **morreu de velho** better safe than sorry; **estar** ~ **de/de que** to be sure of/that; **fazer** ~ to take out an insurance policy; **companhia de** ~**s** insurance company; ~ **contra acidentes/incêndio** accident/fire insurance; ~ **de vida/automóvel** life/car insurance.

seguro-saúde (*pl* **seguros-saúde**) *m* health insurance.

SEI (*BR*) *abr f* = **Secretaria Especial da Informática**.

sei [sej] *vb V* **saber**.

seio ['seju] *m* breast, bosom; (*âmago*) heart; (~ *paranasal*) sinus; **no** ~ **de** in the heart of.

seis [sejʃ] *num* six; *V tb* **cinco**.

seiscentos/as [sejʃ'sētuʃ/aʃ] *num* six hundred.

seita ['sejta] *f* sect.

seiva ['sejva] *f* sap; (*fig*) vigour (*BRIT*), vigor (*US*), vitality.

seixo ['sejʃu] *m* pebble.

seja ['seʒa] *etc vb V* **ser**.

SELA *abr m* = **Sistema Econômico Latino-Americano**.

sela ['sɛla] *f* saddle.

selagem [se'laʒē] *f* (*de cartas*) franking; **máquina de** ~ franking machine.

selar [se'la*] *vt* (*carta*) to stamp; (*documento oficial, pacto*) to seal; (*cavalo*) to saddle; (*fechar*) to shut, seal; (*concluir*) to conclude.

seleção [sele'sāw] (*PT:* **-cç-**: *pl* **-ões**) *f* selection; (*ESPORTE*) team.

selecionado [selesjo'nadu] (*PT:* **-cc-**) *m* (*ESPORTE*) team.

selecionador(a) [selesjona'do*(a)] (*PT:* **-cc-**) *m/f* selector.

selecionar [selesjo'na*] (*PT:* **-cc-**) *vt* to select.

seleções [sele'sōjʃ] *fpl de* **seleção**.

seleta [se'lɛta] (*PT:* **-ct-**) *f* anthology.

seletivo/a [sele'tʃivu/a] (*PT:* **-ct-**) *adj* selective.

seleto/a [se'lɛtu/a] (*PT:* **-ct-**) *adj* select.

selim [se'lī] (*pl* **-ns**) *m* saddle.

selo ['selu] *m* stamp; (*carimbo, sinete*) seal; (*fig*) stamp, mark.

selva ['sɛwva] *f* (*tb fig*) jungle.

selvagem [sew'vaʒē] (*pl* **-ns**) *adj* (*silvestre*) wild; (*feroz*) fierce; (*povo*) savage; (*fig: indivíduo, maneiras*) coarse.

selvageria [sewvaʒe'ria] *f* savagery.

sem [sē] *prep* without ♦ *conj:* ~ **que eu peça** without my asking; **a casa está** ~ **limpar há duas semanas** the house hasn't been cleaned for two weeks; **estar/ficar** ~ **dinheiro/gasolina** to have no/have run out of money/petrol; ~ **quê nem para quê** for no apparent reason.

SEMA (*BR*) *abr f* = **Secretaria Especial do Meio Ambiente**.

semáforo [se'maforu] *m* (*AUTO*) traffic lights *pl*; (*FERRO*) signal.

semana [se'mana] *f* week.

semanada [sema'nada] *f* (*weekly*) wages *pl*; (*mesada*) weekly allowance.

semanal [sema'naw] (*pl* **-ais**) *adj* weekly; **ganha $200 semanais** he earns $200 a week.

semanário [sema'narju] *m* weekly (publication).

semântica [se'mātʃika] *f* semantics *sg*.

semântico/a [se'mātʃiku/a] *adj* semantic.

semblante [sē'blātʃi] *m* face; (*fig*) appearance, look.

semeadura [semja'dura] *f* sowing.

semear [se'mja*] *vt* to sow; (*fig*) to spread; (*espalhar*) to scatter.

semelhança [seme'ʎāsa] *f* similarity, resemblance; **a** ~ **de** like; **ter** ~ **com** to resemble.

semelhante [seme'ʎātʃi] *adj* similar; (*tal*) such ♦ *m* fellow creature.

semelhar [seme'ʎa*] *vi:* ~ **a** to look like, resemble ♦ *vt* to look like, resemble; ~**-se** *vr* to be alike.

sêmen ['semē] *m* semen.

semente [se'mētʃi] *f* seed.

sementeira [semē'tejra] *f* sowing, spreading.

semestral [semeʃ'traw] (*pl* **-ais**) *adj* half-yearly.

semestralmente [semeʃtraw'mētʃi] *adv* every six months.

semestre [se'mɛʃtri] *m* six months; (*EDUC*) semester.

sem-fim *m:* **um** ~ **de perguntas** *etc* endless questions *etc*.

semi... [semi] *prefixo* semi..., half....

semi-aberto/a *adj* half-open.

semi-analfabeto/a *adj* semiliterate.

semibreve [semi'brɛvi] *f* (*MÚS*) semibreve.

semicírculo [semi'sixkulu] *m* semicircle.

semicondutor [semikõdu'to*] *m* semiconductor.

semiconsciente [semikõ'sjētʃi] *adj* semiconscious.

semifinal [semi'finaw] (*pl* -ais) *f* semifinal.

semifinalista [semifina'liʃta] *m/f* semifinalist.

semi-internato *m* day school.

semi-interno/a *m/f* (*tb*: *aluno* ~) day pupil.

seminal [semi'naw] (*pl* -ais) *adj* seminal.

seminário [semi'narju] *m* (*EDUC*, *congresso*) seminar; (*REL*) seminary.

seminarista [semina'riʃta] *m* seminarist.

seminu(a) [semi'nu(a)] *adj* half-naked.

semiótica [se'mjɔtʃika] *f* semiotics *sg*.

semiprecioso/a [semipre'sjozu/ɔza] *adj* semiprecious.

semita [se'mita] *adj* Semitic.

semítico/a [se'mitʃiku/a] *adj* Semitic.

semitom [semi'tõ] *m* (*MÚS*) semitone.

sem-lar *m/f inv* homeless person.

sem-número *m*: **um** ~ **de coisas** loads *pl* of things.

semolina [semo'lina] *f* semolina.

sem-par *adj inv* unequalled, unique.

sempre ['sēpri] *adv* always; **você** ~ **vai?** (*PT*) are you still going?; ~ **que** whenever; **como** ~ as always; **a comida/hora** *etc* **de** ~ the usual food/time *etc*; **a mesma história de** ~ the same old story; **para** ~ forever; **para todo o** ~ for ever and ever; **quase** ~ nearly always.

sem-sal *adj inv* insipid.

sem-terra *m/f inv* landless labourer (*BRIT*) *ou* laborer (*US*).

sem-vergonha *adj inv* shameless ♦ *m/f inv* (*pessoa*) rogue.

Sena ['sɛna] *m*: **o** ~ the Seine.

Senac [se'naki] (*BR*) *abr m* = **Serviço Nacional de Aprendizagem Comercial**.

senado [se'nadu] *m* senate.

senador(a) [sena'do*(a)] *m/f* senator.

Senai [se'naj] (*BR*) *abr m* = **Serviço Nacional de Aprendizagem Industrial**.

senão [se'nãw] (*pl* -ões) *conj* (*do contrário*) otherwise; (*mas sim*) but, but rather ♦ *prep* (*exceto*) except ♦ *m* flaw, defect; ~ **quando** suddenly.

Senav [se'navi] (*BR*) *abr f* = **Superintendência Estadual de Navegação**.

senda ['sēda] *f* path.

Senegal [sene'gaw] *m*: **o** ~ Senegal.

senha ['sɛɲa] *f* (*sinal*) sign; (*palavra de passe*, *COMPUT*) password; (*de caixa automática*) PIN number; (*recibo*) receipt; (*bilhete*) ticket, voucher.

senhor(a) [se'ɲo*(a)] *m* (*homem*) man; (*formal*) gentleman; (*homem idoso*) elderly man; (*REL*) lord; (*dono*) owner; (*tratamento*) Mr(.); (*tratamento respeitoso*) sir ♦ *f* (*mulher*) lady; (*esposa*) wife; (*mulher idosa*) elderly lady; (*dona*) owner; (*tratamento*)

Mrs(.), Ms(.); (*tratamento respeitoso*) madam ♦ *adj* marvellous (*BRIT*), marvelous (*US*); **uma** ~**a gripe** a bad case of flu; **o** ~**/a** ~**a** (*você*) you; **nossa** ~**a!** (*col*) gosh!; **sim,** ~**(a)!** yes indeed; **estar** ~ **de si** to be cool *ou* collected; **estar** ~ **da situação** to be in control of the situation; **ser** ~ **do seu nariz** to be one's own boss; ~ **de engenho** plantation owner.

senhoria [seɲo'ria] *f* (*proprietária*) landlady; **Vossa S**~ (*em cartas*) you.

senhoril [seɲo'riw] (*pl* -is) *adj* (*roupa etc*) gentlemen's/ladies'; (*distinto*) lordly.

senhorio [seɲo'riu] *m* (*proprietário*) landlord; (*posse*) ownership.

senhoris [seɲo'riʃ] *adj pl de* **senhoril**.

senhorita [seɲo'rita] *f* young lady; (*tratamento*) Miss, Ms.; **a** ~ (*você*) you.

senil [se'niw] (*pl* -is) *adj* senile.

senilidade [senili'dadʒi] *f* senility.

senilizar [senili'za*] *vt* to age.

senis [se'niʃ] *adj pl de* **senil**.

senões [se'nõjʃ] *mpl de* **senão**.

sensação [sēsa'sãw] (*pl* -ões) *f* sensation; **a** ~ **de que/uma** ~ **de** the feeling that/a feeling of; **causar** ~ to cause a sensation.

sensacional [sēsasjo'naw] (*pl* -ais) *adj* sensational.

sensacionalismo [sēsasjona'liʒmu] *m* sensationalism.

sensacionalista [sēsasjona'liʃta] *adj* sensationalist.

sensações [sēsa'sõjʃ] *fpl de* **sensação**.

sensatez [sēsa'teʒ] *f* good sense.

sensato/a [sē'satu/a] *adj* sensible.

sensibilidade [sēsibili'dadʒi] *f* sensitivity; (*artística*) sensibility; (*física*) feeling; **estou com muita** ~ **neste dedo** this finger is very sensitive.

sensibilizar [sēsibili'za*] *vt* to touch, move; (*opinião pública*) to influence; ~**-se** *vr* to be moved.

sensitivo/a [sēsi'tʃivu/a] *adj* sensory; (*pessoa*) sensitive.

sensível [sē'sivew] (*pl* -eis) *adj* sensitive; (*visível*) noticeable; (*considerável*) considerable; (*dolorido*) tender.

sensivelmente [sēsivew'mētʃi] *adv* perceptibly, markedly.

senso ['sēsu] *m* sense; (*juízo*) judgement; ~ **comum** *ou* **bom** ~ common sense; ~ **de humor/responsabilidade** sense of humour (*BRIT*) *ou* humor (*US*)/responsibility.

sensorial [sēso'rjaw] (*pl* -ais) *adj* sensory.

sensual [sē'swaw] (*pl* -ais) *adj* sensual, sensuous.

sensualidade [sēswali'dadʒi] *f* sensuality, sensuousness.

sentado/a [sē'tadu/a] *adj* sitting; (*almoço*) sit-down.

NB: *European Portuguese adds the following consonants to certain words:* **b** (sú(b)dito, su(b)til); **c** (a(c)ção, a(c)cionista, a(c)to); **m** (inde(m)ne); **p** (ado(p)ção, ado(p)tar); *for further details see p. xiii.*

sentar [sẽ'ta*] *vt* to seat ♦ *vi* to sit; ~-**se** *vr* to sit down.

sentença [sẽ'tẽsa] *f* (*JUR*) sentence; ~ **de morte** death sentence.

sentenciar [sẽtẽ'sja*] *vt* (*julgar*) to pass judgement on; (*condenar por sentença*) to sentence ♦ *vi* to pass judgement; to pass sentence.

sentidamente [sẽtʃida'mẽtʃi] *adv* (*chorar*) bitterly; (*desculpar-se*) abjectly.

sentido/a [sẽ'tʃidu/a] *adj* (*magoado*) hurt; (*choro, queixa*) heartfelt ♦ *m* sense; (*significação*) sense, meaning; (*direção*) direction; (*atenção*) attention; (*aspecto*) respect; ~**!** (*MIL*) attention!; **em certo** ~ in a sense; **sem** ~ meaningless; **fazer** ~ to make sense; **perder/recobrar os** ~**s** to lose/recover consciousness; (**não**) **ter** ~ (not) to be acceptable; ~ **figurado** figurative sense; "~ **único**" (*PT: sinal*) "one-way".

sentimental [sẽ'tʃimẽ'taw] (*pl* -**ais**) *adj* sentimental; **aventura** ~ romance; **vida** ~ love life.

sentimentalismo [sẽtʃimẽta'liʒmu] *m* sentimentality.

sentimento [sẽtʃi'mẽtu] *m* feeling; (*senso*) sense; ~**s** *mpl* (*pêsames*) condolences; **fazer algo com** ~ to do sth with feeling; **ter bons** ~**s** to be good-natured.

sentinela [sẽtʃi'nɛla] *f* sentry, guard; **estar de** ~ to be on guard duty; **render** ~ to relieve the guard.

sentir [sẽ'tʃi*] *vt* to feel; (*perceber, pressentir*) to sense; (*ser afetado por*) to be affected by; (*magoar-se*) to be upset by ♦ *vi* to feel; (*sofrer*) to suffer; ~-**se** *vr* to feel; (*julgar-se*) to consider o.s. (to be); ~ **a falta de** to miss; ~ **cheiro/gosto** (**de**) to smell/ taste; ~ **tristeza** to feel sad; ~ **vontade de** to feel like; **você sente a diferença?** can you tell the difference?; **sinto muito** I am very sorry.

senzala [sẽ'zala] *f* slave quarters *pl*.

separação [separa'sãw] (*pl* -**ões**) *f* separation.

separado/a [sepa'radu/a] *adj* separate; (*casal*) separated; **em** ~ separately, apart.

separar [sepa'ra*] *vt* to separate; (*dividir*) to divide; (*pôr de lado*) to put aside; ~-**se** *vr* to separate; (*dividir-se*) to be divided; ~-**se de** to separate from.

separata [sepa'rata] *f* offprint.

separatismo [separa'tʃiʒmu] *m* separatism.

séptico/a [' sɛptʃiku/a] *adj* septic.

septuagésimo/a [septwa'ʒɛzimu/a] (*PT*) *num* = setuagésimo.

sepulcro [se'puwkru] *m* tomb.

sepultamento [sepuwta'mẽtu] *m* burial.

sepultar [sepuw'ta*] *vt* to bury; (*esconder*) to hide, conceal; (*segredo*) to keep quiet.

sepultura [sepuw'tura] *f* grave, tomb.

sequei [se'kej] *etc vb V* **secar**.

seqüela [se'kwɛla] *f* sequel; (*conseqüência*) consequence; (*MED*) after-effect.

seqüência [se'kwẽsja] *f* sequence.

seqüencial [sekwẽ'sjaw] (*pl* -**ais**) *adj* (*COMPUT*) sequential.

sequer [se'kɛ*] *adv* at least; (**nem**) ~ not even.

seqüestrador(a) [sekwɛʃtra'do*(a)] *m/f* (*raptor*) kidnapper; (*de avião etc*) hijacker.

seqüestrar [sekwɛʃ'tra*] *vt* (*bens*) to seize, confiscate; (*raptar*) to kidnap; (*avião etc*) to hijack.

seqüestro [se'kwɛʃtru] *m* seizure; (*rapto*) abduction, kidnapping; (*de avião etc*) hijack.

sequidão [seki'dãw] *f* dryness; (*de pessoa*) coldness.

sequioso/a [se'kjozu/ɔza] *adj* (*sedento*) thirsty; (*fig: desejoso*) eager.

séquito ['sɛkitu] *m* retinue.

ser [se*] *vi* to be; (*como aux*): ~ **ferido/ amado** to be injured/loved ♦ *m* being; ~**es** *mpl* creatures; ~ **com** (*dizer respeito a*) to concern; (*estar sob a alçada de*) to be up to; (*depender de*) to be dependent on; (*interessar*): **o futebol é com ele** football is his thing; ~ **de** (*origem*) to be ou come from; (*feito de*) to be made of; (*pertencer*) to belong to; **ela é de uma bondade incrível** she's incredibly kind; ~ **de mentir/briga** (*pessoa*) to be the sort to lie/fight; ~ **por** to be for, be in favour (*BRIT*) ou favor (*US*) of; **a não** ~ except; **a não** ~ **por** but for; **a não** ~ **que** unless; **é** (*resposta afirmativa*) yes; ..., **não é?** isn't it?, don't you? *etc*; **ah, é?** really?; **é ou não é?** am I right?; **que foi?** (*o que aconteceu?*) what happened?; (*qual é o problema?*) what's the matter?; **é que ...** it's just that ...; **nós é que pedimos feijoada** it was us who ordered feijoada; **eu quero é viajar** what I want is to travel; **ele está é danado** he's really angry; **seja ... seja ...** whether it is ... or ...; **ou seja** that is to say; **seja quem for** whoever it may be; **se eu fosse você** if I were you; **se não fosse você**, ... if it hadn't been for you, ...; **será que ...?** I wonder if ...?; **ele vem amanhã — será?** he's coming tomorrow — do you think so?; ~ **humano** human being.

serão [se'rãw] (*pl* -**ões**) *m* (*trabalho noturno*) night work; (*horas extraordinárias*) overtime; **fazer** ~ to work late; (*dormir tarde*) to go to bed late.

sereia [se'reja] *f* mermaid.

serelepe [sere'lɛpi] *adj* frisky.

serenar [sere'na*] *vt* to calm ♦ *vi* (*pessoa*) to calm down; (*mar*) to grow calm; (*dor*) to subside.

serenata [sere'nata] *f* serenade.

serenidade [sereni'dadʒi] *f* serenity, tranquillity.

sereno/a [se'rɛnu/a] *adj* calm; (*olhar*) serene; (*tempo*) fine, clear ♦ *m* (*relento*) damp night air; **no** ~ in the open.

seresta [se'rɛʃta] *f* serenade.

SERFA (*BR*) *abr m* = **Serviço de Fiscalização**

Agrícola.

sergipano/a [sexʒi'panu/a] *adj* from Sergipe ♦ *m/f* person from Sergipe.

seriado/a [se'rjadu/a] *adj* (*número*) serial; (*publicação, filme*) serialized.

serial [se'rjaw] (*pl* **-ais**) *adj* (*COMPUT*) serial.

série ['sɛri] *f* series; (*seqüência*) sequence, succession; (*EDUC*) grade; (*categoria*) category; **fora de** ~ out of order; (*fig*) extraordinary; **fabricar em** ~ to mass-produce.

seriedade [serje'dadʒi] *f* seriousness; (*honestidade*) honesty.

seringa [se'rĩga] *f* syringe.

seringal [serĩ'gaw] (*pl* **-ais**) *m* rubber plantation.

seringalista [serĩga'liʃta] *m* rubber plantation owner.

seringueira [serĩ'gejra] *f* rubber tree; *V tb* **seringueiro**.

seringueiro/a [serĩ'gejru/a] *m/f* rubber tapper.

sério/a ['sɛrju/a] *adj* serious; (*honesto*) honest, decent; (*responsável*) responsible; (*confiável*) reliable; (*roupa*) sober ♦ *adv* seriously; **a** ~ seriously; **falando** ~ ... seriously ...; ~? really?

sermão [sex'mãw] (*pl* **-ões**) *m* sermon; (*fig*) telling-off; **levar um** ~ **de alguém** to get a telling-off from sb; **passar um** ~ **em alguém** to give sb a telling-off.

serões [se'rõjʃ] *mpl de* **serão**.

serpeante [sex'pjãtʃi] *adj* wriggling; (*fig*: *caminho, rio*) winding, meandering.

serpear [sex'pja*] *vi* (*como serpente*) to wriggle; (*fig*: *caminho, rio*) to wind, meander.

serpente [sex'pẽtʃi] *f* snake; (*pessoa*) snake in the grass.

serpentear [sexpẽ'tʃja*] *vi* = **serpear**.

serpentina [sexpẽ'tʃina] *f* (*conduto*) coil; (*fita de papel*) streamer.

serra ['sɛxa] *f* (*montanha*) mountain range; (*TEC*) saw; ~ **circular** circular saw; ~ **de arco** hacksaw; ~ **de cadeia** chain saw; ~ **tico-tico** fret saw.

serrado/a [se'xadu/a] *adj* serrated.

serragem [se'xaʒẽ] *f* (*pó*) sawdust.

Serra Leoa *f* Sierra Leone.

serralheiro/a [sexa'ʎejru/a] *m/f* locksmith.

serrania [sexa'nia] *f* mountain range.

serrano/a [se'xanu/a] *adj* highland ♦ *m/f* highlander.

serrar [se'xa*] *vt* to saw.

serraria [sexa'ria] *f* sawmill.

serrote [se'xɔtʃi] *m* handsaw.

sertanejo/a [sexta'neʒu/a] *adj* rustic, country *atr* ♦ *m/f* inhabitant of the "sertão".

sertão [sex'tãw] (*pl* **-ões**) *m* backwoods *pl*, bush (country).

servente [sex'vẽtʃi] *m/f* (*criado*) servant; (*operário*) assistant; ~ **de pedreiro**

bricklayer's mate.

serventuário/a [sexvẽ'twarju/a] *m/f* (*JUR*) legal official.

serviçal [sexvi'saw] (*pl* **-ais**) *adj* obliging, helpful ♦ *m/f* (*criado*) servant; (*trabalhador*) wage earner.

serviço [sex'visu] *m* service; (*de chá etc*) set; **o** ~ (*emprego*) work; **um** ~ (*trabalho*) a job; **não brincar em** ~ not to waste time; **dar o** ~ (*col*: *confessar*) to blab; **estar de** ~ to be on duty; **matar o** ~ to cut corners; **prestar** ~ to help; ~ **ativo** (*MIL*) active duty; ~ **de informações** (*MIL*) intelligence service; ~ **doméstico** housework; ~ **militar** military service; **S**~ **Nacional de Saúde** National Health Service; **S**~ **Público** Civil Service; ~**s públicos** public utilities.

servidão [sexvi'dãw] *f* servitude, serfdom; (*JUR*: *de passagem*) right of way.

servido/a [sex'vidu/a] *adj* served; ~ **de** (*provido*) supplied with, provided with; **você está** ~? (*num bar*) are you all right for a drink?

servidor(a) [sexvi'do*(a)] *m/f* (*criado*) servant; (*funcionário*) employee; ~ **público** civil servant.

servil [sex'viw] (*pl* **-is**) *adj* servile.

servir [sex'vi*] *vt* to serve ♦ *vi* to serve; (*ser útil*) to be useful; (*ajudar*) to help; (*roupa*: *caber*) to fit; ~**-se** *vr*: ~**-se** (**de**) (*comida, café*) to help o.s. (to); (*meios*) to use, make use of; ~ **de algo** to serve as sth; **para que serve isto?** what is this for?; **ele não serve para trabalhar aqui** he's not suitable to work here; **qualquer ônibus serve** any bus will do.

servis [sex'viʃ] *adj pl de* **servil**.

servível [sex'vivew] (*pl* **-eis**) *adj* serviceable; (*roupa*) wearable.

servo/a ['sɛxvu/a] *m/f* (*feudal*) serf; (*criado*) servant.

servo-croata [sɛxvu'krwata] *m* (*LING*) Serbo-Croat.

Sesc ['sɛʃki] (*BR*) *abr m* = **Serviço Social do Comércio**.

Sesi [se'zi] (*BR*) *abr m* = **Serviço Social da Indústria**.

sessão [se'sãw] (*pl* **-ões**) *f* (*do parlamento etc*) session; (*reunião*) meeting; (*de cinema*) showing; **primeira/segunda** ~ first/second show; ~ **coruja** late show; ~ **da tarde** matinée.

sessenta [se'sẽta] *num* sixty; *V tb* **cinqüenta**.

sessões [se'sõjʃ] *fpl de* **sessão**.

sesta ['sɛʃta] *f* siesta, nap.

set ['sɛtʃi] *m* (*TÊNIS*) set.

set. *abr* (= *setembro*) Sept.

seta ['sɛta] *f* arrow.

sete ['sɛtʃi] *num* seven; **pintar o** ~ (*fig*) to get up to all sorts; *V tb* **cinco**.

setecentos/as [sete'sẽtuʃ/aʃ] *num* seven

hundred.

sete-e-meio *m* seven-and-a-half (*card game similar to pontoon*).

setembro [se'tẽbru] (*PT*: **S-**) *m* September; *V tb* **julho**.

setenta [se'tẽta] *num* seventy; *V tb* **cinqüenta**.

setentrional [setẽtrjo'naw] (*pl* **-ais**) *adj* northern.

sétima ['sɛtʃima] *f* (*MÚS*) seventh.

sétimo/a ['sɛtʃimu/a] *num* seventh; *V tb* **quinto**.

setor [se'to*] *m* sector.

setuagésimo/a [setwa'ʒɛzimu/a] *num* seventieth; *V tb* **quinto**.

seu/sua [sew/'sua] *adj* (*dele*) his; (*dela*) her; (*de coisa*) its; (*deles, delas*) their; (*de você, vocês*) your ♦ *pron* (*dele*) his; (*dela*) hers; (*deles, delas*) theirs; (*de você, vocês*) yours ♦ *m* (*senhor*) Mr(.); **um homem de ~s 60 anos** a man of about sixty; **~ idiota!** you idiot!

Seul [se'uw] *n* Seoul.

severidade [severi'dadʒi] *f* severity, harshness.

severo/a [se'vɛru/a] *adj* severe, harsh.

seviciar [sevi'sja*] *vt* to ill-treat; (*mulher, criança*) to batter.

sevícias [se'visjaʃ] *fpl* (*maus tratos*) ill treatment *sg*; (*desumanidade*) inhumanity *sg*, cruelty *sg*.

Sevilha [se'viʎa] *n* Seville.

sex. *abr* (= *sexta-feira*) Fri.

sexagésimo/a [seksa'ʒɛzimu/a] *num* sixtieth; *V tb* **quinto**.

sexo ['sɛksu] *m* sex; **de ~ feminino/ masculino** female/male.

sexta ['seʃta] *f* (*tb*: **~-feira**) Friday; (*MÚS*) sixth.

sexta-feira (*pl* **sextas-feiras**) *f* Friday; **S~ Santa** Good Friday; *V tb* **terça-feira**.

sexto/a ['seʃtu/a] *num* sixth; *V tb* **quinto**.

sexual [se'kswaw] (*pl* **-ais**) *adj* sexual; (*vida, ato*) sex *atr*.

sexualidade [sekswali'dadʒi] *f* sexuality.

sexy ['sɛksi] (*pl* **~s**) *adj* sexy.

Seychelles [sej'ʃɛliʃ] *f ou fpl*: **a(s) ~** the Seychelles.

sezão [se'zãw] (*pl* **-ões**) *f* (*febre*) (intermittent) fever; (*malária*) malaria.

s.f.f. (*PT*) *abr* = **se faz favor**.

SFH (*BR*) *abr m* = **Sistema Financeiro de Habitação**.

shopping (center) ['ʃɔpĩŋ('sẽte*)] *m* shopping centre (*BRIT*), (shopping) mall (*US*).

short ['ʃɔxtʃi] *m* (pair of) shorts *pl*.

show [ʃow] (*pl* **~s**) *m* show; (*de cantor, conjunto*) concert, gig; **dar um ~** (*fig*) to put on a real show; (*dar escândalo*) to make a scene; **ser um ~** (*col*) to be a sensation.

showroom [ʃow'rũ] (*pl* **~s**) *m* showroom.

si [si] *pron* oneself; (*ele*) himself; (*ela*) herself; (*coisa*) itself; (*PT*: *você*) yourself, you; (: *vocês*) yourselves; (*eles, elas*)

themselves; **em ~** in itself; **fora de ~** beside oneself; **cheio de ~** full of oneself; **voltar a ~** to come round.

siamês/esa [sja'meʃ/eza] *adj* Siamese.

Sibéria [si'bɛrja] *f*: **a ~** Siberia.

sibilar [sibi'la*] *vi* to hiss.

sicário [si'karju] *m* hired assassin.

Sicília [si'silja] *f*: **a ~** Sicily.

sicrano [si'kranu] *m*: **fulano e ~** so-and-so.

SIDA ['sida] (*PT*) *abr f* (= *síndrome de deficiência imunológica adquirida*): **a ~** AIDS.

siderúrgica [side'ruxʒika] *f* steel industry.

siderúrgico/a [side'ruxʒiku/a] *adj* iron and steel *atr*; (**usina**) **siderúrgica** steelworks.

sidra ['sidra] *f* cider.

SIF (*BR*) *abr m* = **Serviço de Inspeção Federal**.

sifão [si'fãw] (*pl* **-ões**) *m* syphon.

sífilis ['sifiliʃ] *f* syphilis.

sifões [si'fõjʃ] *mpl de* **sifão**.

siga ['siga] *etc vb V* **seguir**.

sigilo [si'ʒilu] *m* secrecy; **guardar ~ sobre algo** to keep quiet about sth.

sigiloso/a [siʒi'lozu/ɔza] *adj* secret.

sigla ['sigla] *f* acronym, abbreviation.

signatário/a [signa'tarju/a] *m/f* signatory.

significação [signifika'sãw] *f* significance.

significado [signifi'kadu] *m* meaning.

significante [signifi'kãtʃi] *adj* significant.

significar [signifi'ka*] *vt* to mean, signify.

significativo/a [signifika'tʃivu/a] *adj* significant.

signo ['signu] *m* sign; **~ do zodíaco** sign of the zodiac.

sigo ['sigu] *etc vb V* **seguir**.

sílaba ['silaba] *f* syllable.

silenciar [silẽ'sja*] *vt* (*pessoa*) to silence; (*escândalo*) to hush up ♦ *vi* to remain silent.

silêncio [si'lẽsju] *m* silence, quiet; **~!** silence!; **ficar em ~** to remain silent.

silencioso/a [silẽ'sjozu/ɔza] *adj* silent, quiet ♦ *m* (*AUTO*) silencer (*BRIT*), muffler (*US*).

silhueta [si'ʎweta] *f* silhouette.

silício [si'lisju] *m* silicon.

silicone [sili'kɔni] *m* silicone.

silo ['silu] *m* silo.

silvar [siw'va*] *vi* to hiss; (*assobiar*) to whistle.

silvestre [siw'vɛʃtri] *adj* wild.

silvícola [siw'vikola] *adj* wild.

silvicultura [siwvikuw'tura] *f* forestry.

sim [sĩ] *adv* yes; **creio que ~** I think so; **isso ~** that's it!; **pelo ~, pelo não** just in case; **dar ou dizer o ~** to consent, say yes.

simbólico/a [sĩ'bɔliku/a] *adj* symbolic.

simbolismo [sĩbo'liʒmu] *m* symbolism.

simbolizar [sĩboli'za*] *vt* to symbolise.

símbolo ['sĩbolu] *m* symbol.

simetria [sime'tria] *f* symmetry.

simétrico/a [si'mɛtriku/a] *adj* symmetrical.

similar [simi'la*] *adj* similar.

similaridade [similari'dadʒi] *f* similarity.

símile ['simili] *m* simile.
similitude [simili'tudʒi] *f* similarity.
simpatia [sĩpa'tʃia] *f* (*por alguém, algo*) liking; (*afeto*) affection; (*afinidade, solidariedade*) sympathy; **~s** *fpl* (*inclinações*) sympathies; **com ~** sympathetically; **ser uma ~** to be very nice; **ter** *ou* **sentir ~ por** to like.
simpático/a [sĩ'patʃiku/a] *adj* (*pessoa, decoração etc*) nice; (*lugar*) pleasant, nice; (*amável*) kind ♦ *m* (*ANAT*) nervous system; **ser ~ a** to be sympathetic to.
simpatizante [sĩpatʃi'zãtʃi] *adj* sympathetic ♦ *m/f* sympathizer.
simpatizar [sĩpatʃi'za*] *vi*: **~ com** (*pessoa*) to like; (*causa*) to sympathize with.
simples ['sĩpliʃ] *adj inv* simple; (*único*) single; (*fácil*) easy; (*mero*) mere; (*ingênuo*) naïve ♦ *adv* simply.
simplicidade [sĩplisi'dadʒi] *f* simplicity; (*ingenuidade*) naïveté; (*modéstia*) plainness; (*naturalidade*) naturalness.
simplicíssimo/a [sĩpli'sisimu/a] *adj superl de* **simples**.
simplificação [sĩplifika'sãw] (*pl* **-ões**) *f* simplification.
simplificar [sĩplifi'ka*] *vt* to simplify.
simplíssimo/a [sĩ'plisimu/a] *adj superl de* **simples**.
simplista [sĩ'pliʃta] *adj* simplistic.
simplório/a [sĩ'plɔrju/a] *adj* simple ♦ *m/f* simple person.
simpósio [sĩ'pɔzju] *m* symposium.
simulação [simula'sãw] (*pl* **-ões**) *f* simulation; (*fingimento*) pretence (*BRIT*), pretense (*US*), sham.
simulacro [simu'lakru] *m* (*imitação*) imitation; (*fingimento*) pretence (*BRIT*), pretense (*US*).
simulado/a [simu'ladu/a] *adj* simulated.
simular [simu'la*] *vt* to simulate.
simultaneamente [simuwtanja'mẽtʃi] *adv* simultaneously.
simultâneo/a [simuw'tanju/a] *adj* simultaneous.
sina ['sina] *f* fate, destiny.
sinagoga [sina'gɔga] *f* synagogue.
Sinai [sina'i] *m* Sinai.
sinal [si'naw] (*pl* **-ais**) *m* (*ger*) sign; (*gesto, TEL*) signal; (*na pele*) mole; (: *de nascença*) birthmark; (*depósito*) deposit; (*tb*: **~ luminoso**) traffic light; **~ (de tráfego)** traffic light; **~ rodoviário** road sign; **dar de ~** to give as a deposit; **em ~ de** (*fig*) as a sign of; **por ~** (*por falar nisso*) by the way; (*aliás*) as a matter of fact; **avançar o ~** (*AUTO*) to jump the lights; (*fig*) to jump the gun; **dar ~ de vida** to show up; **fazer ~** to signal; **~ de alarma** alarm; **~ de chamada** (*TEL*) ringing tone; **~ de discar** (*BR*) *ou* **de**

marcar (*PT*) dialling (*BRIT*) *ou* dial (*US*) tone; **~ de ocupado** (*BR*) *ou* **de impedido** (*PT*) engaged tone (*BRIT*), busy signal (*US*); **~ de mais/menos** (*MAT*) plus/minus sign; **~ de perigo** danger signal; **~ de pontuação** punctuation mark; **~ verde** *ou* **aberto/vermelho** *ou* **fechado** green/red light.
sinal-da-cruz *m* sign of the cross; **fazer o ~** to cross o.s.
sinaleiro [sina'lejru] *m* (*FERRO*) signalman; (*aparelho*) traffic lights *pl*.
sinalização [sinaliza'sãw] *f* (*ato*) signalling; (*para motoristas*) traffic signs *pl*; (*FERRO*) signals *pl*.
sinalizar [sinali'za*] *vi* to signal.
sinceridade [sĩseri'dadʒi] *f* sincerity.
sincero/a [sĩ'sɛru/a] *adj* sincere; (*opinião, confissão*) honest.
sincopado/a [sĩko'padu/a] *adj* (*MÚS*) syncopated.
síncope ['sĩkopi] *f* fainting fit.
sincronizar [sĩkroni'za*] *vt* to synchronize.
sindical [sĩdʒi'kaw] (*pl* **-ais**) *adj* (trade) union *atr*.
sindicalismo [sĩdʒika'liʒmu] *m* trade unionism.
sindicalista [sĩdʒika'liʃta] *m/f* trade unionist.
sindicalizar [sĩdʒikali'za*] *vt* to unionize; **~-se** *vr* to become unionized.
sindicância [sĩdʒi'kãsja] *f* inquiry, investigation.
sindicato [sĩdʒi'katu] *m* (*de trabalhadores*) trade union; (*financeiro*) syndicate.
síndico/a ['sĩdʒiku/a] *m/f* (*de condomínio*) manager; (*de massa falida*) receiver.
síndrome ['sĩdromi] *f* syndrome; **~ de deficiência imunológica adquirida** acquired immune deficiency syndrome.
SINE (*BR*) *abr m* = **Sistema Nacional de Empregos**.
sinecura [sine'kura] *f* sinecure.
sineta [si'neta] *f* bell.
sinfonia [sĩfo'nia] *f* symphony.
sinfônica [sĩ'fonika] *f* (*tb*: *orquestra* **~**) symphony orchestra.
sinfônico/a [sĩ'foniku/a] *adj* symphonic.
singeleza [sĩʒe'leza] *f* simplicity.
singelo/a [sĩ'ʒɛlu/a] *adj* simple.
singular [sĩgu'la*] *adj* singular; (*extraordinário*) exceptional; (*bizarro*) odd, peculiar.
singularidade [sĩgulari'dadʒi] *f* peculiarity.
singularizar [sĩgulari'za*] *vt* (*distinguir*) to single out; **~-se** *vr* to stand out, distinguish o.s.
sinistrado/a [siniʃ'tradu/a] *adj* damaged.
sinistro/a [si'niʃtru/a] *adj* sinister ♦ *m* disaster, accident; (*prejuízo*) damage.
sino ['sinu] *m* bell.
sinônimo/a [si'nonimu/a] *adj* synonymous ♦ *m* synonym.

sinopse [si'nɔpsi] *f* synopsis.
sinta ['sĩta] *etc vb* V **sentir**.
sintático/a [sĩ'tatʃiku/a] *adj* syntactic.
sintaxe [sĩ'tasi] *f* syntax.
síntese ['sĩtezi] *f* synthesis; **em** ~ in short.
sintético/a [sĩ'tɛtʃiku/a] *adj* synthetic; *(resumido)* brief.
sintetizar [sĩtetʃi'za*] *vt* to synthesize; *(resumir)* to summarize.
sinto ['sĩtu] *etc vb* V **sentir**.
sintoma [sĩ'tɔma] *m* symptom.
sintomático/a [sĩto'matʃiku/a] *adj* symptomatic.
sintonizador [sĩtoniza'do*] *m* tuner.
sintonizar [sĩtoni'za*] *vt* (*RÁDIO*) to tune ♦ *vi* to tune in; ~ **(com)** *(pessoa)* to get on (with); *(opinião)* to coincide (with).
sinuca [si'nuka] *f* snooker; *(mesa)* snooker table; **estar numa** ~ *(col)* to be snookered.
sinuoso/a [si'nwozu/ɔza] *adj* (*caminho*) winding; *(linha)* wavy.
sinusite [sinu'zitʃi] *f* sinusitis.
sionismo [sjo'niʒmu] *m* Zionism.
sionista [sjo'niʃta] *adj*, *m/f* Zionist.
sirena [si'rena] *f* siren.
sirene [si'reni] *f* = **sirena**.
siri [si'ri] *m* crab; **casquinha de** ~ *(CULIN)* crab au gratin.
sirigaita [siri'gajta] *(col)* *f* floozy.
Síria ['sirja] *f*: **a** ~ Syria.
sírio/a ['sirju/a] *adj*, *m/f* Syrian.
sirvo ['sixvu] *vb* V **servir**.
siso ['sizu] *m* good sense; **dente de** ~ wisdom tooth.
sísmico/a ['siʒmiku/a] *adj* seismic.
sismógrafo [siʒ'mɔgrafu] *m* seismograph.
sistema [siʃ'tema] *m* system; *(método)* method; ~ **operacional** *(COMPUT)* operating system; ~ **solar** solar system.
sistemático/a [siʃte'matʃiku/a] *adj* systematic.
sistematizar [siʃtematʃi'za*] *vt* to systematize.
sisudo/a [si'zudu/a] *adj* serious, sober.
sitiar [si'tʃja*] *vt* to besiege.
sítio ['sitʃju] *m* (*MIL*) siege; *(propriedade rural)* small farm; *(PT: lugar)* place; **estado de** ~ state of siege.
situação [sitwa'sãw] *(pl* **-ões)** *f* situation; *(posição)* position; *(social)* standing.
situado/a [si'twadu/a] *adj* situated; **estar** *ou* **ficar** ~ to be situated.
situar [si'twa*] *vt* (*pôr*) to place, put; *(edifício)* to situate, locate; ~**-se** *vr* (*pôr-se*) to position o.s.; *(estar situado)* to be situated.
SL *abr* = **sobreloja**.
sl *abr* = **sobreloja**.
slogan [iʃ'lɔgã] *(pl* ~**s)** *m* slogan.
smoking [iʒ'mokiʃ] *(pl* ~**s)** *m* dinner jacket (*BRIT*), tuxedo (*US*).
SMTU *(BR)* *abr f* = **Superintendência Municipal de Transportes Urbanos**.
SNI *(BR)* *abr m* (*antes*): = *Serviço Nacional de Informações*) *state intelligence service*.

só [sɔ] *adj* alone; *(único)* single; *(solitário)* solitary ♦ *adv* only; **um** ~ only one; **a** ~**s** alone; **por si** ~ by himself *(ou* herself, itself); **é** ~! that's all!; **é** ~ **discar** all you have to do is dial; **veja/imagine** ~ just look/ imagine; **não** ~ ... **mas também** ... not only ... but also ...; **que** *ou* **como** ~ **ele** *etc* like nobody else; ~ **isso?** is that all?
soalho ['swaʎu] *m* = **assoalho**.
soar [swa*] *vi* to sound; *(cantar)* to sing; *(sinos, clarins)* to ring; *(apito)* to blow; *(boato)* to go round ♦ *vt* (*horas*) to strike; *(instrumento)* to play; ~ **a** to sound like; ~ **bem/mal** *(fig)* to go down well/badly.
sob [sob] *prep* under; ~ **emenda** subject to correction; ~ **juramento** on oath; ~ **medida** *(roupa)* made to measure; *(software)* bespoke; ~ **minha palavra** on my word; ~ **pena de** on pain of.
sobe ['sɔbi] *etc vb* V **subir**.
sobejar [sobe'ʒa*] *vi* (*superabundar*) to abound; *(restar)* to be left over.
sobejos [so'beʒuʃ] *mpl* remains, leftovers.
soberania [sobera'nia] *f* sovereignty.
soberano/a [sobe'ranu/a] *adj* sovereign; *(fig: supremo)* supreme; (: *altivo*) haughty ♦ *m/f* sovereign.
soberba [so'bexba] *f* haughtiness, arrogance.
soberbo/a [so'bexbu/a] *adj* (*arrogante*) haughty, arrogant; *(magnífico)* magnificent, splendid.
sobra ['sɔbra] *f* surplus, remnant; ~**s** *fpl* remains; *(de comida)* leftovers, remains; **ter algo de** ~ to have sth extra; *(tempo, comida, motivos)* to have plenty of sth; **ficar de** ~ to be left over.
sobraçar [sobra'sa*] *vt* (*levar debaixo do braço*) to carry under one's arm; *(meter debaixo do braço)* to put under one's arm.
sobrado [so'bradu] *m* (*andar*) floor; *(casa)* house *(of two or more storeys)*.
sobranceiro/a [sobrã'sejru/a] *adj* (*que está acima de*) lofty, towering; *(proeminente)* prominent; *(arrogante)* haughty, arrogant.
sobrancelha [sobrã'seʎa] *f* eyebrow.
sobrar [so'bra*] *vi* to be left; *(dúvidas)* to remain; **ficar sobrando** *(pessoa)* to be left out; (: *não ter parceiro*) to be the odd one out; **sobram-me cinco** I have five left; **isto dá e sobra** this is more than enough.
sobre ['sobri] *prep* on; *(por cima de)* over; *(acima de)* above; *(a respeito de)* about; **ser meio** ~ **o chato** *(col)* to be a bit boring.
sobreaviso [sobrja'vizu] *m* warning; **estar de** ~ to be alert, be on one's guard.
sobrecapa [sobri'kapa] *f* cover.
sobrecarga [sobri'kaxga] *f* overload.
sobrecarregar [sobrikaxe'ga*] *vt* to overload.
sobreestimar [sobrjeʃtʃi'ma*] *vt* to overestimate.
sobre-humano/a *adj* superhuman.
sobrejacente [sobriʒa'sẽtʃi] *adj*: ~ **a** over.
sobreloja [sobri'lɔʒa] *f* mezzanine (floor).

sobremaneira [sobrema'nejra] adv exceedingly.

sobremesa [sobri'meza] f dessert.

sobremodo [sobri'mɔdu] adv exceedingly.

sobrenatural [sobrinatu'raw] (pl -ais) adj supernatural; (esforço) superhuman ♦ m: o ~ the supernatural.

sobrenome [sobri'nɔmi] (BR) m surname, family name.

sobrepairar [sobripaj'ra*] vi: ~ a to hover above; (crise) to rise above.

sobrepor [sobri'po*] (irreg: como pôr) vt: ~ algo a algo (pôr em cima) to put sth on top of sth; (adicionar) to add sth to sth; (dar preferência) to put sth before sth; ~-se vr: ~-se a (pôr-se sobre) to cover, go on top of; (sobrevir) to succeed.

sobrepujar [sobripu'ʒa*] vt (exceder em altura) to rise above; (superar) to surpass; (obstáculos, perigos) to overcome; (inimigo) to overwhelm.

sobrepunha [sobri'puɲa] etc vb V **sobrepor**.

sobrepus [sobri'pujʃ] etc vb V **sobrepor**.

sobrepuser [sobripu'ze*] etc vb V **sobrepor**.

sobrescritar [sobreʃkri'ta*] vt to address.

sobrescrito [sobreʃ'kritu] m address.

sobressair [sobrisa'i*] vi to stand out; ~-se vr to stand out.

sobressalente [sobrisa'lẽtʃi] adj, m spare.

sobressaltado/a [sobrisaw'tadu/a] adj: **viver** ~ to live in fear; **acordar** ~ to wake up with a start.

sobressaltar [sobrisaw'ta*] vt to startle, frighten; ~-se vr to be startled.

sobressalto [sobri'sawtu] m (movimento brusco) start; (temor) trepidation; **de** ~ suddenly; **o seu** ~ **com aquele estrondo/ aquela notícia** his fright at that noise/his shock at that news; **ter um** ~ to get a fright.

sobretaxa [sobri'taʃa] f surcharge.

sobretudo [sobri'tudu] m overcoat ♦ adv above all, especially.

sobrevir [sobri'vi*] (irreg: como **vir**) vi to occur, arise; ~ **a** (seguir) to follow (on from); **sobreveio-lhe uma doença** he was struck down by illness.

sobrevivência [sobrivi'vẽsja] f survival.

sobrevivente [sobrivi'vẽtʃi] adj surviving ♦ m/f survivor.

sobreviver [sobrivi've*] vi: ~ (a) to survive.

sobrevoar [sobrivo'a*] vt, vi to fly over.

sobriedade [sobrje'dadʒi] f soberness; (comedimento) moderation, restraint.

sobrinho/a [so'briɲu/a] m/f nephew/niece.

sóbrio/a ['sɔbrju/a] adj sober; (moderado) moderate, restrained.

socado/a [so'kadu/a] adj (alho) crushed; (escondido) hidden; (pessoa) stout.

socador [soka'do*] m crusher; ~ **de alho** garlic press.

soçaite [so'sajtʃi] (col) m high society.

socapa [so'kapa] f: **à** ~ furtively, on the sly.

socar [so'ka*] vt (esmurrar) to hit, strike; (calcar) to crush, pound; (massa de pão) to knead.

social [so'sjaw] (pl -ais) adj social; (entrada, elevador) private; (camisa) dress atr.

socialismo [sosja'liʒmu] m socialism.

socialista [sosja'liʃta] adj, m/f socialist.

socialite [sosja'lajtʃi] m/f socialite.

socializar [sosjali'za*] vt to socialize.

sociável [so'sjavew] (pl -eis) adj sociable.

sociedade [sosje'dadʒi] f society; (COM: empresa) company; (: de sócios) partnership; (associação) association; ~ **anônima** joint-stock ou limited company; ~ **anônima aberta/fechada** public/private limited company.

sócio/a ['sɔsju/a] m/f (COM) partner, associate; (de clube) member; ~ **comanditário** (COM) silent partner.

socio-econômico/a adj socio-economic.

sociolingüística [sosjoli'gwiʃtʃika] f sociolinguistics sg.

sociologia [sosjolo'ʒia] f sociology.

sociológico/a [sosjo'lɔʒiku/a] adj sociological.

sociólogo/a [so'sjɔlogu/a] m/f sociologist.

socio-político/a adj socio-political.

soco ['soku] m punch; **dar um** ~ **em** to punch.

soçobrar [soso'bra*] vt (afundar) to sink ♦ vi to sink; (esperanças) to founder; ~ **em** (fig: no vício etc) to sink into.

soco-inglês (pl **socos-ingleses**) m knuckleduster.

socorrer [soko'xe*] vt (ajudar) to help, assist; (salvar) to rescue; ~-se vr: ~-se de to resort to, have recourse to.

socorro [so'koxu] m help, assistance; (reboque) breakdown (BRIT) ou tow (US) truck; **ir em** ~ **de** to come to the aid of; **primeiros** ~s first aid sg; ~! help!; **equipe de** ~ rescue team.

soda ['sɔda] f soda (water); **pedir** ~ (col) to back off, back down; ~ **cáustica** caustic soda.

sódio ['sɔdʒju] m sodium.

sodomia [sodo'mia] f sodomy.

sofá [so'fa] m sofa, settee.

sofá-cama (pl **sofás-camas**) m sofa-bed.

Sófia ['sɔfja] n Sofia.

sofisma [so'fiʒma] m sophism; (col) trick.

sofismar [sofiʒ'ma*] vt (fatos) to twist; (enganar) to swindle, cheat.

sofisticação [sofiʃtʃika'sãw] f sophistication.

sofisticado/a [sofiʃtʃi'kadu/a] adj sophisticated; (afetado) pretentious.

sofisticar [sofiʃtʃi'ka*] vt to refine.

sôfrego/a ['sofregu/a] adj (ávido) keen; (impaciente) impatient; (no comer) greedy.

sofreguidão [sofregi'dãw] f keenness; (im-

NB: European Portuguese adds the following consonants to certain words: **b** (sú(b)dito, su(b)til); **c** (a(c)ção, a(c)cionista, a(c)to); **m** (inde(m)ne); **p** (ado(p)ção, ado(p)tar); for further details see p. xiii.

paciência) impatience; (*no comer*) greed.

sofrer [so'fre*] *vt* to suffer; (*acidente*) to have; (*agüentar*) to bear, put up with; (*experimentar*) to undergo, experience ♦ *vi* to suffer; ~ **de reumatismo/do fígado** to suffer from rheumatism/with one's liver.

sofrido/a [so'fridu/a] *adj* long-suffering.

sofrimento [sofri'mẽtu] *m* suffering.

sofrível [so'frivew] (*pl* **-eis**) *adj* bearable; (*razoável*) reasonable.

soft ['sɔftʃi] (*pl* ~**s**) *m* (*COMPUT*) piece of software, software package.

software [sof'twe*] (*pl* ~**s**) *m* (*COMPUT*) software; **um** ~ a piece of software.

sogro/a ['sogru/'sɔgra] *m/f* father-in-law/ mother-in-law.

sóis [sɔjʃ] *mpl de* **sol**.

soja ['sɔʒa] *f* soya (*BRIT*), soy (*US*); **leite de** ~ soya *ou* soy milk.

sol [sɔw] (*pl* **sóis**) *m* sun; (*luz*) sunshine, sunlight; **ao** *ou* **no** ~ in the sun; **fazer** ~ to be sunny; **pegar** ~ to sunbathe; **tomar (banho de)** ~ to sunbathe.

sola ['sɔla] *f* sole.

solado/a [so'ladu/a] *adj* (*bolo*) flat.

solão [so'lãw] *m* very hot sun.

solapar [sola'pa*] *vt* (*escavar*) to dig into; (*abalar*) to shake; (*fig: arruinar*) to destroy.

solar [so'la*] *adj* solar ♦ *m* manor house ♦ *vt* (*sapato*) to sole ♦ *vi* (*bolo*) not to rise; (*cantor, músico*) to sing (*ou* play) solo.

solavanco [sola'vãku] *m* jolt, bump; **andar aos** ~**s** to jog along.

solda ['sɔwda] *f* solder.

soldado [sow'dadu] *m* soldier; ~ **de chumbo** toy soldier; ~ **raso** private soldier.

soldador(a) [sowda'do*(a)] *m/f* welder.

soldadura [sowda'dura] *f* (*ato*) welding; (*parte soldada*) weld.

soldagem [sow'daʒẽ] *f* welding.

soldar [sow'da*] *vt* to weld; (*fig*) to unite, amalgamate.

soldo ['sowdu] *m* (*MIL*) pay.

soleira [so'lejra] *f* doorstep.

solene [so'lɛni] *adj* solemn.

solenidade [soleni'dadʒi] *f* solemnity; (*cerimônia*) ceremony.

solenizar [soleni'za*] *vt* to solemnize.

solércia [so'lɛxsja] *f* ploy.

soletração [soletra'sãw] *f* spelling.

soletrar [sole'tra*] *vt* to spell; (*ler devagar*) to read out slowly.

solicitação [solisita'sãw] (*pl* **-ões**) *f* request; **solicitações** *fpl* (*apelo*) appeal *sg*.

solicitar [solisi'ta*] *vt* to ask for; (*requerer: emprego etc*) to apply for; (*amizade, atenção*) to seek; ~ **algo a alguém** to ask sb for sth.

solícito/a [so'lisitu/a] *adj* helpful.

solicitude [solisi'tudʒi] *f* (*zelo*) care; (*boa vontade*) concern, thoughtfulness; (*empenho*) commitment.

solidão [soli'dãw] *f* solitude, isolation;

(*sensação*) loneliness; (*de lugar*) desolation; **sentir** ~ to feel lonely.

solidariedade [solidarje'dadʒi] *f* solidarity.

solidário/a [soli'darju/a] *adj* (*pessoas*) who show solidarity; (*a uma causa etc*) sympathetic; (*JUR: obrigação*) mutually binding; (: *devedores*) jointly liable; **ser** ~ **com** to stand by.

solidarizar [solidari'za*] *vt* to bring together; ~**-se** *vr* to join forces.

solidez [soli'deʒ] *f* solidity, strength.

solidificar [solidʒifi'ka*] *vt* to solidify; (*fig*) to consolidate; ~**-se** *vr* to solidify; to be consolidated.

sólido/a ['sɔlidu/a] *adj* solid.

solilóquio [soli'lɔkju] *m* soliloquy.

solista [so'liʃta] *m/f* soloist.

solitária [soli'tarja] *f* (*verme*) tapeworm; (*cela*) solitary confinement.

solitário/a [soli'tarju/a] *adj* lonely, solitary ♦ *m* hermit; (*jóia*) solitaire.

solo ['sɔlu] *m* ground, earth; (*MÚS*) solo.

soltar [sow'ta*] *vt* (*tornar livre*) to set free; (*desatar*) to loosen, untie; (*afrouxar*) to slacken, loosen; (*largar*) to let go of; (*emitir*) to emit; (*grito, risada*) to let out; (*foguete, fogos de artifício*) to set *ou* let off; (*cabelo*) to let down; (*freio, animais*) to release; (*piada*) to tell; ~**-se** *vr* (*desprender-se*) to come loose; (*desinibir-se*) to let o.s. go; ~ **palavrão** to swear.

solteira [sol'tejra] *f* single woman, spinster.

solteirão [sowtej'rãw] (*pl* **-ões**) *m* bachelor.

solteiro/a [sow'tejru/a] *adj* unmarried, single ♦ *m* bachelor.

solteirões [sowtej'rõjʃ] *mpl de* **solteirão**.

solteirona [sowtej'rona] *f* old maid.

solto/a ['sowtu/a] *pp de* **soltar** ♦ *adj* loose; (*livre*) free; (*sozinho*) alone; (*arroz*) fluffy; **à solta** freely.

soltura [sow'tura] *f* looseness; (*liberdade*) release, discharge.

solução [solu'sãw] (*pl* **-ões**) *f* solution.

soluçar [solu'sa*] *vi* (*chorar*) to sob; (*MED*) to hiccup.

solucionar [solusjo'na*] *vt* to solve; (*decidir*) to resolve.

soluço [so'lusu] *m* (*pranto*) sob; (*MED*) hiccup.

soluções [solu'sõjʃ] *fpl de* **solução**.

solúvel [so'luvew] (*pl* **-eis**) *adj* soluble.

solvência [sow'vẽsja] *f* solvency.

solvente [sow'vẽtʃi] *adj*, *m* solvent.

som [sõ] (*pl* **-ns**) *m* sound; (*MÚS*) tone; (*BR: equipamento*) hi-fi, stereo; (: *música*) music; **ao** ~ **de** (*MÚS*) to the accompaniment of.

soma ['sɔma] *f* sum.

Somália [so'malja] *f*: **a** ~ Somalia.

somar [so'ma*] *vt* (*adicionar*) to add (up); (*chegar a*) to add up to, amount to ♦ *vi* to add up.

somatório [soma'tɔrju] *m* sum; (*fig*) sum total.

sombra ['sõbra] *f* shadow; (*proteção*) shade;

(*indício*) trace, sign; **à ~ de** in the shade of; (*fig*) under the protection of; **sem ~ de dúvida** without a shadow of a doubt; **querer ~ e água fresca** (*fig*) to want the good things in life.

sombreado/a [sõ'brjadu/a] *adj* shady ♦ *m* shading.

sombrear [sõ'brja*] *vt* to shade.

sombreiro [sõ'brejru] *m* (*chapéu*) sombrero.

sombrinha [sõ'briɲa] *f* parasol, sunshade; (*BR*) lady's umbrella.

sombrio/a [sõ'briu/a] *adj* (*escuro*) shady, dark; (*triste*) gloomy; (*rosto*) grim.

some ['sɔmi] *etc vb* V **sumir**.

somenos [so'menuʃ] *adj* inferior, poor; **de ~ importância** unimportant.

somente [sɔ'mẽtʃi] *adv* only; **tão ~** only.

somos ['somoʃ] *vb* V **ser**.

sonambulismo [sonãbu'liʒmu] *m* sleepwalking.

sonâmbulo/a [so'nãbulu/a] *adj* sleepwalking ♦ *m/f* sleepwalker.

sonante [so'nãtʃi] *adj*: **moeda ~** cash.

sonata [so'nata] *f* sonata.

sonda ['sõda] *f* (*NÁUT*) plummet, sounding lead; (*MED*) probe; (*de petróleo*) drill; (*de alimentação*) drip; **~ espacial** space probe.

sondagem [sõ'daʒẽ] (*pl* **-ns**) *f* (*NÁUT*) sounding; (*de terreno, opinião*) survey; (*para petróleo*) drilling; (*para minerais*) boring; (*atmosférica*) testing.

sondar [sõ'da*] *vt* to probe; (*opinião etc*) to sound out.

soneca [so'nɛka] *f* nap, snooze; **tirar uma ~** to have a nap.

sonegação [sonega'sãw] *f* withholding; (*furto*) theft; **~ de impostos** tax evasion.

sonegar [sone'ga*] *vt* (*dinheiro, valores*) to conceal, withhold; (*furtar*) to steal, pilfer; (*impostos*) to dodge, evade; (*informações, dados*) to withhold.

soneto [so'netu] *m* sonnet.

sonhador(a) [soɲa'do*(a)] *adj* dreamy ♦ *m/f* dreamer.

sonhar [so'ɲa*] *vt, vi* to dream; **~ com** to dream about; **~ em fazer** to dream of doing; **~ acordado** to daydream; **nem sonhando** *ou* **~!** (*col*) no way!

sonho ['soɲu] *m* dream; (*CULIN*) doughnut.

sono ['sonu] *m* sleep; **estar caindo de ~** to be half-asleep; **estar com** *ou* **ter ~** to be sleepy; **estar sem ~** not to be sleepy; **ferrar no ~** to fall into a deep sleep; **pegar no ~** to fall asleep; **ter o ~ leve/pesado** to be a light/heavy sleeper.

sonolência [sono'lẽsja] *f* drowsiness.

sonolento/a [sono'lẽtu/a] *adj* sleepy, drowsy.

sonoridade [sonori'dadʒi] *f* sound quality.

sonoro/a [so'nɔru/a] *adj* resonant; (*consoante*) voiced.

sonoterapia [sonotera'pia] *f* hypnotherapy.

sons [sõʃ] *mpl de* **som**.

sonso/a ['sõsu/a] *adj* sly, artful.

sopa ['sopa] *f* soup; (*col*) pushover, cinch; **dar ~** (*abundar*) to be plentiful; (*estar disponível*) to go spare; (*descuidar-se*) to be careless; **essa ~ vai acabar** (*col*) all good things come to an end; **~ de legumes** vegetable soup.

sopapear [sopa'pja*] *vt* to slap.

sopapo [so'papu] *m* slap, cuff; **dar um ~ em** to slap.

sopé [so'pɛ] *m* foot, bottom.

sopeira [so'pejra] *f* (*CULIN*) soup dish.

sopitar [sopi'ta*] *vt* (*conter*) to curb, repress.

soporífero/a [sopo'riferu/a] *adj* soporific ♦ *m* sleeping drug.

soporífico/a [sopo'rifiku/a] *adj, m* = **soporífero**.

soprano [so'pranu] *adj, m/f* soprano.

soprar [so'pra*] *vt* to blow; (*balão*) to blow up; (*vela*) to blow out; (*dizer em voz baixa*) to whisper ♦ *vi* to blow.

sopro ['sopru] *m* blow, puff; (*de vento*) gust; (*no coração*) murmur; **instrumento de ~** wind instrument.

soquei [so'kej] *etc vb* V **socar**.

soquete [so'ketʃi] *f* ankle sock.

sordidez [soxdʒi'deʒ] *f* sordidness; (*imundície*) squalor.

sórdido/a ['sɔxdʒidu/a] *adj* sordid; (*imundo*) squalid; (*obsceno*) indecent, dirty.

soro ['soru] *m* (*MED*) serum; (*do leite*) whey.

sóror ['sɔro*] *f* (*REL*) sister.

sorrateiro/a [soxa'tejru/a] *adj* sly, sneaky.

sorridente [soxi'dẽtʃi] *adj* smiling.

sorrir [so'xi*] *vi* to smile.

sorriso [so'xizu] *m* smile; **~ amarelo** forced smile.

sorte ['sɔxtʃi] *f* luck; (*casualidade*) chance; (*destino*) fate, destiny; (*condição*) lot; (*espécie*) sort, kind; **de ~** (*pessoa etc*) lucky; **desta ~** so, thus; **de ~ que** so that; **por ~** luckily; **dar ~** (*trazer sorte*) to bring good luck; (*ter sorte*) to be lucky; **estar com** *ou* **ter ~** to be lucky; **tentar a ~** to try one's luck; **ter a ~ de** to be lucky enough to; **tirar a ~** to draw lots; **tirar a ~ grande** (*tb fig*) to hit the jackpot; **~ grande** big prize.

sorteado/a [sox'tʃjadu/a] *adj* (*pessoa, bilhete*) winning; (*MIL*) conscripted.

sortear [sox'tʃja*] *vt* to draw lots for; (*rifar*) to raffle; (*MIL*) to draft.

sorteio [sox'teju] *m* draw; (*rifa*) raffle; (*MIL*) draft.

sortido/a [sox'tʃidu/a] *adj* (*abastecido*) supplied, stocked; (*variado*) assorted; (*loja*) well-stocked.

sortilégio [soxtʃi'lɛʒu] *m* (*bruxaria*) sorcery; (*encantamento*) charm, fascination.

NB: *European Portuguese adds the following consonants to certain words:* **b** (sú(b)dito, su(b)til); **c** (a(c)ção, a(c)cionista, a(c)to); **m** (inde(m)ne); **p** (ado(p)ção, ado(p)tar); *for further details see p. xiii.*

sortimento [soxtʃi'mɛtu] *m* assortment, stock.

sortir [sox'tʃi*] *vt* (*abastecer*) to supply, stock; (*variar*) to vary, mix.

sortudo/a [sox'tudu/a] (*col*) *adj* lucky ♦ *m/f* lucky beggar.

sorumbático/a [sorũ'batʃiku/a] *adj* gloomy, melancholy.

sorvedouro [soxve'doru] *m* whirlpool; (*abismo*) chasm; **um ~ de dinheiro** (*fig*) a drain on resources.

sorver [sox've*] *vt* (*beber*) to sip; (*inalar*) to inhale; (*tragar*) to swallow up; (*absorver*) to soak up, absorb.

sorvete [sox'vetʃi] (*BR*) *m* (*feito com leite*) ice cream; (*feito com água*) sorbet; **~ de chocolate/creme** chocolate/dairy ice cream.

sorveteiro [soxve'tejru] *m* ice-cream man.

sorveteria [soxvete'ria] *f* ice-cream parlour (*BRIT*) *ou* parlor (*US*).

sorvo ['soxvu] *m* sip.

SOS *abr* SOS.

sósia ['sɔzja] *m/f* double.

soslaio [soz'laju]: **de ~** *adv:* sideways, obliquely; **olhar algo de ~** to squint at sth.

sossegado/a [sose'gadu/a] *adj* peaceful, calm.

sossegar [sose'ga*] *vt* to calm, quieten ♦ *vi* to quieten down.

sossego [so'segu] *m* peace (and quiet).

sotaina [so'tajna] *f* cassock, soutane.

sótão ['sɔtãw] (*pl* ~s) *m* attic, loft.

sotaque [so'taki] *m* accent.

sotavento [sota'vẽtu] *m* (*NÁUT*) lee; **a ~** to leeward.

soterrar [sote'xa*] *vt* to bury.

soturno/a [so'tuxnu/a] *adj* sad, gloomy.

sou [so] *vb* V **ser**.

soube ['sobi] *etc vb* V **saber**.

soutien [su'tʃjã] *m* = **sutiã**.

sova ['sɔva] *f* beating, thrashing; **dar uma ~ em alguém** to beat sb up; **levar uma ~ (de alguém)** to be beaten up (by sb).

sovaco [so'vaku] *m* armpit.

sovaqueira [sova'kejra] *f* body odour (*BRIT*) *ou* odor (*US*).

sovar [so'va*] *vt* (*surrar*) to beat, thrash; (*massa*) to knead; (*uva*) to tread; (*roupa*) to wear out; (*couro*) to soften up.

soviético/a [so'vjɛtʃiku/a] *adj*, *m/f* Soviet.

sovina [so'vina] *m/f* miser, skinflint ♦ *adj* mean, stingy.

sovinice [sovi'nisi] *f* meanness.

sozinho/a [sɔ'ziɲu/a] *adj* (all) alone, by oneself; (*por si mesmo*) by oneself.

SP *abr* = **São Paulo**.

SPI (*BR*) *abr m* = **Serviço de Proteção ao Índio**.

spot [iʃ'pɔtʃi] (*pl* ~s) *m* spotlight.

spray [iʃ'prej] (*pl* ~s) *m* spray.

spread [iʃ'prɛdʒi] *m* (*COM*) spread.

SPU (*BR*) *abr m* = **Serviço de Patrimônio da União**; = **Serviço Psiquiátrico de Urgência**.

squash [iʃ'kweʃ] *m* squash.

Sr. *abr* (= *senhor*) Mr(.).

Sr.ª *abr* (= *senhora*) Mrs(.).

Sri Lanka [ʃri'lãka] *m*: **o ~** Sri Lanka.

Sr.ta *abr* (= *senhorita*) Miss.

SSP (*BR*) *abr f* = **Secretaria de Segurança Pública**.

staff [iʃ'tafi] *m* staff.

standard [iʃ'tãdaxdʒi] *adj inv* standard.

status [iʃ'tatus] *m* status.

STF (*BR*) *abr m* = **Supremo Tribunal Federal**.

STM (*BR*) *abr m* = **Supremo Tribunal Militar**.

sua ['sua] *f de* **seu**.

suado/a ['swadu/a] *adj* sweaty; (*fig: dinheiro etc*) hard-earned.

suadouro [swa'doru] *m* sweat; (*lugar*) sauna.

suar [swa*] *vt ou vi* to sweat; (*fig*): **~ por algo/para conseguir algo** to sweat blood for sth/to get sth; **~ em bicas** to sweat buckets; **~ frio** to come out in a cold sweat.

suástica ['swaʃtʃika] *f* swastika.

suave ['swavi] *adj* gentle; (*música, voz*) soft; (*sabor, vinho*) smooth; (*cheiro*) delicate; (*dor*) mild; (*trabalho*) light; (*prestações*) easy.

suavidade [suavi'dadʒi] *f* gentleness; (*de voz*) softness.

suavizar [swavi'za*] *vt* to soften; (*dor, sofrimento*) to alleviate.

subalimentado/a [subalimẽ'tadu/a] *adj* undernourished.

subalterno/a [subaw'tɛxnu/a] *adj* inferior, subordinate ♦ *m/f* subordinate.

subalugar [subalu'ga*] *vt* to sublet.

subarrendar [subaxẽ'da*] (*PT*) *vt* to sublet.

subconsciência [subkõ'sjẽsja] *f* subconscious.

subconsciente [subkõ'sjẽtʃi] *adj*, *m* subconscious.

subdesenvolvido/a [subdʒizẽvow'vidu/a] *adj* underdeveloped ♦ *m/f* (*pej*) degenerate.

subdesenvolvimento [subdʒizẽvowvi'mẽtu] *m* underdevelopment.

súbdito ['subditu] (*PT*) *m* = **súdito**.

subdividir [subdʒivi'dʒi*] *vt* to subdivide; **~-se** *vr* to subdivide.

subeditor(a) [subedʒi'to*(a)] *m/f* subeditor.

subemprego [subẽ'pregu] *m* low-paid unskilled job.

subentender [subẽtẽ'de*] *vt* to understand, assume.

subentendido/a [subẽtẽ'dʒidu/a] *adj* implied ♦ *m* implication.

subestimar [subeʃtʃi'ma*] *vt* to underestimate.

subida [su'bida] *f* ascent, climb; (*ladeira*) slope; (*de preços*) rise.

subido/a [su'bidu/a] *adj* high.

subir [su'bi*] *vi* to go up; (*preço, de posto etc*) to rise ♦ *vt* (*levantar*) to raise; (*ladeira, escada, rio*) to climb, go up; **~ em** (*morro, árvore*) to climb, go up; (*cadeira, palanque*) to climb onto, get up onto; (*ônibus*) to get on.

súbito/a ['subitu/a] *adj* sudden ♦ *adv* (*tb: de ~*) suddenly.

subjacente [subʒa'sẽtʃi] *adj* (*tb fig*) underlying.

subjetivo/a [subʒe'tʃivu/a] (*PT*: -ct-) *adj* subjective.

subjugar [subʒu'ga*] *vt* to subjugate, subdue; (*inimigo*) to overpower; (*moralmente*) to dominate.

subjuntivo/a [subʒũ'tʃivu/a] *adj* subjunctive ♦ *m* subjunctive.

sublevação [subleva'sãw] (*pl* -ões) *f* (up)rising, revolt.

sublevar [suble'va*] *vt* to stir up (to revolt), incite (to revolt); ~-se *vr* to revolt, rebel.

sublimar [subli'ma*] *vt* (*pessoa*) to exalt; (*desejos*) to sublimate.

sublime [su'blimi] *adj* sublime; (*nobre*) noble; (*música*, *espetáculo*) marvellous (*BRIT*), marvelous (*US*).

sublinhado [subli'ɲadu] *m* underlining.

sublinhar [subli'ɲa*] *vt* (*pôr linha debaixo de*) to underline; (*destacar*) to emphasize, stress.

sublocar [sublo'ka*] *vt*, *vi* to sublet.

sublocatário/a [subloka'tarju/a] *m/f* subtenant.

submarino/a [subma'rinu/a] *adj* underwater ♦ *m* submarine.

submergir [submex'ʒi*] *vt* to submerge; ~-se *vr* to submerge.

submerso/a [sub'mexsu/a] *adj* submerged; (*absorto*): ~ **em** immersed *ou* engrossed in.

submeter [subme'te*] *vt* (*povos*, *inimigo*) to subdue; (*plano*) to submit; (*sujeitar*): ~ **a** to subject to; ~-se *vr*: ~-se **a** to submit to; (*operação*) to undergo.

submirjo [sub'mixju] *etc vb V* **submergir**.

submissão [submi'sãw] *f* submission.

submisso/a [sub'misu/a] *adj* submissive, docile.

submundo [sub'mũdu] *m* underworld.

subnutrição [subnutri'sãw] *f* malnutrition.

subnutrido/a [subnu'tridu/a] *adj* malnourished.

subordinar [suboxdʒi'na*] *vt* to subordinate.

subornar [subox'na*] *vt* to bribe.

suborno [su'boxnu] *m* bribery.

subproduto [subpro'dutu] *m* by-product.

sub-reptício/a [subxep'tʃisju/a] *adj* surreptitious.

subrotina [subxo'tʃina] *f* (*COMPUT*) subroutine.

subscrever [subʃkre've*] *vt* to sign; (*opinião*, *COM*: *ações*) to subscribe to; (*contribuir*) to put in ♦ *vi*: ~ **a** to endorse; ~-se *vr* to sign one's name; ~ **para** to contribute to; **subscrevemo-nos** ... (*COM*: *em cartas*) ≈ we remain ....

subscrição [subʃkri'sãw] (*pl* -ões) *f* subscription; (*contribuição*) contribution.

subscritar [subʃkri'ta*] *vt* to sign.

subscrito/a [sub'ʃkritu/a] *pp de* **subscrever**.

subsecretário/a [subsekre'tarju/a] *m/f* undersecretary.

subseqüente [subse'kwẽtʃi] *adj* subsequent.

subserviente [subsex'vjẽtʃi] *adj* obsequious, servile.

subsidiar [subsi'dʒa*] *vt* to subsidize.

subsidiária [subsi'dʒjarja] *f* (*COM*) subsidiary (company).

subsidiário/a [subsi'dʒjarju/a] *adj* subsidiary.

subsídio [sub'sidʒu] *m* subsidy; (*ajuda*) aid; ~s *mpl* data *sg*, information *sg*.

subsistência [subsiʃ'tẽsja] *f* (*sustento*) subsistence; (*meio de vida*) livelihood.

subsistir [subsiʃ'tʃi*] *vi* (*existir*) to exist; (*viver*) to subsist, live; (*estar em vigor*) to be in force; (*perdurar*) to remain, survive.

subsolo [sub'sɔlu] *m* subsoil; (*de prédio*) basement.

substabelecer [subiʃtabele'se*] *vt* to delegate.

substância [sub'ʃtãsja] *f* substance.

substancial [subʃtã'sjaw] (*pl* -ais) *adj* substantial.

substantivo/a [subʃtã'tʃivu/a] *adj* substantive ♦ *m* noun.

substituição [subʃtʃitwi'sãw] (*pl* -ões) *f* substitution, replacement.

substituir [subʃtʃi'twi*] *vt* to substitute, replace.

substituto/a [subʃti'tutu/a] *adj*, *m/f* substitute.

subterfúgio [subtex'fuʒu] *m* subterfuge.

subterrâneo/a [subite'xanju/a] *adj* subterranean, underground.

subtil *etc* [sub'tiw] (*PT*) = **sutil** *etc*.

subtítulo [sub'tʃitulu] *m* subtitle.

subtrair [subtra'i*] *vt* (*furtar*) to steal; (*deduzir*) to subtract ♦ *vi* to subtract.

subumano/a [subu'manu/a] *adj* subhuman; (*desumano*) inhuman.

suburbano/a [subux'banu/a] *adj* suburban; (*pej*) uncultivated.

subúrbio [su'buxbju] *m* suburb.

subvenção [subvẽ'sãw] (*pl* -ões) *f* subsidy, grant.

subvencionar [subvẽsjo'na*] *vt* to subsidize.

subvenções [subvẽ'sõjʃ] *fpl de* **subvenção**.

subversivo/a [subvex'sivu/a] *adj*, *m/f* subversive.

subverter [subvex'te*] *vt* to subvert; (*povo*) to incite (to revolt); (*planos*) to upset.

Sucam ['sukã] (*BR*) *abr f* = **Superintendência da Campanha de Saúde Pública**.

sucata [su'kata] *f* scrap metal.

sucatar [suka'ta*] *vt* to scrap.

sucção [suk'sãw] *f* suction.

sucedâneo/a [suse'danju/a] *adj* substitute ♦ *m* (*substância*) substitute.

suceder [suse'de*] *vi* to happen ♦ *vt* to succeed; ~-se *vr* to succeed one another; ~ **a** (*num cargo*) to succeed; (*seguir*) to follow; ~ **com** to happen to; ~-se **a** to follow.

sucedido [suse'dʒidu] *m* event, occurrence.

sucessão [suse'sãw] (*pl* -ões) *f* succession.

NB: *European Portuguese adds the following consonants to certain words:* **b** (sú(b)dito, su(b)til); **c** (a(c)ção, a(c)cionista, a(c)to); **m** (inde(m)ne); **p** (ado(p)ção, ado(p)tar); *for further details see p. xiii.*

sucessivo/a [suse'sivu/a] *adj* successive.

sucesso [su'sɛsu] *m* success; *(música, filme)* hit; **com/sem** ~ successfully/unsuccessfully; **de** ~ successful; **fazer** *ou* **ter** ~ to be successful.

sucessor(a) [suse'so*(a)] *m/f* successor.

súcia ['susja] *f* gang, band.

sucinto/a [su'sĩtu/a] *adj* succinct.

suco ['suku] *(BR)* *m* juice; ~ **de laranja** orange juice.

suculento/a [suku'lẽtu/a] *adj* succulent, juicy; *(substancial)* substantial.

sucumbir [sukũ'bi*] *vi (render)* to succumb, yield; *(morrer)* to die, perish.

sucursal [sukux'saw] *(pl* **-ais)** *f (COM)* branch.

Sudam ['sudã] *abr f* = **Superintendência de Desenvolvimento da Amazônia.**

Sudão [su'dãw] *m*: **o** ~ (the) Sudan.

Sudeco [su'dɛku] *(BR)* *abr f* = **Superintendência de Desenvolvimento do Centro-Oeste.**

Sudene [su'dɛni] *(BR)* *abr f* = **Superintendência de Desenvolvimento do Nordeste.**

Sudepe [su'dɛpi] *(BR)* *abr f* = **Superintendência de Desenvolvimento da Pesca.**

sudeste [su'dɛʃtʃi] *adj* southeast ♦ *m*: **o** ~ the South East.

Sudhevea [sude'vɛa] *(BR)* *abr f* = **Superintendência da Borracha.**

súdito ['sudʒitu] *m (de rei etc)* subject.

sudoeste [sud'wɛʃtʃi] *adj* southwest ♦ *m*: **o** ~ the South West.

Suécia ['swɛsja] *f*: **a** ~ Sweden.

sueco/a ['sweku/a] *adj* Swedish ♦ *m/f* Swede ♦ *m (LING)* Swedish.

suéter ['swɛte*] *(BR)* *m ou f* sweater.

Suez [swɛʒ]: **o canal de** ~ the Suez canal.

suficiência [sufi'sjẽsja] *f* sufficiency.

suficiente [sufi'sjẽtʃi] *adj* sufficient, enough; **o** ~ enough.

sufixo [su'fiksu] *m* suffix.

suflê [su'flɛ] *m* soufflé.

sufocante [sufo'kãtʃi] *adj* suffocating; *(calor)* sweltering, oppressive.

sufocar [sufo'ka*] *vt* to suffocate; *(revolta)* to put down ♦ *vi* to suffocate.

sufoco [su'foku] *m (afã)* eagerness; *(ansiedade)* anxiety; *(dificuldade)* hassle.

sufrágio [su'fraʒu] *m* suffrage, vote; ~ **universal** universal suffrage.

sugar [su'ga*] *vt* to suck; *(fig)* to extort.

sugerir [suʒe'ri*] *vt* to suggest.

sugestão [suʒeʃ'tãw] *(pl* **-ões)** *f* suggestion; **dar uma** ~ to make a suggestion.

sugestionar [suʒeʃtʃjo'na*] *vt* to influence; ~-**se** *vr* to be influenced.

sugestionável [suʒeʃtʃjo'navew] *(pl* **-eis)** *adj* impressionable.

sugestivo/a [suʒeʃ'tʃivu/a] *adj* suggestive.

sugestões [suʒeʃ'tõjʃ] *fpl* **de sugestão.**

sugiro [su'ʒiru] *etc vb V* **sugerir.**

suguei [su'gej] *etc vb V* **sugar.**

Suíça ['swisa] *f*: **a** ~ Switzerland.

suíças ['swisaʃ] *fpl* sideburns; *V tb* **suiço.**

suicida [swi'sida] *m/f* suicidal person; *(morto)* suicide ♦ *adj* suicidal.

suicidar-se [swisi'daxsi] *vr* to commit suicide.

suicídio [swisi'dʒju] *m* suicide.

suíço/a ['swisu/a] *adj, m/f* Swiss.

sui generis [swi'ʒeneris] *adj inv* in a class of one's own, unique.

suíno ['swinu] *m* pig, hog ♦ *adj V* **gado.**

Suipa ['swipa] *(BR)* *abr f* = **Sociedade União Internacional Protetora dos Animais.**

suíte ['switʃi] *f (MÚS, em hotel)* suite; *(em residência)* maid's quarters *pl.*

sujar [su'ʒa*] *vt* to dirty; *(fig: honra)* to sully ♦ *vi* to make a mess; ~-**se** *vr* to get dirty; *(fig)* to sully o.s.

sujeição [suʒej'sãw] *f* subjection.

sujeira [su'ʒejra] *f* dirt; *(estado)* dirtiness; *(col)* dirty trick; **fazer uma** ~ **com alguém** to do the dirty on sb.

sujeitar [suʒej'ta*] *vt* to subject; ~-**se** *vr* to submit.

sujeito/a [su'ʒejtu/a] *adj*: ~ **a** subject to ♦ *m (LING)* subject ♦ *m/f* fellow/woman; ~ **a espaço** *(AER)* stand-by.

sujidade [suʒi'dadʒi] *(PT)* *f* dirt; *(estado)* dirtiness.

sujo/a ['suʒu/a] *adj* dirty; *(fig: desonesto)* nasty, dishonest ♦ *m* dirt; **estar/ficar** ~ **com alguém** to be/get into sb's bad books.

sul [suw] *adj inv* south, southern ♦ *m*: **o** ~ the south.

sul-africano/a *adj, m/f* South African.

sul-americano/a *adj, m/f* South American.

sulcar [suw'ka*] *vt* to plough *(BRIT)*, plow *(US)*; *(rosto)* to line, furrow.

sulco [suw'ku] *m* furrow.

sulfato [suw'fatu] *m* sulphate *(BRIT)*, sulfate *(US)*.

sulfúrico/a [suw'furiku/a] *adj V* **ácido.**

sulista [su'liʃta] *adj* Southern ♦ *m/f* Southerner.

sultão/tana [suw'tãw/'tana] *(pl* **-ões/~s)** *m/f* sultan/sultana.

suma ['suma] *f*: **em** ~ in short.

sumamente [suma'mẽtʃi] *adv* extremely.

sumário/a [su'marju/a] *adj (breve)* brief, concise; *(JUR)* summary; *(biquíni)* brief, skimpy ♦ *m* summary.

sumiço [su'misu] *m* disappearance; **dar** ~ **a** *ou* **em** to do away with; *(comida)* to put away.

sumidade [sumi'dadʒi] *f (pessoa)* genius.

sumido/a [su'midu/a] *adj (apagado)* faint, indistinct; *(voz)* low; *(desaparecido)* vanished; *(escondido)* hidden; **ela anda sumida** she's not around much.

sumir [su'mi*] *vi* to disappear, vanish.

sumo/a ['sumu/a] *adj (importância)* extreme; *(qualidade)* supreme ♦ *m (PT)* juice.

sumptuoso/a [sũ'twozu/ɔza] *(PT)* *adj* = **suntuoso/a.**

Sunab [su'nabi] *(BR)* *abr f* = **Superintendência Nacional de Abastecimento.**

Sunamam [suna'mami] (*BR*) *abr f* = **Supe-rintendência Nacional da Marinha Mercante.**
sundae ['sãdej] *m* sundae.
sunga ['sũga] *f* swimming trunks *pl*.
sungar [sũ'ga*] *vt* to hitch up.
suntuoso/a [sũ'twozu/ɔza] *adj* sumptuous.
suor [swɔ*] *m* sweat; (*fig*): **com o meu** ~ by the sweat of my brow.
super- [supe*-] *prefixo* super-; (*col*) really.
superabundante [superabũ'dãtʃi] *adj* over-abundant.
superado/a [supe'radu/a] *adj* (*idéias*) out-moded.
superalimentar [superalimẽ'ta*] *vt* to over-feed.
superaquecer [superake'se*] *vt* to overheat.
superar [supe'ra*] *vt* (*rival*) to surpass; (*ini-migo, dificuldade*) to overcome; (*expectativa*) to exceed.
superávit [supe'ravitʃi] *m* (*COM*) surplus.
superdose [supex'dɔzi] *f* overdose.
superdotado/a [supexdo'tadu/a] *adj* excep-tionally gifted.
superestimar [supereʃtʃi'ma*] *vt* to overesti-mate.
superestrutura [supereʃtru'tura] *f* super-structure.
superficial [supexfi'sjaw] (*pl* **-ais**) *adj* super-ficial; (*pessoa*) shallow.
superfície [supex'fisi] *f* (*parte externa*) sur-face; (*extensão*) area; (*fig*: *aparência*) appearance.
superfino/a [supex'finu/a] *adj* (*de largura*) extra fine; (*de qualidade*) excellent quality *atr*.
supérfluo/a [su'pexflwu/a] *adj* superfluous.
super-homem (*pl* **-ns**) *m* superman.
superintendência [superĩtẽ'dẽsja] *f* (*órgão*) bureau.
superintendente [superĩtẽ'dẽtʃi] *m* super-intendent; (*de empresa*) chief executive.
superintender [superĩtẽ'de*] *vt* to super-intend.
superior [supe'rjo*] *adj* superior; (*mais elevado*) higher; (*quantidade*) greater; (*mais acima*) upper ♦ *m* superior; (*REL*) superior, abbot; ~ **a** superior to; **um número** ~ **a 10** a number greater *ou* higher than 10; **curso/ensino** ~ degree course/higher education; **lá-bio** ~ upper lip.
superiora [supe'rjora] *adj*, *f*: **(madre)** ~ mother superior.
superioridade [superjori'dadʒi] *f* superiority.
superlativo/a [supexla'tʃivu/a] *adj* superlative ♦ *m* superlative.
superlotação [supexlota'sãw] *f* overcrowding.
superlotado/a [supexlo'tadu/a] *adj* (*cheio*) really crowded; (*excessivamente cheio*) over-crowded.
supermercado [supexmex'kadu] *m* super-

market.
supermicro [supex'mikru] *m* (*COMPUT*) super-micro.
supermíni [supex'mini] *m* (*COMPUT*) super-mini.
superpor [supex'po*] (*irreg*: *como* **pôr**) *vt*: ~ **algo a algo** to put sth before sth.
superpotência [supexpo'tẽsja] *f* superpower.
superpovoado/a [supexpo'vwadu/a] *adj* over-populated.
superprodução [supexprodu'sãw] *f* over-production.
superproteger [supexprote'ʒe*] *vt* to over-protect.
superpunha [supex'puɲa] *etc vb* V **superpor.**
superpus [supex'puʃ] *etc vb* V **superpor.**
superpuser [supexpu'ze*] *etc vb* V **superpor.**
supersecreto/a [supexse'krɛtu/a] *adj* top secret.
supersensível [supexsẽ'sivew] (*pl* **-eis**) *adj* oversensitive.
supersimples [supex'sĩpliʃ] *adj inv* extremely simple.
supersônico/a [supex'soniku/a] *adj* super-sonic.
superstição [supexʃtʃi'sãw] (*pl* **-ões**) *f* super-stition.
supersticioso/a [supexʃtʃi'sjozu/ɔza] *adj* superstitious.
superstições [supexʃtʃi'sõjʃ] *fpl de* **supers-tição.**
supervisão [supexvi'zãw] *f* supervision.
supervisionar [supexvizjo'na*] *vt* to supervise.
supervisor(a) [supexvi'zo*(a)] *m/f* supervisor.
supetão [supe'tãw] *m*: **de** ~ all of a sudden.
suplantar [suplã'ta*] *vt* to supplant, supersede.
suplementar [suplemẽ'ta*] *adj* supplementary ♦ *vt* to supplement.
suplemento [suple'mẽtu] *m* supplement.
suplente [su'plẽtʃi] *m/f* substitute.
súplica ['suplika] *f* supplication, plea.
suplicante [supli'kãtʃi] *m/f* supplicant; (*JUR*) plaintiff.
suplicar [supli'ka*] *vt*, *vi* to plead, beg; ~ **algo a** *ou* **de alguém** to beg sb for sth; ~ **a alguém que faça** to beg sb to do.
suplício [su'plisju] *m* torture; (*experiência penosa*) trial.
supor [su'po*] (*irreg*: *como* **pôr**) *vt* to suppose; (*julgar*) to think; **suponhamos que** let us suppose that; **vamos** ~ let us suppose *ou* say; **suponho que sim** I suppose so; **era de** ~ **que** one could assume that.
suportar [supox'ta*] *vt* to hold up, support; (*tolerar*) to bear, tolerate.
suportável [supox'tavew] (*pl* **-eis**) *adj* bear-able, tolerable.
suporte [su'pɔxtʃi] *m* support, stand; ~ **atléti-co** athletic support, jockstrap.
suposição [supozi'sãw] (*pl* **-ões**) *f* supposition,

NB: European Portuguese adds the following consonants to certain words: **b** (sú(b)dito, su(b)til); **c** (a(c)ção a(c)cionista, a(c)to); **m** (inde(m)ne); **p** (ado(p)ção, ado(p)tar); *for further details see p. xiii.*

presumption.

supositório [supozi'tɔrju] *m* suppository.

supostamente [supoʃta'mētʃi] *adv* supposedly.

suposto/a [su'poʃtu/'pɔʃta] *pp de* **supor** ♦ *adj* supposed ♦ *m* assumption.

supracitado/a [suprasi'tadu/a] *adj* foregoing ♦ *m* foregoing.

supra-sumo ['supra-] *m*: **o** ~ **da beleza** *etc* the pinnacle of beauty *etc*.

supremacia [suprema'sia] *f* supremacy.

supremo/a [su'prɛmu/a] *adj* supreme ♦ *m*: **o** **S**~ the Supreme Court; **S**~ **Tribunal Federal** (*BR*) Federal Supreme Court.

supressão [supre'sãw] (*pl* **-ões**) *f* suppression; (*omissão*) omission; (*abolição*) abolition.

suprimento [supri'mētu] *m* supply.

suprimir [supri'mi*] *vt* to suppress; (*frases de um texto*) to delete; (*abolir*) to abolish.

suprir [su'pri*] *vt* (*fazer as vezes de*) to take the place of; ~ **alguém de** to provide *ou* supply sb with; ~ **algo por algo** to substitute sth with sth; ~ **uma quantia** to make up an amount; ~ **a falta de alguém/algo** to make up for sb's absence/the lack of sth; ~ **as necessidades/uma família** to provide for needs/a family.

supunha [su'puɲa] *etc vb V* **supor.**

supus [su'puʃ] *etc vb V* **supor.**

supuser [supu'ze*] *etc vb V* **supor.**

supurar [supu'ra*] *vi* to go septic, suppurate.

surdez [sux'deʒ] *f* deafness; **aparelho de** ~ hearing aid.

surdina [sux'dʒina] *f* (*MÚS*) mute; **em** ~ stealthily, on the quiet.

surdo/a ['suxdu/a] *adj* deaf; (*som*) muffled, dull; (*consoante*) voiceless ♦ *m/f* deaf person; ~ **como uma porta** as deaf as a post.

surdo/a-mudo/a *adj* deaf and dumb ♦ *m/f* deaf-mute.

surfe ['suxfi] *m* surfing.

surfista [sux'fiʃta] *m/f* surfer.

surgir [sux'ʒi*] *vi* to appear; (*problema, dificuldade*) to arise, crop up; (*oportunidade*) to arise, come up; ~ **de** (*proceder*) to come from; ~ **à mente** to come *ou* spring to mind.

Suriname [suri'nami] *m*: **o** ~ Surinam.

surjo ['suxju] *etc vb V* **surgir.**

surpreendente [suxprjē'dētʃi] *adj* surprising.

surpreender [suxprjē'de*] *vt* to surprise; (*pegar de surpresa*) to take unawares ♦ *vi* to be surprising; ~**-se** *vr*: ~**-se** (**de**) to be surprised (at).

surpresa [sux'preza] *f* surprise; **de** ~ by surprise.

surpreso/a [sux'prezu/a] *pp de* **surpreender** ♦ *adj* surprised.

surra ['suxa] *f* (*ger, ESPORTE*) thrashing; **dar uma** ~ **em** to thrash; **levar uma** ~ (**de**) to get thrashed (by).

surrado/a [su'xadu/a] *adj* (*espancado*) beaten up; (*roupa*) worn out.

surrar [su'xa*] *vt* to beat, thrash; (*roupa*) to

wear out.

surrealismo [suxea'liʒmu] *m* surrealism.

surrealista [suxea'liʃta] *adj, m/f* surrealist.

surrupiar [suxu'pja*] *vt* to steal.

sursis [sux'si] *m inv* (*JUR*) suspended sentence.

surte ['suxtʃi] *etc vb V* **sortir.**

surtir [sux'tʃi*] *vt* to produce, bring about; ~ **bem** to turn out well; ~ **efeito** to have an effect.

surto ['suxtu] *m* (*de doença*) outbreak; (*de progresso*) surge.

suscetibilidade [susetʃibili'dadʒi] *f* susceptibility; (*sensibilidade*) sensitivity.

suscetível [suse'tʃivew] (*pl* **-eis**) *adj* susceptible; ~ **de** liable to.

suscitar [susi'ta*] *vt* to arouse; (*admiração*) to cause; (*dúvidas*) to raise; (*obstáculos*) to throw up.

Susep [su'zɛpi] (*BR*) *abr f* = **Superintendência de Seguros Privados.**

suspeição [suʃpej'sãw] (*pl* **-ões**) *f* suspicion.

suspeita [suʃ'pejta] *f* suspicion.

suspeitar [suʃpej'ta*] *vt* to suspect ♦ *vi*: ~ **de algo** to suspect sth; ~ **de alguém** to be suspicious of sb.

suspeito/a [suʃ'pejtu/a] *adj* suspect, suspicious ♦ *m/f* suspect.

suspeitoso/a [suʃpej'tozu/ɔza] *adj* suspicious.

suspender [suʃpē'de*] *vt* (*levantar*) to lift; (*pendurar*) to hang; (*trabalho, pagamento etc*) to suspend, stop; (*funcionário, aluno*) to suspend; (*jornal*) to suspend publication of; (*encomenda*) to cancel; (*sessão*) to adjourn, defer; (*viagem*) to put off.

suspensão [suʃpē'sãw] (*pl* **-ões**) *f* (*ger, AUTO*) suspension; (*de trabalho, pagamento*) stoppage; (*de viagem, sessão*) deferment; (*de encomenda*) cancellation.

suspense [suʃ'pēsi] *m* suspense; **filme de** ~ thriller.

suspenso/a [suʃ'pēsu/a] *pp de* **suspender.**

suspensões [suʃpē'sõjʃ] *fpl de* **suspensão.**

suspensórios [suʃpē'sɔrjuʃ] *mpl* braces (*BRIT*), suspenders (*US*).

suspicácia [suʃpi'kasja] *f* distrust, suspicion.

suspicaz [suʃpi'kajʒ] *adj* (*suspeito*) suspect; (*desconfiado*) suspicious.

suspirar [suʃpi'ra*] *vi* to sigh; ~ **por algo** to long for sth.

suspiro [suʃ'piru] *m* sigh; (*doce*) meringue.

sussurrar [susu'xa*] *vt, vi* to whisper.

sussurro [su'suxu] *m* whisper.

sustância [suʃ'tãsja] *f* (*força*) strength; (*de comida*) nourishment.

sustar [suʃ'ta*] *vt, vi* to stop.

sustenho [suʃ'teɲu] *etc vb V* **suster.**

sustentáculo [suʃtē'takulu] *m* (*tb fig*) support.

sustentar [suʃtē'ta*] *vt* to sustain; (*escorar*) to hold up, support; (*manter*) to maintain; (*financeiramente, acusação*) to support; ~**-se** *vr* (*alimentar-se*) to sustain o.s.; (*financeiramente*) to support o.s.; (*equilibrar-se*) to balance; ~ **que** to maintain that.

sustento [suʃ'tẽtu] *m* sustenance; *(subsistência)* livelihood; *(amparo)* support.

suster [suʃ'te*] *(irreg: como* **ter**) *vt* to support, hold up; *(reprimir)* to restrain, hold back.

susto ['suʃtu] *m* fright, scare; **tomar** *ou* **levar um ~** to get a fright; **que ~!** what a fright!

sutiã [su'tʃjã] *m* bra(ssiere).

sutil [su'tʃiw] *(pl* **-is**) *adj* subtle; *(fino)* fine, delicate.

sutileza [sutʃi'leza] *f* subtlety; *(finura)* fineness, delicacy.

sutilizar [sutʃili'za*] *vt* to refine.

sutis [su'tʃiʃ] *adj pl de* **sutil**.

sutura [su'tura] *f* (*MED*) suture.

suturar [sutu'ra*] *vt, vi* to suture.

T

T, t [te] *(pl* **ts**) *m* T, t; **T de Tereza** T for Tommy.

ta [ta] = **te** + **a**.

tá [ta] *(col) excl* OK; **~ bom** OK, fine; = **está**.

tabacaria [tabaka'ria] *f* tobacconist's (shop).

tabaco [ta'baku] *m* tobacco.

tabefe [ta'bɛfi] *(col) m* slap.

tabela [ta'bɛla] *f* table, chart; *(lista)* list; **por ~** indirectly; **estar caindo pelas ~s** *(fig)* to be feeling low; **~ de preços** price table.

tabelado/a [tabe'ladu/a] *adj (produto)* price-controlled; *(preço)* controlled.

tabelar [tabe'la*] *vt (produto)* to fix the price of; *(preço)* to fix; *(dados)* to tabulate.

tabelião [tabe'ljãw] *(pl* **-ães**) *m* notary public.

taberna [ta'bɛxna] *f* tavern, bar.

tabique [ta'biki] *m* partition.

tablado [ta'bladu] *m* platform; *(para espectadores)* grandstand.

tablete [ta'blɛtʃi] *m (de chocolate)* bar; *(de manteiga)* pat.

tablóide [ta'blɔjdʒi] *m* tabloid.

tabu [ta'bu] *adj, m* taboo.

tábua ['tabwa] *f (de madeira)* plank, board; *(MAT)* list, table; *(de mesa)* leaf; **~ de passar roupa** ironing board; **~ de salvação** *(fig)* last resort.

tabuada [ta'bwada] *f* times table; *(livro)* tables book.

tabulador [tabula'do*] *m* tab(ulator key).

tabular [tabu'la*] *vt* to tabulate.

tabuleiro [tabu'lejru] *m* tray; *(XADREZ)* board.

tabuleta [tabu'leta] *f (letreiro)* sign, signboard.

taça ['tasa] *f* cup; **~ de champanhe** champagne glass *ou* flute.

tacada [ta'kada] *f* shot; **de uma ~** in one go.

tacanho/a [ta'kaɲu/a] *adj* mean, niggardly; *(de idéias curtas)* narrow-minded; *(baixo)* small.

tacar [ta'ka*] *vt (bola)* to hit; *(col: jogar)* to chuck; **~ a mão** *ou* **um soco em alguém** to punch sb.

tacha ['taʃa] *f (prego)* tack; *(em calça jeans)* stud.

tachar [ta'ʃa*] *vt*: **~ algo de** to brand sth as.

tachinha [ta'ʃiɲa] *f* drawing pin *(BRIT)*, thumb tack *(US)*.

tácito/a ['tasitu/a] *adj* tacit, implied.

taciturno/a [tasi'tuxnu/a] *adj* taciturn, reserved.

taco ['taku] *m (de bilhar)* cue; *(de golfe)* club; *(de hóquei)* stick; *(bucha)* plug, wad; *(de assoalho)* parquet block.

táctico/a *etc* ['tatiku/a] *(PT)* = **tático** *etc*.

táctil ['tatiw] *(PT) adj* = **tátil**.

tacto ['tatu] *(PT) m* = **tato**.

tadinho/a [ta'dʒiɲu/a] *(col) excl* poor thing!; **~ dele!** poor him!

tafetá [tafe'ta] *m* taffeta.

tagarela [taga'rɛla] *adj* talkative ♦ *m/f* chatterbox.

tagarelar [tagare'la*] *vi* to chatter.

tagarelice [tagare'lisi] *f* chat, chatter, gossip.

tailandês/esa [tajlã'deʃ/eza] *adj, m/f* Thai ♦ *m (LING)* Thai.

Tailândia [taj'lãdʒja] *f*: **a ~** Thailand.

tailleur [taj'ɛ*] *m* suit.

tainha [ta'iɲa] *f* mullet.

taipa ['tajpa] *f*: **parede de ~** mud wall.

tais [tajʃ] *adj pl de* **tal**.

Taiti [taj'tʃi] *m*: **o ~** Tahiti.

tal [taw] *(pl* **tais**) *adj* such; **~ e coisa** this and that; **um ~ de Sr. X** a certain Mr. X; **que ~?** what do you think?; *(PT)* how are things?; **que ~ um cafezinho?** what about a coffee?; **que ~ nós irmos ao cinema?** what about (us) going to the cinema?; **~ pai, ~ filho** like father, like son; **~ como** such as; *(da maneira que)* just as; **~ qual** just like; **o ~ professor** that teacher; **a ~ ponto** to such an extent; **de ~ maneira** in such a way; **e ~** and so on; **o/a ~** *(col)* the greatest; **o Pedro de ~** Peter what's-his-name; **na rua ~** in such and such a street; **foi um ~ de gente ligar lá para casa** there were people ringing home non-stop.

tala ['tala] *f (MED)* splint.

talão [ta'lãw] *(pl* **-ões**) *m (de recibo)* stub; **~ de cheques** cheque book *(BRIT)*, check book *(US)*.

talco ['tawku] *m* talc; **pó de ~** *(PT)* talcum powder.

NB: European Portuguese adds the following consonants to certain words: **b** (sú(b)dito, su(b)til); **c** (a(c)ção, a(c)cionista, a(c)to); **m** (inde(m)ne); **p** (ado(p)ção, ado(p)tar); *for further details see p. xiii.*

talento [ta'lẽtu] *m* talent; *(aptidão)* ability.
talentoso/a [talẽ'tozu/ɔza] *adj* talented.
talha ['taʎa] *f (corte)* carving; *(vaso)* pitcher; *(NÁUT)* tackle.
talhado/a [ta'ʎadu/a] *adj (apropriado)* appropriate, right; *(leite)* curdled.
talhar [ta'ʎa*] *vt* to cut; *(esculpir)* to carve ♦ *vi (coalhar)* to curdle.
talharim [taʎa'rĩ] *m* tagliatelle.
talhe ['taʎi] *m* cut, shape; *(de rosto)* line.
talher [ta'ʎe*] *m* set of cutlery; **~es** *mpl* cutlery *sg*.
talho ['taʎu] *m (corte)* cutting, slicing; *(PT: açougue)* butcher's (shop).
talismã [taliʒ'mã] *m* talisman.
talo ['talu] *m* stalk, stem; *(ARQ)* shaft.
talões [ta'lõjʃ] *mpl de* **talão**.
talude [ta'ludʒi] *m* slope, incline.
taludo/a [ta'ludu/a] *adj* stocky.
talvez [taw'veʒ] *adv* perhaps, maybe; **~ tenha razão** maybe you're right.
tamanco [ta'mãku] *m* clog, wooden shoe.
tamanduá [tamã'dwa] *m* ant-eater.
tamanho/a [ta'maɲu/a] *adj* such (a) great ♦ *m* size; **em ~ natural** life-size; **de que ~ é?** what size is it?; **uma casa que não tem ~** *(col)* a huge house; **do ~ de um bonde** *(col)* enormous.
tamanho-família *adj inv* family-size; *(fig)* giant-size.
tamanho-gigante *adj inv* giant-size.
tâmara ['tamara] *f* date.
tamarindo [tama'rĩdu] *m* tamarind.
também [tã'bẽj] *adv* also, too, as well; *(além disso)* besides; **~ não** not ... either, nor; **eu ~ me too**; **eu ~ não** nor me, neither do (*ou* did, am, have *etc*) I.
tambor [tã'bo*] *m* drum.
tamborilar [tãbori'la*] *vi (com os dedos)* to drum; *(chuva)* to pitter-pat.
tamborim [tãbo'rĩ] *(pl* **-ns)** *m* tambourine.
Tâmisa ['tamiza] *m*: **o ~** the Thames.
tampa ['tãpa] *f* lid; *(de garrafa)* cap.
tampão [tã'pãw] *(pl* **-ões)** *m* cover; *(rolha)* stopper, plug; *(vaginal)* tampon; *(para curativos)* compress.
tampar [tã'pa*] *vt (lata, garrafa)* to put the lid on; *(cobrir)* to cover.
tampinha [tã'piɲa] *f* lid, top ♦ *m/f (col)* shortly.
tampo ['tãpu] *m* lid; *(MÚS)* sounding board.
tampões [tã'põjʃ] *mpl de* **tampão**.
tampouco [tã'poku] *adv* nor, neither.
tanga ['tãga] *f* loincloth; *(biquíni)* bikini.
tangente [tã'ʒẽtʃi] *f* tangent; *(trecho retilíneo)* straight section; **pela ~** *(fig)* narrowly.
tanger [tã'ʒe*] *vt (MÚS)* to play; *(sinos)* to ring; *(cordas)* to pluck ♦ *vi (sinos)* to ring; **~ a** *(dizer respeito)* to concern; **no que tange a** as regards, with respect to.
tangerina [tãʒe'rina] *f* tangerine.
tangerineira [tãʒeri'nejra] *f* tangerine tree.

tangível [tã'ʒivew] *(pl* **-eis)** *adj* tangible.
tango ['tãgu] *m* tango.
tanjo ['tãʒu] *etc vb V* **tanger**.
tanque ['tãki] *m (reservatório, MIL)* tank; *(de lavar roupa)* sink.
tantã [tã'tã] *(col)* *adj* crazy.
tanto/a ['tãtu/a] *adj, pron (sg)* so much; (: + *interrogativa/negativa)* as much; *(pl)* so many; (: + *interrogativa/negativa)* as many ♦ *adv* so much; **~ melhor/pior** so much the better/more's the pity; **~ ... como ...** both ... and ...; **~ mais ... quanto mais ...** the more ... the more ...; **~ ... quanto ...** as much ... as ...; **~s ... quanto ...** as many ... as ...; **~ tempo** so long; **quarenta e ~s anos** forty-odd years; **vinte e tantas pessoas** twenty-odd people; **~ a Lúcia, quanto o Luís** both Lúcia and Luís; **~ faz** it's all the same to me, I don't mind; **um ~ vinho** some wine; **um outro ~ de vinho** a little more wine; **um ~ (quanto)** *(como advérbio)* rather, somewhat; **as tantas** the small hours; **lá para as tantas** late, in the small hours; **um médico e ~** quite a doctor; **não é para ~** it's not such a big deal; **não ou nem ~ assim** not as much as all that; **~ (assim) que** so much so that.
Tanzânia [tã'zanja] *f*: **a ~** Tanzania.
tão [tãw] *adv* so; **~ rico quanto** as rich as.
tão-só *adv* only.
tapa ['tapa] *f ou m* slap; **no ~** *(col)* by force.
tapado/a [ta'padu/a] *adj (col: bobo)* stupid.
tapar [ta'pa*] *vt* to cover; *(garrafa)* to cork; *(caixa)* to put the lid on; *(ouvidos)* to block; *(orifício)* to block up; *(encobrir)* to block out.
tapeação [tapja'sãw] *f* cheating.
tapear [ta'pja*] *vt, vi* to cheat.
tapeçaria [tapesa'ria] *f* tapestry; *(loja)* carpet shop.
tapetar [tape'ta*] *vt* to carpet.
tapete [ta'petʃi] *m* carpet, rug.
tapioca [ta'pjɔka] *f* tapioca.
tapume [ta'pumi] *m* fencing, boarding.
taquicardia [takikax'dʒia] *f* palpitations *pl*.
taquigrafar [takigra'fa*] *vt, vi* to write in shorthand.
taquigrafia [takigra'fia] *f* shorthand.
taquígrafo/a [ta'kigrafu/a] *m/f* shorthand typist *(BRIT)*, stenographer *(US)*.
tara ['tara] *f* fetish, mania; *(COM)* tare.
tarado/a [ta'radu/a] *adj* manic; *(sexualmente)* perverted ♦ *m/f* maniac; **~ sexual** sex maniac, pervert; **ser ~ por** to be mad about.
tarar [ta'ra*] *vi*: **~ (por)** to be smitten (with).
tardança [tax'dãsa] *f* delay, slowness.
tardar [tax'da*] *vi* to delay, be slow; *(chegar tarde)* to be late ♦ *vt* to delay; **sem mais ~** without delay; **~ a ou em fazer** to take a long time to do; **o mais ~** at the latest.
tarde ['taxdʒi] *f* afternoon ♦ *adv* late; **ele chegou ~ (demais)** he got there too late; **mais cedo ou mais ~** sooner or later; **antes ~ do que nunca** better late than never; **boa ~!**

good afternoon!; **hoje à** ~ this afternoon; **à ou de** ~ in the afternoon; **às três da** ~ at three in the afternoon; ~ **da noite** late at night; **ontem/sexta à** ~ yesterday/(on) Friday afternoon.

tardinha [tax'dʒiɲa] f late afternoon; **de** ~ late in the afternoon.

tardio/a [tax'dʒiu/a] adj late.

tarefa [ta'rɛfa] f task, job; (faina) chore.

tarifa [ta'rifa] f tariff; (para transportes) fare; (lista de preços) price list; ~ **alfandegária** customs duty; ~ **de embarque** (AER) airport tax.

tarimba [ta'rĩba] f bunk; (fig) army life; (: experiência) experience; **ter** ~ to be an old hand.

tarimbado/a [tarĩ'badu/a] adj experienced.

tartamudear [taxtamu'dʒja*] vi, vt to mumble; (gaguejar) to stammer, stutter.

tartamudo/a [taxta'mudu/a] m/f mumbler; (gago) stammerer, stutterer.

tártaro ['taxtaru] m tartar.

tartaruga [taxta'ruga] f turtle; **pente de** ~ tortoiseshell comb.

tas [taʃ] = **te** + **as**.

tasca ['taʃka] (PT) f cheap eating place.

tascar [taʃ'ka*] vt (tapa, beijo) to plant.

tasco ['taʃku] (col) m bit, mouthful.

Tasmânia [taʒ'manja] f: **a** ~ Tasmania.

tatear [ta'tʃja*] vt to touch, feel; (fig) to sound out ♦ vi to feel one's way.

táteis ['tatejʃ] adj pl de **tátil**.

tática ['tatʃika] f tactics pl.

tático/a ['tatʃiku/a] adj tactical.

tátil ['tatʃiw] (pl -eis) adj tactile.

tato ['tatu] m touch; (fig: diplomacia) tact.

tatu [ta'tu] m armadillo.

tatuador(a) [tatwa'do*(a)] m/f tattooist.

tatuagem [ta'twaʒẽ] (pl -ns) f tattoo.

tatuar [ta'twa*] vt to tattoo.

tauromaquia [tawroma'kia] f bullfighting.

tautologia [tawtolo'ʒia] f tautology.

tautológico/a [tawto'lɔʒiku/a] adj tautological.

taxa ['taʃa] f (imposto) tax; (preço) fee; (índice) rate; ~ **de câmbio** exchange rate; ~ **de juros** interest rate; ~ **bancária** bank rate; ~ **de desconto** discount rate; ~ **de matrícula** ou **inscrição** enrol(l)ment ou registration fee; ~ **de exportação** export duty; ~ **rodoviária** road tax; ~ **fixa** (COM) flat rate; ~ **de retorno** (COM) rate of return; ~ **de crescimento** growth rate.

taxação [taʃa'sãw] f taxation; (de preços) fixing.

taxar [ta'ʃa*] vt (fixar o preço de) to fix the price of; (lançar impostos sobre) to tax.

taxativo/a [taʃa'tʃivu/a] adj categorical, firm.

táxi ['taksi] m taxi, cab; ~ **aéreo** air taxi.

taxímetro [tak'simetru] m taxi meter.

taxista [tak'siʃta] m/f taxi driver.

tchã [tʃã] (col) m (toque) special touch; (charme) charm.

tchau [tʃaw] excl bye!

tcheco/a ['tʃɛku/a] adj, m/f Czech.

Tcheco-Eslováquia [tʃɛkuiʒlo'vakja] f = **Tchecoslováquia**.

Tchecoslováquia [tʃeko̜ʒlo'vakja] f: **a** ~ Czechoslovakia.

TCU (BR) abr m = **Tribunal de Contas da União**.

te [tʃi] pron you; (para você) (to) you.

té [tɛ] prep abr de **até**.

tear [tʃja*] m loom.

teatral [tʃja'traw] (pl -ais) adj theatrical; (grupo) theatre atr (BRIT), theater atr (US); (obra, arte) dramatic.

teatralizar [tʃjatrali'za*] vt to dramatize.

teatro ['tʃjatru] m theatre (BRIT), theater (US); (obras) plays pl, dramatic works pl; (gênero, curso) drama; **peça de** ~ play; **fazer** ~ (fig) to be dramatic; ~ **de arena** theatre-in-the-round; ~ **de bolso** small theatre; ~ **de marionetes** puppet theatre; ~ **de variedades** vaudeville theatre; ~ **rebolado** burlesque theatre.

teatrólogo/a [tʃja'trɔlogu/a] m/f playwright, dramatist.

teatro-revista (pl **teatros-revista**) m review theatre (BRIT) ou theater (US).

tecelão/lã [tese'lãw/'lã] (pl **-ões/~s**) m/f weaver.

tecer [te'se*] vt to weave; (fig: intrigas) to weave; (disputas) to cause ♦ vi to weave.

tecido [te'sidu] m cloth, material; (ANAT) tissue.

tecla ['tɛkla] f key; **bater na mesma** ~ (fig) to harp on the same subject; ~ **de controle** (COMPUT) control key; ~ **de função** (COMPUT) function key; ~ **de saída** (COMPUT) exit key.

tecladista [tekla'dʒiʃta] m/f (MÚS) keyboards player; (COMPUT) keyboard operator.

teclado [tek'ladu] m keyboard; ~ **complementar** (COMPUT) keypad.

teclar [tek'la*] vt (dados) to key (in).

tecnicalidade [teknikali'dadʒi] f technicality.

técnica ['tɛknika] f technique; V tb **técnico**.

técnico/a ['tekniku/a] adj technical ♦ m/f technician; (especialista) expert.

tecnicolor [tekniko'lo*] adj technicolour (BRIT), technicolor (US) ♦ m: **em** ~ in technicolo(u)r.

tecnocrata [tekno'krata] m/f technocrat.

tecnologia [teknolo'ʒia] f technology; ~ **de ponta** up-to-the-minute technology.

tecnológico/a [tekno'lɔʒiku/a] adj technological.

teco ['tɛku] m hit; (tiro) shot; (peteleco) flick.

teco-teco (pl **~s**) m small plane, light air-

NB: *European Portuguese adds the following consonants to certain words:* **b** (sú(b)dito, su(b)til); **c** (a(c)ção, a(c)cionista, a(c)to); **m** (inde(m)ne); **p** (ado(p)ção, ado(p)tar); *for further details see p. xiii.*

craft.

tecto ['tɛktu] (*PT*) *m* = **teto**.

tédio ['tɛdʒju] *m* tedium, boredom.

tedioso/a [te'dʒjozu/ɔza] *adj* tedious, boring.

Teerã [tee'rã] *n* Teheran.

teia ['teja] *f* web; (*fig*: *enredo*) intrigue, plot; (: *série*) series; ~ **de aranha** spider's web; ~ **de espionagem** spy ring, web of espionage.

teima ['tejma] *f* insistence.

teimar [tej'ma*] *vi* to insist, keep on; ~ **em** to insist on.

teimosia [tejmo'zia] *f* stubbornness; ~ **em fazer** insistence on doing.

teimoso/a [tej'mozu/ɔza] *adj* obstinate; (*criança*) wilful (*BRIT*), willful (*US*).

teixo ['tejʃu] *m* yew.

Tejo ['teʒu] *m*: **o (rio)** ~ the (river) Tagus.

tel. *abr* (= *telefone*) tel.

tela ['tɛla] *f* (*tecido*) fabric, material; (*de pintar*) canvas; (*CINEMA*, *TV*) screen.

telão [te'lãw] (*pl* **-ões**) *m* big screen.

Telavive [tela'vivi] *n* Tel Aviv.

tele... [tɛle] *prefixo* tele....

telecomandar [telekomã'da*] *vt* to operate by remote control.

telecomando [teleko'mãdu] *m* remote control.

telecomunicação [telekomunika'sãw] (*pl* **-ões**) *f* telecommunication; **telecomunicações** *fpl* telecommunications.

teleférico [tele'fɛriku] *m* cable car.

telefonar [telefo'na*] *vi* to telephone, phone; ~ **para alguém** to (tele)phone sb.

telefone [tele'fɔni] *m* phone, telephone; (*número*) (tele)phone number; (*telefonema*) phone call; **estar/falar no** ~ to be/talk on the phone; ~ **público** public phone; ~ **sem fio** cordless (tele)phone.

telefonema [telefo'nɛma] *m* phone call; **dar um** ~ to make a phone call.

telefônico/a [tele'foniku/a] *adj* telephone *atr*; **mesa telefônica** switchboard; **cabine telefônica** telephone box (*BRIT*) *ou* booth (*US*).

telefonista [telefo'niʃta] *m/f* telephonist; (*na companhia telefônica*) operator.

telegrafar [telegra'fa*] *vt*, *vi* to telegraph, wire.

telegrafia [telegra'fia] *f* telegraphy.

telegráfico/a [tele'grafiku/a] *adj* telegraphic.

telegrafista [telegra'fiʃta] *m/f* telegraph operator.

telégrafo [te'lɛgrafu] *m* telegraph.

telegrama [tele'grama] *m* telegram, cable; **passar um** ~ to send a telegram; ~ **fonado** telemessage.

teleguiado/a [tele'gjadu/a] *adj* remote-controlled.

teleguiar [tele'gja*] *vt* to operate by remote control.

teleimpressor [teleĩpre'so*] *m* teleprinter.

telejornal [teleʒox'naw] (*pl* **-ais**) *m* television news *sg*.

telêmetro [te'lemetru] *m* rangefinder.

telenovela [teleno'vɛla] *f* (TV) soap opera.

teleobjetiva [teleobʒe'tʃiva] (*PT*: **-ct-**) *f* telephoto lens.

telepatia [telepa'tʃia] *f* telepathy.

telepático/a [tele'patʃiku/a] *adj* telepathic.

teleprocessamento [teleprosesa'mẽtu] *m* teleprocessing.

Telerj [te'lɛxʒi] *abr f Rio telephone company*.

telescópico/a [tele'skɔpiku/a] *adj* telescopic.

telescópio [tele'skɔpju] *m* telescope.

Telesp [te'lɛʃpi] *abr f São Paulo telephone company*.

telespectador(a) [teleʃpekta'do*(a)] *m/f* viewer ♦ *adj* (*público*) viewing.

teletexto [tele'teʃtu] *m* teletext.

teletipista [teletʃi'piʃta] *m/f* teletypist.

teletipo [tele'tʃipu] *m* teletype.

televisão [televi'zãw] *f* television; ~ **a cores** colo(u)r television; ~ **a cabo** cable television; **aparelho de** ~ television set.

televisar [televi'za*] *vt* = **televisionar**.

televisionar [televizjo'na*] *vt* to televise.

televisivo/a [televi'zivu/a] *adj* television *atr*.

televisor [televi'zo*] *m* (*aparelho*) television (set), TV (set).

telex [te'lɛks] *m* telex.

telha ['teʎa] *f* tile; (*col*: *cabeça*) head; **ter uma** ~ **de menos** to have a screw loose; **não estar bom da** ~ not to be right in the head; **deu-lhe na** ~ **(de) viajar** he got it into his head to go travel(l)ing.

telhado [te'ʎadu] *m* roof.

telões [te'lõjʃ] *mpl de* **telão**.

tema ['tema] *m* theme; (*assunto*) subject.

temática [te'matʃika] *f* theme.

temático/a [te'matʃiku/a] *adj* thematic.

temer [te'me*] *vt* to fear, be afraid of ♦ *vi* to be afraid; ~ **por** to fear for; ~ **que** to be afraid that; ~ **fazer** to be afraid of doing.

temerário/a [teme'rarju/a] *adj* reckless; (*arriscado*) risky; (*juízo*) unfounded.

temeridade [temeri'dadʒi] *f* recklessness.

temeroso/a [teme'rozu/ɔza] *adj* fearful, afraid; (*pavoroso*) dreadful.

temido/a [te'midu/a] *adj* fearsome, frightening.

temível [te'mivew] (*pl* **-eis**) *adj* fearsome.

temor [te'mo*] *m* fear.

tempão [tẽ'pãw] *m*: **um** ~ a long time, ages *pl* (*col*).

têmpera ['tẽpera] *f* (*de metais*) tempering; (*caráter*) temperament; (*pintura*) distemper, tempera.

temperado/a [tẽpe'radu/a] *adj* (*metal*) tempered; (*clima*) temperate; (*comida*) seasoned.

temperamental [tẽperamẽ'taw] (*pl* **-ais**) *adj* temperamental.

temperamento [tẽpera'mẽtu] *m* temperament, nature.

temperança [tẽpe'rãsa] *f* moderation.

temperar [tẽpe'ra*] *vt* (*metal*) to temper, harden; (*comida*) to season.

temperatura [tẽpera'tura] *f* temperature.

tempero [tẽ'peru] *m* seasoning, flavouring (*BRIT*), flavoring (*US*).

tempestade [tẽpeʃ'tadʒi] *f* storm, tempest; **fazer uma ~ em copo de água** to make a mountain out of a molehill.

tempestuoso/a [tẽpeʃ'twozu/ɔza] *adj* stormy; (*fig*) tempestuous.

templo ['tẽplu] *m* temple; (*igreja*) church.

tempo ['tẽpu] *m* time; (*meteorológico*) weather; (*LING*) tense; **o ~ todo** the whole time; **a ~** on time; **ao mesmo ~** at the same time; **a um ~** at once; **a ~ e a hora** at the appropriate time; **antes do ~** before time; **com ~** in good time; **de ~ em ~** from time to time; **nesse ~** at that time; **nesse meio ~** in the meantime; **em ~ de fazer** about to do; **em ~ recorde** in record time; **em seu devido ~** in due course; **quanto ~?** how long?; **muito/pouco ~** a long/short time; **mais ~** longer; **ganhar/perder ~** to gain/waste time; **já era ~** it's about time; **não dá ~** there isn't time; **dar ~ ao ~** to bide one's time, wait and see; **matar o ~** to kill time; **nos bons ~s** in the good old days; **o maior de todos os ~s** the greatest of all time; **há ~s** for ages; (*atrás*) ages ago; **com o passar do ~** in time; **primeiro/segundo ~** (*ESPORTE*) first/second half; **~ integral** full time; **~ real** (*COMPUT*) real time.

tempo-quente *m* fight, set-to.

têmpora ['tẽpora] *f* (*ANAT*) temple.

temporada [tẽpo'rada] *f* season; (*tempo*) spell; **~ de ópera** opera season.

temporal [tẽpo'raw] (*pl* **-ais**) *adj* worldly ♦ *m* storm, gale.

temporário/a [tẽpo'rarju/a] *adj* temporary, provisional.

tenacidade [tenasi'dadʒi] *f* tenacity.

tenaz [te'najʒ] *adj* tenacious ♦ *f* tongs *pl*.

tenção [tẽ'sãw] (*pl* **-ões**) *f* intention; **fazer ~ de fazer** to decide to do.

tencionar [tẽsjo'na*] *vt* to intend, plan.

tenções [tẽ'sõjʃ] *fpl* de **tenção**.

tenda ['tẽda] *f* (*barraca*) tent; **~ de oxigênio** oxygen tent.

tendão [tẽ'dãw] (*pl* **-ões**) *m* tendon; **~ de Aquiles** Achilles tendon.

tendência [tẽ'dẽsja] *f* tendency; (*da moda etc*) trend; **a ~ de ou em ou a fazer** the tendency to do.

tendencioso/a [tẽdẽ'sjozu/ɔza] *adj* tendentious, bias(s)ed.

tendente [tẽ'dẽtʃi] *adj*: **~ a** tending to.

tender [tẽ'de*] *vi*: **~ para** to tend towards; **~ a fazer** to tend ou have a tendency to do; (*encaminhar-se*) to head towards doing; (*visar*) to aim to do.

tendinha [tẽ'dʒiɲa] *f* (*botequim*) dive; (*birosca*) shop.

tendões [tẽ'dõjʃ] *mpl de* **tendão**.

tenebroso/a [tene'brozu/ɔza] *adj* dark, gloomy; (*fig*) horrible.

tenente [te'nẽtʃi] *m* lieutenant.

tenho ['teɲu] *etc vb* **V ter**.

tênis ['teniʃ] *m inv* (*jogo*) tennis; (*sapatos*) training shoes *pl*; (*um sapato*) training shoe; **~ de mesa** table tennis.

tenista [te'niʃta] *m/f* tennis player.

tenor [te'no*] *adj*, *m* tenor.

tenro/a ['tẽxu/a] *adj* tender; (*macio*) soft; (*delicado*) delicate; (*novo*) young.

tensão [tẽ'sãw] *f* tension; (*pressão*) pressure, strain; (*rigidez*) tightness; (*TEC*) stress; (*ELET*: *voltagem*) voltage; **~ nervosa** nervous tension; **~ pré-menstrual** premenstrual tension.

tenso/a ['tẽsu/a] *adj* tense; (*sob pressão*) under stress, strained.

tentação [tẽta'sãw] *f* temptation.

tentáculo [tẽ'takulu] *m* tentacle.

tentado/a [tẽ'tadu/a] *adj* (*pessoa*) tempted; (*crime*) attempted.

tentador(a) [tẽta'do*(a)] *adj* tempting; (*sedutor*) inviting ♦ *m/f* tempter/temptress.

tentar [tẽ'ta*] *vt* to try; (*seduzir*) to tempt, entice ♦ *vi* to try; **~ fazer** to try to do.

tentativa [tẽta'tʃiva] *f* attempt; **~ de fazer** attempt to do; **~ de homicídio/suicídio/roubo** (*JUR*) attempted murder/suicide/ robbery; **por ~s** by trial and error.

tentativo/a [tẽta'tʃivu/a] *adj* tentative.

tentear [tẽ'tʃja*] *vt* (*tentar*) to try.

tênue ['tenwi] *adj* tenuous; (*fino*) thin; (*delicado*) delicate; (*luz*, *voz*) faint; (*pequeníssimo*) minute.

tenuidade [tenwi'dadʒi] *f* tenuousness.

teologia [teolo'ʒia] *f* theology.

teológico/a [teo'lɔʒiku/a] *adj* theological.

teólogo/a [te'ɔlogu/a] *m/f* theologian.

teor [te'o*] *m* (*conteúdo*) tenor; (*sentido*) meaning, drift; (*fig*: *norma*) system; (: *modo*) way; (*QUÍM*) grade; **~ alcoólico** alcoholic content; **baixo ~ de nicotina** low tar.

teorema [teo'rɛma] *m* theorem.

teoria [teo'ria] *f* theory.

teoricamente [teorika'mẽtʃi] *adv* theoretically, in theory.

teórico/a [te'ɔriku/a] *adj* theoretical ♦ *m/f* theoretician.

teorizar [teori'za*] *vi* to theorize.

tépido/a ['tɛpidu/a] *adj* tepid, lukewarm.

ter [te*] *vt* to have; (*na mão*) to hold; (*considerar*) to consider; (*conter*) to hold, contain; **~ fome/sorte** to be hungry/lucky; **~ frio/calor** to be cold/hot; **ela tem 5 anos** she is 5 years old; **tem 10 metros de largura** it is 10 metres wide; **~ que ou de fazer** to have to do; **~ o que dizer/fazer** to have something

NB: European Portuguese adds the following consonants to certain words: **b** (sú(b)dito, su(b)til); **c** (a(c)ção, a(c)cionista, a(c)to); **m** (inde(m)ne); **p** (ado(p)ção, ado(p)tar); *for further details see p. xiii.*

to say/do; **você tem como chegar lá?** have you got some way of getting there?; ~ **a ver com** to have to do with; **tem** (*impess*) there is/are; **tem 3 dias que não saio de casa** I haven't been out for 3 days; **o que é que ele tem?** what's the matter with him?; **o que é que tem isso?** (*col*) so what?; **não tem de quê** don't mention it; **vai** ~**!** (*col*) there'll be hell to pay!; **ir** ~ **com** to (go and) meet; ~**-se** *vr*: ~**-se por** to consider o.s.

ter. *abr* (= *terça-feira*) Tues.

terapeuta [tera'pewta] *m/f* therapist.

terapêutica [tera'pewtʃika] *f* therapeutics *sg*.

terapêutico/a [tera'pewtʃiku/a] *adj* therapeutic.

terapia [tera'pia] *f* therapy; ~ **ocupacional** occupational therapy; ~ **de reposição de estrogênio** hormone replacement therapy.

terça ['texsa] *f* (*tb*: ~*-feira*) Tuesday.

terça-feira (*pl* **terças-feiras**) *f* Tuesday; ~ **gorda** Shrove Tuesday; ~ **que vem** next Tuesday; ~ **passada/retrasada** last Tuesday/Tuesday before last; **hoje é** ~ **dia 12 de junho** today is Tuesday the 12th of June; **na** ~ on Tuesday; **nas terças-feiras** on Tuesdays; **todas as terças-feiras** every Tuesday; ~ **sim,** ~ **não** every other Tuesday; **na** ~ **de manhã** on Tuesday morning; **o jornal da** ~ Tuesday's newspaper.

terceiranista [texsejra'niʃta] *m/f* third-year.

terceiro/a [tex'sejru/a] *num* third ♦ *m* (*JUR*) third party; ~**s** *mpl* outsiders; **o T**~ **Mundo** the Third World; *V tb* **quinto**.

terciário/a [tex'sjarju/a] *adj* tertiary.

terço ['texsu] *m* third (part).

terçol [tex'sɔw] (*pl* **-óis**) *m* stye.

tergal [tex'gaw] ® *m* Terylene ®.

tergiversar [texʒivex'sa*] *vi* to prevaricate, evade the issue.

termal [tex'maw] (*pl* **-ais**) *adj* thermal.

termas ['texmaʃ] *fpl* bathhouse *sg*.

térmico/a ['texmiku/a] *adj* thermal; **garrafa térmica** (Thermos ®) flask.

terminação [texmina'sãw] (*pl* **-ões**) *f* (*LING*) ending.

terminal [texmi'naw] (*pl* **-ais**) *adj* terminal ♦ *m* (*de rede*, *ELET*, *COMPUT*) terminal ♦ *f* terminal; ~ **de vídeo** monitor, VDU.

terminante [texmi'nãtʃi] *adj* final; (*categórico*) categorical, firm; (*decisivo*) decisive.

terminantemente [texminãtʃi'mẽtʃi] *adv* categorically, expressly.

terminar [texmi'na*] *vt* to finish ♦ *vi* (*pessoa*) to finish; (*coisa*) to end; ~ **de fazer** to finish doing; (*ter feito há pouco*) to have just done; ~ **por algo/fazer algo** to end with sth/end up doing sth.

término ['texminu] *m* (*fim*) end, termination.

terminologia [texminolo'ʒia] *f* terminology.

termo ['texmu] *m* term; (*fim*) end, termination; (*limite*) limit, boundary; (*prazo*) period; (*PT*: *garrafa*) (Thermos ®) flask; **pôr** ~ **a** to put an end to; **meio** ~ compromise;

em ~**s (de)** in terms (of).

termodinâmica [texmodʒi'namika] *f* thermodynamics *sg*.

termômetro [tex'mometru] *m* thermometer.

termonuclear [texmonukle'a*] *adj* thermonuclear ♦ *f* nuclear power station.

termostato [texmoʃ'tatu] *m* thermostat.

terninho [tex'niɲu] *m* trouser suit (*BRIT*), pantsuit (*US*).

terno/a ['texnu/a] *adj* gentle, tender ♦ *m* (*BR*: *roupa*) suit.

ternura [tex'nura] *f* gentleness, tenderness.

terra ['tɛxa] *f* (*mundo*) earth, world; (*AGR*, *propriedade*) land; (*pátria*) country; (*chão*) ground; (*GEO*) soil, earth; (*pó*) dirt; (*ELET*) earth; ~ **firme** dry land; **por** ~ on the ground; **nunca viajei por essas** ~**s** I've never been to those parts; **ela não é da** ~ she's not from these parts; **caminho de** ~ **batida** dirt road; ~ **de ninguém** no man's land; ~ **natal** homeland; ~ **prometida** promised land; **a T**~ **Santa** the Holy Land; ~ **vegetal** black earth; **soltar em** ~ to disembark.

terraço [te'xasu] *m* terrace.

terracota [texa'kɔta] *f* terracotta.

Terra do Fogo *f* Tierra del Fuego.

terramoto [texa'mɔtu] (*PT*) *m* earthquake.

Terra Nova *f*: **a** ~ Newfoundland.

terraplenagem [texaple'naʒẽ] *f* earth-moving.

terreiro [te'xejru] *m* yard, square; (*de macumba*) shrine.

terremoto [texe'mɔtu] *m* earthquake.

terreno/a [te'xenu/a] *m* ground, land; (*porção de terra*) plot of land; (*GEO*) terrain ♦ *adj* earthly; **ganhar/perder** ~ (*fig*) to gain/lose ground; **sondar o** ~ (*fig*) to test the ground; ~ **baldio** (piece of) wasteground.

térreo/a ['tɛxju/a] *adj* ground level *atr*; **andar** ~ (*BR*) ground floor (*BRIT*), first floor (*US*).

terrestre [te'xɛʃtri] *adj* land *atr*; **globo** ~ globe, Earth.

terrificante [texifi'kãtʃi] *adj* terrifying.

terrífico/a [te'xifiku/a] *adj* terrifying.

terrina [te'xina] *f* tureen.

territorial [texito'rjaw] (*pl* **-ais**) *adj* territorial.

território [texi'tɔrju] *m* territory; (*distrito*) district, region.

terrível [te'xivew] (*pl* **-eis**) *adj* terrible, dreadful.

terror [te'xo*] *m* terror, dread.

terrorismo [texo'riʒmu] *m* terrorism.

terrorista [texo'riʃta] *m/f, adj* terrorist.

tertúlia [tex'tulja] *f* gathering (of friends).

tesão [te'zãw] (*pl* **-ões**) (*col!*) *m* randiness; (*pessoa*, *coisa*) turn-on; (*ereção*) hard-on; **sentir** ~ **por alguém** to fancy sb; **estar de** ~ to feel randy; (*ter ereção*) to have a hard-on.

tese ['tɛzi] *f* proposition, theory; (*EDUC*) thesis; **em** ~ in theory.

teso/a ['tezu/a] *adj* (*cabo*) taut; (*rígido*) stiff; **estar** ~ (*col*) to be broke *ou* skint.

tesões [te'zõjʃ] *mpl de* **tesão**.

tesoura [te'zora] *f* scissors *pl*; (*fig*) backbiter; **uma ~** a pair of scissors.

tesourar [tezo'ra*] *vt* to cut; (*col*) to run down.

tesouraria [tezora'ria] *f* treasury.

tesoureiro/a [tezo'rejru/a] *m/f* treasurer.

tesouro [te'zoru] *m* treasure; (*erário*) treasury, exchequer; (*LITERATURA*) thesaurus; **um ~ (de informações)** a treasure trove of information.

testa ['tɛʃta] *f* brow, forehead; **à ~ de** at the head of.

testa-de-ferro (*pl* **testas-de-ferro**) *f* figurehead, dummy.

testamentário/a [teʃtamẽ'tarju/a] *adj* of a will.

testamento [teʃta'mẽtu] *m* will, testament; **Velho/Novo T~** Old/New Testament.

testar [teʃ'ta*] *vt* to test; (*deixar em testamento*) to bequeath.

teste ['tɛʃtʃi] *m* test; **~ de aptidão** aptitude test.

testemunha [teʃte'muɲa] *f* witness; **~ ocular** eyewitness; **~ de acusação** prosecution witness; **~ de Jeová** Jehovah's witness.

testemunhar [teʃtemu'ɲa*] *vi* to testify ♦ *vt* to give evidence about; (*presenciar*) to witness; (*confirmar*) to demonstrate.

testemunho [teʃte'muɲu] *m* evidence, testimony; (*prova*) evidence; **dar ~** to give evidence.

testículo [teʃ'tʃikulu] *m* testicle.

testificar [teʃtʃifi'ka*] *vt* to testify to; (*comprovar*) to attest; (*assegurar*) to maintain.

testudo/a [teʃ'tudu/a] *adj* big-headed.

teta ['tɛta] *f* teat, nipple.

tétano ['tɛtanu] *m* tetanus.

tête-à-tête [tɛta'tɛtʃi] *m* tête-à-tête.

tetéia [te'tɛja] *f* (*pessoa*) gem.

teto ['tɛtu] *m* ceiling; (*telhado*) roof; (*habitação*) home; (*para preço etc*) ceiling; **~ solar** sun roof.

tetracampeão [tetrakã'pjãw] (*pl* **-ões**) *m* four-times champion.

tétrico/a ['tɛtriku/a] *adj* (*lúgubre*) gloomy, dismal; (*horrível*) horrible.

teu/tua [tew/'tua] *adj* your ♦ *pron* yours.

teve ['tevi] *vb V* **ter**.

tevê [te've] *f* telly (*BRIT*), TV.

têxtil ['teʃtʃiw] (*pl* **-eis**) *m* textile.

texto ['teʃtu] *m* text.

textual [teʃ'twaw] (*pl* **-ais**) *adj* textual; **estas são suas palavras textuais** these are his exact words.

textualmente [teʃtwaw'mẽtʃi] *adv* (*exatamente*) exactly, to the letter.

textura [teʃ'tura] *f* texture.

texugo [te'ʃugu] *m* badger.

tez [teʒ] *f* complexion; (*pele*) skin.

TFR (*BR*) *abr m* = **Tribunal Federal de Recursos**.

thriller ['srila*] (*pl* **~s**) *m* thriller.

ti [tʃi] *pron* you.

tia ['tʃia] *f* aunt.

tia-avó (*pl* **tias-avós**) *f* great aunt.

tiara ['tʃjara] *f* tiara.

Tibete [tʃi'betʃi] *m*: **o ~** Tibet.

tíbia ['tʃibja] *f* shinbone.

ticar [tʃi'ka*] *vt* to tick.

tico ['tʃiku] *m*: **um ~ (de)** a little bit (of).

tido/a [t'ʃidu/a] *pp de* **ter** ♦ *adj*: **~ como** *ou* **por** considered to be.

tiete ['tʃjetʃi] (*col*) *m/f* fan.

tifo ['tʃifu] *m* typhoid, typhus.

tigela [tʃi'ʒɛla] *f* bowl; **de meia ~** (*fig, col*) second-rate, small-time.

tigre ['tʃigri] *m* tiger.

tigresa [tʃi'greza] *f* tigress.

tijolo [tʃi'ʒolu] *m* brick; **~ furado** air brick.

til [tʃiw] (*pl* **tis**) *m* tilde.

tilintar [tʃili'ta*] *vt, vi* to jingle ♦ *m* jingling.

timaço [tʃi'masu] (*col*) *m* great team.

timão [tʃi'mãw] (*pl* **-ões**) *m* (*NÁUT*) helm, tiller; (*time*) great team.

timbre ['tʃibri] *m* insignia, emblem; (*selo*) stamp; (*MÚS*) tone, timbre; (*de voz*) tone; (*LING*: *de vogal*) quality; (*em papel de carta*) heading.

time ['tʃimi] (*BR*) *m* team; **de segundo ~** (*fig*) second-rate; **tirar o ~ de campo** (*col*) to get going.

timer ['tajme*] (*pl* **~s**) *m* timer.

timidez [tʃimi'deʒ] *f* shyness, timidity.

tímido/a ['tʃimidu/a] *adj* shy, timid.

timões [tʃi'mõjʃ] *mpl de* **timão**.

timoneiro [tʃimo'nejru] *m* helmsman, coxswain.

tímpano ['tʃĩpanu] *m* eardrum; (*MÚS*) kettledrum.

tina ['tʃina] *f* vat.

tingimento [tʃĩʒi'mẽtu] *m* dyeing.

tingir [tʃĩ'ʒi*] *vt* to dye; (*fig*) to tinge.

tinha ['tʃĩɲa] *etc vb V* **ter**.

tinhoso/a [tʃĩ'ɲozu/oza] *adj* single-minded.

tinido [tʃi'nidu] *m* jingle.

tinir [tʃi'ni*] *vi* to jingle, tinkle; (*ouvidos*) to ring; (*de frio, febre*) to shiver; (*de raiva, fome*) to tremble; **estar tinindo** (*carro, atleta*) to be in tip-top condition.

tinjo ['tʃĩʒu] *etc vb V* **tingir**.

tino ['tʃinu] *m* (*juízo*) discernment, judgement; (*intuição*) intuition; (*prudência*) prudence; **perder o ~** to lose one's senses; **ter ~ para algo** to have a flair for sth.

tinta ['tʃĩta] *f* (*de pintar*) paint; (*de escrever*) ink; (*para tingir*) dye; (*fig*: *vestígio*) shade, tinge; **carregar nas ~s** (*fig*) to exaggerate, embroider; **~ a óleo** oil paint; **~ de impressão** printing ink.

NB: *European Portuguese adds the following consonants to certain words:* **b** (sú(b)dito, su(b)til); **c** (a(c)ção, a(c)cionista, a(c)to); **m** (inde(m)ne); **p** (ado(p)ção, ado(p)tar); *for further details see p. xiii.*

tinteiro [tʃĩ'tejru] *m* inkwell.

tintim [tʃĩ'tʃĩ] *m*: ~! cheers!; ~ **por** ~ blow by blow.

tinto/a ['tʃĩtu/a] *adj* dyed; (*fig*) stained; **vinho** ~ red wine.

tintura [tʃĩ'tura] *f* dye; (*ato*) dyeing; (*fig*) tinge, hint.

tinturaria [tʃĩtura'ria] *f* (*lavanderia a seco*) dry-cleaner's.

tintureiro/a [tʃĩtu'rejru/a] *m/f* dry cleaner ♦ *m* police van.

tio/a ['tʃiu/a] *m/f* uncle/aunt; **meus** ~**s** my uncle and aunt.

tio-avô (*pl* **tios-avôs**) *m* great uncle.

tipa ['tʃipa] (*col: pej*) *f* dolly bird.

tipão [tʃi'pãw] (*col: pl* -**ões**) *m* good looker.

típico/a ['tʃipiku/a] *adj* typical.

tipificar [tʃipifi'ka*] *vt* to typify.

tipo ['tʃipu] *m* type; (*de imprensa*) print; (*de impressora*) typeface; (*classe*) kind; (*col: sujeito*) guy, chap; (*pessoa*) person.

tipões [tʃi'põjʃ] *mpl de* **tipão**.

tipografia [tʃipogra'fia] *f* printing, typography; (*estabelecimento*) printing office, printer's.

tipógrafo [tʃi'pografu] *m* printer.

tipóia [tʃi'pɔja] *f* (*tira de pano*) sling.

tique ['tʃiki] *m* (*MED*) twitch, tic; (*sinal*) tick.

tique-taque [-'taki] (*pl* ~**s**) *m* tick-tock.

tíquete ['tʃiketʃi] *m* ticket.

tiquinho [tʃi'kiɲu] *m*: **um** ~ (**de**) a little bit (of).

tira ['tʃira] *f* strip ♦ *m* (*BR: col*) cop.

tiracolo [tʃira'kɔlu] *m*: **a** ~ slung from the shoulder; **com o marido a** ~ with her husband in tow.

tirada [tʃi'rada] *f* (*dito*) tirade.

tiragem [tʃi'raʒẽ] *f* (*de livro*) print run; (*de jornal, revista*) circulation; (*de chaminé*) draught (*BRIT*), draft (*US*).

tira-gosto (*pl* ~**s**) *m* snack, savoury (*BRIT*).

tira-manchas *m inv* stain remover.

tirania [tʃira'nia] *f* tyranny.

tirânico/a [tʃi'raniku/a] *adj* tyrannical.

tiranizar [tʃirani'za*] *vt* to tyrannize.

tirano/a [tʃi'ranu/a] *adj* tyrannical ♦ *m/f* tyrant.

tirante [tʃi'rãtʃi] *m* (*de arreio*) brace; (*MECÂNICA*) driving rod; (*viga*) tie beam ♦ *prep* except; **uma cor** ~ **a vermelho** *etc* a reddish *etc* colo(u)r.

tirar [tʃi'ra*] *vt* to take away; (*de dentro*) to take out; (*de cima*) to take off; (*roupa, sapatos*) to take off; (*arrancar*) to pull out; (*férias*) to take, have; (*boas notas*) to get; (*salário*) to get, earn; (*curso*) to do, take; (*mancha*) to remove; (*foto, cópia*) to take; (*radiografia*) to have; (*mesa*) to clear; (*música, letra*) to take down; (*libertar*) to get out; ~ **algo a alguém** to take sth from sb; **sem** ~ **nem pôr** exactly, precisely; ~ **proveito/conclusões de** to benefit/draw conclusions from; ~ **alguém para dançar** to ask sb to dance; ~ **a tampa de** to take the lid off.

tiririca [tʃiri'rika] (*col*) *adj* hopping mad.

tiritante [tʃiri'tãtʃi] *adj* shivering.

tiritar [tʃiri'ta*] *vi* to shiver.

tiro ['tʃiru] *m* (*disparo*) shot; (*ato de disparar*) shooting, firing; ~ **ao alvo** target practice; **trocar** ~**s** to fire at one another; **o** ~ **saiu pela culatra** (*fig*) the plan backfired; **dar um** ~ **no escuro** (*fig*) to take a shot in the dark; **ser** ~ **e queda** (*fig*) to be a dead cert.

tirocínio [tʃiro'sinju] *m* apprenticeship, training.

tiroteio [tʃiro'teju] *m* shooting, exchange of shots.

tis [tʃiʃ] *mpl de* **til**.

tísica ['tʃizika] *f* consumption; *V tb* **tísico**.

tísico/a ['tʃiziku/a] *adj*, *m/f* consumptive.

tisnar [tʃiʒ'na*] *vt* (*enegrecer*) to blacken; (*tostar*) to brown.

titânico/a [tʃi'taniku/a] *adj* titanic.

titânio [tʃi'tanju] *m* titanium.

títere ['tʃiteri] *m* (*tb fig*) puppet.

titia [tʃi'tʃia] *f* aunty; **ficar para** ~ to be left on the shelf.

titica [tʃi'tʃika] (*col*) *f* (piece of) junk ♦ *m/f* good-for-nothing.

titio [tʃi'tʃiu] *m* uncle.

titití [tʃitʃi'tʃi] *m* (*tumulto*) hubbub; (*falatório*) gossip, talk.

titubeante [tʃitu'bjãtʃi] *adj* tottering; (*vacilante*) hesitant.

titubear [tʃitu'bja*] *vi* (*cambalear*) to totter, stagger; (*vacilar*) to hesitate.

titular [tʃitu'la*] *adj* titular ♦ *m/f* holder; (*POL*) minister ♦ *vt* to title.

título ['tʃitulu] *m* title; (*COM*) bond; (*universitário*) degree; **a** ~ **de** by way of, as; **a** ~ **de que você fez isso?** what was your reason for doing that?; **a** ~ **de curiosidade** out of curiosity; ~ **ao portador** (*LOM*) bearer bond; ~ **de propriedade** title deed; ~ **de câmbio** (*COM*) bill of exchange.

tive ['tʃivi] *etc vb V* **ter**.

TJ (*BR*) *abr m* = **Tribunal do Júri; Tribunal de Justiça**.

tlim [tʃlĩ] *m* ring.

TO *abr* = **Tocantins**.

to [tu] = **te** + **o**.

toa ['toa] *f* towrope; **à** ~ (*sem reflexão*) at random; (*sem motivo*) for no reason; (*inutilmente*) in vain, for nothing; (*sem ocupação*) with nothing to do; (*sem mais nem menos*) out of the blue; **andar à** ~ to wander aimlessly; **não é à** ~ **que** it is not for nothing that, it is without reason that.

toada [to'ada] *f* tune, melody.

toalete [twa'letʃi] *f* washing and dressing ♦ *m* (*banheiro*) toilet; (*traje*) outfit; **fazer a** ~ to have a wash.

toalha [to'aʎa] *f* towel; ~ **de mesa** tablecloth; ~ **de banho** bath towel; ~ **de rosto** hand towel.

toar [to'a*] *vi* to sound, resound.
tobogã [tobo'gã] *m* toboggan.
toca ['tɔka] *f* burrow, hole; (*fig: refúgio*) bolt-hole; (: *casebre*) hovel.
toca-discos (*BR*) *m inv* record-player.
tocado/a [to'kadu/a] *adj* (*col: alegre*) tipsy; (*expulso*) thrown out.
toca-fitas *m inv* cassette player.
tocaia [to'kaja] *f* ambush.
tocante [to'kãtʃi] *adj* moving, touching; **no ~ a** regarding, concerning.
tocar [to'ka*] *vt* to touch; (*MÚS*) to play; (*campainha*) to ring; (*comover*) to touch; (*programa, campanha*) to conduct; (*ônibus, gado*) to drive; (*expulsar*) to drive out; (*chegar a*) to reach ♦ *vi* to touch; (*MÚS*) to play; (*campainha, sino, telefone*) to ring; (*em carro*) to drive; **~-se** *vr* to touch (each other); (*ir-se*) to head off; (*perceber*) to realize; **~ a** (*dizer respeito*) to concern, affect; **~ em** to touch; (*assunto*) to touch upon; (*NÁUT*) to call at; **~ para alguém** (*telefonar*) to ring sb (up), call sb (up); **~ (o bonde) para frente** (*fig*) to get going, get a move on; **pelo que me toca** as far as I am concerned.
tocha ['tɔʃa] *f* torch.
toco ['toku] *m* (*de cigarro*) stub; (*de árvore*) stump.
todavia [toda'via] *adv* yet, still, however.
todo/a ['todu/'tɔda] *adj* all; (*inteiro*) whole, entire; (*cada*) every; **~s** *mpl* everybody *sg*, everyone *sg*; **a toda (velocidade)** at full speed; **toda a gente** (*PT*), **~ (o) mundo** (*BR*) everyone, everybody; **em toda (a) parte** everywhere; **~s nós** all of us; **~s os dias** *ou* **~ dia** every day; **~ o dia, o dia ~** all day; **ao ~** altogether; (*no total*) in all; **de ~** completely; **não está de ~ ruim** it's not all bad; **para ~ e sempre** for ever more; **em ~ caso** in any case; **~ o Brasil** the whole of Brazil; **como um ~** as a whole; **estar em todas** (*col*) to be all over the place.
todo-poderoso/a *adj* almighty, all-powerful ♦ *m*: **o T~** the Almighty.
tofe ['tɔfi] *m* toffee.
toga ['tɔga] *f* toga; (*EDUC, de magistrado*) gown.
toicinho [toj'siɲu] *m* bacon fat.
toldo ['towdu] *m* awning, sun blind.
toleima [to'lejma] *f* folly, stupidity.
tolerância [tole'rãsja] *f* tolerance.
tolerante [tole'rãtʃi] *adj* tolerant.
tolerar [tole'ra*] *vt* to tolerate.
tolerável [tole'ravew] (*pl* **-eis**) *adj* tolerable, bearable; (*satisfatório*) passable; (*falta*) excusable.
tolher [to'ʎe*] *vt* to impede, hinder; (*voz*) to cut off; **~ alguém de fazer** to stop sb doing.
tolice [to'lisi] *f* stupidity, foolishness; (*ato, dito*) stupid thing.

tolo/a ['tolu/a] *adj* foolish, silly, stupid ♦ *m/f* fool; **fazer alguém/fazer-se de ~** to make a fool of sb/o.s.
tom [tõ] (*pl* **-ns**) *m* tone; (*MÚS: altura*) pitch; (: *escala*) key; (*cor*) shade; **ser de bom ~** to be good manners; **~ agudo/grave** high/low note; **~ maior/menor** (*MÚS*) major/minor key.
tomada [to'mada] *f* capture; (*ELET*) socket; (*CINEMA*) shot; **~ de posse** investiture; **~ de preços** tender.
tomar [to'ma*] *vt* to take; (*capturar*) to capture, seize; (*decisão*) to make; (*bebida*) to drink; **~-se** *vr*: **~-se de** to be overcome with; **~ algo emprestado** to borrow sth; **~ alguém por algo** to take sb for sth; **~ algo como** to take sth as; **toma!** here you are!; **quer ~ alguma coisa?** do you want something to drink?; **~ café (de manhã)** to have breakfast; **toma lá, dá cá** give and take.
tomara [to'mara] *excl*: **~!** if only!; **~ que venha hoje** I hope he comes today.
tomara-que-caia *adj inv*: (**vestido**) **~** strapless dress.
tomate [to'matʃi] *m* tomato.
tombadilho [tõba'dʒiʎu] *m* deck.
tombar [tõ'ba*] *vi* to fall down, tumble down ♦ *vt* to knock down, knock over; (*conservar: edifício*) to list.
tombo ['tõbu] *m* (*queda*) tumble, fall; (*registro*) archives *pl*, records *pl*.
tomilho [to'miʎu] *m* thyme.
tomo ['tɔmu] *m* tome, volume.
tona ['tɔna] *f* surface; **vir à ~** to come to the surface; (*fig*) to emerge; **trazer à ~** to bring up; (*recordações*) to bring back.
tonalidade [tonali'dadʒi] *f* (*de cor*) shade; (*MÚS*) tonality; (: *tom*) key.
tonel [to'nɛw] (*pl* **-éis**) *m* cask, barrel.
tonelada [tone'lada] *f* ton; **uma ~ de** (*fig*) tons of.
tonelagem [tone'laʒẽ] *f* tonnage.
toner ['tone*] *m* toner.
tônica ['tonika] *f* (*água, MÚS*) tonic; (*LING*) stressed syllable; (*fig*) keynote.
tônico/a ['toniku/a] *adj* tonic; (*sílaba*) stressed ♦ *m* tonic; **acento ~** stress.
tonificante [tonifi'kãtʃi] *adj* invigorating.
tonificar [tonifi'ka*] *vt* to tone up.
tons [tõʃ] *mpl de* **tom**.
tontear [tõ'tʃja*] *vt*: **~ alguém** to make sb dizzy; (*suj: barulheira*) to get sb down, give sb a headache; (: *alvoroço, notícia*) to stun sb ♦ *vi* (*pessoa: com bebida*) to get dizzy; (: *com barulho*) to get a headache; (: *com alvoroço*) to be dazed; (*barulho*) to be wearing; (*alvoroço*) to be upsetting; **~ de sono** to be half-asleep.
tonteira [tõ'tejra] *f* dizziness.
tontice [tõ'tʃisi] *f* stupidity, nonsense.

NB: *European Portuguese adds the following consonants to certain words:* **b** (sú(b)dito, su(b)til); **c** (a(c)ção, a(c)cionista, a(c)to); **m** (inde(m)ne); **p** (ado(p)ção, ado(p)tar); *for further details see p. xiii.*

tonto/a ['tõtu/a] *adj* (*tolo*) stupid, silly; (*zonzo*) dizzy, lightheaded; (*atarantado*) flustered; **às tontas** impulsively.

tontura [tõ'tura] *f* dizziness, lightheadedness.

topada [to'pada] *f* trip; **dar uma ~ em** to stub one's toe on.

topar [to'pa*] *vt* to agree to ♦ *vi*: **~ com** to come across; **~-se** *vr* (*duas pessoas*) to run into one another; **~ em** (*tropeçar*) to stub one's toe on; (*esbarrar*) to run into; (*tocar*) to touch; **você topa ir ao cinema?** do you fancy going to the cinema?; **~ que alguém faça** to agree that sb should do.

topa-tudo ['tɔpa-] *m inv* person who can't say no.

topázio [to'pazju] *m* topaz.

tope ['tɔpi] *m* top.

topete [to'petʃi] *m* quiff; **ter o ~ de fazer** (*fig*) to have the cheek to do.

tópico/a ['tɔpiku/a] *adj* topical ♦ *m* topic.

topless [tɔp'les] *adj inv* topless ♦ *m inv* (*na praia*) topless bikini.

topo ['topu] *m* top; (*extremidade*) end, extremity.

topografia [topogra'fia] *f* topography.

topográfico/a [topo'grafiku/a] *adj* topographical.

topônimo [to'ponimu] *m* place name, toponym.

toque ['tɔkɪ] *etc vb V* **tocar** ♦ *m* touch; (*de instrumento musical*) playing; (*de campainha*) ring; (*fig: vestígio*) touch; (*retoque*) finishing touch; **os últimos ~s** the finishing touches; **dar um ~ em alguém** (*col: avisar*) to let sb know; (: *falar com*) to have a word with sb; **a ~ de caixa** in all haste.

Tóquio ['tɔkju] *n* Tokyo.

tora ['tɔra] *f* (*pedaço*) piece; (*de madeira*) log; (*sesta*) nap; **tirar uma ~** to have a nap.

toranja [to'rãʒa] *f* grapefruit.

tórax ['tɔraks] *m inv* thorax.

torção [tox'sãw] (*pl* **-ões**) *m* twist, twisting; (*MED*) sprain.

torcedor(a) [toxse'do*(a)] *m/f* supporter, fan.

torcedura [toxse'dura] *f* twist; (*MED*) sprain.

torcer [tox'se*] *vt* to twist; (*deslocar*) to sprain; (*desvirtuar*) to distort, misconstrue; (*roupa: espremer*) to wring; (: *na máquina*) to spin; (*vergar*) to bend ♦ *vi*: **~ por** (*time*) to support; (*amigo etc*) to keep one's fingers crossed for; **~-se** *vr* (*contorcer-se*) to squirm, writhe; **~ para** *ou* **por** to cheer for; **~ para que tudo dê certo** to keep one's fingers crossed that everything works out right.

torcicolo [toxsi'kɔlu] *m* stiff neck.

torcida [tox'sida] *f* (*pavio*) wick; (*ESPORTE: ato de torcer*) cheering; (: *torcedores*) supporters; **dar uma ~ em algo** to twist sth; (*roupa*) to wring sth out.

torções [tox'sõjʃ] *mpl de* **torção**.

tormenta [tox'mẽta] *f* storm; (*fig*) upset.

tormento [tox'mẽtu] *m* torment, torture; (*angústia*) anguish.

tormentoso/a [toxmẽ'tozu/ɔza] *adj* stormy, tempestuous.

tornado [tox'nadu] *m* tornado.

tornar [tox'na*] *vi* (*voltar*) to return, go back ♦ *vt* to make; **~-se** *vr* to become; **~ algo em algo** to turn *ou* make sth into sth; **~ a fazer algo** to do sth again.

torneado/a [tox'njadu/a] *adj*: **bem ~** (*pernas, pescoço*) shapely.

tornear [tox'nja*] *vt* to turn (on a lathe), shape.

torneio [tox'neju] *m* tournament.

torneira [tox'nejra] *f* tap (*BRIT*), faucet (*US*).

torniquete [toxni'ketʃi] *m* (*MED*) tourniquet; (*PT: roleta*) turnstile.

torno ['toxnu] *m* lathe; (*CERÂMICA*) wheel; **em ~ de** (*ao redor de*) around; (*sobre*) about; **em ~ de 5 milhões** around 5 million.

tornozeleira [toxnoze'lejra] *f* ankle support.

tornozelo [toxno'zelu] *m* ankle.

toró [to'rɔ] *m* (*chuva*) downpour, shower; **caiu um ~** there was a sudden downpour.

torpe ['tɔxpi] *adj* vile.

torpedear [toxpe'dʒja*] *vt* to torpedo.

torpedo [tox'pedu] *m* torpedo.

torpeza [tox'peza] *f* vileness.

torpor [tox'po*] *m* torpor; (*MED*) numbness.

torrada [to'xada] *f* toast.

torradeira [toxa'dejra] *f* toaster.

torrão [to'xãw] (*pl* **-ões**) *m* turf, sod; (*terra*) soil, land; (*de açúcar*) lump; **~ natal** native land.

torrar [to'xa*] *vt* (*pão*) to toast; (*café*) to roast; (*plantação*) to parch; (*dinheiro*) to blow, squander; (*vender*) to sell off cheap; **~ a paciência** *ou* **o saco** (*col*) **de alguém** to try sb's patience; **~ (alguém)** (*col*) to get on sb's nerves.

torre ['toxi] *f* tower; (*XADREZ*) castle, rook; (*ELET*) pylon; **~ de controle** (*AER*) control tower; **~ de vigia** watchtower.

torreão [to'xjãw] (*pl* **-ões**) *m* turret.

torrefação [toxefa'sãw] (*PT*: **-cç-**: *pl* **-ões**) *f* coffee-roasting house.

torrencial [toxẽ'sjaw] (*pl* **-ais**) *adj* torrential.

torrente [to'xẽtʃi] *f* (*tb fig*) torrent.

torreões [to'xjõjʃ] *mpl de* **torreão**.

torresmo [to'xeʒmu] *m* crackling.

tórrido/a ['tɔxidu/a] *adj* torrid.

torrinha [to'xiɲa] *f* (*TEATRO*) gallery; **as ~s** the gods.

torrões [to'xõjʃ] *mpl de* **torrão**.

torrone [to'xɔni] *m* nougat.

torso ['toxsu] *m* torso, trunk.

torta ['tɔxta] *f* pie, tart; **~ de maçã** apple pie.

torto/a ['toxtu/'tɔxta] *adj* twisted, crooked; **a ~ e a direito** indiscriminately; **cometer erros a ~ e a direito** to make mistakes left, right and centre.

tortuoso/a [tox'twozu/ɔza] *adj* winding.

tortura [tox'tura] *f* torture; (*fig*) anguish,

agony.

torturador(a) [toxtura'do*(a)] *m/f* torturer.

torturante [toxtu'rătʃi] *adj* (*sonhos*) haunting; (*dor*) excruciating.

torturar [toxtu'ra*] *vt* to torture; (*fig: afligir*) to torment.

torvelinho [toxve'liɲu] *m* (*de vento*) whirlwind; (*de água*) whirlpool; (*fig: de pensamentos*) swirl.

tos [tuʃ] = **te** + **os**.

tosão [to'zãw] (*pl* -ões) *m* fleece.

tosar [to'za*] *vt* (*ovelha*) to shear; (*cabelo*) to crop.

tosco/a ['toʃku/a] *adj* rough, unpolished; (*grosseiro*) coarse, crude.

tosões [to'zõjʃ] *mpl de* **tosão**.

tosquiar [toʃ'kja*] *vt* (*ovelha*) to shear, clip.

tosse ['tɔsi] *f* cough; ~ **de cachorro** whooping cough; ~ **seca** dry *ou* tickly cough.

tossir [to'si*] *vi* to cough ♦ *vt* to cough up.

tosta ['tɔʃta] (*PT*) *f* toast; ~ **mista** toasted cheese and ham sandwich.

tostado/a [toʃ'tadu/a] *adj* toasted; (*pessoa*) tanned; (*carne*) browned.

tostão [toʃ'tãw] *m* (*dinheiro*) cash; **estar sem um** ~ to be completely penniless.

tostar [toʃ'ta*] *vt* to toast; (*pele, pessoa*) to tan; (*carne*) to brown; ~-**se** *vr* to get tanned.

total [to'taw] (*pl* -**ais**) *adj, m* total.

totalidade [totali'dadʒi] *f* totality, entirety; **em sua** ~ in its entirety; **a** ~ **da população/dos políticos** the entire population/ all politicians.

totalitário/a [totali'tarju/a] *adj* totalitarian.

totalitarismo [totalita'riʒmu] *m* totalitarianism.

totalizar [totali'za*] *vt* to total up.

totalmente [totaw'mẽtʃi] *adv* totally, completely.

touca ['toka] *f* bonnet; (*de freira*) veil; ~ **de banho** bathing hat.

toucador [toka'do*] *m* (*penteadeira*) dressing table.

toucinho [to'siɲu] *m* = **toicinho**.

toupeira [to'pejra] *f* mole; (*fig*) numbskull, idiot.

tourada [to'rada] *f* bullfight.

tourear [to'rja*] *vi* to fight (bulls).

toureiro [to'rejru] *m* bullfighter.

touro ['toru] *m* bull; **T~** (*ASTROLOGIA*) Taurus; **pegar o** ~ **à unha** to take the bull by the horns; **praça de** ~**s** bullring.

toxemia [tokse'mia] *f* blood poisoning.

tóxico/a ['tɔksiku/a] *adj* poisonous, toxic ♦ *m* (*veneno*) poison; (*droga*) drug.

toxina [tok'sina] *f* toxin.

trabalhadeira [trabaʎa'dejra] *f de* **trabalhador**.

trabalhador(a) [trabaʎa'do*(a)] *adj* (*laborioso*) hard-working, industrious; (*POL: classe*) working ♦ *m/f* worker; ~ **braçal** manual worker.

trabalhão [traba'ʎãw] (*pl* -ões) *m* big job.

trabalhar [traba'ʎa*] *vi* to work; (*TEATRO*) to act ♦ *vt* (*terra*) to till, work; (*madeira, metal*) to work; (*texto*) to work at; ~ **com** (*comerciar*) to deal in; ~ **de** *ou* **como** to work as.

trabalheira [traba'ʎejra] *f* big job.

trabalhista [traba'ʎiʃta] *adj* labour *atr* (*BRIT*), labor *atr* (*US*) ♦ *m/f* Labour Party member; **Partido T~** (*BRIT: POL*) Labour Party.

trabalho [tra'baʎu] *m* work; (*emprego, tarefa*) job; (*ECON*) labour (*BRIT*), labor (*US*); (*EDUC: tarefa*) assignment; ~ **braçal** manual work; ~**s forçados** hard labo(u)r, forced labo(u)r; **estar sem** ~ to be out of work; **dar** ~ to need work; **dar** ~ **a alguém** to cause sb trouble; **dar-se o** ~ **de fazer** to take the trouble to do; **um** ~ **ingrato** a thankless task; ~ **doméstico** housework; ~ **de parto** labo(u)r.

trabalhões [traba'ʎõjʃ] *mpl de* **trabalhão**.

trabalhoso/a [traba'ʎozu/ɔza] *adj* laborious, arduous.

traça ['trasa] *f* moth.

traçado [tra'sadu] *m* sketch, plan.

tração [tra'sãw] *f* traction.

traçar [tra'sa*] *vt* to draw; (*determinar*) to set out, outline; (*limites, fronteiras*) to mark out; (*planos*) to draw up; (*escrever*) to compose; (*col: comer, beber*) to guzzle down.

tracçao [tra'sãw] (*PT*) *f* = **tração**.

traço ['trasu] *m* (*linha*) line, dash; (*de lápis*) stroke; (*vestígio*) trace, vestige; (*aspecto*) feature, trait; ~**s** *mpl* (*do rosto*) features; ~ (**de união**) hyphen; (*entre frases*) dash.

tractor [tra'to*] (*PT*) *m* = **trator**.

tradição [tradʒi'sãw] (*pl* -ões) *f* tradition.

tradicional [tradʒisjo'naw] (*pl* -**ais**) *adj* traditional.

tradições [tradʒi'sõjʃ] *fpl de* **tradição**.

tradução [tradu'sãw] (*pl* -ões) *f* translation.

tradutor(a) [tradu'to*(a)] *m/f* translator; ~ **juramentado** legally recognized translator.

traduzir [tradu'zi*] *vt* to translate; ~-**se** *vr* to come across; ~ **do inglês para o português** to translate from English into Portuguese.

trafegar [trafe'ga*] *vi* to move, go.

trafegável [trafe'gavew] (*pl* ~**eis**) *adj* (*rua*) open to traffic.

tráfego ['trafegu] *m* (*trânsito*) traffic; ~ **aéreo/marítimo** air/sea traffic.

traficante [trafi'kãtʃi] *m/f* trafficker, dealer; ~ **de drogas** drug trafficker, pusher (*col*).

traficar [trafi'ka*] *vi*: ~ (**com**) to deal (in), traffic (in).

tráfico ['trafiku] *m* traffic; ~ **de drogas** drug

NB: *European Portuguese adds the following consonants to certain words:* **b** (sú(b)dito, su(b)til); **c** (a(c)ção, a(c)cionista, a(c)to); **m** (inde(m)ne); **p** (ado(p)ção, ado(p)tar); *for further details see p. xiii.*

trafficking.

tragada [tra'gada] *f* (*em cigarro*) drag, puff.

tragar [tra'ga*] *vt* to swallow; (*fumaça*) to inhale; (*suportar*) to tolerate ♦ *vi* to inhale.

tragédia [tra'ʒɛdʒja] *f* tragedy; **fazer ~ de algo** to make a drama out of sth.

trágico/a ['traʒiku/a] *adj* tragic; (*dado a fazer tragédia*) dramatic.

tragicomédia [traʒiko'mɛdʒja] *f* tragicomedy.

tragicômico/a [traʒi'komiku/a] *adj* tragicomic.

trago ['tragu] *etc vb V* **trazer** ♦ *m* mouthful; (*em cigarro*) drag, puff; **tomar um ~** to have a mouthful; (*em cigarro*) to have a drag; **de um ~** in one gulp.

traguei [tra'gej] *etc vb V* **tragar**.

traição [traj'sãw] (*pl* **-ões**) *f* treason, treachery; (*deslealdade*) betrayal, disloyalty; (*infidelidade*) infidelity; **alta ~** high treason.

traiçoeiro/a [traj'swejru/a] *adj* treacherous; (*infiel*) disloyal.

traições [traj'sõjʃ] *fpl de* **traição**.

traidor(a) [traj'do*(a)] *m/f* traitor.

trailer ['trejla*] (*pl* **~s**) *m* trailer; (*tipo casa*) caravan (*BRIT*), trailer (*US*).

traineira [traj'nejra] *f* trawler.

training ['trejnĩŋ] (*pl* **~s**) *m* track suit.

trair [tra'i*] *vt* to betray; (*mulher, marido*) to be unfaithful to; (*esperanças*) not to live up to; **~-se** *vr* to give o.s. away.

trajar [tra'ʒa*] *vt* to wear; **~-se** *vr*: **~-se de preto** to be dressed in black.

traje ['traʒi] *m* dress, clothes *pl*; **~ de banho** bathing costume; **~ de noite** evening gown; **~ a rigor** evening dress; **~ de passeio** smart dress; **~ domingueiro** Sunday best; **em ~s de Adão** in one's birthday suit; **~s menores** smalls, underwear *sg*.

trajeto [tra'ʒɛtu] (*PT*: **-ct-**) *m* course, path.

trajetória [traʒe'tɔrja] (*PT*: **-ct-**) *f* trajectory, path; (*fig*) course.

tralha ['traʎa] *f* fishing net; (*col*) junk.

trama ['trama] *f* (*tecido*) woof; (*enredo, conspiração*) plot.

tramar [tra'ma*] *vt* (*tecer*) to weave; (*maquinar*) to scheme, plot; ♦ *vi*: **~ contra** to conspire against.

trambicar [trãbi'ka*] *vt* to con.

trambique [trã'biki] (*col*) *m* con.

trambiqueiro/a [trãbi'kejru/a] *m/f* con merchant ♦ *adj* slippery.

trambolhão [trãbo'ʎãw] (*pl* **-ões**) *m* tumble; **andar aos trambolhões** to stumble along.

trambolho [trã'boʎu] *m* encumbrance.

trambolhões [trãbo'ʎõjʃ] *mpl de* **trambolhão**.

tramitar [trami'ta*] *vi* to go through the procedure.

trâmites ['tramitʃiʃ] *mpl* procedure *sg*, channels.

tramóia [tra'mɔja] *f* (*fraude*) swindle, trick; (*trama*) plot, scheme.

trampolim [trãpo'lĩ] (*pl* **-ns**) *m* trampoline;

(*de piscina*) diving board; (*fig*) springboard.

trampolinagem [trãpoli'naʒẽ] (*pl* **-ns**) *f* trick, swindle.

trampolineiro [trãpoli'nejru] *m* trickster, swindler.

trampolinice [trãpoli'nisi] *f* trick, swindle.

trampolins [trãpo'lĩʃ] *mpl de* **trampolim**.

tranca ['trãka] *f* (*de porta*) bolt; (*de carro*) lock.

trança ['trãsa] *f* (*cabelo*) plait; (*galão*) braid.

trançado/a [trã'sadu/a] *adj* (*cesto*) woven.

trancafiar [trãka'fja*] *vt* to lock up.

trancão [trã'kãw] (*pl* **-ões**) *m* bump.

trancar [trã'ka*] *vt* to lock; (*matrícula*) to suspend; (*FUTEBOL*) to shove; **~-se** *vr* (*mostrar-se fechado*) to clam up; **~-se no quarto** to lock o.s. (away) in one's room.

trançar [trã'sa*] *vt* to weave; (*cabelo*) to plait, braid ♦ *vi* (*col*) to wander around.

tranco ['trãku] *m* (*solavanco*) jolt; (*esbarrão*) bump; (*de cavalo*) walk; (*col*: admoestação*) put-down; **aos ~s** jolting; **aos ~s e barrancos** with great difficulty; (*aos saltos*) jolting.

trancões [trã'kõjʃ] *mpl de* **trancão**.

tranqüilamente [trãkwila'mẽtʃi] *adv* calmly; (*facilmente*) easily; (*seguramente*) for sure.

tranqüilidade [trãkwili'dadʒi] *f* tranquillity; (*paz*) peace.

tranqüilizador(a) [trãkwiliza'do*(a)] *adj* reassuring; (*música*) soothing.

tranqüilizante [trãkwili'zãtʃi] *adj* = **tranqüilizador** ♦ *m* (*MED*) tranquillizer.

tranqüilizar [trãkwili'za*] *vt* to calm, quieten; (*despreocupar*): **~ alguém** to reassure sb, put sb's mind at rest; **~-se** *vr* to quieten down; (*pessoa preocupada*) to be reassured.

tranqüilo/a [trã'kwilu/a] *adj* peaceful; (*mar, pessoa*) calm; (*criança*) quiet; (*consciência*) clear; (*seguro*) sure, certain ♦ *adv* with no problems.

transa ['trãza] (*BR*: *col*) *f* (*namoro*) affair; (*combinação*) arrangement; (*trama, negócios*) business; (*ligação*) relationship; (*assunto*) matter; **combinar altas ~s** to be into all sorts of things.

transação [trãza'sãw] (*PT*: **-cç-**; *pl* **-ões**) *f* (*COM*) transaction, deal; (*combinação*) arrangement; (*col*: *maquinação*) business.

transada [trã'zada] *f*: **dar uma ~** (*col*) to have sex.

transado/a [trã'zadu/a] *adj*: **bem ~** (*col*: *objeto*) well made; (*relacionamento*) sorted out, healthy; (*pessoa, casa*) classy.

Transamazônica [trãzama'zonika]: **a ~** the trans-Amazonian highway.

transamazônico/a [trãzama'zoniku/a] *adj* trans-Amazonian.

transar [trã'za*] (*col*) *vt* (*combinar*) to arrange; (*tramar*) to plan; (*drogas*) to do ♦ *vi* (*namorar*) to go out; (*ter relação sexual*) to have sex; **~ com** (*relacionar-se*) to hang out with; (*negociar*) to deal in.

transatlântico/a [trãzat'lãtʃiku/a] *adj* transatlantic ♦ *m* (transatlantic) liner.

transbordar [trãʒbox'da*] *vi* to overflow; ~ **de alegria** to burst with happiness.

transbordo [trãʒ'boxdu] *m* (*de viajantes*) change, transfer.

transcendental [trãsẽdẽ'taw] (*pl* -**ais**) *adj* transcendental.

transcender [trãsẽ'de*] *vt, vi:* ~ **(a)** to transcend.

transcorrer [trãʃko'xe*] *vi* to elapse, go by; (*evento*) to pass off.

transcrever [trãʃkre've*] *vt* to transcribe.

transcrição [trãʃkri'sãw] (*pl* -**ões**) *f* transcription.

transcrito/a [trãʃ'kritu/a] *pp de* **transcrever** ♦ *m* transcript.

transe ['trãzi] *m* ordeal; (*lance*) plight; (*hipnótico*) trance; **a todo** ~ at all costs.

transeunte [trã'zjũtʃi] *m/f* passer-by.

transferência [trãʃfe'rẽsja] *f* transfer; (*JUR*) conveyancing.

transferir [trãʃfe'ri*] *vt* to be transferred; (*adiar*) to postpone.

transferível [trãʃfe'rivew] (*pl* -**eis**) *adj* transferable.

transfigurar [trãʃfigu'ra*] *vt* to transfigure, transform; ~-**se** *vr* to be transformed.

transfiro [trãʃ'firu] *etc vb V* **transferir**.

transformação [trãʃfoxma'sãw] (*pl* -**ões**) *f* transformation.

transformador [trãʃfoxma'do*] *m* (*ELET*) transformer.

transformar [trãʃfox'ma*] *vt* to transform, turn; ~-**se** *vr* to turn; ~ **algo em algo** to turn *ou* transform sth into sth.

trânsfuga ['trãʃfuga] *m* (*desertor*) deserter; (*político*) renegade, turncoat; (*da Rússia etc*) defector.

transfusão [trãʃfu'zãw] (*pl* -**ões**) *f* transfusion; ~ **de sangue** blood transfusion.

transgredir [trãʒgre'dʒi*] *vt* to infringe.

transgressão [trãʒgre'sãw] (*pl* -**ões**) *f* transgression, infringement.

transgrido [trãʒ'gridu] *etc vb V* **transgredir**.

transição [trãzi'sãw] (*pl* -**ões**) *f* transition; **período** *ou* **fase de** ~ transition period.

transicional [trãzisjo'naw] (*pl* -**ais**) *adj* transitional.

transições [trãzi'sõjʃ] *fpl de* **transição**.

transido/a [trã'zidu/a] *adj* numb.

transigente [trãzi'ʒẽtʃi] *adj* willing to compromise.

transigir [trãzi'ʒi*] *vi* to compromise, make concessions; ~ **com alguém** to compromise with sb, meet sb halfway.

transistor [trãziʃ'to*] *m* transistor.

transitar [trãzi'ta*] *vi:* ~ **por** to move through; (*rua*) to go along.

transitável [trãzi'tavew] (*pl* -**eis**) *adj* (*caminho*) passable.

transitivo/a [trãzi'tʃivu/a] *adj* (*LING*) transitive.

trânsito ['trãzitu] *m* (*ato*) transit, passage; (*na rua: veículos*) traffic; (: *pessoas*) flow; **em** ~ in transit; **sinal de** ~ traffic signal.

transitório/a [trãzi'tɔrju/a] *adj* transitory, passing; (*período*) transitional.

transladar [trãʒla'da*] *vt* = **trasladar**.

translado [trãʒ'ladu] *m* = **traslado**.

translúcido/a [trãʒ'lusidu/a] *adj* translucent.

transmissão [trãʒmi'sãw] (*pl* -**ões**) *f* transmission; (*RÁDIO, TV*) transmission, broadcast; (*transferência*) transfer; ~ **ao vivo** live broadcast; ~ **de dados** data transmission.

transmissível [trãʒmi'sivew] (*pl* -**eis**) *adj* transmittable.

transmissões [trãʒmi'sõjʃ] *fpl de* **transmissão**.

transmissor(a) [trãʒmi'so*(a)] *adj* transmitting ♦ *m* transmitter.

transmitir [trãʒmi'tʃi*] *vt* to transmit; (*RÁDIO, TV*) to broadcast, transmit; (*transferir*) to transfer; (*recado, notícia*) to pass on; (*aroma, som*) to carry; ~-**se** *vr* (*doença*) to be transmitted; ~ **algo a alguém** (*paz etc*) to bring sb sth.

transparecer [trãʃpare'se*] *vi* to be visible, appear; (*revelar-se*) to be apparent.

transparência [trãʃpa'rẽsja] *f* transparency; (*de água*) clarity.

transparente [trãʃpa'rẽtʃi] *adj* transparent; (*roupa*) see-through; (*água*) clear; (*evidente*) clear, obvious.

transpassar [trãʃpa'sa*] *vt* = **traspassar**.

transpiração [trãʃpira'sãw] *f* perspiration.

transpirar [trãʃpi'ra*] *vi* (*suar*) to perspire; (*divulgar-se*) to become known; (*verdade*) to come out ♦ *vt* to exude.

transplantar [trãʃplã'ta*] *vt* to transplant.

transplante [trãʃ'plãtʃi] *m* transplant.

transpor [trãʃ'po*] (*irreg: como* **pôr**) *vt* to cross; (*inverter*) to transpose.

transportação [trãʃpoxta'sãw] *f* transportation.

transportadora [trãʃpoxta'dora] *f* haulage company.

transportar [trãʃpox'ta*] *vt* to transport; (*levar*) to carry; (*enlevar*) to entrance, enrapture; (*fig: remontar*) to take back; ~-**se** *vr* to be entranced; (*remontar*) to be transported back; **a** ~ (*COM: quantia*) carry forward, c/f.

transporte [trãʃ'pɔxtʃi] *m* transport; (*COM*) haulage; (*em contas*) amount carried forward; (*fig: êxtase*) rapture, delight; **despesas de** ~ transport costs; **Ministério dos T~s** Ministry of Transport (*BRIT*), Department of Transportation (*US*); ~ **rodoviário** road transport; ~**s coletivos** public transport

---

NB: *European Portuguese adds the following consonants to certain words:* **b** (sú(b)dito, su(b)til); **c** (a(c)ção, a(c)cionista, a(c)to); **m** (inde(m)ne); **p** (ado(p)ção, ado(p)tar); *for further details see p. xiii.*

sg.

transposição [trãʃpozi'sãw] f transposition; (de rio) crossing.

transpôs [trãʃ'poʃ] vb V **transpor**.

transposto/a [trãʃ'poʃtu/'pɔʃta] pp de **transpor**.

transpunha [trãʃ'puɲa] etc vb V **transpor**.

transpus [trãʃ'puʃ] etc vb V **transpor**.

transpuser [trãʃpu'ze*] etc vb V **transpor**.

transtornar [trãʃtox'na*] vt to upset; (rotina, reunião) to disrupt; **~-se** vr to get upset; (reunião, rotina) to be disrupted.

transtorno [trãʃ'toxnu] m upset, disruption; (contrariedade) hardship; (mental) distraction.

transversal [trãʒvex'saw] (pl -ais) adj transverse, cross; (rua) ~ cross street.

transverso/a [trãʒ'vɛxsu/a] adj transverse.

transviado/a [trãʒ'vjadu/a] adj wayward, erring.

transviar [trãʒ'vja*] vt to lead astray; **~-se** vr to go astray.

trapaça [tra'pasa] f swindle, fraud.

trapacear [trapa'sja*] vt, vi to swindle.

trapaceiro/a [trapa'sejru/a] adj crooked, cheating ♦ m/f swindler, cheat.

trapalhada [trapa'ʎada] f confusion, mix up.

trapalhão/lhona [trapa'ʎãw/'ʎɔna] (pl -ões/ ~s) m/f bungler, blunderer.

trapézio [tra'pɛzju] m trapeze; (MAT) trapezium.

trapezista [trape'ziʃta] m/f trapeze artist.

trapo ['trapu] m rag; **ser** ou **estar um** ~ (pessoa) to be washed up.

traquéia [tra'kɛja] f windpipe.

traquejo [tra'keʒu] m experience.

traqueotomia [trakjoto'mia] f tracheotomy.

traquinas [tra'kinaʃ] adj inv mischievous.

trarei [tra'rej] etc vb V **trazer**.

trás [trajʃ] prep, adv: **para** ~ backwards; **por** ~ **de** behind; **de** ~ from behind; **a luz de** ~ the back light; **de** ~ **para frente** back to front; **ano** ~ **ano** year after year; **dar para** ~ (fig: pessoa) to go wrong.

traseira [tra'zejra] f rear; (ANAT) bottom.

traseiro/a [tra'zejru/a] adj back, rear ♦ m (ANAT) bottom, behind.

trasladar [traʒla'da*] vt to remove, transfer; (copiar) to transcribe.

traslado [traʒ'ladu] m (cópia) copy; (deslocamento) removal, transference.

traspassar [traʃpa'sa*] vt (rio etc) to cross; (penetrar) to pierce, penetrate; (exceder) to exceed, overstep; (transferir) to transmit, transfer; (PT: sublocar) to sublet.

traspasse [traʃ'pasi] m transfer; (sublocação) sublease, sublet.

traste ['traʃtʃi] m thing; (coisa sem valor) piece of junk; (patife) rogue, rascal; **estar** ou **ficar um** ~ to be devastated.

tratado [tra'tadu] m treaty; (LITERATURA) treatise; ~ **de paz** peace treaty.

tratador(a) [trata'do*(a)] m/f: ~ **de cavalos** groom.

tratamento [trata'mẽtu] m treatment; (título) title; **forma de** ~ form of address; ~ **de choque** shock treatment.

tratante [tra'tãtʃi] m/f rogue.

tratar [tra'ta*] vt to treat; (tema) to deal with, cover; (combinar) to agree ♦ vi: ~ **com** to deal with; (combinar) to agree with; **~-se** com (MED) to take treatment; (cuidar-se) to take care of o.s.; ~ **de** to deal with; ~ **por** ou **de** to address as; **de que se trata?** what is it about?; **trata-se de** it is a question of; ~ **de fazer** (esforçar-se) to try to do; (resolver) to resolve to do; **trate da sua vida!** mind your own business!; **~-se a pão e água** to live on bread and water.

tratável [tra'tavew] (pl -eis) adj treatable; (afável) approachable, amenable.

trato ['tratu] m (tratamento) treatment; (contrato) agreement, contract; **~s** mpl (relações) dealings; **maus ~s** ill-treatment sg; **pessoa de fino** ~ refined person; **dar ~s à bola** to rack one's brains.

trator [tra'to*] m tractor.

traulitada [trawli'tada] f beating.

trauma ['trawma] m trauma.

traumático/a [traw'matʃiku/a] adj traumatic.

traumatizante [trawmatʃi'zãtʃi] adj traumatic, harrowing.

traumatizar [trawmatʃi'za*] vt to traumatize.

travada [tra'vada] f: **dar uma** ~ to put on the brake.

travão [tra'vãw] (PT: pl -ões) m brake.

travar [tra'va*] vt (roda) to lock; (iniciar) to engage in; (conversa) to strike up; (luta) to wage; (carro) to stop; (passagem) to block; (movimentos) to hinder ♦ vi (PT) to brake; ~ **amizade com** to become friendly with, make friends with.

trave ['travi] f beam, crossbeam; (ESPORTE) crossbar; **foi na** ~ (col: resposta etc) (it was) close.

través [tra'vɛʃ] m slant, incline; **de** ~ across, sideways; **olhar de** ~ to look sideways (at).

travessa [tra'vɛsa] f crossbeam, crossbar; (rua) lane, alley; (prato) dish; (para o cabelo) comb, slide.

travessão [trave'sãw] (pl -ões) m (de balança) bar, beam; (pontuação) dash.

travesseiro [trave'sejru] m pillow; **consultar o** ~ to sleep on it.

travessia [trave'sia] f (viagem) journey, crossing.

travesso/a¹ [tra'vɛsu/a] adj cross, transverse.

travesso/a² [tra'vesu/a] adj mischievous, naughty.

travessões [trave'sõjʃ] mpl de **travessão**.

travessura [trave'sura] f mischief, prank; **fazer ~s** to get up to mischief.

travesti [traveʃ'tʃi] m/f transvestite; (artista) drag artist.

travões [tra'võjʃ] mpl de **travão**.

trazer [tra'ze*] vt to bring; (roupa) to wear;

(causar) to bring; *(nome, marcas)* to bear; ~ à **memória** to bring to mind; **o jornal traz uma notícia sobre isso** the newspaper has an item about that; ~ **de volta** to bring back.
TRE *(BR) abr m* = **Tribunal Regional Eleitoral**.
trecho ['treʃu] *m* passage; *(de rua, caminho)* stretch; *(espaço)* space.
treco ['treku] *(col) m (tralha)* thing; *(indisposição)* bad turn; ~**s** *mpl* stuff *sg*; **ter um** ~ *(sentir-se mal)* to be taken bad; *(zangar-se)* to have a fit.
trégua ['trɛgwa] *f* truce; *(descanso)* respite, rest; **não dar** ~ **a** to give no respite to.
treinado/a [trej'nadu/a] *adj (atleta)* fit; *(animal)* trained; *(acostumado)* practised *(BRIT)*, practiced *(US)*.
treinador(a) [trejna'do*(a)] *m/f* trainer.
treinamento [trejna'mẽtu] *m* training.
treinar [trej'na*] *vt* to train; ~**-se** *vr* to train; ~ **seu inglês** to practise *(BRIT)* ou practice *(US)* one's English.
treino ['trejnu] *m* training.
trejeito [tre'ʒejtu] *m (gesto)* gesture; *(careta)* grimace, face.
trela ['trɛla] *f (correia)* lead, leash; *(col: conversa)* chat; **dar** ~ **a** *(col: conversar)* to chat with; *(encorajar)* to lead on.
treliça [tre'lisa] *f* trellis.
trem [trẽj] *(pl* -**ns**) *m* train; *(PT: carruagem)* carriage, coach; **trens** *mpl (col)* gear *sg*, belongings *pl*; **ir de** ~ to go by train; **mudar de** ~ to change trains; **pegar um** ~ to catch a train; **puxar o** ~ *(col)* to make tracks; ~ **de carga/passageiros** freight/passenger train; ~ **correio** mail train; ~ **de aterrissagem** *(avião)* landing gear; ~ **da alegria** *(POL)* jobs *pl* for the boys, nepotism.
trema ['trema] *m* di(a)eresis.
tremedeira [treme'dejra] *f* trembling.
tremelicante [tremeli'kãtʃi] *adj* trembling.
tremelicar [tremeli'ka*] *vi* to tremble, shiver.
tremelique [treme'liki] *m* trembling.
tremeluzir [tremelu'zi*] *vi* to twinkle, glimmer.
tremendo/a [tre'mẽdu/a] *adj* tremendous; *(terrível)* terrible, awful.
tremer [tre'me*] *vi* to shudder, quake; *(terra)* to shake; *(de frio, medo)* to shiver.
tremor [tre'mo*] *m* tremor, trembling; ~ **de terra** earth tremor.
tremular [tremu'la*] *vi (bandeira)* to flutter, wave; *(luz)* to glimmer, flicker.
trêmulo/a ['tremulu/a] *adj* shaky, trembling; *(voz)* faltering.
trena ['trena] *f* tape measure.
trenó [tre'nɔ] *m* sledge *(BRIT)*, sled *(US)*, sleigh.
trens [trẽjʃ] *mpl de* **trem**.
trepadeira [trepa'dejra] *f* creeper, climbing plant.

trepada [tre'pada] *(col!) f* screw *(!)*, fuck *(!)*.
trepar [tre'pa*] *vt* to climb ♦ *vi:* ~ **(com alguém)** *(col!)* to screw *(!)* (sb); ~ **em** to climb.
trepidação [trepida'sãw] *f* shaking.
trepidar [trepi'da*] *vi* to tremble, shake.
trépido/a ['trɛpidu/a] *adj* fearful.
três [treʃ] *num* three; **a** ~ **por dois** every five minutes, all the time; *V tb* **cinco**.
tresloucado/a [treʒlo'kadu/a] *adj* crazy, deranged.
três-quartos *adj inv (saia, manga)* three-quarter-length ♦ *m inv (apartamento)* three-room flat *ou* apartment.
trespassar [treʃpa'sa*] *vt* = **traspassar**.
trespasse [treʃ'pasi] *m* = **traspasse**.
trevas ['trevaʃ] *fpl* darkness *sg*.
trevo ['trevu] *m* clover; *(de vias)* intersection.
treze ['trezi] *num* thirteen; *V vb* **cinco**.
trezentos/as [tre'zẽtuʃ/aʃ] *num* three hundred.
tríade ['triadʒi] *f* triad.
triagem ['trjaʒẽ] *f* selection; *(separação)* sorting; **fazer uma** ~ **de** to make a selection of, sort out.
triangular [trjãgu'la*] *adj* triangular.
triângulo ['trjãgulu] *m* triangle.
tribal [tri'baw] *(pl* -**ais**) *adj* tribal.
tribo ['tribu] *f* tribe.
tribulação [tribula'sãw] *(pl* -**ões**) *f* tribulation, affliction.
tribuna [tri'buna] *f* platform, rostrum; *(REL)* pulpit.
tribunal [tribu'naw] *(pl* -**ais**) *m* court; *(comissão)* tribunal; ~ **de apelação** *ou* **de recursos** court of appeal; **T**~ **de Justiça/Contas** Court of Justice/Accounts; **T**~ **do Trabalho** Industrial Tribunal.
tributação [tributa'sãw] *f* taxation.
tributar [tribu'ta*] *vt* to tax; *(pagar)* to pay.
tributário/a [tribu'tarju/a] *adj* tax *atr* ♦ *m (de rio)* tributary.
tributável [tribu'tavew] *(pl* -**eis**) *adj* taxable.
tributo [tri'butu] *m* tribute; *(imposto)* tax.
tricampeão/peã [trikã'pjãw/'pjã] *(pl* -**ões**/~**s**) *m/f* three-times champion.
tricô [tri'ko] *m* knitting; **artigos de** ~ knitted goods, knitwear *sg*; **ponto de** ~ plain stitch.
tricolor [triko'lo*] *adj* three-coloured *(BRIT)*, three-colored *(US)*.
tricotar [triko'ta*] *vt, vi* to knit.
tridimensional [tridimẽsjo'naw] *(pl* -**ais**) *adj* three-dimensional.
triênio [tri'jenju] *m* three-year period.
trigal [tri'gaw] *(pl* -**ais**) *m* wheat field.
trigêmeo/a [tri'ʒemju/a] *m/f* triplet.
trigésimo/a [tri'ʒɛzimu/a] *adj* thirtieth; *V tb* **quinto**.
trigo ['trigu] *m* wheat.
trigonometria [trigonome'tria] *f* trigonometry.

NB: *European Portuguese adds the following consonants to certain words:* **b** *(sú(b)dito, su(b)til);* **c** *(a(c)ção, a(c)cionista, a(c)to);* **m** *(inde(m)ne);* **p** *(ado(p)ção, ado(p)tar); for further details see p. xiii.*

trigueiro/a [tri'gejru/a] *adj* dark, swarthy.

trilátero/a [tri'lateru/a] *adj* trilateral.

trilha ['triʎa] *f* (*caminho*) path; (*rasto*) track, trail; (*COMPUT*) track; ~ **sonora** soundtrack.

trilhado/a [tri'ʎadu/a] *adj* (*pisado*) well-worn, well-trodden; (*percorrido*) covered.

trilhão [tri'ʎãw] (*pl* **-ões**) *m* billion (*BRIT*), trillion (*US*).

trilhar [tri'ʎa*] *vt* (*vereda*) to tread, wear.

trilho ['triʎu] *m* (*BR*: *FERRO*) rail; (*vereda*) path, track.

trilhões [tri'ʎõjʃ] *mpl de* **trilhão**.

trilíngüe [tri'lĩgwi] *adj* trilingual.

trilogia [trilo'ʒia] *f* trilogy.

trimestral [trimeʃ'traw] (*pl* **-ais**) *adj* quarterly.

trimestralidade [trimeʃtrali'dadʒi] *f* quarterly payment.

trimestralmente [trimeʃtraw'mẽtʃi] *adv* quarterly.

trimestre [tri'mɛʃtri] *m* (*EDUC*) term; (*COM*) quarter.

trinca ['trĩka] *f* set of three; (*col*: *trio*) threesome.

trincar [trĩ'ka*] *vt* to crunch; (*morder*) to bite; (*dentes*) to grit ♦ *vi* to crunch.

trinchar [trĩ'ʃa*] *vt* to carve.

trincheira [trĩ'ʃejra] *f* trench.

trinco ['trĩku] *m* latch.

trindade [trĩ'dadʒi] *f*: **a T~** the Trinity; **~s** *fpl* angelus *sg*.

Trinidad e Tobago [trinidadʒito'bagu] *m* Trinidad and Tobago.

trinta ['trĩta] *num* thirty; *V tb* **cinqüenta**.

trio ['triu] *m* trio; ~ **elétrico** music float.

tripa ['tripa] *f* gut, intestine; **~s** *fpl* bowels, guts; (*CULIN*) tripe *sg*; **fazer das ~s coração** to make a great effort.

tripé [tri'pɛ] *m* tripod.

tríplex ['tripleks] *adj inv* three-storey (*BRIT*), three-story (*US*) ♦ *m inv* three-stor(e)y apartment.

triplicar [tripli'ka*] *vt*, *vi* to treble; **~-se** *vr* to treble.

Trípoli ['tripoli] *n* Tripoli.

tripulação [tripula'sãw] (*pl* **-ões**) *f* crew.

tripulante [tripu'lãtʃi] *m/f* crew member.

tripular [tripu'la*] *vt* to man.

trisavô/vó [triza'vo/'vɔ] *m/f* great-great-grandfather/mother.

triste ['triʃtʃi] *adj* sad; (*lugar*) depressing.

tristeza [triʃ'teza] *f* sadness; (*de lugar*) gloominess; **esse professor é uma ~** (*col*) this teacher is awful.

tristonho/a [triʃ'toɲu/a] *adj* sad, melancholy.

triturar [tritu'ra*] *vt* (*moer*) to grind; (*espancar*) to beat to a pulp; (*afligir*) to beset.

triunfal [trjũ'faw] (*pl* **-ais**) *adj* triumphal.

triunfante [trjũ'fãtʃi] *adj* triumphant.

triunfar [trjũ'fa*] *vi* to triumph.

triunfo ['trjũfu] *m* triumph.

trivial [tri'vjaw] (*pl* **-ais**) *adj* (*comum*) common(place), ordinary; (*insignificante*) trivial, trifling ♦ *m* (*pratos*) everyday food.

trivialidade [trivjali'dadʒi] *f* triviality; **~s** *fpl* trivia *sg*.

triz [triʒ] *m*: **por um ~** by a hair's breadth; **escapar por um ~** to have a narrow escape.

troca ['trɔka] *f* exchange, swap; **em ~ de** in exchange for.

troça ['trɔsa] *f* ridicule, mockery; **fazer ~ de** to make fun of.

trocadilho [troka'dʒiʎu] *m* pun, play on words.

trocado/a [tro'kadu/a] *adj* mixed up ♦ *m*: **~(s)** (small) change.

trocador(a) [troka'do*(a)] *m/f* (*em ônibus*) conductor.

trocar [tro'ka*] *vt* to exchange, swap; (*mudar*) to change; (*inverter*) to change *ou* swap round; (*confundir*) to mix up; **~-se** *vr* to change; **~ dinheiro** to change money; **~ algo por algo** to exchange *ou* swap sth for sth; **~ algo de lugar** to move sth; **~ de roupa/lugar** to change (clothes)/places; **~ de bem/mal** to make up/fall out.

troçar [tro'sa*] *vi*: **~ de** to ridicule, make fun of.

troca-troca (*pl* **~s**) *m* swap.

trocista [tro'siʃta] *m/f* joker.

troco ['troku] *m* (*dinheiro*) change; (*revide*) retort, rejoinder; **a ~ de** at the cost of; (*por causa de*) because of; **em ~ de** in exchange for; **dar o ~ a alguém** (*fig*) to pay sb back.

troço ['trɔsu] (*BR*: *col*) *m* (*coisa inútil*) piece of junk; (*coisa*) thing; **ser ~** (*pessoa*) to be a big-shot; **ser um ~** to be amazing; **ter um ~** (*sentir-se mal*) to be taken bad; (*zangar-se*) to get mad; **senti** *ou* **me deu um ~** I felt bad; **ele é um ~ de feio** he's incredibly ugly; **meus ~s** my things.

troféu [tro'fɛw] *m* trophy.

tromba ['trõba] *f* (*do elefante*) trunk; (*de outro animal*) snout; (*col*) poker face; **estar de ~** (*col*) to be poker-faced.

trombada [trõ'bada] *f* crash; **dar uma ~** to have a crash.

tromba-d'água (*pl* **trombas-d'água**) *f* waterspout; (*chuva*) downpour.

trombadinha [trõba'dʒiɲa] *f* child thief.

trombeta [trõ'beta] *f* (*MÚS*) trumpet.

trombone [trõ'boni] *m* (*MÚS*) trombone; **botar a boca no ~** (*fig*: *col*) to tell the world.

trombose [trõ'bɔzi] *f* thrombosis.

trombudo/a [trõ'budu/a] *adj* (*fig*) poker-faced.

trompa ['trõpa] *f* (*MÚS*) horn; **~ de Falópio** (*ANAT*) fallopian tube.

tronchar [trõ'ʃa*] *vt* to cut off, chop off.

troncho/a ['trõʃu/a] *adj* (*torto*) crooked; **~ de uma perna** one-legged.

tronco ['trõku] *m* (*caule*) trunk; (*ramo*) branch; (*de corpo*) torso, trunk; (*de família*) lineage; (*TEL*) trunkline.

troncudo/a [trõ'kudu/a] *adj* stocky.

trono ['trɔnu] *m* throne.

tropa ['trɔpa] *f* troop, gang; (*MIL*) troop; (*exército*) army; **ir para a** ~ (*PT*) to join the army; ~ **de choque** riot police, riot squad.

tropeção [trope'sãw] (*pl* **-ões**) *m* trip-up; (*fig*) faux pas, slip-up; **dar um** ~ **(em)** to stumble (on).

tropeçar [trope'sa*] *vi* to stumble, trip; (*fig*) to blunder; ~ **em dificuldades** to meet with difficulties.

tropeço [tro'pesu] *m* stumbling block.

tropeções [trope'sõjʃ] *mpl de* **tropeção**.

trôpego/a ['tropegu/a] *adj* shaky, unsteady.

tropel [tro'pɛw] (*pl* **-éis**) *m* (*ruído*) uproar, tumult; (*confusão*) confusion; (*estrépito de pés*) stamping of feet; (*turbamulta*) mob.

tropical [tropi'kaw] (*pl* **-ais**) *adj* tropical.

trópico ['trɔpiku] *m* tropic; **T~ de Câncer/ Capricórnio** Tropic of Cancer/Capricorn.

troquei [tro'kej] *etc vb V* **trocar**.

trotar [tro'ta*] *vi* to trot.

trote ['trɔtʃi] *m* trot; (*por telefone etc*) hoax; (*em calouro*) trick; **passar um** ~ to play a hoax.

trottoir [tro'twa*] *m*: **fazer** ~ to go on the streets (as a prostitute).

trouxa ['troʃa] *adj* (*col*) gullible ♦ *f* bundle of clothes ♦ *m/f* (*col*: *pessoa*) sucker.

trouxe ['trosi] *etc vb V* **trazer**.

trova ['trɔva] *f* ballad, folksong.

trovador [trova'do*] *m* troubadour, minstrel.

trovão [tro'vãw] (*pl* **-ões**) *m* clap of thunder.

trovejar [trove'ʒa*] *vi* to thunder.

trovoada [tro'vwada] *f* thunderstorm.

trovoar [tro'vwa*] *vi* to thunder.

trovões [tro'võjʃ] *mpl de* **trovão**.

TRT (*BR*) *abr m* = **Tribunal Regional do Trabalho**.

TRU (*BR*) *abr f* = **Taxa Rodoviária Única**.

trucidar [trusi'da*] *vt* to butcher, slaughter.

truculência [truku'lẽsja] *f* cruelty, barbarism.

truculento [truku'lẽtʃi] *adj* cruel, barbaric.

trufa ['trufa] *f* truffle.

truísmo [tru'iʒmu] *m* truism.

trumbicar-se [trũbi'kaxsi] (*col*) *vr* to come a cropper.

truncar [trũ'ka*] *vt* to chop off, cut off; (*texto*) to garble.

trunfo ['trũfu] *m* trump card.

truque ['truki] *m* trick; (*publicitário*) gimmick.

truste ['truʃtʃi] *m* trust, monopoly.

truta ['truta] *f* trout.

TSE (*BR*) *abr m* = **Tribunal Superior Eleitoral**.

TST (*BR*) *abr m* = **Tribunal Superior do Trabalho**.

tu [tu] (*PT*) *pron* you.

tua ['tua] *f de* **teu**.

tuba ['tuba] *f* tuba.

tubarão [tuba'rãw] (*pl* **-ões**) *m* shark.

tubário/a [tu'barju/a] *adj V* **gravidez**.

tubarões [tuba'rõjʃ] *mpl de* **tubarão**.

tuberculose [tubexku'lɔzi] *f* tuberculosis, TB.

tuberculoso/a [tubexku'lozu/ɔza] *adj* suffering from tuberculosis ♦ *m/f* TB sufferer.

tubinho [tu'biɲu] *m* tube dress.

tubo ['tubu] *m* tube, pipe; ~ **de ensaio** test tube; **gastar/custar os** ~**s** (*col*) to spend/cost a bomb.

tubulação [tubula'sãw] *f* piping, plumbing; **entrar pela** ~ to come a cropper.

tubular [tubu'la*] *adj* tubular.

tucano [tu'kanu] *m* toucan.

tudo ['tudu] *pron* everything; ~ **quanto** everything that; **antes de** ~ first of all; **apesar de** ~ despite everything; **acima de** ~ above all; **depois de** ~ after all; ~ **ou nada** all or nothing; **estar com** ~ to be sitting pretty.

tufão [tu'fãw] (*pl* **-ões**) *m* typhoon.

tugúrio [tu'gurju] *m* (*cabana*) hut, shack; (*refúgio*) shelter.

tulipa [tu'lipa] *f* tulip; (*copo*) tall glass.

tumba ['tũba] *f* (*sepultura*) tomb; (*lápide*) tombstone.

túmido/a [tu'midu/a] *adj* (*inchado*) swollen.

tumular [tumu'la*] *adj* (*pedra*) tomb *atr*; (*silêncio*) like the grave.

túmulo [tu'mulu] *m* tomb; (*sepultura*) burial; **ser um** ~ (*pessoa*) to be very discreet.

tumor [tu'mo*] *m* tumour (*BRIT*), tumor (*US*); ~ **benigno/maligno** benign/malignant tumo(u)r; ~ **cerebral** brain tumo(u)r.

tumulto [tu'muwtu] *m* (*confusão*) uproar, trouble; (*grande movimento*) bustle; (*balbúrdia*) hubbub; (*motim*) riot.

tumultuado/a [tumuw'twadu/a] *adj* riotous, heated.

tumultuar [tumuw'twa*] *vt* (*fazer tumulto em*) to disrupt; (*amotinar*) to rouse, incite.

tumultuoso/a [tumuw'twozu/ɔza] *adj* tumultuous; (*revolto*) stormy.

tunda ['tũda] *f* thrashing, beating; (*fig*) dressing-down.

túnel ['tunew] (*pl* **-eis**) *m* tunnel.

túnica ['tunika] *f* tunic.

Tunísia [tu'nizja] *f*: **a** ~ Tunisia.

tupi [tu'pi] *m* Tupi (tribe); (*LING*) Tupi ♦ *m/f* Tupi Indian.

tupiniquim [tupini'kĩ] (*pej*: *pl* **-ns**) *adj* Brazilian (Indian).

turba ['tuxba] *f* throng; (*em desordem*) mob.

turbamulta [tuxba'muwta] *f* mob.

turbante [tux'bãtʃi] *m* turban.

turbar [tux'ba*] *vt* (*escurecer*) to darken, cloud; (*perturbar*) to perturb; ~**-se** *vr* to be perturbed.

turbilhão [tuxbi'ʎãw] (*pl* **-ões**) *m* (*de vento*) whirlwind; (*de água*) whirlpool; **um** ~ **de** a whirl of.

turbina [tux'bina] *f* turbine.

turbulência [tuxbu'lẽsja] *f* turbulence.

NB: European Portuguese adds the following consonants to certain words: **b** (sú(b)dito, su(b)til); **c** (a(c)ção, a(c)cionista, a(c)to); **m** (inde(m)ne); **p** (ado(p)ção, ado(p)tar); *for further details see p. xiii.*

turbulento/a [tuxbu'lẽtu/a] *adj* turbulent, stormy; *(pessoa)* disorderly.
turco/a ['tuxku/a] *adj* Turkish ♦ *m/f* Turk ♦ *m* *(LING)* Turkish.
turfa ['tuxfa] *f* peat.
turfe ['tuxfi] *m* horse-racing.
túrgido/a ['tuxʒidu/a] *adj* swollen, bloated.
turíbulo [tu'ribulu] *m* incense-burner.
turismo [tu'riʒmu] *m* tourism; *(indústria)* tourist industry; **fazer** ~ to go sightseeing; **agência de** ~ travel agency.
turista [tu'riʃta] *m/f* tourist; *(aluno)* persistent absentee ♦ *adj* *(classe)* tourist *atr*.
turístico/a [tu'riʃtʃiku/a] *adj* tourist *atr*; *(viagem)* sightseeing *atr*.
turma ['tuxma] *f* group; *(EDUC)* class; **a** ~ **da pesada** *(col)* the in crowd.
turnê [tux'ne] *f* tour.
turnedô [tuxne'do] *m* *(CULIN)* tournedos.
turno ['tuxnu] *m* shift; *(vez)* turn; *(ESPORTE, de eleição)* round; **por** ~**s** alternately, by turns, in turn; ~ **da noite** night shift.
turquesa [tux'keza] *adj inv* turquoise.
Turquia [tux'kia] *f*: **a** ~ Turkey.
turra ['tuxa] *f* *(disputa)* argument, dispute; **andar** *ou* **viver às** ~**s** to be at loggerheads.
turvar [tux'va*] *vt* to cloud; *(escurecer)* to darken; ~**-se** *vr* to become clouded; to darken.
turvo/a ['tuxvu/a] *adj* clouded.
tusso ['tusu] *etc vb V* **tossir**.
tusta ['tuʃta] *(col)* *m*: **nem um** ~ not a penny.
tutano [tu'tanu] *m* *(ANAT)* marrow.
tutela [tu'tela] *f* protection; *(JUR)* guardianship; **estar sob a** ~ **de** *(fig)* to be under the protection of.
tutelar [tute'la*] *adj* protective; *(JUR)* guardian ♦ *vt* to protect; to act as a guardian to.
tutor(a) [tu'to*(a)] *m/f* guardian.
tutu [tu'tu] *m* *(CULIN)* beans, bacon and manioc flour; *(de balé)* tutu; *(col: dinheiro)* cash.
TV [te've] *abr f* (= *televisão*) TV.
TVE *(BR)* *abr f* (= *Televisão Educativa*) educational television station.
TVS *(BR)* *abr f* = **Televisão Stúdio Sílvio Santos**.
tweed ['twidʒi] *m* tweed.

U

U, u [u] *(pl* **us**) *m* U, u; **U de Úrsula** U for Uncle.
uai [waj] *excl* ah.
UBE *abr f* = **União Brasileira de Empresários**.
úbere ['uberi] *adj* fertile ♦ *m* udder.
ubérrimo/a [u'bɛximu/a] *adj superl de* **úbere**.

ubiqüidade [ubikwi'dadʒi] *f* ubiquity.
ubíquo/a [u'bikwu/a] *adj* ubiquitous.
Ucrânia [u'kranja] *f*: **a** ~ the Ukraine.
UD *(BR)* *abr f* = **Feira de Utilidades Domésticas**.
UDN *abr f* (= *União Democrática Nacional*) former Brazilian political party.
ué [wɛ] *excl* what?, just a minute!
UERJ ['wɛxʒi] *abr f* = **Universidade Estadual do Rio de Janeiro**.
ufa ['ufa] *excl* phew!
ufanar-se [ufa'naxsi] *vr*: ~ **de** to take pride in, pride o.s. on.
ufanismo [ufa'niʒmu] *(BR)* *m* boastful nationalism, chauvinism.
Uferj [u'fɛxʒi] *abr f* = **Unidade Fiscal do Estado do Rio de Janeiro**.
UFF *abr f* = **Universidade Federal Fluminense**.
UFMG *abr f* = **Universidade Federal de Minas Gerais**.
UFPE *abr f* = **Universidade Federal de Pernambuco**.
UFRJ *abr f* = **Universidade Federal do Rio de Janeiro**.
Uganda [u'gãda] *m* Uganda.
ugandense [ugã'dẽsi] *adj*, *m/f* Ugandan.
uh [uh] *excl* ooh!; *(de repugnância)* ugh!
ui [ui] *excl* *(de dor)* ouch, ow; *(de surpresa)* oh; *(de repugnância)* ugh.
uísque ['wiʃki] *m* whisky *(BRIT)*, whiskey *(US)*.
uisqueria [wiʃke'ria] *f* whisk(e)y bar.
uivada [wi'vada] *f* howl.
uivante [wi'vãtʃi] *adj* howling.
uivar [wi'va*] *vi* to howl; *(berrar)* to yell.
uivo ['wivu] *m* howl; *(fig)* yell.
úlcera ['uwsera] *f* ulcer.
ulceração [uwsera'sãw] *f* ulceration.
ulcerar [uwse'ra*] *vt*, *vi* to ulcerate; ~**-se** *vr* to ulcerate.
ulceroso/a [uwse'rozu/ɔza] *adj* ulcerous.
ulterior [ulte'rjo*] *adj* *(além)* further, farther; *(depois)* later, subsequent.
ulteriormente [uwteriox'mẽtʃi] *adv* later on, subsequently.
ultimamente [uwtʃima'mẽtʃi] *adv* lately.
ultimar [uwtʃi'ma*] *vt* to finish; *(negócio, compra)* to complete.
ultimato [uwtʃi'matu] *m* ultimatum.
ultimátum [uwtʃi'matũ] *m* = **ultimato**.
último/a ['uwtʃimu/a] *adj* last; *(mais recente)* latest; *(qualidade)* lowest; *(fig)* final; **por** ~ finally; **fazer algo por** ~ to do sth last; **nos** ~**s anos** in recent years; **em** ~ **caso** if the worst comes to the worst; **pela última vez** (for) the last time; **a última** *(notícia)* the latest (news); *(absurdo)* the latest folly; **dizer as últimas a alguém** to insult sb; **estar nas últimas** *(na miséria)* to be down and out; *(agoniando)* to be on one's last legs.
ultra- [uwtra-] *prefixo* ultra-.
ultracheio/a [uwtra'ʃeju/a] *adj* packed.
ultrajante [uwtra'ʒãtʃi] *adj* outrageous; *(que*

insulta) insulting.

ultrajar [uwtra'ʒa*] vt to outrage; (insultar) to insult, offend.

ultraje [uw'traʒi] m outrage; (insulto) insult, offence (BRIT), offense (US).

ultraleve [uwtra'lɛvi] adj ultralight ♦ m microlite.

ultramar [uwtra'ma*] m overseas.

ultramarino/a [uwtrama'rinu/a] adj overseas atr.

ultramoderno/a [uwtramo'dɛxnu/a] adj ultramodern.

ultrapassado/a [uwtrapa'sadu/a] adj (idéias etc) outmoded.

ultrapassagem [uwtrapa'saʒē] f overtaking (BRIT), passing (US).

ultrapassar [uwtrapa'sa*] vt (atravessar) to cross, go beyond; (ir além de) to exceed; (transgredir) to overstep; (AUTO) to overtake (BRIT), pass (US); (ser superior a) to surpass ♦ vi (AUTO) to overtake (BRIT), pass (US).

ultra-secreto/a adj top secret.

ultra-sensível (pl -eis) adj hypersensitive.

ultra-som m ultrasound.

ultra-sônico/a [-'soniku/a] adj ultrasonic; (MED) ultrasound atr.

ultra-sonografia [-sonogra'fia] f ultrasound scanning.

ultravioleta [uwtravjo'leta] adj ultraviolet.

ululante [ulu'lãtʃi] adj howling; (mentira: óbvio) blatant.

ulular [ulu'la*] vi to howl, wail ♦ m howling, wailing.

um(a) [ũ/'uma] (pl uns/~s) art indef (sg) a; (antes de vogal ou 'h' mudo) an; (pl) some ♦ num one ♦ pron one ♦ f (fato, acontecimento) a thing, one; ~ e outro both; ~ a ~ one by one; ~ ao outro one another; (entre dois) each other; à uma at once, at the same time; à uma (hora) at one (o'clock); (aproximadamente): uns 5 about 5; (dando ênfase): estou com uma fome! I'm so hungry!; ~ dia sim, ~ dia não every other day; ela é de uma beleza incrível she's incredibly beautiful; ~ de cada vez one at a time; dar uma de ator etc (col) to do the actor etc bit; V tb cinco.

umbanda [ũ'bãda] m umbanda (Afro-Brazilian cult).

umbigo [ũ'bigu] m navel.

umbilical [ũbili'kaw] (pl -ais) adj V cordão.

umbral [ũ'braw] (pl -ais) m (limiar) threshold.

umedecer [umede'se*] vt to moisten, wet; ~-se vr to get wet.

umedecido/a [umede'sidu/a] adj damp.

umidade [umi'daʒi] f dampness; (clima) humidity.

úmido/a ['umidu/a] adj wet, moist; (roupa) damp; (clima) humid.

unânime [u'nanimi] adj unanimous.

unanimidade [unanimi'dadʒi] f unanimity.

unção [ũ'sãw] f anointing; (REL) unction.

UNE (BR) abr f = **União Nacional de Estudantes**.

UNESCO [u'nɛʃku] abr f UNESCO.

ungir [ũ'ʒi*] vt to rub with ointment; (REL) to anoint.

ungüento [ũ'gwẽtu] m ointment.

unha ['uɲa] f nail; (garra) claw; com ~s e dentes tooth and nail; ser ~ e carne (com) to be hand in glove (with); fazer as ~s to do one's nails; (por outra pessoa) to have one's nails done; ~ encravada (no pé) ingrowing toenail.

unhada [u'ɲada] f scratch.

unha-de-fome (pl unhas-de-fome) m/f miser ♦ adj mean.

unhar [u'ɲa*] vt to scratch.

união [u'ɲjãw] (pl -ões) f union; (ato) joining; (unidade, solidariedade) unity; (casamento) marriage; (TEC) joint; a U~ Soviética the Soviet Union; a ~ faz a força unity is strength; a U~ (no Brasil) the Union, the Federal Government.

unicamente [unika'mẽtʃi] adv only.

único/a ['uniku/a] adj only; (sem igual) unique; (um só) single; mão única (sinal) one-way; ele é o ~ que ... he is the only one who ...; ela é filha única she's an only child; um caso ~ a one-off; preço ~ one price.

unicórnio [uni'kɔxnju] m unicorn.

unidade [uni'dadʒi] f unity; (TEC, COM) unit; ~ de processamento central (COMPUT) central processing unit; ~ de disco (COMPUT) disk drive; ~ de fita (COMPUT) tape streamer.

unido/a [u'nidu/a] adj joined, linked; (fig) united; manter-se ~s to stick together.

Unif [u'nifi] (BR) abr f = **Unidade Fiscal**.

unificação [unifika'sãw] f unification.

unificar [unifi'ka*] vt to unite; ~-se vr to join together.

uniforme [uni'fɔxmi] adj uniform; (semelhante) alike, similar; (superfície) even ♦ m uniform; de ~ uniformly.

uniformidade [unifoxmi'dadʒi] f uniformity.

uniformizado/a [unifoxmi'zadu/a] adj (uniforme) uniform, standardized; (vestido de uniforme) in uniform.

uniformizar [unifoxmi'za*] vt to standardize; (pessoa) to put into uniform; ~-se vr to put on one's uniform.

unilateral [unilate'raw] (pl -ais) adj unilateral.

unilíngüe [uni'lĩgwi] adj monolingual.

uniões [u'ɲjõjʃ] fpl de união.

unir [u'ni*] vt (juntar) to join together; (ligar) to link; (pessoas, fig) to unite; (misturar) to mix together; (atar) to tie together; ~-se vr to come together; (povos etc) to unite; ~-se

a alguém to join forces with sb.
unissex [uni'sɛks] *adj inv* unisex.
uníssono [u'nisonu] *m*: **em ~** in unison.
Unita [u'nita] *abr f* (= *União Nacional pela Libertação de Angola*) Unita.
unitário/a [uni'tarju/a] *adj* (*preço*) unit *atr*; (*POL*) unitarian ♦ *m/f* (*POL, REL*) unitarian.
universal [univex'saw] (*pl* -**ais**) *adj* universal; (*geral*) general; (*mundial*) worldwide; (*espírito*) broad.
universalidade [univexsali'dadʒi] *f* universality.
universalizar [univexsali'za*] *vt* to universalize.
universidade [univexsi'dadʒi] *f* university.
universitário/a [univexsi'tarju/a] *adj* university *atr* ♦ *m/f* (*professor*) lecturer; (*aluno*) university student.
universo [uni'vɛxsu] *m* universe; (*mundo*) world.
unjo ['ũʒu] *etc vb V* ungir.
uno/a ['unu/a] *adj* one.
uns [ũʃ] *mpl de* um.
untar [ũ'ta*] *vt* (*esfregar*) to rub; (*com óleo, manteiga*) to grease.
upa ['upa] *excl* (*quando algo cai*) whoops!; (*para animar a se levantar*) up you get!; (*de espanto*) wow!
UPC (*BR*) *abr f* = **Unidade Padrão de Capital**.
Urais [u'rajʃ] *mpl*: **os ~** the Urals.
urânio [u'ranju] *m* uranium.
Urano [u'ranu] *m* Uranus.
urbanidade [uxbani'dadʒi] *f* courtesy, politeness.
urbanismo [uxba'niʒmu] *m* town planning.
urbanista [uxba'niʃta] *m/f* town planner.
urbanístico/a [uxba'niʃtʃiku/a] *adj* town planning *atr*.
urbanização [uxbaniza'sãw] *f* urbanization.
urbanizado/a [uxbani'zadu/a] *adj* (*zona*) built-up.
urbanizar [uxbani'za*] *vt* to urbanize; (*pessoa*) to refine.
urbano/a [ux'banu/a] *adj* (*da cidade*) urban; (*fig*) urbane.
urbe ['uxbi] *f* city.
urdir [ux'dʒi*] *vt* to weave; (*fig*: *maquinar*) to weave, hatch.
urdu [ux'du] *m* (*LING*) Urdu.
uretra [u'retra] *f* urethra.
urgência [ux'ʒẽsja] *f* urgency; **com toda ~** as quickly as possible; **de ~** urgent; **pedir algo com ~** to ask for sth insistently.
urgente [ux'ʒẽtʃi] *adj* urgent.
urgir [ux'ʒi*] *vi* to be urgent; (*tempo*) to be pressing ♦ *vt* to require urgently; **são providências que urge sejam tomadas** they are steps which urgently need to be taken; **urge fazermos** we must do.
urina [u'rina] *f* urine.
urinado/a [uri'nadu/a] *adj* (*molhado*) soaked with urine; (*manchado*) urine-stained.
urinar [uri'na*] *vi* to urinate ♦ *vt* (*sangue*) to

pass; (*cama*) to wet; **~-se** *vr* to wet o.s.
urinário/a [uri'narju/a] *adj* urinary.
urinol [uri'nɔw] (*pl* -**óis**) *m* chamber pot.
urna ['uxna] *f* urn; **as ~s** *fpl* (*fig*) the polls; **~ eleitoral** ballot box.
urologia [urolo'ʒia] *f* urology.
urologista [urolo'ʒiʃta] *m/f* urologist.
URP (*BR*) *abr f* = **Unidade de Referência de Preços**.
URPE (*BR*) *abr fpl* = **Urgências Pediátricas**.
urrar [u'xa*] *vt, vi* to roar; (*de dor*) to yell.
urro ['uxu] *m* roar; (*de dor*) yell.
ursa ['uxsa] *f* bear; **U~ Maior/Menor** Ursa Major/Minor.
urso ['uxsu] *m* bear.
urso-branco (*pl* **ursos-brancos**) *m* polar bear.
URSS *abr f* (= *União das Repúblicas Socialistas Soviéticas*): **a ~** the USSR.
urticária [uxtʃi'karja] *f* nettle rash.
urtiga [ux'tʃiga] *f* nettle.
urubu [uru'bu] *m* vulture.
urubusservar [urubusex'va*] (*col*) *vt, vi* to watch.
urucubaca [uruku'baka] *f* bad luck; **estar com uma ~** to be unlucky.
Uruguai [uru'gwaj] *m*: **o ~** Uruguay.
uruguaio/a [uru'gwaju/a] *adj, m/f* Uruguayan.
urze ['uxzi] *m* heather.
usado/a [u'zadu/a] *adj* used; (*comum*) common; (*roupa*) worn; (*gasto*) worn out; (*de segunda mão*) second-hand; **~ a** (*acostumado*) accustomed to.
usar [u'za*] *vt* (*servir-se de*) to use; (*vestir*) to wear; (*gastar com o uso*) to wear out; (*barba, cabelo curto*) to have, wear ♦ *vi*: **~ de** to use; **~ fazer** to be in the habit of doing; **modo de ~** directions *pl*.
usina [u'zina] *f* (*fábrica*) factory; (*de energia*) plant; **~ de açúcar** sugar mill; **~ de aço** steelworks; **~ hidrelétrica** hydroelectric power station; **~ termonuclear** nuclear power plant.
usineiro/a [uzi'nejru/a] *adj* plant *atr* ♦ *m/f* sugar mill owner.
uso ['uzu] *m* (*emprego*) use; (*utilização*) usage; (*prática*) practice; (*moda*) fashion; (*costume*) custom; (*vestir*) wearing; **~ e desgaste normal** (*COM*) fair wear and tear.
USP ['uʃpi] *abr f* = **Universidade de São Paulo**.
usual [u'zwaw] (*pl* -**ais**) *adj* usual; (*comum*) common.
usuário/a [u'zwarju/a] *m/f* user; **~ do telefone** telephone subscriber.
usucapião [uzuka'pjãw] *m* (*JUR*) prescription.
usufruir [uzu'frwi*] *vt* to enjoy ♦ *vi*: **~ de** to enjoy.
usufruto [uzu'frutu] *m* (*JUR*) usufruct.
usura [u'zura] *f* (*juro*) interest; (*avareza*) avarice.
usurário/a [uzu'rarju/a] *m/f* (*avaro*) miser; (*col*: *agiota*) loan shark ♦ *adj* avaricious.

usurpar [uzux'pa*] *vt* to usurp.

úteis ['utejʃ] *adj pl de* **útil**.

utensílio [utẽ'silju] *m* utensil.

uterino/a [ute'rinu/a] *adj* uterine.

útero ['uteru] *m* womb, uterus.

UTI ['utʃi] *abr f* (= *Unidade de Terapia Intensiva*) intensive care (unit), ICU.

útil ['utʃiw] (*pl* **-eis**) *adj* useful; (*vantajoso*) profitable, worthwhile; (*tempo*) working; (*prazo*) stipulated; **dias úteis** weekdays, working days; **em que lhe posso ser ~?** how can I be of assistance (to you)?

utilidade [utʃili'dadʒi] *f* usefulness; (*vantagem*) advantage; (*utensílio*) utility.

utilitário/a [utʃili'tarju/a] *adj* utilitarian, practical; (*pessoa*) matter-of-fact, pragmatic; (*veículo*) general purpose *atr*; **programa ~** (*COMPUT*) utilities program.

utilização [utʃiliza'sãw] *f* use.

utilizar [utʃili'za*] *vt* to use; **~-se** *vr*: **~-se de** to make use of.

utilizável [utʃili'zavew] (*pl* **-eis**) *adj* usable.

utopia [uto'pia] *f* Utopia.

utópico/a [u'tɔpiku/a] *adj* Utopian.

uva ['uva] *f* grape; (*col*: *mulher*) peach; (: *coisa*) lovely thing; **ser uma ~** (*pessoa*, *objeto*) to be lovely; **uma ~ de pessoa/ broche** a lovely person/brooch.

úvula ['uvula] *f* uvula.

V

V, v [ve] (*pl* **vs**) *m* V, v; **V de Vera** V for Victor.

v *abr de* **volt**.

vá [va] *etc vb* **V ir**.

vã [vã] *f de* **vão²**.

vaca ['vaka] *f* cow; **carne de ~** beef; **tempo das ~s magras** (*fig*) lean period; **a ~ foi para o brejo** (*fig*) everything went wrong; **voltar à ~ fria** to get back to the subject.

vacância [va'kãsja] *f* vacancy.

vacante [va'kãtʃi] *adj* vacant.

vaca-preta (*pl* **vacas-pretas**) *f* coca-cola *with* ice cream.

vacilação [vasila'sãw] *f* (*hesitação*) hesitation; (*balanço*) swaying.

vacilada [vasi'lada] *f* slip-up; **dar uma ~** (*col*) to slip up.

vacilante [vasi'lãtʃi] *adj* (*hesitante*) hesitant; (*pouco firme*) unsteady; (*luz*) flickering.

vacilar [vasi'la*] *vi* (*hesitar*) to hesitate; (*balançar*) to sway; (*cambalear*) to stagger;

(*luz*) to flicker; (*col*) to slip up.

vacina [va'sina] *f* vaccine.

vacinação [vasina'sãw] (*pl* **-ões**) *f* vaccination.

vacinar [vasi'na*] *vt* to vaccinate; (*fig*) to immunize; **~-se** *vr* to take vaccine.

vacuidade [vakwi'dadʒi] *f* emptiness.

vacum [va'kũ] *adj*: **gado ~** cattle.

vácuo ['vakwu] *m* vacuum; (*fig*) void; (*espaço*) space; **empacotado a ~** vacuum-packed.

vadear [va'dʒja*] *vt* to wade through.

vadiação [vadʒja'sãw] *f* vagrancy.

vadiagem [va'dʒjaʒẽ] *f* vagrancy.

vadiar [va'dʒja*] *vi* to lounge about; (*não trabalhar*) to idle about; (*não estudar*) to skive; (*perambular*) to wander.

vadio/a [va'dʒiu/a] *adj* (*ocioso*) idle, lazy; (*vagabundo*) vagrant ♦ *m/f* idler; (*vagabundo*) vagabond, vagrant.

vaga ['vaga] *f* (*onda*) wave; (*em hotel*, *trabalho*) vacancy; (*em estacionamento*) parking place; **ser bom de ~** to be good at parking.

vagabundear [vagabũ'dʒja*] *vi* to wander about, roam about; (*vadiar*) to laze around.

vagabundo/a [vaga'būdu/a] *adj* vagrant; (*vadio*) lazy, idle; (*de má qualidade*) cheap and cheerful; (*canalha*) rotten; (*mulher*) easy ♦ *m/f* tramp; (*canalha*) bum.

vagalhão [vaga'ʎãw] (*pl* **-ões**) *m* big wave, breaker.

vaga-lume [vaga'lumi] (*pl* **~s**) *m* (*ZOOL*) glow-worm; (*no cinema*) usher.

vagão [va'gãw] (*pl* **-ões**) *m* (*de passageiros*) carriage; (*de cargas*) wagon.

vagão-leito (*pl* **vagões-leitos**) (*PT*) *m* sleeping car.

vagão-restaurante (*pl* **vagões-restaurantes**) *m* buffet car.

vagar [va'ga*] *vi* to wander about, roam about; (*barco*) to drift; (*ficar vago*) to be vacant ♦ *m* slowness; **fazer algo com mais ~** to do sth at a more leisurely pace.

vagareza [vaga'reza] *f* slowness; **com ~** slowly.

vagaroso/a [vaga'rozu/ɔza] *adj* slow.

vagem ['vaʒẽ] (*pl* **-ns**) *f* green bean.

vagido [va'ʒidu] *m* wail.

vagina [va'ʒina] *f* vagina.

vaginal [vaʒi'naw] (*pl* **-ais**) *adj* vaginal.

vago/a ['vagu/a] *adj* (*indefinido*) vague; (*desocupado*) vacant, free; **tempo ~, horas vagas** spare time.

vagões [va'gõjʃ] *mpl de* **vagão**.

vaguear [va'gja*] *vi* to wander, roam; (*passear*) to ramble.

vai [vaj] *etc vb* **V ir**.

vaia ['vaja] *f* boo.

vaiar [va'ja*] *vt*, *vi* to boo, hiss.

vaidade [vaj'dadʒi] *f* vanity; (*futilidade*)

NB: *European Portuguese adds the following consonants to certain words:* **b** (sú(b)dito, su(b)til); **c** (a(c)ção, a(c)cionista, a(c)to); **m** (inde(m)ne); **p** (ado(p)ção, ado(p)tar); *for further details see p. xiii.*

futility.
vai-da-valsa *m*: **ir no** ~ to take life as it comes, go with the flow.
vaidoso/a [vaj'dozu/ɔza] *adj* vain.
vai-e-vem [-vēj] *m inv* = **vaivém**.
vai-não-vai *m inv* shilly-shallying.
vaivém [vaj'vēj] *m* to-and-fro.
vala ['vala] *f* ditch; ~ **comum** pauper's grave.
vale ['vali] *m* valley; (*poético*) vale; (*escrito*) voucher; (*reconhecimento de dívida*) IOU; ~ **postal** postal order.
vale-tudo [vali'tudu] *m inv* (*ESPORTE*) all-in wrestling; (*fig*) anything goes principle.
valentão/tona [valē'tãw/'tɔna] (*pl* -**ões/~s**) *adj* tough ♦ *m/f* tough nut.
valente [va'lētʃi] *adj* brave.
valentia [valē'tʃia] *f* courage, bravery; (*proeza*) feat.
valentões [valē'tójʃ] *mpl de* **valentão**.
valentona [valē'tɔna] *f de* **valentão**.
valer [va'le*] *vi* to be worth; (*ser válido*) to be valid; (*ter influência*) to carry weight; (*servir*) to serve; (*ser proveitoso*) to be useful; ~-**se** *vr*: ~-**se de** to use, make use of; ~ **a pena** to be worthwhile; **não vale a pena** it isn't worth it; **vale a pena fazer** it is worth doing; ~ **a** (*ajudar*) to help; ~ **por** (*equivaler*) to be worth the same as; **para** ~ (*muito*) very much, a lot; (*realmente*) for real, properly; **vale dizer** in other words; **fazer** ~ **os seus direitos** to stand up for one's rights; **vale examinar os detalhes** we should examine the details; **mais vale fazê-lo já (do que ...)** it would be better to do it right away (than ...); **não vale empurrar** (*ESPORTE etc*) you're not allowed to push; **assim não vale!** that's not fair!; **vale tudo** anything goes; **ser para** ~ (*col*) to be for real; **ou coisa que o valha** or something like it; **valeu!** (*col*) you bet!
valeta [va'leta] *f* gutter.
valete [va'letʃi] *m* (*CARTAS*) jack.
valha ['vaʎa] *etc vb V* **valer**.
valia [va'lia] *f* value; **de grande** ~ valuable.
validação [valida'sãw] *f* validation.
validade [vali'dadʒi] *f* validity.
validar [vali'da*] *vt* to validate, make valid.
válido/a ['validu/a] *adj* valid.
valioso/a [va'ljozu/ɔza] *adj* valuable.
valise [va'lizi] *f* case, grip.
valor [va'lo*] *m* value; (*mérito*) merit; (*coragem*) courage; (*preço*) price; (*importância*) importance; ~**es** *mpl* values; (*COM*) securities; **dar** ~ **a** to value; **sem** ~ worthless; **no** ~ **de** to the value of; **objetos de** ~ valuables; ~ **nominal** face value; ~ **contábil** *ou* **contabilizado** (*COM*) book value; ~ **ao par** (*COM*) par value.
valorização [valoriza'sãw] *f* increase in value.
valorizar [valori'za*] *vt* to value; (*aumentar o valor*) to raise the value of; ~-**se** *vr* to go up in value; (*pessoa*) to value o.s.
valoroso/a [valo'rozu/ɔza] *adj* brave.

valsa ['vawsa] *f* waltz.
válvula ['vawvula] *f* valve.
vampe ['vãpi] *f* femme fatale.
vampiro/a [vã'piru/a] *m/f* vampire.
vandalismo [vãda'liʒmu] *m* vandalism.
vândalo/a ['vãdalu/a] *m/f* vandal.
vangloriar-se [vãglo'rjaxsi] *vr*: ~ **de** to boas of *ou* about.
vanguarda [vã'gwaxda] *f* vanguard, forefront; (*arte*) avant-garde; **artista de** ~ avant-garde artist.
vantagem [vã'taʒē] (*pl* -**ns**) *f* advantage; (*ganho*) profit, benefit; **contar** ~ (*col*) t brag, boast; **levar** ~ to get the upper hand; **tirar** ~ **de** to take advantage of.
vantajoso/a [vãta'ʒozu/ɔza] *adj* advantageous, (*lucrativo*) profitable; (*proveitoso*) beneficial.
vão¹ [vãw] *vb V* **ir**.
vão²/vã [vãw/vã] (*pl* ~**s/~s**) *adj* vain; (*fútil*) futile ♦ *m* (*intervalo*) space; (*de porta etc*) opening; (*ARQ*) empty space; **em** ~ in vain.
vapor [va'po*] *m* steam; (*navio*) steamer; (*de gas*) vapour (*BRIT*), vapor (*US*); **cozer no** ~ to steam; **ferro a** ~ steam iron; **a todo o** ~ at full speed.
vaporizador [vaporiza'do*] *m* vaporizer; (*de perfume*) spray.
vaporizar [vapori'za*] *vt* to vaporize; (*perfume*) to spray.
vaporoso/a [vapo'rozu/ɔza] *adj* steamy, misty; (*transparente*) transparent, see-through.
vaqueiro [va'kejru] *m* cowboy, cowhand.
vaquinha [va'kiɲa] *f*: **fazer uma** ~ to have a whip-round.
vara ['vara] *f* (*pau*) stick; (*TEC*) rod; (*JUR*) jurisdiction; (*de porcos*) herd; **salto de** ~ pole vault; ~ **de condão** magic wand.
varal [va'raw] (*pl* -**ais**) *m* clothes line.
varanda [va'rãda] *f* verandah; (*balcão*) balcony; ~ **envidraçada** conservatory.
varão/roa [va'rãw/'roa] (*pl* -**ões/~s**) *adj* male ♦ *m* man, male; (*de ferro*) rod.
varapau [vara'paw] (*col*) *m* (*pessoa*) beanpole.
varar [va'ra*] *vt* (*furar*) to pierce; (*passar*) to cross ♦ *vi* to beach, run aground.
varejar [vare'ʒa*] *vt* (*com vara*) to beat; (*revistar*) to search.
varejeira [vare'ʒejra] *f* bluebottle.
varejista [vare'ʒiʃta] (*BR*) *m/f* retailer ♦ *adj* (*mercado*) retail.
varejo [va'reʒu] (*BR*) *m* (*COM*) retail trade; **loja de** ~ retail store; **a** ~ retail; **preço no** ~ retail price.
variação [varja'sãw] (*pl* -**ões**) *f* variation, change.
variado/a [va'rjadu/a] *adj* varied; (*sortido*) assorted.
variante [va'rjãtʃi] *adj, f* variant.
variar [va'rja*] *vt, vi* to vary; **para** ~ for a change.
variável [va'rjavew] (*pl* -**eis**) *adj* variable; (*tempo, humor*) changeable ♦ *f* variable.

varicela [vari'sɛla] *f* chickenpox.

variedade [varje'dadʒi] *f* variety; ~s *fpl* (*TEATRO*) variety *sg*; **espetáculo/teatro de** ~s variety show/theatre (*BRIT*) *ou* theater (*US*).

Varig ['varigi] *abr f* (= *Viação Aérea Rio-Grandense*) *Brazilian national airline.*

varinha [va'riɲa] *f* wand; ~ **de condão** magic wand.

vário/a ['varju/a] *adj* (*diverso*) varied; (*pl*) various, several; (*COM*) sundry.

varíola [va'riola] *f* smallpox.

varizes [va'riziʃ] *fpl* varicose veins.

varoa [va'roa] *f de* **varão.**

varões [va'rõjʃ] *mpl de* **varão.**

varonil [varo'niw] (*pl* **-is**) *adj* manly, virile.

VAR-Palmares *abr f* (= *Vanguarda Armada Revolucionária*) *former Brazilian terrorist movement.*

varredor(a) [vaxe'do*(a)] *adj* sweeping ♦ *m/f* sweeper; ~ **de rua** road sweeper.

varrer [va'xe*] *vt* to sweep; (*sala*) to sweep out; (*folhas*) to sweep up; (*fig*) to sweep away.

varrido/a [va'xidu/a] *adj*: **um doido** ~ a raving lunatic.

Varsóvia [vax'sɔvja] *n* Warsaw; **pacto de** ~ Warsaw Pact.

várzea ['vaxzja] *f* meadow, field.

vascular [vaʃku'la*] *adj* vascular.

vasculhar [vaʃku'ʎa*] *vt* (*pesquisar*) to research; (*remexer*) to rummage through.

vasectomia [vazekto'mia] *f* vasectomy.

vaselina [vaze'lina] ® *f* vaseline ®; (*col*: *pessoa*) smooth talker.

vasilha [va'ziʎa] *f* (*para líquidos*) jug; (*para alimentos*) dish, container; (*barril*) barrel.

vaso ['vazu] *m* pot; (*para flores*) vase; ~ (**sanitário**) toilet (bowl); ~ **sanguíneo** blood vessel.

Vasp ['vaʃpi] *abr f* (= *Viação Aérea de São Paulo*) *Brazilian internal airline.*

vassoura [va'sora] *f* broom.

vastidão [vaʃtʃi'dãw] *f* vastness, immensity.

vasto/a ['vaʃtu/a] *adj* vast.

vatapá [vata'pa] *m dish of fish or chicken with coconut milk, shrimps, nuts, palm oil and spices.*

Vaticano [vatʃi'kanu] *m*: **o** ~ the Vatican; **a Cidade do** ~ the Vatican City.

vaticinar [vatʃisi'na*] *vt* to foretell, prophesy.

vaticínio [vatʃi'sinju] *m* prophecy.

vau [vaw] *m* ford, river crossing; (*NÁUT*) beam.

vazamento [vaza'mẽtu] *m* leak.

vazante [va'zãtʃi] *f* ebb tide.

vazão [va'zãw] (*pl* **-ões**) *f* flow; (*venda*) sale; **dar** ~ **a** (*expressar*) to give vent to; (*COM*) to clear; (*atender*) to deal with; (*resolver*) to attend to.

vazar [va'za*] *vt* (*tornar vazio*) to empty;

(*derramar*) to spill; (*verter*) to pour out ♦ *vi* to leak; (*maré*) to go out; (*notícia*) to leak; **ser vazado em** (*moldado*) to be modelled on.

vazio/a [va'ziu/a] *adj* empty; (*pessoa*) empty-headed, frivolous; (*cidade*) deserted ♦ *m* (*tb fig*) emptiness; (*deixado por alguém, algo*) void; ~ **de** (*fig*: *sem*) devoid of.

vazões [va'zõjʃ] *fpl de* **vazão.**

VBC (*BR*) *abr m* = **Valor Básico de Custeio.**

vê [ve] *etc vb* V **ver.**

veado ['vjadua] *m* deer; (*BR*: *col*) poof (*BRIT*), fag (*US*); **carne de** ~ venison.

vedado/a [ve'dadu/a] *adj* (*proibido*) forbidden; (*fechado*) enclosed.

vedar [ve'da*] *vt* (*proibir*) to ban, prohibit; (*sangue*) to stop the flow of); (*buraco*) to stop up; (*garrafa*) to cork; (*entrada, passagem*) to block; (*terreno*) to close off.

vedete [ve'dɛtʃi] *f* star.

veemência [vje'mẽsja] *f* vehemence.

veemente [vje'mẽtʃi] *adj* vehement.

vegetação [veʒeta'sãw] *f* vegetation.

vegetal [veʒe'taw] (*pl* **-ais**) *adj* vegetable *atr*; (*reino, vida*) plant *atr* ♦ *m* vegetable; **medicamento** ~ herbal remedy.

vegetar [veʒe'ta*] *vi* to vegetate.

vegetariano/a [veʒeta'rjanu/a] *adj*, *m/f* vegetarian.

vegetativo/a [veʒeta'tʃivu/a] *adj*: **vida vegetativa** (*fig*) insular life.

veia ['veja] *f* (*MED, BOT*) vein; (*fig*: *pendor*) bent.

veicular [vejku'la*] *vt* to convey; (*anúncios*) to distribute.

veículo [ve'ikulu] *m* vehicle; (*fig*: *meio*) means *sg*; ~ **de propaganda** advertising medium.

veio ['veju] *vb* V **vir** ♦ *m* (*de rocha*) vein; (*na mina*) seam; (*de madeira*) grain;* (*eixo*) shaft.

vejo ['veʒu] *etc vb* V **ver.**

vela ['vɛla] *f* candle; (*AUTO*) spark plug; (*NÁUT*) sail; **fazer-se à** *ou* **de** ~ to set sail; **segurar a** ~ (*col*) to play gooseberry; **barco à** ~ sailing boat; ~ **mestra** mainsail.

velar [ve'la*] *vt* (*cobrir*) to veil; (*ocultar*) to hide; (*vigiar*) to keep watch over; (*um doente*) to sit up with ♦ *vi* (*não dormir*) to stay up; (*vigiar*) to keep watch; ~ **por** to look after.

veleidade [velej'dadʒi] *f* (*capricho*) whim, fancy; (*inconstância*) fickleness.

veleiro [ve'lejru] *m* (*barco*) sailing boat.

velejar [vele'ʒa*] *vi* to sail.

velhaco/a [ve'ʎaku/a] *adj* crooked ♦ *m/f* crook.

velha-guarda *f* old guard.

velharia [veʎa'ria] *f* (*os velhos*) old people *pl*; (*coisa*) old thing.

velhice [ve'ʎisi] *f* old age.

velho/a ['vɛʎu/a] *adj* old ♦ *m/f* old man/

woman; (col: pai/mãe) old man/lady; **meus ~s** (col: pais) my folks; **meu ~!** (col) old chap.

velhote/ta [ve'ʌotʃi/ta] adj elderly ♦ m/f elderly man/woman.

velocidade [velosi'dadʒi] f speed, velocity; (PT: AUTO) gear; **a toda ~** at full speed; **trem de alta ~** high-speed train; **"diminua a ~"** "reduce speed now"; **~ máxima** (em estrada) speed limit; **~ de processamento** (COMPUT) processing speed.

velocímetro [velo'simetru] m speedometer.

velocíssimo/a [velo'sisimu/a] adj superl de veloz.

velocista [velo'siʃta] m/f sprinter.

velódromo [ve'lɔdromu] m cycle track.

velório [ve'lɔrju] m wake.

veloz [ve'lɔʒ] adj fast.

velozmente [veloʒ'mētʃi] adv fast.

veludo [ve'ludu] m velvet; **~ cotelê** corduroy.

vencedor(a) [vēse'do*(a)] adj winning ♦ m/f winner.

vencer [vē'se*] vt (num jogo) to beat; (competição) to win; (inimigo) to defeat; (exceder) to surpass; (obstáculos) to overcome; (percorrer) to pass; (dominar) to overcome ♦ vi (num jogo) to win; **~(-se)** (vr) (prazo) to run out; (promissória) to become due; (apólice) to mature.

vencido/a [vē'sidu/a] adj: **dar-se por ~** to give in.

vencimento [vēsi'mētu] m (COM) expiry; (: de letra, dívida) maturation; (data) expiry date; (: de promissória) due date; (salário) salary; (de gêneros alimentícios etc) sell-by date; **~s** mpl earnings.

venda ['vēda] f sale; (pano) blindfold; (mercearia) general store; **à ~** on sale, for sale; **pôr algo à ~** to put sth up for sale; **preço de ~** selling price; **~ a crédito** credit sale; **~ a prazo** ou **prestação** sale in instal(l)ments; **~ à vista** cash sale; **~ por atacado** wholesale; **~ pelo correio** mail-order.

vendar [vē'da*] vt to blindfold.

vendaval [vēda'vaw] (pl -ais) m gale.

vendável [vē'davew] (pl -eis) adj marketable.

vendedor(a) [vēde'do*(a)] m/f seller; (em loja) sales assistant; (de imóvel) vendor; **~ ambulante** street seller.

vender [vē'de*] vt, vi to sell; **~-se** vr (pessoa) to allow o.s. to be bribed; **~ por atacado/a varejo** to sell wholesale/retail; **~ fiado/a prestações** ou **a prazo** to sell on credit/in instal(l)ments; **~ à vista** to sell for cash; **ela está vendendo saúde** she's bursting with health.

vendeta [vē'deta] f vendetta.

vendinha [vē'dʒiɲa] f corner shop.

veneno [ve'nɛnu] m poison; (fig, de serpente) venom; **ser um ~ para** (fig) to be very bad for.

venenoso/a [vene'nozu/ɔza] adj poisonous; (fig) venomous.

veneta [ve'neta] f: **ser de ~** (pessoa) to be moody; **deu-lhe na ~ (que)** he got it into his head (that).

veneração [venera'sãw] f reverence.

venerar [vene'ra*] vt to revere; (REL) to worship.

venéreo/a [ve'nɛrju/a] adj venereal.

Veneza [ve'neza] n Venice.

veneziana [vene'zjana] f (porta) louvre (BRIT) ou louver (US) door; (janela) louvre ou louver window.

Venezuela [vene'zwɛla] f: **a ~** Venezuela.

venezuelano/a [venezwe'lanu/a] adj, m/f Venezuelan.

venha ['vɛɲa] etc vb V **vir**.

vênia ['venja] f (desculpa) forgiveness; (licença) permission.

venial [ve'njaw] (pl -ais) adj venial, forgiveable.

venta ['vēta] f nostril.

ventania [vēta'nia] f gale.

ventar [vē'ta*] vi: **está ventando** it is windy.

ventarola [vēta'rɔla] f fan.

ventas ['vētaʃ] fpl nose sg.

ventilação [vētʃila'sãw] f ventilation.

ventilador [vētʃila'do*] m ventilator; (elétrico) fan.

ventilar [vētʃi'la*] vt to ventilate; (roupa, sala) to air; (fig) to discuss; (: hipótese, possibilidade) to entertain.

vento ['vētu] m wind; (brisa) breeze; **de ~ em popa** (fig) swimmingly, very well.

ventoinha [vē'twiɲa] f (cata-vento) weathercock; (grimpa) weather vane; (PT: AUTO) fan.

ventoso/a [vē'tozu/ɔza] adj windy.

ventre ['vētri] m belly; (literário: útero) womb.

ventríloquo/a [vē'trilokwu/a] m/f ventriloquist.

ventura [vē'tura] f fortune; (felicidade) happiness; **se por ~** if by any chance.

venturoso/a [vētu'rozu/ɔza] adj happy.

Vênus ['venuʃ] f Venus.

ver [ve*] vt to see; (olhar para, examinar) to look at; (resolver) to see to; (televisão) to watch ♦ vi to see ♦ m: **a meu ~** in my opinion; **~-se** vr (achar-se) to be, find o.s.; (no espelho) to see o.s.; (duas pessoas) to see each other; **vai ~ que ...** maybe ...; **viu?** (col) OK?; **deixa eu ~** let me see; **ele tem um carro que só vendo** (col) he's got a car like you wouldn't believe; **não tem nada a ~ (com)** it has nothing to do (with); **não tenho nada que ~ com isto** it is nothing to do with me, it is none of my concern; **~-se com** to settle accounts with; **bem se vê que** it's obvious that; **já se vê** of course; **pelo que se vê** apparently.

veracidade [verasi'dadʒi] f truthfulness.

veranear [vera'nja*] vi to spend the summer; (tirar férias) to take summer holidays (BRIT) ou a summer vacation (US).

veraneio [vera'neju] *m* summer holidays *pl* (*BRIT*) *ou* vacation (*US*).

veranista [vera'niʃta] *m/f* holidaymaker (*BRIT*), (summer) vacationer (*US*).

verão [ve'rãw] (*pl* **-ões**) *m* summer.

veraz [ve'raʒ] *adj* truthful.

verba ['vɛxba] *f* allowance; **~(s)** *f(pl)* (*recursos*) funds *pl*.

verbal [vex'baw] (*pl* **-ais**) *adj* verbal.

verbalizar [vexbali'za*] *vt, vi* to verbalize.

verbete [vex'betʃi] *m* (*num dicionário*) entry.

verbo ['vɛxbu] *m* verb; **deitar o ~** (*col*) to say a few words; **soltar o ~** (*col*) to start talking.

verborragia [vexboxa'ʒia] *f* verbiage, waffle.

verboso/a [vex'bozu/ɔza] *adj* wordy, verbose.

verdade [vex'dadʒi] *f* truth; **na ~** in fact; **é ~** it's true; **é ~?** (*col*) really?; **uma princesa de ~** a real princess; **de ~** (*falar*) truthfully; (*ameaçar etc*) really; **dizer umas ~s a alguém** to tell sb a few home truths; **a ~ nua e crua** the plain truth; **para falar a ~** to tell the truth; ..., **não é ~?** (*col*) ..., isn't that so?

verdadeiramente [vexdadejra'mẽtʃi] *adv* really.

verdadeiro/a [vexda'dejru/a] *adj* true; (*genuíno*) real; (*pessoa*) truthful; **foi um ~ desastre** it was a real disaster.

verde ['vexdʒi] *adj* green; (*fruta*) unripe; (*fig*) inexperienced ♦ *m* green; (*plantas etc*) greenery; **~ de medo** pale with fear; **~ de fome/raiva** terribly hungry/angry; **jogar ~ (para colher maduro)** to fish, ask leading questions; **Partido V~** Green Party.

verde-abacate *adj inv* avocado.

verde-garrafa *adj inv* bottle-green.

verdejar [vexde'ʒa*] *vi* to turn green.

verdor [vex'do*] *m* greenness; (*BOT*) greenery; (*fig*) inexperience.

verdugo [vex'dugu] *m* executioner; (*fig*) beast.

verdura [vex'dura] *f* (*hortaliça*) greens *pl*; (*BOT*) greenery; (*cor verde*) greenness.

verdureiro/a [vexdu'rejru/a] *m/f* greengrocer (*BRIT*), produce dealer (*US*).

vereador(a) [verja'do*(a)] *m/f* councillor (*BRIT*), councilor (*US*).

vereda [ve'reda] *f* path.

veredicto [vere'dʒiktu] *m* verdict.

verga ['vexga] *f* (*vara*) stick; (*de metal*) rod.

vergão [vex'gãw] (*pl* **-ões**) *m* weal.

vergar [vex'ga*] *vt* (*curvar*) to bend ♦ *vi* to bend; (*com um peso*) to sag.

vergões [vex'gõjʃ] *mpl de* **vergão**.

vergonha [vex'gɔɲa] *f* shame; (*timidez*) embarrassment; (*humilhação*) humiliation; (*ato indecoroso*) indecency; (*brio*) self-respect; **é uma ~** it's disgraceful; **ter ~ de** to be ashamed; (*tímido*) to be shy; **ter ~ de fa-** zer to be ashamed of doing; (*ser tímido*) to be too shy to do; **não ter ~ na cara** to have a cheek, have no shame.

vergonhoso/a [vexgo'ɲozu/ɔza] *adj* (*infame*) shameful; (*indecoroso*) disgraceful.

verídico/a [ve'ridʒiku/a] *adj* true, truthful.

verificação [verifika'sãw] *f* (*exame*) checking; (*confirmação*) verification.

verificar [verifi'ka*] *vt* to check; (*confirmar*, *COMPUT*) to verify; **~-se** *vr* (*acontecer*) to happen; (*realizar-se*) to come true; **~ se ...** to check that ....

verme ['vɛxmi] *m* worm.

vermelhidão [vexmeʎi'dãw] *f* redness; (*da pele*) rosiness.

vermelho/a [vex'meʎu/a] *adj* red ♦ *m* red; **estar no ~** to be in the red; **ficar ~** to go red.

vermute [vex'mutʃi] *m* vermouth.

vernáculo/a [vex'nakulu/a] *adj*, *m* vernacular; **língua vernácula** vernacular.

vernissage [vexni'saʒ] *m* opening, vernissage.

verniz [vex'niʒ] *m* varnish; (*couro*) patent leather; (*fig*) whitewash; (: *polidez*) veneer; **sapatos de ~** patent shoes.

verões [ve'rõjʃ] *mpl de* **verão**.

verossímil [vero'simiw] (*PT*: **-osí-**: *pl* **-eis**) *adj* (*provável*) likely, probable; (*crível*) credible.

verossimilhança [verosimi'ʎãsa] (*PT*: **-osi-**) *f* probability.

verruga [ve'xuga] *f* wart.

versado/a [vex'sadu/a] *adj*: **~ em** clever at, good at.

versão [vex'sãw] (*pl* **-ões**) *f* version; (*tradução*) translation.

versar [vex'sa*] *vi*: **~ sobre** to be about, concern.

versátil [vex'satʃiw] (*pl* **-eis**) *adj* versatile.

versatilidade [vexsatʃili'dadʒi] *f* versatility.

versículo [vex'sikulu] *m* (*REL*) verse; (*de artigo*) paragraph.

verso ['vɛxsu] *m* verse; (*linha*) line of poetry; (*da página*) other side, reverse; **vide ~** see over; **~ solto** blank verse; **~s brancos** blank verse *sg*.

versões [vex'sõjʃ] *fpl de* **versão**.

vértebra ['vɛxtebra] *f* vertebra.

vertebrado/a [vexte'bradu/a] *adj* vertebrate ♦ *m* vertebrate.

vertebral [vexte'braw] (*pl* **-ais**) *adj* V **coluna**.

vertente [vex'tẽtʃi] *f* slope.

verter [vex'te*] *vt* to pour; (*por acaso*) to spill; (*traduzir*) to translate; (*lágrimas*, *sangue*) to shed ♦ *vi*: **~ de** to spring from; **~ em** (*rio*) to flow into.

vertical [vextʃi'kaw] (*pl* **-ais**) *adj* vertical; (*de pé*) upright, standing ♦ *f* vertical.

vértice ['vɛxtʃisi] *m* apex.

vertigem [vex'tʃiʒẽ] *f* dizziness.

vertiginoso/a [vextʃiʒi'nozu/ɔza] *adj* dizzy,

NB: *European Portuguese adds the following consonants to certain words:* **b** (sú(b)dito, su(b)til); **c** (a(c)ção, a(c)cionista, a(c)to); **m** (inde(m)ne); **p** (ado(p)ção, ado(p)tar); *for further details see p. xiii.*

giddy; (*velocidade*) frenetic.

verve ['vɛxvi] *f* verve.

vesgo/a ['veʒgu/a] *adj* cross-eyed.

vesícula [ve'zikula] *f*: ~ **(biliar)** gall bladder.

vespa ['veʃpa] *f* wasp.

véspera ['vɛʃpera] *f* the day before; **~s** *fpl* (*REL*) vespers *sg*; **a ~ de Natal** Christmas Eve; **nas ~s de** on the eve of; (*de eleição etc*) in the run-up to; **estar nas ~s de** to be about to.

vesperal [veʃpe'raw] (*pl* **-ais**) *adj* afternoon *atr* ♦ *f* matinée.

vespertino/a [veʃpex'tʃinu/a] *adj* evening *atr*.

veste ['vɛʃtʃi] *f* garment; (*REL*) vestment, robe.

vestiário [veʃ'tʃjarju] *m* (*em casa, teatro*) cloakroom; (*ESPORTE*) changing room; (*de ator*) dressing room.

vestibular [veʃtʃibu'la*] *m* college entrance exam.

vestíbulo [veʃ'tʃibulu] *m* hall(-way), vestibule; (*TEATRO*) foyer.

vestido/a [veʃ'tʃidu/a] *adj* dressed ♦ *m* dress; ~ **de branco** *etc* dressed in white *etc*; ~ **de baile** ball gown; ~ **de noiva** wedding dress.

vestidura [veʃtʃi'dura] *f* (*REL*) robe.

vestígio [veʃ'tʃiʒju] *m* (*rastro*) track; (*fig*) sign, trace.

vestimenta [veʃtʃi'mẽta] *f* (*roupa*) garment; (*REL*) vestment.

vestir [veʃ'tʃi*] *vt* (*uma criança*) to dress; (*pôr sobre si*) to put on; (*trajar*) to wear; (*comprar, dar roupa para*) to clothe; (*fazer roupa para*) to make clothes for; ~**-se** *vr* to dress; (*pôr roupa*) to get dressed; ~**-se de algo** to dress up as sth; **ela se veste naquela butique** she buys her clothes in that boutique; ~**-se de preto** *etc* to dress in black *etc*; **este terno veste bem** this suit is a good fit.

vestuário [veʃ'twarju] *m* clothing.

vetar [ve'ta*] *vt* to veto; (*proibir*) to forbid.

veterano/a [vete'ranu/a] *adj*, *m/f* veteran.

veterinário/a [veteri'narju/a] *adj* veterinary ♦ *m/f* vet(erinary surgeon).

veto ['vɛtu] *m* veto.

véu [vɛw] *m* veil; ~ **do paladar** (*ANAT*) soft palate, velum.

vexame [ve'ʃami] *f* (*vergonha*) shame, disgrace; (*tormento*) affliction; (*humilhação*) humiliation; (*afronta*) insult; **passar um ~** to be disgraced; **dar um ~** to make a fool of o.s.

vexaminoso/a [veʃami'nozu/ɔza] *adj* shameful, disgraceful.

vexar [ve'ʃa*] *vt* (*atormentar*) to upset; (*envergonhar*) to put to shame; ~**-se** *vr* to be ashamed.

vez [veʒ] *f* time; (*turno*) turn; **uma ~** once; **duas ~es** twice; **alguma ~** ever; **algumas ~es, às ~es** sometimes; ~ **por outra** sometimes; **cada ~ (que)** every time; **cada ~ mais/menos** more and more/less and less;

desta ~ this time; **de ~** once and for all; **de uma ~** (*ao mesmo tempo*) at once; (*de um golpe*) in one go; **de ~ em quando** from time to time; **em ~ de** instead of; **fazer as ~es de** (*pessoa*) to stand in for; (*coisa*) to replace; **mais uma ~, outra ~** again, once more; **raras ~es** seldom; **uma ~ que** since; **3 ~es 6** 3 times 6; **de uma ~ por todas** once and for all; **ter ~** (*pessoa*) to have a chance; (*argumento etc*) to apply; **muitas ~es** many times; (*freqüentemente*) often; **mais ~es** more often; **na maioria das ~es** most times; **toda ~ que** every time; **um de cada ~** one at a time; **repetidas ~es** repeatedly; **uma ~ ou outra** once in a while; **uma ~ na vida, outra na morte** once in a blue moon; **era uma ~ ...** once upon a time there was ....

vi [vi] *vb* **V ver**.

via ['via] *etc* *vb* **V ver** ♦ *f* road, route; (*meio*) way; (*documento*) copy; (*conduto*) channel ♦ *prep* via, by way of; ~ **aérea** airmail; ~ **de acesso** access road; ~ **férrea** railway (*BRIT*), railroad (*US*); **V~ Láctea** Milky Way; **primeira ~** (*de documento*) top copy; **chegar às ~s de fato** to come to blows; **em ~s de** about to; **por ~ aérea** by airmail; **por ~ das dúvidas** just in case; **por ~ de regra** generally, as a rule; **por ~ terrestre/marítima** by land/sea.

viabilidade [vjabili'dadʒi] *f* feasibility, viability.

viação [vja'sãw] (*pl* **-ões**) *f* transport; (*companhia de ônibus*) bus (*ou* coach) company; (*conjunto de estradas*) roads *pl*.

viaduto [vja'dutu] *m* viaduct.

viageiro/a [vja'ʒejru/a] *adj* travelling (*BRIT*), traveling (*US*).

viagem ['vjaʒẽ] (*pl* **-ns**) *f* journey, trip; (*o viajar*) travel; (*NÁUT*) voyage; (*com droga*) trip; **viagens** *fpl* travels; ~ **de ida e volta** return trip, round trip; ~ **de núpcias** honeymoon; ~ **de ida** outward trip; ~ **de negócios** business trip; ~ **inaugural** (*NÁUT*) maiden voyage; **boa ~!** bon voyage!, have a good trip!

viajado/a [vja'ʒadu/a] *adj* well-travelled (*BRIT*), well-traveled (*US*).

viajante [vja'ʒãtʃi] *adj* travelling (*BRIT*), traveling (*US*) ♦ *m* traveller (*BRIT*), traveler (*US*); (*COM*) commercial travel(l)er.

viajar [vja'ʒa*] *vi* to travel; ~ **por** to travel, tour.

viário/a ['vjarju/a] *adj* road *atr*.

viatura [vja'tura] *f* vehicle.

viável ['vjavew] (*pl* **-eis**) *adj* feasible, viable.

víbora ['vibora] *f* viper; (*fig: pessoa*) snake in the grass.

vibração [vibra'sãw] (*pl* **-ões**) *f* vibration; (*fig*) thrill.

vibrante [vi'brãtʃi] *adj* vibrant; (*discurso*) stirring.

vibrar [vi'bra*] *vt* (*brandir*) to brandish; (*fazer estremecer*) to vibrate; (*cordas*) to strike

♦ *vi* to vibrate, shake; *(som)* to echo; *(col)* to be thrilled.

vice ['visi] *m/f* deputy.

vice- [visi-] *prefixo* vice-.

vice-campeão/peã *(pl* -ões/~s) *m/f* runner-up.

vicejar [vise'ʒa*] *vi* to flourish.

vice-presidente/a *m/f* vice president.

vice-rei *m* viceroy.

vice-reitor(a) *m/f* deputy head.

vice-versa [-'vɛxsa] *adv* vice-versa.

viciado/a [vi'sjadu/a] *adj* addicted; *(ar)* foul ♦ *m/f* addict; **um ~ em entorpecentes** a drug addict; **~ em algo** addicted to sth.

viciar [vi'sja*] *vt (criar vício em)* to make addicted; *(falsificar)* to falsify; *(taxímetro etc)* to fiddle; **~-se** *vr* to become addicted; **~/~-se em algo** to make/become addicted to sth.

vicinal [visi'naw] *(pl* -ais) *adj* local.

vício ['visju] *m* vice; *(defeito)* failing; *(costume)* bad habit; *(em entorpecentes)* addiction.

vicioso/a [vi'sjozu/ɔza] *adj (defeituoso)* defective; *(círculo)* vicious.

vicissitude [visisi'tudʒi] *f* vicissitude; **~s** *fpl* ups and downs.

viço ['visu] *m* vigour *(BRIT)*, vigor *(US)*; *(da pele)* freshness.

viçoso/a [vi'sozu/ɔza] *adj (plantas)* luxuriant; *(fig)* exuberant.

vida ['vida] *f* life; *(duração)* lifetime; *(fig)* vitality; **com ~** alive; **ganhar a ~** to earn one's living; **modo de ~** way of life; **para toda a ~** forever; **sem ~** dull, lifeless; **na ~ real** in real life; **dar ~ a** *(festa, ambiente)* to liven up; **dar a ~ por algo/por fazer algo** to give one's right arm for sth/to do sth; **estar bem de ~** to be well off; **mete-se com a sua ~** mind your own business; **estar entre a ~ e a morte** to be at death's door; **cair na ~** *(col)* to go on the game; **é a ~!** that's life!; **danado/feliz da ~** really angry/happy; **siga essa rua toda a ~** follow this street as far as you can go; **ele trabalha que não é ~** *(col)* he works really hard; **a ~ mansa** the easy life; **~ civil/privada/pública/sentimental/sexual/social** civilian/private/public/love/sex/social life; **~ conjugal/doméstica** married/home life; **~ útil** *(COM)* useful life.

vidão [vi'dãw] *m* good life.

vide ['vidʒi] *vt* see; **~ verso** see over.

videira [vi'dejra] *f* grapevine.

vidente [vi'dẽtʃi] *m/f* clairvoyant; *(no mundo antigo)* seer.

vídeo ['vidʒju] *m* video; *(televisão)* TV; *(tela)* screen.

videocâmara [vidʒju'kamara] *f* video camera.

videocassete [vidʒuka'sɛtʃi] *m (fita)* video cassette *ou* tape; *(aparelho)* video (recorder).

videoclipe [vidʒju'klipi] *m* video.

videoclube [vidʒju'klubi] *m* video club.

videodisco [vidʒju'dʒiʃku] *m* video disk.

vídeo game [-'gejmi] *(pl* ~s) *m* video game.

videoteipe [vidʒju'tejpi] *m (fita)* video tape; *(processo)* (video-)taping.

videotexto [vidʒju'teʃtu] *m* teletext.

vidraça [vi'drasa] *f* window pane.

vidraçaria [vidrasa'ria] *f* glazier's; *(fábrica)* glass factory; *(conjunto de vidraças)* glasswork.

vidraceiro [vidra'sejru] *m* glazier.

vidrado/a [vi'dradu/a] *adj* glazed; *(porta)* glass *atr*; *(olhos)* glazed, glassy; **estar** *ou* **ser ~ em** *ou* **por** *(col)* to be crazy about.

vidrar [vi'dra*] *vt* to glaze ♦ *vi*: **~ em** *ou* **por** *(col)* to fall in love with.

vidreiro [vi'drejru] *m* glazier, glassmaker.

vidro ['vidru] *m* glass; *(frasco)* bottle; **fibra de ~** fibreglass *(BRIT)*, fiberglass *(US)*; **~ fosco** frosted glass; **~ fumê** tinted glass; **~ de aumento** magnifying glass.

viela ['vjɛla] *f* alley.

Viena ['vjɛna] *n* Vienna.

vier [vje*] *etc vb* V **vir**.

viés [vjɛʃ] *m* slant; *(COSTURA)* bias strip; **ao** *ou* **de ~** diagonally.

vieste ['vjeʃtʃi] *vb* V **vir**.

viga ['viga] *f* beam; *(de ferro)* girder.

Vietnã [vjet'nã] *m*: **o ~** Vietnam.

vietnamita [vjetna'mita] *adj, m/f* Vietnamese.

vigarice [viga'risi] *f* swindle.

vigário [vi'garju] *m* vicar.

vigarista [viga'riʃta] *m* swindler, confidence trickster.

vigência [vi'ʒẽsja] *f* validity; **durante a ~ da lei** while the law is in force.

vigente [vi'ʒẽtʃi] *adj* in force, valid.

viger [vi'ʒe*] *vi* to be in force.

vigésimo/a [vi'ʒɛzimu/a] *num* twentieth; *V tb* **quinto**.

vigia [vi'ʒia] *f (ato)* watching; *(NÁUT)* porthole ♦ *m* night watchman; **de ~** on watch.

vigiar [vi'ʒja*] *vt* to watch, keep an eye on; *(ocultamente)* to spy on; *(velar por)* to keep watch over; *(presos, fronteira)* to guard ♦ *vi* to be on the lookout.

vigilância [viʒi'lãsja] *f* vigilance.

vigilante [viʒi'lãtʃi] *adj* vigilant; *(atento)* alert.

vigília [vi'ʒilja] *f (falta de sono)* wakefulness; *(vigilância)* vigilance.

vigor [vi'go*] *m* energy; **em ~** in force; **entrar/pôr em ~** to take effect/put into effect.

vigorar [vigo'ra*] *vi* to be in force; **a ~ a partir de** effective as of.

vigoroso/a [vigo'rozu/ɔza] *adj* vigorous.

vil [viw] *(pl* **vis**) *adj* vile, low.

NB: *European Portuguese adds the following consonants to certain words:* **b** (sú(b)dito, su(b)til); **c** (a(c)ção, a(c)cionista, a(c)to); **m** (inde(m)ne); **p** (ado(p)ção, ado(p)tar); *for further details see p. xiii.*

vila ['vila] *f* town; (*casa*) villa; (*conjunto de casas*) group of houses round a courtyard; **~ militar** military base.

vilã [vi'lã] *f de* **vilão**.

vilania [vila'nia] *f* villainy.

vilão/lã [vi'lãw/'lã] (*pl* ~s/~s) *m/f* villain.

vilarejo [vila'reʒu] *m* village.

vileza [vi'leza] *f* vileness; (*ação*) mean trick.

vilipendiar [vilipẽ'dʒja*] *vt* to revile; (*desprezar*) to despise.

vim [vĩ] *vb V* **vir**.

vime ['vimi] *m* wicker.

vinagre [vi'nagri] *m* vinegar.

vinagrete [vina'gretʃi] *m* vinaigrette.

vincar [vĩ'ka*] *vt* to crease; (*produzir sulco em*) to furrow; (*rosto*) to line.

vinco ['vĩku] *m* crease; (*sulco*) furrow; (*no rosto*) line.

vincular [vĩku'la*] *vt* to link, tie; ~**-se** *vr* to be linked *ou* tied.

vínculo ['vĩkulu] *m* bond, tie; (*relação*) link; **~ de parentesco** blood tie; **~ empregatício** contract of employment.

vinda ['vĩda] *f* arrival; (*ato de vir*) coming; (*regresso*) return; **dar as boas ~s** to welcome.

vindicar [vĩdʒi'ka*] *vt* to vindicate.

vindima [vĩ'dʒima] *f* grape harvest.

vindique [vĩ'dʒiki] *etc vb V* **vindicar**.

vindouro/a [vĩ'doru/a] *adj* future, coming.

vingador(a) [vĩga'do*(a)] *adj* avenging ♦ *m/f* avenger.

vingança [vĩ'gãsa] *f* vengeance, revenge.

vingar [vĩ'ga*] *vt* to avenge ♦ *vi* (*ter êxito*) to be successful; (*planta*) to grow; ~**-se** *vr*: ~**-se de** to take revenge on.

vingativo/a [vĩga'tʃivu/a] *adj* vindictive.

vingue ['vĩgi] *etc vb V* **vingar**.

vinha ['viɲa] *etc vb V* **vir** ♦ *f* vineyard; (*planta*) vine.

vinha-d'alho (*pl* **vinhas d'alho**) *f* marinade.

vinhedo [vi'ɲedu] *m* vineyard.

vinho ['viɲu] *m* wine ♦ *adj inv* maroon; **~ branco/rosado/tinto** white/rosé/red wine; **~ seco/doce** dry/sweet wine; **~ espumante/de mesa** sparkling/table wine; **~ do Porto** port.

vinícola [vi'nikola] *adj inv* wine-producing.

vinicultor(a) [vinikuw'to*(a)] *m/f* wine grower.

vinicultura [vinikuw'tura] *f* wine-growing, viticulture.

vinil [vi'niw] *m* vinyl.

vinte ['vĩtʃi] *num* twenty; **o século ~** the twentieth century; **as ~** (*col: de cigarro, bebida*) the last bit; *V tb* **cinqüenta**.

vintém [vĩ'tẽj] *m*: **sem um ~** penniless.

vintena [vĩ'tena] *f* twenty, a score.

viola ['vjɔla] *f* viola.

violação [vjola'sãw] (*pl* **-ões**) *f* violation; **~ da lei** lawbreaking; **~ de domicílio** housebreaking.

violão [vjo'lãw] (*pl* **-ões**) *m* guitar.

violar [vjo'la*] *vt* to violate; (*a lei*) to break.

violência [vjo'lẽsja] *f* violence.

violentar [vjolẽ'ta*] *vt* to force; (*mulher*) to rape; (*fig: sentido*) to distort.

violento/a [vjo'lẽtu/a] *adj* violent; (*furioso*) furious.

violeta [vjo'leta] *f* violet ♦ *adj inv* violet.

violinista [vjoli'niʃta] *m/f* violinist, violin player.

violino [vjo'linu] *m* violin.

violões [vjo'lõjʃ] *mpl de* **violão**.

violoncelista [vjolõse'liʃta] *m/f* 'cellist.

violoncelo [vjolõ'sɛlu] *m* 'cello.

VIP ['vipi] *m/f* VIP ♦ *adj* (*sala*) VIP *atr*.

vir [vi*] *etc vb V* **ver** ♦ *vi* to come; ~ **a ser** to turn out to be; **a semana que vem** next week; ~ **abaixo** to collapse; **mandar** ~ to send for; ~ **fazendo algo** to have been doing sth; ~ **fazer** to come to do; ~ **buscar** to come for; ~ **com** (*alegar*) to come up with; **isso não vem ao caso** that's irrelevant; **veio-lhe uma idéia** he had an idea, an idea came to him; ~ **a saber** to come to know; **venha o que vier** come what may; **vem cá!** come here!; (*col: escuta*) listen!; **não vem que não tem!** (*col*) come off it!

viração [vira'sãw] (*pl* **-ões**) *f* breeze.

vira-casaca ['vira-] (*pl* ~s) *m/f* turncoat.

virada [vi'rada] *f* turning; (*guinada*) swerve; (*ESPORTE*) turnaround; **dar uma ~** (*col*) to put on a last burst.

virado/a [vi'radu/a] *adj* (*às avessas*) upside down ♦ *m* (*CULIN*): ~ **(de feijão)** fried beans with sausage and eggs; ~ **para** facing.

vira-lata ['vira-] (*pl* ~s) *m* (*cão*) mongrel; (*pessoa*) bum.

virar [vi'ra*] *vt* to turn; (*página, disco, barco*) to turn over; (*esquina*) to turn; (*bolsos*) to turn inside out; (*copo*) to empty; (*despejar*) to tip; (*fazer mudar de opinião*) to turn round; (*transformar-se em*) to become ♦ *vi* to turn; (*barco*) to turn over, capsize; (*mudar*) to change; ~**-se** *vr* to turn; (*voltar-se*) to turn round; (*defender-se*) to fend for o.s.; ~ **de cabeça para baixo** to turn upside down; ~ **do avesso** to turn inside out; ~ **para** to face; **vira e mexe** every so often; ~**(-se) contra** to turn against; ~**-se para** (*recorrer a*) to turn to; ~**-se de bruços** to turn onto one's stomach.

viravolta [vira'vɔwta] *f* (*fig*) turnabout; (*volta completa*) complete turn; (*giro sobre si mesmo*) about-turn; (*cambalhota*) somersault.

virgem ['vixʒẽ] (*pl* **-ns**) *adj* (*puro*) pure; (*mata*) virgin; (*não usado*) unused; (*: fita*) blank ♦ *f* virgin; **V~** (*ASTROLOGIA*) Virgo; ~ **de** free of.

virgindade [vixʒĩ'dadʒi] *f* virginity.

vírgula ['vixgula] *f* comma; (*decimal*) point; **uma ~!** (*col*) my eye!

virgular [vixgu'la*] *vt*: ~ **com** *ou* **de** (*entremear*) to punctuate with.

viril [vi'riw] (*pl* **-is**) *adj* virile.

virilha [vi'riʎa] *f* groin.
virilidade [virili'dadʒi] *f* virility.
viris [vi'riʃ] *adj pl de* **viril**.
virose [vi'rɔzi] *f* viral illness.
virtual [vix'twaw] (*pl* **-ais**) *adj* virtual; (*potencial*) potential.
virtualmente [vixtwaw'mẽtʃi] *adv* virtually.
virtude [vix'tudʒi] *f* virtue; **em ~ de** owing to, because of.
virtuosidade [vixtwozi'dadʒi] *f* virtuosity.
virtuosismo [vixtwo'ziʒmu] *m* = **virtuosidade**.
virtuoso/a [vix'twozu/ɔza] *adj* virtuous ♦ *m* virtuoso.
virulência [viru'lẽsja] *f* virulence.
virulento/a [viru'lẽtu/a] *adj* virulent.
vírus ['viruʃ] *m inv* virus.
vis [viʃ] *adj pl de* **vil**.
visado/a [vi'zadu/a] *adj* stamped; (*pessoa: pela polícia, imprensa*) under observation.
visão [vi'zãw] (*pl* **-ões**) *f* vision; (*ANAT*) eyesight; (*vista*) sight; (*maneira de perceber*) view; **~ de conjunto** overall view.
visar [vi'za*] *vt* (*alvo*) to aim at; (*ter em vista*) to have in view; (*ter como objetivo*) to aim for; (*passaporte, cheque*) to stamp ♦ *vi*: **~ a** to have in view; to aim for; **~ fazer** to aim to do.
Visc. *abr* = **Visconde**.
vísceras ['viseraʃ] *fpl* innards, bowels; (*fig*) heart *sg*.
visconde [viʃ'kõdʒi] *m* viscount.
viscondessa [viʃkõ'desa] *f* viscountess.
viscoso/a [viʃ'kozu/ɔza] *adj* sticky, viscous.
viseira [vi'zejra] *f* visor.
visibilidade [vizibili'dadʒi] *f* visibility.
visionário/a [vizjo'narju/a] *adj*, *m/f* visionary.
visita [vi'zita] *f* visit, call; (*pessoa*) visitor; **fazer uma ~ a** to visit; **ter ~s** to have company; **~ de médico** (*col*) flying visit; **horário de ~s** visiting hours *pl*.
visitante [vizi'tãtʃi] *adj* visiting ♦ *m/f* visitor.
visitar [vizi'ta*] *vt* to visit; (*inspecionar*) to inspect.
visível [vi'zivew] (*pl* **-eis**) *adj* visible.
vislumbrar [viʒlũ'bra*] *vt* to glimpse, catch a glimpse of.
vislumbre [viʒ'lũbri] *m* glimpse.
visões [vi'zõjʃ] *fpl de* **visão**.
visom [vi'zõ] (*pl* **-ns**) *m* mink; **casaco de ~** mink coat.
visor [vi'zo*] *m* (*FOTO*) viewfinder.
visse ['visi] *etc vb V* **ver**.
vista ['viʃta] *f* sight; (*MED*) eyesight; (*panorama*) view; (*braguilha*) fly; **à** *ou* **em ~ de** in view of; **conhecer de ~** to know by sight; **dar na ~** to attract attention; **dar uma ~ de olhos em** to glance at; **fazer ~ grossa (a)** to turn a blind eye (to); **pôr à ~** to show; **ter em ~** to have in mind; **à primeira ~** at first sight; **à ~** visible, showing; (*COM*) in cash;

até a ~! see you!; **na ~ de todos** in view of everyone; **perder de ~** to lose sight of; **a perder de ~** as far as the eye can (*ou* could) see; (*pagamento*) over a long period; **saltar à ~** to be obvious; **fazer ~** to look nice; **~ cansada/curta** eye strain/shortsightedness.
vista-d'olhos *f* glance, quick look; **dar uma ~ em** to have a quick look at.
visto/a ['viʃtu/a] *etc vb V* **vestir** ♦ *pp de* **ver** ♦ *adj* seen ♦ *m* (*em passaporte*) visa; (*em documento*) stamp; **haja ~** witness; **pelo ~** by the looks of things.
vistoria [viʃto'ria] *f* inspection.
vistoriar [viʃto'rja*] *vt* to inspect.
vistoso/a [viʃ'tozu/ɔza] *adj* eye-catching.
visual [vi'zwaw] (*pl* **-ais**) *adj* visual ♦ *m* (*col: de pessoa*) look; (*aparência*) appearance; (*vista*) view.
visualizar [vizwali'za*] *vt* to visualize.
vital [vi'taw] (*pl* **-ais**) *adj* vital; (*essencial*) essential.
vitalício/a [vita'lisju/a] *adj* for life.
vitalidade [vitali'dadʒi] *f* vitality.
vitalizar [vitali'za*] *vt* to revitalize.
vitamina [vita'mina] *f* vitamin; (*para beber*) fruit crush.
vitaminado/a [vitami'nadu/a] *adj* with added vitamins.
vitamínico/a [vita'miniku/a] *adj* vitamin *atr*.
vitela [vi'tɛla] *f* calf; (*carne*) veal.
viticultura [vitʃikuw'tura] *f* wine growing.
vítima ['vitʃima] *f* victim; **fazer-se de ~** to play the martyr.
vitimar [vitʃi'ma*] *vt* to sacrifice; (*matar*) to kill, claim the life of; (*danificar*) to damage.
vitória [vi'tɔrja] *f* victory; (*ESPORTE*) win.
vitória-régia (*pl* **vitórias-régias**) *f* giant water lily.
vitorioso/a [vito'rjozu/ɔza] *adj* victorious; (*time*) winning.
vitral [vi'traw] (*pl* **-ais**) *m* stained glass window.
vítreo/a ['vitrju/a] *adj* (*feito de vidro*) glass *atr*; (*com o aspecto de vidro*) glassy; (*água*) clear.
vitrina [vi'trina] *f* = **vitrine**.
vitrine [vi'trini] *f* shop window; (*armário*) display case.
vitrola [vi'trɔla] *f* gramophone.
viuvez [vju'veʒ] *f* widowhood.
viúvo/a ['vjuvu/a] *adj* widowed ♦ *m/f* widower/widow.
viva ['viva] *m* cheer; **~!** hurray!; **~ o rei!** long live the king!
vivacidade [vivasi'dadʒi] *f* vivacity; (*energia*) vigour (*BRIT*), vigor (*US*).
vivalma [vi'vawma] *f*: **não ver ~** not to see a (living) soul.
vivamente [viva'mẽtʃi] *adv* animatedly; (*descrever, sentir*) vividly; (*protestar*) loud-

ly.
vivar [vi'va*] *vt, vi* to cheer.
vivaz [vi'vaʒ] *adj* (*animado*) lively.
viveiro [vi'vejru] *m* nursery.
vivência [vi'vẽsja] *f* existence; (*experiência*) experience.
vivenda [vi'vẽda] *f* (*casa*) residence.
vivente [vi'vẽtʃi] *adj* living ♦ *m/f* living being; **os ~s** the living.
vivido/a [vi'vidu/a] *adj* experienced in life.
vívido/a ['vividu/a] *adj* vivid.
viver [vi've*] *vi* to live; (*estar vivo*) to be alive ♦ *vt* (*vida*) to live; (*experimentar*) to have, experience ♦ *m* life; **~ de** to live on; **~ à custa de** to live off; **ela vive viajando/cansada** she's always travel(l)ing/tired; **ele vive resfriado/com dor de estômago** he's always got a cold/stomach ache; **vivendo e aprendendo** live and learn.
víveres ['vivereʃ] *mpl* provisions.
vivificar [vivifi'ka*] *vt* to bring to life.
vivissecção [vivisek'sãw] *f* vivisection.
vivo/a ['vivu/a] *adj* living; (*esperto*) clever; (*cor*) bright; (*criança, debate*) lively ♦ *m*: **os ~s** the living; **televisionar ao ~** to televise live; **estar ~** to be alive.
vizinhança [vizi'ɲãsa] *f* neighbourhood (*BRIT*), neighborhood (*US*).
vizinho/a [vi'ziɲu/a] *adj* neighbouring (*BRIT*), neighboring (*US*); (*perto*) nearby ♦ *m/f* neighbour (*BRIT*), neighbor (*US*).
voador(a) [vwa'do*(a)] *adj* flying.
voar [vo'a*] *vi* to fly; (*explodir*) to blow up, explode; **fazer ~ (pelos ares)** (*dinamitar*) to blow up, blast; **~ para cima de alguém** to fly at sb; **estar voando** (*col*) to be in the dark; **~ alto** (*fig*) to aim high; **fazer algo voando** to do sth in a hurry.
vocabulário [vokabu'larju] *m* vocabulary.
vocábulo [vo'kabulu] *m* word.
vocação [voka'sãw] (*pl* **-ões**) *f* vocation.
vocacional [vokasjo'naw] (*pl* **-ais**) *adj* vocational; (*orientação*) careers *atr*.
vocações [voka'sõjʃ] *fpl de* **vocação**.
vocal [vo'kaw] (*pl* **-ais**) *adj* vocal.
você [vo'se] *pron* you.
vocês [vo'seʃ] *pron pl* you.
vociferação [vosifera'sãw] (*pl* **-ões**) *f* shouting; (*censura*) harangue.
vociferar [vosife'ra*] *vt, vi* to shout, yell; **~ contra** to decry.
vodca ['vɔdʒka] *f* vodka.
voga ['vɔga] *f* (*NÁUT*) rowing; (*moda*) fashion; (*popularidade*) popularity; **em ~** popular, fashionable.
vogal [vo'gaw] (*pl* **-ais**) *f* (*LING*) vowel ♦ *m/f* (*votante*) voting member.
vogar [vo'ga*] *vi* to sail; (*boiar*) to float; (*importar*) to matter; (*estar na moda*) to be popular; (*lei*) to be in force; (*palavra*) to be in use.
voile ['vwali] *m* voile; **cortina de ~** net curtain.

vol. *abr* (= *volume*) vol.
volante [vo'latʃi] *m* (*AUTO*) steering wheel; (*piloto*) racing driver; (*impresso para apostas*) betting slip; (*roda*) flywheel.
volátil [vo'latʃiw] (*pl* **-eis**) *adj* volatile.
vôlei ['volej] *m* volleyball.
voleibol [volej'bɔw] *m* = **vôlei**.
volt ['vɔwtʃi] (*pl* **~s**) *m* volt.
volta ['vɔwta] *f* turn; (*regresso*) return; (*curva*) bend, curve; (*circuito*) lap; (*resposta*) retort; **passagem de ida e ~** return ticket (*BRIT*), round trip ticket (*US*); **dar uma ~ (a pé)** to go for a walk; (*de carro*) to go for a drive; **dar ~s** *ou* **uma ~ (a)** to go round; **estar de ~** to be back; **na ~ do correio** by return (post); **por ~ de** about, around; **à** *ou* **em ~ de** around; **na ~** (*no caminho de* ~) on the way back; **vou resolver isso na ~** I'll sort this out when I get back; **estar** *ou* **andar às ~s com** to be tied up with; **fazer a ~, dar meia ~** (*AUTO*) to do a U-turn; **dar meia ~** (*MIL*) to do an about-turn; **dar a ~ por cima** (*fig*) to get over it, pick o.s. up; **~ e meia** every so often.
voltado/a [vow'tadu/a] *adj*: **estar ~ para** to be concerned with.
voltagem [vow'taʒẽ] *f* voltage.
voltar [vow'ta*] *vt* to turn ♦ *vi* to return, go *ou* come back; **~-se** *vr* to turn round; **~ uma arma contra** to turn a weapon on; **~ a fazer** to do again; **~ a si** to come to; **~ atrás** (*fig*) to backtrack; **~-se para** to turn to; **~-se contra** to turn against.
voltear [vow'tʃja*] *vt* to go round; (*manivela*) to turn ♦ *vi* to spin; (*borboleta*) to flit around.
volubilidade [volubili'dadʒi] *f* fickleness.
volume [vo'lumi] *m* volume; (*tamanho*) bulk; (*pacote*) package.
volumoso/a [volu'mozu/ɔza] *adj* bulky, big; (*som*) loud.
voluntário/a [volũ'tarju/a] *adj* voluntary ♦ *m/f* volunteer.
voluntarioso/a [volũta'rjozu/ɔza] *adj* headstrong.
volúpia [vo'lupja] *f* pleasure, ecstasy.
voluptuoso/a [volup'twozu/ɔza] *adj* voluptuous.
volúvel [vo'luvew] (*pl* **-eis**) *adj* fickle, changeable.
volver [vow've*] *vt* to turn ♦ *vi* to go (*ou* come) back.
vomitar [vomi'ta*] *vt, vi* to vomit; (*fig*) to pour out.
vômito ['vomitu] *m* (*ato*) vomiting; (*efeito*) vomit.
vontade [võ'tadʒi] *f* will; (*desejo*) wish; **boa/má ~** good/ill will; **de boa/má ~** willingly/grudgingly; **frutas à ~** fruit galore; **coma à ~** eat as much as you like; **fique** *ou* **esteja à ~** make yourself at home; **não estar à ~** to be ill at ease *ou* uncomfortable; **com ~** (*com prazer*) with pleasure; (*com gana*) with gusto; **estar com** *ou* **ter ~ de fazer** to feel

like doing; **dar ~ a alguém de fazer** to make sb want to do; **essa música dá ~ de bailar** this music makes you want to dance; **fazer a ~ de alguém** to do what sb wants; **de livre e espontânea ~** of one's own free will; **por ~ própria** off one's own bat; **força de ~** will power; **ser cheio de ~s** to be spoilt.

vôo ['vou] *m* flight; **levantar ~** to take off; **~ cego** flying blind, instrument flying; **~ livre** (*ESPORTE*) hang-gliding; **~ picado** nose dive.

voragem [vo'raʒẽ] (*pl* **-ns**) *f* abyss, gulf; (*de águas*) whirlpool; (*fig*: *de paixões*) maelstrom.

voraz [vo'rajʒ] *adj* voracious, greedy.

vórtice ['vɔxtʃisi] *m* vortex.

vos [vuʃ] *pron* you, to you.

vós [vɔʃ] *pron* you.

vosso/a ['vɔsu/a] *adj* your ♦ *pron*: **(o) ~** yours.

votação [vota'sãw] (*pl* **-ões**) *f* vote, ballot; (*ato*) voting; **submeter algo a ~** to put sth to the vote; **~ secreta** secret ballot.

votado/a [vo'tadu/a] *adj*: **o deputado mais ~** the MP (*BRIT*) *ou* Member of Congress (*US*) with the highest number of votes.

votante [vo'tãtʃi] *m/f* voter.

votar [vo'ta*] *vt* (*eleger*) to vote for; (*aprovar*) to pass; (*submeter a votação*) to vote on; (*dedicar*) to devote ♦ *vi* to vote; **~-se** *vr*: **~-se a** to devote o.s. to; **~ em** to vote for; **~ por/contra** to vote for/against.

voto ['vɔtu] *m* vote; (*promessa*) vow; **~s** *mpl* (*desejos*) wishes; **fazer ~s por** to wish for; **fazer ~s que** to hope that; **fazer ~ de castidade** to take a vow of chastity; **~ nulo** *ou* **em branco** blank vote; **~ de confiança** vote of confidence; **~ secreto** secret ballot.

vou [vo] *vb V* **ir.**

vovó [vo'vɔ] *f* grandma.

vovô [vo'vo] *m* grandad.

voz [vɔʒ] *f* voice; (*clamor*) cry; **a meia ~** in a whisper; **dar ~ de prisão a alguém** to tell sb he is under arrest; **de viva ~** orally; **ter ~ ativa** to have a say; **em ~ baixa** in a low voice; **em ~ alta** aloud; **levantar a ~ para alguém** to raise one's voice to sb; **~ de cana rachada** (*col*) screeching voice; **~ de comando** command, order.

vozearia [vozja'ria] *f* = **vozerio.**

vozeirão [vozej'rãw] (*pl* **-ões**) *m* loud voice.

vozerio [voze'riu] *m* shouting, hullabaloo.

VPR *abr f* (= *Vanguarda Popular Revolucionária*) *former Brazilian revolutionary movement.*

vulcânico/a [vuw'kaniku/a] *adj* volcanic.

vulcão [vuw'kãw] (*pl* **~s** *ou* **-ões**) *m* volcano.

vulgar [vuw'ga*] *adj* (*comum*) common; (*reles*) cheap; (*pej*: *pessoa etc*) vulgar.

vulgaridade [vuwgari'dadʒi] *f* commonness;

(*pej*) vulgarity.

vulgarizar [vuwgari'za*] *vt* to popularize; (*abandalhar*) to cheapen.

vulgarmente [vuwgax'mẽtʃi] *adv* commonly, popularly.

vulgo ['vuwgu] *m* common people *pl* ♦ *adv* commonly known as.

vulnerabilidade [vuwnerabili'dadʒi] *f* vulnerability.

vulnerável [vuwne'ravew] (*pl* **-eis**) *adj* vulnerable.

vulto ['vuwtu] *m* figure; (*volume*) mass; (*fig*) importance; (*pessoa importante*) important person; **obras de ~** important works; **tomar ~** to take shape.

vultoso/a [vuw'tozu/ɔza] *adj* bulky; (*importante*) important; (*quantia*) considerable.

vulva ['vuwva] *f* vulva.

vupt ['vuptʃi] *excl* wham!

W

W, w ['dablju, *PT* ve'duplu] (*pl* **ws**) *m* W, w; **W de William** W for William.

w. *abr* (= *watt*) w.

walkie-talkie [wɔki'tɔki] (*pl* **~s**) *m* walkie-talkie.

watt ['wɔtʃi] (*pl* **~s**) *m* watt.

watt-hora (*pl* **watts-horas**) *m* watt-hour.

western ['wɛʃtɛxn] (*pl* **~s**) *m* western.

windsurfe [wĩ'suxfi] *m* windsurfing.

windsurfista [wĩsux'fiʃta] *m/f* windsurfer.

X

X, x [ʃiʃ] (*pl* **xs**) *m* X, x; **o ~ do problema** the crux of the problem; **X de Xavier** X for Xmas.

xá [ʃa] *m* shah.

xadrez [ʃa'dreʒ] *m* (*jogo*) chess; (*tabuleiro*) chessboard; (*tecido*) checked cloth; (*col*: *cadeia*) clink ♦ *adj inv* check(ered); **tecido de ~** check material.

xale ['ʃali] *m* shawl.

xampu [ʃã'pu] *m* shampoo.

Xangai [ʃã'gaj] *n* Shanghai.

xangô [ʃã'go] *m* (*orixá*) Afro-Brazilian deity; (*culto*) Afro-Brazilian religion.

xará [ʃa'ra] *m/f* namesake; (*companheiro*) mate.

xaropada [ʃaro'pada] (*col*) *f* bore; (*conversa*) boring talk.

xarope [ʃa'rɔpi] *m* syrup; (*para a tosse*) cough syrup.

xavante [ʃa'vãtʃi] *adj*, *m/f* Shavante Indian.

xaveco [ʃa'vɛku] *m* (*coisa sem valor*) piece of junk.

xaxim [ʃa'ʃĩ] *m* plant fibre (*BRIT*) *ou* fiber (*US*) (*used to plant indoor plants*).

xelim [ʃe'lĩ] (*pl* **-ns**) *m* shilling.

xenofobia [ʃenofo'bia] *f* xenophobia.

xenófobo/a [ʃe'nɔfobu/a] *adj* xenophobic ♦ *m/f* xenophobe.

xepa ['ʃepa] (*col*) *f* left-overs *pl*.

xepeiro/a [ʃe'pejru/a] *m/f* rubbish (*BRIT*) *ou* garbage (*US*) picker.

xeque ['ʃɛki] *m* (*XADREZ*) check; (*soberano*) sheikh; **pôr em ~** (*fig*) to call into question.

xeque-mate (*pl* **xeques-mate**) *m* checkmate.

xereta [ʃe'reta] *m/f* busybody ♦ *adj* nosy.

xeretar [ʃere'ta*] *vi* to poke one's nose in.

xerez [ʃe'reʒ] *m* sherry.

xerife [ʃe'rifi] *m* sheriff.

xerocar [ʃero'ka*] *vt* to photocopy, Xerox ®.

xerocópia [ʃero'kɔpja] *f* photocopy.

xerocopiar [ʃeroko'pja*] *vt* = **xerocar**.

xerox [ʃe'rɔks] ® *m* (*copia*) photocopy; (*máquina*) photocopier.

xexelento/a [ʃeʃe'lētu/a] (*col*) *adj* scruffy ♦ *m/f* scruff.

xexéu [ʃe'ʃew] *m* stink.

xi [ʃi] *excl* cor! (*BRIT*), gee! (*US*).

xícara ['ʃikara] (*BR*) *f* cup.

xicrinha [ʃi'kriɲa] *f* little cup.

xiita [ʃi'ita] *adj*, *m/f* Shiite.

xilindró [ʃili'drɔ] (*col*) *m* clink.

xilofone [ʃilo'fɔni] *m* xylophone.

xilografia [ʃilogra'fia] *f* woodcut.

xingação [ʃĩga'sãw] (*pl* **-ões**) *f* curse.

xingamento [ʃĩga'mētu] *m* = **xingação**.

xingar [ʃĩ'ga*] *vt* to swear at ♦ *vi* to swear; **~ alguém de algo** to call sb sth.

xingatório [ʃĩga'tɔrju] *m* stream of invectives.

xinxim [ʃĩ'ʃĩ] *m* (*tb*: **~ de galinha**) chicken ragout.

xixi [ʃi'ʃi] (*col*) *m* wee, pee; **fazer ~** to wee, have a wee.

xô [ʃo] *excl* shoo.

xodó [ʃo'dɔ] *m* (*pessoa*) sweetheart; (*coisa*) passion; **ter ~ por alguém/algo** to have a soft spot for sb/sth.

Z

Z, z [ze] (*pl* **zs**) *m* Z, z; **Z de Zebra** Z for Zebra.

zaga ['zaga] *f* (*FUTEBOL*) fullback position.

zagueiro [za'gejru] *m* (*FUTEBOL*) fullback.

Zaire ['zajri] *m*: **o ~** Zaire.

Zâmbia ['zãbja] *f* Zambia.

zanga ['zãga] *f* (*raiva*) anger; (*irritação*) annoyance.

zangado/a [zã'gadu/a] *adj* angry; (*irritado*) annoyed; (*irritadiço*) bad-tempered; **ele está ~ comigo** (*de relações cortadas*) he's not speaking to me.

zangão [zã'gãw] (*pl* **~s** *ou* **-ões**) *m* (*inseto*) drone.

zangar [zã'ga*] *vt* to annoy, irritate ♦ *vi* to get angry; **~-se** *vr* (*aborrecer-se*) to get annoyed; **~-se com** to get cross with.

zangões [zã'gõjʃ] *mpl de* **zangão**.

zanzar [zã'za*] *vi* to wander.

zarolho/a [za'roʎu/a] *adj* blind in one eye.

zarpar [zax'pa*] *vi* (*navio*) to set sail; (*ir-se*) to set off; (*fugir*) to run away.

Zé [ze] *abr* (= *José*) Joe.

zebra ['zebra] *f* zebra; (*col: pessoa*) silly ass; (*jogo*) upset, turn-up for the books; **deu ~** (*col*) there was an upset.

zebrar [ze'bra*] *vi* to be a turn-up for the books.

zelador(a) [zela'do*(a)] *m/f* caretaker ♦ *adj* caring.

zelar [ze'la*] *vt*, *vi*: **~ (por)** to look after.

zelo ['zelu] *m* devotion, zeal; **~ por alguém/ algo** devotion to sb/sth.

zeloso/a [ze'lozu/ɔza] *adj* zealous; (*diligente*) hard-working.

zen-budismo [zē-] *m* Zen (Buddhism).

zênite ['zenitʃi] *m* zenith.

zé-povinho [-po'viɲu] (*pl* **~s**) *m* the man in the street; (*o povo*) the masses *pl*; (*ralé*) riffraff.

zerar [ze'ra*] *vt* (*conta*, *inflação*) to reduce to zero; (*déficit*) to pay off, wipe out; (*aluno*) to give no marks to ♦ *vi*: **~ em** (*aluno*) to get no marks in.

zerinho/a [ze'riɲu/a] (*col*) *adj* brand new.

zero ['zeru] *num* zero; (*ESPORTE*) nil; **ser um ~ à esquerda** to be useless; **8 graus abaixo/ acima de ~** 8 degrees below/above zero; **reduzir alguém a ~** to clean sb out; **ficar a ~** to lose everything; **começar do ~** (*fig*) to start from nothing.

zero-quilômetro *adj inv* brand new ♦ *m inv* brand new car.

ziguezague [zigi'zagi] *m* zigzag.
ziguezagueante [zigiza'gjãtʃi] *adj* zigzag.
ziguezaguear [zigiza'gja*] *vi* to zigzag.
Zimbábue [zĩ'babwi] *m*: **o ~** Zimbabwe.
zinco ['zĩku] *m* zinc; **folha de ~** corrugated iron.
-zinho/a [-'ziɲu/a] *sufixo* little; **florzinha** little flower.
zipe ['zipi] *m* = **zíper**.
zíper ['zipe*] *m* zip (*BRIT*), zipper (*US*).
ziquizira [ziki'zira] (*col*) *f* lurgy.
zoada ['zwada] *f* = **zoeira**.
zodíaco [zo'dʒiaku] *m* zodiac.
zoeira ['zwejra] *f* din.
zombador(a) [zõba'do*(a)] *adj* mocking ♦ *m/f* mocker.
zombar [zõ'ba*] *vi* to mock; **~ de** to make fun of.
zombaria [zõba'ria] *f* mockery, ridicule.
zona ['zɔna] *f* area; (*de cidade*) district; (*GEO*) zone; (*col: local de meretrício*) red-light district; (: *confusão*) mess; (: *tumulto*) free-for-all; **fazer a ~** to go on the game; **fazer uma ~** to raise hell, make a fuss; **~ eleitoral** electoral district, constituency; **~ franca** free-trade area; **Z~ Norte/Sul** (*do Rio, São Paulo etc*) Northern/Southern District; **a Z~ Sul carioca** *the fashionable middle-class suburbs along the beaches in Rio.*
zonear [zo'nja*] *vt* to divide into districts; (*col*) to make a mess in ♦ *vi* (*col*) to raise hell.

zonzeira [zõ'zejra] *f* dizziness; **dar/sentir ~** to make/feel dizzy.
zonzo/a ['zõzu/a] *adj* dizzy.
zôo ['zou] *m* zoo.
zoologia [zolo'ʒia] *f* zoology.
zoológico/a [zo'lɔʒiku/a] *adj* zoological; **jardim ~** zoo.
zoólogo/a [zo'ɔlogu/a] *m/f* zoologist.
zoom [zũ] *m* = **zum**.
zorra ['zoxa] (*col*) *f* mess.
zuarte ['zwaxtʃi] *m* denim.
zulu [zu'lu] *adj, m/f* Zulu ♦ *m* (*LING*) Zulu.
zum [zũ] *m* zoom.
zumbido [zũ'bidu] *m* buzz(ing); (*de tráfego*) hum; **um ~ no ouvido** a ringing in one's ear.
zumbir [zũ'bi*] *vi* to buzz; (*ouvido*) to ring ♦ *m* buzzing; ringing.
zunido [zu'nidu] *m* (*vento*) whistling; (*inseto*) buzz.
zunir [zu'ni*] *vi* (*vento*) to whistle; (*seta*) to whizz; (*bala*) to zip; (*inseto*) to buzz.
zunzum [zũ'zũ] *m* buzz(ing); (*boato*) rumour (*BRIT*), rumor (*US*).
zunzunzum [zũzũ'zũ] *m* rumour (*BRIT*), rumor (*US*).
zura ['zura] *m/f inv* miser ♦ *adj inv* mean, stingy.
zureta [zu'reta] (*col*) *m/f* loony.
Zurique [zu'riki] *n* Zurich.
zurrapa [zu'xapa] *f* rough wine, plonk (*col*).
zurrar [zu'xa*] *vi* to bray.
zurro ['zuxu] *m* bray.

NB: European Portuguese adds the following consonants to certain words: **b** (sú(b)dito, su(b)til); **c** (a(c)ção, a(c)cionista, a(c)to); **m** (inde(m)ne); **p** (ado(p)ção, ado(p)tar); *for further details see p. xiii.*